ROTHMANS
FOOTBALL
YEARBOOK
1996-97

EDITOR: GLENDA ROLLIN
EXECUTIVE EDITOR: JACK ROLLIN

HEADLINE

First published in 1996
by HEADLINE BOOK PUBLISHING

10 9 8 7 6 5 4 3 2 1

Cover photographs: (top left) Eric Cantona (Manchester United) – *Action Images*; (bottom left) Teddy Sheringham (Tottenham Hotspur) – *Colorsport*; (top right) Keith Curle (Manchester City) and Les Ferdinand (Newcastle United) – *Action Images*; (bottom right) Steve McManaman (Liverpool) – *Action Images*.

British Library Cataloguing in Publication Data
Rothmans Football Yearbook.—1996–97
1. Association Football—Serials
796.334'05

ISBN 0 7472 1696 7 (hardback)
ISBN 0 7472 7781 8 (softback)

Typeset by Wearset, Boldon, Tyne and Wear

Printed and bound in Great Britain by
Mackays of Chatham PLC,
Chatham, Kent

HEADLINE BOOK PUBLISHING
A division of Hodder Headline PLC
338 Euston Road
London NW1 3BH

CONTENTS

EUROPEAN FOOTBALL

NON-LEAGUE FOOTBALL

INFORMATION AND RECORDS

INTRODUCTION

The 27th edition of Rothmans Football Yearbook includes complete coverage of the 1996 European Championship with goalscorers, teams, times of goals, attendances and referees for both the qualifying and final competition.

On the domestic scene, there is a reversion to a player's directory under clubs, with trainees and schoolboys also listed.

Among several new features is a list of foreign international players born outside the UK who played in the FA Premier League and Football League during 1995–96 and increased coverage of reserve team football in the Pontin's League and the Avon Insurance Combination.

The performances of British clubs in Europe are monitored and special articles include those on the Football Trust, Football and the Law plus Referees. Also the special work carried out by Chaplains to clubs is again included.

Amateur, schools, university and women's football plus coverage of non-league soccer, awards, records and the International Directory of all member countries in FIFA are among the regular items.

Transfer fees are given where known. When two clubs have differed as to the amount of a record move, the lower figure has been quoted in both instances. Also the date when a player is signed often varies from one given as his registration.

The Editor would also like to thank Alan Elliott for the Scottish section, Norman Barrett for the Milestones Diary and Ian Vosper for the Obituaries. Thanks are also due to John English who provided his usual painstaking and conscientious reading of the proofs.

The Editor would like to pay tribute to the various organisations who have helped to make this edition complete, especially Sheila Andrew of the Football League, Mike Foster of the FA Premier League and the secretaries of all the FA Premier, Football League and Scottish League clubs for their kind co-operation. The ready availability of Football League secretary David Dent and his staff to answer queries was as usual most appreciated especially Chris Hull and thanks are due in equal measure to the Scottish Football League as well as Adrian Cook and Neil Harrison of the FA Premier League.

ACKNOWLEDGEMENTS

The Editor would also like to express her appreciation of the following individuals and organisations for their co-operation: Glynis Firth, Sandra Whiteside, Lorna Parnell, Debbie Birch (all from the Football League), David C. Thompson of the Scottish League, Alan Dick, Malcolm Brodie, Bob Hennessy, Peter Hughes (English Schools FA), W.P. Goss (AFA), Ken Scott for Vauxhall Conference information, Rev. Nigel Sands, Edward Grayson, Ken Goldman and Grahame Lloyd.

Special thanks are due to Lorraine Jerram of Headline Book Publishing Ltd for her expertise, constant support, unflagging patience, sincerity, understanding and appreciation.

Finally sincere thanks to John Anderson, Simon Dunnington and Geoff Turner and the production staff at Wearset for their efforts in the production of this book which was much appreciated throughout the year.

EDITORIAL

More than 100 full international players born outside the United Kingdom appeared in the FA Carling Premiership and Endsleigh Insurance Football League competitions last season. That figure seems certain to increase during 1996–97.

The trend is likely to accelerate, as borders continue to be pushed aside and the map of Europe merges with itself either through legislation or evolution. There are obvious dangers, not the least of these the possibility that home-grown talent will be stifled. But is that a real threat? Judging by the experience of Manchester United in 1995–96, the development of youth is not only a flourishing exercise, but a rewarding experience. While United's first team achieved the FA Premier League and FA Cup double, the reserves won the Pontin's League and the 'A' team took the Lancashire League.

Apart from a cluster of trainees who became professionals, United signed only three other players during the season, only one of whom a trialist from France appeared in the League team.

Of the first team squad, David Beckham, Nicky Butt, the Neville brothers Gary and Phil, Ryan Giggs and Paul Scholes are all products of United's excellent youth policy.

One of the imports at Old Trafford, Eric Cantona, made the transition from being *l'enfant terrible* to prodigal son after his suspension. He emerged a changed character without losing any of the outstanding attributes as a player which his wayward temperament had been supposed to sustain. His rehabilitation should have set an example to other so-called members of the genius fraternity in other walks of life, that they, too, can conform without losing any of their special gifts.

Naturally, United have added to their already formidable strength by some overseas purchases in the summer months, but are unlikely to abandon their attitude to youth which has contributed to putting them in the forefront of English football and set the degree at which all others have to aim. Then again, others may argue, is youth worth persevering with after the Bosman judgement?

Of course, for financial reasons, the Old Trafford story cannot be repeated everywhere, but as a blueprint for success it almost defies improvement. However, a healthy competitive league cannot be sustained by the monopoly of one club.

Newcastle United went very close to the championship themselves, buoyed by their tremendous support in the north-east. Liverpool too, maintained the high standards which have become to be expected of them and with the huge sums of money which are being generated by television coming into the game, it is hoped that it will provide all-round benefits to enable many clubs to compete on a more level footing and not solely to provide cash for foreign transfers.

With Euro 96 affording a wider view of foreign talent and allowing England the opportunity to compete against Europe's best, expectations will have increased towards the 1998 World Cup as a result of England finishing as semi-finalists.

The 'golden goals' experiment which were designed to eliminate penalty shoot-outs proved unsuccessful in the tournament, but penalty kicks do allow teams to remain 'unbeaten' simply because results invariably do not reflect this lottery manner of dividing teams; an attractive option! Even so, there seems to be only one solution to deciding matches after extra time: play on until somebody scores a goal. Everything else seems to fly in the face of the spirit of the game.

ROTHMANS FOOTBALL HONOURS

This year the Rothmans Football Honours are presented to the team of the 1995–96 season chosen by members of the Football Writers' Association. Players eligible had to have appeared in FA Carling Premiership matches during the season and there were no fewer than 50 different players nominated.

The most favoured formation was 4-4-2 which had almost as many votes as all other systems combined and the players receiving the highest number of votes were Eric Cantona (who had been chosen as the FWA's Footballer of the Year), Peter Schmeichel and Alan Shearer. Others who came close to gaining a place in the final selection were Alan Wright (Aston Villa), Dan Petrescu (Chelsea), David Seaman (Arsenal), Georgi Kinkladze (Manchester C), Philip Neville (Manchester U), Les Ferdinand (Newcastle U) and Mark Wright (Liverpool).

Manchester United players dominated the listings. There were votes for ten of them and an eleventh was among the substitutes mentioned. Seven of United's contingent figured in the final selection.

Aston Villa had six players receiving recommendation while two other clubs Newcastle and Liverpool had five each. There were four from Arsenal and three each representing Blackburn, Chelsea and Nottingham Forest.

Ruud Gullit's appearance in the team of the season is interesting since he was the only player to be chosen in the eleven after just one season in the FA Carling Premiership, following his arrival from Italy. He has succeeded Glenn Hoddle, the new England team manager, as Chelsea's manager.

Gullit was also the only nominee with a London club to make the final selection and Steve Bruce (Manchester U), the lone player without full international honours. He has since joined Birmingham City.

Alex Ferguson of Manchester United received more than five times the number of votes for manager than his nearest rival Kevin Keegan of Newcastle United. Ferguson achieved a League Championship and FA Cup double for the second time in three years. Roy Evans, the Liverpool manager and Harry Redknapp of West Ham were other managers who came into contention.

Rothmans Team of the Season

Peter Schmeichel
(Manchester U)

Gary Neville	Steve Bruce	Gareth Southgate	Denis Irwin
(Manchester U)	*(Manchester U)*	*(Aston Villa)*	*(Manchester U)*

Eric Cantona	Ruud Gullit	Roy Keane	Ryan Giggs
(Manchester U)	*(Chelsea)*	*(Manchester U)*	*(Manchester U)*

Alan Shearer   Robbie Fowler
(Blackburn R)   *(Liverpool)*

Manager:
Alex Ferguson *(Manchester U)*

Substitutes:
John Scales *(Liverpool)*
Steve McManaman *(Liverpool)*
Les Ferdinand *(Newcastle U)*

MILESTONES DIARY 1995–96

June 1995

Jim Smith new Derby boss ... Liverpool pay British record £8.5m for Stan Collymore ... Norway win Women's World Cup ... Dennis Bergkamp for Arsenal ... Paul Ince leaves Man Utd ... Chelsea get Gullit and Hughes ... Dalglish steps upstairs at Blackburn ... David Pleat new Owls boss ... Wales sack Mike Smith

13   Norwich, having agreed compensation with Wycombe, name former star Martin O'Neill as manager. Man Utd refuse Derby permission to talk to their captain Steve Bruce, wanted as manager. Spurs sign a record four-year kit deal with Pony said to be worth £10m. Germany beat England 3-0 in the quarter-finals of the Women's World Cup.

14   Luton manager David Pleat's move to Sheff Wed on a one-year rolling contract is disputed by chairman David Kohler, whose demand for £300,000 compensation is way over the £40,000 offered.

15   Jim Smith, dismissed as Portsmouth manager 5 months ago, takes over at Derby, his eighth club in 23 years. Charlton make Alan Curbishley sole manager, but will honour the remaining two years of his partner Steve Gritt's contract. Former Sunderland manager Mick Buxton is appointed coach of Zimbabwe.

16   Luton win a temporary High Court injunction to prevent David Pleat taking over at Sheff Wed.

17   Liverpool, having beaten off opposition from Everton, break the British transfer record by paying £8.5m for Forest striker Stan Collymore. Sheff Wed chairman Dave Richards accuses Luton of harming football over the Pleat affair, pointing out that his club have not acted illegally.

18   Norway win the Women's World Cup.

20   Manager Bruce Rioch makes his first signing for Arsenal, paying Inter-Milan £7.5m for Dutch star Dennis Bergkamp in a four-year deal. Bolton appoint Roy McFarland as manager. Ossie Ardiles signs as coach for Mexican side Guadalajara.

21   Spurs complete the £4.5m signing of Palace striker Chris Armstrong. Brian Horton, sacked by Man City at the end of last season, is appointed manager of Huddersfield.

22   Man Utd and England midfielder Paul Ince finally makes up his mind and signs for Inter-Milan in a £7m transfer. Neil Warnock takes charge at Plymouth, as expected, after leaving Huddersfield. The Isthmian League, no longer Diadora, sign a four-year sponsorship deal with football-strip manufacturers ICIS worth about £0.5m.

23   Another coup for Chelsea, as they introduce Ruud Gullit (a free transfer from Sampdoria) to the media – they sign Man Utd striker Mark Hughes for £1.5m, much to the chagrin of Old Trafford faithfuls. Villa sign unsettled Gareth Southgate from Palace for £2.5m.

24   Stan Collymore's move to Liverpool is reportedly jeopardised by Forest's refusal to meet his demand for 5% of the £8.5m fee. In the first tie of the unpopular Inter-Toto Cup, Wimbledon, with most of their first team still on holiday, crash 4-0 to Bursaspor, Turkey, in a match played at Brighton. Coventry sign Luton midfielder Paul Telfer, the fee to be determined.

25   A major managerial shuffle at Premiership champions Blackburn sees Kenny Dalglish's role redefined as "director of football", with his No.2 Ray Harford promoted to "team manager", while England striker Alan Shearer agrees to extend his contract another three years to four. Spurs are the second London club to lose an Inter-Toto Cup tie at Brighton, going down 2-0 to Lucerne of Switzerland.

26   Villa break their transfer record, paying £3.5m for Partizan Belgrade striker Savo Milosevic.

27   Luton abandon their court action concerning David Pleat, who can now take up his managerial duties at Sheff Wed.

28   Wales sack manager Mike Smith after their disappointing Euro Championship qualifying results.

29   Alan Smith, sacked a month ago as Palace manager, formally takes over at Wycombe. With regular keeper Steve Ogrizovic out with a broken leg, Coventry sign 45-year-old Peter Shilton on a short-term contract.

30   Forest use some of their Collymore money to sign Arsenal's Kevin Campbell and Sheff Wed's Chris Bart-Williams, the fees to be decided.

July
More power for Kelly ... Ball new Man City boss ... Roberto Baggio costs Milan £12.9m ... Platt signs for Arsenal, Gascoigne for Rangers ... George Graham banned for year ... Fashanu, Grobbelaar and Segers on match-fixing charge

1   Turkish side Galatasaray's manager Graeme Souness signs his third former Liverpool player – after Barry Venison and Mike Marsh – Welsh striker Dean Saunders from Villa for £2.35m. At the FA's summer meeting, chief executive Graham Kelly is made a director and installed on the executive committee, and the Premier League are given a second seat on the executive; Kelly, whose powerful new role will enable decisions to be made more quickly, moots the possibility of introducing a short winter break in the domestic football programme in four or five years.

2   Man City chairman Francis Lee flies to Marbella to sign holidaying Alan Ball on a three-year contract as manager, provided compensation can be agreed, while Southampton director of football Lawrie McMenemy will take over at the Dell until a replacement is found.

3   Luton youth team coach Terry Westley is appointed caretaker manager.

4   Liverpool complete the British record signing of Stan Collymore from Forest for £8.5m. Gillingham appoint former Bournemouth chief Terry Pulis as manager. Wolves defender Brian Law is arrested for taking a bus without permission and drink-driving.

5   AC Milan sign Juventus superstar Roberto Baggio, 28, in a near-record deal worth £12.9m, while Villa pay Leicester £3.25m for midfielder Mark Draper.

6   Newcastle complete the signing of French star David Ginola from Paris St Germain for £2.5m. With manager Steve Thompson taking over at Notts County, Southend appoint Ronnie Whelan as player-manager.

7   Brighton, obliged to sell their Goldstone Ground after 93 years to settle their debts, are set to share Portsmouth's Fratton Park next year until they fix up a new ground.

8   New Maine Road manager Alan Ball appoints former City player Asa Hartford his No.2.

10   Arsenal sign England captain David Platt from Sampdoria for £4.75m, bringing his aggregate transfer fees to a world record £22.15m, while North of the border Rangers sign another England midfielder, dyed-blond, slimline Paul Gascoigne, from Lazio for £4.3m. Meanwhile the FA inquiry into illegal-payment allegations against former Arsenal manager George Graham begins at a Watford hotel, with the FA employing for the first time in such proceedings an independent QC and producing seven boxes of evidence. QPR sign Reading midfielder Simon Osborn for £1.1m.

12   George Graham is found guilty of taking illegal payments amounting to £425,500 in 1991 and 1992 from agent Rune Hauge's company Interclub Ltd in respect of the previous transfers to Arsenal of Scandinavian players Pal Lydersen and John Jensen.

13   George Graham is banned from football for a year for "misconduct", while the FA accept that he did not sign the players in question to obtain any personal gain. Spurs striker Teddy Sheringham voices concern for the future and seemingly implies that Armstrong for the possibly departing Barmby is not his idea of a fruitful replacement up front.

14   Southampton's new manager is Dave Merrington, 50, coach at the Dell for the last 11 years, while former chief Alan Ball makes his first foray into the transfer market, paying Tbilisi £2m for midfielder Georgi Kinkladze. Fiorentina sign Arsenal's Swedish international midfielder Stefan Schwarz for £2m, and West Ham sign Dutch international striker Marco Boogers from Sparta Rotterdam for £1m. Following the Dublin riot last February, UEFA announce that all matches involving English teams abroad will be considered "high risk".

17   FIFA endorse George Graham's one-year FA ban, making it effective worldwide. Everton sign Derby defender Craig Short for £2.4m.

18   1st Div Palace pay £2.25m plus midfielder Ricky Newman for Millwall's U-21 international midfielder Andy Roberts.

19   Sheff Wed complete the signing of Belgium captain Marc Degryse for £1.5m. Arsenal striker Alan Smith, having failed to recover from a long-term knee injury, announces his retirement. The FA slap a suspended two-year ban on 17-year-old Jamie Hughes of Tranmere, who tested positive in a random drug test in April.

21   The Peruvian referee, Alberto Tejada, who allowed Brazil's controversial equalizer against Argentina in the Copa America is sent home after admitting his mistake when TV replays show a clear handball.

22   Spurs slump to an 8-0 defeat in the Inter-Toto Cup to FC Cologne.

23   Hosts Uruguay beat Brazil on penalties after a 1-1 draw in the final of the Copa America.

24   Five people are charged with match-fixing, including Villa striker John Fashanu, Southampton keeper Bruce Grobbelaar and Wimbledon keeper Hans Segers, and all are bailed to appear at Southampton magistrates' court on 11 Oct. Forest complete the £1.8m signing of 6ft 5in striker Andrea Silenzi from Torino. Everton reach an "amicable" agreement for compensation with dismissed manager Mike Walker. FIFA threaten Germany and Portugal with expulsion from the World Cup if they continue to annul the results of matches in which referees have made crucial mistakes.

25   Ruud Gullit, playing as sweeper, enjoys his first outing for Chelsea with a 3-1 victory in a friendly that draws a capacity 10,000 crowd at Gillingham.

26   QPR sign Australia's captain Ned Zelic from Borussia Dortmund for £1.25m. New signing Dennis Bergkamp hits a 6 min hat-trick in Arsenal's 8-1 victory over Kristianstads in Sweden.

28   Celtic sign German international striker Andreas Thom from Bayer Leverkusen for £2.2m, while Rangers complete their £2.5m signing from Valencia of Russian star Oleg Salenko, scorer of a record 5 goals against Cameroon in a 1994 World Cup match.

29   Liverpool slump to a 5-0 defeat at the hands of European champions Ajax in a four-team tournament in Germany.

30   Rangers beat Sampdoria 2-0 to win the Ibrox Tournament. A crowd of nearly 17,000 at Stamford Bridge provide an estimated £250,000 in a benefit game for former Chelsea central defender Paul Elliott (to wipe out his outstanding legal bill in the unsuccessful court case against Dean Saunders) – thanks largely to the appearance of summer signings Ruud Gullit and Mark Hughes; Portuguese champions Porto hold Chelsea to a 1-1 draw.

31   An independent report by accountants Touche Ross for the year 1993-94 discloses a widening gap between Premiership and Endsleigh League clubs, the former enjoying an average 27% increase per club in operating profit to £1.86m while all Endsleigh divisions increased average losses.

August
Barmby signs for Middlesbrough ... Everton win Charity Shield ... Bobby Gould gets Welsh job ... Rangers scrape into Champions' League ... Johnny Carey dies ... Kanchelskis signs for Everton ... Sugar threatens to sell Spurs

1   Bolton pay a club record £1.5m for Barnsley's N.Ireland central defender Gerry Taggart. Peter Beardsley, 34, announces his latest contract with Newcastle ties him to the club for another 3 years. Celtic draw 2-2 at Goodison in Everton keeper Neville Southall's benefit match, from which he will probably collect about £200,000.

2 Villa striker John Fashanu, 31, bailed last week to appear on match-fixing charges, is forced to retire from the game through a knee injury, having started only 12 matches for the club.

3 Coventry finally seal John Salako's signature for £1.5m, after doubts about the Palace winger's back condition are cleared up.

5 Bryan Robson gets his man, as Spurs' coveted England international, Nick Barmby, 21, agrees to join Middlesbrough for £5.2m. But Andrei Kanchelskis's move to Everton could be in jeopardy – apparently the contract has not been signed – with reports that Man Utd are recalling the Russian international because of demands by his previous club Shakhtyor Donetsk for £1m.

6 Coventry complete the transfer of £1m Derby defender Paul Williams in an exchange deal involving Sean Flynn.

7 Everton refer the Kanchelskis dispute to the Premiership for arbitration. FIFA rule that Bayern Munich must pay Spurs £1.4m for Jürgen Klinsmann.

8 Eric Cantona's request for a transfer is turned down by Man Utd, who are later informed by the FA that they will not be taking any action over an alleged breach of the French star's suspension in a training work-out against Rochdale behind closed doors. Forest must pay Sheff Wed £2.5m for Chris Bart-Williams, a tribunal record, but reach a private settlement with Arsenal, who agree to accept £2.8m for Kevin Campbell plus further sums related to appearances.

9 Nervous Rangers take a meagre first-leg lead at Ibrox as they beat Anorthosis Famagusta 1-0 in their European Cup preliminary-round tie. Newcastle pay nearly £1.6m for Reading keeper Shaka Hislop. A Football League tribunal orders Coventry to pay Luton £1.15m for Paul Telfer. Ruud Gullit shines again in Chelsea's 4-0 win at Birmingham.

10 Eric Cantona agrees to stay at Old Trafford, and the FA clear him to play in practice matches behind closed doors. Rangers keeper Andy Goram asks to be withdrawn from the Scottish squad for next week's European Championship qualifier, preferring to preserve himself for his club career. The FA hand out £25,000 suspended fines for bad disciplinary records last season to QPR (4 dismissals, 97 bookings) and Wimbledon (6, 85), and £10,000 suspended to Burnley, Chester and Fulham.

11 Rune Hauge, the Norwegian agent involved in the George Graham "bung" scandal, is suspended by FIFA pending a full investigation of the case.

12 The League season opens with a full programme of Endsleigh League and Scottish Div 1 to 3 matches, but no Premier League fixtures either side of the border. However, Newcastle gain an impressive 2-0 victory over Spurs at White Hart Lane in Gary Mabbutt's testimonial, while English Premiership clubs win 4 of the 6 friendlies played in Scotland, including Coventry's 5-1 victory at Aberdeen, but Man City are thrashed 5-1 at Hearts. In the Endsleigh, goalkeepers score two goals, Hereford's Chris MacKenzie from an 80-yard punt (only the 10th League keeper since the war to score from his own half) and Swansea's Roger Freestone from the penalty spot.

13 Cup-winners Everton beat Champions Blackburn 1-0 at Wembley in a scrappy Charity Shield match.

14 Despite the visit of Man Utd director and solicitor Maurice Watkins to Russia, the Kanchelskis transfer, hinging on the translation of the original contract between United and Donetsk, looks unlikely to be settled in time for him to be registered for Everton's foray into Europe and, with United refusing to accept Premier League arbitration, Everton have asked UEFA to help.

15 Fast-food chain McDonalds sign a £1.75m, 2-year sponsorship deal with the Premier League.

16 Ally McCoist scores an invaluable goal for Scotland with his first touch after coming on as a second-half sub, giving Scotland a 1-0 win over close rivals Greece in Gp 8 of the European Championship qualifiers. Man Utd call off the Kanchelskis transfer to Everton.

17 Bobby Gould, out of management for nearly two seasons, is the surprise choice as Welsh supremo, their fourth manager in less than two years, beating several other candidates, including Ron Atkinson, Howard Kendall and Mike Walker. The Kanchelskis saga is not over yet, as the winger returns from Russian international duty and threatens to train with Everton, while Man Utd agree to let the FA arbitrate.

19 A record-equalling 13 League dismissals in one day (set in December 1985) includes one in the Premiership on its opening day – Blackburn keeper Tim Flowers – although an early Shearer penalty suffices to give the champions the points at Ewood Park against QPR. After two matches, Millwall are the only Div 1 side on 6pts. There are no big surprises in the 2nd round of the Scottish Coca-Cola Cup, where Partick win 7-0 at Berwick and Dundee 6-0 at E.Stirling, McCann hitting 4. The FA reluctantly cancel England's fixture with Croatia scheduled for Wembley on 6 Sep because of the escalation of war in the Balkans.

21 Colombia will replace Croatia as England's next opponents. The "Voice of Football", Len Martin, Grandstand results reader for 37 years, dies at 76. The FA ask Birmingham for a report on winger Ricky Otto's arrest on Sunday (he was cautioned and released without charge) after police found cannabis in his car.

22 In the 1st round of the Coca-Cola Cup Rotherham come back against Scunthorpe from a 4-1 deficit to force extra time and then take the tie 6-4 on aggregate, a feat emulated by Peterborough against Swansea, without the extra time score, so they go through on away goals.

23 Rangers clinch a place in the Champions' League, albeit unconvincingly with a 0-0 draw in Famagusta, while Irish club Glenavon reach the 1st round of the UEFA Cup with a 1-0 victory (1-0 agg) over Hafnarfjordur in Iceland. New Wales manager Bobby Gould enlists the help of Ian Rush and Neville Southall in coaching capacities. Former Man Utd captain and Irish international Johnny Carey dies at 75.

25 The Kanchelskis deal finally goes through, but Man Utd are unhappy about Everton chairman Peter Johnson's criticism. George Graham receives reasons in writing – not made public at this time – for his year's suspension from the FA and has 14 days to appeal.

26 Middlesbrough, after last-minute doubts that their new Cellnet Riverside Stadium would be

ready, celebrate its opening with an inaugural 2-0 victory over Chelsea. Andrei Kanchelskis makes his début for Everton, who beat Southampton 2-0 with goals scored by their other foreign players, Limpar and Amokachi. The Premier League season starts in Scotland.

28 Man Utd beat Blackburn 2-1 despite having Roy Keane sent off for 'diving' in a match which sees referee David Elleray caution 7 players. Spurs chairman Alan Sugar, referring to incidents after Saturday's home defeat by Liverpool, insists he will sell the club if he or his family suffer further abuse from the fans.

29 Coventry winger John Salako makes a surprise return to the England squad, but the absence of Inter's Paul Ince and Southampton's Matt Le Tissier from Terry Venables' immediate midfield plans proves more newsworthy, while up front the omission of Ferdinand and Cole is also cause for comment. England captain David Platt is an immediate withdrawal from the team to play Colombia, as he requires knee surgery.

31 Liverpool striker Stan Collymore withdraws from the England squad with an ankle injury, while Everton's Scottish striker Duncan Ferguson undergoes a second hernia operation which will keep him out for as much as two months, taking him up to his court appeal against a custodial sentence for an onfield incident while a Rangers player. The FA announce that the Technical Control Board will meet soon to consider a winter break for the Premiership, a proposal that is gaining momentum within the game.

September
Higuita performs 'scorpion' at Wembley ... Liverpool sign McAteer ... Spurs' ban on Venables lifted ... Bosman verdict threatens transfer chaos ... Dynamo Kiev thrown out of Europe for bribery ... Dave Bowen dies ... Man Utd out of UEFA Cup

3 In the only European Championship qualifier, N.Ireland help the Republic's cause by holding leaders Portugal to a 1-1 draw in Oporto, thanks largely to a magnificent display of goalkeeping by man-of-the-match Alan Fettis of Hull.

4 The first managerial casualties of the season are Bury's Mike Walsh and Lincoln's Sam Ellis, both in Div 3. Lincoln make Steve Wicks their 7th manager in 8 years, while Walsh's assistant Stan Ternent takes over as caretaker at Bury.

5 Terry Venables' team to play Colombia tomorrow is full of youth and dash, with Liverpool's Jamie Redknapp, 22, winning his first England cap in midfield, where he will join club-mate Steve McManaman, 23, and with Middlesbrough's Nick Barmby, 21, making his first start, complementing Shearer up front. Tony Adams takes over the captaincy from injured Arsenal colleague David Platt, and Rangers' Paul Gascoigne is deemed fit to start. Jack Charlton uncharacteristically also gambles on youth, giving Liverpool reserve winger Mark Kennedy, 19, his international début.

6 The sensation of an international night is not any of the results or goals, but an extraordinary stunt by Colombia's keeper Rene Higuita in their goalless draw at Wembley, when instead of catching an easy ball on his goal-line he makes a gymnastic clearance with his heels from behind his head – his 'scorpion', as he calls it. In the more significant pursuit of qualifying for the Euro finals, Scotland virtually book their passage across the border in '96 with a 1-0 win over Finland at Hampden. Ireland, on the other hand, will now really struggle to qualify after their 3-1 defeat in Austria. Liverpool sign Bolton's Jason McAteer for £4.5m.

7 Bolton put their captain, central defender Alan Stubbs, on the transfer list.

8 Millwall escape punishment for the spanner-throwing incident at Reading last month when the home keeper was narrowly missed by a spanner thrown from the visitors' end, having identified and indefinitely banned the 15-year-old culprit from the New Den.

9 Newcastle lose the last 100% record in the League, going down 1-0 to Southampton at the Dell. Wimbledon beat Liverpool 1-0, a remarkable victory in that Vinnie Jones is sent off (Andy Thorn mistakenly goes, too, amidst great confusion and has to be recalled from the dressing-room!) for the 10th time in his career after 22min, with the score 0-0, yet they manage to defend Harford's 30th-minute goal to the end. A record 14 players are sent off in the four English divisions.

11 Man City sign Portsmouth striker Gerry Creaney in a deal that will exceed £1m when he fulfils certain appearance requirements and which sees Paul Walsh go in the opposite direction.

12 Tony Yeboah hits a superb hat-trick as Leeds win the first leg of their UEFA Cup 1st round tie 3-0 in Monaco, who have two players hurt trying to stop his third goal, the clash of heads between Basile Boli and sub keeper Marc Delaroche resulting in their being taken to hospital, Boli, in a bad way.

13 British sides make a poor start in the Champions League, Blackburn losing 1-0 at home to Spartak Moscow and Rangers, who have central defender Alan McLaren sent off together with an opponent, 1-0 away to Steaua Bucharest.

14 Both British Cup-Winners enjoy 3-2 victories in Europe, Everton at Reykjavik, where Anders Limpar is booked for taking a free-kick too quickly, and Celtic at Dinamo Batumi, in Georgia. Spurs chairman Alan Sugar, placing 'personal considerations to one side', lifts the White Hart Lane ban on England supremo Terry Venables. Harold Shepherdson, England's trainer during the 1966 World Cup, dies at 76.

15 Wimbledon's Vinnie Jones has his sending-off against Liverpool revoked, and changed to a booking, when linesman Ray Gould admits, after seeing video evidence, that there was no head contact and he advised the referee wrongly.

18 In Paris, Diego Maradona and Eric Cantona launch the International Association of Professional Footballers, the brainchild of the former, who is confirmed as president. Stan Ternent, in temporary charge at Bury, is made manager.

19 UEFA, meeting in Oporto, call on various committees to look into the English treatment of the Inter-Toto Cup and deal with the conduct of the clubs. UEFA president Lennart Johansson indi-

cates he will stand for the FIFA presidency in 1998. A patently unfit Paul Gascoigne nevertheless marks his first Old Firm game by making the goal for McCoist that gives Rangers a 1-0 win at Parkhead and puts them into the semi-finals of the Coca-Cola Cup. Wimbledon lose a sensational see-saw tie 5-4 in the English counterpart at home to Div 1 Charlton, for whom teenager Lee Bowyer scores a fine hat-trick.

20 The long-awaited verdict of the European Court of Justice in Luxembourg is given in favour of Belgian star Jean-Marc Bosman's restraint-of-trade claim against his club FC Liège, the Belgian FA and UEFA, and promises far-reaching consequences, with a recommendation that a full tribunal rule the present transfer system illegal – players would become free agents at the end of their contracts and could then sell themselves; the restriction on foreign players would also disappear. The initial Football League reaction is that 75% of the country's full-time players could be out of a job, and others fear that many clubs, particularly in the lower divisions, would lose a prime source of income and go out of business. All this cannot dim the sensational giant-killing feat of York, even by their traditions, who beat Man Utd 3-0 at Old Trafford in the 1st leg of their Coca-Cola Cup tie despite having a man sent off halfway through the second half. Dynamo Kiev are thrown out of the Champions' League for attempting to bribe a referee (nearly £20,000 and two mink coats are the alleged sweeteners), and are banned from European competition for the next two seasons. Plans are unveiled for a new Wembley Stadium, a £168m scheme to demolish the current stadium, retaining only the twin towers, and build an entertainment arena that would also contain an athletics track.

21 Wolves sign out-of-contract Blackburn midfielder Mark Atkins for £1m, 30% of which will go to his former club Scunthorpe. The FA bring a disrepute charge against Norwich striker Robert Fleck, on loan from Chelsea, for an incident a fortnight ago when he was ordered from the dugout in the match against Sheff Utd for allegedly making insulting remarks to a linesman. A cabal of half a dozen Div 1 chairmen meeting at Filbert Street to discuss the 'widening financial gulf' opening up with the Premiership decides to call a meeting of all Div 1 clubs, but incurs the wrath of some of those not involved in this 'clandestine' get-together.

23 Some spectacular scoring in the Premier League is headed by Liverpool's Robbie Fowler with 4 goals in their 5-2 defeat of Bolton, while an Alan Shearer hat-trick is a shot in the arm for ailing champions Blackburn, 5-1 victors over Coventry, and Tony Yeboah scores his second hat-trick in a fortnight for Leeds, including a contender for 'goal of the season', in their 4-2 win at Wimbledon. Dennis Bergkamp finally breaks his duck with 2 splendid goals in Arsenal's 4-2 defeat of Southampton, and Julian Dicks converts 2 penalties to give West Ham their first win of the season, 2-1 over Everton. Rangers lose their 100% record in the Scottish Premier, going down 1-0 at home to Hibs.

25 QPR sign Rangers' former England striker Mark Hateley for £1m pending a medical. Former Arsenal and Wales captain Dave Bowen dies at 67.

26 Four out of five British clubs go through to the UEFA Cup 2nd round, but the most dramatic episode occurs at Old Trafford, where an 89th-minute headed equalizer by keeper Peter Schmeichel fails to keep Man Utd in the competition and they go out on away goals, having conceded 2 early ones to Rotor Volgograd. Ironically, the successful four clubs score only 1 goal between them, a splendid second-half strike from Bryan Roy that enables Forest to beat Malmo on away goals. Referee Gary Willard admits he was wrong to dismiss Henning Berg at Liverpool and the Blackburn defender has his one-match ban rescinded. Sheff Wed manager David Pleat sounds off against agents, the 'scourge' of his profession, after the reported transfer request of Romanian defender Dan Petrescu.

28 Celtic and Everton chalk up comfortable wins in the Cup-Winners Cup.

29 Everton striker Daniel Amokachi needs a brain scan after a clash of heads yesterday, but is given the all-clear. Palace sign Wales U-23 international Gareth Taylor from Bristol R at a fee reduced from £1.8m to £1.2m after medicals reveal possible knee problems.

October
Cantona returns ... York beat Man Utd ... Juninho for Middlesbro ... Duncan Ferguson jailed ... Rangers and Blackburn flop in Champions' League ... Ferdinand record ...Venables attacked in Parliament ... Leeds and Liverpool out of Europe

1 Eric Cantona returns in triumph to Old Trafford after his 8-month suspension and scores a penalty equalizer for Man Utd, who are held 2-2 at home by Liverpool and concede top spot in the Premiership to Newcastle, impressive 3-1 winners away to Everton, where Les Ferdinand scores his 100th goal.

2 England supremo Terry Venables names all-rounders Gareth Southgate (Villa) and Steve Stone (Forest) in his squad for Norway next week.

3 York hold on to clinch their Coca-Cola Cup giant-killing act over Man Utd – beaten 4-3 on aggregate by a team 58 places below them in the League and costing less than £100,000. Villa captain Andy Townsend is banned for one game after his dismissal against Forest, and fined for excessive celebrations after scoring in the same game.

4 Three Premiership sides fail at home and go out of the Coca-Cola Cup to clubs from lower divisions: Div 2 Bradford, with a 3-2 lead, hold Forest 2-2 thanks to a last-ditch equalizer from Ian Ormondroyd; and after 0-0 draws at home Div 1 Stoke and Millwall chalk up fine wins at Chelsea (1-0) and Everton (4-2), respectively, the latter a magnificent performance, with the Lions coming back from 2-0 down to win in extra time. Spurs complete the signing of winger Ruel Fox from Newcastle for £4.2m. Paul Gascoigne pulls out of England's squad with a strained muscle. The FA present a proposed TV deal to the Football League management committee, which, if it goes through, will be worth £250m: It covers both Cups, internationals and the Endsleigh League and

could mean the BBC losing the FA Cup final to ITV from 1998 and Div 1 breaking away from the rest of the Endsleigh League.

5   Venables calls Arsenal central defender Steve Bould into the England squad when Steve Howey pulls out, deciding to allow first-choice replacement Neil Ruddock to sort out his private life.

6   Arsenal midfielder David Hillier is reportedly banned for six matches in the New Year, but the FA refuse to say whether this is in connection with drug tests, which are confidential.

7   Middlesbrough boss Bryan Robson brings off the coup of the season with the signing from São Paulo of little midfielder Juninho, 22, Brazilian Player of the Year, for £4.75m, pending a work permit. Terry Venables reveals he turned down a 'name your price' offer three weeks ago to take over at Inter-Milan.

9   Wigan manager Graham Barrow is fired following Saturday's 6-2 home defeat by Mansfield.

11   England manage a 0-0 draw in Norway, but a big night in Europe sees Scotland, who lose a friendly 2-0 in Sweden, virtually assured of going through to the finals in England because their main rivals in Gp 8, Greece, lose 2-1 to leaders Russia. A depleted Ireland have two John Aldridge goals to thank for keeping them in still with a chance by beating Latvia 2-1. Everton and Scotland striker Duncan Ferguson is jailed for 3 months for head-butting an opponent, the first such punishment for an action on the pitch. Scotland U-21 striker Barry Laverty, St Mirren, is undergoing treatment after failing a random drugs test.

12   Leeds, whose captain Gary McAllister was stretchered off with ligament damage in the 57th minute against Sweden yesterday, are angry with Scottish chief Craig Brown, who they say promised McAllister would play for only half the friendly. Derby sign Croatia's captain, defender Igor Stimac, from Hajduk Split for £1.5m.

13   Chelsea sign Romanian international left-back Dan Petrescu from Sheff Wed for £2.3m, pending a new work permit. Two major transfers are completed, Scottish international Billy McKinlay from Dundee Utd to Blackburn for £1.75m and Yugoslavian international midfielder Dragan Curcic from Partizan Belgrade to Bolton for £1m.

14   Recently transferred Mark Atkins claims in the Wolves programme that the discipline and organization at his new club are far better than at Blackburn, but Wolves' further slide down the Div 1 table with a 4-1 home defeat by Stoke is hardly a good advertisement for their methods.

16   A Scottish footballer, Steve Kirk, 32, of Falkirk, is fined £250 in court after being found guilty of culpably and recklessly kicking a ball into the crowd (in a game at Tynecastle last April), injuring a 12-year-old girl. Bottom League club Lincoln sack manager Steve Wicks after only 41 days, replacing him with former Cambridge boss John Beck. Bobby Robson returns to Porto after two months out, having had a cancerous cyst removed. Croydon-born Roy Hodgson, 48, takes up his new post as 'technical consultant' with Inter-Milan, a title devised to get round the ban in Italy on foreign coaches after the deadline; he will continue to assist the Swiss national team part-time.

17   In the 2nd round of the UEFA Cup, Leeds claw back a 3-1 half-time deficit against PSV Eindhoven, but two goals in the last 8min from Luc Nilis give the Dutch side a 5-3 advantage for their home leg. Brazilian star Juninho is welcomed at Middlesbrough by 5,000 fans and a samba band.

18   Another bad night on the Continent for Britain's champion clubs, Rangers being outclassed 4-1 by Juventus (9pts from 3 matches) in Turin, and Blackburn, still pointless after 3 games, going down 1-0 to Legia Warsaw.

19   West Ham's errant full-back Julian Dicks is banned for 3 matches after being found guilty of stamping on Chelsea's John Spencer. Premier League clubs will be allowed to name 5 subs from next season.

21   Premiership leaders Newcastle beat Wimbledon 6-1 at St James' Park, where Les Ferdinand hits a hat-trick and equals the club's post-war record of scoring in 7 games on the trot held by Len White and Paul Goddard; the Magpies are helped when, at 3-0, Vinnie Jones takes over in goal after keeper Paul Heald is sent off. Birmingham MD Karren Brady receives a full apology from Stoke for alleging she made an illegal approach to their striker Paul Peschisolido, her husband. Rangers beat Hearts 4-1 at Ibrox, where an incident near the end of the match, in which Rangers' central defender Craig Moore is left flattened after a clash with Alan Lawrence, goes unseen by the match officials but is bound to have repercussions.

22   The FA announce a deal with the BBC to turn the Cup draw into a 20min peak-time show, with stars of the past participating in the Lottery-style razzmatazz.

23   Leeds complete the signing of Oldham defender Richard Jobson for £1m. Juninho's work permit is granted.

24   In the Coca-Cola Cup 3rd round, torrential rain at Elm Park saves Reading's faces as the match is abandoned after 28 minutes with 3rd Div Bury 2-0 up and their manager Stan Ternent fuming. Aberdeen, with Billy Dodds scoring twice, surprise Rangers 2-1 at Hampden Park in the semi-finals of the Scottish Coca-Cola Cup. Peterborough manager John Still, disgusted at his treatment by fans, resigns and is replaced by assistant Mick Halsall as caretaker-manager.

25   In the Coca-Cola Cup, Coventry find themselves 2-0 down after only 20min, to Spurs, but 3 2nd-half goals give them a dramatic victory. Les Ferdinand scores for the 8th consecutive game for the Magpies to set a post-war club record. Sheff Wed comfortably beat Millwall 2-0 at the forbidding New Den, where interference from two spectators could mean further trouble for the home side. In the all-1st-Division Scottish Coca-Cola Cup semi, Dundee beat Airdrie 2-1 in Perth.

26   The two spectators, one of whom confronted the Sheffield keeper, who ran onto the pitch at Millwall yesterday are charged under the Football Offences Act and banned for life by the club.

27   Kate Hoey, Labour MP for Vauxhall, discloses in the Commons that England coach Terry Venables is being investigated by the DTI regarding an alleged breach of the Financial Services Act, but the FA play down this latest piece of adverse publicity as nothing new.

28   Arsenal have been promised action by the FA and the Kick Racism out of Football campaign on their complaints regarding Ian Wright's treatment by Barnsley fans (and reportedly stewards) at Oakwell in their Coca-Cola Cup tie.

30   FormerArsenal manager George Graham has brought more scorn on his own head with the publication of his book *The Glory and the Grief*, in which further revelations of 'gifts' from agents who receive (illegally) percentages of transfer fees are likely to be investigated by the FA. The admission that he had been offered first option on Andrei Kanchelskis by agent Rune Hauge but had declined because he felt the Ukrainian winger's lack of English would be a problem, and actually put Hauge on to Man Utd, will not win him any accolades for good judgment.

31   Forest are the only British club to survive the 2nd round of the UEFA Cup, going through 1-0 on aggregate after a goalless draw with Auxerre at the City Ground. Liverpool suffer a rare European defeat at Anfield, Brondby scoring the only goal of the tie with 12min to go. Ossie Ardiles, a year after his sacking from Spurs, loses his job as coach to Mexican side Guadalajara after only 10 games.

November

British clubs' Euro woe ... Man City win a match ... Taylor and Wolves part company ... Rangers-Aberdeen match comes under police scrutiny ... Brolin signs for Leeds ... Batty-Le Saux bust-up ... Aberdeen win Scots Coca-Cola Cup ... Ajax win World Club Championship ... BBC to lose Cup final

1   Yet another miserable night for British representatives in the Champions' League as Juventus give Rangers a 4-0 lesson at Ibrox and Blackburn can only draw 0-0 at home to Legia Warsaw, leaving Rangers very little hope of further progress and Blackburn with none. The BBC sack George Graham from his job as football summarizer for Radio 5 Live.

2   With the failures of Everton and Celtic in the Cup-Winners' Cup, Forest are now the only British club left in Europe. Chelsea director Matthew Harding, who has pumped £25m into the club, resigns from the holding company that owns Chelsea, the latest shot in the growing battle for power between him and chairman Ken Bates.

3   The Foreign Office have expressed dismay to the Dutch authorities over the arrest before the Leeds match in Eindhoven on Tuesday of 123 fans, only 4 of whom had been involved in culpable incidents.

4   Juninho, with the necessary paperwork finally completed, makes an impressive Premiership début and wins the hearts of the Middlesbrough fans even though their side are held 1-1 by Leeds.

6   With Vinnie Jones sent off for the 10th time in his career, Forest stroll to a 4-1 victory over Wimbledon (a club record 7th successive defeat), and remain the only unbeaten team in the country.

7   Terry Venables includes QPR's versatile forward Trevor Sinclair, 22, in the England squad for next week's friendly with Switzerland.

8   With Juninho off to play for Brazil and other midfielders injured, Middlesbrough player-manager Bryan Robson presses himself into service and inspires his side to a 2-0 victory over Palace in their Coca-Cola Cup replay. Blackburn complete the signing of Villa striker Graham Fenton for £1.5m. Everton striker Duncan Ferguson loses his appeal against the Scottish FA's 12-match ban for his on-field assault on Raith's John McStay last April, an offence for which he is currently serving a jail sentence.

9   Angered by the serialization of George Graham's new book, the FA release the disciplinary commission's report on the affair, which reveals that they did not accept his assertion that the payments were unsolicited gifts not connected with transfers. England coach Terry Venables continues to suffer embarrassment as allegations are made in court that tend to associate him with false invoicing in the Teddy Sheringham transfer deal of 1992, when he was Spurs' chief executive. Former Arsenal striker Alan Smith receives £250,000 from his benefit match, in which Arsenal beat Sampdoria 1-0 at Highbury. Brighton play-coach Jimmy Case, at 41 Britain's oldest outfield player, who was carried off with a serious neck injury yesterday during a reserve match, announces his retirement from the playing side of the game.

10   Chelsea chairman Ken Bates bans millionaire owner of Stamford Bridge Matthew Harding from the directors box, claiming that his 'boisterous behaviour' is causing the club embarrassment. The FA withdraw their Sky-backed £120m TV deal when the Football League request another deadline extension.

11   Terry Venables, reveals that he has asked the police to investigate what he calls a 'concerted and organized campaign to discredit him', referring to court cases and newspaper 'exposés' of his business affairs. The first round of the FA Cup produces its usual array of non-League heroics, notably from Blyth Spartans (Unibond), who win 2-0 at Bury. The other side of the coin is seen at Shrewsbury, where Marine (Unibond) crash to an 11-2 defeat, and at Oxford, where Dorchester are slammed 9-1. Fulham, languishing in the lower reaches of Div 3, register their first win in 14 games, a 7-0 victory over Div 2 strugglers Swansea. In the Rangers-Aberdeen 1-1 draw in Scotland, Paul Gascoigne is involved in several confrontational incidents.

13   Former England manager Graham Taylor, under growing pressure from disillusioned fans, now finds himself forced to resign from Wolves, steadily tumbling down the Div 1 table instead of challenging for promotion; assistant Bobby Downes takes temporary charge. Strathclyde police announce they have been instructed by the procurator fiscal to look into incidents that occurred in the Rangers-Aberdeen game on Saturday. Liverpool have reportedly fined Stan Collymore two weeks' wages (£24,000) for remarks he made about the club in a magazine.

14   Sunderland have been given the go-ahead to build a 34,000-seater stadium to be ready for the 1997-98 season.

15   The final round of Euro Championship qualifying matches sees Ireland still in with a chance despite losing 3-0 in Portugal, the winners of the group. N.Ireland's remarkable 5-3 defeat of

Austria in Belfast keeps their visitors from taking 2nd place and means the Republic will play off for the last qualifying place – at Anfield against Holland, who need to beat Norway to stay in, and do so 3-0. Scotland, who finish with a 5-0 win over San Marino, qualify in 2nd place. Meanwhile, England put a smile at last on Terry Venables' face with their encouraging 3-1 defeat of Switzerland in their Wembley friendly. Players and officials from Ancona and Birmingham are involved in a brawl after an Anglo-Italian Cup tie between the two sides in Italy, triggered, it appears, by the actions of home coach Massimo Cacciatori, who allegedly attacked visiting players on the pitch during the match; he sustains a broken jaw and an eye injury. Former Cardiff boss Eddie May takes over the vacant job at Torquay, the League's bottom club.

17 After one or two hiccups, Leeds complete the signing of Swedish midfield star Tomas Brolin from Parma for £4.5m. The Ireland-Holland play-off at Anfield next month will incorporate the 'Golden Goal' rule, namely, that, if extra time is required, the first side to score will win, or, failing that, the tie will be settled on penalties. Brentford manager Dave Webb makes an official complaint to the police concerning a telephone conversation with League secretary David Dent which was reported in full by the *Daily Mirror* as part of a series of allegations against England coach Terry Venables.

18 Forest's 25-game unbeaten run in the Premiership, including 12 this season as the last undefeated club in the League, is brought to an end in no uncertain fashion at Ewood Park, where the sleeping champions Blackburn trounce them 7-0. Ryan Giggs scores in 16sec for Man Utd, who beat Southampton 4-1. Liverpool's progress is halted by Everton, whose 2-1 victory, in which Andrei Kanchelskis scores his first goals for the club, is their first at Anfield for 8 years. The Football League take legal advice on the *Mirror's* publication of a taped conversation with Dave Webb, believed to be an intercepted mobile phone call, and assistant secretary Andy Williamson suggests the affair backs up Venables' view that a dirty-tricks campaign is being waged against him. Meanwhile, new allegations appear in the *Guardian*, from leaked documents, implying that the Dept of Trade and Industry are about to recommend that court proceedings be started against Venables.

20 Following 6 successive Div 2 defeats, Liam Brady's contract at financially strapped Brighton is terminated by mutual agreement, after 2 years, assistant manager Gerry Ryan taking temporary charge. UEFA president Lennart Johansson meets no opposition when he delivers two strategy documents at a FIFA summit meeting in Zurich aiming to reduce the dictatorial powers of FIFA supremo João Havelange and to get FIFA to adopt competitive marketing of the World Cup finals with a more even distribution of the revenues between FIFA, the continental confederations and the national associations. Huddersfield's £15m Alfred McAlpine Stadium, shared with the rugby league club, wins the RIBA Building of the Year Award.

21 Drama at the City Ground as Britain's last hope Forest win their 3rd round 1st leg tie by an 83rd-minute goal from sub Paul McGregor, following up after the visitors' keeper parries Stuart Pearce's spot-kick from a penalty awarded when Florent Laville handled and was sent off.

22 Blackburn plumb the depths in the Champions' League, not only slumping to 3-0 defeat by group winners Spartak Moscow, but suffering the ignominy of an angry on-field clash between two of their own players, England internationals David Batty and Graeme Le Saux, followed by a verbal confrontation between Tim Sherwood and Colin Hendry, and finally the dismissal of Hendry for a foul. Rangers fade out of contention, held by Steaua 1-1 at Ibrox, but Paul Gascoigne scores a breathtaking goal to enthral the crowd. The Met Police terminate their investigations into allegations of criminal conspiracy made by England coach Terry Venables (made as far back as Nov 1994).

23 Cambridge manager Tommy Taylor slaps a nightclub ban on his players after midfielder Russell Stock suffers a fractured eye-socket during a night out. Bobby Charlton launches 'Footwall', an advertising-linked training wall, 1,000 of which are being offered free to clubs and local authorities.

24 FIFA back UEFA's fight against the Bosman ruling, maintaining that regulations must be universally applied within an international organization.

25 Coventry stage a remarkable comeback from 3-1 down against Wimbledon at Highfield Road, scoring the equalizer in the 83rd-minute after being reduced to 9 men through dismissals.

26 Aberdeen enjoy a smooth 2-0 victory over 1st Div Dundee at Hampden Park to win the Coca-Cola Cup and provide manager Roy Aitken with a trophy in his first season as manager.

27 UEFA decide to take no action against Blackburn's sparring team-mates in their last Champions' League match, but Blackburn fine the errant pair, David Batty and Graeme Le Saux, who have offered unreserved apologies for their behaviour, Le Saux receiving the heavier fine as he is seen as the instigator. Stoke manager Lou Macari escapes with a severe censure for bringing the game into disrepute – the offence, insulting the referee Gerald Ashby during the club's Coca-Cola Cup defeat last month by Newcastle. Bradford, with only 1 win in the last 8 League games, sack manager Lennie Lawrence, putting assistant Chris Kamara in charge for the remainder of the season.

28 European champions Ajax win the Toyota World Club Championship, beating Gremio in Tokyo on penalties after a disappointing 0-0 draw in which the Brazilian club have defender Catalino Rivarola dismissed in the second half; after the match Ajax coach Louis van Gaal makes strong complaints about the poor state of the playing surface. When their Coca-Cola Cup tie at Reading is apparently called off, Southampton send their players home, but quickly recall them, all on mobile phones, when a hoax is discovered; they arrive at Elm Park only to get beaten 2-1. Former president of disgraced French club Marseille Bernard Tapie is jailed for match-fixing in 1993, his 8-month sentence suspended because of his immunity as a French and Euro MP.

29 With a late winner from sub Steve Watson, high-flying Newcastle knock holders Liverpool out of the Coca-Cola Cup at Anfield to reach the quarter-finals for the first time since 1976. At

Highbury, Arsenal continue their Cup domination over Sheff Wed with a 2-1 victory, Ian Wright scoring his 250th goal. It emerges that the DTI have sent England coach Terry Venables a notice of intention to apply to the High Court to have him disqualified from acting as a company director, but the FA announce they regard this as his personal matter. As the final details of the FA's TV deal are sorted out, it is confirmed that the three channels involved – BBC, ITV and Sky – will all get a share of the FA Cup, but the final will move from BBC to ITV in 1998. UEFA, having received a report from their match observer, do an about-turn on the Le Saux-Batty affair, and ban the Blackburn pair for two European matches.

30 The Scottish FA hand one-match suspensions to Paul Gascoigne and John Brown of Rangers for offences committed during the game with Aberdeen on 11 Nov, while Alan McLaren (Rangers) and Billy Dodds (Aberdeen) have their cases deferred, as both have been cautioned by the police, who are continuing to investigate incidents in the match. Future TV plans for English football are confirmed and include the extension of Sky's live coverage of England internationals to 2001, and they will also continue to show live FA Cup ties from every round as well as live replays, while ITV will broadcast live ties on Sundays. The overall deal agreed by Sky, ITV and the BBC leaves Sky with a significant balance of power, as they will now control the Premiership, the Endsleigh League, the Coca-Cola Cup and England's home internationals and enjoy considerable access to the FA Cup and most of Scottish football.

December
Forest through to UEFA quarter-finals ... Bates and Harding kiss and make up ... Ireland out of Euro 96 and Jack Charlton retires ... Venables loses court battle ... European transfer situation not clear ... Newcastle have 10pt Christmas lead, but Man Utd reduce gap ... Gascoigne booked for 'booking' ref

1 Wolves, seeking a managerial replacement for Graham Taylor, claim they have been refused permission to speak to Leicester boss Mark McGhee, while Leicester counter-claim that they have not been approached.

2 Southampton suspend Bruce Grobbelaar for two matches and fine him a fortnight's pay for not turning up to play at Anfield after the keeper had promised he would return from international duty with Zimbabwe on time. Darlington manager Dave Hodgson hands in his resignation before their 2-2 FA Cup draw at Rochdale. Brentford, despite losing Barry Ashby (sent off) and Brian Statham (broken leg), win 1-0 at Bournemouth. Manchester businessman Mike McDonald buys out Reg Brearley's 52% stake in Sheff Utd.

4 The police again get involved in Scottish football, and are investigating the dismissal of Aberdeen captain Stewart McKimmie for an alleged elbow offence on Callum Milne at Partick on Saturday.

5 Nottm Forest, Britain's last representatives in Europe, bravely defy everything Lyon throw at them – including an elbow from Florian Maurice, who is sent off – to hold out for a 0-0 draw in France and go through to the UEFA Cup quarter-finals on a 1-0 aggregate. Stewart McKimmie is not to be prosecuted. Morton manager Allan McGraw is comfortable after a mild heart attack.

6 Both British sides have players dismissed on the last night of Champions' League matches, but salvage some pride from their traumatic campaigns, Blackburn with a win and Rangers with a draw. At Ewood Park, where Paul Warhurst is sent off in the second half for two bookable offences, Alan Shearer scores at last in Europe, from a penalty, although Mike Newell is the 9-minute hat-trick hero of Blackburn's 4-1 defeat of Rosenborg, which sees the Norwegians eliminated. Despite losing at home to Spartak, the only 100% team in the competition, Legia go through to the quarter-finals with the Russians. In Gp C, Borussia Dortmund's home point against Rangers makes sure of their further progress, although rivals Steaua are held anyway in Bucharest by the already qualified Juventus. Before Gordon Durie hits a late equalizer in Dortmund, Paul Gascoigne is awarded two yellow cards, the second for a pointless argument with the referee. Earlier in the day, Gascoigne and the other players concerned hear that they will not face prosecution over the Rangers-Aberdeen affair, but the Scottish FA are looking into complaints about a press picture showing Gascoigne allegedly pinching the bottom of a Hearts player! Duncan Ferguson, recently released from jail, has the 7 remaining games of his ban put on hold, Everton having won a judicial review in the New Year.

7 Chelsea chairman Ken Bates and owner Matthew Harding, after several weeks of mud-slinging conducted largely in the tabloids, agree a truce as Bates lifts the directors' box ban on his antagonist in the battle for the club. Mark McGhee, sought by Wolves as their new manager, resigns from Leicester – a year after they lost Brian Little in similar circumstances. The FA charge Gillingham and Fulham with misconduct and failing to control their players in a Div 3 match on 25 Nov in which 10 players were cautioned, 2 dismissed, and Gills' Mark O'Connor suffered a broken leg. N.Ireland extend manager Bryan Hamilton's contract for another 2yr 6mo. A record 3.68-second goal has been scored in Australia by Damian Mori, in Adelaide City's 2-2 home draw with Sydney Utd.

9 Newcastle suffer only their second League defeat, 1-0 at Stamford Bridge, where squabbling Chelsea bosses Bates and Harding kiss and apparently demonstrate they have made up. Tony Adams, set to replace his injured club-mate David Platt as England captain next week, is sent off for a 'professional foul' in Arsenal's 0-0 draw at Southampton. In the battle of the Div 1 leaders, Sunderland smash their way to the top with a 6-0 humiliation of Millwall at Roker Park, 21-year-old Craig Russell scoring 4.

10 Brazilian striker Jardel, Rangers' new £3m signing from S.American champion club Gremio, should not have to wait for one of the 10 work permits granted non-EU players in Scotland, having married a Portuguese model on Friday.

11 Rune Hauge, the Norwegian agent involved in the George Graham 'bung' scandal, has been

suspended indefinitely from football by FIFA. Terry Venables reveals his choice of front men (Sheringham is injured) for the friendly against Portugal tomorrow – Alan Shearer and Les Ferdinand, the leading scorers in the Premiership. Duncan Ferguson makes his Premiership comeback as a 62nd-min sub in Everton's 3-0 win over West Ham at Goodison, but fails to score despite the presence in the visitors' goal of left-back Julian Dicks, replacement for the dismissed Ludek Miklosko. Coventry pay Leeds a club-record £2m for striker Noel Whelan. Work permits have been granted to Sheff Wed's two new Yugoslavian internationals, striker Darko Kovacevic and defender Dejan Stefanovic, who cost them £2m apiece.

12 The draw is made in Paris for the 1998 World Cup qualifying competitions. At Wembley, Forest's Steve Stone is man-of-the-match for the second time in a month, scoring for England in their 1-1 draw with Portugal. The court case involving Venables' club Scribes West continues, and ex-footballer Frank McLintock admits that his cash payment of £50,000 was invoiced to Spurs solely for promotional work in order to get round the League rule banning payments to agents – in a statement disclosed to the court, Venables acknowledges that half this fee was for McLintock's services as an agent. Manager Dave Bassett parts company with struggling Div 1 club Sheff Utd after 8 years, by mutual agreement. In an extraordinary Cup replay at Walsall, Torquay are level 1-1 at half-time and 3-3 after 90min, having been inches from victory when Ian Hathaway's shot hits both posts – but they finish up 8-4 losers. Mick Halsall is appointed Peterborough's new manager. A committee looking into the Ancona-Birmingam fracas bans Brum's Liam Daish, accused of beating up Ancona coach Massimo Cacciatori, for the rest of the Anglo-Italian Tournament pending further investigations.

13 Ireland's European dream is ended at Anfield, where teenage Dutch striker Patrick Kluivert scores two exceptional goals in the 2-0 victory that takes Holland to the finals in England next year. Mark McGhee is duly appointed manager of Wolves, who agree compensation to Leicester of about £1m for their manager and assistants, while Howard Kendall takes up the vacant post at Sheff Utd, appointing another ex-Everton man, Adrian Heath, assistant. Wearing a pair of reading glasses borrowed from the judge, Terry Venables gives evidence in the case being brought for fees allegedly owed by his club Scribes West, and states that he believes claims made by businessman Jeff Fugler against him were linked to Spurs; council for Fugler infers that club chairman Alan Sugar was the 'likely candidate' as the alleged source of key documents.

14 Terry Venables loses his court battle and faces a bill for compensation (to the businessman Jeff Fugler suing him) and legal costs totalling an estimated £160,000, and is scathingly criticized by the judge for his evidence. The England coach, not in court to hear the judgement, faces further actions from Fugler's brother and Spurs chairman Alan Sugar, and in turn is counter-suing Fugler and Sugar. Blackburn complete the signing of Palace defender Chris Coleman for £2.8m.

15 As a sequel to the Bosman case, the European Court of Justice rule that clubs have no right to buy and sell players as commodities at the expiry of their contracts, throwing the multi-million-pound transfer market into confusion; the ruling relates to transfers of players between clubs of different EU countries, but there seems little doubt in some quarters that it will affect domestic transfers, too, while others are confident transfers between clubs of the same country will be unaffected – total confusion.

16 Yugoslav striker Savo Milosevic breaks his home duck with a second-half hat-trick as Villa enjoy a 4-1 victory over Coventry, who once again cede numerical advantage to their opponents, this time when former Villa captain Kevin Richardson walks with two yellow cards. But the performance of the day belongs to Sheff Wed, for their fluent, impressive 6-2 demolition of Leeds, who suffer their heaviest defeat of Howard Wilkinson's tenure. Blackburn's Graeme Le Saux breaks a leg in the game against Middlesbrough and looks like missing most of England's preparation for the Euro finals.

17 The Euro 96 draw takes place in Birmingham, with England and Scotland drawn together in a group with Holland and Switzerland. Norwich manager Martin O'Neill resigns. UEFA clarify the new transfer rulings as affecting only EU nationals no longer under contract with their clubs and transferred between EU countries, in which case no fee is applicable – simple! Newcastle striker Malcolm Allen, a Welsh international, who made only 10 League appearances for them, in 1993, loses his battle against a severe knee problem and is forced to retire at 28.

18 In an effort to halt the decline of English clubs' performances in European competition, the FA plan to allow them more time to prepare for their ties, at least 4 clear days without a domestic fixture, and to allow them to opt out of the Coca-Cola Cup until the 3rd round. Manager Terry Westley leaves Div 1 bottom club Luton after only 5 months by mutual consent.

19 The EU Executive Commission rule that UEFA must scrap their limit on foreigners in matches between clubs of different EU states. The Swiss Football Federation decide that Inter manager Roy Hodgson cannot manage their national side part-time and replace him with Portugal's Artur Jorge.

20 Both of tonight's Coca-Cola Cup replays result in wins for Div 1 sides over Premiership opponents, 6ft 7in striker Kevin Francis scoring both Birmingham goals as they beat Middlesbrough 2-0, and Norwich beating Bolton 3-2 on penalties.

21 Jack Charlton, at 60, curtails growing speculation and announces his retirement as manager of Ireland after nearly 10 years and 93 international matches – the finest period in the country's footballing history – and receives accolades from far and wide. Three new managers are appointed to Div 1 clubs, Martin O'Neill to Leicester, Lennie Lawrence to Luton and, provided compensation can be agreed with Bradford where he has been assistant, former caretaker manager Gary Megson to Norwich in place of O'Neill. An FA Premier League Board decide that Liverpool's Stan Collymore is not entitled to a 5% share of his £8.5m transfer fee from Forest because the club had not instigated the move, but he will receive £150,000, the outstanding instalments of his

signing-on fee agreed when he joined Forest. Bolton sign Welsh international Nathan Blake from Sheff Utd in a £1.2m deal that includes the transfer of Mark Patterson to the Yorkshire club.
22   Mark McGhee makes his first signing for Wolves, midfielder Simon Osborn from QPR for £1m. Norwich pre-empt legal action over their appointment of Gary Megson as manager by agreeing compensation with Bradford.
23   England midfielder Robert Lee hits 2 as Newcastle beat Forest 3-1, their 10th win on the trot to take a 10pt lead in the Premiership. Player-manager Bryan Robson, making his first start of the season because of injury problems, links up in midfield with the brilliant Juninho and Middlesbrough beat West Ham 4-2.
26   Frost exposes the absence of undersoil heating at Premier clubs Villa and West Ham, whose fixtures are postponed. Wimbledon's 2-1 win at Stamford Bridge, their first victory in 15 matches, is marred by Vinnie Jones's dismissal for two bookable offences, the second, on Ruud Gullit, for a rash tackle from behind that upends the Dutchman, who is then accused of 'diving'! Only two games take place in Scotland. Rangers' impending signing of Brazilian star Jardel has been delayed by work-permit problems. With non-Europeans eligible for the first time, Milan's £6m Liberian striker George Weah wins the European Player of the Year award in Paris.
27   Man Utd close the gap on Newcastle to 7pts with a passionate 2-0 victory over their rivals at Old Trafford, where stand-in captain Eric Cantona outshines fellow-Frenchman David Ginola.
28   Vinnie Jones is charged by the FA with bringing the game into disrepute over remarks made about Ruud Gullit and other foreign players in a national newspaper. Liverpool offer free transfers to Jan Molby, Mark Walters and Paul Stewart. West Ham agree terms with Croatian central defender Slaven Bilic, who will join them for £1.3m from Bundesliga club Karlsruhe as soon as a work permit is granted.
29   The 72 Football League clubs meet in London and, although the threatened breakaway of the Div 1 clubs to form their own league does not materialize, the rebellion still smoulders, with all 24 clubs having signed resignation letters and lodging them together. Owing to frost again, 27 of tomorrow's League matches have already been cancelled.
30   Spurs lose the last unbeaten away record in the Premier League, defeated 2-1 at Blackburn, where Alan Shearer becomes the first player to score 100 Premiership goals. Again, Rangers' is the only Premier Division match to survive in Scotland, one of only 3 matches played. They take full advantage to increase their lead over Celtic to 8pts with a thumping 7-0 thrashing of 3rd-placed Hibs at Ibrox, Gordon Durie getting 4. Paul Gascoigne is booked for showing referee Dougie Smith the yellow card – a humourless action on the official's part after the English clown, finding the card on the grass after missing a sitter, shows it to himself for his carelessness and is unable to resist brandishing it at the ref before returning it. The FA charge three Middlesbrough players – manager Bryan Robson, captain Nigel Pearson and defender Neil Cox – with bringing the game into disrepute, after referee Paul Danson informs them of a confrontation outside the dressing-rooms at Ewood Park on 17 Dec following controversial decisions in their match against Blackburn.
31   The Div 1 chairmen decide against resigning from the Football League, although 21 of the 24 clubs abstain from voting on the proposed Sky TV deal. FIFA president João Havelange, still taking it upon himself to make unilateral decisions, promises the 2006 World Cup to Africa, with South Africa favourites to host the tournament. African Nations Cup holders Nigeria have withdrawn from next month's competition in S.Africa because of fears for their players' safety, a consequence of the infamous execution in Nigeria last month of minority-rights activists. Former Millwall stalwart defender Harry Cripps dies of a heart attack at 54.

January 1996
Bolton sack McFarland ... Havelange branded a dictator ... Venables to stand down from England job ... Rangers record for McCoist ... Magpies open 12pt gap, sign Asprilla for £7.5m

1   Spurs dent Man United's title hopes with a 4-1 win at White Hart Lane, United's biggest League defeat for 4 years, leaving them still 4pts behind Newcastle who now have two games in hand. Liverpool stay in the race, 3pts behind United with a game in hand, coming from 2-0 down to beat Forest 4-2, thanks largely to a Boy's Own performance by Collymore after he is taunted by the visiting fans.
2   Newcastle beat Arsenal 2-0 to restore their 7pt Premiership lead. Bolton, floundering 8pts adrift at the bottom of the Premiership, sack manager Roy McFarland, leaving partner Colin Todd in sole charge. FIFA sec Sepp Blatter reveals plans to enlarge the goals.
3   FA chairman Sir Bert Millichip, 81, signals his decision to retire after Euro 96, while UEFA boss Lennart Johansson brands FIFA supremo João Havelange a dictator. Rangers draw 0-0 at Celtic to maintain their 8pt lead in the Scottish Premier.
4   Man City ane, 27, is forced to give up his 5-year 14-op battle against knee injuries. Ian Porterfield joins Bolton to work as coach alongside Colin Todd.
5   Spartak Moscow internationals Sergei Yuran and Vasili Kulkov join 1st Div Millwall on loan until the end of the season.
6   The 3rd round of the Cup provides shocks but no upsets as Eric Cantona saves Man United's blushes at Old Trafford with an 80th-min equaliser against 1st Div Sunderland, Arsenal are held at Highbury by Sheff Utd, 2nd from bottom of Div 1, Pearce scores a late equaliser for Forest at Stoke, and Spurs are held 1-1 at Hereford, who miss a penalty. Sheff Wed go down 2-0 to Div 1 high-flyers Charlton. Top-scorers are Liverpool, a Collymore treble and Rush's record 42nd Cup goal helping them to 7-0 victory over Rochdale, and 1st Div Grimsby, 7-1 conquerors of bottom club Luton. In Scotland, Rangers stay 8pts clear with a 4-0 win at Falkirk.

7   Drama in the Sunday Cup-ties, as Stockport hold Everton at Goodison, Les Ferdinand punishes a ghastly keeping error by Chelsea's Dmitri Kharine at Stamford Bridge to earn Newcastle a replay, and Leeds come back from 2-0 at Derby to win 4-2 with two goals in the last minute. The Football League veto Birmingham's plan to buy a top Irish club.

8   Milan striker George Weah (170pts) is voted FIFA World Player of the Year, over club-mate Paolo Maldini (80) and Klinsmann (58).

9   The FA cite Orient defender Roger Stanislaus for failing a random drug test after a match at Barnet last November; he is the first player in England to test positive for a performance-enhancing drug (cocaine).

10 England's coach Terry Venables is to stand down after Euro 96 because the volume of litigation he is involved in will, he believes, hamper England's World Cup qualifying campaign. In Coca-Cola quarter-finals, Ian Wright's double gives Arsenal a 2-0 win over Newcastle at Highbury, where David Ginola's controversial dismissal leads to a dug-out clash, and Leeds come back from a goal down to beat Reading 2-1.

11 Newcastle boss Kevin Keegan rules himself out for the England job, while 'Boro's Bryan Robson feels he hasn't sufficient experience. Talks in Brussels between the Premier League and the European Commission fail to throw any further light on how the Bosman ruling affects the English transfer system. Arsenal manager Bruce Rioch and Newcastle assistant Terry McDermott will escape with a warning for last night's verbal confrontation.

12 UEFA slap a 1-year European ban on Spurs and Wimbledon for fielding weakened clubs in last summer's despised Inter-Toto Cup, but the clubs' appeal will be strongly backed by the FA and Premier League. Two more managers' Gerry Francis (Spurs) and Glenn Hoddle (Chelsea), rule themselves out of the England job, and QPR's Ray Wilkins expresses self-doubts. Man Utd are found guilty of poaching 16-year-old Matthew Wicks from Arsenal, but escape a fine because the son of former Chelsea defender Steve has indicated his willingness to join the Gunners as a trainee.

13 Man Utd, held 0-0 at home by Villa, slip up in the title chase and now find Spurs a point behind them. Lee Chapman, secured earlier this week on a month's loan from Ipswich, is sent off after 26min of his return to the Premiership at Elland Road, but a Brolin brace gives Leeds victory over West Ham. Alan Knight makes his 601st appearance for Portsmouth, a new League record for a keeper for one club, overtaking Peter Bonetti (Chelsea). Steve White scores 4 in Hereford's Div 3 5-2 defeat of Cambridge. In Scotland, Rangers beat Raith 4-0 to go 7pts clear and Ally McCoist's opener, his 231st League goal for the club, takes him past the previous Rangers record set by Bob McPhail between the wars. A turn-up in Div 3 sees Albion, 5pts adrift at the bottom, win 1-0 at 5pt leaders Livingston.

14 A Steve Watson strike at Coventry stretches Newcastle's Premiership lead to 9pts with still a game in hand over Man U. Celtic's 2-1 win at Aberdeen keeps them in the title race, 5pts behind Rangers with a game in hand. European champions Ajax suffer their first League defeat in 52 games since May 1994.

15 The Scottish FA decide to allow TV evidence in disciplinary cases from next season.

16 In 3rd round Cup replays, Man Utd again come back against 1st Div Sunderland to win 2-1, thanks to a Scholes 70th-minute equaliser and a last gasp winner from the much-criticised Cole, but League champions Blackburn go down at home to Div 1 Ipswich, Paul Mason scoring the only goal 5min from the end of extra time. The Premiership clubs vote to decline an invitation to take part in the next Inter-Toto Cup.

17 There's high drama at St James' Park, with penalties for both sides, the dismissal of Newcastle's Darren Peacock after an hour, and a late Gullit equaliser for Chelsea, who proceed to win 4-2 on penalties and go through to the 4th round. Sheff Utd knock Arsenal out 1-0, but the top clubs survive in the other replays, Everton hair-raisingly 3-2 at Stockport, Man City and Spurs smoothly by 5-0 (Sheringham 3) and 5-1 respectively over Leicester and Hereford, while Wimbledon sub Andy Clarke scores the winner over Watford within 3min of coming on to give Wimbledon their first home victory for more than 4 months. West Ham sign Spurs' World Cup star Ilie Dumitrescu for £1.5m. Celtic reverse a half-time deficit to win 2-1 away for the second time this week, beating Hearts to move within 2pts of Rangers.

18 Tottenham Hotspur plc announce record £7.14m pre-tax profits for the half-year ending 30 Nov, and agree a £1.5m deal with Sheff Wed for Andy Sinton.

19 Man City sign Nigel Clough from Liverpool for £1.5m.

20 Newcastle open up a 12pt Premiership lead over Liverpool and non-playing Man Utd, although their 2-1 win over bottom club Bolton, making it 12 out of 12 at home, is less than convincing. Scottish leaders Rangers, however, crash 3-0 at Ibrox, where Hearts midfielder Alan Johnston is the first visiting player to score a League hat-trick against Rangers since Man Utd boss Alex Ferguson for St Johnstone in Dec 1963! But Celtic fail to take full advantage, drawing 0-0 at Kilmarnock, and are now a point behind. Kenny Dalglish, having already upset some of the Irish interviewing board by saying they don't need to interview him, intimates that he's up for the England job, too.

22 An early Cantona strike is enough for a win at West Ham to keep Man Utd in the title hunt, despite Nicky Butt's sending-off 15min from time.

24 Newcastle provisionally sign Colombian striker Faustino Asprilla from Parma for £7.5m and will pay him £26,000 a week. Mark Hughes is suspended for 5 matches, 2 for reaching 33pts and 3 for his dismissal at Everton 10 days ago, as referee Robbie Hart declined to alter his decision after studying a video provided by Chelsea. Leeds on-loan striker Lee Chapman also loses his appeal against a 3-match ban, and Stan Collymore loses his appeal claiming a £425,000 pay-off from his record transfer from Forest to Liverpool.

26 UEFA overturn the Euro ban on Spurs and Wimbledon, thanks to a high-powered appeal team from the FA, the Premier League and the clubs. The FA plump for a short Far East tour to complete England's preparation for Euro 96 so as to avoid possible trouble with travelling fans.

27 Siberian temperatures producing snow and ice restrict the first-class programme to 3 FA Cup 4th-round ties, 1 Endsleigh League game, 5 Tennents Scottish Cup matches and a solitary Scottish League match, as a total of 55 games in England and Scotland are called off. In the Cup, Man Utd win 3-0 at Reading, but Spurs are held at home to Wolves and Everton at home again to a lower-division side, Port Vale. Rangers make up for the lack of matches in Scotland with a 10-1 win at Pittodrie over Highland League club Keith.

29 A Gullit-inspired Chelsea win their 4th round Cup tie 2-1 at QPR, who miss a penalty. Middlesbrough boss and England assistant coach Bryan Robson, still a contender to take over from Venables, is fined £750 by the FA for bringing the game into disrepute following incidents in the Blackburn tunnel last month. Man Utd are convicted for the second time in a month and fined £20,000 for making an illegal approach to 17-y-o schoolboy David Brown when on Oldham's books.

31 Liverpool's 2-0 win at Villa takes them 2nd in the Premiership, 9pts behind Newcastle and ahead of Man Utd on goal difference.

February
Player booked for crossing himself ... Bob Paisley dies ... Port Vale put Cup-holders out ... Man United win 6-0 at Bolton

1 Orient's Roger Stanislaus, 27, is banned for 1 year for drug abuse, the longest FA suspension for 30 years. Everton striker Duncan Ferguson has the remaining 7 matches of his suspension quashed after a Scottish judge rules the Scottish FA acted beyond their powers.

2 The FA find Birmingham guilty of two spectator-related misconduct charges at their November game with Millwall and order them to play one game behind closed doors if there is further trouble this year.

3 Newcastle beat Sheff Wed 2-0 to stay 9pts clear of Man Utd, 4-2 winners over Wimbledon at Selhurst Park, where Cantona exorcises some of last year's public shame with two important goals. Liverpool, held at home by Spurs, fall behind in the title race. Paul Gascoigne scores both Rangers goals in the 2-1 win at Partick that keeps them a point ahead of Celtic, who beat Hibs 2-1. There are curious incidents at both matches: Partick's scorer Rod McDonald is booked for crossing himself at the half-time whistle, and sent off after the interval for a second yellow card. Gascoigne is booked for celebrating one of his goals, while at Celtic Park ref Archie Roy stops the match when Hibs start to play without a keeper. He had refused injured Jim Leighton permission to return but did not notice stand-in keeper Darren Jackson (scorer of Hibs' goal) going back to his outfield position. He explains it is against the rules to play without a keeper. S.African president Nelson Mandela enjoys another emotional triumph in Johannesburg, after last year's Rugby World Cup, as the national side beat Tunisia 2-0 in the final of the African Nations Cup; both goals are scored within a minute by Mark Williams of Wolves, soon after coming on as sub for Leeds' Phil Masinga.

4 Finally the smoke is white and Millwall manager Mick McCarthy is the new Ireland supremo. Gavin Peacock scores 3 as Chelsea rout Middlesbrough 5-0 at the Bridge. Former West Ham winger Alan Sealey dies of a heart attack at 53.

6 The government is heavily defeated in a Lords debate on TV sporting rights, a victory for the campaign to keep 8 "listed" events on BBC and ITV, including the FA and Scottish Cups and the World Cup. Disgraced Orient player Roger Stanislaus, just starting a year's suspension for testing positive for cocaine, is dismissed by the club, who feel the ban is too lenient.

7 A UEFA summit in Geneva, with delegates from 33 leading European clubs, including Arsenal, Liverpool and Man Utd from England, recommends an expansion of European club competition that would see England and 7 other countries entering 2 clubs in the Champions and Cup-Winners cups and as many as 6 in the UEFA Cup, starting next season or certainly by 1997-98. To add to fixture congestion, 5 of the 6 rescheduled 4th round Cup ties are drawn, most commendably by Crewe, Grimsby and Oxford away to Premiership sides, and there are 3 postponements. Charlton get a late winner over Brentford, and in a replay Spurs win 2-0 at Wolves. None of the 5th round ties is yet known. Swansea's chairman-in-waiting Michael Thompson appoints Kevin Cullis, youth manager of non-League Cradley Town, as their new manager.

8 Raith manager Jimmy Nicholl is snapped up for the vacant Millwall post, while Dave Bassett takes over at Palace for the second time. The DoE refuse to sanction the Dumitrescu and Hottiger transfers as they have not played in 75% of Spurs' and Newcastle's games - a decision West Ham intend to fight.

9 Man Utd sign a new kit deal with Umbro said to be worth £60m over 10 years.

10 Man Utd beat Blackburn 1-0 but make no progress as leaders Newcastle, inspired by the unexpected début of their begloved Colombian sub Asprilla, score an important 2-1 win at Middlesbrough with two late strikes; it is Boro's 7th Premiership defeat on the trot. Arsenal's Dennis Bergkamp ends Forest's unbeaten 26-match sequence at home with the only goal of the game. In Scotland, Celtic, held 0-0 at lowly Falkirk, lose ground on Rangers who scrape past bottom club Motherwell 3-2 thanks to a late McCoist penalty given for a foul on Gascoigne, who receives his 9th booking of the season presumably for a matter arising out of the incident. The Premier League programme is unaffected by the weather, but 3 out of 5 fixtures in the other divisions are postponed.

11 Leeds come back to take a 2-1 lead at Birmingham in the 1st leg of their Coca-Cola Cup semi, marred by missiles thrown at visiting captain Gary McAllister from the crowd. Liverpool keep

their faint Premiership hopes alive with a 2-1 victory at QPR. Former England and Stoke stopper Neil Franklin dies at 74.

12 Thanks to representation from the FA, England manager Terry Venables has gained more time to prepare for the first of his upcoming legal battles, the DTI's case to bar him from acting as a company director being adjourned until 15 July. Burnley sack manager Jimmy Mullen after 5 years.

13 Two Premiership sides survive potentially awkward away replays, Forest winning 3-0 at Oxford thanks to 2 goals in the last 10min, and Southampton scraping through 3-2 at Crewe after leading 3-0 in 26min. Vinnie Jones escapes with a £2,000 penalty for a newspaper article criticising Chelsea's Gullit, his fifth FA fine in 5 years. Arsenal manager Bruce Rioch escapes with an FA warning about his touchline confrontation with Newcastle's Terry McDermott, whose own explanation was accepted. Grimsby's Ivano Bonetti misses tomorrow's Cup replay as it emerges there was a confrontation with player-manager Brian Laws following Saturday's defeat at Luton which resulted in the former Italian international sustaining a fractured cheek-bone.

14 The much-loved Liverpool hero Bob Paisley, arguably the most successful British manager of all time, dies in a nursing home at the age of 77. Shocks for Premiership sides in 4th round Cup replays, as Grimsby thrash West Ham 3-0 and holders Everton are beaten and outplayed 2-1 at Port Vale, while Leeds win their rescheduled tie at Bolton 1-0. Dennis Bergkamp puts Arsenal 2-0 ahead in 32min of their Coca-Cola 1st leg semi at Highbury, but Dwight Yorke's double puts Villa level for the return. The inexperienced Kevin Cullis leaves the Swansea job after just 7 days, and Jimmy Rimmer is appointed for his second stint as caretaker. Norwich manager Gary Megson is fined £1,000 on a disrepute charge relating to an incident at Derby on New Year's Day.

15 Huddersfield striker Craig Whitington is charged by the FA with misconduct and suspended by his club after testing positive for cannabis for the second time in a year, the latest target test in a programme of clinical assessment.

16 The FA announce plans to double their drug-testing programme. Shropshire businessman Michael Thompson pulls out of his proposed takeover of Swansea after the fiasco of his managerial choice, and former chairman Doug Sharpe resumes control. FA of Ireland chief executive Sean Connolly is called to a meeting by the association's officers and leaves having resigned.

17 No shocks in the three Endsleigh v Premier 5th-round Cup ties played, but Wimbledon need an Ekoku double, one in the last minute, to earn a replay after going 2-0 down at Huddersfield and Southampton also get a late equaliser at Div 2 leaders Swindon, while Villa are comfortable 3-1 winners at Ipswich. In the Premiership, bottom club Bolton record their first away success of the season, slamming Middlesbrough 4-1, their 8th consecutive League defeat. In the lower echelons, Bury hit 7, Peterborough 6. The only surprise in the Scottish Cup is Div 3 Caledonian Thistle's 1-0 victory at Div 2 Stenhousemuir, winning them the right to entertain Rangers in the 5th round.

18 Man City make a fight of their 5th round Cup tie at Old Trafford, taking an early lead through Rosler, but Man Utd ride their luck as Cantona converts a disputed penalty and Sharpe scores a late winner. In a 4th-round tie, Liverpool cruise through 4-0 at Shrewsbury.

19 Forest's 5th-round home Cup tie with Spurs is abandoned after 15min when a blizzard hits the City Ground. Ian Branfoot becomes general manager of Fulham, player-coach Micky Adams taking over team affairs. Grade One referee Jim McGilvray, 47, submits his resignation to the Scottish FA after 11 years, claiming FIFA edicts on the laws have turned referees into robots. UEFA bow to the European Commission's ruling and agree to bring an immediate end to restrictions on European club "foreigners".

20 Coventry complete the transfers of Birmingham captain Liam Daish for £1.1m and Scottish international striker Eoin Jess from Aberdeen for £2m. Bottom Div 1 club Watford part company with manager Glenn Roeder 10 days after he signed a new 1-year contract.

21 Arsenal fail to break Villa down at Villa Park and a 0-0 draw after extra time puts Villa through on away goals to Wembley, where they will equal Liverpool's record of 7 League Cup final appearances; a pitch invasion at the end and pockets of brawling send shivers down the FA's spine as they entertain 150 foreign delegates in a Heathrow hotel for a Euro 96 workshop. In the FA Cup 5th round, Div 1 relegation-threatened Port Vale outplay another Premiership side, forcing Leeds to hold on for a 0-0 draw at Elland Road, the same score as in the other tie in which Chelsea are relieved stay alive at Grimsby. There is dramatic action in the Premiership, however, as Man Utd beat Everton 2-0 to move within 6pts of Newcastle, who lose 2-0 at West Ham but still have a game in hand. Former England manager Graham Taylor returns to Vicarage Road to take charge of struggling Watford.

22 Jan Molby, given a free transfer by Liverpool, is appointed Swansea player-manager, their 5th boss this season.

23 Blackburn agree to sell England midfielder David Batty to Premiership leaders Newcastle for £3.75m, taking Keegan's spending to £44m in 4 years, this latest buy, insurance against losing the Premiership race, completing his squad; Batty must serve a 2-match suspension. Villa sign England U-21 international Julian Joachim from Leicester for £1.5m. One of Millwall's on-loan Russians, Sergei Yuran, is arrested for failing to provide a breath test. Former West Germany coach Helmut Schön dies at 80.

24 Newcastle hit 3 equalisers at Maine Road, two from Albert and one from Asprilla, his first goal for the club, but a great match is spoilt by several clashes between Asprilla and City captain Keith Curle, especially an alleged head-butt by the tempestuous Colombian at the final whistle, and the FA will be studying video evidence. Newcastle now go 7pts clear of Man Utd with Liverpool, 3-2 winners at Blackburn, 2pts further back, the leading protagonists all having 11 games to play. Celtic's 4-0 defeat of Partick in the Scots Premier takes them level with gameless Rangers, who have a vastly better goal difference.

25　Man Utd sound a grim warning to Newcastle with an awesome 6-0 win at Bolton, their biggest away win since they beat Blackpool by the same score 36 years ago, and they are now only 4pts behind and on a roll. Leeds beat Birmingham 3-0 for a 5 1 aggregate victory in their Coca-Cola semi to reach Wembley for the first time in 23 years. Rangers regain their 3pt lead in Scotland with a 1-0 win at Aberdeen thanks to a Gascoigne penalty.

26　After studying video evidence, the FA charge both Asprilla and Curle with misconduct.

27　Leeds are through to the FA Cup 6th round thanks to a double from inspirational captain Gary McAllister, after Port Vale, who had dominated the game, had taken the lead.

28　Liverpool reach the last 8 of the Cup with a 2-1 win after Charlton put up a commendable show at Anfield, while Forest are held 2-2 at home by Spurs, Ian Woan topping and tailing Armstrong's double for Spurs with two brilliant free-kicks. Chelsea, Southampton and Wimbledon all have comfortable wins against lower-division teams in replays. Rangers sign Denmark striker Erik Bo Andersen from Aalborg for £1.5m.

March
Newcastle lose 100% home record to rivals ... Proper advantage law for next season ... Man U top Premiership ... Forest hammered 5-1 at home, out of Europe ... Villa win Coca-Cola Cup ... Cantona keeps scoring winners ... It's a Man U v Liverpool final

1　Arsenal and JVC renew their sponsorship for another 3 years, no financial details being disclosed. Leicester sign striker Steve Claridge from Birmingham for £1.2m.

2　Millwall's Sergei Yuran is in more trouble, sent off near the end of their home match with Wolves. Celtic's 4-0 win over Hearts puts them behind Rangers only on goal difference again, the two Glasgow giants standing 22pts above the rest.

3　Thanks to a loophole in the rules, David Batty is free to play for Newcastle in the crunch match against Man Utd tomorrow, having yesterday served half his two-match suspension with Blackburn, he cannot serve the rest with another club. Liverpool beat Villa 3-0, all scored in the first 8min, to keep themselves in the race, 2pts behind Man Utd. Rangers beat Hibs 2-0 at Easter Road where a spectator runs onto the pitch and attacks Rangers keeper Andy Goram.

4　Newcastle choose a bad time to lose their 100% 13-match home record, as a Cantona goal after 51min gives Man Utd a 1-0 win and takes them to within a point of the leaders but with a game fewer to play. Following last month's defeat in the Lords, the government climb down over listed TV sports and announce they will safeguard the BBC and ITV's right to show them. UEFA also climb down - over the new European Commission ruling - and promise that the transfer-fee system for end-of-contract players moving between EU countries will be scrapped.

5　Forest, the last British side in Europe, are beaten 2-1 in Germany by Bayern Munich, not a bad result in their UEFA Cup quarter-final 1st leg. Four out of five FA of Ireland honorary officers resign following allegations of financial mismanagement.

6　UEFA decide not to rush their plans for expanding the club competitions.

7　Adrian Heath is the new Burnley boss, only 10 weeks after leaving the playing staff to assist Howard Kendall at Sheff Utd. West Ham finally complete the Dumitrescu transfer from Spurs.

9　Forest beat Spurs on penalties, thanks to 3 Mark Crossley saves, after a 1-1 draw at White Hart Lane to reach the last 8 of the Cup, while Wimbledon hold Chelsea 2-2 in the quarter-finals. Ipswich provide a contender for comeback of the season with 3 goals in the last 6min to draw 3-3 at Barnsley in Div 1, while Sunderland end Derby's 21-match unbeaten run, their 3-0 win taking them to within 4pts of the leaders with 2 games in hand. Gascoigne scores another 2 in Rangers' 3-0 win at Caledonian to reach the Scottish Cup semis. FIFA, in the guise of the International Football Association Board, abandon the idea of enlarging the goals, but will continue to experiment with kick-ins instead of throw-ins. They finally empower the referee to play a true advantage law (awarding a free-kick if the offended-against side do not gain an advantage). And from next season linesmen will be known as "referee's assistants" (but not in this diary).

10　Leeds and Liverpool are goalless at Elland Road in their FA Cup 6th-round tie. Staring defeat in the face at Parkhead in Div 1 Dundee Utd in the Scottish Cup quarter-finals, Celtic produce goals in the 88th and 89th minutes to win 2-1. The FA of Ireland scandal continues as a vote of no confidence forces president Louis Kilcoyne to step down and officials who resigned last week are reinstated.

11　Cantona keeps Man Utd on course for another double with a goal and an assist as they beat Southampton 2-0 and become the first club to reach the FA Cup semis.

12　Legendary Arsenal goalscorer John Jensen goes back to Brondby on loan for the rest of the season.

13　Making his full début for Villa, Franz Carr scores the only goal of the game at the City Ground against his former club Forest to put Villa into the FA Cup semis and keep them on course for the Cup double. Liverpool suffer a severe blow to their Premiership ambitions, held 2-2 at Anfield by Wimbledon. Arsenal reject Ian Wright's transfer request. Sheff Wed agree a fee of £1.5m with Norwich for Jon Newsome, who began his career with them.

14　Wimbledon striker Mick Harford is charged with misconduct by the FA for his gesture to Chelsea fans at Saturday's Cup tie.

15　Beleaguered Norwich chairman Robert Chase sells another player to keep his bank manager happy, Ashley Ward going to Derby for £1m, and leaves manager Gary Megson fuming.

16　Man Utd go top of the Premiership for the first time since 23 Sep, but only just, as Cantona - again - grabs a last gasp equaliser against relegation-threatened QPR at Loftus Road to take them top on goal difference over Newcastle, who play Monday and have 2 games in hand. Liverpool's 2-0 defeat of Chelsea keeps them in the running, 2pts behind with no games in hand. Alan Shearer completes his 5th hat-trick of the season in injury time at White Hart Lane to give

Blackburn a 3-2 win over Spurs. Bottom club Bolton's 2-0 win at Coventry is their third away victory in succession, after 12 defeats and a draw on the road. Backs-to-the-wall Norwich win 3-0 at Reading in Div 1 to ease their relegation fears.

17 A late header from centre-half John Hughes gives Celtic a 1-1 draw in the crunch match at Ibrox despite finishing with 10 men and keeps them within striking distance of Rangers. Sunderland knock Derby off the top of the Endsleigh Div 1 with a 2-0 win at Birmingham, their 7th win on the trot.

18 A convincing 3-0 win over West Ham puts Newcastle back on top of the Premiership by 3pts.

19 England's last hope, Nottm Forest, go crashing out of the UEFA Cup, hammered 5-1 at home by Bayern Munich, Klinsmann scoring 2. Bordeaux produce the shock of the quarter-finals, reversing a 2-0 deficit to beat AC Milan 3-2 on aggregate.

20 Twenty matches unbeaten now, Liverpool win their quarter-final Cup replay at Anfield 3-0 as Leeds succumb to a second-half battering, while Chelsea join them after beating Wimbledon 3-1 in a thriller at Selhurst Park with two late goals. Man Utd have Cantona to thank again for their 1-0 win over Arsenal at Old Trafford, but it is not quite enough to restore them to the top of the table, Newcastle just shading them now on goal difference. Georgian Mikhail Kavelashvili has been granted a work permit to play for Man City, who have agreed a fee of £1.4m with Spartak Vladikavkaz.

21 Blackburn sign Man City midfielder Garry Flitcroft for £3.5m.

23 Man Utd go back on top without playing, as Newcastle crash 2-0 at Arsenal, while Liverpool miss a great chance to make up ground, losing 1-0 to out-of-sorts Forest. Bolton rise off bottom spot for the first time in nearly 4 months, beating Sheff Wed 2-1 to go above QPR and kindle faint hopes of survival. Top v bottom in Scotland produces a shaky 3-2 win for Rangers over Falkirk, but they go 5pts ahead of Celtic, held to a 0-0 draw at Motherwell.

24 There's only one team in the Coca-Cola Cup final, Aston Villa, who cruise through 3-0 against Leeds, demonstrating why manager Brian Little was given a lucrative 2-year extension on his contract yesterday. A somewhat lucky win at Old Trafford over Spurs puts Man Utd 3pts ahead of Newcastle, thanks to yet another goal from Eric Cantona (his 5th in 5 games), although Newcastle striker Les Ferdinand is voted PFA Player of the Year.

25 Grimsby player-manager Brian Laws is charged with misconduct relating to the dressing-room incident 6 weeks ago in which a thrown plate left Ivano Bonetti with a broken jaw.

27 England's performance in beating Bulgaria 1-0 at Wembley in the first round of Euro 96 preparation friendlies is more impressive than their new grey change strip, while their winger Darren Anderton plays his first competitive game since September, a 45min outing with Spurs reserves. Scotland, with 7 first-choice players missing through injury, beat Australia 1-0 at Hampden, McCoist scoring. In Dublin, Roy Keane, having taken over the Ireland captaincy when Andy Townsend was injured, kicks out at Russia's Omar Tetradze and then throws the ball at him after being dismissed - this 15sec from the end of Ireland's 2-0 defeat.

28 The only seven-figure deals on transfer-deadline day are Kavelashvili's expected signing for Man City and Blackburn's £1m purchase of Grimsby full-back Gary Croft.

29 Chairman Ken Bates announces Chelsea's multi-million pound listing on the Alternative Investment Market and confirms that his former sparring partner Matthew Harding, whose total commitment has now increased to £26.5m, is to become vice-chairman. Another club to go public are WBA.

30 Most of Saturday's Premiership action is in the relegation zone, except for Everton's 3-0 win at Ewood Park, where £3m signing Garry Flitcroft is red-carded only 3min into his Blackburn début. In Scotland, Rangers, 2-1 down at Raith with 7min to go, finish up 4-2 winners as McCoist completes a hat-trick and Durie adds one more. With Celtic inactive, Rangers now lead the Premier League by 8pts.

31 Semi-finals day of the Cup leaves a mouth-watering final, Man Utd v Liverpool, United taking advantage of defensive errors after Gullit had put Chelsea in front, to win a thriller 2-1 at Villa Park; 45min later, Liverpool take on Villa at Old Trafford and beat them 3-0, a travesty of a scoreline for the combative Midlanders, the 2 goals from Robbie Fowler taking his tally to 5 in their 3 defeats of Villa in League and Cup this season.

April
Anfield epic: Liverpool 4 Newcastle 3 ... Rangers end Celtic 30-match run in semi-final ... Man U discard grey strip at half-time ... Shearer makes goalscoring history ... Sunderland and Derby promoted to Premiership ... Cantona Footballer of the Year ... Rush leaves Anfield ... Bolton and QPR down ... 8th title on trot for Rangers ... Gascoigne Scotland's Footballer of the Year ... Keegan upset by Ferguson

1 An impressive 5-0 victory over Aberdeen takes Celtic back to within 5pts of Rangers.

3 In an epic, see-saw encounter at Anfield, Stan Collymore scores a last-minute goal to give Liverpool a 4-3 victory over Newcastle, who, suffering their 4th defeat in 6 matches, now find themselves 3pts behind Man Utd, with an inferior goal difference and now only one game in hand, while Liverpool retain an outside chance, 5pts behind the leaders. Chelsea striker Mark Hughes, booked 11 times this season, escapes with a 2-match suspension for reaching 45pts.

4 Newcastle and England central defender Steve Howey, who limped off during last night's match at Anfield, looks like being out for the rest of the season, a blow to both club and country.

5 Newcastle manager Kevin Keegan is commended by FIFA for his sporting attitude to defeat and is invited to share his philosophy in a future FIFA seminar.

6 Man Utd win a spirited derby at Maine Road 3-2 and Newcastle snatch a 2-1 victory over QPR at St James' thanks to 2 goals from a back-in-form Peter Beardsley, but Liverpool appear to have

blown their title chances with anticlimactic defeat 1-0 at Coventry. Hearts reach the final of the Scottish Cup, beating Aberdeen 2-1 at Hampden with a last-minute Alan Johnston strike, all the goals coming in the last 10min.

7 Rangers reach the Scottish Cup final with a 2-1 win at Hampden over Celtic, whose unbeaten 30-match domestic sequence comes to an end. Paul Ince, booked for applauding fans making racial taunts, scores his first goal in Italy's Serie A as his side Inter win 4-2 at Cremonese.

8 In a full Easter Monday Premiership programme, Man Utd put a 6pt barrier between themselves and Newcastle, thanks again to a Cantona goal as they make hard work of defeating Coventry at Old Trafford, while Newcastle have victory snatched from their grasp by former fan Graham Fenton, whose 2 goals in the last 5min gives Blackburn a 2-1 victory at Ewood Park.

10 Rangers lose their unbeaten away record, going down 2-0 at Hearts, but Celtic miss their chance at home to Kilmarnock, and only scrape a draw with a goal in the last 2min. Leeds chairman of 13 years Leslie Silver, 71, steps down from the board for health reasons.

11 The FA slap a 10-year ticket ban on Ireland manager Mick McCarthy for selling on two Cup final tickets last year which wound up on the black market.

12 Tranmere make John Aldridge player-manager, replacing John King, who has been offered a consultancy role. Huddersfield sack striker Craig Whitington, banned this week by the FA until November after twice testing positive for drugs.

13 Man Utd are stunned at The Dell, where they change their despised grey away strip when 3-0 down at half-time but still lose 3-1 to Southampton, who keep themselves just out of the relegation places. Coventry's 1-0 defeat of QPR virtually condemns the London side to the drop, but Man City's win keeps Coventry below the dreaded line. Mark Hughes scores 3 in Chelsea's 4-1 defeat of hapless Leeds, while Blackburn's 5-1 victory at Forest gives them a 12-1 aggregate over their two matches this season. In Scotland, recent signing from Aalborg Erik Bo Andersen hits 3 as Rangers beat Partick 5-0.

14 Thanks to a Ferdinand strike, Newcastle beat Villa 1-0 and take advantage of Man United's slip-up yesterday, moving 3pts behind with a game in hand. In Scotland, Celtic once more come back from behind to win 2-1, both goals by Van Hooijdonk.

17 It's tight at the top, both Man Utd and Newcastle scraping 1-0 home wins, Man U against Leeds, who have keeper Mark Beeney sent off early on, and the Magpies against Southampton. Alan Shearer makes history with the first of his 2 goals in Blackburn's 3-2 defeat of Wimbledon, becoming the first man to reach 30 goals in the top division in three consecutive seasons since Jimmy Dunne (Sheff Utd) in the 1930s, but tomorrow morning he has a groin op scheduled to get him fit in time for Euro 96. Duncan Ferguson, however, Scotland's chief striker, will miss Euro 96, withdrawn by Everton from the international squad because of a nagging groin injury.

20 On a rest weekend for the Premiership (midweek international), Endsleigh clubs who take the limelight are Sunderland, who win promotion to the top echelon despite not playing (manager Peter Reid is at Darlington and unaware of his triumph), and Swindon, whose draw at 2nd-placed Blackpool is enough to take them to Div 1 (manager Steve McMahon celebrates on the pitch with his team, but an altercation with Blackpool boss Sam Allardyce puts a dampener on the proceedings). There's no change at the top in Scotland as Rangers win 3-1 at Motherwell and Celtic beat Falkirk 4-0 to condemn them to the drop.

21 Eric Cantona's redemption is complete as he is voted Footballer of the Year by the Football Writers' Association, ahead of Ruud Gullit and Robbie Fowler.

23 Watford keep their faint hopes of Div 1 survival alive with a 6-3 win over Grimsby, David Connolly and Craig Ramage sharing the goals. Swindon clinch the Div 2 title with a 3-1 win at Chesterfield, but Brighton's 2-1 defeat at Notts Cty means 3rd Div football for them for the first time in 31 years.

24 England create chances but are held to a 0-0 draw in the Wembley friendly with Croatia. The other home countries and Ireland all lose friendlies, Scotland going down 2-0 in Denmark to goals by Michael Laudrup and his brother, Rangers star Brian.

25 The FA are concerned about the state of the Workers' Stadium pitch in Beijing and coach Terry Venables will fly there to inspect it. Bryan Robson signs a new contract with Middlesbrough that will keep him there until 1999, allaying fans' fears that he might take over the England job from Venables.

26 Galatasaray coach Graeme Souness is charged with ungentlemanly conduct by the Turkish FA for planting a club flag in the centre spot to celebrate Cup final victory over rivals Fenerbahce, and so allegedly inciting a riot.

27 The penultimate Saturday of the season sees Ian Rush wave a tearful goodbye to Anfield fans, as a second-half sub, and several issues settled. Bolton's 1-0 defeat at home to Southampton settles their fate, and QPR go down, too, despite beating West Ham. With Man City and Coventry both winning away as well as Southampton, Sheff Wed, who crash 5-2 at home to Everton (Kanchelskis 3), find themselves only 2pts ahead of the three relegation candidates with one game to play. Sunderland clinch the Div 1 title despite being held 0-0 at Roker Park by West Brom. Luton, beaten 3-1 at home by Barnsley, go down, but Watford's 2-1 win at Norwich earns them a stay of execution. There's trouble at Brighton, already relegated from Div 2, as fans riot and invade the pitch to demonstrate at the sale of the Goldstone Ground, and their match with York has to be abandoned after 15min at 0-0. Notts County's 4-0 defeat of Swansea consign the Welsh club to Div 3. Preston and Gillingham clinch promotion from Div 3, the former as champions. In Scotland, Celtic's 4-2 win at Partick keeps their title hopes alive, at least until tomorrow.

28 Man Utd are almost there, a 5-0 victory over Forest in front of nearly 54,000 fans at Old Trafford leaves Newcastle trailing by 6pts and a 7-goal differential, with games running out. Over the border, Rangers clinch their 8th successive title with a 3-1 win over Aberdeen, and Paul Gascoigne

crowns a brilliant first season in Glasgow with a hat-trick after being named Footballer of the Year by his fellow players. Derby beat Palace 2-1 to clinch the second automatic promotion place from Endsleigh's Div 1.

29 Newcastle win at Leeds, their third 1-0 victory on the trot, to stay in the title race. After the match, their manager Kevin Keegan makes some emotional comments on Sky TV criticising Alex Ferguson for his blatant gamesmanship in stirring up the Leeds side 12 days ago.

30 Newcastle's Asprilla, involved in incidents with Man City's Keith Curle (who is cleared) in February, receives a record £10,000 fine for misconduct, but his 1-match suspension will not take effect until next season. Gascoigne is honoured again, as the Scottish Football Writers' Association Player of the Year. Reading and Oldham win to secure their places in Div 1. York fail to clinch survival in Div 2, losing 1-0 at home to Chesterfield. Brighton will stay at the Goldstone Ground for another season, renting it from the developers.

May
Hoddle new England coach ... Man U pip Newcastle for title ... Arsenal win Europe place ... Man City down, Ball's big blunder ... Trevor Phillips resigns from FA ... Birmingham sack Barry Fry ... Peter Reid Manager of the Year ... Gullit new Chelsea boss, signs Vialli ... Man United first ever double Double ... Rangers' 13th Double, slam Hearts 5-1 in Cup final ... Juventus new European champions ... Leicester promoted ... England players accused of damage on flight home ... new Ireland skipper Keane loses captaincy before he starts ... Nationwide new Football League sponsors ... Japan and S. Korea to share 2002 World Cup

1 With the appointment of Glenn Hoddle as new England coach imminent, Chelsea big guns, Ken Bates and Matthew Harding, make a last-ditch effort to keep their manager, the former by persuasion, the latter by castigating the FA for "violating their own rules" with the stealth of their approach. Former Villa and England forward Eric Houghton dies at 85.

2 Hoddle accepts the England job: he will leave Chelsea after their last match on Sunday; his England contract begins on 1 June, but he will not take over from Venables until after Euro 96. The only consolation for Chelsea fans is Ruud Gullit's assertion that he will not leave. Newcastle's 1-1 draw at Forest leaves Man Utd needing only a draw at Middlesbrough on Sunday to clinch the title even if the Magpies win their last game. Darren Anderton's form after his 7-month absence bodes well for his England return, his 2 goals at Elland Road helping Spurs to 3-1 victory over Leeds, who suffer their 6th defeat on the trot, their worst losing sequence since 1947. Former Man City chairman Peter Swales dies of a heart attack at 62. Norwich chairman of 10 years, Robert Chase, resigns from the board and sells his share holding to club president and former chairman Geoffrey Watling, 83. Turkish Cup-winners Galatasaray sack manager Graeme Souness after a year for not winning the league. Matthew Simmons, 21-y-o Palace supporter, is found guilty of provoking the notorious attack by Eric Cantona at Selhurst Park last year and is fined £500 and banned from all football grounds for 12 months, and is jailed for a week for jumping a bench in court to attack a prosecuting solicitor before sentence could be pronounced!

4 Oxford make sure of promotion to Div 1 with a 4-0 win over Peterborough, leaving rivals Blackpool in the play-offs. Bradford clinch a play-off place with a 3-2 victory at bottom club Hull, where there are disturbances inside and outside the ground as well as a sit-in by disgruntled Hull fans. York, defeated 2-0 at home by Blackpool, find themselves in an intriguing if controversial position, the only fixture left in Div 2 being their rearranged match at Brighton: they know exactly what they have to do to leapfrog over Carlisle to safety. Gillingham ensure the 2nd promotion place in Div 3 with a 1-0 win over Scarborough, while Bury snatch the 3rd by beating Cardiff 3-0, and Darlington, held 3-3 at Scunthorpe, miss out on automatic promotion. Dunfermline clinch the only automatic promotion place from Scottish Div 1, leaving Dundee Utd to play off.

5 Man Utd make no mistake at Middlesbrough on the final day, a 3-0 victory, their 10th away from home, giving them the Premiership title. Newcastle finish 4pts behind after failing to win at St James' for only the second time this season (their first, defeat by Man Utd, turning out to make all the difference), and struggling to take the point from Spurs in a 1-1 draw. Arsenal, needing a win at Highbury over bottom club Bolton to clinch the last UEFA Cup place, go a goal down with 15min left, but goals by summer signings Platt and Bergkamp in the last 8min will help pay off their transfer fees. It's not all good news for Manchester, City going down to Div 1 after coming back from a 2-0 half-time deficit at Maine Road to draw with an uninterested Liverpool: Alan Ball's instructions late in the game to his side to keep possession, because he had "heard a rumour" that one of the other sides in trouble was losing, must go down as the blunder of the season, as both Coventry and Southampton achieve safety with 0-0 home draws. In Div 1, Portsmouth win 1-0 at Huddersfield to save themselves from relegation at the expense of Millwall, whose 0-0 draw at Ipswich also prevents the home side from reaching the play-offs as Leicester do by winning 1-0 at Watford, who now go down.

7 The FA's commercial director Trevor Phillips suddenly resigns, with no one willing to elucidate. Birmingham sack colourful manager Barry Fry. Sunderland's Peter Reid is named League Managers' Association Manager of the Year.

8 Terry Venables announces his squad for the upcoming friendly with Hungary from Beijing, where he appears to be overseeing the work of the national stadium's groundsman, and the good news is that Adams, Anderton and Shearer are all named and presumably close to fitness again. Paris St-Germain win the Cup-Winners Cup, beating Rapid Vienna 1-0 in Brussels, where some 400 fans attack police in the city's central square, about 60 being arrested.

9 It emerges that Trevor Phillips had his own ticket line for the European Championships, involving the possible legitimate distribution of 50,000 tickets, the existence of which was unknown to Euro '96, the FA unit responsible for running the tournament. It was this 'misunderstanding'

within the FA that led to recent police raids on the National Sporting club and other agencies legitimately buying blocks of tickets for hospitality packages, and to some embarrassing arrests in this connection. QPR director Richard Thompson resigns, and the club is up for sale. York win their rescheduled match at Brighton to send Carlisle down to Div 3. Celtic midfielder Paul McStay needs an op and is out of Scotland's Euro 96 squad. Vauxhall Conference champions Stevenage issue a High Court writ against the Football League and Div 3 bottom club Torquay, a last-ditch attempt to win the promotion denied them because their ground did not measure up to requirements by the specified date.

10   Ruud Gullit takes over as player-coach at Chelsea, and Trevor Francis is confirmed as new manager at Birmingham. The transfer of Bolton defender-cum-midfielder Alan Stubbs to Celtic for £3.5m is being investigated by the FA and Scottish FA because his agents are allegedly not registered. Former FA commercial director Trevor Phillips denies he had authorised any companies to resell Euro 96 tickets other than Keith Prowse and Sportsworld, and insists that he told the three companies raided by the police to apply to the official ticket agents, Synchro Systems.

11   Man Utd beat Liverpool 1-0 in the Cup final to bring off an unprecedented double 'Double", and appropriately it's captain Cantona who scores the spectacular winner, although it's a disappointing game.

13   QPR midfielder Ian Holloway returns to Bristol Rovers as player-manager.

14   Bryan Robson signs his third Brazilian at Middlesbrough, 24-y-o midfielder Emerson, for £4m from Portuguese champions Porto.

15   Bayern Munich, with a 2-0 advantage from their home leg, win 3-1 at Bordeaux to take the UEFA Cup. In Endsleigh League play-off 2nd legs, Bradford make a remarkable recovery at Blackpool, winning 3-2 on aggregate after losing 2-0 at home.

16   Alex Ferguson signs a new 4-year contract to stay at Man Utd. Bruce Grobbelaar, 38, has been released by Southampton. In a written parliamentary answer, sports minister Iain Sproat states that over 100,000 Euro 96 tickets might have been improperly allocated. Dundee Utd earn promotion to the Scottish Premier with a goal by Owen Coyle in the 115th minute of their 2nd leg play-off with Premier club Partick, after a 90th-minute strike by Brian Welsh had forced extra time.

17   Liverpool win the FA Youth Cup, beating West Ham 2-1 in the 2nd leg of the final after their 2-0 victory at Upton Park.

18   With Gordon Durie notching the first hat-trick in a Scottish Cup final for 24 years - all by courtesy of Brian Laudrup - Rangers beat Hearts 5-1 to chalk up their 13th League and Cup double. England beat Hungary 3-0 in their friendly at Wembley, with 2 goals from comeback man Darren Anderton, but an injury to defender Mark Wright is another worry for Venables.

19   Llansantffraid-ym-Mechain (pop.954) will have a team in Europe next season after beating Barry Town 3-2 on penalties (3-3 aet) in the Welsh Cup final at Cardiff's National Stadium: they would have qualified anyway, as Barry are Welsh League champions.

20   With Mark Wright definitely out of Euro 96, Venables takes Newcastle's Steve Howey with England's squad to the Far East. Ian Rush, given a free transfer by Liverpool, joins Leeds.

21   Former England manager Bobby Robson, 63, released by Porto after steering them to League success for the last two seasons, takes over at Barcelona from Johan Cruyff, who is still engaged in a slanging match with club president Jose Luis Nuñez at the airport as Robson arrives.

22   Juventus beat holders Ajax 4-2 on penalties after a 1-1 draw in Rome to win the European Cup. Man Utd give captain Steve Bruce, 35, a free transfer to Birmingham, whom he will also skipper and earn around £1m in two years. Graeme Souness accepts substantial undisclosed damages from *The Mail on Sunday* newspaper in the High Court for allegations that he had taken bribes over transfers while manager of Liverpool.

23   Nick Barmby stakes his claim for a place in England's squad with 2 goals in their 3-0 win over China in Beijing, while the impressive Gascoigne scores the other. UEFA finally accept the Bosman ruling, scrapping all restrictions on foreign players in club competitions. S.African striker Phil Masinga, who played only 11 times for Leeds during the season, is refused a work permit and may have to leave the club. With Andy Townsend opting out of Ireland's American tour next month, manager Mike McCarthy has handed the captaincy to Roy Keane.

24   Juventus captain Gianluca Vialli, 31, who cost them £12m in 1992 but is now a free agent, is Ruud Gullit's first signing for Chelsea, at an estimated £1-1.4m a year on a 3-year contract.

25   West Ham agree a 2-year contract said to be worth £1m a year with AC Milan's former Portuguese international Paolo Futre, 30, who for injuries and other reasons played less than a full match for the Italian club during the season. A record 43,431 for a Div 3 play-off, some 30,000 from Devon, see Plymouth beat Darlington 1-0, both teams at Wembley for the first time, but not Argyle manager Neil Warnock, whose 4th trip, and 4th success, this was.

26   Pre-Euro 96 tour matches for the home countries prove far from confidence-boosters as an England XI's struggle to beat a Hong Kong XI 1-0 is matched by Scotland's first defeat in the USA, 2-1 at New Britain, Conn. Bradford beat Notts Cty 2-0 in the Div 2 play-off final at Wembley.

27   As England jet home from their Far East tour, the players know the names of the 5 not selected for Euro 96, but the media know only that Peter Beardsley, 35, is one of them. Leicester come from behind to win a dramatic Div 1 play-off at Wembley, beating Palace 2-1 with a goal from Steve Claridge in the last 2 seconds of extra time. Roy Keane goes missing two days before Ireland start a week of internationals.

28   The England squad hit the headlines for all the wrong reasons, as reports of vandalism inside the Cathay Pacific 747 taking them home begin to emerge. The unlucky last four to be left out of the squad are Robert Lee, Jason Wilcox, Ugo Ehiogu and Dennis Wise. Roy Keane is stripped of his

newly won Ireland captaincy after going on holiday without telling manager Mick McCarthy, and is effectively banned from their next 6 internationals.

29 Allegations by Cathay Pacific that England players caused £5,000 worth of damage to their plane, including smashing two TV screens, have stirred MPs of all parties to demand stringent measures be taken. In home internationals, Ireland lose 1-0 to Portugal, but N.Ireland hold Germany 1-1 as Klinsmann misses a penalty. Blackpool sack manager Sam Allardyce and appoint Vicki Oyston chairman in place of her husband Owen, who is serving 6 years for rape.

30 The tabloids have a field day as it emerges that England's antics on the plane home were allegedly a continuation of a drinking party in Hong Kong to celebrate Paul Gascoigne's 29th birthday. Tales of drunkenness impute several players, and Gascoigne is depicted as lying back in a dentist's chair in a nightclub while a waiter poured tequila into his mouth. On the field, Newcastle's Asprilla gives Colombia a 1-0 victory over Scotland at Miami Beach. Nationwide take over sponsorship of the Football League from Endsleigh with a 3-year deal worth £5.25m.

31 At a FIFA meeting in Zurich, Japan and S.Korea agree to share the 2002 World Cup, after a humiliating climb-down by FIFA president João Havelange, whose patronage of the Japanese bid was of 'over my dead body' proportions. Celtic sign AC Milan winger Paulo Di Canio on a 4-year contract worth over £3m. Man Utd rescue non-League Bishop Auckland from ruin as a result of a £30,000 litigation award to an injured visiting player - thus repaying them for their generous loan of players in 1958 after the Munich air disaster.

June 96
England squad accept collective responsibility for Jumbo damage . . . Premier League agree £743m TV deal . . . Euro 96 opens

1 Terry Venables, in Switzerland to cast an eye on England's first Euro 96 opponents, who lose 2-1 to Czech Rep, promises swift action will be taken against any player found guilty of causing trouble on the flight back from Hong Kong, although he warns against making Gascoigne a scapegoat. France inflict Germany's first defeat in 13 matches, winning 1-0 in Stuttgart to take their own unbeaten run to 22.

2 Wales make an impressive start to their World Cup campaign with a 5-0 win in San Marino. Ireland hold Croatia 2-2 in a friendly at Lansdowne Road.

3 The England squad close ranks over the Cathay Pacific affair, no one admitting to causing any damage and all accepting collective responsibility. Former Arsenal centre-forward Cliff Holton, 67, dies while on holiday in Spain. Controversial compensation of £1.2m is awarded to 14 police officers for psychological trauma endured at the Hillsborough disaster in 1989.

4 Venables describes reports of players' misbehaviour on their flight home as "grossly exaggerated", although the collective responsibility aspect is already wearing thin as Liverpool's McManaman and Fowler have both taken steps to deny press reports naming them as culprits. Holland beat Ireland 3-1 in a friendly, while Germany warm up with 9 goals against Liechtenstein.

6 The Premier League agree a new 4-year contract with Sky for £670m plus £73m from the BBC for recorded highlights. UEFA issue a directive aimed at stamping out illegal tackles and time-wasting in Euro 96, and fine Spain and Italy for withdrawing teams from the Inter-Toto Cup. Div 1 champions Sunderland give manager Peter Reid a new 3-year contract.

8 Euro 96 opens in splendid festival atmosphere at Wembley, and Alan Shearer ends his international goal drought to give England the lead in their opening match, but a disputed penalty allows the Swiss to equalise as England fade in the second half.

9 Germany beat the Czech Republic 2-0 at Old Trafford, the only win in the 4 matches played so far.

10 Scotland earn a brave if lucky 0-0 draw with Holland at Villa Park. UEFA president Lennart Johansson backs the referees as a controversy flares at the flurry of red and yellow cards in the first 3 days of Euro 96.

11 Again, while training at Bisham Abbey, Venables has to defend his players against tabloid allegations of drinking at a nightclub after their draw with Switzerland, and there is further bad news when Steve Howey damages ankle ligaments on a training run and is out of the competition, another centre-half biting the dust for Venables. A Casiraghi double gets Italy off to a good start with a 2-1 victory over Russia at Anfield.

12 It's Venables' assistant Bryan Robson's turn to defend the England players against boozing allegations, criticising the tabloids for making mountains out of innocent molehills.

NORMAN BARRETT

LEAGUE REVIEW

Manchester United overhauled Newcastle in the race for the FA Carling Premiership, even though their north-east rivals held an apparently unassailable lead of 12 points over them in January.

Significantly, United completed the double over Newcastle, the second success on 4 March enabling them to establish a psychological advantage, which was only threatened by a bizarre first-half performance at Southampton. This was United's sole defeat among the last 16 games.

Newcastle faltered from February, picking up only four points out of a possible 18. This disastrous period ended in a 4-3 defeat at Liverpool, a match which was justifiably considered to be a contender for the game of the century.

A goal down in two minutes, Newcastle led 2-1 after 14, and edged ahead 3-2 in the second half just a couple of minutes after Liverpool's equalizer. Liverpool levelled again in the 68th minute and snatched a dramatic injury time winner to the chagrin of the visitors.

Ironically, any outside hopes Liverpool were entertaining of catching the top two evaporated three days later when they lost 1-0 at Coventry. There was not even the consolation of the FA Cup as they were beaten 1-0 by Manchester United in arguably one of the poorest finals on record.

There was cup success for enterprising Aston Villa who beat Leeds 3-0 in the Coca-Cola Final and as comfortably as the scoreline suggested. Their season tailed off somewhat afterwards and their fourth place was almost eroded as Arsenal nearly caught them on the last day.

Arsenal still finished disappointingly having lost only one of their first ten matches but Everton showed marked improvement to finish sixth.

Blackburn, the champions, never recovered from a poor start and failed to make any impression in Europe. Alan Shearer did contribute his usual quota of thirty-plus goals, but even this was not enough. Tottenham reached as high as third place in January shortly after a convincing 4-1 win over Manchester United but were unable to sustain this effort and Nottingham Forest after establishing a Premier League record of 25 unbeaten matches, crashed 7-0 at Blackburn in the next match. However, they did reach further than any other English club in Europe during the season.

Manchester United players celebrate after winning the FA Carling Premiership title.

Steve Bruce (Manchester United) shrugs off a challenge from Newcastle United's David Ginola during the crucial match between the two title contestants in March. Manchester United won 1–0. (Colorsport).

West Ham's results did not always reflect their useful performances and like Chelsea often had problems in the scoring line.

Middlesbrough's run of five successive wins to October promised an exciting season, but the Christmas period saw them go 13 games without a win as injuries contributed to their slide down the table. Leeds started well enough but won only three League games in the second half of the season. Wimbledon's traditional ability to extricate themselves from danger was again in evidence.

A season lacking in sparkle for Sheffield Wednesday brought them into the relegation bracket on the last day of the season, but they escaped along with ever-surviving Coventry and Southampton. Earlier, the Saints had somehow contrived to beat both Manchester United and Newcastle. However, they and Coventry only finished above relegated Manchester City on the number of goals scored as the drama enfolded on the last day. Manchester City merely managed to score 33 all season.

Despite brief flurries from both Queens Park Rangers and Bolton, they too, found themselves relegated.

The last champions of the Endsleigh Insurance First Division proved to be Sunderland, who lost only one of their last 19 games and that when they had already secured promotion. They were joined in automatic promotion by Derby County who recovered from a poor start which had seen them as low as 17th in November. In the play-offs, Leicester emerged successfully after winning their last four League games. Crystal Palace were disappointed not to have clinched a place in the Premier League, but were edged into third place after losing their last two League games.

Stoke were another club who began badly though they did make the play-offs. But any hopes that Charlton had beyond that stage ended with only one win in the last nine. Ipswich were denied a play-off place by drawing goalless in the last game despite finishing the season as leading scorers.

Huddersfield, too, had a poor spell in March picking up only one point in five matches, but Sheffield United hauled themselves off the bottom in January with the arrival of new manager Howard Kendall. Barnsley tailed off after a promising first ten games and West Bromwich still finished in mid-table despite a mid-season run in which they took one point from 14 matches.

Port Vale, who had looked relegation contenders in March improved noticeably, but Tranmere – who were briefly top in August – were inconsistent. Southend were as high as fourth in February, but won only three more games and a run of eight matches without a win ruined Birmingham's hopes of the play-offs, as did a similar spell for Norwich.

Fourteen games without a win mid-season threatened to head Grimsby towards relegation and only a revival from April saved Oldham. Reading were late escapers themselves and Wolves had a see-saw season as high as 11th and as low as 22nd.

Portsmouth avoided the drop with a 1-0 win at Huddersfield on the last day of the season, but Millwall plunged alarmingly from being top in December to finishing third from bottom.

Watford did revive when Graham Taylor returned to the club, but it was too late and apart from leapfrogging neighbours Luton, the pair were relegated.

Swindon were never out of the second division top two all season, did not suffer two defeats in succession and fought off the challenge of Blackpool, who slipped disastrously in April and surrendered automatic promotion to Oxford, winners of six of their last seven matches.

Bradford, who finished sixth, emerged successfully from the play-offs, yet Notts County, who appeared more consistent and Crewe, top for a spell in mid-season, both failed in similar attempts.

Chesterfield scored only eight goals in their last dozen games to miss the play-offs by a point and Wrexham's unimpressive start proved costly as did a mid-season slump by Stockport.

Bristol Rovers several times lost twice in a row and Walsall came to life only in mid-April. Wycombe looked a mid-table team for much of the second half of the season as did Bristol City and Bournemouth, who sufficiently improved after seven games without a win to mid-March.

Savo Milosevic fires in Aston Villa's first goal on the way to a comprehensive 3–0 Coca-Cola Cup Final triumph over Leeds United. (Action Images).

Mick Heathcote and Mark Patterson of Plymouth Argyle (dark shirts) dispute possession with Anthony Carss of Darlington during the Third Division play-off final at Wembley. Argyle won 1–0. (Action Images).

Brentford also revealed a second-half improvement but Rotherham, the Auto Windscreens Shield winners, needed a better April to pull themselves out of trouble.

Burnley won only three of their last fifteen, Shrewsbury just two of their last 22 and Peterborough one of the last twelve.

York had to win at Brighton to avoid relegation, a result which sent Carlisle down after they had hovered in dire straits for most of the season. Swansea were rarely out of the bottom four after Christmas and were relegated with Brighton, second from the bottom most of that time and Hull, who appeared doomed since October.

In division three, Preston established themselves in first place by the end of March and Gillingham's defence, which conceded only 20 goals, helped considerably towards their promotion along with Bury, who looked a better outfit from late October.

They were joined from the play-offs by a Plymouth side who had lost their opening four games.

Darlington missed out from the play-offs despite remaining unbeaten in their last 11 outings as did Hereford with eight wins in their last ten and Colchester, who were as high as fourth in January.

Chester, top at the turn of the year, slipped back and Barnet's improvement was too late.

Wigan drifted out of it in April while Northampton were mid-table from the halfway stage and Scunthorpe's revival after nine games without a win, only took them to 12th.

Doncaster won only two of their last 11, Exeter rarely moved far from mid-table, but Rochdale performed really poorly in the second half of the season.

Cambridge had a spell of 11 games without a win, Fulham an earlier 14 and Lincoln one fewer from early August.

Mansfield drew 20 times and Hartlepool's victories were few and spaced out. Leyton Orient were still third in September but Cardiff won only one of their last 12, Scarborough one of their last sixteen.

Torquay were bottom from November, but were spared demotion by Stevenage not meeting the required ground criteria.

The FOOTBALL TRUST
Helping the game

The Football Trust handed out more than £11 million to 14 English and Scottish League clubs with Sunderland the top beneficiaries and they fittingly gained promotion to the Premier League.

The Trust, founded in 1975 by pools promoters Littlewoods, Vernons and Zetters, gave £2.5 million towards the £12 million cost of the Wearsiders' new stadium.

Sunderland received the biggest grant but at the other end of the country Portsmouth picked up £2 million for their building work on stands at the east and west ends of Fratton Park which cost a total of £2.7 million. Other clubs in the millionaire reception bracket were Barnsley, Carlisle and Raith Rovers. All spent the money on renovation and replacement of stands for the safety and facility of spectators.

The Trusts hand-outs are not confined to League clubs in England and Scotland. It helps soccer at all levels and provides playing strips and equipment for boys' and girls' teams, grants to better the safety and comfort of supporters through family enclosures, new toilets and better access for the disabled.

Grants also go towards curbing hooligans by providing closed circuit television equipment, extra stewarding and better transport facilities.

All genuine supporters of football will applaud the efforts of the Trust to make the game better and safer through their generous award of £138 million since 1990.

TREVOR WILLIAMSON

Major Project Grants Season 1995–96

	£s Project cost	£s Trust Grant	Major project
Barnsley	2,400,000	1,000,000	South Stand
Brentford	95,000	71,250	South Stand Paddock seating
Bristol City	311,717	192,369	Dolman Stand
Caledonian Thistle	3,500,000	500,000	New Stadium
Crewe Alexandra	797,042	581,913	West & East Stands
Carlisle United	2,138,000	1,000,000	East Stand
Hartlepool United	370,000	185,000	South Stand
	11,790	6,000	South Stand
Portsmouth	2,700,000	2,000,000	East & West Stands
Peterborough United	1,400,000	918,307	Glebe Road Stand
Raith Rovers	2,200,000	1,500,000	North & South Stands
Rochdale	1,048,013	350,000	Pearl Street Stand
Stockport County	54,000	40,000	Hardcastle Road Stand
Stenhousemuir	450,823	268,500	South Stand
Sunderland	12,000,000	2,500,000	New Stadium

INTRODUCTION TO THE CLUB SECTION

For this year's Rothmans Football Yearbook there is a further change in the way in which players in the 92 League clubs are presented. The players appear under the club with whom they finished the season and in an A–Z form for easy reference (see pages 402–528). The names of Trainees and Associated Schoolboys are also included under each club's name.

The club section again comprises four pages, the first features the team photograph depicting those players and officials taken at the commencement of the 1995–96 season. On the second page which gives historical and record details for each club there are new entries in the 'Did you know?' series. Record Transfer fees are usually left to the discretion of the club concerned.

The third and fourth pages of this section present a complete record of the League season, including date, venue, opponents, results, half-time score, League position, goalscorers, attendances and complete line-ups including substitutes where used, for every League game in the 1995–96 season.

Squad numbers in the Premier League have been ignored; those used are the familiar ones, 1–11 while the introduction of a third outfield substitute has been recognised as follows:- the first substitute No. 12, the second No. 13 and the third No. 14. However, if there is a substitute goalkeeper he is represented by No. 15 but *only* if he replaces the first choice goalkeeper. Otherwise he adopts one of the other three substitute numbers, as there have been several instances where a goalkeeper has been used as an outfield player because of injuries during the game. Players replaced are respectively noted with superior figures [1], [2], [3] and [g] for goalkeeper. These third and fourth pages also include consolidated lists of goalscorers for the club in League, Coca-Cola Cup and FA Cup matches plus a summary of results in these two main domestic competitions.

The continued increase in the number of matches played on Sundays has resulted in the League positions shown after every League result being taken on that day. Full holiday programmes are also recorded, but the position after mid-week fixtures will not normally have been updated. Attendance figures quoted for the Endsleigh Insurance League are those which appeared in the Press at the time. But those in the FA Carling Premiership are official. The attendance statistics published on pages 569–571 are those officially issued by the FA Premier League and the Football League at the end of the season.

In the totals at the top of each column on page 4, substitute appearances are listed separately by the '+', but have been amalgamated in the totals which feature in the players historical section in the directory mentioned above. Thus these appearances include those as substitute. In fact the directory again features those names appearing on the FA Premier League and Football League's Retained list, which is published at the end of May. Each player's height and weight where known, plus birth place, birth date and source together with total League goals and appearances for each club he has represented, can be found as in previous editions. The player's details remain under the club which retained him at the end of the season. An asterisk '*' by a player's name indicates that he was given a free transfer at the end of the 1995–96 season, a dagger '†' against a name means that he is a non-contract player, a double dagger '‡' indicates that the player's registration was cancelled during the season and a section mark '§' shows the player to be a trainee or associated schoolboy who has made League appearances. Appearances by players in the play-offs are not included in their career totals.

There is also a directory of all League club managers to be found on pages 532–541.

ARSENAL 1995-96 *Back row (left to right):* Gary Lewin (Physio), Scott Marshall, Paul Merson, Lee Harper, Steve Bould, Andy Linighan, David Seaman, Steve Morrow, Nigel Winterburn, Vince Bartram, Ray Parlour, John Hartson, Stewart Houston (Coach), George Armstrong (Reserve Team Coach).
Front row: Chris Kiwomya, Paul Dickov, Eddie McGoldrick, Lee Dixon, John Jensen, Ian Wright, Tony Adams, Bruce Rioch, (Manager) Dennis Bergkamp, Glenn Helder, David Platt, Mark Flatts, David Hillier, Martin Keown, Ian Selley.
(Photograph: Kenneth Prater Photography)

FA Premiership ARSENAL

Arsenal Stadium, Highbury, London N5 1BU. Telephone: (0171) 704 4000. Fax: (0171) 704 4001. Box Office: (0171) 413 3366. Commercial and Marketing: (0171) 704 4100. Recorded information on (0171) 704 4242. Clubline: 0891 202021..

Ground capacity: 38,500 all seated.

Record attendance: 73,295 v Sunderland, Div 1, 9 March 1935.

Record receipts: £392,726.50 v Sampdoria, European Cup-Winners' Cup, semi-final first leg, 6 April 1995.

Pitch measurements: 110yd × 73yd.

Chairman: P. D. Hill-Wood. *Vice-Chairman:* D. Dein.

Directors: Sir Robert Bellinger CBE, DSC, R. G. Gibbs, C. E. B. L. Carr, R. C. L. Carr, D. D. Fiszman.

Managing Director: K. J. Friar.

Manager: Bruce Rioch. *Assistant Manager/Coach:* Stewart Houston/Pat Rice.

Physio: Gary Lewin. *Reserve Coach:* George Armstrong. *Youth Coach:* Pat Rice.

Secretary: K. J. Friar. *Assistant Secretary:* David Miles. *Commercial Manager:* John Hazell. *Marketing Manager:* Phil Carling. *Stadium Manager:* J. Beattie.

Year Formed: 1886. *Turned Professional:* 1891. *Ltd Co.:* 1893.

Previous Names: 1886, Dial Square; 1886–91, Royal Arsenal; 1891–1914, Woolwich Arsenal.

Club Nickname: 'Gunners'.

Previous Grounds: 1886–87, Plumstead Common; 1887–88, Sportsman Ground; 1888–90, Manor Ground; 1890–93, Invicta Ground; 1893–1913, Manor Ground; 1913, Highbury.

Foundation: Formed by workers at the Royal Arsenal, Woolwich in 1886 they began as Dial Square (name of one of the workshops) and included two former Nottingham Forest players Fred Beardsley and Morris Bates. Beardsley wrote to his old club seeking help and they provided the new club with a full set of red jerseys and a ball. The club became known as the "Woolwich Reds" although their official title soon after formation was Woolwich Arsenal.

First Football League game: 2 September 1893, Division 2, v Newcastle U (h) D 2-2 – Williams; Powell, Jeffrey; Devine, Buist, Howat; Gemmell, Henderson, Shaw (1), Elliott (1), Booth.

Record League Victory: 12–0 v Loughborough T, Division 2, 12 March 1900 – Orr; McNichol, Jackson; Moir, Dick (2), Anderson (1); Hunt, Cottrell (2), Main (2), Gaudie (3), Tennant (2).

Record Cup Victory: 11–1 v Darwen, FA Cup 3rd rd, 9 January 1932 – Moss; Parker, Hapgood; Jones, Roberts, John; Hulme (2), Jack (3), Lambert (2), James, Bastin (4).

Record Defeat: 0–8 v Loughborough T, Division 2, 12 December 1896.

Most League Points (2 for a win): 66, Division 1, 1930–31.

Most League Points (3 for a win): 83, Division 1, 1990–91.

Most League Goals: 127, Division 1, 1930–31.

Highest League Scorer in Season: Ted Drake, 42, 1934–35.

Most League Goals in Total Aggregate: Cliff Bastin, 150, 1930–47.

Most Capped Player: Kenny Sansom, 77 (86), England.

Most League Appearances: David O'Leary, 558, 1975–93.

Record Transfer Fee Received: £2,800,000 from Nottingham F for Kevin Campbell, July 1995.

Record Transfer Fee Paid: £7,500,000 to Internazionale for Dennis Bergkamp, June 1995.

Football League Record: 1893 Elected to Division 2; 1904–13 Division 1; 1913–19 Division 2; 1919–92 Division 1; 1992– FA Premier League.

Honours: Football League: Division 1 – Champions 1930–31, 1932–33, 1933–34, 1934–35, 1937–38, 1947–48, 1952–53, 1970–71, 1988–89, 1990–91; Runners-up 1925–26, 1931–32, 1972–73; Division 2 – Runners-up 1903–04. *FA Cup:* Winners 1930, 1936, 1950, 1971, 1979, 1993; Runners-up 1927, 1932, 1952, 1972, 1978, 1980. *Double performed:* 1970–71. *Football League Cup:* Winners 1987, 1993; Runners-up 1968, 1969, 1988. *European Competitions: Fairs Cup:* 1963–64, 1969–70 (winners), 1970–71; *European Cup:* 1971–72, 1991–92; *UEFA Cup:* 1978–79, 1981–82, 1982–83; *European Cup-Winners' Cup:* 1979–80 (runners-up), 1993–94 (winners), 1994–95 (runners-up).

Colours: Red shirts with white sleeves, white shorts, red and white hooped stockings. *Change colours:* Navy shirts with teal sleeves, navy shorts, navy and teal hooped stockings.

Did you know?
On 14 October 1995, Arsenal registered their 6000th competitive goal. Their first in the League had been on 2 September 1893 in a 2-2 draw with Newcastle United.

ARSENAL 1995–96 LEAGUE RECORD

Match No.	Date	Venue	Opponents	Result		H/T Score	Lg. Pos.	Goalscorers	Attendance
1	Aug 20	H	Middlesbrough	D	1-1	1-1	—	Wright	37,308
2	23	A	Everton	W	2-0	0-0	—	Platt, Wright	36,047
3	26	A	Coventry C	D	0-0	0-0	7		20,081
4	29	H	Nottingham F	D	1-1	1-0	—	Platt	38,248
5	Sept 10	A	Manchester C	W	1-0	0-0	6	Wright	23,984
6	16	H	West Ham U	W	1-0	0-0	5	Wright (pen)	38,065
7	23	H	Southampton	W	4-2	2-2	4	Bergkamp 2, Adams, Wright	38,136
8	30	A	Chelsea	L	0-1	0-0	6		31,048
9	Oct 14	A	Leeds U	W	3-0	1-0	3	Merson, Bergkamp, Wright	38,332
10	21	H	Aston Villa	W	2-0	0-0	3	Merson, Wright	38,271
11	30	H	Bolton W	L	0-1	0-1	—		18,682
12	Nov 4	H	Manchester U	W	1-0	1-0	3	Bergkamp	38,317
13	18	A	Tottenham H	L	1-2	1-1	3	Bergkamp	32,894
14	21	H	Sheffield W	W	4-2	1-2	—	Bergkamp, Winterburn, Dickov, Hartson	34,556
15	26	H	Blackburn R	D	0-0	0-0	3		37,695
16	Dec 2	A	Aston Villa	D	1-1	0-0	3	Platt	37,770
17	9	A	Southampton	D	0-0	0-0	3		15,238
18	16	H	Chelsea	D	1-1	0-1	6	Dixon	38,295
19	23	A	Liverpool	L	1-3	1-1	7	Wright (pen)	39,806
20	26	H	QPR	W	3-0	1-0	5	Wright, Merson 2	38,259
21	30	H	Wimbledon	L	1-3	1-1	5	Wright	37,640
22	Jan 2	A	Newcastle U	L	0-2	0-1	—		36,530
23	13	A	Middlesbrough	W	3-2	1-1	5	Merson, Platt, Helder	29,359
24	20	H	Everton	L	1-2	1-0	7	Wright	38,275
25	Feb 3	H	Coventry C	D	1-1	1-1	9	Bergkamp	35,623
26	10	A	Nottingham F	W	1-0	0-0	7	Bergkamp	27,222
27	24	A	West Ham U	W	1-0	1-0	6	Hartson	24,217
28	Mar 2	A	QPR	D	1-1	0-1	7	Bergkamp	17,970
29	5	H	Manchester C	W	3-1	2-0	—	Hartson 2, Dixon	34,519
30	16	H	Wimbledon	W	3-0	0-0	5	Winterburn, Platt, Bergkamp	18,335
31	20	A	Manchester U	L	0-1	0-0	—		50,028
32	23	H	Newcastle U	W	2-0	2-0	5	Marshall, Wright	38,271
33	Apr 6	H	Leeds U	W	2-1	1-0	5	Wright 2	37,619
34	8	A	Sheffield W	L	0-1	0-0	5		24,349
35	15	H	Tottenham H	D	0-0	0-0	—		38,273
36	27	A	Blackburn R	D	1-1	0-1	5	Wright (pen)	29,834
37	May 1	H	Liverpool	D	0-0	0-0	—		38,323
38	5	H	Bolton W	W	2-1	0-0	5	Platt, Bergkamp	38,104

Final League Position: 5

GOALSCORERS

League (49): Wright 15 (3 pens), Bergkamp 11, Platt 6, Merson 5, Hartson 4, Dixon 2, Winterburn 2, Adams 1, Dickov 1, Helder 1, Marshall 1.
Coca-Cola Cup (17): Wright 7 (1 pen), Bergkamp 5, Adams 2, Bould 1, Hartson 1, Keown 1.
FA Cup (1): Wright 1.

Match No.	Seaman D 38	Dixon L 38	Winterburn N 36	Keown M 34	Bould S 19	Adams T 21	Platt D 27+2	Wright I 31	Merson P 38	Bergkamp D 33	Parlour R 20+2	Helder G 15+9	Jensen J 13+2	McGoldrick E —+1	Linighan A 17+1	Hartson J 15+4	Hillier D 3+2	Dickov P 1+6	Morrow S 3+1	Clarke A 4+2	Marshall S 10+1	McGowan G 1	Hughes S —+1	Rose M 1+3	Shaw P —+3
1	1	2	3	4	5	6	7	8	9	10	11[1]	12													
2	1	2	3	4[1]	5	6	7	8	9	10	11		12												
3	1	2[1]	3	4	5	6	7	8	9	10	11[2]	13	12												
4	1	2	3	4	5	6	7	8	9	10	11[1]	12													
5	1	2	3	4	5	6		8	9	10	11[1]		7	12											
6	1	2	3		5	6		8	9	10	4	11	7												
7	1	2	3	4	5	6		8	9	10	7	11													
8	1	2	3	4[2]	5	6		8	9	10	11	12	7[1]		13										
9	1	2	3	4	5	6		8	9	10	7	11													
10	1	2	3	4	5	6		8	9	10	7	11													
11	1	2	3	4[1]	5	6	12	8	9	10	7	11													
12	1	2	3	4	5	6	7	8[1]	9	10		11			12										
13	1	2	3	4	5	6	7		9	10		11[1]				8	12								
14	1	2	3	4	5	6	7		9	10		8				11	12								
15	1	2	3	4[1]	5	6	7		9	10		12				8[2]	11	13							
16	1	2	3		5	6	7	8	9			11[2]	4		10[1]		12	13							
17	1	2	3	4	5	6	7	8	9			11			10[1]					12					
18	1	2	3	4	5	6	7	8	9			12			11[1]	10									
19	1	2	3		5		7	8	9		10[2]	11[1]			4	6				12	13				
20	1	2	3		5	6	7	8	9			11					4	10							
21	1	2	3		5		7	8	9	10	12				11[2]	6				4[1]	13				
22	1	2	3	4	5[1]	6	7	8	9	10	11[2]				12	13									
23	1	2			5	6	7	8	9	10	11										4	3			
24	1	2	3					8	9	10	11	7			6					12	4[1]	5			
25	1	2	3					8	9	10	11	7[1]			6						4	5	12		
26	1	2	3		5			8	9	10	11	7			6				4						
27	1	2	3		5	12			9	10		7			6	8				4[1]	11				
28	1	2	3		5		7		9	10	11				6	8					4[1]			12	
29	1	2	3		5		7		9	10	11				6	8					4				
30	1	2	3	4			7	8	9	10					6	11					5				
31	1	2	3	4			7	8	9[1]	10[2]	12				6	11				13	5				
32	1	2	3[2]	4			7	8[1]	9	10	12	13			6	11					5				
33	1	2	3	4			7	8	9	10					6	11					5				
34	1	2	3	4				8	9	10	11[1]				6	7[2]					5			12	13
35	1	2	3	4			7	8	9[1]	10	11	12			6						5				
36	1	2	3	4			7	8[1]	9	10	11				6[2]	12					5[3]			14	13
37	1	2	3	4			7		9	10	11				6	8					5				
38	1	2	3	4			7	8[1]	9	10	11				6	12					5[2]				13

Coca-Cola Cup

Second Round	Hartlepool U	(a)	3-0
		(h)	5-0
Third Round	Barnsley	(a)	3-0
Fourth Round	Sheffield W	(h)	2-1
Fifth Round	Newcastle U	(h)	2-0
Semi-final	Aston Villa	(h)	2-2
		(a)	0-0

FA Cup

Third Round	Sheffield U	(h)	1-1
		(a)	0-1

ASTON VILLA 1995–96   *Back row (left to right)*: Trevor Berry, Scott Murray, Phil King, Paul Browne, Michael Oakes, Mark Bosnich, Nigel Spink, Riccardo Scimeca, Shaun Teale, Lee Hendrie, Stephen Cowe.

Middle row: Paul Barron (Fitness Consultant), Bryan Small, Neil Davis, Paul McGrath, Gareth Southgate, Ian Taylor, Ugo Ehiogu, Gareth Farrelly, Gary Charles, David Farrell, Tommy Johnson, Jim Walker (Physio).

Front row: Graham Fenton, Steve Staunton, Franz Carr, Mark Draper, Allan Evans (Assistant Manager), Brian Little (Manager), John Gregory (Coach), Savo Milosevic, Dwight Yorke, Andy Townsend, Alan Wright.

(Photograph: Mike Smith)

FA Premiership   ASTON VILLA

Villa Park, Trinity Rd, Birmingham B6 6HE. Telephone: (0121) 327 2299. Fax: (0121) 322 2107. Commercial Dept: (0121) 327 5399. Clubcall: 0891 121148. Ticketline: 0891 121848. Ticket information: (0121) 327 5353. Club shop: (0121) 327 2800.

Ground capacity: 39,339.

Record attendance: 76,588 v Derby Co, FA Cup 6th rd, 2 March 1946.

Record receipts: £1,067,620 Chelsea v Manchester U, FA Cup semi-final, 31 March 1996.

Pitch measurements: 115yd × 72yd.

President: H. J. Musgrove. *Chairman:* H. D. Ellis.

Directors: Dr D. H. Targett, P. D. Ellis, S. M. Stride.

Manager: Brian Little. *Assistant Manager:* Allan Evans. *First Team Coach:* John Gregory.

Secretary: Steven Stride. *Director of Youth:* Peter Withe.

Physio: Jim Walker. *Youth Coach:* Tony McAndrew. *Chief Scout:* Malcolm Beard. *Fitness Consultant:* Paul Barron.

Commercial Manager: Abdul Rashid. *Stadium Manager:* E. Small.

Year Formed: 1874. *Turned Professional:* 1885. *Ltd Co.:* 1896.

Previous Grounds: 1874–76, Aston Park; 1876–97, Perry Barr; 1897, Villa Park.

Club Nickname: 'The Villans'.

Foundation: Cricketing enthusiasts of Villa Cross Wesleyan Chapel, Aston, Birmingham decided to form a football club during the winter of 1873–74. Football clubs were few and far between in the Birmingham area and in their first game against Aston Brook St. Mary's Rugby team they played one half rugby and the other soccer. In 1876 they were joined by a Scottish soccer enthusiast George Ramsay who was immediately appointed captain and went on to lead Aston Villa from obscurity to one of the country's top clubs in a period of less than 10 years.

First Football League game: 8 September 1888, Football League, v Wolverhampton W, (a) D 1-1 – Warner; Cox, Coulton; Yates, H. Devey, Dawson; A. Brown, Green (1), Allen, Garvey, Hodgetts.

Record League Victory: 12–2 v Accrington S, Division 1, 12 March 1892 – Warner; Evans, Cox; Harry Devey, Jimmy Cowan, Baird; Athersmith (1), Dickson (2), John Devey (4), L. Campbell (4), Hodgetts (1).

Record Cup Victory: 13–0 v Wednesbury Old Ath, FA Cup 1st rd, 30 October 1886 – Warner; Coulton, Simmonds; Yates, Robertson, Burton (2); R. Davis (1), A. Brown (3), Hunter (3), Loach (2), Hodgetts (2).

Record Defeat: 1–8 v Blackburn R, FA Cup 3rd rd, 16 February 1889.

Most League Points (2 for a win): 70, Division 3, 1971–72.

Most League Points (3 for a win): 78, Division 2, 1987–88.

Most League Goals: 128, Division 1, 1930–31.

Highest League Scorer in Season: 'Pongo' Waring, 49, Division 1, 1930–31.

Most League Goals in Total Aggregate: Harry Hampton, 215, 1904–15.

Most Capped Player: Paul McGrath, 45 (82), Republic of Ireland.

Most League Appearances: Charlie Aitken, 561, 1961–76.

Record Transfer Fee Received: £5,500,000 from Bari for David Platt, July 1991.

Record Transfer Fee Paid: £3,500,000 to Partizan Belgrade for Savo Milosevic, June 1995.

Football League Record: 1888 Founder Member of the League; 1936–38 Division 2; 1938–59 Division 1; 1959–60 Division 2; 1960–67 Division 1; 1967–70 Division 2; 1970–72 Division 3; 1972–75 Division 2; 1975–87 Division 1; 1987–88 Division 2; 1988–92 Division 1; 1992– FA Premier League.

Honours: FA Premier League: – Runners-up 1992–93. *Football League:* Division 1 – Champions 1893–94, 1895–96, 1896–97, 1898–99, 1899–1900, 1909–10, 1980–81; Runners-up 1888–89, 1902–03, 1907–08, 1910–11, 1912–13, 1913–14, 1930–31, 1932–33, 1989–90; Division 2 – Champions 1937–38, 1959–60; Runners-up 1974–75, 1987–88; Division 3 – Champions 1971–72. *FA Cup:* Winners 1887, 1895, 1897, 1905, 1913, 1920, 1957; Runners-up 1892, 1924. *Double Performed:* 1896–97. *Football League Cup:* Winners 1961, 1975, 1977, 1994, 1996; Runners-up 1963, 1971. **European Competitions:** *European Cup:* 1981–82 (winners), 1982–83; *UEFA Cup:* 1975–76, 1977–78, 1983–84, 1990–91, 1993–94, 1994–95.*World Club Championship:* 1982; European Super Cup: 1982–83 (winners).

Colours: Claret body, sky blue sleeves, sky blue collar with trim, white shorts, claret stockings with sky blue top. *Change colours:* White shirts, claret shorts, white stockings.

Did you know?
Harry Hampton scored seven goals in three games for the Football League representative team, including four against the Irish League at Anfield in October 1911.

ASTON VILLA 1995–96 LEAGUE RECORD

Match No.	Date	Venue	Opponents	Result		H/T Score	Lg. Pos.	Goalscorers	Attendance
1	Aug 19	H	Manchester U	W	3-1	3-0	—	Taylor, Draper, Yorke (pen)	34,655
2	23	A	Tottenham H	W	1-0	0-0	—	Ehiogu	26,598
3	26	A	Leeds U	L	0-2	0-1	6		35,086
4	30	H	Bolton W	W	1-0	0-0	—	Yorke	31,770
5	Sept 9	A	Blackburn R	D	1-1	1-0	5	Milosevic	27,084
6	16	H	Wimbledon	W	2-0	1-0	3	Draper, Taylor	26,928
7	23	H	Nottingham F	D	1-1	0-0	5	Townsend	33,972
8	30	A	Coventry C	W	3-0	1-0	2	Yorke, Milosevic 2	21,004
9	Oct 14	H	Chelsea	L	0-1	0-0	7		34,922
10	21	A	Arsenal	L	0-2	0-0	7		38,271
11	28	H	Everton	W	1-0	0-0	7	Yorke	32,792
12	Nov 4	A	West Ham U	W	4-1	1-0	5	Milosevic 2, Johnson, Yorke	23,637
13	18	H	Newcastle U	D	1-1	1-0	4	Johnson	39,167
14	20	A	Southampton	W	1-0	1-0	—	Johnson	13,582
15	25	A	Manchester C	L	0-1	0-0	4		28,027
16	Dec 2	H	Arsenal	D	1-1	0-0	4	Yorke	37,770
17	10	A	Nottingham F	D	1-1	0-0	6	Yorke	25,790
18	16	H	Coventry C	W	4-1	1-0	4	Johnson, Milosevic 3	28,486
19	23	A	QPR	L	0-1	0-0	6		14,778
20	Jan 1	A	Middlesbrough	W	2-0	2-0	5	Wright, Johnson	28,523
21	13	A	Manchester U	D	0-0	0-0	7		42,667
22	21	H	Tottenham H	W	2-1	1-1	5	McGrath, Yorke	35,666
23	31	A	Liverpool	L	0-2	0-0	—		39,332
24	Feb 3	H	Leeds U	W	3-0	2-0	4	Yorke 2, Wright	35,982
25	10	A	Bolton W	W	2-0	1-0	4	Yorke 2	18,099
26	24	A	Wimbledon	D	3-3	1-1	4	Reeves (og), Yorke (pen), Cunningham (og)	12,193
27	28	H	Blackburn R	W	2-0	0-0	4	Joachim, Southgate	28,008
28	Mar 3	A	Liverpool	L	0-3	0-3	4		39,508
29	6	H	Sheffield W	W	3-2	0-1	—	Milosevic 2, Townsend	27,893
30	9	H	QPR	W	4-2	1-0	4	Milosevic, Yorke 2, Yates (og)	28,221
31	16	A	Sheffield W	L	0-2	0-0	4		22,964
32	19	H	Middlesbrough	D	0-0	0-0	—		23,933
33	Apr 6	A	Chelsea	W	2-1	1-1	4	Milosevic, Yorke	23,530
34	8	H	Southampton	W	3-0	0-0	4	Taylor, Charles, Yorke	34,059
35	14	A	Newcastle U	L	0-1	0-0	4		36,546
36	17	H	West Ham U	D	1-1	0-0	—	McGrath	26,768
37	27	H	Manchester C	L	0-1	0-0	4		39,336
38	May 5	A	Everton	L	0-1	0-0	4		40,127

Final League Position: 4

GOALSCORERS

League (52): Yorke 17 (2 pens), Milosevic 12, Johnson 5, Taylor 3, Draper 2, McGrath 2, Townsend 2, Wright 2, Charles 1, Ehiogu 1, Joachim 1, Southgate 1, own goals 3.
Coca-Cola Cup (16): Yorke 6 (2 pens), Johnson 2, Draper 1, Ehiogu 1, Milosevic 1, Southgate 1, Staunton 1, Taylor 1, Townsend 1, own goal 1.
FA Cup (8): Draper 2, Yorke 2 (1 pen), Carr 1, Johnson 1, Milosevic 1, Taylor 1.

Bosnich M 38	Charles G 34	Wright A 38	Southgate G 31	McGrath P 29+1	Ehiogu U 36	Taylor I 24+1	Draper M 36	Milosevic S 36+1	Townsend A 32+1	Yorke D 35	Johnson T 17+6	Scimeca R 7+10	Fenton G —+3	Staunton S 11+2	Tiler C 1	Spink N —+2	Hendrie L 2+1	Farrelly G 1+4	Joachim J 4+7	Carr F 1	Davis N —+2	Murray S 3	Browne P 2	Match No.
1	2	3	4	5	6	7	8	9^1	10	11^2	12	13												1
1	2	3	4	5	6	7	8	9	10	11														2
1		3	4	5	6	2	8	9	7	11	10^1		12											3
1	2	3	4	5	6	7	8	9	10	11														4
1	2	3	4	5	6	7	8	9	10	11														5
1	2	3	4	5	6	7	8	9	10	11														6
1	2	3	4	5	6	7	8	9^1	10	11	12													7
1	2	3	4		5	7	8	9	10	11					6									8
1	2	3	4	5	6	7	8	9^1	10		12	13	11^2											9
1	2	3	4	5^2	6	7	8^3	14	10	9	12	13	11^1											10
1	2	3	4	5		7	8	9	10	11	12			6^1										11
1	2	3	4	5	6	7	8	9	10^1	11	12													12
1	2	3	4	5	6	7	8	9		11	10													13
1	2	3	4	5	6	7	8	9		11	10													14
1	2	3	4	5	6	7^1	8	9^2		11	10	13	12											15
1	2	3	4	5	6		8	9	11	7	10													16
1	2	3	4		6	7	8	9		11	10			5										17
1	2	3	4	5^2	6	7	8	9	12	11^1	10	13				15								18
1	2	3	4	5^1	6	7^2	8^3	9	11	10	12	13	14											19
1	2	3	4		6		8	9	7	11	10			5										20
1	2	3	4	5	6	7	8	9	11	10^1	12													21
1	2	3	4	5	6	12	8	9	11	7	10^1													22
1	2	3	4	5^1	6		8	9	11	7	10	12												23
1	2	3	4	5		7	8	9	10^1	11	6	12												24
1	2	3	4	5			8	9	11	7	10	6												25
1	2	3	4	12	5		8	9^2	11	7	10^1	6						13						26
1	2	3	4	5		8^1	9	10	11	12	6							13	7^2					27
1	2	3	4	5			9	10	11	7	6^1			8					12					28
1	2	3	4	5	6		9	10	11	7				8										29
1	2	3	4^2	5	6		8	9	10^1	11	7							12	13					30
1	2	3		5	6		8	9	10	11	4^1								12	7				31
1		3		5			8	10	11	6	7	12	9^2				13		2^1	4				32
1	2	3		5	4	7	8	9	10	11	12											6^1		33
1	2	3		5^1	6	7	8	9	4	11	10								12					34
1	2	3		5	6	7	8	9	4	11^2	10^1								12	13				35
1	2^1	3		5	6	7	8	9	4	11^2	10								12	13				36
1		3		5	4		8	9	11	10	6			7^1					12	2				37
1		3	4	5			8	9	10	7^1	11								12			2	6	38

Coca-Cola Cup

Second Round	Peterborough U	(h)	6-0
		(a)	1-1
Third Round	Stockport Co	(h)	2-0
Fourth Round	QPR	(h)	1-0
Fifth Round	Wolverhampton W	(h)	1-0
Semi-final	Arsenal	(a)	2-2
		(h)	0-0
Final (at Wembley)	Leeds U		3-0

FA Cup

Third Round	Gravesend & N (at Villa Park)	(a)	3-0
Fourth Round	Sheffield U	(a)	1-0
Fifth Round	Ipswich T	(a)	3 1
Sixth Round	Nottingham F	(a)	1-0
Semi-final (at Old Trafford)	Liverpool		0-3

BARNET 1995–96 Back row *(left to right)*: Graeme Hall, Paul Smith, Shaun Gale, Mark Cooper, Linvoy Primus, Glen Thomas, Alan Pardew, Alex Dyer.
Middle row: David Mott (Physio), Laird Budge (Kit Manager), Jamie Campbell, Danny Mills, Maik Taylor, Paul Newell, Sean Devine, Lee Hodges, Terry Bullivant (First Team Coach), Terry Harvey (Youth Team Coach), Terry Gibson (Youth Team Manager).
Front row: Terry Robbins, David McDonald, Peter Scott, Ray Clemence (Manager), Paul Wilson, Mickey Tomlinson, Chris Perfimou.

Division 3   **BARNET**

Underhill Stadium, Barnet Lane, Barnet, Herts EN5 2BE. Telephone: (0181) 441 6932. Fax: (0181) 447 0655. Credit Card Bookings: (0181) 441 1677.

Ground capacity: 3887.

Record attendance: 11,026 v Wycombe Wanderers. FA Amateur Cup 4th Round 1951–52.

Record Receipts: £31,202 v Portsmouth, FA Cup 3rd Round, 5 January 1991.

Pitch measurements: 112yd × 72yd.

Chairman: A. Kleanthous. **Vice-Chairman:** D. J. Buchler FCA. **Chief Executive:** D. B. Edwards OBE.

Directors: S. Glynne, F. Higgins FCA.

Manager: Ray Clemence MBE. **Physio:** G. Gilbert-Anderson MSF, MAB Phys.

Coach: Terry Gibson. **Secretary:** Miss Alison Ashworth. **Sales and Commercial Manager:** Brian Wheeler. **Marketing Manager:** Tessa Bills.

Year Formed: 1888. **Turned Professional:** 1965. **Ltd Co:**

Club Nickname: The Bees.

Previous Names: 1906–19 Barnet Alston FC.

Previous Grounds: 1888-1901, Queens Road; 1901-07, Totteridge Lane.

Foundation: Barnet Football Club was formed in 1888, disbanded in 1901. A club known as Alston Works FC was then formed and in 1906 changed its name to Barnet Alston FC. In 1912 it combined with The Avenue to become Barnet and Alston.

First Football League game: 17 August 1991, Division 4, v Crewe Alex (h) L 4-7 – Phillips; Blackford, Cooper (Murphy), Horton, Bodley (Stein), Johnson, Showler, Carter (2), Bull (2), Lowe, Evans.

Record League Victory: 6–0 v Lincoln C (away), Division 4, 4 September 1991 – Pape; Poole, Naylor, Bodley, Howell, Evans (1), Willis (1), Murphy (1), Bull (2), Lowe, Showler (1 og).

Record Defeat: 1–5 v York C, Division 3, 13 March 1993.

Most League Points (3 for a win): 79, Division 3, 1992–93.

Most League Goals: 81, Division 4, 1991–92.

Highest League Scorer in Season: Gary Bull, 20, Division 4, 1991–92.

Most League Goals in Total Aggregate: Gary Bull 37, 1991–96.

Most League Appearances: Paul Wilson, 137, 1991–96.

Record Transfer Fee Received: £800,000 from Crystal Palace for Dougie Freedman, September 1995.

Record Transfer Fee Paid: £40,000 to Barrow for Kenny Lowe, January 1991 and £40,000 to Runcorn for Mark Carter, February 1991.

Football League Record: Promoted to Division 4 from GMVC 1991; 1991–92 Division 4; 1992–93 Division 3; 1993–94 Division 2; 1994– Division 3.

Honours: *Football League:* best season 24th, Division 2, 1993–94. *FA Amateur Cup:* Winners 1946. *GM Vauxhall Conference:* Winners 1990–91. *FA Cup:* best season; never past 3rd rd. *League Cup:* never past 2nd rd.

Colours: Amber and black striped shirts, black shorts, black stockings. **Change colours:** Green and white striped shirts, green shorts, green stockings.

Did you know?
Barnet - then in the Athenian League - reached the third round of the FA Cup for the first time beating Isthmian League Enfield 3-0 after a 4-4 draw in 1964–65.

BARNET 1995–96 LEAGUE RECORD

Match No.	Date	Venue	Opponents	Result	H/T Score	Lg. Pos.	Goalscorers	Attendance
1	Aug 12	A	Hereford U	L	1-4	0-3	—	Hodges	2522
2	19	H	Colchester U	D	1-1	0-0	18	Freedman	1966
3	26	A	Scunthorpe U	L	0-2	0-0	21		1970
4	29	H	Gillingham	L	0-2	0-1	—		3077
5	Sept 2	H	Lincoln C	W	3-1	2-1	20	Cooper, Freedman 2	1813
6	9	A	Cambridge U	D	1-1	0-0	19	Westley (og)	3054
7	12	A	Wigan Ath	L	0-1	0-1	—		1745
8	16	H	Plymouth Arg	L	1-2	0-0	24	Cooper	2557
9	23	A	Bury	D	0-0	0-0	23		2453
10	30	H	Darlington	D	1-1	0-1	23	Robbins	1923
11	Oct 7	H	Exeter C	W	3-2	2-0	23	Devine, Dyer, Cooper	2146
12	14	A	Cardiff C	D	1-1	1-1	21	Cooper	3342
13	21	H	Rochdale	L	0-4	0-0	22		2039
14	28	A	Northampton T	W	2-0	0-0	22	Cooper, Campbell	5376
15	31	A	Hartlepool U	D	0-0	0-0	—		1713
16	Nov 4	H	Doncaster R	D	1-1	1-0	22	Devine	1913
17	18	A	Fulham	D	1-1	0-0	21	Dunwell	4369
18	25	H	Leyton Orient	W	3-0	1-0	17	Dyer, Hodges 2	2850
19	Dec 9	H	Bury	D	0-0	0-0	19		1747
20	16	A	Darlington	D	1-1	0-1	18	Devine	1717
21	23	A	Chester C	W	2-0	1-0	14	Hodges, Devine	3081
22	26	H	Mansfield T	D	0-0	0-0	14		2204
23	Jan 6	H	Preston NE	W	1-0	0-0	13	Wilson	2737
24	9	A	Scarborough	D	1-1	1-1	—	Devine	1310
25	13	A	Colchester U	L	2-3	2-3	15	Primus, Cooper	3252
26	20	H	Hereford U	L	1-3	1-1	16	Hodges	1835
27	Feb 3	H	Scunthorpe U	W	1-0	1-0	15	Hodges	1674
28	6	A	Torquay U	D	1-1	0-0	—	Wilson	2262
29	10	A	Preston NE	W	1-0	0-0	11	Wilson	9974
30	13	A	Gillingham	L	0-1	0-1	—		6433
31	17	H	Wigan Ath	W	5-0	2-0	10	Hodges, Primus, Devine 2, Tomlinson	2059
32	24	A	Plymouth Arg	D	1-1	0-1	11	Gale	6426
33	27	H	Cambridge U	W	2-0	0-0	—	Cooper, Wilson	1849
34	Mar 2	A	Mansfield T	L	1-2	0-0	11	Primus	2146
35	9	H	Chester C	D	1-1	0-0	12	Tomlinson	2195
36	16	H	Torquay U	W	4-0	3-0	11	Devine 2, Simpson, Cooper	1734
37	19	A	Lincoln C	W	2-1	0-0	—	Devine 2	1872
38	23	A	Scarborough	W	1-0	0-0	9	Devine	2054
39	30	A	Exeter C	L	0-1	0-0	9		2726
40	Apr 2	H	Cardiff C	W	1-0	0-0	—	Devine	2107
41	6	H	Northampton T	W	2-0	2-0	9	Primus, Hodges	3135
42	8	A	Rochdale	W	4-0	1-0	8	Hodges 4	1492
43	13	H	Hartlepool U	W	5-1	3-0	7	Hodges 3, Devine 2	2530
44	20	A	Doncaster R	L	0-1	0-0	8		1579
45	27	A	Leyton Orient	D	3-3	2-1	10	Devine 2 (1 pen), Hodges	4006
46	May 4	H	Fulham	W	3-0	1-0	9	Devine 2, Hodges	4332

Final League Position: 9

GOALSCORERS

League (65): Devine 19 (1 pen), Hodges 17, Cooper 8, Primus 4, Wilson 4, Freedman 3, Dyer 2, Tomlinson 2, Campbell 1, Dunwell 1, Gale 1, Robbins 1, Simpson 1, own goal 1.
Coca-Cola Cup (0).
FA Cup (3): Devine 1, Hodges 1, Primus 1.

Taylor M 45	Gale S 44	McDonald D 30 + 2	Pardew A 41	Primus L 42	Thomas G 16	Adams K 1	Freedman D 5	Hodges L 34 + 6	Robbins T 9 + 6	Scott P 19 + 1	Tomlinson M 17 + 8	Campbell J 14 + 10	Cooper M 26 + 7	Dyer A 30 + 5	Wilson P 29 + 4	Stimson M 5	Charles L 2 + 3	Smith G — + 1	Brady M 1 + 1	Mills D 5 + 14	Devine S 35	Simpson P 24	Dunwell R 3 + 10	Newell P 1	Thompson N 1 + 1	Howarth L 19	Codner R 8	Match No.
1	2	3	4	5	6	7^1	8	9	10	11	12																	1
1	7^2	2	4	5	6		8	9^1	10	11	12	3	13															2
1	2		4	5	6		8	9	7^1	11	12	3	10															3
1	2		4	5	6		8	9		11	7	3	10															4
1	2	3	4	5	6		8	9^1		11	7		10	12														5
1	2		4	5	6			9	8^1	11	7	3	10	12														6
1	2	12	4	5	6			9^1	8			3	10	7	11													7
1	2	3	4	5	6			8	11				10	7	9													8
1	2^1	12	4	5	6			13	8		7^3		9	11	3	10^2	14											9
1	2		4		6			12	8			5^1	9	7^2	3	10				11			13					10
1	2	5	4		6			7^3	8	12			9^2	11	3	13	14				10^2							11
1	2	5	4		6			12	7^1	8			9^2	11	3					13	10							12
1	2		4	5	6			9	8^2	7	12			11	3					13	10^1							13
1	2	6	4	5				12					13	3	9	11				7^1	10^2	8						14
1	2	6	4	5				12					13	3	9	11				7^2	10^1	8						15
1	2	6	4	5				12					13	3^3	9	11		14		7^1	10^2	8						16
1	2	6	4	5				12	8			13		3^2	9	11				7^1	10^3		14					17
1	2	6	4	5				7					9	3	11						10	8						18
1	2	6	4	5				7					9^2	3	11					12	10^1	8	13					19
	2	6	4	5				7					9^1	3^2	11					12	10	8		1				20
1	2	6	4	5				7					9	3	11					12	10^1	8						21
1	2	6	4	5				7					9^2	3	11					12	10	8^1	13					22
1	2	6	5	4				7	8					3	11					12	10	9^1						23
1	2	6	5	4				7	8				9^1	3^2	11					12	10		13					24
1	2	6	4	5				7	8			3^1	9		11					12	10							25
1	2	6	4^2	5				7	8^3		12	13	9	3^1	11						10		14					26
1	2		4	5				7	8				9	3	11					12	10^1					6		27
1	2		4	5				7	8				9^1	3	11					12	10					6		28
1	2		4	5				7	8					3	11						10	9				6		29
1	2	3^1	4	5				7	8			13	12^2		11						10	9^3	14			6		30
1	2		4	5				7^2	8		12			3	11						10^1	9	13			6		31
1	2		4	5				7^2	8^1		12	13		3	11						10	9				6		32
1	2		4	5				7	8		12	13		3	11						10^2	9^1				6		33
1	2^1	6	4	5				7	8				9^2	3	11					12	10		13			6		34
1	2	9	4	5				7^1	8					3^3	11^3			14		12	10		13			6		35
1	2	5	4^3					12	8			13	9^3	3	11					7^1	10		14			6		36
1	2	11	4	5				12	8^1				9	3						13	10^2	7				6		37
1	2	11	4	5				12	8^3			13		3						7	10^2	9^1	14			6		38
1	2		4^1	5				9				13		7^2	3					12	10	8				6	11	39
1	2		4	5				9				13		7^1	3					12	10	8^2				6	11	40
1	2		4	5^2				9^1				13		7^3	3					12	10	8	14			6	11	41
1	4	2		5				9^1				13		7^3	3					12	10	8^2	14			6	11	42
1	4	2		5				9						7^1	3					12	10	8				6	11	43
1	4	2		5				9			12			7^1	3						10	8				6	11	44
1	2		4	5				9						7^1	3					12	10	8				6	11	45
1	2		4	5				9						7	3						10	8				6	11	46

Coca-Cola Cup
First Round   Charlton Ath   (h)   0-0
                                                      (a)   0-2

FA Cup
First Round   Woking   (h)   2-2
                                         (a)   1-2

BARNSLEY 1995–96   *Back row (left to right):* Scott Jones, Robert Hanby, Chris Jackson, Russell Harmer, Brendan O'Connell, Glynn Hurst, Steve Davis, Troy Bennett, Charlie Bishop, Dean Fearon, Luke Beckett.
Middle row: Paul Smith (Physio), Eric Winstanley (First Team Coach), Darron Clyde, David Brooke, Andy Rammell, Adam Sollitt, Lee Butler, David Watson, Gerry Taggart, Andrew Liddell, Mark Burton, Colin Walker (Youth Team Coach), Malcolm Shotton (Reserve Team Coach).
Front row: Mark Feeney, Jonathan Perry, Andrew Gregory, Neil Redfearn, Nicky Eaden, Gary Fleming, Danny Wilson (Player/Manager), Andy Payton, Owen Archdeacon, Martin Bullock, Darren Sheridan, Adrian Moses, Simon Bochenski.

Division 1 **BARNSLEY**

Oakwell Ground, Grove St, Barnsley, South Yorkshire S71 1ET. Telephone: (01226) 211211. Fax: (01226) 211444. Clubcall: 0891 121152. Commercial Office: (01226) 211222.

Ground capacity: 19,101.

Record attendance: 40,255 v Stoke C, FA Cup 5th rd, 15 February 1936.

Record receipts: Not disclosed.

Pitch measurements: 110yd × 75yd.

President: Arthur Raynor. *Chairman:* J. A. Dennis.

Directors: C. B. Taylor (Vice-Chairman), C. H. Harrison, M. R. Hayselden, J. N. Kelly, S. M. Hall, I. D. Potter.

Player-Manager: Danny Wilson.

First Team Coach: Eric Winstanley. *Physios:* Michael Tarmey, Paul Smith.

General Manager/Secretary: Michael Spinks. *Lotteries Manager:* Gerry Whewall. *Marketing Manager:* Ian Davies.

Year Formed: 1887. *Turned Professional:* 1888. *Ltd Co.:* 1899.

Previous Name: Barnsley St Peter's, 1887–97.

Club Nickname: 'The Tykes', 'Reds' or 'Colliers'.

Foundation: Many clubs owe their inception to the church and Barnsley are among them, for they were formed in 1887 by the Rev. T. T. Preedy, curate of Barnsley St. Peter's and went under that name until it was dropped in 1897 a year before being admitted to the Second Division of the Football League.

First Football League game: 1 September 1898, Division 2, v Lincoln C (a) L 0–1 – Fawcett; McArtney, Nixon; King, Burleigh, Porteous; Davis, Lees, Murray, McCullough, McGee.

Record League Victory: 9–0 v Loughborough T, Division 2, 28 January 1899 – Greaves; McArtney, Nixon; Porteous, Burleigh, Howard; Davis (4), Hepworth (1), Lees (1), McCullough (1), Jones (2). 9–0 v Accrington S, Division 3 (N), 3 February 1934 – Ellis; Cookson, Shotton; Harper, Henderson, Whitworth; Spence (2), Smith (1), Blight (4), Andrews (1), Ashton (1).

Record Cup Victory: 6–0 v Blackpool, FA Cup 1st rd replay, 20 January 1910 – Mearns; Downs, Ness; Glendinning, Boyle (1), Utley; Bartrop, Gadsby (1), Lillycrop (2), Tufnell (2), Forman. 6–0 v Peterborough U, League Cup 1st rd, 2nd leg, 15 September 1981 – Horn; Joyce, Chambers, Glavin (2), Banks, McCarthy, Evans, Parker (2), Aylott (1), McHale, Barrowclough (1).

Record Defeat: 0–9 v Notts Co, Division 2, 19 November 1927.

Most League Points (2 for a win): 67, Division 3 (N), 1938–39.

Most League Points (3 for a win): 74, Division 2, 1988–89.

Most League Goals: 118, Division 3 (N), 1933–34.

Highest League Scorer in Season: Cecil McCormack, 33, Division 2, 1950–51.

Most League Goals in Total Aggregate: Ernest Hine, 123, 1921–26 and 1934–38.

Most Capped Player: Gerry Taggart, 35, Northern Ireland.

Most League Appearances: Barry Murphy, 514, 1962–78.

Record Transfer Fee Received: £1,500,000 from Nottingham F for Carl Tiler, May 1991.

Record Transfer Fee Paid: £310,000 to Celtic for Andy Payton, November 1993.

Football League Record: 1898 Elected to Division 2; 1932–34 Division 3 (N); 1934–38 Division 2; 1938–39 Division 3 (N); 1946–53 Division 2; 1953–55 Division 3 (N); 1955–59 Division 2; 1959–65 Division 3; 1965–68 Division 4; 1968–72 Division 3; 1972–79 Division 4; 1979–81 Division 3; 1981–92 Division 2; 1992– Division 1.

Honours: Football League: best season: 3rd, Division 2, 1914–15, 1921–22; Division 3 (N) – Champions 1933–34, 1938–39, 1954–55; Runners-up 1953–54; Division 3 – Runners-up 1980–81; Division 4 – Runners-up 1967–68; Promoted 1978–79. *FA Cup:* Winners 1912; Runners-up 1910. *Football League Cup:* best season: 5th rd, 1982.

Colours: Red shirts, white shorts, red stockings. *Change colours:* Royal blue and black striped shirts, black shorts, black stockings.

Did you know?
On 13 January 1996 Barnsley won 1-0 at Oldham, their first win there for 61 years when they succeeded 4-1.

BARNSLEY 1995–96 LEAGUE RECORD

Match No.	Date	Venue	Opponents	Result	H/T Score	Lg. Pos.	Goalscorers	Attendance
1	Aug 12	A	Crystal Palace	L	3-4	1-2	—	Davis, Viveash, Liddell	12,067
2	19	H	Oldham Ath	W	2-1	1-0	8	Payton, Redfearn (pen)	8795
3	26	A	Watford	W	3-2	1-1	3	Rammell 2, Davis	8049
4	29	H	Tranmere R	W	2-1	2-0	—	Payton, Davis	9710
5	Sept 2	H	Birmingham C	L	0-5	0-0	7		11,129
6	9	A	Millwall	W	1-0	1-0	3	Redfearn	9272
7	12	A	Huddersfield T	L	0-3	0-1	—		14,635
8	17	H	Sheffield U	D	2-2	2-0	6	Davis, Payton	7150
9	23	H	Derby Co	W	2-0	2-0	3	Liddell 2	8929
10	30	A	Charlton Ath	D	1-1	0-1	3	Redfearn	11,219
11	Oct 7	H	Leicester C	D	2-2	1-1	4	Payton, Bullock	13,669
12	14	A	Norwich C	L	1-3	1-0	7	Eaden	14,002
13	21	H	Port Vale	D	1-1	1-1	9	Archdeacon	7332
14	28	A	Sunderland	L	1-2	0-1	12	Liddell	17,024
15	Nov 4	H	Wolverhampton W	W	1-0	0-0	7	Redfearn	9668
16	11	A	Grimsby T	L	1-3	1-2	10	Davis	6166
17	18	A	Reading	D	0-0	0-0	11		6695
18	21	H	Portsmouth	D	0-0	0-0	—		6187
19	25	H	Luton T	W	1-0	0-0	11	Redfearn	6437
20	Dec 2	A	Leicester C	D	2-2	2-1	12	Payton 2	15,125
21	9	A	Derby Co	L	1-4	0-1	14	Rammell	14,415
22	16	H	Charlton Ath	L	1-2	0-2	15	Payton	6140
23	22	A	Ipswich T	D	2-2	0-1	—	De Zeeuw, Liddell	11,791
24	26	H	Stoke C	W	3-1	2-0	13	Redfearn, Rammell, Liddell	9229
25	Jan 1	A	Southend U	D	0-0	0-0	14		6537
26	13	A	Oldham Ath	W	1-0	0-0	11	Payton	6029
27	20	H	Crystal Palace	D	1-1	0-1	12	Liddell	6620
28	Feb 3	H	Watford	W	2-1	0-0	8	Archdeacon, Payton	6139
29	10	A	Tranmere R	W	3-1	0-0	6	Payton 2, Redfearn (pen)	6376
30	20	A	Birmingham C	D	0-0	0-0	—		14,168
31	24	A	Sheffield U	L	0-1	0-1	7		14,584
32	27	H	Millwall	W	3-1	0-1	—	Payton 2, Liddell	6331
33	Mar 2	A	Stoke C	L	0-2	0-1	6		12,663
34	9	H	Ipswich T	D	3-3	2-0	8	Redfearn 2 (1 pen), Liddell	7705
35	16	A	WBA	L	1-2	0-2	10	Payton	12,701
36	19	H	Huddersfield T	W	3-0	2-0	—	Eaden, Redfearn, Archdeacon	10,660
37	23	H	Southend U	D	1-1	1-1	9	Payton	6754
38	30	A	Port Vale	L	0-3	0-1	10		7358
39	Apr 2	H	Norwich C	D	2-2	1-1	—	Redfearn, Payton	6375
40	6	H	Sunderland	L	0-1	0-1	11		13,189
41	8	A	Wolverhampton W	D	2-2	1-1	11	Moses, Payton	23,789
42	13	H	Reading	L	0-1	0-0	12		5488
43	20	A	Portsmouth	D	0-0	0-0	14		8744
44	27	A	Luton T	W	3-1	2-0	13	Redfearn 2, O'Connell	6194
45	30	H	WBA	D	1-1	1-1	—	Regis	6981
46	May 4	H	Grimsby T	D	1-1	1-1	10	Redfearn	6108

Final League Position: 10

GOALSCORERS

League (60): Payton 17, Redfearn 14 (3 pens), Liddell 9, Davis 5, Rammell 4, Archdeacon 3, Eaden 2, Bullock 1, De Zeeuw 1, Moses 1, O'Connell 1, Regis 1, Viveash 1.
Coca-Cola Cup (4): Payton 3, Rammell 1.
FA Cup (1): Redfearn 1.

Watson D 45	Eaden N 46	Davis S 27	Bishop C 12+1	Viveash A 2	Kane P 4	Bullock M 25+16	Redfearn N 45	Payton A 37+3	Liddell A 43	Archdeacon O 36+2	Rammell A 11+9	Fleming G 2+1	Shirtliff P 32	Sheridan D 38+3	Butler L 1+2	Jackson C 6+2	Bochenski S —+1	Shotton M 2	Moses A 21+3	Molby J 5	De Zeeuw A 31	Hurst G —+5	O'Connell B 20+5	Regis D 4+8	Jones S 4	Van der Velden C 6+1	Ten-Heuvel L 1+2	Match No.
1	2	3	4	5	6	7^1	8	9	10	11	12																	1
1	2	5	6		4	12	8	9	10^1	11	7	3																2
1	2	5	6		4	12	8	9	10^1	13	7		3	11^2	15													3
1	2	5	6		4	12	8	9^1	10		7		3	11														4
1	2	6	5			7	8	9	10	4			3	11	15													5
1	2	5	6			12	8	9	10	4			3	11		7^1												6
1	2	5	6			10	8	9		4	12		3	11^2		7^1			13									7
	2	5				12	8	9^1	10	4			3^2	11	1	7			6	13								8
1	2	5	6			7^1	8	9	10	11	12		3						4									9
1	2	5	6			12	8	9	10^2	11			3			7^1			4				13					10
1	2	5	6			12	8	9^2	10	11			3^1			7			4				13					11
1	2	5^1	6				8	9^2	10	11	12		3			7			4				13					12
1	2	5^1	6			7	8	9^2	10	11	12		3						4^3	14			13					13
1	2	5				7	8	9	10	11	12		3						4	6^1								14
1	2	5				12	8	9	10^1	11			3			7			4		6							15
1	2	5				12	8	9	10^1	11			3			7			4		6							16
1	2	5				7	8	9	10	11			3						4		6							17
1	2	5				7	8	9^2	10^1	11	12		3						4		6		13					18
1	2	5				7	8	9	10^1	11	12		3						4		6							19
1	2	5				7^2	8	9	10^1	11	12		3						4		6		13					20
1	2					7	8	9	10^1	11	12		3	4^2					5		6		13					21
1	2					7	8	9^1	10	11	12		3	4^2					5		6		13					22
1	2					7^1	8		10	11	12		3						5		6		9		4			23
1	2	5				7	8		10	11			3								6		9		4			24
1	2	5				7^1	8		10	11	12		3								6		9		4			25
1	2	5				7	8		10	11	12		3	4^3							6		9					26
1	2	5				7	8		10	11	12		3^1								6		9		4			27
1	2	5				7^1	8		10	11	12		3	4							6		9					28
1	2	5				7	8		10	11^1	12		3	4							6		9					29
1	2	5				7	8		10	11			3	4							6		9					30
1	2	5^1				7	8		10	11^2	12		3	4							6		9	13				31
1	2	5				7	8		10	11	12		3	4							6		9^1					32
1	2	5				7	8		10	11	12		3	4							6		9^1					33
1	2	5				7	8		10	11			3	4							6		9					34
1	2	5				7	8		10	11	12		3^2	4^1							6		9	13				35
1	2	5				7^2	8		10	11	12		3	4							6		9^1	13				36
1	2	5				7	8		10	11	12		3^2	4							6		9^1	13				37
1	2	5				7^2	8		10	11^1	12		3	4							6		13	9				38
1	2	3				7^1	8		10	11	12			4					5		6			9				39
1	2	5^1				7	8		10	11	12		3	4							6		13	9^2				40
1	2	5				7	8		10	11	12		3^1	4							6			9				41
1	2	5				7	8		10^1	11	12		3^2	4							6		13	9				42
1	2	5					8		10^1	11	12		3	4		7					6			9				43
1	2	5					8		10	11	12		3	4		7					6			9^1				44
1	2	5					8		10	11	12		3	4		7^1					6		13			9^2		45
1	2	5					8		10	11^1	12		3	4		7					6		13			9^2		46

Coca-Cola Cup

Second Round	Huddersfield T	(a)	0-2
		(h)	4-0
Third Round	Arsenal	(h)	0-3

FA Cup

Third Round	Oldham Ath	(h)	0-0
		(a)	1-2

BIRMINGHAM CITY 1995–96   *Back row (left to right):* Lil Fuccillo (Chief Scout), Kenny Lowe, Ken Charlery, Peter Shearer, Dave Barnett, Simon Black, Ryan Price, Liam Daish, Andy Edwards, Chris Whyte, Steve Castle, John Frain, Neil McDiarmid (Physio).

Middle row: David Howell (Reserve Team Manager), Ian Muir, John Bass, Paul Challinor, Steve Claridge, Paul Harding, Ian Bennett, Gary Poole, Ben Sedgemore, Neil Doherty, Steve Finnan, Paul Tait, Edwin Stein (Assistant Manager).

Front row: Richard Forsyth, Ricky Otto, Jason Bowen, Steve Robinson, Jae Martin, Barry Fry (Manager), Jonathon Hunt, Louie Donowa, Mark Ward (Player Coach), Scott Hiley, Gary Cooper.

(Photograph: Roy Smiljanic)

Division 1   **BIRMINGHAM CITY**

St Andrews, Birmingham B9 4NH. Telephone: (0121) 772 0101. Fax: (0121) 766 7866. Lottery Office/Souvenir Shop: (0121) 772 1245. Clubcall: 0891 121188. Club Soccer Shop: (0121) 766 8274.

Ground capacity: 25,936.

Record attendance: 66,844 v Everton, FA Cup 5th rd, 11 February 1939.

Record receipts: £230,000 v Aston Villa, Coca-Cola Cup 2nd rd 1st leg, 21 September 1993.

Pitch measurements: 115yd × 75yd.

Directors: J. F. Wiseman (Chairman), K. R. Brady (Managing Director), D. Sullivan, D. Gold, R. Gold, B. Gold, H. Brandman, A. G. Jones.

Manager: Trevor Francis. *Coach:* Kevan Broadhurst. *Physio:* N. McDiarmid.

Commercial Manager: Allan Robson. *Stadium Manager:* Gary Robotham.

Secretary: A. G. Jones BA, MBA.

Year Formed: 1875. *Turned Professional:* 1885. *Ltd Co.:* 1888.

Previous Names: 1875–88, Small Heath Alliance; 1888, dropped 'Alliance'; became Birmingham 1905; became Birmingham City 1945.

Club Nickname: 'Blues'.

Previous Grounds: 1875, waste ground near Arthur St; 1877, Muntz St, Small Heath; 1906, St Andrews.

Foundation: In 1875 cricketing enthusiasts who were largely members of Trinity Church, Bordesley, determined to continue their sporting relationships throughout the year by forming a football club which they called Small Heath Alliance. For their earliest games played on waste land in Arthur Street, the team included three Edden brothers and two James brothers.

First Football League game: 3 September 1892, Division 2, v Burslem Port Vale (h) W 5-1 – Charsley; Bayley, Speller; Ollis, Jenkyns, Devey; Hallam (1), Edwards (1), Short (1), Wheldon (2), Hands.

Record League Victory: 12–0 v Walsall T Swifts, Division 2, 17 December 1892 – Charsley; Bayley, Jones; Ollis, Jenkyns, Devey; Hallam (2), Walton (3), Mobley (3), Wheldon (2), Hands (2). 12–0 v Doncaster R, Division 2, 11 April 1903 – Dorrington; Goldie, Wassell; Beer, Dougherty (1), Howard; Athersmith (1), Leonard (3), McRoberts (1), Wilcox (4), Field (1). Aston. (1 og).

Record Cup Victory: 9–2 v Burton W, FA Cup 1st rd, 31 October 1885 – Hedges; Jones, Evetts (1); F. James, Felton, A. James (1); Davenport (2), Stanley (4), Simms, Figures, Morris (1).

Record Defeat: 1–9 v Sheffield W, Division 1, 13 December 1930 and v Blackburn R, Division 1, 5 January 1895.

Most League Points (2 for a win): 59, Division 2, 1947–48.

Most League Points (3 for a win): 89, Division 2, 1994–95.

Most League Goals: 103, Division 2, 1893–94 (only 28 games).

Highest League Scorer in Season: Joe Bradford, 29, Division 1, 1927–28.

Most League Goals in Total Aggregate: Joe Bradford, 249, 1920–35.

Most Capped Player: Malcolm Page, 28, Wales.

Most League Appearances: Frank Womack, 491, 1908–28.

Record Transfer Fee Received: £1,100,000 from Coventry C for Liam Daish February 1996.

Record Transfer Fee Paid: £800,000 to Southend U for Ricky Otto, December 1994.

Football League Record: 1892 elected to Division 2; 1894–96 Division 1; 1896–1901 Division 2; 1901–02 Division 1; 1902–03 Division 2; 1903–08 Division 1; 1908–21 Division 2; 1921–39 Division 1; 1946–48 Division 2; 1948–50 Division 1; 1950–1955 Division 2; 1955–65 Division 1; 1965–72 Division 2; 1972–79 Division 1; 1979–80 Division 2; 1980–84 Division 1; 1984–85 Division 2; 1985–86 Division 1; 1986–89 Division 2; 1989–92 Division 3; 1992–94 Division 1; 1994–95 Division 2; 1995– Division 1.

Honours: Football League: Division 1 best season: 6th, 1955–56; Division 2 – Champions 1892–93, 1920–21, 1947–48, 1954–55, 1994–95; Runners-up 1893–94, 1900–01, 1902–03, 1971–72, 1984–85. Division 3 Runners-up 1991–92. *FA Cup:* Runners-up 1931, 1956. *Football League Cup:* Winners 1963. *Leyland Daf Cup:* Winners 1991. *Auto Windscreens Shield:* Winners 1995. **European Competitions:** European Fairs Cup: 1955–58, 1958–60 (runners-up), 1960–61 (runners-up), 1961–62.

Colours: Blue shirts, white shorts, blue and white hooped stockings. *Change colours:* All red.

Did you know?
In the 1995–96 season Birmingham City beat the record for the number of players used in League games for one season. They called upon the services of 46.

BIRMINGHAM CITY 1995–96 LEAGUE RECORD

Match No.	Date	Venue	Opponents	Result	H/T Score	Lg. Pos.	Goalscorers	Attendance
1	Aug 12	H	Ipswich T	W 3-1	0-0	—	Tait, Otto, Bowen	18,910
2	19	A	Charlton Ath	L 1-3	0-0	10	Bowen	9692
3	26	H	Norwich C	W 3-1	1-0	4	Hunt 3 (1 pen)	19,267
4	30	A	Huddersfield T	L 2-4	1-1	—	Ward 2	12,305
5	Sept 2	A	Barnsley	W 5-0	0-0	6	Hunt (pen), Claridge, Charlery, Forsyth, Doherty	11,129
6	9	H	Crystal Palace	D 0-0	0-0	6		19,403
7	12	H	Stoke C	D 1-1	1-0	—	Hunt	19,005
8	17	A	WBA	L 0-1	0-1	11		17,875
9	23	A	Watford	D 1-1	1-1	13	Finnan	9422
10	30	H	Oldham Ath	D 0-0	0-0	12		17,269
11	Oct 8	H	Southend U	W 2-0	1-0	6	Claridge 2	17,491
12	14	A	Portsmouth	W 1-0	1-0	5	Claridge	10,006
13	21	H	Grimsby T	W 3-1	1-0	4	Claridge 2, Charlery	16,445
14	29	A	Port Vale	W 2-1	1-0	2	Tait, Claridge	8875
15	Nov 4	H	Millwall	D 2-2	1-0	3	Castle, Charlery	23,016
16	11	A	Reading	W 1-0	0-0	3	Charlery	10,203
17	18	A	Luton T	D 0-0	0-0	3		7920
18	21	H	Derby Co	L 1-4	1-2	—	Ward (pen)	19,417
19	26	H	Leicester C	D 2-2	1-2	5	Hunt 2 (1 pen)	17,350
20	Dec 2	A	Southend U	L 1-3	1-2	6	Claridge	7770
21	9	H	Watford	W 1-0	0-0	4	Francis	16,970
22	16	A	Oldham Ath	L 0-4	0-1	9		6602
23	23	H	Tranmere R	W 1-0	0-0	4	Hunt	18,439
24	26	A	Sheffield U	D 1-1	1-1	3	Francis	17,668
25	Jan 14	H	Charlton Ath	L 3-4	1-3	7	Hunt (pen), Edwards, Forsyth	18,539
26	20	A	Ipswich T	L 0-2	0-1	10		12,540
27	Feb 4	A	Norwich C	D 1-1	0-0	11	Otto	12,612
28	17	A	Stoke C	L 0-1	0-1	13		15,716
29	20	H	Barnsley	D 0-0	0-0	—		14,168
30	27	A	Crystal Palace	L 2-3	1-1	—	Bowen 2	12,965
31	Mar 2	H	Sheffield U	L 0-1	0-0	16		16,799
32	5	H	Wolverhampton W	W 2-0	2-0	—	Devlin 2 (1 pen)	22,051
33	9	A	Tranmere R	D 2-2	1-1	12	Legg, Hunt	8696
34	12	H	Huddersfield T	W 2-0	1-0	—	Devlin, Barnes P	15,296
35	17	H	Sunderland	L 0-2	0-1	11		23,251
36	20	H	WBA	D 1-1	0-1	—	Hunt	19,147
37	23	A	Wolverhampton W	L 2-3	1-1	12	Devlin 2 (1 pen)	26,256
38	30	A	Grimsby T	L 1-2	1-2	13	Barnes P	5475
39	Apr 2	H	Portsmouth	W 2-0	1-0	—	Barnes P, Devlin (pen)	14,886
40	6	H	Port Vale	W 3-1	2-0	9	Barnes P, Peschisolido, Tait	17,469
41	10	A	Millwall	L 0-2	0-1	—		9271
42	13	H	Luton T	W 4-0	1-0	9	Devlin, Francis, Barnes P 2	15,426
43	16	A	Sunderland	L 0-3	0-2	—		19,831
44	20	A	Derby Co	D 1-1	0-0	9	Breen	16,757
45	27	A	Leicester C	L 0-3	0-2	12		19,702
46	May 5	H	Reading	L 1-2	1-2	15	Barnes P	16,233

Final League Position: 15

GOALSCORERS

League (61): Hunt 11 (4 pens), Claridge 8, Barnes P 7, Devlin 7 (3 pens), Bowen 4, Charlery 4, Francis 3, Tait 3, Ward 3 (1 pen), Forsyth 2, Otto 2, Breen 1, Castle 1, Doherty 1, Edwards 1, Finnan 1, Legg 1, Peschisolido 1.
Coca-Cola Cup (17): Francis 4, Bowen 2, Charlery 2, Daish 2, Hunt 2, Claridge 1, Cooper 1, Edwards 1, Rushfeldt 1, own goal 1.
FA Cup (2): Hunt 1, Poole 1.

Bennett I 24	Poole G 27+1	Frain J 22+1	Ward M 13	Edwards A 36+1	Daish L 16+1	Hunt J 43+2	Claridge S 28	Legg A 9+3	Muir I 1	Forsyth R 12+14	Tait J 23+4	Donowa L 5+8	Otto R 6+12	Bowen J 16+7	Devlin P 16	Cooper G 16+2	Whyte C 4	Barnes P 15	Hiley S 5	Barber F 1	Castle S 12+3	Doherty N —+2	Johnson M 31+2	Granger M 8	Charlery K 8+9	Finnan S 6+6	Cornforth J 8	Martin J 1+6	Richardson I 3+4	Peschisolido P 7+2	Rushfeldt S 3+4	Francis K 11+8	Rea S —+1	Preece D 6	Hill D 5	Lowe K —+2	Sahlin D —+1	Griemink B 20	Bull G 3+3	Sansome P 1	Barnes S —+3	Bass J 5	Samways V 12	Breen G 17+1	Sheridan J 1+1	Match No.
1	2	3	4	5	6	7[2]	8	9[1]	10[3]	11	12	13	14																																	1
1	2	3[1]	4[3]	5	6	7	8[1]			14	11	12	13	9	10																															2
1	2		4[1]		6	7	8				12		10[2]			9	3	5			11	13																								3
1	2		4		6	7[1]	8				12		10[3]			9	3	5			11[2]	13	14																							4
1	2		4	5		7[1]	8				13		12			9[2]	11[3]	3			14	6	10																							5
1	2		4[1]	5	6	7	8				12					9	11					3	10																							6
1	2		4	5	6	7	8					12		13		9	11[2]					3	10[1]																							7
1	2		4	5	6	7	8				12	11[1]				10[3]	9[1]				3[2]	14																							8
1	2		4	5	6	7	8				12	13	3				11				10[2]	9[1]																							9
1	2		4	5	6	7	8				12					10[1]	9[2]	3			11[1]																								10
1	2			5		7	8				12			13	11[3]	3	4	6	10[1]	9[2]	14																								11
1	2			5		7	8[2]					11		12	10[1]	3	4	6	13	9[3]	14																								12
1	2			5		7	8					11		10[2]	3	4[3]	6	12	9[1]	13	14																								13
1	2			5	12	7[1]	8					11			3	4	6	9[3]	13	10[2]	14																								14
1	2			5		7[1]	8					11		10[2]	3	4	6	12	13	9																									15
1	2		4	5	6	7[1]	8					11			3			10[1]	3	13	14	9[2]																							16
1			4	5		7	8					11[2]		10[1]	3	2	6	9	13	12	14																							17
1			4	5	12		8					11[3]		10	3	2	6	13	7[1]	14	9[2]																							18
1		3				7	8	2						5		4[2]	6	12					9[1]	10	11[3]	13	14																	19
1	12	3		5	6	7[2]	8	2	14							4[3]		13					9	10[1]	11																				20
1	2	3		5	6	7	8					13		11							12[2]		9	4	10[1]																				21
1	2[2]	3		5	6	7	8	4				11									12	10	9[1]	13																				22
1		3		5	6	7	8	2			12										11	13	9[2]	4	10[1]																			23
1		3		5	6	7	8	2			12							13			10[3]	14	9[2]	4	11[1]																			24
2	3[1]		5	6	7[2]	8[3]	4			11	12												14	10					9	1														25
		3		5	6	7	8	4	12		10[3]							2[2]			11[1]	13					9			1	14													26
2	3		6		8			4	10[1]		12	11[2]	7					5					9						1		13													27
	3		7[3]							11[1]	12	8[2]	6					9								1	13			2	4	14	10										28
2	3		7[2]	8					4[3]	12	10[1]	9					6									1	13				11	5	14										29
2[1]	3		7				12	13[3]	8									6	14		9[2]						1			11	4													30
	3		7[1]	8	12	13		11[3]	10									6			14					1	9[2]			4	5												31
	3		7[2]	11	12	4		13	8	9[1]								6								1				2	10	5											32
	3		7	11		4			12	8[1]	9		1	6												1				2	10	5											33
	3		7	11		4				8	9			6	12											1				2	10[1]	5											34
	3		7	11	12	4				13	8[3]	9		6	14											1				2[1]	10[2]	5											35
		12	7	3	2	4[3]		13	11[2]	8	9[1]			6											14			1				10	5											36
		7	3	2				8	10	11	6									9					1					4	5											37
	2[1]		7[2]	11				8	9[3]		6	3		10		14	13								1					4	5											38
		2	7					8	9		6	3		10[1]	12										1					4	5											39
		5	7	11				8	9		6	3	4	10										1							2											40
	12		7[1]	14	8			11[3]	9		6	3	4	10[2]	13									1							2											41
2		6	7[1]	14	11[3]			8	9		12	3	4[2]	10	13									1												6							42
2		6	12	10[3]	11			8[2]	9		7[1]	3	4	14	13									1												5							43
2		6	7	13	11			8	9[2]		3	4	10[1]	12									1												5							44
2	3	5[3]	7[1]		12	11		8	9		6		4[2]	10	14									1								13	5										45
2	11	6[2]	7		12			8	9		13	3	4[1]	10[3]									1								14	5										46

Coca-Cola Cup

First Round	Plymouth Arg	(h)	1-0	(a)	2-1
Second Round	Grimsby T	(h)	3-1	(a)	1-1
Third Round	Tranmere R	(h)	1-1	(a)	3-1
Fourth Round	Middlesbrough	(a)	0-0	(h)	2-0
Fifth Round	Norwich C	(a)	1-1	(h)	2-1
Semi-final	Leeds U	(h)	1-2	(a)	0-3

FA Cup

Third Round	Wolverhampton W	(h)	1-1		
		(a)	1-2		

BLACKBURN ROVERS 1995–96 *Back row (left to right):* Kevin Gallacher, Alan Shearer, Graeme Le Saux, Nicky Marker, Stuart Ripley, Ian Pearce, Mike Newell, Tim Sherwood, Mark Atkins, Robbie Slater.

Middle row: Steve Foster (Physio), Chris Sutton, Henning Berg, Jason Wilcox, Paul Warhurst, Bobby Mimms, Colin Hendry, Tim Flowers, Jeff Kenna, Gary Tallon, Lee Makel, David Batty, Tony Parkes (First Team Coach).

Front row: Ken Beamish (Commercial Manager), Iain Stanners (Director), Keith Lee (Director), Richard Matthewman (Vice Chairman), Kenny Dalglish (Director of Football), Jack Walker (Senior Vice President), Ray Harford (Manager), Robert Coar (Chairman), William Bancroft (President), George Root (Director), Milton Jeffries (Vice President), John Howarth (Secretary).

(Photograph: Action Images)

FA Premiership   BLACKBURN ROVERS

Ewood Park, Blackburn BB2 4JF. Telephone: (01254) 698888. Fax: (01254) 671042. Ticket Office: (01254) 671666. Clubcall: 0891 121014. Club Shop-Mail Order: (01254) 672137.

Ground capacity: 31,367.

Record attendance: 61,783 v Bolton W, FA Cup 6th rd, 2 March 1929.

Record receipts: £333,067 v Liverpool, Coca-Cola Cup 4th rd, 30 November 1994.

Pitch measurements: 115yd × 72yd.

Chairman: R. D. Coar BSC. *Vice-Chairman:* R. L. Matthewman. *Directors:* K. C. Lee, I. R. Stanners, G. R. Root FCMA.

Director of Football: Kenny Dalglish MBE. *Manager:* Ray Harford. *Physio:* Steve Foster. *First Team Coach:* Tony Parkes. *Coach:* Derek Fazackerley.

Commercial Manager: Ken Beamish.

Secretary: John W. Howarth FAAI. *Stadium Manager:* M. Highmore.

Year Formed: 1875. *Turned Professional:* 1880. *Ltd Co.:* 1897.

Club Nickname: Rovers.

Previous Grounds: 1875-76, all matches played away; 1876, Oozehead Ground; 1877, Pleasington Cricket Ground; 1878, Alexandra Meadows; 1881, Leamington Road; 1890, Ewood Park.

Foundation: It was in 1875 that some Public School old boys called a meeting at which the Blackburn Rovers club was formed and the colours blue and white adopted. The leading light was John Lewis, later to become a founder of the Lancashire FA, a famous referee who was in charge of two FA Cup Finals, and a vice-president of both the FA and the Football League.

First Football League game: 15 September 1888, Football League, v Accrington (h) D 5-5 – Arthur; Beverley, James Southworth; Douglas, Almond, Forrest; Beresford (1), Walton, John Southworth (1), Fecitt (1), Townley (2).

Record League Victory: 9–0 v Middlesbrough, Division 2, 6 November 1954 – Elvy; Suart, Eckersley; Clayton, Kelly, Bell; Mooney (3), Crossan (2), Briggs, Quigley (3), Langton (1).

Record Cup Victory: 11–0 v Rossendale, FA Cup 1st rd, 13 October 1884 – Arthur; Hopwood, McIntyre; Forrest, Blenkhorn, Lofthouse; Sowerbutts (2), J. Brown (1), Fecitt (4), Barton (3), Birtwistle (1).

Record Defeat: 0–8 v Arsenal, Division 1, 25 February 1933.

Most League Points (2 for a win): 60, Division 3, 1974–75.

Most League Points (3 for a win): 89, FA Premier League, 1994–95.

Most League Goals: 114, Division 2, 1954–55.

Highest League Scorer in Season: Ted Harper, 43, Division 1, 1925–26.

Most League Goals in Total Aggregate: Simon Garner, 168, 1978–92.

Most Capped Player: Bob Crompton, 41, England.

Most League Appearances: Derek Fazackerley, 596, 1970–86.

Record Transfer Fee Received: £3,750,000 from Newcastle U for David Batty, February 1996.

Record Transfer Fee Paid: £5,000,000 to Norwich C for Chris Sutton, July 1994.

Football League Record: 1888 Founder Member of the League; 1936–39 Division 2; 1946–48 Division 1; 1948–58 Division 2; 1958–66 Division 1; 1966–71 Division 2; 1971–75 Division 3; 1975–79 Division 2; 1979–80 Division 3; 1980–92 Division 2; 1992– FA Premier League.

Honours: FA Premier League: – Champions 1994–95; Runners-up 1993–94. *Football League: Division 1* – Champions 1911–12, 1913–14; *Division 2* – Champions 1938–39; Runners-up 1957–58; *Division 3* – Champions 1974–75; Runners-up 1979–80. *FA Cup:* Winners 1884, 1885, 1886, 1890, 1891, 1928; Runners-up 1882, 1960. *Football League Cup:* Semi-final 1962, 1993. *Full Members' Cup:* Winners 1987. **European Competitions:** *European Cup:* 1995–96. *UEFA Cup:* 1994–95.

Colours: Blue and white halved shirts, white shorts with blue trim, white stockings with blue trim. *Change colours:* Yellow and navy.

Did you know?
Last season Alan Shearer became the first player to score 30 or more League goals in three consecutive seasons in the top division since the 1930's.

BLACKBURN ROVERS 1995–96 LEAGUE RECORD

Match No.	Date	Venue	Opponents	Result	H/T Score	Lg. Pos.	Goalscorers	Attendance
1	Aug 19	H	QPR	W 1-0	1-0	—	Shearer (pen)	25,932
2	23	A	Sheffield W	L 1-2	0-1	—	Shearer	25,544
3	26	A	Bolton W	L 1-2	0-1	—	Holmes	20,253
4	28	H	Manchester U	L 1-2	0-0	—	Shearer	29,843
5	Sept 9	H	Aston Villa	D 1-1	0-1	14	Shearer	27,084
6	16	A	Liverpool	L 0-3	0-3	17		39,502
7	23	H	Coventry C	W 5-1	2-1	13	Shearer 3, Hendry, Pearce	24,382
8	30	A	Middlesbrough	L 0-2	0-1	14		29,462
9	Oct 14	H	Southampton	W 2-1	1-0	11	Bohinen, Shearer	26,780
10	21	A	West Ham U	D 1-1	0-1	11	Shearer	21,776
11	28	H	Chelsea	W 3-0	1-0	11	Sherwood, Shearer, Newell	27,733
12	Nov 5	A	Everton	L 0-1	0-1	11		30,097
13	8	A	Newcastle U	L 0-1	0-1	—		36,463
14	18	H	Nottingham F	W 7-0	2-0	10	Shearer 3, Bohinen 2, Newell, Le Saux	27,660
15	26	A	Arsenal	D 0-0	0-0	13		37,695
16	Dec 2	H	West Ham U	W 4-2	3-0	10	Shearer 3 (1 pen), Newell	26,638
17	9	A	Coventry C	L 0-5	0-1	11		13,409
18	16	H	Middlesbrough	W 1-0	1-0	11	Shearer	27,996
19	23	A	Wimbledon	D 1-1	1-0	11	Kimble (og)	7105
20	26	H	Manchester C	W 2-0	1-0	9	Shearer, Batty	28,915
21	30	H	Tottenham H	W 2-1	2-0	9	Marker, Shearer	30,004
22	Jan 1	A	Leeds U	D 0-0	0-0	10		31,285
23	13	A	QPR	W 1-0	0-0	8	Shearer	13,957
24	20	H	Sheffield W	W 3-0	2-0	6	Shearer, Bohinen, Gallacher	24,732
25	Feb 3	H	Bolton W	W 3-1	1-1	6	Shearer 3	30,419
26	10	A	Manchester U	L 0-1	0-1	6		42,681
27	24	H	Liverpool	L 2-3	1-2	9	Wilcox, Sherwood	30,895
28	28	A	Aston Villa	L 0-2	0-0	—		28,008
29	Mar 2	A	Manchester C	D 1-1	0-0	10	Shearer	29,078
30	13	H	Leeds U	W 1-0	0-0	—	Fenton	23,358
31	16	A	Tottenham H	W 3-2	2-0	6	Shearer 3 (1 pen)	31,803
32	30	H	Everton	L 0-3	0-0	8		29,468
33	Apr 6	A	Southampton	L 0-1	0-0	9		14,793
34	8	H	Newcastle U	W 2-1	0-0	9	Fenton 2	30,717
35	13	A	Nottingham F	W 5-1	3-1	8	Shearer, McKinlay, Wilcox 2, Fenton	25,273
36	17	H	Wimbledon	W 3-2	1-1	—	Shearer 2, Fenton	24,174
37	27	H	Arsenal	D 1-1	1-0	7	Gallacher	29,834
38	May 5	A	Chelsea	W 3-2	1-1	7	Sherwood, McKinlay, Fenton	28,436

Final League Position: 7

GOALSCORERS
League (61): Shearer 31 (3 pens), Fenton 6, Bohinen 4, Newell 3, Sherwood 3, Wilcox 3, Gallacher 2, McKinlay 2, Batty 1, Hendry 1, Holmes 1, Le Saux 1, Marker 1, Pearce 1, own goal 1.
Coca-Cola Cup (8): Shearer 5, Newell 1, Sutton 1, own goal 1.
FA Cup (0).

Flowers T 37	Berg H 38	Le Saux G 13 + 1	Batty D 23	Hendry C 33	Pearce I 12	Ripley S 28	Sherwood T 33	Shearer A 35	Sutton C 9 + 4	Gallacher K 14 + 2	Atkins M — + 4	Mimms B 1 + 1	Holmes M 8 + 1	Newell M 26 + 4	Makel L — + 3	Kenna J 32	Warhurst P 1 + 9	Bohinen L 17 + 2	McKinlay B 13 + 6	Marker N 8 + 1	Fenton G 4 + 10	Coleman C 19 + 1	Gudmundsson N 1 + 3	Wilcox J 10	Flitcroft G 3	Match No.
1	2	3	4	5	6	7	8	9	10^1	11^6	12			15												1
1	2	3	4	5	6	7^1	8	9	10^2		12		11	13												2
1	2	3	4	5	6	7^1	8	9	10^2		12		11	13												3
1	2	3	4	5	6	7^2	8	9	10		12		11^1	13												4
	2	3	4	5	6	7	8	9				1	11^1	10	12											5
1	2	3	4	5	6	7^1	8	9	12	10				13										11^2		6
1	2	3^1	4	5	6		8	9	10	7	12													11		7
1	2		4	5	6		8	9	10	11^1				7		3	12									8
1	2		4	5	6	7	8	9	10							3								11		9
1	2		4	5	6	7	8^2	9	10^1	12						3								11	13	10
1	2		4	5	6	7	8	9	10							3								11		11
1	2	13	4	5	6^2	7	8	9	12	10^1						3								11		12
1	6	3	4	5			8^2	9	12	10				13		2		7^1						11		13
1	6	3	4	5		7	8	9	10							2								11		14
1	6	3	4	5		7	8	9	10							2								11		15
1	6	3	4	5^1		7	8	9	10					12		2								11		16
1	2	3	4			7	8	9	6	10^1			12	11^2	13	5										17
1	6	3^1	4	5		7^2	8	9	10					13		2	12							11		18
1	2		4	5		7	8	9	12					10^1		3	7					6		11		19
1	2		4	5		7	8	9						10		3						6		11		20
1	2		4	5		7		9						10^1		3	12^2	8	13	5		6		11		21
1	2		4^1	5		7		9	12					10^2		3		8	11	5	13	6		11		22
1	2		4	5		7		9						10		3		8				6		11		23
1	2		4	5		7^2		9						10^1		3		8	12		6	13		11		24
1	2		4	5		7^1		9						10		3		8	12		6			11		25
1	2		4	5				9	7					10^2		3		8	12	13	6^1	14	11^3			26
1	2		4	5		7^1		9						10		3	12	8^2		13	6		11			27
1	2		4	5				9	7					10^2		3	12	8	13	6		11^1				28
1	2		4	5				9	7				11	10		3		8			6					29
1	2		4	5				9	12	11				10^1		3		8	4	12	6					30
1	2		4	5				9	12	11				10		3		7	4	8^1	6					31
1	2			7	4	10^1		9								3			12	5^2	13	6		11	8	32
1	2			4	9	7			10							3			5^1	12	6			11	8	33
1	2		5	7^1	4	9		12						10^2		3				13	6			11	8	34
1	2		5	7	4	9								10^1		3		8		12	6			11		35
1	2		5	7	4	9								10^1		3		8		12	6			11		36
1	2		5	7^2	4			10								3	12	13	8	6	9^1			11		37
1	2		5	7	4			10^1								3	12	13	8		9^2	6		11		38

Coca-Cola Cup

Second Round	Swindon T	(a)	3-2
		(h)	2-0
Third Round	Watford	(a)	2-1
Fourth Round	Leeds U	(a)	1-2

FA Cup

Third Round	Ipswich T	(a)	0-0
		(h)	0-1

BLACKPOOL 1995–96   *Back row (left to right):* Paul Symons, Darren Bradshaw, Jamie Murphy, Jason Lydiate, Craig Allardyce, Andy Preece, Phil Horner, Tony Ellis, Jon Sunderland, Scott Darton.

Middle row: David Carroll, Stephen Torre, John Hooks, Graeme Craggs, Lee Martin, Tim Carter, Melvin Capleton, James Quinn, David Burke, Robert Ward, Jamie Sheppard.

Front row: Stuart Parkinson, Micky Mellon, Andy Morrison, Chris Beech, Andy Bingham (Director of Football), Sam Allardyce (Manager), Phil Brown (Player Coach), Brian Croft, Andy Gouck, Mark Bonner, Andy Barlow.

Division 2   BLACKPOOL

Bloomfield Rd Ground, Blackpool FY1 6JJ. Telephone: (01253) 404331. Fax: (01253) 405011. Clubcall: 0891 121648.

Ground capacity: 9701.

Record attendance: 38,098 v Wolverhampton W, Division 1, 17 September 1955.

Record receipts: £72,949 v Tottenham H, FA Cup 3rd rd, 5 January 1991.

Pitch measurements: 112yd × 74yd.

Chairman: Mrs V. Oyston. *Deputy Chairman:* W. Bingham MBE (Director of Football).

Managing Director: Mrs G. Bridge.

Directors: G. Warburton, J. Wilde MBE, Mrs R. Bingham, R. Oakley, K. Chadwick, M. Joyce.

Associate Director: C. Muir.

Manager: Gary Megson.

Secretary: Carol Banks.

Commercial Manager: Geoffrey Warburton.

Physio: Mark Taylor MCSP. *Stadium Manager:* John Turner.

Year Formed: 1887. *Turned Professional:* 1887. *Ltd Co.:* 1896.

Previous Name: 'South Shore' combined with Blackpool in 1899, twelve years after the latter had been formed on the breaking up of the old 'Blackpool St John's' club.

Club Nickname: 'The Seasiders'.

Previous Grounds: 1887, Raikes Hall Gardens; 1897, Athletic Grounds; 1899, Raikes Hall Gardens; 1899, Bloomfield Road.

Foundation: Old boys of St. John's School who had formed themselves into a football club decided to establish a club bearing the name of their town and Blackpool FC came into being at a meeting at the Stanley Arms Hotel in the summer of 1887. In their first season playing at Raikes Hall Gardens, the club won both the Lancashire Junior Cup and the Fylde Cup.

First Football League game: 5 September 1896, Division 2, v Lincoln C (a) L 1-3 – Douglas; Parr, Bowman; Stuart, Stirzaker, Norris; Clarkin, Donnelly, R. Parkinson, Mount (1), J. Parkinson.

Record League Victory: 7–0 v Preston NE (away), Division 1, 1 May 1948 – Robinson; Shimwell, Crosland; Buchan, Hayward, Kelly; Hobson, Munro (1), McIntosh (5), McCall, Rickett (1).

Record Cup Victory: 7–1 v Charlton Ath, League Cup 2nd rd, 25 September 1963 – Harvey; Armfield, Martin; Crawford, Gratrix, Cranston; Lea, Ball (1), Charnley (4), Durie (1), Oates (1).

Record Defeat: 1–10 v Small Heath, Division 2, 2 March 1901 and v Huddersfield T, Division 1, 13 December 1930.

Most League Points (2 for a win): 58, Division 2, 1929–30.

Most League Points (3 for a win): 86, Division 4, 1984–85.

Most League Goals: 98, Division 2, 1929–30.

Highest League Scorer in Season: Jimmy Hampson, 45, Division 2, 1929–30.

Most League Goals in Total Aggregate: Jimmy Hampson, 247, 1927–38.

Most Capped Player: Jimmy Armfield, 43, England.

Most League Appearances: Jimmy Armfield, 568, 1952–71.

Record Transfer Fee Received: £750,000 from QPR for Trevor Sinclair, August 1993.

Record Transfer Fee Paid: £245,000 to Blackburn R for Andy Morrison, October 1994.

Football League Record: 1896 Elected to Division 2; 1899 Failed re-election; 1900 Re-elected; 1900–30 Division 2; 1930–33 Division 1; 1933–37 Division 2; 1937–67 Division 1; 1967–70 Division 2; 1970–71 Division 1; 1971–78 Division 2; 1978–81 Division 3; 1981–85 Division 4; 1985–90 Division 3; 1990–92 Division 4; 1992–Division 2.

Honours: Football League: Division 1 – Runners-up 1955–56; Division 2 – Champions 1929–30; Runners-up 1936–37, 1969–70; Division 4 – Runners-up 1984–85. *FA Cup:* Winners 1953; Runners-up 1948, 1951. *Football League Cup:* Semi-final 1962. *Anglo-Italian Cup:* Winners 1971; Runners-up 1972.

Colours: Tangerine shirts with navy and white trim, white shorts, tangerine stockings with navy blue tops. *Change colours:* Navy and sky blue stripes, navy shorts, navy stockings.

Did you know?
In 1995–96 James Quinn became the first Blackpool player to be capped at full international level for Northern Ireland since Derek Spence in 1979–80.

BLACKPOOL 1995–96 LEAGUE RECORD

Match No.	Date	Venue	Opponents	Result	H/T Score	Lg. Pos.	Goalscorers	Attendance
1	Aug 12	A	Bristol C	D 1-1	1-1	—	Quinn	7734
2	19	H	Wrexham	W 2-0	2-0	4	Ellis 2	4799
3	26	A	Hull C	L 1-2	1-1	8	Lydiate	4755
4	29	H	Peterborough U	W 2-1	1-1	—	Preece, Quinn	3902
5	Sept 2	A	Shrewsbury T	W 2-0	2-0	2	Preece 2	3182
6	9	H	Stockport Co	L 0-1	0-1	6		6602
7	12	H	Bournemouth	W 2-1	1-1	—	Preece, Morrison	3884
8	16	A	Brighton & HA	W 2-1	2-0	3	Ellis, Mellon	6158
9	23	H	Crewe Alex	W 2-1	0-1	2	Preece, Ellis	7301
10	30	A	Bradford C	L 1-2	1-0	2	Preece	6820
11	Oct 7	A	Brentford	W 2-1	0-1	2	Preece (pen), Ellis	5313
12	14	H	Chesterfield	D 0-0	0-0	3		6855
13	21	A	Rotherham U	L 1-2	0-0	4	Preece (pen)	3663
14	28	H	Oxford U	D 1-1	0-0	5	Quinn	5303
15	31	H	Bristol R	W 3-0	3-0	—	Gouck, Quinn, Ellis	3877
16	Nov 4	A	Swindon T	D 1-1	0-0	5	Quinn (pen)	12,470
17	18	H	York C	L 1-3	1-1	5	Holden	4514
18	25	A	Walsall	D 1-1	0-0	6	Mellon	4459
19	Dec 9	A	Crewe Alex	W 2-1	1-0	4	Ellis, Watson	4551
20	16	H	Bradford C	W 4-1	1-0	4	Watson 2, Ellis, Bonner	4857
21	23	A	Notts Co	D 1-1	0-0	4	Arkins (og)	5522
22	Jan 1	A	Carlisle U	W 2-1	1-0	3	Bryan, Linighan	7532
23	13	A	Wrexham	D 1-1	0-0	3	Preece	5479
24	20	H	Bristol C	W 3-0	1-0	3	Morrison, Ellis, Preece (pen)	4838
25	23	H	Wycombe W	D 1-1	1-0	—	Preece	3877
26	Feb 3	H	Hull C	D 1-1	1-0	4	Holden	4713
27	10	A	Wycombe W	W 1-0	1-0	3	Watson	5285
28	13	H	Swansea C	W 4-0	2-0	—	Watson, Mellon, Bonner, Preece	3992
29	17	A	Bournemouth	L 0-1	0-0	3		4157
30	20	H	Shrewsbury T	W 2-1	1-0	—	Quinn, Seabury (og)	4210
31	24	H	Brighton & HA	W 2-1	0-1	2	Mellon 2	4937
32	27	A	Stockport Co	D 1-1	0-0	—	Ellis	7711
33	Mar 2	A	Burnley	W 1-0	0-0	2	Preece	10,082
34	9	H	Notts Co	W 1-0	1-0	2	Ellis	7187
35	12	H	Burnley	W 3-1	1-1	—	Mellon, Bonner, Ellis	8941
36	16	A	Swansea C	W 2-0	0-0	1	Ellis, Watson	4478
37	23	H	Carlisle U	W 3-1	1-1	1	Linighan 2, Quinn (pen)	8144
38	26	A	Peterborough U	D 0-0	0-0	—		4425
39	30	H	Brentford	W 1-0	1-0	1	Quinn (pen)	5899
40	Apr 2	A	Chesterfield	L 0-1	0-0	—		7002
41	6	A	Oxford U	L 0-1	0-0	2		7875
42	8	H	Rotherham U	L 1-2	1-1	2	Preece	6850
43	13	A	Bristol R	D 1-1	0-1	2	Linighan	5626
44	20	H	Swindon T	D 1-1	0-1	2	Barlow	9175
45	27	H	Walsall	L 1-2	1-1	3	Quinn (pen)	9148
46	May 4	A	York C	W 2-0	1-0	3	Morrison, Ellis	7147

Final League Position: 3

GOALSCORERS

League (67): Ellis 14, Preece 14 (3 pens), Quinn 9 (4 pens), Mellon 6, Watson 6, Linighan 4, Bonner 3, Morrison 3, Holden 2, Barlow 1, Bryan 1, Gouck 1, Lydiate 1, own goals 2.
Coca-Cola Cup (3): Ellis 2, Mellon 1.
FA Cup (5): Quinn 2, Lydiate 1, Preece 1, Quinn 1.

Capleton M 1	Brown P 5+8	Barlow A 34	Lydiate J 30+2	Mellon M 45	Bradshaw D 25	Quinn J 42+2	Bonner M 41+1	Gouck A 8+8	Ellis T 41+2	Preece A 37+4	Bryan M 44+2	Banks S 24	Brown R 2+1	Beech C 3+15	Darton S 5+4	Morrison A 29	Holden R 19+3	Watson A 14+13	Yallop F 3	Linighan D 29	Barber F 1	Allardyce C —+1	Nixon E 20	Charnock P —+4	Philpott L 4+6	Thorpe L —+1	Pascoe C —+1	Match No.
1		3	4	5	6	7¹	8	9	10	11	12		2															1
		3	4	5	6	7¹		9	10	11	12	1	2	8														2
		3¹	4	5	6	7	13	9²	10	11	2	1	12	8														3
			4	5	6	7¹	8		10	11	2	1				12	3	9										4
			4	5	6	7	8		10	11	2	1				12	3	9¹										5
			4	5¹	6	7	8		10	11	2	1					3	9	12									6
		3	4	5	6	7¹	8		10	11	2	1						9	12									7
	12	3	4	5	6³	13	8¹	14	10	11²	2	1						9	7									8
		3	4	5		6¹	8		10	11	2	1				12		9	7									9
			4	5¹		6²			10	11	2	1				12	3	9	7	13								10
		3	4	5		6	8		10¹	11	2	1				12		9	7									11
		3	4	5		6²	8	12	10¹	11	2	1						9	7	13								12
			4	5		6	8			11	2	1				12	3	9	7	10¹								13
		3	4	5		6	8		10¹	11²	2	1				12		9	7	13								14
		3	4	5		6	8¹	7	10	12	2	1					13	9²	11									15
	12		4¹	5	9	6	8	7	10		2	1						11	3									16
				5		6	8²	7	10		2	1				12		9	11	13	3	4						17
				5	7	6	8¹		10	12	2	1				13		9	11	3²	4							18
	3		7	5		6	8		10		2	1				12		11	9¹	4								19
	3		7	5		6	8¹		10		2					12	13	11²	9	4³	1	14						20
	3		7	5		6	8		10		2	1				9		11		4								21
	3		7	5		6¹	8²		10	12	2	1				13	9	11		4								22
	12	3¹	7	5		6	8		10	13	2	1				9		11²		4								23
	3		7	5		6²	8¹	12	10	11	2	1				9	13			4								24
	3		7	5¹		6	8	12	10	11	2	1				9²	13³	14		4								25
	3¹			5	7	6	8	12	10	11	2	1				9²	13			4								26
	3			5	7	6¹	8			11	2					9	10			4			1	12				27
	3	12		5	7	6	8²			11	2¹					9	10			4			1	13				28
	3³	13		5	7	6²	8	12		11	2					9¹	10			4			1	14				29
	3			5	7	6	8		10¹	11	2			12		9				4			1					30
	3			5	7	6	8	12	10	11	2					9¹				4			1					31
	3²			5	7	6	8		10	11¹	2					9		12		4			1	13				32
	3			5	7	6	8		10	11¹	2					9		12		4			1					33
	3			5	7	6¹	8		10²	11	2			12		9		13		4			1					34
	3			5	7	6	8¹		10	11²	2			12		9		13		4			1					35
	12	3¹		5	7				8	10	11	2		6		9				4			1					36
	3			5	7	6			8	10	11	2				9¹				4			1	12				37
	12	3		5	7¹				10	11	2		13		9	6²				4			1	8				38
	3	7			6	5			10	11	2			12		9				4			1	8¹				39
	12	3¹	7	5		6	8		10	11²	2					9				4			1	13				40
	3	7		5		6	8¹		10	11	2					9				4			1	12				41
	12	3	7³	5		6¹	8		10	11	2					9	13			4²	1			14				42
	3	7		5		6	8	12	10¹	11	2			13						4			1	9²				43
	12	3	7	5		6	8		13	11	2					10¹				4			1	9²				44
	9³	3	7	5	4	6²	8		10	11¹	2									1			12		13	14		45
	3²			5	7	12	8	13	10	11³	2					9¹	6			4			1	14				46

Coca-Cola Cup
First Round   Bradford C   (a) 1-2   (h) 2-3

FA Cup
First Round   Chester C   (h) 2-1
Second Round   Colwyn Bay   (h) 2-0
Third Round   Huddersfield T   (a) 1-2

BOLTON WANDERERS 1995-96   *Back row (left to right)*: Richard Sneekes, Jimmy Phillips, Scott Green, Chris Fairclough, Simon Coleman, Neil McDonald, Andy Todd, Nicky Spooner.
Middle row: Ewan Simpson (Physio), Jason McAteer, Fabian de Freitas, Gudni Bergsson, Keith Branagan, Gerry Taggart, Aidan Davison, Alan Thompson, Mark Patterson, Steve Carroll (Reserve Team Manager), Ian McNeil (Chief Scout)
Front row: David Lee, Owen Coyle, Alan Stubbs, Colin Todd (Assistant Manager), Roy McFarland (Manager), Mixu Paatelainen, John McGinlay, Stewart Whittaker.

Division 1   **BOLTON WANDERERS**

Burnden Park, Bolton BL3 2QR. Telephone: (01204) 389200. Fax: (01204) 382334. Ticket Office: (01204) 521101. Ticket Office Fax: (01204) 392474. Commercial Dept: (01204) 24518.

Ground capacity: 20,500.

Record attendance: 69,912 v Manchester C, FA Cup 5th rd, 18 February 1933.

Record receipts: £159,290.50 v Swindon T, Coca-Cola Cup semi-final, 8 March 1995.

Pitch measurements: 113yd × 76yd.

President: Nat Lofthouse.

Chairman: G. Hargreaves.

Directors: P. A. Gartside, G. Ball, G. Seymour, G. Warburton, W. B. Warburton, B. Scowcroft.

Team Manager: Colin Todd. *Physio:* E. Simpson.

Chief Executive & Secretary: Des McBain. *Commercial Manager:* T. Holland.

Year Formed: 1874. *Turned Professional:* 1880. *Ltd Co.:* 1895.

Previous Name: 1874–77, Christ Church FC; 1877 became Bolton Wanderers.

Club Nickname: 'The Trotters'.

Previous Grounds: Park Recreation Ground and Cockle's Field before moving to Pike's Lane ground 1881; 1895, Burnden Park.

Foundation: In 1874 boys of Christ Church Sunday School, Blackburn Street, led by their master Thomas Ogden, established a football club which went under the name of the school and whose president was Vicar of Christ Church. Membership was 6d (two and a half pence). When their president began to lay down too many rules about the use of church premises, the club broke away and formed Bolton Wanderers in 1877, holding their earliest meetings at the Gladstone Hotel.

First Football League game: 8 September 1888, Football League, v Derby Co (h), L 3–6 – Harrison; Robinson, Mitchell; Roberts, Weir, Bullough, Davenport (2), Milne, Coupar, Barbour, Brogan (1).

Record League Victory: 8–0 v Barnsley, Division 2, 6 October 1934 – Jones; Smith, Finney; Goslin, Atkinson, George Taylor; George T. Taylor (2), Eastham, Milsom (1), Westwood (4), Cook. (1 og).

Record Cup Victory: 13–0 v Sheffield U, FA Cup 2nd rd, 1 February 1890 – Parkinson; Robinson (1), Jones; Bullough, Davenport, Roberts; Rushton, Brogan (3), Cassidy (5), McNee, Weir (4).

Record Defeat: 1–9 v Preston NE, FA Cup 2nd rd, 10 December 1887.

Most League Points (2 for a win): 61, Division 3, 1972–73.

Most League Points (3 for a win): 90, Division 2, 1992–93.

Most League Goals: 96, Division 2, 1934–35.

Highest League Scorer in Season: Joe Smith, 38, Division 1, 1920–21.

Most League Goals in Total Aggregate: Nat Lofthouse, 255, 1946–61.

Most Capped Player: Nat Lofthouse, 33, England.

Most League Appearances: Eddie Hopkinson, 519, 1956–70.

Record Transfer Fee Received: £550,000 from Celtic for Andy Walker, July 1994.

Record Transfer Fee Paid: £450,000 to Leeds U for Chris Fairclough, July 1995.

Football League Record: 1888 Founder Member of the League; 1899–1900 Division 2; 1900–03 Division 1; 1903–05 Division 2; 1905–08 Division 1; 1908–09 Division 2; 1909–10 Division 1; 1910–11 Division 2; 1911–33 Division 1; 1933–35 Division 2; 1935–64 Division 1; 1964–71 Division 2; 1971–73 Division 3; 1973–78 Division 2; 1978–80 Division 1; 1980–83 Division 2; 1983–87 Division 3; 1987–88 Division 4; 1988–92 Division 3; 1992–93 Division 2; 1993–95 Division 1; 1995–96 FA Premier League; 1996– Division 1.

Honours: Football League: Division 1 best season: 3rd, 1891–92, 1920–21, 1924–25, 1994–95; Division 2 – Champions 1908–09, 1977–78; Runners-up 1899–1900, 1904–05, 1910–11, 1934–35, 1992–93; Division 3 – Champions 1972–73. *FA Cup:* Winners 1923, 1926, 1929, 1958; Runners-up 1894, 1904, 1953. *Football League Cup:* Runners-up 1995. *Freight Rover Trophy:* Runners-up 1986. *Sherpa Van Trophy:* Winners 1989.

Colours: White shirts, navy blue shorts, blue stockings. *Change colours:* Dark/sky blue shirts, navy blue shorts, blue stockings.

Did you know?
The first season in which Bolton were unbeaten at home was 1910–11 in Division Two, when they dropped only two points in drawn games.

BOLTON WANDERERS 1995–96 LEAGUE RECORD

Match No.	Date	Venue	Opponents	Result	H/T Score	Lg. Pos.	Goalscorers	Attendance
1	Aug 19	A	Wimbledon	L	2-3	2-2	—	Thompson (pen), De Freitas	9317
2	22	H	Newcastle U	L	1-3	0-1	—	Bergsson	20,243
3	26	H	Blackburn R	W	2-1	1-0	—	De Freitas, Stubbs	20,253
4	30	A	Aston Villa	L	0-1	0-0	—		31,770
5	Sept 9	H	Middlesbrough	D	1-1	1-0	16	McGinlay	18,376
6	16	A	Manchester U	L	0-3	0-2	18		32,812
7	23	A	Liverpool	L	2-5	0-2	19	Todd, Patterson (pen)	40,104
8	30	H	QPR	L	0-1	0-0	19		17,362
9	Oct 14	H	Everton	D	1-1	1-0	19	Paatelainen	20,427
10	21	A	Nottingham F	L	2-3	1-1	19	Sneekes, De Freitas	25,426
11	30	H	Arsenal	W	1-0	1-0	—	McGinlay	18,682
12	Nov 4	A	Manchester C	L	0-1	0-1	18		28,397
13	18	H	West Ham U	L	0-3	0-0	18		19,047
14	22	A	Chelsea	L	2-3	1-1	—	Curcic, Green	17,495
15	25	A	Southampton	L	0-1	0-0	20		14,404
16	Dec 2	H	Nottingham F	D	1-1	0-0	19	De Freitas	17,342
17	9	H	Liverpool	L	0-1	0-0	20		21,042
18	16	A	QPR	L	1-2	1-1	20	Sellars	11,456
19	23	A	Tottenham H	D	2-2	0-0	20	Green, Bergsson	30,702
20	27	H	Leeds U	L	0-2	0-1	—		18,414
21	30	H	Coventry C	L	1-2	1-1	20	McGinlay	16,678
22	Jan 1	A	Sheffield W	L	2-4	0-2	20	Curcic, Taggart	24,872
23	13	H	Wimbledon	W	1-0	1-0	20	McGinlay (pen)	16,216
24	20	A	Newcastle U	L	1-2	1-2	20	Bergsson	36,543
25	Feb 3	A	Blackburn R	L	1-3	1-1	20	Green	30,419
26	10	H	Aston Villa	L	0-2	0-1	20		18,099
27	17	A	Middlesbrough	W	4-1	2-1	20	Blake, Coleman, De Freitas, Lee	29,354
28	25	H	Manchester U	L	0-6	0-2	20		21,381
29	Mar 2	A	Leeds U	W	1-0	1-0	20	Bergsson	30,106
30	16	A	Coventry C	W	2-0	0-0	20	Stubbs 2	17,168
31	20	H	Tottenham H	L	2-3	0-1	—	Stubbs, Sellars	17,829
32	23	H	Sheffield W	W	2-1	1-1	19	Sellars, Curcic	18,368
33	30	H	Manchester C	D	1-1	0-1	20	McGinlay	21,050
34	Apr 6	A	Everton	L	0-3	0-1	20		37,974
35	8	H	Chelsea	W	2-1	2-1	20	McGinlay, Curcic	18,021
36	13	A	West Ham U	L	0-1	0-1	20		23,086
37	27	H	Southampton	L	0-1	0-1	20		18,795
38	May 5	A	Arsenal	L	1-2	0-0	20	Todd	38,104

Final League Position: 20

GOALSCORERS
League (39): McGinlay 6 (1 pen), De Freitas 5, Bergsson 4, Curcic 4, Stubbs 4, Green 3, Sellars 3, Todd 2, Blake 1, Coleman 1, Lee 1, Paatelainen 1, Patterson 1 (pen), Sneekes 1, Taggart 1, Thompson 1 (pen).
Coca-Cola Cup (7): McGinlay 2, Sneekes 2, Curcic 1, Patterson 1, Thompson 1.
FA Cup (3): Curcic 2, McGinlay 1.

Branagan K 31	Green S 26+5	Phillips J 37	McAteer J 4	Bergsson G 34	Stubbs A 24+1	Fairclough C 33	De Freitas F 17+10	Paatelainen M 12+3	Patterson M 12+4	Thompson A 23+3	Lee D 9+9	Coyle O 2+3	Sneekes R 14+3	McGinlay J 29+3	Taggart G 11	Todd A 9+3	McAnespie S 7+2	Curcic S 28	Sellars S 22	Blake N 14+4	Burnett W —+1	Strong G —+1	Coleman S 12	Davison A 2	Ward G 5	Taylor S —+1	Small B 1	Match No.
1	2	3	4	5[1]	6	7	8	9[2]	10	11	12	13																1
1	2	3	4	5	6	7[1]	8		10	11[2]	12	9	13															2
1	2	3	4	5	6	7	8		10	11	12	9[1]																3
1	2[1]	3	4	5	6	7	8	9	11	12		13	10[2]															4
1	2	3		5		7	8	9	11		12			4	10[1]	6												5
1	2	3		5	13	7	8	12	11	9				4	10[1]	6[1]												6
1	2	3		5	6		8	9	11[2]	7	12			4	10[1]	13												7
1		3		5	6		8	9	11	7				4	10		2											8
1	12	3		5	6	7		9[2]	8	11	13			4	10[1]		2											9
1		3		5	6	7	12	9	8[2]	11	13			4	10[1]		2											10
1	12	3		5	6	4	9	13	11[1]	7				10			2	8[2]										11
1	12	3[1]		5	6	4	13	9[3]	14	11	7			10			2	8[2]										12
1	12	3		5	6		9	11	7[1]	8				10	13		2[2]	4										13
1	2	3		5		7		9	11					10	6	8		4										14
1	2	3		5		7		9	11					10	6	8		4										15
1	2	3		5		7	9			11				10	6	8		4										16
1	2	3		5		7	9				12			10	6	8[1]		4	11									17
1	2	3		5		7	9							10	6	8[1]	12	4	11									18
1	2	3		5		7	12						13	10[1]	6	8[2]		4	11	9								19
1	2	3[1]		5		7	12						8[2]	10	6			4	11	9	13							20
1	2	3		5									7	10	6	8		4	11	9								21
1	2	3			5		12						7	10[1]	6	8[2]		4	11	9	13							22
1	2	3		5	6		9				12		7	10				4	11	8[1]								23
1	2[3]	3		5	6		12			7			8	10	13	14		4[1]	11	9[2]								24
1	2	3		5	6	7[1]	9		12	8				10[2]				4	11	13								25
1	2	3		5[1]	6	7	10		12					8	13			4	11[2]	9								26
1	2	3			5	8				11	7							4	10	9			6					27
1	2	3			5	8			10	7[1]				12				4	11	9			6					28
1	2	3		5	8	7	12	9										4	11	10[1]			6					29
1	2	3		5	8	7	12	9										4	11	10[1]			6					30
	2[1]	3	4	8	5	12	9[3]	14		13	7			11				10[2]					6	1				31
		3	2	8	5	9			11					10				4	7				6	1				32
	12	3	2	8	5	9[1]	13	11[3]						10				4	7	14			6	1				33
	2[1]	3	4	8	5	12	9[2]			10								7	11	13			6	1				34
		3	2	8	5					11				10				4	7	9[1]			6	1		12		35
		3	2	8	5	12				11				10				4	7	9[1]			6	1				36
		3	2	8	5[1]	9[1]	12			11	13			10				4	7				6	1				37
1				5	8			9	12	10	11		2			4[1]	7	13					6[2]				3	38

Coca-Cola Cup

Second Round	Brentford	(h)	1-0	
		(a)	3-2	
Third Round	Leicester C	(h)	0-0	
		(a)	3-2	
Fourth Round	Norwich C	(a)	0-0	
		(h)	0-0	

FA Cup

Third Round	Bradford C	(a)	3-0
Fourth Round	Leeds U	(h)	0-1

AFC BOURNEMOUTH 1995–96 *Back row (left to right)*: Mike McElhatton, Matty Holland, Neil Young, Scott Mean, Rob Murray, Jason Brissett. *Middle row*: Larry Clay (Youth & Community Development Officer), Sean O'Driscoll (Youth Development Manager), Steve Fletcher, Adrian Pennock, Alex Watson, Ian Andrews, Neil Moss, Steve Jones, Mark Morris, Jamie Victory, John Williams (Assistant Manager), Steve Hardwick (Physio). *Front row*: Russell Beardsmore, Mark Rawlinson, John Bailey, Mel Machin (Manager), Steve Robinson, Marcus Oldbury, David Town.

Division 2 AFC BOURNEMOUTH

Dean Court Ground, Bournemouth, Dorset BH7 7AF. Telephone: (01202) 395381. Fax: (01202) 309797.
Ground capacity: 11,000.
Record attendance: 28,799 v Manchester U, FA Cup 6th rd, 2 March 1957.
Record receipts: £33,723 v Manchester U, FA Cup 3rd rd, 7 January 1984.
Pitch measurements: 112yd × 75yd.
Chairman: K. Gardiner.
Directors: B. E. Willis (Vice-Chairman), G. M. C. Hayward, E. G. Keep, C. W. Legg, N. Hayward, A. J. C. Griffiths.
Secretary: K. R. J. MacAlister.
Manager: Mel Machin. *Assistant Manager:* John Williams. *Youth Team Coach:* Sean O'Driscoll.
Physio: Steve Hardwick. *Commercial Manager:* Terry Lovell. *Stadium Manager:* S. Baker.
Year Formed: 1899. *Turned Professional:* 1912. *Ltd Co.:* 1914.
Previous Names: Boscombe St Johns, 1890–99; Boscombe FC, 1899–1923; Bournemouth & Boscombe Ath FC, 1923–71.
Club Nickname: 'Cherries'.
Previous Grounds: 1899–1910, Castlemain Road, Pokesdown; 1910, Dean Court.
Foundation: There was a Bournemouth FC as early as 1875, but the present club arose out of the remnants of the Boscombe St John's club (formed 1890). The meeting at which Boscombe FC came into being was held at a house in Gladstone Road in 1899. They began by playing in the Boscombe and District Junior League.
First Football League game: 25 August 1923, Division 3 (S), v Swindon T (a), L 1-3 – Heron; Wingham, Lamb; Butt, C. Smith, Voisey; Miller, Lister (1), Davey, Simpson, Robinson.
Record League Victory: 7–0 v Swindon T, Division 3 (S), 22 September 1956 – Godwin; Cunningham, Keetley; Clayton, Crosland, Rushworth; Siddall (1), Norris (2), Arnott (1), Newsham (2), Cutler (1). 10–0 win v Northampton T at start of 1939–40 expunged from the records on outbreak of war.
Record Cup Victory: 11–0 v Margate, FA Cup 1st rd, 20 November 1971 – Davies; Machin (1), Kitchener, Benson, Jones, Powell, Cave (1), Boyer, MacDougall (9 incl. 1p), Miller, Scott (De Garis).
Record Defeat: 0–9 v Lincoln C, Division 3, 18 December 1982.
Most League Points (2 for a win): 62, Division 3, 1971–72.
Most League Points (3 for a win): 97, Division 3, 1986–87.
Most League Goals: 88, Division 3 (S), 1956–57.
Highest League Scorer in Season: Ted MacDougall, 42, 1970–71.
Most League Goals in Total Aggregate: Ron Eyre, 202, 1924–33.
Most Capped Player: Gerry Peyton, 7 (33), Republic of Ireland.
Most League Appearances: Sean O'Driscoll, 423, 1984–95.
Record Transfer Fee Received: £800,000 from Everton for Joe Parkinson, March 1994.
Record Transfer Fee Paid: £210,000 to Gillingham for Gavin Peacock, August 1989.
Football League Record: 1923 Elected to Division 3 (S). Remained a Third Division club for record number of years until 1970; 1970–71 Division 4; 1971–75 Division 3; 1975–82 Division 4; 1982–87 Division 3; 1987–90 Division 2; 1990–92 Division 3; 1992– Division 2.
Honours: Football League: Division 3 – Champions 1986–87; Division 3 (S) – Runners-up 1947–48. Promotion from Division 4 1970–71 (2nd), 1981–82 (4th). *FA Cup:* best season: 6th rd, 1957. *Football League Cup:* best season: 4th rd, 1962, 1964. *Associate Members' Cup:* Winners 1984.
Colours: Red shirts with black 3" stripe and white pinstripe, white shorts, white stockings. *Change colours:* Blue/yellow halved shirts, blue shorts, yellow stockings.
Did you know?
On 25 November 1995 at Chesterfield, Bournemouth conceded their first goal in 669 minutes of play.

BOURNEMOUTH 1995–96 LEAGUE RECORD

Match No.	Date	Venue	Opponents	Result		H/T Score	Lg. Pos.	Goalscorers	Atten- dance
1	Aug 12	A	Bradford C	L	0-1	0-0	—		5107
2	19	H	Peterborough U	W	3-0	1-0	10	Jones 3	4175
3	26	A	Wycombe W	W	2-1	2-0	6	Jones, Murray	4749
4	29	H	Wrexham	D	1-1	0-1	—	Jones	4825
5	Sept 2	H	Rotherham U	W	2-1	2-1	3	Brissett, Holland	4906
6	9	A	Notts Co	L	0-2	0-0	7		4875
7	12	A	Blackpool	L	1-2	1-1	—	Jones	3884
8	16	H	Crewe Alex	L	0-4	0-2	13		4488
9	24	H	Brighton & HA	W	3-1	2-0	11	Robinson 2, Jones	4560
10	30	A	Stockport Co	L	1-3	0-1	12	Bailey	5655
11	Oct 7	A	Bristol R	W	2-0	1-0	10	Brissett, Bailey	5171
12	14	H	Burnley	L	0-2	0-1	12		4954
13	21	A	Swansea C	D	1-1	1-0	14	Jones	1988
14	28	H	Carlisle U	W	2-0	1-0	9	Brissett, Fletcher	4250
15	31	H	Swindon T	D	0-0	0-0	—		6352
16	Nov 4	A	Walsall	D	0-0	0-0	11		3626
17	18	H	Brentford	W	1-0	0-0	10	Victory	3894
18	25	A	Chesterfield	L	0-3	0-2	13		4034
19	Dec 9	A	Brighton & HA	L	0-2	0-1	13		5414
20	16	H	Stockport Co	W	3-2	1-1	12	Ndah, Jones, Holland	3638
21	23	H	Hull C	W	2-0	1-0	11	Murray, Holland	3491
22	26	A	Oxford U	L	0-2	0-2	13		6347
23	Jan 2	H	Shrewsbury T	L	0-2	0-1	—		3265
24	6	H	Bristol C	D	1-1	0-1	12	Morris	3662
25	13	A	Peterborough U	W	5-4	1-1	11	Ndah, Casper, Mean, Jones 2	4596
26	20	A	Bradford C	W	3-1	1-1	7	Jones, Holland, Robinson	3628
27	Feb 3	H	Wycombe W	L	2-3	2-1	10	Bailey, Holland	4447
28	10	A	Bristol C	L	0-3	0-2	12		6217
29	17	H	Blackpool	W	1-0	0-0	10	Holland	4157
30	20	A	Rotherham U	L	0-1	0-1	—		2092
31	24	A	Crewe Alex	L	0-2	0-0	12		3535
32	27	H	Notts Co	L	0-2	0-1	—		3191
33	Mar 2	H	Oxford U	L	0-1	0-1	13		3996
34	9	A	Hull C	D	1-1	1-1	16	Scott	2853
35	12	A	Wrexham	L	0-5	0-3	—		2004
36	16	H	York C	D	2-2	1-0	16	Robinson 2 (1 pen)	3505
37	23	A	Shrewsbury T	W	2-1	0-1	15	Holland 2	2534
38	26	A	York C	L	1-3	0-1	—	Holland	2055
39	30	H	Bristol R	W	2-1	1-0	14	Robinson (pen), Jones	4607
40	Apr 2	A	Burnley	D	0-0	0-0	—		7941
41	6	A	Carlisle U	L	0-4	0-0	15		5401
42	9	H	Swansea C	W	3-1	1-1	—	Jones, Bailey, Holland	4049
43	13	A	Swindon T	D	2-2	1-1	15	Jones 2	10,508
44	20	H	Walsall	D	0-0	0-0	14		4380
45	27	H	Chesterfield	W	2-0	1-0	14	Robinson, Jones	4483
46	May 4	A	Brentford	L	0-2	0-0	14		6091

Final League Position: 14

GOALSCORERS

League (51): Jones 17, Holland 10, Robinson 7 (2 pens), Bailey 4, Brissett 3, Murray 2, Ndah 2, Casper 1, Fletcher 1, Mean 1, Morris 1, Scott 1, Victory 1.
Coca-Cola Cup (5): Jones 3, Morris 1, Oldbury 1.
FA Cup (1): Robinson 1.

Andrews I 26	Young N 40+1	Beardsmore R 44	Morris M 28+3	Murray R 30+5	Mean S 13+1	Holland M 43	Robinson S 36+5	Jones S 44	Fletcher S 3+4	Brissett J 43	Pennock A 16+1	Victory J 5+11	Bailey J 36+8	Rawlinson M 3+16	Town D 1+6	McElhatton M 2+2	Cureton J —+5	Duberry M 7	Oldbury M 2+11	Ndah G 12	Moss N 7	Howe E 4+1	Santos Y —+3	Casper C 16	Dean M 4+1	Scott K 8	Glass J 13	Strong S —+1	Coll O 8	Cox I 8	Mitchell P 2+2	O'Neill J 2+4	Match No.
1	2	3	4²	5	6	7¹	8³	9	10	11	12	13	14																				1
1	2	3	4	5	6	7	8	9		11			10																				2
1	2	3²	4	5	6	7		9³		11	8¹	12	10	13	14																		3
1	2	3	4	5	6	7		9		11²	8¹	12	10	13																			4
1	2	3	4	5	6	7		9		11	8		10																				5
1	2	3²	4	5	6	12		9		11	8	7²	10¹			13	14																6
1	2²	3	4	5	6	12		9		11	8	13	10			7¹	14																7
1	2	3	4¹	5	6	7	12	9		11	8		10²			13³	14																8
1	2¹	3	4	5	6²	7	8³	9		11			10	12	13		14																9
1		3	4²	5		7	8	9		11³	6¹		10	13		12	2	14															10
1		3	4	5		7	8	9		11	2		10				6																11
1	12	3	4³	5		7	8²	9	13	11	2		10			6¹	14																12
1	2	3	4	12		7	8¹	9		11			10	5	6																		13
	2	3	4	12		7	8¹	9³	14	11²		5	10	13		6					1												14
	2	3	4			7	12	9		11	8	5	10			6					1												15
	2¹	3	4	12		7	13	9²	14	11	8³	5	10			6					1												16
	2	3	4			7¹	8	9		11	6	5	10²	12	14			13³			1												17
	2	3	4²			7	8	9¹	10³	11	12	5			14	6		13			1												18
	2	3	4³	5		7	8	9		11²	6¹		10	12	14			13			1												19
	2	3	4¹	5	12	7	8	9		11	6²		10					13			1												20
1		3	4	5		7	8	9		11	6		10	12		2¹																	21
1		3	4	5		7	8	9		11	6¹		10	12		2²		13															22
1	2	3¹	4	5		7	8	9		11	6²		10	12				13															23
1	2	3	4	5¹	12	7	8	9²		11	6		10					13															24
1	2	3	4³		12	7	8	9		11²	6		10¹		14			13						5									25
1	2	3	4			7	8¹	9		11	6		10					13	12²					5									26
1	2	3	4			7	8	9		11	6		10											5									27
1		3	4			7	8²	9		11	6		10	12	14	2¹		13³						5									28
1	2	3				7		9		11	6		10						12					5	4¹	8							29
1	2	3			12	7		9		11²	6¹		10		14			13						5	4³	8							30
1	2	3	4		12	7		9¹		11²	6		10					13						5		8							31
1	2¹	3	4²		12	7		9		11³	6		10		14			13						5		8							32
1	2	3	4			7		9		11¹	6		10		14			13³	12					5²		8							33
	2	3	4			7	8	9		11¹	6		10						12					5			1						34
	2	3	4			7		9		11¹	6²		10³		14			13	12					5		8	1						35
	2	3	4			7		9		11	6		10											5		8	1						36
	2	3	4			7		9		11	6		10											5		8	1						37
	2²	3	4			7		9		11¹	6³		10		13				12					5		8	1		14				38
	2	3				7		9		11	6¹		10						12					5			1		4	8			39
	2	3				7		9		11²	6¹		10						12					5			1		4	8		13	40
	2²	3				7		9		11³	6		10						12					5¹			1		4	8	13	14	41
	2	3		5		7		9		11	6		10														1		4	8			42
	2	3		5		7		9		11²	6		10¹														1		4	8	13	12	43
	2	3		5		7		0¹		11³	6		10						12								1		4	8	13		44
	2	3		5		7		9		11	6		10														1		4	8			45
	2	13		5²		7		9		11¹	6		10						12								1		4	8		3	46

Coca-Cola Cup

First Round	Luton T	(a)	1-1	
		(h)	2-1	
Second Round	Watford	(a)	1-1	
		(h)	1-1	

FA Cup

First Round	Bristol C	(h)	0-0	
		(a)	1-0	
Second Round	Brentford	(h)	0-1	

BRADFORD CITY 1995-96   *Back row (left to right):* Wayne Benn, Richard Liburd, Scott Jackson, Carl Shutt, Richard Huxford, Andy Kiwomya, Paul Showler, Chris Stabb, Neil Grayston. *Middle row:* Steve Redmond (Physio), Graham Mitchell, John Ford, Nicky Mohan, Ian Ormondroyd, Neil Tolson, Des Hamilton, Steve Smith (Youth Team Coach). *Front row:* Chris Dolby, Wayne Jacobs, Craig Midgley, Lennie Lawrence (Manager), Eddie Youds, Chris Kamara (Assistant Manager), Gary Robson, Shaun Murray, Tommy Wright.

Division 1 BRADFORD CITY

The Pulse Stadium, Bradford BD8 7DY. Telephone: (01274) 773355 (Office). Fax: (01274) 773356.
Ground capacity: 13,500 until December 1995 then 18,100.
Record attendance: 39,146 v Burnley, FA Cup 4th rd, 11 March 1911.
Record receipts: £89,000 v Manchester U, Friendly, 9 August 1995.
Pitch measurements: 110yd × 73yd.
Chairman: Geoffrey Richmond. *Vice-Chairman:* David Thompson FCA.
Directors: David Richmond, Elizabeth Richmond, Terry Goddard.
Manager: Chris Kamara. *Assistant Manager:* M. Hunter. *Coach:* Paul Jewell.
Youth Coach: Steve Smith. *Physio:* S. Redmond.
Secretary: Shaun A. Harvey. *Stadium Manager:* Allan Gilliver.
Year Formed: 1903. *Turned Professional:* 1903. *Ltd Co.:* 1908.
Club Nickname: 'The Bantams'.

Foundation: Bradford was a rugby stronghold around the turn of the century but after Manningham RFC held an archery contest to help them out of financial difficulties in 1903, they were persuaded to give up the handling code and turn to soccer. So they formed Bradford City and continued at Valley Parade. Recognising this as an opportunity of spreading the dribbling code in this part of Yorkshire, the Football League immediately accepted the new club's first application for membership of the Second Division.

First Football League game: 1 September 1903, Division 2, v Grimsby T (a), L 0-2 – Seymour; Wilson, Halliday; Robinson, Millar, Farnall; Guy, Beckram, Forrest, McMillan, Graham.

Record League Victory: 11–1 v Rotherham U, Division 3 (N), 25 August 1928 – Sherlaw; Russell, Watson; Burkinshaw (1), Summers, Bauld; Harvey (2), Edmunds (3), White (3), Cairns, Scriven (2).

Record Cup Victory: 11–3 v Walker Celtic, FA Cup 1st rd (replay), 1 December 1937 – Parker; Rookes, McDermott; Murphy, Mackie, Moore; Bagley (1), Whittingham (1), Deakin (4 incl. 1p), Cooke (1), Bartholomew (4).

Record Defeat: 1–9 v Colchester U, Division 4, 30 December 1961.
Most League Points (2 for a win): 63, Division 3 (N), 1928–29.
Most League Points (3 for a win): 94, Division 3, 1984–85.
Most League Goals: 128, Division 3 (N), 1928–29.
Highest League Scorer in Season: David Layne, 34, Division 4, 1961–62.
Most League Goals in Total Aggregate: Bobby Campbell, 121, 1981–84, 1984–86.
Most Capped Player: Harry Hampton, 9, Northern Ireland.
Most League Appearances: Cec Podd, 502, 1970–84.
Record Transfer Fee Received: £1,850,000 from Wolverhampton W for Dean Richards, June 1995.
Record Transfer Fee Paid: £300,000 to Bristol R for John Taylor, July 1994.

Football League Record: 1903 Elected to Division 2; 1908–22 Division 1; 1922–27 Division 2; 1927–29 Division 3 (N); 1929–37 Division 2; 1937–61 Division 3; 1961–69 Division 4; 1969–72 Division 3; 1972–77 Division 4; 1977–78 Division 3; 1978–82 Division 4; 1982–85 Division 3; 1985–90 Division 2; 1990–92 Division 3; 1992–96 Division 2; 1996– Division 1.

Honours: Football League: Division 1 best season: 5th, 1910–11; Division 2 – Champions 1907–08; Promoted from Division 2 (play-offs) 1995–96; Division 3 – Champions 1984–85; Division 3 (N) – Champions 1928–29; Division 4 – Runners-up 1981–82. *FA Cup:* Winners 1911 (first holders of the present trophy). *Football League Cup:* best season: 5th rd, 1965, 1989.

Colours: Claret and amber striped shirts, black shorts, black stockings. *Change colours:* Light blue shirts and shorts, blue stockings.

Did you know?
On 31 January 1996 against Crewe, Nicky Mohan declined to be substituted after 60 minutes. Seven minutes later he scored in a 2-1 win.

BRADFORD CITY 1995–96 LEAGUE RECORD

Match No.	Date	Venue	Opponents	Result		H/T Score	Lg. Pos.	Goalscorers	Attendance
1	Aug 12	H	Bournemouth	W	1-0	0-0	—	Tolson	5107
2	19	A	Brighton & HA	D	0-0	0-0	9		5471
3	26	H	Shrewsbury T	W	3-1	3-1	3	Youds 2, Shutt	5017
4	29	A	Notts Co	W	2-0	1-0	—	Youds, Showler	6168
5	Sept 2	H	Wycombe W	L	0-4	0-1	4		9748
6	9	A	Wrexham	W	2-1	0-0	2	Shutt, Youds	3268
7	13	A	Swindon T	L	1-4	1-2	—	Showler	8203
8	16	H	Bristol C	W	3-0	1-0	4	Showler, Shutt 2	5165
9	23	A	Peterborough U	L	1-3	1-1	5	Showler	4509
10	30	H	Blackpool	W	2-1	0-1	3	Ormondroyd, Tolson	6820
11	Oct 7	A	Swansea C	L	0-2	0-1	4		2207
12	14	H	Bristol R	L	2-3	1-1	6	Wright (pen), Tolson	5817
13	21	A	Carlisle U	D	2-2	0-2	8	Shutt, Showler	6274
14	28	H	Burnley	D	2-2	1-1	8	Mitchell, Hamilton	8356
15	31	H	Walsall	W	1-0	0-0	—	Tolson	4310
16	Nov 4	A	Chesterfield	L	1-2	1-1	8	Tolson	5490
17	18	H	Hull C	D	1-1	0-1	9	Midgley	5820
18	25	A	Brentford	L	1-2	0-2	11	Murray	4237
19	Dec 9	H	Peterborough U	W	2-1	1-0	11	Showler, Duxbury	4605
20	16	A	Blackpool	L	1-4	0-1	10	Showler	4857
21	23	H	Oxford U	W	1-0	1-0	10	Mohan	4637
22	26	A	York C	W	3-0	1-0	8	Showler (pen), Duxbury, Jewell	5218
23	Jan 10	A	Stockport Co	W	2-1	2-1	—	Jewell, Huxford	6030
24	13	H	Brighton & HA	L	1-3	0-2	7	Ormondroyd	5139
25	20	A	Bournemouth	L	1-3	1-1	8	Stallard	3628
26	23	A	Rotherham U	L	0-2	0-0	—		3052
27	31	H	Crewe Alex	W	2-1	0-0	—	Mohan, Shutt	4095
28	Feb 3	A	Shrewsbury T	D	1-1	0-0	6	Murray	3605
29	10	H	Stockport Co	L	0-1	0-0	6		5290
30	24	A	Bristol C	L	1-2	0-1	11	Wright	5400
31	27	H	Wrexham	W	2-0	2-0	—	Stallard, Jewell	3804
32	Mar 2	H	York C	D	2-2	2-1	10	Mohan 2	5208
33	9	A	Oxford U	L	0-2	0-0	10		5138
34	16	H	Rotherham U	W	2-0	0-0	10	Stallard, Ormondroyd	4047
35	19	H	Notts Co	W	1-0	1-0	—	Stallard	3622
36	23	A	Crewe Alex	W	2-1	1-0	8	Stallard, Liburd	3887
37	26	A	Wycombe W	L	2-5	1-2	—	Kiwomya, Shutt	3021
38	30	H	Swansea C	W	5-1	0-0	8	Edwards (og), Stallard 2, Tolson, Hamilton	4183
39	Apr 2	A	Bristol R	L	0-1	0-0	—		4008
40	6	A	Burnley	W	3-2	2-0	9	Tolson, Winstanley (og), Kiwomya	9714
41	8	H	Carlisle U	W	3-1	1-0	6	Tolson, Ormondroyd, Stallard	6156
42	13	A	Walsall	L	1-2	0-0	8	Wright (pen)	3679
43	20	A	Chesterfield	W	2-1	0-1	7	Hamilton, Ormondroyd	6803
44	26	H	Brentford	W	2-1	1-0	—	Ormondroyd, Duxbury	7730
45	30	H	Swindon T	D	1-1	0-0	—	Wright	9812
46	May 4	A	Hull C	W	3-2	2-2	6	Stallard, Duxbury, Shutt	8965

Final League Position: 6

GOALSCORERS
League (71): Stallard 9, Showler 8 (1 pen), Shutt 8, Tolson 8, Ormondroyd 6, Duxbury 4, Mohan 4, Wright 4 (2 pens), Youds 4, Hamilton 3, Jewell 3, Kiwomya 2, Murray 2, Huxford 1, Liburd 1, Midgley 1, Mitchell 1, own goals 2.
Coca-Cola Cup (13): Showler 4, Ormondroyd 3, Wright 2, Youds 2, Hamilton 1, Tolson 1.
FA Cup (6): Jacobs 2, Showler 2, Ormondroyd 1, Robson 1.

Ward G 36	Huxford R 21+5	Liburd R 33	Robson G 4+2	Mohan N 39	Mitchell G 32+1	Wright T 28+6	Youds E 30	Ormondroyd I 28+9	Shutt C 22+12	Murray S 25+9	Tolson N 12+19	Showler P 29+4	Kiwomya A 7+9	Jacobs W 28	Hamilton D 18+6	Foley S —+1	Ford J 18+1	Midgley C —+5	Harper S 1	Grayston N 2	Duxbury L 30	Jewell P 7+11	Bullimore W 1+1	Brightwell D 21+1	Stallard M 20+1	Kernaghan A 5	Gould J 9	Match No.
1	2	3	4^2	5	6	7	8	9^1	10^3	11	12	13	14															1
1	2	3		5	6	7	8	9	10	11			4															2
1	2			5	6	7^2	8	9^1	10^3	11	12	13	14	3	4													3
1	2			5	6		8	9	10	11		7		3	4													4
1	2^3			5	6		8	9^1	10	11^2	12	7	13	3	4	14												5
1	2			5	12		8	9	10^2	7	13	11^1		3	4		6											6
1	2			5		12	8	9^1	10^2	7	13	11		3	4		6											7
1	2			5		4	7	8^1	9	10	12	11		3			6											8
1	2	3		5		4	7^1	8	9	10^2	12	11	13				6^3	14										9
1	2			5	4	7	8	9	10^1		12^2	11		3	13		6											10
1	2	12		5	4	7	8	9^3			13	14	11	3	10^2		6^1											11
1	2			5	4	7	8	9	10^3	12	14	11^2		3	13		6^1											12
1		2	5^1	4		7	8	13	12	9^2		11		3	10		6											13
1		2	5	4		7	8		9			11		3	10		6											14
1		2	12	5	4	7^2		8^3	9	13	14	11		3	10^1		6											15
1		2		5	4			9		10	8^1	11		3	7		6	12										16
	2		4	5				9		12	10^3	11			8^2		6	13	1	3	7	14						17
1	2^1	3^3	4	5				9		12	10^2	11			8		6	13			7	14						18
1				6	5	10	4	9	2^1			11		3	7						8	12						19
1	2^2			6	5	10	4	12		14	13	11		3							8	9^3		7^1				20
1	7^1	2		6			4	9	12		13	11^2		3							8	10^2	14	5				21
1	7	2		6			4			9		11		3							8	10		5				22
1	7			5	2		4		9			11		3							8	10		6				23
1	7			6	2^3		4	13	9	12		11		3^2							8	10^1		5	14			24
1	2			6	3		4	12	7^2	11	9^3		13								8	14		5	10			25
1	2			6			4		7^3	11	12	9^1	13	3							8^2	14		5	10			26
1	3	2		6	4	12		7	11	13	9										8^2			5^1	10			27
1	3	2			4	7			6^2	11	12	9									8			10^1	5			28
1	3	2			6	7	4^1		13	11^3	12	9									8			10^2	5			29
1	2			4	6	7		12	13	11^2		9^1									8	3		10^3	5			30
1	2			4	6	7	11					9									8	12		10^1	5			31
1	2			4	6^3	7		9	13	12		11^1	14								8	10^2	3		5			32
1	2			4	6^2	7		9^3	12	11			13				5	14			8	10^1	3					33
1	2			4	6	7		9^1		11	12		13				5^2				8	3		10^3				34
1	2			4	6	7		9				11	5								8	3		10				35
1	2			4	6	7^2		9	13	11		12	5^3		3						8	14		10^1				36
1	2			4	6^3	7^1		9^2	13	11		12	5			14					8	3		10				37
	2			5	12	4^2				11	9				7^1	3		13			8		6		10		1	38
	2		4			12	5		13	11^3	9^2				7^1	3		14			8		6		10		1	39
	2			5		12	4	13		11^3	9^2				7	3		14			8		6		10^1		1	40
	2			5		12	4	13		11^3	9^2				7^1	3		14			8		6		10		1	41
12	2^1					7	4	13	14		9^2					3	11		5		8		6^3		10		1	42
12	2					7^1	4	13	6		9^2					3	11		5			10					1	43
12	2		5			7	4^3	9	6		13					3	11^1					14			10^2		1	44
12	2			5		7		9^2	13	4	14					3	11					6			10^3		1	45
12	2			5		7^2		9	13	4^1						3	11					6			10		1	46

Coca-Cola Cup					**FA Cup**			
First Round	Blackpool	(h)	2-1		First Round	Burton Alb	(h)	4-3
		(a)	3-2		Second Round	Preston NE	(h)	2-1
Second Round	Nottingham F	(h)	3-2		Third Round	Bolton W	(h)	0-3
		(a)	2-2					
Third Round	Norwich C	(a)	0-0					
		(h)	3-5					

BRENTFORD 1995-96　*Back row (left to right)*: Joseph Omigie, Gus Hurdle, Jamie Bates, Barry Ashby, Robert Taylor, Carl Asaba, Carl Hutchings, Corey Campbell, Kevin Burke.
Middle row: Bob Booker (Youth Team Manager), Martin Grainger, David McGhee, Paul Smith, Tamer Fernandes, Kevin Dearden, Denny Mundee, Paul Abrahams, Ijah Anderson, Roy Johnson (Physio).
Front row: Jon Hooker, Darren Annon, Lee Harvey, David Webb (Manager), Kevin Lock (Assistant Manager), Nick Forster, Brian Statham, Craig Ravenscroft.

Division 2   **BRENTFORD**

Griffin Park, Braemar Rd, Brentford, Middlesex TW8 0NT. Telephone: (0181) 847 2511. Fax: (0181) 568 9940. Commercial Dept: (0181) 560 6062. Press Office: (0181) 574 3047. Clubcall: 0891 21108.

Ground capacity: 13,870.

Record attendance: 39,626 v Preston NE, FA Cup 6th rd, 5 March 1938.

Record receipts: £79,838 v Tottenham H, Coca-Cola Cup 2nd rd 2nd leg, 7 October 1992.

Pitch measurements: 111yd × 74yd.

President: W. Wheatley.

Chairman: M. M. Lange.

Directors: B. Evans, J. Herting, E. J. Radley-Smith MS, FRCS, LRCP, D. Tana.

Manager: David Webb. *Assistant Manager:* Kevin Lock.

Youth Team Manager: Bob Booker.

Community Officer: Lee Doyle.

Secretary: Polly Kates. *Physio:* R. Johnson.

Safety Officer: Jill Dawson. *Marketing Manager:* Peter Gilham.

Year Formed: 1889. *Turned Professional:* 1899. *Ltd Co.:* 1901.

Club Nickname: 'The Bees'.

Previous Grounds: 1889–91, Clifden Road; 1891–95, Benns Fields, Little Ealing; 1895–98, Shotters Field; 1898–1900, Cross Road, S. Ealing; 1900–04, Boston Park; 1904, Griffin Park.

Foundation: Formed as a small amateur concern in 1889 they were very successful in local circles. They won the championship of the West London Alliance in 1893 and a year later the West Middlesex Junior Cup before carrying off the Senior Cup in 1895. After winning both the London Senior Amateur Cup and the Middlesex Senior Cup in 1898 they were admitted to the Second Division of the Southern League.

First Football League game: 28 August 1920, Division 3, v Exeter C (a), L 0-3 – Young; Rosier, Hodson; Amos, Levitt, Elliott; Henery, Morley, Spredbury, Thompson, Smith.

Record League Victory: 9–0 v Wrexham, Division 3, 15 October 1963 – Cakebread; Coote, Jones; Slater, Scott, Higginson; Summers (1), Brooks (2), McAdams (2), Ward (2), Hales (1). (1 og).

Record Cup Victory: 7–0 v Windsor & Eton (away), FA Cup 1st rd, 20 November 1982 – Roche; Rowe, Harris (Booker), McNichol (1), Whitehead, Hurlock (2), Kamara, Bowles, Joseph (1), Mahoney (3), Roberts.

Record Defeat: 0–7 v Swansea T, Division 3 (S), 8 November 1924 and v Walsall, Division 3 (S), 19 January 1957.

Most League Points (2 for a win): 62, Division 3 (S), 1932–33 and Division 4, 1962–63.

Most League Points (3 for a win): 85, Division 2, 1994–95.

Most League Goals: 98, Division 4, 1962–63.

Highest League Scorer in Season: Jack Holliday, 38, Division 3 (S), 1932–33.

Most League Goals in Total Aggregate: Jim Towers, 153, 1954–61.

Most Capped Player: John Buttigieg, (63), Malta.

Most League Appearances: Ken Coote, 514, 1949–64.

Record Transfer Fee Received: £720,000 from Wimbledon for Dean Holdsworth, August 1992.

Record Transfer Fee Paid: £275,000 to Chelsea for Joe Allon, November 1992.

Football League Record: 1920 Original Member of Division 3; 1921–33 Division 3 (S); 1933–35 Division 2; 1935–47 Division 1; 1947–54 Division 2; 1954–62 Division 3 (S); 1962–63 Division 4; 1963–66 Division 3; 1966–72 Division 4; 1972–73 Division 3; 1973–78 Division 4; 1978–92 Division 3; 1992–93 Division 1; 1993– Division 2.

Honours: Football League: Division 1 best season: 5th, 1935–36; Division 2 – Champions 1934–35; Division 3 – Champions 1991–92; Division 3 (S) – Champions 1932–33; Runners-up 1929–30, 1957–58; Division 4 Champions 1962–63. *FA Cup:* best season: 6th rd, 1938, 1946, 1949, 1989. *Football League Cup:* best season: 4th rd, 1983. *Freight Rover Trophy;* Runners-up 1985.

Colours: Red and white vertical striped shirts, red shorts, red stockings. *Change colours:* Blue shirts, dark blue shorts, dark blue stockings.

Did you know?
Dave McCulloch signed for Brentford at 2 o'clock in the morning of 30 November 1935. Later that day he scored the second goal of a 2-2 draw with Leeds United.

BRENTFORD 1995–96 LEAGUE RECORD

Match No.	Date	Venue	Opponents	Result	H/T Score	Lg. Pos.	Goalscorers	Attendance
1	Aug 12	A	York C	D 2-2	1-0	—	Smith, Forster	3239
2	19	H	Oxford U	W 1-0	1-0	6	Taylor	5516
3	26	A	Burnley	L 0-1	0-1	10		9586
4	29	H	Hull C	W 1-0	0-0	—	Taylor	4535
5	Sept 2	H	Swindon T	L 0-2	0-1	13		7878
6	9	A	Rotherham U	L 0-1	0-1	16		3061
7	12	A	Bristol C	D 0-0	0-0	—		5054
8	16	H	Walsall	W 1-0	1-0	12	Taylor	4717
9	23	A	Bristol R	L 0-2	0-1	14		5131
10	30	H	Chesterfield	L 1-2	0-1	18	McGhee	4734
11	Oct 7	H	Blackpool	L 1-2	1-0	19	McGhee	5313
12	14	A	Stockport Co	D 1-1	0-1	19	Smith	6228
13	21	H	Peterborough U	W 3-0	2-0	16	Bates 2, Grainger (pen)	4565
14	28	A	Crewe Alex	L 1-3	0-2	18	Forster	3835
15	Nov 1	A	Notts Co	L 0-4	0-1	—		4005
16	4	H	Shrewsbury T	L 0-2	0-2	21		4104
17	18	A	Bournemouth	L 0-1	0-0	22		3894
18	25	H	Bradford C	W 2-1	2-0	22	Taylor 2	4237
19	Dec 9	H	Bristol R	D 0-0	0-0	22		5679
20	16	A	Chesterfield	D 2-2	2-0	22	Smith, Ansah	4016
21	22	A	Wrexham	D 2-2	0-2	—	Taylor, Martin	3670
22	26	H	Brighton & HA	L 0-1	0-1	21		5794
23	Jan 13	A	Oxford U	L 1-2	1-1	23	Ashby	5566
24	20	H	York C	W 2-0	1-0	22	Bates, Taylor	3915
25	30	H	Wycombe W	W 1-0	0-0	—	Taylor	4668
26	Feb 3	H	Burnley	W 1-0	0-0	18	Forster	5195
27	10	A	Carlisle U	L 1-2	0-1	19	Bates	5143
28	17	H	Bristol C	D 2-2	1-0	19	McGhee, Taylor	5213
29	21	A	Swindon T	D 2-2	2-2	—	Abrahams 2	8814
30	24	A	Walsall	W 1-0	1-0	19	Abrahams	3506
31	27	H	Rotherham U	D 1-1	0-0	—	Grainger	3446
32	Mar 2	A	Brighton & HA	D 0-0	0-0	19		5914
33	5	A	Hull C	W 1-0	0-0	—	Anderson	2284
34	9	A	Wrexham	W 1-0	1-0	13	Anderson	4579
35	12	A	Swansea C	L 1-2	1-0	—	Forster	3538
36	16	A	Wycombe W	L 1-2	1-1	17	Forster	4912
37	19	H	Carlisle U	D 1-1	1-1	—	Grainger	3104
38	23	H	Swansea C	D 0-0	0-0	16		4378
39	30	A	Blackpool	L 0-1	0-1	16		5899
40	Apr 2	H	Stockport Co	W 1-0	0-0	—	Smith	3274
41	6	H	Crewe Alex	W 2-1	0-1	14	Taylor 2	4408
42	8	A	Peterborough U	W 1-0	0-0	13	McGhee	4343
43	13	H	Notts Co	D 0-0	0-0	14		4588
44	20	A	Shrewsbury T	L 1-2	1-2	15	McGhee	2711
45	26	A	Bradford C	L 1-2	0-1	—	Bent	7730
46	May 4	H	Bournemouth	W 2-0	0-0	15	Asaba 2	6091

Final League Position: 15

GOALSCORERS

League (43): Taylor 11, Forster 5, McGhee 5, Bates 4, Smith 4, Abrahams 3, Grainger 3 (1 pen), Anderson 2, Asaba 2, Ansah 1, Ashby 1, Bent 1, Martin 1.
Coca-Cola Cup (7): Forster 2, Anderson 1, Grainger 1 (pen), Harvey 1, McGhee 1, Taylor 1.
FA Cup (10): Bent 3, Taylor 3, Smith 2, Ashby 1, own goal 1.

Dearden K 41	Statham B 17	Grainger M 33	Ashby B 31 + 2	Bates J 36	Hurdle G 11 + 3	Harvey L 38 + 2	Smith P 46	Forster N 37 + 1	Anderson I 25	Taylor R 42	McGhee D 31 + 5	Mundee D 5 + 1	Annon D — + 1	Asaba C 5 + 5	Hooker J 4	Davis P 5	Hutchings C 20 + 3	Abrahams P 14 + 3	Martin D 14 + 5	Ravenscroft C 1	Fernandes T 5	Bent M 8 + 4	Ansah A 6	Sussex A 3	Omigie J 3 + 7	Canham S 14	Greene D 11	Match No.
1	2	3	4	5	6	7	8	9	10	11																		1
1	2	3	4	5	6	7	8	9	10	11																		2
1	2	3		5	6¹	7	8	9	10	11	4	12																3
1	2	3		5		7	8	9	10	11	4			6														4
1	2	3	12	5		7	8	9¹	10	11	4			6²	13													5
1	2	3	6	5		7	8	9	10¹	11	4						12											6
1	2	3	6	5			8	9		11¹	4					7	12		10									7
1	2	3	6	5			8	9		11						7	10	4										8
1	2	3	6	5			8	9		11		12				7¹	13	10²	4									9
1	2	3	6	5	12		8	9		11						7	10¹	4										10
1	2		6			10	8	9	3	11						7	4¹	5	12									11
1	2	3	6	5		4	8	9		11						7	10											12
1	2	3	6	5	12	4	8¹	9								7	13		10	11²								13
1	2	3	6		5¹	4	8	9		11						7	12		10									14
1	2	3	6			4	8	9		5						7	11		10									15
	2	3				12	8			6			7	11	4¹	5			10		1	9						16
		3		5		2	8			11				6			4		10		1	7	9					17
	2	3	6	5		12	8			11				9²			4		10		1	13	7¹					18
1		3	6	5		2	8	9		11							4		10			12	7¹					19
1		3		5		2	8			11				6			4		10			7	9					20
1		3		5		2	8			11				6			4		10			13	7¹	9				21
1		3		5		2	8			11				6			4		10¹				7	9	12			22
1		3	6	5		2	8¹	9		11							4		10			12		13	7¹			23
1		3	6	5		2	8	9¹		11							4		10¹					12	7			24
1		3	6	5		2	8	9		11							4		10¹			12			7			25
1		3	6	5		2	8	9		11							4		10						7			26
1		3	6	5		2	8	9		11							4		10¹			12			7			27
1				5		2	8	9	3	11				6			4		10²			12		13	7¹			28
1				5		2	8	9	3	11				6			4	7	10									29
1		3	6	5		2	8²	9¹	10	11	4							7	12					13				30
1		3	6	5		2	8	9	10	11	4¹							7	12									31
1		3		5	4	2	8	9	10	11							7										6	32
1		3		5	4	2¹	8	9	10	11							12	7									6	33
1				5	4	2	8	9	10	11	12						3	7¹									6	34
1				5	4	2	8	9	10	11	12						3	7¹									6	35
1		3	4	5		2	8	9	10	11															12	7	6¹	36
1		3	12	5		2	8	9	10	11							4									7	6¹	37
1		3	4	5		2²	8	9¹	6	11	12						13								10	7		38
1					4	2	8	9	3	11¹							5		10						12	7	6	39
1					4	2	8	9	3	11							5		10							7	6	40
1					4	2	8	9	3	11							5		10						12	7	6¹	41
1					4	2	8		3¹	11							5	12	10						9	7	6	42
1			12		4	2	8		13	11							5	3	10						9²	7	6¹	43
1			6		4	2	8	9	3	11							5		10¹						12	7		44
		4¹	5	2			8	9	3	11				6					10		1	7			12			45
		4	5	2			8	9		11				6				3	10¹		1	7			12			46

Coca-Cola Cup

First Round	Walsall	(a)	2-2	
		(h)	3-2	
Second Round	Bolton W	(a)	0-1	
		(h)	2-3	

FA Cup

First Round	Farnborough	(h)	1-1
		(a)	4-0
Second Round	Bournemouth	(a)	1-0
Third Round	Norwich C	(a)	2-1
Fourth Round	Charlton Ath	(a)	2-3

BRIGHTON AND HOVE ALBION 1995-96   *Back row (left to right):* Peter Smith, Stuart Storer, Paul McCarthy, Mark Ormerod, Nicky Rust, Derek Coughlan, Steve Foster, Simon Fox.
Third row: George Petchey (Coach), Gerry Ryan, Ross Johnson, John Byrne, Kevin McGarrigle, Mark Fox, John Ryan, Dean Wilkins, Jimmy Case (Manager), Malcolm Stuart (Physiol).
Second row: Ian Chapman, Stuart Myall, Phil Andrews, Jeff Minton, Liam Brady, Junior McDougald, James Virgo, Stuart Munday, Stuart Tuck.
Front row: John Westcott, Paul Kennett, Ian Earles, Kerry Mayo, Alan Hughes, Jay Pickering, Dominic Shepherd, Robert Cox, Richard Carter.

Division 3   **BRIGHTON & HOVE ALBION**

Goldstone Ground, Newtown Rd, Hove, East Sussex BN3 7DE. Telephone: (01273) 778855 (all departments). Fax: (01273) 321095. Recorded information (team & ticket news etc): Albion Clubline: 0891 440066.

Ground capacity: 13,600.

Record attendance: 36,747 v Fulham, Division 2, 27 December 1958.

Record receipts: £109,615.65 v Crawley T, FA Cup 3rd rd, 4 January 1992.

Pitch measurements: 112yd × 74yd.

President: G. A. Stanley.

Directors: G. A. Stanley, W. E. Archer (Chairman), R. A. Bloom, D. Stanley.

Manager: Jimmy Case.

Secretary: Derek Allan. ***Chief Executive/Deputy Chairman:*** David Bellotti.

Coach: George Petchey. ***Physio:*** Malcolm Stuart. ***Youth Development Officer:*** John Jackson. ***Stadium Manager:*** Brian Harwood.

Year Formed: 1900. ***Turned Professional:*** 1901. ***Ltd Co.:*** 1904.

Previous Grounds: 1901, County Ground; 1902, Goldstone Ground.

Club Nickname: 'The Seagulls'.

Foundation: A professional club Brighton United was formed in November 1897 at the Imperial Hotel, Queen's Road, but folded in March 1900 after less than two seasons in the Southern League at the County Ground. An amateur team, Brighton & Hove Rangers was then formed by some prominent United supporters and after one season at Withdean, decided to turn semi-professional and play at the County Ground. Rangers were accepted into the Southern League but then also folded June 1901. John Jackson the former United manager organised a meeting at the Seven Stars public house, Ship Street on 24 June 1901 at which a new third club Brighton & Hove United was formed. They took over Rangers' place in the Southern League and pitch at County Ground. The name was changed to Brighton & Hove Albion before a match was played because of objections by Hove FC.

First Football League game: 28 August 1920, Division 3, v Southend U (a), L 0-2 – Hayes; Woodhouse, Little; Hall, Comber, Bentley; Longstaff, Ritchie, Doran, Rodgerson, March.

Record League Victory: 9–1 v Newport Co, Division 3 (S), 18 April 1951 – Ball; Tennant (1p), Mansell (1p); Willard, McCoy, Wilson; Reed, McNichol (4), Garbutt, Bennett (2), Keene (1). 9–1 v Southend U, Division 3, 27 November 1965 – Powney; Magill, Baxter; Leck, Gall, Turner; Gould (1), Collins (1), Livesey (2), Smith (3), Goodchild (2).

Record Cup Victory: 10–1 v Wisbech, FA Cup 1st rd, 13 November 1965 – Powney; Magill, Baxter; Collins (1), Gall, Turner; Gould, Smith (2), Livesey (3), Cassidy (2), Goodchild (1). (1 og).

Record Defeat: 0–9 v Middlesbrough, Division 2, 23 August 1958.

Most League Points (2 for a win): 65, Division 3 (S), 1955–56 and Division 3, 1971–72.

Most League Points (3 for a win): 84, Division 3, 1987–88.

Most League Goals: 112, Division 3 (S), 1955–56.

Highest League Scorer in Season: Peter Ward, 32, Division 3, 1976–77.

Most League Goals in Total Aggregate: Tommy Cook, 114, 1922–29.

Most Capped Player: Steve Penney, 17, Northern Ireland.

Most League Appearances: 'Tug' Wilson, 509, 1922–36.

Record Transfer Fee Received: £900,000 from Liverpool for Mark Lawrenson, August 1981.

Record Transfer Fee Paid: £500,000 to Manchester U for Andy Ritchie, October 1980.

Football League Record: 1920 Original Member of Division 3; 1921–58 Division 3 (S); 1958–62 Division 2; 1962–63 Division 3; 1963–65 Division 4; 1965–72 Division 3; 1972–73 Division 2; 1973–77 Division 3; 1977–79 Division 2; 1979–83 Division 1; 1983–87 Division 2; 1987–88 Division 3; 1988–96 Division 2; 1996– Division 3.

Honours: *Football League:* Division 1 best season: 13th, 1981–82; Division 2 – Runners-up 1978–79; Division 3 (S) – Champions 1957–58; Runners-up 1953–54, 1955–56; Division 3 – Runners-up 1971–72, 1976–77, 1987–88; Division 4 – Champions 1964–65. *FA Cup:* Runners-up 1983. *Football League Cup:* best season: 5th rd, 1979.

Colours: Blue and white striped shirts, blue shorts, white stockings. ***Change colours:*** All yellow.

Did you know?
On 1 January 1996 the 1-1 draw with Stockport County was the 1500th League game played at the Goldstone Ground.

BRIGHTON & HOVE ALBION 1995–96 LEAGUE RECORD

Match No.	Date		Venue	Opponents	Result		H/T Score	Lg. Pos.	Goalscorers	Attendance
1	Aug	12	A	Peterborough U	L	1-3	0-1	—	Clark (og)	5394
2		19	H	Bradford C	D	0-0	0-0	20		5471
3		26	A	Wrexham	D	1-1	1-0	19	Berry	2947
4		29	H	Wycombe W	L	1-2	1-1	—	Bull	5360
5	Sept	2	H	Notts Co	W	1-0	0-0	16	McDougald	5267
6		9	A	Bristol C	W	1-0	1-0	14	Berry	7585
7		12	A	Crewe Alex	L	1-3	0-1	—	Bull	3272
8		16	H	Blackpool	L	1-2	0-2	18	Chapman	6158
9		24	A	Bournemouth	L	1-3	0-2	20	Chapman	4560
10		30	H	Shrewsbury T	D	2-2	1-1	20	Foster, Minton	5247
11	Oct	7	A	Rotherham U	L	0-1	0-0	21		2950
12		14	H	Swindon T	L	1-3	0-3	23	McDougald	7808
13		21	A	Burnley	L	0-3	0-3	23		9016
14		28	H	Bristol R	W	2-0	0-0	22	Parris, Mundee (pen)	5658
15		31	H	Swansea C	L	0-2	0-1	—		4230
16	Nov	4	A	Carlisle U	L	0-1	0-0	23		5896
17		18	H	Walsall	L	0-3	0-0	23		4976
18		25	A	York C	L	1-3	1-0	23	McCarthy	3105
19	Dec	9	H	Bournemouth	W	2-0	1-0	23	Myall, Minton	5414
20		16	A	Shrewsbury T	L	1-2	1-1	23	Storer	3697
21		22	H	Chesterfield	L	0-2	0-1	—		3629
22		26	A	Brentford	W	1-0	1-0	23	Wilkins	5794
23	Jan	1	H	Stockport Co	D	1-1	1-1	23	Chapman	5694
24		13	A	Bradford C	W	3-1	2-0	21	Minton, Mundee, McDougald	5139
25		20	H	Peterborough U	L	1-2	1-1	23	Mundee (pen)	5572
26		23	A	Hull C	D	0-0	0-0	—		2421
27	Feb	3	H	Wrexham	D	2-2	1-2	23	Minton 2	4617
28		10	A	Oxford U	D	1-1	0-1	22	McDougald	5967
29		17	A	Crewe Alex	D	2-2	0-2	22	Wilkins, Smith	6561
30		24	A	Blackpool	L	1-2	1-0	22	Storer	4937
31		27	H	Bristol C	L	0-2	0-1	—		4739
32	Mar	2	H	Brentford	D	0-0	0-0	23		5914
33		6	A	Wycombe W	W	2-0	0-0	—	Minton, McGarrigle	3466
34		9	A	Chesterfield	L	0-1	0-0	23		6233
35		12	H	Oxford U	L	1-2	0-1	—	Maskell	3953
36		16	H	Hull C	W	4-0	2-0	23	Maskell 2, Byrne 2	4910
37		23	A	Stockport Co	L	1-3	1-1	23	Parris	5765
38		30	H	Rotherham U	D	1-1	1-1	23	Wilkins	5530
39	Apr	3	A	Swindon T	L	2-3	0-1	—	Minton, Rowe	8610
40		6	A	Bristol R	L	0-1	0-0	23		5385
41		9	H	Burnley	W	1-0	1-0	—	Rowe	5954
42		13	A	Swansea C	L	1-2	1-1	23	Ampadu (og)	2373
43		20	H	Carlisle U	W	1-0	1-0	23	Rowe	6131
44		23	A	Notts Co	L	1-2	1-1	—	Minton	3501
45	May	4	A	Walsall	L	1-2	0-1	23	Myall	4840
46		9	H	York C	L	1-3	1-0	23	Maskell	2106

Final League Position: 23

GOALSCORERS
League (46): Minton 8, McDougald 4, Maskell 4, Chapman 3, Mundee 3 (2 pens), Rowe 3, Wilkins 3, Berry 2, Bull 2, Byrne 2, Myall 2, Parris 2, Storer 2, Foster 1, McCarthy 1, McGarrigle 1, Smith 1, own goals 2.
Coca-Cola Cup (0).
FA Cup (6): McDougald 3, Byrne 2, Smith 1.

Rust N 46	Smith P 28+3	Tuck S 7+1	McGarrigle K 8+6	Foster S 8	McCarthy P 33	Storer S 28+10	Minton J 37+2	McDougald J 34+3	Myall S 27+6	Wilkins D 31+4	Fox M —+2	Fox S —+6	Chapman I 36	Munday S 6+3	Bull G 10	Byrne J 15+10	Berry G 6	Case J —+2	Andrews P —+8	Parris G 38	Osman R 11+1	Mundee D 31+1	Johnson R 19+1	McDonald P 5	Maskell C 15	Coughlan D 1	Hobson G 9	Rowe Z 9	Allan D 8	Match No.
1	2	3	4[2]	5	6	7	8	9	10[1]	11	12	13																		1
1	2	5	8[2]		6	7		11	13		12		3	4[1]	9	10														2
1	2	5	8		6	7[1]			4				3		9	10	11	12												3
1	2	5	8		6	7	12	11		4[1]			3		9	10[2]	13													4
1		5			6	7	10[1]	8	2	4			3		9	12	11[2]		13											5
1	13	5			6	7	10	8	2[2]	4			3		9[3]	12	11[1]	14												6
1		5			6	7	10	8[1]	2	4			3		9	12	11													7
1	12	5			6	7	10	8	2[1]	4			3		9	11[2]			13											8
1	2	5			6	12	10[1]	8		4			3		9	11[2]			13		7									9
1	2	5			6	12	10	8		4[2]			3	13	9[1]						7	11								10
1	2	5			6	12	10	8					3	4[1]	9						7	11								11
1	2	12	6	5[1]	9	10[3]		8	13				3	4[2]					14		7	11								12
1	2				6	7	11[1]	8	9	4		12	3								5	10								13
1	2	3			6	11[1]	8	9		4		12									7	5	10							14
1	2	3[2]			6	11[1]	8	9[3]		4		12							13		7	5	10	14						15
1	2				6	11[1]	12	8	3	4					9						7	5	10							16
1	2				6			9	8	3						11			10	4	5	7								17
1	2				6			9	8	3						11	5		10	4		7								18
1	2				6			9	8	3		12				11[1]			10	4		7	5							19
1	2[2]	12			6	10		9	8	11			3						13	4		7	5[1]							20
1	2				6	10[2]	9	8	12	11			13	3[1]	5					4		7								21
1	2				6	10	9	8		11			3							4	5	7								22
1	2				6	10	9[1]	8	12	11			3							4	5	7								23
1	2				6	10	9	8		11			3							4		7	5							24
1	2				6[1]	10	9	8		11			3							4	12	7	5							25
1	2					10	9	8		11			3							4	5	7	6							26
1	2				6	10	9	8		11			3						12	4		7[1]	5							27
1	2				6	10	9[1]	8	12	11			3						7	4			5							28
1	2				6	12	9	8	13	11[2]			3						7[1]	4			5		10					29
1					6	10	9	8	2				3							4		7	5		11					30
1					6	10	9	12	2			13	3		8[2]					4		7[1]	5		11					31
1	12				6		9	13	2[1]				3		8[2]					4		7	5	11	10					32
1	2[1]	12			6		9	8	13				3							4		7	5	11[2]	10					33
1		12			6[1]	11[2]	9	8	2			13	3							4		7	5		10					34
1		3				11	9	8		2			12						4		7	5		10	6[1]				35
1		6				12	9	11	2				3		8					4		7[1]	5		10					36
1		6				12	9	11[2]	2	13			3		8[1]					4		7	5		10					37
1						11		2	8				3							4		7	5		10		6	9		38
1		12				13	8[2]	2[3]	11[1]				3	14						4		7			10		6	9	5	39
1		12					8	2[3]	13				3	14						4		7[2]	11[1]		10		6	9	5	40
1						7[1]	8	2	11[2]				3	13						4		12			10		6	9	5	41
1		12				8	2	11[2]					3	13						4		7			10		6	9	5	42
1		12				8	2	11[1]					3							4		7			10		6	9	5	43
1		12				8	2[2]					13	3							4		7			10		6	9	5	44
1	2					12		8												11[1]		4	7	3	10		6	9	5	45
1	2[1]					11	12	3	8				14							13		4	7[1]		10		6[2]	9	5	46

Coca-Cola Cup
First Round   Fulham   (a) 0-3
                                                     (h) 0-2

FA Cup
First Round   Canvey Island   (a) 2-2
                                                     (h) 4-1
Second Round   Fulham   (a) 0-0
                                                     (h) 0-0

BRISTOL CITY 1995–96   *Back row (left to right):* Louis Carey, Rob Edwards, Matt Hewlett, Vegard Hansen, Keith Welch, Mark Shail, Phil Kite, Jason Fowler, Scott Paterson, Matt Bryant, Alan McLeary.
Middle row: Dave Bell (Youth Team Coach), Tony Fawthrop (Chief Scout), Jim Brennan, Dominic Barclay, Paul Agostino, Mark Humphries, Wayne Brown, Richard Dryden, Gary Owers, Brian Tinnion, Phil Barber, Mike Gibson (Coach), Buster Footman (Physio), Gerry Sweeney (Coach).
Front row: Stuart Munro, Dean Huggins, Junior Bent, Scott Partridge, Joe Jordan (Manager), John Gorman (Assistant Manager), David Seal, Martin Kuhl, Rodney McAree, Ian Baird.

Division 2   **BRISTOL CITY**

Ashton Gate, Bristol BS3 2EJ. Telephone: (0117) 9632812 (5 lines). Fax: (0117) 9639574. Commercial: (0117) 9633836. Shop: (0117) 9538566. Clubcall: 0891 121176. Supporters Club: (0117) 9665554. Community Dept: (0117) 9664685.

Ground capacity: 17,888.

Record attendance: 43,335 v Preston NE, FA Cup 5th rd, 16 February 1935.

Record receipts: £148,282 v Everton, FA Cup 4th rd, 29 January 1995.

Pitch measurements: 115yd × 75yd.

Chairman: S. Davidson.

Directors: J. Clapp, R. Neale, G. Williams. *Commercial Manager:* John Cox.

Manager: Joe Jordan. *Assistant Manager:* John Gorman.

Physio: H. Footman. *Secretary:* Ian Wilson. *Stadium Manager:* D. Lewis.

Year Formed: 1894. *Turned Professional:* 1897. *Ltd Co.:* 1897. BCFC (1982) Plc.

Previous Name: Bristol South End 1894–97.

Club Nickname: 'Robins'.

Previous Grounds: 1894, St John's Lane; 1904, Ashton Gate.

Foundation: The name Bristol City came into being in 1897 when the Bristol South End club, formed three years earlier, decided to adopt professionalism and apply for admission to the Southern League after competing in the Western League. The historic meeting was held at The Albert Hall, Bedminster. Bristol City employed Sam Hollis from Woolwich Arsenal as manager and gave him £40 to buy players. In 1901 they merged with Bedminster, another leading Bristol club.

First Football League game: 7 September 1901, Division 2, v Blackpool (a) W 2-0 – Moles; Tuft, Davies; Jones, McLean, Chambers; Bradbury, Connor, Boucher, O'Brien (2), Flynn.

Record League Victory: 9–0 v Aldershot, Division 3 (S), 28 December 1946 – Eddols; Morgan, Fox; Peacock, Roberts, Jones (1); Chilcott, Thomas, Clark (4 incl. 1p), Cyril Williams (1), Hargreaves (3).

Record Cup Victory: 11–0 v Chichester C, FA Cup 1st rd, 5 November 1960 – Cook; Collinson, Thresher; Connor, Alan Williams, Etheridge; Tait (1), Bobby Williams (1), Atyeo (5), Adrian Williams (3), Derrick. (1 og).

Record Defeat: 0–9 v Coventry C, Division 3 (S), 28 April 1934.

Most League Points (2 for a win): 70, Division 3 (S), 1954–55.

Most League Points (3 for a win): 91, Division 3, 1989–90.

Most League Goals: 104, Division 3 (S), 1926–27.

Highest League Scorer in Season: Don Clark, 36, Division 3 (S), 1946–47.

Most League Goals in Total Aggregate: John Atyeo, 314, 1951–66.

Most Capped Player: Billy Wedlock, 26, England.

Most League Appearances: John Atyeo, 597, 1951–66.

Record Transfer Fee Received: £1,750,000 from Newcastle U for Andy Cole, March 1993.

Record Transfer Fee Paid: £500,000 to Arsenal for Andy Cole, July 1992.

Football League Record: 1901 Elected to Division 2; 1906–11 Division 1; 1911–22 Division 2; 1922–23 Division 3 (S); 1923–24 Division 2; 1924–27 Division 3 (S); 1927–32 Division 2; 1932–55 Division 3 (S); 1955–60 Division 2; 1960–65 Division 3; 1965–76 Division 2; 1976–80 Division 1; 1980–81 Division 2; 1981–82 Division 3; 1982–84 Division 4; 1984–90 Division 3; 1990–92 Division 2; 1992– Division 1.

Honours: Football League: Division 1 – Runners-up 1906–07; *Division 2* – Champions 1905–06; Runners-up 1975–76; Division 3 (S) – Champions 1922–23, 1926–27, 1954–55; Runners-up 1937–38; Division 3 – Runners-up 1964–65, 1989–90. *FA Cup:* Runners-up 1909. *Football League Cup:* Semi-final 1971, 1989. *Welsh Cup:* Winners 1934. *Anglo-Scottish Cup:* Winners 1978. *Freight Rover Trophy:* Winners 1986; Runners-up 1987.

Colours: Red shirts, white shorts, red and white stockings. *Change colours:* Green, black, red repeat hooped shirts, black shorts with red trim, green stockings with black trim.

Did you know?
On 4 May 1912 Bristol City beat Bristol Rovers 3-1 in the Titanic Disaster Fund. On 11 May 1946 they also beat their neighbours 2-1 in the Bolton Disaster Fund.

BRISTOL CITY 1995–96 LEAGUE RECORD

Match No.	Date	Venue	Opponents	Result	H/T Score	Lg. Pos.	Goalscorers	Atten- dance
1	Aug 12	H	Blackpool	D 1-1	1-1	—	Seal	7734
2	26	H	Stockport Co	W 1-0	1-0	13	Seal	7731
3	29	A	Shrewsbury T	L 1-4	1-0	—	Agostino	2558
4	Sept 2	A	Peterborough U	D 1-1	0-1	17	Seal	4621
5	9	H	Brighton & HA	L 0-1	0-1	22		7585
6	12	H	Brentford	D 0-0	0-0	—		5054
7	16	A	Bradford C	L 0-3	0-1	22		5165
8	23	H	Notts Co	D 2-2	0-0	22	Agostino, Seal	5251
9	30	H	Wycombe W	D 0-0	0-0	22		5564
10	Oct 7	A	Swindon T	L 0-2	0-1	23		11,979
11	14	H	Hull C	W 4-0	1-0	21	Bent 2, Starbuck, Barnard	5354
12	21	A	York C	W 1-0	1-0	19	Nugent	3367
13	28	H	Walsall	L 0-2	0-2	21		6475
14	31	H	Chesterfield	W 2-1	1-1	—	Barnard, Morris (og)	4408
15	Nov 4	A	Oxford U	L 0-2	0-0	19		5665
16	18	H	Carlisle U	D 1-1	0-0	20	Nugent	5423
17	25	A	Rotherham U	W 3-2	1-1	18	Barnard, Owers, Seal	2649
18	Dec 5	A	Crewe Alex	L 2-4	1-0	—	Nugent, Dryden	2977
19	9	H	Notts Co	L 0-2	0-1	20		5617
20	16	A	Wycombe W	D 1-1	0-1	18	Tinnion	4020
21	23	A	Burnley	D 0-0	0-0	17		9327
22	26	H	Swansea C	W 1-0	0-0	17	Kuhl	6845
23	Jan 6	A	Bournemouth	D 1-1	1-0	16	Maskell	3662
24	13	H	Crewe Alex	W 3-2	2-1	16	Paterson, Nugent 2	6790
25	16	H	Bristol R	L 0-2	0-0	—		20,007
26	20	A	Blackpool	L 0-3	0-1	16		4838
27	23	A	Wrexham	D 0-0	0-0	—		2673
28	Feb 10	H	Bournemouth	W 3-0	2-0	17	Seal, Tinnion, Agostino	6217
29	13	H	Shrewsbury T	W 2-0	0-0	—	Agostino 2	5269
30	17	A	Brentford	D 2-2	0-1	15	Agostino, Barnard	5213
31	20	H	Peterborough U	L 0-1	0-0	—		5014
32	24	H	Bradford C	W 2-1	1-0	13	Seal, Kuhl	5400
33	27	A	Brighton & HA	W 2-0	1-0	—	Kuhl 2	4739
34	Mar 2	A	Swansea C	L 1-2	0-2	11	Walker (og)	4109
35	9	H	Burnley	L 0-1	0-0	11		6612
36	16	A	Bristol R	W 4-2	2-1	11	Nugent, Hewlett, Agostino, Seal	8648
37	19	A	Stockport Co	D 0-0	0-0	—		3713
38	23	H	Wrexham	W 3-1	1-0	11	Nugent 2, Tinnion	6141
39	30	H	Swindon T	D 0-0	0-0	12		11,370
40	Apr 2	A	Hull C	W 3-2	0-0	—	Hewlett, Agostino, Seal	2641
41	6	A	Walsall	L 1-2	1-1	12	Seal	4142
42	8	H	York C	D 1-1	0-0	12	Kuhl (pen)	7512
43	13	A	Chesterfield	D 1-1	1-0	11	Owers	4619
44	20	H	Oxford U	L 0-2	0-0	13		7674
45	27	H	Rotherham U	W 4-3	1-1	13	Partridge, Agostino 2, Kuhl	6101
46	May 4	A	Carlisle U	L 1-2	1-2	13	Robinson (og)	5935

Final League Position: 13

GOALSCORERS

League (55): Agostino 10, Seal 10, Nugent 8, Kuhl 6 (1 pen), Barnard 4, Tinnion 3, Bent 2, Hewlett 2, Owers 2, Dryden 1, Maskell 1, Partridge 1, Paterson 1, Starbuck 1, own goals 3.
Coca-Cola Cup (4): Seal 3, Agostino 1.
FA Cup (0).

Welch K 35	Hansen V 7+1	Munro S 3	McLeary A 30+1	Dryden R 17+1	Kuhl M 46	Bent J 33+7	Partridge S 3+6	Seal D 19+11	Agostino P 29+11	Barber P 3	Shail M 9+3	Armstrong G 6	Plummer D 1+10	Bryant M 31+1	Kite P 3+1	Fowler J 6+4	Owers G 34+3	Edwards R 18+1	Starbuck P 5	Dykstra S 8	Baird I 1	Nugent K 29+5	Paterson S 16+2	Barnard D 33+1	Tinnion B 27+3	Carey L 22+1	Hewlett M 27	Maskell C 5	Barclay D —+2	Match No.
1	2	3	4	5	6	7	8	9	10	11																				1
1	2		4	5	6	7	12	9	10[1]	11[2]	3	8	13																	2
1	2		4	5	6	7		9	10	11[2]	3[1]	8	13	12																3
1[6]		3	4[2]	5	6	7	12	9	10				13	8		2	15	11[1]												4
	3			5	6	7	12	9	10[1]			4	8[2]	14	2	1	11[3]	13												5
	2				6	7[2]	12	9	10[1]			4	11	13	5	1	8	3												6
	2		4		6	7		9	12				11	5		1	8[1]	3				10								7
	2		4		6	12		13	10			7[1]		5			8	3	11		1	9[2]								8
	2		4		6	7		12						5			8[1]	3	11			9	10							9
			4		6	7		12						5			8	3	2	1		9	10[1]	11						10
			4		6[2]	7		12						5			8	3	11[1]	1		9	2	10	13					11
			4		6	7		12						5			8	3		1		9	2	10	11[1]					12
			4		6	7		12	13					5			8	3		1		9	2[1]	10	11[2]					13
			4		6	7	12	11[1]						5			8	3		1		9	2	10						14
	2[1]		4		6	7	12	11[2]		3				5			8			1		9		10	13					15
1			4		6	7[2]	11[1]	12						5	13		8	3				9		10	2					16
1			12		6	7	13	11[2]						5[1]	4		8	3				9		10	2					17
1			4		6	7								5			8	3				9		10	11	2				18
1	12		4		6	7	11[2]	13						5[1]			8	3				9		10[3]	14	2				19
1			4		6	7[1]			12					5			8					9		10	11	2	3			20
1			4		6				12			7[1]		5[2]			8					9	13	10	11	2	3			21
1			4		6				12			7[1]	13				8					9	5	10	11	2	3[2]			22
1			4		6	12												3				9	5	10[1]	11	2	8	7		23
1			4		6	10												3				9	5		11	2	8	7		24
1			4		6	12			13								8	3[3]				9	5	14	11	2	10[1]	7[2]		25
1			4		6	12			13								8	3				9	5		11	2	10[1]	7[2]		26
1					6				12								8	3				9	5	4[1]	11	2	10	7		27
1	12		4		6	7[2]		9	10				13	5										3	11	2[1]	8			28
1			4		6	7		9	10					5										3	11	2	8			29
1			4		6	7[1]		9	10					5			12							3	11	2	8			30
1			4		6	7[2]		9	10[3]					5			13					14		3	11	2	8[1]			31
1			4		6	12		9[2]	10					5			7					13		3	11	2[1]	8			32
1			4		6	7		9[1]	10					5			2					12		3	11		8			33
1			4		6	7[1]		9	10					5			2					12		3	11		8			34
1			4		6	7[1]		9	10[2]					5		12	2					13		3	11		8			35
1			4		6	7[2]		12	10[1]					5		13	2					9		3	11		8			36
1			4		6	7[1]			10					5		12	2					9		3	11		8			37
1			4[3]		6	7[2]		12	10[1]					5		13	2					9		3	11	14	8			38
1			4		6	7[1]		12	10					5			2					9		3	11		8			39
1			4		6			12	10[1]					5		7	2					9		3	11		8			40
1			4		6	12		10[2]	13					5		7[1]	2					9			11	3	8			41
1			4		6	7[2]		9[3]	10				13	5[1]			2					12		3	11		8		14	42
1			4		6	12		13	10[2]					7[1]			2					9	5		11		8			43
1			4		6	7			10[2]			12		11[1]			2					9	5	3			8		13	44
1					6	7			10					5								9	4	3	11	2	8			45
1		5			6		12		10								7	13				9	4	3	11[2]	2[1]	8			46

Coca-Cola Cup

First Round	Colchester U	(a)	1-2
		(h)	2-1
Second Round	Newcastle U	(h)	0-5
		(a)	1-3

FA Cup

First Round	Bournemouth	(a)	0-0
		(h)	0-1

BRISTOL ROVERS 1995-96 *Back row (left to right):* Mike Wyatt, Billy Clarke, Gareth Taylor, Shane Higgs, Brian Parkin, Andy Collett, Justin Skinner, Ian McLean, Ian Wright.
Third row: Lee Archer, David Pritchard, Marcus Stewart, Andy Tillson, Marcus Browning, Paul Miller, Worrell Sterling, Justin Channing.
Second row: Roy Dolling (Youth Development Manager), Ray Kendall (Kit Manager), Tony Gill (Youth Team Manager), John Ward (Manager), Steve Cross (Assistant Manager), Terry Connor (Reserve Team Manager), Keith James (Physio).
Front row: Andy Gurney, Jonathan French, Matthew Hayfield, Mike Davis, Martin Paul, Paul Tovey, Tom White, Lee Maddison.

Division 2 — BRISTOL ROVERS

Twerton Park, Twerton, Bath, BA2 1DB. Training Ground: (0117) 861743. Match Day Ticket Office: (01225) 312327. Offices: Avonfields House, Somerdale, Keynsham, Bristol BS18 2DJ. (0117) 9869999. Pirates Hotline: 0891 664422. Fax: (0117) 9864030. Community Office: (0117) 9860809.

Ground capacity: 8943.

Record attendance: 9464 v Liverpool, FA Cup 4th rd, 8 February 1992 (Twerton Park). 38,472 v Preston NE, FA Cup 4th rd, 30 January 1960 (Eastville).

Record receipts: £62,480 v Liverpool, FA Cup 4th rd, 8 February 1992.

Pitch measurements: 110yd × 75yd.

President: Marquis of Worcester.

Vice-Presidents: Dr W. T. Cussen, A. I. Seager, H. E. L. Brown, R. Redmond.

Chairman: D. H. A. Dunford. *Vice-Chairman:* G. M. H. Dunford.

Directors: R. Craig, B. Andrews, V. Stokes.

Manager: Ian Holloway. *Assistant Manager:* Steve Cross.

Reserve Team Manager: Steve Cross. *Physio:* Keith James. *Youth Team Coach:* Tony Gill. *Community Scheme Organiser:* A. Walsh.

Chief Administrator/Club Secretary: Ian Wilson. *Office Manager:* Mrs Angela Mann.

Year Formed: 1883. *Turned Professional:* 1897. *Ltd Co.:* 1896.

Previous Names: 1883, The Purdown Poachers; 1883, Black Arabs; 1884, Eastville Rovers; 1897, Bristol Eastville Rovers; 1898, Bristol Rovers.

Club Nickname: 'Pirates'.

Previous Grounds: 1883, Purdown; Three Acres, Ashley Hill; Rudgeway, Fishponds; 1894 Eastville.

Foundation: Bristol Rovers were formed at a meeting in Stapleton Road, Eastville, in 1883. However, they first went under the name of the Black Arabs (wearing black shirts). Changing their name to Eastville Rovers in their second season, they won the Gloucestershire Senior Cup in 1888–89. Original members of the Bristol & District League in 1892, this eventually became the Western League and Eastville Rovers adopted professionalism in 1897.

First Football League game: 28 August 1920, Division 3, v Millwall (a) L 0-2 – Stansfield; Bethune, Panes; Boxley, Kenny, Steele; Chance, Kenny, Sims, Bell, Palmer.

Record League Victory: 7–0 v Brighton & HA, Division 3 (S), 29 November 1952 – Hoyle; Bamford, Geoff Fox; Pitt, Warren, Sampson; McIlvenny, Roost (2), Lambden (1), Bradford (1), Petherbridge (2). (1 og). 7–0 v Swansea T, Division 2, 2 October 1954 – Radford; Bamford, Watkins; Pitt, Muir, Anderson; Petherbridge, Bradford (2), Meyer, Roost (1), Hooper (2). (2 og). 7–0 v Shrewsbury T, Division 3, 21 March 1964 – Hall; Hillard, Gwyn Jones; Oldfield, Stone (1), Mabbutt; Jarman (2), Brown (1), Biggs (1p), Hamilton, Bobby Jones (2).

Record Cup Victory: 6–0 v Merthyr Tydfil, FA Cup 1st rd, 14 November 1987 – Martyn; Alexander (Dryden), Tanner, Hibbitt, Twentyman, Jones, Holloway, Meacham (1), White (2), Penrice (3) (Reece), Purnell.

Record Defeat: 0–12 v Luton T, Division 3 (S), 13 April 1936.

Most League Points (2 for a win): 64, Division 3 (S), 1952–53.

Most League Points (3 for a win): 93, Division 3, 1989–90.

Most League Goals: 92, Division 3 (S), 1952–53.

Highest League Scorer in Season: Geoff Bradford, 33, Division 3 (S), 1952–53.

Most League Goals in Total Aggregate: Geoff Bradford, 245, 1949–64.

Most Capped Player: Neil Slatter, 10 (22), Wales.

Most League Appearances: Stuart Taylor, 545, 1966–80.

Record Transfer Fee Received: £1,000,000 from Crystal Palace for Nigel Martyn, November 1989.

Record Transfer Fee Paid: £370,000 to QPR for Andy Tillson, November 1992.

Football League Record: 1920 Original Member of Division 3; 1921–53 Division 3 (S); 1953–62 Division 2; 1962–74 Division 3; 1974–81 Division 2; 1981–90 Division 3; 1990–92 Division 2. 1992–93 Division 1; 1993– Division 2.

Honours: Football League: Division 2 best season: 4th, 1994–95; Division 3 (S) – Champions 1952–53; Division 3 – Champions 1989–90; Runners-up 1973–74. *FA Cup:* best season: 6th rd, 1951, 1958. *Football League Cup:* best season: 5th rd, 1971, 1972.

Colours: Blue and white quartered shirts, white shorts, blue stockings. *Change colours:* Green shirts, black shorts, black stockings.

Did you know?
Joe Riley was the first Bristol Rovers player to score a hat-trick on his League debut. He did so on 2 January 1932 in a 4-1 win over Bournemouth.

BRISTOL ROVERS 1995–96 LEAGUE RECORD

Match No.	Date	Venue	Opponents	Result		H/T Score	Lg. Pos.	Goalscorers	Attendance
1	Aug 12	A	Carlisle U	W	2-1	1-1	—	Clark, Stewart	8003
2	19	H	Swansea C	D	2-2	0-1	3	Taylor 2	6689
3	26	A	Walsall	D	1-1	0-0	7	Taylor	4851
4	29	H	Burnley	W	1-0	0-0	—	Taylor	5646
5	Sept 2	H	Wrexham	L	1-2	1-0	6	Stewart	6031
6	9	A	York C	W	1-0	0-0	4	Miller	4047
7	12	A	Rotherham U	L	0-1	0-0	—		2739
8	16	H	Swindon T	L	1-4	1-1	11	Miller	7025
9	23	H	Brentford	W	2-0	1-0	9	Stewart (pen), Paul	5131
10	30	A	Oxford U	W	2-1	2-0	8	Browning, Stewart	6091
11	Oct 7	H	Bournemouth	L	0-2	0-1	9		5171
12	14	A	Bradford C	W	3-2	1-1	5	Gurney, Archer, Stewart	5817
13	21	H	Notts Co	L	0-3	0-1	9		6078
14	28	A	Brighton & HA	L	0-2	0-0	11		5658
15	31	A	Blackpool	L	0-3	0-3	—		3877
16	Nov 4	H	Peterborough U	D	1-1	1-0	13	Gurney	4241
17	18	A	Wycombe W	D	1-1	0-1	14	Gurney	4886
18	25	H	Stockport Co	L	1-3	0-0	15	Miller	4326
19	Dec 9	A	Brentford	D	0-0	0-0	15		5679
20	16	H	Oxford U	W	2-0	0-0	14	Stewart 2	4051
21	23	H	Crewe Alex	L	1-2	0-0	15	Browning	4519
22	26	A	Shrewsbury T	D	1-1	0-0	15	Beadle	4944
23	Jan 6	H	Hull C	W	2-1	2-0	14	Stewart 2	4267
24	13	A	Swansea C	D	2-2	0-2	15	Gurney, Beadle	2956
25	16	A	Bristol C	W	2-0	0-0	—	Beadle 2	20,007
26	20	A	Carlisle U	D	1-1	0-1	12	Stewart	5196
27	Feb 3	H	Walsall	W	2-0	0-0	11	Beadle, Stewart (pen)	4948
28	10	A	Hull C	W	3-1	0-0	7	Stewart, Browning, Beadle	3311
29	17	H	Rotherham U	W	1-0	0-0	6	Stewart	5412
30	20	A	Wrexham	L	2-3	1-1	—	Beadle, Tillson	3235
31	24	A	Swindon T	L	1-2	1-0	9	Stewart	11,697
32	27	H	York C	W	1-0	1-0	—	Stewart	4013
33	Mar 2	H	Shrewsbury T	W	2-1	1-1	7	Gurney, Stewart (pen)	5004
34	9	A	Crewe Alex	W	2-1	0-0	7	French, Stewart	4091
35	16	H	Bristol C	L	2-4	1-2	7	Gurney, Clark	8648
36	23	A	Chesterfield	L	1-2	0-0	10	Stewart	4748
37	26	H	Chesterfield	W	1-0	0-0	—	Beadle	3513
38	30	A	Bournemouth	L	1-2	0-1	9	Miller	4607
39	Apr 2	H	Bradford C	W	1-0	0-0	—	Beadle	4008
40	6	H	Brighton & HA	W	1-0	0-0	8	Beadle	5385
41	9	A	Notts Co	L	2-4	0-1	—	Stewart, Beadle	4661
42	13	H	Blackpool	D	1-1	1-0	10	Beadle	5626
43	20	A	Peterborough U	D	0-0	0-0	10		4884
44	23	A	Burnley	W	1-0	0-0	—	Stewart	9368
45	27	A	Stockport Co	L	0-2	0-1	9		6935
46	May 4	H	Wycombe W	W	2-1	1-0	10	Browning, Stewart	6621

Final League Position: 10

GOALSCORERS

League (57): Stewart 21 (3 pens), Beadle 12, Gurney 6, Browning 4, Miller 4, Taylor 4, Clark 2, Archer 1, French 1, Paul 1, Tillson 1.
Coca-Cola Cup (5): Stewart 4, Miller 1.
FA Cup (1): Archer 1.

Parkin B 20	Pritchard D 12	Gurney A 42 + 1	Browning M 45	Clark B 38 + 1	Tillson A 38	Sterling W 28 + 2	Miller P 37 + 1	Stewart M 44	Skinner J 23 + 5	Taylor G 7	Wright I 15 + 3	Wyatt M 3 + 1	Hayfield M 3 + 3	Archer L 13 + 6	Channing J 35 + 1	McLean I 4 + 3	Paul M 9 + 4	Collett A 26	Davis M 1 + 3	White T — + 2	French J 3 + 7	Beadle P 26 + 1	Tovey P 8	Armstrong C 13 + 1	Matthew D 8	Morgan S 5	Low J — + 1	Match No.
1	2	3	4	5	6	7	8	9	10	11																		1
1	2	3	4	5	6	7	8	9	10	11																		2
1	2	3	4	5		7	8	9	10	11	6																	3
1	2	3	4	5		7	8	9	10	11	6																	4
1	2	3		5		7	8	9	10¹	11	6	4	12															5
1	2	3	4	5		7	8	9	10		6				11¹	12												6
1	2	3²	4	5			8	9	10	11	6	7¹			12		13											7
1	2	3	4	5			8	9	10	11	6					7												8
1	2		4	12	6		8	9	10²		5¹	11	13		3		7											9
1	2	3	4		6	7		9	10		5		12		11		8¹											10
1	2¹	3	4		6	7		9	10		5				12	11	8											11
		3	4		6	7		9	10		5				11	2	8¹	1	12									12
		3	4		6	7		9	10		5				11	2	8¹	1	12									13
		3	4		6	7		9	10		5¹				11	2³	12	13	1		8²	14						14
		3	4		6	7		9	10			12	2	11		5	8¹	1										15
		3	4¹		6	7			10		2		8	11		5		1	12	9								16
1	2	3	4	5	6		12	9	10						7	11						8¹						17
1		3	4	5	6		8	9	10			2			7	11¹	12											18
1		3	4	5	6	7	8	9							2							11¹	12	10				19
1		3	4	5	6	7	8	9							2							11		10				20
1		3	4	5	6	7	8		12						2		9					11¹		10				21
		3¹	4	5	6	7	8	9	12						2	13		1				11		10²				22
1		3	4	5	6	7	8	9	12						2							11¹		10²	13			23
1		7	4	5	6		8	9							2							11			3	10		24
1		3	4	5	6		8	9							2							11			7	10		25
1			4	5	6	7	8	9							2							11			3	10		26
			4	5	6	7	8	9							2			1				11			3	10		27
		3	4	5	6	7	8	9							2	12		1				11				10		28
		3	4	5	6	7	8	9							2			1				11				10		29
		3	4	5	6	7	8	9							2			1				11				10		30
		3	4	5	6	7	8	9							2	11		1								10		31
		3	4¹	5	6	7	8	9							2			1			12	11	10					32
		7	4	5	6	12	8	9	13						2¹			1				11	10²			3		33
		2	4¹	5	6	7	8	9	13							12		1			11²	10				3		34
		2	4	5	6	7	8	9							10¹			1			12	11				3		35
		2¹	4	5		7²	8	9			6				13	10		1			12	11				3		36
		2	4	5	6	12		9							7	10		1			8¹	11				3		37
		2³	4	5	6		8	9				12			7	10		1			13	11			3¹			38
		3	4	5	6		8	9							7¹	10		1			12	11			2			39
		2	4	5	6		8	9	12						7	10		1				11¹			3			40
		2¹	4	5			8	9	12		6				7	10		1				11			3			41
		2	4	5	6		8¹	9	7						12	10		1				11			3			42
		2¹	4	5	6		8	9	7						12	10		1				11			3			43
		2¹	4	5	6		8	9	7							10		1	13	12	11¹				3			44
		2¹	4	5	6		8	9	7						12	10		1				11			3			45
		12	4	5	6		8	9	7						2¹	10³		1			13	11²			3		14	46

Coca-Cola Cup

First Round	Gillingham	(a)	1-1	
		(h)	4-2	
Second Round	West Ham U	(h)	0-1	
		(a)	0-3	

FA Cup

First Round	Hitchin	(a)	1-2

BURNLEY 1995-96   *Back row (left to right):* Ted McMinn, Adrian Randall, Steve Thompson, Nathan Peel, Mark Winstanley, Tony Philliskirk, Peter Swan, John Pender, Glen Davies, Paul Smith.
Middle row: Terry Pashley (Youth Team Coach), Gary Parkinson, Warren Joyce, Alan Harper, Derek Adams, Wayne Dowell, Mar on Beresford, Wayne Russell, Andy Cooke, Kurt Nogan, Matthew Taylor, John Borland, Brian Miller (Chief Scout).
Front row: Harry Wilson (Reserve Team Coach), Adrian Heath, Liam Robinson, Chris Brass, David Eyres, Jamie Hoyland, Jimmy Mullen (Manager), Clive Middlemass (Assistant Manager), Chris Vinnicombe, John Francis, Paul Weller, Gerry Harrison, Andy Jones (Physio).

Division 2   **BURNLEY**

Turf Moor, Burnley BB10 4BX. Telephone: (01282) 700000. Fax: (01282) 700014. Clubcall: 0891 121153. Credit Card Ticket Sales: (0645) 101010. Ticket Office: (01282) 70010. Community Programme: (01282) 70011. Commercial Department: (01282) 70007.

Ground capacity: 22,966.

Record attendance: 54,775 v Huddersfield T, FA Cup 3rd rd, 23 February 1924.

Record receipts: £150,000 v Liverpool, FA Cup 4th rd, 28 January 1995.

Pitch measurements: 114yd × 72yd.

Chairman: F. J. Teasdale.

Vice-Chairman: Dr R. D. Iven MRCS (Eng), LRCP (Lond), MRCGP.

Directors: B. Rothwell JP, C. Holt, R. Blakeborough.

Manager: Adrian Heath. *Assistant Manager:* Clive Middlemass.

Coaches: Harry Wilson, Terry Pashley.

Commercial Manager: T. Skelly. *Physio:* Andy Jones.

Year Formed: 1882. *Turned Professional:* 1883. *Ltd Co.:* 1897.

Previous Name: 1881–82, Burnley Rovers.

Club Nickname: 'The Clarets'.

Previous Grounds: 1881, Calder Vale; 1882, Turf Moor.

Foundation: The majority of those responsible for the formation of the Burnley club in 1881 were from the defunct rugby club Burnley Rovers. Indeed, they continued to play rugby for a year before changing to soccer and dropping "Rovers" from their name. The changes were decided at a meeting held in May 1882 at the Bull Hotel.

First Football League game: 8 September 1888, Football League, v Preston NE (a), L 2-5 – Smith; Lang, Bury, Abrams, Friel, Keenan, Brady, Tait, Poland (1), Gallocher (1), Yates.

Record League Victory: 9–0 v Darwen, Division 1, 9 January 1892 – Hillman; Walker, McFettridge, Lang, Matthews, Keenan, Nicol (3), Bowes, Espie (1), McLardie (3), Hill (2).

Record Cup Victory: 9–0 v Crystal Palace, FA Cup 2nd rd (replay), 10 February 1909 – Dawson; Barron, McLean; Cretney (2), Leake, Moffat; Morley, Ogden, Smith (3), Abbott (2), Smethams (1). 9–0 v New Brighton, FA Cup 4th rd 26 January 1957 – Blacklaw; Angus, Winton; Seith, Adamson, Miller; Newlands (1), McIlroy (3), Lawson (3), Cheesebrough (1), Pilkington (1). 9–0 v Penrith, FA Cup 1st rd, 17 November 1984 – Hansbury; Miller, Hampton, Phelan, Overson (Kennedy), Hird (3 incl. 1p), Grewcock (1), Powell (2), Taylor (3), Biggins, Hutchison.

Record Defeat: 0–10 v Aston Villa, Division 1, 29 August 1925 and v Sheffield U, Division 1, 19 January 1929.

Most League Points (2 for a win): 62, Division 2, 1972–73.

Most League Points (3 for a win): 83, Division 4, 1991–92.

Most League Goals: 102, Division 1, 1960–61.

Highest League Scorer in Season: George Beel, 35, Division 1, 1927–28.

Most League Goals in Total Aggregate: George Beel, 178, 1923–32.

Most Capped Player: Jimmy McIlroy, 51 (55), Northern Ireland.

Most League Appearances: Jerry Dawson, 522, 1907–28.

Record Transfer Fee Received: £750,000 from Luton T for Steve Davis, August 1995.

Record Transfer Fee Paid: £250,000 to Bristol C for Liam Robinson, August 1994 and £250,000 to Brighton & HA for Kurt Nogan, February 1995.

Football League Record: 1888 Original Member of the Football League; 1897–98 Division 2; 1898–1900 Division 1; 1900–13 Division 2; 1913–30 Division 1; 1930–47 Division 2; 1947–71 Division 1; 1971–73 Division 2; 1973–76 Division 1; 1976–80 Division 2; 1980–82 Division 3; 1982–83 Division 2; 1983–85 Division 3; 1985–92 Division 4; 1992–94 Division 2; 1994–95 Division 1; 1995– Division 2.

Honours: Football League: Division 1 – Champions 1920–21, 1959–60; Runners-up 1919–20, 1961–62; Division 2 – Champions 1897–98, 1972–73; Runners-up 1912–13, 1946–47; Division 3 – Champions 1981–82. Division 4 – Champions 1991–92. Record 30 consecutive Division 1 games without defeat 1920–21. *FA Cup:* Winners 1914; Runners-up 1947, 1962. *Football League Cup:* semi-final 1961, 1969, 1983. *Anglo-Scottish Cup:* Winners 1979. *Sherpa Van Trophy:* Runners-up 1988. **European Competitions;** *European Cup:* 1960–61. *European Fairs Cup:* 1966–67.

Colours: Claret and blue quartered shirts, white shorts and stockings. *Change colours:* White shirts with three sky blue stripes, black shorts, sky blue stockings.

Did you know?
Dave Thomas became the youngest player to appear for Burnley when he made his debut at 17 against Everton in the last game of the 1966–67 season.

BURNLEY 1995–96 LEAGUE RECORD

Match No.	Date	Venue	Opponents	Result		H/T Score	Lg. Pos.	Goalscorers	Attendance
1	Aug 12	H	Rotherham U	W	2-1	2-1	—	Eyres (pen), Philliskirk	10,478
2	19	A	Stockport Co	D	0-0	0-0	8		8463
3	26	H	Brentford	W	1-0	1-0	5	Nogan	9586
4	29	A	Bristol R	L	0-1	0-0	—		5646
5	Sept 6	H	Walsall	D	1-1	0-0	—	Joyce	8778
6	9	A	Carlisle U	L	0-2	0-0	15		7318
7	12	A	York C	D	1-1	1-0	—	Cooke	4684
8	16	H	Hull C	W	2-1	1-0	9	Nogan, Allison (og)	10,613
9	23	A	Chesterfield	L	2-4	2-2	13	Nogan, Eyres (pen)	4933
10	30	H	Swansea C	W	3-0	1-0	9	Nogan, Joyce, Eyres	8068
11	Oct 7	H	Wycombe W	D	1-1	1-0	11	Joyce	8029
12	14	A	Bournemouth	W	2-0	1-0	7	Vinnicombe, Nogan	4954
13	21	H	Brighton & HA	W	3-0	3-0	5	Eyres, Swan, Nogan	9016
14	28	A	Bradford C	D	2-2	1-1	6	Harrison, Swan	8356
15	31	H	Peterborough U	W	2-0	2-0	—	McDonald, Swan	4737
16	Nov 4	H	Notts Co	L	3-4	1-2	7	Nogan 2, Cooke	10,511
17	18	A	Shrewsbury T	L	0-3	0-2	8		3914
18	25	H	Wrexham	D	2-2	0-0	8	Nogan, Joyce	8710
19	Dec 2	H	Carlisle U	W	2-0	1-0	4	Nogan 2	8297
20	9	H	Chesterfield	D	2-2	1-1	6	Nogan 2	8459
21	16	A	Swansea C	W	4-2	1-0	5	Eyres, Nogan, Cooke 2	2078
22	23	H	Bristol C	D	0-0	0-0	5		9327
23	Jan 13	H	Stockport Co	W	4-3	2-3	5	Vinnicombe, Cooke, Nogan, Francis	9113
24	20	A	Rotherham U	L	0-1	0-0	6		4018
25	30	H	Oxford U	L	0-2	0-1	—		6815
26	Feb 3	A	Brentford	L	0-1	0-0	8		5195
27	10	A	Crewe Alex	L	0-1	0-1	11		9153
28	17	H	York C	D	3-3	0-2	12	Winstanley, Francis, Nogan	8731
29	24	A	Hull C	L	0-3	0-1	15		4206
30	Mar 2	H	Blackpool	L	0-1	0-0	16		10,082
31	9	A	Bristol C	W	1-0	0-0	15	Nogan	6612
32	12	A	Blackpool	L	1-3	1-1	—	Nogan	8941
33	16	H	Swindon T	D	0-0	0-0	15		9360
34	19	A	Crewe Alex	L	1-3	0-0	—	Winstanley	3393
35	23	A	Oxford U	L	0-5	0-1	18		6529
36	30	A	Wycombe W	L	1-4	0-2	18	Mahorn	4921
37	Apr 2	H	Bournemouth	D	0-0	0-0	—		7941
38	6	H	Bradford C	L	2-3	0-2	20	Robinson, Eyres (pen)	9714
39	9	A	Brighton & HA	L	0-1	0-1	—		5954
40	13	H	Peterborough U	W	2-1	0-0	20	Joyce, Swan	8393
41	17	A	Swindon T	D	0-0	0-0	—		10,480
42	20	A	Notts Co	D	1-1	1-0	20	Swan	5697
43	23	H	Bristol R	L	0-1	0-0	—		9368
44	27	A	Wrexham	W	2-0	2-0	19	Robinson, Nogan	6664
45	30	A	Walsall	L	1-3	0-0	—	Nogan	3411
46	May 4	H	Shrewsbury T	W	2-1	1-1	17	Weller, Winstanley	9729

Final League Position: 17

GOALSCORERS

League (56): Nogan 20, Eyres 6 (3 pens), Cooke 5, Joyce 5, Swan 5, Winstanley 3, Francis 2, Robinson 2, Vinnicombe 2, Harrison 1, McDonald 1, Mahorn 1, Philliskirk 1, Weller 1, own goal 1.
Coca-Cola Cup (4): Nogan 3, Randall 1.
FA Cup (1): Eyres 1.

Beresford M 36	Parkinson G 29	Vinnicombe C 35	Swan P 31 + 1	Pender J 1	Randall A 12 + 3	McMinn T 7 + 3	Joyce W 42 + 1	Philliskirk T 7 + 1	Nogan K 46	Eyres D 39 + 3	Francis J 4 + 18	Brass C 7 + 2	Winstanley M 45	Harper A 3 + 1	Hoyland J 21 + 2	Cooke A 10 + 13	Harrison G 35	Borland J 1	McDonald P 8 + 1	Heath A 5 + 2	Weller P 24 + 1	Adams D — + 2	Russell W 10	Robinson L 11 + 5	Helliwell I 3 + 1	Dowell W 1	Thompson S 18	Smith P 3 + 7	Bishop C 9	Mahorn P 3 + 5	Match No.
1	2	3	4	5	6²	7¹	8	9	10	11	12	13																			1
1	2	3	4		6	11¹	8	9	10		12		5	7																	2
1	2	3	4		6		8	9¹	10	12	11		5		7																3
1	2	3	4		6		8¹	9²	10	11	12		5		7	13															4
1		3	4		6		12	9²	10	11	7	2⁵	5		8	13															5
1		3	4		6		8	9²	10	11	12		5		7	13	2¹														6
1		3	4				8		10¹	11	12		5		6	9	2	7													7
1		3	4¹			7	8	13	10		12		5		6²	9	2		11												8
1	2²	3					6	9¹	10	11	12		5	7	4				13	8											9
1	2	3			6	7	8		10	9			5		4				11												10
1	2	3	4		6	7¹	8		10	9²	12		5			13			11												11
1	2	3	4				8		10	9¹			5		6	12	7		11												12
1	2	3	4			7¹	8		10	9	12		5		13		6		11²												13
1	2¹	3	4			12		8²	10	9	13		5		6	14	7		11³												14
1	2	3	4			12		8¹	10	9			5		6		7		11												15
1	2³	3	4			12	11¹		10	9	13		5		6	14	7			8²											16
1	2	3¹	4³			11²	8		10	9	12	13	5		6	14	7														17
1		3	4		11	12	8		10	9			5		6¹					2	7										18
1		3			6		8		10	11		2	5		4	12					9¹	7									19
1		3			6	12	8		10	11²	13	2	5		4	14					9³	7¹									20
1		3						8¹	10	11		2	5		4	9	6						7	12							21
1		3¹	12			13	8		10	11		2	5		4	9²	6³						7	14							22
1		3	4				8		10	12	13	2	5		7¹	9	6				11²										23
1		3	4				8		10	11	12	2¹	5			9	6				7										24
	2¹	3	4				8		10	11	12		5			9	6²				7			1		13					25
	2¹	3					8		10	11	9		5		4	6					7			1			12				26
	2	3²					8		10	11	12		5		4	13	6				7¹			1		9					27
	2						8		10		7		5		4	12	6				11¹			1		13	9²	3			28
		3	4				8		10		12		5		6		2				7			1			9¹			11	29
1		3	4				8		10	11²	12		5			13	2				7³			1			9¹		6	14	30
1	2	3					8		10	11			5		12				4¹		7			13			6	9²			31
1	2	3					8		10	11			5						4		7¹			9			6	12			32
1	2	3					8		10	11			5			9¹			4		7						6	12			33
1	2	3					8		10	11			5			9			4		7						6				34
1	2	3					8		10	11			5			9¹			4		7						6	12			35
1	2	3²	4						10	11			5				7		9¹	12							8		6	13	36
	2		4		6				10	11			5				7							1			8		3	9	37
			4		6				10	11			5				2				7¹		1	12			8		3	9	38
			4		6				10				5	9¹			2						1	7			8	11	3	12	39
			4		6				10				5				2		12				1	7			8		3	9¹	40
1			4		6				10¹	11			5				2				7			9			8		3	12	41
1	2		4		6				10	11			5								7			9			8		3		42
1	2		4		6				10	11			5								7²			9¹			8	12	3	13	43
1	2		4		6				10	11			5								7			9			8		13		44
1		3	4		6²				10	11			5				2				7¹			9		12	8		13		45
1	2		4¹		6³				10	11²			5		13		3		12		7			9			8			14	46

Coca-Cola Cup

First Round	Mansfield T	(a)	1-0
		(h)	3-1
Second Round	Leicester C	(a)	0-2
		(h)	0-2

FA Cup

First Round	Walsall	(h)	1-3

BURY 1995-96 *Back row (left to right):* Ian Hughes, Mark Sertori, Trevor Matthewson, John Paskin, Ryan Cross, Nick Daws, Chris Lucketti.
Middle row: Alan Raw (Physio), Stan Ternent (Assistant Manager), Andy Woodward, Dave Lancaster, Gary Kelly, Michael Jackson, Lee Bracey, Tony Rigby, Dave Johnson, Cliff Roberts (First Team Coach).
Front row: Phil Stant, Kevin Hulme, Lenny Johnrose, David Pugh, Mike Walsh (Manager), Jimmy Mulligan, Stuart Bimson, Shaun Reid, Mark Carter.

Division 2 **BURY**

Gigg Lane, Bury BL9 9HR. Telephone: (0161) 764 4881. Fax: (0161) 764 5521. Commercial Dept: (0161) 705 2144. Fax: (0161) 763 3103. Clubcall: 0891 121197. Community Programme: (0161) 797 5423. Social Club: (0161) 764 6771.

Ground capacity: 11,936.

Record attendance: 35,000 v Bolton W, FA Cup 3rd rd, 9 January 1960.

Record receipts: £37,000 v Bolton W, Division 3 play-off, 19 May 1991.

Pitch measurements: 112yd × 72yd.

Chairman: T. Robinson. *Vice-Chairman:* Canon J. R. Smith MA.

Directors: C. H. Eaves, J. Smith, F. Mason.

Manager: Stan Ternent. *Assistant Manager:* Sam Ellis. *Coach:* Cliff Roberts. *Physio:* Alan Raw.

Youth Development: W. Joyce. *Stadium Manager:* Wilf Linton.

Assistant Secretary: J. Neville. *Commercial Manager:* Neville Neville.

Year Formed: 1885. *Turned professional:* 1885. *Ltd Co.:* 1897. *Club Nickname:* 'Shakers'.

Club Sponsors: Birthdays.

Foundation: A meeting at the Waggon & Horses Hotel, attended largely by members of Bury Wesleyans and Bury Unitarians football clubs, decided to form a new Bury club. This was officially formed at a subsequent gathering at the Old White Horse Hotel, Fleet Street, Bury on 24 April 1885.

First Football League game: 1 September 1894, Division 2, v Manchester C (h) W 4-2 – Lowe; Gillespie, Davies; White, Clegg, Ross; Wylie, Barbour (2), Millar (1), Ostler (1), Plant.

Record League Victory: 8–0 v Tranmere R, Division 3, 10 January 1970 – Forrest; Tinney, Saile; Anderson, Turner, McDermott; Hince (1), Arrowsmith (1), Jones (4), Kerr (1), Grundy. (1 og).

Record Cup Victory: 12–1 v Stockton, FA Cup 1st rd (replay), 2 February 1897 – Montgomery; Darroch, Barbour; Hendry (1), Clegg, Ross (1); Wylie (3), Pangbourn, Millar (4), Henderson (2), Plant. (1 og).

Record Defeat: 0–10 v Blackburn R, FA Cup preliminary round, 1 October 1887 and v West Ham U, Milk Cup 2nd rd 2nd leg, 25 October 1983.

Most League Points (2 for a win): 68, Division 3, 1960–61.

Most League Points (3 for a win): 84, Division 4, 1984–85.

Most League Goals: 108, Division 3, 1960–61.

Highest League Scorer in Season: Craig Madden, 35, Division 4, 1981–82.

Most League Goals in Total Aggregate: Craig Madden, 129, 1978–86.

Most Capped Player: Bill Gorman, 11 (13), Republic of Ireland and (4), Northern Ireland.

Most League Appearances: Norman Bullock, 506, 1920–35.

Record Transfer Fee Received: £375,000 from Southampton for David Lee, October 1991.

Record Transfer Fee Paid: £175,000 to Shrewsbury T for John McGinlay, July 1990.

Football League Record: 1894 Elected to Division 2; 1895–1912 Division 1; 1912–24 Division 2; 1924–29 Division 1; 1929–57 Division 2; 1957–61 Division 3; 1961–67 Division 2; 1967–68 Division 3; 1968–69 Division 2; 1969–71 Division 3; 1971–74 Division 4; 1974–80 Division 3; 1980–85 Division 4; 1985–96 Division 2; 1996– Division 2.

Honours: Football League: Division 1 best season: 4th, 1925–26; Division 2 – Champions 1894–95; Runners-up 1923–24; Division 3 – Champions 1960–61; Runners-up 1967–68; Promoted from Division 3 (3rd) 1995–96. *FA Cup:* Winners 1900, 1903. *Football League Cup:* Semi-final 1963.

Colours: White shirts, royal blue shorts, royal blue stockings. *Change colours:* Navy/red shirts, white shorts, navy/red stockings.

Did you know?
On 17 February 1996, Bury's 7-1 win over Lincoln City was their highest for 26 years. They had beaten Tranmere 8-0 on 10 January 1970.

BURY 1995–96 LEAGUE RECORD

Match No.	Date	Venue	Opponents	Result		H/T Score	Lg. Pos.	Goalscorers	Atten- dance
1	Aug 12	A	Northampton T	L	1-4	1-1	—	Stant	4487
2	19	H	Chester C	D	1-1	1-1	19	Stant	3211
3	26	A	Hereford U	W	4-3	1-2	10	Carter 2 (1 pen), Johnrose, Rigby	2702
4	29	H	Preston NE	D	0-0	0-0	—		4682
5	Sept 2	H	Plymouth Arg	L	0-5	0-3	14		3040
6	9	A	Wigan Ath	W	2-1	2-1	12	Carter, Stant	3128
7	12	A	Lincoln C	D	2-2	0-0	—	Wanless (og), Johnrose	1851
8	16	H	Cambridge U	L	1-2	1-0	16	Pugh	2672
9	23	H	Barnet	D	0-0	0-0	15		2453
10	30	A	Gillingham	L	0-3	0-0	20		6125
11	Oct 7	H	Leyton Orient	W	2-1	2-1	16	Carter, Rigby	3025
12	14	A	Fulham	D	0-0	0-0	18		3803
13	21	H	Scarborough	L	0-2	0-1	21		2590
14	28	A	Mansfield T	W	5-1	1-1	15	Stant 4, Pugh	2356
15	31	A	Torquay U	W	2-0	1-0	—	Lucketti, Stant	1456
16	Nov 4	H	Darlington	D	0-0	0-0	11		2974
17	18	A	Cardiff C	W	1-0	1-0	9	Johnson	3846
18	25	H	Exeter C	W	2-0	0-0	7	Johnson, Pugh	3597
19	Dec 9	A	Barnet	D	0-0	0-0	9		1747
20	16	H	Gillingham	W	1-0	0-0	8	Rigby	3045
21	23	H	Colchester U	D	0-0	0-0	9		3559
22	Jan 1	H	Hartlepool U	L	0-3	0-0	10		2927
23	6	H	Doncaster R	W	4-1	1-1	6	Pugh, Johnrose, Stant, Rigby	2606
24	13	A	Chester C	D	1-1	0-1	6	Matthews	3283
25	20	H	Northampton T	L	0-1	0-0	8		3074
26	Feb 10	A	Doncaster R	W	1-0	1-0	10	Matthews	2418
27	13	A	Rochdale	D	1-1	0-0	—	Carter	3048
28	17	H	Lincoln C	W	7-1	2-1	6	Matthews, Rigby 2, Pugh, Carter 2, Daws	3096
29	20	A	Plymouth Arg	L	0-1	0-0	—		4536
30	24	A	Cambridge U	W	4-2	1-2	8	Carter 2, Johnson, Pugh	2341
31	27	H	Wigan Ath	W	2-1	0-0	—	Carter (pen), Jackson	3800
32	Mar 2	H	Scunthorpe U	W	3-0	1-0	6	Carter (pen), Johnrose, Pugh	3035
33	9	A	Colchester U	L	0-1	0-0	7		2832
34	16	H	Rochdale	D	1-1	1-1	7	Matthews	3473
35	19	H	Hereford U	W	2-0	0-0	—	Carter, Jackson	2280
36	23	A	Hartlepool U	W	2-1	0-1	5	Jackson, Pugh	1879
37	26	A	Preston NE	D	0-0	0-0	—		12,260
38	30	A	Leyton Orient	W	2-0	1-0	3	Carter 2 (1 pen)	3421
39	Apr 2	H	Fulham	W	3-0	2-0	—	Sertori, Johnrose, West	3371
40	6	H	Mansfield T	L	0-2	0-2	3		3600
41	9	A	Scarborough	W	2-0	2-0	—	Pugh, Johnrose	1773
42	13	H	Torquay U	W	1-0	0-0	3	Carter	3247
43	16	A	Scunthorpe U	W	2-1	0-0	—	Jackson, Johnson	2132
44	20	A	Darlington	L	0-4	0-2	3		4325
45	27	A	Exeter C	D	1-1	1-0	4	Carter (pen)	3508
46	May 4	H	Cardiff C	W	3-0	1-0	3	Pugh, Johnson, Rigby	5658

Final League Position: 3

GOALSCORERS

League (66): Carter 16 (5 pens), Pugh 10, Stant 9, Rigby 7, Johnrose 6, Johnson 5, Jackson 4, Matthews 4, Daws 1, Lucketti 1, Sertori 1, West 1, own goal 1.
Coca-Cola Cup (9): Stant 4, Carter 2 (1 pen), Daws 1, Johnson 1, Rigby 1.
FA Cup (0).

Kelly G 25	Woodward A 1	Bimson S 16	Reid S 20 + 1	Lucketti C 42	Jackson M 31	Richardson N 3 + 2	Carter M 28 + 4	Stant P 27 + 7	Rigby T 33 + 8	Pugh D 42	Mulligan J — + 2	Lancaster D 1 + 4	Bracey L 21	Cross R 13	Hughes I 30 + 2	Johnrose L 34	Daws N 33 + 4	Matthewson T 16	Paskin J — + 12	Sertori M 4 + 7	Hulme K — + 1	Johnson D 21 + 15	West D 32 + 5	Harle M — + 1	Matthews R 11 + 5	Reid N 13 + 5	Edwards P 4	Brabin G 5	Match No.
1	2	3	4	5	6	7¹	8²	9	10	11	12	13																	1
		3	4	5		7¹	8	9²	14	11		13		1	2	6	10³	12											2
		3	4	5		7¹	8	9	12	11				1	2	6	10												3
		3		5	12		8	9²	7	11	13³	14		1	2	6	10	4¹											4
		3	4	5	12		8	9	10	11				1	2	6	7¹												5
		3	4³	5			8²	9¹		11				1	2	10	7	6	12	13	14								6
		3	4¹	5			8	9		11				1	10	7	6	12		2									7
1			4	5	3¹		8	9²	12	11					10	7	6	13	2										8
			4	5			8	9¹	10	11				1	2	3	7	6	12										9
		3²	4	5			8	9¹	10	11				1	2	7	6		12	13									10
1		3¹	4	5			8	9	10	11					2	7	6		12										11
1		3	4²	5			8	9¹	10		12				2	11	6		13	7									12
1		3	4²	5				9	10	8	2³				11	12	6		14	13	7¹								13
1		3	4	5				9	10	11					2	7	6		8¹	12									14
1		3	4	5				9	10	11					7	7¹	12	6	8²	13									15
1		3	4	5				9	10	11²					2	7	6		9¹	13									16
1			4	5	6		12	9	7²	11					3	10	13					8¹	2						17
1			4	5	6			9	7	11					3	10						8	2						18
1			4²	5				9	7	11					3	10	6					8¹	2		13				19
1				5				9	7	11					3	10	4	6				8	2						20
1				5				9	7	11					3	10	4	6				8	2						21
1				5			12	9	7	11					3¹	10	4	6				8	2						22
1				5	6			9	7	11					3	10	4					8	2						23
1		12		5	6			9¹	7	11			1		3	10	4					8²	2		13				24
				5	6			9	7	11			1		3¹	10	4		12			8	2						25
1	10³			5	6		12		7¹	11					9		4					13	2		8²	14	3		26
1	10²			5	6		12		7	11¹					9		4					13	2		8³	14	3		27
1				5	6		9³		7	11					10		4¹	13				14	2		8²	12	3		28
1				5	6		9		7²	11					10		4	12				13	2		8	3¹			29
1	3¹			5	6		9		7²	11					10		4					12	2		8	13			30
1	3²			5	6		9		7	11					10		4	12				2			8¹	13			31
1				5	6		9²		7	11					10		4	12				13	2		8¹				32
1				5	6		9		7²	11					13	10	4		12			14	2		8¹	3²			33
1				5	6		9	12	7	11					10		4					13	2		8²	3			34
1				5	6		8	9²	7	11			1		12	10	4					13	2			3			35
1				5	6		8			11			1		7	10	4		12			9¹	2			3			36
1				5	6		8		12	11			1		7	10	4					9¹	2			3			37
1				5	6		8³		12	11			1		10		4	13				9²	2		14	3		7¹	38
1				5	6			12		11			1		7	10	4		9¹			8²	2		13	3			39
1				5	6			12		11²			1		7¹	10	4		9			8	2		13	3			40
1				5	6		14		12	11			1		10		4	13³				9²	2		7¹	3	8		41
1				5	6		7	12	13	11²			1		10		4¹	14				9²	2			3	8		42
1				5	6		7			11			1		3	10	4		12			9¹	2				8		43
1				5	6		7	12		11			1		3²	10	4¹		13			9²	2		14		8		44
				5			8²	9¹	12	11			1		7	10	4¹	6	13			14	2			3	8		45
1				5	6		8	12	7	11					10		4					9¹	2			3			46

Coca-Cola Cup				
First Round	Chesterfield	(a)	1-0	
		(h)	2-1	
Second Round	Sheffield U	(a)	1-2	
		(h)	4-2	
Third Round	Reading	(a)	1-2	

FA Cup				
First Round	Blyth Spartans	(h)	0-2	

CAMBRIDGE UNITED 1995–96 *Back row (left to right)*: Jody Craddock, Ollie Morah, Steve Butler, Dave Thompson, Shane Westley, Russell Stock, David Adekola, Danny Granville.
Middle row: Tony Richards, Leon Gutzmore, Martin Davies, Colin Vowden, Scott Barrett, Marc Joseph, Lee Palmer.
Front row: Soner Zumutrel, Matthew Joseph, John Fowler, Craig Middleton, Andrew Jeffrey, Lenny Pack, Carlo Corazzin, Michael Kyd.
(Photograph: David Smith)

Division 3   **CAMBRIDGE UNITED**

Abbey Stadium, Newmarket Rd, Cambridge, CB5 8LN. Telephone: (01223) 566500. Fax: (01223) 566502. Abbey Update: 0891 555885.

Ground capacity: 9667.

Record attendance: 14,000 v Chelsea, Friendly, 1 May 1970.

Record receipts: £86,308 v Manchester U, Rumbelows Cup 2nd rd 2nd leg, 9 October 1991.

Pitch measurements: 110yd × 74yd.

Chairman: R. H. Smart. *Vice-Chairman:* R. F. Hunt. *Directors:* G. Harwood, J. Howard, R. Hunt, G. Lowe, R. Summerfield.

Manager: Tommy Taylor. *Assistant Manager:* Paul Clark. *Youth Manager:* David Batch.

Physio: Ken Steggles.

Secretary: Steve Greenall. *Commercial Manager:* Vince Durrant. *Stadium Manager:* Ian Darler.

Year Formed: 1919. *Turned Professional:* 1946. *Ltd Co.:* 1948.

Club Nickname: The 'U's'.

Previous Name: Abbey United until 1949.

Foundation: The football revival in Cambridge began soon after World War II when the Abbey United club (formed 1919) decided to turn professional and in 1949 changed their name to Cambridge United. They were competing in the United Counties League before graduating to the Eastern Counties League in 1951 and the Southern League in 1958.

First Football League game: 15 August 1970, Division 4, v Lincoln C (h) D 1-1 – Roberts; Thompson, Meldrum (1), Slack, Eades, Hardy, Leggett, Cassidy, Lindsey, McKinven, Harris.

Record League Victory: 6–0 v Darlington, Division 4, 18 September 1971 – Roberts; Thompson, Akers, Guild, Eades, Foote, Collins (1p), Horrey, Hollett, Greenhalgh (4), Phillips. (1 og). 6–0 v Hartlepool U, Division 4, 11 February 1989 – Vaughan; Beck, Kimble, Turner, Chapple (1), Daish, Clayton, Holmes, Taylor (3 incl. 1p), Bull (1), Leadbitter (1).

Record Cup Victory: 5–1 v Bristol C, FA Cup 5th rd second replay, 27 February 1990 – Vaughan; Fensome, Kimble, Bailie (O'Shea), Chapple, Daish, Cheetham (Robinson), Leadbitter (1), Dublin (2), Taylor (1), Philpott (1).

Record Defeat: 0–6 v Aldershot, Division 3, 13 April 1974; v Darlington, Division 4, 28 September 1974 and v Chelsea, Division 2, 15 January 1983.

Most League Points (2 for a win): 65, Division 4, 1976–77.

Most League Points (3 for a win): 86, Division 3, 1990–91.

Most League Goals: 87, Division 4, 1976–77.

Highest League Scorer in Season: David Crown, 24, Division 4, 1985–86.

Most League Goals in Total Aggregate: Alan Biley, 74, 1975–80.

Most Capped Player: Tom Finney, 7 (15), Northern Ireland.

Most League Appearances: Steve Spriggs, 416, 1975–87.

Record Transfer Fee Received: £1,000,000 from Manchester U for Dion Dublin, August 1992.

Record Transfer Fee Paid: £190,000 to Luton T for Steve Claridge, November 1992.

Football League Record: 1970 Elected to Division 4; 1973–74 Division 3; 1974–77 Division 4; 1977–78 Division 3; 1978–84 Division 2; 1984–85 Division 3; 1985–90 Division 4; 1990–91 Division 3; 1991–92 Division 2; 1992–93 Division 1; 1993–95 Division 2; 1995– Division 3.

Honours: Football League: Division 2 best season: 5th, 1991–92; Division 3 – Champions 1990–91; Runners-up 1977–78; Division 4 – Champions 1976–77. *FA Cup:* best season: 6th rd, 1990, 1991. *Football League Cup:* 5th rd, 1993.

Colours: Amber and black quartered shirts, black shorts, black and amber hooped stockings. *Change colours:* Blue and green halved shirts, blue shorts, blue and green hooped stockings.

Did you know?
Cambridge United first reached the First Round Proper of the FA Cup in 1953–54 beating Newport County 2-1 after a 2-2 draw. This was their only victory as a non-League club over a Football League team.

CAMBRIDGE UNITED 1995–96 LEAGUE RECORD

Match No.	Date	Venue	Opponents	Result	H/T Score	Lg. Pos.	Goalscorers	Attendance
1	Aug 12	A	Scunthorpe U	W 2-1	0-1	—	Kyd, Butler	2561
2	19	H	Hereford U	D 2-2	2-1	6	Brough (og), Butler	2557
3	26	A	Gillingham	L 0-3	0-0	13		5093
4	29	H	Colchester U	W 3-1	2-0	—	Palmer, Joseph Matthew, Corazzin	3476
5	Sept 2	A	Preston NE	D 3-3	1-1	8	Barrick, Corazzin, Butler	7034
6	9	H	Barnet	D 1-1	0-0	9	Butler	3054
7	12	H	Exeter C	D 1-1	0-0	—	Butler	2365
8	16	A	Bury	W 2-1	0-1	6	Butler, Corazzin	2672
9	23	A	Lincoln C	W 3-1	2-0	3	Perkins, Corazzin 2	2614
10	30	H	Hartlepool U	L 0-1	0-0	6		2849
11	Oct 7	H	Cardiff C	W 4-2	2-0	3	Corazzin 2, Craddock, Adekola	2648
12	14	A	Northampton T	L 0-3	0-2	6		6301
13	21	H	Darlington	L 0-1	0-1	7		2730
14	28	A	Rochdale	L 1-3	0-1	10	Butler	2344
15	30	A	Doncaster R	L 1-2	1-1	—	Watson	1657
16	Nov 4	H	Scarborough	W 4-1	2-0	9	Butler 2, Corazzin, Middleton C	2304
17	18	A	Leyton Orient	L 1-3	1-1	11	Raynor	4142
18	25	H	Torquay U	D 1-1	1-0	11	Butler (pen)	2536
19	Dec 9	H	Lincoln C	W 2-1	1-1	10	Middleton C 2	2472
20	16	A	Hartlepool U	W 2-1	1-1	10	Middleton C, Stock	1612
21	23	A	Plymouth Arg	L 0-1	0-0	10		7135
22	26	H	Wigan Ath	W 2-1	0-0	7	Turner, Joseph Matthew	2855
23	Jan 6	H	Chester C	D 1-1	0-1	7	Turner	2643
24	13	A	Hereford U	L 2-5	1-3	9	Middleton C, Raynor	2548
25	20	H	Scunthorpe U	L 1-2	0-0	11	Turner	2413
26	23	A	Mansfield T	L 1-2	0-1	—	Raynor	1801
27	Feb 3	H	Gillingham	D 0-0	0-0	12		4114
28	13	H	Fulham	D 0-0	0-0	—		2233
29	17	A	Exeter C	L 0-1	0-0	16		2804
30	24	H	Bury	L 2-4	2-1	17	Middleton C, Robinson	2341
31	27	A	Barnet	L 0-2	0-0	—		1849
32	Mar 2	A	Wigan Ath	L 1-3	1-2	22	Craddock	2528
33	9	H	Plymouth Arg	L 2-3	0-1	23	Hyde, Corazzin (pen)	2785
34	16	A	Fulham	W 2-0	1-0	20	Beall, Corazzin	3872
35	19	A	Colchester U	L 1-2	1-1	—	Middleton C	2995
36	23	H	Mansfield T	L 0-2	0-2	22		2302
37	26	A	Chester C	D 1-1	1-0	—	Beall	1623
38	30	A	Cardiff C	D 1-1	0-0	21	Richards	2326
39	Apr 2	H	Northampton T	L 0-1	0-0	—		3631
40	6	H	Rochdale	W 2-1	1-1	21	Craddock, Barnwell-Edinboro	2186
41	8	A	Darlington	D 0-0	0-0	21		3064
42	13	H	Doncaster R	D 2-2	0-0	21	Barnwell-Edinboro, Middleton C	2451
43	16	H	Preston NE	W 2-1	0-1	—	Beall 2	2831
44	20	A	Scarborough	L 0-2	0-1	20		1401
45	27	A	Torquay U	W 3-0	1-0	18	Wanless, Watson (og), Hyde	1853
46	May 4	H	Leyton Orient	W 2-0	1-0	16	Hyde 2 (2 pens)	3858

Final League Position: 16

GOALSCORERS

League (61): Butler 10 (1 pen), Corazzin 10 (1 pen), Middleton C 8, Beall 4, Hyde 4 (2 pens), Craddock 3, Raynor 3, Turner 3, Barnwell-Edinboro 2, Matthew Joseph 2, Adekola 1, Barrick 1, Kyd 1, Palmer 1, Perkins 1, Richards 1, Robinson 1, Stock 1, Wanless 1, Watson 1, own goals 2.
Coca-Cola Cup (2): Corazzin 2 (1 pen).
FA Cup (1): Butler 1.

Barrett S 31	Jeffrey A 20 + 7	Vowden C 22 + 2	Thompson D 14 + 1	Westley S 3	Joseph Matthew 42	Richards T 15 + 4	Middleton C 38 + 2	Butler S 16	Corazzin C 31	Granville D 31 + 4	Craddock J 44 + 2	Fowler J — + 2	Kyd M 3 + 6	Palmer L 30	Pack L 2 + 9	Barrick D 2 + 1	Stock R 15 + 2	Raynor P 35	Adekola D 1 + 4	Perkins D 1 + 1	Hyde M 20 + 4	Rattle J 7 + 2	Watson M 1 + 3	Hayes A 1	Middleton L 1 + 2	Clark P 2	Davies M 15	Howes S — + 1	Joseph Marc 10 + 2	Robinson D 4 + 13	Turner R 10	Beall M 15	Wosahlo B — + 4	Benjamin T — + 5	Gutzmore L — + 2	Wanless P 14	Pick G 2 + 2	Illman N 1 + 4	Barnwell-Edinboro J 7	Match No.
1	2	3	4	5¹	6	7²	8³	9	10	11	12	13	14																											1
1	2		4		6	7²	8	9	10	11¹	5	12		3	13																									2
1	2	3	4	5	6	7²	8		10		12			13			9³	11¹	14																					3
1	2		4		6		8	9	10		5			3	12		11				7¹																			4
1	2		4		6²		8	9	10	12	5			3¹	13		11				7																			5
1	2¹			5	6	12	8	9	10	11²	4			3	13						7																			6
1	2		4		6		8	9	10		5			3							7	11																		7
1		2	4		6		8	9²	10		5			3	12						7¹	11	13																	8
1	12		4		2		8	9	10		5			3	13						7	6¹	11²																	9
1			4		2	12	8	9	10		5			3²	11¹						7	6	13																	10
1	2		4		7²		8	9	10		5			3							6	12	13	11																11
1		2	4				8²	9	10		5			3¹	12						7	6	13	11																12
1	2		4²		7			12		10	8¹	5	13	3							6	9	11																	13
1	2	12	4¹				8	9		13	5	10	3								6²	11	7³	14																14
1		4					8	9		12	5	13	3								6	11¹	7	10²			2													15
1		4			2		8	9	10		5			3							6	11	7																	16
1	4				2¹		6	9	10	12	5			3							7	11	13	8²																17
1	4				2		8	9¹	10		5			3							6	11	12	13	7²															18
						7	8		10	11	5			3			4¹	6			9					1	2	12												19
	12	3				7	9³	8		11	5						4¹	6²			13	14				1	2	10												20
		3²				7		8	10	11	5	12					4¹	6								1	2	13	9											21
		3				7		8	10	11	5	12						6²			4¹	13				1	2	14	9³											22
	7¹	3					8		10	11	5							6			4					1	2	12	9											23
		3				7	8				5							6			4²	11				1	2	12	9	10¹	13									24
	8²	4				7			10	3	5							6			12	11¹				1	2	13	9											25
	12	4				8			10	3	5			11²				6							13	7¹	1	2	9											26
	4					2	8	7	11	5	3						6				10¹					1		9				12								27
	2					7	8	10	3	5				4			6				11¹					1		9	12											28
	2					7	8	10²	3	5				4		12	6				11¹					1		9	13											29
	2	11				7	8		3	5	10²	4			12	6										1		9¹				13								30
	2					7	8		3	5	11²				6¹		4				11					1	12	10³	9				13	14					31
	2²	4				7	8	10	3	5				9¹	6		11									1	13	12												32
	4					7	9²	8	10	3	5				6		12									1		13	11			2¹								33
1	12	4				7	9¹	8	10	3	5				6²													13	11			2								34
1	12	4¹				7	9	8	10	3	5				6													13	11²			2								35
1	12					7	9¹	8	10	3	5	4³	13		6													11²				14	2							36
1	12	4				7	9²	8	10	3	5				6¹													13	11			2								37
1		4¹				7	9	8		3	5				6²													11	12			2	10	13						38
1	12	4¹				7	9	8		3	5				6²													13	11			2	10	6²						39
1						7		8		3	5	4			10¹	6												12	11			2					9			40
1			4			7	12			3	5	4			10²		6										8¹	11				2	13				9			41
1						7	12	8		3	5¹	4			10²	6³	13											11				2	14				9			42
1						7	10¹	12²		3	5	4	13		6		8³											11				2	14				9			43
1		4				7	10¹			3	5				8		6											11				2		12			9			44
1	6					7	10³			3	5	4¹			8							14						11²				2	13				9			45
1¹		13				6	10			3	5	4			8											7		11				12²					9			46

Coca-Cola Cup
First Round   Swindon T   (h)   2-1
                                                  (a)   0-2

FA Cup
First Round   Swindon T   (a)   1-4

CARDIFF CITY 1995-96 *Back row (left to right):* Ian Rodgerson, Tony Bird, Chris Ingram, Andy Evans, Andy Scott, Chris David, Derik Brazil.
Middle row: Gavin Tait (Youth Development Officer), Lee Jarman, Lee Baddeley, Steve Flack, Dave Williams, Steve Williams, Pat Mountain, Simon Haworth, Scott Young, Tony Phillискirk, Jimmy Gardner, Jim Goodfellow (Physio).
Front row: Hayden Fleming, Nathan Wigg, Damon Searle, Paul Harding, Kenny Hibbitt (Chief Coach), Jason Perry, Carl Dale, Chas Oatway, Darren Adams.

Division 3 **CARDIFF CITY**

Ninian Park, Cardiff CF1 8SX. Telephone: (01222) 398636. Fax: (01222) 341148. Newsline: 0891 888603.

Ground capacity: 20,284.

Record attendance: 61,566, Wales v England, 14 October 1961.

Club record: 57,893 v Arsenal, Division 1, 22 April 1953.

Record receipts: £141,756 v Manchester C, FA Cup 4th rd, 29 January 1994.

Pitch measurements: 114yd × 78yd.

Directors: S. Kumar (Chairman), W. Dixon, R. East, D. Henderson.

Director of Football: Kenny Hibbitt.

Chief Executive Director: Joan Hill.

Secretary: Barry Doughty.

Manager: Phil Neal.

Physio: Jimmy Goodfellow.

Year Formed: 1899. *Turned Professional:* 1910. *Ltd Co.:* 1910.

Previous Names: 1899–1902, Riverside; 1902–08, Riverside Albion; 1908, Cardiff City.

Club Nickname: 'Bluebirds'.

Previous Grounds: Riverside, Sophia Gardens, Old Park and Fir Gardens. Moved to Ninian Park, 1910.

Foundation: Credit for the establishment of a first class professional football club in such a rugby stronghold as Cardiff, is due to members of the Riverside club formed in 1899 out of a cricket club of that name. Cardiff became a city in 1905 and in 1908 the local FA granted Riverside permission to call themselves Cardiff City.

First Football League game: 28 August 1920, Division 2, v Stockport Co (a) W 5-2 – Kneeshaw; Brittain, Leyton; Keenor (1), Smith, Hardy; Grimshaw (1), Gill (2), Cashmore, West, Evans (1).

Record League Victory: 9–2 v Thames, Division 3 (S), 6 February 1932 – Farquharson; E. L. Morris, Roberts; Galbraith, Harris, Ronan; Emmerson (1), Keating (1), Jones (1), McCambridge (1), Robbins (5).

Record Cup Victory: 8–0 v Enfield, FA Cup 1st rd, 28 November 1931 – Farquharson; Smith, Roberts; Harris (1), Galbraith, Ronan; Emmerson (2), Keating (3); O'Neill (2), Robbins, McCambridge.

Record Defeat: 2–11 v Sheffield U, Division 1, 1 January 1926.

Most League Points (2 for a win): 66, Division 3 (S), 1946–47.

Most League Points (3 for a win): 86, Division 3, 1982–83.

Most League Goals: 93, Division 3 (S), 1946–47.

Highest League Scorer in Season: Stan Richards, 30, Division 3 (S), 1946–47.

Most League Goals in Total Aggregate: Len Davies, 128, 1920–31.

Most Capped Player: Alf Sherwood, 39 (41), Wales.

Most League Appearances: Phil Dwyer, 471, 1972–85.

Record Transfer Fee Received: £300,000 from Sheffield U for Nathan Blake, February 1994.

Record Transfer Fee Paid: £180,000 to San Jose Earthquakes for Godfrey Ingram, September 1982.

Football League Record: 1920 Elected to Division 2; 1921–29 Division 1; 1929–31 Division 2; 1931–47 Division 3 (S); 1947–52 Division 2; 1952–57 Division 1; 1957–60 Division 2; 1960–62 Division 1; 1962–75 Division 2; 1975–76 Division 3; 1976–82 Division 2; 1982–83 Division 3; 1983–85 Division 2; 1985–86 Division 3; 1986–88 Division 4; 1988–90 Division 3; 1990–92 Division 4; 1992–93 Division 3; 1993–95 Division 2; 1995– Division 3.

Honours: Football League: Division 1 – Runners-up 1923–24; Division 2 – Runners-up 1920–21, 1951–52, 1959–60; Division 3 (S) – Champions 1946–47; Division 3 – Champions 1992–93. Runners-up 1975–76, 1982–83; Division 4 – Runners-up 1987–88. *FA Cup:* Winners 1927 (only occasion the Cup has been won by a club outside England); Runners-up 1925. *Football League Cup:* Semi-final 1966. *Welsh Cup:* Winners 21 times. *Charity Shield:* 1927. **European Competitions:** *European Cup-Winners' Cup:* 1964–65, 1965–66, 1967–68, 1968–69, 1969–70, 1970–71, 1971–72, 1973–74, 1974–75, 1976–77, 1977–78, 1988–89, 1991–92, 1992–93, 1993–94.

Colours: Blue shirts, blue shorts, blue stockings. *Change colours:* Yellow shirts, navy shorts, navy stockings.

Did you know?
In the 1995–96 season Carl Dale scored 21 of Cardiff City's 41 League goals, the first player with the club to achieve more than half the total number of League goals.

CARDIFF CITY 1995–96 LEAGUE RECORD

Match No.	Date	Venue	Opponents	Result		H/T Score	Lg. Pos.	Goalscorers	Atten- dance
1	Aug 12	A	Rochdale	D	3-3	2-2	—	Bird 2, Dale	2321
2	19	H	Northampton T	L	0-1	0-1	15		7872
3	26	A	Doncaster R	D	0-0	0-0	19		2186
4	29	H	Exeter C	L	0-1	0-1	—		3750
5	Sept 2	A	Darlington	W	1-0	1-0	15	Dale (pen)	1895
6	9	H	Torquay U	D	0-0	0-0	16		4281
7	12	H	Scarborough	W	2-1	1-1	—	Todd (og), Dale	2385
8	16	A	Gillingham	L	0-1	0-1	17		5317
9	23	A	Hartlepool U	L	1-2	1-1	20	Dale (pen)	2172
10	30	H	Mansfield T	W	3-0	1-0	15	Ingram, Dale 2 (1 pen)	3468
11	Oct 7	A	Cambridge U	L	2-4	0-2	19	Adams, Bird	2648
12	14	H	Barnet	D	1-1	1-1	19	Dale	3342
13	21	A	Lincoln C	W	1-0	0-0	15	Gardner	2453
14	28	H	Colchester U	L	1-2	1-2	19	Adams	3207
15	31	H	Scunthorpe U	L	0-1	0-1	—		2024
16	Nov 4	A	Plymouth Arg	D	0-0	0-0	21		7434
17	18	H	Bury	L	0-1	0-1	22		3846
18	26	A	Hereford U	W	3-1	0-0	18	Dale 2, Adams	3528
19	Dec 9	H	Hartlepool U	W	2-0	0-0	15	Dale 2	2919
20	16	A	Mansfield T	D	1-1	0-0	14	Searle	2212
21	19	A	Fulham	L	2-4	2-1	—	Dale, Rodgerson	2284
22	26	H	Chester C	D	0-0	0-0	17		6046
23	Jan 1	A	Preston NE	L	0-5	0-1	17		8354
24	6	H	Leyton Orient	D	0-0	0-0	17		2736
25	13	A	Northampton T	L	0-1	0-1	20		4454
26	20	H	Rochdale	W	1-0	0-0	19	Gardner	2230
27	Feb 3	H	Doncaster R	W	3-2	1-0	16	Dale 3	2313
28	10	A	Leyton Orient	L	1-4	1-1	17	Philliskirk	3564
29	17	A	Scarborough	L	0-1	0-1	21		1414
30	20	H	Darlington	L	0-2	0-2	—		2113
31	24	H	Gillingham	W	2-0	0-0	20	Dale, Harris (og)	2994
32	27	A	Torquay U	D	0-0	0-0	—		2004
33	Mar 2	A	Chester C	L	0-4	0-2	21		2308
34	5	H	Wigan Ath	W	3-0	2-0	—	Gardner 2, Philliskirk	1611
35	9	H	Fulham	L	1-4	0-1	18	Dale	3019
36	12	A	Exeter C	L	0-2	0-1	—		2609
37	16	A	Wigan Ath	L	1-3	0-0	19	Flack	2789
38	23	H	Preston NE	L	0-1	0-0	21		3511
39	30	H	Cambridge U	D	1-1	0-0	22	Dale (pen)	2326
40	Apr 2	A	Barnet	L	0-1	0-0	—		2107
41	6	A	Colchester U	L	0-1	0-0	22		3345
42	8	H	Lincoln C	D	1-1	0-0	22	Dale	2657
43	13	A	Scunthorpe U	D	1-1	1-1	22	Dale	2044
44	20	H	Plymouth Arg	L	0-1	0-0	22		3374
45	27	H	Hereford U	W	3-2	2-0	22	Dale, Philliskirk 2	3751
46	May 4	A	Bury	L	0-3	0-1	22		5658

Final League Position: 22

GOALSCORERS

League (41): Dale 21 (4 pens), Gardner 4, Philliskirk 4, Adams 3, Bird 3, Flack 1, Ingram 1, Rodgerson 1, Searle 1, own goals 2.
Coca-Cola Cup (4): Dale 2, Bird 1, Rodgerson 1.
FA Cup (3): Dale 2, Jarman 1.

Williams D 42	Brazil D 19+1	Searle D 41	Harding P 36	Baddeley L 27+3	Perry J 13+1	Wigg N 14+6	Rodgerson I 28+6	Shaw P 6	Dale C 44	Bird A 9+3	Haworth S 7+6	Young S 37+4	Downing K 3+1	Jones I 1	Dobbs G 3	Adams D 8+6	Ingram C 4+4	Gardner J 32+3	Evans A 1+1	Evans T 1+1	Oatway C 2	Jarman L 31+1	Fleming H 20+2	Bolesan M —+1	Harper A 5	Philliskirk T 28	Scully T 13+1	Flack S 5+5	Osman R 14+1	Scott A —+1	McGorry B 7	Johnson G 1+4	Vick L —+2	Williams S 4	Match No.
1	2	3	4	5	6	7	8	9	10	11																									1
1	2	3	4	5¹	6	7	8	9	10	11¹	12	13																							2
1	2	3	4	5	6	7²	8	9	10	11¹	12		13																						3
1	2		4	5	6	12	7	9	10	11¹					8	3																			4
1	2	3	4	5	6	11	7¹	9²	10		12	13			8																				5
1	2	3	4	5	6	12	7	9¹	10						8	11																			6
1	2	3	4	5	6		8		10	11		9				2	7¹																		7
1	2¹	3		5	6		8	4	10	11		9²				12	7	13																	8
1		3	4	5	6		8		10	11¹		9				2	7	12																	9
1		3	4	5	6		8		10			9				2	7	11																	10
1		3	4	5	6		8¹		10			2				12	7²	11	9	13															11
1			4	5	6¹				10			9²			8	3	12	7	11	13			2												12
1	2	3	4	5			7²		10		12	6				8¹		11	9	13															13
1	2	3	4	5			7²		10		12	6				8	13	11	9¹																14
1	2²	3	4					9	10		12	6				8¹	7	11				5	13												15
1	2	3	4					9	10		12	6				8¹	7	11				5													16
1	2¹	3	4			12		9	10²			6				8	13	11				5							7						17
1	2²	3	4			12		9				6				8	13	11				5				10			7¹						18
1		3	4				7		9			6						11				5	2			10	8								19
1		3	4				7¹		9			6				12		11				5	2			10	8								20
1		3	4				7¹		9			6				12		11				5	2			10	8								21
1		3	4				7		9		12	6				8		11				5	2			10¹									22
1		3	4²			12	7		9			6				13		11				5¹	2			10	8								23
1		3	4²			12	7		9		13	6						11¹				5	2			10	8								24
1	11	3	4				7¹		9			6				12						5	2²			10	8	13							25
1	12	3	4				7		9			6						11				5	2¹			10	8								26
1		3	4				7		9¹			6						11				5	2			10	8	12							27
1	7	3	4			12			9			6						11²				5	2			10	8¹	13							28
1		3	4			11	2		9			6					12					5				10	8¹		7						29
1		3	4				8		9			6						11²				5	2¹			10	12	13	7						30
1		3	4				7		9			6						11				5	2			10	8								31
1		3	4				7		9			6				12		11				5	2¹			10	8								32
1	11	3	4				7¹		9			6				12						5	2			10	8								33
1	2	4	3						9			6				12		11				5				10	8¹		7						34
1	2	4¹	3						9			6				12		11				5				10	8²	13	7						35
1	2¹	3	11			12	8		9			6										5				10	4	13	7²						36
1		3	4	2			8¹		9							12						5				10	13	11	7²		6				37
1		3	2	12					9			4					7					5				10	8	11¹			6				38
1		3	4¹	5														11					2			10	12	9²	7		8		13		39
1		3	4						9			6						11¹				5	2			10	8	12	7						40
1		3	4						9			6						11²				5	2¹			10	12	13	7		8				41
1		3	4						9			6						11				5	2			10	8		7						42
		3¹	4						9			6						11				5	2			10	8		7			12		1	43
			4						9			6						11²				5	2	3		10¹	8	13	7			12		1	44
		3	4						9			6						11				5	2			10	8		7					1	45
		3	4³			12			9			6				13		11²				5	2¹			10	8		7				14	1	46

Coca-Cola Cup

First Round	Portsmouth	(a)	2-0
		(h)	1-0
Second Round	Southampton	(h)	0-3
		(a)	1-2

FA Cup

First Round	Rushden & D	(a)	3-1
Second Round	Swindon T	(a)	0-2

CARLISLE UNITED   1995-96 *Back row (left to right):* Marc Cleeland, Jeff Thorpe, Lee Peacock, Rory Delap, Paul Conway, David Currie, Tony Gallimore, Will Varty, Gareth McAlindon, Nathan Murray.

Middle row: David Wilkes (Youth Team Coach), Peter Hampton (Physio), Tony Hopper, Richard Prokas, Darren Edmondson, Tony Caig, Tony Elliott, Jamie Robinson, Glynn Snodin, Rod Thomas, Joe Joyce (Coach), Neil Dalton (Assistant Physio).

Front row: Warren Aspinall, Steve Hayward, David Reeves, Mick Wadsworth (Director of Coaching), Michael Knighton (Chairman & Chief Executive), Mervyn Day (Coach), Dean Walling, Derek Mountfield, Paul Murray.

Division 3   **CARLISLE UNITED**

Brunton Park, Carlisle CA1 1LL. Telephone: (01228) 26237. Fax: (01228) 30138. Commercial Dept: (01228) 24014. Information Line: 0891 230011.

Record attendance: 27,500 v Birmingham C, FA Cup 3rd rd, 5 January 1957 and v Middlesbrough, FA Cup 5th rd, 7 February 1970.

Record receipts: £104,410 v Sunderland, FA Cup 3rd rd replay, 18 January 1994.

Ground capacity: 16,651.

Pitch measurements: 117yd × 72yd.

Directors: M Knighton (Chairman), B. Chaytow, R. McKnight, A. Doweck, A. Jenkins.

Manager: Mervyn Day. *Player-Coach:* Joe Joyce.

Physio: Peter Hampton.

Commercial Manager: Martin Hudson.

Acting Secretary: A. Ritchie.

Year Formed: 1903. *Ltd Co.:* 1921.

Previous Grounds: 1903–05, Milholme Bank; 1905–09, Devonshire Park; 1909– Brunton Park.

Previous Name: Shaddongate United.

Club Nickname: 'Cumbrians' or 'The Blues'.

Foundation: Carlisle United came into being in 1903 through the amalgamation of Shaddongate United and Carlisle Red Rose. The new club was admitted to the Second Division of the Lancashire Combination in 1905–06, winning promotion the following season.

First Football League game: 25 August 1928, Division 3 (N), v Accrington S (a) W 3-2 – Prout; Coulthard, Cook; Harrison, Ross, Pigg; Agar, Hutchison, McConnell (1), Ward (1), Watson (1) o.g.

Record League Victory: 8–0 v Hartlepools U, Division 3 (N), 1 September 1928 – Prout; Smiles, Cook; Robinson (1) Ross, Pigg; Agar (1), Hutchison (1), McConnell (4), Ward (1), Watson. 8–0 v Scunthorpe U, Division 3 (N), 25 December 1952 – MacLaren; Hill, Scott; Stokoe, Twentyman, Waters; Harrison (1), Whitehouse (5), Ashman (2), Duffett, Bond.

Record Cup Victory: 6–1 v Billingham Synthonia, FA Cup 1st rd, 17 November 1956 – Fairley; Hill, Kenny; Johnston, Waters, Thompson; Mooney, Broadis (1), Ackerman (2), Garvie (3), Bond.

Record Defeat: 1–11 v Hull C, Division 3 (N), 14 January 1939.

Most League Points (2 for a win): 62, Division 3 (N), 1950–51.

Most League Points (3 for a win): 91, Division 3, 1994–95.

Most League Goals: 113, Division 4, 1963–64.

Highest League Scorer in Season: Jimmy McConnell, 42, Division 3 (N), 1928–29.

Most League Goals in Total Aggregate: Jimmy McConnell, 126, 1928–32.

Most Capped Player: Eric Welsh, 4, Northern Ireland.

Most League Appearances: Alan Ross, 466, 1963–79.

Record Transfer Fee Received: £275,000 from Vancouver Whitecaps for Peter Beardsley, April 1981.

Record Transfer Fee Paid: £121,000 to Notts Co for David Reeves, December 1993.

Football League Record: 1928 Elected to Division 3 (N); 1958–62 Division 4; 1962–63 Division 3; 1963–64 Division 4; 1964–65 Division 3; 1965–74 Division 2; 1974–75 Division 1; 1975–77 Division 2; 1977–82 Division 3; 1982–86 Division 2; 1986–87 Division 3; 1987–92 Division 4; 1992–95 Division 3; 1995–96 Division 2; 1996– Division 3.

Honours: Football League: Division 1 best season: 22nd, 1974–75; Promoted from Division 2 (3rd) 1973–74; Division 3 – Champions 1964–65, 1994–95; Runners-up 1981–82; Division 4 – Runners-up 1963–64. *FA Cup:* 6th rd 1975. *Football League Cup:* Semi-final 1970. *Auto Windscreens Shield:* Runners-up 1995.

Colours: Blue shirts, white shorts, blue stockings. *Change colours:* Green, red, yellow and white shirts, green shorts, green stockings.

Did you know?
Carlisle United were the first club outside London to install floodlighting which they did in 1952.

CARLISLE UNITED 1995–96 LEAGUE RECORD

Match No.	Date	Venue	Opponents	Result		H/T Score	Lg. Pos.	Goalscorers	Attendance
1	Aug 12	H	Bristol R	L	1-2	1-1	—	Aspinall	8003
2	19	A	Chesterfield	L	0-3	0-2	23		3634
3	26	H	Swindon T	L	0-1	0-0	24		6325
4	29	A	Rotherham U	D	2-2	0-0	—	Reeves 2	3550
5	Sept 1	A	Swansea C	D	1-1	1-0	—	Peacock	3345
6	9	H	Burnley	W	2-0	0-0	20	Aspinall, Conway	7318
7	12	H	Peterborough U	D	1-1	0-1	—	Reeves	6027
8	16	A	Oxford U	L	0-4	0-2	21		5046
9	23	H	Hull C	W	2-0	2-0	17	Reeves 2	6007
10	30	A	Walsall	L	1-2	0-2	21	Thorpe	4214
11	Oct 7	H	Notts Co	D	0-0	0-0	20		6058
12	14	A	Crewe Alex	L	1-2	0-0	22	Delap	4512
13	21	H	Bradford C	D	2-2	2-0	22	Reeves, Edmondson	6274
14	28	A	Bournemouth	L	0-2	0-1	23		4250
15	31	H	Wrexham	L	2-3	0-1	—	Philliskirk, Aspinall	2939
16	Nov 4	H	Brighton & HA	W	1-0	0-0	22	Currie	5896
17	18	A	Bristol C	D	1-1	0-0	21	Currie	5423
18	26	H	Wycombe W	W	4-2	3-1	21	Aspinall, Walling, Reeves, Gallimore (pen)	4459
19	Dec 2	A	Burnley	L	0-2	0-1	21		8297
20	9	A	Hull C	W	5-2	3-2	17	Currie 2, Murray, Reeves, Bennett	3478
21	16	H	Walsall	D	1-1	1-0	17	Bennett	5308
22	26	A	Stockport Co	L	0-2	0-1	18		5941
23	30	A	Shrewsbury T	D	1-1	0-0	18	Currie	2864
24	Jan 1	H	Blackpool	L	1-2	0-1	18	Gallimore (pen)	7532
25	13	H	Chesterfield	D	1-1	0-1	20	Law (og)	5851
26	20	A	Bristol R	D	1-1	1-0	19	Reeves	5196
27	Feb 3	A	Swindon T	L	1-2	0-0	20	Delap	8242
28	10	H	Brentford	W	2-1	1-0	20	Currie, Reeves	5143
29	17	A	Peterborough U	L	1-6	0-4	20	Reeves	4302
30	20	H	Swansea C	W	3-0	2-0	—	Peacock, Bennett, Aspinall	4645
31	24	H	Oxford U	L	1-2	0-0	20	Robinson	5525
32	Mar 2	A	Stockport Co	L	0-1	0-0	22		4849
33	9	A	York C	D	1-1	1-0	22	Currie	3965
34	16	H	Shrewsbury T	D	1-1	1-0	22	Currie	3760
35	19	A	Brentford	D	1-1	1-1	—	Robinson	3104
36	23	A	Blackpool	L	1-3	1-1	22	Reeves	8144
37	26	H	Rotherham U	W	2-0	2-0	—	Bennett, Hayward	4054
38	30	A	Notts Co	L	1-3	0-2	21	Aspinall	4515
39	Apr 2	H	Crewe Alex	W	1-0	0-0	—	Conway	4698
40	6	H	Bournemouth	W	4-0	0-0	21	Currie, Hayward, Delap, Bennett	5401
41	8	A	Bradford C	L	1-3	0-1	21	Hayward	6156
42	13	H	Wrexham	L	1-2	0-1	21	Thomas	7317
43	20	A	Brighton & HA	L	0-1	0-1	22		6131
44	23	H	York C	W	2-0	2-0	—	Walling, Reeves	4813
45	27	A	Wycombe W	L	0-4	0-1	21		3964
46	May 4	H	Bristol C	W	2-1	2-1	20	Conway, Hayward (pen)	5935

Final League Position: 21

GOALSCORERS

League (57): Reeves 13, Currie 9, Aspinall 6, Bennett 5, Hayward 4 (1 pen), Conway 3, Delap 3, Gallimore 2 (2 pens), Peacock 2, Robinson 2, Walling 2, Edmondson 1, Murray 1, Philliskirk 1, Thomas 1, Thorpe 1, own goal 1.
Coca-Cola Cup (4): Reeves 2, Aspinall 1, Walling 1.
FA Cup (1): Reeves 1.

Caig T 33	Edmondson D 40 + 2	Gallimore T 36	Walling D 43	Robinson J 18 + 2	Aspinall W 36 + 6	Thomas R 28 + 8	Currie D 41 + 1	Reeves D 43	Hayward S 36 + 2	Prokas R 17 + 3	Peacock L 12 + 10	Murray P 23 + 5	Conway P 13 + 9	Moore N 13	Thorpe J 16 + 18	Allen C 3	Elliott T 13	Delap R 5 + 14	McAlindon G — + 3	Philliskirk T 3	Bennett G 26	Smart A 3 + 1	Atkinson B 2	Donachie D — + 1	Hopper T 1 + 4	Dowell W 2 + 5	Match No.
1	2	3	4	5	6^1	7	8	9	10	11^2	12	13															1
1	2	3	4	5	6^2	7^1	8	9	10		12	13	11														2
1	2	3	4		10	7^2	8^1	9			6	11	12	5	13												3
1	2	3	4		10	7	8^1	9			6	11		5	12												4
1	2	3	4		10	7^1	8	9			6	11		5	12												5
1	2	3	4		10^3	7^1	8	9	14		6^2	11	13	5	12												6
1	2	3	4		10	7	8	9			12	11^2	6^1	5	13												7
1	2	3^2	4		10	7	8^1	9			6	11	13	5	12												8
1	2	3	4		10	12	8^1	9	6			11		5		7											9
1	2	3	4		10^3	12	8^2	9	6		13	11^1		5	14	7											10
	2	3	4		10	12	8^1	9	6^2			11	13	5	7^1		1										11
	2	3	4		10	12		9			6	11		5	7^1		1	8									12
	2	3	4		10	7^1	8^2	9	11		6			5	12		1		13								13
	2	3	4				8	9			6	11		5	12		1^1			7							14
1	2	3	4	12	10		8	9	6			11		5^1	13				7^1								15
1		3	4	5	10^2		8	9	6	2	12	11			13				7^1								16
1	2	3			10^1	12	8	9	6	7		11			4						5						17
1	2	3	4		10^2	12	8^1	9	6	11		13			14						5	7^3					18
1	13	3	4		10	12	8^1	9	6^2	11		2							7^3		5	14					19
1	12	3	4		10^2		8^1	9	6	11		2	13		14				7^3		5						20
1		3	4		10		8		6	11		2	13		7^1				12		5	9					21
1		3	4		10^2	7	8^1		6		11^3	2	9		12			13	14		5						22
1	11	3	4		10	7^1	8		6			2	9		12						5						23
1	2	3	4		10	12	8	9	6	11^2		13	7^1								5						24
1	2	3	4	6^2	10^3		8	9	12	11^1		7	13				14				5						25
1	2	3	4				8^2	9	10	11		7^1			12		13				5	6					26
1	2		4		12			8	9	10	13	7			3		11				5	6^2					27
1	2	3	4		12			8	9	10^1	7	13			6		11^2				5						28
1	2	3	4		8			9	10	7	12				6^1		11				5						29
	2	3	4		12	7^2		9	10	11	8				6^1	13		1	14		5^3						30
	2	3	4	5	12	7^2	13	9	10^1	11	8		14		6^3		1										31
	2	3	4	5	10^2	7	8^1	9	6		12	11^3					1							13	14		32
		3	4	2	12	7^1	8^2	9	6	10	13						1				5		11				33
	2	3	4	5	10	7	8	9	6			13			11^1		1						12^2				34
	2	3	4	5	10	7	8^1	9	6						11		1	12			11						35
	2	3	4	5	10	7	8^2	9	6				12				1	13		11							36
	2	3		5	10^1	7	8^2	9	6	12					11		1	13			4						37
	2		4	3^1	10	7	8	9	6						11^2		1	12								13	38
1	2		4	3	10^1	7		9	6					8	11						5					12	39
1	2		4	3		7^1	8^2	9	6						10^3			12			5				13	14	40
1	2		4	3		7	8^2	9	6						10			11^1			12					13	41
1	2		4	3^2	12	7	8	9	6	13					10^1		11^3				5					14	42
1	2		4	3^2	10	7	8	9	6	14					11^1			12						13^3			43
1	2		4	3		7^1	8^2	9	6	11					12			13							3		44
1	2		4	12	10	7^2	8	9	6	11^3			14					13			5				3^1		45
1	2		3			7	8^1	9	6						10		11	4	12		5						46

Coca-Cola Cup
First Round   Hull C   (a) 2-1   (h) 2-4

FA Cup
First Round   Preston NE   (h) 1-2

CHARLTON ATHLETIC 1995–96   *Back row (left to right):* Jamie Kyte, Stuart Reynolds, Steve Brown, Richard Rufus, Mike Ammann, Mike Salmon, Andy Petterson, Carl Leaburn,
Dean Chandler, Jamie Stuart, Paul Linger.
Middle row: Neil Banfield (Youth Team Coach), Jimmy Hendry (Physio), Keith Dowson, Shaun Newton, Lee Bowyer, Paul Sturgess, Phil Chapple, Andy Larkin, Kim Grant, Peter Garland,
Steve Watts (Youth Development Officer), Gary Moss (Assistant Physio).
Front row: John Humphrey, David Whyte, Garry Nelson, Keith Jones, Keith Peacock (Reserve Team Coach), Alan Curbishley (Manager), Les Reed (First Team Coach), Stuart Balmer, Colin Walsh,
John Robinson, Mark Robson.
(Photograph: Tom Morris)

Division 1   CHARLTON ATHLETIC

The Valley, Floyd Road, Charlton, London SE7 8BL. Telephone: (0181) 293 4567. Fax: (0181) 853 4001. Box Office: (0181) 858 5888. Clubcall 0891 121146.

Ground capacity: 15,000.

Record attendance: 75,031 v Aston Villa, FA Cup 5th rd, 12 February 1938 (at The Valley).

Record receipts: £135,813 v Brentford, FA Cup 4th rd, 7 February 1996.

Pitch measurements: 110yd × 73yd.

President: R. D. Collins.

Chairman: M. A. Simons. *Vice-Chairman:* R. A. Murray.

Directors: R. N. Alwen, G. P. Bone, S. T. Clarke, R. D. Collins, J. T. T. Fuller, M. C. Stevens, D. G. Ufton.

Manager: Alan Curbishley.

Reserve Team Manager: Keith Peacock. *Youth Team Manager:* Neil Banfield.

Youth Development Officer: Steve Watts. *Physio:* Jimmy Hendry. *Coach:* Les Reed.

Secretary: Chris Parkes.

Marketing Manager: Steve Dixon. *Stadium Manager:* Roy King.

Year Formed: 1905. *Turned Professional:* 1920. *Ltd Co.:* 1919.

Club Nickname: 'Addicks'.

Previous Grounds: 1906, Siemen's Meadow; 1907, Woolwich Common; 1909, Pound Park; 1913, Horn Lane; 1920, The Valley; 1923, Catford (The Mount); 1924, The Valley; 1985 Selhurst Park; 1991 Upton Park; 1992 The Valley.

Foundation: The club was formed on 9 June 1905, by a group of 14 and 15-year-old youths living in streets by the Thames in the area which now borders the Thames Barrier. The club's progress through local leagues was so rapid that after the First World War they joined the Kent League where they spent a season before turning professional and joining the Southern League in 1920. A year later they were elected to the Football League's Division 3 (South).

First Football League game: 27 August 1921, Division 3 (S), v Exeter C (h) W 1-0 – Hughes; Mitchell, Goodman; Dowling (1), Hampson, Dunn; Castle, Bailey, Halse, Green, Wilson.

Record League Victory: 8–1 v Middlesbrough, Division 1, 12 September 1953 – Bartram; Campbell, Ellis; Fenton, Ufton, Hammond; Hurst (2), O'Linn (2), Leary (1), Firmani (3), Kiernan.

Record Cup Victory: 7–0 v Burton A, FA Cup 3rd rd, 7 January 1956 – Bartram; Campbell, Townsend; Hewie, Ufton, Hammond; Hurst (1), Gauld (1), Leary (3), White, Kiernan (2).

Record Defeat: 1–11 v Aston Villa, Division 2, 14 November 1959.

Most League Points (2 for a win): 61, Division 3 (S), 1934–35.

Most League Points (3 for a win): 77, Division 2, 1985–86.

Most League Goals: 107, Division 2, 1957–58.

Highest League Scorer in Season: Ralph Allen, 32, Division 3 (S), 1934–35.

Most League Goals in Total Aggregate: Stuart Leary, 153, 1953–62.

Most Capped Player: John Hewie, 19, Scotland.

Most League Appearances: Sam Bartram, 583, 1934–56.

Record Transfer Fee Received: £750,000 from Newcastle U for Robert Lee, September 1992.

Record Transfer Fee Paid: £600,000 to Chelsea for Joe McLaughlin, August 1989.

Football League Record: 1921 Elected to Division 3 (S); 1929–33 Division 2; 1933–35 Division 3 (S); 1935–36 Division 2; 1936–57 Division 1; 1957–72 Division 2; 1972–75 Division 3; 1975–80 Division 2; 1980–81 Division 3; 1981–86 Division 2; 1986–90 Division 1; 1990–92 Division 2; 1992– Division 1.

Honours: Football League: Division 1 – Runners-up 1936–37; Division 2 – Runners-up 1935–36, 1985–86; Division 3 (S) – Champions 1928–29, 1934–35; Promoted from Division 3 (3rd) 1974–75, 1980–81. *FA Cup:* Winners 1947; Runners-up 1946. *Football League Cup:* best season: 4th rd, 1963, 1966, 1979. *Full Members Cup:* Runners-up 1987.

Colours: Red shirts, white shorts, red stockings. *Change colours:* White shirts, black shorts, white stockings.

Did you know?
Charlton Athletic's 4-3 win at Birmingham on 14 January 1996 was their first such success there since 4 February 1939 when they also won 4-3.

CHARLTON ATHLETIC 1995–96 LEAGUE RECORD

Match No.	Date	Venue	Opponents	Result	H/T Score	Lg. Pos.	Goalscorers	Attendance
1	Aug 12	A	WBA	L	0-1	0-0	—	14,688
2	19	H	Birmingham C	W	3-1	0-0	13	Nelson, Bowyer, Grant	9692
3	26	A	Crystal Palace	D	1-1	1-0	11	Bowyer	14,124
4	29	H	Watford	W	2-1	0-1	—	Bowyer, Leaburn	8442
5	Sept 2	H	Huddersfield T	W	2-1	1-0	4	Newton, Stuart	9570
6	9	A	Tranmere R	D	0-0	0-0	4		7402
7	12	A	Sheffield U	L	0-2	0-1	—		9448
8	16	H	Oldham Ath	D	1-1	0-1	8	Leaburn	8926
9	23	A	Ipswich T	W	5-1	0-1	4	Chapple, Leaburn 3 (1 pen), Linger	12,815
10	30	A	Barnsley	D	1-1	1-0	4	Grant	11,219
11	Oct 7	H	Grimsby T	L	0-1	0-1	8		8994
12	14	A	Leicester C	D	1-1	0-1	9	Leaburn	16,771
13	21	H	Norwich C	D	1-1	0-0	10	Bowyer	13,369
14	29	A	Luton T	W	1-0	1-0	8	Nelson	6270
15	Nov 5	H	Sunderland	D	1-1	1-1	8	Newton	11,626
16	12	A	Wolverhampton W	D	0-0	0-0	9		20,450
17	18	A	Derby Co	L	0-2	0-1	13		12,963
18	21	H	Reading	W	2-1	1-1	—	Chapple, Robinson	7840
19	25	H	Port Vale	D	2-2	0-0	12	Mortimer (pen), Bowyer	10,174
20	Dec 2	A	Grimsby T	W	2-1	1-0	10	Grant, Whyte D (pen)	6881
21	5	A	Millwall	W	2-0	1-0	—	Grant 2	11,350
22	9	H	Ipswich T	L	0-2	0-0	9		10,316
23	16	A	Barnsley	W	2-1	2-0	4	Robinson, Newton	6140
24	26	H	Portsmouth	W	2-1	0-1	2	Newton, Nelson	11,686
25	Jan 14	A	Birmingham C	W	4-3	3-1	2	Edwards (og), Grant, Robinson, Leaburn	18,539
26	20	H	WBA	W	4-1	3-0	2	Robinson 2, Stuart, Mortimer (pen)	11,864
27	Feb 4	H	Crystal Palace	D	0-0	0-0	2		13,560
28	10	A	Watford	W	2-1	0-1	2	Robinson, Bowyer	8394
29	17	H	Sheffield U	D	1-1	0-0	2	Mortimer	11,239
30	20	A	Huddersfield T	D	2-2	1-2	—	Bowyer, Robson (pen)	10,951
31	24	A	Oldham Ath	D	1-1	0-0	2	Grant	6570
32	Mar 2	A	Portsmouth	L	1-2	1-1	3	Butters (og)	9323
33	5	H	Southend U	L	0-3	0-1	—		11,927
34	9	H	Millwall	W	2-0	1-0	3	Bowyer, Leaburn	12,204
35	16	A	Southend U	D	1-1	1-1	4	Mortimer (pen)	7382
36	23	H	Stoke C	W	2-1	0-1	4	Mortimer (pen), Whyte D	12,770
37	30	A	Norwich C	W	1-0	0-0	4	Allen	13,434
38	Apr 2	H	Leicester C	L	0-1	0-1	—		11,287
39	5	H	Luton T	D	1-1	0-1	—	Allen (pen)	14,643
40	8	A	Sunderland	D	0-0	0-0	4		20,914
41	14	A	Derby Co	D	0-0	0-0	4		11,334
42	17	A	Stoke C	L	0-1	0-1	—		12,969
43	20	A	Reading	D	0-0	0-0	5		9778
44	27	A	Port Vale	W	3-1	1-1	5	Balmer, Newton, Allen	8428
45	30	H	Tranmere R	D	0-0	0-0	—		10,936
46	May 5	H	Wolverhampton W	D	1-1	1-0	6	Leaburn	14,023

Final League Position: 6

GOALSCORERS

League (57): Leaburn 9 (1 pen), Bowyer 8, Grant 7, Robinson 6, Mortimer 5 (4 pens), Newton 5, Allen 3 (1 pen), Nelson 3, Chapple 2, Stuart 2, Whyte D 2 (1 pen), Balmer 1, Linger 1, Robson 1 (pen), own goals 2.
Coca-Cola Cup (11): Bowyer 5, Robinson 2, Garland 1, Grant 1, Leaburn 1, Newton 1.
FA Cup (6): Grant 2, Bowyer 1, Mortimer 1 (pen), Robinson 1, Whyte D 1.

Salmon M 27	Humphrey J 28	Sturgess P 13	Jones K 24 + 1	Rufus R 40 + 1	Balmer S 30 + 2	Robson M 11 + 16	Leaburn C 38 + 2	Brown S 17 + 2	Whyte D 11 + 14	Bowyer L 41	Nelson G 12 + 18	Robinson J 43 + 1	Grant K 20 + 10	Walsh C 5 + 1	Chapple P 13 + 3	Stuart J 27	Newton S 39 + 2	Garland P 3	Linger P 2 + 6	Williams P 2 + 7	Ammann M 10 + 1	Mortimer P 13 + 6	Chandler D — + 1	Whyte C 10 + 1	Allen B 10	Jackson M 8	Petterson A 9	Match No.
1	2	3	4	5	6	7[1]	8	9[2]	10	11	12	13																1
1	2	3[1]	4	5	6	7			10[3]	11	8[2]	9	12	13	14													2
1	2		4	5	6		12		10	11	8[1]	9[2]	13			3	7											3
1	2		4	5	6		13		10[1]	11	8	9	12			3[2]	7											4
1	2		4	5[2]	6		10			11	8	9[1]	12		13	3	7											5
1	2	3	4	5	6	13	10[1]			11	8[3]	9[2]	12		14		7											6
1	2	3[1]	4	5	6	13	10			11	8	9	12				7[2]											7
1	2		4[2]	5	6	13	10			11	8	9	12			3[1]	7											8
1	2				6	12	10			11[1]		9	8[2]		5	3	7	4	13									9
1	2				6		10			11		9	8		5	3	7	4[1]	12									10
1	2		14		6[3]	12	10			11	13	9	8[2]		5	3	7[1]	4										11
1	2[2]				6	12	10			11	13	9	8[3]	4[1]	5	3	7					14						12
1	2[2]				6	12	10			11	13	9		4[1]	5	3	7				8							13
1	2				6		10			11	8[1]	9	12	4	5	3	7											14
1[9]	2	13			6	9[2]	10			11[1]	8		12	4	5	3	7					15						15
	2	3	4		6		10			11	12	9	8		5		7[1]				1							16
	2	3	4		6		10		12	11		9	8[2]		5		7[1]				1	13						17
	2	3	4		6		10		12	11		9	8[1]		5		7[2]				1	13						18
	2	3[2]	4		6		10		12	11		9	8		5		7[1]				1	13						19
	2		4		6		10[1]			11		9	8		5	3	7[2]			12	1	13						20
	2		4		6	12	10[3]			11		9	8[2]		5[1]	3	7			13	1	14						21
	2[1]		4	5	6		10			11		9	8[3]			3	7[2]			12	1	13	14					22
	2		4	5	6			8[1]	10[2]	11	12	9				3	7			13	1							23
1	2			5	6			8		12	13	9	10		4[1]	3[2]	7					11						24
1	2			5	6			8			11	12	9	10[1]		3	7					4						25
1				5	6			8	2		11	12	9	10[1]		3	7					4						26
1	2				6			8	5		12	11	9	10[1]		3	7					4						27
1				5	6			8	2	10[1]	11	12	9[2]			3	7				13	4						28
1	2[1]			5	6	12		8		10[2]	11	13	9			3	7					4						29
1	2[2]		4	5	6	12		8	13	11	10	9				3	7[1]											30
1			4	5	6	7			2	10[1]	11	8[2]	9		12	3				13								31
1			4[2]	5	6	7[1]		8	2[3]		12	9	10			3				13	14	11						32
1				5	6[1]	12			2		13	11	14		9	3[3]	7				8[2]	4						33
1	3			5		12		8	2		11	13	9		10[2]		7[1]					4		6				34
1[2]	3[2]			5		12	13	8	2			14	9		10[1]		7				11	4		6				35
	3			5		12		8	2[1]		13	11	9		10[2]		7					4	1	6				36
	3[1]			5		12		8	2[1]		13	11	9				7					4	1	6	10		2	37
	3[2]			5		12		8			13	14	11		9		7[1]					4		6	10	2[2]	1	38
			4	5		7		8	2		12	11[1]	9			3[2]				13			6	10		1	39
			4	5	3	11[1]		8	2			9					7			12				6	10		1	40
			4	5				8	3		12	11	9				7							6	10[1]	2	1	41
			4[2]	5		12		8	11[3]		13		14		9	3[1]	7							6	10	2	1	42
			4[2]	5	6	7		8	3		12	11	9							13					10[1]	2	1	43
				5	6	7		8	3		11	12	9							13	4[2]				10[1]	2	1	44
				5	6	7		8	3[2]		12	11	9							13	4				10[1]	2	1	45
				5	6	7		8			12	11	13		9						4			3	10[1]	2[2]	1	46

Coca-Cola Cup

First Round	Barnet	(a)	0-0
		(h)	2-0
Second Round	Wimbledon	(a)	5-4
		(h)	3-3
Third Round	Wolverhampton W	(a)	0-0
		(h)	1-2

FA Cup

Third Round	Sheffield W	(h)	2-0
Fourth Round	Brentford	(h)	3-2
Fifth Round	Liverpool	(a)	1-2

CHELSEA 1995–96   *Back row (left to right)*: Dave Collyer (Youth Development Officer), Terry Byrne (Assistant Physio), Robert Fleck, Gareth Hall, Michael Duberry, Nigel Spackman, Paul Furlong, Jakob Kjeldbjerg, Erland Johnsen, Paul Hughes, Mussie Izzet, Mark Nicholls, Junior Mendes, Christian McCann, Bernie Dixson (Youth Development Officer), Ian Oliver (Reflexologist).

Middle row: George Price (Reserve Team Physio), Mike Banks (Physio), Scott Minto, Anthony Barness, Zeke Rowe, Andy Myers, Russell Kelly, Dmitri Kharine, Kevin Hitchcock, Steve Clarke, Craig Burley, David Lee, Terry Skiverton, Darren Barnard, Gwyn Williams (Chief Scout/Team Administration Manager), Bob Orsborn (Kit Manager).

Front row: Eddie Niedzwiecki (Reserve Team Manager), Eddie Newton, Mark Stein, Andy Dow, Ruud Gullit, Dennis Wise, Glenn Hoddle (Manager), Peter Shreeves (Assistant Manager), Gavin Peacock, Mark Hughes, David Rocastle, Frank Sinclair, John Spencer, Graham Rix (Youth Team Manager).

(Photograph: Action Images)

FA Premiership

CHELSEA

Stamford Bridge, London SW6 1HS. Telephone: (0171) 385 5545. Fax: (0171) 381 4831. Clubcall: 0891 121159. Ticket News and Promotions: 0891 121011. Ticket Credit Card Service: (0171) 386 7799.

Ground capacity: 31,791 (during ground development); 41,000 (eventually).

Record attendance: 82,905 v Arsenal, Division 1, 12 October 1935.

Record receipts: £488,960 v Liverpool, FA Premier League, 30 December 1995.

Pitch measurements: 113yd × 74yd.

President: G. M. Thomson.

Chairman: K. W. Bates.

Directors: C. Hutchinson (Managing), Ms Y. S. Todd, M. C. Harding.

Team Manager: Ruud Gullit. *Assistant Manager:* Peter Shreeves.

Physio: Michael Banks. *Reserve Team Manager:* Eddie Niedzwiecki.

Company Secretary/Director: Yvonne Todd. *Match Secretary and Safety Officer:* Keith Lacy.

Commercial Manager: Carole Phair. *Stadium Manager:* D. Johnson.

Year Formed: 1905. *Turned Professional:* 1905. *Ltd Co.:* 1905.

Club Nickname: 'The Blues'.

Foundation: Chelsea may never have existed but for the fact that Fulham rejected an offer to rent the Stamford Bridge ground from Mr. H. A. Mears who had owned it since 1904. Fortunately he was determined to develop it as a football stadium rather than sell it to the Great Western Railway and got together with Frederick Parker, who persuaded Mears of the financial advantages of developing a major sporting venue. Chelsea FC was formed in 1905, and when admission to the Southern League was denied, they immediately gained admission to the Second Division of the Football League.

First Football League game: 2 September 1905, Division 2, v Stockport Co (a) L 0-1 – Foulke; Mackie, McEwan; Key, Harris, Miller; Moran, J.T. Robertson, Copeland, Windridge, Kirwan.

Record League Victory: 9–2 v Glossop N E, Division 2, 1 September 1906 – Byrne; Walton, Miller; Key (1), McRoberts, Henderson; Moran, McDermott (1), Hilsdon (5), Copeland (1), Kirwan (1).

Record Cup Victory: 13–0 v Jeunesse Hautcharage, ECWC, 1st rd 2nd leg, 29 September 1971 – Bonetti; Boyle, Harris (1), Hollins (1p), Webb (1), Hinton, Cooke, Baldwin (3), Osgood (5), Hudson (1), Houseman (1).

Record Defeat: 1–8 v Wolverhampton W, Division 1, 26 September 1953.

Most League Points (2 for a win): 57, Division 2, 1906–07.

Most League Points (3 for a win): 99, Division 2, 1988–89.

Most League Goals: 98, Division 1, 1960–61.

Highest League Scorer in Season: Jimmy Greaves, 41, 1960–61.

Most League Goals in Total Aggregate: Bobby Tambling, 164, 1958–70.

Most Capped Player: Ray Wilkins, 24 (84), England.

Most League Appearances: Ron Harris, 655, 1962–80.

Record Transfer Fee Received: £2,200,000 from Tottenham H for Gordon Durie, July 1991.

Record Transfer Fee Paid: £2,300,000 to Sheffield W for Dan Petrescu, November 1995.

Football League Record: 1905 Elected to Division 2; 1907–10 Division 1; 1910–12 Division 2; 1912–24 Division 1; 1924–30 Division 2; 1930–62 Division 1; 1962–63 Division 2; 1963–75 Division 1; 1975–77 Division 2; 1977–79 Division 1; 1979–84 Division 2; 1984–88 Division 1; 1988–89 Division 2; 1989–92 Division 1; 1992– FA Premier League.

Honours: Football League: Division 1 – Champions 1954–55; Division 2 – Champions 1983–84, 1988–89; Runners-up 1906–07, 1911–12, 1929–30, 1962–63, 1976–77. *FA Cup:* Winners 1970; Runners-up 1915, 1967, 1994. *Football League Cup:* Winners 1965; Runners-up 1972. *Full Members' Cup:* Winners 1986. *Zenith Data Systems Cup:* Winners 1990. **European Competitions:** *European Fairs Cup:* 1958–60, 1965–66, 1968–69; *European Cup-Winners' Cup:* 1970–71 (winners), 1971–72, 1994–95.

Colours: Royal blue with white and amber trim shirts and shorts, white stockings with royal blue and amber trim. *Change colours:* Yellow with sky blue/royal blue trim shirts and shorts, yellow stockings with sky blue trim.

Did you know?
Jimmy Greaves scored five goals in each of three League matches in consecutive seasons, 1958–59, 1959–60 and 1960–61 against Wolverhampton Wanderers, Preston North End and West Bromwich Albion respectively.

CHELSEA 1995–96 LEAGUE RECORD

Match No.	Date	Venue	Opponents	Result		H/T Score	Lg. Pos.	Goalscorers	Attendance
1	Aug 19	H	Everton	D	0-0	0-0	—		30,189
2	23	A	Nottingham F	D	0-0	0-0	—		27,007
3	26	A	Middlesbrough	L	0-2	0-1	16		28,826
4	30	H	Coventry C	D	2-2	2-1	—	Wise (pen), Hughes	22,718
5	Sept 11	A	West Ham U	W	3-1	2-0	—	Wise, Spencer 2	19,228
6	16	H	Southampton	W	3-0	0-0	9	Sinclair, Gullit, Hughes	26,237
7	24	A	Newcastle U	L	0-2	0-1	10		36,225
8	30	H	Arsenal	W	1-0	0-0	10	Hughes	31,048
9	Oct 14	A	Aston Villa	W	1-0	0-0	9	Wise	34,922
10	21	H	Manchester U	L	1-4	0-2	10	Hughes	30,192
11	28	A	Blackburn R	L	0-3	0-1	10		27,733
12	Nov 4	H	Sheffield W	D	0-0	0-0	10		23,216
13	18	A	Leeds U	L	0-1	0-0	12		36,133
14	22	H	Bolton W	W	3-2	1-1	—	Lee, Hall, Newton	17,495
15	25	H	Tottenham H	D	0-0	0-0	11		31,059
16	Dec 2	A	Manchester U	D	1-1	0-0	11	Wise	42,019
17	9	H	Newcastle U	W	1-0	1-0	10	Petrescu	31,098
18	16	A	Arsenal	D	1-1	1-0	10	Spencer	38,295
19	23	A	Manchester C	W	1-0	0-0	10	Peacock	28,668
20	26	H	Wimbledon	L	1-2	1-2	11	Petrescu	21,906
21	30	H	Liverpool	D	2-2	2-1	12	Spencer 2	31,137
22	Jan 2	A	QPR	W	2-1	0-0	—	Brazier (og), Furlong	14,904
23	13	A	Everton	D	1-1	1-1	12	Spencer	34,968
24	20	H	Nottingham F	W	1-0	0-0	10	Spencer	24,482
25	Feb 4	H	Middlesbrough	W	5-0	3-0	8	Peacock 3, Spencer, Furlong	21,060
26	10	A	Coventry C	L	0-1	0-1	10		20,629
27	17	H	West Ham U	L	1-2	1-0	10	Peacock	25,252
28	24	A	Southampton	W	3-2	2-2	8	Wise 2 (1 pen), Gullit	15,226
29	Mar 2	A	Wimbledon	D	1-1	1-1	8	Furlong	17,048
30	12	H	Manchester C	D	1-1	1-1	—	Gullit	17,078
31	16	A	Liverpool	L	0-2	0-0	9		40,820
32	23	H	QPR	D	1-1	1-1	10	Spencer	25,590
33	Apr 6	H	Aston Villa	L	1-2	1-1	11	Spencer	23,530
34	8	A	Bolton W	L	1-2	1-2	11	Spencer	18,021
35	13	H	Leeds U	W	4-1	3-0	11	Hughes 3 (1 pen), Spencer	22,131
36	17	A	Sheffield W	D	0-0	0-0	—		25,094
37	27	A	Tottenham H	D	1-1	1-0	10	Hughes	32,918
38	May 5	H	Blackburn R	L	2-3	1-1	11	Wise, Spencer	28,436

Final League Position: 11

GOALSCORERS
League (46): Spencer 13, Hughes 8 (1 pen), Wise 7 (2 pens), Peacock 5, Furlong 3, Gullit 3, Petrescu 2, Hall 1, Lee 1, Newton 1, Sinclair 1, own goal 1.
Coca-Cola Cup (0)
FA Cup (15): Hughes 4, Gullit 3, Duberry 2, Peacock 2, Furlong 1, Petrescu 1, Spencer 1, Wise 1 (pen).

Kharine D 26	Clarke S 21+1	Myers A 20	Gullit R 31	Johnsen E 18+4	Sinclair F 12+1	Spackman N 13+3	Hughes M 31	Stein M 7+1	Peacock G 17+11	Wise D 34+1	Spencer J 23+5	Burley C 16+6	Lee C 29+2	Newton E 21+3	Minto S 10	Furlong P 14+14	Rocastle D 1	Hall G 5	Petrescu D 22+2	Duberry M 22	Phelan T 12	Dow A 1	Hitchcock K 12	Morris J —+1	Match No.
1	2	3	4	5	6	7	8	9^1	10^2	11	12	13													1
1	2	3	4	5	6	7	8	9^1	10^2	11	12	13													2
1	2	3	4	5	6		8	9^2	10^1	11	12			7	13										3
1	2		4	5	6		8		10	11^1	9	12		7		3									4
1	2		4	5	6		8		10^1	11	9	12		7		3									5
1	2		4	5	6		8		10^1	11	9		7	12		3									6
1	2		4	5	6	7	8	9^2	10	11	12			13		3^1									7
1		3	4	5	6	7	8		10^1	11	9			12					2						8
1		3	4	5			8		10	11	9	7		6					2						9
1	2	3	4	5	6		8		10^1	11^2	12	13		7		9									10
1		3	4	5	6^1		8		10	11	12	13	7			9^2			2						11
1			4^1	5	6	7	8	9	10	11	12					3			2						12
1				5^1	6		8	9	10	11	12	7				3			2	4					13
1				5	6		8	9^2	10	11	12	7^1		13		3			2	4					14
1				5	6		8	9	10	11	12	7^1				3			2	4					15
1	5						8		10	11	9^1	7		6		12			2	4	3				16
1	5						8		10	11	9	7		6					2	4	3				17
1	5						8		10	11	9^2	7	13	6		12			2	4	3^1				18
1	5						8		10	11	9	7		6	3				2	4					19
1	5						8		10^1	11	9	7		6	3	12			2	4					20
1							8		10	11	9^1	7		6	3	12		5	2	4					21
1	5						8		10	11	9^2	7^1	13	6	3	12			2	4					22
	5						8		10	11^1	9	7		6		12			2	4	3		1		23
	5						8^2		10	11	9^1	7	13	6		12			2	4	3		1		24
	5		6^1				8^2		10	11	9	7				12			2	4	3		1	13	25
	5		6^1				8^2		10	11	9	7	13			12			2	4	3		1		26
	5						8^1		10	11	9	7		6		12			2	4	3		1		27
	5						8		10	11	9^2	7	13	6		12			2	4^1	3		1		28
	5^1		6				8		10	11	9	7				12			2	4	3		1		29
	5						8		10^1	11	9	7		6		12			2	4	3		1		30
	5						8^1		10	11	9	7		6		12			2	4	3		1		31
	5						8^3		10	11	9^2	7	13	6^1		12			2	4	3		1	14	32
	5						8		10^1	11	9	7	13	6	3	12			2	4			1		33
	5						8		10	11	9	7	13	6	3^1	12			2^2	4			1		34
1	5						8		10	11	9^1	7		6		12			2	4	3				35
1	5						8		10	11	9	7		6		12			2	4^1	3				36
1	5						8		10	11	9^1	7	13	6		12			2^2	4	3				37
1	5						8		10^1	11	9	7	13	6^2		12			2^3	4	3			14	38

Coca-Cola Cup
Second Round   Stoke C   (a)   0-0
                                       (h)   0-1

FA Cup
Third Round   Newcastle U   (h)   1-1
                                         (a)   2-2
Fourth Round   QPR   (a)   2-1
Fifth Round   Grimsby T   (a)   0-0
                                         (h)   4-1
Sixth Round   Wimbledon   (h)   2-2
                                         (a)   3-1
Semi-final (at Villa Park)
         Manchester U   1-2

CHESTER CITY 1995–96 *Back row (left to right):* Scott Blenchley, John Murphy, Spencer Whelan, Julian Alsford, David Rogers, Andrew Milner.
Middle row: Stuart Walker (Physiol), Jason Burnham, Edward Bishop, Ray Newlands, Leroy Chambers, William Steward, Stuart Rimmer, Cyrille Regis, Derek Mann (Youth Coach/Physiol).
Front row: David Flitcroft, Iain Jenkins, Roger Preece, Kevin Ratcliffe (Manager), Gary Shelton (Player/Coach), Peter Jackson, Christopher Priest, Neil Fisher.

Division 3   CHESTER CITY

The Deva Stadium, Bumpers Lane, Chester CH1 4LT. Telephone: (01244) 371376, 371809. Fax: (01244) 390265. Commercial: (01244) 390243.

Ground capacity: 6000.

Record attendance: 20,500 v Chelsea, FA Cup 3rd rd (replay), 16 January 1952 (at Sealand Road).

Record receipts: £30,609 v Sheffield W, FA Cup 4th rd, 31 January 1987.

Pitch measurements: 115yd×75yd.

Club Patron: Duke of Westminster. *Honorary President:* C. Thompson.

Chairman: M. S. Guterman. *Director:* I. G. Morris. *Manager:* Kevin Ratcliffe.

General Manager: Bill Wingrove. *Honorary Vice-Presidents:* J. F. Kane, L. Lloyd, Dr. M. D. Swallow.

Secretary: Derek Barber JP, AMITD. *Physio:* Stuart Walker.

Year Formed: 1884. *Turned Professional:* 1902. *Ltd Co.:* 1909.

Previous Name: Chester until 1983.

Club Nickname: 'Blues' and 'City'.

Previous Grounds: Faulkner Street; Old Showground; 1904, Whipcord Lane; 1906, Sealand Road; 1990, Moss Rose Ground, Macclesfield; 1992, The Stadium, Bumpers Lane.

Foundation: All students of soccer history have read about the medieval games of football in Chester, but the present club was not formed until 1884 through the amalgamation of King's School Old Boys with Chester Rovers. For many years Chester were overshadowed in Cheshire by Northwich Victoria and Crewe Alexandra who had both won the Senior Cup several times before Chester's first success in 1894–95.

First Football League game: 2 September 1931, Division 3 (N), v Wrexham (a) D 1-1 – Johnson; Herod, Jones; Keeley, Skitt, Reilly; Thompson, Ranson, Jennings (1), Cresswell, Hedley.

Record League Victory: 12–0 v York C, Division 3 (N), 1 February 1936 – Middleton; Common, Hall; Wharton, Wilson, Howarth; Horsman (2), Hughes, Wrightson (4), Cresswell (2), Sargeant (4).

Record Cup Victory: 6–1 v Darlington, FA Cup 1st rd, 25 November 1933 – Burke; Bennett, Little; Pitcairn, Skitt, Duckworth; Armes (3), Whittam, Mantle (2), Cresswell (1), McLachlan.

Record Defeat: 2–11 v Oldham Ath, Division 3 (N), 19 January 1952.

Most League Points (2 for a win): 56, Division 3 (N), 1946–47 and Division 4, 1964–65.

Most League Points (3 for a win): 84, Division 4, 1985–86.

Most League Goals: 119, Division 4, 1964–65.

Highest League Scorer in Season: Dick Yates, 36, Division 3 (N), 1946–47.

Most League Goals in Total Aggregate: Stuart Rimmer, 123, 1985–88, 1991–96.

Most Capped Player: Bill Lewis, 7 (30), Wales.

Most League Appearances: Ray Gill, 408, 1951–62.

Record Transfer Fee Received: £300,000 from Liverpool for Ian Rush, May 1980.

Record Transfer Fee Paid: £94,000 to Barnsley for Stuart Rimmer, August 1991.

Football League Record: 1931 Elected Division 3 (N); 1958–75 Division 4; 1975–82 Division 3; 1982–86 Division 4; 1986–92 Division 3; 1992–93 Division 2; 1993–94 Division 3; 1994–95 Division 2; 1995– Division 3.

Honours: Football League: Division 3 – Runners-up 1993–94; Division 3 (N) – Runners-up 1935–36; Division 4 – Runners-up 1985–86. *FA Cup:* best season: 5th rd, 1977, 1980. *Football League Cup:* Semi-final 1975. *Welsh Cup:* Winners 1908, 1933, 1947. *Debenhams Cup:* Winners 1977.

Colours: Blue and white striped shirts, blue shorts, blue stockings. *Change colours:* Yellow shirts, royal blue shorts, yellow stockings.

Did you know?
When Chester City beat Lincoln City 5-1 on 16 September 1995 they led their opponents with 23 wins to 22 in 59 meetings.

CHESTER CITY 1995–96 LEAGUE RECORD

Match No.	Date	Venue	Opponents	Result	H/T Score	Lg. Pos.	Goalscorers	Attendance
1	Aug 12	H	Hartlepool U	W	2-0	1-0	—	Bishop, Priest	2286
2	19	A	Bury	D	1-1	1-1	8	Bishop	3211
3	26	H	Plymouth Arg	W	3-1	1-0	5	Bishop 2, Regis	2660
4	29	A	Wigan Ath	L	1-2	1-1	—	Rimmer	2555
5	Sept 2	H	Hereford U	W	2-1	2-0	4	Regis, Noteman	3385
6	9	A	Colchester U	W	2-1	0-0	2	Priest, Regis	3422
7	12	A	Scunthorpe U	W	2-0	2-0	—	Richardson, Priest (pen)	1875
8	16	H	Lincoln C	W	5-1	3-1	1	Burnham, Fisher, Milner, Priest (pen), Murphy	3049
9	23	H	Gillingham	D	1-1	0-0	1	Flitcroft	3886
10	30	A	Preston NE	L	0-2	0-0	2		8544
11	Oct 7	H	Doncaster R	L	0-3	0-0	2		2374
12	14	A	Leyton Orient	W	2-0	2-0	2	Regis, Noteman	6037
13	21	H	Fulham	D	1-1	1-0	3	Bishop	2752
14	28	A	Scarborough	D	0-0	0-0	5		1847
15	31	A	Rochdale	W	3-1	1-0	—	Regis, Noteman, Shelton	3018
16	Nov 4	H	Torquay U	W	4-1	2-0	2	Regis, Milner, Whelan, Noteman (pen)	2535
17	18	A	Mansfield T	W	4-3	2-1	1	Rimmer 3, Noteman	2415
18	25	H	Darlington	W	4-1	1-0	1	Rimmer 2, Priest 2 (1 pen)	2652
19	Dec 16	H	Preston NE	D	1-1	1-1	1	Richardson	5004
20	23	H	Barnet	L	0-2	0-1	2		3081
21	26	A	Cardiff C	D	0-0	0-0	2		6046
22	30	A	Exeter C	W	2-1	2-0	1	Rimmer, Noteman	3324
23	Jan 6	A	Cambridge U	D	1-1	1-0	1	Rimmer	2643
24	9	A	Gillingham	L	1-3	0-0	—	Kenworthy	9191
25	13	H	Bury	D	1-1	1-0	3	Regis	3283
26	20	A	Hartlepool U	L	1-2	1-1	3	Rimmer	1864
27	Feb 3	A	Plymouth Arg	L	2-4	0-3	3	Priest, Richardson	5114
28	17	H	Scunthorpe U	W	3-0	1-0	3	Noteman, Fisher, Jackson	2401
29	20	A	Hereford U	L	0-1	0-0	—		1827
30	24	A	Lincoln C	D	0-0	0-0	3		2533
31	27	H	Colchester U	D	1-1	0-0	—	Richardson	2001
32	Mar 2	H	Cardiff C	W	4-0	2-0	5	Davidson, Priest, Rogers (pen), Rimmer	2308
33	9	A	Barnet	D	1-1	0-0	5	Priest	2195
34	16	H	Exeter C	D	2-2	1-1	6	Priest, Blake (og)	2043
35	19	H	Wigan Ath	D	0-0	0-0	—		2825
36	23	A	Northampton T	L	0-1	0-1	8		4810
37	26	H	Cambridge U	D	1-1	0-1	—	Noteman	1623
38	30	H	Doncaster R	W	2-1	0-1	7	Whelan, Murphy	1548
39	Apr 2	H	Leyton Orient	D	1-1	1-1	—	Rimmer	2097
40	6	H	Scarborough	W	5-0	3-0	6	Milner 2, Noteman, Priest, Rimmer	2485
41	8	A	Fulham	L	0-2	0-2	7		3777
42	13	A	Rochdale	L	1-2	1-1	9	Ryan (pen)	2158
43	20	A	Torquay U	D	1-1	0-0	10	Priest	2549
44	23	H	Northampton T	W	1-0	0-0	—	Murphy	1674
45	27	A	Darlington	L	1-3	0-0	9	Rimmer	4510
46	May 4	H	Mansfield T	W	2-1	0-0	8	Chambers, Priest	2935

Final League Position: 8

GOALSCORERS

League (72): Priest 13 (3 pens), Rimmer 13, Noteman 9 (1 pen), Regis 7, Bishop 5, Milner 4, Richardson 4, Murphy 3, Fisher 2, Whelan 2, Burnham 1, Chambers 1, Davidson 1, Flitcroft 1, Jackson 1, Kenworthy 1, Rogers 1 (pen), Ryan 1 (pen), Shelton 1, own goal 1.
Coca-Cola Cup (8): Milner 3, Bishop 2, Chambers 1, Murphy 1, Whelan 1.
FA Cup (1): Milner 1.

Stewart B 45	Jenkins I 12+1	Burnham J 40	Preece R 1	Jackson P 36	Whelan S 35+4	Fisher N 43+1	Priest C 38+1	Regis C 29	Milner A 35+7	Bishop E 7+2	Murphy J 1+17	Flitcroft D 7+2	Shelton G 10+1	Alsford J 22+2	Rimmer S 30+11	Chambers L 2+6	Noteman K 27+6	Richardson N 36+1	Rogers D 14+6	Kenworthy J 5+2	Brown G 1+2	Davidson R 19	Ryan J 2+2	Brien T 8	Cutler N 1	Match No.
1	2	3	4²	5	6	7	8	9¹	10	11	12	13														1
1		3			6	7	8	9	10¹	11				2	4	5	12									2
1	4	3		5		7	8	9²	10¹	11	13	2			6	12										3
1	4	3		5	12	7	8	9					2⁵	11²	6	10	13									4
1	2	3		5	6¹	4	8	9	13			7²		12	10		11									5
1	2³	3		5	6	4	8	9¹	10²			13		14	12		11	7								6
1	2	3		5	6	4	8	9²	10¹			13	11		12			7								7
1	2	3		5	6	4	8	9²	10¹			13	11		12			7								8
1		3		5			4	8		10¹	11²	12	7	2	9			6	13							9
1		3		5			2	8	9		7	12		6	10		11¹	4								10
1		3		5	6	4		9	12	11			8²	2	10¹	13		7								11
1		3		5	6	4		9²	10¹	13			8	2	12		11	7								12
1		3		5	6	4		9	10¹	11			8	2	12			7								13
1		3		5	2	4	12	9²	10				8¹	6		13	11	7								14
1		3		5	2		4	9²	10	12			8¹	6		13	11	7								15
1	13	3		5²	2		4	9³	10				8	6	12	14	11	7¹								16
1		3		5	2	8	4	9						6	10		11	7								17
1		3		5	2	8	4	9¹						6	10	12	11	7								18
1		3		5	12	2		9	13				4¹	6	10		11	7		8²						19
1	3³			5	2	4		9			12			6²	10		11	8	13	7¹	14					20
1	3			5	2	8		9							10		11	4	7	6						21
1	3			5	6	2	8	9							10		11	4¹	7	12						22
1	3				2	4	7	9	8					6	10		11¹	5	12							23
1	3			5	2	8		9¹	12					6	10		11	7	4²	13						24
1	3				6	2	8	9	12					5	10¹		11	7²	4	13						25
1	3			5	2	8		9	12					6	10		11	4	7¹							26
1	3³			5	6	7	8	9²	13				4¹		10		11	12	14			2				27
1				5	6	4	8	9¹	10						12		11	7	3			2				28
1				5	6	4	8	9	10								11	7	3			2				29
1	11			5	6	4	8		10						9			7	3			2				30
1	11²			5	6	4	8		10					12	9¹		13	7	3			2				31
1				5	6	4¹	8		10					12	9		11	7	3			2				32
1	11			5¹		4	8		10				6		9	12		7	3			2				33
1	6					4	8	9¹	10					5	11	12		7	3			2				34
1	6			5		4	8	9¹	10						12			7	3			2	11			35
1	11				6	4	8		10		12				9		13	7	3²			2¹	5			36
1	3				6	4	8	9							10		11	7				2	5			37
1	3			5	6	12	8	9²	10				14				13	11³	7¹			2	4			38
1	3			5	12	6	8	7¹	9²						10		11³	13				2	14	4		39
1	3			5¹	12	4	8		10				13		9²		11	7				2³	14	6		40
1	3			5	11²	4	8¹		10³				12		9		13	7	14			2		6		41
1	3	11¹		5		4			10		12				9			7				2	8	6		42
	3			5		4	8		10		12				9		11¹	7				2		6	1	43
1	3			5	6	4	8		10		12				9		11¹	7				2				44
1	2	3¹		5	6	4	8		10		12			5	9	11		7				2				45
1	3			5	6	4	8		10		12			9	11¹	13		7²				2				46

Coca-Cola Cup
First Round   Wigan Ath   (h) 4-1
(a) 3-1
Second Round   Tottenham H   (a) 0-4
(h) 1-3

FA Cup
First Round   Blackpool   (a) 1-2

CHESTERFIELD 1995–96 *Back row (left to right):* Mark Williams, Kevin Davies, Andy Beasley, Chris Marples, Darren Roberts, Tony Lormor.
Middle row: Mark Stewart, Jonathan Howard, Darren Carr, David Moss, Andy Morris, Nicky Law, Shaun Dyche, Dez Hazel, Phil Robinson, Lee Rogers.
Front row: Mark Jules, Tom Curtis, Chris Perkins, Dave Rushbury, John Duncan (Manager), Kevin Randall (Assistant Manager), John Narbett, Wayne Fairclough, Jamie Hewitt.

Division 2   **CHESTERFIELD**

Recreation Ground, Chesterfield S40 4SX. Telephone: (01246) 209765. Fax: (01246) 556799. Commercial Dept: (01246) 231535. Spireites Hotline: (0891) 555818.

Ground capacity: 8880.

Record attendance: 30,968 v Newcastle U, Division 2, 7 April 1939.

Record receipts: £45,000 v Mansfield T, Division 3 play-off semi-final, 17 May 1995.

Pitch measurements: 113yd × 71yd.

President: His Grace the Duke of Devonshire MC, DL, JP.

Chairman: J. Norton Lea. *Vice-Chairman:* B. W. Hubbard.

Directors: R. F. Pepper, M. L. Warner.

Manager: John Duncan. *Executive Manager:* M. Horton.

Physio: Dave Rushbury. *Assistant Manager:* Kevin Randall.

Secretary: Mick Horton. *Commercial Manager:* Jim Brown. *Stadium Manager:* W. W. Kenworthy.

Year Formed: 1866. *Turned Professional:* 1891. *Ltd Co:* 1871.

Previous Names: Chesterfield Town.

Club Nickname: 'Blues' or 'Spireites'.

Foundation: Chesterfield are fourth only to Stoke, Notts County and Nottingham Forest in age for they can trace their existence as far back as 1866, although it is fair to say that they were somewhat casual in the first few years of their history playing only a few friendlies a year. However, their rules of 1871 are still in existence showing an annual membership of 2s (10p), but it was not until 1891 that they won a trophy (the Barnes Cup) and followed this a year later by winning the Sheffield Cup, Barnes Cup and the Derbyshire Junior Cup.

First Football League game: 2 September 1899, Division 2, v Sheffield W (a) L 1-5 – Hancock; Pilgrim, Fletcher; Ballantyne, Bell, Downie; Morley, Thacker, Gooing, Munday (1), Geary.

Record League Victory: 10–0 v Glossop NE, Division 2, 17 January 1903 – Clutterbuck; Thorpe, Lerper; Haig, Banner, Thacker; Tomlinson (2), Newton (1), Milward (3), Munday (2), Steel (2).

Record Cup Victory: 5–0 v Wath Ath (away), FA Cup 1st rd, 28 November 1925 – Birch; Saxby, Dennis; Wass, Abbott, Thompson; Fisher (1), Roseboom (1), Cookson (2), Whitfield (1), Hopkinson.

Record Defeat: 0–10 v Gillingham, Division 3, 5 September 1987.

Most League Points (2 for a win): 64, Division 4, 1969–70.

Most League Points (3 for a win): 91, Division 4, 1984–85.

Most League Goals: 102, Division 3 (N), 1930–31.

Highest League Scorer in Season: Jimmy Cookson, 44, Division 3 (N), 1925–26.

Most League Goals in Total Aggregate: Ernie Moss, 161, 1969–76, 1979–81 and 1984–86.

Most Capped Player: Walter McMillen, 4 (7), Northern Ireland.

Most League Appearances: Dave Blakey, 613, 1948–67.

Record Transfer Fee Received: £200,000 from Wolverhampton W for Alan Birch, August 1981.

Record Transfer Fee Paid: £150,000 to Carlisle U for Phil Bonnyman, March 1980.

Football League Record: 1899 Elected to Division 2; 1909 failed re-election; 1921–31 Division 3 (N); 1931–33 Division 2; 1933–36 Division 3 (N); 1936–51 Division 2; 1951–58 Division 3 (N); 1958–61 Division 3; 1961–70 Division 4; 1970–83 Division 3; 1983–85 Division 4; 1985–89 Division 3; 1989–92 Division 4; 1992–95 Division 3; 1995– Division 2.

Honours: Football League: Division 2 best season: 4th, 1946–47; Division 3 (N) – Champions 1930–31, 1935–36; Runners-up 1933–34; Division 4 – Champions 1969–70, 1984–85. *FA Cup:* best season: 5th rd, 1933, 1938, 1950. *Football League Cup:* best season: 4th rd, 1965. *Anglo-Scottish Cup:* Winners 1981.

Colours: Blue shirts, white shorts, blue stockings. *Change colours:* Green and white striped shirts, navy shorts, navy stockings.

Did you know?
Jimmy Cookson scored in eight consecutive Division Three (North) League games during 1926–27. His total in this sequence was 12 goals.

CHESTERFIELD 1995–96 LEAGUE RECORD

Match No.	Date	Venue	Opponents	Result		H/T Score	Lg. Pos.	Goalscorers	Attendance
1	Aug 12	A	Oxford U	L	0-1	0-0	—		5563
2	19	H	Carlisle U	W	3-0	2-0	11	Lormor, Robinson, Morris	3634
3	26	A	Swansea C	L	2-3	0-2	16	Davies 2	3492
4	29	H	York C	W	2-1	0-1	—	Morris, Lormor	3419
5	Sept 2	H	Hull C	D	0-0	0-0	11		4345
6	9	A	Swindon T	D	1-1	1-0	12	Davies	8687
7	12	A	Wycombe W	L	0-1	0-1	—		3617
8	16	H	Rotherham U	W	3-0	1-0	10	Lormor, Jules, Law (pen)	5146
9	23	H	Burnley	W	4-2	2-2	7	Hewitt, Robinson, Lormor, Morris	4933
10	30	A	Brentford	W	2-1	1-0	7	Ashby (og), Robinson	4734
11	Oct 7	H	Crewe Alex	L	1-2	0-0	7	Morris	4981
12	14	A	Blackpool	D	0-0	0-0	9		6855
13	21	H	Shrewsbury T	W	1-0	1-0	6	Law	3920
14	28	A	Stockport Co	W	1-0	1-0	4	Law (pen)	6287
15	31	A	Bristol C	L	1-2	1-1	—	Robinson	4408
16	Nov 4	H	Bradford C	W	2-1	1-1	6	Law 2 (2 pens)	5490
17	18	A	Notts Co	L	1-4	1-2	7	Law (pen)	6747
18	25	H	Bournemouth	W	3-0	2-0	4	Robinson 2, Lormor	4034
19	Dec 9	A	Burnley	D	2-2	1-1	7	Davies, Lormor	8459
20	16	H	Brentford	D	2-2	0-2	7	Bates (og), Morris	4016
21	22	A	Brighton & HA	W	2-0	1-0	—	Robinson 2	3629
22	26	H	Peterborough U	D	1-1	0-1	4	Williams	6017
23	Jan 13	A	Carlisle U	D	1-1	1-0	6	Narbett	5851
24	20	H	Oxford U	W	1-0	1-0	5	Lormor	4589
25	Feb 3	H	Swansea C	W	3-2	2-2	5	Holland, Lormor 2	4050
26	17	H	Wycombe W	W	3-1	3-0	5	Williams, Robinson, Lormor	4571
27	24	A	Rotherham U	W	1-0	0-0	4	Jules	5712
28	Mar 2	A	Peterborough U	W	1-0	1-0	5	Howard	6105
29	5	A	Wrexham	L	0-3	0-3	—		2656
30	9	H	Brighton & HA	W	1-0	0-0	5	Williams	6233
31	12	A	Hull C	D	0-0	0-0	—		2832
32	16	A	Walsall	L	0-3	0-0	6		4172
33	19	A	Wrexham	D	1-1	0-0	—	Lormor	3760
34	23	H	Bristol R	W	2-1	0-0	6	Howard, Lormor	4748
35	26	A	Bristol R	L	0-1	0-0	—		3513
36	30	A	Crewe Alex	L	0-3	0-2	6		4073
37	Apr 2	H	Blackpool	W	1-0	0-0	—	Holland	7002
38	6	H	Stockport Co	L	1-2	0-1	6	McDougald	6090
39	9	A	Shrewsbury T	D	0-0	0-0	—		3035
40	13	H	Bristol C	D	1-1	0-1	6	McDougald	4619
41	16	H	Walsall	D	1-1	0-1	—	Lormor	4508
42	20	A	Bradford C	L	1-2	1-0	9	McDougald	6803
43	23	H	Swindon T	L	1-3	1-2	—	Hewitt	5523
44	27	A	Bournemouth	L	0-2	0-1	10		4483
45	30	A	York C	W	1-0	0-0	—	Lund	2839
46	May 4	H	Notts Co	W	1-0	0-0	7	Law (pen)	6708

Final League Position: 7

GOALSCORERS

League (56): Lormor 13, Robinson 9, Law 7 (6 pens), Morris 5, Davies 4, McDougald 3, Williams 3, Hewitt 2, Holland 2, Howard 2, Jules 2, Lund 1, Narbett 1, own goals 2.
Coca-Cola Cup (1): Roberts 1.
FA Cup (4): Davies 2, Lormor 2.

Beasley A 11	Jules M 28 + 4	Perkins C 18 + 4	Curtis T 46	Williams M 42	Madden L 1	Robinson P 38 + 1	Davies K 28 + 2	Lormor T 38 + 3	Howard J 16 + 14	Dyche S 39 + 2	Morris A 14 + 2	Hewitt J 23 + 5	Narbett J 11 + 6	Roberts D 6 + 8	Rogers L 20 + 1	Law N 38	Moss D 6 + 7	Carr D 1	Hazel D 16 + 5	Pierce D 1	Mercer B 34	Lund G 6 + 2	Fairclough W — + 2	Holland P 16 + 1	McDougald J 9	Match No.
1	2	3[1]	4	5	6[2]	7	8	9	10[5]	11	12	13	14													1
1		3	4	5		7	8[1]	9	12	6	10[2]	2	11	13												2
1	12		4	5		7[3]	8	9	13	11	2	14			3[1]	6	10[2]									3
1		3	4			7	8	9	12	5	10	2	11[1]			6										4
1	12	11	4			7	8[2]	9[1]	13	5	10	2			14	3[1]	6									5
1[3]	13		4			7[2]	8	9	12	10		2	14		3	6		5	11[1]							6
	12		4	5		7[1]	8	9		10	13	2			3	6			11[2]	1						7
	11		4			7	8	9		5	10	2			3	6				1						8
	11		4	5		7	8[1]	9	12	6	10	2			3					1						9
	11[1]	12	4[2]	5		7	8	9[1]	13	6	10	2	14		3					1						10
			4	5		7[2]	8	9	12	11	10	2	13		3[1]	6				1						11
	11		4	5		7	8	9[1]	12	3	10	2				6				1						12
			4	5		7	8	12	11	3	10			9[1]	2	6			12	1						13
			4	5		7	8	9[1]	11	3	10	2				6			12	1						14
	12		4	5		7	8	13	11[1]	3	10[2]			9[3]	2	6			14	1						15
			4	5		7	8	9[1]	11	3	10	2				6			12	1						16
1			4	5		7	8	9	11	3	10	2				6										17
1			4	5		7	8	9		3	10	2				6			11							18
1			4	5		7	8	9		3		2				6			11							19
	12		4	5		7	8	9		3	10[2]	2				6			11[1]		1	13				20
	3	6	4	5		7	8	9[2]	12		10[1]	2				6			11		1	13				21
	3	6	4	5		7	8[3]	9[2]			12	13				6			11[1]		1	10	14			22
	3	2	4	5		12	13				8	9[1]	11			6					1	10[2]	7			23
	3	2	4	5				8	9			11				6			12		1	10[1]	7			24
	3[2]	2	4	5		7	8[1]	9	11			12				6					1		13	10		25
	3	2	4	5		7[1]	8	9	11	12		13				6					1			10[2]		26
	3	2	4	5		7	8[1]	9	11	13	10[2]					6	12				1					27
11	2	4	5			7	8[2]	9	10[1]	3		13				6	12				1					28
11	2	4	5			7[1]	8[1]	9	12	3	14	10				6[3]	13				1					29
	3		4	5		7[2]		9	10	2			11		8[1]	6	12				1			13		30
	3		4	5			9			2		7	11	8[1]		6	12				1			10		31
	3	7	4	5			9			2			11			6	8				1			10		32
	3		4	5			9		6	2		11				8			7		1			10	8	33
	3		4	5		7[2]		9	11[1]	2			12			6	13		8		1			10	8	34
	3		4	5		7		9[1]	10	2						6	12		8		1			11		35
	3		4	5		7		12		2		13			14	6[2]			8[1]		1		9[2]	10	11	36
	3	12	4	5		7[1]			11			2				6	8				1			10	9	37
	3		4	5		7			11			2				6	8				1			10	9	38
1	3		4	5		7[2]			12	11		2			13	6	8[1]							10	9	39
1	11		4	5			9			3		2				6			7					10	8	40
11			4	5			9		3			2				6			7	1				10	8	41
11			4	5		12[2]		9	13	3		2				6			7					10[1]	8	42
	2		4	5		7		9			11				10	3	6				1				8	43
	3[2]		4	5		7		9	10	11		2		12		6			13	1					8[1]	44
	3	2	4	5		7			10	6		8					2		11		1	9				45
	3		4	5		7	13	9	11	6		12[2]				2			8[1]		1	10				46

Coca-Cola Cup
First Round   Bury   (h)   0-1
               (a)   1-2

FA Cup
First Round   Scarborough   (a)   2-0
Second Round   Wrexham   (a)   2-3

COLCHESTER UNITED 1995-96 *Back row (left to right):* Adam Locke, Steve Ball, Tony McCarthy, Carl Emberson, Peter Cawley, Mark Kinsella, Simon Betts.
Middle row: Steve Foley (Youth Team Manager), Tony English, Michael Cheetham, Chris Fry, Robbie Reinelt, Nicky Haydon, Paul Gibbs, Brian Owen (Physio).
Front row: Kelvin Wagner (Kit Man), Gus Caesar, Tony Dennis, Steve Mardenborough, Steve Wignall (Manager), Steve Whitton (Assistant Manager), James Siddons, Tony Lock, Jean Dalli, Paul Dyer (Chief Scout).

Division 3   COLCHESTER UNITED

Layer Rd Ground, Colchester, Essex CO2 7JJ. Telephone: (01206) 574042. Fax: (01206) 48700. Club Shop: (01206) 561180. Soccer Centre: (01206) 571581. Lottery: (01206) 47754.

Ground capacity: 7190.

Record attendance: 19,072 v Reading, FA Cup 1st rd, 27 November 1948.

Record receipts: £26,330 v Barrow, GM Vauxhall Conference, 2 May 1992.

Pitch measurements: 110yd × 71yd.

Patron: The Mayor of Colchester.

Directors: Gordon Parker (Chairman), Peter Heard (Vice-Chairman), John Worsp, Peter Powell.

Chief Executive: Richard Summers.

Manager: Steve Wignall. *Assistant Manager/Coach:* Steve Whitton. *Youth Coach:* Steve Foley.

Physio: Brian Owen. *Consultant Physio:* Ray Cole.

Secretary: Mrs Marie Partner.

Commercial Manager: Marie Partner. *Lottery Manager:* Liz Blacknall. *Stadium Manager:* David Blacknall.

Year Formed: 1937. *Turned Professional:* 1937. *Ltd Co.:* 1937.

Club Nickname: 'The U's'.

Foundation: Colchester United was formed in 1937 when a number of enthusiasts of the much older Colchester Town club decided to establish a professional concern as a limited liability company. The new club continued at Layer Road which had been the amateur club's home since 1909.

First Football League game: 19 August 1950, Division 3 (S), v Gillingham (a) D 0-0 – Wright; Kettle, Allen; Bearryman, Stewart, Elder; Jones, Curry, Turner, McKim, Church.

Record League Victory: 9–1 v Bradford C, Division 4, 30 December 1961 – Ames; Millar, Fowler; Harris, Abrey, Ron Hunt; Foster, Bobby Hunt (4), King (4), Hill (1), Wright.

Record Cup Victory: 7–1 v Yeovil T (away), FA Cup 2nd rd (replay), 11 December 1958 – Ames; Fisher, Fowler; Parker, Milligan, Hammond; Williams (1), McLeod (2), Langman (4), Evans, Wright.

Record Defeat: 0–8 v Leyton Orient, Division 4, 15 October 1989.

Most League Points (2 for a win): 60, Division 4, 1973–74.

Most League Points (3 for a win): 81, Division 4, 1982–83.

Most League Goals: 104, Division 4, 1961–62.

Highest League Scorer in Season: Bobby Hunt, 38, Division 4, 1961–62.

Most League Goals in Total Aggregate: Martyn King, 130, 1956–64.

Most Capped Player: None.

Most League Appearances: Micky Cook, 613, 1969–84.

Record Transfer Fee Received: £100,000 from Birmingham C for Steve McGavin, January 1994.

Record Transfer Fee Paid: £40,000 to Lokeren for Dale Tempest, August 1987.

Football League Record: 1950 Elected to Division 3 (S); 1958–61 Division 3; 1961–62 Division 4; 1962–65 Division 3; 1965–66 Division 4; 1966–68 Division 3; 1968–74 Division 4; 1974–76 Division 3, 1976–77 Division 4; 1977–81 Division 3; 1981–90 Division 4; 1990–92 GM Vauxhall Conference; 1992– Division 3.

Honours: Football League: Division 3 (S) best season: 3rd , 1956–57; Division 4 – Runners-up 1961–62. *FA Cup:* best season: 1971, 6th rd (record for a Fourth Division club shared with Oxford United and Bradford City). *Football League Cup:* best season: 5th rd, 1975. *GM Vauxhall Conference:* Winners: 1991–92. *FA Trophy:* Winners: 1992.

Colours: Blue and white striped shirts, white shorts, white stockings. *Change colours:* White shirts, black shorts, black stockings white trim.

Did you know?
When winning 3-2 at Torquay on 1 January 1996, Colchester United scored 15 seconds from the kick-off and again 15 seconds from the end.

COLCHESTER UNITED 1995–96 LEAGUE RECORD

Match No.	Date	Venue	Opponents	Result		H/T Score	Lg. Pos.	Goalscorers	Attendance
1	Aug 12	H	Plymouth Arg	W	2-1	1-0	—	Betts, Locke	3585
2	19	A	Barnet	D	1-1	0-0	9	Adcock	1966
3	26	H	Lincoln C	W	3-0	2-0	6	Dennis 2, Mardenborough	2939
4	29	A	Cambridge U	L	1-3	0-2	—	Adcock	3476
5	Sept 2	A	Gillingham	W	1-0	0-0	5	Adcock	7667
6	9	H	Chester C	L	1-2	0-0	8	Whitton	3422
7	12	H	Preston NE	D	2-2	1-0	—	Fry, Whitton	2869
8	16	A	Darlington	D	2-2	2-0	9	Dennis, Cheetham	1685
9	23	H	Hereford U	W	2-0	1-0	7	Reinelt 2	2596
10	30	A	Scunthorpe U	L	0-1	0-1	9		2051
11	Oct 7	H	Hartlepool U	W	4-1	3-0	7	Locke 2, Adcock, Reinelt	2618
12	14	A	Rochdale	D	1-1	1-0	7	Reinelt	2193
13	21	H	Northampton T	W	1-0	0-0	6	Kinsella	3823
14	28	A	Cardiff C	W	2-1	2-1	4	Adcock 2	3207
15	31	A	Fulham	D	1-1	1-0	—	Mardenborough	2870
16	Nov 4	H	Exeter C	D	1-1	1-0	5	Kinsella	3377
17	18	A	Doncaster R	L	2-3	1-2	5	Cheetham, Adcock	1603
18	25	H	Mansfield T	L	1-3	0-1	6	Adcock (pen)	2819
19	Dec 9	A	Hereford U	D	1-1	0-0	8	Betts	3324
20	16	H	Scunthorpe U	W	2-1	2-0	7	Ball, Kinsella	2138
21	23	A	Bury	D	0-0	0-0	7		3559
22	26	H	Leyton Orient	D	0-0	0-0	5		4965
23	Jan 1	A	Torquay U	W	3-2	1-1	5	Kinsella, Duguid, Betts	2425
24	13	H	Barnet	W	3-2	3-2	4	Betts (pen), Abrahams 2	3252
25	20	A	Plymouth Arg	D	1-1	0-1	5	Greene	5800
26	30	A	Wigan Ath	L	0-2	0-2	—		2101
27	Feb 3	A	Lincoln C	D	0-0	0-0	6		2531
28	6	H	Scarborough	D	1-1	1-0	—	Cawley	2299
29	10	H	Wigan Ath	L	1-2	0-0	6	Adcock	3082
30	17	A	Preston NE	L	0-2	0-2	8		9335
31	24	H	Darlington	D	1-1	1-0	9	Adcock	2653
32	27	A	Chester C	D	1-1	0-0	—	Gibbs	2001
33	Mar 2	A	Leyton Orient	W	1-0	1-0	8	Adcock (pen)	4049
34	9	H	Bury	W	1-0	0-0	8	Caesar	2832
35	16	A	Scarborough	D	0-0	0-0	8		1201
36	19	H	Cambridge U	W	2-1	1-1	—	Adcock, McGleish	2995
37	23	H	Torquay U	W	3-1	1-0	7	Fry, McGleish, Betts (pen)	2888
38	30	A	Hartlepool U	L	1-2	1-1	8	Gibbs	1364
39	Apr 2	H	Rochdale	W	1-0	0-0	—	Reinelt	3021
40	6	H	Cardiff C	W	1-0	0-0	8	Kinsella	3345
41	8	A	Northampton T	L	1-2	0-0	9	Reinelt	5021
42	13	H	Fulham	D	2-2	1-1	8	McGleish 2	3795
43	16	H	Gillingham	D	1-1	0-0	—	McGleish	4952
44	20	A	Exeter C	D	2-2	1-2	9	Caesar, McGleish	2788
45	27	A	Mansfield T	W	2-1	0-0	7	Reinelt, Dunne	2073
46	May 4	H	Doncaster R	W	1-0	1-0	7	Gibbs	5038

Final League Position: 7

GOALSCORERS

League (61): Adcock 12 (2 pens), Reinelt 7, McGleish 6, Betts 5 (2 pens), Kinsella 5, Dennis 3, Gibbs 3, Locke 3, Abrahams 2, Caesar 2, Cheetham 2, Fry 2, Mardenborough 2, Whitton 2, Ball 1, Cawley 1, Duguid 1, Dunne 1, Greene 1.
Coca-Cola Cup (3): Adcock 1, Cheetham 1, Kinsella 1.
FA Cup (0).

Emberson C 41	Locke A 22 + 3	Betts S 45	McCarthy T 44	Caesar G 23	Cawley P 42	Kinsella M 45	English T 20 + 1	Whiton S 10 + 2	Adcock T 41	Cheetham M 25 + 3	Dennis T 24 + 8	Reinelt R 12 + 10	Fry C 35 + 3	Mardenborough S 4 + 8	Gibbs P 13 + 11	Lewis B 1 + 1	Ball S 6 + 2	Boyce R — + 2	Greene D 14	Duguid K 7 + 9	Abrahams P 8	Gregory D 7 + 3	McGleish S 10 + 5	Petterson A 5	Dunne J 2 + 3	Match No.
1	2	3	4	5	6	7	8	9	10	11^1	12															1
1	2	3	4	5	6	7	8	9	10^1	11		12														2
1	2	3	4	5^1	6	7		9	10	11^1	8		12	13												3
1	2	3	4	5^1	6	7	12	9	10	11	8^2			13												4
1	2	3	4		6	7	5	9	10	11^1	8			12												5
1	2^1	3	4		6	7	5	9	10	11^2	8	13	12													6
1	2^1	3	4			7	5	9	10	11	8	12	6													7
1		3	4		6	7	5	9^1	10	11	8^2		2	12	13											8
1	2	3	4		6	7	5		10	11^2			9^1	8	12	13										9
1	2^3	3	4		6	7			10	11			9^2	8^1	13	12	5	14								10
1	2	3	4		6	7	5		10	11			9	8												11
1	2^1	3	4		6	7^3	5		10	11^2	12		9	8	13	14										12
1		3	4	5^1	6	7	8		10	11	12		9	2												13
1		3	4	5	6	7^1	2		10	11	8		9^2	12	13											14
1	2		4		6	7	5		10	11	8		9^1	3	12											15
1		3	4		6	7	5		10	11	8	12	2	9^1												16
1		3	4	5	6	7	8		10	11^1			2	9			12									17
1	3^2		4		6	7	8		10	11			9^1	2	12	13			5							18
1		3	4		6	7	8		10	11			2		9^1				5	12						19
1		3	4		6	7	8		10	11	12		2		9^1				5							20
1		3	4		6	7	8		10	11	12		2		9^1				5							21
1	12	3	4		6	7	8		10	11^1	13		2		9^2				5							22
1		3	4		6	7	8		10				2^1	9					5	12	11					23
1	8^1	3	4		6	7				11	12		2						5	13		9^2	10			24
1		3	4		6	7			10	12	8^2		2^1						5	13	9	11				25
1		3	4		6	7			10	12	8^2		2^1						5	13	9	11				26
1	2	3	4		6	7			10		12						8^1		5		9	11				27
1	2	3	4		6	7			10		8								5		9	11				28
1	2	3	4		6	7			10		8^1	12				13			5		9	11^2				29
1	3^1		4			7			10	12	8		2	13			6^2		5	14	9	11^3				30
1	6^1	3	4			7			10		8		2				11		5	9			12			31
1		3	4	5	6	7			10	12	8		2							9^1	11					32
1		3	4	5	6	7			10		8		2^1							9	11^2	12	13			33
1		3	4	5	6	7			10		8	12	2								11^1	9^2	13		1	34
1		3	4	5	6	7			10		8^1	14	2								11^2	9^3	13		1	35
1	8	3	4	5	6^1	7			10				2								11	9^2	12	13	1	36
1	8	3	4	5	6	7		12	10^1				2								11^2	13	9		1	37
1	8	3	4	5	6	7			10^3	12			2								11^2	13	9^1	1	14	38
1	8	3	4	5	6		7		10^1	12			2								11		9			39
1	8	3	4	5	6	7			10	12			2								11^1		9			40
1	8^1	3	4	5	6^3	7			10	12			2				11					13	9^2		14	41
1			4	5		7			10	6	11		8		3								9		2	42
1		3	4	5	6	7			10^1		8		2								11	12	9			43
1		3	4	5^1	6	7			10		8		2^1							12	11^2	13	9		14	44
1	12	3	4		6	7			10	13	8		2^2							11^1			9		5	45
1	12	3	4	5^1	6	7			10^2	13	8		2							11			9			46

Coca-Cola Cup
First Round   Bristol C   (h) 2-1
(a) 1-2

FA Cup
First Round   Gravesend & N   (a) 0-2

COVENTRY CITY 1995–96   *Back row (left to right):* Isaias, David Burrows, Iyseden Christie, John Filan, Steve Ogrizovic, Jonathan Gould, Peter Shilton, Gary Gillespie, Leigh Jenkinson, Carlita.
Middle row: Trevor Gould (Youth Team Manager), Jim Blythe (Goalkeeping Coach), George Dalton (Physio), Paul Williams, Marcus Hall, John Williams, David Busst, Steve Morgan, Paul Cook, David Rennie, Willie Boland, Gary Pendry (Coach), Brian Roberts (Reserve Team Manager).
Front row: Julian Darby, Brian Borrows, Kevin Richardson, Dion Dublin, Ron Atkinson (Manager), Gordon Strachan (Assistant Manager), John Salako, Peter Ndlovu, Paul Telfer, Ally Pickering.
(Photograph: Action Images)

FA Premiership COVENTRY CITY

Highfield Road Stadium, King Richard Street, Coventry CV2 4FW. Telephone: (01203) 234000. Fax: (01203) 234099. Ticket Office: (01203) 234020. Ticket Office Fax: (01203) 234023. Sales & Marketing: (01203) 234010. Clubcall: 0891 121166.

Ground capacity: 23,500.

Record attendance: 51,455 v Wolverhampton W, Division 2, 29 April 1967.

Record receipts: £272,134 v Tottenham H, Coca-Cola Cup 3rd Rd, 25 October 1995.

Pitch measurements: 110yd × 75yd.

President: E. W. Grove.

Chairman: B. A. Richardson. *Deputy Chairman:* M. C. McGinnity.

Directors: A. M. Jepson, J. F. W Reason, G. Robinson MP.

Secretary: Graham Hover.

Manager: Ron Atkinson. *Assistant Manager:* Gordon Strachan. *Coach:* Gary Pendrey.

Physio: George Dalton.

Sales & Marketing Manager: Mark Jones. *Stadium Manager:* Don Blair.

Club Statistician: Jim Brown.

Year Formed: 1883. *Turned Professional:* 1893. *Ltd Co.:* 1907.

Previous Names: 1883–98, Singers FC; 1898, Coventry City FC.

Club Nickname: 'Sky Blues'.

Previous Grounds: Binley Road, 1883–87; Stoke Road, 1887–99; Highfield Road, 1899–.

Foundation: Workers at Singers' cycle factory formed a club in 1883. The first success of Singers' FC was to win the Birmingham Junior Cup in 1891 and this led in 1894 to their election to the Birmingham and District League. Four years later they changed their name to Coventry City and joined the Southern League in 1908 at which time they were playing in blue and white quarters.

First Football League game: 30 August 1919, Division 2, v Tottenham H (h) L 0-5 – Lindon; Roberts, Chaplin, Allan, Hawley, Clarke, Sheldon, Mercer, Sambrooke, Lowes, Gibson.

Record League Victory: 9–0 v Bristol C, Division 3 (S), 28 April 1934 – Pearson; Brown, Bisby; Perry, Davidson, Frith; White (2), Lauderdale, Bourton (5), Jones (2), Lake.

Record Cup Victory: 7–0 v Scunthorpe U, FA Cup 1st rd, 24 November 1934 – Pearson; Brown, Bisby; Mason, Davidson, Boileau; Birtley (2), Lauderdale (2), Bourton (1), Jones (1), Liddle (1).

Record Defeat: 2–10 v Norwich C, Division 3 (S), 15 March 1930.

Most League Points (2 for a win): 60, Division 4, 1958–59 and Division 3, 1963–64.

Most League Points (3 for a win): 63, Division 1, 1986–87.

Most League Goals: 108, Division 3 (S), 1931–32.

Highest League Scorer in Season: Clarrie Bourton, 49, Division 3 (S), 1931–32.

Most League Goals in Total Aggregate: Clarrie Bourton, 171, 1931–37.

Most Capped Player: Peter Ndlovu 26 (37) Zimbabwe.

Most League Appearances: George Curtis, 486, 1956–70.

Record Transfer Fee Received: £3,750,000 from Liverpool for Phil Babb, September 1994.

Record Transfer Fee Paid: £2,000,000 to Leeds U for Noel Whelan, December 1995.

Football League Record: 1919 Elected to Division 2; 1925–26 Division 3 (N); 1926–36 Division 3 (S); 1936–52 Division 2; 1952–58 Division 3 (S); 1958–59 Division 4; 1959–64 Division 3; 1964–67 Division 2; 1967–92 Division 1; 1992– FA Premier League.

Honours: Football League: Division 1 best season: 6th, 1969–70; Division 2 – Champions 1966–67; Division 3 – Champions 1963–64; Division 3 (S) – Champions 1935–36; Runners-up 1933–34; Division 4 – Runners-up 1958–59. *FA Cup:* Winners 1987. *Football League Cup:* best season: Semi-final 1981, 1990. **European Competitions:** *European Fairs Cup:* 1970–71.

Colours: Sky blue and navy stripes, navy shorts, navy stockings. *Change colours:* Red and navy check, navy shorts, red stockings.

Did you know?
Coventry City won the 1935–36 Division Three (South) Cup beating Swindon Town 5-2 on aggregate in the two-legged final.

COVENTRY CITY 1995–96 LEAGUE RECORD

Match No.	Date	Venue	Opponents	Result	H/T Score	Lg. Pos.	Goalscorers	Attendance
1	Aug 19	A	Newcastle U	L	0-3	0-1	—	36,485
2	23	H	Manchester C	W	2-1	1-0	—	Telfer, Dublin	16,568
3	26	H	Arsenal	D	0-0	0-0	11		20,081
4	30	A	Chelsea	D	2-2	1-2	—	Isaias, Ndlovu	22,718
5	Sept 9	H	Nottingham F	D	1-1	1-1	11	Dublin	17,238
6	16	A	Middlesbrough	L	1-2	0-0	14	Isaias	27,882
7	23	A	Blackburn R	L	1-5	1-2	16	Ndlovu	24,382
8	30	H	Aston Villa	L	0-3	0-1	16		21,004
9	Oct 14	A	Liverpool	D	0-0	0-0	16		39,079
10	21	H	Sheffield W	L	0-1	0-1	17		14,002
11	28	A	Leeds U	L	1-3	1-2	18	Dublin	30,025
12	Nov 4	H	Tottenham H	L	2-3	1-2	19	Dublin, Williams	17,567
13	19	A	QPR	D	1-1	0-1	19	Dublin	11,189
14	22	H	Manchester U	L	0-4	0-1	—		23,344
15	25	H	Wimbledon	D	3-3	1-2	19	Heald (og), Dublin, Rennie	12,496
16	Dec 4	A	Sheffield W	L	3-4	2-2	—	Dublin 3	16,229
17	9	H	Blackburn R	W	5-0	1-0	19	Busst, Dublin, Rennie, Ndlovu, Salako	13,409
18	16	A	Aston Villa	L	1-4	0-1	19	Dublin	28,486
19	23	H	Everton	W	2-1	0-0	19	Busst, Whelan	16,638
20	30	A	Bolton W	W	2-1	1-1	17	Whelan, Salako (pen)	16,678
21	Jan 1	H	Southampton	D	1-1	0-0	17	Whelan	16,822
22	14	H	Newcastle U	L	0-1	0-1	17		20,532
23	20	A	Manchester C	D	1-1	0-0	17	Dublin	25,710
24	31	A	West Ham U	L	2-3	0-0	—	Dublin, Whelan	18,884
25	Feb 3	A	Arsenal	D	1-1	1-1	18	Whelan	35,623
26	10	H	Chelsea	W	1-0	1-0	17	Whelan	20,629
27	24	H	Middlesbrough	D	0-0	0-0	17		17,979
28	Mar 2	H	West Ham U	D	2-2	2-2	16	Salako, Whelan	17,448
29	9	A	Everton	D	2-2	1-2	15	Daish, Williams	34,517
30	16	A	Bolton W	L	0-2	0-0	16		17,168
31	25	A	Southampton	L	0-1	0-1	—		14,461
32	30	A	Tottenham H	L	1-3	1-0	19	Dublin	26,808
33	Apr 6	H	Liverpool	W	1-0	1-0	18	Whelan	23,037
34	8	A	Manchester U	L	0-1	0-0	19		50,332
35	13	H	QPR	W	1-0	0-0	18	Jess	22,906
36	17	A	Nottingham F	D	0-0	0-0	—		24,629
37	27	A	Wimbledon	W	2-0	0-0	16	Ndlovu 2	15,796
38	May 5	H	Leeds U	D	0-0	0-0	16		22,757

Final League Position: 16

GOALSCORERS
League (42): Dublin 14, Whelan 8, Ndlovu 5, Salako 3 (1 pen), Busst 2, Isaias 2, Rennie 2, Williams 2, Daish 1, Jess 1, Telfer 1, own goal 1.
Coca-Cola Cup (7): Lamptey 2, Busst 1, Ndlovu 1 (pen), Richardson 1, Salako 1, Williams P 1.
FA Cup (6): Dublin 2, Pickering 1, Salako 1, Telfer 1, Whelan 1.

Filan J 13	Borrows B 21	Burrows D 11	Williams P 30 + 2	Rennie D 9 + 2	Richardson K 33	Telfer P 31	Ndlovu P 27 + 5	Dublin D 34	Hall M 24 + 1	Salako J 34 + 3	Pickering A 26 + 4	Isaias 9 + 2	Barnwell-Edinboro J — + 1	Cook P 2 + 1	Christie I — + 1	Busst D 16 + 1	Strachan G 5 + 7	Lampley N 3 + 3	Boland W 2 + 1	Ogrizovic S 25	Shaw R 21	Whyte C 1	Whelan N 21	Daish L 11	Jess E 9 + 3	Match No.
1	2	3	4	5	6	7	8	9	10[1]	11	12															1
1	5		4		6	7	8	9	3	11	2	10														2
1	5	3	4		6	7	8	9		11	2	10														3
1	5	3	4		6	7	8	9		11	2	10														4
1	5	3	4		6	7	8	9		11	2	10														5
1	5		4		6	7	8	9[1]	3	11	2	10	12													6
1	5		4		6	7	8		3	11	2	10		9[1]	12											7
1	5		4		8	7	9		3	11	2[1]	10				6	12									8
1	3		4		6	7	8			11	2					5	9	10								9
1	3		4		6	7	8		12	11	2					5	10	9[1]								10
1		10	5		6	7	8[1]	9	3	11	2					4	12									11
1	2[1]	10	5	4		7		9	3	11	12	13				6	8[2]									12
	4	5	6		7[1]	8	9		3	11		10					12			1	2					13
	4	5	6			8	9		3	11				12	10[1]		7			1	2					14
	4	5	6		7	8	9		3	11[2]	13			12	10[1]					1	2					15
		6	5[1]		10	7	8	9	3	11	2						12			1	4					16
			5		10	7	8	9	3	11	2					6				1		4				17
1		6	12	4		7	8[2]	9	3	11	13					5					2		10			18
	4	12	10			7	9		3	11	2[1]					6				1	5		8			19
	4		7				9		3	11	2					6		10		1	5		8			20
	4	10	7[1]				9		3	11	2					6	12			1	5		8			21
	4	10	7[1]	12			9		3	11	2					6				1	5		8			22
	6		4			7	8	9	3	11	2									1	5		10			23
	6	8[2]	4[1]			7	12	9	3	11	2						13			1	5		10			24
	2		4			7	12	9	3	11						6	8[1]			1	5		10			25
	2	12	4			7	8[1]	9	3	11										1	5		10			26
		3	4			7[1]		9		11	2[2]						12	13		1	5		10	6	8	27
	2	3	12	4			8	9		11										1	5		10	6	7	28
	2		4			7[2]	12	9		11						5	13			1	3		10[1]	6	8	29
	2	3	4				8[1]	9		11							12			1	5		10	6	7	30
	2	3	4			7	12	9		11[1]										1	5		10	6	8	31
	2	3	11	4			8	9			12						13			1	5		10	6	7[2]	32
	2[1]	11	4			7	8[2]	9			12		3			5				1			10	6	13	33
		3	4			7[2]	8	9		11	2					5[1]	12			1			10	6	13	34
		11	5[1]	4			8	9	3		2						7			1			10	6	12	35
			5	4			8	9	3		12	2					7[1]			1			10	6	11	36
	4					7	8	6	3	11	2									1	5		9	10		37
	4					7		9	3	11	2									1	5		10	6	8	38

Coca-Cola Cup

Second Round	Hull C	(h)	2-0	
		(a)	1-0	
Third Round	Tottenham H	(h)	3-2	
Fourth Round	Wolverhampton W	(a)	1-2	

FA Cup

Third Round	Plymouth Arg	(a)	3-1
Fourth Round	Manchester C	(h)	2-2
		(a)	1-2

CREWE ALEXANDRA 1995-96 *Back row (left to right):* Anthony Hughes, Steve Macauley, Dave Ridings, Danny Collier, Simon Turpin, Francis Tierney, Mark Rivers, Justin Parker.
Middle row: John Fleet (Kit Man), Steve Holland (Youth Team Coach), Rob Edwards, Bill Barr, Lee Unsworth, Steven Pope, Mark Sayle, Mark Smith, Dele Adebola, Ashley Westwood, Shaun Smith, Dario Gradi (Manager), Neil Baker (Assistant Manager).
Front row: Phil Clarkson, Dale Hawtin, Martyn Booty, Neil Lennon, Robbie Savage, Gareth Whalley, Steve Garvey, Wayne Collins, Danny Murphy.
(Photograph: Steve Finch L.R.P.S.)

Division 2   **CREWE ALEXANDRA**

Football Ground, Gresty Rd, Crewe CW2 6EB. Telephone: (01270) 213014.

Ground capacity: 6000.

Record attendance: 20,000 v Tottenham H, FA Cup 4th rd, 30 January 1960.

Record receipts: £41,093 v Liverpool, FA Cup 3rd rd, 6 January 1992.

Pitch measurements: 112yd × 74yd.

President: N. Rowlinson.

Chairman: J. Bowler. *Vice-Chairman:* N. Hassall.

Directors: K. Potts, D. Rowlinson, R. Clayton, J. McMillan, E. Weetman, J. R. Holmes, D. Gradi.

Manager: Dario Gradi.

Secretary: Mrs Gill Palin. *Marketing Manager:* Alison Bowler.

Year Formed: 1877. *Turned Professional:* 1893. *Ltd Co.:* 1892.

Club Nickname: 'Railwaymen'.

Foundation: Crewe Alexandra played cricket before they decided to form a football club in 1877. They took the name "Alexandra" after Princess Alexandra. Crewe's first trophy was the Crewe and District Cup in 1887 and it is worth noting that they reached the semi-finals of the FA Cup the following year.

First Football League game: 3 September 1892, Division 2, v Burton Swifts (a) L 1-7 – Hickton; Moore, Cope; Linnell, Johnson, Osborne; Bennett, Pearson (1), Bailey, Barnett, Roberts.

Record League Victory: 8–0 v Rotherham U, Division 3 (N), 1 October 1932 – Foster; Pringle, Dawson; Ward, Keenor (1), Turner (1); Gillespie, Swindells (1), McConnell (2), Deacon (2), Weale (1).

Record Cup Victory: 7–1 v Gresley R, FA Cup 1st rd, 12 November 1994 – Smith M; Booty, Smith S (1), Wilson, Macauley, Whalley, Garvey (1), Collins, Ward (3), Lennon, Rowbotham (2).

Record Defeat: 2–13 v Tottenham H, FA Cup 4th rd replay, 3 February 1960.

Most League Points (2 for a win): 59, Division 4, 1962–63.

Most League Points (3 for a win): 83, Division 2, 1994–95.

Most League Goals: 95, Division 3 (N), 1931–32.

Highest League Scorer in Season: Terry Harkin, 35, Division 4, 1964–65.

Most League Goals in Total Aggregate: Bert Swindells, 126, 1928–37.

Most Capped Player: Bill Lewis, 12 (30), Wales.

Most League Appearances: Tommy Lowry, 436, 1966–78.

Record Transfer Fee Received: £600,000 from Liverpool for Rob Jones, October 1991.

Record Transfer Fee Paid: £80,000 to Barnsley for Darren Foreman, March 1990.

Football League Record: 1892 Original Member of Division 2; 1896 Failed re-election; 1921 Re-entered Division 3 (N); 1958–63 Division 4; 1963–64 Division 3; 1964–68 Division 4; 1968–69 Division 3; 1969–89 Division 4; 1989–91 Division 3; 1991–92 Division 4; 1992–94 Division 3; 1994– Division 2.

Honours: Football League: Division 2 best season: 3rd, 1994–95. *FA Cup:* best season: semi-final 1888. *Football League Cup:* best season: 3rd rd, 1975, 1976, 1979, 1993. *Welsh Cup:* Winners 1936, 1937.

Colours: Red shirts, white shorts, red stockings. *Change colours:* Navy shirts with gold trim, navy shorts, gold stockings.

Did you know?
Eight different players scored for Crewe Alexandra in the 8-0 Auto Windscreens Shield win over Hartlepool United on 17 October 1995, the first time in the club's history as many players had appeared on the scoresheet.

CREWE ALEXANDRA 1995–96 LEAGUE RECORD

Match No.	Date	Venue	Opponents	Result	H/T Score	Lg. Pos.	Goalscorers	Attendance
1	Aug 12	A	Wycombe W	D 1-1	1-0	—	Murphy	5281
2	26	A	York C	W 3-2	1-1	9	Savage, Adebola 2	3880
3	29	H	Walsall	W 1-0	0-0	—	Edwards	4377
4	Sept 2	A	Stockport Co	D 1-1	0-0	7	Tierney	6125
5	9	H	Shrewsbury T	W 3-0	1-0	3	Savage, Tierney, Westwood	3747
6	12	H	Brighton & HA	W 3-1	1-0	—	Murphy, Savage, Macauley	3272
7	16	A	Bournemouth	W 4-0	2-0	2	Whalley, Morris (og), Murphy, Savage (pen)	4488
8	23	A	Blackpool	L 1-2	1-0	3	Murphy	7301
9	30	H	Notts Co	D 2-2	0-0	4	Westwood, Macauley	4260
10	Oct 7	A	Chesterfield	W 2-1	0-0	3	Savage, Macauley	4901
11	14	H	Carlisle U	W 2-1	0-0	2	Savage (pen), Edwards	4512
12	21	A	Swindon T	L 1-2	0-0	3	Garvey	12,633
13	28	H	Brentford	W 3-1	2-0	2	Rivers 2, Westwood	3835
14	31	H	Hull C	W 1-0	1-0	—	Edwards	3609
15	Nov 4	A	Rotherham U	D 2-2	1-1	2	Savage, Macauley	3328
16	18	H	Swansea C	W 4-1	2-1	2	Edwards 2, Rivers, Murphy	3608
17	25	A	Oxford U	L 0-1	0-1	3		5287
18	Dec 5	H	Bristol C	W 4-2	0-1	—	Adebola, Booty, Lennon, Edwards	2977
19	9	H	Blackpool	L 1-2	0-1	3	Edwards	4551
20	16	A	Notts Co	W 1-0	1-0	2	Macauley	5869
21	23	A	Bristol R	W 2-1	0-0	1	Murphy, Rivers	4519
22	26	H	Wrexham	D 0-0	0-0	1		5177
23	Jan 13	A	Bristol C	L 2-3	1-2	2	Booty, Westwood	6790
24	20	H	Wycombe W	W 2-0	2-0	2	Rivers, Lennon	4150
25	31	A	Bradford C	L 1-2	0-0	—	Adebola	4095
26	Feb 10	A	Burnley	W 1-0	1-0	2	Edwards	9153
27	17	A	Brighton & HA	D 2-2	2-0	2	Edwards 2	6561
28	20	H	Stockport Co	L 0-1	0-0	—		4241
29	24	H	Bournemouth	W 2-0	0-0	3	Collins, Edwards	3535
30	27	A	Shrewsbury T	W 3-2	2-2	—	Murphy, Edwards, Rivers	3745
31	Mar 2	A	Wrexham	W 3-2	2-1	3	Edwards 3	6112
32	5	H	York C	D 1-1	0-1	—	Adebola	3431
33	9	H	Bristol R	L 1-2	0-0	3	Rivers	4091
34	12	A	Walsall	L 2-3	2-1	—	Blissett, Whalley	3171
35	16	A	Peterborough U	L 1-3	0-2	3	Smith (pen)	5004
36	19	H	Burnley	W 3-1	1-0	—	Garvey, Adebola, Rivers	3393
37	23	H	Bradford C	L 1-2	0-1	3	Adebola	3887
38	30	H	Chesterfield	W 3-0	2-0	3	Adebola, Murphy 2	4073
39	Apr 2	A	Carlisle U	L 0-1	0-0	—		4698
40	6	A	Brentford	L 1-2	1-0	3	Macauley	4408
41	8	H	Swindon T	L 0-2	0-1	4		5162
42	13	A	Hull C	W 2-1	0-0	3	McAllister, Murphy	3497
43	20	H	Rotherham U	L 0-2	0-1	5		3685
44	27	A	Oxford U	L 1-2	0-1	5	Macauley	4605
45	30	H	Peterborough U	W 2-1	2-0	—	Rivers, Little	3206
46	May 4	A	Swansea C	L 1-2	0-1	5	Rivers	2604

Final League Position: 5

GOALSCORERS

League (77): Edwards 15, Murphy 10, Rivers 10, Adebola 8, Macauley 7, Savage 7 (2 pens), Westwood 4, Booty 2, Garvey 2, Lennon 2, Tierney 2, Whalley 2, Blissett 1, Collins 1, Little 1, McAllister 1, Smith 1 (pen), own goal 1.
Coca-Cola Cup (9): Edwards 4, Adebola 1, Collins 1, Lennon 1, Unsworth 1, Whalley 1.
FA Cup (11): Rivers 3, Adebola 2, Edwards 2, Booty 1, Murphy 1, Unsworth 1, Westwood 1.

Gayle M 46	Booty M 21	Unsworth L 16+13	Westwood A 31+2	Macauley S 27+2	Whalley G 44	Tierney F 21+1	Collins W 37+5	Savage R 28+2	Lennon N 25	Murphy D 41+1	Adebola D 20+9	Edwards R 29+3	Garvey S 18+11	Clarkson P 1+4	Rivers M 24+9	Smith S 24+5	Ridings D 1	Collier D 2+4	Barr B 15+2	Little C 7+5	McAllister B 13	Blissett G 10	Lightfoot C 5+1	Ellison L —+1	Match No.
1	2	3²	4	5	6	7²	8	9¹	10	11	12	13	14												1
1	2	3	4	5	6	7	8	9²	10	12	11¹	13													2
1		3	4	5	6	7	8	9	10	2	11¹	12													3
1	3		4	5	6	7	8	9		2	12	11				10¹									4
1	3	12	4	5	6	7²	8¹	9	10	2	11		13												5
1	3	12	4	5	6	7	8¹	9	10	2	11²		13												6
1	3¹	12	4	5	6		8	9	10	2	11²	7	13												7
1	3		4	5	6		8	9	10	2	11	7													8
1	3		4	5	6		8	9	10	2	11	7													9
1	3	2¹	4	5	6		12	9	10	8	11	7													10
1	3	12	4	5	6		2	9	10	8	11¹	7													11
1	3		4	5	6		2	9	10	8	11	7													12
1	3		4	5	6		2	9	10	8	11				7										13
1	3	12	4	5	6		2		10	8	11				7²	13	9¹								14
1	3		4	5	6		2	9	10	8	11				7¹	12									15
1	3	10	4	5	6		2	9²		8	13	11	12		7¹										16
1	3	12	4	5			2	9	10	8	6	11²			7¹	13									17
1	3	12	4²	5			2	6¹	10	8	9	11			7	13									18
1	3	5¹	4		6		2		10	8	9	11			7	12									19
1	3²		4	5	6		2		10	8	9³	11	12		7¹	13		14							20
1			4	5	6		2		10	8	9¹	11	7²	12	13	3									21
1	10		4	5	6		2			8	9	11	12		7¹	3									22
1	3	12	4		6		2		10	8¹	9	11²	13		7				5						23
1	12		4		6		2		10	8	9	11¹	13		7²	3			5						24
1	8		4		6		2		10		9	11¹	12		7	3			5						25
1	12				6¹		8	2	10		9	11²	13		7	3			5		4				26
1	12		4		6		8²	2¹	10	9	11	13	14		7³	3			5						27
1			4		6		8¹	2	10	9	11	12			7	3			5						28
1			4		6		8	2	10	9	11				7¹	3			5	12					29
1	12		4		6		8¹	2	10³	9		11²	13	14	7	3			5						30
1	2	4¹			6		8				9²	11	7³		13	3		12	5	14					31
1	2		4		6		8	9¹	10	12	11				7²	3		13	5		4				32
1					6		8¹	2	12	10	9	7²			11	3			5	13	4				33
1					6		8¹	2	10	12		7				3	13		5		4²	9			34
1	4				6		8	2	10	12	11				7¹	3			5			9			35
1	2				6		8³		10	12	11	14			3			13	5²	7¹	4	9			36
1	2				6		8²			10²	11				7	13		3	5		4	9			37
1	2	12			6		8		13	10²	11				7	3				4		9¹	5		38
1	2				6		8	12	10	9³	11				7²	13		3			14	4	5¹		39
1	2		4		6		8¹	12	10		11²				7	13		3				5	9		40
1			4		6			2	8		11	10¹			7	3				12	5	9			41
1			4		6			2	8	10		12			11¹	3				13	7	5	9²		42
1			4		6			2	8	10	12				11	3				7¹	5	9²	13		43
1		12	13		6		7	8¹	9			11			3					7	5	10²	4		44
1		12	13	9	6		2	8²	10			11			3					7¹	5		4		45
1	3	2	9		6³		12		8	10		11			13				7¹	5²			4	14	46

Coca-Cola Cup

First Round	Darlington	(h)	4-0
		(a)	1-1
Second Round	Sheffield W	(h)	2-2
		(a)	2-5

FA Cup

First Round	Altrincham	(a)	2-0
Second Round	Mansfield T	(h)	2-0
Third Round	WBA	(h)	4-3
Fourth Round	Southampton	(a)	1-1
		(h)	2-3

CRYSTAL PALACE 1995-96 *Back row (left to right):* Danny Boxall, Bjorn Enqvist, Rory Ginty, Jason Harris, Robert Quinn, Paul Sparrow.
Third row: Richard Shaw, George Ndah, Brian Launders, Andy Roberts, Jimmy Glass, Damian Matthew, Marc Edworthy, Jamie Vincent.
Second row: Brian Sparrow, Peter McClean (Physio), Simon Rodger, Ian Cox, David Hopkin, Steve Taylor, Nigel Martyn, Rhys Wilmot, Bruce Dyer, Anthony Scully, Gareth Davies,
Vic Bettonelli (Kit Manager), Steve Kember (Reserve Team Manager).
Front row: Darren Patterson, Dean Gordon, Ray Houghton, Ray Lewington (First Team Coach), Steve Coppell (Technical Director), Peter Nicholas (First Team Coach), Iain Dowie, Darren Pitcher,
Chris Coleman.

Division 1   **CRYSTAL PALACE**

Selhurst Park, London SE25 6PU. Telephone: (0181) 768 6000. Fax: (0181) 771 5311. Lottery Office: (0181) 768 6094. Club Shop: (0181) 653 5584. Dial-A-Seat Ticketline: (0181) 771 8841. Palace Publications: (0181) 768 6093. Fax: (0181) 653 6312. Palace Clubline: 0891 400 333. Palace Ticket Line: 0891 400 334 (normal 0891 charges apply for these services).

Ground capacity: 26,400.

Record attendance: 51,482 v Burnley, Division 2, 11 May 1979.

Record receipts: £327,124 v Manchester U, FA Premier League, 21 April 1993 (League); £336,583 v Chelsea, Coca-Cola Cup 5th rd, 6 January 1993.

Pitch measurements: 110yd × 74yd.

Chairman: R. G. Noades.

Directors: R. G. Noades (Chairman and Managing), B. Coleman OBE, A. S. C. De Souza, M. E. Lee, S. Hume-Kendall, P. H. J. Norman, R. E. Anderson, V. E. Murphy, S. R. Ebbs MS, FRCS, D. A. Miller, P. L. Morley CBE, JP.

Manager: Dave Bassett. *First Team Coaches:* Ray Lewington, Peter Nicholas.

Physio: Peter McClean. *Stadium Manager:* Vic Worrall.

Company Secretary: Doug Miller. *Club Secretary:* Mike Hurst. *Assistant Secretary:* Terry Byfield.

Year Formed: 1905. *Turned Professional:* 1905. *Ltd Co.:* 1905.

Club Nickname: 'The Eagles'.

Club Sponsor: TDK.

Previous Grounds: 1905, Crystal Palace; 1915, Herne Hill; 1918, The Nest; 1924, Selhurst Park.

Foundation: There was a Crystal Palace club as early as 1861 but the present organisation was born in 1905 after the formation of a club by the company that controlled the Crystal Palace (building), had been rejected by the FA who did not like the idea of the Cup Final hosts running their own club. A separate company had to be formed and they had their home on the old Cup Final ground until 1915.

First Football League game: 28 August 1920, Division 3, v Merthyr T (a) L 1-2 – Alderson; Little, Rhodes; McCracken, Jones, Feebury; Bateman, Conner, Smith, Milligan (1), Whibley.

Record League Victory: 9–0 v Barrow, Division 4, 10 October 1959 – Rouse; Long, Noakes; Truett, Evans, McNichol; Gavin (1), Summersby (4 incl. 1p), Sexton, Byrne (2), Colfar (2).

Record Cup Victory: 8–0 v Southend U, Rumbelows League Cup 2nd rd (1st leg), 25 September 1990 – Martyn; Humphrey (Thompson (1)), Shaw, Pardew, Young, Thorn, McGoldrick, Thomas, Bright (3), Wright (3), Barber (Hodges (1)).

Record Defeat: 0–9 v Burnley, FA Cup 2nd rd replay, 10 February 1909 and 0–9 v Liverpool, Division 1, 12 September 1990.

Most League Points (2 for a win): 64, Division 4, 1960–61.

Most League Points (3 for a win): 90, Division 1, 1993–94.

Most League Goals: 110, Division 4, 1960–61.

Highest League Scorer in Season: Peter Simpson, 46, Division 3 (S), 1930–31.

Most League Goals in Total Aggregate: Peter Simpson, 153, 1930–36.

Most Capped Player: Eric Young, 19 (21), Wales.

Most League Appearances: Jim Cannon, 571, 1973–88.

Record Transfer Fee Received: £4,500,000 from Tottenham H for Chris Armstrong, June 1995.

Record Transfer Fee Paid: £2,250,000 to Millwall for Andy Roberts, July 1995.

Football League Record: 1920 Original Members of Division 3; 1921–25 Division 2; 1925–58 Division 3 (S); 1958–61 Division 4; 1961–64 Division 3; 1964–69 Division 2; 1969–73 Division 1; 1973–74 Division 2; 1974–77 Division 3; 1977–79 Division 2; 1979–81 Division 1; 1981–89 Division 2; 1989–92 Division 1; 1992–93 FA Premier League; 1993–94 Division 1; 1994–95 FA Premier League; 1995– Division 1.

Honours: Football League: Division 1 – Champions 1993–94; 3rd 1990–91; Division 2 – Champions 1978–79; Runners-up 1968–69; Division 3 – Runners-up 1963–64; Division 3 (S) – Champions 1920–21; Runners-up 1928–29, 1930–31, 1938–39; Division 4 – Runners-up 1960–61. *FA Cup:* best season: Runners-up 1990. *Football League Cup:* best season; semi-final 1993, 1995. *Zenith Data Systems Cup:* Winners: 1991.

Colours: Red and blue shirts, white shorts, white stockings. *Change colours:* White shirts, blue shorts, blue stockings.

Did you know?
Phil Hoadley was Crystal Palace's youngest ever Football League debutant when he came on as substitute on 27 April 1968 at the age of 16.

CRYSTAL PALACE 1995–96 LEAGUE RECORD

Match No.	Date	Venue	Opponents	Result		H/T Score	Lg. Pos.	Goalscorers	Attendance
1	Aug 12	H	Barnsley	W	4-3	2-1	—	Houghton, Dowie 2, Gordon (pen)	12,067
2	19	A	Ipswich T	L	0-1	0-1	11		12,681
3	26	H	Charlton Ath	D	1-1	0-1	9	Dyer	14,124
4	29	A	Sheffield U	W	3-2	0-0	—	Dyer 2, Gordon	10,378
5	Sept 9	A	Birmingham C	D	0-0	0-0	14		19,403
6	12	A	Watford	D	0-0	0-0	—		8780
7	16	H	Huddersfield T	D	0-0	0-0	15		15,645
8	23	A	Oldham Ath	L	1-3	1-0	17	Hopkin	6586
9	30	H	Stoke C	D	1-1	1-1	18	Freedman	14,613
10	Oct 7	H	Sunderland	L	0-1	0-0	20		13,754
11	15	A	Port Vale	W	2-1	0-0	18	Freedman, Gordon	6935
12	22	H	Millwall	L	1-2	1-2	20	Gordon	14,338
13	28	A	Leicester C	W	3-2	2-0	17	Dyer 2, Hopkin	18,376
14	Nov 4	H	Reading	L	0-2	0-2	19		16,058
15	11	A	Norwich C	L	0-1	0-1	20		14,156
16	19	A	Southend U	D	1-1	0-0	19	Lapper (og)	5089
17	22	H	Wolverhampton W	W	3-2	2-0	—	Freedman 3	12,571
18	25	H	Derby Co	D	0-0	0-0	17		13,506
19	Dec 3	A	Sunderland	L	0-1	0-1	18		12,777
20	9	H	Oldham Ath	D	2-2	2-0	18	Davies, Freedman	12,709
21	16	A	Stoke C	W	2-1	1-0	16	Freedman, Taylor	12,090
22	23	A	WBA	W	3-2	3-0	16	Gordon 3 (2 pens)	13,103
23	Jan 1	A	Portsmouth	W	3-2	2-0	15	Hopkin 2, Freedman	12,926
24	13	A	Ipswich T	D	1-1	1-0	15	Davies	14,097
25	20	A	Barnsley	D	1-1	1-0	15	Gordon	6620
26	Feb 4	A	Charlton Ath	D	0-0	0-0	16		13,560
27	10	H	Sheffield U	D	0-0	0-0	15		15,883
28	17	H	Watford	W	4-0	2-0	14	Freedman 2, Dyer 2	13,235
29	20	A	Tranmere R	W	3-2	0-2	—	Freedman, Boere, Houghton	5253
30	24	A	Huddersfield T	L	0-3	0-3	11		13,041
31	27	H	Birmingham C	W	3-2	1-1	—	Dyer 3	12,965
32	Mar 2	A	Luton T	D	0-0	0-0	9		8478
33	5	H	Grimsby T	W	5-0	5-0	—	Freedman 3, Hopkin, Houghton	11,548
34	9	H	WBA	W	1-0	1-0	5	Freedman	18,336
35	12	H	Tranmere R	W	2-1	1-1	—	Ndah, Hopkin	13,183
36	16	A	Grimsby T	W	2-0	1-0	3	Ndah, Tuttle	5059
37	19	H	Luton T	W	2-0	0-0	—	Dyer 2	13,609
38	23	H	Portsmouth	D	0-0	0-0	3		17,039
39	30	A	Millwall	W	4-1	0-0	3	Hopkin, Brown, Ndah 2	13,214
40	Apr 2	H	Port Vale	D	2-2	2-0	—	Freedman 2	14,180
41	6	A	Leicester C	L	0-1	0-1	3		17,331
42	8	A	Reading	W	2-0	1-0	3	Freedman, Houghton	12,576
43	13	H	Southend U	W	2-0	1-0	3	Freedman 2	15,672
44	20	A	Wolverhampton W	W	2-0	1-0	3	Hopkin, Dyer	24,350
45	28	A	Derby Co	L	1-2	1-1	3	Brown	17,041
46	May 5	H	Norwich C	L	0-1	0-1	3		19,354

Final League Position: 3

GOALSCORERS

League (67): Freedman 20, Dyer 13, Gordon 8 (3 pens), Hopkin 8, Houghton 4, Ndah 4, Brown 2, Davies 2, Dowie 2, Boere 1, Taylor 1, Tuttle 1, own goal 1.
Coca-Cola Cup (6): Hopkin 4, McKenzie 1, Vincent 1.
FA Cup (3): Cox 1, Dyer 1, Taylor 1.

Martyn N 46	Edworthy M 44	Gordon D 34	Hopkin D 41+1	Coleman C 17	Shaw R 15	Houghton R 41	Pitcher D 36	Dowie I 4	Dyer B 21+14	Ndah G 17+6	Cox I 11+3	Matthew D 4+4	Scully T —+2	Rodger S 14+10	Vincent J 19+6	Freedman D 37+2	Roberts A 36+2	Taylor G 18+2	Launders B —+2	McKenzie L 4+8	Sparrow P 1	Davies G 17+3	Boere J —+8	Cundy J 4	Andersen L 12+4	Gale T 2	Tuttle D 9+1	Veart C 5+7	Brown K 5+1	Boxall D 1	Quinn R 1	Match No.
1	2	3	4	5	6	7	8	9	10	11¹	12																					1
1	2	3	4¹	5	6	7	8	9	10	11²	12	13																				2
1	2	3	4	5	6	7	8¹	9	10	11²	12	13																				3
1	2	3	4	5	6	7	8²	9	10	11¹	12	13																				4
1	2		4	5	6	7	8		10		12	11²				13	3	9¹														5
1	2	11	4	5	6	7	8²	9	10		12					13	3¹	9														6
1	2	3	4	5	6		8		10¹		12	11²				13	7²	14	9													7
1	2	3	4	5¹	6	7	8		10¹	11²	12	13						9	14													8
1	2	11	4	5	6	7	8¹									3²	9	12	10	13												9
1	2¹	11	7	5	6		8				12					3²	9	4	10			13										10
1		3	7	5	6		8			11		12				2¹	9	4	10													11
1	2¹	3	7	5	6		8				12		13			11²	9	4	10													12
1	2	3	7	5	6		8	11	9¹								12	4	10													13
1	2¹	3	7	5	6		8	11	9								12	4	10													14
1	2		7	5	6			8	11¹							3	9	4	10	12												15
1	2	3	11	5¹			8	7	10²							9	4	12		13	6											16
1	2	3	6			8	7									11	9¹	4	10²			12			5		13					17
1	2¹	3	6			8	7									11	9¹	4	10			12			5							18
1	2	3	6			8	7									11¹	9¹	4	10			12			5		13					19
1	2	3	6¹	5			7		12								9	4	10²		11				8		13					20
1	2	3				8	7		12							6	9	4	10²	11¹					13		5					21
1	2	3	12			8	7									6	9	4	10²	11¹					13		5					22
1	2	3	6¹			8	7									11²	9	4	10		12	13			5							23
1	2	3	6			8	7		12							13	9¹	4	10³	14		11²			5							24
1	2	3				8	7	11	12							6	9	4	10¹			5										25
1	2	3				8	7		12							6	9	4	10	11¹		5										26
1	2	3				8	7	11	12							6	13	9¹	4	10¹		5										27
1	2	3	6¹			8	7		10	12						11²	13	9³	4						14		5					28
1	2	3	6			8	7		10¹	12						11²		9	4						13		14	5³				29
1	2	3	6			8			10²							11¹		9	4			13	12		7	5						30
1	2	3	6			8		11	10¹							12		9	4			5			7							31
1	2	3	6			8		11¹	10							7²	9	4	12			5			13							32
1	2	3	6			8¹	7			10²						12	9	4		13		5			11							33
1	2	3	6			8	7		12	10¹							9	4				5²			11		13					34
1	2	3	6			8	7²		12	10³						13	9¹	4							11			5	14			35
1	2	3	6				7			10						8	9¹	4							11			5	12			36
1	2		6			8	7		12	10						3	9¹	4							11²			5	13			37
1	2		6			8	7		12	10³						3	9¹	4				13			11²			5	14			38
1	2		6			8	7			10						3		4				5						9	11			39
1	2		6			8	7¹		13	10						12	9²	4				5						11	3			40
1	2		6			8	7		9	10³						12	3	4							11			5¹	13			41
1	2		6			8			12							7		9²	4			5			13			11	10¹	3		42
1	2		6			8			12							7		9	4			5²			13			11	10¹	3		43
1	2		6				8		12							7	3	9¹	4						5			11	12			44
1	2		6			8	7		10²	12						11	13	9³	4						5¹				14	3		45
1			6						9	10						7¹		3				5					4	11	12	2	8	46

Coca-Cola Cup

Second Round	Southend U	(a)	2-2
		(h)	2-0
Third Round	Middlesbrough	(h)	2-2
		(a)	0-2

FA Cup

Third Round	Port Vale	(h)	0-0
		(a)	3-4

DARLINGTON 1995–96   *Back row (left to right):* Bernard Lowery (Chairman), Michael Pugh, Robbie Painter, Simon Shaw, Andy Crosby, Sean Gregan, Steve Gaughan, Gavin Worboys, David Hodgson (Director of Coaching).
Front row: Anthony Carrs, Peter Kirkham, Paul Olsson, Nigel Carnell (Physio), Mike Pollitt, Robbie Blake, Gary Bannister (Player/Coach), Philip Brumwell, Matty Appleby, Paul Mattison.

Division 3   **DARLINGTON**

Feethams Ground, Darlington DL1 5JB. Telephone: (01325) 465097. Fax: (01325) 381377.

Ground capacity: 7046.

Record attendance: 21,023 v Bolton W, League Cup 3rd rd, 14 November 1960.

Record receipts: £32,300 v Rochdale, Division 4, 11 May 1991.

Pitch measurements: 110yd × 74yd.

President: A. Noble.

Chairman: S. Weeks. *Vice-Chairman:* G. Hodgson.

Director: S. Morgon.

Manager: Jim Platt. *Coach:* J. Hope.

Chief Executive: T. D. Hughes.

Secretary: S. Morgon.

Year Formed: 1883. *Turned Professional:* 1908. *Ltd Co.:* 1891.

Club Nickname: 'The Quakers'.

Foundation: A football club was formed in Darlington as early as 1861 but the present club began in 1883 and reached the final of the Durham Senior Cup in their first season, losing to Sunderland in a replay after complaining that they had suffered from intimidation in the first. The following season Darlington won this trophy and for many years were one of the leading amateur clubs in their area.

First Football League game: 27 August 1921, Division 3 (N), v Halifax T (h) W 2-0 – Ward; Greaves, Barbour; Dickson (1), Sutcliffe, Malcolm; Dolphin, Hooper (1), Edmunds, Wolstenholme, Winship.

Record League Victory: 9–2 v Lincoln C, Division 3 (N), 7 January 1928 – Archibald; Brooks, Mellen; Kelly, Waugh, McKinnell; Cochrane (1), Gregg (1), Ruddy (3), Lees (3), McGiffen (1).

Record Cup Victory: 7–2 v Evenwood T, FA Cup 1st rd, 17 November 1956 – Ward; Devlin, Henderson; Bell (1p), Greener, Furphy; Forster (1), Morton (3), Tulip (2), Davis, Moran.

Record Defeat: 0–10 v Doncaster R, Division 4, 25 January 1964.

Most League Points (2 for a win): 59, Division 4, 1965–66.

Most League Points (3 for a win): 85, Division 4, 1984–85.

Most League Goals: 108, Division 3 (N), 1929–30.

Highest League Scorer in Season: David Brown, 39, Division 3 (N), 1924–25.

Most League Goals in Total Aggregate: Alan Walsh, 90, 1978–84.

Most Capped Player: None.

Most League Appearances: Ron Greener, 442, 1955–68.

Record Transfer Fee Received: £200,000 from Leicester C for Jim Willis, December 1991.

Record Transfer Fee Paid: £95,000 to Motherwell for Nick Cusack, January 1992.

Football League Record: 1921 Original Member Division 3 (N); 1925–27 Division 2; 1927–58 Division 3 (N); 1958–66 Division 4; 1966–67 Division 3; 1967–85 Division 4; 1985–87 Division 3; 1987–89 Division 4; 1989–90 GM Vauxhall Conference; 1990–91 Division 4; 1991– Division 3.

Honours: Football League: Division 2 best season: 15th, 1925–26; Division 3 (N) – Champions 1924–25; Runners-up 1921–22; Division 4 – Champions 1990–91; Runners-up 1965–66. *FA Cup:* best season: 3rd rd, 1911, 5th rd, 1958. *Football League Cup:* best season: 5th rd, 1968. *GM Vauxhall Conference:* Champions 1989–90.

Colours: Black and white. *Change colours:* All red.

Did you know?
In 1968–69, Darlington were unbeaten in their opening 14 matches in Division Four. They finished fifth.

DARLINGTON 1995–96 LEAGUE RECORD

Match No.	Date	Venue	Opponents	Result	H/T Score	Lg. Pos.	Goalscorers	Attendance
1	Aug 12	A	Exeter C	W 1-0	1-0	—	Olsson	2934
2	19	H	Rochdale	L 0-1	0-0	14		2139
3	26	A	Leyton Orient	D 1-1	0-0	15	Crosby	4034
4	29	H	Fulham	D 1-1	0-1	—	Carss	1906
5	Sept 2	H	Cardiff C	L 0-1	0-1	17		1895
6	9	A	Hartlepool U	D 1-1	0-0	17	Carss	2705
7	12	A	Mansfield T	D 2-2	2-1	—	Bannister, Olsson	2190
8	16	H	Colchester U	D 2 2	0 2	18	Muir, Bannister	1686
9	23	H	Scarborough	L 1-2	0-1	21	Himsworth	2046
10	30	A	Barnet	D 1-1	1-0	22	Bannister	1923
11	Oct 7	A	Lincoln C	W 2-0	1-0	18	Appleby, Olsson	2564
12	14	H	Gillingham	W 1-0	1-0	13	Bannister	2043
13	21	A	Cambridge U	W 1-0	1-0	11	Painter	2730
14	28	H	Plymouth Arg	W 2-0	0-0	7	Himsworth, Naylor	2352
15	31	H	Wigan Ath	W 2-1	1-0	—	Shaw, Appleby	2076
16	Nov 4	A	Bury	D 0-0	0-0	7		2974
17	18	H	Scunthorpe U	D 0-0	0-0	8		2078
18	25	A	Chester C	L 1-4	0-1	8	Barnard	2652
19	Dec 9	A	Scarborough	W 2-1	0-1	6	Bannister, Worboys	1585
20	16	H	Barnet	D 1-1	1-0	9	Guinan	1717
21	23	A	Torquay U	W 1-0	1-0	5	Bannister	2045
22	Jan 6	H	Northampton T	L 1-2	0-2	8	Worboys	1943
23	13	A	Rochdale	W 2-1	0-1	7	Appleby (pen), Olsson	1945
24	16	H	Doncaster R	L 1-2	0-1	—	Painter	1502
25	20	H	Exeter C	W 1-0	0-0	6	Blake	1723
26	30	H	Preston NE	L 1-2	1-0	—	Himsworth	2599
27	Feb 3	H	Leyton Orient	W 2-0	0-0	4	Blake, McMahon	1880
28	10	A	Northampton T	D 1-1	1-1	4	Painter	4926
29	17	H	Mansfield T	D 1-1	0-0	4	Bannister	2598
30	20	A	Cardiff C	W 2-0	2-0	—	Barnard, Blake	2113
31	24	A	Colchester U	D 1-1	0-1	4	Blake	2653
32	27	H	Hartlepool U	W 1-0	0-0	—	Gaughan	4332
33	Mar 2	A	Doncaster R	W 2-1	1-1	3	Bannister, Blake	2209
34	5	A	Fulham	D 2-2	2-0	—	Blake 2	2534
35	9	H	Torquay U	L 1-2	0-2	4	Appleby	2861
36	16	A	Preston NE	D 1-1	1-1	5	Bannister	11,419
37	23	H	Hereford U	W 1-0	0-0	6	Painter	1708
38	30	H	Lincoln C	W 3-2	2-1	4	Gaughan 2, Blake	2146
39	Apr 2	A	Gillingham	D 0-0	0-0	—		6426
40	6	A	Plymouth Arg	W 1-0	1-0	5	Painter	8990
41	8	H	Cambridge U	D 0-0	0-0	4		3064
42	13	A	Wigan Ath	D 1-1	1-0	6	Appleby	4473
43	20	H	Bury	W 4-0	2-0	5	Carmichael, Blake, Painter 2	4325
44	23	A	Hereford U	W 1-0	1-0	—	Carmichael	5359
45	27	H	Chester C	W 3-1	0-0	3	Blake, Painter, Bannister	4510
46	May 4	A	Scunthorpe U	D 3-3	0-2	5	Appleby (pen), Blake, Barnard	4847

Final League Position: 5

GOALSCORERS

League (60): Blake 11, Bannister 10, Painter 8, Appleby 6 (2 pens), Olsson 4, Barnard 3, Gaughan 3, Himsworth 3, Carmichael 2, Carss 2, Worboys 2, Crosby 1, Guinan 1, McMahon 1, Muir 1, Naylor 1, Shaw 1.
Coca-Cola Cup (1): Carss 1.
FA Cup (6): Bannister 1, Brumwell 1, Gaughan 1, Olsson 1, Painter 1, Shaw 1.

Pollitt M 15	Appleby M 42+1	Shaw S 38+5	Gaughan S 34+7	Crosby A 45	Gregan S 38	Paulo P 4+2	Olsson P 34	Bannister G 39+2	Blake R 23+6	Carss A 13+15	Worboys G 6+8	Himsworth G 26+2	Brumwell P 16+12	Neves R 3+2	Barnard M 37	Muir I 4	Stephenson A 1	Painter R 33+2	Quitongo J 1	Naylor G 3+1	Burridge J 3	Robinson P —+4	Lucas D 6	Guinan S 3	McMahon S 6+4	Mattison P 1+6	Newell P 21	Carmichael M 11+2	Twynham G 2	Match No.
1	2	3	4	5	6	7^2	8	9^1	10	11^3	12	13	14																	1
1	2^3		4	5	6	7	8	9	10^2	11^1	12	3	14	13																2
1	2	3	4	5	6	7^2	8^3	9	13	12	11	14	10^1																	3
1		3^1	4	5	6	7^2	8^1	10	12	14	9	11		2	13															4
1	2^1	3^2	4	5	6	13	8	10				9	11	12	7															5
1	13		4	5	6		8	11	14	12				2^2	7	10^1	3^3	9												6
1	12	13	4	5	6		8	10	11^2			9		2^1	3			7												7
	2	13	4^3	5	6		8	10	12	11		9^1	14	3^2		1		7												8
1	2	12		5	6	13	8	10	11^1			14			7	4^3	3^2	9												9
	4	2	10	5	6		8	11^2			12	14	7^1	13	3			9^3												10
1	4	2	10	5	6		8	11				7			3			9												11
1	4	2	10	5	6		8	11				7			3			9												12
1	4	2	10^1	5	6		8	11				7			3			9	12											13
1	4	2	12	5	6		8	11				7			3			9^1	10											14
1	4	2		5	6		8	11^1			12	7			3			9	10											15
1	4	2		5	6		8	11			12	7			3			9^1	10											16
	4	2	10^2	5	6		8	11			12	7		13	3			9^1			1									17
	4	2	8^2	5	6		10^1	11			12	7			3			9			1	13								18
	4	2	12	5			8	11	10	13	14	7^2	6^1		3			9^3			1									19
	4	2	12	5			8	11				9^1	7	6	3			13					1		10^2					20
	4	2	12	5	6		8	11^1			13	7			3			9					1		10^2					21
	4	2	12	5	6^2		8	9^1	13	14		7			3			10					1		11^3					22
	4	2	11^1	5	6		8	10	10^2	7	12				3			9					1							23
	4	2		5	6		8^1	12				7^2	11		3			9					1		10			13		24
	4	2			6		8		11^1		7	5			3			9					1		10			12		25
	4	2	6	5			8^1	11	12			7			3			9							10		1			26
	4	2^1	11	5	6		8	10				7			3			9							12		1			27
	4	2	11	5	6		8	12				7			3			9							10^1		1			28
	4	2	8	5	6			7	10	11					3			9^1							12		1			29
	4	2^1	8	5			11	7	10			6			3			9								12	1			30
	4	2	8^2	5			11	7	10	12		6^1			3			9^3		13					14	1				31
	4	2	8	5			6	12	10	11					3			9							7^1	1				32
	4	2	8	5			11	7	10	12		6^2			3			9^1								1	13			33
	4	2	11	5	6		8	7	10^1	12					3			13								1	9^2			34
	4	2		5	6^2		8^3	7	10^1	11		12			3			14					13	1	9					35
	4	2	8	5	6			7	10	3					9^1									12		1	11			36
	4	2	8	5	6			7	10^1	3					9									12		1	11			37
	$4	2^1	8	5	6			7	10			12	3		9											1	11			38
	4		8	5	6			7	10^1	12		2	3		9											1	11			39
	4		8	5	6			12	10^1			2	3		9											1	11			40
	$4	2^2	8	5	6			7	10	12		13	3^1		9											1	14	11^3		41
	4		8	5	6			7		11		2	3		9			12								1	10^1			42
		12	8	5	6			7	10	11^2		2^1	3		9									13		1	4		43
	4	12	8	5	6			7^2	10	13		2^1	3		9											1	11			44
	4	2	8	5	6			7	10				3		9											1	11			45
	4	2	8	5	6			7	10	12			3		9											1	11^1			46

Coca-Cola Cup

First Round	Crewe Alex	(a)	0-4
		(h)	1-1

FA Cup

First Round	Hartlepool U	(a)	4-2
Second Round	Rochdale	(a)	2-2
		(h)	0-1

DERBY COUNTY 1995-96   *Back row (left to right):* Peter Melville (Physio), Lee Carsley, Jason Kavanagh, Darren Wassall, Gary Rowett, Dean Yates, Darryl Powell, Shane Nicholson, Andrew Tretton, Mark Stallard.

Third row: Steve McLaren (Assistant to Manager), Billy McEwan (Coach), Paul Trollope, Matt Warren, Ian Ashbee, Russell Hoult, Martin Taylor, Steve Sutton, Craig Smith, John Harkes, Sean Flynn, Eric Steele (Goalkeeping Coach), Gordon Guthrie (Assistant to Physio).

Second row: Steve Round, Wayne Sutton, Dean Sturridge, Paul Simpson, Marco Gabbiadini, Jim Smith (Manager), Robin van der Laan, Ron Willems, Chris Boden, Will Davies.

Front row: Nick Wright, Darren Wrack, Carl Cunningham, Matt Green, Steve Powell, Kevin Cooper.

(Photograph: Raymonds Press Agency)

FA Premiership   **DERBY COUNTY**

Baseball Ground, Shaftesbury Crescent, Derby DE23 8NB. Telephone: (01332) 340105. Fax: (01332) 360988.
Ticket Information: (01332) 203030. Clubcall: 0891 121187.

Ground capacity: 18,000 (all seated).

Record attendance: 41,826 v Tottenham H, Division 1, 20 September 1969.

Record receipts: £146,651 v Aston Villa, FA Cup 4th rd, 5 February 1992.

Pitch measurements: 110yd × 71yd.

Chairman: L. V. Pickering. *Vice-Chairman:* P. J. Gadsby.

Directors: J. N. Kirkland, A. S. Webb.

Manager: Jim Smith. *Chief Scout:* Bobby Roberts.

First Team Coach: Steve McClaren. *Physio:* Peter Melville. *Stadium Manager:* D. Hollands.

Secretary: Keith Pearson. *Chief Executive:* Keith Loring. *Commercial Manager:* Colin Tunnicliffe.

Year Formed: 1884. *Turned Professional:* 1884. *Ltd Co.:* 1896.

Club Nickname: 'The Rams'.

Previous Grounds: 1884–95, Racecourse Ground; 1895, Baseball Ground.

Foundation: Derby County was formed by members of the Derbyshire County Cricket Club in 1884, when football was booming in the area and the cricketers thought that a football club would help boost finances for the summer game. To begin with, they sported the cricket club's colours of amber, chocolate and pale blue, and went into the game at the top immediately entering the FA Cup.

First Football League game: 8 September 1888, Football League, v Bolton W (a) W 6-3 – Marshall; Latham, Ferguson, Williamson; Monks, W. Roulstone; Bakewell (2), Cooper (2), Higgins, H. Plackett, L. Plackett (2).

Record League Victory: 9–0 v Wolverhampton W, Division 1, 10 January 1891 – Bunyan; Archie Goodall, Roberts; Walker, Chalmers, Roulston (1); Bakewell, McLachlan, Johnny Goodall (1), Holmes (2), McMillan (5). 9–0 v Sheffield W, Division 1, 21 January 1899 – Fryer; Methven, Staley; Cox, Archie Goodall, May; Oakden (1), Bloomer (6), Boag, McDonald (1), Allen. (1 og).

Record Cup Victory: 12–0 v Finn Harps, UEFA Cup 1st rd 1st leg, 15 September 1976 – Moseley; Thomas, Nish, Rioch (1), McFarland, Todd (King), Macken, Gemmill, Hector (5), George (3), James (3).

Record Defeat: 2–11 v Everton, FA Cup 1st rd, 1889–90.

Most League Points (2 for a win): 63, Division 2, 1968–69 and Division 3 (N), 1955–56 and 1956–57.

Most League Points (3 for a win): 84, Division 3, 1985–86 and Division 3, 1986–87.

Most League Goals: 111, Division 3 (N), 1956–57.

Highest League Scorer in Season: Jack Bowers, 37, Division 1, 1930–31 and Ray Straw, 37 Division 3 (N), 1956–57.

Most League Goals in Total Aggregate: Steve Bloomer, 292, 1892–1906 and 1910–14.

Most Capped Player: Peter Shilton, 34 (125), England.

Most League Appearances: Kevin Hector, 486, 1966–78 and 1980–82.

Record Transfer Fee Received: £2,900,000 from Liverpool for Dean Saunders, July 1991.

Record Transfer Fee Paid: £2,500,000 to Notts Co for Craig Short, September 1992.

Football League Record: 1888 Founder Member of the Football League; 1907–12 Division 2; 1912–14 Division 1; 1914–15 Division 2; 1915–21 Division 1; 1921–26 Division 2; 1926–53 Division 1; 1953–55 Division 2; 1955–57 Division 3 (N); 1957–69 Division 2; 1969–80 Division 1; 1980–84 Division 2; 1984–86 Division 3; 1986–87 Division 2; 1987–91 Division 1; 1991–92 Division 2; 1992–96 Division 1; 1996– FA Premier League.

Honours: Football League: Division 1 – Champions 1971–72, 1974–75; Runners-up 1895–96, 1929–30, 1935–36, 1995–96; Division 2 – Champions 1911–12, 1914–15, 1968–69, 1986–87; Runners-up 1925–26; Division 3 (N) Champions 1956–57; Runners-up 1955–56. *FA Cup:* Winners 1946; Runners-up 1898, 1899, 1903. *Football League Cup:* Semi-final 1968. *Texaco Cup:* 1972. **European Competitions:** *European Cup:* 1972–73, 1975–76; *UEFA Cup:* 1974–75, 1976–77. *Anglo-Italian Cup:* Runners-up 1993.

Colours: White shirts, black shorts, white stockings. *Change colours:* Maroon shirts, white shorts, maroon and white stockings.

Did you know?
In the 1995–96 season Derby County established a club record of 17 matches without defeat which was subsequently extended to 20 games.

DERBY COUNTY 1995–96 LEAGUE RECORD

Match No.	Date	Venue	Opponents	Result	H/T Score	Lg. Pos.	Goalscorers	Attendance
1	Aug 13	H	Port Vale	D	0-0	0-0	—	10,869
2	19	A	Reading	L	2-3	0-1	20	Sturridge, Preece	9280
3	26	H	Grimsby T	D	1-1	0-0	21	Sturridge	10,564
4	30	A	Wolverhampton W	L	0-3	0-3	—		26,053
5	Sept 2	A	Luton T	W	2-1	1-1	16	Sturridge 2	6427
6	10	H	Leicester C	L	0-1	0-1	19		11,767
7	13	H	Southend U	W	1-0	1-0	—	Sturridge	9242
8	16	A	Portsmouth	D	2-2	1-1	17	Van Der Laan, Flynn	14,434
9	23	A	Barnsley	L	0-2	0-2	21		8929
10	Oct 1	H	Millwall	D	2-2	1-2	20	Willems, Van Der Laan	9590
11	7	A	Sheffield U	W	2-0	1-0	16	Gabbiadini, Willems	12,721
12	14	H	Ipswich T	D	1-1	1-1	17	Gabbiadini	13,034
13	22	A	Stoke C	D	1-1	0-0	17	Van Der Laan	9435
14	28	H	Oldham Ath	W	2-1	1-0	14	Van Der Laan, Simpson	11,545
15	Nov 4	A	Tranmere R	L	1-5	0-3	17	Stimac	8565
16	11	H	WBA	W	3-0	2-0	14	Gabbiadini 2, Sturridge (pen)	13,765
17	18	H	Charlton Ath	W	2-0	1-0	10	Willems, Gabbiadini	12,963
18	21	A	Birmingham C	W	4-1	2-1	—	Sturridge, Willems, Gabbiadini, Powell D	19,417
19	25	A	Crystal Palace	D	0-0	0-0	10		13,506
20	Dec 2	H	Sheffield U	W	4-2	1-1	8	Sturridge, Willems 2 (1 pen), Gabbiadini	13,841
21	9	H	Barnsley	W	4-1	1-0	2	Carsley, Gabbiadini, Sturridge, Willems (pen)	14,415
22	16	A	Millwall	W	1-0	1-0	2	Sturridge	7694
23	23	H	Sunderland	W	3-1	1-1	1	Gabbiadini, Willems (pen), Sturridge	16,882
24	26	A	Huddersfield T	W	1-0	0-0	1	Willems	18,495
25	Jan 1	H	Norwich C	W	2-1	1-0	1	Willems, Gabbiadini	16,714
26	13	H	Reading	W	3-0	0-0	1	Sturridge 2, Flynn	15,123
27	20	A	Port Vale	D	1-1	1-0	1	Sturridge	11,947
28	Feb 3	A	Grimsby T	D	1-1	0-1	1	Powell D	7818
29	10	H	Wolverhampton W	D	0-0	0-0	1		17,460
30	17	A	Southend U	W	2-1	0-1	1	Simpson, Willems	8331
31	21	H	Luton T	D	1-1	0-0	—	Powell D	14,825
32	24	H	Portsmouth	W	3-2	0-0	1	Yates, Sturridge, Gabbiadini	16,120
33	28	A	Leicester C	D	0-0	0-0	1		20,911
34	Mar 2	H	Huddersfield T	W	3-2	2-1	1	Simpson 2, Van Der Laan	17,097
35	5	A	Watford	D	0-0	0-0	—		8306
36	9	A	Sunderland	L	0-3	0-2	1		21,644
37	16	H	Watford	D	1-1	0-1	2	Simpson (pen)	15,939
38	23	A	Norwich C	L	0-1	0-0	2		15,341
39	30	H	Stoke C	W	3-1	0-1	2	Sturridge 2, Powell D	17,245
40	Apr 2	A	Ipswich T	L	0-1	0-1	—		16,210
41	6	A	Oldham Ath	W	1-0	0-0	2	Simpson (pen)	8119
42	8	H	Tranmere R	W	6-2	1-1	2	Powell D, Yates, Simpson 3, Sturridge	16,723
43	14	A	Charlton Ath	D	0-0	0-0	2		11,334
44	20	H	Birmingham C	D	1-1	0-0	2	Simpson	16,757
45	28	H	Crystal Palace	W	2-1	1-1	2	Sturridge, Van Der Laan	17,041
46	May 5	A	WBA	L	2-3	1-2	2	Sturridge, Ward	23,858

Final League Position: 2

GOALSCORERS

League (71): Sturridge 20 (1 pen), Gabbiadini 11, Willems 11 (3 pens), Simpson 10 (2 pens), Van der Laan 6, Powell D 5, Flynn 2, Yates 2, Carsley 1, Preece 1, Stimac 1, Ward 1.
Coca-Cola Cup (4): Gabbiadini 1, Simpson 1, Stallard 1, Willems 1.
FA Cup (2): Gabbiadini 1, Simpson 1.

Sutton S 6	Flynn S 29+13	Wassall D 16+1	Rowett G 34+1	Powell D 37	Harkes J 7+1	Van der Laan R 39	Trollope P 7+10	Stallard M 3	Gabbiadini M 33+6	Simpson P 21+18	Preece D 10+3	Sturridge D 33+6	Willems R 31+2	Kavanagh J 8+1	Nicholson S 19+1	Webster S 3	Carsley L 31+4	Hoult R 40+1	Yates D 38	Wrack D 2+8	Stimac I 27	Boden C 4	Powell C 19	Hodges G 1+8	Carbon M 2+4	Ward A 5+2	Sutton W 1	Cooper K —+1	Match No.
	12	4^1	2	7		8				10		9^2	13		3		11		5		6		3						1
	12	4	2	7		8^3			14	10		9^2	13		3		11^1		5		6		3						2
	12	4	2	7		8				10		9	13		3^2		11^1		5		6								3
	12	4	2	7		8				10		9^1			3		11		5		6								4
	12	4	2	7		8				10		9^1	13		3		11	1	5		6^2								5
	12	4^3	2	7		8			14	10		9	13		3		11^1	1	5^2		6								6
	12	4	2	7		8				10^1		9			3		11	1	5		6								7
	12	4	2	7		8^3			14	10^2		9	13		3		11^1	1	5		6								8
	12	4	2	7		8^1				10		9			3		11	1	5		6								9
	12	4	2	7		8				10		9	13		3		11^2	1	5		6^1								10
	12	4	2	7		8				10^1		9^2	13		3		11	1	5		6								11
	12	4	2	7		8^2				10		9	13		3		11^1	1	5		6								12
	12	4^2	2	7		8^1				10		9	13		3		11	1	5		6								13
	12	4	2	7		8				10^1		9			3		11	1	5		6								14
	12	4	2	7		8^1				10		9			3		11	1	5		6								15
	12	4	2	7		8				10^1		9					11	1	5		6		3						16
	12	4	2	7		8				10^1		9					11	1	5		6		3						17
	12	4^1	2	7^2		8				10		9	13				11	1	5		6		3						18
	12	4	2	7		8				10		9					11	1	5		6		3^1						19
	12	4	2	7		8				10^1		9	13		3^2		11	1	5		6								20
	12	4^1	2	7		8			14	10^2		9^3	13		3		11	1	5		6								21
	12	4	2	7		8				10^1		9			3		11	1	5		6								22
	12	4	2	7		8				10		9^1			3		11	1	5		6								23
	12	4	2	7^1		8			14	10^3		9	13		3^2		11	1	5		6								24
	12	4	2	7^2		8			14	10^3		9	13		3		11^1	1	5		6								25
		4	2	7		8				10		9			3		11	1	5		6								26
	12	4	2	7		8				10^1		9			3		11	1	5		6								27
	12	4	2	7		8				10^1		9					11	1	5		6		3						28
		4	2	7		8				10		9					11	1	5		6		3						29
	12	4	2	7		8				10		9	13				11^1	1	5		6		3^2						30
	12	4	2	7^1		8			14	10^3		9	13				11^2	1	5		6		3						31
	12	4	2	7^2		8				10		9	13				11	1	5		6		3^1						32
	12	4	2	7		8				10^1		9^2	13				11	1	5		6		3						33
	12	4	2	7^2		8			14	10^3		9^1	13				11	1	5		6		3						34
	12	4	2	7^1		8				10		9^2	13				11	1	5		6		3						35
	12	4	2	7^1		8			14	10		9^2	13				11	1	5^3		6		3						36
	12	4^1	2^2	7		8				10		9	13				11	1	5		6		3						37
	12	4^2	2	7		8			14	10^3		9	13				11	1	5		6		3^1						38
	12	4	2	7		8^1				10		9	13				11	1	5		6^2		3						39
	12	4^1	2	7		8			14	10		9^2	13				11	1	5		6		3^3						40
	12	4^2	2	7		8^1				10		9	13				11	1	5		6		3						41
	12	4	2	7^1		8			14	10		9	13				11	1	5		6^3		3^2						42
	12	4^1	2	7		8			14	10^3		9	13				11^2	1	5		6		3						43
	12	4	2	7^2		8			14	10^1		9	13				11^3	1	5		6		3						44
	12	4	2	7		8				10^1		9^2	13				11	1	5		6		3						45
	12	4	2	7^1		8				10		9	13				11	1	5		6		3^2						46

Coca-Cola Cup

Second Round	Shrewsbury T	(a)	3-1
		(h)	1-1
Third Round	Leeds U	(h)	0-1

FA Cup

Third Round	Leeds U	(h)	2-4

DONCASTER ROVERS 1995–96 *Back row (left to right):* Jason Knight, Kevin Noteman, Mark Proctor, Paul Marquis, Micky Norbury, Perry Suckling, Graeme Jones, Lee Warren, Darren Moore, Hakan Hayrettin.
Middle row: Jon Schofield, Ian Measham, Mark McCluskie, Warren Hackett, Lee Saunders, Sean Parrish, Paul Haywood, Ryan Kirby.
Front row: Scott Maxfield, James Meara, Steve Gallen, Ian Clark, Russ Wilcox, Scott Colcombe, Duane Darby, Steve Harper, Gary Brabin.

Division 3 DONCASTER ROVERS

Belle Vue Ground, Doncaster DN4 5HT. Telephone: (01302) 539441. Fax: (01302) 539679. Commercial: (01302) 535093.

Ground capacity: 8608.

Record attendance: 37,149 v Hull C, Division 3 (N), 2 October 1948.

Record receipts: £22,000 v QPR, FA Cup 3rd rd, 5 January 1985.

Pitch measurements: 110yd × 76yd.

Vice-Chairman: K. Haran. *Directors:* C. Dunn, L. Mabbett, J. Richardson, D. Hicken (Managing), R. Ashworth.

Manager: Sammy Chung. *Assistant Manager:* Steve Beaglehole. *Coaches:* Jimmy Neighbour/George Foster.

Secretary: Mrs K. J. Oldale. *Physio:* Phil McLoughlin. *Youth Team Coach:* Jim Golze.

Commercial Executive: Terry Burdass. *Stadium Manager:* Peter White.

Year Formed: 1879. *Turned Professional:* 1885. *Ltd Co.:* 1905 and 1920.

Club Nickname: 'Rovers'.

Previous Grounds: 1880–1916, Intake Ground; 1920–22, Benetthorpe Ground; 1922, Low Pasture, Belle Vue.

Foundation: In 1879 Mr. Albert Jenkins got together a team to play a game against the Yorkshire Institution for the Deaf. The players stuck together as Doncaster Rovers joining the Midland Alliance in 1889 and the Midland Counties League in 1891.

First Football League game: 7 September 1901, Division 2, v Burslem Port Vale (h) D 3-3 – Eggett; Simpson, Layton; Longden, Jones, Wright; Langham, Murphy, Price, Goodson (2), Bailey (1).

Record League Victory: 10–0 v Darlington, Division 4, 25 January 1964 – Potter; Raine, Meadows; Windross (1), White, Ripley (2); Robinson, Book (2), Hale (4), Jeffrey, Broadbent (1).

Record Cup Victory: 7–0 v Blyth Spartans, FA Cup 1st rd, 27 November 1937 – Imrie; Shaw, Rodgers; McFarlane, Bycroft, Cyril Smith; Burton (1), Kilourhy (4), Morgan (2), Malam, Dutton.

Record Defeat: 0–12 v Small Heath, Division 2, 11 April 1903.

Most League Points (2 for a win): 72, Division 3 (N), 1946–47.

Most League Points (3 for a win): 85, Division 4, 1983–84.

Most League Goals: 123, Division 3 (N), 1946–47.

Highest League Scorer in Season: Clarrie Jordan, 42, Division 3 (N), 1946–47.

Most League Goals in Total Aggregate: Tom Keetley, 180, 1923–29.

Most Capped Player: Len Graham, 14, Northern Ireland.

Most League Appearances: Fred Emery, 417, 1925–36.

Record Transfer Fee Received: £250,000 from QPR for Rufus Brevett, February 1991.

Record Transfer Fee Paid: £62,500 to Torquay U for Darren Moore, July 1995.

Football League Record: 1901 Elected to Division 2; 1903 Failed re-election; 1904 Re-elected; 1905 Failed re-election; 1923 Re-elected to Division 3 (N); 1935–37 Division 2; 1937–47 Division 3 (N); 1947–48 Division 2; 1948–50 Division 3 (N); 1950–58 Division 2; 1958–59 Division 3; 1959–66 Division 4; 1966–67 Division 3; 1967–69 Division 4; 1969–71 Division 3; 1971–81 Division 4; 1981–83 Division 3; 1983–84 Division 4; 1984–88 Division 3; 1988–92 Division 4; 1992– Division 3.

Honours: Football League: Division 2 best season: 7th, 1901–02; Division 3 (N) Champions 1934–35, 1946–47, 1949–50; Runners-up 1937–38, 1938–39; Division 4 – Champions 1965–66, 1968–69; Runners-up 1983–84. Promoted 1980–81 (3rd). *FA Cup:* best season: 5th rd, 1952, 1954, 1955, 1956. *Football League Cup:* best season: 5th rd, 1976.

Colours: All red. *Change colours:* All blue.

Did you know?
During 1923–24, Doncaster Rovers' first season in Division Three (North), their average attendance was 7285.

Doncaster Rovers Football Club Ltd.
(Founded 1879)

DONCASTER ROVERS 1995–96 LEAGUE RECORD

Match No.	Date	Venue	Opponents	Result	H/T Score	Lg. Pos.	Goalscorers	Atten- dance
1	Aug 12	H	Scarborough	W 1-0	0-0	—	Parrish	2523
2	19	A	Torquay U	W 2-1	0-0	3	Noteman, Jones	2086
3	26	H	Cardiff C	D 0-0	0-0	7		2186
4	29	A	Mansfield T	D 0-0	0-0	—		2944
5	Sept 2	H	Hartlepool U	W 1-0	0-0	2	Brodie	2304
6	9	A	Fulham	L 1-3	1-2	5	Brabin	2879
7	12	A	Plymouth Arg	L 1-3	1-2	—	Hill (og)	4858
8	16	H	Northampton T	W 1-0	1-0	5	Brabin	2353
9	23	H	Rochdale	L 0-3	0-1	8		2217
10	30	A	Leyton Orient	L 1-3	0-2	11	Darby	5524
11	Oct 7	A	Chester C	W 3-0	0-0	9	Maxfield, Darby, Carmichael	2374
12	14	H	Hereford U	D 0-0	0-0	10		1961
13	21	A	Gillingham	L 0-4	0-1	12		6307
14	28	H	Preston NE	D 2-2	1-1	11	Darby, Jones	4413
15	30	H	Cambridge U	W 2-1	1-1	—	Parrish, Darby	1657
16	Nov 4	A	Barnet	D 1-1	0-1	8	Moore	1913
17	18	H	Colchester U	W 3-2	2-1	7	Colcombe, Jones 2	1603
18	25	A	Wigan Ath	L 0-2	0-2	9		2879
19	Dec 2	H	Exeter C	W 2-0	1-0	6	Brabin, Jones	1429
20	9	A	Rochdale	L 0-1	0-1	7		2168
21	16	H	Leyton Orient	W 4-1	2-1	6	Colcombe, Jones 3 (1 pen)	1633
22	Jan 6	A	Bury	L 1-4	1-1	11	Carmichael	2606
23	13	H	Torquay U	W 1-0	0-0	8	Carmichael	1807
24	16	A	Darlington	W 2-1	1-0	—	Parrish, Carmichael	1502
25	20	A	Scarborough	W 2-0	0-0	4	Cramb 2	1661
26	Feb 3	A	Cardiff C	L 2-3	0-1	7	Jones, Colcombe	2313
27	5	H	Lincoln C	D 1-1	1-0	—	Parrish	2083
28	10	H	Bury	L 0-1	0-1	7		2418
29	17	H	Plymouth Arg	D 0-0	0-0	7		2338
30	20	A	Hartlepool U	W 1-0	0-0	—	Cramb (pen)	1367
31	24	A	Northampton T	D 3-3	1-2	7	Schofield (pen), Cramb 2	4738
32	26	H	Fulham	L 0-2	0-2	—		2331
33	Mar 2	H	Darlington	L 1-2	1-1	9	Moore	2209
34	9	A	Exeter C	L 0-1	0-1	10		3175
35	16	H	Scunthorpe U	W 2-0	0-0	9	Marquis, Parrish	1920
36	23	A	Lincoln C	L 0-4	0-4	11		3240
37	25	H	Mansfield T	D 0-0	0-0	—		1657
38	30	H	Chester C	L 1-2	1-0	12	Williams P	1548
39	Apr 2	A	Hereford U	L 0-1	0-1	—		2060
40	6	A	Preston NE	L 0-1	0-0	14		12,773
41	8	H	Gillingham	L 0-1	0-1	14		1783
42	13	A	Cambridge U	D 2-2	0-0	15	Jones, Schofield	2451
43	20	H	Barnet	W 1-0	0-0	15	Clark	1579
44	23	A	Scunthorpe U	D 2-2	1-1	—	Cramb 2	2614
45	27	H	Wigan Ath	W 2-1	1-1	13	Schofield 2 (1 pen)	2122
46	May 4	A	Colchester U	L 0-1	0-1	13		5038

Final League Position: 13

GOALSCORERS
League (49): Jones 10 (1 pen), Cramb 7 (1 pen), Parrish 5, Carmichael 4, Darby 4, Schofield 4 (2 pens), Brabin 3, Colcombe 3, Moore 2, Brodie 1, Clark 1, Marquis 1, Maxfield 1, Noteman 1, Williams PA 1, own goal 1.
Coca-Cola Cup (1): Wilcox 1.
FA Cup (2): Carmichael 1, Jones 1 (pen).

Suckling P 21	Kirby R 32 + 4	Hackett W 7	Moore D 35	Wilcox R 4	Parrish S 39 + 2	Schofield J 40 + 1	Noteman K 4	Jones G 31 + 1	Darby D 8 + 9	Clark I 14 + 9	Warren L 40 + 2	Measham 17 + 3	Harper S — + 1	Carmichael M 19 + 8	Colcombe S 21 + 9	Maxfield S 12 + 7	Brabin G 31	Norbury M 2 + 3	Brodie S 5	Knight J 1 + 3	Murphy J 17 + 6	Williams D 17	Barker R 5 + 1	Robertson P 12 + 4	Cramb C 20 + 1	Marquis P 15	O'Connor G 8	Doling S — + 1	Smith M 12 + 1	Peel N 2	Meara J — + 1	Wright J 13	Gore 15	Ashley K 3	Williams P 2 + 1	Utley D 1	Speight M 1	Match No.
1	2²	3	4	5	6	7	8	9	10	11¹	12	13																										1
1	3¹	4	5	6	7	8²	9	10		11	2	12		13																								2
1	12		4		6	7	8	10	9	11		2¹		5	3																							3
1	2		4			7	8		10²	12	11			5	3	6¹	9	13																				4
1	2		4		3	7		6¹			11			5	12		8	10	9																			5
1	2³		4		3	7		9		6¹	11			5	13		8	12	10²	14																		6
1	2²		4	5	3	7		9			11			6¹	12		8	10	13																			7
1	12	3	4	5	6	7¹		9		11	13	2					8	10²																				8
1	3		4		6	7			10¹	12	11	13		5	2³		8²			14	9																	9
	2	3	4	12		7				9²	11	13		5			8				6		1	10¹														10
1	2	3	4		6	7		9¹		12	11			5	13		8	10²																				11
1	2	3	4		6²	7		9¹		12	11			5	10		8							13														12
1			4		3	7		9		12	11¹	2		5	6		8						13	10²														13
1			4		3	7		9		12	2			5	6¹		8							11	10													14
1	5		4		3	7		9	6	12	11²	2		13			8							10¹														15
1	5		4³		3	7		9¹	6	12	2										14			10²	11													16
1	2							9		12	7²	10	13	5	4	3¹	8				6			11														17
	2			12		7		9	13	10				5	4²	3¹	8				6		1	11														18
	12		4			7²		9		10	2			5	13	3	8				6		1	11¹														19
	2	3	4			7		9		10¹				5	12		8				6		1	11														20
	2	3	4			7		9						5			8				6		1	11	10													21
	2					7		9¹			11		4	12	13	14	8				6³		1	3	10²	5												22
	2		4			7					11			12	9	5	8				6¹		1	3	10													23
	2					7				11	12		6	4	9²	5¹	8			13				3	10													24
	2					7				11			6	4	9	5¹	8				12		1	3	10													25
	2					7		9		11			6	4			8				12			3	10¹	5	1											26
	2		4			7				11	3	6		12	5		8								10		1											27
	2		4			7		9		11	3	6²		12	5		8			13					10¹		1											28
1	10	3	4			7		9				6		5			8				2¹											12	11					29
1	9	3	4			7						6		2	5														10				11					30
1	5	3²	4			7						6		2	13		8									12							11¹	9				31
1	5	3	4			7						6		2			8									12						10	11¹	9²	13			32
1	5²	3	4			7		9				6		12	2¹		8							13	14	10³							11					33
	2	3	4			7		9	5¹			6		12			8						1		6				10				11					34
		3	4			7		9	12						8¹	5							1		6				10				11		2¹			35
		3	4			7		9	12			2¹			8	5							1		6				10				11					36
		3	4			7		9	12	5					8								1		6							10¹	11	2				37
		3	4			12		9							8								1	13	6				7				11	5	2¹	10²		38
	12		4²			3		7					8		13								1		11²	6							9	5	2¹	10		39
		4²				3		7	9³				8		13		12					1		6			11					10	5	2¹	14			40
	2					3		7	9				12		8						4	1			6				11			10¹	5					41
						3		7	9				8								4			6	1				11	10						2	5¹	42
	2					3		7	9				8								4		10		6	1			11¹				5					43
	2					3		7		12			8		9						4	13	10¹		6	1			11²				5					44
	2					3		7		12			8		9						4	13	10		6	1			11¹				5²					45
	2	5				11	7	12					8		9						4		3²	10	6¹	1			13									46

Coca-Cola Cup
First Round   Shrewsbury T   (h) 1-1 / (a) 0-0

FA Cup
First Round   Mansfield T   (a) 2-4

EVERTON 1995-96 *Back row (left to right)*: Graham Stuart, John Ebbrell, Paul Holmes, Jason Kearton, Craig Short, Neville Southall, Joe Parkinson, Paul Rideout, Andy Hinchcliffe.
Middle row: Jim Martin (Kit Manager), Jim Gabriel (Reserve Team Coach), Matthew Jackson, Vinny Samways, Neil Moore, Tony Grant, Earl Barrett, Andrei Kanchelskis, Willie Donachie (First Team Coach), Les Helm (Physio).
Front row: David Unsworth, Stuart Barlow, Gary Ablett, Barry Horne, Joe Royle (Manager), Dave Watson, Duncan Ferguson, Daniel Amokachi, Anders Limpar.

FA Premiership **EVERTON**

Goodison Park, Liverpool L4 4EL. Telephone: (0151) 330 2200. Fax: (0151) 286 9112. Ticket Infoline: 0891 121599. Clubcall 0891 121199. Dial-A-Seat Service: (0151) 471 8000.

Ground capacity: 40,200.

Record attendance: 78,299 v Liverpool, Division 1, 18 September 1948.

Record receipts: £450,000 v Liverpool, FA Premier League, 16 April 1996.

Pitch measurements: 112yd × 78yd.

Chairman: Peter R. Johnson.

Directors: Sir Desmond Pitcher, Clifford Finch, Richard Hughes, Sir Philip Carter CBE, Dr. David M. Marsh, Keith Tamlin, Bill Kenwright, Arthur Abercromby, Lord Grantchester.

Manager: Joe Royle. ***First Team Coach:*** Willie Donachie.

Physio: Les Helm.

Secretary: Michael J. Dunford.

Commercial Manager: Andrew Watson. ***Sales Promotion Manager:*** Colum Whelan.

Stadium Manager: A. Bowen.

Year Formed: 1878. ***Turned Professional:*** 1885. ***Ltd Co.:*** 1892.

Previous Name: St Domingo FC, 1878–79.

Club Nickname: 'The Toffees'.

Previous Grounds: 1878, Stanley Park; 1882, Priory Road; 1884, Anfield Road; 1892, Goodison Park.

Foundation: St. Domingo Church Sunday School formed a football club in 1878 which played at Stanley Park. Enthusiasm was so great that in November 1879 they decided to expand membership and changed the name to Everton playing in black shirts with a white sash and nicknamed the "Black Watch". After wearing several other colours, royal blue was adopted in 1901.

First Football League game: 8 September 1888, Football League, v Accrington (h) W 2-1 – Smalley; Dick, Ross; Holt, Jones, Dobson; Fleming (2), Waugh, Lewis, E. Chadwick, Farmer.

Record League Victory: 9–1 v Manchester C, Division 1, 3 September 1906 – Scott; Balmer, Crelley; Booth, Taylor (1), Abbott (1); Sharp, Bolton (1), Young (4), Settle (2), George Wilson. 9–1 v Plymouth Arg, Division 2, 27 December 1930 – Coggins; Williams, Cresswell; McPherson, Griffiths, Thomson; Critchley, Dunn, Dean (4), Johnson (1), Stein (4).

Record Cup Victory: 11–2 v Derby Co, FA Cup 1st rd, 18 January 1890 – Smalley; Hannah, Doyle (1); Kirkwood, Holt (1), Parry; Latta, Brady (3), Geary (3), Chadwick, Millward (3).

Record Defeat: 4–10 v Tottenham H, Division 1, 11 October 1958.

Most League Points (2 for a win): 66, Division 1, 1969–70.

Most League Points (3 for a win): 90, Division 1, 1984–85.

Most League Goals: 121, Division 2, 1930–31.

Highest League Scorer in Season: William Ralph 'Dixie' Dean, 60, Division 1, 1927–28 (All-time League record).

Most League Goals in Total Aggregate: William Ralph 'Dixie' Dean, 349, 1925–37.

Most Capped Player: Neville Southall, 86, Wales.

Most League Appearances: Neville Southall, 532, 1981–96.

Record Transfer Fee Received: £2,750,000 from Barcelona for Gary Lineker, July 1986.

Record Transfer Fee Paid: £5,500,000 to Manchester U for Andrei Kanchelskis, August 1995.

Football League Record: 1888 Founder Member of the Football League; 1930–31 Division 2; 1931–51 Division 1; 1951–54 Division 2; 1954–92 Division 1; 1992– FA Premier League.

Honours: *Football League:* Division 1 – Champions 1890–91, 1914–15, 1927–28, 1931–32, 1938–39, 1962–63, 1969–70, 1984–85, 1986–87; Runners-up 1889–90, 1894–95, 1901–02, 1904–05, 1908–09, 1911–12, 1985–86; Division 2 – Champions 1930–31; Runners-up 1953–54. *FA Cup:* Winners 1906, 1933, 1966, 1984, 1995; Runners-up 1893, 1897, 1907, 1968, 1985, 1986, 1989. *Football League Cup:* Runners-up 1977, 1984. *League Super Cup:* Runners-up 1986. *Simod Cup:* Runners-up 1989. *Zenith Data Systems Cup:* Runner-up 1991. **European Competitions:** *European Cup:* 1963–64, 1970–71. *European Cup-Winners' Cup:* 1966–67, 1984–85 (winners), 1995–96. *European Fairs Cup:* 1962–63, 1964–65, 1965–66. *UEFA Cup:* 1975–76, 1978–79, 1979–80.

Colours: Royal blue shirts with white and black trim, white shorts with blue and black trim, blue stockings with black rings. ***Change colours:*** Amber shirts with black stripes, black shorts, amber stockings.

Did you know?
Everton were the first club to win the Second Division, First Division and FA Cup in successive seasons from 1931 to 1933.

EVERTON 1995–96 LEAGUE RECORD

Match No.	Date	Venue	Opponents	Result	H/T Score	Lg. Pos.	Goalscorers	Attendance
1	Aug 19	A	Chelsea	D	0-0	0-0	1		30,189
2	23	H	Arsenal	L	0-2	0-0	—		36,047
3	26	H	Southampton	W	2-0	2-0	10	Limpar, Amokachi	33,676
4	30	A	Manchester C	W	2-0	0-0	—	Parkinson, Amokachi	28,432
5	Sept 9	H	Manchester U	L	2-3	1-1	10	Limpar, Rideout	39,496
6	17	A	Nottingham F	L	2-3	0-2	12	Rideout 2	24,786
7	23	A	West Ham U	L	1-2	1-2	14	Samways	21,085
8	Oct 1	H	Newcastle U	L	1-3	0-1	15	Limpar	33,026
9	14	A	Bolton W	D	1-1	0-1	14	Rideout	20,427
10	22	H	Tottenham H	D	1-1	1-1	15	Stuart	33,629
11	28	A	Aston Villa	L	0-1	0-0	16		32,792
12	Nov 5	H	Blackburn R	W	1-0	1-0	13	Stuart	30,097
13	18	A	Liverpool	W	2-1	0-0	13	Kanchelskis 2	40,818
14	22	H	QPR	W	2-0	2-0	—	Stuart, Rideout	30,000
15	25	H	Sheffield W	D	2-2	1-2	12	Kanchelskis, Amokachi	35,898
16	Dec 2	A	Tottenham H	D	0-0	0-0	12		32,894
17	11	H	West Ham U	W	3-0	2-0	—	Stuart, Unsworth (pen), Ebbrell	31,778
18	16	A	Newcastle U	L	0-1	0-1	12		36,557
19	23	A	Coventry C	L	1-2	0-0	12	Rideout	16,638
20	26	H	Middlesbrough	W	4-0	2-0	12	Short, Stuart 2, Kanchelskis	40,091
21	30	H	Leeds U	W	2-0	1-0	11	Wetherall (og), Kanchelskis	40,009
22	Jan 1	A	Wimbledon	W	3-2	3-0	9	Ebbrell, Ferguson 2	11,121
23	13	H	Chelsea	D	1-1	1-1	10	Unsworth (pen)	34,968
24	20	A	Arsenal	W	2-1	0-1	9	Stuart, Kanchelskis	38,275
25	Feb 3	A	Southampton	D	2-2	0-0	10	Stuart, Horne	15,126
26	10	H	Manchester C	W	2-0	1-0	8	Parkinson, Hinchcliffe (pen)	37,354
27	21	A	Manchester U	L	0-2	0-1	—		42,459
28	24	H	Nottingham F	W	3-0	1-0	7	Kanchelskis, Watson, Ferguson	33,163
29	Mar 2	A	Middlesbrough	W	2-0	2-0	6	Grant, Hinchcliffe (pen)	29,805
30	9	H	Coventry C	D	2-2	2-1	7	Ferguson 2	34,517
31	17	A	Leeds U	D	2-2	1-2	6	Stuart, Kanchelskis	29,422
32	23	H	Wimbledon	L	2-4	1-1	7	Short, Kanchelskis	31,282
33	30	A	Blackburn R	W	3-0	0-0	7	Amokachi, Kanchelskis 2	29,468
34	Apr 6	H	Bolton W	W	3-0	1-0	6	Hottiger, Kanchelskis, Amokachi	37,974
35	8	A	QPR	L	1-3	0-2	7	Ebbrell	18,349
36	16	H	Liverpool	D	1-1	1-0	6	Kanchelskis	40,120
37	27	A	Sheffield W	W	5-2	3-1	6	Amokachi, Ebbrell, Kanchelskis 3	32,724
38	May 5	H	Aston Villa	W	1-0	0-0	6	Parkinson	40,127

Final League Position: 6

GOALSCORERS

League (64): Kanchelskis 16, Stuart 9, Amokachi 6, Rideout 6, Ferguson 5, Ebbrell 4, Limpar 3, Parkinson 3, Hinchcliffe 2 (2 pens), Short 2, Unsworth 2 (2 pens), Grant 1, Horne 1, Hottiger 1, Samways 1, Watson 1, own goal 1.
Coca-Cola Cup (2): Hinchcliffe 1 (pen), Stuart 1.
FA Cup (8): Stuart 3, Ferguson 2, Ablett 1, Amokachi 1, Ebbrell 1.

Southall N 38	Barrett E 8	Hinchcliffe A 23 + 5	Unsworth D 28 + 3	Watson D 34	Ablett G 13	Limpar A 22 + 6	Horne B 25 + 1	Ferguson D 16 + 2	Rideout P 19 + 6	Parkinson J 28	Samways V 3 + 1	Amokachi D 17 + 8	Barlow S — + 3	Kanchelskis A 32	Holmes P 1	Short C 22 + 1	Grant T 11 + 2	Stuart G 27 + 2	Ebbrell J 24 + 1	Jackson M 14	O'Connor J 3 + 1	Branch M 1 + 2	Hottiger M 9	Match No.
1	2	3	4	5	6	7[1]	8	9	10	11	12													1
1	2	3	4	5	6	7[1]	8	9	10	11[2]		12	13											2
1	2		4	5	3	11	8		10	6		9		7										3
1	2	12	4	5	3	11[1]	8		10	6		9		7										4
1	12		4	5	3	11	8		10	6		9		7[1]	2									5
1	2	11		5	3[2]	7[1]	8		10	4		9	12			6	13							6
1	2	3		5	12		8		10[2]	4	7	9				6	11[1]	13						7
1	2	3	4	5	12		7		10	11[1]							8	9	6					8
1	2	3			6[1]	12	8		10			9	13	7[2]		5		11	4					9
1	11[1]			5	3	12	8		10	4				7		6		9		2				10
1		3[1]	13		5	6	12		10		11	9[2]		7			8	4		2				11
1				5	3	11			10	8		12		7		6		9[1]	4	2				12
1		12		5	3[1]	11			10	8				7		6		9	4	2				13
1			3	5		11			10	8				7		6		9	4	2				14
1		3	6	5		11			10[1]	8		12		7				9	4	2				15
1	12	3		5		11	8					9		7		6[1]		10	4	2				16
1		3		5		11[1]	12		8			9		7		6		10	4	2				17
1		3		5		11	12	13	8[1]			9		7		6		10	4	2[2]				18
1		3		5		11[1]		12	8			9		7		6		10	4	2				19
1		3		5		11	8		10	4				7		6		9		2				20
1	12	3		5			8	9[1]	10	4				7		6		11		2				21
1	12	3		5			8	9	10	4				7[1]		6		11		2				22
1		3[1]	4		6	11	8		10			12		7		5		9		2				23
1	12			5	3		8	9	10[1]	4				7		6		11		2				24
1		3		5		11[1]	8	9	10	4	12			7		6				2				25
1	11	3		5		7	8	9		4						6		10		2				26
1		3	6	5			8					9		7		11[1]		10	4	2	12		2	27
1		3	6	5			8	9[1]				12		7		11		10	4	2			2	28
1		3	6	5			8	9						7		11		10	4	2			2	29
1		3	6				8[1]	9			12			7		5[2]	11	10	4	2	13		2	30
1		3	6			11	8	9						7		5		10	4				2	31
1		3		5		11	8	9				12	13	7		6		10[2]	4[1]				2	32
1		3	4	5		11[1]	8	9				12[2]	13	7		6		10					2	33
1		3	6	5			8	9		4				7		10		11[1]			12		2	34
1		3	6[1]	5		11[3]	8[2]	9	10					7		12	13		4	14			2	35
1		3	6	5			8	9	10[1]					7		11	12		4				2	36
1		3		5							12	9		7		6	8	11	4			10[1]	2	37
1		3	6	5	12		8	13		4		9[2]		7		11[1]		10					2	38

Coca-Cola Cup
Second Round Millwall (a) 0-0 (h) 2-4

FA Cup
Third Round Stockport Co (h) 2-2 (a) 3-2
Fourth Round Port Vale (h) 2-2 (a) 1-2

EXETER CITY 1995-96 *Back row (left to right):* Mark Cooper, Mark Gavin, Russell Coughlin, Anthony Thirlby, Jamie Morgan, Barry McConnell, Neil Parsley, Richard Neno.
Middle row: Eammon Dolan, Robbie Turner, Mark Came, Mike Cecere, Ross Bellotti, Jon Richardson, Matthew Hare, Colin Anderson, Gary Rice.
Front row: Richard Pears, Danny Bailey, Mike Chapman (Physio), George Kent (Chief Scout), Peter Fox (Manager), Noel Blake (Assistant Manager), Mike Radford (Youth Team Manager), Martin Phillips, Nicky Medlin.

Division 3   EXETER CITY

St James Park, Exeter EX4 6PX. Telephone: (01392) 54073. Fax: (01392) 425885. Training Ground: (01395) 232784.

Ground capacity: 10,570.

Record attendance: 20,984 v Sunderland, FA Cup 6th rd (replay), 4 March 1931.

Record receipts: £59,862.98 v Aston Villa, FA Cup 3rd rd, 8 January 1994.

Pitch measurements: 114yd × 73yd.

Honorary President: W. C. Hill.

Chairman: A. I. Doble.

Directors: P. Carter, I. M. Couch, S. W. Dawe, L. G. Vallance, M. Shalbourne (Associate Director)

Manager: Peter Fox. *Assistant Manager/Coach:* Noel Blake. *Physio:* Mike Chapman MCSP.

Secretary: Margaret Bond. *Company Secretary:* P. Carter.

Commercial Manager: David Bird.

Year Formed: 1904. *Turned Professional:* 1908. *Ltd Co.:* 1908.

Club Nickname: 'The Grecians'.

Foundation: Exeter City was formed in 1904 by the amalgamation of St. Sidwell's United and Exeter United. The club first played in the East Devon League and then the Plymouth & District League. After an exhibition match between West Bromwich Albion and Woolwich Arsenal was held to test interest as Exeter was then a rugby stronghold, Exeter City decided at a meeting at the Red Lion Hotel to turn professional in 1908.

First Football League game: 28 August 1920, Division 3, v Brentford (h) W 3-0 – Pym; Coleburne, Feebury (1p); Crawshaw, Carrick, Mitton; Appleton, Makin, Wright (1), Vowles (1), Dockray.

Record League Victory: 8–1 v Coventry C, Division 3 (S), 4 December 1926 – Bailey; Pollard, Charlton; Pullen, Pool, Garrett; Purcell (2), McDevitt, Blackmore (2), Dent (2), Compton (2). 8–1 v Aldershot, Division 3 (S), 4 May 1935 – Chesters; Gray, Miller; Risdon, Webb, Angus; Jack Scott (1), Wrightson (1), Poulter (3), McArthur (1), Dryden (1). (1 og).

Record Cup Victory: 9–1 v Aberdare, FA Cup 1st rd, 26 November 1927 – Holland; Pollard, Charlton; Phoenix, Pool, Gee; Purcell (2), McDevitt, Dent (4), Vaughan (2), Compton (1).

Record Defeat: 0–9 v Notts Co, Division 3 (S), 16 October 1948 and v Northampton T, Division 3 (S), 12 April 1958.

Most League Points (2 for a win): 62, Division 4, 1976–77.

Most League Points (3 for a win): 89, Division 4, 1989–90.

Most League Goals: 88, Division 3 (S), 1932–33.

Highest League Scorer in Season: Fred Whitlow, 33, Division 3 (S), 1932–33.

Most League Goals in Total Aggregate: Tony Kellow, 129, 1976–78, 1980–83, 1985–88.

Most Capped Player: Dermot Curtis, 1 (17), Eire.

Most League Appearances: Arnold Mitchell, 495, 1952–66.

Record Transfer Fee Received: £500,000 from Rangers for Chris Vinnicombe, November 1989 and £500,000 from Manchester C for Martin Phillips, November 1995.

Record Transfer Fee Paid: £65,000 to Blackpool for Tony Kellow, March 1980.

Football League Record: 1920 Elected Division 3; 1921–58 Division 3 (S); 1958–64 Division 4; 1964–66 Division 3; 1966–77 Division 4; 1977–84 Division 3; 1984–90 Division 4; 1990–92 Division 3; 1992–94 Division 2; 1994– Division 3.

Honours: Football League: Division 3 best season: 8th, 1979–80; Division 3 (S) – Runners-up 1932–33; Division 4 – Champions 1989–90; Runners-up 1976–77. *FA Cup:* best season: 6th rd replay, 1931. *Football League Cup:* never beyond 4th rd. *Division 3 (S) Cup:* Winners 1934.

Colours: Red and white striped shirts, black shorts, red stockings. *Change colours:* Blue and white striped shirts, blue shorts, blue stockings.

Did you know?
Jim 'Daisy' Bell was Exeter City's top scorer in three Southern League seasons from 1908–09 to 1910–11 with 23, 15 and 14 goals respectively.

EXETER CITY 1995–96 LEAGUE RECORD

Match No.	Date	Venue	Opponents	Result	H/T Score	Lg. Pos.	Goalscorers	Attendance
1	Aug 12	H	Darlington	L	0-1	0-1	—	2934
2	19	A	Hartlepool U	D	0-0	0-0	20	2311
3	26	H	Scarborough	W	2-0	0-0	14	Came 2	2439
4	29	A	Cardiff C	W	1-0	1-0	—	Pears	3750
5	Sept 2	H	Scunthorpe U	W	1-0	1-0	6	Bailey	2893
6	9	A	Northampton T	D	0-0	0-0	6		5625
7	12	A	Cambridge U	D	1-1	0-0	—	Turner	2365
8	16	H	Fulham	W	2-1	1-0	4	Cooper, Phillips	4420
9	23	H	Leyton Orient	D	2-2	2-1	5	Pears, Cooper	5507
10	30	A	Rochdale	L	2-4	0-3	7	Phillips, Cecere	2052
11	Oct 7	A	Barnet	L	2-3	0-2	10	Turner 2	2146
12	14	H	Wigan Ath	L	0-4	0-1	12		3870
13	21	A	Hereford U	D	2-2	0-0	13	Blatherwick (og), Buckle	2249
14	28	H	Lincoln C	D	1-1	1-1	13	Phillips	3252
15	31	H	Gillingham	D	0-0	0-0	—		3024
16	Nov 4	A	Colchester U	D	1-1	0-1	14	Pears	3377
17	18	H	Preston NE	D	1-1	1-0	14	Saville (og)	3550
18	25	A	Bury	L	0-2	0-0	14		3597
19	Dec 2	A	Doncaster R	L	0-2	0-1	14		1429
20	9	A	Leyton Orient	W	3-0	2-0	12	Ross, Bradbury 2	3471
21	16	H	Rochdale	W	2-0	1-0	12	Richardson, Gavin	3152
22	26	H	Torquay U	D	0-0	0-0	12		6182
23	30	H	Chester C	L	1-2	0-2	12	Ross	3324
24	Jan 1	A	Plymouth Arg	D	2-2	2-0	12	Came, Buckle	12,427
25	6	A	Mansfield T	D	1-1	1-0	12	Bradbury	1853
26	20	A	Darlington	L	0-1	0-0	15		1723
27	30	H	Hartlepool U	W	1-0	1-0	—	Cooper	2468
28	Feb 3	A	Scarborough	D	0-0	0-0	14		1307
29	13	H	Mansfield T	D	2-2	1-2	—	Bradbury, Hackett (og)	2507
30	17	H	Cambridge U	W	1-0	0-0	12	Blake	2804
31	24	A	Fulham	L	1-2	0-1	12	Braithwaite	4048
32	27	H	Northampton T	L	1-2	1-1	—	Gavin	2663
33	Mar 2	A	Torquay U	W	2-0	1-0	12	Bradbury, Cooper (pen)	4038
34	9	H	Doncaster R	W	1-0	1-0	13	Braithwaite	3175
35	12	H	Cardiff C	W	2-0	1-0	—	Pears, Cooper (pen)	2609
36	16	A	Chester C	D	2-2	1-1	12	Came, Cooper	2043
37	23	A	Plymouth Arg	D	1-1	1-1	12	Logan (og)	6185
38	26	A	Scunthorpe U	L	0-4	0-0	—		1615
39	30	H	Barnet	W	1-0	0-0	11	Pears	2726
40	Apr 2	A	Wigan Ath	L	0-1	0-0	—		2744
41	6	A	Lincoln C	W	1-0	1-0	12	Sharpe	2723
42	8	H	Hereford U	L	0-2	0-1	12		3191
43	13	A	Gillingham	L	0-1	0-0	12		7698
44	20	H	Colchester U	D	2-2	2-1	12	Braithwaite, Chamberlain	2788
45	27	A	Bury	D	1-1	0-1	14	Blake	3508
46	May 4	A	Preston NE	L	0-2	0-1	14		18,700

Final League Position: 14

GOALSCORERS
League (46): Cooper 6 (2 pens), Bradbury 5, Pears 5, Came 4, Braithwaite 3, Phillips 3, Turner 3, Blake 2, Buckle 2, Gavin 2, Ross 2, Bailey 1, Cecere 1, Chamberlain 1, Richardson 1, Sharpe 1, own goals 4.
Coca-Cola Cup (1): Richardson 1.
FA Cup (0).

Fox P 46	Parsley N 29 + 3	Anderson C 5 + 8	Cooper M 26 + 1	Blake N 44	Richardson J 43	Chamberlain M 29 + 4	Bailey D 41 + 1	Turner R 6 + 6	Cecere M 5 + 8	Phillips M 11 + 2	Gavin M 24 + 4	Rice G 17 + 2	Came M 38	Coughlin R 6 + 2	Pears R 19 + 3	Hare M 10 + 3	Morgan J 2 + 4	McConnell B 1 + 7	Buckle P 22	Medlin N 2 + 4	Hughes D 25 + 1	Ross M 7	Braithwaite L 14 + 9	Bradbury L 14	Sharpe J 9 + 5	Foster A 4 + 3	Myers C 7 + 1	Thirtby A — + 2	Match No.
1	2	3	4	5	6	7	8	9	10	11[1]	12																		1
1	2		4	5	6	7[1]	8	10		12	11[2]	3	9	13															2
1	2	12	4	5	6	7	8					3	11[1]	10	9														3
1	2[1]	12	4	5	6	7	8					3	11[2]	10	9	13													4
1			4	5	6	7	8					3	11	10	9		2												5
1	2		4	5	6	7	8	12				13	3	10[2]	9[1]	11													6
1	2		4	5	6	7	8	12	13	10		3[3]	9[2]	11[1]	14														7
1	2		4	5	6	7[1]	8	12	13	10		9[2]	11	3															8
1	2		4[1]	5	6	7	8	13		10		3	12	9[2]	11														9
1	2	3		5	6	7[2]	8	12	9	10		4	11[1]	13															10
1	2			6	7[1]	8[2]	5	9	11	12	3	4	10	13															11
1	2[1]			6	7	8	5	9	11	12	3[2]	10	13	4															12
1	12			5	6	8	13	11[1]	7	3	10	9[2]	2	4															13
1				5	6	8	12	11	7	3[1]	10	9[2]	13	4															14
1	3			5	6	8	9[2]	11	7	10	13	2[1]	12	4															15
1	2	3		5	6	8		11		10	9	4	7[1]	12															16
1	2			5	6	8	9[1]		7		10	12	4	3	11														17
1	2	12		5	6	8		7		10		4	11[1]	3	9[2]	13													18
1	2			5	6	12	8[1]	13	7	11		4	3	9[2]	10														19
1	2			5	6	8		7		11		4	3	10[1]	12	9													20
1	2			5	6	8	12	7		11		4	3	10[1]		9													21
1	2			5	6	8	12	7[2]		11		4	3	10[1]	13	9													22
1	2[2]	6[1]	5			8	12	7		11		4	3	10	13	9													23
1	2	12	6	5		10		7		11		4	3		9				8[1]										24
1	2	12	8	5	6	10	13			11[1]	7[3]	4	3	14	9[2]														25
1	2	7	8[2]	5	6[1]	10				11		4	12	3	13	9													26
1	12	13	8	5	6	2[1]	10	7		11		4	3[2]		9														27
1	2			5	6	10	12			11		4	13	3	8[1]	9	7[2]												28
1	2	12	5	6[2]	13	10[1]				11		4	3	8	9	7													29
1		8	5	6	2	10[1]		7[2]		11		4	3	12	9	13													30
1	12	8	5	6	2[3]	10		7		11		4[1]	3	13	9[2]	14													31
1		8	5	6	2	10		7		11		4	3	9															32
1		8	5		2	10		7		11		4[1]	12	3	9	6													33
1		8	5	6	2	10		7	12	11			3	9	4[1]														34
1	12	8	5	6	2[1]	10		7		11	4[2]		13	3	9														35
1	2	8	5	6		10		7		11	4[1]		12	3	9														36
1	2	13	8	5	6		10			7		11		3	9	12[2]	4[1]												37
1	2	8	5	6		10		7[2]	13	11	12		4		9[3]	14	3[1]												38
1	2	8	5	6	12	10[1]	7			11	13		3[3]		14	9[2]	4												39
1	2	8	5	6	12		7	3		11	13		10[1]	9[2]	4														40
1			5	6	2	8		7		11	9		3	7	10	4													41
1	4		5	6	2[2]	8[3]	7	3	11	9[1]	13		10	12	14														42
1			5[2]	6	2[1]	8		3	11	9	13	12		7	10	4													43
1			5	6	2	8	12	3	11	9[2]			7	10[1]	13	4[3]	14												44
1			5	6	2	8		3		9[1]	13	11[3]		7	10[2]	17	4	14											45
1			5	6	2	8		3[1]	11	9		12		10	7		4												46

Coca-Cola Cup
First Round   Torquay U   (a)   0-0
                                          (h)   1-1

FA Cup
First Round   Peterborough U   (h)   0-1

FULHAM 1995–96 *Back row (left to right):* Tony Lange, Lee Harrison.
Third row: Lea Barkus, Carl Williams, Danny Bolt, Tony Finnigan, Danny Bower, Rory Hamill, Paul Brooker.
Second row: Len Walker (Assistant Manager), Chris Smith (Physio), Martin Thomas, Nicky Andrews, Carl Bartley, Michael Mison, Mike Conroy, Terry Angus, Duncan Jupp, David Smith,
Alan Cork (Youth Manager), Micky Adams (First Team Coach).
Front row: Gary Brazil, Nick Cusack, Kevin Moore, Ian Branfoot (Manager), Simon Morgan, Mark Blake, Robbie Herrera.

Division 3   FULHAM

Craven Cottage, Stevenage Rd, Fulham, London SW6 6HH. Telephone: (0171) 736 6561. Fax: (0171) 731 7047. Call Line: 0891 440044.

Ground capacity: 14,969.

Record attendance: 49,335 v Millwall, Division 2, 8 October 1938.

Record receipts: £80,247 v Chelsea, Division 2, 8 October 1983.

Pitch measurements: 110yd × 75yd.

Chief Executive: R.J. Summers.

Chairman: Jimmy Hill.

Directors: W. F. Muddyman (Vice-Chairman), C. A. Swain, A. M. Muddyman, T. W. Wilson, D. E. Shrimpton.

Team Manager: Micky Adams. *General Manager:* Ian Branfoot. *Assistant Manager:* Len Walker. *Player-Coach:* Micky Adams. *Reserve Team Coach:* Alan Cork. *Youth Team Coach:* John Marshall. *Physio:* Chris Smith, Grad. Dip. Phys. MCSP. *Community Officer:* Gary Mulcahey (0171) 384 3552.

Club Secretary: Mrs Janice O'Doherty. *Corporate Affairs Manager:* Mrs Annie Bassett.

Communications Manager: Ken Myers. *Club Safety Officer:* Kevin Moore.

Year Formed: 1879. *Turned Professional:* 1898. *Ltd Co.:* 1903. *Reformed:* 1987.

Club Nickname: 'Cottagers'.

Previous Name: 1879–88, Fulham St Andrew's.

Previous Grounds: 1879 Star Road, Fulham; c.1883 Eel Brook Common, 1884 Lillie Road; 1885 Putney Lower Common; 1886 Ranelagh House, Fulham; 1888 Barn Elms, Castelnau; 1889 Purser's Cross (Roskell's Field), Parsons Green Lane; 1891 Eel Brook Common; 1891 Half Moon, Putney; 1895 Captain James Field, West Brompton; 1896 Craven Cottage.

Foundation: Churchgoers were responsible for the foundation of Fulham, which first saw the light of day as Fulham St. Andrew's Church Sunday School FC in 1879. They won the West London Amateur Cup in 1887 and the championship of the West London League in its initial season of 1892–93. The name Fulham had been adopted in 1888.

First Football League game: 3 September 1907, Division 2, v Hull C (h) L 0–1 – Skene; Ross, Lindsay; Collins, Morrison, Goldie; Dalrymple, Freeman, Bevan, Hubbard, Threlfall.

Record League Victory: 10–1 v Ipswich T, Division 1, 26 December 1963 – Macedo; Cohen, Langley; Mullery (1), Keetch, Robson (1); Key, Cook (1), Leggat (4), Haynes, Howfield (3).

Record Cup Victory: 6–0 v Wimbledon (away), FA Cup 1st rd (replay), 3 December 1930 – Iceton; Gibbon, Lilley; Oliver, Dudley, Barrett; Temple, Hammond (1), Watkins (1), Gibbons (2), Penn (2). 6–0 v Bury, FA Cup 3rd rd, 7 January 1938 – Turner; Bacuzzi, Keeping; Evans, Dennison, Tompkins; Higgins, Worsley, Rooke (6), O'Callaghan, Arnold.

Record Defeat: 0–10 v Liverpool, League Cup 2nd rd 1st leg, 23 September 1986.

Most League Points (2 for a win): 60, Division 2, 1958–59 and Division 3, 1970–71.

Most League Points (3 for a win): 78, Division 3, 1981–82.

Most League Goals: 111, Division 3 (S), 1931–32.

Highest League Scorer in Season: Frank Newton, 43, Division 3 (S), 1931–32.

Most League Goals in Total Aggregate: Gordon Davies, 159, 1978–84, 1986–91.

Most Capped Player: Johnny Haynes, 56, England.

Most League Appearances: Johnny Haynes, 594, 1952–70.

Record Transfer Fee Received: £333,333 from Liverpool for Richard Money, May 1980.

Record Transfer Fee Paid: £150,000 to Orient for Peter Kitchen, February 1979, and to Brighton & HA for Teddy Maybank, December 1979.

Football League Record: 1907 Elected to Division 2; 1928–32 Division 3 (S); 1932–49 Division 2; 1949–52 Division 1; 1952–59 Division 2; 1959–68 Division 1, 1968–69 Division 2; 1969–71 Division 3; 1971–80 Division 2; 1980–82 Division 3; 1982–86 Division 2; 1986–92 Division 3; 1992–94 Division 2; 1994– Division 3.

Honours: Football League: Division 1 best season: 10th, 1959–60; Division 2 – Champions 1948–49; Runners-up 1958–59; Division 3 (S) – Champions 1931–32; Division 3 – Runners-up 1970–71. *FA Cup:* Runners-up 1975. *Football League Cup:* best season: 5th rd, 1968, 1971.

Colours: White shirts, red and black trim, black shorts, white stockings red and black trim. *Change colours:* Red and black halved shirts, white shorts, black stockings with red trim.

Did you know?
On 14 December 1995, goalkeeper Tony Lange converted a penalty in a 4-1 FA Cup shoot-out win over Brighton & Hove Albion, having remained unbeaten during the match.

FULHAM 1995–96 LEAGUE RECORD

Match No.	Date	Venue	Opponents	Result	H/T Score	Lg. Pos.	Goalscorers	Attendance
1	Aug 12	H	Mansfield T	W	4-2	1-1	—	Mison 2, Thomas 2	4909
2	19	A	Scarborough	D	2-2	2-1	5	Adams, Thomas	1946
3	26	H	Torquay U	W	4-0	1-0	2	Barkus, Adams, Hamill, Barrow (og)	4764
4	29	A	Darlington	D	1-1	1-0	—	Conroy	1906
5	Sept 2	A	Leyton Orient	L	0-1	0-0	7		7244
6	9	H	Doncaster R	W	3-1	2-1	3	Conroy, Blake (pen), Cusack	
7	12	H	Rochdale	D	1-1	1-1	—	Morgan	3848
8	16	A	Exeter C	L	1-2	0-1	7	Moore	4420
9	23	H	Preston NE	D	2-2	1-1	9	Thomas, Morgan	5209
10	30	A	Northampton T	L	0-2	0-0	12		5778
11	Oct 7	A	Plymouth Arg	L	0-3	0-2	12		6681
12	14	H	Bury	D	0-0	0-0	16		3803
13	21	A	Chester C	D	1-1	0-1	16	Conroy	2752
14	28	H	Hereford U	D	0-0	0-0	17		3631
15	31	H	Colchester U	D	1-1	0-1	—	Cusack	2870
16	Nov 4	A	Wigan Ath	D	1-1	1-1	17	Angus	2438
17	18	H	Barnet	D	1-1	0-0	17	Brazil	4369
18	25	A	Gillingham	L	0-1	0-0	20		7704
19	Dec 9	A	Preston NE	D	1-1	1-0	20	Bolt (pen)	8422
20	16	H	Northampton T	L	1-3	1-2	20	Angus	3421
21	19	H	Cardiff C	W	4-2	1-2	—	Bolt (pen), Harding (og), Mison, Morgan	2284
22	26	A	Lincoln C	L	0-4	0-2	20		3693
23	Jan 13	H	Scarborough	W	1-0	1-0	18	Cusack	3557
24	20	A	Mansfield T	L	0-1	0-0	21		2025
25	30	H	Scunthorpe U	L	1-3	0-1	—	Blake	2176
26	Feb 3	A	Torquay U	L	1-2	1-1	23	Conroy	2594
27	10	H	Hartlepool U	D	2-2	1-0	23	Barber, Blake	3700
28	13	A	Cambridge U	D	0-0	0-0	—		2233
29	17	A	Rochdale	D	1-1	1-1	23	Conroy	1923
30	24	H	Exeter C	W	2-1	1-0	22	Scott 2	4048
31	26	A	Doncaster R	W	2-0	2-0	—	Thomas, Cusack	2331
32	Mar 2	H	Lincoln C	L	1-2	1-2	23	McAree	4245
33	5	H	Darlington	D	2-2	0-2	—	Cusack, Mison	2534
34	9	A	Cardiff C	W	4-1	1-0	15	McAree, Scott, Conroy 2	3019
35	12	A	Hartlepool U	L	0-1	0-1	—		1198
36	16	H	Cambridge U	L	0-2	0-1	17		3872
37	23	A	Scunthorpe U	L	1-3	0-1	20	Blake (pen)	1919
38	26	H	Leyton Orient	W	2-1	0-0	—	Blake, Brooker	3636
39	30	H	Plymouth Arg	W	4-0	1-0	17	Scott, Morgan, Conroy, Brooker	5667
40	Apr 2	A	Bury	L	0-3	0-2	—		3371
41	6	A	Hereford U	L	0-1	0-1	18		3276
42	8	H	Chester C	W	2-0	2-0	17	Morgan, Scott	3777
43	13	A	Colchester U	D	2-2	1-1	16	Morgan, Conroy	3795
44	20	H	Wigan Ath	W	1-0	0-0	16	Hamill	4657
45	27	H	Gillingham	D	0-0	0-0	16		10,320
46	May 4	A	Barnet	L	0-3	0-1	17		4332

Final League Position: 17

GOALSCORERS

League (57): Conroy 9, Morgan 6, Blake 5 (2 pens), Cusack 5, Scott 5, Thomas 5, Mison 4, Adams 2, Angus 2, Bolt 2 (2 pens), Brooker 2, Hamill 2, McAree 2, Barber 1, Barkus 1, Brazil 1, Moore 1, own goals 2.
Coca-Cola Cup (6): Conroy 2, Barkus 1, Brazil 1, Cusack 1, Mison 1.
FA Cup (9): Conroy 3, Angus 1, Brooker 1, Cusack 1, Hamill 1, Jupp 1, Thomas 1.

Lange T 41	Jupp D 35+1	Herrera R 42+1	Mison M 16+7	Angus T 30+1	Blake M 35+3	Thomas M 32+5	Morgan S 41	Conroy M 38+2	Brazil G 17+1	Adams M 5	Cusack N 38+4	Barkus L 3+6	Hamill R 6+19	Bolt D 7+4	Moore K 17+3	Taylor M 7	Finnigan T 1+1	Harrison L 5	Bower D 4	Brooker P 9+11	Gray M 6	Williams C 2+11	Marshall J 14+2	Scott R 21	McAree R 16+1	Barber P 13	Simpson G 5+2	Hansher J —+3	Match No
1	2	3	4	5	6	7	8	9[1]	10[2]	11	12	13																	1
1	2	3	4	5	6	7[2]	8	9	10[1]	11	12	13																	2
1	2	3	4	5	6	7		9	11	10	8[1]			12															3
1	2	3	4	5	6	7	8	9	10	11																			4
1	2	3	4	5	6	7	8	10	9[1]	11[2]	13				12														5
1	2	3	4	5	6	7	8	10	9	11																			6
1	2	3	4	5	6	7[1]	8	10	9	11						12													7
1	2	3	4	5	6		8	10	9	11				7[1]	12														8
1	2	3	4	5	6	7	8	10[1]	9	11				12															9
1	2[2]	3	4	5	6	7	8	10[1]		11	12								9	13									10
1	2		4	5	6[1]	7	8	10	9		12		13		11	3[2]													11
			4	5		7[1]	8	10	11		9[2]	12			3	2	1			6	13								12
1	2					7	8[1]	10	9[2]		11	13	12		5	3				6			4						13
1	2	12				7[3]	8	10[2]	9		11	14	13		5	3[1]				6			4						14
1	2	3	6[2]			7	8	12	9		11				10[1]	5				13			4						15
1	2	3	6			7	8	10	9		11[1]				12	5							4						16
1	2	3	6	12			8	10	9		11[1]		13			5				7[2]			4						17
1	2	3	6			7	8	10	9[1]		11				12[2]	5				13			4						18
1	2	3	8		6			10			7[1]	9[2]	11		5	4					12			13					19
1	2	3		6	12		8	10[3]			9	7[2]	11		5[1]	4					13		14						20
1	2	3	4	6[1]	12	7	8	9[2]			10				11	5							13						21
1	2	3		6	12	7	8	10			4[2]	13	11[3]		5[1]						14	9							22
	2	3		5	6	7	8	12			9	13	11[2]		1							4[1]	10						23
	2[2]	3		5[1]	6	7[3]	8				9	13			12		1					4	10	14	11				24
	2	3		5[1]	6	7[2]	8				9		13		12		1					10	4	11					25
1	2	3		6	7[1]		9				4	12			5							13	10[2]	8	11				26
1	2[1]	3		6			9				4	12			5							7	10	8	11				27
1	2	3		6		4	12	9			5[1]											13	7	10[2]	8	11			28
1	2	3		6		4	9	5[2]			12											13	7	10	8[1]	11			29
1		3		6	7	4	9	5			12											13	2	10	8[2]	11[1]			30
1		3	12	6	7	4	9	5														13	2	10	8[1]	11[2]			31
1		3	12	6	7	4	9	5															2	10	8	11[1]			32
1		3	12	6	7	4	9	5				2[2]			13					14			10	8[3]	11[1]				33
1		3		6	7	4	9	5			12				13							2[1]	10[2]	8	11				34
1	2[3]	3	12	6	7	4	9	5			13											14	10	8[1]	11[2]				35
1	2	3	12	6		4	9	5							13						14	8[2]	10		11[1]				36
1	2	3		5	6	12	4	9			8		11[1]		7								10						37
1	2	3	12	5	6	13	4				8		9		7								10[2]	11[1]					38
1	2	3		5[2]	6		4	9			8		12		7								10	11[1]		13			39
1	2	3	12	5[2]	6		4	9			8				7								10[3]	11[1]		13	14		40
1	2[3]	3	11[2]	5[1]	6	12	4	9			8				13								10		7		14		41
1		3		5	6	7	4				9				8								2	10			11		42
1		3		5	6	7	4	9							8								2	10[1]			11		43
	12	3		5	6	7		9			4	10							1	8[2]	13	2[1]					11		44
1		3	12		6		4	9[1]			8	10[3]			5					13	14	2		7[2]		11			45
1		3			6[3]	12	4	9			8		13		5				10	11		2[1]		7[2]			14		46

Coca-Cola Cup

First Round — Brighton & HA — (h) 3-0, (a) 2-0

Second Round — Wolverhampton W — (a) 0-2, (h) 1-5

FA Cup

First Round — Swansea C — (h) 7-0, (a) 0-0

Second Round — Brighton & HA — (h) 0-0, (a) 0-0

Third Round — Shrewsbury T — (h) 1-1, (a) 1-2

GILLINGHAM 1995–96 *Back row (left to right)*: Dominic Naylor, Joseph Dunne, Neil Smith, Richard Carpenter, Jim Stannard, Steven Brown, Scott Lindsey, Gary Micklewhite, Mark O'Connor. *Middle row*: Wayne Jones (Physio), Andrew Arnott, Darren Freeman, David Martin, Tony Butler, Mark Harris, Richard Green, Simon Ratcliffe, Kevin Bremner (Youth Team Manager). *Front row*: Paul Watson, Leo Fortune-West, Paul Wilson, Tony Pulis (Manager), Paul Scally (Chairman & Chief Executive), Lindsay Parsons (Assistant Manager), Dennis Bailey, Adrian Foster, Kevin Rattray.

(Photograph: Keith Slater)

Division 2   GILLINGHAM

Priestfield Stadium, Gillingham, ME7 4DD. Telephone: (01634) 851854/576828. Fax: (01634) 850986.

Ground capacity: 10,600.

Record attendance: 23,002 v QPR, FA Cup 3rd rd, 10 January 1948.

Record receipts: £80,184 v Sheffield W, FA Cup 3rd rd, 7 January 1995.

Pitch measurements: 114yd × 75yd.

President: J. W. Leech. *Vice-Presidents:* G. B. Goodere, G. V. W. Lukehurst.

Chairman/Chief Executive: P. D. P. Scally.

Directors: A. Smith FRICS, J. Paulley (Associate).

Manager: Tony Pulis. *Assistant Manager:* Lindsay Parsons. *Coach:* Gary Micklewhite.

Physio: W. Jones.

Acting Secretary: Mrs G. E. Poynter. *Commercial/Lotteries Manager:* M. Ling.

Year Formed: 1893. *Turned Professional:* 1894. *Ltd Co.:* 1893.

Club Nickname: 'The Gills'.

Previous Name: New Brompton, 1893–1913.

Foundation: The success of the pioneering Royal Engineers of Chatham excited the interest of the residents of the Medway Towns and led to the formation of many clubs including Excelsior. After winning the Kent Junior Cup and the Chatham District League in 1893, Excelsior decided to go for bigger things and it was at a meeting in the Napier Arms, Brompton, in 1893 that New Brompton FC came into being as a professional concern, securing the use of a ground in Priestfield Road.

First Football League game: 28 August 1920, Division 3, v Southampton (h) D 1-1 – Branfield; Robertson, Sissons; Battiste, Baxter, Wigmore; Holt, Hall, Gilbey (1), Roe, Gore.

Record League Victory: 10–0 v Chesterfield, Division 3, 5 September 1987 – Kite; Haylock, Pearce, Shipley (2) (Lillis), West, Greenall (1), Pritchard (2), Shearer (2), Lovell, Elsey (2), David Smith (1).

Record Cup Victory: 10–1 v Gorleston, FA Cup 1st rd, 16 November 1957 – Brodie; Parry, Hannaway; Riggs, Boswell, Laing; Payne, Fletcher (2), Saunders (5), Morgan (1), Clark (2).

Record Defeat: 2–9 v Nottingham F, Division 3 (S), 18 November 1950.

Most League Points (2 for a win): 62, Division 4, 1973–74.

Most League Points (3 for a win): 83, Division 3, 1984–85 and Division 3, 1995–96.

Most League Goals: 90, Division 4, 1973–74.

Highest League Scorer in Season: Ernie Morgan, 31, Division 3 (S), 1954–55 and Brian Yeo, 31, Division 4, 1973–74.

Most League Goals in Total Aggregate: Brian Yeo, 135, 1963–75.

Most Capped Player: Tony Cascarino, 3 (63), Republic of Ireland.

Most League Appearances: John Simpson, 571, 1957–72.

Record Transfer Fee Received: £300,000 from Tottenham H for Peter Beadle, June 1992.

Record Transfer Fee Paid: £102,500 to Tottenham H for Mark Cooper, October 1987.

Football League Record: 1920 Original Member of Division 3; 1921 Division 3 (S); 1938 Failed re-election; Southern League 1938–44; Kent League 1944–46; Southern League 1946–50; 1950 Re-elected to Division 3 (S); 1958–64 Division 4; 1964–71 Division 3; 1971–74 Division 4; 1974–89 Division 3; 1989–92 Division 4; 1992–96; Division 3; 1996– Division 2.

Honours: Football League: Division 3 best season: Runners-up 1995-96; Division 4 – Champions 1963–64; Runners-up 1973–74. *FA Cup:* best season: 5th rd, 1970. *Football League Cup:* best season: 4th rd, 1964.

Colours: Blue shirts, white shorts, white stockings. *Change colours:* Red shirts, white shorts, red stockings.

Did you know?
Jim Stannard kept 29 clean sheets during the 1995–96 season beating goalkeeper John Simpson's 24 in 1963–64.

GILLINGHAM 1995–96 LEAGUE RECORD

Match No.	Date	Venue	Opponents	Result		H/T Score	Lg. Pos.	Goalscorers	Attendance
1	Aug 12	H	Wigan Ath	W	2-1	0-1	—	Foster, Fortune-West	3901
2	19	A	Lincoln C	W	3-0	1-0	1	Fortune-West, Bailey, Brightwell (og)	2822
3	26	H	Cambridge U	W	3-0	0-0	1	Fortune-West, Bailey, Rattray	5093
4	29	A	Barnet	W	2-0	1-0	—	Rattray, Naylor	3077
5	Sept 2	H	Colchester U	L	0-1	0-0	1		7667
6	9	A	Scunthorpe U	D	1-1	1-1	1	Bailey	2423
7	12	A	Hereford U	D	0-0	0-0	—		1747
8	16	H	Cardiff C	W	1-0	1-0	2	Fortune-West	5317
9	23	A	Chester C	D	1-1	0-0	2	Martin	3886
10	30	H	Bury	W	3-0	0-0	1	Bailey, Fortune-West 2	6125
11	Oct 7	H	Rochdale	W	1-0	1-0	1	Watson A	7785
12	14	A	Darlington	L	0-1	0-1	1		2043
13	21	H	Doncaster R	W	4-0	1-0	1	O'Connor, Ratcliffe, Bailey, Harris	6307
14	28	A	Hartlepool U	D	1-1	1-0	1	Bailey (pen)	2355
15	31	A	Exeter C	D	0-0	0-0	—		3024
16	Nov 4	H	Northampton T	D	0-0	0-0	3		7207
17	18	A	Scarborough	W	2-0	2-0	2	Green, Fortune-West	1546
18	25	H	Fulham	W	1-0	0-0	2	Fortune-West	7704
19	Dec 16	A	Bury	L	0-1	0-0	3		3045
20	23	A	Preston NE	D	0-0	0-0	3		10,669
21	26	H	Plymouth Arg	W	1-0	0-0	1	Butler S (pen)	9651
22	Jan 1	A	Leyton Orient	W	1-0	1-0	1	Fortune-West	7098
23	9	H	Chester C	W	3-1	0-0	—	Butler S 3	9191
24	13	H	Lincoln C	W	2-0	1-0	1	Fortune-West, Ratcliffe	8047
25	20	A	Wigan Ath	L	1-2	1-1	1	Green	2773
26	30	H	Mansfield T	W	2-0	2-0	—	Rattray, Butler T	6116
27	Feb 3	A	Cambridge U	D	0-0	0-0	1		4114
28	10	H	Torquay U	W	2-0	2-0	1	Smith, Ratcliffe	7110
29	13	H	Barnet	W	1-0	1-0	—	Butler S	6433
30	17	H	Hereford U	D	1-1	0-1	1	Castle	6993
31	24	A	Cardiff C	L	0-2	0-0	1		2994
32	27	H	Scunthorpe U	D	0-0	0-0	—		5557
33	Mar 2	A	Plymouth Arg	L	0-1	0-0	1		8485
34	9	H	Preston NE	D	1-1	0-0	1	Harris	10,602
35	12	A	Torquay U	D	0-0	0-0	—		2406
36	16	A	Mansfield T	W	1-0	1-0	1	Gayle	2698
37	23	H	Leyton Orient	D	1-1	0-0	1	Gayle	8071
38	30	A	Rochdale	L	0-2	0-2	2		2098
39	Apr 2	H	Darlington	D	0-0	0-0	—		6426
40	6	H	Hartlepool U	W	2-0	1-0	2	Butler T, Bailey	6267
41	8	A	Doncaster R	W	1-0	1-0	2	Bailey	1783
42	13	H	Exeter C	W	1-0	0-0	2	Puttnam	7698
43	16	A	Colchester U	D	1-1	0-0	—	Gayle	4952
44	20	A	Northampton T	D	1-1	1-0	2	Fortune-West	7427
45	27	A	Fulham	D	0-0	0-0	2		10,320
46	May 4	H	Scarborough	W	1-0	1-0	2	Fortune-West	10,421

Final League Position: 2

GOALSCORERS

League (49): Fortune-West 12, Bailey 8 (1 pen), Butler S 5 (1 pen), Gayle 3, Ratcliffe 3, Rattray 3, Butler T 2, Green 2, Harris 2, Castle 1, Foster 1, Martin 1, Naylor 1, O'Connor 1, Puttnam 1, Smith 1, Watson A 1, own goal 1.
Coca-Cola Cup (3): Bailey 1, Fortune-West 1, Naylor 1.
FA Cup (6): Fortune-West 2, Bailey 1, Martin 1, Ratcliffe 1, own goal 1.

Stannard J 46	Dunne J 1+1	Naylor D 30+1	Butler T 34+2	Harris M 44	Green R 35	Martin D 27+4	Ratcliffe S 41	Fortune-West L 36+4	Foster A 1+10	O'Connor M 18	Arnott A —+1	Brown S —+1	Smith N 36+1	Bailey D 40+5	Watson P 3+5	Rattray K 18+8	Carpenter R 7+5	Micklewhite G 17+14	Watson A 10	Puttnam D 10+16	Freeman D 4+6	Butler S 14+6	Thomas G 14+1	Manuel B 6+4	Castle S 5+1	Gayle J 9	Ansah A —+2	Match No.
1	2	3²	4	5	6¹	7	8	9	10²	11	12	13		14														1
1		3	4²	5	6	7³	8	9¹	12	11			2	10	13	14												2
1		3	4	5	6		8	9		11			2	10		7												3
1		3	4	5	6		8	9	12	11			2	10¹		7												4
1		3	4	5	6	13	8	9	12	11			2¹	10		7²												5
1		3	4²	5	6		8	9	12	11			2	10¹		7	13											6
1		3		5	6		8	9	12	11			2	10		7¹	4											7
1		3		5	6		8	9¹	12	11			2	10		7	4											8
1		3¹		5	6	13	8	9	12	11			2	10		7²	4											9
1		3		5	6	13	8	9	12	11			2³	10¹		7²	14	4										10
1		3		5	6	7¹	8	9		11			2	10				4	12									11
1		3	12	5	6	7²	8	9		11¹			2	10		13		4³	14									12
1		3		5		7	8	9		11			2	10				6	4									13
1		3²	6	5		7¹	8	9³		11			2	10		13		4	12	14								14
1		3²	6	5			8	9		11			2	10	12	7		4¹	13									15
1		3		5	6	7²	8		12	11			2	10		13		4	9¹									16
1			5	6	7	8¹	9³		11				4	10	3	12	2²	13	14									17
1		12		5	6	7	8	9		11¹			4	10	3²	2		13										18
1		3	4	5	2	7¹	8	9					10		6²	12		13	11									19
1		3	4	5	6	7	8	12					10		2	11¹		9										20
1		3	4	5	6	7	8	12	13				10		2	11¹		9										21
1		3	6	5	2	7	8	11					4	10¹		12		9										22
1		3	6¹	5	2	7	8	9					4	10		12	13	11²										23
1		3	6	5	2	7²	8	9³					4	10¹	12	13	14	11										24
1			8		5		8	9					10	12	4	13	2	7²		11¹	3							25
1		6		2			8	9¹					10		3	4	12	7²		13	11³	5	14					26
1	12		6	5	2		8	9					10¹	13		7	14	4²		11³		3						27
1			6	5	2		8	9					4	10		7		12		11¹	3							28
1			6	5	2	12	8	9¹					4	10²		7³	14	13		11	3							29
1	12		6	5	2	7²							4	10		11		13	14	9³	3¹	8						30
1		3	6	5	2	7							4	10		11¹		12	9			8						31
1		3	6	5	2	7		12					4	10¹		11²		13	9			8						32
1		3	6	5	2²	7		9					4	12	13	11			10¹			8						33
1		3	6²	5	2	7		9¹					4	10	12	11		13	14			8³						34
1		3	6	5		7²	8	9¹					4	10		11	12			2	13							35
1		3³	6	5		7	8	10¹					4	12		11²	14	13				2		9				36
1			6	5	2	7	8						4	10¹		11²	12			3	13		9					37
1		3	6	5	2		8						14	12	7	4¹	11	9		10²				13³				38
1			5	2			8	9²	12				6	7²	4	11		10¹		3	13		14					39
1			6	5	2³	8	12						4	13	7	14	11	10²		3			9¹					40
1		3²	6	5		8	10						4	11	7		12	2	13	9								41
1			6	5		8	12						4	10	7²	2		11	13	3			9¹					42
1			6	5		7	8	10¹					4	11		13		12	2	3²	9							43
1			6	5		7³	8	10²					4	11	12	14		13	2	3¹	9							44
1			5			7	8	10¹					4	11²	6	3	13	12	7		0							45
1			6¹	5		7²	8	10					4	13	2	11	14	12	3	9³								46

Coca-Cola Cup
First Round   Bristol R   (h) 1-1
                                      (a) 2-4

FA Cup
First Round   Wycombe W   (a) 1-1
                                            (h) 1-0
Second Round   Hitchin   (h) 3-0
Third Round   Reading   (a) 1-3

GRIMSBY TOWN 1995–96   *Back row (left to right):* Simon Buckley, Neil Woods, Jim Neil, Peter Handyside, Paul Crichton, Jason Pearcey, Graham Rodger. Stewart Petchey, Mark Lever, Jobie Gowshall, Mark Brookes.
Middle row: Mike Bielby (Kit Manager), Nicky Southall, Tommy Watson, Craig Shakespeare, Jack Lester, Steve Livingstone, Ashley Fickling, Jim Dobbin, Paul Groves, Gerry Delahunt (Physio). *Front row:* Kevin Jobling, Clive Mendonca, Gary Childs, Kenny Swain (Assistant Manager), Brian Laws (Manager), John Cockerill (Youth Coach), John McDermott, Gary Croft.

Division 1 GRIMSBY TOWN

Blundell Park, Cleethorpes, North East Lincolnshire DN35 7PY. Telephone: (01472) 697111. Fax: (01472) 693665. Mariners Hotline: 0891 555 855.

Ground capacity: 8686.

Record attendance: 31,657 v Wolverhampton W, FA Cup 5th rd, 20 February 1937.

Record receipts: £119,799 v Aston Villa, FA Cup 4th rd, 29 January 1994.

Pitch measurements: 111yd × 75yd.

Presidents: T. J. Lindley, T. Wilkinson.

Chairman: W. H. Carr. *Vice-Chairman:* T. A. Aspinall.

Directors: G. Lamming, J. Mager, J. Teanby.

Manager: Brian Laws. *Assistant Manager:* Kenny Swain.

Youth Team Coach: John Cockerill.

Chief Executive/Company Secretary: Ian Fleming. *Commercial Manager:* Tony Richardson.

Assistant Commercial Manager/Lottery Manager: T. E. Harvey.

Physio: Gerry Delahunt, FA Treatment of Injuries, MCSP, FSMT, RST.

Year Formed. 1878. *Turned Professional:* 1890. *Ltd Co.:* 1890.

Previous Name: Grimsby Pelham.

Club Nickname: 'The Mariners'.

Previous Grounds: Clee Park; Abbey Park.

Foundation: Grimsby Pelham FC as they were first known, came into being at a meeting held at the Wellington Arms in September 1878. Pelham is the family name of big landowners in the area, the Earls of Yarborough. The receipts for their first game amounted to 6s. 9d. (approx. 39p). After a year, the club name was changed to Grimsby Town.

First Football League game: 3 September 1892, Division 2, v Northwich Victoria (h) W 2-1 – Whitehouse; Lundie, T. Frith; C. Frith, Walker, Murrell; Higgins, Henderson, Brayshaw, Riddoch (2), Ackroyd.

Record League Victory: 9–2 v Darwen, Division 2, 15 April 1899 – Bagshaw; Lockie, Nidd; Griffiths, Bell (1), Nelmes; Jenkinson (3), Richards (1), Cockshutt (3), Robinson, Chadburn (1).

Record Cup Victory: 8–0 v Darlington, FA Cup 2nd rd, 21 November 1885 – G. Atkinson; J. H. Taylor, H. Taylor; Hall, Kimpson, Hopewell; H. Atkinson (1), Garnham, Seal (3), Sharman, Monument (4).

Record Defeat: 1–9 v Arsenal, Division 1, 28 January 1931.

Most League Points (2 for a win): 68, Division 3 (N), 1955–56.

Most League Points (3 for a win): 83, Division 3, 1990–91.

Most League Goals: 103, Division 2, 1933–34.

Highest League Scorer in Season: Pat Glover, 42, Division 2, 1933–34.

Most League Goals in Total Aggregate: Pat Glover, 180, 1930–39.

Most Capped Player: Pat Glover, 7, Wales.

Most League Appearances: Keith Jobling, 448, 1953–69.

Record Transfer Fee Received: £1,000,000 from Blackburn R for Gary Croft, March 1996.

Record Transfer Fee Paid: £180,000 to Carlisle U for Tony Gallimore, March 1996.

Football League Record: 1892 Original Member Division 2; 1901–03 Division 1; 1903 Division 2; 1910 Failed re-election; 1911 re-elected Division 2; 1920–21 Division 3; 1921–26 Division 3 (N); 1926–29 Division 2; 1929–32 Division 1; 1932–34 Division 2; 1934–48 Division 1; 1948–51 Division 2; 1951–56 Division 3 (N); 1956–59 Division 2; 1959–62 Division 3; 1962–64 Division 2; 1964–68 Division 3; 1968–72 Division 4; 1972–77 Division 3; 1977–79 Division 4; 1979–80 Division 3; 1980–87 Division 2; 1987–88 Division 3; 1988–90 Division 4; 1990–91 Division 3; 1991–92 Division 2; 1992– Division 1.

Honours: Football League: Division 1 best season: 5th, 1934–35; Division 2 – Champions 1900–01, 1933–34; Runners-up 1928 29; Division 3 (N) – Champions 1925–26, 1955–56; Runners-up 1951–52; Division 3 – Champions 1979–80; Runners-up 1961–62; Division 4 – Champions 1971–72; Runners-up 1978–79; 1989–90. *FA Cup:* Semi-finals, 1936, 1939. *Football League Cup:* best season: 5th rd, 1980, 1985. *League Group Cup:* Winners 1982.

Colours: Black and white striped shirts, black shorts, white stockings. *Change colours:* All blue.

Did you know?
Clive Mendonca scored a hat-trick in only his second full appearance for Grimsby Town against Ipswich Town on 8 April 1996 after 15 months out with injury.

GRIMSBY TOWN 1995–96 LEAGUE RECORD

Match No.	Date	Venue	Opponents	Result		H/T Score	Lg. Pos.	Goalscorers	Attendance
1	Aug 12	A	Millwall	L	1-2	0-2	—	Livingstone	8546
2	19	H	Portsmouth	W	2-1	0-0	14	Laws, Croft	4515
3	26	A	Derby Co	D	1-1	0-0	12	Shakespeare (pen)	10,564
4	29	H	Luton T	D	0-0	0-0	—		4289
5	Sept 2	H	Watford	D	0-0	0-0	14		3993
6	9	A	Wolverhampton W	L	1-4	1-1	18	Groves	23,656
7	12	H	Reading	W	2-0	1-0	—	Woods, Livingstone	7283
8	16	H	Port Vale	W	1-0	1-0	10	Livingstone	4066
9	23	H	Norwich C	D	2-2	2-1	12	Childs, Southall	5901
10	30	A	Southend U	L	0-1	0-0	14		4977
11	Oct 7	A	Charlton Ath	W	1-0	1-0	12	Jewell	8994
12	14	H	Oldham Ath	D	1-1	0-1	11	Dobbin	5509
13	21	A	Birmingham C	L	1-3	0-0	12	Woods	16,445
14	28	H	Stoke C	W	1-0	0-0	10	Groves	5477
15	Nov 4	A	Ipswich T	D	2-2	0-2	12	Woods, Dobbin	10,250
16	11	H	Barnsley	W	3-1	2-1	8	Lever, De Zeeuw (og), Livingstone	6166
17	18	H	WBA	W	1-0	0-0	7	Bonetti	8155
18	21	A	Sheffield U	W	2-1	0-0	—	Southall, Childs	9884
19	25	A	Tranmere R	W	1-0	1-0	3	Bonetti	7500
20	Dec 2	A	Charlton Ath	L	1-2	0-1	5	Groves	6881
21	9	A	Norwich C	D	2-2	1-1	6	Livingstone, Groves	13,283
22	16	H	Southend U	D	1-1	0-0	6	Forrester	5269
23	23	H	Leicester C	D	2-2	1-0	7	Walsh (og), Dobbin	7713
24	Jan 1	H	Huddersfield T	D	1-1	1-0	8	Livingstone	7524
25	13	A	Portsmouth	L	1-3	0-2	10	Groves	6958
26	20	H	Millwall	L	1-2	1-0	13	Livingstone	5218
27	24	A	Sunderland	L	0-1	0-0	—		14,656
28	Feb 3	H	Derby Co	D	1-1	1-0	13	Bonetti	7818
29	10	A	Luton T	L	2-3	1-1	14	Forrester 2	7158
30	17	H	Reading	D	0-0	0-0	15		6546
31	Mar 3	H	Sunderland	L	0-4	0-1	17		5318
32	5	A	Crystal Palace	L	0-5	0-5	—		11,548
33	9	A	Leicester C	L	1-2	0-1	19	Livingstone	13,784
34	12	H	Wolverhampton W	W	3-0	0-0	—	Shakespeare, Groves, Forrester	5013
35	16	H	Crystal Palace	L	0-2	0-1	17		5059
36	24	A	Huddersfield T	W	3-1	1-1	17	Livingstone, Childs, Groves	12,090
37	30	A	Birmingham C	W	2-1	2-1	15	Groves, Livingstone	5475
38	Apr 2	A	Oldham Ath	L	0-1	0-0	—		5037
39	6	A	Stoke C	W	2-1	0-1	15	Groves, Gallimore	12,524
40	8	H	Ipswich T	W	3-1	0-0	13	Mendonca 3	5904
41	13	A	WBA	L	1-3	1-2	14	Forrester	16,116
42	16	A	Port Vale	L	0-1	0-0	—		5796
43	20	H	Sheffield U	L	0-2	0-2	17		7685
44	23	A	Watford	L	3-6	1-4	—	Groves, Livingstone, Walker	8909
45	27	H	Tranmere R	D	1-1	1-0	16	Mendonca (pen)	5408
46	May 4	A	Barnsley	D	1-1	1-1	17	McDermott	6108

Final League Position: 17

GOALSCORERS

League (55): Livingstone 11, Groves 10, Forrester 5, Mendonca 4 (1 pen), Bonetti 3, Childs 3, Dobbin 3, Woods 3, Shakespeare 2 (1 pen), Southall 2, Croft 1, Gallimore 1, Jewell 1, Laws 1, Lever 1, McDermott 1, Walker 1, own goals 2.
Coca-Cola Cup (2): Southall 1, Woods 1.
FA Cup (12): Forrester 3, Livingstone 2, Woods 2, Bonetti 1, Childs 1, Groves 1, Laws 1, Southall 1.

Crichton P 44	Laws B 21 + 6	Jobling K 3	Handyside P 30	Rodger G 14 + 2	Groves P 46	Croft G 36	Shakespeare C 24 + 4	Woods N 24 + 9	Livingstone S 33 + 5	Southall N 28 + 5	Lester J — + 5	Jewell P 2 + 3	Dobbin J 21 + 5	Lever M 23 + 1	Fickling A 5 + 6	Pearcey J 2	McDermott J 27 + 1	Childs G 33 + 2	Smith R 18	Watson T — + 2	Bonetti I 19	Forrester J 23 + 5	Warner V 3	Butler P 3	Gambaro E — + 1	Gallimore T 10	Flatts M 4 + 1	Mendonca C 8	Clare D — + 1	Walker J 1 + 1	Neil J 1	Match No.
1	2^1	3	4	5	6	7	8	9	10	11	12																					1
1	2	3	4	5	6	7	8	9	10	11																						2
1	2	3^2	4	5	6	7	8	9	10	11^1	12	13																				3
1	2		4		6	7	8	9	10	11			3^1	5	12																	4
	2^3		4		6	3	8	9	10	11	12	13		5^2		1	14	7^1														5
1			4		6	3	8^1	9^2	10	11	12	13					2	7	5													6
1	12		4		6	3	8	9	10	11							2^1	7	5													7
1	2		4		6	3	8^1	9	10	11				12				7^2	5	13												8
1			4		6	3		9	10	11				8			2	7^1	5	12												9
1			4		6	3	12	9		11	13	10^2	8				2	7^1	5													10
1	2		4		6	3				11		9	8					7	5		10											11
1	2^1		4		6	3		9		11	12		8					7	5		10											12
1	2		4		6	3		9		11^2			8	12				7	5^1		10	13										13
1	2		4		6	3		9	12	11^2			0	5				7^1			10	13										14
1	2		4		6	3		9	12	11			8	5				7			10^1											15
1	2		4		6	3		9	10				8	5				7				11										16
1	2		4		6	3			10				8	5				7			11	9										17
1			4		6	3	12		10	11^1			8	5			2	7				9										18
1	12			4	6	3			10				8	5			2	7			11	9^1										19
1				4	6	3	12		10				8	5			2	7			11	9										20
1	12		4		6	3			10				8	5			2	7			11	9^1										21
1	2		4		6	3	12		10^1				8	5				7			11	9										22
1	2		4		6	3			10	11			8	5				7				9										23
1	2		4		6	3	12		10				8	5				7			11	9^1										24
1	2		4	5^1	6	3	13	14	10				8^2	12				7			11	9^3										25
1	12			4^1	6	3	13		10		14		8^2	5			2	7			11	9^3										26
1	8		4		6	3	7		12	10				5			2			13	11^1	9^2										27
1			12		6	3		9			13			5^1			2	7			11					10^2	4	8				28
1	2				6	3		9			12	13		5				7^1			11					10^2	4	8				29
1					6	3	8	9	12	11				5	4		2	7								10^1						30
1	12				6	3		13	10	11				5			2	7^2				9^1					4	8				31
1				4	6	3	8	9	10	11				5			2	7														32
1	12			4	6	3	8	9	10	11^1				5			2	7^2							13							33
1	11		12		6	3	8		10					5^1			2	7	4			9										34
1	11			5	6	3^2	8		10	12				13			2	7	4			9										35
1				5	6	3	8		10	11							2	7	4			9										36
1				5	6		8		10	11							2		4			9				3	7					37
1				5	6		8	12	10	11^2							2	13	4			9^1				3	7					38
1	5				6		8	9		12				13			2^2	11	4			14				3	7^1	10^2				39
1	5				6		8^1	9		12				13			2	11^2	4^3			14				3	7	10				40
1					6		8	9	12	11				5			2	7^2	4							3	13	10				41
1	5				6		8	9			7						2		4		11					3		10				42
1	5				6		8	9			7^2			12			2			4^1	11					3		10	13			43
1	4^2				6		8	12	9		7	5		13			2				11					3		10		14		44
1	5				6		8	9		7				12			2			4	11^1					3		10				45
1	5				6			9	12				8	4		1	2			13						3		10		11^2	7^1	46

Coca-Cola Cup

Second Round	Birmingham C	(a)	1-3
		(h)	1-1

FA Cup

Third Round	Luton T	(h)	7-1
Fourth Round	West Ham U	(a)	1-1
		(h)	3-0
Fifth Round	Chelsea	(h)	0-0
		(a)	1-4

HARTLEPOOL UNITED 1995-96 *Back row (left to right):* Sean McAuley, Chris Homer, Chris Lynch, Neil Maughan, Ian McGuckin, Damian Henderson, Denny Ingram, Ian Gallagher.
Third row: Gary Henderson, Stephen Farnaby, Graeme Lee, Richard Maxwell, Brian Horne, Steve Jones, Jamie Allinson, Stuart Levine, Lee Hainsworth.
Brian Honour (Assistant Youth Team Coach).
Second row: Billy Horner (Youth Team Coach), Keith Oliver, Stephen Halliday, Mick Tait (Player/Coach), Keith Houchen (Player/Manager), Tony Canham, Scott Sloan, Shane Reddish.
Front row: Glen Downey, Darren Slater, Carl Thexton, Stephen Hutt, Paul Walton, Danny Hyson, Paul Conlon, Craig Winstanley, Lee Foster.
(Photograph: F. L. Reid)

Division 3 **HARTLEPOOL UNITED**

Victoria Park, Clarence Road, Hartlepool, Cleveland TS24 8B2. Telephone: (01429) 272584. Commercial Dept: (01429) 222077. Fax: (01429) 863007. Football in the Community: (01429) 272584.

Ground capacity: 7229.

Record attendance: 17,426 v Manchester U, FA Cup 3rd rd, 5 January 1957.

Record receipts: £42,300 v Tottenham H, Rumbelows Cup 2nd rd 2nd leg, 9 October 1990.

Pitch measurements: 110yd × 75yd.

President: E. Leadbitter.

Chairman: H. Hornsey.

Directors: A. Bamford, D. Jukes.

Manager: Keith Houchen. *Coach:* Mick Tait.

Youth Coach: Billy Horner. *Physio:* Gary Hinchley. *Commercial Manager:* Frank Baggs.

Secretary: Stuart Bagnall. *Football in the Community Officer:* Brian Honour. *Safety Officer:* Maurice Russell.

Year Formed: 1908. *Turned Professional:* 1908. *Ltd Co.:* 1908.

Club Nickname: 'The Pool'.

Previous Names: Hartlepools United until 1968; Hartlepool until 1977.

Foundation: The inspiration for the launching of Hartlepool United was the West Hartlepool club which won the FA Amateur Cup in 1904–05. They had been in existence since 1881 and their Cup success led in 1908 to the formation of the new professional concern which first joined the North-Eastern League. In those days they were Hartlepools United and won the Durham Senior Cup in their first two seasons.

First Football League game: 27 August 1921, Division 3 (N), v Wrexham (a) W 2-0 – Gill; Thomas, Crilly; Dougherty, Hopkins, Short; Kessler, Mulholland (1), Lister (1), Robertson, Donald.

Record League Victory: 10–1 v Barrow, Division 4, 4 April 1959 – Oakley; Cameron, Waugh; Johnson, Moore, Anderson; Scott (1), Langland (1), Smith (3), Clark (2), Luke (2). (1 og).

Record Cup Victory: 6–0 v North Shields, FA Cup 1st rd, 30 November 1946 – Heywood; Brown, Gregory; Spelman, Lambert, Jones; Price, Scott (2), Sloan (4), Moses, McMahon.

Record Defeat: 1–10 v Wrexham, Division 4, 3 March 1962.

Most League Points (2 for a win): 60, Division 4, 1967–68.

Most League Points (3 for a win): 82, Division 4, 1990–91.

Most League Goals: 90, Division 3 (N), 1956–57.

Highest League Scorer in Season: William Robinson, 28, Division 3 (N), 1927–28 and Joe Allon, 28, Division 4, 1990–91.

Most League Goals in Total Aggregate: Ken Johnson, 98, 1949–64.

Most Capped Player: Ambrose Fogarty, 1 (11), Republic of Ireland.

Most League Appearances: Wattie Moore, 447, 1948–64.

Record Transfer Fee Received: £300,000 from Chelsea for Joe Allon, August 1991.

Record Transfer Fee Paid: £60,000 to Barnsley for Andy Saville, March 1992.

Football League Record: 1921 Original Member of Division 3 (N); 1958–68 Division 4; 1968–69 Division 3; 1969–91 Division 4; 1991–92 Division 3; 1992–94 Division 2; 1994– Division 3.

Honours: Football League: Division 3 best season: 22nd, 1968–69; Division 3 (N) – Runners-up 1956–57. *FA Cup:* best season: 4th rd, 1955, 1978, 1989, 1993. *Football League Cup,* best season: 4th rd, 1975.

Colours: Blue and white striped shirts. *Change colours:* Red shirts with white trim.

Did you know?
Hartlepool United had two players sent off at Torquay on 17 February 1996, the first after 20 minutes, the second after 32 minutes but still managed to draw 0-0.

HARTLEPOOL UNITED 1995–96 LEAGUE RECORD

Match No.	Date	Venue	Opponents	Result		H/T Score	Lg. Pos.	Goalscorers	Attendance
1	Aug 12	A	Chester C	L	0-2	0-1	—		2286
2	19	H	Exeter C	D	0-0	0-0	21		2311
3	26	A	Rochdale	L	0-4	0-1	22		1794
4	29	H	Northampton T	W	2-1	1-0	—	Hughes (og), Henderson	2390
5	Sept 2	A	Doncaster R	L	0-1	0-0	23		2304
6	9	H	Darlington	D	1-1	0-0	22	Houchen	2705
7	12	H	Torquay U	D	2-2	1-0	—	Houchen, Lowe	1945
8	16	A	Leyton Orient	L	1-4	0-2	22	Houchen	4519
9	23	H	Cardiff C	W	2-1	1-1	19	Lowe 2	2172
10	30	H	Cambridge U	W	1-0	0-0	16	Howard	2849
11	Oct 7	A	Colchester U	L	1-4	0-3	20	Howard	2618
12	14	H	Scunthorpe U	W	2-0	0-0	14	Howard, Henderson	2608
13	21	A	Wigan Ath	L	0-1	0-0	18		2104
14	28	H	Gillingham	D	1-1	0-1	20	Halliday	2355
15	31	H	Barnet	D	0-0	0-0	—		1713
16	Nov 4	A	Lincoln C	D	1-1	0-1	19	Allon	2939
17	18	H	Plymouth Arg	D	2-2	0-2	18	Ingram, Howard	1830
18	25	A	Preston NE	L	0-3	0-1	22		9449
19	Dec 9	A	Cardiff C	L	0-2	0-0	22		2919
20	16	H	Cambridge U	L	1-2	1-1	22	Allon	1612
21	23	A	Mansfield T	W	3-0	1-0	22	Houchen 2, Halliday	1982
22	Jan 1	A	Bury	W	3-0	1-0	18	Houchen, Halliday, McGuckin	2927
23	6	H	Scarborough	D	1-1	0-1	16	Allon	2252
24	20	H	Chester C	W	2-1	1-1	18	Halliday, Tait	1864
25	30	A	Exeter C	L	0-1	0-1	—		2468
26	Feb 3	H	Rochdale	D	1-1	0-0	20	Tait	1927
27	10	A	Fulham	D	2-2	0-1	21	Allon 2	3700
28	17	A	Torquay U	D	0-0	0-0	20		2580
29	20	H	Doncaster R	L	0-1	0-0	—		1367
30	24	H	Leyton Orient	W	4-1	2-0	18	Conlon, Allon, McGuckin, Lynch	1915
31	27	A	Darlington	L	0-1	0-0	—		4332
32	Mar 2	A	Scarborough	W	2-1	1-1	15	Conlon 2	2419
33	5	H	Hereford U	L	0-1	0-1	—		1473
34	9	H	Mansfield T	D	1-1	1-0	17	Howard	1758
35	12	H	Fulham	W	1-0	1-0	—	Conlon	1198
36	19	H	Northampton T	D	0-0	0-0	—		3537
37	23	H	Bury	L	1-2	1-0	16	Ingram	1879
38	30	H	Colchester U	W	2-1	1-1	16	Halliday, Howard	1364
39	Apr 2	A	Scunthorpe U	L	1-2	1-1	—	Halliday	2100
40	6	A	Gillingham	L	0-2	0-1	17		6267
41	8	H	Wigan Ath	L	1-2	1-0	19	Canham	1877
42	13	A	Barnet	L	1-5	0-3	19	Halliday	2530
43	20	H	Lincoln C	W	3-0	1-0	19	Henderson, Allon 2	3012
44	27	H	Preston NE	L	0-2	0-1	20		5076
45	30	A	Hereford U	L	1-4	0-1	—	Howard	3942
46	May 4	A	Plymouth Arg	L	0-3	0-1	20		11,526

Final League Position: 20

GOALSCORERS

League (47): Allon 8, Halliday 7, Howard 7, Houchen 6, Conlon 4, Henderson 3, Lowe 3, Ingram 2, McGuckin 2, Tait 2, Canham 1, Lynch 1, own goal 1.
Coca-Cola Cup (1): McGuckin 1.
FA Cup (2): Halliday 1, Sloan 1.

Jones S 7 + 2	Ingram D 32 + 1	McAuley S 46	Billing P 35 + 1	McGuckin I 40	Howard S 32 + 7	Halliday S 36 + 3	Tait M 38 + 1	Houchen K 36 + 2	Henderson D 33 + 3	Canham T 25 + 4	Horne B 32	Lynch C 13 + 6	Oliver K 7 + 6	Sloan S 1 + 5	Foster L — + 1	Reddish S 18 + 2	Homer C 1 + 4	Lowe K 13	Ford G 2 + 1	Debont A 1	Allon J 22	Roberts B 4	Dixon A 3	Key L 1	Lee G 3 + 3	Conlon P 11 + 4	Stokoe G 8	Allinson J 3 + 1	Walton P 1 + 5	Slater D — + 1	O'Connor P 1	Gallagher I 1	Hutt S — + 1	Match No.
1	2	3	4	5	6	7	8	9	10	11																								1
	2	3	4	5	6	10	8	12	9	11	1	7¹																						2
		3	4		7²	10	8	9¹	5	2	1	11	6	12	13																			3
		3²	4	5	6¹	10	8		9	11	1	7	12			2	13																	4
		3	4	5		7¹	8	9	10	11	1	12				2					6													5
		3	4	5		7	8	9	10¹	11	1					2					6	12												6
		3	4	5		10	8	9		11	1	12	13			2					6²	7¹												7
		3	4	5		10	8	9	12	11	1					2					6	7¹												8
		11	4	5		10	8	9¹	12	7	1	3	13			2²					6													9
15	12	3		5	11	10	8	9	4	2¹	1⁶		7								6													10
1	2	3	4	5	11	10	8		9		7¹						12	6																11
	2	3	4	5	11	10	8		9								12	6	1		7¹													12
	2	3	4	5	11		8	9¹	12								10	6			7	1												13
	2	3	4	5	11²	12	8	9	10¹							13		6			7	1												14
	2	3	4	5	12	11	9¹	6				13				8²	10				7	1												15
	2	3	4	5	12	13	8	9¹	6							11¹	10				7	1												16
	2	3	4	5	12	10	14	13	6	11¹					7²		8³							9										17
	2	3	4	5	11	10³	8	9	6	12²	1				14	13								7¹										18
	2	6	4		11	10	8	9	5		1	3			12									7¹										19
	2	3	4	5	11¹	10	8	9								12		6			7		1											20
	2	3	4	5		10	8¹	9	6							1	11	12			7													21
		3	4	5	7¹	10		9²				1	11	8	13		2	12								6								22
		3	4	5	9	10						1	11	8	12		2									6¹								23
	2	11	4	5	12	10	8¹	9				1	3			6										7								24
	2	11	4	5	12	10	8	9				1	3¹			6										7								25
	2	3	4	5	11	10	8	9				1		12		6										7¹								26
	2	3	4	5	11	10³	8	9				1		12		6										7								27
		3		5¹	6		9	4	11		1	10	8			2						7²				12	13							28
	4	3			6		8	9¹	5	12	1	11	10²			2						7				13								29
	2	3		5	12		8	9¹	4	11²	1	13										7				10	6							30
	2	3		5	12		8	9	4	11	1	13										7¹				10²	6							31
	2	3	4	5			8	9	7	11	1															10	6							32
	2	3	4	5	9		8			11	1											7				10	6							33
	2	3	4	5	9	12	8			11	1											7				10¹	6							34
	2	3		5	11	10	8	9	4		1											7	6											35
	2	3		5	11	10	8	9	4	12	1											7¹	6											36
	2	3		5	11	10	8	9	4	12	1											7¹	6											37
	2¹	3	12	5²	6	10	8	9	4	11	1											7³				13	14							38
	3	2			6	10	8	9	4	11	1											12	7¹			5²	13							39
15	2¹	3	7		6	10	8	9	4	11	1⁶															5	12							40
1		3	2		6	10	8	9	4	11													7¹			5²	12	13						41
1		3	2	5	6	10	8	9	4	11								7																42
	2	3	8	5	6	10		9²	4¹	11								7					12	13					1					43
1	2	3		5	9	8	9		4	11								7																44
1	8	3	2	5	6	7		4	10								9						12				11¹							45
1	2²	3		5	9	10			4	11							7				6				12				8¹	13				46

Coca-Cola Cup
First Round   Scarborough   (a)   0-1   (h)   1-0
Second Round   Arsenal   (h)   0-3   (a)   0-5

FA Cup
First Round   Darlington   (h)   2-4

HEREFORD UNITED 1995-96   *Back row (left to right):* Dean Clarke, Steve White, John Brough, Tony James, Chris MacKenzie, Neil Lyne, Kevin Lloyd, Robert Warner. *Front row:* Phil Preedy, Murray Fishlock, Andy Reece, Gary Pick, Graham Turner (Manager), Dean Smith, Richard Wilkins, Nicky Cross, Tim Steele.

Division 3   **HEREFORD UNITED**

Edgar Street, Hereford HR4 9JU. Telephone: (01432) 276666. Fax: (01432) 341359.

Ground capacity: 8843.

Record attendance: 18,114 v Sheffield W, FA Cup 3rd rd, 4 January 1958.

Record receipts: £103,224 v Tottenham H, FA Cup 3rd rd, 6 January 1996.

Pitch measurements: 110yd × 74yd.

Chairman: P. S. Hill FRICS.

Directors: J. W. T. Duggan, D. H. Vaughan, R. A. Fry, J. Simmons, K. Benjamin (Assoc).

Manager: Graham Turner. *Assistant Manager:* Dick Bate.

Physio: S. Shakesaft. *Coach:* S. Ritchie.

Secretary: J. Fennessy. *Commercial Manager:* J. Pulling. *Stadium Manager:* W. Adamson.

Year Formed: 1924. *Turned Professional:* 1924. *Ltd Co.:* 1939.

Club Nickname: 'United'.

Foundation: A number of local teams amalgamated in 1924 under the chairmanship of Dr. E. W. Maples to form Hereford United and joined the Birmingham Combination. They graduated to the Birmingham League four years later.

First Football League game: 12 August 1972, Division 4, v Colchester U (a) L 0-1 – Potter; Mallender, Naylor; Jones, McLaughlin, Tucker; Slattery, Hollett, Owen, Radford, Wallace.

Record League Victory: 6–0 v Burnley (away), Division 4, 24 January 1987 – Rose; Rodgerson, Devine, Halliday, Pejic, Dalziel, Harvey (1p), Wells, Phillips (3), Kearns (2), Spooner.

Record Cup Victory: 6–1 v QPR, FA Cup 2nd rd, 7 December 1957 – Sewell; Tomkins, Wade; Masters, Niblett, Horton (2p); Reg Bowen (1), Clayton (1), Fidler, Williams (1), Cyril Beech (1).

Record Defeat: 1-7 v Mansfield T, Division 3, 26 December 1994.

Most League Points (2 for a win): 63, Division 3, 1975–76.

Most League Points (3 for a win): 77, Division 4, 1984–85.

Most League Goals: 86, Division 3, 1975–76.

Highest League Scorer in Season: Dixie McNeil, 35, 1975–76.

Most League Goals in Total Aggregate: Stewart Phillips, 93, 1980–88, 1990–91.

Most Capped Player: Brian Evans, 1 (7), Wales.

Most League Appearances: Mel Pejic, 412, 1980–92.

Record Transfer Fee Received: £440,000 from QPR for Darren Peacock, December 1990.

Record Transfer Fee Paid: £80,000 to Walsall for Dean Smith, June 1994.

Football League Record: 1972 Elected to Division 4; 1973–76 Division 3; 1976–77 Division 2; 1977–78 Division 3; 1978–92 Division 4; 1992– Division 3.

Honours: Football League: Division 2 best season: 22nd, 1976–77; Division 3 – Champions 1975–76; Division 4 – Runners-up 1972–73. *FA Cup:* best season: 4th rd, 1972, 1977, 1982, 1990. *Football League Cup:* best season: 3rd rd, 1975. *Welsh Cup:* Winners 1990.

Colours: White and black shirts, black shorts, white stockings. *Change colours:* Red and black striped shirts, white shorts, white stockings.

Did you know?
During the 1995–96 season Hereford United established a club record of six successive wins.

HEREFORD UNITED 1995–96 LEAGUE RECORD

Match No.	Date	Venue	Opponents	Result		H/T Score	Lg. Pos.	Goalscorers	Attendance
1	Aug 12	H	Barnet	W	4-1	3-0	—	Smith (pen), Brough, Mackenzie, Pounder	2522
2	19	A	Cambridge U	D	2-2	1-2	4	Fishlock, Lyne	2557
3	26	H	Bury	L	3-4	2-1	9	White 2, Preedy	2702
4	29	A	Plymouth Arg	W	1-0	1-0	—	White	5608
5	Sept 2	A	Chester C	L	1-2	0-2	11	Pounder	3385
6	9	H	Preston NE	L	0-1	0-0	14		3124
7	12	H	Gillingham	D	0-0	0-0	—		1747
8	16	A	Scarborough	D	2-2	1-0	14	Stoker, Cross	1449
9	23	A	Colchester U	L	0-2	0-1	17		2596
10	30	H	Wigan Ath	D	2-2	1-1	17	Wilkins, White	2198
11	Oct 7	H	Torquay U	W	2-1	1-0	14	White, Wilkins	2143
12	14	A	Doncaster R	D	0-0	0-0	17		1961
13	21	H	Exeter C	D	2-2	0-0	17	White, Blatherwick	2249
14	28	A	Fulham	D	0-0	0-0	18		3631
15	31	A	Leyton Orient	W	1-0	0-0	—	Cross	3567
16	Nov 4	H	Mansfield T	L	0-1	0-0	15		2193
17	18	A	Rochdale	D	0-0	0-0	15		2619
18	26	H	Cardiff C	L	1-3	0-0	16	White	3528
19	Dec 9	H	Colchester U	D	1-1	0-0	17	Smith	3324
20	16	A	Wigan Ath	L	1-2	1-0	19	Cross	1962
21	19	H	Scunthorpe U	W	3-0	1-0	—	Cross, White 2	2516
22	26	A	Northampton T	D	1-1	0-0	15	Smith	5222
23	Jan 13	A	Cambridge U	W	5-2	3-1	16	White 4, Smith (pen)	2548
24	20	A	Barnet	W	3-1	1-1	13	Stoker, Cross, White	1835
25	Feb 13	A	Lincoln C	L	1-2	1-0	—	White	1884
26	17	A	Gillingham	D	1-1	1-0	19	Smith	6993
27	20	H	Chester C	W	1-0	0-0	—	White	1827
28	24	H	Scarborough	D	0-0	0-0	16		2551
29	27	A	Preston NE	D	2-2	1-1	—	Fishlock, Smith	9761
30	Mar 2	H	Northampton T	W	1-0	0-0	14	James	2822
31	5	A	Hartlepool U	W	1-0	1-0	—	Smith	1473
32	9	A	Scunthorpe U	W	1-0	0-0	11	Hargreaves	1903
33	19	A	Bury	L	0-2	0-0	—		2280
34	23	A	Darlington	L	0-1	0-0	14		1708
35	27	H	Lincoln C	W	1-0	0-0	—	Cross	1631
36	30	A	Torquay U	D	1-1	1-1	14	White	2034
37	Apr 2	H	Doncaster R	W	1-0	1-0	—	White	2060
38	6	H	Fulham	W	1-0	1-0	10	James	3276
39	8	A	Exeter C	W	2-0	1-0	10	White 2	3191
40	13	A	Leyton Orient	W	3-2	1-0	10	Wilkins, White 2	3459
41	16	H	Plymouth Arg	W	3-0	2-0	—	White 3 (1 pen)	4739
42	20	A	Mansfield T	W	2-1	1-1	7	White (pen), Hargreaves	2358
43	23	H	Darlington	L	0-1	0-1	—		5359
44	27	A	Cardiff C	L	2-3	0-2	8	White, Fishlock	3751
45	30	H	Hartlepool U	W	4-1	1-0	—	White, Smith (pen), Cross, Stoker	3942
46	May 4	H	Rochdale	W	2-0	1-0	6	Cross, White	5880

Final League Position: 6

GOALSCORERS

League (65): White 29 (2 pens), Cross 8, Smith 8 (3 pens), Fishlock 3, Stoker 3, Wilkins 3, Hargreaves 2, James 2, Pounder 2, Blatherwick 1, Brough 1, Lyne 1, Mackenzie 1, Preedy 1.
Coca-Cola Cup (2): Reece 1, Smith 1.
FA Cup (6): White 3, Brough 1, Cross 1, Stoker 1.

MacKenzie C 38	Stoker G 30 + 3	Lloyd K 25 + 2	Smith D 39 + 1	Brough J 22	Reece A 6	Pounder T 31 + 3	Wilkins R 42	Lyne N 22 + 10	White S 39 + 1	Fishlock M 26 + 1	Cross N 32 + 5	Pick G 10 + 4	Preedy P 5 + 8	Clarke D 5	Hall L — + 1	Blatherwick S 10	Evans D 24	Downing K 29	Steele T — + 7	Watkiss S 19	Pitman J 12 + 1	Hargreaves C 15 + 2	James T 17	Debont A 8	Match No.
1	2	3	4	5	6	7	8	9	10	11															1
1	2	3	4	5^2	6	7	8	9^1	10	11	12	13													2
1	2	3^2	4		6	7	8	9	10	11	12	5^1	13												3
1			4		6	7	8	9	10^1	11	5	12	3	2											4
1	5		4		6	7	8	9^1	3	10	12	11	2												5
1	5	11	4		6^2	7	8	9	3	10	12	2^1	13												6
1	6	3	4			7	8	9		11	10		2			5									7
1	11^1		4			7	8	9	3	10	12					5	2	6							8
1	11^1	3	4			7	8	9		10	13	12				5	2	6^2							9
1	11^1	3	4			7	8	9	10		12					5		6							10
1	11	3	4			7^1	8		10		9	12				5	2	6							11
1	11	3	4				8		10		9	7				5	2	6							12
1	11^1	3	4			7	8		10		9	12				5	2	6							13
1		3	4			7	8	12	10		9^1	11				5	2	6							14
1		3	4			7	8		10		9	11				5	2	6							15
1	12	3	4			7	8		10		9	11^1	13			5	2	6^2							16
1	5		4			7	8		10	3	9	6	11				2								17
1	5		4			7	8	12	10	3	9	6^2	11^1				2	13							18
1	5	3	4		6	7	8	12	10^1		9						2			11					19
1	5^1		4		6	7	8	12	10	3	9						2			11					20
1			4		6	7^1	8	5	10	3	9						2			11	12				21
1			4		6	7	8	5	10	3	9						2			11					22
1	12		4		6	7	8	5	10	3	9^2						2			11^1	13				23
1	8	3	4		6	7		5	10		9	11					2								24
1	8^1	3	4		6	7		5	10		9	11					2	12							25
1	8		4		6			5^2	9^1	10	3	12	11					7	13	2					26
1	8		4		6			5	9	10	3							7		2	11^1	12			27
1			4	5	6		8	12	10	3							11	7		2		9^1			28
1			4	5	6		8	12	10	3							11	7		2		9			29
1			4	5^1			8	12	10	3	13						11	7		2		9^2	6		30
1			4				8	9	10	3	5						11	7		2			6		31
1			4				8	9		3	5						11	7		2		10	6		32
1	12		4	5^2			8	9		3		13					11^3	7		2	14	10	6^1		33
	12		4	5^3			8	9		3^1		13	14					7		2	11	10	6^2	1	34
		3	4	5			8	9			12							7		2	11	10^1	6	1	35
	12	3	4	5			8	9			10							7		2^1	11		6	1	36
	7	3	4	5			8	9			10									2	11		6	1	37
1	7	3	4	5^1			8	9			10									2	11	12	6		38
1	7	3	4				8	9			10									2	11	5	6		39
1	7	3	4				8	9									5			2	11	10	6		40
1	7	3	4				8	12			9^2						5	13		2	11	10^1	6	1	41
1	7	3	4				8	9									5	12		2	11^1	10	6	1	42
1	7	3^1	4				8	12			9	13					5	11^2		2^1		10	6	1	43
1	7	12	4				8	9		3		13					5	11^2		2^1		10	6	1	44
1	7		4				8	9		3	5^1									2	11	10	6		45
1	7		4				8	9		3	5									2	11	10	6		46

Coca-Cola Cup
First Round — Oxford U — (h) 0-2 / (a) 2-3

FA Cup
First Round — Stevenage B — (h) 2-1
Second Round — Sutton U — (h) 2-0
Third Round — Tottenham H — (h) 1-1 / (a) 1-5

HUDDERSFIELD TOWN 1995-96 *Back row (left to right)*: Simon Baldry, Iain Dunn, Chris Billy, Jon Whitney, Ronnie Jepson, Andrew Booth, Simon Collins, Kevin Gray. *Middle row*: Dennis Booth (Coach), David Moss (Youth Team Coach), Craig Whitington, Simon Trevitt, Richard Logan, Tony Norman, Steve Francis, Jonathan Dyson, Patrick Scully, Dave Wilson (Physio). *Front row*: Rodney Rowe, Tom Cowan, Darren Bullock, Lee Sinnott, Brian Horton (Manager), Paul Reid, Lee Duxbury, Gary Crosby, Gary Clayton.

Division 1 HUDDERSFIELD TOWN

The Alfred McAlpine Stadium, Leeds Rd, Huddersfield HD1 6PX. Telephone: (01484) 420335. Fax: (01484) 515122. Ticket Office: (01484) 424444. Club Shop: (01484) 534867. Recorded Information: 0891 121635.

Ground capacity: 19,500.

Record attendance: 67,037 v Arsenal, FA Cup 6th rd, 27 February 1932 (at new ground): 18,775 v Birmingham C, Division 2, 6 May 1995.

Record receipts: £89,081 v Arsenal, Coca-Cola Cup 2nd rd lst leg, 21 September 1993. (At new ground): £155,149 v Wimbledon, FA Cup 5th rd, 17 February 1996.

Pitch measurements: 115yd × 76yd.

President: Lawrence Batley OBE. *Chairman:* D. G. Headey.

Directors: M. Asquith, D. Taylor, R. Whiteley.

Associate Director: T. J. Cherry.

Manager: Brian Horton. *First Team Coach:* Dennis Booth. *Coach:* David Moss.

Secretary: Alan D. Sykes. *Assistant Secretary:* Ann Hough. *Commercial Manager:* Alan Stevenson.

Physio: Dave Wilson. *Stadium Manager:* Brian Buckley.

Year Formed: 1908. *Turned Professional:* 1908. *Ltd Co.:* 1908.

Club Nickname: 'The Terriers'.

Foundation: A meeting, attended largely by members of the Huddersfield & District FA, was held at the Imperial Hotel in 1906 to discuss the feasibility of establishing a football club in this rugby stronghold. However, it was not until a man with both the enthusiasm and the money to back the scheme came on the scene, that real progress was made. This benefactor was Mr. Hilton Crowther and it was at a meeting at the Albert Hotel in 1908, that the club formally came into existence with a capital of £2,000 and joined the North-Eastern League.

First Football League game: 3 September 1910, Division 2, v Bradford PA (a) W 1-0 – Mutch; Taylor, Morris; Beaton, Hall, Bartlett; Blackburn, Wood, Hamilton (1), McCubbin, Jee.

Record League Victory: 10–1 v Blackpool, Division 1, 13 December 1930 – Turner; Goodall, Spencer; Redfern, Wilson, Campbell; Bob Kelly (1), McLean (4), Robson (3), Davies (1), Smailes (1).

Record Cup Victory: 7–1 v Chesterfield (away), FA Cup 3rd rd, 12 January 1929 – Turvey; Goodall, Wadsworth; Evans, Wilson, Naylor: Jackson (1), Kelly, Brown (3), Cumming (2), Smith. (1 og).

Record Defeat: 1–10 v Manchester C, Division 2, 7 November 1987.

Most League Points (2 for a win): 66, Division 4, 1979–80.

Most League Points (3 for a win): 82, Division 3, 1982–83.

Most League Goals: 101, Division 4, 1979–80.

Highest League Scorer in Season: Sam Taylor, 35, Division 2, 1919–20; George Brown, 35, Division 1, 1925–26.

Most League Goals in Total Aggregate: George Brown, 142, 1921–29 and Jimmy Glazzard, 142, 1946–56.

Most Capped Player: Jimmy Nicholson, 31 (41), Northern Ireland.

Most League Appearances: Billy Smith, 520, 1914–34.

Record Transfer Fee Received: £375,000 from Southampton for Simon Charlton, June 1993.

Record Transfer Fee Paid: £250,000 to Bradford C for Lee Duxbury, December 1994.

Football League Record: 1910 Elected to Division 2; 1920–52 Division 1; 1952–53 Division 2; 1953–56 Division 1; 1956–70 Division 2; 1970–72 Division 1; 1972–73 Division 2; 1973–75 Division 3; 1975–80 Division 4; 1980–83 Division 3; 1983–88 Division 2; 1988–92 Division 3; 1992–95 Division 2; 1995– Division 1.

Honours: Football League: Division 1 – Champions 1923–24, 1924–25, 1925–26; Runners-up 1926–27, 1927–28, 1933–34; Division 2 – Champions 1969–70; Runners-up 1919–20, 1952–53; Division 4 – Champions 1979–80. *FA Cup:* Winners 1922; Runners-up 1920, 1928, 1930, 1938. *Football League Cup:* Semi-final 1968. *Autoglass Trophy:* Runners-up 1994.

Colours: Blue and white striped shirts, white shorts, white stockings. *Change colours:* White shirts with black sleeves, black shorts, white stockings.

Did you know?
In May 1951, Huddersfield Town beat PSV Eindhoven 4-1 and Rennes 5-1 in Festival of Britain matches.

HUDDERSFIELD TOWN 1995–96 LEAGUE RECORD

Match No.	Date	Venue	Opponents	Result		H/T Score	Lg. Pos.	Goalscorers	Attendance
1	Aug 12	A	Oldham Ath	L	0-3	0-1	—		10,259
2	19	H	Watford	W	1-0	0-0	18	Jepson	10,556
3	26	A	Tranmere R	L	1-3	0-0	20	Cowan	9072
4	30	H	Birmingham C	W	4-2	1-1	—	Dalton 2, Jepson, Bullock	12,305
5	Sept 2	A	Charlton Ath	L	1-2	0-1	12	Booth	9570
6	9	H	Ipswich T	W	2-1	2-0	10	Collins, Sedgley (og)	12,057
7	12	H	Barnsley	W	3-0	1-0	—	Jepson, Collins, Booth	14,635
8	16	A	Crystal Palace	D	0-0	0-0	7		15,645
9	24	H	Sheffield U	L	1-2	0-2	10	Jepson	12,840
10	30	A	WBA	W	2-1	2-1	5	Cowan, Booth	15,945
11	Oct 7	H	Port Vale	L	0-2	0-1	10		11,554
12	14	A	Reading	L	1-3	1-1	14	Booth	8534
13	21	H	Sunderland	D	1-1	0-0	11	Booth	16,054
14	28	A	Southend U	D	0-0	0-0	13		5128
15	Nov 4	H	Norwich C	W	3-2	1-0	11	Jepson, Jenkins, Dalton	13,747
16	11	A	Portsmouth	D	1-1	1-1	12	Scully	6876
17	18	A	Millwall	D	0-0	0-0	12		9402
18	21	H	Leicester C	W	3-1	1-1	—	Bullock 2, Dalton	14,300
19	25	H	Wolverhampton W	W	2-1	2-0	8	Booth, Dalton	16,423
20	Dec 2	A	Port Vale	L	0-1	0-1	11		7701
21	9	A	Sheffield U	W	2-0	1-0	10	Booth, Bullock	12,126
22	16	H	WBA	W	4-1	0-0	5	Turner, Jepson 2, Booth	12,664
23	23	A	Luton T	D	2-2	0-1	5	Booth, Makel	7076
24	26	H	Derby Co	L	0-1	0-0	7		18,495
25	30	H	Stoke C	D	1-1	0-0	6	Prudhoe (og)	15,071
26	Jan 1	A	Grimsby T	D	1-1	0-1	4	Jepson (pen)	7524
27	13	A	Watford	W	1-0	0-0	3	Bullock	7568
28	20	H	Oldham Ath	D	0-0	0-0	3		13,013
29	Feb 3	H	Tranmere R	W	1-0	0-0	3	Collins	12,041
30	20	H	Charlton Ath	D	2-2	2-1	—	Booth, Rowe	10,951
31	24	H	Crystal Palace	W	3-0	3-0	4	Booth, Jepson (pen), Makel	13,041
32	Mar 2	A	Derby Co	L	2-3	1-2	5	Booth, Thornley	17,097
33	9	H	Luton T	W	1-0	0-0	6	Edwards	11,950
34	12	A	Birmingham C	L	0-2	0-1	—		15,296
35	16	A	Stoke C	D	1-1	0-0	6	Edwards	13,157
36	19	A	Barnsley	L	0-3	0-2	—		10,660
37	24	H	Grimsby T	L	1-3	1-1	7	Jepson (pen)	12,090
38	30	A	Sunderland	L	2-3	1-1	8	Edwards, Booth	20,131
39	Apr 2	H	Reading	W	3-1	0-1	—	Edwards 2, Booth	11,828
40	6	H	Southend U	W	3-1	0-0	6	Jepson, Edwards, Booth	11,558
41	8	A	Norwich C	L	0-2	0-0	6		13,021
42	13	H	Millwall	W	3-0	1-0	7	Jepson (pen), Edwards, Booth	11,206
43	20	A	Leicester C	L	1-2	0-1	8	Bullock	17,619
44	27	A	Wolverhampton W	D	0-0	0-0	8		25,290
45	May 1	A	Ipswich T	L	1-2	1-1	—	Thornley	17,473
46	5	H	Portsmouth	L	0-1	0-1	8		14,091

Final League Position: 8

GOALSCORERS

League (61): Booth 16, Jepson 12 (4 pens), Edwards 7, Bullock 6, Dalton 5, Collins 3, Cowan 2, Makel 2, Thornley 2, Jenkins 1, Rowe 1, Scully 1, Turner 1, own goals 2.
Coca-Cola Cup (6): Booth 3, Bullock 1, Collins 1, Dalton 1.
FA Cup (7): Booth 2, Jepson 2 (1 pen), Bullock 1, Cowan 1, Rowe 1.

Francis S 43	Trevitt S 4	Cowan T 43	Bullock D 42	Scully P 25	Sinnott L 32	Dalton P 29	Duxbury L 3	Booth A 43	Jepson R 40 + 3	Reid P 8 + 5	Collins S 18 + 12	Dunn I 3 + 11	Whitney J 3 + 1	Crosby G — + 1	Logan R 2	Gray K 38	Baldry S 3 + 11	Brown K 5	Dyson J 15 + 2	Norman T 3	Makel L 33	Rowe R 6 + 8	Jenkins S 31	Turner A 2 + 3	Thornley B 12	Edwards R 13	Ward M 7 + 1	Match No.
1	2	3	4	5	6	7	8	9	10	11^1	12																	1
1	2	3	4	5	6	7	8^1	9	10		11	12																2
1	2^1	3	4	5	6	7		9	10		11		8	12														3
1		3	4	5	6	7		9	10		11		2			8												4
1		3	4	5^7	6	7		9	10		11	12			8^1	2	13											5
1		3^1	4	5	6	7		9	10	8	11	12				2												6
1		3	4	5	6	7		9	10	8	11					2												7
1			4	5	6	7		9	10	8	11		3			2												8
		3	4	5	6	7		9	10	8^1	11^2	12				2	13			1								9
1		3	4	5	6	7		9	10	8	11					2												10
1		3^2	4		6	7^1		9	10	8	11^3	12	14			2	13	5										11
1	2	3	4		6	7^2		9	10	11^1	12	13				8		5										12
1		3	4	5		7	12	9	10^1							6	11^2				2	13	8					13
1		3	4	5		7		9	10		12					6	11^1				2		8					14
1		3	4	5		7		9	10		12					6					2^1	11	8					15
1		3	4	5		7		9	10							6					2	11	8					16
1		3	4	5		7^1	12	9	10							6					2^2	13	8		11			17
1		3	4	5		7	12	9								6					2	10^1	8		11			18
1		3	4	5		7	12	9								6					2^1	10	8		11			19
1		3	4	5		7^2	12	9								6					2	10^1	8	13	11			20
1		3	4	5		7		9	10							6					2		8		11			21
1		3	4	5		7^1	12	9	10							6					2^2		8	13	11			22
1		3^1	4	5		7	12	9	10							6					2		8		11			23
1		3	4^2	5		7^1	12	9	10			13				6					2		8		11			24
1		3	4	5		7^1		9	10							6			12		2^2		8	13	11			25
1		3	4	5		7^1	12	9	10							6					2^2		8	13	11			26
1		3	4	5		7		9	10							6	11^1		12		2		8					27
1		3	4	5		7	12	9	10							6					2		8		11^1			28
1		3	4	5		7	12	9	10^2			13				6					2		8		11^1			29
1		3	4	5		7^2	12	9	10			13				6	11^1				2		8					30
1		3	4	5		7^1	12	9	10							6					2		8		11			31
1		3	4	5		7^2	12	9^1	10			13				6		4			2		8		11			32
1		3	4	5		7		9	10							6					2		8		11			33
1		3	4	5		7		9	10							6					2		8		11			34
1		3	4	5		7		9	10^1							6					2		8		11			35
1		3	4	5		7		9	10^1			13				6			12		2		8		11^2			36
		3	4	5				9	10^1		12	13				6				1	2		8		11	7	9^2	37
		3	4	5				9	10							6			2	1			8		11	7		38
1		3	4	5				9	10							6	11				2				11	7	8	39
1		3	4	5				9	10							6					2				11	7	8	40
1		3		5				9	10		12					6					2		8		11^1	7	4	41
1		3	4^1	5				9	10^3		12	13				6					2		8^2	14	11	7		42
1		3	4	5				9	10^3		12	13				6					2		8^2	14	11^1	7		43
1		3	4	5				9	10		12					6					2		8		11	7^1		44
1		3	4	5				9	10							6			12		2		8		11^2	7	13	45
1		3	4	5				9^2	10		12	13				6					2		8^1		11	7		46

Coca-Cola Cup

First Round	Port Vale	(h)	1-2	
		(a)	3-1	
Second Round	Barnsley	(h)	2-0	
		(a)	0-4	

FA Cup

Third Round	Blackpool	(h)	2-1
Fourth Round	Peterborough U	(h)	2-0
Fifth Round	Wimbledon	(h)	2-2
		(a)	1-3

HULL CITY 1995–96 *Back row (left to right):* Andy Williams, Neil Allison, Rob Dewhurst, Alan Fettis, Steve Wilson, Gary Hobson, Andrew Mason, Paul Fewings.
Middle row: Billy Legg (U16 Manager), Bernard Ellison (Youth Team Coach), Chris Lee, Linton Brown, Neil Mann, Richard Peacock, Simon Dakin, Gavin Haigh, Craig Lawford, Adam Lowthorpe, Rod Arnold (Goalkeeping Coach), Jeff Radcliffe (Physio).
Front row: Ian Plant, Michael Quigley, Dean Windass, Terry Dolan (Manager), Martin Fish (Chairman), Jeff Lee (Assistant Manager), Greg Abbott, Jimmy Graham, David Chambers.
(Photograph: Innes Photographers)

Division 3 HULL CITY

Boothferry Park, Hull HU4 6EU. Telephone: (01482) 351119. Fax: (01482) 565752. Commercial Manager: (01482) 566050. Football in the Community Office: (01482) 565088.

Ground capacity: 16,564.

Record attendance: 55,019 v Manchester U, FA Cup 6th rd, 26 February 1949.

Record receipts: £79,604 v Liverpool, FA Cup 5th rd, 18 February 1989.

Pitch measurements: 115yd × 75yd.

President: T. C. Waite FIMI, MIRTE.

Honorary Vice-Presidents: D. Robinson, H. Bermitz, J. Johnson BA, DPA.

Vice-Presidents: R. Beercock, K. Davis, N. Howe, R. Booth, A. Fetiveau, W. Law.

Chairman: M. W. Fish MCA. *Vice-Chairman:* R. M. Chetham.

Directors: G. H. C. Needler MA, FCA.

Manager: Terry Dolan. *Assistant Manager:* Jeff Lee.

Secretary: M. W. Fish. *Physio:* Jeff Radcliffe MCSP, SRP.

Commercial Manager: Simon Cawkill. *Stadium Manager:* John Cooper.

Ticket Office/Gate Manager: Wilf Rogerson. *Hon. Medical Officers:* G. Hoyle, MBCHB, FRCS, Dr. B. Kell, MBBS.

Year Formed: 1904. *Turned Professional:* 1905. *Ltd Co.:* 1905.

Club Nickname: 'The Tigers'.

Previous Grounds: 1904, Boulevard Ground (Hull RFC); 1905, Anlaby Road (Hull CC); 1944–45 Boulevard Ground; 1946, Boothferry Park.

Foundation: The enthusiasts who formed Hull City in 1904 were brave men indeed. More than that they were audacious for they immediately put the club on the map in this Rugby League fortress by obtaining a three-year agreement with the Hull Rugby League club to rent their ground! They had obtained quite a number of conversions to the dribbling code, before the Rugby League forbade the use of any of their club grounds by Association Football clubs. By that time, Hull City were well away having entered the FA Cup in their initial season and the Football League, Second Division after only a year.

First Football League game: 2 September 1905, Division 2, v Barnsley (h) W 4-1 – Spendiff; Langley, Jones; Martin, Robinson, Gordon (2); Rushton, Spence (1), Wilson (1), Howe, Raisbeck.

Record League Victory: 11–1 v Carlisle U, Division 3 (N), 14 January 1939 – Ellis; Woodhead, Dowen; Robinson (1), Blyth, Hardy; Hubbard (2), Richardson (2), Dickinson (2), Davies (2), Cunliffe (2).

Record Cup Victory: 8–2 v Stalybridge Celtic (away), FA Cup 1st rd, 26 November 1932 – Maddison; Goldsmith, Woodhead; Gardner, Hill (1), Denby; Forward (1), Duncan, McNaughton (1), Wainscoat (4), Sargeant (1).

Record Defeat: 0–8 v Wolverhampton W, Division 2, 4 November 1911.

Most League Points (2 for a win): 69, Division 3, 1965–66.

Most League Points (3 for a win): 90, Division 4, 1982–83.

Most League Goals: 109, Division 3, 1965–66.

Highest League Scorer in Season: Bill McNaughton, 39, Division 3 (N), 1932–33.

Most League Goals in Total Aggregate: Chris Chilton, 195, 1960–71.

Most Capped Player: Terry Neill, 15 (59), Northern Ireland.

Most League Appearances: Andy Davidson, 520, 1952–67.

Record Transfer Fee Received: £750,000 from Middlesbrough for Andy Payton, November 1991.

Record Transfer Fee Paid: £200,000 to Leeds U for Peter Swan, March 1989.

Football League Record: 1905 Elected to Division 2; 1930–33 Division 3 (N); 1933–36 Division 2; 1936–49 Division 3 (N); 1949–56 Division 2; 1956–58 Division 3 (N); 1958–59 Division 3; 1959–60 Division 2; 1960–66 Division 3; 1966–78 Division 2; 1978–81 Division 3; 1981–83 Division 4; 1983–85 Division 3; 1985–91 Division 2; 1991–92 Division 3; 1992–96 Division 2; 1996– Division 3.

Honours: Football League: Division 2 best season: 3rd, 1909–10; Division 3 (N) – Champions 1932–33, 1948–49; Division 3 – Champions 1965–66; Runners-up 1958–59; Division 4 – Runners-up 1982–83. *FA Cup:* best season: Semi-final 1930. *Football League Cup:* best season: 4th, 1974, 1976, 1978. *Associate Members' Cup:* Runners-up 1984.

Colours: Black and amber striped shirts, black shorts, amber stockings with two black hoops and black turnover. *Change colours:* White and jade.

Did you know?
In reaching the semi-final of the FA Cup in 1930, Hull City beat Plymouth Argyle, Blackpool, Manchester City and Newcastle United.

HULL CITY 1995–96 LEAGUE RECORD

Match No.	Date	Venue	Opponents	Result	H/T Score	Lg. Pos.	Goalscorers	Atten-dance
1	Aug 12	H	Swindon T	L	0-1	0-0	—	6525
2	19	A	Rotherham U	D	1-1	0-0	19	Windass	3754
3	26	H	Blackpool	W	2-1	1-1	11	Brown, Mason	4755
4	29	A	Brentford	L	0-1	0-0	—	4535
5	Sept 2	A	Chesterfield	D	0-0	0-0	18		4345
6	9	H	Oxford U	D	0-0	0-0	19		4608
7	12	H	Swansea C	D	0-0	0-0	—		3519
8	16	A	Burnley	L	1-2	0-1	20	Fewings	10,613
9	23	A	Carlisle U	L	0-2	0-2	23		6007
10	30	H	York C	L	0-3	0-2	23		5273
11	Oct 7	H	Shrewsbury T	L	2-3	0-1	24	Abbott, Windass (pen)	3266
12	14	A	Bristol C	L	0-4	0-1	24		5354
13	21	H	Stockport Co	D	1-1	0-1	24	Abbott	3496
14	28	A	Wycombe W	D	2-2	1-0	24	Windass, Lee	5021
15	31	A	Crewe Alex	L	0-1	0-1	—		3609
16	Nov 4	H	Wrexham	D	1-1	0-0	24	Abbott	3515
17	18	A	Bradford C	D	1-1	1-0	24	Windass	5820
18	25	H	Peterborough U	L	2-3	1-1	24	Davison, Peacock	3642
19	Dec 9	A	Carlisle U	L	2-5	2-3	24	Peacock 2	3478
20	16	A	York C	W	1-0	0-0	24	Fewings	3593
21	23	A	Bournemouth	L	0-2	0-1	24		3491
22	Jan 6	A	Bristol R	L	1-2	0-2	24	Davison (pen)	4267
23	13	H	Rotherham U	L	1-4	0-1	24	Abbott	3678
24	20	A	Swindon T	L	0-3	0-0	24		8118
25	23	H	Brighton & HA	D	0-0	0-0	—		2421
26	Feb 3	A	Blackpool	D	1-1	0-1	24	Allison	4713
27	10	H	Bristol R	L	1-3	0-0	24	Davison	3311
28	17	A	Swansea C	D	0-0	0-0	24		1909
29	24	H	Burnley	W	3-0	1-0	24	Peacock 2, Davison	4206
30	27	A	Oxford U	L	0-2	0-1	—		4650
31	Mar 2	A	Notts Co	L	0-1	0-0	24		4528
32	5	H	Brentford	L	0-1	0-0	—		2284
33	9	H	Bournemouth	D	1-1	1-1	24	Graham	2853
34	12	H	Chesterfield	D	0-0	0-0	—		2832
35	16	A	Brighton & HA	L	0-4	0-2	24		4910
36	23	H	Walsall	W	1-0	0-0	24	Abbott	3060
37	26	H	Notts Co	D	0-0	0-0	—		2589
38	30	A	Shrewsbury T	D	1-1	1-0	24	Peacock	2347
39	Apr 2	H	Bristol C	L	2-3	0-0	—	Gordon, Mann	2641
40	6	H	Wycombe W	W	4-2	3-0	24	Wilkinson, Peacock, Quigley, Abbott	3065
41	8	A	Stockport Co	D	0-0	0-0	24		5043
42	13	H	Crewe Alex	L	1-2	0-0	24	Gordon	3497
43	20	A	Wrexham	L	0-5	0-2	24		3400
44	23	A	Walsall	L	0-3	0-1	—		2752
45	27	A	Peterborough U	L	1-3	0-0	24	Allison	6649
46	May 4	H	Bradford C	L	2-3	2-2	24	Gordon, Darby	8965

Final League Position: 24

GOALSCORERS

League (36): Peacock 7, Abbott 6, Davison 4 (1 pen), Windass 4 (1 pen), Gordon 3, Allison 2, Fewings 2, Brown 1, Darby 1, Graham 1, Lee 1, Mann 1, Mason 1, Quigley 1, Wilkinson 1.
Coca-Cola Cup (5): Windass 3, Allison 1, Fewings 1.
FA Cup (0).

Wilson S 19	Lowthorpe A 15 + 4	Graham J 24	Hobson G 28 + 1	Dewhurst R 16	Quigley M 9 + 4	Peacock R 39 + 6	Lee C 25 + 3	Brown L 21 + 2	Windass D 16	Mann N 34 + 4	Mason A 10 + 10	Allison N 33 + 2	Lawford C 20 + 11	Fewings P 16 + 9	Humphries G 9 + 3	Fettis A 4 + 3	Williams A 33 + 1	Abbott G 31	Gordon G 3 + 10	Watson T 4	Dakin S 2 + 4	Trevitt S 25	Davison B 11	Fidler R — + 1	Gilbert K 6 + 7	Carroll R 23	Marks J 4 + 1	Wharton P 7 + 2	Wilkinson I 8	Darby D 8	Maxfield S 3 + 1	Match No.
1	2	3	4	5	6	7	8	9^1	10^2	11	12	13																				1
1		3	4	5	6^1	7^2	8	9	10	11		2	12	13																		2
1		3	4	5		8	7^1		11	10		2	6	9	12																	3
1		3	4	5		12^2	8	7^3		11	10		2	6	9^1	13	14															4
1		3	4			12	8	9^2	10	11	13		2	6^1		5		7														5
1		3		5		7	8^1	9^2	10	11	13^3	2	12		4	14	6															6
1	12	3	4	5		7	8		10	11	9	2^1					6															7
1		3		5		7^2	8^1		10	11	9	2	12	13	4		6															8
1	2	3^1	4	5		12	8^2		10	13		11	9			7	6															9
1	2^3		4	5		12				8^1	3	9	14	13	7	6^2																10
1	2		4			7^3		9	10	11^2		12	3	8	5^1	13	6	14														11
1	12		4^2			7^1	13	9^2	10	11			3	14	5	8	6		2													12
			5			12	8		10^1	13	11	4	3^2	9		1	7	6	2													13
			5			11	8	12	10	3	9^1	4				1	7	6	2^1													14
8			5			11			10	3^1	9	4		12		1	7	6	2													15
2			5^1			11^2	8	9^1	10	3	12	4		13		1	7	6		14												16
1	2	12	5			11^1	8	9	10^2	3	13			4		7	6															17
1		5				12	8	9	10	13		3			7^1	6^2		4	2	11												18
1	8	4				10		9^2				12	5	3^3		7^1	6		13	2	11	14										19
1	12	3	5			7				13	4	11	10^2		8	6^1		2	9													20
1	6^1	3	5^2			7				12	4	11	10		8		13	2	9													21
1		4				7	3	12			11	10	5		8^1	6		2	9													22
1	11^2	4^3				7	8	9			3	10	5^1		6	13	12	2		14												23
	12	4				7	8		13	5	3^1	10^2	6		2	9	11					1										24
	3	4				7	8^2		13	5	12	10	6			2	9^1	11	1													25
	3	4				7	10	8	5			6				2	9	11	1													26
	3	4				7	10^1	8	12	5	11	13				6^2		2	9	11	1											27
	3					7	10^1	8	5	12		4	6			2	9	11	1													28
	3	4				7	8^1		10^2	5	12		11	6			2	9	13	1												29
5^1	3	4	6^3	7	8	9^1	10			12	13		11				2		14	1												30
	3	4	12	7	8		10		5	10^2	9		11	6^1			2		13	1												31
	3	4	12	7	8^1	9	10		5	13			11	6^2			2		1													32
	3	4	12	7		9	10^1			13			11	6^3			2		14	1	5^2	8										33
	3	4		7		9	10			11			6				2		12	1	5^1	8										34
	3^1	4		10		9	11		12			6				2			1	7	8	5										35
	3	4		7		10	5		9^1	11		6	12				2		1		8											36
	3		12	7		10	5		9^2	11		6	13				2		1		8^1	4										37
	3			7	12	10			13	11		6^1	14	4	2^3		2		1		8	5	9^2									38
	3	6		7		10	5	12	9	2^1	11	13					2		1		8^2	4										39
	3	8		7		10	5		11	6^2	12	2^1					2		1		13	4	9									40
	3	8^1		7		10	5		11	6	12	2					1					4	9									41
	3^1	8^2		7		10	5	4	11	6	12	2					1		13				9									42
	3^2	8	7^2	12		10	5		11	6	13	2^1					1		4			9	14									43
			7	8		10	4	5	6			11					2	1					9	3								44
			7	8		10	4	5	6			11					2^1	1	12		2^2		6^1	9	3							45
			8	7	10		4	5	12			11					13	1	2^2				6^1	9	3							46

Coca-Cola Cup

First Round	Carlisle U	(h)	1-2
		(a)	4-2
Second Round	Coventry C	(a)	0-2
		(h)	0-1

FA Cup

First Round	Wrexham	(h)	0-0
		(a)	0-0

IPSWICH TOWN 1995–96 *Back row (left to right):* Leo Cotterell, Steve Palmer, Simon Portrey, Lee Chapman, Claus Thomsen, James Scowcroft, Kevin Ellis, Frank Yallop.
Middle row: Bryan Klug (Coach), Geraint Williams, Simon Milton, David Linighan, Steve Sedgley, Richard Wright, Craig Forrest, Clive Baker, Richard Naylor, Chris Swailes, Tony Vaughan, Adam Tanner, Dale Roberts (Coach).
Front row: Mauricio Taricco, Stuart Slater, Ian Marshall, Paul Mason, Alex Mathie, George Burley (Manager), John Wark, Neil Gregory, Mick Stockwell, Neil Thompson, Lee Norfolk, Lee Durrant.
(Photograph: Allsport)

Division 1 IPSWICH TOWN

Portman Road, Ipswich, Suffolk IP1 2DA. Telephone: (01473) 219211 (4 lines). Fax: (01473) 226835. Ticket Office: (01473) 221133. Sales & Marketing Dept: (01473) 212202.

Ground capacity: 22,600.

Record attendance: 38,010 v Leeds U, FA Cup 6th rd, 8 March 1975.

Record receipts: £105,950 v AZ 67 Alkmaar, UEFA Cup Final 1st leg, 6 May 1981.

Pitch measurements: 112yd × 70yd.

Chairman: David Sheepshanks.

Vice-Presidents: Kenneth H. Brightwell, Harold R. Smith.

Directors: P. Hope-Cobbold, J. Kerridge, R. Moore, John Kerr MBE, R. J. Finbow.

Manager: George Burley. *Assistant Manager:* Dale Roberts. *Reserve Team Coach:* Bryan Klug.

Youth Team Coach: Paul Goddard. *Chief Scout:* Charlie Woods. *Director of Coaching:* Colin Suggett.

Physio: Dave Williams.

Secretary: David C. Rose.

Commercial Manager: C. Turner. *Sales & Promotions Manager:* Mike Noye.

Year Formed: 1878. *Turned Professional:* 1936. *Ltd Co.:* 1936.

Club Nickname: 'Blues' or 'Town'.

Foundation: Considering that Ipswich Town only reached the Football League in 1938, many people outside of East Anglia may be surprised to learn that this club was formed at a meeting held in the Town Hall as far back as 1878 when Mr. T. C. Cobbold, MP, was voted president. Originally it was the Ipswich Association FC to distinguish it from the older Ipswich Football Club which played rugby. These two amalgamated in 1888 and the handling game was dropped in 1893.

First Football League game: 27 August 1938, Division 3 (S), v Southend U (h) W 4-2 – Burns; Dale, Parry; Perrett, Fillingham, McLuckie; Williams, Davies (1), Jones (2), Alsop (1), Little.

Record League Victory: 7–0 v Portsmouth, Division 2, 7 November 1964 – Thorburn; Smith, McNeil; Baxter, Bolton, Thompson; Broadfoot (1), Hegan (2), Baker (1), Leadbetter, Brogan (3). 7–0 v Southampton, Division 1, 2 February 1974 – Sivell; Burley, Mills (1), Morris, Hunter, Beattie (1), Hamilton (2), Viljoen, Johnson, Whymark (2), Lambert (1) (Woods). 7–0 v WBA, Division 1, 6 November 1976 – Sivell; Burley, Mills, Talbot, Hunter, Beattie (1), Osborne, Wark (1), Mariner (1) (Bertschin), Whymark (4), Woods.

Record Cup Victory: 10–0 v Floriana, European Cup Prel. rd, 25 September 1962 – Bailey; Malcolm, Compton; Baxter, Laurel, Elsworthy (1); Stephenson, Moran (2), Crawford (5), Phillips (2), Blackwood.

Record Defeat: 1–10 v Fulham, Division 1, 26 December 1963.

Most League Points (2 for a win): 64, Division 3 (S), 1953–54 and 1955–56.

Most League Points (3 for a win): 84, Division 1, 1991–92.

Most League Goals: 106, Division 3 (S), 1955–56.

Highest League Scorer in Season: Ted Phillips, 41, Division 3 (S), 1956–57.

Most League Goals in Total Aggregate: Ray Crawford, 203, 1958–63 and 1966–69.

Most Capped Player: Allan Hunter, 47 (53), Northern Ireland.

Most League Appearances: Mick Mills, 591, 1966–82.

Record Transfer Fee Received: £1,900,000 from Tottenham H for Jason Dozzell, August 1993.

Record Transfer Fee Paid: £1,000,000 to Tottenham H for Steve Sedgley, June 1994.

Football League Record: 1938 Elected to Division 3 (S); 1954–55 Division 2; 1955–57 Division 3 (S); 1957–61 Division 2; 1961–64 Division 1; 1964–68 Division 2; 1968–86 Division 1; 1986–92 Division 2; 1992–95 FA Premier League; 1995– Division 1.

Honours: Football League: Division 1 – Champions 1961–62; Runners-up 1980–81, 1981–82; Division 2 – Champions 1960–61, 1967–68, 1991–92; Division 3 (S) – Champions 1953–54, 1956–57. *FA Cup:* Winners 1978. *Football League Cup:* best season: Semi-final 1982, 1985. *Texaco Cup:* 1973. **European Competitions:** *European Cup:* 1962–63. *European Cup-Winners' Cup:* 1978–79. *UEFA Cup:* 1973–74, 1974–75, 1975–76, 1977–78, 1979–80, 1980–81 (winners), 1981–82, 1982–83.

Colours: Blue shirts, white shorts, blue stockings. *Change colours:* Black and cream striped shirts with red piping, black shorts, cream stockings with a red and black hoop, or Jade shirts with maroon sleeves, maroon shorts with jade stripe, maroon stockings with jade hoop.

Did you know?
On 9 March 1996 at Barnsley, Ipswich Town scored three goals in the 85th, 88th and 89th minutes to draw 3-3.

IPSWICH TOWN 1995–96 LEAGUE RECORD

Match No.	Date	Venue	Opponents	Result	H/T Score	Lg. Pos.	Goalscorers	Attendance
1	Aug 12	A	Birmingham C	L	1-3	0-0	—	Marshall	18,910
2	19	H	Crystal Palace	W	1-0	1-0	16	Mathie	12,681
3	26	A	WBA	D	0-0	0-0	17		14,470
4	30	H	Stoke C	W	4-1	1-0	—	Slater 2, Mathie 2	10,848
5	Sept 2	H	Sunderland	W	3-0	2-0	3	Mathie 3	12,390
6	9	A	Huddersfield T	L	1-2	0-2	7	Sedgley (pen)	12,057
7	12	A	Oldham Ath	D	1-1	0-0	—	Marshall	5622
8	16	H	Watford	W	4-2	2-1	4	Gregory 2, Thomsen, Uhlenbeek	11,441
9	23	H	Charlton Ath	L	1-5	1-0	8	Thomsen	12,815
10	30	A	Sheffield U	D	2-2	0-2	7	Marshall 2	12,557
11	Oct 7	H	Wolverhampton W	L	1-2	1-2	13	Sedgley (pen)	15,335
12	14	A	Derby Co	D	1-1	1-1	13	Sedgley	13,034
13	22	H	Luton T	L	0-1	0-1	14		9123
14	28	A	Reading	W	4-1	1-0	11	Uhlenbeek, Mathie, Mason, Williams	10,281
15	Nov 4	H	Grimsby T	D	2-2	2-0	13	Mason 2	10,250
16	11	A	Millwall	L	1-2	1-1	15	Mason	11,360
17	19	A	Norwich C	L	1-2	0-1	15	Wark (pen)	17,862
18	22	H	Southend U	D	1-1	0-0	—	Uhlenbeek	9757
19	25	H	Portsmouth	W	3-2	2-1	14	Milton, Marshall, Thompson	10,286
20	Dec 3	A	Wolverhampton W	D	2-2	1-0	15	Marshall, Mowbray	20,867
21	9	A	Charlton Ath	W	2-0	0-0	13	Stockwell, Marshall	10,316
22	16	H	Sheffield U	D	1-1	0-0	14	Tuttle (og)	9630
23	22	H	Barnsley	D	2-2	1-0	—	Marshall, Mathie	11,791
24	Jan 1	H	Port Vale	W	5-1	0-0	12	Milton, Sedgley, Marshall, Mathie 2	9926
25	13	A	Crystal Palace	D	1-1	0-1	13	Mathie	14,097
26	20	H	Birmingham C	W	2-0	1-0	11	Milton 2	12,540
27	Feb 3	H	WBA	W	2-1	1-0	6	Marshall, Mowbray	10,798
28	10	A	Stoke C	L	1-3	0-1	9	Scowcroft	12,239
29	20	A	Sunderland	L	0-1	0-1	—		14,052
30	24	A	Watford	W	3-2	0-2	10	Uhlenbeek, Mathie 2	11,872
31	Mar 3	H	Leicester C	W	4-2	3-0	7	Wark, Milton, Marshall 2	9817
32	9	A	Barnsley	D	3-3	0-2	10	Marshall 2, Milton	7705
33	13	A	Leicester C	W	2-0	2-0	—	Marshall, Mathie	17,783
34	16	H	Tranmere R	L	1-2	1-0	7	Marshall	11,759
35	19	H	Oldham Ath	W	2-1	0-0	—	Mason 2	9674
36	23	A	Port Vale	L	1-2	1-1	6	Marshall	7277
37	30	A	Luton T	W	2-1	1-0	5	Milton 2	9151
38	Apr 2	H	Derby Co	W	1-0	1-0	—	Vaughan	16,210
39	6	H	Reading	L	1-2	0-1	5	Mathie	17,328
40	8	A	Grimsby T	L	1-3	0-0	5	Scowcroft	5904
41	14	H	Norwich C	W	2-1	1-0	6	Marshall, Ullathorne (og)	20,355
42	17	A	Tranmere R	L	2-5	1-1	—	Mason, Marshall	6008
43	20	A	Southend U	L	1-2	1-1	7	Milton	8363
44	27	A	Portsmouth	W	1-0	0-0	7	Mathie	12,954
45	May 1	H	Huddersfield T	W	2-1	1-1	—	Mathie 2	17,473
46	5	H	Millwall	D	0-0	0-0	7		17,290

Final League Position: 7

GOALSCORERS
League *(79):* Marshall 19, Mathie 18, Milton 9, Mason 7, Sedgley 4 (2 pens), Uhlenbeek 4, Gregory 2, Mowbray 2, Scowcroft 2, Slater 2, Thomsen 2, Wark 2 (1 pen), Stockwell 1, Thompson 1, Vaughan 1, Williams 1, own goals 2.
Coca-Cola Cup (2): Sedgley 1, Thomsen 1.
FA Cup (3): Mason 3.

Forrest C 21	Stockwell M 33 + 4	Thompson N 5	Vaughan T 19 + 6	Wark J 13 + 1	Sedgley S 40	Uhlenbeek G 37 + 3	Williams G 42	Mathie A 39	Marshall I 35	Thomsen C 36 + 1	Chapman L 2 + 4	Yallop F 3 + 4	Milton S 34 + 3	Palmer S 5	Slater S 11 + 6	Gregory N 5 + 12	Taricco M 36 + 3	Tanner A 3 + 7	Swailes C 4 + 1	Wright R 23	Mowbray T 19	Scowcroft J 13 + 10	Petterson A 1	Linighan D 2	Mason P 24 + 2	Barber F 1	Appleby R — + 3	Match No.
1	2	3²	4	5¹	6	7	8	9	10	11	12	13²	14															1
1	2	3	5	4	7	6	9	10	8	11																		2
1	2	3		4	7	6	9¹		10				8	5	11²	12	13											3
1	2	3		4	7	6¹	9		10				8²	5	11	12	13											4
1	2	3¹		4	7	6	9						8²	5	11	12	13											5
1	2			4	7	6	9¹	10	13	12				5	11		3	8²										6
1	2	13		4	7	6		10	8	12				5	11²	9¹	3											7
1	2	12	5¹	4	7	6		10	8						11	9	3											8
1¹		3	5²	4	7	6	9		8	12	11	10	2		13													9
				4	7	6	9	10	8	3	11	12	2		5¹	1												10
	2			4	7	6	9		8	12	11		3¹		1	5	10											11
	2				8	7¹	6²	9	10	3	12	11	13		14	5		1	4³									12
1	2				8²	7	6	9¹	10	11	12	3	13		5		4											13
1	2	4			7	8	9	10	0	12	13	3			5²		11¹											14
1	2	4			7	6	9	10¹	8²	12	3	13			5		11											15
1	2	4			6	9¹	10	7		12	3	8			5		11											16
1	2	3	5		9²	6	10	7		8¹	12	13			4		11											17
1	2	5			7	6	9	8		10²	3	12			4	13	11¹											18
1	12	3			7¹	6	9	10	4	11			2	8	5													19
	7¹	3		4	12	9	10	11	6	8			2²		5							13	1					20
1	7¹	3			8	12	6	9	10	4	11		2		5													21
1	7	3			8	12	6	9	10	4	11		2¹		5													22
1	2				8	7¹	6	9	10	4	12	11	3		5²										13			23
1	2				8	7¹	6	9	10	4	3	11			5										12			24
	2	12			8		6	9	10	4	11		3¹		1	5									7			25
	3				8	2	6	9		4	12	11	10²		1	5	13					7¹						26
	12				8	2	6		10	4	11	9²	3		1	5	13					7¹						27
	12				8	2	6		10	4	11¹	13	3		1	5	9					7²						28
	6	12			8	2			10²	4	11	13	3		1	5¹	9					7						29
	6²	5			8	2	9¹	10		4	11	12	3		1		13					7						30
		5			8	2	6	9	10	4	11		3		1		12					7¹						31
	12	5¹			8	2	6	9	10	4	11		3		1		13					7²						32
	7¹	5			8	2	6	9	10	4	11		3		1		12											33
	7¹	5			8	2	6	9²	10	4	11		3		1		13					12						34
		5			8	2	6	9		4	11		3		1		10					7						35
	12	5²			8	2¹	6	9	10³	4	11	13	3		1		14					7						36
	7				8	2	6	9	10	4	11¹	12	3		1		5											37
	11				8	2	6	9		4			3	5	1		10					7¹						38
	11				8	2	6	9		4	12		3	5¹	1		10					7						39
	5				8	2	6	9¹		4	11		12	3	1		10					7						40
	4²	12	5¹		8	2	6		10	11			3		1		9					7		13				41
	11	5			8	2¹	6		10	4	12		3		1		9					7						42
1	3				8		6	9¹	10	4	11		12	2			5					7						43
	2				5	8		9	10	4	11		3		1		6					7						44
	2				5	8		9	10	4	11	12	3¹		1		6					7						45
	2	12	5¹		8		6	9	10	4	11		3		1		13					7²						46

Coca-Cola Cup
Second Round	Stockport Co	(a)	1-1	
		(h)	1-2	

FA Cup
Third Round	Blackburn R	(h)	0-0
		(a)	1-0
Fourth Round	Walsall	(h)	1-0
Fifth Round	Aston Villa	(h)	1-3

LEEDS UNITED 1995-96   *Back row (left to right):* David White, Brian Deane, Carlton Palmer, John Lukic, David Wetherall, Mark Beeney, Philemon Masinga, Lucas Radebe, Paul Beesley.
Middle row: Mike Hennigan (Assistant Manager), Matthew Smithard, Mark Ford, Noel Whelan, Robert Bowman, Mark Tinkler, Andy Couzens, Kevin Sharp, Tony Dorigo, Nigel Worthington, David O'Leary, David Williams (Coach), Geoff Ladley (Physio).
Front row: Rod Wallace, Anthony Yeboah, Gary McAllister, Howard Wilkinson (Manager), John Pemberton, Gary Speed, Gary Kelly.

FA Premiership LEEDS UNITED

Elland Road, Leeds LS11 0ES. Telephone: (0113) 2716037 (4 lines). Fax: (0113) 2720370. Ticket Information: 0891 121680. Clubcall: 0891 121180.

Ground capacity: 40,000.

Record attendance: 57,892 v Sunderland, FA Cup 5th rd (replay), 15 March 1967.

Record receipts: £314,063 v Oldham Ath, FA Cup 4th rd, 28 January 1995.

Pitch measurements: 110yd × 72yd.

President: The Right Hon The Earl of Harewood LLD.

Executive Directors: P. J. Gilman (Vice-Chairman); W. J. Fotherby (Acting Chairman).

Directors: J. W. G. Marjason, R. Barker, A. Hudson, P. Ridsdale, K. J. Woolmer.

Manager: Howard Wilkinson. *Assistant Manager:* Mick Hennegan.

Company/Club Secretary: Nigel Pleasants.

General Manager: Alan Roberts.

Coach: David Williams.

Physio: Geoff Ladley.

Commercial Manager: Bob Baldwin. *Stadium Manager:* William Butterworth.

Year Formed: 1919, as Leeds United after disbandment (by FA order) of Leeds City (formed in 1904).

Turned Professional: 1920. *Ltd Co.:* 1920.

Club Nickname: 'United'.

Foundation: Immediately the Leeds City club (founded in 1904) was wound up by the FA in October 1919, following allegations of illegal payments to players, a meeting was called by a Leeds solicitor, Mr. Alf Masser, at which Leeds United was formed. They joined the Midland League playing their first game in that competition in November 1919. It was in this same month that the new club had discussions with the directors of a virtually bankrupt Huddersfield Town who wanted to move to Leeds in an amalgamation. But Huddersfield survived even that crisis.

First Football League game: 28 August 1920, Division 2, v Port Vale (a) L 0-2 – Down; Duffield, Tillotson; Musgrove, Baker, Walton; Mason, Goldthorpe, Thompson, Lyon, Best.

Record League Victory: 8–0 v Leicester C, Division 1, 7 April 1934 – Moore; George Milburn, Jack Milburn; Edwards, Hart, Copping; Mahon (2), Firth (2), Duggan (2), Furness (2), Cochrane.

Record Cup Victory: 10–0 v Lyn (Oslo), European Cup 1st rd 1st leg, 17 September 1969 – Sprake; Reaney, Cooper, Bremner, Charlton, Hunter, Madeley, Clarke (2), Jones (3), Giles (2) (Bates), O'Grady (1).

Record Defeat: 1–8 v Stoke C, Division 1, 27 August 1934.

Most League Points (2 for a win): 67, Division 1, 1968–69.

Most League Points (3 for a win): 85, Division 2, 1989–90.

Most League Goals: 98, Division 2, 1927–28.

Highest League Scorer in Season: John Charles, 42, Division 2, 1953–54.

Most League Goals in Total Aggregate: Peter Lorimer, 168, 1965–79 and 1983–86.

Most Capped Player: Billy Bremner, 54, Scotland.

Most League Appearances: Jack Charlton, 629, 1953–73.

Record Transfer Fee Received: £3,500,000 from Everton for Gary Speed, June 1996.

Record Transfer Fee Paid: £4,500,000 to Parma for Tomas Brolin, 23 November 1995.

Football League Record: 1920 Elected to Division 2; 1924–27 Division 1; 1927–28 Division 2; 1928–31 Division 1; 1931–32 Division 2; 1932–47 Division 1; 1947–56 Division 2; 1956–60 Division 1; 1960–64 Division 2; 1964–82 Division 1; 1982–90 Division 2; 1990–92 Division 1; 1992– FA Premier League.

Honours: Football League: Division 1 – Champions 1968–69, 1973–74, 1991–92; Runners-up 1964–65, 1965–66, 1969–70, 1970–71, 1971–72; Division 2 – Champions 1923–24, 1963–64, 1989–90; Runners-up 1927–28, 1931–32, 1955–56. *FA Cup:* Winners 1972; Runners-up 1965, 1970, 1973. *Football League Cup:* Winners 1968; Runners-up 1996. **European Competitions:** *European Cup:* 1969–70, 1974–75 (runners-up), 1992–93. *European Cup-Winners' Cup:* 1972–73 (runners-up). *European Fairs Cup:* 1965–66, 1966–67 (runners-up), 1967–68 (winners), 1968–69, 1970–71 (winners). *UEFA Cup:* 1971–72, 1973–74, 1979–80, 1995–96.

Colours: White with yellow and blue trim. *Change colours:* Yellow with white and blue trim.

Did you know?
Lucas Radebe played in goal during an emergency in the second half against Middlesbrough on 30 March 1996 and kept a clean sheet, then restricted Manchester United to one goal in a similar situation for 72 minutes on 17 April.

LEEDS UNITED 1995–96 LEAGUE RECORD

Match No.	Date	Venue	Opponents	Result		H/T Score	Lg. Pos.	Goalscorers	Attendance
1	Aug 19	A	West Ham U	W	2-1	0-1	—	Yeboah 2	22,901
2	21	H	Liverpool	W	1-0	0-0	—	Yeboah	36,007
3	26	H	Aston Villa	W	2-0	1-0	2	Speed, White	35,086
4	30	A	Southampton	D	1-1	0-0	—	Dorigo	15,212
5	Sept 9	A	Tottenham H	L	1-2	0-1	4	Yeboah	30,034
6	16	H	QPR	L	1-3	0-2	6	Wetherall	31,505
7	23	A	Wimbledon	W	4-2	3-1	6	Palmer, Yeboah 3	13,307
8	30	H	Sheffield W	W	2-0	1-0	5	Yeboah, Speed	33,899
9	Oct 14	H	Arsenal	L	0-3	0-1	8		38,332
10	21	A	Manchester C	D	0-0	0-0	8		26,390
11	28	H	Coventry C	W	3-1	2-1	8	McAllister 3 (1 pen)	30,025
12	Nov 4	A	Middlesbrough	D	1-1	1-1	8	Deane	29,467
13	18	H	Chelsea	W	1-0	0-0	5	Yeboah	36,133
14	25	A	Newcastle U	L	1-2	1-0	8	Deane	36,572
15	Dec 2	H	Manchester C	L	0-1	0-0	9		33,249
16	9	H	Wimbledon	D	1-1	0-1	9	Jobson	27,994
17	16	A	Sheffield W	L	2-6	1-3	9	Brolin, Wallace	24,573
18	24	H	Manchester U	W	3-1	2-1	9	McAllister (pen), Yeboah, Deane	39,801
19	27	A	Bolton W	W	2-0	1-0	—	Brolin, Wetherall	18,414
20	30	A	Everton	L	0-2	0-1	10		40,009
21	Jan 1	H	Blackburn R	D	0-0	0-0	11		31,285
22	13	H	West Ham U	W	2-0	1-0	9	Brolin 2	30,472
23	20	A	Liverpool	L	0-5	0-1	11		40,254
24	31	A	Nottingham F	L	1-2	0-1	—	Palmer	24,465
25	Feb 3	A	Aston Villa	L	0-3	0-2	11		35,982
26	Mar 2	H	Bolton W	L	0-1	0-1	12		30,106
27	6	A	QPR	W	2-1	2-1	—	Yeboah 2	13,991
28	13	A	Blackburn R	L	0-1	0-0	—		23,358
29	17	H	Everton	D	2-2	2-1	12	Deane 2	29,422
30	30	H	Middlesbrough	L	0-1	0-1	12		31,788
31	Apr 3	H	Southampton	W	1-0	0-0	—	Deane	26,077
32	6	A	Arsenal	L	1-2	0-1	12	Deane	37,619
33	8	H	Nottingham F	L	1-3	1-2	13	Wetherall	29,220
34	13	A	Chelsea	L	1-4	0-3	13	McAllister	22,131
35	17	A	Manchester U	L	0-1	0-1	—		48,382
36	29	H	Newcastle U	L	0-1	0-1	—		38,562
37	May 2	H	Tottenham H	L	1-3	1-2	—	Wetherall	30,024
38	5	A	Coventry C	D	0-0	0-0	13		22,757

Final League Position: 13

GOALSCORERS

League (40): Yeboah 12, Deane 7, McAllister 5 (2 pens), Brolin 4, Wetherall 4, Palmer 2, Speed 2, Dorigo 1, Jobson 1, Wallace 1, White 1.
Coca-Cola Cup (13): Speed 3, Yeboah 3, Deane 2, Masinga 2, Couzens 1, McAllister 1, own goal 1.
FA Cup (7): McAllister 3, Deane 1, Speed 1, Wallace 1, Yeboah 1.

Lukic J 28	Kelly G 34	Dorigo T 17	Palmer C 35	Wetherall D 34	Pemberton J 16+1	Yeboah T 22	Wallace R 12+12	Deane B 30+4	McAllister G 36	Speed G 29	Whelan N 3+5	Worthington N 12+4	Beesley P 8+2	White D 1+3	Masinga P 5+4	Tinkler M 5+4	Couzens A 8+6	Jobson R 12	Sharp K —+1	Ford M 12	Brolin T 17+2	Bowman R 1+2	Beeney M 10	Radebe L 10+3	Chapman L 2	Gray A 12+3	Harte I 2+2	Maybury A 1	Kewell H 2	Blunt J 2+1	Jackson M —+1	Match No.
1	2	3²	4³	5	6	7	8¹	9	10	11	12	13	14																			1
1	2	3	4	5	6	7	8¹	9	10	11	12																					2
1	2	3	4	5	6	7	8¹	9	10	11				12																		3
1	2	3	4	5	6	7²	8¹	9	10	11			13	12																		4
1	2	3	4	5	6		8	9	10	11	12				7¹																	5
1	2		4	5	6		8	9	10	11	7¹	3²	13	12																		6
1	2		4	5	6		8	9	10	11			3		7¹	12																7
1	2		4	5			8	12	10	11			3		9¹	6	7															8
1	2	3	4	5	6		8	12	9	11					7¹	10																9
1	2		4	5	6	7	8¹	9	10		12		3			11																10
1	2		4	5	3	7		9¹	10	11					8²	12	6	13														11
1	2		4	5	3		8	9	10						7	11		6														12
1	2	3	4	5			8	12	9	10	11				7¹			6														13
1	2	3⁴	4	5			8	9	10	11								6		7¹	12	13										14
1	2	3	4	5	12		8	9	10			13						6		7¹	11²											15
1		3	4	5	2		8	12	9¹	10	11							6		7												16
1	2¹	3	4	5				9¹	10	11	12	13			8			6		7												17
	2	3	4	5			8¹	12	9	10	11							6		7			1									18
	2	3		5			8	9	10	11								6		7¹			1	4	12							19
	2	3²		5	12			9	10	11		13			8¹			6		7			1	4								20
	2		4				8	12	9	10	11							6		7¹			1	5			3					21
	2	3¹	4	5					10	11					8²		12	6		7³			1			9	13	14				22
	2		4	5			8	12	10	11								6		7¹		13	1			9²	3					23
	2	3³	4				8	9	10	11							12	6		7¹	14	13	1	5²								24
		3	4	5¹			8	9	10	11		13					12	6					1		2	7²						25
1			4		6			9		10	11				8						7			5	12		3¹	2²	13			26
1	2		4		6		8		10¹	11	9										7			5	12		3					27
1	2		4		6			9	10		11				8						7			5¹	12		3					28
1	2		4	5				9	10	11					8¹		12	6				13				7²	3					29
1²	2		4	5	6³			9	10	11							12				7					8¹	3		13	14		30
1	2		4	5					10	11					8¹		12	6			7	13				9²	3					31
1	2		4	5				9	10	11					8			6			7						3					32
1	2		4	5				9	10	11					8		12				3²			6¹		7			13			33
1	2		4	5	6¹			9	10	11					8						12					7	3					34
	2		4		6			9¹	10	11					8²		12				14		1	5		7³	3		13			35
	2		4		6			9	10	11¹					8²		12				7	13	1	5			3					36
1	2		4		6			9	10						8		12	6		7¹	11			5			3					37
1	2		4	5				9	10						8		12	6			7					11¹	3					38

Coca-Cola Cup

Second Round	Notts Co	(h)	0-0
		(a)	3-2
Third Round	Derby Co	(a)	1-0
Fourth Round	Blackburn R	(h)	2-1
Fifth Round	Reading	(h)	2-1
Semi-final	Birmingham C	(a)	2-1
		(h)	3-0
Final (at Wembley)	Aston Villa		0-3

FA Cup

Third Round	Derby Co	(a)	4-2
Fourth Round	Bolton W	(a)	1-0
Fifth Round	Port Vale	(h)	0-0
		(a)	2-1
Sixth Round	Liverpool	(h)	0-0
		(a)	0-3

LEICESTER CITY 1995–96 *Back row (left to right):* Jamie Lawrence, Lee Philpott, Garry Parker, Simon Grayson, Colin Hill, Mark Blake, Phil Gee, Craig Hallam.
Middle row: Mark McGhee (Manager), Colin Lee (Assistant Manager), Richard Smith, Jimmy Willis, Iwan Roberts, Kevin Poole, Steve Walsh, Brian Carey, Mike Whitlow, Mike Hickman (First Team Coach), Alan Smith (Physio).
Front row: Taff Davies (Kit Manager), Julian Joachim, Sam McMahon, Neil Lewis, David Lowe, Scott Taylor, Mark Robins, Paul Bedder, Mick Yoeman (Physio).

FA Premiership LEICESTER CITY

City Stadium, Filbert St, Leicester LE2 7FL. Telephone: (0116) 2555000 and (0116) 2854000. Fax: (0116) 2470585. Ticket Office: (0116) 2915232. Clubcall: 0891 121185.

Ground capacity: 22,517.

Record attendance: 47,298 v Tottenham H, FA Cup 5th rd, 18 February 1928.

Record receipts: £215,270 v Manchester C, FA Cup 3rd rd, 6 January 1996.

Pitch measurements: 110yd × 76yd.

President: K. R. Brigstock.

Chairman: T. Smeaton. *Vice-Chairman:* John Elson FCA.

Chief Executive: Barrie Pierpoint.

Directors: R. W. Parker, J. E. Sharp, T. W. Shipman, W. K. Shooter FCA, M. F. George.

Manager: Martin O'Neill. *Coaches:* Paul Franklin and Steve Walford.

Youth Team Coach: David Nish.

Football Secretary: Ian Silvester.

Company Secretary: Steve Kind.

Head of Publicity/Press Officer: Paul Mace.

Physio: Alan Smith. *General Sales Manager:* Charles Rayner. *Stadium Manager:* Mark Brown.

Year Formed: 1884.

Club Nickname: 'Filberts' or 'Foxes'.

Previous Grounds: 1884, Victoria Park; 1887, Belgrave Road; 1888, Victoria Park; 1891, Filbert Street.

Previous Name: 1884–1919, Leicester Fosse.

Foundation: In 1884 a number of young footballers who were mostly old boys of Wyggeston School, held a meeting at a house on the Roman Fosse Way and formed Leicester Fosse FC. They collected 9d (less than 4p) towards the cost of a ball, plus the same amount for membership. Their first professional, Harry Webb from Stafford Rangers, was signed in 1888 for 2s 6d (12p) per week, plus travelling expenses.

First Football League game: 1 September 1894, Division 2, v Grimsby T (a) L 3-4 – Thraves; Smith, Bailey; Seymour, Brown, Henrys; Hill, Hughes, McArthur (1), Skea (2), Priestman.

Record League Victory: 10–0 v Portsmouth, Division 1, 20 October 1928 – McLaren; Black, Brown; Findlay, Carr, Watson; Adcock, Hine (3), Chandler (6), Lochhead, Barry (1).

Record Cup Victory: 8–1 v Coventry C (away), League Cup 5th rd, 1 December 1964 – Banks; Sjoberg, Norman (2); Roberts, King, McDerment; Hodgson (2), Cross, Goodfellow, Gibson (1), Stringfellow (2). (1 og).

Record Defeat: 0–12 (as Leicester Fosse) v Nottingham F, Division 1, 21 April 1909.

Most League Points (2 for a win): 61, Division 2, 1956–57.

Most League Points (3 for a win): 77, Division 2, 1991–92.

Most League Goals: 109, Division 2, 1956–57.

Highest League Scorer in Season: Arthur Rowley, 44, Division 2, 1956–57.

Most League Goals in Total Aggregate: Arthur Chandler, 259, 1923–35.

Most Capped Player: John O'Neill, 39, Northern Ireland.

Most League Appearances: Adam Black, 528, 1920–35.

Record Transfer Fee Received: £3,250,000 from Aston Villa for Mark Draper, July 1995.

Record Transfer Fee Paid: £1,250,000 to Notts Co for Mark Draper, July 1994.

Football League Record: 1894 Elected to Division 2; 1908–09 Division 1; 1909–25 Division 2; 1925–35 Division 1; 1935–37 Division 2; 1937–39 Division 1; 1946–54 Division 2; 1954–55 Division 1; 1955–57 Division 2; 1957–69 Division 1; 1969–71 Division 2; 1971–78 Division 1; 1978–80 Division 2; 1980–81 Division 1; 1981–83 Division 2; 1983–87 Division 1; 1987–92 Division 2; 1992–94 Division 1; 1994–95 FA Premier League; 1995–96 Division 1; 1996– FA Premier League.

Honours: Football League: Division 1 – Runners-up 1928–29; Promoted from Division 1 1995–96 (play-offs) *Division 2* – Champions 1924–25, 1936–37, 1953–54, 1956–57, 1970–71, 1979–80; Runners-up 1907–08. *FA Cup:* Runners-up 1949, 1961, 1963, 1969. *Football League Cup:* Winners 1964; Runners-up 1965. **European Competitions:** *European Cup-Winners' Cup:* 1961–62.

Colours: Royal blue shirts, white shorts, blue stockings. *Change colours:* Jade and navy.

Did you know?
Between 3 September and 29 December 1906, Leicester City won 13 consecutive home matches in Division Two.

LEICESTER CITY 1995–96 LEAGUE RECORD

Match No.	Date	Venue	Opponents		Result	H/T Score	Lg. Pos.	Goalscorers	Attendance
1	Aug 12	A	Sunderland	W	2-1	1-1	—	Corica, Robins	18,593
2	19	H	Stoke C	L	2-3	0-3	12	Walsh, Parker (pen)	17,719
3	26	A	Luton T	D	1-1	0-1	10	Parker	7612
4	30	H	Portsmouth	W	4-2	4-1	—	Roberts 3, Parker	15,170
5	Sept 2	H	Wolverhampton W	W	1-0	1-0	2	Whitlow	18,441
6	10	A	Derby Co	W	1-0	1-0	1	Joachim	11,767
7	12	A	Port Vale	W	2-0	1-0	—	McMahon, Roberts	8814
8	16	H	Reading	D	1-1	0-1	1	Roberts	19,103
9	23	H	Southend U	L	1-3	1-2	1	Lowe	15,276
10	30	A	Norwich C	W	1-0	0-0	1	Heskey	18,435
11	Oct 7	A	Barnsley	D	2-2	1-1	1	Robins, Walsh	13,669
12	14	H	Charlton Ath	D	1-1	1-0	1	Lowe	16,771
13	21	A	Sheffield U	W	3-1	1-1	1	Roberts, Taylor, Lowe	13,100
14	28	H	Crystal Palace	L	2-3	0-2	3	Robins, Taylor	18,376
15	Nov 5	A	WBA	W	3-2	3-0	2	Taylor 2, Roberts	16,071
16	11	H	Watford	W	1-0	1-0	2	Roberts	16,230
17	19	H	Tranmere R	L	0-1	0-0	2		13,125
18	21	A	Huddersfield T	L	1-3	1-1	—	Robins	14,300
19	26	A	Birmingham C	D	2-2	2-1	4	Roberts, Grayson	17,350
20	Dec 2	H	Barnsley	D	2-2	1-2	3	Roberts, Grayson	15,125
21	9	A	Southend U	L	1-2	1-1	8	Roberts	5835
22	17	H	Norwich C	W	3-2	1-2	3	Whitlow, Roberts, Heskey	14,251
23	23	A	Grimsby T	D	2-2	0-1	3	Roberts, Walsh	7713
24	Jan 1	A	Millwall	D	1-1	1-0	3	Corica	9953
25	13	A	Stoke C	L	0-1	0-1	5		13,669
26	21	H	Sunderland	D	0-0	0-0	5		16,130
27	Feb 3	H	Luton T	D	1-1	0-0	7	Roberts	14,821
28	10	A	Portsmouth	L	1-2	1-1	10	Roberts	9003
29	17	H	Port Vale	D	1-1	1-0	8	Taylor	13,758
30	21	A	Wolverhampton W	W	3-2	1-2	—	Roberts, Heskey 2	27,381
31	24	A	Reading	D	1-1	0-0	6	Lewis	9817
32	28	H	Derby Co	D	0-0	0-0	—		20,911
33	Mar 3	A	Ipswich T	L	2-4	0-3	8	Roberts 2	9817
34	9	H	Grimsby T	W	2-1	1-0	7	Heskey 2	13,784
35	13	H	Ipswich T	L	0-2	0-2	—		17,783
36	16	A	Oldham Ath	L	1-3	0-1	8	Whitlow	5582
37	23	H	Millwall	W	2-1	1-1	8	Carey, Taylor	12,543
38	30	H	Sheffield U	L	0-2	0-0	9		15,230
39	Apr 2	A	Charlton Ath	W	1-0	1-0	—	Claridge	11,287
40	6	A	Crystal Palace	W	1-0	1-0	7	Roberts	17,331
41	9	H	WBA	L	1-2	0-1	—	Robins	17,889
42	13	A	Tranmere R	D	1-1	1-0	8	Robins	8882
43	17	H	Oldham Ath	W	2-0	0-0	—	Claridge 2	12,790
44	20	H	Huddersfield T	W	2-1	1-0	6	Walsh, Claridge	17,619
45	27	H	Birmingham C	W	3-0	2-0	6	Claridge, Heskey, Lennon	19,702
46	May 5	A	Watford	W	1-0	0-0	5	Izzet	20,089

Final League Position: 5

GOALSCORERS

League (66): Roberts 19, Heskey 7, Robins 6, Taylor 6, Claridge 5, Walsh 4, Lowe 3, Parker 3 (1 pen), Whitlow 3, Corica 2, Grayson 2, Carey 1, Izzet 1, Joachim 1, Lennon 1, Lewis 1, McMahon 1.
Coca-Cola Cup (6): Robins 4, Joachim 1, Roberts 1.
FA Cup (0).

Poole K 45	Grayson S 39 + 2	Whitlow M 41 + 1	Willis J 11 + 1	Walsh S 37	Parker G 36 + 4	Joachim J 14 + 8	Taylor S 39	Robins M 19 + 12	Corica S 16	Lawrence J 10 + 5	Roberts I 34 + 3	Hill C 24 + 7	Philpott L 1 + 5	Lewis N 10 + 4	Lowe D 21 + 7	Blake M 6 + 2	Gee P 1 + 1	McMahon S 1 + 2	Heskey E 20 + 10	Rolling F 17	Carey B 16 + 3	Kalac Z 1	Kamark P 1	Smith R 1	Lennon N 14 + 1	Claridge S 14	Watts J 9	Izzet M 8 + 1	Match No.
1	2	3	4^2	5	6	7	8	9^1	10	11^3	12	13	14																1
1	2^2	3	4^1	5	6	7	8	9	10	11^3	12	13		14															2
1		3	4	5	6	7	8	9^1	11		10	2			12														3
1		3	4	5	6	7	8		11		9	2			10														4
1	2	3	4^2	5	6	7^1	8		11		9			12	10	13													5
1	12	3	4	5	6	7^2	8	13	11		10	2^1			9^3			14											6
1	2	3	4	5	6	7	8		11^1		10				9				12										7
1	2	3	4	5	6	7^1	8	12			10				9				11^2	13									8
1	2	3	4	5	6	7^3	8	12			10	13			9^2				11^1	14									9
1	2	3		5	6	7	8	10^1		11					9				12	4									10
1	2	3		5	6	7^1	10			11^2		4			9	8			12		13								11
1	2	3		5	6		8^3	7^2	12		10	4			9				11^1	13	14								12
1	2	3		5	6		8				10	4			9						11								13
1	2	3			6		8	12			10	4	13		9	7^2				11	5^1								14
		3			6	7		9			10	4			8^1	12					11	5	1	2					15
1	2^1	3			6	12	8	9			10	13			7	11^2				4	5								16
1	2^1	3			6	12		9			10	11	8^2	13	7					4	5								17
1	12	3			6	11^1	8^2	9			10	2			7				13	4	5								18
1	2	3			6		8	9^1			10	11			7				12	4	5								19
1	2	3			6	12	8	9^1	11		10	4			7^2				13		5								20
1	2	3			6	12	8	13	11		10	4			9^2	7^1					5								21
1		3		5	6	12	8	9^1	7		10	2							13	11^2	4								22
1		3		5	6	13	8	12	7^3		10	2^1		14					9^2	11	4								23
1	2	3		5	6	12	8		7^2		10	4							13	9^1	11								24
1	2	3		5	6	12	8^1	9^2	7		10	4	13						14						11^3				25
1	2	3		5	6	9^1	8				10	4			7				12	11									26
1	2			5	6	12	8^1				10	4	13	3^2	7				9	11									27
1	2			5	6	9^1	8	12			10	4^2		3	7				11	13									28
1	2	3		5	6		8^2	12	7		10	4			11^1	13			9										29
1	2	12		5	6		8		7		10	4^1		11					9	3									30
1	2	3		5	6		8	12	7^2		10				11				9^1		4				13				31
1	2	3		5	6		8				10				11				9		4				7				32
1	2	3		5	6		8^1	12				10			11^2				13		4				7	9			33
1	2		4	5	6		8								11				10	3					7	9			34
1	2		4	5	6	12	8								11^2	13			10	3^1					7	9			35
1	2	3	12	5	6		8^3	13						14	11^2				10	4^1					7	9			36
1	2	3		5	6		8				12	11^1							10		4				7	9			37
1	2	3		5			8^1		7			11		12					10		4					9^2	6	13	38
1	2	3		5			7^1				12	11							10						8	9	4	6	39
1	2	3		5			8				12	10							11						7	9	4	6^1	40
1	2	3		5			8	12				10^1							11						7	9	4	6	41
1	2	3		5			8	10											11						7	9	4	6	42
1	2	3				12	8^1	10						5					11						7	9	4	6	43
1	2	3		5		12	8	10^1											11						7	9	4	6	44
1	2	3		5		12	8^1	10											11						7	9	4	6	45
1	2	3		5		12	8	10^1											11						7	9	4	6	46

Coca-Cola Cup

Second Round	Burnley	(h)	2-0
		(a)	2-0
Third Round	Bolton W	(a)	0-0
		(h)	2-3

FA Cup

Third Round	Manchester C	(h)	0-0
		(a)	0-5

LEYTON ORIENT 1995–96 *Back row (left to right):* Danny Chapman, Ian Hendon, Lee Shearer, Peter Caldwell, Colin West, Mark Warren, Kevin Austin. *Middle row:* Tommy Cunningham (Director of Coaching), Roger Stanislaus, Barry Lakin, Glen Wilkie, Darren Purse, Paul Hague, Alex Inglethorpe, Joseph Baker, Andy Taylor (Physio). *Front row:* Tony Flynn (Kit Man/Assistant Physio), Lee Williams, Tony Kelly, Glenn Cockerill, Pat Holland (Manager), Gary Bellamy, Shaun Brooks, Andy Gray, Steve Shorey (Chief Scout/Youth Development Officer).

Division 3   **LEYTON ORIENT**

Leyton Stadium, Brisbane Road, Leyton, London E10 5NE. Telephone: (0181) 539 2223/4. Fax: (0181) 539 4390. Clubcall: 0891 121150.

Ground capacity: 12,573.

Record attendance: 34,345 v West Ham U, FA Cup 4th rd, 25 January 1964.

Record receipts: £87,867.92 v West Ham U, FA Cup 3rd rd, 10 January 1987.

Pitch measurements: 110yd × 80yd.

Chairman: Barry Hearn.

Directors: D. L. Weinrabe, Tony Wood, Harry Linney, V. Marsh, J. Goldsmith FR, BA.

Team Manager: Pat Holland. *Assistant Manager:* Tommy Cunningham. *Physio:* A. Taylor.

Secretary: David Burton. *Assistant Secretary:* Mrs Sue Tilling. *Commercial Manager:* Frank Woolf.

Stadium Manager: Janet Hasler.

Year Formed: 1881. *Turned Professional:* 1903. *Ltd Co.:* 1906.

Club Nickname: 'The O's'.

Previous Names: 1881–86, Glyn Cricket and Football Club; 1886–88, Eagle Football Club; 1888–98, Orient Football Club; 1898–1946, Clapton Orient; 1946–66, Leyton Orient; 1966–87, Orient.

Previous Grounds: Glyn Road, 1884–96; Whittles Athletic Ground, 1896–1900; Millfields Road, 1900–30; Lea Bridge Road, 1930–37.

Foundation: There is some doubt about the foundation of Leyton Orient, and, indeed, some confusion with clubs like Leyton and Clapton over their early history. As regards the foundation, the most favoured version is that Leyton Orient was formed originally by members of Homerton Theological College who established Glyn Cricket Club in 1881 and then carried on through the following winter playing football. Eventually many employees of the Orient Shipping Line became involved and so the name Orient was chosen in 1888.

First Football League game: 2 September 1905, Division 2, v Leicester Fosse (a) L 1-2 – Butler; Holmes, Codling; Lamberton, Boden, Boyle; Kingaby (1), Wootten, Leigh, Evenson, Bourne.

Record League Victory: 8–0 v Crystal Palace, Division 3 (S), 12 November 1955 – Welton; Lee, Earl; Blizzard, Aldous, McKnight; White (1), Facey (3), Burgess (2), Heckman, Hartburn (2). 8–0 v Rochdale, Division 4, 20 October 1987 – Wells; Howard, Dickenson (1), Smalley (1), Day, Hull, Hales (2), Castle (Sussex), Shinners (2), Godfrey (Harvey), Comfort (2). 8–0 v Colchester U, Division 4, 15 October 1988 – Wells; Howard, Dickenson, Hales (1p), Day (1). Sitton (1), Baker (1), Ward, Hull (3). Juryeff, Comfort (1).

Record Cup Victory: 9–2 v Chester, League Cup 3rd rd, 15 October 1962 – Robertson; Charlton, Taylor; Gibbs, Bishop, Lea; Deeley (1), Waites (3), Dunmore (2), Graham (3), Wedge.

Record Defeat: 0–8 v Aston Villa, FA Cup 4th rd, 30 January 1929.

Most League Points (2 for a win): 66, Division 3 (S), 1955–56.

Most League Points (3 for a win): 75, Division 4, 1988–89.

Most League Goals: 106, Division 3 (S), 1955–56.

Highest League Scorer in Season: Tom Johnston, 35, Division 2, 1957–58.

Most League Goals in Total Aggregate: Tom Johnston, 121, 1956–58, 1959–61.

Most Capped Player: John Chiedozie, 8 (10), Nigeria.

Most League Appearances: Peter Allen, 432, 1965–78.

Record Transfer Fee Received: £600,000 from Notts Co for John Chiedozie, August 1981.

Record Transfer Fee Paid: £175,000 to Wigan Ath for Paul Beesley, October 1989.

Football League Record: 1905 Elected to Division 2; 1929–56 Division 3 (S); 1956–62 Division 2; 1962–63 Division 1; 1963–66 Division 2; 1966–70 Division 3; 1970–82 Division 2; 1982–85 Division 3; 1985–89 Division 4; 1989–92 Division 3; 1992–95 Division 2; 1995– Division 3.

Honours: Football League: Division 1 best season: 22nd, 1962–63; Division 2 – Runners-up 1961–62; Division 3 – Champions 1969–70; Division 3 (S) – Champions 1955–56; Runners-up 1954–55. *FA Cup:* Semi-final 1978. *Football League Cup:* best season: 5th rd, 1963.

Colours: Red shirts with white pinstripe, white shorts, red stockings. *Change colours:* Blue and yellow.

Did you know?
On 26 May 1996, Leyton Orient defeated Wales 2-1 in a friendly at Brisbane Road watched by a crowd of 5000.

LEYTON ORIENT 1995–96 LEAGUE RECORD

Match No.	Date	Venue	Opponents	Result		H/T Score	Lg. Pos.	Goalscorers	Atten- dance
1	Aug 12	H	Torquay U	W	1-0	0-0	—	Brooks	8221
2	19	A	Mansfield T	D	0-0	0-0	10		2565
3	26	H	Darlington	D	1-1	0-0	8	Inglethorpe	4034
4	30	A	Scarborough	L	1-2	1-1	—	Cockerill	1796
5	Sept 2	H	Fulham	W	1-0	0-0	10	Inglethorpe	7244
6	9	A	Plymouth Arg	D	1-1	0-1	11	Watson	6292
7	12	A	Northampton T	W	2-1	0-1	—	Hendon, Inglethorpe	5072
8	16	H	Hartlepool U	W	4-1	2-0	3	Inglethorpe, Bellamy, West 2	4519
9	23	A	Exeter C	D	2-2	1-2	4	Inglethorpe 2	5507
10	30	H	Doncaster R	W	3-1	2-0	3	West, Kelly, Chapman	5524
11	Oct 7	A	Bury	L	1-2	1-2	5	West	3025
12	14	H	Chester C	L	0-2	0-2	8		6037
13	21	A	Scunthorpe U	L	0-2	0-1	9		2315
14	28	H	Wigan Ath	D	1-1	1-1	9	Brooks	4562
15	31	H	Hereford U	L	0-1	0-0	—		3567
16	Nov 4	A	Preston NE	L	0-4	0-0	13		9823
17	18	H	Cambridge U	W	3-1	1-1	10	West 2, Inglethorpe	4142
18	25	A	Barnet	L	0-3	0-1	12		2850
19	Dec 9	A	Exeter C	L	0-3	0-2	14		3471
20	16	A	Doncaster R	L	1-4	1-2	16	Chapman	1633
21	22	H	Rochdale	W	2-0	1-0	—	West 2	5399
22	26	A	Colchester U	D	0-0	0-0	13		4965
23	Jan 1	H	Gillingham	L	0-1	0-1	13		7098
24	6	A	Cardiff C	D	0-0	0-0	15		2736
25	13	H	Mansfield T	W	1-0	0-0	13	Kelly	3461
26	16	A	Lincoln C	L	0-1	0-1	—		1841
27	20	A	Torquay U	L	1-2	1-0	14	Hendon	2212
28	Feb 3	A	Darlington	L	0-2	0-0	19		1880
29	10	H	Cardiff C	W	4-1	1-1	15	West 3 (1 pen), Inglethorpe	3564
30	17	H	Northampton T	W	2-0	1-0	13	West, Arnott	4444
31	24	A	Hartlepool U	L	1-4	0-2	13	Kelly	1915
32	27	H	Plymouth Arg	L	0-1	0-0	—		3374
33	Mar 2	H	Colchester U	L	0-1	0-1	18		4049
34	9	A	Rochdale	L	0-1	0-1	21		1934
35	16	H	Lincoln C	W	2-0	0-0	16	Austin, Inglethorpe	3129
36	19	H	Scarborough	W	1-0	0-0	—	Warren	2121
37	23	A	Gillingham	D	1-1	0-0	15	Arnott	8071
38	26	A	Fulham	L	1-2	0-0	—	Shearer	3636
39	30	H	Bury	L	0-2	0-1	19		3421
40	Apr 2	A	Chester C	D	1-1	1-1	—	West	2097
41	6	A	Wigan Ath	L	0-1	0-0	20		3081
42	8	H	Scunthorpe U	D	0-0	0-0	20		2814
43	13	A	Hereford U	L	2-3	0-1	20	West 2	3459
44	20	H	Preston NE	L	0-2	0-1	21		5170
45	27	H	Barnet	D	3-3	1-2	21	Hanson, Arnott, West	4006
46	May 4	A	Cambridge U	L	0-2	0-1	21		3858

Final League Position: 21

GOALSCORERS

League (44): West 16 (1 pen), Inglethorpe 9, Arnott 3, Kelly T 3, Brooks 2, Chapman 2, Hendon 2, Austin 1, Bellamy 1, Cockerill 1, Hanson 1, Shearer 1, Warren 1, Watson 1.
Coca-Cola Cup (2): Austin 1, West 1 (pen).
FA Cup (0).

Caldwell P 28	Warren M 15 + 7	Austin K 32 + 8	Chapman D 38	Hendon I 38	Bellamy G 32	Brooks S 34 + 7	Cockerill G 38	Inglethorpe A 30	Gray A 3 + 4	Stanislaus R 20 + 1	Baker J 4 + 16	McCarthy A 40 + 3	Kelly T 32 + 2	West C 39	Shearer L 5 + 3	Watson M — + 1	Purse D 9 + 3	Hanson D 7 + 4	Lakin B 5 + 3	Fearon R 18	Currie D 9 + 1	Williams L 1 + 2	Arnott A 19	Berry G 4 + 3	Kelly R 5 + 1	Ayorinde S 1	Match No.
1	2	3¹	4	5	6	7	8	9	10	11	12																1
1	2	3	4	5			11	8	9¹		12	6	7	10													2
1		3	4	5	2	11	8	9¹			12	6	7	10													3
1		3	4¹	5		11	8	9			12	6	7	10	2												4
1			4	2	5	11	8	9	3			6	7	10													5
1	12		4	2¹	5	11	8	9²	3			6	7	10	13												6
1			4	2	5	11	8¹	9	3	12		6	7	10													7
1			4	2	5	11	8	9	3			6	7	10													8
1	12	13	4	2	5	11²	8	9	3			6	7¹	10													9
1	12	13	4	2	5	11²	8	9	3			6	7¹	10													10
1	2	11¹	4	8	5			9		3		6	7²	10			12	13									11
1	2	12	4	6	5¹			9	3	13	11	7	10²				8										12
1	11	8	4	2	5			9¹	3	12		6	7				10										13
1	12	13	4²	2	5¹	11	8	9	3			6	7	10													14
1	2		4	5		11	8	9	3			6	7				10										15
1	12	3	4	5		11	8			13	7²	6	9				2	10¹									16
	6		2	5	4¹	8	9²		3		12	7	10							1	11	13					17
	6		2	5	4²	8	9		3		12		10				7¹	1	11	13							18
	6			5	12	8	9	13	3			10					2	4¹	1	11	7²						19
	7³		4	2	5	12	8	9	3		6		10					1	11								20
		2	4	5		8	9		3		6	7	10					1	11								21
	11¹			5	4³	8	9	12	3		6	7	10				2	13	1								22
				5	4	8	9¹		3		6	7	10				2	12	1	11							23
	12			5	4	8		10¹	3		6	7					2	9	1	11							24
		3	2	4	5³	12	8		13		6	7	10				14	9¹	1	11²							25
		3	2	7	5	4	8¹		9²	12	6	11	10						1	13							26
		3	2	7	5	4		9	12	13	6	11²					8		1	10¹							27
1	12		4	5	11	8	9		13	3	7¹	10					2²					6					28
	3		2	5	10	8¹	11			6	7	9					12				1	4					29
	3	11	2	5		8	9			6	7	10									1	4					30
	3	11	2	5	12	8	9¹			6	7	10									1	4					31
	3	11²	2	5	12	8	9¹		13	6	7	10									1	4					32
	12	3	11	2	5	9	8			6	7¹	10									1	4					33
1	9	3	4		5	11¹	8²			12	7	10	13	2								6					34
1	11	3	4		5	12		9		13	8	7²		2¹	10							6					35
1	11	3	4	2	5	12		9²		6	7¹	10		13								8					36
1	7³	3	4¹	2		11	8			6	12	10	5		13							9²	14				37
1	7¹	3	4	2		11²	8			6	12	10	5									9	13				38
1		3	4	2		7¹	8			12	6		10	5								9	11²	13			39
1	7¹	3	4	2		11	8			12	6		10									9	5				40
1	11	3	4		7¹	8				12	6		10				2²					5	13	9			41
1	12	3¹	4	2		8				7	6		10									5	9	11			42
1	11	3	4		7					12	6		10	8			2¹					5	9				43
1		3¹	4²	2	7	8				12	6		10				13					5	9	11			44
	12	3	4	2	7	8²				11	6¹		10	14			9³	13	1			5					45
	6	12	4	2	7²	8				11			10	13					1			5		3¹	9		46

Coca-Cola Cup

First Round   Wycombe W   (a)   0-3
                                    (h)   2-0

FA Cup

First Round   Torquay U   (a)   0-1

LINCOLN CITY 1995–96 *Back row (left to right):* Colin Alcide, Jason Minett, Andy Leaning, Jonathon Whitney, Barry Richardson, Paul Wanless, Alan Johnson.
Middle row: Roger Cleary (Physio), Neil Davies, Steve Williams, Phil Daley, Grant Brown, Matt Carbon, David Johnson, John Robertson.
Front row: Terry Fleming, Gareth Ainsworth, Jason Barnett, John Beck (Manager), John Still (Assistant Manager), Ben Dixon, Steve Brown, Tony Daws, Paul Mudd.

Division 3 LINCOLN CITY

Sincil Bank, Lincoln LN5 8LD. Telephone: (01522) 522224. Fax: (01522) 520564. Commercial: (01522) 536966. Community Officer: (01522) 539671.

Ground capacity: 10,918.

Record attendance: 23,196 v Derby Co, League Cup 4th rd, 15 November 1967.

Record receipts: £44,184.46 v Everton, Coca-Cola Cup 2nd rd 1st leg, 21 September 1993.

Pitch measurements: 110yd × 75yd.

Hon. Life Presidents: V. C. Withers, D. W. L. Bocock.

President: H. Dove.

Chairman: K. J. Reames. *Vice-Chairman:* G. R. Davey (and Managing).

Directors: H. C. Sills, J. Hicks, Mrs E. C. Reames, N. Woolsey, C. J. Thomas, P. Jackson.

Hon. Consultant Surgeon: Mr Brian Smith. *Hon. Club Doctor:* Nick Huntley.

Company Secretary: G. R. Davey.

Team Manager: John Beck. *Assistant Manager:* John Still. *Physio:* M. Hudson BSC (Hons) MSC, MCSP.

Commercial Manager: G. R. Davey. *Stadium Manager:* Nigel Dennis.

Year Formed: 1883. *Turned Professional:* 1892. *Ltd Co.:* 1892.

Club Nickname: 'The Red Imps'.

Previous Grounds: 1883, John O'Gaunt's; 1894, Sincil Bank.

Foundation: Although there was a Lincoln club as far back as 1861, the present organisation was formed in 1883 winning the Lincolnshire Senior Cup in only their fourth season. They were founder members of the Midland League in 1889 and that competition's first champions.

First Football League game: 3 September 1892, Division 2, v Sheffield U (a) L 2-4 – W. Gresham; Coulton, Neill; Shaw, Mettam, Moore; Smallman, Irving (1), Cameron (1), Kelly, J. Gresham.

Record League Victory: 11–1 v Crewe Alex, Division 3 (N), 29 September 1951 – Jones; Green (1p), Varney; Wright, Emery, Grummett (1); Troops (1), Garvey, Graver (6), Whittle (1), Johnson (1).

Record Cup Victory: 8–1 v Bromley, FA Cup 2nd rd, 10 December 1938 – McPhail; Hartshorne, Corbett; Bean, Leach, Whyte (1); Hancock, Wilson (1), Ponting (3), Deacon (1), Clare (2).

Record Defeat: 3–11 v Manchester C, Division 2, 23 March 1895.

Most League Points (2 for a win): 74, Division 4, 1975–76.

Most League Points (3 for a win): 77, Division 3, 1981–82.

Most League Goals: 121, Division 3 (N), 1951–52.

Highest League Scorer in Season: Allan Hall, 42, Division 3 (N), 1931–32.

Most League Goals in Total Aggregate: Andy Graver, 144, 1950–55 and 1958–61.

Most Capped Player: David Pugh, 3 (7), Wales and George Moulson, 3, Republic of Ireland.

Most League Appearances: Tony Emery, 402, 1946–59.

Record Transfer Fee Received: £400,000 plus increments from Newcastle U for Darren Huckerby, November 1995.

Record Transfer Fee Paid: £63,000 to Leicester C for Grant Brown, January 1990.

Football League Record: 1892 Founder member of Division 2. Remained in Division 2 until 1920 when they failed re-election but also missed seasons 1908–09 and 1911–12 when not re-elected. 1921–32 Division 3 (N); 1932–34 Division 2; 1934–48 Division 3 (N); 1948–49 Division 2; 1949–52 Division 3 (N); 1952–61 Division 2; 1961–62 Division 3; 1962–76 Division 4; 1976–79 Division 3; 1979–81 Division 4; 1981–86 Division 3; 1986–87 Division 4; 1987–88 GM Vauxhall Conference; 1988–92 Division 4; 1992– Division 3.

Honours: Football League: Division 2 best season: 5th, 1901–02; Division 3 (N) – Champions 1931–32, 1947–48, 1951–52; Runners-up 1927–28, 1930–31, 1936–37; Division 4 – Champions 1975–76; Runners-up 1980–81. *FA Cup:* best season: 1st rd of Second Series (5th rd equivalent), 1887, 2nd rd (5th rd equivalent), 1890, 1902. *Football League Cup:* best season: 4th rd, 1968. *GM Vauxhall Conference:* Champions 1987–88.

Colours: Red and white striped shirts, black shorts, red stockings with white trim. *Change colours:* Jade shirts, black shorts, jade stockings.

Did you know?
In 1995–96 Lincoln City's six successive home matches without conceding a goal taking the total to 621 minutes, equalled a 64 year old club record.

LINCOLN CITY 1995–96 LEAGUE RECORD

Match No.	Date	Venue	Opponents	Result	H/T Score	Lg. Pos.	Goalscorers	Attendance
1	Aug 12	A	Preston NE	W 2-1	1-1	—	Puttnam, West	7813
2	19	H	Gillingham	L 0-3	0-1	13		2822
3	26	A	Colchester U	L 0-3	0-2	17		2939
4	28	H	Scunthorpe U	D 2-2	0-0	—	Daws, Onwere (pen)	2674
5	Sept 2	A	Barnet	L 1-3	1-2	21	Huckerby	1813
6	9	H	Rochdale	L 1-2	0-1	24	Onwere	2408
7	12	H	Bury	D 2-2	0-0	—	Onwere (pen), Daws	1851
8	16	A	Chester C	L 1-5	1-3	23	Daws	3049
9	23	H	Cambridge U	L 1-3	0-2	24	Johnson D	2614
10	30	A	Plymouth Arg	L 0-3	0-3	24		6643
11	Oct 7	H	Darlington	L 0-2	0-1	24		2564
12	14	A	Scarborough	D 0-0	0-0	24		1848
13	21	H	Cardiff C	L 0-1	0-0	24		2453
14	28	A	Exeter C	D 1-1	1-1	24	Barnett	3252
15	Nov 1	A	Mansfield T	W 2-1	1-0	—	Onwere (pen), Holmes	2398
16	4	H	Hartlepool U	D 1-1	1-0	23	Huckerby	2939
17	18	A	Torquay U	W 2-0	1-0	23	Ainsworth 2	2553
18	25	H	Northampton T	W 1-0	0-0	23	Brown S	3287
19	Dec 9	A	Cambridge U	L 1-2	1-1	23	Westley	2472
20	16	H	Plymouth Arg	D 0-0	0-0	23		2801
21	23	A	Wigan Ath	D 1-1	0-0	23	Brown S	2334
22	26	H	Fulham	W 4-0	2-0	22	Brown S, Ainsworth 2, Whitney	3693
23	Jan 13	A	Gillingham	L 0-2	0-1	23		8047
24	16	H	Leyton Orient	W 1-0	1-0	—	Carbon	1841
25	20	H	Preston NE	D 0-0	0-0	22		5185
26	Feb 3	H	Colchester U	D 0-0	0-0	22		2531
27	5	A	Doncaster R	D 1-1	0-1	—	Minett (pen)	2083
28	13	H	Hereford U	W 2-1	0-1	—	Minett (pen), Whitney	1884
29	17	A	Bury	L 1-7	1-2	22	Carbon	3096
30	24	H	Chester C	D 0-0	0-0	23		2533
31	27	A	Rochdale	D 3-3	1-2	—	Carbon, Ainsworth, Stuart (og)	1253
32	Mar 2	A	Fulham	W 2-1	2-1	20	Ainsworth 2	4245
33	5	A	Scunthorpe U	W 3-2	1-0	—	Ainsworth 2, Daley	2411
34	9	H	Wigan Ath	L 2-4	1-1	16	Alcide, Ainsworth	3282
35	16	A	Leyton Orient	L 0-2	0-0	18		3129
36	19	H	Barnet	L 1-2	0-0	—	Bos	1872
37	23	H	Doncaster R	W 4-0	4-0	17	Alcide 2, Minett 2	3240
38	27	H	Hereford U	L 0-1	0-0	—		1631
39	30	A	Darlington	L 2-3	1-2	20	Bos, Ainsworth	2146
40	Apr 2	H	Scarborough	W 3-1	2-1	—	Bos 2, Ainsworth	2010
41	6	H	Exeter C	L 0-1	0-1	19		2723
42	8	A	Cardiff C	D 1-1	0-0	18	Alcide	2657
43	13	H	Mansfield T	W 2-1	0-0	17	Eustace (og), Bos	2992
44	20	A	Hartlepool U	L 0-3	0-1	18		3012
45	27	A	Northampton T	D 1-1	0-0	19	Minett (pen)	5166
46	May 4	H	Torquay U	W 5-0	1-0	18	Alcide 2, Barnett (pen), Storey, Holmes	5814

Final League Position: 18

GOALSCORERS

League (57): Ainsworth 12, Alcide 6, Bos 5, Minett 5 (3 pens), Onwere 4 (3 pens), Brown S 3, Carbon 3, Daws 3, Barnett 2 (1 pen), Holmes 2, Huckerby 2, Whitney 2, Daley 1, Johnson D 1, Puttnam 1, Storey 1, West 1, Westley 1, own goals 2.
Coca-Cola Cup (0).
FA Cup (0).

Key L 5	Minett J 39+3	Dixon B 10+2	Megson G 2	Storey B —+2	Greenall C 4	Brightwell D 5	West D 7+1	Onwere U 33+2	Allon J 3+1	Huckerby D 16	Puttnam D 4+1	Mudd P 2+2	Platnauer N —+1	Carbon M 26	Daws T 8+3	Williams S 1+2	Dyer A 1	Johnson D 14+10	Brown G 34	Wanless P 7+1	Leaning A 7	Davis D 3	Bound M 3+1	Appleton M 4	Johnson A 17+5	Hulme K 4+1	Westley S 9	Brown S 22+4	Daley P 6+6	Richardson B 34	Holmes S 23	Barnett J 27+5	Whitney J 25+1	Ainsworth G 31	Alcide C 22+5	Fleming T 17+5	Robertson J 21+1	Bos G 10+1	Match No.
1	2	3	4		5	6	7	8	9[2]	10	11[1]	12	13																											1
1	2	3	4		5	6	7	8	9[1]	10				11[2]	12	13																								2
1	2	3			5	6	7	8		10	4[2]			11	12				9[1]	13																				3
1	2	3			5	6	7	8		10			9[1]	11	12			4																						4
1	2	3				6	7	8		10		12		11			9[2]	4	5[1]	13																				5
	2	3					7	8	11					5	10			9	4			1	6																6
	2	3				12	8			7	11[1]			5	10			9	4			1		6															7
	2	3				12				7	11[2]			5	10[3]	13		9	4			1	6				8												8
14		3			2				9[1]	11		13[3]		7	10			12	4			1	6	5[2]			8												9
	2				12			8		10				5				9	4			1	6	11		3	7[1]												10
		3[1]						8		7								9[2]	4			1		12	2	6	11	5	10	13									11
		2						8											6									3	4	5	1	2		7	11	9			12
								8											6									3	4[1]	10	1	2	12	7		9	5		13
								8[2]											6									3	13	10	1	2	12	7	11[1]	9	5		14
								8											6									3		10	1	2	12	7[2]	11	9	5		15
								8											6									3[1]		10	1	2		7	11	9	5		16
								8											6									3		10	1	2		7	11	9	5		17
								8											6									3		10	1	2		7	11	9	5		18
4								8										9[1]	6									3	13	10[2]	1	2	12	7	11	9	5		19
4								8										9[1]	6									3[7]	13	10	1	2	12	7	11	9[1]	5		20
4								8										9[2]	6									3	13	10	1	2	12	7	11[1]	9[2]	5		21
4								8											6									3	13	10	1	2	12	7	11	9[2]	5		22
4								8											6									3		10	1	2[1]	12	7	11	9	5		23
4								8											6									3	13	10[1]	1	2	12	7	11	9[2]	5		24
4								8											6									3		10	1	2	12	7[1]	11	9	5		25
4								8											6									3		10	1	2		7	11	9	5		26
4								8											6									3		10[1]	1	2	12	7	11	9	5		27
4								8											6									3		10	1	2	12	7[1]	11	9	5		28
4								8											6									3		10	1	2[1]	12	7	11	9	5		29
4								8											6									3		10[1]	1	2	12	7	11	9	5		30
4								8											6									3	13	10[1]	1	2	12	7	11	9[2]	5		31
								8[2]											6									3	13	10	1	2	12	7	11	9[1]	5		32
								8											6									3	13	10[2]	1	2	12	7	11	9[1]	5		33
4[1]								8											6									3	13	10	1	2	12	7	11	9[2]	5		34
4								8											6									3	13	10	1	2	12	7[2]	11[1]	9	5		35
4								8											6									3		10	1	2	12	7	11	9[1]	5	9	36
4								8											6						14			3[2]	13	10[1]	1	2	12	7[3]	11	9	5	9[2]	37
4								8											6									3	13	10[1]	1	2	12	7	11	9	5	9[2]	38
4								8											6									3		10	1	2	12	7	11[1]	9	5	9	39
4								8											6									3		10[1]	1	2	12	7	11	9	5	9	40
4								8											6									3		10	1	2		7	11	9	5	9	41
4								8[1]											6									3		10[2]	1	2	12	7	11	9	5	9	42
4				13				8[1]											6									3		10	1	2	12	7	11[2]	9	5	9	43
4								8											6									3		10	1	2	12	7	11	9[1]	5	9	44
4								8											6[2]									3	13	10	1	2	12	7	11	9[1]	5	9	45
4[1]				12				8											6									3		10	1	2		7	11	9	5	9	46

Coca-Cola Cup
First Round Notts Co (a) 0-2
(h) 0-2

FA Cup
First Round Stockport Co (a) 0-5

LIVERPOOL 1995–96   *Back row (left to right):* Doug Livermore (Assistant Manager), Lee Jones, Rob Jones, John Scales, David James, Michael Stensgaard, Anthony Warner, Mark Wright, Mark Walters, Dominic Matteo, Sammy Lee (Coach).
Middle row: Joe Corrigan (Goalkeeping Coach), Ronnie Moran (Coach), Michael Thomas, Stig Bjornebye, Stan Collymore, Phil Babb, John Barnes, Jan Molby, Mark Leather (Physio).
Front row: Mark Kennedy, Robbie Fowler, Steve Harkness, Neil Ruddock, Roy Evans (Manager), Ian Rush (Manager), Jamie Redknapp, Steve McManaman, Nigel Clough.

FA Premiership **LIVERPOOL**

Anfield Road, Liverpool L4 0TH. Telephone: (0151) 263 2361. Fax: (0151) 260 8813. Clubcall: 0891 121184. Ticket and Match Information: (0151) 260 9999 (24-hour service) or (0151) 260 8680 (office hours) Credit Card Bookings.

Ground Capacity: 41,000.

Record attendance: 61,905 v Wolverhampton W, FA Cup 4th rd, 2 February 1952.

Record receipts: £496,000 v Newcastle U, Coca-Cola Cup 4th rd, 29 November 1995.

Pitch measurements: 111yd × 74yd.

Chairman: D. R. Moores.

Directors: J. T. Cross, N. White FSCA, T. D. Smith, T. W. Saunders, P. B. Robinson, K. E. B. Clayton FCA.

Vice-Presidents: C. J. Hill, H. E. Roberts, W. D. Corkish FCA.

Team Manager: Roy Evans. *Assistant Manager:* Doug Livermore. *Coach:* Ronnie Moran. *Physio:* Mark Leather.

Chief Executive/General Secretary: Peter B. Robinson. *Commercial Manager:* Mike Turner.

Year Formed: 1892. *Turned Professional:* 1892. *Ltd Co.:* 1892.

Club Nickname: 'Reds' or 'Pool'.

Foundation: But for a dispute between Everton FC and their landlord at Anfield in 1892, there may never have been a Liverpool club. This dispute persuaded the majority of Evertonians to quit Anfield for Goodison Park, leaving the landlord, Mr. John Houlding, to form a new club. He originally tried to retain the name "Everton" but when this failed, he founded Liverpool Association FC on 15 March 1892.

First Football League game: 2 September 1893, Division 2, v Middlesbrough Ironopolis (a) W 2-0 – McOwen; Hannah, McLean; Henderson, McQue (1), McBride; Gordon, McVean (1), M. McQueen, Stott, H. McQueen.

Record League Victory: 10–1 v Rotherham T, Division 2, 18 February 1896 – Storer; Goldie, Wilkie, McCarthy, McQueen, Holmes; McVean (3), Ross (2), Allan (4), Becton (1), Bradshaw.

Record Cup Victory: 11–0 v Stromsgodset Drammen, ECWC 1st rd 1st leg, 17 September 1974 – Clemence; Smith (1), Lindsay (1p), Thompson (2), Cormack (1), Hughes (1), Boersma (2), Hall, Heighway (1), Kennedy (1), Callaghan (1).

Record Defeat: 1–9 v Birmingham C, Division 2, 11 December 1954.

Most League Points (2 for a win): 68, Division 1, 1978–79.

Most League Points (3 for a win): 90, Division 1, 1987–88.

Most League Goals: 106, Division 2, 1895–96.

Highest League Scorer in Season: Roger Hunt, 41, Division 2, 1961–62.

Most League Goals in Total Aggregate: Roger Hunt, 245, 1959–69.

Most Capped Player: Ian Rush, 67 (73), Wales.

Most League Appearances: Ian Callaghan, 640, 1960–78.

Record Transfer Fee Received: £2,750,000 from Juventus for Ian Rush, June 1986.

Record Transfer Fee Paid: £8,500,000 to Nottingham F for Stan Collymore, June 1995.

Football League Record: 1893 Elected to Division 2; 1894–95 Division 1; 1895–96 Division 2; 1896–1904 Division 1; 1904–05 Division 2; 1905–54 Division 1; 1954–62 Division 2; 1962–92 Division 1; 1992– FA Premier League.

Honours: **Football League:** Division 1 – Champions 1900–01, 1905–06, 1921–22, 1922–23, 1946–47, 1963–64, 1965–66, 1972–73, 1975–76, 1976–77, 1978–79, 1979–80, 1981–82, 1982–83, 1983–84, 1985–86, 1987–88, 1989–90 (Liverpool have a record number of 18 League Championship wins); Runners-up 1899–99, 1909–10, 1968–69, 1973–74, 1974–75, 1977–78, 1984–85, 1986–87, 1988–89, 1990–91; Division 2 – Champions 1893–94, 1895–96, 1904–05, 1961–62. *FA Cup:* Winners 1965, 1974, 1986, 1989, 1992; Runners-up 1914, 1950, 1971, 1977, 1988, 1995–96; *Football League Cup:* Winners 1981, 1982, 1983, 1984, 1995; Runners-up 1978, 1987. *League Super Cup:* Winners 1986. **European Competitions:** *European Cup:* 1964–65, 1966–67, 1973–74, 1976–77 (winners), 1977–78 (winners), 1978–79, 1979–80, 1980–81 (winners), 1981–82, 1982–83, 1983–84 (winners), 1984–85 (runners-up); *European Cup-Winners' Cup:* 1965–66 (runners-up), 1971–72, 1974–75, 1992–93; *European Fairs Cup:* 1967–68, 1968–69, 1969–70, 1970–71; *UEFA Cup:* 1972–73 (winners), 1975–76 (winners), 1991–92, 1995–96; *Super Cup:* 1977 (winners), 1978, 1984; *World Club Championship:* 1981 (runners-up).

Colours: All red. *Change colours:* Ecru shirts, black shorts, ecru stockings.

Did you know?
When Ian Rush scored a 59th minute goal against Rochdale in 1995–96, he broke Denis Law's post-war record of FA Cup goals with the 42nd of his career.

LIVERPOOL 1995–96 LEAGUE RECORD

Match No.	Date	Venue	Opponents	Result		H/T Score	Lg. Pos.	Goalscorers	Atten-dance
1	Aug 19	H	Sheffield W	W	1-0	0-0	—	Collymore	40,535
2	21	A	Leeds U	L	0-1	0-0	—		36,007
3	26	A	Tottenham H	W	3-1	2-0	4	Barnes 2, Fowler	31,254
4	30	H	QPR	W	1-0	1-0	—	Ruddock	37,548
5	Sept 9	A	Wimbledon	L	0-1	0-1	7		19,530
6	16	H	Blackburn R	W	3-0	3-0	4	Redknapp, Fowler, Collymore	39,502
7	23	H	Bolton W	W	5-2	2-0	3	Fowler 4, Harkness	40,104
8	Oct 1	A	Manchester U	D	2-2	1-1	4	Fowler 2	34,934
9	14	H	Coventry C	D	0-0	0-0	5		39,079
10	22	A	Southampton	W	3-1	1-1	5	McManaman 2, Redknapp	15,245
11	28	H	Manchester C	W	6-0	2-0	3	Rush 2, Redknapp, Fowler 2, Ruddock	39,267
12	Nov 4	A	Newcastle U	L	1-2	1-1	4	Rush	36,547
13	18	H	Everton	L	1-2	0-0	7	Fowler	40,818
14	22	A	West Ham U	D	0-0	0-0	—		24,324
15	25	A	Middlesbrough	L	1-2	0-1	7	Ruddock	29,390
16	Dec 2	H	Southampton	D	1-1	0-0	8	Collymore	38,007
17	9	A	Bolton W	W	1-0	0-0	7	Collymore	21,042
18	17	H	Manchester U	W	2-0	1-0	5	Fowler 2	40,546
19	23	H	Arsenal	W	3-1	1-1	3	Fowler 3	39,806
20	30	A	Chelsea	D	2-2	1-2	3	McManaman 2	31,137
21	Jan 1	H	Nottingham F	W	4-2	2-2	3	Fowler 2, Collymore, Cooper (og)	39,206
22	13	A	Sheffield W	D	1-1	0-1	4	Rush	32,747
23	20	H	Leeds U	W	5-0	1-0	2	Ruddock 2, Fowler 2 (1 pen), Collymore	40,254
24	31	A	Aston Villa	W	2-0	0-0	—	Collymore, Fowler	39,332
25	Feb 3	H	Tottenham H	D	0-0	0-0	3		40,628
26	11	A	QPR	W	2-1	2-0	3	Wright, Fowler	18,405
27	24	A	Blackburn R	W	3-2	2-1	3	Collymore 2, Thomas	30,895
28	Mar 3	H	Aston Villa	W	3-0	3-0	3	McManaman, Fowler 2	39,508
29	13	H	Wimbledon	D	2-2	1-0	—	McManaman, Collymore	34,063
30	16	H	Chelsea	W	2-0	0-0	3	Wright, Fowler	40,820
31	23	A	Nottingham F	L	0-1	0-1	3		29,058
32	Apr 3	H	Newcastle U	W	4-3	1-2	—	Fowler 2, Collymore 2	40,702
33	6	A	Coventry C	L	0-1	0-1	3		23,037
34	8	H	West Ham U	W	2-0	2-0	3	Collymore, Barnes	40,326
35	16	A	Everton	D	1-1	0-1	—	Fowler	40,120
36	27	H	Middlesbrough	W	1-0	0-0	3	Collymore	40,782
37	May 1	A	Arsenal	D	0-0	0-0	—		38,323
38	5	A	Manchester C	D	2-2	2-0	3	Lomas (og), Rush	31,436

Final League Position: 3

GOALSCORERS

League (70): Fowler 28 (1 pen), Collymore 14, McManaman 6, Ruddock 5, Rush 5, Barnes 3, Redknapp 3, Wright 2, Harkness 1, Thomas 1, own goals 2.
Coca-Cola Cup (7): Fowler 2, Harkness 1, McManaman 1, Rush 1, Scales 1, Thomas 1.
FA Cup (19): Fowler 6, Collymore 5, McAteer 3, McManaman 2, Rush 1, own goals 2.

James D 38	Jones R 33	Harkness S 23 + 1	Babb P 28	Wright M 28	Matteo D 5	McManaman S 38	Redknapp J 19 + 4	Rush I 10 + 10	Barnes J 36	Collymore S 30 + 1	Fowler R 36 + 2	Thomas M 18 + 9	Ruddock N 18 + 2	McAteer J 27 + 2	Scales J 27	Kennedy M 1 + 3	Clough N 1 + 1	Bjornebye S 2	Match No.
1	2	3	4	5	6	7	8	9[1]	10	11[2]	12	13							1
1	2	3	4	5	6[2]	7	8	9	10	11[1]	12	13							2
1	2	3	4	5		7[1]	8	9	10	11	12		6						3
1	2	3	4	5		7	8	9	10	11			6						4
1	2	3[1]	4	5		7	8		10	9	11	12	6						5
1	2	3	4	5		7	8[1]		10[2]	9	11	12	6	13					6
1	2	3	4	5		7	8		10	9	11		6						7
1		3		5		7	8	9	11	10			6	4	2				8
1	2[1]	3	4	5		7	8	13	10	9[1]	11		6		12				9
1		3	4	5		7	8	9	10	11				2	6				10
1		3	4	5		7	8	9	10[1]	11	12			2	6[2]	13			11
1	2	3	6	5		7	8	9[1]	10	12	11			4					12
1	2	3[2]	6[1]	5		7		9	10	11	12	13	8	4					13
1	2	3	4	5		7			10	9	11		6	8					14
1	2[1]	3	4	5		7			10	9	11	12	6	8					15
1	2[1]	3	6			7			10	9	8			4	5	11	12		16
1	2		6	5		7			10	9	11			4			8	3	17
1	3		6	5		7			10	9	11	8		2	4				18
1	2	3		5		7			10	9	11	8		4	6				19
1	2	3		5		7			10	9	11	8		4	6				20
1	2	3	5			7			10	9	11	8		4	6				21
1	3[1]			5		7		12	10	9	11	8	6	2	4				22
1	3			5		7			10	9	11	8	6	2	4				23
1	3			5		7			10	9	11	8	6	2	4				24
1	3[1]		6	5		7		12	10	9	11	8		2	4				25
1	3		6	5		7		12	10	9	11[1]	8		2	4				26
1	3		6	5		7			10	9	11	8		2	4				27
1	3		6	5[2]		7	13	12	10	9[1]	11	8		2	4				28
1	3[1]		6	5		7		12	10	9	11	8		2	4				29
1	2	3		5		7			10	9	11	8		4	6				30
1				5	3[1]	7	12	13	10	9[2]	11	8	6	2	4				31
1	3[2]	12		5[1]		7	8	13	10	9	11		6	2	4				32
1	3[2]	5[1]	6			7	8	13	10	9	11	12		2	4				33
1				5		7	8		10	9	11		6	2	4			3	34
1	3			5		7	8[1]	12	10	9	11	13	6[2]	2	4				35
1	2			5		7	8	12	10	9	11[1]	3[2]	6	4		13			36
1	3			5		7	8	12	10	9[1]	11		6	2	4				37
1	3		4	5		7	8[1]	9	10		11		6	2	12				38

Coca-Cola Cup

Second Round	Sunderland	(h)	2-0
		(a)	1-0
Third Round	Manchester C	(h)	4-0
Fourth Round	Newcastle U	(h)	0-1

FA Cup

Third Round	Rochdale	(h)	7-0
Fourth Round	Shrewsbury T	(a)	4-0
Fifth Round	Charlton Ath	(h)	2-1
Sixth Round	Leeds U	(a)	0-0
		(h)	3-0
Semi-final (at Old Trafford)	Aston Villa		3-0
Final at Wembley	Manchester U		0-1

LUTON TOWN 1995–96   *Back row (left to right):* Ben Chenery, Danny Power, Gary Simpson, Fred Barber, Paul McLaren, Rob Matthews, Gavin Johnson, David Greene, Steve Davis, Kelvin Davis, John Taylor, Trevor Peake, Julian James.

Middle row: Chris Green (Director), Cliff Bassett (Director), Clive Goodyear (Physio), Paul Lowe (Youth Development Officer), Richard Harvey, Aaron Skelton, David Oldfield, Mitchell Thomas, Des Linton, Marvin Johnson, Bontcho Guentchev, Matthew Woolgar, Wayne Turner (First Team Coach), John Moore (Youth Team Coach), Les Shannon (Scouting Co-ordinator), Nigel Terry (Director).

Front row: Jamie Woodsford, Gary Waddock, Tony Thorpe, Ceri Hughes, Mick McGiven, David Kohler (Chairman), Terry Westley, Scott Oakes, Nathan Jones, Graham Alexander, Dwight Marshall.

Division 2   LUTON TOWN

Kenilworth Road Stadium, 1 Maple Rd, Luton, Beds LU4 8AW. Telephone: (01582) 411622. Ticket Office: (01582) 416976. Credit Hotline: (01582) 30748 (24 hrs). Banqueting: (01582) 411526. Clubcall: 0891 121123.

Ground capacity: 9975.

Record attendance: 30,069 v Blackpool, FA Cup 6th rd replay, 4 March 1959.

Record receipts: £115,541.20 v West Ham U, FA Cup 6th rd, 23 March 1994.

Pitch measurements: 110yd × 72yd.

Chairman & Managing Director: D. A. Kohler BSC (HONS), ARICS.

Directors: C. S. Bassett, C. T. F. Green, N. S. Terry.

Secretary: Cherry Newbery.

Commercial Manager: Kathy Leather.

Manager: Lennie Lawrence. **Stadium Manager:** Geoff Lovell. **First Team Coach:** Wayne Turner. **Coaches:** Trevor Peake, John Moore.

Physio: Clive Goodyear.

Year Formed: 1885. **Turned Professional:** 1890. **Ltd Co.:** 1897.

Club Nickname: 'The Hatters'.

Previous Grounds: 1885, Excelsior, Dallow Lane; 1897, Dunstable Road; 1905, Kenilworth Road.

Foundation: Formed by an amalgamation of two leading local clubs, Wanderers and Excelsior a works team, at a meeting in Luton Town Hall in April 1885. The Wanderers had three months earlier changed their name to Luton Town Wanderers and did not take too kindly to the formation of another Town club but were talked around at this meeting. Wanderers had already appeared in the FA Cup and the new club entered in its inaugural season.

First Football League game: 4 September 1897, Division 2, v Leicester Fosse (a) D 1-1 – Williams; McCartney, McEwen; Davies, Stewart, Docherty; Gallacher, Coupar, Birch, McInnes, Ekins (1).

Record League Victory: 12–0 v Bristol R, Division 3 (S), 13 April 1936 – Dolman; Mackey, Smith; Finlayson, Nelson, Godfrey; Rich, Martin (1), Payne (10), Roberts (1), Stephenson.

Record Cup Victory: 9–0 v Clapton, FA Cup 1st rd (replay after abandoned game), 30 November 1927 – Abbott; Kingham, Graham; Black, Rennie, Fraser; Pointon, Yardley (4), Reid (2), Woods (1), Dennis (2).

Record Defeat: 0–9 v Small Heath, Division 2, 12 November 1898.

Most League Points (2 for a win): 66, Division 4, 1967–68.

Most League Points (3 for a win): 88, Division 2, 1981–82.

Most League Goals: 103, Division 3 (S), 1936–37.

Highest League Scorer in Season: Joe Payne, 55, Division 3 (S), 1936–37.

Most League Goals in Total Aggregate: Gordon Turner, 243, 1949–64.

Most Capped Player: Mal Donaghy, 58 (91), Northern Ireland.

Most League Appearances: Bob Morton, 494, 1948–64.

Record Transfer Fee Received: £2,500,000 from Arsenal for John Hartson, January 1995.

Record Transfer Fee Paid: £850,000 to Odense for Lars Elstrup, August 1989.

Football League Record: 1897 Elected to Division 2; 1900 Failed re-election; 1920 Division 3; 1921–37 Division 3 (S); 1937–55 Division 2; 1955–60 Division 1; 1960–63 Division 2; 1963–65 Division 3; 1965–68 Division 4; 1968–70 Division 3; 1970–74 Division 2; 1974–75 Division 1; 1975–82 Division 2; 1982–96 Division 1; 1996– Division 2.

Honours: *Football League:* Division 1 best season: 7th, 1986–87; Division 2 – Champions 1981–82; Runners-up 1954–55, 1973–74; Division 3 – Runners-up 1969–70; Division 4 – Champions 1967–68; Division 3 (S) – Champions 1936–37; Runners-up 1935–36. *FA Cup:* Runners-up 1959. *Football League Cup:* Winners 1988; Runners-up 1989. *Simod Cup:* Runners-up 1988.

Colours: White shirts with blue sleeves with white and orange trim, blue collar with orange trim, blue shorts with orange and white trim, blue and white hooped stockings with orange trim. **Change colours:** Black and orange vertical striped shirts, with black collar and orange trim, black shorts with orange stripe down side, black stockings with orange turnover.

Did you know?
Luton Town's first full international player was left-half Bob Hawkes capped for England in 1907. He was already an established amateur international.

LUTON TOWN 1995–96 LEAGUE RECORD

Match No.	Date	Venue	Opponents	Result		H/T Score	Lg. Pos.	Goalscorers	Atten-dance
1	Aug 13	H	Norwich C	L	1-3	0-1	—	Guentchev (pen)	7848
2	19	A	Southend U	W	1-0	0-0	17	Thorpe	4630
3	26	H	Leicester C	D	1-1	1-0	16	Hughes	7612
4	29	A	Grimsby T	D	0-0	0-0	—		4289
5	Sept 2	H	Derby Co	L	1-2	1-1	17	Marshall	6427
6	9	A	Reading	L	1-3	1-1	20	Marshall	8550
7	13	A	Millwall	L	0-1	0-0	—		7076
8	16	H	Sunderland	L	0-2	0-0	23		6955
9	23	A	Wolverhampton W	D	0-0	0-0	24		23,659
10	30	H	Portsmouth	W	3-1	2-1	23	Marshall, Davis, Guentchev (pen)	7795
11	Oct 7	A	Tranmere R	L	0-1	0-1	24		6680
12	14	H	WBA	L	1-2	1-0	24	Harvey	8042
13	22	A	Ipswich T	W	1-0	1-0	21	Oldfield	9123
14	29	H	Charlton Ath	L	0-1	0-1	22		6270
15	Nov 4	A	Stoke C	L	0-5	0-1	24		9382
16	11	H	Oldham Ath	D	1-1	1-0	23	Douglas	6047
17	18	H	Birmingham C	D	0-0	0-0	23		7920
18	21	A	Watford	D	1-1	1-0	—	Davis	10,042
19	25	A	Barnsley	L	0-1	0-0	23		6437
20	Dec 2	H	Tranmere R	W	3-2	1-1	23	Marshall 2, McLaren	6025
21	10	A	Wolverhampton W	L	2-3	1-3	24	Oakes, Marshall	6997
22	16	A	Portsmouth	L	0-4	0-3	24		7012
23	23	H	Huddersfield T	D	2-2	1-0	24	Marshall, Oldfield	7076
24	Jan 13	H	Southend U	W	3-1	1-0	24	Guentchev, Oakes 2	6566
25	20	A	Norwich C	W	1-0	1-0	23	Guentchev (pen)	12,474
26	31	H	Sheffield U	W	1-0	1-0	—	Guentchev	6995
27	Feb 3	A	Leicester C	D	1-1	0-0	21	Thorpe	14,821
28	10	H	Grimsby T	W	3-2	1-1	20	Alexander, Guentchev, Marshall	7158
29	17	A	Millwall	W	1-0	0-0	19	Thorpe (pen)	7308
30	21	A	Derby Co	D	1-1	0-0	—	Marshall	14,825
31	24	A	Sunderland	L	0-1	0-1	19		16,693
32	27	H	Reading	L	1-2	1-1	—	Guentchev (pen)	6683
33	Mar 2	H	Crystal Palace	D	0-0	0-0	20		8478
34	9	A	Huddersfield T	L	0-1	0-0	20		11,950
35	19	A	Crystal Palace	L	0-2	0-0	—		13,609
36	23	A	Sheffield U	L	0-1	0-0	23		14,935
37	30	H	Ipswich T	L	1-2	0-1	23	Grant	9151
38	Apr 2	H	WBA	W	2-0	1-0	—	Guentchev, Grant	15,131
39	5	A	Charlton Ath	D	1-1	1-0	—	Thorpe	14,643
40	9	H	Stoke C	L	1-2	1-0	—	Grant	7689
41	13	A	Birmingham C	L	0-4	0-1	23		15,426
42	20	A	Watford	D	0-0	0-0	24		9454
43	23	A	Port Vale	L	0-1	0-1	—		6054
44	27	H	Barnsley	L	1-3	0-2	24	Thorpe	6194
45	30	H	Port Vale	W	3-2	1-1	—	Thorpe 2, Guentchev	5443
46	May 5	A	Oldham Ath	L	0-1	0-0	24		6623

Final League Position: 24

GOALSCORERS
League (40): Guentchev 9 (4 pens), Marshall 9, Thorpe 7 (1 pen), Grant 3, Oakes 3, Davis S 2, Oldfield 2, Alexander 1, Douglas 1, Harvey 1, Hughes 1, McLaren 1.
Coca-Cola Cup (2): Johnson 1, Marshall 1.
FA Cup (1): Marshall 1.

Davis K 6	Thomas M 25+2	Johnson M 34+2	Waddock G 32+4	Hughes C 21+2	Peake T 15+3	Alexander G 35+2	Oldfield D 23+11	Thorpe T 23+10	Guentchev B 25+10	Harvey R 28+8	Taylor J 18+10	Sumner J 2	James J 23+4	Davis S 36	Marshall D 23+3	Johnson G 4+1	Linton D 6+4	Woodsford J 1+2	Feuer T 38	Vilstrup J 6+1	McLaren P 9+3	Oakes S 26+3	Riseth V 6+5	Douglas S 3+5	Patterson D 21+2	Tomlinson G 1+6	Wilkinson P 3	Grant K 10	Chenery B 2	Evers S 1	Match No.
1	2	3	4	5	6	7	8	9[1]	10	11	12																				1
	12	3	13	5		7[1]	6	14	10[2]	11	9	1	2	4	8[3]																2
		3		5	14	6[2]	12	13	11	9[1]		1	2[3]	4	8	10	7														3
1		3	13	5		6[3]	8	11	12				2	4	9[1]	10	7[2]	14													4
1		3	12	5[1]		6[2]	13	8[3]	11	9			2	4	7	10		14													5
1		3	4	5		9	12	11					2	6	8	10	7[1]														6
		3[1]	4			2		9	10	11	12			5	8		7		1	6											7
		4[1]	10				2	9	13	11	12		3	5	8		7[2]		1	6											8
		3	12	5			2	7	13	10	11		9[2]	4	8				1	6[1]											9
		3	12	5			2	7[2]	10	11	9		13	4	8				1	6[1]											10
		3		5			2	7	12	10[1]	11			4	8				1	6	9										11
		3		5	6		2[1]	7	9	11	12			4	8	10			1												12
		3	12	5			2	7	9	13	11			4		10[2]		14	1	6[1]	8[3]										13
		3	6[1]	5[3]			2	7[2]	9	13	11			4		10	12	14	1		8										14
		3		5			2	7	12		11			4		10			1	6[1]	8	9									15
		3		5			2	7	12		11			4					1	6[2]	8[1]	9	10	13							16
		3		5			2	7	12		11			4		10[1]			1	6[2]	8	9		13							17
		3		5			2	7[1]	12		11			4[2]		10[3]			1	6	8	9	14	13							18
		3		5			2	7	12	13	11			4		10[1]			1	6[3]	8	9[2]	14								19
		3	4	5			2	9			11					10	7		1	6	8										20
1		3	4	5[1]				9	12	13	11		2			10	7				6[2]	8									21
	12	3		5			7[1]	9		13	11[2]		2	4		10			1	6		8									22
		3	4	6			12	11[1]	14	13	9[3]		2	5		10	7[1]		1			8									23
		3	4	6			10	7	12	13	11		2	5					1		8[2]	9[1]									24
		3	4	6			10	7	12		11		2	5					1		8[1]	9									25
		3	4	6[1]			12	10		13	11[3]		2	5			7		1		8[2]	9		14							26
		3	4	6[1]			10	7	12		11		2	5					1		8[2]	9[3]	13	14							27
		3	4				10	7	12		11[2]		2	5					1	6	8	9[1]	13								28
		3	4				10[1]	7[2]	12		11		2	5					1	6	8	9[3]	13	14							29
		3	4				10	9	12		11[1]		2	5			7[2]		1	6	8		13								30
		3	4	6			10	7	12		11[1]		2	5					1		8[2]	9[3]	13	14							31
		3	4[1]	6			10	7	12		11[3]		2	5					1		8	9[2]	13	14							32
		3	4	6			10	7[1]	12		11[2]		2	5					1		8	9[3]	13	14							33
		3	4[1]				10[2]	7	12		11		2	5					1	6	8	9	13								34
		3	4				10	7[1]	12		11		2	5					1	6	8	9[2]	13								35
		3	4				10[2]	7[3]	12		11[1]		2	5					1	6	8	9	13	14							36
		3	4[1]					7[2]	12		11		2	5					1	6	8[3]	9	13	14				10			37
		3	4[1]					7	12		11[2]		2	5					1	6	8	9	13					10			38
		3	4					7	12		11[3]		2	5					1	6	8[1]	9	13	14				10[2]			39
		3	4					7	12		11		2	5					1	6	8[2]	9[1]	13					10			40
		3	4[2]					7[1]	12		11		2	5					1	6	8	9[3]	13	14				10			41
		3	4					7	12		11		2	5					1	6	8[1]	9[2]	13					10			42
		3	4	6				7	12		11		2	5					1		8[1]	9						10			43
		3	4	6				9	12		11[3]		2	5					1		8[1]		13	14				10[2]			44
1		3	4	6			8		12		11		2	5			7[1]					9	13	14				10[3]	11[3]		45
		3	4	6				7	12		11		2[1]	5					1		8	9	13					10[2]			46

Coca-Cola Cup
First Round   Bournemouth   (h) 1-1
                                        (a) 1-2

FA Cup
Third Round   Grimsby T   (a) 1-7

MANCHESTER CITY 1995-96 *Back row (left to right):* Niall Quinn, Garry Flitcroft, Kit Symons, Michel Vonk.
Middle row: Tony Book (First Team Coach), Les Chapman (Reserve Team Coach), Roy Bailey (Physio), Uwe Rosler, Gerry Creaney, Eike Immel, Tony Coton, Martyn Margetson, Andy Dibble, Steve Lomas, Ian Brightwell, Ronnie Evans (Assistant Physio), Neil McNab (Youth Team Coach), Asa Hartford (Assistant Manager).
Front row: Terry Phelan, Nick Summerbee, Peter Beagrie, Scott Thomas, Georgiou Kinkladze, Alan Ball (Manager), Keith Curle, John Foster, Michael Brown, Richard Edghill, Rae Ingram.
(Photograph: Paul Marriott Photography)

Division 1   MANCHESTER CITY

Maine Road, Moss Side, Manchester M14 7WN. Telephone: (0161) 224 5000. Fax: (0161) 248 8449. Ticket Office: (0161) 226 2224. Dial-A-Seat: (0161) 227 9229. Development Office: (0161) 226 3143. Clubcall: 0891 121191. Ticketcall: 0891 121591.

Ground capacity: 31,257.

Record attendance: 84,569 v Stoke C, FA Cup 6th rd, 3 March 1934 (British record for any game outside London or Glasgow).

Record receipts: £512,235 Manchester U v Oldham Ath, FA Cup semi-final replay, 13 April 1994.

Pitch measurements: 117yd × 78yd.

Chairman: F. H. Lee. *Vice-Chairman:* F. Pye. *Managing Director:* C. J. Barlow.

Directors: I. L. G. Niven, J. G. Dunkerley, W. A. Miles, G. Doyle, B. Turnbull, J. Greibach, D. A. Holt, A. M. Lewis, G. J. Grant, B. Jervis.

General Secretary: J. B. Halford. *Commercial Manager:* Geoff Durbin.

Manager: Alan Ball. *Assistant Manager:* Asa Hartford. *First Team Coach:* Tony Book. *Physio:* Roy Bailey. *Youth Team Coach:* Neil McNab.

Year Formed: 1887 as Ardwick FC; 1894 as Manchester City.

Turned Professional: 1887 as Ardwick FC. *Ltd Co.:* 1894. *Club Nickname:* 'Blues' The Citizens.

Previous Names: 1887–94, Ardwick FC (formed through the amalgamation of West Gorton and Gorton Athletic, the latter having been formed in 1880).

Previous Grounds: 1880–81, Clowes Street; 1881–82, Kirkmanshulme Cricket Ground; 1882–84, Queens Road; 1884–87, Pink Bank Lane; 1887–1923, Hyde Road (1894–1923, as City); 1923, Maine Road.

Foundation: Manchester City was formed as a Limited Company in 1894 after their predecessors Ardwick had been forced into bankruptcy. However, many historians like to trace the club's lineage as far back as 1880 when St. Mark's Church, West Gorton added a football section to their cricket club. They amalgamated with Gorton Athletic in 1884 as Gorton FC. Because of a change of ground they became Ardwick in 1887.

First Football League game: 3 September 1892, Division 2, v Bootle (h) W 7-0 – Douglas; McVickers, Robson; Middleton, Russell, Hopkins; Davies (3), Morris (2), Angus (1), Weir (1), Milarvie.

Record League Victory: 10-1 v Huddersfield T, Division 2, 7 November 1987 – Nixon; Gidman, Hinchcliffe, Clements, Lake, Redmond, White (3), Stewart (3), Adcock (3), McNab (1) Simpson.

Record Cup Victory: 10-1 v Swindon T, FA Cup 4th rd, 29 January 1930 – Barber; Felton, McCloy; Barrass, Cowan, Heinemann; Toseland, Tait (3), Marshall (5), Johnson (1), Brook (1).

Record Defeat: 1–9 v Everton, Division 1, 3 September 1906.

Most League Points (2 for a win): 62, Division 2, 1946–47.

Most League Points (3 for a win): 82, Division 2, 1988–89.

Most League Goals: 108, Division 2, 1926–27.

Highest League Scorer in Season: Tommy Johnson, 38, Division 1, 1928–29.

Most League Goals in Total Aggregate: Tommy Johnson, 158, 1919–30.

Most Capped Player: Colin Bell, 48, England.

Most League Appearances: Alan Oakes, 565, 1959–76.

Record Transfer Fee Received: £1,700,000 from Tottenham H for Paul Stewart, June 1988.

Record Transfer Fee Paid: £2,500,000 to Wimbledon for Keith Curle, August 1991.

Football League Record: 1892 Ardwick elected founder member of Division 2; 1894 Newly-formed Manchester C elected to Division 2; Division 1 1899–1902, 1903–09, 1910–26, 1928–38, 1947–50, 1951–63, 1966–83, 1985–87, 1989–92; Division 2 1902–03, 1909–10, 1926–28, 1938–47, 1950–51, 1963–66, 1983–85, 1987–89; 1992–96 FA Premier League; 1996– Division 1.

Honours: Football League: Division 1 – Champions 1936–37, 1967–68; Runners-up 1903–04, 1920–21, 1976–77; Division 2 – Champions 1898–99, 1902–03, 1909–10, 1927–28, 1946–47, 1965–66; Runners-up 1895–96, 1950–51, 1987–88. *FA Cup:* Winners 1904, 1934, 1956, 1969; Runners-up 1926, 1933, 1955, 1981. *Football League Cup:* Winners 1970, 1976; Runners-up 1974. **European Competitions:** *European Cup:* 1968–69. *European Cup-Winners' Cup:* 1969–70 (winners), 1970–71. *UEFA Cup:* 1972–73, 1976–77, 1977–78, 1978–79.

Colours: Sky blue shirts, white shorts, white stockings. *Change colours:* Red and black striped shirts, black shorts, black stockings with white top.

Did you know?
Manchester City became the first English club to field as many as four foreign players born outside the UK in one match during the 1995–96 season.

MANCHESTER CITY 1995–96 LEAGUE RECORD

Match No.	Date	Venue	Opponents	Result	H/T Score	Lg. Pos.	Goalscorers	Attendance
1	Aug 19	H	Tottenham H	D 1-1	0-1	—	Rosler	30,827
2	23	A	Coventry C	L 1-2	0-1	—	Rosler	16,568
3	26	A	QPR	L 0-1	0-1	18		14,212
4	30	H	Everton	L 0-2	0-0	—		28,432
5	Sept 10	H	Arsenal	L 0-1	0-0	20		23,984
6	16	A	Newcastle U	L 1-3	0-2	20	Creaney	36,501
7	23	H	Middlesbrough	L 0-1	0-1	20		25,865
8	30	A	Nottingham F	L 0-3	0-1	20		25,620
9	Oct 14	A	Manchester U	L 0-1	0-1	20		35,707
10	21	H	Leeds U	D 0-0	0-0	20		26,390
11	28	H	Liverpool	L 0-6	0-2	20		39,267
12	Nov 4	H	Bolton W	W 1-0	1-0	20	Summerbee	28,397
13	18	A	Sheffield W	D 1-1	0-1	20	Lomas	24,422
14	22	H	Wimbledon	W 1-0	0-0	—	Quinn	23,617
15	25	A	Aston Villa	W 1-0	0-0	17	Kinkladze	28,027
16	Dec 2	A	Leeds U	W 1-0	0-0	15	Creaney	33,249
17	9	A	Middlesbrough	L 1-4	1-1	16	Kinkladze	29,469
18	18	H	Nottingham F	D 1-1	0-1	—	Rosler	24,287
19	23	H	Chelsea	L 0-1	0-0	17		28,668
20	26	A	Blackburn R	L 0-2	0-1	18		28,915
21	Jan 1	H	West Ham U	W 2-1	1-0	18	Quinn 2	26,024
22	13	A	Tottenham H	L 0-1	0-0	18		31,438
23	20	H	Coventry C	D 1-1	0-0	18	Rosler	25,710
24	31	A	Southampton	D 1-1	0-0	—	Rosler	15,172
25	Feb 3	H	QPR	W 2-0	1-0	17	Clough, Symons	27,509
26	10	A	Everton	L 0-2	0-1	18		37,354
27	24	H	Newcastle U	D 3-3	1-1	18	Quinn 2, Rosler	31,115
28	Mar 2	H	Blackburn R	D 1-1	0-0	17	Lomas	29,078
29	5	A	Arsenal	L 1-3	0-2	—	Creaney	34,519
30	12	A	Chelsea	D 1-1	1-1	—	Clough	17,078
31	16	H	Southampton	W 2-1	2-0	15	Kinkladze 2	29,550
32	23	A	West Ham U	L 2-4	0-1	16	Quinn 2	24,017
33	30	A	Bolton W	D 1-1	1-0	16	Quinn	21,050
34	Apr 6	H	Manchester U	L 2-3	1-2	17	Kavelashvili, Rosler	29,688
35	8	A	Wimbledon	L 0-3	0-1	17		11,844
36	13	H	Sheffield W	W 1-0	0-0	17	Rosler	30,898
37	27	A	Aston Villa	W 1-0	0-0	18	Lomas	39,336
38	May 5	H	Liverpool	D 2-2	0-2	18	Rosler (pen), Symons	31,436

Final League Position: 18

GOALSCORERS

League (33): Rosler 9 (1 pen), Quinn 8, Kinkladze 4, Creaney 3, Lomas 3, Clough 2, Symons 2, Kavelashvili 1, Summerbee 1.
Coca-Cola Cup (4): Rosler 2, Curle 1 (pen), Quinn 1.
FA Cup (10): Quinn 2, Rosler 2, Clough 1, Creaney 1, Flitcroft 1, Kinkladze 1, Lomas 1, own goal 1.

Immel E 38	Edghill R 13	Phelan T 9	Lomas S 32 + 1	Symons K 38	Brightwell I 26 + 3	Summerbee N 33 + 4	Walsh P 3	Rosler U 34 + 2	Flitcroft G 25	Kinkladze G 37	Quinn N 24 + 8	Kernaghan A 4 + 2	Foster J 4	Brown M 16 + 5	Ingram R 5	Kerr D — + 1	Curle K 32	Beagrie P 4 + 1	Creaney G 6 + 9	Ekelund R 2 + 2	Phillips M 2 + 9	Frontzeck M 11 + 1	Clough N 15	Hiley S 2 + 4	Mazzarelli G — + 2	Kavelashvili M 3 + 1	Match No.
1	2	3	4	5	6	7	8	9[1]	10	11	12																1
1	2	3	4[1]	5	6[2]	7	8	9	10	11	12	13															2
1		3	4[2]	5		7	8[1]	9	10	11	12	6	2	13													3
1		3		5		7		9	10	11	8	12	2	6[2]	4[1]	13											4
1	2	3		5	6	7		9	10	11[1]	12						4	8									5
1	2	3	13	5	6	12		9	10[2]	7[1]							4	11	8								6
1	2	3	10	5	6	12		9		11[1]				7[2]			4	13	8								7
1		10	5	3	12			9		7			2	6			4	11	8[1]								8
1	2	3	6	5		12		9	10	7	8[2]						4	11[1]	13								9
1	2	3[2]	6	5	12	7		9	10[1]	11	8						4	13									10
1	2		6	5	3[1]	7		9	10	11[2]	8			13			4	12									11
1		3	6	5		7		9	10[2]	11	8			2[1]	13		4	12									12
1	2		6	5	3	7		9	10	11	8						4										13
1	2[1]		6	5	3	7		9	10	11	8						4	12									14
1	2		6	5	3	7		9	10	11	8						4										15
1	2[1]		6	5	3	7		9	10	11	8						4	12									16
1			6	5	2	7				11	9			8	3		4	10									17
1		10	5		2	7		9		11	8	6[1]		12	3		4										18
1			5		2	7		9[1]		11	8			6	3		4	10	12								19
1			5	3	2			9	10	11	8			6			4	12	7[1]								20
1		7	5	3	2			9[2]	10[1]	11	8			6			4		12	13							21
1			6	5		2		9	10	11	8			12	3		4			7[1]							22
1		7[1]	5	3	2			9	10	11	8			6			4				12						23
1			6	5	12	2		9	10	11	8[2]						4				13	3[1]	7				24
1			6[1]	5	12	2		9[2]	10	11							4		13		7	3	8				25
1			6	5		2		9	10		12			7[2]			4		13		11[1]	3	8				26
1			6	5		2		9	10	11				7			4						8	3			27
1			6	5		2		9	10	11	8[1]						4				12	3[2]	7	13			28
1			6	5		2[1]		9	10	11							4			8	12	3[2]	7	13			29
1		8	5	6		2[1]		9	10	11												3	7		12		30
1		8[1]	5	6		2		9	10	11	12						4					3[2]	7	13			31
1		10	5	6		2[3]		9[1]		11	12						4					3[2]	8	13	14		32
1		10	5	6		2				11	8			7			4						12	9		3[1]	33
1			5	6		2				11		12					4				13	3[2]	9			10[1]	34
1			6	5		2	7[2]			11		12		8[1]			4				13	3	9			10	35
1			6	5		2		9		11	12			7			4				13	3[2]	8			10[1]	36
1		10	5	6		2		9		11	8			3			4						7				37
1		10	5	6		2		9		11	8[1]			3			4				12		7[2]			13	38

Coca-Cola Cup

Second Round	Wycombe W	(a)	0-0
		(h)	4-0
Third Round	Liverpool	(a)	0-4

FA Cup

Third Round	Leicester C	(a)	0-0
		(h)	5-0
Fourth Round	Coventry C	(a)	2-2
		(h)	2-1
Fifth Round	Manchester U	(a)	1-2

MANCHESTER UNITED 1995-96   *Back row (left to right):* Norman Davies (Kit Manager), Ryan Giggs, Roy Keane, Nicky Butt, David May, John O'Kane, Phil Neville, Gary Neville, Andy Cole, David Fevre (Physio).
Middle row: David Beckham, Patrick McGibbon, Eric Cantona, Gary Walsh, Peter Schmeichel, Kevin Pilkington, Gary Pallister, Lee Sharpe, Chris Casper.
Front row: Paul Parker, Brian McClair, Steve Bruce, Alex Ferguson (Manager), Brian Kidd (Assistant Manager), Denis Irwin, Ben Thornley, Paul Scholes.

FA Premiership   MANCHESTER UNITED

Sir Matt Busby Way, Old Trafford, Manchester M16 0RA. Telephone: (0161) 872 1661, (0161) 930 1968. Fax: (0161) 876 5502. Ticket and Match Information: (0161) 872 0199. Membership Enquiries and Supporters Club: (0161) 872 5208. Clubcall: 0891 121161.

Ground capacity: 54,000.

Record attendance: 76,962 Wolverhampton W v Grimsby T, FA Cup semi-final, 25 March 1939.

Club record: 70,504 v Aston Villa, Division 1, 27 December 1920.

Record receipts: £576,494.50 v Southampton, FA Cup 6th rd, 11 March 1996.

Pitch measurements: 116yd × 76yd.

Chairman/Chief Executive: C. M. Edwards.

Directors: J. M. Edelson, Sir Bobby Charlton CBE, E. M. Watkins LL.M., R. L. Olive, R. P. Launders.

Manager: Alex Ferguson CBE. *Assistant Manager:* Brian Kidd. *Physio:* D. Fevre MCSP, SRP.

Secretary: Kenneth Merrett. *Commercial Manager:* Danny McGregor. *Stadium Manager:* E. Cassin.

Year Formed: 1878 as Newton Heath LYR; 1902, Manchester United.

Turned Professional: 1885. *Ltd Co.:* 1907.

Previous Name: Newton Heath, 1880–1902.

Club Nickname: 'Red Devils'.

Previous Grounds: 1880–93, North Road, Monsall Road; 1893, Bank Street; 1910, Old Trafford (played at Maine Road 1941–49).

Foundation: Manchester United was formed as comparatively recently as 1902 after their predecessors, Newton Heath, went bankrupt. However, it is usual to give the date of the club's foundation as 1878 when employees of the Lancashire and Yorkshire Railway Company formed Newton Heath L and YR Cricket and Football Club. They won the Manchester Cup in 1886 and as Newton Heath FC were admitted to the Second Division in 1892.

First Football League game: 3 September 1892, Division 1, v Blackburn R (a) L 3-4 – Warner; Clements, Brown; Perrins, Stewart, Erentz; Farman (1), Coupar (1), Donaldson (1), Carson, Mathieson.

Record League Victory (as Newton Heath): 10–1 v Wolverhampton W, Division 1, 15 October 1892 – Warner; Mitchell, Clements; Perrins, Stewart (3), Erentz; Farman (1), Hood (1), Donaldson (3), Carson (1), Hendry (1).

Record League Victory (as Manchester U): 9–0 v Ipswich T, FA Premier League, 4 March 1995 – Schmeichel; Keane (1) (Sharpe), Irwin, Bruce (Butt), Kanchelskis, Pallister, Cole (1), Ince (1), McClair, Hughes (2), Giggs.

Record Cup Victory: 10–0 v RSC Anderlecht, European Cup Prel. rd (2nd leg), 26 September 1956 – Wood; Foulkes, Byrne; Colman, Jones, Edwards; Berry (1), Whelan (2), Taylor (3), Viollet (4), Pegg.

Record Defeat: 0–7 v Blackburn R, Division 1, 10 April 1926 and v Aston Villa, Division 1, 27 December 1930 and v Wolverhampton W, Division 2, 26 December 1931.

Most League Points (2 for a win): 64, Division 1, 1956–57.

Most League Points (3 for a win): 92, FA Premier League, 1993–94.

Most League Goals: 103, Division 1, 1956–57 and 1958–59.

Highest League Scorer in Season: Dennis Viollet, 32, 1959–60.

Most League Goals in Total Aggregate: Bobby Charlton, 199, 1956–73.

Most Capped Player: Bobby Charlton, 106, England.

Most League Appearances: Bobby Charlton, 606, 1956–73.

Record Transfer Fee Received: £7,000,000 from Internazionale for Paul Ince, June 1995.

Record Transfer Fee Paid: £6,250,000 to Newcastle U for Andy Cole, January 1995.

Football League Record: 1892 Newton Heath elected to Division 1; 1894–1906 Division 2; 1906–22 Division 1; 1922–25 Division 2; 1925–31 Division 1; 1931–36 Division 2; 1936–37 Division 1; 1937–38 Division 2; 1938–74 Division 1; 1974–75 Division 2; 1975–92 Division 1; 1992– FA Premier League.

Honours: FA Premier League: – Champions 1992–93, 1993–94, 1995–96; Runners-up 1994–95. *Football League:* Division 1 – Champions 1907–08, 1910–11, 1951–52, 1955–56, 1956–57, 1964–65, 1966–67; Runners-up 1946–47, 1947–48, 1948–49, 1950–51, 1958–59, 1963–64, 1967–68, 1979–80, 1987–88, 1991–92. Division 2 – Champions 1935–36, 1974–75; Runners-up 1896–97, 1905–06, 1924–25, 1937–38. *FA Cup:* Winners 1909, 1948, 1963, 1977, 1983, 1985, 1990, 1994, 1996; Runners-up 1957, 1958, 1976, 1979, 1995. *Football League Cup:* Winners 1992, 1983 (Runners-up), 1991 (Runners-up), 1994 (Runners-up). **European Competitions:** *European Cup:* 1956–57 (s-f), 1957–58 (s-f), 1965–66 (s-f), 1967–68 (winners), 1968–69 (s-f), 1993–94, 1994–95. *European Cup-Winners' Cup:* 1963–64, 1977–78, 1983–84, 1990–91 (winners). 1991–92. *European Fairs Cup:* 1964–65. *UEFA Cup:* 1976–77, 1980–81, 1982–83, 1984–85, 1992–93, 1995–96. *World Club Championship:* 1968. *Super Cup:* 1991 (winners).

Colours: Red shirts, white shorts, black stockings. *Change colours:* All white.

Did you know?
Eric Cantona became the first foreign player born outside the UK to captain an FA Cup winning team which he did in the 1995–96 season.

MANCHESTER UNITED 1995–96 LEAGUE RECORD

Match No.	Date	Venue	Opponents	Result	H/T Score	Lg. Pos.	Goalscorers	Attendance
1	Aug 19	A	Aston Villa	L 1-3	0-3	—	Beckham	34,655
2	23	H	West Ham U	W 2-1	0-0	—	Scholes, Keane	31,966
3	26	H	Wimbledon	W 3-1	1-0	5	Keane 2, Cole	32,226
4	28	A	Blackburn R	W 2-1	0-0	—	Sharpe, Beckham	29,843
5	Sept 9	A	Everton	W 3-2	1-1	2	Sharpe 2, Giggs	39,496
6	16	H	Bolton W	W 3-0	2-0	2	Scholes 2, Giggs	32,812
7	23	A	Sheffield W	D 0-0	0-0	2		34,101
8	Oct 1	H	Liverpool	D 2-2	1-1	3	Butt, Cantona (pen)	34,934
9	14	H	Manchester C	W 1-0	1-0	2	Scholes	35,707
10	21	A	Chelsea	W 4-1	2-0	2	Scholes 2, Giggs, McClair	30,192
11	28	H	Middlesbrough	W 2-0	1-0	2	Pallister, Cole	36,580
12	Nov 4	H	Arsenal	L 0-1	0-1	2		38,317
13	18	H	Southampton	W 4-1	3-0	2	Giggs 2, Scholes, Cole	39,301
14	22	A	Coventry C	W 4-0	1-0	—	Irwin, McClair 2, Beckham	23,344
15	27	A	Nottingham F	D 1-1	0-1	—	Cantona (pen)	29,263
16	Dec 2	H	Chelsea	D 1-1	0-0	2	Beckham	42,019
17	9	H	Sheffield W	D 2-2	1-0	2	Cantona 2	41,849
18	17	A	Liverpool	L 0-2	0-1	2		40,546
19	24	A	Leeds U	L 1-3	1-2	2	Cole	39,801
20	27	H	Newcastle U	W 2-0	1-0	—	Cole, Keane	42,024
21	30	H	QPR	W 2-1	1-0	2	Cole, Giggs	41,890
22	Jan 1	A	Tottenham H	L 1-4	1-2	2	Cole	32,852
23	13	H	Aston Villa	D 0-0	0-0	2		42,667
24	22	A	West Ham U	W 1-0	1-0	—	Cantona	24,197
25	Feb 3	A	Wimbledon	W 4-2	2-0	2	Cole, Perry (og), Cantona 2 (1 pen)	25,423
26	10	H	Blackburn R	W 1-0	1-0	2	Sharpe	42,681
27	21	H	Everton	W 2-0	1-0	—	Keane, Giggs	42,459
28	25	H	Bolton W	W 6-0	2-0	2	Beckham, Bruce, Cole, Scholes 2, Butt	21,381
29	Mar 4	A	Newcastle U	W 1-0	0-0	—	Cantona	36,584
30	16	A	QPR	D 1-1	0-0	1	Cantona	18,817
31	20	H	Arsenal	W 1-0	0-0	—	Cantona	50,028
32	24	H	Tottenham H	W 1-0	0-0	1	Cantona	50,508
33	Apr 6	A	Manchester C	W 3-2	2-1	1	Cantona (pen), Cole, Giggs	29,688
34	8	H	Coventry C	W 1-0	0-0	1	Cantona	50,332
35	13	A	Southampton	L 1-3	0-3	1	Giggs	15,262
36	17	H	Leeds U	W 1-0	0-0	—	Keane	48,382
37	28	A	Nottingham F	W 5-0	2-0	1	Scholes, Beckham 2, Giggs, Cantona	53,926
38	May 5	A	Middlesbrough	W 3-0	1-0	1	May, Cole, Giggs	29,922

Final League Position: 1

GOALSCORERS

League (73): Cantona 14 (4 pens), Cole 11, Giggs 11, Scholes 10, Beckham 7, Keane 6, Sharpe 4, McClair 3, Butt 2, Bruce 1, Irwin 1, May 1, Pallister 1, own goal 1.
Coca-Cola Cup (3): Scholes 2, Cooke 1.
FA Cup (14): Cantona 5 (1 pen), Cole 2, Sharpe 2, Beckham 1, Butt 1, Giggs 1, Parker 1, Scholes 1.

Schmeichel P 36	Neville P 21 + 3	Irwin D 31	Parker P 5 + 1	Neville G 30 + 1	Pallister G 21	Butt N 31 + 1	Keane R 29	McClair B 12 + 10	Scholes P 16 + 10	Sharpe L 21 + 10	Beckham D 26 + 7	O'Kane J — + 1	Bruce S 30	Cole A 32 + 2	Thornley B — + 1	Giggs R 30 + 3	Davies S 1 + 5	Cooke T 1 + 3	Cantona E 30	May D 11 + 5	Pilkington K 2 + 1	Prunier W 2	Match No.
1	2^1	3	4	5	6^2	7	8	9	10	11	12	13											1
1		3		2	6	7	8	9^2	10^1	5	11		4	12	13								2
1		3		2	6	7	8		10^2	5	11		4	9^1		12	13						3
1		3		2	6	7	8		10^1	5	11^2		4	9		12	13						4
1		3		2	6	7	8		10^1	5	11		4	9^2		12	13						5
1		3		2		6	7		9	5	10		4			11			12	8^1			6
1		3		2		6	7		5	9	10		4			11			8^1	12			7
1	3^1			2		6	10^2	8	12	5	13		4	9		11			7				8
1	3			2		6	7	5^1	12	10^2	13	8	4	9		11			7				9
1		3		2		6		8	5	12	10^1		4	9		11			7				10
1		3		2		6		8	5	12	10^1		4	9		11			7				11
1	3^2			2		6		8^1	5	13	10^3	12	14	4		9			11	7			12
1	12	3^1		2		6	8		5	13	10^2	14	4	9		11^3			7				13
1	12	3		2^1		6	10^2		8	13	5		4^3	9		11			7	14			14
1		3		2		6	5		8^1	12	13	10^2	4	9		11			7				15
		3		2			8		10	5	11		4	9^1		12	7	6			1		16
	3			2			8		10^1	5^2	11		4	9		12	13		7	6	1		17
1		3		2		8	12		5	10			4	9^1		11			7	6			18
1	13	3	6^3	2		10	5	8	12		11^1		4^2	9					7	14			19
1	2	3				6	10	8	12		5			9		11			7	4^1			20
1	3^1	2	12	6			10	5	13		14	8^3		9^2		11			7		4		21
$1^?$	3^2		2	4		10	5^1	12		13	8		9		11			7	15	6		22
1	3	2			6	10	8		12	5^1			4	9		11			7				23
1	6	3		2		10	8		5	12			4	9^1		11			7				24
1	3	2		6		10	8		5	12			4^1	9		11			7				25
1	3	2		6		8			5	10				9		11			7	4			26
1	3	2		6		10	8		5^1	12			4	9		11			7				27
1	3	2		6		10	8	12	13	5			4	9		11^1			7^2				28
1	3	2		6		10	8		5				4	9		11			7				29
1		3		2		12	5	8^2	13	14	10^3		4	9		11			7	6^1			30
1	3			2		10	8	12	5				4	9^1		11			7	6			31
1	3^2			2		10	8	12	5	13			4	9^1		11			7	6			32
1	3	2		6		10	5	12	8				4^2	9^1		11			7	13			33
1	2			5		10	8		3	4				9		11			7	6			34
1	2			5		10^1	8	12	3^2	6			4	9		11			7	13			35
1	3	2		6			5		8^1	12	13	10	4^3	9^2		11			7	14			36
1	3^1	2	12	6			8	9	5	10						11			7	4			37
1	3	2		6		10	5		9^1		8			12		11			7	4			38

Coca-Cola Cup
Second Round · York C · (h) 0-3 · (a) 3-1

FA Cup
Third Round · Sunderland · (h) 2-2 · (a) 2-1
Fourth Round · Reading · (a) 3-0
Fifth Round · Manchester C · (h) 2-1
Sixth Round · Southampton · (h) 2-0
Semi-final (at Villa Park)
· Chelsea · 2-1
Final at Wembley · Liverpool · 1-0

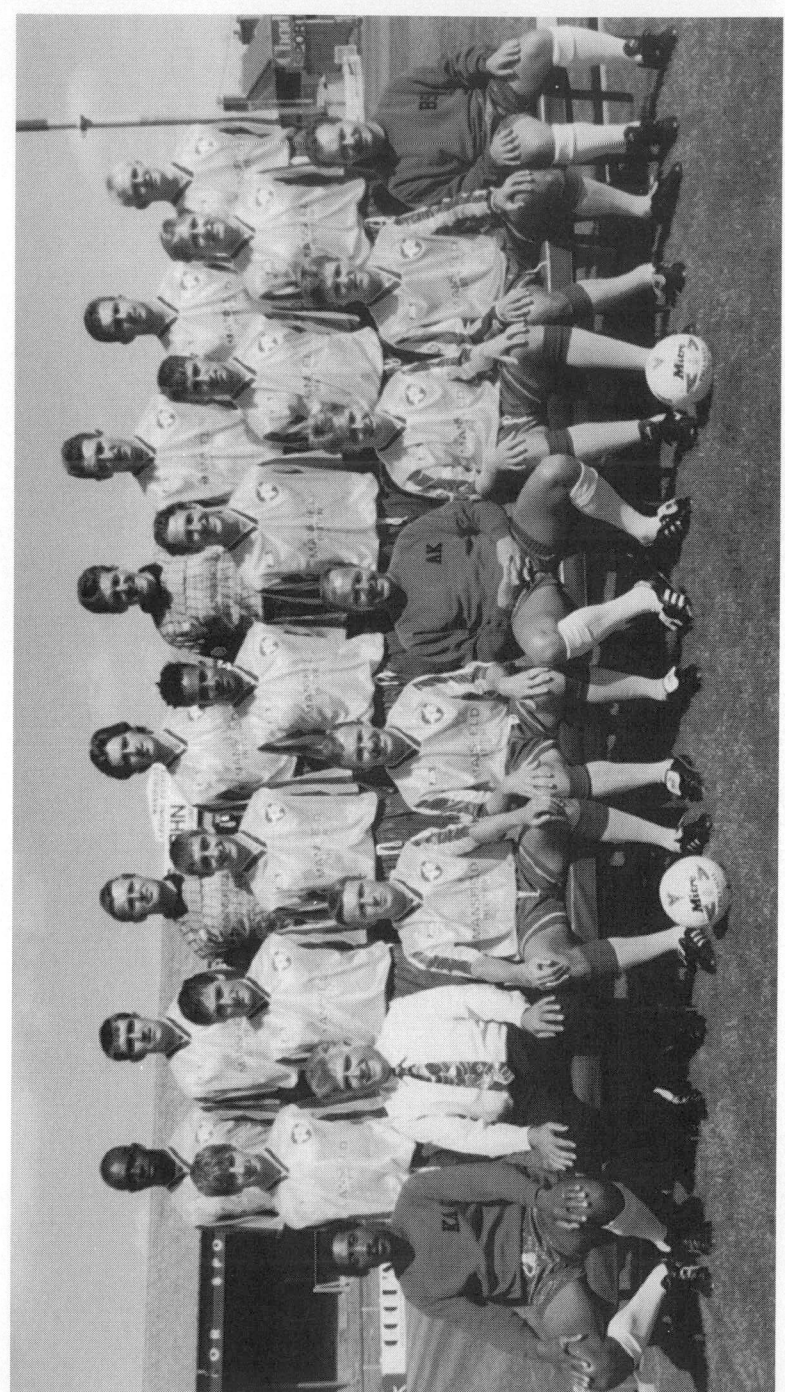

MANSFIELD TOWN 1995-96 *Back row (left to right)*: Iffem Onuora, Matt Carmichael, Jason Trinder, Lee Howarth, Ian Bowling, Mark Sale, Mark Peters, Kevin Lampkin.
Middle row: Paul Handford, John Doolan, Chris Timons, Scott Eustace, Ian Baraclough, Steve Slawson, Stewart Hadley.
Front row: Keith Alexander (Assistant Manager), Bob Shaw (Chief Scout), Aidy Boothroyd, Steve Parkin, Andy King (Manager), Paul Sherlock, Simon Ireland, Barry Statham (Physio).

Division 3   **MANSFIELD TOWN**

Field Mill Ground, Quarry Lane, Mansfield NG18 5DA. Telephone: (01623) 23567. Fax: (01623) 25014. Marketing: (01623) 658070. Football in the Community: (01623) 25197.

Ground capacity: 7033.

Record attendance: 24,467 v Nottingham F, FA Cup 3rd rd, 10 January 1953.

Record receipts: £46,915 v Sheffield W, FA Cup 3rd rd, 5 January 1991.

Pitch measurements: 115yd × 70yd.

Chairman/Chief Executive: Keith Haslam.

Director: Mrs M. Haslam. *Associate Directors:* T. Hewson, D. Wardman, K. Woodcock, S. Whetton.

Manager: Andy King. *Coach:* Steve Parkin.

Physio: Barry Statham.

Community Scheme Organiser: D. Bentley Tel: (01623) 25197.

Secretary: Christine Reynolds. *Marketing Manager:* Mick Saxby.

Year Formed: 1910. *Turned Professional:* 1910. *Ltd Co.:* 1921.

Previous Name: Mansfield Wesleyans 1891–1910.

Club Nickname: 'The Stags'.

Foundation: Many records give the date of Mansfield Town's formation as 1905. But the present club did not come into being until 1910 when the Mansfield Wesleyans (formed 1891) and playing in the Notts and District League, decided to spread their wings and changed their name to Mansfield Town, joining the new Central Alliance in 1911.

First Football League game: 29 August 1931, Division 3 (S), v Swindon T (h) W 3-2 – Wilson; Clifford, England; Wake, Davis, Blackburn; Gilhespy, Readman (1), Johnson, Broom (2), Baxter.

Record League Victory: 9–2 v Rotherham U, Division 3 (N), 27 December 1932 – Wilson; Anthony, England; Davies, S. Robinson, Slack; Prior, Broom, Readman (3), Hoyland (3), Bowater (3).

Record Cup Victory: 8–0 v Scarborough (away), FA Cup 1st rd, 22 November 1952 – Bramley; Chessell, Bradley; Field, Plummer, Lewis; Scott, Fox (3), Marron (2), Sid Watson (1), Adam (2).

Record Defeat: 1–8 v Walsall, Division 3 (N), 19 January 1933.

Most League Points (2 for a win): 68, Division 4, 1974–75.

Most League Points (3 for a win): 81, Division 4, 1985–86.

Most League Goals: 108, Division 4, 1962–63.

Highest League Scorer in Season: Ted Harston, 55, Division 3 (N), 1936–37.

Most League Goals in Total Aggregate: Harry Johnson, 104, 1931–36.

Most Capped Player: John McClelland, 6 (53), Northern Ireland.

Most League Appearances: Rod Arnold, 440, 1970–83.

Record Transfer Fee Received: £500,000 from Middlesbrough for Simon Coleman, September 1989.

Record Transfer Fee Paid: £80,000 to Leicester C for Steve Wilkinson, September 1989.

Football League Record: 1931 Elected to Division 3 (S); 1932–37 Division 3 (N); 1937–47 Division 3 (S); 1947–58 Division 3 (N); 1958–60 Division 3; 1960–63 Division 4; 1963–72 Division 3; 1972–75 Division 4; 1975–77 Division 3; 1977–78 Division 2; 1978–80 Division 3; 1980–86 Division 4; 1986–91 Division 3; 1991–92 Division 4; 1992–93 Division 2; 1993– Division 3.

Honours: Football League: Division 2 best season: 21st, 1977–78; Division 3 – Champions 1976–77; Division 4 – Champions 1974–75; Division 3 (N) – Runners-up 1950–51. *FA Cup:* best season: 6th rd, 1969. *Football League Cup:* best season: 5th rd, 1976. *Freight Rover Trophy:* Winners 1987.

Colours: Amber shirts with royal blue stripe down side, royal blue collar, amber shorts with royal blue stripe down sides, royal blue stockings with amber trim. *Change colours:* White shirts and shorts with thin blue stripe, white stockings with blue stripe.

Did you know?
Former Olympic decathlete Daley Thompson was Mansfield Town's unused substitute against Cardiff City on 16 December 1995.

MANSFIELD TOWN 1995–96 LEAGUE RECORD

Match No.	Date	Venue	Opponents	Result	H/T Score	Lg. Pos.	Goalscorers	Attendance
1	Aug 12	A	Fulham	L	2-4	1-1	—	Carmichael, Sherlock	4909
2	19	H	Leyton Orient	D	0-0	0-0	17		2565
3	26	A	Northampton T	D	3-3	2-1	18	Sale 2, Baraclough	4797
4	29	H	Doncaster R	D	0-0	0-0	—		2944
5	Sept 2	A	Torquay U	D	1-1	1-1	19	Sale	2203
6	9	H	Scarborough	W	2-0	0-0	15	Baraclough, Hadley	2419
7	12	H	Darlington	D	2-2	1-2	—	Slawson, Sale	2190
8	16	A	Rochdale	D	1-1	0-0	15	Slawson	2173
9	23	H	Scunthorpe U	D	1-1	0-0	14	Ireland	2478
10	30	A	Cardiff C	L	0-3	0-1	18		3468
11	Oct 7	A	Wigan Ath	W	6-2	2-1	13	Hadley 3, Peters, Harper, Doolan	2084
12	14	H	Plymouth Arg	D	1-1	1-1	15	Ireland	3164
13	21	A	Preston NE	L	0-6	0-3	19		8989
14	28	H	Bury	L	1-5	1-1	21	Doolan	2356
15	Nov 1	H	Lincoln C	L	1-2	0-1	—	Sale	2398
16	4	A	Hereford U	W	1-0	0-0	20	Harper	2193
17	18	H	Chester C	L	3-4	1-2	20	Hadley 3	2415
18	25	A	Colchester U	W	3-1	1-0	15	Hadley, Boothroyd (pen), Ireland	2819
19	Dec 9	A	Scunthorpe U	D	1-1	0-0	16	Barber	2552
20	16	H	Cardiff C	D	1-1	0-0	17	Parkin	2212
21	23	H	Hartlepool U	L	0-3	0-1	21		1982
22	26	A	Barnet	D	0-0	0-0	18		2204
23	Jan 6	A	Exeter C	D	1-1	0-1	19	Harper	1853
24	13	A	Leyton Orient	L	0-1	0-0	22		3461
25	20	H	Fulham	W	1-0	0-0	20	Slawson	2025
26	23	H	Cambridge U	W	2-1	1-0	—	Sale, Sherlock	1801
27	30	A	Gillingham	L	0-2	0-2	—		6116
28	Feb 3	H	Northampton T	D	0-0	0-0	18		2981
29	13	A	Exeter C	D	2-2	2-1	—	Hackett, Onuora	2507
30	17	A	Darlington	D	1-1	0-0	18	Ireland	2598
31	27	A	Scarborough	D	1-1	1-1	—	Slawson	1304
32	Mar 2	H	Barnet	W	2-1	0-0	17	Hackett, Peters	2146
33	9	A	Hartlepool U	D	1-1	0-1	19	Slawson	1758
34	16	H	Gillingham	L	0-1	0-1	21		2698
35	23	A	Cambridge U	W	2-0	2-0	18	Timons, Sale	2302
36	25	A	Doncaster R	D	0-0	0-0	—		1657
37	30	H	Wigan Ath	W	1-0	0-0	18	Hackett	2369
38	Apr 2	A	Plymouth Arg	L	0-1	0-0	—		6375
39	6	A	Bury	W	2-0	2-0	16	Harper, Wood	3600
40	8	H	Preston NE	D	0-0	0-0	16		4661
41	13	A	Lincoln C	L	1-2	0-0	18	Ireland	2992
42	16	H	Rochdale	D	2-2	1-0	—	Boothroyd (pen), Williams	1814
43	20	H	Hereford U	L	1-2	1-1	17	Harper	2358
44	23	A	Torquay U	W	2-0	1-0	—	Williams 2	1674
45	27	H	Colchester U	L	1-2	0-0	17	Eustace	2073
46	May 4	A	Chester C	L	1-2	0-0	19	Robinson	2935

Final League Position: 19

GOALSCORERS

League (54): Hadley 8, Sale 7, Harper 5, Ireland 5, Slawson 5, Hackett 3, Williams 3, Baraclough 2, Boothroyd 2 (2 pens), Doolan 2, Peters 2, Sherlock 2, Barber 1, Carmichael 1, Eustace 1, Onuora 1, Parkin 1, Robinson 1, Timons 1, Wood 1.
Coca-Cola Cup (1): Sale 1.
FA Cup (4): Doolan 1, Harper 1, Parkin 1, Sherlock 1.

Bowling I 44	Boothroyd A 42 + 1	Baraclough I 11	Sherlock P 14 + 4	Howarth L 17	Doolan J 42	Ireland S 38 + 1	Carmichael M 1	Varadi I 1	Sale M 24 + 3	Slawson S 21 + 8	Parkin S 25 + 1	Hadley S 27 + 6	Peters M 21	Robinson I 4 + 5	Sedgemore B 4 + 5	Harper S 29	Lampkin K 2 + 4	Eustace S 25 + 2	Kerr D 4 + 1	Hackett W 32	Peel N 2	Onuora I 7 + 7	Barber P 4	Trinder J 1	Kilcline B 18 + 1	Alexander K — + 1	Williams R 5 + 5	Todd M 10 + 2	Brien T 4	Timons C 16 + 1	Weaver N 1	Wood S 9 + 1	Clarke D 1 + 2	Match No.
1	2	3	4	5	6	7	8¹	9²	10	11	12	13																						1
1	2	3	4	5	6	7			9	11	8	10																						2
1	2	3		5	4	7			10	11¹	8	9	6	12																				3
1	2	3		5	4	7			10	12²	8	9	6		13			11¹																4
1		3	12	5	2	7			10	11¹	8	13	6		4	9¹																		5
1	13	3	4³	5	2	7			10	12	8²	11	6		14	9¹																		6
1	2	3		5	4	7			10	11		12			8	9¹		6																7
1	2	3		5	4	7			10	11	8		6		12	9¹																		8
1	2	3		5	4	7			10	11		12	6		13	9¹		8²																9
1	2	3		5	4				10		8	11	6		7¹	9		12																10
1	2	3	12	5	4³	7				13	8	10²	6		14	9		11¹																11
1	2			5	4	7					8	10	6			9				3		11												12
1	2			5	4	7				12	8	10	6			9²	13	11¹		3														13
1	2	11		5	4	7					8		6			9				3		10¹	12											14
1	2	11			4	7			12	13	8³		6			9²		5		3		10¹	14											15
1	2	10		5	4	7					8					9		6		3		11												16
	2	11	5¹		4	7			12		8	10	6			9²				3		13	1											17
1	2	4	5								8	10	6			9				3		11												18
1	2	4			7						8	10	6			9				3		11			5									19
1	2	11			4	7					8	10	6			9				3					5									20
1	2	11²			4	7				12	8	10¹	6			9	13			3					5									21
1	2				4	7					8	10	6			9		11		3					5									22
1	2	12			4						8	10			7²	9		6		3		11			5¹		13							23
1	2	11¹			4					12	8	10			7²	9		6		3					5		13							24
1	2	12			4				7	11	8	10²				9¹		6		3		13			5									25
1	2	9			4				7	11¹	8	10						6		3		12			5									26
1	2	9¹			4				7	11	8	10						6		3		12			5									27
1	2				4	7¹			10	12	8	13						6		3		9			5					11²				28
1	2				4				10	7	8							6		3		9			5					11				29
1	2				9				10	7	8							6		3					5¹					11	4	12		30
1	2				12				10¹		8		6					7		3		9					13	11²	4	5				31
1					4	7			10	11			6						2	3		9							8	5				32
1					4	7			10²	11				6¹	13				2	3		9					12		8	5				33
1	2				4	7			10	11								6		3		8						9		5				34
	2				4	7			10	11¹					9			6		3		8						12		5		1		35
	2				4	7			10	11¹		12			9			6		3		8²								5		13		36
1	2				4	7				11¹		10			9					3								12	8	5		6		37
1	2				4	7				11¹		10	12		9					3									8	5		6		38
1	2				4	7						10				9	12	6									8			11¹		5	3	39
1	2				4	7²									13	9	12	6		3								10		11¹		5	8	40
1	2				4	7				12		10¹				9		6		3							8			11		5		41
1	2				4	7						10²				9	12	6		3								13		11¹		5	8	42
1	2				4	7¹						11				9²		6		3								10	12	5		8	13	43
1	2				4	7				10¹					11		12	6		3		12						9		5		8²	13	44
1	2				4	7									11¹		12	6		3		9						10		5		8		45
1	2				4¹	7²						10		12		8				9					5		13			6		11	3	46

Coca-Cola Cup

First Round	Burnley	(h)	0-1	
		(a)	1-3	

FA Cup

First Round	Doncaster R	(h)	4-2	
Second Round	Crewe Alex	(a)	0-2	

MIDDLESBROUGH 1995-96 *Back row (left to right):* John Hendrie, Jaime Moreno, Michael Barron, Craig Liddle, Phil Stamp, Craig Hignett, Jamie Pollock, Derek Whyte, Alan Moore, Keith O'Halloran.

Middle row: Gordon McQueen (Reserve Team Coach), David Geddis (Youth Team Coach), Jan Fjortoft, Steve Vickers, Phil Whelan, Alan Miller, Ben Roberts, Paul Wilkinson, Robbie Mustoe, Curtis Fleming, Tommy Johnson (Kit Man), Mike Kelly (Goalkeeping Coach).

Front row: Bob Ward (Physio), Chris Morris, Graham Kavanagh, Bryan Robson (Player/Manager), Nigel Pearson, Viv Anderson (Assistant Manager), Clayton Blackmore, Neil Cox, John Pickering (First Team Coach).

FA Premiership   **MIDDLESBROUGH**

Cellnet Riverside Stadium, Middlesbrough, Cleveland TS3 6RS. Telephone: (01642) 227227. Fax: (01642) 248450. Boro Livewire: 0891 424200. Ticket Office: (01642) 207014.

Ground capacity: 30,500.

Record attendance: 53,596 v Newcastle U, Division 1, 27 December 1949. (Riverside Stadium): 30,011 v Newcastle U, FA Premier League, 10 February 1996.

Record receipts: £200,351 v Newcastle U, Coca-Cola Cup 2nd rd 2nd leg, 7 October 1992.

Pitch measurements: 115yd × 74yd.

Chairman: S. Gibson.

Director: G. Cooke.

Chief Executive: Keith Lamb. ***Secretary:*** Karen Nelson.

Manager: Bryan Robson. ***Assistant Manager:*** Viv Anderson.

Physio: Bob Ward. ***Coach:*** John Pickering. ***Head of Marketing and Commercial:*** John Knox.

Youth Development Officer: Ron Bone. ***Public Relations Officer:*** Dave Allan.

Stadium Manager: Terry Tasker.

Year Formed: 1876. ***Turned Professional:*** 1889; became amateur 1892, and professional again, 1899. ***Ltd Co:*** 1892.

Club Nickname: 'Boro'.

Previous Grounds: 1877, Old Archery Ground, Albert Park; 1879, Breckon Hill; 1882, Linthorpe Road Ground; 1903, Ayresome Park; 1995, Cellnet Riverside Stadium.

Foundation: A previous belief that Middlesbrough Football Club was founded at a tripe supper at the Corporation Hotel has proved to be erroneous. In fact, members of Middlesbrough Cricket Club were responsible for forming it at a meeting in the gymnasium of the Albert Park Hotel in 1875.

First Football League game: 2 September 1899, Division 2, v Lincoln C (a) L 0-3 – Smith; Shaw, Ramsey; Allport, McNally, McCracken; Wanless, Longstaffe, Gettins, Page, Pugh.

Record League Victory: 9–0 v Brighton & HA, Division 2, 23 August 1958 – Taylor; Bilcliff, Robinson; Harris (2 p), Phillips, Walley; Day, McLean, Clough (5), Peacock (2), Holliday.

Record Cup Victory: 9–3 v Goole T, FA Cup 1st rd, 9 January 1915 – Williamson; Haworth, Weir; Davidson, Cook, Malcolm; Wilson, Carr (3), Elliott (3), Tinsley (3), Davies.

Record Defeat: 0–9 v Blackburn R, Division 2, 6 November 1954.

Most League Points (2 for a win): 65, Division 2, 1973–74.

Most League Points (3 for a win): 94, Division 3, 1986–87.

Most League Goals: 122, Division 2, 1926–27.

Highest League Scorer in Season: George Camsell, 59, Division 2, 1926–27 (Second Division record).

Most League Goals in Total Aggregate: George Camsell, 326, 1925–39.

Most Capped Player: Wilf Mannion, 26, England.

Most League Appearances: Tim Williamson, 563, 1902–23.

Record Transfer Fee Received: £2,300,000 from Manchester United for Gary Pallister, August 1989.

Record Transfer Fee Paid: £5,250,000 to Tottenham H for Nick Barmby, August 1995.

Football League Record: 1899 Elected to Division 2; 1902–24 Division 1; 1924–27 Division 2; 1927–28 Division 1; 1928–29 Division 2; 1929–54 Division 1; 1954–66 Division 2; 1966–67 Division 3; 1967–74 Division 2; 1974–82 Division 1; 1982–86 Division 2; 1986–87 Division 3; 1987–88 Division 2; 1988–89 Division 1; 1989–92 Division 2; 1992–93 FA Premier League; 1993–95 Division 1; 1995– FA Premier League.

Honours: *Football League:* Division 1 – Champions 1994–95. Division 2 – Champions 1926–27, 1928–29, 1973–74; Runners-up 1901–02, 1991–92. Division 3 – Runners-up 1966–67, 1986–87. *FA Cup:* best season: 6th rd, 1936, 1947, 1970, 1975, 1977, 1978; old last eight 1901, 1904. *Football League Cup:* Semi-final 1976. *Amateur Cup:* Winners 1895, 1898, *Anglo-Scottish Cup:* Winners 1976.

Colours: Red and white. ***Change colours:*** White and royal blue.

Did you know?
In the 1914–15 season three players shared the Middlesbrough goals in a 9-3 FA Cup win over Goole Town: John Carr, George Elliott amd Walter Tinsley.

MIDDLESBROUGH 1995–96 LEAGUE RECORD

Match No.	Date	Venue	Opponents	Result		H/T Score	Lg. Pos.	Goalscorers	Attendance
1	Aug 20	A	Arsenal	D	1-1	1-1	—	Barmby	37,308
2	26	H	Chelsea	W	2-0	1-0	9	Hignett, Fjortoft	28,826
3	30	A	Newcastle U	L	0-1	0-0	—		36,483
4	Sept 9	A	Bolton W	D	1-1	0-1	12	Hignett	18,376
5	12	H	Southampton	D	0-0	0-0	—		29,181
6	16	H	Coventry C	W	2-1	0-0	10	Vickers, Fjortoft	27,882
7	23	A	Manchester C	W	1-0	1-0	7	Barmby	25,865
8	30	H	Blackburn R	W	2-0	1-0	7	Barmby, Hignett	29,462
9	Oct 15	A	Sheffield W	W	1-0	0-0	4	Hignett (pen)	21,177
10	21	H	QPR	W	1-0	1-0	4	Hignett (pen)	29,283
11	28	A	Manchester U	L	0-2	0-1	6		36,580
12	Nov 4	H	Leeds U	D	1-1	1-1	6	Fjortoft	29,467
13	18	A	Wimbledon	D	0-0	0-0	8		13,780
14	21	H	Tottenham H	L	0-1	0-0	—		29,487
15	25	H	Liverpool	W	2-1	1-0	6	Cox, Barmby	29,390
16	Dec 2	A	QPR	D	1-1	1-1	6	Morris	17,546
17	9	H	Manchester C	W	4-1	1-1	4	Barmby 2, Stamp, Juninho	29,469
18	16	A	Blackburn R	L	0-1	0-1	7		27,996
19	23	H	West Ham U	W	4-2	3-0	5	Fjortoft, Cox, Morris, Hendrie	28,640
20	26	A	Everton	L	0-4	0-2	6		40,091
21	30	A	Nottingham F	L	0-1	0-1	7		27,027
22	Jan 1	H	Aston Villa	L	0-2	0-2	8		28,523
23	13	H	Arsenal	L	2-3	1-1	11	Juninho, Stamp	29,359
24	20	A	Southampton	L	1-2	1-0	12	Barmby	15,115
25	Feb 4	A	Chelsea	L	0-5	0-3	12		21,060
26	10	H	Newcastle U	L	1-2	1-0	12	Beresford (og)	30,011
27	17	H	Bolton W	L	1-4	1-2	13	Pollock	29,354
28	24	A	Coventry C	D	0-0	0-0	13		17,979
29	Mar 2	H	Everton	L	0-2	0-2	13		29,805
30	9	A	West Ham U	L	0-2	0-1	13		23,850
31	16	H	Nottingham F	D	1-1	0-0	13	Mustoe	29,392
32	19	A	Aston Villa	D	0-0	0-0	—		23,933
33	30	A	Leeds U	W	1-0	1-0	13	Kavanagh (pen)	31,788
34	Apr 5	H	Sheffield W	W	3-1	0-0	—	Fjortoft 2, Freestone	29,751
35	8	A	Tottenham H	D	1-1	0-0	12	Whelan	32,036
36	13	H	Wimbledon	L	1-2	1-1	12	Fleming	29,176
37	27	A	Liverpool	L	0-1	0-0	12		40,782
38	May 5	H	Manchester U	L	0-3	0-1	12		29,922

Final League Position: 12

GOALSCORERS

League (35): Barmby 7, Fjortoft 6, Hignett 5 (2 pens), Cox 2, Juninho 2, Morris 2, Stamp 2, Fleming 1, Freestone 1, Hendrie 1, Kavanagh 1 (pen), Mustoe 1, Pollock 1, Vickers 1, Whelan 1, own goal 1.
Coca-Cola Cup (7): Fjortoft 2, Hignett 2, Barmby 1, Mustoe 1, Vickers 1.
FA Cup (2): Barmby 1, Pollock 1.

Miller A 6	Cox N 35	Morris C 22+1	Vickers S 32	Pearson N 36	Whyte D 24+1	Barmby N 32	Pollock J 31	Fjortoft J 27+1	Mustoe R 21	Hignett C 17+5	Whelan P 9+4	Moreno J 2+5	Walsh G 32	Hendrie J 7+6	Moore A 5+7	Liddle C 12+1	Juninho 20+1	Stamp P 11+1	Robson B 1+1	Fleming C 13	Blackmore C 4+1	O'Halloran K 2+1	Wilkinson P 2+1	Kavanagh G 6+1	Barron M 1	Branco 5+2	Freestone C 2+1	Campbell A 1+1	Summerbell M —+1	Match No.
1	2	3	4	5	6	7	8¹	9	10	11	12																			1
1	2	3	4	5	6	7	8	9	10	11																				2
1	2	3	4	5	6	7	8	9	10	11¹		12																		3
	2	3	4	5	6	7	8	9	10	11			1																	4
	2	3	4	5	6	7	8	9	10	11			1																	5
	2	3	4	5	6	7	8	9	10	11			1																	6
	2	3	4	5	6	7	8	9	10	11			1																	7
	2	3	4	5	6	7	8	9	10	11			1																	8
	2	3	4	5	6	7	8	9¹	10	11			1			12														9
	2	3	4	5	6²	7	8	9	10	11¹		13	1			12														10
	2	3²	4	5		7	8	9¹	10	11	6	12	1				13													11
		3	4	5		7	8	9	6²	11		13	1		12	2	10¹													12
	2	3	4	5		7	8	9					1		6		10	11												13
	2	3	4	5		7	8²	9¹			12		1		6		10	11	13											14
	2	3	4	5		7	8	9					1		6		10	11												15
	2	3	4	5		7	8				12	9	1		6		10¹	11												16
	2		4	5	6	7	8	9					1			3	10	11												17
	2		4	5	6	7		9¹					1		12	8	10	11	3											18
	2	3	4	5	6		8	9					1			11	10			7										19
	2	12³	4	5	6¹		8	9				13	1	7	14	11	10²		3											20
	2		4	5			8						1	9	11	7	10			3	6									21
	2		4	5¹			8			12	11		1	9²	13	6	10	7		3²	14									22
			4	5		7	8¹	9				6	1		12	2	10	11		3										23
	2	3	4	5		7					12	6	1				11¹			8²	10	13	9							24
	2	3	4	5		7		9¹		11			1				10				6	8	12							25
	2	3	4	5		7	8				12	6	1						13	10¹	11²		9							26
	2	3	4	5¹	12	7	8	9		11	6²		1						13		14		10³							27
	2		4	5		7	8	9	10			6	1							3						11				28
	2				6		8	9	10	7¹			1		12			11		3			4²	5	13					29
		4	2³	5	6		8	9²	10	7¹			1		12			11	13	3	14									30
	2			5	6	7	8			11			1		9		10			3	4									31
	2			5	6	7	8			11	12		1		9		10¹			3						13	4²			32
	2			5	6	7	8			10	4		1		9					3						11				33
			4	5	6		9	8			12		1		10			11¹	2	3						7²	13			34
1	2			5	6		8¹							7	4	11	10			3								9	12	35
1	2		4	5		7	8								6	11	10			3						9¹		12		36
1	2		4	5¹	6	7	8							13	12		10	11		3						9²				37
	2		4	5	6	7	8¹	9		11			1				10	13	12							3²				38

Coca-Cola Cup

Second Round	Rotherham U	(h)	2-1	
		(a)	1-0	
Third Round	Crystal Palace	(a)	2-2	
		(h)	2-0	
Fourth Round	Birmingham C	(h)	0-0	
		(a)	0-2	

FA Cup

Third Round	Notts Co	(a)	2-1
Fourth Round	Wimbledon	(h)	0-0
		(a)	0 1

MILLWALL 1995–96　*Back row (left to right):* Mickey Bennett, Kerry Dixon, Tony Witter, Uwe Fuchs, Jason van Blerk, Chris Malkin, Greg Berry, Anton Rogan, Damian Webber.
Middle row: Keith Johnstone (Physio), Michael Harle, Keith Stevens, Ricky Newman, Dave Savage, Jimmy Nielsen, Kasey Keller, Dave Wietecha, Alistair Edwards, Bobby Bowry, Maurice Doyle, Richard Cadette, Ian McDonald (Coach).
Front row: Phil O'Neil, Ben Thatcher, Scott Taylor, Alex Rae, Mick McCarthy (Manager), Ian Evans (First Team Coach), Steve Forbes, Lee McRobert, James Connor, Mark Beard.

Division 2   **MILLWALL**

Millwall Football & Athletic Company (1985) plc, The Den, Zampa Road, Bermondsey SE16 3LN. Telephone: (0171) 232 1222. Ticket Office: (0171) 231 9999. Club Shop: (0171) 231 5881. Fax: (0171) 231 3663.

Ground capacity: 20,146 (all-seater).

Record Attendance: 20,093 v Arsenal, FA Cup 3rd rd, 10 January 1994.

Pitch measurements: 100 metres × 68m.

President: Lord Mellish of Bermondsey.

Chairman: Peter W. Mead. *Directors:* R. I. Burr, J. D. Burnige, B. E. Mitchell, Cllr. David Sullivan, J. M. R. Berardo.

Chief Executive/Secretary: Graham Hortop. *Assistant Secretary:* Yvonne Haines.

Manager: Jimmy Nicholl. *Assistant Manager:* Martin Harvey. *First Team Coach:* Ian Evans.

Reserve Team Coach and Youth Coach: Ian McDonald. *Chief Scout:* Ron Howard. *Youth Development Officer:* Allen Batsford. *Physio:* Keith Johnstone. *Hon. Medical Officer:* Dr. Daniel Baron.

Sales & Promotions Manager: Mike Sullivan. *Commercial Manager:* Billy Neil.

Stadium Manager: Colin Sayer. *Marketing Manager:* D. Frazer.

Year Formed: 1885. *Turned Professional:* 1893. *Ltd Co.:* 1894.

Previous Names: 1885, Millwall Rovers; 1889, Millwall Athletic.

Club Nickname: 'The Lions'.

Previous Grounds: 1885, Glengall Road, Millwall; 1886, Back of 'Lord Nelson'; 1890, East Ferry Road; 1901, North Greenwich; 1910, The Den, Cold Blow Lane; 1993, The Den, Bermondsey.

Foundation: Formed in 1885 as Millwall Rovers by employees of Morton & Co, a jam and marmalade factory in West Ferry Road. The founders were predominantly Scotsmen. Their first headquarters was The Islanders pub in Tooke Street, Millwall. Their first trophy was the East End Cup in 1887.

First Football League game: 28 August 1920, Division 3, v Bristol R (h) W 2-0 – Lansdale; Fort, Hodge; Voisey (1), Riddell, McAlpine; Waterall, Travers, Broad (1), Sutherland, Dempsey.

Record League Victory: 9–1 v Torquay U, Division 3 (S), 29 August 1927 – Lansdale; Tilling, Hill; Amos, Bryant (3), Graham; Chance, Hawkins (3), Landells (1), Phillips (2), Black. 9–1 v Coventry C, Division 3 (S), 19 November 1927 – Lansdale; Fort, Hill; Amos, Collins (1), Graham; Chance, Landells (4), Cock (2), Phillips (2), Black.

Record Cup Victory: 7–0 v Gateshead, FA Cup 2nd rd, 12 December 1936 – Yuill; Ted Smith, Inns; Brolly, Hancock, Forsyth; Thomas (1), Mangnall (1), Ken Burditt (2), McCartney (2), Thorogood (1).

Record Defeat: 1–9 v Aston Villa, FA Cup 4th rd, 28 January 1946.

Most League Points (2 for a win): 65, Division 3 (S), 1927–28 and Division 3, 1965–66.

Most League Points (3 for a win): 90, Division 3, 1984–85.

Most League Goals: 127, Division 3 (S), 1927–28.

Highest League Scorer in Season: Richard Parker, 37, Division 3 (S), 1926–27.

Most League Goals in Total Aggregate: Teddy Sheringham, 93, 1984–91.

Most Capped Player: Eamonn Dunphy, 22 (23), Republic of Ireland.

Most League Appearances: Barry Kitchener, 523, 1967–82.

Record Transfer Fee Received: £2,300,000 from Liverpool for Mark Kennedy, March 1995.

Record Transfer Fee Paid: £800,000 to Derby Co for Paul Goddard, December 1989.

Football League Record: 1920 Original Members of Division 3; 1921 Division 3 (S); 1928–34 Division 2; 1934–38 Division 3 (S); 1938–48 Division 2; 1948–58 Division 3 (S); 1958–62 Division 4; 1962–64 Division 3; 1964–65 Division 4; 1965–66 Division 3; 1966–75 Division 2; 1975–76 Division 3; 1976–79 Division 2; 1979–85 Division 3; 1985–88 Division 2; 1988–90 Division 1; 1990–92 Division 2; 1992–96 Division 1; 1996– Division 2.

Honours: Football League: Division 1 best season: 7th 1992–93; Division 2 – Champions 1987–88; Division 3 (S) – Champions 1927–28, 1937–38; Runners-up 1952–53; Division 3 – Runners–up 1965–66, 1984–85; Division 4 – Champions 1961–62; Runners-up 1964–65. *FA Cup:* Semi-final 1900, 1903, 1937 (first Division 3 side to reach semi-final). *Football League Cup:* best season: 5th rd, 1974, 1977, 1995. *Football League Trophy:* Winners 1983.

Colours: Blue shirts, white shorts, blue stockings. *Change colours:* Green and white shirts, green shorts, green stockings.

Did you know?
Up to 25 November 1995, Millwall had established a club record equalling nine away games without defeat.

MILLWALL 1995–96 LEAGUE RECORD

Match No.	Date	Venue	Opponents	Result	H/T Score	Lg. Pos.	Goalscorers	Attendance
1	Aug 12	H	Grimsby T	W 2-1	2-0	—	Rae (pen), Malkin	8546
2	19	A	Port Vale	W 1-0	0-0	1	Dixon	8202
3	26	H	Southend U	D 0-0	0-0	2		11,536
4	29	A	Reading	W 2-1	0-1	—	Rae (pen), Dixon	10,143
5	Sept 2	A	Portsmouth	W 1-0	1-0	1	Dixon	8023
6	9	H	Barnsley	L 0-1	0-1	2		9272
7	13	H	Luton T	W 1-0	0-0	—	Malkin	7076
8	16	A	Norwich C	D 0-0	0-0	2		15,962
9	23	H	Sunderland	L 1-2	0-1	2	Stevens	8691
10	Oct 1	A	Derby Co	D 2-2	2-1	2	Rae, Black	9590
11	7	A	Watford	W 1-0	0-0	2	Rae	8918
12	14	H	Tranmere R	D 2-2	0-0	2	Dixon (pen), Stevens	9293
13	22	A	Crystal Palace	W 2-1	2-1	2	Malkin, Fuchs	14,338
14	28	H	WBA	W 2-1	1-1	1	Malkin, Fuchs	9717
15	Nov 4	A	Birmingham C	D 2-2	0-1	1	Dixon, Rae	23,016
16	11	H	Ipswich T	W 2-1	1-1	1	Malkin, Witter	11,360
17	18	H	Huddersfield T	D 0-0	0-0	1		9402
18	21	A	Oldham Ath	D 2-2	0-1	—	Rae, Malkin	6161
19	25	A	Stoke C	L 0-1	0-0	1		12,590
20	Dec 2	H	Watford	L 1-2	1-2	1	Malkin	8389
21	5	H	Charlton Ath	L 0-2	0-1	—		11,350
22	9	A	Sunderland	L 0-6	0-2	7		18,951
23	16	H	Derby Co	L 0-1	0-1	10		7694
24	26	A	Wolverhampton W	D 1-1	0-1	10	Malkin	25,593
25	Jan 1	H	Leicester C	D 1-1	0-1	10	Malkin	9953
26	13	H	Port Vale	L 1-2	1-1	12	Rae	14,220
27	20	A	Grimsby T	W 2-1	0-1	8	Rae 2 (1 pen)	5218
28	27	H	Portsmouth	D 1-1	1-0	6	Van Blerk	7710
29	Feb 3	A	Southend U	L 0-2	0-1	9		7302
30	10	H	Reading	D 1-1	0-1	8	Newman	8875
31	13	A	Sheffield U	L 0-2	0-1	—		10,007
32	17	A	Luton T	L 0-1	0-0	9		7308
33	24	H	Norwich C	W 2-1	0-0	9	Bowry, Fuchs	8218
34	27	A	Barnsley	L 1-3	1-0	—	Fuchs	6331
35	Mar 2	H	Wolverhampton W	L 0-1	0-0	11		9131
36	9	A	Charlton Ath	L 0-2	0-1	13		12,204
37	16	H	Sheffield U	W 1-0	0-0	12	Fuchs	7795
38	23	A	Leicester C	L 1-2	1-1	15	Rae	12,543
39	30	H	Crystal Palace	L 1-4	0-0	17	Rae (pen)	13,214
40	Apr 2	A	Tranmere R	D 2-2	1-0	—	Yuran, Malkin	5850
41	6	A	WBA	L 0-1	0-0	20		13,793
42	10	H	Birmingham C	W 2-0	1-0	—	Bowry, Malkin	9271
43	13	A	Huddersfield T	L 0-3	0-1	18		11,206
44	20	H	Oldham Ath	L 0-1	0-0	19		9574
45	27	H	Stoke C	L 2-3	0-2	19	Rae 2 (1 pen)	10,105
46	May 5	A	Ipswich T	D 0-0	0-0	22		17,290

Final League Position: 22

GOALSCORERS

League *(43):* Rae 13 (5 pens), Malkin 11, Dixon 5 (1 pen), Fuchs 5, Bowry 2, Stevens 2, Black 1, Newman 1, Van Blerk 1, Witter 1, Yuran 1.
Coca-Cola Cup (4): Taylor 2, Rae 1 (pen), Savage 1.
FA Cup (3): Rae 2, Malkin 1.

Keller K 42	Bennett M 1+1	Thatcher B 41+1	Doyle M 15+3	Witter T 30+1	Stevens K 39	Savage D 17+10	Rae A 37	Dixon K 15+7	Malkin C 39+4	Van Blerk J 42	Newman R 34+2	Bowry B 33+5	Taylor S 12+10	Rogan A 4+4	Fuchs U 21+11	McRobert L 1+6	Forbes S —+4	Black K 1+2	Webber D 8+8	Lavin G 18+2	Connor J 7+1	Berry G 1	Carter T 4	Kulkov V 6	Yuran S 13	Neill L 5+8	Dolby T 6+4	Gordon D 6	Weir M 8	Cadette R —+1	Match No.
1	2	3	4	5	6	7	8	9	10	11																					1
1		3	4	5	6	7^{3}	8	10^{2}	9	11^{1}	2	12	13	14																	2
1		3	4	5	6^{1}	7	8	10^{2}	9	11^{3}	2	12			13	14															3
1		3	4^{2}	5	6	7^{3}	8	10	9^{1}	11	2	13			14	12															4
1		3	13	5	6	7^{2}	8^{3}	10	12	11	2	4			14	9^{1}															5
1		3	13	5	6	7^{2}	8	10^{1}	12	11^{3}	2	4			9	14															6
1		3	8	5	6	7^{3}		10	12	11^{2}	2	4			9^{1}	13	14														7
1		3	8^{1}	5	6			10	9	11	2	4			12	7^{2}	13														8
1		3	7^{3}	5	6		8	10^{2}	9	11^{1}	2	4	12		13	14															9
1		3		5	6	13	8	12	9^{1}	7	2	4			10				11^{2}												10
1		3		5	6	12	8^{3}	13	9	11	2	4	7^{2}		10^{1}				14												11
1	12		11	5	6		8^{3}	13	10	3	2	4	7^{1}		9^{2}				14												12
1			11	5	6	7	8	12	10^{1}	3	2	4			9^{2}				13												13
1			11	5^{1}	6		8		10	3	2	4	7		9				12												14
1	12		11^{1}	5	6		8	13	10	3	2	4	7		9^{2}																15
1		3		5	6	12	8	9^{2}	10	11	2	4	7^{1}		13																16
1		3		5	6	12	8	9	10^{1}	11	2	4	7^{2}		13																17
1		3		5^{2}	6	12	8	9	10	11	2	4			7^{1}				13												18
1		3			6	12	8	9^{1}	10	11		4			7				13	5	2										19
1		3			6	7^{2}	8	12	10	11		4^{1}	9		13					5	2										20
1		3	12		6		8^{1}		10	11	4^{3}		7^{2}	5	9	13	14		2												21
1		3	4		6	7	8		10^{2}	11		13	5^{1}	9	12				2												22
1		3	4^{2}	5	6		8	12	10	11			7		9^{1}				2	13											23
1		3		5		7	8	10	9	11	2	4							6												24
1		3		5			8	10^{2}	9		2	4	12		13				6	7						11^{1}					25
		3		5			8^{2}		9	11	2	4	12			14		6^{3}	13		1	7^{1}	10								26
		3		5	6	7	8		9	11	2									1	4	10									27
		3		5	6	7^{1}		9	11	2		12						8		1	4	10									28
		3		5	6	7		11	2		9	12				13	8	1	4^{2}	10^{1}											29
1		3			6	12	8	10	11	13	7^{1}	14		9^{3}					5	2	4^{2}										30
1		3		4	6	12	8^{2}	10		13	14		9					5^{1}	2	7	11^{3}	9									31
1		3		5	4	8		9	11		6	10^{1}					2							7	12						32
1		3		5	6^{1}		11	13	4		12	9				2			8^{2}	10^{3}	7	14									33
1		3		5		11	8	12	6	2	4	9^{2}							10	7^{1}	13										34
1		3		6		8	7	5	2	4^{2}	12	9^{1}							10	13	11										35
1		3^{2}		6	12	8		5	10	4^{1}	7^{3}	9	13	2	14						11										36
1		3		8	10	5	7^{1}	4	9	6	2	12								11											37
1		3		6	8	10	5	12	13	9	14	2^{3}	4		11^{2}	7^{1}															38
1		3		6	8	9	5	12	13	2	4^{1}	10^{2}	7	11																	39
1		3		6	8	10	5	4	12	2	9	7	11^{1}																		40
1		3		6	10	5	8	4	2	9^{1}	12	11	7																		41
1		3		6	10	5	8	4	12	2	9	7^{1}	11																		42
1		3		8	10	6	4	5	2	9	12	13	7^{2}	11^{1}																	43
1		2^{2}	6	8	10	11^{3}	4	3^{1}	12	5	9	13	7	14																	44
1		3	6	12	8	9	5	4	10^{2}	2	13	11^{1}	7																		45
1		3	10	12	6	8^{2}	9	5	2	4	7	13	11^{1}																		46

Coca-Cola Cup

Second Round	Everton	(h)	0-0
		(a)	4-2
Third Round	Sheffield W	(h)	0-2

FA Cup

Third Round	Oxford U	(h)	3-3
		(a)	0-1

NEWCASTLE UNITED 1995-96 *Back row (left to right):* Pavel Srnicek, Steve Watson, Robbie Elliott, Steve Howey, Paul Kitson, Philippe Albert, Darren Peacock, David Ginola, Shaka Hislop. *Front row:* Scott Sellars, Warren Barton, Keith Gillespie, John Beresford, Robert Lee, Peter Beardsley, Lee Clark, Marc Hottiger, Darren Huckerby, Les Ferdinand.

FA Premiership　　NEWCASTLE UNITED

St James' Park, Newcastle-upon-Tyne NE1 4ST. Telephone: (0191) 201 8400. Club Fax: (0191) 201 8600. Lottery Office: (0191) 201 8502. Commercial Dept: (0191) 201 8422. Ticket Office Hotline: (0191) 261 1571. Club Shop: (0191) 201 8426. Club Shop Mail Order Answering Service: (0191) 262 6878. Football in the Community Scheme: (0191) 261 9715. Conference and Banqueting: (0191) 201 8525. Clubcall: 0891 121590. Clubcall Main Line: 0891 121190. Ticket Line: 0891 121590. Club Shop numbers: St James' Park Club Shop: (0191) 201 8426. Metro Centre Club Shop: (0191) 461 0000; (Russell Way): (0191) 460 3509; Within Asda, Metro Centre (0191) 460 3974; Asda, Gosforth (0191) 213 0638; Asda, Blyth (01670) 351653; Club Shop at Newcastle Airport: (0191) 271 2631. Eldon Square Club Shop: (0191) 230 0808. Travel Club: (0191) 201 8550. Junior Magpies: (0191) 201 8467.

Ground capacity: 36,610.

Record attendance: 68,386 v Chelsea, Division 1, 3 September 1930.

Record receipts: £359,112.12 v Swansea C, FA Cup 4th rd, 28 January 1995.

Pitch measurements: 114yd × 74yd.

President: T. L. Bennett.

Chairman: Sir John Hall.

Vice-Chairman: W. F. Shepherd. *Chief Executive:* A. O. Fletcher.

Directors: D. S. Hall, R. Jones, T. L. Bennett.

Manager: Kevin Keegan. *Assistant Manager:* Terry McDermott.

Coaches: Arthur Cox, Chris McMenemy and Jeff Clarke. *Physios:* Derek Wright, Paul Ferris.

General Manager/Secretary: R. Cushing. *Operations Manager:* P. W. Stevens.

Assistant Secretary: A. Toward. *Marketing Control:* Trevor Garwood.

Year Formed: 1881. *Turned Professional:* 1889. *Ltd Co.:* 1890.

Club Nickname: 'Magpies'.

Previous Names: Stanley 1881; Newcastle East End 1882–92.

Previous Grounds: South Byker, 1881; Chillingham Road, Heaton, 1886–92.

Foundation: It stemmed from a newly formed club called Stanley in 1881. In October 1882 they changed their name to Newcastle East End to avoid confusion with Stanley in Co. Durham. Shortly afterwards another club Rosewood merged with them. Newcastle West End had been formed in August 1882 and they played on a ground which is now St. James' Park. In 1889, West End went out of existence after a bad run and the remaining committee men invited East End to move to St. James' Park. They accepted and at a meeting in Bath Lane Hall in 1892, changed their name to Newcastle United.

First Football League game: 2 September 1893, Division 2, v Royal Arsenal (a) D 2-2 – Ramsay; Jeffery, Miller; Crielly, Graham, McKane; Bowman, Crate (1), Thompson, Sorley (1), Wallace. Graham and not Crate scored according to some reports.

Record League Victory: 13–0 v Newport Co, Division 2, 5 October 1946 – Garbutt; Cowell, Graham; Harvey, Brennan, Wright; Milburn (2), Bentley (1), Wayman (4), Shackleton (6), Pearson.

Record Cup Victory: 9–0 v Southport (at Hillsborough) FA Cup 4th rd, 1 February 1932 – McInroy; Nelson, Fairhurst; McKenzie, Davidson, Weaver (1); Boyd (1), Jimmy Richardson (3), Cape (2), McMenemy (1), Lang (1).

Record Defeat: 0–9 v Burton Wanderers, Division 2, 15 April 1895.

Most League Points (2 for a win): 57, Division 2, 1964–65.

Most League Points (3 for a win): 96, Division 1, 1992–93.

Most League Goals: 98, Division 1, 1951–52.

Highest League Scorer in Season: Hughie Gallacher, 36, Division 1, 1926–27.

Most League Goals in Total Aggregate: Jackie Milburn, 177, 1946–57.

Most Capped Player: Alf McMichael, 40, Northern Ireland.

Most League Appearances: Jim Lawrence, 432, 1904–22.

Record Transfer Fee Received: £6,250,000 from Manchester U for Andy Cole, January 1995.

Record Transfer Fee Paid: £7,500,000 to Parma for Faustino Asprilla, February 1996.

Football League Record: 1893 Elected to Division 2; 1898–1934 Division 1; 1934–48 Division 2; 1948–61 Division 1; 1961–65 Division 2; 1965–78 Division 1; 1978–84 Division 2; 1984–89 Division 1; 1989–92 Division 2; 1992–93 Division 1; 1993– FA Premier League.

Honours: FA Premier League: Runners-up 1995–96. *Football League:* Division 1 – Champions 1904–05, 1906–07, 1908–09, 1926–27, 1992–93; Division 2 – Champions 1964–65; Runners-up 1897–98, 1947–48. *FA Cup:* Winners 1910, 1924, 1932, 1951, 1952, 1955; Runners-up 1905, 1906, 1908, 1911, 1974. *Football League Cup:* Runners-up 1976. *Texaco Cup:* Winners 1974, 1975. **European Competitions:** *European Fairs Cup:* 1968–69 (winners), 1969–70, 1970–71. *UEFA Cup:* 1977–78, 1994–95. *Anglo-Italian Cup:* Winners 1972–73.

Colours: Black and white striped shirts, black shorts, black stockings. *Change colours:* Gorge.

Did you know?
Les Ferdinand's hat-trick for Newcastle United on 21 October 1995 equalled a post-war eight consecutive scoring games for the club.

NEWCASTLE UNITED 1995–96 LEAGUE RECORD

Match No.	Date	Venue	Opponents	Result		H/T Score	Lg. Pos.	Goalscorers	Attendance
1	Aug 19	H	Coventry C	W	3-0	1-0	—	Lee, Beardsley (pen), Ferdinand	36,485
2	22	A	Bolton W	W	3-1	1-0	—	Ferdinand 2, Lee	20,243
3	27	A	Sheffield W	W	2-0	0-0	1	Ginola, Beardsley	24,815
4	30	H	Middlesbrough	W	1-0	0-0	—	Ferdinand	36,483
5	Sept 9	A	Southampton	L	0-1	0-0	1		15,237
6	16	H	Manchester C	W	3-1	2-0	1	Beardsley (pen), Ferdinand 2	36,501
7	24	H	Chelsea	W	2-0	1-0	1	Ferdinand 2	36,225
8	Oct 1	A	Everton	W	3-1	1-0	1	Ferdinand, Lee (pen), Kitson	33,026
9	14	A	QPR	W	3-2	0-1	1	Gillespie 2, Ferdinand	18,254
10	21	H	Wimbledon	W	6-1	3-0	1	Howey, Ferdinand 3, Clark, Albert	36,434
11	29	A	Tottenham H	D	1-1	0-1	1	Ginola	32,257
12	Nov 4	H	Liverpool	W	2-1	1-1	1	Ferdinand, Watson	36,547
13	8	H	Blackburn R	W	1-0	0-0	—	Lee	36,463
14	18	A	Aston Villa	D	1-1	0-1	1	Ferdinand	39,167
15	25	H	Leeds U	W	2-1	0-1	1	Lee, Beardsley	36,572
16	Dec 3	A	Wimbledon	D	3-3	3-2	1	Ferdinand 2, Gillespie	18,002
17	9	A	Chelsea	L	0-1	0-1	1		31,098
18	16	H	Everton	W	1-0	1-0	1	Ferdinand	36,557
19	23	H	Nottingham F	W	3-1	2-1	1	Lee 2, Ginola	36,531
20	27	A	Manchester U	L	0-2	0-1	—		42,024
21	Jan 2	H	Arsenal	W	2-0	1-0	—	Ginola, Ferdinand	36,530
22	14	A	Coventry C	W	1-0	1-0	1	Watson	20,532
23	20	H	Bolton W	W	2-1	2-1	1	Kitson, Beardsley	36,543
24	Feb 3	H	Sheffield W	W	2-0	0-0	1	Ferdinand, Clark	36,567
25	10	A	Middlesbrough	W	2-1	0-1	1	Watson, Ferdinand	30,011
26	21	A	West Ham U	L	0-2	0-1	—		23,843
27	24	A	Manchester C	D	3-3	1-1	1	Albert 2, Asprilla	31,115
28	Mar 4	H	Manchester U	L	0-1	0-0	—		36,584
29	18	H	West Ham U	W	3-0	1-0	—	Albert, Asprilla, Ferdinand	36,331
30	23	A	Arsenal	L	0-2	0-2	2		38,271
31	Apr 3	A	Liverpool	L	3-4	2-1	—	Ferdinand, Ginola, Asprilla	40,702
32	6	H	QPR	W	2-1	0-0	2	Beardsley 2	36,583
33	8	A	Blackburn R	L	1-2	0-0	2	Batty	30,717
34	14	H	Aston Villa	W	1-0	0-0	2	Ferdinand	36,546
35	17	H	Southampton	W	1-0	1-0	—	Lee	36,554
36	29	A	Leeds U	W	1-0	1-0	—	Gillespie	38,562
37	May 2	A	Nottingham F	D	1-1	1-0	—	Beardsley	28,280
38	5	H	Tottenham H	D	1-1	0-0	2	Ferdinand	36,589

Final League Position: 2

GOALSCORERS

League (66): Ferdinand 25, Lee 8 (1 pen), Beardsley 8 (2 pens), Ginola 5, Albert 4, Gillespie 4, Asprilla 3, Watson 3, Clark 2, Kitson 2, Batty 1, Howey 1.
Coca-Cola Cup (13): Ferdinand 3, Beardsley 2, Peacock 2, Albert 1, Barton 1, Gillespie 1, Lee 1, Sellars 1, Watson 1.
FA Cup (3): Albert 1, Beardsley 1 (pen), Ferdinand 1.

Hislop S 24	Barton W 30 + 1	Beresford J 32 + 1	Clark L 22 + 6	Peacock D 33 + 1	Howey S 28	Lee R 36	Beardsley P 35	Ferdinand L 37	Ginola D 34	Gillespie K 26 + 2	Fox R 2 + 2	Kitson P 2 + 5	Watson S 15 + 8	Sellars S 2 + 4	Albert P 19 + 4	Hottiger M — + 1	Smicek P 14 + 1	Elliott R 5 + 1	Huckerby D — + 1	Asprilla F 11 + 3	Batty D 11	Match No.
1	2	3	4	5	6	7	8	9	10^1	11	12											1
1	2	3	4	5	6	7	8	9	10	11												2
1	2	3	4	5	6	7	8	9	10	11												3
1	2	3	4	5	6	7	8	9	10	11												4
1	2	3	4	5	6	7		9	10	11		8^1	12									5
1	2^2	3^3	4	5	6	7	8^1	9	10	11	12			13	14							6
1	2^1	3	4	5	6	7		9	10^2	11	8		12	13	11							7
1	2	3	4	5	6	7		9	10^2	8^1		13	12	11								8
1	2	3	4	5	6	7	8	9	10^1	11					12							9
1	2	3	4^1	5	6^2	7^3	8	9	10	11			12	13	14							10
1	2	3		5	6	7	8	9	4	10			11									11
1	2	3		5	6	7	8	9	10	11^1			4	12								12
1	2	3		5	6	7	8	9	10	11			4									13
1	2	3	12	5	6	7	8	9^2	10	11			4^1	13								14
1	2	3	4	5	6	7	8	9	10	11												15
1	2	3	4	5	6	7	8	9	10	11												16
1^6	2	3	4	5	6	7	8	9	10	11							15					17
	2	3	4	5	6	7	8	9	10	11^1					12		1					18
	2	12	4	5	6	7	8	9	10	11^2			13		3^1		1					19
	2	3	4^2	5	6	7	8	9	10	11^1			13	12			1					20
	2	12		5	6	7^1	8	9	10				11^2	13	3		1	4				21
	2	3	4	5		7	8	9	10				11		6		1					22
	2	3	4	5		7	8		10			9^1	11		6		1	12				23
	2	3	4		6	7	8	9		11^1		12	10		5		1					24
	2	3	4	5		7	8	9		11^1			10		6		1		12			25
	2	3	10	5	6		8	9		11^1	12				4		1		7			26
	2	3	11	5	6		8	9	10						4		1		7			27
	2	3			6	7	8	9	10						5		1			11	4	28
	2^1	3			6	7	8	9	10				12		5		1			11	4	29
	2^1	3			6	7	8	9	10				12		5		1			11	4	30
		3	12		6^1	7	8	9	10				2		5		1			11	4	31
1		3		5		7^1	8	9	10	12			2		6					11	4	32
1		3		5		7	8	9	10	12			2		6					11	4	33
1		3^1		5		7	8	9	10				2		6			12		11	4	34
1		12		5		7	8	9	10				2		6		3			11^1	4	35
1	12	13		5		7	8	9		11^1			2		6		3			10^2	4	36
1		12		5		7	8	9	10^1	11^2			2		6		3			13	4	37
1		12		5		7	8^2	9	10	11^1			2		6		3			13	4	38

Coca-Cola Cup

Second Round	Bristol C	(a)	5-0
		(h)	3-1
Third Round	Stoke C	(a)	4-0
Fourth Round	Liverpool	(a)	1-0
Fifth Round	Arsenal	(a)	0-2

FA Cup

Third Round	Chelsea	(a)	1-1
		(h)	2-2

NORTHAMPTON TOWN 1995-96   *Back row (left to right)*: Michael Warner, Martin Aldridge, Ollie Cahill, Jason White, Darren Hughes, Christian Lee.
Middle row: Denis Casey (Physio), Jason Beckford, Dean Peer, Andy Woodman, Chris Burns, Billy Turley, Ian Sampson, Gary Thompson, Paul Curtis (Youth Team Coach).
Front row: Gareth Williams, Neil Grayson, Ray Warburton, Ian Atkins (Manager), Danny O'Shea, Lee Colkin, David Norton.
(Photograph: Pete Norton)

Division 3   **NORTHAMPTON TOWN**

Sixfields Stadium, Upton Way, Northampton NN5 4EG. Telephone: (01604) 757773. Fax: (01604) 751613/754960. Ticket Office: (01604) 588338. Soccer Line: 0839 664477.

Ground capacity: 7653 (all seating).

Record attendance (at County Ground): 24,523 v Fulham, Division 1, 23 April 1966. (Sixfields Stadium): 7461 v Barnet, Division 3, 15 October 1994.

Record receipts (at County Ground): £52,373 v WBA, Coca-Cola Cup 1st rd, 2nd leg, 22 August 1995.

Pitch measurements: 116yd × 72yd.

Chairman: B. J. Ward.

Directors: B. Stonhill, B. Hancock, M. Church, D. Kerr, B. Collins, B. Lomax.

Secretary: Mrs Rebecca Kerr. *Company Secretary:* Barry W. Collins.

Manager: Ian Atkins. *Coach:* Danny O'Shea.

Physio: Dennis Casey. *Commercial Manager:* Bob Gorrill. *Stadium Manager:* Martin Girvan (Pall Mall Services).

Year Formed: 1897. *Turned Professional:* 1901. *Ltd Co.:* 1901.

Previous Ground: County Ground.

Club Nickname: 'The Cobblers'.

Foundation: Formed in 1897 by school teachers connected with the Northampton and District Elementary Schools' Association, they survived a financial crisis at the end of their first year when they were £675 in the red and became members of the Midland League – a fast move indeed for a new club. They achieved Southern League membership in 1901.

First Football League game: 28 August 1920, Division 3, v Grimsby T (a) L 0-2 – Thorpe; Sproston, Hewison; Jobey, Tomkins, Pease; Whitworth, Lockett, Thomas, Freeman, MacKechnie.

Record League Victory: 10–0 v Walsall, Division 3 (S), 5 November 1927 – Hammond; Watson, Jeffs; Allen, Brett, Odell; Daley, Smith (3), Loasby (3), Hoten (1), Wells (3).

Record Cup Victory: 10–0 v Sutton T, FA Cup Prel rd, 7 December 1907 – Cooch; Drennan, Lloyd Davies, Tirrell (1), McCartney, Hickleton, Badenock (3), Platt (3), Lowe (1), Chapman (2), McDiarmid.

Record Defeat: 0–11 v Southampton, Southern League, 28 December 1901.

Most League Points (2 for a win): 68, Division 4, 1975–76.

Most League Points (3 for a win): 99, Division 4, 1986–87.

Most League Goals: 109, Division 3, 1962–63 and Division 3 (S), 1952–53.

Highest League Scorer in Season: Cliff Holton, 36, Division 3, 1961–62.

Most League Goals in Total Aggregate: Jack English, 135, 1947–60.

Most Capped Player: E. Lloyd Davies, 12 (16), Wales.

Most League Appearances: Tommy Fowler, 521, 1946–61.

Record Transfer Fee Received: £265,000 from Watford for Richard Hill, July 1987.

Record Transfer Fee Paid: £85,000 to Manchester C for Tony Adcock, January 1988.

Football League Record: 1920 Original Member of Division 3; 1921 Division 3 (S); 1958–61 Division 4; 1961–63 Division 3; 1963–65 Division 2; 1965–66 Division 1; 1966–67 Division 2; 1967–69 Division 3; 1969–76 Division 4; 1976–77 Division 3; 1977–87 Division 4; 1987–90 Division 3; 1990–92 Division 4; 1992– Division 3.

Honours: Football League: Division 1 best season: 21st, 1965–66; Division 2 – Runners-up 1964–65; Division 3 – Champions 1962–63; Division 3 (S) – Runners-up 1927–28, 1949–50; Division 4 – Champions 1986–87; Runners-up 1975–76. *FA Cup:* best season: 5th rd, 1934, 1950, 1970. *Football League Cup:* best season: 5th rd, 1965, 1967.

Colours: Claret with white shirts, yellow shoulder panel (Lotto logo), white shorts, claret stockings. *Change colours:* Reverse of (home) first choice.

Did you know?
When Northampton Town beat Sutton Town 10-0 in an FA Cup tie in 1907–08, Herbert Chapman scored twice and had three other goals disallowed.

NORTHAMPTON TOWN 1995–96 LEAGUE RECORD

Match No.	Date	Venue	Opponents	Result		H/T Score	Lg. Pos.	Goalscorers	Attendance
1	Aug 12	H	Bury	W	4-1	1-1	—	Grayson 3, Burns (pen)	4487
2	19	A	Cardiff C	W	1-0	1-0	2	Peer	7872
3	26	H	Mansfield T	D	3-3	1-2	4	White, Burns 2 (1 pen)	4797
4	29	A	Hartlepool U	L	1-2	0-1	—	Thompson	2390
5	Sept 2	A	Rochdale	W	2-1	1-0	3	Burns, White	2193
6	9	H	Exeter C	D	0-0	0-0	4		5625
7	12	H	Leyton Orient	L	1-2	1-0	—	Williams	5072
8	16	A	Doncaster R	L	0-1	0-1	11		2353
9	23	A	Torquay U	L	0-3	0-1	13		2314
10	30	H	Fulham	W	2-0	0-0	10	Grayson, White	5778
11	Oct 7	A	Scunthorpe U	D	0-0	0-0	11		2455
12	14	H	Cambridge U	W	3-0	2-0	9	Grayson, Burns, Colkin	6301
13	21	A	Colchester U	L	0-1	0-0	10		3823
14	28	H	Barnet	L	0-2	0-0	12		5376
15	31	H	Preston NE	L	1-2	0-1	—	Gibb	4695
16	Nov 4	A	Gillingham	D	0-0	0-0	16		7207
17	18	H	Wigan Ath	D	0-0	0-0	16		4102
18	25	A	Lincoln C	L	0-1	0-0	19		3287
19	Dec 9	H	Torquay U	D	1-1	1-0	18	White	3656
20	16	A	Fulham	W	3-1	2-1	13	Thompson, White 2	3421
21	23	A	Scarborough	L	1-2	0-0	16	White	1404
22	26	H	Hereford U	D	1-1	0-0	16	White	5222
23	Jan 6	A	Darlington	W	2-1	2-0	14	White 2	1943
24	13	H	Cardiff C	W	1-0	1-0	12	Armstrong	4454
25	20	A	Bury	W	1-0	0-0	10	White	3074
26	30	H	Plymouth Arg	W	1-0	1-0	—	Sampson	3911
27	Feb 3	A	Mansfield T	D	0-0	0-0	9		2981
28	10	H	Darlington	D	1-1	1-1	9	White	4926
29	17	A	Leyton Orient	L	0-2	0-1	11		4444
30	20	H	Rochdale	W	2-1	0-0	—	Warburton, Worboys	3090
31	24	H	Doncaster R	D	3-3	2-1	10	Sampson, Doherty, White (pen)	4738
32	27	A	Exeter C	W	2-1	1-1	—	Warburton, Grayson	2663
33	Mar 2	A	Hereford U	L	0-1	0-0	10		2822
34	9	H	Scarborough	W	2-0	1-0	9	White, Sampson	4621
35	16	A	Plymouth Arg	L	0-1	0-0	10		7001
36	19	H	Hartlepool U	D	0-0	0-0	—		3537
37	23	H	Chester C	W	1-0	1-0	10	Burns	4810
38	30	H	Scunthorpe U	L	1-2	0-0	10	Grayson	4290
39	Apr 2	A	Cambridge U	W	1-0	0-0	—	White	3631
40	6	A	Barnet	L	0-2	0-2	11		3135
41	8	H	Colchester U	W	2-1	0-0	11	Grayson, Gibb	5021
42	13	A	Preston NE	W	3-0	1-0	11	Grayson 3	11,774
43	20	H	Gillingham	D	1-1	0-1	11	Burns	7427
44	23	A	Chester C	L	0-1	0-0	—		1674
45	27	A	Lincoln C	D	1-1	0-0	11	Warburton	5166
46	May 4	A	Wigan Ath	W	2-1	1-1	11	Sampson, White	5089

Final League Position: 11

GOALSCORERS

League (51): White 16 (1 pen), Grayson 11, Burns 7 (2 pens), Sampson 4, Warburton 3, Gibb 2, Thompson 2, Armstrong 1, Colkin 1, Doherty 1, Peer 1, Williams 1, Worboys 1.
Coca-Cola Cup (3): Burns 1 (pen), Colkin 1, Peer 1.
FA Cup (1): Warburton 1.

Woodman A 44	Norton D 42 + 2	Hughes D 7 + 1	O'Shea D 37 + 1	Warburton R 44	Sampson I 30 + 3	Peer D 37 + 5	Williams G 25 + 10	Grayson N 37 + 5	Burns C 40 + 3	Colkin L 14 + 10	Thompson G 21 + 13	Hunter R 26 + 8	Smith T 2	White J 40 + 5	Beckford J — + 1	Gibb A 12 + 11	Maddison L 21	Lee C 1 + 4	Mountfield D 4	Taylor S 1 + 1	Scott R 5	Cahill O 2 + 1	Turley B 2	Armstrong G 4	Worboys G 4 + 9	Doherty N 3 + 6	Taylor M 1	Match No.
1	2	3[2]	4	5	6	7	8	9[1]	10	11	12	13																1
1	2		4	5	6	7	8[2]	9[1]	10	11	12	13		3														2
1	2	12	4	5	6[2]	7	13		10	11	8			9			3[1]											3
1	2	3[1]	4	5	6	7	8		10	11	12	13		9														4
1	2	3	4	5	6	7	8[1]		10	11	13	12		9[2]														5
1	2	3	4[2]	5	6	7	8	12	10	11		13		9[1]														6
1	2	3		5	6	7	8[2]	4	10	11[1]	12	13		9														7
1	2	3	4	5	6	7[2]	11[1]	8	10	13	12			9														8
1	2	3	4	5	6	12	8		10	11[2]	13			9		7[1]												9
1	2	12		5	6	4		11	10	13		8[2]		9[2]		7[1]	3	14										10
1	2			5	4	12	8		10	11				9		7[1]	3	6										11
1	2			5	14	4	12	11	10	13		8[2]		9[3]		7[1]	3	6										12
1	2[3]			5	9[1]	4	13	8	10	11[2]		14		12		7	3	6										13
1	2[3]			5[1]	12	4	14	11	10	13				9		7	3	6	8[2]									14
1	2			5	6	9[2]	8		10	11[1]		13		12		7[1]	3			14								15
1	2		9	5	6	4	13	8	10	11[2]	14			12		7[1]	3[3]											16
1	2		6	5	4		8		10	11[1]				9		7	3				12							17
1	2		6	5	4		8		10	12	7			9[1]			3				11							18
1	2		6	5	4		8		10	12	13			9			3				11[2]			7[1]				19
1	2		6	5	4		8	9	10	11[2]	12	13				7[1]	3											20
1	2		6	5	4		8	9	10	12	13					7[2]	3				11[1]							21
1	2		6	5	4		8		10	12	13			9[1]		7	3				11[2]							22
1	2			5	4		8			12	13	10[2]		9		7[1]	3	6			11							23
1	2		6	5	4		8[3]		10	12	13			9[2]		7[1]	3			14	11							24
1			6	5	2	7	8	12	10	11		4		9			3											25
		12	6	5	2		8		10	11[1]		4		9[2]		7	3						1		13			26
1		11	6	5	2		8		10	12	13	4		9[1]		7[2]	3											27
1		11	6	5	2[1]	7	8		10	12		4	14	9[2]			3								13[3]			28
1	2[2]		6	5	4	7	8[1]	11	10	12	13			9[3]			3								14			29
1	2		6	5	4		8	11	10	12				9[3]		7[2]	3[1]								13	14		30
1	2[3]		6	5	4	3	8	11[2]	10	12	13			9[1]		7									14			31
1	2		6	5	4		8[1]	11	10	12				9		7	3											32
1	2		6	5	4	7	8[1]	11	10	12	13			9[2]			3											33
1	2		6	5	4	7	8	11	10					9			3											34
1	2		6	5	4	7	8	11[1]	10	12				9[2]			3[3]								13	14		35
1	2		6	5	4	7	8	11[3]	10	12				9[1]			3[2]								13	14		36
1	2		6	5	4	7	8	11	10	12				9[2]			3[1]								13			37
1	2[1]		6	5	4	7	8[2]	11	10	12				9[3]			3								13	14		38
1	2		6	5	4	7	8	11	10	12				9[1]			3											39
1	2[1]		6	5	4	7[2]	8	11	10	12				9[3]			3								13	14		40
1	2[1]		6	5	4	7	8	11	10[3]	12				9[2]		7	3								13	14		41
1	2		6	5	9	7	8	11	10			4					3											42
1	2[2]		6	5	9	7	8[1]	11	10	12		4					3								13			43
1	2		6	5	9	7	8[1]	11[2]	10[3]	12	13	4					3									14		44
1	2[1]	12	6	5	9	7	8[2]	11	10		13	4					3											45
1	4		6	5	9	7	8	11	10	12	13						3[2]					2[1]						46

Coca-Cola Cup
First Round   WBA   (a) 1-1   (h) 2-4

FA Cup
First Round   Hayes   (h) 1-0
Second Round   Oxford U   (a) 0-2

NORWICH CITY 1995-96 *Back row (left to right):* Ade Akinbiyi, Daryl Sutch, Mike Sheron, Ashley Ward, Rob Newman, Lee Bray, Jon Newsome, Spencer Prior, Andy Johnson, Keith O'Neill, Danny Mills.
Middle row: Tim Sheppard (Physio), Stacey Kreft, Johnny Wright, Shaun Carey, Jeremy Goss, Andrew Brownrigg, Steve Walford (Reserve Team Manager), Paul Franklin (Assistant Manager), John Faulkner (Coach), Carl Bradshaw, Mark Bowen, Robert Ullathorne, Ali Gibb, Justin Harrington, Keith Webb (Youth Team Manager).
Front row: Darren Eadie, Neil Adams, Karl Simpson, John Polston, Bryan Gunn, Martin O'Neill (Manager), Andy Marshall, Ian Crook, Mike Milligan, Jamie Cureton, Jamie Mitchell.

Division 1 NORWICH CITY

Carrow Road, Norwich NR1 1JE. Telephone: (01603) 760760. Fax: (01603) 665510. Box Office: (01603) 761661. Canary Call: 0891 424212.

Ground capacity: 21,994.

Record attendance: 43,984 v Leicester C, FA Cup 6th rd, 30 March 1963.

Record receipts: £261,918 v Internazionale, UEFA Cup 3rd rd 1st leg, 24 November 1993.

Pitch measurements: 114yd × 74yd.

President: G. C. Watling.

Chairman: Robert T. Chase JP. *Company Secretary:* T. Nicholls.

Directors: B. W. Lockwood, G. A. Paterson.

Manager: Mike Walker.

Youth Team Coach: Steve Walford.

Commercial Manager: Ray Cossey.

Physio: Tim Sheppard MCSP, SRP.

Secretary: A. R. W. Neville.

Year Formed: 1902. *Turned Professional:* 1905. *Ltd Co.:* 1905.

Club Nickname: 'The Canaries'.

Previous Grounds: 1902, Newmarket Road; 1908–35, The Nest, Rosary Road.

Foundation: Formed in 1902, largely through the initiative of two local schoolmasters who called a meeting at the Criterion Cafe, they were shocked by an FA Commission which in 1904 declared the club professional and ejected them from the FA Amateur Cup. However, this only served to strengthen their determination. New officials were appointed and a professional club established at a meeting in the Agricultural Hall in March 1905.

First Football League game: 28 August 1920, Division 3, v Plymouth Arg (a) D 1-1 – Skermer; Gray, Gadsden; Wilkinson, Addy, Martin; Laxton, Kidger, Parker, Whitham (1), Dobson.

Record League Victory: 10–2 v Coventry C, Division 3 (S), 15 March 1930 – Jarvie; Hannah, Graham; Brown, O'Brien, Lochhead (1); Porter (1), Anderson, Hunt (5), Scott (2), Slicer (1).

Record Cup Victory: 8–0 v Sutton U, FA Cup 4th rd, 28 January 1989 – Gunn; Culverhouse, Bowen, Butterworth, Linighan, Townsend (Crook), Gordon, Fleck (3), Allen (4), Phelan, Putney (1).

Record Defeat: 2–10 v Swindon T, Southern League, 5 September 1908.

Most League Points (2 for a win): 64, Division 3 (S), 1950–51.

Most League Points (3 for a win): 84, Division 2, 1985–86.

Most League Goals: 99, Division 3 (S), 1952–53.

Highest League Scorer in Season: Ralph Hunt, 31. Division 3 (S), 1955–56.

Most League Goals in Total Aggregate: Johnny Gavin, 122, 1945–54, 1955–58.

Most Capped Player: Mark Bowen, 35 (37), Wales.

Most League Appearances: Ron Ashman, 592, 1947–64.

Record Transfer Fee Received: £5,000,000 from Blackburn R for Chris Sutton, July 1994.

Record Transfer Fee Paid: £1,000,000 to Leeds U for Jon Newsome, June 1994.

Football League Record: 1920 Original Member of Division 3; 1921 Division 3 (S): 1934–39 Division 2; 1946–58 Division 3 (S); 1958–60 Division 3; 1960–72 Division 2; 1972–74 Division 1; 1974–75 Division 2; 1975–81 Division 1; 1981–82 Division 2; 1982–85 Division 1; 1985–86 Division 2; 1986–92 Division 1; 1992–95 FA Premier League; 1995– Division 1.

Honours: FA Premier League: best season: 3rd 1992–93. *Football League:* Division 2 – Champions 1971–72, 1985–86. Division 3 (S) – Champions 1933–34; Division 3 – Runners-up 1959–60. *FA Cup:* Semi-finals 1959, 1989, 1992. *Football League Cup:* Winners 1962, 1985; Runners-up 1973, 1975. **European Competitions:** *UEFA Cup:* 1993–94.

Colours: Yellow shirts, green shorts, yellow stockings. *Change colours:* All blue.

Did you know?
When Norwich City won the Division Three (South) title in 1933–34, they were captained by left-back Stan Ramsey.

NORWICH CITY FC

NORWICH CITY 1995–96 LEAGUE RECORD

Match No.	Date	Venue	Opponents	Result		H/T Score	Lg. Pos.	Goalscorers	Attendance
1	Aug 13	A	Luton T	W	3-1	1-0	—	Newsome 2, Adams	7848
2	19	H	Sunderland	D	0-0	0-0	5		16,739
3	26	A	Birmingham C	L	1-3	0-1	13	Sheron	19,267
4	30	H	Oldham Ath	W	2-1	0-0	—	Bowen, Johnson	14,816
5	Sept 2	H	Port Vale	W	2-1	2-1	5	Johnson, Fleck	13,908
6	9	A	Sheffield U	L	1-2	1-1	8	Ward	11,205
7	13	A	Wolverhampton W	W	2-0	0-0	—	Johnson, Ward	27,064
8	16	H	Millwall	D	0-0	0-0	5		15,962
9	23	A	Grimsby T	D	2-2	1-2	5	Fleck, Akinbiyi	5901
10	30	H	Leicester C	L	0-1	0-0	9		18,435
11	Oct 7	A	Stoke C	D	1-1	1-0	11	Akinbiyi	12,016
12	14	H	Barnsley	W	3-1	0-1	6	Newsome, Johnson, Fleck	14,002
13	21	A	Charlton Ath	D	1-1	0-0	8	Bowen	13,369
14	29	H	Tranmere R	D	1-1	1-0	7	Johnson	15,513
15	Nov 4	A	Huddersfield T	L	2-3	0-1	10	Ward 2	13,747
16	11	H	Crystal Palace	W	1-0	1-0	6	Johnson	14,156
17	19	H	Ipswich T	W	2-1	1-0	6	Newsome, Fleck	17,862
18	21	A	WBA	W	4-1	1-1	—	Fleck, Scott, Adams, Ward	13,680
19	26	A	Watford	W	2-0	1-0	2	Ward, Scott	7798
20	Dec 2	H	Stoke C	L	0-1	0-0	4		15,707
21	9	H	Grimsby T	D	2-2	1-1	3	Ward, Eadie	13,283
22	17	A	Leicester C	L	2-3	2-1	7	Eadie, Fleck	14,251
23	23	A	Portsmouth	L	0-1	0-0	9		9960
24	26	H	Southend U	L	0-1	0-0	11		17,029
25	30	H	Reading	D	3-3	1-1	10	Johnson, Ward, Fleck	13,556
26	Jan 1	A	Derby Co	L	1-2	0-1	11	Fleck	16,714
27	14	A	Sunderland	W	1-0	1-0	6	Ward	14,983
28	20	H	Luton T	L	0-1	0-1	9		12,474
29	Feb 4	H	Birmingham C	D	1-1	0-0	10	Ward	12,612
30	10	A	Oldham Ath	L	0-2	0-1	12		5604
31	17	H	Wolverhampton W	L	2-3	2-2	12	Crook, Eadie	14,691
32	24	A	Millwall	L	1-2	0-0	14	Milligan	8218
33	28	H	Sheffield U	D	0-0	0-0	—		10,945
34	Mar 2	A	Southend U	D	1-1	0-1	13	Bradshaw	6208
35	9	H	Portsmouth	D	1-1	1-1	14	Milligan	13,004
36	16	A	Reading	W	3-0	1-0	13	Prior, Eadie, O'Neill	8501
37	20	A	Port Vale	L	0-1	0-1	—		6085
38	23	H	Derby Co	W	1-0	0-0	11	Goss	15,341
39	30	H	Charlton Ath	L	0-1	0-0	14		13,434
40	Apr 2	A	Barnsley	D	2-2	1-1	—	Fleck, Newman	6375
41	6	A	Tranmere R	D	1-1	1-0	16	Eadie	6613
42	8	H	Huddersfield T	W	2-0	0-0	14	Fleck, Akinbiyi	13,021
43	14	A	Ipswich T	L	1-2	0-1	15	Cureton	20,355
44	20	H	WBA	D	2-2	0-1	16	Cureton, Eadie	14,667
45	27	H	Watford	L	1-2	0-1	17	Crook	14,188
46	May 5	A	Crystal Palace	W	1-0	1-0	16	Hopkin (og)	19,354

Final League Position: 16

GOALSCORERS

League (59): Fleck 10, Ward 10, Johnson 7, Eadie 6, Newsome 4, Akinbiyi 3, Adams 2, Bowen 2, Crook 2, Cureton 2, Milligan 2, Scott 2, Bradshaw 1, Goss 1, Newman 1, O'Neill 1, Prior 1, Sheron 1, own goal 1.
Coca-Cola Cup (16): Ward 3, Akinbiyi 2, Fleck 2, Sheron 2, Crook 1, Eadie 1, Johnson 1, Mills 1, Molby 1, Ullathorne 1, own goal 1.
FA Cup (1): Newsome 1.

Gunn B 43	Mills D 8+6	Bowen M 30+1	Milligan M 21+7	Newsome J 26+1	Prior S 42+2	Adams N 40+2	Akinbiyi A 13+9	Ward A 28	Johnson A 23+3	Eadie D 29+2	Sutch D 7+6	Polston J 27+3	Sheron M 2+5	Newman R 15+8	Rush M —+1	Cureton J 4+8	Ullathorne R 26+3	Fleck R 37+4	Crook I 27+1	Marshall A 3	O'Neill K 12+7	Simpson J 1	Bradshaw C 18+3	Scott K 5+7	Carey S 6+3	Goss J 9+7	Molby J 3	Wright J 1	Match No.
1	2	3	4^{3}	5	6	7	8	9	10^{1}	11^{2}	12	13		14															1
1	2	3	4	6	5	7	8		10^{2}	11			9^{1}	12	13														2
1	2	3	4^{1}	5	6	7	9		10^{2}	11	12			8			13												3
1		3		4		7		9	10	11		2	5	12			6	8^{1}											4
1		3	13	5		7		9	10^{1}	11		2	6^{2}	12			4	8											5
1	2	3	12	5	6	7	13	9	10^{2}	11				14				8^{3}	4^{1}										6
1	2	3	12	5	6	7		9	10	11								8	4^{1}										7
1	2	3	12	5	6	7	13	9^{2}	10	11								8	4^{1}										8
		3		5	6	7^{2}		9	10	11		2^{1}		13	14		12	8^{3}	4	1									9
		3		5	6	7^{2}		9	10	11					12		2	8^{1}	4	1			13						10
1		3	12	5	6		7^{1}	9	10				13	14			2	8^{3}	4		11^{2}								11
1		3	12	5	6			9	10								2	8	4		11		7^{1}						12
1		3	7	5	6			9	10								2	8	4		11								13
1		3^{1}	12	5	6		14	9	10	7		13					2	8^{2}	4^{1}		11								14
1	7			5	6		8^{1}	9	10	11		3		2	12				4										15
1	7			5	6	12	13	9	10^{2}	11							3	8	4^{1}				2						16
1	7	10^{1}	4	5	6	12		9				13					3	8			11		2^{2}						17
1	7^{2}			5	6	12	11	9				2	4				3	8^{1}						10	13				18
1	7			5	6		11^{2}	9		12		2^{3}	4				3	8^{1}	13					14	10				19
1	7		4	5	6	12		9		11		2^{1}					3	8						10					20
1	7		4	5	6			9		11		2					3	8^{1}						12	10				21
1	7	4		5	6	12		9		11^{1}		2					3	8^{2}						13	10				22
1		3		5	6	7		9	10^{1}		12	2					11	8^{2}					13	4					23
1	2	4^{3}		5	6	7		9	10			12					3	8^{2}			11^{1}		13	14					24
1	2			5	6	7		9	10^{2}				12				3	8			11				13	4^{1}			25
1		3	12		6^{2}	7		9				2	5	13		10	14		11^{1}					4^{3}	8				26
1		3			6	7		9	10				5				12	8^{2}			11^{1}		2	13			4		27
1		3^{1}			6	7		9	10^{3}				5	12				8			11		2^{2}	13		14		4	28
1		3^{1}			6	7	11^{2}	9	10^{3}				5	12				8	4				2	13		14			29
	12				6	7	11^{2}	9	10				5	3	13			8^{3}	4^{1}	1			2			14			30
1		3			6	7		9	10	11			5				12	8^{1}	4^{2}				2	13					31
1		3	10		6	7^{2}	12	9^{1}		11			5				2		4^{2}		8					13			32
1			10		6	7^{2}	9^{1}		8	11			5				2		12		4		13	3					33
1			12		6	7		9		11			5				2		4				3	10^{1}	8				34
1			10	5	6	7		9		11			3				12		4		2				8^{1}				35
1	12		10		6	7				11^{2}			5				3	8	4^{1}		13		2		9				36
1	12		10		6	7		13					5				3	8^{3}	4^{2}		11		2		9^{1}	14			37
1	12		10		6	7	13						5				11^{2}	8^{3}	4^{1}		14		2		9				38
1	12	10			6	7						13	5				3	11^{1}	8	4			2		9^{2}				39
1	12		10		6	7				11^{1}			5				4	13	8^{2}				2		9^{3}				40
1		10			6	7^{2}				11			5				3	8	4		12		2	9^{1}		13			41
1	12		10			7		9^{2}				11^{1}	14	5		6	13	3	8	4^{3}			2						42
1		10^{2}	12	7			9^{3}		13	11		5^{1}		6		14	3	8	4				2						43
1		10^{1}	2	7			12			11		5^{2}		6		14	3	8	4				13	9^{3}					44
1		10	2	7								5		6	9^{1}		3	8	4^{3}		13		12		14	11^{2}			45
	4	10		6	7							12	5			9	3	8		1			11			2		2^{1}	46

Coca-Cola Cup

Second Round	Torquay U	(h)	6-1
		(a)	3-2
Third Round	Bradford C	(h)	0-0
		(a)	5-3
Fourth Round	Bolton W	(h)	0-0
		(a)	0-0
Fifth Round	Birmingham C	(h)	1-1
		(a)	1-2

FA Cup

Third Round	Brentford	(h)	1-2

NOTTINGHAM FOREST 1995–96   *Back row (left to right):* Scot Gemmill, Paul McGregor, Lars Bohinen, Alf Haaland, Chris Bart-Williams, Kingsley Black, Neil Webb.
Middle row: Richard Money (Reserve Coach), Liam O'Kane (Coach), Andrea Silenzi, Jason Lee, Carl Tiler, Mark Crossley, Tommy Wright, Robert Rosario, Stephen Chettle, Kevin Campbell, John Haseldon (Physio), Peter Edwards (Fitness Consultant).
Front row: Des Lyttle, Stephen Stone, Bryan Roy, Frank Clark (Manager), Stuart Pearce, Alan Hill (Assistant Manager), Ian Woan, David Phillips, Colin Cooper.

FA Premiership NOTTINGHAM FOREST

City Ground, Nottingham NG2 5FJ. Telephone: (0115) 9526000. Fax: (0115) 9526003. Information Desk: (0115) 9526016. Commercial Office: (0115) 9526006. Commercial Office Fax: (0115) 9526007. Ticket Office: (0115) 9526002. Souvenir Shop: (0115) 9526026. Junior Reds: (0115) 9526001. Lottery Office: (0115) 9526005. Clubcall: 0891 121174.

Ground capacity: 30,602.

Record attendance: 49,946 v Manchester U, Division 1, 28 October 1967.

Record receipts: £272,735 v Sheffield W, FA Cup 3rd rd replay, 19 January 1994.

Pitch measurements: 116yd × 77yd.

Chairman: Fred Reacher. *Vice-Chairman:* I. I. Korn.

Directors: G. E. Macpherson, R. W. Dove, C. Wootton, K. Gibson, R. A. Fairhall.

Manager: Frank Clark. *Assistant Manager:* Alan Hill.

Secretary: Paul White. *Commercial Manager:* David Pullan.

Coach: Liam O'Kane. *Physio:* John Haselden.

Year Formed: 1865. *Turned Professional:* 1889. *Ltd Co.:* 1982.

Club Nickname: 'Reds'.

Previous Grounds: 1865, Forest Racecourse; 1879, The Meadows; 1880, Trent Bridge Cricket Ground; 1882, Parkside, Lenton; 1885, Gregory, Lenton; 1890, Town Ground; 1898, City Ground.

Foundation: One of the oldest football clubs in the world, Nottingham Forest was formed at a meeting in the Clinton Arms in 1865. Known originally as the Forest Football Club, the game which first drew the founders together was "shinney" a form of hockey. When they determined to change to football in 1865, one of their first moves was to buy a set of red caps to wear on the field.

First Football League game: 3 September 1892, Division 1, v Everton (a) D 2-2 – Brown; Earp, Scott; Hamilton, A. Smith, McCracken; McCallum, W. Smith, Higgins (2), Pike, McInnes.

Record League Victory: 12–0 v Leicester Fosse, Division 1, 12 April 1909 – Iremonger; Dudley, Maltby; Hughes (1), Needham, Armstrong; Hooper (3), Marrison, West (3), Morris (2), Spouncer (3 incl. 1p).

Record Cup Victory: 14–0 v Clapton (away), FA Cup 1st rd, 17 January 1891 – Brown; Earp, Scott; A. Smith, Russell, Jeacock; McCallum (2), 'Tich' Smith (1), Higgins (5), Lindley (4), Shaw (2).

Record Defeat: 1–9 v Blackburn R, Division 2, 10 April 1937.

Most League Points (2 for a win): 70, Division 3 (S), 1950–51.

Most League Points (3 for a win): 83, Division 1, 1993–94.

Most League Goals: 110, Division 3 (S), 1950–51.

Highest League Scorer in Season: Wally Ardron, 36, Division 3 (S), 1950–51.

Most League Goals in Total Aggregate: Grenville Morris, 199, 1898–1913.

Most Capped Player: Stuart Pearce, 70, England.

Most League Appearances: Bob McKinlay, 614, 1951–70.

Record Transfer Fee Received: £8,500,000 from Liverpool for Stan Collymore, June 1995.

Record Transfer Fee Paid: £2,900,000 to Foggia for Bryan Roy, August 1994.

Football League Record: 1892 Elected to Division 1; 1906–07 Division 2; 1907–11 Division 1; 1911–22 Division 2; 1922–25 Division 1; 1925–49 Division 2; 1949–51 Division 3 (S); 1951–57 Division 2; 1957–72 Division 1; 1972–77 Division 2; 1977–92 Division 1; 1992–93 FA Premier League; 1993–94 Division 1; 1994– FA Premier League.

Honours: Football League: Division 1 – Champions 1977–78; Runners-up 1966–67, 1978–79; Division 2 – Champions 1906–07, 1921–22; Runners-up 1956–57; Division 3 (S) – Champions 1950–51. *FA Cup:* Winners 1898, 1959; Runners-up 1991. *Anglo-Scottish Cup:* Winners 1977; *Football League Cup:* Winners 1978, 1979, 1989, 1990; Runners-up 1980, 1992. *Simod Cup:* Winners 1989. *Zenith Data Systems Cup:* Winners: 1992. *European Competitions: Fairs Cup:* 1961–62, 1967–68. *European Cup:* 1978–79 (winners), 1979–80 (winners), 1980–81. *Super Cup:* 1979–80 (winners), 1980–81 (runners-up). *World Club Championship:* 1980. *UEFA Cup:* 1983–84, 1984–85, 1995–96.

Colours: Red shirts with black shoulders, white shorts, red stockings. *Change colours:* Yellow and navy.

Did you know?
On 21 October 1995, Nottingham Forest beat Bolton Wanderers 3-2 to establish a new Premier League record of 23 unbeaten matches subsequently extended to 25.

NOTTINGHAM FOREST 1995–96 LEAGUE RECORD

Match No.	Date	Venue	Opponents	Result	H/T Score	Lg. Pos.	Goalscorers	Attendance
1	Aug 19	A	Southampton	W 4-3	3-1	—	Cooper, Woan, Roy 2	15,164
2	23	H	Chelsea	D 0-0	0-0	—		27,007
3	26	H	West Ham U	D 1-1	1-1	8	Pearce (pen)	26,645
4	29	A	Arsenal	D 1-1	0-1	—	Campbell	38,248
5	Sept 9	A	Coventry C	D 1-1	1-1	8	Roy	17,238
6	17	H	Everton	W 3-2	2-0	6	Watson (og), Lee, Woan	24,786
7	23	A	Aston Villa	D 1-1	0-0	8	Lyttle	33,972
8	30	H	Manchester C	W 3-0	1-0	8	Lee 2, Stone	25,620
9	Oct 14	A	Tottenham H	W 1-0	0-0	6	Stone	32,876
10	21	H	Bolton W	W 3-2	1-1	6	Roy, Lee, Cooper	25,426
11	28	A	QPR	D 1-1	0-0	5	Lee	17,549
12	Nov 6	H	Wimbledon	W 4-1	2-1	—	Roy, Pearce, Lee, Gemmill	20,810
13	18	A	Blackburn R	L 0-7	0-2	6		27,660
14	27	H	Manchester U	D 1-1	1-0	—	McGregor	29,263
15	Dec 2	A	Bolton W	D 1-1	0-0	7	Cooper	17,342
16	10	H	Aston Villa	D 1-1	0-0	8	Stone	25,790
17	18	A	Manchester C	D 1-1	1-0	—	Campbell	24,287
18	23	A	Newcastle U	L 1-3	1-2	8	Woan	36,531
19	26	H	Sheffield W	W 1-0	1-0	8	Lee	27,810
20	30	H	Middlesbrough	W 1-0	1-0	6	Pearce (pen)	27,027
21	Jan 1	A	Liverpool	L 2-4	2-2	7	Stone, Woan	39,206
22	13	H	Southampton	W 1-0	1-0	6	Cooper	23,321
23	20	A	Chelsea	L 0-1	0-0	8		24,482
24	31	H	Leeds U	W 2-1	1-0	—	Campbell, Roy (pen)	24,465
25	Feb 3	A	West Ham U	L 0-1	0-1	7		21,651
26	10	H	Arsenal	L 0-1	0-0	9		27,222
27	24	A	Everton	L 0-3	0-0	10		33,163
28	Mar 2	A	Sheffield W	W 3-1	1-0	9	Howe, McGregor, Roy	21,930
29	16	A	Middlesbrough	D 1-1	0-0	10	Allen	29,392
30	23	H	Liverpool	W 1-0	1-0	9	Stone	29,058
31	30	A	Wimbledon	L 0-1	0-0	9		9807
32	Apr 6	H	Tottenham H	W 2-1	1-0	8	Stone, Woan	27,053
33	8	A	Leeds U	W 3-1	2-1	8	Cooper, Lee, Woan	29,220
34	13	H	Blackburn R	L 1-5	1-3	9	Woan	25,273
35	17	H	Coventry C	D 0-0	0-0	—		24,629
36	28	A	Manchester U	L 0-5	0-2	9		53,926
37	May 2	H	Newcastle U	D 1-1	0-1	—	Woan	28,280
38	5	H	QPR	W 3-0	1-0	9	Stone, Roy, Howe	22,910

Final League Position: 9

GOALSCORERS

League (50): Lee 8, Roy 8 (1 pen), Woan 8, Stone 7, Cooper 5, Campbell 3, Pearce 3 (2 pens), Howe 2, McGregor 2, Allen 1, Gemmill 1, Lyttle 1, own goal 1.
Coca-Cola Cup (4): Bohinen 2, Pearce 1, Silenzi 1.
FA Cup (10): Campbell 3, Woan 3 (1 pen), Pearce 2 (1 pen), Roy 1, Silenzi 1.

Crossley M 38	Lyttle D 32 + 1	Pearce S 31	Cooper C 37	Chettle S 37	Stone S 34	Phillips D 14 + 4	Roy B 25 + 3	Bohinen L 7	Campbell K 21	Woan I 33	Lee J 21 + 7	Gemmill S 26 + 5	Silenzi A 3 + 7	Bart-Williams C 33	Haaland A 12 + 5	McGregor P 7 + 7	Howe S 4 + 5	Irving R — + 1	Black K 1 + 1	Allen C 1 + 2	Guinan S 1 + 1	Match No.
1	2	3	4	5	6	7	8[2]	9	10[1]	11	12	13										1
1	2	3	4	5	6	7	8	9	10[1]	11	12											2
1	2	3	4	5	6	7	8[1]	9[2]	10	11	12	13										3
1	2	3	4	5	6	7	8[1]		10	11	12	9										4
1	2	3	4	5	6	7	8	9[1]	10[2]	11		12	13									5
1	2		4	5	6	3	8[1]	9		11	10	12		7								6
1	2		4	5	6		8	9		11	10			7		3						7
1	2	3	4	5	6		8[2]	9[1]		11	10	12	13	7								8
1	2	3	4	5	6			9[1]		11	10	8		7		12						9
1	2	3	4	5	6			9		11	10	8		7								10
1	2	3	4	5	6			9		11	10	8		7								11
1	2	3	4	5	6			9		11	10[1]	8	12	7								12
1	2	3	4[1]	5	6	12				11	10[2]	8	13	7	9							13
1	2	3	4	5	6					11		8		7	12	10[1]	9[2]	13				14
1	2[1]	3	4		6					11		8	9	7	5	10	12					15
1	2	3	4	5	6				10			8	12	7		11	9[1]					16
1		3	4	5	6	2		9[1]		11	10	8	12	7								17
1	2	3	4	5	6	7[1]		9		11	10	8			12							18
1	2	3	4	5	6	12		9[1]		11	10	8		7								19
1	2	3	4	5	6	12		9		11	10[1]	8		7								20
1	2	3	4	5	6	12		9		11				7	8	10[1]						21
1	2	3	4	5	6	10		9[1]		11		8	12	7								22
1	2	3	4	5	6	10		9		11		8[1]	12	7								23
1	2		4	5		3			10	11	7	8	9[2]	6[1]	12	13						24
1	2		4	5		3			10	11	7	8[1]	9	6	12							25
1	2		4	5	6	3			10	9		8[2]	12	7	13				11[1]			26
1	2		4	5	6	3		9	10	11[1]		8		7	12							27
1	2			5		3		9	10			8	6	4	7[2]	11[1]	12	13				28
1	2	3	4	5		7		9				8[1]		6	10	12	11					29
1	2	3	4	5	6	12			10[2]	11	9	8[1]		7		13						30
1	2	3	4	5	6				10		9	8		7	12					11[1]		31
1	2	3	4	5	6		8[1]			11	9			7	12	10[2]				13		32
1		3	4	5	6			9[1]		11	10	8		7	2	12						33
1	2[1]	3	4	5	6		8			11	9			7	10	12						34
1		3	4	5	6	12		9[2]		11	10	8[1]		7	2	13						35
1		3	4	5	6				10	11	9	8		7	2							36
1		3	4	5	6				10[2]	11	9	8[1]		7	2	12				13		37
1	12	3	4	5	6[2]	13		8		11			14	7	2[1]	10[3]	9					38

Coca-Cola Cup

Second Round	Bradford C	(a)	2-3
		(h)	2-2

FA Cup

Third Round	Stoke C	(a)	1-1
		(h)	2-0
Fourth Round	Oxford U	(h)	1-1
		(a)	3-0
Fifth Round	Tottenham H	(h)	2-2
		(a)	1-1
Sixth Round	Aston Villa	(h)	0-1

NOTTS COUNTY 1995-96   *Back row (left to right):* Colin Hoyle, Gary Strodder, Graham Hogg, Darren Ward, Tony Agana, Paul Reece, Devon White, Matthew Redmile, Michael Forsyth.
Middle row: John Gaunt (Youth Manager), Chris Marsden, James Hunt, Michael Johnson, Chris Short, Gary Mills, Nigel Jemson, Gary Lund, Shaun Murphy, Richard Walker, Michael Emenalo, Dennis Pettitt (Physio).
Front row: Michael Simpson, Paul Devlin, Mick Galloway, Gary McSwegan, Phil Turner, Colin Murphy (General Manager), Derek Pavis (Chairman), Steve Thompson (Manager), Ian Ridgway, Tommy Gallagher, Peter Butler, Andy Legg, Chris Pearson.
(Photograph: Empics)

Division 2 NOTTS COUNTY

County Ground, Meadow Lane, Nottingham NG2 3HJ. Telephone: (0115) 9529000. Fax: (0115) 9553994. Ticket Office: (0115) 9557210. Clubline: 0891 888684. Football in the Community: (0115) 955 7215. Supporters Club: (0115) 9557255.

Ground capacity: 20,300.

Record attendance: 47,310 v York C, FA Cup 6th rd, 12 March 1955.

Record receipts: £124,539.10 v Manchester C, FA Cup 6th rd, 16 February 1991.

Pitch measurements: 114yd × 74yd.

Chairman: D. C. Pavis. *Vice-Chairman:* J. Mounteney.

Directors: D. Ward, F. Sherwood (President), Mrs V. Pavis, M. Youdell, W. Barrowcliffe.

General Manager: Colin Murphy. *Team Manager:* Steve Thompson.

Advertising & Sponsorship Executive: Miss F. Ball. *Sales & Marketing Executive:* John Hackett. *Conference & Banqueting Executive:* Miss S. Wright.

Secretary: Ian Moat. *Coaches:* Mark Smith, John Gaunt.

Physio: Dennis Pettitt. *Stadium Manager:* Bob Davy.

Year Formed: 1862 *(see Foundation).*

Turned Professional: 1885. *Ltd Co.:* 1888.

Club Nickname: 'Magpies'.

Previous Grounds: 1862, The Park; 1864, The Meadows; 1877, Beeston Cricket Ground; 1880, Castle Ground; 1883, Trent Bridge; 1910, Meadow Lane.

Foundation: For many years the foundation date of the Football League's oldest club was given as 1862 and the club celebrated its centenary in 1962. However, the researches of Keith Warsop have since shown that the club was on a very haphazard basis at that time, playing little more than practice matches. The meeting which put it on a firm footing was held at the George IV Hotel in December 1864, when they became known as the Notts Football Club.

First Football League game: 15 September 1888, Football League, v Everton (a) L 1-2 – Holland; Guttridge, McLean; Brown, Warburton, Shelton; Hodder, Harker, Jardine, Moore (1), Wardle.

Record League Victory: 11–1 v Newport Co, Division 3 (S), 15 January 1949 – Smith; Southwell, Purvis; Gannon, Baxter, Adamson; Houghton (1), Sewell (4), Lawton (4), Pimbley, Johnston (2).

Record Cup Victory: 15–0 v Rotherham T (at Trent Bridge), FA Cup 1st rd, 24 October 1885 – Sherwin; Snook, H. T. Moore; Dobson (1), Emmett (1), Chapman; Gunn (1), Albert Moore (2), Jackson (3), Daft (2), Cursham (4). (1 og).

Record Defeat: 1–9 v Blackburn R, Division 1, 16 November 1889 and v Aston Villa, Division 1, 29 September 1888 and v Portsmouth, Division 2, 9 April 1927.

Most League Points (2 for a win): 69, Division 4, 1970–71.

Most League Points (3 for a win): 87, Division 3, 1989–90.

Most League Goals: 107, Division 4, 1959–60.

Highest League Scorer in Season: Tom Keetley, 39, Division 3 (S), 1930–31.

Most League Goals in Total Aggregate: Les Bradd, 124, 1967–78.

Most Capped Player: Kevin Wilson, 15 (42), Northern Ireland.

Most League Appearances: Albert Iremonger, 564, 1904–26.

Record Transfer Fee Received: £2,500,000 from Derby Co for Craig Short, September 1992.

Record Transfer Fee Paid: £685,000 to Sheffield U for Tony Agana, November 1991.

Football League Record: 1888 Founder Member of the Football League; 1893–97 Division 2; 1897–1913 Division 1; 1913–14 Division 2; 1914–20 Division 1; 1920–23 Division 2; 1923–26 Division 1; 1926–30 Division 2; 1930–31 Division 3 (S); 1931–35 Division 2; 1935–50 Division 3 (S); 1950–58 Division 2; 1958–59 Division 3; 1959–60 Division 4; 1960–64 Division 3; 1964–71 Division 4; 1971–73 Division 3; 1973–81 Division 2; 1981–84 Division 1; 1984–85 Division 2; 1985–90 Division 3; 1990–91 Division 2; 1991–95 Division 1; 1995– Division 2.

Honours: Football League: Division 1 best season: 3rd, 1890–91, 1900–01; Division 2 – Champions 1896–97, 1913–14, 1922–23; Runners-up 1894–95, 1980–81; Division 3 (S) – Champions 1930–31, 1949–50; Runners-up 1936–37; Division 3 – Runners-up 1972-73; Division 4 – Champions 1970–71; Runners-up 1959–60. *FA Cup:* Winners 1894; Runners-up 1891. *Football League Cup:* best season: 5th rd, 1964, 1973, 1976. *Anglo-Italian Cup:* Winners 1995; Runners-up 1994.

Colours: Black and white striped shirts, white shorts, black stockings. *Change colours:* Tartan shirts, black shorts, tartan stockings.

Did you know?
Paddy Mills scored five goals for Notts County in a 9-0 win over Barnsley on 19 November 1927.

NOTTS COUNTY 1995–96 LEAGUE RECORD

Match No.	Date	Venue	Opponents	Result	H/T Score	Lg. Pos.	Goalscorers	Attendance
1	Aug 12	A	Wrexham	D 1-1	1-0	—	Turner	4281
2	19	H	Wycombe W	W 2-0	0-0	5	Legg, White	5552
3	26	A	Peterborough U	W 1-0	1-0	4	White	5618
4	29	H	Bradford C	L 0-2	0-1	—		6168
5	Sept 2	A	Brighton & HA	L 0-1	0-0	12		5267
6	9	H	Bournemouth	W 2-0	0-0	8	White 2 (1 pen)	4875
7	12	H	Stockport Co	W 1-0	0-0	—	Devlin	4588
8	16	A	Shrewsbury T	W 1-0	0-0	5	White	2892
9	23	H	Bristol C	D 2-2	0-0	4	Legg, White	5251
10	30	A	Crewe Alex	D 2-2	0-0	6	Agana, White	4260
11	Oct 7	A	Carlisle U	D 0-0	0-0	5		6058
12	14	H	Rotherham U	W 2-1	1-1	4	Devlin, Gallagher	5478
13	21	A	Bristol R	W 3-0	1-0	2	Nicol, Arkins, Legg	6078
14	28	H	Swindon T	L 1-3	1-2	3	Legg	8725
15	Nov 1	H	Brentford	W 4-0	1-0	—	Devlin, Arkins 2, Murphy	4005
16	4	A	Burnley	W 4-3	2-1	3	Arkins, Devlin 2 (1 pen), Baraclough	10,511
17	18	H	Chesterfield	W 4-1	2-1	3	Gallagher, Strodder, Nicol, Arkins	6747
18	25	A	Swansea C	D 0-0	0-0	2		2327
19	Dec 9	A	Bristol C	W 2-0	1-0	2	Strodder, White	5617
20	16	H	Crewe Alex	L 0-1	0-1	3		5869
21	23	H	Blackpool	D 1-1	0-0	3	Arkins	5522
22	Jan 13	A	Wycombe W	D 1-1	0-0	4	Rogers	4980
23	20	H	Wrexham	W 1-0	0-0	4	Arkins	5014
24	Feb 3	H	Peterborough U	W 1-0	0-0	3	Battersby	5067
25	10	A	Walsall	D 0-0	0-0	4		4378
26	17	A	Stockport Co	L 0-2	0-0	4		6179
27	24	H	Shrewsbury T	D 1-1	1-1	5	Rogers	4559
28	27	A	Bournemouth	W 2-0	1-0	—	Devlin, Hunt	3191
29	Mar 2	H	Hull C	W 1-0	0-0	4	Battersby	4528
30	6	H	Walsall	W 2-1	1-1	—	Battersby, Jones	4050
31	9	A	Blackpool	L 0-1	0-1	4		7187
32	12	H	York C	D 2-2	2-2	—	Jones, Battersby	3462
33	16	H	Oxford U	D 1-1	0-1	4	Martindale	5140
34	19	A	Bradford C	L 0-1	0-1	—		3622
35	23	A	York C	W 3-1	1-1	5	Martindale 2, Jones	3126
36	26	A	Hull C	D 0-0	0-0	—		2589
37	30	H	Carlisle U	W 3-1	2-0	4	Jones 2, Martindale	4515
38	Apr 2	A	Rotherham U	L 0-2	0-0	—		3215
39	6	A	Swindon T	L 0-1	0-0	5		10,926
40	9	H	Bristol R	W 4-2	1-0	—	Strodder, Martindale, Baraclough, Finnan	4661
41	13	A	Brentford	D 0-0	0-0	5		4588
42	16	A	Oxford U	D 1-1	0-1	—	Murphy	6934
43	20	H	Burnley	D 1-1	0-1	4	Battersby	5697
44	23	H	Brighton & HA	W 2-1	1-1	—	Battersby 2	3501
45	27	H	Swansea C	W 4-0	0-0	4	Murphy, Agana, Martindale, Finnan	5051
46	May 4	A	Chesterfield	L 0-1	0-0	—		6708

Final League Position: 4

GOALSCORERS
League (63): White 8 (1 pen), Arkins 7, Battersby 7, Devlin 6 (1 pen), Martindale 6, Jones 5, Legg 4, Murphy 3, Strodder 3, Agana 2, Baraclough 2, Finnan 2, Gallagher 2, Nicol 2, Rogers 2, Hunt 1, Turner 1.
Coca-Cola Cup (6): White 6 (1 pen).
FA Cup (4): Legg 2, Gallagher 1, Rogers 1.

Ward D 46	Mills G 11+2	Walker R 11	Turner P 12	Strodder G 43	Hogg G 10	Devlin P 26	Marsden C 3	White D 18+2	Agana T 20+9	Legg A 24+1	McSwegan G —+3	Nicol S 13	Galloway M 7+2	Simpson M 18+5	Jemson N 2+1	Gallagher T 21+1	Murphy S 39	Arkins V 17+6	Short C —+2	Baraclough I 35	Battersby T 14+7	Rogers P 21	Wilder C 9	Richardson I 15	Hunt J 10	Jones G 16+2	Hoyle C 2	Finnan S 14+3	Martindale G 13+3	Derry S 12	Ashcroft L 4+2	Match No.
1	2	3	4	5	6	7	8	9	10[1]	11	12																					1
1	2	3	4	5	6	7	8	9	10[1]	11	12																					2
1	2	3	4	5		7[2]		9	12	11			6	8	13	10[1]																3
1	2	3	4	5		7		9		11	12		6	8		10[1]																4
1	2	3	4	5		7	8	9	10[1]	11			6		12																	5
1		3	4	5		7		9	12	11[1]			6	10			2	8														6
1		3	4	5		7		9	12	11[1]			6[2]		13	10	2	8														7
1		3	4	5		7		9	12	11[1]					8[2]	10	2	6		13												8
1		3		5				9	12	11[1]			4	8[2]		7	2	6	10	13												9
1		3		5				9	11	12			4[1]	8		7	2	6	10[2]	13												10
1		3		5		7		9[1]		11			4	8		10	2	6	12													11
1				5		7		9		11			4	8			2	6	10	3												12
1	12			5		7		9		11			4	8			2[1]	6	10	3												13
1				5		7		9		11			4	8			2	6	10	3												14
1	12			5		7		9[2]	13	11			4[3]	14		8	2[1]	6	10	3												15
1	2			5				9	12	11			4	8		7		6	10	3[1]												16
1	2			5				9		11			4	8		7		6	10	3												17
1	2	4		5				9		11				8		7		6	10	3												18
1	2	4		5				9	12	11[2]				8	13	7[1]		6	10	3												19
1	2	4		5				9	12	11				8		7[1]		6	10	3												20
1	2	4		5	6	7		9		11[1]				8	12				10	3												21
1				5	6		8	9		11							2	4		3	10	7										22
1				5		7[2]		9		11					12		4	13		3	10[1]	8	2	6								23
1					6	7				11					12		4			3	10	8[1]	2	5		9						24
1					6	7				11							4	2		3	10	8		5		9						25
1				5				9		11				6		7	4	10		3	2	8										26
1				5				9		11				6		7	4	10[1]		3	12	8	2									27
1				5				9		11						7	4			3	10	8	2	6								28
1				5						11				12		7[1]	4			3	10	8	2	6		9						29
1				5						11				4			12			3	10[1]	8	6			9	2	7				30
1				5						11				4						3	10	8	6			9	2[1]	12	7			31
1				5			8			11				4						3	10		6			9	7[1]	12	2			32
1				5						11				4						3	10[1]	8	6			9	7	12	2			33
1				5						11				4		2				3	10[1]	8	6			9	12	7				34
1				5						11				4						3		8	11	6		9	7	10	2			35
1			4	5						11										3		8	11	6		9	7	10	2			36
1			4	5										4						3	12	8	6			9	7	10[1]	2	11		37
1				5										4						3		8	6			9	7	10	2	11		38
1				5	6									7		4				3	12	8			13	10[1]	2	11[2]				39
1				5					12					4						3	13	8	2	6		9[2]	7	10	11[1]			40
1				5						11				4						3	12	8	2	6		9[1]	7	10				41
1				5						11				4	12					3[1]	13	8	6			9[2]	7	10	2			42
1				5						11[2]				4						3	12	8	6			9	7	10	2	13		43
1			5							11				12			4			3	10	6[1]	8			9[2]	7	13	2			44
1				5						11				4						3	10[1]	8	6		12	7	9	2				45
1				5						11[1]				4	13					3	10	8	6	12	7	9[3]	2[5]	14				46

Coca-Cola Cup

First Round	Lincoln C	(h)	2-0
		(a)	2-0
Second Round	Leeds U	(a)	0-0
		(h)	2-3

FA Cup

First Round	York C	(a)	1-0
Second Round	Telford U	(a)	2-0
Third Round	Middlesbrough	(h)	1-2

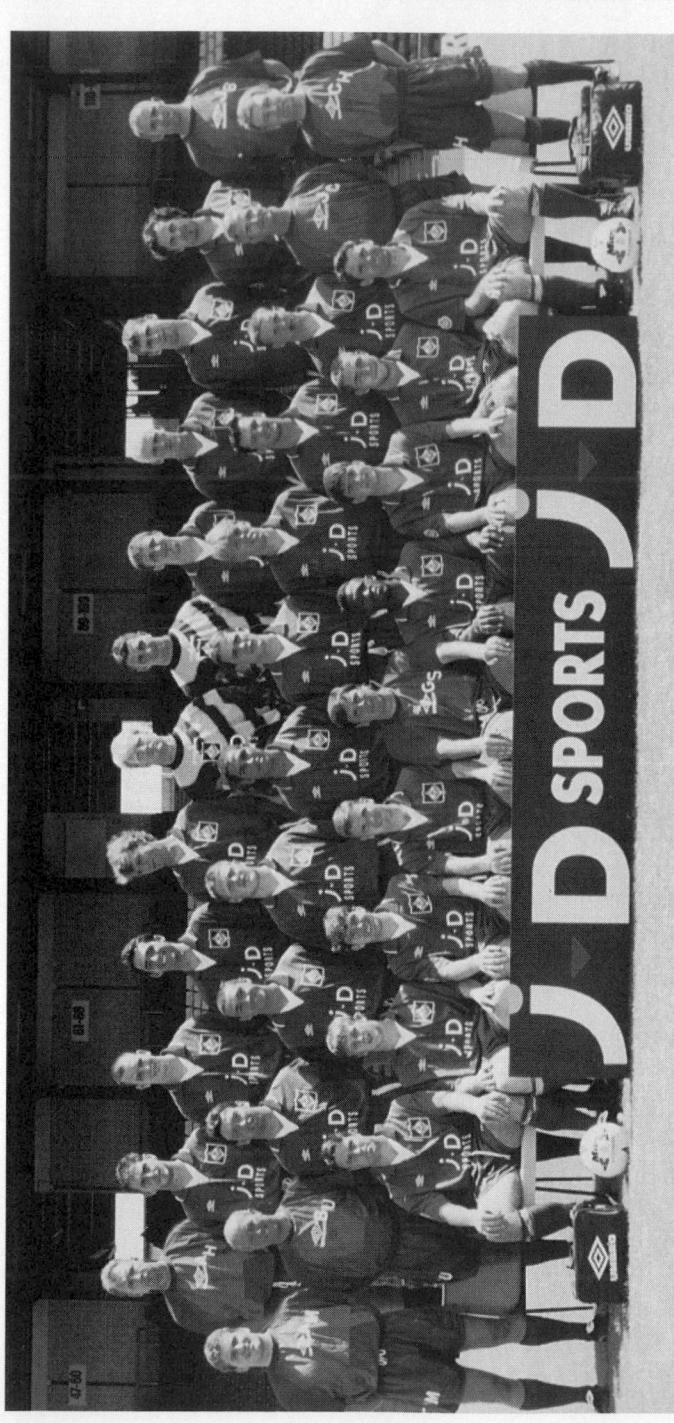

OLDHAM ATHLETIC 1995–96   *Back row (left to right):* Andy Holden (Reserve Team Coach), Steve Redmond, Richard Graham, Craig Fleming, Richard Jobson, Jon Hallworth, Paul Gerrard, Simon Kay, Ian Olney, Ricky Evans, Lee Richardson, John Bowden (Kit Manager).
Middle row: Alexis Moreno (Physio), Billy Urmson (Youth Coach), Rick Holden, Carl Serrant, Darren Lonergan, Martin Pemberton, Paul Bernard, Gunnar Halle, Nicky Banger, David Beresford, Jim Cassell (Chief Scout), Colin Harvey (First Team Coach).
Front row: Sean McCarthy, Paul Rickers, Mark Brennan, Nick Henry, Graeme Sharp (Manager), Darren Beckford, Ian Snodin, Chris Makin, Neil Pointon.

Division 1 　　　　OLDHAM ATHLETIC

Boundary Park, Oldham OL1 2PA. Telephone: (0161) 624 4972. Fax: (0161) 627 5915. Ticket Call: 0891 121582. Commercial Office: (0161) 627 1802 Fax: (0161) 652 6501. Clubcall: 0891 121142.

Ground capacity: 13,700.

Record attendance: 47,671 v Sheffield W, FA Cup 4th rd, 25 January 1930.

Record receipts: £138,680 v Manchester U, FA Premier League, 29 December 1993.

Pitch measurements: 110yd × 74yd.

President: R. Schofield.

Chairman & Chief Executive: I. H. Stott, *Vice-Chairman:* D. A. Brierley.

Directors: G. T. Butterworth, R. Adams, D. R. Taylor, P. Chadwick, J. Slevin, N. Holden.

Manager: Graeme Sharp. *Assistant Manager:* Colin Harvey.

Secretary: Terry Cale. *Commercial Manager:* Alan Hardy. *Public Relations Office:* Gordon A. Lawton *Stadium Manager:* Stuart Oddy.

Coaches: Bill Urmson, Andy Holden. *Physio:* Alex Moreno MCSP SRP.

Year Formed: 1895. *Turned Professional:* 1899. *Ltd Co.:* 1906.

Previous Name: 1895, Pine Villa; 1899, Oldham Athletic.

Club Nickname: 'The Latics'.

Previous Ground: Sheepfoot Lane; 1905, Boundary Park.

Foundation: It was in 1895 that John Garland, the landlord of the Featherstall and Junction Hotel, decided to form a football club. As Pine Villa they played in the Oldham Junior League. In 1899 the local professional club Oldham County, went out of existence and one of the liquidators persuaded Pine Villa to take over their ground at Sheepfoot Lane and change their name to Oldham Athletic.

First Football League game: 9 September 1907, Division 2, v Stoke (a) W 3-1 – Hewitson; Hodson, Hamilton; Fay, Walders, Wilson; Ward, W. Dodds (1), Newton (1), Hancock, Swarbrick (1).

Record League Victory: 11–0 v Southport, Division 4, 26 December 1962 – Hollands; Branagan, Marshall; McCall, Williams, Scott; Ledger (1), Johnstone, Lister (6), Colquhoun (1), Whitaker (3).

Record Cup Victory: 10–1 v Lytham, FA Cup 1st rd, 28 November 1925 – Gray; Wynne, Grundy; Adlam, Heaton, Naylor (1), Douglas, Pynegar (2), Ormston (2), Barnes (3), Watson (2).

Record Defeat: 4–13 v Tranmere R, Division 3 (N), 26 December 1935.

Most League Points (2 for a win): 62, Division 3, 1973–74.

Most League Points (3 for a win): 88, Division 2, 1990–91.

Most League Goals: 95, Division 4, 1962–63.

Highest League Scorer in Season: Tom Davis, 33, Division 3 (N), 1936–37.

Most League Goals in Total Aggregate: Roger Palmer, 141, 1980–94.

Most Capped Player: Gunnar Halle, (51), Norway.

Most League Appearances: Ian Wood, 525, 1966–80.

Record Transfer Fee Received: £1,700,000 from Aston Villa for Earl Barrett, February 1992.

Record Transfer Fee Paid: £750,000 to Aston Villa for Ian Olney, June 1992.

Football League Record: 1907 Elected to Division 2; 1910–23 Division 1; 1923–35 Division 2; 1935–53 Division 3 (N); 1953–54 Division 2; 1954–58 Division 3 (N); 1958–63 Division 4; 1963–69 Division 3; 1969–71 Division 4; 1971–74 Division 2; 1974–91 Division 2; 1991–92 Division 1; 1992–94 FA Premier League; 1994– Division 1.

Honours: Football League: Division 1 – Runners-up 1914–15; Division 2 – Champions 1990–91; Runners-up 1909–10; Division 3 (N) – Champions 1952–53; Division 3 – Champions 1973–74; Division 4 – Runners-up 1962–63. *FA Cup:* Semi-final 1913, 1990. *Football League Cup:* Runners-up 1990.

Colours: Blue and red hooped shirts, white shorts, blue and red hooped stockings. *Change colours:* Green and navy shirts, navy shorts, green stockings.

Did you know?
Jimmy Fay, later to become a key figure in the Players Union, was top scorer for Oldham Athletic in 1909–10 with 26 League goals.

OLDHAM ATHLETIC 1995–96 LEAGUE RECORD

Match No.	Date	Venue	Opponents	Result		H/T Score	Lg. Pos.	Goalscorers	Attendance
1	Aug 12	H	Huddersfield T	W	3-0	1-0	—	Brennan 2, Richardson	10,259
2	19	A	Barnsley	L	1-2	0-1	9	McCarthy	8795
3	26	H	Sheffield U	W	2-1	0-0	5	Banger, McCarthy	6851
4	30	A	Norwich C	L	1-2	0-0	—	Halle	14,816
5	Sept 2	A	Stoke C	W	1-0	0-0	8	Overson (og)	8663
6	9	H	WBA	L	1-2	1-1	9	Bernard	8397
7	12	H	Ipswich T	D	1-1	0-0	—	McCarthy	5622
8	16	A	Charlton Ath	D	1-1	1-0	12	McCarthy	8926
9	23	H	Crystal Palace	W	3-1	0-1	9	McCarthy, Brennan, Banger	6586
10	30	A	Birmingham C	D	0-0	0-0	8		17,269
11	Oct 7	H	Portsmouth	D	1-1	0-0	9	McCarthy	5937
12	14	A	Grimsby T	D	1-1	1-0	10	Richardson	5509
13	21	H	Reading	W	2-1	1-1	7	Richardson, Beresford	5709
14	28	A	Derby Co	L	1-2	0-1	9	McCarthy	11,545
15	Nov 5	H	Port Vale	D	2-2	1-1	9	Wilkinson, Richardson (pen)	5138
16	11	A	Luton T	D	1-1	0-1	11	Halle	6047
17	18	A	Wolverhampton W	W	3-1	0-1	8	Makin, McCarthy, Beresford	23,128
18	21	H	Millwall	D	2-2	1-0	—	McCarthy, Barlow	6161
19	25	H	Southend U	L	0-1	0-0	13		6474
20	Dec 2	A	Portsmouth	L	1-2	1-1	14	Beckford	6002
21	9	A	Crystal Palace	D	2-2	0-2	15	Vonk, Redmond	12,709
22	16	H	Birmingham C	W	4-0	1-0	12	Poole (og), Francis (og), Barlow, Halle	6602
23	23	H	Watford	D	0-0	0-0	12		5878
24	26	A	Tranmere R	L	0-2	0-0	14		9787
25	Jan 13	H	Barnsley	L	0-1	0-0	17		6029
26	20	A	Huddersfield T	D	0-0	0-0	17		13,013
27	Feb 3	A	Sheffield U	L	1-2	1-1	17	Hughes	10,956
28	10	H	Norwich C	W	2-0	1-0	16	Makin, Barlow	5604
29	24	H	Charlton Ath	D	1-1	0-0	18	Richardson (pen)	6570
30	27	A	WBA	L	0-1	0-1	—		10,959
31	Mar 3	H	Tranmere R	L	1-2	0-1	21	Graham	4225
32	9	A	Watford	L	1-2	0-1	21	McCarthy	10,961
33	12	H	Sunderland	L	1-2	1-1	—	Richardson	7149
34	16	H	Leicester C	W	3-1	1-0	19	Barlow, Serrant, Richardson (pen)	5582
35	19	A	Ipswich T	L	1-2	0-0	—	Richardson (pen)	9674
36	23	A	Sunderland	L	0-1	0-0	22		20,631
37	30	A	Reading	L	0-2	0-1	22		7025
38	Apr 2	H	Grimsby T	W	1-0	0-0	—	Barlow	5037
39	6	H	Derby Co	L	0-1	0-0	22		8119
40	8	A	Port Vale	W	3-1	1-0	22	Barlow, Beckford, Richardson (pen)	7796
41	13	H	Wolverhampton W	D	0-0	0-0	22		7592
42	17	A	Leicester C	L	0-2	0-0	—		12,790
43	20	A	Millwall	W	1-0	0-0	22	Richardson (pen)	9574
44	27	A	Southend U	D	1-1	1-0	20	Creaney	5397
45	30	H	Stoke C	W	2-0	1-0	—	Richardson (pen), Creaney	10,271
46	May 5	H	Luton T	W	1-0	0-0	18	Barlow	6623

Final League Position: 18

GOALSCORERS

League (54): Richardson 11 (7 pens), McCarthy 10, Barlow 7, Brennan 3, Halle 3, Banger 2, Beckford 2, Beresford 2, Creaney 2, Makin 2, Bernard 1, Graham 1, Hughes 1, Redmond 1, Serrant 1, Vonk 1, Wilkinson 1, own goals 3.
Coca-Cola Cup (1): Halle 1.
FA Cup (2): Beckford 2 (1 pen).

Gerrard P 36	Snodin I 24 + 2	Makin C 39	Henry N 14	Jobson R 12	Fleming C 21 + 1	Halle G 37	Bernard P 7	McCarthy S 30 + 5	Richardson L 27	Brennan M 23 + 2	Pointon N 3 + 1	Beckford D 12 + 8	Redmond S 37 + 3	Banger N 8 + 5	Rickers P 23	McNiven S 14 + 1	Hallworth J 10 + 1	Pemberton M — + 2	Graham R 31 + 1	Beresford D 8 + 20	Olney I 1	Wilkinson P 4	Vonk M 5	Hughes A 10 + 5	Barlow S 21 + 5	Orlygsson T 15 + 1	Serrant C 20	Gannon J 5	Creaney G 8 + 1	Lonergan D 1 + 1	Match No.
1	2^1	3	4	5	6	7	8	9	10	11	12																				1
1	2		4	5	6	7	8	9	10	11^1	3	12																			2
1		3	4	5	6	7	8	9	10^1	11			2	12																	3
1		3	4^2	5	6	7		9		11	10		2	12	8^1	13															4
	2		4	5		7	8	9		11	3		6	10^1			1	12													5
		3	4	5	6	7	8	9	10^1				2	12			1	11													6
		3	4	5	6	7	8	9		11^1			10		2		1		12												7
1		3	4	5	6	7	8	9		11			10^1		2				12												8
1		3	4	5	6	7		9		11			10		2			8													9
1		3	4	5		7		9		11			6	10^1	2				8	12											10
1	12	3	4	5		7		9		11		13	6		2				10^1	8^2											11
1	6	3	4	5		7		9^2	10	11		13			2				8^1	12											12
1	6	3	4			7		9	10	11^1		8^2	12		2				5	13											13
1	6	3	4					9	10^2	11^1		12			2				5	13				8							14
1	2	3		5		7		9^1	10	11			6		4				12					8							15
1	2	3		5		7		9	10	11			6		4				12					8^1							16
1	2	3			6	7		9^1	10				4		8				11					5	12						17
	2	3			6	7		9^1			12		4		8		1		11					5	10						18
1	2	3			6	7		9^2	10	11					4^1				8	13				12	5						19
1	2	3			6	7^1		9	10				4		8			12	11					5							20
1	2	3			6^1	7		9^1	10	11			4		8				13	12				5^2	14	10					21
1	2	3				7		9		11			6		8				5					4	10						22
1	2^2	3				7		9		11^1			6		8				5	12				4	10	13					23
1		3				7		9			12		6		2^1			11	5	13				4	10	8^2					24
1		3				7		9^2			12		6		2			11	5	13				4	10	8^1					25
1	2					7		9		11			6						5	13				4	10	8	3				26
1	2					7	12	9		11			6						5					4	10^1	8	3				27
1	2					7	12	9^1		11			6						5					4	10	8	3				28
1	2					7	4	9					6	12				11^2	5	13					10^1	8	3				29
1	2					7	4	9					6	12				11^2	5						10^1	13	8	3			30
1	2					7^1	4	9					6	10				11	5						13	12	3^2				31
1	2		8			7	4	9					6	10^1				5						12	13	3^2	11				32
1	2	3		5		7	9	8					6		4				12	13					10^2	11^1					33
1	2			5		7	9	8					6		4^1				11	12					10	3					34
1	2					7	9	8					6	4^1					5	12					10	3	11				35
1	2					7	9	8					6	4					5	12					10	3	11^1				36
1		4				12	8						6	9^1	7	2^2			5	13					10	3		11			37
1		4					8						6			2			5	7					10	3	9	11			38
1		4^2				12	8				13		6		7	2^3			5	14					10	9	3	11^1			39
1	4	2					8	11					6	7					5						10	9^1	3			12	40
1^3	2	12						11					6	7	8				5	13					10^2	9	3	14		4^1	41
	4	2					8						6		7	1			5	13					10	9^1	3	11^2			42
	4^2	2		5			10^1	9					6		7	1			8						13	12	3	11			43
	4	2					8						9	6	7	1			5						10	3	11			44
		2	4				7						0	11	6	1			5						9	3	10			45
	12					4	2	13	8				9^1	6	7	1			5						14	10^1	3	11^2			46

Coca-Cola Cup
Second Round   Tranmere R   (a) 0-1
                              (h) 1-3

FA Cup
Third Round   Barnsley   (a) 0-0
                           (h) 2-1
Fourth Round   Swindon T   (a) 0-1

OXFORD UNITED 1995-96   *Back row (left to right):* Mickey Lewis, Matt Murphy, Paul Milsom, Elliot Jackson, Phil Whitehead, Danny Cullip, Mark Druce, Chris Allen. *Middle row:* John Clinkard (Physio), Maurice Evans (General Manager), Simon Marsh, Alex Dyer, Steve Wood, Paul Moody, Matt Elliott, Phil Gilchrist, Malcolm Elias (Youth Development Officer), Mark Harrison (Reserve & Youth Team Manager). *Front row:* Bobby Ford, Stuart Massey, Wayne Biggins, Les Robinson, Denis Smith (Manager), Malcolm Crosby (Assistant Manager), Mike Ford, David Smith, David Rush.

Division 1 **OXFORD UNITED**

Manor Ground, Headington, Oxford OX3 7RS. Telephone: (01865) 61503. Fax: (01865) 741820. Supporters Club: (01865) 63063. Clubline: 0891 440055.

Ground capacity: 9572.

Record attendance: 22,750 v Preston NE, FA Cup 6th rd, 29 February 1964.

Record receipts: £103,411 v Leeds U, FA Cup 4th rd, 29 January 1994.

Pitch measurements: 110yd × 75yd.

President: The Duke of Marlborough.

Directors: G. E. Coppock, K. A. Cox, N. J. W. Harris, D. Smith.

Chairman: R. J. Herd CBE.

Manager: Denis Smith. *Assistant Manager:* Malcolm Crosby. *Coach:* Mark Harrison. *Physio:* John Clinkard.

Secretary: Mick Brown. *Commercial Manager:* Trevor Baxter. *Stadium Manager:* Mick Moore.

Year Formed: 1893. *Turned Professional:* 1949. *Ltd Co.:* 1949.

Club Nickname: 'The U's'.

Previous Names: 1893, Headington; 1894, Headington United; 1960, Oxford United.

Previous Grounds: 1893–94 Headington Quarry; 1894–98 Wootten's Field; 1898–1902 Sandy Lane Ground; 1902–09 Britannia Field; 1909–10 Sandy Lane; 1910–14 Quarry Recreation Ground; 1914–22 Sandy Lane; 1922–25 The Paddock Manor Road; 1925– Manor Ground.

Foundation: There had been an Oxford United club around the time of World War I but only in the Oxfordshire Thursday League and there is no connection with the modern club which began as Headington in 1893, adding "United" a year later. Playing first on Quarry Fields and subsequently Wootten's Fields, they owe much to a Dr. Hitchings for their early development.

First Football League game: 18 August 1962, Division 4, v Barrow (a) L 2-3 – Medlock; Beavon, Quartermain; R. Atkinson, Kyle, Jones; Knight, G. Atkinson (1), Houghton (1), Cornwell, Colfar.

Record League Victory: 7–0 v Barrow, Division 4, 19 December 1964 – Fearnley; Beavon, Quartermain; R. Atkinson (1), Kyle, Jones; Morris, Booth (3), Willey (1), G. Atkinson (1), Harrington (1).

Record Cup Victory: 6–0 v Gillingham, League Cup 2nd rd (1st leg), 24 September 1986 – Judge; Langan, Trewick, Phillips (Brock), Briggs, Shotton, Houghton (1), Aldridge (4 incl. 1p), Charles (Leworthy), Hebberd, Slatter. (1 og).

Record Defeat: 0–6 v Liverpool, Division 1, 22 March 1986.

Most League Points (2 for a win): 61, Division 4, 1964–65.

Most League Points (3 for a win): 95, Division 3, 1983–84.

Most League Goals: 91, Division 3, 1983–84.

Highest League Scorer in Season: John Aldridge, 30, Division 2, 1984–85.

Most League Goals in Total Aggregate: Graham Atkinson, 77, 1962–73.

Most Capped Player: Jim Magilton, 18 (32), Northern Ireland.

Most League Appearances: John Shuker, 478, 1962–77.

Record Transfer Fee Received: £1,190,000 from Derby Co for Dean Saunders, October 1988.

Record Transfer Fee Paid: £285,000 to Gillingham for Colin Greenall, February 1988.

Football League Record: 1962 Elected to Division 4; 1965–68 Division 3; 1968–76 Division 2; 1976–84 Division 3; 1984–85 Division 2; 1985–88 Division 1; 1988–92 Division 2; 1992–94 Division 1; 1994–96 Division 2; 1996– Division 1.

Honours: Football League: Division 1 best season: 18th, 1985–86, 1986–87; Division 2 – Champions 1984–85; Runners-up 1995–96; Division 3 – Champions 1967–68, 1983–84; Division 4 – Promoted 1964–65 (4th). *FA Cup:* best season: 6th rd, 1964 (record for 4th Division club). *Football League Cup:* Winners 1986.

Colours: Gold shirts with blue sleeves, blue shorts, blue stockings. *Change colours:* Red and black striped shirts, black shorts, black stockings.

Did you know?
When Oxford United drew 1-1 with Notts County on 16 April 1996, it was the first goal they had conceded at home in 10 hours, 44 minutes of play.

OXFORD UNITED
F.C.

OXFORD UNITED 1995–96 LEAGUE RECORD

Match No.	Date	Venue	Opponents	Result	H/T Score	Lg. Pos.	Goalscorers	Attendance
1	Aug 12	H	Chesterfield	W	1-0	0-0	—	Allen	5563
2	19	A	Brentford	L	0-1	0-1	14		5516
3	26	H	Rotherham U	D	1-1	0-1	15	Ford M	4282
4	30	A	Swindon T	D	1-1	0-1	—	Moody	13,041
5	Sept 3	H	York C	W	2-0	2-0	9	Elliott, Biggins (pen)	4304
6	9	A	Hull C	D	0-0	0-0	9		4608
7	12	A	Walsall	D	2-2	0-1	—	Gilchrist, Rush	3905
8	16	H	Carlisle U	W	4-0	2-0	6	Gilchrist, Ford B, Rush, Murphy	5046
9	23	A	Swansea C	D	1-1	1-0	8	Ford B	2505
10	30	H	Bristol R	L	1-2	0-2	10	Allen	6091
11	Oct 7	H	Stockport Co	W	2-1	2-1	8	Gilchrist, Moody	5646
12	14	A	Wrexham	L	1-2	0-1	11	Elliott	3189
13	21	H	Wycombe W	L	1-4	0-3	12	Smith	7731
14	28	A	Blackpool	D	1-1	0-0	13	Rush	5303
15	31	A	Shrewsbury T	L	0-2	0-1	—		2186
16	Nov 4	H	Bristol C	W	2-0	0-0	12	Angel, Murphy	5665
17	18	A	Peterborough U	D	1-1	1-0	13	Ford M	4720
18	25	H	Crewe Alex	W	1-0	1-0	12	Rush	5287
19	Dec 9	H	Swansea C	W	5-1	0-0	10	Moody 3, Elliott 2	4674
20	16	A	Bristol R	L	0-2	0-0	11		4051
21	23	A	Bradford C	L	0-1	0-1	13		4637
22	26	H	Bournemouth	W	2-0	2-0	12	Ford B, Massey	6347
23	Jan 13	A	Brentford	W	2-1	1-1	12	Aldridge 2	5566
24	20	A	Chesterfield	L	0-1	0-1	14		4589
25	30	A	Burnley	W	2-0	1-0	—	Massey, Allen	6815
26	Feb 3	A	Rotherham U	L	0-1	0-0	13		2842
27	10	H	Brighton & HA	D	1-1	1-0	13	Elliott	5967
28	17	H	Walsall	W	3-2	0-1	9	Moody (pen), Aldridge 2	4369
29	20	A	York C	L	0-1	0-0	—		2112
30	24	A	Carlisle U	W	2-1	0-0	8	Elliott, Aldridge	5525
31	27	H	Hull C	W	2-0	1-0	—	Rush 2	4650
32	Mar 2	A	Bournemouth	W	1-0	1-0	6	Beauchamp	3996
33	9	H	Bradford C	W	2-0	0-0	6	Moody, Aldridge	5138
34	12	A	Brighton & HA	W	2-1	1-0	—	Murphy 2	3953
35	16	A	Notts Co	D	1-1	1-0	5	Rush	5140
36	19	H	Swindon T	W	3-0	1-0	—	Elliott, Aldridge, Beauchamp	8585
37	23	H	Burnley	W	5-0	1-0	4	Aldridge, Moody 3, Beauchamp	6529
38	30	A	Stockport Co	L	2-4	1-2	5	Beauchamp, Aldridge	6096
39	Apr 2	H	Wrexham	D	0-0	0-0	—		5554
40	6	H	Blackpool	W	1-0	0-0	4	Beauchamp	7875
41	8	A	Wycombe W	W	3-0	1-0	3	Rush, Massey, Moody	6727
42	16	H	Notts Co	D	1-1	1-0	—	Moody (pen)	6934
43	20	A	Bristol C	W	2-0	0-0	3	Rush, Moody	7674
44	23	H	Shrewsbury T	W	6-0	2-0	—	Moody 2, Massey, Rush, Beauchamp, Murphy	5799
45	27	A	Crewe Alex	W	2-1	1-0	2	Moody, Beauchamp	4605
46	May 4	H	Peterborough U	W	4-0	0-0	2	Grazioli (og), Moody, Elliott, Rush	7535

Final League Position: 2

GOALSCORERS
League (76): Moody 17 (2 pens), Rush 11, Aldridge 9, Elliott 8, Beauchamp 7, Murphy 5, Massey 4, Allen 3, Ford B 3, Gilchrist 3, Ford M 2, Angel 1, Biggins 1 (pen), Smith 1, own goal 1.
Coca-Cola Cup (7): Allen 2, Biggins 1 (pen), Moody 1, Murphy 1, Robinson 1, Smith 1.
FA Cup (16): Moody 5, Massey 4, Ford B 2, Wood 2, Beauchamp 1, Ford M 1, Rush 1.

Carter T 12	Robinson L 40 + 1	Ford M 43 + 1	Smith D 45	Elliott M 45	Wood S 10 + 1	Rush D 41 + 2	Biggins W 8 + 2	Moody P 30 + 12	Ford B 26 + 2	Allen C 13 + 11	Murphy M 13 + 21	Angel M 16 + 11	Gilchrist P 42	Massey S 33 + 2	Lewis M 5 + 14	Beauchamp J 25 + 7	Marsh S 2 + 3	Whitehead P 34	Aldridge M 15 + 3	Druce M 1 + 7	Powell P 1 + 2	Gray M 6 + 1	Match No.
1	2	3	4¹	5	6	7	8²	9	10	11	12	13											1
1	2	3	4	5			13	8	9		11	12	6	7¹	10²								2
1	2	3	4	5		7	8	9	12	11²	10¹	13	6										3
1	2	3	4	5		7	8	9	10	11¹	12		6										4
1	2	3	4	5		7²	8	9¹	10	11	12	13	6										5
1	2	3	4	5		7¹	8²	9	10	11	13		6	12									6
1	2	3	4	5		7		9	10	11²	12	13	6	8¹									7
1	2	3	4	5		7		9¹	10	11	12		6	8									8
1	2	3	4	5		7			10	11	9	12	6	8¹									9
1	2	3	4	5		7		12	10	11	9¹	13	6	8²									10
1	2¹	3	4	5		7		9²	10	11	13	12	6			8							11
1		3	4	5		7	12	9	10	11²	2		6			8¹	13						12
	2	3	4	5		7¹	12	9	10	11²	13	14	6			8³		1					13
	2	3	4	5	6	7		9¹	10	13	12	11²				8		1					14
	2²	3	4³	5	13	7		9¹	12	10		11	6	8		14		1					15
	2²	3	4	5		7¹		9	10		12	11	6	8		13		1					16
		3	4	5	2	7		9¹	10		12	11	6	8				1					17
		3	4	5	2	7¹		9	10		12	11²	6	8		13		1					18
		3	4	5	2	7¹		9	10			11	6	8		12		1					19
		3	4	5	2	7¹		9	10		12	11	6	8²		13		1					20
12		3		5	2	7		9	10		4¹	11	6	8²		13		1					21
	2	3	4	5		7²		9	10	12		11¹	6	8				1	13				22
	2	3²	4	5				9		12		11	6	8	13	7¹		1	10³	14			23
	2		4	5		7³		9	10			6		8¹	12	11		1	13	14		3²	24
	2		4	5		7		9	10	12			6¹	8		11²	3	1		13			25
	2	12	4	5	6	7³		9²	10	13				8		11	3¹	1		14			26
	2	3	4	5	6³	7¹		9²	10	12	13			8		11		1		14			27
	2	3	4	5				12	10²		11³		6	8	14	13		1	9	7¹			28
	2	3	4	5		12		7	10²	13		11	6	8				1	9¹				29
	2	3	4	5		7¹				12	11³	6	8	13	10²		1	9		14			30
	2	3	4²	5		7¹	12	13		11	6	8	10³			1	9						31
	2	3	4	5		7³	12		13	11²	6	8	14	10		1	9¹						32
	2	3	4	5		7¹	12		13	11²	6		8	10	14	1	9³						33
	2	3	4	5		7³	12		11	6		8	10²	13	1	9¹	14						34
	2	3	4	5		7¹			11		6	8	12	10²		1	9	13					35
	2	3	4	5		7²	12		11		6	8	13	10³		1	9¹		14				36
	2	3	4	5		7¹	12		11³	13	6	8²	14	10		1	9						37
	2	3	4		5	7¹	12		13	11²	6	8³	14	10		1	9						38
	2	3	4	5		7²	12		11¹	13	6		14	10		1	9³				8		39
	2	3	4	5		7³		9		12	11¹	6		13	10	1	14				8²		40
	2	3	4	5		7²	12		13	11³	6	14	8	10		1	9¹						41
	2	3	4	5			11		12	13³	6	7	8	10¹		1	9²		14				42
	2	3	4	5		7	9				6	11		10		1					8		43
	2	3	4	5		7²	9		12	13	6	11¹		10		1					8		44
	2	3	4	5		7²	9		12		6	11	13	10¹		1					0		45
	2	3	4	5		7	9				6	11	12	10		1					8¹		46

Coca-Cola Cup

First Round	Hereford U	(a)	2-0
		(h)	3-2
Second Round	QPR	(h)	1-1
		(a)	1-2

FA Cup

First Round	Dorchester	(h)	9-1
Second Round	Northampton T	(h)	2-0
Third Round	Millwall	(a)	3-3
		(h)	1-0
Fourth Round	Nottingham F	(a)	1-1
		(h)	0-3

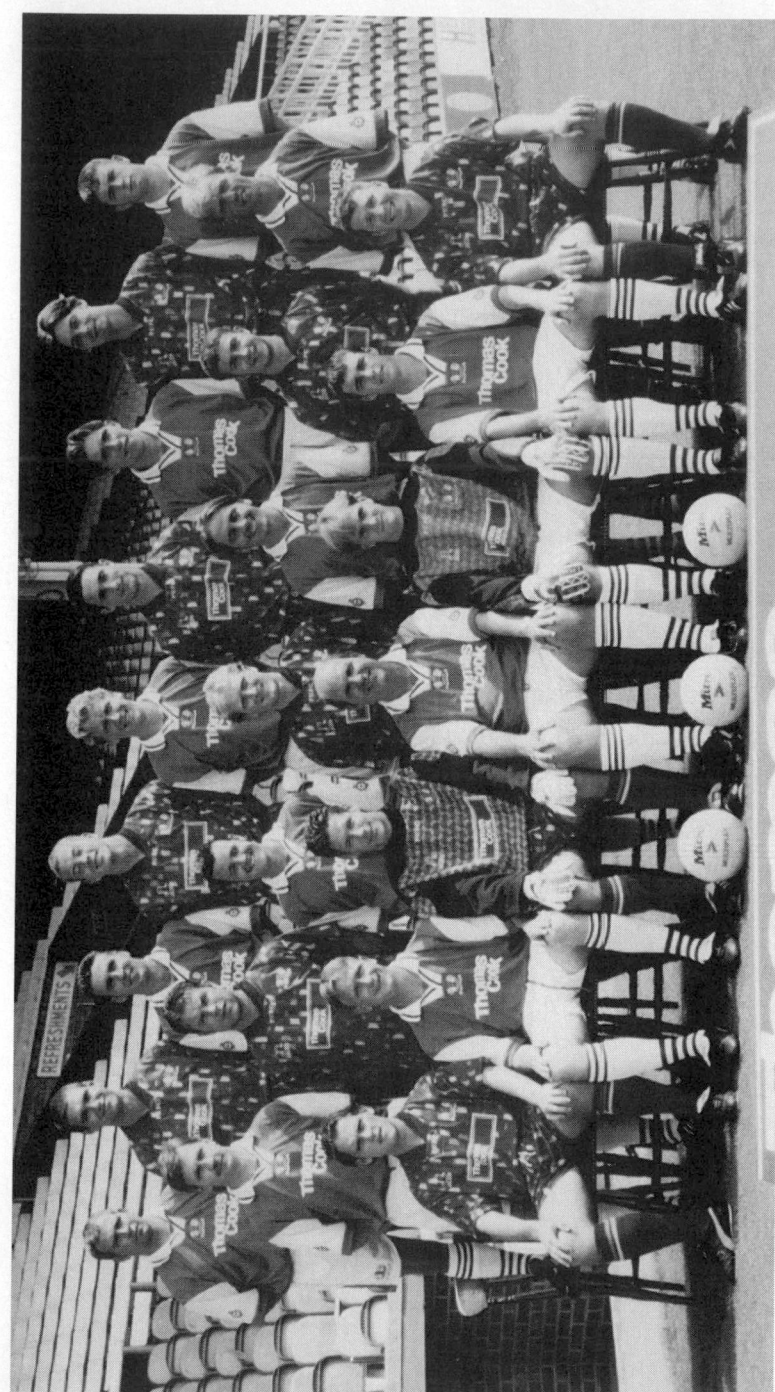

PETERBOROUGH UNITED 1995-96 *Back row (left to right):* Kevin Ashley, Simon Clark, Danny Carter, Greg Heald, Lee Power, David Morrison, Neil LeBihan, Gary Breen, Ryan Semple. *Middle row:* Keith Oakes (Physio), Sean Farrell, David Gregory, Marcus Ebdon, Billy Manuel, Andy Furnell, Michael Halsall (Assistant Manager). *Front row:* Lee Williams, Gary Martindale, Mark Tyler, John Still (Manager), Jon Sheffield, Scott McGleish, Tony Spearing.

Division 2 **PETERBOROUGH UNITED**

London Road Ground, Peterborough PE2 8AL. Telephone: (01733) 63947. Fax: (01733) 577210.

Ground capacity: 15,500.

Record attendance: 30,096 v Swansea T, FA Cup 5th rd, 20 February 1965.

Record receipts: £51,315 v Brighton & HA, FA Cup 5th rd, 15 February 1986.

Pitch measurements: 112yd × 75yd.

Chairman: R. Terrell.

Directors: A Hand, N Hards, P. Sagar. *Company Secretary:* Miss Caroline Hand.

Chief Executive: Iain Russell.

Director of Football: Barry Fry. *Assistant Manager:* Lil Fuccillo. *First Team Coach:* Mick Halsall.

Physio: Keith Oakes.

Commercial Manager: Michael Vincent.

Year Formed: 1934. *Turned Professional:* 1934. *Ltd Co.:* 1934.

Club Nickname: 'The Posh'.

Foundation: The old Peterborough & Fletton club, founded in 1923, was suspended by the FA during season 1932–33 and disbanded. Local enthusiasts determined to carry on and in 1934 a new professional club Peterborough United was formed and entered the Midland League the following year.

First Football League game: 20 August 1960, Division 4, v Wrexham (h) W 3-0 – Walls; Stafford, Walker; Rayner, Rigby, Norris; Hails, Emery (1), Bly (1), Smith, McNamee (1).

Record League Victory: 8–1 v Oldham Ath, Division 4, 26 November 1969 – Drewery; Potts, Noble; Conmy, Wile, Wright; Moss (1), Price (3), Hall (4), Halliday, Robson.

Record Cup Victory: 6–0 v Redditch, FA Cup 1st rd (replay), 22 November 1971 – Drewery; Carmichael, Brookes; Oakes, Turner, Wright; Conmy, Price (1), Hall (2), Barker (2), Robson (1).

Record Defeat: 1–8 v Northampton T, FA Cup 2nd rd (2nd replay), 18 December 1946.

Most League Points (2 for a win): 66, Division 4, 1960–61.

Most League Points (3 for a win): 82, Division 4, 1981–82.

Most League Goals: 134, Division 4, 1960–61.

Highest League Scorer in Season: Terry Bly, 52, Division 4, 1960–61.

Most League Goals in Total Aggregate: Jim Hall, 122, 1967–75.

Most Capped Player: Tony Millington, 8 (21), Wales.

Most League Appearances: Tommy Robson, 482, 1968–81.

Record Transfer Fee Received: £400,000 from Notts Co for David Robinson, October 1992.

Record Transfer Fee Paid: £225,000 to Portsmouth for Carl Griffiths, February 1996.

Football League Record: 1960 Elected to Division 4; 1961–68 Division 3, when they were demoted for financial irregularities; 1968–74 Division 4; 1974–79 Division 3; 1979–91 Division 4; 1991–92 Division 3; 1992–94 Division 1; 1994– Division 2.

Honours: Football League: Division 1 best season: 10th Division 1 1992–93; Division 4 – Champions 1960–61, 1973–74. *FA Cup:* best season: 6th rd, 1965. *Football League Cup:* Semi-final 1966.

Colours: Royal blue shirts, white shorts, white stockings. *Change colours:* All red.

Did you know?
Mick Drewery, the Peterborough United goalkeeper, kept seven consecutive clean sheets from 6 October to 10 November 1973.

PETERBOROUGH UNITED 1995–96 LEAGUE RECORD

Match No.	Date		Venue	Opponents	Result		H/T Score	Lg. Pos.	Goalscorers	Attendance
1	Aug	12	H	Brighton & HA	W	3-1	1-0	—	Clark, Farrell, Martindale	5394
2		19	A	Bournemouth	L	0-3	0-1	12		4175
3		26	H	Notts Co	L	0-1	0-1	17		5618
4		29	A	Blackpool	L	1-2	1-1	—	Heald	3902
5	Sept	2	H	Bristol C	D	1-1	1-0	19	Farrell	4621
6		9	A	Wycombe W	D	1-1	0-1	21	Farrell	5637
7		12	A	Carlisle U	D	1-1	1-0	—	Martindale	6027
8		16	H	Wrexham	W	1-0	0-0	16	Martindale	3817
9		23	H	Bradford C	W	3-1	1-1	12	Heald, Manuel, Martindale	4509
10		30	A	Rotherham U	L	1-5	0-2	15	Power	2863
11	Oct	7	A	Walsall	D	1-1	0-0	16	Power	3768
12		14	H	Swansea C	D	1-1	1-0	15	Carter	3834
13		21	A	Brentford	L	0-3	0-2	17		4565
14		28	H	York C	W	6-1	3-0	15	Martindale 2, Morrison 2, Power, Shaw	4605
15		31	H	Burnley	L	0-2	0-2	—		4737
16	Nov	4	A	Bristol R	D	1-1	0-1	16	Shaw	4241
17		18	H	Oxford U	D	1-1	0-1	17	Shaw	4720
18		25	H	Hull C	W	3-2	1-1	14	Martindale 3	3642
19	Dec	9	A	Bradford C	L	1-2	0-1	16	Farrell	4605
20		16	H	Rotherham U	W	1-0	0-0	15	Spearing	3847
21		19	H	Stockport Co	L	0-1	0-0	—		3267
22		26	A	Chesterfield	D	1-1	1-0	16	Heald	6017
23	Jan	13	H	Bournemouth	L	4-5	1-1	17	Farrell 2, Martindale 2	4596
24		20	A	Brighton & HA	W	2-1	1-1	17	Shaw 2	5572
25	Feb	3	A	Notts Co	L	0-1	0-0	19		5067
26		10	H	Shrewsbury T	D	2-2	0-0	18	Martindale, Basham	4986
27		17	H	Carlisle U	W	6-1	4-0	18	Charlery 2, Ebdon, Farrell 2, Martindale (pen)	4302
28		20	A	Bristol C	W	1-0	0-0	—	Charlery	5014
29		24	A	Wrexham	L	0-1	0-0	17		4012
30		27	H	Wycombe W	W	3-0	1-0	—	Martindale 2, Foran	3670
31	Mar	2	H	Chesterfield	L	0-1	0-1	15		6105
32		5	H	Swindon T	L	0-2	0-1	—		4196
33		9	A	Stockport Co	W	1-0	0-0	14	Power (pen)	5915
34		16	H	Crewe Alex	W	3-1	2-0	14	Charlery 2, Power	5004
35		19	A	Shrewsbury T	D	1-1	0-1	—	Ansah	2291
36		23	H	Swindon T	L	0-2	0-2	13		8780
37		26	H	Blackpool	D	0-0	0-0	—		4425
38		30	H	Walsall	L	2-3	2-2	15	Griffiths, Charlery	4954
39	Apr	2	A	Swansea C	D	0-0	0-0	—		3805
40		6	A	York C	L	1-3	1-2	16	Ebdon (pen)	3261
41		8	H	Brentford	L	0-1	0-0	17		4343
42		13	A	Burnley	L	1-2	0-0	19	Heald	8393
43		20	H	Bristol R	D	0-0	0-0	18		4884
44		27	H	Hull C	W	3-1	1-0	18	Power, Farrell, Charlery	6649
45		30	A	Crewe Alex	L	1-2	0-2	—	Grazioli	3206
46	May	4	A	Oxford U	L	0-4	0-0	19		7535

Final League Position: 19

GOALSCORERS

League (59): Martindale 15 (1 pen), Farrell 9, Charlery 7, Power 6 (1 pen), Shaw 5, Heald 4, Ebdon 2 (1 pen), Morrison 2, Ansah 1, Basham 1, Carter 1, Clark 1, Foran 1, Grazioli 1, Griffiths 1, Manuel 1, Spearing 1.
Coca-Cola Cup (5): Manuel 3, Le Bihan 1, Martindale 1.
FA Cup (6): Farrell 3, Le Bihan 2, Ebdon 1.

Sheffield J 46	Williams L 32 + 1	Spearing T 9	Ebdon M 39	Breen G 25	Clark S 39 + 1	Carter D 30 + 7	Manuel B 13	Power L 25 + 13	Martindale G 26 + 5	Morrison D 21 + 3	Farrell S 20 + 6	Le Bihan N 16 + 9	McGleish S 3 + 9	Rioch G 13 + 5	Heald G 40	Gregory D — + 3	Ashley K 9	Shaw P 12	Furnell A — + 1	Hooper D 4	Sedgemore B 13 + 4	Basham M 13 + 1	Dobson T 4	Foran M 17	Charlery K 19	Williams S — + 3	Codner R 1 + 1	Ansah A — + 2	Robinson S 5	Grazioli G 2 + 1	Griffiths C 4	Blount M 4 + 1	Meredith T 1 + 1	Irman N 1	Drury A — + 1	Match No.
1	2	3	4	5	6	7	8	9¹	10	11²	12	13																								1
1	2	3	4	5	6	7²	8	9¹	10³	11	12	13	14																							2
1	2		4	5		12	8	13	9²	11	10	7¹		3	6																					3
1	2		4	5		12	8	13	9²	11¹	10	7	14	3	6³																					4
1	2		4	5		12	8	9²	13	11¹	10	7³	14	3	6																					5
1	2		4	5		12	8	9²	13	11¹	10	7		3	6																					6
1	2³		4	5	7	8	11	12	9²		10¹	13		3	6	14																				7
1			4	5	2	8¹	11	10²	9	12		7³	13	3	6	14																				8
1	2		4	5²	8	7¹	11	9	10	12				3	6	13																				9
1	2		5	4	7	8		9	10	11				3	6																					10
1		8	5	4	7	3		9	10	12		11¹			6		2																			11
1		8	5	4	7	3		9¹	10	11		12			6		2																			12
1	7	8²	5	4	12	11¹		9³				13	14	3	6		2	10																		13
1	7		5	3	12	10¹		9³	11²	8		13			6		2	4	14																	14
1	7¹		5	3	12			9	10	11²	8	13			6		2	4																		15
1	7		5	3	11¹			10	9	8		12			6		2	4																		16
1	12		4	5	3	10²		9	13	8¹	11				6		2	7																		17
1	8		4	5	3			9	10	11					6		2	7																		18
1	8		4	5	3	12		9	10	11¹					6		2	7																		19
1	8	11	4	5	3	12		9¹	10						6		7	2																		20
1	8¹	11	4²	5	3	12		9	10	13					6		7	2																		21
1	11	4	5	3	8			9¹	12	10					6		7	2																		22
1	2	3		5	7			9	10	4					6		8	11¹	12																	23
1	2	3		5		11	12	9²	10¹	13					6		8	7	4																	24
1	2²		8	5	3	11		13	12	10		9¹			6			7	4																	25
1	2		8	3¹				12	11	9		7			6						4				5	10										26
1			8	3	11¹			13	7	9	12				6						4	2		5	10²											27
1			8	3	11				7	9					6						4	2		5	10											28
1			8	3	11			12	7	9¹					6						4	2		5	10											29
1			8	3	11			10²	9	7¹	13				6						4	2		5	12											30
1			8	3	11			10	9	7²	12				6						4¹	2		5	13											31
1			8	3	11			9	7³	12	13				6						4¹	2²	5	10	14											32
1	2		8	3	11			9	7						6						12			5	10	4¹										33
1	2		8	3	11¹			9	7						6									5	10	12	4									34
1	2		8	3	11			9¹	7						6									5	10	12	4									35
1	2¹		8	3	11			9³	7						6								12	5	10	13		4²	14							36
1	2		8	3	11				7		9				6										5	10		4								37
1	2		8	3	11	12		7¹							6						13	6		5	10			4²	9						38
1	7		8	3	11										6						4			5	10				9	2					39
1	7¹		8	3	11			13			12	6			6						4			5	10				9²	2					40
	3		8		11	12		7¹	9	4	13	6			6									5	10					2²					41
1	2	3¹	8		7			11		9	4	12	6		6									5	10										42
1	2		7	12	13			9	4	3¹	6				6						8	5			10							11⁷				43
1	2		8	3	11	7		9	4	5	5				6							5			10										44
1			8	3		7		12	4²		6³	13									13	5			10			9		2	14	11¹			45
1			8	3	11	7³		12			6										4²	5			10			9¹		13	2			14	46

Coca-Cola Cup

First Round	Swansea C	(a)	1-4
		(h)	3-0
Second Round	Aston Villa	(a)	0-6
		(h)	1-1

FA Cup

First Round	Exeter C	(a)	1-0
Second Round	Bognor Regis	(h)	4-0
Third Round	Wrexham	(h)	1-0
Fourth Round	Huddersfield T	(a)	0-2

PLYMOUTH ARGYLE 1995-96 *Back row (left to right):* Andy Comyn, Keith Hill, Mick Heathcote, Kevin Blackwell, Nicky Hammond, Kevin Nugent, Adrian Viveash, Michael Evans.
Middle row: Mick Jones (Assistant Manager), Wayne Burnett, Steve McCall, Chris Twiddy, James Dungey, Ronnie Mauge, Mark Patterson, Chris Leadbitter, Norman Medhurst (Physio).
Front row: Mark Saunders, Paul Williams, Micky Ross, Neil Warnock (Manager), Dan McCauley (Chairman), Martin Barlow, Adrian Littlejohn, Sam Shilton.

Division 2   **PLYMOUTH ARGYLE**

Home Park, Plymouth, Devon PL2 3DQ. Telephone: (01752) 562561. Fax: (01752) 606167. Marketing Department: (01752) 569597. Lottery Shop: (01752) 561041. Pilgrim Shop: (01752) 558292.

Ground capacity: 19,630.

Record attendance: 43,596 v Aston Villa, Division 2, 10 October 1936.

Record receipts: £128,000 v Burnley, Division 2 play-off, 18 May 1994.

Pitch measurements: 110yd × 72yd.

President: S. J. Rendell.

Chairman: D. McCauley. *Vice-Chairman:* P. Bloom.

Directors: D. Angilley, G. Jasper, I. Jones.

Manager: Neil Warnock. *Assistant Manager:* Mike Jones. *Physio:* Norman Medhurst.

Secretary: Michael Holladay.

Year Formed: 1886. *Turned Professional:* 1903. *Ltd Co.:* 1903.

Club Nickname: 'The Pilgrims'.

Previous Name: 1886–1903, Argyle Athletic Club.

Foundation: The club was formed in September 1886 as the Argyle Football Club by former public and private school pupils who wanted to continue playing the game. The meeting was held in a room above the Borough Arms (a Coffee House), Bedford Street, Plymouth. It was common then to choose a local street/terrace as a club name and Argyle or Argyll was a fashionable name throughout the land due to Queen Victoria's great interest in Scotland.

First Football League game: 28 August 1920, Division 3, v Norwich C (h) D 1-1 – Craig; Russell, Atterbury; Logan, Dickinson, Forbes; Kirkpatrick, Jack, Bowler, Heeps (1), Dixon.

Record League Victory: 8–1 v Millwall, Division 2, 16 January 1932 – Harper; Roberts, Titmuss; Mackay, Pullan, Reed; Grozier, Bowden (2), Vidler (3), Leslie (1), Black (1). (1 og). 8–1 v Hartlepool U (a), Division 2, 7 May 1994 – Nicholls; Patterson (Naylor), Hill, Burrows, Comyn, McCall, Barlow, Castle, Landon, Marshall, Dalton.

Record Cup Victory: 6–0 v Corby T, FA Cup 3rd rd, 22 January 1966 – Leiper; Book, Baird; Williams, Nelson, Newman; Jones (1), Jackson (1), Bickle (3), Piper (1), Jennings.

Record Defeat: 0–9 v Stoke C, Division 2, 17 December 1960.

Most League Points (2 for a win): 68, Division 3 (S), 1929–30.

Most League Points (3 for a win): 87, Division 3, 1985–86.

Most League Goals: 107, Division 3 (S), 1925–26 and 1951–52.

Highest League Scorer in Season: Jack Cock, 32, Division 3 (S), 1925–26.

Most League Goals in Total Aggregate: Sammy Black, 180, 1924–38.

Most Capped Player: Moses Russell, 20 (23), Wales.

Most League Appearances: Kevin Hodges, 530, 1978–92.

Record Transfer Fee Received: £350,000 from Southend U for Gary Poole, July 1993.

Record Transfer Fee Paid: £250,000 to Hartlepool U for Paul Dalton, June 1992.

Football League Record: 1920 Original Member of Division 3; 1921–30 Division 3 (S); 1930–50 Division 2; 1950–52 Division 3 (S); 1952–56 Division 2; 1956–58 Division 3 (S); 1958–59 Division 3; 1959–68 Division 2; 1968–75 Division 3; 1975–77 Division 2; 1977–86 Division 3; 1986–95 Division 2; 1995–96 Division 3; 1996– Division 2.

Honours: Football League: Division 2 best season: 4th, 1931–32, 1952–53; Division 3 (S) – Champions 1929–30, 1951–52; Runners-up 1921–22, 1922–23, 1923–24, 1924–25, 1925–26, 1926–27 (record of six consecutive years); Division 3 – Champions 1958–59; Runners-up 1974–75, 1985–86, Promoted 1995–96 (play-offs). *FA Cup:* best season: Semi-final 1984. *Football League Cup:* Semi-final 1965, 1974.

Colours: Green and black striped shirts, black shorts, black stockings. *Change colours:* All white.

Did you know?
On 2 January 1927, Plymouth Argyle beat Aberdare Athletic 6-5 away in a Division Three (South) match.

PLYMOUTH ARGYLE 1995–96 LEAGUE RECORD

Match No.	Date	Venue	Opponents	Result	H/T Score	Lg. Pos.	Goalscorers	Attendance
1	Aug 12	A	Colchester U	L	1-2	0-1	—	Littlejohn	3585
2	19	H	Preston NE	L	0-2	0-0	24		6862
3	26	A	Chester C	L	1-3	0-1	23	Williams	2660
4	29	H	Hereford U	L	0-1	0-1	—		5608
5	Sept 2	A	Bury	W	5-0	3-0	24	Evans 2, Clayton, Billy, Littlejohn	3040
6	9	H	Leyton Orient	D	1-1	1-0	23	Evans	6292
7	12	H	Doncaster R	W	3-1	2-1	—	Evans, Billy, Littlejohn	4858
8	16	A	Barnet	W	2-1	0-0	13	Evans (pen), Littlejohn	2557
9	23	A	Wigan Ath	W	1-0	0-0	10	Littlejohn	2631
10	30	H	Lincoln C	W	3-0	3-0	5	Minett (og), Evans, Littlejohn	6643
11	Oct 7	H	Fulham	W	3-0	2-0	4	Littlejohn, Baird 2	6681
12	14	A	Mansfield T	D	1-1	1-1	4	Heathcote	3164
13	21	H	Torquay U	W	4-3	2-3	4	Littlejohn 3, Mauge	11,695
14	28	A	Darlington	L	0-2	0-0	6		2352
15	31	A	Scarborough	D	2-2	1-0	—	Leadbitter, Littlejohn	1876
16	Nov 4	H	Cardiff C	D	0-0	0-0	6		7434
17	18	A	Hartlepool U	D	2-2	2-0	6	Evans (pen), Mauge	1830
18	25	H	Rochdale	W	2-0	0-0	5	Littlejohn, Evans	6558
19	Dec 9	H	Wigan Ath	W	3-1	1-1	4	Barlow, Littlejohn 2	5931
20	16	A	Lincoln C	D	0-0	0-0	4		2801
21	23	H	Cambridge U	W	1-0	0-0	4	Mauge	7135
22	26	A	Gillingham	L	0-1	0-0	4		9651
23	Jan 1	H	Exeter C	D	2-2	0-2	4	Mauge, Baird	12,427
24	13	A	Preston NE	L	2-3	1-2	5	Heathcote, Saunders	11,126
25	20	H	Colchester U	D	1-1	1-0	7	Baird	5800
26	23	H	Scunthorpe U	L	1-3	0-2	—	Logan	4712
27	30	A	Northampton T	L	0-1	0-1	—		3911
28	Feb 3	H	Chester C	W	4-2	3-0	5	Barlow, Mauge, Partridge, Williams	5114
29	10	A	Scunthorpe U	D	1-1	1-1	5	Evans	2789
30	17	A	Doncaster R	D	0-0	0-0	5		2338
31	20	H	Bury	W	1-0	0-0	—	Heathcote	4536
32	24	H	Barnet	D	1-1	1-0	5	Partridge	6426
33	27	A	Leyton Orient	W	1-0	0-0	—	Logan	3374
34	Mar 2	H	Gillingham	W	1-0	0-0	4	Barlow	8485
35	9	A	Cambridge U	W	3-2	1-0	3	Billy, Logan, Baird	2785
36	16	H	Northampton T	W	1-0	0-0	3	Evans	7001
37	23	A	Exeter C	D	1-1	1-1	3	Clayton	6185
38	30	A	Fulham	L	0-4	0-1	5		5667
39	Apr 2	H	Mansfield T	W	1-0	0-0	—	Corazzin (pen)	6375
40	6	H	Darlington	L	0-1	0-1	7		8990
41	8	A	Torquay U	W	2-0	1-0	5	Mauge, Littlejohn	4269
42	13	H	Scarborough	W	5-1	1-0	5	Mauge, Barlow 2, Littlejohn 2	6949
43	16	A	Hereford U	L	0-3	0-2	—		4739
44	20	A	Cardiff C	W	1-0	0-0	4	Evans	3374
45	27	A	Rochdale	W	1-0	0-0	5	Evans	2355
46	May 4	H	Hartlepool U	W	3-0	1-0	4	Billy, Heathcote, Logan	11,526

Final League Position: 4

GOALSCORERS

League (68): Littlejohn 17, Evans 12 (2 pens), Mauge 7, Baird 5, Barlow 5, Billy 4, Heathcote 4, Logan 4, Clayton 2, Partridge 2, Williams 2, Corazzin 1 (pen), Leadbitter 1, Saunders 1, own goal 1.
Coca-Cola Cup (1): Heathcote 1.
FA Cup (5): Baird 1, Heathcote 1, Leadbitter 1, Littlejohn 1, own goal 1.

Hammond N 4	Patterson M 42 + 1	Williams P 46	Burnett W 6	Heathcote M 44	Hill K 21 + 3	Billy C 22 + 10	Mauge R 36 + 1	Littlejohn A 40 + 2	Nugent K 4 + 2	Leadbitter C 29 + 4	Twiddy C 1 + 1	Evans M 41 + 4	Hodgson D 3 + 2	Clayton G 32 + 4	O'Hagan D — + 6	Saunders M 4 + 6	Blackwell K 20	Shifton S — + 1	Barlow M 25 + 3	Baird I 24 + 3	Magee K — + 4	Logan R 25 + 6	Wotton P — + 1	Curran C 6 + 2	Petterson A 6	Partridge S 6 + 1	Cherry S 16	Corazzin C 1 + 5	McCall S 2 + 2	Match No.
1	2^2	3	4	5	6^3	7	8	9	10	11^1	12	13	14																	1
1	2^1	3	4	5	6^3	7	8	9	10	12		13	14	11^2																2
1		3	4^1	5	6	7	8	9	10^3	12	2^2	13		11	14															3
1	12	3		5		7	8	9	10^2	11^3		13	6	4	14	2^1														4
	2	3		5		7	8^1	9^2	11			10	6	4	13	12	1													5
	2	3		5		7	8	9^3	11^2			10	6	4^1	12	13	1	14												6
	2	3	4	5	6	7	8	9	11			10					1													7
	2	3	4^2	5	6	7^1	8	9	12	11		10			13		1													8
	2	3	4^2	5	6	7	8	9	12	11		10^1			13		1													9
	2	3		5	6		8^1	9		11		10		12			1		4^2	7	13									10
	2^1	3		5	6		8	9		11		10		12			1		4	7										11
	2	3		5	6		8	9		11		10		12			1		4^1	7										12
	2	3		5	6		8	9		11^2		10		12			1		4^1	7	13									13
	2	3		5	6		8^3	9		11		10		4^1			1		12	7^2	13	14								14
	2	3			6		8	9		11		10^1		4			1		7	12		5^2	13							15
	2	3		6	12	8	9		11^2		10		4			1		7^1		13	5									16
	2	3		5	6	7^1	8	9		11		10		4			1			12										17
	2	3		5	6	7^2	8	9		11		10		4^1	12	1		13												18
	2	3		5	6			9		11		10		4			1		8	7										19
	2	3		5	6			9		11		10		4			1		7	8										20
	2	3		5	6		8^1	9		11^2		10		4			1		7	12	13									21
	2	3		5	6	12	8^2	9^1		11		10		4			1		7	13										22
	2	3		5	6^3	12	8	9		11^1		10		4^2			1		7	13	14									23
		3		5	12		2	8	9	11^1		10				7	1		12	4	6									24
		3		5	12		2	8	9^1	11^2		10		13			1		7	4	6									25
	2	3		5		11^3	8^2	9^1				10		4	13		1		7	12	6		14							26
	2^1	3		5	12							10		6					11			7		8			1	9		27
	2	3		5	12							10		6^1	13				11			7		8			1	9^2		28
	2	3		5								10		6					11			7		8			1	9		29
	2	3		5	12							10		6					11			7		8			1	9^1		30
	2	3		5	12		4		13			10^2		6^3					11			7		8		9^1	1			31
	2	3		5			4	9						6					11			7		8		10	1			32
	2	3		5			4	9				10		6					11			7		8			1			33
	2	3		5			4	9				10		6					11			7		8			1			34
	2	3		5			4		9			10		6					11^1			7		8			1			35
	2	3		5			4		9			10		6					11			7		8			1			36
	2	3		5			4		9			10		6					11			7		8			1			37
	2	3		5	12		4		9^1			10		6					11			7^2		8			1	13		38
	2	3		5		7^2	4		9^1			10		6					11					8			1	12	13	39
	2	3^3		5	6^2	12	4	13		14		10							11^1					8			1	9	7	40
	2	3		5			4		9	7		10		6					11					8			1			41
	2	3		5	12		4		9	7^1		10^2		6^3					11					8			1	13	14	42
	2	3^1		5	12	13	4		9	7		10^3							11^2					8			1	14	6	43
	2	3		5			4		9	7		10		6					12					8		11	1			44
	2	3		5			4		9	7		10		6^1					12					8		11	1			45
	2	3		5^1			4	12	9	7^2		10^3		13					6					8		11	1	14		46

Coca-Cola Cup

First Round	Birmingham C	(a)	0-1
		(h)	1-2

FA Cup

First Round	Slough	(a)	2-0
Second Round	Kingstonian	(a)	2-1
Third Round	Coventry C	(h)	1-3

PORTSMOUTH 1995-96   *Back row (left to right):* Danny Hounsell, Alan McLoughlin, Mark Stimson, Kevin Braybrook, Aaron Flahavan, Tony Dobson, Jimmy Carter, Jimmy Frazer, Deon Burton, Alex Totten.

Middle row: Gordon Neave (Kit Manager), Neil Sillett (Physio), Jason Rees, Lloyd McGrath, Mart Poom, Keith Waldon (First Team Coach), Alan Knight, Guy Butters, Russell Perrett, Larry May (Youth Team Coach), Martin Hinshelwood (Reserve Team Coach).

Front row: Sam Igoe, Paul Hall, Andy Awford, Simon Barnard, David Waterman, Gerry Creaney, Terry Fenwick (Manager), Kit Symons, John Durnin, Paul Wood, Lee Russell, Robbie Pethick, Anthony Tilley.

Division 1 **PORTSMOUTH**

Fratton Park, Frogmore Rd, Portsmouth PO4 8RA. Telephone: (01705) 731204. Fax: (01705) 734129. Commercial Dept: (01705) 827111. Ticket Office: (01705) 750825. Lottery Office: (01705) 825016. Clubcall: 0891 121182.

Ground capacity: 26,452.

Record attendance: 51,385 v Derby Co, FA Cup 6th rd, 26 February 1949.

Record receipts: £214,000 v Manchester U, Coca-Cola Cup 5th rd replay, 26 January 1994.

Pitch measurements: 114yd × 72yd.

Managing Director: M. H. Gregory.

Directors: R. E. Smith, V. Jenner, F. Dinenage, T. Brady.

Manager: Terry Fenwick. *First Team Coach:* Keith Waldon.

Secretary: Paul Weld. *Marketing Manager:* Julie Baker.

Reserve Team Coach: Martin Hinshelwood.

Physio: Neil Sillett. *Youth Team Coach:* Larry May.

Year Formed: 1898. *Turned Professional:* 1898. *Ltd Co.:* 1898.

Club Nickname: 'Pompey'.

Foundation: At a meeting held in his High Street, Portsmouth offices in 1898, solicitor Alderman J. E. Pink and five other business and professional men agreed to buy some ground close to Goldsmith Avenue for £4,950 which they developed into Fratton Park in record breaking time. A team of professionals was signed up by manager Frank Brettell and entry to the Southern League obtained for the new club's September 1899 kick-off.

First Football League game: 28 August 1920, Division 3, v Swansea T (h) W 3-0 – Robson; Probert, Potts; Abbott, Harwood, Turner; Thompson, Stringfellow (1), Reid (1), James (1), Beedie.

Record League Victory: 9–1 v Notts Co, Division 2, 9 April 1927 – McPhail; Clifford, Ted Smith; Reg Davies (1), Foxall, Moffat; Forward (1), Mackie (2), Haines (3), Watson, Cook (2).

Record Cup Victory: 7–0 v Stockport Co, FA Cup 3rd rd, 8 January 1949 – Butler; Rookes, Ferrier; Scoular, Flewin, Dickinson; Harris (3), Barlow, Clarke (2), Phillips (2), Froggatt.

Record Defeat: 0–10 v Leicester C, Division 1, 20 October 1928.

Most League Points (2 for a win): 65, Division 3, 1961–62.

Most League Points (3 for a win): 91, Division 3, 1982–83.

Most League Goals: 91, Division 4, 1979–80.

Highest League Scorer in Season: Guy Whittingham, 42, Division 1, 1992–93.

Most League Goals in Total Aggregate: Peter Harris, 194, 1946–60.

Most Capped Player: Jimmy Dickinson, 48, England.

Most League Appearances: Jimmy Dickinson, 764, 1946–65.

Record Transfer Fee Received: £2,000,000 from Tottenham H for Darren Anderton, May 1992.

Record Transfer Fee Paid: £650,000 to Celtic for Gerry Creaney, January 1994.

Football League Record: 1920 Original Member of Division 3; 1921 Division 3 (S); 1924–27 Division 2; 1927–59 Division 1; 1959–61 Division 2; 1961–62 Division 3; 1962–76 Division 2; 1976–78 Division 3; 1978–80 Division 4; 1980–83 Division 3; 1983–87 Division 2; 1987–88 Division 1; 1988–92 Division 2; 1992– Division 1.

Honours: Football League: Division 1 – Champions 1948–49, 1949–50; Division 2 – Runners-up 1926–27, 1986–87; Division 3 (S) – Champions 1923–24; Division 3 – Champions 1961–62, 1982–83. *FA Cup:* Winners 1939; Runners-up 1929, 1934. *Football League Cup:* best season: 5th rd, 1961, 1986.

Colours: Blue shirts, white shorts, red stockings. *Change colours:* Red and black shirts, black shorts, red stockings.

Did you know?
Alan Knight established a record number of League appearances for a goalkeeper with one club when he played his 601st game on 13 January 1996.

PORTSMOUTH 1995–96 LEAGUE RECORD

Match No.	Date	Venue	Opponents	Result		H/T Score	Lg. Pos.	Goalscorers	Attendance
1	Aug 12	H	Southend U	W	4-2	2-1	—	Creaney 2, Tilson (og), Rees	10,630
2	19	A	Grimsby T	L	1-2	0-0	7	McLoughlin (pen)	4515
3	26	H	Reading	D	0-0	0-0	8		9917
4	30	A	Leicester C	L	2-4	1-4	—	Creaney (pen), Hall	15,170
5	Sept 2	H	Millwall	L	0-1	0-1	21		8023
6	9	A	Port Vale	W	2-0	1-0	16	Burton, Griffiths (pen)	7374
7	12	A	Sunderland	D	1-1	0-1	—	McLoughlin (pen)	12,282
8	16	H	Derby Co	D	2-2	1-1	16	Gittens, McLoughlin	14,434
9	23	H	Tranmere R	L	0-2	0-0	18		11,127
10	30	A	Luton T	L	1-3	1-2	22	Walsh	7795
11	Oct 7	A	Oldham Ath	D	1-1	0-0	22	Simpson	5937
12	14	H	Birmingham C	L	0-1	0-1	22		10,006
13	21	H	WBA	L	1-2	0-0	24	McLoughlin (pen)	16,257
14	28	H	Watford	W	4-2	2-0	21	Stimson, Simpson, Allen, Carter	7025
15	Nov 4	A	Sheffield U	L	1-4	1-2	22	Simpson	11,281
16	11	H	Huddersfield T	D	1-1	1-1	22	Simpson (pen)	6876
17	18	H	Stoke C	D	3-3	2-1	22	McLoughlin 2 (1 pen), Walsh	8030
18	21	A	Barnsley	D	0-0	0-0	—		6187
19	25	A	Ipswich T	L	2-3	1-2	22	Walsh, Allen	10,286
20	Dec 2	H	Oldham Ath	W	2-1	1-1	20	Allen, McLoughlin (pen)	6002
21	9	A	Tranmere R	W	2-1	2-0	19	Durnin, Hall	6678
22	16	H	Luton T	W	4-0	3-0	17	Hall 2, Walsh, Carter	7012
23	23	H	Norwich C	W	1-0	0-0	17	Durnin	9960
24	26	A	Charlton Ath	L	1-2	1-0	17	Hall	11,686
25	30	A	Wolverhampton W	D	2-2	0-2	16	Carter, Burton	25,291
26	Jan 1	H	Crystal Palace	L	2-3	0-2	17	Butters, Simpson	12,926
27	13	H	Grimsby T	W	3-1	2-0	16	Walsh, Wood, Carter	6958
28	20	A	Southend U	L	1-2	1-0	16	Hall	5560
29	27	A	Millwall	D	1-1	0-1	16	Burton	7710
30	Feb 4	H	Reading	W	1-0	0-0	14	McLoughlin	7924
31	10	H	Leicester C	W	2-1	1-1	11	Burton, Hall	9003
32	17	H	Sunderland	D	2-2	1-1	11	Hall, Griffiths	12,241
33	24	A	Derby Co	L	2-3	0-0	12	Hall, McLoughlin (pen)	16,120
34	Mar 2	H	Charlton Ath	W	2-1	1-1	12	Burton 2	9323
35	9	A	Norwich C	D	1-1	1-1	11	Hall	13,004
36	16	H	Wolverhampton W	L	0-2	0-2	15		11,732
37	23	A	Crystal Palace	D	0-0	0-0	16		17,039
38	27	H	Port Vale	L	1-2	1-2	—	Allen	6335
39	30	H	WBA	L	0-2	0-1	18		8126
40	Apr 2	A	Birmingham C	L	0-2	0-1	—		14,886
41	6	A	Watford	W	2-1	1-1	18	Awford, McLoughlin	8226
42	8	H	Sheffield U	L	1-2	0-2	18	Durnin	8978
43	13	A	Stoke C	L	1-2	0-1	21	Butters	11,471
44	20	H	Barnsley	D	0-0	0-0	21		8744
45	27	H	Ipswich T	L	0-1	0-0	22		12,954
46	May 5	A	Huddersfield T	W	1-0	1-0	21	Burton	14,091

Final League Position: 21

GOALSCORERS
League (61): Hall 10, McLoughlin 10 (6 pens), Burton 7, Simpson 5 (1 pen), Walsh 5, Allen 4, Carter 4, Creaney 3 (1 pen), Durnin 3, Butters 2, Griffiths 2 (1 pen), Awford 1, Gittens 1, Rees 1, Stimson 1, Wood 1, own goal 1.
Coca-Cola Cup (0).
FA Cup (0).

Poom M 4	Pethick R 30 + 8	Russell L 17 + 2	McLoughlin A 38 + 2	Symons K 1	Butters G 37	Carter J 31 + 4	Durnin J 30 + 11	Hall P 44 + 2	Creaney G 3	Rees J 15 + 6	Burton D 24 + 8	Awford A 17 + 1	Igoe S 4 + 18	Simpson F 27 + 3	Dobson T 7 + 2	Gittens J 14 + 1	Griffiths C 2 + 12	Bradbury L 3 + 9	Knight A 42	Allen M 27	Walsh P 21	Wood P 13 + 2	Stinson M 14	Perrett R 8 + 1	Whitbread A 13	Thomson A 15 + 1	Hinshelwood D 5	Match No.
1	2	3	4^2	5	6	7^3	8	9^1	10	11	12	13	14															1
1	2	3	4^2		6		8	9	10^1	11	12	5	14			7^3	13											2
1	2	3			6	7^1	8	9	10	11^2	12	4	5	13														3
1	2	3				7^4	8	9	10^1	11	12	13	4	6	5													4
	2	3	4			7^1		9	11	10^2	12	8	6^1	5	13	14			1									5
	2	3	4		6	7		9^1	10^2		8	5	12	13	1													6
	2	3	12		6	7^2	13	9		11^1	10	8	5	14		1	4^3											7
	2^3	3	12		6	13	9	11^1	10^2	8	5	14	1	4	7													8
	2^1	3^3	4		6	12	9	11	10^2	8	5	13	1	7	14													9
	2^3	3	4^2		6	12	9	11^1		13	8	5	10	1	7	14												10
12		4	6		2	13		11^3		14	8	3	5	10^2	1	7^1	9											11
12		4	6		2	13		11^1				8^2	3	5	14	10^3	1	7	9									12
12		4	6		2	10^1		13				8	3	5		1	11	7^2	9									13
12		4	6		13	2^1	10					8	3	5		1	11	7		9^2								14
12	6	4			13	2	10^1					8	3		1	11	7		9^2	5								15
12	6				13	2^1	10	3^3				9	8	5^2	14	1	11	7			4							16
	2	3	4		6	11^1	9	10				12				1	8	7			5							17
	2	3	4		6	11^2	9^3	10	13	12	14		7^1			1	8				5							18
	2	4^3			6	11^1	9	10^2	12		13	14				1	8	7		3	5							19
	2		4		6	12	9	10			8					1	11	7		3^1	5							20
	2				6	11^2	9	10	13				8	12		1	4	7^1		3	5							21
	2				6	11	9	10						8		1	7			3	5							22
			4		6	11^1	9	10		12				2		1	8	7		3	5							23
		2	4		6	11^2	9	10^1	12				13			1	8	7		3	5							24
	2		4		6	11	9^2	10		7^1		12	13			1	8			3	5							25
	2		4		6	11^1	13	10	12				14	9^3		1	8	7		3^2	5							26
	2		4		6	11	9	10			12					1		7	8^1	3	5							27
	2		4		6	11	9^1	10			12					1		7	8	3	5							28
	2		4		6	11^2	9^3	10	13	12						1		7^1	8	3	5	14						29
	2		4		6	11	12	10		9		13		7^1		1			8^2	3	5							30
	2^2		4		6	11	12	10		9	3	13				1		7^1	8					5				31
	2		4		6	11	7	10		9^2	3		12		13	1			8^1					5				32
	2		4		6	11^1	12	10		9	3				13	1	7^2		8					5				33
	2		4		6	11	7	10		9	3				13	1			8					5				34
	2		4		6	11	12	10		9^2	3				13	1	7		8^1					5				35
	2^1		4		6^3	11	12	10		9^2	3				13	1	7		8		14			5				36
			4^1			11	12	10		9^2	3		8		13	1	7				6			5		2		37
						11^2	4	10		12	9	3	13	8^1		14	1	7			6			5		2^3		38
12	2^5					4^2	10			9	3	11	8			13	1	7			6			5				39
12			4			11	10			9	3	11	13	8^2		13	1	7			6			5		2		40
			4			11	10			9	3		8			1	7				6			5		2		41
12			4		6	11	10			9	3		8			1	7							5		2^1		42
	2		4		6	11^1	8	10		9	3		12			1	7							5				43
	2^5	5	4		6	11		10	12		9^2	3	8		13	1	7											44
	17	4			6	11^1		10	7	9	3	2^7	0		13	1								5				45
		4			6	11		10	2	9	3		8			1	7							5				46

Coca-Cola Cup
First Round   Cardiff C   (h)   0-2
                                         (a)   0-1

FA Cup
Third Round   Southampton   (a)   0-3

PORT VALE 1995–96   *Back row (left to right)*: Martin Foyle, Allen Tankard, Stewart Talbot, Jermaine Holwyn, Paul Musselwhite, Gareth Griffiths, Arjan van Heusden, Lee Mills, Neil Aspin, Dean Glover, Steve Guppy.

Middle row: Mark Grew (Youth Team Coach), Stan Nicholls (Kit Manager), John Jeffers, Ray Walker, Wayne Corden, Kevin Kent, Richard Eyre, Bradley Sandeman, Jim Cooper (Community Officer), Rick Carter (Physio).

Front row: John Rudge (Manager), Ian Bogie, Craig Lawton, John McCarthy, Tony Naylor, Andy Porter, Dean Stokes, Dean Cunningham, Bill Dearden (First Team Coach).

Division 1 **PORT VALE**

Vale Park, Burslem, Stoke-on-Trent ST6 1AW. Telephone: (01782) 814134. Fax: (01782) 834981. Commercial Dept: (01782) 835524. Clubcall: 0891 121636. Commercial Fax: (01782) 836875. Valiant Leisure Shop: (01782) 818718. Community: (01782) 575594

Ground capacity: 22,356.

Record attendance: 49,768 v Aston Villa, FA Cup 5th rd, 20 February 1960.

Record receipts: £170,349 v Everton, FA Cup 4th rd, 14 February 1996.

Pitch measurements: 116yd × 76yd.

President: J. Burgess.

Chairman: W. T. Bell TECH. ENG, MIMI.

Directors: A. Belfield, I. McPherson, D. Bundy (Vice-Chairman).

Manager: John Rudge. *Secretary:* R. A. Allan. *Commercial Manager:* Mrs Margaret Moran-Smith.

Coach: Bill Dearden. *Physio:* Rick Carter. *Medical Officer:* Dr. D. Phillips. *Stadium Manager:* F. W. Lodey. *Groundsman:* R. Fairbanks. *Community Scheme Officer:* Jim Cooper (01782 575594).

Year Formed: 1876. *Turned Professional:* 1885. *Ltd Co.:* 1911.

Club Nickname: 'Valiants'.

Previous Name: Burslem Port Vale; became Port Vale, 1909.

Previous Grounds: 1876, Limekin Lane, Longport; 1881, Westport; 1884, Moorland Road, Burslem; 1886, Athletic Ground, Cobridge; 1913, Recreation Ground, Hanley; 1950, Vale Park.

Foundation: Formed in 1876 as Port Vale, adopting the prefix 'Burslem' in 1884 upon moving to that part of the city. It was dropped in 1909.

First Football League game: 3 September 1892, Division 2, v Small Heath (a) L 1-5 – Frail; Clutton, Elson; Farrington, McCrindle, Delves; Walker, Scarratt, Bliss (1), Jones. (Only 10 men).

Record League Victory: 9–1 v Chesterfield, Division 2, 24 September 1932 – Leckie; Shenton, Poyser; Sherlock, Round, Jones; McGrath, Mills, Littlewood (6), Kirkham (2), Morton (1).

Record Cup Victory: 7–1 v Irthlingborough, FA Cup 1st rd, 12 January 1907 – Matthews; Dunn, Hamilton; Eardley, Baddeley, Holyhead; Carter, Dodds (2), Beats, Mountford (2), Coxon (3).

Record Defeat: 0–10 v Sheffield U, Division 2, 10 December 1892 and v Notts Co, Division 2, 26 February 1895.

Most League Points (2 for a win): 69, Division 3 (N), 1953–54.

Most League Points (3 for a win): 89, Division 2, 1992–93.

Most League Goals: 110, Division 4, 1958–59.

Highest League Scorer in Season: Wilf Kirkham 38, Division 2, 1926–27.

Most League Goals in Total Aggregate: Wilf Kirkham, 154, 1923–29, 1931–33.

Most Capped Player: Sammy Morgan, 7 (18), Northern Ireland.

Most League Appearances: Roy Sproson, 761, 1950–72.

Record Transfer Fee Received: £1,000,000 from Sheffield W for Ian Taylor, August 1994.

Record Transfer Fee Paid: £450,000 to York C for Jon McCarthy, July 1995.

Football League Record: 1892 Original Member of Division 2. Failed re-election in 1896; Re-elected 1898; Resigned 1907; Returned in Oct, 1919, when they took over the fixtures of Leeds City; 1929–30 Division 3 (N); 1930–36 Division 2; 1936–38 Division 3 (N); 1938–52 Division 3 (S); 1952–54 Division 3 (N); 1954–57 Division 2; 1957–58 Division 3 (S); 1958–59 Division 4; 1959–65 Division 3; 1965–70 Division 4; 1970–78 Division 3; 1978–83 Division 4; 1983–84 Division 3; 1984–86 Division 4; 1986–89 Division 3; 1989–94 Division 2; 1994– Division 1.

Honours: Football League: Division 2 – Runners-up 1993–94; Division 3 (N) – Champions 1929–30, 1953–54; Runners-up 1952–53; Division 4 – Champions 1958–59; Promoted 1969–70 (4th). *FA Cup:* Semi-final 1954, when in Division 3. *Football League Cup:* 3rd rd 1991–92. *Autoglass Trophy:* Winners: 1993. *Anglo-Italian Cup:* Runners-up: 1996.

Colours: White shirts, black shorts, black and white stockings. *Change colours:* All yellow.

Did you know?
In the 1995–96 season, Port Vale completed a League double over neighbours Stoke City, their first such success for 70 years.

PORT VALE 1995–96 LEAGUE RECORD

Match No.	Date	Venue	Opponents	Result		H/T Score	Lg. Pos.	Goalscorers	Attendance
1	Aug 13	A	Derby Co	D	0-0	0-0	—		10,869
2	19	H	Millwall	L	0-1	0-0	22		8202
3	27	A	Stoke C	W	1-0	0-0	18	Bogie	14,283
4	30	H	Sunderland	D	1-1	1-0	—	Porter	7693
5	Sept 2	A	Norwich C	L	1-2	1-2	20	Mills	13,908
6	9	H	Portsmouth	L	0-2	0-1	22		7374
7	12	H	Leicester C	L	0-2	0-1	—		8814
8	16	A	Grimsby T	L	0-1	0-1	24		4066
9	23	A	Reading	D	2-2	2-1	23	Mills, Glover L	7819
10	30	H	Wolverhampton W	D	2-2	1-2	24	Richards (og), Porter (pen)	11,550
11	Oct 7	A	Huddersfield T	W	2-0	1-0	23	McCarthy, Guppy	11,554
12	15	H	Crystal Palace	L	1-2	0-0	23	Glover L	6935
13	21	A	Barnsley	D	1-1	1-1	23	Guppy	7332
14	29	A	Birmingham C	L	1-2	0-1	24	Porter (pen)	8875
15	Nov 5	A	Oldham Ath	D	2-2	1-1	23	Mills 2	5138
16	11	H	Sheffield U	L	2-3	1-1	24	Naylor, Mills	7284
17	18	H	Watford	D	1-1	0-1	24	Samuel	6265
18	22	A	Tranmere R	L	1-2	0-1	—	Naylor	6681
19	25	A	Charlton Ath	D	2-2	0-0	24	Porter, Griffiths	10,174
20	Dec 2	H	Huddersfield T	W	1-0	1-0	24	Foyle	7701
21	9	H	Reading	W	3-2	3-1	21	Foyle, Guppy, Porter (pen)	6376
22	16	A	Wolverhampton W	W	1-0	1-0	21	Porter	23,329
23	20	A	Southend U	L	1-2	1-2	—	Naylor	4506
24	26	H	WBA	W	3-1	0-0	18	Naylor, Foyle, Guppy	10,807
25	Jan 1	A	Ipswich T	L	1-5	0-0	19	Naylor	9926
26	13	A	Millwall	W	2-1	1-1	18	Foyle, Naylor	14,220
27	20	H	Derby Co	D	1-1	0-1	19	Naylor	11,947
28	Feb 10	A	Sunderland	D	0-0	0-0	21		15,954
29	17	A	Leicester C	D	1-1	0-1	21	McCarthy	13,758
30	Mar 2	A	WBA	D	1-1	0-1	23	McCarthy	13,707
31	9	H	Southend U	W	2-1	1-1	23	McCarthy, Glover L	6222
32	12	H	Stoke C	W	1-0	1-0	—	Bogie	16,737
33	20	H	Norwich C	W	1-0	1-0	—	Foyle	6085
34	23	H	Ipswich T	W	2-1	1-1	18	Bogie (pen), McCarthy	7277
35	27	A	Portsmouth	W	2-1	2-1	—	Naylor, Griffiths	6335
36	30	H	Barnsley	W	3-0	1-0	12	Foyle, Porter, Naylor	7358
37	Apr 2	A	Crystal Palace	D	2-2	0-2	—	McCarthy, Foyle	14,180
38	6	A	Birmingham C	L	1-3	0-2	12	Porter	17,469
39	8	H	Oldham Ath	L	1-3	0-1	16	Mills	7796
40	13	A	Watford	L	2-5	1-2	17	Porter (pen), Foyle	9066
41	16	H	Grimsby T	W	1-0	0-0	—	Aspin	5796
42	20	H	Tranmere R	D	1-1	0-0	12	Naylor	7419
43	23	H	Luton T	W	1-0	1-0	—	Mills	6054
44	27	H	Charlton Ath	L	1-3	1-1	10	McCarthy	8428
45	30	A	Luton T	L	2-3	1-1	—	Porter, Mills	5443
46	May 4	A	Sheffield U	D	1-1	0-0	12	Naylor	18,741

Final League Position: 12

GOALSCORERS

League (59): Naylor 11, Porter 10 (4 pens), Foyle 8, Mills 8, McCarthy 7, Guppy 4, Bogie 3 (1 pen), Glover L 3, Griffiths 2, Aspin 1, Samuel 1, own goal 1.
Coca-Cola Cup (3): Glover D 1, Glover L 1, Mills 1.
FA Cup (9): Bogie 2, Foyle 2, Walker 2, McCarthy 1, Naylor 1, Porter 1 (pen).

Musselwhite P 39	Aspin N 22	Tankard A 28 + 1	Walker R 21 + 14	Griffiths G 40 + 1	Glover D 27 + 2	McCarthy J 44 + 1	Porter A 44 + 1	Foyle M 24 + 1	Glover L 17 + 7	Guppy S 43 + 1	Mills L 20 + 12	Bogie I 27 + 5	Stokes D 16 + 2	Hill A 35	Naylor T 30 + 9	Sandeman B 1	Talbot S 8 + 12	Van Heusden A 7	Kent K — + 1	Samuel R 9	Lawton C 2	Corden W 2	Match No.
1	2	3	4	5	6	7	8	9	10¹	11	12												1
1	2²	3	4	5³	6	7	8	9	10¹	11	12	13	14										2
1		3		5	6	7	8		10¹	11	9	4		2	12								3
1		3		5	6	7	8		10	11	9¹	4		2	12								4
1		3	12	5	6	7²	8		10	11	9	4¹		2	13								5
1		3		5	6	7	8		10	11	9¹	4²	12	2	13								6
1		3	9	5	6	7²	8		10	11¹	12	4³		2	13		14						7
		3	12	5	6	7	8		10	11²		4¹		2			9	1	13				8
		3	4²	5	6	7	8		10	11¹	9			2	12		13	1					9
		3	4	5	6	7	8		10¹	11	9			2	12			1					10
		3	4	5	6	7	8		10	11	9			2				1					11
			4	5	6	7²	8		10	11	9¹		3	2	12		13	1					12
1		3	4	5	6	7	8		10	11	12			2	9¹								13
1		3	4²	5	6	7³	8		10¹	11	12	13		2	9		14						14
1		3		5	6¹	7	8			11	9	12		2	10	4							15
1		3	12	5	6	7²	2		13	11	9	4			10		8¹						16
1		3	12		6	7	2	13		11	9²	4¹			10		8			5			17
1		3	12	4	6	7	2¹		13	11	9²				10		8			5			18
1		3	4	5	6	7	8	9							10		11			2			19
1		3	4	5	6	7	8	9		11					10					2			20
1		3	4	5	6	7	8	9		11¹					10					2			21
1			4	5	6	7	8	9		11	12		3		10¹					2			22
1	12		4	5	6	7	8			11	9		3		10					2¹			23
1		3		5	6	7	8	9		11		4		2	10								24
1		3		5	6	7	8	9		11		4¹		2	10		12						25
1		3			6	7	8	9		11		4		2	10		5						26
1	6	3	4	12	7	8	9		11¹		13		2	10		5²						27
1	6	3	12	5	7	8	9	13	11		4¹		2	10²								28
1	6	3	13	5	7	8	9		11	12	4²		2	10¹								29
1	6	3	2	5	7	8	10¹	11	9	4			12										30
1	6	12	5	7	8	9	10	11¹	4	3	2												31
1	6	12	5	7	8	9	10²	11	4¹	3	2	13											32
1	6	8	5	7¹	9	11	4	3	2	10	12												33
1	6	8¹	5	7	12	9	13	11	4	3	2	10²											34
1	6	7	5	12	8	9	11	13	4¹	3	2	10²											35
1	6	12	5	7	8	9	11	13	4¹	3	2	10²											36
1	6	5²	7	8¹	9	11	12	4	3	2	10	13											37
1	6	12	7²	8	9	11	13	4¹	3	2	10²	14					5						38
1	6	12	7	8	9	11	13	4¹	3	2	10²	14					5³						39
1	6	2	5	7	8	9	12	11	4	3	10¹												40
1	6	3¹	5	12	7	8	9	11	10	4	2												41
1	6	12	5	7	8	13	11	9²	4¹	3	2	10											42
	6		5	12	8		11	9		3	2	10	13	1			4¹			7²			43
	6		5	7	8	13	11	9	12	3	2	10		1			4²			11¹			44
1	6	12	5	7	8	13	11	9²	4¹	3	2	10											45
1	6	4	5	7	8	11	9	3	2	10													46

Coca-Cola Cup

First Round	Huddersfield T	(a)	2-1	
		(h)	1-3	

FA Cup

Third Round	Crystal Palace	(a)	0-0	
		(h)	4-3	
Fourth Round	Everton	(a)	2-2	
		(h)	2-1	
Fifth Round	Leeds U	(a)	0-0	
		(h)	1-2	

PRESTON NORTH END 1995-96   *Back row (left to right):* Gareth Ainsworth, Lee Cartwright, Simon Davey, Allan Smart, Barry Richardson, David Lucas, John Vaughan, Steve Wilkinson, Kevin Magee, Graeme Atkinson.

Middle row: Geoff McDougle (Chief Scout), Brian Hickson (Kit Manager), Paul Raynor, Ryan Kidd, Andy Saville, Jamie Squires, John Calligan, Steve Holmes, Kevin Kilbane, Mick Rathbone (Physio), Jim Parker (Youth Physio).

Front row: Joe Jakub (Youth Development Officer), Chris Borwick, Terry Fleming, Andy Fensome, David Moyes (Player/Coach), Gary Peters (Manager), Ian Bryson, Graham Lancashire, Mickey Brown, Raymond Sharp, Chris Sulley (Youth Manager).

(Photograph: Karen Pearson)

Division 2   **PRESTON NORTH END**

Deepdale, Preston PR1 6RU. Telephone: (01772) 902020. Fax: (01772) 653266. Ticket Enquiries: (01772) 902000. Commercial/Shop: (01772) 902001.

Ground capacity: 18,700.

Record attendance: 42,684 v Arsenal, Division 1, 23 April 1938.

Record receipts: £68,650 v Sheffield W, FA Cup 3rd rd, 4 January 1992.

Pitch measurements: 110yd × 77yd.

President: Tom Finney OBE, JP.

Vice-President: T. C. Nicholson JP, FCIOB.

Chairman: Bryan M. Gray.

Directors: K. W. Leeming, (Vice-Chairman), M. J. Woodhouse (snr) (Vice-Chairman), D. Shaw (Managing), L. King (Company Secretary).

Manager: Gary Peters. *Assistant Manager:* David Moyes. *Coach:* Steve Harrison.

Secretary: Mrs Audrey Shaw.

Year Formed: 1881. *Turned Professional:* 1885. *Ltd Co.:* 1893.

Club Nicknames: 'The Lilywhites' or 'North End'.

Foundation: North End Cricket and Rugby Club which was formed in 1863, indulged in most sports before taking up soccer in about 1879. In 1881 they decided to stick to football to the exclusion of other sports and even a 16–0 drubbing by Blackburn Rovers in an invitation game at Deepdale, a few weeks after taking this decision, did not deter them for they immediately became affiliated to the Lancashire FA.

First Football League game: 8 September 1888, Football League, v Burnley (h) W 5-2 – Trainer; Howarth, Holmes; Robertson, W. Graham, J. Graham; Gordon (1), Ross (2), Goodall, Dewhurst (2), Drummond.

Record League Victory: 10–0 v Stoke, Division 1, 14 September 1889 – Trainer; Howarth, Holmes; Kelso, Russell (1), Graham; Gordon, Jimmy Ross (2), Nick Ross (3), Thomson (2), Drummond (2).

Record Cup Victory: 26–0 v Hyde, FA Cup 1st rd, 15 October 1887 – Addison; Howarth, Nick Ross; Russell (1), Thomson (5), Graham (1); Gordon (5), Jimmy Ross (8), John Goodall (1), Dewhurst (3), Drummond (2).

Record Defeat: 0–7 v Blackpool, Division 1, 1 May 1948.

Most League Points (2 for a win): 61, Division 3, 1970–71.

Most League Points (3 for a win): 90, Division 4, 1986–87.

Most League Goals: 100, Division 2, 1927–28 and Division 1, 1957–58.

Highest League Scorer in Season: Ted Harper, 37, Division 2, 1932–33.

Most League Goals in Total Aggregate: Tom Finney, 187, 1946–60.

Most Capped Player: Tom Finney, 76, England.

Most League Appearances: Alan Kelly, 447, 1961–75.

Record Transfer Fee Received: £765,000 from Manchester C for Michael Robinson, June 1979.

Record Transfer Fee Paid: £200,000 to Tranmere R for Gary Bennett, March 1996.

Football League Record: 1888 Founder Member of League; 1901–04 Division 2; 1904–12 Division 1; 1912–13 Division 2; 1913–14 Division 1; 1914–15 Division 2; 1919–25 Division 1; 1925–34 Division 2; 1934–49 Division 1; 1949–51 Division 2; 1951–61 Division 1; 1961–70 Division 2; 1970–71 Division 3; 1971–74 Division 2; 1974–78 Division 3; 1978–81 Division 2; 1981–85 Division 3; 1985–87 Division 4; 1987–92 Division 3; 1992–93 Division 2; 1993–96 Division 3; 1996– Division 2.

Honours: Football League: Division 1 – Champions 1888–89 (first champions), 1889–90; Runners-up 1890–91, 1891–92, 1892–93, 1905–06, 1952–53, 1957–58; *Division 2* – Champions 1903–04, 1912–13, 1950–51; Runners-up 1914–15, 1933–34; *Division 3* – Champions 1970–71, 1995–96; *Division 4* – Runners-up 1986–87. *FA Cup:* Winners 1889, 1938; Runners-up 1888, 1922, 1937, 1954, 1964. *Double Performed:* 1888–89. *Football League Cup:* best season: 4th rd, 1963, 1966, 1972, 1981.

Colours: White and navy shirts, navy shorts, navy stockings. *Change colours:* Red/navy.

Did you know?
In the 1995–96 season, Preston North End became the last club to lose its away record in a sequence of 21 unbeaten games.

PRESTON NORTH END FC

PRESTON NORTH END 1995–96 LEAGUE RECORD

Match No.	Date	Venue	Opponents	Result	H/T Score	Lg. Pos.	Goalscorers	Atten- dance
1	Aug 12	H	Lincoln C	L	1-2	1-1	—	Saville	7813
2	19	A	Plymouth Arg	W	2-0	0-0	11	Hammond (og), Bryson	6862
3	26	H	Wigan Ath	D	1-1	1-1	11	Atkinson	6837
4	29	A	Bury	D	0-0	0-0	—		4682
5	Sept 2	H	Cambridge U	D	3-3	1-1	13	Saville, Wilkinson, Lancashire	7034
6	9	A	Hereford U	W	1-0	0-0	10	Saville	3124
7	12	A	Colchester U	D	2-2	0-1	—	Cartwright, Bryson	2869
8	16	H	Scunthorpe U	D	2-2	1-0	12	Atkinson, Bryson	7391
9	23	A	Fulham	D	2-2	1-1	11	Bryson (pen), Davey	5209
10	30	H	Chester C	W	2-0	0-0	8	Wilkinson, Saville	8544
11	Oct 7	H	Scarborough	W	3-2	1-1	8	Saville, Wilkinson, Davey	7702
12	14	A	Torquay U	W	4-0	2-0	3	Bryson 2, Saville 2	4058
13	21	H	Mansfield T	W	6-0	3-0	2	Wilkinson 3, Saville 3	8989
14	28	A	Doncaster R	D	2-2	1-1	2	Davey 2	4413
15	31	A	Northampton T	W	2-1	1-0	—	Wilcox, Saville	4695
16	Nov 4	H	Leyton Orient	W	4-0	0-0	1	Saville 3, Davey	9823
17	18	A	Exeter C	D	1-1	0-1	3	Moyes	3550
18	25	H	Hartlepool U	W	3-0	1-0	3	Moyes, Atkinson, Saville	9449
19	Dec 9	A	Fulham	D	1-1	0-1	2	Bryson	8422
20	16	A	Chester C	D	1-1	1-1	2	Wilkinson	5004
21	23	H	Gillingham	D	0-0	0-0	1		10,669
22	Jan 1	H	Cardiff C	W	5-0	1-0	3	Davey, Brown, Saville 2, Atkinson	8354
23	6	A	Barnet	L	0-1	0-0	3		2737
24	13	H	Plymouth Arg	W	3-2	2-1	2	Bryson, Davey, Cartwright	11,126
25	20	A	Lincoln C	D	0-0	0-0	2		5185
26	30	A	Darlington	W	2-1	0-1	—	Cartwright, Saville (pen)	2599
27	Feb 3	A	Wigan Ath	W	1-0	0-0	2	Kilbane	5567
28	10	H	Barnet	L	0-1	0-0	2		9974
29	17	H	Colchester U	W	2-0	2-0	2	Saville 2	9335
30	24	A	Scunthorpe U	W	2-1	0-0	2	Saville, Lancashire	3638
31	27	H	Hereford U	D	2-2	1-1	—	Atkinson, Saville	9761
32	Mar 2	H	Rochdale	L	1-2	1-2	2	Saville	9698
33	9	A	Gillingham	D	1-1	0-0	2	Davey	10,602
34	12	A	Rochdale	W	3-0	2-0	—	Birch, Wilkinson, Moyes	4597
35	16	H	Darlington	D	1-1	1-1	2	Bryson	11,419
36	23	A	Cardiff C	W	1-0	0-0	2	Saville	3511
37	26	H	Bury	D	0-0	0-0	—		12,260
38	30	A	Scarborough	W	2-1	1-0	1	Davey, Bennett	3771
39	Apr 2	H	Torquay U	W	1-0	1-0	—	Wilkinson	11,965
40	6	H	Doncaster R	W	1-0	0-0	1	Birch	12,773
41	8	A	Mansfield T	D	0-0	0-0	1		4661
42	13	H	Northampton T	L	0-3	0-1	1		11,774
43	16	A	Cambridge U	L	1-2	1-0	—	Saville	2831
44	20	A	Leyton Orient	W	2-0	1-0	1	Saville 2	5170
45	27	A	Hartlepool U	W	2-0	1-0	1	Davey, Saville	5076
46	May 4	H	Exeter C	W	2-0	1-0	1	Saville, Wilkinson	18,700

Final League Position: 1

GOALSCORERS

League (78): Saville 29 (1 pen), Davey 10, Wilkinson 9, Bryson 9 (1 pen), Atkinson 5, Cartwright 3, Moyes 3, Birch 2, Lancashire 2, Bennett 1, Brown 1, Kilbane 1, Wilcox 1, own goal 1.
Coca-Cola Cup (3): Bryson 1, Cartwright 1, Kidd 1.
FA Cup (3): Cartwright 1, Wilcox 1, Wilkinson 1.

Vaughan J 40	Fensome A 20	Fleming T 5	Davey S 37+1	Kidd R 23+7	Moyes D 41	Raynor P 2+1	Bryson I 44	Saville A 44	Wilkinson S 36+6	Atkinson G 42+2	Lancashire G 2+4	Sharp R 1	Magee K 4+1	Ainsworth G —+2	Squires J 3+4	Holmes S 8	Cartwright L 22+4	Brown M 6+4	Richardson B 3	Johnson A 2	Barrick D 39+1	Smart A —+2	Wilcox R 27	Kibane K 7+4	McDonald N 8+3	Bishop C 4	Moilanen T 2	Sparrow P 13	Birch P 11	Grant T —+1	Bennett G 5+3	Gage K 4+3	Lucas D 1	Match No.
1	2¹	3	4	5	6	7	8	9	10	11	12																							1
1	2¹		7	5	6		8	9	10	4²		3	11	12	13																			2
1	2	3			6		8	9	10	4			11¹	12		5	7																	3
1	2	3			6		8	9	10	4			11			5	7																	4
1	2	3		13	6¹		8	9	10	4	12		11²		14	5	7³																	5
	2	3	11				8	9	10	4						5	7		1	6														6
	2¹	3					8	9	10³	4	12			14	13	5	7	11²	1	6														7
	2		12		6		8	9	10	4					13	5	7²	11¹	1		3													8
1	2		7		6		8¹	9	10	4	12						11				3		5											9
1	2		7		6		8	9	10	4	12						11¹				3		5											10
1	2		7	12	6		8	9	10	4					13		11²				3		5¹											11
1	2		7	12	6		8	9	10	4²					13		11				3		5¹											12
1	2		7¹		6		8	9	10	4	12						11				3		5											13
1	2		7	12	6		8	9	10	4							11				3		5¹											14
1	2		7		6		8	9	10	4	12						11¹				3		5											15
1	2		7		6		8	9	10	4							11				3		5											16
1	2		7	12	6		8	9	10	4					13		11²				3		5¹											17
1	2		7		6		8	9	10	4							11				3		5											18
1	2¹		7		6		8	9	10	4	12						11				3		5											19
1	2		7		6		8	9	10¹	4	12						11				3		5											20
1	2		7		6		8	9	10	4							11				3		5											21
1	2		7		6		8	9		4	12						11				3		5¹		10									22
1	2¹		7²		6		8	9		4	12				13		11				3		5		10									23
1			7		6		8	9	10	4							11				3		5					2						24
			7		6		8¹	9		4	12						11				3		5		10		1	2						25
			7		6		8¹	9		4	12				13		11				3		5		10²		1	2						26
1			7		6		8²	9	10	4	12				13		11				3		5¹					2						27
1			7		6		8	9		4¹	12						11				3		5		10			2						28
1			7		6		8	9	10	4							11				3		5					2						29
1			7		6		8	9	10	4	12						11¹				3		5					2						30
1			7		6¹		8	9	10²	4³	12			14	13		11				3		5					2						31
1			7		6		8	9	10¹	4	12			14	13		11²				3		5					2³						32
1			7		6		8	9	10	4											3		5					2	11					33
1			7		6		8	9	10	4											3		5					2	11					34
1			7¹		6		8	9	10	4											3		5					2	11		12			35
1			7		6		8	9	10	4	12										3		5¹					2	11					36
1			7		6		8	9	10	4											3		5					2	11					37
1			7		6		8	9	10	4											3		5					2¹	11					38
1			7		6		8	9	10	4											3		5					2¹	11			12		39
1			7		6		8	9	10												3		5					2	11					40
1			7		6		8	9	10	4	12				13						3		5					2²	11¹					41
1			7		6		8	9	10	4²	12				13						3		5					2	11¹					42
1			7		6		8	9	10	4¹	12				13						3		5					2	11²					43
1			7		6		8	9	10	4¹											3		5					2	11			12		44
			7		6		8	9	10	4											3		5					2	11				1	45
1			7		6		8	9	10	4²	12				13						3		5					2	11¹					46

Coca-Cola Cup
First Round   Sunderland   (h) 1-1
                            (a) 2-3

FA Cup
First Round   Carlisle U   (a) 2-1
Second Round   Bradford C   (a) 1-2

QUEENS PARK RANGERS 1995-96   *Back row (left to right):* John Cross, Danny Maddix, Karl Ready, Chris Plummer, Daniele Dichio, Tony Roberts, Richard Hurst, Alan McDonald, Alan McCarthy, Kevin Gallen, Simon Osborn, Steven Parmenter.

Middle row: Brian Morris (Physio), Terry Warren (Assistant Physio), Les Boyle (Kit Manager), Matthew Lockwood, David Bardsley, Michael Mahoney-Johnson, Trevor Sinclair, Sieb Dykstra, Steve Yates, Dennis Bailey, Graeme Power, Nigel Quashie, Phil Parkes (Goalkeeping Coach), Billy Bonds (Youth Team Manager), John Nolan (Assistant Kit Manager), John Hollins (Reserve Team Manager).

Front row: Andrew McDermott, Mark Graham, Bradley Allen, Matthew Brazier, Steve Hodge, Andrew Impey, Ray Wilkins (Player/Manager), Frank Sibley (Assistant Manager), Simon Barker, Gary Penrice, Trevor Challis, Rufus Brevett, Ian Holloway, Lee Charles.

(Photograph: Action Images)

Division 1   QUEENS PARK RANGERS

South Africa Road, London W12 7PA. Telephone: (0181) 743 0262. Fax: (0181) 749 0994. Box Office: (0181) 749 5744 (24 hour information service 0181 749 7798). Supporters Club: (0181) 749 6771. Club Shop: (0181) 749 6862. Marketing: (0181) 740 8737.

Ground capacity: 19,148.

Record attendance: 35,353 v Leeds U, Division 1, 27 April 1974.

Record receipts: £218,475 v Manchester U, FA Premier League, 5 February 1994.

Pitch measurements: 112yd × 72yd.

Chairman: P. D. Ellis.

Directors: R. B. Copus ACA, A. Ellis, A. Ingham, R. C. Thompson.

Manager: Ray Wilkins MBE. *Assistant Manager/Coach:* Frank Sibley.

Secretary: Miss S. F. Marson. *Commercial Controller:* Leon Gold.

Reserve Team Coach: John Hollins MBE.

Physio: Brian Morris.

Year Formed: 1885 *(see Foundation). Turned Professional:* 1898. *Ltd Co.:* 1899.

Club Nicknames: 'Rangers' or 'Rs'. *Previous Name:* 1885–87, St Jude's.

Previous Grounds: 1885 *(see Foundation)*, Welford's Fields; 1888–99; London Scottish Ground, Brondesbury, Home Farm, Kensal Rise Green, Gun Club Wormwood Scrubs, Kilburn Cricket Ground; 1899, Kensal Rise Athletic Ground; 1901, Latimer Road, Notting Hill; 1904, Agricultural Society, Park Royal; 1907, Park Royal Ground; 1917, Loftus Road; 1931, White City; 1933, Loftus Road; 1962, White City; 1963, Loftus Road.

Foundation: There is an element of doubt about the date of the foundation of this club, but it is believed that in either 1885 or 1886 it was formed through the amalgamation of Christchurch Rangers and St. Jude's Institute FC. The leading light was George Wodehouse, whose family maintained a connection with the club until comparatively recent times. Most of the players came from the Queen's Park district so this name was adopted after a year as St. Jude's Institute.

First Football League game: 28 August 1920, Division 3, v Watford (h) L 1-2 – Price; Blackman, Wingrove; McGovern, Grant, O'Brien; Faulkner, Birch (1), Smith, Gregory, Middlemiss.

Record League Victory: 9–2 v Tranmere R, Division 3, 3 December 1960 – Drinkwater; Woods, Ingham; Keen, Rutter, Angell; Lazarus (2), Bedford (2), Evans (2), Andrews (1), Clark (2).

Record Cup Victory: 8–1 v Bristol R (away), FA Cup 1st rd, 27 November 1937 – Gilfillan; Smith, Jefferson; Lowe, James, March; Cape, Mallett, Cheetham (3), Fitzgerald (3) Bott (2). 8–1 v Crewe Alex, Milk Cup 1st rd, 3 October 1983 – Hucker; Neill, Dawes, Waddock (1), McDonald (1), Fenwick, Micklewhite (1), Stewart (1), Allen (1), Stainrod (3), Gregory.

Record Defeat: 1–8 v Mansfield T, Division 3, 15 March 1965 and v Manchester U, Division 1, 19 March 1969.

Most League Points (2 for a win): 67, Division 3, 1966–67.

Most League Points (3 for a win): 85, Division 2, 1982–83.

Most League Goals: 111, Division 3, 1961–62.

Highest League Scorer in Season: George Goddard, 37, Division 3 (S), 1929–30.

Most League Goals in Total Aggregate: George Goddard, 172, 1926–34.

Most Capped Player: Alan McDonald, 52, Northern Ireland.

Most League Appearances: Tony Ingham, 519, 1950–63.

Record Transfer Fee Received: £6,000,000 from Newcastle U for Les Ferdinand, June 1995.

Record Transfer Fee Paid: £1,500,000 to Rangers for Mark Hateley, November 1995.

Football League Record: 1920 Original Members of Division 3; 1921–48 Division 3 (S); 1948–52 Division 2; 1952–58 Division 3 (S); 1958–67 Division 3; 1967–68 Division 2; 1968–69 Division 1; 1969–73 Division 2; 1973–79 Division 1; 1979–83 Division 2; 1983–92 Division 1; 1992–96 FA Premier League; 1996– Division 1.

Honours: Football League: Division 1 – Runners-up 1975–76; Division 2 – Champions 1982–83; Runners-up 1967–68, 1972–73; Division 3 (S) – Champions 1947–48; Runners-up 1946–47; Division 3 – Champions 1966–67. *FA Cup:* Runners-up 1982. *Football League Cup:* Winners 1967; Runners-up 1986. (In 1966–67 won Division 3 and Football League Cup). **European Competitions:** *UEFA Cup:* 1976–77, 1984–85.

Colours: Blue and white hooped shirts, white shorts, white stockings. *Change colours:* All red with black trim.

Did you know?
Queens Park Rangers first capped player was right-half Evelyn Lintott who played three times for England and in November 1908 was transferred to Bradford City for £1000.

QUEENS PARK RANGERS 1995–96 LEAGUE RECORD

Match No.	Date	Venue	Opponents	Result		H/T Score	Lg. Pos.	Goalscorers	Attendance
1	Aug 19	A	Blackburn R	L	0-1	0-1	—		25,932
2	23	H	Wimbledon	L	0-3	0-1	—		11,837
3	26	H	Manchester C	W	1-0	1-0	15	Barker	14,212
4	30	A	Liverpool	L	0-1	0-1	—		37,548
5	Sept 9	H	Sheffield W	L	0-3	0-0	18		12,659
6	16	A	Leeds U	W	3-1	2-0	15	Dichio 2, Sinclair	31,505
7	25	H	Tottenham H	L	2-3	1-0	—	Dichio, Impey	15,659
8	30	A	Bolton W	W	1-0	0-0	12	Dichio	17,362
9	Oct 14	H	Newcastle U	L	2-3	1-0	13	Dichio 2	18,254
10	21	A	Middlesbrough	L	0-1	0-1	16		29,283
11	28	H	Nottingham F	D	1-1	0-0	14	Sinclair	17,549
12	Nov 4	A	Southampton	L	0-2	0-1	16		15,137
13	19	H	Coventry C	D	1-1	1-0	16	Barker	11,189
14	22	A	Everton	L	0-2	0-2	—		30,009
15	25	A	West Ham U	L	0-1	0-0	18		21,504
16	Dec 2	H	Middlesbrough	D	1-1	1-1	18	McDonald	17,546
17	9	A	Tottenham H	L	0-1	0-1	18		28,851
18	16	H	Bolton W	W	2-1	1-1	16	Osborn, Impey	11,456
19	23	H	Aston Villa	W	1-0	0-0	16	Gallen	14,778
20	26	A	Arsenal	L	0-3	0-1	17		38,259
21	30	A	Manchester U	L	1-2	0-1	18	Dichio	41,890
22	Jan 2	H	Chelsea	L	1-2	0-0	—	Allen	14,904
23	13	H	Blackburn R	L	0-1	0-0	19		13,957
24	20	A	Wimbledon	L	1-2	0-1	19	Hateley	9123
25	Feb 3	A	Manchester C	L	0-2	0-1	19		27,509
26	11	H	Liverpool	L	1-2	0-2	19	Dichio	18,405
27	17	A	Sheffield W	W	3-1	1-1	19	Barker 2, Goodridge	22,442
28	Mar 2	H	Arsenal	D	1-1	1-0	19	Gallen	17,970
29	6	H	Leeds U	L	1-2	1-2	—	Gallen	13,991
30	9	A	Aston Villa	L	2-4	0-1	19	Dichio, Gallen	28,221
31	16	H	Manchester U	D	1-1	0-0	19	Irwin (og)	18,817
32	23	A	Chelsea	D	1-1	1-1	20	Barker	25,590
33	30	H	Southampton	W	3-0	1-0	18	Brevett, Dichio, Gallen	17,615
34	Apr 6	A	Newcastle U	L	1-2	0-0	19	Holloway	36,583
35	8	H	Everton	W	3-1	2-0	18	Gallen, Hateley, Impey	18,349
36	13	A	Coventry C	L	0-1	0-0	19		22,906
37	27	H	West Ham U	W	3-0	0-0	19	Ready, Gallen 2	18,828
38	May 5	A	Nottingham F	L	0-3	0-1	19		22,910

Final League Position: 19

GOALSCORERS

League (38): Dichio 10, Gallen 8, Barker 5, Impey 3, Hateley 2, Sinclair 2, Allen 1, Brevett 1, Goodridge 1, Holloway 1, McDonald 1, Osborn 1, Ready 1, own goal 1.
Coca-Cola Cup (6): Dichio 1, Gallen 1, Impey 1, Ready 1, Sinclair 1, own goal 1.
FA Cup (3): Quashie 2, Sinclair 1.

Roberts T 5	Bardsley D 28 + 1	Brevett R 27	Barker S 33	McDonald A 25 + 1	Maddix D 20 + 2	Impey A 28 + 1	Holloway I 26 + 1	Dichio D 21 + 8	Gallen K 26 + 4	Sinclair T 37	Osborn S 6 + 3	Zelic N 3 + 1	Wilkins R 11 + 4	Penrice G — + 3	Sommer J 33	Ready K 16 + 6	Allen B 5 + 3	Yates S 30	Goodridge G — + 7	Brazier M 6 + 5	Challis T 10 + 1	Charles L — + 4	Hateley M 10 + 4	Quashie N 11	Murray P 1	Plummer C — + 1	Match No.
1	2^1	3	4	5	6	7	8	9	10	11	12																1
1	2	3	4^2	5^1	6	7	8	9	10	11			12	13													2
1	2	3	4	5	6	7	8	9	10^1	11				12													3
1	2	3	4	5	6	7		9	10	11			8^1	12													4
1	2	3^1	4	5	6	7	8	9	10	11				12													5
	2	3	4	5	6		8	9		11	10				1	7											6
		3	4	5	6	7	8	9		11	10^1				1	2	12										7
		3	4	5	6	7	8^1	9		11	10		12		1	2											8
		3	4		6	7	8	9		11	10^1				1	2		5	12								9
	2	3^1	10		6	7	8	9	12	11					1	4		5									10
	2	3	10^2		6	7^3		9		11	12		8		1	4^1		5	13	14							11
	2	3	10		6			9	12	11		7	8		1	4^1		5									12
		3^2	4		6	7		9	10	11^1		8	12		1	2		5			13						13
		8	12		6	7		13	10	11^2			4		1	2		5	3	9^1							14
		4	6	12		7^2	8	9	10	11^1					1	2		5	3		13						15
		4		6		7	8	12	10^1	11					1	2		5				3	9				16
	2	4^2	6			7	8		10^1	11	12				1			5			3	13	9				17
	2		4		6	7	8		12	11	10^1				1	13		5				3^2	9				18
	2	3	4		6	7			10^3	11			8^2		1	12	13	5					9^1				19
	2	3	4		6	7	12	13	10^1	11			8^2		1			5					9				20
	2^2	3			6	7	8	12		11					1	13	10^1	5		4			9				21
12					6	7	8	13		11					1	2^1	10	5		4	3		9^2				22
	2		6	12	7^2					11			8^1		1		10	5	13	4^3	3	14	9				23
	2		8	6				12		11					1		10^1	5	13	4	3^2		9	7			24
		4	5	6		8	12	13		11					1	10^2	2		14		3		9^1	7^3			25
	2	3	4		6		8	9	10	11					1			5						7			26
	2	3	4		6		7^2	8	10^1	11					1	12		5			13		9				27
	2		4			7^1	8	12	10	11					1	6		5				3	9				28
	2		4^1				8	9	10^2	11					1	6		5	13	12	3			7			29
	2	3	4				8	9	10	11					1	6		5			12			7^1			30
	2	3	4		6	12	8	9^1	10^2	11					1	13		5					14	7^1			31
	2	3	8		6	4^1	7	9	10^3	11					1	12		5^2			13		14				32
	2	3	4		6	7	8	9	10	11					1			5									33
	2	3			6	7	8	9^1	10	11			4		1			5					12				34
	2	3			6	7	8		10	11			4		1			5					9				35
	2	3			6	7	8		10	11			12		1			5					9^1				36
		3	4		6	7			10	11		8			1	2		5				12	9^1				37
	2^1	3	4		6^3			9	10	11			8^2		1	12		5			13			7		14	38

Coca-Cola Cup

Second Round	Oxford U	(a)	1-1
		(h)	2-1
Third Round	York C	(h)	3-1
Fourth Round	Aston Villa	(a)	0-1

FA Cup

Third Round	Tranmere R	(a)	2-0
Fourth Round	Chelsea	(h)	1-2

READING 1995-96   *Back row (left to right):* Trevor Morley, Jeff Hopkins, Michael Thorp, Matthew Stowell, Ron Grant (Kit Man), Stuart Lovell, David Bass, Martin Williams, Alan Carey.
Middle row: Lee Nogan, Michael Murphy, Michael Gilkes, Andy Bernal, Stuart Jones, Phil Parkinson, Simon Sheppard, Keith McPherson, Michael Meaker, Paul Holsgrove, Dylan Kerr.
Front row: Phil Holder (Coach), Derek Simpson, James Lambert, Steve Swales, Jimmy Quinn (Joint Player/Manager), Adrian Williams, Mick Gooding (Joint Player/Manager), Dariusz Wdowczyk, Tom Jones, Gareth Randell, Paul Turner (Physio).

Division 1 **READING**

Elm Park, Norfolk Road, Reading RG30 2EF. Telephone: (01189) 507878. Fax: (01189) 566628. Community Office: (01189) 560898. Promotions Office: (01189) 464008.

Ground capacity: 15,000.

Record attendance: 33,042 v Brentford, FA Cup 5th rd, 19 February 1927.

Record receipts: £110,741 v Manchester U, FA Cup 4th rd, 27 January 1996.

Pitch measurements: 112yd × 77yd.

Life President: J. H. Brooks.

Chairman: John Madejski.

Directors: G. Denton, I. Wood-Smith.

General Manager: Adrian Porter.

Joint Managers: Jimmy Quinn/Mick Gooding.

Coach: Phil Holder. *Youth Development Officer:* Bobby Williams.

Physio: Paul Turner.

Commercial Manager: Kevin Girdler.

Secretary: Ms Andrea Barker.

Year Formed: 1871. *Turned Professional:* 1895. *Ltd Co.:* 1895.

Club Nickname: 'The Royals'.

Previous Grounds: 1871, Reading Recreation; Reading Cricket Ground; 1882, Coley Park; 1889, Caversham Cricket Ground; 1896, Elm Park.

Foundation: Reading was formed as far back as 1871 at a public meeting held at the Bridge Street Rooms. They first entered the FA Cup as early as 1877 when they amalgamated with the Reading Hornets. The club was further strengthened in 1889 when Earley FC joined them. They were the first winners of the Berks and Bucks Cup in 1878–79.

First Football League game: 28 August 1920, Division 3, v Newport Co (a) W 1-0 – Crawford; Smith, Horler; Christie, Mavin, Getgood; Spence, Weston, Yarnell, Bailey (1), Andrews.

Record League Victory: 10–2 v Crystal Palace, Division 3 (S), 4 September 1946 – Groves; Glidden, Gulliver; McKenna, Ratcliffe, Young; Chitty, Maurice Edelston (3), McPhee (4), Barney (1), Deverell (2).

Record Cup Victory: 6–0 v Leyton, FA Cup 2nd rd, 12 December 1925 – Duckworth; Eggo, McConnell; Wilson, Messer, Evans; Smith (2), Braithwaite (1), Davey (1), Tinsley, Robson (2).

Record Defeat: 0–18 v Preston NE, FA Cup 1st rd, 1893–94.

Most League Points (2 for a win): 65, Division 4, 1978–79.

Most League Points (3 for a win): 94, Division 3, 1985–86.

Most League Goals: 112, Division 3 (S), 1951–52.

Highest League Scorer in Season: Ronnie Blackman, 39, Division 3 (S), 1951–52.

Most League Goals in Total Aggregate: Ronnie Blackman, 158, 1947–54.

Most Capped Player: Jimmy Quinn, 17 (46), Northern Ireland.

Most League Appearances: Martin Hicks, 500, 1978–91.

Record Transfer Fee Received: £1,575,000 from Newcastle U for Shaka Hislop, August 1995.

Record Transfer Fee Paid: £700,000 to Tottenham H for Darren Caskey, February 1996.

Football League Record: 1920 Original Member of Division 3; 1921–26 Division 3 (S); 1926–31 Division 2; 1931–58 Division 3 (S); 1958–71 Division 3; 1971–76 Division 4; 1976–77 Division 3; 1977–79 Division 4; 1979–83 Division 3; 1983–84 Division 4; 1984–86 Division 3; 1986–88 Division 2; 1988–92 Division 3; 1992–94 Division 2; 1994– Division 1.

Honours: Football League: Division 1 – Runners-up 1994–95; Division 2 – Champions 1993–94; Division 3 – Champions 1985–86. Division 3 (S) – Champions 1925–26; Runners-up 1931–32, 1934–35, 1948–49, 1951–52; Division 4 – Champions 1978–79. *FA Cup:* Semi-final 1927. *Football League Cup:* best season: 5th rd. 1996. *Simod Cup:* Winners 1988.

Colours: Royal blue and white hooped shirts, white shorts, white stockings. *Change colours:* Toro red and white shirts, Toro red shorts, Toro red/white stockings.

Did you know?
On 2 December 1995 during Reading's 3-1 win over West Bromwich Albion, Jimmy Quinn was a second-half emergency goalkeeper. It was their first win over Albion since 1928.

READING 1995–96 LEAGUE RECORD

Match No.	Date	Venue	Opponents	Result		H/T Score	Lg. Pos.	Goalscorers	Attendance
1	Aug 12	A	Stoke C	D	1-1	0-1	—	Williams A	11,932
2	19	H	Derby Co	W	3-2	1-0	3	Lovell, Morley, Nogan	9280
3	26	A	Portsmouth	D	0-0	0-0	6		9917
4	29	H	Millwall	L	1-2	1-0	—	Gooding	10,143
5	Sept 1	A	Southend U	D	0-0	0-0	13		4962
6	9	H	Luton T	W	3-1	1-1	11	Nogan 2, Lovell (pen)	8550
7	12	H	Grimsby T	L	0-2	0-1	—		7283
8	16	A	Leicester C	D	1-1	1-0	14	Bernal	19,103
9	23	H	Port Vale	D	2-2	1-2	14	Lambert 2	7819
10	30	A	Sunderland	D	2-2	0-0	16	Lovell, Kerr	17,503
11	Oct 7	A	WBA	L	0-2	0-0	18		12,956
12	14	H	Huddersfield T	W	3-1	1-1	15	Lambert, Williams A, Quinn	8534
13	21	A	Oldham Ath	L	1-2	1-1	15	Lovell	5709
14	28	A	Ipswich T	L	1-4	0-1	18	Lovell	10,281
15	Nov 4	A	Crystal Palace	W	2-0	2-0	16	Shaw (og), Nogan	16,058
16	11	H	Birmingham C	L	0-1	0-0	17		10,203
17	18	H	Barnsley	D	0-0	0-0	17		6695
18	21	A	Charlton Ath	L	1-2	1-1	—	Brown	7840
19	25	A	Sheffield U	D	0-0	0-0	18		9737
20	Dec 2	H	WBA	W	3-1	2-1	17	Morley, Holsgrove, Nogan	7910
21	9	A	Port Vale	L	2-3	1-3	17	Morley, Quinn (pen)	6376
22	16	H	Sunderland	D	1-1	0-1	18	Quinn	9431
23	30	A	Norwich C	D	3-3	1-1	19	Lambert, Nogan, Kerr	13,556
24	Jan 1	A	Tranmere R	W	1-0	0-0	18	Morley	8421
25	13	A	Derby Co	L	0-3	0-0	19		15,123
26	20	H	Stoke C	W	1-0	0-0	18	Gooding	8082
27	Feb 4	H	Portsmouth	L	0-1	0-0	19		7924
28	10	A	Millwall	D	1-1	1-0	19	Bowry (og)	8875
29	17	A	Grimsby T	D	0-0	0-0	20		6546
30	24	H	Leicester C	D	1-1	0-0	21	Lovell (pen)	9817
31	27	A	Luton T	W	2-1	1-1	—	Booty, Lovell	6683
32	Mar 2	H	Watford	D	0-0	0-0	19		8933
33	9	A	Wolverhampton W	D	1-1	1-1	18	Gooding	25,954
34	16	H	Norwich C	L	0-3	0-1	22		8501
35	19	H	Southend U	D	3-3	1-0	—	Nogan 3	5321
36	23	A	Tranmere R	L	1-2	1-1	21	Caskey	6249
37	30	H	Oldham Ath	W	2-0	1-0	21	Quinn 2	7025
38	Apr 2	A	Huddersfield T	L	1-3	1-0	—	Williams A	11,828
39	6	A	Ipswich T	W	2-1	1-0	21	Bernal, Quinn	17,328
40	8	H	Crystal Palace	L	0-2	0-1	21		12,576
41	13	A	Barnsley	W	1-0	0-0	20	Quinn (pen)	5488
42	16	A	Watford	L	2-4	0-2	—	Caskey, Quinn	8113
43	20	H	Charlton Ath	D	0-0	0-0	20		9778
44	27	H	Sheffield U	L	0-3	0-0	21		9769
45	30	H	Wolverhampton W	W	3-0	2-0	—	Williams M, Quinn 2	12,828
46	May 5	A	Birmingham C	W	2-1	2-1	19	Nogan, Quinn	16,233

Final League Position: 19

GOALSCORERS

League (54): Quinn 11 (2 pens), Nogan 10, Lovell 7 (2 pens), Lambert 4, Morley 4, Gooding 3, Williams A 3, Bernal 2, Caskey 2, Kerr 2, Booty 1, Brown 1, Holsgrove 1, Williams M 1, own goals 2.
Coca-Cola Cup (10): Quinn 4 (1 pen), Lovell 2, Lambert 1, Morley 1, Nogan 1, own goal 1.
FA Cup (3): Quinn 2, Morley 1.

M.No	Sheppard S 18	Bernal A 34	Gooding M 37+3	Parkinson P 36+6	Williams A 31	McPherson K 16	Gilkes M 36+8	Jones T 13+8	Nogan L 32+7	Lovell S 28+7	Williams M 11+4	Morley T 14+3	Wdowczyk D 29+1	Meaker M 15+6	Swales S 4+5	Quinn J 20+15	Lambert J 10+5	Holsgrove P 27+3	Thorp M 2	Mikhailov B 16	Codner R 3+1	Kerr D 4+4	Gordon N —+1	Woods C 5	Brown K 12	Hammond N 5	Sutton S 2	Booty M 17	Hopkins J 14	Caskey D 15	Freeman A —+1	Match No.
1	1	2²	3	4	5	6	7	8	9¹	10	11	12	13																			1
2	1		3	8	5	6	7²	2	9	10		11	4	12	13																	2
3	1	2	3	8	5	6	7²		9	10		11¹	4	12	13																	3
4	1	2	3	8¹	5	6	12		9	10²	13		4	11	7																	4
5	1	2	3	8	5	6	12		9³	10	13		4	11²	7¹	14																5
6	1	2	3²	6	5				7	12	9	10	8		4¹	11		13														6
7	1	2	3	6	5			7	4	9	10	8²		11¹			12	13														7
8	1	2	3		5	6	7	11	9	10							4	8														8
9		2		12		6	7	11	9	10			13³		5²	3	4		1	8¹	14											9
10		2	3	8			7		9¹	10			6		12	11²	4³	5	1	14	13											10
11	1	2	3	8	5		7			10			6		9¹	11	4					12										11
12		2	12	8	5		7			10			6		9	11	4¹		1		3											12
13	1	2	12	8	5		7		13	10			6¹		9	11²	4				3											13
14		6	8		5		7		12	10	13			11³		9¹	14				4⁷	3		1	2							14
15		3	8	5	6		7	12	9	10						11					4¹			1	2							15
16	5	3	8		6	7			9	10¹				12		4	11							1	2							16
17	5	3	8		6	7²	13	9¹	12		10					4	11							1	2							17
18	5	3	8		6	7	12		9²	10			13			4¹	11							1	2							18
19	1	5	3¹	8		6	12	7		10			9²	4			11								2							19
20	1²	5³	3	8		6	12	7	10				9	4¹		14	13		11						2							20
21			8		6	7	5³	10	13	14		9	4			3¹	12	11²		1					2							21
22			8³	5	6	7²	3¹	10				9	4			12	13	11				14			2	1						22
23			8	5	6¹	7²	13	10				9	4			12	3¹	11				14			2	1						23
24		6	8	5			12	10¹	13			9²	4			7	14	11				3³			2	1						24
25	4	3	8	5		12	6¹	10²	13			9				7		11							2	1						25
26	2	3	8	5		12		10				9²	4¹			7	13	11									1	6				26
27	4	3	8	5		6	12	13	14				9³	7¹	11									1			2					27
28		3		5		6	8¹	10	4	12	9			7	11										1		2					28
29		3		5			7	8	10		9¹	4	12				11		1									2	6			29
30		3	9	5		12		8	10		4	7					11¹		1									2	6			30
31	3		9	5		12		8²	10		4¹	7	13				11		1									2	6			31
32	3	12	9¹	5		11		8				7	10				13		1									2	6	4		32
33	3	8	9	5		11		12	10¹			7					13		1									2	6	4²		33
34	1	3¹	8	9²	5		11		10				7				13	12										2	6	4		34
35		8	12	5		11¹		9	10²				3	7	13				1									2	6	4		35
36		8	12	5		11		9	10¹				3	7²	13				1									2	6	4		36
37	1	2	8	12	5		11		9²	10			3¹	7	13														6	4		37
38	1	2	3	8¹	5		11		10				7	12	9		6													4		38
39	1	6	8	11	5¹		7			13	10²	3		9		12											2			4		39
40	1	6	8	11³			7		12	13	10²	3	14	9¹		5											2			4		40
41		6	8	11			7		12		10	3		9¹				1									2	5		4		41
42		6	11³				7²	12	8		10¹	3	13	9				1									2	5	4	14		42
43		6	8	11			7	12			10¹	3		9				1									2	5	4			43
44		6	3	8¹			7		12		10		11	9				1									2	5	4			44
45		6	3	12			7		8		10	2		9		11		1										5	4¹			45
46	1		3	12			7	2	8		10		6		5	9		11											4¹			46

Coca-Cola Cup

Second Round	WBA	(h)	1-1
		(a)	4-2
Third Round	Bury	(h)	2-1
Fourth Round	Southampton	(h)	2-1
Fifth Round	Leeds U	(a)	1-2

FA Cup

Third Round	Gillingham	(h)	3-1
Fourth Round	Manchester U	(h)	0-3

ROCHDALE 1995–96   *Back row (left to right):* Steve Whitehall, Mark Stuart, Paul Butler, Paul Williams, Ian Thompstone, Peter Valentine, Dave Bayliss.
Middle row: Jimmy Robson (Youth & Reserve Manager), Graham Shaw, Darren Ryan, Ian Gray, Chris Clarke, Dean Martin, John Deary, Mick Docherty (Manager).
Front row: Derek Hall, Jason Peake, Dave Thompson, Kevin Formby, Alex Russell, Jamie Taylor, Andy Thackeray.
(Photograph: Alpha Photography)

Division 3 **ROCHDALE**

Spotland, Sandy Lane, Rochdale OL11 5DS. Telephone: (01706) 44648. Fax: (01706) 48466. Commercial: (01706) 47521.

Ground capacity: 6448.

Record attendance: 24,231 v Notts Co, FA Cup 2nd rd, 10 December 1949.

Record receipts: £46,000 v Burnley, Division 4, 5 May 1992.

Pitch measurements: 114yd × 76yd.

President: Mrs L. Stoney.

Chairman: D. F. Kilpatrick.

Directors: G. R. Brierley, T. Butterworth, C. Dunphy, M. Mace, J. Marsh, G. Morris.

Manager: Graham Barrow.

Secretary: Miss Karen Smyth. *Coach:* Jimmy Robson. *Commercial Manager:* S. Walmsley.

Advertising & Sponsorship Manager: L. Duckworth. *Stadium Manager:* Ronnie Cowgill.

Physio: J. Dawson.

Year Formed: 1907. *Turned Professional:* 1907. *Ltd Co.:* 1910.

Club Nickname: 'The Dale'.

Foundation: Considering the love of rugby in their area, it is not surprising that Rochdale had difficulty in establishing an Association Football club. The earlier Rochdale Town club formed in 1900 went out of existence in 1907 when the present club was immediately established and joined the Manchester League, before graduating to the Lancashire Combination in 1908.

First Football League game: 27 August 1921, Division 3 (N), v Accrington Stanley (h) W 6-3 – Crabtree; Nuttall, Sheehan; Hill, Farrer, Yarwood; Hoad, Sandiford, Dennison (2), Owens (3), Carney (1).

Record League Victory: 8–1 v Chesterfield, Division 3 (N), 18 December 1926 – Hill; Brown, Ward; Hillhouse, Parkes, Braidwood; Hughes, Bertram, Whitehurst (5), Schofield (2), Martin (1).

Record Cup Victory: 8–2 v Crook T, FA Cup 1st rd, 26 November 1927 – Moody; Hopkins, Ward; Braidwood, Parkes, Barker; Tompkinson, Clennell (3) Whitehurst (4), Hall, Martin (1).

Record Defeat: 1–9 v Tranmere R, Division 3 (N), 25 December 1931.

Most League Points (2 for a win): 62, Division 3 (N), 1923–24.

Most League Points (3 for a win): 67, Division 4, 1991–92.

Most League Goals: 105, Division 3 (N), 1926–27.

Highest League Scorer in Season: Albert Whitehurst, 44, Division 3 (N), 1926–27.

Most League Goals in Total Aggregate: Reg Jenkins, 119, 1964–73.

Most Capped Player: None.

Most League Appearances: Graham Smith, 317, 1966–74.

Record Transfer Fee Received: £300,000 from Wimbledon for Alan Reeves, September 1994.

Record Transfer Fee Paid: £80,000 to Scunthorpe U for Andy Flounders, August 1991.

Football League Record: 1921 Elected to Division 3 (N); 1958–59 Division 3; 1959–69 Division 4; 1969–74 Division 3; 1974–92 Division 4; 1992– Division 3.

Football League: Division 3 best season: 9th, 1969–70; Division 3 (N) – Runners-up 1923–24, 1926–27. *FA Cup:* best season: 5th rd, 1990. *Football League Cup:* Runners-up 1962 (record for 4th Division club).

Colours: Blue with red and white chevrons. *Change colours:* White shirts, white shorts, blue stockings.

Did you know?
On 21 October 1995, Rochdale won 4-0 at Barnet, their first away win against any club in the London area.

ROCHDALE 1995–96 LEAGUE RECORD

Match No.	Date	Venue	Opponents	Result	H/T Score	Lg. Pos.	Goalscorers	Atten- dance
1	Aug 12	H	Cardiff C	D	3-3	2-2	—	Whitehall 2 (1 pen), Thompson	2321
2	19	A	Darlington	W	1-0	0-0	7	Whitehall (pen)	2139
3	26	H	Hartlepool U	W	4-0	1-0	3	Taylor 3, Thompson	1794
4	29	A	Torquay U	L	0-1	0-0	—		2139
5	Sept 2	H	Northampton T	L	1-2	0-1	12	Butler	2193
6	9	A	Lincoln C	W	2-1	1-0	7	Whitehall (pen), Stuart	2408
7	12	A	Fulham	D	1-1	1-1	—	Deary	3848
8	16	H	Mansfield T	D	1-1	0-0	8	Stuart	2173
9	23	A	Doncaster R	W	3-0	1-0	6	Whitehall (pen), Schofield (og), Stuart	2217
10	30	H	Exeter C	W	4-2	3-0	4	Stuart, Deary, Whitehall, Peake	2052
11	Oct 7	A	Gillingham	L	0-1	0-1	6		7785
12	14	H	Colchester U	D	1-1	0-1	5	Stuart	2193
13	21	A	Barnet	W	4-0	0-0	5	Peake, Stuart 2, Whitehall	2039
14	28	A	Cambridge U	W	3-1	1-0	3	Moulden, Whitehall 2	2344
15	31	H	Chester C	L	1-3	0-1	—	Peake	3018
16	Nov 4	A	Scunthorpe U	W	3-1	2-0	4	Stuart, Whitehall 2	3003
17	18	H	Hereford U	D	0-0	0-0	4		2619
18	25	A	Plymouth Arg	L	0-2	0-0	4		6558
19	Dec 9	H	Doncaster R	W	1-0	1-0	5	Whitehall (pen)	2168
20	16	A	Exeter C	L	0-2	0-1	5		3152
21	22	A	Leyton Orient	L	0-2	0-1	—		5399
22	Jan 2	A	Wigan Ath	L	0-2	0-0	—		2624
23	13	H	Darlington	L	1-2	1-0	10	Whitehall (pen)	1945
24	20	A	Cardiff C	L	0-1	0-0	12		2230
25	23	A	Scarborough	D	1-1	0-0	—	Peake	1400
26	Feb 3	A	Hartlepool U	D	1-1	0-0	13	Whitehall	1927
27	10	H	Scarborough	L	0-2	0-0	14		1662
28	13	H	Bury	D	1-1	0-0	—	Butler	3048
29	17	H	Fulham	D	1-1	1-1	15	Stuart	1923
30	20	A	Northampton T	L	1-2	0-0	—	Thompstone	3090
31	27	H	Lincoln C	D	3-3	2-1	—	Whitehall (pen), Stuart 2	1253
32	Mar 2	A	Preston NE	W	2-1	2-1	13	Whitehall, Stuart	9698
33	9	H	Leyton Orient	W	1-0	1-0	14	Lancaster	1934
34	12	H	Preston NE	L	0-3	0-2	—		4597
35	16	A	Bury	D	1-1	1-1	14	Butler	3473
36	19	A	Torquay U	W	3-0	1-0	—	Deary, Whitehall (pen), Thompson	1206
37	23	H	Wigan Ath	L	0-2	0-1	13		2870
38	30	H	Gillingham	W	2-0	2-0	13	Stuart, Thompson	2098
39	Apr 2	A	Colchester U	L	0-1	0-0	—		3021
40	6	A	Cambridge U	L	1-2	1-1	15	Lancaster	2186
41	8	H	Barnet	L	0-4	0-1	15		1492
42	13	A	Chester C	W	2-1	1-1	14	Whitehall 2	2158
43	16	A	Mansfield T	D	2-2	0-1	—	Hall, Whitehall	1814
44	20	H	Scunthorpe U	D	1-1	1-0	14	Deary	1654
45	27	H	Plymouth Arg	L	0-1	0-1	15		2355
46	May 4	A	Hereford U	L	0-2	0-1	15		5880

Final League Position: 15

GOALSCORERS
League (57): Whitehall 20 (8 pens), Stuart 13, Deary 4, Peake 4, Thompson 4, Butler 3, Taylor 3, Lancaster 2, Hall 1, Moulden 1, Thompstone 1, own goal 1.
Coca-Cola Cup (3): Shaw 1, Thompstone 1, own goal 1.
FA Cup (8): Deary 2, Moulden 2, Peake 2, Martin 1, Whitehall 1 (pen).

Gray I 20	Russell A 20+5	Formby K 18	Thompstone I 11+14	Valentine P 22+1	Butler P 38	Thompson D 43	Martin D 33+4	Shaw G 9+9	Whitehall S 46	Peake J 45+1	Williams P 1+11	Ryan D 4+3	Bayliss D 25+3	Hall D 9+5	Deary J 36	Taylor J 8+8	Moulden P 6+10	Hardy J 5+2	Stuart M 32+2	Thackeray A 27+2	Mitchell N 3+1	Clarke C 6	Price J 3	Pilkington K 6	Lancaster D 13+1	Key L 14	Powell F —+2	Proctor J 1+2	Barlow N 1+1	Lyons P 1+2	Match No.
1	2	3	4	5	6	7	8[2]	9[1]	10	11	12	13																			1
1	2	3	4[3]	5	6	7[2]		9[1]	10	11	12	13	8	14																	2
1	2	3			6	7	8		10[2]	11	12		5		4		9[1]	13													3
1	2	3	12		6	7	8[3]		10	11		13	5[2]		4		9[1]		14												4
1	2				6	7	8		10	11			5[2]		4		9[1]	12	3	13											5
1	2[1]	3			6	7[2]	8	13	10	11	12		5		4				9												6
1					6		8	7	10	11	9[1]		5		4		12		3		2										7
1	12		13		6	7	8[1]	9[2]	10	11[3]			5		4				3	14	2										8
1	12		13		6	7[3]	8	14	10[2]	11			5	3[1]	4				9		2										9
1		3			6	7	13	8	10	11	12		5		4				9[1]		2[2]										10
1	12	3			6	7	8[2]	13	10[3]	11[1]			5		4		14		9		2										11
1		3	12		6	7		8[1]	10	11			5[2]		4		13		9		2										12
1		3		5	6	7	8		10	11					4				9		2										13
1		3		5	6	7			10	11					4			8	9		2										14
1		3[1]	13	5	6	7			12	10	11				4		8[2]		9		2										15
1		3	8	5	6	7		4	12	10	11								9		2[1]										16
1		3	11[1]	5	6	7		4	13	10	12		9					8			2[2]										17
1		3	2		6	7		4	9	10	11[1]		5	12[2]	8		13														18
1		3	2		5	6		12	8[2]	10	11	13	9		4							7[1]									19
	2	3		5		7	8	12	10[2]	11	13	9[3]	6			14				4[1]	1										20
	2	3		5	6	7	8		10	11	12	4[1]					9[2]			13	1										21
	2[2]	3		5	6	7	8		10	11[1]	13		14		4				12	9[3]	1										22
		12	5	6		7[2]	4	13	10	11[3]					8	14	9[1]	3		2				1							23
	2			3	5		7	8	12	10	11		6[2]	13					4[1]	14	9[3]			1							24
1	2			5		7	4	8	10	11			6						9				3								25
	2		12	5[1]	6	7	8[2]		10	11			14		4	13			9				3[1]	1							26
	2		12	5	6	7	13		10	11			4				8[1]		9				3[2]	1							27
	2		9		6	7	8		10	3			5		4				11					1							28
	2		9	12	6[1]	7	8[2]		10	3			5[3]		4	14	13		11					1							29
	2		12	5		7	8		10	3			6		4				11[1]					1	9						30
	2		12	5		7	8[1]		10	3			6[2]		4				11	13				1	9						31
				5	6	7	8		10	3					4				11	2					9	1					32
12[3]	13	5[2]	6	7	8				10[1]	3		14			4				11	2					9	1					33
12	13	5[1]	6	7	8[2]				10[3]	3		14			4				11	2					9	1					34
9		5[1]			6	7			10	3				12	4		8		11	2						1					35
8					6	7			10	3			5		4		12		11	2					9[1]	1					36
8[1]					6	7	12		10	3			5		4				11	2					9	1					37
		5[1]			6	7	8		10	3			12[2]	13	4				11	2					9	1					38
					7	5			10[1]	9					6	4	8[2]	12	3[1]	11	2					1	14	13			39
					7	4			10	3			6		5		12		11[3]	2					9	1	13	8[2]	14		40
					7	4			10	8			5		14		12		11	2					9	1	13[3]	6[2]	3[1]		41
					6	7	8		10	3			5	9	4				11	2						1					42
					6	7	8[1]		10	3			5	9	4	12[2]			11	2					13	1					43
		12			6	7[1]			10	3			5	8	4[2]				11	2					9	1				13	44
		12			6	7			10	3			5[1]	8	4				11	2					9	1					45
		5			6				10	3			8		4	7[2]		12	11	2[1]	1				9					13	46

Coca-Cola Cup
| First Round | York C | (h) | 2-1 |
| | | (a) | 1-5 |

FA Cup
First Round	Rotherham U	(h)	5-3
Second Round	Darlington	(h)	2-2
		(a)	1-0
Third Round	Liverpool	(a)	0-7

ROTHERHAM UNITED 1995–96 *Back row (left to right):* Mark Monington, Neil Richardson, Mark Haran, Matthew Clarke, Steve Farrelly, John McGlashan, Ian Breckin, Andy Hayward.
Middle row: Bobby Davison, Paul Hurst, Scott Smith, Nicky Viljoen, Shaun Goater, Matthew Ayrton, Kris Boucken, Darren Garner, Ian Bailey (Physio).
Front row: Martin Pike, Martin James, Chris Wilder, Shaun Goodwin, John McGovern (Joint Manager), Archie Gemmill (Joint Manager), Paul Blades, Andy Roscoe, Mike Jeffrey, Gary Bowyer.

Division 2   ROTHERHAM UNITED

Millmoor Ground, Rotherham S60 1HR. Telephone: (01709) 512434. Fax: (01709) 512762. Commercial Dept: (01709) 512760. Fax: (01709) 512763. Football in the Community: (01709) 512761.

Ground Capacity: 11,514.

Record attendance: 25,170 v Sheffield U, Division 2, 13 December 1952 and v Sheffield W, Division 2, 26 January 1952.

Record receipts: £79,155 v Newcastle U, FA Cup 4th rd, 23 January 1993.

Pitch measurements. 115yd × 75yd.

President: Sir J. Layden.

Chairman: K. F. Booth.

Directors: R. Hull (Vice-Chairman), C. A. Luckock, J. A. Webb. *Chief Executive:* Phil Henson.

Joint Managers: Archie Gemmill/John McGovern. *Assistant Manager/Coach:* John Breckin. *Physio:* Ian Bailey. *Coach:* Billy Russell.

Secretary: N. Darnill. *Stadium Manager/Safety Officer:* David Sumner.

Commercial Manager: D. Nicholls.

Year Formed: 1870. *Turned Professional:* 1905. *Ltd Co.:* 1920.

Club Nickname: 'The Merry Millers'.

Previous Names: 1877, Thornhill United; 1905, Rotherham County; 1925, amalgamated with Rotherham Town under Rotherham United.

Previous Ground: Red House Ground; 1907, Millmoor.

Foundation: Rotherham were formed in 1870 before becoming Town in the late 1880s. Thornhill United were founded in 1877 and changed their name to Rotherham County in 1905. The Town amalgamated with Rotherham County to form Rotherham United in 1925.

First Football League game: 2 September 1893, Division 2, Rotherham T v Lincoln C (a) D 1-1 – McKay; Thickett, Watson; Barr, Brown, Broadhead; Longden, Cutts, Leatherbarrow, McCormick, Pickering. (1 og) 30 August 1919, Division 2, Rotherham Co v Nottingham F (h) W 2-0 – Branston; Alton, Baines; Bailey, Coe, Stanton; Lee (1), Cawley (1), Glennon, Lees, Lamb.

Record League Victory: 8–0 v Oldham Ath, Division 3 (N), 26 May 1947 – Warnes; Selkirk, Ibbotson; Edwards, Horace Williams, Danny Williams; Wilson (2), Shaw (1), Ardron (3), Guest (1), Hainsworth (1).

Record Cup Victory: 6–0 v Spennymoor U, FA Cup 2nd rd, 17 December 1977 – McAlister; Forrest, Breckin, Womble, Stancliffe, Green, Finney, Phillips (3), Gwyther (2) (Smith), Goodfellow, Crawford (1). 6–0 v Wolverhampton W, FA Cup 1st rd, 16 November 1985 – O'Hanlon; Forrest, Dungworth, Gooding (1), Smith (1), Pickering, Birch (2), Emerson, Tynan (1), Simmons (1), Pugh.

Record Defeat: 1–11 v Bradford C, Division 3 (N), 25 August 1928.

Most League Points (2 for a win): 71, Division 3 (N), 1950–51.

Most League Points (3 for a win): 82, Division 4, 1988–89.

Most League Goals: 114, Division 3 (N), 1946–47.

Highest League Scorer in Season: Wally Ardron, 38, Division 3 (N), 1946–47.

Most League Goals in Total Aggregate: Gladstone Guest, 130, 1946–56.

Most Capped Player: Shaun Goater, 18, Bermuda.

Most League Appearances: Danny Williams, 459, 1946–62.

Record Transfer Fee Received: £255,000 from Fortuna Sittard for Mike Jeffrey, January 1996.

Record Transfer Fee Paid: £150,000 to Millwall for Tony Towner, August 1980.

Football League Record: 1893 Rotherham Town elected to Division 2; 1896 Failed re-election; 1919 Rotherham County elected to Division 2; 1923–51 Division 3 (N); 1951–68 Division 2; 1968–73 Division 3; 1973–75 Division 4; 1975–81 Division 3; 1981–83 Division 2; 1983–88 Division 3; 1988–89 Division 4; 1989–91 Division 3; 1991–92 Division 4; 1992– Division 2.

Honours: Football League: Division 2 best season: 3rd, 1954–55 (equal points with champions and runners-up); Division 3 – Champions 1980–81; Division 3 (N) – Champions 1950–51; Runners-up 1946–47, 1947–48, 1948–49; Division 4 – Champions 1988–89; Runners-up 1991–92. *FA Cup:* best season: 5th rd, 1953, 1968. *Football League Cup:* Runners-up 1961. *Auto Windscreens Shield:* Winners 1996.

Colours: Red and white. *Change colours:* White shirts with black sleeves, black shorts, black stockings.

Did you know?
In 1950–51, during their Division Three (North) title winning season, Rotherham United completed 15 League and Cup matches without defeat.

ROTHERHAM UNITED 1995–96 LEAGUE RECORD

Match No.	Date	Venue	Opponents	Result	H/T Score	Lg. Pos.	Goalscorers	Attendance
1	Aug 12	A	Burnley	L	1-2	1-2	—	Goater (pen)	10,478
2	19	H	Hull C	D	1-1	0-0	15	Goater (pen)	3754
3	26	A	Oxford U	D	1-1	1-0	16	Murphy (og)	4282
4	29	H	Carlisle U	D	2-2	0-0	—	Goater 2 (1 pen)	3550
5	Sept 2	A	Bournemouth	L	1-2	1-2	21	Goater	4906
6	9	H	Brentford	W	1-0	1-0	17	Berry	3061
7	12	H	Bristol R	W	1-0	0-0	—	Jeffrey	2739
8	16	A	Chesterfield	L	0-3	0-1	17		5146
9	23	A	Swindon T	L	0-1	0-0	18		8473
10	30	H	Peterborough U	W	5-1	2-0	13	Goater 2, Berry, Jeffrey, Roscoe	2863
11	Oct 7	A	Brighton & HA	W	1-0	0-0	12	Jeffrey	2950
12	14	A	Notts Co	L	1-2	1-1	13	Goater	5478
13	21	H	Blackpool	W	2-1	0-0	11	Jeffrey 2	3663
14	28	A	Shrewsbury T	L	1-3	1-0	14	Garner	2632
15	31	A	Stockport Co	D	1-1	1-0	—	Goater	4070
16	Nov 4	H	Crewe Alex	D	2-2	1-1	15	Goater, Blades	3328
17	18	A	Wrexham	L	0-7	0-3	15		3227
18	25	H	Bristol C	L	2-3	1-1	19	Goater 2	2649
19	Dec 2	A	Swansea C	D	0-0	0-0	17		1788
20	9	H	Swindon T	L	0-2	0-0	19		3042
21	16	A	Peterborough U	L	0-1	0-0	20		3847
22	26	H	Walsall	L	0-1	0-0	20		3694
23	Jan 6	H	York C	D	2-2	2-0	20	Goater (pen), Richardson	2695
24	13	A	Hull C	W	4-1	1-0	18	Berry, Goater, Goodwin, Viljoen	3678
25	20	H	Burnley	W	1-0	0-0	18	Berry	4018
26	23	H	Bradford C	W	2-0	0-0	—	Breckin, Roscoe	3052
27	Feb 3	H	Oxford U	W	1-0	0-0	15	Viljoen	2842
28	10	A	York C	D	2-2	0-1	16	Richardson (pen), Goodwin	3299
29	17	A	Bristol R	L	0-1	0-0	17		5412
30	20	H	Bournemouth	W	1-0	1-0	—	Hayward	2092
31	24	H	Chesterfield	L	0-1	0-0	16		5712
32	27	A	Brentford	D	1-1	0-0	—	Jemson	3446
33	Mar 2	A	Walsall	L	1-3	1-1	17	Jemson	3001
34	9	H	Swansea C	D	1-1	1-0	18	Jemson	2714
35	16	A	Bradford C	L	0-2	0-0	19		4047
36	23	H	Wycombe W	D	0-0	0-0	19		2775
37	26	A	Carlisle U	L	0-2	0-2	—		4054
38	30	A	Brighton & HA	D	1-1	1-1	20	Goater	5530
39	Apr 2	H	Notts Co	W	2-0	0-0	—	Hurst, Berry	3215
40	6	H	Shrewsbury T	D	2-2	2-1	18	Goater, Goodwin	2973
41	8	A	Blackpool	W	2-1	1-1	16	McGlashan, Berry	6850
42	16	A	Wycombe W	D	1-1	1-0	—	Goater	2936
43	20	A	Crewe Alex	W	2-0	1-0	17	Goodwin, Jemson (pen)	3685
44	23	H	Stockport Co	W	2-0	0-0	—	Goater (pen), Hayward	6920
45	27	A	Bristol C	L	3-4	1-1	15	Jemson, Berry, McGlashan	6101
46	May 4	H	Wrexham	L	0-1	0-0	16		4419

Final League Position: 16

GOALSCORERS

League (54): Goater 18 (4 pens), Berry 7, Jeffrey 5, Jemson 5 (1 pen), Goodwin 4, Hayward 2, McGlashan 2, Richardson 2 (1 pen), Roscoe 2, Viljoen 2, Blades 1, Breckin 1, Garner 1, Hurst 1, own goal 1.
Coca-Cola Cup (7): Goater 3, Hayward 2, Jeffrey 1, McGlashan 1.
FA Cup (3): Goater 2 (1 pen), McGlashan 1.

Clarke M 40	Wilder C 18	Bowyer G 23+4	Garner D 31	Monington M 7+4	Blades P 34	Hayward A 22+14	Goodwin S 25+1	Jeffrey M 22	Goater S 44	Roscoe A 44+1	McGlashan J 13+3	Breckin J 37+2	Pettinger P —+1	Hurst P 32+8	James M —+1	Berry T 33+3	Richardson N 23+2	Muggleton C 6	Smith S 11+3	Viljoen N 5+3	McLean I 9	Jemson N 16	Moore N 10+1	Pike M —+2	Davison B 1	Match No.
1	2	3	4[1]	5	6	7	8	9	10	11	12															1
1	2	3	4	5[6]	6[2]	7[1]	8	9	10	11	12	13		15												2
1	2		4		6	7[1]	12	9	10	11	8	5		3												3
1	2		4		6	7	8	9	10	11		5		3												4
1	2		4		6	7[1]	8	9	10	11		5		3	12											5
1	2		4		6			9	10	11	8	5		3		7[1]	12									6
1	2		4		6			9	10	11	8	5		3		7[1]	12									7
1	2	12	4[1]		6			9	10	11	8	5		3		13	7[2]									8
1	2	3	4[1]	13	6		8	9	10	11[2]		5		12		7										9
1	2	3[1]		12	6	13	8[2]	9	10	11		5				7	4									10
1	2	3		12	6		8[1]	9	10	11		5				7	4									11
1	2	3[1]		7	6	13	8	9	10	11		5		12		4[2]										12
1	2		4		6	7	8	9	10	11		5		3												13
1	2		4		6	7	8	9	10	11		5		3												14
1	2		4		6	7[1]	8	9	10	11	12	5		3												15
	2		4		6	7		9	10	11	8	5		3				1								16
			4		6	12		9	10	11[1]	8	5		3		7		1	2							17
			4	5	6			9	10	11	8			3		7		1	2							18
			4	5	2	7		9	10		8			3		11	6	1								19
2			4[1]	5			10	9	11[2]	8	12			3		7	6	1	13							20
		12			6	13	8	9	10	11		5		3[1]		7[4]	4	1	2							21
1	2	12			6	13	8	9	10	11[1]		5		3		7[2]	4									22
1			4		6	12	8		10	11		5		3		7[1]	9		2							23
1		3	4				8		10	11[1]		5		12		7	6		2	9						24
1	8		4					9	10	11	2			3		7	6					5				25
1			4				8		10	11	2			3		7	6				9	5				26
1			4			12	8		10	11[1]	2			3		7	6				9	5				27
1		3	4			2	12	8	10	11[2]		13		7		6					9[1]	5				28
1[2]		3			9	2	12	8	10	11[1]		5		13		7	6					4				29
1		3	4			2		9	10	11		6		12		7[1]					5	8				30
1			4		2	7[2]			10	11[1]		6		3		12	9		13		5	8				31
1		3		12		7[1]			11	6	13	4		10					2		9[2]	5	8			32
1		3	4			2			10	11		6				7	9				5	8				33
1	9	5[1]			2	7			10	11		6		3		4					12	8				34
1	9				2	7			10	11[1]		6		3		4					12	5	8			35
1	9					12			10	11[1]		6		3		7	5		2			8	4			36
1			4		2	7			10	11				3		9	5					8	6			37
1			4		5	7			10	11[1]				3		9			2			8	6	12		38
1			4		2[2]	12	8		10	11		6		3		9	5					7[1]	13			39
1			4		2	12	8		10	11[1]		6		3		9						7	5			40
1		3	4		2	7	8		10	12	9[1]	6				11[2]					13		5			41
1	12		4				8		10	11[1]	2			3		9	6					7	5			42
1		3		12		8[2]			10	11	4	6		13		9[1]			2			7	5			43
1		4[2]				7			10	11	2			3		8	6		12			5	13	9[1]		44
1					8			9	10	11[1]	4	5		3		12			2			7	6			45
1			4			12	8		10	11[1]		5		3		9			2			7	6			46

Coca-Cola Cup

First Round	Scunthorpe U	(a)	1-4
		(h)	5-0
Second Round	Middlesbrough	(a)	1-2
		(h)	0-1

FA Cup

First Round	Rochdale	(a)	3-5

SCARBOROUGH 1995-96   *Back row (left to right):* Don Page, Lee Thew, Craig Boardman, Kevin Martin, Gavin Kelly, Stuart Hicks, Ian Ironside, Jason Rockett, Lee Harper, Neil Trebble.
Front row: Oliver Heald, Steve Charles, David D'Auria, Andy Ritchie, Ian Kerr, Phil Chambers (Assistant Manager), Ray McHale (Manager), John Murray (Physio), Darren Knowles, Mark Wells, Richard Lucas, Alex Willgrass.

Division 3   **SCARBOROUGH**

The McCain Stadium, Seamer Road, Scarborough YO12 4HF. Telephone: (01723) 375094. Fax: (01723) 378733.

Ground capacity: 6899.

Record Attendance: 11,130 v Luton T, FA Cup 3rd rd, 8 January 1938. Football League: 7314 v Wolverhampton W, Division 4, 15 August 1987.

Record receipts: £37,609.50 v Arsenal, Coca-Cola Cup 4th rd, 6 January 1993.

Pitch measurements: 114yd × 74yd.

President and Chief Executive: John Birley.

Chairman: J. Russell.

Director: Mrs G. Russell.

Manager: Mick Wadsworth. *Assistant Manager:* Phil Chambers.

Secretary: Mrs Gillian Russell. *Physio:* J. Murray.

Year Formed: 1879. *Turned Professional:* 1926. *Ltd Co.:* 1933.

Club Nickname: 'The Boro'.

Previous Grounds: 1879–87, Scarborough Cricket Ground; 1887–98, Recreation Ground; 1898– Athletic Ground.

Foundation: Scarborough came into being as early as 1879 when they were formed by members of the town's cricket club and went under the name of Scarborough Cricketers' FC with home games played on the North Marine Road Cricket Ground.

First Football League game: 15 August 1987, Division 4, v Wolverhampton W (h) D 2-2 – Blackwell; McJannet, Thompson, Bennyworth, Richards, Kendall, Hamill, Moss, McHale (1), Mell (1), Graham.

Record League Victory: 4–0 v Bolton W, Division 4, 29 August 1987 – Blackwell; McJannet, Thompson, Bennyworth (Walker), Richards (1) (Cook), Kendall, Hamill (1), Moss, McHale, Mell (1), Graham. (1 og). 4–0 v Newport Co (away), Division 4, 12 April 1988 – Ironside; McJannet, Thompson, Kamara, Richards (1), Short (1), Adams (Cook 1), Brook, Outhart (1), Russell, Graham.

Record Cup Victory: 6–0 v Rhyl Ath, FA Cup 1st rd, 29 November 1930 – Turner; Severn, Belton; Maskell, Robinson, Wallis; Small (1), Rand (2), Palfreman (2), A. D. Hill (1), Mickman.

Record Defeat: 1–16 v Southbank, Northern League, 15 November 1919.

Most League Points (3 for a win): 77, Division 4, 1988–89.

Most League Goals: 69, Division 4, 1990–91.

Highest League Scorer in Season: Darren Foreman, 27, Division 4, 1992–93.

Most League Goals in Total Aggregate: Darren Foreman, 35, 1991–95.

Most Capped Player: None.

Most League Appearances: Ian Ironside, 144, 1988–91, 1992, 1994–96.

Record Transfer Fee Received: £240,000 from Notts Co for Chris Short, September 1990.

Record Transfer Fee Paid: £102,000 to Leicester C for Martin Russell, March 1989.

Football League Record: Promoted to Division 4 1987; 1992– Division 3.

Honours: Football League: Division 4 best season: 5th, 1988–89. *FA Cup:* best seasons: 3rd rd, 1931, 1938, 1976, 1978, 1995. *Football League Cup:* best season: 4th rd 1993. *FA Trophy:* Winners 1973, 1976, 1977. *GM Vauxhall Conference:* Winners 1986–87.

Colours: Red and white. *Change colours:* Yellow and black.

Did you know?
Scarborough's first League victims in the FA Cup, whilst they were members of the Midland League, were Lincoln City beaten 6-4 on 13 December 1930 in a Second Round tie.

SCARBOROUGH 1995–96 LEAGUE RECORD

Match No.	Date	Venue	Opponents	Result		H/T Score	Lg. Pos.	Goalscorers	Atten- dance
1	Aug 12	A	Doncaster R	L	0-1	0-0	—		2523
2	19	H	Fulham	D	2-2	1-2	16	Ritchie, Heald	1946
3	26	A	Exeter C	L	0-2	0-0	20		2439
4	30	H	Leyton Orient	W	2-1	1-1	—	Page 2	1796
5	Sept 2	H	Wigan Ath	D	0-0	0-0	16		1949
6	9	A	Mansfield T	L	0-2	0-0	20		2419
7	12	A	Cardiff C	L	1-2	1-1	—	Charles	2385
8	16	H	Hereford U	D	2-2	0-1	21	Rockett, Gardner	1449
9	23	A	Darlington	W	2-1	1-0	18	Page, Rockett	2046
10	30	H	Torquay U	W	2-1	1-0	14	Charles, D'Auria	1455
11	Oct 7	A	Preston NE	L	2-3	1-1	17	Page, Ritchie	7702
12	14	H	Lincoln C	D	0-0	0-0	20		1848
13	21	A	Bury	W	2-0	1-0	14	Page, Todd	2590
14	28	H	Chester C	D	0-0	0-0	16		1847
15	31	H	Plymouth Arg	D	2-2	0-1	—	Charles, Trebble	1876
16	Nov 4	A	Cambridge U	L	1-4	0-2	18	Ritchie	2304
17	18	H	Gillingham	L	0-2	0-2	19		1546
18	25	A	Scunthorpe U	D	3-3	0-2	21	Trebble, Wells, Rockett	2231
19	Dec 9	H	Darlington	L	1-2	1-0	21	Charles	1585
20	16	A	Torquay U	D	0-0	0-0	21		1680
21	23	H	Northampton T	W	2-1	0-0	20	Trebble, Ritchie	1404
22	Jan 6	A	Hartlepool U	D	1-1	1-0	20	Magee	2252
23	9	H	Barnet	D	1-1	1-1	—	Ritchie	1310
24	13	A	Fulham	L	0-1	0-1	21		3557
25	20	H	Doncaster R	L	0-2	0-0	23		1661
26	23	H	Rochdale	D	1-1	0-0	—	Trebble	1400
27	Feb 3	H	Exeter C	D	0-0	0-0	21		1307
28	6	A	Colchester U	D	1-1	0-1	—	Trebble	2299
29	10	A	Rochdale	W	2-0	0-0	20	Toman, Midgley	1662
30	17	H	Cardiff C	W	1-0	1-0	17	Toman	1414
31	20	A	Wigan Ath	L	0-2	0-2	—		2208
32	24	H	Hereford U	D	0-0	0-0	19		2551
33	27	H	Mansfield T	D	1-1	1-1	—	Ritchie (pen)	1304
34	Mar 2	H	Hartlepool U	L	1-2	1-1	19	Hicks	2419
35	9	A	Northampton T	L	0-2	0-1	22		4621
36	16	H	Colchester U	D	0-0	0-0	23		1201
37	19	A	Leyton Orient	L	0-1	0-0	—		2121
38	23	A	Barnet	L	0-1	0-0	23		2054
39	30	H	Preston NE	L	1-2	0-1	23	Ritchie	3771
40	Apr 2	A	Lincoln C	L	1-3	1-2	—	Robertson (og)	2010
41	6	A	Chester C	L	0-5	0-3	23		2485
42	9	H	Bury	L	0-2	0-2	—		1773
43	13	A	Plymouth Arg	L	1-5	0-1	23	Ritchie (pen)	6949
44	20	H	Cambridge U	W	2-0	1-0	23	Rockett, Charles	1401
45	27	H	Scunthorpe U	L	1-4	1-3	23	Knowles	1738
46	May 4	A	Gillingham	L	0-1	0-1	23		10,421

Final League Position: 23

GOALSCORERS

League (39): Ritchie 8 (2 pens), Charles 5, Page 5, Trebble 5, Rockett 4, Toman 2, D'Auria 1, Gardner 1, Heald 1, Hicks 1, Knowles 1, Magee 1, Midgley 1, Todd 1, Wells 1, own goal 1.
Coca-Cola Cup (1): D'Auria 1.
FA Cup (0).

Ironside I 40	Knowles D 46	Lucas R 44	D'Auria D 18	Hicks S 39+2	Rockett J 39	Thew L 9+5	Todd M 23	Page D 26+11	Ritchie A 33+4	Charles S 41	Kelly G 6	Heald O 1+8	Trebble N 25+7	Boardman C 6+3	Gardner J 5+1	Kinnaird P 3	Robinson R 1	Wells M 10+4	Magee K 26+2	Midgley C 14+2	Myers C 8+1	Curtis A 3+2	Toman A 12+4	Anthony G 2	Partridge S 5+2	Willgrass A 2+5	Sansam C 5+1	O'Riordan D 1	Foreman M 1+3	Fairclough W 7	Sunderland J 3+3	Cook M 2	Match No.
1	2	3	4	5	6	7	8	9	10	11																							1
	2	3	4	5	6	7	8^1	9	10	11	1	12																					2
	2	3	4	5^1	6	7	8^2	12	10	11	1	13	9^1	14																			3
	2	3	4	5	6	7^2	8	9	10^1	11	1	12				13																	4
	2	3	4	5	6	12	8^1	9	10	11	1						7																5
	2	3	4	5	6	12	8	9^2		11^1	1	13	10				7																6
	2	3	4^1	5	6		8	9	10	11	1	12					7																7
1	2	3	4	5	6	12	8^1	9	10^2	11		13					7																8
1	2	3	4		6		8		10	11			9	5	7																		9
1	2	3	4	5	6	7	8	9^1	10^2	11		13	12																				10
1	2	3	4	5	6	7^3	8	9^1	10^2	11		13	12	14																			11
1	2	3	4	5	6	7^1	8	9	10	11		12																					12
1	2	3	4	5	6		8	9	10				7					11															13
1		3	4	5	6		8	9^2	10^1				7	13	12			11															14
1	2	3	4	5	6		8	9^1	12				7					10	11														15
1	2	11	4^2	5	6	13	8	12	10^3	7			9	14		3^1																	16
1	2	3	4	5	6		8	7		11			10					9															17
1	2	3	4	5	6	12	8	7^1	10	11^2								9	13														18
1	2	3		5	6	4	12	10^1	8	9								11	7														19
1	2	3		5	6	4	10	8	9									11	7														20
1	2	3		5	6	4	10	8	9									11	7														21
1	2	3			6	4	10	8	9									5	11	7													22
1	2	3			6	4^1	10	8	9									5	12	11	7												23
1	2	3	12		6	4^1	13	10	8	9^2								5	14	11^3	7												24
1	2	3	12		6	4^1	13	10	8	9								5^3	14	11	7^2												25
1	2	6		5			10^1	12	8	9								3^3	11	13			4	14	7^2								26
1	2	3		5	6		10	8	9	11									12				4		7^1								27
1	2	3		5	6		10^1	12	8	9									11		7		4										28
1	2	3		5	6		10	8	9										11		7		4										29
1	2	3		5	6		10	8^1	9										11		7	12	4										30
1	2	3		5	6		10^1	12	9										11		7^2	8	13	4									31
1	2	3		5	6		10	9											11		7	8	4										32
1	2	3		5	6		12	10^2	9										11^1		7	8	13	4									33
1	2	3		5	6		10	9											11		7	8	4										34
1	2	3			6		10	12											11		8		7^1	5^2	4	9	13						35
1	2				6		13	7^2	5									10	3	11		8^1	4		9		12						36
1	2			5	6		12	8	9									3^2	11				4^1		10		7		13				37
1	2			5	6		8^1	12										3	11		7^2		9		13		10		4^3	14			38
1	2	3		5			9	6^2	10										8^2		12		11^1		13		4		14	7			39
1	2		4	5			12	9	11										3^1		13		8^2		10		7		6				40
1	2			5	6		10	9	11										3^2		12		8^1		13^3		14		4	7			41
1	2	3		5	6^1		12	9	8										11				13		14		10^3		4	7^2			42
1		3		5	6^1		12	9	4										7		11				10^2				8	13			43
1	2	3		5	6		10	9	8										7		11								4				44
1	2	3		5			10	9	8										7		11^2		12		6^1				4	13	3		45
1	2	3		5	6		9	8	4^1										10		11		12		13					7^2			46

Coca-Cola Cup
First Round Hartlepool U   (h) 1-0
                            (a) 0-1

FA Cup
First Round Chesterfield   (h) 0-2

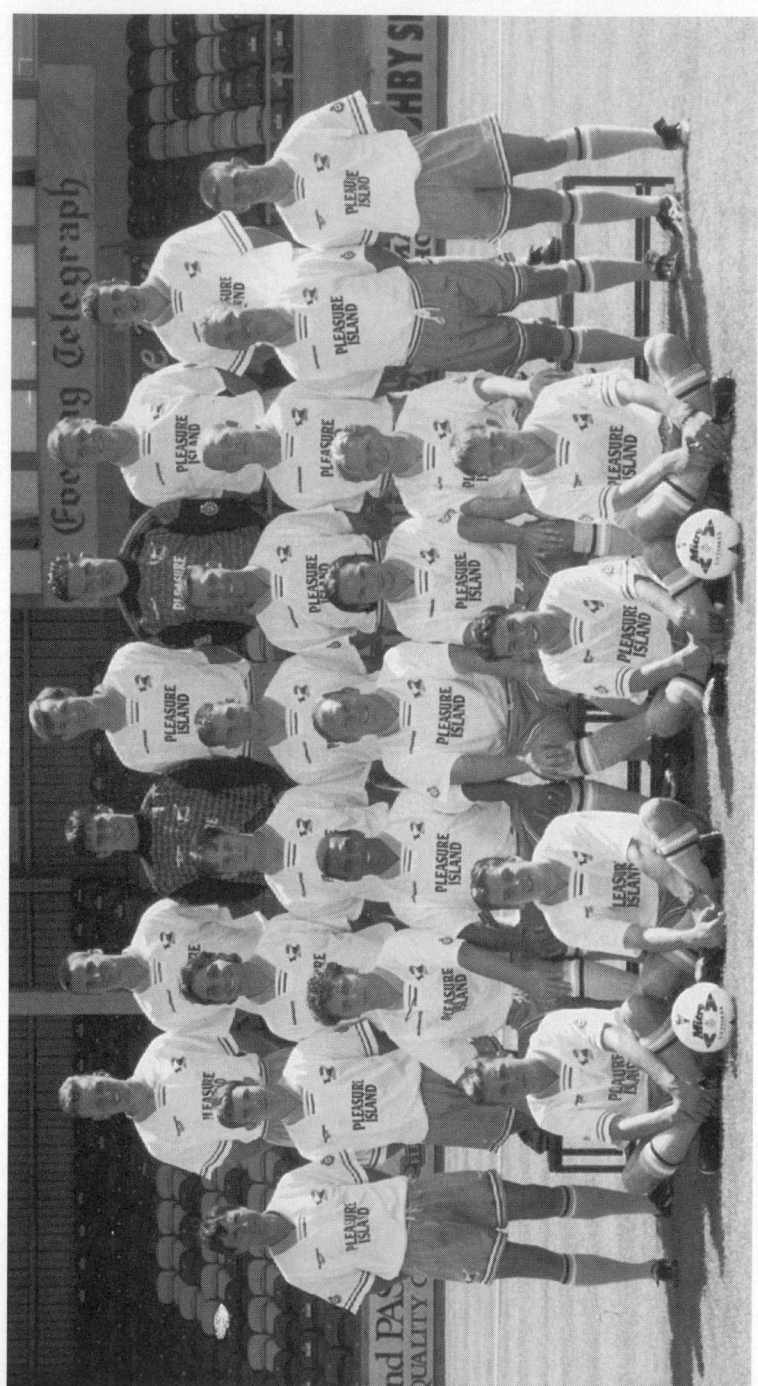

SCUNTHORPE UNITED 1995-96 *Back row (left to right):* Ryan Wake, Chris Hope, Mario Ziccardi, Alan Knill, Mark Samways, Russell Bradley, Andrew Murfin.
Third row: Ian Whyte, Lee Field, Christian Sansam, Michael Walsh, Steven Housham, Lee Turnbull, Wayne Bullimore, Stephen Thornber, John Exley.
Second row: Stuart Young, Tony Ford, David Moore (Manager), John Eyre, Max Nicholson.
Front row: Ryan Vickers, Simon Heath, Peter Wilson, Phillip Spark.

Division 3   **SCUNTHORPE UNITED**

Glanford Park, Scunthorpe, South Humberside DN15 8TD. Telephone: (01724) 848077. Fax: (01724) 857986.
Ground capacity: 9183.

Record attendance: Old Showground: 23,935 v Portsmouth, FA Cup 4th rd, 30 January 1954. Glanford Park: 8775 v Rotherham U, Division 4, 1 May 1989.

Record receipts: £44,481.50 v Leeds U, Rumbelows Cup 2nd rd 1st leg, 24 September 1991.

Pitch measurements: 110yd × 71yd.

Vice-Presidents: I. T. Botham, G. Johnson, A. Harvey, R. Ashman.

Chairman: K. Wagstaff.

Vice-Chairman: R. Garton.

Directors: J. B. Borrill, C. Plumtree, S. Wharton, B. Collen, J. A. C. Godfrey.

Team Manager: Mick Buxton.

Chief Executive/Secretary: A. D. Rowing. *Commercial Manager:* A. D. Rowing.

*Year Formed:*1899. *Turned Professional:* 1912. *Ltd Co.:* 1912.

Club Nickname: 'The Iron'.

Previous Names: Amalgamated first with Brumby Hall then North Lindsey United to become Scunthorpe & Lindsey United, 1910; dropped '& Lindsey' in 1958.

Previous ground: Old Showground to 1988.

Foundation: The year of foundation for Scunthorpe United has often been quoted as 1910, but the club can trace its history back to 1899 when Brumby Hall FC, who played on the Old Showground, consolidated their position by amalgamating with some other clubs and changing their name to Scunthorpe United. The year 1910 was when that club amalgamated with North Lindsey United as Scunthorpe and Lindsey United. The link is Mr. W. T. Lockwood whose chairmanship covers both years.

First Football League game: 19 August 1950, Division 3 (N), v Shrewsbury T (h) D 0-0 – Thompson; Barker, Brownsword; Allen, Taylor, McCormick; Mosby, Payne, Gorin, Rees, Boyes.

Record League Victory: 8–1 v Luton T, Division 3, 24 April 1965 – Sidebottom; Horstead, Hemstead; Smith, Neale, Lindsey; Bramley (1), Scott, Thomas (5), Mahy (1), Wilson (1).

Record Cup Victory: 9–0 v Boston U, FA Cup 1st rd, 21 November 1953 – Malan; Hubbard, Brownsword; Sharpe, White, Bushby; Mosby (1), Haigh (3), Whitfield (2), Gregory (1), Mervyn Jones (2).

Record Defeat: 0–8 v Carlisle U, Division 3 (N), 25 December 1952.

Most League Points (2 for a win): 66, Division 3 (N), 1956–57, 1957–58.

Most League Points (3 for a win): 83, Division 4, 1982–83.

Most League Goals: 88, Division 3 (N), 1957–58.

Highest League Scorer in Season: Barrie Thomas, 31, Division 2, 1961–62.

Most League Goals in Total Aggregate: Steve Cammack, 110, 1979–81, 1981–86.

Most Capped Player: None.

Most League Appearances: Jack Brownsword, 595, 1950–65.

Record Transfer Fee Received: £350,000 from Aston Villa for Neil Cox, February 1991.

Record Transfer Fee Paid: £80,000 to York C for Ian Helliwell, August 1991.

Football League Record: 1950 Elected to Division 3 (N); 1958–64 Division 2; 1964–68 Division 3; 1968–72 Division 4; 1972–73 Division 3; 1973–83 Division 4; 1983–84 Division 3; 1984–92 Division 4; 1992– Division 3.

Honours: Football League: Division 2 best season: 4th, 1961–62; Division 3 (N) – Champions 1957–58. *FA Cup:* best season: 5th rd, 1958, 1970. *Football League Cup:* never past 3rd rd.

Colours: Sky blue shirt with three vertical claret stripes, sky blue shorts, claret trim, sky blue stockings, claret trim. *Change colours:* Navy and yellow quarters, navy shorts, navy and yellow hooped stockings.

Did you know?
Scunthorpe United's eight away goals in their victory at Torquay United on 28 October 1995 established a club record.

SCUNTHORPE UNITED 1995–96 LEAGUE RECORD

Match No.	Date	Venue	Opponents	Result	H/T Score	Lg. Pos.	Goalscorers	Attendance
1	Aug 12	H	Cambridge U	L	1-2	1-0	—	Eyre	2561
2	19	A	Wigan Ath	L	1-2	1-1	22	Turnbull	3153
3	26	H	Barnet	W	2-0	0-0	16	Thomas (og), McFarlane	1970
4	28	A	Lincoln C	D	2-2	0-0	—	Graham, Eyre	2674
5	Sept 2	A	Exeter C	L	0-1	0-1	18		2893
6	9	H	Gillingham	D	1-1	1-1	18	Hope	2423
7	12	H	Chester C	L	0-2	0-2	—		1875
8	16	A	Preston NE	D	2-2	0-1	20	Bullimore (pen), Sansam	7391
9	23	A	Mansfield T	D	1-1	0-0	22	McFarlane	2478
10	30	H	Colchester U	W	1-0	1-0	19	Eyre	2051
11	Oct 7	H	Northampton T	D	0-0	0-0	21		2455
12	14	A	Hartlepool U	L	0-2	0-0	22		2608
13	21	H	Leyton Orient	W	2-0	1-0	20	Paterson, Hope	2315
14	28	A	Torquay U	W	8-1	4-1	14	McFarlane 4, Eyre 2, Knill, Ford	2137
15	31	H	Cardiff C	W	1-0	1-0	—	McFarlane	2024
16	Nov 4	H	Rochdale	L	1-3	0-2	12	Ford	3003
17	18	A	Darlington	D	0-0	0-0	13		2078
18	25	H	Scarborough	D	3-3	2-0	13	Ford, Clarkson, Bullimore (pen)	2231
19	Dec 9	H	Mansfield T	D	1-1	0-0	13	McFarlane	2552
20	16	A	Colchester U	L	1-2	0-2	15	Young	2138
21	19	A	Hereford U	L	0-3	0-1	—		2516
22	Jan 13	H	Wigan Ath	W	3-1	1-0	17	Jones, D'Auria, McFarlane	2288
23	20	A	Cambridge U	W	2-1	0-0	17	McFarlane, Wilson (pen)	2413
24	23	A	Plymouth Arg	W	3-1	2-0	—	Hope, Turnbull, McFarlane	4712
25	30	A	Fulham	W	3-1	1-0	—	D'Auria, Jones, Paterson	2176
26	Feb 3	A	Barnet	L	0-1	0-1	11		1674
27	10	H	Plymouth Arg	D	1-1	1-1	12	McFarlane	2789
28	17	A	Chester C	L	0-3	0-1	14		2401
29	24	H	Preston NE	L	1-2	0-0	14	Jones	3638
30	27	A	Gillingham	D	0-0	0-0	—		5557
31	Mar 2	A	Bury	L	0-3	0-1	16		3035
32	5	H	Lincoln C	L	2-3	0-1	—	Eyre, Clarkson	2411
33	9	H	Hereford U	L	0-1	0-0	20		1903
34	16	A	Doncaster R	L	0-2	0-0	22		1920
35	23	H	Fulham	W	3-1	1-0	19	Knill, Ford, D'Auria	1919
36	26	H	Exeter C	W	4-0	0-0	—	Eyre 2, Ford, McFarlane	1615
37	30	A	Northampton T	W	2-1	0-0	15	Clarkson, McFarlane	4290
38	Apr 2	H	Hartlepool U	W	2-1	1-1	—	Ford, Bradley	2100
39	6	H	Torquay U	W	1-0	1-0	13	Ford	2247
40	8	A	Leyton Orient	D	0-0	0-0	13		2814
41	13	A	Cardiff C	D	1-1	1-1	13	Knill	2044
42	16	H	Bury	L	1-2	0-0	—	Nicholson	2132
43	20	A	Rochdale	D	1-1	0-1	13	Clarkson	1654
44	23	H	Doncaster R	D	2-2	1-1	—	Turnbull, Clarkson	2614
45	27	A	Scarborough	W	4-1	3-1	12	McFarlane, Clarkson, D'Auria 2 (1 pen)	1738
46	May 4	A	Darlington	D	3-3	2-0	12	Eyre 2, McFarlane	4847

Final League Position: 12

GOALSCORERS

League (67): McFarlane 16, Eyre 10, Ford 7, Clarkson 6, D'Auria 5 (1 pen), Hope 3, Jones 3, Knill 3, Turnbull 3, Bullimore 2 (2 pens), Paterson 2, Bradley 1, Graham 1, Nicholson 1, Sansam 1, Wilson 1 (pen), Young 1, own goal 1.
Coca-Cola Cup (4): Eyre 2, Ford 1, McFarlane 1.
FA Cup (5): McFarlane 2, Eyre 1, Ford 1, Paterson 1.

Samways M 33	Walsh M 22+3	Wilson P 40	Thornber S 14+2	Knill A 38	Bradley R 36+2	Ford T 35+3	Turnbull L 16+7	McFarlane A 41+5	Eyre J 36+3	Nicholson M 13+23	Hope C 38+2	Bullimore W 11+3	Young S 7+7	Housham S 21+7	Graham D 1+2	Murfin A 1	Sansam C 2+3	Varadi I —+2	Paterson J 23+3	Clarkson P 21+3	D'Auria D 27	Jones R 11	Butler L 2	Germaine G 11	O'Halloran K 6+1	Match No.
1	2	3	4	5	6	7	8	9	10	11																1
1	2	3	4^1		6	7	8	9^2	10	11^1	5	12	13	14												2
1		3	4	7	6			9	10	11	5	8		2												3
1		3	4	7	6^1			9	10	11	5	8		2	12											4
1	3		4	5				9^1	10		6	8	12	2	7	11										5
1		3	4	5	6	12		9^2	10	11^1	7	8	13	2												6
1		3	4^2	5	6^3	14		9	10	11	7	8	12	2^1	13											7
1	2	3		5	13	4		12	10^1	11^2	6	8	9^3	7			14									8
1	2^1	3		5	12	4		13	10	11^2	6	8	9^3	7			14									9
1		3	8	5	6	4		12	10^1	13	2		9^2	7			11^3		14							10
1		3	8	5	6	4		12	10^1	13	2		9^2	7			11^3		14							11
1		3^1	8^3	5	6	4		13	10		2	12	9^2	7			14		11							12
1		3	6	5		4		9^1	10	13	2	8	12	7					11^2							13
1	12	3	7	5		4		9^2	10	14	6^3	8^1	13	2					11							14
1	12	3	7	5	6	4		9	10	13				2^1					11^7		8					15
1		3	7	5	6^1	4		9	10	12				2					11		8					16
1	2^1	3	12	5	6	4		9	10			8							11			7				17
1	2	3		5^2	6	4		9	10	12	13	8^1							11			7				18
1	2	3			6	4	12	9^2	10	7^1	5	13							11		8					19
1	2	3^1			6	4	7	9	12	5	10								11		8					20
1	2^1	3	12		6	4	7	9	13	5	10^2								11		8					21
1	2	3			6	4	12	9	10	13	5								11^2		8	7^1				22
1	2	3			6	4	12	9	10^1	13	5								11^2		8	7				23
1	2	3			6	4	10	9		11	5	12									8	7^1				24
1	2	3			6	4	10^1	9	12	5	13								11		8	7^2				25
1	2	3			6	4	10^2	9	12	8^1	5	13							11			7				26
	2	3		5	6	12		9	10^1										11	4	8	7	1			27
	2	3^1			6	4		9	12	5									11	10	8	7	1			28
1	2^3			5	6	4		9^2	13	12	3						14		11	10	8	7^1				29
1				5	6	4		9	10		2	3							11	7	8					30
1	12			5	6	4	13	9	10	14	2^2	3							11^3		8	7^1				31
1	2	3		5	6	4	12	9	10	13									11^2		8	7^1				32
	2	3		5^1	6	4^3	13	9	10	14	12								11		8	7^2	1			33
	2^1	3		5	6	4	12	9	10	11^2	7		13								8			1		34
		3^1		5	6	4	7	9	10	2	12								11		8			1		35
1		3		5	6	4	7^1	9	10	2	12										8				11	36
		3		5	6	4	7	9	10	2									11		8			1		37
		3		5	6	4		9	10	2									11		8			1	7	38
		3		5		4^1		9^2	10	12	2			6					13	11	8			1	7	39
		3		5		7		9	10	12	2			6^1	4				11		8			1		40
		3		5		4^1	7	9	10^2	12	2	13							11		8			1	6	41
		3		5	6	4^2	7^1	9	12	2									11	13	8			1	10	42
		3^2		5	6	7^1		9	12	2	13						10		11		8			1	4	43
1				5	6^1	7		9	10	12	2	3^2	4						11		8^2				13	44
1		3		5	6			9^1	12	10	2		4				13		11		8^2			1		45
		3		5	6			9	10	12	2^1		4	7					11		8			1		46

Coca-Cola Cup

First Round	Rotherham U	(h)	4-1
		(a)	0-5

FA Cup

First Round	Northwich Vic	(a)	3-1
Second Round	Shrewsbury T	(h)	1-1
		(a)	1-2

SHEFFIELD UNITED 1995–96   *Back row (left to right):* Denis Circuit (Physio), Rob Scott, Doug Hodgson, Brian Gayle, Mark Foran, Alan Kelly, Jostein Flo, Dave Tuttle, Paul Rogers, Andy Scott, Brian Eastick (Coach).

Middle row: Derek French (Physio), John Greaves (Kit Man), Mark Blount, Phil Starbuck, Carl Veart, Billy Mercer, Glyn Hodges, Salvatore Bibbo, Charlie Hartfield, Roger Nilsen, Nathan Blake, Geoff Taylor (Assistant Manager).

Front row: John Reed, Paul Holland, Dane Whitehouse, Dave Bassett (Manager), Mitch Ward, Kevin Gage, Ross Davidson.

Division 1 SHEFFIELD UNITED

Bramall Lane Ground, Sheffield S2 4SU. Telephone: (0114) 2738955. Fax: (0114) 2723030. Ticket Office: (0114) 2766771. Pools Office: (0114) 2727901. Club Shop: (0114) 2750596. Community Scheme: (0114) 2769314. Executive Suite: (0114) 2755277. Ticket info line: 0891 332950.

Ground capacity: 23,459 (increasing to 30,200).

Record attendance: 68,287 v Leeds U, FA Cup 5th rd, 15 February 1936.

Record receipts: £261,758 v Manchester U, FA Cup 5th rd, 14 February 1993.

Pitch measurements: 112yd × 72yd.

Chairman: A. M. McDonald. *Vice-Chairman:* S. L. Hinchliffe.

Directors: A. H. Laver, B. Proctor, J. A. Plant JP, K. C. McCabe.

Manager: Howard Kendall. *Assistant Manager:* Geoff Taylor. *Coach:* Viv Busby.

Youth Team Manager: Keith Mincher.

Physios: Derek French, Denis Circuit.

Secretary: D. Capper AFA. *Commercial Manager:* Andy R. Daykin.

Youth Development Officer: John Dungworth. *Stadium Manager:* Roy Mitchell.

Community Programme Organiser: Tony Currie, Tel: (0114) 2769314.

Year Formed: 1889. *Turned Professional:* 1889. *Ltd Co.:* 1899.

Club Nickname: 'The Blades'.

Foundation: In March 1889, Yorkshire County Cricket Club formed Sheffield United six days after an FA Cup semi-final between Preston North End and West Bromwich Albion had finally convinced Charles Stokes, a member of the cricket club, that the formation of a professional football club would prove successful at Bramall Lane. The United's first secretary, Mr. J. B. Wostinholm was also secretary of the cricket club.

First Football League game: 3 September 1892, Division 2, v Lincoln C (h) W 4-2 – Lilley; Witham, Cain; Howell, Hendry, Needham (1); Wallace, Dobson, Hammond (3), Davies, Drummond.

Record League Victory: 10–0 v Burslem Port Vale (away), Division 2, 10 December 1892 – Howlett; Witham, Lilley; Howell, Hendry, Needham; Drummond (1), Wallace (1), Hammond (4), Davies (2), Watson (2).

Record Cup Victory: 5–0 v Newcastle U (away), FA Cup 1st rd, 10 January 1914 – Gough; Cook, English; Brelsford, Howley, Sturgess; Simmons (2), Gillespie (1), Kitchen (1), Fazackerley, Revill (1). 5–0 v Corinthians, FA Cup 1st rd, 10 January 1925 – Sutcliffe; Cook, Milton; Longworth, King, Green; Partridge, Boyle (1), Johnson (4), Gillespie, Tunstall. 5–0 v Barrow, FA Cup 3rd rd, 7 January 1956 – Burgin; Coldwell, Mason; Fountain, Johnson, Iley; Hawksworth (1), Hoyland (2), Howitt, Wragg (1), Grainger (1).

Record Defeat: 0–13 v Bolton W, FA Cup 2nd rd, 1 February 1890.

Most League Points (2 for a win): 60, Division 2, 1952–53.

Most League Points (3 for a win): 96, Division 4, 1981–82.

Most League Goals: 102, Division 1, 1925–26.

Highest League Scorer in Season: Jimmy Dunne, 41, Division 1, 1930–31.

Most League Goals in Total Aggregate: Harry Johnson, 205, 1919–30.

Most Capped Player: Billy Gillespie, 25, Northern Ireland.

Most League Appearances: Joe Shaw, 629, 1948–66.

Record Transfer Fee Received: £2,700,000 from Leeds U for Brian Deane, July 1993.

Record Transfer Fee Paid: £1,200,000 to West Ham U for Don Hutchison, January 1996.

Football League Record: 1892 Elected to Division 2; 1893–1934 Division 1; 1934–39 Division 2; 1946–49 Division 1; 1949–53 Division 2; 1953–56 Division 1; 1956–61 Division 2; 1961–68 Division 1; 1968–71 Division 2; 1971–76 Division 1; 1976–79 Division 2; 1979–81 Division 3; 1981–82 Division 4; 1982–84 Division 3; 1984–88 Division 2; 1988–89 Division 3; 1989–90 Division 2; 1990–92 Division 1; 1992–94 FA Premier League; 1994–Division 1.

Honours: Football League: Division 1 – Champions 1897–98; Runners-up 1896–97, 1899–1900; Division 2 – Champions 1952–53; Runners-up 1892–93, 1938–39, 1960–61, 1970–71, 1989–90; Division 4 – Champions 1981–82. *FA Cup:* Winners 1899, 1902, 1915, 1925; Runners-up 1901, 1936. *Football League Cup:* best season: 5th rd, 1962, 1967, 1972.

Colours: Broad red, thin white striped shirts with large white diamond overlay, black shorts with red/white trim, black stockings with red/white trim. *Change colours:* Purple and yellow halved shirts with matching trim, yellow shorts with purple trim, yellow stockings with purple trim.

Did you know?
Jimmy Dunne's record of scoring 30 or more goals in three successive seasons in the top flight stood for over sixty years until 1995–96.

SHEFFIELD UNITED 1995–96 LEAGUE RECORD

Match No.	Date	Venue	Opponents	Result		H/T Score	Lg. Pos.	Goalscorers	Atten- dance
1	Aug 12	A	Watford	L	1-2	1-2	—	Blake	8687
2	19	H	Tranmere R	L	0-2	0-1	24		11,247
3	26	A	Oldham Ath	L	1-2	0-0	24	Blake	6851
4	29	H	Crystal Palace	L	2-3	0-0	—	Flo, Whitehouse	10,378
5	Sept 2	A	WBA	L	1-3	0-2	24	Scott R	14,377
6	9	H	Norwich C	W	2-1	1-1	24	Blake, Veart	11,205
7	12	H	Charlton Ath	W	2-0	1-0	—	Blake 2	9448
8	17	A	Barnsley	D	2-2	0-2	21	Blake 2	7150
9	24	A	Huddersfield T	W	2-1	2-0	16	Flo, Hodges	12,840
10	30	H	Ipswich T	D	2-2	2-0	17	Blake, Whitehouse (pen)	12,557
11	Oct 7	H	Derby Co	L	0-2	0-1	19		12,721
12	14	A	Southend U	L	1-2	1-1	21	Holland	5292
13	21	H	Leicester C	L	1-3	1-1	22	Flo	13,100
14	28	A	Wolverhampton W	L	0-1	0-1	23		23,881
15	Nov 4	H	Portsmouth	W	4-1	2-1	21	Veart 2, Flo, Battersby	11,281
16	11	A	Port Vale	W	3-2	1-1	19	Blake 2, Hodges	7284
17	18	A	Sunderland	L	0-2	0-0	20		16,640
18	21	H	Grimsby T	L	1-2	0-0	—	Blake	9884
19	25	H	Reading	D	0-0	0-0	19		9737
20	Dec 2	A	Derby Co	L	2-4	1-1	22	Blake, Veart	13,841
21	9	H	Huddersfield T	L	0-2	0-1	23		12,126
22	16	A	Ipswich T	D	1-1	0-0	23	Starbuck	9630
23	23	A	Stoke C	D	2-2	1-1	23	Patterson, White	12,265
24	26	A	Birmingham C	D	1-1	1-1	23	Patterson	17,668
25	Jan 13	A	Tranmere R	D	1-1	0-0	23	Hodges	7321
26	20	H	Watford	D	1-1	0-0	24	Tuttle	12,782
27	31	A	Luton T	L	0-1	0-1	—		6995
28	Feb 3	H	Oldham Ath	W	2-1	1-1	22	White 2	10,956
29	10	A	Crystal Palace	D	0-0	0-0	23		15,883
30	13	H	Millwall	W	2-0	1-0	—	Veart, Hutchison	10,007
31	17	A	Charlton Ath	D	1-1	0-0	22	White	11,239
32	20	H	WBA	L	1-2	1-2	—	Angell	10,944
33	24	H	Barnsley	W	1-0	1-0	20	Angell	14,584
34	28	A	Norwich C	D	0-0	0-0	—		10,945
35	Mar 2	A	Birmingham C	W	1-0	0-0	18	Walker	16,799
36	9	H	Stoke C	D	0-0	0-0	17		14,468
37	16	H	Millwall	L	0-1	0-0	20		7795
38	23	H	Luton T	W	1-0	0-0	20	Hutchison	14,935
39	30	A	Leicester C	W	2-0	0-0	20	Walker, Ward (pen)	15,230
40	Apr 2	H	Southend U	W	3-0	3-0	—	White, Walker 2	11,319
41	6	H	Wolverhampton W	W	2-1	2-1	14	Taylor, White	16,658
42	8	A	Portsmouth	W	2-1	2-0	12	Whitehouse (pen), White	8978
43	13	H	Sunderland	D	0-0	0-0	10		20,050
44	20	A	Grimsby T	W	2-0	2-0	10	Walker, Taylor	7685
45	27	A	Reading	W	3-0	1-0	9	Walker 2, Whitehouse	9769
46	May 4	H	Port Vale	D	1-1	0-0	9	Walker	18,741

Final League Position: 9

GOALSCORERS

League (57): Blake 12, Walker 8, White 7, Veart 5, Flo 4, Whitehouse 4 (2 pens), Hodges 3, Angell 2, Hutchison 2, Patterson 2, Taylor 2, Battersby 1, Holland 1, Scott R 1, Starbuck 1, Tuttle 1, Ward 1 (pen).
Coca-Cola Cup (4): Flo 1, Holland 1, Veart 1, Whitehouse 1 (pen).
FA Cup (2): Veart 1, Whitehouse 1.

Kelly A 34 + 1	Ward M 39 + 3	Scott A 3 + 4	Holland P 11 + 7	Tuttle D 26	Nilsen R 39	Rogers P 13 + 3	Veart C 17 + 10	Scott R 2 + 3	Blake N 20 + 2	Whitehouse D 36 + 2	Flo J 17 + 2	Starbuck P 5 + 6	Gayle B 3 + 2	Beard M 13 + 7	Mercer B 1	Blount M 7 + 1	Hodges G 15 + 7	Hawes S 1 + 1	Hodgson D 12 + 4	Battersby T 3 + 7	Foran M 6 + 1	Davidson R 1	Gannon J 12	Gage K 2 / Muggleton C — + 1	Tracey S 11 / Reed J — + 2	White D 24 + 4	Fitzgerald S 6	Heath A — + 4	Vonk M 17	Patterson M 21	Short C 13 + 2	Hutchison D 18 + 1	Cowans G 18 + 2	Angell B 6	Walker A 12 + 2	Ablett G 12	Taylor G 10	Match No.
1	2	3³	4²	5	6	7	8	9¹	10	11	12	13	14																									1
1	2	3	4	5	6	7¹	12	8²	10	11	9			13																								2
1	7	13	10	6	3	4	8			12	11	9²	5	2¹																								3
	7	12			3	4	8³	13	10	11	9²		5	2		6¹	14																					4
1	7			3	4²	8¹	12	9	11			5	2		6	10	13																					5
1	7		12	5²	3	4¹	13		9	11	8			2		6	10																					6
1	7		12		3	4	13		9	11	8³			2²		6	10		5	14																		7
1	7¹		13		3	4²	12		9	11				2		6	10		5	8																		8
1		12	7	6	3	4			9¹	11	8			2		10					5																	9
1		12	13	6	3	4	14		9³	11	8²		7¹	2		10					5																	10
1	12		4	6	3				13	9	11	8²				10	7¹		14	5	2³																	11
1	2		7	6¹	3	12	11²	13	14	8						10			9³	5		4																12
1	2		7	6	3				9		8	11				10				5		4																13
1	12	5	13	6	3		7		9		8	11¹				10				4²	2																	14
1	11		4	6	3		9³	5	8	13				12		10²			14		2¹																	15
	11		12	6	3²		7		9	5	8			2		10¹	13			4	1																	16
1	11	10¹			6		7²		9	3	8			2	12	5			4			13																17
1	11		6			12	7¹		9	3	8³			2		13	5	14	4²			10																18
1	11		6			12	4		9²	3	8			2¹		10			13			7	5															19
1	12		6¹			10			9	11	8³			2		13	3	14	4²			7	5															20
	12		3			8			9	11²	13			2		10³		14	5		4	1	7¹	6														21
1	11		10	6	3	2	8¹		9²				13			12			4			7	5															22
1	11		10	6		2										12		9	4²			7	3	13	5¹	8												23
1	11		6	3	2				9¹							10			12			4²		7	5	13	8											24
1	3		6						11		9¹					12	13		4²			7				5		2	10	8								25
1	10¹		6	3					13		11²					12						7				5	4	2	9	8								26
1	2		6	3		12			11													7¹		13	5	4			10	8²	9							27
1	2		6¹	3		12			11													7			5	4			10	8	9							28
1	3		6						11¹							12						7		13	5	4	2	10	8	9²								29
1	3		6		9¹				11	12												7			5	4	2	10	8									30
1	11		6	3¹	9				12													7			5	4	2	10	8									31
1	3		6						8	11												7			5	4	2	10		9								32
1	2		6	3		12			11													7			5	4	13		8	9²	10¹							33
1	2		6¹	3		11			12													7			5	8	13		4	9	10²							34
1	8		3			11¹	9									5						7				2	10	4			12	6						35
1	8		3			11										5						7				2	10¹	4			12	6	9					36
1	2		3			11	12									5										8		13	4¹		10	6	9²					37
	7		3			11³	12									5						1	13			4	2¹	8	14		10	6	9²					38
	7		3																			1	12			5	11	2¹	8	4	10	6	9					39
	2		3													12						1	7¹			5	11		8	4	10	6	9					40
	2		3				12		13							5						1	7¹			11		8	4¹		10	6	9					41
	2¹		3				11		12							5						1	7			4		8	13		10²	6	9					42
	2		3				11									12						1	7			5	9	8	4		10¹	6						43
	7		3				11															1	12			5	4	2	8		10¹	6	9					44
	7¹		3				11							12		6¹						14	13	1		5	8	2³	4	4²	10	6	9²					45
15							11					12				6¹						13	1⁶			5	8	2	7	4²	10	3	9					46

Coca-Cola Cup
Second Round	Bury	(h)	2-1
		(a)	2-4

FA Cup
Third Round	Arsenal	(a)	1-1
		(h)	1-0
Fourth Round	Aston Villa	(h)	0-1

SHEFFIELD WEDNESDAY 1995–96 *Back row (left to right):* Andy Pearce, Mark Bright, Kevin Pressman, Julian Watts, Klas Ingesson, Chris Woods, Ryan Jones, Chris Waddle.
Middle row: Danny Bergara (First Team Coach), Mark Pembridge, Peter Atherton, John Sheridan, Michael Williams, Lee Briscoe, Ian Nolan, Guy Whittingham, Dave Galley (Physio).
Front row: David Pleat (Manager), Graham Hyde, Marc Degryse, Dan Petrescu, Des Walker, Andy Sinton, David Hirst, Richie Barker (Football Development/Manager's Assistant).
(Photograph: Steve Ellis)

FA Premiership   **SHEFFIELD WEDNESDAY**

Hillsborough, Sheffield S6 1SW. Telephone: (0114) 2343122. Fax: (0114) 2337145. Ticket Office: (0114) 2337233. Clubcall: 0891 121186.

Ground capacity: 39,814.

Record attendance: 72,841 v Manchester C, FA Cup 5th rd, 17 February 1934.

Record receipts: £533,918 Sunderland v Norwich C, FA Cup semi-final, 5 April 1992.

Pitch measurements: 115yd × 76yd.

Chairman: D. G. Richards. *Vice-Chairman:* K. T. Addy.

Directors: G. K. Hulley, R. M. Grierson FCA, J. Ashton MP, G. A. Thorpe, H. E. Culley.

Manager: David Pleat. *Assistant Manager:* Danny Bergara.

Physio: David Galley.

Secretary: Graham Mackrell FCCA. *Commercial Manager:* Sean O'Toole. *Stadium Manager:* T. Grayson.

Year Formed: 1867 (fifth oldest League club).

Turned Professional: 1887. *Ltd Co.:* 1899.

Former Names: The Wednesday until 1929.

Club Nickname: 'The Owls'.

Previous Grounds: 1867, Highfield; 1869, Myrtle Road; 1877, Sheaf House; 1887, Olive Grove; 1899, Owlerton (since 1912 known as Hillsborough). Some games were played at Endcliffe in the 1880s. Until 1895 Bramall Lane was used for some games.

Foundation: Sheffield, being one of the principal centres of early Association Football, this club was formed as long ago as 1867 by the Sheffield Wednesday Cricket Club (formed 1825) and their colours from the start were blue and white. The inaugural meeting was held at the Adelphi Hotel and the original committee included Charles Stokes who was subsequently a founder member of Sheffield United.

First Football League game: 3 September 1892, Division 1, v Notts Co (a) W 1-0 – Allan; Tom Brandon (1), Mumford; Hall, Betts, Harry Brandon; Spiksley, Brady, Davis, R.N. Brown, Dunlop.

Record League Victory: 9–1 v Birmingham, Division 1, 13 December 1930 – Brown; Walker, Blenkinsop; Strange, Leach, Wilson; Hooper (3), Seed (2), Ball (2), Burgess (1), Rimmer (1).

Record Cup Victory: 12–0 v Halliwell, FA Cup 1st rd, 17 January 1891 – Smith; Thompson, Brayshaw; Harry Brandon (1), Betts, Cawley (2); Winterbottom, Mumford (2), Bob Brandon (1), Woolhouse (5), Ingram (1).

Record Defeat: 0–10 v Aston Villa, Division 1, 5 October 1912.

Most League Points (2 for a win): 62, Division 2, 1958–59.

Most League Points (3 for a win): 88, Division 2, 1983–84.

Most League Goals: 106, Division 2, 1958–59.

Highest League Scorer in Season: Derek Dooley, 46, Division 2, 1951–52.

Most League Goals in Total Aggregate: Andy Wilson, 199, 1900–20.

Most Capped Player: Nigel Worthington, 50 (64), Northern Ireland.

Most League Appearances: Andy Wilson, 502, 1900–20.

Record Transfer Fee Received: £2,650,000 from Blackburn R for Paul Warhurst, September 1993.

Record Transfer Fee Paid: £2,750,000 to Sampdoria for Des Walker, July 1993 and £2,750,000 to QPR for Andy Sinton, August 1993.

Football League Record: 1892 Elected to Division 1; 1899–1900 Division 2; 1900–20 Division 1; 1920–26 Division 2; 1926–37 Division 1; 1937–50 Division 2; 1950–51 Division 1; 1951–52 Division 2; 1952–55 Division 1; 1955–56 Division 2; 1956–58 Division 1; 1958–59 Division 2; 1959–70 Division 1; 1970–75 Division 2; 1975–80 Division 3; 1980–84 Division 2; 1984–90 Division 1; 1990–91 Division 2; 1991–92 Division 1; 1992– FA Premier League.

Honours: Football League: Division 1 – Champions 1902–03, 1903–04, 1928–29, 1929–30; Runners-up 1960–61; Division 2 – Champions 1899–1900, 1925–26, 1951–52, 1955–56, 1958–59; Runners-up 1949–50, 1983–84. *FA Cup:* Winners 1896, 1907, 1935; Runners-up 1890, 1966, 1993. *Football League Cup:* Winners 1991; Runners-up 1993. **European Competitions:** *Fairs Cup:* 1961–62, 1963–64, 1992–93.

Colours: Blue and white striped shirts, blue shorts, blue stockings. *Change colours:* Green shirts, white shorts, white stockings.

Did you know?
In 1902–03, Sheffield Wednesday won five trophies: the First Division, Midland League, Sheffield Challenge Cup, Wharncliffe Charity Cup and the Plymouth Bowl.

SHEFFIELD WEDNESDAY 1995–96 LEAGUE RECORD

Match No.	Date	Venue	Opponents	Result	H/T Score	Lg. Pos.	Goalscorers	Attendance
1	Aug 19	A	Liverpool	L 0-1	0-0	—		40,535
2	23	H	Blackburn R	W 2-1	1-0	—	Waddle, Pembridge	25,544
3	27	H	Newcastle U	L 0-2	0-0	14		24,815
4	30	A	Wimbledon	D 2-2	1-1	—	Degryse, Hirst	6352
5	Sept 9	A	QPR	W 3-0	0-0	9	Bright 2, Donaldson	12,659
6	16	H	Tottenham H	L 1-3	1-1	13	Hirst	26,565
7	23	H	Manchester U	D 0-0	0-0	12		34,101
8	30	A	Leeds U	L 0-2	0-1	13		33,899
9	Oct 15	H	Middlesbrough	L 0-1	0-0	15		21,177
10	21	A	Coventry C	W 1-0	1-0	12	Whittingham	14,002
11	28	H	West Ham U	L 0-1	0-1	13		23,917
12	Nov 4	A	Chelsea	D 0-0	0-0	14		23,216
13	18	H	Manchester C	D 1-1	1-0	14	Hirst (pen)	24,422
14	21	A	Arsenal	L 2-4	2-1	—	Hirst, Waddle	34,556
15	25	A	Everton	D 2-2	2-1	15	Bright 2	35,898
16	Dec 4	H	Coventry C	W 4-3	2-2	—	Whittingham, Hirst, Degryse, Bright	16,229
17	9	A	Manchester U	D 2-2	0-1	14	Bright, Whittingham	41,849
18	16	H	Leeds U	W 6-2	3-1	14	Degryse 2, Whittingham, Bright, Hirst 2	24,573
19	23	H	Southampton	D 2-2	1-1	14	Hirst 2 (2 pens)	25,115
20	26	A	Nottingham F	L 0-1	0-1	14		27,810
21	Jan 1	H	Bolton W	W 4-2	2-0	13	Kovacevic 2, Hirst 2 (1 pen)	24,872
22	13	H	Liverpool	D 1-1	1-0	13	Kovacevic	32,747
23	20	A	Blackburn R	L 0-3	0-2	13		24,732
24	Feb 3	A	Newcastle U	L 0-2	0-0	14		36,567
25	10	H	Wimbledon	W 2-1	0-0	13	Degryse, Watts	19,085
26	17	H	QPR	L 1-3	1-1	14	Hyde	22,442
27	24	A	Tottenham H	L 0-1	0-1	14		32,047
28	Mar 2	A	Nottingham F	L 1-3	0-1	14	Kovacevic	21,930
29	6	A	Aston Villa	L 2-3	1-0	—	Blinker 2	27,893
30	16	H	Aston Villa	W 2-0	0-0	14	Whittingham, Hirst	22,964
31	20	H	Southampton	W 1-0	1-0	—	Degryse	13,216
32	23	A	Bolton W	L 1-2	1-1	14	Whittingham	18,368
33	Apr 5	A	Middlesbrough	L 1-3	0-0	—	Whyte (og)	29,751
34	8	H	Arsenal	W 1-0	0-0	14	Degryse	24,349
35	13	A	Manchester C	L 0-1	0-0	15		30,898
36	17	H	Chelsea	D 0-0	0-0	—		25,094
37	27	H	Everton	L 2-5	1-3	15	Hirst, Degryse	32,724
38	May 5	A	West Ham U	D 1-1	0-0	15	Newsome	23,790

Final League Position: 15

GOALSCORERS

League (48): Hirst 13 (4 pens), Degryse 8, Bright 7, Whittingham 6, Kovacevic 4, Blinker 2, Waddle 2, Donaldson 1, Hyde 1, Newsome 1, Pembridge 1, Watts 1, own goal 1.
Coca-Cola Cup (10): Degryse 4, Bright 3, Hirst 1, Pembridge 1, Whittingham 1.
FA Cup (0).

Pressman K 30	Petrescu D 8	Nolan I 29	Atherton P 36	Watts J 9+2	Walker D 36	Hyde G 14+12	Waddle C 23+9	Bright M 15+10	Pembridge M 24+1	Sheridan J 13+4	Hirst D 29+1	Sinton A 7+3	Degryse M 30+4	Ingesson K 3+2	Donaldson O 1+2	Humphreys R 1+4	Whittingham G 27+2	Pearce A 3	Briscoe L 22+4	Williams M 2+3	Nicol S 18+1	Kovacevic D 8+8	Stefanovic D 5+1	Woods C 8	Platts M —+2	Blinker R 9	Newsome J 8	Match No.
1	2	3¹	4	5	6	7	8²	9	10	11	12	13																1
1	2	3	4	5	6		8¹	10	7	11	9	12																2
1	2³	3	4	5	6	13		10	7	11²	9¹	12	8	14														3
1	2	3	4	5	6			10	7	11	9¹		8	12														4
1	2	3	4	5	6		8	9	7	11							10¹	12										5
1	2	3	4	5¹	6	12	10		7	11²	9		8				13											6
1	2	3	4		6	7	8	12	11²		9¹		10								5	13						7
1	2³	3²	4		6	7	8	12	11	13	9		10¹								5	14						8
1	2			5	6	7¹	8	9	4	12			11				10²		13		3							9
1	2			5	6	12	8¹	9	4				11	7			10		3²		13							10
1		3		5			8	12	7	11	9	13	4				10¹				2²							11
1	2			5	6	7¹	8	12	4	11	9		10						3									12
1	2		4	5	6¹	7	8	12		11	9		10						3									13
1	2		4	5	6¹	7	8	13	12²	11	9		10						3									14
1	2			5	6	7	8	9		11		13	10						3¹		12²	4						15
1	2			5	6	12	8¹		7	11	9		10						3		4							16
1	2			5	6	12	8¹		7	11	9		10						3		4							17
1	2			5	6	12	8		7	11¹	9		10						3		4							18
1	2			5	6	12	8		7¹	11	9		10²						3		4	13						19
1	2			5	6	12	8		7	11	9¹		10						3²		4	13						20
1	2			5	6	12	8		7	11	9		4				10²		3									21
	2			5	6	12	8		7¹	11	9	13	10²						3		4			1				22
	2			5	6	13	8¹		7	11	9		10						3³		4	14	17²	1				23
1	2	3		5	6		8	12	7	11	9¹		10								4							24
1	2			5	6	12	8³	9	7²	11		13	10						3¹		4	14						25
1	2			5	6	10¹	8	12	7	11	9								3		4							26
1	2			5	6	12	8¹		7²		9	13	10						3³		4			1			14	27
	2	3		5	6	12	8¹		7	11³	9	13	10	14							4			1²				28
	2³			5	6	10¹	8		4	11	9²	12					13		3			14		1		7		29
					6	12			4¹	11	9²		7				10		3		2	13		1		8	5	30
					6	12			4	11	9²		7				10		3		2	13		1		8¹	5	31
1	2				6	12		13	4	11¹	9³		7				10		3			14	8²				5	32
1	2				6	12			4	11¹	9³		7				10		13			3²	14			8	5	33
1	2				6	12			4	11	9²		7				10		3			13				8¹	5	34
1		4			6	12			11²	13	9		7³	14			10		3		2¹					8	5	35
1	2				6	12			4	11	9		7				10		3							8¹	5	36
1		5			6	12	13		4¹	11²	9³		7	14			10		3		2					8		37
1	2				6	10	12		4	9			7²	13			11		3							8¹	5	38

Coca-Cola Cup

Second Round	Crewe Alex	(a)	2-2
		(h)	5-2
Third Round	Millwall	(a)	2-0
Fourth Round	Arsenal	(a)	1-2

FA Cup

Third Round	Charlton Ath	(a)	0-2

SHREWSBURY TOWN 1995–96 *Back row (left to right):* Darren Rowbotham, Ian Stevens, Darren Simkin, Martin Jefferies, Ray Woods, Austin Berkley, Nathan King.
Middle row: Malcolm Musgrove (Physio), Dean Spink, Shaun Wray, Mark Hughes, Tony Grenham, Tim Clarke, Paul Edwards, Tommy Lynch, Dave Walton, Steve Anthrobus, Kevin Summerfield.
Front row: Chris Withe, Ian Reed, Paul Evans, Mark Taylor, Fred Davies (Manager), Kevin Seabury, Richard Scott, Lee Martin, Mark Dempsey.

Division 2 **SHREWSBURY TOWN**

Gay Meadow, Shrewsbury SY2 6AB. Telephone: (01743) 360111. Commercial Dept: (01743) 56316. Clubcall: 0891 121194.

Ground capacity: 8000.

Record attendance: 18,917 v Walsall, Division 3, 26 April 1961.

Record receipts: £80,610 v Arsenal, FA Cup 5th rd, 27 February 1991.

Pitch measurements: 116yd × 76yd.

Vice-President: Dr J. Millard Bryson.

Chairman: R. Bailey.

Directors: F. C. G. Fry, M. J. Starkey, W. H. Richards, K. R. Woodhouse.

Manager: Fred Davies. *Commercial Manager:* M. Thomas.

Physio: Malcolm Musgrove. *Coaches:* Kevin Summerfield, D. Pratley.

Secretary: M. J. Starkey. *Stadium Manager:* R. Ashton.

Club Nickname: 'Town' or 'Shrews'.

Year Formed: 1886. *Turned Professional:* 1905 (approx). *Ltd Co.:* 1936.

Previous Ground: Old Shrewsbury Racecourse.

Foundation: Shrewsbury School having provided a number of the early England and Wales international players it is not surprising that there was a Town club as early as 1876 which won the Birmingham Senior Cup in 1879. However, the present Shrewsbury Town club was formed in 1886 and won the Welsh FA Cup as early as 1891.

First Football League game: 19 August 1950, Division 3 (N), v Scunthorpe U (a) D 0-0 – Eggleston; Fisher, Lewis; Wheatley, Depear, Robinson; Griffin, Hope, Jackson, Brown, Barker.

Record League Victory: 7–0 v Swindon T, Division 3 (S), 6 May 1955 – McBride; Bannister, Skeech; Wallace, Maloney, Candlin; Price, O'Donnell (1), Weigh (4), Russell, McCue (2).

Record Cup Victory: 7–1 v Banbury Spencer, FA Cup 1st rd, 4 November 1961 – Gibson; Walters, Skeech; Wallace, Pountney, Harley; Kenning (2), Pragg, Starkey (1), Rowley (2), McLaughlin (2).

Record Defeat: 1–8 v Norwich C, Division 3 (S), 1952–53 and v Coventry C, Division 3, 22 October 1963.

Most League Points (2 for a win): 62, Division 4, 1974–75.

Most League Points (3 for a win): 79, Division 3, 1993–94.

Most League Goals: 101, Division 4, 1958–59.

Highest League Scorer in Season: Arthur Rowley, 38, Division 4, 1958–59.

Most League Goals in Total Aggregate: Arthur Rowley, 152, 1958–65 (thus completing his League record of 434 goals).

Most Capped Player: Jimmy McLaughlin, 5 (12), Northern Ireland and Bernard McNally, 5, Northern Ireland.

Most League Appearances: Colin Griffin, 406, 1975–89.

Record Transfer Fee Received: £385,000 from WBA for Bernard McNally, July 1989.

Record Transfer Fee Paid: £100,000 to Aldershot for John Dungworth, November 1979 and £100,000 to Southampton for Mark Blake, August 1990.

Football League Record: 1950 Elected to Division 3 (N); 1951–58 Division 3 (S); 1958–59 Division 4; 1959–74 Division 3; 1974–75 Division 4; 1975–79 Division 3; 1979–89 Division 2; 1989–94 Division 3; 1994– Division 2.

Honours: Football League: Division 2 best season: 8th, 1983–84, 1984–85; Division 3 – Champions 1978–79, 1993–94; Division 4 – Runners-up 1974–75. *FA Cup:* best season: 6th rd, 1979, 1982. *Football League Cup:* Semi-final 1961. *Welsh Cup:* Winners 1891, 1938, 1977, 1979, 1984, 1985; Runners-up 1931, 1948, 1980. *Auto Windscreens Shield:* Runners-up 1996.

Colours: Blue shirts, white trim, blue shorts, blue stockings, white trim. *Change colours:* Red shirts, white shorts, red stockings.

Did you know?
On 25 November 1995, Shrewsbury Town equalled a club record with seven consecutive wins in all competitions, subsequently extended to seven in the League alone.

SHREWSBURY TOWN 1995–96 LEAGUE RECORD

Match No.	Date	Venue	Opponents	Result	H/T Score	Lg. Pos.	Goalscorers	Attendance
1	Aug 12	A	Swansea C	L	1-3	0-2	—	Anthrobus	3498
2	19	H	Walsall	L	0-2	0-0	24		4019
3	26	A	Bradford C	L	1-3	1-3	23	Reed	5017
4	29	H	Bristol C	W	4-1	0-1	—	Reed, Spink, Dempsey, Rowbotham	2558
5	Sept 2	H	Blackpool	L	0-2	0-2	22		3182
6	9	A	Crewe Alex	L	0-3	0-1	23		3747
7	12	A	Wrexham	D	1-1	1-1	—	Taylor	3298
8	16	H	Notts Co	L	0-1	0-0	24		2892
9	23	H	Stockport Co	L	1-2	0-0	24	Anthrobus	2588
10	30	A	Brighton & HA	D	2-2	1-1	24	Whiston, Rowbotham	5247
11	Oct 7	A	Hull C	W	3-2	1-0	22	Rowbotham 2, Spink	3266
12	14	H	York C	W	2-1	1-0	20	Lynch (pen), Spink	2827
13	21	A	Chesterfield	L	0-1	0-1	21		3920
14	28	H	Rotherham U	W	3-1	0-1	19	Whiston, Spink 2	2632
15	31	H	Oxford U	W	2-0	1-0	—	Evans, Lynch (pen)	2186
16	Nov 4	A	Brentford	W	2-0	2-0	14	Lynch (pen), Scott	4104
17	18	H	Burnley	W	3-0	2-0	11	Evans 2 (1 pen), Scott	3914
18	25	A	Swindon T	W	1-0	0-0	9	Scott	9306
19	Dec 9	A	Stockport Co	W	2-0	1-0	8	Rowbotham, Dempsey	5530
20	16	H	Brighton & HA	W	2-1	1-1	8	Rowbotham 2 (1 pen)	3697
21	23	A	Wycombe W	L	0-2	0-1	9		4131
22	26	H	Bristol R	D	1-1	0-0	10	Stevens	4944
23	30	H	Carlisle U	D	1-1	0-0	8	Spink	2864
24	Jan 2	A	Bournemouth	W	2-0	1-0	—	Rowbotham (pen), Anthrobus	3265
25	13	A	Walsall	L	0-3	0-1	8		5008
26	20	H	Swansea C	L	1-2	1-1	9	Stevens	6532
27	Feb 3	H	Bradford C	D	1-1	0-0	9	Berkley	3605
28	10	A	Peterborough U	D	2-2	0-0	8	Anthrobus, Currie	4986
29	13	A	Bristol C	L	0-2	0-0	—		5269
30	20	A	Blackpool	L	1-2	0-1	—	Anthrobus	4210
31	24	H	Notts Co	D	1-1	1-1	14	Anthrobus	4559
32	27	H	Crewe Alex	L	2-3	2-2	—	Stevens 2	3745
33	Mar 2	A	Bristol R	L	1-2	1-1	14	Stevens	5004
34	9	H	Wycombe W	D	1-1	1-1	17	Stevens	2866
35	16	A	Carlisle U	D	1-1	0-1	18	Anthrobus	3760
36	19	H	Peterborough U	D	1-1	1-0	—	Stevens	2291
37	23	H	Bournemouth	L	1-2	1-0	17	Stevens	2534
38	30	H	Hull C	D	1-1	0-1	17	Anthrobus	2347
39	Apr 2	A	York C	W	2-1	1-1	—	Scott, Stevens	2767
40	6	A	Rotherham U	D	2-2	1-2	17	Anthrobus, Stevens (pen)	2973
41	9	H	Chesterfield	D	0-0	0-0	—		3035
42	17	H	Wrexham	D	2-2	2-1	—	Anthrobus, Stevens	4094
43	20	H	Brentford	W	2-1	2-1	16	Scott 2	2711
44	23	A	Oxford U	L	0-6	0-2	—		5799
45	27	A	Swindon T	L	1-2	1-1	17	Currie	4233
46	May 4	A	Burnley	L	1-2	1-1	18	Stevens	9729

Final League Position: 18

GOALSCORERS

League (58): Stevens 12 (1 pen), Anthrobus 10, Rowbotham 8 (2 pens), Scott 6, Spink 6, Evans 3 (1 pen), Lynch 3 (3 pens), Currie 2, Dempsey 2, Reed 2, Whiston 2, Berkley 1, Taylor 1.
Coca-Cola Cup (3): Lynch 1 (pen), Rowbotham 1 (pen), Seabury 1.
FA Cup (17): Scott 3, Spink 3, Dempsey 2, Evans 2, Whiston 2, Anthrobus 1, Rowbotham 1 (pen), Stevens 1, Withe 1, own goal 1.

Clarke T 15	Scott R 36	Withe C 30 + 2	Taylor M 38	Hughes M 2	Stewart S 4	Woods R 18 + 5	Evans P 25 + 9	Spink D 32 + 2	Rowbotham D 20 + 6	Dempsey M 17 + 11	Anthrobus S 27 + 12	Seabury K 26 + 8	Walton D 35	Berkley A 36 + 2	Reed I 9 + 2	Stevens I 27 + 5	Lynch T 22 + 3	Megson G 2	Whiston P 28	Edwards P 31	Boden C 5	Watson M 1	Currie D 11 + 2	Kay J 7	Robinson C 2 + 2	Summerfield K — + 1	Wray S — + 3	Jackson D — + 1	Cope J — + 1	Match No.
1	2	3	4	5	6	7²	8	9	10¹	11	12	13																		1
1	2	3³	4		5	12	8	9	13	11¹	7²	6	10	14																2
1	2		4			13		9		5	11	12	3	10		7¹	6	8²												3
1	2	5	4		6			9	8	11				10		7	3													4
1	2	5	4		6²		12	9	8	11³		10		7	3¹	14	13													5
1	2	3	4	5¹		9		8	11		12	7	13	6	10²															6
1	2		4			12		8¹	13	9	6	7	11	3	10²	5														7
1	2		4¹			10		8	12	9	6	7	11	3		5														8
1	2		4			12		9		11¹	8	6	10	7		3														9
1	2¹	12	4			7		9	8	13	6	10	11²	7		3														10
	6		4			7	9²	8	12		2	10	11¹	13	3					5	1									11
	6		4			7	9		12	13	2	10	11¹	8²	3					5	1									12
	6		4¹			7	9	8²	12	13	2	10	11		3					5	1									13
	7	6²				7	4	12	8¹		13	10	11	9	3					5	1									14
	6					7	4	9		12	2	10	11	8¹	3					5	1									15
	6					7	4	9		12	13	2	10	11¹	8²	3				5	1									16
	6	3				7	4	9	12		10	2		11	8¹					5	1									17
	6	3	7			4	9	8	5	12	2	10	11¹								1									18
	6	3	7			4	9	8	11	10	2									5	1									19
	6	3	7			4	9	8	11	10	2									5	1									20
	6	3	7			5¹	4	9	8		10	2		11	12						1									21
	6	3	7			10²	9	8		12	2³	4	11¹	14	13					5	1									22
	6	3	4				9	8	11	7	10	2								5	1									23
	2	3	7			4¹	6		8²	12	9	10	11	13						5	1									24
	6	3	4			7¹	2	9²		5	12	13	10	11	8						1									25
1	6		4			7	2			9	12	10¹	11	8					5		3									26
	6		4			7¹			12		2	10	11	8	13			9²	5	1	3									27
	6	3	4				9²		12	13	2	10	11	8			7¹		5	1										28
	6		4			12			7	9	2	10	11¹	8			3		5	1										29
1		3	4			12	6	9¹		11	13	2	10	8					5		7²									30
1		5	4			12	6		13	9	2	10	11	8			3			7¹										31
1		5	4			7	6			9	2	10	11	8			3													32
1		3	4			7¹	6	12	13		9	2³	10	11²		8	14		5											33
		3	4²			6	9¹	13		12		10	11	8	2	5	1			7										34
		3				4	5	7	11	9	12	10	13	6²	8¹	2				1										35
	2					6¹	4	12	11	9		10		8	3		5	1		7										36
	4	3²				5	12		9	13	10	11¹	6	8	2		1		7											37
	6	5	4			12		7³	8²	9		10	11		3¹		1				13	2	14							38
	6	3	4¹			12			9		10	11²	8		5	1						2	7	13						39
	6	3	4			12	10		9		11²		8		5	1	13				2	7¹								40
	6	5	4			7¹	10	11	9			8	3		1						2	12								41
	6		4			12		9		10	11¹	8	3	5	1		7	2												42
	6		4¹			12	5	9		10	11	8	3		1		7	2												43
	6²	12	4			13	5	9		10	11²	8	3		1		7	2				14								44
	6²					4	5	9	12	10	11	8	3¹	2	1		7					13								45
			4			6³	5	9	2	10		11¹	8	3²		1		7				12	13	14						46

Coca-Cola Cup

First Round	Doncaster R	(a)	1-1
		(h)	0-0
Second Round	Derby Co	(h)	1-3
		(a)	1-1

FA Cup

First Round	Marine	(h)	11-2
Second Round	Scunthorpe U	(a)	1-1
		(h)	2-1
Third Round	Fulham	(a)	1-1
		(h)	2-1
Fourth Round	Liverpool	(h)	0-4

SOUTHAMPTON 1995–96 *Back row (left to right):* Frankie Bennett, Alan Neilson, Neil Shipperley, Dave Beasant, Ken Monkou, Richard Hall, Peter Whiston, Neil Heaney.
Middle row: Paul McDonald, Craig Maskell, Gordon Watson, Simon Charlton, Jason Dodd, Tommy Widdrington, David Hughes, Paul Tisdale, Paul Allen.
Front row: Lew Chatterley (Assistant Manager), Neil Maddison, Matthew Le Tissier, Lawrie McMenemy (Director of Football), Dave Merrington (Manager), Francis Benali, Jim Magilton, Jim Joyce (Physio).

FA Premiership SOUTHAMPTON

The Dell, Milton Road, Southampton SO15 2XH. Telephone: (01703) 220505. Fax: (01703) 330360. Recorded Ticket Information: (01703) 228575. Clubcall: 0891 121178.

Ground capacity: 15,000.

Record attendance: 31,044 v Manchester U, Division 1, 8 October 1969.

Record receipts: £215,450 v Portsmouth, FA Cup 3rd rd, 7 January 1996.

Pitch measurements: 110yd × 72yd.

Chairman: F. G. L. Askham FCA.

Vice-Chairman: K. St. J. Wiseman.

Directors: I. L. Gordon, B. H. D. Hunt, L. McMenemy, M. R. Richards FCA.

President: J. Corbett. *Vice-President:* E. T. Bates. *Manager:* Graeme Souness.

Joint Assistant Managers: John Mortimore, Lew Chatterley.

Coach: Alan Murray. *Physios:* Don Taylor, Jim Joyce.

Secretary: Brian Truscott.

Year Formed: 1885. *Turned Professional:* 1894. *Ltd Co.:* 1897.

Club Nickname: 'The Saints'.

Previous Name: Southampton St Mary's until 1885.

Previous Grounds: 1885, Antelope Ground; 1897, County Cricket Ground; 1898, The Dell.

Foundation: Formed largely by players from the Deanery FC, which had been established by school teachers in 1880. Most of the founders were connected with the young men's association of St. Mary's Church. At the inaugural meeting held in November 1885 the club was named Southampton St. Mary's and the church's curate was elected president.

First Football League game: 28 August 1920, Division 3, v Gillingham (a) D 1-1 – Allen; Parker, Titmuss; Shelley, Campbell, Turner; Barratt, Dominy (1), Rawlings, Moore, Foxall.

Record League Victory: 9–3 v Wolverhampton W, Division 2, 18 September 1965 – Godfrey; Jones, Williams; Walker, Knapp, Huxford; Paine (2), O'Brien (1), Melia, Chivers (4), Sydenham (2).

Record Cup Victory: 7–1 v Ipswich T, FA Cup 3rd rd, 7 January 1961 – Reynolds; Davies, Traynor; Conner, Page, Huxford; Paine (1), O'Brien (3 incl. 1p), Reeves, Mulgrew (2), Penk (1).

Record Defeat: 0–8 v Tottenham H, Division 2, 28 March 1936 and v Everton, Division 1, 20 November 1971.

Most League Points (2 for a win): 61, Division 3 (S), 1921–22 and Division 3, 1959–60.

Most League Points (3 for a win): 77, Division 1, 1983–84.

Most League Goals: 112, Division 3 (S), 1957–58.

Highest League Scorer in Season: Derek Reeves, 39, Division 3, 1959–60.

Most League Goals in Total Aggregate: Mike Channon, 185, 1966–77, 1979–82.

Most Capped Player: Peter Shilton, 49 (125), England.

Most League Appearances: Terry Paine, 713, 1956–74.

Record Transfer Fee Received: £3,300,000 from Blackburn R for Alan Shearer, July 1992.

Record Transfer Fee Paid: £1,200,000 to Chelsea for Neil Shipperley, January 1995 and to Sheffield W for Gordon Watson, March 1995.

Football League Record: 1920 Original Member of Division 3; 1921–22 Division 3 (S); 1922–53 Division 2; 1953–58 Division 3 (S); 1958–60 Division 3; 1960–66 Division 2; 1966–74 Division 1; 1974–78 Division 2; 1978–92 Division 1; 1992– FA Premier League.

Honours: Football League: Division 1 – Runners-up 1983–84; Division 2 – Runners-up 1965–66, 1977–78; Division 3 (S) – Champions 1921–22; Runners-up 1920–21; Division 3 – Champions 1959–60. *FA Cup:* Winners 1976; Runners-up 1900, 1902. *Football League Cup:* Runners-up 1979. *Zenith Data Systems Cup:* Runners-up 1992. **European Competitions:** *European Fairs Cup:* 1969–70. *UEFA Cup:* 1971–72, 1981–82, 1982–83, 1984–85. *European Cup-Winners' Cup:* 1976–77.

Colours: Red and white striped shirts, black shorts, red and white hooped stockings. *Change colours:* Blue and yellow striped shirts, blue shorts, blue and yellow hooped stockings.

Did you know?
In 1966–67, Ron Davies scored exactly half of Southampton's 74 First Division goals, the first Saints player to achieve this League feat.

SOUTHAMPTON 1995–96 LEAGUE RECORD

Match No.	Date	Venue	Opponents	Result	H/T Score	Lg. Pos.	Goalscorers	Attendance
1	Aug 19	H	Nottingham F	L	3-4	1-3	—	Le Tissier 3 (2 pens)	15,164
2	26	A	Everton	L	0-2	0-2	20		33,676
3	30	H	Leeds U	D	1-1	0-0	—	Widdrington	15,212
4	Sept 9	H	Newcastle U	W	1-0	0-0	15	Magilton	15,237
5	12	A	Middlesbrough	D	0-0	0-0	—		29,181
6	16	A	Chelsea	L	0-3	0-0	16		26,237
7	23	A	Arsenal	L	2-4	2-2	18	Watson, Monkou	38,136
8	Oct 2	H	West Ham U	D	0-0	0-0	—		13,568
9	14	A	Blackburn R	L	1-2	0-1	18	Maddison	26,780
10	22	H	Liverpool	L	1-3	1-1	18	Watson	15,245
11	28	A	Wimbledon	W	2-1	1-0	17	Shipperley 2	7982
12	Nov 4	H	QPR	W	2-0	1-0	15	Dodd, Le Tissier	15,137
13	18	A	Manchester U	L	1-4	0-3	15	Shipperley	39,301
14	20	H	Aston Villa	L	0-1	0-1	—		13,582
15	25	H	Bolton W	W	1-0	0-0	14	Hughes	14,404
16	Dec 2	A	Liverpool	D	1-1	0-0	14	Shipperley	38,007
17	9	H	Arsenal	D	0-0	0-0	15		15,238
18	16	A	West Ham U	L	1-2	1-0	15	Bishop (og)	18,501
19	23	A	Sheffield W	D	2-2	1-1	15	Heaney, Magilton (pen)	25,115
20	26	H	Tottenham H	D	0-0	0-0	15		15,238
21	Jan 1	A	Coventry C	D	1-1	0-0	16	Heaney	16,822
22	13	A	Nottingham F	L	0-1	0-1	16		23,321
23	20	H	Middlesbrough	W	2-1	0-1	16	Shipperley, Hall	15,115
24	31	H	Manchester C	D	1-1	0-0	—	Shipperley	15,172
25	Feb 3	H	Everton	D	2-2	0-0	15	Watson, Magilton	15,126
26	24	H	Chelsea	L	2-3	2-2	15	Widdrington, Clarke (og)	15,226
27	Mar 2	A	Tottenham H	L	0-1	0-0	18		26,320
28	16	A	Manchester C	L	1-2	0-2	18	Tisdale	29,550
29	20	H	Sheffield W	L	0-1	0-1	—		13,216
30	25	H	Coventry C	W	1-0	1-0	—	Dodd	14,461
31	30	A	QPR	L	0-3	0-1	17		17,615
32	Apr 3	A	Leeds U	L	0-1	0-0	—		26,077
33	6	H	Blackburn R	W	1-0	0-0	16	Le Tissier (pen)	14,793
34	8	A	Aston Villa	L	0-3	0-0	16		34,059
35	13	H	Manchester U	W	3-1	3-0	16	Monkou, Shipperley, Le Tissier	15,262
36	17	A	Newcastle U	L	0-1	0-1	—		36,554
37	27	A	Bolton W	W	1-0	1-0	17	Le Tissier	18,795
38	May 5	H	Wimbledon	D	0-0	0-0	17		15,182

Final League Position: 17

GOALSCORERS

League (34): Le Tissier 7 (3 pens), Shipperley 7, Magilton 3 (1 pen), Watson 3, Dodd 2, Heaney 2, Monkou 2, Widdrington 2, Hall 1, Hughes 1, Maddison 1, Tisdale 1, own goals 2.
Coca-Cola Cup (8): Le Tissier 2, Shipperley 2, Watson 2, Hall 1, Monkou 1.
FA Cup (10): Shipperley 3, Magilton 2, Dodd 1, Hall 1, Le Tissier 1, Oakley 1, Watson 1.

Beasant D 36	Dodd J 37	Benali F 28+1	Magilton J 31	Hall R 30	Monkou K 31+1	Le Tissier M 34	Watson G 18+7	Shipperley N 37	Maddison N 13+2	Heaney N 15+2	Hughes D 6+5	Charlton S 24+2	Widdrington T 20+1	Neilson A 15+3	Bennett F 5+6	Warren C 1+6	Tisdale P 5+4	Maskell C —+1	Venison B 21+1	Oakley M 5+5	Robinson M —+5	McDonald P —+1	Walters M 4+1	Grobbelaar B 2	Match No.
1	2	3	4	5	6	7	8	9	10	11^1	12														1
1	2	3	4	5	6^1	9	8^2	10		12		7	11	13											2
1	2	3	4	5		9		8	10			7^1	11	6	12										3
1	2	3	4	5		9		8	10		12	11	6	7^1											4
1	2	3	4	5		9	12	8	10			7^1	11	6											5
1	2	3	4	5	13	9	12	8	10				11	6^2	7^1										6
1	2	3^1	4	5	6	7	8	9^2	10	12		11	13												7
1	2	3	4	5	6	9		8	10			7^1	11	12											8
1	2	3		5	6	7	8^1	9	10			4	12	11^2	13										9
1	2	3		5		7		8	9^2	12		4	11	6^1		10	13								10
1	2	3		5	6	7	8	9		11^1		10^2	12	13			4								11
1	2	3	10	5	6	7	8^1	9		11			12				4								12
1	2	3	4	5	6		8^1	9	12	11^2		10	7	13											13
1	2	3	4^1	5	6	7	8	9		11		10	12												14
1	2	3	4	5	6	7	8^2	9		12			11^1	13					10						15
1	2	3	4	5	6	7		9				10	11^1						8	12					16
1	2	3^1	4	5	6	7	12	9				11^2	10						8	13					17
1	2	3	4^1	5	6	7		9	12			13	10						8	11^2					18
1	2		4	5	6			9	10^1	11^2		3		8	12					7	13				19
1	2		4	5	6	7^1		9		11		3					12		8	10					20
1	2	12	8	5	6			9	10	11		3^1			4				7						21
1	5		4		6	7	12	9	10^1			3			2	11^2			8		13		10		22
1	2		4	5	6	7	12	9^2				3			13				8	11^1			10		23
1	2	3	4	5	6	7	8	9											10	12			11^1		24
1	2		4	5	6	7	8	9				3							10	12			11^1		25
1	2		4	5	6	7	8	9				3	10							12			11^1		26
1	2		4	5	6	7	8^1	9				3^2	11						12	10	13				27
1	2			5	6	7	12	9			8	3	4^1						10	11^2	13				28
1	2		4	5^2	6	7	8	9^1				3	11				12		10	13					29
1	2		4		6	7	8^1	9		11		3			5		12		10						30
1	2	3^1	8		6			9		11		4			5		7		10			12			31
1	4	3			6^2	7		9				11^1		5	2		12		8	10	13				32
	5	3				7		8	9	11^1	6	12	4		2				10					1	33
	5	3				7	12	9				11	4	6	2				8	10^1				1	34
1	5	3	4		6	7		9				11	10		2				8						35
1	5	3	4		6	7		9				11^2	10	12	2^1				8		13				36
1	2	3	4	5	6	7	8	9	10^1				11				12								37
1	4	3	8	5	6	7		9				11			2				10						38

Coca-Cola Cup

Second Round	Cardiff C	(a)	3-0
		(h)	2-1
Third Round	West Ham U	(h)	2-1
Fourth Round	Reading	(a)	1-2

FA Cup

Third Round	Portsmouth	(h)	3-0
Fourth Round	Crewe Alex	(h)	1-1
		(a)	3-2
Fifth Round	Swindon T	(a)	1-1
		(h)	2-0
Sixth Round	Manchester U	(a)	0-2

SOUTHEND UNITED 1995-96 *Back row (left to right):* Dominic Iorfa, Luke Morrish, Andy Sussex, Paul Sansome, Dave Regis, Simon Royce, Mark Hone, Daniel Foot, Leo Roget. *Middle row:* Danny Greaves (Youth Team Coach), Ijah Anderson, Declan Perkins, Gary Jones, Roger Willis, Phil Gridelet, Steve Tilson, Keith Dublin, John Gowans (Physio). *Front row:* Andy Ansah, Andy Thomson, Theo Foley (Assistant Manager), Mick Bodley, Ronnie Whelan (Manager), Julian Halls, Chris Powell.

Division 1 SOUTHEND UNITED

Roots Hall Football Ground, Victoria Avenue, Southend-on-Sea SS2 6NQ. Telephone: (01702) 304050. Fax: (01702) 330164. Commercial: (01702) 304050. Soccerline: 0839 664444. Ticket Office: (01702) 304090. Infoline: 0839 664443.

Ground capacity: 12,485.

Record attendance: 31,090 v Liverpool, FA Cup 3rd rd, 10 January 1979.

Record receipts: £83,999 v West Ham U, Division 1, 7 April 1993.

Pitch measurements: 110yd × 74yd.

President: N. J. Woodcock.

Chairman and Managing Director: V. T. Jobson. *Vice-Chairman and Chief Executive:* J. W. Adams.

Secretary: J. W. Adams.

Directors: J. A. Bridge, B. R. Gunner, W. R. Kelleway, C. Wooldridge, D. M. Markscheffel.

Associate Directors: A. W. Jobson, R. J. Osborne, W. E. Parsons.

Manager: Ronnie Whelan. *Assistant Manager:* Theo Foley.

Physio: John Cowens. *Commercial Manager:* C. Wooldridge. *Stadium Manager:* David Jobson.

Club Nickname: 'The Blues' or 'The Shrimpers'.

Year Formed: 1906. *Turned Professional:* 1906. *Ltd Co.:* 1919.

Previous Grounds: 1906, Roots Hall, Prittlewell; 1920, Kursaal; 1934, Southend Stadium; 1955, Roots Hall Football Ground.

Foundation: The leading club in Southend around the turn of the century was Southend Athletic, but they were an amateur concern. Southend United was a more ambitious professional club when they were founded in 1906, employing Bob Jack as secretary-manager and immediately joining the Second Division of the Southern League.

First Football League game: 28 August 1920, Division 3, v Brighton & HA (a) W 2-0 – Capper; Reid, Newton; Wileman, Henderson, Martin; Nicholls, Nuttall, Fairclough (2), Myers, Dorsett.

Record League Victory: 9–2 v Newport Co, Division 3 (S), 5 September 1936 – McKenzie; Nelson, Everest (1); Deacon, Turner, Carr; Bolan, Lane (1), Goddard (4), Dickinson (2), Oswald (1).

Record Cup Victory: 10–1 v Golders Green, FA Cup 1st rd, 24 November 1934 – Moore; Morfitt, Kelly; Mackay, Joe Wilson, Carr (1); Lane (1), Johnson (5), Cheesmuir (2), Deacon (1), Oswald. 10–1 v Brentwood, FA Cup 2nd rd, 7 December 1968 – Roberts; Bentley, Birks; McMillan (1) Beesley, Kurila; Clayton, Chisnall, Moore (4), Best (5), Hamilton. 10–1 v Aldershot, Leyland Daf Cup Prel rd, 6 November 1990 – Sansome; Austin, Powell, Cornwell, Prior (1), Tilson (3), Cawley, Butler, Ansah (1), Benjamin (1), Angell (4).

Record Defeat: 1–9 v Brighton & HA, Division 3, 27 November 1965.

Most League Points (2 for a win): 67, Division 4, 1980–81.

Most League Points (3 for a win): 85, Division 3, 1990–91.

Most League Goals: 92, Division 3 (S), 1950–51.

Highest League Scorer in Season: Jim Shankly, 31, 1928–29 and Sammy McCrory, 1957–58, both in Division 3 (S).

Most League Goals in Total Aggregate: Roy Hollis, 122, 1953–60.

Most Capped Player: George Mackenzie, 9, Eire.

Most League Appearances: Sandy Anderson, 451, 1950–63.

Record Transfer Fee Received: £2,000,000 from Nottingham F for Stan Collymore, June 1993.

Record Transfer Fee Paid: £400,000 to Galatasaray for Mike Marsh, August 1995.

Football League Record: 1920 Original Member of Division 3; 1921–58 Division 3 (S); 1958–66 Division 3; 1966–72 Division 4; 1972–76 Division 3; 1976–78 Division 4; 1978–80 Division 3; 1980–81 Division 4; 1981–84 Division 3; 1984–87 Division 4; 1987–89 Division 3; 1989–90 Division 4; 1990–91 Division 3; 1991–92 Division 2; 1992– Division 1.

Honours: Football League: Best season: 15th, Division 1, 1993–94. Division 3 – Runners-up 1990–91; Division 4 – Champions 1980–81; Runners-up 1971–72, 1977–78. *FA Cup:* best season: old 3rd rd, 1921, 5th rd, 1926, 1952, 1976, 1993. *Football League Cup:* never past 3rd rd.

Colours: All royal blue. *Change colours:* All red.

Did you know?
On 1 January 1996, Southend United established a club record nine games without defeat in a 0-0 draw against Barnsley.

SOUTHEND UNITED 1995–96 LEAGUE RECORD

Match No.	Date	Venue	Opponents	Result	H/T Score	Lg. Pos.	Goalscorers	Attendance
1	Aug 12	A	Portsmouth	L	2-4	1-2	—	Thomson 2	10,630
2	19	H	Luton T	L	0-1	0-0	23		4630
3	26	A	Millwall	D	0-0	0-0	23		11,536
4	29	H	WBA	W	2-1	1-1	—	Thomson, Regis	4621
5	Sept 1	H	Reading	D	0-0	0-0	18		4962
6	9	A	Sunderland	L	0-1	0-1	21		13,805
7	13	A	Derby Co	L	0-1	0-1	—		9242
8	16	H	Wolverhampton W	W	2-1	1-1	20	Gridelet, Jones	6322
9	23	A	Leicester C	W	3-1	2-1	15	Hails 3	15,276
10	30	H	Grimsby T	W	1-0	0-0	11	Regis	4977
11	Oct 8	A	Birmingham C	L	0-2	0-1	14		17,491
12	14	H	Sheffield U	W	2-1	1-1	12	Regis, Tilson	5292
13	21	A	Tranmere R	L	0-3	0-1	13		6584
14	28	H	Huddersfield T	D	0-0	0-0	15		5128
15	Nov 4	A	Watford	D	2-2	1-1	14	Regis, Read	7091
16	11	H	Stoke C	L	2-4	1-1	16	Belsvik, Hails	5967
17	19	H	Crystal Palace	D	1-1	0-0	16	Regis	5089
18	22	A	Ipswich T	D	1-1	0-0	—	Regis	9757
19	25	A	Oldham Ath	W	1-0	0-0	16	Snodin (og)	6474
20	Dec 2	H	Birmingham C	W	3-1	2-1	13	Bodley, Regis, Byrne	7770
21	9	H	Leicester C	W	2-1	1-1	12	Dublin, Gridelet	5835
22	16	A	Grimsby T	D	1-1	0-0	11	Byrne	5269
23	20	H	Port Vale	W	2-1	2-1	—	Marsh 2 (1 pen)	4506
24	26	A	Norwich C	W	1-0	0-0	6	Jones	17,029
25	Jan 1	H	Barnsley	D	0-0	0-0	7		6537
26	13	A	Luton T	L	1-3	0-1	9	Byrne	6566
27	20	H	Portsmouth	W	2-1	0-1	4	McNally, Tilson	5560
28	Feb 3	H	Millwall	W	2-0	1-0	4	McNally, Regis	7302
29	10	A	WBA	L	1-3	0-1	4	Marsh	12,906
30	17	H	Derby Co	L	1-2	1-0	6	Thomson	8331
31	24	A	Wolverhampton W	L	0-2	0-1	8		24,677
32	27	H	Sunderland	L	0-2	0-0	—		5786
33	Mar 2	H	Norwich C	D	1-1	1-0	10	Byrne	6208
34	5	A	Charlton Ath	W	3-0	1-0	—	Dublin, Tilson, Thomson	11,927
35	9	A	Port Vale	L	1-2	1-1	9	Boere	6222
36	16	H	Charlton Ath	D	1-1	1-1	9	Thomson	7382
37	19	A	Reading	D	3-3	0-1	—	Willis 2, Rammell	5321
38	23	A	Barnsley	D	1-1	1-1	10	Rammell	6754
39	30	H	Tranmere R	W	2-0	0-0	7	Byrne, Boere	4738
40	Apr 2	A	Sheffield U	L	0-3	0-3	—		11,319
41	6	A	Huddersfield T	L	1-3	0-0	10	Willis	11,558
42	8	H	Watford	D	1-1	0-1	9	Roget	5348
43	13	A	Crystal Palace	L	0-2	0-1	11		15,672
44	20	H	Ipswich T	W	2-1	1-1	11	Dublin, Marsh	8363
45	27	H	Oldham Ath	D	1-1	0-1	11	Marsh (pen)	5397
46	May 5	A	Stoke C	L	0-1	0-1	14		18,897

Final League Position: 14

GOALSCORERS

League (52): Regis 8, Thomson 6, Byrne 5, Marsh 5 (2 pens), Hails 4, Dublin 3, Tilson 3, Willis 3, Boere 2, Gridelet 2, Jones 2, McNally 2, Rammell 2, Belsvik 1, Bodley 1, Read 1, Roget 1, own goal 1.
Coca-Cola Cup (2): Byrne 1, Jones 1.
FA Cup (0).

Royce S 46	Dublin K 42 + 1	Powell C 27	Bodley M 38 + 1	Lapper M 23 + 1	Hails J 39 + 3	Iorfa D 1 + 1	Whelan R 1	Jones G 14 + 9	Thomson A 22 + 11	Tilson S 23 + 5	Regis D 25 + 4	Gridelet P 37 + 3	Hone M 11 + 5	Ansah A — + 4	Byrne P 38 + 3	Marsh M 40	Sussex A 1 + 1	Read P 3 + 1	Belsvik P 3	McNally M 20	Charlery K 2 + 1	Barness A 5	Rammell A 6 + 1	Roget L 4 + 4	Brown K 6	Boere J 6	Stimson M 10	Willis R 9 + 1	Turner A 4 + 2	Match No.
1	2	3	4	5	6	7¹	8	9	10	11	12																			1
1	2¹	3	4	5	12	14		7²	10	11	9	6			8³	13														2
1	2	3	4	5	7				10	11	9	6			8															3
1	2	3	4	5	7²			12	10¹	11	9	6		13	8															4
1	2	3	4	5	7				10¹	11	9	6		12	8															5
1	2	3	4	5	13			12	10¹	11²	9	6	14		8³	7														6
1	5	3	4		11²			12	10	9¹		6		2	8	7	13													7
1	5	3	4		11			10		9		6		2	8	7														8
1	2	3	5	4	11			10		9¹	12	6			8	7														9
1	2	3	5	4	11			10		9¹	12	6²	13		8	7														10
1	2	3	5	4	11			12	10²			6	13	14	8³	7				9¹										11
1	2	3²	5	4	11			13	12	6	9¹	10			8	7														12
1	5	3	4		11²			12	10¹	9		6		2	8	7	13													13
1	5	3	4	2				12	11		9	6			8	7				10¹										14
1	2	3	5	4	11			12		9		6			8¹	7				10										15
1	2	3	5	4	11²			12		9		6			8	7			13	10¹										16
1	2	3	5	4	11			12		9		6			8	7				10¹										17
1	2	3	5	4	11			12		9		6			8	7				10¹										18
1	2	3	5	4	11			10		9		6			8	7														19
1	2	3	5	4	11			10		9		6			8	7														20
1	2	3	5	4	11			10		9		6			8	7														21
1	2	3	5	4	11			10¹	12	9		6			8	7														22
1	2	3	5	4	11			10		9		6			8	7														23
1	2	3		4	11			10		9		6		12	8	7			5											24
1	2	3	5		11			10¹	12	9		6			8	7				4										25
1	2²	3	5		11			10³	12	9		6¹	13		8	7				4	14									26
1		3	5		11			12		9		6¹		2	8	7				4	10									27
1			5		11					9		6		2	8	7				4	10	3								28
1			5		11			10	12	9		6		2	8	7				4¹		3								29
1	4		5		11			12	10²	9		6		2	8¹	7		13				3								30
1	4		5		11			10				6		2	8¹	7						3	9							31
1	4²		5		11			12	10¹			6		2	8	7						3	9	13						32
1	3		5		11			12				6			8	7				4				10¹	2	9				33
1	3				11			10	6						8	7				4				5	2	9				34
1	3	12			11			10	6			13			8²	7				4				5	2	9¹				35
1		5			11¹			10	6			12			8	7				4				2		9²	3	13		36
1	12	5			13			10¹	11³	14					8²	7				4				9	2		3	6		37
1	11	5						10¹				8	12			7				4				9	2		3	6		38
1	2²	5						10¹	12			8				7				4			13			9	3	6	11	39
1	11	5						12				8				7	10		2	4²						9	3	6¹	13	40
1		5	2					9¹	12			8			6	7				4							3	10	11	41
1	9	5	2						12			8			6¹	7				4			13				3	10	11²	42
1	9	5	2						3			8	12		11	7				4			6¹				3	10³	13	43
1	9	5	2						6			8				7				4							3	10	11	44
1	9	5	2						6	11		0				7				4			12				3	10¹		45
1	9	5	12	2					11			6			8¹	7				4			10²	13			3			46

Coca-Cola Cup
Second Round   Crystal Palace   (h)   2-2
                                  (a)   0-2

FA Cup
Third Round   West Ham U   (a)   0-2

STOCKPORT COUNTY 1995–96 *Back row (left to right):* Alun Armstrong, Tony Dinning, Richard Landon, Ian Helliwell, Jim Gannon, Matthew Bound, Jeff Eckhardt.
Middle row: Rodger Wylde (Physio), Tom Bennett, Michael Oliver, Neil Edwards, John Sainty (Assistant Manager), Matt Dickins, Chris Beaumont, Paul Ware, Dave Philpotts (Youth Manager).
Front row: Sean Connelly, Phil Johnson, Gavin Allen, Martyn Chalk, Dave Jones (Manager), Michael Flynn, Michael Chalk, Lee Marshall, Lee Todd, Marc Lloyd Williams.

Division 2   STOCKPORT COUNTY

Edgeley Park, Hardcastle Road, Stockport, Cheshire SK3 9DD. Telephone: (0161) 286 8888. Fax: (0161) 286 8900. Club Shop: (0161) 286 8899. Clubcall: 0891 121638.

Ground capacity: 12,086

Record attendance: 27,833 v Liverpool, FA Cup 5th rd, 11 February 1950.

Record receipts: £116,747 v Everton, FA Cup 3rd rd replay, 17 January 1996.

Pitch measurements: 111yd × 72yd.

Hon. Vice-Presidents: Mike Yarwood OBE, Freddie Pye, Andrew Barlow.

Chairman: Brendan Elwood. *Vice-Chairman:* Grahame White.

Directors: Mike Baker, Michael Rains, Brian Taylor, David Jolley.

Secretary: Gary Glendenning BA (HONS), ACCA.

Manager: Dave Jones. *Assistant Manager:* John Sainty.

Physio: Rodger Wylde.

Assistant Secretary: Andrea Dawson. *Commercial Manager:* John Rutter.

Marketing Manager and Programme Editor: Steve Bellis.

Year Formed: 1883. *Turned Professional:* 1891. *Ltd Co.:* 1908.

Club Nicknames: 'County' or 'Hatters'.

Previous Names: Heaton Norris Rovers, 1883–88; Heaton Norris, 1888–90.

Previous Grounds: 1883 Heaton Norris Recreation Ground; 1884 Heaton Norris Wanderers Cricket Ground; 1885 Chorlton's Farm, Chorlton's Lane; 1886 Heaton Norris Cricket Ground; 1887 Wilkes' Field, Belmont Street; 1889 Nursery Inn, Green Lane; 1902 Edgeley Park.

Foundation: Formed at a meeting held at Wellington Road South by members of Wycliffe Congregational Chapel in 1883, they called themselves Heaton Norris Rovers until changing to Stockport County in 1890, a year before joining the Football Combination.

First Football League game: 1 September 1900, Division 2, v Leicester Fosse (a) D 2-2 – Moores; Earp, Wainwright; Pickford, Limond, Harvey; Stansfield, Smith (1), Patterson, Foster, Betteley (1).

Record League Victory: 13–0 v Halifax T, Division 3 (N), 6 January 1934 – McGann; Vincent (1p), Jenkinson; Robinson, Stevens, Len Jones; Foulkes (1), Hill (3), Lythgoe (2), Stevenson (2), Downes (4).

Record Cup Victory: 6–2 v West Auckland T (away), FA Cup 1st rd, 14 November 1959 – Lea; Betts (1), Webb; Murray, Hodder, Porteous; Wilson (1), Holland, Guy (2), Ritchie (1), Davock (1).

Record Defeat: 1–8 v Chesterfield, Division 2, 19 April 1902.

Most League Points (2 for a win): 64, Division 4, 1966–67.

Most League Points (3 for a win): 85, Division 2, 1993–94.

Most League Goals: 115, Division 3 (N), 1933–34.

Highest League Scorer in Season: Alf Lythgoe, 46, Division 3 (N), 1933–34.

Most League Goals in Total Aggregate: Jack Connor, 132, 1951–56.

Most Capped Player: Harry Hardy, 1, England.

Most League Appearances: Andy Thorpe, 489, 1978–86, 1988–92.

Record Transfer Fee Received: £800,000 from Birmingham C for Kevin Francis, January 1995.

Record Transfer Fee Paid: £150,000 to Preston NE for Mike Flynn, March 1993.

Football League Record: 1900 Elected to Division 2; 1904 Failed re-election; 1905–21 Division 2; 1921–22 Division 3 (N); 1922–26 Division 2; 1926–37 Division 3 (N); 1937–38 Division 2; 1938–58 Division 3 (N); 1958–59 Division 3; 1959–67 Division 4; 1967–70 Division 3; 1970–91 Division 4; 1991–92 Division 3; 1992– Division 2.

Honours: Football League: Division 2 best season: 10th, 1905–06; Division 3 (N) – Champions 1921–22, 1936–37; Runners-up 1928–29, 1929-30; Division 4 – Champions 1966–67; Runners-up 1990–91. *FA Cup:* best season: 5th rd, 1935, 1950. *Football League Cup:* best season: 4th rd, 1973. *Autoglass Trophy:* Runners-up 1992, 1993.

Colours: White shirts with double royal pinstripe, white shorts with double royal pinstripe, white stockings. *Change colours:* Red and black striped shirts, black shorts, red and black stockings.

Did you know?
On 26 December 1995, Tony Dinning kept a clean sheet when deputising for injured goalkeeper Neil Edwards during 55 minutes of a 2-0 win against Carlisle.

STOCKPORT COUNTY 1995–96 LEAGUE RECORD

Match No.	Date	Venue	Opponents	Result	H/T Score	Lg. Pos.	Goalscorers	Attendance
1	Aug 12	A	Walsall	W 2-0	2-0	—	Helliwell 2	4884
2	19	H	Burnley	D 0-0	0-0	7		8463
3	26	A	Bristol C	L 0-1	0-1	14		7731
4	29	H	Swansea C	W 2-0	1-0	—	Helliwell, Armstrong	4433
5	Sept 2	H	Crewe Alex	D 1-1	0-0	8	Armstrong	6125
6	9	A	Blackpool	W 1-0	1-0	5	Armstrong	6602
7	12	A	Notts Co	L 0-1	0-0	—		4588
8	16	H	Wycombe W	D 1-1	1-1	8	Helliwell	5588
9	23	A	Shrewsbury T	W 2-1	0-0	6	Armstrong 2	2588
10	30	H	Bournemouth	W 3-1	1-0	5	Helliwell 2, Eckhardt	5655
11	Oct 7	A	Oxford U	L 1-2	1-2	6	Ware	5646
12	14	H	Brentford	D 1-1	1-0	8	Landon	6228
13	21	A	Hull C	D 1-1	1-0	10	Landon	3496
14	28	H	Chesterfield	L 0-1	0-1	12		6287
15	31	H	Rotherham U	D 1-1	0-1	—	Gannon	4070
16	Nov 4	A	York C	D 2-2	1-0	10	Helliwell, Oliver	3101
17	18	H	Swindon T	D 1-1	0-1	12	Helliwell	7196
18	25	A	Bristol R	W 3-1	0-0	10	Thornley, Armstrong, Eckhardt	4326
19	Dec 9	A	Shrewsbury T	L 0-2	0-1	12		5530
20	16	A	Bournemouth	L 2-3	1-1	13	Flynn 2	3638
21	19	A	Peterborough U	W 1-0	0-0	—	Bennett (pen)	3267
22	26	H	Carlisle U	W 2-0	1-0	11	Armstrong, Jeffers	5941
23	Jan 1	A	Brighton & HA	D 1-1	1-1	11	Eckhardt	5694
24	10	A	Bradford C	L 1-2	1-2	—	Jeffers	6030
25	13	A	Burnley	L 3-4	3-2	13	Bound, Flynn, Helliwell	9113
26	20	H	Walsall	L 0-1	0-1	15		5870
27	Feb 6	A	Swansea C	W 3-0	2-0	—	Eckhardt, Bound, Armstrong	1938
28	10	A	Bradford C	W 1-0	0-0	9	Landon	5290
29	13	H	Wrexham	L 2-3	1-1	—	Landon 2	4688
30	17	H	Notts Co	W 2-0	0-0	7	Armstrong, Williams	6179
31	20	A	Crewe Alex	W 1-0	0-0	—	Eckhardt	4241
32	24	A	Wycombe W	L 1-4	0-3	7	Flynn	4246
33	27	H	Blackpool	D 1-1	0-0	—	Armstrong	7711
34	Mar 2	A	Carlisle U	W 1-0	0-0	8	Ware	4849
35	9	H	Peterborough U	L 0-1	0-0	9		5915
36	16	H	Wrexham	W 3-2	1-0	9	Eckhardt, Armstrong 2	4081
37	19	H	Bristol C	D 0-0	0-0	—		3713
38	23	H	Brighton & HA	W 3-1	1-1	7	Bound (pen), Ware, Mutch	5765
39	30	H	Oxford U	W 4-2	2-1	7	Mutch 3, Marsden	6096
40	Apr 2	A	Brentford	L 0-1	0-0	—		3274
41	6	A	Chesterfield	W 2-1	1-0	7	Jeffers, Bound	6090
42	8	H	Hull C	D 0-0	0-0	7		5043
43	20	H	York C	W 3-0	2-0	8	Flynn 2, Bound (pen)	6286
44	23	A	Rotherham U	L 0-2	0-0	—		6920
45	27	H	Bristol R	W 2-0	1-0	7	Armstrong, Dinning	6935
46	May 4	A	Swindon T	D 0-0	0-0	9		14,697

Final League Position: 9

GOALSCORERS

League (61): Armstrong 13, Helliwell 9, Eckhardt 6, Flynn 6, Bound 5 (2 pens), Landon 5, Mutch 4, Jeffers 3, Ware 3, Bennett 1 (pen), Dinning 1, Gannon 1, Marsden 1, Oliver 1, Thornley 1, Williams 1.
Coca-Cola Cup (6): Armstrong 2, Chalk 1, Eckhardt 1, Gannon 1, Helliwell 1.
FA Cup (11): Eckhardt 4, Armstrong 3, Bound 1, Helliwell 1, own goals 2.

Edwards N 45	Connelly S 42 + 1	Todd L 42	Bennett T 24	Flynn M 46	Gannon J 22 + 1	Beaumont C 38 + 5	Ware P 22 + 5	Helliwell I 18 + 4	Armstrong A 44 + 2	Chalk M 5 + 5	Williams M 12 + 5	Eckhardt J 30 + 5	Mike A 4 + 4	Dinning T 1 + 9	Landon R 7 + 4	Oliver M 7 + 2	Croft B — + 3	Thornley B 8 + 2	Jeffers J 21 + 2	Bound M 26	Marsden C 19 + 1	Durkan K 11 + 5	Dickins M 1	Mutch A 11	Match No.
1	2	3	4	5	6	7^1	8	9	10	11	12														1
1	2	3	4	5	6	7	8	9	10		11														2
1	2	3	4	5	6	7	8	9^1	10		11^2	12	13												3
1	2^1	3	4	5	6	7		9	10		11	8	12												4
1	2	3	4	5	6	7		9	10	12	11^1	8													5
1	2	3	4	5	6	7	8	9^2	10		11^1	12			13										6
1	2	3	4	5	6	7	8	9	10		11^1	12													7
1	2	3	4	5	6	7	8	9	10		11														8
1	2	3	4	5	6	7	8	9	10	11	12														9
1	2	3	4	5^1	6	7	8	9	10		11	12													10
1	2	3	4	5	6	7	8	9^1	10	13	11				12^2										11
1	2	3	4	5	6	7	8		10		11	12			9^1										12
1	2	3	4	5	6	7	8		10		11				9^1	12									13
1	2	3	4	5	6	7	8^2		10		11				9^1	12		13							14
1	2	3	4	5	6	7			10		11^2	12			9^1	8		13							15
1	2	3	4^1	5	6	7	12	9^2	10		11	8						13							16
1	2^1	3	4	5	6	7	12		10						9	8			11^2		13				17
1	2		4	5	6	7	12		10^1						9	8		3	11						18
1	2^2	3	4	5	6^1	7	12		10						9	8			11		13				19
1	2	3	4	5		7	12		10^2					13	9	8^1			11	6					20
1	2	3	4	5		12			10^2			8		13	9			7^1	11	6					21
1^1	2	3	4	5				9	10			8		12				7	11	6					22
1	2	3	4	5		12		9^2	10			8		13					11^1	6	7				23
	2	3		5				9	10			8		12					11	6	4	7^1	1		24
1	2	3		5		7		9	10			8		12					11^1	6	4				25
1	2	3		5		7^2		9^1	10			8		12				13	11	6	4^3	14			26
1	2	3		5		7^1		9	10			8		12					11	6	4				27
1	2	3		5		7^1		9	10			8		12				13	11^2	6	4				28
1	2	3		5		7		9	10			8		12					11^1	6	4				29
1	2	3		5		7^1		9	10			8							11	6	4				30
1	2	3		5		7		9	10			8							11	6	4				31
	2	3		5		7		9^2	10			8		13				12	11	6	4^1		1		32
1	2	3		5		7		9^1	10			8		12					11	6	4				33
1	2	3		5		7		9^1	10			8		12					11	6	4				34
1	2	3		5		7^1		9	10			8		12					11	6	4				35
1	2	3		5		12	13		10			8^2		14					11	6	4^3	7		9^1	36
1	2	3		5					10			8							11	6	4	7		9	37
1	2	3		5		12			10			8							11	6	4	7^1		9	38
1	2	3		5		12			10			8^2		13					11	6	4	7^1		9	39
1	2	3		5					10			8		12					11	6	4	7^1		9	40
1	2	3		5		7			10			8							11	6	4			9	41
1	2			5		7^2			10			8^1		12				3	11	6	4	13		9	42
1	2	3		5	12	7	8		10^2										11^1	6	4	13		9	43
1		3	2^2	5		7	8^1		10					12					11	6	4	13		9	44
1		3	2^2	5		7	8^1		10^2					12					11	6	4	13		9	45
1	12	3	4^2	5	2^1	7^3	13		10			8							11	6	8	14		9	46

Coca-Cola Cup

First Round	Wrexham	(h)	1-0
		(a)	2-2
Second Round	Ipswich T	(h)	1-1
		(a)	2-1
Third Round	Aston Villa	(a)	0-2

FA Cup

First Round	Lincoln C	(h)	5-0
Second Round	Blyth Spartans	(h)	2-0
Third Round	Everton	(a)	2-2
		(h)	2-3

STOKE CITY 1995–96   *Back row (left to right):* Graham Potter, Lee Sandford, Vince Overson, John Gayle, Ian Cranson, John Dreyer, Larus Sigurdsson.
Middle row: Martin Carruthers, Carl Muggleton, Mark Prudhoe, Ronnie Sinclair, Nigel Gleghorn.
Front row: Toddy Orlygsson, Ray Wallace, Paul Peschisolido, Simon Sturridge, Kevin Keen, Ian Clarkson.

Division 1   STOKE CITY

Victoria Ground, Stoke-on-Trent ST4 4EG. Telephone: (01782) 413511. Fax: (01782) 745340. Commercial Dept: (01782) 45840. Soccerline Information: 0891 700278. Football in the Community: (01782) 744347.

Ground capacity: 24,054.

Record attendance: 51,380 v Arsenal, Division 1, 29 March 1937.

Record receipts: £160,000 v Newcastle U, Coca-Cola Cup 3rd rd, 25 October 1995.

Pitch measurements: 116yd × 75yd.

Vice-President: J. A. M. Humphries.

Chairman: P. Coates. *Vice-Chairman:* K. A. Humphreys.

Directors: D. J. Edwards, M. E. Moors.

Manager: Lou Macari. *Assistant Manager:* Chic Bates. *Coach:* Mike Pejic.

Physio: I. Liversedge MCSP, SRP.

Secretary: M. J. Potts. *Stadium Manager/Safety Officer:* J. Alcock.

Chief Executive: Jez Moxey F. INST SMM.

Year Formed: 1863 *(see Foundation).*

Turned Professional: 1885. *Ltd Co.:* 1908.

Club Nickname: 'The Potters'.

Previous Name: Stoke.

Previous Grounds: 1875, Sweeting's Field; 1878, Victoria Ground (previously known as the Athletic Club Ground).

Foundation: The date of the formation of this club has long been in doubt. The year 1863 was claimed, but more recent research by Wade Martin has uncovered nothing earlier than 1868, when a couple of Old Carthusians, who were apprentices at the local works of the old North Staffordshire Railway Company, met with some others from that works, to form Stoke Ramblers. It should also be noted that the old Stoke club went bankrupt in 1908 when a new club was formed.

First Football League game: 8 September 1888, Football League, v WBA (h) L 0-2 – Rowley; Clare, Underwood; Ramsey, Shutt, Smith; Sayer, McSkimming, Staton, Edge, Tunnicliffe.

Record League Victory: 10–3 v WBA, Division 1, 4 February 1937 – Doug Westland; Brigham, Harbot; Tutin, Turner (1p); Kirton; Matthews, Antonio (2), Freddie Steele (5), Jimmy Westland, Johnson (2).

Record Cup Victory: 7–1 v Burnley, FA Cup 2nd rd (replay), 20 February 1896 – Clawley; Clare, Eccles; Turner, Grewe, Robertson; Willie Maxwell, Dickson, A. Maxwell (3), Hyslop (4), Schofield.

Record Defeat: 0–10 v Preston NE, Division 1, 14 September 1889.

Most League Points (2 for a win): 63, Division 3 (N), 1926–27.

Most League Points (3 for a win): 93, Division 2, 1992–93.

Most League Goals: 92, Division 3 (N), 1926–27.

Highest League Scorer in Season: Freddie Steele, 33, Division 1, 1936–37.

Most League Goals in Total Aggregate: Freddie Steele, 142, 1934–49.

Most Capped Player: Gordon Banks, 36 (73), England.

Most League Appearances: Eric Skeels, 506, 1958–76.

Record Transfer Fee Received: £1,500,000 from Chelsea for Mark Stein, October 1993.

Record Transfer Fee Paid: £580,000 to Birmingham C for Paul Peschisolido, July 1994.

Football League Record: 1888 Founder Member of Football League; 1890 Not re-elected; 1891 Re-elected; relegated in 1907, and after one year in Division 2, resigned for financial reasons; 1919 re-elected to Division 2; 1922–23 Division 1; 1923–26 Division 2; 1926–27 Division 3 (N); 1927–33 Division 2; 1933–53 Division 1; 1953–63 Division 2; 1963–77 Division 1; 1977–79 Division 2; 1979–85 Division 1; 1985–90 Division 2; 1990–92 Division 3; 1992–93 Division 2; 1993– Division 1.

Honours: Football League: Division 1 best season: 4th, 1935–36, 1946–47; Division 2 – Champions 1932–33, 1962–63, 1992–93; Runners-up 1921–22; Promoted 1978–79 (3rd); Division 3 (N) – Champions 1926–27. *FA Cup:* Semi-finals 1899, 1971, 1972. *Football League Cup:* Winners 1972. *Autoglass Trophy:* Winners: 1992. *European Competitions:* UEFA Cup: 1972–73, 1974–75.

Colours: Red and white striped shirts, white shorts, white stockings with a red and black band at top. *Change colours:* Green and black striped shirts, black shorts, black stockings.

Did you know?
Mike Sheron scored in seven successive League games during the 1995–96 season, the best sequence for the club in modern times.

STOKE CITY 1995–96 LEAGUE RECORD

Match No.	Date	Venue	Opponents	Result	H/T Score	Lg. Pos.	Goalscorers	Attendance
1	Aug 12	H	Reading	D 1-1	1-0	—	Wallace	11,932
2	19	A	Leicester C	W 3-2	3-0	4	Peschisolido 2, Gleghorn	17,719
3	27	H	Port Vale	L 0-1	0-0	14		14,283
4	30	A	Ipswich T	L 1-4	0-1	—	Peschisolido	10,848
5	Sept 2	H	Oldham Ath	L 0-1	0-0	23		8663
6	9	A	Watford	L 0-3	0-2	23		7130
7	12	A	Birmingham C	D 1-1	0-1	—	Carruthers	19,005
8	16	H	Tranmere R	D 0-0	0-0	22		8618
9	24	H	WBA	W 2-1	1-0	22	Keen, Peschisolido	9612
10	30	A	Crystal Palace	D 1-1	1-1	21	Carruthers	14,613
11	Oct 7	H	Norwich C	D 1-1	0-1	21	Wallace	12,016
12	14	A	Wolverhampton W	W 4-1	2-0	16	Gleghorn, Potter, Wallace, Carruthers	26,483
13	22	H	Derby Co	D 1-1	0-0	16	Keen	9435
14	28	A	Grimsby T	L 0-1	0-0	19		5477
15	Nov 4	H	Luton T	W 5-0	1-0	15	Peschisolido, Sturridge 2, Gayle, Gleghorn	9382
16	11	A	Southend U	W 4-2	1-1	13	Sturridge 3, Gleghorn	5967
17	18	A	Portsmouth	D 3-3	1-2	14	Gayle 2, Sturridge	8030
18	22	H	Sunderland	W 1-0	1-0	—	Wallace	11,754
19	25	H	Millwall	W 1-0	1-0	9	Gleghorn	12,590
20	Dec 2	A	Norwich C	W 1-0	0-0	7	Gleghorn	15,707
21	9	A	WBA	W 1-0	1-0	5	Peschisolido	14,819
22	16	H	Crystal Palace	L 1-2	0-1	8	Sheron	12,090
23	23	H	Sheffield U	D 2-2	1-1	8	Gleghorn, Sheron	12,265
24	26	A	Barnsley	L 1-3	0-2	9	Gleghorn	9229
25	30	A	Huddersfield T	D 1-1	0-0	8	Sheron	15,071
26	Jan 13	H	Leicester C	W 1-0	1-0	4	Sturridge	13,669
27	20	A	Reading	L 0-1	0-0	6		8082
28	Feb 10	H	Ipswich T	W 3-1	1-0	7	Sheron 2, Gleghorn	12,239
29	17	H	Birmingham C	W 1-0	1-0	3	Sturridge	15,716
30	24	A	Tranmere R	D 0-0	0-0	5		8312
31	28	H	Watford	W 2-0	0-0	—	Cranson, Wallace	10,114
32	Mar 2	H	Barnsley	W 2-0	1-0	4	Keen, Sheron	12,663
33	9	A	Sheffield U	D 0-0	0-0	4		14,468
34	12	A	Port Vale	L 0-1	0-1	—		16,737
35	16	H	Huddersfield T	D 1-1	0-0	5	Sturridge	13,157
36	23	A	Charlton Ath	L 1-2	1-0	5	Sheron	12,770
37	30	A	Derby Co	L 1-3	1-0	6	Sheron	17,245
38	Apr 3	H	Wolverhampton W	W 2-0	1-0	—	Sheron, Sturridge	16,361
39	6	H	Grimsby T	L 1-2	1-0	8	Sheron	12,524
40	9	A	Luton T	W 2-1	0-1	—	Sturridge, Sheron	7689
41	13	H	Portsmouth	W 2-1	1-0	5	Wallace, Sheron	11,471
42	17	H	Charlton Ath	W 1-0	1-0	—	Sheron	12,969
43	21	A	Sunderland	D 0-0	0-0	4		21,276
44	27	A	Millwall	W 3-2	2-0	4	Sheron, Sturridge 2 (1 pen)	10,105
45	30	A	Oldham Ath	L 0-2	0-1	—		10,271
46	May 5	H	Southend U	W 1-0	1-0	4	Sheron	18,897

Final League Position: 4

GOALSCORERS

League (60): Sheron 15, Sturridge 13 (1 pen), Gleghorn 9, Peschisolido 6, Wallace 6, Carruthers 3, Gayle 3, Keen 3, Cranson 1, Potter 1.
Coca-Cola Cup (1): Peschisolido 1.
FA Cup (1): Sturridge 1.

Muggleton C 6	Clarkson I 43	Sandford L 46	Sigurdsson L 46	Overson V 18	Orlygsson T 6+1	Keen K 27+6	Wallace R 44	Peschisolido P 20+6	Scott K 6+1	Gleghorn N 46	Sturridge S 30+11	Gayle J 5+5	Potter G 38+3	Sinclair R 1	Carruthers M 10+14	Dreyer J 4+15	Devlin M 5+5	Brightwell D —+1	Prudhoe M 39	Cranson I 23+1	Whittle J 7+1	Sheron M 23+5	Beeston C 13+3	Match No.
1	2	3	4	5	6	7	8	9[1]	10	11	12													1
1	2	3	4	5	6	7	8	9[1]	10[2]	11	12	13												2
1	2	3	4	5	6[1]	7	8	9	10[2]	11	12		13											3
1	2	3	4	5	6	7[1]	8	9	10	11	12													4
1	2	3	4	5	6	7[1]	8	9	10	11	12													5
	2	3[1]	4	5	6[2]	7[3]	8	9	12	11				1	10	13	14							6
1	2	3	4	5		7[1]	8	9	10[2]	11[3]	12		6		13		14							7
	2	3	4	5	12	7[1]	8	9		11			6		10				1					8
	2	3	4	5		7	8	9		11	12		6		10[1]				1					9
	2	3	4	5		7	8	9[1]		11	12		6		10				1					10
	2	3	4	5			8	9		11	7		6		10				1					11
	2	3	4	5		7	8	9		11	12		6		10[1]				1					12
	2	3[1]	4	5		7	8	9		11			6		10	12			1					13
	2	3	4	5		7[1]	8	9		11	12		6		10				1					14
	2[3]	3	4	5		7	8	9[2]		11	12	13	6		10[1]				1		14			15
		3	4	5		7	8[2]			11[3]	10	9[1]	6		12	13			1	2	14			16
		3	4	5		7	8			11	10	9	6[1]		12				1	2[2]	13			17
	2	3	4	5[3]		7	8			11	10[1]	9	6[2]		12	13			1		14			18
	2	3	4			7[1]	8			11	10[3]	9[1]	6		12	13			1	5		14		19
	2	3	4				8	9[1]		11	10		6[2]		7				1	5		12	13	20
	2	3	4			12	8[1]	9[3]		11	10[2]		6		13	7			1	5		14		21
	2	3	4			7[1]	8	12		11	10		6						1	5		9		22
	2	3	4				8	9		11	10		6		12				1	5		7[1]		23
	2[1]	3	4				8	9		11			6		7	12			1	5		10		24
	2	3	4			7	8	9[1]		11	12		6		13				1	5		10[2]		25
	2	3	4			7[3]	8			11	9	12	6[2]		10[1]	13			1	5		14		26
	2	3	4			7	8	12		11	10	9[1]	6						1	5				27
	2	3	4				8	12		11	10[1]		6[2]			13			1	5		9	7	28
	2	3	4			12	8			11	10		6[2]			13			1	5		9	7[1]	29
	2	3	4				8	12		11	10		6						1	5		9[1]	7	30
	2	3	4			12	8[1]	13		11	10		6						1	5		9[2]	7	31
	2	3	4				8			11	10		6[1]		12				1	5		9	7	32
	2	3	4				8	12		11	10		6[2]			13			1	5		9[1]	7	33
	2	3	4				8[2]			11	10		6		13	12			1	5		9	7[1]	34
	2	3	4				8			11	10		6						1	5		9	7	35
	2	3	4			12	8			11	10		6[1]			13			1	5		9[2]	7	36
	2	4	3				8			11	10		6[1]		12				1	5		9	7	37
	2	3	4			12	8			11	10		6[2]		14	13			1	5		9[3]	7[1]	38
	2	3	4			7[1]	8			11[2]	10		6		12				1	5		9	13	39
	2	3	4			12	8			11	10		6[2]		13	14			1	5		9[1]	7[3]	40
	2	3	4				8			11	10		6		12				1	5		9	7[1]	41
	2	3	4				8			11	10		6[1]		12	7			1	5		9		42
	2	3	4				8			11	10		6[2]		12	13	7		1	5		9[1]		43
	2	3	4				8			11	10		6[2]		12	13	7		1	5		9[1]		44
	2[1]	3	4				8			11	10		6		12	7			1	5		9		45
	2	3	4				8			11	10		6[1]		12	7			1	5		9		46

Coca-Cola Cup

Second Round	Chelsea	(h)	0-0
		(a)	1-0
Third Round	Newcastle U	(h)	0-4

FA Cup

Third Round	Nottingham F	(h)	1-1
		(a)	0-2

SUNDERLAND 1995-96 *Back row (left to right):* Martin Smith, Gary Bennett, Gordon Armstrong, Brett Angell, Richard Ord, Andy Melville, Lee Howey.
Middle row: Mick Ferguson, Gordon Ellis, Paul Bracewell, Derek Ferguson, Brian Atkinson, John Kay, Alec Chamberlain, David Preece, Michael Gray, Steve Agnew, Phil Gray, Martin Gray, Martin Scott, Steven Grant, Bobby Saxton, Pop Robson, Steve Smelt.
Front row: Ricky Sbragia, Scott Coates, Christopher Lawless, Paul Heckingbottom, Dariusz Kubicki, Kevin Ball, Peter Reid, Craig Russell, David Mawson, Stephen Brodie, Sam Aiston, Joey McGiven, Stephen Pickering, John Cooke.

FA Premiership   **SUNDERLAND**

Roker Park Ground, Sunderland, Tyne and Wear SR6 9SW. Telephone: (0191) 514 0332. Fax: (0191) 514 5854.
Ground capacity: 22,657.
Record attendance: 75,118 v Derby Co, FA Cup 6th rd replay, 8 March 1933.
Record receipts: £187,000 v Manchester U, FA Cup 3rd rd replay, 16 January 1996.
Pitch measurements: 113yd × 74yd.
Chairman: R. S. Murray.
Director: John Fickling (Chief Executive). *Associate Directors:* J. R. Featherstone, G. S. Wood, J. G. Wood.
Manager: Peter Reid. *Assistant Manager:* Paul Bracewell. *General Manager/Secretary:* Mark Blackbourne.
Chief Coach: Bobby Saxton. *Physio:* Nigel Carnell. *Youth Team Coach:* Ricky Sbragia. *Director of Youth:* Mick Ferguson.
Director of Marketing and Commercial Development: Grahame McDonnell. *Stadium Manager:* Fred Bailey
Year Formed: 1879. *Turned Professional:* 1886. *Ltd Co.:* 1906.
Club Nickname: 'Rokermen'.
Previous Name: 1879–80, Sunderland and District Teacher's AFC.
Previous Grounds: 1879, Blue House Field, Hendon; 1882, Groves Field, Ashbrooke; 1883, Horatio Street; 1884, Abbs Field, Fulwell; 1886, Newcastle Road; 1898, Roker Park.
Foundation: A Scottish schoolmaster named James Allan, working at Hendon Boarding School, took the initiative in the foundation of Sunderland in 1879 when they were formed as The Sunderland and District Teachers' Association FC at a meeting in the Adults School, Norfolk Street. Due to financial difficulties, they quickly allowed members from outside the teaching profession and so became Sunderland AFC in October 1880.
First Football League game: 13 September 1890, Football League, v Burnley (h) L 2-3 – Kirtley; Porteous, Oliver; Wilson, Auld, Gibson; Spence (1), Miller, Campbell (1), Scott, D. Hannah.
Record League Victory: 9–1 v Newcastle U (away), Division 1, 5 December 1908 – Roose; Forster, Melton; Daykin, Thomson, Low; Mordue, Hogg (4), Brown, Holley (3), Bridgett (2).
Record Cup Victory: 11–1 v Fairfield, FA Cup 1st rd, 2 February 1895 – Doig; McNeill, Johnston; Dunlop, McCreadie (1), Wilson; Gillespie (1), Millar (5), Campbell, Hannah (3), Scott (1).
Record Defeat: 0–8 v West Ham U, Division 1, 19 October 1968 and v Watford, Division 1, 25 September 1982.
Most League Points (2 for a win): 61, Division 2, 1963–64.
Most League Points (3 for a win): 93, Division 3, 1987–88.
Most League Goals: 109, Division 1, 1935–36.
Highest League Scorer in Season: Dave Halliday, 43, Division 1, 1928–29.
Most League Goals in Total Aggregate: Charlie Buchan, 209, 1911–25.
Most Capped Player: Martin Harvey, 34, Northern Ireland.
Most League Appearances: Jim Montgomery, 537, 1962–77.
Record Transfer Fee Received: £1,500,000 from Crystal Palace for Marco Gabbiadini, September 1991.
Record Transfer Fee Paid: £1,000,000 to Millwall for Alex Rae, June 1996.
Football League Record: 1890 Elected to Division 1; 1958–64 Division 2; 1964–70 Division 1; 1970–76 Division 2; 1976–77 Division 1; 1977–80 Division 2; 1980–85 Division 1; 1985–87 Division 2; 1987–88 Division 3; 1988–90 Division 2; 1990–91 Division 1; 1991–92 Division 2; 1992–96 Division 1; 1996– FA Premier League.
Honours: Football League: Division 1 – Champions 1891–92, 1892–93, 1894–95, 1901–02, 1912–13, 1935–36, 1995-96; Runners-up 1893–94; 1897–98, 1900–01, 1922–23, 1934–35; Division 2 – Champions 1975–76; Runners-up 1963–64; 1979–80; Division 3 – Champions 1987–88. *FA Cup:* Winners 1937; 1973; Runners-up 1913, 1992. *Football League Cup:* Runners-up 1985. **European Competitions:** Cup-Winners' Cup: 1973–74.
Colours: Red and white striped shirts, black shorts, red stockings, white turnover. *Change colours:* White shirts with red trim, white shorts with red trim, red and white hooped stockings.
Did you know?
In the 1995–96 season, Sunderland established a club record of 18 undefeated League games beating their previous run of 16 in 1922–23.

SUNDERLAND 1995–96 LEAGUE RECORD

Match No.	Date	Venue	Opponents	Result		H/T Score	Lg. Pos.	Goalscorers	Attendance
1	Aug 12	H	Leicester C	L	1-2	1-1	—	Agnew	18,593
2	19	A	Norwich C	D	0-0	0-0	21		16,739
3	26	H	Wolverhampton W	W	2-0	2-0	15	Melville, Gray P	16,816
4	30	A	Port Vale	D	1-1	0-1	—	Gray P	7693
5	Sept 2	A	Ipswich T	L	0-3	0-2	19		12,390
6	9	H	Southend U	W	1-0	1-0	15	Russell	13,805
7	12	H	Portsmouth	D	1-1	1-0	—	Melville	12,282
8	16	A	Luton T	W	2-0	0-0	9	Mullin, Gray P	6955
9	23	A	Millwall	W	2-1	1-0	7	Scott (pen), Smith	8691
10	30	H	Reading	D	2-2	0-0	6	Kelly, Melville	17,503
11	Oct 7	A	Crystal Palace	W	1-0	0-0	3	Kelly	13,754
12	14	H	Watford	D	1-1	0-0	4	Scott	17,790
13	21	A	Huddersfield T	D	1-1	0-0	5	Gray P	16,054
14	28	H	Barnsley	W	2-1	1-0	5	Russell, Howey	17,024
15	Nov 5	A	Charlton Ath	D	1-1	1-1	4	Gray Michael	11,626
16	18	H	Sheffield U	W	2-0	0-0	4	Gray P 2	16,640
17	22	A	Stoke C	L	0-1	0-1	—		11,754
18	25	A	WBA	W	1-0	1-0	6	Howey	15,931
19	Dec 3	H	Crystal Palace	W	1-0	1-0	2	Scott (pen)	12,777
20	9	H	Millwall	W	6-0	2-0	1	Scott (pen), Russell 4, Gray P	18,951
21	16	A	Reading	D	1-1	1-0	1	Smith	9431
22	23	A	Derby Co	L	1-3	1-1	2	Gray Michael	16,882
23	Jan 14	H	Norwich C	L	0-1	0-1	8		14,983
24	21	A	Leicester C	D	0-0	0-0	7		16,130
25	24	H	Grimsby T	W	1-0	0-0	—	Ord	14,656
26	30	H	Tranmere R	D	0-0	0-0	—		17,616
27	Feb 3	A	Wolverhampton W	L	0-3	0-2	5		26,537
28	10	H	Port Vale	D	0-0	0-0	5		15,954
29	17	A	Portsmouth	D	2-2	1-1	5	Agnew, Howey	12,241
30	20	H	Ipswich T	W	1-0	1-0	—	Russell	14,052
31	24	H	Luton T	W	1-0	1-0	3	James (og)	16,693
32	27	A	Southend U	W	2-0	0-0	—	Scott (pen), Bridges	5786
33	Mar 3	A	Grimsby T	W	4-0	1-0	2	Ball, Russell, Gray P, Bridges	5318
34	9	H	Derby Co	W	3-0	2-0	2	Russell 2, Agnew	21,644
35	12	A	Oldham Ath	W	2-1	1-1	—	Gray Michael, Ball	7149
36	17	A	Birmingham C	W	2-0	1-0	1	Agnew, Melville	23,251
37	23	H	Oldham Ath	W	1-0	0-0	1	Scott	20,631
38	30	H	Huddersfield T	W	3-2	1-1	1	Ball, Bridges 2	20,131
39	Apr 2	A	Watford	D	3-3	3-1	—	Agnew, Ball, Russell	11,195
40	6	A	Barnsley	W	1-0	1-0	1	Russell	13,189
41	8	H	Charlton Ath	D	0-0	0-0	1		20,914
42	13	A	Sheffield U	D	0-0	0-0	1		20,050
43	16	H	Birmingham C	W	3-0	2-0	—	Gray Michael, Stewart, Russell	19,831
44	21	H	Stoke C	D	0-0	0-0	1		21,276
45	27	H	WBA	D	0-0	0-0	1		22,027
46	May 5	A	Tranmere R	L	0-2	0-1	1		16,193

Final League Position: 1

GOALSCORERS

League (59): Russell 13, Gray P 8, Scott 6 (4 pens), Agnew 5, Ball 4, Bridges 4, Michael Gray 4, Melville 4, Howey 3, Kelly 2, Smith 2, Mullin 1, Ord 1, Stewart 1, own goal 1.
Coca-Cola Cup (4): Howey 2, Angell 1, own goal 1.
FA Cup (3): Agnew 1, Gray P 1, Russell 1.

Chamberlain A 29	Kubicki D 46	Scott M 43	Bracewell P 38	Ball K 35 + 1	Ord R 41 + 1	Gray Michael 46	Agnew S 26 + 3	Smith M 9 + 11	Gray P 28 + 4	Angell B 2	Russell C 35 + 6	Armstrong G —+1	Gray Martin 4 + 3	Atkinson B 5 + 2	Howey L 17 + 10	Melville A 40	Mullin J 5 + 5	Stewart P 11 + 1	Aiston S 4 + 10	Kelly D 9 + 1	Hall G 8 + 6	Given S 17	Cooke T 6	Bridges M 2 + 13	Match No.
1	2	3	4	5	6	7	8^2	9	10	11^1	12	13													1
1	2		4	5	6	7		9^1	10	11^2	12		3	8	13										2
1	2	3	4	5		7		12	10^2	11^1				8	9	6	13								3
1	2	3	4	5		7^1		12	10	11				8^2	9	6	13								4
1	2	3	4	5	12	7^3		10		11^2					9	6	13	8^1	14						5
1	2	3	4	5	8	7^1		12^2	10	11				14	9^3	6		13							6
1	2	3	4	5	8	7			10	11^1						6	9	12							7
1	2	3	4	5	8	7		12	10	11^1					13	6	9^2								8
1	2	3	4		8	7		12	10				11			6	9^1		5						9
1	2	3	4	14	8^3	7		13	10		12		11^1			6	9^2		5						10
1	2	3	4	8	9	11		7^1	10		12					6			5						11
1	2	3	4	5	8	7		11^2	10		12					6	9^1	13							12
1	2	3	4	5^1	9	7	12		10		13			14		6		11^2	8^3						13
1	2	3	4	5	8	7	12		10		9^2				13	6		11^1							14
1	2	3	4	5	8	7			10	11^1						6		12	9						15
1	2	3	4	5	8	7		12	10	11^1						6			9						16
1	2	3	4^2	5	8	7		13	10	11^1					12	6		14	9^3						17
1	2	3		5	8	7	4	12	10						9	6		11^1							18
1	2	3		5	8	7	4	11^2	12			13	9^1			6		10							19
1	2	3			8	7	4	11	10		9	5				6									20
1	2	3			8	7	4	11	10		9	5				6									21
1	2	3			8	7	4^3	11^2	10		9	5^1				6		13	12	14					22
1	2^1	3	4		8	7	5	13	10		9			12		6		11^2							23
	2	3	4^1		8	7	5		10		9^2		12	13		6					11	1			24
	2	3			8	7^1	5		10		9		12			6	13	11^2			4	1			25
	2	3			8	7	5^1		10		9		12			6					4	1	11		26
	2	3	4^1		8	7	12		10^2		9					6	13				5	1	11		27
	2	3	4	5		7			10^1		9			8		6						1	11	12	28
	2		4	5		7^1	10	12			9^3			8		6	13		3			1	11^2	14	29
	2		4	5	8	7					9			10		6			3			1	11		30
	2	3	4	5	8	7					9			10^1		6						1	11	12	31
	2	3	4	5	8	7	11		10					9^1		6						1		12	32
	2	3	4	5	8	7	11^1		10		9^2					6			12			1		13	33
	2	3	4	5	8	7^2	11		12		9					6	10^1				13	1			34
	2	3	4	5	8	7	11				9					6	10					1			35
	2	3	4	5	8	7	11		12^2		9^3					6	10^1				13	1		14	36
	2	3	4	5	8	7	11				9^1			12		6	10^2					1		13	37
	2	3	4	5	8	7	11				9^1					6	10					1		12	38
	2	3	4	5	8	7	11^1				9^2					6	10		12			1		13	39
	2	3	4	5	8	7	11				9^1			13		6	10					1		12^2	40
1	2	3	4	5	8	7	11^2							12		6	10	13						9^1	41
1	2	3	4	5	8	7	11				9^1					6	10							12	42
1	2	3	4	5	8	7	11				9					6	10								43
1	2	3^1	4	5	8	7	11^2				9^3			10		6		13		12				14	44
1	2	3	4		8	7	11				9			10^1		6			5					12	45
1	2	3		5	8	7^1	11	12			9					6		13	4					10^2	46

Coca-Cola Cup

First Round	Preston NE	(a)	1-1
		(h)	3-2
Second Round	Liverpool	(a)	0-2
		(h)	0-1

FA Cup

Third Round	Manchester U	(a)	2-2
		(h)	1-2

SWANSEA CITY 1995–96   *Back row (left to right):* Denis Spiteri, Darren Perrett, Lee Jones, Roger Freestone, Ben Miles, David Barnhouse, Jamie Rickard.
Middle row: Mark Clode, David Thomas, Michael Basham, Christian Edwards, Stephen Torpey, Carl Heggs, Keith Walker, Jason Price, Shaun Chapple.
Front row: David Beresford, Jonathan Coates, John Hodge, Colin Pascoe, John Cornforth, David Penney, Andy Cook, Kwame Ampadu, Stephen Jenkins.
(Photograph: Reg Pike)

Division 3   **SWANSEA CITY**

Vetch Field, Swansea SA1 3SU. Telephone: (01792) 474114. Fax: (01792) 646120. Club Shop: 33 William St, Swansea SA1 3QS. Telephone: (01792) 462584.

Ground capacity: 16,540.

Record attendance: 32,796 v Arsenal, FA Cup 4th rd, 17 February 1968.

Record receipts: £36,477.42 v Liverpool, Division 1, 18 September 1982.

Pitch measurements: 112yd × 74yd.

President: I. C. Pursey MBE.

Chairman: D. J. Sharpe.

Directors: D. G. Hammond FCA, MBIM (Vice-Chairman), M. Griffiths.

Chief Executive: Robin Sharpe.

Manager: Jan Molby. *Assistant Manager:* Billy Ayre. *Coach:* Ronnie Walton.

Youth Team Manager: Alan Curtis. *Physio:* Mike Davenport. *Stadium Manager:* David Healey.

Programme Editor: Major Reg Pike (01792) 474114.

Year Formed: 1912. *Turned Professional:* 1912. *Ltd Co.:* 1912.

Secretary: George Taylor.

Previous Name: Swansea Town until February 1970.

Club Nickname: 'The Swans'.

Foundation: The earliest Association Football in Wales was played in the Northern part of the country and no international took place in the South until 1894, when a local paper still thought it necessary to publish an outline of the rules and an illustration of the pitch markings. There had been an earlier Swansea club, but this has no connection with Swansea Town (now City) formed at a public meeting in June 1912.

First Football League game: 28 August 1920, Division 3, v Portsmouth (a) L 0-3 – Crumley; Robson, Evans; Smith, Holdsworth, Williams; Hole, I. Jones, Edmundson, Rigsby, Spottiswood.

Record League Victory: 8–0 v Hartlepool U, Division 4, 1 April 1978 – Barber; Evans, Bartley, Lally (1) (Morris), May, Bruton, Kevin Moore, Robbie James (3 incl. 1p), Curtis (3), Toshack (1), Chappell.

Record Cup Victory: 12–0 v Sliema W (Malta), ECWC 1st rd 1st leg, 15 September 1982 – Davies; Marustik, Hadziabdic (1), Irwin (1), Kennedy, Rajkovic (1), Loveridge (2) (Leighton James), Robbie James, Charles (2), Stevenson (1), Latchford (1) (Walsh (3)).

Record Defeat: 0–8 v Liverpool, FA Cup 3rd rd, 9 January 1990.

Most League Points (2 for a win): 62, Division 3 (S), 1948–49.

Most League Points (3 for a win): 73, Division 2, 1992–93.

Most League Goals: 90, Division 2, 1956–57.

Highest League Scorer in Season: Cyril Pearce, 35, Division 2, 1931–32.

Most League Goals in Total Aggregate: Ivor Allchurch, 166, 1949–58, 1965–68.

Most Capped Player: Ivor Allchurch, 42 (68), Wales.

Most League Appearances: Wilfred Milne, 585, 1919–37.

Record Transfer Fee Received: £375,000 from Nottingham F for Des Lyttle, July 1993.

Record Transfer Fee Paid: £340,000 to Liverpool for Colin Irwin, August 1981.

Football League Record: 1920 Original Member of Division 3; 1921–25 Division 3 (S); 1925–47 Division 2; 1947–49 Division 3 (S); 1949–65 Division 2; 1965–67 Division 3; 1967–70 Division 4; 1970–73 Division 3; 1973–78 Division 4; 1978–79 Division 3; 1979–81 Division 2; 1981–83 Division 1; 1983–84 Division 2; 1984–86 Division 3; 1986–88 Division 4; 1988–92 Division 3; 1992–96 Division 2; 1996– Division 3.

Honours: Football League: Division 1 best season: 6th, 1981–82; Division 2 – Promoted 1980–81 (3rd); Division 3 (S) – Champions 1924–25, 1948–49; Division 3 – Promoted 1978–79 (3rd); Division 4 – Promoted 1969–70 (3rd), 1977–78 (3rd). *FA Cup:* Semi-finals 1926, 1964. *Football League Cup:* best season: 4th rd, 1965, 1977. *Welsh Cup:* Winners 9 times; Runners-up 8 times. *Autoglass Trophy:* Winners 1994. **European Competitions:** *European Cup-Winners' Cup:* 1961–62, 1966–67, 1981–82, 1982–83, 1983–84, 1989–90, 1991–92.

Colours: White shirts with black double pin stripes, black sleeve with red, white shorts with red trim, white stockings with black top. *Change colours:* Black shirts with red stripes, black shorts with red trim, red stockings with black/white hooped tops.

Did you know?
Swansea City's first game in Division Two was on 29 August 1925, their first in the First Division was on 29 August 1981.

SWANSEA CITY 1995–96 LEAGUE RECORD

Match No.	Date	Venue	Opponents	Result	H/T Score	Lg. Pos.	Goalscorers	Atten- dance
1	Aug 12	H	Shrewsbury T	W 3-1	2-0	—	Heggs, Cornforth, Freestone (pen)	3498
2	19	A	Bristol R	D 2-2	1-0	2	Torpey, Basham	6689
3	26	H	Chesterfield	W 3-2	2-0	2	Freestone (pen), Torpey, Edwards	3492
4	29	A	Stockport Co	L 0-2	0-1	—		4433
5	Sept 1	H	Carlisle U	D 1-1	0-1	—	Heggs	3345
6	9	A	Walsall	L 1-4	0-2	10	Palmer (og)	3788
7	12	A	Hull C	D 0-0	0-0	—		3519
8	16	H	York C	L 0-1	0-1	15		2422
9	23	H	Oxford U	D 1-1	0-1	15	Heggs	2505
10	30	A	Burnley	L 0-3	0-1	19		8068
11	Oct 7	H	Bradford C	W 2-0	1-0	17	Torpey 2	2207
12	14	A	Peterborough U	D 1-1	0-1	16	Ampadu	3834
13	21	H	Bournemouth	D 1-1	0-1	15	Heggs	1988
14	28	A	Wrexham	L 0-1	0-1	17		4002
15	31	A	Brighton & HA	W 2-0	1-0	—	Torpey, Lampard	4230
16	Nov 4	H	Wycombe W	L 1-2	0-0	17	Torpey	2809
17	18	A	Crewe Alex	L 1-4	1-2	19	Pascoe	3608
18	25	A	Notts Co	D 0-0	0-0	20		2327
19	Dec 2	H	Rotherham U	D 0-0	0-0	20		1788
20	9	A	Oxford U	L 1-5	0-0	21	Torpey	4674
21	16	H	Burnley	L 2-4	0-1	21	Hurst, Torpey	2078
22	26	A	Bristol C	L 0-1	0-1	22		6845
23	Jan 10	A	Swindon T	L 0-3	0-1	—		6555
24	13	H	Bristol R	D 2-2	2-0	22	Torpey, Edwards	2956
25	20	A	Shrewsbury T	W 2-1	1-1	21	Heggs, Cornforth	6532
26	Feb 3	A	Chesterfield	L 2-3	2-2	22	Torpey 2	4050
27	6	H	Stockport Co	L 0-3	0-2	—		1938
28	10	H	Swindon T	L 0-1	0-1	23		4452
29	13	A	Blackpool	L 0-4	0-2	—		3992
30	17	H	Hull C	D 0-0	0-0	23		1909
31	20	A	Carlisle U	L 0-3	0-2	—		4645
32	24	A	York C	D 0-0	0-0	23		2786
33	27	H	Walsall	W 2-1	1-0	—	Torpey, Hodge	3546
34	Mar 2	H	Bristol C	W 2-1	2-0	21	Chapple, Molby	4109
35	9	A	Rotherham U	D 1-1	0-1	21	Torpey	2714
36	12	H	Brentford	W 2-1	0-1	—	Chapple, Molby (pen)	3538
37	16	H	Blackpool	L 0-2	0-0	21		4478
38	23	A	Brentford	D 0-0	0-0	20		4378
39	30	A	Bradford C	L 1-5	0-0	22	Chapman	4183
40	Apr 2	H	Peterborough U	D 0-0	0-0	—		3805
41	6	H	Wrexham	L 1-3	0-1	22	Torpey	4256
42	9	A	Bournemouth	L 1-3	1-1	—	Chapman	4049
43	13	H	Brighton & HA	W 2-1	1-1	22	Ampadu, Chapman	2373
44	20	A	Wycombe W	W 1-0	0-0	21	Chapman	3672
45	27	A	Notts Co	L 0-4	0-0	22		5051
46	May 4	H	Crewe Alex	W 2-1	1-0	22	Torpey, Thomas	2604

Final League Position: 22

GOALSCORERS

League (43): Torpey 15, Heggs 5, Chapman 4, Ampadu 2, Chapple 2, Cornforth 2, Edwards 2, Freestone 2 (2 pens), Molby 2 (1 pen), Basham 1, Hodge 1, Hurst 1, Lampard 1, Pascoe 1, Thomas 1, own goal 1.
Coca-Cola Cup (4): Hodge 2, Ampadu 1, Torpey 1.
FA Cup (0).

Freestone R 45	Jenkins S 15	Barnhouse D 12 + 3	Walker K 32 + 1	Edwards C 36 + 2	Pascoe C 9 + 4	Coates J 7 + 11	Heggs C 28 + 4	Torpey S 41 + 1	Comforth J 17	Hodge J 34 + 7	Ampadu K 40 + 3	Beresford D 4 + 2	Basham M 9 + 2	Cook A 30 + 3	Clode M 25 + 5	Thomas D 3 + 13	Perrett D 2 + 2	Lampard F 8 + 1	Dennison R 9	Chapple S 15 + 7	Jones S 16 + 1	Penney D 28 + 1	Mardenborough S 1	Hurst G 2	Barnwell-Edinboro J 2 + 2	Molby J 12	Garnett S 9	McDonald C 3 + 5	Brown L 3 + 1	Chapman L 7	O'Leary K 1	Jones L 1	Match No.
1	2	3	4	5	6^1	7^2	8	9	10	11	12	13																					1
1	2	3	4	5		12	8	9	10	11^1	6	7^2	13																				2
1	2		4	5			8	9	10	11	6	7		3																			3
1	2	12		5			8	9	10	11	6	13	4^2	3	7^1																		4
1	2			5		12	8	9	10^2	11	6	7^1	4	3	13																		5
1	10	2	6^2	5		12		9		11^1	8	7	4	3	13																		6
1	10		6	5			8			11	9^1	4	3	2	12	7																	7
1	2		4		6^1	12	8			11	10	5	3^2	13	9	7																	8
1	6	2	4	5		7^1	8	9		11	10		3	12																			9
1	6	2	4	5		7^1	8	9		11	10		3	12																			10
1	2		4	5^1			8	9		11	10	13	3		12	14				6^2	7^3												11
1	2	13	4	5	14		8	9^1		7	10		3		12					6^2	11^3												12
1	2	12		5^1	13	14	8^2	9		7	10	4	3^3							6	11												13
1	4	2^1				12	8	9		7	10	5	3							6^2	11	13											14
1	3	2		5		7^1				8^3	9		10		4		12	6^2	7	13													15
1	2			5	1^1	3^2	8^3	9		12	10	4	13		14					6	11												16
1	2			5	10	8	9	12		3										6	11					4	7						17
1		4	5	10	12	8^1	9	13		3^2										6	11					2	7						18
1		4	5	6		9				10	3	8^1								12	11					2	7						19
1		4	4^1	5	6	11	9			13	10	3								12^2	2	7	8										20
1		4	5	6^2	11^1		9			12	10	3								2	13		7	8									21
1		4	5	12				9	10	8		3								13	2	6^2	7^1	11									22
1	2	4	5	12	11^3	9	10	13	7		3^1									6	8^2	14											23
1		4	5	8	11	9	10	7	6		3^1									12	2												24
1		4	12		8	9	10^2	7	6	11	3^3									13	5^1	2	14										25
1		4		12	8	9	10	7^1	6	11	3									5	2												26
1		4	5	12	8	9	10^2	7	6	11	3^1									13	2												27
1		4	5	8	9			7	6^1	3	12									10	2	11											28
1	2^1			5	8	9		7		3	6	12								10	4	11											29
1		4	5	8	9			7	6	3	2									10		11											30
1		4	5	12	8^2	9		7	6	3	2	13								10^1		11											31
1			5		9	10	7	12		3	2	8^1								6		11					4						32
1			5		9	10	7^1	6		3	2	12								8		11					4						33
1	12		5^1	13	9	10	7^3	6^2		3	2	14								8		11					4						34
1	3		5		9	10	7	6		2										8		11					4						35
1			5	12	9	10	7^1	6		2										8		11					4	3					36
1			5	12	9	10	7^1	6		2										8		11					4	3					37
1	7		5	9			12			3^1	2^2									8		11					4	6	13	10			38
1			5	12		7^2	11			2										8							4	6	13	10	9	3^1	39
1		5	7	12			3			13	2									8		11					4	6^3	14	10^2	9^1		40
1		5		10	7	3^1				12	2									8^2		11					4	6	13	9			41
1		4		10	12	3				11^2	13									8	5	2						6	7^1	9			42
1		4	13		12^2	10	7^1	8			3									14	2	6						5	11^3	9			43
1		4			10	7	8			3^2	2									5	11					6			9			44
1		4			10	7	8			3	12									2	11					6	5^1	13	9^2			45
	6	4	5			9^2	7	10		3^1	12	14								2	8							11^3	13			1	46

Coca-Cola Cup
First Round   Peterborough U   (h)   4-1
                                                          (a)   0-3

FA Cup
First Round   Fulham   (a)   0-7

SWINDON TOWN 1995-96   *Back row left to right*: Wayne Allison, Paul Bodin, Shaun Taylor, Fraser Digby, Mark Seagraves, Andy Thomson, Peter Thorne.
Middle row: Ian Culverhouse, Kevin Horlock, Jason Drysdale, Stephen Finney, Dean Hooper, Mark Robinson, Luc Nijholt, Ty Gooden, Edwin Murray.
Front row: Martin Ling, Wayne O'Sullivan, Andy Rowland (First Team Coach), Steve McMahon (Player/Manager), Andy Rowland (Player/Manager), Ross MacLaren (Reserve Team Coach), Jonathan Trigg (Physio), Jamie Pitman,
Ben Worrall.

Division 1   SWINDON TOWN

County Ground, Swindon, Wiltshire SN1 2ED. Telephone: (01793) 430430. Fax: (01793) 536170. Marketing: (01793) 532121. Marketing Fax: (01793) 423771. Superstore: (01793) 423030. Community Office: (01793) 421303. Clubcall: 0891 121640.

Ground capacity: 15,760.

Record attendance: 32,000 v Arsenal, FA Cup 3rd rd, 15 January 1972.

Record receipts: £149,371 v Bolton W, Coca-Cola Cup semi-final 1st leg, 12 February 1995.

Pitch measurements: 110yd × 70yd.

President: C. J. Green.

Chairman: J. M. Spearman. *Vice-Chairman:* P. T. Archer.

Directors: Sir Seton Willis Bt, C. J. Puffett, J. R. Hunt (Associate), P. R. Godwin CBE.

Manager: Steve McMahon. *Assistant Manager:* Andy Rowland.

Coach: Ross MacLaren. *Physio:* Jonathan Trigg.

Chief Executive/Secretary: Steve Jones. *Assistant Club Secretary:* Michelle McDonald.

Youth Team Manager: Thomas Wheeldon.

Marketing Manager: Martin Stevens. *Community Officers:* Clive Maguire and John Holloway.

Year Formed: 1881 *(see Foundation). Turned Professional:* 1894. *Ltd Co.:* 1894.

Club Nickname: 'Robins'.

Previous Ground: 1881–96, The Croft.

Foundation: It is generally accepted that Swindon Town came into being in 1881, although there is no firm evidence that the club's founder, Rev. William Pitt, captain of the Spartans (an offshoot of a cricket club) changed his club's name to Swindon Town before 1883, when the Spartans amalgamated with St. Mark's Young Men's Friendly Society.

First Football League game: 28 August 1920, Division 3, v Luton T (h) W 9-1 – Nash; Kay, Macconachie; Langford, Hawley, Wareing; Jefferson (1), Fleming (4), Rogers, Batty (2), Davies (1). (1 og).

Record League Victory: 9–1 v Luton T, Division 3 (S), 28 August 1920 – Nash; Kay, Macconachie; Langford, Hawley, Wareing; Jefferson (1), Fleming (4), Rogers, Batty (2), Davies (1). (1 og).

Record Cup Victory: 10–1 v Farnham U Breweries (away), FA Cup 1st rd (replay), 28 November 1925 – Nash; Dickenson, Weston, Archer, Bew, Adey; Denyer (2), Wall (1), Richardson (4), Johnson (3), Davies.

Record Defeat: 1–10 v Manchester C, FA Cup 4th rd (replay), 25 January 1930.

Most League Points (2 for a win): 64, Division 3, 1968–69.

Most League Points (3 for a win): 102, Division 4, 1985–86 (League record).

Most League Goals: 100, Division 3 (S), 1926–27.

Highest League Scorer in Season: Harry Morris, 47, Division 3 (S), 1926–27.

Most League Goals in Total Aggregate: Harry Morris, 216, 1926–33.

Most Capped Player: Rod Thomas, 30 (50), Wales.

Most League Appearances: John Trollope, 770, 1960–80.

Record Transfer Fee Received: £1,300,000 from Middlesbrough for Jan-Aage Fjortoft, March 1995.

Record Transfer Fee Paid: £800,000 to West Ham U for Joey Beauchamp, August 1994.

Football League Record: 1920 Original Member of Division 3; 1921–58 Division 3 (S); 1958–63 Division 3; 1963–65 Division 2; 1965–69 Division 3; 1969–74 Division 2; 1974–82 Division 3; 1982–86 Division 4; 1986–87 Division 3; 1987–92 Division 2; 1992–93 Division 1; 1993–94 FA Premier League; 1994–95 Division 1; 1995–96 Division 2; 1996– Division 1.

Honours: FA Premier League: best season: 22nd 1993–94; *Football League:* Division 2 – Champions 1995–96. Division 3 – Runners-up 1962–63, 1968–69; Division 4 – Champions 1985–86 (with record 102 points). *FA Cup:* Semi-finals 1910, 1912. *Football League Cup:* Winners 1969. *Anglo-Italian Cup:* Winners 1970.

Colours: All red. *Change colours:* Black/blue shirts, blue shorts, blue stockings.

Did you know?
Archie Bown was top scorer for Swindon Town in four consecutive Southern League seasons from 1911–12 to 1914–15.

SWINDON TOWN FC

SWINDON TOWN 1995–96 LEAGUE RECORD

Match No.	Date		Venue	Opponents	Result		H/T Score	Lg. Pos.	Goalscorers	Attendance
1	Aug 12	A	Hull C		W	1-0	0-0	—	Finney	6525
2	19	H	York C		W	3-0	2-0	1	Finney 2, Bodin (pen)	7746
3	26	A	Carlisle U		W	1-0	0-0	1	Murray	6325
4	30	H	Oxford U		D	1-1	1-0	—	Allison	13,041
5	Sept 2	A	Brentford		W	2-0	1-0	1	O'Sullivan, Finney	7878
6	9	H	Chesterfield		D	1-1	0-1	1	Allison	8687
7	13	H	Bradford C		W	4-1	2-1	—	Robinson, Allison, Finney, Horlock	8203
8	16	A	Bristol R		W	4-1	1-1	1	Horlock 3, Taylor	7025
9	23	H	Rotherham U		W	1-0	0-0	1	Gooden	8473
10	30	A	Wrexham		L	3-4	2-1	1	Allison 2, Thorne	4296
11	Oct 7	H	Bristol C		W	2-0	1-0	1	O'Sullivan, Allison	11,979
12	14	A	Brighton & HA		W	3-1	3-0	1	Finney 2, Horlock	7808
13	21	H	Crewe Alex		W	2-1	0-0	1	Allison, Finney (pen)	12,633
14	28	A	Notts Co		W	3-1	2-1	1	Taylor 2, Bodin	8725
15	31	A	Bournemouth		D	0-0	0-0	—		6352
16	Nov 4	H	Blackpool		D	1-1	0-0	1	Finney	12,470
17	18	A	Stockport Co		D	1-1	1-0	1	Allison	7196
18	25	H	Shrewsbury T		L	0-1	0-0	1		9306
19	Dec 9	A	Rotherham U		W	2-0	0-0	1	Finney 2	3042
20	16	H	Wrexham		D	1-1	0-0	1	O'Sullivan	8418
21	23	A	Walsall		D	0-0	0-0	2		5624
22	26	H	Wycombe W		D	0-0	0-0	2		12,976
23	Jan 10	A	Swansea C		W	3-0	1-0	—	Allison, Thorne 2	6555
24	13	A	York C		L	0-2	0-0	1		3613
25	20	H	Hull C		W	3-0	0-0	1	Thorne, Grant, Horlock	8118
26	Feb 3	H	Carlisle U		W	2-1	0-0	1	Thorne, Allison	8242
27	10	A	Swansea C		W	1-0	1-0	1	Taylor	4452
28	21	H	Brentford		D	2-2	2-2	—	Allison, Gooden (pen)	8814
29	24	H	Bristol R		W	2-1	0-1	1	Allison, Taylor	11,697
30	Mar 2	A	Wycombe W		W	2-1	2-0	1	Gooden, Thorne	6457
31	5	A	Peterborough U		W	2-0	1-0	—	Allison, Finney	4196
32	9	H	Walsall		D	1-1	0-0	1	Taylor	9559
33	16	A	Burnley		D	0-0	0-0	2		9360
34	19	A	Oxford U		L	0-3	0-1	—		8585
35	23	H	Peterborough U		W	2-0	2-0	2	Allison, Thorne	8780
36	30	A	Bristol C		D	0-0	0-0	2		11,370
37	Apr 3	H	Brighton & HA		W	3-2	1-0	—	Thorne 2, Allison	8610
38	6	H	Notts Co		W	1-0	0-0	1	Horlock	10,926
39	8	A	Crewe Alex		W	2-0	1-0	1	Horlock, Preece	5162
40	13	H	Bournemouth		D	2-2	1-1	1	Horlock 2 (1 pen)	10,508
41	17	H	Burnley		D	0-0	0-0	—		10,480
42	20	A	Blackpool		D	1-1	1-0	1	Horlock	9175
43	23	A	Chesterfield		W	3-1	2-1	—	Cowe, Thorne, Allison	5523
44	27	A	Shrewsbury T		W	2-1	1-1	1	Horlock, Taylor	4233
45	30	A	Bradford C		D	1-1	0-0	—	Allison	9812
46	May 4	H	Stockport Co		D	0-0	0-0	1		14,697

Final League Position: 1

GOALSCORERS

League (71): Allison 17, Finney 12 (1 pen), Horlock 12 (1 pen), Thorne 10, Taylor 7, Gooden 3 (1 pen), O'Sullivan 3, Bodin 2 (1 pen), Cowe 1, Grant 1, Murray 1, Preece 1, Robinson 1.
Coca-Cola Cup (5): Allison 1, Beauchamp 1, Finney 1, Gooden 1, Horlock 1.
FA Cup (10): Horlock 3, Allison 2, Finney 2, Allen 1, Bodin 1, Ling 1.

Given S 5	Culverhouse I 46	Drysdale J 10 + 3	McMahon S 20 + 1	Seagraves M 25 + 3	Taylor S 43	Robinson M 46	O'Sullivan W 27 + 7	Finney S 22 + 8	Allison W 43 + 1	Gooden T 14 + 12	Bodin P 32 + 1	Horlock K 44 + 1	Murray E 3 + 2	Beauchamp J 1 + 2	Talia F 16	Thorne P 22 + 4	Digby F 25	Allen P 25 + 2	Ling M 12 + 4	Smith A 2 + 6	Grant T 3	Collins L 2 + 3	Preece D 7	Cowe S 4 + 7	Leitch D 7	Match No.
1	2	3[1]	4	5	6	7	8	9	10	11	12															1
1	2		4[1]	5	6	7	8	9	10	11	3	12														2
1	2		4	5	6	7	8	9			3	10	11													3
1	2		4[2]	5	6	7[1]	8	9	10		3	11	12	13												4
1	2		4[1]	5	6	7	8	9	10		3	11	12													5
	2		4	5	6	7	8	9	10	12	3[1]	11			1											6
	2		4[2]	5	6	7	8	9	10[1]	12	3	11		13	1											7
	2		4	5	6	7	8	9		12	3	11	10[1]		1											8
	2		4	5	6	7	8	9[2]	10	12	3[1]	11			1	13										9
	2		4	5	6	7	8	12	10	11	3				1	9[1]										10
	2		4	5	6	7	8	9	10		3	11			1											11
	2		4[1]	5	6	7	8	9	10		3	11					1	12								12
	2		4		6	7	8	9	10		3	11					1	5								13
	2		4		6	7	8	9	10		3	11					1	5								14
	2		4		6	7	8[1]	9	10	12	3	11					1	5								15
	2	12			6	7	8[2]	9	10	4	3[1]	11					1	5	13							16
	2		4		6	7	8	9[1]	10		3	11	12				1	5								17
	2	3	4		6	7	8[1]	9	10	12		11	13				1	5[2]								18
	2	3	4	5[1]	6	7		9	10	12		11					1	8								19
	2	3	4		6	7	12	9[1]	10[2]	8		11	13				1	5								20
	2	3	4[1]	5	6	7[2]	13		10	12		11				9	1	8								21
	2			5	6	7	4[1]		10	12	3	11				9	1	8								22
	2			5[2]		7	8	12	10	13	3	11				9	1	8	4[1]							23
	2				6[1]	7	5[2]	12	10	13	3	11[3]				9	1	8	4	14						24
	2					7	12	13	10	4	3[3]	11				9	1	5[1]	6[2]	14		8				25
	2				6	7	12		10[1]	4	3	11				9	1	5				8				26
	2				6	7			10	4	3	11				9	1	5				8				27
	2	3			6	7	12		10	4		11				9	1	5				8[1]				28
	2	3	12		6	7	13		10	4[2]		11				9	1	5[1]				8				29
	2	3		5	6	7	12		10	4		11			1	9[1]						8				30
	2	3		5	6	7		9	10	4		11			1			8								31
	2	3		5	6	7		9	10	4		11[1]			1			8					12			32
	2			5	6	7		9[1]	10	4	3	11			1			8	12							33
	2			5[2]	6	7	12		10	13	3	11[3]			1	9		8	4[1]	14						34
	2				6	7	8[1]		10		3	11			1	9[2]		5	12				4	13		35
	2				6	7	8		10		3	11			1	9		5					4			36
	2	12			6	7[1]	13		10		3[2]	11			1			8	5				4	14	9[3]	37
	2				6	7	12		10		3	11			1	9[2]		5					4	13	8[1]	38
	2				6	7			10[2]		3	11			1	9		5	12				4	13	8[1]	39
	2				6	7			10		3[1]	11			1	9[2]		5	12				4	13	8	40
	2				6	7			10		3	11				9	1	5				4[1]	12		8	41
	2	12			6	7	13		10		3	11				9[3]	1	5[1]	4	14					8[2]	42
	2			5	6	7	4		10		3	11				9	1		12			8[1]				43
	2	12		5	6	7	8[3]	13				11[1]				9[2]	1	4	3	14		10		8[1]		44
	2	12		5	6	7	8[2]		10			11					1	4	3[1]			13		9		45
	2	12		5[2]	6	7	8[1]		10		3[3]	11					1		13	4		14		9		46

Coca-Cola Cup

First Round	Cambridge U	(a)	1-2
		(h)	2-0
Second Round	Blackburn R	(h)	2-3
		(a)	0-2

FA Cup

First Round	Cambridge U	(h)	4-1
Second Round	Cardiff C	(h)	2-0
Third Round	Woking	(h)	2-0
Fourth Round	Oldham Ath	(h)	1-0
Fifth Round	Southampton	(h)	1-1
		(a)	0-2

TORQUAY UNITED 1995-96 *Back row (left to right):* Chris Curran, Simon Travis, Lee Barrow, Ellis Laight, Scott Stamps, Paul Buckle, Mark Hawthorne.
Middle row: Damien Davey (Physio), Paul Compton (Youth Development Officer), Jamie Ndah, David Byng, Ashley Bayes, Ian Gore, Richard Hancox, John James (Scout), Kevin Hodges (Coach).
Front row: Neil Povey, Steve Winter, Mark Hall, Don O'Riordan (Manager), Mike Bateson (Chairman), Tom Kelly, Ian Hathaway, Lee Setter.

Division 3   **TORQUAY UNITED**

Plainmoor Ground, Torquay, Devon TQ1 3PS. Telephone: (01803) 328666. Fax: (01803) 323976. Clubcall: 0891 121641.

Ground capacity: 6000.

Record attendance: 21,908 v Huddersfield T, FA Cup 4th rd, 29 January 1955.

Record receipts: £26,205 v Exeter C, Division 3, 1 January 1992.

Pitch measurements: 112yd × 74yd.

President: A. J. Boyce.

Chairman/Managing Director: M. Bateson. *Directors:* Mrs S. Bateson, M. Beer, M. Benney, I. Hayman, Miss H. Kindeleit, T. Lilley, B. Palk, W. Rogers, D. Turner.

Manager: Kevin Hodges. *Physio:* D. Davey.

Company Secretary: Miss H. Kindeleit.

Secretary/General Manager: D. F. Turner.

Year Formed: 1899. *Turned Professional:* 1921. *Ltd Co.:* 1921.

Previous Name: 1910, Torquay Town; 1921, Torquay United.

Nickname: 'The Gulls'.

Previous Grounds: 1899, Teignmouth Road; 1900, Torquay Recreation Ground; 1904, Cricket Field Road; 1906–10, Torquay Cricket Ground.

Foundation: The idea of establishing a Torquay club was agreed by old boys of Torquay College and Torbay College, while sitting in Princess Gardens listening to the band. A proper meeting was subsequently held at Tor Abbey Hotel at which officers were elected. This was in 1898 and the club's first competition was the Eastern League (later known as the East Devon League).

First Football League game: 27 August 1927, Division 3 (S), v Exeter C (h) D 1-1 – Millsom; Cook, Smith; Wellock, Wragg, Connor, Mackey, Turner (1), Jones, McGovern, Thomson.

Record League Victory: 9–0 v Swindon T, Division 3 (S), 8 March 1952 – George Webber; Topping, Ralph Calland; Brown, Eric Webber, Towers; Shaw (1), Marchant (1), Northcott (2), Collins (3), Edds (2).

Record Cup Victory: 7–1 v Northampton T, FA Cup 1st rd, 14 November 1959 – Gill; Penford, Downs; Bettany, George Northcott, Rawson; Baxter, Cox, Tommy Northcott (1), Bond (3), Pym (3).

Record Defeat: 2–10 v Fulham, Division 3 (S), 7 September 1931 and v Luton T, Division 3 (S), 2 September 1933.

Most League Points (2 for a win): 60, Division 4, 1959–60.

Most League Points (3 for a win): 77, Division 4, 1987–88.

Most League Goals: 89, Division 3 (S), 1956–57.

Highest League Scorer in Season: Sammy Collins, 40, Division 3 (S), 1955–56.

Most League Goals in Total Aggregate: Sammy Collins, 204, 1948–58.

Most Capped Player: None.

Most League Appearances: Dennis Lewis, 443, 1947–59.

Record Transfer Fee Received: £180,000 from Manchester U for Lee Sharpe, May 1988.

Record Transfer Fee Paid: £60,000 to Dundee for Wes Saunders, July 1990.

Football League Record: 1927 Elected to Division 3 (S); 1958–60 Division 4; 1960–62 Division 3; 1962–66 Division 4; 1966–72 Division 3; 1972–91 Division 4; 1991– Division 3.

Honours: Football League: Division 3 best season: 4th, 1967–68; Division 3 (S) – Runners-up 1956–57; Division 4 – Promoted 1959–60 (3rd), 1965–66 (3rd), 1990–91 (Play-offs). *FA Cup:* best season: 4th rd, 1949, 1955, 1971, 1983, 1990. *Football League Cup:* never past 3rd rd. *Sherpa Van Trophy:* Runners-up 1989.

Colours: Yellow and navy striped shirts, navy shorts, yellow stockings. *Change colours:* Blue and white striped shirts, white shorts, blue stockings.

Did you know?
Jimmy Trotter's 26 League goals for Torquay United in 1930–31 stood for 25 years as a club record.

TORQUAY UNITED 1995–96 LEAGUE RECORD

Match No.	Date	Venue	Opponents	Result	H/T Score	Lg. Pos.	Goalscorers	Atten-dance
1	Aug 12	A	Leyton Orient	L	0-1	0-0	—		8221
2	19	H	Doncaster R	L	1-2	0-0	3	Buckle (pen)	2086
3	26	A	Fulham	L	0-4	0-1	24		4764
4	29	H	Rochdale	W	1-0	0-0	—	Stamps	2139
5	Sept 2	H	Mansfield T	D	1-1	1-1	22	Buckle (pen)	2203
6	9	A	Cardiff C	D	0-0	0-0	21		4281
7	12	A	Hartlepool U	D	2-2	0-1	—	Gore, Buckle (pen)	1945
8	16	H	Wigan Ath	D	1-1	0-1	19	Curran	2188
9	23	H	Northampton T	W	3-0	1-0	16	Ndah, Mateu, Buckle (pen)	2314
10	30	A	Scarborough	L	1-2	0-1	21	Hicks (og)	1455
11	Oct 7	A	Hereford U	L	1-2	0-1	22	Hathaway	2143
12	14	H	Preston NE	L	0-4	0-2	23		4058
13	21	A	Plymouth Arg	L	3-4	3-2	23	Ndah 2, Partridge	11,695
14	28	H	Scunthorpe U	L	1-8	1-4	23	Partridge	2137
15	31	H	Bury	L	0-2	0-1	—		1456
16	Nov 4	A	Chester C	L	1-4	0-2	24	Laight	2535
17	18	H	Lincoln C	L	0-2	0-1	24		2553
18	25	A	Cambridge U	D	1-1	0-1	24	Gore	2536
19	Dec 9	A	Northampton T	D	1-1	0-1	24	Newhouse	3656
20	16	H	Scarborough	D	0-0	0-0	24		1680
21	23	H	Darlington	L	0-1	0-1	24		2045
22	26	A	Exeter C	D	0-0	0-0	24		6182
23	Jan 1	H	Colchester U	L	2-3	1-1	24	Jack, Newhouse	2425
24	13	A	Doncaster R	L	0-1	0-0	24		1807
25	20	H	Leyton Orient	W	2-1	0-1	24	Baker, Watson	2212
26	Feb 3	H	Fulham	W	2-1	1-1	24	Baker, Garner	2594
27	6	H	Barnet	D	1-1	0-0	—	Baker (pen)	2262
28	10	A	Gillingham	L	0-2	0-2	24		7110
29	17	H	Hartlepool U	D	0-0	0-0	24		2580
30	24	A	Wigan Ath	L	0-3	0-1	24		2697
31	27	H	Cardiff C	D	0-0	0-0	—		2004
32	Mar 2	H	Exeter C	L	0-2	0-1	24		4038
33	9	A	Darlington	W	2-1	2-0	24	Watson, Jack	2861
34	12	H	Gillingham	D	0-0	0-0	—		2406
35	16	A	Barnet	L	0-4	0-3	24		1734
36	19	A	Rochdale	L	0-3	0-1	—		1206
37	23	A	Colchester U	L	1-3	0-1	24	Laight	2888
38	30	H	Hereford U	D	1-1	1-1	24	Hancox	2034
39	Apr 2	A	Preston NE	L	0-1	0-1	—		11,965
40	6	A	Scunthorpe U	L	0-1	0-1	24		2247
41	8	H	Plymouth Arg	L	0-2	0-1	24		4269
42	13	A	Bury	L	0-1	0-0	24		3247
43	20	H	Chester C	D	1-1	0-0	24	Baker	2549
44	23	A	Mansfield T	L	0-2	0-1	—		1674
45	27	H	Cambridge U	L	0-3	0-1	24		1853
46	May 4	A	Lincoln C	L	0-5	0-1	24		5814

Final League Position: 24

GOALSCORERS

League (30): Baker 4 (1 pen), Buckle 4 (4 pens), Ndah 3, Gore 2, Jack 2, Laight 2, Newhouse 2, Partridge 2, Watson 2, Curran 1, Garner 1, Hancox 1, Hathaway 1, Mateu 1, Stamps 1, own goal 1.
Coca-Cola Cup (4): Barrow 2, Hathaway 1, Hawthorne 1.
FA Cup (6): Barrow 1, Byng 1, Gore 1, Hathaway 1, Hawthorne 1, Mateu 1.

Bayes A 28	Curran C 17 + 2	Stamps S 20 + 3	Kelly T 26 + 5	Barrow L 35 + 6	Gore J 25	Hawthorne M 17 + 5	Buckle P 11	Laight E 8 + 12	Hathaway I 22 + 4	Byng D 4 + 10	Hancox R 15 + 10	Preston M 4 + 4	Travis S 4 + 4	Croft B — + 1	Ndah J 16	Hall M 22 + 7	O'Riordan D 6 + 2	Winter S 36	Thomas W 1 + 5	Barnes B — + 1	Bedeau A 1 + 3	Povey N 3	Williams P 9	Gregg M 1	Mateu J 5 + 5	Coughlin R 22 + 3	Jack R 12 + 2	Partridge S 5	Haddaoui R — + 2	Cooke J 1	Hodges K 1 + 1	Monk G 4 + 1	Canham S 3	Moors C — + 1	Ramsey P 18	Watson A 29	Newhouse A 4	Oatway C 24	Newland R 17	Baker P 20	Garner S 10 + 1	Match No.
1	2	3	4	5	6	7	8²	9¹	10	11	12	13																														1
1	2	3³	4	5	6	7	8²	11¹	10	12	9	14	13																													2
1	2		4	5	6	7	8		12	13	9³	3				10²	11	14																								3
1	6	3³	7	5		12	8		10	13			14			9	11²	4¹	2																							4
1	6	3	7	5			8		10¹	12						9	11	4²	2	13																						5
1	6	3	7	12	5		8	10		13						9¹	11¹		2		14	4²																			6
1²	6	3	7	12	5		8	10¹		13						9	11		2			4																			7
	6	3	7	13	5		8		10¹	12						9	11	14	2²			4³	1																		8
1	6		7¹	5		3	8		10	13	12					9²	14	4	2						11³																	9
1	12		3	6	5	7	8³		10	14						9	13	4²	2¹						11																	10
1	12	4	3	6	5	7³	8²	9	10		13	2¹				11									14																	11
1		3	6	5	11		12	10			2														4	7	8	9¹														12
1	2		3	6	5	10		12								11²	4¹								8	7	9	13														13
1	2	13	3	6	5	10		14	12							11	4								8²	7¹	9³															14
1	4	3		6	5	10		7¹	12			13	14			11²		2³							8	9																15
1	4	3²		6				10³				13	2			11¹	12								8	9			5	7	14											16
1	4		3	5					12	11	9²	13	2			8										7¹					10				6							17
1	4		3		2	10¹			11	13	9					8		2								12						7²			6	5						18
1	4		3			10			11	12						8¹		2								13	7²								6	5	9					19
1	4	11¹	3							10						7		2								12	8								6	5	9					20
1		3	12	4	13				11		9³	10²				7		2								8	14								6¹	5						21
1		3	12	4	8				11							7		2¹									10								6	5	9					22
1	12	3	4						11							7		2									10								6	5	9	8¹				23
	4	3							11		9¹					7		2	12		10														6	5		8		1		24
	12	3¹	13	4					11							7²		2																	6	5		8	1		9	25
	3		7	4¹					11²			13				12		2								7¹									6	5		8	1	9	10	26
	3		4						11			12						2								7¹									6	5		8	1	9	10	27
	3	12	4						13	11¹			7²					2																	6	5		8	1	9	10	28
	3	12	4						11²		13	7¹						2																	6	5		8	1	9	10	29
	3		4	6					11²							7¹		2	13						12										5		8	1	9	10	30
	3²		4	6					12									2							11¹	7							13		5		8	1	9	10	31
	3		4	2¹					12							11										7									6	5		8	1	9	10	32
		4	2	12					7³							9²		3	13						11	10¹									6	5		8	1		10	33
		2	4													9¹		3							12	11	10								6	5		8	1	14		34
		2	4															12	3							11	7								6	5	8¹		1	9	7	35
		7²	4	2					13	12						10¹		3								11									6	5	8		1	9	10	36
1		3	4		12				13	11						7¹			10²							6		2								5	8		9			37
1		3¹	12	4							11					7²		2				10				6		13								5	8		9			38
1		3	12	4					13		11					7²		2¹				10				6										5	8		9			39
1		3	12	4					13		11³					7		2				10				6¹		14								5	8		9²			40
1		3¹		4					11		7²					12		2				10				6	13									5	8		9			41
1			4	11²					3	14	7³					12		2				10¹			13	6										5	8		9			42
			4	11¹					3	7³						2	13				10				12	6										5	8	1	9			43
			4	12					3	7¹						2	13	11				10²	6													5	8	1	9			44
			4⁴						12	11	14					3	13	8	7¹			6				2										5	9	1	10²			45
				11					12	3	14					2	13	10²				6³				7	4									5	8	1	9¹			46

Coca-Cola Cup

First Round	Exeter C	(h)	0-0
		(a)	1-1
Second Round	Norwich C	(a)	1-6
		(h)	2-3

FA Cup

First Round	Leyton Orient	(h)	1-0
Second Round	Walsall	(h)	1-1
		(a)	4-8

TOTTENHAM HOTSPUR 1995-96　*Back row (left to right):* Andy Turner, Jason Cundy, Ronny Rosenthal, Darren Anderton, Erik Thorstvedt, Ian Walker, Kevin Scott, Colin Calderwood, Jason Dozzell, Stuart Nethercott (Physio).

Middle row: Tony Lenaghan (Physio), Danny Hill, Gerry McMahon, Clive Wilson, Ilie Dumitrescu, Chris Day, David Howells, Chris Armstrong, Justin Edinburgh, Gary Mabbutt, Gerry Francis (Manager), Roger Cross (Assistant Manager), Teddy Sheringham, Dean Austin, Sol Campbell, Darren Caskey, Chris Hughton (Reserve Team Manager).

Front row: Pat Jennings (Goalkeeping Coach), David Kerslake, Chris Armstrong, Justin Edinburgh, Gary Mabbutt, Gerry Francis (Manager), Roger Cross (Assistant Manager), Teddy Sheringham, Kevin Watson, Steve Carr, Roy Reyland (Kit Manager).

(Photograph: Action Images)

FA Premiership **TOTTENHAM HOTSPUR**

748 High Rd, Tottenham, London N17 0AP. Telephone: (0181) 365 5000. Fax: (0181) 365 5005. Commercial Dept: (0181) 365 5010. Ticketline: 0891 335566. Telephone Bookings: (0171) 396 4567. Ticket Office: (0181) 365 5050. Spurs Line: 0891 335555. Members Ticketline: (0181) 365 5100. Additional Recorded Information: (0181) 365 5060.

Ground capacity: 33,083.

Record attendance: 75,038 v Sunderland, FA Cup 6th rd, 5 March 1938.

Record receipts: £336,702 v Manchester U, Division 1, 28 September 1991.

Pitch measurements: 110yd × 73yd.

Directors: A. M. Sugar (Chairman), C. Littner (Chief Executive), J. Sedgwick (Finance). *Non-Executive:* A. G. Berry (Deputy Chairman), D. A. Alexiou, I. Yawetz, C. T. Sandy.

President: W. E. Nicholson OBE. *Vice-President:* N. Solomon.

Manager: Gerry Francis. *Assistant Manager:* Roger Cross. *Coach:* Chris Hughton. *Physio:* Tony Lenaghan. *Secretary:* Peter Barnes. *Commercial Manager:* Mike Rollo. *PRO:* John Fennelly.

Year Formed: 1882. *Turned Professional:* 1895. *Ltd Co.:* 1898.

Club Nickname: 'Spurs'.

Previous Name: 1882–85, Hotspur Football Club.

Previous Grounds: 1882, Tottenham Marshes; 1885, Northumberland Park; 1898, White Hart Lane.

Foundation: The Hotspur Football Club was formed from an older cricket club in 1882. Most of the founders were old boys of St. John's Presbyterian School and Tottenham Grammar School. The Casey brothers were well to the fore as the family provided the club's first goalposts (painted blue and white) and their first ball. They soon adopted the local YMCA as their meeting place, but after a couple of moves settled at the Red House, which is still their headquarters, although now known simply as 748 High Road.

First Football League game: 1 September 1908, Division 2, v Wolverhampton W (h) W 3-0 – Hewitson; Coquet, Burton; Morris (1), D. Steel, Darnell; Walton, Woodward (2), Macfarlane, R. Steel, Middlemiss.

Record League Victory: 9–0 v Bristol R, Division 2, 22 October 1977 – Davies; Naylor, Holmes, Hoddle (1), McAllister, Perryman, Pratt, McNab, Morris (3), Lee (4), Taylor (1).

Record Cup Victory: 13–2 v Crewe Alex, FA Cup 4th rd (replay), 3 February 1960 – Brown; Hills, Henry; Blanchflower, Norman, Mackay; White, Harmer (1), Smith (4), Allen (5), Jones (3 incl. 1p).

Record Defeat: 0–7 v Liverpool, Division 1, 2 September 1978.

Most League Points (2 for a win): 70, Division 2, 1919–20.

Most League Points (3 for a win): 77, Division 1, 1984–85.

Most League Goals: 115, Division 1, 1960–61.

Highest League Scorer in Season: Jimmy Greaves, 37, Division 1, 1962–63.

Most League Goals in Total Aggregate: Jimmy Greaves, 220, 1961–70.

Most Capped Player: Pat Jennings, 74 (119), Northern Ireland.

Most League Appearances: Steve Perryman, 655, 1969–86.

Record Transfer Fee Received: £5,500,000 from Lazio for Paul Gascoigne, May 1992.

Record Transfer Fee Paid: £4,500,000 to Crystal Palace for Chris Armstrong, June 1995.

Football League Record: 1908 Elected to Division 2; 1909–15 Division 1; 1919–20 Division 2; 1920–28 Division 1; 1928–33 Division 2; 1933–35 Division 1; 1935–50 Division 2; 1950–77 Division 1; 1977–78 Division 2; 1978–92 Division 1; 1992– FA Premier League.

Honours: Football League: Division 1 – Champions 1950–51, 1960–61; Runners-up 1921–22, 1951–52, 1956–57, 1962–63; Division 2 – Champions 1919–20, 1949–50; Runners-up 1908–09, 1932–33; Promoted 1977–78 (3rd). *FA Cup:* Winners 1901 (as non-League club), 1921, 1961, 1962, 1967, 1981, 1982, 1991 (8 wins stands as the record); Runners-up 1987. *Football League Cup:* Winners 1971, 1973; Runners-up 1982. **European Competitions:** *European Cup:* 1961–62. *European Cup-Winners' Cup:* 1962–63 (winners), 1963–64, 1967–68, 1981–82, 1982–83, 1991–92. *UEFA Cup:* 1971–72 (winners), 1972–73, 1973–74 (runners-up), 1983–84 (winners), 1984–85.

Colours: White shirts, navy blue shorts, navy blue stockings. *Change colours:* All yellow.

Did you know?
On 25 May 1968, Tottenham Hotspur beat the Cypriot National team 3-0 in Nicosia during an unbeaten tour of Greece and Cyprus.

TOTTENHAM HOTSPUR 1995–96 LEAGUE RECORD

Match No.	Date	Venue	Opponents	Result	H/T Score	Lg. Pos.	Goalscorers	Atten- dance
1	Aug 19	A	Manchester C	D	1-1	1-0	—	Sheringham	30,827
2	23	H	Aston Villa	L	0-1	0-0	—		26,598
3	26	H	Liverpool	L	1-3	0-2	19	Barnes (og)	31,254
4	30	A	West Ham U	D	1-1	0-1	—	Rosenthal	23,516
5	Sept 9	H	Leeds U	W	2-1	1-0	13	Howells, Sheringham	30,034
6	16	A	Sheffield W	W	3-1	1-1	11	Sheringham 2 (1 pen), Walker (og)	26,565
7	25	A	QPR	W	3-2	0-1	—	Sheringham 2 (1 pen), Dozzell	15,659
8	30	H	Wimbledon	W	3-1	2-1	9	Sheringham 2, Elkins (og)	25,321
9	Oct 14	H	Nottingham F	L	0-1	0-0	10		32,876
10	22	A	Everton	D	1-1	1-1	9	Armstrong	33,629
11	29	H	Newcastle U	D	1-1	1-0	9	Armstrong	32,257
12	Nov 4	A	Coventry C	W	3-2	2-1	9	Fox, Sheringham, Howells	17,567
13	18	H	Arsenal	W	2-1	1-1	9	Sheringham, Armstrong	32,894
14	21	A	Middlesbrough	W	1-0	0-0	—	Armstrong	29,487
15	25	A	Chelsea	D	0-0	0-0	5		31,059
16	Dec 2	H	Everton	D	0-0	0-0	5		32,894
17	9	H	QPR	W	1-0	1-0	5	Sheringham	28,851
18	16	A	Wimbledon	W	1-0	0-0	3	Fox	16,193
19	23	H	Bolton W	D	2-2	0-0	4	Sheringham, Armstrong	30,702
20	26	A	Southampton	D	0-0	0-0	3		15,238
21	30	A	Blackburn R	L	1-2	0-2	4	Sheringham	30,004
22	Jan 1	H	Manchester U	W	4-1	2-1	4	Sheringham, Campbell, Armstrong 2	32,852
23	13	H	Manchester C	W	1-0	0-0	3	Armstrong	31,438
24	21	A	Aston Villa	L	1-2	1-1	4	Fox	35,666
25	Feb 3	A	Liverpool	D	0-0	0-0	5		40,628
26	12	H	West Ham U	L	0-1	0-1	—		29,781
27	24	H	Sheffield W	W	1-0	1-0	5	Armstrong	32,047
28	Mar 2	H	Southampton	W	1-0	0-0	5	Dozzell	26,320
29	16	H	Blackburn R	L	2-3	0-2	7	Sheringham, Armstrong	31,803
30	20	A	Bolton W	W	3-2	1-0	6	Howells, Fox, Armstrong	17,829
31	24	A	Manchester U	L	0-1	0-0	6		50,508
32	30	H	Coventry C	W	3-1	0-1	6	Sheringham, Fox 2	26,808
33	Apr 6	A	Nottingham F	L	1-2	0-1	7	Armstrong	27,053
34	8	H	Middlesbrough	D	1-1	0-0	6	Armstrong	32,036
35	15	A	Arsenal	D	0-0	0-0	—		38,273
36	27	H	Chelsea	D	1-1	0-1	8	Armstrong	32,918
37	May 2	A	Leeds U	W	3-1	2-1	—	Armstrong, Anderton 2	30,024
38	5	A	Newcastle U	D	1-1	0-0	8	Dozzell	36,589

Final League Position: 8

GOALSCORERS

League (50): Sheringham 16 (2 pens), Armstrong 15, Fox 6, Dozzell 3, Howells 3, Anderton 2, Campbell 1, Rosenthal 1, own goals 3.
Coca-Cola Cup (9): Armstrong 3, Sheringham 3, Howells 1, Rosenthal 1, own goal 1.
FA Cup (12): Sheringham 5, Armstrong 4, Rosenthal 2, Wilson 1.

Walker I 38	Austin D 28	Edinburgh J 15 + 7	Nethercott S 9 + 4	Howells D 29	Mabbutt G 32	Kerslake D 2	Dumitrescu I 5	Armstrong C 36	Sheringham T 38	Rosenthal R 26 + 7	Scott K — + 2	Calderwood C 26 + 3	McMahon G 7 + 7	Wilson C 28	Dozzell J 24 + 4	Anderton D 6 + 2	Campbell S 31	Fox R 26	Slade S 1 + 4	Caskey D 3	Sinton A 8 + 1	Cundy J — + 1	Match No.
1	2	3^1	4	5	6	7	8	9	10	11	12												1
1	2	3		4	6	7^1	8	9	10	11		5	12										2
1		2		4	6		8	9	10	11		5	7^1	3	12								3
1	2			4	6			9	10	11		5	7^1	3	8	12							4
1	2		4^2		6			9	10	11	12	5	13	3	8	7^1							5
1	2	12			6			9	10	11		5	8	3		7	4^1						6
1	2	12		4	6			9	10	11		5		3	8	7^1							7
1	2		4^1		6			9	10	11		5	8	3	12		7						8
1	2			4	6				10	11		5	8	3	12		7^1	9					9
1	2			4	6			9	10	12		5	8^1	3	13		7^2	11					10
1	2			4	6			9	10	11^2	12	13	3	8			5^1	7					11
1	2			4	6			9	10	11^1		12		3	8		5	7					12
1	2			4	6			9	10	11^1		5	12		8		3	7					13
1	2			4	6			9	10	11		5			8		3	7					14
1	2			4	6			9	10	11		5	12		8		3	7					15
1	2			4	6			9	10	11^1		5	12		8		3	7					16
1	12			4	6			9	10	11		5		3	8		2^1	7					17
1	12			4	6			9	10	11		5		3	8^1		2^2	7	13				18
1	3	12	4^1		6			9	10	8		5		11			2	7					19
1	2	3			6			9	10	8		5	4^1	11				7		12			20
1	2	3	4		6		8	9	10	7		5				11							21
1	2	3	4				8^1	9	10	11		5	12			6				7			22
1	2	3	4		6			9	10	11				8		5				7			23
1	2	3	4					9	10	11		5				6		7		8			24
1	2	3	12		6			9	10	13		5		8			4^1	7			11^2		25
1	2				6			9	10	11^1		5		3	8		4	7			12		26
1				4	6			9	10	12		5		3	8		2	7^1			11		27
1				4	6				10	12		5		3	8		2	7	9^1		11		28
1	2	3	4		6			9	10			5^1		8				7			11	12	29
1	2	12		4	6			9	10			5^1		3	8		11	7^2	13				30
1	2	12		4	6^1			9	10					3	8		5	7			11		31
1	2			4	6			9	10					3	8		5	7			11		32
1	2	12		4	6^1			9	10	13				3	8		5	7			11^2		33
1	2	12		4	6^1			9	10^2	11				3	8		5	7	13				34
1	2	12		4	6			9	10	11				3	8^2	13	5^1	7					35
1	2				6			9	10	12				3	8	7	5	4			11^1		36
1	2			4	6			9	10					3	8	7	5	11					37
1	2			4	6			9	10	12		13		3	8	7	5^2	11^1					38

Coca-Cola Cup

Second Round	Chester C	(h)	4-0	
		(a)	3-1	
Third Round	Coventry C	(a)	2-3	

FA Cup

Third Round	Hereford U	(a)	1-1	
		(h)	5-1	
Fourth Round	Wolverhampton W	(h)	1-1	
		(a)	2-0	
Fifth Round	Nottingham F	(a)	2-2	
		(h)	1-1	

TRANMERE ROVERS 1995–96 *Back row (left to right):* Alan Morgan, John McGreal, David Challinor, Graham Branch, Jamie Jardine, Shaun Garnett, Gary Jones, Gary Bennett, Kenny Irons, John Morrissey.

Middle row: Norman Wilson (Secretary), Warwick Rimmer (Youth Development Officer), Kenny Jones (Trainer), Alan Rogers, Dave Higgins, James Hughes, Martin Jones, Eric Nixon, Danny Coyne, Mick Edwards, Ian Moore, Phil Davies, Ronnie Moore (First Team Coach), Les Parry (Physio), Ray Mathias (Reserve Coach).

Front row: Alan Mahon, Ged Brannan, Tony Thomas, Gary Stevens, Steve Mungall, John King (Manager), John Aldridge, Pat Nevin, Jon Kenworthy, Liam O'Brien, Billy Woods.

Division 1   TRANMERE ROVERS

Prenton Park, Prenton Road West, Birkenhead L42 9PN. Telephone: (0151) 608 3677. Fax: (0151) 608 4385. Commercial: (0151) 608 0371. Valley Road Training Centre: (0151) 652 2578. Shop: (0151) 608 0438. Ticket Office: (0151) 609 0137.

Ground capacity: 16,789 (all seated).

Record attendance: 24,424 v Stoke C, FA Cup 4th rd, 5 February 1972.

Record receipts: £114,150 v Aston Villa, Coca-Cola Cup semi-final, 16 February 1994.

Pitch measurements: 110yd × 70yd.

President: H. B. Thomas.

Chairman and Chief Executive: F. D. Corfe.

Directors: Norman Wilson FAAI, A. J. Adams BDS, G. E. H. Jones LLB, F. J. Williams, J. J. Holsgrove FCA.

Secretary: Norman Wilson FAAI. *Commercial Manager:* Janet Ratcliffe.

Player-Manager: John Aldridge. *Trainer:* Kenny Jones.

Youth Development Officer: Warwick Rimmer.

Coach: Ronnie Moore. *Physio:* Les Parry.

Year Formed: 1884. *Turned Professional:* 1912. *Ltd Co.:* 1920.

Previous Name: Belmont AFC, 1884–85.

Club Nickname: 'The Rovers'.

Previous Grounds: 1884, Steeles Field; 1887, Ravenshaws Field/Old Prenton Park; 1912, Prenton Park.

Foundation: Formed in 1884 as Belmont they adopted their present title the following year and eventually joined their first league, the West Lancashire League in 1889–90, the same year as their first success in the Wirral Challenge Cup. The club almost folded in 1899–1900 when all the players left en bloc to join a rival club, but they survived the crisis and went from strength to strength winning the 'Combination' title in 1907–08 and the Lancashire Combination in 1913–14. They joined the Football League in 1921 from the Central League.

First Football League game: 27 August 1921, Division 3 (N), v Crewe Alex (h) W 4-1 – Bradshaw; Grainger, Stuart (1); Campbell, Milnes (1), Heslop; Moreton, Groves (1), Hyam, Ford (1), Hughes.

Record League Victory: 13–4 v Oldham Ath, Division 3 (N), 26 December 1935 – Gray; Platt, Fairhurst; McLaren, Newton, Spencer; Eden, MacDonald (1), Bell (9), Woodward (2), Urmson (1).

Record Cup Victory: 13–0 v Oswestry U, FA Cup 2nd prel rd, 10 October 1914 – Ashcroft; Stevenson, Bullough, Hancock, Taylor, Holden (1), Moreton (1), Cunningham (2), Smith (5), Leck (3), Gould (1).

Record Defeat: 1–9 v Tottenham H, FA Cup 3rd rd (replay), 14 January 1953.

Most League Points (2 for a win): 60, Division 4, 1964–65.

Most League Points (3 for a win): 80, Division 4, 1988–89 and Division 3, 1989–90.

Most League Goals: 111, Division 3 (N), 1930–31.

Highest League Scorer in Season: Bunny Bell, 35, Division 3 (N), 1933–34.

Most League Goals in Total Aggregate: Ian Muir, 141, 1985–95.

Most Capped Player: John Aldridge, 29 (68), Republic of Ireland.

Most League Appearances: Harold Bell, 595, 1946–64 (incl. League record 401 consecutive appearances).

Record Transfer Fee Received: £1,500,000 from Sheffield W for Ian Nolan, August 1994.

Record Transfer Fee Paid: £350,000 to Celtic for Tommy Coyne, March 1993 and £350,000 to Rangers for Gary Stevens, October 1994.

Football League Record: 1921 Original Member of Division 3 (N): 1938–39 Division 2; 1946–58 Division 3 (N); 1958–61 Division 3; 1961–67 Division 4; 1967–75 Division 3; 1975–76 Division 4; 1976–79 Division 3; 1979–89 Division 4; 1989–91 Division 3; 1991–92 Division 2; 1992– Division 1.

Honours: Football League Division 1 best season: 4th, 1992–93; Division 3 (N) – Champions 1937–38; Promotion to 3rd Division: 1966–67, 1975–76; Division 4 – Runners-up 1988–89. *FA Cup:* best season: 5th rd, 1968. *Football League Cup:* best season: semi-final 1994. *Welsh Cup:* Winners 1935; Runners-up 1934. *Leyland Daf Cup:* Winners 1990; Runners-up 1991.

Colours: All white. *Change colours:* Yellow and black striped shirts, black shorts, black stockings.

Did you know?
Harold Atkinson scored six goals for Tranmere Rovers against Ashington in a First Round FA Cup tie on 22 November 1952 in an 8-1 win.

TRANMERE ROVERS 1995–96 LEAGUE RECORD

Match No.	Date	Venue	Opponents	Result	H/T Score	Lg. Pos.	Goalscorers	Attendance
1	Aug 12	H	Wolverhampton W	D	2-2	0-1	—	O'Brien, Aldridge	11,880
2	19	A	Sheffield U	W	2-0	1-0	2	Aldridge 2	11,247
3	26	H	Huddersfield T	W	3-1	0-0	1	O'Brien, Aldridge, Moore	9072
4	29	A	Barnsley	L	1-2	0-2	—	Aldridge	9710
5	Sept 9	H	Charlton Ath	D	0-0	0-0	13		7402
6	12	H	WBA	D	2-2	1-0	—	Bennett, Aldridge	7196
7	16	A	Stoke C	D	0-0	0-0	13		8618
8	23	A	Portsmouth	W	2-0	0-0	11	Nevin, Bennett	11,127
9	30	H	Watford	L	2-3	1-1	13	Bennett, Aldridge	7041
10	Oct 7	H	Luton T	W	1-0	1-0	7	Aldridge	6680
11	14	A	Millwall	D	2-2	0-0	8	Moore, Bennett	9293
12	21	A	Southend U	W	3-0	1-0	6	Moore 2, Bennett	6584
13	29	A	Norwich C	D	1-1	0-1	6	Moore	15,513
14	Nov 4	H	Derby Co	W	5-1	3-0	5	Nevin, Moore, Aldridge 2, Bennett	8565
15	19	A	Leicester C	W	1-0	0-0	5	Moore	13,125
16	22	H	Port Vale	W	2-1	1-0	—	Aldridge 2	6681
17	25	H	Grimsby T	L	0-1	0-1	7		7500
18	Dec 2	A	Luton T	L	2-3	1-1	9	Bennett, Jones	6025
19	9	H	Portsmouth	L	1-2	0-2	11	Moore	6678
20	16	A	Watford	L	0-3	0-1	13		7257
21	23	A	Birmingham C	L	0-1	0-0	14		18,439
22	26	H	Oldham Ath	W	2-0	0-0	12	Aldridge 2	9787
23	Jan 1	A	Reading	L	0-1	0-0	13		8421
24	13	H	Sheffield U	D	1-1	0-0	14	Moore	7321
25	20	A	Wolverhampton W	L	1-2	0-1	14	Aldridge	24,173
26	30	A	Sunderland	D	0-0	0-0	—		17,616
27	Feb 3	A	Huddersfield T	L	0-1	0-0	15		12,041
28	10	H	Barnsley	L	1-3	0-0	17	Aldridge	6376
29	17	A	WBA	D	1-1	0-1	16	Branch	15,014
30	20	H	Crystal Palace	L	2-3	2-0	—	Bennett, Aldridge	5253
31	24	H	Stoke C	D	0-0	0-0	17		8312
32	Mar 3	A	Oldham Ath	W	2-1	1-0	15	Nevin, Aldridge	4225
33	9	H	Birmingham C	D	2-2	1-1	16	Aldridge, Rogers	8696
34	12	A	Crystal Palace	L	1-2	1-1	—	Branch	13,183
35	16	A	Ipswich T	W	2-1	0-1	16	Aldridge, Bennett	11,759
36	23	H	Reading	W	2-1	1-1	14	Aldridge, Hopkins (og)	6249
37	30	A	Southend U	L	0-2	0-0	16		4738
38	Apr 2	H	Millwall	D	2-2	0-1	—	Rogers, Aldridge (pen)	5850
39	6	H	Norwich C	D	1-1	0-1	17	Aldridge	6613
40	8	A	Derby Co	L	2-6	1-1	17	Cook, Aldridge (pen)	16,723
41	13	H	Leicester C	D	1-1	0-1	19	Lennon (og)	8882
42	17	H	Ipswich T	W	5-2	1-1	—	O'Brien, Irons 2, Aldridge, Morgan	6008
43	20	A	Port Vale	D	1-1	0-0	15	O'Brien	7419
44	27	A	Grimsby T	D	1-1	0-1	15	Aldridge	5408
45	30	A	Charlton Ath	D	0-0	0-0	—		10,936
46	May 5	H	Sunderland	W	2-0	1-0	13	Irons, Aldridge (pen)	16,193

Final League Position: 13

GOALSCORERS

League (64): Aldridge 27 (3 pens), Bennett 9, Moore 9, O'Brien 4, Irons 3, Nevin 3, Branch 2, Rogers 2, Cook 1, Jones 1, Morgan 1, own goals 2.
Coca-Cola Cup (6): Aldridge 2, Jones 2, Brannan 1, Moore 1.
FA Cup (0).

Coyne D 46	Stevens G 33 + 1	Teale S 29	McGreal J 32	Garnett S 17 + 1	O'Brien L 18 + 4	Bennett G 26 + 3	Brannan G 44	Aldridge J 45	Irons K 25 + 7	Nevin P 39 + 1	Mungall S 2 + 4	Moore I 27 + 9	Thomas T 31	Morrissey J 8 + 8	Jones G 17 + 6	Kenworthy J — + 4	Branch G 11 + 10	Rogers A 25 + 1	Higgins D 16 + 1	Mahon A — + 2	Cook P 15	Morgan A — + 4	Match No.
1	2¹	3	4	5²	6	7	8	9	10	11	12	13											1
1	2		4	5	6	7	8	9	10	11				3									2
1	2		4	5	6	7	8	9	10¹	11		12		3									3
1	2		4	5	6	7	8	9	10	11				3									4
1	12	5	4		6	9	8	2	10	11				3	7¹								5
1	2	5	4		6	9	8		10	11				3	7								6
1	2²	5	4		6¹	9	8	7	10	11	12			3	13								7
1	2		4	5¹		9	8²	7	10	11	12			3	6	13							8
1	2¹	5	4			9	8	7	10	11²	12			3	6	13							9
1	2	5	4			9¹	8	7	10	11	12			3	6								10
1	2	5	4			9	8¹	7		11			10	3	6		12						11
1	2	5	4			9	8	7		11			10	3	6								12
1	2	5	4			9	8	7		11			10	3	6								13
1	2	5	4			9	8	7		11			10	3	6								14
1	2	5	4			9	8	7		11			10¹	3	6		12						15
1	2¹		4	5		9	8	7	12	11			10	3	6								16
1			4	5		9	8	7	2²	11¹			10	3	6		12	13					17
1			4	5¹	12	9²	8	7		11			10	3	6		13	2					18
1			4		12	9		7		11			10	3	13		6¹	8²	2	5			19
1			4		12	9	8	7	13	11²			10¹	3	6			2		5			20
1		5				9	8	7		11			10	3	6			2	4				21
1		5				9¹	8	7		11			10	3	12		6	2	4				22
1		5				9	8	7		11¹			10	3	12		6	2	4				23
1		4	5	6		8	7	10²		13		9	3		12		11²	2					24
1		4	5	6		8	7		11			9	3		12			2		10¹			25
1	2		4	6¹		8	7	10	11²	12		9	3				13	5					26
1	2		4	6²		8		10	11	7¹		9	3				13	5	12				27
1	2		4			8		10³	11²	7		9	3¹		12		13	6	5	14			28
1	2	5	4¹	12		8	7	10					6		11	3							29
1	2	4	5	6		9	8	7	10					12			11¹	3					30
1	2	4	5¹	6²		9³	8	7	10			12				13	14	11	3				31
1	2		5				12	8	7	13		10		9	3		11¹	4³	14	6²			32
1	2¹		5				8	7	12	10		9				13	11²	3	4	6			33
1	2	5					12	8	7	10		9		3			11¹	4	6				34
1	2	5					12	8	7	13		10²		9	3		11¹	4	6				35
1	2	5	4				8	7	12	10¹		9		3²		13	11	6					36
1	2	5	4				8	7	3¹	10		9				12	11	6					37
1	2	5	4				8	7	12	10		9				13	11²	3	6¹				38
1	2	5	4				8	7	3¹	10		9				12	11	6					39
1	2	5	4				8	7		10		9				12	11¹	3	6				40
1	2		4		12		8²	10	11¹	9				7³	13	14		3	5	6			41
1	2		4		10		8	9	11	12				7¹				3²	5	6	13		42
1	2		4		10		8¹	3	11²	9				7	12				5	6	13		43
1	2		4		10		8¹	3	11	9²		12		7					5	6	13		44
1	2		4		10		8¹	9	11	12				7				3²	5	6	13		45
1	2		4		10		8	9	11¹	12				7				3	5	6			46

Coca-Cola Cup						**FA Cup**			
Second Round	Oldham Ath	(h)	1-0			Third Round	QPR	(h)	0-2
		(a)	3-1						
Third Round	Birmingham C	(a)	1-1						
		(h)	1-3						

WALSALL 1995–96   *Back row (left to right):* Charlie Ntamark, Wayne Evans, Chris Marsh, James Walker, Adrian Thompson, Trevor Wood, Ian Roper, Stuart Ryder, Darren Bradley.
Middle row: Eric McManus (Youth Team Coach), Stuart Watkiss, Charlie Palmer, Kyle Lightbourne, David Richards, Darren Rogers, Martin Butler, James Rollo, Ray Daniels, Tom Bradley (Physiol).
Front row: Colin Gibson, Scott Houghton, Kevin Wilson, Chris Nicholl (Manager), Martin O'Connor, John Keister, Chris Smith.

Division 2   WALSALL

Bescot Stadium, Bescot Crescent, Walsall WS1 4SA. Telephone: (01922) 22791. Fax: (01922) 613202. Commercial Dept: (01922) 30696. Saddlers Hotline: 0891 555800.

Ground capacity: 9000.

Record attendance: 10,628 B International, England v Switzerland, 20 May 1991.

Record receipts: £98,828 v Leeds U, FA Cup 3rd rd, 7 January 1995.

Pitch measurements: 110yd × 73yd.

Chairman: J. W. Bonsor.

Directors: M. N. Lloyd, K. R. Whalley, C. Welch, R. M. Tisdale.

Manager: Chris Nicholl. *General Manager:* Paul Taylor. *Physio:* Tom Bradley. *Coach:* Kevin Wilson.

Secretary/Commercial Manager: Roy Whalley.

Year Formed: 1888. *Turned Professional:* 1888. *Ltd Co.:* 1921.

Club Nickname: 'The Saddlers'.

Previous Names: Walsall Swifts (founded 1877) and Walsall Town (founded 1879) amalgamated in 1888 and were known as Walsall Town Swifts until 1895.

Previous Grounds: Fellows Park to 1990.

Foundation: Two of the leading clubs around Walsall in the 1880s were Walsall Swifts (formed 1877) and Walsall Town (formed 1879). The Swifts were winners of the Birmingham Senior Cup in 1881, while the Town reached the 4th round (5th round modern equivalent) of the FA Cup in 1883. These clubs amalgamated as Walsall Town Swifts in 1888, becoming simply Walsall in 1895.

First Football League game: 3 September 1892, Division 2, v Darwen (h) L 1-2 – Hawkins; Withington, Pinches; Robinson, Whitrick, Forsyth; Marshall, Holmes, Turner, Gray (1), Pangbourn.

Record League Victory: 10–0 v Darwen, Division 2, 4 March 1899 – Tennent; E. Peers (1), Davies; Hickinbotham, Jenkyns, Taggart; Dean (3), Vail (2), Aston (4), Martin, Griffin.

Record Cup Victory: 6–1 v Leytonstone (away), FA Cup 1st rd, 30 November 1946 – Lewis; Netley, Skidmore; Crutchley, Foulkes, Newman; Maund (1), Talbot, Darby (1), Wilshaw (2), Davies (2). 6–1 v Margate, FA Cup 1st rd (replay), 24 November 1955 – Davies; Haddington, Vinall; Dorman, McPherson, Crook; Morris, Walsh (3), Richards (2), McLaren (1), Moore.

Record Defeat: 0–12 v Small Heath, 17 December 1892 and v Darwen, 26 December 1896, both Division 2.

Most League Points (2 for a win): 65, Division 4, 1959–60.

Most League Points (3 for a win): 83, Division 3, 1994–95.

Most League Goals: 102, Division 4, 1959–60.

Highest League Scorer in Season: Gilbert Alsop, 40, Division 3 (N), 1933–34 and 1934–35.

Most League Goals in Total Aggregate: Tony Richards, 184, 1954–63, and Colin Taylor, 184, 1958–63, 1964–68, 1969–73.

Most Capped Player: Mick Kearns, 15 (18), Republic of Ireland.

Most League Appearances: Colin Harrison, 467, 1964–82.

Record Transfer Fee Received: £600,000 from West Ham U for David Kelly, July 1988.

Record Transfer Fee Paid: £175,000 to Birmingham C for Alan Buckley, June 1979.

Football League Record: 1892 Elected to Division 2; 1895 Failed re-election; 1896–1901 Division 2; 1901 Failed re-election; 1921 Original Member of Division 3 (N); 1927–31 Division 3 (S); 1931–36 Division 3 (N); 1936–58 Division 3 (S); 1958–60 Division 4; 1960–61 Division 3; 1961–63 Division 2; 1963–79 Division 3; 1979–80 Division 4; 1980–88 Division 3; 1988–89 Division 2; 1989–90 Division 3; 1990–92 Division 4; 1992–95 Division 3; 1995– Division 2.

Honours: Football League: Division 2 best season: 6th, 1898–99; Division 3 – Runners-up 1960–61, 1994–95; Division 4 – Champions 1959–60; Runners-up 1979–80. FA Cup: best season: 5th rd, 1939, 1975, 1978, and last 16 1889. Football League Cup: Semi-final 1984.

Colours: Red shirts, black shorts, white stockings. *Change colours:* Jade and white squares, jade shorts, jade stockings.

Did you know?
Michael Ricketts scored with his first touch of the ball in his first League game after coming on as a substitute in the 68th minute against Brighton on 4 May 1996 .

WALSALL 1995–96 LEAGUE RECORD

Match No.	Date	Venue	Opponents	Result	H/T Score	Lg. Pos.	Goalscorers	Attendance
1	Aug 12	H	Stockport Co	L	0-2	0-2	—	4884
2	19	A	Shrewsbury T	W	2-0	0-0	13	Lightbourne, Stewart (og)	4019
3	26	H	Bristol R	D	1-1	0-0	12	Wright (og)	4851
4	29	A	Crewe Alex	L	0-1	0-0	—		4377
5	Sept 6	A	Burnley	D	1-1	0-0	—	Lightbourne	8778
6	9	H	Swansea C	W	4-1	2-0	13	Houghton, O'Connor, Edwards (og), Wilson	3788
7	12	H	Oxford U	D	2-2	1-0	—	O'Connor, Wilson	3905
8	16	A	Brentford	L	0-1	0-1	14		4717
9	23	A	York C	L	0-1	0-0	16		3541
10	30	H	Carlisle U	W	2-1	2-0	14	O'Connor (pen), Wilson	4214
11	Oct 7	H	Peterborough U	D	1-1	0-0	15	Lightbourne	3768
12	14	A	Wycombe W	L	0-1	0-1	18		4724
13	21	H	Wrexham	L	1-2	0-0	20	Wilson	4020
14	28	A	Bristol C	W	2-0	2-0	16	Houghton, Wilson	6475
15	31	A	Bradford C	L	0-1	0-0	—		4310
16	Nov 4	H	Bournemouth	D	0-0	0-0	18		3626
17	18	A	Brighton & HA	W	3-0	0-0	16	Wilson, Houghton 2	4976
18	25	H	Blackpool	D	1-1	0-0	17	Wilson	4459
19	Dec 9	H	York C	W	2-0	2-0	14	Mountfield, Marsh	3193
20	16	A	Carlisle U	D	1-1	0-1	16	Wilson	5308
21	23	H	Swindon T	D	0-0	0-0	14		5624
22	26	A	Rotherham U	W	1-0	0-0	14	Wilson	3694
23	Jan 13	H	Shrewsbury T	W	3-0	1-0	14	Wilson, O'Connor (pen), Lightbourne	5008
24	20	A	Stockport Co	W	1-0	1-0	13	Houghton	5870
25	Feb 3	A	Bristol R	L	0-2	0-0	14		4948
26	10	H	Notts Co	D	0-0	0-0	15		4378
27	17	A	Oxford U	L	2-3	1-0	16	Butler 2	4369
28	24	H	Brentford	L	0-1	0-1	18		3506
29	27	A	Swansea C	L	1-2	0-1	—	Lightbourne	3546
30	Mar 2	H	Rotherham U	W	3-1	1-1	18	Lightbourne 2, Wilson	3001
31	6	A	Notts Co	L	1-2	1-1	—	Lightbourne	4050
32	9	A	Swindon T	D	1-1	0-0	19	Houghton	9559
33	12	H	Crewe Alex	W	3-2	1-2	—	Wilson, Marsh, Lightbourne	3171
34	16	H	Chesterfield	W	3-0	0-0	13	Lightbourne, O'Connor 2 (1 pen)	4172
35	23	A	Hull C	L	0-1	0-0	14		3060
36	30	A	Peterborough U	W	3-2	2-2	13	O'Connor 2, Wilson	4954
37	Apr 2	H	Wycombe W	L	0-1	0-0	—		3252
38	6	H	Bristol C	W	2-1	1-1	13	Nugent (og), Bradley	4142
39	8	A	Wrexham	L	0-3	0-1	14		3309
40	13	H	Bradford C	W	2-1	0-0	13	Lightbourne 2	3679
41	16	A	Chesterfield	D	1-1	1-0	—	Lightbourne	4508
42	20	A	Bournemouth	D	0-0	0-0	12		4380
43	23	H	Hull C	W	3-0	1-0	—	Butler, Lightbourne, Platt	2752
44	27	A	Blackpool	W	2-1	1-1	11	Butler, O'Connor	9148
45	30	H	Burnley	W	3-1	0-0	—	Wilson, Platt, Lightbourne	3411
46	May 4	H	Brighton & HA	W	2-1	1-0	11	Wilson, Ricketts	4840

Final League Position: 11

GOALSCORERS

League (60): Lightbourne 15, Wilson 15, O'Connor 9 (3 pens), Houghton 6, Butler 4, Marsh 2, Platt 2, Bradley 1, Mountfield 1, Ricketts 1, own goals 4.
Coca-Cola Cup (4): Evans 1, Houghton 1, O'Connor 1, Wilson 1.
FA Cup (13): Lightbourne 3, Bradley 2, Houghton 2, Marsh 2, Wilson 2, O'Connor 1, own goal 1.

Walker J 26	Evans W 20+4	Daniel R 23+2	Ryder S 1+2	Marsh C 39+2	Watkiss S 14+1	O'Connor M 41	Ntamark C 34+8	Lightbourne K 37+6	Wilson K 46	Bradley D 45	Palmer C 15	Houghton S 38+2	Keister J 9+12	Rogers D 23+2	Butler M 13+15	Wood T 20	Viveash A 31	Roper I 3+2	Mountfield D 28	Kerr J —+1	Smith C —+4	Platt C —+4	Ricketts M —+1	Match No.
1	2	3	4	5	6	7	8	9	10	11														1
1	2	3		5¹	4	7	8	9	10	11	6	12												2
1	2	3		5	4	7		9	10	8	6	11												3
1	2	3		5	4			9	10	8	6	11	7											4
1	2	3	12	5	4		13	9³	10¹	8	6	11²	7		14									5
1	2	3		5	4²	7	12	9	10³	8	6	11¹		13	14									6
1	2	3		5	4	7	12	9	10	8	6	11¹												7
1	2¹	3	12	5¹	4	7	13	9³	10	8	6	11			14									8
1	2	3²		5¹	4	7	12	9	10	8	6	11		13										9
	2	3		5	4	7	11	12	10¹	8	6	13			9²	1								10
	2	3		5¹	4	7	11	12	10	8²	6		13		9	1								11
	2			5¹	4	7	12	11	10	8	6			3	9	1								12
	2			5		7	12	11	10	8	6			3	9¹	1	4							13
1	2²			5	12	7	13	9	10	8¹	6¹	11		3	14		4							14
1				5	6	7	2	9	10	8		11		3			4							15
1				5	6	7	2	12	10	8²		11	13	3	9¹		4							16
1				5		7	2	9	10	8²		11¹	13	3	12		4		6					17
1				5		7	2	9¹	10	8²		11	13	3	12		4		6					18
1				5		7¹	2	12	10²	8		11	9	3	13		4		6					19
1				5¹		7	2	9	10	8		11		3	12		4		6					20
1				5		7	2	9	10	8		11		3			4		6					21
				5		7	2	9	10	8		11¹		3	12	1	4		6					22
	12			5¹		7	2	9²	10	8		11	14	3¹	13	1	4		6					23
				5¹		7	2		10	8	4	11		3	9	1		12	6					24
	12			5²		7	2	9³	10	8		4¹	11	13	3	1			6			14		25
		3		5		7	2	9	10	8		11				1	4	12	6¹					26
	2	3		5		7			10	8		11			9	1	4		6					27
	2	3¹		5				12	10	8		11	7		9²	1	4		6			13		28
				5¹		7²	2	12	10	8		11	13	3	9	1	4		6					29
				5		7	2	9	10	8²		11¹	13	3	12	1	4		6					30
				5		7	2	9	10	8		11		3		1	4		6					31
				5		7	2	9	10	8		11		3¹	12	1	4		6					32
	3			5		7	2	9	10	8		11				1	4		6					33
	3			5		7	2	9	10	8		11				1	4		6					34
	3					7	2	9	10	8		11			5	1	4		6					35
	5	3				7	2	9	10	8¹		11	12			1	4		6					36
	5	3				7²	2¹	9	10	8		11	13		12	1	4		6					37
1	5	3	12				2¹	9	10	8		11	7				4		6					38
1	5¹	3	12				2	9	10	8		11	7				4		6					39
1		3		5		7	2	9	10			11¹	8		12		4		6					40
1		3		5		7	2	9	10	8		11					4		6					41
1	14			5		7¹	2		10³	8		11²	9	3	12		4		6			13		42
1	12			5		7	2	9¹	10³	8²			13	3	11		4		6		14			43
1				5		7	2	9	10	8				3	11		4		6					44
1	12					7²	2	9	10	8¹		11³	13	3	5		4		6			14		45
1	12					7¹	2³	9	10²	8		11	5	3			4		6			13	14	46

Coca-Cola Cup

First Round	Brentford	(h)	2-2
		(a)	2-3

FA Cup

First Round	Burnley	(a)	3-1
Second Round	Torquay U	(a)	1-1
		(h)	8-4
Third Round	Wigan Ath	(h)	1-0
Fourth Round	Ipswich T	(a)	0-1

WATFORD 1995-96 *Back row (left to right):* John McDermott, David Barnes, Gary Fitzgerald, Robert Page, Colin Simpson, Peter Beadle, Colin Foster, Keith Millen, Robert Calderhead, Richard Johnson, Jamie Moralee, Billy Hails (Physio).

Middle row: Len Cheesewright (Chief Scout), Ken Brooks (Kit Manager), Dominic Ludden, Kevin Phillips, Darren Bazeley, Steve Cherry, Kevin Miller, Paul Wilkerson, David Holdsworth, Craig Ramage, Gerard Lavin, Stuart Murdoch (Reserve Team Manager), Robert Marshall (Football in the Community Assistant)

Front row: Kenny Sansom (Player/Coach), John White, Gary Porter, Nigel Gibbs, Glenn Roeder (Manager), Andy Hessenthaler, Tommy Mooney, David Connolly, Derek Payne, Kenny Jackett (Youth Team Manager).

Division 2   **WATFORD**

Vicarage Road Stadium, Watford WD1 8ER. Telephone: (01923) 496000. Fax: (01923) 496001. Hornet Hotline: 0891 104104. Ticket Office: (01923) 496010. Club Shop: (01923) 496005. Catering: (01923) 221457. Football in the Community: (01923) 440449. Junior Hornets Club: (01923) 496000. Marketing: (01923) 496006.

Ground capacity: 22,000.

Record attendance: 34,099 v Manchester U, FA Cup 4th rd (replay), 3 February 1969.

Record receipts: £115,000 v Leeds U, Coca-Cola Cup 3rd rd, 10 November 1992.

Pitch measurements: 115yd × 75yd.

Life President: Elton John CBE.

Chairman: Dr. S. R. Timperley PHD.

Directors: G. Smith (Vice-Chairman). G. S. Lawson Rogers, C. D. Lissack, J. Petchey, E. Plumley FAAI.

Secretary: John Alexander.

General Manager: Graham Taylor. *Team Manager:* Kenny Jackett. *Assistant Manager:* Luther Blissett.

Director of Marketing: Brian Blower. *Public Relations Manager:* Ed Coan.

Head of Sales and Marketing: Mark Devlin. *Youth Development Officer:* Jimmy Gilligan.

Stadium Manager: Mick Buttle.

Year Formed: 1891*(see Foundation). *Turned Professional:* 1897. *Ltd Co.:* 1909.

Club Nickname: 'The Hornets'.

Previous Name: West Herts.

Previous Ground: 1899, Cassio Road; 1922, Vicarage Road.

Foundation: Tracing this club's foundation proves difficult. Nowadays it is suggested that Watford was formed as Watford Rovers in 1891. Another version is that Watford Rovers were not forerunners of the present club whose history began in 1898 with the amalgamation of West Herts and Watford St. Mary's.

First Football League game: 28 August 1920, Division 3, v QPR (a) W 2-1 – Williams; Horseman, F. Gregory; Bacon, Toone, Wilkinson; Bassett, Ronald (1), Hoddinott, White (1), Waterall.

Record League Victory: 8–0 v Sunderland, Division 1, 25 September 1982 – Sherwood; Rice, Rostron, Taylor, Terry, Bolton, Callaghan (2), Blissett (4), Jenkins (2), Jackett, Barnes.

Record Cup Victory: 10–1 v Lowestoft T, FA Cup 1st rd, 27 November 1926 – Yates; Prior, Fletcher (1); F. Smith, 'Bert' Smith, Strain; Stephenson, Warner (3), Edmonds (2), Swan (2), Daniels (1). (1 og).

Record Defeat: 0–10 v Wolverhampton W, FA Cup 1st rd (replay), 13 January 1912.

Most League Points (2 for a win): 71, Division 4, 1977–78.

Most League Points (3 for a win): 80, Division 2, 1981–82.

Most League Goals: 92, Division 4, 1959–60.

Highest League Scorer in Season: Cliff Holton, 42, Division 4, 1959–60.

Most League Goals in Total Aggregate: Luther Blissett, 158, 1976–83, 1984–88, 1991–92.

Most Capped Player: John Barnes, 31 (79), England and Kenny Jackett, 31, Wales.

Most League Appearances: Luther Blissett, 415, 1976–83, 1984–88, 1991–92.

Record Transfer Fee Received: £2,300,000 from Chelsea for Paul Furlong, May 1994.

Record Transfer Fee Paid: £550,000 to AC Milan for Luther Blissett, August 1984.

Football League Record: 1920 Original Member of Division 3; 1921–58 Division 3 (S); 1958–60 Division 4; 1960–69 Division 3; 1969–72 Division 2; 1972–75 Division 3; 1975–78 Division 4; 1978–79 Division 3; 1979–82 Division 2; 1982–88 Division 1; 1988–92 Division 2; 1992–96 Division 1; 1996– Division 2.

Honours: Football League: Division 1 – Runners-up 1982–83; Division 2 – Runners-up 1981–82; Division 3 – Champions 1968–69; Runners-up 1978–79; Division 4 – Champions 1977–78; Promoted 1959–60 (4th). *FA Cup:* Runners-up 1984. *Football League Cup:* Semi-final 1979. **European Competitions:** *UEFA Cup:* 1983–84.

Colours: Yellow shirts, black shorts, black stockings. *Change colours:* Burgundy/jade shirts, burgundy shorts, burgundy stockings.

Did you know?
Goalkeeper Kevin Miller saved three shoot-out penalties against Bournemouth in a Coca-Cola Cup tie on 3 October 1995. Watford won 6-5 on penalties.

WATFORD 1995–96 LEAGUE RECORD

Match No.	Date	Venue	Opponents	Result		H/T Score	Lg. Pos.	Goalscorers	Atten-dance
1	Aug 12	H	Sheffield U	W	2-1	2-1	—	Payne, Johnson	8687
2	19	A	Huddersfield T	L	0-1	0-0	15		10,556
3	26	H	Barnsley	L	2-3	1-1	19	Phillips 2 (1 pen)	8049
4	29	A	Charlton Ath	L	1-2	1-0	—	Mooney	8442
5	Sept 2	A	Grimsby T	D	0-0	0-0	22		3993
6	9	H	Stoke C	W	3-0	2-0	17	Ramage 2, Mooney	7130
7	12	H	Crystal Palace	D	0-0	0-0	—		8780
8	16	A	Ipswich T	L	2-4	1-2	19	Phillips, Pitcher	11,441
9	23	H	Birmingham C	D	1-1	1-1	20	Moralee	9422
10	30	A	Tranmere R	W	3-2	1-1	15	Foster, Moralee, Mooney	7041
11	Oct 7	H	Millwall	L	0-1	0-0	17		8918
12	14	A	Sunderland	D	1-1	0-0	20	Moralee	17,790
13	21	H	Wolverhampton W	D	1-1	0-1	19	Holdsworth	11,319
14	28	A	Portsmouth	L	2-4	0-2	20	Phillips, Ramage	7025
15	Nov 4	H	Southend U	D	2-2	1-1	20	Caskey, Phillips	7091
16	11	A	Leicester C	L	0-1	0-1	21		16,230
17	18	A	Port Vale	D	1-1	1-0	21	Ramage	6265
18	21	H	Luton T	D	1-1	0-1	—	Phillips	10,042
19	26	H	Norwich C	L	0-2	0-1	21		7798
20	Dec 2	A	Millwall	W	2-1	2-1	19	Phillips 2	8389
21	9	A	Birmingham C	L	0-1	0-0	22		16,970
22	16	H	Tranmere R	W	3-0	1-0	20	Phillips 2 (1 pen), Foster	7257
23	23	A	Oldham Ath	D	0-0	0-0	19		5878
24	Jan 13	H	Huddersfield T	L	0-1	0-0	22		7568
25	20	A	Sheffield U	D	1-1	0-0	22	Bazeley	12,782
26	Feb 3	A	Barnsley	L	1-2	0-0	24	Penrice	6139
27	10	H	Charlton Ath	L	1-2	1-0	24	Phillips	8394
28	17	A	Crystal Palace	L	0-4	0-2	24		13,235
29	24	H	Ipswich T	L	2-3	2-0	24	White, Palmer	11,872
30	28	A	Stoke C	L	0-2	0-0	—		10,114
31	Mar 2	A	Reading	D	0-0	0-0	24		8933
32	5	H	Derby Co	D	0-0	0-0	—		8306
33	9	H	Oldham Ath	W	2-1	1-0	24	Ramage 2	10,961
34	12	A	WBA	D	4-4	2-3	—	Ramage 2, Foster 2	11,836
35	16	A	Derby Co	D	1-1	1-0	24	Foster	15,939
36	23	H	WBA	D	1-1	0-0	24	Ramage	10,334
37	30	A	Wolverhampton W	L	0-3	0-2	24		25,885
38	Apr 2	H	Sunderland	D	3-3	1-3	—	Mooney 2, Ramage	11,195
39	6	H	Portsmouth	L	1-2	1-1	24	Mooney (pen)	8226
40	8	A	Southend U	D	1-1	1-0	24	Ramage	5348
41	13	H	Port Vale	W	5-2	2-1	24	Connolly 3 (1 pen), White 2	9066
42	16	H	Reading	W	4-2	2-0	—	White 2, Connolly, Ramage	8113
43	20	A	Luton T	D	0-0	0-0	23		9454
44	23	H	Grimsby T	W	6-3	4-1	—	Ramage 3, Connolly 3	8909
45	27	A	Norwich C	W	2-1	1-0	23	Connolly (pen), Porter	14,188
46	May 5	H	Leicester C	L	0-1	0-0	23		20,089

Final League Position: 23

GOALSCORERS

League (62): Ramage 15, Phillips 11 (2 pens), Connolly 8 (2 pens), Mooney 6 (1 pen), Foster 5, White 5, Moralee 3, Bazeley 1, Caskey 1, Holdsworth 1, Johnson 1, Palmer 1, Payne 1, Penrice 1, Pitcher 1, Porter 1.
Coca-Cola Cup (3): Bazeley 1, Johnson 1, Phillips 1.
FA Cup (1): Mooney 1.

Miller K 42	Lavin G 16	Johnson R 17 + 3	Millen K 32 + 1	Holdsworth D 26 + 1	Gibbs N 8 + 1	Hessenthaler A 30	Payne D 9 + 3	Beadle P 3	Porter G 28 + 1	Phillips K 26 + 1	Mooney T 38 + 4	Bazeley D 35 + 6	Cherry S 4	Connolly D 7 + 4	Foster C 26	Ramage C 34 + 2	Moralee J 17 + 8	Pitcher G 2 + 7	Palmer S 35	Caskey D 6	Penrice G 4 + 3	Wilkinson P 4	Hodge S 2	Page R 16 + 3	Ludden D 9 + 3	Dixon K 8 + 3	Neill W 1	White D 9 + 7	Hill D 1	Barnes D 10	Andrews W — + 1	Simpson C — + 1	Ward D 1	Match No.
1	2	3	4	5	6	7	8		9¹	10	11	12																						1
1	2	3	4	5	6	7	8		9¹	10	11²	12	13																					2
	2	3	4	5	6²	7¹	8		10	11	12	9	1		13																			3
	2	7	4²	5	12		8		10¹	11	9	3	1	13	6																			4
		3		5	2		8		10	11		7	1	9¹	4	6	12																	5
1		3		5	2		8		10	11	9¹	7²			4	6	12	13																6
1	2	3		5			8		10	11	9	7			4	6																		7
1	2	3¹		5			8		10	11	9	7			4	6	12																	8
1	2	3		5	12		8²		10		9	7		13	4	6	11¹																	9
1	2	3		5	7				10		9	12			4	6	11¹		8															10
1	2	3		5	7				10	12	9²	13			4	6²	11¹	14	8															11
1	2			5		7				11	9	3			4	6	10		8															12
1	2			5		7				11	9	3			4	6	10		8															13
	2			5		7				11	12	3¹	1		4	6	10²	13	8	9														14
1	2			5		7				11	9				4	6	10		8	3														15
1	2	12	4	5		7				11	9					6¹	10		8	3														16
1	2	12	4	5		7				11	9					6¹	10²		8	3	13													17
1	2		4	5		7				11	9					6	12		8	3	10¹													18
1			4	5						11	9	2				6	10		8	3														19
1		3		5		7	12		10¹	11	9	2			4	6			8															20
1		3		5		7				11	9	2			4	6	10¹		8	12														21
1	7	3		5						11	9	2			4	6			8					10										22
1	7	3		5						11	9	2			4	12	6²		8					10¹	13									23
1	12	3¹		5			10			11		2			4	6		13	8²					7		9								24
1	8	3		5							9	2¹			4	6				12				7	10	11								25
1		3				7					9	2			4	6	8¹	11		12				5	10									26
1	9¹	3		5		7				11		2			4	6			8	12					10									27
1				5	2¹	7			10²	11		3			4	6	12		8					13		9								28
1	6		4	5	2					11	10¹			13					8	12			7²			9		3						29
1	6		4	5	2					11	10¹								8	12			7²		13	9		3						30
1	6		4						10	11¹									8					5	7	9²		3						31
1	6		4			7¹			10	11²	9	2							8	12				5				3		13				32
1			4			7			10	11¹	9	2				6			8	12				5				3						33
1			4			7			10²	11¹	9	2				6			8	12				5	13			3						34
1		3	4			7			10	11¹	9	2				6			8	12				5										35
1		3	4			7¹			10	11²	9	2				6			8	12				5	13									36
1	6		4						10	11¹	9	2					12²		8					5	7			3		13				37
1	6		4						10		9	2					12		8					5	7¹			3		11				38
1	6		4			7²			10		9	2							8	12				5				3		11⁵		13		39
1	6		4			7			10		9	2							8					5				3		11				40
1	6	12	4			7¹			10		9²	2		13					8					5	14			3		11³				41
1			4			7			10		9	2				6¹			8	12				5	13			3²		11				42
1		12	4			7¹			10		9	2				6²			8						13			3		11			5	43
1			4			7			10		9	2				6			8					5				3		11				44
1			4			7			10		9	2				6			8	12				5				3¹		11				45
1	12		4¹			7			10		9	2				6²			8					5	13			3		11				46

Coca-Cola Cup

Second Round	Bournemouth	(h)	1-1	
		(a)	1-1	
Third Round	Blackburn R	(h)	1-2	

FA Cup

Third Round	Wimbledon	(h)	1-1	
		(a)	0-1	

WEST BROMWICH ALBION 1995–96 *Back row (left to right):* Tony Brien, Daryl Burgess, Andy Hunt, Paul Raven, Bob Taylor, Mike Phelan, Paul Agnew.
Middle row: Richard O'Kelly (Youth Team Coach), Paul Mitchell (Physio), Ian Hamilton, Stuart Naylor, Gary Germaine, Chris Hargreaves, Ronnie Allen (Coach), John Trewick (Reserve Team Coach).
Front row: Tony Rees, Stacy Coldicott, Lee Ashcroft, Arthur Mann (Assistant Manager), Paul Mardon, Alan Buckley (Manager), Paul Edwards, Kevin Donovan, David Smith.
(Photograph: Action Images)

Division 1 WEST BROMWICH ALBION

The Hawthorns, West Bromwich B71 4LF. Telephone: (0121) 525 8888 (all Depts). Fax: (0121) 553 6634.
Registered Office: 'The Tom Silk Building', Halfords Lane, West Bromwich, West Midlands B71 4BR.

Ground capacity: 25,296 (all seated).

Record attendance: 64,815 v Arsenal, FA Cup 6th rd, 6 March 1937.

Record receipts: £244,501 v Coventry C, FA Cup 3rd rd, 18 January 1995.

Pitch measurements: 115yd × 75yd.

President: Sir F. A. Millichip. *Vice-President:* John G. Silk LL.B (Lond).

Chairman: A. B. Hale.

Directors: C. M. Stapleton, P. Thompson, J. W. Brandrick, T. K. Guy, B. Hurst.

Manager: Alan Buckley. *Assistant Manager:* Arthur Mann. *Coach:* John Trewick. *Physio:* Paul Mitchell.

Secretary: Dr. John J. Evans BA, PHD. (Wales).

Club Statistician: Tony Matthews. *Commercial Manager:* Tom Cardall. *Stadium Manager:* Andy Williamson.

Year Formed: 1878. *Turned Professional:* 1885. *Ltd Co.:* 1892. *plc:* 1996.

Previous Name: 1878–81, West Bromwich Strollers.

Club Nicknames: 'Throstles', 'Baggies', 'Albion'.

Previous Grounds: 1878, Coopers Hill; 1879, Dartmouth Park; 1881, Bunns Field, Walsall Street; 1882, Four Acres (Dartmouth Cricket Club); 1885, Stoney Lane; 1900, The Hawthorns.

Foundation: There is a well known story that when employees of Salter's Spring Works in West Bromwich decided to form a football club, they had to send someone to the nearby Association Football stronghold of Wednesbury to purchase a football. A weekly subscription of 2d (less than 1p) was imposed and the name of the new club was West Bromwich Strollers.

First Football League game: 8 September 1888, Football League, v Stoke (a) W 2-0 – Roberts; J. Horton, Green; E. Horton, Perry, Bayliss; Bassett, Woodhall (1), Hendry, Pearson, Wilson (1).

Record League Victory: 12–0 v Darwen, Division 1, 4 April 1892 – Reader; J. Horton, McCulloch; Reynolds (2), Perry, Groves; Bassett (3), McLeod, Nicholls (1), Pearson (4), Geddes (1). (1 og).

Record Cup Victory: 10–1 v Chatham (away), FA Cup 3rd rd, 2 March 1889 – Roberts; J. Horton, Green; Timmins (1), Charles Perry, E. Horton; Bassett (2), Perry (1), Bayliss (2), Pearson, Wilson (3). (1 og).

Record Defeat: 3–10 v Stoke C, Division 1, 4 February 1937.

Most League Points (2 for a win): 60, Division 1, 1919–20.

Most League Points (3 for a win): 85, Division 2, 1992–93.

Most League Goals: 105, Division 2, 1929–30.

Highest League Scorer in Season: William 'Ginger' Richardson, 39, Division 1, 1935–36.

Most League Goals in Total Aggregate: Tony Brown, 218, 1963–79.

Most Capped Player: Stuart Williams, 33 (43), Wales.

Most League Appearances: Tony Brown, 574, 1963–80.

Record Transfer Fee Received: £1,500,000 from Manchester U for Bryan Robson, October 1981.

Record Transfer Fee Paid: £748,000 to Manchester C for Peter Barnes, July 1979.

Football League Record: 1888 Founder Member of Football League; 1901–02 Division 2; 1902–04 Division 1; 1904–11 Division 2; 1911–27 Division 1; 1927–31 Division 2; 1931–38 Division 1; 1938–49 Division 2; 1949–73 Division 1; 1973–76 Division 2; 1976–86 Division 1; 1986–91 Division 2; 1991–92 Division 3; 1992–93 Division 2; 1993– Division 1.

Honours: Football League: Division 1 – Champions 1919–20; Runners-up 1924–25, 1953–54; Division 2 – Champions 1901–02, 1910–11; Runners-up 1930–31, 1948–49; Promoted to Division 1 1975–76 (3rd). *FA Cup:* Winners 1888, 1892, 1931, 1954, 1968; Runners-up 1886, 1887, 1895, 1912, 1935. *Football League Cup:* Winners 1966; Runners-up 1967, 1970. **European Competitions:** *European Cup-Winners' Cup:* 1968–69; *European Fairs Cup:* 1966–67; *UEFA Cup:* 1978–79, 1979–80, 1981–82.

Colours: Navy blue and white striped shirts, white shorts, blue and white stockings. *Change colours:* Yellow shirts with sky blue sleeves, sky blue shorts, yellow stockings.

Did you know?
In successive games in October 1995, West Bromwich Albion recorded their 1000th home win and their 500th away.

WEST BROMWICH ALBION 1995–96 LEAGUE RECORD

Match No.	Date	Venue	Opponents	Result		H/T Score	Lg. Pos.	Goalscorers	Attendance
1	Aug 12	H	Charlton Ath	W	1-0	0-0	—	Gilbert	14,688
2	20	A	Wolverhampton W	D	1-1	0-0	6	Taylor	26,329
3	26	H	Ipswich T	D	0-0	0-0	7		14,470
4	29	A	Southend U	L	1-2	1-1	—	Raven	4621
5	Sept 2	H	Sheffield U	W	3-1	2-0	9	Burgess, Hamilton, Hunt	14,377
6	9	A	Oldham Ath	W	2-1	1-0	5	Taylor, Gilbert	8397
7	12	A	Tranmere R	D	2-2	0-1	—	Hunt, Ashcroft (pen)	7196
8	17	H	Birmingham C	W	1-0	1-0	3	Hunt	17,875
9	24	A	Stoke C	L	1-2	0-1	6	Hunt (pen)	9612
10	30	H	Huddersfield T	L	1-2	1-2	10	Taylor	15,945
11	Oct 7	H	Reading	W	2-0	0-0	5	Gilbert, Taylor	12,956
12	14	A	Luton T	W	2-1	0-1	3	Ashcroft, Hunt	8042
13	21	H	Portsmouth	W	2-1	0-0	3	Ashcroft, Hunt	16,257
14	28	A	Millwall	L	1-2	1-1	4	Hunt	9717
15	Nov 5	H	Leicester C	L	2-3	0-3	6	Hamilton, Raven	16,071
16	11	A	Derby Co	L	0-3	0-2	7		13,765
17	18	A	Grimsby T	L	0-1	0-0	9		8155
18	21	H	Norwich C	L	1-4	1-1	—	Hunt	13,680
19	25	H	Sunderland	L	0-1	0-1	15		15,931
20	Dec 2	A	Reading	L	1-3	1-2	16	Ashcroft	7910
21	9	H	Stoke C	L	0-1	0-1	16		14,819
22	16	A	Huddersfield T	L	1-4	0-0	19	Hamilton	12,664
23	23	H	Crystal Palace	L	2-3	0-3	20	Hunt, Darby	13,103
24	26	A	Port Vale	L	1-3	0-0	19	Gilbert	10,807
25	Jan 13	H	Wolverhampton W	D	0-0	0-0	21		21,642
26	20	A	Charlton Ath	L	1-4	0-3	21	Hunt (pen)	11,864
27	Feb 3	A	Ipswich T	L	1-2	0-1	23	Taylor	10,798
28	10	A	Southend U	W	3-1	1-0	22	Hunt, Taylor 2	12,906
29	17	H	Tranmere R	D	1-1	1-0	23	Hunt (pen)	15,014
30	20	A	Sheffield U	W	2-1	2-1	—	Burgess, Hunt	10,944
31	27	H	Oldham Ath	W	1-0	1-0	—	Taylor	10,959
32	Mar 2	H	Port Vale	D	1-1	1-0	22	Taylor	13,707
33	9	A	Crystal Palace	L	0-1	0-1	22		18,336
34	12	H	Watford	D	4-4	3-2	—	Taylor 3, Sneekes	11,836
35	16	A	Barnsley	W	2-1	2-0	18	Raven, Sneekes	12,701
36	20	A	Birmingham C	D	1-1	1-0	—	Sneekes	19,147
37	23	A	Watford	D	1-1	0-0	19	Taylor	10,334
38	30	A	Portsmouth	W	2-0	1-0	19	Sneekes 2	8126
39	Apr 2	H	Luton T	L	0-2	0-1	—		15,131
40	6	H	Millwall	W	1-0	0-0	19	Sneekes	13,793
41	9	A	Leicester C	W	2-1	1-0	—	Sneekes, Raven	17,889
42	13	H	Grimsby T	W	3-1	2-1	13	Taylor 2, Sneekes	16,116
43	20	A	Norwich C	D	2-2	1-0	13	Taylor, Sneekes	14,667
44	27	H	Sunderland	D	0-0	0-0	14		22,027
45	30	A	Barnsley	D	1-1	1-1	—	Gilbert	6981
46	May 5	H	Derby Co	W	3-2	2-1	11	Hunt, Sneekes, Taylor	23,858

Final League Position: 11

GOALSCORERS

League (60): Taylor 17, Hunt 14 (3 pens), Sneekes 10, Gilbert 5, Ashcroft 4 (1 pen), Raven 4, Hamilton 3, Burgess 2, Darby 1.
Coca-Cola Cup (8): Taylor 3, Burgess 2, Donovan 2, Hunt 1.
FA Cup (3): Coldicott 1, Hunt 1, Raven 1.

Naylor S 27	Burgess D 45	Edwards P 13+3	Cunnington S 8+1	Mardon P 35+4	Raven P 40	Donovan K 28+6	Gilbert D 35+5	Taylor B 39+3	Hunt A 44+1	Coldicott S 21+12	Smith D 9+7	Hamilton I 39+2	Ashcroft L 11+15	Rees T 3+6	Brien T 2	Agnew P 3	King P 4	Reece P 1	Fettis A 3	Darby J 19+3	Hargreaves C —+1	Phelan M 1	Holmes P 18	Spink N 15	Nicholson S 18	Sneekes R 13	Butler P 9	Angell B —+3	Comyn A 3	Match No.
1	2	3	4^1	5	6	7	8	9	10	11	12																			1
1	2	3		5	6	7	8	9	10	4		11																		2
1	2	3		5	6	7	8^1	9	10	4		11	12																	3
1	2	3		5	6	7^2	8	9	10^1	4		11	12	13																4
1	2	3		5	6^1	7	8	9	10	4		11	12																	5
1	2	3		5		7	8	9	10	4		11			6															6
1	2			5	6	7		9	10	4	8^1	11	13	12		3^2														7
1	2	3		5	6	7	8	9	10	4		11																		8
1	2	3^3		5	6	7	8	9^2	10	4		11	12	13																9
1	2		4^1	5	6	7	8	9	10	12		11	13			3^2														10
1	2	11		5	6	7	8	9		4		10				3														11
1	2	11		5	6	7	8^1	9	12	4	13	10				3^2														12
1	2	3	11^1	5	6	7^2	13	9	10	4	12	8																		13
1	2	3^1		5	6		8	9	10	4	12	11	7^2	13																14
1	2	12		5	6		8	9	10	4		11	7				3^1													15
1	2^2		4^1	5	6	7	8	9	10	12		11	13				3													16
	2	12	4	5	6	7^2	8	14	10			11	13	9^2			3^1	1												17
	2	12^2		5	6	7	8	9^2	10	4	14	11		13			3^1													18
	2			5^1	6	7	8^2		10	12	3	11		9					1	4			13							19
	2	3			6	7^1	8		10	5	12	11		9					1	4										20
1	2			5	6	12	8^1	9	10	13	3	7	11^2							4										21
1	2	3		5	6	7^2	8	9^1	10	13		11	12							4										22
1	2	14		5	6	13	8^3	12	10	3		11	9^1							4					7^2					23
1	2			5	6	7	8^1	9	10	3		11	12							4										24
1	2			5	6	7	11	9		4		3								10				8						25
1	2			5^1	6	7	12	9^3	10	4^2		3	13	14						11				8						26
	5		4^1		6	7	8^3	13	10	12		3	14	9^2						11			2	1						27
				5	6	7	8	9	10			11								4			2	1	3					28
				5^1	6	7	8^2	9	10	12		11	14	13						4^3			2	1	3					29
				5	6	7	8	9	10^1	12		11								4			2	1	3					30
		12		5	6		8^1	9	10	13		11	7							4^2			2	1	3					31
				5	6			9^1	10^2	12	8	11	7	13						4			2	1	3					32
1		12		5^3	6	7	8^2	9	10	13	14	11								4^1			2		3					33
		12		5	6	7^2	8^1	9	10			11								13			2	1	3	4				34
				5	6		8	9	10	12		11								7^1			2	1	3	4				35
1				5	6		8	9	10^2	12		11	13							7^1			2		3	4				36
1				5	6		8	9	10^1	12		11	7^2							13			2		3	4				37
1				5	6		8^1	9	10	12		11								13			2^2		3	4	7			38
1	2			5	6^1		13	9	10	12		11^2								7^3					3	4	8	14		39
		12		5			8	9	10			11											2^1	1	3	4	7		6	40
	2			5	6		8^1	9	10	12		11												1	3	4	7			41
	2			5	6		8	9	10			11												1	3	4	7			42
	2	12		5	6		8	9	10^2			11											8	1	3	4^1	7	13		43
	2			5^1			8		10			11			3								9	1		4	7	12	6	44
	2	12		5			8		10			11											9	1	3	4	7	6^1		45
				5	6		8	9	10			11											2	1	3	4	7			46

Coca-Cola Cup

First Round	Northampton T	(h)	1-1
		(a)	4-2
Second Round	Reading	(a)	1-1
		(h)	2-4

FA Cup

Third Round	Crewe Alex	(a)	3-4

WEST HAM UNITED 1995-96　*Back row (left to right):* Simon Webster, Ian Feuer, Marc Rieper, Ludek Miklosko, Jeroen Boere, Les Sealey, Alvin Martin.
Middle row: Eddie Gillam, Marco Boogers, Adrian Whitbread, Kenny Brown, Tim Breacker, Dale Gordon, John Moncur, Mark Watson, Matthew Rush, Danny Williamson, Martin Allen, John Green (Physio).
Front row: Keith Rowland, Tony Cottee, Don Hutchison, Harry Redknapp (Manager), Steve Potts, Frank Lampard (Assistant Manager), Julian Dicks, Ian Bishop, Matthew Holmes.

FA Premiership WEST HAM UNITED

Boleyn Ground, Green Street, Upton Park, London E13 9AZ. Telephone General Office: (0181) 548 2748. Ticket Office: (0181) 548 2700. Merchandise Shop: (0181) 548 2722. Fax: (0181) 548 2758. Membership Office: (0181) 548 2727. Promotions: (0181) 548 2777. Dial-a-seat: (0181) 548 2700. Football in the Community: (0181) 548 2707. Clubcall: 0891 121165.

Ground capacity: 25,985.

Record attendance: 42,322 v Tottenham H, Division 1, 17 October 1970.

Record receipts: £339,420 gross v Liverpool, FA Premier League, 22 November 1995.

Pitch measurements: 112yd × 72yd.

Chairman: T. W. Brown FCIS, AII, FCCA. *Vice-Chairman:* M. W. Cearns ACIB.

Directors: C. J. Warner, P. J. Storrie (Managing).

Manager: Harry Redknapp. *Assistant Manager:* Frank Lampard. *Coaches:* Frank Burrows, Tony Carr.
Physio: John Green BSC (hons) MCSP, SRP.

Secretary: Richard Skirrow. *Stadium Manager:* John Ball.

Year Formed: 1895. *Turned Professional:* 1900. *Ltd Co.:* 1900.

Previous Name: Thames Ironworks FC, 1895–1900.

Club Nickname: 'The Hammers'.

Previous Ground: Memorial Recreation Ground, Canning Town: 1904 Boleyn Ground.

Foundation: Thames Ironworks FC was formed by employees of this shipbuilding yard in 1895 and entered the FA Cup in their initial season at Chatham and the London League in their second. Short of funds, the club was wound up in June 1900 and relaunched a month later as West Ham United. Connection with the Ironworks was not finally broken until four years later.

First Football League game: 30 August 1919, Division 2, v Lincoln C (h) D 1-1 – Hufton; Cope, Lee; Lane, Fenwick, McCrae; D. Smith, Moyes (1), Puddefoot, Morris, Bradshaw.

Record League Victory: 8–0 v Rotherham U, Division 2, 8 March 1958 – Gregory; Bond, Wright; Malcolm, Brown, Lansdowne; Grice, Smith (2), Keeble (2), Dick (4), Musgrove. 8–0 v Sunderland, Division 1, 19 October 1968 – Ferguson; Bonds, Charles; Peters, Stephenson, Moore (1); Redknapp, Boyce, Brooking (1), Hurst (6), Sissons.

Record Cup Victory: 10–0 v Bury, League Cup 2nd rd (2nd leg), 25 October 1983 – Parkes; Stewart (1), Walford, Bonds (Orr); Martin (1), Devonshire (2), Allen, Cottee (4), Swindlehurst, Brooking (2), Pike.

Record Defeat: 2–8 v Blackburn R, Division 1, 26 December 1963.

Most League Points (2 for a win): 66, Division 2, 1980–81.

Most League Points (3 for a win): 88, Division 1, 1992–93.

Most League Goals: 101, Division 2, 1957–58.

Highest League Scorer in Season: Vic Watson, 42, Division 1, 1929–30.

Most League Goals in Total Aggregate: Vic Watson, 298, 1920–35.

Most Capped Player: Bobby Moore, 108, England.

Most League Appearances: Billy Bonds, 663, 1967–88.

Record Transfer Fee Received: £2,000,000 from Everton for Tony Cottee, July 1988.

Record Transfer Fee Paid: £1,500,000 to Liverpool for Don Hutchison, August 1994.

Football League Record: 1919 Elected to Division 2; 1923–32 Division 1; 1932–58 Division 2; 1958–78 Division 1; 1978–81 Division 2; 1981–89 Division 1; 1989–91 Division 2; 1991–93 Division 1; 1993– FA Premier League.

Honours: Football League: Division 1 best season: 3rd, 1985–86; Division 2 – Champions 1957–58, 1980–81; Runners-up 1922–23, 1990–91. *FA Cup:* Winners 1964, 1975, 1980; Runners-up 1923. *Football League Cup:* Runners-up 1966, 1981. **European Competitions:** *European Cup-Winners' Cup:* 1964–65 (winners), 1965–66, 1975–76 (runners-up), 1980–81.

Colours: Claret shirts with blue sleeves, white shorts, light blue with claret hooped stockings. *Change colours:* Ecru shirts and shorts, navy stockings.

Did you know?
Julian Dicks became the first West Ham United full-back to finish as equal top scorer in League games with ten goals in the 1995–96 season.

WEST HAM UNITED 1995–96 LEAGUE RECORD

Match No.	Date		Venue	Opponents	Result		H/T Score	Lg. Pos.	Goalscorers	Attendance
1	Aug	19	H	Leeds U	L	1-2	1-0	—	Williamson	22,901
2		23	A	Manchester U	L	1-2	0-0	—	Bruce (og)	31,966
3		26	A	Nottingham F	D	1-1	1-1	17	Allen	26,645
4		30	H	Tottenham H	D	1-1	1-0	—	Hutchison	23,516
5	Sept	11	H	Chelsea	L	1-3	0-2	—	Hutchison	19,228
6		16	A	Arsenal	L	0-1	0-0	19		38,065
7		23	H	Everton	W	2-1	2-1	17	Dicks 2 (2 pens)	21,085
8	Oct	2	A	Southampton	D	0-0	0-0	—		13,568
9		16	A	Wimbledon	W	1-0	1-0	—	Cottee	9411
10		21	H	Blackburn R	D	1-1	1-0	13	Dowie	21,776
11		28	A	Sheffield W	W	1-0	1-0	12	Dowie	23,917
12	Nov	4	H	Aston Villa	L	1-4	0-1	12	Dicks (pen)	23,637
13		18	A	Bolton W	W	3-0	0-0	11	Bishop, Cottee, Williamson	19,047
14		22	H	Liverpool	D	0-0	0-0	—		24,324
15		25	H	QPR	W	1-0	0-0	10	Cottee	21,504
16	Dec	2	A	Blackburn R	L	2-4	0-3	13	Dicks (pen), Slater	26,638
17		11	A	Everton	L	0-3	0-2	—		31,778
18		16	H	Southampton	W	2-1	0-1	13	Cottee, Dowie	18,501
19		23	A	Middlesbrough	L	2-4	0-3	13	Cottee, Dicks	28,640
20	Jan	1	A	Manchester C	L	1-2	0-1	14	Dowie	26,024
21		13	A	Leeds U	L	0-2	0-1	14		30,472
22		22	H	Manchester U	L	0-1	0-1	—		24,197
23		31	H	Coventry C	W	3-2	0-0	—	Rieper, Cottee, Dowie	18,884
24	Feb	3	H	Nottingham F	W	1-0	1-0	13	Slater	21,651
25		12	A	Tottenham H	W	1-0	1-0	—	Dani	29,781
26		17	A	Chelsea	W	2-1	0-1	12	Dicks, Williamson	25,252
27		21	H	Newcastle U	W	2-0	1-0	—	Williamson, Cottee	23,843
28		24	H	Arsenal	L	0-1	0-1	11		24,217
29	Mar	2	A	Coventry C	D	2-2	2-2	11	Cottee, Rieper	17,448
30		9	H	Middlesbrough	W	2-0	1-0	11	Dowie, Dicks (pen)	23,850
31		18	A	Newcastle U	L	0-3	0-1	—		36,331
32		23	H	Manchester C	W	4-2	1-0	11	Dowie 2, Dicks, Dani	24,017
33	Apr	6	H	Wimbledon	D	1-1	1-1	10	Dicks	20,462
34		8	A	Liverpool	L	0-2	0-2	10		40,326
35		13	H	Bolton W	W	1-0	1-0	10	Cottee	23,086
36		17	H	Aston Villa	D	1-1	0-1	—	Cottee	26,768
37		27	A	QPR	L	0-3	0-0	11		18,828
38	May	5	H	Sheffield W	D	1-1	0-0	10	Dicks	23,790

Final League Position: 10

GOALSCORERS

League (43): Cottee 10, Dicks 10 (5 pens), Dowie 8, Williamson 4, Dani 2, Hutchison 2, Rieper 2, Slater 2, Allen 1, Bishop 1, own goal 1.
Coca-Cola Cup (5): Cottee 2, Bishop 1, Dicks 1 (pen), Moncur 1.
FA Cup (3): Dowie 1, Hughes 1, Moncur 1.

Miklosko L 36	Breacker T 19 + 3	Dicks J 34	Potts S 34	Rieper M 35 + 1	Williamson D 28 + 1	Moncur J 19 + 1	Bishop I 35	Cottee T 30 + 3	Hutchison D 8 + 4	Rowland K 19 + 4	Martin A 10 + 4	Boogers M — + 4	Allen M 3	Slater R 16 + 6	Boere J — + 1	Dowie I 33	Lazaridis S 2 + 2	Sealey L 1 + 1	Hughes M 28	Harkes J 6 + 5	Finn N 1	Brown K 3	Whitbread A — + 2	Lampard F — + 2	Dani 3 + 6	Bilic S 13	Gordon D — + 1	Dumitrescu 12 + 1	Watson M — + 1	Ferdinand R — + 1	Match No.
1	2	3	4	5	6¹	7	8	9	10	11²	12	13																			1
1	2	3	4	5	11¹	7	8	9	10			12	6																		2
1	2	3	4	5		7	8	9¹	10			12		6		11															3
1	2	3	4	5		7	8	9	10¹					6		11	12														4
1	2	3	4	5		7	6¹	9	10							11			8	12											5
1	2	3	4	5		7³	6	9¹	10²			12				11			8	13	14										6
1	2	3	4¹	12	13	7	6	9²			5					11			8	10											7
1	2		4			7	6	12	10	3	5					11			9	8¹											8
1	3	2	4			7	6	9			5					10	8			11											9
1	3	2	4			7	6	9	12		5					10¹	8			11											10
1	3	2	4			7¹	6	9	12		5					10²	8			11	13										11
1	3	2	4				6	9	10¹		5	12				7²	8			11	13										12
1		2	4	10			6	9		3	5					8				11	7										13
1		2	4	10			6	9		3	5					8				11	7										14
1	12	2	4	10			6	9		3¹	5			13		8				11	7²										15
1	2	3	4	5	10		6¹	9⁴	12			14		13		8				11	7²										16
1	2	3	4	5	10		6	9¹		12				7		8				11											17
1	12	3	2	4	10	7²	6	9		5¹				13		8				11											18
1	2	3	4	5	10	7¹	6	9		12				13		8				11²											19
		3	4	5	10¹	7	6		12					8		9				11	2	1									20
1	6	2	5	4	7	8	9		3¹					12		10				11											21
1		3	4	5	10	7	6	9		12				11¹		8							2								22
1		3	4	5	10	7²	6	9¹								8				11				2	12	13					23
1		3	4	5	10		6	9²						7¹		8				11				2	12		13				24
1		3	2	5	10		6	12		11						8				7²	13				9¹	4					25
1		3	2	5	10		6	12		11						8				7					9¹	4					26
1		3	2	5	10		6	9²		11						8				7	12				4¹	13					27
1		3	4	5	10		6	9		11						8				7	2¹			12		4					28
1		3	2	5	10		6	9¹		11						8				7	12					4					29
1	2	3	4		10		6	9¹		11						8				7				5		12					30
12	3	2	5	10			6¹			11						8	1			7				13	4	9²					31
1	2	3		5	10		6			11						8				7				12	4	9¹					32
1	2	3		5	10		6			11¹				12		8				7				9	4						33
1	2	3		5	10		6			11				9		8				7¹				12	4						34
1	2	3		5	10	12	6	9		13				7²		8				11¹				4							35
1	2	3	4¹	5	10		7			9				11		8								12	6						36
1	2	3	4	5	10	8¹		9		11						7								6				12			37
1	2	3	4	5	10			9³		11²	12			8¹		7				13				6						14	38

Coca-Cola Cup

Second Round	Bristol R	(a)	1-0	
		(h)	3-0	
Third Round	Southampton	(a)	1-2	

FA Cup

Third Round	Southend U	(h)	2-0	
Fourth Round	Grimsby T	(h)	1-1	
		(a)	0-3	

WIGAN ATHLETIC 1995-96   *Back row (left to right):* Ian Benjamin, John Butler, Neil Ogden, Chris Lightfoot, Simon Farnworth, David Felgate, Martin Haley, David Miller, Mark Leonard, John Robertson.

Middle row: Joe Hinnigan (Coach), Paul Tait, Roberto Martinez, Ian Kilford, Tony Kelly, Paul West, John Doolan, Andy Lyons, Michael Millett, David Crompton (Youth Development Officer), Alex Cribley (Coach/Physio).

Front row: Tony Black, Jesus Seba, Neill Rimmer, Graham Barrow (Manager), Andy Farrell, Isidro Diaz, Matthew Carragher.
(Photograph: Derek Davies)

Division 3   **WIGAN ATHLETIC**

Springfield Park, Wigan WN6 7BA. Telephone: (01942) 244433. Fax: (01942) 494654. Commercial Dept: (01942) 243067. Latics Clubcall: 0891 121655. Football in the Community: (01942) 824599.

Ground capacity: 6901.

Record attendance: 27,500 v Hereford U, 12 December 1953.

Record receipts: £40,577 v Leeds U, FA Cup 6th rd, 15 March 1987.

Pitch measurements: 114yd × 72yd.

President: T. Hitchen.

Chairman: David Whelan.

Directors: S. Jackson, J. Winstanley, C. Ronnie, D. Sharp, D. Whelan., P. Williams.

Chief Executive/Secretary: Mrs Brenda Spencer. *Assistant Secretary:* Gordon Allan. *Football Co-Ordinator:* Frank Lord.

Manager: John Deehan. *Assistant Manager:* John Benson. *Physio/Coach:* Alex Cribley. *Safety Officer:* David Johnson. *Groundsman:* David Pinch.

Year Formed: 1932.

Club Nickname: 'The Latics'.

Foundation: Following the demise of Wigan Borough and their resignation from the Football League in 1931, a public meeting was called in Wigan at the Queen's Hall in May 1932 at which a new club Wigan Athletic, was founded in the hope of carrying on in the Football League. With this in mind, they bought Springfield Park for £2,250, but failed to gain admission to the Football League until 46 years later.

First Football League game: 19 August 1978, Division 4, v Hereford U (a) D 0-0 – Brown; Hinnigan, Gore, Gillibrand, Ward, Davids, Corrigan, Purdie, Houghton, Wilkie, Wright.

Record League Victory: 7–2 v Scunthorpe U (away), Division 4, 12 March 1982 – Tunks; McMahon, Glenn, Wignall, Cribley, Methven (1), O'Keefe, Barrow (1), Bradd (3), Houghton (2), Evans.

Record Cup Victory: 6–0 v Carlisle U (away), FA Cup 1st rd, 24 November 1934 – Caunce; Robinson, Talbot; Paterson, Watson, Tufnell; Armes (2), Robson (1), Roberts (2), Felton, Scott (1).

Record Defeat: 1–6 v Bristol R, Division 3, 3 March 1990.

Most League Points (2 for a win): 55, Division 4, 1978–79 and 1979–80.

Most League Points (3 for a win): 91, Division 4, 1981–82.

Most League Goals: 80, Division 4, 1981–82.

Highest League Scorer in Season: Warren Aspinall, 21, Division 3, 1985–86.

Most League Goals in Total Aggregate: Peter Houghton, 62, 1978–84.

Most Capped Player: None.

Most League Appearances: Kevin Langley, 317, 1981–86, 1990–94.

Record Transfer Fee Received: £329,000 from Coventry C for Peter Atherton, August 1991.

Record Transfer Fee Paid: £100,000 to Leeds U for Kevin Sharp, November 1995.

Football League Record: 1978 Elected to Division 4; 1982–92 Division 3; 1992–93 Division 2; 1993– Division 3.

Honours: Football League: Best season in Division 3: 4th, 1985–86, 1986–87; Division 4 – Promoted (3rd) 1981–82. *FA Cup:* 6th rd 1987. *Football League Cup:* best season: 4th rd, 1982. *Freight Rover Trophy:* Winners 1985.

Colours: Blue and white striped shirts, black shorts, blue stockings. *Change colours:* Burgundy with gold trim.

Did you know?
In 1995–96, Wigan Athletic became the first English club to field three Spanish players in the Football League, two of them finishing as leading scorers.

WIGAN ATHLETIC 1995–96 LEAGUE RECORD

Match No.	Date	Venue	Opponents		Result	H/T Score	Lg. Pos.	Goalscorers	Attendance
1	Aug 12	A	Gillingham	L	1-2	1-0	—	Martinez	3901
2	19	H	Scunthorpe U	W	2-1	1-1	12	Seba, Lightfoot	3153
3	26	A	Preston NE	D	1-1	1-1	12	Mutch	6837
4	29	H	Chester C	W	2-1	1-1	—	Diaz, Lyons	2555
5	Sept 2	A	Scarborough	D	0-0	0-0	9		1949
6	9	H	Bury	L	1-2	1-2	13	Kilford	3128
7	12	H	Barnet	W	1-0	1-0	—	Kilford	1745
8	16	A	Torquay U	D	1-1	1-0	10	Diaz	2188
9	23	H	Plymouth Arg	L	0-1	0-0	12		2631
10	30	A	Hereford U	D	2-2	1-1	13	Diaz, Greenall	2198
11	Oct 7	H	Mansfield T	L	2-6	1-2	15	Diaz 2	2084
12	14	A	Exeter C	W	4-0	1-0	11	Diaz, Seba 2, Leonard	3870
13	21	H	Hartlepool U	W	1-0	0-0	8	Diaz	2104
14	28	A	Leyton Orient	D	1-1	1-1	8	Martinez	4562
15	31	A	Darlington	L	1-2	0-1	—	Butler	2076
16	Nov 4	H	Fulham	D	1-1	1-1	10	Robertson	2438
17	18	A	Northampton T	D	0-0	0-0	12		4102
18	25	H	Doncaster R	W	2-0	2-0	10	Leonard, Biggins	2879
19	Dec 9	A	Plymouth Arg	L	1-3	1-1	11	Farrell	5931
20	16	H	Hereford U	W	2-1	0-1	11	Sharp, Martinez	1962
21	23	H	Lincoln C	D	1-1	0-0	11	Martinez	2334
22	26	A	Cambridge U	L	1-2	0-0	11	Kilford	2855
23	Jan 2	A	Rochdale	W	2-0	0-0	—	Diaz, Martinez	2624
24	13	A	Scunthorpe U	L	1-3	0-1	11	Sharp	2288
25	20	H	Gillingham	W	2-1	1-1	9	Lancashire, Diaz	2773
26	30	H	Colchester U	W	2-0	2-0	—	Johnson 2	2101
27	Feb 3	H	Preston NE	L	0-1	0-0	8		5567
28	10	A	Colchester U	W	2-1	0-0	8	Lancashire 2	3082
29	17	A	Barnet	L	0-5	0-2	9		2059
30	20	H	Scarborough	W	2-0	2-0	—	Martinez 2	2208
31	24	H	Torquay U	W	3-0	1-0	6	Diaz, Black, Pender	2697
32	27	A	Bury	L	1-2	0-0	—	Black	3800
33	Mar 2	H	Cambridge U	W	3-1	2-1	7	Martinez (pen), Sharp, Barnwell-Edinboro	2528
34	5	A	Cardiff C	L	0-3	0-2	—		1611
35	9	A	Lincoln C	W	4-2	1-1	6	Greenall, Johnson, Sharp (pen), Leonard	3282
36	16	H	Cardiff C	W	3-1	0-0	4	Sharp 2, Leonard	2789
37	19	A	Chester C	D	0-0	0-0	—		2825
38	23	A	Rochdale	W	2-0	1-0	4	Peake (og), Biggins (pen)	2870
39	30	H	Mansfield T	L	0-1	0-0	6		2369
40	Apr 2	H	Exeter C	W	1-0	0-0	—	Leonard	2744
41	6	H	Leyton Orient	W	1-0	0-0	4	Lowe	3081
42	8	A	Hartlepool U	W	2-1	0-1	3	Lowe, Leonard	1877
43	13	H	Darlington	D	1-1	0-1	4	Lowe	4473
44	20	A	Fulham	L	0-1	0-0	6		4657
45	27	A	Doncaster R	L	1-2	1-1	6	Martinez	2122
46	May 4	H	Northampton T	L	1-2	1-1	10	Leonard	5089

Final League Position: 10

GOALSCORERS

League (62): Diaz 10, Martinez 9 (1 pen), Leonard 7, Sharp 6 (1 pen), Johnson 3, Kilford 3, Lancashire 3, Lowe 3, Seba 3, Biggins 2 (1 pen), Black 2, Greenall 2, Barnwell-Edinboro 1, Butler 1, Farrell 1, Lightfoot 1, Lyons 1, Mutch 1, Pender 1, Robertson 1, own goal 1.
Coca-Cola Cup (2): Lyons 1 (pen), Martinez 1.
FA Cup (9): Martinez 3, Black 2, Diaz 2, Leonard 1, own goal 1.

Felgate D 3	Butler J 33	Farrell A 21+2	Miller D 4+3	Robertson J 14	Martinez R 42	Seba J 8+12	Lightfoot C 11+3	Leonard M 32+3	Doolan J 2+1	Lyons A 14+8	Carragher M 22+6	Diaz I 31+6	Pender J 40+1	Black T 8+13	Mutch A 7	Farnworth S 43	Rimmer N 27+3	Kilford J 18+7	Ogden N 10	Greenall C 37	Benjamin I 1+2	Kelly T 2	Biggins W 15+3	Sharp K 20	Johnson G 27	Lancashire G 5	Barnwell-Edinboro J 2+8	Lowe D 7	Match No.
1	2	3	4	5	6	7	8	9	10²	11¹	12	13																	1
1		3		5	6	7¹	8	9		10	2	11	4	12															2
1		3	10	5	6	12	8			11	2	7¹	4		9														3
		3	10	5	6		8			11	2	7¹	4	12	9	1													4
		3	10	5	6	12	8			11¹	2²	7	4		9	1	13												5
		3	10	4	5	12				13	11¹	2	7	14	9	1	8³	6²											6
		2	4	5	6					10		12		11	9	1	8¹	7	3										7
		2	10	5	6							12	4	11	9	1	8¹	7	3										8
		2			6	12	8			13	11¹	5		9³		1	10²	7¹	3	4	14								9
					6						2	11	12	7	5	1	10	3¹	4	9	8								10
		2			6			9				11¹		7	5	1	10	3²	4	13	8								11
		2		5	6	11	10¹	9				7	13			1	12	8	3²	4									12
		2		5	6	11¹		9²		12		7	10	13		1		8	3	4									13
		2		5	6	11		9				7	10			1		8	3	4									14
		2		5	6	11²		9		12		7	10	13		1		8¹	3	4									15
		2		5	6¹		12	9		11		7	10²	13		1		8	3	4									16
		3		5	10			12	13		14	2	7³	6	11²	1		8		4¹			9						17
	5	3				8		4	9		11	2	7¹	6	12	1							10						18
3¹	6					8			9		2	7²	5	12		1		13		4			10	11					19
2	6					8			9				5	12		1		7		4			10¹	11	3				20
						8			9	11	2	12	5	7¹		1	13	10²		4				6	3				21
	7¹	6				8			9	11	2	12	5			1	13			4²				10	3				22
						8			9	11	2	7	5			1	10			4				6	3				23
	12	13				8²	14	9³		11¹	2	7	5			1				4				6	3	10			24
						8¹		9		12	2	7	5			1	11			4				6	3	10			25
						8		9			2	7	5			1	11			4			12	6	3	10¹			26
						8		9			2	7	5			1	11			4			10	6¹	3		12		27
	7					8					2		5			1	11			4			10¹	6	3	9	12		28
	7					8²		9	13	2¹	12	5				1	11			4			10³	6	3		14		29
2						8		9				7	5	10¹		1	11			4				6	3		12		30
2						8²		9				7	5	12		1	11	13		4			10¹	6	3³		14		31
2						8		7²	9				12	5	10	1	11			4				6¹	3		13		32
2²						8		12	9			7	5¹	10³		1	11	13		4				6	3		14		33
	12					8		5	9¹			2	7			10				4			13	6	3		11²		34
2	8						11	12				13	5	7¹		1				4			10	6	3	9¹			35
2	8¹		12				9					7	5	10³		1	11²	13		4			14	6	3				36
2	6		8				9¹					5				1	11	7		4			10		3		12		37
2	6		8²								12	5	13			1	11	7		4			10		3	9¹			38
2	6²		8¹	14							12	5	13²			1	11	9		4			10		3		7		39
2				8	12		13					7¹	5			1	11	6²		4			10		3		9		40
2				7			9				12	5				1	11	13		4			10¹	6²	3		8		41
2	12			6¹	13		9			10		5				1	11	7²		4					3		8		42
2²			12	6	13		9			10	7¹	5				1	11			4					3		8		43
	10¹	8		6	12		9²			2		5				1	11	13		4					3		7		44
9	5			6	7					2						1	11	8		4			10		3				45
2²				6	12		9			13	7	5				1	11			4				8¹	3		10		46

Coca-Cola Cup

First Round	Chester C	(a)	1-4
		(h)	1-3

FA Cup

First Round	Runcorn	(a)	1-1
		(h)	4-2
Second Round	Barrow	(a)	4-0
Third Round	Walsall	(a)	0-1

WIMBLEDON 1995–96 *Back row (left to right):* Danny Hodges, Scott Fitzgerald, Steve Talboys, Gary Blissett, Hans Segers, Paul Heald, Brian McAllister, Dean Blackwell, Peter Fear, Chris Perry.

Middle row: Terry Burton (Assistant Manager), Mark Thomas, Oyvind Leonhardsen, Mick Harford, Andy Thorn, Kenny Cunningham, Alan Reeves, Marcus Gayle, Neal Ardley, Robbie Earle, Aidan Newhouse, Steve Allen (Physio).

Front row: Andy Clarke, Justin Skinner, Jon Goodman, Vinnie Jones, Joe Kinnear (Manager), Dean Holdsworth, Gary Elkins, Jason Euell, Alan Kimble.

FA Premiership **WIMBLEDON**

Selhurst Park, South Norwood, London SE25 6PY. Telephone: (0181) 771 2233. Fax: (0181) 768 0640. Box Office: (0181) 771 8841.

Ground capacity: 26,309.

Record attendance: 30,115 v Manchester U, FA Premier League, 9 May 1993.

Record receipts: £312,024 v Manchester U, FA Premier League, 16 April 1994.

Pitch measurements: 110yd × 74yd.

Chairman: S. G. Reed. **Vice-Chairman:** J. Lelliott.

Managing Director: S. Hammam.

Directors: P. Cork, P. R. Cooper, N. N. Hammam, P. Miller.

Chief Executive: David Barnard.

Manager: Joe Kinnear. **Assistant Manager:** Terry Burton. **Physio:** Steve Allen. **Stadium Manager:** Vic Worrall.

Secretary: Steve Rooke. **Marketing Manager:** Sharon Sillitoe. **Press Manager:** Reg Davis.

Year Formed: 1889. **Turned Professional:** 1964. **Ltd Co.:** 1964.

Previous Name: Wimbledon Old Centrals, 1899–1905.

Previous Ground: Plough Lane.

Club Nickname: 'The Dons'.

Foundation: Old boys from Central School formed this club as Wimbledon Old Centrals in 1889. Their earliest successes were in the Clapham League before switching to the Southern Suburban League in 1902.

First Football League game: 20 August 1978, Division 4, v Halifax T (h) D 3-3 – Guy; Bryant (1), Galvin, Donaldson, Aitken, Davies, Galliers, Smith, Connell (1), Holmes, Leslie (1).

Record League Victory: 6–0 v Newport Co, Division 3, 3 September 1983 – Beasant; Peters, Winterburn, Galliers, Morris, Hatter, Evans (2), Ketteridge (1), Cork (3 incl. 1p), Downes, Hodges (Driver).

Record Cup Victory: 7–2 v Windsor & Eton, FA Cup 1st rd, 22 November 1980 – Beasant; Jones, Armstrong, Galliers, Mick Smith (2), Cunningham (1), Ketteridge, Hodges, Leslie, Cork (1), Hubbick (3).

Record Defeat: 0–8 v Everton, League Cup 2nd rd, 29 August 1978.

Most League Points (2 for a win): 61, Division 4, 1978–79.

Most League Points (3 for a win): 98, Division 4, 1982–83.

Most League Goals: 97, Division 3, 1983–84.

Highest League Scorer in Season: Alan Cork, 29, 1983–84.

Most League Goals in Total Aggregate: Alan Cork, 145, 1977–92.

Most Capped Player: Terry Phelan, 8 (35), Republic of Ireland.

Most League Appearances: Alan Cork, 430, 1977–92.

Record Transfer Fee Received: £4,000,000 from Newcastle U for Warren Barton, June 1995.

Record Transfer Fee Paid: £920,000 to Norwich C for Efan Ekoku, October 1994.

Football League Record: 1977 Elected to Division 4; 1979–80 Division 3; 1980–81 Division 4; 1981–82 Division 3; 1982–83 Division 4; 1983–84 Division 3; 1984–86 Division 2; 1986–92 Division 1; 1992– FA Premier League.

Honours: *FA Premier League* : best season: 6th, 1993–94; *Football League:* Division 3 – Runners-up 1983–84; Division 4 – Champions 1982–83. *FA Cup:* Winners 1988. *Football League Cup:* best season: 4th rd, 1980, 1984, 1989. *League Group Cup:* Runners-up 1982. *Amateur Cup:* Winners 1963; Runners-up 1935, 1947.

Colours: All navy blue with yellow trim. **Change colours:** White shirts with black trim, black shorts and stockings with white trim.

Did you know?
Between 1921 and 1964 when members of the Isthmian League, Wimbledon were champions eight times, twice reached the FA Amateur Cup Final and won it in 1963.

WIMBLEDON 1995–96 LEAGUE RECORD

Match No.	Date	Venue	Opponents	Result	H/T Score	Lg. Pos.	Goalscorers	Attendance
1	Aug 19	H	Bolton W	W	3-2	2-2	—	Ekoku, Earle, Holdsworth	9311
2	23	A	QPR	W	3-0	1-0	—	Leonhardsen, Holdsworth, Goodman	11,837
3	26	A	Manchester U	L	1-3	0-1	3	Earle	32,226
4	30	H	Sheffield W	D	2-2	1-1	—	Goodman, Holdsworth (pen)	6352
5	Sept 9	H	Liverpool	W	1-0	1-0	3	Harford	19,530
6	16	A	Aston Villa	L	0-2	0-1	7		26,928
7	23	H	Leeds U	L	2-4	1-3	9	Holdsworth, Reeves	13,307
8	30	A	Tottenham H	L	1-3	1-2	11	Earle	25,321
9	Oct 16	H	West Ham U	L	0-1	0-1			9411
10	21	A	Newcastle U	L	1-6	0-3	14	Gayle	36,434
11	28	H	Southampton	L	1-2	0-1	15	Euell	7982
12	Nov 6	A	Nottingham F	L	1-4	1-2	—	Jones	20,810
13	18	H	Middlesbrough	D	0-0	0-0	17		13,780
14	22	A	Manchester C	L	0-1	0-0	—		23,617
15	25	A	Coventry C	D	3-3	2-1	16	Jones (pen), Goodman, Leonhardsen	12,496
16	Dec 3	H	Newcastle U	D	3-3	2-3	17	Holdsworth 2, Ekoku	18,002
17	9	A	Leeds U	D	1-1	1-0	17	Leonhardsen	27,994
18	16	H	Tottenham H	L	0-1	0-0	18		16,193
19	23	H	Blackburn R	D	1-1	0-1	18	Earle	7105
20	26	A	Chelsea	W	2-1	2-1	16	Earle, Ekoku	21,906
21	30	A	Arsenal	W	3-1	1-1	15	Earle 2, Holdsworth	37,640
22	Jan 1	H	Everton	L	2-3	0-3	16	Holdsworth, Ekoku	11,121
23	13	A	Bolton W	L	0-1	0-1	15		16,216
24	20	H	QPR	W	2-1	1-0	14	Leonhardsen, Clarke	9123
25	Feb 3	H	Manchester U	L	2-4	0-2	16	Gayle, Euell	25,423
26	10	A	Sheffield W	L	1-2	0-0	16	Gayle	19,085
27	24	H	Aston Villa	D	3-3	1-1	16	Goodman 2, Harford	12,193
28	Mar 2	H	Chelsea	D	1-1	1-1	15	Clarke (og)	17,048
29	13	A	Liverpool	D	2-2	0-1	—	Ekoku, Holdsworth	34,063
30	16	H	Arsenal	L	0-3	0-0	17		18,335
31	23	A	Everton	W	4-2	1-1	15	Gayle, Castledine, Clarke, Goodman	31,282
32	30	H	Nottingham F	W	1-0	0-0	15	Holdsworth	9807
33	Apr 6	A	West Ham U	D	1-1	1-1	15	Jones	20,462
34	8	H	Manchester C	W	3-0	1-0	15	Earle 2, Ekoku	11,844
35	13	A	Middlesbrough	W	2-1	1-1	14	Earle, Ekoku	29,176
36	17	A	Blackburn R	L	2-3	1-1	—	Earle, Gayle	24,174
37	27	H	Coventry C	L	0-2	0-0	14		15,796
38	May 5	A	Southampton	D	0-0	0-0	14		15,182

Final League Position: 14

GOALSCORERS

League (55): Earle 11, Holdsworth 10 (1 pen), Ekoku 7, Goodman 6, Gayle 5, Leonhardsen 4, Jones 3 (1 pen), Clarke 2, Euell 2, Harford 2, Castledine 1, Reeves 1, own goal 1.
Coca-Cola Cup (7): Holdsworth 4 (1 pen), Earle 2, Clarke 1.
FA Cup (11): Ekoku 3, Goodman 3, Holdsworth 2, Clarke 1, Earle 1, Leonhardsen 1.

Heald P 18	Perry C 35+2	Kimble A 31	Jones V 27+4	Reeves A 21+3	Thorn A 11+3	Fear P 4	Earle R 37	Ekoku E 28+3	Holdsworth D 31+2	Leonhardsen O 28+1	Goodman J 9+18	Elkins G 7+3	Blissett G —+4	Talboys S 3+2	Gayle M 21+13	Cunningham K 32+1	Harford M 17+4	Clarke A 9+9	Fitzgerald S 2+2	McAllister B 2	Skinner J 1	Euell J 4+5	Tracey S 1	Pearce A 6+1	Segers H 3+1	Sullivan N 16	Ardley N 4+2	Castledine S 2+2	Blackwell D 8	Match No.
1	2	3²	4	5	6	7	8	9¹	10³	11	12	13	14																	1
1	2	3	4	5	6	7²	8	9¹	10	11²	12	13	14																	2
1	11	3	4	5	6		8	9¹	10	7²	12	2¹	14	13																3
1	2	3	4	5	6¹		8	9¹	10	11²	7	13	14		12															4
1	13	3	4	5	6²		8	10³	11	12						7¹	2	9	14											5
1	6	3	4	5			8²	10	12	11	13					7³	2	9¹	14											6
1	6		4	5	11²		8	12	10				13	3		7¹	2	9												7
1	5		4		6	7¹	8		10	11²	12			3		9	2	13												8
1	3		4		6³		8		10	11¹	7					12	2	13	14	5	9²									9
1	11¹		4	5			8		10	13	12²		14			7	2	9	6	3³										10
1	3		12				8	10	11					5	4¹	9²	2	13	6			7								11
	5		4		6		8	10¹	11						3	9²	2	12				13		7	1					12
1	5		4		6		8	9¹	10	11					3	12	2							7						13
1	13	3	4		6		8	9¹	10¹	11			14			2⁴	12					7	5							14
1	2	3	4				8	7¹	10	11			14		12⁵	9³		13	5											15
1	6	3	12				8	11²	10					4	7	13	2	9	5¹											16
1	6	3	12	5			8	11	10					4	7	13	2	9²												17
1	6	3	12	5			8	11	10					4	7¹	13	2	9²												18
1⁶	6	3	12	5			8	11²	10					4	7¹	13	2	9								15				19
1	6	3	4	5			8	7³	10²	11	12				13	2	9¹	14					1							20
1	6	3	4	5			8	7¹	10	11	12				13	2	9²						1							21
1	6	3	4	5			8	7	10	11					12	2¹	9¹					13	1							22
1	6	3		5			8	11	10¹	4					7	2	9					12				1				23
1	6	3		5			8	12²	10	4					7¹	2	9	11				13	1			1				24
1	6	3		5			10²		4	12	7				9	2	8					13		11¹		1				25
1	6	3					8	13	10¹	4					7	2	9²					14	5			1			11³	26
	3	12	5				8		4	7					10¹	2	9	11²				13				1			6	27
	6	3	4				8	9		11	10¹				7	2	12									1			5	28
	6	3	4		12		8	7	10¹	11	13				2	9²										1			5	29
	6	3	4		12		8	11	10¹	13	7				2	9²										1			5	30
	6	3	4²				8	9¹	11	12	7				2	10										1		13	5	31
	6	3	4				8¹	9	12	7					2	11										1	10		5	32
	6	3	4				8	9	10	12	7¹	11²				2										1	2	13	5	33
	6	3	4				8	9¹	10	12	7²				2	13									5	1	11			34
	6	3	4	12			8	9	10	7²					2	13									5¹	1	11			35
	6	3	4	5			8	9	10²	12	7				2	11¹										1	13			36
	6	3	4	5			8	9	10	12	7¹				2	13	11²									1				37
	7	3	4	5			8	9	10²	11¹	12				2	13										1			6	38

Coca-Cola Cup
Second Round   Charlton Ath   (h)   4-5
                              (a)   3-3

FA Cup
Third Round   Watford   (a)   1-1
                        (h)   1-0
Fourth Round   Middlesbrough   (a)   0-0
                               (h)   1-0
Fifth Round   Huddersfield T   (a)   2-2
                               (h)   3-1
Sixth Round   Chelsea   (a)   2-2
                        (h)   1-3

WOLVERHAMPTON WANDERERS 1995–96 *Back row (left to right):* James Smith, Gordon Cowans, Darren Ferguson, Geoff Thomas, Mike Stowell, Paul Jones, Neil Emblen, Neil Masters, Jermaine Wright, Robbie Dennison.
Middle row: Barry Holmes (Physio), Andy Thompson, Don Goodman, Brian Law, Dean Richards, Andy Debont, David Kelly, James Kelly, Mark Rankine, Paul Birch, Dave Hancock (Assistant Physio).
Front row: Chris Evans (Youth Development Officer), Ian Miller (Reserve Team Manager), Steve Froggatt, Tony Daley, Peter Shirtliff, Graham Taylor (First Team Manager), Bobby Downes (First Team Assistant Manager), John De Wolf, Mark Venus, Steve Bull, Robert Kelly (Youth Team Manager), Steve Harrison (First Team Coach).
(Photograph: Action Images)

Division 1   WOLVERHAMPTON WANDERERS

Molineux Grounds, Wolverhampton WV1 4QR. Telephone: (01902) 655000; Fax: (01902) 687006.
Ground capacity: 28,525.
Record attendance: 63,315 v Liverpool, FA Cup 5th rd, 11 February 1939.
Record receipts: £276,168 v Tottenham H, FA Cup 4th rd, 7 February 1996.
Pitch measurements: 110yd × 75yd.
President: Sir Jack Hayward.
Chairman: Jonathan Hayward.
Directors: Jack Harris, John Harris, Nic Stones, John Richards.
Manager: Mark McGhee. *Assistant Manager:* Colin Lee. *Stadium Manager:* Clive Mountford.
Coach: Mike Hickman. *Physio:* Barry Holmes.
Secretary: Tom Finn. *Commercial Director:* D. Clayton.
Year Formed: 1877*(see Foundation).* *Turned Professional:* 1888. *Ltd Co.:* 1982.
Club Nickname: 'Wolves'.
Previous Grounds: 1877, Goldthorn Hill; 1879, John Harper's Field; 1881, Dudley Road; 1889, Molineux.
Previous Names: 1880, St Luke's, Blakenhall combined with Blakenhall Wanderers to become Wolverhampton Wanderers (1923) Ltd until 1982.
Foundation: Another club where precise details of information are confused, due in part to the existence of an earlier Wolverhampton club which played rugby. However, it is now considered likely that it came into being in 1879 when players from St. Luke's (founded 1877) and Goldthorn (founded 1876) broke away to form Wolverhampton Wanderers Association FC.
First Football League game: 8 September 1888, Football League, v Aston Villa (h) D 1-1 – Baynton; Baugh, Mason; Fletcher, Allen, Lowder; Hunter, Cooper, Anderson, White, Cannon. Scorer – Cox (og).
Record League Victory: 10–1 v Leicester C, Division 1, 15 April 1938 – Sidlow; Morris, Dowen; Galley, Cullis, Gardiner; Maguire (1), Horace Wright, Westcott (4), Jones (1), Dorsett (4).
Record Cup Victory: 14–0 v Cresswell's Brewery, FA Cup 2nd rd, 13 November 1886 – I. Griffiths; Baugh, Mason; Pearson, Allen (1), Lowder; Hunter (4), Knight (2), Brodie (4), B. Griffiths (2), Wood. Plus one goal 'scrambled through'.
Record Defeat: 1–10 v Newton Heath, Division 1, 15 October 1892.
Most League Points (2 for a win): 64, Division 1, 1957–58.
Most League Points (3 for a win): 92, Division 4, 1988–89.
Most League Goals: 115, Division 2, 1931–32.
Highest League Scorer in Season: Dennis Westcott, 38, Division 1, 1946–47.
Most League Goals in Total Aggregate: Steve Bull, 217, 1986–96.
Most Capped Player: Billy Wright, 105, England (70 consecutive).
Most League Appearances: Derek Parkin, 501, 1967–82.
Record Transfer Fee Received: £1,150,000 from Manchester C for Steve Daley, September 1979.
Record Transfer Fee Paid: £1,850,000 to Bradford C for Dean Richards, May 1995.
Football League Record: 1888 Founder Member of Football League: 1906–23 Division 2; 1923–24 Division 3 (N); 1924–32 Division 2; 1932–65 Division 1; 1965–67 Division 2; 1967–76 Division 1; 1976–77 Division 2; 1977–82 Division 1; 1982–83 Division 2; 1983–84 Division 1; 1984–85 Division 2; 1985–86 Division 3; 1986–88 Division 4; 1988–89 Division 3; 1989–92 Division 2; 1992– Division 1.
Honours: Football League: Division 1 – Champions 1953–54, 1957–58, 1958–59; Runners-up 1937–38, 1938–39, 1949–50, 1954–55, 1959–60; Division 2 – Champions 1931–32, 1976–77; Runners-up 1966–67, 1982–83; Division 3 (N) – Champions 1923–24; Division 3 – Champions 1988–89; Division 4 – Champions 1987–88. *FA Cup:* Winners 1893, 1908, 1949, 1960; Runners-up 1889, 1896, 1921, 1939. *Football League Cup:* Winners 1974, 1980. *Texaco Cup:* Winners: 1971. *Sherpa Van Trophy:* Winners 1988. **European Competitions:** *European Cup:* 1958–59, 1959–60. *European Cup-Winners' Cup:* 1960–61. *UEFA Cup:* 1971–72 (runners-up), 1973–74, 1974–75, 1980–81.
Colours: Gold shirts, black shorts, gold stockings. *Change colours:* All teal.
Did you know?
From 26 October 1938 to 6 April 1963, England played 148 peacetime internationals and Wolverhampton Wanderers were represented in each one.

WOLVERHAMPTON WANDERERS 1995–96 LEAGUE RECORD

Match No.	Date	Venue	Opponents	Result	H/T Score	Lg. Pos.	Goalscorers	Attendance
1	Aug 12	A	Tranmere R	D	2-2	1-0	—	Bull, Goodman	11,880
2	20	H	WBA	D	1-1	0-0	19	Mardon (og)	26,329
3	26	A	Sunderland	L	0-2	0-2	22		16,816
4	30	H	Derby Co	W	3-0	3-0	—	Daley, Goodman, De Wolf	26,053
5	Sept 2	A	Leicester C	L	0-1	0-1	15		18,441
6	9	H	Grimsby T	W	4-1	1-1	12	Bull 2, Goodman 2	23,656
7	13	H	Norwich C	L	0-2	0-0	—		27,064
8	16	A	Southend U	L	1-2	1-1	18	Goodman	6322
9	23	H	Luton T	D	0-0	0-0	19		23,659
10	30	A	Port Vale	D	2-2	2-1	19	Goodman, Daley	11,550
11	Oct 7	A	Ipswich T	W	2-1	2-1	15	Goodman, Atkins	15,335
12	14	H	Stoke C	L	1-4	0-2	19	Thompson (pen)	26,483
13	21	A	Watford	D	1-1	1-0	18	Daley	11,319
14	28	H	Sheffield U	W	1-0	1-0	16	Bull	23,881
15	Nov 4	A	Barnsley	L	0-1	0-0	18		9668
16	12	H	Charlton Ath	D	0-0	0-0	18		20,450
17	18	H	Oldham Ath	L	1-3	1-0	18	Emblen	23,128
18	22	A	Crystal Palace	L	2-3	0-2	—	Thompson (pen), Young	12,571
19	25	A	Huddersfield T	L	1-2	0-2	20	Bull	16,423
20	Dec 3	H	Ipswich T	D	2-2	0-1	21	Goodman 2	20,867
21	10	A	Luton T	W	3-2	3-1	20	Richards, Goodman, Bull	6997
22	16	H	Port Vale	L	0-1	0-1	22		23,329
23	26	A	Millwall	D	1-1	1-0	22	Bull	25,593
24	30	H	Portsmouth	D	2-2	2-0	20	Bull, Goodman	25,291
25	Jan 13	A	WBA	D	0-0	0-0	20		21,642
26	20	H	Tranmere R	W	2-1	1-0	20	Bull, Goodman	24,173
27	Feb 3	H	Sunderland	W	3-0	2-0	18	Thompson (pen), Goodman, Atkins	26,537
28	10	A	Derby Co	D	0-0	0-0	18		17,460
29	17	A	Norwich C	W	3-2	2-2	17	Bull 2, Goodman	14,691
30	21	H	Leicester C	L	2-3	2-1	—	Bull, Law	27,381
31	24	H	Southend U	W	2-0	1-0	16	Young, Thompson	24,677
32	Mar 2	A	Millwall	W	1-0	0-0	14	Bull	9131
33	5	A	Birmingham C	L	0-2	0-2	—		22,051
34	9	H	Reading	D	1-1	1-1	15	Atkins	25,954
35	12	A	Grimsby T	L	0-3	0-0	—		5013
36	16	A	Portsmouth	W	2-0	2-0	14	Emblen, Goodman	11,732
37	23	H	Birmingham C	W	3-2	1-1	13	Goodman, Thompson (pen), Bull	26,256
38	30	H	Watford	W	3-0	2-0	11	Froggatt, Osborn 2	25,885
39	Apr 3	A	Stoke C	L	0-2	0-1	—		16,361
40	6	A	Sheffield U	L	1-2	1-2	13	Thompson (pen)	16,658
41	8	H	Barnsley	D	2-2	1-1	15	Bull, Ferguson (pen)	23,789
42	13	A	Oldham Ath	D	0-0	0-0	16		7592
43	20	H	Crystal Palace	L	0-2	0-1	18		24,350
44	27	H	Huddersfield T	D	0-0	0-0	18		25,290
45	30	A	Reading	L	0-3	0-2	—		12,828
46	May 5	A	Charlton Ath	D	1-1	0-1	20	Crowe	14,023

Final League Position: 20

GOALSCORERS

League (56): Goodman 16, Bull 15, Thompson 6 (5 pens), Atkins 3, Daley 3, Emblen 2, Osborn 2, Young 2, Crowe 1, De Wolf 1, Ferguson 1 (pen), Froggatt 1, Law 1, Richards 1, own goal 1.
Coca-Cola Cup (11): Goodman 3, Atkins 2, Daley 1, Emblen 1, Ferguson 1, Venus 1, Williams 1, Wright 1.
FA Cup (4): Bull 2, Ferguson 1, Goodman 1.

Jones P 8	Thompson A 45	Masters N 3	Emblen N 30+3	Shirtliff P 2	Richards D 36+1	Daley T 16+2	Kelly D 3+2	Bull S 42+2	Cowans G 10+6	Goodman D 43+1	Stowell M 38	Froggatt S 13+5	Rankine M 27+5	De Wolf J 14+1	Thomas G —+2	Ferguson D 26+7	Pearce D 3+2	Smith J 10+3	Young E 30	Atkins M 26+6	Wright J 4+3	Williams M 5+7	Venus M 19+3	Birch P 5+2	Foley D 1+4	Law B 5+2	Osborn S 21	Samways V 3	Corica S 17	Crowe G 1+1	Match No.
1	2	3	4	5	6	7	8	9	10	11																					1
	2	3	4	5	6	7	8[1]	9	10	11	1	12																			2
	2		3[2]		6	12	8	9	10	7[1]	1	11	4	5	13																3
	3		4		6	7		9		8	1	11				2[1]		10	5	12											4
	3		4[2]		6	7[1]	12	9		8	1					2		13	5	10		11									5
	2				6	7		9	12	8	1	11	4	5				10	3[1]												6
	2		12		6	7	13	9	14	8[2]	1	11	4	5				10[3]	3[1]												7
	3				6	7		9		8	1	11	4			10			2	5											8
	3				6	7		9	12	8	1					2			10	5	4[1]	11[2]	13								9
	3				6	7		9		8	1					2			10	5	4	11[1]	12								10
	3				6	7[1]	12			8	1					2			10	5	4	13	11[2]	9							11
	3		2		6	12	13			8	1					14		10[1]	5	4	7	11	9[2]								12
1	3				6	7		9	10	8						2			5	4			11								13
1	3	12	6[1]					9	10	8						2			5	4	7		11								14
1	3	12				7[1]		9	10	8						2	6		5	4	13		11[2]								15
1	3		9			7			12	10	8					2[1]	6		5	4	13		11[2]								16
1	3		4			11[2]		9	10	8						2	6		5	12	13[3]		7	14							17
1	3		4			12		9	10	8						2	6		5	11[1]			7[2]	13							18
1	3		4		6			9		8						2			5	12		10	7	11[1]							19
	3		11[1]		6			9		8	1					2				4		10	7	12		5					20
	3		11		6			9		8	1					2				4		10	7			5					21
	3		11		6	12		9		8	1					2			5[1]	4		10[2]	7	13							22
	3	5			6	7[2]		9	12	8	1		14			13				4[2]		2					10	11[1]			23
	3	5			6	7[1]		9		8	1		13			12				4		2					10	11[2]			24
	3				6			9		8	1					2		10[1]		4	12		5	13			7	11[2]			25
	3				6			9		8	1					2		10		4	11		5				7				26
	3	5						9		8	1					2		10		4	11		6				7				27
	2	5						9		8	1					6		10		4	11		3				7				28
	2	5						9		8	1					6[1]		10		3	4			12		11	7				29
	2	5				12		9		8	1							10		4	3	13				6[2]	11		7[1]		30
	2	5						9		8	1							10		4	3					6	11		7		31
	2	5			6[1]			9		8	1							10		4	3		12				11		7		32
	2	5			6	12		9		8	1							10		4	3[1]	13					11		7		33
	2	5	6			12		9		8	1							10[1]		4	3						11		7		34
	2	5[1]						9		8	1		13			10		12		4	7[2]	14	3[3]				11				35
	3	5	6					9		8	1					10		2		4							11		7		36
	3	5	6					9		8	1					10		2		4[1]	12						11		7		37
	3	5[2]			6			9		8	1					10		12	2	4		13					11		7[1]		38
	3		6					9		8	1		10			12	13		2[3]	4	14		5[2]				11[1]		7		39
2[2]			6					9		8	1		3			12		5[3]		11	13	4	10[1]	14			7				40
			6					9		8	1		3			5		11		2	4	10[1]	12				7				41
	3	5	6					9		8[2]	1		10			12			11	2	4	13					7[1]				42
	2	5	6					9	12		1		3[2]			8[3]	13		10[1]	4		14					11		7		43
	2	5	6					9		8[1]	1		7	12					3	4							11		10		44
	2	5	6					9			1		7[1]			8[2]			3	12			4				11		10	13	45
	2		6[2]					9		8[2]	1		10[3]			12	13		3	5	14		4				11		7[1]	8	46

Coca-Cola Cup

Second Round	Fulham	(h)	2-0
		(a)	5-1
Third Round	Charlton Ath	(h)	0-0
		(a)	2-1
Fourth Round	Coventry C	(h)	2-1
Fifth Round	Aston Villa	(a)	0-1

FA Cup

Third Round	Birmingham C	(a)	1-1
		(h)	2-1
Fourth Round	Tottenham H	(a)	1-1
		(h)	0-2

WREXHAM 1995-96   *Back row (left to right):* Lewis Coady, Karl Connolly, Scott Williams, Barry Jones, Mark Cartwright, Barry Hunter, Andy Marriott, Mark McGregor, Ken Dixon, Paul Jones, Jonathan Cross, Stephen Futcher, Gareth Owen.

Middle row: Mel Pejic (Player/Physio), Joey Jones (Coach), Steve Morris, Kieron Durkan, Peter Ward, Wayne Phillips, Mike Cody, Steve Watkin, David Ridler, Craig Skinner, Richard Barnes, Kevin Russell, Mike Buxton (Schoolboy Development Officer), Cliff Sear (Youth Development Officer).

Front row: Steve Weaver (Community Scheme Officer), Bryan Hughes, David Brammer, Tony Humes, Kevin Reeves (Assistant Manager), Brian Flynn (Manager), Phil Hardy, Deryn Brace, Richard Rawlins, Dudley Hall (Reserve Team Physio).

Division 2 **WREXHAM**

Racecourse Ground, Mold Road, Wrexham LL11 2AN. Telephone: (01978) 262129. Fax: (01978) 357821. Commercial Dept: (01978) 352536. Community Office: (01978) 358545. Clubcall: 0891 121642.

Ground capacity: 9200.

Record attendance: 34,445 v Manchester U, FA Cup 4th rd, 26 January 1957.

Record receipts: £126,012 v West Ham U, FA Cup 4th rd, 4 February 1992.

Pitch measurements: 111yd × 71yd.

Chairman: W. P. Griffiths.

Managing Director: D. L. Rhodes.

Directors: C. Griffiths, S. Mackreth, G. Paletta, B. Williams (Vice-Chairman), P. Griffiths.

Manager: Brian Flynn. *Assistant Manager:* Kevin Reeves.

Secretary: D. L. Rhodes. *Player-Coach:* Joey Jones.

Commercial Manager: P. Stokes. *Physio:* Mel Pejic.

Year Formed: 1873 (oldest club in Wales).

Turned Professional: 1912. *Ltd Co.:* 1912.

Previous Ground: Acton Park.

Club Nickname: 'Robins'.

Foundation: The oldest club still in existence in Wales, Wrexham was founded in 1873 by a group of local businessmen initially to play a 17-a-side game against the Provincial Insurance team. By 1875 their team formation was reduced to 11 men and a year later they were among the founders of the Welsh FA.

First Football League game: 27 August 1921, Division 3 (N), v Hartlepools U (h) L 0-2 – Godding; Ellis, Simpson; Matthias, Foster, Griffiths; Burton, Goode, Cotton, Edwards, Lloyd.

Record League Victory: 10–1 v Hartlepool U, Division 4, 3 March 1962 – Keelan; Peter Jones, McGavan; Tecwyn Jones, Fox, Ken Barnes; Ron Barnes (3), Bennion (1), Davies (3), Ambler (3), Ron Roberts.

Record Cup Victory: 6–0 v Gateshead, FA Cup 1st rd, 20 November 1976 – Lloyd; Evans, Whittle, Davis, Roberts, Thomas (Hill), Shinton (3 incl. 1p), Sutton, Ashcroft (2), Lee (1), Griffiths. 6–0 v Charlton Ath, FA Cup 3rd rd, 5 January 1980 – Davies; Darracott, Kenworthy, Davis, Jones (Hill), Fox, Vinter (3), Sutton, Edwards (1), McNeil (2), Carrodus.

Record Defeat: 0–9 v Brentford, Division 3, 15 October 1963.

Most League Points (2 for a win): 61, Division 4, 1969–70 and Division 3, 1977–78.

Most League Points (3 for a win): 80, Division 3, 1992–93.

Most League Goals: 106, Division 3 (N), 1932–33.

Highest League Scorer in Season: Tom Bamford, 44, Division 3 (N), 1933–34.

Most League Goals in Total Aggregate: Tom Bamford, 175, 1928–34.

Most Capped Player: Dai Davies, 28 (51), Wales.

Most League Appearances: Arfon Griffiths, 592, 1959–61, 1962–79.

Record Transfer Fee Received: £300,000 from Manchester U for Mickey Thomas, November 1978, from Manchester C for Bobby Shinton, July 1979 and from Liverpool for Lee Jones, March 1992.

Record Transfer Fee Paid: £210,000 to Liverpool for Joey Jones, October 1978.

Football League Record: 1921 Original Member of Division 3 (N); 1958–60 Division 3; 1960–62 Division 4; 1962–64 Division 3; 1964–70 Division 4; 1970–78 Division 3; 1978–82 Division 2; 1982–83 Division 3; 1983–92 Division 4; 1992–93 Division 3; 1993– Division 2.

Honours: Football League: Division 2 best season: 15th, 1978–79; Division 3 – Champions 1977–78; Division 3 (N) – Runners-up 1932–33; Division 4 – Runners-up 1969–70. *FA Cup:* best season: 6th rd, 1974, 1978. *Football League Cup:* best season: 5th rd, 1961, 1978. *Welsh Cup:* Winners 23 times. Runners-up 22 times (record). **European Competition:** *European Cup-Winners' Cup:* 1972–73, 1975–76, 1978–79, 1979–80, 1984–85, 1986–87, 1990–91, 1995–96.

Colours: Red shirts, white shorts, red stockings. *Change colours:* Gold shirts, black shorts, black stockings.

Did you know?
On 18 November 1995, Wrexham beat Rotherham United 7-0, their biggest win in 33 years. They had defeated Hartlepool United 10-1 on 3 March 1962.

WREXHAM 1995–96 LEAGUE RECORD

Match No.	Date	Venue	Opponents	Result	H/T Score	Lg. Pos.	Goalscorers	Attendance
1	Aug 12	H	Notts Co	D	1-1	0-1	—	Watkin (pen)	4281
2	19	A	Blackpool	L	0-2	0-2	21		4799
3	26	H	Brighton & HA	D	1-1	0-1	20	Connolly	2947
4	29	A	Bournemouth	D	1-1	1-0	—	Russell	4825
5	Sept 2	A	Bristol R	W	2-1	0-1	15	Owen, Watkin	6031
6	9	H	Bradford C	L	1-2	0-0	18	Watkin	3268
7	12	H	Shrewsbury T	D	1-1	1-1	—	Watkin	3298
8	16	A	Peterborough U	L	0-1	0-0	19		3817
9	23	A	Wycombe W	D	1-1	1-1	19	Brammer	4649
10	30	H	Swindon T	W	4-3	1-2	16	Connolly 3, Hunter	4296
11	Oct 7	A	York C	L	0-1	0-0	18		3512
12	14	H	Oxford U	W	2-1	1-0	14	Humes, Phillips	3189
13	21	A	Walsall	W	2-1	0-0	13	Connolly (pen), Hunter	4020
14	28	H	Swansea C	W	1-0	1-0	10	Connolly (pen)	4002
15	31	H	Carlisle U	W	3-2	1-0	—	Russell 2, Brammer	2939
16	Nov 4	A	Hull C	D	1-1	0-0	9	McGregor	3515
17	18	H	Rotherham U	W	7-0	3-0	6	Connolly 2, Garner (og), Ward, Skinner, Watkin 2	3227
18	25	A	Burnley	D	2-2	0-0	7	Skinner, Ward	8710
19	Dec 9	A	Wycombe W	W	1-0	1-0	5	Connolly	3468
20	16	A	Swindon T	D	1-1	0-0	6	Connolly (pen)	8418
21	22	H	Brentford	D	2-2	2-0	—	Russell, Connolly	3670
22	26	A	Crewe Alex	D	0-0	0-0	7		5177
23	Jan 13	A	Blackpool	D	1-1	0-0	9	Watkin	5479
24	20	A	Notts Co	L	0-1	0-0	10		5014
25	23	H	Bristol C	D	0-0	0-0	—		2673
26	Feb 3	A	Brighton & HA	D	2-2	2-1	12	Skinner, Phillips	4617
27	13	A	Stockport Co	W	3-2	1-1	—	Ward, Connolly (og), Humes	4688
28	20	H	Bristol R	W	3-2	1-1	—	Hunter, Channing (og), Jones L	3235
29	24	H	Peterborough U	W	1-0	0-0	6	Brace	4012
30	27	A	Bradford C	L	0-2	0-2	—		3804
31	Mar 2	H	Crewe Alex	L	2-3	1-2	9	Chalk, Humes	6112
32	5	H	Chesterfield	W	3-0	3-0	—	Phillips, Chalk, Connolly (pen)	2656
33	9	A	Brentford	L	0-1	0-1	8		4579
34	12	H	Bournemouth	W	5-0	3-0	—	Ward, Jones L 2, Connolly, Russell	2004
35	16	H	Stockport Co	L	2-3	0-0	8	Jones L 2	4081
36	19	A	Chesterfield	D	1-1	0-0	—	Ward	3760
37	23	A	Bristol C	L	1-3	0-1	9	Connolly	6141
38	30	H	York C	L	2-3	1-2	10	Russell, Morris	2923
39	Apr 2	A	Oxford U	D	0-0	0-0	—		5554
40	6	A	Swansea C	W	3-1	1-0	10	Owen, Jones L 2	4256
41	8	H	Walsall	W	3-0	1-0	10	Chalk, Phillips, Connolly	3309
42	13	A	Carlisle U	W	2-1	1-0	7	Connolly, Jones L	7317
43	17	A	Shrewsbury T	D	2-2	1-2	—	Chalk, Jones L	4094
44	20	H	Hull C	W	5-0	2-0	6	Connolly 2, Russell, Phillips, Morris	3400
45	27	H	Burnley	L	0-2	0-2	8		6664
46	May 4	A	Rotherham U	W	1-0	0-0	8	Morris	4419

Final League Position: 8

GOALSCORERS

League (76): Connolly 18 (4 pens), Jones L 9, Russell 7, Watkin 7 (1 pen), Phillips 5, Ward 5, Chalk 4, Humes 3, Hunter 3, Morris 3, Skinner 3, Brammer 2, Owen 2, Brace 1, McGregor 1, own goals 3.
Coca-Cola Cup (2): Russell 1, Watkin 1.
FA Cup (3): Connolly 1 (pen), Hunter 1, Watkin 1.

Marriott A 46	Brace D 16	Hardy P 41 + 1	Hughes B 11 + 11	Hunter B 30 + 1	Jones B 39 + 1	Skinner C 21 + 2	Ward P 33 + 1	Connolly K 45 + 1	Watkin S 16 + 13	Russell K 37 + 3	Phillips W 43 + 1	Morris S 4 + 9	Owen G 11 + 8	Durkan K 6 + 2	McGregor M 27 + 5	Brammer D 11	Cross J 4 + 3	Humes T 26 + 1	Jones L 20	Chalk M 19	Match No.
1	2	3	4	5	6	7	8	9	10	11											1
1	2	3	4	5	6	7	8	9	10²	11	12	13									2
1		3	4¹	5	6	7²	8	9		11³	2	10	12	13	14						3
1		3		5	6		8²	9	12	11	2	10	4	7	13						4
1		3			6			9	12	11	2	10¹	8	7	5	4					5
1		3		5	6	12		9	10	11²	2		8	7¹		4	13				6
1		3		5	6			9	10	11¹	2		8	7	13	4²	12				7
1		3	12	5	6	13		9	10	11¹	4		8¹	7²	2		14				8
1		3	11	5	6	7		9	10¹	12	4				2	8					9
1		3	11		6		7¹	9	10		4		12		2	8		5			10
1		3	11		6		7	9	10		4				2	8		5			11
1		3	11¹		6		7	9	10²		4	13	12		2	8		5			12
1		3	11³		6	12	7¹	9	10²		4	13			2	8	14	5			13
1		3			6		7	9¹	10	11	4		12		2	8		5			14
1		3			6		7	9	10	11	4				2	8		5			15
1		3			6		7	9	10	11	4		12		2	8¹		5			16
1		3	12		6		7	9	10²	11	4	13			2	8		5¹			17
1		3	12		6		7	9	10	11	4		8¹		2			5¹			18
1		3			6	2	7	9	10	11	8		4		12			5¹			19
1		3			6	2	7	9	10	11	8		4					5			20
1	3				6	2	7	9	10¹	8	4	12			13			5²			21
1		3	12		6	2	7	9	10	8¹	4							5			22
1	2	3	12	6	5	7	11	9	10²	8	4¹	13						14			23
1	2	3	12	6	5	7	11¹	9	10²	8¹	4	13						14			24
1	2	3	11		5	7		9	10	8¹	4²	13	12		6						25
1	2	3	12		6	7¹	11	9	13	8²	4							5	10		26
1	3				6		11	9	12	8	4			7	2			5	10¹		27
1	3		5		6		11	9		8	4				2				10	7	28
1	3		12	5	6		11	9		8	4¹				2				10	7	29
1	3³	12	14	5¹	2		11	9²	13	8	4							6	10	7	30
1	2	3	12		6		11	9	13	8¹	4²							5	10	7	31
1	2	3			6		11	9		8	4							5	10	7	32
1	2¹	3	13		6		11	9	12	8	4²							5	10	7	33
1	2	3			6		11	9		8	4							5	10	7	34
1	2	3	11²		6			9	12	8	4		13					5	10	7	35
1		3			6		11	9	12	8	4				2¹			5	10	7	36
1		3²	13		6		11	9	12	8	4¹				2			5	10	7	37
1		3			6		11	9²	8¹	4		12	13		2			5	10	7	38
1		3			6		11	12	9¹	8	4	13	14		2			5	10²	7³	39
1		3		5	6		11	9		4	8				2				10	7	40
1		3		5	6		11	9		4	8				2				10	7	41
1		3		5	6		11	9		4	8				2				10	7	42
1		3	11	5	6			9		4	8				2				10	7	43
1		3		5	6			9		8	4	12	11		2				10¹	7	44
1		3		5	6		11	9		8	4²	12	13		2¹				10	7	45
1		3		5			11¹	9		8	4	10	12		2			6		7	46

Coca-Cola Cup				
First Round	Stockport Co	(a)	0-1	
		(h)	2-2	

FA Cup				
First Round	Hull C	(a)	0-0	
		(h)	0-0	
Second Round	Chesterfield	(h)	3-2	
Third Round	Peterborough U	(a)	0-1	

WYCOMBE WANDERERS 1995–96   *Back row (left to right):* Jason Soloman, Shaun Stevens, Terry Howard, Paul Hyde, Terry Evans, Chuck Moussaddik, Matt Crossley, Simon Stapleton, Gary Patterson.
Third row: David Jones (Physio), Jim Melvin (Youth Officer), Miguel De Souza, Anthony Hemmings, Keith Ryan, Jason Cousins, David Carroll, Steve Thompson, David Kemp (Assistant Manager), Neil Smillie (Youth Team Manager).
Second row: Steve Brown, Mickey Bell, Paul Hardyman, Alan Smith (Manager), Anthony Clark, Simon Garner, Steve McGavin.
Front row: Lewis Craker, Aaron Patton, James Glynn, Lee Allan, Lee Passmore, Tom Keys, Gary Wraight, Maurice Harkin, Allan Beeton, Stuart Cowie.

Division 2   **WYCOMBE WANDERERS**

Adams Park, Hillbottom Road, Sands, High Wycombe HP12 4HJ. Telephone (01494) 472100. Fax: (01494) 527633. Credit Card Hotline: (01494) 441118. Information Line 0891 446855.

Ground Capacity: 9650.

Record attendance: 9007 v West Ham U, FA Cup 3rd rd, 7 January 1995.

Record receipts: £61,221 (net of VAT) v West Ham U, FA Cup 3rd rd, 7 January 1995.

Pitch measurements: 115yd × 75yd.

Patron: J. Adams.

President: M. E. Seymour.

Chairman: I. L. Beeks.

Directors: G. Peart (Financial), G. Richards, B. R. Lee, A. Parry, A. Thibault, G. Cox.

Associate Director: J. Goldsworthy.

Manager: Alan Smith. *Assistant Manager:* David Kemp. *Secretary:* John Reardon.

Physio: David Jones. *Marketing Manager:* Mark Austin. *Promotions Manager:* Mike Phillips.

Year Formed: 1884. *Turned professional:* 1974. *Club Nicknames:* 'Chairboys' (after High Wycombe's tradition of furniture making), 'The Blues'.

Previous Ground: 1887 The Rye; 1893 Spring Meadow; 1895 Loakes Park, 1899 Daws Hill Park; 1901 Loakes Park; 1990 Adams Park.

Foundation: In 1884 a group of young furniture trade workers started playing together informally under the name of North Town Wanderers, the area of the town where they lived. They decided to better themselves by entering junior football and in 1887 Jim Ray, secretary, and Datchett Webb, captain, called a meeting at the Steam Engine public house. Wycombe Wanderers FC was formed and probably named after the famous FA Cup winners, The Wanderers, who had visited the town in 1877 for a tie with the original High Wycombe club.

First Football League game: 14 August 1993, Division 3 v Carlisle U (a), D 2-2: Hyde; Cousins, Horton (Langford), Kerr, Crossley, Ryan, Carroll, Stapleton, Thompson, Scott, Guppy (1) (Hutchinson). Wycombe's first goal was an own goal by Chris Curran.

Record League Victory: 4–0 v Scarborough (h), Division 3, 2 November 1993: Hyde; Cousins, Horton, Crossley (1), Evans T, Ryan, Carroll (1), Hayrettin, Thompson (Hemmings), Scott (2), Guppy.

Record Cup Victory: 4–0 v Boston U (h), FA Cup 1st rd replay, 21 November 1990: Granville; Crossley, Walford, Kerr, Creaser (1), Carroll, Blackler, Stapleton (Smith), West (2), Evans N (Ryan (1)), Hutchinson.

Most League points: 70, Division 3, 1993–94.

Most League goals: 66, Division 3, 1993–94.

Highest League goalscorer in season: Miguel De Souza 18, 1995–96.

Most League appearances: Dave Carroll, 128, 1993–96.

Record Transfer Fee Received: £375,000 from Swindon T for Keith Scott, November 1993.

Record Transfer Fee Paid: £140,000 to Birmingham C for Steve McGavin, March 1995.

Football League Record: Promoted to Division 3 from GMVC in 1993; 1993–94 Division 3; 1994– Division 2.

Honours: Football League: Division 2 best season: 6th, 1994–95; *FA Amateur Cup:* Winners 1931; *FA Trophy:* Winners 1991, 1993; *GM Vauxhall Conference:*Winners 1992–93; *FA Cup:* best season: 3rd rd 1975, 1986, 1994, 1995; *Football League Cup:* never beyond 2nd rd.

Colours: Light & dark blue striped quartered shirts, light blue shorts, light blue stockings. *Change colours:* All white.

Did you know?
Wycombe Wanderers won the FA Amateur Cup in 1931, beating Hayes 1-0 at Highbury.

Founded 1884

WYCOMBE WANDERERS 1995–96 LEAGUE RECORD

Match No.	Date		Venue	Opponents	Result		H/T Score	Lg. Pos.	Goalscorers	Attendance
1	Aug	12	H	Crewe Alex	D	1-1	0-1	—	McGavin (pen)	5281
2		19	A	Notts Co	L	0-2	0-0	22		5552
3		26	H	Bournemouth	L	1-2	0-2	22	De Souza	4749
4		29	A	Brighton & HA	W	2-1	1-1	—	De Souza 2	5360
5	Sept	2	A	Bradford C	W	4-0	1-0	10	De Souza 3, Castledine	9748
6		9	H	Peterborough U	D	1-1	1-0	11	Garner	5637
7		12	H	Chesterfield	W	1-0	1-0	—	Castledine	3617
8		16	A	Stockport Co	D	1-1	1-1	7	Castledine	5588
9		23	H	Wrexham	D	1-1	1-1	10	De Souza	4649
10		30	A	Bristol C	D	0-0	0-0	11		5564
11	Oct	7	A	Burnley	D	1-1	0-1	13	Williams	8029
12		14	H	Walsall	W	1-0	1-0	10	Carroll	4724
13		21	A	Oxford U	W	4-1	3-0	7	Farrell, Howard, De Souza, McGavin (pen)	7731
14		28	H	Hull C	D	2-2	0-1	7	Evans, Bell	5021
15		31	H	York C	W	2-1	0-0	—	De Souza (pen), Garner	4038
16	Nov	4	A	Swansea C	W	2-1	0-0	4	Farrell, Carroll	2809
17		18	H	Bristol R	D	1-1	1-0	4	Farrell	4886
18		26	A	Carlisle U	L	2-4	1-3	5	Carroll, Farrell (pen)	4459
19	Dec	9	A	Wrexham	L	0-1	0-1	9		3468
20		16	H	Bristol C	D	1-1	1-0	9	Blissett	4020
21		23	H	Shrewsbury T	W	2-0	1-0	8	Blissett, Howard	4131
22		26	A	Swindon T	D	0-0	0-0	9		12,976
23	Jan	13	H	Notts Co	D	1-1	0-0	10	Williams	4980
24		20	A	Crewe Alex	L	0-2	0-2	11		4150
25		23	A	Blackpool	D	1-1	0-1	—	De Souza	3877
26		30	A	Brentford	L	0-1	0-0	—		4668
27	Feb	3	H	Bournemouth	W	3-2	1-2	7	Williams 2, Patterson	4447
28		10	H	Blackpool	L	0-1	0-1	10		5285
29		17	A	Chesterfield	L	1-3	0-3	14	De Souza	4571
30		24	H	Stockport Co	W	4-1	3-0	10	Williams 3, Carroll	4246
31		27	A	Peterborough U	L	0-3	0-1	—		3670
32	Mar	2	H	Swindon T	L	1-2	0-2	12	De Souza	6457
33		6	H	Brighton & HA	L	0-2	0-0	—		3466
34		9	A	Shrewsbury T	D	1-1	1-1	12	Ryan	2866
35		16	H	Brentford	W	2-1	1-1	12	Carroll, Evans	4912
36		23	A	Rotherham U	D	0-0	0-0	12		2775
37		26	H	Bradford C	W	5-2	2-1	—	De Souza 3, Ryan, Evans	3021
38		30	H	Burnley	W	4-1	2-0	11	Ryan 2, De Souza, Farrell	4921
39	Apr	2	A	Walsall	W	1-0	0-0	—	Carroll (pen)	3252
40		6	H	Hull C	L	2-4	0-3	11	Carroll (pen), De Souza	3065
41		8	H	Oxford U	L	0-3	0-1	11		6727
42		13	A	York C	L	1-2	1-1	12	Skiverton	3113
43		16	H	Rotherham U	D	1-1	0-1	—	De Souza	2936
44		20	A	Swansea C	L	0-1	0-0	11		3672
45		27	H	Carlisle U	W	4-0	1-0	12	Crossley, Williams, Farrell 2	3964
46	May	4	A	Bristol R	L	1-2	0-1	12	Carroll	6621

Final League Position: 12

GOALSCORERS

League (63): De Souza 18 (1 pen), Carroll 8 (2 pens), Williams 8, Farrell 7 (1 pen), Ryan 4, Castledine 3, Evans 3, Blissett 2, Garner 2, Howard 2, McGavin 2 (2 pens), Bell 1, Crossley 1, Patterson 1, Skiverton 1.
Coca-Cola Cup (3): De Souza 2, Crossley 1.
FA Cup (1): Patterson 1.

Hyde P 17	Cousins J 28 + 2	Hardyman P 12 + 3	Crossley M 12	Foran M 5	Brown S 38	Carroll D 46	Bell M 40 + 1	De Souza M 38 + 5	McGavin S 22 + 9	Soloman J 6 + 1	Garner S 8 + 5	Howard T 36 + 3	McGorry B — + 4	Hennings T — + 3	Castledine S 7	Clark T 1 + 2	Moussaddik C 1	Patterson G 31 + 6	Rowbotham J 27	Farrell D 27 + 6	Williams J 23 + 6	Evans T 26 + 2	Roberts B 15	Blissett G 4	Ryan K 18 + 5	Lawrence M 1 + 5	Markman D — + 2	Dykstra S 13	Skiverton T 3 + 1	Stapleton S 1	Match No.
1	2	3	4	5	6	7^1	8	9^2	10	11	12	13																			1
1	2	3	4	5	6	7	8^1	9	10^2	11^3		13	12	14																	2
1		3^1		5	6	7	8^3	9	10^2	4	12	2	13	14	11																3
1		3		5	6	7	13	9	12	4	10^1	2				8	11^2														4
1		3	5		6	7	11	9	12	2	10^1	4				8															5
			5	3		7	11^3	9	12	2	10^1	4	13	14	8		1	6^2													6
1		3	5^1			7		9	10			4	12		8			6	2	11											7
1		3	5			7		10				4			8			6	2	11	9										8
1	5	3			8	7		9	12			4			6^1			2	11	10											9
1	5	3			8	7		9	12			4			6			2	11	10^1											10
1	5	3			6	7		9	10			4			12			2	11	8^1											11
1	5				6	7	3	9	10			4						12	2	11	8^1										12
1	5				6	7	3	9^2	10			4				13		12	2	11	8^1										13
1	5^1				6^7	7	3	9	10^2		12	4				13		13	2	11	8	14									14
1	12				6	7	3	9				10	4					13	2	11	8^2	5^1									15
1	5				6	7	3	9	12			10^1	4					13	2	11	8^2										16
1	5				6	7	3	9	12			10^1	4					8^2	2	11	13										17
1	5				6^1	7	3	9	12			10^2	4					8^3	2	11		14									18
	6					7	3	9				12	4					8^1	2^2	11	13	5	1		10						19
	6					7	3	9	12			8^1	4						2	11		5	1		10						20
						7	3	9^2			8^1	13	12	4				6	2	11		5	1		10						21
					6	7	3			9			4					8	2	11		5	1		10						22
					6	7	3	10^3	9^1				4					8	2	11	12	5	1		13						23
					6^2	7	3	10^1	9				4					8	2^3	11	12	5	1		13	14					24
					6	7	3	12	9^1				4					8	2	11	10^2	5	1		13						25
5^1					6	7	3	10	9				4					8^2	2	11	12		1		13						26
11					6	7	3	12					4^1					8	2		10	5	1		9						27
11					6	7	3	9					4					8	2	12	10	5	1		4^1						28
11^2					6	7	3	10				12						8	2	13	9	5	1		4^1						29
12					6	7	3	9					4					8	2	11	10	5^1	1								30
5					6	7	3	9					4					8^1	2	11	10		1		12						31
2					6	7	3	9					4							11	10	5		1	8						32
2	12				6	7	3	9^2					4							11^3	10	5		1	8	13					33
2					6	7	3	12	9^1				4					11			10	5			8	1					34
2	6					7	3		9				4					11			10	5			8	1					35
2	6					7	3	12	9				4					11			10^1	5			8	1					36
2					6	7	3	9	10				4					11				5			8	1					37
2					6	7	3	9^1	10				4					11	12			5			8	1					38
2	12				6	7	3^1	9	10				4					11				5			8	1					39
2					6	7	3	9	10^1				4^2					11	12			5			8	1	13				40
2		4			6	7	3	9	10^1									11				5			8	1					41
		4			6	7	3	9										11^1	12	10^2		5			8	13	1	5	2		42
		4			6	7	3	9										11	12			5			8	10^1	1	2		43
		4			6	7	3	9										11	10			5			8	1?	1	2^1		44
	12	4			6^1	7	3											11	2	9	10	5			8		1			45
		4			6	7	3	12										11	2	9^1	10	5			8		1			46

Coca-Cola Cup

First Round	Leyton Orient	(h)	3-0
		(a)	0-2
Second Round	Manchester C	(h)	0-0
		(a)	0-4

FA Cup

First Round	Gillingham	(h)	1-1
		(a)	0-1

YORK CITY 1995-96   *Back row (left to right):* Scott Oxley, Neil Campbell, Paul Baker (Player/Coach) Nick Scaife, Dean Kiely, Andy Warrington, Tony Barras, Steve Tutill, Wayne Osborne, Paul Atkin (Player/Coach).

Middle row: Paul Stancliffe (Assistant Manager), Paul Wilson, Paul Barnes, Jon McCarthy, Nigel Pepper, Graeme Murty, Andy McMillan, Glenn Naylor, Nick Peverell, Jeff Miller (Physio).

Front row: Darren Williams, Wayne Hall, Scott Jordan, Alan Little (Manager), Steve Bushell, Jason Cutler, Andy Curtis.

Division 2   YORK CITY

Bootham Crescent, York YO3 7AQ. Telephone: (01904) 624447. Fax: (01904) 631457.

Ground capacity: 9534.

Record attendance: 28,123 v Huddersfield T, FA Cup 6th rd, 5 March 1938.

Record receipts: £63,680 v Manchester U, Coca-Cola Cup 2nd rd 2nd leg, 3 October 1995.

Pitch measurements: 115yd × 74yd.

Chairman: D. M. Craig OBE, JP, BSC, FICE, FI, MUN E, FCI ARB, M CONS E

Directors: B. A. Houghton, C. Webb, E. B. Swallow, J. E. H. Quickfall FCA.

Manager: Alan Little. *Assistant Manager:* Paul Stancliffe.

Secretary: Keith Usher. *Commercial Manager:* Mrs Maureen Leslie.

Physio: Jeff Miller.

Hon. Orthopaedic Surgeon: Mr Peter De Boer MA, FRCS. *Medical Officer:* Dr R. Porter.

Year Formed: 1922. *Turned Professional:* 1922. *Ltd Co.:* 1922.

Club Nickname: 'Minstermen'.

Previous Ground: 1922, Fulfordgate; 1932, Bootham Crescent.

Foundation: Although there was a York City club formed in 1903 by a soccer enthusiast from Darlington, this has no connection with the modern club because it went out of existence during World War I. Unlike many others of that period who restarted in 1919, York City did not re-form until 1922 and the tendency now is to ignore the modern club's pre-1922 existence.

First Football League game: 31 August 1929, Division 3 (N), v Wigan Borough (a) W 2-0 – Farmery, Archibald, Johnson; Beck, Davis, Thompson; Evans, Gardner, Cowie (1), Smailes, Stockhill (1).

Record League Victory: 9–1 v Southport, Division 3 (N), 2 February 1957 – Forgan; Phillips, Howe; Brown (1), Cairney, Mollatt; Hill, Bottom (4 incl. 1p), Wilkinson (2), Wragg (1), Fenton (1).

Record Cup Victory: 6–0 v South Shields (away), FA Cup 1st rd, 16 November 1968 – Widdowson; Baker (1p), Richardson; Carr, Jackson, Burrows; Taylor, Ross (3), MacDougall (2), Hodgson, Boyer.

Record Defeat: 0–12 v Chester, Division 3 (N), 1 February 1936.

Most League Points (2 for a win): 62, Division 4, 1964–65.

Most League Points (3 for a win): 101, Division 4, 1983–84.

Most League Goals: 96, Division 4, 1983–84.

Highest League Scorer in Season: Bill Fenton, 31, Division 3 (N), 1951–52; Arthur Bottom, 31, Division 3 (N), 1954–55 and 1955–56.

Most League Goals in Total Aggregate: Norman Wilkinson, 125, 1954–66.

Most Capped Player: Peter Scott, 7 (10), Northern Ireland.

Most League Appearances: Barry Jackson, 481, 1958–70.

Record Transfer Fee Received: £450,000 from Port Vale for Jon McCarthy, July 1995.

Record Transfer Fee Paid: £140,000 to Burnley for Adrian Randall, December 1995.

Football League Record: 1929 Elected to Division 3 (N); 1958–59 Division 4; 1959–60 Division 3; 1960–65 Division 4; 1965–66 Division 3; 1966–71 Division 4; 1971–74 Division 3; 1974–76 Division 2; 1976–77 Division 3; 1977–84 Division 4; 1984–88 Division 3; 1988–92 Division 4; 1992–93 Division 3; 1993– Division 2.

Honours: Football League: Division 2 best season: 15th, 1974–75; Division 3 – Promoted 1973–74 (3rd); Division 4 – Champions 1983–84. *FA Cup:* Semi-finals 1955, when in Division 3. *Football League Cup:* best season: 5th rd, 1962.

Colours: Red shirts, blue shorts, red stockings. *Change colours:* All blue.

Did you know?
York City knocked out Manchester United in the Coca-Cola Cup during 1995–96, but had to wait until the last match of the season to avoid relegation.

YORK CITY 1995–96 LEAGUE RECORD

Match No.	Date		Venue	Opponents	Result		H/T Score	Lg. Pos.	Goalscorers	Attendance
1	Aug	12	H	Brentford	D	2-2	0-1	—	Baker, Barnes	3239
2		19	A	Swindon T	L	0-3	0-2	16		7746
3		26	H	Crewe Alex	L	2-3	1-1	21	Baker, Barnes	3880
4		29	A	Chesterfield	L	1-2	1-0	—	Pepper	3419
5	Sept	3	A	Oxford U	L	0-2	0-2	24		4304
6		9	H	Bristol R	L	0-1	0-0	24		4047
7		12	H	Burnley	D	1-1	0-1	—	Barnes	4684
8		16	A	Swansea C	W	1-0	1-0	23	Thomas (og)	2422
9		23	H	Walsall	W	1-0	0-0	21	Barnes	3541
10		30	A	Hull C	W	3-0	2-0	17	Barnes 2 (1 pen), Peverell	5273
11	Oct	7	H	Wrexham	W	1-0	0-0	14	Barras	3512
12		14	A	Shrewsbury T	L	1-2	0-1	17	Pepper	2827
13		21	H	Bristol C	L	0-1	0-1	18		3367
14		28	A	Peterborough U	L	1-6	0-3	20	Baker	4605
15		31	A	Wycombe W	L	1-2	0-0	—	Barnes	4038
16	Nov	4	H	Stockport Co	D	2-2	0-1	20	Barnes 2 (1 pen)	3101
17		18	A	Blackpool	W	3-1	1-1	18	Barnes, Matthews, Baker	4514
18		25	H	Brighton & HA	W	3-1	0-1	16	Barnes 2, Baker	3105
19	Dec	9	A	Walsall	L	0-2	0-2	18		3193
20		16	H	Hull C	L	0-1	0-0	19		3593
21		26	H	Bradford C	L	0-3	0-1	19		5218
22	Jan	6	A	Rotherham U	D	2-2	0-2	19	Barnes 2	2695
23		13	H	Swindon T	W	2-0	0-0	19	Naylor, McMillan	3613
24		20	A	Brentford	L	0-2	0-1	20		3915
25	Feb	10	A	Rotherham U	D	2-2	1-0	21	Pepper, Naylor	3299
26		17	A	Burnley	D	3-3	2-0	21	Pepper (pen), Naylor, Murty	8731
27		20	H	Oxford U	W	1-0	0-0	—	Barnes	2112
28		24	H	Swansea C	D	0-0	0-0	21		2786
29		27	A	Bristol R	L	0-1	0-1	—		4013
30	Mar	2	A	Bradford C	D	2-2	1-2	20	Pepper (pen), Cresswell	5208
31		5	A	Crewe Alex	D	1-1	1-0	—	Murty	3431
32		9	H	Carlisle U	D	1-1	0-1	20	Stephenson	3965
33		12	A	Notts Co	D	2-2	2-2	—	Baraclough (og), Barras	3462
34		16	A	Bournemouth	D	2-2	0-1	20	Barras, Pepper	3505
35		23	H	Notts Co	L	1-3	1-1	21	Bull	3126
36		26	H	Bournemouth	W	3-1	1-0	—	Himsworth, Naylor 2	2055
37		30	A	Wrexham	W	3-2	2-1	19	Bull 3	2923
38	Apr	2	H	Shrewsbury T	L	1-2	1-1	—	Pepper	2767
39		6	H	Peterborough U	W	3-1	2-1	19	Naylor, Pepper, Bull	3261
40		8	A	Bristol C	D	1-1	0-0	19	Bull	7512
41		13	H	Wycombe W	W	2-1	1-1	16	Bull (pen), Naylor	3113
42		20	A	Stockport Co	L	0-3	0-2	19		6286
43		23	A	Carlisle U	L	0-2	0-2	—		4813
44		30	H	Chesterfield	L	0-1	0-0	—		2839
45	May	4	H	Blackpool	L	0-2	0-1	21		7147
46		9	A	Brighton & HA	W	3-1	0-1	20	Bull, Stephenson, Jordan	2106

Final League Position: 20

GOALSCORERS

League (58): Barnes 15 (2 pens), Bull 8 (1 pen), Pepper 8 (2 pens), Naylor 7, Baker 5, Barras 3, Murty 2, Stephenson 2, Cresswell 1, Himsworth 1, Jordan 1, McMillan 1, Matthews 1, Peverell 1, own goals 2.
Coca-Cola Cup (11): Barnes 5, Baker 2, Barras 1, Jordan 1, Pepper 1, Peverell 1.
FA Cup (0).

Kiely D 40	McMillan A 46	Osborne W 5+1	Pepper N 39+1	Tutill S 25	Barras T 32	Murty G 31+4	Jordan S 18+8	Barnes P 30	Baker P 11+7	Stephenson P 24+3	Atkin P 25+4	Williams D 16+2	Hall W 21+2	Oxley S 1+1	Peverell N 11+9	Naylor G 20+5	Matthews R 14+3	Warrington A 6	Scaife N —+1	Bushell S 17+6	Curtis A —+1	Atkinson P 20+2	Randall A 13+3	Cresswell R 9+7	Himsworth G 7+1	Bull G 15	Sharples J 10	Match No.
1	2	3	4²	5	6	7	8¹	9	10	11	12	13																1
1	2		4	5	6	12		9	10	11			8	3	7¹													2
1	2		4	5		7		9	10	11		6	8	3														3
1	2	12	4²	5		7	13	9	10	11		6	8³	3¹	14													4
1	2		4	5		7	12	9	10²			6	8¹	3	11	13												5
1	2		4	5	6¹	7		9	10²			12	8	3	11		13											6
1	2		4	5	6	7		9					8	3	10	11												7
1	2		4	5	6	7	12	9					8	3	10²	13	11¹											8
1	2		4	5	6			11	9	12			8	3	10	7¹												9
1¹	2		4	5	6			11	9	12			8	3	10	7												10
	2		4	5	6			11	9²				8	3	10¹	12	7	1	13									11
	2		4	5	6		12	11²	9	13			8	3	10¹		7	1										12
	2			5	6	11	4²		9	12			8	3	10		7¹	1		13								13
	2	12	5			11	4		9	13		6	8¹	3	10³	14		1		7²								14
	2		4	5	6	11¹	13	9					12	3	10		7¹	1		8²	14							15
	2		4	5	6			9	10				11	3	7			1		8								16
1	2		4	5	6			8	9	10	11			3	7													17
1	2		4	5	6			8	9	10	11			3	7¹							12						18
1	2		4²	5	6	12		8	9	10¹	11			3	7					13								19
1	2		4	5		7		9		10¹	11	6		3						8								20
1	2		4	5		7		9¹	12	11		6		3	13	10²				8								21
1	2		4	5		7		9	12	11²		6		3¹		10				13		8						22
	2			5		7	12	9				6	11¹	13		10				4		3²	8					23
	2	5²				7	12	9				6	11³	13	14	10				4	3	8		10¹				24
1	2		4	5		7		9				6			12	10				3		8	11¹					25
1	2		4	5²		7		9				6			12	10				3		8	11¹					26
1	2		4	5		7		9				6			12	10¹				13	3	8²	11³	14				27
1	2		4	5				9				6			12	10¹				7	3	8	11					28
1	2				6	7		9	12	5					10					4	3	8	11¹					29
1	2		4	5		7	12	9				6			10²					8¹	3		13	11				30
1	2¹		4	5		7	13					12			14	10³				8²	3		9	11				31
1	2		4	5		7						12	6							8	3		9	11¹	10			32
1	2	3	4	5		7						11	6		12					8		9		10¹				33
1	2	3	4	5		7						11	6		12					8²	13	9¹	10					34
1	2	3	4	5								11	6		9²					12	8¹	13	7	10				35
1	2	3	4	5								11	6		9					12	8		7	10				36
1	2		4									11	6		9²		12			3	8¹	13	7	10	5			37
1	2		4		6	7						11			9					3	8			10	5			38
1	2		4		6	7	8					11			9					3				10	5			39
1	2		4		6	7²	8					11¹			12	9				13	3			10	5			40
1	2				6	7	8					11								4	3	9		10	5			41
1	2				6	7	8					11			12	9				4²	3¹	13		10	5			42
1	2		4		6¹	7³	8					11³	12		9					3	13	14		10	5			43
1	2		4				8	6				11			9¹					3	7	12		10	5			44
1	2		4				8	6		12		11			9²					3	7	13		10	5			45
1	2		4			7	8	6	12			11			9²					3	13			10	5			46

Coca-Cola Cup

First Round	Rochdale	(a)	1-2
		(h)	5-1
Second Round	Manchester U	(a)	3-0
		(h)	1-3
Third Round	QPR	(a)	1-3

FA Cup

First Round	Notts Co	(h)	0-1

ENGLISH LEAGUE PLAYERS DIRECTORY

Player	Ht	Wt	Pos	Birth Date	Place	Source	Clubs	League App	Gls
							ARSENAL		
Adams Tony	6 3	13 11	D	10 10 66	London	Apprentice	Arsenal	367	24
Bartram Vince	6 2	13 07	G	7 8 68	Birmingham	Local	Wolverhampton W	5	—
							Blackpool (loan)	9	—
							WBA (loan)	—	—
							Bournemouth	132	—
							Arsenal	11	—
Bergkamp Dennis	6 0	12 05	F	18 5 69	Amsterdam		Ajax	185	103
							Internazionale	52	11
							Arsenal	33	11
Black Michael	5 8	11 08	M	6 10 76	Chigwell	Trainee	Arsenal	—	—
Bould Steve	6 4	14 02	D	16 11 62	Stoke	Apprentice	Stoke C	183	6
							Torquay U (loan)	9	—
							Arsenal	211	5
Clarke Adrian	5 10	11 00	F	28 9 74	Suffolk	Trainee	Arsenal	7	—
Crowe Jason			M	30 9 78	Sidcup	Trainee	Arsenal	—	—
Dickov Paul	5 5	11 09	F	1 11 72	Glasgow	Trainee	Arsenal	20	3
							Luton T (loan)	15	1
							Brighton & HA (loan)	8	5
Dixon Lee	5 8	11 08	D	17 3 64	Manchester	Local	Burnley	4	—
							Chester	57	1
							Bury	45	5
							Stoke C	71	5
							Arsenal	292	18
Flatts Mark*	5 6	9 08	M	14 10 72	Haringey	Trainee	Arsenal	16	—
							Cambridge U (loan)	5	1
							Brighton & HA (loan)	10	1
							Bristol C (loan)	6	—
							Grimsby T (loan)	5	—
Griggs Timmy*			D	9 11 76	Bexley	Trainee	Arsenal	—	—
Harper Lee	6 1	13 11	G	30 10 71	London	Sittingbourne	Arsenal	—	—
Hartson John	6 1	14 06	F	5 4 75	Swansea	Trainee	Luton T	54	11
							Arsenal	34	11
Helder Glenn	5 11	11 07	F	28 10 68	Leiden		Sparta	93	9
							Vitesse	52	12
							Arsenal	37	1
Hillier David	5 10	12 05	M	19 12 69	Blackheath	Trainee	Arsenal	102	2
Howell Jamie*			M	19 2 77	Rustington	Trainee	Arsenal	—	—
Hughes Stephen	6 0	12 08	M	18 9 76	Wokingham	Trainee	Arsenal	2	—
Imber Noel*			G	4 12 76	London	Trainee	Arsenal	—	—
Jensen John*	5 10	12 06	M	3 5 65	Denmark	Brondby	Arsenal	98	1
Keown Martin	6 1	12 04	D	24 7 66	Oxford	Apprentice	Arsenal	22	—
							Brighton & HA (loan)	16	—
							Brighton & HA (loan)	7	1
							Aston Villa	112	3
							Everton	96	—
							Arsenal	114	1
Kiwomya Chris	5 9	10 07	F	2 12 69	Huddersfield	Trainee	Ipswich T	225	51
							Arsenal	14	3
Linighan Andy	6 4	13 10	D	18 6 62	Hartlepool	Smiths BC	Hartlepool U	110	4
							Leeds U	66	3
							Oldham Ath	87	6
							Norwich C	86	8
							Arsenal	107	4
Macdonald James	6 0	12 05	M	21 2 79	Inverness	Trainee	Arsenal	—	—
Marshall Scott	6 1	12 05	D	1 5 73	Edinburgh	Trainee	Arsenal	13	1
							Rotherham U (loan)	10	1
							Oxford U (loan)	—	—
							Sheffield U (loan)	17	—
McGoldrick Eddie	5 10	11 07	F	30 4 65	London	Nuneaton, Kettering T	Northampton T	107	9
							Crystal Palace	147	11
							Arsenal	38	—
McGowan Gavin	5 8	11 07	M	16 1 76	Blackheath	Trainee	Arsenal	4	—
Merson Paul	6 0	13 02	F	20 3 68	London	Apprentice	Arsenal	295	72
							Brentford (loan)	7	—

Morrow Steve	5 11	12 02	D	2 7 70	Belfast	Trainee	Arsenal	48	1
							Reading (loan)	10	—
							Watford (loan)	8	—
							Reading (loan)	3	—
							Barnet (loan)	1	—
O'Brien Roy*	6 1	12 00	D	27 11 74	Cork	Trainee	Arsenal	—	—
Owen Dafydd‡			D	3 6 77	Bangor	Trainee	Arsenal	—	—
Parlour Ray	5 10	11 12	M	7 3 73	Romford	Trainee	Arsenal	106	4
Platt David	5 10	11 12	F	10 6 66	Chadderton	Chadderton	Manchester U	—	—
							Crewe Alex	134	55
							Aston Villa	121	50
							Bari	29	11
							Juventus	16	3
							Sampdoria	55	17
							Arsenal	29	6
Rankin Isiah	5 10	11 00	F	22 5 78	London	Trainee	Arsenal	—	—
Read Paul	5 11	12 06	F	25 9 73	Harlow	Trainee	Arsenal	—	—
							Leyton Orient (loan)	11	—
							Southend U (loan)	4	1
Rose Matthew	5 11	11 01	D	24 9 75	Dartford	Trainee	Arsenal	4	—
Seaman David	6 4	14 10	G	19 9 63	Rotherham	Apprentice	Leeds U	—	—
							Peterborough U	91	—
							Birmingham C	75	—
							QPR	141	—
							Arsenal	227	—
Selley Ian	5 9	10 01	M	14 6 74	Chertsey	Trainee	Arsenal	40	—
Shaw Paul	5 11	12 02	F	4 9 73	Burnham	Trainee	Arsenal	4	—
							Burnley (loan)	9	4
							Cardiff C (loan)	6	—
							Peterborough U (loan)	12	5
Smith Alan‡	6 3	12 13	F	21 11 62	Birmingham	Alvechurch	Leicester C	191	73
							Leicester C (loan)	9	3
							Arsenal	264	86
Taylor Ross	5 10	11 12	D	14 1 77	Southend	Trainee	Arsenal	—	—
Wicks Matthew	6 2	13 05	D	8 9 78	Reading	Manchester U	Arsenal	—	—
Winterburn Nigel	5 8	11 04	D	11 12 63	Coventry	Local	Birmingham C	—	—
							Oxford U	—	—
							Wimbledon	165	8
							Arsenal	308	7
Woolsey Jeff§	5 11	12 03	D	8 11 77	Upminster	Trainee	Arsenal	—	—
Wright Ian	5 9	11 08	F	3 11 63	Woolwich	Greenwich Borough	Crystal Palace	225	89
							Arsenal	162	95

Trainees
Coffey, Christopher J; Donaldson, David; Goddard-Crawley, Richard; Hollingsworth, Orlando; Richardson, Lee; Smith, Ben P; Tello, Gregory; Thorogood, Marc T; Woolsey, Jeffrey A; Wynter, Jermaine.

Associated Schoolboys
Boateng, Daniel; Chilvers, Liam C; Cowell, Clayden; Halls, John; Harper, James A J; Jeanne, Leon; Johnson, Lee D; Noble, David J; Stack, Graham; Taylor, Stuart J; Weston, Rhys D.

Associated Schoolboys who have accepted the club's offer of a Traineeship/Contract
Black, Tom; Bowes, Terry D; Clark, Peter J; Day, Jamie R; Douglas, Andrew R; Gray, Julian R; Lincoln, Greg D; Livermore, David; Lopez, Rik; McLeod, Allan J; Perna, Ferdinando A; Riza, Omer; Vernazza, Paolo.

ASTON VILLA

Atkinson Dalian‡	6 0	13 10	F	21 3 68	Shrewsbury		Ipswich	60	18
							Sheffield W	38	10
							Real Sociedad	26	12
							Aston Villa	87	23
Bosnich Mark	6 1	13 07	G	13 1 72	Fairfield	Croatia Sydney	Manchester U	3	—
							Aston Villa	114	1
Brock Stuart	6 1	12 07	G	26 9 76	Birmingham	Trainee	Aston Villa	—	—
Browne Paul	6 1	12 00	D	17 2 75	Glasgow	Trainee	Aston Villa	2	—
Burchell Lee	5 7	10 06	M	12 11 76	Birmingham	Trainee	Aston Villa	—	—
Byfield Darren	5 11	11 04	F	29 9 76	Birmingham	Trainee	Aston Villa	—	—
Carr Franz	5 6	11 12	F	24 9 66	Preston	Apprentice	Blackburn R	—	—
							Nottingham F	131	17
							Sheffield W (loan)	12	—
							West Ham U (loan)	3	—
							Newcastle U	25	3
							Sheffield U	18	4
							Leicester C (loan)	13	1
							Aston Villa	3	—

Name	Ht	Wt	Pos	Born	Birthplace	Source	Clubs	Apps	Gls
Charles Gary	5 9	11 08	D	13 4 70	London	Trainee	Nottingham F	56	1
							Leicester C (loan)	8	—
							Derby Co	61	3
							Aston Villa	50	1
Davis Neil	5 8	11 00	F	15 8 73	Bloxwich	Redditch U	Aston Villa	2	—
Draper Mark	5 10	12 04	F	11 11 70	Long Eaton	Trainee	Notts Co	222	40
							Leicester C	39	5
							Aston Villa	36	2
Ehiogu Ugo	6 2	13 03	D	3 11 72	London	Trainee	WBA	2	—
							Aston Villa	104	4
Farrelly Gareth	6 0	12 07	M	28 8 75	Dublin	Home Farm	Aston Villa	5	—
							Rotherham U (loan)	10	2
Hendrie Lee	5 9	10 03	F	18 5 77	Birmingham	Trainee	Aston Villa	3	—
Hines Leslie	6 5	9 08	M	7 1 77	Germany	Trainee	Aston Villa	—	—
Impey Jamie*	6 3	11 11	M	28 7 77	Bournemouth	Trainee	Aston Villa	—	—
Joachim Julian	5 6	12 11	F	20 9 74	Peterborough	Trainee	Leicester C	99	25
							Aston Villa	11	1
Johnson Tommy	5 11	12 04	F	15 1 71	Newcastle	Trainee	Notts Co	118	47
							Derby Co	98	30
							Aston Villa	37	9
King Phil	5 8	11 09	D	28 12 67	Bristol	Apprentice	Exeter C	27	—
							Torquay U	24	3
							Swindon T	116	4
							Sheffield W	129	2
							Notts Co (loan)	6	—
							Aston Villa	16	—
							WBA (loan)	4	—
Kirby Alan	5 7	9 11	M	8 9 77	Waterford	Trainee	Aston Villa	—	—
Lee Alan	6 2	13 04	F	21 8 78	Galway	Trainee	Aston Villa	—	—
McGrath Paul	6 2	14 00	D	4 12 59	Ealing	St Patrick's Ath	Manchester U	163	12
							Aston Villa	253	9
Middleton Darren			M	28 12 78	Lichfield	Trainee	Aston Villa	—	—
Milosevic Savo	6 1	13 05	F	2 9 73	Bijelina		Partizan Belgrade	67	50
							Aston Villa	37	12
Mitchell Andrew*	6 0	12 00	D	12 9 76	Rotherham	Trainee	Aston Villa	—	—
Moore David*	6 0	14 00	M	23 11 76	Birmingham	Trainee	Aston Villa	—	—
Murray Scott	5 10	11 00	F	26 5 74	Aberdeen	Fraserburgh	Aston Villa	3	—
Oakes Michael	6 1	12 07	G	30 10 73	Northwich	Trainee	Aston Villa	—	—
							Scarborough (loan)	1	—
							Tranmere R (loan)	—	—
Petty Ben	6 0	12 06	D	22 3 77	Solihull	Trainee	Aston Villa	—	—
Rachel Adam	5 11	12 00	G	10 12 76	Birmingham	Trainee	Aston Villa	—	—
Saunders Dean‡	5 8	10 06	F	21 6 64	Swansea	Apprentice	Swansea C	49	12
							Cardiff C (loan)	4	—
							Brighton & HA	72	21
							Oxford U	59	22
							Derby Co	106	42
							Liverpool	42	11
							Aston Villa	112	37
Scimeca Riccardo	6 1	12 09	D	13 6 75	Leamington Spa	Trainee	Aston Villa	17	—
Southgate Gareth	6 0	12 08	M	3 9 70	Watford	Trainee	Crystal Palace	152	15
							Aston Villa	31	1
Staunton Steve	6 0	12 04	D	19 1 69	Drogheda	Dundalk	Liverpool	65	—
							Bradford C (loan)	8	—
							Aston Villa	151	13
Taylor Ian	6 1	12 00	M	4 6 68	Birmingham	Moor Green	Port Vale	83	28
							Sheffield W	14	1
							Aston Villa	47	4
Tiler Carl	6 4	12 10	D	11 2 70	Sheffield	Trainee	Barnsley	71	3
							Nottingham F	69	1
							Swindon T (loan)	2	—
							Aston Villa	1	—
Townsend Andy	5 11	12 07	M	27 7 63	Maidstone	Welling and Weymouth	Southampton	83	5
							Norwich C	71	8
							Chelsea	110	12
							Aston Villa	97	6
Walker Richard			M	8 11 77	Birmingham	Trainee	Aston Villa	—	—
Wright Alan	5 4	9 05	D	28 9 71	Ashton under Lyme	Trainee	Blackpool	98	—
							Blackburn R	74	1
							Aston Villa	46	2
Yorke Dwight	5 11	11 13	F	3 11 71	Tobago	Tobago	Aston Villa	163	44

Trainees
Burgess, Richard D; Collins, Lee D; Elias, Phillip; George, Matthew; Hadland, Guy W; Hazell, Reuben; Hickman, John A; Hughes, Robert D; Jaszczun, Antony J; Lescott, Aaron A; Miley, Jonathan H.

Associated Schoolboys
Brayley, Albert P; Britton, Jonathan A; Brown, Christopher; Bull, Nikki; Court, David J; Crowe, Michael W; Evans, Stephen G; Folds, Liam J; Ghent, Matthew I; Halliday, James S; Harding, David M; Jones, Mark A; McDonald, Marcus; Price, Michael; Reeves, Martin L; Ridgway, David J; Stock, Stephen A; Thornley, Stuart; Wickett, Neil R; Williams, Joseph S.

Associated Schoolboys who have accepted the club's offer of a Traineeship/Contract
Appleby, Mark; Blackwood, Michael; Meredith, Alex D; Reece, Dominic M A; Ridley, Martin J; Tongue, Philip; Vassell, Darius.

BARNET

Player				Pos	DOB	Birthplace	Source	Clubs	Apps	Gls
Adams Kieran§	5 10	11 06	M	20 10 77	St Ives	Trainee	Barnet	5	—
Brady Matthew§	6 0	10 04	M	27 10 77	London	Trainee	Barnet	3	—
Campbell Jamie	6 2	12 11	F	21 10 72	Birmingham	Trainee	Luton T	36	1
								Mansfield T (loan)	3	1
								Cambridge U (loan)	12	—
								Barnet	24	1
Codner Robert	5 11	13 01	M	23 1 65	Walthamstow	Barnet	Brighton & HA	266	39
								Reading	4	—
								Peterborough U	2	—
								Barnet	8	—
Cooper Mark§	6 4	14 00	F	5 4 67	Cambridge	Apprentice	Cambridge U	71	17
								Tottenham H	—	—
								Shrewsbury T	6	2
								Gillingham	49	11
								Leyton Orient	150	45
								Barnet	67	19
Devine Sean	6 0	13 00	F	6 9 72	Lewisham	Omonia	Barnet	35	19
Dunwell Richard	6 0	13 00	F	17 6 71	Islington	Collier Row	Barnet	13	1
Dyer Alex‡	6 0	13 04	M	14 11 65	West Ham	Watford	Blackpool	108	19
								Hull C	60	14
								Crystal Palace	17	2
								Charlton Ath	78	13
								Oxford U	76	6
								Lincoln C	1	—
								Barnet	35	2
Gale Shaun	6 1	11 10	D	8 10 69	Reading	Trainee	Portsmouth	3	—
								Barnet	71	3
Gallagher Kieran	5 8	10 03	M	23 12 76	Barnet	Trainee	Barnet	—	—
Hall Graeme‡	6 3	13 12	D	22 11 75	Stockton	Trainee	Arsenal	—	—
								Barnet	—	—
Hamlet Alan	6 0	11 03	D	30 9 77	Watford	Trainee	Barnet	3	—
Hodges Lee	6 0	12 01	F	4 9 73	Epping	Trainee	Tottenham H	4	—
								Plymouth Arg (loan)	7	2
								Wycombe W (loan)	4	—
								Barnet	74	21
Howarth Lee	6 3	13 08	D	3 1 68	Bolton	Chorley	Peterborough U	62	—
								Mansfield T	57	2
								Barnet	19	—
McDonald David	5 10	12 05	D	2 1 71	Dublin	Trainee	Tottenham H	2	—
								Gillingham (loan)	10	—
								Bradford C (loan)	7	—
								Reading (loan)	11	—
								Peterborough U	29	—
								Barnet	77	—
Mills Danny	5 11	11 06	M	13 2 75	Sidcup	Trainee	Charlton Ath	—	—
								Barnet	19	—
Moussaddik Chuck‡	6 0	13 00	G	23 2 70	Morocco	Wimbledon	Wycombe W	1	—
								Barnet	—	—
Pardew Alan	6 1	12 04	M	18 7 61	Wimbledon	Yeovil	Crystal Palace	128	8
								Charlton Ath	104	24
								Barnet	41	—
Perifimou Chris‡	5 8	11 07	M	27 11 75	Enfield	Trainee	Leyton Orient	4	—
								Barnet	—	—
Primus Linvoy	6 0	13 08	D	14 9 73	Stratford	Trainee	Charlton Ath	4	—
								Barnet	81	4
Robbins Terry‡	5 7	10 08	F	18 7 65	London	Welling U	Barnet	15	1
Scott Peter*	5 9	12 03	M	1 10 63	London	Apprentice	Fulham	277	27
								Bournemouth	10	—
								Barnet	78	2
Simpson Philip	5 9	11 12	M	18 10 69	London	Stevenage B	Barnet	24	1

Smith Gary‡	5 10	12 09	M	3 12 68	Harlow	Apprentice	Fulham	1	—
							Colchester U	11	—
						Enfield, Wycombe	Barnet	14	—
						W, Welling U			
Smith Paul‡	6 1	11 12	M	2 11 71	Lewisham	Horsham	Barnet	—	—
Taylor Maik	6 5	13 08	G	4 9 71	Germany	Farnborough T	Barnet	45	—
Thompson Neil§			D	30 4 78	Hackney	Trainee	Barnet	2	—
Tomlinson Micky	5 8	11 00	M	15 9 72	Lambeth	Trainee	Leyton Orient	14	1
							Barnet	63	3
Wilson Paul	5 9	12 00	D	29 6 64	London	Barking	Barnet	137	11

Trainees
Adams, Kieren C; Archer, Aaron A; Brady, Matthew J; Constantinou, Anthony; Cowen, Benjamin J; Evans, Richard W; Field, Marc I; Foster, Craig; Goodhind, Warren E; Hamlet, Alan G; Harvey, Michael J; McMenemy, Thomas; Morris, Nicky P; Pearce, Lee C; Thompson, Neil P.

BARNSLEY

Archdeacon Owen	5 7	10 09	M	4 3 66	Glasgow	Gourock U	Celtic	76	7
							Barnsley	233	23
Beckett Luke	5 11	11 02	F	25 11 76	Sheffield	Trainee	Barnsley	—	—
Bennett Troy	5 9	11 13	M	25 12 75	Barnsley	Trainee	Barnsley	2	—
Bishop Charlie	5 9	13 07	D	16 2 68	Nottingham	Stoke C	Watford	—	—
							Bury	114	6
							Barnsley	130	1
							Preston NE (loan)	4	—
							Burnley (loan)	9	—
Bochenski Simon	5 8	11 13	F	6 12 75	Worksop	Trainee	Barnsley	1	—
Brooke David*	5 8	11 02	M	23 11 75	Barnsley	Trainee	Barnsley	—	—
Bullock Martin	5 4	10 09	M	5 3 75	Derby	Eastwood T	Barnsley	70	1
Burton Mark‡	5 7	11 11	M	7 5 73	Barnsley	Trainee	Barnsley	5	—
Butler Lee*	6 1	14 04	G	30 5 66	Sheffield	Haworth Colliery	Lincoln C	30	—
							Aston Villa	8	—
							Hull C (loan)	4	—
							Barnsley	120	—
							Scunthorpe U (loan)	2	—
Clyde Darran	6 4	11 13	D	26 3 76	N Ireland	Trainee	Barnsley	—	—
Davis Steve	5 11	12 12	D	26 7 65	Birmingham	Stoke C	Crewe Alex	145	1
							Burnley	147	11
							Barnsley	83	7
De Zeeuw Arjan	6 2	12 12	D	16 4 70	Holland	Telstar	Barnsley	31	1
Eaden Nicky	5 8	11 09	D	12 12 72	Sheffield	Trainee	Barnsley	130	5
Fearon Dean	6 1	13 12	D	9 1 76	Barnsley	Schoolboy	Barnsley	—	—
Feeney Mark‡	5 7	11 00	M	26 7 74	Derry	Trainee	Barnsley	2	—
Fleming Gary	5 7	11 09	D	17 2 67	Derry	Apprentice	Nottingham F	74	—
							Manchester C	14	—
							Notts Co (loan)	3	—
							Barnsley	239	—
Gregory Andrew	5 8	10 09	M	8 10 76	Barnsley	Trainee	Barnsley	—	—
Hanby Robert*	5 8	11 09	D	24 12 74	Pontefract	Trainee	Barnsley	—	—
Harmer Russell*	5 10	11 09	M	29 10 76	Doncaster	Trainee	Barnsley	—	—
Hurst Glynn	5 10	11 06	D	17 1 76	Barnsley	Tottenham H	Barnsley	7	—
							Swansea C (loan)	2	1
Jackson Chris	5 9	11 06	F	16 1 76	Barnsley	Trainee	Barnsley	23	2
Jones Scott	5 10	11 06	D	1 5 75	Sheffield	Trainee	Barnsley	4	—
Liddell Andrew	5 6	10 09	F	28 6 73	Leeds	Trainee	Barnsley	126	25
Moses Adrian	5 8	12 08	D	4 5 75	Doncaster	School	Barnsley	28	1
O'Connell Brendan	5 9	12 01	F	12 11 66	London		Portsmouth	—	—
							Exeter C	81	19
							Burnley	64	17
							Huddersfield T (loan)	11	1
							Barnsley	240	35
Payton Andy	5 7	11 13	F	23 10 67	Burnley	Apprentice	Hull C	144	55
							Middlesbrough	19	3
							Celtic	36	15
							Barnsley	108	41
Perry Jonathan	6 0	11 11	D	22 11 76	Hamilton	Trainee	Barnsley	—	—
Prendergast Rory§	5 9	12 00	M	6 4 78	Pontefract	Rochdale	Barnsley	—	—

Redfearn Neil	5 8	12 00	M	20 6 65	Dewsbury	Nottingham F	Bolton W	35	1
							Lincoln C (loan)	10	1
							Lincoln C	90	12
							Doncaster R	46	14
							Crystal Palace	57	10
							Watford	24	3
							Oldham Ath	62	16
							Barnsley	212	44
Regis Dave	6 1	13 06	F	3 3 64	Paddington	Barnet	Notts Co	46	15
							Plymouth Arg	31	4
							Bournemouth (loan)	6	2
							Stoke C	63	15
							Birmingham C	6	2
							Southend U	38	9
							Barnsley	12	1
Rose Karl	5 10	11 00	M	12 10 78	Barnsley		Barnsley	—	—
Sheridan Darren	5 4	10 12	M	8 12 67	Manchester	Winsford	Barnsley	79	2
Shirtliff Peter	6 1	12 02	D	6 4 61	Barnsley	Apprentice	Sheffield W	188	4
							Charlton Ath	103	7
							Sheffield W	104	4
							Wolverhampton W	69	—
							Barnsley	32	—
Shotton Malcolm†	6 3	13 12	D	16 2 57	Newcastle	Apprentice	Leicester C	—	—
						Nuneaton	Oxford U	263	12
							Portsmouth	10	—
							Huddersfield T	16	1
							Barnsley	66	6
							Hull C	59	2
							Ayr U	73	3
							Barnsley	10	1
Sollitt Adam	6 0	10 09	G	22 6 77	Sheffield	Trainee	Barnsley	—	—
Ten-Heuvel Laurens	6 0	10 09	F	6 6 76	Amsterdam	Den Bosch	Barnsley	3	—
Van der Velden Carel	5 9	13 00	M	3 8 72	Arnhem	Den Bosch	Barnsley	7	—
Watson David	5 11	12 03	G	10 11 73	Barnsley	Trainee	Barnsley	96	—
Wilson Danny	5 6	11 00	M	1 1 60	Wigan	Wigan Ath	Bury	90	8
							Chesterfield	100	13
							Nottingham F	10	1
							Scunthorpe U (loan)	6	3
							Brighton & HA	135	33
							Luton T	110	24
							Sheffield W	98	11
							Barnsley	77	2

Trainees
Bagshaw, Paul J; Beckett, Duane L; Clayton, Steven; Clyde, Glynn N; Coleano, Rudi A; Harris, Christopher; Hayes, Shaun A; Hulson, Shane E; Hume, Mark A; Jones, Dean S; McClare, Sean P; Morgan, Christopher P; Prendergast, Rory; Shaw, Ian; Shenton, Daniel R; Ward, Kevin N; Webster, Stephen.

Non-Contract
Shotton, Malcolm.

Associated Schoolboys
Barraclough, Carl; Bird, Martin P; Cooper, Ian; Crossfield, Richard; Dixon, Lee; Donoghue, Matthew J; Foulstone, Thomas N; Goodyear, Craig; Greensmith, Adam A; Heckingbottom, Marc; Horbury, Russell; Jackson, Paul S; Kirby, Jonathan; Lee, Robin; Pressley, Mark; Rhodes, Gavin I; Rogers, Adrian A; Sidebottom, Frazer; Taylor, David J; Toone, Leigh S; Wilkinson, Craig; Winter, Damian.

BIRMINGHAM CITY

Barber Fred‡	5 10	12 00	G	26 8 63	Ferryhill	Apprentice	Darlington	135	—
							Everton	—	—
							Walsall	153	—
							Peterborough U (loan)	6	—
							Chester (loan)	8	—
							Blackpool (loan)	2	—
							Peterborough U	68	—
							Colchester U (loan)	10	—
							Chesterfield (loan)	—	—
							Luton T	—	—
							Ipswich T (loan)	1	—
							Blackpool (loan)	1	—
							Birmingham C	1	—
Barnes Paul	5 10	12 00	F	16 11 67	Leicester	Apprentice	Notts Co	53	14
							Stoke C	24	3
							Chesterfield (loan)	1	—
							York C	148	76
							Birmingham C	15	7
Barnes Steve	5 4	10 05	M	5 1 76	Harrow	Welling U	Birmingham C	3	—

Name	Ht	Wt	Pos	Date	Birthplace	From	Clubs	Apps	Gls
Barnett Dave	6 0	12 00	D	16 4 67	London	Windsor & Eton	Colchester U	20	—
							WBA	—	—
							Walsall	5	—
						Kidderminster H	Barnet	59	3
							Birmingham C	40	—
Bass Jonathan	6 0	12 02	D	1 7 76	Weston Super Mare	Trainee	Birmingham C	5	—
Bennett Ian	6 0	12 00	G	10 10 71	Worksop	Newcastle U	Peterborough U	72	—
							Birmingham C	92	—
Black Simon‡	6 1	12 00	F	9 11 75	Marston Green	Trainee	Birmingham C	2	—
Bloxham Robert‡	5 7	10 12	F	9 10 76	Solihull		Birmingham C	—	—
Bowen Jason	5 6	8 10	M	24 8 72	Merthyr	Trainee	Swansea C	124	26
							Birmingham C	23	4
Breen Gary	6 2	11 12	D	12 12 73	London	Charlton Ath	Maidstone U	19	—
							Gillingham	51	—
							Peterborough U	69	1
							Birmingham C	18	1
Bunch James	5 9	11 05	D	5 12 76	Sandwell	Trainee	Birmingham C	—	—
Castle Steve	5 10	12 07	M	17 5 66	Barkingside	Apprentice	Orient	243	55
							Plymouth Arg	101	35
							Birmingham C	15	1
							Gillingham (loan)	6	1
Challinor Paul‡	6 1	12 02	D	6 4 76	Newcastle under Lyme	Trainee	Birmingham C	—	—
Cooper Gary‡	5 8	11 00	D	20 11 65	Edgware	Fisher Ath	QPR	1	—
							Brentford (loan)	10	—
							Torquay U	—	—
							Maidstone U	60	7
							Peterborough U	88	10
							Birmingham C	62	2
Cornforth John	6 1	12 08	M	7 10 67	Whitley Bay	Apprentice	Sunderland	32	2
							Doncaster R (loan)	7	3
							Shrewsbury T (loan)	3	—
							Lincoln C (loan)	9	1
							Swansea C	149	16
							Birmingham C	8	—
Devlin Paul	5 8	11 05	F	14 4 72	Birmingham	Stafford R	Notts Co	141	25
							Birmingham C	16	7
Doherty Neil	5 8	10 09	M	21 2 69	Barrow	Trainee	Watford	—	—
						Barrow	Birmingham C	23	2
							Northampton T (loan)	9	1
Dominguez Jose‡	5 3	10 00	F	16 2 74	Lisbon	Benfica	Birmingham C	35	3
Donowa Lou	5 9	11 00	F	24 9 64	Ipswich	Apprentice	Norwich C	62	11
							Stoke C (loan)	4	1
						Coruna, Willem II	Ipswich T	23	1
							Bristol C	24	3
							Birmingham C	112	18
							Crystal Palace (loan)	—	—
							Burnley (loan)	4	—
							Shrewsbury T (loan)	4	—
Edwards Andy	6 2	12 00	D	17 9 71	Epping	Trainee	Southend U	147	5
							Birmingham C	37	1
Finnan Steve	5 9	10 09	M	20 4 76	Chelmsford	Welling U	Birmingham C	12	1
							Notts Co (loan)	17	2
Forsyth Richard	5 10	12 04	M	3 10 70	Dudley	Kidderminster H	Birmingham C	26	2
Frain John	5 7	11 00	M	8 10 68	Birmingham	Apprentice	Birmingham C	273	23
Francis Kevin	6 7	15 00	F	6 12 67	Moseley	Mile Oak R	Derby Co	10	—
							Stockport Co	152	88
							Birmingham C	34	11
Grainger Martin	5 10	11 07	D	23 8 72	Enfield	Trainee	Colchester U	46	7
							Brentford	101	12
							Birmingham C	8	—
Griemink Bart	6 4	15 04	G	29 3 72	Holland	WKE	Birmingham C	20	—
Hatton Paul§			M	2 11 78	Kidderminster	Trainee	Birmingham C	—	—
Hiles Paul*	6 0	11 06	D	27 9 76	Bristol	Trainee	Birmingham C	—	—
Howell David‡	6 0	12 00	D	10 10 58	London	Enfield	Barnet	57	3
							Southend U	6	—
							Birmingham C	2	—
Hughes Lee‡			M	19 6 77	Walsall	Trainee	Birmingham C	—	—
Hunt Jonathan	5 10	11 00	M	2 11 71	London	Slough T	Barnet	33	—
							Southend U	49	6
							Birmingham C	65	16
Johnson Michael	5 10	11 12	D	7 7 73	Nottingham	Trainee	Notts Co	107	—
							Birmingham C	33	—

Name	Ht	Wt	Pos	Date/Born	Birthplace	Source	Club	Apps	Gls
Jones Ian‡	5 7	10 02	M	25 10 76	Birmingham	Trainee	Birmingham C	—	—
Legg Andy	5 8	10 07	M	28 7 66	Neath	Briton Ferry	Swansea C	163	29
							Notts Co	89	9
							Birmingham C	12	1
Lowe Kenny‡	6 1	11 13	M	6 11 64	Sedgefield	Apprentice	Hartlepool U	54	3
						Barrow	Scarborough	4	—
						Barrow	Barnet	72	5
							Stoke C	9	—
							Birmingham C	21	3
							Carlisle U (loan)	2	—
							Hartlepool U (loan)	13	3
Martin Jae	5 10	12 04	F	5 2 76	London	Trainee	Southend U	8	—
							Leyton Orient (loan)	4	—
							Birmingham C	7	—
Muir Ian	5 8	11 00	F	5 5 63	Coventry	Apprentice	QPR	2	2
							Burnley (loan)	2	1
							Birmingham C	1	—
							Brighton & HA	4	—
							Swindon T (loan)	2	—
							Tranmere R	314	141
							Birmingham C	1	—
							Darlington (loan)	4	1
Otto Ricky	5 10	11 00	M	9 11 67	Hackney	Dartford	Leyton Orient	56	13
							Southend U	64	17
							Birmingham C	42	6
Peschisolido Paul	5 7	10 12	F	25 5 71	Canada	Toronto Blizzard	Birmingham C	43	16
							Stoke C	66	19
							Birmingham C	9	1
Poole Gary	6 0	11 00	D	11 9 67	Stratford	Arsenal	Tottenham H	—	—
							Cambridge U	43	—
						Barnet	Barnet	40	2
							Plymouth Arg	39	5
							Southend U	44	2
							Birmingham C	62	—
Price Ryan‡	6 4	14 00	G	13 3 70	Stafford	Stafford R	Birmingham C	—	—
Rea Simon	6 1	13 00	D	20 9 76	Coventry	Trainee	Birmingham C	1	—
Robinson Steve	5 9	11 03	M	17 1 75	Nottingham	Trainee	Birmingham C	6	—
							Peterborough U (loan)	5	—
Round Steven‡	5 9	11 00	M	8 10 76	Wolverhampton	Trainee	Birmingham C	—	—
Rushfeldt Sigurd‡	6 3	13 00	F	11 12 72	Tromso	Tromso	Birmingham C	7	—
Sahlin Dan‡			F	18 4 67	Falun	Hammarby	Birmingham C	1	—
Shearer Peter*	6 0	11 00	F	4 2 67	Birmingham	Apprentice	Birmingham C	4	—
							Rochdale	1	—
						Cheltenham T	Bournemouth	85	10
							Birmingham C	25	7
Tait Paul	6 1	10 00	M	31 1 71	Sutton	Trainee	Birmingham C	144	14
							Millwall (loan)	—	—
Thomas Jason‡	5 8	10 12	F	22 2 77	Swansea		Birmingham C	—	—
Webb Matthew	5 8	9 12	M	24 9 76	Bristol	Trainee	Birmingham C	1	—
Weston Richard*	5 11	11 02	G	2 3 77	Bristol	Trainee	Birmingham C	—	—

Trainees
Bryan, Simon M; Burden, Neil S; Crockett, Daniel J; Dandy, Richard; Dyer, Wayne; Dyson, James G; Francis, Delton M O; Hatton, Paul M; Hinton, Craig; Homer, Paul L; Lutz, Steven G; McKenzie, Christy G; Sandland, Paul N; Tilley, Dean J; Unitt, David T; White, Paul; Worrall, Dean J.

Associated Schoolboys
Burns, Robert J; Cozens, Leon; Dunn, Matthew J; Dutfield, Luke P; Feely, Michael D; Hawkins, Peter L; Johnson, Andrew; Lanns, Jason M; McLinden, Andrew J; Sedgemore, Jacob O; Sumnall, Keith T J.

Associated Schoolboys who have accepted the club's offer of a Traineeship/Contract
Butler, Stuart; Dukes, Lee; Powell, Jason D.

BLACKBURN ROVERS

Name	Ht	Wt	Pos	Date/Born	Birthplace	Source	Club	Apps	Gls
Beattie James	6 1	12 00	F	27 2 78	Lancaster	Trainee	Blackburn R	—	—
Benson Mark	5 5	10 05	D	7 8 78	Dublin	Trainee	Blackburn R	—	—
Berg Henning	6 0	12 04	D	1 9 68	Eidsvoll	Lillestrom	Blackburn R	123	2
Bohinen Lars	6 1	12 01	M	8 9 69	Vadso		Valerengen	33	5
							Viking	10	—
							Young Boys	58	6
							Nottingham F	64	7
							Blackburn R	19	4
Broomes Marlon	6 0	12 12	D	28 11 77	Birmingham	Trainee	Blackburn R	—	—
Cassin Graham	5 10	11 07	F	24 3 78	Dublin	Belvedere	Blackburn R	—	—
Chisholm Craig	5 11	10 08	M	21 9 77	Glasgow	Trainee	Blackburn R	—	—

Coleman Chris	6 2	14 03	D	10 6 70	Swansea	Apprentice	Swansea C	160	2
							Crystal Palace	154	13
							Blackburn R	20	—
Coughlan Graham	6 2	13 04	D	18 11 74	Dublin	Bray Wanderers	Blackburn R	—	—
Croft Gary	5 9	11 08	D	17 2 74	Stafford	Trainee	Grimsby T	149	3
							Blackburn R	—	—
Duff Damien	5 10	9 07	F	2 3 79	Ballyboden		Blackburn R	—	—
Fenton Graham	5 10	12 10	F	22 5 74	Wallsend	Trainee	Aston Villa	32	3
							WBA (loan)	7	3
							Blackburn R	14	6
Flitcroft Garry	6 0	12 09	M	6 11 72	Bolton	Trainee	Manchester C	115	13
							Bury (loan)	12	—
							Blackburn R	3	—
Flowers Tim	6 3	14 04	G	3 2 67	Kenilworth	Apprentice	Wolverhampton W	63	—
							Southampton (loan)	—	—
							Southampton	192	—
							Swindon T (loan)	2	—
							Swindon T (loan)	5	—
							Blackburn R	105	—
Gallacher Kevin	5 8	11 03	F	23 11 66	Clydebank	Duntocher BC	Dundee U	131	27
							Coventry C	100	28
							Blackburn R	56	15
Gill Wayne	5 10	11 04	M	28 11 75	Chorley	Trainee	Blackburn R	—	—
Given Shay	6 1	12 10	G	20 4 76	Lifford	Celtic	Blackburn R	—	—
							Swindon T (loan)	—	—
							Swindon T (loan)	5	—
							Sunderland (loan)	17	—
Goodall Danny*	5 9	10 09	D	3 9 75	Bury	Trainee	Blackburn R	—	—
Gudmundsson Niklas			F	29 2 72	Sweden	Halmstad	Blackburn R	4	—
Harford Paul	6 4	13 12	F	21 10 74	Kent	Trainee	Blackburn R	—	—
							Wigan Ath (loan)	3	—
							Shrewsbury T (loan)	6	—
Hendry Colin	6 1	12 07	D	7 12 65	Keith	Islavale	Dundee	41	2
							Blackburn R	102	22
							Manchester C	63	5
							Blackburn R	165	10
Hitchen Steve	5 10	11 04	D	28 11 76	Salford	Trainee	Blackburn R	—	—
Holmes Matt	5 7	11 00	F	1 8 69	Luton	Trainee	Bournemouth	114	8
							Cardiff C (loan)	1	—
							West Ham U	76	4
							Blackburn R	9	1
Holt Michael*	5 9	10 09	F	28 7 77	Burnley	Trainee	Blackburn R	—	—
Hope Richard	6 2	12 06	D	22 6 78	Stockton	Trainee	Blackburn R	—	—
Johnson Damien	5 9	10 00	M	18 11 78	Blackburn	Trainee	Blackburn R	—	—
Kenna Jeff	5 11	12 03	D	28 8 70	Dublin	Trainee	Southampton	114	4
							Blackburn R	41	1
Le Saux Graeme	5 10	12 02	D	17 10 68	Jersey	St Pauls	Chelsea	90	8
							Blackburn R	103	6
Malone Chris	5 11	10 02	F	29 12 75	Drogheda		Blackburn R	—	—
Marker Nicky	6 0	13 00	D	3 5 65	Exeter	Apprentice	Exeter C	202	3
							Plymouth Arg	202	13
							Blackburn R	47	1
McCrone Chris	6 1	12 07	G	5 2 77	Preston	Trainee	Blackburn R	—	—
McKinlay Billy	5 8	11 04	M	22 4 69	Glasgow	Hamilton T	Dundee U	222	23
							Blackburn R	19	2
Mimms Bobby*	6 4	14 04	G	12 10 63	York	Halifax T	Rotherham U	83	—
							Everton	29	—
							Notts Co (loan)	2	—
							Sunderland (loan)	4	—
							Blackburn R (loan)	6	—
							Manchester C (loan)	3	—
							Tottenham H	37	—
							Aberdeen (loan)	6	—
							Blackburn R	128	—
Morgan Thomas	5 8	10 08	M	30 3 77	Dublin	Belvedere	Blackburn R	—	—
Newell Mike	6 2	12 00	F	27 1 65	Liverpool	Liverpool	Crewe Alex	3	—
							Wigan Ath	72	25
							Luton T	63	18
							Leicester C	81	21
							Everton	68	15
							Blackburn R	130	28
Pearce Ian	6 4	14 04	D	7 5 74	Bury St Edmunds	Schoolboy	Chelsea	4	—
							Blackburn R	45	2

Reed Adam	6 0	11 00	D	18 2 75	Bishop Auckland	Trainee	Darlington	52	1
							Blackburn R	—	—
Ripley Stuart	6 0	13 00	F	20 11 67	Middlesbrough	Apprentice	Middlesbrough	249	26
							Bolton W (loan)	5	1
							Blackburn R	145	11
Shearer Alan	5 11	12 06	F	13 8 70	Newcastle	Trainee	Southampton	118	23
							Blackburn R	138	112
Sherwood Tim	6 1	12 09	M	2 2 69	St Albans	Trainee	Watford	32	2
							Norwich C	71	10
							Blackburn R	159	14
Staton Luke	5 7	9 10	M	10 3 79	Doncaster	Trainee	Blackburn R	—	—
Sutton Chris	6 3	13 07	F	10 3 73	Nottingham	Trainee	Norwich C	102	35
							Blackburn R	53	15
Tallon Gary‡	5 10	11 12	F	5 9 73	Drogheda	Trainee	Blackburn R	—	—
Warhurst Paul	6 0	11 04	D	26 9 69	Stockport	Trainee	Manchester C	—	—
							Oldham Ath	67	2
							Sheffield W	66	6
							Blackburn R	46	2
Whealing Anthony	5 9	10 02	D	3 9 76	Manchester	Trainee	Blackburn R	—	—
Wilcox Jason	6 0	11 00	F	15 7 71	Bolton	Trainee	Blackburn R	160	22
Worrell David	5 10	11 08	D	12 1 78	Dublin	Trainee	Blackburn R	—	—

Trainees
Brewer, Benjamin R; Fitzpatrick, Lee G; Hewitt, Scott P; McAvoy, Andrew D; Obeng, Junior L; Owler, Lee R; Rimmer, Martin J; Ryan, Ciaran; Taylor, Philip M; Thomas, James A; Trudgill, Paul C; Watkins, Steven L; Williams, Anthony S.

Associated Schoolboys
Baldacchino, Ryan L; Dunning, Darren; Dunning, Richard; Hardy, Lee; Hawe, Steven J; Howson, Stuart L; Irving, Michael J; Topley, Jonathan W.

Associated Schoolboys who have accepted the club's offer of a Traineeship/Contract
Berry, Adam; Connolly, Patrick J; Dunn, David J I; Featherstone, James L; Harding, John M; Lomax, Michael J; Pierce, Iddon; Richards, Ian; Richardson, Leam N; Scates, Garth; Stewart, Gareth J; Taylor, Martin; Whittle, Christopher T.

BLACKPOOL

Allardyce Craig	6 3	13 07	D	9 6 75	Bolton	Trainee	Preston NE	1	—
							Blackpool	1	—
Banks Steven	6 0	13 02	G	9 2 72	Hillingdon	Trainee	West Ham U	—	—
							Gillingham	67	—
							Blackpool	24	—
Barlow Andy	5 9	11 01	D	24 11 65	Oldham		Oldham Ath	261	5
							Bradford C (loan)	2	—
							Blackpool	34	1
Beech Chris	5 10	11 00	M	16 9 74	Blackpool	Trainee	Blackpool	82	4
Bonner Mark	5 10	11 00	M	7 6 74	Ormskirk	Trainee	Blackpool	117	10
Bradshaw Darren	5 11	11 04	M	19 3 67	Sheffield	Matlock T	Chesterfield	18	—
							York C	59	3
							Newcastle U	38	—
							Peterborough U	73	1
							Plymouth Arg (loan)	6	1
							Blackpool	51	1
Brown Phil*	5 11	11 08	D	30 5 59	South Shields	Local	Hartlepool U	217	8
							Halifax T	135	19
							Bolton W	256	14
							Blackpool	44	5
Brown Richard‡	5 10	11 02	D	13 1 67	Nottingham	Ilkeston T	Sheffield W	—	—
						Kettering T	Blackburn R	28	—
							Maidstone U (loan)	3	—
							Stockport Co	1	—
							Blackpool	3	—
Bryan Marvin	6 0	12 02	F	2 8 75	Paddington	Trainee	QPR	—	—
							Doncaster R (loan)	5	1
							Blackpool	46	1
Burke David‡	5 10	11 06	D	6 8 60	Liverpool	Apprentice	Bolton W	69	1
							Huddersfield T	189	3
							Crystal Palace	81	—
							Bolton W	106	—
							Blackpool	23	—
Capleton Mel*	5 11	12 00	G	24 10 73	London	Trainee	Southend U	—	—
							Blackpool	11	—
Carroll David*			M	25 9 76	Blackpool	Trainee	Blackpool	—	—
Craggs Graham*	6 1	13 06	D	5 6 76	Ashington	Trainee	Blackpool	—	—
Darton Scott	5 11	11 02	D	27 3 75	Ipswich	Trainee	WBA	15	—
							Blackpool	27	—

Name							Club	Apps	Goals
Ellis Tony	5 11	11 00	F	20 10 64	Salford	Northwich Vic	Oldham Ath	8	—
							Preston NE	86	26
							Stoke C	77	19
							Preston NE	72	48
							Blackpool	83	31
Gouck Andy	5 9	11 02	M	8 6 72	Blackpool	Trainee	Blackpool	148	12
Holden Rick*	5 11	12 07	F	9 9 64	Skipton		Burnley	1	—
							Halifax T	67	12
							Watford	42	8
							Oldham Ath	129	19
							Manchester C	50	3
							Oldham Ath	60	9
							Blackpool	22	2
Hooks John	5 8	11 07	D	10 2 77	Armagh	Southampton	Blackpool	—	—
Horner Philip*	6 1	12 07	F	10 11 66	Leeds	Lincoln C	Leicester C	10	—
							Rotherham U (loan)	4	—
							Halifax T	72	4
							Blackpool	187	22
Jones Stephen*			M	25 10 76	Derry		Blackpool	—	—
Linighan David	6 2	12 06	D	9 1 65	Hartlepool	Local	Hartlepool U	91	5
							Leeds U (loan)	—	—
							Derby Co	—	—
							Shrewsbury T	65	1
							Ipswich T	277	12
							Blackpool	29	4
Lydiate Jason	5 11	12 04	D	29 10 71	Manchester	Trainee	Manchester U	—	—
							Bolton W	30	—
							Blackpool	43	1
Martin Lee	6 0	13 00	G	9 9 68	Huddersfield	Trainee	Huddersfield T	54	—
							Blackpool	98	—
							Bradford C (loan)	—	—
Mellon Michael	5 9	11 03	M	18 3 72	Paisley	Trainee	Bristol C	35	1
							WBA	45	6
							Blackpool	71	10
Mitchell Neil	5 6	10 00	M	7 11 74	Lytham	Trainee	Blackpool	67	8
							Rochdale (loan)	4	—
Morrison Andy	5 11	13 10	D	30 7 70	Inverness	Trainee	Plymouth Arg	113	6
							Blackburn R	5	—
							Blackpool	47	3
Parkinson Stuart*	5 8	10 04	F	18 2 76	Blackpool	Trainee	Blackpool	1	—
Pascoe Colin	5 10	12 00	F	9 4 65	Bridgend	Apprentice	Swansea C	174	39
							Sunderland	126	22
							Swansea C (loan)	15	4
							Swansea C	81	11
							Blackpool	1	—
Philpott Lee	5 9	11 08	F	21 2 70	Hackney	Trainee	Peterborough U	4	—
							Cambridge U	134	17
							Leicester C	75	3
							Blackpool	10	—
Preece Andy	6 1	12 00	M	27 3 67	Evesham	Evesham	Northampton T	1	—
						Worcester C	Wrexham	51	7
							Stockport Co	97	42
							Crystal Palace	20	4
							Blackpool	41	14
Quinn James	6 1	12 10	F	15 12 74	Coventry	Trainee	Birmingham C	4	—
							Blackpool	99	20
							Stockport Co (loan)	1	—
Sheppard James‡	5 8	10 10	M	18 9 75	Preston	Trainee	Blackpool	—	—
Symons Paul	5 11	12 00	F	20 4 76	North Shields	Trainee	Blackpool	1	—
Thorpe Lee	6 0	11 06	F	14 12 75	Wolverhampton	Trainee	Blackpool	3	—
Ward Robert*	5 8	11 04	D	16 3 77	Blackpool	Trainee	Blackpool	—	—
Watson Andy	5 9	11 02	D	1 4 67	Huddersfield	Harrogate T	Halifax T	83	15
							Swansea C	14	1
							Carlisle U	56	22
							Blackpool	115	43

Trainees
Ashcroft, Paul R; Best, Christopher J; Carden, Paul; Cross, James R; Gabriel, Nathan K; Greer, Matthew J; Haddow, Paul A; Hall, Gary A; Hall, Lee D; Heighton, Henry P; Howard, Mark D; Johnstone, Paul S; Mairs, Paul S A; Smith, Adam T; Vickers, Ian.

Associated Schoolboys
Bridge, Simon; Carlisle, Clark J; Dickinson, Ian J; Lazenby, Mark; Longworth, Steven P; McCarthy, John; Munday, Jason; Nicholls, Thomas; Nowland, Adam C; Pepper, Carl; Porter, Benjamin T; Pygrum, Adam K; Riley, Neil; Robinson, Philip D; Ryan, Paul; Shockledge, Lee S; Sidebotham, Paul; Thompson, Philip.

BOLTON WANDERERS

Name	Ht	Wt	Pos	Birthdate	Birthplace	Signed from	Club	Apps	Gls
Bergsson Gudni	6 1	12 03	D	21 7 65	Reykjavik	Valur	Tottenham H	71	2
							Bolton W	42	4
Blake Nathan	5 11	13 12	F	27 1 72	Cardiff	Chelsea	Cardiff C	131	35
							Sheffield U	69	34
							Bolton W	18	1
Branagan Keith	6 0	13 02	G	10 7 66	Fulham		Cambridge U	110	—
							Millwall	46	—
							Brentford (loan)	2	—
							Gillingham (loan)	1	—
							Fulham (loan)	—	—
							Bolton W	130	—
Burnett Wayne	5 11	12 01	M	4 9 71	London	Trainee	Leyton Orient	40	—
							Blackburn R	—	—
							Plymouth Arg	70	3
							Bolton W	1	—
Coleman Simon	6 0	10 08	D	13 6 68	Worksop		Mansfield T	96	7
							Middlesbrough	55	2
							Derby Co	70	2
							Sheffield W	16	1
							Bolton W	34	5
Curcic Sasa	5 9	10 07	M	14 2 72	Belgrade	Partizan Belgrade	Bolton W	28	4
Davison Aidan	6 1	13 12	G	11 5 68	Sedgefield	Billingham Syn	Notts Co	1	—
							Leyton Orient (loan)	—	—
							Bury	—	—
							Chester C (loan)	—	—
							Blackpool (loan)	—	—
							Millwall	34	—
							Bolton W	37	—
De Freitas Fabian	6 1	12 09	F	28 7 72	Paramaribo	Volendam	Bolton W	40	7
Fairclough Chris	5 11	11 02	D	12 4 64	Nottingham	Apprentice	Nottingham F	107	1
							Tottenham H	60	5
							Leeds U	193	21
							Bolton W	33	—
Feeney Gareth			M	5 12 78	Manchester	Trainee	Bolton W	—	—
Green Scott	5 10	12 05	M	15 1 70	Walsall	Trainee	Derby Co	—	—
							Bolton W	208	24
Hallows Marcus*	6 1	12 09	M	7 7 75	Bolton	Leigh RMI	Bolton W	—	—
Lee David	5 7	11 00	M	5 11 67	Whitefield	Blackburn Schools	Bury	208	35
							Southampton	20	—
							Bolton W	130	15
McAnespie Steve	5 9	10 07	D	1 2 72	Kilmarnock	Vasterhauringe	Raith R	40	—
							Bolton W	9	—
McGinlay John	5 9	11 04	F	8 4 64	Inverness	Elgin C	Shrewsbury T	60	27
							Bury	25	9
							Millwall	34	10
							Bolton W	142	63
McKay Andrew‡	5 10	11 10	D	16 1 75	Bolton	Trainee	Bolton W	—	—
Paatelainen Mixu	6 0	13 11	F	3 2 67	Helsinki	Valkeakosken Haka	Dundee U	133	33
							Aberdeen	75	23
							Bolton W	59	13
Phillips Jimmy	6 0	12 07	D	8 2 66	Bolton	Apprentice	Bolton W	108	2
							Rangers	25	
							Oxford U	79	8
							Middlesbrough	139	6
							Bolton W	125	1
Rhodes Andy	6 1	13 06	G	23 8 64	Doncaster	Apprentice	Barnsley	36	—
							Doncaster R	106	—
							Oldham Ath	69	—
							Dunfermline Ath	79	—
							St Johnstone	107	—
							Bolton W (loan)	—	—
Sellars Scott	5 7	9 10	M	27 11 65	Sheffield	Apprentice	Leeds U	76	12
							Blackburn R	202	35
							Leeds U	7	—
							Newcastle U	61	5
							Bolton W	22	3
Small Bryan	5 9	11 09	D	15 11 71	Birmingham	Trainee	Aston Villa	36	—
							Birmingham C (loan)	3	—
							Bolton W	1	—
Spooner Nicky	5 10	11 09	D	5 6 71	Manchester	Trainee	Bolton W	23	2
Strong Greg	6 2	11 12	D	5 9 75	Bolton	Trainee	Wigan Ath	35	3
							Bolton W	1	—
Stubbs Alan	6 2	13 10	D	6 10 71	Kirkby	Trainee	Bolton W	202	9

Taggart Gerry	6 1	12 03	D	18 10 70	Belfast	Trainee	Manchester C	12	1
							Barnsley	212	16
							Bolton W	11	1
Taylor Scott	5 10	11 04	F	5 5 76	Chertsey	Staines	Millwall	28	—
							Bolton W	1	—
Thompson Alan	6 0	12 08	M	22 12 73	Newcastle	Trainee	Newcastle U	16	—
							Bolton W	90	14
Todd Andy	5 10	10 11	D	21 9 74	Derby	Trainee	Middlesbrough	8	—
							Swindon T (loan)	13	—
							Bolton W	12	2
Ward Gavin	6 3	14 05	G	30 6 70	Sutton Coldfield	Aston Villa	Shrewsbury T	—	—
							WBA	—	—
							Cardiff C	59	—
							Leicester C	38	—
							Bradford C	36	—
							Bolton W	5	—
Whitehead Stuart	5 11	12 04	M	17 7 76	Bromsgrove	Bromsgrove R	Bolton W	—	—
Whittaker Stuart	5 7	9 03	M	2 1 75	Liverpool	Liverpool	Bolton W	3	—

Trainees
Aljofree, Hasney; Bowman, Matthew S; Doherty, Martin A; Glennon, Matthew; Gregory, Christopher; Haley, Craig; Hallat, Christopher J; Marsh, Neil D; Marston, Neil J; Martin, Shaun A; McLeod, James; Minchella, Marco; Potter, Lee; Proctor, Daniel R; Quinn, Stephen.

Associated Schoolboys
Bell, Phillip S; Buggie, Lee D; Challoner, Michael J; Chiswala, Tendai J; Crompton, Peter; Croxton, Liam T; Darby, Philip; Derbyshire, Robert W; Entwistle, Adam; Fox, Matthew J; Omalley, Carl; Parkinson, Neil F; Smith, Sean; Spencer, Steven L; Tagoe, Darrel J; Willett, Ryan T; Wilson, Scott A.

Associated Schoolboys who have accepted the club's offer of a Traineeship/Contract
Fagan, Steven J; Morrison, Peter A; Pryers, Lee M.

BOURNEMOUTH

Andrews Ian	6 2	14 01	G	1 12 64	Nottingham	Apprentice	Leicester C	126	—
							Swindon T (loan)	1	—
							Celtic	5	—
							Leeds U (loan)	1	—
							Southampton	10	—
							Bournemouth	64	—
Bailey John	5 8	10 02	M	6 5 69	London	Enfield	Bournemouth	44	4
Beardsmore Russell	5 8	10 04	M	28 9 68	Wigan	Apprentice	Manchester U	56	4
							Blackburn R (loan)	2	—
							Bournemouth	111	3
Brissett Jason	5 9	12 00	M	7 9 74	Redbridge	Arsenal	Peterborough U	35	—
							Bournemouth	68	3
Coll Owen	6 0	11 07	D	9 4 76	Donegal	Amateur	Tottenham H	—	—
							Bournemouth	8	—
Cotterill Steve‡	6 1	12 02	F	20 7 64	Cheltenham	Burton Alb	Wimbledon	17	6
							Brighton & HA (loan)	11	4
							Bournemouth	45	15
Cox Ian	6 0	12 00	M	25 3 71	Croydon	Carshalton Ath	Crystal Palace	15	—
							Bournemouth	8	—
Dean Michael§			D	9 3 78	Weymouth	Trainee	Bournemouth	5	—
Fletcher Steve	6 2	14 09	F	26 7 72	Hartlepool	Trainee	Hartlepool U	32	4
							Bournemouth	114	17
Glass Jimmy	6 1	13 04	G	1 8 73	Epsom	Trainee	Crystal Palace	—	—
							Portsmouth (loan)	3	—
							Bournemouth	13	—
Holland Matthew	5 9	11 12	M	11 4 74	Bury	Trainee	West Ham U	—	—
							Bournemouth	59	11
Howe Eddie§			D	29 11 77	Amersham	Trainee	Bournemouth	5	—
Kearn Stewart‡			G	1 12 75	Salisbury		Sheffield W	—	—
							Bournemouth	—	—
McElhatton Mike	6 1	12 08	D	16 4 75	Co. Kerry	Trainee	Bournemouth	42	2
Mean Scott	5 11	13 08	M	13 12 73	Crawley	Trainee	Bournemouth	74	8
Mitchell Paul*	5 10	12 00	D	20 10 71	Bournemouth	Trainee	Bournemouth	12	—
							West Ham U	1	—
							Bournemouth	4	—
Morris Mark	6 1	14 02	D	26 9 62	Morden	Apprentice	Wimbledon	168	9
							Aldershot (loan)	14	—
							Watford	41	1
							Sheffield U	56	3
							Bournemouth	193	8
Murray Robert	5 11	12 07	F	31 10 74	Hammersmith	Trainee	Bournemouth	111	10

Name	Ht	Wt	Pos	Date	Birthplace	Source	Club	Apps	Gls
O'Neill Jon	5 11	12 00	F	2 1 74	Glasgow	Queen's Park BC	Queen's Park	91	30
							Celtic	1	—
							Bournemouth	6	—
Oldbury Marcus	5 7	11 13	M	29 3 76	Bournemouth	Trainee	Norwich C	—	—
							Bournemouth	13	—
Pennock Adrian	5 11	13 06	D	27 3 71	Ipswich	Trainee	Norwich C	1	—
							Bournemouth	131	9
Rawlinson Mark	5 10	11 04	M	9 6 75	Bolton	Trainee	Manchester U	—	—
							Bournemouth	19	—
Robinson Steve	5 9	11 03	F	10 12 74	Lisburn	Trainee	Tottenham H	2	—
							Leyton Orient (loan)	—	—
							Bournemouth	73	12
Santos Yazalde*			F	30 7 75	Jersey		Bournemouth	3	—
Strong Steve§			F	15 3 78	Watford	Trainee	Bournemouth	2	—
Town David	5 7	11 13	F	9 12 76	Bournemouth	Trainee	Bournemouth	13	—
Victory Jamie*	5 11	12 02	D	14 11 75	London	Trainee	West Ham U	—	—
							Bournemouth	16	1
Watson Mark	5 9	11 00	F	28 12 73	Birmingham	Sutton U	West Ham U	1	—
							Leyton Orient (loan)	1	1
							Cambridge U (loan)	4	1
							Shrewsbury T (loan)	1	—
							Bournemouth	1	—
Wells David§			G	29 12 77	Portsmouth	Trainee	Bournemouth	1	—
Young Neil	5 9	12 00	D	31 8 73	Harlow	Trainee	Tottenham H	—	—
							Bournemouth	73	—

Trainees
Bowers, Tyronne G; Camfield, Adam J; Cox, Robert S; Dean, Michael J; Fricker, Matthew; Griffin, Antony R; Hayter, James E; Howe, Edward J F; Jenkins, Jamie; Smith, Mark L; Stone, Nicholas J; Strong, Steven G; Wells, David P; Williams, Gary L.

Associated Schoolboys
Baines, Simon A; Birmingham, David P; Black, Ryan-Zico; Farnham, Russell A; Game, Samuel; George, Mark; Holland, Christopher J; Leaver, Matthew L; Martin, Jamie G; Saunders, Steele; Trickey, Steven I.

Associated Schoolboys who have accepted the club's offer of a Traineeship/Contract
Broadhurst, Karl M; Hughes, Daniel R; Jenkins, Jody D.

BRADFORD CITY

Name	Ht	Wt	Pos	Date	Birthplace	Source	Club	Apps	Gls
Benn Wayne‡	5 10	11 12	D	7 8 76	Pontefract	Trainee	Bradford C	10	—
Brightwell David	6 1	13 04	D	7 1 71	Lutterworth	Trainee	Manchester C	43	1
							Chester C (loan)	6	—
							Lincoln C (loan)	5	—
							Stoke C (loan)	1	—
							Bradford C	22	—
Bullimore Wayne	5 9	12 01	M	12 9 70	Mansfield	Trainee	Manchester U	—	—
							Barnsley	35	1
							Stockport Co	—	—
							Scunthorpe U	67	11
							Bradford C	2	—
Dolby Chris*	5 8	10 03	F	4 9 74	Dewsbury	Trainee	Rotherham U	3	—
							Bradford C	—	—
Duxbury Lee	5 9	12 00	M	7 10 69	Keighley	Trainee	Bradford C	209	25
							Rochdale (loan)	10	—
							Huddersfield T	29	2
							Bradford C	30	4
Foley Steve‡	5 7	11 03	M	4 10 62	Liverpool	Apprentice	Liverpool	—	—
							Fulham (loan)	3	—
							Grimsby T	31	2
							Sheffield U	66	14
							Swindon T	151	23
							Stoke C	107	10
							Lincoln C	16	—
							Bradford C	1	—
Ford John	6 2	13 04	M	12 4 68	Birmingham	Cradley T	Swansea C	160	7
							Bradford C	19	—
Franks Michael‡	6 5	12 10	G	20 4 77	Edmonton		Bradford C	—	—
Grayston Neil*	5 8	11 00	D	25 11 75	Keighley	Trainee	Bradford C	7	—
Hamilton Derrick	5 10	12 13	M	15 8 76	Bradford	Trainee	Bradford C	56	5
Hansen Glenn			M	20 9 72	Oslo	Drobak	Bradford C	—	—
Huxford Richard	6 0	12 02	D	25 7 69	Scunthorpe	Kettering T	Barnet	33	1
							Millwall	32	—
							Birmingham C (loan)	5	—
							Bradford C	59	2
Jackson Scott‡	6 1	11 08	M	6 1 77	Leeds	Trainee	Bradford C	—	—

Jacobs Wayne	5 10	11 02	D	3 2 69	Sheffield	Apprentice	Sheffield W	6	—
							Hull C	129	4
							Rotherham U	42	2
							Bradford C	66	1
Jewell Paul	5 8	12 01	F	28 9 64	Liverpool	Apprentice	Liverpool	—	—
							Wigan Ath	137	35
							Bradford C	269	56
							Grimsby T (loan)	5	1
Kamara Chris‡	6 1	12 10	M	25 12 57	Middlesbrough	Apprentice	Portsmouth	63	7
							Swindon T	147	21
							Portsmouth	11	—
							Brentford	152	28
							Swindon T	87	6
							Stoke C	60	5
							Leeds U	20	1
							Luton T	49	—
							Sheffield U (loan)	8	—
							Middlesbrough (loan)	5	—
							Sheffield U	16	—
							Bradford C	23	3
Kiwomya Andrew	5 11	10 10	F	1 10 67	Huddersfield	Trainee	Barnsley	1	—
							Sheffield W	—	—
					Retired injury	Dundee	21	1
							Rotherham U	7	—
					Halifax T	Scunthorpe U	9	3
							Bradford C	16	2
Liburd Richard	5 10	11 01	D	26 9 73	Nottingham	Forest Athletic	Middlesbrough	41	1
							Bradford C	42	2
Megson Gary‡	5 10	12 00	M	2 5 59	Manchester	Apprentice	Plymouth Arg	78	10
							Everton	22	2
							Sheffield W	123	13
							Nottingham F	—	—
							Newcastle U	24	1
							Sheffield W	110	12
							Manchester C	82	2
							Norwich C	46	1
							Lincoln C	2	—
							Shrewsbury T	2	—
							Bradford C	—	—
Midgley Craig	5 8	10 11	F	24 5 76	Bradford	Trainee	Bradford C	8	1
							Scarborough (loan)	16	1
Mitchell Graham	6 2	12 13	D	16 2 68	Shipley	Apprentice	Huddersfield T	244	2
							Bournemouth (loan)	4	—
							Bradford C	59	1
Mohan Nicky	6 2	14 00	D	6 10 70	Middlesbrough	Trainee	Middlesbrough	99	4
							Hull C (loan)	5	1
							Leicester C	23	—
							Bradford C	39	4
Murray Shaun	5 8	10 11	M	7 2 70	Newcastle	Trainee	Tottenham H	—	—
							Portsmouth	34	1
							Millwall (loan)	—	—
							Scarborough	29	5
							Bradford C	75	7
Ormondroyd Ian	6 5	13 07	F	22 9 64	Bradford	Thackley	Bradford C	87	20
							Oldham Ath (loan)	10	1
							Aston Villa	56	6
							Derby Co	25	8
							Leicester C	77	7
							Hull C (loan)	10	6
							Bradford C	37	6
Robson Gary‡	5 9	11 10	M	6 7 65	Durham	Apprentice	WBA	218	28
							Bradford C	75	3
Showler Paul	5 7	11 00	M	10 10 66	Doncaster	Altrincham	Barnet	71	12
							Bradford C	88	15
Shutt Carl	5 10	12 10	F	10 10 61	Sheffield	Spalding U	Sheffield W	40	16
							Bristol C	46	10
							Leeds U	79	17
							Birmingham C	26	4
							Manchester C (loan)	6	—
							Bradford C	66	12
Stabb Chris‡	5 9	11 11	D	12 10 76	Bradford	Trainee	Bradford C	1	—
Stallard Mark	6 0	12 09	F	24 10 74	Derby	Trainee	Derby Co	27	2
							Fulham (loan)	4	3
							Bradford C	21	9
Tolson Neil	6 2	11 12	F	25 10 73	Wordley	Trainee	Walsall	9	1
							Oldham Ath	3	—
							Bradford C	63	12
							Chester C (loan)	4	—

Tomlinson Paul‡	6 2	14 04	G	22 2 64	Brierley Hill	Middlewood R	Sheffield U	37	—
							Birmingham C (loan)	11	—
							Bradford C	293	—
Wright Tommy	5 7	11 04	F	10 1 66	Dunfermline	Apprentice	Leeds U	81	24
							Oldham Ath	112	23
							Leicester C	129	22
							Middlesbrough	53	5
							Bradford C	34	4
Youds Eddie	6 3	14 00	D	3 5 70	Liverpool	Trainee	Everton	8	—
							Cardiff C (loan)	1	—
							Wrexham (loan)	20	2
							Ipswich T	50	1
							Bradford C	47	7

Trainees
Brown, Paul M; Davey, Benjamin J N; Edwards, Gavin P; Langhorn, Richard; Mazurke, Shane; McDonald, Philip J; McLean, Ian J; O'Brien, Andrew J; Payne, Dean; Rickers, John D; Shields, Antony J.

Associated Schoolboys
Bennett, Niel R; Briggs, Ian M; Brook, Matthew; Brown, Liam; Clark, Gareth A; Coonan, Gavin; Devine, Ian J; Edwards, Ian D; Grant, Gareth M; Kinch, Liam D; Lambert, Mark; Long, Alastair D; Lonsdale, Jonathan; Meehan, Mark; Oakes, Michael; Pallister, Timothy J; Palmer, Dean; Preston, Matthew; Senior, Mark A; Smith, David M; Trainor, Mark; Walker, Lee; Wilson, James D.

Associated Schoolboys who have accepted the club's offer of a Traineeship/Contract
Airdrie, Stewart W; Bates, Craig A; Bolland, Paul G; Bower, Mark J; Machell, Richard A; Verity, Daniel R.

BRENTFORD

Abrahams Paul	5 8	11 03	F	31 10 73	Colchester	Trainee	Colchester U	55	8
							Brentford	27	6
							Colchester U (loan)	8	2
Anderson Ijah	5 7	10 02	D	30 12 75	Hackney	Tottenham H	Southend U	—	—
							Brentford	25	2
Annon Darren‡	5 5	10 11	M	17 2 72	London	Carshalton Ath	Brentford	20	2
Asaba Carl	6 1	12 12	F	28 1 73	London	Dulwich Hamlet	Brentford	10	2
							Colchester U (loan)	12	2
Ashby Barry	6 2	12 02	D	21 11 70	London	Trainee	Watford	114	3
							Brentford	81	3
Bates Jamie	6 1	12 12	D	24 2 68	London	Trainee	Brentford	315	14
Bent Marcus	6 3	11 13	F	19 5 78	Hammersmith	Trainee	Brentford	12	1
Campbell Corey‡	5 10	11 06	D	6 3 76	London	Trainee	Brentford	—	—
Cleary Kevin‡			D	7 9 76	Isleworth	Trainee	Brentford	—	—
Davis Paul	5 9	10 08	M	9 12 61	London	Apprentice	Arsenal	351	30
							Brentford	5	—
Dearden Kevin	5 11	12 06	G	8 3 70	Luton	Trainee	Tottenham H	1	—
							Cambridge U (loan)	15	—
							Hartlepool U (loan)	10	—
							Oxford U (loan)	—	—
							Swindon T (loan)	1	—
							Peterborough U (loan)	7	—
							Hull C (loan)	3	—
							Rochdale (loan)	2	—
							Birmingham C (loan)	12	—
							Portsmouth (loan)	—	—
							Brentford	119	—
Fernandes Tamer	6 3	13 05	G	7 12 74	London	Trainee	Brentford	10	—
Forster Nick	5 9	10 12	F	8 9 73	Oxted	Horley T	Gillingham	67	24
							Brentford	84	29
Harvey Lee	5 11	11 07	M	21 12 66	Harlow	Harrow	Leyton Orient	184	23
							Nottingham F	2	—
							Brentford	91	6
Hooker Jon*	5 6	11 00	M	31 3 72	London	Hertford T	Gillingham	—	—
							Brentford	5	—
Hurdle Gus	5 7	11 01	D	14 10 73	London	Fulham	Brentford	23	—
Hutchings Carl	5 11	11 00	M	24 9 74	London	Trainee	Brentford	91	—
Martin Dean‡	5 7	10 06	F	31 8 72	Islington	Fisher Ath	West Ham U	2	—
							Colchester U (loan)	8	2
						Iceland	Brentford	19	1
McGhee David	5 9	11 04	F	19 6 76	Sussex	Trainee	Brentford	43	6
Omigie Joe	6 2	13 00	F	13 6 72	Hammersmith	Donna	Brentford	10	—
Ravenscroft Craig*	5 6	9 04	F	20 12 74	London	Trainee	Brentford	9	1
Smith Paul	5 11	14 00	M	18 9 71	Lenham	Trainee	Southend U	20	1
							Brentford	113	10

Statham Brian	5 11	11 00	D	21 5 69	Zimbabwe	Apprentice	Tottenham H	24	—
							Reading (loan)	8	—
							Bournemouth (loan)	2	—
							Brentford (loan)	18	—
							Brentford	129	1
Taylor Robert	6 1	13 08	F	30 4 71	Norwich	Trainee	Norwich C	—	—
							Leyton Orient (loan)	3	1
							Birmingham C	—	—
							Leyton Orient	73	20
							Brentford	90	36

Trainees
Adcock, Brady R; Cotter, John M; Denys, Ryan; Duffy, Gary; Green, Darren J; Mills, Paul T; Mitchell, Terry F; O'Neill, Stephen M; Rapley, Kevin J; Ray, Damian L; Smith, Mark A; Weedon, Mark N.

Associated Schoolboys
French, Steven A; McLoughlin, Ross.

Associated Schoolboys who have accepted the club's offer of a Traineeship/Contract
Brooks, Leyton C.

BRIGHTON & HOVE ALBION

Andrews Philip	5 11	10 06	F	14 9 76	Andover	Trainee	Brighton & HA	18	—
Byrne John*	6 0	12 13	F	1 2 61	Manchester	Apprentice	York C	175	55
							QPR	126	30
						Le Havre	Brighton & HA	51	14
							Sunderland	33	8
							Millwall	17	1
							Brighton & HA (loan)	7	2
							Oxford U	55	18
							Brighton & HA	39	6
Case Jimmy†	5 9	12 12	M	18 5 54	Liverpool	South Liverpool	Liverpool	186	23
							Brighton & HA	127	10
							Southampton	215	10
							Bournemouth	40	1
							Halifax T	21	2
							Wrexham	4	—
							Darlington	1	—
						Sittingbourne	Brighton & HA	32	—
Chapman Ian*	5 9	12 05	M	31 5 70	Brighton	Trainee	Brighton & HA	281	14
Coughlan Derek*	6 4	13 10	D	2 1 77	Cork	Trainee	Brighton & HA	1	—
Foster Steve*	6 1	14 00	D	24 9 57	Portsmouth	Apprentice	Portsmouth	109	6
							Brighton & HA	172	6
							Aston Villa	15	3
							Luton T	163	11
							Oxford U	95	9
							Brighton & HA	115	7
Fox Mark	5 11	10 05	M	17 11 75	Basingstoke	Trainee	Brighton & HA	23	1
Fox Simon	5 10	9 08	F	28 8 77	Basingstoke	Trainee	Brighton & HA	9	—
Hobson Gary	6 1	13 03	D	12 11 71	North Ferriby	Trainee	Hull C	142	—
							Brighton & HA	9	—
Johnson Ross	6 0	12 04	D	2 1 76	Brighton	Trainee	Brighton & HA	22	—
Maskell Craig	5 10	11 10	F	10 4 68	Aldershot	Apprentice	Southampton	6	1
							Swindon T (loan)	—	—
							Huddersfield T	87	43
							Reading	72	26
							Swindon T	47	22
							Southampton	17	1
							Bristol C (loan)	5	1
							Brighton & HA	15	4
McCarthy Paul	6 0	13 06	D	4 8 71	Cork	Trainee	Brighton & HA	181	6
McDonald Paul	5 6	10 00	F	20 4 68	Motherwell	Merry Street BC	Hamilton A	215	26
							Southampton	3	—
							Burnley (loan)	9	1
							Brighton & HA	5	—
McDougald Junior	5 11	12 06	F	12 1 75	Big Spring	Trainee	Tottenham H	—	—
							Brighton & HA	78	14
							Chesterfield (loan)	9	3
McGarrigle Kevin	5 11	11 00	D	9 4 77	Newcastle	Trainee	Brighton & HA	32	1
Minton Jeffrey	5 6	10 13	M	28 12 73	Hackney	Trainee	Tottenham H	2	1
							Brighton & HA	78	13
Munday Stuart*	5 11	11 00	D	28 9 72	Newham	Trainee	Brighton & HA	95	4
Mundee Denny	5 10	13 00	F	10 10 68	Swindon	Apprentice	QPR	—	—
							Swindon T	—	—
							Bournemouth	100	6
							Torquay U (loan)	9	—
							Brentford	84	16
							Brighton & HA	32	3

Myall Stuart*	5 10	12 12	M	12 11 74	Eastbourne	Trainee	Brighton & HA	80	4
Ormerod Mark	6 0	12 11	G	5 2 76	Bournemouth	Trainee	Brighton & HA	—	—
Parris George	5 9	13 00	D	11 9 64	Ilford	Apprentice	West Ham U	239	12
							Birmingham C	39	1
							Brentford (loan)	5	—
							Bristol C (loan)	6	—
							Brighton & HA (loan)	18	2
							Brighton & HA	38	2
Rust Nicky	6 0	13 01	G	25 9 74	Ely	Arsenal	Brighton & HA	136	—
Ryan John‡	5 8	11 06	F	7 12 75	Cork	Cork C	Brighton & HA	—	—
Smith Peter	6 0	12 01	D	12 7 69	Stone	Alma Swanley	Brighton & HA	69	2
Storer Stuart	5 11	12 13	F	16 1 67	Harborough	Local	Mansfield T	1	—
							Birmingham C	8	—
							Everton	—	—
							Wigan Ath (loan)	12	—
							Bolton W	123	12
							Exeter C	77	8
							Brighton & HA	40	3
Tuck Stuart	5 11	11 02	D	1 10 74	Brighton	Trainee	Brighton & HA	42	—
Virgo James	5 10	12 10	D	21 12 76	Brighton	Trainee	Brighton & HA	—	—
Wilkins Dean*	5 10	12 04	M	12 7 62	Hillingdon	Apprentice	QPR	6	—
							Brighton & HA	312	25
							Orient (loan)	10	—

Trainees
Armstrong, Paul G; Carter, Richard A J; Earles, Ian J; Hughes, Alan D; Kennett, Paul J; Mayo, Kerry; McNally, Ross J; O'Brien, David; Pickering, Jay T; Rowlands, James S; Saul, Eric M; Shepherd, Dominic M W; Westcott, John P J.

Non-Contract
Case, James R

Associated Schoolboys
Kirkland, Joel M.

BRISTOL CITY

Agostino Paul	5 11	12 12	F	9 6 75	Woodville		Young Boys	29	3
							Bristol C	40	10
Barber Phil‡	5 11	12 06	M	10 6 65	Tring	Aylesbury	Crystal Palace	234	35
							Millwall	110	12
							Plymouth Arg (loan)	4	—
							Bristol C	3	—
							Mansfield T (loan)	4	1
							Fulham (loan)	13	1
Barclay Dominic	5 10	11 07	F	5 9 76	Bristol	Trainee	Bristol C	4	—
Barnard Darren	5 10	11 00	D	30 11 71	Rinteln	Wokingham	Chelsea	29	2
							Reading (loan)	4	—
							Bristol C	34	4
Bent Junior	5 6	10 09	F	1 3 70	Huddersfield	Trainee	Huddersfield T	36	6
							Burnley (loan)	9	3
							Bristol C	159	17
							Stoke C (loan)	1	—
Brennan Jim	5 9	12 05	M	8 5 77	Toronto	Sora Lazio	Bristol C	—	—
Brown Wayne*	6 1	11 06	G	14 1 77	Southampton	Trainee	Bristol C	1	—
Bryant Matthew	6 0	13 02	D	21 9 70	Bristol	Trainee	Bristol C	203	7
							Walsall (loan)	13	—
Carey Louis	5 11	11 05	D	22 1 77	Bristol	Trainee	Bristol C	23	—
Dryden Richard	6 0	13 00	D	14 6 69	Stroud	Trainee	Bristol R	13	—
							Exeter C	51	7
							Manchester C (loan)	—	—
							Notts Co	31	1
							Plymouth Arg (loan)	5	—
							Birmingham C	48	—
							Bristol C	37	2
Edwards Robert	6 0	12 02	D	1 7 73	Kendal	Trainee	Carlisle U	48	5
							Bristol C	125	3
Fowler Jason	6 1	11 13	M	20 8 74	Bristol	Trainee	Bristol C	25	—
Hansen Vergard	6 2	12 07	D	8 8 69	Drammen	Stromsgodset	Bristol C	37	—
Hewlett Matthew	6 1	11 03	M	25 2 76	Bristol	Trainee	Bristol C	40	2
Huggins Dean	5 10	11 00	D	21 11 76	Cardiff	Trainee	Bristol C	—	—

Name	Ht	Wt	Pos	Born	Birthplace	Source	Club	Apps	Gls
Kite Phil*	6 2	15 04	G	26 10 62	Bristol	Apprentice	Bristol R	96	—
							Tottenham H (loan)	—	—
							Southampton	4	—
							Middlesbrough (loan)	2	—
							Gillingham	70	—
							Bournemouth	7	—
							Sheffield U	11	—
							Mansfield T (loan)	11	—
							Plymouth Arg (loan)	2	—
							Rotherham U (loan)	1	—
							Crewe Alex (loan)	5	—
							Stockport Co (loan)	5	—
							Cardiff C	18	—
							Bristol C	6	—
Kuhl Martin	5 10	12 08	M	10 1 65	Frimley	Apprentice	Birmingham C	111	5
							Sheffield U	38	4
							Watford	4	—
							Portsmouth	157	27
							Derby Co	68	1
							Notts Co (loan)	2	—
							Bristol C	63	7
McKop Henry‡	5 11	12 00	D	8 7 67	Zimbabwe	Bonner Sport Club	Bristol C	5	—
McLeary Alan	5 10	10 06	D	6 10 64	Lambeth	Apprentice	Millwall	307	5
							Sheffield U (loan)	3	—
							Wimbledon (loan)	4	—
							Charlton Ath	66	3
							Bristol C	31	—
Nugent Kevin	6 1	12 04	F	10 4 69	Edmonton	Trainee	Leyton Orient	94	20
							Cork C (loan)	—	—
							Plymouth Arg	131	32
							Bristol C	34	8
Owers Gary	6 0	12 07	M	3 10 68	Newcastle	Apprentice	Sunderland	268	25
							Bristol C	58	4
Partridge Scott	5 8	11 01	F	13 10 74	Leicester	Trainee	Bradford C	5	—
							Bristol C	51	7
							Torquay U (loan)	5	2
							Plymouth Arg (loan)	7	2
							Scarborough (loan)	7	—
Paterson Scott	6 2	12 08	M	13 5 72	Aberdeen	Cove Rangers	Liverpool	—	—
							Bristol C	21	1
Plummer Dwayne	5 10	10 09	F	12 5 78	Bristol	Trainee	Bristol C	11	—
Seal David	5 11	12 01	F	26 1 72	Penrith NSW	Aalst	Bristol C	39	10
Shail Mark	6 1	13 03	D	15 10 66	Sweden	Yeovil	Bristol C	90	4
Tinnion Brian	6 1	13 00	D	23 2 68	Stanley	Apprentice	Newcastle U	32	2
							Bradford C	145	22
							Bristol C	117	12
Welch Keith	6 1	13 07	G	3 10 68	Bolton	Trainee	Bolton W	—	—
							Rochdale	205	—
							Bristol C	195	—

Trainees
Alderman, Scott G; Dibble, Anthony J; Doherty, Thomas E; Edwards, Shaun P; Fowler, Paul M; Greaves, James E; Hale, Matthew J; Hobbs, Darren J; Kentish, Neil A; Langan, Kevin; Loydon, Gareth J A; Perry, Richard A; Rogers, Scott P; Rutkowski, Alexei J; Smith, Dwayne D; Vanes, Michael A; Waters, Andrew J.

Associated Schoolboys
Badman, Mark; Ball, Alex; Burnell, Joseph M; Claridge, Jamie; Clarke, Robert; Coles, Daniel; Farmer, Christopher; Hill, Matthew C; Poynter, Christopher; Reynolds, Nicholas; Sammut, Benjamin; Saunders, Mark; Turner, Daniel J; Vaughan, Ian; Whittington, Geoffrey.

Associated Schoolboys who have accepted the club's offer of a Traineeship/Contract
Brown, Aaron; Morrison, Scott; Ridge, Neil; Sloan, Christopher J; Wilmot, Ellis J.

BRISTOL ROVERS

Name	Ht	Wt	Pos	Born	Birthplace	Source	Club	Apps	Gls
Archer Lee	5 6	9 06	M	6 11 72	Bristol	Trainee	Bristol R	105	13
Beadle Peter	6 2	13 07	F	13 5 72	London	Trainee	Gillingham	67	14
							Tottenham H	—	—
							Bournemouth (loan)	9	2
							Southend U (loan)	8	1
							Watford	23	1
							Bristol R	27	12
Bowey Steven	5 8	10 09	M	10 7 74	Durham	Forest Green R	Bristol R	—	—
Browning Marcus	5 11	13 00	F	22 4 71	Bristol	Trainee	Bristol R	148	11
							Hereford U (loan)	7	5
Channing Justin	5 11	11 07	D	19 11 68	Reading	Apprentice	QPR	55	5
							Bristol R	130	10
Clark Billy	6 0	12 03	D	19 5 67	Christchurch	Trainee	Bournemouth	4	—
							Bristol R	221	13

Player	Ht	Wt	Pos	Born	Birthplace	From	Club	Apps	Gls
Collett Andy	6 0	13 00	G	28 10 73	Middlesbrough	Trainee	Middlesbrough	2	—
							Bristol R	30	—
Davis Mike*	6 0	12 00	F	19 10 74	Bristol	Yate T	Bristol R	17	1
							Hereford U (loan)	1	1
French John	5 10	10 10	F	25 9 76	Bristol	Trainee	Bristol R	10	1
Gurney Andy	5 7	10 07	D	25 1 74	Bristol	Trainee	Bristol R	84	7
Hayfield Matthew	5 10	11 07	M	8 8 75	Bristol	Trainee	Bristol R	6	—
Higgs Shane	6 2	12 12	G	13 5 77	Oxford	Trainee	Bristol R	—	—
Low Joshua§			M	15 2 79	Bristol	Trainee	Bristol R	1	—
McLean Ian*	6 2	13 02	D	13 8 66	Paisley	Metroford	Bristol R	35	2
							Cardiff C (loan)	4	—
							Rotherham U (loan)	9	—
Miller Paul	6 0	11 07	F	31 1 68	Bisley	Trainee	Wimbledon	80	10
							Newport Co (loan)	6	2
							Bristol C (loan)	3	—
							Bristol R	80	20
Parkin Brian*	6 2	13 00	G	12 10 65	Birkenhead	Local	Oldham Ath	6	—
							Crewe Alex (loan)	12	—
							Crewe Alex	86	—
							Crystal Palace (loan)	—	—
							Crystal Palace	20	—
							Bristol R	241	—
Paul Martin*	5 8	9 07	F	2 2 75	Whalley	Trainee	Bristol R	22	1
Pritchard David	5 7	11 04	D	27 5 72	Wolverhampton	Telford U	WBA	5	—
						Telford U	Bristol R	66	—
Skinner Justin	6 0	11 03	M	30 1 69	Hounslow	Apprentice	Fulham	135	23
							Bristol R	149	10
Sterling Worrell*	5 7	11 02	M	8 6 65	Bethnal Green	Apprentice	Watford	94	14
							Peterborough U	193	29
							Bristol R	119	6
Stewart Marcus	5 10	10 06	F	7 11 72	Bristol	Trainee	Bristol R	171	57
Tillson Andy	6 2	12 10	D	30 6 66	Huntingdon	Kettering T	Grimsby T	105	5
							QPR	29	2
							Grimsby T (loan)	4	—
							Bristol R	120	3
Tovey Paul*	5 8	10 10	M	5 12 73	Wokingham	Trainee	Bristol R	9	—
White Tom	5 11	12 02	D	26 1 76	Bristol	Trainee	Bristol R	6	—
Wright Ian*	6 0	12 07	D	10 3 72	Lichfield	Trainee	Stoke C	6	—
							Bristol R	54	1
Wyatt Mike*	5 10	11 03	F	12 9 74	Bristol	Trainee	Bristol C	13	—
							Bristol R	4	—

Trainees
Atkinson, David J; Brown, Justin C; Davey, James A; De-Long, Nicholas M; Harte, Stuart G; Hope, David J; Low, Joshua D; Morgan, Ryan S; Parkinson, Matthew S; Pritchard, Justin; Sanderson, Jonathan; Sefton, Sheridan E; Serjeant, Philip R; Teague, Simon J; Uren, Paul; Westlake, Tristan M; Zabek, Lee K.

Associated Schoolboys
Adams, Michael J; Annetts, Stephen J; Beales, Nicholas J; Gitson, Lee A; Holmes, Jamie; Pendry, Dean; Shaughnessy, Peter J; Trought, Michael; Watts, David J; Zabek, James K.

Associated Schoolboys who have accepted the club's offer of a Traineeship/Contract
Claridge, Robert R; Lloyd, Andrew P; White, Jonathon.

BURNLEY

Player	Ht	Wt	Pos	Born	Birthplace	From	Club	Apps	Gls
Adams Derek	5 10	11 12	M	25 6 75	Aberdeen	Aberdeen	Burnley	2	—
Beresford Marlon	6 1	13 05	G	2 9 69	Lincoln	Trainee	Sheffield W	—	—
							Bury (loan)	1	—
							Ipswich T (loan)	—	—
							Northampton T (loan)	13	—
							Crewe Alex (loan)	3	—
							Northampton T (loan)	15	—
							Burnley	166	—
Borland John	5 8	11 06	M	28 1 77	Lancaster	Trainee	Burnley	1	—
Brass Chris	5 9	12 06	D	24 7 75	Easington	Trainee	Burnley	14	—
							Torquay U (loan)	7	—
Cooke Andy	5 11	12 08	F	2 1 74	Shrewsbury	Newtown	Burnley	23	5
Davies Glen*	6 1	12 10	D	20 2 76	Brighton	Trainee	Burnley	—	—
Dowell Wayne	5 9	12 06	D	28 12 73	Co Durham	Trainee	Burnley	6	—
							Carlisle U (loan)	7	—
Eyres David	5 9	11 10	F	26 2 64	Liverpool	Rhyl	Blackpool	158	38
							Burnley	126	33

Name							Clubs	Apps	Gls
Francis John‡	5 8	12 13	F	12 11 63	Dewsbury	Emley	Halifax T	4	—
							Sheffield U	42	6
							Burnley	101	26
							Cambridge U	29	3
							Burnley	76	10
Harper Alan*	5 9	11 09	M	1 11 60	Liverpool	Apprentice	Liverpool	—	—
							Everton	127	4
							Sheffield W	35	—
							Manchester C	50	1
							Everton	51	—
							Luton T	41	1
							Burnley	31	—
							Cardiff C (loan)	5	—
Harrison Gerry	5 9	12 03	M	15 4 72	Lambeth	Trainee	Watford	9	—
							Bristol C	38	1
							Cardiff C (loan)	10	1
							Hereford U (loan)	6	—
							Huddersfield T	—	—
							Burnley	54	3
Heath Adrian†	5 6	11 00	F	11 1 61	Newcastle under Lyme	Apprentice	Stoke C	95	16
							Everton	226	71
						Espanol	Aston Villa	9	—
							Manchester C	75	4
							Stoke C	6	—
							Burnley	115	29
							Sheffield U	4	—
							Burnley	3	—
Helliwell Ian	6 4	14 08	F	7 11 62	Rotherham	Matlock T	York C	160	40
							Scunthorpe U	80	22
							Rotherham U	52	4
							Stockport Co	39	13
							Burnley	4	—
Hoyland Jamie	6 0	14 00	M	23 1 66	Sheffield	Apprentice	Manchester C	2	—
							Bury	172	35
							Sheffield U	89	6
							Bristol C (loan)	6	—
							Burnley	53	2
Joyce Warren	5 8	12 04	M	20 1 65	Oldham	Local	Bolton W	184	17
							Preston NE	177	34
							Plymouth Arg	30	3
							Burnley	70	9
							Hull C (loan)	9	3
McMinn Ted‡	6 0	13 08	F	28 9 62	Castle Douglas	Glenafton Athletic	Q of S	22	1
							Queen of the S	40	4
							Rangers	63	4
						Seville	Derby Co	123	9
							Birmingham C	22	—
							Burnley	46	3
Nogan Kurt	5 11	11 11	F	9 9 70	Cardiff	Trainee	Luton T	33	3
							Peterborough U	—	—
							Brighton & HA	97	49
							Burnley	61	23
Parkinson Gary	5 11	13 00	D	10 1 68	Thornaby	Everton	Middlesbrough	202	5
							Southend U (loan)	6	—
							Bolton W	3	—
							Burnley	92	3
Peel Nathan*	6 1	13 03	F	17 5 72	Blackburn	Trainee	Preston NE	10	1
							Sheffield U	1	—
							Halifax T (loan)	3	—
							Burnley	16	2
							Rotherham U (loan)	9	4
							Mansfield T (loan)	2	—
							Doncaster R (loan)	2	—
Robinson Liam	5 7	12 07	F	20 12 65	Bradford	Nottingham F	Huddersfield T	21	2
							Tranmere R (loan)	4	3
							Bury	262	89
							Bristol C	41	4
							Burnley	55	9
Russell Wayne	6 2	12 12	G	29 11 67	Cardiff	Ebbw Vale	Burnley	18	—
Smith Paul	6 0	13 03	F	22 1 76	Easington	Trainee	Burnley	11	—
Swan Peter	6 3	15 09	D	28 9 66	Leeds	Local	Leeds U	49	11
							Hull C	80	24
							Port Vale	111	5
							Plymouth Arg	27	2
							Burnley	32	5
Taylor Matthew*	5 7	11 12	D	6 3 76	Maidstone	Trainee	Burnley	—	—

Thompson Steve	5 11	13 05	M	2 11 64	Oldham	Apprentice	Bolton W	335	49
							Luton T	5	—
							Leicester C	127	18
							Burnley	30	—
Vinnicombe Chris	5 8	10 12	M	20 10 70	Exeter		Exeter C	39	1
							Rangers	23	1
							Burnley	64	3
Weller Paul	5 8	11 02	F	6 3 75	Brighton	Trainee	Burnley	25	1
Winstanley Mark	6 1	12 08	D	22 1 68	St Helens	Trainee	Bolton W	220	3
							Burnley	89	5

Trainees
Bowden, Paul A; Carr-Lawton, Colin; Ciaraldi, Craig; Cotton, David P; Duerden, Ian C; Dugdale, Gordon T; Eastwood, Philip J; Elsworth, Patrick D; Fogarty, Richard P; Francis, Martin N; Gray, Adam R; Heffernan, Jason T; Lee, Patrick D; Mawson, Craig J; Mutton, Thomas J; O'Leary, Daniel W J; Pennington, Lee D; Richardson, Lee M; Smith, Carl P; Webster, Philip J; West, Gareth E.

Non-Contract
Heath, Adrian P.

Associated Schoolboys
Costello, John; Gardiner, Marc; Heavyside, John R; Holt, David S; Kelly, Eamonn; Lillis, Adam D; Maylett, Bradley; McCoy, James J; Stevens, Barry J.

Associated Schoolboys who have accepted the club's offer of a Traineeship/Contract
Heywood, Matthew S; Pates, Bradley J; Scott, Christopher.

BURY

Berry Damien‡			D	30 3 77	Bury	Trainee	Bury	—	—
Bimson Stuart	5 11	12 00	D	29 9 69	Liverpool	Macclesfield	Bury	35	—
Brabin Gary	5 11	15 01	M	9 12 70	Liverpool	Trainee	Stockport Co	2	—
						Runcorn	Doncaster R	59	11
							Bury	5	—
Bracey Lee	6 0	13 07	G	11 9 68	Ashford	Trainee	West Ham U	—	—
							Swansea C	99	—
							Halifax T	73	—
							Bury	67	—
Carter Mark	5 10	12 07	F	17 12 60	Liverpool	Runcorn	Barnet	82	30
							Bury	94	50
Cross Ryan*	6 0	13 08	D	11 10 72	Plymouth	Trainee	Plymouth Arg	19	—
							Hartlepool U	50	2
							Bury	42	—
Dale Geoff*	5 8	11 06	D	27 9 76	Manchester	Trainee	Bury	—	—
Daws Nick	5 11	13 03	D	15 3 70	Manchester	Altrincham	Bury	144	5
Hughes Ian	5 11	12 08	M	2 8 74	Bangor	Trainee	Bury	140	1
Jackson Michael	6 0	13 10	D	4 12 73	West Cheshire	Trainee	Crewe Alex	5	—
							Bury	94	6
Johnrose Lenny	5 10	12 04	F	29 11 69	Preston	Trainee	Blackburn R	42	11
							Preston NE (loan)	3	1
							Hartlepool U	66	11
							Bury	74	10
Johnson David	5 6	12 05	F	15 8 76	Kingston	Trainee	Manchester U	—	—
							Bury	36	5
Kelly Gary	5 10	13 06	G	3 8 66	Fulwood	Apprentice	Newcastle U	53	—
							Blackpool (loan)	5	—
							Bury	236	—
							West Ham U (loan)	—	—
Lancaster David	6 3	15 00	F	8 9 61	Preston	Colne Dynamoes	Blackpool	8	1
							Chesterfield (loan)	12	4
							Chesterfield	69	16
							Rochdale	40	14
							Bury	10	1
							Rochdale (loan)	14	2
Lucketti Chris	6 0	13 04	D	28 9 71	Littleborough	Trainee	Rochdale	1	—
							Stockport Co	—	—
							Halifax T	78	2
							Bury	108	5
Matthews Rob	5 11	13 00	F	14 10 70	Slough	Loughborough Univ	Notts Co	43	11
							Luton T	11	—
							York C	17	1
							Bury	16	4
Matthewson Trevor*	6 4	13 06	D	12 2 63	Sheffield	Apprentice	Sheffield W	3	—
							Newport Co	75	—
							Stockport Co	80	—
							Lincoln C	43	2
							Birmingham C	168	12
							Preston NE	12	1
							Bury	34	—

Player	Ht	Wt	Pos	Date	Birthplace	Source	Club	Apps	Gls
Mulligan James‡	5 6	11 07	F	21 4 74	Dublin	Trainee	Stoke C	—	—
							Bury (loan)	3	1
							Bury	17	2
Oakes Andrew‡			G	11 1 77	Crewe		Bury	—	—
Paskin John*	6 1	13 08	F	1 2 62	Capetown	Seiko	WBA	25	5
							Wolverhampton W	34	3
							Stockport Co (loan)	5	1
							Birmingham C (loan)	10	3
							Shrewsbury T (loan)	1	—
							Wrexham	51	11
							Bury	38	8
Pugh David	6 2	13 02	F	19 9 64	Liverpool	Runcorn	Chester C	179	23
							Bury	84	26
Reid Nicky	5 10	12 04	D	30 10 60	Ormston	Apprentice	Manchester C	217	2
							Blackburn R	174	9
							Bristol C (loan)	4	—
							WBA	20	—
							Wycombe W	8	—
						Woking	Bury	18	—
Reid Shaun	5 8	12 00	M	13 10 65	Huyton	Local	Rochdale	133	4
							Preston NE (loan)	3	—
							York C	106	7
							Rochdale	107	10
							Bury	21	—
Rigby Tony	5 10	12 12	M	10 8 72	Ormskirk	Barrow	Bury	125	18
Sertori Mark*	6 2	14 02	M	1 9 67	Manchester		Stockport Co	4	—
							Lincoln C	50	9
							Wrexham	110	3
							Bury	13	1
Shuttleworth Barry	5 8	11 00	F	9 7 77	Accrington	Trainee	Bury	—	—
Stant Phil	5 11	13 04	F	13 10 62	Bolton	Camberley Army	Reading	4	2
							Hereford U	89	38
							Notts Co	22	6
							Blackpool (loan)	12	5
							Lincoln C (loan)	4	—
							Huddersfield T (loan)	5	1
							Fulham	19	5
							Mansfield T	57	32
							Cardiff C	79	34
							Mansfield T (loan)	4	1
							Bury	54	22
Steele Winnie	5 8	11 02	M	28 2 77	Basildon	Trainee	Bury	—	—
Swailes Matthew‡			F	28 10 76	Bolton	Trainee	Bury	—	—
Taylor Paul*	5 10	12 02	D	5 8 77	Manchester	Trainee	Bury	—	—
Thomson Peter	6 3	13 04	F	30 6 77	Bury	Stand Ath	Bury	—	—
Titterton David‡	5 11	13 08	D	25 9 71	Hatton	Trainee	Coventry C	2	—
							Hereford U	51	1
							Wycombe W	19	1
							Bury	—	—
West Dean	5 8	12 02	D	5 12 72	Wakefield	Leeds U	Lincoln C	119	20
							Bury	37	1
Winter Paul*	5 10	12 03	M	15 8 76	Salford		Bury	—	—
Woodward Andy	6 0	13 06	D	23 9 73	Stockport	Trainee	Crewe Alex	20	—
							Bury	9	—

Trainees
Andrew, Steven P; Forrest, Martyn W; Fraser, Christopher J W; Green, Andrew; Hines, Rowan J; Horne, Matthew S M; Jones, John D; Kane, Marvin A; Lindley, Stuart; McCann, Steven J; McNally, Daniel S; Nuttall, Mark; Phillips, Paul D; Rawlinson, Craig A; Shaw, James A; Stevens, Richard A; Stockton, Anthony P; Swailes, Daniel; Warner, Daniel G; Winrow, Brian.

Non-Contract
Newall, Andrew; Radcliffe, Matthew S.

Associated Schoolboys
Bourne, Gareth J; Buckley, Matthew T H; Bury, Daniel J; Connell, Lee A; Halford, Stephen P; Hanson, Peter V; Hill, Nicholas D; Hughes, Paul; Hutchinson, Ian P A; Manivannan, Paul; Menzies, Anton M; Newall, Steven C; Popiolek, John P; Roberts, Reece; Smith, Andrew J; Sturtivant, David M; Thompson, Nicholas A; Wakes, Jeffrey R A; Wardle, Darren C.

Associated Schoolboys who have accepted the club's offer of a Traineeship/Contract
Denney, Philip M; Green, Alexander J; Wright, Gary J; Young, Ian T.

CAMBRIDGE UNITED

Player	Ht	Wt	Pos	Date	Birthplace	Source	Club	Apps	Gls
Adekola David‡	6 0	12 10	F	19 5 68	Lagos		Bury	35	12
							Exeter C (loan)	3	1
							Bournemouth	—	—
							Wigan Ath	4	—
							Hereford U	—	—
							Cambridge U	5	1

Name	Ht	Wt	Pos	Born	Birthplace	Source	Club	Apps	Gls
Barnwell-Edinboro Jamie	5 10	11 09	F	26 12 75	Hull	Trainee	Coventry C	1	—
							Swansea C (loan)	4	—
							Wigan Ath (loan)	10	1
							Cambridge U	7	2
Barrett Scott	6 0	13 13	G	2 4 63	Derby	Ilkeston T	Wolverhampton W	30	—
							Stoke C	51	—
							Colchester U (loan)	13	—
							Stockport Co (loan)	10	—
							Colchester U	—	—
							Gillingham	51	—
							Cambridge U	31	—
Beall Matthew	5 7	10 06	F	4 12 77	Enfield	Trainee	Cambridge U	15	4
Benjamin Trevor§			M	8 2 79	Cambridge	Trainee	Cambridge U	5	—
Clark Paul‡	5 9	13 13	M	14 9 58	Benfleet	Apprentice	Southend U	33	1
							Brighton & HA	79	9
							Reading (loan)	2	—
							Southend U	276	3
							Gillingham	90	1
							Cambridge U	2	—
Craddock Jody	6 2	11 13	D	25 7 75	Redditch	Christchurch	Cambridge U	104	3
Davies Martin	6 2	13 04	G	28 6 74	Swansea	Trainee	Coventry C	—	—
							Cambridge U	15	—
Fowler John‡	5 10	12 03	M	27 10 74	Preston	Trainee	Cambridge U	41	—
							Preston NE (loan)	6	—
Granville Danny	6 0	12 01	M	19 1 75	Islington	Trainee	Cambridge U	62	7
Gutzmore Leon‡			F	30 10 76	London	Trainee	Cambridge U	2	—
Hayes Adi§	6 1	11 10	M	22 5 78	Norwich	Trainee	Cambridge U	1	—
Howes Shaun§	5 10	11 02	M	7 11 77	Norwich	Trainee	Cambridge U	1	—
Hyde Micah	5 10	11 07	M	10 11 74	Newham	Trainee	Cambridge U	69	6
Jeffrey Andrew*	5 10	12 08	D	15 1 72	Bellshill	Cambridge C	Cambridge U	95	2
Joseph Marc	6 1	12 05	D	10 11 76	Leicester	Trainee	Cambridge U	12	—
Joseph Matthew	5 8	10 05	D	30 9 72	Bethnal Green	Trainee	Arsenal	—	—
							Gillingham	—	—
							Cambridge U	108	6
Kyd Michael	5 9	12 08	M	21 5 77	Hackney	Trainee	Cambridge U	28	2
Lomas Andrew†			G	26 4 65	Hartlepool		Cambridge U (loan)	2	—
						Rushden & Diamonds	Cambridge U	—	—
Middleton Craig*	5 10	11 02	M	10 9 70	Nuneaton	Trainee	Coventry C	3	—
							Cambridge U	59	10
Middleton Lee‡	5 9	11 09	M	10 9 70	Nuneaton	Trainee	Coventry C	2	—
							Swindon T	—	—
							Cambridge U	3	—
Morah Ollie‡	6 1	13 04	F	30 9 72	Islington	Trainee	Tottenham H	—	—
							Hereford U (loan)	2	—
							Swindon T	—	—
						Sutton U	Cambridge U	14	2
							Torquay U (loan)	2	—
Pack Lenny	5 9	12 08	M	27 9 76	Salisbury	Trainee	Cambridge U	14	—
Palmer Lee	6 0	12 07	D	19 9 70	Croydon	Trainee	Gillingham	120	5
							Cambridge U	30	1
Pick Gary*	5 9	11 10	M	9 7 71	Leicester	Leicester U	Stoke C	—	—
							Hereford U	43	2
							Cambridge U	4	—
Rattle Jon‡	5 8	12 09	D	22 7 76	Melton	Trainee	Cambridge U	15	—
Raynor Paul	5 11	12 08	M	29 4 66	Nottingham	Apprentice	Nottingham F	3	—
							Bristol R (loan)	8	—
							Huddersfield T	50	9
							Swansea C	191	27
							Wrexham (loan)	6	—
							Cambridge U	49	2
							Preston NE	80	9
							Cambridge U	35	3
Richards Tony	6 1	13 01	F	17 9 73	Newham	Sudbury T	Cambridge U	19	1
Robinson David†	6 0	13 02	F	27 11 69	Newcastle	Gateshead	Cambridge U	17	1
Stock Russell*	6 1	13 01	M	25 6 77	Great Yarmouth	Trainee	Cambridge U	17	1
Thompson David	6 2	13 02	D	20 11 68	Ashington	Trainee	Millwall	92	6
							Bristol C	17	—
							Brentford	10	1
							Blackpool	17	—
							Cambridge U	22	—

Turner Robbie	6 2	13 12	M	18 9 66	Durham	Apprentice	Huddersfield T	1	—
							Cardiff C	39	8
							Hartlepool U (loan)	7	1
							Bristol R	26	2
							Wimbledon	10	—
							Bristol C	52	12
							Plymouth Arg	66	17
							Notts Co	8	1
							Shrewsbury T (loan)	9	—
							Exeter C	45	7
							Cambridge U	10	3
Vowden Colin	6 1	13 00	D	13 9 71	Newmarket	Cambridge C	Cambridge U	24	—
Walker Richard‡			M	14 3 77	Cambridge	Trainee	Cambridge U	—	—
Wosahlo Bradley‡	5 10	10 06	M	14 2 75	Ipswich	Trainee	Brighton & HA	1	—
							Cambridge U	4	—
Zumrutel Soner‡	5 6	11 00	F	6 10 74	Islington	Trainee	Arsenal	—	—
							Cambridge U	—	—

Trainees
Benjamin, Trevor J; Brown, Dwight C; Hassan, Hassan H; Hayes, Adrian M; Howes, Shaun C; Huckstepp, Kris; Kett, Jamie C; Kriehn, Christopher T; Marshall, Shaun A; Reid, Darren S; Rutter, Aron J; Thompson, Kristian P; Wilde, Adam.

Non-Contract
Lomas, Andrew J; Robinson, David J.

Associated Schoolboys
Church, Michael; Fox, Karl; Gibson, Mark A; Gill, Matthew J; Haines, Darren G; Haniver, Matthew G; Hann, Matthew; Holliday, Dean P; Lake, Daniel J; Newbery, Martin B; Turner, Daniel P J; Waldron, Matthew; Youngs, Thomas A J.

Associated Schoolboys who have accepted the club's offer of a Traineeship/Contract
Dolby, Lee R; Eagle, Philip; King, Stuart; Scales, Jamie; Webb, Darren.

CARDIFF CITY

Adams Darren	5 7	10 07	F	12 1 74	Newham	Danson Furnace	Cardiff C	34	4
Baddeley Lee	6 1	12 07	D	12 7 74	Cardiff	Trainee	Cardiff C	124	1
Bird Anthony‡	5 10	10 07	F	1 9 74	Cardiff	Trainee	Cardiff C	75	13
Bolesan Mirko‡			F	6 5 75	Genoa	Sestrese	Cardiff C	1	—
Brazil Derek*	5 11	10 06	D	14 12 68	Dublin	Rivermount BC	Manchester U	2	—
							Oldham Ath (loan)	1	—
							Swansea C (loan)	12	1
							Cardiff C	115	1
Dale Carl	5 8	10 07	F	29 4 66	Colwyn Bay	Bangor C	Chester C	116	41
							Cardiff C	155	59
Davis Chris*			D	17 10 76	Cardiff	Trainee	Cardiff C	—	—
Evans Andy‡	6 1	12 01	F	25 11 75	Aberystwyth	Trainee	Cardiff C	15	—
Evans Terry‡	5 8	10 07	D	8 1 76	Pontypridd	Trainee	Cardiff C	14	—
Flack Steve	6 1	11 04	F	29 5 71	Cambridge	Cambridge C	Cardiff C	10	1
Fleming Hayden§			D	14 3 78	Islington	Trainee	Cardiff C	22	—
Gardner Jimmy	5 10	10 02	D	27 9 67	Dunfermline	Ayresome North	Queen's Park	2	—
							Motherwell	16	—
							St Mirren	41	1
							Scarborough	6	1
							Cardiff C	35	4
Harding Paul	5 10	12 05	M	6 3 64	Mitcham	Barnet	Notts Co	54	1
							Southend U (loan)	5	—
							Watford (loan)	2	—
							Birmingham C	22	—
							Cardiff C	36	—
Haworth Simon	6 3	11 05	F	30 3 77	Cardiff	Trainee	Cardiff C	13	—
Ingram Chris*			F	5 12 76	Cardiff	Trainee	Cardiff C	8	1
Jarman Lee	6 1	10 10	D	16 12 77	Cardiff	Trainee	Cardiff C	32	—
Johnson Glenn	5 10	11 10	F	16 7 72	Sydney	Blacktown City	Cardiff C	5	—
Jones Ian‡			D	26 8 76	Germany	Trainee	Cardiff C	3	—
Osman Russell‡	5 11	12 01	D	14 2 59	Repton	Apprentice	Ipswich T	294	17
							Leicester C	108	8
							Southampton	96	6
							Bristol C	70	3
							Plymouth Arg	—	—
							Brighton & HA	12	—
							Cardiff C	15	—
Perry Jason	5 11	10 09	D	2 4 70	Caerphilly	Trainee	Cardiff C	246	5

Philliskirk Tony	6 1	13 02	F	10	2 6 65	Sunderland	Amateur	Sheffield U	80	20
								Rotherham U (loan)	6	1
								Oldham Ath	10	1
								Preston NE	14	6
								Bolton W	141	51
								Peterborough U	43	15
								Burnley	40	9
								Carlisle U (loan)	3	1
								Cardiff C	28	4
Rodgerson Ian	5 8	10 07	M	9	4 6 66	Hereford	Pegasus Juniors	Hereford U	100	6
								Cardiff C	99	4
								Birmingham C	95	13
								Sunderland	10	—
								Cardiff C	34	1
Scott Andy	6 0	12 11	D	27	6 7 75	Manchester	Trainee	Blackburn R	—	—
								Cardiff C	14	1
Searle Damon*	5 11	10 04	D	26	10 71	Cardiff	Trainee	Cardiff C	234	3
Vick Leigh§			M	8	1 7 8	Cardiff	Trainee	Cardiff C	4	—
Wigg Nathan	5 8	11 03	M	27	9 7 4	Newport	Trainee	Cardiff C	58	1
Williams David*	6 0	12 00	G	18	9 6 8	Liverpool	Trainee	Oldham Ath	—	—
								Burnley	24	—
								Rochdale (loan)	6	—
								Crewe Alex (loan)	—	—
								Cardiff C	82	—
Williams Steven	6 3	12 12	G	16	10 74	Aberystwyth	Coventry C	Cardiff C	28	—
Young Scott	6 2	12 04	F	14	1 7 6	Tonypandy	Trainee	Cardiff C	69	—

Trainees
Butler, David M; Clark, Allan A; Dennis, Richard O; Fleming, Hayden V; Greedy, Mark J; Hill, John A; Jeremiah, Jerome; Misbah, Samir; Phillips, Lee; Pugh, Richard G; Rendell, John D; Street, Lee J; Vick, Leigh.

Associated Schoolboys
Downs, Robert; George, Stephen A; Hicks, Mike; Howse, Ian; Kelly, Philip; McCarthy, James; Owen, Philip; Parnell, Blake; Phillips, Darryl J; Skelly, Lee; Vaughan, Daniel.

Associated Schoolboys who have accepted the club's offer of a Traineeship/Contract
Cadette, Nathan D; Loveless, Ian; Roberts, Christian J; Smith, Gavin; Thomas, Danny; Wedgbury, Karl.

CARLISLE UNITED

Allen Clive‡	5 11	12 07	F	20	5 5 61	London	Apprentice	QPR	49	32
								Arsenal	—	—
								Crystal Palace	25	9
								QPR	87	40
								Tottenham H	105	60
								Bordeaux	19	13
								Manchester C	53	16
								Chelsea	16	7
								West Ham U	38	17
								Millwall	12	—
								Carlisle U	3	—
Aspinall Warren	5 9	12 10	F	13	9 6 67	Wigan	Apprentice	Wigan Ath	10	1
								Everton	7	—
								Wigan Ath (loan)	41	21
								Aston Villa	44	14
								Portsmouth	132	21
								Swansea C (loan)	5	—
								Bournemouth	33	9
								Carlisle U (loan)	7	1
								Carlisle U	42	6
Bennett Gary*	6 1	12 01	D	4	12 61	Manchester	Amateur	Manchester C	—	—
								Cardiff C	87	11
								Sunderland	369	23
								Carlisle U	26	5
Caig Tony	6 0	13 04	G	11	4 7 4	Whitehaven	Trainee	Carlisle U	94	—
Cleeland Marc‡	5 8	10 00	M	15	12 75	Whitehaven	Trainee	Carlisle U	—	—
Conway Paul‡	6 1	12 10	M	17	4 7 0	London	Oldham Ath	Carlisle U	64	13
Currie David	5 11	12 13	F	27	11 62	Stockton	Local	Middlesbrough	113	31
								Darlington	76	33
								Barnsley	80	30
								Nottingham F	8	1
								Oldham Ath	31	3
								Barnsley	75	12
								Rotherham U (loan)	5	2
								Huddersfield T (loan)	7	1
								Carlisle U	80	13

Name					Birthplace	Source	Clubs	Apps	Gls
Day Mervyn	6 2	14 13	G	26 6 55	Chelmsford	Apprentice	West Ham U	194	—
							Orient	170	—
							Aston Villa	30	—
							Leeds U	227	—
							Coventry C (loan)	—	—
							Luton T (loan)	4	—
							Sheffield U (loan)	1	—
							Carlisle U	16	—
Delap Rory	6 0	12 03	M	6 7 76	Coldfield	Trainee	Carlisle U	24	3
Donachie Danny*	5 11	12 00	M	17 5 73	Manchester	Radcliffe	Carlisle U	1	—
Edmondson Darren	6 0	12 11	M	4 11 71	Coniston	Trainee	Carlisle U	194	8
Elliott Tony‡	6 0	13 04	G	30 11 69	Nuneaton		Birmingham C	—	—
							Hereford U	75	—
							Huddersfield T	15	—
							Carlisle U	22	—
Hayward Steve	5 11	12 03	M	8 9 71	Walsall	Trainee	Derby Co	26	1
							Carlisle U	47	6
Hopper Tony	5 10	11 13	M	31 5 76	Carlisle	Trainee	Carlisle U	11	—
Jansen Matthew			M	20 10 77	Carlisle	Trainee	Carlisle U	—	—
Joyce Joe	5 9	11 01	D	18 3 61	Consett	School	Barnsley	334	4
							Scunthorpe U	91	2
							Carlisle U	50	—
							Darlington (loan)	4	—
McAlindon Gareth	5 9	12 09	F	6 4 77	Hexham	Newcastle U	Carlisle U	3	—
Murray Nathan‡	6 1	12 07	D	10 9 75	South Shields	Trainee	Newcastle U	—	—
							Carlisle U	—	—
Peacock Lee	6 0	12 05	F	9 10 76	Paisley	Trainee	Carlisle U	30	2
Prokas Richard	5 9	11 04	M	22 1 76	Penrith	Trainee	Carlisle U	59	1
Reeves David	6 0	12 08	F	19 11 67	Birkenhead	Heswall	Sheffield W	17	2
							Scunthorpe U (loan)	4	2
							Scunthorpe U (loan)	6	4
							Burnley (loan)	16	8
							Bolton W	134	29
							Notts Co	13	2
							Carlisle U	119	45
Robinson Jamie	6 1	12 08	D	22 2 72	Liverpool	Trainee	Liverpool	—	—
							Barnsley	9	—
							Carlisle U	50	4
Snodin Glynn‡	5 6	11 00	D	14 2 60	Rotherham	Apprentice	Doncaster R	309	61
							Sheffield W	59	1
							Leeds U	94	10
							Oldham Ath (loan)	8	1
							Rotherham U	3	—
							Hearts	34	—
							Barnsley	25	—
							Carlisle U	—	—
Thomas Rod	5 6	11 02	F	10 10 70	London	Trainee	Watford	84	9
							Gillingham (loan)	8	1
							Carlisle U	110	16
Thorpe Jeff	5 11	12 08	M	17 11 72	Whitehaven	Trainee	Carlisle U	131	6
Varty Will	6 0	12 04	D	1 10 76	Workington	Trainee	Carlisle U	—	—
Walling Dean	5 11	11 10	D	17 4 69	Leeds		Leeds U	—	—
							Rochdale	65	8
						Guiseley	Carlisle U	184	19

Trainees
Armstrong, Gavin; Boertien, Paul; Corrieri, Stephen J; Day, Richard M; Dixon, George; Dixon, Lee D P; Dobie, Robert S; Hodgson, Michael A; Knighton, Mark M; Lancaster, Ian R; Mellon, Marc R; Moore, David G; Sandwith, Kevin; Taylor, Lee R.

Non-Contract
Conway, Paul J; Dalton, Neil J; Wilkes, David A.

Associated Schoolboys
Benson, Jon K; Clark, Barry J; Hampton, James; Heath, Jamie; Hetherington, Philip M; Holmes, Gareth; Jenkinson, Peter M; Kelleher, Christopher; Skelton, Gavin; Thurston, Mark R; Thwaites, Adam; Wilson, Christopher.

Associated Schoolboys who have accepted the club's offer of a Traineeship/Contract
Burton, Lee R; Douglas, Andrew S; Jones, Mark A; Thompson, Craig.

CHARLTON ATHLETIC

Name					Birthplace	Source	Clubs	Apps	Gls
Allen Bradley	5 7	10 07	F	13 9 71	Harold Wood	School	QPR	81	27
							Charlton Ath	10	3
Ammann Mike*	6 2	14 04	G	8 2 71	California	Cal State Univ	Charlton Ath	30	—
Balmer Stuart	6 1	12 04	D	20 9 69	Falkirk	Celtic BC	Celtic	—	—
							Charlton Ath	179	6
Bowyer Lee	5 9	9 09	M	3 1 77	London	Trainee	Charlton Ath	46	8
Brown Steve	6 1	13 10	D	13 5 72	Brighton	Trainee	Charlton Ath	81	3

Name							Club	Apps	Gls
Chandler Dean	6 1	11 02	D	6 5 76	Ilford	Trainee	Charlton Ath	2	1
Chapple Phil	6 2	12 07	D	26 11 66	Norwich	Apprentice	Norwich C	—	—
							Cambridge U	187	19
							Charlton Ath	81	9
Curbishley Alan	5 10	11 07	M	8 11 57	Forest Gate	Apprentice	West Ham U	85	5
							Birmingham C	130	11
							Aston Villa	36	1
							Charlton Ath	63	6
							Brighton & HA	116	13
							Charlton Ath	28	—
Dowson Keith‡			F	14 9 76	London	Trainee	Charlton Ath	—	—
Garland Peter‡	5 10	12 00	M	20 1 71	Croydon	Trainee	Tottenham H	1	—
							Newcastle U	2	—
							Charlton Ath	53	2
							Wycombe W (loan)	5	—
Gritt Steve‡	5 9	10 10	D	31 10 57	Bournemouth	Apprentice	Bournemouth	6	3
							Charlton Ath	347	24
							Walsall	20	1
							Charlton Ath	33	1
Humphrey John*	5 10	11 04	D	31 1 61	Paddington	Apprentice	Wolverhampton W	149	3
							Charlton Ath	194	3
							Crystal Palace	160	2
							Reading (loan)	8	—
							Charlton Ath	28	—
Jones Keith	5 9	10 11	M	14 10 65	Dulwich	Apprentice	Chelsea	52	7
							Brentford	169	13
							Southend U	90	11
							Charlton Ath	56	1
Kyte Jamie*	5 7	10 00	M	17 9 77	Erith	Trainee	Charlton Ath	—	—
Larkin Andy*	6 1	11 09	D	24 9 77	Kent	Trainee	Charlton Ath	—	—
Leaburn Carl	6 3	13 00	F	30 3 69	Lewisham	Apprentice	Charlton Ath	264	42
							Northampton T (loan)	9	—
Linger Paul	5 6	10 03	M	20 12 74	Stepney	Trainee	Charlton Ath	23	1
Mortimer Paul	5 11	11 03	M	8 5 68	Kensington	Fulham	Charlton Ath	113	17
							Aston Villa	12	1
							Crystal Palace	22	2
							Brentford (loan)	6	—
							Charlton Ath	45	9
Nelson Garry*	5 10	11 10	F	16 1 61	Braintree	Amateur	Southend U	129	17
							Swindon T	79	7
							Plymouth Arg	74	20
							Brighton & HA	144	46
							Notts Co (loan)	2	—
							Charlton Ath	185	37
Newton Shaun	5 8	11 00	M	20 8 75	Camberwell	Trainee	Charlton Ath	88	7
Nicholls Kevin			M	2 1 79	Newham	Trainee	Charlton Ath	—	—
Petterson Andy	6 2	14 12	G	26 9 69	Fremantle		Luton T	19	—
							Swindon T (loan)	—	—
							Ipswich T (loan)	—	—
							Ipswich T (loan)	1	—
							Charlton Ath	18	—
							Bradford C (loan)	3	—
							Ipswich T (loan)	1	—
							Plymouth Arg (loan)	6	—
							Colchester U (loan)	5	—
Robinson John	5 10	11 02	M	29 8 71	Bulawayo	Apprentice	Brighton & HA	62	6
							Charlton Ath	107	12
Robson Mark	5 7	10 02	M	22 5 69	Newham	Trainee	Exeter C	26	7
							Tottenham H	8	—
							Reading (loan)	7	—
							Watford (loan)	1	—
							Plymouth Arg (loan)	7	—
							Exeter C (loan)	8	1
							West Ham U	47	8
							Charlton Ath	90	6
Rufus Richard	6 1	10 05	D	12 1 75	Lewisham	Trainee	Charlton Ath	69	—
Salmon Marc*			M	10 2 73	Edmonton	Harlow T	Charlton Ath	—	—
Salmon Mike	6 2	12 12	G	14 7 64	Leyland	Local	Blackburn R	1	—
							Chester C (loan)	16	—
							Stockport Co	118	—
							Bolton W	26	—
							Wrexham (loan)	17	—
							Wrexham	83	—
							Charlton Ath	114	—
Stuart Jamie	5 10	11 00	D	15 10 76	Southwark	Trainee	Charlton Ath	39	2
Sturgess Paul	5 11	12 05	D	4 8 75	Dartford	Trainee	Charlton Ath	48	—

Walsh Colin‡	5 9	11 00	M	22 7 62	Hamilton	Apprentice	Nottingham F	139	32
							Charlton Ath	242	21
							Peterborough U (loan)	5	1
							Middlesbrough (loan)	13	1
Whyte Chris*	6 1	12 00	D	2 9 61	London	Amateur	Arsenal	90	8
							Crystal Palace (loan)	13	—
						Los Angeles R	WBA	84	7
							Leeds U	113	5
							Birmingham C	68	1
							Coventry C (loan)	1	—
							Charlton Ath	11	—
Whyte David	5 8	10 07	F	20 4 71	Greenwich	Greenwich	Crystal Palace	27	4
						Borough	Charlton Ath (loan)	8	2
							Charlton Ath	63	21
Williams Paul*	5 7	10 09	F	16 8 65	London	Woodford T	Charlton Ath	82	23
							Brentford (loan)	7	3
							Sheffield W	93	25
							Crystal Palace	46	7
							Sunderland (loan)	3	—
							Birmingham C (loan)	11	—
							Charlton Ath	9	—
							Torquay U (loan)	9	—
Wright Robert			G	17 9 77	London	QPR	Charlton Ath	—	—

Trainees
Campbell, Paul I; Cella, Nicholas D; Crane, Paul S; Foley, Westley A; Frampton, Stephen G; Kearley, Dean R; Lee, Matthew A; Lisbie, Kevin A; McCann, Lawrence; Minors, Dwayne J; Mpele, John; Notley, Jay D; Oakey, Steven R; Odum-Jones, Bobby C; Pierou, Christopher C; Terry, Paul E; Tindall, Jason; Watkins, Jake A; Way, James W.

Associated Schoolboys
Allman, Anthony; Beale, Michael; Cook, Paul; Day, Aaron A; Hockley, David; Izzet, Kemal; Konchesky, Paul; Parker, Scott; Tucker, Lyndon A; Turner, Sam.

Associated Schoolboys who have accepted the club's offer of a Traineeship/Contract
Carnegie, Daniel I; Goldup, Robert; Hawkins, John A; Osborn, Scott; Richardson, Craig; Toms, Frazer P.

CHELSEA

Barness Anthony	5 10	12 01	D	25 2 72	Lewisham	Trainee	Charlton Ath	27	1
							Chelsea	14	—
							Middlesbrough (loan)	—	—
							Southend U (loan)	5	—
Burley Craig	6 1	12 13	M	24 9 71	Ayr	Trainee	Chelsea	82	5
Clarke Steve	5 10	12 05	D	29 8 63	Saltcoats	Beith J	St Mirren	151	6
							Chelsea	273	6
Clement Neil	5 10	10 00	D	3 10 78	Reading	Trainee	Chelsea	—	—
Colgan Nick	6 1	13 06	G	19 9 73	Eire	Drogheda	Chelsea	—	—
							Crewe Alex (loan)	—	—
							Grimsby T (loan)	—	—
							Millwall (loan)	—	—
Duberry Michael	6 1	13 06	D	14 10 75	Enfield	Trainee	Chelsea	23	—
							Bournemouth (loan)	7	—
Furlong Paul	6 0	13 08	F	1 10 68	London	Enfield	Coventry C	37	4
							Watford	79	37
							Chelsea	64	13
Gullit Ruud	6 2	12 00	F	1 9 62	Surinam	DWS Amsterdam	Haarlem	91	32
							Feyenoord	85	30
							PSV Eindhoven	68	46
							AC Milan	117	35
							Sampdoria	31	15
							AC Milan	8	3
							Sampdoria	22	9
							Chelsea	31	3
Hitchcock Kevin	6 1	13 04	G	5 10 62	Custom House	Barking	Nottingham F	—	—
							Mansfield T (loan)	14	—
							Mansfield T	168	—
							Chelsea	81	—
							Northampton T (loan)	17	—
							West Ham U (loan)	—	—
Hoddle Glenn*	6 0	11 06	M	27 10 57	Hayes	Apprentice	Tottenham H	377	88
						Monaco	Chelsea	—	—
							Swindon T	64	1
							Chelsea	31	1
Hughes Mark	6 0	12 04	F	1 11 63	Wrexham	Apprentice	Manchester U	89	37
							Barcelona	28	4
							Bayern Munich (loan)	18	6
							Manchester U	256	82
							Chelsea	31	8
Hughes Paul	6 0	11 07	M	19 4 76	Hammersmith	Trainee	Chelsea	—	—

Name	Ht	Wt	Pos	DOB	Birthplace	Source	Club	Apps	Gls
Izzet Muzzy	5 10	10 12	M	31 10 74	Mile End	Trainee	Chelsea	—	—
							Leicester C (loan)	9	1
Johnsen Erland	6 1	14 04	D	5 4 67	Fredrikstad	Bayern Munich	Chelsea	127	1
Kelly Russell*	5 10	11 00	M	10 8 76	Ballymoney	Trainee	Leyton Orient (loan)	6	—
Kharine Dmitri	6 2	13 09	G	16 8 68	Moscow		Torpedo Moscow	63	—
							Dynamo Moscow	40	—
							CSKA Moscow	34	—
							Chelsea	102	—
Kjeldbjerg Jakob	6 3	13 08	D	21 10 69	Frederiks	Silkeborg	Chelsea	52	2
Lee David	6 3	15 01	D	26 11 69	Kingswood	Trainee	Chelsea	149	10
							Reading (loan)	5	5
							Plymouth Arg (loan)	9	1
							Portsmouth (loan)	5	—
McCann Chris	5 8	10 05	D	28 11 76	Plaistow	Trainee	Chelsea	—	—
Mendes Junior‡	5 8	10 00	M	15 9 76	Balham	Trainee	Chelsea	—	—
Minto Scott	5 10	12 07	D	6 8 71	Cheshire	Trainee	Charlton Ath	180	7
							Chelsea	29	—
Morris Jody	5 5	9 00	M	22 12 78	London	Trainee	Chelsea	1	—
Myers Andy	5 10	12 11	M	3 11 73	Hounslow	Trainee	Chelsea	53	1
Newton Eddie	6 0	12 08	F	13 12 71	Hammersmith	Trainee	Chelsea	125	8
							Cardiff C (loan)	18	4
Nicholls Mark	5 9	9 10	F	30 5 77	Hillingdon	Trainee	Chelsea	—	—
Norman Craig‡	5 11	11 11	D	21 3 75	Perivale	Trainee	Chelsea	—	—
Peacock Gavin	5 9	11 09	M	18 11 67	Welling	Apprentice	QPR	17	1
							Gillingham	70	11
							Bournemouth	56	8
							Newcastle U	105	35
							Chelsea	103	17
Petrescu Dan	5 8	9 05	M	22 12 67	Bucharest	Genoa	Sheffield W	37	3
							Chelsea	24	2
Phelan Terry	5 7	9 00	D	16 3 67	Manchester	Trainee	Leeds U	14	—
							Swansea C	45	—
							Wimbledon	159	1
							Manchester C	103	1
							Chelsea	12	—
Rix Graham‡	5 9	11 00	F	23 10 57	Doncaster	Apprentice	Arsenal	351	41
							Brentford (loan)	6	—
						Caen, Le Havre	Dundee	14	2
							Chelsea	1	—
Rocastle David	5 9	12 10	F	2 5 67	Lewisham	Apprentice	Arsenal	218	24
							Leeds U	25	2
							Manchester C	21	2
							Chelsea	29	—
Rowe Zeke*	5 10	11 08	M	30 10 73	Stoke Newington	Trainee	Chelsea	—	—
							Barnet (loan)	10	2
							Brighton & HA (loan)	9	3
Sinclair Frank	5 9	12 09	D	3 12 71	Lambeth	Trainee	Chelsea	127	5
							WBA (loan)	6	1
Spackman Nigel*	6 1	13 04	M	2 12 60	Romsey	Andover	Bournemouth	119	10
							Chelsea	141	12
							Liverpool	51	—
							QPR	29	1
							Rangers	100	1
							Chelsea	67	—
Spencer John	5 6	11 07	F	11 9 70	Glasgow	Rangers Am BC	Rangers	13	2
							Morton (loan)	4	1
							Chelsea	99	36
Stein Mark	5 6	11 09	F	29 1 66	S. Africa		Luton T	54	19
							Aldershot (loan)	2	1
							QPR	33	4
							Oxford U	82	18
							Stoke C	94	50
							Chelsea	50	21
Wise Dennis	5 6	10 00	F	16 12 66	Kensington	Southampton	Wimbledon	135	27
							Chelsea	187	40

Trainees
Aggrey, James E; Crittenden, Nicholas J; Hampshire, Steven G; Hams, Neil; Hanlon, Ritchie K; Harrison, Gavin A; Potter, Daniel R J; Quinn, Paul J; Sakala, Mavuto; Sexton, Richard L; Sheerin, Joseph E; Ullah, Ainsley B; Wilkinson, Jeffrey M.

Associated Schoolboys
Demetrious, Shayne; Evans, Rhys K; Hajgato, Geza; King, John S; Martin, Paul; Nichols, Paul D; Osborne, Steven J; Parkes, Lee W; Rattray, John W; Royal, Mark; Terry, John G.

Associated Schoolboys who have accepted the club's offer of a Traineeship/Contract
Broad, Stephen; Dixon, Kevin R; Harley, Jonathon; Richardson, Jay G; Wolleaston, Robert A.

CHESTER CITY

Player	Ht	Wt	Pos	Birthdate	Birthplace	Source	Club	Apps	Gls
Alsford Julian	6 2	13 07	D	24 12 72	Poole	Trainee	Watford	13	1
							Chester C	59	—
Bagnall John*	6 0	12 00	G	23 11 73	Southport	Preston NE	Chester C	—	—
							Wigan Ath	—	—
							Bury	—	—
							Chester C	—	—
Bishop Eddie*	5 10	12 06	M	28 11 62	Liverpool	Runcorn	Tranmere R	76	19
							Chester C	115	28
							Crewe Alex (loan)	3	—
Brenchley Scott‡			M	22 12 76	Hull	Liverpool	Chester C	—	—
Brown Greg§			D	31 7 78	Manchester	Trainee	Chester C	3	—
Burnham Jason*	5 10	13 03	D	8 5 73	Mansfield	Notts County	Northampton T	88	2
							Chester C	64	1
Chambers Leroy*	5 11	12 00	F	25 10 72	Sheffield	Trainee	Sheffield W	—	—
							Chester C	21	1
Davidson Ross	5 8	11 06	D	13 11 73	Chertsey	Walton & Hersham	Sheffield U	2	—
							Chester C	19	1
Fisher Neil	5 10	11 00	M	7 11 70	St Helens	Trainee	Bolton W	24	1
							Chester C	44	2
Flitcroft David	5 11	13 05	M	14 1 74	Bolton	Trainee	Preston NE	8	2
							Lincoln C (loan)	2	—
							Chester C	49	2
Jackson Peter	6 0	13 06	D	6 4 61	Bradford	Apprentice	Bradford C	278	24
							Newcastle U	60	3
							Bradford C	58	5
							Huddersfield T	155	3
							Chester C	68	2
Jenkins Iain	5 9	11 10	D	24 11 72	Whiston	Trainee	Everton	5	—
							Bradford C (loan)	6	—
							Chester C	87	—
Milner Andy	6 0	11 00	F	10 2 67	Kendal	Netherfield	Manchester C	—	—
							Rochdale	127	25
							Chester C	78	12
Murphy John	6 1	14 00	F	18 10 76	Whiston	Trainee	Chester C	23	3
Noteman Kevin	5 10	12 02	F	15 10 69	Preston	Trainee	Leeds U	1	—
							Doncaster R	106	20
							Mansfield T	95	15
							Doncaster R	4	1
							Chester C	33	9
Preece Roger	5 8	10 11	M	9 6 69	Much Wenlock	Coventry C	Wrexham	110	12
							Chester C	170	4
Priest Chris	5 10	10 10	M	18 10 73	Leigh	Trainee	Everton	—	—
							Chester C	63	14
Ratcliffe Kevin	6 1	13 06	D	12 11 60	Mancot	Apprentice	Everton	359	2
							Dundee	4	—
							Everton	—	—
							Cardiff C	25	1
							Nottingham F	—	—
							Derby Co	6	—
							Chester C	23	—
Regis Cyrille	6 0	13 04	F	9 2 58	French Guyana	Moseley, Hayes	WBA	237	82
							Coventry C	238	47
							Aston Villa	52	12
							Wolverhampton W	19	2
							Wycombe W	35	9
							Chester C	29	7
Richardson Nick	6 1	12 06	M	11 4 67	Halifax	Local	Halifax T	101	17
							Cardiff C	111	13
							Wrexham (loan)	4	2
							Chester C (loan)	6	1
							Bury	5	—
							Chester C	37	4
Rimmer Stuart	5 7	11 00	F	12 10 64	Southport	Apprentice	Everton	3	—
							Chester C	114	67
							Watford	10	1
							Notts Co	4	2
							Walsall	88	31
							Barnsley	15	1
							Chester C	188	56
							Rochdale (loan)	3	—
							Preston NE (loan)	2	—
Rogers Dave	6 1	12 00	M	25 8 75	Liverpool	Trainee	Tranmere R	—	—
							Chester C	20	1

Name	Ht	Wt	Pos	DOB	Birthplace	Source	Club	Apps	Gls
Ryan Darren‡	5 9	11 00	M	3 7 72	Oswestry	Trainee	Shrewsbury T	4	—
							Chester C	17	2
							Stockport Co	36	6
							Rochdale	32	2
							Chester C	4	1
Shelton Gary	5 7	11 00	M	21 3 58	Nottingham	Apprentice	Walsall	24	—
							Aston Villa	24	7
							Notts Co (loan)	8	—
							Sheffield W	198	18
							Oxford U	65	1
							Bristol C	150	24
							Rochdale (loan)	3	—
							Chester C	44	3
Stewart Billy*	5 11	11 07	G	1 1 65	Liverpool	Apprentice	Liverpool	—	—
							Wigan Ath	14	—
							Chester C	272	—
							Northampton T	27	—
							Chesterfield (loan)	1	—
							Chester C	45	—
Whelan Spencer	6 2	13 00	D	17 9 71	Liverpool	Liverpool	Chester C	155	3

Trainees
Barlow, Brett; Briggs, Gregory M; Brown, Greg J; Cannon, Ian; Cattell, Mark P; Clench, Philip R; Dobson, Ryan A; Giles, Martin W; Hussaney, James A; Jones, Jonathan B; Quinn, Philip; Smith, Paul; Turner, David J; Warrington, Craig A.

Associated Schoolboys
Doughty, Matthew L; McKay, Matthew P.

Associated Schoolboys who have accepted the club's offer of a Traineeship/Contract
Kinsey, Benjamin; Kinsey, Joel; Williams, Scott J; Wright, Darren.

CHESTERFIELD

Name	Ht	Wt	Pos	DOB	Birthplace	Source	Club	Apps	Gls
Beasley Andrew	6 1	12 10	G	5 2 64	Sedgley	Apprentice	Luton T	—	—
							Mansfield T (loan)	—	—
							Gillingham (loan)	—	—
							Mansfield T	94	—
							Peterborough U (loan)	7	—
							Scarborough (loan)	4	—
							Bristol R (loan)	1	—
							Doncaster R	37	—
							Chesterfield	32	—
Carr Darren	6 3	13 07	D	4 9 68	Bristol	Trainee	Bristol R	30	—
							Newport Co	9	—
							Sheffield U	13	1
							Crewe Alex	104	5
							Chesterfield	64	3
Castledine Gary‡	5 8	11 12	F	27 3 70	Dumfries	Shirebrook	Mansfield T	66	3
							Chesterfield	—	—
Curtis Tom	5 8	11 07	M	1 3 73	Exeter	School	Derby Co	—	—
							Chesterfield	122	5
Davies Kevin	6 0	13 05	F	26 3 77	Sheffield	Trainee	Chesterfield	95	19
Dyche Sean	6 0	13 02	D	28 6 71	Kettering	Trainee	Nottingham F	—	—
							Chesterfield	195	8
Fairclough Wayne*	5 10	12 02	D	27 4 68	Nottingham	Apprentice	Notts Co	71	—
							Mansfield T	141	12
							Chesterfield	15	—
							Scarborough (loan)	7	—
Hazel Des*	5 10	11 10	M	15 7 67	Bradford	Apprentice	Sheffield W	6	—
							Grimsby T (loan)	9	2
							Rotherham U	238	30
							Chesterfield	21	—
Hewitt Jamie	5 10	11 04	M	17 5 68	Chesterfield	School	Chesterfield	249	14
							Doncaster R	33	—
							Chesterfield	95	8
Holland Paul	5 10	12 03	M	8 7 73	Lincoln	School	Mansfield T	149	25
							Sheffield U	18	1
							Chesterfield	17	2
Howard Jonathan	5 10	12 00	F	7 10 71	Sheffield	Trainee	Rotherham U	36	5
							Chesterfield	42	3
Jules Mark	5 9	11 00	F	5 9 71	Bradford	Trainee	Bradford C	—	—
							Scarborough	77	16
							Chesterfield	88	3
Law Nicky	6 0	13 07	D	8 9 61	London	Apprentice	Arsenal	—	—
							Barnsley	114	1
							Blackpool	66	1
							Plymouth Arg	38	5
							Notts Co	47	4
							Scarborough (loan)	12	—
							Rotherham U	128	4
							Chesterfield	104	10

Lormor Tony	6 0	12 10	F	29 10 70	Ashington	Trainee	Newcastle U	8	3
							Norwich C (loan)	—	—
							Lincoln C	100	30
							Peterborough U	5	—
							Chesterfield	64	23
Lund Gary	6 1	12 08	F	13 9 64	Grimsby	School	Grimsby T	60	24
							Lincoln C	44	13
							Notts Co	248	62
							Hull C (loan)	11	3
							Hull C (loan)	11	3
							Chesterfield	8	1
Madden Lawrie‡	5 10	13 00	D	28 9 55	Hackney	Arsenal Amateur	Mansfield T	10	—
						Manchester Univ	Charlton Ath	113	7
							Millwall	47	2
							Sheffield W	212	2
							Leicester C (loan)	3	—
							Wolverhampton W	67	1
							Darlington	5	—
							Chesterfield	37	1
Marples Chris‡	6 0	13 10	G	3 8 64	Chesterfield	Goole	Chesterfield	84	—
							Stockport Co	57	—
							York C	138	—
							Scunthorpe U (loan)	1	—
							Chesterfield	57	—
Mercer Billy	6 2	13 03	G	22 5 69	Liverpool	Trainee	Liverpool	—	—
							Rotherham U	104	—
							Sheffield U	4	—
							Nottingham F (loan)	—	—
							Chesterfield	34	—
Morris Andy	6 4	15 10	F	17 11 67	Sheffield		Rotherham U	7	—
							Chesterfield	234	51
							Exeter C (loan)	7	2
Moss David*	6 2	13 03	F	15 11 68	Doncaster	Boston U	Doncaster R	18	5
							Chesterfield	71	16
Narbett Jon*	5 10	12 02	M	21 11 68	Birmingham	Apprentice	Shrewsbury T	26	3
							Hereford U	149	31
							Leicester C (loan)	—	—
							Oxford U	15	—
							Chesterfield	20	1
Perkins Chris	5 11	11 00	M	9 1 74	Nottingham	Trainee	Mansfield T	8	—
							Chesterfield	40	—
Pierce David‡			G	4 10 75	Manchester	Rotherham U	Chesterfield	1	—
Roberts Darren*	6 0	12 04	F	12 10 69	Birmingham	Burton Alb	Wolverhampton W	21	5
							Hereford U (loan)	6	5
							Doncaster R	—	—
							Chesterfield	25	1
Robinson Philip	5 9	11 07	M	6 1 67	Stafford	Apprentice	Aston Villa	3	1
							Wolverhampton W	71	8
							Notts Co	66	5
							Birmingham C (loan)	9	—
							Huddersfield T	75	5
							Northampton T (loan)	14	—
							Chesterfield	61	17
Rogers Lee	5 11	12 00	D	28 10 66	Doncaster	Doncaster R	Chesterfield	314	1
Williams Mark	6 0	13 00	D	28 9 70	Stalybridge	Newtown	Shrewsbury T	102	3
							Chesterfield	42	3

Trainees
Bamford, Paul G; Bowater, Jason; Deakin, Mark; Kuchta, Andrew S; Lomas, James D; Partridge, Paul G; Sheppard, Jody.

COLCHESTER UNITED

Adcock Tony	5 10	11 09	F	27 2 63	Bethnal Green	Apprentice	Colchester U	210	98
							Manchester C	15	5
							Northampton T	72	30
							Bradford C	38	6
							Northampton T	35	10
							Peterborough U	111	35
							Luton T	2	—
							Colchester U	41	12
Ball Steve‡	5 11	13 00	M	2 9 69	Colchester	Trainee	Arsenal	—	—
							Colchester U	4	—
							Norwich C	2	—
							Colchester U	64	7
Betts Simon	5 7	11 00	D	3 3 73	Middlesbrough	Trainee	Ipswich T	—	—
							Scarborough	—	—
							Colchester U	136	8
Boyce Robert*			F	7 1 74	Islington	Enfield	Colchester U	2	—

Name			Pos	D.O.B.	Birthplace	Source	Club	Apps	Gls
Burley George	5 10	11 00	D	3 6 56	Cumnock	Apprentice	Ipswich T	394	5
							Sunderland	54	—
							Gillingham	46	2
							Motherwell	54	—
							Ayr U	67	—
							Falkirk	1	—
							Motherwell	5	—
							Colchester U	7	—
Caesar Gus*	6 0	12 09	D	5 3 66	London	Apprentice	Arsenal	44	—
							QPR (loan)	5	—
							Cambridge U	—	—
							Bristol C	10	—
							Airdrieonians	57	1
							Colchester U	62	3
Caldwell Garrett			G	6 11 73	Princeton		Colchester U	—	—
Cawley Peter	6 4	15 07	D	15 9 65	London	Chertsey	Wimbledon	1	—
							Bristol R (loan)	10	—
							Fulham (loan)	5	—
							Bristol R	3	—
							Southend U	7	1
							Exeter C	7	—
							Barnet	3	—
							Colchester U	125	7
Cheetham Michael*	5 9	12 03	M	30 6 67	Amsterdam	Army	Ipswich T	4	—
							Cambridge U	132	22
							Chesterfield	5	—
							Colchester U	37	3
Cook Anthony§			M	17 9 76	Hemel Hempstead	Trainee	Colchester U	2	—
Dalli Jean‡			D	13 8 76	Enfield		Colchester U	1	—
Dennis Tony*	5 7	10 02	M	1 12 63	Eton	Slough	Cambridge U	111	10
							Chesterfield	10	—
							Colchester U	65	5
Duguid Karl§	5 11	11 09	F	21 3 78	Hitchin	Trainee	Colchester U	16	1
Dunne Joe	5 8	11 06	D	25 5 73	Dublin	Trainee	Gillingham	115	1
							Colchester U	5	1
Emberson Carl	6 1	14 09	G	13 7 73	Epsom	Trainee	Millwall	—	—
							Colchester U (loan)	13	—
							Colchester U	61	—
English Tony	6 0	12 07	D	19 10 66	Luton	Coventry C	Colchester U	351	42
Fry Chris	5 8	10 07	F	23 10 69	Cardiff	Trainee	Cardiff C	55	1
							Hereford U	90	10
							Colchester U	88	10
Gibbs Paul	5 10	11 03	D	26 10 72	Gorleston	Diss T	Colchester U	33	3
Gregory David	5 9	12 08	M	23 1 70	Colchester	Trainee	Ipswich T	32	2
							Hereford U (loan)	2	—
							Peterborough U	3	—
							Colchester U	10	—
Haydon Nicky	5 9	11 07	M	10 8 78	Barking	Trainee	Colchester U	—	—
Kinsella Mark	5 9	11 05	M	12 8 72	Dublin	Home Farm	Colchester U	173	25
Lewis Ben	5 10	12 04	D	22 6 77	Chelmsford	Trainee	Colchester U	2	—
Lock Tony	5 10	13 00	M	3 9 76	Harlow	Trainee	Colchester U	3	1
Locke Adam	5 11	12 07	M	20 8 70	Croydon	Trainee	Crystal Palace	—	—
							Southend U	73	4
							Colchester U (loan)	4	—
							Colchester U	47	4
McCarthy Tony	6 1	12 06	D	9 11 69	Dublin	Shelbourne	Millwall	21	1
							Crewe Alex (loan)	2	—
							Colchester U	54	1
Reinelt Robbie	5 10	12 07	M	11 3 74	Epping	Trainee	Aldershot	5	—
							Gillingham	52	5
							Colchester U	27	7
Whitton Steve	6 0	13 07	M	4 12 60	East Ham	Apprentice	Coventry C	74	21
							West Ham U	39	6
							Birmingham C (loan)	8	2
							Birmingham C	95	28
							Sheffield W	32	4
							Ipswich T	88	15
							Colchester U	56	14

Trainees
Armitage, Gavin L; Bates, Robert C; Cook, Anthony M; Craft, Daryl J; Duguid, Karl A; Kingshott, Daryll N; McCormack, Francis P; O'Donnell, Daniel J; Palfreyman, Andrew M; Rainford, David J; Trigg, Darryl; Walsh, Marc D.

Associated Schoolboys
Atkinson, Robert P; Delaney, Paul M; Sinclair, Simon; Slatter, Daniel C; Taylor, Andrew D; Watkins, John.

COVENTRY CITY

Name			Pos	Birth	Birthplace	Source	Club	Apps	Gls
Blake Tim	6 2	13 00	D	25 9 75	Merthyr	Trainee	Coventry C	—	—
Boland Willie	5 9	11 02	M	6 8 75	Ennis	Trainee	Coventry C	43	—
Borrows Brian	5 10	11 12	D	20 12 60	Liverpool	Amateur	Everton	27	—
							Bolton W	95	—
							Coventry C	386	11
							Bristol C (loan)	6	—
Burrows David	5 10	11 08	D	25 10 68	Dudley	Apprentice	WBA	46	1
							Liverpool	146	3
							West Ham U	29	1
							Everton	19	—
							Coventry C	22	—
Busst David	6 1	12 10	D	30 6 67	Birmingham	Moor Green	Coventry C	50	4
Carlita	5 9	10 06	M	20 12 70	Angola	Farense	Coventry C	—	—
Christie Iyseden	6 0	12 06	F	14 11 76	Coventry	Trainee	Coventry C	1	—
Costello Lorcan	5 9	11 02	D	11 11 76	Dublin	Trainee	Coventry C	—	—
Daish Liam	6 2	13 05	D	23 9 68	Portsmouth	Apprentice	Portsmouth	1	—
							Cambridge U	139	4
							Birmingham C	73	3
							Coventry C	11	1
Dublin Dion	6 2	12 04	F	22 4 69	Leicester		Norwich C	—	—
							Cambridge U	156	52
							Manchester U	12	2
							Coventry C	65	27
Ducros Andrew	5 4	9 08	F	16 9 77	Evesham	Trainee	Coventry C	—	—
Ekelund Ronnie‡	5 10	12 06	M	21 8 72	Denmark	Barcelona	Southampton	17	5
							Manchester C	4	—
							Coventry C	—	—
Filan John	5 11	13 02	G	8 2 70	Sydney	Budapest St George	Cambridge U	68	—
							Nottingham F (loan)	—	—
							Coventry C	15	—
Gillespie Gary	6 2	12 07	D	5 7 60	Stirling	School	Falkirk	22	—
							Coventry C	172	6
							Liverpool	156	14
							Celtic	69	2
							Coventry C	3	—
Goodwin Scott	5 9	11 08	D	13 9 78	Hull	Trainee	Coventry C	—	—
Gould Jonathan*	6 1	12 07	G	18 7 68	Paddington	Clevedon T	Halifax T	32	—
							WBA	—	—
							Coventry C	25	—
							Bradford C (loan)	9	—
Hall Marcus	6 1	12 02	D	24 3 76	Coventry	Trainee	Coventry C	30	—
Hawkins Colin	6 1	12 06	G	17 8 77	Galway		Coventry C	—	—
Healy Brett	5 8	10 08	M	6 10 77	Coventry	Trainee	Coventry C	—	—
Hurst Lee*	6 0	11 09	M	21 9 70	Nuneaton	Trainee	Coventry C	49	2
Isaias	5 10	12 10	M		Brazil	Benfica	Coventry C	11	2
Jenkinson Leigh‡	6 0	12 02	F	9 7 69	Thorne	Trainee	Hull C	130	13
							Rotherham U (loan)	7	—
							Coventry C	32	1
							Birmingham C (loan)	3	—
Jess Eoin	5 10	11 07	F	13 12 70	Aberdeen	Rangers	Aberdeen	201	50
							Coventry C	12	1
Lamptey Nii	5 8	11 04	F	10 12 74	Accra		Anderlecht	30	9
							PSV Eindhoven	22	9
							Aston Villa	6	—
							Coventry C	6	—
Lovelock Andrew*	5 9	10 12	F	20 12 76	Swindon	Trainee	Coventry C	—	—
Mitten Paul	5 8	10 12	F	22 12 75	Stockport	Manchester U	Stockport Co	—	—
							Coventry C	—	—
Morgan Steve*	5 9	11 00	D	19 9 68	Oldham	Apprentice	Blackpool	144	10
							Plymouth Arg	121	6
							Coventry C	68	2
							Bristol R (loan)	5	—
Ndlovu Peter	5 8	10 2	F	25 2 73	Zimbabwe	Highlanders	Coventry C	157	36
O'Toole Gavin	5 9	11 00	M	19 9 75	Dublin	Trainee	Coventry C	—	—
Ogrizovic Steve	6 5	15 00	G	12 9 57	Mansfield	ONRYC	Chesterfield	16	—
							Liverpool	4	—
							Shrewsbury T	84	—
							Coventry C	440	1

Pickering Ally	5 11	11 00	D	22 6 67	Manchester	Buxton	Rotherham U	88	2
							Coventry C	65	—
Prenderville Barry	6 0	12 08	D	16 10 76	Dublin	Trainee	Coventry C	—	—
Rennie David*	6 0	12 00	D	29 8 64	Edinburgh	Apprentice	Leicester C	21	1
							Leeds U	101	5
							Bristol C	104	8
							Birmingham C	35	4
							Coventry C	82	3
Richardson Kevin	5 7	11 07	M	4 12 62	Newcastle	Apprentice	Everton	109	16
							Watford	39	2
							Arsenal	96	5
						Real Sociedad	Aston Villa	143	13
							Coventry C	47	—
Salako John	5 9	12 03	F	11 2 69	Nigeria	Trainee	Crystal Palace	215	22
							Swansea C (loan)	13	3
							Coventry C	37	3
Shaw Richard	5 9	12 08	D	11 9 68	Brentford	Apprentice	Crystal Palace	207	3
							Hull C (loan)	4	—
							Coventry C	21	—
Shilton Sam	5 10	11 06	M	21 7 78	Nottingham	Schoolboy	Plymouth Arg	3	—
							Coventry C	—	—
Strachan Gordon	5 6	10 06	M	9 2 57	Edinburgh		Dundee	60	13
							Aberdeen	183	55
							Manchester U	160	33
							Leeds U	197	37
							Coventry C	17	—
Telfer Paul	5 9	11 06	M	21 10 71	Edinburgh	Trainee	Luton T	144	19
							Coventry C	31	1
Wegerle Roy‡	5 11	11 00	F	19 3 64	South Africa	Tampa Bay R	Chelsea	23	3
							Swindon T (loan)	7	1
							Luton T	45	10
							QPR	75	29
							Blackburn R	34	6
							Coventry C	53	9
Whelan Noel	6 2	12 03	F	30 12 74	Leeds	Trainee	Leeds U	48	7
							Coventry C	21	8
Williams Jamie	5 7	9 06	M	21 2 77	Coventry	Trainee	Coventry C	—	—
Williams Paul	6 0	12 10	D	26 3 71	Burton	Trainee	Derby Co	160	26
							Lincoln C (loan)	3	—
							Coventry C	32	2
Willis Adam	6 1	12 02	M	21 9 76	Nuneaton	Trainee	Coventry C	—	—

Trainees
Andrews, John H; Barnett, Christopher J; Faulconbridge, Craig M; Hunwick, Colin J; McGregor, Scott C; Morgan, Leon R; Nolan, Carl N; Quinn, Barry S; Strachan, Gavin D; Sumner, Jed; Ward, Alan.

Associated Schoolboys
Dagnan, Kieran; Downing, Roy J; English, Mark M; Eribenne, Chutwun Y; Fearn, Mark D; Gough, Steven; Hall, Daniel; Padmore, Stephen R; Pead, Craig G; Pearson, David; Steane, Ben; Thompson, Nathan; Watson, Steven; Woollaston, Gregory J.

Associated Schoolboys who have accepted the club's offer of a Traineeship/Contract
Bindley, Christopher J; Burrows, Mark; Colwell, Richard; Mullen, Nicky R; Williams, Jamie L.

CREWE ALEXANDRA

Adebola Dele	6 3	12 06	F	23 6 75	Lagos	Trainee	Crewe Alex	65	16
Barr Billy	5 11	10 08	M	21 1 69	Halifax	Trainee	Halifax T	196	13
						Halifax T	Crewe Alex	51	2
Collier Danny*	6 1	11 00	D	15 1 74	Eccles	Trainee	Wolverhampton W	—	—
							Crewe Alex	11	—
Collins Wayne	6 0	12 00	M	4 3 69	Manchester	Winsford U	Crewe Alex	117	14
Ellison Lee*	5 10	10 00	F	13 1 73	Bishop Auckland	Trainee	Darlington	72	17
							Hartlepool U (loan)	4	1
							Leicester C	—	—
							Crewe Alex	1	—
Garvey Steve	5 9	10 09	F	22 11 73	Tameside	Trainee	Crewe Alex	79	6
Gavin Patt‡	6 0	12 00	F	5 6 67	Hammersmith	Hanwell T	Gillingham	13	7
							Leicester C	3	—
							Gillingham (loan)	34	1
							Peterborough U	23	5
							Barnet	—	—
							Northampton T	14	4
							Wigan Ath	42	8
							Crewe Alex	—	—
Gayle Mark	6 2	12 03	G	21 10 69	Bromsgrove	Trainee	Leicester C	—	—
							Blackpool	—	—
						Worcester C	Walsall	75	—
							Crewe Alex	79	—
							Liverpool (loan)	—	—

Hawtin Dale*	5 11	11 00	D	28 12 75	Crewe	Trainee	Crewe Alex	—	—
Hopper Neil‡	6 1	12 08	G	27 1 76	Southampton	Trainee	Southampton	—	—
							Blackpool	—	—
							Crewe Alex	—	—
Hughes Anthony‡	6 0	12 05	D	3 10 73	Liverpool	Trainee	Crewe Alex	23	1
Lightfoot Chris	6 1	13 03	M	1 4 70	Warrington	Trainee	Chester C	277	32
							Wigan Ath	14	1
							Crewe Alex	6	—
Little Colin	5 8	10 00	F	4 11 72	Wythenshaw	Hyde U	Crewe Alex	12	1
Macauley Steve	6 1	12 00	D	4 3 69	Lytham	Fleetwood	Crewe Alex	123	18
Murphy Danny	5 9	10 08	M	18 3 77	Chester	Trainee	Crewe Alex	89	17
Parker Justin*			D	11 11 76	Stoke	Trainee	Crewe Alex	—	—
Pope Steven	5 11	11 00	D	8 9 76	Mow Cop	Trainee	Crewe Alex	—	—
Ridings Dave*	6 1	11 08	F	27 2 70	Farnworth	Curzon Ashton	Halifax T	21	4
							Lincoln C	10	—
						Curzon Ashton	Rochdale	—	—
							Crewe Alex	1	—
Rivers Mark	5 11	10 08	D	26 11 75	Crewe	Trainee	Crewe Alex	33	10
Savage Rob	6 0	10 01	F	18 10 74	Wrexham	Trainee	Manchester U	—	—
							Crewe Alex	36	9
Smith Mark*	6 1	13 09	G	2 1 73	Birmingham	Trainee	Nottingham F	—	—
							Crewe Alex	63	—
Smith Shaun	5 10	11 00	D	9 4 71	Leeds	Trainee	Halifax T	7	—
							Crewe Alex	157	20
Sund Ulf‡			M	28 12 78	Finland	IFK Vasa	Crewe Alex	—	—
Tierney Francis	5 10	11 00	M	10 9 75	Liverpool	Trainee	Crewe Alex	51	7
Turpin Simon	6 3	11 08	D	11 8 75	Blackburn		Crewe Alex	—	—
Unsworth Lee	6 0	11 00	D	25 2 73	Eccles	Ashton U	Crewe Alex	29	—
Westwood Ashley	5 10	10 08	D	31 8 76	Bridgnorth	Trainee	Manchester U	—	—
							Crewe Alex	33	4
Whalley Gareth	5 10	11 06	M	19 12 73	Manchester	Trainee	Crewe Alex	124	5
Wilkinson Ian‡	5 11	13 04	G	2 7 73	Warrington	Trainee	Manchester U	—	—
							Stockport Co	—	—
							Crewe Alex	3	—
							Doncaster R (loan)	—	—

Trainees
Bell, Christopher G; Collins, James I; Cox, Lee A; Critchley, Neil; Edwards, Gareth J; Green, Jonathan M; Hibbs, John R; Johnson, Seth A M; Knight, Darren P; Morse, Peter R; Mottram, Paul G; Murray, David R; Percival, Christopher; Richardson, Paul M; Smith, Aaran P; Smith, Peter L; Street, Kevin; Whittaker, David A; Wolstenholme, Michael D.

Non-Contract
Simpson, Wesley L.

Associated Schoolboys
Angell, Barry; Arrowsmith, Paul; Beeston, Mark A; Bostock, Andrew M; Burke, Andrew J; Foster, Stephen J; Hoult, Stephen R; Jones, John P; Jones, Robert A; Laurie, Carl A; Marsh, Nicholas J; McCready, Christopher J; Scheuber, Stuart M; Walker, Richard S.

Associated Schoolboys who have accepted the club's offer of a Traineeship/Contract
Allen, Christopher D; Baker, Ryan J; Brown, Christopher; Chadwick, Gareth; Hulse, Robert W; Jones, Andrew J; Lunt, Kenny V; Webster, Colin J L; Wright, David.

CRYSTAL PALACE

Andersen Leif	6 5	14 10	D	19 4 71	Fredrikstad	Moss	Crystal Palace	16	—
Boxall Danny	5 8	10 05	D	24 8 77	Croydon	Trainee	Crystal Palace	1	—
Burton Sagi	6 2	13 00	D	25 11 77	Birmingham	Trainee	Crystal Palace	—	—
Cyrus Andrew	5 8	10 07	D	30 9 76	Lambeth	Trainee	Crystal Palace	—	—
Davies Gareth	6 1	11 12	D	11 12 73	Hereford	Trainee	Hereford U	95	1
							Crystal Palace	20	2
Dyer Bruce	5 11	11 03	F	13 4 75	Ilford	Trainee	Watford	31	6
							Crystal Palace	62	14
Edworthy Marc	5 8	11 10	D	24 12 72	Barnstaple	Trainee	Plymouth Arg	69	1
							Crystal Palace	44	—
Enqvist Bjorn	5 10	10 09	M	12 10 77	Lund	Malmo	Crystal Palace	—	—
Folan Anthony	5 10	10 13	M	18 9 78	Lewisham	Trainee	Crystal Palace	—	—
Freedman Dougie	5 9	11 00	F	21 1 74	Glasgow	Trainee	QPR	—	—
							Barnet	47	27
							Crystal Palace	39	20
Gale Tony‡	6 1	13 07	D	19 11 59	London	Apprentice	Fulham	277	19
							West Ham U	300	5
							Blackburn R	15	—
							Crystal Palace	2	—

Ginty Rory	5 9	10 02	F	23 1 77	Galway	Trainee	Crystal Palace	—	—
Gordon Dean	6 0	13 04	D	10 2 73	Thornton Heath	Trainee	Crystal Palace	134	15
Hall Kevin‡	5 10	11 00	M	7 2 76	Edinburgh	Trainee	Crystal Palace	—	—
Harris Jason	6 1	11 07	F	24 11 76	Sutton	Trainee	Crystal Palace	—	—
Hopkin David	5 9	10 03	M	21 8 70	Greenock	Pt Glasgow R BC	Morton	18	—
							Chelsea	40	1
							Crystal Palace	42	8
Houghton Ray	5 7	10 10	M	9 1 62	Glasgow	Amateur	West Ham U	1	—
							Fulham	129	16
							Oxford U	83	10
							Liverpool	153	28
							Aston Villa	95	6
							Crystal Palace	51	6
Launders Brian*	5 10	11 10	M	8 1 76	Dublin	Trainee	Crystal Palace	4	—
							Oldham Ath (loan)	—	—
Martyn Nigel	6 2	14 07	G	11 8 66	St Austell	St Blazey	Bristol R	101	—
							Crystal Palace	272	—
Matthew Damian	5 11	10 10	M	23 9 70	Islington	Trainee	Chelsea	21	—
							Luton T (loan)	5	—
							Crystal Palace	24	1
							Bristol R (loan)	8	—
McKenzie Leon	5 10	11 02	M	17 5 78	Croydon	Trainee	Crystal Palace	12	—
Ndah George	6 1	11 04	M	23 12 74	Camberwell	Trainee	Crystal Palace	49	5
							Bournemouth (loan)	12	2
Parry David	5 10	11 02	M	12 3 78	Belfast	Trainee	Crystal Palace	—	—
Pitcher Darren	5 9	12 02	M	12 10 69	London	Trainee	Charlton Ath	173	8
							Galway (loan)	—	—
							Crystal Palace	61	—
Quinn Robert	5 11	11 02	D	8 11 76	Sidcup	Trainee	Crystal Palace	1	—
Roberts Andy	5 10	13 00	M	20 3 74	Dartford	Trainee	Millwall	138	5
							Crystal Palace	38	—
Rodger Simon	5 9	11 09	M	3 10 71	Shoreham	Trainee	Crystal Palace	115	5
Scully Tony	5 7	11 12	F	12 6 76	Dublin	Trainee	Crystal Palace	2	—
							Bournemouth (loan)	10	—
							Cardiff C (loan)	14	—
Thomson Steven	5 8	10 09	M	23 1 78	Glasgow	Trainee	Crystal Palace	—	—
Tuttle David	6 2	12 10	D	6 2 72	Reading	Trainee	Tottenham H	13	—
							Peterborough U (loan)	7	—
							Sheffield U	63	1
							Crystal Palace	10	1
Veart Carl	5 10	11 05	F	21 5 70	Whyalla	Adelaide C	Sheffield U	66	15
							Crystal Palace	12	—
Vincent Jamie	5 10	11 09	D	18 6 75	London	Trainee	Crystal Palace	25	—
							Bournemouth (loan)	8	—
Wales Danny	5 10	10 12	M	17 11 77	London	Trainee	Crystal Palace	—	—
Wilmot Rhys*	6 1	12 00	G	21 2 62	Newport	Apprentice	Arsenal	8	—
							Hereford U (loan)	9	—
							Orient (loan)	46	—
							Swansea C (loan)	16	—
							Plymouth Arg (loan)	17	—
							Plymouth Arg	116	—
							Grimsby T	33	—
							Crystal Palace	6	—

Trainees
Bruce, John P; Dillon, Leion A; Garland, Mark D; Graham, Gareth L; Kennedy, Richard J M; Morrison, Clinton H; Mullins, Hayden; Noonan, Samuel T M; Small-King, Shane O P; Stevens, David P.

Non-Contract
Ormshaw, Gareth D.

Associated Schoolboys
Bibby, Matthew J; Boardman, Jonathan G; Dsane, Roscoe; Fowler, Michael D; Gooding, Scott; Hankin, Sean A; Harris, Richard; Hughes, Robert; Kendall, Lee M; Manby, David J; Shevel, Steven W; Wilde, Bobby.

Associated Schoolboys who have accepted the club's offer of a Traineeship/Contract
Carlisle, Wayne T; Harney, Michael D; Hibbert, James; Loughran, Kieran; Martin, Andrew P; Sears, Paul M; Woozley, David J.

DARLINGTON

Appleby Matty	5 10	11 10	D	16 4 72	Middlesbrough	Trainee	Newcastle U	20	—
							Darlington (loan)	10	1
							Darlington	79	7
Bannister Gary	5 8	11 06	F	22 7 60	Warrington	Apprentice	Coventry C	22	3
							Sheffield W	118	55
							QPR	136	56
							Coventry C	43	11

Player	Ht	Wt	Pos	Born	Birthplace	Source	Club	Apps	Gls
							WBA	72	18
							Oxford U (loan)	10	2
							Nottingham F	31	8
							Stoke C	15	2
					Hong Kong		Lincoln C	29	7
							Darlington	41	10
Barnard Mark	5 10	11 07	D	27 11 75	Sheffield	Trainee	Rotherham U	—	—
							Darlington	37	3
Blake Robbie	5 9	11 07	F	4 3 76	Middlesbrough	Trainee	Darlington	38	11
Brumwell Phil	5 8	11 00	M	8 8 75	Darlington	Trainee	Sunderland	—	—
							Darlington	28	—
Carmichael Matt	6 1	13 02	F	13 5 64	Singapore	Army	Lincoln C	133	18
							Scunthorpe U	62	20
							Barnet (loan)	3	—
							Preston NE	10	3
							Mansfield T	1	1
							Doncaster R	27	4
							Darlington	13	2
Carss Anthony	5 9	11 05	M	31 3 76	Alnwick	Bradford C	Blackburn R	—	—
							Darlington	28	2
Crosby Andy	6 2	13 07	D	3 3 73	Rotherham	Leeds U	Doncaster R	51	—
							Darlington	105	1
Gaughan Steve	6 0	13 08	M	14 4 70	Doncaster	Hatfield Main	Doncaster R	67	3
							Sunderland	—	—
							Darlington	171	15
Gregan Sean	6 2	14 00	D	29 3 74	Cleveland	Trainee	Darlington	120	4
Innes Lee‡	6 2	11 10	F	28 2 76	Co Durham	Trainee	Sheffield U	—	—
							Darlington	—	—
Johnson Frank	6 3	13 00	G	24 2 77	South Shields		Darlington	—	—
Kirkham Peter*	5 11	11 07	M	28 10 74	Newcastle	Newcastle U	Darlington	13	—
Mattison Paul*	5 8	11 00	M	24 4 73	Wakefield	North Ferriby U	Darlington	17	—
McMahon Steve*	6 4	14 07	D	22 4 70	Glasgow	Foshan	Partick T	1	—
							Darlington	10	1
Neves Rui‡			F	10 3 65	Portugal	Famalicao	Darlington	5	—
Newell Paul*	6 2	14 07	G	23 2 69	Greenwich	Trainee	Southend U	15	—
							Leyton Orient	61	—
							Colchester U (loan)	14	—
							Barnet	16	—
							Darlington	21	—
Olsson Paul	6 0	12 10	M	24 12 65	Hull	Apprentice	Hull C	—	—
							Exeter C (loan)	8	—
							Exeter C	35	2
							Scarborough	48	5
							Hartlepool U	171	13
							Darlington	76	8
Painter Robbie	5 10	12 02	M	26 1 71	Ince	Trainee	Chester C	84	8
							Maidstone U	30	5
							Burnley	26	2
							Darlington	109	28
Paulo Pedro‡			M	21 11 73	Portugal		Darlington	6	—
Pepper Graham*	5 7	11 00	M	19 8 77	Darlington	Newcastle U	Darlington	—	—
Pugh Michael*	5 7	11 07	M	27 3 77	Stockton	Trainee	Darlington	—	—
Quitongo Jose‡			F	18 11 74	Angola		Darlington	1	—
Robinson Paul§			F	20 11 78	Sunderland	Trainee	Darlington	4	—
Shaw Simon	5 11	11 02	M	21 9 73	Teeside	Trainee	Darlington	107	7
Stephenson Ashlyn‡			G	6 7 74	South Africa		Birmingham C	—	—
							Darlington	1	—
Twynham Gary	6 0	12 01	M	8 2 76	Manchester	Trainee	Manchester U	—	—
							Darlington	2	—

Trainees
Alderson, Simon J; Anderson, Peter M; Carfoot, Jamie; Dann, Steven W; Darke, Peter; Elliott, Mark T; Henwood, Mark D; Key, Daniel C; Manuel, Jed A; Nicholson, Christopher M; Nixon, Philip; Pickersgill, Stephen; Richards, Mark D; Robinson, Paul D; Roxby, John P; Syms, Gareth; Tarrant, Neil K.

Associated Schoolboys
Carter, Michael D; Carter, Sean C P; Harris, Paul; Wild, Christopher I.

Associated Schoolboys who have accepted the club's offer of a Traineeship/Contract
Campbell, Paul A; Christie, David.

DERBY COUNTY

Player	Ht	Wt	Pos	Birthdate	Birthplace	Status	Club	Apps	Gls
Ashbee Ian	6 0	13 07	D	6 9 76	Birmingham	Trainee	Derby Co	1	—
Boden Chris	5 9	11 12	D	13 10 73	Wolverhampton	Trainee	Aston Villa	1	—
							Barnsley (loan)	4	—
							Derby Co	10	—
							Shrewsbury T (loan)	5	—
Carbon Matthew	6 3	13 12	D	8 6 75	Nottingham	Trainee	Lincoln C	69	10
							Derby Co	6	—
Carsley Lee	5 9	12 07	D	28 2 74	Birmingham	Trainee	Derby Co	58	3
Cooper Kevin	5 7	10 07	M	8 2 75	Derby	Trainee	Derby Co	2	—
Cunningham Carl*	5 5	11 11	M	19 4 77	Derby	Trainee	Derby Co	—	—
Davies Will	6 2	13 01	F	27 9 75	Derby	Trainee	Derby Co	2	—
Flynn Sean	5 7	11 10	M	13 3 68	Birmingham	Halesowen T	Coventry C	97	9
							Derby Co	42	2
Gabbiadini Marco	5 10	13 00	F	20 1 68	Nottingham	Apprentice	York C	60	14
							Sunderland	157	74
							Crystal Palace	15	5
							Derby Co	174	50
Green Matt‡	5 8	11 10	M	22 10 75	Northampton	Trainee	Derby Co	—	—
Hodges Glyn*	6 1	12 03	M	30 4 63	Streatham	Apprentice	Wimbledon	232	49
							Newcastle U	7	—
							Watford	86	15
							Crystal Palace	7	—
							Sheffield U	147	19
							Derby Co	9	—
Hoult Russell	6 4	14 05	G	22 11 72	Leicester	Trainee	Leicester C	10	—
							Lincoln C (loan)	2	—
							Blackpool (loan)	—	—
							Bolton W (loan)	4	—
							Lincoln C (loan)	15	—
							Derby Co (loan)	15	—
							Derby Co	41	—
Kavanagh Jason	5 9	12 07	D	23 11 71	Birmingham	Birmingham C	Derby Co	99	1
Kozluk Robert			M	5 8 77	Mansfield	Trainee	Derby Co	—	—
Powell Chris	5 10	11 07	D	8 9 69	Lambeth	Trainee	Crystal Palace	3	—
							Aldershot (loan)	11	—
							Southend U	248	3
							Derby Co	19	—
Powell Darryl	6 1	11 02	F	15 1 71	Lambeth	Trainee	Portsmouth	132	16
							Derby Co	37	5
Powell Stephen*	5 9	11 05	M	14 12 76	Derby	Trainee	Derby Co	—	—
Preece David	5 5	10 12	M	28 5 63	Bridgnorth	Apprentice	Walsall	111	5
							Luton T	336	21
							Derby Co	13	1
							Birmingham C (loan)	6	—
							Swindon T (loan)	7	1
Quy Andy	5 11	13 02	G	4 7 76	Harlow	Tottenham H	Derby Co	—	—
Radzki Lee			M	14 11 78	Mansfield	Trainee	Derby Co	—	—
Round Steve‡	5 10	10 12	D	9 11 70	Buxton	Trainee	Derby Co	9	—
Rowett Gary	6 1	12 06	F	6 3 74	Bromsgrove	Trainee	Cambridge U	63	9
							Everton	4	—
							Blackpool (loan)	17	—
							Derby Co	35	—
Simpson Paul	5 6	11 09	F	26 7 66	Carlisle	Apprentice	Manchester C	121	18
							Oxford U	144	43
							Derby Co	166	46
Smith Craig	6 1	13 07	M	2 8 76	Mansfield	Trainee	Derby Co	—	—
Stimac Igor	6 2	13 02	D	6 9 67	Croatia	Hajduk Split	Derby Co	27	1
Sturridge Dean	5 7	11 13	F	27 7 73	Birmingham	Trainee	Derby Co	62	21
							Torquay U (loan)	10	5
Sutton Steve	6 1	14 08	G	16 4 61	Hartington	Apprentice	Nottingham F	199	—
							Mansfield T (loan)	8	—
							Derby Co (loan)	14	—
							Coventry C (loan)	1	—
							Luton T (loan)	14	—
							Derby Co	61	—
							Reading (loan)	2	—
Sutton Wayne	6 0	13 09	D	1 10 75	Derby	Trainee	Derby Co	7	—
Taylor Martin	5 11	13 09	G	9 12 66	Tamworth	Mile Oak R	Derby Co	94	—
							Carlisle U (loan)	10	—
							Scunthorpe U (loan)	8	—
Tretton Andrew	6 0	12 08	D	9 10 76	Derby	Trainee	Derby Co	—	—

Name							Club	Apps	Gls
Trollope Paul	5 9	11 09	M	3 6 72	Swindon	Trainee	Swindon T	—	—
							Torquay U (loan)	10	—
							Torquay U	96	16
							Derby Co	41	4
Van der Laan Robin	5 11	13 08	F	5 9 68	Schiedam	Wageningen	Port Vale	176	24
							Derby Co	39	6
Ward Ashley	6 2	11 09	F	24 11 70	Manchester	Trainee	Manchester C	1	—
							Wrexham (loan)	4	2
							Leicester C	10	—
							Blackpool (loan)	2	1
							Crewe Alex	61	25
							Norwich C	53	18
							Derby Co	7	1
Warren Matt*	5 10	13 06	D	14 2 76	Derby	Trainee	Derby Co	—	—
Wassall Darren	6 0	12 07	D	27 6 68	Edgbaston		Nottingham F	27	—
							Hereford U (loan)	5	—
							Bury (loan)	7	1
							Derby Co	98	—
Willems Ron	6 0	12 11	F	20 9 66	Epe		PEC Zwolle	43	7
							Twente	85	16
							Ajax	47	15
							Grasshoppers	56	18
							Derby Co	33	11
Wrack Darren	5 9	12 00	F	5 5 76	Cleethorpes	Trainee	Derby Co	26	1
Wright Nick	5 9	11 07	F	15 10 75	Derby	Trainee	Derby Co	—	—
Yates Dean	6 2	12 06	D	26 10 67	Leicester	Apprentice	Notts Co	314	33
							Derby Co	49	3

Trainees
Bridge-Wilkinson, Marc; Broadhurst, Neil O; Brown, Duane C; Elliott, Steven W; Green, Steven A; Hofford, Mark F M; Lyons, Patrick M; Murphy, Leroy A; Murphy, Shaun P; Owen, Craig; Owen, Steve; Rattray, Vincent M; Rowntree, Martyn E; Wilson, Mark A; Yates, Tom W.

Associated Schoolboys
Banks, Steven J; Bate, Christopher T; Evatt, Ian R; Gummer, Sean M; Hanson, Craig P; Madley, Paul J; Mills, Jonathan; Murray, Adam D; North, Brent A; Paling, David A; Pitter, Dominic J; Roome, Stephen; Ryan, Mark; Sidhu, Amrit S; Smith, Matthew E; Thompson, Mitchell G; Wraith, Paul J.

Associated Schoolboys who have accepted the club's offer of a Traineeship/Contract
Greenhill, Ross F; Macdonald, Jamie; Messina, Robert P; Thornhill, Wayne; Wall, James T.

DONCASTER ROVERS

Name							Club	Apps	Gls
Ashley Kevin‡	5 7	11 10	D	31 12 68	Birmingham	Apprentice	Birmingham C	57	1
							Wolverhampton W	88	1
							Peterborough U	36	—
							Doncaster R	3	—
Byng David	6 2	13 12	F	9 7 77	Walsgrave	Trainee	Torquay U	24	3
							Doncaster R	—	—
Clark Ian	5 11	11 02	M	23 10 74	Cleveland		Doncaster R	23	1
Colcombe Scott	5 6	10 04	F	15 12 71	West Bromwich	Trainee	WBA	—	—
							Torquay U	89	1
							Doncaster R	30	3
Cramb Colin	6 0	13 00	F	23 6 74	Lanark	Hamilton A BC	Hamilton A	48	10
							Southampton	1	—
							Falkirk	8	1
							Hearts	6	1
							Doncaster R	21	7
Doling Stuart	5 7	11 07	M	28 10 72	Newport, IOW	Trainee	Portsmouth	37	4
							Torquay U	—	—
							Doncaster R	1	—
Gallen Stephen‡	6 2	13 00	D	21 11 73	Acton	Trainee	QPR	—	—
							Doncaster R	—	—
Gore Ian	5 11	12 04	M	10 1 68	Whiston		Birmingham C	—	—
						Southport	Blackpool	200	—
							Torquay U	25	2
							Doncaster R	5	—
Hayrettin Hakan	5 9	12 04	M	4 2 70	London	Trainee	Leyton Orient	—	—
						Barnet	Barnet	6	—
							Torquay U (loan)	4	—
							Wycombe W	19	1
							Cambridge U	17	—
							Doncaster R	—	—
Haywood Paul‡	5 11	10 02	D	4 10 75	Barnsley	Trainee	Nottingham F	—	—
							Doncaster R	—	—
Hoy Kristian‡	5 11	12 00	F	27 4 76	Doncaster		Doncaster R	1	—
Jones Graeme	6 0	12 12	F	13 3 70	Gateshead	Bridlington T	Doncaster R	92	26

Name	Ht	Wt	Pos	Date	Birthplace	Source	Club	Apps	Gls
Kirby Ryan*	6 0	12 00	D	6 9 74	Chingford	Trainee	Arsenal	—	—
							Doncaster R	78	—
Knight Jason‡	6 1	11 09	M	16 9 74	Australia	West Ham U	Doncaster R	4	—
Leach Gavin*	6 1	13 06	M	9 8 77	Middlesbrough	Stockton	Doncaster R	—	—
Marquis Paul	6 2	12 04	D	29 8 72	Enfield	Trainee	West Ham U	1	—
							Doncaster R	26	1
McCluskie Mark‡	5 11	11 03	F	23 10 76	Ogar		Doncaster R	—	—
Meara Jim‡	5 9	11 02	M	7 10 72	London	Trainee	Watford	2	—
							Doncaster R	16	1
Measham Ian*	5 11	11 09	D	14 12 64	Barnsley	Apprentice	Huddersfield T	17	—
							Lincoln C (loan)	6	—
							Rochdale (loan)	12	—
							Cambridge U	46	—
							Burnley	182	2
							Doncaster R	32	—
Moore Darren	6 2	15 00	D	22 4 74	Birmingham	Trainee	Torquay U	103	8
							Doncaster R	35	2
Murphy Jamie	6 1	13 00	D	25 2 73	Manchester	Trainee	Blackpool	55	1
							Doncaster R	23	—
Norbury Mike‡	6 1	11 10	F	22 1 69	Hemsworth	Bridlington	Cambridge U	26	3
							Preston NE	42	13
							Doncaster R	27	5
O'Connor Gary	6 3	13 00	G	7 4 74	Newtongrange	Dalkeith T	Hearts	—	—
							Berwick R	39	—
							Hearts	3	—
							Doncaster R	8	—
Parrish Sean	5 10	10 00	M	14 3 72	Wrexham	Trainee	Shrewsbury T	3	—
							Telford U		
							Doncaster R	66	8
Robertson Paul	5 7	11 08	D	5 2 72	Stockport	York C	Stockport Co	10	—
							Bury	8	—
							Runcorn		
							Doncaster R	16	—
Robinson Earl*	6 3	12 05	M	8 10 78	Birmingham		Doncaster R	—	—
Saunders Lee‡	5 10	12 03	D	23 3 77	Nuneaton	Trainee	Doncaster R	—	—
Schofield Jon	5 11	11 08	M	16 5 65	Barnsley	Gainsborough T	Lincoln C	231	11
							Doncaster R	68	5
Smith Mike	5 11	11 07	M	28 9 73	Liverpool	Runcorn	Doncaster R	13	—
Speight Martyn§			D	26 7 78	Stockton	Trainee	Doncaster R	1	—
Suckling Perry‡	6 2	13 02	G	12 10 65	Leyton	Apprentice	Coventry C	27	—
							Manchester C	39	—
							Crystal Palace	59	—
							West Ham U (loan)	6	—
							Brentford (loan)	8	—
							Watford	39	—
							Doncaster R	30	—
Utley Darren	6 0	10 09	M	28 9 77	Barnsley	Trainee	Doncaster R	1	—
Warren Lee	6 0	12 00	M	28 2 69	Manchester	Trainee	Leeds U	—	—
							Rochdale	31	1
							Hull C	153	1
							Lincoln C (loan)	3	1
							Doncaster R	56	2
Wheeler Adam			M	29 11 77	Sheffield	Newcastle U	Doncaster R	—	—
Williams Dean P	6 1	12 09	G	5 1 72	Lichfield	Tamworth	Brentford	7	—
							Doncaster R	52	—
Williams Paul‡	5 11	12 02	D	25 9 70	Liverpool	Trainee	Sunderland	9	—
							Swansea C (loan)	12	1
							Doncaster R	8	—
Williams Philip‡			G	1 10 78	Salford		Doncaster R	—	—

Trainees
Clarke, Gary; Hammond, Andrew B; Hawthorne, Mark; Hilton, Steven; Hodgkinson, James A; Horan, Mark A; Knott, Richard; Lawrence, Carl M M; Ramsay, John W; Speight, Martyn S.

Associated Schoolboys
Beal, Phillip L; Cawthorne, Ian; Corry, David; Fairham, Steven J; Gilberthorpe, Matthew J; Lewkowicz, Wayne S; Maw, Paul; Walker, Leigh D.

Associated Schoolboys who have accepted the club's offer of a Traineeship/Contract
Combellack, Brian; Donnelly, Mark P; Howe, Jamie I; Pollard, Steven R; Robinson, Andrew; Robinson, Tobias.

EVERTON

Name	Ht	Wt	Pos	Date	Birthplace	Source	Club	Apps	Gls
Ablett Gary	6 2	12 02	D	19 11 65	Liverpool	Apprentice	Liverpool	109	1
							Derby Co (loan)	6	—
							Hull C (loan)	5	—
							Everton	128	5
							Sheffield U (loan)	12	—

Name	Ht	Wt	Pos	D.O.B.	Birthplace	Source	Club	Apps	Gls
Allen Graham	6 1	11 12	D	8 4 77	Bolton	Trainee	Everton	—	—
Amokachi Daniel	5 10	13 00	F	30 12 72	Nigeria		FC Brugge	81	35
							Everton	43	10
Barrett Earl	5 9	11 07	D	28 4 67	Rochdale	Apprentice	Manchester C	3	—
							Chester C (loan)	12	—
							Oldham Ath	183	7
							Aston Villa	119	1
							Everton	25	—
Branch Michael	5 9	11 00	F	18 10 78	Liverpool	Trainee	Everton	3	—
Ebbrell John	5 9	11 09	M	1 10 69	Bromborough		Everton	210	13
Ferguson Duncan	6 3	13 08	F	27 12 71	Stirling	Carse T	Dundee U	77	28
							Rangers	14	2
							Everton	41	12
Grant Tony	5 9	10 00	M	14 11 74	Liverpool	Trainee	Everton	18	1
							Swindon T (loan)	3	1
Grugel Mark	5 8	10 00	M	9 3 76	Liverpool	Local	Everton	—	—
Hennigan Gerard*			M	2 8 77	Liverpool	Trainee	Everton	—	—
Hills John	5 8	10 08	M	21 4 78	Blackpool	Trainee	Blackpool	—	—
							Everton	—	—
Hinchcliffe Andy	5 10	13 07	D	5 2 69	Manchester	Apprentice	Manchester C	112	8
							Everton	147	6
Holcroft Peter	5 9	11 00	M	3 1 76	Liverpool	Trainee	Everton	—	—
Horne Barry	5 10	12 01	M	18 5 62	St Asaph	Rhyl	Wrexham	136	17
							Portsmouth	70	7
							Southampton	112	6
							Everton	123	3
Hottiger Marc	5 9	11 00	D	7 11 67	Lausanne		Lausanne	123	5
							Sion	67	13
							Newcastle U	39	1
							Everton	9	1
Jackson Matthew	6 1	12 09	D	19 10 71	Leeds	School	Luton T	9	—
							Preston NE (loan)	4	—
							Everton	138	4
							Charlton Ath (loan)	8	—
Kanchelskis Andrei	5 10	12 12	F	23 1 69	Kirovograd		Dynamo Kiev	22	1
							Donetsk	21	3
							Manchester U	123	28
							Everton	32	16
Kearton Jason	5 11	12 00	G	9 7 69	Ipswich (Aus)	Brisbane Lions	Everton	6	—
							Stoke C (loan)	16	—
							Blackpool (loan)	14	—
							Notts Co (loan)	10	—
							Preston NE (loan)	—	—
Limpar Anders	5 8	11 02	F	24 9 65	Solna		Brommapojkarna	77	12
							Orgryte	47	9
							Young Boys	17	6
							Cremonese	24	3
							Arsenal	96	17
							Everton	64	5
McCann Gavin	5 11	11 00	M	10 1 78	Blackpool	Trainee	Everton	—	—
Moore Neil	6 1	12 07	D	21 9 72	Liverpool	Trainee	Everton	5	—
							Blackpool (loan)	7	—
							Oldham Ath (loan)	5	—
							Carlisle U (loan)	13	—
							Rotherham U (loan)	11	—
Moore Richard	6 2	13 07	G	2 9 77	Scunthorpe	Trainee	Everton	—	—
O'Connor Jonathan	6 0	11 00	M	29 10 76	Darlington	Trainee	Everton	4	—
Parkinson Joe	6 1	13 00	D	11 6 71	Eccles	Trainee	Wigan Ath	119	6
							Bournemouth	30	1
							Everton	62	3
Price Chris	5 9	11 09	M	24 10 75	Liverpool	Trainee	Everton	—	—
Quayle Mark	5 9	10 02	F	2 10 78	Liverpool	Trainee	Everton	—	—
Rideout Paul	5 11	12 00	F	14 8 64	Bournemouth	Apprentice	Swindon T	95	38
							Aston Villa	54	19
							Bari	99	23
							Southampton	75	19
							Swindon T (loan)	9	1
							Notts Co	11	3
							Rangers	12	1
							Everton	102	29
Samways Vinny	5 8	11 02	M	27 10 68	Bethnal Green	Apprentice	Tottenham H	193	11
							Everton	23	2
							Wolverhampton W (loan)	3	—
							Birmingham C (loan)	12	—

Short Craig	6 3	13 08	D	25 6 68	Bridlington	Pickering T	Scarborough	63	7
							Notts Co	128	6
							Derby Co	118	9
							Everton	23	2
Southall Neville	6 0	14 00	G	16 9 58	Llandudno	Winsford	Bury	39	—
							Everton	532	—
							Port Vale (loan)	9	—
Speare James	6 1	13 00	G	5 11 76	Liverpool	Trainee	Everton	—	—
Stuart Graham	5 9	11 09	F	24 10 70	Tooting, London	Trainee	Chelsea	87	14
							Everton	87	15
Unsworth David	6 0	14 00	F	16 10 73	Preston	Trainee	Everton	82	6
Watson Dave	6 0	13 07	D	20 11 61	Liverpool	Amateur	Liverpool	—	—
							Norwich C	212	11
							Everton	340	22
Weathers Andrew*			M	14 11 76	Liverpool	Trainee	Everton	—	—
Woods Matthew*			D	9 9 76	Gosport	Trainee	Everton	—	—

Trainees
Davies, Paul; Denton, Adam M; Dunne, Richard P; Gabrielson, Daniel J; Hardman, Christopher S; Hussin, Edward W; Jevons, Phillip; Knight, Christopher D; Lane, Christopher; Maguire, John; McHugh, Bartholomew; O'Toole, John; Roscoe, Christopher J; Townsend, Richard P; Tynan, Robert L; West, Andrew; Wood, Robert D.

Associated Schoolboys
Abel, Graeme F; Burgess, Benjamin K; Butler, Kieran J L; Clarke, Peter M; Curran, Damien M; Hibbert, Anthony J; Howarth, Carl J; Jeffers, Francis; Kearney, Thomas J; Knowles, David J; Lloyd, David; Logan, Damian G; McLeod, Kevin A; O'Brien, Edward; Osman, Leon; Pilkington, George E; Rhodes, Tristan M; Tuft, Dean K; Wright, Johngeorge.

Associated Schoolboys who have accepted the club's offer of a Traineeship/Contract
Ball, Michael J; Cadamarteri, Daniel L; Eaton, Adam P; Farley, Adam J; Holmes, Neil; Hulbert, Robin J; McDermott, Wayne; Milligan, Jamie; Obrien, Michael G; Poppleton, David J; Regan, Carl A; Williams, David P.

EXETER CITY

Anderson Colin‡	5 10	11 11	M	26 4 62	Newcastle	Apprentice	Burnley	6	—
							Torquay U	109	11
							QPR (loan)	—	—
							WBA	140	10
							Walsall	26	2
							Hereford U	70	1
							Exeter C	34	1
Bailey Danny	5 8	12 11	M	21 5 64	Leyton	Apprentice	Bournemouth	2	—
						Local	Torquay U	1	—
						Wealdstone	Exeter C	64	2
							Reading	50	2
							Fulham (loan)	3	—
							Exeter C	117	2
Bellotti Ross§			G	15 5 78	Pembury	Trainee	Exeter C	2	—
Blake Noel	6 2	14 02	D	12 1 62	Jamaica	Sutton Coldfield T	Aston Villa	4	—
							Shrewsbury T (loan)	6	—
							Birmingham C	76	5
							Portsmouth	144	10
							Leeds U	51	4
							Stoke C	75	3
							Bradford C (loan)	6	—
							Bradford C	39	3
							Dundee	54	2
							Exeter C	44	2
Braithwaite Leon			F	17 12 72	Hackney	Bishops Stortford	Exeter C	23	3
Buckle Paul	5 7	10 10	M	16 12 70	Hatfield	Trainee	Brentford	57	1
							Torquay U	59	9
							Exeter C	22	2
Came Mark	6 1	14 03	D	14 9 61	Exeter	Winsford U	Bolton W	195	7
							Chester C	47	1
							Exeter C	70	5
Cecere Michele‡	6 0	12 12	F	4 1 68	Chester	Apprentice	Oldham Ath	52	8
							Huddersfield T	54	8
							Stockport Co (loan)	1	—
							Walsall	112	32
							Exeter C	43	11
Chamberlain Mark†	5 9	12 00	M	19 11 61	Stoke	Apprentice	Port Vale	96	17
							Stoke C	112	17
							Sheffield W	66	8
							Portsmouth	167	20
							Brighton & HA	19	2
							Exeter C	33	1

Cooper Mark‡	5 8	10 10	M	18 12 68	Wakefield	Trainee	Bristol C	—	—
							Exeter C	50	12
							Southend U (loan)	5	—
							Birmingham C	39	4
							Fulham	14	—
							Huddersfield T (loan)	10	4
							Wycombe W	2	1
							Exeter C	88	20
Fox Peter	5 11	13 10	G	5 7 57	Scunthorpe	Apprentice	Sheffield W	49	—
							West Ham U (loan)	—	—
							Barnsley (loan)	1	—
							Stoke C	409	—
							Wrexham (loan)	—	—
							Exeter C	103	—
Gavin Mark‡	5 9	11 01	M	10 12 63	Bailleston	Apprentice	Leeds U	30	3
							Hartlepool U (loan)	7	—
							Carlisle U	13	1
							Bolton W	49	3
							Rochdale	23	6
							Hearts	9	—
							Bristol C	69	6
							Watford	13	—
							Bristol C	41	2
							Exeter C	77	4
Hare Matthew	6 2	13 00	D	26 12 76	Barnstaple	Trainee	Exeter C	13	—
Hughes Darren†	5 11	13 01	D	6 10 65	Prescot	Apprentice	Everton	3	—
							Shrewsbury T	37	1
							Brighton & HA	26	2
							Port Vale	184	4
							Northampton T	21	—
							Exeter C	26	—
McConnell Barry	5 11	10 03	F	1 1 77	Exeter	Trainee	Exeter C	8	—
Medlin Nicky	5 7	10 01	M	23 11 76	Camborne	Trainee	Exeter C	6	—
Morgan Jamie‡	5 11	12 00	M	1 10 75	Plymouth	Trainee	Plymouth Arg	11	—
							Exeter C	6	—
Myers Chris‡	5 10	11 10	M	1 4 69	Yeovil	Apprentice	Torquay U	105	7
							Dundee U	6	—
							Torquay U (loan)	6	—
							Wrexham	—	—
							Scarborough	9	—
							Exeter C	8	—
Parsley Neil	5 10	11 08	D	25 4 66	Liverpool	Witton Alb	Leeds U	—	—
							Chester C (loan)	6	—
							Huddersfield T	57	—
							Doncaster R (loan)	3	—
							WBA	43	—
							Exeter C	32	—
Pears Richard	5 10	12 07	F	16 7 76	Exeter	Trainee	Exeter C	52	7
Rice Gary	5 9	11 10	D	29 9 75	Zambia	Trainee	Exeter C	29	—
Richardson Jon	6 1	12 05	M	29 8 75	Nottingham	Trainee	Exeter C	88	2
Thirlby Anthony*	5 8	10 05	M	4 3 76	Germany	Trainee	Exeter C	39	2

Trainees
Ahearn, Jamie P; Bellotti, Ross C; Derham, Roger K; Edwards, Wayne A; Ghazghazi, Sufyan; Grant, Christopher S; Littley, James M; Neno, Richard J; Rollason, Andrew J; Steer, Richard; Thomas, William N; Vittles, James M S; White, Stevie; Wilkinson, John C.

Non-Contract
Chamberlain, Mark V; Hughes, Darren J.

Associated Schoolboys
Bennett, Troy M; Bray, Adam; Frankland, Damien R; Hillson, Bradley; Hughes, Paul M; Jee, Russell; Melhuish, Stuart A; Wainwright, Thomas W; Walker, David; Watts, Shaun R.

Associated Schoolboys who have accepted the club's offer of a Traineeship/Contract
Harris, Daniel; Holmes, Mark; Rendle, Daniel L; Walker, Scott.

FULHAM

Adams Micky	5 8	11 04	M	8 11 61	Sheffield	Apprentice	Gillingham	92	5
							Coventry C	90	9
							Leeds U	73	2
							Southampton	144	7
							Stoke C	10	3
							Fulham	26	9
Andrews Nicky‡	5 10	11 05	D	10 10 75	London	Trainee	Fulham	—	—
Angus Terry	6 0	13 10	D	14 1 66	Coventry	VS Rugby	Northampton T	116	6
							Fulham	90	4
Barkus Lea	5 6	10 10	F	7 12 74	Reading	Trainee	Reading	15	1
							Fulham	9	1
Bartley Carl‡	6 2	12 13	F	6 10 76	Lambeth	Trainee	Fulham	1	—

Name	Ht	Wt	Pos	Birth date	Birthplace	Source	Club	Apps	Gls
Blake Mark	6 0	12 06	D	17 12 67	Portsmouth	Apprentice	Southampton	18	2
							Colchester U (loan)	4	1
							Shrewsbury T (loan)	10	—
							Shrewsbury T	132	3
							Fulham	73	8
Bolt Danny*	5 7	11 06	M	5 2 76	Wandsworth	Trainee	Fulham	13	2
Bower Danny*			D	20 11 76	Woolwich	Trainee	Fulham	4	—
Brazil Gary*	5 11	11 04	F	19 9 62	Tunbridge Wells	Crystal Palace	Sheffield U	62	9
							Port Vale (loan)	6	3
							Preston NE	166	58
							Newcastle U	23	2
							Fulham	213	47
Brooker Paul	5 8	9 13	M	25 11 76	Hammersmith	Trainee	Fulham	20	2
Conroy Mike	6 0	13 03	F	31 12 65	Glasgow	Apprentice	Coventry C	—	—
							Clydebank	114	38
							St Mirren	10	1
							Reading	80	7
							Burnley	77	30
							Preston NE	57	22
							Fulham	40	9
Cusack Nick	6 0	12 08	F	24 12 65	Rotherham	Alvechurch	Leicester C	16	1
							Peterborough U	44	10
							Motherwell	77	17
							Darlington	21	6
							Oxford U	61	10
							Wycombe W (loan)	4	—
							Fulham	69	12
Gregory John‡			G	16 5 77	Hounslow	Trainee	Fulham	1	—
Hamill Rory	5 10	12 02	F	4 5 76	Coleraine	Portstewart	Fulham	48	7
Hamsher John§			D	14 1 78	Lambeth	Trainee	Fulham	3	—
Harrison Lee*	6 2	12 07	G	12 9 71	Billericay	Trainee	Charlton Ath	—	—
							Fulham (loan)	—	—
							Gillingham (loan)	2	—
							Fulham (loan)	—	—
							Fulham	12	—
Herrera Robbie	5 6	10 07	D	12 6 70	Torbay	Trainee	QPR	6	—
							Torquay U (loan)	11	—
							Torquay U (loan)	5	—
							Fulham	93	1
Hurlock Terry‡	5 9	14 01	M	22 9 58	Hackney	Leytonstone/Ilford	Brentford	220	18
							Reading	29	—
							Millwall	104	8
							Rangers	29	2
							Southampton	61	—
							Millwall	13	—
							Fulham	27	1
Jupp Duncan	6 0	12 11	D	25 1 75	Guildford	Trainee	Fulham	105	2
Lange Tony	6 0	14 06	G	10 12 64	London	Apprentice	Charlton Ath	12	—
							Aldershot (loan)	7	—
							Aldershot	125	—
							Wolverhampton W	8	—
							Aldershot (loan)	2	—
							Torquay U (loan)	1	—
							Portsmouth (loan)	—	—
							WBA	48	—
							Fulham	41	—
Marshall John*	5 10	12 04	M	18 8 64	Surrey	Apprentice	Fulham	411	28
McAree Rod	5 7	10 02	D	19 8 74	Dungannon	Trainee	Liverpool	—	—
							Bristol C	6	—
							Fulham	17	2
Mison Michael	6 3	14 00	M	8 11 75	London	Trainee	Fulham	51	5
Moore Kevin*	5 11	12 12	D	29 4 58	Grimsby	Local	Grimsby T	400	27
							Oldham Ath	13	1
							Southampton	148	10
							Bristol R (loan)	7	—
							Bristol R (loan)	4	1
							Fulham	51	4
Morgan Simon	5 10	12 05	M	5 9 66	Birmingham	Trainee	Leicester C	160	3
							Fulham	227	34
Scott Rob	6 1	11 10	F	15 8 73	Epsom	Sutton U	Sheffield U	6	1
							Scarborough (loan)	8	3
							Northampton T (loan)	5	—
							Fulham	21	5
Smith David‡	5 11	11 07	D	13 9 76	Lambeth	Trainee	Fulham	—	—
Thomas Martin	5 8	11 04	F	12 9 73	Lyndhurst	Trainee	Southampton	—	—
							Leyton Orient	5	2
							Fulham	60	8
Williams Carl*	5 7	12 06	M	14 1 77	Cambridge	Trainee	Fulham	13	—

Trainees
Bjurstrom, Paul A; Buckley, Jamie J; Edwards, Ross P; Fitzgerald, Philip J; Grover, Adam A; Hamsher, John J; Jennings, Gary B; Jones, Lee P; Newby, Peter A; Probets, Clayton; Rouse, Mark B; Smith, Kevin A; Symons, Shaun P; Taylor, Mark P; Ware, Christopher; Wareing, Andrew J.

Associated Schoolboys
Moore, Garry.

Associated Schoolboys who have accepted the club's offer of a Traineeship/Contract
Wilkinson, Jamie S.

GILLINGHAM

Name			Pos	DOB	Birthplace	Previous club	Clubs	Apps	Gls
Ansah Andy‡	5 9	11 03	F	19 3 69	Lewisham	Crystal Palace	Brentford	8	2
							Southend U	157	33
							Brentford (loan)	3	1
							Brentford (loan)	6	1
							Peterborough U	2	1
							Gillingham	2	—
Bailey Dennis	5 10	11 04	F	13 11 65	Lambeth	Farnborough T	Crystal Palace	5	1
							Bristol R (loan)	17	9
							Birmingham C	75	23
							Bristol R (loan)	6	1
							QPR	39	10
							Charlton Ath (loan)	4	—
							Watford (loan)	8	4
							Brentford (loan)	6	3
							Gillingham	45	8
Butler Steve	6 2	13 00	F	27 1 62	Birmingham	Wokingham	Brentford	97	44
							Watford	62	9
							Bournemouth (loan)	1	—
							Cambridge U	109	51
							Gillingham	20	5
Butler Tony	6 2	12 02	D	28 9 72	Stockport	Trainee	Gillingham	148	5
Carpenter Richard	5 11	13 02	M	30 9 72	Sheppey	Trainee	Gillingham	121	4
Fortune-West Leo	6 3	13 10	F	9 4 71	Newham	Stevenage Borough	Gillingham	40	12
Foster Adrian*	5 9	11 00	F	19 3 71	Kidderminster	Trainee	WBA	27	2
							Torquay U	75	24
							Gillingham	40	9
							Exeter C (loan)	7	—
Freeman Darren	5 10	13 01	F	22 8 73	Brighton	Horsham T	Gillingham	12	—
Green Richard	6 1	13 07	D	22 11 67	Wolverhampton	Apprentice	Shrewsbury T	125	5
							Swindon T	—	—
							Gillingham	162	14
Harris Mark	6 2	14 07	M	15 7 63	Reading	Wokingham	Crystal Palace	2	—
							Burnley (loan)	4	—
							Swansea C	228	14
							Gillingham	44	2
Hunt Kevin‡	5 10	11 00	M	4 7 75	Chatham		Gillingham	—	—
Lindsey Scott‡	5 9	11 10	D	4 5 72	Walsall	Bridlington T	Gillingham	12	—
Manuel Billy†	5 8	12 04	D	28 6 69	Hackney	Apprentice	Tottenham H	—	—
							Gillingham	87	5
							Brentford	94	1
							Cambridge U	10	—
							Peterborough U	27	2
							Gillingham	10	—
Martin Dave	6 1	13 02	M	25 4 63	East Ham	Apprentice	Millwall	140	6
							Wimbledon	35	3
							Southend U	221	19
							Bristol C	38	1
							Northampton T (loan)	7	1
							Gillingham	31	1
Martin Eliot‡	5 6	10 00	D	27 9 72	Plumstead	Trainee	Gillingham	60	1
Micklewhite Gary*	5 7	10 04	M	21 3 61	Southwark	Apprentice	Manchester U	—	—
							QPR	106	11
							Derby Co	240	31
							Gillingham	95	3
Naylor Dominic	5 9	12 12	D	12 8 70	Watford	Trainee	Watford	—	—
							Halifax T	6	1
						Barnet	Barnet	51	—
							Plymouth Arg	85	—
							Gillingham	31	1
O'Connor Mark	5 7	10 11	M	10 3 63	Rochdale	Apprentice	QPR	3	—
							Exeter C (loan)	38	1
							Bristol R	80	10
							Bournemouth	128	12
							Gillingham	116	8
							Bournemouth	58	3
							Gillingham	18	1

Pettinger Paul*	6 0	13 07	G	1 10 75	Sheffield	Barnsley	Leeds U	—	—
							Torquay U (loan)	3	—
							Rotherham U (loan)	1	—
							Gillingham	—	—
Pike Chris‡	6 2	13 07	F	19 10 61	Cardiff	Barry T	Fulham	42	4
							Cardiff C (loan)	6	2
							Cardiff C	148	65
							Hereford U	38	18
							Gillingham	27	13
Puttnam Dave	5 10	12 02	M	3 2 67	Leicester	Leicester U	Leicester C	7	—
							Lincoln C	177	21
							Gillingham	26	1
Ratcliffe Simon	5 11	13 08	M	8 2 67	Davyhulme	Apprentice	Manchester U	—	—
							Norwich C	9	—
							Brentford	214	14
							Gillingham	41	3
Rattray Kevin	5 9	11 05	M	6 10 68	London	Woking	Gillingham	26	3
Smillie Neil‡	5 6	10 07	F	19 7 58	Barnsley	Apprentice	Crystal Palace	83	7
							Brentford (loan)	3	—
							Brighton & HA	75	2
							Watford	16	3
							Reading	39	—
							Brentford	172	18
							Gillingham	53	3
Smith Neil	5 9	12 05	M	30 9 71	London	Trainee	Tottenham H	—	—
							Gillingham	170	9
Stannard Jim	6 2	15 08	G	6 10 62	London	Local	Fulham	41	—
							Charlton Ath (loan)	1	—
							Southend U (loan)	17	—
							Southend U	92	—
							Fulham	348	1
							Gillingham	46	—
Thomas Glen	6 1	13 03	D	6 10 67	Hackney	Apprentice	Fulham	251	6
							Peterborough U	8	—
							Barnet	23	—
							Gillingham	15	—
Watson Paul	5 8	10 08	D	4 1 75	Hastings	Trainee	Gillingham	62	2
Wilson Paul‡			F	22 2 77	Maidstone	Trainee	Gillingham	2	—

Trainees
Barnes, Mark A J; Butler, Thomas P; Clark, Scott A; Clifford, Kevin D; Cole, Jody; Edge, Roland; Eggleton, Russell; Flanagan, Adam M; Halls, Christopher J; Norman, Steven D; Pinnock, James E; Quigley, Lee P; Roser, Craig M; Saunders, Jay L; Smith, Darren K; Tydeman, Samuel.

Non-Contract
Bremner, Kevin J; Manuel, William A J; Scally, Paul D P.

GRIMSBY TOWN

Bonetti Ivano‡			M	1 8 64	Brescia	Torino	Grimsby T	19	3
Brookes Mark*	5 9	10 06	M	19 9 75	Nottingham	Trainee	Grimsby T	—	—
Childs Gary	5 7	10 08	M	19 4 64	Birmingham	Apprentice	WBA	3	—
							Walsall	131	17
							Birmingham C	55	2
							Grimsby T	206	25
Clare Daryl	5 8	10 06	M	1 8 78	Jersey	Trainee	Grimsby T	1	—
Crichton Paul	6 0	12 05	G	3 10 68	Pontefract	Apprentice	Nottingham F	—	—
							Notts Co (loan)	5	—
							Darlington (loan)	5	—
							Peterborough U (loan)	4	—
							Darlington (loan)	3	—
							Swindon T (loan)	4	—
							Rotherham U (loan)	6	—
							Torquay U (loan)	13	—
							Peterborough U	47	—
							Doncaster R	77	—
							Grimsby T	133	—
Dobbin Jim*	5 10	10 07	M	17 9 63	Dunfermline	Whitburn BC	Celtic	2	—
							Motherwell (loan)	2	—
							Doncaster R	64	13
							Barnsley	129	12
							Grimsby T	164	21
Fickling Ashley	5 10	11 06	D	15 11 72	Sheffield	Trainee	Sheffield U	—	—
							Darlington (loan)	14	—
							Darlington (loan)	1	—
							Grimsby T	12	—
Forrester Jamie	5 6	10 00	F	1 11 74	Bradford	Auxerre	Leeds U	9	—
							Southend U (loan)	5	—
							Grimsby T (loan)	9	1
							Grimsby T	28	5

Player	Ht	Wt	Pos	Birth date	Birthplace	From	Clubs	Apps	Gls
Futcher Paul‡	6 0	12 03	D	25 9 56	Chester	Apprentice	Chester	20	—
							Luton T	131	1
							Manchester C	37	—
							Oldham Ath	98	1
							Derby Co	35	—
							Barnsley	230	—
							Halifax T	15	—
							Grimsby T	132	—
Gallimore Tony	5 11	12 12	D	21 2 72	Crewe	Trainee	Stoke C	11	—
							Carlisle U (loan)	16	—
							Carlisle U (loan)	8	1
							Carlisle U	116	8
							Grimsby T	10	1
Gambaro Enzo‡			M	23 2 66	Genoa	Bolton W	Grimsby T	1	—
Gowshall Joby	5 11	13 00	D	7 8 75	Louth	Trainee	Grimsby T	—	—
Groves Paul	5 11	11 05	M	28 2 66	Derby	Burton Alb	Leicester C	16	1
							Lincoln C (loan)	8	1
							Blackpool	107	21
							Grimsby T	184	38
Handyside Peter	6 1	12 03	D	31 7 74	Dumfries	Trainee	Grimsby T	89	—
Jobling Kevin	5 9	10 11	M	1 1 68	Sunderland	Apprentice	Leicester C	9	—
							Grimsby T	227	9
							Scunthorpe U (loan)	—	—
Laws Brian†	5 8	11 05	D	14 10 61	Wallsend	Apprentice	Burnley	125	12
							Huddersfield T	56	1
							Middlesbrough	107	12
							Nottingham F	147	4
							Grimsby T	43	2
Lester Jack	5 10	11 00	F	8 10 75	Sheffield	Trainee	Grimsby T	12	—
Lever Mark	6 3	12 08	D	29 3 70	Beverley	Trainee	Grimsby T	243	8
Livingstone Steve	6 1	11 04	F	8 9 69	Middlesbrough	Trainee	Coventry C	31	5
							Blackburn R	30	10
							Chelsea	1	—
							Port Vale (loan)	5	—
							Grimsby T	99	22
McDermott John	5 7	10 00	D	3 1 69	Middlesbrough	Trainee	Grimsby T	304	5
Mendonca Clive	5 10	10 07	F	9 9 68	Islington	Apprentice	Sheffield U	13	4
							Doncaster R (loan)	2	—
							Rotherham U	84	27
							Sheffield U	10	1
							Grimsby T (loan)	10	3
							Grimsby T	111	39
Neil James	5 9	10 05	D	28 2 76	Bury St Edmunds	Trainee	Grimsby T	1	—
Pearcey Jason	6 1	13 12	G	23 7 71	Leamington Spa	Trainee	Mansfield T	77	—
							Grimsby T	5	—
Petchey Stewart‡			D	22 1 77	Grimsby	Trainee	Grimsby T	—	—
Rodger Graham	6 2	11 13	D	1 4 67	Glasgow	Apprentice	Wolverhampton W	1	—
							Coventry C	36	2
							Luton T	28	2
							Grimsby T	107	9
Shakespeare Craig	5 10	12 05	M	26 10 63	Birmingham	Apprentice	Walsall	284	45
							Sheffield W	17	—
							WBA	112	12
							Grimsby T	80	8
Smith Richard	5 11	13 03	D	3 10 70	Leicester	Trainee	Leicester C	98	1
							Cambridge U (loan)	4	—
							Grimsby T	18	—
Southall Nicky	5 10	12 12	F	28 1 72	Teeside	Trainee	Hartlepool U	138	24
							Grimsby T	33	2
Walker John	5 6	11 06	M	12 12 73	Glasgow	Clydebank BC	Rangers	—	—
							Clydebank	27	2
							Grimsby T	2	1
Watson Tommy*	5 8	10 10	M	29 9 69	Liverpool	Trainee	Grimsby T	172	24
							Hull C (loan)	4	—
Woods Neil	6 0	12 11	F	30 7 66	York	Apprentice	Doncaster R	65	16
							Rangers	3	—
							Ipswich T	27	5
							Bradford C	14	2
							Grimsby T	192	41

Trainees
Brown, James K; Burdon, Andrew J; Carinci, Pietro; Chapman, Ben; Fraser, Steven M; Hamnett, John C; Harsley, Paul; Jarvis, Paul W; Louth, Daniel J; Love, Andrew M; Mundell, Andrew A; Oster, John M; Stephenson, Lee; Welton, Guy E.

Non-Contract
Laws, Brian.

Associated Schoolboys
Bloomer, Matthew B; Brown, Kevin; Crew, Lee N; Meenaghan, Matthew.

Associated Schoolboys who have accepted the club's offer of a Traineeship/Contract
Hanslip, Nicolas; Oakes, Andrew; Oswin, Matthew S W; Rockhill, Antony J; Soley, Martin R F.

HARTLEPOOL UNITED

Name	Ht	Wt	Pos	Born	Birthplace	Source	Club	Apps	Gls
Allinson Jamie§	6 1	12 00	D	15 6 78	Stockton	Trainee	Hartlepool U	4	—
Allon Joe	5 11	13 06	F	12 11 66	Gateshead	Trainee	Newcastle U	9	2
							Swansea C	34	11
							Hartlepool U	112	50
							Chelsea	14	2
							Port Vale (loan)	6	—
							Brentford	45	19
							Southend U (loan)	3	—
							Port Vale	23	9
							Lincoln C	4	—
							Hartlepool U	22	8
Billing Peter*	6 0	13 12	D	24 10 64	Liverpool	South Liverpool	Everton	1	—
							Crewe Alex	88	1
							Coventry C	58	1
							Port Vale (loan)	12	—
							Port Vale	14	—
							Hartlepool U	36	—
Canham Tony*	5 8	11 04	M	8 6 60	Leeds	Harrogate Railway	York C	347	57
							Hartlepool U	29	1
Conlon Paul§	5 9	11 08	F	5 1 78	Sunderland	Trainee	Hartlepool U	15	4
Dixon Andy‡	5 9	10 00	F	5 8 68	Hartlepool	Mons	Hartlepool U	3	—
Ford Gary‡	5 8	12 05	M	8 2 61	York	Apprentice	York C	366	52
							Leicester C	16	2
							Port Vale	75	12
							Walsall (loan)	13	2
							Mansfield T	88	6
						Tromso, Harstad	Hartlepool U	3	—
Foster Lee§			F	21 10 77	Bishop Auckland	Trainee	Hartlepool U	1	—
Gallagher Ian§			M	30 5 78	Hartlepool	Trainee	Hartlepool U	1	—
Halliday Stephen	5 10	12 03	F	3 5 76	Sunderland	Charlton Ath	Hartlepool U	78	12
Henderson Damian*	6 2	13 12	F	12 5 73	Leeds	Trainee	Leeds U	—	—
							Scarborough	17	5
							Scunthorpe U	37	4
							Hereford U (loan)	5	—
							Hartlepool U (loan)	12	3
							Hartlepool U	36	3
Homer Chris	5 9	10 05	M	16 4 77	Stockton	Trainee	Hartlepool U	6	—
Horne Brian‡	5 10	14 00	G	5 10 67	Billericay	Apprentice	Millwall	163	—
							Watford (loan)	—	—
							Middlesbrough (loan)	4	—
							Stoke C (loan)	1	—
							Portsmouth	3	—
							Hartlepool U	73	—
Houchen Keith	6 2	13 04	F	25 7 60	Middlesbrough	Chesterfield	Hartlepool U	170	65
							Orient	76	20
							York C	67	19
							Scunthorpe U	9	3
							Coventry C	54	7
							Hibernian	57	11
							Port Vale	49	10
							Hartlepool U	104	27
Howard Steve	6 1	13 08	M	10 5 76	Durham	Tow Law T	Hartlepool U	39	7
Hutt Stephen§			F	19 2 79	Middlesbrough	Trainee	Hartlepool U	1	—
Ingram Denny	5 10	12 01	D	27 6 76	Sunderland	Trainee	Hartlepool U	81	2
Jones Steve*	5 11	13 04	G	31 1 74	Teeside	Trainee	Hartlepool U	48	—
Lee Graeme§	6 2	12 07	M	31 5 78	Middlesbrough	Trainee	Hartlepool U	6	—
Linyard Paul‡	6 1	12 00	G	18 7 77	Keighley	Trainee	Hartlepool U	—	—
Lynch Chris‡	6 0	11 07	F	18 11 74	Middlesbrough	Halifax T	Hartlepool U	50	2
McAuley Sean	5 10	11 03	D	23 6 72	Sheffield	Trainee	Manchester U	—	—
							St Johnstone	62	—
							Chesterfield (loan)	1	1
							Hartlepool U	46	—
McGuckin Ian	6 2	14 00	D	24 4 73	Middlesbrough	Trainee	Hartlepool U	130	8
O'Connor Paul†			G	17 8 71	Easington	Blyth Spartans	Hartlepool U	1	—
Oliver Keith*	5 8	11 00	M	15 1 76	South Shields	Trainee	Hartlepool U	32	—

Name							Club	Apps	Gls
Reddish Shane‡	5 10	11 10	M	5 5 71	Bolsover	Trainee	Doncaster R	60	3
							Carlisle U	37	1
							Chesterfield (loan)	3	—
							Hartlepool U	43	—
Slater Darren§			D	4 1 79	Bishop Auckland	Trainee	Hartlepool U	1	—
Sloan Scott‡	5 10	12 01	F	14 12 67	Wallsend	Ponteland	Berwick R	61	20
							Newcastle U	16	1
							Falkirk	64	11
							Cambridge U (loan)	4	1
							Hartlepool U	35	2
Tait Mick	5 11	12 10	M	30 9 56	Wallsend	Apprentice	Oxford U	64	23
							Carlisle U	106	20
							Hull C	33	3
							Portsmouth	240	30
							Reading	99	9
							Darlington	79	2
							Hartlepool U	120	3
Walton Paul§			F	2 7 79	Sunderland	Trainee	Hartlepool U	6	—

Trainees

Allinson, Jamie; Conlon, Paul R; Farnaby, Stephend C; Foster, Lee; Gallagher, Ian; Goodwin, Marc T; Hainsworth, Lee D; Hutt, Stephen G; Hyson, Daniel J; Irvine, Stuart C; Lee, Graeme B; Maxwell, Richard S; Miller, Thomas W; Slater, Darren; Thexton, Carl; Walton, Paul A; Winstanley, Craig J.

Non-Contract
O'Connor, Paul D.

Associated Schoolboys

Associated Schoolboys who have accepted the club's offer of a Traineeship/Contract
Forster, Alan C; Timmons, Darren.

HEREFORD UNITED

Name							Club	Apps	Gls
Brough John	6 0	12 11	D	8 1 73	Heanor	Trainee	Notts Co	—	—
							Shrewsbury T	16	1
						Telford U	Hereford U	40	2
Clarke Dean*	5 9	11 04	F	28 7 77	Hereford	Trainee	Hereford U	11	—
Cross Nicky*	5 10	12 09	F	7 2 61	Birmingham	Apprentice	WBA	105	15
							Walsall	109	45
							Leicester C	58	15
							Port Vale	144	39
							Hereford U	65	14
Downing Keith	5 9	11 05	M	23 7 65	Oldbury	Mile Oak R	Notts Co	23	1
							Wolverhampton W	191	8
							Birmingham C	1	—
							Stoke C	16	—
							Cardiff C	4	—
							Hereford U	29	—
Evans Darren*	5 11	12 00	D	30 9 74	Wolverhampton	Trainee	Aston Villa	—	—
							Hereford U	24	—
Fishlock Murray	5 8	10 09	D	23 9 73	Marlborough	Trowbridge T	Hereford U	41	3
Hall Leigh‡			F	10 6 75	Hereford		Hereford U	2	—
James Tony	6 3	14 05	D	27 6 67	Sheffield	Gainsborough T	Lincoln C	29	—
							Leicester C	107	11
							Hereford U	35	4
Lloyd Kevin*	6 0	12 04	D	26 9 70	Llanidloes	Caersws	Hereford U	51	3
Lyne Neil*	6 1	13 01	F	4 4 70	Leicester	Leicester U	Nottingham F	—	—
							Walsall (loan)	7	—
							Shrewsbury T (loan)	16	6
							Shrewsbury T	64	11
							Cambridge U	17	—
							Chesterfield (loan)	6	1
							Hereford U	63	2
MacKenzie Chris	6 0	12 06	G	14 5 72	Northampton	Corby T	Hereford U	60	1
Pitman Jamie	5 8	10 12	M	6 1 76	Warminster	Trainee	Swindon T	3	—
							Hereford U	13	—
Pounder Tony*	5 9	11 01	M	11 3 66	Yeovil	Weymouth	Bristol R	113	10
						Weymouth	Hereford U	62	4
Preedy Phil	5 10	11 02	M	20 11 75	Hereford	Trainee	Hereford U	42	2
Reece Andy‡	5 10	12 02	M	5 9 62	Shrewsbury	Willenhall	Bristol R	239	17
							Walsall (loan)	9	1
							Walsall (loan)	6	—
							Hereford U	71	5
Smith Dean	6 0	13 00	D	19 3 71	West Bromwich	Trainee	Walsall	142	2
							Hereford U	75	11

Steele Tim*	5 10	11 04	F	1 12 67	Coventry	Apprentice	Shrewsbury T	61	5
							Wolverhampton W	75	7
							Stoke C (loan)	7	1
							Bradford C	11	—
							Hereford U	32	2
Stoker Gareth	5 10	10 12	M	22 2 73	Bishop Auckland	Leeds U	Hull C	30	2
							Hereford U	43	3
Warner Rob	5 10	11 06	D	20 4 77	Stratford	Trainee	Hereford U	16	—
Watkiss Stuart*	6 1	13 09	D	8 5 66	Wolverhampton	Apprentice	Wolverhampton W	2	—
						Rushall Olympic	Walsall	62	2
							Hereford U	19	—
White Steve	5 11	12 06	F	2 1 59	Chipping Sodbury	Mangotsfield U	Bristol R	50	20
							Luton T	72	25
							Charlton Ath	29	12
							Lincoln C (loan)	3	—
							Luton T (loan)	4	—
							Bristol R	101	24
							Swindon T	244	83
							Hereford U	76	44
Wilkins Richard	6 0	12 01	M	28 5 65	Streatham	Haverhill R	Colchester U	152	22
							Cambridge U	81	7
							Hereford U	77	5

Trainees
Bristow, Andrew; Cook, Garry J; Davies, Sean J; Hibbard, Mark A; Jackson, Scott S; Jordan, Roy A; King, Christopher A; Medford, Mark; Naylor, Martyn P; Ogiesby, Andrew; Piper, Christopher J; Reeves, Dominic S B; Relish, Lee D; Sims, Christopher J; Smith, Colin S; Woods, Simon A.

HUDDERSFIELD TOWN

Baldry Simon	5 10	11 06	F	12 2 76	Huddersfield	Trainee	Huddersfield T	35	2
Booth Andrew	6 1	12 06	F	17 3 73	Huddersfield	Trainee	Huddersfield T	123	54
Bullock Darren	5 8	12 07	M	12 2 69	Worcester	Nuneaton	Huddersfield T	101	15
Collins Sam	6 2	13 07	D	5 6 77	Pontefract	Trainee	Huddersfield T	—	—
Collins Simon	6 0	13 02	M	16 12 73	Pontefract	Trainee	Huddersfield T	36	3
Cowan Tom	5 8	11 10	D	28 8 69	Bellshill	Netherdale BC	Clyde	16	2
							Rangers	12	—
							Sheffield U	45	—
							Stoke C (loan)	14	—
							Huddersfield T (loan)	10	—
							Huddersfield T	80	4
Crosby Gary	5 8	9 00	F	8 5 64	Sleaford	Lincoln U	Lincoln C	7	—
						Grantham	Nottingham F	152	12
							Grimsby T (loan)	3	—
							Huddersfield T	20	4
Dalton Paul	5 11	12 06	M	25 4 67	Middlesbrough	Brandon	Manchester U	—	—
							Hartlepool U	151	37
							Plymouth Arg	98	25
							Huddersfield T	29	5
Dunn Iain	5 10	12 00	F	1 4 70	Derwent	School	York C	77	11
							Chesterfield	13	1
						Goole T	Huddersfield T	115	14
Dyson Jon	6 1	12 09	D	18 12 71	Mirfield	School	Huddersfield T	82	2
Edwards Rob	5 9	12 04	F	23 2 70	Manchester	Trainee	Crewe Alex	155	44
							Huddersfield T	13	7
Francis Steve	6 1	14 00	G	29 5 64	Billericay	Apprentice	Chelsea	71	—
							Reading	216	—
							Huddersfield T	132	—
Gray Kevin	6 0	14 00	D	7 1 72	Sheffield	Trainee	Mansfield T	141	3
							Huddersfield T	43	—
Heary Thomas	5 9	11 03	M	14 2 79	Dublin	Trainee	Huddersfield T	—	—
Illingworth Jeremy	5 10	11 11	M	20 5 77	Huddersfield	Trainee	Huddersfield T	—	—
Jenkins Steve	5 11	12 03	D	16 7 72	Merthyr	Trainee	Swansea C	165	1
							Huddersfield T	31	1
Jepson Ronnie	6 0	13 07	F	12 5 63	Stoke	Nantwich	Port Vale	22	—
							Peterborough U (loan)	18	5
							Preston NE	38	8
							Exeter C	54	21
							Huddersfield T	107	36
Kelly Mark	6 0	11 10	M	5 10 76	Gibraltar	Trainee	Huddersfield T	—	—
Lawson Ian	5 11	11 05	F	4 11 77	Huddersfield	Trainee	Huddersfield T	—	—
Makel Lee	5 9	11 05	M	11 1 73	Sunderland	Trainee	Newcastle U	12	1
							Blackburn R	6	—
							Huddersfield T	33	2
Murphy Stephen	5 11	12 00	M	5 4 78	Dublin	Belvedere	Huddersfield T	—	—

Norman Tony	6 1	13 08	G	24 2 58	Mancot	Amateur	Burnley	—	—
							Hull C	372	—
							Sunderland	198	—
							Huddersfield T	3	—
O'Connor Derek	5 11	12 01	G	9 3 78	Dublin	Crumplin U	Huddersfield T	—	—
O'Keeffe Darren‡			M	29 8 78	Dublin	Trainee	Huddersfield T	—	—
Reid Paul	5 8	11 08	M	19 1 68	Oldbury	Apprentice	Leicester C	162	21
							Bradford C (loan)	7	—
							Bradford C	82	15
							Huddersfield T	55	6
Rowe Rodney	5 9	12 04	F	30 7 75	Huddersfield	Trainee	Huddersfield T	27	2
							Scarborough (loan)	14	1
							Bury (loan)	3	—
Ryan Robbie	5 10	12 00	D	11 8 76	Dublin	Belvedere	Huddersfield T	—	—
Scully Pat	6 1	13 07	D	23 6 70	Dublin	Trainee	Arsenal	—	—
							Preston NE (loan)	13	1
							Northampton T (loan)	15	—
							Southend U	115	6
							Huddersfield T	74	2
Sinnott Lee	6 1	13 07	D	12 7 65	Pelsall	Apprentice	Walsall	40	2
							Watford	78	2
							Bradford C	173	6
							Crystal Palace	55	—
							Bradford C	34	1
							Huddersfield T	57	1
Ward Mark*	5 6	10 00	M	10 10 62	Prescot	Northwich Vic	Oldham Ath	84	12
							West Ham U	165	12
							Manchester C	55	14
							Everton	83	6
							Birmingham C (loan)	9	1
							Birmingham C	54	6
							Huddersfield T	8	—
Whitington Craig‡	5 11	13 03	F	3 9 70	Brighton	Crawley T	Scarborough	27	10
							Huddersfield T	1	—
							Rochdale (loan)	1	—

Trainees
Cuss, Paul M; Dougan, James M; Gonsalves, Ryan M; Kaye, Peter J; Sanders, Steven; Smith, Steve D; Stansfield, James E; Stott, Michael J; Sweet, Benjamin J; Sykes, James A; Tully, Jamie P.

Associated Schoolboys
Atkinson, Robert F; Bainbridge, Lee; Cartwright, Christopher; Clarke, Doni J; Connor, Mark; Fowler, Adam M; Gray, Liam G; Horsley, Jamie L; Patterson, Andrew; Senior, Michael G; Tindle, James P.

Associated Schoolboys who have accepted the club's offer of a Traineeship/Contract
Bemrose, Daniel S; Callaghan, Billy; Facey, Delroy M; Scott, Paul; Walker, Richard J; Williams, Adam R.

HULL CITY

Abbott Greg*	5 9	10 07	M	14 12 63	Coventry	Apprentice	Coventry C	—	—
							Bradford C	281	38
							Halifax T	28	1
						Guiseley	Hull C	124	16
Allison Neil	6 2	11 10	D	20 10 73	Hull	Trainee	Hull C	95	3
Brown Andrew	6 3	13 00	F	11 11 76	Edinburgh	Trainee	Leeds U	—	—
							Hull C	—	—
Carroll Roy	6 2	11 09	G	30 9 77	Northern Ireland	Trainee	Hull C	23	—
Chambers David*	5 11	10 10	F	16 9 76	Chesterfield	Trainee	Hull C	—	—
Dakin Simon*	5 9	11 02	D	30 11 74	Nottingham	Derby Co	Hull C	36	1
Darby Duane	5 11	11 02	F	17 10 73	Birmingham	Trainee	Torquay U	108	26
							Doncaster R	17	4
							Hull C	8	1
Dewhurst Rob	6 3	12 02	D	10 9 71	Keighley	Trainee	Blackburn R	13	—
							Darlington (loan)	11	1
							Huddersfield T (loan)	7	—
							Hull C	84	10
Fewings Paul	5 11	11 07	F	18 2 78	Hull	Trainee	Hull C	27	2
Fidler Richard‡	5 9	10 09	M	26 10 76	Sheffield	Leeds U	Hull C	1	—
Gilbert Kenny	5 8	10 11	F	8 3 75	Aberdeen	East End A	Aberdeen	—	—
							Hull C	13	—
Gordon Gavin§	6 1	11 05	F	24 6 79	Manchester	Trainee	Hull C	13	3
Graham Jimmy*	5 10	11 05	D	5 11 69	Glasgow	Trainee	Bradford C	7	—
							Rochdale (loan)	11	—
							Rochdale	126	1
							Hull C	63	1
Haigh Gavin*	5 10	11 08	M	9 2 77	Doncaster	Trainee	Hull C	—	—

Humphries Glenn*	6 0	12 00	D	11 8 64	Hull	Apprentice	Doncaster R	180	8
							Lincoln C (loan)	9	—
							Bristol C	85	—
							Scunthorpe U	72	5
					Golden		Hull C	12	—
Laister Jamie			M	9 2 79	Newport		Hull C	—	—
Lawford Craig*	5 10	11 00	M	25 11 72	Dewsbury	Trainee	Bradford C	20	1
							Hull C	62	3
Lee Chris*	5 9	11 05	M	18 6 71	Halifax	Trainee	Bradford C	—	—
							Rochdale	26	2
							Scarborough	78	3
							Hull C	116	5
Lowthorpe Adam	5 7	10 06	D	7 8 75	Hull	Trainee	Hull C	44	—
Mann Neil	5 10	12 01	M	19 11 72	Nottingham	Grantham T	Hull C	74	3
Marks Jamie	5 10	10 13	D	18 3 77	Belfast	Trainee	Leeds U	—	—
							Hull C	5	—
Mason Andy	5 11	11 11	F	22 11 74	Bolton	Trainee	Bolton W	—	—
							Hull C	20	1
Maxfield Scott	5 9	10 09	D	13 7 76	Doncaster	Trainee	Doncaster R	29	1
							Hull C	4	—
Peacock Richard	5 10	11 00	F	29 10 72	Sheffield	Sheffield FC	Hull C	93	13
Plant Ian*	5 11	12 02	D	15 5 77	Hull	Trainee	Hull C	—	—
Quigley Michael	5 7	10 00	M	2 10 70	Manchester	Trainee	Manchester C	12	—
							Wrexham (loan)	4	—
							Hull C	13	1
Trevitt Simon	5 11	12 06	D	20 12 67	Dewsbury	Apprentice	Huddersfield T	229	3
							Hull C	25	—
Wharton Paul	5 4	9 09	M	26 6 77	Newcastle	Trainee	Leeds U	—	—
							Hull C	9	—
Wilkinson Ian§	6 2	13 00	D	19 9 77	Ferriby	Trainee	Hull C	8	1
Williams Andy*	6 0	11 10	M	19 7 62	Birmingham	Dudley and	Coventry C	9	—
						Solihull B	Rotherham U	87	13
							Leeds U	46	3
							Port Vale (loan)	5	—
							Notts Co	39	2
							Huddersfield T (loan)	6	—
							Rotherham U	51	2
							Hull C	34	—
Wilson Steve	5 10	10 10	G	24 4 74	Hull	Trainee	Hull C	79	—

Trainees
Ainsley, Stuart; Capuano, Julian; Dickinson, Patrick J; Gordon, Kenyatta G; Hennessy, Simon P; Hunter, Glenn W P; Hurst, Liam J J; Laister, Jamie R; Norton, Daniel P; O'Brien, Kieron J; Ogle, Gareth D; Powell, Graham A; Pridmore, Lee C; Stock, Nicholas; Sykes, Simon J; Waddley, Kevin; Wilkinson, Ian J.

Associated Schoolboys
Artymiuk, Michael J; Blythe, Michael; Bolder, Adam P; Brough, Steven P; Longthorn, Russell A L; Thacker, Martin; Waters, Paul A.

Associated Schoolboys who have accepted the club's offer of a Traineeship/Contract
Edwards, Michael; Evans, James N.

IPSWICH TOWN

Appleby Ritchie*	5 8	10 06	M	18 9 75	Middlesbrough	Trainee	Newcastle U	—	—
							Darlington (loan)	—	—
							Ipswich T	3	—
Baker Clive‡	5 9	11 00	G	14 3 59	North Walsham	Amateur	Norwich C	4	—
							Barnsley	291	—
							Coventry C	—	—
							Ipswich T	48	—
Bell Leon§			M	23 9 77	Ipswich	Trainee	Ipswich T	—	—
Brown Wayne§			M	20 8 77	Barking	Trainee	Ipswich T	—	—
Cotterell Leo*	5 9	10 00	D	2 9 74	Cambridge	Trainee	Ipswich T	2	—
Durrant Lee*	5 10	11 07	M	18 12 73	Gt Yarmouth	Trainee	Ipswich T	7	—
Ellis Kevin	6 2	12 07	D	12 5 77	Gt Yarmouth	Trainee	Ipswich T	1	—
Forrest Craig	6 5	14 00	G	20 9 67	Vancouver	Apprentice	Ipswich T	257	—
							Colchester U (loan)	11	—
Gaughan Kevin			D	6 3 78	Glasgow		Ipswich T	—	—
Gregory Neil	5 11	11 10	F	7 10 72	Zambia	Trainee	Ipswich T	20	2
							Chesterfield (loan)	3	1
							Scunthorpe U (loan)	10	7
Hollman James§			M	22 3 78	Canterbury	Trainee	Ipswich T	—	—
Marshall Ian	6 1	12 12	F	20 3 66	Liverpool	Apprentice	Everton	15	1
							Oldham Ath	170	36
							Ipswich T	82	32

Mason Paul	5 9	12 01	M	3 9 63	Liverpool	Groningen	Aberdeen	158	27
							Ipswich T	69	13
Mathie Alex	5 10	11 07	F	20 12 68	Bathgate	Celtic BC	Celtic	11	—
							Morton	74	31
							Port Vale (loan)	3	—
							Newcastle U	25	4
							Ipswich T	52	20
McCrindle Scott‡			M	30 9 77	Stranraer	Trainee	Ipswich T	—	—
Milton Simon	5 10	11 05	M	23 8 63	Fulham	Bury St Edmunds	Ipswich T	238	48
							Exeter C (loan)	2	3
							Torquay U (loan)	4	1
Mowbray Tony	6 1	13 00	D	22 11 63	Saltburn	Apprentice	Middlesbrough	348	25
							Celtic	78	6
							Ipswich T	19	2
Naylor Richard	6 1	13 07	F	28 2 77	Leeds	Trainee	Ipswich T	—	—
Norfolk Lee	5 10	11 03	M	17 10 75	Dunedin NZ	Trainee	Ipswich T	3	—
Portrey Simon*	6 2	12 07	M	2 11 76	Wakefield	Trainee	Ipswich T	—	—
Scowcroft James	6 1	12 02	F	15 11 75	Bury St Edmunds	Trainee	Ipswich T	23	2
Sedgley Steve	6 1	13 13	M	26 5 68	Enfield	Apprentice	Coventry C	84	3
							Tottenham H	164	8
							Ipswich T	66	8
Slater Stuart	5 9	11 06	M	27 3 69	Sudbury	Apprentice	West Ham U	141	11
							Celtic	43	3
							Ipswich T	72	4
Stockwell Mick	5 9	11 04	M	14 2 65	Chelmsford	Apprentice	Ipswich T	352	21
Swailes Chris	6 2	12 07	D	19 10 70	Gateshead	Bridlington T	Doncaster R	49	—
							Ipswich T	5	—
Tanner Adam	6 0	12 01	M	25 10 73	Maldon	Trainee	Ipswich T	20	2
Taricco Mauricio	5 8	11 05	D	10 3 73	Buenos Aires	Argentinos Juniors	Ipswich T	39	—
Thompson Neil*	5 11	13 08	D	2 10 63	Beverley	Nottingham F	Hull C	31	—
						Scarborough	Scarborough	87	15
							Ipswich T	206	19
Thomsen Claus	6 3	13 06	M	31 5 70	Aarhus	Aarhus	Ipswich T	70	7
Uhlenbeek Gus			M	20 8 70	Paramaribo		Ipswich T	40	4
Vaughan Tony	6 1	11 02	D	11 10 75	Manchester	Trainee	Ipswich T	35	1
Wark John	5 11	12 12	D	4 8 57	Glasgow	Apprentice	Ipswich T	296	94
							Liverpool	70	28
							Ipswich T	89	23
							Middlesbrough	32	2
							Ipswich T	152	18
Williams Geraint	5 7	12 06	M	5 1 62	Cwmpare	Apprentice	Bristol R	141	8
							Derby Co	277	9
							Ipswich T	151	2
Wright Richard	6 2	13 00	G	5 11 77	Ipswich	Trainee	Ipswich T	26	—
Yallop Frank‡	5 11	12 00	D	4 4 64	Watford	Apprentice	Ipswich T	316	7
							Blackpool (loan)	3	—

Trainees
Bell, Leon C; Brown, Wayne L; Burgess, Mark P; Crawford, Graeme D; Dyer, Kieron C; Hollman, James N T; Keeble, Christopher M; Kennedy, John N; May, Robert D; Midgley, Neil A; Niven, Stuart T; Pearson, Craig D; Theobald, David J.

Associated Schoolboys
Farrington, Louie M; Gill, James O; Hehir, Samuel J; Logan, Richard J; Miller, Adam E; Stearn, Carl; Supple, Michael J; Wright, Carl A J.

Associated Schoolboys who have accepted the club's offer of a Traineeship/Contract
Beckham, Michael J; Coburn, Neil; Lowes, Brendan.

LEEDS UNITED

Beeney Mark	6 3	15 08	G	30 12 67	Pembury		Gillingham	2	—
							Maidstone U	50	—
							Aldershot (loan)	7	—
							Brighton & HA	69	—
							Leeds U	33	—
Beesley Paul	6 1	12 07	D	21 9 65	Liverpool	Marine	Wigan Ath	155	3
							Leyton Orient	32	1
							Sheffield U	168	7
							Leeds U	10	—
Blunt Jason	5 8	11 07	M	16 8 77	Penzance	Trainee	Leeds U	3	—
Bowman Robert	6 1	12 07	D	21 11 75	Durham	Trainee	Leeds U	7	—
Boyle Wesley			M	30 3 79	Portadown	Trainee	Leeds U	—	—

Name	Ht	Wt	Pos	Born	Birthplace	Source	Club	Apps	Gls
Brolin Tomas	5 8	12 07	M	29 11 69	Hudiksvall		Sundsvall	54	13
							Norrkoping	11	7
							Parma	133	20
							Leeds U	19	4
Byrne Nicky			M	9 10 78	Dublin		Leeds U	—	—
Couzens Andrew	5 9	11 06	D	4 6 75	Shipley	Trainee	Leeds U	18	—
Deane Brian	6 3	14 04	F	7 2 68	Leeds	Apprentice	Doncaster R	66	12
							Sheffield U	197	82
							Leeds U	110	27
Dorigo Tony	5 8	11 00	D	31 12 65	Melbourne	Apprentice	Aston Villa	111	1
							Chelsea	146	11
							Leeds U	153	5
Evans Paul	6 3	13 12	G	28 12 73	South Africa	Witts Univ	Leeds U	—	—
							Crystal Palace (loan)	—	—
Ford Mark	5 7	10 13	M	10 10 75	Pontefract	Trainee	Leeds U	13	—
Foster Martin	5 6	10 07	M	29 10 77	Sheffield	Trainee	Leeds U	—	—
Gray Andrew	6 1	13 06	M	15 11 77	Harrogate	Trainee	Leeds U	15	—
Harte Ian	5 10	12 05	D	31 8 77	Drogheda	Trainee	Leeds U	4	—
Heath Stephen*			D	15 11 77	Hull	Trainee	Leeds U	—	—
Jackson Mark	6 1	11 13	D	30 9 77	Leeds	Trainee	Leeds U	1	—
Jaques Daniel			M	18 1 78	North Ormesby	Trainee	Leeds U	—	—
Jobson Richard	6 2	13 06	D	9 5 63	Hull	Burton Alb	Watford	28	4
							Hull C	221	17
							Oldham Ath	189	10
							Leeds U	12	1
Kelly Gary	5 9	11 00	D	9 7 74	Drogheda	Home Farm	Leeds U	120	—
Kewell Harry			M	22 9 78	Australia		Leeds U	2	—
Lukic John*	6 4	13 12	G	11 12 60	Chesterfield	Apprentice	Leeds U	146	—
							Arsenal	223	—
							Leeds U	209	—
Masinga Phil	6 2	12 07	F	28 6 69	Johannesburg	Mamelodi Sundowns	Leeds U	31	5
Matthews Lee			M	16 1 79	Middlesbrough	Trainee	Leeds U	—	—
Maybury Alan			M	8 8 78	Dublin	Trainee	Leeds U	1	—
McAllister Gary	6 0	12 07	M	25 12 64	Motherwell	Fir Park BC	Motherwell	59	6
							Leicester C	201	47
							Leeds U	231	31
Moody Jimmy*	5 10	11 02	D	16 11 77	Hull	Trainee	Leeds U	—	—
O'Leary David‡	6 1	13 09	D	2 5 58	London	Apprentice	Arsenal	558	10
							Leeds U	10	—
O'Shea Alan‡	5 10	10 12	D	21 7 77	Dublin	Trainee	Leeds U	—	—
Palmer Carlton	6 3	12 13	D	5 12 65	Oldbury	Trainee	WBA	121	4
							Sheffield W	205	14
							Leeds U	74	5
Pemberton John	5 11	13 04	D	18 11 64	Oldham	Chadderton	Rochdale	1	—
							Crewe Alex	121	1
							Crystal Palace	78	2
							Sheffield U	68	—
							Leeds U	53	—
Radebe Lucas	6 0	11 09	M	12 4 69	Johannesburg	Kaiser Chiefs	Leeds U	25	—
Shepherd Paul	6 0	11 04	F	17 11 77	Leeds	Trainee	Leeds U	—	—
Smithard Matthew*	5 9	10 09	F	13 6 76	Leeds	Trainee	Leeds U	—	—
Speed Gary	5 9	12 10	M	8 9 69	Hawarden	Trainee	Leeds U	248	39
Tinkler Mark	6 0	13 06	M	24 10 74	Bishop Auckland	Trainee	Leeds U	22	—
Wallace Rodney	5 7	11 07	F	2 10 69	Lewisham	Trainee	Southampton	128	45
							Leeds U	159	40
Wetherall David	6 3	13 11	D	14 3 71	Sheffield	School	Sheffield W	—	—
							Leeds U	118	9
Worthington Nigel*	5 11	12 08	D	4 11 61	Ballymena	Ballymena U	Notts Co	67	4
							Sheffield W	338	12
							Leeds U	43	1
Wright Andrew			M	21 10 78	Leeds	Trainee	Leeds U	—	—
Yeboah Tony	5 11	14 09	F	6 6 66	Kumasi	Okwawu U	Saarbrucken	65	26
							Eintracht Frankfurt	123	68
							Leeds U	40	24

Trainees
Briggs, Simon J; Brown, Matthew; Butler, John; Davies, Lawrence; McPhail, Stephen; Morgan, Simon R.

Associated Schoolboys
Beeton, Lee J; Crawford, Dale; Davis, Neil; Dufton, Thomas S; Evans, Gareth J; Evans, Kevin; Francis, Ruben M; Froggatt, Jonathan P; Hackett, Kristian S; Hart, Jonathon; Henderson, Darius A; Jones, Matthew G; Lockwood, Adam B; Manousios, Nicholas G;

Rothmans Football Yearbook 1996–97

Miller, Scott R J; Monkhouse, Andrew W; Montgomery, Nicholas A; Moore, Ben K; Price, Jamie B; Ravenhill, Richard J; Singh, Harpal; Smith, Alan; Southern, Keith W; Watson, David S; Wrankmore, Luke.

Associated Schoolboys who have accepted the club's offer of a Traineeship/Contract
Hackworth, Anthony; Jackson, Daniel M D; Robinson, Paul W; Woodgate, Jonathan S.

LEICESTER CITY

Name	Ht	Wt	Pos	Birthdate	Birthplace	Source	Clubs	Apps	Gls
Bedder Paul*	5 8	11 03	M	8 3 77	Leicester	Trainee	Leicester C	—	—
Blake Mark*	5 11	12 09	M	16 12 70	Nottingham	Trainee	Aston Villa	31	2
							Wolverhampton W (loan)	2	—
							Portsmouth	15	—
							Leicester C	49	4
Carey Brian	6 3	13 12	D	31 5 68	Cork	Cork C	Manchester U	—	—
							Wrexham (loan)	3	—
							Wrexham (loan)	13	1
							Leicester C	58	1
Claridge Steve	6 0	12 10	F	10 4 66	Portsmouth	Fareham	Bournemouth	7	1
						Weymouth	Crystal Palace	—	—
							Aldershot	62	19
							Cambridge U	79	28
							Luton T	16	2
							Cambridge U	53	18
							Birmingham C	88	35
							Leicester C	14	5
Doherty James‡			M	10 3 77	Leicester		Leicester C	—	—
Gee Phil*	5 11	12 06	F	19 12 64	Pelsall	Gresley R	Derby Co	124	26
							Leicester C	53	9
							Plymouth Arg (loan)	6	—
Gordon Alan‡			M	7 9 77	Glasgow	Rochedale R	Doncaster R	—	—
							Leicester C	—	—
Grayson Simon	6 0	12 06	D	16 12 69	Ripon	Trainee	Leeds U	2	—
							Leicester C	152	4
Hallam Craig	5 10	12 05	F	11 11 76	Leicester	Trainee	Leicester C	—	—
Heskey Emile	6 2	13 02	M	11 1 78	Leicester	Trainee	Leicester C	31	7
Hill Colin	6 0	12 07	D	12 11 63	Hillingdon	Apprentice	Arsenal	46	1
							Brighton & HA (loan)	—	—
						Maritimo	Colchester U	69	—
							Sheffield U	82	1
							Leicester C (loan)	10	—
							Leicester C	128	—
Hyde Paul*	6 1	14 00	G	7 4 63	Hayes	Hayes	Wycombe W	105	—
							Leicester C	—	—
Kalac Zeljko	6 7	14 03	G	16 12 72	Camperdown	Sydney United	Leicester C	1	—
Kamark Pontus	5 10	12 03	D	5 4 69	Sweden	IFK Gothenburg	Leicester C	1	—
Lawrence Jamie	6 0	12 06	F	8 3 70	Balham	Cowes	Sunderland	4	—
							Doncaster R	25	3
							Leicester C	32	1
Lennon Neil	5 10	12 12	D	25 6 71	Lurgan	Trainee	Manchester C	1	—
							Crewe Alex	147	15
							Leicester C	15	1
Lewis Neil	5 8	10 05	M	28 6 74	Wolverhampton	Trainee	Leicester C	61	1
McMahon Sam	5 10	11 06	M	10 2 76	Newark	Trainee	Leicester C	4	1
Parker Garry	6 0	13 02	M	7 9 65	Oxford	Apprentice	Luton T	42	3
							Hull C	84	8
							Nottingham F	103	17
							Aston Villa	95	13
							Leicester C	54	5
Poole Kevin	5 10	12 06	G	21 7 63	Bromsgrove	Apprentice	Aston Villa	28	—
							Northampton T (loan)	3	—
							Middlesbrough	34	—
							Hartlepool U (loan)	12	—
							Leicester C	156	—
Roberts Iwan	6 2	14 04	F	26 6 68	Bangor	Trainee	Watford	63	9
							Huddersfield T	142	50
							Leicester C	100	41
Robins Mark	5 8	11 08	F	22 12 69	Ashton under Lyme	Apprentice	Manchester U	48	11
							Norwich C	67	20
							Leicester C	48	11
Rolling Frank	6 1	13 00	D	23 8 68	Colnar	FC Pau	Ayr U	35	2
							Leicester C	17	—
Taylor Scott	5 9	11 00	M	28 11 70	Portsmouth	Trainee	Reading	207	24
							Leicester C	39	6

Walsh Steve	6 3	14 06	D	3 11 64	Fulwood	Local	Wigan Ath	126	4
							Leicester C	287	45
Watts Julian	6 3	13 07	D	17 3 71	Sheffield	Trainee	Rotherham U	20	1
							Sheffield W	16	1
							Shrewsbury T (loan)	9	—
							Leicester C	9	—
Whitlow Mike	6 0	13 03	D	13 1 68	Northwich	Witton Alb	Leeds U	77	4
							Leicester C	130	8
Willis Jimmy	6 2	12 04	D	12 7 68	Liverpool	Blackburn R	Halifax T	—	—
							Stockport Co	10	—
							Darlington	90	6
							Leicester C	60	3
							Bradford C (loan)	9	1

Trainees
Arcos-Diaz, Miguel; Branston, Guy P B; Campbell, Stuart P; Davies, Lee S; Dodds, Andrew R; Emerson, Paul G; Fox, Martin R; Jaffa, Graeme C; Johnson, Owen R; Mitchell, Ross J; Neil, Gary D C; Oakes, Stefan T; Quincey, Lee P; Skeldon, Kevin; Wenlock, Stephen; Wilson, Stevie J; Wilson, Stuart K.

Associated Schoolboys
Amoroso, Roberto P; Bacon, Carl R; Harrison, Andrew J; Heath, Matthew P; Heggs, Gareth L; Noble, Craig P; Nurse, Matthew J; Piper, Matthew J; Ratcliffe, David P; Saddington, David; Salter, Alex; Weale, Richard J; White, Christopher I.

Associated Schoolboys who have accepted the club's offer of a Traineeship/Contract
Goodwin, Tommy N; Hodges, John K; Jackson, Matthew; McCann, Timothy.

LEYTON ORIENT

Arnott Andy	6 1	12 02	F	18 10 73	Chatham	Trainee	Gillingham	73	12
							Manchester U (loan)	—	—
							Leyton Orient	19	3
Austin Kevin	6 1	14 00	D	12 2 73	Hackney	Saffron Walden	Leyton Orient	109	3
Ayorinde Sam	6 0	12 07	F	20 10 74	Lagos		Leyton Orient	1	—
Baker Joe	5 7	10 03	M	19 4 77	London	Charlton Ath	Leyton Orient	20	—
Bellamy Gary*	6 2	11 05	D	4 7 62	Worksop	Apprentice	Chesterfield	184	7
							Wolverhampton W	136	9
							Cardiff C (loan)	9	—
							Leyton Orient	132	6
Brooks Shaun*	5 8	11 00	M	9 10 62	London	Apprentice	Crystal Palace	54	4
							Orient	148	26
							Bournemouth	129	13
							Stockport C (loan)	—	—
							Leyton Orient	50	2
Caldwell Peter	6 1	13 00	G	5 6 72	Dorchester	Trainee	QPR	—	—
							Leyton Orient	28	—
Chapman Danny	5 10	11 06	M	21 11 74	Peckham	Trainee	Millwall	12	—
							Leyton Orient	38	2
Cockerill Glenn*	5 10	12 06	M	25 8 59	Grimsby	Louth U	Lincoln C	71	10
							Swindon T	26	1
							Lincoln C	115	25
							Sheffield U	62	10
							Southampton	287	32
							Leyton Orient	90	7
Everitt Dave*			M	30 12 76	Chertsey		Leyton Orient	—	—
Fearon Ron*	6 0	11 12	G	19 11 60	Romford	QPR	Reading	61	—
						Sutton	Ipswich T	28	—
							Brighton & HA (loan)	7	—
							Leyton Orient	—	—
							Ipswich T	—	—
							Walsall (loan)	1	—
							Southend U	—	—
							Leyton Orient	18	—
Gray Andy‡	5 6	10 10	F	25 10 73	Southampton	Trainee	Reading	17	3
							Leyton Orient	32	3
Hague Paul‡	6 3	13 03	D	16 9 72	Consett	Trainee	Gillingham	9	—
							Leyton Orient	18	1
Hanson Dave	6 1	13 01	F	19 11 68	Huddersfield	Farsley Celtic	Bury	1	—
						Hednesford	Leyton Orient	11	1
Hendon Ian	6 0	12 10	D	5 12 71	Ilford	Trainee	Tottenham H	4	—
							Portsmouth (loan)	4	—
							Leyton Orient (loan)	6	—
							Barnsley (loan)	6	—
							Leyton Orient	103	4
							Birmingham C (loan)	4	—
Inglethorpe Alex	5 11	11 07	F	14 11 71	Epsom	School	Watford	12	2
							Barnet (loan)	6	3
							Leyton Orient	30	9

Kelly Tony	5 11	11 08	F	14 2 66	Meridan		Bristol C	6	1
						St Albans C	Stoke C	58	5
							Hull C (loan)	6	1
							Cardiff C (loan)	5	1
							Bury	57	10
							Leyton Orient	34	3
Lakin Barry*	5 9	12 02	M	19 9 73	Dartford	Trainee	Leyton Orient	54	2
McCarthy Alan	5 11	12 10	D	11 1 72	London	Trainee	QPR	11	—
							Watford (loan)	9	—
							Plymouth Arg (loan)	2	—
							Leyton Orient	43	—
Purse Darren	6 2	12 08	D	14 2 77	London	Trainee	Leyton Orient	55	3
Rufus Marvin‡			M	11 9 76	Lewisham	Charlton Ath	Leyton Orient	7	—
Shearer Lee	6 4	12 01	D	23 10 77	Southend	Trainee	Leyton Orient	10	1
Stanislaus Roger‡	5 11	13 02	D	2 11 68	Hammersmith	Trainee	Arsenal	—	—
							Brentford	111	4
							Bury	176	5
							Leyton Orient	21	—
Warren Mark	6 05	11 07	D	12 11 74	Clapton	Trainee	Leyton Orient	74	4
							West Ham U (loan)	—	—
West Colin	6 0	13 12	F	13 11 62	Wallsend	Apprentice	Sunderland	102	21
							Watford	45	20
							Rangers	10	2
							Sheffield W	45	8
							WBA	73	22
							Port Vale (loan)	5	1
							Swansea C	33	12
							Leyton Orient	112	39
Wilkie Glen*			D	22 1 77	Stepney	Trainee	Leyton Orient	11	—
Williams Lee‡			F	13 3 77	Essex		Leyton Orient	3	—

Trainees
Bird, Matthew W; Brazier, Jeffery C; Doe, Steven R; Everingham, William L; Harrington, Daniel J; Haynes, David J; Honeyball, Scott R; Jones, Anthony S; Jones, David; Martin, Gary D; Phillips, Wayne D; Pike, David A; Sopp, Darryl J; Sugg, Darren W; Warren, Kevin; Weaver, Luke D S; Whybrow, Daniel S; Williams, Michael J.

Associated Schoolboys
Antoine, Marlon A.

Associated Schoolboys who have accepted the club's offer of a Traineeship/Contract
Cockerill, David; Morris, Jamie B.

LINCOLN CITY

Ainsworth Gareth	5 9	11 09	M	10 5 73	Blackburn	Blackburn R	Preston NE	5	—
							Cambridge U	4	1
							Preston NE	82	12
							Lincoln C	31	12
Alcide Colin	6 2	12 09	F	14 4 72	Huddersfield	Emley	Lincoln C	27	6
Barnett Jason	5 9	12 04	F	21 4 76	Shrewsbury	Trainee	Wolverhampton W	—	—
							Lincoln C	32	2
Bos Gijsbert	6 4	12 07	F	22 3 73	Spakenburg	Ijsselmeervogels	Lincoln C	11	5
Brown Grant	6 0	11 12	D	19 11 69	Sunderland	Trainee	Leicester C	14	—
							Lincoln C	254	11
Brown Steve	6 0	12 07	F	6 12 73	Southend	Trainee	Southend U	10	2
							Scunthorpe U	—	—
							Colchester U	62	17
							Gillingham	9	2
							Lincoln C	26	3
Daley Phil*	6 2	12 09	F	12 4 67	Walton	Newtown	Wigan Ath	161	39
							Lincoln C	32	5
Davies Neil	6 2	14 02	F	9 11 76	Liverpool	Fleetwood T	Lincoln C	—	—
Davis Darren‡	6 0	11 00	D	5 2 67	Sutton in Ashfield	Apprentice	Notts Co	92	1
							Lincoln C	102	4
							Maidstone U	31	2
						Frickley Ath	Scarborough	48	3
							Lincoln C	3	—
Daws Tony*	5 8	11 10	F	10 9 66	Sheffield	Apprentice	Notts Co	8	1
							Sheffield U	11	3
							Scunthorpe U	183	63
							Grimsby T	16	1
							Lincoln C	51	13
Dixon Ben	6 1	11 00	F	16 9 74	Lincoln	Trainee	Lincoln C	43	—
Fleming Terry	5 9	10 09	D	5 1 73	Marston Green	Trainee	Coventry C	13	—
							Northampton T	31	1
							Preston NE	32	2
							Lincoln C	22	—

Name	Ht	Wt	Pos	Birthdate	Birthplace	From	Club	Apps	Gls
Holmes Steve	6 2	13 00	D	13 1 71	Middlesbrough	Guisborough T	Preston NE	13	1
							Hartlepool U (loan)	5	2
							Lincoln C	23	2
Hulme Kevin‡	5 10	13 07	F	7 12 67	Farnworth	Radcliffe Borough	Bury	110	21
							Chester C (loan)	4	—
							Doncaster R	34	8
							Bury	29	—
							Lincoln C	5	—
Johnson Alan*	6 0	12 00	D	19 2 71	Ince	Trainee	Wigan Ath	180	13
							Lincoln C	63	—
							Preston NE (loan)	2	—
Johnson David*	6 2	13 08	F	29 10 70	Rother Valley	Trainee	Sheffield W	6	—
							Hartlepool U (loan)	7	2
							Hartlepool U (loan)	3	—
							Lincoln C	89	13
Leaning Andy*	6 0	13 00	G	18 5 63	York	Rowntree Mackintosh	York C	69	—
							Sheffield U	21	—
							Bristol C	75	—
							Lincoln C	36	—
Minett Jason	5 10	10 02	M	12 8 71	Peterborough	Trainee	Norwich C	3	—
							Exeter C (loan)	12	—
							Exeter C	76	3
							Lincoln C	42	5
Mudd Paul‡	5 9	11 04	D	13 11 70	Hull	Trainee	Hull C	1	—
							Scarborough	98	2
							Scunthorpe U	68	4
							Lincoln C	4	—
Onwere Udo*	6 0	11 03	M	9 11 71	Hammersmith	Trainee	Fulham	85	7
							Lincoln C	43	4
Platnauer Nicky‡	5 11	12 10	D	10 6 61	Leicester	Bedford T	Bristol R	24	7
							Coventry C	44	6
							Birmingham C	28	2
							Reading (loan)	7	—
							Cardiff C	115	6
							Notts Co	57	1
							Port Vale (loan)	14	—
							Leicester C	35	—
							Scunthorpe U	14	2
							Mansfield T	25	—
							Lincoln C	27	—
Richardson Barry	6 1	12 01	G	5 8 69	Wallsend	Trainee	Sunderland	—	—
							Scunthorpe U	—	—
							Scarborough	30	—
							Northampton T	96	—
							Preston NE	20	—
							Lincoln C	34	—
Robertson John	6 2	12 08	D	8 1 74	Liverpool	Trainee	Wigan Ath	112	4
							Lincoln C	22	—
Storey Brett†			M	7 7 77	Sheffield	Trainee	Sheffield U	—	—
							Lincoln C	2	1
Wanless Paul	6 1	13 04	M	14 12 73	Banbury	Trainee	Oxford U	32	—
							Lincoln C	8	—
							Cambridge U (loan)	14	1
Westley Shane	6 2	13 08	D	16 6 65	Canterbury	Apprentice	Charlton Ath	8	—
							Southend U	144	10
							Norwich C (loan)	—	—
							Wolverhampton W	50	2
							Brentford	64	1
							Southend U (loan)	5	—
							Cambridge U	3	—
							Lincoln C	9	1
Whitney Jonathan	5 10	12 03	D	23 12 70	Nantwich	Winsford	Huddersfield T	18	—
							Wigan Ath (loan)	12	—
							Lincoln C	26	2

Trainees
Bartlett, Darren S; Crossland, Mark D; Davie, Lee T; Davis, Matthew D; Dilnot, John C; Dixon, Andrew S; Farrell, Lee D; Gibson, Lee P; Gresham, Robert K; Hubbard, Christopher R; Huckerby, Scott I; McGill, Andrew J; O'Callaghan, Sean; Smith, Matthew P; Wareham, Scott J; Wilkins, Adam L.

Non-Contract
Storey, Brett B.

Associated Schoolboys
Addlesee, Jason D; Foster, Mark N.

Associated Schoolboys who have accepted the club's offer of a Traineeship/Contract
Lynn, Daniel J; Wilkins, Ian J.

LIVERPOOL

Name	Ht	Wt	Pos	Born	Birthplace	Source	Club	Apps	Gls
Babb Phil	6 0	12 03	D	30 11 70	Lambeth	Trainee	Millwall	—	—
							Bradford C	80	14
							Coventry C	77	3
							Liverpool	62	—
Barnes John	5 11	12 07	M	7 11 63	Jamaica	Sudbury Court	Watford	233	65
							Liverpool	279	80
Bjornebye Stig Inge	5 10	11 09	D	11 12 69	Norway	Rosenborg	Liverpool	53	—
Brazier Philip§			D	3 9 77	Liverpool	Trainee	Liverpool	—	—
Brunskill Iain*	5 10	12 05	D	5 11 76	Ormskirk	Trainee	Liverpool	—	—
Brydon Lee*	5 11	11 00	D	15 11 74	Stockton	Trainee	Liverpool	—	—
Carragher James			M	28 1 78	Bootle	Trainee	Liverpool	—	—
Cassidy Jamie	5 9	10 08	M	21 11 77	Liverpool	Trainee	Liverpool	—	—
Charnock Phil	5 11	11 02	M	14 2 75	Southport	Trainee	Liverpool	—	—
							Blackpool (loan)	4	—
Clegg David*	5 9	10 01	M	23 10 76	Liverpool	Trainee	Liverpool	—	—
Collymore Stan	6 3	14 10	F	22 1 71	Stone	Stafford R	Crystal Palace	20	1
							Southend U	30	15
							Nottingham F	65	41
							Liverpool	31	14
Culshaw Thomas	5 10	12 02	M	10 10 78	Liverpool	Trainee	Liverpool	—	—
Fowler Robbie	5 11	11 10	F	9 4 75	Liverpool	Trainee	Liverpool	108	65
Friars Sean§			M	15 5 79	Derry	Trainee	Liverpool	—	—
Harkness Steve	5 10	11 02	M	27 8 71	Carlisle	Trainee	Carlisle U	13	—
							Liverpool	64	2
							Huddersfield T (loan)	5	—
							Southend U (loan)	6	—
Harris Andrew*	5 10	11 11	D	26 2 77	Springs	Trainee	Liverpool	—	—
James David	6 5	14 02	G	1 8 70	Welwyn	Trainee	Watford	89	—
							Liverpool	123	—
Jones Lee	5 8	10 08	F	29 5 73	Wrexham	Trainee	Wrexham	39	10
							Liverpool	1	—
							Crewe Alex (loan)	8	1
							Wrexham (loan)	20	9
Jones Rob	5 8	11 00	D	5 11 71	Wrexham	Trainee	Crewe Alex	75	2
							Liverpool	160	—
Kennedy Mark	5 11	11 00	F	15 5 76	Dublin	Belvedere	Millwall	43	9
							Liverpool	10	—
Matteo Dominic	6 1	11 10	D	24 4 74	Dumfries	Trainee	Liverpool	23	—
							Sunderland (loan)	1	—
McAteer Jason	5 11	11 10	M	18 6 71	Birkenhead	Marine	Bolton W	114	8
							Liverpool	29	—
McManaman Steve	6 0	10 06	F	11 2 72	Liverpool	School	Liverpool	171	24
Neal Ashley	6 0	11 10	M	16 12 74	Liverpool	Trainee	Liverpool	—	—
Pears Steve*	6 0	13 07	G	22 1 62	Brandon	Apprentice	Manchester U	4	—
							Middlesbrough (loan)	12	—
							Middlesbrough	327	—
							Liverpool	—	—
Prior Lee§			D	30 10 77	Liverpool	Trainee	Liverpool	—	—
Quinn Mark§			M	7 10 77	Warrington	Trainee	Liverpool	—	—
Quinn Stuart§			M	11 12 77	Whiston	Trainee	Liverpool	—	—
Redknapp Jamie	6 0	12 10	M	25 6 73	Barton on Sea	Trainee	Bournemouth	13	—
							Liverpool	134	13
Roberts Gareth§			D	6 2 78	Wrexham	Trainee	Liverpool	—	—
Ruddock Neil	6 2	12 12	D	9 5 68	London	Apprentice	Millwall	—	—
							Tottenham H	9	—
							Millwall	2	1
							Southampton	107	9
							Tottenham H	38	3
							Liverpool	96	10
Rush Ian*	6 0	12 06	F	20 10 61	St Asaph	Apprentice	Chester C	1	—
							Chester	33	14
							Liverpool	224	139
							Juventus	29	7
							Liverpool	245	90
							Leeds U	—	—
Scales John	6 2	13 05	D	4 7 66	Harrogate		Leeds U	—	—
							Bristol R	72	2
							Wimbledon	240	11
							Liverpool	62	2

Name	Ht	Wt	Pos	Date	Birthplace	Source	Club	Apps	Gls
Stensgaard Michael	6 2	13 04	G	1 9 74	Denmark	Hvidovre	Liverpool	—	—
Thomas Michael	5 9	12 06	M	24 8 67	Lambeth	Apprentice	Arsenal	163	24
							Portsmouth (loan)	3	—
							Liverpool	82	5
Thompson David	5 7	10 00	M	12 9 77	Birkenhead	Trainee	Liverpool	—	—
Turkington Edmond§			M	15 5 78	Merseyside	Trainee	Liverpool	—	—
Warner Anthony	6 4	13 09	G	11 5 74	Liverpool	School	Liverpool	—	—
Whitehead Russell	5 8	10 04	D				Liverpool	—	—
Wright Mark	6 2	13 03	D	1 8 63	Dorchester	Amateur	Oxford U	10	—
							Southampton	170	7
							Derby Co	144	10
							Liverpool	119	5

Trainees
Brazier, Philip; Burghall, Terence R; Byrne, Niall P; Friars, Sean M; Hessey, Sean P; Johnson, Michael P; Jones, Jason A W; Larmour, David J; Moore, Michael A; Naylor, Roy; Parkinson, Andrew J; Prior, Lee J; Proctor, Paul; Quinn, Mark P; Quinn, Stuart; Rigoglioso, Adriano; Roberts, Gareth W; Turkington, Edmond B; Williams, Daniel I L.

Associated Schoolboys
Armstrong, Ian; Beesley, Mark A; Bishop, David S; Boardman, John S; Boggan, John R; Cass, Matthew; Cavanagh, Peter J; De Arostegui, Daniel; Evans, Gareth J; Gregson, Neil R; Hadland, Phillip J; Jones, Eifion P; Miles, John F; Mitchell, Craig; Navarro, Alan; Newby, Jon P R; Obrien, Christopher T; Olsen, James P; Owen, Michael J; Porter, Stephen; Roberts, John P; Torpey, Stephen R; Warnock, Stephen; Williams, Robert.

Associated Schoolboys who have accepted the club's offer of a Traineeship/Contract
Andrews, Lee; Dunbavin, Ian S; Gerrard, Steven G; Maxwell, Layton J; McGrath, Anthony; Murphy, Neil A; Wright, Stephen J; Yates, Michael A.

LUTON TOWN

Name	Ht	Wt	Pos	Date	Birthplace	Source	Club	Apps	Gls
Abbey Nathanael			G	11 7 78	Islington	Trainee	Luton T	—	—
Alexander Graham	5 10	12 02	M	10 10 71	Coventry	Trainee	Scunthorpe U	159	18
							Luton T	37	1
Chenery Ben	6 1	12 05	D	28 1 77	Ipswich	Trainee	Luton T	2	—
Davis Kelvin	6 0	14 00	G	29 9 76	Bedford	Trainee	Luton T	16	—
							Torquay U (loan)	2	—
Davis Steve	6 2	14 07	D	30 10 68	Hexham	Trainee	Southampton	7	—
							Burnley (loan)	9	—
							Notts Co (loan)	2	—
							Burnley	162	22
							Luton T	36	2
Douglas Stuart§	5 8	11 05	F	9 4 78	London	Trainee	Luton T	8	1
Evers Sean	5 9	9 11	M	10 10 77	Hitchin	Trainee	Luton T	1	—
Feuer Tony	6 6	15 06	G	20 5 71	Las Vegas	Los Angeles Salsa	West Ham U	—	—
							Peterborough U (loan)	16	—
							Luton T	38	—
Grant Kim	5 10	10 12	F	25 9 72	Ghana	Trainee	Charlton Ath	123	18
							Luton T	10	3
Greene David	6 2	13 05	D	26 10 73	Luton	Trainee	Luton T	19	—
							Colchester U (loan)	14	1
							Brentford (loan)	11	—
Guentchev Bontcho	5 10	11 07	F	7 7 64	Bulgaria	Sporting Lisbon	Ipswich T	61	6
							Luton T	35	9
Harvey Richard	5 10	11 12	D	17 4 69	Letchworth	Apprentice	Luton T	153	4
							Blackpool (loan)	5	—
Hughes Ceri	5 10	12 07	M	26 2 71	Pontypridd	Trainee	Luton T	139	13
James Julian	5 10	12 04	M	22 3 70	Tring	Trainee	Luton T	214	12
							Preston NE (loan)	6	—
Johnson Marvin	6 1	13 06	D	29 10 68	Wembley	Apprentice	Luton T	202	4
Jones Nathan‡			M	28 5 73	Rhondda	Merthyr T	Luton T	—	—
Kean Robert			M	3 6 78	Luton	Trainee	Luton T	—	—
Linton Des	6 1	13 10	D	5 9 71	Birmingham	Trainee	Leicester C	11	—
							Luton T	76	1
Marshall Dwight	5 7	11 02	F	3 10 65	Jamaica	Grays Ath	Plymouth Arg	99	27
							Middlesbrough (loan)	3	—
							Luton T	71	20
McLaren Paul	6 1	13 04	D	17 11 76	High Wycombe	Trainee	Luton T	13	1
Oakes Scott	5 11	11 11	F	5 8 72	Leicester	Trainee	Leicester C	3	—
							Luton T	173	27
Oldfield David	6 0	13 04	M	30 5 68	Perth, Australia	Apprentice	Luton T	29	4
							Manchester C	26	6
							Leicester C	188	26
							Millwall (loan)	17	6
							Luton T	34	2

Name	Ht	Wt	Pos	DOB	Birthplace	Source	Clubs	Apps	Gls
Patterson Darren	6 1	12 10	D	15 10 69	Belfast	Trainee	WBA	—	—
							Wigan Ath	97	6
							Crystal Palace	22	1
							Luton T	23	—
Peake Trevor	6 0	12 09	D	10 2 57	Nuneaton	Nuneaton	Lincoln C	171	7
							Coventry C	278	6
							Luton T	178	—
Power Danny*	5 10	12 00	D	24 11 76	Haverfordwest	Trainee	Luton T	—	—
Riseth Vidar	6 2	12 07	F	21 4 72	Levanger	Kongsvinger	Luton T	11	—
Simpson Gary	6 3	13 11	D	14 2 76	Ashford	Trainee	Luton T	—	—
							Fulham (loan)	7	—
Skelton Aaron	6 0	12 06	M	22 11 74	Welwyn	Trainee	Luton T	5	—
Taylor John	6 3	13 09	F	24 10 64	Norwich	Local	Colchester U	—	—
						Sudbury	Cambridge U	160	46
							Bristol R	95	44
							Bradford C	36	11
							Luton T	37	3
Thomas Mitchell	6 2	13 00	D	2 10 64	Luton	Apprentice	Luton T	107	1
							Tottenham H	157	6
							West Ham U	38	3
							Luton T	83	1
Thorpe Tony	5 9	12 04	F	10 4 74	Leicester	Leicester C	Luton T	51	8
Upson Matthew	6 1	11 05	D	18 4 79	Eye	Trainee	Luton T	—	—
Vilstrup Johnny	6 0	13 02	M	27 2 69	Copenhagen	Lyngby	Luton T	7	—
Waddock Gary	5 10	12 05	M	17 3 62	Alperton	Apprentice	QPR	203	8
						Charleroi	Millwall	58	2
							QPR	—	—
							Swindon T (loan)	6	—
							Bristol R	71	1
							Luton T	76	1
Willmott Chris			D	30 9 77	Bedford	Trainee	Luton T	—	—
Woodsford Jamie	5 10	12 00	F	9 11 76	Ipswich	Trainee	Luton T	10	—
Woolgar Matthew‡	5 10	11 10	M	5 1 76	Bedford	Trainee	Luton T	—	—

Trainees
Augustine, Steve K; Barr, Andrew R; Douglas, Stuart A; George, Liam B; Jones, Ian; Sharpe, Robert L; Smith, Andrew P; Sweeney, Terry N; Thomas, Jay D P; Turner, Samuel; Webb, Nicholas M.

Associated Schoolboys
Ayres, James M; Challinor, Jon; Curran, Shaun; Howe, Darren; Lewis, Graeme; Robert, Steven; Roberts, Ben; Tate, Daniel A.

Associated Schoolboys who have accepted the club's offer of a Traineeship/Contract
Boyce, Emerson; Cox, James; Doherty, Gary M; Lawes, Russell I; Spring, Matthew J.

MANCHESTER CITY

Name	Ht	Wt	Pos	DOB	Birthplace	Source	Clubs	Apps	Gls
Beagrie Peter	5 8	12 00	M	28 11 65	Middlesbrough	Local	Middlesbrough	33	2
							Sheffield U	84	11
							Stoke C	54	7
							Everton	114	11
							Sunderland (loan)	5	1
							Manchester C	51	3
Beech Chris	5 9	11 00	F	5 11 75	Congleton	Trainee	Manchester C	—	—
Bentley Jim	6 1	13 00	D	11 6 76	Liverpool	Trainee	Manchester C	—	—
Brennan Steve*	5 9	11 00	F	24 9 76	Bury	Trainee	Manchester C	—	—
Brightwell Ian	5 10	12 05	M	9 4 68	Lutterworth	Congleton T	Manchester C	263	16
Brown Michael	5 8	11 08	M	25 1 77	Hartlepool	Trainee	Manchester C	21	—
Callaghan Anthony			D	11 1 78	Manchester	Trainee	Manchester C	—	—
Clough Nigel	5 10	12 03	M	19 3 66	Sunderland	AC Hunters	Nottingham F	311	101
							Liverpool	39	7
							Manchester C	15	2
Creaney Gerry	5 11	13 06	F	13 4 70	Coatbridge	Celtic BC	Celtic	113	36
							Portsmouth	60	32
							Manchester C	15	3
							Oldham Ath (loan)	9	2
Crooks Lee	5 11	12 01	M	14 1 78	Wakefield	Trainee	Manchester C	—	—
Curle Keith	6 0	12 12	D	14 11 63	Bristol	Apprentice	Bristol R	32	4
							Torquay U	16	5
							Bristol C	121	1
							Reading	40	—
							Wimbledon	93	3
							Manchester C	171	11

Name	Ht	Wt	Pos	Born	Birthplace	Source	Club	Apps	Gls
Dibble Andy	6 2	16 02	G	8 5 65	Cwmbran	Apprentice	Cardiff C	62	—
							Luton T	30	—
							Sunderland (loan)	12	—
							Huddersfield T (loan)	5	—
							Manchester C	102	—
							Aberdeen (loan)	5	—
							Middlesbrough (loan)	19	—
							Bolton W (loan)	13	—
							WBA (loan)	9	—
							Oldham Ath (loan)	—	—
Edghill Richard	5 9	11 03	D	23 9 74	Oldham	Trainee	Manchester C	49	—
Evans Gareth*	5 8	10 08	M	8 3 77	Deeside	Trainee	Manchester C	—	—
Foster John	5 11	13 02	D	19 9 73	Manchester	Trainee	Manchester C	16	—
Freeman Nathan			G	5 8 77	Portsmouth	Trainee	Manchester C	—	—
Frontzeck Michael	5 11	12 12	D	26 3 64	Germany	Odenkirchen	Moenchengladbach	190	17
							Stuttgart	163	16
							Bochum	28	2
							Moenchengladbach	8	—
							Manchester C	12	—
Gardner David*	5 9	11 00	M	17 9 76	Salford	Manchester U	Manchester C	—	—
Gaudino Maurizio‡	5 11	12 02	M	12 12 66	Brule	Eintracht Frankfurt	Manchester C	20	3
Greenacre Chris	5 11	12 08	F	23 12 77	Wakefield	Trainee	Manchester C	—	—
Harkin Joe*	5 10	11 04	D	9 12 75	Derry	Trainee	Manchester C	—	—
Harris Sammy			D	2 4 78	Stockport	Trainee	Manchester C	—	—
Hiley Scott	5 9	11 05	M	27 9 68	Plymouth	Trainee	Exeter C	210	12
							Birmingham C	49	—
							Manchester C	6	—
Immel Eike	6 2	13 05	G	27 11 60	Marburg/Lahn	Stadtallendorf	Borussia Dortmund	247	—
							Stuttgart	287	—
							Manchester C	38	—
Ingram Rae	5 11	12 08	D	6 12 74	Manchester	Trainee	Manchester C	5	—
Kavelashvili Mikhail	5 11	12 01	M	22 7 71	Tbilisi	Spartak Vladikavkaz	Manchester C	4	1
Kelly Ray	5 11	12 00	F	29 12 76	Athlone	Athlone T	Manchester C	—	—
Kernaghan Alan	6 2	14 01	D	25 4 67	Otley	Apprentice	Middlesbrough	212	16
							Charlton Ath (loan)	13	—
							Manchester C	52	1
							Bolton W (loan)	11	—
							Bradford C (loan)	5	—
Kerr David	5 10	12 07	M	6 9 74	Dumfries	Trainee	Manchester C	6	—
							Mansfield T (loan)	5	—
Kielty Ged*	5 8	10 11	M	1 9 76	Manchester	Trainee	Manchester C	—	—
Kinkladze Georgiou	5 8	10 09	M	6 7 73	Tbilisi	Dynamo Tbilisi	Manchester C	37	4
Lake Paul‡	6 0	12 02	M	28 10 68	Manchester	Trainee	Manchester C	110	7
Lomas Steve	6 0	11 09	M	18 1 74	Hanover	Trainee	Manchester C	76	5
Margetson Martyn	6 0	14 00	G	8 9 71	West Neath	Trainee	Manchester C	6	—
							Bristol R (loan)	3	—
							Bolton W (loan)	—	—
							Luton T (loan)	—	—
Mazzarelli Guiseppe*			M	14 8 72	Switzerland		Manchester C	2	—
McGlinchey Brian			M	26 10 77	Derry	Trainee	Manchester C	—	—
Morley David			D	25 9 77	St Helens	Trainee	Manchester C	—	—
Nurse David*			G	12 10 76	Kings Lynn	Trainee	Manchester C	—	—
Phillips Martin	5 9	10 03	F	13 3 76	Exeter	Trainee	Exeter C	52	5
							Manchester C	11	—
Quinn Niall	6 4	15 10	F	6 10 66	Dublin		Arsenal	67	14
							Manchester C	203	66
Rosler Uwe	6 1	12 06	F	15 11 68	Attenburg	Chemie Leipzig	Magdeburg	62	22
							Dynamo Dresden	33	4
							Nuremberg	28	—
							Dynamo Dresden	7	—
							Manchester C	79	29
Rowlands Aled	5 8	10 13	M	9 6 78	Anglesey	Trainee	Manchester C	—	—
Sharpe John*	5 11	11 06	M	9 8 75	Birmingham	Trainee	Manchester C	—	—
							Exeter C (loan)	14	1
Smith Ian*	6 0	12 00	D	28 11 76	Bury	Trainee	Manchester C	—	—
Summerbee Nicky	5 11	12 08	F	26 8 71	Altrincham	Trainee	Swindon T	112	6
							Manchester C	78	2
Symons Kit	6 1	13 07	D	8 3 71	Basingstoke	Trainee	Portsmouth	161	10
							Manchester C	38	2
Tarpey Ged	6 0	13 00	D	28 4 77	Manchester	Trainee	Manchester C	—	—

Thomas Scott	5 9	11 02	M	30 10 74	Bury	Trainee	Manchester C	2	—
Whitley Jeffrey			M	14 4 75	Zambia	Trainee	Manchester C	—	—
Whitley Jim	5 9	11 00	M	14 4 75	Zambia	Trainee	Manchester C	—	—

Trainees
Bailey, Alan; Blore, Darren L; Brisco, Neil A; Gallagher, Benn S; Maddocks, Marc N; Mason, Gary; Morley, Neil T; Muir, Alexander I; Pridham, Christopher; Rimmer, Stephen A; Rishworth, Stephen P; Sailesman, Neil A; Wardley, Andrew; Wills, David J.

Associated Schoolboys
Carter, John G; Daly, Lee C; Duff, Greg J; Garfield, Darren; Hodgson, Steven G; Holmes, Sean; Hunter, Darren T; Laycock, David; McNab, Joe; McNab, Neil; Mike, Leon J; O'Keefe, Gerald J; Price, Kevin.

Associated Schoolboys who have accepted the club's offer of a Traineeship/Contract
Acton, Richard F; Burrows, Benjamin A; Docherty, George; Fenton, Anthony B; Fenton, Nicholas L.

MANCHESTER UNITED

Appleton Michael	5 9	11 13	M	4 12 75	Salford	Trainee	Manchester U	—	—
							Lincoln C (loan)	4	—
Baker Desmond*	5 7	11 00	F	25 8 77	Dublin	Trainee	Manchester U	—	—
Beckham David	6 0	11 02	M	2 5 75	Leytonstone	Trainee	Manchester U	37	7
							Preston NE (loan)	5	2
Brebner Grant	5 9	11 03	M	6 12 77	Edinburgh	Trainee	Manchester U	—	—
Brightwell Stuart	5 6	10 09	F	31 1 79	Easington	Trainee	Manchester U	—	—
Brown David	5 9	12 06	F	2 10 78	Bolton	Trainee	Manchester U	—	—
Bruce Steve	6 0	13 00	D	31 12 60	Newcastle	Apprentice	Gillingham	205	29
							Norwich C	141	14
							Manchester U	309	36
Butt Nicky	5 10	11 03	M	21 1 75	Manchester	Trainee	Manchester U	56	3
Cantona Eric	6 2	14 03	F	24 5 66	Paris		Auxerre	13	2
							Martigues	—	—
							Auxerre	68	21
							Marseille	22	5
							Bordeaux	11	6
							Montpellier	33	10
							Marseille	18	8
							Nimes	17	2
							Leeds U	28	9
							Manchester U	107	53
Casper Chris	6 0	11 11	D	28 4 75	Burnley	Trainee	Manchester U	—	—
							Bournemouth (loan)	16	1
Clegg Michael	5 8	11 08	D	3 7 77	Tameside	Trainee	Manchester U	—	—
Cole Andy	5 11	11 02	F	15 10 71	Nottingham	Trainee	Arsenal	1	—
							Fulham (loan)	13	3
							Bristol C (loan)	12	8
							Bristol C	29	12
							Newcastle U	70	55
							Manchester U	52	23
Cooke Terry	5 7	9 09	F	5 8 76	Marston Green	Trainee	Manchester U	4	—
							Sunderland (loan)	6	—
Coton Tony	6 2	13 07	G	19 5 61	Tamworth	Mile Oak	Birmingham C	94	—
							Hereford U (loan)	—	—
							Watford	233	—
							Manchester C	164	—
							Manchester U	—	—
Culkin Nick	6 2	12 13	G	6 7 78	York	York C	Manchester U	—	—
Curtis John	5 9	11 03	D	3 9 78	Nuneaton	Trainee	Manchester U	—	—
Davies Simon	6 0	11 11	M	23 4 74	Middlewich	Trainee	Manchester U	11	—
							Exeter C (loan)	6	1
Duncan Andrew§	5 11	13 04	D	20 10 77	Hexham		Manchester U	—	—
Gibson Paul	6 2	13 04	G	1 11 76	Sheffield	Trainee	Manchester U	—	—
Giggs Ryan	5 11	10 07	F	29 11 73	Cardiff	School	Manchester U	181	39
Hall Danny*	5 9	10 13	D	18 8 77	Bletchley	Trainee	Manchester U	—	—
Hilton David	5 11	10 10	D	10 11 77	Barnsley	Trainee	Manchester U	—	—
Irwin Denis	5 8	10 08	D	31 10 65	Cork	Apprentice	Leeds U	72	1
							Oldham Ath	167	4
							Manchester U	225	14
Keane Roy	5 10	12 10	M	10 8 71	Cork	Cobh Ramblers	Nottingham F	114	22
							Manchester U	91	13
Kirovski Jovan†			F	18 3 76	Escondido		Manchester U	—	—
Macken Jonathan§	5 10	12 10	F	7 9 77	Manchester		Manchester U	—	—
May David	6 0	12 10	D	24 6 70	Oldham	Trainee	Blackburn R	123	3
							Manchester U	35	3

Name	Ht	Wt	Pos	Born	Birthplace	Source	Club	Apps	Gls
McClair Brian	5 10	12 12	F	8 12 63	Airdrie	Apprentice	Aston Villa	—	—
							Motherwell	39	15
							Celtic	145	99
							Manchester U	323	88
McGibbon Patrick	6 1	13 02	D	6 9 73	Lurgan	Portadown	Manchester U	—	—
Mulryne Philip	5 8	10 04	F	1 1 78	Belfast	Trainee	Manchester U	—	—
Murdock Colin	6 3	12 13	D	2 7 75	Ballymena	Trainee	Manchester U	—	—
Mustoe Neil	5 8	12 00	F	5 11 76	Gloucester	Trainee	Manchester U	—	—
Neville Gary	5 10	11 11	D	18 2 75	Bury	Trainee	Manchester U	50	—
Neville Philip	5 10	11 10	D	21 1 77	Bury	Trainee	Manchester U	26	—
O'Kane John	5 10	12 02	D	15 11 74	Nottingham	Trainee	Manchester U	1	—
							Wimbledon (loan)	—	—
Pallister Gary	6 4	14 13	D	30 6 65	Ramsgate	Billingham	Middlesbrough	156	5
							Darlington (loan)	7	—
							Manchester U	257	9
Parker Paul*	5 7	11 07	D	4 4 64	West Ham	Apprentice	Fulham	153	2
							QPR	125	1
							Manchester U	105	1
Pilkington Kevin	6 0	13 00	G	8 3 74	Hitchin	Trainee	Manchester U	4	—
							Rochdale (loan)	6	—
Prunier William‡	6 0	12 08	D	14 8 67	Montreuil		Auxerre	221	20
							Marseille	35	4
							Bordeaux	20	—
							Manchester U	2	—
Schmeichel Peter	6 4	15 13	G	18 11 63	Gladsaxe		Hvidovre	88	6
							Brondby	119	2
							Manchester U	190	—
Scholes Paul	5 7	11 00	F	16 11 74	Salford	Trainee	Manchester U	43	15
Sharpe Lee	6 0	12 06	F	27 5 71	Halesowen	Trainee	Torquay U	14	3
							Manchester U	193	21
Smith Tommy	5 9	10 10	M	25 11 77	Northampton	Trainee	Manchester U	—	—
Teather Paul	5 11	11 02	M	26 12 77	Rotherham	Trainee	Manchester U	—	—
Thornley Ben	5 9	11 12	F	21 4 75	Bury	Trainee	Manchester U	2	—
							Stockport Co (loan)	10	1
							Huddersfield T (loan)	12	2
Tomlinson Graeme	5 9	11 05	F	10 12 75	Watford	Trainee	Bradford C	17	6
							Manchester U	—	—
							Luton T (loan)	7	—
Trees Robert§	5 10	11 05	M	18 12 77	Manchester		Manchester U	—	—
Twiss Michael§	5 10	12 10	F	26 12 77	Salford		Manchester U	—	—
Wallwork Ronnie	5 9	12 09	D	10 9 77	Manchester	Trainee	Manchester U	—	—
Whittam Philip*	5 8	9 08	D	12 8 76	Bolton	Trainee	Manchester U	—	—
Wilson Mark	5 11	12 01	F	9 2 79	Scunthorpe	Trainee	Manchester U	—	—

Trainees
Bickerton, Gary; Byers, Alexander J; Calderone, Christopher J; Duncan, Andrew; Ford, Ryan; Higginbotham, Daniel J; Macken, Jonathan P; Maxon, Heath R; Millard, Ross J; Naylor, Gavin E; Notman, Alexander M; Phillips, Jonathan J; Trees, Robert V; Twiss, Michael J; Wood, Jamie.

Associated Schoolboys
Chadwick, Luke H; Clegg, George G; Dickman, Jonjo; Dodd, Ashley M; Evans, Wayne A; Fitzpatrick, Ian M; Gaff, Gerard A; Gardiner, Gareth; Hickson, Jason M; Jolley, Craig S; Macklin, Gareth; Newham, Stephen J C; O'Kane, Barry; Parkinson, Simon A; Roche, Lee P; Rose, Stephen D; Strange, Gareth A; Studley, Dominic P; Webber, Daniel V; Wheatcroft, Paul M.

Associated Schoolboys who have accepted the club's offer of a Traineeship/Contract
Brown, Wesley M; Healy, David J; Mills, Leon J; Ryan, Michael S P; Wellens, Richard P.

MANSFIELD TOWN

Name	Ht	Wt	Pos	Born	Birthplace	Source	Club	Apps	Gls
Alexander Keith†	6 4	14 08	F	14 11 58	Nottingham	Barnet	Grimsby T	83	26
							Stockport Co	11	—
							Lincoln C	45	4
							Mansfield T	3	—
Boothroyd Aidy*	5 9	11 07	D	8 2 71	Bradford	Trainee	Huddersfield T	10	—
							Bristol R	16	—
							Hearts	4	—
							Mansfield T	102	3
Bowling Ian	6 4	14 04	G	27 7 65	Sheffield	Gainsborough T	Lincoln C	59	—
							Hartlepool U (loan)	1	—
							Bradford C (loan)	7	—
							Bradford C	29	—
							Mansfield T	44	—
Clarke Darrell§	5 10	12 00	D	16 12 77	Mansfield	Trainee	Mansfield T	3	—
Clifford Mark§			D	11 9 77	Nottingham	Trainee	Mansfield T	1	—
Doolan John	6 0	13 00	D	7 5 74	Liverpool	Trainee	Everton	—	—
							Mansfield T	66	3

Name							Club	Apps	Gls
Eustace Scott	6 1	14 02	D	13 6 75	Leicester	Trainee	Leicester C	1	—
							Mansfield T	27	1
Hackett Warren	6 0	12 05	D	16 12 71	Newham	Tottenham H	Leyton Orient	72	3
							Doncaster R	46	2
							Mansfield T	32	3
Hadley Stewart	6 1	13 03	F	30 12 73	Dudley	Halesowen	Derby Co	—	—
							Mansfield T	86	27
Handford Paul*			D	24 3 77	Chesterfield	Trainee	Mansfield T	—	—
Harper Steve	5 10	11 12	F	3 2 69	Stoke	Trainee	Port Vale	28	2
							Preston NE	77	10
							Burnley	69	8
							Doncaster R	65	11
							Mansfield T	29	5
Ireland Simon	5 10	10 10	M	23 11 71	Barnstaple	School	Huddersfield T	19	—
							Wrexham (loan)	5	—
							Blackburn R	1	—
							Mansfield T (loan)	9	1
							Mansfield T	79	10
Kilcline Brian	6 2	12 10	D	7 5 62	Nottingham	Apprentice	Notts Co	158	9
							Coventry C	173	28
							Oldham Ath	8	—
							Newcastle U	32	—
							Swindon T	17	—
							Mansfield T	19	—
Lampkin Kevin*	6 0	12 02	M	20 12 72	Liverpool	Trainee	Liverpool	—	—
							Huddersfield T	13	—
							Mansfield T	42	3
Onuora Iffy	6 1	13 10	F	28 7 67	Glasgow	British Univ	Huddersfield T	165	30
							Mansfield T	28	8
Parkin Steve	5 6	11 01	M	7 11 65	Mansfield	Apprentice	Stoke C	113	5
							WBA	48	2
							Mansfield T	87	3
Peters Mark	6 1	13 00	D	6 7 72	St Asaph	Trainee	Manchester C	—	—
							Norwich C	—	—
							Peterborough U	19	—
							Mansfield T	47	6
Robinson Ian§	5 10	11 10	M	25 8 78	Nottingham	Trainee	Mansfield T	9	1
Sale Mark	6 5	14 04	F	27 2 72	Burton-on-Trent	Trainee	Stoke C	2	—
							Cambridge U	—	—
							Birmingham C	21	—
							Torquay U	44	8
							Preston NE	13	7
							Mansfield T	27	7
Sherlock Paul	5 11	11 05	D	17 11 73	Wigan	Trainee	Notts Co	12	1
							Mansfield T	20	2
Slawson Steve‡	6 0	12 11	F	13 11 72	Nottingham	Trainee	Notts Co	38	4
							Burnley (loan)	5	2
							Shrewsbury T (loan)	6	—
							Mansfield T	29	5
Stark Wayne‡			M	14 10 76	Derby	Trainee	Mansfield T	1	—
Timons Chris*	6 1	12 07	D	8 12 74	Longworth	Clipstone Welfare	Mansfield T	39	2
Todd Mark‡	5 9	10 04	M	4 12 67	Belfast	Trainee	Manchester U	—	—
							Sheffield U	70	5
							Wolverhampton W (loan)	7	—
							Rotherham U	64	7
							Scarborough	23	1
							Mansfield T	12	—
Trinder Jason‡	5 11	14 03	G	3 3 70	Leicester	Grimsby T	Mansfield T	8	—
Weaver Nicky§	6 4	14 00	G	2 3 79	Sheffield	Trainee	Mansfield T	1	—
Williams Ryan§	5 3	9 10	F	31 8 78	Sutton	Trainee	Mansfield T	10	3
Wood Simon	5 9	11 08	M	24 9 76	Hull	Trainee	Coventry C	—	—
							Mansfield T	10	1

Trainees
Clarke, Darrell J; Clifford, Mark R; Cooper, Dale J; Dunkley, Marlon J; Holbrook, Leigh W; Hopley, Dean C; Ingram, Aaron D; Jenkinson, Matthew; Morris, David; Roberts, Duncan A; Robinson, Ian B; Sisson, Michael A; Spink, Neil D; Weaver, Nicholas J; Williams, Ryan N.

Non-Contract
Alexander, Keith.

Associated Schoolboys
Footitt, Nicholas A; Jervis, David J; Smith, Mark J; Wiggington, Mark.

Associated Schoolboys who have accepted the club's offer of a Traineeship/Contract
Hutchinson, James A; Leech, James; Rankin, Darrel A; Sedlan, Jason M.

MIDDLESBROUGH

Name			Pos	DOB	Birthplace	Signed from	Clubs	Apps	Gls
Anderson Viv	6 1	13 00	D	29 8 56	Nottingham	Apprentice	Nottingham F	328	15
							Arsenal	120	9
							Manchester U	54	2
							Sheffield W	70	8
							Barnsley	20	3
							Middlesbrough	2	—
Bagayoko Salif	6 0	12 00	F	9 5 77	Manosque	Trainee	Middlesbrough	—	—
Barmby Nick	5 7	11 04	F	11 2 74	Hull	Trainee	Tottenham H	87	20
							Middlesbrough	32	7
Barron Michael	5 11	11 09	D	22 12 74	Chester le Street	Trainee	Middlesbrough	3	—
Blackmore Clayton	5 8	11 12	M	23 9 64	Neath	Apprentice	Manchester U	186	19
							Middlesbrough	35	2
Branco			D	4 4 64	Bage	Internacional	Middlesbrough	7	—
Byrne Wesley*	5 9	11 03	D	9 2 77	Dublin	Trainee	Middlesbrough	—	—
Campbell Andrew§			F	18 4 79	Stockton	Trainee	Middlesbrough	2	—
Cox Neil	6 0	13 02	D	8 10 71	Scunthorpe	Trainee	Scunthorpe U	17	1
							Aston Villa	42	3
							Middlesbrough	75	3
Cummins Michael			M	1 6 78	Dublin	Trainee	Middlesbrough	—	—
Fjortoft Jan-Aage	6 3	13 04	F	10 1 67	Aalesund		Hamar	22	10
							Lillestrom	35	20
							Rapid Vienna	128	62
							Swindon T	72	28
							Middlesbrough	36	9
Fleming Curtis	5 10	12 09	D	8 10 68	Manchester	St Patrick's Ath	Middlesbrough	126	1
Freestone Chris			F	4 9 71	Nottingham	Arnold T	Middlesbrough	4	1
Hendrie John	5 8	12 05	F	24 10 63	Lennoxtown	Apprentice	Coventry C	21	2
							Hereford U (loan)	6	—
							Bradford C	173	46
							Newcastle U	34	4
							Leeds U	27	5
							Middlesbrough	192	44
Hignett Craig	5 9	11 10	M	12 1 70	Whiston	Liverpool	Crewe Alex	121	42
							Middlesbrough	98	22
Juninho	5 5	9 10	F	22 2 73	Sao Paulo	Sao Paulo	Middlesbrough	21	2
Kavanagh Graham	5 10	12 08	M	2 12 73	Dublin	Home Farm	Middlesbrough	35	3
							Darlington (loan)	5	—
Lee Paddy			M	2 8 77	Dublin	Manchester U	Middlesbrough	—	—
Liddle Craig	5 11	12 03	M	21 10 71	Chester le Street	Blyth Spartans	Middlesbrough	14	—
McGargle Stephen	5 9	11 00	F	24 10 75	Gateshead	Trainee	Middlesbrough	—	—
Miller Alan	6 3	14 08	G	29 3 70	Epping	Trainee	Arsenal	8	—
							Plymouth Arg (loan)	13	—
							WBA (loan)	3	—
							Birmingham C (loan)	15	—
							Middlesbrough	47	—
Moore Alan	5 9	10 08	F	25 11 74	Dublin	Rivermount	Middlesbrough	93	14
Moreno Jaime	5 9	11 09	F	19 1 74	Bolivia	Blooming	Middlesbrough	21	1
Morris Chris	5 11	11 11	D	24 12 63	Newquay		Sheffield W	74	1
							Celtic	163	8
							Middlesbrough	78	3
Mustoe Robbie	5 10	11 10	M	28 8 68	Oxford		Oxford U	91	10
							Middlesbrough	180	13
O'Halloran Keith	5 9	11 06	D	10 11 75	Ireland	Cherry Orchard	Middlesbrough	4	—
							Scunthorpe U (loan)	7	—
Ormerod Anthony			M	31 3 79	Middlesbrough	Trainee	Middlesbrough	—	—
Pearson Nigel	6 1	14 03	D	21 8 63	Nottingham	Heanor T	Shrewsbury T	153	5
							Sheffield W	180	14
							Middlesbrough	69	3
Pollock Jamie	5 10	14 01	M	16 2 74	Stockton	Trainee	Middlesbrough	155	17
Richardson Paul	6 0	13 00	F	22 7 77	Durham	Trainee	Middlesbrough	—	—
Roberts Ben	6 1	12 11	G	22 6 75	Bishop Auckland	Trainee	Middlesbrough	—	—
							Hartlepool U (loan)	4	—
							Wycombe W (loan)	15	—
Robson Bryan	5 9	12 05	M	11 1 57	Witton Gilbert	Apprentice	WBA	197	39
							Manchester U	345	74
							Middlesbrough	24	1
Skingsley Ross*	5 11	12 00	M	10 1 77	Woolwich	Trainee	Middlesbrough	—	—
Stamp Philip	5 10	12 05	M	12 12 75	Middlesbrough	Trainee	Middlesbrough	25	2

Name							Club	Apps	Gls
Summerbell Mark	5 10	11 09	M	30 10 76	Durham	Trainee	Middlesbrough	1	—
Swalwell Andrew			M	29 3 79	Middlesbrough	Trainee	Middlesbrough	—	—
Vickers Steve	6 1	12 12	D	13 10 67	Bishop Auckland	Spennymoor U	Tranmere R	311	11
							Middlesbrough	102	7
Walsh Gary	6 3	14 13	G	21 3 68	Wigan	Apprentice	Manchester U	50	—
							Airdrie (loan)	3	—
							Oldham Ath (loan)	6	—
							Middlesbrough	32	—
Ward Richard*	5 11	13 00	M	6 1 77	Middlesbrough	Trainee	Middlesbrough	—	—
Whelan Phil	6 4	14 01	D	7 8 72	Stockport		Ipswich T	82	2
							Middlesbrough	13	1
White Alan			D	22 3 76	Darlington		Middlesbrough	—	—
White Darren			M	13 1 79	Easington	Trainee	Middlesbrough	—	—
Whyte Derek	5 11	12 11	D	31 8 68	Glasgow	Celtic BC	Celtic	216	7
							Middlesbrough	138	2
Wilkinson Paul	6 1	12 04	F	30 10 64	Louth	Apprentice	Grimsby T	71	27
							Everton	31	7
							Nottingham F	34	5
							Watford	134	52
							Middlesbrough	166	49
							Oldham Ath (loan)	4	1
							Watford (loan)	4	—
							Luton T (loan)	3	—

Trainees
Baker, David A; Baker, Steven R; Brumpton, David M; Campbell, Andrew P; Carter, Graeme J; Cole, Benjamin L; Connor, Paul; Cosgrove, Antony; Harrison, Craig; Harrison, Paul; Howarth, Andrew J; Mowbray, Darren K; Naisbitt, Daniel J; Patterson, Mark; Payne, Lee J; Riggall, Paul J; Trevor, Kris A.

Associated Schoolboys
Allon, Wayne; Boase, Leon A; Booth, Gregory; Greenwood, David; Hudson, Mark; McStea, Anthony C; Rice, Dominic A; Rogers, Nicholas G; Taylor, Andrew; Todd, Michael W.

Associated Schoolboys who have accepted the club's offer of a Traineeship/Contract
Dunn, Thomas; Jones, Thomas A M; Kell, Richard; Middleton, James R; Reeve, Christopher J; Stockdale, Robert; Terrell, Paul A; Walklate, Steven.

MILLWALL

Name							Club	Apps	Gls
Aris Steven			D	27 4 78	London		Millwall	—	—
Bennett Mickey*	5 10	11 11	M	22 7 69	Camberwell	Apprentice	Charlton Ath	35	2
							Wimbledon	18	2
							Brentford	46	4
							Charlton Ath	24	1
							Millwall	2	—
Berry Greg	6 1	12 00	F	5 3 71	Essex	East Thurrock	Leyton Orient	80	14
							Wimbledon	7	1
							Millwall	20	1
							Brighton & HA (loan)	6	2
							Leyton Orient (loan)	7	—
Bowry Bobby	5 10	10 08	M	19 5 71	Croydon		Crystal Palace	50	1
							Millwall	38	2
Cadette Richard	5 7	12 00	F	21 3 65	Hammersmith	Wembley	Orient	21	4
							Southend U	90	48
							Sheffield U	28	7
							Brentford	87	20
							Bournemouth (loan)	8	1
							Falkirk	92	32
							Millwall	17	4
Canoville Dean			M	30 11 78	Perivale	Trainee	Millwall	—	—
Carter Tim	6 2	13 11	G	5 10 67	Bristol	Apprentice	Bristol R	47	—
							Newport Co (loan)	1	—
							Carlisle U (loan)	4	—
							Sunderland	37	—
							Bristol C (loan)	3	—
							Birmingham C (loan)	2	—
							Hartlepool U	18	—
							Millwall	4	—
							Oxford U	12	—
							Millwall	4	—
Connor James	6 0	13 00	M	22 8 74	Middlesbrough	Trainee	Millwall	9	—
Dawes Ian‡	5 7	11 10	D	22 2 63	Croydon	Apprentice	QPR	229	3
							Millwall	225	5
Dolby Tony	5 11	12 08	F	16 4 74	Greenwich	Trainee	Millwall	45	1
							Barnet (loan)	16	2

Name	Ht	Wt	Pos	Born	Birthplace	Source	Club	Apps	Gls
Doyle Maurice	5 8	10 07	F	17 10 69	Ellesmere Port	Trainee	Crewe Alex	8	2
							QPR	6	—
							Crewe Alex (loan)	7	2
							Wolverhampton W (loan)	—	—
							Millwall	18	—
Edwards Alistair‡	6 1	12 06	F	21 6 68	Wyalla	Sydney Olympic	Brighton & HA	1	—
						Selangor	Millwall	4	—
Forbes Steve	6 2	12 06	M	24 12 75	London	Sittingbourne	Millwall	5	—
Fuchs Uwe	6 2	12 00	F	23 7 66	Germany	Pirmasens	Homburg	60	9
							Stuttgart Kickers	10	2
							Fortuna Cologne	67	36
							Fortuna Dusseldorf	25	7
							Cologne	19	4
							Kaiserslautern	19	3
							Middlesbrough	15	9
							Millwall	32	5
Harle Mike	6 0	12 06	D	31 10 72	Lewisham	Sittingbourne	Millwall	—	—
							Bury (loan)	1	—
Haworth Robert‡	6 2	13 04	F	21 11 75	Edgware	Trainee	Fulham	21	1
							Millwall	—	—
Iga Andrew			G	9 12 77	Kampala	Trainee	Millwall	—	—
Keller Kasey	6 1	12 07	G	27 1 69	Washington	Portland Univ	Millwall	176	—
Keown Darren			F	28 2 78	Chertsey	Trainee	Millwall	—	—
Kulkov Vasili‡			M	11 6 66	Moscow	Porto	Millwall	6	—
Lavin Gerard	5 10	11 00	M	5 2 74	Corby	Trainee	Watford	126	3
							Millwall	20	—
Malkin Chris	6 3	12 07	F	4 6 67	Bebington	Overpool	Tranmere R	232	60
							Millwall	43	11
Markey Brendan			F	19 5 76	Ireland	Bohemians	Millwall	—	—
McCarthy Mick‡	6 2	13 12	D	7 2 59	Barnsley	Apprentice	Barnsley	272	7
							Manchester C	140	2
							Celtic	48	—
						Lyon	Millwall	35	2
McRobert Lee	5 9	10 12	M	4 10 72	Bromley	Sittingbourne	Millwall	14	1
Neill Lucas	6 1	12 00	M	9 3 78	Australia		Millwall	13	—
Newman Ricky	5 10	12 06	M	5 8 70	Guildford	Trainee	Crystal Palace	48	3
							Maidstone U (loan)	10	1
							Millwall	36	1
Nielsen Jimmi‡	6 3	12 11	G	6 8 77	Aalborg	Aalborg	Millwall	—	—
Nightingale Lewis			M	25 3 79	Greenwich	Trainee	Millwall	—	—
O'Neil Phil*	5 10	12 00	M	22 10 77	Sidcup	Trainee	Millwall	—	—
Rae Alex	5 9	11 11	M	30 9 69	Glasgow	Bishopbriggs	Falkirk	83	20
							Millwall	218	63
Roche Stephen			M	2 10 78	Dublin	Belvedere	Millwall	—	—
Rogan Anton	6 1	13 00	D	25 3 66	Belfast	Distillery	Celtic	127	4
							Sunderland	46	1
							Oxford U	58	3
							Millwall	8	—
Savage Dave	6 2	12 07	M	30 7 73	Dublin	Longford T	Millwall	64	2
Stevens Keith	6 0	12 12	D	21 6 64	Merton	Apprentice	Millwall	449	9
Thatcher Ben	5 11	12 07	D	30 11 75	Swindon	Trainee	Millwall	90	1
Van Blerk Jason	6 1	13 00	M	16 3 68	Sydney	Go Ahead	Millwall	69	2
Webber Damien	6 4	14 00	D	8 10 68	Rustington	Bognor Regis T	Millwall	38	2
Weir Micky	5 4	10 03	M	16 1 66	Edinburgh	Portobello T	Hibernian	48	5
							Luton T	8	—
							Hibernian	150	24
							Millwall (loan)	8	—
Wietecha Dave*	6 3	15 00	G	1 11 74	Colchester		Millwall	—	—
							Crewe Alex (loan)	—	—
							Rotherham U (loan)	—	—
Witter Tony	6 2	13 02	D	12 8 65	London	Grays Ath	Crystal Palace	—	—
							QPR	1	—
							Millwall (loan)	—	—
							Plymouth Arg (loan)	3	1
							Reading (loan)	4	—
							Millwall	58	2
Yuran Sergei*			F	11 6 69	Kiev	Porto	Millwall	13	1

Trainees
Bircham, Marc S J; Dillon, Warren D; Hirst, Matthew; Hockton, Danny J; Johnson, Steven L; Kelly, Steven; Poulter, Simon; Stevens, Shaun D; Thompson, Samuel J; Venables, Ross; White, Darren J.

Non-Contract
Nicholl, James M.

Associated Schoolboys
Barnard, Richard M; Bubb, Byron J; Canoville, Lee; Davies, Laurence T; Davies, Robert M; Davis, Duane; Dodds, Jammes; Edwards, Daniel; Edwards, Owain L; Harrison, Chris; Highton, Robert; Holsgrove, Lee; Leach, Nicholas; Little, Joseph G; McCord, Glenn M; O'Dunsi, Leke; Pittwood, Adam; Powell, Terry M; Reid, Steven J; Squires, Oliver H; Starbrook, Ian S; Williams, Leon K.

Associated Schoolboys who have accepted the club's offer of a Traineeship/Contract
Field, Lewis M; Jenkins, Stuart; Smith, Anthony P.

NEWCASTLE UNITED

Name	Ht	Wt	Pos	Born	Birthplace	Source	Clubs	Apps	Gls
Albert Philippe	6 3	13 00	D	10 8 67	Bouillon		Charleroi	65	7
							Mechelen	87	5
							Anderlecht	50	9
							Newcastle U	40	6
Allen Malcolm	5 8	11 08	F	21 3 67	Dioniolen	Apprentice	Watford	39	5
							Aston Villa (loan)	4	—
							Norwich C	35	8
							Millwall	81	24
							Newcastle U	10	5
Arnison Paul	5 9	10 12	M	18 9 77	Hartlepool	Trainee	Newcastle U	—	—
Asprilla Faustino	5 9	11 03	F	10 11 69	Tulua	Nacional	Parma	84	25
							Newcastle U	14	3
Barton Warren	5 11	12 00	D	19 3 69	Stoke Newington	Leytonstone/Ilford	Maidstone U	42	—
							Wimbledon	180	10
							Newcastle U	31	—
Batty David	5 8	12 00	M	2 12 68	Leeds	Trainee	Leeds U	211	4
							Blackburn R	54	1
							Newcastle U	11	1
Beardsley Peter	5 8	11 07	F	18 1 61	Newcastle	Wallsend BC	Carlisle U	104	22
						Vancouver Whitecaps	Manchester U	—	—
						Vancouver Whitecaps	Newcastle U	147	61
							Liverpool	131	46
							Everton	81	25
							Newcastle U	104	41
Beresford John	5 5	10 12	M	4 9 66	Sheffield	Apprentice	Manchester C	—	—
							Barnsley	88	5
							Portsmouth	107	8
							Newcastle U	142	1
Brayson Paul	5 4	10 10	F	16 9 77	Newcastle	Trainee	Newcastle U	—	—
Clark Lee	5 7	11 07	M	27 10 72	Wallsend	Trainee	Newcastle U	170	21
Crawford Jimmy	5 11	11 06	M	1 5 73	USA	Bohemians	Newcastle U	—	—
Eatock David	5 4	10 05	F	11 11 76	Blackrod	Chorley	Newcastle U	—	—
Elliott Robbie	5 10	10 13	D	25 12 73	Newcastle	Trainee	Newcastle U	50	2
Elliott Stuart	5 8	11 05	D	27 8 77	London	Trainee	Newcastle U	—	—
Ferdinand Les	5 11	13 05	F	18 12 66	Acton	Hayes	QPR	163	80
							Brentford (loan)	3	—
							Besiktas (loan)	—	—
							Newcastle U	37	25
Gillespie Keith	5 9	11 05	F	18 2 75	Lame	Trainee	Manchester U	9	1
							Wigan Ath (loan)	8	4
							Newcastle U	45	6
Ginola David	6 0	11 10	F	25 1 67	Gassin		Toulon	81	4
							Racing Paris	61	8
							Brest	50	10
							Paris St Germain	115	32
							Newcastle U	34	5
Harper Steve	6 0	12 03	G	3 2 70	Easington	Seaham Red Star	Newcastle U	—	—
							Bradford C (loan)	1	—
Hislop Shaka	6 3	14 04	G	22 2 69	London	Howard Un	Reading	104	—
							Newcastle U	24	—
Holland Chris	5 9	11 05	M	11 9 75	Whalley	Trainee	Preston NE	1	—
							Newcastle U	3	—
Hooper Mike*	6 3	13 05	G	10 2 64	Bristol	Mangotsfield	Bristol C	1	—
							Wrexham (loan)	20	—
							Wrexham	14	—
							Liverpool	51	—
							Leicester C (loan)	14	—
							Newcastle U	25	—
							Sunderland (loan)	—	—
Howey Steve	6 1	11 12	M	26 10 71	Sunderland	Trainee	Newcastle U	146	5
Huckerby Darren	5 10	11 11	M	23 4 76	Nottingham	Trainee	Lincoln C	28	5
							Newcastle U	1	—

Keen Peter	6 0	11 09	G	16 11 76	Middlesbrough	Trainee	Newcastle U	—	—
Kitson Paul	5 10	10 12	F	9 1 71	Murton	Trainee	Leicester C	50	6
							Derby Co	105	36
							Newcastle U	33	10
Lee Robert	5 10	11 13	F	1 2 66	West Ham	Hornchurch	Charlton Ath	298	59
							Newcastle U	148	34
Peacock Darren	6 2	12 12	D	3 2 68	Bristol	Apprentice	Newport Co	28	—
							Hereford U	59	4
							QPR	126	6
							Newcastle U	78	1
Srnicek Pavel	6 2	14 07	G	10 3 68	Ostrava	Banik Ostrava	Newcastle U	126	—
Thornton Mark‡			D	17 11 76	Newcastle	Trainee	Newcastle U	—	—
Watson Steve	6 1	12 07	D	1 4 74	North Shields	Trainee	Newcastle U	136	10

Trainees
Asiamah, Anthony; Barrett, Paul D; Beharall, David; Burt, David C; Garrity, James K; Gibson, Barry J; Main, Paul; McClen, James D; Milbourne, Ian; Paris, Stephen; Shutt, Matthew J; Talbot, Paul M; Winskill, Neil.

Associated Schoolboys
Anderson, Ross; Burt, Jamie P; Collins, Shaun T; Cowan, David R; D'Amore, David R; Donnelly, Paul A; Fisher, Darren T; Gallant, Paul K; Green, Stuart; Hogg, Graham; Parry, Anthony; Porter, Karl; Pringle, Andrew S; Tremble, David G; Warwick, Stephen J.

Associated Schoolboys who have accepted the club's offer of a Traineeship/Contract
Broadbent, David; Hughes, Aaron W; Muir, Karl J; Peterson, Owen; Tait, Jordan A; Woodcock, Chris.

NORTHAMPTON TOWN

Atkins Ian‖	5 11	12 06	M	16 1 57	Birmingham	Apprentice	Shrewsbury T	278	58
							Sunderland	77	6
							Everton	7	1
							Ipswich T	77	4
							Birmingham C	93	6
							Colchester U	—	—
							Birmingham C	8	—
							Cambridge U	2	—
							Sunderland	—	—
							Doncaster R	7	—
							Northampton T	—	—
Beckford Jason*	5 9	14 03	F	14 2 70	Manchester	Trainee	Manchester C	20	1
							Blackburn R (loan)	4	—
							Port Vale (loan)	5	1
							Birmingham C	7	2
							Bury (loan)	3	—
							Stoke C	4	—
							Millwall	9	—
							Northampton T	1	—
Burns Chris	6 1	14 01	M	9 11 67	Manchester	Cheltenham T	Portsmouth	90	9
							Swansea C (loan)	4	—
							Bournemouth (loan)	14	1
							Swansea C	5	—
							Northampton T	60	9
Cahill Ollie	5 10	11 01	F	29 9 75	Clonmel	Clonmel	Northampton T	11	1
Colkin Lee	5 11	12 04	D	15 7 74	Nuneaton	Trainee	Northampton T	93	3
Gibb Ali	5 9	11 07	M	17 2 76	Salisbury	Trainee	Norwich C	—	—
							Northampton T	23	2
Grayson Neil	5 10	12 09	F	1 11 64	York	Rowntree Mackintosh	Doncaster R	29	6
							York C	1	—
							Chesterfield	15	—
						Boston U	Northampton T	80	19
Harmon Darren‡	5 5	9 12	M	30 1 73	Northampton	Trainee	Notts Co	—	—
							Shrewsbury T	6	2
							Northampton T	89	12
							Cambridge U (loan)	—	—
Harrison Gary‡	5 9	11 05	F	12 3 75	Northampton	Aston Villa	Northampton T	7	—
Hunter Roy	5 10	12 08	M	29 10 73	Cleveland	Trainee	WBA	9	1
							Northampton T	34	—
Lee Christian	6 1	11 07	F	8 10 76	Aylesbury	Doncaster R	Northampton T	5	—
Maddison Lee	5 11	12 04	D	5 10 72	Bristol	Trainee	Bristol R	73	—
							Northampton T	21	—
Matthews Martin‡	5 10	11 03	D	22 12 75	Peterborough	Trainee	Derby Co	—	—
							Northampton T	—	—

Name			Pos	DOB	Birthplace	Source	Club	Apps	Gls
Mehew David‡	5 10	12 06	M	29 10 67	Camberley	Trainee	Leeds U	—	—
							Bristol R	222	63
							Exeter C (loan)	7	—
							Walsall	13	—
							Northampton T	—	—
Norton David*	5 8	11 12	M	3 3 65	Cannock	Apprentice	Aston Villa	44	2
							Notts Co	27	1
							Rochdale (loan)	9	—
							Hull C (loan)	15	—
							Hull C	134	5
							Northampton T	82	—
O'Shea Danny	6 0	13 02	D	26 3 63	Kennington	Apprentice	Arsenal	6	—
							Charlton Ath (loan)	9	—
							Exeter C	45	2
							Southend U	118	12
							Cambridge U	203	1
							Northampton T	45	1
Peer Dean	6 2	12 05	M	8 8 69	Dudley	Trainee	Birmingham C	120	8
							Mansfield T (loan)	10	—
							Walsall	45	8
							Northampton T	42	1
Sampson Ian	6 2	13 03	D	14 11 68	Wakefield	Goole T	Sunderland	17	1
							Northampton T (loan)	8	—
							Northampton T	75	6
Smith Tony‡	5 11	11 09	D	21 9 71	Sunderland	Trainee	Sunderland	20	—
							Hartlepool U (loan)	5	—
							Northampton T	2	—
Taylor Mark‡	6 2	13 10	D	8 11 74	Saltburn	Trainee	Middlesbrough	—	—
							Darlington (loan)	8	—
							Fulham	7	—
							Northampton T	1	—
Taylor Steve‡	6 0	12 08	F	7 1 70	Stone	Bromsgrove R	Northampton T	2	—
Thompson Garry	6 1	14 04	F	7 10 59	Birmingham	Apprentice	Coventry C	134	38
							WBA	91	39
							Sheffield W	36	7
							Aston Villa	60	17
							Watford	34	8
							Crystal Palace	20	3
							QPR	19	1
							Cardiff C	43	5
							Northampton T	49	6
Turley Billy	6 3	14 12	G	15 7 73	Wolverhampton	Evesham	Northampton T	2	—
Turner Mark‡	6 1	12 09	M	4 10 72	Bebbington	Trainee	Wolverhampton W	1	—
							Northampton T	4	—
Warburton Ray	6 0	12 13	D	7 10 67	Rotherham	Apprentice	Rotherham U	4	—
							York C	90	9
							Northampton T (loan)	17	1
							Northampton T	83	6
Warner Michael	5 9	10 10	M	17 1 74	Harrogate	Tamworth	Northampton T	—	—
White Jason	6 0	12 10	F	19 10 71	Meriden	Derby Co	Scunthorpe U	68	16
							Darlington (loan)	4	1
							Scarborough	63	20
							Northampton T	45	16
Williams Gareth*	6 0	12 02	F	12 3 67	Isle of Wight	Gosport Borough	Aston Villa	12	—
							Barnsley	34	6
							Hull C (loan)	4	—
							Hull C (loan)	16	2
							Bournemouth	1	—
							Northampton T	50	1
Woodman Andy	6 3	13 07	G	11 8 71	Denmark Hill	Apprentice	Crystal Palace	—	—
							Exeter C	6	—
							Northampton T	54	—
Worboys Gavin*	6 2	12 00	F	14 7 74	Doncaster	Trainee	Doncaster R	7	2
							Notts Co	—	—
							Exeter C (loan)	4	1
							Darlington	41	8
							Northampton T	13	1

Trainees
Bedford, Grant E; Bott, Graham; Boxford, Edward M C; Burden, Anthony P; Coles, Michael; De Vito, Claudio G; Jakes, Simon C; King, James J; Leczynski, Alexander J; Martin, Stephen J; Potter, Daniel; Preekel, Garry; Wagstaff, Paul; Whittaker, Michael A.

Non-Contract
Atkins, Ian L.

Associated Schoolboys
Binder, Paul M; Dedman, Adam L; Finlay, Mathew D; Gascoyne, Murray; Palmiero, Dino; Richardson, Wayne D; Silvestri, Lorenzo; Williams, Marc T.

Associated Schoolboys who have accepted the club's offer of a Traineeship/Contract
Ahern, John; Isaac, Lee R; Sutton, Brian.

NORWICH CITY

Name							Club	Apps	Gls
Adams Neil	5 8	10 12	M	23 11 65	Stoke	Local	Stoke C	32	4
							Everton	20	—
							Oldham Ath (loan)	9	—
							Oldham Ath	129	23
							Norwich C	89	5
Akinbiyi Ade	6 1	12 09	F	10 10 74	Hackney	Trainee	Norwich C	37	3
							Hereford U (loan)	4	2
							Brighton & HA (loan)	7	4
Bowen Mark*	5 8	11 07	D	7 12 63	Neath	Apprentice	Tottenham H	17	2
							Norwich C	320	24
Bradshaw Carl	5 10	11 11	D	2 10 68	Sheffield	Apprentice	Sheffield W	32	4
							Barnsley (loan)	6	1
							Manchester C	5	—
							Sheffield U	147	8
							Norwich C	47	2
Bray Lee*	6 1	12 00	G	21 9 76	Great Yarmouth	Trainee	Norwich C	—	—
Brownrigg Andrew	6 0	11 12	D	2 8 76	Sheffield	Trainee	Hereford U	8	—
							Norwich C	—	—
Carey Shaun	5 9	10 10	M	13 5 76	Kettering	Trainee	Norwich C	9	—
Crook Ian*	5 8	10 07	M	18 1 63	Romford	Apprentice	Tottenham H	20	1
							Norwich C	304	16
Cureton Jamie	5 8	10 07	F	28 8 75	Bristol	Trainee	Norwich C	29	6
							Bournemouth (loan)	5	—
Eadie Darren	5 7	11 00	F	10 6 75	Chippenham	Trainee	Norwich C	72	11
Fleck Robert	5 8	11 09	F	11 8 65	Glasgow	Possil YM	Partick T	2	1
							Rangers	85	29
							Norwich C	143	40
							Chelsea	40	3
							Bolton W (loan)	7	1
							Bristol C (loan)	10	1
							Norwich C	41	10
Goss Jeremy*	5 9	11 08	M	11 5 65	Oekolia	Amateur	Norwich C	188	14
Gunn Bryan	6 2	13 08	G	22 12 63	Thurso	Invergordon BC	Aberdeen	15	—
							Norwich C	347	—
Harrington Justin*	5 9	11 00	F	18 6 75	Truro	Trainee	Norwich C	—	—
Johnson Andy	6 1	12 02	M	2 5 74	Bristol	Trainee	Norwich C	39	8
Kreft Stacey*	5 9	11 00	D	2 2 76	Southampton	Trainee	Norwich C	—	—
Marshall Andy	6 2	13 00	G	14 4 75	Bury	Trainee	Norwich C	24	—
Milligan Mike	5 8	11 00	M	20 2 67	Manchester	Trainee	Oldham Ath	162	17
							Everton	17	1
							Oldham Ath	117	6
							Norwich C	54	4
Mills Danny	5 11	11 11	D	18 5 77	Norwich	Trainee	Norwich C	14	—
Mitchell Jamie*	5 6	9 10	M	6 11 76	Glasgow	Trainee	Norwich C	—	—
Newman Rob	6 2	13 02	D	13 12 63	Bradford on Avon	Apprentice	Bristol C	394	52
							Norwich C	146	13
O'Neill Keith	6 1	11 09	M	16 2 76	Dublin	Trainee	Norwich C	20	1
Polston John	5 11	11 12	D	10 6 68	Walthamstow	Apprentice	Tottenham H	24	1
							Norwich C	172	6
Prior Spencer	6 3	12 12	D	22 4 71	Rochford	Trainee	Southend U	135	3
							Norwich C	74	1
Ramasut Tom*	5 9	10 07	M	30 8 77	Cardiff		Norwich C	—	—
Rush Matthew	5 11	12 06	M	6 8 71	Dalston	Trainee	West Ham U	48	5
							Cambridge U (loan)	10	—
							Swansea C (loan)	13	—
							Norwich C	1	—
Scott Keith	6 3	14 00	F	9 6 67	London	Leicester U	Lincoln C	16	2
						Wycombe W	Wycombe W	15	10
							Swindon T	51	12
							Stoke C	25	3
							Norwich C	12	2
							Bournemouth (loan)	8	1
Shore Jamie	5 9	10 09	M	1 9 77	Bristol	Trainee	Norwich C	—	—
Simpson Karl	5 11	11 06	D	12 10 76	Newmarket	Trainee	Norwich C	1	—
Sutch Daryl	6 0	12 02	M	11 9 71	Lowestoft	Trainee	Norwich C	81	3
Ullathorne Robert	5 8	11 03	M	11 10 71	Wakefield	Trainee	Norwich C	94	7
Woodman Clayton‡			D	6 2 77	Bristol	Trainee	Norwich C	—	—
Wright Johnny	5 9	11 05	D	24 11 75	Belfast	Trainee	Norwich C	3	—

Trainees
Barber, Paul; Bellamy, Craig D; Broughton, Drewe O; Coote, Adrian; Davis, Kori M; Forbes, Adrian E; Green, Joseph A; Hilton, Damian A; Kenton, Darren E; Lewis, Craig K; Llewellyn, Christopher M; McCullough, Stephen P; O'Connor, Westley M; Roach, Stewart D C; Tipple, Gaven L; Wigger, Christopher J; Wilson, Che C; Winston, Samuel A.

Associated Schoolboys
Belgrave, Barrington; Blois, Lewis, P; Carr, Shaun L; Culbertson, Richard D J; Etunmu, Anayo S; Goreham, Paul M; Green, Robert P; Irwin, Paul J M; Joynson, Matthew; Karim, Alexis W; McKeaveney, Paul J; Ngopwani, Pitshou M; Roberts, Michael A; Russell, Darel F; Scantlebury, Dean I J.

Associated Schoolboys who have accepted the club's offer of a Traineeship/Contract
Allen, Alexander R; Andrews, Bradley J; Henderson, Tommy S; Parker, Kevin J; Walker, Trevor M; Way, Darren.

NOTTINGHAM FOREST

Name	Ht	Wt	Pos	Birthdate	Birthplace	Source	Clubs	App	Gls
Archer Paul	5 7	9 04	M	25 4 78	Leicester	Trainee	Nottingham F	—	—
Armstrong Craig	5 11	12 10	D	23 5 75	South Shields	Trainee	Nottingham F	—	—
							Burnley (loan)	4	—
							Bristol R (loan)	14	—
Atkinson Craig	6 0	11 02	M	29 9 77	Rotherham	Trainee	Nottingham F	—	—
Barber Andrew	5 9	9 08	D	4 2 79	Darlington	Trainee	Nottingham F	—	—
Barrett Richard‡	5 6	9 08	D	1 11 77	Sutton	Trainee	Nottingham F	—	—
Bart-Williams Chris	5 11	11 00	M	16 6 74	Freetown	Trainee	Leyton Orient	36	2
							Sheffield W	124	16
							Nottingham F	33	—
Black Kingsley	5 9	11 12	M	22 6 68	Luton	School	Luton T	127	26
							Nottingham F	98	14
							Sheffield U (loan)	11	2
							Millwall (loan)	3	1
Blatherwick Steve	6 1	14 14	D	20 9 73	Nottingham	Notts Co	Nottingham F	3	—
							Wycombe W (loan)	2	—
							Hereford U (loan)	10	1
Bough Gareth	5 10	12 01	G	17 10 78	Nottingham	Trainee	Nottingham F	—	—
Burns John	5 8	10 08	M	4 12 77	Dublin	Belvedere	Nottingham F	—	—
Campbell Kevin	6 1	13 08	F	4 2 70	Lambeth	Trainee	Arsenal	166	46
							Leyton Orient (loan)	16	9
							Leicester C (loan)	11	5
							Nottingham F	21	3
Carbone Anthony‡	5 10	11 13	M	13 10 74	Perth	Perth Italia	Nottingham F	—	—
Chettle Steve	6 1	13 01	D	27 9 68	Nottingham	Apprentice	Nottingham F	293	7
Clark Richard	5 11	13 04	G	6 4 77	Nuneaton	Trainee	Nottingham F	—	—
Cooper Colin	5 9	11 09	D	28 2 67	Durham		Middlesbrough	188	6
							Millwall	77	6
							Nottingham F	109	13
Cowling Lee	5 8	9 04	M	22 9 77	Doncaster	Trainee	Nottingham F	—	—
Crossley Mark	6 0	16 00	G	16 6 69	Barnsley	Trainee	Nottingham F	238	—
							Manchester U (loan)	—	—
Dawson Andrew	5 9	10 02	M	20 10 78	Northallerton	Trainee	Nottingham F	—	—
Fettis Alan	6 1	11 08	G	1 2 71	Belfast	Ards	Hull C	135	2
							WBA (loan)	3	—
							Nottingham F	—	—
Finnigan John	5 8	10 11	M	28 3 76	Wakefield	Trainee	Nottingham F	—	—
Fitchett Scott	5 8	9 06	M	20 1 79	Manchester	Trainee	Nottingham F	—	—
Gemmill Scot	5 11	11 06	M	2 1 71	Paisley	School	Nottingham F	157	19
George Daniel	6 1	12 01	D	22 10 78	Lincoln	Trainee	Nottingham F	—	—
Grim Robert	5 11	11 08	M	10 9 78	London	Trainee	Nottingham F	—	—
Guinan Stephen	6 1	13 07	F	24 12 75	Birmingham	Trainee	Nottingham F	2	—
							Darlington (loan)	3	1
Haaland Alf-Inge	5 10	12 12	M	23 11 72	Stavanger	Bryne	Nottingham F	40	1
Henry David			G	12 9 77	Nottingham		Nottingham F	—	—
Howe Stephen	5 7	10 06	M	6 1 73	Annitsford	Trainee	Nottingham F	13	2
Hurst Matthew‡	5 7	10 03	F	3 11 77	Farnborough	Trainee	Nottingham F	—	—
Irving Richard	5 8	10 07	F	10 9 75	Halifax	Trainee	Manchester U	—	—
							Nottingham F	1	—
Lee Jason	6 3	13 03	F	9 5 71	Newham	Trainee	Charlton Ath	1	—
							Stockport Co (loan)	2	—
							Lincoln C	93	21
							Southend U	24	3
							Nottingham F	63	13
Lyttle Des	5 8	12 13	D	26 9 71	Wolverhampton	Worcester C	Swansea C	46	1
							Nottingham F	108	2
McGregor Paul	5 10	11 06	F	17 12 74	Liverpool	Trainee	Nottingham F	25	3

Melton Stephen	5 11	10 11	M	3 10 78	Lincoln	Trainee	Nottingham F	—	—
Morgan Ian	6 2	12 10	D	11 10 77	Birmingham	Trainee	Nottingham F	—	—
O'Neill Shane	5 10	12 00	M	20 6 78	Limavady	Trainee	Nottingham F	—	—
Orr Stephen	5 7	10 00	F	19 1 78	Belper	Trainee	Nottingham F	—	—
Pearce Stuart	5 10	12 12	D	24 4 62	London	Wealdstone	Coventry C	51	4
							Nottingham F	368	58
Phillips David	5 9	12 05	M	29 7 63	Wegberg	Apprentice	Plymouth Arg	73	15
							Manchester C	81	13
							Coventry C	100	8
							Norwich C	152	18
							Nottingham F	99	5
Poole Darren*	5 8	10 03	F	9 11 77	Northampton	Trainee	Nottingham F	—	—
Rigby Malcolm	6 1	12 03	G	13 3 76	Nottingham	Notts Co	Nottingham F	—	—
Rosario Robert*	6 4	14 10	F	4 3 66	Hammersmith	Hillingdon Bor	Norwich C	126	18
							Wolverhampton W (loan)	2	1
							Coventry C	59	8
							Nottingham F	27	3
Roy Bryan	5 10	10 10	M	12 2 69	Amsterdam		Ajax	126	17
							Foggia	50	14
							Nottingham F	65	21
Silenzi Andrea	6 3	11 13	F	10 2 66	Rome	Torino	Nottingham F	10	—
Smith Paul	5 11	11 07	M	25 1 76	Hastings	Hastings	Nottingham F	—	—
Stone Steve	5 8	12 05	M	20 8 71	Gateshead	Trainee	Nottingham F	133	18
Stratford Lee	5 10	10 09	M	11 11 75	Barnsley	Trainee	Nottingham F	—	—
Thom Stuart	6 2	11 12	D	27 12 76	Dewsbury	Trainee	Nottingham F	—	—
Todd Andrew			M	22 2 79	Nottingham	Trainee	Nottingham F	—	—
Turner Barry	5 9	10 03	M	1 12 78	Nottingham	Trainee	Nottingham F	—	—
Turner Darren‡	5 3	8 00	M	23 12 77	Derby	Trainee	Nottingham F	—	—
Walker Justin	5 10	12 12	M	6 9 75	Nottingham	Trainee	Nottingham F	—	—
Walley Mark	5 10	11 01	F	17 9 76	Barnsley	Trainee	Nottingham F	—	—
Warner Vance	6 0	13 02	D	3 9 74	Leeds	Trainee	Nottingham F	2	—
							Grimsby T (loan)	3	—
Webb Neil*	6 0	14 07	M	30 7 63	Reading	Apprentice	Reading	72	22
							Portsmouth	123	34
							Nottingham F	146	47
							Manchester U	75	8
							Nottingham F	30	3
							Swindon T (loan)	6	—
Whitney Scott			D	10 3 79	Northampton	Trainee	Nottingham F	—	—
Woan Ian	5 10	12 02	M	14 12 67	Wirral	Runcorn	Nottingham F	155	29
Wright Dale*	6 0	12 01	D	21 12 74	Middlesbrough	Trainee	Nottingham F	—	—
Wright Tommy	6 1	14 05	G	29 8 63	Belfast	Linfield	Newcastle U	73	—
							Hull C (loan)	6	—
							Nottingham F	10	—

Trainees
Follett, Richard J; Freeman, David; Harewood, Marlon A; Porteous, Andrew G; Winters, Kris J.

Associated Schoolboys
Ashley, Neil; Dawson, Kevin E; Donlon, Jason A; Gibbons, Scott P; Higgins, Paul K; Howarth, Paul; Kearney, Martin R; Mitchell, Dean J; Rees, Daniel D; Sherwood, Benjamin D; Simpson, Mark; Thomas, Danny J; Wright-Phillips, Shaun C.

Associated Schoolboys who have accepted the club's offer of a Traineeship/Contract
Anderson, Dale R; Browne, Bevan; Cooper, Richard A; Cox, Christopher A; Goodlad, Mark; Hodgson, Richard J; Macari, Jonathan; Wood, Scott T.

NOTTS COUNTY

Agana Tony	6 0	12 02	F	2 10 63	London	Weymouth	Watford	15	1
							Sheffield U	118	42
							Notts Co	122	12
							Leeds U (loan)	2	—
Arkins Vinny	6 2	11 10	F	18 9 70	Dublin	Home Farm	Dundee U	—	—
						Shamrock R	St Johnstone	48	11
						Shelbourne	Notts Co	23	7
Baraclough Ian	6 1	12 02	D	4 12 70	Leicester	Trainee	Leicester C	—	—
							Wigan Ath (loan)	9	2
							Grimsby T (loan)	4	—
							Grimsby T	1	—
							Lincoln C	73	10
							Mansfield T	47	5
							Notts Co	35	2

Battersby Tony	6 0	12 07	F	30 8 75	Doncaster	Trainee	Sheffield U	10	1
							Southend U (loan)	8	1
							Notts Co	21	7
Butler Peter	5 9	11 02	M	27 8 66	Halifax	Apprentice	Huddersfield T	5	—
							Cambridge U (loan)	14	1
							Bury	11	—
							Cambridge U	55	9
							Southend U	142	9
							Huddersfield T (loan)	7	—
							West Ham U	70	3
							Notts Co	20	—
							Grimsby T (loan)	3	—
							WBA (loan)	9	—
Derry Shaun	5 10	10 13	D	6 12 77	Nottingham	Trainee	Notts Co	12	—
Emenalo Michael‡	5 11	11 04	D	14 7 65	Nigeria	Eintracht Trier	Notts Co	7	—
Forsyth Mike	5 11	12 02	D	20 3 66	Liverpool	Apprentice	WBA	29	—
							Northampton T (loan)	—	—
							Derby Co	325	8
							Notts Co	7	—
Gallagher Tommy	5 10	10 08	D	25 8 74	Nottingham	Trainee	Notts Co	42	2
Galloway Mick	5 11	11 05	M	13 10 74	Nottingham	Trainee	Notts Co	16	—
Hogg Graeme	6 1	12 04	D	17 6 64	Aberdeen	Apprentice	Manchester U	83	1
							WBA (loan)	7	—
							Portsmouth	100	2
							Hearts	58	3
							Notts Co	27	—
Hoyle Colin*	5 11	12 03	D	15 1 72	Derby	Trainee	Arsenal	—	—
							Chesterfield (loan)	3	—
							Barnsley	—	—
							Bradford C	62	1
							Notts Co	5	—
							Mansfield T (loan)	5	—
Hunt James	5 8	10 03	M	17 12 76	Nottingham	Trainee	Notts Co	10	1
Jemson Nigel	5 10	12 10	F	10 8 69	Hutton	Trainee	Preston NE	32	8
							Nottingham F	47	13
							Bolton W (loan)	5	—
							Preston NE (loan)	9	2
							Sheffield W	51	9
							Grimsby T (loan)	6	2
							Notts Co	14	1
							Watford (loan)	4	—
							Coventry C (loan)	—	—
							Rotherham U (loan)	16	5
Jones Gary	6 1	12 09	F	6 4 69	Huddersfield	Rossington Main	Doncaster R	20	2
						Boston U	Southend U	70	16
							Lincoln C (loan)	4	2
							Notts Co	18	5
Martindale Gary	6 0	12 00	F	24 6 71	Liverpool	Burscough	Bolton W	—	—
							Peterborough U	31	15
							Notts Co	16	6
Mills Gary*	5 9	11 10	D	11 11 61	Northampton	Apprentice	Nottingham F	58	8
						Seattle S	Derby Co	18	1
						Seattle S	Nottingham F	79	4
							Notts Co	75	8
							Leicester C	200	15
							Notts Co	47	—
Murphy Shaun	6 1	12 00	D	5 11 70	Sydney	Perth Italia	Notts Co	93	5
Pearson Chris‡	5 6	10 06	F	5 1 76	Leicester	Trainee	Notts Co	—	—
Pollitt Michael	6 4	14 00	G	29 2 72	Bolton	Trainee	Manchester U	—	—
							Oldham Ath (loan)	—	—
							Bury	—	—
							Lincoln C	57	—
							Darlington	55	—
							Notts Co	—	—
Redmile Matthew	6 0	14 01	D	12 11 76	Nottingham	Trainee	Notts Co	—	—
Richardson Ian	5 10	11 01	M	22 10 70	Barking	Dagenham &	Birmingham C	7	—
						Redbridge			
							Notts Co	15	—
Ridgeway Ian	5 8	10 06	M	28 12 75	Nottingham	Trainee	Notts Co	1	—
Rogers Paul	6 0	11 13	M	21 3 65	Portsmouth	Sutton U	Sheffield U	125	10
							Notts Co	21	2
Simpson Michael	5 9	10 08	M	28 2 74	Nottingham	Trainee	Notts Co	48	3
Strodder Gary	6 1	13 03	D	1 4 65	Cleckheaton	Apprentice	Lincoln C	132	6
							West Ham U	65	2
							WBA	140	8
							Notts Co	43	3

Turner Phil	5 8	11 00	M	12 2 62	Sheffield	Apprentice	Lincoln C	241	19
							Grimsby T	62	8
							Leicester C	24	2
							Notts Co	237	16
Walker Richard	6 0	12 00	D	9 11 71	Derby	Trainee	Notts Co	51	4
							Mansfield T (loan)	4	—
Ward Darren	5 11	12 09	G	11 5 74	Worksop	Trainee	Mansfield T	81	—
							Notts Co	46	—
Wilder Chris	5 11	10 10	D	23 9 67	Stocksbridge	Apprentice	Southampton	—	—
							Sheffield U	93	1
							Walsall (loan)	4	—
							Charlton Ath (loan)	1	—
							Charlton Ath (loan)	2	—
							Leyton Orient (loan)	16	1
							Rotherham U	132	11
							Notts Co	9	—

Trainees
Beckford-Quailey, Damion A; Eaton, Jamie; Fitzgerald, Louis; Folwell, John A; Gee, Christopher; Hickling, Graham J; Kelly, Daniel T; Marshall, James A; Matthews, Jamie L; Mitchell, Paul; Patton, Nigel; Randall, Dean; Smith, Richard; Wilkes, Timothy C; Williams, Anthony C; Wilson, Scott R.

Associated Schoolboys
Broome, Iain G; Christian, Dale T; Clarkson, Jonathan T; Cockerill, Colin P; Holmes, Richard; Kerr, Simon J; Lindley, James E; Norwood, Andrew M; Wall, Ryan D; Wigginton, Steven.

Associated Schoolboys who have accepted the club's offer of a Traineeship/Contract
Bateman, Neal S; Best, Russell S; Diuk, Wayne J; Dudley, Craig B; Henshaw, Terrence R; Jones, Kevin P; Lancaster, Mathew D; Marshall, Ben; Newton, Richard J; Smith, Neil S.

OLDHAM ATHLETIC

Allott Mark	5 10	11 01	F	3 10 77	Manchester	Trainee	Oldham Ath	—	—
Banger Nicky	5 8	10 07	F	25 2 71	Southampton	Trainee	Southampton	55	8
							Oldham Ath	41	5
Barlow Stuart	5 10	11 01	F	16 7 68	Liverpool		Everton	71	10
							Rotherham U (loan)	—	—
							Oldham Ath	26	7
Beckford Darren	6 1	11 01	F	12 5 67	Manchester	Apprentice	Manchester C	11	—
							Bury (loan)	12	5
							Port Vale (loan)	11	4
							Port Vale	167	68
							Norwich C	38	8
							Oldham Ath	52	11
Beresford David	5 7	10 09	F	11 11 76	Middlesbrough	Trainee	Oldham Ath	31	2
							Swansea C (loan)	6	—
Brennan Mark*	5 9	11 01	M	4 10 65	Rossendale	Apprentice	Ipswich T	168	19
							Middlesbrough	65	6
							Manchester C	29	6
							Oldham Ath	90	7
Darnbrough Lee			G	15 9 77	Ashton	Trainee	Oldham Ath	—	—
Evans Richard*			M	24 9 76	Wrexham	Trainee	Oldham Ath	—	—
Fleming Craig	6 0	11 07	D	6 10 71	Calder	Trainee	Halifax T	57	—
							Oldham Ath	120	1
Gannon John	5 8	10 10	M	18 12 66	Wimbledon	Apprentice	Wimbledon	16	2
							Crewe Alex (loan)	15	—
							Sheffield U (loan)	16	1
							Sheffield U	158	5
							Middlesbrough (loan)	7	—
							Oldham Ath	5	—
Gerrard Paul	6 2	13 01	G	22 1 73	Heywood	Trainee	Oldham Ath	119	1
Graham Richard	6 1	11 02	M	28 11 74	Dewsbury	Trainee	Oldham Ath	69	4
Halle Gunnar	5 11	11 02	D	11 8 65	Oslo	Lillestrom	Oldham Ath	168	14
Hallworth Jon	6 2	12 11	G	26 10 65	Stockport	School	Ipswich T	45	—
							Swindon T (loan)	—	—
							Fulham (loan)	—	—
							Bristol R (loan)	2	—
							Oldham Ath	170	—
Henry Nick	5 9	10 09	M	21 2 69	Liverpool	Trainee	Oldham Ath	251	18
Holden Andy	6 1	13 02	D	14 9 62	Flint	Rhyl	Chester C	100	17
							Wigan Ath	49	4
							Oldham Ath	22	4
Hughes Andrew	5 11	11 01	M	2 1 78	Manchester	Trainee	Oldham Ath	15	1
Innes Mark			D	27 9 78	Bellshill	Trainee	Oldham Ath	—	—
Kay Simon*			D	10 6 77	Rochdale	Trainee	Oldham Ath	—	—
Kenny Billy‡	5 8	11 00	M	19 9 73	Liverpool	Trainee	Everton	17	1
							Oldham Ath	4	—

Lonergan Darren	6 0	12 04	D	28 1 74	Cork	Waterford	Oldham Ath	2	—
Makin Chris	5 10	10 12	D	8 5 73	Manchester	Trainee	Oldham Ath	94	4
							Wigan Ath (loan)	15	2
McCarthy Sean	6 1	11 05	F	12 9 67	Bridgend	Bridgend	Swansea C	91	25
							Plymouth Arg	70	19
							Bradford C	131	60
							Oldham Ath	94	32
McNiven David	5 10	11 06	F	27 5 78	Leeds	Trainee	Oldham Ath	—	—
McNiven Scott	5 10	11 10	D	27 5 78	Leeds	Trainee	Oldham Ath	16	—
Olney Ian‡	6 1	12 04	F	17 12 69	Luton	Trainee	Aston Villa	88	16
							Oldham Ath	45	13
Orlygsson Thorvaldur	5 11	10 12	M	2 8 66	Odense	FC Akureyi	Nottingham F	37	2
							Stoke C	90	16
							Oldham Ath	16	—
Pemberton Martin	5 11	11 02	M	1 2 76	Bradford	Trainee	Oldham Ath	2	—
Redmond Steven	5 11	11 05	D	2 11 67	Liverpool	Apprentice	Manchester C	235	7
							Oldham Ath	147	2
Richardson Lee	5 11	10 11	M	12 3 69	Halifax		Halifax T	56	2
							Watford	41	1
							Blackburn R	62	3
							Aberdeen	64	6
							Oldham Ath	57	17
Richardson Lloyd			M	7 10 77	Dewsbury	Trainee	Oldham Ath	—	—
Rickers Paul	5 9	10 09	M	9 5 75	Pontefract	Trainee	Oldham Ath	27	1
Serrant Carl	5 11	11 06	D	12 9 75	Bradford	Trainee	Oldham Ath	20	1
Sharp Graeme	6 1	11 06	F	16 10 60	Glasgow	Eastercraigs	Dumbarton	40	17
							Everton	322	111
							Oldham Ath	109	30
Snodin Ian	5 11	12.06	M	15 8 63	Rotherham	Apprentice	Doncaster R	188	25
							Leeds U	51	6
							Everton	148	3
							Sunderland (loan)	6	—
							Oldham Ath	43	—
Sundgot Ole‡			M	21 3 72	Norway	Molde	Oldham Ath	—	—

Trainees
Agg, Nathan V; Carroll, Stephen A; Clark, Allan M; Clitheroe, Lee; Dixon, Alan J; Earnshaw, Mark; Gorman, Darren A; Hart, Barrie R; Holt, Andrew; Hotte, Mark S; Jablonski, Mark P; Johnson, Alan; Levendis, Andreas D; Mather, Gregg R; Morrison, Alastair J; Murphy, Gerard P M; Oldham, Gavin P; Ramsden, Gavin S; Randall, Lee E; Salt, Phillip T; Sandbach, Steven B; Stott, Lee; Swan, Iain; Yorke-Robinson, David.

Associated Schoolboys
Boshell, Daniel K; Clark, Liam; Harris, Gareth H; Hartley, Adrian L; Hodgkinson, Anthony L; Johnston, Patrick; Lush, Simon; McLean, Michael J; Park, Stephen M; Pashley, Adam; Pemberton, John; Roberts, Glen R; Saunders, John J; Wharton, Nathan; Wright, Matthew.

Associated Schoolboys who have accepted the club's offer of a Traineeship/Contract
Fairhurst, Scott; Jeffries, Paul; Selfe, Oliver; Tipton, Matthew; Walsh, Daniel G; Zarac, Neil.

OXFORD UNITED

Aldridge Martin	5 11	12 02	F	6 12 74	Northampton	Trainee	Northampton T	70	17
							Oxford U	18	9
Allen Chris	6 0	12 02	F	18 11 72	Oxford	Trainee	Oxford U	150	12
							Nottingham F (loan)	3	1
Angel Mark	5 10	11 01	F	23 8 75	Newcastle	Trainee	Sunderland	—	—
							Oxford U	27	1
Beauchamp Joey	5 10	12 05	M	13 3 71	Oxford	Trainee	Oxford U	124	20
							Swansea C (loan)	5	2
							West Ham U	—	—
							Swindon T	45	3
							Oxford U	32	7
Cullip Danny*	6 1	12 07	M	17 9 76	Bracknell	Trainee	Oxford U	—	—
Druce Mark	5 11	12 08	F	3 3 74	Oxford	Trainee	Oxford U	52	4
Elliott Matt	6 3	14 10	D	1 11 68	Epsom	Epsom & Ewell	Charlton Ath	—	—
							Torquay U	124	15
							Scunthorpe U (loan)	8	1
							Scunthorpe U	53	7
							Oxford U	122	17
Ford Bobby	5 9	10 08	M	22 9 74	Bristol	Trainee	Oxford U	65	5
Ford Mike	6 0	12 06	D	9 2 66	Bristol	Apprentice	Leicester C	—	—
						Devizes	Cardiff C	145	13
							Oxford U	225	12

Gilchrist Phil	6 0	13 04	D	25 8 73	Stockton	Trainee	Nottingham F	—	—
							Middlesbrough	—	—
							Hartlepool U	82	—
							Oxford U	60	4
Gray Martin	5 9	11 05	M	17 8 71	Stockton	Trainee	Sunderland	64	1
							Aldershot (loan)	5	—
							Fulham (loan)	6	—
							Oxford U	7	—
Lewis Mickey	5 7	12 06	M	15 2 65	Birmingham	School	WBA	24	—
							Derby Co	43	1
							Oxford U	300	7
Marsh Simon	5 11	11 06	D	29 1 77	Ealing	Trainee	Oxford U	13	—
Massey Stuart	5 10	12 07	M	17 11 64	Crawley	Sutton U	Crystal Palace	2	—
							Oxford U	57	4
Milsom Paul‡	6 1	13 01	F	5 10 74	Bristol	Trainee	Bristol C	3	—
							Cardiff C	3	—
							Oxford U	—	—
Moody Paul	6 3	14 07	F	13 6 67	Portsmouth	Waterlooville	Southampton	12	—
							Reading (loan)	5	1
							Oxford U	98	45
Murphy Matt	6 0	12 02	F	20 8 71	Northampton	Corby	Oxford U	58	12
Powell Paul§	5 8	11 00	D	30 6 78	Wallingford	Trainee	Oxford U	3	—
Reeves Steve	5 11	13 00	G	24 9 74	Dagenham	Trainee	Everton	—	—
							Chelsea	—	—
							Oxford U	—	—
Robinson Les	5 10	12 04	D	1 3 67	Shirebrook	Local	Mansfield T	15	—
							Stockport Co	67	3
							Doncaster R	82	12
							Oxford U	210	2
Rush David	5 10	11 02	F	15 5 71	Sunderland	Trainee	Sunderland	59	12
							Hartlepool U (loan)	8	2
							Peterborough U (loan)	4	1
							Cambridge U (loan)	2	—
							Oxford U	77	20
Smith David	5 10	12 02	M	26 12 70	Liverpool	Trainee	Norwich C	18	—
							Oxford U	87	1
Whitehead Phil	6 2	15 04	G	17 12 69	Halifax	Trainee	Halifax T	42	—
							Barnsley	16	—
							Halifax T (loan)	9	—
							Scunthorpe U (loan)	8	—
							Scunthorpe U (loan)	8	—
							Bradford C (loan)	6	—
							Oxford U	111	—
Wood Steve*	6 1	13 00	D	2 2 63	Bracknell	Apprentice	Reading	219	9
							Millwall	110	—
							Southampton	46	—
							Oxford U	13	—

Trainees
Concannon, Ian D; Cook, James S; Davis, Paul; Greason, Craig S; Hayter, Jonathon R; Jackson, Elliot; Lumsden, Todd M; McGregor, Marc R; Michael, James D; Powell, Paul; Robertson, Andrew; Rose, Andrew M; Whelan, Paul L.

Associated Schoolboys
Anderson, Simon P; Davies, Alex; Davies, Mathew; Davies, Simon L; Devonald, Steven E; Forde, Justin L; Jones, Michael; Richards, Andrew; Ricketts, Sam D; Shepheard, Jonathan; Stevens, Mark R; Townsend, Ben; Twine, Richard; Whitehead, Dean; Wickens, Gary J.

Associated Schoolboys who have accepted the club's offer of a Traineeship/Contract
Best, Gavin; Clarke, Daniel; Davies, Gary L; Emsden, Nigel G; Evans, David A; Folland, Robert; Grey, Iain M; Shepherd, Sam; Weatherstone, Simon.

PETERBOROUGH UNITED

Basham Michael	6 2	13 02	M	27 9 73	Barking	Trainee	West Ham U	—	—
							Colchester U (loan)	1	—
							Swansea C	29	1
							Peterborough U	14	1
Blount Mark‡	5 10	12 04	M	5 1 74	Derby	Gresley R	Sheffield U	13	—
							Peterborough U	5	—
Carter Danny	5 9	12 01	M	29 6 69	Hackney	Billericay	Leyton Orient	188	22
							Peterborough U	37	1
Charlery Ken	6 0	12 00	F	28 11 64	Stepney	Beckton U	Maidstone U	59	11
							Peterborough U	51	19
							Watford	48	13
							Peterborough U	70	24
							Birmingham C	17	4
							Southend U (loan)	3	—
							Peterborough U	19	7

Name	Ht	Wt	Pos	Birthdate	Birthplace	Source	Club	Apps	Gls
Clark Simon	6 0	12 12	D	12 3 67	London	Stevenage Bor	Peterborough U	73	1
Drury Adams§			D	29 8 78	Cambridge	Trainee	Peterborough U	1	—
Dunphy Nick‡	5 11	12 06	D	3 8 74	Birmingham	Hednesford	Peterborough U	2	—
Ebdon Marcus	5 10	11 07	M	17 10 70	Pontypool	Trainee	Everton	—	—
							Peterborough U	127	14
Farrell Sean	6 1	13 03	F	28 2 69	Watford	Apprentice	Luton T	25	1
							Colchester U (loan)	9	1
							Northampton T (loan)	4	1
							Fulham	94	31
							Peterborough U	59	17
Foran Mark	6 4	14 03	D	30 10 73	Aldershot	Trainee	Millwall	—	—
							Sheffield U	11	1
							Rotherham U (loan)	3	—
							Wycombe W (loan)	5	—
							Peterborough U	17	1
Furnell Andy*	5 10	12 05	F	13 2 77	Peterborough	Trainee	Peterborough U	19	1
Grazioli Guiliano	5 11	12 00	F	23 3 75	London	Wembley	Peterborough U	3	1
Griffiths Carl	6 0	12 06	F	15 7 71	Oswestry	Trainee	Shrewsbury T	143	54
							Manchester C	18	4
							Portsmouth	14	2
							Peterborough U	4	1
Heald Greg	6 2	13 01	D	26 9 71	London	Enfield	Peterborough U	69	4
Inman Niall§			M	6 2 78	Wakefield	Trainee	Peterborough U	1	—
Le Bihan Neil	6 0	12 03	M	14 3 76	London	Tottenham H	Peterborough U	29	—
McGleish Scott	5 9	11 04	F	10 2 74	London	Edgware T	Charlton Ath	6	—
							Leyton Orient (loan)	6	1
							Peterborough U	12	—
							Colchester U (loan)	15	6
Meredith Tom§			D	27 10 77	Enfield	Trainee	Peterborough U	2	—
Moran Paul‡	5 10	12 07	F	22 5 68	Enfield	Trainee	Tottenham H	36	2
							Portsmouth (loan)	3	—
							Leicester C (loan)	10	1
							Newcastle U (loan)	1	—
							Southend U (loan)	1	—
							Cambridge U (loan)	—	—
							Peterborough U	7	—
Morrison David	5 11	12 10	F	30 11 74	Waltham Forest	Chelmsford C	Peterborough U	66	10
Power Lee	5 10	12 00	F	30 6 72	Lewisham	Trainee	Norwich C	44	10
							Charlton Ath (loan)	5	—
							Sunderland (loan)	3	—
							Portsmouth (loan)	2	—
							Bradford C	30	5
							Millwall (loan)	—	—
							Peterborough U	38	6
Rioch Greg*	5 10	12 12	D	24 6 75	Sutton	Trainee	Luton T	—	—
							Barnet (loan)	3	—
							Peterborough U	18	—
Sedgemore Ben	6 0	12 04	M	5 8 75	Wolverhampton	Trainee	Birmingham C	—	—
							Northampton T (loan)	1	—
							Mansfield T (loan)	9	—
							Peterborough U	17	—
Semple Ryan‡			M	2 7 77	Derry	Trainee	Peterborough U	2	—
Sheffield Jon	6 0	12 08	G	1 2 69	Bedworth		Norwich C	1	—
							Aldershot (loan)	11	—
							Ipswich T (loan)	—	—
							Aldershot (loan)	15	—
							Cambridge U (loan)	2	—
							Cambridge U	54	—
							Colchester U (loan)	6	—
							Swindon T (loan)	2	—
							Hereford U (loan)	8	—
							Peterborough U	46	—
Spearing Tony	5 7	12 00	D	7 10 64	Romford	Apprentice	Norwich C	69	—
							Stoke C (loan)	9	—
							Oxford U (loan)	5	—
							Leicester C	73	1
							Plymouth Arg	35	—
							Peterborough U	98	2
Tyler Mark	5 11	12 00	G	2 4 77	Norwich	Trainee	Peterborough U	5	—
Williams Lee*	5 7	11 07	M	3 2 73	Birmingham	Trainee	Aston Villa	—	—
							Shrewsbury T (loan)	3	—
							Peterborough U	91	1
Williams Steven*	6 1	11 07	F	3 11 75	Sheffield	Trainee	Lincoln C	17	2
							Peterborough U	3	—

Trainees
Ackroft, Robert D; Cleaver, Christopher W; Drury, Adam J; Edwards, Michael R; Houston, Norman N; Inman, Niall E; Koogi, Anders B; McCafferty, Sean T P; McKeever, Mark A; Meredith, Thomas J A; Miller, Neil C; O'Donnell, Noel G; Raitt, Dion S T; Wilson, Simon M.

Associated Schoolboys
Alcraft, Kevin S R; Bellwood, Philip R; Cable, Aaron P; Davis, Craig A; Dunton, Dominic P; Ferguson, Scott J; Heuze, Michael; Jelleyman, Gareth A; McCarron, Gerald R; McCormick, Charles; Mitchell, Robert S; Smith, Wayne M; Sturmey, Paul J; Thorne, Jonathan M; Williamson, Ian P.

Associated Schoolboys who have accepted the club's offer of a Traineeship/Contract
Benfield, William W; Billington, David J; Costick, Paul; Davies, Simon; French, Daniel J; Haley, Grant R; Kenna, Warren J; Pendleton, Matthew; Shields, Tony.

PLYMOUTH ARGYLE

Player	Ht	Wt	Pos	DOB	Birthplace	From	Club	Apps	Gls
Baird Ian	6 0	12 12	F	1 4 64	Rotherham	Apprentice	Southampton	22	5
							Cardiff C (loan)	12	6
							Newcastle U (loan)	5	1
							Leeds U	85	33
							Portsmouth	20	1
							Leeds U	77	17
							Middlesbrough	63	19
							Hearts	64	15
							Bristol C	57	11
							Plymouth Arg	27	5
Barlow Martin	5 7	10 01	M	25 6 71	Barnstable	Trainee	Plymouth Arg	180	14
Billy Chris	5 11	10 09	D	2 1 73	Huddersfield	Trainee	Huddersfield T	94	4
							Plymouth Arg	32	4
Blackwell Kevin	5 10	12 10	G	21 12 58	Luton	Barnet	Scarborough	44	—
							Notts Co	—	—
							Torquay U	18	—
							Huddersfield T	5	—
							Plymouth Arg	20	—
Clayton Gary	5 10	12 03	M	2 2 63	Sheffield	Burton Alb	Doncaster R	35	5
							Cambridge U	179	17
							Peterborough U (loan)	4	—
							Huddersfield T	19	1
							Plymouth Arg	36	2
Corazzin Carlo	5 11	12 07	F	25 12 71	Canada	Vancouver 86ers	Cambridge U	105	39
							Plymouth Arg	6	1
Curran Chris	5 11	12 04	D	17 9 71	Birmingham	Trainee	Torquay U	152	4
							Plymouth Arg	8	—
Dawe Simon*	5 10	11 06	D	16 3 77	Plymouth	Trainee	Plymouth Arg	4	—
Dungey James	5 10	12 00	G	7 2 78	Plymouth	Trainee	Plymouth Arg	4	—
Evans Mike	6 0	13 04	F	1 1 73	Plymouth	Trainee	Plymouth Arg	130	26
							Blackburn R (loan)	—	—
Heathcote Mike	6 2	12 06	D	10 9 65	Durham	Spennymoor U	Sunderland	9	—
							Halifax T (loan)	7	1
							York C (loan)	3	—
							Shrewsbury T	44	6
							Cambridge U	128	13
							Plymouth Arg	44	4
Hill Keith*	6 0	12 06	D	17 5 69	Bolton	Apprentice	Blackburn R	96	3
							Plymouth Arg	123	2
Hodge Martin*	6 2	15 03	G	4 2 59	Southport	Apprentice	Plymouth Arg	43	—
							Everton	25	—
							Preston NE (loan)	28	—
							Oldham Ath (loan)	4	—
							Gillingham (loan)	4	—
							Preston NE (loan)	16	—
							Sheffield W	197	—
							Leicester C	75	—
							Hartlepool U	69	—
							Rochdale	42	—
							Plymouth Arg	17	—
Illman Neil	5 9	11 00	F	29 4 75	Doncaster	Eastwood T	Plymouth Arg	—	—
							Cambridge U (loan)	5	—
Leadbitter Chris	5 9	10 07	F	17 10 67	Middlesbrough	Apprentice	Grimsby T	—	—
							Hereford U	36	1
							Cambridge U	176	18
							Bournemouth	54	3
							Plymouth Arg	33	1
Littlejohn Adrian	5 9	10 04	F	26 9 70	Wolverhampton	WBA	Walsall	44	1
							Sheffield U	69	12
							Plymouth Arg	42	17
Logan Richard	6 0	13 03	M	24 5 69	Barnsley	Gainsborough T	Huddersfield T	45	1
							Plymouth Arg	31	4

Name					Birthplace	Source	Club	Apps	Gls
Mauge Ron	5 10	11 10	M	10 3 69	Islington	Trainee	Charlton Ath	—	—
							Fulham	50	2
							Bury	108	10
							Manchester C (loan)	—	—
							Plymouth Arg	37	7
McCall Steve*	5 10	12 06	M	15 10 60	Carlisle	Apprentice	Ipswich T	257	7
							Sheffield W	29	2
							Carlisle U (loan)	6	—
							Plymouth Arg	100	5
O'Hagan Danny	6 1	13 08	F	24 4 76	Padstow	Trainee	Plymouth Arg	9	1
Patterson Mark	5 10	12 04	D	13 9 68	Leeds	Trainee	Carlisle U	22	—
							Derby Co	51	3
							Plymouth Arg	122	3
Payne Ian‡	5 9	11 00	D	19 1 77	Crawley	Trainee	Plymouth Arg	1	—
Ross Mike‡	5 6	9 13	F	2 9 71	Southampton	Trainee	Portsmouth	4	—
							Exeter C	28	9
							Plymouth Arg	17	—
							Exeter C (loan)	7	2
Saunders Mark	5 10	11 12	M	23 7 71	Reading	Tiverton	Plymouth Arg	10	1
Twiddy Chris*	5 10	11 06	M	19 1 76	Pontyridd	Trainee	Plymouth Arg	17	1
Williams Paul	5 7	10 00	F	11 9 69	Leicester	Trainee	Leicester C	—	—
							Stockport Co	70	4
							Coventry C	14	—
							WBA (loan)	5	—
							Huddersfield T (loan)	9	—
							Plymouth Arg	46	2
Wotton Paul	5 10	12 00	D	17 8 77	Plymouth	Trainee	Plymouth Arg	8	—

Trainees
Ashton, Jon F; Beswetherick, Jonathan B; Bushby, Ryan; Dann, Craig A; Davies, Nicholas J; Fox, Lee G; Francis, Kevin; Glover, Arron M; Latham, Matthew J; Lovett, Jay; Richardson, Dominic K; Sargent, Andrew D; Turpin, Paul.

Non-Contract
Craven, Daniel F T.

Associated Schoolboys
Adams, Stephen M; Hampton, Andrew J; Hill, Andrew J; Jordan, John E; Nichols, Jonathan A; Phillips, Lee P; Sobey, Billy.

Associated Schoolboys who have accepted the club's offer of a Traineeship/Contract
Ford, Liam A.

PORTSMOUTH

Name					Birthplace	Source	Club	Apps	Gls
Allen Martin	5 10	11 00	M	14 8 65	Reading	School	QPR	136	16
							West Ham U	190	25
							Portsmouth	27	4
Awford Andy	5 9	11 09	D	14 7 72	Worcester	Worcester C	Portsmouth	164	1
Bradbury Lee			F	3 7 75	Isle of Wight	Cowes	Portsmouth	12	—
							Exeter C (loan)	14	5
Braybrook Kevin‡			M	11 2 77	Basingstoke	Trainee	Portsmouth	—	—
Burton Deon	5 8	10 09	F	25 10 76	Ashford	Trainee	Portsmouth	41	9
Butters Guy	6 3	13 00	D	30 10 69	Hillingdon	Trainee	Tottenham H	35	1
							Southend U (loan)	16	3
							Portsmouth	147	6
							Oxford U (loan)	3	1
Carter Jimmy	5 10	11 02	M	9 11 65	London	Apprentice	Crystal Palace	—	—
							QPR	—	—
							Millwall	110	10
							Liverpool	5	—
							Arsenal	25	2
							Oxford U (loan)	5	—
							Oxford U (loan)	4	—
							Portsmouth	35	4
Dobson Tony	6 1	11 12	D	5 2 69	Coventry	Apprentice	Coventry C	54	1
							Blackburn R	41	—
							Portsmouth	47	2
							Oxford U (loan)	5	—
							Peterborough U (loan)	4	—
Durnin John	5 10	11 10	F	18 8 65	Bootle	Waterloo Dock	Liverpool	—	—
							WBA (loan)	5	2
							Oxford U	161	44
							Portsmouth	85	11
Fenwick Terry†	5 10	11 12	D	17 11 59	Co. Durham	Apprentice	Crystal Palace	70	—
							QPR	256	33
							Tottenham H	93	8
							Leicester C (loan)	8	1
							Swindon T	28	—
							Portsmouth	—	—
Flahavan Aaron	6 1	11 12	G	15 12 75	Southampton	Trainee	Portsmouth	—	—

Fraser James*			F	22 10 76	Swindon		Portsmouth	—	—
Gittens Jon*	6 0	12 06	D	22 1 64	Moseley	Paget R	Southampton	18	—
							Swindon T	126	6
							Southampton	19	—
							Middlesbrough (loan)	12	1
							Middlesbrough	13	—
							Portsmouth	83	2
Hall Paul	5 9	10 02	F	3 7 72	Manchester	Trainee	Torquay U	93	1
							Portsmouth	117	19
Hinshelwood Danny	5 9	11 14	D	4 12 75	Bromley	Trainee	Nottingham F	—	—
							Portsmouth	5	—
Hounsell Daniel*			D	11 10 76	Southampton	Trainee	Portsmouth	—	—
Igoe Sammy	5 6	10 08	M	30 9 75	Spelthorne	Trainee	Portsmouth	23	—
Knight Alan	6 1	13 11	G	3 6 61	Balham	Apprentice	Portsmouth	620	—
McGrath Lloyd	5 8	12 05	M	24 2 65	Birmingham	Apprentice	Coventry C	214	4
							Portsmouth	18	—
McLoughlin Alan	5 8	10 10	M	20 4 67	Manchester	Local	Manchester U	—	—
							Swindon T	9	—
							Torquay U	24	4
							Swindon T	97	19
							Southampton	24	1
							Aston Villa (loan)	—	—
							Portsmouth	176	33
Perrett Russell	6 2	13 00	D	18 6 73	Barton on Sea	AFC Lymington	Portsmouth	9	—
Pethick Robbie	5 10	11 11	M	8 9 70	Tavistock	Weymouth	Portsmouth	100	1
Poom Mart‡	6 4	13 07	G	3 2 72	Tallinn	FC Wil	Portsmouth	4	—
Rees Jason	5 5	9 10	F	22 12 69	Pontypridd	Trainee	Luton T	82	—
							Mansfield T (loan)	15	1
							Portsmouth	40	2
Russell Lee	5 10	11 09	D	3 9 69	Southampton	Trainee	Portsmouth	95	1
							Bournemouth (loan)	3	—
Simpson Fitzroy	5 6	10 04	M	26 2 70	Trowbridge	Trainee	Swindon T	105	9
							Manchester C	71	4
							Bristol C (loan)	4	—
							Portsmouth	30	5
Thomson Andrew	6 3	14 12	D	28 3 74	Swindon	Trainee	Swindon T	22	—
							Portsmouth	16	—
Tilley Anthony			F	11 2 77	Zambia		Portsmouth	—	—
Totten Alex‡	5 8	10 07	M	1 10 76	Southampton	Trainee	Portsmouth	4	—
Walsh Paul	5 8	10 04	F	1 10 62	Plumstead	Apprentice	Charlton Ath	87	24
							Luton T	80	24
							Liverpool	77	25
							Tottenham H	128	19
							QPR (loan)	2	—
							Portsmouth	73	14
							Manchester C	53	16
							Portsmouth	21	5
Waterman David	5 10	12 00	D	16 5 77	Guernsey	Trainee	Portsmouth	—	—
Wood Paul	5 9	11 06	F	1 11 64	Middlesbrough	Apprentice	Portsmouth	47	6
							Brighton & HA	92	8
							Sheffield U	28	3
							Bournemouth (loan)	21	—
							Bournemouth	78	18
							Portsmouth	32	3

Trainees
Ahmet, Jason J; Barker, Daniel T; Bundy, Scott D; Burrows, Marc P; Campbell, Stuart; Guile, Neil R; Hawley, Jonathan A; Jukes, Nathan B; Karimzadeh, Ashkan; Orman, James D; Porter, Daniel J; Rees, Gavin R; Thompson, Mark; Williams, Adam L.

Non-Contract
Fenwick, Terence W.

Associated Schoolboys
Brown, James R; Connolly, Gary M; Craggs, Christopher R; Davis, Adam R; Eastman, Wayne; Farndell, Lee R; Fisher, Daniel; Godden, Ian J; Griffin, Joe; Hawkins, David J; Holbrook, Adam P; Hussey, Stuart R; Irwin, Andrew R; Leaves, Jay; Linpow, Steven J; Pettefer, Carl J; Scott, Wayne; Vipond, Neil I J; Webb, Arthur G; Wyatt, John.

Associated Schoolboys who have accepted the club's offer of a Traineeship/Contract
Cook, Aaron; Macdonald, Gary; Tardif, Christopher L; Waterman, Lee; Wright, David S; Wyatt, Nicky.

PORT VALE

Aspin Neil	6 0	12 06	D	12 4 65	Gateshead	Apprentice	Leeds U	207	5
							Port Vale	259	3
Bogie Ian	5 7	10 02	M	6 12 67	Newcastle	Apprentice	Newcastle U	14	—
							Preston NE	79	12
							Millwall	51	1
							Leyton Orient	65	5
							Port Vale	41	5

Name			Pos	Birth date	Birthplace	Source	Club	Apps	Gls
Corden Wayne	5 9	10 06	M	1 11 75	Leek	Trainee	Port Vale	3	—
Cunningham Dean	5 5	9 0	F	28 5 77	Stoke	Trainee	Port Vale	—	—
Eyre Richard	5 9	10 12	F	15 9 76	Stockport	Trainee	Port Vale	—	—
Foyle Martin	5 10	11 02	F	2 5 63	Salisbury	Amateur	Southampton	12	1
							Blackburn R (loan)	—	—
							Aldershot	98	35
							Oxford U	126	36
							Port Vale	163	57
Glover Dean	5 11	11 02	D	29 12 63	West Bromwich	Apprentice	Aston Villa	28	—
							Sheffield U (loan)	5	—
							Middlesbrough	50	5
							Port Vale	296	12
Glover Lee	5 10	12 01	F	24 4 70	Kettering	Trainee	Nottingham F	76	9
							Leicester C (loan)	5	1
							Barnsley (loan)	8	—
							Luton T (loan)	1	—
							Port Vale	52	7
Griffiths Gareth	6 4	14 00	D	10 4 70	Winsford	Rhyl	Port Vale	65	4
Guppy Steve	5 11	10 10	M	29 3 69	Winchester	Southampton	Wycombe W	41	8
							Newcastle U	—	—
							Port Vale	71	6
Hill Andy	5 11	12 00	D	20 1 65	Maltby	Apprentice	Manchester U	—	—
							Bury	264	10
							Manchester C	98	6
							Port Vale	35	—
Holwyn Jermaine	5 10	11 08	D	16 4 73	Amsterdam	Ajax	Port Vale	—	—
Kent Kevin‡	5 8	11 00	F	19 3 65	Stoke	Apprentice	WBA	2	—
							Newport Co	33	1
							Mansfield T	229	36
							Port Vale	115	7
Lawton Craig*	5 7	10 03	M	5 1 72	Mancot	Trainee	Manchester U	—	—
							Port Vale	3	—
McCarthy Jon	5 9	11 05	M	18 8 70	Middlesbrough	Shepshed	Hartlepool U	1	—
							York C	199	31
							Port Vale	45	7
Mills Lee	6 1	12 11	F	10 7 70	Mexborough	Stocksbridge	Wolverhampton W	25	2
							Derby Co	16	7
							Port Vale	32	8
Musselwhite Paul	6 2	12 09	G	22 12 68	Portsmouth		Portsmouth	—	—
							Scunthorpe U	132	—
							Port Vale	170	—
Naylor Tony	5 6	9 00	F	29 3 67	Manchester	Droylsden	Crewe Alex	122	45
							Port Vale	72	20
O'Reilly Justin			M	29 6 73	Derby	Gresley R	Port Vale	—	—
Porter Andy	5 9	11 02	M	17 9 68	Holmes Chapel	Trainee	Port Vale	272	17
Samuel Randy*			D	23 12 63	Trinidad	Fortuna Sittard	Port Vale	9	1
Sandeman Bradley*	5 10	10 08	M	24 2 70	Northampton	Trainee	Northampton T	58	3
							Maidstone U	57	8
							Port Vale	69	1
Stokes Dean	5 9	10 05	D	23 5 70	Birmingham	Halesowen	Port Vale	42	—
Talbot Stuart	5 11	11 00	F	14 6 73	Birmingham	Moor Green	Port Vale	22	—
Tankard Allen	5 10	11 07	D	21 5 69	Islington	Trainee	Southampton	5	—
							Wigan Ath	209	4
							Port Vale	94	1
Van Heusden Arjan	6 4	12 09	G	11 12 72	Alphen	Noordwijk	Port Vale	9	—
Walker Ray	5 10	12 00	M	28 9 63	North Shields	Apprentice	Aston Villa	23	—
							Port Vale (loan)	15	1
							Port Vale	334	33
							Cambridge U (loan)	5	—

Trainees
Bloor, Darren G; Boyd, Stephen J; Brown, Mark A; Burns, Liam; Butler, Robert J; Commander, Andrew P; Davis, Neal N; Hancock, Darren K; Male, Andrew S; McShane, Antony M; Plant, Robert A; Reynolds, Craig J; Rochester, Daniel D; Williams, Stephen J; Worth, Matthew J.

Non-Contract
Boswell, Matthew H.

Associated Schoolboys
Blount, Ivan G W; Donnelly, Paul M; Gardner, Anthony; Rowland, Stephen J.

Associated Schoolboys who have accepted the club's offer of a Traineeship/Contract
Smolenski, Andrew.

PRESTON NORTH END

Atkinson Graeme	5 8	11 02	M	11 11 71	Hull	Trainee	Hull C	149	23
							Preston NE	59	6
Barrick Dean	5 9	12 05	D	30 9 69	Hemsworth	Trainee	Sheffield W	11	2
							Rotherham U	99	7
							Cambridge U	91	3
							Preston NE	40	—
Bennett Gary	5 11	12 00	F	20 9 63	Kirby	Kirby T	Wigan Ath	20	3
							Chester C	126	36
							Southend U	42	6
							Chester C	80	15
							Wrexham	121	77
							Tranmere R	29	9
							Preston NE	8	1
Borwick Chris*	5 10	12 07	M	30 10 76	Preston	Trainee	Preston NE	—	—
Brown Mickey	5 8	11 12	F	8 2 68	Birmingham	Apprentice	Shrewsbury T	190	9
							Bolton W	33	3
							Shrewsbury T	67	11
							Preston NE	10	1
Bryson Ian	5 10	12 10	M	26 11 62	Kilmarnock		Kilmarnock	215	40
							Sheffield U	155	36
							Barnsley	16	3
							Preston NE	110	16
Calligan John*	6 4	13 13	F	15 8 77	Preston	Trainee	Preston NE	—	—
Cartwright Lee	5 9	11 00	M	19 9 72	Rossendale	Trainee	Preston NE	182	13
Davey Simon	5 9	11 08	M	1 10 70	Swansea	Trainee	Swansea C	49	4
							Carlisle U	105	18
							Preston NE	51	13
Fensome Andy*	5 8	11 02	D	18 2 69	Northampton	Trainee	Norwich C	—	—
							Newcastle U (loan)	—	—
							Cambridge U	126	1
							Preston NE	93	1
Gage Kevin	5 9	11 07	D	21 4 64	Chiswick	Apprentice	Wimbledon	168	15
							Aston Villa	115	8
							Sheffield U	112	7
							Preston NE	7	—
Grant Tony	5 9	11 04	D	20 8 76	Louth	Trainee	Leeds U	—	—
							Preston NE	1	—
Jakub Joe‡	5 6	9 06	M	7 12 56	Falkirk	Apprentice	Burnley	42	—
							Bury	265	27
						AZ Alkmaar	Chester C	42	1
							Burnley	163	8
							Chester C	36	—
							Wigan Ath	16	—
							Preston NE	—	—
Kidd Ryan	6 1	13 03	D	6 10 71	Radcliffe	Trainee	Port Vale	1	—
							Preston NE	113	4
Kilbane Kevin	5 11	12 10	M	1 2 77	Preston	Trainee	Preston NE	12	1
Lucas David	6 1	12 04	G	23 11 77	Preston	Trainee	Sheffield U	10	—
							Preston NE	51	—
							Lincon C (loan)	4	—
							Darlington (loan)	6	—
McDonald Neil	5 11	12 08	D	2 11 65	Wallsend	Wallsend BC	Newcastle U	180	24
							Everton	90	4
							Oldham Ath	24	1
							Bolton W	4	—
							Preston NE	11	—
McKenna Paul			M	20 10 77	Chorley	Trainee	Preston NE	—	—
Moilanen Teuvo	6 3	12 05	G	12 12 73	Oulu		Preston NE	2	—
Moyes David	6 1	12 09	D	25 4 63	Glasgow	Drumchapel A	Celtic	24	
							Cambridge U	79	1
							Bristol C	83	6
							Shrewsbury T	96	11
							Dunfermline Ath	105	13
							Hamilton A	5	—
							Preston NE	108	11
Saville Andy	6 1	12 11	F	12 12 64	Hull	Local	Hull C	100	18
							Walsall	38	5
							Barnsley	82	21
							Hartlepool U	37	13
							Birmingham C	59	17
							Burnley (loan)	4	1
							Preston NE	44	29

Sharp Ray	5 11	12 04	D	16 11 69	Stirling	Gairdoch U	Dunfermline Ath	151	1
							Stenhousemuir (loan)	5	—
							Preston NE	22	—
Smart Allan	6 2	12 10	F	8 7 74	Perth		Caledonian Th	4	—
							Preston NE	21	6
							Carlisle U (loan)	4	—
Sparrow Paul	6 0	11 07	D	24 3 75	London	Trainee	Crystal Palace	1	—
							Preston NE	13	—
Squires Jamie	6 1	13 11	D	15 11 75	Preston	Trainee	Preston NE	22	—
Sulley Chris‡	5 8	10 00	D	3 12 59	Camberwell	Apprentice	Chelsea	—	—
							Bournemouth	206	3
							Dundee U	7	—
							Blackburn R	134	3
							Port Vale	40	1
							Preston NE	21	1
Vaughan John*	5 10	13 01	G	26 6 64	Isleworth	Apprentice	West Ham U	—	—
							Charlton Ath (loan)	6	—
							Bristol R (loan)	6	—
							Wrexham (loan)	4	—
							Bristol C (loan)	2	—
							Fulham	44	—
							Bristol C (loan)	3	—
							Cambridge U	178	—
							Charlton Ath	6	—
							Preston NE	66	—
Wilcox Russ	6 0	12 10	D	25 3 64	Hemsworth	Apprentice	Doncaster R	1	—
						Cambridge U,	Northampton T	138	9
						Frickley Ath	Hull C	100	7
							Doncaster R	81	6
							Preston NE	27	1
Wilkinson Steve	5 10	11 07	F	1 9 68	Lincoln	Apprentice	Leicester C	9	1
							Rochdale (loan)	—	—
							Crewe Alex (loan)	5	2
							Mansfield T	232	83
							Preston NE	42	10

Trainees
Barnes, Stephen W; Bingham, Stuart J; Brooks, Gilbert I; Cliff, Stuart J; Harrison, Spencer K; Hayton, Kyle; Heys, Daniel J; McCrone, Paul D; Miller, Jamie; Morgan, Mark P T; Numberson, Kevin R; Potts, Colin E; Smith, Gary A; Southworth, Brian J; Stewart, Simon D S; Subachus, Anthony V; Sutton, Christopher W.

Non-Contract
Jakub, Yanek; Peters, Gary; Stewart, Steven; Sulley, Christopher S.

Associated Schoolboys
Berry, Peter; Boardman, Roger J; Chapman, Andrew J; Connolly, James M; Houldsworth, Matthew; Roberts, Karl M; Thompson, Gary K L; Underwood, Jeffrey H; Wright, Mark S; Wright, Ronnie M.

Associated Schoolboys who have accepted the club's offer of a Traineeship/Contract
Boase, Marc; Hutchinson, Russell D; Ollerton, Neil; Turner, John.

QUEENS PARK RANGERS

Bardsley David	5 10	11 07	D	11 9 64	Manchester	Apprentice	Blackpool	45	—
							Watford	100	7
							Oxford U	74	7
							QPR	241	4
Barker Simon	5 9	11 07	M	4 11 64	Farnworth	Apprentice	Blackburn R	182	35
							QPR	254	26
Brazier Matthew	5 8	11 06	D	2 7 76	Whipps Cross	Trainee	QPR	11	—
Brevett Rufus	5 8	11 04	D	24 9 69	Derby	Trainee	Doncaster R	109	3
							QPR	85	1
Challis Trevor	5 8	11 00	D	23 10 75	Paddington	Trainee	QPR	11	—
Charles Lee	5 11	12 04	F	20 8 71	Hillingdon	Chertsey T	QPR	4	—
							Barnet (loan)	5	—
Cross John*	5 9	12 03	M	6 4 76	Barking	Trainee	QPR	—	—
Dichio Daniele	6 3	12 03	F	19 10 74	Hammersmith	Trainee	QPR	38	13
							Barnet (loan)	9	2
Dykstra Sieb	6 5	14 10	G	20 10 66	Kerkrade	Roda JC	Motherwell	80	—
							QPR	11	—
							Bristol C (loan)	8	—
							Wycombe W (loan)	13	—
Gallen Kevin	5 11	12 10	F	21 9 75	Hammersmith	Trainee	QPR	67	18
Goodridge Greg	5 6	10 00	F	10 7 71	Barbados	Lambada	Torquay U	38	4
							QPR	7	1
Graham Mark	5 7	10 12	F	24 10 74	Newry	Trainee	QPR	—	—

Name	Ht	Wt	Pos	Born	Birthplace	Source	Club	Apps	Gls
Hateley Mark	6 1	11 07	F	7 11 61	Liverpool	Apprentice	Coventry C	93	25
							Portsmouth	38	22
							AC Milan	66	17
							Monaco	59	22
							Rangers	165	85
							QPR	14	2
Holloway Ian*	5 7	10 10	M	12 3 63	Kingswood	Apprentice	Bristol R	111	14
							Wimbledon	19	2
							Brentford (loan)	13	2
							Brentford	17	—
							Torquay U (loan)	5	—
							Bristol R	179	26
							QPR	147	4
Hurst Richard	6 0	13 00	G	23 12 76	Hammersmith	Trainee	QPR	—	—
Impey Andrew	5 8	11 02	F	13 9 71	Hammersmith	Yeading	QPR	155	11
Lockwood Matthew*	5 9	10 12	M	17 10 76	Rochford	Trainee	QPR	—	—
Maddix Danny	5 11	11 07	D	11 10 67	Ashford	Apprentice	Tottenham H	—	—
							Southend U (loan)	2	—
							QPR	188	7
Mahoney-Johnson Michael	5 10	12 00	F	6 11 76	Paddington	Trainee	QPR	—	—
McDermott Andrew	5 9	11 03	M	20 3 77	Sydney	Aust Inst of Sport	QPR	—	—
McDonald Alan	6 2	13 11	D	12 10 63	Belfast	Apprentice	QPR	363	11
							Charlton Ath (loan)	9	—
Murray Paul	5 9	10 03	M	31 8 76	Carlisle	Trainee	Carlisle U	41	1
							QPR	1	—
Parmenter Steven*	5 9	11 00	M	22 1 77	Chelmsford	Trainee	QPR	—	—
Perry Mark	5 10	11 03	M	19 10 78	London	Trainee	QPR	—	—
Plummer Chris	6 2	12 09	D	12 10 76	Isleworth	Trainee	QPR	1	—
Power Graeme*	5 9	10 10	D	7 3 77	Northwick Park	Trainee	QPR	—	—
Quashie Nigel	5 9	11 00	F	20 7 78	Nunhead	Trainee	QPR	11	—
Ready Karl	6 1	13 03	D	14 8 72	Neath	Trainee	QPR	61	3
Roberts Tony	6 0	13 11	G	4 8 69	Bangor	Trainee	QPR	99	—
Sharp Lee	6 2	14 00	G	18 12 76	Lincoln	Lincoln U	QPR	—	—
Sinclair Trevor	5 10	12 05	M	2 3 73	Dulwich	Trainee	Blackpool	112	15
							QPR	102	10
Sommer Jurgen	6 5	15 12	G	27 2 69	New York		Luton T	82	—
							Brighton & HA (loan)	1	—
							Torquay U (loan)	10	—
							QPR	33	—
Wilkins Ray†	5 8	11 00	M	14 9 56	Hillingdon	Apprentice	Chelsea	179	30
							Manchester U	160	7
							AC Milan	73	2
						Paris St Germain	Rangers	70	2
							QPR	154	7
							Crystal Palace	1	—
							QPR	17	—
Yates Steve	5 10	12 02	D	29 1 70	Bristol	Trainee	Bristol R	197	—
							QPR	82	1
Zelic Ned‡	6 2	13 00	M	4 7 71	Australia	Aust Inst	Borussia Dortmund	41	1
							QPR	4	—

Trainees
Bruce, Paul M; Conlon, Barry J; Dobson, Warren E; Harris, Jonathan; Hart, Paul A; Kingsmith, Benjamin L A; McGoff, Alan D; McVeigh, Mark A; Murray, Frazer W G.

Non-Contract
Wilkins, Raymond C.

Associated Schoolboys
Brown, Carlos D; Browne, Ricky D; Bubb, Alvin R; Burgess, Oliver D; Campbell, Dudley J; Cochrane, Justin V; Kyriacou, Paul; Mills, Christopher M; Norman, Brian P; Rustem, Adam R; Shelton, Richard; Smillie, Allan D; Taylor, Steven A; Wright, Daniel J.

Associated Schoolboys who have accepted the club's offer of a Traineeship/Contract
Ashton, Lee; Currie, Michael J; Franklin, Damien M; Graham, Richard S; Langley, Richard; Lione, Angelo M; Lusardi, Mario; Owen, Karl R; Purser, Wayne M; Robinson, Nicky J; Roostan, Benjamin L; Spiller, Richard B.

READING

Name	Ht	Wt	Pos	Born	Birthplace	Source	Club	Apps	Gls
Bass David	5 11	12 07	M	29 11 74	Frimley	Trainee	Reading	9	—
Bernal Andy	5 10	12 05	D	16 7 66	Canberra	Sporting Gijon	Ipswich T	9	—
						Sydney Olympic	Reading	67	2
Booty Martyn	5 8	11 02	D	30 5 71	Kirby Muxloe	Trainee	Coventry C	5	—
							Crewe Alex	96	5
							Reading	17	1
Carey Alan	5 7	10 10	D	21 8 75	Greenwich	Trainee	Reading	3	—

Name	Ht	Wt	Pos	Date of birth	Birthplace	Source	Clubs	Apps	Gls
Caskey Darren	5 8	11 09	M	21 8 74	Basildon	Trainee	Tottenham H	32	4
							Watford (loan)	6	1
							Reading	15	2
Freeman Andy§			F	8 9 77	Reading	Crystal Palace	Reading	1	—
Gilkes Michael	5 8	10 10	F	20 7 65	Hackney	Leicester C	Reading	361	42
							Chelsea (loan)	1	—
							Southampton (loan)	6	—
Gooding Mick	5 9	10 07	M	12 4 59	Newcastle	Bishop Auckland	Rotherham U	102	10
							Chesterfield	12	—
							Rotherham U	156	33
							Peterborough U	47	21
							Wolverhampton W	44	4
							Reading	271	26
Gordon Neville*	5 10	11 00	F	15 11 75	Greenwich	Trainee	Millwall	—	—
							Reading	1	—
Hammond Nicky	6 0	11 13	G	7 9 67	Hornchurch	Apprentice	Arsenal	—	—
							Bristol R (loan)	3	—
							Peterborough U (loan)	—	—
							Aberdeen (loan)	—	—
							Swindon T	67	—
							Plymouth Arg	4	—
							Reading	5	—
Holsgrove Paul	6 1	11 10	F	26 8 69	Wellington	Trainee	Aldershot	3	—
							Wimbledon (loan)	—	—
							WBA (loan)	—	—
					Wokingham	Luton T	2	—
					Heracles	Millwall	11	—
							Reading	54	4
Hopkins Jeff	6 0	12 11	D	14 4 64	Swansea	Apprentice	Fulham	219	4
							Crystal Palace	70	2
							Plymouth Arg (loan)	8	—
							Bristol R	6	—
							Reading	113	3
Jones Tom*	5 10	11 07	M	7 10 64	Aldershot	Weymouth	Aberdeen	28	3
							Swindon T	168	12
							Reading	79	2
Kerr Dylan	5 9	11 04	D	14 1 67	Valetta	Arcadia Shepherds	Leeds U	13	—
							Doncaster R (loan)	7	1
							Blackpool (loan)	12	1
							Reading	89	5
Lambert James	5 7	10 04	F	14 9 73	Henley	School	Reading	59	8
Lovell Stuart	5 10	11 00	M	9 1 72	Sydney	Trainee	Reading	186	52
McPherson Keith	5 11	11 00	D	11 9 63	Greenwich	Apprentice	West Ham U	1	—
							Cambridge U (loan)	11	1
							Northampton T	182	8
							Reading	193	6
Meaker Michael	5 11	11 00	M	18 8 71	Greenford	Trainee	QPR	34	1
							Plymouth Arg (loan)	4	—
							Reading	21	—
Mikhailov Bobby	6 1	12 04	G	12 2 63	Bulgaria	Botev Plovdiv	Reading	16	—
Morley Trevor	5 11	12 01	F	20 3 61	Nottingham	Nuneaton	Northampton T	107	39
							Manchester C	72	18
							West Ham U	178	57
							Reading	17	4
Nogan Lee	5 10	10 08	F	21 5 69	Cardiff	Apprentice	Oxford U	64	10
							Brentford (loan)	11	2
							Southend U (loan)	6	1
							Watford	105	26
							Southend U (loan)	5	—
							Reading	59	20
Parkinson Phil	6 0	11 06	M	1 12 67	Chorley	Apprentice	Southampton	—	—
							Bury	145	5
							Reading	154	7
Quinn Jimmy	6 0	11 06	F	18 11 59	Belfast	Oswestry T	Swindon T	49	10
							Blackburn R	71	17
							Swindon T	64	30
							Leicester C	31	6
							Bradford C	35	14
							West Ham U	47	18
							Bournemouth	43	19
							Reading	158	68
Randell Gareth*	5 5	9 07	F	11 8 77	Salisbury	Trainee	Reading	—	—
Sheppard Simon*	6 4	14 03	G	7 8 73	Clevedon	Trainee	Watford	23	—
							Scarborough (loan)	9	—
							Reading	18	—
Simpson Derek	5 10	10 09	M	23 12 78	Lanark	Trainee	Reading	—	—

	Ht	Wt	Pos	DOB	Birthplace	Source	Club	Apps	Gls
Stowell Matthew*	6 0	12 00	D	1 3 77	Reading	Trainee	Reading	—	—
Swales Steve	5 8	10 03	D	26 12 73	Whitby	Trainee	Scarborough	54	1
							Reading	9	—
Thorp Michael	6 0	11 07	D	5 12 75	Wallington	Trainee	Reading	2	—
Wdowczyk Dariusz	5 11	11 11	D	21 9 62	Warsaw	Legia Warsaw	Celtic	116	4
							Reading	68	—
Williams Adrian	6 2	12 06	D	16 8 71	Reading	Trainee	Reading	196	14
Williams Martin	5 9	11 12	F	12 7 73	Luton	Leicester C	Luton T	40	2
							Colchester U (loan)	3	—
							Reading	15	1

Trainees
Curtis, Richard S; Dowling, Luke J; Forbes, Andrew J; Freeman, Andrew J; Glasgow, Byron F; Holloway, Neil S; Jones, Matthew; Jones, Russell; Jones, Stuart C; Lough, Lee A; Lyttle, Clive A; May, Steven J; Roach, Neville; Sanders, Guy B.

Associated Schoolboys who have accepted the club's offer of a Traineeship/Contract
Norris, Jordan; Rooke, Maxwell J.

ROCHDALE

	Ht	Wt	Pos	DOB	Birthplace	Source	Club	Apps	Gls
Barlow Neil§			D	24 3 78	Bury	Trainee	Rochdale	2	—
Bayliss David	5 11	12 04	D	8 6 76	Liverpool	Trainee	Rochdale	29	—
Butler Paul	6 2	13 00	D	2 11 72	Manchester	Trainee	Rochdale	158	10
Clarke Chris*	6 1	12 10	G	1 5 74	Barnsley	Trainee	Bolton W	—	—
							Rochdale	30	—
Deary John	5 8	12 07	M	18 10 62	Ormskirk	Apprentice	Blackpool	303	43
							Burnley	215	23
							Rochdale	53	5
Formby Kevin	5 9	11 04	D	22 7 71	Ormskirk	Burscough	Rochdale	51	—
Gray Ian	6 2	12 00	G	25 2 75	Manchester	Trainee	Oldham Ath	—	—
							Rochdale (loan)	12	—
							Rochdale	20	—
Hall Derek*	5 8	11 12	M	5 1 65	Manchester	Apprentice	Coventry C	1	—
							Torquay U (loan)	10	2
							Torquay U	45	4
							Swindon T	10	—
							Southend U	123	15
							Halifax T	49	4
							Hereford U	103	18
							Rochdale	23	2
Hardy Jason*	5 9	11 07	M	14 12 69	Burnley	Trainee	Burnley	43	1
							Halifax T (loan)	4	—
							Halifax T	22	2
						Halifax T	Rochdale	7	—
Lyons Paul	5 6	10 11	M	24 6 77	Leigh		Rochdale	3	—
Martin Dean	5 11	11 09	M	9 9 67	Halifax	Apprentice	Halifax T	153	7
							Scunthorpe U	106	7
							Rochdale	52	—
Moulden Paul*	5 8	11 03	F	6 9 67	Farnworth	Apprentice	Manchester C	64	18
							Bournemouth	32	13
							Oldham Ath	38	4
							Brighton & HA (loan)	11	5
							Birmingham C	20	6
							Huddersfield T	2	—
							Rochdale	16	1
Peake Jason	5 11	12 08	M	29 9 71	Leicester	Trainee	Leicester C	8	1
							Hartlepool U (loan)	6	1
							Halifax T	33	1
							Rochdale	95	6
Powell Francis*	6 1	12 00	F	17 6 77	Burnley	Burnley	Rochdale	2	—
Price James§			D	1 2 78	Preston	Trainee	Rochdale	3	—
Proctor James*	5 8	11 07	M	25 10 76	Doncaster	Bradford C	Rochdale	3	—
Russell Alex	5 8	11 07	M	17 3 73	Crosby	Burscough	Rochdale	32	1
Shaw Graham*	5 9	11 04	F	7 6 67	Newcastle under Lyme	Apprentice	Stoke C	99	18
							Preston NE	121	29
							Stoke C	36	5
							Plymouth Arg (loan)	6	—
							Rochdale	22	—
Stuart Mark	5 10	11 03	D	15 12 66	Hammersmith	QPR	Charlton Ath	107	28
							Plymouth Arg	57	11
							Ipswich T (loan)	5	2
							Bradford C	29	5
							Huddersfield T	15	3
							Rochdale	107	28
Taylor Jamie	5 6	9 12	F	11 1 77	Bury	Trainee	Rochdale	35	4

Player				DOB	Birthplace	Source	Clubs	Apps	Gls
Thackeray Andy	5 9	11 00	M	13 2 68	Huddersfield		Manchester C	—	—
							Huddersfield T	2	—
							Newport Co	54	4
							Wrexham	152	14
							Rochdale	148	13
Thompson David	5 8	11 12	D	27 5 62	Manchester	Local	Rochdale	155	13
							Manchester U (loan)	—	—
							Notts Co	55	8
							Wigan Ath	108	14
							Preston NE	46	4
							Chester C	80	9
							Rochdale	83	10
Thompstone Ian*	6 0	13 00	F	17 1 71	Manchester	Trainee	Manchester C	1	1
							Oldham Ath	—	—
							Exeter C	15	3
							Halifax T	31	9
							Scunthorpe U	60	8
							Rochdale	25	1
Valentine Peter*	6 0	12 09	D	16 6 63	Huddersfield	Apprentice	Huddersfield T	19	1
							Bolton W	68	1
							Bury	319	16
							Carlisle U	29	2
							Rochdale	50	2
Whitehall Steve	5 9	11 05	F	8 12 66	Bromborough	Southport	Rochdale	203	66
Williams Paul A*	6 3	14 08	F	8 9 63	Sheffield	Nuneaton	Preston NE	1	—
							Newport Co	26	3
							Sheffield U	8	—
							Hartlepool U	8	—
							Stockport Co	24	14
							WBA	44	5
							Coventry C (loan)	2	—
							Stockport Co	16	3
							Rochdale	37	7
							Doncaster R (loan)	3	1

Trainees
Adams, Paul; Barlow, Neil K; Hill, Paul S; Matthews, Lee A; Ogden, John; Price, James R; Shore, Philip A; Stanley, Ian; Swettenham, Andrew B; Taylor, Neil; Woods, Daniel M.

Non-Contract
Hill, James R; Irwin, Nicholas J.

Associated Schoolboys
Bywater, Stephen M; Gilks, Daniel; Hicks, Graham; Loft, Paul; O'Reilly, Gareth; Preston, Michael A; Riley, Peter; Rudd, Paul G; Staniland, Ryan; Taylor, Carl D; Taylor, Christopher J; Westmoreland, Darren P.

Associated Schoolboys who have accepted the club's offer of a Traineeship/Contract
Brannelly, Ashley; Lambert, Dale L.

ROTHERHAM UNITED

Player				DOB	Birthplace	Source	Clubs	Apps	Gls
Ayrton Matthew*	5 9	10 11	M	16 12 76	Rotherham	Trainee	Rotherham U	—	—
Berry Trevor	5 7	10 08	F	1 8 74	Haslemere	Bournemouth	Aston Villa	—	—
							Rotherham U	36	7
Blades Paul	6 0	12 00	D	5 1 65	Peterborough	Apprentice	Derby Co	166	1
							Norwich C	47	—
							Wolverhampton W	107	2
							Rotherham U	34	1
Boucken Kriss‡	5 9	12 00	F	7 2 77	Raratonga	Trainee	Rotherham U	—	—
Bowyer Gary	6 1	13 04	D	26 6 71	Manchester		Hereford U	14	2
							Nottingham F	—	—
							Rotherham U	27	—
Breckin Ian	5 11	11 07	D	24 7 75	Rotherham	Trainee	Rotherham U	90	3
Clarke Matthew	6 3	11 05	G	3 11 73	Sheffield	Trainee	Rotherham U	124	—
Davison Bobby*	5 9	11 10	F	17 7 59	South Shields	Seaham CW	Huddersfield T	2	—
							Halifax T	63	29
							Derby Co	206	83
							Leeds U	91	31
							Derby Co (loan)	10	8
							Sheffield U (loan)	11	4
							Leicester C	25	6
							Sheffield U	12	1
							Rotherham U	22	4
							Hull C (loan)	11	4
Farrelly Stephen	6 5	15 07	G	27 3 65	Liverpool	Macclesfield T	Rotherham U	—	—
Garner Darren	5 9	12 07	M	10 12 71	Plymouth	Dorchester T	Rotherham U	31	1
Goater Shaun	6 0	12 00	F	25 2 70	Bermuda		Manchester U	—	—
							Rotherham U	209	70
							Notts Co (loan)	1	—
Goodwin Shaun	5 8	11 04	M	14 6 69	Rotherham	Trainee	Rotherham U	259	34

Haran Mark*	6 1	12 00	D	21 1 77	Barnsley	Trainee	Rotherham U	—	—
Hayward Andy	6 0	11 00	F	21 6 70	Barnsley	Frickley Ath	Rotherham U	73	8
Hurst Paul	5 4	9 00	D	25 9 74	Sheffield	Trainee	Rotherham U	57	1
James Martin*	5 10	11 10	M	18 5 71	Formby	Trainee	Preston NE	98	11
							Stockport Co	32	—
							Rotherham U	41	—
Jeffrey Mike‡	6 1	11 09	F	11 8 71	Liverpool	Trainee	Bolton W	15	—
							Doncaster R (loan)	11	6
							Doncaster R	38	13
							Newcastle U	2	—
							Rotherham U	22	5
McGlashan John	6 2	13 00	F	3 6 67	Dundee	Dundee Violet	Montrose	68	11
							Millwall	16	—
							Cambridge U (loan)	1	—
							Fulham (loan)	5	1
							Peterborough U	46	3
							Rotherham U	43	5
Monington Mark	6 1	14 02	D	21 10 70	Bilsthorpe	School	Burnley	84	5
							Rotherham U	36	2
Pike Martin*	5 11	12 09	D	21 10 64	South Shields	Apprentice	WBA	—	—
							Peterborough U	126	8
							Sheffield U	129	5
							Tranmere R (loan)	2	—
							Bolton W (loan)	5	1
							Fulham	190	14
							Rotherham U	9	—
Richardson Neil	6 0	13 00	D	3 3 68	Sunderland	Brandon U	Rotherham U	127	6
Roscoe Andy	5 10	11 08	M	4 6 73	Liverpool	Trainee	Liverpool	—	—
							Bolton W	3	—
							Rotherham U	76	6
Smith Scott	5 8	11 00	D	6 3 75	Christchurch	Trainee	Rotherham U	25	—
Viljoen Nik	5 10	12 00	F	3 12 76	New Zealand	Trainee	Rotherham U	8	2

Trainees
Ashcroft, Richard G; Barnes, Philip K; Davis, Craig; Dillon, Paul W; Gordon, James D; Hobson, Daniel D; Hudson, Daniel R; Kelly, Christopher; McIntosh, Andrew P; McKenzie, Robert A; Pell, Robert A; Spiby, Dale K; Trower, Kevin J.

Associated Schoolboys
Allen, Paul C; Beesley, Darren; Capill, Stephen L; Gamble, Jonathan; Grieve, Christopher; Hawke, Richard J; Hensman, Matthew D; Jenkinson, Thomas A F; Lax, Ryan A; Merris, David A; Ollivant, Glenn; Reynolds, Steven J; Roden, Craig; Sandland, Guy; Stanley, Peter B; Thompson, David M.

Associated Schoolboys who have accepted the club's offer of a Traineeship/Contract
Bagshaw, Neil D; Barton, Warren L; Hall, Matthew D; Howard, Daniel R; Ingledow, Jamie G; Levers, Roger; Sedgwick, Christopher E; Smith, Jamie M.

SCARBOROUGH

Boardman Craig*	6 1	12 02	D	30 11 70	Barnsley	Trainee	Nottingham F	—	—
							Peterborough U	—	—
						Halifax T	Scarborough	9	—
Calvert Mark‡	5 9	11 08	M	11 9 70	Consett	Trainee	Hull C	30	1
							Scarborough	72	5
Charles Steve*	5 11	12 02	M	10 5 60	Sheffield	Sheffield Univ	Sheffield U	123	10
							Wrexham	113	37
							Mansfield T	237	39
							Scunthorpe U (loan)	4	—
							Scarborough	134	20
Cook Mitch‡	6 0	12 00	M	15 10 61	Scarborough	Scarborough	Darlington	34	4
							Middlesbrough	6	—
							Scarborough	81	10
							Halifax T	54	2
							Scarborough (loan)	9	1
							Darlington (loan)	9	—
							Darlington	27	3
							Blackpool	68	—
							Hartlepool U	24	—
							Scarborough	2	—
Curtis Andy‡	5 8	12 00	F	2 12 72	Doncaster	Trainee	York C	12	—
							Peterborough U	11	1
							York C	1	—
							Scarborough	5	—
Foreman Matt‡	6 0	12 04	D	15 2 75	Gateshead	Trainee	Sheffield U	—	—
							Scarborough	4	—
Harper Lee‡	5 11	12 05	D	24 3 75	Bridlington	York C	Scarborough	2	—
Heald Oliver‡	6 0	11 13	F	13 3 75	Vancouver		Port Vale	—	—
							Scarborough	9	1

Hicks Stuart	6 1	13 03	D	30 5 67	Peterborough	Wisbech	Colchester U	64	—
							Scunthorpe U	67	1
							Doncaster R	36	—
							Huddersfield T	22	1
							Preston NE	12	—
							Scarborough	47	1
Ironside Ian	6 2	13 10	G	8 3 64	Sheffield	N Ferriby U	Scarborough	88	—
							Middlesbrough	13	—
							Scarborough (loan)	7	—
							Stockport Co	19	—
							Scarborough	49	—
Kelly Gavin*	6 0	13 13	G	29 9 68	Beverley	Trainee	Hull C	11	—
							Bristol R (loan)	—	—
							Bristol R	30	—
							Scarborough	30	—
Kinnaird Paul‡	5 8	10 10	F	11 11 66	Glasgow	Apprentice	Norwich C	—	—
							Dundee U	18	—
							Motherwell	34	—
							St Mirren	57	4
							Partick T	33	3
							Shrewsbury T	4	1
							St Johnstone	8	—
							Partick T	3	—
							Dunfermline Ath	9	—
							Ayr U	18	2
							Scarborough	3	—
Knowles Darren	5 6	11 01	D	8 10 70	Sheffield	Trainee	Sheffield U	—	—
							Stockport Co	63	—
							Scarborough	127	2
Lucas Richard	5 10	12 06	M	22 9 70	Sheffield	Trainee	Preston NE	—	—
							Scarborough	44	—
Magee Kevin‡	5 10	11 05	F	10 4 71	Edinburgh	Armadale T	Partick T	11	—
							Preston NE	26	1
							Plymouth Arg	4	—
							Scarborough	28	1
Martin Kevin	6 1	12 09	G	22 6 76	Bromsgrove	Trainee	Scarborough	3	—
O'Riordan Don‡	6 0	12 07	D	14 5 57	Dublin	Apprentice	Derby Co	6	1
							Doncaster R (loan)	2	—
						Tulsa	Preston NE	158	8
							Carlisle U	84	18
							Middlesbrough	41	2
							Grimsby T	86	14
							Notts Co	109	5
							Mansfield T (loan)	6	—
							Torquay U	79	3
							Scarborough	1	—
Page Don*	5 10	11 03	F	18 1 64	Manchester	Runcorn	Wigan Ath	74	15
							Rotherham U	55	13
							Rochdale (loan)	4	1
							Doncaster R	22	4
							Chester C	30	5
							Scarborough	37	5
Ritchie Andy	5 10	12 09	F	28 11 60	Manchester	Apprentice	Manchester U	33	13
							Brighton & HA	89	23
							Leeds U	136	40
							Oldham Ath	217	82
							Scarborough	37	8
Robinson Ronnie‡	5 9	13 06	D	22 10 66	Sunderland	SC Vaux	Ipswich T	—	—
						Vaux Breweries	Leeds U	27	—
							Doncaster R	78	5
							WBA	1	—
							Rotherham U	86	2
							Peterborough U	47	—
							Exeter C	39	1
							Huddersfield T (loan)	2	—
							Scarborough	1	—
Rockett Jason	6 1	13 04	D	26 9 69	London		Rotherham U	—	—
							Scarborough	100	4
Sansam Christian‡	6 0	11 00	F	26 12 75	Hull	Trainee	Scunthorpe U	21	1
							Scarborough	6	—
Sunderland Jon	6 0	11 13	M	2 11 75	Newcastle	Trainee	Blackpool	2	—
							Scarborough	6	—
Thew Lee‡	5 10	12 08	M	23 10 74	Sunderland	Trainee	Doncaster R	32	2
							Scarborough	14	—
Toman Andy*	5 10	12 06	M	7 3 62	Northallerton	Bishop Auckland	Lincoln C	24	4
							Hartlepool U	112	28
							Darlington	115	10
							Scarborough (loan)	6	—
							Scunthorpe U	15	5
							Scarborough	35	3

Trebble Neil‡	6 3	13 10	F	16 2 69	Hitchin	Stevenage Borough	Scunthorpe U	14	2
							Preston NE	19	4
							Scarborough	47	8
Wells Mark*	5 8	11 02	M	17 10 71	Leicester	Trainee	Notts Co	2	—
							Huddersfield T	23	4
							Scarborough	32	2
Willgrass Alex	5 10	11 06	M	8 4 76	Scarborough		Scarborough	7	—

Trainees
Carr, Graeme; Connor, Joseph P; Corking, Neil M; Coulson, Alec; Dawson, Paul M; Gamble, Crawford S; Hooper, Christopher; Hopps, Paul M; Lee, Mark; Lewis, Paul D; Macauley, Dean; Russell, Matthew L.

Associated Schoolboys who have accepted the club's offer of a Traineeship/Contract
Gredziak, Wayne; Jackson, Richard; Radigan, Neil.

SCUNTHORPE UNITED

Bradley Russell	6 1	12 07	D	28 3 66	Birmingham	Dudley T	Nottingham F	—	—
							Hereford U (loan)	12	1
							Hereford U	77	3
							Halifax T	56	3
							Scunthorpe U	97	4
Clarkson Phil	5 8	11 02	M	13 11 68	Hambleton	Fleetwood	Crewe Alex	98	27
							Scunthorpe U	24	6
D'Auria David	5 8	11 11	M	26 3 70	Swansea	Trainee	Swansea C	45	6
						Barry T	Scarborough	52	8
							Scunthorpe U	27	5
Eyre John	6 0	12 07	F	9 10 74	Humberside	Trainee	Oldham Ath	10	1
							Scunthorpe U (loan)	9	8
							Scunthorpe U	39	10
Ford Tony*	5 10	13 00	D	14 5 59	Grimsby	Apprentice	Grimsby T	354	54
							Sunderland (loan)	9	1
							Stoke C	112	13
							WBA	114	14
							Grimsby T	68	3
							Bradford C (loan)	5	—
							Scunthorpe U	76	9
Graham Deniol‡	5 10	10 05	F	4 10 69	Cannock	Trainee	Manchester U	2	—
							Barnsley	38	2
							Preston NE (loan)	8	—
							Carlisle U (loan)	2	1
							Stockport Co	11	2
							Scunthorpe U	3	1
Hope Chris	6 0	12 02	D	14 11 72	Sheffield	Darlington	Nottingham F	—	—
							Scunthorpe U	105	3
Housham Steven	5 10	11 00	D	24 2 76	Gainsborough T	Trainee	Scunthorpe U	32	—
Knill Alan	6 4	13 02	D	8 10 64	Slough	Apprentice	Southampton	—	—
							Halifax T	118	6
							Swansea C	89	3
							Bury	144	8
							Cardiff C (loan)	4	—
							Scunthorpe U	102	8
McFarlane Andy	6 3	13 07	F	30 11 66	Wolverhampton	Cradley T	Portsmouth	2	—
							Swansea C	55	8
							Scunthorpe U	46	16
Murfin Andrew†			M	26 11 77	Doncaster		Scunthorpe U	1	—
Nicholson Max*	5 11	12 07	F	3 10 71	Leeds	Trainee	Doncaster R	27	2
							Hereford U	63	7
							Torquay U	1	—
							Scunthorpe U	51	5
Paterson Jamie	5 4	10 04	F	26 4 73	Dumfries	Trainee	Halifax T	86	18
							Falkirk	4	—
							Scunthorpe U	26	2
Samways Mark	6 3	13 07	G	11 11 68	Doncaster	Trainee	Doncaster R	121	—
							Scunthorpe U (loan)	8	—
							Scunthorpe U	147	—
Thornber Stephen‡	5 9	11 07	M	11 10 65	Dewsbury	Local	Halifax T	104	4
							Swansea C	117	6
							Blackpool	24	—
							Scunthorpe U	77	7
Turnbull Lee	6 0	12 07	M	27 9 67	Stockton	Local	Middlesbrough	16	4
							Aston Villa	—	—
							Doncaster R	123	21
							Chesterfield	87	26
							Doncaster R	11	1
							Wycombe W	11	1
							Scunthorpe U (loan)	10	3
							Scunthorpe U	23	3

Varadi Imre‡	5 9	12 03	F	8 7 59	Paddington	Letchworth GC	Sheffield U	10	4
							Everton	26	6
							Newcastle U	81	39
							Sheffield W	76	33
							WBA	32	9
							Manchester C	65	26
							Sheffield W	22	3
							Leeds U	26	5
							Luton T (loan)	6	1
							Oxford U (loan)	5	—
							Rotherham U	67	25
							Mansfield T	1	—
							Scunthorpe U	2	—
Walsh Michael	6 0	12 07	D	5 8 77	Rotherham	Trainee	Scunthorpe U	28	—
Wilson Paul	5 11	12 00	D	2 8 68	Bradford	Trainee	Huddersfield T	15	—
							Norwich C		
							Northampton T	141	6
							Halifax T	45	7
							Burnley	31	—
							York C	22	—
							Scunthorpe U	40	1
Young Stuart‡	5 10	12 10	F	16 12 72	Hull	Arsenal	Hull C	19	2
							Northampton T	8	2
							Scarborough	41	10
							Scunthorpe U	28	3

Trainees
Heath, Simon T; Spark, Phillip J; Wilson, Peter E; Ziccardi, Mariano L.

Non-Contract
Murfin, Andrew J; Wilson, Paul D.

Associated Schoolboys who have accepted the club's offer of a Traineeship/Contract
Mitchell, Barry S; Render, Craig; Stones, Craig.

SHEFFIELD UNITED

Andison Gary*	5 11	12 00	D	12 12 76	Gateshead	Trainee	Sheffield U	—	—
Anthony Graham	5 8	10 08	M	9 8 75	Jarrow	Trainee	Sheffield U	1	—
							Scarborough (loan)	2	—
Beard Mark	5 11	11 03	D	8 10 74	Roehampton	Trainee	Millwall	45	2
							Sheffield U	20	—
Bettney Chris			M	27 10 77	Chesterfield	Trainee	Sheffield U	—	—
Bibbo Sal*	6 2	13 05	G	24 8 74	Basingstoke	Bournemouth	Sheffield U	—	—
							Chesterfield (loan)	1	—
Cowans Gordon*	5 7	10 07	M	27 10 58	Durham	Apprentice	Aston Villa	286	42
							Bari	94	3
							Aston Villa	117	7
							Blackburn R	50	2
							Aston Villa	11	—
							Derby Co	36	—
							Wolverhampton W	37	—
							Sheffield U	20	—
Dyer Liam			M	2 5 78	Doncaster	Trainee	Sheffield U	—	—
Evans Tom‡	6 0	12 10	G	31 12 76	Doncaster	Trainee	Sheffield U	—	—
Flo Jostein‡	6 4	15 03	F	3 10 64	Norway	Sogndal	Sheffield U	84	19
Gayle Brian*	6 2	13 12	D	6 3 65	Kingston		Wimbledon	83	3
							Manchester C	55	3
							Ipswich T	58	4
							Sheffield U	117	9
Hartfield Charles	6 0	13 00	D	4 9 71	London	Trainee	Arsenal	—	—
							Sheffield U	54	1
Hawes Steve	5 8	11 04	M	17 7 78	Wycombe	Trainee	Sheffield U	2	—
Hocking Matthew			M	30 1 78	Boston	Trainee	Sheffield U	—	—
Hodgson Doug	6 2	13 09	M	27 2 69	Frankston	Heidelberg	Sheffield U	17	—
							Plymouth Arg (loan)	5	—
Hutchison Don	6 2	11 04	F	9 5 71	Gateshead	Trainee	Hartlepool U	24	2
							Liverpool	45	7
							West Ham U	35	11
							Sheffield U	19	2
Kelly Alan	6 3	14 03	G	11 8 68	Preston	Trainee	Preston NE	142	—
							Sheffield U	136	—
Marston Marvin*	6 5	13 02	D	27 8 76	London	Notts Co	Sheffield U	—	—
Nilsen Roger	5 11	12 02	D	8 8 69	Norway	Viking Stavanger	Sheffield U	94	—

Patterson Mark	5 6	11 04	M	24 5 65	Darwen	Apprentice	Blackburn R	101	20
							Preston NE	55	19
							Bury	42	10
							Bolton W	169	11
							Sheffield U	21	2
Pearson Gary‡	5 10	12 05	M	7 12 76	Co Durham	Trainee	Sheffield U	—	—
Powell Craig‡	5 10	12 04	F	10 6 77	Doncaster	Trainee	Sheffield U	—	—
Quinn Wayne	5 10	11 08	M	19 11 76	Cornwall		Sheffield U	—	—
Reed John	5 8	11 07	F	27 8 72	Rotherham	Trainee	Sheffield U	15	2
							Scarborough (loan)	14	6
							Scarborough (loan)	6	—
							Darlington (loan)	10	2
							Mansfield T (loan)	13	2
Scott Andy	6 1	11 05	F	2 8 72	Epsom	Sutton U	Sheffield U	61	5
Short Chris	5 10	12 04	D	9 5 70	Munster	Pickering T	Scarborough	43	1
							Manchester U (loan)	—	—
							Notts Co	94	2
							Huddersfield T (loan)	6	—
							Sheffield U	15	—
Starbuck Phil	5 10	13 03	F	24 11 68	Nottingham	Apprentice	Nottingham F	36	2
							Birmingham C (loan)	3	—
							Hereford U (loan)	6	—
							Blackburn R (loan)	6	1
							Huddersfield T	137	36
							Sheffield U	34	2
							Bristol C (loan)	5	1
Taylor Gareth	6 2	12 05	F	25 2 73	Weston Super Mare	Southampton	Bristol R	47	16
							Crystal Palace	20	1
							Sheffield U	10	2
Thomson Martin‡	5 10	11 08	D	3 10 74	Bradford	Trainee	Sheffield U	—	—
Thorpe Andrew*	5 11	12 02	D	9 3 77	Sheffield	Trainee	Sheffield U	—	—
Tracey Simon	6 0	13 08	G	9 12 67	Woolwich	Apprentice	Wimbledon	1	—
							Sheffield U	154	—
							Manchester C (loan)	3	—
							Norwich C (loan)	1	—
							Wimbledon (loan)	1	—
Vine Darren*	5 11	12 08	F	22 12 76	Sheffield	Trainee	Sheffield U	—	—
Vonk Michael	6 3	13 05	D	28 10 68	Alkmaar	SW/Dordrecht	Manchester C	91	3
							Oldham Ath (loan)	5	1
							Sheffield U	17	—
Walker Andy	5 8	10 07	F	6 4 65	Glasgow	Baillieston J	Motherwell	76	17
							Celtic	108	30
							Newcastle U (loan)	2	—
							Bolton W	67	44
							Celtic	42	9
							Sheffield U	14	8
Ward Mitch	5 8	10 12	M	19 6 71	Sheffield	Trainee	Sheffield U	114	6
							Crewe Alex (loan)	4	1
White David	6 1	12 09	F	30 10 67	Manchester		Manchester C	285	79
							Leeds U	42	9
							Sheffield U	28	7
Whitehouse Dane	5 9	11 10	M	14 10 70	Sheffield	Trainee	Sheffield U	184	30
Wood Paul			M	14 10 77	Sheffield	Trainee	Sheffield U	—	—

Trainees
Capper, David A; Collins, Michael T; Davies, Kevin J; Elton, Paul; Heritage, Paul W; Hewitt, Craig P G; James, Owen; Lewin, Karlda D; Litten, Thomas N; Ludlam, Ryan; Mays, Ross A; Metcalf, Ian R; Mincher, Kevin L; Spooner, Daniel; Summerell, Stewart D; Tracey, Richard S.

Associated Schoolboys
Burke, Paul; Camm, Liam M; East, Paul M; Gray, Jonathan; Henderson, Ewan; Hudson, Jamie R; Joel, Christopher D; Mosley, Matthew J; Munnings, Simon; Nixon, Adam R C; Parkin, Andrew T; Patterson, Jamie; Strickland, Steven J.

Associated Schoolboys who have accepted the club's offer of a Traineeship/Contract
Bamforth, Liam A; Doane, Ben N; Eastwood, Mark; Johnson, David S M; Morris, Lee; Strickland, Robert P; Thurlby, Simon E; Woodhouse, Curtis.

SHEFFIELD WEDNESDAY

Aldous Richard*	6 2	13 00	G	2 9 76	Sheffield	Trainee	Sheffield W	—	—
Atherton Peter	5 7	13 07	D	6 4 70	Wigan	Trainee	Wigan Ath	149	1
							Coventry C	114	—
							Sheffield W	77	1
Bailey Gavin*	5 8	11 07	F	10 10 76	Chesterfield	Trainee	Sheffield W	—	—
Barker Richard	6 1	13 05	F	30 5 75	Sheffield	Trainee	Sheffield W	—	—
							Doncaster R (loan)	6	—

Name			Pos	Date	Birthplace	Source	Club	Apps	Gls
Batty Mark			M	30 1 79	Nottingham	Trainee	Sheffield W	—	—
Blinker Regi	5 8	11 07	F	4 6 69	Surinam		Feyenoord	51	3
							Den Bosch	25	6
							Feyenoord	187	42
							Sheffield W	9	2
Bright Mark	6 1	13 00	F	6 6 62	Stoke	Leek T	Port Vale	29	10
							Leicester C	42	6
							Crystal Palace	227	92
							Sheffield W	132	48
Briscoe Lee	5 11	11 05	F	30 9 75	Pontefract	Trainee	Sheffield W	33	—
Burrows Marc*	5 9	10 00	D	20 12 75	Sheffield	Trainee	Sheffield W	—	—
Daly Matthew	6 3	13 07	F	8 10 76	Derby		Sheffield W	—	—
Degryse Marc	5 8	10 13	F	4 9 65	Belgium	Ardooie	FC Brugge	182	93
							Anderlecht	170	65
							Sheffield W	34	8
Donaldson O'Neill	5 11	11 07	F	24 11 69	Birmingham	Hinckley	Shrewsbury T	28	4
							Doncaster R	9	2
							Mansfield T (loan)	4	6
							Sheffield W	4	1
Faulkner David*	6 1	12 13	D	8 10 75	Sheffield	Trainee	Sheffield W	—	—
Guest Mark*	5 8	10 13	F	21 1 76	Mexborough	Trainee	Sheffield W	—	—
Hirst David	6 0	13 08	F	7 12 67	Barnsley	Apprentice	Barnsley	28	9
							Sheffield W	263	100
Holmes Darren*	5 10	11 07	M	30 1 75	Sheffield	Trainee	Sheffield W	—	—
Humphreys Richie			M	30 11 77	Sheffield	Trainee	Sheffield W	5	—
Hyde Graham	5 8	11 11	M	10 11 70	Doncaster	Trainee	Sheffield W	130	8
Ingesson Klas‡	6 3	14 00	M	20 8 68	Odeshog	PSV Eindhoven	Sheffield W	18	2
Jackson Kirk‡	5 11	11 06	F	16 10 76	Barnsley	Trainee	Sheffield W	—	—
Jones Ryan	6 3	13 08	M	23 7 73	Sheffield	Trainee	Sheffield W	41	6
							Scunthorpe U (loan)	11	3
Key Lance*	6 3	14 13	G	13 5 68	Kettering	Histon	Sheffield W	—	—
							York C (loan)	—	—
							Oldham Ath (loan)	2	—
							Portsmouth (loan)	—	—
							Oxford U (loan)	6	—
							Lincoln C (loan)	5	—
							Hartlepool U (loan)	1	—
							Rochdale (loan)	14	—
Kovacevic Darko	6 2	12 06	F	18 11 73	Yugoslavia	Red Star Belgrade	Sheffield W	16	4
Linighan Brian	6 3	12 10	D	2 11 73	Hartlepool	Trainee	Sheffield W	1	—
Ludlam Craig*	5 11	11 05	M	8 11 76	Sheffield	Trainee	Sheffield W	—	—
Mason Richard*	5 11	11 11	D	5 6 77	Sheffield	Trainee	Sheffield W	—	—
Newsome Jon	6 3	13 10	D	6 9 70	Sheffield	Trainee	Sheffield W	7	—
							Leeds U	76	3
							Norwich C	62	7
							Sheffield W	8	1
Nicol Steve	5 10	12 06	D	11 12 61	Irvine	Ayr U BC	Ayr U	70	7
							Liverpool	343	36
							Notts Co	32	2
							Sheffield W	19	—
Nolan Ian	5 11	11 11	D	9 7 70	Liverpool	Marine	Tranmere R	88	1
							Sheffield W	71	3
Pass Steven*	5 11	11 06	F	15 9 76	Leigh	Trainee	Sheffield W	—	—
Pembridge Mark	5 7	11 11	M	29 11 70	Merthyr Tydfil	Trainee	Luton T	60	6
							Derby Co	110	28
							Sheffield W	25	1
Platts Mark§			M	23 5 79	Sheffield	Trainee	Sheffield W	2	—
Poric Adem	5 10	12 06	M	22 4 73	London	St George's Budapest	Sheffield W	10	—
Pressman Kevin	6 1	14 13	G	6 11 67	Fareham	Apprentice	Sheffield W	158	—
							Stoke C (loan)	4	—
Scargill Jon	6 1	14 02	G	9 4 77	Dewsbury	Trainee	Sheffield W	—	—
Sheridan John	5 10	12 01	M	1 10 64	Stretford	Local	Leeds U	230	47
							Nottingham F	—	—
							Sheffield W	195	25
							Birmingham C (loan)	2	—
Smith Gavin			F	24 9 77	Sheffield	Trainee	Sheffield W	—	—
Stefanovic Dejan	6 2	12 10	D	28 10 74	Yugoslavia	Red Star Belgrade	Sheffield W	6	—
Stewart Simon*	6 2	13 08	D	1 11 73	Leeds	Trainee	Sheffield W	6	—
							Shrewsbury T (loan)	4	—
Sykes Paul*	6 2	12 00	D	13 1 77	Pontefract	Trainee	Sheffield W	—	—

Waddle Chris	6 1	13 03	F	14 12 60	Hedworth	Tow Law T	Newcastle U	170	46
							Tottenham H	138	33
							Marseille	107	22
							Sheffield W	109	10
Walker Des	5 11	11 11	D	26 11 65	Hackney	Apprentice	Nottingham F	264	1
							Sampdoria	30	—
							Sheffield W	116	—
Whittingham Guy	5 10	12 00	F	10 11 64	Evesham	Yeovil and Army	Portsmouth	160	88
							Aston Villa	25	5
							Wolverhampton W (loan)	13	8
							Sheffield W	50	15
Williams Michael	5 11	11 04	M	21 11 69	Bradford	Maltby	Sheffield W	22	1
							Halifax T (loan)	9	1
Woods Chris‡	6 2	14 12	G	14 11 59	Boston	Apprentice	Nottingham F	—	—
							QPR	63	—
							Norwich C (loan)	10	—
							Norwich C	206	—
							Rangers	173	—
							Sheffield W	107	—
							Reading (loan)	5	—

Trainees
Bowler, Martin S; Hiner, Daniel; Hutchinson, Sean A; James, Mark B; Kirkpatrick, Matthew R; Lenagh, Steven M; Platts, Mark A; Pringle, Alan J; Sharman, Samuel J; Simpkins, James M; Simpkins, Michael J; Smith, Daniel J; Stevens, Andrew E; Thorpe, Steven M; Todd, Luke G; Weaver, Simon D; Wood, Scott R; Woodward, Jonathan J.

Associated Schoolboys
Coubrough, James R; Davison, Mark J; Hamshaw, Matthew T; Haslam, Nathan L; Hutton, John; Kotylo, Krystof J; McDermott, Darren G; Nicholson, Kevin J; Quinn, Andrew J; Sherwood, David.

Associated Schoolboys who have accepted the club's offer of a Traineeship/Contract
Bettney, Scott; Davis, Ryan L; Harkin, Thomas E; Haslam, Steven R; Hibbins, John J; King, Christopher; Powell, Vill W; Siddall, Christopher J; Wainwright, Jody.

SHREWSBURY TOWN

Anthrobus Steve	6 3	14 11	F	10 11 68	Lewisham		Millwall	21	4
							Southend U (loan)	—	—
							Wimbledon	28	—
							Peterborough U (loan)	2	—
							Chester C (loan)	7	—
							Shrewsbury T	39	10
Berkley Austin	5 8	11 06	M	28 1 73	Gravesend	Trainee	Gillingham	3	—
							Swindon T	1	—
							Shrewsbury T	38	1
Clarke Tim*	6 3	13 07	G	19 9 68	Stourbridge	Halesowen	Coventry C	—	—
							Huddersfield T	70	—
							Rochdale (loan)	2	—
							Shrewsbury T	31	—
Cope James§			M	4 10 77	Solihull	Trainee	Shrewsbury T	1	—
Currie Darren	5 7	11 10	M	29 11 74	Hampstead	Trainee	West Ham U	—	—
							Shrewsbury T (loan)	17	2
							Leyton Orient (loan)	10	—
							Shrewsbury T	13	2
Dempsey Mark	5 6	12 05	M	10 12 72	Dublin	Trainee	Gillingham	48	2
							Leyton Orient	43	1
							Shrewsbury T	28	2
Edwards Paul	6 0	13 02	G	22 2 65	Liverpool	St. Helens T	Crewe Alex	29	—
							Shrewsbury T	146	—
Evans Paul	5 6	12 00	M	1 9 74	Oswestry	Trainee	Shrewsbury T	85	8
Grenham Tony‡			G	22 6 77	Brighton	Trainee	Shrewsbury T	—	—
Hughes Mark‡	6 0	13 00	D	3 2 62	Port Talbot	Apprentice	Bristol R	74	3
							Torquay U (loan)	9	1
							Swansea C	12	—
							Bristol C	22	—
							Tranmere R	266	9
							Shrewsbury T	22	—
Jackson David§			D	22 8 78	Solihull	Trainee	Shrewsbury T	1	—
Jefferis Martin‡			D	22 8 76	Shrewsbury	Trainee	Shrewsbury T	—	—
King Nathan*	6 0	12 06	D	1 8 75	West Bromwich	Trainee	Shrewsbury T	—	—
Lynch Tom	6 0	13 03	D	10 10 64	Limerick	Limerick	Sunderland	4	—
							Shrewsbury T	234	14
Martin Lee*	5 10	12 00	M	3 10 76	Birmingham	Trainee	Shrewsbury T	—	—
Reed Ian	5 8	11 04	M	4 9 75	Lichfield	Trainee	Shrewsbury T	15	2

Player	Ht	Wt	Pos	DoB	Birthplace	From	Club	App	Gls
Rowbotham Darren	5 10	12 13	M	22 10 66	Cardiff	Trainee	Plymouth Arg	46	2
							Exeter C	118	47
							Torquay U	14	3
							Birmingham C	36	6
							Hereford U (loan)	8	2
							Mansfield T (loan)	4	—
							Crewe Alex	61	21
							Shrewsbury T	26	8
Scott Richard	5 9	12 08	D	29 9 74	Dudley	Trainee	Birmingham C	12	—
							Shrewsbury T	44	7
Seabury Kevin	5 9	11 11	D	24 11 73	Shrewsbury	Trainee	Shrewsbury T	65	—
Simkin Darren	6 0	13 08	D	24 3 70	Walsall	Blakenall	Wolverhampton W	15	—
							Shrewsbury T	12	—
Spink Dean	6 1	14 08	F	22 1 67	Birmingham	Halesowen	Aston Villa	—	—
							Scarborough (loan)	3	2
							Bury (loan)	6	1
							Shrewsbury T	232	48
Stevens Ian	5 9	12 04	F	21 10 66	Malta	Trainee	Preston NE	11	2
							Stockport Co	2	—
						Lancaster C	Bolton W	47	7
							Bury	110	38
							Shrewsbury T	70	20
Summerfield Kevin*	5 11	11 00	M	7 1 59	Walsall	Apprentice	WBA	9	4
							Birmingham C	5	1
							Walsall	54	17
							Cardiff C	10	1
							Plymouth Arg	139	26
							Exeter C (loan)	4	—
							Shrewsbury T	163	22
Taylor Mark	5 9	12 05	M	22 2 66	Walsall	Local	Walsall	113	4
							Sheffield W	9	—
							Shrewsbury T (loan)	19	2
							Shrewsbury T	194	12
Walton David	6 1	14 01	D	10 4 73	Bedlingham	Trainee	Sheffield U	—	—
							Shrewsbury T	98	8
Whiston Peter	6 0	12 02	D	4 1 68	Widnes		Plymouth Arg	10	—
							Torquay U (loan)	8	1
							Torquay U	32	—
							Exeter C	85	7
							Southampton	1	—
							Shrewsbury T	28	2
Withe Chris*	5 10	11 12	D	25 9 62	Liverpool	Apprentice	Newcastle U	2	—
							Bradford C	143	2
							Notts Co	80	3
							Bury	31	1
							Chester C (loan)	2	—
							Mansfield T (loan)	11	—
							Mansfield T	65	5
							Shrewsbury T	89	2
Woods Ray*	5 10	11 09	F	7 6 65	Birkenhead	Apprentice	Tranmere R	7	2
						Colne D	Wigan Ath	28	3
							Coventry C	21	1
							Wigan Ath (loan)	13	—
							Shrewsbury T (loan)	9	1
							Shrewsbury T	42	—
Wray Shaun	6 0	12 11	F	14 3 78	Birmingham	Trainee	Shrewsbury T	3	—

Trainees
Berry, Paul; Briscoe, Anthony M; Campbell, William J; Clark, David M; Cope, James A; Corns, Stuart R; Dignam, Michael G; Green, Adam B; Hill, Paul D; Jackson, David K G; Murrell, Scott N; Pemberton, Stephen J; Smith, Dean; Stephens, Philip P; Turpie, Sam R; Ward, Nicholas J.

Associated Schoolboys
Green, Stewart C; Harman, Jeremy; Jones, Matthew N; Neville, Mark; Sidaway, Carl J; Tilt, Matthew A; Woodley, Frederick R.

SOUTHAMPTON

Player	Ht	Wt	Pos	DoB	Birthplace	From	Club	App	Gls
Allan Derek*	6 0	12 01	D	24 12 74	Irving	Ayr U BC	Ayr U	5	—
							Southampton	1	—
							Brighton & HA (loan)	8	—
Beasant Dave	6 4	14 03	G	20 3 59	Ealing	Edgware T	Wimbledon	340	—
							Newcastle U	20	—
							Chelsea	133	—
							Grimsby T (loan)	6	—
							Wolverhampton W (loan)	4	—
							Southampton	74	—
Benali Francis	5 10	10 13	D	30 12 68	Southampton	Apprentice	Southampton	202	—
Bennett Frankie	5 7	12 01	F	3 1 69	Birmingham	Halesowen T	Southampton	19	1

Player	Ht	Wt	Pos	Born	Birthplace	Source	Club	Apps	Gls
Blamey Nathan	5 10	11 05	D	10 6 77	Plymouth	Trainee	Southampton	—	—
Charlton Simon	5 8	11 10	D	25 10 71	Huddersfield	Trainee	Huddersfield T	124	1
							Southampton	84	2
Dodd Jason	5 11	12 03	D	2 11 70	Bath	Bath C	Southampton	172	5
Everest Anthony‡	5 6	10 00	M	20 9 76	Maidstone	Trainee	Southampton	—	—
Grobbelaar Bruce*	6 1	14 02	G	6 10 57	Durban	Vancouver Whitecaps	Crewe Alex	24	1
							Liverpool	440	—
							Stoke C (loan)	4	—
							Southampton	32	—
Hall Richard	6 2	13 11	D	14 3 72	Ipswich	Trainee	Scunthorpe U	22	3
							Southampton	126	12
Heaney Neil	5 9	11 07	F	3 11 71	Middlesbrough	Trainee	Arsenal	7	—
							Hartlepool U (loan)	3	—
							Cambridge U (loan)	13	4
							Southampton	53	4
Hughes David	5 10	11 08	M	30 12 72	St Albans	Trainee	Southampton	25	3
Le Tissier Matthew	6 1	13 08	F	14 10 68	Guernsey	Trainee	Southampton	326	127
Liney Andrew‡	5 11	13 02	M	18 7 77	Frimley	Trainee	Southampton	—	—
Maddison Neil	5 11	11 06	M	2 10 69	Darlington	Trainee	Southampton	145	17
Magilton Jim	6 1	14 02	M	6 5 69	Belfast	Apprentice	Liverpool	—	—
							Oxford U	150	34
							Southampton	88	9
Monkou Ken	6 3	14 05	D	29 11 64	Surinam	Feyenoord	Chelsea	94	2
							Southampton	131	8
Moss Neil	6 2	12 13	G	10 5 75	New Milton	Trainee	Bournemouth	22	—
							Southampton	—	—
Neilson Alan	5 11	12 09	D	26 9 72	Wegburg	Trainee	Newcastle U	42	1
							Southampton	18	—
Oakley Matthew	5 10	12 01	F	17 8 77	Peterborough	Trainee	Southampton	11	—
Robinson Matthew	5 10	11 03	M	23 12 74	Exeter	Trainee	Southampton	6	—
Sheerin Paul	5 10	12 00	M	28 8 74	Edinburgh	Whitehill Welfare	Alloa	9	—
							Southampton	—	—
Shipperley Neil	6 1	13 11	F	30 10 74	Chatham	Trainee	Chelsea	37	7
							Watford (loan)	6	1
							Southampton	56	11
Tisdale Paul	5 9	11 13	M	14 1 73	Malta	School	Southampton	16	1
							Northampton T (loan)	5	—
Venison Barry	5 10	12 03	D	16 8 64	Consett	Apprentice	Sunderland	173	2
							Liverpool	110	1
							Newcastle U	109	1
						Galatasaray	Southampton	22	—
Walters Mark‡	5 9	11 08	M	2 6 64	Birmingham	Apprentice	Aston Villa	181	39
							Rangers	106	32
							Liverpool	94	14
							Stoke C (loan)	9	2
							Wolverhampton W (loan)	11	3
							Southampton	5	—
Warren Christer	5 10	11 04	M	10 10 74	Bournemouth	Cheltenham T	Southampton	7	—
Watson Gordon	5 10	12 09	F	20 3 71	Sidcup	Trainee	Charlton Ath	31	7
							Sheffield W	66	15
							Southampton	37	6
Widdrington Tommy	5 10	11 12	D	1 10 71	Newcastle	Trainee	Southampton	75	3
							Wigan Ath (loan)	6	—

Trainees
Basham, Steven; Batchelor, Adam; Care, Simon J; Catley, Andrew; Davis, Neil; Deegan, Christopher M; Desborough, Daniel; Flahavan, Darryl J; Hazlehurst, Daniel R; Homer, Gareth; Piper, David; Spedding, Duncan; Stockley, Sam; Sullivan, Andrew; Warner, Philip; Williams, Andrew P.

Associated Schoolboys
Ashford, Ryan M; Blake, Dean; Canavan, Michael G; Cleife, Lloyd R; Copp, Christopher G; Curtis, Darren D; Hayden, Ben; Jordan, James A; Lashley, Simon D; Liddon, Paul G; Madgwick, Benjamin; Malessa, Antony G; Morse, Richard; Sims, Adam D; Wallace, Adam; Waller, Andrew P; Webber, Lloyd E; Wilson, Richard S.

Associated Schoolboys who have accepted the club's offer of a Traineeship/Contract
Bevan, Scott; Bradley, Shane; Bridge, Wayne; Collins, Christopher; Gibbons, Kevin; Jenkins, Stephen M; McCarthy, Craig.

SOUTHEND UNITED

Player	Ht	Wt	Pos	Born	Birthplace	Source	Club	Apps	Gls
Belsvik Peter‡			F	2 10 67	Lillehammer	IK Start	Southend U	3	1
Bodley Mick	6 1	13 01	D	14 9 67	Hayes	Apprentice	Chelsea	6	1
							Northampton T	20	—
							Barnet	69	3
							Southend U	67	2
							Gillingham (loan)	7	—
							Birmingham C (loan)	3	—

Name			Pos	DOB	Birthplace	Source	Club	Apps	Gls
Boere Jeroen	6 3	13 02	F	18 11 67	Arnheim	Go Ahead	West Ham U	25	6
							Portsmouth (loan)	5	—
							WBA (loan)	5	—
							Crystal Palace	8	1
							Southend U	6	2
Byrne Paul	5 11	13 00	M	30 6 72	Dublin	Trainee	Oxford U	6	—
						Bangor	Celtic	28	4
							Brighton & HA (loan)	8	1
							Southend U	41	5
Dublin Keith	6 0	12 10	D	29 1 66	Wycombe	Apprentice	Chelsea	51	—
							Brighton & HA	132	5
							Watford	168	2
							Southend U	83	5
Foot Danny*	6 0	11 04	D	6 9 75	Edmonton	Tottenham H	Southend U	3	—
Gridelet Phil	5 11	13 00	M	30 4 67	Edgware	Barnet	Barnsley	6	—
							Rotherham U (loan)	9	—
							Southend U	98	7
Hails Julian	5 10	11 02	F	20 11 67	Lincoln	Hemel Hempstead	Fulham	109	12
							Southend U	68	6
Hayes Martin‡	6 0	12 04	F	21 3 66	Walthamstow	Apprentice	Arsenal	102	26
							Celtic	7	—
							Wimbledon (loan)	2	—
							Swansea C	61	8
							Southend U	—	—
Hone Mark*	6 1	13 01	D	31 3 68	Croydon	Trainee	Crystal Palace	4	—
						Welling	Southend U	56	—
Lapper Mike	6 0	12 02	D	28 8 70	California	USSF	Southend U	24	—
Marsh Mike	5 8	11 00	F	21 7 69	Liverpool	Kirkby T	Liverpool	69	2
							West Ham U	49	1
							Coventry C	15	2
						Galatasaray	Southend U	40	5
McNally Mark	5 10	12 02	D	10 3 71	Bellshill	Celtic BC	Celtic	123	3
							Southend U	20	2
Morrish Luke*	6 1	11 00	D	14 11 77	Greenwich	Trainee	Southend U	—	—
Perkins Declan*	5 11	12 04	F	17 10 75	Ilford	Trainee	Southend U	6	—
							Cambridge U (loan)	2	1
Rammell Andy	6 2	13 10	F	10 2 67	Nuneaton	Atherstone U	Manchester U	—	—
							Barnsley	185	44
							Southend U	7	2
Roche David	6 0	13 02	M	13 12 70	Newcastle	Trainee	Newcastle U	36	—
							Peterborough U (loan)	4	—
							Doncaster R	50	8
							Southend U	4	—
Roget Leo	6 1	12 02	D	1 8 77	Ilford	Trainee	Southend U	8	1
Royce Simon	6 2	12 10	G	9 9 71	Forest Gate	Heybridge Swifts	Southend U	69	—
Sansome Paul	6 0	13 06	G	6 10 61	N Addington	Crystal Palace	Millwall	156	—
							Southend U	305	—
							Birmingham C (loan)	1	—
Stimson Mark	5 10	12 06	D	27 12 67	Plaistow	Trainee	Tottenham H	2	—
							Leyton Orient (loan)	10	—
							Gillingham (loan)	18	—
							Newcastle U	86	2
							Portsmouth (loan)	4	—
							Portsmouth	58	2
							Barnet (loan)	5	—
							Southend U	10	—
Sussex Andy	6 3	13 08	M	23 11 64	Islington	Apprentice	Orient	144	17
							Crewe Alex	102	24
							Southend U	76	14
							Brentford (loan)	3	—
Thomson Andy	5 10	10 12	F	1 4 71	Motherwell	Jerviston BC	Q of S	175	93
							Southend U	72	17
Tilson Steve	5 11	12 10	M	27 7 66	Wickford	Burnham	Southend U	211	25
							Brentford (loan)	2	—
Whelan Ronnie	5 9	12 03	M	25 9 61	Dublin	Home Farm	Liverpool	362	46
							Southend U	34	1
Willis Roger*	6 1	12 00	D	17 6 67	Sheffield		Grimsby T	9	—
						Barnet	Barnet	44	13
							Watford	36	2
							Birmingham C	19	5
							Southend U	31	7

Trainees
Farmer, Stephen P; Kinseley, Mark; Leggatt, Philip D; Pike, Gregory J; Taylor, Paul S.

Non-Contract
Jones, Mark.

Associated Schoolboys who have accepted the club's offer of a Traineeship/Contract
Morrish, Adam; Thurley, Westley S.

STOCKPORT COUNTY

Player	Ht	Wt	Pos	Born	Birthplace	Source	Club	Apps	Gls
Allen Gavin‡	6 0	10 05	F	17 6 76	Bangor	Trainee	Tranmere R	—	—
							Stockport Co	—	—
Armstrong Alun	6 0	12 00	F	22 2 75	Gateshead	School	Newcastle U	—	—
							Stockport Co	91	27
Beaumont Chris	5 11	11 07	F	5 12 65	Sheffield	Denaby	Rochdale	34	7
							Stockport Co	258	39
Bennett Tom	5 11	11 08	D	12 12 69	Falkirk	Trainee	Aston Villa	—	—
							Wolverhampton W	115	2
							Stockport Co	24	1
Bound Matthew	6 2	13 09	D	9 11 72	Trowbridge	Trainee	Southampton	5	—
							Hull C (loan)	7	1
							Stockport Co	40	5
							Lincoln C (loan)	4	—
Connelly Sean	5 10	11 10	D	26 6 70	Sheffield	Hallam	Stockport Co	121	—
Croft Brian‡	5 9	10 10	M	27 9 67	Chester	Trainee	Chester C	59	3
							Cambridge U	17	2
							Chester C	114	3
							QPR	—	—
							Shrewsbury T (loan)	4	—
							Torquay U	1	—
							Stockport Co	3	—
Davenport Peter‡	5 10	11 06	F	24 3 61	Birkenhead	Everton	Nottingham F	118	54
							Manchester U	92	22
							Middlesbrough	59	7
							Sunderland	99	15
							Airdrie	38	9
							St Johnstone	22	4
							Stockport Co	6	1
Dickins Matt*	6 4	14 00	G	3 9 70	Sheffield	Trainee	Sheffield U	—	—
							Leyton Orient (loan)	—	—
							Lincoln C	27	—
							Blackburn R	1	—
							Blackpool (loan)	19	—
							Lincoln C (loan)	—	—
							Grimsby T (loan)	—	—
							Rochdale (loan)	4	—
							Stockport Co	13	—
Dinning Tony	5 11	12 00	D	12 4 75	Wallsend	Trainee	Newcastle U	—	—
							Stockport Co	50	2
Durkan Kieron	5 10	10 05	M	1 12 73	Chester	Trainee	Wrexham	50	3
							Stockport Co	16	—
Eckhardt Jeff	6 0	11 07	D	7 10 65	Sheffield		Sheffield U	74	2
							Fulham	249	25
							Stockport Co	62	7
Edwards Neil	5 8	11 02	G	5 12 70	Aberdare	Trainee	Leeds U	—	—
							Huddersfield T (loan)	—	—
							Stockport Co	164	—
Flynn Mike	6 0	11 02	D	23 2 69	Oldham	Trainee	Oldham Ath	40	1
							Norwich C	—	—
							Preston NE	136	7
							Stockport Co	145	9
Gannon Jim	6 2	13 00	D	7 9 68	Southwark	Dundalk	Sheffield U	—	—
							Halifax T (loan)	2	—
							Stockport Co	240	47
							Notts Co (loan)	2	—
Jeffers John	5 10	11 10	F	5 10 68	Liverpool	Trainee	Liverpool	—	—
							Port Vale	180	10
							Shrewsbury T (loan)	3	1
							Stockport Co	23	3
Johnson Phil*	5 7	10 06	D	7 4 75	Liverpool	Trainee	Tranmere R	—	—
							Stockport Co	—	—
Landon Richard	6 3	13 05	F	22 3 70	Worthing	Bedworth U	Plymouth Arg	30	12
							Stockport Co	11	5
Marsden Chris	6 0	10 12	M	3 1 69	Sheffield	Trainee	Sheffield U	16	1
							Huddersfield T	121	9
							Coventry C (loan)	7	—
							Wolverhampton W	8	—
							Notts Co	10	—
							Stockport Co	20	1
Marshall Lee*	5 9	9 12	F	1 8 75	Nottingham	Trainee Grantham	Nottingham F	—	—
							Stockport Co	1	—
Mike Adie	6 0	11 06	F	16 11 73	Manchester	Trainee	Manchester C	16	2
							Bury (loan)	7	1
							Stockport Co	8	—

Mutch Andy	5 10	11 00	F	28 12 63	Liverpool	Southport	Wolverhampton W	289	96
							Swindon T	50	6
							Wigan Ath (loan)	7	1
							Stockport Co	11	4
Oliver Michael‡	5 10	12 04	M	2 8 75	Cleveland	Trainee	Middlesbrough	—	—
							Stockport Co	22	1
Todd Lee	5 5	10 03	D	7 3 72	Hartlepool	Hartlepool U	Stockport Co	184	2
Ware Paul	5 9	11 05	M	7 11 70	Congleton	Trainee	Stoke C	115	10
							Stockport Co	46	4
Williams Marc‡	5 11	11 10	F	8 2 73	Bangor	Bangor C	Stockport Co	18	1

Trainees
Ansell, Gary S; Atterton, Lee M; Baker, Andrew C; Barrow, Paul S; Bennett, Thomas W F; Carden, Simon; Cross, Jonathan R; Gray, Kevin J; Hare, Rudi J; Honeyman, Ryan M; Jones, Lea D; Jones, Paul H; Kilduff, Daniel T; King, John P; Knight, Robert T; Lewis, Gary S; Shearer, Lee C; Smith, Stephen P; Yongo, Daniel T T A.

Non-Contract
O'Driscoll, Barry J.

Associated Schoolboys
Brown, Clive C; France, Oliver J.

Associated Schoolboys who have accepted the club's offer of a Traineeship/Contract
Green, Robert J.

STOKE CITY

Bailey Mark*	5 9	10 12	M	12 8 76	Stoke	Trainee	Stoke C	—	—
Beeston Carl	5 10	12 03	M	30 6 67	Stoke	Apprentice	Stoke C	218	13
Birch Mark	5 10	12 05	D	5 1 77	Stoke	Trainee	Stoke C	—	—
Callan Aiden	5 9	10 12	M	8 10 76	Stoke	Trainee	Stoke C	—	—
Carruthers Martin	5 11	11 07	F	7 8 72	Nottingham	Trainee	Aston Villa	4	—
							Hull C (loan)	13	6
							Stoke C	90	13
Clarkson Ian	5 10	12 02	D	4 12 70	Birmingham	Trainee	Birmingham C	136	—
							Stoke C	75	—
Cranson Ian	6 0	13 05	D	2 7 64	Easington	Apprentice	Ipswich T	131	5
							Sheffield W	30	—
							Stoke C	217	9
Devlin Mark	5 10	11 05	M	18 1 73	Irvine	Trainee	Stoke C	34	2
Dreyer John	6 1	12 13	D	11 6 63	Alnwick	Wallingford T	Oxford U	60	2
							Torquay U (loan)	5	—
							Fulham (loan)	12	2
							Luton T	214	13
							Stoke C	37	2
							Bolton W (loan)	2	—
Gayle John	6 3	15 00	F	30 7 64	Birmingham	Burton Alb	Wimbledon	20	2
							Birmingham C	44	10
							Walsall (loan)	4	1
							Coventry C	3	—
							Burnley	14	3
							Stoke C	14	3
							Gillingham (loan)	9	3
Gleghorn Nigel	6 0	13 07	M	12 8 62	Seaham	Seaham Red Star	Ipswich T	66	11
							Manchester C	34	7
							Birmingham C	142	33
							Stoke C	166	26
Hawkes Marc*	6 0	11 05	F	22 9 76	Stoke	Trainee	Stoke C	—	—
Holden Mark*	5 7	11 06	D	2 4 76	Tamworth	Trainee	Stoke C	—	—
Keen Kevin	5 7	10 10	M	25 2 67	Amersham	Apprentice	West Ham U	219	21
							Wolverhampton W	42	7
							Stoke C	54	5
Leslie Steven‡	5 6	10 00	M	6 2 76	Dumfries	Trainee	Stoke C	1	—
Macari Michael	5 7	10 10	F	4 2 73	Kilwinning	Trainee	West Ham U	—	—
							Stoke C	—	—
Macari Paul	5 8	11 03	F	23 8 76	Manchester	Trainee	Stoke C	—	—
Morgan Philip	6 1	13 00	G	18 12 74	Stoke	Trainee	Ipswich T	1	—
							Stoke C	—	—
Muggleton Carl	6 1	12 13	G	13 9 68	Leicester	Apprentice	Leicester C	46	—
							Chesterfield (loan)	17	—
							Blackpool (loan)	2	—
							Hartlepool U (loan)	8	—
							Stockport Co (loan)	4	—
							Liverpool (loan)	—	—
							Stoke C (loan)	6	—
							Sheffield U (loan)	—	—

Name			Pos	D.O.B.	Birthplace	Source	Club	Apps	Gls
							Celtic	12	—
							Stoke C	30	—
							Rotherham U (loan)	6	—
							Sheffield U (loan)	1	—
Overson Vince	6 2	14 13	D	15 5 62	Kettering	Apprentice	Burnley	211	6
							Birmingham C	182	3
							Stoke C	170	6
Potter Graham	6 1	11 08	D	20 5 75	Solihull	Trainee	Birmingham C	25	2
							Wycombe W (loan)	3	—
							Stoke C	45	1
Prudhoe Mark	6 0	14 00	G	8 11 63	Washington	Apprentice	Sunderland	7	—
							Hartlepool U (loan)	3	—
							Birmingham C	1	—
							Walsall	26	—
							Doncaster R (loan)	5	—
							Sheffield W (loan)	—	—
							Grimsby T (loan)	8	—
							Hartlepool U (loan)	13	—
							Bristol C (loan)	3	—
							Carlisle U	34	—
							Darlington	146	—
							Stoke C	69	—
							Peterborough U (loan)	6	—
							Liverpool (loan)	—	—
Sandford Lee	6 0	13 03	D	22 4 68	Basingstoke	Apprentice	Portsmouth	72	1
							Stoke C	258	8
Sheron Mike	5 10	11 12	F	11 1 72	Liverpool	Trainee	Manchester C	100	24
							Bury (loan)	5	1
							Norwich C	28	2
							Stoke C	28	15
Sigurdsson Larus	6 0	12 06	D	4 6 73	Akuveyni	Thor	Stoke C	69	1
Sinclair Ron*	5 11	12 03	G	19 11 64	Stirling	Apprentice	Nottingham F	—	—
							Wrexham (loan)	11	—
							Derby Co (loan)	—	—
							Sheffield U (loan)	—	—
							Leeds U (loan)	—	—
							Leeds U	8	—
							Halifax T (loan)	4	—
							Halifax T (loan)	10	—
							Bristol C	44	—
							Walsall (loan)	10	—
							Stoke C	80	—
							Bradford C (loan)	—	—
Stokoe Graham	6 1	12 02	M	17 12 75	Newcastle	Birmingham C	Stoke C	—	—
							Hartlepool U (loan)	8	—
Sturridge Simon	5 5	10 09	F	9 12 69	Birmingham	Trainee	Birmingham C	150	30
							Stoke C	62	14
Talbot David*	6 3	11 05	D	12 10 76	Stoke	Trainee	Stoke C	—	—
Wallace Ray	5 7	11 04	D	2 10 69	Lewisham	Trainee	Southampton	35	—
							Leeds U	7	—
							Swansea C (loan)	2	—
							Reading (loan)	3	—
							Stoke C	64	7
							Hull C (loan)	7	—
Whittle Justin	6 1	12 08	D	18 3 71	Derby	Celtic	Stoke C	8	—
Woods Stephen	5 11	11 12	D	15 12 76	Davenham	Trainee	Stoke C	—	—

Trainees
Brownsword, Andrew; Carter, Richard J; Clarke, Clive R; Crowe, Dean A; Dickin, David A; Drury, Adrian D; Griffin, Andrew; Hawtin, Mark A; Jagielka, Stephen; O'Connor, James K; Ruscoe, Scott; Simpson, Andrew P; Wade, Robert S; Watson, David I; Williams, Darrell J.

Non-Contract
Heath, Robert; Mackenzie, Neil D.

Associated Schoolboys
Bullock, Matthew; Dixon, Calvin G; Willis, David A.

Associated Schoolboys who have accepted the club's offer of a Traineeship/Contract
Cartwright, James P; Godbold, Jamie T; Taaffe, Steven; Woolliscroft, Ashley.

SUNDERLAND

Name			Pos	D.O.B.	Birthplace	Source	Club	Apps	Gls
Agnew Steve	5 10	11 01	M	9 11 65	Shipley	Apprentice	Barnsley	194	29
							Blackburn R	2	—
							Portsmouth (loan)	5	—
							Leicester C	56	4
							Sunderland	45	7
Aiston Sam	6 0	12 10	M	21 11 76	Newcastle	Newcastle U	Sunderland	14	—

Name										
Angell Brett	6 2	13 10	F	20 8 68	Marlborough	Cheltenham T	Derby Co	—	—
							Stockport Co	70	28
							Southend U	115	47
							Everton (loan)	1	—
							Everton	19	1
							Sunderland	10	—
							Sheffield U (loan)	6	2
							WBA (loan)	3	—
Armstrong Gordon	6 0	12 10	M	15 7 67	Newcastle	Apprentice	Sunderland	349	50
							Bristol C (loan)	6	—
							Northampton T (loan)	4	1
Atkinson Brian	5 9	12 02	M	19 1 71	Darlington	Trainee	Sunderland	141	4
							Carlisle U (loan)	2	—
Ball Kevin	5 10	12 05	D	12 11 64	Hastings	Apprentice	Portsmouth	105	4
							Sunderland	223	13
Bracewell Paul	5 10	12 05	M	19 7 62	Stoke	Apprentice	Stoke C	129	5
							Sunderland	38	4
							Everton	95	7
							Sunderland	113	2
							Newcastle U	73	3
							Sunderland	38	—
Bridges Michael	6 0	11 00	F	5 8 78	Whitley Bay	Trainee	Sunderland	15	4
Brodie Steve	5 6	10 08	F	14 1 73	Sunderland	Trainee	Sunderland	12	—
							Doncaster R (loan)	5	1
Chamberlain Alec	6 2	13 06	G	30 6 64	Ramsey	Ramsey T	Ipswich T	—	—
							Colchester U	184	—
							Everton	—	—
							Tranmere R (loan)	15	—
							Luton T	138	—
							Chelsea (loan)	—	—
							Sunderland	90	—
							Liverpool (loan)	—	—
Coates Scott‡			D	7 9 76	Consett	Trainee	Sunderland	—	—
Grant Stephen	5 10	11 07	F	14 4 77	Birr	Athlone T	Sunderland	—	—
Gray Michael	5 8	10 08	D	3 8 74	Sunderland	Trainee	Sunderland	111	7
Gray Phil	5 9	12 09	F	2 10 68	Belfast	Apprentice	Tottenham H	9	—
							Barnsley (loan)	3	—
							Fulham (loan)	3	—
							Luton T	59	22
							Sunderland	115	34
Hall Gareth	5 8	12 00	D	12 3 69	Croydon	Apprentice	Chelsea	138	4
							Sunderland	14	—
Heckingbottom Paul	5 11	12 00	M	17 7 77	Barnsley		Sunderland	—	—
Holloway Darren			D	3 10 77	Bishop Auckland	Trainee	Sunderland	—	—
Howey Lee	6 2	13 08	F	1 4 69	Sunderland	AC Hemptinne	Sunderland	57	8
Kay John*	5 9	11 08	D	29 1 64	Sunderland	Apprentice	Arsenal	14	—
							Wimbledon	63	2
							Middlesbrough (loan)	8	—
							Sunderland	199	—
							Shrewsbury T (loan)	7	—
Kelly David	5 11	12 01	F	25 11 65	Birmingham	Alvechurch	Walsall	147	63
							West Ham U	41	7
							Leicester C	66	22
							Newcastle U	70	35
							Wolverhampton W	83	26
							Sunderland	10	2
Kubicki Dariusz	5 11	11 12	D	6 6 63	Kozuchow	Legia Warsaw	Aston Villa	25	—
							Sunderland (loan)	15	—
							Sunderland	92	—
Lawless Chris*	5 8	11 01	M	4 10 74	Dublin	Home Farm	Sunderland	—	—
Mawson David	5 11	12 05	F	4 3 77	Sunderland	Trainee	Sunderland	—	—
McGiven Joseph‡			M	8 6 77	Newcastle	Watford	Sunderland	—	—
Melville Andy	6 0	13 10	D	29 11 68	Swansea	School	Swansea C	175	22
							Oxford U	135	13
							Sunderland	120	9
Mullin John	6 0	11 08	F	11 8 75	Bury	School	Burnley	18	2
							Sunderland	10	1
Ord Richard	6 2	13 03	D	3 3 69	Easington	Trainee	Sunderland	196	5
							York C (loan)	3	—
Pickering Steven	5 10	9 13	M	25 9 76	Sunderland	Trainee	Sunderland	—	—
Preece David	6 2	12 03	G	28 8 76	Sunderland	Trainee	Sunderland	—	—
Russell Craig	5 10	12 06	F	4 2 74	Jarrow	Trainee	Sunderland	118	27

Scott Martin	5 10	11 08	M	7 1 68	Sheffield	Apprentice	Rotherham U	94	3
							Nottingham F (loan)	—	—
							Bristol C	171	14
							Sunderland	67	6
Smith Martin	5 11	12 03	F	13 11 74	Sunderland	Trainee	Sunderland	84	20
Stewart Paul	5 11	11 10	M	7 10 64	Manchester	Apprentice	Blackpool	201	56
							Manchester C	51	26
							Tottenham H	131	28
							Liverpool	32	1
							Crystal Palace (loan)	18	3
							Wolverhampton W (loan)	8	2
							Burnley (loan)	6	—
							Sunderland	12	1

Trainees
Barnes, Liam; Barton, Michael R; Beavers, Paul M; Dickman, Elliott; Johnston, Michael; Knight, Robert G; Lloyd, Gary P; Naisbett, Philip; Parker, Neal; Peters, Stephen; Provan, John A; Somerville, John F; Thirlwell, Paul.

Associated Schoolboys
Brunton, Daniel J; Convery, Mark; Downey, Gareth; Gildea, Alex; Johnson, Neil; Lamb, Kris A; Maley, Mark; Parmley, Lee J; Proctor, Michael A; Stewart, Craig M; Vyse, Brian.

Associated Schoolboys who have accepted the club's offer of a Traineeship/Contract
Frampton, Kevin W; Gibson, Daniel; Lumsden, Christopher; Wright, Andrew.

SWANSEA CITY

Ampadu Kwame	5 10	11 10	F	20 12 70	Bradford	Belvedere	Arsenal	2	—
							Plymouth Arg (loan)	6	1
							WBA (loan)	7	1
							WBA	42	3
							Swansea C	100	8
Barnhouse David*	5 8	10 09	D	19 3 75	Swansea	Trainee	Swansea C	23	—
Brown Linton	5 9	11 00	F	12 4 68	Driffield	Guiseley	Halifax T	3	—
							Hull C	121	23
							Swansea C	4	—
Chapman Lee‡	6 2	13 00	F	5 12 59	Lincoln	Amateur	Stoke C	99	34
							Plymouth Arg (loan)	4	—
							Arsenal	23	4
							Sunderland	15	3
							Sheffield W	149	63
						Niort	Nottingham F	48	15
							Leeds U	137	62
							Portsmouth	5	2
							West Ham U	40	7
							Southend U (loan)	1	1
							Ipswich T	22	1
							Leeds U (loan)	2	—
							Swansea C	7	4
Chapple Shaun	5 11	12 03	M	14 2 73	Swansea	Trainee	Swansea C	85	9
Clode Mark	5 10	10 10	D	24 2 73	Plymouth	Trainee	Plymouth Arg	—	—
							Swansea C	91	2
Coates Jonathan	5 8	10 04	F	27 6 75	Swansea	Trainee	Swansea C	27	1
Cook Andy	5 9	12 00	D	10 8 69	Romsey	Apprentice	Southampton	16	1
							Exeter C	70	1
							Swansea C	62	—
Edwards Christian	6 2	11 09	D	23 11 75	Caerphilly	Trainee	Swansea C	47	2
Freestone Roger	6 3	14 06	G	19 8 68	Newport	Trainee	Newport Co	13	—
							Chelsea	42	—
							Swansea C (loan)	14	—
							Hereford U (loan)	8	—
							Swansea C	224	3
Garnett Shaun	6 3	13 04	D	22 11 69	Wallasey	Trainee	Tranmere R	112	5
							Chester C (loan)	9	—
							Preston NE (loan)	10	2
							Wigan Ath (loan)	13	1
							Swansea C	9	—
Heggs Carl	6 1	12 10	F	11 10 70	Leicester	Paget R	WBA	40	3
							Bristol R (loan)	5	1
							Swansea C	32	5
Hodge John	5 7	11 03	F	1 4 69	Ormskirk	Exmouth	Exeter C	65	10
							Swansea C	112	10
Jones Lee	6 3	14 04	G	9 8 70	Pontypridd	Porth	Swansea C	3	—
							Crewe Alex (loan)	—	—
Jones Steve	5 10	12 02	D	25 12 70	Bristol	Cheltenham T	Swansea C	17	—

Mardenborough Steve‡	5 8	11 09	F	11 9 64	Birmingham	Apprentice	Coventry C	—	—
							Wolverhampton W	9	1
							Cambridge C (loan)	6	—
							Swansea C	36	7
							Newport Co	64	11
							Cardiff C	32	1
							Hereford U	27	—
							Darlington	106	18
							Lincoln C	21	2
							Scarborough	1	—
							Colchester U	12	2
							Swansea C	1	—
McDonald Colin	5 7	11 04	F	10 4 74	Edinburgh		Hibernian	—	—
							Falkirk	56	11
							Swansea C	8	—
Miles Ben‡	6 1	11 07	G	13 4 76	Middlesex	Trainee	Swansea C	—	—
Molby Jan	6 1	14 07	M	4 7 63	Kolding	Ajax	Liverpool	218	44
							Barnsley (loan)	5	—
							Norwich C (loan)	3	—
							Swansea C	12	2
Morgan Matthew*			D	24 2 77	Swansea		Swansea C	—	—
O'Leary Kristian§			D	30 8 77	Neath	Trainee	Swansea C	1	—
Penney David	5 10	12 00	M	17 8 64	Wakefield	Pontefract	Derby Co	19	—
							Oxford U	110	15
							Swansea C (loan)	12	3
							Swansea C (loan)	11	2
							Swansea C	64	5
Perrett Darren‡	5 8	11 06	F	29 12 69	Cardiff	Cheltenham T	Swansea C	30	1
Price Jason	6 2	11 05	M	12 4 77	Pontypridd	Aberaman	Swansea C	—	—
Spiteri Denis*			D	16 10 76	Cardiff	Trainee	Swansea C	—	—
Thomas David	5 10	11 07	F	26 9 75	Caerphilly	Trainee	Swansea C	20	1
Torpey Steve	6 3	14 03	F	8 12 70	Islington	Trainee	Millwall	7	—
							Bradford C	96	22
							Swansea C	123	35
Walker Keith	6 0	12 08	M	17 4 66	Edinburgh	ICI Juveniles	Stirling Albion	91	17
							St Mirren	43	6
							Swansea C	199	5

Trainees
Casey, Ryan; Cunningham, Barry L; Cunningham, John L; Davies, Dewi O; Freeman, Stuart; Graham, David; Grey, Jonathan R; Harris, Gareth; James, Rhys A; Jenkins, Lee D; Jones, Christopher J; Jones, Lee E; King, Robert D; Lacey, Damian J; Lewis, Huw A W; Llewellyn, Lee M; Mackay, James S; Milsom, Greg H; O'Leary, Kristian D; Rosselli, Dean A.

Associated Schoolboys
Barwood, Daniel D; De-Vulgt, Leigh S; Howard, Martin; Jones, Huw R; Jones, Mathew; Kern, Jamie T; Mackennall, Paul; Morgan, Ian K; Todd, Christopher; Watkins, David J.

Associated Schoolboys who have accepted the club's offer of a Traineeship/Contract
Mainwaring, Andrew; Phillips, Gareth; Roberts, Stuart I.

SWINDON TOWN

Allen Paul	5 7	10 04	M	28 8 62	Aveley	Apprentice	West Ham U	152	6
							Tottenham H	292	23
							Southampton	43	1
							Luton T (loan)	4	—
							Stoke C (loan)	17	1
							Swindon T	27	—
Allison Wayne	6 1	12 06	F	16 10 68	Huddersfield		Halifax T	84	23
							Watford	7	—
							Bristol C	195	48
							Swindon T	44	17
Bodin Paul*	6 0	13 01	D	13 9 64	Cardiff	Chelsea	Newport Co	—	3
							Cardiff C	57	3
						Bath C	Newport Co	6	1
							Swindon T	93	9
							Crystal Palace	9	—
							Newcastle U (loan)	6	—
							Swindon T	146	28
Collins Lee	5 8	10 02	M	3 2 74	Bellshill	Possil U	Albion R	45	1
							Swindon T	5	—
Cowe Steve	5 7	10 02	M	29 9 74	Gloucester	Trainee	Aston Villa	—	—
							Swindon T	11	1
Culverhouse Ian	5 10	11 02	D	22 9 64	Bishop's Stortford	Apprentice	Tottenham H	2	—
							Norwich C	296	1
							Swindon T	55	

Digby Fraser	6 1	12 12	G	23 4 67	Sheffield	Apprentice	Manchester U	—	—
							Oldham Ath (loan)	—	—
							Swindon T (loan)	—	—
							Swindon T	348	—
							Manchester U (loan)	—	—
Drysdale Jason	5 10	12 00	D	17 11 70	Bristol	Trainee	Watford	145	11
							Newcastle U	—	—
							Swindon T	14	—
Finney Stephen	5 10	12 00	F	31 10 73	Hexham	Trainee	Preston NE	6	1
							Manchester C	—	—
							Swindon T	30	12
Gooden Ty	5 8	12 06	M	23 10 72	Canvey Island	Wycombe W	Swindon T	46	5
Hamon Chris‡	6 1	13 07	F	27 4 70	Jersey	St Peter	Swindon T	8	1
Holloway Jonathan‡	5 10	12 04	D	11 2 77	Swindon	Trainee	Swindon T	—	—
Hooper Dean	5 10	12 08	M	13 4 71	Harefield	Hayes	Swindon T	4	—
							Peterborough U (loan)	4	—
Horlock Kevin	6 0	12 00	D	1 11 72	Plumstead	Trainee	West Ham U	—	—
							Swindon T	135	14
Laidlaw Jamie‡	5 10	12 03	M	14 11 75	Irvine	Trainee	Swindon T	—	—
Leitch Scott	5 9	11 08	D	6 10 69	Motherwell	Shettleston J	Dunfermline Ath	89	16
							Hearts	55	2
							Swindon T (loan)	7	—
Ling Martin*	5 7	10 08	M	15 7 66	West Ham	Apprentice	Exeter C	116	14
							Swindon T	2	—
							Southend U	138	31
							Mansfield T (loan)	3	—
							Swindon T (loan)	1	—
							Swindon T	149	10
Maclaren Ross	5 10	12 12	M	14 4 62	Edinburgh	Rangers	Shrewsbury T	161	18
							Derby Co	122	4
							Swindon T	197	9
McMahon Steve	5 9	11 08	M	20 8 61	Liverpool	Apprentice	Everton	100	11
							Aston Villa	75	7
							Liverpool	204	29
							Manchester C	87	1
							Swindon T	38	—
Murray Edwin	5 11	12 00	D	31 8 73	Redbridge	Trainee	Swindon T	12	1
O'Sullivan Wayne	5 8	10 06	D	25 2 74	Akrotiri	Trainee	Swindon T	64	3
Robinson Mark	5 9	11 08	D	21 11 68	Rochdale	Trainee	WBA	2	—
							Barnsley	137	6
							Newcastle U	25	—
							Swindon T	86	1
Seagraves Mark	6 0	13 04	D	22 10 66	Bootle	Apprentice	Liverpool	—	—
							Norwich C (loan)	3	—
							Manchester C	42	—
							Bolton W	157	7
							Swindon T	28	—
Smith Alex	5 8	9 09	D	15 2 76	Liverpool	Trainee	Everton	—	—
							Swindon T	8	—
Talia Frank	6 1	13 04	G	20 7 72	Melbourne	Sunshine GC	Blackburn R	—	—
							Hartlepool U (loan)	14	—
							Swindon T	16	—
Taylor Shaun	6 1	13 00	D	26 2 63	Plymouth	Bideford	Exeter C	200	16
							Swindon T	210	30
Thorne Gary‡	5 8	11 07	D	22 3 77	Reading	Trainee	Swindon T	—	—
Thorne Peter	6 0	12 00	F	21 6 73	Manchester	Trainee	Blackburn R	—	—
							Wigan Ath (loan)	11	—
							Swindon T	46	19
Worrall Ben‡	5 7	11 06	M	7 12 75	Swindon	Trainee	Swindon T	3	—

Trainees
Campbell, Stephen J; Coupe, Matthew W E; Finlayson, Alexander J; Haines, Jonathan J; Harvey, Iain D; Hunt, Daniel J; Mildenhall, Stephen J; Organ, Christopher D; Pattimore, Michael R; Pearce, Graham R; Souter, Ryan; Thomas, Steven J; Wheeldon, Thomas V; Wimble, Shaun M; Woodman, Scott C.

Associated Schoolboys
Murphy, Lee J; Peters, Bradley S.

Associated Schoolboys who have accepted the club's offer of a Traineeship/Contract
Betterton, Anthony G; Davis, Sol S; Hodson, Stuart M; O'Connell, Christopher W; Thorne, Wayne P.

TORQUAY UNITED

Player			Pos	DOB	Birthplace	Source	Club	Apps	Gls
Baker Paul	6 0	13 00	F	5 1 63	Newcastle	Bishop Auckland	Southampton	—	—
							Carlisle U	71	11
							Hartlepool U	197	67
							Motherwell	9	1
							Gillingham	62	16
							York C	48	18
							Torquay U	20	4
Barnes Bobby‡	5 7	10 09	F	17 12 62	Kingston	Apprentice	West Ham U	43	5
							Scunthorpe U (loan)	6	—
							Aldershot	49	26
							Swindon T	45	13
							Bournemouth	14	—
							Northampton T	98	37
							Peterborough U	49	9
							Partick T	7	—
						Hong Kong	Torquay U	1	—
Barrow Lee	5 11	13 00	D	1 5 73	Worksworth	Trainee	Notts Co	—	—
							Scarborough	11	—
							Torquay U	116	5
Bayes Ashley*	6 1	13 05	G	19 4 72	Lincoln	Trainee	Brentford	4	—
							Torquay U	97	—
Bedeau Anthony§	5 9	11 01	M	24 3 79	Hammersmith	Trainee	Torquay U	4	—
Cooke Jason‡			F	13 7 71	Birmingham		Preston NE	—	—
						Brierley Hill	Torquay U	1	—
Coughlin Russell*	5 8	11 07	M	15 2 60	Swansea	Apprentice	Manchester C	—	—
							Blackburn R	24	—
							Carlisle U	130	13
							Plymouth Arg	131	18
							Blackpool	102	8
							Shrewsbury T (loan)	5	—
							Swansea C	101	2
							Exeter C	68	—
							Torquay U	25	—
Gregg Matt§			G	30 11 78	Cheltenham	Trainee	Torquay U	1	—
Haddaoui Riffi‡			F	24 3 71	Copenhagen	Avarta	Torquay U	2	—
Hall Mark*	5 7	10 09	M	13 1 73	Islington	Tottenham H	Southend U	12	—
							Barnet (loan)	3	—
							Torquay U	29	—
Hancox Richard	5 10	13 00	F	4 10 70	Stourbridge	Stourbridge S	Torquay U	71	10
Hardy Paul‡	5 8	10 05	M	29 8 75	Plymouth	Trainee	Torquay U	1	—
Hathaway Ian	5 6	10 10	M	22 8 68	Wordsley	Bedworth U	Mansfield T	44	2
							Rotherham U	13	1
							Torquay U	105	13
Hawthorne Mark*	5 8	11 09	M	31 10 73	Glasgow	Trainee	Crystal Palace	—	—
							Sheffield U	—	—
							Walsall	—	—
							Torquay U	24	—
Hodges Kevin*	5 7	11 01	M	12 6 60	Bridport	Apprentice	Plymouth Arg	530	81
							Torquay U (loan)	3	—
							Torquay U	67	4
Jack Rodney	5 6	10 08	F	28 9 72	Kingston,Lambada		Torquay U	14	2
Kelly Tom*	5 9	12 07	D	28 3 64	Bellshill	Hibs	Hartlepool U	15	—
							Torquay U	120	—
							York C	35	2
							Exeter C	88	9
							Torquay U	117	8
Laight Ellis*	5 10	11 02	F	30 6 76	Birmingham	Trainee	Torquay U	31	2
Mateu Jose-Luis‡	5 11	11 06	F	15 1 66	Castellon	Castellon	Torquay U	10	1
Monk Garry§	5 11	11 13	D	6 3 79	Bedford	Trainee	Torquay U	5	—
Moors Christopher‡			D	18 8 76	Yeovil	West Ham U	Torquay U	1	—
Ndah Jamie	6 2	11 13	F	5 8 71	East Dulwich	Kingstonian	Torquay U	16	3
Newland Ray	6 2	12 02	G	19 7 71	Liverpool	Everton	Plymouth Arg	26	—
							Chester C	10	—
							Torquay U	17	—
Oatway Charlie	5 6	10 04	M	28 11 73	Hammersmith	Yeading	Cardiff C	32	—
							Torquay U	24	—
Povey Neil‡	5 8	10 00	M	26 6 77	Birmingham	Trainee	Torquay U	11	—
Preston Michael§	5 7	10 02	M	22 11 77	Plymouth	Trainee	Torquay U	8	—
Ramsey Paul*	5 10	12 00	D	3 9 62	Londonderry	Apprentice	Leicester C	290	13
							Cardiff C	69	7
							St Johnstone	33	—
							Cardiff C (loan)	11	—
							Torquay U	18	—

Setter Lee‡	5 6	10 10	M	10 10 76	Torquay	Trainee	Torquay U	—	—
Stamps Scott	5 10	11 02	D	20 3 75	Edgbaston	Trainee	Torquay U	56	2
Thomas Wayne§	5 11	11 10	F	28 8 78	Walsall	Trainee	Torquay U	6	—
Thornley Timothy‡			G	3 3 77	Leicester	Trainee	Torquay U	1	—
Travis Simon‡			F	22 3 77	Preston	Trainee	Torquay U	8	—
Watson Alex	6 2	13 00	D	15 4 68	Liverpool	Apprentice	Liverpool	4	—
							Derby Co (loan)	5	—
							Bournemouth	151	5
							Gillingham (loan)	10	1
							Torquay U	29	2
Winter Steve	5 8	10 10	D	26 10 73	Bristol	Taunton T	Torquay U	36	—

Trainees
Aggett, Neil R P; Bedeau, Anthony C O; Beswick, Paul L; Gregg, Matthew S; Hockley, Wayne; Hogg, Christopher; Jennings, Paul C; Male, Neil J; Monk, Garry A; Preston, Michael J; Thomas, Wayne J R; Tucker, Lee A; Wright, Matthew P.

Associated Schoolboys
Medlin, Daniel L.

Associated Schoolboys who have accepted the club's offer of a Traineeship/Contract
Froude, Paul T; Gomm, Richard A; Hapgood, Leon D; Newell, Justin J; Smillie, Duncan; Tully, Stephen R.

TOTTENHAM HOTSPUR

Allen Rory			F	17 10 77	Beckenham	Trainee	Tottenham H	—	—
Anderton Darren	6 1	12 00	F	3 3 72	Southampton	Trainee	Portsmouth	62	7
							Tottenham H	116	19
Arber Mark			D	9 10 77	South Africa	Trainee	Tottenham H	—	—
Armstrong Chris	6 0	13 03	F	19 6 71	Newcastle	Llay Welfare	Wrexham	60	13
							Millwall	28	5
							Crystal Palace	118	45
							Tottenham H	36	15
Austin Dean	6 0	11 06	D	26 4 70	Hemel Hempstead	St. Albans C	Southend U	96	2
							Tottenham H	109	—
Brady Garry	5 8	10 02	M	7 9 76	Glasgow	Trainee	Tottenham H	—	—
Brown Simon	6 2	13 00	G	3 12 76	Chelmsford	Trainee	Tottenham H	—	—
Calderwood Colin	6 0	12 12	D	20 1 65	Glasgow	Amateur	Mansfield T	100	1
							Swindon T	330	20
							Tottenham H	91	2
Campbell Sol	6 1	14 01	M	18 9 74	Newham	Trainee	Tottenham H	96	2
Carr Steve	5 7	12 02	D	29 8 76	Dublin	Trainee	Tottenham H	1	—
Clapham Jamie	5 9	10 08	M	7 12 75	Lincoln	Trainee	Tottenham H	—	—
Clemence Stephen	5 11	12 00	M	31 3 78	Liverpool	Trainee	Tottenham H	—	—
Cundy Jason	6 1	13 13	D	12 11 69	Wimbledon	Trainee	Chelsea	41	1
							Tottenham H (loan)	10	—
							Tottenham H	16	1
							Crystal Palace (loan)	4	—
D'Arcy Ross	6 0	12 00	D	21 3 78	Balbriggan	Trainee	Tottenham H	—	—
Davies Darren§			D	13 8 78	Port Talbot	Trainee	Tottenham H	—	—
Day Chris	6 2	13 06	G	28 7 75	Whipps Cross	Trainee	Tottenham H	—	—
Dozzell Jason	6 1	13 08	M	9 12 67	Ipswich	School	Ipswich T	332	52
							Tottenham H	67	11
Edinburgh Justin	5 10	11 08	D	18 12 69	Brentwood	Trainee	Southend U	37	—
							Tottenham H (loan)	—	—
							Tottenham H	149	1
Fenn Neale	5 10	11 06	F	18 1 77	Edmonton	Trainee	Tottenham H	—	—
Fox Ruel	5 6	10 00	M	14 1 68	Ipswich	Apprentice	Norwich C	172	22
							Newcastle U	58	12
							Tottenham H	26	6
Gain Peter	6 1	12 09	M	11 11 76	Hammersmith	Trainee	Tottenham H	—	—
Hazard Mickey‡	5 8	11 08	M	5 2 60	Sunderland	Apprentice	Tottenham H	91	13
							Chelsea	81	9
							Portsmouth	8	1
							Swindon T	119	17
							Tottenham H	28	2
Hill Danny	5 9	11 03	M	1 10 74	Edmonton	Trainee	Tottenham H	10	—
							Birmingham C (loan)	5	—
							Watford (loan)	1	—
Howells David	5 11	12 04	M	15 12 67	Guildford	Trainee	Tottenham H	225	20
Janney Mark§			F	2 12 77	Romford	Trainee	Tottenham H	—	—

Name							Club	Apps	Gls
Kerslake David	5 9	12 03	D	19 6 66	Stepney	Apprentice	QPR	58	6
							Swindon T	135	1
							Leeds U	8	—
							Tottenham H	37	—
Knott Gareth*	5 8	11 04	F	19 1 76	Blackwood	Trainee	Tottenham H	—	—
							Gillingham (loan)	5	—
Mabbutt Gary	5 9	12 09	D	23 8 61	Bristol	Apprentice	Bristol R	131	10
							Tottenham H	465	27
Maher Kevin	6 0	13 06	D	17 10 76	Ilford	Trainee	Tottenham H	—	—
Mahorn Paul	5 8	11 06	F	13 8 73	Whipps Cross	Trainee	Tottenham H	1	—
							Fulham (loan)	3	—
							Burnley (loan)	8	1
Mannix Alan	5 8	10 09	M	23 10 77	Castle Knock	Trainee	Tottenham H	—	—
McMahon Gerard	5 11	11 00	F	29 12 73	Belfast	Glenavon	Tottenham H	16	—
							Barnet (loan)	10	2
McVeigh Paul§			M	6 12 77	Belfast	Trainee	Tottenham H	—	—
Nethercott Stuart	5 11	13 08	D	21 3 73	Chadwell Heath	Trainee	Tottenham H	45	—
							Maidstone U (loan)	13	1
							Barnet (loan)	3	—
Rosenthal Ronny	5 11	12 13	F	11 10 63	Haifa	Standard Liege	Luton T (loan)	—	—
							Liverpool (loan)	8	7
							Liverpool	66	14
							Tottenham H	68	3
Scott Kevin	6 2	14 03	D	17 12 66	Easington	Middlesbrough	Newcastle U	227	8
							Tottenham H	18	1
							Port Vale (loan)	17	1
Sheringham Teddy	6 0	12 05	F	2 4 66	Highams Park	Apprentice	Millwall	220	93
							Aldershot (loan)	5	—
							Nottingham F	42	14
							Tottenham H	137	69
Simpson Robert*	5 9	10 07	F	3 3 76	Luton	Trainee	Tottenham H	—	—
Sinton Andy	5 8	11 05	M	19 3 66	Newcastle	Apprentice	Cambridge U	93	13
							Brentford	149	28
							QPR	160	22
							Sheffield W	60	3
							Tottenham H	9	—
Slade Steve	5 10	10 10	F	6 10 75	Romford	Trainee	Tottenham H	5	—
Spencer Simon	5 10	11 04	M	10 9 76	Islington	Trainee	Tottenham H	—	—
Thorstvedt Erik*	6 4	14 03	G	28 10 62	Stavanger	IFK Gothenburg	Tottenham H	173	—
Townley Leon	6 0	12 09	D	16 2 76	Loughton	Trainee	Tottenham H	—	—
Turner Andy	5 9	11 07	M	23 5 75	Woolwich	Trainee	Tottenham H	20	3
							Wycombe W (loan)	4	—
							Doncaster R (loan)	4	1
							Huddersfield T (loan)	5	1
							Southend U (loan)	6	—
Walker Ian	6 1	12 09	G	31 10 71	Watford	Trainee	Tottenham H	126	—
							Oxford U (loan)	2	—
							Ipswich T (loan)	—	—
Watson Kevin*	5 9	12 06	M	3 1 74	Hackney	Trainee	Tottenham H	5	—
							Brentford (loan)	3	—
							Bristol C (loan)	2	—
							Barnet (loan)	13	—
Webb Simon	5 11	12 02	M	19 1 78	Castle Bar	Trainee	Tottenham H	—	—
Wilson Clive	5 7	10 00	M	13 11 61	Manchester	Local	Manchester C	98	9
							Chester (loan)	21	2
							Chelsea	81	5
							Manchester C (loan)	11	—
							QPR	172	12
							Tottenham H	28	—
Wormull Simon	5 10	12 03	M	1 12 76	Crawley	Trainee	Tottenham H	—	—

Trainees
Bunn, James T; Davies, Darren J; Delicata, Julian; Evans, James M; Gower, Mark; Janney, Mark; Kersey, Lee D; Marriott, Alan; McVeigh, Paul; Outram, Ross P; Samways, Shane A; Shave, Arran L; Southgate, Glenn S; Spencer, Ryan L; Warrington, Russell C; Young, Luke P.

Associated Schoolboys
Bernard, Narada M; Carter, James F; Clist, Simon J; Crouch, Peter J; Elliott, Anthony R; Hunt, Nicholas G; Jackson, Johnnie; King, Ledley; Mills, Stephen J; Saker, Blake M; Stonebridge, Ian R; White, Ross A.

Associated Schoolboys who have accepted the club's offer of a Traineeship/Contract
Dobson, Stephen G; Dormer, James S; Hillier, Ian M; Lee, David J; Piercy, John W; Sinclair, Jamie; Stone, Gavin; Vaughan, Wayne S R.

TRANMERE ROVERS

Name					Birthplace	Source	Clubs	Apps	Gls
Aldridge John	5 11	12 03	F	18 9 58	Liverpool	South Liverpool	Newport Co	170	69
							Oxford U	114	72
							Liverpool	83	50
							Real Sociedad	63	33
							Tranmere R	185	115
Branch Graham	6 2	12 12	F	12 2 72	Liverpool	Heswall Ath	Tranmere R	42	2
							Bury (loan)	4	1
Brannan Ged	6 0	12 05	D	15 1 72	Liverpool	Trainee	Tranmere R	204	14
Challinor Dave	6 1	12 12	D	2 10 75	Chester	Bromburgh Pool	Tranmere R	—	—
Cook Paul	5 11	10 10	M	22 2 67	Liverpool	Marine	Wigan Ath	83	14
							Norwich C	6	—
							Wolverhampton W	193	19
							Coventry C	37	3
							Tranmere R	15	1
Coyne Danny	5 11	13 00	G	27 8 73	Prestatyn	Trainee	Tranmere R	57	—
Crawford Keith			F	31 10 78	Dublin	Belvedere	Tranmere R	—	—
Davies Phil‡	5 11	12 00	M	5 8 76	Bangor	Trainee	Tranmere R	—	—
Edwards Mike*	6 0	12 00	M	10 9 74	Bebbington	Trainee	Tranmere R	3	—
Higgins Dave	6 0	11 07	D	19 8 61	Liverpool	Eagle	Tranmere R	325	10
Hughes Jamie*	6 0	11 00	F	5 4 77	Liverpool	Trainee	Tranmere R	—	—
Irons Kenny	5 10	12 02	M	4 11 70	Liverpool	Trainee	Tranmere R	224	30
Jardine Jamie	5 10	12 00	M	1 2 77	Liverpool		Tranmere R	—	—
Jones Gary	6 3	13 12	F	10 5 75	Chester	Trainee	Tranmere R	48	6
Jones Martin	6 1	13 03	G	27 3 75	Liverpool	Trainee	Tranmere R	—	—
Jones Paul			D	3 6 78	Liverpool	Trainee	Tranmere R	—	—
Kenworthy Jon	5 8	11 00	F	18 8 74	St Asaph	Trainee	Tranmere R	26	2
							Chester C (loan)	7	1
Mahon Alan	5 10	10 09	M	4 4 78	Dublin		Tranmere R	2	—
McGreal John	5 11	12 08	D	2 6 72	Birkenhead	Trainee	Tranmere R	93	1
Moore Ian	6 0	11 10	F	26 8 76	Birkenhead	Trainee	Tranmere R	37	9
Morgan Alan	5 10	11 02	D	2 11 73	Aberystwyth	Trainee	Tranmere R	4	1
Morrissey John	5 8	11 10	F	8 3 65	Liverpool	Apprentice	Everton	1	—
							Wolverhampton W	10	1
							Tranmere R	378	47
Mungall Steve	5 8	11 12	D	22 5 58	Bellshill		Motherwell	20	—
							Tranmere R	512	13
Nevin Pat	5 6	10 07	F	6 9 63	Glasgow	Gartcosh U	Clyde	73	17
							Chelsea	193	36
							Everton	109	16
							Tranmere R (loan)	8	—
							Tranmere R	172	28
Nixon Eric	6 4	15 07	G	4 10 62	Manchester	Curzon Ashton	Manchester C	58	—
							Wolverhampton W (loan)	16	—
							Bradford C (loan)	3	—
							Southampton (loan)	4	—
							Carlisle U (loan)	16	—
							Tranmere R (loan)	8	—
							Tranmere R	308	—
							Blackpool (loan)	20	—
O'Brien Liam	6 1	13 07	M	5 9 64	Dublin	Shamrock R	Manchester U	31	2
							Newcastle U	151	19
							Tranmere R	77	6
Rogers Alan	5 10	11 09	D	3 1 77	Liverpool	Trainee	Tranmere R	26	2
Scott Gary			D	3 2 78	Liverpool	Trainee	Tranmere R	—	—
Stevens Gary	5 11	12 07	D	27 3 63	Barrow	Apprentice	Everton	208	8
							Rangers	187	8
							Tranmere R	71	1
Teale Shaun	6 0	14 00	D	10 3 64	Southport	Weymouth	Bournemouth	100	4
							Aston Villa	147	2
							Tranmere R	29	—
Thomas Tony	5 11	13 00	D	12 7 71	Liverpool	Trainee	Tranmere R	227	12
Woods Billy	6 0	12 00	F	24 10 73	Cork	Cork C	Tranmere R	—	—

Trainees
Ball, David B; Baxter, Brett R; Blundell, Gregg S; Gedman, James; Haworth, Martin; Hill, Clinton S; Howard, Michael A; Hynes, Martin R; Kinsella, Michael E; Lampkin, Ricky J; Marsden, Thomas A; McIntyre, Kevin; Moran, Stephen; Simonsen, Steven P A; Taylor, John; Tippett, Ryan; Tynan, Paul S; Walker, Robert F; Waters, Anthony P; Webster, Christopher R; Williams, Mark T.

Non-Contract
Gladwin, Duncan H.

Associated Schoolboys
Davies, Kevin M; Douglas, Michael; Fofana, Brian; Hay, Alexander; Hinds, Richard P; Jones, Gwyn E; Morgan, David B R; O'Brien, Paul; Poole, David H; Sharps, Ian W; Taylor, Perry L.

Associated Schoolboys who have accepted the club's offer of a Traineeship/Contract
Edge, Christopher; Gibson, Neil D; Graves, Stuart R; Holmes, Thomas M; Jones, Darren J; Sexton, Warren.

WALSALL

Player	Ht	DOB	Pos	Birthplace	Source	Club	Apps	Gls
Bradley Darren	5 11	13 02	D	24 11 65	Birmingham	Apprentice	Aston Villa	20	—
							WBA	254	9
							Walsall	45	1
Butler Martin	5 11	11 09	F	15 9 74	Dudley	Trainee	Walsall	51	7
Daniel Ray	5 8	12 05	D	10 12 64	Luton	Apprentice	Luton T	22	4
							Gillingham (loan)	5	—
							Hull C	58	3
							Cardiff C	56	1
							Portsmouth	100	4
							Notts Co (loan)	5	—
							Walsall	25	—
Evans Wayne	5 10	12 05	D	25 8 71	Abermule	Welshpool	Walsall	101	—
Gibson Colin‡	5 8	11 04	D	6 4 60	Bridport	Apprentice	Aston Villa	185	10
							Manchester U	79	9
							Port Vale (loan)	6	2
							Leicester C	59	4
							Blackpool	2	—
							Walsall	33	—
Houghton Scott	5 6	12 01	F	22 10 71	Hitchin	Trainee	Tottenham H	10	2
							Ipswich T (loan)	8	1
							Cambridge U (loan)	—	—
							Gillingham (loan)	3	—
							Charlton Ath (loan)	6	—
							Luton T	16	1
							Walsall	78	14
Keister John	5 8	10 06	M	11 11 70	Manchester	Fawah FC	Walsall	54	1
Kerr John‡	5 8	11 05	F	6 3 65	Toronto	Harrow Borough	Portsmouth	4	—
							Peterborough U (loan)	10	1
						San Diego Sockers	Millwall	43	8
							Walsall	1	—
Lightbourne Kyle	6 2	12 04	F	29 9 68	Bermuda		Scarborough	19	3
							Walsall	120	45
Marsh Chris	5 10	13 04	M	14 1 70	Dudley	Trainee	Walsall	236	21
Mountfield Derek	6 0	13 06	D	2 11 62	Liverpool	Apprentice	Tranmere R	26	1
							Everton	106	19
							Aston Villa	90	9
							Wolverhampton W	83	4
							Carlisle U	31	3
							Northampton T	4	—
							Walsall	28	1
Ntamark Charlie	5 9	11 09	M	22 7 64	Paddington	Boreham Wood	Walsall	238	11
O'Connor Martin	5 10	12 10	M	10 12 67	Walsall	Bromsgrove R	Crystal Palace	2	—
							Walsall (loan)	10	1
							Walsall	94	21
Palmer Charlie*	5 11	13 01	D	10 7 63	Aylesbury	Apprentice	Watford	10	1
							Derby Co	51	2
							Hull C	70	1
							Notts Co	182	7
							Walsall	54	2
Platt Clive§			F	27 10 77	Wolverhampton	Trainee	Walsall	4	2
Richards Dave*	6 0	12 02	M	31 12 76	Birmingham	Trainee	Walsall	—	—
Ricketts Michael§			F	4 12 78	Birmingham	Trainee	Walsall	1	1
Rogers Darren	5 11	12 11	D	9 4 70	Birmingham	Trainee	WBA	14	1
							Birmingham C	18	—
							Wycombe W (loan)	1	—
							Walsall	52	—
Rollo James‡	5 11	10 10	M	22 5 76	Wisbech	Trainee	Walsall	—	—
Roper Ian	6 2	13 04	D	20 6 77	Nuneaton	Trainee	Walsall	5	—
Ryder Stuart	6 0	12 05	D	6 11 73	Sutton	Trainee	Walsall	87	5
Smith Chris*	5 7	11 01	F	3 1 77	Birmingham	Trainee	Walsall	1	—
Thompson Adrian*	5 9	11 12	G	13 3 77	Sydney	Trainee	Walsall	—	—
Viveash Adrian	6 1	11 09	D	30 9 69	Swindon	Trainee	Swindon T	54	2
							Reading (loan)	5	—
							Reading (loan)	6	—
						Trainee	Barnsley (loan)	2	1
							Walsall	31	—

Walker James	5 11	13 03	G	9	7 73	Sutton in Ashfield	Trainee	Notts Co Walsall	— 61	— —
Wilson Kevin	5 8	11 03	F	18	4 61	Banbury	Banbury U	Derby Co Ipswich T Chelsea Notts Co Bradford C (loan) Walsall	122 98 152 69 5 88	30 34 42 3 — 31
Wood Trevor	6 0	13 04	G	3	11 68	Jersey	Apprentice	Brighton & HA Port Vale Walsall	— 42 59	— — —

Trainees
Baldwin, David J; Bentley, Gavin; Blakeley, Andrew P; Brant, Gavin J; Davies, Stuart J; Derry, Leighton W; Edwards, Gavin D; Jones, Daniel; Jones, Darren; Keates, Dean S; Langley, James T; Mountford, Paul J; Perry, Mark; Platt, Clive L; Ricketts, Michael B; Rowland, Stephen J; Sault, Christopher A; Thomas, Wayne.

Non-Contract
Da Silva, Chiwale S.

Associated Schoolboys
Edwards, Gary S; Gozzard, Paul J; Hodgetts, Andrew J; Scott, Ben.

WATFORD

Andrews Wayne§			M	25 11 77	Paddington	Trainee	Watford	1	—
Barnes David*	5 10	11 01	D	16 11 61	London	Apprentice	Coventry C Ipswich T Wolverhampton W Aldershot Sheffield U Watford	9 17 88 69 82 16	— — 4 1 1 —
Bazeley Darren	5 10	11 02	F	5 10 72	Northampton	Trainee	Watford	143	13
Calderhead Robert*	5 11	12 00	M	8 12 76	Liverpool	Trainee	Watford	—	—
Cherry Steve*	6 1	13 00	G	5 8 60	Nottingham	Apprentice	Derby Co Port Vale (loan) Walsall Plymouth Arg Chesterfield (loan) Notts Co Watford Plymouth Arg (loan)	77 4 71 73 10 266 4 16	— — — — — — — —
Connolly David	5 8	10 09	F	6 6 77	Willesden	Trainee	Watford	13	8
Dixon Kerry	6 0	13 10	F	24 7 61	Luton	Dunstable	Reading Chelsea Southampton Luton T (loan) Luton T Millwall Watford	116 335 9 17 58 31 11	51 147 2 3 16 9 —
Fitzgerald Gary‡	6 1	11 07	D	27 10 76	Hampstead	Trainee	Watford	1	—
Foster Colin	6 4	14 01	D	16 7 64	Chislehurst	Apprentice	Orient Nottingham F West Ham U Notts Co (loan) Watford	174 72 93 9 66	10 5 5 — 8
Gibbs Nigel*	5 7	11 01	D	20 11 65	St Albans	Apprentice	Watford	291	3
Hessenthaler Andy	5 7	11 05	M	17 8 65	Gravesend	Redbridge Forest	Watford	195	11
Hodge Steve‡	5 8	11 03	M	25 10 62	Nottingham	Apprentice	Nottingham F Aston Villa Tottenham H Nottingham F Leeds U Derby Co (loan) QPR Watford	123 53 45 82 54 10 15 2	30 12 7 20 10 2 — —
Holdsworth David	6 1	12 04	D	8 11 68	Walthamstow	Trainee	Watford	258	10
Johnson Richard	5 10	11 13	M	27 4 74	Kurri Kurri	Trainee	Watford	85	4
Lowndes Nathan	5 11	10 04	F	2 6 77	Salford	Trainee	Leeds U Watford	— —	— —
Ludden Dominic	5 7	10 09	D	30 3 74	Basildon	Trainee	Leyton Orient Watford	58 13	1 —
Millen Keith	6 2	12 04	D	26 9 66	Croydon	Juniors	Brentford Watford	305 74	17 1
Miller Kevin	6 1	13 00	G	15 3 69	Falmouth	Newquay	Exeter C Birmingham C Watford	163 24 86	— — —

Name	Ht	Wt	Pos	Birthdate	Birthplace	Source	Club	Apps	Gls
Mooney Tommy	5 11	12 06	F	11 8 71	Teesside North	Trainee	Aston Villa	—	—
							Scarborough	107	30
							Southend U	14	5
							Watford (loan)	10	2
							Watford	71	9
Moralee Jamie*	5 11	11 00	F	2 12 71	Wandsworth	Trainee	Crystal Palace	6	—
							Millwall	67	19
							Watford	49	7
Neill Warren‡	5 9	11 05	M	21 11 62	Acton	Apprentice	QPR	181	3
							Portsmouth	218	2
							Watford	1	—
Page Robert	6 0	12 05	D	3 9 74	Llwynpia	Trainee	Watford	28	—
Palmer Steve	6 1	12 13	M	31 3 68	Brighton	Cambridge Univ	Ipswich T	111	2
							Watford	35	1
Payne Derek*	5 6	10 08	M	26 4 67	Edgware	Hayes	Barnet	51	6
							Southend U	35	—
							Watford	36	1
Penrice Gary	5 8	10 06	F	23 3 64	Bristol	Bristol C	Bristol R	188	54
							Watford	43	18
							Aston Villa	20	1
							QPR	82	20
							Watford	7	1
Phillips Kevin	5 7	11 00	F	25 7 73	Hitchin	Baldock T	Watford	43	20
Pitcher Geoffrey*	5 6	10 13	M	15 8 75	Sutton	Trainee	Millwall	—	—
							Watford	13	2
Porter Gary	5 6	11 00	M	6 3 66	Sunderland	Apprentice	Watford	394	47
Ramage Craig	5 9	11 08	M	30 3 70	Derby	Trainee	Derby Co	42	4
							Wigan Ath (loan)	10	2
							Watford	93	24
Simpson Colin	6 1	11 05	F	30 4 76	Oxford	Trainee	Watford	1	—
Ward Darran§			D	13 9 78	Kenton	Trainee	Watford	1	—
White Devon	6 3	14 00	F	2 3 64	Nottingham	Arnold T	Lincoln C	29	4
						Boston U	Bristol R	202	53
							Cambridge U	22	4
							QPR	26	9
							Notts Co	40	15
							Watford	16	5
White John*	5 8	11 03	M	9 9 74	Honiton	Trainee	Watford	—	—
Wilkerson Paul*	6 3	13 11	G	11 12 74	Hertford		Watford	—	—

Trainees
Andrews, Wayne M H; Belgrave, Kevin M; Cave, Vincent K; Easton, Clint J; Grieves, Daniel L; Johnson, Andrew; Johnson, Christopher; Jones, Mark C; Pearl, Craig M; Pluck, Colin I; Robinson, Paul P; Rogers, David A; Rooney, Mark J; Walton, David G J; Ward, Darren P.

Associated Schoolboys
Bethell, James; Birch, Alan; Brathwaite, Daniel S; Brown, Daniel; Dickie, James P; Dobson, Michael J; Farley, Craig; Fattorusso, Jay D; Fisken, Gary S; Gates, Matthew; Langston, Matthew J; Marsh, David K; Maynard, Stuart A C; Murphy, Mitchell E; Neill, Thomas E; Nix, Lee; Piper, Christopher O; Reynolds, Adam T.

Associated Schoolboys who have accepted the club's offer of a Traineeship/Contract
Boyce, Mark; Cornock, Grant L W; Noel-Williams, Gifton; Panayi, James; Perpetuini, David P; Smith, Thomas W.

WEST BROMWICH ALBION

Name	Ht	Wt	Pos	Birthdate	Birthplace	Source	Club	Apps	Gls
Agnew Paul	5 9	10 07	D	15 8 65	Lisburn	Cliftonville	Grimsby T	241	3
							WBA	17	1
Ashcroft Lee	5 10	11 02	F	7 9 72	Preston	Trainee	Preston NE	91	13
							WBA	85	17
							Notts Co (loan)	6	—
Brien Tony	5 11	11 09	D	10 2 69	Dublin	Apprentice	Leicester C	16	1
							Chesterfield	204	8
							Rotherham U	43	2
							WBA	2	—
							Mansfield T (loan)	4	—
							Chester C (loan)	8	—
Buckley Simon‡	5 10	11 00	F	29 2 76	Stafford	Trainee	Grimsby T	—	—
							WBA	—	—
Burgess Daryl	5 11	12 03	D	20 4 71	Birmingham	Trainee	WBA	223	7
Clarke Stuart*			M	10 3 77	Leamington	Trainee	WBA	—	—
Coldicott Stacy	5 8	11 04	D	29 4 74	Worcester	Trainee	WBA	63	—
Comyn Andy†	6 1	11 12	D	2 6 68	Manchester	Alvechurch	Aston Villa	15	—
							Derby Co	63	1
							Plymouth Arg	76	5
							Preston NE	—	—
							WBA	3	—

Cunnington Shaun	5 9	11 04	M	4 1 66	Bourne	Bourne T	Wrexham	199	12
							Grimsby T	182	13
							Sunderland	58	8
							WBA	9	—
Cutler Neil	6 1	12 00	G	3 9 76	Birmingham	Trainee	WBA	—	—
							Coventry C (loan)	—	—
							Chester C (loan)	1	—
Darby Julian	6 0	11 04	M	3 10 67	Bolton	Trainee	Bolton W	270	36
							Coventry C	55	5
							WBA	22	1
Donovan Kevin	5 8	11 02	F	17 12 71	Halifax	Trainee	Huddersfield T	20	1
							Halifax T (loan)	6	—
							WBA	136	19
Edwards Paul R*	5 11	11 00	D	25 12 63	Birkenhead	Altrincham	Crewe Alex	86	6
							Coventry C	36	—
							Wolverhampton W	46	—
							WBA	51	—
							Bury (loan)	4	—
Germaine Gary	6 0	11 07	G	2 8 76	Birmingham	Trainee	WBA	—	—
							Scunthorpe U (loan)	11	—
Gilbert Dave	5 4	10 08	M	22 6 63	Lincoln	Apprentice	Lincoln C	30	1
							Scunthorpe U	1	—
						Boston U	Northampton T	120	21
							Grimsby T	259	41
							WBA	40	5
Hamilton Ian	5 9	11 03	F	14 12 67	Stevenage	Apprentice	Southampton	—	—
							Cambridge U	24	1
							Scunthorpe U	145	18
							WBA	164	17
Hargreaves Christian	5 11	12 02	F	12 5 72	Cleethorpes	Trainee	Grimsby T	51	5
							Scarborough (loan)	3	—
							Hull C	49	—
							WBA	1	—
							Hereford U (loan)	17	2
Hayter Robert*			D	20 4 77	London	Trainee	WBA	—	—
Herbert Craig	5 10	11 00	D	9 11 75	Coventry	Torquay U	WBA	8	—
Holmes Paul	5 10	11 00	D	18 2 68	Wortley	Apprentice	Doncaster R	47	1
							Torquay U	138	4
							Birmingham C	12	—
							Everton	21	—
							WBA	18	—
Hunt Andy	6 0	11 12	F	9 6 70	Thurrock	Kettering T	Newcastle U	43	11
							WBA (loan)	10	9
							WBA	119	39
Mardon Paul	6 0	12 00	D	14 9 69	Bristol	Trainee	Bristol C	42	—
							Doncaster R (loan)	3	—
							Birmingham C	64	—
							WBA	89	2
Naylor Stuart*	6 4	12 02	G	6 12 62	Wetherby	Yorkshire A	Lincoln C	49	—
							Peterborough U (loan)	8	—
							Crewe Alex (loan)	38	—
							Crewe Alex (loan)	17	—
							WBA	355	—
Nicholson Shane	5 10	11 00	D	3 6 70	Newark	Trainee	Lincoln C	133	6
							Derby Co	74	1
							WBA	18	—
Phelan Mike‡	5 11	11 01	D	24 9 62	Nelson	Apprentice	Burnley	168	9
							Norwich C	156	9
							Manchester U	102	2
							WBA	21	—
Raven Paul	6 1	12 11	D	28 7 70	Salisbury	School	Doncaster R	52	4
							WBA	179	13
							Doncaster R (loan)	7	—
Reece Paul	5 10	12 08	G	16 7 68	Nottingham	Kettering T	Grimsby T	54	—
							Doncaster R	1	—
							Oxford U	39	—
							Notts Co	11	—
							WBA	1	—
Rees Tony*	5 10	12 02	F	1 8 64	Merthyr Tydfil	Apprentice	Aston Villa	—	—
							Birmingham C	95	12
							Peterborough U (loan)	5	2
							Shrewsbury T (loan)	2	—
							Barnsley	31	3
							Grimsby T	141	33
							WBA	23	2
Rodosthenous Michael	5 11	11 02	F	25 8 76	Islington	Trainee	WBA	—	—

Smith David	5 8	10 08	M	29 3 68	Gloucester		Coventry C	154	19
							Bournemouth (loan)	1	—
							Birmingham C	38	3
							WBA	56	—
Sneekes Richard	5 11	12 03	M	30 10 68	Amsterdam		Ajax	3	—
							Volendam	31	7
							Fortuna Sittard	126	20
						Locarno	Bolton W	55	7
							WBA	13	10
Spink Nigel	6 2	14 06	G	8 8 58	Chelmsford	Chelmsford C	Aston Villa	361	—
							WBA	15	—
Taylor Bob	5 9	11 13	F	3 2 67	Horden	Horden CW	Leeds U	42	9
							Bristol C	106	50
							WBA	191	84

Trainees
Adamson, Christopher; Bowman, Darren M; Buckley, Adam C; Cleverley, Jay; Craven, Dean; Cunningham, Darren; Heath, Dominic; James, Anthony; Knight, Lee K; O'Brien, Scott L; Prosser, Gareth B; Tranter, Carl; Williams, Richard; Wills, James D.

Non-Contract
Comyn, Andrew J.

Associated Schoolboys
Abercrombie, Garry B; Chambers, Adam C; Chambers, James A; Davies, Gareth W; Dealtry, Russell J; Joynson, Dean; Oliver, Adam.

WEST HAM UNITED

Bilic Slaven	6 2	13 06	D	11 9 68	Croatia		Hajduk Split	109	13
							Karlsruhe	54	5
							West Ham U	13	—
Bishop Ian	5 9	10 12	M	29 5 65	Liverpool	Apprentice	Everton	1	—
							Crewe Alex (loan)	4	—
							Carlisle U	132	14
							Bournemouth	44	2
							Manchester C	19	2
							West Ham U	222	11
Blaney Steven	6 0	13 00	D	24 3 77	Orsett	Trainee	West Ham U	—	—
Boogers Marco	6 1	12 00	M	12 1 67	Dordrecht		DS 79	60	18
							Utrecht	60	15
							RKC	33	14
							Fortuna Sittard	29	13
							RKC	71	32
							Sparta	25	11
							West Ham U	4	—
Breacker Tim	5 11	13 00	D	2 7 65	Bicester		Luton T	210	3
							West Ham U	192	8
Brown Kenny	5 10	11 06	D	11 7 67	Barking	Apprentice	Norwich C	25	—
							Plymouth Arg	126	4
							West Ham U	63	5
							Huddersfield T (loan)	5	—
							Reading (loan)	12	1
							Southend U (loan)	6	—
							Crystal Palace (loan)	6	2
Canham Scott	5 8	10 13	M	5 11 74	London	Trainee	West Ham U	—	—
							Torquay U (loan)	3	—
							Brentford (loan)	14	—
Cottee Tony	5 7	11 03	F	11 7 65	West Ham	Apprentice	West Ham U	212	92
							Everton	184	72
							West Ham U	64	23
Coyne Christopher	6 1	13 10	D	20 12 78	Brisbane	Perth SC	West Ham U	—	—
Dani			M	2 11 76	Lisbon	Sporting Lisbon	West Ham U	9	2
Dicks Julian	5 10	13 00	D	8 8 68	Bristol	Apprentice	Birmingham C	89	1
							West Ham U	159	29
							Liverpool	24	3
							West Ham U	63	15
Dowie Iain	6 1	13 07	F	9 1 65	Hatfield	Hendon	Luton T	66	16
							Fulham (loan)	5	1
							West Ham U	12	4
							Southampton	122	30
							Crystal Palace	19	6
							West Ham U	33	8
Dumitrescu Ilie	5 8	10 07	M	6 1 69	Bucharest		FC Olt	32	1
							Steaua	163	71
							Tottenham H	18	4
							West Ham U	3	—
Ferdinand Rio	6 2	12 00	D	7 11 78	London	Trainee	West Ham U	1	—
Finn Neil§			G	29 12 78	London	Trainee	West Ham U	1	—

Name	Ht	Wt	Pos	Birth	Birthplace	Prev	Club	Apps	Gls
Gordon Dale*	5 10	11 08	F	9 1 67	Gt Yarmouth	Apprentice	Norwich C	206	31
							Rangers	45	6
							West Ham U	9	1
							Peterborough U (loan)	6	1
							Millwall (loan)	6	—
Harkes John‡	5 10	11 12	M	8 3 67	New Jersey	USSF	Sheffield W	81	7
							Derby Co	74	2
							West Ham U	11	—
Hodges Lee	5 5	10 02	F	2 3 78	Newham	Trainee	West Ham U	—	—
Hughes Michael	5 7	10 13	F	2 8 71	Larne	Carrick R	Manchester C	26	1
							Strasbourg	83	9
							West Ham U (loan)	45	2
Jones Steve	5 11	12 00	F	17 3 70	Cambridge	Billericay	West Ham U	16	4
							Bournemouth	74	26
							West Ham U	—	—
Kydd Peter‡	5 8	10 00	M	20 1 78	Bournemouth	Trainee	West Ham U	—	—
Lampard Frank	6 0	13 07	M	21 6 78	Romford	Trainee	West Ham U	2	—
							Swansea C (loan)	9	1
Lazaridis Stan	5 9	11 12	M	16 8 72	Perth	West Adelaide	West Ham U	4	—
Martin Alvin*	6 1	13 07	D	29 7 58	Bootle	Apprentice	West Ham U	469	27
Mautone Steve	6 1	12 00	G	10 8 70	Myrtleford	Canberra Cosmos	West Ham U	—	—
McPherson Malcolm‡	5 10	12 00	F	9 12 74	Glasgow	Yeovil	West Ham U	—	—
Miklosko Ludek	6 5	14 00	G	9 12 61	Ostrava	Banik Ostrava	West Ham U	266	—
Moncur John	5 7	9 10	M	22 9 66	Stepney	Apprentice	Tottenham H	21	1
							Cambridge U (loan)	4	—
							Doncaster R (loan)	4	—
							Portsmouth (loan)	7	—
							Brentford (loan)	5	1
							Ipswich T (loan)	6	—
							Nottingham F (loan)	—	—
							Swindon T	58	5
							West Ham U	50	2
Moore Jason	5 8	11 04	D	16 2 79	Dover	Trainee	West Ham U	—	—
Omoyimni Emmanuel	5 6	10 07	M	28 12 77	Nigeria	Trainee	West Ham U	—	—
Philson Graeme	5 10	10 11	D	24 3 75	Ireland	Coleraine	West Ham U	—	—
Potts Steve	5 7	10 11	D	7 5 67	Hartford (USA)	Apprentice	West Ham U	312	1
Rieper Marc	6 3	14 00	D	5 6 68	Denmark	Brondby	West Ham U	57	3
Rowland Keith	5 10	10 00	M	1 9 71	Portadown	Trainee	Bournemouth	72	2
							Coventry C (loan)	2	—
							West Ham U	58	—
Sealey Les	6 1	13 06	G	29 9 57	Bethnal Green	Apprentice	Coventry C	158	—
							Luton T	207	—
							Plymouth Arg (loan)	6	—
							Manchester U (loan)	2	—
							Manchester U	31	—
							Aston Villa	18	—
							Coventry C (loan)	2	—
							Birmingham C (loan)	12	—
							Manchester U	—	—
							Blackpool	7	—
							West Ham U	2	—
Shilton Peter*	6 1	14 00	G	18 9 49	Leicester	Apprentice	Leicester C	286	1
							Stoke C	110	—
							Nottingham F	202	—
							Southampton	188	—
							Derby Co	175	—
							Plymouth Arg	34	—
							Wimbledon	—	—
							Bolton W	1	—
							Coventry C	—	—
							West Ham U	—	—
Shipp Danny	5 11	11 13	F	25 9 76	Romford	Trainee	West Ham U	—	—
Slater Robbie	5 11	12 05	M	26 11 64	Ormskirk	Lens	Blackburn R	18	—
							West Ham U	22	2
Webster Simon‡	6 0	11 07	D	20 1 64	Earl Shilton	Apprentice	Tottenham H	3	—
							Exeter C (loan)	26	—
							Norwich C (loan)	—	—
							Huddersfield T	118	4
							Sheffield U	37	3
							Charlton Ath	127	7
							West Ham U	5	—
							Oldham Ath (loan)	7	—
							Derby Co (loan)	3	—

Whitbread Adrian	6 2	11 13	D	22 10 71	Epping	Trainee	Leyton Orient	125	2
							Swindon T	36	1
							West Ham U	10	—
							Portsmouth (loan)	13	—
Williamson Danny	5 10	11 06	M	5 12 73	London	Trainee	West Ham U	36	5
							Doncaster R (loan)	13	1

Trainees
Bowen, Justin J R; Boylan, Lee M; Finn, Neil E; Goodwin, Lee J; Keith, Joseph R; McFarlane, Anthony Z; Partridge, David W; Richardson, Stuart J; Sains, Christopher F; Sweeting, Daniel B.

Associated Schoolboys
Angus, Stevland; Briggs, Ryan D; Byrne, Shaun R; Gray, Edward; Newton, Adam L.

Associated Schoolboys who have accepted the club's offer of a Traineeship/Contract
Bartley, Danny R; Fernley, Daniel P; Henry, Anthony F; McCann, Grant S; Miller, Robert; Wells, Andrew.

WIGAN ATHLETIC

Benjamin Ian‡	5 11	13 04	F	11 12 61	Nottingham	Apprentice	Sheffield U	5	3
							WBA	2	—
							Notts Co	—	—
							Peterborough U	80	14
							Northampton T	150	59
							Cambridge U	25	2
							Chester C	22	2
							Exeter C	32	4
							Southend U	122	33
							Luton T	13	2
							Brentford	15	2
							Wigan Ath	20	6
Biggins Wayne	5 11	11 00	F	20 11 61	Sheffield	Apprentice	Lincoln C	8	1
						Matlock Town	Burnley	78	29
						and King's Lynn			
							Norwich C	79	16
							Manchester C	32	9
							Stoke C	122	46
							Barnsley	47	16
							Celtic	9	—
							Stoke C	27	6
							Luton T (loan)	7	1
							Oxford U	10	1
							Wigan Ath	18	2
Black Tony	5 8	11 01	F	15 7 69	Barrow	Bamber Bridge	Wigan Ath	30	2
Butler John	5 11	12 01	D	7 2 62	Liverpool	Prescot Cables	Wigan Ath	245	15
							Stoke C	262	7
							Wigan Ath	33	1
Carragher Matthew	5 9	10 07	D	14 1 76	Liverpool	Trainee	Wigan Ath	101	—
Diaz Isidro	5 7	9 04	M	15 5 72	Valencia	Balaguer	Wigan Ath	37	10
Doolan John*	5 9	11 05	M	10 11 68	South Liverpool	Knowsley U	Wigan Ath	38	1
Farnworth Simon	5 11	13 04	G	28 10 63	Chorley	Apprentice	Bolton W	113	—
							Stockport Co (loan)	10	—
							Tranmere R (loan)	7	—
							Bury	105	—
							Preston NE	81	—
							Wigan Ath	126	—
Farrell Andy*	5 11	12 03	D	7 10 65	Colchester	School	Colchester U	105	5
							Burnley	257	19
							Wigan Ath	54	1
Felgate David*	6 1	15 00	G	4 3 60	Blaenau Ffestiniog	Blaenau Ffestiniog	Bolton W	—	—
							Rochdale (loan)	35	—
							Bradford C (loan)	—	—
							Crewe Alex (loan)	14	—
							Rochdale (loan)	12	—
							Lincoln C	198	—
							Cardiff C (loan)	4	—
							Grimsby T (loan)	12	—
							Grimsby T	12	—
							Bolton W	238	—
							Rotherham U (loan)	—	—
							Bury	—	—
							Wolverhampton W	—	—
							Chester C	72	—
							Wigan Ath	3	—
Furlong Carl‡	5 11	12 06	F	18 10 76	Liverpool	Trainee	Wigan Ath	3	1

Player	Ht	Wt	Pos	Born	Birthplace	Source	Clubs	Apps	Gls
Greenall Colin	5 11	12 12	D	30 12 63	Billinge	Apprentice	Blackpool	183	9
							Gillingham	62	4
							Oxford U	67	2
							Bury (loan)	3	—
							Bury	68	5
							Preston NE	29	1
							Chester C	42	1
							Lincoln C	43	3
							Wigan Ath	37	2
Haley Martin‡	5 10	10 05	G	22 11 76	Salford	Trainee	Wigan Ath	—	—
Johnson Gavin	5 11	11 07	D	10 10 70	Eye	Trainee	Ipswich T	132	11
							Luton T	5	—
							Wigan Ath	27	3
Kelly Tony‡	5 10	14 07	M	1 10 64	Prescot	Liverpool	Derby Co	—	—
							Wigan Ath	101	15
							Stoke C	36	4
							WBA	26	1
							Chester C (loan)	5	—
							Colchester U (loan)	13	2
							Shrewsbury T	101	15
							Bolton W	106	5
							Port Vale	4	1
							Millwall	2	—
							Wigan Ath	—	—
							Peterborough U	13	2
							Wigan Ath	2	—
Kilford Ian	5 10	11 00	M	6 10 73	Bristol	Trainee	Nottingham F	1	—
							Wigan Ath (loan)	8	3
							Wigan Ath	60	8
Lancashire Graham	5 10	11 12	F	19 10 72	Blackpool	Trainee	Burnley	31	8
							Halifax T (loan)	2	—
							Chester C (loan)	11	7
							Preston NE	23	2
							Wigan Ath	5	3
Leonard Mark*	5 11	13 03	F	27 9 62	St Helens	Witton Albion	Everton	—	—
							Tranmere R (loan)	7	—
							Crewe Alex	54	15
							Stockport Co	73	24
							Bradford C	157	29
							Rochdale	9	1
							Preston NE	22	1
							Chester C	32	8
							Wigan Ath	64	12
Love Michael	5 11	12 04	M	27 11 73	Stockport	Hinckley Ath	Wigan Ath	—	—
Lowe David	5 10	11 04	F	30 8 65	Liverpool	Apprentice	Wigan Ath	188	40
							Ipswich T	134	37
							Port Vale (loan)	9	2
							Leicester C	94	22
							Port Vale (loan)	19	5
							Wigan Ath	7	3
Martinez Roberto	5 11	11 12	M	13 7 73	Balaguer	Balaguer	Wigan Ath	42	9
Miller David*	5 11	11 13	M	8 1 64	Burnley	Apprentice	Burnley	32	3
							Crewe Alex (loan)	3	—
							Tranmere R	29	1
							Preston NE	58	2
							Burnley (loan)	4	—
							Carlisle U	109	7
							Stockport Co	81	1
							Wigan Ath	38	3
Millett Mike (Deceased)	5 10	11 07	D	22 9 77	Wigan	Trainee	Wigan Ath	3	—
Ogden Neil‡	5 10	11 07	M	29 11 75	Billinge	Trainee	Wigan Ath	15	—
Pender John	6 0	13 09	D	19 11 63	Luton	Apprentice	Wolverhampton W	117	3
							Charlton Ath	41	—
							Bristol C	83	3
							Burnley	171	8
							Wigan Ath	41	1
Rimmer Neill*	5 6	10 05	M	13 11 67	Liverpool	Apprentice	Everton	1	—
							Ipswich T	22	3
							Wigan Ath	190	10
Seba Jesus	5 6	9 13	M	11 4 74	Zaragoza	Zaragoza	Wigan Ath	20	3
Sharp Kevin	5 9	10 07	M	19 9 74	Ontario	Auxerre	Leeds U	17	—
							Wigan Ath	20	6
Statham Mark*	6 2	13 03	G	7 3 76	Daveyhulme	Trainee	Nottingham F	—	—
							Wigan Ath	2	—
Tait Paul‡	6 1	10 13	F	24 10 74	Newcastle	Trainee	Everton	—	—
							Wigan Ath	5	—
West Paul‡	5 11	12 07	D	22 6 70	Birmingham	Alcester T	Port Vale	—	—
							Bradford C	—	—
							Wigan Ath	3	—

Trainees
Elwell, Steven P; Fearns, Terence P; Fitzhenry, Neil; Foulds, Jason J; Gallagher, Damien J; Hall, Stephen J; Hilton, Darren J; Hogg, Russell S; Just, Paul G; Lloyd, Neil E; Lynch, Paul E; McKie, Tony; Moore, Andrew P; Moss, Steven J; Salt, Daniel J; Slater, Stewart J; Tyrrell, Kevin M; Weston, Steven M.

Associated Schoolboys
Barratt, Andrew; Brennan, Daniel T; Brittain, Jonathan; Court, Mark; Coyne, John; Crompton, Paul; Donachie, Stuart G; Forsyth, Anthony J; Jones, Philip A; Jones, Richard; McLean, Alan; Rhead, Michael; Sing, Stephen; Smith, David; Stubbs, David J; Turner, Mark D; Wiswell, Gareth.

Associated Schoolboys who have accepted the club's offer of a Traineeship/Contract
Alexander, Paul; Baccino, Stephen D; Birch, Christopher J; Cunliffe, David A; Hatton, Barry.

WIMBLEDON

Name					Birthplace	Previous club	Clubs	Apps	Gls
Ardley Neal	5 11	11 09	M	1 9 72	Epsom	Trainee	Wimbledon	71	6
Blackwell Dean	6 1	12 10	D	5 12 69	Camden	Trainee	Wimbledon	92	1
							Plymouth Arg (loan)	7	—
Blissett Gary	6 0	12 07	F	29 6 64	Manchester	Altrincham	Crewe Alex	122	39
							Brentford	233	79
							Wimbledon	31	3
							Wycombe W (loan)	4	2
							Crewe Alex (loan)	10	1
Castledine Stewart	6 1	12 13	M	22 1 73	Wandsworth	Trainee	Wimbledon	15	3
							Wycombe W (loan)	7	3
Clarke Andy	5 10	11 07	F	22 7 67	Islington	Barnet	Wimbledon	145	16
Cunningham Kenny	5 11	11 02	D	28 6 71	Dublin	Tolka R	Millwall	136	1
							Wimbledon	61	—
Dobbs Gerald*	5 8	11 07	D	24 1 71	Lambeth	Trainee	Wimbledon	33	1
							Cardiff C (loan)	3	—
Earle Robbie	5 9	10 10	F	27 1 65	Newcastle under Lyme	Stoke C	Port Vale	294	77
							Wimbledon	170	41
Ekoku Efan	6 1	12 00	F	8 6 67	Manchester	Sutton U	Bournemouth	62	21
							Norwich C	37	15
							Wimbledon	55	16
Elkins Gary	5 9	11 13	M	4 5 66	Wallingford	Apprentice	Fulham	104	2
							Exeter C (loan)	5	—
							Wimbledon	110	3
Euell Jason	5 11	11 02	F	6 2 77	South London	Trainee	Wimbledon	9	2
Fear Peter	5 10	11 07	D	10 9 73	London	Trainee	Wimbledon	45	2
Fitzgerald Scott	6 0	12 02	D	13 8 69	London	Trainee	Wimbledon	106	1
							Sheffield U (loan)	6	—
Futcher Andy	5 7	10 07	D	10 2 78	Enfield	Trainee	Wimbledon	—	—
Gayle Marcus	6 1	12 09	M	27 9 70	Hammersmith	Trainee	Brentford	156	22
							Wimbledon	67	7
Goodman Jon	6 0	12 03	F	2 6 71	Walthamstow	Bromley	Millwall	109	35
							Wimbledon	46	10
Harford Mick	6 3	14 05	F	12 2 59	Sunderland	Lambton St BC	Lincoln C	115	41
							Newcastle U	19	4
							Bristol C	30	11
							Birmingham C	92	25
							Luton T	139	57
							Derby Co	58	15
							Luton T	29	12
							Chelsea	28	9
							Sunderland	11	2
							Coventry C	1	1
							Wimbledon	48	8
Heald Paul	6 2	12 05	G	20 9 68	Wath on Dearne	Trainee	Sheffield U	—	—
							Leyton Orient	176	—
							Coventry C (loan)	2	—
							Crystal Palace (loan)	—	—
							Swindon T (loan)	2	—
							Wimbledon	18	—
Hodges Danny	6 0	12 07	D	14 9 76	Greenwich	Trainee	Wimbledon	—	—
Holdsworth Dean	5 11	11 13	F	8 11 68	Walthamstow	Trainee	Watford	16	3
							Carlisle U (loan)	4	1
							Port Vale (loan)	6	2
							Swansea C (loan)	5	1
							Brentford (loan)	7	1
							Brentford	110	53
							Wimbledon	139	53
Jones Vinnie	6 0	11 12	M	5 1 65	Watford	Wealdstone	Wimbledon	77	9
							Leeds U	46	5
							Sheffield U	35	2
							Chelsea	42	4
							Wimbledon	124	9

Joseph Roger*	5 11	11 10	D	24 12 65	Paddington	Juniors	Brentford	104	2
							Wimbledon	162	—
							Millwall (loan)	5	—
Kimble Alan	5 10	12 04	D	6 8 66	Poole		Charlton Ath	6	—
							Exeter C (loan)	1	—
							Cambridge U	299	24
							Wimbledon	71	—
Laidlaw Iain	6 2	12 07	D	10 12 76	Newcastle	Trainee	Wimbledon	—	—
Leonhardsen Oyvind	5 10	11 02	M	17 8 70	Norway	Rosenborg	Wimbledon	49	8
McAllister Brian	5 11	12 05	D	30 11 70	Glasgow	Trainee	Wimbledon	55	—
							Plymouth Arg (loan)	8	—
							Crewe Alex (loan)	13	1
Murphy Brendan	5 11	11 12	G	19 8 75	Wexford	Bradford C	Wimbledon	—	—
Newhouse Aidan	6 2	13 05	M	23 5 72	Wallasey	Trainee	Chester C	44	6
							Wimbledon	23	2
							Tranmere R (loan)	—	—
							Port Vale (loan)	2	—
							Portsmouth (loan)	6	1
							Torquay U (loan)	4	2
Payne Grant	5 9	11 04	F	25 12 75	Woking	Trainee	Wimbledon	—	—
Pearce Andy	6 4	14 11	D	20 4 66	Bradford on Avon	Halesowen	Coventry C	71	4
							Sheffield W	69	3
							Wimbledon	7	—
Perry Chris	5 8	10 08	D	26 4 73	London	Trainee	Wimbledon	61	—
Piper Len	5 6	9 09	M	8 8 77	London	Trainee	Wimbledon	—	—
Reeves Alan	6 0	12 00	D	19 11 67	Birkenhead	Heswall	Norwich C	—	—
							Gillingham (loan)	18	—
							Chester C	40	2
							Rochdale	121	9
							Wimbledon	55	4
Segers Hans*	5 11	12 07	G	30 10 61	Eindhoven	PSV Eindhoven	Nottingham F	58	—
							Stoke C (loan)	1	—
							Sheffield U (loan)	10	—
							Dunfermline Ath (loan)	4	—
							Wimbledon	267	—
Skinner Justin*	5 8	10 12	D	17 9 72	London	Trainee	Wimbledon	2	—
							Bournemouth (loan)	16	—
							Wycombe W (loan)	5	—
Sullivan Neil	6 0	12 01	G	24 2 70	Sutton	Trainee	Wimbledon	32	—
							Crystal Palace (loan)	1	—
Talboys Steve*	5 10	11 06	M	18 9 66	Bristol	Gloucester C	Wimbledon	26	1
Thomas Mark*	5 9	10 10	M	22 11 74	Tooting	Trainee	Wimbledon	—	—
Thorn Andy	6 0	11 05	D	12 11 66	Carshalton	Apprentice	Wimbledon	107	2
							Newcastle U	36	2
							Crystal Palace	128	3
							Wimbledon	37	1

Trainees
Boyle Renner, Victor D; Cameron, Justin W J; Cort, Carl E R; Francis, Damien J; Gardner, James F; Hawkins, Peter S; Hinds, Leigh M; Joseph, Stacy L; Longman, Luke J; Lyons, Danny; Miller, Paul J; O'Connor, Richard; O'Neill, Daniel H; Odlum, Gary M; Petrovic, Timotije; Reynolds, Paul; Rothon, John D.

Associated Schoolboys
Agyemang, Patrick; Gray, Wayne; Mawhinney, Paul; McLernon, Trevor J W; Okikiolu, Kola S.

Associated Schoolboys who have accepted the club's offer of a Traineeship/Contract
Owusu, Ansah O; Vella, Simon.

WOLVERHAMPTON WANDERERS

Atkins Mark	6 1	12 00	D	14 8 68	Doncaster		Scunthorpe U	48	2
							Blackburn R	257	35
							Wolverhampton W	32	3
Birch Paul	5 6	10 04	M	20 11 62	West Bromwich	Apprentice	Aston Villa	173	16
							Wolverhampton W	142	15
							Preston NE (loan)	11	2
Bull Steve	5 11	11 04	F	28 3 65	Tipton	Apprentice	WBA	4	2
							Wolverhampton W	385	217
Bytheway Matthew*	5 11	13 00	D	11 3 77	Wolverhampton	Trainee	Wolverhampton W	—	—
Corica Steve	5 8	10 10	F	24 3 73	Cairns	Marconi	Leicester C	16	2
							Wolverhampton W	17	—
Crowe Glen§	5 10	13 01	F	30 9 78	Kent	Trainee	Wolverhampton W	2	1
Daley Tony	5 8	10 08	F	18 10 67	Birmingham	Apprentice	Aston Villa	233	31
							Wolverhampton W	19	3
De Jong Davy			M	26 4 75	Rotterdam		Wolverhampton W	—	—
De Wolf John	6 2	14 03	D	10 12 62	Schiedam	Feyenoord	Wolverhampton W	28	5

							Club		
Debont Andy	6 2	15 06	G	7 2 74	Wolverhampton	Trainee	Wolverhampton W	—	—
							Hartlepool U (loan)	1	—
							Hereford U (loan)	8	—
Dennison Robbie	5 7	11 00	F	30 4 63	Banbridge	Glenavon	WBA	16	1
							Wolverhampton W	279	39
							Swansea C (loan)	9	—
Emblen Neil	6 2	13 03	D	19 6 71	Bromley	Sittingbourne	Millwall	12	—
							Wolverhampton W	60	9
Ferguson Darren	5 10	10 04	M	9 2 72	Glasgow	Trainee	Manchester U	27	—
							Wolverhampton W	71	1
Flash Richard*	5 9	11 08	M	8 4 76	Birmingham	Trainee	Manchester U	—	—
							Wolverhampton W	—	—
Foley Dominic	6 1	12 08	M	7 7 76	Dublin	St James Gate	Wolverhampton W	5	—
Froggatt Steve	5 10	11 00	M	9 3 73	Lincoln	Trainee	Aston Villa	35	2
							Wolverhampton W	38	3
Goodman Don	5 10	12 12	F	9 5 66	Leeds	School	Bradford C	70	14
							WBA	158	60
							Sunderland	116	40
							Wolverhampton W	68	19
Jones Paul	6 3	14 00	G	18 4 67	Chirk	Kidderminster H	Wolverhampton W	33	—
Kelly Jimmy‡	5 7	11 10	M	14 2 73	Liverpool	Trainee	Wrexham	21	—
							Wolverhampton W	7	—
							Walsall (loan)	10	2
							Wrexham (loan)	9	—
Law Brian	6 2	14 00	D	1 1 70	Merthyr	Apprentice	QPR	20	—
							Wolverhampton W	24	1
Mahon Gavin*	6 0	13 02	M	2 1 77	Birmingham	Trainee	Wolverhampton W	—	—
Masters Neil	6 1	13 00	D	25 5 72	Lisburn	Trainee	Bournemouth	38	2
							Wolverhampton W	12	—
Osborn Simon	5 10	11 04	M	19 1 72	New Addington	Apprentice	Crystal Palace	55	5
							Reading	32	5
							QPR	9	1
							Wolverhampton W	21	2
Pearce Dennis	5 9	11 00	F	10 9 74	Wolverhampton	Trainee	Aston Villa	—	—
							Wolverhampton W	5	—
Piearce Stephen*	5 11	10 10	F	29 9 74	Sutton Coldfield	Trainee	Wolverhampton W	—	—
Rankine Mark	5 10	11 01	M	30 9 69	Doncaster	Trainee	Doncaster R	164	20
							Wolverhampton W	132	1
Richards Dean	6 2	13 07	D	9 6 74	Bradford	Trainee	Bradford C	86	4
							Wolverhampton W (loan)	10	2
							Wolverhampton W	37	1
Robinson Carl	6 3	12 05	M	13 10 76	Llandrudod	Trainee	Wolverhampton W	—	—
							Shrewsbury T (loan)	4	—
Smith James	5 6	10 08	F	17 9 74	Birmingham	Trainee	Wolverhampton W	38	—
Stowell Mike	6 2	13 10	G	19 4 65	Preston	Leyland Motors	Preston NE	—	—
							Everton	—	—
							Chester C (loan)	14	—
							York C (loan)	6	—
							Manchester C (loan)	14	—
							Port Vale (loan)	7	—
							Wolverhampton W (loan)	7	—
							Preston NE (loan)	2	—
							Wolverhampton W	232	—
Thomas Geoff	6 1	12 03	M	5 8 64	Manchester	Local	Rochdale	11	1
							Crewe Alex	125	20
							Crystal Palace	195	26
							Wolverhampton W	24	5
Thompson Andy	5 4	10 06	D	9 11 67	Cannock	Apprentice	WBA	24	1
							Wolverhampton W	344	41
Townsend Quentin*	6 1	13 00	D	13 2 77	Worcester	Trainee	Wolverhampton W	—	—
Venus Mark	6 0	11 08	D	6 4 67	Hartlepool		Hartlepool U	4	—
							Leicester C	61	1
							Wolverhampton W	247	7
Westwood Chris	6 0	13 00	D	13 2 77	Dudley	Trainee	Wolverhampton W	—	—
Williams Mark	5 10	11 03	F	11 8 66	Johannesburg	RWD Molenbeek.	Wolverhampton W	12	—
Wright Jermaine	5 9	10 03	F	21 10 75	Greenwich	Trainee	Millwall	—	—
							Wolverhampton W	13	—
							Doncaster R (loan)	13	—
Young Eric	6 3	13 04	D	25 3 60	Singapore	Slough T	Brighton & HA	126	10
							Wimbledon	99	9
							Crystal Palace	161	15
							Wolverhampton W	30	2

Trainees
Biddle, Steven J; Cotterill, John R; Crowe, Glen M; Davis, Paul; Harper, Lee N; Hill, Daniel F; Holmes, Martin L; Hook, Lee; Leadbeater, Richard P; Nwadike, Chukwuemeka I; Owen, Mark T; Sawyers, Robert; Smith, Darryl C; Stimpson, Ben N; Willoughby, John M; Wilson, Christopher J; Wright, Ian J.

Associated Schoolboys
Bray, Justin; Burke, Andrew; Clark, David; Clegg, Dean R; Gioia, Luigi; Pinches, Scott; Spittle, Stephen.

Associated Schoolboys who have accepted the club's offer of a Traineeship/Contract
Hampton, Richard P; Naylor, Lee M; Turpin, Jamie L; Winstone, Alexander.

WREXHAM

Name	Ht	Wt	Pos	Birth date	Birthplace	Signed from	Club	Apps	Gls
Barnes Richard*	5 10	11 06	F	6 9 75	Wrexham	Trainee	Wrexham	1	—
Brace Deryn	5 7	10 12	D	15 3 75	Haverfordwest	Trainee	Norwich C	—	—
							Wrexham	31	1
Brammer David	5 10	12 00	M	28 2 75	Bromborough	Trainee	Wrexham	49	5
Cartwright Mark	6 2	13 06	G	13 1 73	Chester	York C	Wrexham	—	—
Chalk Martyn	5 6	10 00	F	30 8 69	Swindon	Louth U	Derby Co	7	1
							Stockport Co	43	6
							Wrexham	19	4
Coady Lewis	6 1	11 05	F	20 9 76	Liverpool	Trainee	Wrexham	2	—
Connolly Karl	5 9	11 00	F	9 2 70	Prescot	Napoli (Liverpool)	Wrexham	208	47
Cross Jonathan	5 10	11 07	M	2 3 75	Wallasey	Trainee	Wrexham	99	10
Dixon Ken	6 0	11 03	G	24 2 76	Knowsley	Trainee	Wrexham	—	—
Futcher Stephen			M	24 10 76	Chester	Trainee	Wrexham	—	—
Hardy Phil	5 7	11 08	D	9 4 73	Chester	Trainee	Wrexham	218	—
Hughes Bryan	5 11	11 02	M	19 6 76	Liverpool	Trainee	Wrexham	71	9
Humes Tony	6 0	12 00	D	19 3 66	Blyth	Apprentice	Ipswich T	120	10
							Wrexham	129	4
Hunter Barry	6 3	12 09	D	18 11 68	Coleraine	Crusaders	Wrexham	91	4
Jones Barry	5 11	11 12	D	20 6 70	Prescot	Prescot T	Liverpool	—	—
							Wrexham	159	4
Marriott Andy	6 1	12 08	G	11 10 70	Nottingham	Trainee	Arsenal	—	—
							Nottingham F	11	—
							WBA (loan)	3	—
							Blackburn R (loan)	2	—
							Colchester U (loan)	10	—
							Burnley (loan)	15	—
							Wrexham	128	—
McGregor Mark	5 11	11 05	D	16 2 77	Chester	Trainee	Wrexham	33	1
Morris Steve	5 10	12 00	F	13 5 76	Liverpool	Liverpool	Wrexham	25	5
Owen Gareth	5 7	12 00	M	21 10 71	Chester	Trainee	Wrexham	191	20
Pejic Mel*	5 9	11 05	D	27 4 59	Chesterton	Local	Stoke C	1	—
							Hereford U	412	14
							Wrexham	106	3
Phillips Wayne	5 10	11 02	M	15 12 70	Bangor	Trainee	Wrexham	161	10
Russell Kevin	5 9	10 12	F	6 12 66	Portsmouth	Brighton	Portsmouth	4	1
							Wrexham	84	43
							Leicester C	43	10
							Peterborough U (loan)	7	3
							Cardiff C (loan)	3	—
							Hereford U (loan)	3	1
							Stoke C (loan)	5	1
							Stoke C	40	5
							Burnley	28	6
							Bournemouth	30	1
							Notts Co	11	—
							Wrexham	40	7
Skinner Craig	5 10	11 00	F	21 10 70	Bury	Trainee	Blackburn R	16	—
							Plymouth Arg	53	4
							Wrexham	23	3
Ward Peter	5 10	11 07	F	15 10 64	Durham	Chester-le-Street	Huddersfield T	37	2
							Rochdale	84	10
							Stockport Co	142	10
							Wrexham	34	5
Watkin Steve	5 10	11 10	F	16 6 71	Wrexham	School	Wrexham	171	47
Williams Scott	6 0	12 00	D	7 8 74	Bangor	Trainee	Wrexham	25	—

Trainees
Brown, Terence R; Davies, Andrew M; Edwards, Leigh; Ellison, Barry J; Griffiths, Andrew; Hughes, Gareth E; McNeil, Jamie S; Melarangi, Philip; Morris, Robert I; Nall, Darren; Owens, Robert J; Pepper, Julian M; Roberts, Neil W; Shone, Gareth; Stewart,

John R; Swanick, David; Taylor, Paul A; Thomas, Andrew P; Thomas, Stephen; Wainwright, Neil; Walsh, David; Williams, Robert V; Wilson, Gareth E; Wright, Anthony.

Non-Contract
Jones, Paul P; Ridler, David G.

Associated Schoolboys
Andrews, Carl; Graham, Adam; Jones, Adam; Owen, Adam L; Taylor, Michael J; Whitley, John; Williams, David P; Williams, Gavin P.

Associated Schoolboys who have accepted the club's offer of a Traineeship/Contract
Cooper, Steven D; Hooson, David J; Jones, Phillip B; Roberts, Stephen W; Williams, Daniel F.

WYCOMBE WANDERERS

Bell Mick	5 10	11 08	D	15 11 71	Newcastle	Trainee	Northampton T	153	10
							Wycombe W	72	4
Brown Steve	6 0	11 08	D	6 7 66	Northampton		Northampton T	158	19
							Wycombe W	87	3
Carroll David	6 0	11 09	F	20 9 66	Paisley	Ruislip Manor	Wycombe W	128	20
Cheesewright John†	6 0	12 03	G	12 1 73	Hornchurch	Tottenham H	Southend U	—	—
							Birmingham C	1	—
						Braintree T	Colchester U	40	—
							Wimbledon	—	—
							Wycombe W	—	—
Clark Anthony	5 7	11 00	F	7 4 77	London		Wycombe W	4	—
Cousins Jason	5 10	12 05	D	14 10 70	Hayes	Trainee	Brentford	21	—
						Wycombe W	Wycombe W	108	3
Crossley Matt	6 1	13 12	D	18 3 68	Basingstoke	Overton U	Wycombe W	87	3
De Souza Miguel	5 11	13 08	F	11 2 70	Newham	Dagenham	Birmingham C	15	—
							Bury (loan)	3	—
							Wycombe W	50	24
Evans Terry	6 4	15 04	D	12 4 65	Hammersmith	Hillingdon	Brentford	229	23
							Wycombe W	94	13
Farrell Dave	5 10	11 07	F	11 11 71	Birmingham	Redditch U	Aston Villa	6	—
							Scunthorpe U (loan)	5	1
							Wycombe W	33	7
Garner Simon*	5 8	13 00	F	23 11 59	Boston	Apprentice	Blackburn R	484	168
							WBA	33	8
							Wycombe W	66	14
							Torquay U (loan)	11	1
Hardyman Paul*	5 8	11 04	D	11 3 64	Portsmouth	Waterford	Portsmouth	117	3
							Sunderland	106	9
							Bristol R	67	5
							Wycombe W	15	—
Hemmings Tony‡	5 10	12 09	F	21 9 67	Burton	Northwich Vic	Wycombe W	49	12
Howard Terry*	6 1	14 00	D	26 2 66	Stepney	Apprentice	Chelsea	6	—
							Crystal Palace (loan)	4	—
							Chester C (loan)	2	—
							Leyton Orient	328	31
							Wycombe W	59	2
Lawrence Matthew	5 10	11 04	M	19 6 74	Northampton	Grays Ath	Wycombe W	3	—
Markman Damien†			F	7 1 78	Ascot		Wycombe W	2	—
McGavin Steve	5 9	12 08	F	24 1 69	North Walsham	Sudbury	Colchester U	58	17
							Birmingham C	23	2
							Wycombe W	43	4
McGorry Brian	5 10	12 05	M	16 4 70	Liverpool	Weymouth	Bournemouth	61	11
							Peterborough U	52	6
							Wycombe W	4	—
							Cardiff C (loan)	7	—
Patterson Gary	6 0	12 05	M	27 11 72	Newcastle	Trainee	Notts Co	—	—
							Shrewsbury T	57	2
							Wycombe W	50	2
Rowbotham Jason	5 8	11 05	D	3 1 69	Cardiff	Trainee	Plymouth Arg	9	—
							Shrewsbury T	—	—
							Hereford U	5	1
							Raith R	56	1
							Wycombe W	27	—
Ryan Keith	5 11	12 07	M	25 6 70	Northampton	Berkhamsted T	Wycombe W	89	9
Sargent Dave‡	5 10	12 00	D	22 12 77	Wembley	Watford	Wycombe W	—	—
Skiverton Terry	5 11	11 06	D	26 6 75	Mile End	Trainee	Chelsea	—	—
							Wycombe W (loan)	10	—
							Wycombe W	4	1

Name	Ht	Wt	Pos	Birth date	Birthplace	Source	Club	Apps	Gls
Soloman Jason*	6 0	12 02	M	6 10 70	Welwyn	Trainee	Watford	100	5
							Peterborough U (loan)	4	—
							Wycombe W	13	1
Stapleton Simon*	6 0	13 01	M	10 12 68	Oxford	Portsmouth	Bristol R	5	—
						Wycombe W	Wycombe W	49	3
Stevens Shaun*	5 10	11 07	D	8 3 76	Chertsey		Wycombe W	—	—
Thompson Steve‡	5 7	11 09	M	12 1 63	Plymouth	Saltash U	Bristol C	12	1
							Torquay U	1	—
						Slough T	Wycombe W	62	3
Williams John	6 0	13 01	M	11 5 68	Birmingham	Cradley T	Swansea C	39	11
							Coventry C	80	11
							Notts Co (loan)	5	2
							Stoke C (loan)	4	—
							Swansea C (loan)	7	2
							Wycombe W	29	8

Trainees
Allen, Lee S; Beeton, Alan M; Cowie, Stuart G; Craker, Lewis D; Glynn, James A R; Harkin, Maurice P; Keys, Thomas E; Passmore, Lee M; Patton, Aaron A; Wraight, Gary P.

Non-Contract
Cheesewright, John; Hall, Graham A; Markman, Damien L.

Associated Schoolboys
Colley, Daniel P; James, Matthew; Moakes, Daniel G; Nye, Timothy J; Rama- Dominguez, James.

YORK CITY

Name	Ht	Wt	Pos	Birth date	Birthplace	Source	Club	Apps	Gls
Atkin Paul	6 0	13 00	D	3 9 69	Nottingham	Trainee	Notts Co	—	—
							Bury	21	1
							York C	141	3
Atkinson Paddy	5 9	11 06	D	22 5 70	Singapore	Workington	York C	22	—
Barras Tony	6 0	13 00	D	29 3 71	Stockton	Trainee	Hartlepool U	12	—
							Stockport Co	99	5
							Rotherham U (loan)	5	1
							York C	63	4
Bull Gary	5 10	12 02	F	12 6 66	West Bromwich		Southampton	—	—
							Cambridge U	19	4
						Barnet	Barnet	83	37
							Nottingham F	12	1
							Birmingham C (loan)	10	6
							Brighton & HA (loan)	10	2
							Birmingham C (loan)	6	—
							York C	15	8
Bushell Steve	5 9	11 05	M	28 12 72	Manchester	Trainee	York C	103	5
Campbell Neil	5 10	13 00	F	26 1 77	Middlesbrough	Trainee	York C	—	—
Cresswell Richard			F	20 9 77	Bridlington	Trainee	York C	16	1
Cutler Jason*	5 7	9 06	D	8 9 76	Cleveland	Trainee	York C	—	—
Hall Wayne	5 9	10 06	D	25 10 68	Rotherham	Darlington	York C	259	8
Himsworth Gary	5 8	11 00	D	19 12 69	Appleton	Trainee	York C	88	8
							Scarborough	92	6
							Darlington	94	8
							York C	8	1
Jordan Scott	5 10	11 05	M	19 7 75	Newcastle	Trainee	York C	64	4
Kiely Dean	6 0	13 05	G	10 10 70	Salford	WBA	Coventry C	—	—
							Ipswich T (loan)	—	—
							York C (loan)	—	—
							York C	210	—
McMillan Andy	5 11	11 02	D	22 6 68	Bloemfontein		York C	312	4
Murty Graeme	5 10	11 12	M	13 11 74	Middlesbrough	Trainee	York C	56	4
Naylor Glenn	5 11	11 00	F	11 8 72	York	Trainee	York C	110	30
							Darlington (loan)	4	1
Osborne Wayne	5 10	11 07	D	14 1 77	Stockton	Trainee	York C	6	—
Oxley Scott	5 9	12 00	M	22 11 77	Sheffield	Trainee	York C	2	—
Pepper Nigel	5 10	12 04	M	25 4 68	Rotherham	Apprentice	Rotherham U	45	1
							York C	206	27
Peverell Nick*	5 10	11 02	F	28 4 73	Middlesbrough	Trainee	Middlesbrough	—	—
							Hartlepool U	36	3
							York C	29	2
Pouton Alan	6 0	12 02	M	1 2 77	Newcastle	Newcastle U	Oxford U	—	—
							York C	—	—

Randall Adrian	5 10	12 05	M	10 11 68	Amesbury	Apprentice	Bournemouth	3	—
							Aldershot	107	12
							Burnley	125	8
							York C	16	—
Scaife Nicky‡	6 1	13 13	M	14 5 75	Middlesbrough	Whitby	York C	2	—
Sharples John	6 01	11 03	D	26 1 73	Bury	Manchester U	Hearts	—	—
							Ayr U	53	4
							York C	10	—
Stancliffe Paul‡	6 2	13 04	D	5 5 58	Sheffield	Apprentice	Rotherham U	285	8
							Sheffield U	278	12
							Rotherham U (loan)	5	—
							Wolverhampton W	17	—
							York C	91	3
Stephenson Paul	5 9	12 05	M	2 1 68	Wallsend	Apprentice	Newcastle U	61	1
							Millwall	98	6
							Gillingham (loan)	12	2
							Brentford	70	2
							York C	27	2
Tutill Steve	5 10	12 01	D	1 10 69	Derwent	Trainee	York C	284	6
Warrington Andy	6 3	12 11	G	10 6 76	Sheffield	Trainee	York C	6	—
Williams Darren	5 8	11 00	M	28 4 77	Middlebrough	Trainee	York C	19	—

Trainees
Boyes, Scott; Gibson, David E; Greening, Jonathan; Lamb, Stephen C; Lee, Stuart; Massey, Miles G; Middleditch, Stephen J; Murr, Michael; Pledger, Darren A; Reed, Martin J; Render, Patrick J L; Rennison, Graham L; Rich, Oliver C; Rose, Richard; Tate, Christopher D.

Associated Schoolboys
Batchelor, Peter; Bullock, Lee; Clough, Ian; Dibie, Michael; Farley, Michael C; Fox, Christian; Mohan, John; Rennison, Shaun; Taylor, Ian; Taylor, Kirk; Urwin, Jonathan G; Walters, Steven K.

Associated Schoolboys who have accepted the club's offer of a Traineeship/Contract
Abblett, Mark P; Cruddas, David A; Siddle, James D.

THE FOREIGN (INTERNATIONAL) LEGION

The following full international players born outside the UK played in the FA Premier League and Endsleigh League in 1995–96.

	Player	*Club*	*From*	*Fee £s*
AUSTRALIA	Andy Bernal	Reading	Sydney Olympic	30,000
	Mark Bosnich	Aston Villa	Croatia Sydney	Free
	Steve Corica	Wolverhampton W	Leicester C	1,100,000
	Zeljko Kalac	Leicester C	Sydney United	760,000
	Stan Lazaridis	West Ham U	West Adelaide	300,000
	Robbie Slater	West Ham U	Blackburn R	600,000
	Jason Van Blerk	Millwall	Go Ahead	300,000
	Carl Veart	Crystal Palace	Sheffield U	200,000
BARBADOS	Greg Goodridge	QPR	Torquay U	350,000
BELGIUM	Philippe Albert	Newcastle U	Anderlecht	2,650,000
	Marc Degryse	Sheffield W	Anderlecht	1,500,000
BERMUDA	Shaun Goater	Rotherham U	Manchester U	Free
	Kyle Lightbourne	Walsall	Scarborough	Free
BOLIVIA	Jaime Moreno	Middlesbrough	Blooming	250,000
BRAZIL	Branco	Middlesbrough	Internacional	Free
	Isaias	Coventry C	Benfica	500,000
	Juninho	Middlesbrough	Sao Paulo	4,750,000
BULGARIA	Boncho Guentchev	Luton T	Ipswich T	Free
	Bobby Mikhailov	Reading	Botev Plovdiv	300,000
CAMEROON	Charlie Ntamark	Walsall	Boreham Wood	Free
CANADA	Carlo Corazzin	Plymouth Arg	Cambridge U	150,000
	Craig Forrest	Ipswich T	Trainee	
	Ian McLean	Bristol R	Metroford	Free
	Paul Peschisolido	Birmingham C	Stoke C	400,000
	Randy Samuel	Port Vale	Fortuna Sittard	undisclosed
	Frank Yallop	Ipswich T	Trainee	
COLOMBIA	Faustino Asprilla	Newcastle U	Parma	7,500,000
CROATIA	Slaven Bilic	West Ham U	Karlsruhe	1,650,000
	Igor Stimac	Derby Co	Hajduk Split	1,500,000
CZECH REPUBLIC	Ludek Miklosko	West Ham U	Banik Ostrava	300,000
	Pavel Srnicek	Newcastle U	Banik Ostrava	350,000
DENMARK	John Jensen	Arsenal	Brondby	1,100,000
	Jan Molby	Swansea C	Liverpool	Free
	Marc Rieper	West Ham U	Brondby	1,000,000
	Peter Schmeichel	Manchester U	Brondby	550,000
	Claus Thomsen	Ipswich T	Aarhus	250,000
ESTONIA	Mart Poom	Portsmouth	FC Wil	200,000
FINLAND	Mixu Paatelainen	Bolton W	Aberdeen	300,000
FRANCE	Eric Cantona	Manchester U	Leeds U	1,200,000
	David Ginola	Newcastle U	Paris St Germain	2,500,000
GEORGIA	Mikhail Kavelashvili	Manchester C	Spartak Vladikavkaz	1,400,000
	Georgi Kinkladze	Manchester C	Dynamo Tbilisi	2,000,000
GERMANY	Michael Frontzeck	Manchester C	Moenchengladbach	350,000
	Eike Immel	Manchester C	Stuttgart	400,000
	Uwe Rosler	Manchester C	Dynamo Dresden	750,000

GHANA

Nii Lamptey	Coventry C	Aston Villa	Free
Tony Yeboah	Leeds U	Eintracht Frankfurt	3,400,000

HOLLAND

Dennis Bergkamp	Arsenal	Inter Milan	7,500,000
Regi Blinker	Sheffield W	Feyenoord	275,000
John De Wolf	Wolverhampton W	Feyenoord	600,000
Ruud Gullit	Chelsea	Sampdoria	Free
Glenn Helder	Arsenal	Vitesse	2,300,000
Bryan Roy	Nottingham F	Foggia	2,500,000

ICELAND

Gudni Bergsson	Bolton W	Tottenham H	65,000
Thorvaldur Orlygsson	Oldham Ath	Stoke C	180,000

ISRAEL

Ronny Rosenthal	Tottenham H	Liverpool	250,000

ITALY

Andrea Silenzi	Nottingham F	Torino	1,800,000

NIGERIA

Daniel Amokachi	Everton	FC Brugge	3,000,000
Efan Ekoku	Wimbledon	Norwich C	900,000

NORWAY

Henning Berg	Blackburn R	Lillestrom	400,000
Stig Inge Bjornebye	Liverpool	Rosenborg	600,000
Lars Bohinen	Blackburn R	Nottingham F	700,000
Jan Aage Fjortoft	Middlesbrough	Swindon T	1,300,000
Jostein Flo	Sheffield U	Sogndal	400,000
Alf Inge Haaland	Nottingham F	Young Boys	250,000
Gunnar Halle	Oldham Ath	Lillestrom	280,000
Erland Johnsen	Chelsea	Bayern Munich	300,000
Oyvind Leonhardsen	Wimbledon	Rosenborg	400,000
Roger Nilsen	Sheffield U	Viking Stavanger	550,000
Sigurd Rushfeldt	Birmingham C	Tromso	Loan

POLAND

Dariusz Kubicki	Sunderland	Aston Villa	100,000
Dariusz Wdowczyk	Reading	Celtic	Free

PORTUGAL

Dani	West Ham U	Sporting Lisbon	Loan

ROMANIA

Illie Dumitrescu	West Ham U	Tottenham H	1,500,000
Dan Petrescu	Chelsea	Sheffield W	2,300,000

RUSSIA

Andrei Kanchelskis	Everton	Manchester U	5,500,000
Dmitri Kharine	Chelsea	CSKA Moscow	200,000
Vasili Kulkov	Millwall	Spartak Moscow	Loan
Sergi Yuran	Millwall	Spartak Moscow	Loan

SOUTH AFRICA

Phil Masinga	Leeds U	Mamelodi Sundowns	275,000
Lucas Radebe	Leeds U	Kaiser Chiefs	250,000
Mark Williams	Wolverhampton W	RWD Molenbeek	300,000

ST VINCENT

Rodney Jack	Torquay U	Lambada	Free

SWEDEN

Tomas Brolin	Leeds U	Parma	4,500,000
Niklas Gudmundsson	Blackburn R	Halmstad	Loan
Pontus Kamark	Leicester C	IFK Gothenburg	840,000
Anders Limpar	Everton	Arsenal	1,600,000

SWITZERLAND

Marc Hottiger	Everton	Newcastle U	700,000

TRINIDAD & TOBAGO

Dwight Yorke	Aston Villa	Signal Hill	120,000

USA

Ian Feuer	Luton T	West Ham U	580,000
John Harkes	West Ham U	USSF	Loan
Kasey Keller	Millwall	Portland Univ	Free
John Kerr	Walsall	Millwall	Free
Michael Lapper	Southend U	USSF	150,000
Jurgen Sommer	QPR	Luton T	600,000

YUGOSLAVIA

Sasa Curcic	Bolton W	Partizan Belgrade	1,000,000
Darko Kovacevic	Sheffield W	Red Star Belgrade	2,000,000
Savo Milosevic	Aston Villa	Partizan Belgrade	3,500,000
Dejan Stefanovic	Sheffield W	Red Star Belgrade	2,000,000

ZIMBABWE

Bruce Grobbelaar	Southampton	Liverpool	Free
Peter Ndlovu	Coventry C	Highlanders	10,000

LEADING GOALSCORERS 1995-96

	League	FA Cup	Coca-Cola Cup	Other Cups	Total
FA CARLING PREMIERSHIP					
Alan Shearer *(Blackburn R)*	31	0	5	1	37
Robbie Fowler *(Liverpool)*	28	6	2	0	36
Les Ferdinand *(Newcastle U)*	25	1	3	0	29
Dwight Yorke *(Aston Villa)*	17	2	6	0	25
Teddy Sheringham *(Tottenham H)*	16	5	3	0	24
Andrei Kanchelskis *(Everton)*	16	0	0	0	16
Ian Wright *(Arsenal)*	15	1	7	0	23
Chris Armstrong *(Tottenham H)*	15	4	3	0	22
Eric Cantona *(Manchester U)*	14	5	0	0	19
Stan Collymore *(Liverpool)*	14	5	0	0	19
Dion Dublin *(Coventry C)*	14	2	0	0	16
David Hirst *(Sheffield W)*	13	0	1	0	14
John Spencer *(Chelsea)*	13	1	0	0	14
Tony Yeboah *(Leeds U)*	12	1	3	3	19
Savo Milosevic *(Aston Villa)*	12	1	1	0	14
ENDSLEIGH INSURANCE DIVISION 1					
John Aldridge *(Tranmere R)*	27	0	2	0	29
Dougie Freedman *(Crystal Palace)*	23	0	0	0	23
(Includes three League goals for Barnet)					
Paul Barnes *(Birmingham C)*	22	0	5	2	29
(All except seven League goals for York C)					
Rob Edwards *(Huddersfield T)*	22	2	4	0	28
(All except seven League goals for Crewe Alex)					
Dean Sturridge *(Derby Co)*	20	0	0	0	20
Iwan Roberts *(Leicester C)*	19	0	1	0	20
Ian Marshall *(Ipswich T)*	19	0	0	0	19
Alex Mathie *(Ipswich T)*	18	0	0	1	19
Bob Taylor *(WBA)*	17	0	3	3	23
Andy Payton *(Barnsley)*	17	0	3	0	20
Andy Booth *(Huddersfield T)*	16	2	3	0	21
Don Goodman *(Wolverhampton W)*	16	1	3	0	20
Mike Sheron *(Stoke C)*	16	0	2	0	18
(Includes one League, two Coca-Cola Cup goals for Norwich C)					
Steve Bull *(Wolverhampton W)*	15	2	0	0	17
Craig Ramage *(Watford)*	15	0	0	0	15
DIVISION 2					
Marcus Stewart *(Bristol R)*	21	0	4	5	30
Gary Martindale *(Notts Co)*	21	0	1	4	26
(All except six League goals for Peterborough U)					
Kurt Nogan *(Burnley)*	20	0	3	3	26
Shaun Goater *(Rotherham U)*	18	2	3	1	24
Karl Connolly *(Wrexham)*	18	1	0	2	21
Miguel De Souza *(Wycombe W)*	18	0	2	0	20
Paul Moody *(Oxford U)*	17	5	1	1	24
Wayne Allison *(Swindon T)*	17	2	1	0	20
Steve Jones *(Bournemouth)*	17	0	3	0	20
Kyle Lightbourne *(Walsall)*	15	3	0	6	24
Kevin Wilson *(Walsall)*	15	2	1	1	19
Steve Torpey *(Swansea C)*	15	0	1	1	17
Tony Ellis *(Blackpool)*	14	0	2	1	17
DIVISION 3					
Steve White *(Hereford U)*	29	3	0	1	33
Andy Saville *(Preston NE)*	29	0	0	1	30
Carl Dale *(Cardiff C)*	21	2	3	5	31
Steve Whitehall *(Rochdale)*	20	1	0	3	24
Sean Devine *(Barnet)*	19	1	0	0	20
Lee Hodges *(Barnet)*	17	1	0	0	18
Adrian Littlejohn *(Plymouth Arg)*	17	1	0	0	18
Andy McFarlane *(Scunthorpe U)*	16	2	1	2	21
Mark Carter *(Bury)*	16	0	2	0	18
Colin West *(Leyton Orient)*	16	0	1	0	17
Jason White *(Northampton T)*	16	0	0	0	16

ENGLISH LEAGUE MANAGERS

GM General Manager, CC Chief Coach, HC Head Coach, DoC Director of Coaching, DoF Director of Football.

ARSENAL
Sam Hollis 1894–97, Tom Mitchell 1897–98, George Elcoat 1898–99, Harry Bradshaw 1899–1904, Phil Kelso 1904–08, George Morrell 1908–15, Leslie Knighton 1919–25, Herbert Chapman 1925–34, George Allison 1934–47, Tom Whittaker 1947–56, Jack Crayston 1956–58, George Swindin 1958–62, Billy Wright 1962–66, Bertie Mee 1966–76, Terry Neill 1976–83, Don Howe 1984–86, George Graham 1986–95, Bruce Rioch June 1995– .

ASTON VILLA
George Ramsay 1884–1926*, W. J. Smith 1926–34*, Jimmy McMullan 1934–35, Jimmy Hogan 1936–44, Alex Massie 1945–50, George Martin 1950–53, Eric Houghton 1953–58, Joe Mercer 1958–64, Dick Taylor 1965–67, Tommy Cummings 1967–68, Tommy Docherty 1968–70, Vic Crowe 1970–74, Ron Saunders 1974–82, Tony Barton 1982–84, Graham Turner 1984–86, Billy McNeill 1986–87, Graham Taylor 1987–90, Dr. Jozef Venglos 1990–91, Ron Atkinson 1991–94, Brian Little November 1994– .

BARNET
Lester Finch, George Wheeler, Dexter Adams, Tommy Coleman, Gerry Ward, Gordon Ferry, Brian Kelly, Bill Meadows, Barry Fry, Roger Thompson, Don McAllister, Barry Fry, Edwin Stein, Gary Phillips (player-manager) 1993–94, Ray Clemence January 1994– .

BARNSLEY
Arthur Fairclough 1898–1901*, John McCartney 1901–04*, Arthur Fairclough 1904–12, John Hastie 1912–14, Percy Lewis 1914–19, Peter Sant 1919–26, John Commins 1926–29, Arthur Fairclough 1929–30, Brough Fletcher 1930–37, Angus Seed 1937–53, Tim Ward 1953–60, Johnny Steele 1960–71 (continued as GM), John McSeveney 1971–72, Johnny Steele (GM) 1972–73, Jim Iley 1973–78, Allan Clarke 1978–80, Norman Hunter 1980–84, Bobby Collins 1984–85, Allan Clarke 1985–89, Mel Machin 1989–93, Viv Anderson 1993–94, Danny Wilson June 1994– .

BIRMINGHAM CITY
Alfred Jones 1892–1908*, Alec Watson 1908–10, Bob McRoberts 1910–15, Frank Richards 1915–23, Billy Beer 1923–27, Leslie Knighton 1928–33, George Liddell 1933–39, Harry Storer 1945–48, Bob Brocklebank 1949–54, Arthur Turner 1954–58, Pat Beasley 1959–60, Gil Merrick 1960–64, Joe Mallett 1965, Stan Cullis 1965–70, Fred Goodwin 1970–75, Willie Bell 1975–77, Jim Smith 1978–82, Ron Saunders 1982–86, John Bond 1986–87, Garry Pendrey 1987–89, Dave Mackay 1989–1991, Lou Macari 1991, Terry Cooper 1991–93, Barry Fry 1993–96, Trevor Francis May 1996– .

BLACKBURN ROVERS
Thomas Mitchell 1884–96*, J. Walmsley 1896–1903*, R. B. Middleton 1903–25, Jack Carr 1922–26 (TM under Middleton to 1925), Bob Crompton 1926–30 (Hon. TM), Arthur Barritt 1931–36 (had been Sec. from 1927), Reg Taylor 1936–38, Bob Crompton 1938–41, Eddie Hapgood 1944–47, Will Scott 1947, Jack Bruton 1947–49, Jackie Bestall 1949–53, Johnny Carey 1953–58, Dally Duncan 1958–60, Jack Marshall 1960–67, Eddie Quigley 1967–70, Johnny Carey 1970–71, Ken Furphy 1971–73, Gordon Lee 1974–75, Jim Smith 1975–78, Jim Iley 1978, John Pickering 1978–79, Howard Kendall 1979–81, Bobby Saxton 1981–86, Don Mackay 1987–91, Kenny Dalglish 1991–95, Ray Harford June 1995– .

BLACKPOOL
Tom Barcroft 1903–33* (Hon. Sec.), John Cox 1909–11, Bill Norman 1919–23, Maj. Frank Buckley 1923–27, Sid Beaumont 1927–28, Harry Evans 1928–33 (Hon. TM), Alex "Sandy" Macfarlane 1933–35, Joe Smith 1935–58, Ronnie Suart 1958–67, Stan Mortensen 1967–69, Les Shannon 1969–70, Bob Stokoe 1970–72, Harry Potts 1972–76, Allan Brown 1976–78, Bob Stokoe 1978–79, Stan Ternent 1979–80, Alan Ball 1980–81, Allan Brown 1981–82, Sam Ellis 1982–89, Jimmy Mullen 1989–90, Graham Carr 1990, Bill Ayre 1990–94, Sam Allardyce 1994–96, Gary Megson July 1996– .

BOLTON WANDERERS
Tom Rawthorne 1874–85*, J. J. Bentley 1885–86*, W. G. Struthers 1886–87*, Fitzroy Norris 1887*, J. J. Bentley 1887–95*, Harry Downs 1895–96*, Frank Brettell 1896–98*, John Somerville 1898–1910, Will Settle 1910–15, Tom Mather 1915–19, Charles Foweraker 1919–44, Walter Rowley 1944–50, Bill Ridding 1951–68, Nat Lofthouse 1968–70, Jimmy McIlroy 1970, Jimmy Meadows 1971, Nat Lofthouse 1971 (then admin. man. to 1972), Jimmy Armfield 1971–74, Ian Greaves 1974–80, Stan Anderson 1980–81, George Mulhall 1981–82, John McGovern 1982–85, Charlie Wright 1985, Phil Neal 1985–92, Bruce Rioch 1992–95, Roy McFarland 1995–96, Colin Todd January 1996– .

AFC BOURNEMOUTH
Vincent Kitcher 1914–23*, Harry Kinghorn 1923–25, Leslie Knighton 1925–28, Frank Richards 1928–30, Billy Birrell 1930–35, Bob Crompton 1935–36, Charlie Bell 1936–39, Harry Kinghorn 1939–47, Harry Lowe 1947–50, Jack Bruton 1950–56, Fred Cox 1956–58, Don Welsh 1958–61, Bill McGarry 1961–63, Reg Flewin 1963–65, Fred Cox 1965–70, John Bond 1970–73, Trevor Hartley 1974–78, John Benson 1975–78, Alec Stock 1979–80, David Webb 1980–82, Don Megson 1983, Harry Redknapp 1983–92, Tony Pulis 1992–94, Mel Machin August 1994– .

BRADFORD CITY
Robert Campbell 1903–05, Peter O'Rourke 1905–21, David Menzies 1921–26, Colin Veitch 1926–28, Peter O'Rourke 1928–30, Jack Peart 1930–35, Dick Ray 1935–37, Fred Westgarth 1938–43, Bob Sharp 1943–46, Jack Barker 1946–47, John Milburn 1947–48, David Steele 1948–52, Albert Harris 1952, Ivor Powell 1952–55, Peter Jackson 1955–61, Bob Brocklebank 1961–64, Bill Harris 1965–66, Willie Watson 1966–69, Grenville Hair 1967–68, Jimmy Wheeler 1968–71,

Bryan Edwards 1971–75, Bobby Kennedy 1975–78, John Napier 1978, George Mulhall 1978–81, Roy McFarland 1981–82, Trevor Cherry 1982–87, Terry Dolan 1987–89, Terry Yorath 1989–90, John Docherty 1990–91, Frank Stapleton 1991–94, Lennie Lawrence 1994–95, Chris Kamara November 1995– .

BRENTFORD

Will Lewis 1900–03*, Dick Molyneux 1903–06, W. G. Brown 1906–08, Fred Halliday 1908–26 (only secretary to 1922), Ephraim Rhodes 1912–15, Archie Mitchell 1921–22, Harry Curtis 1926–49, Jackie Gibbons 1949–52, Jimmy Blain 1952–53, Tommy Lawton 1953, Bill Dodgin Snr 1953–57, Malcolm Macdonald 1957–65, Tommy Cavanagh 1965–66, Billy Gray 1966–67, Jimmy Sirrel 1967–69, Frank Blunstone 1969–73, Mike Everitt 1973–75, John Docherty 1975–76, Bill Dodgin Jnr 1976–80, Fred Callaghan 1980–84, Frank McLintock 1984–87, Steve Perryman 1987–90, Phil Holder 1990–93, David Webb May 1993– .

BRIGHTON & HOVE ALBION

John Jackson 1901–05, Frank Scott-Walford 1905–08, John Robson 1908–14, Charles Webb 1919–47, Tommy Cook 1947, John Slade 1947–51, George Curtis 1961–63, Archie Macaulay 1963–68, Fred Goodwin 1968–70, Pat Saward 1970–73, Brian Clough 1973–74, Peter Taylor 1974–76, Alan Mullery 1976–81, Mike Bailey 1981–82, Jimmy Melia 1982–83, Chris Cattlin 1983–86, Alan Mullery 1986–87, Barry Lloyd 1987–93, Liam Brady 1993–95, Jimmy Case November 1995– .

BRISTOL CITY

Sam Hollis 1897–99, Bob Campbell 1899–1901, Sam Hollis 1901–05, Harry Thickett 1905–10, Sam Hollis 1911–13, George Hedley 1913–15, Jack Hamilton 1915–19, Joe Palmer 1919–21, Alex Raisbeck 1921–29, Joe Bradshaw 1929–32, Bob Hewison 1932–49 (under suspension 1938–39), Bob Wright 1949–50, Pat Beasley 1950–58, Peter Doherty 1958–60, Fred Ford 1960–67, Alan Dicks 1967–80, Bobby Houghton 1980–82, Roy Hodgson 1982, Terry Cooper 1982–88 (Director from 1983), Joe Jordan 1988–90, Jimmy Lumsden 1990–92, Denis Smith 1992–93, Russell Osman 1993–94, Joe Jordan November 1994– .

BRISTOL ROVERS

Alfred Homer 1899–1920 (continued as secretary to 1928), Ben Hall 1920–21, Andy Wilson 1921–26, Joe Palmer 1926–29, Dave McLean 1929–30, Albert Prince-Cox 1930–36, Percy Smith 1936–37, Brough Fletcher 1938–49, Bert Tann 1950–68 (continued as GM to 1972), Fred Ford 1968–69, Bill Dodgin Snr 1969–72, Don Megson 1972–77, Bobby Campbell 1978–79, Harold Jarman 1979–80, Terry Cooper 1980–81, Bobby Gould 1981–83, David Williams 1983–85, Bobby Gould 1985–87, Gerry Francis 1987–91, Martin Dobson 1991, Dennis Rofe 1992, Malcolm Allison 1992–93, John Ward 1993–96, Ian Holloway May 1996– .

BURNLEY

Arthur F. Sutcliffe 1893–96*, Harry Bradshaw 1896–99*, Ernest Magnall 1899–1903*, Spen Whittaker 1903–10, R. H. Wadge 1910–11*, John Haworth 1911–25, Albert Pickles 1925–32, Tom Bromilow 1932–35, Alf Boland 1935–39*, Cliff Britton 1945–48, Frank Hill 1948–54, Alan Brown 1954–57, Billy Dougall 1957–58, Harry Potts 1958–70 (GM to 1972), Jimmy Adamson 1970–76, Joe Brown 1976–77, Harry Potts 1977–79, Brian Miller 1979–83, John Bond 1983–84, John Benson 1984–85, Martin Buchan 1985, Tommy Cavanagh 1985–86, Brian Miller 1986–89, Frank Casper 1989–91, Jimmy Mullen 1991–96, Adrian Heath March 1996– .

BURY

T. Hargreaves 1887*, H. S. Hamer 1887–1907*, Archie Montgomery 1907–15, William Cameron 1919–23, James Hunter Thompson 1923–27, Percy Smith 1927–30, Arthur Paine 1930–34, Norman Bullock 1934–38, Jim Porter 1944–45, Norman Bullock 1945–49, John McNeil 1950–53, Dave Russell 1953–61, Bob Stokoe 1961–65, Bert Head 1965–66, Les Shannon 1966–69, Jack Marshall 1969, Les Hart 1970, Tommy McAnearney 1970–72, Alan Brown 1972–73, Bobby Smith 1973–77, Bob Stokoe 1977–78, David Hatton 1978–79, Dave Connor 1979–80, Jim Iley 1980–84, Martin Dobson 1984–89, Sam Ellis 1989–90, Mike Walsh 1990–95, Stan Ternent September 1995– .

CAMBRIDGE UNITED

Bill Whittaker 1949–55, Gerald Williams 1955, Bert Johnson 1955–59, Bill Craig 1959–60, Alan Moore 1960–63, Roy Kirk 1964–66, Bill Leivers 1967–74, Ron Atkinson 1974–78, John Docherty 1978–83, John Ryan 1984–85, Ken Shellito 1985, Chris Turner 1985–90, John Beck 1990–1992, Ian Atkins 1992–93, Gary Johnson 1993–95, Tommy Taylor May 1995– .

CARDIFF CITY

Davy McDougall 1910–11, Fred Stewart 1911–33, Bartley Wilson 1933–34, B. Watts-Jones 1934–37, Bill Jennings 1937–39, Cyril Spiers 1939–46, Billy McCandless 1946–48, Cyril Spiers 1948–54, Trevor Morris 1954–58, Bill Jones 1958–62, George Swindin 1962–64, Jimmy Scoular 1964–73, Frank O'Farrell 1973–74, Jimmy Andrews 1974–78, Richie Morgan 1978–82, Len Ashurst 1982–84, Jimmy Goodfellow 1984, Alan Durban 1984–86, Frank Burrows 1986–89, Len Ashurst 1989–91, Eddie May 1991–94, Terry Yorath 1994–95, Eddie May 1995, Kenny Hibbitt (CC), 1995, Phil Neal January 1996– .

CARLISLE UNITED

Harry Kirkbride 1904–05*, McCumiskey 1905–06*, Jack Houston 1906–08*, Bert Stansfield 1908–10, Jack Houston 1910–12, Davie Graham 1912–13, George Bristow 1913–30, Billy Hampson 1930–33, Bill Clarke 1933–35, Robert Kelly 1935–36, Fred Westgarth 1936–38, David Taylor 1938–40, Howard Harkness 1940–45, Bill Clark 1945–46*, Ivor Broadis 1946–49, Bill Shankly 1949–51, Fred Emery 1951–58, Andy Beattie 1958–60, Ivor Powell 1960–63, Alan Ashman 1963–67, Tim Ward 1967–68, Bob Stokoe 1968–70, Ian MacFarlane 1970–72, Alan Ashman 1972–75, Dick Young 1975–76, Bobby Moncur 1976–80, Martin Harvey 1980, Bob Stokoe 1980–85, Bryan "Pop" Robson 1985, Bob Stokoe

1985–86, Harry Gregg 1986–87, Cliff Middlemass 1987–91, Aidan McCaffery 1991–92, David McCreery 1992–93, Mick Wadsworth (Director of Coaching) 1993–96, Mervyn Day January 1996– .

CHARLTON ATHLETIC

Bill Rayner 1920–25, Alex McFarlane 1925–27, Albert Lindon 1928, Alex McFarlane 1928–32, Jimmy Seed 1933–56, Jimmy Trotter 1956–61, Frank Hill 1961–65, Bob Stokoe 1965–67, Eddie Firmani 1967–70, Theo Foley 1970–74, Andy Nelson 1974–79, Mike Bailey 1979–81, Alan Mullery 1981–82, Ken Craggs 1982, Lennie Lawrence 1982–91, Steve Gritt/Alan Curbishley 1991–95, Alan Curbishley June 1995– .

CHELSEA

John Tait Robertson 1905–07, David Calderhead 1907–33, Leslie Knighton 1933–39, Billy Birrell 1939–52, Ted Drake 1952–61, Tommy Docherty 1962–67, Dave Sexton 1967–74, Ron Suart 1974–75, Eddie McCreadie 1975–77, Ken Shellito 1977–78, Danny Blanchflower 1978–79, Geoff Hurst 1979–81, John Neal 1981–85 (Director to 1986), John Hollins 1985–88, Bobby Campbell 1988–91, Ian Porterfield 1991–93, David Webb 1993, Glenn Hoddle 1993–96, Ruud Gullit May 1996– .

CHESTER CITY

Charlie Hewitt 1930–36, Alex Raisbeck 1936–38, Frank Brown 1938–53, Louis Page 1953–56, John Harris 1956–59, Stan Pearson 1959–61, Bill Lambton 1962–63, Peter Hauser 1963–68, Ken Roberts 1968–76, Alan Oakes 1976–82, Cliff Sear 1982, John Sainty 1982–83, John McGrath 1984, Harry McNally 1985–92, Graham Barrow 1992–94, Mike Pejic 1994–95, Derek Mann 1995, Kevin Ratcliffe April 1995– .

CHESTERFIELD

E. Russell Timmeus 1891–95*, Gilbert Gillies 1895–1901, E. F. Hind 1901–02, Jack Hoskin 1902–06, W. Furness 1906–07, George Swift 1907–10, G. H. Jones 1911–13, R. L. Weston 1913–17, T. Callaghan 1919, J. J. Caffrey 1920–22, Harry Hadley 1922, Harry Parkes 1922–27, Alec Campbell 1927, Ted Davison 1927–32, Bill Harvey 1932–38, Norman Bullock 1938–45, Bob Brocklebank 1945–48, Bobby Marshall 1948–52, Ted Davison 1952–58, Duggie Livingstone 1958–62, Tony McShane 1962–67, Jimmy McGuigan 1967–73, Joe Shaw 1973–76, Arthur Cox 1976–80, Frank Barlow 1980–83, John Duncan 1983–87, Kevin Randall 1987–88, Paul Hart 1988–91, Chris McMenemy 1991–93, John Duncan February 1993– .

COLCHESTER UNITED

Ted Fenton 1946–48, Jimmy Allen 1948–53, Jack Butler 1953–55, Benny Fenton 1955–63, Neil Franklin 1963–68, Dick Graham 1968–72, Jim Smith 1972–75, Bobby Roberts 1975–82, Allan Hunter 1982–83, Cyril Lea 1983–86, Mike Walker 1986–87, Roger Brown 1987–88, Jock Wallace 1989, Mick Mills 1990. Ian Atkins 1990–91, Roy McDonough 1991–94, George Burley 1994, Steve Wignall January 1995– .

COVENTRY CITY

H. R. Buckle 1909–10, Robert Wallace 1910–13*, Frank Scott-Walford 1913–15, William Clayton 1917–19, H. Pollitt 1919–20, Albert Evans 1920–24, Jimmy Kerr 1924–28, James McIntyre 1928–31, Harry Storer 1931–45, Dick Bayliss 1945–47, Billy Frith 1947–48, Harry Storer 1948–53, Jack Fairbrother 1953–54, Charlie Elliott 1954–55, Jesse Carver 1955–56, Harry Warren 1956–57, Billy Frith 1957–61, Jimmy Hill 1961–67, Noel Cantwell 1967–72, Bob Dennison 1972, Joe Mercer 1972–75, Gordon Milne 1972–81, Dave Sexton 1981–83, Bobby Gould 1983–84, Don Mackay 1985–86, George Curtis 1986–87 (became MD), John Sillett 1987–90, Terry Butcher 1990–92, Don Howe 1992, Bobby Gould 1992–93, Phil Neal 1993–95, Ron Atkinson February 1995– .

CREWE ALEXANDRA

W. C. McNeill 1892–94*, J. G. Hall 1895–96*, R. Roberts* (1st team sec.) 1897, J. B. Bromerley 1898–1911* (continued as Hon. Sec. to 1925), Tom Bailey 1925–38, George Lillicrop 1938–44, Frank Hill 1944–48, Arthur Turner 1948–51, Harry Catterick 1951–53, Ralph Ward 1953–55, Maurice Lindley 1955–58, Harry Ware 1958–60, Jimmy McGuigan 1960–64, Ernie Tagg 1964–71 (continued as secretary to 1972), Dennis Viollet 1971, Jimmy Melia 1972–73, Ernie Tagg 1974, Harry Gregg 1975–78, Warwick Rimmer 1978–79, Tony Waddington 1979–81, Arfon Griffiths 1981–82, Peter Morris 1982–83, Dario Gradi June 1983– .

CRYSTAL PALACE

John T. Robson 1905–07, Edmund Goodman 1907–25 (had been secretary since 1905 and afterwards continued in this position to 1933). Alec Maley 1925–27, Fred Mavin 1927–30, Jack Tresadern 1930–35, Tom Bromilow 1935–36, R. S. Moyes 1936, Tom Bromilow 1936–39, George Irwin 1939–47, Jack Butler 1947–49, Ronnie Rooke 1949–50, Charlie Slade and Fred Dawes (joint managers) 1950–51, Laurie Scott 1951–54, Cyril Spiers 1954–58, George Smith 1958–60, Arthur Rowe 1960–62, Dick Graham 1962–66, Bert Head 1966–72 (continued as GM to 1973), Malcolm Allison 1973–76, Terry Venables 1976–80, Ernie Walley 1980, Malcolm Allison 1980–81, Dario Gradi 1981, Steve Kember 1981–82, Alan Mullery 1982–84, Steve Coppell 1984–93, Alan Smith 1993–95, Steve Coppell (TD) 1995–96, Dave Bassett February 1996– .

DARLINGTON

Tom McIntosh 1902–11, W. L. Lane 1911–12*, Dick Jackson 1912–19, Jack English 1919–28, Jack Fairless 1928–33, George Collins 1933–36, George Brown 1936–38, Jackie Carr 1938–42, Jack Surtees 1942, Jack English 1945–46, Bill Forrest 1946–50, George Irwin 1950–52, Bob Gurney 1952–57, Dick Duckworth 1957–60, Eddie Carr 1960–64, Lol Morgan 1964–66, Jimmy Greenhalgh 1966–68, Ray Yeoman 1968–70, Len Richley 1970–71, Frank Brennan 1971, Ken Hale 1971–72, Allan Jones 1972, Ralph Brand 1972–73, Dick Conner 1973–74, Billy Horner 1974–76, Peter Madden 1976–78, Len Walker 1978–79, Billy Elliott 1979–83, Cyril Knowles 1983–87, Dave Booth 1987–89, Brian Little 1989–91, Frank Gray 1991–92, Ray Hankin 1992, Billy McEwan 1992–93, Alan Murray 1993–95, Paul Futcher 1995, David Hodgson/ Jim Platt (Directors of Coaching) 1995, Jim Platt December 1995– .

DERBY COUNTY

Harry Newbould 1896–1906, Jimmy Methven 1906–22, Cecil Potter 1922–25, George Jobey 1925–41, Ted Magner 1944–46, Stuart McMillan 1946–53, Jack Barker 1953–55, Harry Storer 1955–62, Tim Ward 1962–67, Brian Clough 1967–73, Dave Mackay 1973–76, Colin Murphy 1977, Tommy Docherty 1977–79, Colin Addison 1979–82, Johnny Newman 1982, Peter Taylor 1982–84, Roy McFarland 1984, Arthur Cox 1984–93, Roy McFarland 1993–95, Jim Smith June 1995– .

DONCASTER ROVERS

Arthur Porter 1920–21*, Harry Tufnell 1921–22, Arthur Porter 1922–23, Dick Ray 1923–27, David Menzies 1928–36, Fred Emery 1936–40, Bill Marsden 1944–46, Jackie Bestall 1946–49, Peter Doherty 1949–58, Jack Hodgson and Sid Bycroft (joint managers) 1958, Jack Crayston 1958–59 (continued as Sec-Man to 1961), Jackie Bestall (TM) 1959–60, Norman Curtis 1960–61, Danny Malloy 1961–62, Oscar Hold 1962–64, Bill Leivers 1964–66, Keith Kettleborough 1966–67, George Raynor 1967–68, Lawrie McMenemy 1968–71, Maurice Setters 1971–74, Stan Anderson 1975–78, Billy Bremner 1978–85, Dave Cusack 1985–87, Dave Mackay 1987–89, Billy Bremner 1989–91, Steve Beaglehole 1991–93, Ian Atkins 1994, Sammy Chung July 1994– .

EVERTON

W. E. Barclay 1888–89*, Dick Molyneux 1889–1901*, William C. Cuff 1901–18*, W. J. Sawyer 1918–19*, Thomas H. McIntosh 1919–35*, Theo Kelly 1936–48, Cliff Britton 1948–56, Ian Buchan 1956–58, Johnny Carey 1958–61, Harry Catterick 1961–73, Billy Bingham 1973–77, Gordon Lee 1977–81, Howard Kendall 1981–87, Colin Harvey 1987–90, Howard Kendall 1990–93, Mike Walker 1994, Joe Royle November 1994– .

EXETER CITY

Arthur Chadwick 1910–22, Fred Mavin 1923–27, Dave Wilson 1928–29, Billy McDevitt 1929–35, Jack English 1935–39, George Roughton 1945–52, Norman Kirkman 1952–53, Norman Dodgin 1953–57, Bill Thompson 1957–58, Frank Broome 1958–60, Glen Wilson 1960–62, Cyril Spiers 1962–63, Jack Edwards 1963–65, Ellis Stuttard 1965–66, Jock Basford 1966–67, Frank Broome 1967–69, Johnny Newman 1969–76, Bobby Saxton 1977–79, Brian Godfrey 1979–83, Gerry Francis 1983–84, Jim Iley 1984–85, Colin Appleton 1985–87, Terry Cooper 1988–91, Alan Ball 1991–94, Terry Cooper 1994–95, Peter Fox June 1995– .

FULHAM

Harry Bradshaw 1904–09, Phil Kelso 1909–24, Andy Ducat 1924–26, Joe Bradshaw 1926–29, Ned Liddell 1929–31, Jim MacIntyre 1931–34, Jimmy Hogan 1934–35, Jack Peart 1935–48, Frank Osborne 1948–64 (was secretary-manager or GM for most of this period), Bill Dodgin Snr 1949–53, Duggie Livingstone 1956–58, Bedford Jezzard 1958–64 (GM for last two months), Vic Buckingham 1965–68, Bobby Robson 1968, Bill Dodgin Jnr 1969–72, Alec Stock 1972–76, Bobby Campbell 1976–80, Malcolm Macdonald 1980–84, Ray Harford 1984–96, Ray Lewington 1986–90, Alan Dicks 1990–91, Don Mackay 1991–94, Ian Branfoot 1994–96 (continued as GM), Micky Adams February 1996– .

GILLINGHAM

W. Ironside Groombridge 1896–1906* (previously financial secretary), Steve Smith 1906–08, W. I. Groombridge 1908–19*, George Collins 1919–20, John McMillan 1920–23, Harry Curtis 1923–26, Albert Hoskins 1926–29, Dick Hendrie 1929–31, Fred Mavin 1932–37, Alan Ure 1937–38, Bill Harvey 1938–39, Archie Clark 1939–58, Harry Barratt 1958–62, Freddie Cox 1962–65, Basil Hayward 1966–71, Andy Nelson 1971–74, Len Ashurst 1974–75, Gerry Summers 1975–81, Keith Peacock 1981–87, Paul Taylor 1988, Keith Burkinshaw 1988–89, Damien Richardson 1989–93, Mike Flanagan 1993–95, Neil Smillie 1995, Tony Pulis June 1995– .

GRIMSBY TOWN

H. N. Hickson 1902–20*, Haydn Price 1920, George Fraser 1921–24, Wilf Gillow 1924–32, Frank Womack 1932–36, Charles Spencer 1937–51, Bill Shankly 1951–53, Billy Walsh 1954–55, Allenby Chilton 1955–59, Tim Ward 1960–62, Tom Johnston 1962–64, Jimmy McGuigan 1964–67, Don McEvoy 1967–68, Bill Harvey 1968–69, Bobby Kennedy 1969–71, Lawrie McMenemy 1971–73, Ron Ashman 1973–75, Tom Casey 1975–76, Johnny Newman 1976–79, George Kerr 1979–82, David Booth 1982–85, Mike Lyons 1985–87, Bobby Roberts 1987–88, Alan Buckley 1988–94, Brian Laws November 1994– .

HARTLEPOOL UNITED

Alfred Priest 1908–12, Percy Humphreys 1912–13, Jack Manners 1913–20, Cecil Potter 1920–22, David Gordon 1922–24, Jack Manners 1924–27, Bill Norman 1927–31, Jack Carr 1932–35 (had been player-coach since 1931), Jimmy Hamilton 1935–43, Fred Westgarth 1943–57, Ray Middleton 1957–59, Bill Robinson 1959–62, Allenby Chilton 1962–63, Bob Gurney 1963–64, Alvan Williams 1964–65, Geoff Twentyman 1965, Brian Clough 1965–67, Angus McLean 1967–70, John Simpson 1970–71, Len Ashurst 1971–74, Ken Hale 1974–76, Billy Horner 1976–83, Johnny Duncan 1983, Mike Docherty 1983, Billy Horner 1984–86, John Bird 1986–88, Bobby Moncur 1988–89, Cyril Knowles 1989–91, Alan Murray 1991–93, Viv Busby 1993, John MacPhail 1993–94, David McCreery 1994–95, Keith Houchen April 1995– .

HEREFORD UNITED

Eric Keen 1939, George Tranter 1948–49, Alex Massie 1952, George Tranter 1953–55, Joe Wade 1956–62, Ray Daniels 1962–63, Bob Dennison 1963–67, John Charles 1967–71, Colin Addison 1971–74, John Sillett 1974–78, Mike Bailey 1978–79, Frank Lord 1979–82, Tommy Hughes 1982–83, Johnny Newman 1983–87, Ian Bowyer 1987–90, Colin Addison 1990–91, John Sillett 1991–92, Greg Downs 1992–94, John Layton 1994–95, Graham Turner (DoF) August 1995– .

HUDDERSFIELD TOWN

Fred Walker 1908–10, Richard Pudan 1910–12, Arthur Fairclough 1912–19, Ambrose Langley 1919–21, Herbert Chapman 1921–25, Cecil Potter 1925–26, Jack Chaplin 1926–29, Clem Stephenson 1929–42, David Steele 1943–47, George Stephenson 1947–52, Andy Beattie 1952–56, Bill Shankly 1956–59, Eddie Boot 1960–64, Tom Johnston

1964–68, Ian Greaves 1968–74, Bobby Collins 1974, Tom Johnston 1975–78 (had been GM since 1975), Mike Buxton 1978–86, Steve Smith 1986–87, Malcolm Macdonald 1987–88, Eoin Hand 1988–92, Ian Ross 1992–93, Neil Warnock 1993–95, Brian Horton June 1995– .

HULL CITY
James Ramster 1904–05*, Ambrose Langley 1905–13, Harry Chapman 1913–14, Fred Stringer 1914–16, David Menzies 1916–21, Percy Lewis 1921–23, Bill McCracken 1923–31, Haydn Green 1931–34, John Hill 1934–36, David Menzies 1936, Ernest Blackburn 1936–46, Major Frank Buckley 1946–48, Raich Carter 1948–51, Bob Jackson 1952–55, Bob Brocklebank 1955–61, Cliff Britton 1961–70 (continued as GM to 1971), Terry Neill 1970–74, John Kaye 1974–77, Bobby Collins 1977–78, Ken Houghton 1978–79, Mike Smith 1979–82, Bobby Brown 1982, Colin Appleton 1982–84, Brian Horton 1984–88, Eddie Gray 1988–89, Colin Appleton 1989, Stan Ternent 1989–91, Terry Dolan February 1991– .

IPSWICH TOWN
Mick O'Brien 1936–37, Scott Duncan 1937–55 (continued as secretary), Alf Ramsey 1955–63, Jackie Milburn 1963–64, Bill McGarry 1964–68, Bobby Robson 1969–82, Bobby Ferguson 1982–87, Johnny Duncan 1987–90, John Lyall 1990–94, George Burley December 1994– .

LEEDS UNITED
Dick Ray 1919–20, Arthur Fairclough 1920–27, Dick Ray 1927–35, Bill Hampson 1935–47, Willis Edwards 1947–48, Major Frank Buckley 1948–53, Raich Carter 1953–58, Bill Lambton 1958–59, Jack Taylor 1959–61, Don Revie 1961–74, Brian Clough 1974, Jimmy Armfield 1974–78, Jock Stein 1978, Jimmy Adamson 1978–80, Allan Clarke 1980–82, Eddie Gray 1982–85, Billy Bremner 1985–88, Howard Wilkinson October 1988– .

LEICESTER CITY
William Clark 1896–97, George Johnson 1898–1907*, James Blessington 1907–09, Andy Aitken 1909–11, John William Bartlett 1912–14, Peter Hodge 1919–26, William Orr 1926–32, Peter Hodge 1932–34, Andy Lochhead 1934–36, Frank Womack 1936–39, Tom Bromilow 1939–45, Tom Mather 1945–46, Johnny Duncan 1946–49, Norman Bullock 1949–55, David Halliday 1955–58, Matt Gillies 1959–68, Frank O'Farrell 1968–71, Jimmy Bloomfield 1971–77, Frank McLintock 1977–78, Jock Wallace 1978–82, Gordon Milne 1982–86, Bryan Hamilton 1986–87, David Pleat 1987–91, Brian Little 1991–94, Mark McGhee 1994–95, Martin O'Neill December 1995– .

LEYTON ORIENT
Sam Omerod 1905–06, Ike Ivenson 1906, Billy Holmes 1907–22, Peter Proudfoot 1922–29, Arthur Grimsdell 1929–30, Peter Proudfoot 1930–31, Jimmy Seed 1931–33, David Pratt 1933–34, Peter Proudfoot 1935–39, Tom Halsey 1939, Bill Wright 1939–45, Willie Hall 1945, Bill Wright 1945–46, Charlie Hewitt 1946–48, Neil McBain 1948–49, Alec Stock 1949–56, 1957–57, 1958–59, Johnny Carey 1961–63, Benny Fenton 1963–64, Dave Sexton 1965, Dick Graham 1966–68, Jimmy Bloomfield 1968–71, George Petchey 1971–77, Jimmy Bloomfield 1977–81, Paul Went 1981, Ken Knighton 1981, Frank Clark 1982–91 (MD), Peter Eustace 1991–94, Chris Turner/John Sitton 1994–95, Pat Holland May 1995– .

LINCOLN CITY
David Calderhead 1900–07, John Henry Strawson 1907–14 (had been secretary), George Fraser 1919–21, David Calderhead Jnr. 1921–24, Horace Henshall 1924–27, Harry Parkes 1927–36, Joe McClelland 1936–46, Bill Anderson 1946–65 (GM to 1966), Roy Chapman 1965–66, Ron Gray 1966–70, Bert Loxley 1970–71, David Herd 1971–72, Graham Taylor 1972–77, George Kerr 1977–78, Willie Bell 1977–78, Colin Murphy 1978–85, John Pickering 1985, George Kerr 1985–87, Peter Daniel 1987, Colin Murphy 1987–90, Allan Clarke 1990, Steve Thompson 1990–93, Keith Alexander 1993–94, Sam Ellis 1994–95, Steve Wicks (HC) 1995, John Beck October 1995– .

LIVERPOOL
W. E. Barclay 1892–96, Tom Watson 1896–1915, David Ashworth 1920–22, Matt McQueen 1923–28, George Patterson 1928–36 (continued as secretary), George Kay 1936–51, Don Welsh 1951–56, Phil Taylor 1956–59, Bill Shankly 1959–74, Bob Paisley 1974–83, Joe Fagan 1983–85, Kenny Dalglish 1985–91, Graeme Souness 1991–94, Roy Evans January 1994–

LUTON TOWN
Charlie Green 1901–28*, George Thomson 1925, John McCartney 1927–29, George Kay 1929–31, Harold Wightman 1931–35, Ted Liddell 1936–38, Neil McBain 1938–39, George Martin 1939–47, Dally Duncan 1947–58, Syd Owen 1959–60, Sam Bartram 1960–62, Bill Harvey 1962–64, George Martin 1965–66, Allan Brown 1966–68, Alec Stock 1968–72, Harry Haslam 1972–78, David Pleat 1978–86, John Moore 1986–87, Ray Harford 1987–89, Jim Ryan 1900–91, David Pleat 1991–95, Terry Westley 1995, Lennie Lawrence December 1995– .

MANCHESTER CITY
Joshua Parlby 1893–95*, Sam Omerod 1895–1902, Tom Maley 1902–06, Harry Newbould 1906–12, Ernest Magnall 1912–24, David Ashworth 1924–25, Peter Hodge 1926–32, Wilf Wild 1932–46 (continued as secretary to 1950), Sam Cowan 1946–47, John "Jock" Thomson 1947–50, Leslie McDowall 1950–63, George Poyser 1963–65, Joe Mercer 1965–71 (continued as GM to 1972), Malcolm Allison 1972–73, Johnny Hart 1973, Ron Saunders 1973–74, Tony Book 1974–79, Malcolm Allison 1979–80, John Bond 1980–83, John Benson 1983, Billy McNeill 1983–86, Jimmy Frizzell 1986–87 (continued as GM), Mel Machin 1987–89, Howard Kendall 1990, Peter Reid 1990–93, Brian Horton 1993–95, Alan Ball July 1995– .

MANCHESTER UNITED
Ernest Magnall 1900–12, John Robson 1914–21, John Chapman 1921–26, Clarence Hildrith 1926–27, Herbert Bamlett 1927–31, Walter Crickmer 1931–32, Scott Duncan 1932–37, Jimmy Porter 1938–44, Walter Crickmer 1944–45*, Matt Busby 1945–69 (continued as GM then Director), Wilf McGuinness 1969–70, Frank O'Farrell 1971–72, Tommy Docherty 1972–77, Dave Sexton 1977–81, Ron Atkinson 1981–86, Alex Ferguson November 1986– .

MANSFIELD TOWN

John Baynes 1922–25, Ted Davison 1926–28, Jack Hickling 1928–33, Henry Martin 1933–35, Charlie Bell 1935, Harold Wightman 1936, Harold Parkes 1936–38, Jack Poole 1938–44, Lloyd Barke 1944–45, Roy Goodall 1945–49, Freddie Steele 1949–51, George Jobey 1952–53, Stan Mercer 1953–55, Charlie Mitten 1956–58, Sam Weaver 1958–60, Raich Carter 1960–63, Tommy Cummings 1963–67, Tommy Eggleston 1967–70, Jock Basford 1970–71, Danny Williams 1971–74, Dave Smith 1974–76, Peter Morris 1976–78, Billy Bingham 1978–79, Mick Jones 1979–81, Stuart Boam 1981–83, Ian Greaves 1983–89, George Foster 1989–93, Andy King November 1993– .

MIDDLESBROUGH

John Robson 1899–1905, Alex Mackie 1905–06, Andy Aitken 1906–09, J. Gunter 1908–10*, Andy Walker 1910–11, Tom McIntosh 1911–19, Jimmy Howie 1920–23, Herbert Bamlett 1923–26, Peter McWilliam 1927–34, Wilf Gillow 1934–44, David Jack 1944–52, Walter Rowley 1952–54, Bob Dennison 1954–63, Raich Carter 1963–66, Stan Anderson 1966–73, Jack Charlton 1973–77, John Neal 1977–81, Bobby Murdoch 1981–82, Malcolm Allison 1982–84, Willie Maddren 1984–86, Bruce Rioch 1986–90, Colin Todd 1990–91, Lennie Lawrence 1991–94, Bryan Robson May 1994– .

MILLWALL

William Henderson 1894–99*, E. R. Stopher 1899–1900, George Saunders 1900–11, Herbert Lipsham 1911–19, Robert Hunter 1919–33, Bill McCracken 1933–36, Charlie Hewitt 1936–40, Bill Voisey 1940–44, Jack Cock 1944–48, Charlie Hewitt 1948–56, Ron Gray 1956–57, Jimmy Seed 1958–59, Reg Smith 1959–61, Ron Gray 1961–63, Billy Gray 1963–66, Benny Fenton 1966–74, Gordon Jago 1974–77, George Petchey 1978–80, Peter Anderson 1980–82, George Graham 1982–86, John Docherty 1986–90, Bob Pearson 1990, Bruce Rioch 1990–92, Mick McCarthy 1992–96, Jimmy Nicholl February 1996– .

NEWCASTLE UNITED

Frank Watt 1895–32*, Andy Cunningham 1930–35, Tom Mather 1935–39, Stan Seymour 1939–47 (Hon-manager), George Martin 1947–50, Stan Seymour 1950–54 (Hon-manager), Duggie Livingstone 1954–56, Stan Seymour 1956–58 (Hon-manager), Charlie Mitten 1958–61, Norman Smith 1961–62, Joe Harvey 1962–75, Gordon Lee 1975–77, Richard Dinnis 1977, Bill McGarry 1977–80, Arthur Cox 1980–84, Jack Charlton 1984, Willie McFaul 1985–88, Jim Smith 1988–91, Ossie Ardiles 1991–92, Kevin Keegan February 1992– .

NORTHAMPTON TOWN

Arthur Jones 1897–1907*, Herbert Chapman 1907–12, Walter Bull 1912–13, Fred Lessons 1913–19, Bob Hewison 1920–25, Jack Tresadern 1925–30, Jack English 1931–35, Syd Puddefoot 1935–37, Warney Cresswell 1937–39, Tom Smith 1939–49, Bob Dennison 1949–54, Dave Smith 1954–59, David Bowen 1959–67, Tony Marchi 1967–68, Ron Flowers 1968–69, Dave Bowen 1969–72 (continued as GM and secretary to 1985 when joined the board), Billy Baxter 1972–73, Bill Dodgin Jnr 1973–76, Pat Crerand 1976–77, Bill Dodgin Jnr 1977, John Petts 1977–78, Mike Keen 1978–79, Clive Walker 1979–80, Bill Dodgin Jnr 1980–82, Clive Walker 1982–84, Tony Barton 1984–85, Graham Carr 1985–90, Theo Foley 1990–92, Phil Chard 1992–93, John Barnwell 1993–95, Ian Atkins January 1995– .

NORWICH CITY

John Bowman 1905–07, James McEwen 1907–08, Arthur Turner 1909–10, Bert Stansfield 1910–15, Major Frank Buckley 1919–20, Charles O'Hagan 1920–21, Albert Gosnell 1921–26, Bert Stansfield 1926, Cecil Potter 1926–29, James Kerr 1929–33, Tom Parker 1933–37, Bob Young 1937–39, Jimmy Jewell 1939, Bob Young 1939–45, Cyril Spiers 1946–47, Duggie Lochhead 1947–50, Norman Low 1950–55, Tom Parker 1955–57, Archie Macaulay 1957–61, Willie Reid 1961–62, George Swindin 1962, Ron Ashman 1962–66, Lol Morgan 1966–69, Ron Saunders 1969–73, John Bond 1973–80, Ken Brown 1980–87, Dave Stringer 1987–92, Mike Walker 1992–94, John Deehan 1994–95, Martin O'Neill 1995, Gary Megson 1995–96, Mike Walker June 1996– .

NOTTINGHAM FOREST

Harry Radford 1889–97*, Harry Haslam 1897–1909*, Fred Earp 1909–12, Bob Masters 1912–25, John Baynes 1925–29, Stan Hardy 1930–31, Noel Watson 1931–36, Harold Wightman 1936–39, Billy Walker 1939–60, Andy Beattie 1960–63, Johnny Carey 1963–68, Matt Gillies 1969–72, Dave Mackay 1972, Allan Brown 1973–75, Brian Clough 1975–93, Frank Clark May 1993– .

NOTTS COUNTY

Edwin Browne 1883–93*, Tom Featherstone 1893*, Tom Harris 1893–1913*, Albert Fisher 1913–27, Horace Henshall 1927–34, Charlie Jones 1934–35, David Pratt 1935, Percy Smith 1935–36, Jimmy McMullan 1936–37, Harry Parkes 1938–39, Tony Towers 1939–42, Frank Womack 1942–43, Major Frank Buckley 1944–46, Arthur Stollery 1946–49, Eric Houghton 1949–53, George Poyser 1953–57, Tommy Lawton 1957–58, Frank Hill 1958–61, Tim Coleman 1961–63, Eddie Lowe 1963–65, Tim Coleman 1965–66, Jack Burkitt 1966–67, Andy Beattie (GM 1967), Billy Gray 1967–68, Jimmy Sirrel 1969–75, Ron Fenton 1975–77, Jimmy Sirrel 1978–82 (continued as GM to 1984), Howard Wilkinson 1982–83, Larry Lloyd 1983–84, Richie Barker 1984–85, Jimmy Sirrel 1985–87, John Barnwell 1987–88, Neil Warnock 1989–93, Mick Walker 1993–94, Russell Slade 1994–95, Howard Kendall 1995, Colin Murphy June 1995 (continued as GM), Steve Thompson May 1996– .

OLDHAM ATHLETIC

David Ashworth 1906–14, Herbert Bamlett 1914–21, Charlie Roberts 1921–22, David Ashworth 1923–24, Bob Mellor 1924–27, Andy Wilson 1927–32, Jimmy McMullan 1933–34, Bob Mellor 1934–45 (continued as secretary to 1953), Frank Womack 1945–47, Billy Wootton 1947–50, George Hardwick 1950–56, Ted Goodier 1956–58, Norman Dodgin 1958–60, Jack Rowley 1960–63, Les McDowall 1963–65, Gordon Hurst 1965–66, Jimmy McIlroy 1966–68, Jack Rowley 1968–69, Jimmy Frizzell 1970–82, Joe Royle 1982–94, Graeme Sharp November 1994– .

OXFORD UNITED
Harry Thompson 1949–58 (Player-Manager 1949-51), Arthur Turner 1959–69 (continued as GM to 1972), Ron Saunders 1969, George Summers 1969–75, Mike Brown 1975–79, Bill Asprey 1979–80, Ian Greaves 1980–82, Jim Smith 1982–85, Maurice Evans 1985–88, Mark Lawrenson 1988, Brian Horton 1988–93, Denis Smith September 1993– .

PETERBOROUGH UNITED
Jock Porter 1934–36, Fred Taylor 1936–37, Vic Poulter 1937–38, Sam Madden 1938–48, Jack Blood 1948–50, Bob Gurney 1950–52, Jack Fairbrother 1952–54, George Swindin 1954–58, Jimmy Hagan 1958–62, Jack Fairbrother 1962–64, Gordon Clark 1964–67, Norman Rigby 1967–69, Jim Iley 1969–72, Noel Cantwell 1972–77, John Barnwell 1977–78, Billy Hails 1978–79, Peter Morris 1979–82, Martin Wilkinson 1982–83, John Wile 1983–86, Noel Cantwell 1986–88 (continued as GM), Mick Jones 1988–89, Mark Lawrenson 1989–90, Chris Turner 1991–92, Lil Fuccillo 1992–93, John Still 1994–95, Mick Halsall 1995–96, Barry Fry May 1996– .

PLYMOUTH ARGYLE
Frank Brettell 1903–05, Bob Jack 1905–06, Bill Fullerton 1906–07, Bob Jack 1910–38, Jack Tresadern 1938–47, Jimmy Rae 1948–55, Jack Rowley 1955–60, Neil Dougall 1961, Ellis Stuttard 1961–63, Andy Beattie 1963–64, Malcolm Allison 1964–65, Derek Ufton 1965–68, Billy Bingham 1968–70, Ellis Stuttard 1970–72, Tony Waiters 1972–77, Mike Kelly 1977–78, Malcolm Allison 1978–79, Bobby Saxton 1979–81, Bobby Moncur 1981–83, Johnny Hore 1983–84, Dave Smith 1984–88, Ken Brown 1988–90, David Kemp 1990–92, Peter Shilton 1992–95, Steve McCall 1995, Neil Warnock June 1995– .

PORTSMOUTH
Frank Brettell 1898–1901, Bob Blyth 1901–04, Richard Bonney 1905–08, Bob Brown 1911–20, John McCartney 1920–27, Jack Tinn 1927–47, Bob Jackson 1947–52, Eddie Lever 1952–58, Freddie Cox 1958–61, George Smith 1961–70, Ron Tindall 1970–73 (GM to 1974), John Mortimore 1973–74, Ian St. John 1974–77, Jimmy Dickinson 1977–79, Frank Burrows 1979–82, Bobby Campbell 1982–84, Alan Ball 1984–89, John Gregory 1989–90, Frank Burrows 1990–1991, Jim Smith 1991–95, Terry Fenwick February 1995– .

PORT VALE
Sam Gleaves 1896–1905*, Tom Clare 1905–11, A. S. Walker 1911–12, H. Myatt 1912–14, Tom Holford 1919–24 (continued as trainer), Joe Schofield 1924–30, Tom Morgan 1930–32, Tom Holford 1932–35, Warney Cresswell 1936–37, Tom Morgan 1937–38, Billy Frith 1945–46, Gordon Hodgson 1946–51, Ivor Powell 1951, Freddie Steele 1951–57, Norman Low 1957–62, Freddie Steele 1962–65, Jackie Mudie 1965–67, Sir Stanley Matthews (GM) 1965–68, Gordon Lee 1968–74, Roy Sproson 1974–77, Colin Harper 1977, Bobby Smith 1977–78, Dennis Butler 1978–79, Alan Bloor 1979, John McGrath 1980–83, John Rudge March 1984– .

PRESTON NORTH END
Charlie Parker 1906–15, Vincent Hayes 1919–23, Jim Lawrence 1923–25, Frank Richards 1925–27, Alex Gibson 1927–31, Lincoln Hayes 1931–1932 (run by committee 1932–36), Tommy Muirhead 1936–37, (run by committee 1937–49), Will Scott 1949–53, Scot Symon 1953–54, Frank Hill 1954–56, Cliff Britton 1956–61, Jimmy Milne 1961–68, Bobby Seith 1968–70, Alan Ball Sr 1970–73, Bobby Charlton 1973–75, Harry Catterick 1975–77, Nobby Stiles 1977–81, Tommy Docherty 1981, Gordon Lee 1981–83, Alan Kelly 1983–85, Tommy Booth 1985–86, Brian Kidd 1986, John McGrath 1986–90, Les Chapman 1990–92, John Beck 1992–94, Gary Peters December 1994– .

QUEENS PARK RANGERS
James Cowan 1906–13, Jimmy Howie 1913–20, Ted Liddell 1920–24, Will Wood 1924–25 (had been secretary since 1903), Bob Hewison 1925–30, John Bowman 1930–31, Archie Mitchell 1931–33, Mick O'Brien 1933–35, Billy Birrell 1935–39, Ted Vizard 1939–44, Dave Mangnall 1944–52, Jack Taylor 1952–59, Alec Stock 1959–65 (GM to 1968), Bill Dodgin Jnr 1968, Tommy Docherty 1968, Les Allen 1968–71, Gordon Jago 1971–74, Dave Sexton 1974–77, Frank Sibley 1977–78, Steve Burtenshaw 1978–79, Tommy Docherty 1979–80, Terry Venables 1980–84, Gordon Jago 1984, Alan Mullery 1984, Frank Sibley 1984–85, Jim Smith 1985–88, Trevor Francis 1988–90, Don Howe 1990–91, Gerry Francis 1991–94, Ray Wilkins November 1994– .

READING
Thomas Sefton 1897–1901*, James Sharp 1901–02, Harry Matthews 1902–20, Harry Marshall 1920–22, Arthur Chadwick 1923–25, H. S. Bray 1925–26 (secretary only since 1922 and 1926–35), Andrew Wylie 1926–31, Joe Smith 1931–35, Billy Butler 1935–39, John Cochrane 1939, Joe Edelston 1939–47, Ted Drake 1947–52, Jack Smith 1952–55, Harry Johnston 1955–63, Roy Bentley 1963–69, Jack Mansell 1969–71, Charlie Hurley 1972–77, Maurice Evans 1977–84, Ian Branfoot 1984–89, Ian Porterfield 1989–91, Mark McGhee 1991–94, Jimmy Quinn/Mick Gooding December 1994– .

ROCHDALE
Billy Bradshaw 1920, (run by committee 1920–22), Tom Wilson 1922–23, Jack Peart 1923–30, Will Cameron 1930–31, Herbert Hopkinson 1932–34, Billy Smith 1934–35, Ernest Nixon 1935–37, Sam Jennings 1937–38, Ted Goodier 1938–52, Jack Warner 1952–53, Harry Catterick 1953–58, Jack Marshall 1958–60, Tony Collins 1960–68, Bob Stokoe 1967–68, Len Richley 1968–70, Dick Conner 1970–73, Walter Joyce 1973–76, Brian Green 1976–77, Mike Ferguson 1977–78, Doug Collins 1979, Bob Stokoe 1979–80, Peter Madden 1980–83, Jimmy Greenhoff 1983–84, Vic Halom 1984–86, Eddie Gray 1986–88, Danny Bergara 1988–89, Terry Dolan 1989–91, Dave Sutton 1991–94, Mick Docherty 1995–96, Graham Barrow May 1996– .

ROTHERHAM UNITED
Billy Heald 1925–29 (secretary only for long spell), Stanley Davies 1929–30, Billy Heald 1930–33, Reg Freeman 1934–52, Andy Smailes 1952–58, Tom Johnston 1958–62, Danny Williams 1962–65, Jack Mansell 1965–67, Tommy Docherty 1967–68, Jimmy McAnearney 1968–73, Jimmy McGuigan 1973–79, Ian Porterfield 1979–81, Emlyn Hughes 1981–83, George Kerr 1983–85, Norman Hunter 1985–87, Dave Cusack 1987–88, Billy McEwan 1988–91, Phil Henson 1991–94, Archie Gemmill/ John McGovern September 1994– .

SCARBOROUGH
B. Chapman 1945–47*, George Hall 1946–47, Harold Taylor 1947–48, Frank Taylor 1948–50, A. C. Bell (Director & Hon. TM) 1950–53, Reg Halton 1953–54, Charles Robson (Hon. TM) 1954–57, George Higgins 1957–58, Andy Smailes 1959–61, Eddie Brown 1961–64, Albert Franks 1964–65, Stuart Myers 1965–66, Graham Shaw 1968–69, Colin Appleton 1969–73, Ken Houghton 1974–75, Colin Appleton 1975–81, Jimmy McAnearney 1981–82, John Cottam 1982–84, Harry Dunn 1984–86, Neil Warnock 1986–88, Colin Morris 1989, Ray McHale 1989–93, Phil Chambers 1993, Steve Wicks 1993–94, Billy Ayre 1994, Ray McHale 1994–96, Mitch Cook (DoC) 1996, Mick Wadsworth June 1996– .

SCUNTHORPE UNITED
Harry Allcock 1915–53*, Tom Crilly 1936–37, Bernard Harper 1946–48, Leslie Jones 1950–51, Bill Corkhill 1952–56, Ron Suart 1956–58, Tony McShane 1959, Bill Lambton 1959, Frank Soo 1959–60, Dick Duckworth 1960–64, Fred Goodwin 1964–66, Ron Ashman 1967–73, Ron Bradley 1973–74, Dick Rooks 1974–76, Ron Ashman 1976–81, John Duncan 1981–83, Allan Clarke 1983–84, Frank Barlow 1984–87, Mick Buxton 1987–91, Bill Green 1991–93, Richard Money 1993–94, David Moore 1994–96, Mick Buxton March 1996– .

SHEFFIELD UNITED
J. B. Wostinholm 1889–1899*, John Nicholson 1899–1932, Ted Davison 1932–52, Reg Freeman 1952–55, Joe Mercer 1955–58, Johnny Harris 1959–68 (continued as GM to 1970), Arthur Rowley 1968–69, Johnny Harris (GM resumed TM duties) 1969–73, Ken Furphy 1973–75, Jimmy Sirrel 1975–77, Harry Haslam 1978–81, Martin Peters 1981, Ian Porterfield 1981–86, Billy McEwan 1986–88, Dave Bassett 1988–95, Howard Kendall December 1995– .

SHEFFIELD WEDNESDAY
Arthur Dickinson 1891–1920*, Robert Brown 1920–33, Billy Walker 1933–37, Jimmy McMullan 1937–42, Eric Taylor 1942–58 (continued as GM to 1974), Harry Catterick 1958–61, Vic Buckingham 1961–64, Alan Brown 1964–68, Jack Marshall 1968–69, Danny Williams 1969–71, Derek Dooley 1971–73, Steve Burtenshaw 1974–75, Len Ashurst 1975–77, Jackie Charlton 1977–83, Howard Wilkinson 1983–88, Peter Eustace 1988–89, Ron Atkinson 1989–91, Trevor Francis 1991–95, David Pleat June 1995– .

SHREWSBURY TOWN
W. Adams 1905–12*, A. Weston 1912–34*, Jack Roscamp 1934–35, Sam Ramsey 1935–36, Ted Bousted 1936–40, Leslie Knighton 1945–49, Harry Chapman 1949–50, Sammy Crooks 1950–54, Walter Rowley 1955–57, Harry Potts 1957–58, Johnny Spuhler 1958, Arthur Rowley 1958–68, Harry Gregg 1968–72, Maurice Evans 1972–73, Alan Durban 1974–78, Richie Barker 1978, Graham Turner 1978–84, Chic Bates 1984–87, Ian McNeill 1987–90, Asa Hartford 1990–91, John Bond 1991–93, Fred Davies February 1994 (previously caretaker-manager from May 1993)– .

SOUTHAMPTON
Cecil Knight 1894–95*, Charles Robson 1895–97, E. Arnfield 1897–1911* (continued as secretary), George Swift 1911–12, Ernest Arnfield 1912–19, Jimmy McIntyre 1919–24, Arthur Chadwick 1925–31, George Kay 1931–36, George Gross 1936–37, Tom Parker 1937–43, J. R. Sarjantson stepped down from the board to act as secretary-manager 1943–47 with the next two listed being team managers during this period, Arthur Dominy 1943–46, Bill Dodgin Snr 1946–49, Sid Cann 1949–51, George Roughton 1952–55, Ted Bates 1955–73, Lawrie McMenemy 1973–85, Chris Nicholl 1985–91, Ian Branfoot 1991–94, Alan Ball 1994–95, Dave Merrington 1995–96, Graeme Souness July 1996– .

SOUTHEND UNITED
Bob Jack 1906–10, George Molyneux 1910–11, O. M. Howard 1911–12, Joe Bradshaw 1912–19, Ned Liddell 1919–20, Tom Mather 1920–21, Ted Birnie 1921–34, David Jack 1934–40, Harry Warren 1946–56, Eddie Perry 1956–60, Frank Broome 1960, Ted Fenton 1961–65, Alvan Williams 1965–67, Ernie Shepherd 1967–69, Geoff Hudson 1969–70, Arthur Rowley 1970–76, Dave Smith 1976–83, Peter Morris 1983–84, Bobby Moore 1984–86, Dave Webb 1986–87, Dick Bate 1987, Paul Clark 1987–88, Dave Webb (GM) 1988–92, Colin Murphy 1992–93, Barry Fry 1993, Peter Taylor 1993–95, Steve Thompson 1995, Ronnie Whelan July 1995– .

STOCKPORT COUNTY
Fred Stewart 1894–1911, Harry Lewis 1911–14, David Ashworth 1914–19, Albert Williams 1919–24, Fred Scotchbrook 1924–26, Lincoln Hyde 1926–31, Andrew Wilson 1932–33, Fred Westgarth 1934–36, Bob Kelly 1936–38, George Hunt 1938–39, Bob Marshall 1939–49, Andy Beattie 1949–52, Dick Duckworth 1952–56, Billy Moir 1956–60, Reg Flewin 1960–63, Trevor Porteous 1963–65, Bert Trautmann (GM) 1965–66, Eddie Quigley (TM) 1965–66, Jimmy Meadows 1966–69, Wally Galbraith 1969–70, Matt Woods 1970–71, Brian Doyle 1972–74, Jimmy Meadows 1974–75, Roy Chapman 1975–76, Eddie Quigley 1976–77, Alan Thompson 1977–78, Mike Summerbee 1978–79, Jimmy McGuigan 1979–82, Eric Webster 1982–85, Colin Murphy 1985, Les Chapman 1985–86, Jimmy Melia 1986, Colin Murphy 1986–87, Asa Hartford 1987–89, Danny Bergara 1989–95, Dave Jones March 1995– .

STOKE CITY
Tom Slaney 1874–83*, Walter Cox 1883–84*, Harry Lockett 1884–90, Joseph Bradshaw 1890–92, Arthur Reeves 1892–95, William Rowley 1895–97, H. D. Austerberry 1897–1908, A. J. Barker 1908–14, Peter Hodge 1914–15, Joe Schofield 1915–19, Arthur Shallcross 1919–23, John "Jock" Rutherford 1923, Tom Mather 1923–35, Bob McGrory 1935–52, Frank Taylor 1952–60, Tony Waddington 1960–77, George Eastham 1977–78, Alan A'Court 1978, Alan Durban 1978–81, Richie Barker 1981–83, Bill Asprey 1984–85, Mick Mills 1985–89, Alan Ball 1989–91, Lou Macari 1991–93, Joe Jordan 1993–94, Lou Macari September 1994– .

SUNDERLAND
Tom Watson 1888–96, Bob Campbell 1896–99, Alex Mackie 1899–1905, Bob Kyle 1905–28, Johnny Cochrane 1928–39, Bill Murray 1939–57, Alan Brown 1957–64, George Hardwick 1964–65, Ian McColl 1965–68, Alan Brown 1968–72, Bob Stokoe 1972–76, Jimmy Adamson 1976–78, Ken Knighton 1979–81, Alan Durban 1981–84, Len Ashurst 1984–85,

Lawrie McMenemy 1985–87, Denis Smith 1987–91, Malcolm Crosby 1992–93, Terry Butcher 1993, Mick Buxton 1993–95, Peter Reid March 1995– .

SWANSEA CITY

Walter Whittaker 1912–14, William Bartlett 1914–15, Joe Bradshaw 1919–26, Jimmy Thomson 1927–31, Neil Harris 1934–39, Haydn Green 1939–47, Bill McCandless 1947–55, Ron Burgess 1955–58, Trevor Morris 1958–65, Glyn Davies 1965–66, Billy Lucas 1967–69, Roy Bentley 1969–72, Harry Gregg 1972–75, Harry Griffiths 1975–77, John Toshack 1978–83 (resigned October re-appointed in December) 1983–84, Colin Appleton 1984, John Bond 1984–85, Tommy Hutchison 1985–86, Terry Yorath 1986–89, Ian Evans 1989–90, Terry Yorath 1990–91, Frank Burrows 1991–95, Kevin Cullis 1996, Jan Molby February 1996– .

SWINDON TOWN

Sam Allen 1902–33, Ted Vizard 1933–39, Neil Harris 1939–41, Louis Page 1945–53, Maurice Lindley 1953–55, Bert Head 1956–65, Danny Williams 1965–69, Fred Ford 1969–71, Dave Mackay 1971–72, Les Allen 1972–74, Danny Williams 1974–78, Bobby Smith 1978–80, John Trollope 1980–83, Ken Beamish 1983–84, Lou Macari 1984–89, Ossie Ardiles 1989–91, Glenn Hoddle 1991–93, John Gorman 1993–94, Steve McMahon November 1994– .

TORQUAY UNITED

Percy Mackrill 1927–29, A. H. Hoskins 1929*, Frank Womack 1929–32, Frank Brown 1932–38, Alf Steward 1938–40, Billy Butler 1945–46, Jack Butler 1946–47, John McNeil 1947–50, Bob John 1950, Alex Massie 1950–51, Eric Webber 1951–65, Frank O'Farrell 1965–68, Alan Brown 1969–71, Jack Edwards 1971–73, Malcolm Musgrove 1973–76, Mike Green 1977–81, Frank O'Farrell 1981–82 (continued as GM to 1983), Bruce Rioch 1982–84, Dave Webb 1984–85, John Sims 1985, Stuart Morgan 1985–87, Cyril Knowles 1987–89, Dave Smith 1989–91, John Impey 1991–92, Ivan Golac 1992, Paul Compton 1992–93, Don O'Riordan 1993–95, Eddie May 1995–96, Kevin Hodges (HC) June 1996– .

TOTTENHAM HOTSPUR

Frank Brettell 1898–99, John Cameron 1899–1906, Fred Kirkham 1907–08, Peter McWilliam 1912–27, Billy Minter 1927–29, Percy Smith 1930–35, Jack Tresadern 1935–38, Peter McWilliam 1938–42, Arthur Turner 1942–46, Joe Hulme 1946–49, Arthur Rowe 1949–55, Jimmy Anderson 1955–58, Bill Nicholson 1958–74, Terry Neill 1974–76, Keith Burkinshaw 1976–84, Peter Shreeves 1984–86, David Pleat 1986–87, Terry Venables 1987–91, Peter Shreeves 1991–92, Ossie Ardiles 1993–94, Gerry Francis November 1994– .

TRANMERE ROVERS

Bert Cooke 1912–35, Jackie Carr 1935–36, Jim Knowles 1936–39, Bill Ridding 1939–45, Ernie Blackburn 1946–55, Noel Kelly 1955–57, Peter Farrell 1957–60, Walter Galbraith 1961, Dave Russell 1961–69, Jackie Wright 1969–72, Ron Yeats 1972–75, John King 1975–80, Bryan Hamilton 1980–85, Frank Worthington 1985–87, Ronnie Moore 1987, John King 1987–96, John Aldridge April 1996– .

WALSALL

H. Smallwood 1888–91*, A. G. Burton 1891–93, J. H. Robinson 1893–95, C. H. Ailso 1895–96*, A. E. Parsloe 1896–97*, L. Ford 1897–98*, G. Hughes 1898–99*, L. Ford 1899–1901*, J. E. Shutt 1908–13*, Haydn Price 1914–20, Joe Burchell 1920–26, David Ashworth 1926–27, Jack Torrance 1927–28, James Kerr 1928–29, Sid Scholey 1929–30, Peter O'Rourke 1930–32, Bill Slade 1932–34, Andy Wilson 1934–37, Tommy Lowes 1937–44, Harry Hibbs 1944–51, Tony McPhee 1951, Brough Fletcher 1952–53, Major Frank Buckley 1953–55, John Love 1955–57, Billy Moore 1957–64, Alf Wood 1964, Reg Shaw 1964–68, Dick Graham 1968, Ron Lewin 1968–69, Billy Moore 1969–72, John Smith 1972–73, Doug Fraser 1973–77, Dave Mackay 1977–78, Alan Ashman 1978, Frank Sibley 1979, Alan Buckley 1979–86, Neil Martin (joint manager with Buckley) 1981–82, Tommy Coakley 1986–88, John Barnwell 1989–90, Kenny Hibbitt 1990–94, Chris Nicholl September 1994– .

WATFORD

John Goodall 1903–10, Harry Kent 1910–26, Fred Pagnam 1926–29, Neil McBain 1929–37, Bill Findlay 1938–47, Jack Bray 1947–48, Eddie Hapgood 1948–50, Ron Gray 1950–51, Haydn Green 1951–52, Len Goulden 1952–55 (GM to 1956), Johnny Paton 1955–56, Neil McBain 1956–59, Ron Burgess 1959–63, Bill McGarry 1963–64, Ken Furphy 1964–71, George Kirby 1971–73, Mike Keen 1973–77, Graham Taylor 1977–87, Dave Bassett 1987–88, Steve Harrison 1988–90, Colin Lee 1990, Steve Perryman 1990–93, Glenn Roeder 1993–96, Graham Taylor (GM) February 1996– . Kenny Jackett May 1996– .

WEST BROMWICH ALBION

Louis Ford 1890–92*, Henry Jackson 1892–94*, Edward Stephenson 1894–95*, Clement Keys 1895–96*, Frank Heaven 1896–1902*, Fred Everiss 1902–48, Jack Smith 1948–52, Jesse Carver 1952, Vic Buckingham 1953–59, Gordon Clark 1959–61, Archie Macaulay 1961–63, Jimmy Hagan 1963–67, Alan Ashman 1967–71, Don Howe 1971–75, Johnny Giles 1975–77, Ronnie Allen 1977, Ron Atkinson 1978–81, Ronnie Allen 1981–82, Ron Wylie 1982–84, Johnny Giles 1984–85, Ron Saunders 1986–87, Ron Atkinson 1987–88, Brian Talbot 1988–91, Bobby Gould 1991–92, Ossie Ardiles 1992–93, Keith Burkinshaw 1993–94, Alan Buckley October 1994– .

WEST HAM UNITED

Syd King 1902–32, Charlie Paynter 1932–50, Ted Fenton 1950–61, Ron Greenwood 1961–74 (continued as GM to 1977), John Lyall 1974–89, Lou Macari 1989–90, Billy Bonds 1990–94, Harry Redknapp August 1994– .

WIGAN ATHLETIC

Charlie Spencer 1932–37, Jimmy Milne 1946–47, Bob Pryde 1949–52, Ted Goodier 1952–54, Walter Crook 1954–55, Ron Suart 1955–56, Billy Cooke 1956, Sam Barkas 1957, Trevor Hitchen 1957–58, Malcolm Barrass 1958–59, Jimmy Shirley 1959, Pat Murphy 1959–60, Allenby Chilton 1960, Johnny Ball 1961–63, Allan Brown 1963–66, Alf Craig

1966–67, Harry Leyland 1967–68, Alan Saunders 1968, Ian McNeill 1968–70, Gordon Milne 1970–72, Les Rigby 1972–74, Brian Tiler 1974–76, Ian McNeill 1976–81, Larry Lloyd 1981–83, Harry McNally 1983–85, Bryan Hamilton 1985–86, Ray Mathias 1986–89, Bryan Hamilton 1989–93, Dave Philpotts 1993, Kenny Swain 1993–94, Graham Barrow 1994–95, John Deehan November 1995– .

WIMBLEDON
Les Henley 1955–71, Mike Everitt 1971–73, Dick Graham 1973–74, Allen Batsford 1974–78, Dario Gradi 1978–81, Dave Bassett 1981–87, Bobby Gould 1987–90, Ray Harford 1990–91, Peter Withe 1991, Joe Kinnear January 1992– .

WOLVERHAMPTON WANDERERS
George Worrall 1877–85*, John Addenbrooke 1885–1922, George Jobey 1922–24, Albert Hoskins 1924–26 (had been secretary since 1922), Fred Scotchbrook 1926–27, Major Frank Buckley 1927–44, Ted Vizard 1944–48, Stan Cullis 1948–64, Andy Beattie 1964–65, Ronnie Allen 1966–68, Bill McGarry 1968–76, Sammy Chung 1976–78, John Barnwell 1978–81, Ian Greaves 1982, Graham Hawkins 1982–84, Tommy Docherty 1984–85, Bill McGarry 1985, Sammy Chapman 1985–86, Brian Little 1986, Graham Turner 1986–94, Graham Taylor 1994–95, Mark McGhee December 1995– .

WREXHAM
Ted Robinson 1912–25* (continued as secretary to 1930), Charlie Hewitt 1925–29, Jack Baynes 1929–31, Ernest Blackburn 1932–36, Jimmy Logan 1937–38, Arthur Cowell 1938, Tom Morgan 1938–40, Tom Williams 1940–49, Les McDowall 1949–50, Peter Jackson 1951–54, Cliff Lloyd 1954–57, John Love 1957–59, Billy Morris 1960–61, Ken Barnes 1961–65, Billy Morris 1965, Jack Rowley 1966–67, Alvan Williams 1967–68, John Neal 1968–77, Arfon Griffiths 1977–81, Mel Sutton 1981–82, Bobby Roberts 1982–85, Dixie McNeil 1985–89, Brian Flynn November 1989– .

WYCOMBE WANDERERS
First coach appointed 1951. Prior to Brian Lee's appointment in 1969, the team was selected by a Match Committee which met every Monday evening. James McCormack 1951–52, Sid Cann 1952–61, Graham Adams 1961–62, Don Welsh 1962–64, Barry Darvill 1964–68, Brian Lee 1969–76, Ted Powell 1976–77, John Reardon 1977–78, Andy Williams 1978–80, Mike Keen 1980–84, Paul Bence 1984–86, Alan Gane 1986–87, Peter Suddaby 1987–88, Jim Kelman 1988–90, Martin O'Neill 1990–95, Alan Smith June 1995– .

YORK CITY
Bill Sherrington 1924–60 (was secretary for most of this time but virtually secretary-manager for a long pre-war spell), John Collier 1929–36, Tom Mitchell 1936–50, Dick Duckworth 1950–52, Charlie Spencer 1952–53, Jimmy McCormick 1953–54, Sam Bartram 1956–60, Tom Lockie 1960–67, Joe Shaw 1967–68, Tom Johnston 1968–75, Wilf McGuinness 1975–77, Charlie Wright 1977–80, Barry Lyons 1980–81, Denis Smith 1982–87, Bobby Saxton 1987–88, John Bird 1988–91, John Ward 1991–93, Alan Little March 1993– .

Alex Ferguson the Manchester United manager congratulates Eric Cantona after the Cup Final. Gary Pallister (left) and David Beckham (right) are in attendance. (Colorsport)

The things they said ...

Luton chairman David Kohler, after winning a High Court injunction putting a temporary stop on manager David Pleat's switch to Sheff Wed:
"Someone has to stand up and set an example to fans. It seems that the only loyalty left in football comes from fans and directors. Players and managers don't seem to give a damn."

Alan Thorne, George Graham's former chairman at Millwall, after not being called to give evidence to the FA commission which found the sacked Arsenal manager guilty of accepting "bungs":
"I'm shocked and disgusted. It's typical of the FA. They're run just like masons. George is the most honourable man I have known."

Brazilian sports minister Pele, horrified at the escalating violence in his country's football:
"The time has gone for persuasion - punishment is necessary."

Man City manager Alan Ball:
"Players of today aren't facing up to their responsibilities in return for their salaries and adulation. I speak to other managers and they're saying the same thing."

Spurs chairman Alan Sugar, dismayed by criticism from fans and from former star Jürgen Klinsmann:
"I've worked my nuts off for this club. I will not stand for this abuse. If there's someone out there who thinks they can do better and put up more money than I have for the club, then good luck to them. But put up or shut up."

Former Spurs star Jürgen Klinsmann:
"There is a big question mark over whether his heart is in the club and football. I would not have wanted to leave Spurs if Sugar had shown more ambition."

Spurs chairman Alan Sugar, brandishing Klinsmann's shirt at a TV interview:
"He signed it 'To Alan, with a very special thankyou'. I'm bloody sure it's a very special thankyou. I'm the blooming mug that relaunched his career. I wouldn't wash my car with that shirt now. You can auction it among your viewers for charity."

George Graham's reasons for not appealing against his one-year ban:
"I do not have a bottomless pocket ... I feel in my heart I would not get a fair hearing ... and lastly I want to get on with the rest of my life.... My aim is to be back in football management within the year."

Wimbledon manager Joe Kinnear, after captain Vinnie Jones had a dismissal revoked:
"I'm very glad to see that common sense has prevailed. I'm pleased that the linesman has seen the video and agreed he made a mistake. It proves that referees and linesmen are human after all."

Everton's Anders Limpar, on being booked in a Cup-Winners Cup match by referee Roger Phillipe (Luxembourg) for taking a free-kick too quickly:
"I have never heard of anything like this. You won't find it in the rule book ... If the opposition has been penalized, you are entitled to expect some advantage from a free-kick."

The Football League reaction to the Bosman ruling:
"We expect to maintain the present-day system, as we believe that three-quarters of full-time footballers would lose their jobs under the proposed arrangements."

The reaction of PFA chief executive Gordon Taylor:
"While I'm concerned about the consequences, there are obviously great opportunities for star players to capitalise on their ability."

Sheff Wed manager David Pleat:
"If there is no incentive for Endsleigh League clubs to produce quality players, that will be a very bad thing for the game in this country."

Premier League chief executive Rick Parry:
"There has been a bizarre, hysterical reaction even by football standards.... Our system will survive in some form. It isn't a bad model, and what happened with Bosman in Belgium couldn't have happened here."

Wolves manager Graham Taylor after another lack-lustre performance, a home draw against bottom club Luton, leaves them floundering near the relegation zone:
"At the end of the day it's results-oriented, this game, and our results aren't anything like we would like them to be."

Sheff Wed manager David Pleat, on the reported transfer request of Romanian defender Dan Petrescu, who has three years of his contract still to run:
"If he doesn't want to be in our first team, perhaps he can play in our reserves. I am very unhappy. The club will not be held to ransom. Dan has not been knocking at my door. It is his agent who is demanding more money."

Manager Bruce Rioch, on FIFA referee Martin Bodenham after Arsenal lose their unbeaten record at Chelsea:

"He's past his sell-by date. This is the first time I've ever criticised an official and it will be the last, but he didn't give right decisions and he let far too much go. He was poor by Premier League standards."

Everton manager Joe Royle on the jailing in Scotland of striker Duncan Ferguson for a head-butting incident while playing for Rangers:
"Anyone who knows him will tell you he's a very pleasant young man and isn't a bad lad at all. He's been guilty sometimes of stupidity, but mostly of immaturity. Consider that a young man who is certainly no danger to society is now behind bars with hardened criminals."

Wolves owner Sir Jack Hayward, speaking in the Bahamas of manager Graham Taylor (before their 4-1 home defeat by Stoke):
"The more I see of Graham, the more I meet him, the more impressed I am with him. I held the view he was the best man available when we appointed him and it is a view I continue to hold.... He's not just a manager, he's a psychiatrist who is able to think his way around matters."

Torquay player-manager Don O'Riordan, sacked after their 8-1 home defeat by Scunthorpe:
"I don't understand it. We did everything right in training, but yesterday every time they came near our goal they scored. I'm very disappointed. I still think I'm a good manager."

UEFA president Lennart Johansson on the judgment in the European Court on the Bosman case:
"The transfer system may not be the perfect model, but the last thing any of us need is some dictate from a European court which turns our sport upside-down."

The FA commission investigating the George Graham "bung" allegations:
"Mr Graham gave evidence about the payments [£140,500 in £50 notes and a banker's draft for £285,000] being unsolicited. However, even if this is right, as a respected manager ... we find that he must have known how serious a matter it was for him to be receiving this amount from an agent. ... Mr Graham told us that he did not declare the payments to Arsenal because he did not consider them to be connected to transfers. We do not accept this. When he received the bundles of cash in the Park Lane Hotel, he must have reflected on the fact that he had only really succeeded in negotiating a cut for Mr Hauge in relation to the Lydersen deal."

Chelsea Chairman Ken Bates, in a letter to Matthew Harding, owner of Stamford Bridge:
"Being a director brings responsibilities, duties and privileges. In view of your behaviour, your privileges are being withdrawn."

Birmingham manager Barry Fry, following the Anglo-Italian Cup tie in Italy after which his side were involved in altercations with Ancona coach Massimo Cacciatori:
"He [Cacciatori] attacked three players during the match and at the end he wanted to fight anyone in sight. It was disgraceful. If I'd done that in England, I would be banned for life."

Marine manager Roly Howard, after his side's narrow 11-2 defeat in the FA Cup by Shrewsbury:
"It may sound daft, but until we let in those three goals just before half-time I thought we were the better side."

Coventry manager Ron Atkinson on the joys of football despite getting knocked out of the Coca-Cola Cup by Wolves:
"Once you've had a taste of it you never have enough. You tell me a better way to spend Wednesday night - under the floodlights at a cracking stadium, big game, plenty at stake. Not even Coronation Street is that good."

FA chief executive Graham Kelly, continuing to support much-harassed England coach Terry Venables:
"I don't know of anybody in football who has had to suffer such a constant barrage of adverse comment, which must have affected his reputation, not as a football coach, but as a person. I think that's sad. If things can be proved, fine. But it's very far from that at the moment as far as I can see. ... We appointed him as the England coach, and I've seen nothing in his coaching to question that decision. Nor have I seen very much that really affects him from outside. He seems to have a remarkable ability to focus and do the job very well."

The Recorder of London County Court, when ruling in favour of a businessman suing England coach Terry Venables as a debtor:
"I do not accept his [Venables'] evidence as entirely reliable, to put it at its most charitable.... Unfortunately for Mr Venables and the defendant's company [Scribes West], his evidence under oath contradicts what he said not only in liquidation proceedings but in his own published autobiography."

Louis Kilcoyne, president of the FA of Ireland, on manager Jack Charlton's retirement:
"The FAI and the people of Ireland owe Jack a huge debt of gratitude for all he has done for football and the country in the last 10 years. Jack has steered our international team to levels of success never before achieved. In doing this he has helped to expand the game into every corner of Ireland.... Thanks Jack, you have been a manager in a million."

Wimbledon captain Vinnie Jones, likening Chelsea's Ruud Gullit to two pot-bellied pigs he owns, after being sent off at Stamford Bridge when he was given a second yellow card for a foul on the Dutchman:
"They don't squeal as much as him."

A Wimbledon spokesman after studying a video of the foul on Ruud Gullit that resulted in the 11th dismissal of Vinnie Jones's career and caused him to squeal about the referee's decision:
"We believe referee Dermot Gallagher had no alternative but to take the action he did. We have stood by Vinnie in the past when we felt he was being unfairly treated, but it is not something we do blindly."

UEFA president Lennart Johansson, on FIFA leader João Havelange's assertion that the 2006 World Cup will go to Africa:
"That decision will not be taken for another four years and is a matter for the whole of FIFA, not just the president. ... It is dictatorial. It is not for the president to travel around the world deciding where the World Cup should be held ... this simply had to stop."

UEFA chairman Lennart Johansson, on Arsenal vice-chairman David Dein's 'blueprint for a European League':
"I will read the proposal tonight - if I can keep awake."

Bolton manager Colin Todd, in his programme notes for the match with Villa:
"I am not wishing to highlight any particular official and I am not moaning because of the position in which we find ourselves in the League table. But the standard of refereeing in the Premiership is appalling."

Spurs chairman Alan Sugar on UEFA's move to expand European club competitions, proposals for a Super League, and the growing elitism of the top clubs:
"You would have thought that [the £30-40m a year ploughed into football by Sky] was an amazing windfall for the 20 clubs, but what happens is that the money seems to flow into escalating transfer fees, escalating players' salaries, and no one ever seems to win. If the [new] deal is worth £150m or £200m, I think the clever thing is to allocate some of that money to the development of the game."

Scottish referee Jim McGilvray, critical of FIFA's edicts, on why he resigned:
"The day I had to book Gascoigne for celebrating scoring a goal was the last straw - that was the day I decided to pack it in."

Newcastle manager Kevin Keegan rationalising the incidents in the Premiership match at Maine Road that persuaded the FA to bring misconduct charges against his new Colombian signing Faustino Asprilla:
"He's from Latin America. That's the way they are."

Norwich manager Gary Megson, after chairman Robert Chase sold two players to reduce the club's overdraft from £4.5m to £1.9m:
"I'm furious, flabbergasted and bewildered. It's ludicrous what the board have done. This has got absolutely nothing to do with football and I can't see what they're trying to achieve. I didn't sanction the moves, and I'm not party to either transfer. ... It's me and the players now against the world. ... Things couldn't be any worse, but we will just have to adopt a siege mentality, ... I've no intention of resigning. ... I've never quit in my life."

Manchester United's Roy Keane, the day before his sending off for Ireland against Russia:
"I think I've only been booked a couple of times in the last dozen games, which is good for me. I had better not say any more about that, or I'll probably be sent off next week."

From a faxed letter to Kevin Keegan from FIFA secretary Sepp Blatter, moved by the Newcastle manager's sporting reaction to their devastating defeat in the 4-3 epic at Anfield:
"I have been greatly impressed by your remarks regarding your commitment to attacking football and about referees' rights to make human errors. Allow me, on behalf of FIFA, and those who believe in fair play, to commend you for the positive attitude you bring to our game with comments such as these - especially in the disappointment of defeat in such an important match."

Martin Prothero, Umbro promotions director, after Man United abandon their grey away strip, costing his company many millions of pounds:
"We had a difficulty with that particular shade of grey and its configuration with the other colours. The problem was that we tested it on a really dark day, whereas every game in which the kit was used was a bright day. The different hue it produced was incredible."

Tim Gardiner, Umbro International's marketing manager, stressing that England's change strip, unlike Man United's, is not grey but indigo blue, and rejecting the theory that England played in it against Bulgaria last month to advertise the availability of a colour designed to go with jeans:
"It's an interpretation of something that England have worn before, the pale blue which was really popular during the Mexico World Cup [of 1986]."

Man Utd manager Alex Ferguson, after 10-man Leeds had eschewed their dreadful form and pushed the Premiership leaders all the way before Roy Keane scored a late winner:
"If they played like that every week, they would be up near the top. You wonder if it is just because they are playing Manchester United. Pathetic, I think. We can accept any club coming here and trying their hardest as long as they do it every week. No wonder managers get the sack."

Newcastle manager Kevin Keegan, after his side win at Leeds:
"You don't say what he [Ferguson] said about Leeds. You just don't say that in football. He's gone down a lot in my estimation. ... United have not won it yet. ... I'd love to beat them now, love to."

Glenn Hoddle, on accepting the job as England coach:
"It has been a heart-rending time for me, these last few days. Chelsea have done everything right. They offered me a super contract, but it is just an ambition I have had. The only job I would have left Chelsea for was the national job, and that goes for any club in Britain and Europe."

Man Utd manager Alex Ferguson, whose first thoughts are for Newcastle after his team clinch the title:
"I feel for them. I feel for the whole club. Newcastle have had a fantastic season. Their supporters were brilliant to us when we played up there. There was no bitterness, no spite. We are not gloating, but we are quietly satisfied. We have done the right thing by the kids and stuck with them."

Man Utd captain Steve Bruce, echoing his manager's sentiments:
"We have been in Newcastle's situation twice in the last five years. We know what it feels like. They've been a credit to English football."

Kevin Keegan, in final defeat:
"Our congratulations go to Manchester United and their supporters. Everyone has talked about our collapse, but that doesn't do justice to what they have achieved in turning round what looked an impossible situation."

Eric Cantona, breaking his 15-month silence on last season's moment of madness at Selhurst Park:
"Before that night I was behaving like a child. I was prepared to repeat the same mistake again and again. After it, I realised that was an irresponsible habit. ... I don't think of him [Simmons] much, only that his assault on the lawyer last Thursday speaks for itself."

Carlisle chairman Michael Knighton, as his club's survival in Division 2 depends on the result of the match between Brighton and York to be replayed after the end of the season because the original fixture had to be abandoned:
"They [the Football League] are messing about with our livelihoods and I will not stand back and watch this absurd degree of ineptitude by our administrators. I shall be calling for resignations, and a High Court writ for negligence is a real possibility."

Birmingham joint owner David Sullivan, insisting there was nothing sinister about the sacking of manager Barry Fry:
"We feel Barry has taken the club as far as he can [15th in Div 1]. ... After three years and 61 players, we think it is time someone else is entitled to a go."

Barry Fry's answerphone message the same day:
"Kristine's gone shopping as usual and I've gone to the JobCentre looking for new employment. Funny ol' game, innit?"

David Willis of the National Sporting Club, which was raided by the police investigating alleged irregularities in ticket sales for Euro 96:
"It is now very clear that the right hand at the FA did not know what the left hand was doing. We, as a reputable organisation, legitimately offered hospitality packages for Euro 96 on the basis that we were on the approved FA commercial directors' ticket list. But it seems that down the corridor at the FA, the tournament director Mr Kirton and other officials did not know anything about that list."

Former FA commercial director Trevor Phillips, who resigned because of allegations he described as spurious:
"I did not tell them [Sportsworld and two other companies whose premises were raided by the police] that they were authorised to resell tickets and I am very surprised to see it suggested, by one report at least. ... At no time did I give any such authorisation nor, indeed, would it have been my responsibility to do so."

FA chief executive Graham Kelly, when asked if commercial director Trevor Phillips had resigned:
"Not necessarily."

Eric Cantona, commenting on his omission from France's Euro 96 squad:
"Since I was not completely dead and since I even resurrected, they have done everything they could to make sure I died a second time."

England coach Terry Venables, after quizzing his players regarding the damage to their plane on the way back from Hong Kong: *"The England squad has accepted collective responsibility. The matter is now being dealt with internally."*

Former referee Clive Thomas on the flurry of red and yellow cards at the start of Euro 96:
"They are refereeing like headmasters, not using man management. They are under pressure [from UEFA], but I blame them for not demanding to be given the leeway to use their common sense. We have inconsistent refereeing, but consistent yellow-carding."

England's assistant coach Bryan Robson, defending the squad against lurid tabloid tales of debauchery:
"The young players are frightened to death to play for England because of the publicity they get for absolutely anything. Paul Ince goes to a private barbecue and there's a photo of him on the front page of a national newspaper. He's had two bottles of Budweiser."

END OF SEASON PLAY-OFFS 1995-96

Semi-finals, First Leg

12 MAY

DIVISON 1

Charlton Ath (1) 1 *(Newton)*
Crystal Palace (0) 2 *(Brown, Veart)*   14,618
Charlton Ath: Petterson; Jackson, Whyte C,Newton,
Rufus, Balmer, Robson (Whyte D), Leaburn, Robinson,
Allen (Nelson), Bowyer.
Crystal Palace: Martyn; Edworthy, Brown, Roberts,
Andersen (Quinn), Veart, Pitcher, Houghton, Freedman,
Ndah, Tuttle.

Leicester C (0) 0
Stoke C (0) 0   20,325
Leicester C: Poole; Grayson, Whitlow, Watts, Walsh,
Izzet, Lennon, Taylor, Claridge, Robins (Parker),
Heskey.
Stoke C: Prudhoe; Clarkson, Sandford, Sigurdsson,
Whittle, Potter, Devlin, Wallace, Sheron, Sturridge,
Gleghorn.

DIVISION 2

Bradford C (0) 0
Blackpool (0) 2 *(Ellis, Bonner)*   14,273
Bradford C: Gould; Liburd (Huxford), Jacobs, Youds,
Mohan, Brightwell (Kiwomya), Shutt, Duxbury,
Ormondroyd, Stallard (Tolson), Hamilton.
Blackpool: Nixon; Bryan, Gouck, Linighan, Mellon,
Watson, Bradshaw, Bonner, Morrison, Ellis, Preece
(Quinn).

Crewe Alex (2) 2 *(Little, Rivers)*
Notts Co (0) 2 *(Finnan, Martindale)*   4931
Crewe Alex: Gayle; Westwood, Unsworth, Lightfoot,
McAllister, Whalley (Collins), Little, Savage, Macauley,
Murphy (Blissett), Rivers (Tierney).
Notts Co: Ward; Derry, Baraclough, Murphy, Strodder,
Richardson, Finnan, Rogers, Jones (Martindale),
Battersby, Agana.

DIVISION 3

Colchester U (1) 1 *(Kinsella)*
Plymouth Arg (0) 0   6511
Colchester U: Emberson; Fry, Betts, McCarthy, Caesar,
Cawley, Kinsella, Dennis, McGleish, Reinelt (Whitton),
Gibbs (Locke).
Plymouth Arg: Cherry; Patterson, Williams, Billy,
Heathcote, Barlow (Mauge), Leadbitter, Logan,
Littlejohn, Evans (Corazzin), Curran.

Hereford U (1) 1 *(Smith)*
Darlington (2) 2 *(Gregan, Blake)*   6622
Hereford U: MacKenzie; Watkiss, Fishlock, Smith, Cross,
James, Stoker, Wilkins, White, Hargreaves (Lyne),
Pitman.
Darlington: Newell; Carmichael, Barnard, Appleby,
Crosby, Gregan, Bannister, Gaughan, Painter, Blake
(Mattison), Carss (Brumwell).

Semi-finals, Second Leg

15 MAY

DIVISION 1

Crystal Palace (1) 1 *(Houghton)*
Charlton Ath (0) 0   22,880
Crystal Palace: Martyn; Edworthy, Brown, Roberts,
Quinn, Veart, Pitcher, Houghton, Freedman (Dyer),
Ndah, Tuttle.
Charlton Ath: Petterson; Jackson (Allen), Whyte C
(Whyte D), Newton, Rufus, Balmer, Brown, Leaburn,
Robinson, Nelson (Stuart), Bowyer.

Stoke C (0) 0
Leicester C (0) 1 *(Parker)*   21,037
Stoke C: Prudhoe; Clarkson, Sandford, Sigurdsson,
Whittle, Potter (Carruthers), Devlin, Wallace, Sheron,
Sturridge, Gleghorn.
Leicester C: Poole; Grayson, Whitlow, Watts, Walsh,
Izzet, Lennon, Taylor, Claridge, Parker, Heskey.

Leicester's match-winner Steve Claridge celebrates after the First Division play-off win over Crystal Palace.
(Action Images).

Mark Stallard (striped shirt) scores Bradford City's second goal in their 2-0 victory over Notts County.
(Action Images).

DIVISION 2

Blackpool (0) 0
Bradford C (1) 3 *(Shutt, Hamilton, Stallard)*   9593
Blackpool: Nixon; Bryan, Gouck (Philpott), Linighan, Mellon, Watson (Brown P), Bradshaw, Bonner, Morrison, Ellis, Preece (Quinn).
Bradford C: Gould; Huxford, Jacobs, Mitchell, Mohan, Brightwell, Kiwomya, Duxbury, Shutt, Stallard, Hamilton.

Notts Co (0) 1 *(Martindale)*
Crewe Alex (0) 0   9640
Notts Co: Ward; Derry, Baraclough, Murphy, Strodder, Richardson, Finnan, Rogers, Martindale, Battersby, Agana.
Crewe Alex: Gayle; Westwood, Unsworth, Lightfoot, McAllister, Savage, Ridings (Barr), Collins (Tierney), Blissett (Rivers), Macauley, Adebola.

DIVISION 3

Darlington (1) 2 *(Painter, Appleby (pen))*
Hereford U (0) 1 *(James)*   6584
Darlington: Newell; Carmichael, Barnard, Appleby, Crosby, Gregan, Bannister, Gaughan, Painter, Blake, Brumwell.
Hereford U: MacKenzie; Watkiss (Brough), Fishlock, Smith, Cross, James, Stoker, Wilkins, White, Lyne, Pitman (Pounder).

Plymouth Arg (2) 3 *(Evans, Leadbitter, Williams)*
Colchester U (0) 1 *(Kinsella)*   14,525
Plymouth Arg: Cherry; Patterson, Williams, Mauge, Heathcote, Barlow, Leadbitter, Logan, Littlejohn, Evans, Curran.
Colchester U: Emberson; Fry, Betts, McCarthy, Caesar (Locke), Cawley, Kinsella, Dennis, McGleish, Reinelt (Adcock), Gibbs (Whitton).

Finals (at Wembley)

25 MAY

DIVISION 3

Darlington (0) 0
Plymouth Arg (0) 1 *(Mauge)*   43,431
Darlington: Newell; Brumwell, Barnard, Appleby, Crosby, Gregan, Bannister, Gaughan (Carmichael), Painter, Blake, Carss.
Plymouth Arg: Cherry; Patterson, Williams, Mauge, Heathcote, Barlow, Leadbitter, Logan, Littlejohn, Evans, Curran.

26 MAY

DIVISION 2

Bradford C (1) 2 *(Hamilton, Stallard)*
Notts Co (0) 0   39,972
Bradford C: Gould; Huxford, Jacobs, Mitchell, Mohan, Youds, Kiwomya (Wright), Duxbury, Shutt, Stallard, Hamilton (Ormondroyd).
Notts Co: Ward; Derry, Baraclough, Murphy, Strodder, Richardson, Finnan, Rogers, Martindale, Battersby (Jones), Agana.

27 MAY

DIVISION 1

Crystal Palace (1) 1 *(Roberts)*
Leicester C (0) 2 *(Parker (pen), Claridge) aet*   73,573
Crystal Palace: Martin; Edworthy, Brown, Roberts, Quinn, Hopkin (Veart), Pitcher, Houghton, Freedman (Dyer), Ndah, Tuttle (Rodger).
Leicester C: Poole (Kalac); Grayson, Whitlow, Watts, Walsh (Hill), Izzet, Lennon, Taylor (Robins), Claridge, Parker, Heskey.

FA Carling Premiership

		P	W	D	L	F	A	W	D	L	F	A	GD	Pts
			Home			Goals		Away			Goals			
1	Manchester U	38	15	4	0	36	9	10	3	6	37	26	+38	82
2	Newcastle U	38	17	1	1	38	9	7	5	7	28	28	+29	78
3	Liverpool	38	14	4	1	46	13	6	7	6	24	21	+36	71
4	Aston Villa	38	11	5	3	32	15	7	4	8	20	20	+17	63
5	Arsenal	38	10	7	2	30	16	7	5	7	19	16	+17	63
6	Everton	38	10	5	4	35	19	7	5	7	29	25	+20	61
7	Blackburn R	38	14	2	3	44	19	4	5	10	17	28	+14	61
8	Tottenham H	38	9	5	5	26	19	7	8	4	24	19	+12	61
9	Nottingham F	38	11	6	2	29	17	4	7	8	21	37	−4	58
10	West Ham U	38	9	5	5	25	21	5	4	10	18	31	−9	51
11	Chelsea	38	7	7	5	30	22	5	7	7	16	22	+2	50
12	Middlesbrough	38	8	3	8	27	27	3	7	9	8	23	−15	43
13	Leeds U	38	8	3	8	21	21	4	4	11	19	36	−17	43
14	Wimbledon	38	5	6	8	27	33	5	5	9	28	37	−15	41
15	Sheffield W	38	7	5	7	30	31	3	5	11	18	30	−13	40
16	Coventry C	38	6	7	6	21	23	2	7	10	21	37	−18	38
17	Southampton	38	7	7	5	21	18	2	4	13	13	34	−18	38
18	Manchester C	38	7	7	5	21	19	2	4	13	12	39	−25	38
19	QPR	38	6	5	8	25	26	3	1	15	13	31	−19	33
20	Bolton W	38	5	4	10	16	31	3	1	15	23	40	−32	29

Endsleigh Insurance League Division 1

		P	W	D	L	F	A	W	D	L	F	A	GD	Pts
			Home			Goals		Away			Goals			
1	Sunderland	46	13	8	2	32	10	9	9	5	27	23	+26	83
2	Derby Co	46	14	8	1	48	22	7	8	8	23	29	+20	79
3	Crystal Palace	46	9	9	5	34	22	11	6	6	33	26	+19	75
4	Stoke C	46	13	6	4	32	15	7	7	9	28	34	+11	73
5	Leicester C	46	9	7	7	32	29	10	7	6	34	31	+6	71
6	Charlton Ath	46	8	11	4	28	23	9	9	5	29	22	+12	71
7	Ipswich T	46	13	5	5	45	30	6	7	10	34	39	+10	69
8	Huddersfield T	46	14	4	5	42	23	3	8	12	19	35	+3	63
9	Sheffield U	46	9	7	7	29	25	7	7	9	28	29	+3	62
10	Barnsley	46	9	10	4	34	28	5	8	10	26	38	−6	60
11	WBA	46	11	5	7	34	29	5	7	11	26	39	−8	60
12	Port Vale	46	10	5	8	30	29	5	10	8	29	37	−7	60
13	Tranmere R	46	9	9	5	42	29	5	8	10	22	31	+4	59
14	Southend U	46	11	8	4	30	22	4	6	13	22	39	−9	59
15	Birmingham C	46	11	7	5	37	23	4	6	13	24	41	−3	58
16	Norwich C	46	7	9	7	26	24	7	6	10	33	31	+4	57
17	Grimsby T	46	8	10	5	27	25	6	4	13	28	44	−14	56
18	Oldham Ath	46	10	7	6	33	20	4	7	12	21	30	+4	56
19	Reading	46	8	7	8	28	30	5	10	8	26	33	−9	56
20	Wolverhampton W	46	8	9	6	34	28	5	7	11	22	34	−6	55
21	Portsmouth	46	8	8	6	34	32	5	7	11	27	37	−8	52
22	Millwall	46	7	6	10	23	28	6	7	10	20	35	−20	52
23	Watford	46	7	8	8	40	33	3	10	10	22	37	−8	48
24	Luton T	46	7	6	10	30	34	4	6	13	10	30	−24	45

Endsleigh Insurance League Division 2

		P	W	D	L	F	A	W	D	L	F	A	GD	Pts
			Home			**Goals**		**Away**			**Goals**			
1	Swindon T	46	12	10	1	37	16	13	7	3	34	18	+37	92
2	Oxford U	46	17	4	2	52	14	7	7	9	24	25	+37	83
3	Blackpool	46	14	5	4	41	20	9	8	6	26	20	+27	82
4	Notts Co	46	14	6	3	42	21	7	9	7	21	18	+24	78
5	Crewe Alex	46	13	3	7	40	24	9	4	10	37	36	+17	73
6	Bradford C	46	15	4	4	41	25	7	3	13	30	44	+2	73
7	Chesterfield	46	14	6	3	39	21	6	6	11	17	30	+5	72
8	Wrexham	46	12	6	5	51	27	6	10	7	25	28	+21	70
9	Stockport Co	46	8	9	6	30	20	11	4	8	31	27	+14	70
10	Bristol R	46	12	4	7	29	28	8	6	9	28	32	−3	70
11	Walsall	46	12	7	4	38	20	7	5	11	22	25	+15	69
12	Wycombe W	46	9	8	6	36	26	6	7	10	27	33	+4	60
13	Bristol C	46	10	6	7	28	22	5	9	9	27	38	−5	60
14	AFC Bournemouth	46	12	5	6	33	25	4	5	14	18	45	−19	58
15	Brentford	46	12	6	5	24	15	3	7	13	19	34	−6	58
16	Rotherham U	46	11	7	5	31	20	3	7	13	23	42	−8	56
17	Burnley	46	9	8	6	35	28	5	5	13	21	40	−12	55
18	Shrewsbury T	46	7	8	8	32	29	6	6	11	26	41	−12	53
19	Peterborough U	46	9	6	8	40	27	4	7	12	19	39	−7	52
20	York C	46	8	6	9	28	29	5	7	11	30	44	−15	52
21	Carlisle U	46	11	6	6	35	20	1	7	15	22	52	−15	49
22	Swansea C	46	8	8	7	27	29	3	6	14	16	50	−36	47
23	Brighton & HA	46	6	7	10	25	31	4	3	16	21	38	−23	40
24	Hull C	46	4	8	11	26	37	1	8	14	10	41	−42	31

Endsleigh Insurance League Division 3

		P	W	D	L	F	A	W	D	L	F	A	GD	Pts
			Home			**Goals**		**Away**			**Goals**			
1	Preston NE	46	11	8	4	44	22	12	9	2	34	16	+40	86
2	Gillingham	46	16	6	1	33	6	6	11	6	16	14	+29	83
3	Bury	46	11	6	6	33	21	11	7	5	33	27	+18	79
4	Plymouth Arg	46	14	5	4	41	20	8	7	8	27	29	+19	78
5	Darlington	46	10	6	7	30	21	10	12	1	30	21	+18	78
6	Hereford U	46	13	5	5	40	22	7	9	7	25	25	+18	74
7	Colchester U	46	13	7	3	37	22	5	11	7	24	29	+10	72
8	Chester C	46	11	9	3	45	26	7	7	9	27	31	+19	70
9	Barnet	46	13	6	4	40	19	5	10	8	25	26	+20	70
10	Wigan Ath	46	15	3	5	36	21	5	7	11	26	35	+6	70
11	Northampton	46	9	10	4	32	22	9	3	11	19	22	+7	67
12	Scunthorpe U	46	8	8	7	36	30	7	7	9	31	31	+6	60
13	Doncaster R	46	11	6	6	25	19	5	5	13	24	41	−11	59
14	Exeter C	46	9	9	5	25	22	4	9	10	21	31	−7	57
15	Rochdale	46	7	8	8	32	33	7	5	11	25	28	−4	55
16	Cambridge U	46	8	8	7	34	30	6	4	13	27	41	−10	54
17	Fulham	46	10	9	4	39	26	2	8	13	18	37	−6	53
18	Lincoln C	46	8	7	8	32	26	5	7	11	25	47	−16	53
19	Mansfield T	46	6	10	7	25	29	5	10	8	29	35	−10	53
20	Hartlepool U	46	8	9	6	30	24	4	4	15	17	43	−20	49
21	Leyton Orient	46	11	4	8	29	22	1	7	15	15	41	−19	47
22	Cardiff C	46	8	6	9	24	22	3	6	14	17	42	−23	45
23	Scarborough	46	5	11	7	22	28	3	5	15	17	41	−30	40
24	Torquay U	46	4	9	10	17	36	1	5	17	13	48	−54	29

In the Endsleigh Insurance League, goals scored determine League positions where clubs are level on points. If teams still cannot be separated, the team that has conceded fewer goals is placed higher.

FA CHARITY SHIELD WINNERS 1908–95

1908	Manchester U v QPR	4-0 after 1-1 draw		1959	Wolverhampton W v Nottingham F	3-1
1909	Newcastle U v Northampton T	2-0		1960	Burnley v Wolverhampton W	2-2*
1910	Brighton v Aston Villa	1-0		1961	Tottenham H v FA XI	3-2
1911	Manchester U v Swindon T	8-4		1962	Tottenham H v Ipswich T	5-1
1912	Blackburn R v QPR	2-1		1963	Everton v Manchester U	4-0
1913	Professionals v Amateurs	7-2		1964	Liverpool v West Ham U	2-2*
1920	WBA v Tottenham H	2-0		1965	Manchester U v Liverpool	2-2*
1921	Tottenham H v Burnley	2-0		1966	Liverpool v Everton	1-0
1922	Huddersfield T v Liverpool	1-0		1967	Manchester U v Tottenham H	3-3*
1923	Professionals v Amateurs	2-0		1968	Manchester C v WBA	6-1
1924	Professionals v Amateurs	3-1		1969	Leeds U v Manchester C	2-1
1925	Amateurs v Professionals	6-1		1970	Everton v Chelsea	2-1
1926	Amateurs v Professionals	6-3		1971	Leicester C v Liverpool	1-0
1927	Cardiff C v Corinthians	2-1		1972	Manchester C v Aston Villa	1-0
1928	Everton v Blackburn R	2-1		1973	Burnley v Manchester C	1-0
1929	Professionals v Amateurs	3-0		1974	Liverpool† v Leeds U	1-1
1930	Arsenal v Sheffield W	2-1		1975	Derby Co v West Ham U	2-0
1931	Arsenal v WBA	1-0		1976	Liverpool v Southampton	1-0
1932	Everton v Newcastle U	5-3		1977	Liverpool v Manchester U	0-0*
1933	Arsenal v Everton	3-0		1978	Nottingham F v Ipswich T	5-0
1934	Arsenal v Manchester C	4-0		1979	Liverpool v Arsenal	3-1
1935	Sheffield W v Arsenal	1-0		1980	Liverpool v West Ham U	1-0
1936	Sunderland v Arsenal	2-1		1981	Aston Villa v Tottenham H	2-2*
1937	Manchester C v Sunderland	2-0		1982	Liverpool v Tottenham H	1-0
1938	Arsenal v Preston NE	2-1		1983	Manchester U v Liverpool	2-0
1948	Arsenal v Manchester U	4-3		1984	Everton v Liverpool	1-0
1949	Portsmouth v Wolverhampton W	1-1*		1985	Everton v Manchester U	2-0
1950	World Cup Team v Canadian Touring Team	4-2		1986	Everton v Liverpool	1-1*
1951	Tottenham H v Newcastle U	2-1		1987	Everton v Coventry C	1-0
1952	Manchester U v Newcastle U	4-2		1988	Liverpool v Wimbledon	2-1
1953	Arsenal v Blackpool	3-1		1989	Liverpool v Arsenal	1-0
1954	Wolverhampton W v WBA	4-4*		1990	Liverpool v Manchester U	1-1*
1955	Chelsea v Newcastle U	3-0		1991	Arsenal v Tottenham H	0-0*
1956	Manchester U v Manchester C	1-0		1992	Leeds U v Liverpool	4-3
1957	Manchester U v Aston Villa	4-0		1993	Manchester U† v Arsenal	1-1
1958	Bolton W v Wolverhampton W	4-1		1994	Manchester U v Blackburn R	2-0

* Each club retained shield for six months.   † Won on penalties.

FA CHARITY SHIELD 1995

Everton (0) 1, Blackburn R (0) 0

At Wembley, 12 August 1995, attendance 40,149

Everton: Southall; Barrett, Hinchcliffe, Parkinson, Unsworth, Ablett, Samways, Horne, Grant (Watson), Rideout, Limpar.

Scorer: Samways.

Blackburn R: Flowers; Kenna (Atkins), Le Saux, Batty, Pearce, Sutton, Ripley (Makel), Sherwood, Shearer, Newell, Gallacher (Marker).

Referee: D. Gallagher (Banbury).

FOOTBALL LEAGUE 1888–89 to 1995–96

FA PREMIER LEAGUE
Maximum points: 126

	First	*Pts*	*Second*	*Pts*	*Third*	*Pts*
1992–93	Manchester U	84	Aston Villa	74	Norwich C	72
1993–94	Manchester U	92	Blackburn R	84	Newcastle U	77
1994–95	Blackburn R	89	Manchester U	88	Nottingham F	77
1995–96	Manchester U	82	Newcastle U	78	Liverpool	71

FIRST DIVISION
Maximum points: 138

1992–93	Newcastle U	96	West Ham U*	88	Portsmouth††	88
1993–94	Crystal Palace	90	Nottingham F	83	Millwall††	74
1994–95	Middlesbrough	82	Reading††	79	Bolton W	77
1995–96	Sunderland	83	Derby Co	79	Crystal Palace††	75

SECOND DIVISION
Maximum points: 138

1992–93	Stoke C	93	Bolton W	90	Port Vale††	89
1993–94	Reading	89	Port Vale	88	Plymouth Arg*††	85
1994–95	Birmingham C	89	Brentford††	85	Crewe Alex††	83
1995–96	Swindon T	92	Oxford U	83	Blackpool††	82

THIRD DIVISION
Maximum points: 126

1992–93	Cardiff C	83	Wrexham	80	Barnet	79
1993–94	Shrewsbury T	79	Chester C	74	Crewe Alex	73
1994–95	Carlisle U	91	Walsall	83	Chesterfield	81
1995–96	Preston NE	86	Gillingham	83	Bury	79

††*Not promoted after play-offs.*

FOOTBALL LEAGUE
Maximum points: a 44; b 60

	First	*Pts*	*Second*	*Pts*	*Third*	*Pts*
1888–89a	Preston NE	40	Aston Villa	29	Wolverhampton W	28
1889–90a	Preston NE	33	Everton	31	Blackburn R	27
1890–91a	Everton	29	Preston NE	27	Notts Co	26
1891–92b	Sunderland	42	Preston NE	37	Bolton W	36

FIRST DIVISION to 1991–92
Maximum points: a 44; b 52; c 60; d 68; e 76; f 84; g 126; h 120; k 114.

1892–93c	Sunderland	48	Preston NE	37	Everton	36
1893–94c	Aston Villa	44	Sunderland	38	Derby Co	36
1894–95c	Sunderland	47	Everton	42	Aston Villa	39
1895–96c	Aston Villa	45	Derby Co	41	Everton	39
1896–97c	Aston Villa	47	Sheffield U*	36	Derby Co	36
1897–98c	Sheffield U	42	Sunderland	37	Wolverhampton W*	35
1898–99d	Aston Villa	45	Liverpool	43	Burnley	39
1899–1900d	Aston Villa	50	Sheffield U	48	Sunderland	41
1900–01d	Liverpool	45	Sunderland	43	Notts Co	40
1901–02d	Sunderland	44	Everton	41	Newcastle U	37
1902–03d	The Wednesday	42	Aston Villa*	41	Sunderland	41
1903–04d	The Wednesday	47	Manchester C	44	Everton	43
1904–05d	Newcastle U	48	Everton	47	Manchester C	46
1905–06e	Liverpool	51	Preston NE	47	The Wednesday	44
1906–07e	Newcastle U	51	Bristol C	48	Everton*	45
1907–08e	Manchester U	52	Aston Villa*	43	Manchester C	43
1908–09e	Newcastle U	53	Everton	46	Sunderland	44
1909–10e	Aston Villa	53	Liverpool	48	Blackburn R*	45
1910–11e	Manchester U	52	Aston Villa	51	Sunderland*	45
1911–12e	Blackburn R	49	Everton	46	Newcastle U	44
1912–13e	Sunderland	54	Aston Villa	50	Sheffield W	49
1913–14e	Blackburn R	51	Aston Villa	44	Middlesbrough*	43
1914–15e	Everton	46	Oldham Ath	45	Blackburn R*	43
1919–20f	WBA	60	Burnley	51	Chelsea	49
1920–21f	Burnley	59	Manchester C	54	Bolton W	52
1921–22f	Liverpool	57	Tottenham H	51	Burnley	49
1922–23f	Liverpool	60	Sunderland	54	Huddersfield T	53
1923–24f	Huddersfield T*	57	Cardiff C	57	Sunderland	53
1924–25f	Huddersfield T	58	WBA	56	Bolton W	55
1925–26f	Huddersfield T	57	Arsenal	52	Sunderland	48
1926–27f	Newcastle U	56	Huddersfield T	51	Sunderland	49
1927–28f	Everton	53	Huddersfield T	51	Leicester C	48
1928–29f	Sheffield W	52	Leicester C	51	Aston Villa	50
1929–30f	Sheffield W	60	Derby Co	50	Manchester C*	47
1930–31f	Arsenal	66	Aston Villa	59	Sheffield W	52
1931–32f	Everton	56	Arsenal	54	Sheffield W	50
1932–33f	Arsenal	58	Aston Villa	54	Sheffield W	51
1933–34f	Arsenal	59	Huddersfield T	56	Tottenham H	49
1934–35f	Arsenal	58	Sunderland	54	Sheffield W	49
1935–36f	Sunderland	56	Derby Co*	48	Huddersfield T	48
1936–37f	Manchester C	57	Charlton Ath	54	Arsenal	52
1937–38f	Arsenal	52	Wolverhampton W	51	Preston NE	49

*Won or placed on goal average, goal difference or most goals scored.

	First	Pts	Second	Pts	Third	Pts
1938–39f	Everton	59	Wolverhampton W	55	Charlton Ath	50
1946–47f	Liverpool	57	Manchester U*	56	Wolverhampton W	56
1947–48f	Arsenal	59	Manchester U*	52	Burnley	52
1948–49f	Portsmouth	58	Manchester U*	53	Derby Co	53
1949–50f	Portsmouth*	53	Wolverhampton W	53	Sunderland	52
1950–51f	Tottenham H	60	Manchester U	56	Blackpool	50
1951–52f	Manchester U	57	Tottenham H*	53	Arsenal	53
1952–53f	Arsenal*	54	Preston NE	54	Wolverhampton W	51
1953–54f	Wolverhampton W	57	WBA	53	Huddersfield T	51
1954–55f	Chelsea	52	Wolverhampton W*	48	Portsmouth*	48
1955–56f	Manchester U	60	Blackpool*	49	Wolverhampton W	49
1956–57f	Manchester U	64	Tottenham H*	56	Preston NE	56
1957–58f	Wolverhampton W	64	Preston NE	59	Tottenham H	51
1958–59f	Wolverhampton W	61	Manchester U	55	Arsenal*	50
1959–60f	Burnley	55	Wolverhampton W	54	Tottenham H	53
1960–61f	Tottenham H	66	Sheffield W	58	Wolverhampton W	57
1961–62f	Ipswich T	56	Burnley	53	Tottenham H	52
1962–63f	Everton	61	Tottenham H	55	Burnley	54
1963–64f	Liverpool	57	Manchester U	53	Everton	52
1964–65f	Manchester U*	61	Leeds U	61	Chelsea	56
1965–66f	Liverpool	61	Leeds U*	55	Burnley	55
1966–67f	Manchester U	60	Nottingham F*	56	Tottenham H	56
1967–68f	Manchester C	58	Manchester U	56	Liverpool	55
1968–69f	Leeds U	67	Liverpool	61	Everton	57
1969–70f	Everton	66	Leeds U	57	Chelsea	55
1970–71f	Arsenal	65	Leeds U	64	Tottenham H*	52
1971–72f	Derby Co	58	Leeds U*	57	Liverpool*	57
1972–73f	Liverpool	60	Arsenal	57	Leeds U	53
1973–74f	Leeds U	62	Liverpool	57	Derby Co	48
1974–75f	Derby Co	53	Liverpool*	51	Ipswich T	51
1975–76f	Liverpool	60	QPR	59	Manchester U	56
1976–77f	Liverpool	57	Manchester C	56	Ipswich T	52
1977–78f	Nottingham F	64	Liverpool	57	Everton	55
1978–79f	Liverpool	68	Nottingham F	60	WBA	59
1979–80f	Liverpool	60	Manchester U	58	Ipswich T	52
1980–81f	Aston Villa	60	Ipswich T	56	Arsenal	53
1981–82g	Liverpool	87	Ipswich T	83	Manchester U	78
1982–83g	Liverpool	82	Watford	71	Manchester U	70
1983–84g	Liverpool	80	Southampton	77	Nottingham F*	74
1984–85g	Everton	90	Liverpool*	77	Tottenham H	77
1985–86g	Liverpool	88	Everton	86	West Ham U	84
1986–87g	Everton	86	Liverpool	77	Tottenham H	71
1987–88h	Liverpool	90	Manchester U	81	Nottingham F	73
1988–89k	Arsenal*	76	Liverpool	76	Nottingham F	64
1989–90k	Liverpool	79	Aston Villa	70	Tottenham H	63
1990–91k	Arsenal†	83	Liverpool	76	Crystal Palace	69
1991–92g	Leeds U	82	Manchester U	78	Sheffield W	75

No official competition during 1915–19 and 1939–46.
†2 pts deducted

SECOND DIVISION to 1991–92

Maximum points: a 44; b 56; c 60; d 68; e 76; f 84; g 126; h 132; k 138.

	First	Pts	Second	Pts	Third	Pts
1892–93a	Small Heath	36	Sheffield U	35	Darwen	30
1893–94b	Liverpool	50	Small Heath	42	Notts Co	39
1894–95c	Bury	48	Notts Co	39	Newton Heath*	38
1895–96c	Liverpool*	46	Manchester C	46	Grimsby T*	42
1896–97c	Notts Co	42	Newton Heath	39	Grimsby T	38
1897–98c	Burnley	48	Newcastle U	45	Manchester C	39
1898–99d	Manchester C	52	Glossop NE	46	Leicester Fosse	45
1899–1900d	The Wednesday	54	Bolton W	52	Small Heath	46
1900–01d	Grimsby T	49	Small Heath	48	Burnley	44
1901–02d	WBA	55	Middlesbrough	51	Preston NE*	42
1902–03d	Manchester C	54	Small Heath	51	Woolwich A	48
1903–04d	Preston NE	50	Woolwich A	49	Manchester U	48
1904–05d	Liverpool	58	Bolton W	56	Manchester U	53
1905–06e	Bristol C	66	Manchester U	62	Chelsea	53
1906–07e	Nottingham F	60	Chelsea	57	Leicester Fosse	48
1907–08e	Bradford C	54	Leicester Fosse	52	Oldham Ath	50
1908–09e	Bolton W	52	Tottenham H*	51	WBA	51
1909–10e	Manchester C	54	Oldham Ath*	53	Hull C*	53
1910–11e	WBA	53	Bolton W	51	Chelsea	49
1911–12e	Derby Co*	54	Chelsea	54	Burnley	52
1912–13e	Preston NE	53	Burnley	50	Birmingham	46
1913–14e	Notts Co	53	Bradford PA*	49	Woolwich A	49
1914–15e	Derby Co	53	Preston NE	50	Barnsley	47
1919–20f	Tottenham H	70	Huddersfield T	64	Birmingham	56
1920–21f	Birmingham*	58	Cardiff C	58	Bristol C	51
1921–22f	Nottingham F	56	Stoke C*	52	Barnsley	52
1922–23f	Notts Co	53	West Ham U*	51	Leicester C	51
1923–24f	Leeds U	54	Bury*	51	Derby Co	51
1924–25f	Leicester C	59	Manchester U	57	Derby Co	55

Won or placed on goal average/goal difference.

	First	Pts	Second	Pts	Third	Pts
1925–26f	Sheffield W	60	Derby Co	57	Chelsea	52
1926–27f	Middlesbrough	62	Portsmouth*	54	Manchester C	54
1927–28f	Manchester C	59	Leeds U	57	Chelsea	54
1928–29f	Middlesbrough	55	Grimsby T	53	Bradford PA*	48
1929–30f	Blackpool	58	Chelsea	55	Oldham Ath	53
1930–31f	Everton	61	WBA	54	Tottenham H	51
1931–32f	Wolverhampton W	56	Leeds U	54	Stoke C	52
1932–33f	Stoke C	56	Tottenham H	55	Fulham	50
1933–34f	Grimsby T	59	Preston NE	52	Bolton W*	51
1934–35f	Brentford	61	Bolton W*	56	West Ham U	56
1935–36f	Manchester U	56	Charlton Ath	55	Sheffield U*	52
1936–37f	Leicester C	56	Blackpool	55	Bury	52
1937–38f	Aston Villa	57	Manchester U*	53	Sheffield U	53
1938–39f	Blackburn R	55	Sheffield U	54	Sheffield W	53
1946–47f	Manchester C	62	Burnley	58	Birmingham C	55
1947–48f	Birmingham C	59	Newcastle U	56	Southampton	52
1948–49f	Fulham	57	WBA	56	Southampton	55
1949–50f	Tottenham H	61	Sheffield W*	52	Sheffield U*	52
1950–51f	Preston NE	57	Manchester C	52	Cardiff C	50
1951–52f	Sheffield W	53	Cardiff C*	51	Birmingham C	51
1952–53f	Sheffield U	60	Huddersfield T	58	Luton T	52
1953–54f	Leicester C*	56	Everton	56	Blackburn R	55
1954–55f	Birmingham C*	54	Luton T*	54	Rotherham U	54
1955–56f	Sheffield W	55	Leeds U	52	Liverpool*	48
1956–57f	Leicester C	61	Nottingham F	54	Liverpool	53
1957–58f	West Ham U	57	Blackburn R	56	Charlton Ath	55
1958–59f	Sheffield W	62	Fulham	60	Sheffield U*	53
1959–60f	Aston Villa	59	Cardiff C	58	Liverpool*	50
1960–61f	Ipswich T	59	Sheffield U	58	Liverpool	52
1961–62f	Liverpool	62	Leyton Orient	54	Sunderland	53
1962–63f	Stoke C	53	Chelsea*	52	Sunderland	52
1963–64f	Leeds U	63	Sunderland	61	Preston NE	56
1964–65f	Newcastle U	57	Northampton T	56	Bolton W	50
1965–66f	Manchester C	59	Southampton	54	Coventry C	53
1966–67f	Coventry C	59	Wolverhampton W	58	Carlisle U	52
1967–68f	Ipswich T	59	QPR*	58	Blackpool	58
1968–69f	Derby Co	63	Crystal Palace	56	Charlton Ath	50
1969–70f	Huddersfield T	60	Blackpool	53	Leicester C	51
1970–71f	Leicester C	59	Sheffield U	56	Cardiff C*	53
1971–72f	Norwich C	57	Birmingham C	56	Millwall	55
1972–73f	Burnley	62	QPR	61	Aston Villa	50
1973–74f	Middlesbrough	65	Luton T	50	Carlisle U	49
1974–75f	Manchester U	61	Aston Villa	58	Norwich C	53
1975–76f	Sunderland	56	Bristol C*	53	WBA	53
1976–77f	Wolverhampton W	57	Chelsea	55	Nottingham F	52
1977–78f	Bolton W	58	Southampton	57	Tottenham H*	56
1978–79f	Crystal Palace	57	Brighton & HA*	56	Stoke C	56
1979–80f	Leicester C	55	Sunderland	54	Birmingham C*	53
1980–81f	West Ham U	66	Notts Co	53	Swansea C*	50
1981–82g	Luton T	88	Watford	80	Norwich C	71
1982–83g	QPR	85	Wolverhampton W	75	Leicester C	70
1983–84g	Chelsea*	88	Sheffield W	88	Newcastle U	80
1984–85g	Oxford U	84	Birmingham C	82	Manchester C	74
1985–86g	Norwich C	84	Charlton Ath	77	Wimbledon	76
1986–87g	Derby Co	84	Portsmouth	78	Oldham Ath††	75
1987–88h	Millwall	82	Aston Villa*	78	Middlesbrough	78
1988–89k	Chelsea	99	Manchester C	82	Crystal Palace	81
1989–90k	Leeds U*	85	Sheffield U	85	Newcastle U††	80
1990–91k	Oldham Ath	88	West Ham U	87	Sheffield W	82
1991–92k	Ipswich T	84	Middlesbrough	80	Derby Co	78

No competition during 1915–19 and 1939–46.
††Not promoted after play-offs.

THIRD DIVISION to 1991–92
Maximum points: 92; 138 from 1981–82.

	First	Pts	Second	Pts	Third	Pts
1958–59	Plymouth Arg	62	Hull C	61	Brentford*	57
1959–60	Southampton	61	Norwich C	59	Shrewsbury T*	52
1960–61	Bury	68	Walsall	62	QPR	60
1961–62	Portsmouth	65	Grimsby T	62	Bournemouth*	59
1962–63	Northampton T	62	Swindon T	58	Port Vale	54
1963–64	Coventry C*	60	Crystal Palace	60	Watford	58
1964–65	Carlisle U	60	Bristol C*	59	Mansfield T	59
1965–66	Hull C	69	Millwall	65	QPR	57
1966–67	QPR	67	Middlesbrough	55	Watford	54
1967–68	Oxford U	57	Bury	56	Shrewsbury T	55
1968–69	Watford*	64	Swindon T	64	Luton T	61
1969–70	Orient	62	Luton T	60	Bristol R	56
1970–71	Preston NE	61	Fulham	60	Halifax T	56
1971–72	Aston Villa	70	Brighton & HA	65	Bournemouth*	62
1972–73	Bolton W	61	Notts Co	57	Blackburn R	55
1973–74	Oldham Ath	62	Bristol R*	61	York C	61
1974–75	Blackburn R	60	Plymouth Arg	59	Charlton Ath	55

Won or placed on goal average/goal difference.

	First	Pts	Second	Pts	Third	Pts
1975–76	Hereford U	63	Cardiff C	57	Millwall	56
1976–77	Mansfield T	64	Brighton & HA	61	Crystal Palace*	59
1977–78	Wrexham	61	Cambridge U	58	Preston NE*	56
1978–79	Shrewsbury T	61	Watford*	60	Swansea C	60
1979–80	Grimsby T	62	Blackburn R	59	Sheffield W	58
1980–81	Rotherham U	61	Barnsley*	59	Charlton Ath	59
1981–82	Burnley*	80	Carlisle U	80	Fulham	78
1982–83	Portsmouth	91	Cardiff C	86	Huddersfield T	82
1983–84	Oxford U	95	Wimbledon	87	Sheffield U*	83
1984–85	Bradford C	94	Millwall	90	Hull C	87
1985–86	Reading	94	Plymouth Arg	87	Derby Co	84
1986–87	Bournemouth	97	Middlesbrough	94	Swindon T	87
1987–88	Sunderland	93	Brighton & HA	84	Walsall	82
1988–89	Wolverhampton W	92	Sheffield U*	84	Port Vale	84
1989–90	Bristol R	93	Bristol C	91	Notts Co	87
1990–91	Cambridge U	86	Southend U	85	Grimsby T*	83
1991–92	Brentford	82	Birmingham C	81	Huddersfield T	78

FOURTH DIVISION (1958–1992)
Maximum points: 92; 138 from 1981–82.

	First	Pts	Second	Pts	Third	Pts	Fourth	Pts
1958–59	Port Vale	64	Coventry C*	60	York C	60	Shrewsbury T	58
1959–60	Walsall	65	Notts Co*	60	Torquay U	60	Watford	57
1960–61	Peterborough U	66	Crystal Palace	64	Northampton T*	60	Bradford PA	60
1961–62†	Millwall	56	Colchester U	55	Wrexham	53	Carlisle U	52
1962–63	Brentford	62	Oldham Ath*	59	Crewe Alex	59	Mansfield T*	57
1963–64	Gillingham*	60	Carlisle U	60	Workington	59	Exeter C	58
1964–65	Brighton & HA	63	Millwall*	62	York C	62	Oxford U	61
1965–66	Doncaster R*	59	Darlington	59	Torquay U	58	Colchester U*	56
1966–67	Stockport Co	64	Southport*	59	Barrow	59	Tranmere R	58
1967–68	Luton T	66	Barnsley	61	Hartlepools U	60	Crewe Alex	58
1968–69	Doncaster R	59	Halifax T	57	Rochdale*	56	Bradford C	56
1969–70	Chesterfield	64	Wrexham	61	Swansea C	60	Port Vale	59
1970–71	Notts Co	69	Bournemouth	60	Oldham Ath	59	York C	56
1971–72	Grimsby T	63	Southend U	60	Brentford	59	Scunthorpe U	57
1972–73	Southport	62	Hereford U	58	Cambridge U	57	Aldershot*	56
1973–74	Peterborough U	65	Gillingham	62	Colchester U	60	Bury	59
1974–75	Mansfield T	68	Shrewsbury T	62	Rotherham U	59	Chester*	57
1975–76	Lincoln C	74	Northampton T	68	Reading	60	Tranmere R	58
1976–77	Cambridge U	65	Exeter C	62	Colchester U*	59	Bradford C	59
1977–78	Watford	71	Southend U	60	Swansea C*	56	Brentford	56
1978–79	Reading	65	Grimsby T*	61	Wimbledon*	61	Barnsley	61
1979–80	Huddersfield T	66	Walsall	64	Newport Co	61	Portsmouth*	60
1980–81	Southend U	67	Lincoln C	65	Doncaster R	56	Wimbledon	55
1981–82	Sheffield U	96	Bradford C*	91	Wigan Ath	91	Bournemouth	88
1982–83	Wimbledon	98	Hull C	90	Port Vale	88	Scunthorpe U	83
1983–84	York C	101	Doncaster R	85	Reading*	82	Bristol C	82
1984–85	Chesterfield	91	Blackpool	86	Darlington	85	Bury	84
1985–86	Swindon T	102	Chester C	84	Mansfield T	81	Port Vale	79
1986–87	Northampton T	99	Preston NE	90	Southend U	80	Wolverhampton W††	79
1987–88	Wolverhampton W	90	Cardiff C	85	Bolton W	78	Scunthorpe U††	77
1988–89	Rotherham U	82	Tranmere R	80	Crewe Alex	78	Scunthorpe U††	77
1989–90	Exeter C	89	Grimsby T	79	Southend U	75	Stockport Co††	74
1990–91	Darlington	83	Stockport Co*	82	Hartlepool U	82	Peterborough U	80
1991–92†*	Burnley	83	Rotherham U*	77	Mansfield T	77	Blackpool	76

†*Maximum points:* 88 owing to Accrington Stanley's resignation.   ††*Not promoted after play-offs.*
†**Maximum points:* 126 owing to Aldershot being expelled.

THIRD DIVISION—SOUTH (1920–1958)
Maximum points: a 84; b 92.

	First	Pts	Second	Pts	Third	Pts
1920–21a	Crystal Palace	59	Southampton	54	QPR	53
1921–22a	Southampton*	61	Plymouth Arg	61	Portsmouth	53
1922–23a	Bristol C	59	Plymouth Arg*	53	Swansea T	53
1923–24a	Portsmouth	59	Plymouth Arg	55	Millwall	54
1924–25a	Swansea T	57	Plymouth Arg	56	Bristol C	53
1925–26a	Reading	57	Plymouth Arg	56	Millwall	53
1926–27a	Bristol C	62	Plymouth Arg	60	Millwall	56
1927–28a	Millwall	65	Northampton T	55	Plymouth Arg	53
1928–29a	Charlton Ath*	54	Crystal Palace	54	Northampton T*	52
1929–30a	Plymouth Arg	68	Brentford	61	QPR	51
1930–31a	Notts Co	59	Crystal Palace	51	Brentford	50
1931–32a	Fulham	57	Reading	55	Southend U	53
1932–33a	Brentford	62	Exeter C	58	Norwich C	57
1933–34a	Norwich C	61	Coventry C*	54	Reading*	54
1934–35a	Charlton Ath	61	Reading	53	Coventry C	51
1935–36a	Coventry C	57	Luton T	56	Reading	54
1936–37a	Luton T	58	Notts Co	56	Brighton & HA	53
1937–38a	Millwall	56	Bristol C	55	QPR*	53
1938–39a	Newport Co	55	Crystal Palace	52	Brighton & HA	49
1939–46	Competition cancelled owing to war.					

* *Won or placed on goal average/goal difference.*

	First	Pts	Second	Pts	Third	Pts
1946–47a	Cardiff C	66	QPR	57	Bristol C	51
1947–48a	QPR	61	Bournemouth	57	Walsall	51
1948–49a	Swansea T	62	Reading	55	Bournemouth	52
1949–50a	Notts Co	58	Northampton T*	51	Southend U	51
1950–51b	Nottingham F	70	Norwich C	64	Reading*	57
1951–52b	Plymouth Arg	66	Reading*	61	Norwich C	61
1952–53b	Bristol R	64	Millwall*	62	Northampton T	62
1953–54b	Ipswich T	64	Brighton & HA	61	Bristol C	56
1954–55b	Bristol C	70	Leyton Orient	61	Southampton	59
1955–56b	Leyton Orient	66	Brighton & HA	65	Ipswich T	64
1956–57b	Ipswich T*	59	Torquay U	59	Colchester U	58
1957–58b	Brighton & HA	60	Brentford*	58	Plymouth Arg	58

THIRD DIVISION—NORTH (1921–1958)
Maximum points: a 76; b 84; c 80; d 92.

	First	Pts	Second	Pts	Third	Pts
1921–22a	Stockport Co	56	Darlington*	50	Grimsby T	50
1922–23a	Nelson	51	Bradford PA	47	Walsall	46
1923–24b	Wolverhampton W	63	Rochdale	62	Chesterfield	54
1924–25b	Darlington	58	Nelson*	53	New Brighton	53
1925–26b	Grimsby T	61	Bradford PA	60	Rochdale	59
1926–27b	Stoke C	63	Rochdale	58	Bradford PA	55
1927–28b	Bradford PA	63	Lincoln C	55	Stockport Co	54
1928–29g	Bradford C	63	Stockport Co	62	Wrexham	52
1929–30b	Port Vale	67	Stockport Co	63	Darlington*	50
1930–31b	Chesterfield	58	Lincoln C	57	Wrexham*	54
1931–32c	Lincoln C*	57	Gateshead	57	Chester	50
1932–33b	Hull C	59	Wrexham	57	Stockport Co	54
1933–34b	Barnsley	62	Chesterfield	61	Stockport Co	59
1934–35b	Doncaster R	57	Halifax T	55	Chester	54
1935–36b	Chesterfield	60	Chester*	55	Tranmere R	55
1936–37b	Stockport Co	60	Lincoln C	57	Chester	53
1937–38b	Tranmere R	56	Doncaster R	54	Hull C	53
1938–39b	Barnsley	67	Doncaster R	56	Bradford C	52
1939–46	Competition cancelled owing to war.					
1946–47b	Doncaster R	72	Rotherham U	60	Chester	56
1947–48b	Lincoln C	60	Rotherham U	59	Wrexham	50
1948–49b	Hull C	65	Rotherham U	62	Doncaster R	50
1949–50b	Doncaster R	55	Gateshead	53	Rochdale*	51
1950–51d	Rotherham U	71	Mansfield T	64	Carlisle U	62
1951–52d	Lincoln C	69	Grimsby T	66	Stockport Co	59
1952–53d	Oldham Ath	59	Port Vale	58	Wrexham	56
1953–54d	Port Vale	69	Barnsley	58	Scunthorpe U	57
1954–55d	Barnsley	65	Accrington S	61	Scunthorpe U*	58
1955–56d	Grimsby T	68	Derby Co	63	Accrington S	59
1956–57d	Derby Co	63	Hartlepools U	59	Accrington S*	58
1957–58d	Scunthorpe U	66	Accrington S	59	Bradford C	57

* Won or placed on goal average.

PROMOTED AFTER PLAY-OFFS
(Not accounted for in previous section)

1986–87	Aldershot to Division 3.
1987–88	Swansea C to Division 3.
1988–89	Leyton Orient to Division 3.
1989–90	Cambridge U to Division 3; Notts Co to Division 2; Sunderland to Division 1.
1990–91	Notts Co to Division 1; Tranmere R to Division 2; Torquay U to Division 3.
1991–92	Blackburn R to Premier League; Peterborough U to Division 1.
1992–93	Swindon T to Premier League; WBA to Division 1; York C to Division 2.
1993–94	Leicester C to Premier League; Burnley to Division 1; Wycombe W to Division 2.
1994–95	Huddersfield T to Division 1.
1995–96	Leicester C to Premier League; Bradford C to Division 1; Plymouth Arg to Division 2.

LEAGUE TITLE WINS

FA PREMIER LEAGUE – Manchester U 3, Blackburn R 1.

LEAGUE DIVISION 1 – Liverpool 18, Arsenal 10, Everton 9, Manchester U 7, Aston Villa 7, Sunderland 7, Newcastle U 5, Sheffield W 4, Huddersfield T 3, Leeds U 3, Wolverhampton W 3, Blackburn R 2, Portsmouth 2, Preston NE 2, Burnley 2, Manchester C 2, Tottenham H 2, Derby Co 2, Chelsea, Crystal Palace, Sheffield U, WBA, Ipswich T, Nottingham F, Middlesbrough 1 each.

LEAGUE DIVISION 2 – Leicester C 6, Manchester C 6, Sheffield W 5, Birmingham C (one as Small Heath) 5, Derby Co 4, Liverpool 4, Ipswich T 3, Leeds U 3, Notts Co 3, Preston NE 3, Middlesbrough 3, Stoke C 3, Grimsby T 2, Norwich C 2, Nottingham F 2, Tottenham H 2, WBA 2, Aston Villa 2, Burnley 2, Chelsea 2, Manchester U 2, West Ham U 2, Wolverhampton W 2, Bolton W 2, Swindon T, Huddersfield T, Bristol C, Brentford, Bury, Bradford C, Everton, Fulham, Sheffield U, Newcastle U, Coventry C, Blackpool, Blackburn R, Sunderland, Crystal Palace, Luton T, QPR, Oxford U, Millwall, Oldham Ath, Reading 1 each.

LEAGUE DIVISION 3 – Portsmouth 2, Oxford U 2, Shrewsbury T 2, Carlisle U 2, Preston NE 2, Plymouth Arg, Southampton, Bury, Northampton T, Coventry C, Hull C, QPR, Watford, Leyton Orient, Aston Villa, Bolton W, Oldham Ath, Blackburn R, Hereford U, Mansfield T, Wrexham, Grimsby T, Rotherham U, Burnley, Bradford C, Bournemouth, Reading, Sunderland, Wolverhampton W, Bristol R, Cambridge U, Brentford, Cardiff C 1 each.

LEAGUE DIVISION 4 – Chesterfield 2, Doncaster R 2, Peterborough U 2, Port Vale, Walsall, Millwall, Brentford, Gillingham, Brighton & HA, Stockport Co, Luton T, Notts Co, Grimsby T, Southport, Mansfield T, Lincoln C, Cambridge U, Watford, Reading, Huddersfield T, Southend U, Sheffield U, Wimbledon, York C, Swindon T, Northampton T, Wolverhampton W, Rotherham U, Exeter C, Darlington, Burnley 1 each.

To 1957–58

DIVISION 3 (South) – Bristol C 3; Charlton Ath, Ipswich T, Millwall, Notts Co, Plymouth Arg, Swansea T 2 each; Brentford, Bristol R, Cardiff C, Crystal Palace, Coventry C, Fulham, Leyton Orient, Luton T, Newport Co, Nottingham F, Norwich C, Portsmouth, QPR, Reading, Southampton, Brighton & HA 1 each.

DIVISION 3 (North) – Barnsley, Doncaster R, Lincoln C 3 each; Chesterfield, Grimsby T, Hull C, Port Vale, Stockport Co 2 each; Bradford PA, Bradford C, Darlington, Derby Co, Nelson, Oldham Ath, Rotherham U, Stoke C, Tranmere R, Wolverhampton W, Scunthorpe U 1 each.

RELEGATED CLUBS

1891–92 League extended. Newton Heath, Sheffield W and Nottingham F admitted. *Second Division formed* including Darwen.

1892–93 In Test matches, Sheffield U and Darwen won promotion in place of Notts Co and Accrington S.

1893–94 In Tests, Liverpool and Small Heath won promotion. Newton Heath and Darwen relegated.

1894–95 After Tests, Bury promoted, Liverpool relegated.

1895–96 After Tests, Liverpool promoted, Small Heath relegated.

1896–97 After Tests, Notts Co promoted, Burnley relegated.

1897–98 Test system abolished after success of Stoke C and Burnley. League extended. Blackburn R and Newcastle U elected to First Division. *Automatic promotion and relegation introduced.*

FA PREMIER LEAGUE TO DIVISION 1

1992–93 Crystal Palace, Middlesbrough, Nottingham F
1993–94 Sheffield U, Oldham Ath, Swindon T
1994–95 Crystal Palace, Norwich C, Leicester C, Ipswich T
1995–96 Manchester C, QPR, Bolton W

DIVISION 1 TO DIVISION 2

1898–99 Bolton W and Sheffield W
1899–1900 Burnley and Glossop
1900–01 Preston NE and WBA
1901–02 Small Heath and Manchester C
1902–03 Grimsby T and Bolton W
1903–04 Liverpool and WBA
1904–05 League extended. Bury and Notts Co, two bottom clubs in First Division, re-elected.
1905–06 Nottingham F and Wolverhampton W
1906–07 Derby Co and Stoke C
1907–08 Bolton W and Birmingham C
1908–09 Manchester C and Leicester Fosse
1909–10 Bolton W and Chelsea
1910–11 Bristol C and Nottingham F
1911–12 Preston NE and Bury
1912–13 Notts Co and Woolwich Arsenal
1913–14 Preston NE and Derby Co
1914–15 Tottenham H and Chelsea*
1919–20 Notts Co and Sheffield W
1920–21 Derby Co and Bradford PA
1921–22 Bradford C and Manchester U
1922–23 Stoke C and Oldham Ath
1923–24 Chelsea and Middlesbrough
1924–25 Preston NE and Nottingham F
1925–26 Manchester C and Notts Co
1926–27 Leeds U and WBA
1927–28 Tottenham H and Middlesbrough
1928–29 Bury and Cardiff C
1929–30 Burnley and Everton
1930–31 Leeds U and Manchester U
1931–32 Grimsby T and West Ham U
1932–33 Bolton W and Blackpool
1933–34 Newcastle U and Sheffield U
1934–35 Leicester C and Tottenham H
1935–36 Aston Villa and Blackburn R
1936–37 Manchester U and Sheffield W
1937–38 Manchester C and WBA
1938–39 Birmingham C and Leicester C
1946–47 Brentford and Leeds U
1947–48 Blackburn R and Grimsby T
1948–49 Preston NE and Sheffield U
1949–50 Manchester C and Birmingham C
1950–51 Sheffield W and Everton
1951–52 Huddersfield T and Fulham

1952–53 Stoke C and Derby Co
1953–54 Middlesbrough and Liverpool
1954–55 Leicester C and Sheffield W
1955–56 Huddersfield T and Sheffield U
1956–57 Charlton Ath and Cardiff C
1957–58 Sheffield W and Sunderland
1958–59 Portsmouth and Aston Villa
1959–60 Luton T and Leeds U
1960–61 Preston NE and Newcastle U
1961–62 Chelsea and Cardiff C
1962–63 Manchester C and Leyton Orient
1963–64 Bolton W and Ipswich T
1964–65 Wolverhampton W and Birmingham C
1965–66 Northampton T and Blackburn R
1966–67 Aston Villa and Blackpool
1967–68 Fulham and Sheffield U
1968–69 Leicester C and QPR
1969–70 Sunderland and Sheffield W
1970–71 Burnley and Blackpool
1971–72 Huddersfield T and Nottingham F
1972–73 Crystal Palace and WBA
1973–74 Southampton, Manchester U, Norwich C
1974–75 Luton T, Chelsea, Carlisle U
1975–76 Wolverhampton W, Burnley, Sheffield U
1976–77 Sunderland, Stoke C, Tottenham H
1977–78 West Ham U, Newcastle U, Leicester C
1978–79 QPR, Birmingham C, Chelsea
1979–80 Bristol C, Derby Co, Bolton W
1980–81 Norwich C, Leicester C, Crystal Palace
1981–82 Leeds U, Wolverhampton W, Middlesbrough
1982–83 Manchester C, Swansea C, Brighton & HA
1983–84 Birmingham C, Notts Co, Wolverhampton W
1984–85 Norwich C, Sunderland, Stoke C
1985–86 Ipswich T, Birmingham C, WBA
1986–87 Leicester C, Manchester C, Aston Villa
1987–88 Chelsea**, Portsmouth, Watford, Oxford U
1988–89 Middlesbrough, West Ham U, Newcastle U
1989–90 Sheffield W, Charlton Ath, Millwall
1990–91 Sunderland and Derby Co
1991–92 Luton T, Notts Co, West Ham U
1992–93 Brentford, Cambridge U, Bristol R
1993–94 Birmingham C, Oxford U, Peterborough U
1994–95 Swindon T, Burnley, Bristol C, Notts Co
1995–96 Millwall, Watford, Luton T

**Relegated after play-offs.
*Subsequently re-elected to Division 1 when League was extended after the War.

DIVISION 2 TO DIVISION 3

1920–21 Stockport Co
1921–22 Bradford PA and Bristol C
1922–23 Rotherham Co and Wolverhampton W
1923–24 Nelson and Bristol C
1924–25 Crystal Palace and Coventry C
1925–26 Stoke C and Stockport Co
1926–27 Darlington and Bradford C
1927–28 Fulham and South Shields
1928–29 Port Vale and Clapton Orient
1929–30 Hull C and Notts Co
1930–31 Reading and Cardiff C
1931–32 Barnsley and Bristol C
1932–33 Chesterfield and Charlton Ath
1933–34 Millwall and Lincoln C

1934–35 Oldham Ath and Notts Co
1935–36 Port Vale and Hull C
1936–37 Doncaster R and Bradford C
1937–38 Barnsley and Stockport Co
1938–39 Norwich C and Tranmere R
1946–47 Swansea T and Newport Co
1947–48 Doncaster R and Millwall
1948–49 Nottingham F and Lincoln C
1949–50 Plymouth Arg and Bradford PA
1950–51 Grimsby T and Chesterfield
1951–52 Coventry C and QPR
1952–53 Southampton and Barnsley
1953–54 Brentford and Oldham Ath
1954–55 Ipswich T and Derby Co

1955–56 Plymouth Arg and Hull C	1976–77 Carlisle U, Plymouth Arg, Hereford U
1956–57 Port Vale and Bury	1977–78 Blackpool, Mansfield T, Hull C
1957–58 Doncaster R and Notts Co	1978–79 Sheffield U, Millwall, Blackburn R
1958–59 Barnsley and Grimsby T	1979–80 Fulham, Burnley, Charlton Ath
1959–60 Bristol C and Hull C	1980–81 Preston NE, Bristol C, Bristol R
1960–61 Lincoln C and Portsmouth	1981–82 Cardiff C, Wrexham, Orient
1961–62 Brighton & HA and Bristol R	1982–83 Rotherham U, Burnley, Bolton W
1962–63 Walsall and Luton T	1983–84 Derby Co, Swansea C, Cambridge U
1963–64 Grimsby T and Scunthorpe U	1984–85 Notts Co, Cardiff C, Wolverhampton W
1964–65 Swindon T and Swansea T	1985–86 Carlisle U, Middlesbrough, Fulham
1965–66 Middlesbrough and Leyton Orient	1986–87 Sunderland**, Grimsby T, Brighton & HA
1966–67 Northampton T and Bury	1987–88 Huddersfield T, Reading, Sheffield U**
1967–68 Plymouth Arg and Rotherham U	1988–89 Shrewsbury T, Birmingham C, Walsall
1968–69 Fulham and Bury	1989–90 Bournemouth, Bradford C, Stoke C
1969–70 Preston NE and Aston Villa	1990–91 WBA and Hull C
1970–71 Blackburn R and Bolton W	1991–92 Plymouth Arg, Brighton & HA, Port Vale
1971–72 Charlton Ath and Watford	1992–93 Preston NE, Mansfield T, Wigan Ath, Chester C
1972–73 Huddersfield T and Brighton & HA	1993–94 Fulham, Exeter C, Hartlepool U, Barnet
1973–74 Crystal Palace, Preston NE, Swindon T	1994–95 Cambridge U, Plymouth Arg, Cardiff C, Chester
1974–75 Millwall, Cardiff C, Sheffield W	C, Leyton Orient
1975–76 Oxford U, York C, Portsmouth	1995–96 Carlisle U, Swansea C, Brighton & HA, Hull C

DIVISION 3 TO DIVISION 4

1958–59 Rochdale, Notts Co, Doncaster R, Stockport Co	1974–75 Bournemouth, Tranmere R, Watford, Huddersfield T
1959–60 Accrington S, Wrexham, Mansfield T, York C	1975–76 Aldershot, Colchester U, Southend U, Halifax T
1960–61 Chesterfield, Colchester U, Bradford C, Tranmere R	1976–77 Reading, Northampton T, Grimsby T, York C
1961–62 Newport Co, Brentford, Lincoln C, Torquay U	1977–78 Port Vale, Bradford C, Hereford U, Portsmouth
1962–63 Bradford PA, Brighton & HA, Carlisle U, Halifax T	1978–79 Peterborough U, Walsall, Tranmere R, Lincoln C
1963–64 Millwall, Crewe Alex, Wrexham, Notts Co	1979–80 Bury, Southend U, Mansfield T, Wimbledon
1964–65 Luton T, Port Vale, Colchester U, Barnsley	1980–81 Sheffield U, Colchester U, Blackpool, Hull C
1965–66 Southend U, Exeter C, Brentford, York C	1981–82 Wimbledon, Swindon T, Bristol C, Chester
1966–67 Doncaster R, Workington, Darlington, Swansea T	1982–83 Reading, Wrexham, Doncaster R, Chesterfield
1967–68 Scunthorpe U, Colchester U, Grimsby T, Peterborough U (demoted)	1983–84 Scunthorpe U, Southend U, Port Vale, Exeter C
1968–69 Oldham Ath, Crewe Alex, Hartlepool, Northampton T	1984–85 Burnley, Orient, Preston NE, Cambridge U
1969–70 Bournemouth, Southport, Barrow, Stockport Co	1985–86 Lincoln C, Cardiff C, Wolverhampton W, Swansea C
1970–71 Reading, Bury, Doncaster R, Gillingham	1986–87 Bolton W**, Carlisle U, Darlington, Newport Co
1971–72 Mansfield T, Barnsley, Torquay U, Bradford C	1987–88 Doncaster R, York C, Grimsby T, Rotherham U**
1972–73 Rotherham U, Brentford, Swansea C, Scunthorpe U	1988–89 Southend U, Chesterfield, Gillingham, Aldershot
1973–74 Cambridge U, Shrewsbury T, Southport, Rochdale	1989–90 Cardiff C, Northampton T, Blackpool, Walsall
	1990–91 Crewe Alex, Rotherham U, Mansfield T
	1991–92 Bury, Shrewsbury T, Torquay U, Darlington

** *Relegated after play-offs.*

APPLICATIONS FOR RE-ELECTION
FOURTH DIVISION

Eleven: Hartlepool U.
Seven: Crewe Alex.
Six: Barrow (lost League place to Hereford U 1972), Halifax T, Rochdale, Southport (lost League place to Wigan Ath 1978), York C.
Five: Chester C, Darlington, Lincoln C, Stockport Co, Workington (lost League place to Wimbledon 1977).
Four: Bradford PA (lost League place to Cambridge U 1970), Newport Co, Northampton T.
Three: Doncaster R, Hereford U.
Two: Bradford C, Exeter C, Oldham Ath, Scunthorpe U, Torquay U.
One: Aldershot, Colchester U, Gateshead (lost League place to Peterborough U 1960), Grimsby T, Swansea C, Tranmere R, Wrexham, Blackpool, Cambridge U, Preston NE.
Accrington S resigned and Oxford U were elected 1962.
Port Vale were forced to re-apply following expulsion in 1968.

THIRD DIVISIONS NORTH & SOUTH

Seven: Walsall.
Six: Exeter C, Halifax T, Newport Co.
Five: Accrington S, Barrow, Gillingham, New Brighton, Southport.
Four: Rochdale, Norwich C.
Three: Crystal Palace, Crewe Alex, Darlington, Hartlepool U, Merthyr T, Swindon T.
Two: Aberdare Ath, Aldershot, Ashington, Bournemouth, Brentford, Chester, Colchester U, Durham C, Millwall, Nelson, QPR, Rotherham U, Southend U, Tranmere R, Watford, Workington.
One: Bradford C, Bradford PA, Brighton & HA, Bristol R, Cardiff C, Carlisle U, Charlton Ath, Gateshead, Grimsby T, Mansfield T, Shrewsbury T, Torquay U, York C.

LEAGUE STATUS FROM 1986–87

RELEGATED FROM LEAGUE	PROMOTED TO LEAGUE
	Scarborough
1986–87 Lincoln C	Lincoln C
1987–88 Newport Co	Maidstone U
1988–89 Darlington	Darlington
1989–90 Colchester U	Barnet
1990–91 —	Colchester U
1991–92 —	Wycombe W
1992–93 Halifax T	—
1993–94 —	—
1994–95 —	—
1995–96 —	—

TRANSFERS 1995–96

June 1995

	From	To	Fee in £s
30 Armstrong, Christopher P.	Crystal Palace	Tottenham Hotspur	4,500,000
7 Barton, Warren D.	Wimbledon	Newcastle United	4,000,000
7 Bennett, Thomas M.	Wolverhampton Wanderers	Stockport County	75,000
19 Butler, John E.	Stoke City	Wigan Athletic	Free
21 Carter, Darren S.	Leyton Orient	Peterborough United	25,000
29 Clarke, Matthew L.	Halesowen Harriers	Halesowen Town	undisclosed
30 Cuggy, Michael S.	Margate	Hastings Town	undisclosed
15 Edworthy, Marc	Plymouth Argyle	Crystal Palace	350,000
12 Eustace, Scott D.	Leicester City	Mansfield Town	Free
9 Ferdinand, Leslie	Queens Park Rangers	Newcastle United	6,000,000
12 Finnan, Stephen J.	Welling United	Birmingham City	100,000
16 Finney, Stephen K.	Manchester City	Swindon Town	Free
5 Fisher, Neil J.	Bolton Wanderers	Chester City	Free
26 Garner, Darren	Dorchester Town	Rotherham United	30,000
19 Griffiths, Bryan K.	Telford United	Southport	undisclosed
20 Holland, Paul	Mansfield Town	Sheffield United	250,000
22 Jeffrey, Michael R.	Newcastle United	Rotherham United	100,000
23 Muir, Ian J.	Tranmere Rovers	Birmingham City	125,000
1 Neilson, Alan B.	Newcastle United	Southampton	500,000
15 Payne, Stephen R.	Crawley Town	Sutton United	undisclosed
23 Rattray, Kevin	Woking	Gillingham	5,000
2 Richards, Dean I.	Bradford City	Wolverhampton Wanderers	1,850,000
6 Seagraves, Mark	Bolton Wanderers	Swindon Town	100,000
24 Taylor, Stephen C.	Bromsgrove Rovers	Crystal Palace	90,000
7 Turnbull, Lee M.	Wycombe Wanderers	Scunthorpe United	12,000
15 Vansittart, Jonathan	Crawley Town	Sutton United	undisclosed
15 White, Jason G.	Scarborough	Northampton Town	35,000
16 Wilkinson, Stephen J.	Mansfield Town	Preston North End	90,000
12 Wilson, Clive	Queens Park Rangers	Tottenham Hotspur	Free
12 Yates, Jason	Bridgnorth Town	Clevedon Town	undisclosed

TEMPORARY TRANSFERS

	From	To	
19 Appleton, Michael A.	Manchester United	Wimbledon	
19 O'Kane, John A.	Manchester United	Wimbledon	
22 O'Shea, Daniel E.	Northampton Town	Wimbledon	
22 Sampson, Ian	Northampton Town	Wimbledon	
19 Tomlinson, Graham	Manchester United	Tottenham Hotspur	

JULY 1995

	From	To	
10 Alexander, Graham	Scunthorpe United	Luton Town	100,000
25 Allison, Wayne	Bristol City	Swindon Town	475,000
24 Allon, Joseph B.	Port Vale	Lincoln City	42,500
31 Anderson, Ijah M.	Southend United	Brentford	Free
10 Aspinall, Warren	AFC Bournemouth	Carlisle United	Free
5 Bailey, John A.	Enfield	AFC Bournemouth	10,000
15 Barber, Philip A.	Millwall	Bristol City	Free
3 Barkus, Lea P.	Reading	Fulham	20,000
1 Bart-Williams, Chris	Sheffield Wednesday	Nottingham Forest	2,500,000
14 Bennett, Gary M.	Wrexham	Tranmere Rovers	300,000
18 Blades, Paul A.	Wolverhampton Wanderers	Rotherham United	110,000
21 Bowen, Jason P.	Swansea City	Birmingham City	275,000
4 Bowry, Robert	Crystal Palace	Millwall	220,000
3 Caldwell, Peter J.	Queens Park Rangers	Leyton Orient	Free
1 Campbell, Kevin J.	Arsenal	Nottingham Forest	2,800,000
21 Castle, Stephen C.	Plymouth Argyle	Birmingham City	225,000
3 Charlery, Kenneth	Peterborough United	Birmingham City	350,000
3 Collymore, Stanley V.	Nottingham Forest	Liverpool	8,500,000
19 Darby, Duane A.	Torquay United	Doncaster Rovers	35,000
5 Davies, Gareth M.	Hereford United	Crystal Palace	120,000
13 Davis, Stephen M.	Burnley	Luton Town	750,000
3 Dempsey, Mark A.	Leyton Orient	Shrewsbury Town	Free
5 Draper, Mark A.	Leicester City	Aston Villa	3,250,000
10 Edwards, Andrew D.	Southend United	Birmingham City	400,000
5 Eyre, John R.	Oldham Athletic	Scunthorpe United	40,000
4 Fairclough, Courtney H.	Leeds United	Bolton Wanderers	500,000
13 Farrelly, Stephen	Macclesfield Town	Rotherham United	20,000
7 Felgate, David W.	Chester City	Wigan Athletic	Free
25 Ford, Jonathan S.	Swansea City	Bradford City	210,000
13 Forsyth, Richard	Kidderminster Harriers	Birmingham City	50,000
17 Gray, Ian J.	Oldham Athletic	Rochdale	20,000
20 Hannigan, Al J.	Enfield	Rushden & Diamonds	undisclosed
28 Heald, Paul A.	Leyton Orient	Wimbledon	125,000
27 Heathcote, Michael	Cambridge United	Plymouth Argyle	70,000
27 Heggs, Carl S.	West Bromwich Albion	Swansea City	60,000
21 Hopkin, David	Chelsea	Crystal Palace	850,000
13 Hoult, Russell	Leicester City	Derby County	200,000
12 Hyatt, Frederick	Wokingham Town	Hayes	undisclosed
19 Irving, Richard J.	Manchester United	Nottingham Forest	75,000
13 Kelly, Anthony G.	Peterborough United	Wigan Athletic	Free
6 Kelly, Anthony O. N.	Bury	Leyton Orient	30,000
13 Landon, Richard J.	Plymouth Argyle	Stockport County	30,000
7 Lightfoot, Christopher I.	Chester City	Wigan Athletic	87,500
13 Malkin, Christopher G.	Tranmere Rovers	Millwall	400,000
31 Mauge, Ronald C.	Bury	Plymouth Argyle	40,000
13 Meaker, Michael J.	Queens Park Rangers	Reading	500,000
18 Mohan, Nicholas	Leicester City	Bradford City	225,000
19 Moore, Darren M.	Torquay United	Doncaster Rovers	62,500
21 Newman, Richard A.	Crystal Palace	Millwall	500,000
18 Oldfield, David C.	Leicester City	Luton Town	150,000
18 Ormondroyd, Ian	Leicester City	Bradford City	75,000
11 Osborn, Simon E.	Reading	Queens Park Rangers	600,000

	From	To	Fee in £s
20 Pembridge, Mark A.	Derby County	Sheffield Wednesday	900,000
28 Powell, Darryl A.	Portsmouth	Derby County	750,000
27 Power, Lee M.	Bradford City	Peterborough United	80,000
5 Preece, Andrew P.	Crystal Palace	Blackpool	200,000
13 Reid, Shaun	Rochdale	Bury	15,000
21 Roberts, Andrew J.	Millwall	Crystal Palace	2,250,000
21 Rowett, Gary	Everton	Derby County	300,000
21 Russell, Kevin J.	Notts County	Wrexham	60,000
26 Sale, Mark D.	Preston North End	Mansfield Town	50,000
29 Saville, Andrew V.	Birmingham City	Preston North End	100,000
24 Sheffield, Jonathan	Cambridge United	Peterborough United	150,000
21 Short, Craig J.	Derby County	Everton	2,400,000
21 Skinner, Craig R.	Plymouth Argyle	Wrexham	50,000
13 Southall, Leslie N.	Hartlepool United	Grimsby Town	40,000
1 Southgate, Gareth	Crystal Palace	Aston Villa	2,500,000
20 Stanislaus, Roger E. P.	Bury	Leyton Orient	50,000
13 Strodder, Gary J.	West Bromwich Albion	Notts County	145,000
26 Sugrue, James S.	Kingstonian	Aldershot Town	750
13 Swales, Stephen C.	Scarborough	Reading	70,000
13 Taylor, Scott D.	Reading	Leicester City	500,000
11 Telfer, Paul N.	Luton Town	Coventry City	1,150,000
13 Ward, Darren	Mansfield Town	Notts County	150,000
18 Ward, Gavin J.	Leicester City	Bradford City	175,000
19 Ward, Peter	Stockport County	Wrexham	Free
27 Westwood, Ashley M.	Manchester United	Crewe Alexandra	40,000

TEMPORARY TRANSFERS

21 Galloway, Michael	Celtic	Leicester City	

AUGUST 1995

9 Allon, Andrew	Margate	Ashford Town	undisclosed
9 Anthrobus, Stephen A.	Wimbledon	Shrewsbury Town	25,000
15 Bailey, Dennis L.	Queens Park Rangers	Gillingham	25,000
18 Banks, Steven	Gillingham	Blackpool	60,000
10 Barber, Philip A.	Millwall	Bristol City	Free
8 Barmby, Nicholas J.	Tottenham Hotspur	Middlesbrough	5,250,000
18 Beard, Mark	Millwall	Sheffield United	117,000
4 Beesley, Paul	Sheffield United	Leeds United	250,000
11 Billy, Christopher A.	Huddersfield Town	Plymouth Argyle	exch
19 Birch, Troy J.	Hayes	Wealdstone	undisclosed
22 Bradford, Lee T.	Dorchester Town	Weymouth	undisclosed
11 Bryan, Marvin L.	Queens Park Rangers	Blackpool	Free
25 Byrne, Paul P.	Celtic	Southend United	80,000
11 Clayton, Gary	Huddersfield Town	Plymouth Argyle	exch
11 Conroy, Michael K.	Preston North End	Fulham	75,000
11 Cunnington, Shaun G.	Sunderland	West Bromwich Albion	220,000
11 Dalton, Paul	Plymouth Argyle	Huddersfield Town	125,000
11 Flynn, Sean M.	Coventry City	Derby County	225,000
10 Gilbert, David J.	Grimsby Town	West Bromwich Albion	65,000
16 Goodridge, Gregory R.S.	Torquay United	Queens Park Rangers	100,000
18 Griffiths, Carl B.	Manchester City	Portsmouth	200,000
16 Grocutt, Darren	Burton Albion	Bromsgrove Rovers	undisclosed
10 Hammond, Nicholas D.	Swindon Town	Plymouth Argyle	40,000
25 Hill, Andrew R.	Manchester City	Port Vale	150,000
11 Hislop, Neil S.	Reading	Newcastle United	1,575,000
18 Hodgson, Philip	Morecambe	Netherfield	undisclosed
15 Holmes, Matthew J.	West Ham United	Blackburn Rovers	600,000
25 Kanchelskis, Andrei	Manchester United	Everton	5,500,000
15 McCarthy, Alan J.	Queens Park Rangers	Leyton Orient	undisclosed
1 McCarthy, Jonathan D.	York City	Port Vale	450,000
7 McFarlane, Andrew A.	Swansea City	Scunthorpe United	15,000
16 McGorry, Brian P.	Peterborough United	Wycombe Wanderers	Free
1 MacKenzie, Stuart M.	Yeading	Farnborough Town	undisclosed
3 Marshall, Shaun	Hitchin Town	Stevenage Borough	undisclosed
18 May, Leroy A.	Stafford Rangers	Kidderminster Harriers	undisclosed
23 Mike, Adrian R.	Manchester City	Stockport County	60,000
3 Mills, Rowan L.	Derby County	Port Vale	200,000
17 Morton, Neil	Altrincham	Barrow	undisclosed
14 Mullin, John	Burnley	Sunderland	40,000
22 Ndah, Jamie	Kingstonian	Torquay United	20,000
21 Patterson, Darren J.	Crystal Palace	Luton Town	230,000
18 Pender, John P.	Burnley	Wigan Athletic	30,000
15 Reed, Adam M.	Darlington	Blackburn Rovers	200,000
7 Richardson, Nicholas J.	Cardiff City	Bury	22,500
2 Ross, Brian J.	Marine	Chorley	undisclosed
18 Rush, Matthew J.	West Ham United	Norwich City	330,000
7 Salako, John A.	Crystal Palace	Coventry City	1,500,000
21 Salmon, Marc R.	Harlow Town	Charlton Athletic	undisclosed
22 Saunders, Mark P.	Tiverton Town	Plymouth Argyle	undisclosed
25 Shirtliff, Peter A.	Wolverhampton Wanderers	Barnsley	200,000
18 Simpson, Fitzroy	Manchester City	Portsmouth	200,000
15 Slater, Robert D.	Blackburn Rovers	West Ham United	600,000
10 Smith, Malcolm A.	Ashford Town	Margate	undisclosed
15 Smith, Neil	Cheltenham Town	Rushden & Diamonds	undisclosed
29 Sommer, Jurgen P.	Luton Town	Queens Park Rangers	600,000
17 Sperry, Gary	Bognor Regis Town	Ryde	undisclosed
8 Stephenson, Paul	Brentford	York City	undisclosed
14 Strong, Greg	Wigan Athletic	Bolton Wanderers	undisclosed
11 Swan, Peter H.	Plymouth Argyle	Burnley	200,000
18 Symons, Christopher J.	Portsmouth	Manchester City	1,200,000
2 Taggart, Gerald P.	Barnsley	Bolton Wanderers	1,500,000
11 Teal, Shaun	Aston Villa	Tranmere Rovers	500,000
1 Todd, Andrew	Middlesbrough	Bolton Wanderers	250,000
15 Ullathorne, Simon	Gloucester City	Hastings Town	undisclosed
3 Van der Laan, Robertus P.	Port Vale	Derby County	475,000

	From	To	Fee in £s
11 Walsh, Gary	Manchester United	Middlesbrough	250,000
15 Williams, Karl I.	Warrington Town	Macclesfield Town	undisclosed
11 Williams, Mark S.	Shrewsbury Town	Chesterfield	20,000
11 Williams, Paul D.	Derby County	Coventry City	750,000
2 Williams, Paul R.C.	Coventry City	Plymouth Argyle	50,000
10 Wilson, Paul A.	York City	Scunthorpe United	undisclosed
8 Woods, Billy	Cork City	Tranmere Rovers	50,000

TEMPORARY TRANSFERS

25 Armstrong, Gordon I.	Sunderland	Bristol City
11 Beresford, David	Oldham Athletic	Swansea City
24 Berry, Greg J.	Millwall	Brighton & Hove Albion
11 Brightwell, David J.	Manchester City	Lincoln City
31 Brodie, Stephen E.	Sunderland	Doncaster Rovers
17 Bull, Gary W.	Nottingham Forest	Brighton & Hove Albion
25 Castledine, Stewart M.	Wimbledon	Wycombe Wanderers
29 Fleck, Robert	Chelsea	Norwich City
11 Foran, Mark J.	Sheffield United	Wycombe Wanderers
7 Given, Seamus J.J.	Blackburn Rovers	Swindon Town
11 Harmon, Darren J.	Northampton Town	Cambridge United
11 Harris, Mark A.	Swansea City	Gillingham
21 Heywood, David I.	Hailsowen Town	Bilston Town
10 Hodgson, Douglas J.H.	Sheffield United	Plymouth Argyle
21 Jardine, Jamie	Tranmere Rovers	Chorley
16 Jewell, Paul	Bradford City	Grimsby Town
3 Kane, Paul	Aberdeen	Barnsley
11 Key, Lance	Sheffield Wednesday	Lincoln City
29 Lowe, Kenneth	Birmingham City	Hartlepool United
26 Martin, Eliot J.	Gillingham	Margate
19 Monk, Ian L.	Macclesfield Town	Leigh RMI
25 Moore, Neil	Everton	Carlisle United
25 Morah, Olisa H.	Cambridge United	Braintree Town
24 Mutch, Andrew T.	Swindon Town	Wigan Athletic
11 Oatway, Anthony	Cardiff City	Coleraine
11 Pettinger, Paul A.	Leeds United	Rotherham United
26 Reilly, James L.	Sudbury Town	Purfleet
25 Sedgemore, Benjamin R.	Birmingham City	Mansfield Town
11 Shaw, Paul	Arsenal	Cardiff City
11 Shipp, Daniel A.	West Ham United	Dagenham & Redbridge
11 Simpson, Gary	Luton Town	Aylesbury United
29 Stewart, Paul A.	Liverpool	Sunderland
11 Stewart, Simon A.	Sheffield Wednesday	Shrewsbury Town
2 Stuart, Mark R.	Rochdale	Chesterfield
4 Swan, Peter H.	Plymouth Argyle	Burnley
19 Timons, Christopher	Mansfield Town	Halifax Town
10 Tracey, Simon P.	Sheffield United	Nottingham Forest
10 Viveash, Adrian L.	Swindon Town	Barnsley
29 Webster, Simon P.	West Ham United	Derby County

SEPTEMBER 1995

30 Arkins, Vincent	Shelbourne	Notts County	undisclosed
21 Atkins, Mark N.	Blackburn Rovers	Wolverhampton Wanderers	1,000,000
11 Barrick, Dean	Cambridge United	Preston North End	exch
19 Beard, Simon A.	Sittingbourne	Hastings Town	undisclosed
29 Bernard, Paul R.J.	Oldham Athletic	Aberdeen	800,000
7 Boere, Jeroen W.J.	West Ham United	Crystal Palace	375,000
29 Carruthers, Matthew J.	Dover Athletic	Ashford Town	undisclosed
14 Creaney, Gerard	Portsmouth	Manchester City	1,500,000
8 Dowie, Iain	Crystal Palace	West Ham United	125,000
11 Farrell, David	Aston Villa	Wycombe Wanderers	100,000
7 Ferguson, Derek	Sunderland	Falkirk	150,000
29 Fleck, Robert	Chelsea	Norwich City	650,000
7 Foley, Dominic	St James Gate	Wolverhampton Wanderers	undisclosed
8 Freedman, Douglas A.	Barnet	Crystal Palace	800,000
20 Greenall, Colin A.	Lincoln City	Wigan Athletic	undisclosed
29 Hackett, Brendan	Hednesford Town	Rushden & Diamonds	undisclosed
1 Harper, Steven J.	Doncaster Rovers	Mansfield Town	20,000
14 Harris, Mark A.	Swansea City	Gillingham	undisclosed
29 Hume, Kevin	Bury	Lincoln City	exch
12 Humphreys, Delwyn J.	Kidderminster Harriers	Northwich Victoria	undisclosed
1 Johnson, Michael O.	Notts County	Birmingham City	225,000
14 Keast, Douglas W.	Rushden & Diamonds	Burton Albion	undisclosed
20 Kelly, David T.	Wolverhampton Wanderers	Sunderland	900,000
26 Masters, Paul J.	Havant Town	Salisbury City	undisclosed
8 Matthews, Robert D.	Luton Town	York City	90,000
6 McAteer, Jason W.	Bolton Wanderers	Liverpool	4,500,000
14 Murphy, James A.	Blackpool	Doncaster Rovers	undisclosed
7 Newbery, Richard J.	Woking	Wokingham Town	undisclosed
29 Nugent, Kevin P.	Plymouth Argyle	Bristol City	75,000
28 O'Neill, Steven A.	Altrincham	Bamber Bridge	undisclosed
28 Palmer, Stephen L.	Ipswich Town	Watford	135,000
11 Raynor, Paul J.	Preston North End	Cambridge United	exch
7 Richardson, Nicholas J.	Bury	Chester City	40,000
11 Rowbotham, Jason	Raith Rovers	Wycombe Wanderers	undisclosed
29 Taylor, Gareth K.	Bristol Rovers	Crystal Palace	1,250,000
14 Walsh, Paul A.	Manchester City	Portsmouth	500,000
21 Warner, Ashley S.	Gloucester City	VS Rugby	undisclosed
21 Watson, Liam	Marine	Witton Albion	undisclosed
29 West, Dean	Lincoln City	Bury	exch
22 Wilcox, Russell	Doncaster Rovers	Preston North End	undisclosed
14 Williams, John	Coventry City	Wycombe Wanderers	150,000

TEMPORARY TRANSFERS

11 Allen, Martin J.	West Ham United	Portsmouth
15 Appleton, Michael A.	Manchester United	Lincoln City

	From	To	Fee in £s
11 Arkins, Vincent	Shelbourne	Notts County	
29 Barker, Richard I.	Sheffield Wednesday	Doncaster Rovers	
29 Barton, Stuart A.	Bamber Bridge	Atherton LR	
8 Berry, Trevor J.	Aston Villa	Rotherham United	
29 Black, Kingsley	Nottingham Forest	Millwall	
11 Blatherwick, Steven S.	Nottingham Forest	Hereford United	
11 Bound, Matthew T.	Stockport County	Lincoln City	
11 Brightwell, David J.	Manchester City	Stoke City	
7 Brown, Kenneth J.	West Ham United	Huddersfield Town	
15 Browne, Corey	Dover Athletic	Stevenage Borough	
17 Bull, Gary W.	Nottingham Forest	Brighton & Hove Albion	
22 Charles, Lee	Queens Park Rangers	Barnet	
22 Cole, Peter	Ashton United	Netherfield	
29 Colgan, Nicholas V.	Chelsea	Millwall	
11 Collier, Daniel J.	Crewe Alexandra	York City	
8 Cureton, Jamie	Norwich City	AFC Bournemouth	
8 Dobbs, Gerald F.	Wimbledon	Cardiff City	
29 Dewberry, Michael W.	Chelsea	AFC Bournemouth	
22 Dykstra, Sieb	Queens Park Rangers	Bristol City	
29 Edwards, Matthew D.	Kettering Town	Walton & Hersham	
22 Evans, Richard J.	Marlow	Yeading	
11 Feuer, Antony I.	West Ham United	Luton Town	
27 Foot, Daniel F.	Southend United	Dover Athletic	
14 Freeman, Mark W.	Hednesford Town	Gloucester City	
22 Gibb, Alistair S.	Norwich City	Northampton Town	
12 Goodacre, Samuel D.	Stalybridge Celtic	Gainsborough Town	
28 Hague, Paul	Leyton Orient	Dagenham & Redbridge	
18 Harper, Stephen A.	Newcastle United	Bradford City	
25 Jardine, Jamie	Tranmere Rovers	Chorley	
18 Jewell, Paul	Bradford City	Grimsby Town	
1 Johnson, Alan K.	Lincoln City	Preston North End	
4 Jones, Martin	Tranmere Rovers	Altrincham	
15 Joseph, Marc E.	Cambridge United	Cambridge City	
22 Kerr, David W.	Manchester City	Mansfield Town	
18 Ludlow, Lee	Halifax Town	Spennymoor United	
22 Maddison, Lee R.	Bristol Rovers	Northampton Town	
15 Marquis, Paul R.	Doncaster Rovers	Gateshead	
14 McDonald, Paul	Southampton	Burnley	
15 Mercer, William	Sheffield United	Chesterfield	
22 Molby, Jan	Liverpool	Barnsley	
18 Monk, Ian L.	Macclesfield Town	Leigh RMI	
26 Moore, Neil	Everton	Carlisle United	
7 Morah, Olisa	Cambridge United	Braintree Town	
29 Morah, Olisa	Cambridge United	Welling United	
8 Muir, Ian J.	Birmingham City	Darlington	
1 Omigie, Joseph	Brentford	Woking	
15 Parker, Adam	Stevenage Borough	Hitchin Town	
15 Parsons, Mark C.	Kettering Town	Aylesbury United	
15 Penman, Jon D.	Southport	Marine	
22 Perkins, Declan O.	Southend United	Cambridge United	
26 Petterson, Andrew K.	Charlton Athletic	Ipswich Town	
22 Quy, Andrew	Derby County	Stalybridge Celtic	
1 Ridout, John	Enfield	Purfleet	
4 Rolling, Frank	Ayr United	Leicester City	
19 Savage, Robert T.	Bashley	Fareham Town	
24 Sedgemore, Benjamin R.	Birmingham City	Mansfield Town	
9 Simpson, Gary	Luton Town	Aylesbury United	
8 Smith, Richard G.	Leicester City	Grimsby Town	
15 Starbuck, Philip M.	Sheffield United	Bristol City	
21 Stimson, Mark	Portsmouth	Barnet	
8 Talia, Francesco	Blackburn Rovers	Swindon Town	
19 Thorpe, Lee A.	Blackpool	Bangor	
11 Watson, Alexander F.	AFC Bournemouth	Gillingham	
4 Watson, Mark L.	West Ham United	Leyton Orient	
25 Wells, Mark	Scarborough	Dagenham & Redbridge	
11 Whiston, Peter	Southampton	Shrewsbury Town	

OCTOBER 1995

	From	To	Fee in £s
9 Allon, Joseph B.	Lincoln City	Hartlepool United	50,000
27 Arnold, Ian	Kettering Town	Stalybridge Celtic	undisclosed
13 Baraclough, Ian R.	Mansfield Town	Notts County	150,000
6 Barnard, Darren S.	Chelsea	Bristol City	75,000
9 Barnes, Steven L.	Welling United	Birmingham City	75,000
26 Barnett, Jason V.	Wolverhampton Wanderers	Lincoln City	undisclosed
12 Beauchamp, Joseph D.	Swindon Town	Oxford United	300,000
13 Berry, Trevor J.	Aston Villa	Rotherham United	20,000
14 Bohinen, Lars	Nottingham Forest	Blackburn Rovers	700,000
6 Brown, Steven R.	Gillingham	Lincoln City	exch
13 Coughlin, Russell J.	Exeter City	Torquay United	Free
30 Doling, Stuart J.	Lymington AFC	Doncaster Rovers	Free
13 Edey, Cecil	Witton Albion	Macclesfield Town	undisclosed
6 Fox, Ruel A.	Newcastle United	Tottenham Hotspur	4,200,000
20 Hackett, Warren J.	Doncaster Rovers	Mansfield Town	50,000
4 Hanson, David	Hednesford Town	Leyton Orient	50,000
27 Hoddle, Carl	Woking	Enfield	undisclosed
25 Jobson, Richard I.	Oldham Athletic	Leeds United	1,000,000
27 Lay, David A.	Slough Town	Chesham United	undisclosed
26 Logan, Richard A.	Huddersfield Town	Plymouth Argyle	20,000
5 Lowndes, Nathan P.	Leeds United	Watford	40,000
6 McSwegan, Gary J.	Notts County	Dundee United	375,000
27 Maddison, Lee R.	Bristol Rovers	Northampton Town	Free
13 Makel, Lee R.	Blackburn Rovers	Huddersfield Town	300,000
6 Mowbray, Anthony	Celtic	Ipswich Town	300,000
20 Munro, Stuart	Bristol City	Falkirk	undisclosed

		From	*To*	*Fee in £s*
2	Perrett, Russell	Lymington AFC	Portsmouth	undisclosed
9	Pointon, Neil G.	Oldham Athletic	Heart of Midlothian	30,000
7	Puttnam, David P.	Lincoln City	Gillingham	exch
20	Richardson, Barry	Preston North End	Lincoln City	20,000
27	Simpson, Philip M.	Stevenage Borough	Barnet	undisclosed
3	Smart, Stephen J.	Sutton United	Aylesbury United	undisclosed
17	Thompson, Steven	Wycombe Wanderers	Woking	undisclosed
19	Tierling, Lee A.	Woking	Welling United	undisclosed
28	Tiler, Carl	Nottingham Forest	Aston Villa	750,000
6	Walker, David J.	Dover Athletic	Gravesend & Northfleet	undisclosed
6	Westley, Shane L.M.	Cambridge United	Lincoln City	undisclosed
24	Whiston, Peter	Southampton	Shrewsbury Town	50,000
31	Whitney, John D.	Huddersfield Town	Lincoln City	20,000

TEMPORARY TRANSFERS

4	Beauchamp, Joseph D.	Swindon Town	Oxford United	
13	Blake, Robert J.	Darlington	Waterford United	
9	Brown, Dereck	Walton & Hersham	St Albans City	
27	Brown, Kenneth J.	West Ham United	Reading	
13	Buckle, Paul J.	Torquay United	Exeter City	
12	Burnett, Wayne	Plymouth Argyle	Bolton Wanderers	
30	Capleton, Melvin D.R.	Blackpool	Cork City	
27	Caskey, Darren M.	Tottenham Hotspur	Watford	
30	Clarkson, Phillip I.	Crewe Alexandra	Scunthorpe United	
17	Cobb, Paul M.	Enfield	Purfleet	
20	Collinson, David	Ashford Town	Margate	
5	Cullip, Daniel	Oxford United	Kettering Town	
28	Cutler, Neil A.	West Bromwich Albion	Coventry City	
13	Debont, Andrew	Wolverhampton Wanderers	Hartlepool United	
5	Dennison, Robert	Wolverhampton Wanderers	Swansea City	
30	Dunphy, Nicholas	Peterborough United	Cheltenham Town	
20	Fowler, John A.	Cambridge United	Cambridge City	
28	Gorman, Paul M.	Welling United	Fisher 93	
20	Gray, Martin D.	Sunderland	Fulham	
21	Greene, Dennis B.	Dagenham & Redbridge	Chelmsford City	
5	Higgs, Shane P.	Bristol Rovers	York City	
20	Holmes, Steven P.	Preston North End	Lincoln City	
31	Hooper, Michael D.	Newcastle United	Sunderland	
27	Horner, Phillip M.	Blackpool	Southport	
5	Jones, Lee	Swansea City	Crewe Alexandra	
24	Keys, Martin	Bilston Town	Solihull Borough	
20	King, Nathan P.	Shrewsbury Town	Stafford Rangers	
30	King, Phillip G.	Aston Villa	West Bromwich Albion	
13	Kirkham, Peter J.	Darlington	Waterford United	
6	Lampard, Frank J.	West Ham United	Swansea City	
7	Lawrence, Stephen P.	Dover Athletic	Margate	
6	Lomas, Andrew J.	Rushden & Diamonds	Slough Town	
20	Martin, Lee C.	Shrewsbury Town	Stafford Rangers	
13	Mattison, Paul A.	Darlington	Cork City	
16	McDonald, Paul	Southampton	Burnley	
6	Morgan, Philip J.	Stoke City	Macclesfield Town	
13	Naylor, Glenn	York City	Darlington	
13	Ndah, George E.	Crystal Palace	AFC Bournemouth	
1	Oghani, George W.	Northwich Victoria	Guiseley	
13	Partridge, Scott M.	Bristol City	Torquay United	
12	Paterson, James	Falkirk	Scunthorpe United	
27	Peel, Nathan J.	Burnley	Mansfield Town	
27	Perifimou, Christopher	Barnet	Hendon	
26	Petterson, Andrew K.	Charlton Athletic	Ipswich Town	
26	Philiskirk, Anthony	Burnley	Carlisle United	
6	Read, Paul C.	Arsenal	Sheffield United	
23	Rhodes, Andrew C.	St Johnstone	Preston North End	
19	Roberts, Ben J.	Middlesbrough	Hartlepool United	
24	Sharp, Lee	Queens Park Rangers	Lincoln United	
20	Shaw, Paul	Arsenal	Peterborough United	
13	Simkin, Darren S.	Shrewsbury Town	Telford United	
12	Sunderland, Jonathan	Blackpool	Northwich Victoria	
27	Taylor, Stephen C.	Crystal Palace	Northampton Town	
21	Tobin, Steven R.	Macclesfield Town	Hyde United	
26	Tovey, Paul	Bristol Rovers	Sligo Rovers	
27	Watson, Mark L.	West Ham United	Cambridge United	
13	Watson, Thomas R.	Grimsby Town	Hull City	
26	Wilkinson, Paul	Middlesbrough	Oldham Athletic	
27	Williams, Karl I.	Macclesfield Town	Ashton United	
27	Woods, Christopher C.	Sheffield Wednesday	Reading	
17	Wood, Simon O.	Coventry City	VS Rugby	

NOVEMBER 1995

1	Ainsworth, Gareth	Preston North End	Lincoln City	25,000
21	Barlow, Stuart	Everton	Oldham Athletic	350,000
17	Bartlett, Richard	Newport (IW)	Weymouth	undisclosed
17	Beadle, Peter C.	Watford	Bristol Rovers	30,000
16	Bennett, Gary E.	Sunderland	Carlisle United	Free
11	Brown, Dereck	Waltham & Hersham	Welling United	undisclosed
3	Buckle, Paul J.	Torquay United	Exeter City	Free
4	Bywater, Paul R.	Bridgnorth Town	Stafford Rangers	undisclosed
17	Chenoweth, Paul	Bath City	Cheltenham Town	undisclosed
16	Collins, Lee	Albion Rovers	Swindon Town	15,000
24	Darby, Julian T.	Coventry City	West Bromwich Albion	200,000
16	Duxbury, Lee E.	Huddersfield Town	Bradford City	135,000
8	Fenton, Graham A.	Aston Villa	Blackburn Rovers	1,500,000
14	Grant, Anthony	Leeds United	Preston North End	Free
30	Hercules, Cliff N.	Aylesbury United	Slough Town	undisclosed
3	Hills, John D.	Blackpool	Everton	undisclosed

	From	To	Fee in £s
10 Huckerby, Darren C.	Lincoln City	Newcastle United	500,000
3 Jenkins, Stephen R.	Swansea City	Huddersfield Town	275,000
24 Lavin, Gerard	Watford	Millwall	400,000
6 McDonald, Neil R.	Bolton Wanderers	Preston North End	40,000
7 Mayers, Kenneth	Bamber Bridge	Chorley	undisclosed
24 Nicol, Stephen	Notts County	Sheffield Wednesday	Free
3 Paterson, James	Falkirk	Scunthorpe United	18,000
22 Pearce, Andrew J.	Sheffield Wednesday	Wimbledon	600,000
16 Penrice, Gary K.	Queens Park Rangers	Watford	300,000
18 Petrescu, Dan V.	Sheffield Wednesday	Chelsea	2,300,000
15 Phelan, Terrence M.	Manchester City	Chelsea	900,000
24 Phillips, Martin J.	Exeter City	Manchester City	500,000
14 Pollitt, Michael F.	Darlington	Notts County	75,000
3 Price, Ryan	Birmingham City	Macclesfield Town	undisclosed
3 Rolling, Frank	Ayr United	Leicester City	100,000
15 Scott, Keith	Stoke City	Norwich City	exch
30 Sharp, Kevin P.	Leeds United	Wigan Athletic	100,000
16 Shaw, Richard E.	Crystal Palace	Coventry City	650,000
15 Sheron, Michael N.	Norwich City	Stoke City	exch
10 Talia, Francesco	Blackburn Rovers	Swindon Town	150,000
6 Trundle, Lee C.	Burscough	Chorley	undisclosed
24 Watson, Alexander F.	AFC Bournemouth	Torquay United	50,000
24 Williams, Nicholas B.	Yeovil Town	Newport (IW)	undisclosed
7 Wood, Jeffrey J.	Barking	Aldershot Town	3,000

TEMPORARY TRANSFERS

	From	To	
15 Ansah, Andrew	Southend United	Brentford	
10 Barber, Frederick	Luton Town	Ipswich Town	
3 Barber, Philip A.	Bristol City	Mansfield Town	
1 Barker, Richard I.	Sheffield Wednesday	Doncaster Rovers	
11 Bensted, David T.	Harrow Borough	Aylesbury United	
17 Biggins, Wayne	Oxford United	Wigan Athletic	
11 Blatherwick, Steven S.	Nottingham Forest	Hereford United	
27 Brown, Kenneth J.	West Ham United	Reading	
3 Burnett, Wayne	Plymouth Argyle	Bolton Wanderers	
3 Canham, Scott W.	West Ham United	Torquay United	
25 Cartwright, Mike N.	Wrexham	Runcorn	
17 Cobb, Paul M.	Enfield	Purfleet	
30 Colgan, Nicholas V.	Chelsea	Millwall	
16 Currie, Darren P.	West Ham United	Leyton Orient	
20 Davis, Michael	Bristol Rovers	Bangor	
24 Davison, Robert	Rotherham United	Hull City	
20 Fettis, Alan	Hull City	West Bromwich Albion	
24 Fitzgerald, Scott B.	Wimbledon	Sheffield United	
13 Gentle, Dominic	Boreham Wood	Purfleet	
20 Gray, Martin	Sunderland	Fulham	
1 Grazioli, Giuliano	Peterborough United	Yeovil Town	
24 Greene, David M.	Luton Town	Colchester United	
2 Hague, Paul	Leyton Orient	Dagenham & Redbridge	
11 Haines, Danny	Cheltenham Town	Evesham United	
24 Harper, Alan	Burnley	Cardiff City	
24 Hill, Daniel R.L.	Tottenham Hotspur	Birmingham City	
22 Holmes, Steven P.	Preston North End	Lincoln City	
27 Horner, Philip M.	Blackpool	Southport	
17 Keys, Martin	Bilston Town	Solihull Borough	
17 Kyd, Michael R.	Cambridge United	Bishops Stortford	
6 Lawrence, Stephen P.	Dover Athletic	Margate	
17 Linighan, David	Ipswich Town	Blackpool	
24 Martin, Kevin	Scarborough	Guiseley	
30 Morah, Olisa H.	Cambridge United	Welling United	
8 Morgan, Philip J.	Stoke City	Macclesfield Town	
1 Muggleton, Carl D.	Stoke City	Rotherham United	
14 Ndah, George E.	Crystal Palace	AFC Bournemouth	
17 Norbury, Michael S.	Doncaster Rovers	Linfield	
10 Powell, Jay	Kidderminster Harriers	Bridgnorth Town	
24 Preece, David W.	Derby County	Birmingham City	
7 Read, Paul	Arsenal	Southend United	
13 Rea, Simon	Birmingham City	Kettering Town	
9 Richards, Tony S.	Cambridge United	Sligo Rovers	
17 Ross, Michael P.	Plymouth Argyle	Exeter City	
3 Russell, Alexander J.	Rochdale	Glenavon	
24 Scott, Robert	Sheffield United	Northampton Town	
20 Shaw, Paul	Arsenal	Peterborough United	
10 Simkin, Darren S.	Shrewsbury Town	Telford United	
24 Smart, Allan A.C.	Preston North End	Carlisle United	
20 Theodosiou, Andrew	Dover Athletic	Chesham United	
6 Thornley, Benjamin L.	Manchester United	Stockport County	
18 Tobin, Steven R.	Macclesfield Town	Hyde United	
1 Tracey, Simon P.	Sheffield United	Wimbledon	
24 Trevitt, Simon	Huddersfield Town	Hull City	
28 Turner, Andrew P.	Tottenham Hotspur	Huddersfield Town	
17 Vonk, Michel C.	Manchester City	Oldham Athletic	
24 Wardley, Stuart	Bishop Stortford	Saffron Walden Town	
18 Washington, Darren T.	Leek Town	Ashton United	
9 Whitbread, Adrian R.	West Ham United	Portsmouth	
17 White, David	Leeds United	Sheffield United	
3 Yallop, Frank W.	Ipswich Town	Blackpool	

DECEMBER 1995

5 Alcide, Colin J.	Emley	Lincoln City	undisclosed
22 Aldridge, Martin J.	Northampton Town	Oxford United	Free
18 Basham, Michael	Swansea City	Peterborough United	Free
18 Biggins, Wayne	Oxford United	Wigan Athletic	undisclosed
24 Birkby, Dean	Bath City	Yeovil Town	undisclosed

	From	To	Fee in £s
23 Blake, Nathan A.	Sheffield United	Bolton Wanderers	1,200,000
29 Brightwell, David J.	Manchester City	Bradford City	30,000
29 Bull, Gary W.	Nottingham Forest	Birmingham City	Free
15 Bullimore, Wayne A.	Scunthorpe United	Bradford City	Free
15 Butler, Stephen	Cambridge United	Gillingham	100,000
16 Coleman, Christopher	Crystal Palace	Blackburn Rovers	2,800,000
29 Cowans, Gordon S.	Wolverhampton Wanderers	Sheffield United	Free
16 Cramb, Colin	Heart of Midlothian	Doncaster Rovers	undisclosed
22 Curran, Christopher	Torquay United	Plymouth Argyle	50,000
6 D'Auria, David A.	Scarborough	Scunthorpe United	Free
8 Dawber, Mark	Chertsey Town	Hendon	undisclosed
14 Feuer, Anthony I.	West Ham United	Luton Town	580,000
7 Fleming, Terry M.	Preston North End	Lincoln City	undisclosed
22 Green, Andrew J.	Altrincham	Barrow	undisclosed
15 Heath, Adrian P.	Burnley	Sheffield United	Free
22 Heritage, Peter M.	Stamco	Margate	undisclosed
21 McDonald, Tony	Chorley	Witton Albion	undisclosed
8 McNally, Mark	Celtic	Southend United	50,000
12 Mercer, William	Sheffield United	Chesterfield	100,000
15 Monk, Ian L.	Macclesfield Town	Morecambe	undisclosed
20 Moss, Neil G.	AFC Bournemouth	Southampton	250,000
28 Oatway, Anthony P.D.	Cardiff City	Torquay United	Free
22 Orlygsson, Thorvaldur	Stoke City	Oldham Athletic	Tribunal
22 Osborn, Simon E.	Queens Park Rangers	Wolverhampton Wanderers	1,000,000
22 Patterson, Mark A.	Bolton Wanderers	Sheffield United	300,000
7 Philliskirk, Anthony	Burnley	Cardiff City	60,000
22 Pritchard, Dean B.	Witton Albion	Altrincham	undisclosed
28 Randall, Adrian J.	Burnley	York City	140,000
5 Robertson, John N.	Wigan Athletic	Lincoln City	undisclosed
29 Rogers, Paul A.	Sheffield United	Notts County	exch
7 Sellars, Scott	Newcastle United	Bolton Wanderers	750,000
29 Short, Christian M.	Notts County	Sheffield United	exch
14 Stott, Steve T.W.	Kettering Town	Rushden & Diamonds	undisclosed
29 Thomson, Andrew	Swindon Town	Portsmouth	75,000
21 Trevitt, Simon	Huddersfield Town	Hull City	Free
21 Vonk, Michel C.	Manchester City	Sheffield United	350,000
22 Whalley, David N.	Altrincham	Witton Albion	undisclosed
16 Whelan, Noel D.	Leeds United	Coventry City	2,000,000
29 White, David	Leeds United	Sheffield United	500,000
8 Williams, Dean A.	Aylesbury United	Hayes	undisclosed
1 Windass, Dean	Hull City	Aberdeen	700,000
20 Wingfield, Philip	Kingstonian	Farnborough Town	undisclosed

TEMPORARY TRANSFERS

	From	To
29 Abrahams, Paul	Brentford	Colchester United
9 Aldridge, Martin J.	Northampton Town	Dagenham & Redbridge
15 Barber, Frederick	Luton Town	Blackpool
3 Barber, Philip A.	Bristol City	Mansfield Town
15 Barnwell-Edinboro, Jamie	Coventry City	Swansea City
15 Bateman, Robert S.	Slough Town	Berkhamsted Town
7 Blissett, Gary P.	Wimbledon	Wycombe Wanderers
1 Bradbury, Lee	Portsmouth	Exeter City
22 Brightwell, David J.	Manchester City	Bradford City
28 Brown, Kenneth J.	West Ham United	Reading
1 Brownrigg, Andrew D.	Norwich City	Kettering Town
5 Burnett, Wayne	Plymouth Argyle	Bolton Wanderers
15 Coates, Daniel	Hednesford Town	Halesowen Town
22 Cobb, Paul M.	Enfield	Purfleet
14 Cundy, Jason V.	Tottenham Hotspur	Crystal Palace
8 Cunningham, Carl M.	Derby County	Buxton
16 Currie, Darren	West Ham United	Leyton Orient
9 Cutler, Neil	West Bromwich Albion	Tamworth
1 Davies, William	Derby County	Buxton
29 Davison, Robert	Rotherham United	Hull City
2 Edwards, Michael	Tranmere Rovers	Northwich Victoria
1 Evans, David A.	Cardiff City	Pontypridd Town
8 Evans, Terry	Cardiff City	Barry Town
26 Fleming, David	Enfield	Bromley
13 Flory, Andrew	Yeovil Town	Weymouth
21 Fowler, John A.	Cambridge United	Cambridge City
19 Freeman, Darren B.A.	Gillingham	Glenavon
15 Fuff, Glen B.	Rushden & Diamonds	Rothewell Town
4 Furnell, Andrew P.	Peterborough United	VS Rugby
20 Gentle, Dominic	Boreham Wood	Grays Athletic
9 Germaine, Gary	West Bromwich Albion	Telford United
21 Glass, James R.	Crystal Palace	Gillingham
1 Grazioli, Giuliano	Peterborough United	Yeovil Town
24 Greene, David M.	Luton Town	Colchester United
14 Guinan, Stephen	Nottingham Forest	Darlington
11 Haines, Danny	Cheltenham Town	Evesham United
15 Hall, Derek R.	Rochdale	Altrincham
20 Hall, Gareth D.	Chelsea	Sunderland
13 Hammond, Nicholas D.	Plymouth Argyle	Reading
8 Harle, Michael J.L.	Millwall	Bury
24 Hill, Daniel R.L.	Tottenham Hotspur	Birmingham City
23 Holmes, Steven P.	Preston North End	Lincoln City
15 Hooper, Dean R.	Swindon Town	Peterborough United
1 Hooper, Michael D.	Newcastle United	Sunderland
27 Horner, Philip M.	Blackpool	Southport
15 Hurst, Glynn	Barnsley	Swansea City
15 Johnson, Gavin	Luton Town	Wigan Athletic
22 Kellman, David	Hayes	Molesey
8 Kenworthy, Jonathan R.	Tranmere Rovers	Chester City
15 Key, Lance W.	Sheffield Wednesday	Hartlepool United

		From	To	Fee in £s
17	Linighan, David	Ipswich Town	Blackpool	
14	Lucas, David A.	Preston North End	Darlington	
28	Maskell, Craig D.	Southampton	Bristol City	
7	Midgley, Craig S.	Bradford City	Scarborough	
8	Mitchell, Neil N.	Blackpool	Rochdale	
29	Molby, Jan	Liverpool	Norwich City	
5	Muggleton, Carl D.	Stoke City	Rotherham United	
14	Ndah, George E.	Crystal Palace	AFC Bournemouth	
7	Newhouse, Aidan R.	Wimbledon	Torquay United	
15	Nicholls, Mark	Chelsea	Chertsey Town	
22	Petterson, Andrew K.	Charlton Athletic	Bradford City	
15	Pickett, Ross	Slough Town	Chesham United	
12	Powell, Jay	Kidderminster Harriers	Bridgnorth Town	
25	Preece, David W.	Derby County	Birmingham City	
8	Roberts, Ben J.	Middlesbrough	Wycombe Wanderers	
15	Robinson, Steven	Birmingham City	Kidderminster Harriers	
29	Rogers, Paul A.	Sheffield United	Notts County	
1	Roget, Leo T.E.	Sheffield United	Dover Athletic	
20	Ross, Michael P.	Plymouth Argyle	Exeter City	
21	Samways, Vincent	Everton	Wolverhampton Wanderers	
1	Scott, Andrew M.	Cardiff City	Pontypridd Town	
24	Scott, Robert	Sheffield United	Northampton Town	
8	Senior, Trevor J.	Farnborough Town	Newport (IW)	
20	Shaw, Paul	Arsenal	Peterborough United	
8	Simkin, Darren S.	Shrewsbury Town	Telford United	
22	Simpson, Derek	Reading	Bangor	
7	Smart, Erskine	St Albans City	Hendon	
12	Sussex, Andrew R.	Southend United	Brentford	
6	Thornley, Benjamin L.	Manchester United	Stockport County	
14	Titterton, David S.	Hednesford Town	Burton Albion	
16	Tobin, Steven R.	Macclesfield Town	Hyde United	
19	Turner, Robert P.	Exeter City	Cambridge United	
30	Twigg, Darren	Leek Town	Stafford Rangers	
25	Wardley, Stuart	Bishops Stortford	Saffron Walden Town	
7	Warren, Matthew T.	Derby County	VS Rugby	
14	Whitbread, Adrian R.	West Ham United	Portsmouth	
21	White, David	Leeds United	Sheffield United	
9	Whyte, Christopher A.	Birmingham City	Coventry City	
1	Wilkinson, Paul	Middlesbrough	Watford	
22	Williams, Martin	Reading	Bangor	
1	Williams, Richard J.	Hednesford Town	Atherstone United	
9	Wollen, Andrew J.	Gloucester Town	Whitney Town	

JANUARY 1996

		From	To	Fee in £s
26	Arnott, Andrew J.	Gillingham	Leyton Orient	10,000
19	Baker, David P.	York City	Torquay United	25,000
16	Barber, Frederick	Luton Town	Birmingham City	Free
8	Battersby, Anthony	Sheffield United	Notts County	200,000
19	Biggins, Wayne	Oxford United	Wigan Athletic	Free
19	Booty, Martyn J.	Crewe Alexandra	Reading	75,000
3	Burnett, Wayne	Plymouth Argyle	Bolton Wanderers	undisclosed
24	Clough, Nigel H.	Liverpool	Manchester City	1,500,000
23	Coton, Anthony P.	Manchester City	Manchester United	500,000
12	Dixon, Kerry M.	Millwall	Watford	undisclosed
12	Fettis, Alan	Hull City	Nottingham Forest	250,000
19	Hall, Gareth D.	Chelsea	Sunderland	300,000
10	Hammond, Nicholas D.	Plymouth Argyle	Reading	40,000
8	Hobbs, Paul	Aylesbury United	Hendon	undisclosed
8	Holland, Paul	Sheffield United	Chesterfield	200,000
11	Hutchison, Donald	West Ham United	Sheffield United	1,200,000
26	Linighan, David	Ipswich Town	Blackpool	90,000
12	Matthews, Robert D.	York City	Bury	100,000
2	McBean, Peter	Bridgnorth Town	Hinckley Town	undisclosed
29	Newell, Paul C.	Barnet	Darlington	Free
12	Newland, Raymond J.	Chester City	Torquay United	Free
18	O'Connor, Gary	Heart of Midlothian	Doncaster Rovers	25,000
31	Powell, Christopher G.	Southend United	Derby County	800,000
10	Scott, Robert	Sheffield United	Fulham	30,000
10	Sedgemore, Benjamin R.	Birmingham City	Peterborough United	Free
23	Sinton, Andrew	Sheffield Wednesday	Tottenham Hotspur	1,500,000
12	Smith, Alex P.	Everton	Swindon Town	Free
31	Spink, Nigel P.	Aston Villa	West Bromwich Albion	Free
18	Stallard, Mark	Derby County	Bradford City	110,000
15	Thomas, Glen A.	Barnet	Gillingham	15,000
3	Thomson, Andrew J.	Swindon Town	Portsmouth	75,000
11	Titterton, David S.	Hednesford Town	Burton Albion	undisclosed
18	Walters, Mark E.	Liverpool	Southampton	Free
10	Weaver, Steven A.	Salisbury City	Clevedon Town	undisclosed
3	Wilder, Christopher J.	Rotherham United	Notts County	130,000
18	Worboys, Gavin A.	Darlington	Northampton Town	Free

TEMPORARY TRANSFERS

		From	To	
30	Angell, Brett	Sunderland	Sheffield United	
5	Armstrong, Craig	Nottingham Forest	Bristol Rovers	
5	Armstrong, Gordon I.	Sunderland	Northampton Town	
19	Atkinson, Brian	Sunderland	Carlisle United	
19	Barber, Philip A.	Bristol City	Fulham	
11	Barclay, Dominic	Bristol City	Bangor	
23	Barton, Stuart A.	Bamber Bridge	Netherfield	
12	Bishop, Darren C.	Barnsley	Preston North End	
19	Boden, Christopher D.	Derby County	Shrewsbury Town	
25	Bolton, James L.	Kingstonian	Hendon	
4	Brownrigg, Andrew D.	Norwich City	Kettering Town	
31	Butler, Peter J.	Notts County	Grimsby Town	

	From	To	Fee in £s
19 Canham, Scott W.	West Ham United	Brentford	
11 Casper, Christopher M.	Manchester United	AFC Bournemouth	
10 Chapman, Lee R.	Ipswich Town	Leeds United	
12 Charlery, Kenneth	Birmingham City	Southend United	
19 Clark, Anthony J.	Wycombe Wanderers	Hitchin Town	
29 Cooke, Terence J.	Manchester United	Sunderland	
27 Cooper, Simon	Cheltenham Town	Dorchester Town	
9 Cutler, Neil	West Bromwich Albion	Tamworth	
26 Davidson, Ross J.	Sheffield United	Chester City	
1 Davies, William	Derby County	Buxton	
30 Davison, Robert	Rotherham United	Hull City	
29 Dobson, Anthony J.	Portsmouth	Peterborough United	
12 Forbes, Scott	Bishops Stortford	Saffron Walden Town	
4 Furnell, Andrew P.	Peterborough United	VS Rugby	
19 Garner, Simon	Wycombe Wanderers	Torquay United	
7 Germaine, Gary	West Bromwich Albion	Telford United	
5 German, David	Macclesfield Town	Ashton United	
12 Gilbert, Kenneth	Aberdeen	Hull City	
19 Given, Seamus J.J.	Blackburn Rovers	Sunderland	
31 Glass, James R.	Crystal Palace	Burnley	
18 Grant, Anthony J.	Everton	Swindon Town	
1 Grazioli, Giuliano	Peterborough United	Yeovil Town	
6 Haines, Danny	Cheltenham Town	Evesham United	
12 Holmes, Paul	Everton	West Bromwich Albion	
26 Howarth, Lee	Mansfield Town	Barnet	
16 Johnson, Gavin	Luton Town	Wigan Athletic	
26 Jones, Philip L.	Liverpool	Wrexham	
12 Jones, Ryan A.	Sheffield Wednesday	Scunthorpe United	
12 Lancashire, Graham	Preston North End	Wigan Athletic	
17 Linighan, David	Ipswich Town	Blackpool	
5 Marginson, Karl K.	Macclesfield Town	Ashton United	
12 Marsden, Christopher	Notts County	Stockport County	
5 Martin, Kevin	Scarborough	Guiseley	
25 Martin, Lee B.	Blackpool	Bradford City	
12 Matthew, Damian	Crystal Palace	Bristol Rovers	
19 McLean, Ian	Bristol Rovers	Rotherham United	
9 Nixon, Eric W.	Tranmere Rovers	Reading	
22 Partridge, Scott M.	Bristol City	Plymouth Argyle	
19 Petterson, Andrew K.	Charlton Athletic	Plymouth Argyle	
9 Powell, Jay	Kidderminster Harriers	Bridgnorth Town	
26 Richards, David S.	Walsall	Leicester United	
19 Richardson, Ian G.	Birmingham City	Notts County	
5 Roberts, Ben J.	Middlesbrough	Wycombe Wanderers	
26 Samuels, Dean	Boreham Wood	Bromley	
9 Sansome, Paul E.	Southend United	Birmingham City	
12 Scargill, Jonathan M.	Sheffield Wednesday	Matlock Town	
5 Scully, Anthony D.T.	Crystal Palace	Cardiff City	
8 Smithard, Matthew P.	Leeds United	Northampton Town	
12 Stallard, Mark	Derby County	Bradford City	
19 Sutton, Stephen J.	Derby County	Reading	
26 Thomas, Mark L.	Wimbledon	Dulwich Hamlet	
25 Tyler, Mark R.	Peterborough United	Billericay Town	
26 Wanless, Paul S.	Lincoln City	Woking	
7 Warren, Matthew T.	Derby County	VS Rugby	
12 Whyte, Christopher A.	Birmingham City	West Ham United	
1 Williams, Richard J.	Hednesford Town	Atherstone United	
6 Wollen, Andrew J.	Gloucester City	Newport (IW)	

FEBRUARY 1996

22 Allen, Martin J.	West Ham United	Portsmouth	500,000
9 Breen, Gary	Peterborough United	Birmingham City	250,000
9 Burton, Nicholas J.	Yeovil Town	Aldershot Town	undisclosed
6 Byng, David G.	Torquay United	Doncaster Rovers	Free
28 Caskey, Darren M.	Tottenham Hotspur	Reading	700,000
20 Chalk, Martyn P.G.	Stockport County	Wrexham	exch
9 Charlery, Kenneth	Birmingham City	Peterborough United	exch
16 Corica, Stephen C.	Leicester City	Wolverhampton Wanderers	1,100,000
8 Currie, Darren P.	West Ham United	Shrewsbury Town	70,000
24 Daish, Liam S.	Birmingham City	Coventry City	1,100,000
5 Daly, Stephen	Wembley	Boreham Wood	undisclosed
16 Durkan, Kieron J.	Wrexham	Stockport County	70,000
2 Eriemo, Soloman	Aldershot Town	Carshalton Athletic	undisclosed
9 Foran, Mark J.	Sheffield United	Peterborough United	30,000
5 Gibb, Alistair S.	Norwich City	Northampton Town	15,000
16 Gilbert, Kenneth R.	Aberdeen	Hull City	Free
9 Haines, Danny	Cheltenham Town	Evesham United	undisclosed
9 Helliwell, Ian	Stockport County	Burnley	25,000
16 Himsworth, Gary P.	Darlington	York City	25,000
29 Hinshelwood, Danny M.	Nottingham Forest	Portsmouth	Free
15 Hodges, Glyn P.	Sheffield United	Derby County	Free
15 Holmes, Paul	Everton	West Bromwich Albion	80,000
29 Howarth, Lee	Mansfield Town	Barnet	undisclosed
1 Iorfa, Dominic	Southend United	Falkirk	undisclosed
24 Joachim, Julian K.	Leicester City	Aston Villa	1,500,000
16 Johnson, Gavin	Luton Town	Wigan Athletic	15,000
23 Lennon, Neil F.	Crewe Alexandra	Leicester City	750,000
16 Marsden, Christopher	Notts County	Stockport County	70,000
2 McCue, James G.	West Bromwich Albion	Partick Thistle	Free
16 McDonald, Paul	Southampton	Brighton & Hove Albion	25,000
16 Mintram, Spencer	Worthing	Farnborough Town	undisclosed
23 Molby, Jan	Liverpool	Swansea City	Free
16 Pitman, Jamie R.	Swindon Town	Hereford United	Free
22 Rammell, Andrew V.	Barnsley	Southend United	exch
22 Regis, David	Southend United	Barnsley	exch
29 Russell, Keith D.	Atherstone United	Hednesford Town	undisclosed

	From	To	Fee in £s
2 Stanborough, Nicholas	Gresley Rovers	Hinckley Athletic	undisclosed
14 Tinson, Darren L.	Northwich Victoria	Macclesfield Town	undisclosed
23 Walker, Andrew F.	Celtic	Sheffield United	500,000
16 Watkiss, Stuart P.	Walsall	Hereford United	Free
16 White, Devon W.	Notts County	Watford	100,000
26 Williams, Steven R.	Lincoln City	Peterborough United	Free

TEMPORARY TRANSFERS

	From	To
24 Allen, Christopher	Oxford United	Nottingham Forest
19 Barber, Philip A.	Bristol City	Fulham
2 Barness, Anthony	Chelsea	Southend United
2 Barnwell-Edinburgh, Jamie	Coventry City	Wigan Athletic
23 Black, Simon A.	Birmingham City	Ilkeston Town
19 Boden, Christopher D.	Derby County	Shrewsbury Town
6 Bradbury, Lee	Portsmouth	Exeter City
16 Braybrook, Kevin P.	Portsmouth	Yeovil Town
16 Brien, Anthony J.	West Bromwich Albion	Mansfield Town
23 Brown, Wayne L.	Bristol City	Salisbury City
5 Butler, Lee S.	Barnsley	Scunthorpe United
25 Canham, Scott W.	West Ham United	Brentford
11 Casper, Christopher M.	Manchester United	AFC Bournemouth
15 Castle, Stephen	Birmingham City	Gillingham
9 Charlery, Kenneth L.	Birmingham City	Peterborough United
9 Charnock, Philip A.	Liverpool	Blackpool
19 Cherry, Steven R.	Watford	Plymouth Argyle
17 Clark, Anthony J.	Wycombe Wanderers	Hitchin Town
29 Cook, Paul A.	Coventry City	Tranmere Rovers
22 Cottrill, Ian T.	Worcester City	Moor Green
8 Cutler, Neil	West Bromwich Albion	Tamworth
26 Davidson, Ross	Sheffield United	Chester City
2 Davies, William	Derby County	Bangor
29 Dobson, Anthony J.	Portsmouth	Peterborough United
16 Doherty, Neil	Birmingham City	Northampton Town
5 Edwards, Paul R.	West Bromwich Albion	Bury
9 Ellison, Anthony L.	Crewe Alexandra	Stalybridge Celtic
16 Forbes, Scott	Bishops Stortford	Saffron Walden Town
23 Furnell, Andrew P.	Peterborough United	Chertsey Town
20 Garner, Simon	Wycombe Wanderers	Torquay United
5 Germaine, Gary	West Bromwich Albion	Telford United
15 German, David	Macclesfield Town	Winsford United
20 Given, Seamus J.J.	Blackburn Rovers	Sunderland
1 Glass, James R.	Crystal Palace	Burnley
2 Glenister, Andrew A.	Alfreton Town	Matlock Town
16 Goodwin, Nicholas J.	Telford United	Cheltenham Town
2 Gordon, Neville	Reading	Woking
23 Gray, Andrew	Leyton Orient	Enfield
10 Grazioli, Giuliano	Peterborough United	Enfield
2 Green, Matthew R.	Derby County	Bangor
2 Hannigan, Al J.	Rushden & Diamonds	Yeovil Town
16 Hanson, David	Leyton Orient	Welling United
19 Hargreaves, Christian	West Bromwich Albion	Hereford United
23 Hiley, Scott	Birmingham City	Manchester City
15 Hill, Daniel R.L.	Tottenham Hotspur	Watford
15 Jemson, Nigel B.	Notts County	Rotherham United
10 Jennings, Gareth J.	Hednesford Town	Stafford Rangers
14 Jones, Ryan A.	Sheffield Wednesday	Scunthorpe United
3 Kellman, David	Hayes	Waltham & Hersham
2 Kernaghan, Alan N.	Manchester City	Bradford City
19 Lancaster, David	Bury	Rochdale
7 Lemoine, Adrian D.	Ashford Town	Tonbridge
16 Lemoine, Matthew B.	Ashford Town	Tonbridge
9 Marginson, Karl K.	Macclesfield Town	Ashton United
12 Marsden, Christopher	Notts County	Stockport County
14 Martin, Lee A.	Celtic	Coventry City
25 Martin, Lee B.	Blackpool	Bradford City
12 Matthew, Damien	Crystal Palace	Bristol Rovers
23 McGleish, Scott	Peterborough United	Colchester United
17 McLean, Ian	Bristol Rovers	Rotherham United
7 Midgley, Craig S.	Bradford City	Scarborough
23 Miles, Benjamin D.	Swansea City	Slough Town
8 Morgan, Philip J.	Stoke City	Macclesfield Town
9 Nicholson, Shane M.	Derby County	West Bromwich Albion
5 Nixon, Eric W.	Tranmere Rovers	Blackpool
19 Osgood, David R.	Aldershot Town	Bracknell Town
23 Peel, Nathan J.	Burnley	Doncaster Rovers
2 Pilkington, Kevin W.	Manchester United	Rochdale
2 Procopi, Carl	Hendon	Leighton Town
19 Restarick, Stephen L.	Dover Athletic	Crawley Town
29 Richards, David S.	Walsall	Leicester United
17 Richardson, Ian G.	Birmingham City	Notts County
9 Samways, Vincent	Everton	Birmingham City
16 Scargill, Jonathan M.	Sheffield Wednesday	Matlock Town
16 Scott, Keith	Norwich City	AFC Bournemouth
1 Sharpe, John J.	Manchester City	Exeter City
23 Shepherd, George J.	Macclesfield Town	Droylsden
9 Sheridan, John J.	Sheffield Wednesday	Birmingham City
23 Stokoe, Graham	Stoke City	Hartlepool United
22 Taylor, Stephen C.E.	Crystal Palace	Rushden & Diamonds
19 Theodosiou, Andrew	Dover Athletic	Crawley Town
22 Thornley, Benjamin L.	Manchester United	Huddersfield Town
16 Tobin, Steven R.	Macclesfield Town	Droylsden
25 Tyler, Mark R.	Peterborough United	Billericay Town
16 Warner, Michael	Northampton Town	Telford United
2 Warner, Vance	Nottingham Forest	Grimsby Town

	From	To	Fee in £s
6 Warren, Matthew T	.Derby County	VS Rugby	
26 Waters, Jamie S.	Cheltenham Town	Witney Town	
2 Watson, Mark L.	West Ham United	Shrewsbury Town	

MARCH 1996

	From	To	Fee in £s
28 Alford, Carl P.	Kettering Town	Rushden & Diamonds	85,000
28 Allen, Bradley J.	Queens Park Rangers	Charlton Athletic	400,000
4 Barnes, Paul L.	York City	Birmingham City	350,000
29 Barnwell-Edinboro, Jamie	Coventry City	Cambridge United	Free
2 Batty, David	Blackburn Rovers	Newcastle United	3,750,000
27 Bennett, Gary M.	Tranmere Rovers	Preston North End	200,000
21 Bennett, Ian	Leicester United	Tamworth	undisclosed
1 Boere, Jeroen W.J.	Crystal Palace	Southend United	150,000
29 Brabin, Gary	Doncaster Rovers	Bury	125,000
22 Brown, Linton	Hull City	Swansea City	60,000
22 Campbell, David A.	Leicester United	Tamworth	undisclosed
8 Carbon, Matthew P.	Lincoln City	Derby County	400,000
28 Chapman, Lee R.	Ipswich Town	Swansea City	Free
1 Claridge, Stephen E.	Birmingham City	Leicester City	1,200,000
28 Coll, Owen O.	Tottenham Hotspur	AFC Bournemouth	Free
29 Cook, Paul A.	Coventry City	Tranmere Rovers	250,000
1 Cooper, Simon	Cheltenham Town	Gloucester City	undisclosed
28 Corazzin, Giancarlo M.	Cambridge United	Plymouth Argyle	150,000
26 Cornforth, John M.	Swansea City	Birmingham City	350,000
28 Cowe, Steven M.	Aston Villa	Swindon Town	100,000
28 Cox, Ian G.	Crystal Palace	AFC Bournemouth	Free
29 Croft, Gary	Grimsby Town	Blackburn Rovers	1,000,000
28 Darby, Duane A.	Doncaster Rovers	Hull City	25,000 (combined fee)
26 Davidson, Ross J.	Sheffield United	Chester City	Free
1 Devlin, Paul J.	Notts County	Birmingham City	500,000 (combined fee)
15 Dudley, Derek A.	Halesowen Town	Telford United	undisclosed
9 Dumitrescu, Ilie	Tottenham Hotspur	West Ham United	1,500,000
8 Edwards, Robert	Crewe Alexandra	Huddersfield Town	150,000
26 Flitcroft, Garry	Manchester City	Blackburn Rovers	3,525,000
28 Gallimore, Anthony M.	Carlisle United	Grimsby Town	180,000
8 Gannon, John S.	Sheffield United	Oldham Athletic	Free
11 Garnett, Shaun M.	Tranmere Rovers	Swansea City	200,000
8 Glass, James R.	Crystal Palace	AFC Bournemouth	Free
22 Gore, Ian G.	Torquay United	Doncaster Rovers	5000
26 Grainger, Martin R.	Brentford	Birmingham City	400,000
28 Grant, Kim T.	Charlton Athletic	Luton Town	250,000
22 Gray, Andrew	Leyton Orient	Slough Town	5000
28 Gray, Martin D.	Sunderland	Oxford United	100,000
28 Griffiths, Carl B.	Portsmouth	Peterborough United	225,000
27 Hobson, Gary	Hull City	Brighton & Hove Albion	60,000
15 Holmes, Steven P.	Preston North End	Lincoln City	30,000
9 Hottiger, Marc	Newcastle United	Everton	750,000
27 Illman, Neil D.	Eastwood Town	Plymouth Argyle	undisclosed
25 Johnson, David D.	Rushden & Diamonds	Gloucester City	undisclosed
1 Jones, Gary	Southend United	Notts County	140,000
8 Lancashire, Graham	Preston North End	Wigan Athletic	35,000
23 Lee, Justin D.	Abingdon Town	Oxford City	undisclosed
1 Legg, Andrew	Notts County	Birmingham City	500,000 (combined fee)
22 Lightfoot, Christopher I.	Wigan Athletic	Crewe Alexandra	50,000
28 Lowe, David A.	Leicester City	Wigan Athletic	125,000
29 Lynch, Anthony J.	Stevenage Borough	Yeovil Town	undisclosed
1 Lyons, Andrew	Wigan Athletic	Partick Thistle	undisclosed
7 Martindale, Gary	Peterborough United	Notts County	175,000
1 Maskell, Craig D.	Southampton	Brighton & Hove Albion	40,000
27 Maxfield, Scott	Doncaster Rovers	Hull City	25,000 (combined fee)
22 McDonald, Colin	Falkirk	Swansea City	40,000
28 Mitchell, Paul R.	West Ham United	AFC Bournemouth	Free
13 Newbery, Richard J.	Wokingham Town	Gravesend & Northfleet	undisclosed
15 Newsome, Jon	Norwich City	Sheffield Wednesday	1,600,000
1 Nicholson, Shane M.	Derby County	West Bromwich Albion	150,000
25 Norbury, Michael S.	Guiseley	Stafford Rangers	undisclosed
28 O'Neill, Jon J.	Celtic	AFC Bournemouth	Free
28 O'Reilly, Justin	Gresley Rovers	Port Vale	30,000
28 Paris, Alan	Slough Town	Stevenage Borough	undisclosed
29 Peschisolido, Paolo _.	Stoke City	Birmingham City	400,000
22 Phillips, Leslie M.	Marlow	Oxford City	undisclosed
22 Philpott, Lee	Leicester City	Blackpool	75,000
25 Pick, Gary	Hereford United	Cambridge United	Free
21 Powell, Darren K.	Bashley	Weymouth	undisclosed
22 Richardson, Ian G.	Birmingham City	Notts County	200,000
28 Sharples, John	Ayr United	York City	undisclosed
11 Smith, Richard G.	Leicester City	Grimsby Town	50,000
12 Sneekes, Richard	Bolton Wanderers	West Bromwich Albion	400,000
15 Sparrow, Paul	Crystal Palace	Preston North End	undisclosed
6 Stewart, Paul A.	Liverpool	Sunderland	Free
15 Stimson, Mark	Portsmouth	Southend United	25,000
12 Sugure, James S.	Aldershot Town	Hayes	2000
28 Sunderland, Jonathan P.	Blackpool	Scarborough	Free
8 Taylor, Gareth K.	Crystal Palace	Sheffield United	exch
29 Taylor, Scott J.	Millwall	Bolton Wanderers	150,000
16 Tompkins, Mark	Tooting & Mitcham United	Bromley	undisclosed
27 Trebble, Neil D.	Scarborough	Stevenage Borough	Free
8 Tuttle, David P.	Sheffield United	Crystal Palace	300,000
8 Veart, Thomas C.	Sheffield United	Crystal Palace	200,000
21 Ward, Ashley S.	Norwich City	Derby County	1,000,000
29 Ward, Gavin J.	Bradford City	Bolton Wanderers	300,000
22 Ward, Mark W.	Birmingham City	Huddersfield Town	Free
29 Watts, Julian	Sheffield Wednesday	Leicester City	210,000
2 Williams, Richard J.	Hednesford Town	Atherstone United	undisclosed
18 Wood, Simon O.	Coventry City	Mansfield Town	Free

	From	To	Fee in £s
TEMPORARY TRANSFERS			
1 Ablett, Gary I.	Everton	Sheffield United	
31 Acteson, Robert	Hendon	Berkhamsted Town	
29 Adams, Darren S.	Cardiff City	Woking	
28 Allan, Derek T.	Southampton	Brighton & Hove Albion	
28 Angell, Brett A.M.	Sunderland	West Bromwich Albion	
1 Anthony, Graham J.	Sheffield United	Scarborough	
28 Armstrong, Craig	Nottingham Forest	Bristol Rovers	
28 Ashcroft, Lee	West Bromwich Albion	Notts County	
29 Ashenden, Scott	Boreham Wood	Grays Athletic	
8 Bailey, Gavin I.	Sheffield Wednesday	Matlock Town	
4 Barnwell-Edinboro, Jamie	Coventry City	Wigan Athletic	
30 Bellingham, Mark	Chelmsford City	Halesowen Town	
22 Berry, Greg J.	Millwall	Leyton Orient	
7 Birch, Paul	Wolverhampton Wanderers	Preston North End	
28 Bishop, Charles D.	Barnsley	Burnley	
30 Black, Simon A.	Birmingham City	Gloucester City	
11 Blissett, Gary P.	Wimbledon	Crewe Alexandra	
22 Brien, Anthony J.	West Bromwich Albion	Chester City	
1 Brown, Kenneth J.	West Ham United	Southend United	
28 Brown, Kenneth J.	West Ham United	Crystal Palace	
28 Butler, Peter J.F.	Notts County	West Bromwich Albion	
11 Casper, Christopher M.	Manchester United	AFC Bournemouth	
26 Cherry, Steve R.	Watford	Plymouth Argyle	
21 Clark, Anthony J.	Wycombe Wanderers	Hitchin Town	
1 Cooper, Simon	Cheltenham Town	Dorchester Town	
22 Cottrill, Ian T.	Worcester City	Moor Green	
22 Cowe, Steven M.	Aston Villa	Swindon Town	
28 Creaney, Gerard	Manchester City	Oldham Athletic	
1 Cross, Jonathan N.	Wrexham	Cliftonville	
27 Cutler, Neil A.	West Bromwich Albion	Chester City	
15 Daws, Anthony	Lincoln City	Halifax Town	
21 De Bont, Andrew C.	Wolverhampton Wanderers	Hereford United	
16 Doherty, Neil	Birmingham City	Northampton Town	
29 Dowell, Wayne A.	Burnley	Carlisle United	
7 Dykstra, Sieb	Queens Park Rangers	Wycombe Wanderers	
29 Ellitts, Justin S.	Telford United	Stafford Rangers	
18 Evans, Paul A.	Leeds United	Crystal Palace	
28 Fairclough, Wayne R.	Chesterfield	Scarborough	
5 Finnan, Stephen	Birmingham City	Notts County	
28 Flatts, Mark	Arsenal	Grimsby Town	
25 Foreman, Darren	Hednesford Town	Barrow	
22 Foster, Adrian M.	Gillingham	Exeter City	
14 Gayle, John	Stoke City	Gillingham	
8 Germaine, Gary	West Bromwich Albion	Scunthorpe United	
15 German, David	Macclesfield Town	Winsford United	
22 Given, Shamus J.J.	Blackburn Rovers	Sunderland	
17 Goodwin, Nicholas J.	Telford United	Cheltenham Town	
21 Gordon, Dale A.	West Ham United	Millwall	
29 Gould, Jonathan A.	Coventry City	Bradford City	
1 Greene, David M.	Luton Town	Brentford	
1 Grime, Nicholas	Stevenage Borough	Berkhamsted Town	
22 Hanson, David	Leyton Orient	Welling United	
20 Hargreaves, Christian	West Bromwich Albion	Hereford United	
1 Harris, Jason A.	Crystal Palace	Dover Athletic	
28 Hathaway, Ian A.	Torquay United	Chesterfield	
30 Hawtin, Dale C.	Crewe Alexandra	Hyde United	
29 Hollamby, Ian	Bishops Stortford	Saffron Walden Town	
25 Holmes, David J.	Gloucester City	Rushden & Diamonds	
18 Howell, Ian R.	Cheltenham Town	Gloucester City	
28 Illman, Neil D.	Plymouth Argyle	Cambridge United	
28 Izzet, Mustafa K.	Chelsea	Leicester City	
27 Jackson, Matthew A.	Everton	Charlton Athletic	
20 Jemson, Nigel B.	Notts County	Rotherham United	
11 Jennings, Gareth J.	Hednesford Town	Stafford Rangers	
30 Jones, Alexander	Stalybridge Celtic	Chorley	
29 Joseph, Marc E.	Cambridge United	Coventry City	
28 Kay, John	Sunderland	Shrewsbury Town	
21 Kearton, Jason B.	Everton	Preston North End	
28 Kelly, Russell	Chelsea	Leyton Orient	
1 Key, Lance W.	Sheffield Wednesday	Rochdale	
30 Knight, Keith	Gloucester City	Cheltenham Town	
20 Lancaster, David	Bury	Rochdale	
28 Launders, Brian T.	Crystal Palace	Oldham Athletic	
28 Leitch, Donald S.	Heart of Midlothian	Swindon Town	
5 Lemoine, Adrian D.	Ashford Town	Tonbridge	
15 Lemoine, Matthew B.	Ashford Town	Tonbridge	
15 Lock, Anthony	Colchester United	Chelmsford City	
28 Mahorn, Paul G.	Tottenham Hotspur	Burnley	
28 Martin, Lee C.	Shrewsbury Town	Bridgnorth Town	
23 Mason, Richard M.	Sheffield Wednesday	Boston United	
8 McAllister, Brian	Wimbledon	Crewe Alexandra	
28 McDougald, David E.J.	Brighton & Hove Albion	Chesterfield	
28 McGleish, Scott	Peterborough United	Colchester United	
22 McGorry, Brian P.	Wycombe Wanderers	Cardiff City	
22 Mean, Scott	AFC Bournemouth	West Ham United	
28 Mitchell, Neil N.	Blackpool	Southport	
20 Moore, Neil	Everton	Rotherham United	
1 Morgan, Stephen A.	Coventry City	Bristol Rovers	
15 Mudd, Paul	Lincoln City	Halifax Town	
28 Muggleton, Carl D.	Stoke City	Sheffield United	
8 Murray, Paul	Carlisle United	Queens Park Rangers	
5 Nixon, Eric W.	Tranmere Rovers	Blackpool	
25 O'Halloran, Keith J.	Middlesbrough	Scunthorpe United	
19 Osgood, David R.	Aldershot Town	Bracknell Town	

	From	To	Fee in £s
8 Partridge, Scott	Bristol City	Scarborough	
8 Petterson, Andrew K.	Charlton Athletic	Colchester United	
1 Phillips, Mark	Stevenage Borough	Berkhamsted Town	
28 Piearce, Stephen	Wolverhampton Wanderers	Hednesford Town	
8 Powell, Jay	Kidderminster Harriers	Bedworth United	
30 Preddie, Delroy E.	Slough Town	Walton & Hersham	
21 Preece, David W.	Derby County	Swindon Town	
31 Procopi, Carl	Hendon	Molesey	
1 Reece, Paul J.	West Bromwich Albion	Ilkeston Town	
20 Restarick, Stephen L.	Dover Athletic	Crawley Town	
28 Ridings, David J.	Crewe Alexandra	Hednesford Town	
28 Robinson, Carl P.	Wolverhampton Wanderers	Shrewsbury Town	
15 Robinson, Steven E.	Birmingham City	Peterborough United	
28 Rowe, Ezekiel B.	Chelsea	Brighton & Hove Albion	
15 Scargill, Jonathan M.	Sheffield Wednesday	Matlock Town	
29 Scott, Andrew M.	Cardiff City	Bath City	
1 Setori, Mark A.	Bury	Whitton Albion	
1 Sharpe, John J.	Manchester City	Exeter City	
29 Simpkins, John P.	Newport (IW)	Salisbury City	
28 Simpson, Gary	Luton Town	Fulham	
8 Sparrow, Paul	Crystal Palace	Preston North End	
29 Spencer, Michael	Bath City	Salisbury City	
20 Theodosiou, Andrew	Dover Athletic	Crawley Town	
25 Thornley, Benjamin L.	Manchester United	Huddersfield Town	
22 Tomlinson, Graeme M.	Manchester United	Luton Town	
1 Tucker, Andrew L.	Cheltenham Town	Gloucester City	
28 Turner, Andrew P.	Tottenham Hotspur	Southend United	
19 Tiler, Mark R.	Peterborough United	Billericay Town	
8 Wanless, Paul S.	Lincoln City	Cambridge United	
16 Warner, Michael	Northampton Town	Telford United	
27 Waters, Jamie S.	Cheltenham Town	Whitney Town	
28 Weir, Michael	Hibernian	Millwall	
28 Wilkinson, Paul	Middlesbrough	Luton Town	
2 Williams, Dean A.	Hayes	Chesham United	
29 Williams, Dean A.	Hayes	Hitchin Town	
28 Williams, Paul A.	Rochdale	Doncaster Rovers	
28 Williams, Paul A.	Charlton Athletic	Torquay United	
29 Williams, Steven R.	Peterborough United	Cambridge City	
1 Woodsford, Jamie	Luton Town	Portadown	
1 Wright, Jermaine M.	Wolverhampton Wanderers	Doncaster Rovers	

APRIL 1996

	From	To	Fee in £s
3 Barnwell-Edinboro, Jamie	Coventry City	Cambridge United	undisclosed
1 Hiley, Scott P.	Birmingham City	Manchester City	200,000

TEMPORARY TRANSFERS

	From	To	Fee in £s
3 Abblet, Gary I.	Everton	Sheffield United	
4 Bibbo, Salvatore	Sheffield United	Ards	
1 Black, Simon A.	Birmingham City	Gloucester City	
11 Blissett, Gary P.	Wimbledon	Crewe Alexandra	
27 Cutler, Neil	West Bromwich Albion	Chester City	
7 Dean, Craig	Tamworth	Hinckley Town	
22 Debont, Andrew	Wolverhampton Wanderers	Hereford United	
22 Evans, Paul A.	Leeds United	Crystal Palace	
2 Finnan, Stephen J.	Birmingham City	Notts County	
9 Germaine, Gary	West Bromwich Albion	Scunthorpe United	
23 Gordon, Dale A.	West Ham United	Millwall	
1 Greene, David M.	Luton Town	Brentford	
1 Grime, Nicholas	Stevenage Borough	Berkhamsted Town	
21 Hargreaves, Christian	West Bromwich Albion	Hereford United	
1 Harris, Jason A.	Crystal Palace	Dover Athletic	
9 Hathaway, Ian A.	Torquay United	Chesterfield	
30 Hawtin, Dale	Crewe Alexandra	Hyde United	
30 Izzet, Mustafa K.	Chelsea	Leicester City	
28 Jackson, Matthew A.	Everton	Charlton Athletic	
11 Jennings, Gareth J.	Hednesford Town	Stafford Rangers	
1 Key, Lance W.	Sheffield Wednesday	Rochdale	
16 Lemoine, Adrian D.	Ashford Town	Tonbridge	
24 Mason, Richard M.	Sheffield Wednesday	Boston United	
11 McAllister, Brian	Wimbledon	Crewe Alexandra	
10 McDougald, David E.	Brighton & Hove Albion	Chesterfield	
22 Moore, Neil	Everton	Rotherham United	
5 Nixon, Eric W.	Tranmere Rovers	Blackpool	
17 Osgood, David R.	Aldershot Town	Bracknell Town	
1 Reece, Paul J.	West Bromwich Albion	Ilkeston Town	
1 Sharpe, John J.	Manchester City	Exeter City	
22 Tomlinson, Graeme	Manchester United	Luton Town	
11 Wanless, Paul S.	Lincoln City	Cambridge United	
2 Wright, Jermaine M.	Wolverhampton Wanderers	Doncaster Rovers	

MAY 1996

	From	To	Fee in £s
19 Cherry, Steve R.	Watford	Plymouth Argyle	undisclosed
16 Jones, Stephen G.	AFC Bournemouth	West Ham United	undisclosed
2 Murray, Paul	Carlisle United	Queens Park Rangers	300,000
24 Rush, Ian J.	Liverpool	Leeds United	Free
13 Smart, Stephen J.	Aylesbury United	Hendon	undisclosed
31 Tucker, Mark J.	Woking	Rushden & Diamonds	undisclosed
16 Watson, Mark L.	West Ham United	AFC Bournemouth	undisclosed

TEMPORARY TRANSFERS

	From	To	Fee in £s
7 Allan, Derek T.	Southampton	Brighton & Hove Albion	
9 Brown, Kenneth J.	West Ham United	Crystal Palace	
5 Gould, Jonathan A.	Coventry City	Bradford City	

LEAGUE ATTENDANCES SINCE 1946–47

Season	Matches	Total	Div. 1	Div. 2	Div. 3 (S)	Div. 3 (N)
1946–47	1848	35,604,606	15,005,316	11,071,572	5,664,004	3,863,714
1947–48	1848	40,259,130	16,732,341	12,286,350	6,653,610	4,586,829
1948–49	1848	41,271,414	17,914,667	11,353,237	6,998,429	5,005,081
1949–50	1848	40,517,865	17,278,625	11,694,158	7,104,155	4,440,927
1950–51	2028	39,584,967	16,679,454	10,780,580	7,367,884	4,757,109
1951–52	2028	39,015,866	16,110,322	11,066,189	6,958,927	4,880,428
1952–53	2028	37,149,966	16,050,278	9,686,654	6,704,299	4,708,735
1953–54	2028	36,174,590	16,154,915	9,510,053	6,311,508	4,198,114
1954–55	2028	34,133,103	15,087,221	8,988,794	5,996,017	4,051,071
1955–56	2028	33,150,809	14,108,961	9,080,002	5,692,479	4,269,367
1956–57	2028	32,744,405	13,803,037	8,718,162	5,622,189	4,601,017
1957–58	2028	33,562,208	14,468,652	8,663,712	6,097,183	4,332,661

Season	Matches	Total	Div. 1	Div. 2	Div. 3	Div. 4
1958–59	2028	33,610,985	14,727,691	8,641,997	5,946,600	4,276,697
1959–60	2028	32,538,611	14,391,227	8,399,627	5,739,707	4,008,050
1960–61	2028	28,619,754	12,926,948	7,033,936	4,784,256	3,874,614
1961–62	2015	27,979,902	12,061,194	7,453,089	5,199,106	3,266,513
1962–63	2028	28,885,852	12,490,239	7,792,770	5,341,362	3,261,481
1963–64	2028	28,535,022	12,486,626	7,594,158	5,419,157	3,035,081
1964–65	2028	27,641,168	12,708,752	6,984,104	4,436,245	3,512,067
1965–66	2028	27,206,980	12,480,644	6,914,757	4,779,150	3,032,429
1966–67	2028	28,902,596	14,242,957	7,253,819	4,421,172	2,984,648
1967–68	2028	30,107,298	15,289,410	7,450,410	4,013,087	3,354,391
1968–69	2028	29,382,172	14,584,851	7,382,390	4,339,656	3,075,275
1969–70	2028	29,600,972	14,868,754	7,581,728	4,223,761	2,926,729
1970–71	2028	28,194,146	13,954,337	7,098,265	4,377,213	2,764,331
1971–72	2028	28,700,729	14,484,603	6,769,308	4,697,392	2,749,426
1972–73	2028	25,448,642	13,998,154	5,631,730	3,737,252	2,081,506
1973–74	2027	24,982,203	13,070,991	6,326,108	3,421,624	2,163,480
1974–75	2028	25,577,977	12,613,178	6,955,970	4,086,145	1,992,684
1975–76	2028	24,896,053	13,089,861	5,798,405	3,948,449	2,059,338
1976–77	2028	26,182,800	13,647,585	6,250,597	4,152,218	2,132,400
1977–78	2028	25,392,872	13,255,677	6,474,763	3,332,042	2,330,390
1978–79	2028	24,540,627	12,704,549	6,153,223	3,374,558	2,308,297
1979–80	2028	24,623,975	12,163,002	6,112,025	3,999,328	2,349,620
1980–81	2028	21,907,569	11,392,894	5,175,442	3,637,854	1,701,379
1981–82	2028	20,006,961	10,420,793	4,750,463	2,836,915	1,998,790
1982–83	2028	18,766,158	9,295,613	4,974,937	2,943,568	1,552,040
1983–84	2028	18,358,631	8,711,448	5,359,757	2,729,942	1,557,484
1984–85	2028	17,849,835	9,761,404	4,030,823	2,667,008	1,390,600
1985–86	2028	16,488,577	9,037,854	3,551,968	2,490,481	1,408,274
1986–87	2028	17,379,218	9,144,676	4,168,131	2,350,970	1,715,441
1987–88	2030	17,959,732	8,094,571	5,341,599	2,751,275	1,772,287
1988–89	2036	18,464,192	7,809,993	5,887,805	3,035,327	1,791,067
1989–90	2036	19,445,442	7,883,039	6,867,674	2,803,551	1,891,178
1990–91	2036	19,508,202	8,618,709	6,285,068	2,835,759	1,768,666
1991–92	2064*	20,487,273	9,989,160	5,809,787	2,993,352	1,694,974

Season	Matches	Total	FA Premierx Div. 1	Div. 2	Div. 3	
1992–93	2028	20,657,327	9,759,809	5,874,017	3,483,073	1,540,428
1993–94	2028	21,683,381	10,644,551	6,487,104	2,972,702	1,579,024
1994–95	2028	21,856,020	11,213,168	6,044,293	3,037,752	1,560,807
1995–96	2036	21,844,416	10,469,107	6,566,349	2,843,652	1,965,308

Figures include matches played by Aldershot.

LEAGUE ATTENDANCES 1995–96

FA CARLING PREMIERSHIP STATISTICS

	Average Gate			Season 1995/96	
	1994/95	1995/96	+/–%	Highest	Lowest
Arsenal	35,330	37,568	+6.3	38,323	34,519
Aston Villa	29,756	32,614	+9.6	39,336	23,933
Blackburn Rovers	25,272	27,714	+9.7	30,895	23,358
Bolton Wanderers	13,029	18,822	+44.5	21,381	16,216
Chelsea	21,057	25,466	+20.9	31,137	17,078
Coventry City	15,980	18,507	+15.8	23,344	12,496
Everton	31,291	35,435	+13.2	40,127	30,009
Leeds United	32,925	32,578	–1.1	39,801	26,077
Liverpool	34,176	39,553	+15.7	40,820	34,063
Manchester City	22,725	27,869	+22.6	31,436	23,617
Manchester United	43,681	41,700	–4.5	53,926	31,966
Middlesbrough	18,807	29,283	+55.7	30,011	27,882
Newcastle United	34,690	36,507	+5.2	36,589	36,225
Nottingham Forest	23,633	25,916	+9.7	29,263	20,810
Queens Park Rangers	14,613	15,683	+7.3	18,828	11,189
Sheffield Wednesday	26,572	24,877	–6.4	34,101	16,229
Southampton	14,685	14,820	+0.9	15,262	13,216
Tottenham Hotspur	27,259	30,510	+11.9	32,918	25,321
West Ham United	20,118	22,340	+11.0	24,324	18,501
Wimbledon	10,230	13,246	+29.5	25,423	6,352

ENDSLEIGH INSURANCE LEAGUE: DIVISION ONE ATTENDANCES

	Average Gate			Season 1995/96	
	1994/95	1995/96	+/–%	Highest	Lowest
Barnsley	6,509	8,086	+24.2	13,669	5,440
Birmingham City	16,983	18,090	+6.5	23,251	14,168
Charlton Athletic	10,211	11,185	+9.5	14,515	7,849
Crystal Palace	14,992	15,248	+1.7	20,664	12,166
Derby County	13,589	14,327	+5.4	17,460	9,242
Grimsby Town	5,921	5,992	+1.2	8,155	3,993
Huddersfield Town	11,665	13,151	+12.7	18,495	10,556
Ipswich Town	16,818	12,604	–25.1	20,083	9,157
Leicester City	19,532	16,530	–15.4	21,565	12,790
Luton Town	7,350	7,223	–1.7	9,454	5,443
Millwall	7,685	9,571	+24.5	14,501	7,354
Norwich City	18,625	14,581	–21.7	18,435	10,945
Oldham Athletic	8,444	6,634	–21.4	10,271	4,225
Port Vale	9,174	8,227	–10.3	16,737	5,796
Portsmouth	8,269	9,406	+13.8	14,434	6,002
Reading	9,350	8,918	–4.6	12,828	5,321
Sheffield United	14,462	12,901	–10.8	20,050	9,448
Southend United	5,146	5,898	+14.6	8,272	4,506
Stoke City	12,910	12,275	–4.9	18,881	8,609
Sunderland	15,344	17,482	+13.9	22,027	12,282
Tranmere Rovers	8,906	7,861	–11.7	16,188	5,253
Watford	8,125	9,457	+16.4	20,089	7,091
West Bromwich Albion	15,200	15,061	–0.9	23,821	10,956
Wolverhampton Wanderers	25,940	24,786	–4.4	27,381	20,450

ENDSLEIGH INSURANCE LEAGUE: DIVISION TWO ATTENDANCES

	Average Gate			Season 1995/96	
	1994/95	1995/96	+/-%	Highest	Lowest
AFC Bournemouth	4,391	4,213	−4.1	6,352	3,191
Blackpool	4,771	5,818	+21.9	9,175	3,877
Bradford City	6,152	5,708	−7.2	9,812	3,622
Brentford	6,536	4,768	−27.1	7,878	3,102
Brighton & Hove Albion	7,563	5,448	−28.0	9,852	3,629
Bristol City	8,005	7,017	−12.3	20,007	4,408
Bristol Rovers	5,173	5,279	+2.0	8,622	3,505
Burnley	12,135	9,064	−25.3	10,613	6,814
Carlisle United	7,422	5,704	−23.1	8,003	3,760
Chesterfield	3,528	4,884	+38.4	7,002	3,419
Crewe Alexandra	4,239	3,974	−6.3	5,177	2,977
Hull City	4,721	3,803	−19.4	8,965	2,284
Notts County	7,195	5,130	−28.7	8,725	3,462
Oxford United	6,148	5,876	−4.4	8,585	4,282
Peterborough United	5,055	4,655	−7.9	6,649	3,267
Rotherham United	3,278	3,413	+4.1	6,912	2,092
Shrewsbury Town	4,013	3,348	−16.6	7,983	2,186
Stockport County	4,525	5,903	+30.5	8,463	3,713
Swansea City	3,582	2,996	−16.4	4,478	1,788
Swindon Town	9,744	10,602	+8.8	15,062	6,704
Walsall	4,071	3,982	−2.1	5,624	2,740
Wrexham	4,071	3,705	−9.0	6,709	2,003
Wycombe Wanderers	5,856	4,573	−21.9	6,727	2,836
York City	3,685	3,538	−4.0	7,147	2,055

ENDSLEIGH INSURANCE LEAGUE: DIVISION THREE ATTENDANCES

	Average Gate			Season 1995/96	
	1994/95	1995/96	+/-%	Highest	Lowest
Barnet	2,201	2,282	+3.7	4,332	1,674
Bury	3,223	3,262	+1.2	5,658	2,280
Cambridge United	3,443	2,767	−19.6	4,114	2,186
Cardiff City	4,543	3,420	−24.7	7,772	1,611
Chester City	2,388	2,674	+12.0	5,004	1,623
Colchester United	3,280	3,274	−0.2	5,038	2,138
Darlington	2,346	2,408	+2.6	4,474	1,502
Doncaster Rovers	2,585	2,090	−19.1	4,413	1,429
Exeter City	2,484	3,442	+38.6	6,185	2,439
Fulham	4,207	4,191	−0.4	10,320	2,284
Gillingham	3,206	7,198	+124.5	10,595	4,099
Hartlepool United	1,953	2,072	+6.1	5,076	1,198
Hereford United	2,367	2,973	+25.6	5,838	1,728
Leyton Orient	3,436	4,478	+30.3	7,881	2,121
Lincoln City	3,276	2,870	−12.4	5,814	1,841
Mansfield Town	2,946	2,415	−18.0	4,626	1,674
Northampton Town	5,086	4,831	−5.0	7,427	3,090
Plymouth Argyle	5,832	7,120	+22.1	12,427	4,457
Preston North End	8,469	10,012	+18.2	18,700	6,837
Rochdale	2,184	2,214	+1.4	4,597	1,206
Scarborough	1,771	1,714	−3.2	3,772	1,201
Scunthorpe United	2,917	2,434	−16.6	4,847	1,615
Torquay United	2,968	2,454	−17.3	4,269	1,456
Wigan Athletic	1,748	2,856	+63.4	5,567	1,745

LEAGUE CUP FINALISTS 1961–96

Played as a two-leg final until 1966. All subsequent finals at Wembley.

Year	Winners	Runners-up	Score
1961	Aston Villa	Rotherham U	0-2, 3-0 (aet)
1962	Norwich C	Rochdale	3-0, 1-0
1963	Birmingham C	Aston Villa	3-1, 0-0
1964	Leicester C	Stoke C	1-1, 3-2
1965	Chelsea	Leicester C	3-2, 0-0
1966	WBA	West Ham U	1-2, 4-1
1967	QPR	WBA	3-2
1968	Leeds U	Arsenal	1-0
1969	Swindon T	Arsenal	3-1 (aet)
1970	Manchester C	WBA	2-1 (aet)
1971	Tottenham H	Aston Villa	2-0
1972	Stoke C	Chelsea	2-1
1973	Tottenham H	Norwich C	1-0
1974	Wolverhampton W	Manchester C	2-1
1975	Aston Villa	Norwich C	1-0
1976	Manchester C	Newcastle U	2-1
1977	Aston Villa	Everton	0-0, 1-1 (aet), 3-2 (aet)
1978	Nottingham F	Liverpool	0-0 (aet), 1-0
1979	Nottingham F	Southampton	3-2
1980	Wolverhampton W	Nottingham F	1-0
1981	Liverpool	West Ham U	1-1 (aet), 2-1

MILK CUP

Year	Winners	Runners-up	Score
1982	Liverpool	Tottenham H	3-1 (aet)
1983	Liverpool	Manchester U	2-1 (aet)
1984	Liverpool	Everton	0-0 (aet), 1-0
1985	Norwich C	Sunderland	1-0
1986	Oxford U	QPR	3-0

LITTLEWOODS CUP

Year	Winners	Runners-up	Score
1987	Arsenal	Liverpool	2-1
1988	Luton T	Arsenal	3-2
1989	Nottingham F	Luton T	3-1
1990	Nottingham F	Oldham Ath	1-0

RUMBELOWS LEAGUE CUP

Year	Winners	Runners-up	Score
1991	Sheffield W	Manchester U	1-0
1992	Manchester U	Nottingham F	1-0

COCA-COLA CUP

Year	Winners	Runners-up	Score
1993	Arsenal	Sheffield W	2-1
1994	Aston Villa	Manchester U	3-1
1995	Liverpool	Bolton W	2-1
1996	Aston Villa	Leeds U	3-0

LEAGUE CUP WINS
Aston Villa 5, Liverpool 5, Nottingham F 4, Arsenal 2, Manchester C 2, Norwich C 2, Tottenham H 2, Wolverhampton W 2, Birmingham C 1, Chelsea 1, Leeds U 1, Leicester C 1, Luton T 1, Manchester U 1, Oxford U 1, QPR 1, Sheffield W 1, Stoke C 1, Swindon T 1, WBA 1.

APPEARANCES IN FINALS
Aston Villa 7, Liverpool 7, Nottingham F 6, Arsenal 5, Manchester U 4, Norwich C 4, Manchester C 3, Tottenham H 3, WBA 3, Chelsea 2, Everton 2, Leeds U 2, Leicester C 2, Luton T 2, QPR 2, Sheffield W 2, Stoke C 2, West Ham U 2, Wolverhampton W 2, Birmingham C 1, Bolton W 1, Newcastle U 1, Oldham Ath 1, Oxford U 1, Rochdale 1, Rotherham U 1, Southampton 1, Sunderland 1, Swindon T 1.

APPEARANCES IN SEMI-FINALS
Aston Villa 10, Liverpool 9, Arsenal 8, Tottenham H 8, Manchester U 7, West Ham U 7, Nottingham F 6, Chelsea 5, Leeds U 5, Manchester C 5, Norwich C 5, WBA 4, Birmingham C 3, Burnley 3, Everton 3, QPR 3, Sheffield W 3, Swindon T 3, Wolverhampton W 3, Blackburn R 2, Bolton W 2, Bristol C 2, Coventry C 2, Crystal Palace 2, Ipswich T 2, Leicester C 2, Luton T 2, Middlesbrough 2, Oxford U 2, Plymouth Arg 2, Southampton 2, Stoke C 2, Sunderland 2, Blackpool 1, Bury 1, Cardiff C 1, Carlisle U 1, Chester C 1, Derby Co 1, Huddersfield T 1, Newcastle U 1, Oldham Ath 1, Peterborough U 1, Rochdale 1, Rotherham U 1, Shrewsbury T 1, Tranmere R 1, Walsall 1, Watford 1.

COCA-COLA CUP 1995–96

FIRST ROUND FIRST LEG

14 AUG

Doncaster R (0) 1 *(Wilcox)*
Shrewsbury T (1) 1 *(Seabury)* 1580
Doncaster R: Suckling; Measham, Hackett, Moore, Wilcox, Parrish, Schofield, Noteman (Clark), Jones, Darby (Norbury), Warren.
Shrewsbury T: Clarke; Scott, Withe, Taylor, Hughes, Seabury, Anthrobus, Evans, Spink (Rowbotham), Walton, Dempsey.

15 AUG

Barnet (0) 0
Charlton Ath (0) 0 1893
Barnet: Taylor; McDonald, Campbell, Pardew, Primus, Thomas, Gale, Freedman, Hodges (Cooper), Robbins (Tomlinson), Scott.
Charlton Ath: Salmon; Humphrey, Sturgess, Jones, Rufus (Robinson), Balmer, Robson, Nelson, Brown, Whyte, Bowyer.

Birmingham C (1) 1 *(Cooper)*
Plymouth Arg (0) 0 7964
Birmingham C: Bennett; Poole, Cooper, Ward (Forsyth), Edwards, Whyte, Donowa, Claridge (Muir), Bowen, Otto, Tait (Hunt).
Plymouth Arg: Hammond; Patterson, Williams, Burnett, Heathcote, Hill, Billy, Mauge, Littlejohn, Nugent, Clayton.

Bradford C (2) 2 *(Showler, Wright)*
Blackpool (0) 1 *(Ellis)* 3670
Bradford C: Ward; Huxford, Liburd, Showler, Mohan, Mitchell, Wright, Youds, Ormondroyd (Tolson), Shutt (Kiwomya), Murray.
Blackpool: Capleton; Brown R (Beech), Barlow, Lydiate, Mellon, Bradshaw, Quinn, Bonner (Bryan), Gouck, Ellis, Preece.

Cambridge U (1) 2 *(Corazzin 2 (1 pen))*
Swindon T (1) 1 *(Gooden)* 2530
Cambridge U: Barrett; Jeffrey (Fowler), Vowden, Thompson, Craddock, Matthew Joseph, Kyd (Granville), Middleton C, Adekola (Pack), Corazzin, Barrick.
Swindon T: Mildenhall; Culverhouse, Bodin, McMahon (Nijholt), Seagraves, Taylor, Robinson (Horlock), O'Sullivan, Finney, Allison, Gooden.

Chester C (2) 4 *(Whelan, Bishop, Milner, Murphy)*
Wigan Ath (0) 1 *(Martinez)* 2626
Chester C: Stewart; Flitcroft, Burnham, Shelton (Brenchley), Alsford, Whelan, Fisher, Priest, Regis (Murphy), Milner, Bishop (Rimmer).
Wigan Ath: Felgate; Farrell, Butler (Carragher), Miller, Robertson, Martinez, Seba, Lightfoot, Leonard, Doolan (Lyons), Diaz.

Chesterfield (0) 0
Bury (0) 1 *(Stant)* 2821
Chesterfield: Beasley; Hewitt, Perkins, Curtis, Williams, Dyche, Robinson, Davies, Lormor (Morris), Howard, Hazel (Narbett).
Bury U: Bracey; Cross, Bimson (Rigby), Reid, Lucketti, Jackson (Hughes), Richardson, Carter, Stant, Johnrose, Pugh.

Colchester U (2) 2 *(Adcock, Kinsella)*
Bristol C (1) 1 *(Seal)* 2831
Colchester U: Emberson; Locke, Betts, McCarthy, Caesar, Cawley, Kinsella, English, Whitton, Adcock, Cheetham.
Bristol C: Welch; Hansen, Munro (Shail), McLeary, Dryden, Kuhl, Bent, Partridge (Kite), Seal, Agostino, Barber.

Fulham (1) 3 *(Mison, Conroy, Barkus)*
Brighton & HA (0) 0 4380
Fulham: Lange; Jupp, Herrera, Mison, Angus, Blake, Thomas (Barkus), Morgan, Conroy, Brazil (Cusack), Adams.
Brighton & HA: Rust; Smith (Andrews), Tuck, McGarrigle (Chapman), Munday, McCarthy, Storer, Minton, McDougald (Byrne), Myall, Wilkins.

Gillingham (0) 1 *(Naylor)*
Bristol R (0) 1 *(Stewart)* 3827
Gillingham: Stannard; Dunne (Foster), Naylor, Butler, Harris, Green, Martin, Ratcliffe, Fortune-West, Bailey, O'Connor.
Bristol R: Parkin; Pritchard, Gurney, Browning, Clark, Tillson, Sterling, Miller, Stewart, Skinner, Taylor.

Hereford U (0) 0
Oxford U (1) 2 *(Biggins (pen), Murphy)* 3021
Hereford U: MacKenzie; Stoker, Lloyd, Smith, Brough, Reece, Pounder, Wilkins, Lyne, White, Fishlock.
Oxford U: Carter; Robinson, Ford M, Smith, Elliott, Gilchrist, Massey, Biggins (Murphy), Moody, Ford R, Allen.

Huddersfield T (1) 1 *(Dalton)*
Port Vale (1) 2 *(Glover D, Mills)* 5363
Huddersfield T: Francis; Trevitt, Cowan, Bullock, Scully, Sinnott, Dalton, Duxbury (Dunn), Booth, Jepson, Collins.
Port Vale: Musselwhite; Aspin, Tankard, Bogie, Griffiths, Glover D, McCarthy, Porter, Mills, Glover L, Guppy.

Hull C (0) 1 *(Windass)*
Carlisle U (0) 2 *(Walling, Aspinall)* 2779
Hull C: Wilson; Lowthorpe, Graham, Hobson, Dewhurst, Quigley (Mason), Peacock, Lee (Lawford), Brown (Fewings), Windass, Mann.
Carlisle U: Caig; Edmondson, Gallimore, Walling, Mountfield, Aspinall, Thomas, Currie (Robinson), Reeves, Hayward, Murray (Conway).

Luton T (0) 1 *(Marshall)*
Bournemouth (1) 1 *(Jones)* 2728
Luton T: Sommer; Thomas, Johnson, Davis S, Hughes, Oldfield, Alexander, Marshall (Thorpe), Taylor, Guentchev, Harvey.
Bournemouth: Andrews; Young, Beardsmore, Morris, Murray, Mean, Holland, Robinson (McElhatton), Jones, Fletcher (Bailey), Brissett.

Mansfield T (0) 0
Burnley (1) 1 *(Nogan)* 2544
Mansfield T: Bowling; Boothroyd, Baraclough, Sherlock (Lampkin), Howarth, Doolan, Ireland, Parkin, Hadley, Sale, Slawson.
Burnley: Beresford; Parkinson, Vinnicombe, Swan, Pender, Borland, Harper, Joyce, Philliskirk, Nogan, Eyres (Francis).

Notts Co (2) 2 *(White 2)*
Lincoln C (0) 0 3494
Notts Co: Ward; Mills, Walker, Turner, Strodder, Hogg, Devlin, Marsden, White, Agana (McSwegan), Legg.
Lincoln C: Leaning; Minett, Dixon, Megson, Greenall, Brightwell, West, Onwere, Allon, Huckerby, Puttnam (Mudd) (Williams).

Preston NE (0) 1 *(Kidd)*
Sunderland (0) 1 *(Angell)* 6323
Preston NE: Vaughan; Fensome, Sharp, Atkinson, Kidd, Moyes, Fleming (Magee), Bryson, Saville, Wilkinson, Raynor (Ainsworth).
Sunderland: Chamberlain; Kubicki, Scott, Bracewell, Ball, Ord, Michael Gray, Agnew (Armstrong), Smith (Russell), Gray P, Angell.

Rochdale (1) 2 *(Shaw, Thompstone)*
York C (0) 1 *(Baker)* 1390
Rochdale: Gray; Russell, Formby, Thompstone, Valentine, Butler, Thompson, Bayliss, Shaw, Whitehall, Peake.
York C: Kiely; McMillan, Hall, Pepper, Tutill, Barras, Oxley, Jordan (Williams), Barnes, Baker, Stephenson.

Scarborough (0) 1 *(D'Auria)*
Hartlepool U (0) 0 1555
Scarborough: Kelly; Knowles, Lucas, D'Auria (Willgrass), Hicks, Rockett, Thew, Todd, Page, Ritchie (Heald), Charles.
Hartlepool U: Jones; Ingram (Lynch), McAuley, Billing, McGuckin, Howard, Halliday, Tait, Houchen, Henderson (Oliver), Canham.

Scunthorpe U (1) 4 *(Eyre 2, McFarlane, Ford)*
Rotherham U (1) 1 *(Hayward)* 2110
Scunthorpe U: Samways; Walsh, Wilson, Thornber (Bullimore), Knill (Hope), Bradley, Ford, Turnbull, McFarlane, Eyre, Nicholson (Young).
Rotherham U: Clarke; Wilder, Bowyer, Garner, Monington, Blades, Hayward, Goodwin, Davison, Goater, Roscoe.

Stockport Co (1) 1 *(Armstrong)*
Wrexham (0) 0 3493
Stockport Co: Edwards; Connelly, Todd, Bennett, Flynn, Gannon, Beaumont (Dinning), Ware, Helliwell, Armstrong, Chalk (Williams).
Wrexham: Marriott; Brace, Hardy, Hughes (Phillips), Hunter, Jones, Skinner (Durkan), Ward, Connolly, Watkin (Morris), Russell.

Swansea C (2) 4 *(Ampadu, Hodge 2, Torpey)*
Peterborough U (0) 1 *(Manuel)* 1862
Swansea C: Freestone; Jenkins, Barnhouse, Walker (Clode), Edwards, Ampadu, Coates (Perrett), Heggs, Torpey, Cornforth, Hodge.
Peterborough U: Sheffield; Williams, Spearing, Ebdon, Breen, Clark, Carter, Manuel, Power, Martindale (Le Bihan), Morrison (Farrell).

Torquay U (0) 0
Exeter C (0) 0 2473
Torquay U: Bayes; Curran, Stamps, Kelly, Barrow, Gore, Hawthorne, Buckle (Croft), Hancox, Hathaway, Byng (Laight).
Exeter C: Fox; Parsley, Rice, Cooper, Blake, Richardson, Chamberlain, Bailey, Came, Cecere, Gavin.

Walsall (2) 2 *(Wilson, O'Connor)*
Brentford (1) 2 *(Harvey, Forster)* 2405
Walsall Walker; Evans, Daniel, Ryder, Marsh, Watkiss, O'Connor, Ntamark, Lightbourne, Wilson, Bradley.
Brentford: Dearden; Statham, Grainger, Ashby, Bates, Hurdle, Harvey, Smith, Forster, Anderson, Taylor.

WBA (1) 1 *(Taylor)*
Northampton T (0) 1 *(Colkin)* 6489
WBA: Naylor; Burgess, Edwards, Coldicott, Mardon, Raven, Donovan, Gilbert, Taylor, Hunt (Rees), Brien (Smith).
Northampton T: Woodman; Norton, Smith, O'Shea, Warburton, Sampson, Peer, Williams, Grayson (Thompson), Burns, Colkin.

Wycombe W (2) 3 *(De Souza 2, Crossley)*
Leyton Orient (0) 0 3310
Wycombe W: Hyde; Cousins, Hardyman, Crossley, Foran, Brown, Carroll, Bell, De Souza (Hemmings), McGavin (Garner), Soloman.
Leyton Orient: Caldwell; Warren, Austin, Chapman, Hendon, Bellamy, Brooks, Cockerill, Inglethorpe, Shearer, Stanislaus (Baker).

16 AUG
Portsmouth (0) 0
Cardiff C (1) 2 *(Dale, Bird)* 4203
Portsmouth: Knight; Pethick, Russell, McLoughlin, Awford, Butters, Carter (Igoe), Durnin, Hall, Creaney (Burton), Rees.
Cardiff C: Williams D; Brazil, Searle, Harding, Baddeley, Perry, Wigg, Rodgerson, Haworth (Evans), Dale, Bird.

FIRST ROUND SECOND LEG
22 AUG
Blackpool (0) 2 *(Mellon, Ellis)*
Bradford C (0) 3 *(Wright, Hamilton, Youds)* 4553
Blackpool: Banks; Brown R, Barlow (Bonner), Lydiate, Mellon, Bradshaw, Quinn, Beech, Gouck (Bryan), Ellis, Preece.
Bradford C: Ward; Huxford, Liburd, Hamilton, Mohan, Mitchell, Wright, Youds, Ormondroyd, Shutt (Kiwomya), Murray.
Bradford C won 5-3 on aggregate.

Bournemouth (1) 2 *(Jones, Morris)*
Luton T (1) 1 *(Johnson M)* 4884
Bournemouth: Andrews; Young, Beardsmore, Morris, Murray, Mean, Holland, Pennock (Victory), Jones, Bailey, Brissett (Town) (Rawlinson).
Luton T: Sommer; James, Johnson M, Davis S, Waddock, Oldfield (Matthews), Alexander, Marshall, Taylor (Thorpe), Guentchev, Harvey (Thomas).
aet; Bournemouth won 3-2 on aggregate.

Brentford (2) 3 *(Taylor, Anderson, McGhee)*
Walsall (1) 2 *(Evans, Houghton)* 3149
Brentford: Dearden; Statham, Grainger, Ashby (McGhee), Bates, Hurdle (Mundee), Harvey, Smith, Forster, Anderson, Taylor.
Walsall: Walker; Evans, Daniel, Watkiss, Marsh, Palmer, O'Connor, Ntamark, Lightbourne (Houghton), Wilson, Bradley.
Brentford won 5-4 on aggregate.

Brighton & HA (0) 0
Fulham (0) 2 *(Conroy, Brazil)* 3799
Brighton & HA: Rust; Smith (Fox S), Chapman, Myall, Tuck, McCarthy, Storer, McGarrigle (Virgo), Andrews, Byrne, Wilkins.
Fulham: Lange; Jupp, Herrera, Mison, Angus, Blake, Thomas, Barkus (Brazil), Conroy, Cusack, Adams.
Fulham won 5-0 on aggregate.

Bristol C (1) 2 *(Seal 2)*
Colchester U (0) 1 *(Cheetham)* 3648
Bristol C: Welch; Hansen (Bryant), Shail, McLeary, Dryden, Kuhl, Bent, Fowler, Seal, Agostino (Partridge), Barber (Plummer).
Colchester U: Emberson; Locke, Betts, McCarthy, Caesar, Cawley, Kinsella, English, Whitton, Adcock (Fry), Cheetham (Reinelt).
aet; Bristol C won 5-3 on penalties.

Burnley (1) 3 *(Randall, Nogan 2)*
Mansfield T (0) 1 *(Sale)* 4673
Burnley: Beresford; Parkinson, Vinnicombe, Swan (Francis), Winstanley, Randall, Hoyland, Joyce, Philliskirk, Nogan, Borland.
Mansfield T: Bowling; Boothroyd, Baraclough, Doolan, Howarth, Peters, Ireland (Robinson), Parkin, Hadley, Sale, Slawson (Alexander).
Burnley won 4-1 on aggregate.

Cardiff C (0) 1 *(Dale)*
Portsmouth (0) 0 4347
Cardiff C: Williams D; Brazil, Searle, Harding (Downing), Baddeley, Perry, Wigg, Rodgerson, Haworth (Young), Dale, Bird.
Portsmouth: Poom; Pethick, Russell, Simpson, Awford (Igoe), Butters, Burton, Durnin, Hall, Creaney (Carter), Rees (Griffiths).
Cardiff C won 3-0 on aggregate.

Carlisle U (0) 2 *(Reeves 2)*
Hull C (2) 4 *(Allison, Windass 2, Fewings)* 4250
Carlisle U: Caig; Edmondson, Gallimore, Walling, Joyce, Aspinall (Thomas), Conway (Peacock), Currie, Reeves, Hayward, Murray.
Hull C: Wilson; Allison, Graham, Hobson, Dewhurst, Lawford, Peacock, Lee, Fewings, Windass (Mason), Mann.
Hull C won 5-4 on aggregate.

Charlton Ath (1) 2 *(Bowyer 2)*
Barnet (0) 0 4418
Charlton Ath: Salmon; Humphrey, Stuart, Jones, Rufus, Balmer, Robson (Walsh), Nelson, Robinson, Whyte (Grant), Bowyer.
Barnet: Taylor; McDonald, Campbell, Pardew, Primus, Thomas, Gale, Freedman, Hodges (Cooper), Robbins (Tomlinson), Scott.
Charlton Ath won 2-0 on aggregate.

Hartlepool U (1) 1 *(McGuckin)*
Scarborough (0) 0 2134
Hartlepool U: Horne; Ingram (Lynch), McAuley, Billing, McGuckin, Howard (Oliver), Halliday, Tait, Houchen, Henderson, Canham.
Scarborough: Kelly; Knowles, Lucas, D'Auria, Hicks, Rockett, Thew, Todd, Page, Ritchie (Heald), Charles.
aet; Hartlepool U won 7-6 on penalties.

Leyton Orient (1) 2 *(Austin, West (pen))*
Wycombe W (0) 0 2478
Leyton Orient: Caldwell; Warren (Shearer), Austin, Chapman, Hendon, McCarthy, Kelly, Cockerill, Inglethorpe, West, Brooks (Baker).
Wycombe W: Hyde; Cousins (Hemmings), Hardyman, Crossley, Foran, Brown, Carroll, McGorry (Moussaddik), De Souza, McGavin (Garner), Howard.
Wycombe W won 3-2 on aggregate.

Lincoln C (0) 0
Notts Co (0) 2 *(White 2)* 2636
Lincoln C: Leaning; Minett, Dixon, Megson, Greenall, Brightwell, West, Onwere, Carbon, Huckerby, Dyer.
Notts Co: Ward; Mills, Walker, Turner, Strodder, Hogg, Simpson, Nicol, White, Jemson, Legg.
Notts Co won 4-0 on aggregate.

Northampton T (0) 2 *(Burns (pen), Peer)*
WBA (1) 4 *(Taylor 2, Donovan, Hunt)* 7083
Northampton T: Woodman; Norton, Smith, O'Shea, Warburton, Sampson, Peer, Williams (Thompson), Grayson (White), Burns, Colkin.
WBA: Naylor; Burgess, Edwards, Coldicott, Mardon, Raven, Donovan, Gilbert, Taylor, Hunt (Rees), Hamilton.
WBA won 5-3 on aggregate.

Oxford U (3) 3 *(Allen, Smith, Moody)*
Hereford U (0) 2 *(Reece, Smith)* 3571
Oxford U: Carter; Robinson, Ford M, Smith, Elliott, Gilchrist, Rush, Biggins, Moody (Angell), Murphy (Marsh), Allen.
Hereford U: MacKenzie; Stoker, Lloyd, Smith, Pick, Reece, Pounder, Wilkins, Lyne (Cross), White, Fishlock (Preedy).
Oxford U won 5-2 on aggregate.

Peterborough U (1) 3 *(Manuel 2, Le Bihan)*
Swansea C (0) 0 1871
Peterborough U: Sheffield; Williams, Rioch, Ebdon, Breen, Heald, Le Bihan, Manuel, Martindale (McGleish), Farrell, Morrison (Power).
Swansea C: Freestone; Jenkins, Barnhouse (Clode), Walker, Edwards, Ampadu, Chapple, Heggs, Torpey, Cornforth, Hodge (Coates).
aet; Peterborough U won on away goals.

Plymouth Arg (1) 1 *(Heathcote)*
Birmingham C (0) 2 *(Edwards, Hunt)* 6529
Plymouth Arg: Hammond; Twiddy, Williams, Burnett (Evans), Heathcote, Hill, Billy, Mauge, Littlejohn, Nugent (O'Hagan), Clayton (Saunders).
Birmingham C: Bennett; Poole, Cooper, Ward (Donowa), Edwards, Whyte, Hunt (Forsyth), Claridge, Bowen, Castle, Hiley (Doherty).
Birmingham C won 3-1 on aggregate.

Port Vale (0) 1 *(Glover L)*
Huddersfield T (2) 3 *(Bullock, Booth 2)* 4380
Port Vale: Musselwhite; Sandeman (Stokes), Tankard, Walker, Bogie, Glover D, McCarthy, Porter, Foyle (Glover L), Mills, Guppy.
Huddersfield T: Francis; Trevitt, Cowan, Bullock, Scully, Sinnott, Dalton (Whitney), Crosby, Booth, Jepson, Collins.
Huddersfield T won 4-3 on aggregate.

Rotherham U (1) 5 *(Goater 2, McGlashan, Hayward, Jeffrey)*
Scunthorpe U (0) 0 2206
Rotherham U: Clarke; Wilder, Hurst, Garner, Breckin, Richardson, Hayward, McGlashan, Jeffrey, Goater, Roscoe.
Scunthorpe U: Samways; Walsh, Wilson, Thornber, Hope, Bradley, Ford (Bullimore), Turnbull, McFarlane, Eyre (Young), Nicholson.
aet; Rotherham U won 6-4 on aggregate.

Shrewsbury T (0) 0
Doncaster R (0) 0 1842
Shrewsbury T: Clarke; Scott, Reed, Taylor, Hughes, Seabury, Berkley (Evans), Rowbotham (Anthrobus), Spink, Walton, Dempsey.
Doncaster R: Suckling; Measham, Hackett, Moore, Wilcox, Parrish (Harper) (Clark), Schofield, Noteman, Jones, Darby (Carmichael), Warren.
aet; Shrewsbury T won on away goals.

Wigan Ath (0) 1 *(Lyons (pen))*
Chester C (2) 3 *(Milner 2, Bishop)* 2061
Wigan Ath: Felgate; Carragher, Farrell, Miller (Ogden), Robertson, Martinez, Seba (Millett), Lightfoot, Leonard, Lyons, Diaz.
Chester C: Stewart; Flitcroft (Rimmer), Burnham, Jenkins (Rogers), Jackson, Alsford, Fisher, Priest, Regis (Murphy), Milner, Bishop.
Chester C won 7-2 on aggregate.

York C (1) 5 *(Baker, Barnes 2, Pepper, Peverell)*
Rochdale (0) 1 *(Tutill (og))* 2130
York C: Kiely; McMillan, Hall, Pepper, Tutill, Barras (Atkin), Murty, Williams, Barnes, Baker (Peverell), Stephenson (Jordan).
Rochdale: Gray; Russell, Formby, Deary, Valentine, Butler (Martin), Thompson, Bayliss (Ryan), Williams, Whitehall, Peake.
aet; York C won 6-3 on aggregate.

23 AUG

FIRST ROUND FIRST LEG

Crewe Alex (0) 4 *(Unsworth, Whalley, Collins, Adebola)*
Darlington (0) 0 2850
Crewe Alex: Gayle; Booty, Unsworth, Westwood, Macauley, Whalley, Tierney, Collins, Savage, Lennon, Murphy (Adebola).
Darlington: Pollitt; Shaw (Worboys), Himsworth, Gaughan, Crosby, Gregan, Paulo, Olsson, Bannister, Neves (Blake), Carrs (Brumwell).

FIRST ROUND SECOND LEG

Bristol R (1) 4 *(Stewart 3, Miller)*
Gillingham (1) 2 *(Bailey, Fortune-West)* 3601
Bristol R: Parkin; Pritchard, Gurney, Browning, Clark, Tillson (Wright), Sterling, Miller, Stewart, Taylor, Skinner.
Gillingham: Stannard; Green, Naylor, Smith, Harris, Butler, Rattray (Foster), Ratcliffe, Fortune-West, Bailey, O'Connor.
Bristol R won 5-3 on aggregate

Exeter C (1) 1 *(Richardson)*
Torquay U (1) 1 *(Hawthorne)* 3721
Exeter C: Fox; Parsley, Rice (Pears), Cooper, Blake, Richardson, Chamberlain (Phillips), Bailey (Thirlby), Turner, Coughlin, Came.
Torquay U: Bayes; Curran, Travis, Kelly (O'Riordan), Barrow, Gore, Hawthorne, Buckle, Hancox (Byng), Hathaway, Hall (Ndah).
Torquay U won on away goals

Sunderland (0) 3 *(Howey 2, Kidd (og))*
Preston NE (2) 2 *(Cartwright, Bryson)* 7407
Sunderland: Chamberlain; Kubicki, Martin Gray, Bracewell, Ball, Ord (Melville), Michael Gray (Smith), Atkinson, Russell, Gray P, Howey.
Preston NE: Vaughan; Fleming, Sharp, Atkinson, Kidd, Moyes, Cartwright, Bryson, Saville, Wilkinson, Magee (Ainsworth).
Sunderland won 4-3 on aggregate

Swindon T (0) 2 *(Beauchamp, Horlock)*
Cambridge U (0) 0 6724
Swindon T: Mildenhall; Culverhouse, Bodin, McMahon, Seagraves (Hooper), Taylor, Murray, O'Sullivan, Thorne (Beauchamp), Finney, Horlock.
Cambridge U: Barrett; Vowden, Palmer, Thompson, Westley, Matthew Joseph, Stock, Middleton C, Adekola (Granville), Corrazin (Kyd), Pack.
Swindon T won 3-2 on aggregate

5 SEPT

Bury (0) 2 *(Carter (pen), Daws)*
Chesterfield (1) 1 *(Roberts)* 2565
Bury: Bracey; Cross, Bimson, Reid S, Lucketti, Matthewson, Daws, Carter, Stant, Johnrose, Pugh.
Chesterfield: Beasley; Hewitt, Rogers, Curtis, Carr, Law, Narbett, Davies (Morris), Lormor, Roberts, Dyche.
Bury won 3-1 on aggregate

Darlington (0) 1 *(Carss)*
Crewe Alex (0) 1 *(Edwards)* 1084
Darlington: Pollitt; Shaw (Paulo), Barnard, Gaughan, Crosby, Brumwell, Himsworth, Bannister, Worboys, Neves (Blake), Carss.
Crewe Alex: Gayle; Murphy, Booty, Westwood, Macauley, Whalley, Tierney, Collins, Adebola (Clarkson), Lennon, Edwards.
Crewe Alex won 5-1 on aggregate

Wrexham (1) 2 *(Russell, Watkin)*
Stockport Co (0) 2 *(Eckhardt, Helliwell)* 2764
Wrexham: Marriott; Phillips, Hardy, Brammer, Hunter, Jones, Durkan, Owen, Connolly, Morris (Watkin), Russell.
Stockport Co: Edwards; Connelly, Todd, Bennett, Flynn, Gannon, Beaumont, Eckhardt, Helliwell, Armstrong, Chalk (Williams).
Stockport Co won 3-2 on aggregate

SECOND ROUND FIRST LEG

19 SEPT

Bolton W (0) 1 *(Sneekes)*
Brentford (0) 0 5243
Bolton W: Branagan; Green, Phillips, Patterson (Todd), Bergsson, Fairclough, Lee, Sneekes, De Freitas (Coyle), McGinlay, Thompson.
Brentford: Dearden; Statham, Grainger, Davis, Bates, Ashby, Mundee, Smith, Forster, Hooker, Taylor.

Bradford C (1) 3 *(Showler, Youds, Ormondroyd)*
Nottingham F (1) 2 *(Bohinen 2)* 9288
Bradford C: Ward; Huxford, Jacobs, Mitchell (Liburd), Mohan, Ford, Wright, Youds, Ormondroyd, Shutt, Showler.
Nottingham F: Crossley; Lyttle, Phillips, Cooper, Chettle, Stone, Bart-Williams, Roy, Bohinen, Lee, Woan.

Bristol C (0) 0 15,592
Newcastle U (3) 5 *(Peacock, Sellars, Ferdinand, Gillespie, Lee)*
Bristol C: Kite; Hansen, Edwards, Munro, Bryant, Dryden, Bent, Kuhl, Seal, Agostino, Plummer (Hewlett).
Newcastle U: Hislop (Srnicek); Barton (Watson), Elliott, Fox, Peacock, Howey, Lee, Gillespie (Hottiger), Ferdinand, Ginola, Sellars.

Cardiff C (0) 0
Southampton (1) 3 *(Le Tissier 2, Shipperley)* 9041
Cardiff C: Williams D; Young, Searle, Harding (Rodgerson), Baddeley, Perry, Dobbs (Adams), Wigg, Haworth, Dale, Bird.
Southampton: Beasant; Dodd, Benali, Magilton, Hall, Monkou, Widdrington, Shipperley, Le Tissier, Maddison, Heaney.

Crewe Alex (1) 2 *(Edwards 2)*
Sheffield W (2) 2 *(Degryse 2)* 5702
Crewe Alex: Gayle; Murphy, Booty, Westwood, Macauley, Whalley, Garvey (Unsworth), Collins, Savage, Lennon, Edwards.
Sheffield W: Pressman; Atherton, Nolan, Pembridge, Pearce, Walker, Whittingham (Hyde), Waddle, Bright, Degryse, Sinton.

Hartlepool U (0) 0
Arsenal (2) 3 *(Adams 2, Wright)* 4945
Hartlepool U: Horne; Reddish, Lynch (Oliver), Billing, McGuckin, Lowe (Ford), Canham, Tait, Houchen (Henderson), Halliday, McAuley.
Arsenal: Seaman; Dixon, Winterburn, Parlour, Bould, Adams, Jensen, Wright, Merson, Bergkamp, Helder.

Huddersfield T (1) 2 *(Collins, Booth)*
Barnsley (0) 0 8264
Huddersfield T: Norman; Dyson, Cowan, Bullock, Scully, Sinton, Dalton, Reid, Booth, Dunn (Rowe), Collins.
Barnsley: Watson; Eaden, Bishop, Archdeacon, Davis, Shotton (Moses), Bullock, Redfearn, Payton, Liddell, Sheridan.

Leeds U (0) 0
Notts Co (0) 0 12,384
Leeds U: Lukic; Kelly, Worthington (Beesley), Palmer, Wetherall, Pemberton, White (Gray), Yeboah, Deane, McAllister, Speed.
Notts Co: Ward; Short (Arkins), Walker, Turner, Murphy, Galloway, Devlin, Simpson, White, Agana, Legg.

Oxford U (0) 1 *(Allen)*
QPR (1) 1 *(Dichio)* 7477
Oxford U: Carter; Robinson, Ford M, Smith, Elliott, Gilchrist, Rush, Massey, Biggins (Murphy), Ford R, Allen.
QPR: Roberts; Ready, Brevett, Barker, McDonald, Maddix, Impey, Holloway, Dichio, Osborn, Sinclair.

Shrewsbury T (1) 1 *(Lynch (pen))*
Derby Co (2) 3 *(Simpson, Stallard, Gabbiadini)*   3170
Shrewsbury T: Clarke; Scott, Lynch, Taylor, Hughes, Seabury, Berkley, Anthrobus, Spink, Evans, Reed (Dempsey).
Derby Co: Hoult; Kavanagh, Nicholson, Preece (Trollope), Yates, Wassall, Van der Laan, Stallard, Flynn (Wrack), Gabbiadini, Simpson.

Southend U (1) 2 *(Byrne, Jones)*
Crystal Palace (0) 2 *(Hopkin 2)*   4031
Southend U: Royce; Dublin, Powell, Lapper (Hone), Bodley, Gridelet, Marsh, Byrne, Thomson, Jones, Sussex (Hails).
Crystal Palace: Martyn; Edworthy, Vincent, Hopkin, Coleman, Shaw, Rodger (Ndah), Houghton, Matthew (Roberts), Dyer, Gordon (Pitcher).

Stockport Co (1) 1 *(Chalk)*
Ipswich T (1) 1 *(Sedgley)*   4865
Stockport Co: Edwards; Connolly, Todd, Bennett, Flynn, Gannon, Beaumont (Allen), Ware (Eckhardt), Helliwell, Armstrong, Chalk.
Ipswich T: Forrest; Stockwell, Taricco, Sedgley, Wark, Williams, Uhlenbeek, Thomsen, Gregory, Chapman, Slater (Milton).

Tramere R (0) 1 *(Aldridge)*
Oldham Ath (0) 0   5223
Tranmere R: Coyne; Stevens, Thomas, McGreal, Teale, Brannan, Morrissey (Moore), Aldridge, Bennett, Irons, Nevin.
Oldham Ath: Gerrard; McNiven, Makin, Henry, Jobson, Fleming, Halle, Bernard, McCarthy, Graham, Brennan (Beresford).

Watford (0) 1 *(Johnson)*
Bournemouth (1) 1 *(Jones)*   5037
Watford: Miller; Bazeley, Johnson, Foster, Millen, Ramage, Pitcher, Beadle, Mooney, Porter, Phillips (Moralee).
Bournemouth: Andrews; Young, Beardsmore, Morris, Murray, Mean, Holland, Robinson, Jones, Pennock, Brissett.

Wimbledon (1) 4 *(Holdsworth 2, Earle, Clarke)*
Charlton Ath (2) 5 *(Garland, Bowyer 3, Grant)*   3717
Wimbledon: Heald; Cunningham, Kimble, Jones, Reeves, Perry, Gayle, Earle, Ekoku (Clarke), Holdsworth, Leonhardsen (Goodman).
Charlton Ath: Salmon; Humphrey, Stuart, Garland, Rufus, Balmer, Newton, Nelson (Robson), Robinson (Grant), Leaburn, Bowyer.

Wycombe W (0) 0
Manchester C (0) 0   7443
Wycombe W: Hyde; Rowbotham, Hardyman, Crossley, Howard, Patterson, Carroll, Brown, De Souza, Williams, Farrell.
Manchester C: Immel; Edghill, Phelan, Curle, Symons, Brightwell, Kinkladze (Summerbee), Quinn, Rosler, Lomas, Beagrie.

20 SEPT

Aston Villa (3) 6 *(Draper, Yorke 2 (2 pens), Johnson, Heald (og), Southgate)*
Peterborough U (0) 0   19,602
Aston Villa: Bosnich; Charles, Wright, Southgate, McGrath, Ehiogu, Taylor (Fenton), Draper, Johnson, Townsend (Farrelly), Yorke.
Peterborough U: Sheffield; Williams, Rioch, Ebdon, Breen, Heald, Gregory, Carter (Morrison), Martindale (Power), Clark, Manuel.

Birmingham C (2) 3 *(Claridge, Hunt, Daish)*
Grimsby T (1) 1 *(Woods)*   7446
Birmingham C: Bennett; Poole, Cooper, Castle, Edwards, Daish, Hunt, Claridge, Finnan (Bowen), Charlery (Otto), Tait.

Grimsby T: Crichton; Laws (Lester), Croft, Handyside, Fickling, Groves, Watson, Dobbin, Woods, Livingstone, Southall.

Bristol R (0) 0
West Ham U (1) 1 *(Moncur)*   7103
Bristol R: Parkin; Pritchard, Gurney, Browning, Wright, Tillson, Skinner, Miller, Stewart, Channing (Wyatt), Taylor.
West Ham U: Miklosko; Breaker, Dicks, Potts, Martin, Bishop, Moncur, Dowie (Rieper), Cottee, Lazaridis, Slater (Williamson).

Coventry C (2) 2 *(Richardson, Lamptey)*
Hull C (0) 0   8915
Coventry C: Gould; Pickering, Hall, Williams, Borrows, Richardson, Telfer, Ndlovu, Lamptey, Isaias, Salako.
Hull C: Wilson; Lowthorpe, Lawford, Humphries (Hobson), Dewhurst, Abbott, Williams, Fewings (Fettis), Mason (Gordon), Windass, Mann.

Leicester C (1) 2 *(Robins, Joachim)*
Burnley (0) 0   11,142
Leicester C: Poole; Grayson, Whitlow, Willis, Walsh (Hill), Parker, Joachim, Taylor (McMahon), Lowe (Heskey), Roberts, Robins.
Burnley: Beresford; Parkinson, Vinnicombe, Harrison, Winstanley, Joyce, Harper, Heath, Philliskirk, Nogan, Eyres.

Liverpool (1) 2 *(McManaman, Thomas)*
Sunderland (0) 0   25,579
Liverpool: James; Jones, Harkness, Babb, Wright, Ruddock, McManaman, Redknapp, Collymore (Thomas), McAteer, Fowler.
Sunderland: Chamberlain; Kubicki, Scott, Bracewell, Ball (Smith), Melville, Michael Gray, Ord, Mullin, Gray P (Russell), Atkinson (Martin Gray).

Manchester U (0) 0
York C (1) 3 *(Barnes 2 (1 pen), Barras)*   29,049
Manchester U: Pilkington; Parker, Irwin, McGibbon, Sharpe, Pallister, Neville P (Cooke), Beckham, McClair, Davies (Bruce), Giggs.
York C: Kiely; McMillan, Hall, Pepper, Tutill, Barras, Murty, Williams, Barnes (Atkin), Peverell (Baker), Jordan.

Middlesbrough (2) 2 *(Mustoe, Fjortoft)*
Rotherham U (1) 1 *(Goater)*   13,280
Middlesbrough: Walsh; Cox, Morris, Vickers, Whyte, Whelan, Barmby, Pollock, Fjortoft, Mustoe, Moreno.
Rotherham U: Clarke; Wilder, Bowyer, Garner, Breckin, Blades, Goodwin, McGlashan, Jeffrey, Goater, Roscoe.

Millwall (0) 0
Everton (0) 0   12,053
Millwall: Keller; Newman, Thatcher, Bowry, Witter, Stevens, Van Blerk, Doyle, Malkin, Dixon (Fuchs), McRobert (Forbes).
Everton: Southall; Barrett, Hinchcliffe, Parkinson, Watson, Short, Samways, Horne, Amokachi, Rideout, Grant.

Norwich C (3) 6 *(Akinbiyi 2, Crook, Sheron 2, Gore (og))*
Torquay U (0) 1 *(Hathaway)*   7542
Norwich C: Marshall; Sutch, Bowen, Crook (Carey), Newsome, Prior, Simpson, Sheron, Akinbiyi, Johnson (Mills), Eadie (O'Neill).
Torquay U: Bayes; Barrow, Stamps, O'Riordan, Gore, Curran, Kelly, Buckle, Ndah (Hancox), Hathaway, Hall.

Reading (0) 1 *(Lovell)*
WBA (0) 1 *(Burgess)*   6948
Reading: Sheppard; Bernal, Lambert, Holsgrove (Quinn), Thorp (Williams M) (Kerr), McPherson, Gilkes, Parkinson, Nogan, Lovell, Jones.
WBA: Naylor; Burgess, Edwards, Coldicott, Mardon, Raven, Donovan, Gilbert, Taylor, Hunt, Hamilton.

Sheffield U (1) 2 *(Whitehouse (pen), Veart)*
Bury (0) 1 *(Stant)* 4075
Sheffield U: Kelly; Beard, Nilsen, Holland, Hodgson (Hodges), Blount, Ward, Battersby (Veart), Blake, Anthony (Rogers), Whitehouse.
Bury: Bracey; Sertori, Hulme (Rigby), Reid, Lucketti, Matthewson, Dawes, Carter, Stant (Johnson), Johnrose (Lancaster), Pugh.

Stoke C (0) 0
Chelsea (0) 0 15,574
Stoke C: Prudhoe; Clarkson, Sandford, Sigurdsson, Overson, Potter, Keen, Wallace, Peschisolido, Carruthers, Gleghorn.\
Chelsea: Kharine; Clarke, Minto, Gullitt, Johnsen, Sinclair, Newton, Hughes, Spencer (Furlong), Burley, Wise.

Swindon T (2) 2 *(Allison, Finney)*
Blackburn R (2) 3 *(Sutton, Shearer 2)* 14,740
Swindon T: Digby; Culverhouse, Bodin, McMahon (Gooden), Seagraves, Taylor, Robinson, O'Sullivan, Finney, Allison, Horlock.
Blackburn R: Flowers; Berg, Le Saux, Batty, Hendry, Pearce, Newell, Sherwood, Shearer, Sutton, Kenna.

Tottenham H (3) 4 *(Armstrong 2, Sheringham, Rosenthal)*
Chester C (0) 0 17,645
Tottenham H: Walker; Austin, Wilson, McMahon (Edinburgh), Calderwood (Scott), Mabbutt, Anderton, Dozzell, Armstrong, Sheringham, Rosenthal.
Chester C: Stewart; Jenkins (Alsford), Burnham, Fisher, Jackson, Whelan, Flitcroft, Priest, Rimmer, Murphy, Bishop.

Wolverhampton W (1) 2 *(Goodman, Wright)*
Fulham (0) 0 20,381
Wolverhampton W: Stowell; Smith (Emblen), Thompson, Rankine, Young, Richards, Daley (Williams), Goodman, Bull, Ferguson, Wright.
Fulham: Lange; Jupp, Herrera, Mison (Cusack), Angus, Blake, Thomas, Morgan, Brazil, Conroy, Hamill.

SECOND ROUND SECOND LEG

3 OCT
Arsenal (2) 5 *(Bergkamp 2, Wright 3)*
Hartlepool U (0) 0 27,194
Arsenal: Seaman; Dixon, Winterburn, Keown, Bould, Adams, Jensen, Wright, Merson (Helder), Bergkamp (Hartson), Parlour.
Hartlepool U: Jones; Ingram (Lynch), McAuley, Billing, McGuckin, Lowe, Oliver, Tait (Lee), Henderson, Halliday, Howard (Homer).
Arsenal won 8-0 on aggregate

Barnsley (1) 4 *(Payton 3, Rammell)*
Huddersfield T (0) 0 8192
Barnsley: Watson; Eaden, Moses (Bullock), Sheridan, Davis, Bishop, Rammell, Redfearn, Payton, Jackson, Archdeacon.
Huddersfield T: Francis; Dyson, Cowan, Bullock, Gray, Sinnott, Dalton (Dunn), Reid, Booth, Jepson, Collins (Baldry).
Barnsley won 4-2 on aggregate

Bournemouth (0) 1 *(Oldbury)*
Watford (0) 1 *(Bazeley)* 4365
Bournemouth: Andrews; Pennock, Beardsmore, Morris, Murray, Victory, Holland, Robinson, Jones (Town), Bailey, Brissett (Oldbury).
Watford: Miller; Lavin, Johnson, Foster, Millen, Ramage, Holdsworth, Palmer, Mooney, Porter (Bazeley), Moralee (Pitcher).
aet; Watford won 6-5 on penalties

Brentford (1) 2 *(Forster, Grainger (pen))*
Bolton W (0) 3 *(Patterson, McGinlay, Thompson)* 4861
Brentford: Dearden; Statham, Grainger, Davis (Harvey), Bates, Ashby, McGhee, Smith, Forster, Asaba, Taylor.
Bolton W: Branagan; McAnespie, Phillips, Sneekes (Todd), Bergsson, Stubbs, Fairclough, Lee, Patterson, McGinlay, Thompson (Green).
Bolton W won 4-2 on aggregate

Burnley (0) 0
Leicester C (0) 2 *(Robins 2)* 4553
Burnley: Beresford; Parkinson, Vinnicombe, Harrison, Winstanley, Randall, Weller (Francis), Joyce, Eyres, Nogan, McMinn.
Leicester C: Poole; Grayson, Whitlow, Rolling (Willis), Walsh, Parker, Joachim (Lewis), Blake, Lowe, Heskey (Robbins), Hill.
Leicester C won 4-0 on aggregate

Bury (2) 4 *(Stant 2, Carter, Johnson)*
Sheffield U (0) 2 *(Flo, Holland)* 2888
Bury: Kelly; Cross, Bimson, Reid, Lucketti, Matthewson, Hughes, Carter, Stant (Johnson), Rigby, Pugh.
Sheffield U: Kelly; Blount, Scott A (Hodges), Rogers, Nilsen, Tuttle, Beard (Battersby), Veart, Flo, Holland, Whitehouse.
Bury won 5-4 on aggregate

Charlton Ath (1) 3 *(Newton, Leaburn, Robinson)*
Wimbledon (1) 3 *(Holdsworth 2 (1 pen), Earle)* 9823
Charlton Ath: Salmon; Humphrey, Stuart, Garland (Robson), Chapple, Balmer, Newton, Grant (Linger), Robinson, Leaburn, Bowyer.
Wimbledon: Heald; Cunningham (Clarke), Elkins, Jones, Perry, Thorn, Ardley, Earle (Leonhardsen), Gayle (Harford), Holdsworth, Talboys.
aet; Charlton Ath won 8-7 on aggregate

Crystal Palace (1) 2 *(Vincent, McKenzie)*
Southend U (0) 0 6588
Crystal Palace: Martyn; Edworthy, Vincent, Roberts, Coleman, Shaw, Dyer (Launders), Houghton, McKenzie, Gordon, Hopkin.
Southend U: Royce; Dublin, Powell, Lapper, Bodley, Tilson (Hone), Marsh, Byrne (Thomson), Regis (Ansah), Jones, Hails.
Crystal Palace won 4-2 on aggregate

Fulham (0) 1 *(Cusack)*
Wolverhampton W (1) 5 *(Daley, Williams, Atkins, Goodman 2)* 6625
Fulham: Lange; Finnigan, Herrera, Mison (Jupp), Angus, Blake, Thomas, Morgan, Brazil, Conroy (Cusack), Hamill.
Wolverhampton W: Stowell; Rankine, Thompson, Atkins, Young, Richards, Daley, Goodman, Venus, Ferguson, Williams.
Wolverhampton W won 7-1 on aggregate

Grimsby T (0) 1 *(Southall)*
Birmingham C (0) 1 *(Bowen)* 3280
Grimsby T: Crichton; Laws, Croft, Handyside, Fickling, Groves, Childs (Clare), Dobbin, Jewell, Bonetti, Southall.
Birmingham C: Bennett; Poole, Cooper, Forsyth (Claridge), Edwards, Daish, Castle, Bowen, Finnan (Hunt), Otto (Ward), Charlery.
Birmingham C won 4-2 on aggregate

Ipswich T (1) 1 *(Thomsen)*
Stockport Co (0) 2 *(Armstrong, Gannon)* 8250
Ipswich T: Wright; Yallop, Taricco, Sedgley, Linighan, Williams (Milton), Ulhenbeek, Thomsen, Mathie, Gregory (Scowcroft), Slater.
Stockport Co: Edwards; Connelly, Todd, Bennett (Oliver), Flynn (Dinning), Gannon, Beaumont, Ware, Helliwell (Chalk), Armstrong, Eckhardt.
aet; Stockport Co won 3-2 on aggregate

Notts Co (1) 2 *(White 2 (1 pen))*
Leeds U (1) 3 *(McAllister, Couzens, Speed)*   12,477
Notts Co: Ward; Short, Legg, Walker, Strodder, Murphy, Gallagher, Galloway, White, Arkins (Jemson), Agana.
Leeds U: Lukic; Kelly, Beesley, Palmer, Wetherall, Couzens, Tinkler (Worthington), Yeboah, Deane, McAllister (Wallace), Speed.
Leeds U won 3-2 on aggregate

Peterborough U (1) 1 *(Martindale)*
Aston Villa (0) 1 *(Staunton)*   5745
Peterborough U: Sheffield; Ashley, Manuel, Clark, Breen, Heald, Carter, Le Bihan, Power, Martindale, Morrison.
Aston Villa: Bosnich; Charles, Wright, Southgate, McGrath, Ehiogu, Taylor, Draper (Fenton), Milosevic, Townsend, Yorke (Staunton).
Aston Villa won 7-1 on aggregate

QPR (0) 2 *(Ready, Gallen)*
Oxford U (1) 1 *(Robinson)*   9207
QPR: Roberts; Ready, Brevett, Barker (Wilkins), Maddix, McDonald (Goodridge), Impey, Holloway, Dichio, Gallen, Osborn (Brazier).
Oxford U: Carter; Robinson, Ford M, Smith, Elliott, Gilchrist, Rush (Marsh), Murphy, Moody (Biggins), Ford R, Allen.
aet; QPR won 3-2 on aggregate

Rotherham U (0) 0
Middlesbrough (0) 1 *(Vickers)*   6867
Rotherham U: Clarke; Wilder, Bowyer, Richardson, Breckin, Blades, Monington, Goodwin, Jeffrey, Goater, Roscoe.
Middlesbrough: Walsh; Cox (Liddle), Whelan, Vickers, Pearson, Whyte, Barmby, Pollock, Fjortoft, Mustoe, Hignett.
Middlesbrough won 3-1 on aggregate

WBA (1) 2 *(Burgess, Donovan)*   8163
Reading (1) 4 *(Lovell, Quinn 2 (1 pen), Lambert)*
WBA: Naylor; Burgess, Agnew, Coldicott, Mardon, Raven, Donovan, Gilbert (Smith), Taylor, Hunt (Ashcroft), Cunnington.
Reading: Sheppard; Bernal, Gooding, Holsgrove, Williams A, Wdowczyk, Gilkes, Parkinson, Quinn, Lovell, Lambert.
Reading won 5-3 on aggregate

York C (1) 1 *(Jordan)*
Manchester U (2) 3 *(Scholes 2, Cooke)*   9386
York C: Warrington; McMillan, Hall, Pepper, Tutill, Barras, Atkin, Williams, Barnes (Baker), Peverell (Naylor), Jordan.
Manchester U: Schmeichel; Neville G, Sharpe (Neville P), Bruce, Cooke (Keane), Pallister, Cantona, Beckham, Cole, Scholes, Giggs.
York C won 4-3 on aggregate

4 OCT

Blackburn R (1) 2 *(Shearer 2)*
Swindon T (0) 0   16,924
Blackburn R: Mimms; Berg, Kenna, Batty (Warhurst), Hendry, Pearce, Ripley, Sherwood, Shearer, Sutton, Newell.
Swindon T: Digby; Culverhouse, Bodin, McMahon, Seagraves, Taylor, Robinson, O'Sullivan, Finney, Allison, Horlock.
Blackburn R won 5-2 on aggregate

Chelsea (0) 0
Stoke C (0) 1 *(Peschisolido)*   16,272
Chelsea: Kharine; Burley, Barness, Gullit, Johnsen, Sinclair, Spackman (Stein), Hughes, Furlong, Peacock (Lee), Wise.
Stoke C: Prudhoe; Clarkson, Sandford, Sigurdsson, Oversson, Potter, Sturridge, Wallace, Peschisolido, Carruthers, Gleghorn.
Stoke C won 1-0 on aggregate

Chester C (1) 1 *(Chambers)*
Tottenham H (2) 3 *(Sheringham 2, Howells)*   5372
Chester C: Stewart; Alsford, Burnham, Fisher, Jackson, Whelan, Chambers (Quinn), Shelton, Regis (Rogers), Rimmer, Bishop (Barlow).
Tottenham H: Walker; Austin, Edinburgh, Howells, Calderwood, Mabbutt, Campbell (Dozzell), McMahon (Slade), Armstrong, Sheringham, Wilson.
Tottenham H won 7-1 on aggregate

Derby Co (1) 1 *(Willems)*
Shrewsbury T (0) 1 *(Rowbotham (pen))*   8825
Derby Co: Sutton S; Carsley, Nicholson, Preece, Yates, Rowett, Van der Laan, Willems, Flynn, Gabbiadini (Wrack), Powell.
Shrewsbury T: Edwards; Seabury, Lynch, Taylor, Withe, Woods (Dempsey), Rowbotham (Martin), King, Spink, Walton, Berkeley.
Derby Co won 4-2 on aggregate

Everton (0) 2 *(Hinchcliffe (pen), Stuart)*
Millwall (0) 4 *(Taylor 2, Rae (pen), Savage)*   14,891
Everton: Southall; Jackson (Unsworth), Barrett, Ablett, Short, Hinchcliffe, Grant, Horne, Stuart (Barlow), Rideout, Limpar.
Millwall: Keller; Newman, Thatcher (Taylor), Bowry, Witter, Stevens, Savage, Rae, Malkin (Webber), Fuchs (Dixon), Van Blerk.
aet; Millwall won 4-2 on aggregate

Hull C (0) 0
Coventry C (1) 1 *(Lamptey)*   6929
Hull C: Wilson; Lowthorpe, Lawford, Hobson, Humphries, Abbott, Williams (Peacock), Fewings (Mann), Brown (Gordon), Windass, Mann.
Coventry C: Filan; Hall, Burrows, Richardson, Busst, Williams, Telfer, Ndlovu (Christie), Lamptey, Strachan, Salako.
Coventry C won 3-0 on aggregate

Manchester C (2) 4 *(Rosler 2, Quinn, Curle (pen))*
Wycombe W (0) 0   11,474
Manchester C: Immel; Edghill (Margetson), Brightwell, Curle, Symons, Lomas, Kinkladze (Summerbee), Quinn, Rosler, Flitcroft (Brown), Beagrie.
Wycombe W: Hyde; Rowbotham, Hardyman, Howard, Cousins, Patterson, Carroll, Brown (McGavin), De Souza, Williams, Farrell.
Manchester C won 4-0 on aggregate

Newcastle U (0) 3 *(Barton, Albert, Ferdinand)*
Bristol C (1) 1 *(Agostino)*   36,357
Newcastle U: Hislop; Hottiger, Albert, Clark, Peacock, Watson, Barton, Brayson (Crawford), Ferdinand, Gillespie, Sellars (Holland).
Bristol C: Kite; Hansen, Edwards, Dryden, Bryant, Kuhl, Bent, Owers, Seal (Partridge), Agostino (Plummer), Paterson.
Newcastle U won 8-1 on aggregate

Nottingham F (1) 2 *(Pearce, Silenzi)*
Bradford C (0) 2 *(Showler, Ormondroyd)*   15,321
Nottingham F: Crossley; Lyttle, Pearce, Cooper, Chettle, Stone, Bart-Williams, Gemmill, Silenzi, Lee, Woan.
Bradford C: Ward; Huxford, Jacobs, Mitchell, Mohan, Ford, Wright, Youds, Ormondroyd, Hamilton, Showler.
Bradford C won 5-4 on aggregate

Oldham Ath (1) 1 *(Halle)*
Tranmere R (1) 3 *(Jones 2, Brannan)*   5335
Oldham Ath: Gerrard; McNiven, Makin, Henry, Jobson, Redmond, Halle, Graham (Olney), McCarthy, Beresford, Brennan.
Tranmere R: Coyne; Stevens, Thomas, McGreal, Teale, Garnett, Brannan, Jones, Bennett, Irons, Moore.
Tranmere R won 4-1 on aggregate

Sheffield W (3) 5 *(Degryse, Hirst, Bright 3)*
Crewe Alex (2) 2 *(Edwards, Lennon)* 　　　12,039
Sheffield W: Pressman; Atherton, Nolan, Pembridge, Briscoe, Walker, Hyde, Waddle, Hirst (Williams), Bright, Degryse (Whittingham).
Crewe Alex: Gayle; Murphy, Booty, Westwood, Macauley, Whalley, Garvey, Unsworth (Pope), Savage (Rivers), Lennon, Edwards.
Sheffield W won 7-4 on aggregate

Southampton (0) 2 *(Watson, Hall)*
Cardiff C (1) 1 *(Rodgerson)* 　　　12,709
Southampton: Beasant; Dodd, Benali (Charlton), Magilton, Hall, Monkou, Le Tissier, Watson, Shipperley, Maddison, Widdrington (Bennett).
Cardiff C: Williams D; Young, Searle, Harding, Baddeley, Perry (Evans T), Ingram, Rogerson, Haworth, Dale, Adams (Evans A).
Southampton won 5-1 on aggregate

Sunderland (0) 0
Liverpool (1) 1 *(Fowler)* 　　　20,560
Sunderland: Chamberlain; Kubicki, Scott, Bracewell, Kelly, Melville, Michael Gray (Russell), Ball, Smith, Gray P, Atkinson (Aiston).
Liverpool: James; Jones, Harkness, Scales, Babb, Ruddock, McManaman, Redknapp, Rush (Collymore), Barnes, Fowler (McAteer).
Liverpool won 3-0 on aggregate

Torquay U (0) 2 *(Barrow 2)*
Norwich C (0) 3 *(Ullathorne, Eadie, Mills)* 　　　1790
Torquay U: Bayes; Winter, Kelly, Stamps, Gore, Barrow, Hawthorne, Buckle, Ndah (Byng) (Laight), Hathaway, Hall (Mateu).
Norwich C: Gunn; Mills, Ullathorne, Carey, Newman, Polston, Adams, Sheron (Eadie), Akinbiyi (Fleck), Milligan, O'Neill.
Norwich won 9-3 on aggregate

West Ham U (0) 3 *(Dicks (pen), Bishop, Cottee)*
Bristol R (0) 0 　　　15,375
West Ham U: Miklosko; Breaker, Dicks, Potts, Rieper, Bishop, Moncur, Dowie, Cottee, Slater, Hughes.
Bristol R: Parkin; Pritchard, Gurney, Browning, Wright, Tillson, Sterling, Paul, Stewart, Skinner, Channing (Davis).
West Ham U won 4-0 on aggregate

THIRD ROUND

24 OCT
Barnsley (0) 0
Arsenal (2) 3 *(Bould, Bergkamp, Keown)* 　　　18,429
Barnsley: Watson; Eaden, Moses, Sheridan, Davis (Rammell), Bishop, Bullock, Redfearn, Payton, Liddell, Archdeacon.
Arsenal: Seaman; Dixon, Winterburn, Keown, Bould, Adams, Jensen (Hughes), Wright (Hartson), Merson, Bergkamp, Helder.

Birmingham C (1) 1 *(McGreal (og))*
Tranmere R (0) 1 *(Moore)* 　　　13,752
Birmingham C: Bennett; Poole, Cooper, Castle (Richardson), Edwards, Johnson, Hunt, Claridge, Charlery, Otto (Finnan), Tait.
Tranmere R: Coyne; Stevens, Thomas, McGreal, Teale, Jones, Brannan, Aldridge, Bennett (Branch), Moore, Nevin.

Bolton W (0) 0
Leicester C (0) 0 　　　9166
Bolton W: Branagan; McAnespie, Phillips, Sneekes, Bergsson, Stubbs, Fairclough, Patterson (Lee), Paatelainen (De Freitas), McGinlay, Thompson.
Leicester C: Poole; Grayson, Whitlow, Hill, Carey, Parker, Blake, Taylor, Lowe, Roberts, Rolling.

Reading (0)
Bury (2) *(Stant, Rigby)* 　　　6500
match abandoned 29 minutes, pitch waterlogged

Watford (1) 1 *(Phillips)*
Blackburn R (0) 2 *(Shearer, Newell)* 　　　17,035
Watford: Miller; Lavin, Bazeley, Foster, Millen, Ramage, Holdsworth, Palmer, Mooney, Moralee, Phillips.
Blackburn R: Flowers; Berg, Kenna, Batty, Hendry, Pearce, Ripley, Sherwood, Shearer, Newell, Warhurst.

25 OCT
Aston Villa (0) 2 *(Ehiogu, Yorke)*
Stockport Co (0) 0 　　　17,679
Aston Villa: Bosnich; Charles, Wright, Southgate, Ehiogu, Scimeca, Taylor, Draper, Milosevic, Townsend, Yorke.
Stockport Co: Edwards; Connelly, Todd, Bennett (Oliver), Flynn, Gannon, Beaumont, Ware, Williams (Landon), Armstrong, Chalk.

Coventry C (0) 3 *(Ndlovu (pen), Busst, Salako)*
Tottenham H (2) 2 *(Armstrong, Busst (og))* 　　　18,227
Coventry C: Filan; Borrows (Pickering), Hall, Williams J, Busst, Richardson, Telfer, Ndlovu, Lamptey, Strachan (Dublin), Salako.
Tottenham H: Walker; Austin, Wilson, Howells, Calderwood (Dozzell), Mabbutt, Campbell, McMahon, Armstrong, Sheringham, Rosenthal.

Crystal Palace (2) 2 *(Hopkin 2)*
Middlesbrough (2) 2 *(Barmby, Hignett)* 　　　11,873
Crystal Palace: Martyn; Edworthy, Gordon, Roberts, Coleman, Shaw, Hopkin, Houghton, Dyer, McKenzie, Pitcher.
Middlesbrough: Walsh; Cox, Morris, Vickers, Pearson, Whelan, Barmby, Pollock, Fjortoft (Hendrie), Mustoe, Hignett (Moore).

Derby Co (0) 0
Leeds U (0) 1 *(Speed)* 　　　16,030
Derby Co: Hoult; Carsley, Nicholson, Trollope, Yates, Rowett, Van der Laan, Flynn (Powell), Willems, Gabbiadini, Simpson (Wrack).
Leeds U: Lukic; Kelly, Worthington, Palmer, Wetherall, Pemberton, Beesley, Yeboah (Whelan), Deane, McAllister, Speed.

Liverpool (1) 4 *(Scales, Fowler, Rush, Harkness)*
Manchester C (0) 0 　　　29,394
Liverpool: James; McAteer, Harkness, Babb, Wright, Scales, McManaman, Redknapp (Ruddock), Rush, Barnes, Fowler (Collymore).
Manchester C: Immel; Edghill, Brightwell, Curle, Symons, Lomas, Foster, Quinn, Rosler (Brown), Summerbee, Kinkladze.

Millwall (0) 0
Sheffield W (1) 2 *(Pembridge, Whittingham)* 　　　12,822
Millwall: Keller; Newman, Van Blerk, Bowry, Witter, Stevens, Savage (Taylor), Rae, Fuchs (Dixon), Malkin, Doyle (Black).
Sheffield W: Pressman; Williams, Nolan, Atherton, Ingesson, Walker, Pembridge, Waddle, Hirst (Bright), Whittingham, Sinton.

Norwich C (0) 0
Bradford C (0) 0 　　　11,649
Norwich C: Gunn; Ullathorne, Bowen, Crook, Newsome, Prior, Milligan (Fleck), Eadie, Ward, Johnson, O'Neill.
Bradford C: Ward; Liburd, Jacobs, Mitchell, Mohan, Ford, Wright (Murray), Youds, Ormondroyd (Shutt), Hamilton, Showler.

QPR (1) 3 *(Sinclair, Impey, Atkin (og))*
York C (1) 1 *(Barnes)* 12,972
QPR: Roberts; Bardsley, Brevett, Ready, Yates, Maddix, Impey, Wilkins, Dichio, Barker, Sinclair.
York C: Warrington; McMillan, Hall, Jordan, Tutill, Barras (Atkin), Matthews, Williams, Barnes, Peverell, Murty.

Southampton (1) 2 *(Watson, Shipperley)*
West Ham U (1) 1 *(Cottee)* 11,059
Southampton: Beasant; Dodd, Benali, Venison, Hall, Monkou, Le Tissier, Watson, Shipperley, Hughes, Heaney.
West Ham U: Miklosko; Potts, Dicks, Rieper, Martin, Bishop, Moncur, Dowie, Cottee, Slater, Hughes.

Stoke C (0) 0
Newcastle U (2) 4 *(Beardsley 2, Ferdinand, Peacock)* 23,000
Stoke C: Prudhoe; Clarkson, Sandford, Sigurdsson, Oversson, Potter (Cranson), Keen, Wallace, Peschisolido, Carruthers, Gleghorn.
Newcastle U: Hislop; Barton, Elliott, Clark, Peacock, Howey (Albert), Lee (Watson), Beardsley, Ferdinand, Ginola, Gillespie.

Wolverhampton W (0) 0
Charlton Ath (0) 0 22,481
Wolverhampton W: Jones; Rankine, Thompson, Atkins, Young, Richards, Daley, Goodman, Bull, Cowans, Birch (Wright).
Charlton Ath: Salmon; Humphrey, Stuart, Walsh, Chapple, Rufus, Newton, Nelson, Robinson (Grant), Leaburn, Bowyer.

7 NOV
Reading (0) 2 *(Lucketti (og), Quinn)*
Bury (0) 1 *(Rigby)* 10,329
Reading: Sheppard; Brown, Gooding, Codner (Lambert), Bernal, McPherson, Gilkes, Parkinson, Nogan, Lovell (Quinn), Holsgrove.
Bury: Kelly; Cross, Bimson, Reid, Lucketti, Matthewson, Hughes, Johnson (Carter), Stant, Rigby (Daws), Pugh.

THIRD ROUND REPLAYS

Bradford C (1) 3 *(Showler, Ormondroyd, Tolson) aet*
Norwich C (2) 5 *(Ward 3, Fleck, Johnson)* 8665
Bradford C: Ward; Huxford (Liburd), Jacobs, Mitchell, Mohan, Ford, Wright (Murray), Hamilton, Ormondroyd, Tolson (Robson), Showler.
Norwich C: Gunn; Bradshaw, Ullathorne, Crook, Newman (Akinbiyi), Prior (Mills), Milligan, Fleck, Ward, Johnson, Eadie.

8 NOV
Charlton Ath (0) 1 *(Robinson) aet*
Wolverhampton W (1) 2 *(Emblen, Atkins)* 10,909
Charlton Ath: Ammann; Humphrey, Stuart, Walsh (Jones), Chapple, Rufus, Newton (Grant), Nelson, Robinson, Leaburn, Bowyer.
Wolverhampton W: Jones; Rankine, Thompson, Atkins, Young, De Wolf (Birch), Daley, Williams (Bull), Goodman, Emblen, Cowans.

Leicester C (0) 2 *(Robins, Roberts)*
Bolton W (1) 3 *(McGinlay, Sneekes, Curcic)* 14,884
Leicester C: Kalac; Kamark (Grayson), Whitlow, Hill, Carey (Joachim), Parker, Lowe, Taylor, Robins, Roberts, Rolling.
Bolton W: Branagan; McAnespie, Powell, Curcic, Bergsson, Stubbs (Patterson), Lee, Sneekes (Green), Fairclough, McGinlay, Thompson.

Middlesbrough (1) 2 *(Hignett, Fjortoft)*
Crystal Palace (0) 0 16,150
Middlesbrough: Walsh; Liddle, Morris, Vickers, Pearson, Pollock, Robson, Moreno, Fjortoft, Hignett (Blackmore), Moore.
Crystal Palace: Martyn; Edworthy, Gordon (Vincent), Roberts, Coleman, Shaw (Sparrow), Hopkin, Houghton (Matthew), Dyer, McKenzie, Pitcher.

Tranmere R (0) 1 *(Aldridge) aet*
Birmingham C (0) 3 *(Rushfeldt, Charley 2)* 9151
Tranmere R: Coyne; Stevens, Thomas, McGreal, Teale, Jones, Brannan, Aldridge, Bennett (Branch), Moore, Nevin.
Birmingham C: Bennett; Poole, Johnson, Ward, Edwards, Daish, Hunt (Otto), Claridge, Rushfeldt (Charley), Castle (Finnan), Tait.

FOURTH ROUND

28 NOV
Reading (1) 2 *(Nogan, Morley)*
Southampton (1) 1 *(Moncur)* 13,742
Reading: Sheppard; Brown, Gooding, Wdowczyk, Bernal (Swales), McPherson, Jones (Gilkes), Parkinson, Morley (Quinn), Nogan, Holsgrove.
Southampton: Beasant; Dodd, Benali (Watson), Magilton (Maddison), Hall, Moncur, Le Tissier, Venison, Shipperley, Hughes, Warren (Heaney).\

29 NOV
Arsenal (1) 2 *(Wright (pen), Hartson)*
Sheffield W (1) 1 *(Degryse)* 35,361
Arsenal: Seaman; Dixon, Winterburn, Jensen, Bould, Adams, Platt, Wright, Merson, Bergkamp (Helder), Hartson.
Sheffield W: Pressman; Atherton, Nolan, Degryse, Watts, Walker, Hyde, Waddle, Bright (Hirst), Whittingham, Sinton.

Aston Villa (0) 1 *(Townsend)*
QPR (0) 0 24,951
Aston Villa: Bosnich; Charles, Wright, Southgate, McGrath, Ehiogu, Yorke, Draper (Scimeca), Milosevic, Johnson (Staunton), Townsend.
QPR: Roberts; Bardsley, Brazier, Barker, Yates, McDonald, Impey, Wilkins, Gallen (Hateley), Ready, Sinclair.

Leeds U (2) 2 *(Deane, Yeboah)*
Blackburn R (0) 1 *(Kelly (og))* 26,006
Leeds U: Lukic; Kelly, Dorigo, Palmer, Wetherall, Ford, Brolin (Whelan), Yeboah, Deane, McAllister, Speed (Bowman).
Blackburn R: Flowers; Kenna, Le Saux, Batty, Hendry, Berg, McKinlay (Warhurst), Sherwood, Shearer, Newell (Sutton), Ripley.

Liverpool (0) 0
Newcastle U (0) 1 *(Watson)* 40,077
Liverpool: James; Jones, Harkness, Babb, Wright, Ruddock (Kennedy), McManaman, McAteer, Collymore, Barnes, Fowler.
Newcastle U: Hislop; Barton, Beresford, Clark, Peacock, Howey, Lee, Beardsley, Ferdinand (Watson), Ginola, Gillespie.

Middlesbrough (0) 0
Birmingham C (0) 0 28,031
Middlesbrough: Walsh; Cox, Morris, Vickers, Pearson, Liddle, Barmby, Pollock, Fjortoft (Hignett), Juninho, Stamp.
Birmingham C: Bennett; Forsyth, Johnson (Donowa), Castle, Edwards, Daish, Hunt, Claridge, Francis, Hill, Frain.

Norwich C (0) 0
Bolton W (0) 0   13,820
Norwich C: Gunn; Crook (Scott), Ullathorne, Polston, Newsome, Prior, Bowen, Fleck, Ward, Eadie, Adams.
Bolton W: Branagan; Green, Phillips, Curcic, Bergsson, Taggart, Fairclough, Todd, Patterson, McGinlay, Thompson.

Wolverhampton W (2) 2 *(Venus, Ferguson)*
Coventry C (0) 1 *(Williams)*   24,628
Wolverhampton W: Stowell; Rankine, Thompson, Ferguson, Law, Richards, Venus, Goodman, Bull, Atkins, Birch.
Coventry C: Ogrizovic; Pickering (Lamptey), Hall, Richardson, Rennie, Williams, Telfer, Ndlovu, Dublin, Isaias (Gould), Strachan.

FOURTH ROUND REPLAYS

20 DEC
Birmingham C (2) 2 *(Francis 2)*
Middlesbrough (0) 0   19,878
Birmingham C: Bennett; Poole, Frain, Forsyth, Edwards, Daish, Hunt, Claridge, Francis (Donowa), Hill, Richardson (Barnes).
Middlesbrough: Walsh; Cox, Fleming (Moore), Vickers, Pearson, White, Stamp, Pollock, Fjortoft, Juninho, Hendrie.

Bolton W (0) 0
Norwich C (0) 0   8736
Bolton W: Branagan; Green, Phillips (Whittaker), Curcic, Bergsson, Taggart, Fairclough, Todd, De Freitas, McGinlay, Patterson.
Norwich C: Gunn; Polston, Ullathorne, Milligan, Newsome, Prior, Bowen, Fleck (Adams), Ward, Carey, Sutch.
aet; Norwich C won 3-2 on penalties.

FIFTH ROUND

10 JAN
Arsenal (1) 2 *(Wright 2)*
Newcastle U (0) 0   37,857
Arsenal: Seaman; Dixon, Winterburn, Keown, Bould (Jensen), Adams, Platt, Wright, Merson, Bergkamp, Helder.
Newcastle U: Srnicek; Barton, Albert, Beresford, Peacock, Howey, Lee, Beardsley, Ferdinand, Ginola, Watson.

Aston Villa (0) 1 *(Johnson)*
Wolverhampton W (0) 0   39,277
Aston Villa: Bosnich; Charles, Wright, Southgate, McGrath, Ehiogu, Yorke, Draper, Milosevic, Johnson (Taylor), Townsend.
Wolverhampton W: Stowell; Thompson (Law), Young, Atkins, Venus (Foley), Richards, Rankine, Goodman, Bull, Ferguson, Pearce (Dennison).

Leeds U (2) 2 *(Masinga, Speed)*
Reading (1) 1 *(Quinn)*   21,023
Leeds U: Beeney; Kelly, Dorigo, Palmer, Wetherall, Ford, Brolin, Wallace (Couzens), Masinga (Harte), McAllister, Speed.
Reading: Nixon; Brown, Gooding, Parkinson (Lambert), Williams A, Jones, Quinn, Thorp (Gilkes), Morley, Nogan, Holsgrove.

Norwich C (0) 1 *(Fleck)*
Birmingham C (0) 1 *(Francis)*   13,028
Norwich C: Gunn; Bradshaw, Bowen, Molby, Newsome (Prior), Polston, Adams, Fleck, Ward (Scott), Eadie, O'Neill (Ullathorne).
Birmingham C: Sansome; Poole, Frain, Forsyth, Edwards, Daish, Hunt (Bowen), Claridge, Francis, Richardson (Cooper), Donowa.

FIFTH ROUND REPLAY

24 JAN
Birmingham C (0) 2 *(Bowen, Daish)*
Norwich C (0) 1 *(Molby)*   21,097
Birmingham C: Griemink; Poole, Frain, Forsyth, Edwards, Daish, Donowa, Claridge, Francis (Bull), Castle (Tait), Doherty (Bowen).
Norwich C: Gunn; Bradshaw, Bowen, Molby, Polston, Prior, Adams, Fleck, Ward, Eadie (Johnson), O'Neill.

SEMI-FINAL FIRST LEG

11 FEB
Birmingham C (1) 1 *(Francis)*
Leeds U (0) 2 *(Yeboah, Whyte (og))* 24,781
Birmingham C: Griemink; Bass, Frain, Forsyth (Otto), Whyte, Johnson, Hunt, Claridge, Francis, Sheridan (Bowen), Cooper (Donowa).
Leeds U: Lukic; Kelly, Dorigo, Palmer, Beesley, Wetherall, Ford (Radebe), Wallace (Deane), Yeboah, McAllister, Speed.

14 FEB
Arsenal (2) 2 *(Bergkamp 2)*
Aston Villa (1) 2 *(Yorke 2)*   37,562
Arsenal: Seaman; Dixon, Winterburn, Hillier, Keown, Linigan, Jensen, Wright, Merson, Bergkamp, Helder (Parlour).
Aston Villa: Bosnic; Charles, Wright, Southgate, Ehiogu, Staunton, Yorke, Draper, Milosevic, Johnson, Townsend.

SEMI-FINAL SECOND LEG

21 FEB
Aston Villa (0) 0
Arsenal (0) 0   39,334
Aston Villa: Bosnich; Charles, Wright, Southgate, Ehiogu, Staunton (Scimeca), Taylor (McGrath), Draper, Milosevic, Townsend, Yorke.
Arsenal: Seaman; Dixon, Winterburn (Platt), Hillier, Keown, Linighan, Parlour, Wright, Merson, Bergkamp, Morrow.
aet; Aston Villa won on away goals
.

25 FEB
Leeds U (0) 3 *(Masinga, Yeboah, Deane)*
Birmingham C (0) 0   35,435
Leeds U: Lukic; Kelly, Dorigo (Radebe), Palmer, Beesley, Wetherall, Masinga (Brolin), Wallace, Yeboah, McAllister, Deane.
Birmingham C: Griemink; Poole, Whyte (Hunt), Forsyth (Donowa), Edwards, Johnson, Richardson, Claridge, Francis (Bowen), Sheridan, Frain.
Leeds U won 5-1 on aggregate.

FINAL (AT WEMBLEY)

24 MAR
Aston Villa (1) 3 *(Milosevic, Taylor, Yorke)*
Leeds U (0) 0   77,056
Aston Villa: Bosnich; Charles, Wright, Southgate, McGrath, Ehiogu, Taylor, Draper, Milosevic, Townsend, Yorke.
Leeds U: Lukic; Kelly, Radebe (Brolin), Palmer, Wetherall, Pemberton, Gray, Ford (Deane), Yeboah, McAllister, Speed.
Referee: R. Hart (Darlington).

FOOTBALL LEAGUE COMPETITION ATTENDANCES

LEAGUE CUP ATTENDANCES

Totals	Season	Attendances	Games	Average
	1960/61	1,204,580	112	10,755
	1961/62	1,030,534	104	9,909
	1962/63	1,029,893	102	10,097
	1963/64	945,265	104	9,089
	1964/65	962,802	98	9,825
	1965/66	1,205,876	106	11,376
	1966/67	1,394,553	118	11,818
	1967/68	1,671,326	110	15,194
	1968/69	2,064,647	118	17,497
	1969/70	2,299,819	122	18,851
	1970/71	2,035,315	116	17,546
	1971/72	2,397,154	123	19,489
	1972/73	1,935,474	120	16,129
	1973/74	1,722,629	132	13,050
	1974/75	1,901,094	127	14,969
	1975/76	1,841,735	140	13,155
	1976/77	2,236,636	147	15,215
	1977/78	2,038,295	148	13,772
	1978/79	1,825,643	139	13,134
	1979/80	2,322,866	169	13,745
	1980/81	2,051,576	161	12,743
	1981/82	1,880,682	161	11,681
	1982/83	1,679,756	160	10,498
	1983/84	1,900,491	168	11,312
	1984/85	1,876,429	167	11,236
	1985/86	1,579,916	163	9,693
	1986/87	1,531,498	157	9,755
	1987/88	1,539,253	158	9,742
	1988/89	1,552,780	162	9,585
	1989/90	1,836,916	168	10,934
	1990/91	1,675,496	159	10,538
	1991/92	1,622,337	164	9,892
	1992/93	1,558,031	161	9,677
	1993/94	1,744,120	163	10,700
	1994/95	1,530,478	157	9,748
	1995/96	1,776,060	162	10,963

COCA-COLA CUP 1995–96 GATES BREAKDOWN

Round	Aggregate	Games	Average
One	197,112	56	3,520
Two	672,978	64	10,515
Three	323,854	22	14,721
Four	235,230	10	23,523
Five	132,282	5	26,456
Semi-finals	137,548	4	34,387
Final	77,056	1	77,056
Total	1,776,060	162	10,963

AUTO WINDSCREENS SHIELD 1995–96 GATES BREAKDOWN

Round	Aggregate	Games	Average
One	86,358	48	1,799
Two	37,651	16	2,353
Area q/f	21,155	8	2,644
Area s/f	18,437	4	4,609
Area finals	25,812	4	6,453
Final	35,235	1	35,235
Total	224,648	81	2,773

ANGLO-ITALIAN CUP 1995–96 GATES BREAKDOWN

(Games played in England only)

Round	Aggregate	Games	Average
One	93,045	16	5,815
Semi-final	14,681	2	7,341
Domestic-final	18,476	2	9,238
Final	12,663	1	12,663
Total	138,865	21	6,613

ANGLO-ITALIAN CUP 1995–96

INTERNATIONAL STAGE

5 SEPT

GROUP A

Ancona (0) 1 *(Lemme)*
Oldham Ath (0) 0   311
Ancona: Orlandoni; Franchini, Esposito, Ricci, Pellegrini, Bartolini (Magnani), Tentoni, Sesia, Artistico, Modica, Lemme.
Oldham Ath: Hallworth; McNiven, Makin, Henry (Redmond), Jobson, Fleming, Halle, Bernard, McCarthy, Richardson (Banger), Brennan (Rickers).

Birmingham C (2) 2 *(Bowen 2)*
Genoa (2) 3 *(Bortolazzi, Nappi 2)*   20,430
Birmingham C: Bennett; Hiley, Whyte, Ward, Edwards, Johnson, Hunt, Castle (Doherty), Bowen, Charley (Martin), Cooper (Forsyth).
Genoa: Spagnulo; Torrente, Francesconi (Rossi), Delli Carri, Nappi, Bortolazzi, Montella, Van't Schip (Corrado), Turrone, Ruotolo (Magoni), Onorati.

Cesena (1) 2 *(Hubner, Comandini)*
Port Vale (0) 2 *(Glover L, Mills)*   820
Cesena: Santarelli; Codispoti, Favi (Piangerelli), Teodorani, Ponzo, Hubner (Comandini), Maenza (Farabegoli), Bizzarri, Viali, Rivalta, Ceccarelli.
Port Vale: Musslewhite; Hill (Talbot), Tankard, Bogie, Griffiths, Glover D, McCarthy, Porter, Mills, Glover L, Guppy.

Luton T (1) 1 *(Guentchev (pen))*   2352
Perugia (2) 4 *(Negri 2 (1 pen), Comacchini, Cottini)*
Luton T: Davis K; James, Skelton, Davis S, Evers, Thorpe (Marshall), Linton, Guentchev (Woodsford), Oldfield (Waddock), Hughes, Harvey.
Perugia: Fabbri; Tedesco, Atzori, Pagano (Baiocco), Cottini (Beghetto), Tasso, Negri, Materassi, Cornacchini (Meacci), Camplone, Notaristefano.

GROUP B

Foggia (0) 1 *(Bresciani)*
Stoke C (0) 1 *(Peschisolido)*   4200
Foggia: Brunner; Gasparini, Parisi, Sciacca (Tedesco), Oshadogan, Bucaro, Baglieri (Bresciani), Giacobbo, Amoruso (Grandini), Consagra, Anastasi.
Stoke C: Sinclair; Clarkson, Potter, Sigurdsson, Oversson, Orlygsson, Keane (Gayle), Wallace, Peschisolido (Scott), Carruthers, Gleghorn.

Ipswich T (0) 2 *(Mathie, Tanner)*
Reggiana (1) 1 *(Di Costanzo)*   9525
Ipswich T: Forest; Stockwell, Tarrico, Sedgeley, Palmer, Williams, Uhlenbeek, Tanner, Mathie, Chapman (Gregory), Slater (Milton).
Reggiana: Gandini; Tamgorra (Caini), Orfei, Ziliani (Cevoli), La Spada, Schenardi, Di Mauro (Simutenkov), Sgarbossa, Strada, Di Costanzo, Pietranera.

Salernitana (0) 0
WBA (0) 0   2200
Salernitana: Franzone; Cudini, Grassadonia, Amore (De Silvestro), Frezza, Landini, Juliano, Bevo (Grimaudo), Martinelli (Pirri), Bachini, Logarzo.
WBA: Naylor; Smith, Edwards, Coldicott, Mardon, Brien, Donovan, Gilbert, Taylor, Hunt (Ashcroft), Hamilton.

Southend U (0) 0
Brescia (0) 0   2849
Southend U: Royce; Dublin, Powell, Bodley, Lapper (Hone), Gridelet, Marsh (Tilson), Byrne, Jones, Ansah, Hayes (Iorfa).
Brescia: Cusin; Costi, Savino, Mezzanotti, Luzardi, Bonometti, Neri, Volpi, Lunini (Campolonghi) Giunta, Ambrosetti.

11 OCT

GROUP A

Oldham Ath (0) 0
Cesena (0) 0   4766
Oldham Ath: Gerrard; McNiven, Serrant, Snodin, Jobson, Graham, Halle, Richardson, Beckford, Olney, Beresford.
Cesena: Santarelli; Farabegoli S, Viali, Codispoti, Medri (Scugugia), Affatigato, Piraccini, Teodorani (Comandini), Maenza, Ponzo, Hubner (Bombardini).

Port Vale (0) 2 *(Talbot, Guppy)*
Ancona (0) 0   3440
Port Vale: Van Heusden; Hill, Tankard (Stokes), Talbot (Walker), Griffiths, Glover D, McCarthy (Porter), Bogie, Mills, Naylor, Guppy.
Ancona: Vinti; Corino, Cornacchia, Iacobelli, Tomei, Tentoni, Cavaliere (Pellegrini), Sesia, Lemme, Esposito (Modica), Lucidi (Artistico).

Genoa (3) 4 *(Skuhravy, Montella 2, Nicola)*
Luton T (0) 0   1000
Genoa: Pastine (Spagnulo); Francesconi, Delli Carri, Cavallo, Montella, Skuhravy, Van't Schip (Pagliarini), Turrone, Nicola, Onorati, Rossi (Corrado).
Luton T: Davis K; James (Alexander), Johnson, Davis S, McLaren, Pedersen, Linton, Oakes, Oldfield (Thorpe), Guentchev (Woodsford), Harvey.

Perugia (0) 0
Birmingham C (0) 1 *(Castle)*   1200
Perugia: Braglia; Camplone, Materazzi, Tasso, Cottini, Lombardo, Rocco, Goretti (Tedesco), Negri, Baiocco, Russo (Meacci).
Birmingham C: Bennett; Poole, Cooper, Castle, Edwards, Johnson, Hunt (Martin), Claridge, Rae (Tait), Otto (Richardson), Finnan.

GROUP B

Brescia (1) 2 *(Lunini, Ambrosetti)*
Ipswich T (0) 2 *(Sedgley, Mason)*   1000
Brescia: Di Sarno; Filippini E, Savino, Volpi (Baronio), Adani, Luzardi, Filippini A, Campolonghi, Lunini (Pirlo), Lerda (Neri), Ambrosetti.
Ipswich T: Wright; Uhlenbeek, Yallop, Sedgeley, Mowbray, Linighan, Milton (Gregory), Mason, Mathie, Scowcroft (Tanner), Slater.

Reggiana (0) 1 *(Palombo)*
Southend U (0) 1 *(Tilson)*   800
Reggiana: Gandini; Cevoli, Mazzola, Strada (La Spada), Mozzini (Caini), Pietranera, Orfei, Di Costanzo (Palombo), Colucci, Tarivello, Di Mauro.
Southend U: Royce; Hone, Powell, Lapper, Bodley, Tilson, Marsh, Byrne, Regis, Jones (Ansah) (Iorfa), Hails.

Stoke C (1) 2 *(Peschisolido, Wallace)*
Salernitana (1) 2 *(Amore (pen), Logarzo (pen))*   5071
Stoke C: Prudhoe; Clarkson, Sandford, Brightwell (Devlin), Dreyer, Potter, Sturridge, Wallace, Peschisolido, Carruthers, Gleghorn.
Salernitana: Franzone; Grassadonia, Breda, Gattuso (Grimaudo), Cudini, Amore, Frezza, Landini (Ricchetti), Pirri, Logarzo, Ferrante (Spinelli).

WBA (1) 1 *(Herbert)*
Foggia (1) 2 *(Sciacca (pen), Marazzini)* 8155
WBA: Naylor; Burgess, Smith, Coldicott, Herbert (Hunt),Raven, Donovan, Gilbert, Taylor, Ashcroft (Rees), Cunnington.
Foggia: Brunner; Gasparini (Parisi), Anastasi (Grandini), Sciacca, Oshadogan, Bianchini, Marazzina, Giacobbo, Baglieri, Zanchetta, Consagra (Diorcia).

8 NOV

GROUP A

Cesena (0) 2 *(Maenza, Scugugia)*
Luton T (0) 1 *(Marshall)* 461
Cesena: Santarelli; Albonetti, Codispoti, Affatigato, Aloisi (Scugugia), Medri, Maenza, Farabegoli, Bombardini (Comandini), Pensalfini (Viroli), Bizzarri.
Luton T: Davis K; Patterson (Simpson), Upson, Davis S, McLaren, Vilstrup, Alexander, Oakes (Douglas), Riseth, Marshall, Harvey.

Oldham Ath (2) 2 *(McCarthy, Wilkinson)*
Perugia (0) 0 3760
Oldham Ath: Hallworth; McNiven, Serrant, Rickers, Redmond, Fleming, Halle, Wilkinson (Makin), McCarthy (Beckford), Richardson (Hughes), Beresford.
Perugia: Fabbri; Camplone, Beghetto (Lombardo), Goretti, Cottini, Atzori, Pagano, Allegri, Meacci, Giunti, Russo (Di Maio).

Port Vale (0) 0
Genoa (0) 0 3282
Port Vale: Musselwhite; Hill (Glover L), Tankard (Guppy), Talbot, Stokes, Bogie, McCarthy, Porter, Mills, Naylor (Foyle), Lawton.
Genoa: Pastine; Francesconi, Delli Carri, Cavallo, Nappi, Skuhravy, Van't Schip (Bortolazzi), Turrone, Nicola, Ruotolo, Onorati.

GROUP B

Foggia (0) 0
Ipswich T (1) 1 *(Mason)* 2000
Foggia: Brunner; Gasparini, Parisi (Grandini), Sciacca, Oshadogan, Di Bari, Anastasi, Giacobbo, Amoruso (Kolyvanov), Di Corcia, Marazzina (De Vincenzo).
Ipswich T: Forrest; Stockwell, Tarrico, Wark, Mowbray, Williams, Milton, Tanner (Thomsen), Chapman, Gregory (Slater), Mason.

Salernitana (1) 2 *(Landini 2)*
Southend U (0) 1 *(Regis)* 2000
Salernitana: Franzone; Gattuso, Cudini, Frezza, Landini (Breda), Juliano, Rachini, Ricchetti (De Silvestro), Pirri, Logarzo, Ferrante (Spinelli).
Southend U: Royce; Hone, Powell, Lapper, Bodley, Gridelet, Tilson, Byrne (Regis), Belsvik, Read (Thomson), Hails.

Stoke C (0) 1 *(Dreyer)*
Brescia (0) 1 *(Neri)* 4193
Stoke C: Prudhoe; Cranson, Sandford, Sigurdsson, Oversson, Potter (Dreyer), Keane (Devlin), Wallace, Gayle, Sturridge, Gleghorn.
Brescia: Cusin; Luzardi (Neri), Battistini, Sabau, Saurini, Mezzanotti, Lerda, Filippini A, Ambrozetti, Volpi (Filippini E), Francini (Adani).

WBA (0) 2 *(Hunt, Taylor)*
Reggiana (1) 1 *(Simutenkov)* 6009
WBA: Naylor; Burgess, King, Coldicott, Marden, Raven, Donovan (Taylor), Gilbert, Ashcroft, Hunt, Hamilton.
Reggiana: Gandini; Orfei, Caini (Ziwi), La Spada, Orlandini, Taribello, Ziliani, Colucci (Schenardi), Mencuccini, Simutenkov, (Pietranera), Di Costanzo.

GROUP A

15 NOV

Ancona (0) 1 *(Sesia)*
Birmingham C (2) 2 *(Edwards, Tentoni (og)* 1500
Ancona: Orlandoni; Corino (Magnani), Esposito, Cornacchia, Tomei, Tentoni, Cavaliere (Bartolini), Sesia, Lemme (Artistico), Modica, Lucidi.
Birmingham C: Bennett; Forsyth, Johnson (Cooper), Castle (Richardson), Edwards, Daish, Hunt, Charlery, Rushfeldt, Otto, Tait (Finnan).

13 DEC

GROUP A

Birmingham C (1) 3 *(Claridge, Tamburini (og), Hunt)*
Cesena (0) 1 *(Comndini)* 7813
Birmingham C: Bennett (Griemink); Poole, Frain, Forsyth, Edwards (Rae), Richardson, Hunt, Claridge, Francis (Charlery), Preece, Donowa.
Cesena: Sardini; Zanetti, Tamburini, Medri, Albonetti, Farabegoli, Maenza, Piraccini (Affatigato), Comandini (Chiaretti), Favi (Ponzo), Teodorani.

Genoa (0) 0
Oldham Ath (0) 0 1500
Genoa: Spagnulo; Francesconi, Delli Carri, Galante, Cavallo, Van't Schip (Bortolazzi), Turrone, Magoni, Ruotolo, Pagliarini (Nappi), Niola (Montella).
Oldham: Gerrard; McNiven, Serrant, Richardson, Graham, Fleming, Halle (Rickers), Brennan (Hughes), McCarthy, Barlow (Pemberton), Beresford.

Luton T (1) 5 *(Oakes, Marshall, Taylor, Thorpe, Guentchev)*
Ancona (0) 0 2091
Luton T: Davis K; Patterson, Johnson, Davis S, Waddock, McLaren (Thorpe), Linton (Guentchev), Oakes, Taylor, Marshall, Harvey (Thomas).
Ancona: Orlandoni; Tittarelli, Cornacchia, Ruggiero, Paci, Innocentin (Dorbini), Iacobelli, Bartolini (Fontana), Fini, Magnani (Ventura), Lemme.

Perugia (1) 3 *(Suppa, Rocco, Allegri)*
Port Vale (3) 5 *(Porter, McCarthy, Mills 3)* 200
Perugia: Fabbri; Cottini (Beghetto), Montesanto (Giunti), Goretti, Dicara, Lombardo, Briaschi (Allegri), Rocco, Meacci, Suppa, Russo.
Port Vale: Musselwhite; Hill, Stokes (Lawton), Bogie, Griffiths, Samuel, McCarthy, Porter, Mills, Naylor (Glover L), Guppy.

GROUP B

Brescia (0) 0
WBA (0) 1 *(Taylor)* 300
Brescia: Cusin; Adani, Bonometti, Luzardi, Mezzanotti, Filippini E, Filippini A, Volpi, Campolonghi (Lunini), Barollo (Neri), Saurini.
WBA: Naylor; Burgess, Smith, Darby, Edwards, Raven, Donovan (Coldicott), Gilbert, Taylor, Rees (Hargreaves), Hamilton.

Ipswich T (2) 2 *(Mowbray, Gregory)*
Salernitana (0) 0 6429
Ipswich T: Forrest; Tarrico, Vaughan (Yallop), Thomsen, Mowbray, Norfolk, Uhlenbeek, Milton, Mathie, Gregory, Appleby (Durrant).
Salernitana: Franzone; Grimaudo, Gattuso, Amore (De Silvestro), Frezza, Landini, Juliano, Rachini, Pirri, Logarzo (Ferrante), Spinelli (Facci).

Southend U (1) 1 *(Marsh (pen))*
Foggia (0) 2 *(Zanchetta, Sano)* 2570
Southend U: Royce; Dublin, Powell (Hone), Lapper, Bodley, Gridelet, Marsh, Byrne, Thomson (Iorfa), Willis (Regis), Hails.

Foggia: Botticella; Gasparini, Anastasi (Di Bari), Sciacca, Parisi, Bianchini, Marazzina, Sano, Kolyvanov, Zanchetta (Consagra), Di Corca (Giacobbo).
Reggiana v Stoke C not played .

SEMI-FINALS

10 JAN

Foggia (0) 0
Cesena (0) 0   1230
Foggia: Botticella; Gasparini, Anastasi, Sano, Oshadogan, Parisi, Marazzina (Kolyvanov), Giacobbo (Tedesco), Baglieri, Zanchetta, Consagra (Di Bari).
Cesena: Sardini; Zanetti, Codispoti, Affatigato, Farabegoli S, Medri, Maenza, Teodorani (Farabegoli A), Comandini (Pensalfini), Piraccini, Bombardini (Alteri).
aet; Cesena won 2-1 on penalties.

17 JAN

Genoa (0) 0
Salernitana (0) 0   1400
Genoa: Pastine; Torrente, Francesconi, Cavallo (Bortolazzi), Nappi, Montella, Van't Schip (Pagliarini), Turrone, Nicola, Magoni (Ruotolo), Onorati.
Salernitana: Franzone; Grimaudo, Breda, Gattuso, Cudini, Amore (Pirri), Frezza (Rachini), Juliano, Logarzo, Spinelli (Landini), Ferrante.

23 JAN

Ipswich T (1) 2 *(Gregory, Mason)*
Port Vale (2) 4 *(Naylor 3, Foyle)*   5831
Ipswich T: Wright; Uhlenbeek, Vaughan, Thomsen, Wark (Scowcroft), Tanner (Yallop), Mason, Sedgeley, Mathie (Slater), Gregory, Milton.
Port Vale: Van Heusden; Porter, Tankard, Bogie, Griffiths, Aspin, McCarthy, Walker, Foyle, Naylor, Guppy (Stokes).

30 JAN

Birmingham C (0) 2 *(Poole, Bull)*
WBA (1) 2 *(Rees, Raven)*   9113
Birmingham C: Griemink; Poole, Frain, Forsyth, Edwards, Johnson, Hunt, Bowen (Barnes S), Bull, Otto (Claridge), Finnan (Tait).
WBA: Naylor; Holmes, Smith, Cunnington (Coldicott), Burgess, Raven, Donovan, Gilbert (Taylor), Rees (Ashcroft), Hunt, Darby.

ITALIAN FINAL, FIRST LEG

31 JAN

Cesena (0) 0   1521
Genoa (2) 4 *(Montella 2, Nappi, Pagliarini)*
Cesena: Sardini; Scugugia, Codispoti, Albonetti, Farabegoli S, Affatigato, Teodorani, Piraccini

(Farabegoli A), Binotto (Pensalfini), Maenza, Alteri (Chiaretti).
Genoa: Spinetta; Torrente, Francesconi, Galante, Cavallo, Nappi, Bortolazzi, Montella (Pagliarini), Magoni (Balducci), Ruotolo, Onorati.

ITALIAN FINAL, SECOND LEG

8 FEB

Genoa (0) 1 *(Foschi (og))*
Cesena (0) 0   1753
Genoa: Pastine; Francesconi, Galante, Cavallo, Nappi, Bortolazzi, Van't Schip (Balducci), Nicola, Ruotolo, Onorati, Pagliarini (Magoni).
Cesena: Sardini; Scugugia, Codispoti, Medri, Foschi, Piangerelli, Teodorani, Piraccini (Ponzo), Binotto, Favi (Fornetti), Bizzarri (Hubner).

ANGLO-FINAL, FIRST LEG

24 FEB

WBA (0) 0
Port Vale (0) 0   10,862
WBA: Spink; Holmes, Nicholson, Darby, Burgess, Raven, Donovan (Ashcroft), Gilbert, Taylor, Hunt (Rees), Hamilton.
Port Vale: Musselwhite; Hill, Stokes, Bogie (Talbot), Griffiths, Walker, McCarthy, Porter, Mills (Glover L), Naylor, Guppy (Tankard).

5 MAR

Port Vale (1) 3 *(McCarthy, Glover L, Foyle)*
WBA (0) 1 *(Taylor)*   7640
Port Vale: Musselwhite; Porter, Tankard (Stokes) (Foyle), Bogie, Griffiths, Aspin, McCarthy, Walker, Mills, Glover L, Guppy.
WBA: Spink; Holmes, Nicholson, Darby (Smith), Burgess, Raven, Ashcroft, Gilbert, Taylor, Hunt, Hamilton.

FINAL (AT WEMBLEY)

17 MAR

Genoa (3) 5 *(Ruotolo 3, Galante, Montella)*
Port Vale (0) 2 *(Foyle 2)*   12,683
Genoa: Pastine (Spagnulo); Magoni, Delli Carri, Cavallo, Galante, Nicola (Van't Schip), Onorati (Torrente), Bortolazzi, Ruotolo, Nappi, Montella.
Port Vale: Musselwhite; Hill, Stokes (Walker), Bogie, Griffiths, Aspin, McCarthy, Porter, Foyle, Glover L (Naylor), Guppy (Talbot).
Referee: I. Koho (Finland).

AUTO WINDSCREENS SHIELD 1995–96

FIRST ROUND

25 SEPT   NORTHERN SECTION

Doncaster R (1) 1 *(Clarke)*
Bradford C (1) 1 *(Murray)*   1014
Doncaster R: Williams D; Kirby, Hackett, Moore, Carmichael, Maxfield, Schofield, Colcombe, Clark, Darby (Norbury), Warren.
Bradford C: Ward; Huxford, Liburd, Mitchell, Mohan, Ford, Wright, Youds, Ormondroyd (Shutt), Murray, Showler.

26 SEPT

Blackpool (1) 1 *(Quinn)*
Crewe Alex (0) 0   2560
Blackpool: Banks; Bryan, Barlow, Lydiate, Mellon, Quinn (Beech), Holden, Bonner, Morrison, Ellis (Gouck), Preece.
Crewe Alex: Gayle; Clarkson (Murphy), Booty, Unsworth, Macauley, Whalley, Garvey, Collins, Savage, Lennon, Adebola (Ellison).

Chester C (0) 0
Rotherham U (0) 1 *(Roscoe)*   774
Chester C: Newland; Fisher, Burnham, Richardson, Jackson, Alsford, Flitcroft, Priest, Murphy (Noteman), Rimmer, Bishop.
Rotherham U: Clarke; Blades, Bowyer, Richardson, Breckin, Monington, Berry (Hayward), Goodwin, Jeffrey, Goater, Roscoe.

Lincoln C (1) 4 *(Huckerby 2, Johnson D 2)*
Rochdale (1) 3 *(Whitehall, Peake, Deary)* 1238
Lincoln C: Leaning; Minett, Mudd, Wanless, Carbon (Daley), Bound, Davis, Appleton, Johnson D, Huckerby, Dixon.
Rochdale: Gray; Thackeray, Formby, Deary, Bayliss, Butler, Thompson, Martin (Williams), Stuart, Whitehall, Peake.

Mansfield T (1) 2 *(Hadley, Doolan)*
Wrexham (1) 2 *(Hughes, Connolly)*   1037
Mansfield T: Trinder; Boothroyd, Baraclough, Doolan, Eustace, Peters, Kerr, Sedgemore, Harper, Hadley, Slawson (Ireland).
Wrexham: Marriott; McGregor, Hardy, Phillips, Humes, Jones, Skinner, Brammer, Connolly, Russell (Cross), Hughes.

Scarborough (0) 0
Hull C (1) 2 *(Lawford, Mann)*   893
Scarborough: Ironside; Knowles, Lucas, D'Auria, Hicks, Rockett (Boardman), Heald (Todd), Thew (Willgrass), Trebble, Page, Charles.
Hull C: Wilson; Lowthorpe, Lawford, Hobson, Dewhurst, Abbott, Williams, Allison, Mason (Peacock), Windass (Gordon), Mann.

Stockport Co (0) 1 *(Ware)*
Chesterfield (0) 1 *(Lormor)*   2152
Stockport Co: Edwards; Connelly, Todd, Bennett, Flynn, Gannon, Beaumont, Ware, Helliwell, Armstrong (Williams), Chalk.
Chesterfield: Mercer; Hewitt; Rogers, Curtis (Narbett), Williams, Dyche, Robinson, Davies (Howard), Lormor, Morris (Roberts), Jules.

Wigan Ath (0) 1 *(Benjamin)*
Scunthorpe U (0) 1 *(Housham)*   1064
Wigan Ath: Farnworth; Butler, Ogden, Greenall, Pender, Kelly, Diaz, Lightfoot, Benjamin, Kilford, Lyons.
Scunthorpe U: Samways; Hope, Wilson, Ford, Knill, Bradley, Housham, Thornber, McFarlane, Young (Nicholson), Sansam.

SOUTHERN SECTION

Cambridge U (0) 1 *(Adekola)*   1438
Brighton & HA (1) 4 *(McCarthy, Bull 2 (1 pen), McDougald)*
Cambridge U: Barrett; Jeffrey, Granville, Vowden, Pack, Richards, Stock, Fowler, Adekola, Kyd, Zumrutel (Beall).
Brighton & HA: Rust; Storer (Smith), Chapman (Andrews), Wilkins (Myall), Osman, McCarthy, Parris, McDougald, Bull, Minton, McGarrigle.

Colchester U (2) 5 *(Adcock 3, Reinelt, Cawley)*
Torquay U (0) 2 *(Hathaway (pen), Stamps)*   1122
Colchester U: Emberson; Locke (Ball), Betts, McCarthy, English, Cawley, Kinsella, Fry, Reinelt, Adcock, Cheetham.
Torquay U: Bayes; Winter, Barrow, O'Riordan, Gore, Curran (Stamps), Hawthorne, Kaasikmae, Hancox (Laight), Hathaway, Mateu (Hall).

Hereford U (0) 3 *(Wilkins 2, Smith)*
Cardiff C (1) 3 *(Dale 2, Adams)*   1411
Hereford U: MacKenzie; Evans, Lloyd, Smith, Blatherwick, Downing, Pounder, Wilkins, Lyne, Cross (White), Stoker.
Cardiff C: Williams D; Young, Searle, Harding, Baddeley, Perry, Ingram, Rodgerson, Haworth (Evans A), Dale, Adams (Evans T).

Oxford U (3) 3 *(Rush 2, Murphy)*
Bristol C (0) 0   2557
Oxford U: Carter; Robinson, Ford M, Smith, Elliott, Gilchrist, Rush (Milsom), Massey (Angel), Murphy, Ford R, Allen.
Bristol C: Dykstra; Hansen, Edwards, Dryden, Bryant, Kuhl, Bent, Owers, Baird (Munro), Agostino (Seal), Starbuck.

Plymouth Arg (0) 0
Peterborough U (1) 3 *(Clark, McGleish, Power)* 1682
Plymouth Arg: Dungey; Wotton (Payne), Leadbitter, Clayton (Dawe), Heathcote, Hill, Ross, Mauge (Richardson), Nugent, Evans, Twiddy.
Peterborough U: Sheffield; Williams, Rioch, Gregory, Clark, Heald, Carter (Furnell), Manuel, Power, McGleish, Le Bihan (Morrison).

Shrewsbury T (0) 1 *(Woods)*
Swansea C (0) 1 *(Torpey)*   943
Shrewsbury T: Clarke; Scott, Lynch, Taylor, Withe (Rowbotham), Seabury, Woods, Anthrobus (Stevens), Spink, Walton, Dempsey.
Swansea C: Freestone; Barnhouse, Clode (Basham), Walker, Edwards, Jenkins, Coates, Heggs, Torpey, Ampadu, Hodge.

27 SEPT

Bournemouth (0) 0
Brentford (1) 1 *(Taylor)*   1092
Bournemouth: Andrews; Young, Beardsmore, Morris (Bailey), Murray, Victory, Holland, Robinson (Town), Jones, Pennock, Brissett (Cureton).
Brentford: Dearden; Statham, Grainger, Davis, Bates, Ashby, McGhee, Smith, Forster, Asaba, Taylor.

10 OCT

Wycombe W (1) 1 *(Howard)*
Fulham (1) 1 *(Conroy)*   2756
Wycombe W: Hyde; Rowbotham, Hardyman (Bell), Howard, Cousins, Brown, Carroll, Williams, De Souza, McGavin, Farrell.
Fulham: Harrison; Finnigan, Taylor, Mison, Angus, Bower, Thomas, Morgan, Cusack, Conroy, Brazil.

16 OCT

Peterborough U (0) 0
Northampton T (0) 0 3045
Peterborough U: Sheffield; Ashley, Clark, Manuel, Breen, Heald, Williams, Gregory, Martindale, McGleish, Morrison.
Northampton T: Woodman; Hunter, Hughes, Peer, Warburton, Sampson, Gibb, Lee (Beckford), Williams, Burns, Colkin.

17 OCT

Swansea C (0) 0
Leyton Orient (0) 0 1562
Swansea C: Freestone; Barnhouse, Cook, Walker (Basham), Edwards, Lampard, Dennison, Heggs (Pascoe), Torpey, Ampadu, Hodge (Perrett).
Leyton Orient: Caldwell; Hendon, Stanislaus, Chapman, Bellamy, McCarthy (Baker), Kelly T, Lakin, Inglethorpe, Hanson, Warren.

Cardiff C (1) 3 *(Dale 2, Adams)*
Gillingham (1) 2 *(Freeman, Foster (pen))* 1034
Cardiff C: Williams D; Young, Searle, Harding, Baddeley (Jarman), Brazil, Wigg, Bird (Adams), Haworth (Ingram), Dale, Gardner.
Gillingham: Stannard; Carpenter, Watson P, Rattray (Dunne), Butler T, Green, Martin, Micklewhite, Freeman, Foster (Arnott), Puttnam (Smith).

Fulham (1) 2 *(Morgan 2)* 1315
Walsall (2) 5 *(Butler 2, Wilson, Lightbourne, O'Connor)*
Fulham: Harrison; Finnigan (Hamill), Herrera, Mison (Bolt), Angus, Bowyer, Thomas, Morgan, Brazil, Conroy, Barkus (Cusack).
Walsall: Wood; Evans (Rollo), Rogers, Keister, Marsh, Viveash, O'Connor (Ntamark), Roper (Palmer), Butler, Wilson, Lightbourne.

Brentford (1) 1 *(Forster)*
Exeter C (1) 1 *(Came)* 1431
Brentford: Dearden; Statham, Grainger, Harvey, Bates, Ashby, McGhee (Anderson), Smith, Forster, Martin, Taylor (Hutchings).
Exeter C: Fox; Medlin, Rice, Buckle, Hare, Richardson, Chamberlain (Morgan), Bailey, Pears, Came, Gavin.

Brighton & HA (0) 0
Bristol R (0) 2 *(Archer, Davis)* 1191
Brighton & HA: Rust; Smith, Chapman (Fox S), Wilkins, Johnson, Tuck (McGarrigle), Parris, McDougald, Andrews, Myall, Osman.
Bristol R: Collett; Channing, Gurney, Browning, Wright, McLean, Sterling (Davis), Paul, Stewart (Hayfield), Skinner, Archer (Hope).

Bristol C (1) 2 *(Seal (pen), Edwards)*
Barnet (0) 0 1830
Bristol C: Dykstra; Paterson, Edwards, Dryden, Bryant, Kuhl (Plummer), Bent, Owers, Agostino (Tinnion), Barnard, Seal.
Barnet: Taylor; Gale, Stimson, Pardew, McDonald, Thomas, Hodges, Scott (Charles), Cooper (Mills), Devine, Wilson.

Torquay U (1) 1 *(Curran)*
Swindon T (1) 1 *(Ling)* 1135
Torquay U: Bayes; Curran, Kelly O'Riordan, Gore, Barrow, Jack, Coughlin, Mateu (Laight), Byng (Cooke), Hawthorne.
Swindon T: Digby; Murray, Bodin, Allen, Seagraves (Thorne G), Taylor, Robinson (Horlock), Ling (O'Sullivan), Finney, Allison, Gooden.

NORTHERN SECTION

17 OCT

Crewe Alex (4) 8 *(Collins, Ingram (og), Macauley, Whalley, Savage, Garvey, Murphy, Rivers (pen))*
Hartlepool U (0) 0 2344
Crewe Alex: Gayle; Collins, Booty, Westwood (Unsworth), Macauley, Whalley, Garvey, Murphy, Savage (Rivers), Lennon, Edwards.
Hartlepool U: Jones; Ingram, McAuley, Billing, McGuckin, Canham, Allon, Tait, Henderson, Halliday (Homer), Howard.

Rotherham U (0) 1 *(Hayward)*
Burnley (1) 1 *(Nogan)* 1539
Rotherham U: Clarke; Wilder, Hirst, Garner, Breckin, Blades, Hayward, Goodwin, Jeffrey, Goater, Roscoe.
Burnley: Beresford; Parkinson, Vinnicombe, Swan, Winstanley, Hoyland, Harrison, Joyce, Cooke (Francis), Nogan, McDonald.

Chesterfield (2) 2 *(Robinson, Roberts)*
Notts Co (0) 1 *(White)* 2150
Chesterfield: Mercer; Rogers, Dyche, Curtis, Williams, Law (Perkins), Robinson, Davies, Roberts (Narbett), Morris, Howard.
Notts Co: Ward; Short, Walker (Hunt), Gallagher, Murphy, Redmile, Galloway (Devlin), Simpson, White, Arkins (Legg), Agana.

Scunthorpe U (1) 4 *(McFarlane 2, Matthewson (og), Eyre)*
Bury (0) 0 877
Scunthorpe U: Samways; Hope, Thornber, Ford (Sansam), Knill, Bradley (Nicholson), Housham, Bullimore, McFarlane, Eyre, Paterson (Young).
Bury: Kelly; Cross, Bimson, Reid, Lucketti, Matthewson, West (Sertori), Carter (Johnson), Stant (Lancaster), Rigby, Hughes.

Wrexham (0) 1 *(Connolly)*
York C (0) 0 1411
Wrexham: Marriott; McGregor, Hardy, Phillips, Humes, Jones, Skinner, Brammer, Connolly, Cross, Hughes (Owen).
York C: Warrington; McMillan, Hall, Murty, Tutill, Barras, Matthews, Williams, Barnes, Baker, Jordan (Bushell).

Hull C (0) 1 *(Fewings)*
Preston NE (0) 0 753
Hull C: Fettis; Watson, Lawford, Allison, Humphries, Abbott, Williams, Lee, Brown (Fewings), Windass, Mann.
Preston NE: Richardson; Fensome (Fleming), Sharp (Squires), Atkinson, Kidd, Moyes, Davey, Bryson, Kilbane, Wilkinson (Smart), Cartwright.

Bradford C (1) 1 *(Tolson)*
Carlisle U (0) 1 *(Thomas)* 1287
Bradford C: Ward; Huxford, Jacobs, Mitchell, Mohan (Hamilton), Robson (Shutt), Wright (Ormondroyd), Youds, Tolson, Murray, Showler.
Carlisle U: Elliott; Edmondson, Gallimore, Walling, Moore (Robinson), Peacock, Thomas, Delap (Currie), Reeves, Aspinall, Murray.

24 OCT

Rochdale (2) 5 *(Whitehall, Gregan (og), Moulden 3)*
Darlington (1) 2 *(Olsson, Appleby)* 1055
Rochdale: Gray; Thackeray, Formby, Deary (Martin), Valentine, Butler, Thompson (Shaw), Moulden, Stuart, Whitehall (Thompstone), Peake.
Darlington: Pollitt; Shaw (Worboys), Barnard, Appleby, Crosby, Gregan, Himsworth, Olsson, Painter, Gaughan (Naylor), Bannister (Brumwell).

SOUTHERN SECTION

7 NOV

Leyton Orient (0) 1 *(Hendon)*
Shrewsbury T (2) 3 *(Dempsey, Stevens 2)*   1437
Leyton Orient: Fearon; Hendon, Austin, Chapman, Bellamy, McCarthy, Kelly T, Cockerill, Williams, Hanson (Purse), Brooks (Baker).
Shrewsbury T: Edwards; Seabury, Withe, Evans, Whiston, Scott, Berkley (Woods), Stevens (Summerfield), Spink, Anthrobus, Dempsey.

Gillingham (2) 2 *(Butler, Foster)*
Hereford U (0) 2 *(Stoker, Smith D (pen))*   1866
Gillingham: Nicholls; Dunne, Naylor, Butler, Carpenter, Green, Rattray, Micklewhite, Foster (Bremner), Freeman, Watson P.
Hereford U: MacKenzie; Evans, Lloyd, Smith D, Blatherwick, Downing, Pounder, Wilkins, Cross (Preedy), White, Pick (Stoker).

Northampton T (1) 1 *(Burns (pen))*
Plymouth Arg (0) 0   2109
Northampton T: Woodman; Norton, Hunter, Peer, Warburton, Sampson (O'Shea), Gibb, Lee (Aldridge), White, Burns, Colkin.
Plymouth Arg: Hammond; Patterson, Williams, Barlow, Logan, Hill (Leadbitter), Billy, Wotton, Ross (Richardson), Evans, Magee (Twiddy).

Walsall (4) 5 *(Lightbourne 4, Viveash)*
Wycombe W (0) 0   2592
Walsall: Walker; Ntamark, Rogers, Viveash, Marsh, Mountfield, Keister, Bradley (Richards), Lightbourne (Butler), Wilson (Smith), Houghton.
Wycombe W: Hyde; Rowbotham, Bell, Howard, Cousins, Brown, Carroll (McGavin), Williams, Desouza, Garner (Patterson), Farrell.

Exeter C (0) 0
Bournemouth (0) 2 *(Brissett 2 (1 pen))*   1898
Exeter C: Fox; Parsley (Cecere), Anderson, Buckle, Hare, Richardson, Gavin, Bailey, Pears, Came, Phillips.
Bournemouth: Moss; Fletcher, Beardsmore, Bailey, Pennock, Dewbury, Holland, Robinson, Jones, Ndah, Brissett.

Bristol R (1) 3 *(Stewart 2, French)*
Cambridge U (0) 0   1805
Bristol R: Collett; Wright, Gurney, French, McLean, Tillson, Sterling, Hayfield (White), Stewart, Skinner, Archer (Paul).
Cambridge U: Davies; Joseph, Palmer, Vowden, Craddock, Granville, Rattle, Middleton, Richards (Adekola), Watson (Kyd), Hyde.

Barnet (0) 2 *(Cooper, Robbins)*
Oxford U (0) 3 *(Pardew (og), Murphy, Moody)*   1072
Barnet: Taylor; Gale (Robbins), Dyer, Pardew, Primus, McDonald, Tomlinson, Scott, Cooper, Devine, Wilson (Hodges).
Oxford U: Whitehead; Wood, Ford M, Smith, Elliott, Gilchrist (Beauchamp), Rush (Biggins), Murphy, Moody, Ford R, Angel (Powell).

NORTHERN SECTION

7 NOV

Hartlepool U (2) 3 *(Howard 3, Allon)*
Blackpool (2) 2 *(Beech, Quinn (pen))*   888
Hartlepool U: Roberts (Horne); Ingram, Allinson (Lee), Billing, Henderson, Lynch, Allon (Sloan), Oliver, Howard, Halliday, McAuley.
Blackpool: Banks; Bryan, Yallop, Lydiate, Beech, Quinn, Gouck, Bonner (Holden), Bradshaw, Watson, Preece.

Burnley (1) 1 *(Nogan)*
Chester C (0) 1 *(Richardson)*   3225
Burnley: Beresford; Parkinson, Vinnicombe, Swan, Winstanley, Hoyland, Harrison (Robinson), Randall, Eyres (Cooke), Nogan, McDonald (Francis).
Chester C: Stewart; Jenkins, Burnham, Priest (Brown), Whelan, Alsford, Richardson, Rogers, Rimmer (Jones), Milner (Chambers), Noteman.

Notts Co (1) 1 *(Devlin)*
Stockport Co (0) 0   2015
Notts Co: Ward; Mills, Legg (Short), Nicol, Strodder, Galloway (Hunt), Gallagher, Simpson, Devlin (White), Arkins, Agana.
Stockport Co: Edwards; Connelly, Todd, Bennett, Flynn, Gannon, Beaumont, Oliver, Eckhardt, Armstrong (Chalk), Thornley.

Darlington (0) 0
Lincoln (0) 1 *(Brown G)*   984
Darlington: Pollitt; Shaw, Barnard, Appleby, Crosby, Gregan, Brumwell (Pugh), Gaughan, Worboys (Andersson), Naylor, Carss (Bannister).
Lincoln: Leaning; Barnett, Whitney, Onwere, Holmes, Brown G, Ainsworth, Hulme, Johnson D, Brown S, Minett.

York C (0) 1 *(Barras)*
Mansfield T (0) 0   1571
York C: Warrington; McMillan, Osborne, Pepper, Tutill, Barras, Matthews (Peverell), Bushell (Jordan), Barnes, Baker (Curtis), Williams.
Mansfield T: Bowling; Boothroyd, Peel (Slawson), Doolan, Howarth, Eustace, Ireland, Parkin, Harper, Sale (Hadley), Barber.

Preston NE (1) 2 *(Atkinson, Kidd)*
Scarborough (0) 1 *(Heald)*   5639
Preston NE: Vaughan; Fensome, Barrick, Atkinson (Cartwright), Wilcox (Kidd), Moyes, Davey, Bryson (Kilbane), Saville, Wilkinson, McDonald.
Scarborough: Ironside; Knowles, Robinson, Thew, Hicks, Boardman, Toman, Wells, Trebble, Heald, Lee (Willgrass).

Carlisle U (0) 1 *(Currie)*
Doncaster R (1) 1 *(Colcombe)*   4421
Carlisle U: Caig; Prokas, Gallimore (Thorpe), Walling, Moore (Peacock), Hayward, Thomas (Conway), Currie, Reeves, Aspinall, Murray.
Doncaster R: Suckling; Measham, Colcombe (Darby), Murphy, Kirby, Clark (Carmichael), Schofield, Brabin, Jones (Barker), Warren, Robertson.

SOUTHERN SECTION

8 NOV

Swindon T (0) 2 *(Thorne, Finney)*
Colchester U (0) 0   6222
Swindon: Digby; Hooper, Drysdale (McMahon), Gooden, Thorne G, Taylor, Robinson, Ling (O'Sullivan), Finney, Allison (Thorne P), Horlock.
Colchester U: Caldwell; Betts, Gibbs, McCarthy, Lewis, Caesar (English), Kinsella, Dennis, Mardenborough, Fry, Cheetham.

NORTHERN SECTION

14 NOV

Bury (0) 0
Wigan Ath (0) 0   1471
Bury: Kelly; Cross, Hughes (West), Reid S, Lucketti, Matthewson, Rigby, Johnson, Stant, Johnrose, Pugh.
Wigan Ath: Farnworth; Carragher, Butler, Greenall, Pender, Martinez, Diaz (Black), Kilford, Leonard, Lightfoot, Lyons.

SECOND ROUND
NORTHERN SECTION
27 NOV

Doncaster R (0) 1 *(Moore)*
Notts Co (0) 3 *(Murphy, Agana, Devlin)*   1714
Doncaster R: Williams; Measham, Parrish, Moore, Carmichael, Murphy, Clark, Brabin, Jones, Warren, Robertson.
Notts Co: Ward; Mills, Legg, Hogg, Strodder, Murphy, Gallagher (White), Galloway, Devlin, Arkins, Agana.

28 NOV

Chesterfield (0) 2 *(Roberts, Robinson)*
Rochdale (1) 1 *(Whitehall)* 2344
Chesterfield: Beasley; Perkins, Dyche, Curtis, Williams, Law, Robinson, Davies, Lormor (Roberts), Morris, Howard (Narbett).
Rochdale: Gray; Thompstone, Formby, Martin, Bayliss, Butler, Thompson, Deary, Moulden (Ryan), Whitehall, Shaw.

Hull C (0) 1 *(Windass (pen))*
Blackpool (0) 2 *(Beech, Mellon)* 1422
Hull C: Wilson; Trevitt, Lawford, Hobson, Allison, Dakin (Mason), Peacock, Lee (Mann), Brown, Windass, Davison.
Blackpool: Banks; Bryan, Barlow, Linighan, Mellon, Quinn, Bradshaw, Preece (Watson), Gouck (Beech), Ellis, Holden (Darton).

Lincoln C (0) 2 *(Onwere, Brown S)*
Preston NE (0) 1 *(Saville)* 1729
Lincoln C: Leaning; Wanless (Hulme), Whitney, Minett, Westley, Brown G, Ainsworth, Onwere, Carbon, Brown S, Barnett.
Preston NE: Vaughan; Squires, Barrick, Atkinson (Lancashire), Kidd, Moyes, Davey, Bryson, Saville, Brown (Cartwright), McDonald.

Rotherham U (0) 0
Wigan Ath (0) 0 1008
Rotherham U: Muggleton; Smith, Hurst, Garner (Richardson), Monington, Blades, Hayward, McGlashan, Jeffrey, Goater, Berry.
Wigan Ath: Farnworth; Carragher, Butler, Lightfoot (Greenall), Farrell (Miller), Pender, Diaz, Martinez, Leonard, Seba, Lyons.
(aet; Rotherham U won 4-1 on penalties).

Scunthorpe U (0) 0
York C (2) 3 *(Barnes 2, Stephenson)* 1734
Scunthorpe U: Samways; Walsh, Wilson, Ford, Hope (Nicholson), Bradley, Turnbull, Bullimore (Young), McFarlane, Eyre, Paterson.
York C: Kiely; McMillan, Hall, Pepper, Tutill, Barras, Matthews, Jordan (Bushell), Barnes, Baker (Peverell), Stephenson (Murty).

Wrexham (1) 1 *(Ward)*
Carlisle U (1) 2 *(Bennett, Aspinall)* 2522
Wrexham: Marriott; McGregor (Morris), Hardy, Phillips, Humes, Jones, Skinner, Russell, Connolly, Watkin, Ward.
Carlisle U: Caig; Murray, Gallimore, Walling, Bennett, Hayward, Thorpe, Currie (Peacock), Reeves, Aspinall, Prokas.

SOUTHERN SECTION

Brentford (0) 0
Fulham (0) 1 *(Jupp)* 3760
Brentford: Fernandes; Statham, Grainger, Hutchings, Bates, Ashby, Ansah, Smith, Bent (McGhee), Martin, Taylor.
Fulham: Lange; Jupp, Taylor, Gray, Moore, Angus, Barkus (Brooker), Morgan, Hamill (Bartley), Cusack, Bolt (Herrera).

Bristol R (1) 2 *(Tillson, Browning)*
Bournemouth (0) 1 *(Robinson)* 1979
Bristol R: Parkin; Channing, Gurney, Browning, Clark, Tillson, Sterling, Miller, Stewart, Tovey (French), Paul.
Bournemouth: Moss; Young, Beardsmore, Morris (Santos), McElhatton (Victory), Pennock, Bailey, Robinson, Rawlinson, Oldbury, Brissett (Stephens).

Cardiff C (0) 1 *(Dale (pen))*
Northampton T (1) 2 *(Hunter, Grayson)* 1450
Cardiff C: Williams D; Baddeley; Searle, Rodgerson, Jarman, Young (Bird), Fleming, Adams, Dale, Harper, Gardner.

Northampton T: Woodman; Norton, Maddison, Peer, Warburton, O'Shea, Hunter, Williams (Aldridge) (Beckford), White, Grayson, Scott.

Oxford U (1) 1 *(Angel)*
Colchester U (1) 2 *(Adcock, Betts (pen))* 1943
Oxford U: Whitehead; Wood (Murphy), Ford M, Smith (Powell), Elliott, Gilchrist, Rush (Beauchamp), Massey, Moody, Ford R, Angel.
Colchester U: Emberson; Fry, Betts, McCarthy, Greene, Cawley, Kinsella, English, Ball (Dennis), Adcock, Cheetham.

Peterborough U (0) 1 *(Farrell)*
Swansea C (0) 0 1952
Peterborough U: Sheffield; Ashley, Clark, Ebdon, Breen, Heald, Shaw, Williams, Martindale, McGleish (Farrell), Rioch (Le Bihan).
Swansea C: Freestone; Jones, Cook, Walker, Edwards, Pascoe, Penney, Coates (Hodge), Torpey, Ampadu, Dennison (Lampard).
(aet; Peterborough U won in sudden-death).

Shrewsbury T (0) 0
Bristol C (0) 0 2258
Shrewsbury T: Edwards; Seabury, Withe, Evans, Dempsey, Scott, Anthrobus (Taylor), Rowbotham, Spink, Walton, Berkley.
Bristol C: Welch; Carey, Edwards, Bryant, Shail, Kuhl, Bent, Owers, Tinnion (Agostino), Barnard, Seal.
(aet; Shrewsbury T won 7-6 on penalties).

Walsall (1) 1 *(Lightbourne)*
Brighton & HA (1) 2 *(Storer, Mundee (pen))* 3454
Walsall: Walker; Ntamark (Keister), Rogers, Viveash, Marsh, Mountfield, O'Connor, Bradley, Lightbourne (Butler) (Kerr), Wilson, Houghton.
Brighton & HA: Rust; Smith, Myall, Parris, Munday, Johnson, Storer, McDougald, Minton, Mundee, Chapman.

29 NOV

Swindon T (0) 0
Hereford U (1) 1 *(White)* 6650
Swindon T: Digby; Culverhouse (Robinson), Drysdale, Collins, Seagraves, Taylor, Hooper (Horlock), Ling (Finney), Thorne P, Allison, Gooden.
Hereford U: MacKenzie; Evans, Lloyd, Smith D, Stoker, Brough, Lyne, Wilkins, Cross, White (Pounder), Downing.

NORTHERN SECTION

Crewe Alex (0) 0
Burnley (0) 1 *(Nogan)* 2596
Crewe Alex: Gayle; Collins, Smith S (Unsworth), Westwood, Macauley, Whalley, Rivers (Adebola), Murphy, Savage (Garvey), Lennon, Edwards.
Burnley: Beresford; Brass, Vinnicombe, Swan, Winstanley, Harrison, Weller, Joyce, Heath (Cooke), Nogan, Eyres.
(aet; Burnley won in sudden-death).

NORTHERN SECTION QUARTER-FINALS

6 JAN

Carlisle U (3) 5 *(Edmondson 2, Reeves 3)*
Burnley (0) 0 5169
Carlisle U: Caig; Edmondson (Delap), Gallimore, Walling, Bennett, Hayward (Robinson), Murray, Currie (Conway), Reeves, Aspinall, Prokas.
Burnley: Beresford; Brass, Vinnicombe, Hoyland, Winstanley, Harrison, Weller (Francis), Joyce, Swan, Nogan, Cooke (McMinn).

9 JAN

Blackpool (0) 0
Chesterfield (0) 1 *(Law (pen))* 2469
Blackpool: Banks; Bryan, Barlow, Linighan, Mellon, Preece, Lydiate, Bonner (Beech), Morrison, Ellis, Watson.

Chesterfield: Mercer; Perkins, Jules, Curtis, Williams, Law, Robinson (Lormor), Narbett, Howard, Lund, Hazel (Roberts).

Rotherham U (2) 3 *(Goodwin 2, Berry)*
Lincoln C (0) 1 *(Ainsworth)* 1825
Rotherham U: Clarke; Smith, Hurst, Bowyer (Hayward), Breckin, Richardson, Berry, Goodwin, Garner, Goater, Roscoe.
Lincoln C: Leaning; Holmes, Whitney, Minett, Robertson, Johnson A, Ainsworth, Onwere, Alcide, Brown S, Barnett (Carbon).

York C (0) 1 *(Williams)*
Notts Co (0) 0 2075
York C: Kiely; McMillan, Atkinson, Bushell, Tutill, Atkin, Murty, Williams, Barnes, Baker, Peverell (Jordan).
Notts Co: Ward; Mills (Gallagher), Legg, Murphy, Strodder, Hogg, Simpson (Agana), Rogers, Devlin, Battersby, Arkins.

SOUTHERN SECTION QUARTER-FINALS

Fulham (1) 1 *(Jupp)*
Bristol R (1) 2 *(Stewart 2)* 2479
Fulham: Lange; Jupp, Herrera, Marshall (McAree), Angus, Blake, Thomas, Morgan, Brazil (Hamill), Conroy (Cusack), Bolt.
Bristol R: Parkin; Channing, Gurney, Browning, Clark, Tillson, Sterling, Miller, Stewart, Skinner (Tovey), Beadle.
aet; Bristol R won on sudden death.

Hereford U (1) 1 *(Cross)*
Northampton T (0) 0 2905
Hereford U: MacKenzie; Evans, Fishlock, Smith D, Pounder (Steele), Brough, Lyne, Wilkins, Cross, White, Downing.
Northampton T: Woodman; Norton, Maddison, Hunter, Warburton, O'Shea, Burns (Thompson), Grayson, Peer (Williams), White, Armstrong.

Peterborough U (1) 3 *(Martindale 2, McGleish)*
Colchester U (0) 2 *(Betts, Kinsella)* 2460
Peterborough U: Sheffield; Williams, Spearing, Le Bihan, Breen, Heald, Carter, Shaw, Martindale, Farrell (McGleish), Morrison (Rioch).
Colchester U: Emberson; Locke, Betts, McCarthy, Greene, Cawley, Kinsella, English, Fry, Adcock, Abrahams (Duguid).

Shrewsbury T (1) 4 *(Stevens 3, Evans (pen))*
Brighton & HA (1) 2 *(Scott (og), McDougald)* 2559
Shrewsbury T: Edwards; Evans, Withe, Taylor, Whiston, Scott, Woods, Stevens, Spink, Walton, Berkley.
Brighton & HA: Rust; Smith, Chapman (Byrne), Parris, Osman, McCarthy, Mundee, McDougald, Minton, Storer, Wilkins.

NORTHERN SECTION SEMI-FINAL

30 JAN

Carlisle U (1) 1 *(Hayward)*
Chesterfield (0) 0 5511
Carlisle U: Caig; Edmondson, Gallimore (Prokas), Walling, Bennett, Atkinson, Delap, Currie (Peacock), Reeves, Hayward, Thorpe (Conway).
Chesterfield: Mercer; Perkins, Jules, Curtis, Williams, Law, Robinson (Fairclough), Davics, Lormor, Holland, Narbett (Howard) (Roberts).

SOUTHERN SECTION SEMI-FINAL

31 JAN

Shrewsbury T (0) 4 *(Scott, Stevens, Brough (og), Walton)*
Hereford U (0) 1 *(Cross)* 4545
Shrewsbury T: Edwards; Seabury, Withe, Taylor, Whiston, Scott, Woods, Stevens, Spink (Dempsey), Walton, Berkley.
Hereford U: MacKenzie; Evans, Fishlock, Smith D, Pounder, Brough, Lyne, Stoker, Cross, White, Pick (Steele).

13 FEB

Peterborough U (0) 0
Bristol R (0) 1 *(Stewart (pen))* 3761
Peterborough U: Sheffield; Williams, Clark, Le Bihan, Foran, Heald, Martindale, Ebdon, Farrell, Charlery, Carter.
Bristol R: Collett; Channing, Gurney, Browning, Clark, Tillson, Sterling, Miller, Stewart, Matthew, Beadle.

NORTHERN SECTION

Rotherham U (2) 4 *(Hayward, Roscoe, Garner, Goodwin)*
York C (1) 1 *(Peverell)* 3913
Rotherham U: Clarke; Blades, Bowyer, Garner, Breckin, Richardson, Berry, Goodwin (Hurst), Hayward, Goater (Viljoen), Roscoe.
York C: Kiely; McMillan, Atkinson, Pepper (Jordan), Tutill, Atkin, Murty, Bushell, Barnes, Peverell (Stephenson), Cresswell (Barras).

NORTHERN SECTION FINAL, FIRST LEG

5 MAR

Rotherham U (0) 2 *(Goater, Richardson (pen))*
Carlisle U (0) 0 6858
Rotherham U: Clarke; Blades, Hurst, Garner, Richardson, Breckin, Berry (Hayward), Jemson, Bowyer, Goater, Roscoe (Viljoen).
Carlisle U: Elliott; Robinson, Gallimore, Walling, Bennett, Hayward, Thomas, Currie, Reeves, Delap, Prokas.

SOUTHERN SECTION FINAL, FIRST LEG

Shrewsbury T (0) 1 *(Taylor)*
Bristol R (0) 1 *(Matthew)* 5212
Shrewsbury T: Edwards; Lynch, Withe, Taylor, Whiston, Evans, Woods (Spink), Stevens, Anthrobus, Walton, Berkley (Rowbotham).
Bristol R: Collett; Gurney, Morgan, Browning, Clark, Tillson, Sterling, Miller, Stewart, Matthew, French (Wright).

NORTHERN SECTION FINAL, SECOND LEG

12 MAR

Carlisle U (0) 0
Rotherham U (2) 2 *(Jemson 2)* 6692
Carlisle U: Elliott; Robinson, Gallimore, Walling, Bennett (Thorpe), Hayward, Thomas, Currie, Reeves, Prokas (Aspinall), Hopper.
Rotherham U: Clarke; Blades, Hurst, Berry, Richardson, Breckin, Hayward, Jemson, Bowyer, Goater, Roscoe.

SOUTHERN SECTION FINAL, SECOND LEG

Bristol R (0) 0
Shrewsbury T (0) 1 *(Stevens)* 7050
Bristol R: Collett; Gurney, Morgan, Browning, Clark, Tillson, Channing, Miller, Stewart, Tovey, Beadle.
Shrewsbury T: Edwards; Lynch, Reed (Seabury), Taylor (Rowbotham), Whiston, Evans, Spink, Stevens, Anthrobus, Walton, Dempsey.

FINAL (AT WEMBLEY)

14 APR

Rotherham U (1) 2 *(Jemson 2)*
Shrewsbury T (0) 1 *(Taylor)* 35,235
Rotherham U: Clarke; Blades, Hurst, Garner, Richardson, Breckin, Jemson, Goodwin, Berry, Goater, Roscoe.
Shrewsbury T: Edwards; Kay, Withe, Taylor, Whiston, Scott, Robinson (Lynch), Stevens, Spink (Anthrobus), Walton, Berkley.
Referee: D. Allison (Lancaster).

FA CUP FINALS 1872–1996

1872 and 1874–92	Kennington Oval	1911	Replay at Old Trafford
1873	Lillie Bridge	1912	Replay at Bramall Lane
1886	Replay at Derby (Racecourse Ground)		
1893	Fallowfield, Manchester	1915	Old Trafford, Manchester
1894	Everton	1920–22	Stamford Bridge
1895–1914	Crystal Palace	1923 to date	Wembley
1901	Replay at Bolton	1970	Replay at Old Trafford
1910	Replay at Everton		

Year	Winners	Runners-up	Score
1872	Wanderers	Royal Engineers	1-0
1873	Wanderers	Oxford University	2-0
1874	Oxford University	Royal Engineers	2-0
1875	Royal Engineers	Old Etonians	2-0 (after 1-1 draw aet)
1876	Wanderers	Old Etonians	3-0 (after 1-1 draw aet)
1877	Wanderers	Oxford University	2-1 (aet)
1878	Wanderers*	Royal Engineers	3-1
1879	Old Etonians	Clapham R	1-0
1880	Clapham R	Oxford University	1-0
1881	Old Carthusians	Old Etonians	3-0
1882	Old Etonians	Blackburn R	1-0
1883	Blackburn Olympic	Old Etonians	2-1 (aet)
1884	Blackburn R	Queen's Park, Glasgow	2-1
1885	Blackburn R	Queen's Park, Glasgow	2-0
1886	Blackburn R†	WBA	2-0 (after 0-0 draw)
1887	Aston Villa	WBA	2-0
1888	WBA	Preston NE	2-1
1889	Preston NE	Wolverhampton W	3-0
1890	Blackburn R	Sheffield W	6-1
1891	Blackburn R	Notts Co	3-1
1892	WBA	Aston Villa	3-0
1893	Wolverhampton W	Everton	1-0
1894	Notts Co	Bolton W	4-1
1895	Aston Villa	WBA	1-0
1896	Sheffield W	Wolverhampton W	2-1
1897	Aston Villa	Everton	3-2
1898	Nottingham F	Derby Co	3-1
1899	Sheffield U	Derby Co	4-1
1900	Bury	Southampton	4-0
1901	Tottenham H	Sheffield U	3-1 (after 2-2 draw)
1902	Sheffield U	Southampton	2-1 (after 1-1 draw)
1903	Bury	Derby Co	6-0
1904	Manchester C	Bolton W	1-0
1905	Aston Villa	Newcastle U	2-0
1906	Everton	Newcastle U	1-0
1907	Sheffield W	Everton	2-1
1908	Wolverhampton W	Newcastle U	3-1
1909	Manchester U	Bristol C	1-0
1910	Newcastle U	Barnsley	2-0 (after 1-1 draw)
1911	Bradford C	Newcastle U	1-0 (after 0-0 draw)
1912	Barnsley	WBA	1-0 (aet, after 0-0 draw)
1913	Aston Villa	Sunderland	1-0
1914	Burnley	Liverpool	1-0
1915	Sheffield U	Chelsea	3-0
1920	Aston Villa	Huddersfield T	1-0 (aet)
1921	Tottenham H	Wolverhampton W	1-0
1922	Huddersfield T	Preston NE	1-0
1923	Bolton W	West Ham U	2-0
1924	Newcastle U	Aston Villa	2-0
1925	Sheffield U	Cardiff C	1-0
1926	Bolton W	Manchester C	1-0
1927	Cardiff C	Arsenal	1-0
1928	Blackburn R	Huddersfield T	3-1
1929	Bolton W	Portsmouth	2-0
1930	Arsenal	Huddersfield T	2-0
1931	WBA	Birmingham	2-1
1932	Newcastle U	Arsenal	2-1
1933	Everton	Manchester C	3-0
1934	Manchester C	Portsmouth	2-1
1935	Sheffield W	WBA	4-2
1936	Arsenal	Sheffield U	1-0
1937	Sunderland	Preston NE	3-1
1938	Preston NE	Huddersfield T	1-0 (aet)
1939	Portsmouth	Wolverhampton W	4-1
1946	Derby Co	Charlton Ath	4-1 (aet)
1947	Charlton Ath	Burnley	1-0 (aet)
1948	Manchester U	Blackpool	4-2
1949	Wolverhampton W	Leicester C	3-1
1950	Arsenal	Liverpool	2-0
1951	Newcastle U	Blackpool	2-0
1952	Newcastle U	Arsenal	1-0

Year	Winners	Runners-up	Score
1953	Blackpool	Bolton W	4-3
1954	WBA	Preston NE	3-2
1955	Newcastle U	Manchester C	3-1
1956	Manchester C	Birmingham C	3-1
1957	Aston Villa	Manchester U	2-1
1958	Bolton W	Manchester U	2-0
1959	Nottingham F	Luton T	2-1
1960	Wolverhampton W	Blackburn R	3-0
1961	Tottenham H	Leicester C	2-0
1962	Tottenham H	Burnley	3-1
1963	Manchester U	Leicester C	3-1
1964	West Ham U	Preston NE	3-2
1965	Liverpool	Leeds U	2-1 (aet)
1966	Everton	Sheffield W	3-2
1967	Tottenham H	Chelsea	2-1
1968	WBA	Everton	1-0 (aet)
1969	Manchester C	Leicester C	1-0
1970	Chelsea	Leeds U	2-1 (aet)
	(after 2-2 draw, after extra time, at Wembley)		
1971	Arsenal	Liverpool	2-1 (aet)
1972	Leeds U	Arsenal	1-0
1973	Sunderland	Leeds U	1-0
1974	Liverpool	Newcastle U	3-0
1975	West Ham U	Fulham	2-0
1976	Southampton	Manchester U	1-0
1977	Manchester U	Liverpool	2-1
1978	Ipswich T	Arsenal	1-0
1979	Arsenal	Manchester U	3-2
1980	West Ham U	Arsenal	1-0
1981	Tottenham H	Manchester C	3-2
	(after 1-1 draw, after extra time, at Wembley)		
1982	Tottenham H	QPR	1-0
	(after 1-1 draw, after extra time, at Wembley)		
1983	Manchester U	Brighton & HA	4-0
	(after 2-2 draw, after extra time, at Wembley)		
1984	Everton	Watford	2-0
1985	Manchester U	Everton	1-0 (aet)
1986	Liverpool	Everton	3-1
1987	Coventry C	Tottenham H	3-2 (aet)
1988	Wimbledon	Liverpool	1-0
1989	Liverpool	Everton	3-2 (aet)
1990	Manchester U	Crystal Palace	1-0
	(after 3-3 draw, after extra time, at Wembley)		
1991	Tottenham H	Nottingham F	2-1 (aet)
1992	Liverpool	Sunderland	2-0
1993	Arsenal	Sheffield W	2-1 (aet)
	(after 1-1 draw, after extra time, at Wembley)		
1994	Manchester U	Chelsea	4-0
1995	Everton	Manchester U	1-0
1996	Manchester U	Liverpool	1-0

* Won outright, but restored to the Football Association.
† A special trophy was awarded for third consecutive win.

FA CUP WINS

Manchester U 9, Tottenham H 8, Aston Villa 7, Arsenal 6, Blackburn R 6, Newcastle U 6, Everton 5, Liverpool 5, The Wanderers 5, WBA 5, Bolton W 4, Manchester C 4, Sheffield U 4, Wolverhampton W 4, Sheffield W 3, West Ham U 3, Bury 2, Nottingham F 2, Old Etonians 2, Preston NE 2, Sunderland 2, Barnsley 1, Blackburn Olympic 1, Blackpool 1, Bradford C 1, Burnley 1, Cardiff C 1, Charlton Ath 1, Chelsea 1, Clapham R 1, Coventry C 1, Derby Co 1, Huddersfield T 1, Ipswich T 1, Leeds U 1, Notts Co 1, Old Carthusians 1, Oxford University 1, Portsmouth 1, Royal Engineers 1, Southampton 1, Wimbledon 1.

APPEARANCES IN FINALS

Manchester U 14, Arsenal 12, Everton 12, Liverpool 11, Newcastle U 11, WBA 10, Aston Villa 9, Tottenham H 9, Blackburn R 8, Manchester C 8, Wolverhampton W 8, Bolton W 7, Preston NE 7, Old Etonians 6, Sheffield U 6, Sheffield W 6, Huddersfield T 5, *The Wanderers 5, Chelsea 4, Derby Co 4, Leeds U 4, Leicester C 4, Oxford University 4, Royal Engineers 4, Sunderland 4, West Ham U 4, Blackpool 3, Burnley 3, Nottingham F 3, Portsmouth 3, Southampton 3, Barnsley 2, Birmingham C 2, *Bury 2, Cardiff C 2, Charlton Ath 2, Clapham R 2, Notts Co 2, Queen's Park (Glasgow) 2, *Blackburn Olympic 1, *Bradford C 1, Brighton & HA 1, Bristol C 1, *Coventry C 1, Crystal Palace 1, Fulham 1, *Ipswich T 1, Luton T 1, *Old Carthusians 1, QPR 1, Watford 1, *Wimbledon 1.
* Denotes undefeated.

APPEARANCES IN SEMI-FINALS

Everton 23, Manchester U 21, Liverpool 20, WBA 19, Arsenal 18, Aston Villa 18, Blackburn R 16, Sheffield W 16, Tottenham H 15, Derby Co 13, Newcastle U 13, Wolverhampton W 13, Bolton W 12, Nottingham F 12, Chelsea 12, Sheffield U 11, Sunderland 11, Manchester C 10, Preston NE 10, Southampton 10, Birmingham C 9, Burnley 8, Leeds U 8, Huddersfield T 7, Leicester C 7, Old Etonians 6, Oxford University 6, West Ham U 6, Fulham 5, Notts Co 5, Portsmouth 5, The Wanderers 5, Luton T 4, Queen's Park (Glasgow) 4, Royal Engineers 4, Blackpool 3, Cardiff C 3, Clapham R 3, Crystal Palace (professional club) 3, Ipswich T 3, Millwall 3, Norwich C 3, Old Carthusians 3, Oldham Ath 3, Stoke C 3, The Swifts 3, Watford 3, Barnsley 2, Blackburn Olympic 2, Bristol C 2, Bury 2, Charlton Ath 2, Grimsby T 2, Swansea T 2, Swindon T 2, Bradford C 1, Brighton & HA 1, Cambridge University 1, Coventry C 1, Crewe Alex 1, Crystal Palace (amateur club) 1, Darwen 1, Derby Junction 1, Glasgow R 1, Hull C 1, Marlow 1, Old Harrovians 1, Orient 1, Plymouth Arg 1, Port Vale 1, QPR 1, Reading 1, Shropshire W 1, Wimbledon 1, York C 1.

FA CUP 1995–96
SPONSORED BY LITTLEWOODS POOLS

PRELIMINARY AND QUALIFYING ROUNDS

Preliminary Round

Liversedge v Blackpool (Wren) Rovers	1-4
Guisborough Town v Gretna	1-0
Willington v Dunston Federation Brewery	0-0, 2-5
Prudhoe Town v Consett	1-3
(at Consett)	
South Shields v Pickering Town	3-4
Netherfield v Evenwood Town	10-1
RTM Newcastle v Harrogate Railway	1-2
Brandon United v Chester-Le-Street Town	1-4
Seaham Red Star v Billingham Town	1-2
Esh Winning v Stockton	3-1
Workington v Hebburn	8-1
Alnwick Town v Glasshoughton Welfare	1-3
Whitley Bay v Easington Colliery	3-0
Tadcaster Albion v Bedlington Terriers	1-1, 0-3
Ryhope CA v Morpeth Town	2-2, 1-3
Shotton Comrades v Shildon	1-1, 1-2
Washington v Garforth Town	1-0
(Washington removed for fielding a suspended player; Garforth Town re-instated)	
Darlington Cleveland Society v Billingham Synthonia	0-3
Prescot Cables v Atherton Collieries	3-0
Chadderton v Eastwood Town	0-1
Lincoln United v Stocksbridge Park Steels	3-2
Burscough v Northallerton 1994	2-2, 2-1
Eccleshill United v Atherton LR	3-2
Arnold Town v Maine Road	2-0
Glossop North End v Nantwich Town	1-2
Radcliffe Borough v Alfreton Town	3-2
Sheffield w.o. v Caernarfon Town withdrew	
Belper Town v Worksop Town	2-3
North Ferriby United v Heanor Town	2-4
Maltby MW v Mossley	3-3, 0-4
Leigh RMI v Flixton	2-0
Brigg Town v Clitheroe	1-1, 0-1
Farsley Celtic v Oldham Town	2-2, 2-0
Blidworth MW v Rossendale United	0-0, 0-3
St Helens Town v Bootle	1-2
Winterton Rangers v Darwen	2-0
Denaby United v Hucknall Town	4-0
Trafford v Fleetwood	2-1
Crook Town v Kimberley Town	3-2
Ossett Town v Castleton Gabriels	3-2
Armthorpe Welfare v Bradford (Park Avenue)	1-1, 0-1
Goole Town v Great Harwood Town	2-2, 2-3
(after abandoned match; floodlight failure 50 minutes at 1-0)	
Ossett Albion v Hatfield Main	1-3
Immingham Town v Rossington Main	1-1, 4-1
Louth United v Harworth CI	4-0
Salford City v Newcastle Town	1-2
Pontefract Collieries v Oakham United	4-1
Hinckley Athletic v Ashton United	1-1, 3-1
Thackley v Cheadle Town	5-2
Yorkshire Amateur v Borrowash Victoria	2-4
Bilston Town v Blakenall	0-0, 1-2
Redditch United v Bridgnorth Town	2-2, 4-1
Desborough Town v Rocester	0-0, 4-2
Shifnal Town v Willenhall Town	0-0, 1-0
West Midlands Police v Raunds Town	1-1, 2-3
Stourport Swifts v Armitage	0-1
Chasetown v Halesowen Harriers	2-1
Tamworth v Hinckley Town	3-1
Westfields v Corby Town	1-1, 5-7
Wellingborough Town v Bolehall Swifts	0-4
Shepshed Dynamo v Grantham Town	0-1
Stapenhill v Lye Town	1-2
Northampton Spencer v Cogenhoe United	2-2, 0-1
Pelsall Villa v Dudley Town	1-1, 0-1
Brierley Hill Town v Sandwell Borough	0-0, 3-5
Pershore Town v Evesham United	1-1, 2-3
Newport Pagnell Town v Boldmere St Michaels	0-2
Leicester United v Barwell	0-0, 1-1, 4-3
Wednesfield v Banbury United	2-2, 3-0

Oldbury United v Darlaston	4-0
Long Buckby v Stewarts & Lloyds	2-1
Knypersley Victoria v Stratford Town	0-3
(at Newcastle Town)	
Rothwell Town v Rushall Olympic	2-0
East Thurrock United v Tiptree United	1-1, 2-6
Gorleston v Diss Town	1-5
Halstead Town v Stamford	1-1, 3-3, 2-1
Wisbech Town v Tring Town	4-0
Eynesbury Rovers v Witham Town	4-1
Wroxham v Canvey Island	0-0, 1-3
Spalding United v Harwich & Parkeston	2-3
Kings Lynn v Wivenhoe Town	3-0
Newmarket Town v Boston Town	0-1
Basildon United v Saffron Walden Town	1-2
Aveley v Stowmarket Town	0-0, 4-3
Great Yarmouth Town v Bourne Town	2-1
Burnham Ramblers v Holbeach United	1-3
Bury Town v Collier Row	1-2
March Town United v Fakenham Town	1-0
Leyton Pennant v Clacton Town	2-2, 4-0
East Ham United v Sudbury Wanderers	0-7
Hertford Town v Ware	2-1
Cheshunt v Wealdstone	0-1
Tufnell Park v Potton United	1-0
Felixstowe Town v Burnham	1-1, 3-2
Bedford Town v Edgware Town	1-4
Hillingdon Borough v Cornard United	2-0
Hornchurch v Bowers United	3-0
Biggleswade Town v Berkhamsted Town	0-4
(at Langford)	
Lowestoft Town v Chalfont St Peter	2-2, 1-4
Haverhill Rovers v Hampton	0-1
Uxbridge v Kempston Rovers	4-0
Brook House v Welwyn Garden City	0-0, 2-0
Northwood v Ford United	3-2
Hadleigh United v Southall	1-0
Soham Town Rangers v Stotfold	1-1, 1-4
Tilbury v Woodbridge Town	1-2
Brimsdown Rovers v Barton Rovers	0-2
Harefield United v Hoddesdon Town	0-1
Metropolitan Police v Viking Sports	7-0
Concord Rangers v Wootton Blue Cross	2-1
Clapton v Leighton Town	2-1
Flackwell Heath v Potters Bar Town	1-0
Barking v Royston Town	1-0
Bedfont v Langford	0-0, 1-1, 0-4
Hanwell Town v Wingate & Finchley	2-4
Harlow Town v Thamesmead Town	2-3
Milton Keynes v Leatherhead	0-4
Bracknell Town v Kingsbury Town	0-0, 0-0, 1-1, 3-2
Three Bridges v Camberley Town	0-5
Corinthian-Casuals v Stamco	3-0
Lewes v Lancing	2-1
Dartford v Egham Town	3-1
(at Egham Town)	
Fisher v Merstham	0-0, 2-0
Tonbridge v Croydon Athletic	3-1
Croydon v Dorking	5-2
Folkestone Invicta v Peacehaven & Telscombe	1-1, 1-4
Shoreham v Corinthian	4-2
Epsom & Ewell v Tooting & Mitcham United	0-4
Littlehampton Town v Southwick	1-1, 0-1
Chatham Town v Whyteleafe	3-1
Banstead Athletic v Burgess Hill Town	3-1
Bognor Regis Town v Whitehawk	4-3
Raynes Park Vale v Canterbury City	3-0
Redhill v Tunbridge Wells	3-1
Chipstead v Horsham	0-4
Wick v Portfield	3-2
Herne Bay v Horsham YMCA	1-1, 4-1
Sheppey United v Arundel	2-0
Slade Green v Langney Sports	0-2
Whitstable Town v Hailsham Town	3-2
Crowborough Athletic v Godalming & Guildford	1-3

Bicester Town v Ringmer   0-1
(at Ringmer)
Aldershot Town v Selsey   5-0
Steyning Town v Cove   3-0
Newbury Town removed from competition v
  Buckingham Town w.o.
Thatcham Town v Oakwood   2-1
Hungerford Town v Poole Town   5-0
Abingdon Town v Andover   3-2
Totton AFC v Fleet Town   3-1
Witney Town v BAT Sports   5-0
Thame United v Maidenhead United   4-0
Bournemouth v Wimborne Town   0-4
Westbury United v Basingstoke Town   2-2, 1-5
Fareham Town v Weymouth   1-1, 2-3
Lymington AFC v Calne Town   0-2
(at Calne Town)
Bemerton Heath Harlequins v Ryde   2-3
Brockenhurst v Swanage Town & Herston   0-0, 1-1, 1-0
Melksham Town v Bridport   1-2
Welton Rovers v Odd Down   2-0
Gosport Borough v Eastleigh   2-0
Chippenham Town v Paulton Rovers   0-0, 1-1, 0-2
Devizes Town v Bristol Manor Farm   1-1, 1-3
Glastonbury v Tuffley Rovers   1-5
Clevedon Town v Mangotsfield United   1-5
Worcester City v Yate Town   1-2
Forest Green Rovers v Exmouth Town   4-0
Backwell United v Elmore   0-1
Saltash United v Torrington   3-2
Weston-Super-Mare v St Blazey   7-0
Barnstaple Town v Minehead   2-0
Falmouth Town v Frome Town   3-0

First Qualifying Round
Durham City v Blackpool (Wren) Rovers   1-1, 5-1
Barrow v Consett   3-0
Gateshead v Dunston Federation Brewery   3-2
Guisborough Town v Murton   1-0
Lancaster City v Pickering Town   2-1
Tow Law Town v Chester-Le-Street Town   3-3, 3-1
Bishop Auckland v Harrogate Railway   2-1
Netherfield v Peterlee Newtown   2-4
Whitby Town v Billingham Town   0-1
Spennymoor United v Glasshoughton Welfare   1-0
Whitley Bay v Workington   1-2
Esh Winning v West Auckland Town   1-2
Harrogate Town v Bedlington Terriers   1-2
Blyth Spartans v Garforth Town   6-0
Billingham Synthonia v Shildon   3-1
Morpeth Town v Whickham   1-2
Frickley Athletic v Prescot Cables   0-0, 2-2, 1-0
(at St Helens Town)
Northwich Victoria v Burscough   5-0
Eccleshill United v Lincoln United   2-3
Eastwood Town v Buxton   2-1
Gainsborough Trinity v Arnold Town   2-0
Morecambe v Sheffield   7-0
Worksop Town v Radcliffe Borough   4-0
Nantwich Town v Droylsden   3-0
Bamber Bridge v Heanor Town   4-1
Leek Town v Clitheroe   1-1, 2-2, 0-0, 1-0
Guiseley v Leigh RMI   3-0
Mossley v Hallam   1-0
Chorley v Farsley Celtic   2-2, 2-1
Hyde United v Winterton Rangers   6-0
(at Curzon Ashton)
Denaby United v Bootle   3-0
Rossendale United v Colwyn Bay   1-4
Warrington Town v Trafford   2-2, 3-4
Knowsley United v Bradford (Park Avenue)   0-0, 2-3
(at Bootle)
Accrington Stanley v Ossett Town   2-1
Crook Town v Curzon Ashton   1-1, 1-2
Matlock Town v Great Harwood Town   5-2
Marine v Louth United   4-0
Newcastle Town v Immingham Town   5-0
Hatfield Main v Ilkeston Town   0-2
Congleton Town v Pontefract Collieries   3-1
Winsford United v Borrowash Victoria   1-0
Emley v Thackley   6-0
Hinckley Athletic v Kidsgrove Athletic   3-1
Halesowen Town v Blakenall   3-2
Telford United v Shifnal Town   4-0
Raunds Town v Desborough Town   3-0
Redditch United v Moor Green   1-3

Atherstone United v Armitage   2-2, 3-3, 4-5
Hednesford Town v Corby Town   3-1
Bolehall Swifts v Tamworth   0-1
Chasetown v Solihull Borough   1-3
Rushden & Diamonds v Grantham Town   4-1
Gresley Rovers v Dudley Town   1-2
Sandwell Borough v Cogenhoe United   2-1
Lye Town v Eastwood Hanley   1-2
Stourbridge v Evesham United   2-2, 0-3
Paget Rangers v Wednesfield   1-0
VS Rugby v Leicester United   1-2
Boldmere St Michaels v Bedworth United   1-2
Racing Club Warwick v Oldbury United   1-0
Stafford Rangers v Rothwell Town   6-1
Burton Albion v Stratford Town   4-0
Long Buckby v Sutton Coldfield Town   2-1
Sudbury Town v Tiptree United   3-0
Boston United v Wisbech Town   1-2
Eynesbury Rovers v Halstead Town   7-1
Diss Town v Heybridge Swifts   0-2
Cambridge City v Canvey Island   2-3
Bishop's Stortford v Boston Town   2-2, 2-5
Saffron Walden Town v Kings Lynn   0-2
Harwich & Parkeston v Braintree Town   0-1
Billericay Town v Aveley   2-0
Chelmsford City v Collier Row   1-0
March Town United v Holbeach United   0-3
Great Yarmouth Town v Mirrlees Blackstone   2-1
Arlesy Town v Leyton Pennant   3-0
Grays Athletic v Wealdstone   2-2, 3-4
Tufnell Park v Hertford Town   2-2, 1-5
Sudbury Wanderers v Watton United   3-1
Purfleet v Felixstowe Port & Town   4-0
Dagenham & Redbridge v Hornchurch   4-0
Berkhamsted Town v Hillingdon Borough   3-2
Edgware Town v Chesham United   0-1
Boreham Wood v Chalfont St Peter   1-0
Stevenage Borough v Brook House   0-0, 5-1
Northwood v Uxbridge   0-5
Hampton v Staines Town   1-2
Romford v Hadleigh United   1-0
St Albans City v Barton Rovers   4-1
Hoddesdon Town v Woodbridge Town   0-2
Stotfold v Hemel Hempstead   2-1
Baldock Town v Metropolitan Police   2-1
Hendon v Flackwell Heath   8-0
Barking v Clapton   1-3
Concord Rangers v Hayes   0-3
Wembley v Langford   3-0
Harrow Borough v Leatherhead   2-1
Bracknell Town v Thamesmead Town   1-1, 3-2
Wingate & Finchley v Ruislip Manor   2-3
Walton & Hersham v Camberley Town   4-0
Farnborough Town v Dartford   1-0
Fisher v Lewes   7-0
Corinthian-Casuals v Margate   2-5
Ashford Town v Tonbridge   2-0
Chertsey Town v Shoreham   2-2, 3-1
Tooting & Mitcham United v
  Peacehaven & Telscombe   0-0, 1-0
Croydon v Hastings Town   2-3
Dulwich Hamlet v Southwick   7-1
Dover Athletic v Bognor Regis Town   1-2
Raynes Park Vale v Banstead Athletic   1-2
Chatham Town v Ramsgate   1-1, 2-0
Erith & Belvedere v Redhill   4-1
Bromley v Herne Bay   3-1
Welling United v Wick   2-0
Horsham v Sittingbourne   0-5
Carshalton Athletic v Sheppey United   3-1
Gravesend & Northfleet v Godalming & Guildford   7-0
Molesey v Whitstable Town   4-1
Langney Sports v Windsor & Eton   1-3
Wokingham Town v Ringmer   3-1
Worthing v Buckingham Town   1-1, 0-0, 2-2, 1-6
Thatcham Town v Steyning Town   5-1
Aldershot Town v Pagham   4-0
Salisbury City v Hungerford Town   5-2
Oxford City v Witney Town   1-1, 1-3
Thame United v Totton AFC   1-1, 4-0
Abingdon Town v Newport (IW)   2-3
Dorchester Town v Wimborne Town   2-2, 2-0
Waterlooville v Calne Town   5-0
Ryde v Weymouth   1-1, 1-2
Basingstoke Town v Havant Town   2-1
Newport AFC v Brockenhurst   5-0

Trowbridge Town v Gosport Borough	8-1
Paulton Rovers v Welton Rovers	1-1, 1-2
Bridport v Merthyr Tydfil	0-3
Gloucester City v Bristol Manor Farm	8-0
Cheltenham Town v Yate Town	5-0
Forest Green Rovers v Mangotsfield United	2-1
Tuffley Rovers v Cinderford Town	0-4
Bideford v Elmore	2-2, 6-2
Tiverton Town v Barnstaple Town	9-0
Falmouth Town v Weston-Super-Mare	1-1, 0-5
Saltash United v Taunton Town	1-2

Second Qualifying Round

Durham City v Guisborough Town	2-1
Gateshead v Barrow	2-2, 0-1
Lancaster City v Peterlee Newtown	3-0
Bishop Auckland v Tow Law Town	2-1
Billingham Town v West Auckland Town	1-0
Workington v Spennymoor United	2-4
Bedlington Terriers v Whickham	1-0
Billingham Synthonia v Blyth Spartans	0-2
Frickley Athletic v Eastwood Town	2-4
Lincoln United v Northwich Victoria	1-4
Gainsborough Trinity v Nantwich Town	5-0
Worksop Town v Morecambe	2-3
Bamber Bridge v Mossley	0-2
Guiseley v Leek Town	4-0
Chorley v Colwyn Bay	1-2
Denaby United v Hyde United	1-2
Trafford v Curzon Ashton	1-2
Accrington Stanley v Bradford (Park Avenue)	1-2
Matlock Town v Ilkeston Town	1-2
Newcastle Town v Marine	0-1
Congleton Town v Hinckley Athletic	1-1, 0-1
Emley v Winsford United	1-1, 1-2
Halesowen Town v Moor Green	1-0
Raunds Town v Telford United	1-2
Armitage v Solihull Borough	2-3
Tamworth v Hednesford Town	1-2
Rushden & Diamonds v Eastwood Hanley	1-0
Sandwell Borough v Dudley Town	2-1
Evesham United v Bedworth United	2-0
Leicester United v Paget Rangers	3-2
Racing Club Warwick v Long Buckby	2-0
Burton Albion v Stafford Rangers	1-1, 3-2
Sudbury Town v Heybridge Swifts	2-1
Eynesbury Rovers v Wisbech Town	3-3, 1-6
Canvey Island v Braintree Town	2-0
Kings Lynn v Boston Town	5-1
Billericay Town v Great Yarmouth Town	2-0
Holbeach United v Chelmsford City	0-0, 1-3
Arlesey Town v Sudbury Wanderers	1-2
Hertford Town v Wealdstone	1-0
Purfleet v Chesham United	3-1
Berkhamsted Town v Dagenham & Redbridge	1-2
Boreham Wood v Staines Town	0-1
Uxbridge v Stevenage Borough	0-1
Romford v Stotfold	4-1
Woodbridge Town v St Albans City	1-1, 0-2
Baldock Town v Hayes	0-1
Clapton v Hendon	2-3
Wembley v Ruislip Manor	3-0
Bracknell Town v Harrow Borough	2-1
Walton & Hersham v Margate	2-2, 1-0
Fisher v Farnborough Town	1-4
Ashford Town v Hastings Town	3-1
Tooting & Mitcham United v Chertsey Town	2-2, 2-1
Dulwich Hamlet v Chatham Town	2-1
Banstead Athletic v Bognor Regis Town	0-3
Erith & Belvedere v Sittingbourne	2-2, 1-6
Welling United v Bromley	2-2, 3-3, 1-2
Carshalton Athletic v Windsor & Eton	4-3
Molesey v Gravesend & Northfleet	0-6
Wokingham Town v Aldershot Town	1-2
Thatcham Town v Buckingham Town	0-1
Salisbury City v Newport (IW)	1-3
Thame United v Witney Town	1-1, 3-2
Dorchester Town v Basingstoke Town	2-0

Weymouth v Waterlooville	1-0
Newport AFC v Merthyr Tydfil	3-3, 2-1
Welton Rovers v Trowbridge Town	1-2
Gloucester City v Cinderford Town	0-1
Forest Green Rovers v Cheltenham Town	3-0
Bideford v Taunton Town	4-3
Weston-Super-Mare v Tiverton Town	1-1, 0-1

Third Qualifying Round

Barrow v Durham City	1-1, 1-0
Bishop Auckland v Lancaster City	0-1
Spennymoor United v Billingham Town	6-1
Blyth Spartans v Bedlington Terriers	3-1
Northwich Victoria v Eastwood Town	0-0, 2-1
Morecambe v Gainsborough Trinity	6-2
Guiseley v Mossley	6-1
Hyde United v Colwyn Bay	1-2
(at Curzon Ashton)	
Bradford (Park Avenue) v Curzon Ashton	2-1
Marine v Ilkeston Town	0-0, 2-1
Winsford United v Hinckley Athletic	3-2
Telford United v Halesowen Town	4-1
Hednesford Town v Solihull Borough	2-2, 2-1
Sandwell Borough v Rushden & Diamonds	1-6
Leicester United v Evesham United	0-1
Burton Albion v Racing Club Warwick	2-0
Wisbech Town v Sudbury Town	1-0
Kings Lynn v Canvey Island	1-0
Chelmsford City v Billericay Town	1-1, 1-2
Hertford Town v Sudbury Wanderers	0-2
Dagenham & Redbridge v Purfleet	1-1, 1-2
Stevenage Borough v Staines Town	2-0
St Albans City v Romford	3-1
Hendon v Hayes	0-3
Bracknell Town v Wembley	4-1
Farnborough Town v Walton & Hersham	3-2
Tooting & Mitcham United v Ashford Town	0-1
Bognor Regis Town v Dulwich Hamlet	4-2
Bromley v Sittingbourne	1-1, 2-3
Gravesend & Northfleet v Carshalton Athletic	2-1
Buckingham Town v Aldershot Town	0-1
Thame United v Newport (IW)	1-1, 1-3
Weymouth v Dorchester Town	2-3
Trowbridge Town v Newport AFC	2-0
Forest Green Rovers v Cinderford Town	1-1, 1-1, 1-3
Tiverton Town v Bideford	4-1

Fourth Qualifying Round

Blyth Spartans v Guiseley	2-0
Spennymoor United v Lancaster City	1-0
Marine Town v Bradford (Park Avenue)	2-0
Telford United v Southport	3-0
Winsford United v Barrow	0-3
Macclesfield Town v Northwich Victoria	0-1
Witton Albion v Morecambe	3-2
Stalybridge Celtic v Colwyn Bay	2-2, 0-3
Runcorn v Halifax Town	2-1
Purfleet v Rushden & Diamonds	1-1, 1-3
Canvey Island v Hednesford Town	2-0
(Kings Lynn removed from the competition for fielding a suspended player)	
Aylesbury United v Stevenage Borough	1-3
Nuneaton Borough v Evesham United	6-1
Billericay Town v Wisbech Town	1-1, 0-2
Hayes v Sudbury Wanderers	4-0
Burton Albion v Bracknell Town	3-1
Hitchin Town v St Albans City	2-1
Kettering Town v Bromsgrove Rovers	0-0, 2-2 1-2
Kingstonian v Trowbridge Town	3-1
Tiverton Town v Bognor Regis Town	1-4
Farnborough Town v Yeovil Town	2-1
Newport (IW) v Bashley	1-1, 3-2
Yeading v Slough Town	0-2
Sutton United v Crawley Town	4-1
Gravesend & Northfleet v Marlow	1-1, 1-1, 4-0
Sittingbourne v Dorchester Town	1-2
Ashford Town v Aldershot Town	2-0
Cinderford Town v Bath City	3-2

FA CUP 1995–96
SPONSORED BY LITTLEWOODS POOLS

COMPETITION PROPER

FIRST ROUND

10 NOV

Burnley (1) 1 *(Eyres)*
Walsall (1) 3 *(Bradley, Wilson, Houghton)*   6525
Burnley: Beresford; Parkinson, Vinnicombe, Swan, Winstanley, Hoyland (Cooke), Harrison, Randall (Borland), Eyres, Nogan, McMinn (Francis).
Walsall: Walker; Ntamark, Rogers, Viveash, Marsh, Watkiss, O'Connor, Bradley (Roper), Lightbourne (Keister), Wilson, Houghton (Butler).

11 NOV

Barnet (2) 2 *(Primus, Devine)*
Woking (2) 2 *(Hay, Steele)*   3034
Barnet: Taylor; Gale, Campbell, Pardew, Primus, McDonald (Hodges), Mills (Dyer), Scott, Cooper, Devine (Tomlinson), Wilson.
Woking: Batty; Tucker, Timothy (Wye), Fielder, Brown, Crumplin, Thompson, Ellis, Steele, Hay, Walker.

Barrow (2) 2 *(Morton, Dobie)*
Nuneaton (1) 1 *(Simpson)*   2869
Barrow: Deegan; Speak, Kennedy J, Harold, Parker, Brown (Kennedy E), Todhunter, Humphries, Dobie, Morton, Hoskin.
Nuneaton: Hayward; Donald, Luby, Statham, Williams, Crowley, Andersen, Carr, Straw, Drewitt (Donnelly), Simpson.

Blackpool (0) 2 *(Quinn, Lydiate)*
Chester C (0) 1 *(Milner)*   5004
Blackpool: Banks; Bryan, Brown P, Lydiate, Mellon, Quinn, Gouck (Watson), Bonner, Morrison, Ellis (Preece), Holden.
Chester C: Stewart; Whelan, Burnham (Jenkins), Priest, Jackson, Alsford, Richardson, Fisher, Regis, Milner, Noteman.

Bognor Regis (0) 1 *(Birmingham)*
Ashford T (1) 1 *(Allon)*   2200
Bognor Regis: Matthews; Pullen P, Beazeley, Pearce D (Eastland), Marriner, Pullen M, Rutherford, Birmingham, Rice, Cormack, Miles (Pearce R).
Ashford T: Munden; White, Lemoine A, Pearson, Warrillo, Wynter, Wheeler, Allon, Arter, Stanton (Curruthers), Ross.

Bournemouth (0) 0
Bristol C (0) 0   5304
Bournemouth: Moss; Young, Beardsmore, Morris, Murray, Pennock, Holland, Bailey (Robinson), Jones, Fletcher, Brissett.
Bristol C: Welch; Paterson, Edwards, Dryden, Shail, Kuhl, Bent (Partridge), Owers, Nugent, Barnard, Carey.

Bradford C (3) 4 *(Showler 2, Robson, Ormondroyd)*
Burton Alb (3) 3 *(Rhodes (pen), Stride 2)*   4920
Bradford C: Ward; Liburd, Jacobs (Huxford), Robson, Mohan, Ford, Murray (Midgley), Hamilton, Ormondroyd, Tolson, Showler.
Burton Alb: Acton; Davies, Williams, Smith R, Smith M, Keast, Stride, Redfern, Rhodes, Devaney, Gretton.

Brentford (1) 1 *(Bent)*
Farnborough (0) 1 *(Senior)*   4711
Brentford: Fernandes; Harvey, Grainger, Hutchings, Bates, McGhee, Asaba, Smith, Forster (Hooker), Martin, Bent.
Farnborough: McKenzie; Baker S, Stemp, Coney, McAndy, Robson, Boothe, Harlow, Senior, Denny, Baker K.

Bury (0) 0
Blyth Spartans (1) 2 *(Bond, Ditchburn)*   3076
Bury: Kelly; Cross, West, Reid, Lucketti, Matthewson, Hughes (Sertori), Carter, Stant, Rigby (Johnson), Pugh.
Blyth Spartans: O'Conner; Curry, Teasdale, Walker, Raffell, Gamble, Telfer, Sokoluk, Ditchburn, Bond, Hays.

Carlisle U (1) 1 *(Reeves)*
Preston NE (0) 2 *(Cartwright, Wilcox)*   7046
Carlisle U: Caig; Prokas, Gallimore, Walling, Robinson, Thorpe, Thomas (Peacock), Currie, Reeves, Aspinall (Conway), Murray.
Preston NE: Vaughan; Fensome, Barrick, Atkinson, Wilcox, Moyes, Davey, Bryson, Saville, Wilkinson, Cartwright.

Cinderford T (1) 2 *(Price, Hill)*
Bromsgrove R (0) 1 *(Skelding (pen))*   1850
Cinderford T: Bowles; Price (Criddle), Wilton, Boxall, Howells, Cole, Hamilton, Crouch, Hill (Townsend), Thomas, Smith.
Bromsgrove R: Taylor; Skelding, Brighton, Richardson, Randall, Dowling (Carter), Smith, Grocutt, Dale, Crisp, Radburn (Power).

Exeter C (0) 0
Peterborough U (1) 1 *(Le Bihan)*   3783
Exeter C: Fox; Parsley, Hughes, Buckle, Blake, Richardson, Gavin, Bailey (Anderson), Pears (Hare), Came (Turner), Phillips.
Peterborough U: Sheffield; Ashley, Clark, Ebdon, Breen, Heald, Gregory, Le Bihan (Furnell), Martindale (Farrell), Power (Williams), Rioch.

Fulham (3) 7 *(Conroy 3, Jupp, Cusack, Brooker, Thomas)*
Swansea C (0) 0   4798
Fulham: Lange; Jupp, Herrera, Barkus (Brooker), Moore, Angus, Thomas, Morgan, Brazil (Hamill), Conroy (Bolt), Cusack.
Swansea C: Freestone; Barnhouse, Cook, Basham (Perrett), Edwards, Pascoe, Hodge, Heggs, Torpey, Chapple, Coates.

Gravesend & N (1) 2 *(Jackson, Mortley)*
Colchester U (0) 0   3120
Gravesend & N: Turner; Walker, Lamb, Gubbins, Mortley, Jackson, Best (Gooding), Cotter (Bourne), Blewden, Munday, Powell.
Colchester U: Emberson; Fry, Betts, McCarthy, Caesar (Gibbs), Cawley, Kinsella, English, Mardenborough, Adcock, Cheetham.

Hartlepool U (1) 2 *(Sloan, Halliday)* 3834
Darlington (2) 4 *(Brumwell, Gaughan, Bannister, Painter)*
Hartlepool U: Horne; Ingram, Allinson (Lynch), Billing, McGuckin, Henderson, Sloan, Tait (Oliver), Howard, Halliday, McAuley.
Darlington: Pollitt; Shaw, Brumwell, Appleby, Crosby, Gregan, Himsworth, Olsson, Painter, Gaughan (Robinson), Bannister.

Hereford U (0) 2 *(White, Cross)*
Stevenage B (1) 1 *(Crawshaw)* 3321
Hereford U: Mackenzie; Evans, Fishlock, Smith D, Stoker, Pick, Pounder, Wilkins, Cross, White, Preedy.
Stevenage B: Gallagher; Webster, Mutchell, Sodje, Nugent, Barrowcliffe, Beevor (Berry), Browne, Crawshaw (Venables), Lynch, Hayles.

Hitchin (2) 2 *(Conroy, Burns)*
Bristol R (1) 1 *(Archer)* 3001
Hitchin: Sylvester; McMonamin, Covington, Burke, Bone, Scott, Burns, Conroy, Williams, Cooper, Gillard.
Bristol R: Collett; Pritchard, Gurney, Hayfield (Channing), McLean, Tillson, Sterling, Wright, Stewart, Skinner, Archer.

Hull C (0) 0
Wrexham (0) 0 3724
Hull C: Wilson; Lowthorpe, Mann, Allison, Dewhurst, Pridmore (Hobson), Williams, Lee, Fewings (Brown), Windass, Peacock.
Wrexham: Marriott; McGregor, Hardy, Phillips (Hughes), Humes, Jones, Durkan, Brammer, Connolly, Russell (Watkin), Ward.

Kidderminster H (1) 2 *(Hughes, Webb (pen))*
Sutton U (0) 2 *(Hynes, Vansittart)* 2513
Kidderminster H: Steadman; Hodson, Bancroft, Weir, Brindley, Yates, Shepherd, Webb, May, Davies, Hughes.
Sutton U: McCann; Gates, Benning, Marchant, Costello, Green, Payne, Hynes, Vansittart, Feltham, Dack.

Kingstonian (0) 5 *(Wingfield 2, Riley, Warden, Akuamoah)*
Wisbech (1) 1 *(McLaughlin)* 1396
Kingstonian: Root; Brooker (Jasper), Riley, Finch, Nebbeling, Fisher, Warmington, Luckett (Stevens), Warden, Akuamoah, Wingfield (Kane).
Wisbech: Cross; Shelton, Lindsay, Munns, Slade, Massingham (Garner), Parrott, McLaughlin, De'ath (Wales), Gallagher, Topliss.

Mansfield T (3) 4 *(Harper, Sherlock, Parkin, Doolan)*
Doncaster R (0) 2 *(Jones (pen), Carmichael)* 3116
Mansfield T: Bowling; Boothroyd, Hackett, Doolan, Eustace, Peters, Ireland, Parkin, Harper, Hadley (Onuora), Sherlock.
Doncaster R: Suckling; Measham (Carmichael), Colcombe, Moore, Kirby, Clark, Schofield, Brabin (Darby), Jones, Warren, Parrish.

Newport (IW) (1) 1 *(Fearon)*
Enfield (1) 1 *(Abbott)* 1818
Newport (IW): Simpkins; Wickens, Hughes, Leader, Phillips, Male (Bartlett), Gee, Ritchie, Webb, Soares, Fearon (Barsdell).
Enfield: Pape; Blackford, May, Hoddle, Terry, Ridout, Adams, Sayer, Abbott, Nolan (Cooper), Gentle (Fleming).

Northampton T (0) 1 *(Warburton)*
Hayes (0) 0 5389
Northampton T: Woodman; Norton, Maddison, Peer, Warburton, O'Shea, Lee (Colkin), Grayson, White, Burns, Hunter.
Hayes: Meara; Wilkinson, Stevens, Kelly W, Cox, Denton, Baker (Brady), Kellman, Kelly T (Knight), Pearce (Hyatt), Goodliffe.

Northwich Vic (0) 1 *(Cooke)*
Scunthorpe U (0) 3 *(Ford, McFarlane 2)* 2685
Northwich Vic: Greygoose; Burgess, Jones, Tinson, Simpson, Walters, Williams, Butler, Cooke, Clayton (Vicary), Duffy.
Scunthorpe U: Samways; Housham, Wilson, Ford (Nicholson), Knill, Bradley, Thornber, Bullimore, McFarlane, Eyre, Paterson.

Oxford U (2) 9 *(Ford M, Wood 2, Rush, Ford R, Moody 3, Beauchamp)*
Dorchester (0) 1 *(Killick (pen))* 3819
Oxford U: Whitehead; Wood, Ford M, Smith, Elliott, Gilchrist, Rush, Massey (Murphy), Moody, Ford R, Angel (Beauchamp).
Dorchester: Veysey; Coates, Morgan, Tallon, Reeve, Wilkinson, Richardson, Taylor, Killick, Pickard (Milner), Evans (Jordan).

Rochdale (3) 5 *(Moulden 2, Whitehall (pen), Peake 2)*
Rotherham U (0) 3 *(Goater 2 (1 pen), McGlashan)* 3817
Rochdale: Gray; Thackeray, Formby, Martin, Valentine (Bayliss), Butler, Thompson (Thompstone), Moulden, Stuart (Shaw), Whitehall, Peake.
Rotherham U: Davis; Wilder, Hurst (Hayward), Garner, Breckin, Blades, Berry, McGlashan, Jeffrey, Goater, Roscoe.

Runcorn (0) 1 *(Bignall)*
Wigan Ath (1) 1 *(Martinez)* 2844
Runcorn: Morris; Bates, Rutter, Ellis, Byrne, Brady, Clowes (Taylor), Doherty N, Farrington, Bignall, Smith.
Wigan Ath: Farnworth; Carragher, Butler, Greenall, Robertson, Martinez, Diaz, Lightfoot, Leonard, Pender, Black (Lyons).

Rushden & D (0) 1 *(Hannigan)*
Cardiff C (2) 3 *(Dale 2, Jarman)* 4212
Rushden & D: Benstead; Wooding, Ashby, Peaks (Spooner), Smith, Hannigan, Kirkup, Butterworth, Nuttell (Watkins), Wilkin, Collins.
Cardiff C: Williams D; Brazil (Oatway), Searle, Rodgerson, Jarman, Young, Fleming, Adams (Evans A), Dale, Wigg, Gardner.

Scarborough (0) 0
Chesterfield (0) 2 *(Lormor 2)* 2354
Scarborough: Ironside; Knowles, Lucas, D'Auria, Hicks, Boardman, Charles, Todd, Page, Ritchie (Heald), Kinnaird (Trebble).
Chesterfield: Beasley; Rogers, Dyche, Curtis, Williams, Law, Robinson, Davies, Lormor, Roberts (Hazel), Howard.

Shrewsbury T (4) 11 *(Proctor (og), Spink 3, Withe, Scott, Whiston 2, Evans, Stevens, Dempsey)*
Marine (0) 2 *(Penman, Rowlands)* 2845
Shrewsbury T: Edwards; Seabury (Dempsey), Withe, Evans, Whiston, Scott, Woods, Stevens, Spink (Anthrobus), Walton, Berkley.
Marine: O'Brien; Baines, Proctor, Murray, Draper, Ward (Moss), Lundon (Hollywood), Rowlands, Grant, Penman, Rooney.

Slough (0) 0
Plymouth Arg (0) 2 *(Harvey (og), Heathcote)* 3013
Slough: Preddie; Honor, Clement, Paris, Baron, Harvey, Catlin, Bushay (Lee), West, Pickett (Blackman), Fiore (Rake).
Plymouth Arg: Blackwell; Patterson, Williams, Clayton, Heathcote, Hill, Billy (Logan), Mauge, Littlejohn, Evans, Leadbitter.

Spennymoor U(0) 0
Colwyn Bay (0) 1 *(Nicholas)* 824
Spennymoor U: Swan; O'Hara (Goodrick), Skedd, Coatsworth, Saunders, Healy, Alderson (Cowell), Ainsley, Gorman, Ludlow (Watson), Veart.
Colwyn Bay: Roberts R; McCoch, Mann, Harley, Woods (Dulson), Price, Nicholas, Roberts G, Drury, Donnelly, Rigby.

Stockport Co (3) 5 *(Eckhardt 3, Barnett (og), Armstrong)*
Lincoln C (0) 0 3952
Stockport Co: Edwards; Connelly, Todd, Bennett, Flynn, Gannon (Dinning), Beaumont, Oliver (Ware), Eckhardt, Armstrong (Mike), Chalk.
Lincoln C: Richardson; Barnett, Whitney, Minett, Westley, Brown G, Ainsworth, Onwere, Johnson D, Hulme (Daley) (Mudd), Brown S.

Swindon T (2) 4 *(Horlock 2, Finney, Allen)*
Cambridge U (0) 1 *(Butler)* 7383
Swindon T: Digby; Culverhouse, Bodin (Drysdale), McMahon (Gooden), Allen, Taylor, Robinson, O'Sullivan, Finney, Allison (Thorne), Horlock.
Cambridge U: Barrett; Joseph, Palmer, Jeffrey, Craddock, Raynor, Rattle (Kyd), Middleton C (Granville), Butler, Corazzin, Hyde.

Telford U (1) 2 *(Foster, Langford)*
Witton Alb (1) 1 *(Watson)* 1277
Telford U: Goodwin; Gardiner (Langford), Fowler, Ramsay, Foster, Niblett, Myers, Clarke, Gray, Bignot, Robinson.
Witton Alb: Oakes; Macauley, Albiston, McNeilis, Pritchard B, Ranson, Rodwell, Rose, Thomas (Pritchard D), Morley (Camden), Watson.

Torquay U (0) 1 *(Byng)*
Leyton Orient (0) 0 2434
Torquay U: Bayes; Travis, Kelly, Curran, Laight, Barrow, Jack, Coughlin (Hodges), Moores (Hall), Hathaway, Ndah (Byng).
Leyton Orient: Fearon; Hendon, Stanislaus, Chapman, Bellamy, Austin, Kelly T, Cockerill, Williams, West, Brooks (Baker).

12 NOV

Canvey Island (1) 2 *(Porter, Brett)*
Brighton & HA (2) 2 *(McDougald 2)* 3403
Canvey Island: Keeley; Lee, Martin (Blakebrough), Joscelyn, Porter, Brett, Pennyfather, Pizzey, Britnell, Jones, Mahoney (Harding).
Brighton & HA: Rust; Smith, Myall, Parris, Osman, McCarthy, Mundee (Munday), McDougald, Minton, Byrne, Wilkins.

York C (0) 0
Notts Co (1) 1 *(Legg)* 4228
York C: Warrington; McMillan, Osborne, Pepper, Tutill, Barras, Matthews, Williams (Curtis), Barnes, Baker, Jordan.
Notts Co: Ward; Mills, Baraclough, Nicol, Strodder, Murphy, Gallagher, Devlin, Simpson, Arkins, Legg.

13 NOV

Wycombe W (0) 1 *(Patterson)*
Gillingham (0) 1 *(Bailey)* 5064
Wycombe W: Hyde; Rowbotham, Bell, Howard, Cousins, Brown, Carroll, Patterson, De Souza, Garner, Farrell.
Gillingham: Stannard; Micklewhite (Puttnam), Naylor, Smith, Harris, Green, Martin, Ratcliffe, Rattray (Freeman), Bailey, O'Connor.

FIRST ROUND REPLAYS

21 NOV

Ashford (0) 0
Bognor Regis (0) 1 *(Pearce D)* 2542
Ashford: Munden; Morris, Lemoine A, Pearson, Allon, Wynter, Wheeler, White (Griffiths) (Lemoine M), Arter, Carruthers (Stanton), Ross.
Bognor Regis: Matthews; Pullen P, Beazeley, Pearce R (Pearce D), Easterland, Pullen M, Rutherford, Birmingham, Rice, Cormack (Ford), Miles.

Brighton & HA (1) 4 *(Byrne 2, McDougald, Smith)*
Canvey Island (0) 1 *(Pennyfather)* 7008
Brighton & HA: Rust; Smith, Myall, Parris, Osman (Munday), McCarthy, Mundee, McDougald, Minton, Byrne, Wilkins.
Canvey Island: Keeley; Lee, Joscelyn, Blakeborough (Martin), Porter, Brett, Pennyfather, Pizzey, Mahoney, Jones, Harding.

Bristol C (0) 0
Bournemouth (1) 1 *(Robinson)* 5069
Bristol C: Welch; Carey, Edwards, Bryant, Shail, Kuhl, Bent, Owers (Tinnion), Nugent, Barnard, Seal.
Bournemouth: Moss; Young, Beardsmore, Morris, Murray, Pennock, Bailey, Robinson, Jones, Fletcher, Brissett (Mean).

Enfield (1) 2 *(Abbott 2 (1 pen))*
Newport (IW) (0) 1 *(Leader)* 2034
Enfield: Pape; Blackford, May, Hoddle, Terry, Kerr, Ridout, Sayer, Abbott, Nolan (Richardson), Gentle.
Newport (IW): Simpkins; Wickens, Hughes K, Leader, Phillips, Male, Gee, Ritchie (Hughes J), Puckett, Soares (Webb), Fearon.

Gillingham (1) 1 *(Howard (og))*
Wycombe W (0) 0 8585
Gillingham: Stannard; Micklewhite, Watson, Smith, Harris, Green, Martin, Rattray (Puttnam), Fortune-West, Bailey, O'Connor.
Wycombe W: Hyde; Rowbotham, Bell, Howard, Cousins, Brown, Carroll, Patterson (Garner), De Souza, Williams (McGavin), Farrell.

Sutton U (0) 1 *(Payne)*
Kidderminster H (1) 1 *(Casey)* 1804
Sutton U: McCann; Gates, Golley, Marchant, Costello, Green, Payne, Hynes, Vansittart, Feltham, Dack.
Kidderminster H: Steadman; Hodson, Bancroft, Wier, Brindley, Yates, Webb, Casey, May (Shepherd), Davies (Dearlove), Hughes.
aet; Sutton U won 3-2 on penalties.

Wigan Ath (2) 4 *(Leonard, Diaz, Martinez, Thomson (og))*
Runcorn (2) 2 *(Ruffer, Smith (pen))* 3224
Wigan Ath: Farnworth; Carragher, Butler, Lightfoot, Robertson (Farrell), Pender, Diaz, Kilford (Seba), Leonard, Martinez, Lyons.
Runcorn: Thomson; Bates (Doherty M) (McInerney), Warder, Ellis, Byrne, Ruffer, Taylor, Doherty N, Farrington (Clowes), Bignall, Smith.

Woking (1) 2 *(Hay, Steele)*
Barnet (1) 1 *(Hodges)aet* 3535
Woking: Batty; Tucker, Wye, Fielder, Brown, Timothy (Alexander), Thompson, Ellis, Steele, Hay, Walker.
Barnet: Taylor; Gale (Mills), Campbell (Tomlinson), Pardew, Primus, McDonald, Hodges, Scott, Cooper, Devine, Wilson.

Wrexham (0) 0
Hull C (0) 0 4522
Wrexham: Marriott; McGregor, Hardy, Phillips, Humes (Hunter), Jones B, Skinner, Brammer (Hughes), Connolly, Watkin, Ward.
Hull C: Wilson; Lowthorpe (Lawford), Mann, Humphries (Dakin), Dewhurst, Abbott, Hobson, Lee, Brown, Fewings, Peacock.
aet; Wrexham won 3-1 on penalties.

22 NOV

Altrincham (0) 0
Crewe Alex (0) 2 *(Adebola, Unsworth)* 3062
Altrincham: Collings; Cross, Heesom, France, Hardy, Reid, Terry, Whalley, Zumrutel (Royle), Anderson, Sharratt.
Crewe Alex: Gayle; Unsworth, Booty, Westwood, Macauley, Whalley (Adebola), Rivers, Murphy, Savage, Lennon, Edwards (Smith).

FIRST ROUND REPLAY

Farnborough T (0) 0 3581
Brentford (1) 4 *(Smith, Taylor 2, Bent)*
Farnborough T: McKenzie; Stemp, Day (Juryeff), Coney (Horton), Baker K, Baker S, Robson, Harlow, Senior, Boothe, Denny.
Brentford: Fernandes; Harvey, Grainger, Smith, Bates, Ashby, Bent, Hutchings, McGhee (Hooker), Martin, Taylor.

SECOND ROUND

2 DEC

Barrow (0) 0
Wigan Ath (0) 4 *(Diaz, Martinez, Black 2)* 3500
Barrow: Deegan; Speak, Kennedy J (Kennedy E), Harold, Parker, Kenny, Todhunter (Foley), Humphries, Dobie, Morton, Hoskin.
Wigan Ath: Farnworth; Carragher, Butler, Greenall, Farrell, Pender (Kilford), Diaz, Martinez, Leonard, Black, Lyons.

Blackpool (0) 2 *(Preece, Quinn)*
Colwyn Bay (0) 0 4581
Blackpool: Banks; Bryan, Barlow, Lydiate, Mellon, Quinn (Brown P), Bradshaw, Bonner, Preece, Ellis, Holden (Watson).
Colwyn Bay: Roberts R; McCosh, Mann, Harley, Woods, Price, Nicholas (Dulson), Roberts G, Drury, Donnelly, Rigby (Morgan).

Bournemouth (0) 0
Brentford (1) 1 *(Taylor)* 4451
Bournemouth: Moss; Young, Beardsmore, Morris (Strong), McElhatton (Oldbury), Pennock, Holland, Robinson, Rawlinson, Bailey, Brissett.
Brentford: Dearden; Statham (Anderson), Grainger, Hutchings, Bates, Ashby, Bent, Smith, McGhee, Martin (Harvey), Taylor.

Bradford C (1) 2 *(Jacobs 2)*
Preston NE (0) 1 *(Wilkinson)* 7602
Bradford C: Ward; Shutt (Midgley), Jacobs, Youds, Mitchell, Ford, Hamilton, Duxbury, Ormondroyd (Tolson), Wright, Showler (Murray).
Preston NE: Vaughan; Fensome (Cartwright), Barrick, Atkinson, Kidd, Moyes, Davey, Bryson, Saville, Wilkinson, McDonald.

Cinderford T (0) 1 *(Thomas)*
Gravesend & N (0) 1 *(Blewden)* 2064
Cinderford T: Bowles; Price (Smith), Wilton, Boxall, Howells, Cole, Hamilton, Criddle (Townsend), Hill, Thomas, Harris.
Gravesend & N: Turner; Walker, Lamb, Gubbins, Mortley, Jackson, Bourne, Cotter, Blewden, Munday (Reynolds), Powell (Wilson).

Crewe Alex (1) 2 *(Edwards, Rivers)*
Mansfield T (0) 0 3694
Crewe Alex: Gayle; Collins, Booty, Westwood, Macauley, Whalley, Rivers, Murphy, Adebola, Lennon, Edwards (Unsworth).
Mansfield T: Bowling; Boothroyd, Hackett, Sherlock, Howarth, Peters, Ireland, Parkin, Sale, Hadley, Harper.

Enfield (1) 1 *(Gentle)*
Woking (0) 1 *(Walker)* 3477
Enfield: Pape; Blackford, May, Richardson (Fleming), Terry, Kerr, Ridout, Sayer, Abbott, Carstairs, Gentle.
Woking: Batty; Tucker, Wye, Fielder, Brown, Crumplin, Thompson, Ellis, Timothy, Hay, Walker.

Fulham (0) 0
Brighton & HA (0) 0 8057
Fulham: Lange; Jupp, Herrera, Mison (Williams), Moore, Angus, Thomas, Barkus (Brooker), Bolt, Conroy, Cusack.
Brighton & HA: Rust; Smith, Myall, Parris, Johnson, McCarthy, Mundee, Minton, Storer, Byrne (Andrews), Chapman.

Gillingham (0) 3 *(Fortune-West 2, Ratcliffe)*
Hitchin (0) 0 7142
Gillingham: Stannard; Micklewhite, Naylor, Smith, Harris (Butler), Green, Martin, Ratcliffe, Fortune-West, Bailey, Watson P.
Hitchin: Sylvester; McMonamin, Covington, Burke, Bone, Scott, Byrnes, Conroy (Roberts), Williams, Thompson (Ryan), Gillard.

Hereford U (1) 2 *(White 2)*
Sutton U (0) 0 2908
Hereford U: Mackenzie; Evans, Lloyd, Smith D, Stoker, Brough, Lyne, Wilkins, Cross (Pounder), White, Downing.
Sutton U: McCann; Gates, Benning, Marchant, Costello, Golley, Payne, Hynes, Vansittart (Lempriere), Feltham, Dack.

Oxford U (1) 2 *(Massey, Moody)*
Northampton T (0) 0 6355
Oxford U: Whitehead; Wood, Ford M, Smith, Elliott, Gilchrist, Murphy, Massey, Moody, Ford R (Beauchamp), Angel.
Northampton T: Woodman; Norton (Beckford), Maddison, Peer, Warburton, O'Shea, Williams (Lee), Hunter, White, Byrnes, Colkin (Cahill).

Peterborough U (3) 4 *(Farrell 3, Ebdon)*
Bognor Regis (0) 0 5004
Peterborough U: Sheffield; Ashley (McGleish), Clark, Ebdon (Manuel), Breen, Heald, Le Bihan, Williams, Martindale, Farrell (Power), Rioch.
Bognor Regis: Matthews; Pullen P, Beazeley, Pearce D (Kilpatrick), Marriner (Pearce R), Pullen M, Rutherford, Birmingham, Rice, Eastland, Miles (Cormack).

Rochdale (0) 2 *(Deary 2)*
Darlington (1) 2 *(Shaw, Olsson)* 3732
Rochdale: Gray; Thompstone, Formby, Deary, Valentine, Butler, Thompson, Martin (Ryan), Moulden (Shaw), Whitehall, Peake.
Darlington: Burridge; Shaw, Carss, Appleby, Crosby, Gregan, Himsworth, Olsson, Painter (Blake), Brumwell, Bannister.

Scunthorpe U (0) 1 *(Eyre)*
Shrewsbury T (0) 1 *(Scott)* 2718
Scunthorpe U: Samways; Walsh, Wilson, Ford, Hope, Bradley, Turnbull, Nicholson, McFarlane, Eyre, Paterson.
Shrewsbury T: Edwards; Seabury, Withe, Evans, Dempsey, Scott, Taylor, Rowbotham, Spink, Walton, Berkley (Anthrobus).

Stockport Co (2) 2 *(Eckhardt, Raffell (og))*
Blyth Spartans (0) 0 5693
Stockport Co: Edwards; Connelly, Todd, Bennett, Flynn, Gannon, Beaumont (Chalk), Oliver, Eckhardt, Armstrong, Jeffers.
Blyth Spartans: O'Connor; Curry, Hays, Raffell, Gamble, Ditchburn, Bond, Proctor, Moat, Pyle (Pearson), Walker (Telford).

Swindon T (0) 2 *(Allison, Finney)*
Cardiff C (0) 0 8274
Swindon T: Digby; Culverhouse, Drysdale, McMahon, Seagraves, Taylor, Robinson, Allen, Finney, Allison, Horlock.
Cardiff C: Williams D; Baddeley, Searle, Harding (Wigg), Jarman, Young, Fleming, Rodgerson, Dale, Adams (Bird), Gardner.

Telford U (0) 0
Notts Co (1) 2 *(Gallagher, Legg)* 2831
Telford U: Goodwin; Gardiner (Gray), Fowler, Wilcox, Niblett, Kearney, Myers, Clarke, Adams, Bignot, Langford.
Notts Co: Ward; Mills, Baraclough, Turner, Strodder, Murphy, Gallagher, Simpson, Devlin, Arkins (White), Legg.

Torquay U (1) 1 *(Hathaway)*
Walsall (0) 1 *(Lightbourne)* 3552
Torquay U: Bayes; Winter, Barrow, Curran, Watson, Coughlin, Jack, Hall (Mateu), Byng, Hawthorne (Laight), Hathaway.
Walsall: Walker; Ntamark, Rogers, Viveash, Marsh, Mountfield, O'Connor, Bradley, Butler (Lightbourne), Wilson, Houghton.

Wrexham (2) 3 *(Watkin, Hunter, Connolly (pen))*
Chesterfield (0) 2 *(Davies 2)* 4943
Wrexham: Marriott; Jones B, Hardy, Phillips, Humes, Hunter, Skinner, Russell, Connolly, Watkin, Ward (Hughes).
Chesterfield: Beasley; Perkins, Dyche, Curtis, Williams, Law, Robinson, Davies, Lormor (Howard), Morris (Roberts), Narbett.

3 DEC

Kingstonian (1) 1 *(Warden)*
Plymouth Arg (1) 2 *(Leadbitter, Littlejohn)* 2961
Kingstonian: Root; Brooker, Riley, Finch, Nebbling, Fisher, Warmington, Luckett (Stevens), Warden, Akuamoah, Wingfield (Bolton).
Plymouth Arg: Blackwell; Patterson, Williams, Clayton (Logan), Heathcote, Hill, Billy (Magee), Mauge, Littlejohn, Evans, Leadbitter (Baird).

SECOND ROUND REPLAYS

12 DEC

Darlington (0) 0
Rochdale (0) 1 *(Martin)* 4131
Darlington: Burridge; Shaw, Himsworth, Appleby, Crosby, Brumwell (Carss), Gaughan, Olsson, Worboys, Blake (Painter), Bannister.
Rochdale: Gray; Thompstone (Russell), Formby, Deary, Valentine, Bayliss, Thompson, Martin, Ryan, Whitehall, Peake.

Shrewsbury T (2) 2 *(Scott, Rowbotham (pen))*
Scunthorpe U (0) 1 *(Paterson)* 3313
Shrewsbury T: Edwards; Seabury, Withe, Evans, Whiston (Anthrobus), Scott, Taylor, Rowbotham, Spink, Walton, Dempsey.
Scunthorpe U: Samways; Walsh, Wilson, Ford, Hope, Bradley, Turnbull, Bullimore, Young, Eyre (Nicholson), Paterson.

Walsall (1) 8 *(Marsh 2, Wilson, Bradley, Lightbourne 2, O'Connor, Houghton)*
Torquay U (1) 4 *(Hawthorne, Barrow, Gore, Mateu) aet* 3230
Walsall: Walker; Ntamark, Rogers, Viveash, Marsh, Mountfield (Watkiss), O'Connor, Bradley, Keister (Lightbourne), Wilson, Houghton.
Torquay U: Bayes; Gore, Barrow, Curran, Watson, Coughlin, Jack (Mateu), Hall (Bedeau), Hancox, Hawthorne, Hathaway.

Woking (0) 2 *(Hay 2)*
Enfield (0) 1 *(Abbott)* 2253
Woking: Batty; Tucker, Wye, Fielder, Brown, Timothy, Thompson, Ellis, Steele, Hay, Dowe.
Enfield: Pape; Blackford, May, Carstairs (Nolan), Terry, Kerr, Ridout, Sayer (Adams), Abbott, Richardson (Fleming), Gentle.

14 DEC

Brighton & HA (0) 0
Fulham (0) 0 6209
Brighton & HA: Rust; Smith, Myall (Wilkins), Parris, Johnson, McCarthy, Mundee (Storer), McDougald, Minton, Andrews, Chapman.
Fulham: Lange; Jupp, Herrera, Taylor, Moore, Angus, Brooker (Barkus), Cusack (Mison), Hamill, Conroy, Bolt.
(aet; Fulham won 4-1 on penalties)

Gravesend & N (1) 3 *(Best, Munday, Powell)*
Cinderford T (0) 0 2851
Gravesend & N: Turner; Walker, Lamb, Gubbins (Gibbs), Mortley, Jackson, Best, Cotter (Gooding), Blewden, Munday, Powell.
Cinderford T: Bowles; Price (Townsend), Wilton, Boxall, Howells, Cole, Hamilton (Criddle), Crouch, Hill, Thomas, Smith (Harris).

THIRD ROUND

6 JAN

Arsenal (0) 1 *(Wright)*
Sheffield U (0) 1 *(Whitehouse)* 33,453
Arsenal: Seaman; Dixon, Winterburn, Clarke, Keown, Adams, Jensen, Wright, Merson, Hartson, Helder.
Sheffield U: Kelly; Short, Ward, Gannon (Hodgson), Vonk, Nilsen, White, Cowans, Starbuck (Heath), Hodges, Whitehouse.

Barnsley (0) 0
Oldham Ath (0) 0 9751
Barnsley: Watson; Eaden, Shirtliff, Sheridan (Bullock), Davis, De Zeeuw, Liddell (Payton), Redfearn, O'Connell, Rammell, Archdeacon.
Oldham Ath: Gerrard; McNiven, Makin, Hughes, Graham, Redmond, Halle, Orlygsson, McCarthy, Barlow, Rickers.

Birmingham C (0) 1 *(Poole)*
Wolverhampton W (1) 1 *(Bull)* 21,349
Birmingham C: Bennett; Poole, Frain, Forsyth, Edwards, Daish, Hunt (Bowen), Claridge, Francis (Bull), Richardson, Donowa.
Wolverhampton W: Stowell; Thompson, Young, Atkins, Emblen (Rankine) (Foley), Richards, Williams, Goodman, Bull, Osborn, Pearce (Ferguson).

Bradford C (0) 0
Bolton W (1) 3 *(McGinlay, Curcic 2)* 10,265
Bradford C: Ward; Mitchell (Murray), Jacobs, Youds, Brightwell, Mohan, Huxford, Duxbury, Tolson (Shutt), Jewell (Ormondroyd), Showler.
Bolton W: Branagan; Green, Phillips, Curcic, Stubbs, Taggart, Fairclough, Sneekes, Blake, McGinlay, Sellars.

Charlton Ath (2) 2 *(Grant, Mortimer (pen))*
Sheffield W (0) 0 13,815
Charlton Ath: Salmon; Humphrey, Stuart, Mortimer, Rufus, Balmer, Newton, Grant (Nelson), Robinson, Leaburn, Bowyer.
Sheffield W: Pressman; Nolan, Stefanovic, Degryse, Atherton, Walker, Whittingham, Waddle, Hirst, Kovacevic, Sinton.

Crewe Alex (3) 4 *(Adebola, Rivers, Booty, Murphy)*
WBA (1) 3 *(Hunt, Raven, Coldicott)* 5750
Crewe Alex: Gayle; Collins, Booty, Westwood, Macauley, Whalley, Rivers (Clarkson), Murphy, Adebola (Smith), Lennon, Edwards.
WBA: Naylor; Burgess, Edwards (Smith), Coldicott, Mardon, Raven, Donovan, Gilbert (Ashcroft), Taylor, Hunt, Darby (Hamilton).

Crystal Palace (0) 0
Port Vale (0) 0 10,456
Crystal Palace: Martyn; Edworthy, Gordon, Roberts, Davies, Hopkin (Rodger), Pitcher, Houghton, Freedman, Taylor, Vincent (McKenzie).
Port Vale: Musslewhite; Hill, Tankard, Bogie, Talbot (Walker), Glover D, McCarthy, Porter, Foyle, Naylor, Guppy.

Fulham (0) 1 *(Angus)*
Shrewsbury T (0) 1 *(Evans)* 7265
Fulham: Lange; Jupp, Herrera, Marshall (Moore), Angus, Blake, Thomas, Morgan, Brazil, Conroy (Cusack), Bolt (Hamill).
Shrewsbury T: Edwards; Evans, Withe, Taylor, Whiston, Scott, Woods (Dempsey), Rowbotham (Spink), Anthrobus, Walton, Berkley.

Gravesend & N (0) 0 *at Villa Park*
Aston Villa (1) 3 *(Draper, Milosevic, Johnson)* 26,021
Gravesend & N: Turner; Walker (Harrop), Lamb, Gubbins, Mortley, Jackson, Gibbs, Cotter (Best), Blewden, Munday, Powell (Gooding).
Aston Villa: Bosnich; Charles, Wright, Southgate, Scimeca, Ehiogu, Yorke, Draper, Milosevic, Johnson, Townsend.

Grimsby T (4) 7 *(Forrester 2, Livingstone 2, Bonetti, Southall, Woods)*
Luton T (1) 1 *(Marshall)* 5387
Grimsby T: Crichton; Laws, Croft, Handyside, Rodger, Groves, Childs (Southall), Dobbin (Shakespeare), Forrester, Livingstone (Woods), Bonetti.
Luton T: Feuer; Patterson, Thomas, Waddock, James; Johnson, Guentchev (Thorpe), Oakes, Oldfield, McLaren (Alexander), Marshall.

Hereford U (0) 1 *(Brough)*
Tottenham H (1) 1 *(Rosenthal)* 8806
Hereford U: Mackenzie; Evans, Fishlock, Smith D, Pounder, Brough, Lyne, Wilkins, Cross, White, Downing.
Tottenham H: Walker; Austin, Edinburgh, Nethercott, Campbell, Mabbutt, Fox (Dozzell), Caskey, Armstrong, Sheringham, Rosenthal.

Huddersfield T (1) 2 *(Jepson 2 (1 pen))*
Blackpool (1) 1 *(Quinn)* 12,424
Huddersfield T: Francis; Jenkins, Cowan, Bullock, Sinnott (Collins), Gray, Rowe, Makel, Booth, Jepson, Dunn (Dalton).
Blackpool: Banks; Bryan, Barlow (Gouck), Bradshaw (Brown P), Mellon, Quinn (Preece), Lydiate, Bonner, Morrison, Ellis, Watson.

Ipswich T (0) 0
Blackburn R (0) 0 22,146
Ipswich T: Forrest; Yallop (Uhlenbeek), Taricco, Thomsen, Mowbray, Williams, Stockwell, Sedgley, Mathie, Marshall, Milton.
Blackburn R: Flowers; Berg, Kenna, Sherwood, Hendry, Coleman, Ripley, McKinlay, Shearer, Newell, Gallacher.

Leicester C (0) 0
Manchester C (0) 0 20,640
Leicester C: Poole; Grayson, Smith, Hill, Walsh, Parker, Corica (Joachim), Taylor, Robins, Roberts, Philpott.
Manchester C: Immel; Summerbee, Brightwell, Curle, Symons, Brown, Ekelund, Quinn, Rosler, Flitcroft, Lomas.

Liverpool (3) 7 *(Fowler, Collymore 3, Valentine (og), Rush, McAteer)*
Rochdale (0) 0 28,126
Liverpool: James; Jones (Rush), Harkness, McAteer, Wright (Matteo), Scales, McManaman, Thomas, Collymore, Barnes, Fowler.
Rochdale: Clarke; Thackeray, Formby, Deary, Valentine, Butler, Thompson (Thompstone), Martin, Moulden (Shaw), Whitehall, Peake (Ryan).

Manchester U (1) 2 *(Butt, Cantona)*
Sunderland (0) 2 *(Agnew, Russell)* 41,563
Manchester U: Pilkington; Neville G (Neville P), Irwin, Bruce, Keane, Pallister, Cantona, Butt, Cole, Beckham (Sharpe), Giggs.
Sunderland: Chamberlain; Kubicki, Scott, Bracewell, Ball (Agnew), Melville, Michael Gray, Ord, Russell, Gray P (Howey), Kelly (Smith).

Millwall (0) 3 *(Rae 2, Malkin)*
Oxford U (1) 3 *(Massey, Moody, Ford R)* 7564
Millwall: Keller; Newman, Thatcher, Bowry, Witter, Webber, Lavin (Forbes), Rae, Malkin, Dixon (Fuchs), Berry (Taylor).
Oxford U: Whitehead; Robinson, Ford M, Smith, Elliott, Gilchrist, Rush (Allen), Massey, Moody (Aldridge), Ford R, Angel.

Norwich C (0) 1 *(Newsome)*
Brentford (1) 2 *(Newsome (og), Bent)* 10,082
Norwich C: Gunn; Bradshaw (Prior), Bowen (Sutch), Ullathorne, Newsome, Polston, Adams, Fleck (Eadie), Ward, Goss, O'Neill.
Brentford: Dearden; Harvey (Martin), Grainger, Hutchings, Bates, Ashby, McGhee, Smith, Forster, Bent (Anderson), Taylor.

Notts Co (0) 1 *(Rogers)*
Middlesbrough (0) 2 *(Pollock, Barmby)* 12,621
Notts Co: Ward; Gallagher (Agana), Baraclough, Turner (Simpson), Strodder, Hogg, Rogers, Murphy, Devlin, Arkins, Legg (White).
Middlesbrough: Walsh; Liddle, Fleming (Stamp), Vickers, Pearson, Whelan, Barmby (Moreno), Pollock, Wilkinson, Juninho, Robson.

Peterborough U (0) 1 *(Le Bihan)*
Wrexham (0) 0 5983
Peterborough U: Sheffield; Williams, Clark, Ebdon, Breen, Heald, Carter (Spearing), Manuel (Le Bihan), Martindale, Farrell, Morrison.
Wrexham: Marriott; Jones B, Hardy, Phillips, Humes, Hunter, Skinner (McGregor), Russell, Connolly, Morris (Durkan), Ward.

Plymouth Arg (1) 1 *(Baird)*
Coventry C (0) 3 *(Pickering, Salako, Telfer)* 17,721
Plymouth Arg: Blackwell; Billy, Williams, Logan, Heathcote, Hill, Baird (Twiddy), Mauge (Saunders), Littlejohn, Evans, Leadbitter.
Coventry C: Ogrizovic; Pickering, Hall, Williams, Shaw, Busst, Telfer, Whelan, Dublin, Richardson, Salako.

Reading (0) 3 *(Morley, Quinn 2)*
Gillingham (1) 1 *(Martin)* 10,324
Reading: Mikhailov; Swales (Lambert), Gooding, Thorp, Williams A, Jones, Quinn (Lovell), Parkinson, Morley, Nogan, Holsgrove.
Gillingham: Stannard; Green, Naylor (Carpenter), Smith, Harris, Butler T, Martin, Ratcliffe (Dunne), Fortune-West, Bailey, Micklewhite (Puttnam).

Stoke C (1) 1 *(Sturridge)*
Nottingham F (0) 1 *(Pearce)* 17,947
Stoke C: Prudhoe; Clarkson, Sandford, Sigurdsson, Dreyer, Potter, Keen, Wallace, Sturridge, Carruthers, Gleghorn.
Nottingham F: Crossley; Lyttle, Pearce, Cooper, Chettle, Stone, Bart-Williams, Gemmill, Campbell, Roy (Lee), Woan.

Swindon T (1) 2 *(Allison, Bodin)*
Woking (0) 0 10,322
Swindon T: Digby; Culverhouse, Bodin, Ling, Seagraves, Taylor (McMahon), Robinson, Allen, Thorne (Finney), Allison, Horlock.
Woking: Batty; Tucker, Wye, Fielder, Brown, Crumplin, Thompson, Ellis, Steele, Hay, Walker.

Tranmere R (0) 0
QPR (0) 2 *(Quashie, Sinclair)* 10,230
Tranmere R: Coyne; Rogers, Thomas, McGreal, Garnett, Jones (O'Brien), Morrissey, Aldridge, Brannan, Moore, Nevin.
QPR: Sommer; Ready (Goodridge), Challis, Brazier, Yates (Maddix), McDonald, Impey, Wilkins, Quashie, Allen (Dichio), Sinclair.

Walsall (0) 1 *(Pender (og))*
Wigan Ath (0) 0 5626
Walsall: Wood; Ntamark, Rogers, Viveash, Marsh (Keister), Mountfield, O'Connor, Bradley, Lightbourne (Butler), Wilson, Houghton.
Wigan Ath: Farnworth; Carragher, Sharp, Greenall, Pender, Farrell (Ogden), Diaz, Martinez, Leonard, Rimmer (Seba), Lyons.

Watford (1) 1 *(Mooney)*
Wimbledon (1) 1 *(Leonhardsen)* 11,187
Watford: Miller; Bazeley, Millen, Foster, Holdsworth, Ramage, Johnson, Pitcher (Payne), Mooney (Ludden), Moralee, Phillips.
Wimbledon: Sullivan; Cunningham, Kimble, Leonhardsen, Reeves, Perry, Gayle, Earle, Harford, Holdsworth, Ekoku (Euell).

West Ham U (0) 2 *(Moncur, Hughes)*
Southend U (0) 0 23,284
West Ham U: Miklosko; Harkes, Dicks, Potts, Rieper, Bishop, Moncur, Dowie, Cottee, Williamson, Hughes.
Southend U: Royce; Dublin, Powell, McNally, Bodley, Gridelet, Marsh, Byrne, Regis, Jones (Thomson), Hails.

7 JAN

Chelsea (1) 1 *(Hughes)*
Newcastle U (0) 1 *(Ferdinand)* 25,151
Chelsea: Kharine; Petrescu (Clarke), Phelan, Duberry, Myers, Lee, Newton, Furlong, Spencer, Hughes, Wise.
Newcastle U: Srnicek; Barton, Albert, Elliott, Peacock, Howey, Lee (Clark), Beardsley, Ferdinand, Ginola, Kitson.

Derby Co (0) 2 *(Gabbiadini, Simpson)* 16,155
Leeds U (0) 4 *(Deane, McAllister, Speed, Yeboah)*
Derby Co: Hoult; Rowett, Nicholson, Kavanagh, Yates, Stimac (Trollope), Van der Laan, Flynn, Willems, Gabbiadini (Wrack), Simpson.
Leeds U: Beeney; Kelly, Dorigo, Palmer, Wetherall (Wallace), Jobson, Ford, Yeboah, Deane, McAllister, Speed.

Everton (2) 2 *(Ablett, Stuart)*
Stockport Co (1) 2 *(Armstrong, Helliwell)* 28,921
Everton: Southall; Jackson, Unsworth, Ebbrell (Hinchcliffe), Watson, Ablett, Kanchelskis, Horne, Stuart, Rideout, Limpar (Grant).
Stockport Co: Edwards; Connolly, Todd, Bennett (Dinning), Flynn, Bound, Beaumont (Chalk), Eckhardt, Helliwell, Armstrong, Jeffers.

Southampton (1) 3 *(Magilton 2, Shipperley)*
Portsmouth (0) 0 15,236
Southampton: Beasant; Dodd, Charlton, Magilton, Neilson, Moncur, Le Tissier, Watson (Maddison), Shipperley, Venison, Heaney (McDonald).
Portsmouth: Knight; Pethick, Stimson, McLoughlin, Gittens, Butters, Walsh, Simpson, Durnin, Hall (Burton), Wood (Carter).

THIRD ROUND REPLAYS

16 JAN

Blackburn R (0) 0 aet
Ipswich T (0) 1 *(Mason)* 19,606
Blackburn R: Flowers; Berg, Kenna, Batty (Sherwood), Hendry, Coleman, Ripley, Bohinen, Shearer, Newell (McKinlay), Gallacher.
Ipswich T: Wright; Wark, Vaughan, Thomsen, Mowbray, Williams, Uhlenbeek, Sedgley, Mathie, Marshall (Gregory), Milton (Mason).

Oxford U (0) 1 *(Massey)*
Millwall (0) 0 8122
Oxford U: Whitehead; Robinson, Marsh (Rush), Smith, Elliott, Gilchrist, Aldridge, Massey, Moody, Ford R, Angel (Allen).
Millwall: Carter; Newman, Thatcher, Bowry, Witter, Van Blerk, Savage, Rae, Malkin, Taylor, McRobert (Keown).

Port Vale (2) 4 *(Walker 2, Porter (pen), Foyle)*
Crystal Palace (1) 3 *(Taylor, Cox, Dyer)aet* 6754
Port Vale: Musslewhite; Hill, Tankard, Bogie, Talbot, Glover D (Walker), McCarthy, Porter, Foyle, Naylor (Mills), Guppy.
Crystal Palace: Martyn; Edworthy, Gordon, Roberts, Davies, Gale (Dyer), Pitcher, Houghton, Freedman (Rodger), Taylor, McKenzie (Cox).

Shrewsbury T (0) 2 *(Anthrobus, Dempsey)*
Fulham (1) 1 *(Hamill)* 7983
Shrewsbury T: Edwards; Evans, Withe, Taylor, Whiston, Scott, Woods, Rowbotham (Dempsey), Anthrobus, Walton, Berkley.
Fulham: Lange; Jupp, Herrera, Marshall, Angus (Moore), Blake, Thomas, Morgan, Cusack, Hamill, Bolt.

Sunderland (1) 1 *(Gray P)*
Manchester U (0) 2 *(Scholes, Cole)* 21,378
Sunderland: Chamberlain; Kubicki, Scott, Bracewell (Howey), Agnew (Martin Gray), Melville, Michael Gray, Ord, Russell, Gray P, Smith (Mullin).
Manchester U: Schmeichel; Parker (Sharpe), Irwin, Bruce, Neville P, Neville G, Cantona, Keane, Cole, Butt (Scholes), Giggs.

17 JAN

Manchester C (2) 5 *(Rosler, Kinkladze, Quinn, Lomas, Creaney)*
Leicester C (0) 0 19,980
Manchester C: Immel; Summerbee, Ingram, Curle, Symons, Brown, Lomas, Quinn (Creaney), Rosler, Flitcroft (Ekelund), Kinkladze.
Leicester C: Poole; Grayson, Whitlow, Hill, Walsh, Parker, Lowe, Corica, Joachim (Robins), Roberts, Philpott (Rolling).

Newcastle U (1) 2 *(Albert, Beardsley (pen))*
Chelsea (0) 2 *(Wise (pen), Gullit)*   36,535
Newcastle U: Srnicek; Barton, Beresford, Clark, Peacock, Albert, Watson, Beardsley, Ferdinand (Huckerby), Ginola, Kitson (Elliott).
Chelsea: Hitchcock; Petrescu, Phelan, Duberry, Myers (Clarke), Lee, Gullit, Hughes (Furlong), Spencer (Peacock), Newton, Wise.
aet; Chelsea won 4-2 on penalties.

Nottingham F (1) 2 *(Campbell, Pearce (pen))*
Stoke C (0) 0   17,372
Nottingham F: Crossley; Lyttle, Pearce, Cooper, Chettle, Stone, Bart-Williams, Gemmill, Campbell (Lee), Roy (Phillips), Woan.
Stoke C: Prudhoe; Clarkson, Sandford, Sigurdsson, Cranson, Potter, Keen, Wallace, Sturridge, Peschisolido (Gayle), Gleghorn.

Sheffield U (0) 1 *(Veart)*
Arsenal (0) 0   22,255
Sheffield U: Kelly; Short, Nilsen, Patterson, Vonk, Tuttle, White, Cowans, Veart, Ward, Whitehouse (Hodges).
Arsenal: Seaman; Dixon (Linighan), McGowan, Jensen (Clarke), Keown, Adams, Platt, Wright, Merson, Bergkamp, Helder.

Stockport Co (1) 2 *(Bound, Armstrong)*
Everton (0) 3 *(Ferguson, Stuart, Ebbrell)*   11,283
Stockport Co: Edwards; Connelly, Todd, Ware, Flynn, Bound, Beaumont (Chalk), Eckhardt, Helliwell, Armstrong, Jeffers.
Everton: Southall; Ebbrell, Ablett, Parkinson, Watson, Short, Kanchelskis, Horne, Ferguson, Stuart, Limpar (Amokachi).

Tottenham H (2) 5 *(Sheringham 3, Armstrong 2)*
Hereford U (0) 1 *(Stoker)*   31,534
Tottenham H: Walker; Austin, Edinburgh (Wilson), Nethercott, Campbell, Mabbutt, Fox, Caskey, Armstrong, Sheringham, Rosenthal (Slade).
Hereford U: Mackenzie; Evans, Fishlock, Smith D, Pounder (Steele), Brough, Lyne, Wilkins, Cross (Stoker), White, Downing.

Wimbledon (0) 1 *(Clarke)*
Watford (0) 0   5142
Wimbledon: Sullivan; Cunningham, Kimble, Leonhardsen (Pearce), Reeves, Perry, Gayle (Clarke), Earle, Harford, Euell, Ekoku (Ardley).
Watford: Miller; Bazeley, Millen, Page, Holdsworth, Ramage, Ludden, Johnson, Moralee, Pitcher (Connolly), Phillips.

Wolverhampton W (1) 2 *(Ferguson, Bull)*
Birmingham C (0) 1 *(Hunt)*   28,088
Wolverhampton W: Stowell; Rankine, Thompson, Young, Venus, Law, Osborn, Goodman, Bull, Ferguson, Atkins.
Birmingham C: Griemink; Poole, Frain, Forsyth, Edwards, Daish, Castle (Hunt), Claridge, Francis (Bull), Richardson (Bowen), Johnson.

23 JAN

Oldham Ath (1) 2 *(Beckford 2 (1 pen))*
Barnsley (0) 1 *(Redfearn)*   6670
Oldham Ath: Gerrard; Makin, Serrant, Hughes, Graham, Redmond, Halle, Orlygsson (Rickers), Beckford, Barlow, Brennan.
Barnsley: Watson; Eaden, Moses, Sheridan, Davis (Bochenski), De Zeeuw, Liddell, Redfearn, O'Connell (Bullock), Payton, Archdeacon.

FOURTH ROUND

27 JAN

Everton (1) 2 *(Amokachi, Ferguson)*
Port Vale (0) 2 *(Foyle, Bogie)*   33,168
Everton: Southall; Ebbrell, Ablett (Hinchcliffe), Parkinson, Watson, Short, Kanchelskis, Horne, Ferguson, Amokachi (Limpar), Stuart.
Port Vale: Musslewhite; Hill (Bogie), Tankard, Walker, Griffiths, Aspin, McCarthy, Porter, Foyle, Naylor, Guppy.

Reading (0) 0
Manchester U (1) 3 *(Giggs, Parker, Cantona)*   14,780
Reading: Hammond; Jones, Gooding, Bernal, Williams A, Gilkes, Quinn (Lovell), Parkinson (Meaker), Morley, Nogan (Lambert), Holsgrove.
Manchester U: Schmeichel; Neville G, Irwin, Bruce, Sharpe, Neville P (Parker), Cantona, Keane, Cole, Butt, Giggs.

Tottenham H (1) 1 *(Wilson)*
Wolverhampton W (1) 1 *(Goodman)*   32,812
Tottenham H: Walker; Austin, Edinburgh, Campbell, Calderwood, Mabbutt, Fox, Caskey, Armstrong, Sheringham, Wilson.
Wolverhampton W: Stowell; Rankine, Thompson, Young, Emblen, Richards, Atkins, Goodman, Bull, Ferguson, Osborn.

28 JAN

Sheffield U (0) 0
Aston Villa (0) 1 *(Yorke (pen))*   18,749
Sheffield U: Kelly; Short, Nilsen, Patterson, Hodgson, Tuttle, White, Cowans (Hodges), Hutchison (Veart), Ward, Whitehouse.
Aston Villa: Bosnich; Charles, Wright, Southgate, McGrath, Ehiogu, Yorke, Draper, Milosevic, Johnson, Townsend.

29 JAN

QPR (0) 1 *(Quashie)*
Chelsea (2) 2 *(Peacock, Furlong)*   18,542
QPR: Sommer; Bardsley (Maddix), Challis, Impey, Yates, McDonald, Quashie, Holloway, Hateley, Allen, Sinclair.
Chelsea: Hitchcock; Petrescu, Phelan, Duberry, Clarke, Lee, Gullit, Spencer, Furlong, Peacock, Newton.

6 FEB

Huddersfield T (0) 2 *(Bullock, Booth)*
Peterborough U (0) 0   11,629
Huddersfield T: Francis; Jenkins, Cowan, Bullock, Sinnott, Gray, Dalton, Makel, Booth, Rowe, Reid.
Peterborough U: Sheffield; Williams, Spearing (Rioch), Sedgemore, Green, Clark, Morrison, Ebdon, Martindale, Farrell, Carter (Power).

7 FEB

Charlton Ath (2) 3 *(Robinson, Bowyer, Whyte D)*
Brentford (1) 2 *(Ashby, Smith)*   15,000
Charlton Ath: Salmon; Humphrey (Nelson), Stuart, Mortimer, Brown, Balmer, Newton, Leaburn, Robinson, Grant (Whyte D), Bowyer.
Brentford: Dearden; Harvey, Grainger, Hutchings, Bates, Ashby, Anderson, Smith, Forster, Martin, Taylor.

Coventry C (1) 2 *(Whelan, Dublin)*
Manchester C (1) 2 *(Busst (og), Flitcroft)*   18,709
Coventry C: Ogrizovic; Borrows, Hall, Richardson, Shaw, Busst, Telfer (Ndlovu), Strachan, Dublin, Whelan, Salako.
Manchester C: Immel; Summerbee, Brightwell, Curle, Symons, Lomas, Brown, Clough, Rosler, Flitcroft, Kinkladze.

Middlesbrough (0) 0
Wimbledon (0) 0   28,915
Middlesbrough: Walsh; Cox, Morris, Vickers, Pearson, Whelan, Barmby, Pollock, Wilkinson, Juninho (Freestone), O'Halloran.
Wimbledon: Sullivan; Cunningham, Kimble, Castledine, Reeves (Pearce), Perry, Gayle, Clarke (Ardley), Harford, Holdsworth (Euell), Talboys.

Nottingham F (0) 1 *(Campbell)*
Oxford U (0) 1 *(Massey)*   15,050
Nottingham F: Crossley; Lyttle, Phillips, Cooper, Chettle, Bart-Williams, Campbell, Gemmill, Silenzi, Roy, Woan.
Oxford U: Whitehead; Robinson, Ford M, Smith, Elliott, Wood, Beauchamp, Massey, Moody, Ford R, Allen (Murphy).

Southampton (0) 1 *(Le Tissier)*
Crewe Alex (1) 1 *(Rivers)*   13,736
Southampton: Beasant; Dodd, Charlton, Magilton, Hall, Monkou, Le Tissier, Watson, Shipperley, Venison (Maddison), Walters (Oakley).
Crewe Alex: Gayle; Collins, Smith, Westwood, Barr, Whalley, Rivers (Garvey), Unsworth (Tierney), Adebola, Lennon, Edwards.

West Ham U (1) 1 *(Dowie)*
Grimsby T (1) 1 *(Laws)*   22,020
West Ham U: Miklosko; Potts, Dicks, Rieper, Whitbread, Bishop, Slater (Lazaridis) (Rowland), Dowie, Cottee, Williamson, Hughes.
Grimsby T: Crichton; McDermott, Croft, Laws, Lever, Groves, Childs, Shakespeare, Forrester, Woods (Livingstone), Bonetti (Southall).

FOURTH ROUND REPLAY

Wolverhampton W (0) 0
Tottenham H (2) 2 *(Rosenthal, Sheringham)*   27,846
Wolverhampton W: Stowell; Rankine (Daly), Thompson, Young, Emblen, Venus, Atkins, Goodman, Bull, Ferguson, Osborn.
Tottenham H: Walker; Austin, Wilson, Campbell, Calderwood, Mabbutt, Fox, Dozzell, Armstrong, Sheringham, Rosenthal.

FOURTH ROUND

12 FEB

Swindon T (0) 1 *(Ling)*
Oldham Ath (0) 0   9508
Swindon T: Digby; Culverhouse, Bodin, Gooden, Allen, Taylor, Robinson, McMahon (Ling), Thorne, Allison (Finney), Horlock.
Oldham Ath: Gerrard; Snodin, Serrant, Hughes, Graham, Redmond, Halle, Orlygsson, McCarthy (Banger), Barlow, Brennan.

13 FEB

Ipswich T (1) 1 *(Mason)*
Walsall (0) 0   18,489
Ipswich T: Wright; Stockwell (Uhlenbeek), Taricco, Wark, Mowbray, Williams, Mason, Sedgley, Scowcroft, Marshall, Milton.
Walsall: Wood; Ntamark (Evans), Daniel, Viveash, Marsh, Roper, O'Connor, Bradley, Lightbourne (Kerr), Wilson, Houghton (Butler).

FOURTH ROUND REPLAYS

Crewe Alex (0) 2 *(Edwards, Westwood)*
Southampton (3) 3 *(Shipperley, Hall, Dodd)*   5579
Crewe Alex: Gayle; Unsworth, Smith, Westwood, Collier (Garvey), Barr, Rivers, Collins, Adebola, Lennon, Edwards.
Southampton: Beasant; Dodd, Widdrington, Magilton, Hall, Monkou, Le Tissier, Watson (Hughes), Shipperley, Charlton, Walters.

Oxford U (0) 0
Nottingham F (1) 3 *(Campbell, Woan (pen), Silenzi)* 7978
Oxford U: Whitehead; Robinson, Ford M, Smith (Angel), Elliott, Gilchrist, Murphy (Rush), Massey, Moody (Aldridge), Ford R, Beauchamp.
Nottingham F: Crossley; Lyttle, Phillips, Cooper, Chettle, Stone, Bart-Williams, Gemmill, Silenzi, Campbell, Woan.

Wimbledon (0) 1 *(Holdsworth)*
Middlesbrough (0) 0   5220
Wimbledon: Sullivan; Cunningham, Kimble, Leonhardsen, Reeves, Perry, Gayle, Earle, Harford, Holdsworth, Ekoku (Euell).
Middlesbrough: Walsh; Cox (Hignett), Morris, Vickers, Pearson, Whelan, Barmby, Pollock, Wilkinson, Juninho, O'Halloran.

FOURTH ROUND

14 FEB

Bolton W (0) 0
Leeds U (1) 1 *(Wallace)*   16,694
Bolton W: Branagan; Green, Phillips, Stubbs, Fairclough, Taggart, Lee (McGinlay), Curcic, Blake (Patelainen), De Freitas, Thompson.
Leeds U: Lukic; Kelly, Dorigo, Palmer, Beesley, Wetherall, Ford, Wallace (Deane), Yeboah (Radebe), McAllister, Speed.

FOURTH ROUND REPLAYS

Grimsby T (1) 3 *(Childs, Woods, Forrester)*
West Ham U (0) 0   8382
Grimsby T: Crichton; McDermott, Croft, Fickling, Lever, Groves, Childs (Livingstone), Shakespeare, Woods, Forrester, Southall.
West Ham U: Miklosko; Potts, Dicks, Rieper, Martin (Gordon), Bishop, Hughes, Dowie, Cottee, Williamson, Rowland (Harkes).

Manchester C (1) 2 *(Clough, Quinn)*
Coventry C (0) 1 *(Dublin)*   22,419
Manchester C: Immel; Summerbee, Lomas, Curle (Creaney), Symons, Brown, Clough, Quinn, Rosler, Flitcroft, Kinkladze.
Coventry C: Ogrizovic; Pickering, Burrows, Richardson, Shaw, Busst, Telfer (Lamptey), Strachan, Dublin, Whelan, Salako.

Port Vale (1) 2 *(Bogie, McCarthy)*
Everton (1) 1 *(Stuart)*   19,197
Port Vale: Musselwhite; Hill, Tankard, Bogie, Griffiths, Aspin, McCarthy, Porter, Foyle, Naylor, Guppy (Walker).
Everton: Southall; Jackson (Limpar), Unsworth (Rideout) Ebbrell, Watson, Short, Kanchelskis, Horne, Amokachi, Stuart, Hinchcliffe.

FIFTH ROUND

17 FEB

Huddersfield T (1) 2 *(Rowe, Cowan)*
Wimbledon (0) 2 *(Ekoku 2)*   17,307
Huddersfield T: Francis; Jenkins (Collins), Cowan, Bullock, Sinnott, Gray, Dalton, Makel, Booth, Rowe (Dunn), Reid.
Wimbledon: Sullivan; Cunningham, Kimble, Leonhardsen, Reeves, Perry, Gayle (Euell), Earle, Harford, Holdsworth (Clarke), Ekoku.

Ipswich T (0) 1 *(Mason)*
Aston Villa (2) 3 *(Draper, Yorke, Taylor)*   20,748
Ipswich T: Wright; Stockwell (Uhlenbeek), Taricco, Thomsen, Mowbray, Williams, Mason, Sedgley, Scowcroft, Marshall, Milton.
Aston Villa: Bosnich; Charles, Wright, Southgate, Ehiogu, Staunton, Yorke, Draper (McGrath), Milosevic, Johnson (Taylor), Townsend.

Swindon T (1) 1 *(Horlock)*
Southampton (0) 1 *(Watson)* 15,035
Swindon T: Digby; Culverhouse, Bodin (Drysdale), Gooden, Allen, Taylor, Robinson, Ling (Seagraves), Thorne, Allison (Finney), Horlock.
Southampton: Beasant; Dodd, Benali (Maskell), Magilton, Hall, Monkou, Le Tissier, Watson, Shipperley, Widdrington, Charlton.

FOURTH ROUND

18 FEB

Shrewsbury T (0) 0 7752
Liverpool (1) 4 *(Collymore, Walton (og), Fowler, McAteer)*
Shrewsbury T: Edwards; Seabury, Withe, Taylor, Whiston, Evans, Woods (Reed), Dempsey, Anthrobus, Walton (Stevens), Berkley.
Liverpool: James; McAteer, Jones, Scales, Wright, Babb, McManaman, Thomas, Collymore, Barnes, Fowler.

FIFTH ROUND

Manchester U (1) 2 *(Cantona (pen), Sharpe)*
Manchester C (1) 1 *(Rosler)* 42,692
Manchester U: Schmeichel; Irwin, Neville P, Bruce, Sharpe, Pallister, Cantona, Keane, Cole, Butt, Giggs.
Manchester C: Immel; Summerbee, Frontzeck, Curle, Symons, Lomas, Clough, Quinn (Creaney), Rosler, Brown, Kinkladze.

19 FEB

Nottingham F (0)
Tottenham H (0) 17,009
Abandoned after 15 minutes; snow.

21 FEB

Grimsby T (0) 0
Chelsea (0) 0 9448
Grimsby T: Crichton; McDermott, Croft, Laws, Lever, Groves, Childs, Shakespeare, Woods, Livingstone, Southall.
Chelsea: Hitchcock; Petrescu, Phelan, Duberry, Clarke, Lee, Gullit, Spencer (Spackman), Furlong, Peacock, Wise.

Leeds U (0) 0
Port Vale (0) 0 18,607
Leeds U: Lukic; Kelly, Dorigo, Palmer, Beesley, Wetherall, Ford, Wallace, Yeboah, McAllister, Speed (Deane).
Port Vale: Musselwhite; Hill, Tankard, Bogie, Griffiths, Aspin, McCarthy, Walker, Naylor, Porter, Guppy.

FIFTH ROUND REPLAY

27 FEB

Port Vale (1) 1 *(Naylor)*
Leeds U (0) 2 *(McAllister 2)* 14,023
Port Vale: Musselwhite; Hill (Talbot), Tankard, Bogie, Griffiths, Aspin, McCarthy, Porter, Walker, Naylor (Mills), Guppy.
Leeds U: Lukic; Worthington, Radebe, Palmer, Beesley, Wetherall, Masinga (Brolin), Wallace (Gray), Yeboah, McAllister, Deane.

FIFTH ROUND

28 FEB

Liverpool (1) 2 *(Fowler, Collymore)*
Charlton Ath (0) 1 *(Grant)* 36,818
Liverpool: James; McAteer, Jones, Scales, Wright, Babb, McManaman, Thomas, Collymore (Rush), Barnes, Fowler.
Charlton Ath: Salmon; Brown (Grant), Stuart, Jones, Rufus, Balmer, Robson, Leaburn, Robinson, Nelson (Newton), Bowyer.

Nottingham F (1) 2 *(Woan 2)*
Tottenham H (2) 2 *(Armstrong 2)* 18,600
Nottingham F: Crossley; Lyttle, Phillips, Cooper (Haaland), Chettle, Stone (Silenzi), Bart-Williams, Gemmill, Campbell, Roy, Woan.
Tottenham H: Walker; Campbell, Wilson, Howells, Calderwood, Mabbutt, Fox, Dozzell, Armstrong (McMahon), Sheringham, Rosenthal.

FIFTH ROUND REPLAYS

Chelsea (1) 4 *(Duberry, Hughes, Spencer, Peacock)*
Grimsby T (0) 1 *(Groves)* 28,545
Chelsea: Hitchcock; Petrescu, Phelan, Duberry, Clarke, Lee, Gullit (Spackman), Hughes (Furlong), Spencer, Peacock, Wise.
Grimsby T: Crichton; McDermott, Croft, Laws (Fickling), Lever, Groves, Childs (Dobbin), Shakespeare, Woods, Livingstone, Southall (Forrester).

Southampton (0) 2 *(Oakley, Shipperley)*
Swindon T (0) 0 13,962
Southampton: Beasant; Widdrington, Charlton, Magilton, Hall, Monkou, Oakley, Watson, Shipperley, Venison, Walters (Robinson).
Swindon T: Digby; Culverhouse, Drysdale, Gooden, Seagraves, Taylor, Robinson, Collins (Finney), Thorne, Allison, Horlock.

Wimbledon (2) 3 *(Ekoku, Goodman 2)*
Huddersfield T (1) 1 *(Booth)* 7015
Wimbledon: Sullivan; Cunningham, Kimble, Jones, Reeves, Blackwell, Gayle, Earle, Ekoku (Euell), Goodman, Leonhardsen (Clarke).
Huddersfield T: Francis; Jenkins, Cowan, Bullock, Sinnott, Gray, Dalton (Rowe), Makel, Booth, Jepson, Collins.

9 MAR

Tottenham H (1) 1 *(Sheringham)*
Nottingham F (1) 1 *(Roy)* 31,055
Tottenham H: Walker; Edinburgh (Nethercott), Wilson, Howells, Calderwood, Mabbutt, Fox, Campbell, Armstrong (Slade), Sheringham, Rosenthal.
Nottingham F: Crossley; Lyttle, Pearce, Haaland (Phillips), Chettle, Stone (McGregor), Bart-Williams, Gemmill, Campbell (Lee), Roy, Woan.
aet; Nottingham F won 3-1 on penalties.

SIXTH ROUND

Chelsea (0) 2 *(Hughes, Gullit)*
Wimbledon (0) 2 *(Earle, Holdsworth)* 30,805
Chelsea: Hitchcock; Petrescu, Phelan, Duberry, Clarke, Johnsen, Gullit, Spencer (Peacock), Furlong (Spackman), Hughes, Wise.
Wimbledon: Sullivan; Cunningham, Kimble, Jones, Blackwell, Perry, Ekoku, Earle, Harford (Gayle), Goodman (Holdsworth), Leonhardsen.

10 MAR

Leeds U (0) 0
Liverpool (0) 0 24,632
Leeds U: Lukic; Kelly, Worthington, Palmer, Beesley, Wetherall, Radebe, Brolin (Deane), Yeboah, McAllister, Ford (Pemberton).
Liverpool: James; McAteer, Jones, Scales, Wright, Babb, McManaman, Thomas, Collymore, Barnes (Redknapp), Fowler.

11 MAR

Manchester U (0) 2 *(Cantona, Sharpe)*
Southampton (0) 0 45,446
Manchester U: Schmeichel; Neville P, Irwin, Bruce, Sharpe, Neville G, Cantona, Keane, Cole, Butt, Giggs.
Southampton: Beasant; Dodd, Charlton, Magilton, Hall, Monkou, Le Tissier, Widdrington, Shipperley, Walters (Robinson), Oakley.

13 MAR

Nottingham F (0) 0
Aston Villa (1) 1 *(Carr)* 21,067
Nottingham F: Crossley; Lyttle, Pearce, Bart-Williams, Chettle, Stone, Phillips, Gemmill, Campbell, Roy (McGregor), Woan (Lee).
Aston Villa: Bosnich; Charles, Wright, Scimeca, McGrath, Ehiogu, Carr (Davis), Draper, Milosevic, Taylor, Yorke.

SIXTH ROUND REPLAYS

20 MAR

Liverpool (0) 3 *(McManaman 2, Fowler)*
Leeds U (0) 0 30,812
Liverpool: James; McAteer, Jones, Scales, Wright, Ruddock, McManaman, Thomas, Collymore, Barnes, Fowler.
Leeds U: Lukic; Kelly, Worthington, Palmer, Radebe, Pemberton, Ford (Gray), Yeboah, Deane, McAllister, Speed.

Wimbledon (1) 1 *(Goodman)* 21,380
Chelsea (1) 3 *(Petrescu, Duberry, Hughes)*
Wimbledon: Sullivan; Cunningham (Castledine), Kimble, Jones, Blackwell, Perry, Ekoku, Earle, Harford (Gayle), Goodman, Leonhardsen.
Chelsea: Hitchcock; Petrescu, Phelan, Duberry, Clarke, Lee, Gullit (Furlong), Hughes, Spencer (Peacock), Burley, Wise.

SEMI-FINALS

31 MAR

Aston Villa (0) 0 39,021
Liverpool (1) 3 *(Fowler 2, McAteer)* (at Old Trafford)
Aston Villa: Bosnich; Charles, Wright, Southgate (Staunton), McGrath, Ehiogu, Taylor, Draper, Milosevic (Johnson), Townsend, Yorke.
Liverpool: James; McAteer, Jones, Scales, Wright, Ruddock, McManaman, Redknapp, Collymore (Rush), Barnes, Fowler.

Chelsea (1) 1 *(Gullit)* 38,421
Manchester U (0) 2 *(Cole, Beckham)* (at Villa Park)
Chelsea: Hitchcock; Clarke (Johnsen), Phelan (Peacock), Duberry, Myers, Lee (Furlong), Gullit, Hughes, Spencer, Burley, Wise.
Manchester U: Schmeichel; Neville P, Sharpe, Keane, Neville G, May, Cantona, Beckham, Cole, Butt, Giggs.

FINAL (AT WEMBLEY)

11 MAY

Liverpool (0) 0
Manchester U (0) 1 *(Cantona)* 79,007
Liverpool: James; McAteer, Jones (Thomas), Scales, Wright, Babb, McManaman, Redknapp, Collymore (Rush), Barnes, Fowler.
Manchester U: Schmeichel; Irwin, Neville P, May, Keane, Pallister, Cantona, Beckham (Neville G), Cole (Scholes), Butt, Giggs.
Referee: D. Gallagher (Banbury).

Eric Cantona drives in the only goal of the 1996 FA Cup Final to clinch a League and Cup double for Manchester United. Liverpool's Steve McManaman (17) is an onlooker. (Colorsport).

THE SCOTTISH SEASON 1995-96

The League programme this season has been of great interest. The usual comments have been flying around at the appropriate time: Why not have a winter break? (But they never say when, unless it is for the whole of December, January and February. Why doesn't someone explain to them that we do not have a continental climate?) We must get back to a bigger Premier division. (So that we can be in it, and stay comfortably somewhere out of relegation's reach.) It is so hard for the players and the managers. (Well, they're getting paid enough for it; and no one needs to be a manager if he does not want to.) And so on.

The Premier Division maintained its interest until the end: at the top, Rangers assumed their customary position, but this time they were harried by a Celtic team which at last was regaining some style and class: note that the Bhoys lost only one game in the season; but, of course, they had too many draws; that, and the fact that Rangers came out on top of the Titans clashes (one win and three draws), was enough to see Rangers home for their 8th consecutive title. But we are all looking forward to next season already.

The top two soon left the rest far astern, and the whole division broke into several groups. The second group of Aberdeen and Hearts, two teams with ambitious and effective managers, slogged it out to see who would achieve third place: it was all fairly academic, for Aberdeen were already in Europe by Christmas, whilst Hearts were assured of their place when they reached the Cup Final as soon as Rangers were League champions. Hibs promised early in the season, but rather lost their way and finished down the order. Raith Rovers always seemed just about safe from the threat of relegation, but Motherwell flirted with the bottom of the table until their manager clearly said a few necessary words, and the team won six games out of seven in a row and shot clear of danger. Kilmarnock produced some good results when needed, and the two bottom places were left to Partick and Falkirk. The troubled Falkirk looked doomed as the cold winds and snows of February gave way to the cold winds and snows of March; and so it turned out, with Partick at least giving themselves a chance in the play-off.

There was an intriguing battle at the top of the First Division: when Airdrie dropped gradually out of the running, it left five teams seeking the top: for a while Dundee held their own and looked likely promotion candidates, but they faltered badly. All along it was Dundee United and Dunfermline who seemed to have the edge, but Greenock Morton made a strong challenge, and St Johnstone, too, with their new routines, were not far away. It all boiled up nicely in the last few weeks with the contenders locked against each other: Dundee United, apparently anchored at the top, blew two chances to stay there when they lost to both the Saints and the Pars. It was the latter who at last, after three years of disappointment, took the one promotion place. Greenock Morton v Dundee United on the last afternoon of the League season was a game of immense significance; in the end, United, thanks to a very favourable goal difference, grabbed the point they needed and advanced to the play-off against Partick. Morton, newly promoted into the First Division, did very well to challenge for a further move up. Next season's First Division is looking like being very lively already.

The play-off between Partick Thistle and Dundee United for the right to the last place in the Premier Division was an epic: in the first match, at Firhill, Thistle took an early lead, and it was only five minutes from the end when United snatched the equaliser - which gave them perhaps a slight edge for the return home fixture. However, at Tannadice a tense first half brought no goals but plenty to keep the fans in fine voice. Then, in 72 minutes, Partick scored with a penalty, and as the time ticked away, it looked to be all over. Within a few seconds of full time, there was another equaliser. So to extra time: that, too, was almost spent and the dreaded penalty shoot-out looked imminent, when United produced an exquisite move which gave them victory. It was hard luck on a Thistle side which gave its all, and particularly for their manager who watched in disbelief as, for the third time, the plum was tweaked from his mouth. The United manager, too, had a traumatic time; so did many of each side's supporters. Both games were played to packed grounds. It is hard to argue against this being what the public wants to see, albeit at great strain to everyone's nerves!

At the lower end of the First Division, Dumbarton failed to take a grip, and were for the drop at a very early date. In the other relegation place came Hamilton Accies who, after a disastrous start to the season, very nearly reached safety. It is not easy without one's own ground, and they will surely settle down once their new home is ready.

Stirling Albion were the team of the Second Division. After a sloppy start, they rapidly took the Division apart and proved themselves far and away the best. East Fife started well, and managed to hold their own through the long season, always with a little in hand over Berwick Rangers, who none the less put in a determined push for promotion. Stirling Albion look to have the class to do well in the First Division, whilst hopefully the Fifers can remain afloat in their new ground in the middle of Methil Docks.

The lower end of the Second Division did not lack interest. Stranraer, having had their fling in the First Division, very nearly ran straight through into the Third Division, but a timely win in their last game kept their status. Forfar Athletic, having a mid-table place earlier, had slowly sunk until it was too late: a determined effort in the last games nearly saved them; but it was not enough. They joined Montrose who had a rather miserable league season bringing up the rear. So the two teams that came up this season returned downward for the next season.

Meantime, the reverse was happening in the Third Division. Last season Meadowbank Thistle and Brechin City went down. This time, they return to the Second Division. Now, however, Thistle have transformed to Livingston, and, with a new ground and vastly increased crowds, they have done well. True, it took them some time before they could bring a win to Almondvale, but, with the Bard in good voice and verse, they put forward a major challenge which none of the others could match. Brechin City had good, solid performances when it mattered, and both the Highland clubs missed their opportunities.

The first of the cups to be contested was the Coca-Cola (League) Cup: in the early rounds most of the results were predictable, though Livingston held St Johnstone at McDiarmid Park and won on penalties. Airdrie removed Hibs, and Dundee removed Kilmarnock, whilst Rangers, coasting along happily against Stirling Albion, lost two goals in the last ten minutes and were glad to hear the final whistle, still a goal ahead. In the quarter-finals, Dundee beat Hearts 5-4 on penalties after sharing eight goals in full and extra time. Aberdeen beat Rangers in the first semi-final, whilst Dundee won the clash of First Division clubs against Airdrie: in the rather low key final, Dundee could not find their best form and Aberdeen's two goals proved to be more than enough.

The League Challenge Cup: Livingston and Stirling Albion again did well, but it was Stenhousemuir who took the headlines, disposing of Dundee and Stirling Albion in the later rounds. In the final Stenhousemuir and Dundee United could score no goals, and in the end it was Stenhousemuir who triumphed in the penalty shoot-out: it was their first trophy, and a just reward for some stirring cup performances over the last few seasons.

The Tennent's Scottish Cup provided its ration of exciting matches, and gave several clubs the opportunity of taking on the Old Firm - with predictable results both in goals and cash. The Police rightly took good care of possible crowd difficulties at some grounds: Keith's match against Rangers was transferred to Pittodrie, whilst Celtic took on Whitehill Welfare at Easter Road. Subsequently Caledonian Thistle, having defeated the redoubtable Stenhousemuir, played Rangers at Tannadice in the quarter-final round, a notable 'first' for the Highlanders. Caledonian Thistle were disappointed not to be able to host the game at Telford Street, but the Ibrox manager has mentioned the possibility of coming north with a team to take on Caley when their new ground by the firth opens. Another quarter-final game brought heartbreak to Dundee United. For an hour they led Celtic by a single goal, only to lose two goals in the final minutes. Aberdeen and Celtic lost in the semi-finals, and Hearts could look forward to their first final since 1986. They had not won the Cup since 1956. In the final, Hearts lost their captain in the 7th minute, and they were never able to match Rangers, for whom Laudrup was involved in all five goals.

Motherwell were hit too early in the season, but even a fine second-leg performance away from home could not retrieve them. Raith Rovers came well through two rounds, but then came across too stiff competition in Bayern Munich - though they played pluckily, and came away with much credit from the encounter. Celtic did well in their first match, but then lost to Paris St Germain in both legs of the next. Rangers overcame a difficult opponent in the preliminary round of the European Cup, but failed to impress in the league section. In general, though there were some stout performances, our representatives could not match the top continental opponents. We can but look forward to next season.

It was quite a different matter at International level. Scotland cannot pretend to any players of tremendous skill and ability to match some of the European sides, but they can show great tenacity and endurance, and Craig Brown has given the team a belief in itself which has produced results far exceeding the hopes of many. It was indeed a triumph to reach the European finals in England; and, if we were desperately disappointed to miss out on the qualification for the quarter-finals by the smallest of margins, yet the fans could rejoice in three matches undertaken with energy, planning, purpose. We could indeed be proud of them. The Under 21 team, too, has achieved much. World Cup qualifying games are ahead, and we are in a tough group: we can be assured that, come what may, our side will give of its best.

ALAN ELLIOTT

ABERDEEN   Premier Division

Year Formed: 1903. *Ground & Address:* Pittodrie Stadium, Pittodrie St, Aberdeen AB2 1QH. *Telephone:* 01224 632328.
Ground Capacity: all seated: 21,634. All. *Size of Pitch:* 110yd × 72yd.
Chairman: Ian R. Donald. *Secretary:* Ian J. Taggart. *General Manager:* David Johnston.
Manager: Roy Aitken. *Coach:* Tommy Craig. *Physios:* David Wylie, John Sharp.
Managers since 1975: Ally MacLeod; Billy McNeill; Alex Ferguson; Ian Porterfield; Alex Smith and Jocky Scott; Willie
Miller. *Club Nicknames(s):* The Dons. *Previous Grounds:* None.
Record Attendance: 45,061 v Hearts, Scottish Cup 4th rd; 13 Mar, 1954.
Record Transfer Fee received: £1.75 million for Eoin Jess to Coventry City (February 1996).
Record Transfer Fee paid: £1m+ for Paul Bernard from Oldham Athletic (September 1995).
Record Victory: 13-0 v Peterhead, Scottish Cup; 9 Feb, 1923.
Record Defeat: 0-8 v Celtic, Division 1; 30 Jan, 1965.
Most Capped Players: Alex McLeish, 77, Scotland.
Most League Appearances: 556: Willie Miller, 1973-90.
Most League Goals in Season (Individual): 38: Benny Yorston, Division I; 1929-30.
Most Goals Overall (Individual): 199: Joe Harper.

ABERDEEN 1995–96 LEAGUE RECORD

Match No.	Date	Venue	Opponents	Result	H/T Score	Lg. Pos.	Goalscorers	Attendance
1	Aug 26	A	Falkirk	W 3-2	2-0	—	Inglis, Dodds, Booth	6647
2	Sept 10	H	Celtic	L 2-3	2-3	—	Boyd (og), Jess	16,489
3	16	A	Hibernian	D 1-1	0-0	6	Shearer	11,161
4	23	A	Kilmarnock	W 2-1	2-0	4	Miller, Woodthorpe	7198
5	30	H	Raith R	W 3-0	2-0	2	Booth 2, Miller	13,983
6	Oct 4	A	Hearts	W 2-1	1-1	—	Dodds, Booth	10,927
7	7	H	Rangers	L 0-1	0-0	3		20,351
8	14	A	Motherwell	L 1-2	1-1	3	Booth	6842
9	21	H	Partick Th	W 3-0	1-0	3	Craig (og), Jess, Bernard	12,719
10	28	A	Celtic	L 0-2	0-1	4		32,275
11	Nov 4	A	Hibernian	L 1-2	0-1	4	Glass	14,774
12	8	H	Falkirk	W 3-1	2-1	—	Dodds, Miller, McGowan (og)	11,214
13	11	A	Rangers	D 1-1	1-1	4	Jess	45,427
14	18	A	Raith R	L 0-1	0-1	4		5786
15	Dec 2	A	Partick Th	L 0-1	0-0	5		4286
16	9	H	Motherwell	W 1-0	0-0	4	Shearer	11,299
17	13	H	Kilmarnock	W 4-1	2-1	—	Miller 3, Windass	14,060
18	16	H	Hearts	L 1-2	1-0	4	Windass	12,308
19	Jan 8	A	Hibernian	W 2-1	2-0	—	Miller, Dodds	8191
20	14	H	Celtic	L 1-2	1-0	—	Dodds	16,760
21	16	A	Falkirk	D 1-1	0-1	—	Windass	4003
22	20	H	Partick Th	W 1-0	0-0	4	Dodds	9149
23	23	A	Kilmarnock	D 1-1	1-0	—	Irvine	6703
24	Feb 7	H	Raith R	W 1-0	1-0	—	Windass	6628
25	10	A	Hearts	W 3-1	2-1	3	Windass, Shearer, Glass	14,314
26	13	A	Motherwell	L 0-1	0-0	—		5090
27	25	H	Rangers	L 0-1	0-1	—		19,842
28	Mar 2	H	Kilmarnock	W 3-0	1-0	3	Booth 2, Miller	7177
29	16	A	Raith R	D 2-2	1-2	3	Miller, Buchan	4932
30	23	H	Hibernian	W 2-1	0-1	3	Dodds, Booth	10,924
31	Apr 1	A	Celtic	L 0-5	0-2	—		35,284
32	13	H	Motherwell	W 2-1	0-1	3	McCart (og), Irvine	8943
33	16	A	Partick Th	D 1-1	1-1	—	Booth	4568
34	20	H	Hearts	D 1-1	0-0	3	Windass	11,303
35	28	A	Rangers	L 1-3	1-1	—	Irvine	47,247
36	May 4	H	Falkirk	W 2-1	1-1	3	Glass, McGowan (og)	11,831

Final League Position: 3

Honours
League Champions: Division I 1954-55. Premier Division 1979-80, 1983-84, 1984-85; *Runners-up:* Division I 1910-11, 1936-37, 1955-56, 1970-71, 1971-72. Premier Division 1977-78, 1980-81, 1981-82, 1988-89, 1989-90, 1990-91, 1992-93, 1993-94.
Scottish Cup Winners: 1947, 1970, 1982, 1983, 1984, 1986, 1990; *Runners-up:* 1937, 1953, 1954, 1959, 1967, 1978, 1993.
League Cup Winners: 1955-56, 1976-77, 1985-86, 1989-90, (Coca Cola cup) 1995-96; *Runners-up:* 1946-47, 1978-79, 1979-80, 1987-88, 1988-89, 1992-93.
Drybrough Cup Winners: 1971, 1980.

European: *European Cup* 12 matches (1980-81, 1984-85, 1985-86); *Cup Winners Cup Winners:* 1982-83. Semi-finals 1983-84. 37 matches (1967-68, 1970-71, 1978-79, 1982-83, 1983-84, 1986-87, 1990-91, 1993-94); *UEFA Cup* 36 matches (*Fairs Cup:* 1968-69. *UEFA Cup:* 1971-72, 1972-73, 1973-74, 1977-78, 1979-80, 1981-82, 1987-88, 1988-89, 1989-90, 1991-92, 1994-95).
Club colours: Shirt, Shorts, Stockings: Red with white trim.

Goalscorers: *League (52):* Booth 9, Miller 9, Dodds 8, Windass 6, Glass 3, Irvine 3, Jess 3, Shearer 3, Bernard 1, Buchan 1, Inglis 1, Woodthorpe 1, own goals 5. *Scottish Cup (7):* Shearer 3, Windass 3, Bernard 1. *Coca-Cola Cup (13):* Dodds 5, Booth 3, Inglis 1, Miller 1, Shearer 1, Woodthorpe 1, own goal 1.

Sneiders T 6+1	McKimmie S 29	Woodthorpe C 15	Hetherston P 9+2	Inglis J 24	Smith G 33	Miller J 31	Jess E 25	Booth S 20+4	Dodds W 28+3	Glass S 32	Thomson S —+4	Shearer D 15+15	McKinnon R —+1	Watt M 30	Christie K —+2	Bernard P 27+4	Grant B 22+3	Robertson H 5+6	Windass D 19+1	Irvine B 17+1	Buchan J 1+3	Rowson D 7+2	Kpedekpo M 1+4	Craig M —+1	Match No.
1	2	3	4	5	6	7^1	8	9	10	11	12														1
1	2	3	4^2	5	6	7^1	8	9	10	11		12	13												2
1	2	3	4	5	6	7	8	9^1	10	11		12													3
	2	3	4	5	6	7^1	8	9^2	10	11		12		1	13										4
	2	3	4	5	6	7^1	8	9	10^2	11			13	1	12										5
	2	3	4	5	6	7^1	8	9^2	10	11			13	1	12										6
	2	3	4^2	5	6	7	8	9	10^1	11		12		1	13										7
	2	3^2	4	5	6	7	8	9	10^1	11		12		1	13										8
	2^1			5	6	7	11		10	3^2	12	8		1		9	4								9
15	2	13		5	6	7^1	11	9	10	3^2	12	8		1^8			4								10
1	2			5	6	7	11	9^1	10	3	12	8					4								11
1	2	13		5	6	7	11		10^2	3^1	12	8				9	4								12
1	2			5	6	7	11	9	10^1	3	12	8					4								13
	2		11^2	5	6	7		9	10^1	3	12	8					4	13							14
	2			5	6	7^2	11^1		10	13		8				9	4	3	12						15
					6	7	11		10	3		8		1		4	2	9	5						16
	2				6	7^2	11		10^1	3		8		1		4	12	13	9	5					17
					6	7	11		10^1	3		8		1		4	2	12	9	5					18
	2			5	6	7	11		10	3				1		9	4		8						19
	2			5	6	7^1	11		10	3	12			1		9	4		8						20
	2			5	6	7	11^1		10	3^2	12			1		9	4	13	8						21
	2			5^1	6	7	11		10^2	3		13		1		9	4		8	12					22
	2				6	7	11		10	3		13		1	12	9	4^1		8	5					23
	2				6	7	11	12	10	3		8^1		1		9	4			5					24
	2				6	7	11^1	12	10	3		8		1		9	4			5					25
	2				6	7	11^1	12	10	3		8		1		9	4			5					26
	2^1				6	7	12	11	10	3		8		1		9	4			5					27
		3			6	7^1		9	10	11^2				1		4	2		8	5	12	13			28
		3			6	7		9	12			8^1		1		2	11^2	10		5	13	4			29
		3			6	7		9^2	12			8^1		1		10	2	11		5	13	4			30
		3			6	7		9^2	10	11^1				1		4	2	12	8	5					31
	2	3			6		13	10^2	11^1	8^1		7	12	1		9	5			4			14		32
	2	3			6			9^1	10	12		7	11^2	1		8	5			4		13			33
	2	3^1			6			9^2	11			7	12	1		10	5			4		13			34
	2		6	3				9	10	11		7^1		1		8	5			4		12			35
			6	4				9^2		11		7^1	12	1		8	5	2	3	10		13			36

AIRDRIEONIANS
First Division

Year Formed: 1878. *Ground & Address:* Broadwood Stadium, Cumbernauld G68 9NE. Address for all correspondence:
32 Stirling Street, Airdrie, ML6 0AH *Telephone:* 01236 762067.
Ground Capacity: all seated: 6300. *Size of Pitch:* 112yd × 76yd.
Chairman and Secretary: George W. Peat CA.
Manager: Alex MacDonald. *Assistant Manager:* John McVeigh. *Physio:* Ian Constable. *Coach:* John Binnie.
Managers since 1975: I. McMillan; J. Stewart; R. Watson; W. Munro; A. MacLeod; D. Whiteford; G. McQueen; J. Bone.
Club Nickname(s): The Diamonds or The Waysiders. *Previous Grounds:* Mavisbank, Broomfield Park.
Record Attendance: 24,000 v Hearts, Scottish Cup; 8 Mar, 1952.
Record Transfer Fee received: £200,000 for Sandy Clark to West Ham U, May 1982.
Record Transfer Fee paid: £175,000 for Owen Coyle from Clydebank, February 1990.
Record Victory: 15-1 v Dundee Wanderers, Division I; 1 Dec, 1894.
Record Defeat: 1-11 v Hibernian, Division I; 24 Oct, 1959.
Most Capped Player: Jimmy Crapnell, 9, Scotland.
Most League Appearances: 523: Paul Jonquin, 1962-79.
Most League Goals in Season (Individual): 53, Hugh Baird, Division II, 1954-55. *Most Goals Overall (Individual):* —

AIRDRIEONIANS 1995–96 LEAGUE RECORD

Match No.	Date	Venue	Opponents	Result		H/T Score	Lg. Pos.	Goalscorers	Atten- dance
1	Aug 12	H	Dunfermline Ath	L	0-1	0-0	—		2719
2	26	A	Dundee	D	1-1	0-1	7	Duffield	3536
3	Sept 2	H	St Mirren	L	1-2	0-1	8	Cooper	2142
4	9	A	Dumbarton	W	2-1	2-0	8	Boyle, McIntyre T	1320
5	16	H	Morton	W	3-2	3-1	5	McIntyre J 2, Wylie (og)	1927
6	23	A	Dundee U	W	2-1	0-0	3	Duffield, Cooper	6005
7	30	H	Hamilton A	D	0-0	0-0	4		1586
8	Oct 7	A	St Johnstone	L	0-1	0-1	7		2839
9	14	H	Clydebank	D	1-1	1-0	6	Davies	1306
10	21	A	St Mirren	W	2-1	1-1	5	McIntyre J, Harvey	2459
11	28	H	Dundee	L	2-3	1-1	6	Duffield 2	1925
12	Nov 4	A	Morton	L	1-2	1-1	6	Black (pen)	3856
13	11	H	Dumbarton	W	2-1	1-0	6	Davies, Black	1205
14	18	A	Hamilton A	W	2-1	1-1	6	Smith, Sandison	1169
15	25	H	Dundee U	D	1-1	0-0	6	McIntyre J	2504
16	Dec 2	H	St Johnstone	D	1-1	0-0	5	McIntyre J	1660
17	16	A	Dunfermline Ath	L	0-2	0-0	6		4687
18	30	A	Dundee U	D	2-2	2-1	6	Winters (og), McIntyre J	5855
19	Jan 9	A	Clydebank	D	1-1	0-0	—	McIntyre J	865
20	13	A	Dumbarton	W	2-1	2-0	6	Duffield, McIntyre J	1045
21	16	H	St Mirren	L	1-3	1-1	—	Duffield	1554
22	20	A	St Johnstone	D	0-0	0-0	6		2761
23	23	H	Morton	L	0-2	0-1	—		1605
24	Feb 10	H	Dunfermline Ath	L	1-2	0-0	7	Davies	2453
25	13	H	Clydebank	D	1-1	1-0	—	Boyle	851
26	24	A	Dundee	L	0-2	0-2	7		2116
27	Mar 2	H	Dundee U	D	1-1	0-1	7	Cooper	1810
28	6	H	Hamilton A	W	3-0	3-0	—	Harvey, Smith, Cooper	1021
29	16	A	Hamilton A	L	1-4	1-1	7	McIntyre J	909
30	23	A	Morton	L	0-3	0-1	7		2889
31	30	H	Dumbarton	W	5-1	1-1	7	Smith, McIntyre T, Connolly P 2, Hetherston	1062
32	Apr 6	H	St Johnstone	L	1-3	1-1	7	Hetherston	2018
33	13	A	Clydebank	L	1-2	1-1	7	Hetherston	831
34	20	A	St Mirren	L	1-2	1-2	7	Connolly P	2117
35	27	H	Dundee	D	0-0	0-0	7		1454
36	May 4	A	Dunfermline Ath	L	1-2	0-1	8	Hetherston	13,183

Final League Position: 8

Honours
League Champions: Division II 1902-03, 1954-55, 1973-74; *Runners-up:* Division I 1922-23, 1923-24, 1924-25, 1925-26. First Division 1979-80, 1989-90, 1990-91. Division II 1900-01, 1946-47, 1949-50, 1965-66.
Scottish Cup Winners: 1924; *Runners-up:* 1975, 1992, 1995. *Scottish Spring Cup Winners:* 1976.
League Cup semi-finalists: 1991-92, 1994-95.
B&Q Cup Winners:R: 1994-95.

European: *UEFA Cup* 2 matches (1992-93).
Club colours: Shirt: White with red diamond. Shorts: White. Stockings: Red.

Goalscorers: *League (43):* McIntyre J 9, Duffield 6, Cooper 4, Hetherston 4, Connolly P 3, Davies 3, Smith 3, Black 2 (1 pen), Boyle 2, Harvey 2, McIntyre T 2, Sandison 1, own goals 2. *Scottish Cup (6):* Duffield 3, Bonar 1, Cooper 1, Smith 1. *Coca-Cola Cup (7):* Boyle 2, Duffield 2, Cooper 1, McIntyre J 1, own goal 1. *League Challenge Cup (2):* Boyle 1, McIntyre J 1.

Martin J 20	Boyle J 36	Jack P 9+5	Sandison J 30	McIntyre T 12+5	Black K 33	Davies J 33+2	Harvey P 27+7	Cooper S 24	Duffield P 19+5	Stewart A 30	McIntyre J 22+7	Sweeney S 24	Smith A 28+3	Wilson M 8+5	Connelly G —+8	Rhodes A 16	Bonar P 9+3	Tait S 2+2	Hetherston P 7+1	Connolly P 6	McClelland J 1+2	McPeak A —+1	Match No.
1	2	3	4	5	6	7	8^1	9	10	11	12												1
1	2		4	13	6^2	8	12	9^1	10	3	7	5	11										2
1	7	12	4	5		6	10	9		2	11	3	8^1										3
1	7	3	4	5^1	6	8	10	9^2		2	11		12			13							4
1	7	3	4		6	8^2	10^3	9^1	14	2	11	5	12	13									5
1	7		4	2	6	8	10^1	9	12		11	5	3										6
1	7	3	4		6	8	10^1	9	12	2	11	5											7
1	7	3	4	13	6	8^2	11		10	2^1	9	5	12										8
1	2	4^1		5	6	8	12	9	10	3	7		11										9
1	7		4		6	8	12	9	10^1	2	11	5	3										10
1	7		4		6	8	10		11	2	9	5	3										11
1	7			4	6	8	10		9	2	11	5	3										12
1	7			4	6	8	10	9^1	12	2	11^2	5	3		13								13
1	7		4		6	8	11^1	9	10	2	12	5	3										14
1	7		4	13	6	8	11^2	9	10	2	12	5	3^1										15
1	7		4	3	6	8	11^1		10	2	9	5		12									16
	7		4	5^1	6	8	11		10	2	9		3			1	12						17
	7		4		6	8	11^1		10	2	9		3	12	13	1	5^2						18
	7	12	4		6	8	11		10	2	9		3			1	5^1						19
	7	5	4		6	8	12	9	10	2	11^1		3			1							20
	7^2		4		6	8	12	9^1	10		11		3		13	1	5	2					21
	7		4		6	13	11^2	9^1	10		12		3	8		1	5	2					22
	7^1		4		6	12	10^2	9	13		11	2	3	8		1	5^3	14					23
	7		4		6^1	11	13	9	10^2	2	12	5	3	8		1							24
	7		4		6	11	13	9^1	10^2	2	12	5	3	8		1							25
1	7		4		6	11		9	10	2^2	12	5	3	8^1			13						26
1	7		4			6^1	8	10	9^3	2	11	5					3		8				27
1	7		4		6^1	8	10	9^3		2^2	11	5	3	12	14		13						28
1	7		4		6	8	10	9		2	11	5					3						29
	7	12			6	8	11^3	9		2		5^2	4	10^1	14	1	3		13				30
	7	2		12	6^3	8	10			5	3^2	14	13	1	4^1				11	9			31
	7	2^1		4	6	8	10			5	3			1					11	9	12		32
	7	12	4^2	13	6	8		10^1		2		5	3	1					11	9			33
	7	12	4		6	8	10			2		5^1	3	1					11	9			34
	7		4	5			11			2		3	8^1	1					10	9	6	12	35
	7		4	5^1	6^3	8	10			2		3	13	1					12	11	9	14	36

ALBION ROVERS   Third Division

Year Formed: 1882. *Ground & Address:* Cliftonhill Stadium, Main St, Coatbridge ML5 3RB. *Telephone:* 01236 606334.
Ground capacity: total: 1238, seated: 538. *Size of Pitch:* 110yd × 70yd.
Chairman: David Shanks, BSc. *Secretary:* John Hughes FCCA. *Commercial Manager:* Gordon Dishington.
Manager: Vinnie Moore. *Assistant Manager:* Tom O'Neil. *Coaches:* David Byrne, Robert Russell.
Physio: William Cowan. *Managers since 1975:* G. Caldwell; S. Goodwin; H. Hood; J. Baker; D. Whiteford; M. Ferguson;
W. Wilson; B. Rooney; A. Ritchie; T. Gemmell; D. Provan; M. Oliver; B. McLaren; T. Gemmell; T Spence; J. Crease.
Club Nickname(s): The Wee Rovers. *Previous Grounds:* Cowheath Park, Meadow Park, Whifflet.
Record Attendance: 27,381 v Rangers, Scottish Cup 2nd rd; 8 Feb, 1936.
Record Transfer Fee received: £40,000 from Motherwell for Bruce Cleland.
Record Transfer Fee paid: £7000 for Gerry McTeague to Stirling Albion, September 1989.
Record Victory: 12-0 v Airdriehill, Scottish Cup; 3 Sept, 1887.
Record Defeat: 1-11 v Partick T, League Cup, 11 August 1993.
Most Capped Player: Jock White, 1 (2), Scotland.
Most League Appearances: 399, Murdy Walls, 1921-36.
Most League Goals in Season (Individual): 41: Jim Renwick, Division II; 1932-33.
Most Goals Overall (Individual): 105: Bunty Weir, 1928-31.

ALBION ROVERS 1995–96 LEAGUE RECORD

Match No.	Date	Venue	Opponents		Result	H/T Score	Lg. Pos.	Goalscorers	Atten- dance
1	Aug 12	H	Arbroath	L	0-2	0-0	—		378
2	26	A	Alloa	L	2-3	2-2	9	Young, Scott	427
3	Sept 2	H	Caledonian Th	D	2-2	1-2	8	McBride, Young	284
4	9	H	Cowdenbeath	L	2-3	0-1	9	Collins, McBride	680
5	16	A	Ross Co	L	1-5	0-1	9	Young	1419
6	23	A	Livingston	L	1-2	1-1	10	Young	229
7	30	H	Queen's P	W	3-1	3-1	9	Young 2, McBride	378
8	Oct 7	A	Brechin C	W	1-0	0-0	8	Young	341
9	14	H	East Stirling	L	1-2	0-2	8	Young	334
10	21	A	Caledonian Th	L	1-6	0-6	10	McEwan	1222
11	28	H	Alloa	W	2-1	0-1	8	McBride, Young	427
12	Nov 4	H	Ross Co	L	3-4	1-2	9	Young, McBride, Speirs	399
13	11	A	Cowdenbeath	L	1-4	0-1	10	McDonald	166
14	18	A	Queen's P	L	1-4	0-2	10	Strain	467
15	25	H	Livingston	L	0-2	0-1	10		433
16	Dec 2	H	Brechin C	W	1-0	0-0	10	Willock	289
17	19	A	East Stirling	L	1-5	0-2	—	Willock	245
18	Jan 1	A	Queen's P	L	1-5	0-2	—	Crawford	617
19	6	A	Arbroath	L	0-2	0-1	10		306
20	13	A	Livingston	W	1-0	0-0	10	Crawford	2509
21	20	A	Brechin C	L	0-1	0-1	10		296
22	Feb 17	H	Cowdenbeath	W	2-0	2-0	10	Young, Moore	348
23	24	A	Alloa	L	1-3	1-1	10	Reilly J	342
24	28	H	Caledonian Th	L	0-2	0-1	—		364
25	Mar 2	H	Arbroath	D	1-1	1-1	10	Moore	237
26	6	A	Ross Co	D	1-1	0-1	—	Byrne	1031
27	9	H	Livingston	L	0-1	0-1	10		623
28	16	H	Queen's P	L	0-2	0-1	10		387
29	20	H	East Stirling	D	2-2	0-1	—	Strain, Watson	199
30	23	H	Ross Co	L	0-3	0-2	10		364
31	30	A	Cowdenbeath	D	1-1	0-1	10	MacFarlane	173
32	Apr 6	H	Brechin C	D	0-0	0-0	10		329
33	13	A	East Stirling	D	1-1	0-1	10	Young	293
34	20	A	Caledonian Th	D	1-1	1-1	10	Reilly R	769
35	27	H	Alloa	W	1-0	1-0	9	McInally	454
36	30	A	Arbroath	L	1-2	0-1	10	MacFarlane	350

Final League Position: 10

Honours
League Champions: Division II 1933-34, Second Division 1988-89; *Runners-up:* Division II 1913-14, 1937-38, 1947-48.
Scottish Cup Runners-up: 1920. *League Cup:* —.
Club Colours: Shirt: Yellow with black trim. Shorts: Black. Stockings: Black.

Goalscorers: *League (37):* Young 12, McBride 5, Crawford 2, MacFarlane 2, Moore 2, Strain 2, Willock 2, Byrne 1, Collins 1, McDonald 1, McEwan 1, McNally 1, Reilly J 1, Reilly R 1, Scott 1, Speirs 1, Watson 1. *Scottish Cup (0) Coca-Cola Cup (0) League Challenge Cup (3):* Crawford 1, McBride 1, Scott 1.

Mooney D 4	Riley D 1	Gallagher J 33	Shanks C 17 + 2	Ryan M 20 + 3	Strain B 20 + 6	Deeley B 15 + 5	Collins L 8	Scott M 3	Reilly J 7 + 3	McBride J 12 + 1	Young G 32	Seggie D 2 + 4	Crawford P 11 + 13	McDonald D 24 + 1	Wright A 1	Percy A 1	Bell D 17 + 4	Duncan M 1 + 2	Robertson S 1	Russell R 5 + 7	Osborne M 9	Morrison A 1	Lavery J 4	Quinn K — + 1	Richardson J 1	Brown M 7	Speirs C 9	Willock A 12 + 5	Watson B 1	McEwan A 5 + 2	Thompson D 7	McNally A 6	McConville R 1	Reilly R 3	Friar P 5	Yule R 1 + 1	Moffat J 21	Smith B 3 + 1	Miller D 2	Byrne D 17	Moore V 8	Henderson B 3 + 4	MacFarlane C 16	Pickering M 8 + 1	Clark M 11	Match No.
1	2	3	4	5¹	6	7	8	9²	10	11	12	13																																		1
1		3	6		4	5	8	9		11¹	12		2		7²	10	13																													2
1		3	6	5	4	7	8	9	10	11	12		2¹																																3
1		3	6		4	5	8	10	11	13	9¹	2²		7		12																													4
		3		5	4	6	8		10	11	9¹			7	1	2	12																												5
		3	6		4		8		10	9	12	2	7		11¹	1		5																											6
		3	6		4		8		10	9	12	2	7			1			5	11¹																									7
		3	6		4		8		10¹	9		2	7	12		1			5	11																									8
			6	12	3	4			9	10³	13	2	7	8²		1			5¹	11	14																								9
		3		5					13	9	10	12	2	7		1				11²	8	4	6¹																						10
			4			6			10	9		2	7		12	1			5	11	13	8¹		3²																					11
			6		2	4			10²	9			7		13	1			5	11¹		8		3	12																				12
		3		6	4				10	9		12	7		8¹	1			5			2			11																				13
		3	6²	13	4	5			10	9		12	2	7³		14				11¹	1	8																							14
		3	8		6				10	9		12	2	7²		13			5		11¹	4			1																				15
10	6		4²	13						9		12	2						5	11		7	3		1	8¹																			16
10	6	4		13						9		12	2						5	11	8		3²		1	7¹																			17
8	4			3¹						9		13	2	7						11²	10			5	1	12	6																		18
		3	6	5		11				9		10	2	8				4						1			7																		19
		7	13	5		3				9		12	2	8				6						1				4	10²	11¹															20
		7		6		13				9		11¹	2	8				3²						1				4	10	12	5														21
		7		6				11		9			2											1				4	10		5	3	8												22
		7		6¹	9	13				11³			12	2										14				4	10		5	3²	8												23
		7	14			6	12			11²			13	2					8¹							9³			4	10		5	3												24
		7		6	14								2	13	11³									12					8	10	9¹	5	3	4²											25
		7		6	12								2	13				1						11²					8	10		5	3	4											26
		7		6	12					11²		9³	2	13										14					8¹	10		5	3	4											27
		7		12	6³				14	9			8²	13		11								1			3¹	10			5	2	4											28
		7			6				12	9			14	8³								2	13	11			1	10			5²	3	4¹											29
		7	8¹	6	12	3			10²	9		12	2										13				1	4			5													30
		7		6	8	3				9		11										2				10		1	4		5													31
		7		4	6					9		11										2				10	8	1	3		5													32
		7		4						9		11¹										2				8	10¹	1	3		5		12	6										33
		7		4		12				9		11²										2				8		1	3		13	5		6										34
		7		4	13				10¹	9		11²										2				8	10¹	1	3		12	5		6										35
		7		4	12				8¹	9		11²				14						2				10		1	3			5	13	6³										36

ALLOA
Third Division

Year Formed: 1883. *Ground & Address:* Recreation Park, Clackmannan Rd, Alloa FK10 1RR. *Telephone:* 01259 722695.
Ground Capacity: total: 4100, seated: 424. *Size of Pitch:* 110yd × 75yd.
Chairman: Pat Lawlor. *Secretary:* E. G. Cameron. *Commercial Manager:* William McKie.
Manager: Tom Hendrie. *Assistant Manager:* John Coughlin. *Physio:* Alan Anderson.
Managers since 1975: H. Wilson; A. Totten; W. Garner; J. Thomson; D. Sullivan; G. Abel; B. Little; H. McCann; W. Lamont; Pat McAuley. *Club Nickname(s):* The Wasps. *Previous Grounds:* None.
Record Attendance: 13,000 v Dunfermline Athletic, Scottish Cup 3rd rd replay; 26 Feb, 1939.
Record Transfer Fee received: £60,000 for Paul Sheerin to Southampton (1992).
Record Transfer Fee paid: £10,000 for Douglas Lawrie from Stirling Albion.
Record Victory: 9-2 v Forfar Ath, Division II; 18 Mar, 1933.
Record Defeat: 0-10 v Dundee, Division II; 8 Mar, 1947: v Third Lanark, League Cup, 8 Aug, 1953.
Most Capped Player: Jock Hepburn, 1, Scotland.
Most League Appearances: —.
Most League Goals in Season (Individual): 49: William 'Wee' Crilley, Division II; 1921-22.
Most Goals Overall (Individual): —.

ALLOA 1995–96 LEAGUE RECORD

Match No.	Date	Venue	Opponents		Result	H/T Score	Lg. Pos.	Goalscorers	Attendance
1	Aug 12	A	Cowdenbeath	L	0-1	0-0	—		281
2	26	H	Albion R	W	3-2	2-2	4	Moffat, Bennett, Nixon	427
3	Sept 2	A	Brechin C	W	1-0	1-0	5	Moffat	355
4	9	H	Arbroath	L	0-2	0-2	6		475
5	16	A	Livingston	L	0-2	0-1	7		249
6	23	H	Caledonian Th	L	0-5	0-2	8		387
7	30	A	East Stirling	D	2-2	1-0	7	Whyte, Newbigging	305
8	Oct 7	A	Queen's P	D	0-0	0-0	7		483
9	14	H	Ross Co	W	1-0	0-0	7	Whyte	501
10	21	H	Brechin C	W	3-2	2-0	5	Watters, Rixon, Moffat	371
11	28	A	Albion R	L	1-2	1-0	7	McAneny	427
12	Nov 4	A	Livingston	L	0-2	0-2	7		548
13	11	A	Arbroath	D	1-1	1-0	7	Gilmour	508
14	18	H	East Stirling	L	1-3	0-2	7	Moffat	357
15	25	A	Caledonian Th	D	1-1	0-0	7	Rixon	1181
16	Dec 2	H	Queen's P	D	0-0	0-0	7		352
17	16	A	Ross Co	D	2-2	0-1	8	Cadden, Rixon	1303
18	Jan 13	H	Caledonian Th	L	0-2	0-1	9		410
19	16	H	Cowdenbeath	L	2-3	0-1	—	Moffat, Hannah	289
20	20	A	Queen's P	D	0-0	0-0	9		467
21	23	A	Brechin C	L	0-3	0-2	—		349
22	31	A	East Stirling	L	0-1	0-0	—		310
23	Feb 3	H	Ross Co	L	0-4	0-1	9		373
24	10	A	Livingston	L	0-1	0-1	9		2066
25	17	H	Arbroath	L	0-3	0-3	9		360
26	24	H	Albion R	W	3-1	1-1	9	Rixon, Gilmour, Johnston	342
27	Mar 2	A	Cowdenbeath	L	0-3	0-3	9		190
28	12	A	Caledonian Th	D	0-0	0-0	—		1162
29	16	H	East Stirling	D	2-2	2-0	9	Mackay 2	309
30	23	H	Livingston	D	1-1	1-0	9	Morrison	541
31	30	A	Arbroath	L	0-1	0-1	9		397
32	Apr 6	H	Queen's P	L	0-1	0-0	9		403
33	13	A	Ross Co	D	0-0	0-0	9		1068
34	20	H	Brechin C	L	0-3	0-0	9		369
35	27	A	Albion R	L	0-1	0-1	10		454
36	30	H	Cowdenbeath	W	2-1	1-1	9	Morrison, McCulloch	260

Final League Position: 9

Honours
League Champions: Division II 1921-22; *Runners-up:* Division II 1938-39. Second Division 1976-77, 1981-82, 1984-85, 1988-89.
Scottish Cup: —.
League Cup: —.
Club colours: Shirt: Gold with black trim. Shorts: Black. Stockings: Gold.

Goalscorers: *League (26):* Moffat 5, Rixon 5, Gilmour 2, Mackay 2, Morrison 2, Whyte 2, Bennett 1, Cadden 1, Hannah 1, Johnston 1, McAnenay 1, McCulloch 1, Newbigging 1, Watters 1. *Scottish Cup (1):* Rixon. *Coca-Cola Cup (2):* Moffat 1, Rixon 1. *League Challenge Cup (4):* Moffat 3, Diver 1.

Graham P 9	Newbigging W 15+1	Bennett N 25	McCormack J 15+4	Lawrie D 5	Conway V 7+1	Cadden S 13+3	Diver D 11+1	Rixon S 17+9	Whyte M 18+7	Morrison S 21+5	Kirkham D 2+1	McKenzie C 3+2	Wylie R 14+5	Cully D 4+4	Moffat B 33+2	Smith G 14+2	Nelson M 16+5	Gilmour J 20+5	Hannah K 6+4	Johnston N 9+7	Lamont W 1	Balfour R 26	McAneny P 29	Watters W 3+1	McAvoy N 17	McCulloch K 12+1	Mackay S 16+1	Little T 8+6	Stewart W 1	McCardle R 1	Cummings P 1	Kane K 4	Match No.
1	2	3	4	5	6	7³	8	9	10²	11¹	12	13	14																				1
1	2	3		5		6	8	10	12	7²		11¹		4	9	13																	2
1	2	3		5		8	10	7		11¹					9²	6	4	12	13														3
1	2	3		5		12	8	10³	11²	7			14		9	6¹	4	13															4
1	2²	3	4			11³	8	10¹	12	14			7	5	9	13	6																5
1		3		5			8	10²	11¹	7			6		9	12	4	2	13														6
	4	6	3			11	8	10						5	9¹	2		7	12		1												7
	4	6	2			11	12							3	9		8¹	7				1	5	10									8
	4	3	6			8		9²	14	7³				5¹	12	10	2					1	11		13								9
	4	3	6					9¹		7				5	12	2	11					1	8		10								10
	4	3	12			8				7				5	13	9	2	6¹				1	11²		10								11
	3	4	6¹					10²		7³			8	14	9	2	13	11	12			1	5										12
	4	3				7				8				6	11	2	10	9				1	5										13
	4	3				8				7²		12	13	6	11	2	10	9¹				1	5										14
		3				8				11				5	7	2	10	9				1	4		6								15
		3	12			8²				11			13	5	7	2¹	10	9³				1	4		6	14							16
		3	2			8²		9¹		11				5	12	13	10					1	4		6	7							17
		3³	2			6¹		9		12		13	14		11²	4	10	8				1	5			7							18
		3	2					10		8					9	4	6	12	11¹			1	5			7							19
		3				8³				12		11¹	13	4	9	2	10²	7				1	5		6	14							20
		3				8				11			14	12	4²	9	2¹	10	7			1	5		6³	13							21
1		3												5	9	2	6	12					4		8	7	13	10¹	11²				22
1		3	6²			8				13	11			5	9	2		12					4		10	7¹							23
1		3	13			12				8				6²	9	2		7	11¹				4		10	5							24
		3	12					10		8			13		9²	2		7¹	11			1	4		6	5							25
						7	13	10¹		8²			14		9	3	6	12				1	2		4	5³	11						26
						7²	12	10³		8					9	3	6¹	14				1	2		4	5	13	11					27
	12	2¹								13				8⁴	9	14	10²					1	5		3	4	6	7		11			28
	2		12							7¹			14	8²	9	13	10³					1	5		3	4	6	11					29
	4												7	6	9	3						1	2		10	5	8	11					30
	6¹		12							13			7²	8	5	9	4	14				1	2		3	10	11³						31
						8				13				7¹	2³	9	14	10²				1	5		3	4	6	12			11		32
			12			8²				7				2	9	13		10¹				1	5		3	4	6				11		33
						8		9		7¹				2²	10³		12	14				1	5		3	4	6	13				11	34
	4		6¹							14			7³	13	9	3	10²					1	2			5	8	12				11	35
										10				2	9	3						1	5		6	4	8	11				7	36

ARBROATH   Third Division

Year Formed: 1878. *Ground & Address:* Gayfield Park, Arbroath DD11 1QB. *Telephone and Fax:* 01241 872157.
Ground Capacity: 6488. seated: 715. *Size of Pitch:* 115yd × 71yd.
President: John D. Christison. *Secretary:* Charles Kinnear. *Commercial Manager:* Sandy Watt.
Manager: John Brogan. *Assistant Manager:* Jim Kerr. *Physio:* William Shearer. *Coaches:* John Martin, Tom Fairweather.
Managers since 1975: A. Henderson; I. J. Stewart; G. Fleming; J. Bone; J. Young; W. Borthwick; M. Lawson, D. McGrain MBE, J. Scott.
Club Nickname(s): The Red Lichties. *Previous Grounds:* None.
Record Attendance: 13,510 v Rangers, Scottish Cup 3rd rd; 23 Feb, 1952.
Record Transfer Fee received: £120,000 for Paul Tosh to Dundee (Aug 1993).
Record Transfer Fee paid: £20,000 for Douglas Robb from Montrose (1981).
Record Victory: 36-0 v Bon Accord, Scottish Cup 1st rd; 12 Sept, 1885.
Record Defeat: 1-9 v Celtic, League Cup 3rd rd; 25 Aug 1993.
Most Capped Player: Ned Doig, 2 (5), Scotland.
Most League Appearances: 445: Tom Cargill, 1966-81.
Most League Goals in Season (Individual): 45: Dave Easson, Division II; 1958-59.
Most Goals Overall (Individual): 120: Jimmy Jack; 1966-71.

ARBROATH 1995–96 LEAGUE RECORD

Match No.	Date	Venue	Opponents	Result	H/T Score	Lg. Pos.	Goalscorers	Atten- dance
1	Aug 12	A	Albion R	W 2-0	0-0	—	McCormick, Porteous	378
2	26	H	Livingston	L 1-3	1-0	4=	McCormick	721
3	Sept 2	A	Ross Co	L 2-4	2-1	4=	Pew 2	1400
4	9	A	Alloa	W 2-0	2-0	5	Pew, McCormick	475
5	16	H	Caledonian Th	W 2-1	1-0	4	McCormick, Pew	579
6	23	H	East Stirling	D 2-2	1-1	4	Porteous, Kennedy	570
7	30	A	Brechin C	D 1-1	0-0	4	Sexton	632
8	Oct 7	A	Cowdenbeath	D 1-1	0-1	4	Gardner	308
9	17	H	Queen's P	D 1-1	1-0	—	Kennedy	361
10	21	H	Ross Co	L 1-2	1-2	6	Porteous	603
11	28	A	Livingston	W 1-0	0-0	5	McCormick	236
12	Nov 4	A	Caledonian Th	L 1-5	0-2	5	Porteous	1525
13	11	H	Alloa	D 1-1	0-1	6	Elder	508
14	18	H	Brechin C	D 1-1	1-0	6	McCormick	572
15	25	A	East Stirling	W 1-0	1-0	6	Gardner	335
16	Dec 2	H	Cowdenbeath	W 2-1	1-0	5	Waters M, Watters W	464
17	16	A	Queen's P	L 0-2	0-1	6		464
18	Jan 6	H	Albion R	W 2-0	1-0	5	Watters W 2	306
19	10	A	Ross Co	D 0-0	0-0	—		944
20	13	H	East Stirling	W 2-1	0-0	4	Waters M, Pew	447
21	20	A	Cowdenbeath	W 2-1	2-1	4	Elliot 2	223
22	31	A	Brechin C	W 1-0	0-0	—	Ward	777
23	Feb 3	H	Queen's P	D 1-1	1-0	2	Gardner	572
24	17	A	Alloa	W 3-0	3-0	3	Elliot, Pew 2	360
25	21	H	Caledonian Th	L 1-2	0-0	—	Elliot	703
26	24	H	Livingston	L 1-2	0-1	4	McCormick	772
27	Mar 2	A	Albion R	D 1-1	1-1	5	McCormick	237
28	9	A	East Stirling	L 0-1	0-0	5		358
29	16	H	Brechin C	L 0-1	0-0	5		605
30	23	A	Caledonian Th	D 1-1	0-0	5	Roberts	1105
31	30	H	Alloa	W 1-0	1-0	5	Elliot	397
32	Apr 6	H	Cowdenbeath	D 0-0	0-0	5		387
33	13	A	Queen's P	D 0-0	0-0	5		401
34	20	H	Ross Co	D 1-1	1-0	5	Pew	439
35	27	A	Livingston	L 0-3	0-3	5		2993
36	30	H	Albion R	W 2-1	1-0	5	Roberts, Elder	350

Final League Position: 5

Honours
League Champions Runners-up: Division II 1934-35, 1958-59, 1967-68, 1971-72.
Scottish Cup: Quarter-finals: 1993.
League Cup: —.
Club colours: Shirt: Maroon with white and sky blue trim. Shorts: White. Stockings: Maroon with white and sky blue hooped tops.

Goalscorers: *League (41):* McCormick 8, Pew 8, Elliot 5, Porteous 4, Gardner 3, Watters W 3, Elder 2, Kennedy 2, Roberts 2, Waters M 2, Sexton 1, Ward 1. *Scottish Cup (2):* McCormick 1, Pew 1. *Coca-Cola Cup (3):* McCormick 2, Lindsay 1. *League Challenge Cup (0)*

Hinchcliffe C 11	McMillan T 5+2	Florence S 8+3	Peters S 31+2	Fowler J 5+9	Clark P 13+1	Lindsay J 7+3	Porteous I 10+6	McCormick S 28+3	Kennedy A 7+3	McAulay J 33+2	Pew D 32+4	Sexton B 2+5	Kerr J 4+4	Crawford J 19+2	Elliot D 13+11	Gardner L 15+2	McLean C —+1	Dunn G 25+1	Middleton A 15+1	Elder S 29+1	Welsh B 2+4	McCabe G 12+7	Waters M 14+3	Watters W 20+3	Ward J 18	Phinn J 5	Roberts P 4+7	McVicar D 8	Kerr R 1	Scott S —+1	Match No.
1	2	3	4	5	6	7¹	8	9³	10²	11	12	13	14																		1
1	2	3	11	5	4²		8	9	12	13	7¹			6	10																2
1	2		4	5¹	8²	13		9	10	11	6	3	7³	12	14																3
			5	12		14	13	9	10²	2	8			6	7³	11¹		1	3	4											4
			5	12		13	14	9	8	2	11			6	7²	10³		1	3	4¹											5
		3	6				12	8	9¹	10	2		7²	5	13	11		1		4											6
1	3	12	14		6		8	10²	7		9			5		11¹				4³		13									7
1		11	12		6		8	9	13	2¹	7²			3	5	10				4											8
1	3		12		6		8	9	10²	2	7			5	13	11				4¹											9
1	3¹	10	2²		6		8	9	14	13	7			5		11³			12	4											10
	3		12		6		8	9		2	7²			13	5	11		1		4		10¹									11
		10	6				8	9		2	7²			13	5	11¹		1		4		3	12								12
		5					8	9		2	7			6	11			1		3		4		10							13
		5			6	7	13	9		2²	12			14		11¹		1	3	4		8²		10							14
		6	5			7¹		9³		2	12			13	14	11		1	3	4		8²		10							15
		6	5							2	7²			12	13	11		1	3	4		8¹	9	10							16
	6	3					13	9²		2	7			5¹	14	11		1		4		12	8²	10							17
1	2			8¹			13	9		6	7			3		11				4²		12		10	5						18
1	14	2					8	9²		6	7¹			3³		11			13	4		12		10	5						19
1	2			8²				9¹		6	7			3	13	11²		1		4		12	14	10	5						20
10	2						13			6	7			3	9	11²	15			4		12	8¹	10	5						21
	13	2	12					9¹		6	7			3		11²		1		4			8	10	5						22
	13	2	14					9³		6	7			3		11²		1		4		12	8¹	10	5						23
		2	13					9		6³	8		14	7²		11¹		1		4		12		10	5		3				24
		2	14					9		6	8³			13		11¹		1		4²		12		10	5		3				25
		2	12					9²		6	8			7		11¹		1		4		13	14	10	5		3³				26
		2						9		6	7			11				1		4		8		10	5		3				27
		2						9		7				6		11		1		4³		12	13	8²	10		5		3¹	14	28
		2						9²			7			6²		11¹		1		4		12	14	8	10	13	3				29
		2						10¹		6	7			13		11²		1		4		12		8	5		9	3			30
	14	2						10		6	7³			11				1		4		12	9¹		5	13	3	8²			31
	14	2						12		6	7			11				1		4		10³	9¹		5	13	3	8²			32
		2	10					9¹		6				11				1		4³		12	7²		5	13	3	8		14	33
	11³	2	14							6	7							1		4²		12	9	10¹	5	13	3	8			34
	11¹	2								6	7							1		4		12	9	10²	5	13	3	8			35
		2								6	7			13		11¹		1		4		12	5³	9	10		3	8²		14	36

AYR UNITED   Second Division

Year Formed: 1910. *Ground & Address:* Somerset Park, Tryfield Place, Ayr KA8 9NB. *Telephone:* 01292 263435.
Ground Capacity: 12,128. seated: 1450. *Size of Pitch:* 110yd × 72yd.
Chairman: W. J. Barr. *Secretary:* J. E. Eyley. *Sales and Marketing:* Mrs Angela Smith.
Manager: Gordon Dalziel. *Assistant Manager:* Alistair Dawson.
Managers since 1975: Alex Stuart; Ally MacLeod; Willie McLean; George Caldwell; Ally MacLeod; George Burley;
Simon Stainrod. *Club Nickname(s):* The Honest Men. *Previous Grounds:* None.
Record Attendance: 25,225 v Rangers, Division I; 13 Sept, 1969.
eltic*Record Transfer Fee received:* £300,000 for Steven Nicol to Liverpool (Oct 1981).
Record Transfer Fee paid: £50,000 for Peter Weir from St Mirren, June 1990.
Record Victory: 11-1 v Dumbarton, League Cup; 13 Aug, 1952.
Record Defeat: 0-9 in Division I v Rangers (1929); v Hearts (1931); v Third Lanark (1954).
Most Capped Player: Jim Nisbet, 3, Scotland.
Most League Appearances: 371: Ian McAllister, 1977-90.
Most League Goals in Season (Individual): 66: Jimmy Smith, 1927-28.
Most Goals Overall (Individual): —.

AYR UNITED 1995–96 LEAGUE RECORD

Match No.	Date	Venue	Opponents	Result		H/T Score	Lg. Pos.	Goalscorers	Attendance
1	Aug 12	H	Clyde	D	1-1	0-1	—	Moore	1963
2	26	A	East Fife	L	0-1	0-1	8		684
3	Sept 2	H	Berwick R	L	1-4	1-1	9	Sharples	1221
4	9	H	Forfar Ath	L	1-3	1-1	9	Dalziel	1152
5	16	A	Stirling A	L	0-2	0-0	9		760
6	23	A	Montrose	W	1-0	0-0	9	Chalmers	409
7	30	H	Stranraer	D	0-0	0-0	8		1455
8	Oct 7	A	Queen of the S	D	0-0	0-0	8		1147
9	14	H	Stenhousemuir	L	1-2	1-0	9	Wilson W	1106
10	21	A	Clyde	W	2-1	1-1	8	Moore, Bilsland	1125
11	28	H	East Fife	L	0-1	0-1	9		1278
12	Nov 4	H	Stirling A	L	1-2	1-1	9	Bilsland	1233
13	11	A	Forfar Ath	L	1-2	0-1	9	George	534
14	18	A	Stranraer	L	0-2	0-1	9		891
15	25	H	Montrose	W	2-0	2-0	9	Dalziel 2	1166
16	Dec 2	A	Queen of the S	W	2-0	1-0	8	Smith, Steele	1434
17	16	A	Stenhousemuir	D	1-1	0-1	8	Dalziel	525
18	Jan 13	A	Montrose	W	1-0	1-0	8	Bilsland	587
19	16	A	Berwick R	D	2-2	0-1	—	Bilsland, Balfour	355
20	20	A	Queen of the S	D	2-2	2-1	8	Sharples, Hood	1264
21	27	H	Stranraer	D	0-0	0-0	8		1919
22	Feb 3	H	Stenhousemuir	D	1-1	1-1	8	Bilsland	1181
23	14	A	Stirling A	L	0-2	0-2	—		834
24	24	A	East Fife	D	1-1	1-0	9	Henderson	834
25	27	H	Clyde	W	2-1	0-1	—	Hood, Sharples	1378
26	Mar 2	H	Berwick R	W	5-0	4-0	8	Paavola 2, Diver 3	907
27	5	H	Forfar Ath	D	1-1	1-1	—	Kinnaird	1322
28	9	H	Montrose	W	2-0	0-0	6	Kinnaird, Diver	1326
29	16	A	Stranraer	D	1-1	1-0	6	Henderson	806
30	23	H	Stirling A	D	2-2	1-0	7	English, Sharples	1732
31	30	A	Forfar Ath	L	0-1	0-1	7		442
32	Apr 6	H	Queen of the S	W	3-0	3-0	6	Jamieson, English 2	1764
33	13	A	Stenhousemuir	W	1-0	1-0	5	Henderson	559
34	20	A	Clyde	L	0-2	0-0	5		1075
35	27	H	East Fife	W	1-0	1-0	5	English	1304
36	May 4	A	Berwick R	L	1-2	1-1	6	English	681

Final League Position: 6

Honours
League Champions: Division II 1911-12, 1912-13, 1927-28, 1936-37, 1958-59, 1965-66. Second Division 1987-88;
Runners-up: Division II 1910-11, 1955-56, 1968-69.
Scottish Cup: —. *League Cup:* —.
*B&Q Cup: Runners-up:*1990-91, 1991-92.
Club colours: Shirt: White with black trim. Shorts: White. Stockings: White.

Goalscorers: *League (40):* Bilsland 5, English 5, Dalziel 4, Diver 4, Sharples 4, Henderson 3, Hood 2, Kinnaird 2, Moore 2, Paavola 2, Balfour 1, Chalmers 1, George 1, Jamieson 1, Smith M 1, Steele 1, Wilson W 1. *Scottish Cup (0) Coca-Cola Cup* (0). *League Challenge Cup (1):* Bilsland 1.

Lamont W 4	Biggart K 9+16	Boyce D 4	Diver D 9	George D 24+1	English I 8	Rolling F 2	Coyle R 4	Sharples J 26	Shepherd A 10+1	Dalziel G 16+7	Wilson S 7+1	Stainrod S 2	Moore V 11	Law R 6	MacFarlane C 3+2	Bilsland B 15+6	Bell R 4+1	Tannock R 12+2	Byrne D 8+2	Traynor J 20+4	McKilligan N 7+3	Nolan J 1	Chalmers P 5	Connie C 10+3	Burns G —+1	Agnew S 2+1	Connelly S 1+1	Duncan C 21	Yule R 1+1	Wilson W 9+1	Smith M 8+2	Hood G 19+1	Clarke J 7+2	Mooney S 1	Steele T 10+5	Balfour E 12+2	Jamieson W 20	Barnstaple K 2+3	Napier C 10	Scott M 7	Kinnaird P 16+2	Smith H 9	Paavola T 3	Henderson D 11	Match No.
1	2¹	3	4	5	6	7	8	9²	10	11	12	13																																	1
1	12	3		5	6	7	8¹	10		4	9	2	11																																2
1		3		6²	4	10³	9	8¹	7	13	12	11	2	5	14																													3
1	14	3²		7	8¹	9		6	2³	4	13	5	10	11	12																													4
	3		8¹		4		7	6	2	5	12	9	10	11	1																													5
	3		8	11¹	6		12	4	7	5	2	9	10	1																														6
	3	12	8¹	7		6	4	5	2	11	10	13	1	9²																														7
13	11		5	7	8¹		10		12	6	2⁴	4	3	9	1																													8
14			5	7	8¹	12		10		9²	6	2³	4	3	1	13	11																											9
	7		5	8			10		9	6		4	3	12	1	2²	11¹	13																										10
12	7²		5	8			10		9	6		4	3¹	13	1	2	11																											11
3	7¹		6	13	12		8	5	9²		4	2	10	1	11																													12
	7		6	4	13		8	5	9		2		1	12	11	3²	10¹																											13
	8		5	4			11		12	6		2	1	9¹	3	7	10																											14
	10		6	9¹			7	13	12	3		1	11	2	4²	8	5																											15
	10		6	9¹			7	13	12	3		1⁶	11⁷	2	4	8	5	15																										16
12	10		6	9²			7	2	3		13		1	11	4¹	8	5																											17
13	7		6	10¹			8		4	2	12							5	1	3	9	11²																						18
	7		6	13			8		4	2²	12	10	5	1	3¹	9	11																											19
	7		6	12			8	13	4	2	10	5	3	9¹	11²																												20
13	7		6	9¹			12		4	2	10²	5	3	8	11	1																												21
	7		6	8¹			9	12	4	2	5	3	10	11	1																													22
13	7		6	8			9	10¹	4	3	2	5	15	11²	12	1⁶																												23
	7	6									8		1	4	2	5	3	11		9	10																							24
12	7	6									8		1	4	13	2¹	5	3	11	9²	10																							25
13	8	6	12								3		1	4⁶	7²	5¹	15	2	11	9	10																							26
2	8	6	12								10		1	4	7	5	3	11	9¹																									27
12	8	7	6								3¹		1	4	13	5	9²	11	10	3²																								28
2	8	7	9	6									1	4	13	12	10¹	5	11																									29
3	8	7	9	6	4								1	2	12	10	5	11¹																										30
12		7	9		4²				3	11		13							2	6	14	10¹	5			1																		31
	8²	7	9²					13	3	12		6							2	4		5		11	1		10¹																32
3	8	7¹	9						6			5							2	13	4	12	11	1	10																		33
12	8		9	4²					3	7		5							2	13	6	11	1	10¹																			34
12	8		9	4					3	7	13	8²							2	6	5	11¹	1	10																			35
12			9			7		3	11²	6	8¹	13							2⁰	4	5	14	1	10																			36

BERWICK RANGERS Second Division

Year Formed: 1881. *Ground & Address:* Shielfield Park, Tweedmouth, Berwick-upon-Tweed TD15 2EF. *Telephone:* 01289 307424. *Fax (to Secretary):* 01289 307623. Club 24 hour hotline 01891 800697. *Ground Capacity:* 4131. seated: 1366. *Size of Pitch:* 112yd × 76yd.
Chairman: Roy McDowell. *Vice-chairman:* Tom Davidson. *Company Secretary:* Sheila Stoddart. *Club Secretary:* Dennis McCleary.
Manager: Ian Ross. *Physio:* Glynn Jones. *Coaches:* Ian Oliver, Ian Smith
Managers since 1975: H. Melrose; G. Haig; W. Galbraith; D. Smith; F. Connor; J. McSherry; E. Tait; J. Thomson; J. Jefferies; J. Anderson, J. Crease, T. Hendrie.
Club Nickname(s): The Borderers. *Previous Grounds:* Bull Stob Close, Pier Field, Meadow Field, Union Park, Old Shielfield.
Record Attendance: 13,365 v Rangers, Scottish Cup 1st rd; 28 Jan, 1967.
Record Victory: 8-1 v Forfar Ath. Division II; 25 Dec, 1965: v Vale of Leithen, Scottish Cup; Dec, 1966.
Record Defeat: 1-9 v Hamilton A, First Division; 9 Aug, 1980.
Most Capped Player: —.
Most League Appearances: 435;: Eric Tait, 1970-87.
Most League Goals in Season (Individual): 38: Ken Bowron, Division II; 1963-64.
Most Goals Overall (Individual): 115: Eric Tait, 1970-87.

BERWICK RANGERS 1995–96 LEAGUE RECORD

Match No.	Date	Venue	Opponents	Result		H/T Score	Lg. Pos.	Goalscorers	Atten-dance
1	Aug 12	A	Stranraer	D	0-0	0-0	—		507
2	26	H	Stirling A	W	3-0	2-0	4	Irvine 2, Fraser	434
3	Sept 2	A	Ayr U	W	4-1	1-1	2	Irvine 2, Banks (pen), Rutherford	1221
4	9	A	Clyde	L	1-3	1-1	3	Irvine	1103
5	16	H	Stenhousemuir	W	3-1	1-0	3	Rutherford, Irvine 2	362
6	23	H	Forfar Ath	W	1-0	1-0	2	Graham	450
7	30	A	Queen of the S	W	4-1	2-1	2	Cole, Fraser 2, Cowan	1056
8	Oct 7	H	East Fife	L	0-1	0-0	2		655
9	14	A	Montrose	W	3-1	1-1	2	Fraser, Irvine 2	503
10	21	H	Stranraer	W	4-0	1-0	2	Irvine, Neil, Forrester, Fraser	433
11	28	A	Stirling A	L	0-1	0-1	2		811
12	31	A	Stenhousemuir	L	1-4	0-3	—	Fraser	402
13	Nov 11	H	Clyde	D	0-0	0-0	2		468
14	21	H	Queen of the S	D	0-0	0-0	—		324
15	25	A	Forfar Ath	W	4-1	3-1	2	Fraser, Irvine, Neil, Kane	523
16	Dec 2	A	East Fife	L	0-1	0-1	3		903
17	16	H	Montrose	D	2-2	1-1	3	Banks, Reid	314
18	Jan 10	A	Stranraer	W	3-0	1-0	—	McGlynn 3	433
19	16	A	Ayr U	D	2-2	1-0	—	Cowan, Irvine (pen)	355
20	20	H	East Fife	L	1-2	0-1	4	Neil	382
21	23	A	Queen of the S	L	0-3	0-0	—		840
22	30	H	Forfar Ath	W	1-0	1-0	—	Neil	309
23	Feb 3	A	Montrose	W	2-1	0-0	3	Graham, Neil	520
24	10	H	Stenhousemuir	W	2-1	2-0	3	Irvine, Banks	333
25	18	A	Clyde	L	1-2	0-0	—	Walton	667
26	24	H	Stirling A	L	0-3	0-1	3		483
27	Mar 2	A	Ayr U	L	0-5	0-4	3		907
28	9	A	Forfar Ath	W	3-1	2-0	3	Walton, McGlynn, Forrester	440
29	16	H	Queen of the S	W	4-1	3-0	3	Forrester 3, McGlynn	363
30	23	A	Stenhousemuir	W	3-0	2-0	3	Walton 2, Forrester	419
31	30	H	Clyde	L	2-3	1-2	3	Banks, Forrester	433
32	Apr 6	A	East Fife	D	0-0	0-0	3		1603
33	13	H	Montrose	W	4-1	0-0	3	Forrester 3, Reid	367
34	20	H	Stranraer	W	1-0	0-0	3	Banks (pen)	373
35	27	A	Stirling A	L	3-4	2-2	3	Graham, McGlynn, Cowan	1238
36	May 4	H	Ayr U	W	2-1	1-1	3	Wilson, Walton	681

Final League Position: 3

Honours
League Champions: Second Division 1978-79. *Runners-up* Second Division 1993-94.
Scottish Cup: —.
League Cup: Semi-final 1963-64.
Club colours: Shirt: Gold with black seams, shoulders and collar. Shorts: Black, gold trim. Stockings: Black.

Goalscorers: *League (64):* Irvine 13 (1 pen), Forrester 10, Fraser 7, McGlynn 6, Banks 5 (2 pens), Neil 5, Walton 5, Cowan 3, Graham 3, Reid 2, Rutherford 2, Cole 1, Kane 1, Wilson 1. *Scottish Cup (6):* Kane 2, Fraser 1, Irvine 1, Reid 1, own goal 1. *Coca-Cola Cup (1):* Clegg. *League Challenge Cup (1):* Cole 1.

Young N 31	Valentine C 31	Banks A 26 + 4	Reid A 23 + 1	Cowan M 25 + 1	Fraser G 36	Forrester P 25 + 10	Neil M 33 + 2	Rutherford P 6 + 3	Irvine W 35	Graham T 33	Kane K 22 + 6	Walton K 13 + 10	Clegg N — + 6	Cole A 8	Wilson M 17 + 8	Clarke J 3 + 2	Thomson M 1	Govan M — + 1	Coughlin J 3	McQueen D 15 + 1	McGlynn J 5 + 1	Thomson M 1	Chivers D — + 1	Gallacher J 4	Match No.
1	2	3	4	5	6	7	8	9¹	10	11	12														1
1	2	3	4	5	6	7	8	9¹	10	11	12														2
1	2	3	4	5	6	7¹	8	9	10	11	12														3
1	2	3	4	5	6	7²	8	9	10	11¹		12	13												4
1	2		4	5	6	7¹	8	9²	10	11	13			3	12										5
1	2		4	5	6		8	9	10	11	7			3											6
1	2		4	5	6²	9³	8		10	11	7	13	14	3¹	12										7
1	2		4	5	6	9³	8		10	11²	7	13		3¹	12	14									8
1	2		4	5¹	6	9	8³		10	11	7	14		3²	13	12									9
1	5¹	12	4		6	9	8		10	11	7²			3	13	2									10
1		12	4	5	6	9³	8²		10	11	7	14		3¹	13	2									11
1		13	5		6	9¹	8		10	11	7			3²		2	4	12							12
1		3	5		4	10¹	8			11	9	6	12		7				2						13
1		3	4	5	6	12	8	13	10	11²	9			7¹				2							14
1	2	3²	4	5	6	7	8	12	10¹	11	9	13													15
	4	3	5		6	13	8	12	10		9	11¹		7²				2	1						16
1	2	3	4	5	6	12	8		10	11¹	9			7											17
1	4	3¹		5	6	13	8		10	11	7	12		2						9²					18
1	3		4	5	6	12	8²		10	11	7¹	13		2						9					19
1	4	3		5	6	12	8		10	11	7			2						9¹					20
1	5	13	4		6	8²	12		10	11	7	3		2						9¹					21
1	4	3		5	6¹	12	8		10	11	7			2						9					22
	4	3	5		6	12	8		10	11	7			2					1	9¹					23
1⁶	2	3	4		6	12	8		10	11²	9¹			7						15	13	5			24
	2	3¹	4	5	6²	13	8³		10	11	9	12		7						1	14				25
	4	3		5	6	9	8		10	11¹	7²	12	13	2						1					26
	2	3	4	5	6	9	8		10		7²	11	12							1		13			27
1	2	3		5	9	4		10	11	12	6									8				7¹	28
1	2	3		5	8	4		10	11		6			12						9				7¹	29
1	2	3	12	5	8	4		10	11	13	6			7¹						9²					30
1	2	3		5	8	4		10	11		6									9		7			31
1	2	3		5	6	9	4		10	11		8								7					32
1	2	3	13	5	4	8			10	11		6		12						9²				7¹	33
1	2	3		5	4	8	12		10	11¹		6		7						9					34
1		3		5	4	8	7		10	11		6¹	12	2						9					35
1	2	3		5	4	8	7		10			6		11						9					36

BRECHIN CITY   Second Division

Year Formed: 1906. *Ground & Address:* Glebe Park, Trinity Rd, Brechin, Angus DD9 6BJ. *Telephone:* 01356 622856.
Fax (to Secretary): 01356 625524.
Ground Capacity: total: 3980. seated: 1518. *Size of Pitch:* 110yd × 67yd.
Chairman: Hugh Campbell Adamson. *Secretary:* Ken Ferguson.
Manager: John Young. *Assistant Manager:* Cammy Evans. *Physio:* Tom Gilmartin.
Managers since 1975: Charlie Dunn; Ian Stewart; Doug Houston; Ian Fleming; John Ritchie, Ian Redford. *Club Nickname(s):* The City. *Previous Grounds:* Nursery Park.
Record Attendance: 8122 v Aberdeen, Scottish Cup 3rd rd; 3 Feb, 1973.
Record Transfer Fee received: £100,000 for Scott Thomson to Aberdeen (1991).
Record Transfer Fee paid: £16,000 for Sandy Ross from Berwick Rangers (1991).
Record Victory: 12-1 v Thornhill, Scottish Cup 1st rd; 28 Jan, 1926.
Record Defeat: 0-10 v Airdrieonians, Albion R and Cowdenbeath, all in Division II; 1937-38.
Most Capped Player: —.
Most League Appearances: 459: David Watt, 1975-89.
Most League Goals in Season (Individual): 26: W. McIntosh, Division II; 1959-60.
Most Goals Overall (Individual): 131: Ian Campbell.

BRECHIN CITY 1995–96 LEAGUE RECORD

Match No.	Date		Venue	Opponents	Result		H/T Score	Lg. Pos.	Goalscorers	Atten- dance
1	Aug	12	H	East Stirling	W	3-1	1-1	—	Price 2, Brand	326
2		26	A	Caledonian Th	W	2-1	0-1	2	Smith R, Ross	1029
3	Sept	2	H	Alloa	L	0-1	0-1	3		355
4		9	H	Ross Co	W	2-1	0-1	3	Ross, Brown	479
5		16	A	Cowdenbeath	W	1-0	0-0	3	Brand	251
6		23	A	Queen's P	W	2-0	0-0	2	Brand 2	422
7		30	H	Arbroath	D	1-1	0-0	2	McKellar	632
8	Oct	7	H	Albion R	L	0-1	0-0	2		341
9		14	A	Livingston	D	0-0	0-0	2		273
10		21	A	Alloa	L	2-3	0-2	4	McNeill, Ross	371
11		28	H	Caledonian Th	D	0-0	0-0	4		374
12	Nov	4	H	Cowdenbeath	W	2-1	1-0	4	Farnan, McKellar	338
13		11	A	Ross Co	D	0-0	0-0	4		1653
14		18	A	Arbroath	D	1-1	0-1	4	Ferguson	572
15		25	H	Queen's P	W	1-0	0-0	3	Mitchell	306
16	Dec	2	A	Albion R	L	0-1	0-0	4		289
17		9	H	East Stirling	W	4-1	2-1	2	Christie, Brown R, Cairney, Farnan	253
18		16	H	Livingston	W	2-0	1-0	2	Cairney, McKellar	419
19	Jan	13	A	Queen's P	D	0-0	0-0	3		505
20		20	H	Albion R	W	1-0	1-0	3	Ross	296
21		23	A	Alloa	W	3-0	2-0	—	Ross 2, McNeill	349
22		31	H	Arbroath	L	0-1	0-0	—		777
23	Feb	3	A	Livingston	W	1-0	0-0	1	Buick	2386
24		14	A	Cowdenbeath	D	0-0	0-0	—		160
25		17	A	Ross Co	D	0-0	0-0	2		506
26		24	A	Caledonian Th	W	1-0	1-0	2	Sorbie	2514
27	Mar	2	A	East Stirling	L	0-2	0-1	2		268
28		9	H	Queen's P	W	4-0	1-0	2	McNeill 2, Mitchell, Christie	363
29		16	A	Arbroath	W	1-0	0-0	2	Ross	605
30		23	H	Cowdenbeath	W	2-0	0-0	2	Ross, McNeill	368
31		30	A	Ross Co	W	2-1	1-0	1	McNeill 2	2362
32	Apr	6	A	Albion R	D	0-0	0-0	2		329
33		13	H	Livingston	L	0-1	0-0	2		768
34		20	A	Alloa	W	3-0	0-0	2	Brand 2, Buick	369
35		27	H	Caledonian Th	L	0-1	0-1	2		656
36		30	A	East Stirling	L	0-3	0-2	2		305

Final League Position: 2

Honours
League Champions: Second Division 1982-83. C Division 1953-54. Second Division 1989-90. *Runners-up:* 1992-93. Third Division Runners-up 1995-96
Scottish Cup: —.
League Cup: —.
Club colours: Shirt, Shorts, Stockings: Red with white trimmings.

Goalscorers: *League (41):* Ross 8, McNeill 7, Brand 6, McKellar 3, Brown 2, Buick 2, Cairney 2, Christie 2, Farnan 2, Mitchell 2, Price 2, Ferguson 1, Smith 1, Sorbie 1. *Scottish Cup (3):* Cairney 1 (pen), Christie 1, Mitchell 1. *Coca-Cola Cup (2):* Brand 2. *League Challenge Cup (4):* Brand 2, Brown 1, Mearns 1.

Allan R 33	Mitchell B 36	Christie G 25 + 2	Brown R 36	Conway F 30	Mearns G 8	Smith R 9 + 5	Farnan C 35	Price G 1	Brand R 9 + 5	Marr S 1	Cairney H 33	Scott D 21	Ferguson S 20 + 1	Ross A 23 + 3	McNeill W 28 + 3	McKellar J 18 + 4	Garden S 1 + 1	Reid S — + 1	Brown B 1	Balfour D 1	Graham R 1 + 1	Buick G 12	Baillie R 2 + 6	Kerrigan S 2 + 4	Sorbie S 3	Heddle I 7 + 1	Match No.
1	2	3	4	5	6	7	8	9	10	11																	1
1	2	6	3	5		9	8		7[1]		4	10	11	12													2
1	2	6	3	5	8	7			12		4	10	11[1]	9													3
1	2	6	3	5		7	8		12		4	10	11[1]	9													4
1	2		3	5	10	7[1]	8		11		4		6	9	12												5
1	2		3	5	10		8		11		4		6[1]	9	12	7											6
1	2		3	5	10		8		11[1]		4		6	9	12	7											7
1	2		3	5	10		8				4		6[1]	9	11	7	16	12									8
	2		3	5			8				4	10	6	9	11	7	1			1							9
	2	12	3	5[1]			8				4	10	6	9	11	7			1								10
	2	5	3			12	8				4	10	6		11[1]	7					1	9					11
1	2	5	3		10	11	8				4		6		9[1]	7						12					12
1	2	5	3		10	9[1]	8				4		6	12	11	7											13
1	2	5	3			9[1]	8				4		6	12	11	7						10					14
1	2	5	3			12	8				4		6	9	11[1]	7						10					15
1	2	5	3			12	8				4		6	9[1]	11	7						10					16
1	2	5	3	6[1]			8				4			9	11	7						10	12				17
1	2	5	3	6			8				4			9	11	7						10					18
1	2	6	3	5		13	8				4	10	12	9	11[2]	7[1]											19
1	2	5	3	4[1]			8					10	6	9	11	7						12					20
1	2	5	3	4		12	8						6	9	11	7[1]						10					21
1	2	6	3	5			8				4	10		9	11							7[1]	12				22
1	2	6	3	5			8				4	10		9[1]	11							7	12				23
1	2	6	3	5		7	8		12		4	10			11									9[1]			24
1	2	6	3	5			8		12		4	10		9[1]	11	7											25
1	2	6	3	5			8				4	10			11							7		9			26
1	2	6	3	5			8		12		4[2]	10			11							7	13	9[1]			27
1	2	6	3	5			8		9[2]		4[1]	10			11	7						12	13				28
1	2	6	3	5			8				4	10		9		7										11	29
1	2	6	3	5[2]			8				4	10		9		7[1]						12	13			11	30
1	2	6	3	5			8				4	10		9		7						12				11[1]	31
1	2		3	5			8				4	10		9		7						6				11[1]	32
1	2		3	5			8				4	10	6	9		7						12				11[1]	33
1	2		3	5[1]			8				4		6			7						10	12			11	34
1	2		3	5			8		9[1]		4		6	7	11[2]							10	12			13	35
1	2	13	3	5					10	9[0]	4		6		12								8[1]		7	11	36

CELTIC   Premier Division

Year Formed: 1888. *Ground & Address:* Celtic Park, 95 Kerrydale St, Glasgow G40 3RE. *Telephone:* 0141 556 2611.
Ground Capacity: all seated: 47,500. *Size of Pitch:* 115yd × 75yd.
Managing Director Fergus McCann. *Secretary:* Dominic Keane. *Chief Scout* Davie Hay.
Manager: Tommy Burns. *Assistant Manager:* Billy Stark. *Physio:* Brian Scott. *Coaches:* Frank Connor, Tom McAdam,
Willie McStay.
Managers since 1975: Jock Stein, Billy McNeill, David Hay, Billy McNeill, Liam Brady, Lou Macari. *Club Nickname(s):*
The Bhoys. *Previous Grounds:* None.
Record Attendance: 92,000 v Rangers, Division I; 1 Jan, 1938.
Record Transfer Fee received: £1,400,000 for Paul Elliott to Chelsea, July 1991.
Record Transfer Fee paid: £1,750,000 for Phil O'Donnell from Motherwell, September 1994.
Record Victory: 11-0 Dundee, Division I; 26 Oct, 1895.
Record Defeat: 0-8 v Motherwell, Division I; 30 Apr, 1937.
Most Capped Player: Paul McStay, 73, Scotland.
Most League Appearances: 486: Billy McNeill 1957-75.
Most League Goals in Season (Individual): 50: James McGrory, Division I; 1935-36.
Most Goals Overall (Individual): 397: James McGrory; 1922-39.

CELTIC 1995–96 LEAGUE RECORD

Match No.	Date	Venue	Opponents	Result		H/T Score	Lg. Pos.	Goalscorers	Attendance
1	Aug 26	A	Raith R	W	1-0	0-0	—	Van Hooijdonk	9300
2	Sept 10	A	Aberdeen	W	3-2	3-2	—	Collins 2, Thom	16,489
3	16	H	Motherwell	D	1-1	1-0	2	O'Donnell	31,365
4	23	A	Hearts	W	4-0	2-0	1	McLaughlin 2, Walker 2	13,696
5	30	H	Rangers	L	0-2	0-1	3		33,296
6	Oct 4	A	Falkirk	W	1-0	0-0	—	Hughes	9053
7	7	H	Partick Th	W	2-1	0-0	2	Van Hooijdonk, Collins	29,950
8	14	H	Hibernian	D	2-2	1-1	2	Collins, Van Hooijdonk	31,738
9	21	A	Kilmarnock	D	0-0	0-0	2		14,011
10	28	H	Aberdeen	W	2-0	1-0	2	McLaughlin, Van Hooijdonk (pen)	32,275
11	Nov 4	A	Motherwell	W	2-0	0-0	2	Donnelly, Collins	12,077
12	8	H	Raith R	D	0-0	0-0	—		28,832
13	11	A	Partick Th	W	2-1	1-1	2	Van Hooijdonk 2 (1 pen)	12,223
14	19	A	Rangers	D	3-3	1-1	—	Thom, Collins (pen), Van Hooijdonk	46,640
15	25	H	Hearts	W	3-1	1-0	2	Collins 3 (1 pen)	34,032
16	Dec 2	H	Kilmarnock	W	4-2	2-2	2	Thom, Grant, Van Hooijdonk 2	33,660
17	9	A	Hibernian	W	4-0	2-0	2	McNamara, O'Donnell, Van Hooijdonk, Donnelly	13,626
18	16	H	Falkirk	W	1-0	1-0	2	Van Hooijdonk	34,466
19	Jan 3	H	Rangers	D	0-0	0-0	—		36,719
20	6	H	Motherwell	W	1-0	1-0	2	Van Hooijdonk	34,629
21	9	A	Raith R	W	3-1	2-0	—	O'Donnell, Collins, Van Hooijdonk	9300
22	14	A	Aberdeen	W	2-1	0-1	—	Collins, Van Hooijdonk	16,760
23	17	A	Hearts	W	2-1	0-1	—	Van Hooijdonk, Walker	15,871
24	20	A	Kilmarnock	D	0-0	0-0	2		16,024
25	Feb 3	H	Hibernian	W	2-1	0-1	2	Van Hooijdonk, McStay	36,976
26	10	A	Falkirk	D	0-0	0-0	2		10,366
27	24	H	Partick Th	W	4-0	2-0	2	Grant, Van Hooijdonk 2 (1 pen), Wieghorst	36,421
28	Mar 2	H	Hearts	W	4-0	3-0	2	McStay, Van Hooijdonk, McLaughlin, Donnelly	37,034
29	17	A	Rangers	D	1-1	0-1	—	Hughes	47,312
30	Mar 23	A	Motherwell	D	0-0	0-0	2		12,394
31	Apr 1	H	Aberdeen	W	5-0	2-0	—	Donnelly 2, Van Hooijdonk 2, Cadete	35,284
32	10	H	Kilmarnock	D	1-1	0-1	—	Van Hooijdonk	36,476
33	14	A	Hibernian	W	2-1	0-0	—	Van Hooijdonk 2	10,742
34	20	H	Falkirk	W	4-0	2-0	2	Thom 2, Cadete, Donnelly	35,692
35	27	A	Partick Th	W	4-2	1-2	2	Van Hooijdonk 2 (1 pen), Cadete, Mackay	14,693
36	May 4	H	Raith R	W	4-1	3-0	2	Cadete 2, Gray, Grant	37,318

Final League Position: 2

Honours

League Champions: (35 times) Division I 1892-93, 1893-94, 1895-96, 1897-98, 1904-05, 1905-06, 1906-07, 1907-08, 1908-09, 1909-10, 1913-14, 1914-15, 1915-16, 1916-17, 1918-19, 1921-22, 1925-26, 1935-36, 1937-38, 1953-54, 1965-66, 1966-67, 1967-68, 1968-69, 1969-70, 1970-71, 1971-72, 1972-73, 1973-74. Premier Division 1976-77, 1978-79, 1980-81, 1981-82, 1985-86, 1987-88. *Runners-up:* 23 times.
Scottish Cup Winners: (30 times) 1892, 1899, 1900, 1904, 1907, 1908, 1911, 1912, 1914, 1923, 1925, 1927, 1931, 1933, 1937, 1951, 1954, 1965, 1967, 1969, 1971, 1972, 1974, 1975, 1977, 1980, 1985, 1988, 1989, 1995; *Runners-up:* 16 times.
League Cup Winners: (9 times) 1956-57, 1957-58, 1965-66, 1966-67, 1967-68, 1968-69, 1969-70, 1974-75, 1982-83; *Runners-up:* 10 times.

European: *European Cup Winners:* 1966-67. 78 matches (1966-67 winners, 1967-68, 1968-69, 1969-70 runners-up, 1970-71, 1971-72 semi-finals, 1972-73, 1973-74 semi-finals, 1974-75, 1977-78, 1979-80, 1981-82, 1982-83, 1986-87, 1988-89); *Cup Winners Cup:* 39 matches (1963-64 semi-finals, 1965-66 semi-finals, 1975-76, 1980-81, 1984-85, 1985-86, 1989-90, 1995-96); *UEFA Cup:* 28 matches (*Fairs Cup:* 1962-63, 1964-65. UEFA Cup: 1976-77, 1983-84, 1987-88, 1991-92, 1992-93, 1993-94).
Club colours: Shirt: Green and white hoops. Shorts: White. Stockings: White.

Goalscorers: *League (74):* Van Hooijdonk 26 (4 pens), Collins 11 (2 pens), Donnelly 6, Cadete 5, Thom 5, McLaughlin 4, Grant 3, O'Donnell 3, Walker 3, Hughes 2, McStay 2, Gray 1, Mackay 1, McNamara 1, Wieghorst 1. *Scottish Cup (8):* Van Hooijdonk 4, Donnelly 2, McLaughlin 1, Thom 1. *Coca-Cola Cup (5):* Van Hooijdonk 2, Collins 1 (pen), Donnelly 1, Thom 1.

Marshall G 36	Boyd T 34	McKinlay T 32	Vata R 5+1	Hughes J 26	Grant P 30	O'Donnell P 14+1	Donnelly S 35	Van Hooijdonk P 34	Thom A 31+1	Collins J 26+3	McLaughlin B 11+15	Mackay M 9+2	Walker A 4+12	McStay P 29+1	Falconer W —+2	Hay C 1+3	Gray S 3+2	McQuilken J 3+1	McNamara J 26	Wieghorst M 2+9	O'Neil B 3+2	Cadete J 2+4	Match No.
1	2	3	4	5	6	7	8[1]	9	10	11	12												1
1	2	3[1]	4	5	6	7	8	9[2]	10[3]	11	14	12	13										2
1	2	3	4		6	7		10		11	13	5	9[2]	8[1]	12								3
1	2	3	4	5	6	7[1]				11				9	8	13	10[2]	12					4
1	2	3	4[2]	5	6[1]	7		9	10	11	12	13		8									5
1	2			5	6	7		9	10	11				8			3		4				6
1	2			5	6	7		9[2]	10[1]	11				8	13	12	3		4				7
1	2			5	6	7		9	10	11				8			3		4				8
1	2	3		5	6		8	9[2]	10	11	7[1]				13	12			4				9
1	2	3	12	5	6	7[2]		9		11	10[1]			8	13				4				10
1	2	3		5	6	7		9	10	12	11[1]			8					4				11
1	2	3		5	6	7		9[1]	10		6	11	12	8					4				12
1	2	3		5	6	7		9	10	11				8					4				13
1	2	3		5	6	7[1]		9[2]	10	11	12	13		8					4				14
1	2	3		5	6	7		9	10	11				8					4				15
1	2	3		5	6	7[2]		9	10[1]	11	13			8	12				4				16
1	2	3			6[1]	7		9[2]	10[3]	11	14	5	13	8					4	12			17
1	2	3			6	7		9	10[1]	11		5		8	12				4				18
1	2	3			6	7[1]		9	10[2]	11	12	5	13	8					4				19
1	2	3			6	7[1]		9	10	11	12	5		8					4				20
1	2	3	5	4	6	7		9	10[2]	11	13			8[1]	12								21
1	2	3	5	4	6	7		9	10[1]	11	12			8									22
1	2	3	5	4	6	7[2]		9	10[1]	11	13	12		8									23
1	2	3	5	4	6[1]	7[2]		9		11	13	10		8						12			24
1	2	3		5	6	7		9[1]	10	11	12			8					4				25
1	2	3		5	6	7		9	10[2]	11				8					4	12			26
1		3		5[4]	6	7		9	10[2]	11[1]	13	14		8					4	12	2		27
1		3		5	6	7		9	10[1]	11	13			8[2]					4	12	2		28
1	2	3		5	6	7		9	10[2]	11[1]	12			8					4	13			29
1	2	3[1]		5	6	4	7	9	10	11[2]				8					12	13			30
1	2	3		5	6	7		9	10[1]	11				8[2]					4		13	12	31
1	2	3			6	7		9	10	11[1]				8					4	13	5[2]	12	32
1	2	3			6	7[2]		9	12	11[1]		5		8					4	10	13		33
1	2	3			6	7		9	10[2]	12		5		8					4	11[1]	13		34
1	2				6	7[2]		9	10	12	13	5		8			3		4	11[1]			35
1	2	3			6[2]	7[1]		9	10	12		5		8					4	13	11		36

CLYDE   Second Division

Year Formed: 1878. *Ground & Address:* Broadwood Stadium, Cumbernauld, G68 9NE. *Telephone:* 01236 451511.
Ground Capacity: total: 8200 all seated. *Size of Pitch:* 112yd × 76yd.
Chairman: John F. McBeth FRICS. *Secretary:* John D. Taylor. *Commercial Manager:* John Donnelly.
Manager: Alex Smith. *Assistant Manager:* John Brownlie. *Physio:* J. Watson. *Coach:* Gardner Speirs.
Managers since 1975: S. Anderson; C. Brown; J. Clark. *Club Nickname(s):* The Bully Wee. *Previous Grounds:*
Barrowfield & Shawfield Stadium.
Record Attendance: 52,000 v Rangers, Division I; 21 Nov, 1908.
Record Transfer Fee received: £95,000 for Pat Nevin to Chelsea (July 1983).
Record Transfer Fee paid: £14,000 for Harry Hood from Sunderland (1966).
Record Victory: 11-1 v Cowdenbeath, Division II; 6 Oct, 1951.
Record Defeat: 0-11 v Dumbarton, Scottish Cup 4th rd, 22 Nov, 1879; v Rangers, Scottish Cup 4th rd, 13 Nov, 1880.
Most Capped Player: Tommy Ring, 12, Scotland.
Most League Appearances: 428: Brian Ahern.
Most League Goals in Season (Individual): 32: Bill Boyd, 1932-33.
Most Goals Overall (Individual): —.

CLYDE 1995–96 LEAGUE RECORD

Match No.	Date	Venue	Opponents	Result		H/T Score	Lg. Pos.	Goalscorers	Atten- dance
1	Aug 12	A	Ayr U	D	1-1	1-0	—	Nicholas	1963
2	26	H	Forfar Ath	L	1-2	1-2	7	Annand	1163
3	Sept 2	A	Queen of the S	W	3-0	1-0	4	Nicholas, Annand, Harrison	1897
4	9	H	Berwick R	W	3-1	1-1	4	Harrison, Nicholas, Annand	1103
5	16	A	Montrose	D	0-0	0-0	5		763
6	23	H	Stenhousemuir	L	0-1	0-0	5		1088
7	30	A	Stirling A	D	1-1	0-1	5	McConnell	1011
8	Oct 7	H	Stranraer	D	1-1	1-0	7	Patterson	1048
9	14	A	East Fife	D	0-0	0-0	7		1128
10	21	H	Ayr U	L	1-2	1-1	7	Annand	1125
11	28	A	Forfar Ath	L	0-1	0-1	7		645
12	Nov 4	H	Montrose	W	3-0	0-0	7	Falconer, Annand 2	849
13	11	A	Berwick R	D	0-0	0-0	7		468
14	18	H	Stirling A	L	1-2	1-1	7	Annand	1200
15	25	A	Stenhousemuir	W	1-0	1-0	7	McCarron	714
16	Dec 2	A	Stranraer	D	0-0	0-0	7		683
17	16	H	East Fife	L	0-1	0-0	7		982
18	Jan 13	H	Stenhousemuir	W	3-0	2-0	7	Annand 2, Angus	958
19	20	H	Stranraer	D	2-2	1-2	6	Annand (pen), Nisbet	942
20	24	A	Stirling A	L	0-3	0-2	—		1068
21	Feb 3	A	East Fife	D	1-1	1-1	7	Annand	774
22	18	H	Berwick R	W	2-1	0-0	—	Annand 2	667
23	24	H	Forfar Ath	W	3-1	2-0	6	Knox, Annand, O'Neill	878
24	27	A	Ayr U	L	1-2	1-0	—	Annand	1378
25	Mar 2	A	Queen of the S	L	1-2	1-1	7	Thomson	877
26	5	H	Queen of the S	W	2-1	2-0	—	Thomson, Harrison	776
27	9	A	Stenhousemuir	L	0-1	0-1	7		674
28	12	A	Montrose	W	3-2	3-0	—	Nicholas, McCheyne, Harrison	226
29	16	H	Stirling A	L	1-3	1-2	5	O'Neill	1183
30	23	H	Montrose	L	1-3	1-0	6	Angus	791
31	30	A	Berwick R	W	3-2	2-1	5	Annand 2 (1 pen), McCluskey	433
32	Apr 6	A	Stranraer	D	2-2	0-0	5	McCluskey, McConnell	655
33	13	H	East Fife	D	2-2	1-0	6	McCluskey, Nicholas	1145
34	20	H	Ayr U	W	2-0	0-0	5	Annand 2	1075
35	27	A	Forfar Ath	L	2-4	2-2	6	Annand 2	472
36	May 4	H	Queen of the S	D	0-0	0-0	5		1095

Final League Position: 5

Honours
League Champions: Division II 1904-05, 1951-52, 1956-57, 1961-62, 1972-73. Second Division 1977-78, 1981-82, 1992-93.
Runners-up: Division II 1903-04, 1905-06, 1925-26, 1963-64.
Scottish Cup Winners: 1939, 1955, 1958; *Runners-up:* 1910, 1912, 1949.
League Cup: —
Club colours: Shirt: White with red and black trim. Shorts: Black. Stockings: Black with red and white tops.

Goalscorers: *League (47):* Annand 21 (3 pens), Nicholas 5, Harrison 4, McCluskey 3, Angus 2, McConnell 2, O'Neill 2, Thomson 2, Falconer 1, Knox 1, McCarron 1, McCheyne 1, Nisbet 1, Patterson 1. *Scottish Cup (9):* Annand 3, Nicholas 2, Angus 1, Harrison 1, McCheyne 1, McConnell 1. *Coca-Cola Cup (1):* Annand 1. *League Challenge Cup (0)*

Hillcoat J 25	Ferguson G 26 + 1	Angus I 33	Gillies K 30	Knox K 28 + 1	Brown J 9	O'Neill M 19 + 4	Nicholas C 31	Annand E 35	Harrison T 21 + 6	Parks G 1	McCarron J 1 + 1	McCluskey G 5 + 11	Watson G 25	McLay J 9 + 2	McCheyne G 11 + 10	Nisbet I 4 + 12	Patterson P 4 + 9	McQueen J 11	Thomson J 24	McConnell I 15 + 5	Dickson J 5 + 8	Prunty J 11 + 8	Falconer M 2 + 7	Brownlie P 2 + 2	Dawson R 8	Muir J — + 1	Campbell P — + 2	McEwan C 1	Coleman S — + 1	Match No.
1	2	3	4	5	6	7	8	9	10¹	11²	12	13																		1
1		3		5	6	7¹	8	9	10				2	4	11²	12	13													2
		3	4	2	6	7¹	8	9²	10				13		11	12			1	5										3
		3²	4	2	6	7¹	8	9	10				12		11¹	13			1	5										4
		3	4	2	6	7¹	8	9	10				12		11²	13			1	5										5
		3	4²	2	6	7	8	9	10				12		11	13			1	5										6
	11	3	4	2			8	9²	10¹			7			13		12		1	5	6									7
1	11	3²	4	2	6		8¹	9²				7	12		13		10			5	14									8
	11	3		2	6		8	9	10²			13			7¹				1	5	12									9
	11	3	4²	2			8	9	10			12			6³				1	5	14	7¹								10
	11	3		2	6		8²	9				10³	4		12	13			1	5	14	7¹								11
	11	3	4	2				9	10³				8¹		13				1	5	14	7²	6	12						12
	11	3	4	2				9³	10				8²		13				1	5	14	12	6	7¹						13
		3	4	2				9							7¹	12	13	10²	1	5	8	11	6²	14						14
1		3	4	2			8²	9¹		11	14	10			6	12				5	7¹	13								15
1	11		4	2			8	9²				13	10		6	7¹				5	3	12								16
1	11	3²	4	2			8	9					10		6					5	7¹	12	13							17
1	11	3		2			8³	9¹	14			13	10		6²					4	5	12	7							18
1	11	3¹	10²	2				9³					12		6	13				4	5	7								19
1	11			2			13	8	9	10					7					6	5²	12	3¹							20
1	11			2		7	8	9	10²						3¹	13	12			5		6								21
1	11	3	4	2		7¹	8	9	6²				10		13	12				5										22
1	11	3³	4	2		7²	8	9	6¹				10		13	12				5			14							23
1	11	3¹	4	2		7	8	9	6²				10		12					5			13							24
1	11	3	4	2¹		7³	8	9	14				6				10²			5	13	12								25
1	11	3	4²			12	8	9	7³				6		13		14			5		10¹		2						26
1	11	3³					7	8	9	13			10		6²	4¹	14			5		12		2						27
1	11	3						8	9¹	7			10		6²	13	12			5		4		2						28
1	11	3	4¹				7	8	10³				6		9²					5	12	13		2	14					29
1		3	4				7²	8	9				6		10¹	13				5	14	11¹	12	2						30
1	11	3	4³				8	9	7¹			10²	6		14					5	12	13		2						31
1	11	3	4¹				12	8	9	7²		10	6		14					5		13		2³						32
11¹		3²	4	12			7	8	9	13		10	6							5				2						33
1		3	4	2			7	8	9				10¹	6			11²			5	13	12								34
1	12	3³	4	2			7¹		9			8²	6	10	13					5		11				14				35
1	11	3	4³	2			7		9¹			13								5		6	10²			14	8	12		36

CLYDEBANK
First Division

Year Formed: 1965. *Club Address:* Burnbrae, Milngavie, Glasgow G62 6HX. *Telephone:* 0141 955 9048. *Fax:* 0141 955 9049
Home matches at Boghead Park, Dumbarton in 1996-97. *Ground Capacity:* 5503. *Size of Pitch:* 110yd × 68yd.
Chairman: C.G.Steedman. *Secretary:* A.Steedman. *Commercial Manager:* David Curwood.
Managing Director: I.C.Steedman. *Physio:* Peter Salila. *Coach:* Brian Wright.
Managers since 1975: William Munro, J.S.Steedman. *Club Nickname(s):* The Bankies. *Previous Grounds:* None.
Record Attendance: 14,900 v Hibernian, Scottish Cup 1st rd; 10 Feb, 1965.
Record Transfer Fee received: £175,000 for Owen Coyle from Airdrieonians, (Feb 1990).
Record Transfer Fee paid: £50,000 for Gerry McCabe from Clyde.
Record Victory: 8-1 Arbroath, First Division; 3 Jan 1977.
Record Defeat: 1-9 v Gala Fairydean, Scottish Cup qual rd; 15 Sept, 1965.
Most Capped Player: —.
Most League Appearances: 620: Jim Fallon; 1968-86.
Most League Goals in Season (Individual): 29: Ken Eadie, First Division, 1990-91.
Most League Goals Overall (Individual): 138, Ken Eadie 1988-95.

CLYDEBANK 1995–96 LEAGUE RECORD

Match No.	Date		Venue	Opponents	Result		H/T Score	Lg. Pos.	Goalscorers	Atten- dance
1	Aug	12	H	St Mirren	D	1-1	0-1	—	Eadie	1886
2		26	A	Hamilton A	W	2-0	2-0	—	Eadie, Robertson	845
3	Sept	2	H	Dundee	D	1-1	0-0	3	Connell	1467
4		9	A	Dunfermline Ath	L	1-2	0-2	6	Robertson	4410
5		16	H	Dundee U	L	1-2	1-1	8	Grady	1949
6		23	A	St Johnstone	D	2-2	0-0	7	Nicholls, Eadie	2482
7		30	H	Dumbarton	W	2-1	1-0	6	Grady, Sutherland	913
8	Oct	7	H	Morton	W	1-0	0-0	4	Eadie	2343
9		14	A	Airdrieonians	D	1-1	0-1	5	Grady	1306
10		21	A	Dundee	D	1-1	0-1	6	Bowman	2708
11		28	H	Hamilton A	W	2-0	1-0	5	Robertson, Eadie	814
12		31	A	Dundee U	L	0-3	0-3	—		5428
13	Nov	11	H	Dunfermline Ath	L	0-4	0-1	7		1304
14		18	A	Dumbarton	W	2-1	1-0	7	Grady, Eadie	1043
15		25	H	St Johnstone	W	2-0	2-0	5	Sutherland, Eadie	923
16	Dec	2	A	Morton	L	0-3	0-0	6		3002
17		16	A	St Mirren	L	1-2	1-1	7	Robertson	1828
18	Jan	6	H	Dundee U	D	1-1	0-1	7	Lovering	1383
19		9	H	Airdrieonians	D	1-1	0-0	—	Robertson	865
20		13	A	Dunfermline Ath	L	3-4	1-3	7	Grady 2, Connell	6642
21		16	H	Dundee	L	0-1	0-0	—		644
22		20	H	Morton	L	0-1	0-1	8		1685
23		23	A	St Johnstone	L	1-3	1-1	—	Grady	2167
24	Feb	10	H	St Mirren	L	1-2	0-1	8	Bowman	1515
25		13	A	Airdrieonians	D	1-1	0-1	—	Nicholls	851
26		17	H	Dumbarton	W	1-0	0-0	8	Grady	612
27		24	A	Hamilton A	D	1-1	1-1	8	Nicholls	835
28	Mar	2	H	St Johnstone	L	1-2	0-2	8	Eadie	705
29		16	A	Dumbarton	W	1-0	0-0	8	Flannigan	654
30		23	A	Dundee U	L	0-6	0-3	8		5973
31		30	H	Dunfermline Ath	L	2-3	1-1	8	Grady 2	1298
32	Apr	6	A	Morton	D	0-0	0-0	8		3001
33		13	A	Airdrieonians	W	2-1	1-1	8	Irons, Flannigan	831
34		20	A	Dundee	L	0-3	0-1	8		1403
35		27	H	Hamilton A	L	1-3	1-2	8	Eadie	3665
36	May	4	A	St Mirren	W	2-1	1-0	7	Grady, Teale	1657

Final League Position: 7

Honours
League Champions: Second Division 1975-76; *Runners-up:* First Division 1976-77, 1984-85.
Scottish Cup: Semi-finalists 1990. *League Cup:* —.
Club colours: Shirt: White with red shoulder band with black trim. Shorts: White with red trim. Stockings: White with red trim.

Goalscorers: *League (39):* Grady 11, Eadie 9, Robertson 5, Nicholls 3, Bowman 2, Connell 2, Flannigan 2, Sutherland 2, Irons 1, Lovering 1, Teale 1. *Scottish Cup (0) Coca-Cola Cup (1):* Robertson 1. *League Challenge Cup (5):* Grady 2, Kerrigan 2, Nicholls.

Matthews G 36	Tomlinson C 14	Sutherland C 25+1	Murdoch S 27+1	Currie T 27+1	Nicholls D 35	Robertson J 25+6	Connell G 34	Eadie K 26+2	Grady J 35+1	Bowman G 33	Miller S 3+4	Lovering P 11+10	Teale G 9+7	Kerrigan S —+1	Flannigan C 8+17	Agnew P 4+3	Lansdowne A 10+4	Dunn R 3+2	Connelly D 3+4	Jack S 14+4	Melvin W —+1	Crawford D —+1	McLaughlin 11	Keane G —+1	Irons D 8	Brannigan K 5	Hardie D —+1	Match No.
1	2	3	4	5	6	7¹	8	9	10	11		12																1
1	2	3¹	4	5	6	7²	8	9²	10	11		12	13	14														2
1	2	3	4	5	6	7	8	9	10	11																		3
1	2¹	3	4	5	6	7²	8	9	10	11		12				13												4
1	2²	3	4³	5	6	7¹	8	9	10	11		14				12	13											5
1	2	3		5	6	7²	8	12	9	11		14	13			10¹	4³											6
1	2	3		5	6	7	8	9	10³	11		14	12				4²	13										7
1	2	3	4	5	6	7¹	8	9	10²	11						12	13											8
1	2	3¹	4	5	6		8	9³	10	11		12	7²			14	13											9
1	2		4	5	6	7¹	8	9	10	11		3				12												10
1	2		4¹	5	6	7²	8	9	10	11		3				13	12											11
1	2			5	6	13	8	9	10	11		3				7²			4¹	12								12
1	2	3	4²	5	6	7	8	9¹	10	11						12			13									13
1		3	4	5	6	7	8	9	10	11¹		13				12			2²									14
1		3	4	5	6	7¹	8	9	10	11		2	12															15
1		3¹	4	5	6	7	8²	9	10	11³		2	14						12	13								16
1			4	5	6	7¹	8		10	11	13				9²				2	3	12							17
1	2¹		4	5	6	9	8		10	11		7	3							7		12						18
1	12		4	5	6	9	8		10	11		7¹	3							2								19
1		3¹	4	5	6	7	8	9²	10	11			2	13						12								20
1		3²	4³	5	6	7	8¹	13	9	11			2	10	14					12								21
1		3	4	5	6	12			10	11			7		9¹	8²		13	2									22
1		3	4	5	6		8	9	10		12	14			7³		13	11¹	2²									23
1		4		5	7	8			10	11	9	3			12				6			2¹						24
1		4			6	13	8	9	10	11³	14	3¹					5			2			7²	12				25
1		3	4		6	7¹	8	9	10	11²						12	2	13	5									26
1		3	4		6	7¹	8	9	10	11²						12	2	13	5									27
1		3			5	6	7¹	8	9	10						12	4	11	2									28
1					5	6	7	8	9	10	11¹					12	2		3						4			29
1					5	6	11¹	8²	9	7		13				12	10	2	3						4			30
1						6	3		8²	9	10	11			7	13	12		2¹						4	5		31
1		3				6			8	9¹	10	11			7	12	2								4	5		32
1		3	13			6	14	8		10	11				7	9³	2²		12						4	5¹		33
1		3	2			6	12	8		10	11²				13	7	9		5¹						4			34
1		3	6				13	8	9	12	11				7¹	10²	2								4	5		35
1		3³	4	12	6				10	11		9²	14	7		2¹									8	5	13	36

COWDENBEATH   Third Division

Year Formed: 1881. *Ground & Address:* Central Park, Cowdenbeath KY4 9EY. *Telephone:* 01383 610166. *Fax:* 01383 512132.
Ground Capacity: total: 5268. seated: 1622. *Size of Pitch:* 107yd × 66yd.
Chairman: Gordon McDougall. *Secretary:* Tom Ogilvie. *Commercial Manager:* Joe McNamara.
Manager: Thomas Steven. *Coaches:* William Aitchison, Samuel Conn, Bert Oliver. *Physio:* Brian McNeill
Managers since 1975: D. McLindon; F. Connor; P. Wilson; A. Rolland; H. Wilson; W. McCulloch; J. Clark; J. Craig; R. Campbell; J. Blackley; J. Brownlie, A. Harrow, J. Reilly, P Dolan. *Previous Grounds:* North End Park, Cowdenbeath.
Record Attendance: 25,586 v Rangers, League Cup quarter-final; 21 Sept, 1949.
Record Transfer Fee received: £30,000 for Nicky Henderson to Falkirk, (March 1994).
Record Transfer Fee paid: —
Record Victory: 12-0 v Johnstone, Scottish Cup 1st rd; 21 Jan, 1928.
Record Defeat: 1-11 v Clyde, Division II; 6 Oct, 1951.
Most Capped Player: Jim Paterson, 3, Scotland.
Most League and Cup Appearances: 491 Ray Allan 1972-75, 1979-89.
Most League Goals in Season (Individual): 53, Rab Walls, Division II, 1938-39.
Most Goals Overall (Individual): 120, Willie Devlin, 1922-26, 1929-30.

COWDENBEATH 1995–96 LEAGUE RECORD

Match No.	Date	Venue	Opponents	Result		H/T Score	Lg. Pos.	Goalscorers	Atten- dance
1	Aug 12	H	Alloa	W	1-0	0-0	—	Buckley	281
2	26	A	Queen's P	L	1-3	0-2	7	McMahon	444
3	Sept 2	H	East Stirling	W	4-2	4-2	4	Scott 3, Yardley	203
4	9	A	Albion R	W	3-2	1-0	4	Buckley, Wood, Yardley	680
5	16	H	Brechin C	L	0-1	0-0	5		251
6	23	A	Ross Co	D	2-2	0-1	5	Wood, Buckley	1571
7	30	H	Livingston	L	0-1	0-1	5		340
8	Oct 7	H	Arbroath	D	1-1	1-0	6	Scott	308
9	14	A	Caledonian Th	L	2-3	1-2	6	Scott 2	1378
10	21	A	East Stirling	L	1-3	1-1	7	Soutar	284
11	28	H	Queen's P	W	3-2	2-0	6	Scott 2, Malloy	222
12	Nov 4	A	Brechin C	L	0-2	0-1	6		338
13	11	H	Albion R	W	4-1	1-0	5	Wood 3, Conn	166
14	18	A	Livingston	W	1-0	0-0	5	Bowmaker	3880
15	25	H	Ross Co	W	2-0	0-0	5	Conn 2	318
16	Dec 2	A	Arbroath	L	1-2	0-1	6	Humphreys	464
17	16	A	Caledonian Th	D	0-0	0-0	5		230
18	Jan 9	H	East Stirling	L	1-4	1-1	—	Humphreys	154
19	13	A	Ross Co	L	1-4	1-1	6	Mackenzie	1369
20	16	A	Alloa	W	3-2	1-0	6	Mackenzie 2, Wood	289
21	20	H	Arbroath	L	1-2	1-2	6	Meldrum	223
22	Feb 3	H	Caledonian Th	W	2-1	0-1	6	Steven 2	229
23	14	H	Brechin C	D	0-0	0-0	—		160
24	17	A	Albion R	L	0-2	0-2	6		348
25	24	A	Queen's P	L	1-2	0-0	6	Steven	468
26	28	H	Livingston	L	0-3	0-1	—		272
27	Mar 2	H	Alloa	W	3-0	3-0	6	O'Neill, Winter, Meldrum	190
28	9	H	Ross Co	D	1-1	1-1	6	Scott	290
29	16	A	Livingston	L	1-2	0-0	6	Scott	2147
30	23	A	Brechin C	L	0-2	0-0	7		368
31	30	H	Albion R	D	1-1	1-0	7	O'Neill	173
32	Apr 6	A	Arbroath	D	0-0	0-0	7		387
33	13	A	Caledonian Th	L	0-2	0-1	8		721
34	20	A	East Stirling	D	1-1	0-0	8	Scott	294
35	27	H	Queen's P	L	2-3	0-2	8	Winter, Wood	231
36	30	A	Alloa	L	1-2	1-1	8	Bowmaker	260

Final League Position: 8

Honours
League Champions: Division II 1913-14, 1914-15, 1938-39; *Runners-up:* Division II 1921-22, 1923-24, 1969-70. Second Division 1991-92.
Scottish Cup: Quarter-finals: 1931.
League Cup: Semi-finals: 1959-60, 1970-71.
Club colours: Shirt: Royal blue 1" vertical stripe with red piping on sleeve seam. Shorts: White with blue side stripe. Stockings: Royal blue.

Goalscorers: *League (45):* Scott 11, Wood 7, Buckley 3, Conn 3, Mackenzie 3, Steven 3, Bowmaker 2, Humphreys 2, Meldrum 2, O'Neill 2, Winter 2, Yardley 2, McMahon 1, Malloy 1, Soutar 1. *Scottish Cup (1):* Maratea 1. *Coca-Cola Cup (1):* Scott 1. *League Challenge Cup (0)*

The following table records, for each match, the shirt number worn by each player (superscript figures denote goals scored).

Russell N 32+1	Steven S 36	Meldrum G 35	McMahon B 28	Malloy B 18	Maratea D 13+2	Winter C 32	Wood G 30+1	Wardell S 1	Smith C 2+4	Hutchison K 1+1	Buckley G 6+9	Demelo A 1+5	Humphreys M 35	Scott D 26+2	Yardley M 4	Petrie E 3+2	Chapman G —+1	Soutar G 3+5	Bowmaker K 16+5	Brock J 4+6	Mackenzie A 8	O'Neill H 16+2	Conn S 16+2	Hamilton A 12+3	Brough G 3+4	Millar G 6+7	Oliver S 4+1	Stewart W 3+9	Spence J —+3	McGregor S 2	Match No.
1	2	3	4	5	6^{1}	7	8		9^{1}	10	11	12	13																		1
1	8	3	5	6		7	4				11	12	13	2^{2}	9^{1}	10															2
1	7	3^{2}	6	5	14	4	8				13		11^{1}	2	9^{2}	10	12														3
1	2^{1}	3	5	6		8	7				13		11^{2}	4	9	10	12														4
1	8^{1}	3	5	6		4	7				11			2	9	10		12													5
1	10	3	5	6		2	7					13	11	8^{2}	4	9^{1}		12													6
1	8	3	5	6		2	7						11^{2}	14	4	9^{3}		13	10^{1}		12										7
1	2^{1}	3	5	6		8	7				12	13		4	9			11^{2}	10												8
1	2	3	6		5		7^{2}					13	12	4	9			8^{1}	10		11										9
1	2	3	6	5		7								4	9				11		10	8									10
1	2	3	6	5		8	7				12	14	4	9^{3}					11^{1}		13	10^{2}									11
1	8	3	6	5		4	7						2	9					10^{1}		12	11^{2}	13								12
1	6	11	4	5		8	7^{3}				12	14	2	9^{1}					13		10	3^{2}									13
1	10	3	6	5		11	7^{2}					13	2	9^{2}				12	14		8^{1}	4									14
1	7	3	5						10			13	2	9				11^{2}	12		8^{1}	4	6^{2}	14							15
1	7	3	5	6		11						13	4	9				10	12		8^{2}	2^{1}									16
1	6	3			2	8		5	9									12	11^{1}		10					7					17
1	7^{2}	3			2	10	13	11^{1}	5									12	6		9^{3}	4	14	8							18
1	7	3			6	2	8	9^{2}		5								12	11^{1}		10	4	13								19
	8	3	6	5	2	11	10	4											9	7							1				20
1	8	3	6	5	2^{1}	11	10	4											12	9		7^{2}	13								21
1	11	3	5		2	8	9	4											10	6			7								22
1	9^{2}	3	5		2	7	10	6	13										11			4^{1}	8	12							23
1	8	3	6		2	9	10	4	12										11^{2}			5	7^{1}	13							24
1	11	3	6		2	8	9	4											10	5^{3}	12	7^{2}	13								25
1	6	3	5		9^{1}	7	8	4											11	10^{2}	2	13	12								26
1	10	3	5		6	8^{2}		4	9^{1}										11	7	2	13	12								27
1	10	3	5		7	6		4	9										8^{1}	2	12	11^{2}	13								28
1	8	3	5		7			4	9	6^{1}									11^{2}	10	2	13	12								29
14	8^{1}	3	5		7^{2}			4	9	6^{3}									11	13	2	12	1	10							30
	8	3	5		4	9	6^{2}	11^{1}	7	2	1	12	13	10																	31
1	5	3			6	8		4	9										11^{1}	10^{2}	7	2	12	13							32
1^{6}	5	3			6	8^{1}		4	9										12	10	7	2	11^{2}	15	13						33
1	2				6	8	7^{2}	4	9										12	11^{1}	5	10	3	13							34
	4^{6}	3			6^{1}	7	8	2	9										12	11^{1}	5	13	14	1	10						35
1	5	3			6	14	7^{3}	4	9^{2}										8	13	2	11			17				10^{1}		36

DUMBARTON   Second Division

Year Formed: 1872. *Ground & Address:* Boghead Park, Miller St, Dumbarton G82 2JA. *Telephone:* 01389 762569/767864. *Fax:* 01389 762629
Ground Capacity: total: 5503. seated: 303. *Size of Pitch:* 110yd × 68yd.
Chairman: D. Dalglish. *Company Secretary:* Colin J. Hosie.
Manager: Jim Fallon. *Assistant Manager:* Alistair MacLeod. *Coach:* Sam McGivern. *Physio:* David Stobie.
Managers since 1975: A. Wright; D. Wilson; S. Fallon; W. Lamont; D. Wilson; D. Whiteford; A. Totten; M. Clougherty; R. Auld; J. George; W. Lamont; M. MacLeod. *Club Nickname(s):* The Sons. *Previous Grounds:* Broadmeadow, Ropework Lane.
Record Attendance: 18,000 v Raith Rovers, Scottish Cup; 2 Mar, 1957.
Record Transfer Fee received: £125,000 for Graeme Sharp to Everton (March 1982).
Record Transfer Fee paid: £50,000 for Charlie Gibson from Stirling Albion (1989).
Record Victory: 13-2 v Kirkintilloch Cl. 1st Rd; 1 Sept, 1888.
Record Defeat: 1-11 v Albion Rovers, Division II; 30 Jan, 1926: v Ayr United, League Cup; 13 Aug, 1952.
Most Capped Player: John Lindsay, 8, Scotland; James McAulay, 8, Scotland.
Most League Appearances: 297: Andy Jardine, 1957-67.

DUMBARTON 1995–96 LEAGUE RECORD

Match No.	Date	Venue	Opponents	Result		H/T Score	Lg. Pos.	Goalscorers	Attendance
1	Aug 12	H	Hamilton A	W	1-0	0-0	—	Burns	1191
2	26	A	Morton	W	2-1	2-0	2	Mooney M, Charnley	2612
3	Sept 2	H	Dunfermline Ath	L	0-4	0-1	2		1952
4	9	H	Airdrieonians	L	1-2	0-2	4	Martin	1320
5	16	A	St Johnstone	L	1-4	0-2	6	McKinnon	2273
6	23	H	Dundee	L	1-5	0-2	9	McGarvey	1207
7	30	A	Clydebank	L	1-2	0-1	9	Gibson	913
8	Oct 7	H	Dundee U	W	1-0	0-0	8	Mooney M	2013
9	14	A	St Mirren	L	2-3	1-2	9	Mooney M (pen), McGarvey	2377
10	21	A	Dunfermline Ath	L	1-3	1-2	9	Gibson	3842
11	28	H	Morton	L	0-2	0-2	9		2378
12	Nov 4	H	St Johnstone	L	1-3	1-0	9	Mooney M	1050
13	11	A	Airdrieonians	L	1-2	0-1	9	Boyle (og)	1205
14	18	H	Clydebank	L	1-2	0-1	9	Mooney M	1043
15	Dec 2	A	Dundee U	L	0-8	0-3	9		5285
16	5	A	Dundee	D	1-1	0-0	—	Dallas	2804
17	9	H	St Mirren	D	0-0	0-0	9		1461
18	16	A	Hamilton A	L	0-3	0-3	9		762
19	Jan 6	A	St Johnstone	L	0-3	0-0	9		2448
20	13	H	Airdrieonians	L	1-2	0-2	10	Granger	1045
21	20	H	Dundee U	L	1-3	1-2	10	Ward	1354
22	23	H	Dundee	L	1-2	1-0	—	Ward	761
23	Feb 3	A	St Mirren	L	0-5	0-1	10		1838
24	13	H	Hamilton A	L	1-2	0-1	—	Granger	654
25	17	A	Clydebank	L	0-1	0-0	10		612
26	24	A	Morton	L	0-2	0-2	10		2833
27	Mar 2	A	Dundee	L	0-3	0-1	10		1712
28	9	H	Dunfermline Ath	L	0-3	0-2	10		1477
29	16	H	Clydebank	L	0-1	0-0	10		654
30	23	H	St Johnstone	L	0-3	0-2	10		903
31	30	A	Airdrieonians	L	1-5	1-1	10	Foster	1062
32	Apr 6	A	Dundee U	L	1-6	1-4	10	Sharpe	7142
33	13	H	St Mirren	L	0-1	0-1	10		1139
34	20	A	Dunfermline Ath	L	1-4	1-0	10	Dallas	5971
35	27	H	Morton	L	0-1	0-1	10		2733
36	May 4	A	Hamilton A	L	1-2	1-1	10	Granger (pen)	657

Final League Position: 10

Most Goals in Season (Individual): 38: Kenny Wilson, Division II; 1971-72.
Most Goals Overall (Individual): 169: Hughie Gallacher, 1954-62 (including C Division 1954-55).

Honours
League Champions: Division I 1890-91 (shared with Rangers), 1891-92. Division II 1910-11, 1971-72. Second Division 1991-92; *Runners-up:* First Division 1983-84. Division II 1907-08.
Scottish Cup Winners: 1883; *Runners-up:* 1881, 1882, 1887, 1891, 1897. *League Cup:* —.
Club colours: Shirt: Gold. Shorts: Gold. Stockings: Gold and black.

Goalscorers: *League (23):* Mooney M 5 (1 pen), Granger 3 (1 pen), Dallas 2, Gibson 2, McGarvey 2, Ward 2, Burns 1, Charnley 1, Foster 1, McKinnon 1, Martin 1, Sharpe 1, own goal 1. *Scottish Cup (1):* Mooney M 1. *Coca-Cola Cup (0)*
League Challenge Cup (0)

MacFarlane I 22	Burns H 10+1	Fabiani R 19+1	Meechan J 31+1	Martin P 12	Marsland J 18	Mooney M 31+5	King T 27+1	McGivern S 9+2	Charnley J 16+2	Granger A 20+11	McGarvey M 14+10	Gibson C 23+6	Gow S 20+1	McKinnon S 31+2	Melvin M 32+1	Hamilton J 3	Foster A 10+2	Dallas S 8+14	Dennison P 2	Meechan K 12+1	Ward H 10+4	Sharpe L 14+1	Glancy M 1	Goldie J 1+1	Match No.
1	2	3	4	5	6	7	8	9²	10	11¹	12	13													1
1	2	3		5	6	7	8¹	9²	11	13	12			4	10										2
1	2¹	3	10³	5	6	7	8	9²	14	13				4	11	12									3
1	3²		5	6	7	8	9		11	12		13		10	4			2¹							4
1	3		5	6	7	8¹	9²		11	12		13		10	4			2							5
1		13	5²	6	7¹		11	10	12	9				8	4	2	3								6
1			5	6	12	8			11	10	2	9		7¹	4		3								7
1	12	4	5¹	6	13	8			11	7³	14	9²		10	2		3								8
1	13	3²	5	6	7	8¹	14		11	12		9		4³	2	10									9
1		3	4		6	7			11	10¹	12	9	5	8	2										10
1		3	4		6	7			11¹	10	12	9	5	8	2										11
1		3	2	5	6	7		4	11	10		9		8											12
1		3	4	5	6	7¹	10	12	11	9				8	2²		13								13
		3	4	5	6	7	12	10²	11¹	9				8	2		13	1							14
		3³	4	5	6	13	8²	12	14	9				7¹	2		11	10	1						15
		3	5	6	7	4		11	12		8			10¹	9			1							16
		3	5	6	7²	2		11	13	10	12			8¹	4			9	1						17
1		3	5	6³	7²	2		11	13	10	14			8	4¹		12	9							18
1	2	3	6		7				10	9	5	8		4			11¹	12							19
1	2	3	6		7			12	10¹	9	5	8		4			11								20
1	2	3²	6		7¹			10	12	14	9	5		8	4		13	11²							21
	2¹	3²	6		7			10	12	9	5	8		4			14	1		11³	13				22
	2		5		7			6	8	14	12	13		4	10³		9²	1		11		3			23
			5		7			10¹	12	6	9			2	8		4	11				3			24
			5		7			6	8		9	2	10¹		4		12			11		3			25
			5		7			6	10		9	2	8		4		12			11¹		3			26
			5		7			6	10	11	9²	2	8¹		4		13			12		3			27
6			5		7				10	8	9	2			4		12			11¹		3			28
	2		5		7		9¹		8		6	12		4			13			11²		3	10		29
			5		7²			8	6	9	2	12		4			10	13		11¹		3			30
			5		7¹	6		11		9	2	8		4			10²	13	1			3		12	31
1			5		7¹	6		11	10	9²	2	8		4			13	12				3			32
1			5		7¹	6	9	11	10		2	8		4			12					3			33
1⁹			5		13	6	9	7	10			8		4			2¹	11		15	12²	3			34
1			5		7	6		8		9	2	10		4			11¹	12				3			35
1			5		12	6		11	10	9¹	2	7²		4			13					3		8	36

DUNDEE
First Division

Year Formed: 1893. *Ground & Address:* Dens Park Stadium, Sandeman St, Dundee DD3 7JY. *Telephone:* 01382 826104.
Fax: 01382 832284.
Ground Capacity: 14,177. seated: 10,877. *Size of Pitch:* 110yd × 72yd.
Chairman: Ron Dixon. *Vice-chairman:* Malcolm Reid.*Secretary:* Andrew Drummond. *Managing Director:* Nigel Squire.
Manager: Jim Duffy. *Coaches:* John McCormack, Harry Hay. *Physio:* J. Crosbie.
Managers since 1975: David White; Tommy Gemmell; Donald Mackay; Archie Knox; Jocky Scott; Dave Smith; Gordon
Wallace; Iain Munro, Simon Stainrod. *Club Nickname(s):* The Dark Blues or The Dee. *Previous Grounds:* Carolina
Port 1893-98.
Record Attendance: 43,024 v Rangers, Scottish Cup; 1953.
Record Transfer Fee received: £500,000 for Tommy Coyne to Celtic (March 1989).
Record Transfer Fee paid: £200,000 for Jim Leighton (Feb 1992).
Record Victory: 10-0 Division II v Alloa; 9 Mar, 1947 and v Dunfermline Ath; 22 Mar, 1947.
Record Defeat: 0-11 v Celtic, Division I; 26 Oct, 1895.
Most Capped Player: Alex Hamilton, 24, Scotland.
Most League Appearances: 341: Doug Cowie 1945-61.
Most League Goals in Season (Individual): 52: Alan Gilzean, 1963-64.
Most Goals Overall (Individual): 113: Alan Gilzean.

DUNDEE 1995–96 LEAGUE RECORD

Match No.	Date	Venue	Opponents	Result		H/T Score	Lg. Pos.	Goalscorers	Attendance
1	Aug 12	A	St Johnstone	W	2-0	1-0	—	Main (og), Britton	5236
2	26	H	Airdrieonians	D	1-1	1-0	3	Cargill	3536
3	Sept 2	H	Clydebank	D	1-1	0-0	4	Hamilton	1467
4	9	A	Morton	D	2-2	2-0	3	Tosh, Farningham	3384
5	16	H	Hamilton A	D	1-1	1-1	3	Shaw	2395
6	23	A	Dumbarton	W	5-1	2-0	2	Shaw 2, Martin (og), Bain, Hamilton	1207
7	30	H	Dundee U	L	2-3	1-1	5	Hamilton 2	10,395
8	Oct 7	H	St Mirren	W	3-1	1-0	2	Tosh, Hamilton, Wieghorst	3555
9	14	A	Dunfermline Ath	W	1-0	0-0	2	Tosh	6700
10	21	H	Clydebank	D	1-1	1-1	4	Duffy C	2708
11	28	A	Airdrieonians	W	3-2	1-1	4	Wieghorst 2, Hamilton	1925
12	Nov 4	A	Hamilton A	W	2-1	1-0	4	Tosh, Duffy C	1131
13	11	H	Morton	D	0-0	0-0	4		4060
14	18	A	Dundee U	W	3-2	2-0	2	Shaw 2, Wieghorst	10,752
15	Dec 2	A	St Mirren	W	2-1	2-0	4	Shaw, Tosh	2278
16	5	H	Dumbarton	D	1-1	0-0	—	Tosh	2804
17	9	H	Dunfermline Ath	L	2-4	2-3	4	Shaw, Hamilton	4642
18	16	H	St Johnstone	L	0-1	0-0	4		3034
19	Jan 6	H	Hamilton A	W	2-1	2-1	3	Charnley, Farningham	2020
20	9	A	Dundee U	L	0-2	0-1	—		9199
21	13	A	Morton	L	0-1	0-1	4		3163
22	16	A	Clydebank	W	1-0	0-0	—	Britton	644
23	20	H	St Mirren	L	1-2	0-1	4	Charnley	2698
24	23	A	Dumbarton	W	2-1	0-1	—	Hamilton 2	761
25	Feb 13	A	St Johnstone	L	2-3	0-2	—	McKeown, Farningham	3960
26	24	H	Airdrieonians	W	2-0	2-0	5	McCann, Hamilton	2116
27	Mar 2	H	Dumbarton	W	3-0	1-0	5	Hamilton 2, Tosh	1712
28	6	A	Dunfermline Ath	D	1-1	1-1	—	Duffy C	5580
29	16	A	Dundee U	L	0-2	0-1	5		9831
30	23	A	Hamilton A	W	1-0	1-0	5	Tosh	828
31	30	H	Morton	D	1-1	1-0	5	Tosh	2734
32	Apr 6	A	St Mirren	L	1-2	1-2	5	Hamilton	2175
33	13	H	Dunfermline Ath	D	1-1	0-0	5	O'Driscoll	3218
34	20	H	Clydebank	W	3-0	1-0	5	Charnley, Hamilton, McCann	1403
35	27	A	Airdrieonians	D	0-0	0-0	5		1454
36	May 4	H	St Johnstone	D	0-0	0-0	5		2710

Final League Position: 5

Honours
League Champions: Division I 1961-62. First Division 1978-79, 1991-92. Division II 1946-47; *Runners-up:* Division I 1902-03, 1906-07, 1908-09, 1948-49, 1980-81.
Scottish Cup Winners: 1910; *Runners-up:* 1925, 1952, 1964.
League Cup Winners: 1951-52, 1952-53, 1973-74; *Runners-up:* 1967-68, 1980-81. *(Coca-Cola Cup):* 1995–96.
B&Q (Centenary) Cup: Winners: 1990-91 *Runners-up:* 1994-95.

European: *European Cup:* 1962-63 (semi-final). *Cup Winners:* 1964-65.
UEFA Cup: (Fairs Cup 1967-68 semi-final), 1971-72, 1973-74, 1974-75.
Club colours: Shirt: Dark blue with red and white trim. Shorts: White. Stockings: Blue and white.

Goalscorers: *League (73):* Brewster 17, McSwegan 17, Winters 7, Coyle 5, Johnson 4, McKinlay 4, McLaren 3, Bett 2, Malpas 2, Perry 2, Pressley 2, Connolly 1, Dailly 1, Hannah 1, Shannon 1, Welsh 1, own goals 3. *Scottish Cup (4):* Coyle 3, Brewster 1. *Coca-Cola Cup (5):* Connolly 2, Caldwell 1, McKinlay 1, Winters 1. *League Challenge Cup (4):* Brewster 1, Dailly 1, Honeyman 1, McKinlay 1.

Pageaud M 35	Bain K 7 + 3	Cargill A 11 + 7	Manley R 17	Wieghorst M 14	Duffy C 31	Tosh P 29 + 1	Vrto D 25 + 2	Britton G 15 + 10	Hamilton J 30 + 3	McCann N 22	Shaw G 33 + 3	Anderson J 9 + 8	McQueen T 21	Farningham R 13 + 5	McBain R 3 + 3	Teasdale M 1	Duffy J 19	McKeown G 13 + 4	Smith B 20	Charnley J 12	Adamczuk D 8 + 5	Magee D — + 1	Mathers P 1	Rae G 4 + 2	O'Driscoll J 1 + 4	Tully C 2	Hutchison M — + 1	Match No.
1	2	3	4	5²	6	7	8¹	9	10	11	12	13																1
1	2	6	4	5		7	8	9	10¹	11	12		3															2
1	2	5¹	4		6	9²	8		10	11	7	13	3	12														3
1	2	4²		5¹	6	9	8		10	11	7	13	3	12														4
1		5	4¹		6	9	8		10	11	7	13	3	2	12²													5
1	8	13		5	6	9¹			12	11	7	10²	3			2	4											6
1		5	4	8	6	9		12	10	11	7		3	2¹														7
1	8			5	6	9²		12	10¹	11	7	13	3	2			4											8
1		4	8	6	9			12	10¹	11	7		3	2			5											9
1		4	8²	6¹	9	12	7	10	11	13		3	2				5											10
1		4	5			8	10	12	11	7	9¹	3	2				6											11
1			5	6	9	8	10		11	7		3	2				4											12
1		4	5	6	8	8	10¹	12	11	7		3					2											13
1		4	5	6	9	8	12	10¹	11	7		3					2											14
1			5	6	9	8¹	14	10³		7	11²	3	2	13			4	12										15
1	8	4	5	6	9		10			7	11¹	3	2	12														16
1	14	5²	4³		6	9		11	10		7	13	3	8			12	2¹										17
1	5	12			6		8	10			7	11¹	3	9			4	2										18
1		12		4		8	11	10		7	9¹	3					5	2	6									19
1	12	13		4¹	9	8		10		7			3				5	11²	2	6								20
1		13			9	8	11	10		7		3	6	11¹			5	4²	2									21
1		13			9	8	11	10		7		3	12				5	4¹	2	6²								22
1			4	9¹	8	11²	10		7		3	13				5	2	6	12								23
1	11¹		4	9	8		10		7		3	6²				5	2		12	13							24
1		3²	4	9	8	11	10		7			13				12	2	6	5¹		1						25
1	13		6	9	8	12	10¹	11	7							3	4²	2	5								26
1		14	6	9	8	12	10	11	7							3	4	2²	5³	13							27
1			6	9	8		10	7								3	4	2	5	11							28
1			4	9		12	10		7	11¹						5	8	2	6	3							29
1	4¹	5	6	9		8	10		7	11²							2		3			12	13				30
1		4		9		12	10	11	7	13						5¹	8²	2		6		3					31
1		6¹	4		12	9	10	11	7²								5	2		8		3	13				32
1		4¹	6	12	8		10	11	7								5	2		9²		3	13				33
1			4¹		8		10	11	7	9²							6	2	5	12		3	13				34
1			4	9²	8		10	11	7								12	2	5	6¹				3	13		35
1		4²		6		8¹		10	11	7	14							2	5	13			12	9²	3		36

DUNDEE UNITED   Premier Division

Year Formed: 1909 (1923). *Ground & Address:* Tannadice Park, Tannadice St, Dundee DD3 7JW. *Telephone:* 01382 833166. *Fax:* 01382 882689. *Ground Capacity:* total: 12,616 all seated: stands: east 2868, west 2104, south 2201, George Fox 5151, executive boxes 292.
Size of Pitch: 110yd × 74yd.
Chairman: James Y. McLean. *Company Secretary:* Miss Priti Trivedi. *Commercial Manager:* Bill Campbell.
Manager: Billy Kirkwood. *Assistant Manager:* Maurice Malpas. *Physio:* David Rankin. *Coach:* Gordon Wallace.
Managers since 1975: J. McLean, I.Golac. *Club Nickname(s):* The Terrors. *Previous Grounds:* None.
Record Attendance: 28,000 v Barcelona, Fairs Cup; 16 Nov, 1966.
Record Transfer Fee received: £4,000,000 for Duncan Ferguson from Rangers (July 1993).
Record Transfer Fee paid: £600,000 for Gordon Petric from Partizan Belgrade (Nov 1993).
Record Victory: 14-0 v Nithsdale Wanderers, Scottish Cup 1st rd; 17 Jan, 1931.
Record Defeat: 1-12 v Motherwell, Division II; 23 Jan, 1954.
Most Capped Player: Maurice Malpas, 55, Scotland.
Most League Appearances: 612, Dave Narey; 1973-94.
Most Appearances in European Matches: 76, Dave Narey (record for Scottish player).
Most League Goals in Season (Individual): 41: John Coyle, Division II; 1955-56.
Most Goals Overall (Individual): 158: Peter McKay.

DUNDEE UNITED 1995–96 LEAGUE RECORD

Match No.	Date	Venue	Opponents	Result		H/T Score	Lg. Pos.	Goalscorers	Atten-dance
1	Aug 12	H	Morton	D	1-1	1-0	—	Brewster	6927
2	26	A	Dunfermline Ath	L	0-3	0-0	9		7933
3	Sept 2	H	Hamilton A	W	2-1	0-1	7	Pressley, Connolly	5194
4	9	H	St Mirren	W	1-0	0-0	2	Fullarton (og)	6159
5	16	A	Clydebank	W	2-1	1-1	2	Bett, McKinlay	1949
6	23	H	Airdrieonians	L	1-2	0-0	4	Perry	6005
7	30	A	Dundee	W	3-2	1-1	2	McKinlay 3	10,395
8	Oct 7	A	Dumbarton	L	0-1	0-0	3		2013
9	14	H	St Johnstone	W	2-1	2-0	3	Bett, Coyle	7572
10	21	A	Hamilton A	W	1-0	0-0	2	McSwegan	1719
11	28	H	Dunfermline Ath	W	3-1	1-1	2	Coyle, McLaren, McSwegan	9703
12	31	H	Clydebank	W	3-0	3-0	—	Winters, Johnson, McLaren	5428
13	Nov 11	A	St Mirren	D	1-1	1-1	2	Winters	3556
14	18	H	Dundee	L	2-3	0-2	3	Brewster, Malpas	10,752
15	25	A	Airdrieonians	D	1-1	0-0	4	Malpas	2504
16	Dec 2	H	Dumbarton	W	8-0	3-0	3	Brewster 4, Johnson, Melvin (og), Coyle, McSwegan	5285
17	9	A	St Johnstone	D	0-0	0-0	3		5966
18	16	A	Morton	W	2-1	2-0	2	Johnson, McSwegan	4660
19	26	H	Hamilton A	D	1-1	0-0	—	Brewster	6109
20	30	H	Airdrieonians	D	2-2	1-2	2	Brewster, Hannah	5855
21	Jan 6	A	Clydebank	D	1-1	1-0	2	Winters	1383
22	9	H	Dundee	W	2-0	1-0	—	Winters 2	9199
23	13	H	St Mirren	W	2-1	2-0	1	McSwegan 2	6523
24	20	A	Dumbarton	W	3-1	2-1	1	Brewster, Shannon, McSwegan	1354
25	Feb 3	H	St Johnstone	L	1-3	0-2	1	Pressley	7478
26	24	A	Dunfermline Ath	D	2-2	1-2	2	McSwegan, Brewster	8400
27	27	H	Morton	W	4-0	0-0	—	Brewster 2, McSwegan, Coyle	6768
28	Mar 2	A	Airdrieonians	D	1-1	1-0	2	McSwegan	1810
29	16	H	Dundee	W	2-0	1-0	2	McSwegan, Brewster	9831
30	23	H	Clydebank	W	6-0	3-0	2	Brewster 3, McSwegan 2, Coyle	5973
31	30	A	St Mirren	W	3-1	3-0	2	Winters, McLaren, Smith (og)	4347
32	Apr 6	H	Dumbarton	W	6-1	4-1	1	McSwegan 4, Perry, Brewster	7142
33	13	A	St Johnstone	L	0-1	0-1	1		9973
34	22	A	Hamilton A	W	2-0	0-0	—	Johnson, Dailly	3291
35	27	H	Dunfermline Ath	L	0-1	0-1	2		12,384
36	May 4	A	Morton	D	2-2	1-0	2	Welsh, Winters	12,523

Final League Position: 2

Honours
League Champions: Premier Division 1982-83. Division II 1924-25, 1928-29; *Runners-up:* Division II 1930-31, 1959-60. First Division Runners-up 1995-96.
Scottish Cup Winners: 1994; *Runners-up:* 1974, 1981, 1985, 1987, 1988, 1991.
League Cup Winners: 1979-80, 1980-81;*Runners-up:* 1981-82, 1984-85.
Summer Cup Runners-up: 1964-65. *Scottish War Cup Runners-up:* 1939-40.

European: *European Cup:* 8 matches: 1983-84 (semi-finals), 1988-89; *Cup Winners Cup:* 4 matches: 1974-75; *UEFA Cup Runners-up:* 1986-87. *Fairs Cup:* 10 matches: 1966-67, 1969-70, 1970-71. *UEFA Cup:* 70 matches:1971-72, 1975-76, 1977-78, 1978-79, 1979-80, 1980-81, 1981-82, 1982-83, 1984-85, 1985-86, 1986-87, 1987-88, 1989-90, 1990-91, 1993-94.
Club colours: Tangerine jersey, Black shorts. Change colours: White with two black hoops with mauve trim, black and white with mauve trim shorts.

Goalscorers: *League (53):* Hamilton 14, Tosh 9, Shaw 7, Wieghorst 4, Charnley 3, Duffy C 3, Farningham 3, Britton 2, McCann 2, Bain 1, Cargill 1, McKeown 1, O'Driscoll 1, own goals 2. *Scottish Cup (1):* Duffy C 1. *Coca-Cola Cup (15):* McCann 5, Shaw 3, Wieghorst 3, Hamilton 2, Tosh 2. *League Challenge Cup (8):* Hamilton 3, Anderson 2, Cargill 2, Shaw 1.

Maxwell A 35	Perry M 18+2	Shannon R 26	Malpas M 30	Pressley S 35	Hannah D 4+3	McLaren A 23+7	Robertson A 1+3	Winters R 34+1	Brewster C 23+7	Caldwell N 2	Connolly P 3+3	Walker P —+2	Welsh B 21+2	Bowman D 16+1	McKinlay W 5	Daily C 20+9	Bett J 23	Crabbe S 1+1	Johnson G 25+3	O'Hanlon K 1	McSwegan G 19+6	Honeyman B —+1	Coyle O 20+8	McKinnon R 5+4	McQuilken J 6+3	Keith M —+4	Match No.
1	2	3	4	5	6	7	8	9²	10	11¹	12	13															1
1	2	3	4			7		9²	12	11¹	10		5	6	8		13										2
1		2	3	4		7		9				12		8		5	6		10	11¹							3
1		2	3	5		7		9			13		6	11¹		8	4		10	12²							4
2²	3	6	4			7¹		9			11		12		8	5	10			13	1						5
1	2	3	6	4		7		9			11¹	12			8	5	10										6
1	2	3	6	4		7	11							8	5	10		9									7
1	2	3	6	4		7	12				11		5²	10¹	8		9	13									8
1		2	3	4		7		11	13			12		5	6	8¹	9²	10									9
1		2	3	4		7		11	12					5	6	8	9¹	10									10
1		2	3	4		7		11	12					5	6	8	9	10¹									11
1	13	2	3	4		7¹		11²	12					5	6	8	9	10									12
1		2	3	4		7		11	12					5	6	8¹	9²	10	13								13
1		2	3	4		7		11	12					5	6	8²	13	10¹	9								14
1		2	3	4		7		11	9³			5²		12	6	8	14	13	10¹								15
1		2	3	4				7	9²			5		6	8	12	10¹		11	13							16
1		2	3	4	13			7²	9³			5		14	6	8	12	10¹	11								17
1		2	3	4	12	13		7	10			5		6³	8	9²	14	11¹									18
1		2³	3	4	13	11¹		7	10			5		14	6²	8	9	12									19
1			3¹	4		7		11	10			5	13		2	6³	8²	9	14	12							20
1			3	4	11			7	10			5	8		2	6		9¹				12					21
1			3	4	13	9		7³	10			5	8		2	6²		12	14	11¹							22
1	4	3				11¹		7³	10			5	8		2	6	13	9	14	12							23
1	14	3		4		7²		11³	10¹			5	8		2	6		9	13				12				24
1			3	4	9	7¹		11	10			5³			2	6²	8	12	13	14							25
1	2	3¹	6	4		13		12	10					5			8	9	11²	6³	11						26
1	2		3	4	13	14		7²	10			5¹				12	9	8	6¹	11							27
1	2		3	4	13			7	10²					12		5	9	8	6¹	11							28
1	2		3	4	12			11¹	10			5	8²				6	9	7	13							29
1	2		3	4	12			11¹	10			5	8				6²	9	7	13							30
1	2		3	4		9¹		11	10			5	8		12		6		7								31
1	2		3	4				11	10			5	8				6	9	7								32
1	2	5	3	4		9		11	10²				8		12		6		7¹				13				33
1	2		3	4				11	10			5	8		12		6	9¹	7								34
1	2²		3	4	13			11	10			5	8		12		6	9¹	7								35
1	2		3	4		9¹		11	10			5	8		6				7	12							36

DUNFERMLINE ATHLETIC Premier Division

Year Formed: 1885. *Ground & Address:* East End Park, Halbeath Rd, Dunfermline KY12 7RB. *Telephone:* 01383 724295. *Fax:* 01383 723468.
Ground Capacity: total: 18,328. seated: 4008. *Size of Pitch:* 115yd × 68yd.
Chairman: C. R. Woodrow. *Secretary:* P. A. M. D'Mello. *Commercial Manager:* Audrey Kelly.
Manager: Bert Paton. *Assistant Manager:* Dick Campbell.
Physio: Philip Yeates, MCSP.
Managers since 1975: G. Miller; H. Melrose; P. Stanton; T. Forsyth; J. Leishman; I. Munro; J. Scott. *Club Nickname(s):* The Pars. *Previous Grounds:* None.
Record Attendance: 27,816 v Celtic, Division I, 30 April, 1968.
Record Transfer Fee received: £200,000 for Ian McCall to Rangers (Aug 1987).
Record Transfer Fee paid: £540,000 for Istvan Kozma from Bordeaux (Sept 1989).
Record Victory: 11-2 v Stenhousemuir, Division II, 27 Sept, 1930.
Record Defeat: 1-11 v Hibernian, Scottish Cup, 3rd rd replay, 26 Oct, 1889.
Most Capped Player: Istvan Kozma, 13 (29), Hungary.
Most League Appearances: 360: Bobby Robertson, 1977-88.
Most League Goals in Season (Individual): 53: Bobby Skinner, Division II, 1925-26.
Most Goals Overall (Individual): 154: Charles Dickson.

DUNFERMLINE ATHLETIC 1995–96 LEAGUE RECORD

Match No.	Date	Venue	Opponents	Result		H/T Score	Lg. Pos.	Goalscorers	Atten- dance
1	Aug 12	A	Airdrieonians	W	1-0	0-0	—	Shaw	2719
2	26	H	Dundee U	W	3-0	0-0	1	Petrie, Shaw, Moore	7933
3	Sept 2	A	Dumbarton	W	4-0	1-0	1	McNamara, Shaw, Gow (og), Petrie	1952
4	9	H	Clydebank	W	2-1	2-0	1	Moore, Tod	4410
5	16	A	St Mirren	W	2-0	1-0	1	McCathie, Petrie	3479
6	23	A	Morton	L	0-2	0-1	1		3794
7	30	H	St Johnstone	W	2-1	0-1	1	Petrie, Shaw	5737
8	Oct 7	A	Hamilton A	W	3-1	2-1	1	Petrie, Moore, Robertson	1473
9	14	H	Dundee	L	0-1	0-0	1		6700
10	21	H	Dumbarton	W	3-1	2-1	1	Petrie, Shaw 2	3842
11	28	A	Dundee U	L	1-3	1-1	1	Shaw	9703
12	Nov 4	H	St Mirren	D	1-1	0-1	1	Watson (og)	4578
13	11	A	Clydebank	W	4-0	1-0	1	McCathie, Fleming, Bingham 2	1304
14	18	A	St Johnstone	L	0-1	0-0	1		4559
15	25	H	Morton	L	0-2	0-2	1		4857
16	Dec 2	H	Hamilton A	W	4-0	3-0	1	Shaw, Fleming, Petrie, Tod	3284
17	9	A	Dundee	W	4-2	3-2	1	McCathie, Petrie, Tod, Fleming	4642
18	16	H	Airdrieonians	W	2-0	0-0	1	Moore, Petrie	4687
19	Jan 6	A	St Mirren	L	1-2	1-2	1	Robertson	3380
20	13	H	Clydebank	W	4-3	3-1	2	Tod, Smith A 2, Robertson	6642
21	20	A	Hamilton A	D	0-0	0-0	2		1556
22	Feb 10	A	Airdrieonians	W	2-1	0-0	3	Petrie, Bingham	2453
23	24	H	Dundee U	D	2-2	2-1	3	Den Bieman, French	8400
24	28	H	St Johnstone	W	3-2	1-2	—	Smith A, Clark, Tod	6348
25	Mar 2	H	Morton	W	4-1	2-1	1	Smith A, French, Hegarty, Robertson	4547
26	6	H	Dundee	D	1-1	1-1	—	Petrie	5580
27	9	A	Dumbarton	W	3-0	2-0	1	Shaw 2, Smith A	1477
28	16	A	St Johnstone	D	2-2	2-1	1	Shaw, Smith A	5239
29	19	A	Morton	D	1-1	0-0	—	Millar M	3170
30	23	H	St Mirren	D	2-2	2-0	1	Robertson, Millar M	4936
31	30	A	Clydebank	W	3-2	1-1	1	Petrie, Millar M 2 (1 pen)	1298
32	Apr 6	H	Hamilton A	L	1-3	1-2	2	French	4542
33	13	A	Dundee	D	1-1	0-0	2	Smith A	3218
34	20	H	Dumbarton	W	4-1	0-1	1	French, Smith A, Moore, Shaw	5971
35	27	A	Dundee U	W	1-0	1-0	1	Petrie	12,384
36	May 4	H	Airdrieonians	W	2-1	1-0	1	Smith A, Millar M (pen)	13,183

Final League Position: 1

Honours
League Champions: First Division 1988-89, 1995-96. Division II 1925-26. Second Division 1985-86; *Runners-up:* First Division 1986-87, 1993-94, 1994-95. Division II 1912-13, 1933-34, 1954-55, 1957-58, 1972-73. Second Division 1978-79.
Scottish Cup Winners: 1961, 1968; *Runners-up:* 1965.
League Cup Runners-up: 1949-50, 1991-92.
European: European Cup: —. *Cup Winners Cup:* 1961-62, 1968-69 (semi-finals). *UEFA Cup:* 1962-63, 1964-65, 1965-66, 1966-67, 1969-70 (*Fairs Cup*).
Club colours: Shirt: Black and white vertical stripes, stippled with red dots. Shorts: Black with white side panel. Stockings: White with red chevrons.

Goalscorers: *League (73):* Petrie 13, Shaw 12, Smith A 9, Millar M 5 (1 pen), Moore 5, Robertson 5, Tod 5, French 4, Bingham 3, Fleming 3, McCathie 3, Clark 1, Den Bieman 1, Hegarty 1, McNamara 1, own goals 2. *Scottish Cup (3):* Bingham 1, Petrie 1, Smith A 1. *Coca-Cola Cup (4):* Den Bieman 1, McCathie 1, Moore 1, Petrie 1. *League Challenge Cup (6):* Shaw 2, McNamara 1, Millar M 1, Petrie 1, Tod 1.

After the death of Norrie McCathie, his No. 4 shirt was not used for the remainder of the season. Instead the No. 12 shirt was used. This number is used for the first substitute in these tables; thus No. 21 is used to show the player in the normal No. 4 position in the team lists.

Van De Kamp G 26	Den Bieman I 16+10	Millar M 24	McCathie N 18	Tod A 36	Smith P 10+1	Moore A 28	McNamara J 7	Shaw G 17+11	Petrie S 31+3	Kinnaird P 6+3	McCulloch M 4+6	Fleming D 25+8	Cooper N 2+2	Robertson C 27+1	Fenwick P —+1	Bingham D 12+3	Farrell G 4+2	French H 21+2	Rice B 5+1	Miller C 25	Rissanen K 1+1	Hegarty R 3+6	Ferguson S —+1	Smith A 17+2	Callaghan T —+3	Clark J 11	Westwater I 10+1	Ireland C 10	Match No.
1	2	3	4	5	6	7	8	9	10	11^1	12																		1
1	2	3	4	5	6^1	7^2	8	9	10	11	12	13																	2
1	2	3	4	5^2	6	7	8	9	10	11		12	13																3
1	2^2	3	4	5	6^1	7	8	9	10	11^3		14	12	13															4
1	2	3	4	5	6	7^1	8	9	10	11^2	12	13																	5
1	2	3	4	5	6	7	8	9	10^2	11^1	12					13													6
1	7		4	5	13		2	9	10^2		12	6		3		8		11^1											7
1	12		4	5	6	7^1		9	10^3	13	14			3		8		11^2		2									8
1^1	13		4	5	6	7		9^3	10	14	12			3		8		11		2^2									9
1	7		4	5	6			9	10					3		8		11^1		2	12								10
1	2		4	5	6			9	10	7				3	12			11^1		8									11
1	8		4	5	7^2			9	10	12				3				11^1		6	2	13							12
1	7		4	5				9	10					3		8		12		6^1	2	11							13
1	11			5					10			6^1		3		8		9	2		4		7	12					14
1	12	10	4	5	7							6^1		3		8		11^2		9	2	13							15
1	12	6	4	5	7			9^2	10^1					3		8		11		2	13								16
1	13	6	4	5	7				10^2					3		8		11^1		9	2	12							17
1	13	6	4	5	7				10					3		8^1		11^2		9	2	12							18
1	12	6	4	5	7^1				10					3^2		8		11		9	2	13							19
1	7			5					10					3	21	8		11^1		6	2	12		9					20
1	2			5	7^1				10					11^2	21	8		6		3	12			9	13				21
1	13	3		5	7^1				10^2			11				8		12		6				9^6		21	15		22
1	11			5	7^2			13	12			3^1				8		10		2				9		21		6	23
1	11			5	7^1			13	12			3				8		10		2				9^2		21		6	24
1				5				12	11			3				8		10		2			7^1	9		21		6	25
1				5				12	11			3				8^1		10		2			7	9		21		6	26
	12			5	7^1		8	11	10^4	13		3								2				9		21	1	6	27
	3			5				11^2	13			12				8		10		2				9		21^1	1	6	28
	3			5	7^2			11^1	10	13						8		12		2				9		21	1	6	29
	3			5	7			12	11^1							8		10		2				9		21	1	6	30
	3			5	7^2			12	11			8		13		10				2				9^1		21	1	6	31
	3			5	7			12	11	12		8				10				2				9^2		21	1	6^1	32
21	3^1			5	7			13	11			6				8		10^2		2				9	12		1		33
14	3			5	7^3			13	11			6				8		10	21^1	2				9^6	12		1		34
21	3			5	7^1			13	11			6				8		10	12	2				9^2			1		35
21	3			5			7	11^2	12			6				8		10		2		13		9^3			1		36

EAST FIFE   First Division

Year Formed: 1903. *Ground & Address:* Bayview Park, Methil, Fife KY8 3AG (moving during 1996–97). *Telephone:* 01333 426323. *Fax:* 01333 426376.
Ground Capacity: total: 5385. seated: 600. *Size of Pitch:* 110yd × 71yd.
Chairman: James Baxter. *Managing Director:* Julian Danskin. *Secretary:* Mrs Leona Walker. *Commercial Manager:* James Bonthrone.
Manager: Steve Archibald. *Assistant Manager:* Alan Sneddon. *Physio:* Alex MacQueen. *Coach:* Gordon Rae.
Managers since 1975: Frank Christie; Roy Barry; David Clarke; Gavin Murray, Alex Totten. *Club Nickname(s):* The Fifers. *Previous Grounds:* None.
Record Attendance: 22,515 v Raith Rovers, Division I; 2 Jan, 1950.
Record Transfer Fee received: £150,000 for Paul Hunter from Hull C (March 1990).
Record Transfer Fee paid: £70,000 for John Sludden from Kilmarnock (July 1991).
Record Victory: 13-2 v Edinburgh City, Division II; 11 Dec, 1937.
Record Defeat: 0-9 v Hearts, Division I; 5 Oct, 1957.
Most Capped Player: George Aitken, 5 (8), Scotland.
Most League Appearances: 517: David Clarke, 1968-86.
Most League Goals in Season (Individual): 41: Jock Wood, Division II; 1926-27 and Henry Morris, Division II; 1947-48.
Most Goals Overall (Individual): 225: Phil Weir (215 in League).

EAST FIFE 1995–96 LEAGUE RECORD

Match No.	Date	Venue	Opponents	Result		H/T Score	Lg. Pos.	Goalscorers	Attendance
1	Aug 12	A	Forfar Ath	W	2-0	0-0	—	Beaton, Hutcheon	711
2	26	H	Ayr U	W	1-0	1-0	1	Scott	684
3	Sept 2	A	Stirling A	W	2-0	2-0	1	Beaton, Cusick	942
4	9	H	Montrose	W	3-0	2-0	1	Cusick, Scott 2	702
5	16	A	Stranraer	L	0-2	0-0	1		634
6	23	H	Queen of the S	W	2-1	0-1	1	Donaghy, Allan	700
7	30	A	Stenhousemuir	W	1-0	0-0	1	Dwarika	789
8	Oct 7	A	Berwick R	W	1-0	0-0	1	Archibald	655
9	14	H	Clyde	D	0-0	0-0	1		1128
10	21	A	Forfar Ath	D	1-1	1-1	1	Scott	794
11	28	A	Ayr U	W	1-0	1-0	1	Scott	1278
12	Nov 4	H	Stranraer	D	3-3	1-0	1	Beaton (pen), Hutcheon, Archibald	850
13	11	A	Montrose	W	2-1	0-0	1	Hutcheon 2	802
14	18	H	Stenhousemuir	L	0-2	0-2	1		815
15	25	A	Queen of the S	W	2-0	1-0	1	Scott, Dwarika	1081
16	Dec 2	H	Berwick R	W	1-0	1-0	1	Donaghy	903
17	16	A	Clyde	W	1-0	0-0	1	Allan	982
18	Jan 9	A	Forfar Ath	W	2-0	0-0	—	Archibald, Gartshore	621
19	17	H	Stirling A	L	0-3	0-2	—		1529
20	20	A	Berwick R	W	2-1	1-0	1	Beaton, Allan	382
21	23	A	Stenhousemuir	D	2-2	1-1	—	Dwarika, Gibb	594
22	31	H	Queen of the S	L	1-2	1-1	—	Dwarika	732
23	Feb 3	H	Clyde	D	1-1	1-1	2	Archibald	774
24	10	A	Stranraer	D	0-0	0-0	2		531
25	21	H	Montrose	W	7-0	3-0	—	Allan, Scott 3, Chalmers, Donaghy, Gartshore	425
26	24	H	Ayr U	D	1-1	0-1	2	Archibald	834
27	Mar 2	A	Stirling A	D	2-2	0-1	2	McStay, Archibald	1166
28	9	A	Queen of the S	L	0-1	0-0	2		1476
29	16	H	Stenhousemuir	W	3-1	1-0	2	Dwarika 2, Scott	621
30	23	H	Stranraer	W	2-1	2-0	2	Dwarika 2	738
31	30	A	Montrose	W	1-0	1-0	2	Scott	696
32	Apr 6	H	Berwick R	D	0-0	0-0	2		1603
33	13	A	Clyde	D	2-2	0-1	2	Chalmers 2	1145
34	20	H	Forfar Ath	W	1-0	0-0	2	Chalmers	1462
35	27	A	Ayr U	L	0-1	0-1	2		1304
36	May 4	H	Stirling A	L	0-1	0-0	2		1185

Final League Position: 2

Honours
League Champions: Division II 1947-48; *Runners-up:* Division II 1929-30, 1970-71. Second Division 1983-84., 1995-96
Scottish Cup Winners: 1938; *Runners-up:* 1927, 1950.
League Cup Winners: 1947-48, 1949-50, 1953-54.
Club colours: Shirt: Amber with black collar and cuffs. Shorts: Amber with black flashes. Stockings: Amber with 3 black stripes on top.

Goalscorers: *League (50):* Scott 11, Dwarika 8, Archibald 6, Allan 4, Beaton 4 (1 pen), Chalmers 4, Hutcheon 4, Donaghy 3, Cusick 2, Gartshore 2, Gibb 1, McStay 1. *Scottish Cup (4):* Allan 1, Dwarika 1, Gibb 1, Scott 1. *Coca-Cola Cup (5):* Scott 3, Allan 1, Hutcheon 1. *League Challenge Cup (2):* Scott 2.

Hamilton L 35	McStay J 34	Hamill A 12+3	Cusick J 33	Beaton D 32+1	Balmain K 1	Hildersley R 5	Andrew B 10+6	Scott R 32+2	Allan G 36	Hope D 18+7	Hutcheon S 7+18	Gartshore P 6+4	Donaghy M 32	Archibald S 29+2	Struthers D —+2	Hunter P —+3	Gibb R 24	Dwarika A 12+10	Robertson D 1	Dixon A 17+3	Sneddon A —+3	Demmin C 3	Chalmers P 6+2	Brodie J 6	Ferguson P 5+1	Winiarski S —+1	Match No.
1	2	3	4	5	6	7	8	9¹	10	11	12																1
1	2		5				7	10	9	4	11	14	3¹	6²			8³	12		13							2
1	2		4	5			7	12	9	10	11¹	13	3³	6			8²	14									3
1	2¹		4	5			7	12	9²	10	11	14	3	6			8³	13									4
1	2		4	5			7	9	10	11			3¹	6			8	12									5
1	2		4	5				9	10	11	13	7¹	6	8²			3	12									6
1	2		4	5				9	10	11	13	7¹	6	8²			3	12									7
1	2		4	5				9	10	11	13	7¹	6	8²			3	12									8
1	2		4	5				9	10	11	13	7¹	6	8²			3	12									9
	2		4	5				9	10	11	12	7¹	6	8			3		1								10
1	2		4	5			7	9	10¹	11			6	8			3	12									11
1	2		4	5			7²	9	10	11	13		6	8			3	12									12
1	2		4	5			7	9²	10		13		6	8¹			3	12									13
1	2		4	5				9	10		11²	7¹	6	8			3	12		13							14
1	2	11	4	5				9	10			7¹	6	8²			3	12		13							15
1	2		4	5				9	10		11²	7¹	6	8			3	13		12							16
1	2	11	7	5				9¹	10			14	6	8			3	12³		4²	13						17
1	2	11	7	5				9	10				6	8¹			3	12		4							18
1	2		7	5				9	10	11			6	8			3¹	12		4							19
1	2	11³	4²	5				9	10			14	6	8			3	12		13			7¹				20
1	2	11²	4¹	5				9	10		13		6	8			3	12					7				21
1	2	11²	7	5				9¹	10		13	14	6	8			3³	12		4							22
1	2		7	5				9	10				6	8			3	12		4			11¹				23
1	2		4	5				9¹	10	11		7	6	8²			3	12		13							24
1	2	13		5				9	10			7	6²	8³			3	12		4	14		11¹				25
1	2	12		5				9	10¹			7	6	8			3			4			11				26
1	2²		7	5				9	10		13		6	8			3	12		4			11¹				27
1	2	6		5				9¹	10	11	12	7		8			3			4							28
1	2	11	6	5				9	10			7		8			3			4							29
1	6¹	11	4	5				9	10			7		8²			3	12		2							30
1	4	3		5				9	10	11		7	6	8						2							31
1	2	3		5				9	10¹				6	8				7²		4			13	11	12		32
1	2	3		5				9¹	10				6	13				7²		4			12	11	8		33
1	2	3		5			12		10				6	8			13			4²			9	11	7		34
1	11³	14	4¹	5			12	9	10		13		6²	8			3			2			7				35
1	4	3		5			12		10¹		13		6²	8			11			2			9³		7	14	36

EAST STIRLINGSHIRE　　　Third Division

Year Formed: 1880. *Ground & Address:* Firs Park, Firs St, Falkirk FK2 7AY. *Telephone:* 01324 623583. *Fax:* 01324 637 862
Ground Capacity: total: 1880. seated: 200. *Size of Pitch:* 112yd × 72yd.
Chairman: William C. White. *Secretary:* Margaret Thomson.
Manager: Billy Little. *Assistant Manager/Coach:* Lenny Reid. *Physio:* Angus Williamson.
Managers since 1975: I. Ure; D. McLinden; W. P. Lamont; A. Ferguson; W. Little; D. Whiteford; D. Lawson; J. D.
Connell; A. Mackin; Dom Sullivan, Bobby McCulley. *Club Nickname(s):* The Shire. *Previous Grounds:* Burnhouse,
Randyford Park, Merchiston Park, New Kilbowie Park.
Record Attendance: 12,000 v Partick T, Scottish Cup 3rd rd; 19 Feb 1921.
Record Transfer Fee received: £35,000 for Jim Docherty to Chelsea (1978).
Record Transfer Fee paid: £6,000 for Colin McKinnon from Falkirk (March 1991).
Record Victory: 11-2 v Vale of Bannock, Scottish Cup 2nd rd; 22 Sept, 1888.
Record Defeat: 1-12 v Dundee United, Division II; 13 Apr, 1936.
Most Capped Player: Humphrey Jones, 5 (14), Wales.
Most League Appearances: 379: Gordon Simpson, 1968-80.
Most League Goals in Season (Individual): 36: Malcolm Morrison, Division II; 1938-39.
Most Goals Overall (Individual): —.

EAST STIRLINGSHIRE 1995–96 LEAGUE RECORD

Match No.	Date	Venue	Opponents	Result	H/T Score	Lg. Pos.	Goalscorers	Attendance
1	Aug 12	A	Brechin C	L	1-3	1-1	—	MacLean	326
2	26	H	Ross Co	L	1-2	1-0	—	Bellshaw (og)	478
3	Sept 2	A	Cowdenbeath	L	2-4	2-4	10	MacLean 2	203
4	9	H	Livingston	L	1-2	0-2	10	Dwyer	409
5	16	A	Queen's P	L	0-1	0-0	10		627
6	23	A	Arbroath	D	2-2	1-1	9	Neill, Geraghty	570
7	30	H	Alloa	D	2-2	0-1	10	Lee I, McBride	305
8	Oct 7	H	Caledonian Th	L	0-5	0-1	10		381
9	14	A	Albion R	W	2-1	2-0	10	Geraghty 2	334
10	21	H	Cowdenbeath	W	3-1	1-1	9	Hunter 2, Watt	284
11	28	A	Ross Co	D	1-1	0-0	9	Hunter	1646
12	Nov 4	H	Queen's P	L	1-2	0-1	10	Abercromby	407
13	11	A	Livingston	D	1-1	0-0	9	MacLean	4000
14	18	A	Alloa	W	3-1	2-0	9	Dwyer 2, Hunter	357
15	25	H	Arbroath	L	0-1	0-1	9		335
16	Dec 2	A	Caledonian Th	D	1-1	0-1	9	Lamont	1142
17	9	A	Brechin C	L	1-4	1-2	9	Lee I	253
18	19	H	Albion R	W	5-1	2-0	—	Dwyer 4, Gallagher (og)	245
19	Jan 9	A	Cowdenbeath	W	4-1	1-1	—	Dwyer 2, McBride, Lamont	154
20	13	A	Arbroath	L	1-2	0-0	8	Watt	447
21	20	H	Caledonian Th	L	1-5	0-3	8	Lee I	353
22	31	H	Alloa	W	1-0	0-0	—	Dwyer	310
23	Feb 10	A	Queen's P	D	2-2	2-0	8	McBride, Dwyer	522
24	17	H	Livingston	L	0-3	0-2	8		472
25	24	H	Ross Co	L	2-4	0-1	8	Dwyer, Neill	353
26	Mar 2	H	Brechin C	W	2-0	1-0	8	Dwyer 2	268
27	9	H	Arbroath	W	1-0	0-0	8	Sneddon	358
28	16	A	Alloa	D	2-2	0-2	8	Sneddon, Watt	309
29	20	A	Albion R	D	2-2	1-0	—	Lee I, Dwyer	199
30	23	H	Queen's P	L	1-2	0-1	8	Dwyer	364
31	30	A	Livingston	D	1-1	0-0	8	Dwyer	2084
32	Apr 6	A	Caledonian Th	W	3-0	3-0	8	McBride, Dwyer, MacLean	1071
33	13	H	Albion R	D	1-1	1-0	7	Abercromby	293
34	20	H	Cowdenbeath	D	1-1	0-0	7	McBride	294
35	27	A	Ross Co	W	3-1	2-0	7	McBride 2, Dwyer	914
36	30	H	Brechin C	W	3-0	2-0	7	Dwyer 2, McBride	305

Final League Position: 7

Honours
League Champions: Division II 1931-32; C Division 1947-48. *Runners-up:* Division II 1962-63. Second Division 1979-80. Division Three 1923-24.
Scottish Cup: —.
League Cup: —.
Club colours: Shirt: Black and white stripes. Shorts: Black and white. Stockings: Black with 3 tangerine bands on top.

Goalscorers: *League (58):* Dwyer 21, McBride 8, MacLean 5, Hunter 4, Lee I 4, Geraghty 3, Watt 3, Abercromby 2, Lamont 2, Neill 2, Sneddon 2, own goals 2. *Scottish Cup (0) Coca-Cola Cup (2):* Abercromby 2 (1 pen). *League Challenge Cup (0)*

McDougall G 28	Orr J 6+1	Lee R 34	MacLean S 18+8	Ross B 20+1	Neill A 31+2	McBride M 28+3	Hunter M 12+2	Geraghty M 11	Abercromby M 17+5	Dwyer P 31	Watt D 28+2	Millar G 3+1	Sneddon S 23	Scott C 3	McKenna T 3+1	Moffat J 8	Lee I 31+2	Lamont P 6+7	Russell G 30	Cameron D —+6	Stirling D 11+15	Cuthbert L —+2	Lawrie D 1	Farquhar A 5+3	Frater A 1+2	Docherty R 4+2	Murray N 3+2	Dodds J —+1	Match No.
1	2	3	4	5	6	7	8	9	10	11																			1
1		3			6	7		9	8¹	11	2	4	5	10	12														2
	2³	3	8		6	7²	4¹	9	14	11		13	5	10		1	12												3
	6	3	8	13		7		9		11	2	4²	5	10¹		1	12												4
	6	3	4		12	7²		9¹	14	10	2		5¹		11	1	8	13											5
	6	3	4¹	5		12		9	8²		2				11³	1	10		7	13	14								6
	6¹	3	4²	5		7	14	9		10					11³	1	8		2	13	12								7
		3		6	5	7	8	9	4	11						1	10		2¹	12									8
	3¹	8²	6			7³	9	14	11		2		5			1	10		4	13	12								9
		3		6	10	7¹	9		11		2	8	5			1		4	12										10
1		3		6²	8		7	9	13	11	2¹		5				10		4	12									11
1		3		6¹	8	12		9	11		2		5				10	13	4	7²									12
1		3	8		6	7		9	11		5						10¹	12	2	4									13
1		3	8¹		6	7		9²	11	12	5						10	13	2	4									14
1		3	8¹		6²	14	7	9	11	12	5						10	13	2³	4									15
1		3	13	12	6		7	11²	8		5						10	9⁵	2¹	14	4								16
1		3			6	13	7		9¹	11	10		5				8	12	2²		4								17
1		3	13		6	4	7	8³		11	2¹		5²				10	9	14	12									18
1		3	7		6	5	4¹	9									8	11	2	12									19
1		3	7		6	5	10		9	4²							8	11¹	2	13	12								20
1		3	13		6	7¹		11	8		5						10		2	12	4²	9							21
1		3	8		6	7		9	2		5						10	11	4	5¹	12								22
1		3	8	6¹	5	7		9	4								10	2	12	11²	13								23
1		3	12		5	11			2								10	7¹	6	4		9²	8	13					24
1		3		6	5	7¹		9	2								10	12	4	13		11²	8						25
1		3	8¹	6	5	7		9	4								10	2	12			11							26
1		3		6	7	11	12	9	2		5¹						10	4				8							27
1		3³	14	6	7	11		9¹	2		5						10	4	13		12	8²							28
1		8¹	6	3	7			9	11	2	5						10	4			12								29
1		13	6	5	4			8²	11	2	9						10	3	12		7¹								30
1		3		6	7	8		9¹	11	2	5						10	4	12										31
1		3	11		6	7		9	2		5						10	4²	8¹							12	13		32
1		3	11		6	7		9	2		5						10	4	8¹							12			33
1		3	12		6	7		9²	11	2	5						10	4	13							8¹			34
1	13	3			5	7		9	11	2							10¹	4	6		12²	R							35
1		3	13	6¹	5	7		9	11	2							10	4			12	8²							36

FALKIRK

First Division

Year Formed: 1876. *Ground & Address:* Brockville Park, Hope St, Falkirk FK1 5AX. *Telephone:* 01324 624121/632487.
Fax: 01324 612418.
Ground Capacity: total: 13,401. seated: 2661. *Size of Pitch:* 110yd × 72yd.
Chairman: G. J. Fulston. *Secretary:* A. D. Moffat. *Commercial Executive:* George Miller.
Manager: Eamonn Bannon. *Physio:* Bob McCallum. *Coach:* Willie Wilson.
Managers since 1975: J. Prentice; G. Miller; W. Little; J. Hagart; A. Totten; G. Abel; W. Lamont; D. Clarke; J. Duffy;
J. Jefferies; J. Lambie. *Club Nickname(s):* The Bairns. *Previous Grounds:* Randyford; Blinkbonny Grounds; Hope Street.
Record Attendance: 23,100 v Celtic, Scottish Cup 3rd rd; 21 Feb, 1953.
Record Transfer Fee received: £380,000 for John Hughes to Celtic (Aug 1995).
Record Transfer Fee paid: £225,000 to Chelsea for Kevin McAllister (Aug 1991).
Record Victory: 12-1 v Laurieston, Scottish Cup 2nd rd; 23 Mar, 1893.
Record Defeat: 1-11 v Airdrieonians, Division I; 28 Apr, 1951.
Most Capped Player: Alex Parker, 14 (15), Scotland.
Most League Appearances: (post-war): John Markie, 349.
Most League Goals in Season (Individual): 43: Evelyn Morrison, Division I; 1928-29.
Most Goals Overall (Individual): Dougie Moran, 86.

FALKIRK 1995–96 LEAGUE RECORD

Match No.	Date	Venue	Opponents	Result		H/T Score	Lg. Pos.	Goalscorers	Attendance
1	Aug 26	H	Aberdeen	L	2-3	0-2	—	McLaughlin, Kirk	6647
2	Sept 9	A	Hearts	L	1-4	1-2	8	McDonald	11,531
3	16	H	Rangers	L	0-2	0-1	9		11,480
4	23	H	Motherwell	D	0-0	0-0	9		4246
5	30	A	Partick Th	D	1-1	0-0	9	Johnston M	4078
6	Oct 4	H	Celtic	L	0-1	0-0	—		9053
7	7	A	Hibernian	L	1-2	0-1	10	MacKenzie	8356
8	14	H	Kilmarnock	L	0-2	0-2	10		4878
9	21	A	Raith R	W	1-0	1-0	10	McGrillen	4715
10	28	H	Hearts	W	2-0	1-0	8	Weir, Johnston M	6858
11	Nov 4	A	Rangers	L	0-2	0-2	10		42,059
12	8	A	Aberdeen	L	1-3	1-2	—	McGrillen	11,214
13	11	H	Hibernian	W	2-0	0-0	9	Johnston M 2	6046
14	18	H	Partick Th	L	0-1	0-0	10		4127
15	25	A	Motherwell	D	1-1	0-0	10	Clark (pen)	5201
16	Dec 2	H	Raith R	W	2-1	0-0	8	McGrillen 2	4442
17	9	A	Kilmarnock	L	0-4	0-2	9		6017
18	16	A	Celtic	L	0-1	0-1	9		34,466
19	Jan 6	H	Rangers	L	0-4	0-3	10		10,348
20	9	A	Partick Th	W	3-0	2-0	—	Craig, McGowan, Weir	2708
21	13	A	Hearts	L	1-2	0-1	9	Kirk	11,560
22	16	A	Aberdeen	D	1-1	1-0	—	Clark	4003
23	20	A	Raith R	L	0-1	0-0	9		4123
24	23	H	Motherwell	L	0-1	0-1	—		3845
25	Feb 3	A	Kilmarnock	W	4-2	2-2	9	Finnigan, Craig, Iorfa, Kirk	4143
26	10	H	Celtic	D	0-0	0-0	8		10,366
27	24	A	Hibernian	L	1-2	0-0	9	Kirk	7609
28	Mar 2	A	Motherwell	L	0-1	0-1	9		5037
29	16	H	Partick Th	L	1-2	0-1	10	Weir	3711
30	23	A	Rangers	L	2-3	0-2	10	Johnston M, James	46,361
31	30	H	Hearts	L	0-2	0-1	10		5164
32	Apr 6	H	Raith R	L	2-3	2-1	10	James, Craig	3766
33	13	A	Kilmarnock	L	0-1	0-0	10		6505
34	20	A	Celtic	L	0-4	0-2	10		35,692
35	27	H	Hibernian	D	1-1	0-0	10	McGrillen	2813
36	May 4	A	Aberdeen	L	1-2	1-1	10	McGrillen	11,831

Final League Position: 10

Honours
League Champions: Division II 1935-36, 1969-70, 1974-75. First Division 1990-91, 1993-94. Second Division 1979-80;
Runners-up: Division I 1907-08, 1909-10. First Division 1985-86, 1988-89. Division II 1904-05, 1951-52, 1960-61.
Scottish Cup Winners: 1913, 1957. *League Cup Runners-up:* 1947-48. *B&Q Cup Winners:* 1993-94.
Club colours: Shirt: Dark blue with white flashings. Shorts: White. Stockings: Red.

Goalscorers: *League (31):* McGrillen 6, Johnston M 5, Kirk 4, Craig 3, Weir 3, Clark 2 (1 pen), James 2, Finnigan 1, Iorfa 1, McDonald 1, McGowan 1, Mackenzie 1, McLaughlin 1. *Scottish Cup (0) Coca-Cola Cup (3):* Johnston M 2, Henderson 1.

Parks A 28	Clark J 14+3	Napier C 3+1	Oliver N 3	McLaughlin J 15+1	Rice B 1+4	McGowan J 27+2	Kirk S 16+4	McDonald C 4+5	Johnston M 31	Elliot D 31+1	McGraw M 2+7	Inglis N 1	Weir D 34	MacKenzie S 27+3	Ferguson D 26	Henderson N —+9	Fulton S 4+1	McGrillen P 24+6	Lamont W 7	Hagen D 21+4	Munro S 13	Johnston F 3+3	Wright G 1+1	James K 10+3	Gray A 16	Craig A 14	Finnigan A 8+1	Iorfa D 3+1	Graham A 8	Seaton A —+1	Whiteside G —+2	Lawrie A 1	Hamilton G —+1	Abbott G —+1	Match No.
1	2	3	4	5	6^1	7	8	9	10	11	12																								1
	13	3^1		5		2	7	9^2	10	11			1	4	6	8	12																		2
1	2	3^1		5			7	9^2	10	11				4	6	8	13	12																	3
1	2	14		12		3	7^3		10	11	13		5	4	8			6^1		9^2															4
1^6	2			12		3	7	15	10	11			5	4	8			6		9^1															5
	2^1			12	13	3	7	9^3	10	11			5	4	8			6^2		14	1														6
	3			5			7^2	12	10	11			2	4	8	13		6		9^1	1														7
	3^3			5	12	4	7^2		10	11			2		6	8^1	13			14	1	9													8
				5		4	7^1	13	10	11			2		6			9^2		1	8	3	12												9
				5		4			10	11			2		6	8	12	9^1		1	7	3													10
	12			5		4			10	11			2		6^2	8^1	13	9		1	7	3													11
1	4			5		8		12	10				2		6			9^1		11	3	7													12
1				5		4			10	11			2		6			9		7	3	8													13
1	14			5		4	13		10	11			2		6	12		9^1		7	3^3	8^2													14
1	4			5		8			10	11			2		6	12		9^1		7	3														15
1	4			5		12			10	11^3			2		6	8		9		7	3														16
1	4			5		6			10	11			2	3^1	8	12		9		7															17
1	4^1			5					10	11	13		2		8			9^2		7	3			6	12										18
1	4			5					10	12			2		8			9^1		11	3			6	7										19
1	4					3	13		10^2	11^3			2		6	8		12		7^1				14	5	9									20
1	4					5	12	3	10^1				2		6	8				7					11	9									21
1	4							10^1		11			2		8			9			12	3	13		5	6^2	7								22
1		5						10^1		11			2		8			9			12	3			6	4	7								23
1		5					13		10	11^1			2		8			9			12	3			6	4	7^2								24
1						3	7		10	13			2	12	8						11				5	6^1	4	9^2							25
1						3	7		10				2	13	8^2			12			11				5	6	4	9^1							26
1						3	7	12		11			4		6	8		10							5		2	9^1							27
1						3				10			4		6	8		11^1		7					5		2	12	9						28
1						3				10	6^1		2		4	8		11		7			12		5				9						29
1						13				10	3	14	2	12	8			11^2							5	4	6^3	7^1	9						30
	6^1									10	3		2	7	8			12	1		11				5	4			9						31
1						4				10	3	14	2	7	8^2			11^1			12				5	6	13	9^3							32
1										10	3	13	4	7				8^2		11^1	14				5	6	2	9^2	12						33
1						3				10	11	7^2	2^1		6						13		12		5	4	8	9							34
1						3				10	11		4		7^1			9							5	6	8	2			12				35
1						3					11^3				7			10							5	6	8	2^7		9^1	12	4	13	14	36

FORFAR ATHLETIC

Third Division

Year Formed: 1885. *Ground & Address:* Station Park, Carseview Road, Forfar. *Telephone:* 01307 463576/462259.
Fax: 01307 466956.
Ground Capacity: total: 8732. seated: 739. *Size of Pitch:* 115yd × 69yd.
Chairman: George Enston. *Secretary:* David McGregor.
Manager: Tommy Campbell. *Assistant Manager:* Brian McLaughlin. *Physio:* Jim Peacock. *Coaches:* Gordon Arthur,
Tom McCallum.
Managers since 1975: Jerry Kerr; Archie Knox; Alex Rae; Doug Houston; Henry Hall; Bobby Glennie; Paul Hegarty.
Club Nickname(s): Loons. *Previous Grounds:* None.
Record Attendance: 10,780 v Rangers, Scottish Cup 2nd rd; 2 Feb, 1970.
Record Transfer Fee received: £57,000 for Craig Brewster to Raith R (July 1991).
Record Transfer Fee paid: £50,000 for Ian McPhee from Airdrieonians (1991).
Record Victory: 14-1 v Lindertis, Scottish Cup 1st rd; 1 Sept 1988.
Record Defeat: 2-12 v King's Park, Division II; 2 Jan, 1930.
Most Capped Player: —.
Most League Appearances: 376: Alex Brash, 1974-86.

FORFAR ATHLETIC 1995–96 LEAGUE RECORD

Match No.	Date	Venue	Opponents	Result		H/T Score	Lg. Pos.	Goalscorers	Atten- dance
1	Aug 12	H	East Fife	L	0-2	0-0	—		711
2	26	A	Clyde	W	2-1	2-1	6	Bingham, Craig	1163
3	Sept 2	H	Stenhousemuir	W	1-0	1-0	3	Morgan	542
4	9	A	Ayr U	W	3-1	1-1	2	Bingham, Hannigan 2	1152
5	16	H	Queen of the S	W	2-1	0-0	2	Bingham, Mann	589
6	23	A	Berwick R	L	0-1	0-1	3		450
7	30	H	Montrose	D	0-0	0-0	3		660
8	Oct 7	H	Stirling A	L	0-6	0-3	4		624
9	14	A	Stranraer	D	1-1	0-1	5	Higgins	635
10	21	A	East Fife	D	1-1	1-1	4	Higgins	794
11	28	H	Clyde	W	1-0	1-0	3	Higgins	645
12	Nov 4	A	Queen of the S	D	1-1	0-0	5	Morgan	1147
13	11	H	Ayr U	W	2-1	1-0	4	Higgins, Hannigan	534
14	18	A	Montrose	L	0-1	0-0	6		730
15	25	H	Berwick R	L	1-4	1-3	6	Hannigan	523
16	Dec 2	A	Stirling A	L	1-4	0-2	6	Bowes	734
17	16	H	Stranraer	D	0-0	0-0	6		430
18	Jan 9	H	East Fife	L	0-2	0-0	—		621
19	16	A	Stenhousemuir	L	1-3	1-1	—	Morgan	381
20	20	H	Stirling A	L	1-4	1-3	7	Mann	611
21	23	H	Montrose	W	2-1	1-0	—	Hannigan, Bowes	589
22	30	A	Berwick R	L	0-1	0-1	—		309
23	Feb 3	A	Stranraer	L	0-1	0-0	6		476
24	13	H	Queen of the S	L	0-3	0-1	—		427
25	24	A	Clyde	L	1-3	0-2	8	Hannigan	878
26	Mar 2	H	Stenhousemuir	W	3-1	2-0	9	Higgins 3	371
27	5	A	Ayr U	D	1-1	1-1	—	Allison	1322
28	9	H	Berwick R	L	1-3	0-2	9	Morgan	440
29	16	A	Montrose	L	1-3	0-2	9	Morgan	585
30	23	A	Queen of the S	L	1-4	0-1	9	Inglis	1279
31	30	H	Ayr U	W	1-0	1-0	9	Inglis	442
32	Apr 6	A	Stirling A	L	0-1	0-0	9		788
33	13	H	Stranraer	D	2-2	1-1	9	Higgins 2	388
34	20	A	East Fife	L	0-1	0-0	9		1462
35	27	H	Clyde	W	4-2	2-2	9	Morgan, Craig, Higgins 2	472
36	May 4	A	Stenhousemuir	W	2-0	0-0	9	Higgins, Mann	431

Final League Position: 9

Most League Goals in Season (Individual): 45: Dave Kilgour, Division II; 1929-30.
Most Goals Overall (Individual): 124, John Clark.

Honours
League Champions: Second Division 1983-84. Third Division 1994-95. C Division 1948-49.
Scottish Cup: Semi-finals 1982.
League Cup: Semi-finals 1977-78.
Club colours: Shirt: Sky Blue with narrow Navy vertical stripe. Shorts: Navy. Stockings: Navy.

Goalscorers: *League (37):* Higgins 12, Hannigan 6, Morgan 6, Bingham 3, Mann 3, Bowes 2, Craig 2, Inglis 2, Allison 1. *Scottish Cup (8):* Bowes 3, Inglis 2, Morgan 2, Mann 1. *Coca-Cola Cup (1):* Loney 1. *League Challenge Cup (2):* Bingham 1, Mann 1.

Arthur G 33	Bowes M 27 + 2	Craig D 27 + 1	Mann R 25 + 1	McKillop A 22	Glennie S 24 + 1	Morgan A 34	McPhee I 19	Paterson A 2 + 6	McVicar D 23	Bingham D 5	Loney J 2 + 3	Hannigan P 21 + 12	Irvine N 16 + 3	O'Neill H 4 + 2	Higgins G 24 + 2	Allison J 22 + 4	Inglis G 18 + 5	Archibald E 9	Donegan J 3 + 4	Christie S + 2	Henderson D 5	Heddle I 6 + 2	Hamilton J 19	Strain J 1 + 2	Sexton B 5 + 2	Match No.
1	2	3	4	5	6	7[1]	8	9[2]	10	11	12	13														1
1	8	6	4	5	2	7		12	3	10		9[1]	11													2
1	8	6	4	5	2	7[1]	11	12	3	10		9[1]			13											3
1	8	6	4	5		7	11	12	3	10	13	9[1]			2[2]											4
1	8	6	4	5		7	11	9[1]	3	10	12				2											5
1	8[1]	6	4	5		7	11	13	3			9[2]			2	10	12									6
1	8	6	4	5	2[1]	7	3	13			11	9[2]			12	10										7
1	8[2]		5	4	7			13	3		11	12			6[1]	9	2	10								8
1		11	4	5	2	7	3				6	12			9		10[1]	8								9
1	2	11	4	5		7	3				6				9		10	8								10
1[9]	2	11	4	5		7	3				6	12			9		10[1]	8	15							11
1	2	11[2]	4	5	3	7					6	12			9	13	10[1]	8								12
1	2	11	4	5		7					6	10			9	3		8								13
1	2	11[1]		5	4	7					6	10	12		9	3[2]	13	8								14
1	2[1]	12	4		6	7[2]				3		10	8		9	11		5	13							15
1	2	3	4	5		7[1]	10					12	8		9	11		6[1]	13							16
1	10			5		4	7	6				12			9[1]	2	8				3	11				17
1	10	5	4		6[2]	7						13	11		9		8				3[1]	12	2			18
1	10	5[2]	4		2	7[1]				3		12	11		9	13	8					6				19
1[9]	8		4			7	6	3				9			10				15		5	11	2			20
	10		5		6	7	4		3			9			8			1				11	2			21
1	10	6	5			7[1]	4		3			9			12	8						11	2			22
1	10	6		5			4		3			9	12		7[2]	8[1]	13					11	2			23
1		4		5	13		8[1]		3			9	10			7	12	6				11	2[2]			24
	10		5			6[1]	7	4	3			9	12		8	11[2]					1	13	2			25
1				5		7						9	8	10	4	11						6	2		3	26
1[9]	6			5		7		3				9	8	10	4	11[1]			15				2		12	27
1	11			6[2]	5	7				3[1]		9	8	10	4	12							2		13	28
1	6	3	4		5	7						9	8		10	11[1]							2		12	29
1	6[2]			5	2	10						9	8	13	7	12						3[1]	4		11	30
1	10			6	5	2	7					13	8		9[2]	12	11						4		3[1]	31
1		2	6	5		7						12	8		9	10	11						4		3[1]	32
1		3	6	5		7	10					8			9	2[1]	11						4		12	33
1		3	6	5[1]	8	7	10					12			9	2	11						4			34
1[9]	12	3		5		7						11	8[1]		9	4	10		15					2	6	35
13	3	12		5		7						11	8		9	4[2]	10		1					2	6[1]	36

GREENOCK MORTON First Division

Year Formed: 1874. *Ground & Address:* Cappielow Park, Sinclair St, Greenock. *Telephone:* 01475 723571.
Ground Capacity: total: 14,267. seated: 5257. *Size of Pitch:* 110yd × 71yd.
Chairman: John Wilson. *Secretary:* Mrs Jane Rankin.
Manager: Allan McGraw. *Assistant Manager:* Peter Cormack, Sr. *Physio:* John Tierney. *Coach:* John McMaster.
Managers since 1975: Joe Gilroy; Benny Rooney; Alex Miller; Tommy McLean; Willie McLean. *Club Nickname(s):* The Ton. *Previous Grounds:* Grant Street 1874, Garvel Park 1875, Cappielow Park 1879, Ladyburn Park 1882, (Cappielow Park 1883).
Record Attendance: 23,500 v Celtic; 1922.
Record Transfer Fee received: £350,000 for Neil Orr to West Ham U.
Record Transfer Fee paid: £150,000 for Allan Mahood from Nottingham Forest.
Record Victory: 11-0 v Carfin Shamrock, Scottish Cup 1st rd; 13 Nov, 1886.
Record Defeat: 1-10 v Port Glasgow Ath, Division II; 5 May, 1894 and v St Bernards, Division II; 14 Oct, 1933.
Most Capped Player: Jimmy Cowan, 25, Scotland.
Most League Appearances: 358: David Hayes, 1969-84.
Most League Goals in Season (Individual): 58: Allan McGraw, Division II; 1963-64.
Most Goals Overall (Individual): —.

GREENOCK MORTON 1995–96 LEAGUE RECORD

Match No.	Date	Venue	Opponents	Result		H/T Score	Lg. Pos.	Goalscorers	Attendance
1	Aug 12	A	Dundee U	D	1-1	0-1	—	Mahood	6927
2	26	H	Dumbarton	L	1-2	0-2	6	Lilley	2612
3	Sept 2	A	St Johnstone	W	2-0	1-0	6	Lilley 2	3134
4	9	H	Dundee	D	2-2	0-2	5	Lilley 2	3384
5	16	A	Airdrieonians	L	2-3	1-3	7	Hawke 2	1927
6	23	H	Dunfermline Ath	W	2-0	1-0	5	McInnes, Hawke	3794
7	30	A	St Mirren	W	4-1	2-1	3	Hawke 2, Lilley, Rajamaki	5436
8	Oct 7	A	Clydebank	L	0-1	0-0	5		2343
9	14	H	Hamilton A	W	2-0	1-0	4	Mahood, Hawke	2875
10	21	H	St Johnstone	W	4-0	2-0	3	Anderson, Hawke 3	3313
11	28	A	Dumbarton	W	2-0	2-0	3	Hawke 2	2378
12	Nov 4	H	Airdrieonians	W	2-1	1-1	3	Rajamaki, Mahood	3856
13	11	A	Dundee	D	0-0	0-0	3		4060
14	18	H	St Mirren	L	0-3	0-1	4		6217
15	25	A	Dunfermline Ath	W	2-0	2-0	2	Lilley, Hawke	4857
16	Dec 2	H	Clydebank	W	3-0	0-0	2	Lilley, Rajamaki 2	3002
17	9	A	Hamilton A	W	3-2	2-0	2	Collins, Lilley, Anderson	1813
18	16	H	Dundee U	L	1-2	0-2	3	Lilley	4660
19	Jan 9	A	St Johnstone	L	1-6	0-3	—	Lindberg	3253
20	13	H	Dundee	W	1-0	1-0	3	Anderson	3163
21	20	A	Clydebank	W	1-0	1-0	3	Hawke	1685
22	23	A	Airdrieonians	W	2-0	1-0	3	Lilley, Lindberg	1605
23	31	A	St Mirren	W	1-0	0-0	—	Cormack	5312
24	Feb 24	H	Dumbarton	W	2-0	2-0	1	Lilley, Mahood	2833
25	27	A	Dundee U	L	0-4	0-3	—		6768
26	Mar 2	H	Dunfermline Ath	L	1-4	1-2	4	Rajamaki	4547
27	9	H	Hamilton A	W	4-1	1-1	3	Johnstone, Rajamaki, Cormack, Laing	2560
28	16	H	St Mirren	L	1-2	1-2	3	Rajamaki	4204
29	19	H	Dunfermline Ath	D	1-1	0-0	—	Rajamaki	3170
30	23	A	Airdrieonians	W	3-0	1-0	3	Lilley, McCahill, Rajamaki	2889
31	30	A	Dundee	D	1-1	0-1	3	Lilley	2734
32	Apr 6	H	Clydebank	D	0-0	0-0	4		3001
33	13	A	Hamilton A	W	1-0	1-0	4	Rajamaki	1519
34	20	H	St Johnstone	W	1-0	1-0	3	Johnstone	5808
35	27	A	Dumbarton	W	1-0	1-0	3	Anderson	2733
36	May 4	H	Dundee U	D	2-2	0-1	3	Johnstone, Rajamaki	12,523

Final League Position: 3

Honours
League Champions: First Division 1977-78, 1983-84, 1986-87. Division II 1949-50, 1963-64, 1966-67. Second Division 1994-95. *Runners-up:* Division 1 1916-17, Division II 1899-1900, 1928-29, 1936-37.
Scottish Cup Winners: 1922; *Runners-up:* 1948. *League Cup Runners-up:* 1963-64.
B&Q Cup: Runners-up: 1992-93.
European: *UEFA Cup (Fairs):* 1968-69.
Club colours: Shirt: Royal blue and white 4" Hoops. Shorts: White with royal blue panel down side. Stockings: Royal blue and white hoops.

Goalscorers: *League (57):* Lilley 14, Hawke 13, Rajamaki 11, Anderson 4, Mahood 4, Johnstone 3, Cormack 2, Lindberg 2, Collins 1, Laing 1, McCahill 1, McInnes 1. *Scottish Cup (3):* Cormack 1, Lilley 1, Rajamaki 1. *Coca-Cola Cup (0).* League Challenge Cup (0)

Wylie D 33	Johnstone D 27+2	Collins D 36	Anderson J 29+1	McCahill S 24	Lindberg J 26	Lilley D 35	Mahood A 31	Hawke W 34+1	McInnes D 12	Rajamaki M 34+2	Blair P 3+15	Laing D 3+23	McArthur S 17+6	McPherson C 17+7	Cormack P 23+2	Blaikie A —+3	Hunter J —+1	Boe A 3	Reid B 9	Match No.
1	2	3	4	5	6	7	8[1]	9	10	11[2]	12	13								1
1	3	2	4	5	6	7	8	9	10	11										2
1	4	2		5	6	7[3]	8	9[1]	10	11[2]	13	12	3	14						3
1	4	2	13	5	6	7[3]	8	9[1]	10	11[2]	12	14	3							4
1		2	4	5	6	7	8	9	10	11[1]	13	12	3[2]							5
1		2	4	5	6	7[2]	8	9	10	11[1]	13	12	3							6
1		2	4	5	6	7	8	9	10	11			3							7
1	12	2	4	5[1]	6	7[3]	8	9	10	11[2]	14	13	3							8
1	5	2[2]	4		6	7	8	9	10	11			3[1]	13	12					9
1	5	2	4		6	7	8	9	10[1]	11	12				3					10
1	5	2	4		6	7	8	9		11	10[1]	12			3					11
1	5	2	4		6	7	8	9	10	11					3					12
1	5	2	4		6	7	8	9	10	11[1]	12				3					13
1	5	2	4	10[1]	6	7	8	9		11		12			3					14
1	5	2	4		6	7	8	9		11[1]		12	3	10						15
1	5	2	4		6[3]	7	8[1]	9[2]		11		12	3	10		13	14			16
1	5	2	4		6	7	8	9[1]		11		12	3	10[2]		13				17
1	5	2	4		6	7	8			11		9	3	10[1]	12					18
1	5	2	4		6	7	8[3]	9		11[1]	12	13	14	10[2]	3					19
1		2	4	5	6	7	8[1]	9		11[2]		12	3	13	10					20
1		2	4	5	6	7[2]	8	9		11[1]		13	3	12	10					21
1		2	4	5	6	7[3]	8	9[2]		11[1]		13	3	12	10	14				22
1	12	2	4[1]	5	6	7		9		11[2]	8[3]	13	3	14	10					23
	5	2	4		6	7[2]	8	9[3]	12	11[1]		13	3	14	10			1		24
	5	2	4		6	7	8	9[2]	12			13	3[1]	11	10			1		25
		2	4	5	6[1]	7	8	9[2]		11		13	12	3	10			1		26
1	3	2	4	5			8	9		11			7	6	10					27
1	3[1]	2		5		7	8	12		11			9	6	10[1]				4	28
1	3	2		5		7	8	9		11	12			6	10[1]				4	29
1	3	2		5		7[2]	8	9		11[3]	14	13	12	6[1]	10				4	30
1	3	2		5		7	8	9		11	13		12	6[2]	10[1]				4	31
1	3	2		5		7[2]	8[1]	9		11	12	13		6	10				4	32
1	3	2	6	5		7		9[2]		11[1]	13	12		8	10				4	33
1	3	2	6	5		7		9		11[2]		13	12	8	10[1]				4	34
1	3	2	6	5		7		9		11				8	10				4	35
1	3	2	6[2]	5		7		9		11	12		13	8	10[1]				4	36

HAMILTON ACADEMICAL   Second Division

Year Formed: 1874. *Ground:* Cliftonhill Stadium, Main St. Coatbridge ML5 9XX. *Telephone (match days only):* 01236 606 334. *Club Address:* Douglas Park, Hamilton ML3 0DF. *Telephone:* 01698 286103. *Fax:* 01698 285422.
Ground Capacity: 1238, seated: 538. *Size of Pitch:* 110yd × 70yd.
Chairman: David Campbell. *Secretary:* Scott A. Struthers BA. *Commercial Manager:* Sandy Clark.
Manager: Iain Munro. *Physios:* Douglas Lauchlan and Michael McBride.
Managers since 1975: J. Éric Smith; Dave McParland; John Blackley; Bertie Auld; John Lambie; Jim Dempsey; John Lambie; Billy McLaren. *Club Nickname(s):* The Accies. *Previous Grounds:* Bent Farm, South Avenue, South Haugh.
Record Attendance: 28,690 v Hearts, Scottish Cup 3rd rd; 3 Mar, 1937.
Record Transfer Fee received: £380,000 for Paul Hartley to Millwall (July 1996).
Record Transfer Fee paid: £60,000 for Paul Martin from Kilmarnock (Oct 1988) and for John McQuade from Dumbarton (Aug 1993).
Record Victory: 11-1 v Chryston, Lanarkshire Cup; 28 Nov, 1885.
Record Defeat: 1-11 v Hibernian, Division I; 6 Nov, 1965.
Most Capped Player: Colin Miller, 29 (53), Canada, 1988-96.
Most League Appearances: 447: Rikki Ferguson, 1974-88.
Most League Goals in Season (Individual): 34: David Wilson, Division I; 1936-37.
Most Goals Overall (Individual): 246: David Wilson, 1928-39.

HAMILTON ACADEMICAL 1995–96 LEAGUE RECORD

Match No.	Date	Venue	Opponents	Result	H/T Score	Lg. Pos.	Goalscorers	Atten-dance
1	Aug 12	A	Dumbarton	L	0-1	0-0	—		1191
2	26	H	Clydebank	L	0-2	0-2	—		845
3	Sept 2	A	Dundee U	L	1-2	1-0	10	McQuade	5194
4	9	H	St Johnstone	L	0-3	0-2	10		803
5	16	A	Dundee	D	1-1	1-1	10	Hartley	2395
6	23	H	St Mirren	D	2-2	2-2	10	McEntegart, Hartley	1451
7	30	A	Airdrieonians	D	0-0	0-0	10		1586
8	Oct 7	H	Dunfermline Ath	L	1-3	1-2	10	Clark	1473
9	14	A	Morton	L	0-2	0-1	10		2875
10	21	H	Dundee U	L	0-1	0-0	10		1719
11	28	A	Clydebank	L	0-2	0-1	10		814
12	Nov 4	H	Dundee	L	1-2	0-1	10	McIntosh (pen)	1131
13	11	A	St Johnstone	L	0-2	0-1	10		2348
14	18	A	Airdrieonians	L	1-2	1-1	10	McStay	1169
15	25	A	St Mirren	W	3-0	1-0	10	Quitongo, Geraghty, Hartley	2546
16	Dec 2	A	Dunfermline Ath	L	0-4	0-3	10		3284
17	9	H	Morton	L	2-3	0-2	10	Clark, McStay	1813
18	16	H	Dumbarton	W	3-0	3-0	10	Hartley, McStay, Clark	762
19	26	A	Dundee U	D	1-1	0-0	—	Renicks	6109
20	Jan 6	A	Dundee	L	1-2	1-2	10	McStay	2020
21	13	H	St Johnstone	W	2-1	1-0	9	Hartley, McEntegart	1197
22	20	H	Dunfermline Ath	D	0-0	0-0	9		1556
23	24	H	St Mirren	W	3-0	1-0	—	McEntegart, Geraghty 2	1531
24	Feb 13	A	Dumbarton	W	2-1	1-0	—	Hartley 2	654
25	24	H	Clydebank	D	1-1	1-1	9	McCulloch	835
26	Mar 2	A	St Mirren	W	1-0	1-0	9	Craig	1243
27	6	A	Airdrieonians	L	0-3	0-3	—		1021
28	9	A	Morton	L	1-4	1-1	9	Quitongo	2560
29	16	A	Airdrieonians	W	4-1	1-1	9	Quitongo, Hartley 2, Sweeney (og)	909
30	23	H	Dundee	L	0-1	0-1	9		828
31	30	A	St Johnstone	L	1-4	0-1	9	Sherry	2614
32	Apr 6	A	Dunfermline Ath	W	3-1	2-1	9	McEntegart, Hartley, Quitongo	4542
33	13	H	Morton	L	0-1	0-1	9		1519
34	22	H	Dundee U	L	0-2	0-0	—		3291
35	27	A	Clydebank	W	3-1	2-1	9	Geraghty 2, Baptie	3665
36	May 4	H	Dumbarton	W	2-1	1-1	9	Hartley, Geraghty	657

Final League Position: 9

Rothmans Football Yearbook 1996–97

Honours
League Champions: First Division 1985-86, 1987-88. Division II 1903-04; *Runners-up:* Division II 1952-53, 1964-65.
Scottish Cup Runners-up: 1911, 1935. *League Cup:* Semi-finalists three times.
B&Q Cup Winners: 1991-92 and 1992-93.
Club colours: Shirt: Red and white hoops. Shorts: White. Stockings: White.

Goalscorers: *League (40):* Hartley 11, Geraghty 6, McEntegart 4, McStay 4, Quitongo 4, Clark 3, Baptie 1, Craig 1, McCulloch 1, McIntosh 1 (pen), McQuade 1, Renicks 1, Sherry 1, own goal 1. *Scottish Cup (0) Coca-Cola Cup (0) League Challenge Cup (2):* Clark 2.

Cormack D 10+1	Renicks S 29+1	McInulty S 17+2	Thomson S 19+2	Paterson C 9	McIntosh C 23	Hartley P 29+2	McEntegart S 28+1	Chalmers P 1	McQuade J 9+4	McCulloch S 4+6	Clark G 14+3	Lorimer D 5+10	McKenzie P 11+12	Sherry J 24+1	Baptie C 31	McCormick S 5+4	McParland I —+1	McCarrison D —+3	Ferguson A 26	Hillcoat C 31	McStay R 16+4	McCloy S 1+4	Geraghty M 17+3	Quitongo J 18+4	Craig D 17	Diver D 1+3	Tighe M 1	Macfarlane D —+1	Match No.
1	2	3	4	5	6	7	8	9[1]	10	11[2]	12	13																	1
1		3		5	6		4		10[3]	13	7	14	2[2]	8	9	11[1]	12												2
1	12			5	6	13	4		10	11[1]	7[1]	8[2]	3	2	9				14										3
	3		9[2]	5	6	12	4		10		7	11[1]	2	8					13	1									4
	3		8[1]	5	6	7[2]	4		10				11		9				13	1	2	12							5
	3		8[2]	5	6	7	4		13		10				9	11[1]				1	2	12							6
	3		8	5[2]	6	7	4		10		13	11[1]			9					1	2	12							7
	3		8[3]	5[1]	6	7	4[2]		13		10	14	11		9					1	2	12							8
	3		8		6	7			10[2]		12	4	11		5					1	2	13	9[1]						9
	3	11	8		6[1]	12			10			4	7		5					1	2	13	9[2]						10
	3		8		6	11			10[2]		12	4	7		5					1	2	13	9[1]						11
	3		8[2]	5[1]	6	7			13			14	11		9[3]	12				1	2	4	10						12
	3	11[3]	8[1]		6	7			13			14	12	10	5					1	2	4[2]	9						13
	3				6	7[1]	8		13		10	11[3]	14		5					1	2	4[2]	9	12					14
	3				6	11[2]	8		10		12		13		5					1	2	4	9	7[1]					15
	3	13			6	11	8		10		12				5	9[2]				1	2	4[1]		7					16
	3	11			6	9			10[2]		12	4			5[1]	13				1	2	8		7					17
	3				6	11	8		10						5	9				1	2	4		7					18
15	3	12			6		8[1]		10		7				5	13				1	2	4	9	11[2]					19
1	3	11					8		10[1]		7				5						2	4	9	12	6				20
1	3	13					8		10[3]		12	14	7[2]		5						2	4[1]	9	11	6				21
1	3	11	4				8		10				13		5						2		9[1]	7[2]	6	12			22
1	3	11	4				8[3]		10[2]				13	14	5						2		9	7[1]	6	12			23
2	3		4	5		7	8						11[2]		12				13	1		10			6	9[1]			24
	3	10				7	8					4	11[1]		5	9[2]				1	2	13		12	6				25
	3	11					8		10		12				5					1	2	4	9[1]	7	6				26
	3[1]	11	13				8[2]		10[3]		12	14			5					1	2	4	9	7	6				27
	3					7	8		10		12				5					1	2	4[1]	9	11	6				28
	3		4			11	8		10						5					1	2	12	9[1]	7	6				29
	3		9	4		11	8		10[1]						5					1	2	12		7	6				30
1	3	10	4			11	8				12				5						2		9[1]	7	6				31
1	3			5		11			10						8						2	4		7	6				32
1	3	9[1]		5		11			10		14				8[2]						2	4[3]	13	7	6				33
	3			5		11	8		10[2]						4	9				1	2		13	12	6	7[1]			34
	3			5[1]		11	8				12			4		9				1	2		10	7	6				35
	3			5		11			12				4		9[1]					1	2	8	10[2]	7	6			13	36

HEART OF MIDLOTHIAN   Premier Division

Year Formed: 1874. *Ground & Address:* Tynecastle Park, Gorgie Rd, Edinburgh EH11 2NL. *Telephone:* 0131 337 6132.
Fax: 0131 346 0699.
Ground Capacity: 16,613. *Size of Pitch:* 108yd × 73yd.
Chairman: Christopher P.Robinson. *Secretary:* L. W. Porteous. *Commercial Manager:* Tommy Dickson.
Manager: Jim Jefferies. *Assistant Manager:* Billy Brown.
Physio: Alan Rae. *Coach:* Paul Hegarty.
Managers since 1975: J. Hagart; W. Ormond; R. Moncur; T. Ford; A. MacDonald; A. MacDonald & W. Jardine; A.
MacDonald; J. Jordan, S. Clark, T. McLean.
Club Nickname(s): Hearts. *Previous Grounds:* The Meadows 1874, Powderhall 1878, Old Tynecastle 1881, (Tynecastle
Park, 1886).
Record Attendance: 53,396 v Rangers, Scottish Cup 3rd rd; 13 Feb, 1932.
Record Transfer Fee received: for Alan McLaren from Rangers (October 1994).
Record of Transfer paid: £750,000 for Derek Ferguson to Rangers (July 1990).
Record Victory: 21-0 v Anchor, EFA Cup 30th October 1880.
Record Defeat: 1-8 v Vale of Leven, Scottish Cup, 1888.
Most Capped Player: Bobby Walker, 29, Scotland.
Most League Appearances: 488: Gary Mackay, 1980-96.
Most League Goals in Season (Individual): 44: Barney Battles.
Most Goals Overall (Individual): 206: Jimmy Wardhaugh, 1946-59.

HEART OF MIDLOTHIAN 1995–96 LEAGUE RECORD

Match No.	Date	Venue	Opponents		Result	H/T Score	Lg. Pos.	Goalscorers	Attendance
1	Aug 26	H	Motherwell	D	1-1	0-0	—	Hagan	10,971
2	Sept 9	H	Falkirk	W	4-1	2-1	2	Lawrence 2, Colquhoun, Robertson (pen)	11,531
3	16	A	Partick Th	L	0-2	0-1	5		5396
4	23	H	Celtic	L	0-4	0-2	8		13,696
5	Oct 1	A	Hibernian	D	2-2	1-0	—	McPherson, Robertson	12,374
6	4	H	Aberdeen	L	1-2	1-1	—	Robertson	10,927
7	7	A	Kilmarnock	L	1-3	1-2	8	Lawrence	6721
8	14	H	Raith R	W	4-2	2-0	7	Millar J, Lawrence 2, Robertson	10,133
9	21	A	Rangers	L	1-4	0-3	8	Millar J	45,155
10	28	A	Falkirk	L	0-2	0-1	10		6858
11	Nov 4	H	Partick Th	W	3-0	1-0	7	McWilliams (og), Millar J, Eskilson	10,094
12	7	A	Motherwell	D	0-0	0-0	—		5595
13	11	H	Kilmarnock	W	2-1	0-0	5	Locke, Robertson	10,442
14	19	H	Hibernian	W	2-1	1-0	—	Millar J, Johnston (pen)	12,074
15	25	A	Celtic	L	1-3	0-1	6	Bruno	34,032
16	Dec 2	H	Rangers	L	0-2	0-0	6		15,105
17	9	A	Raith R	D	1-1	0-1	6	Robertson	6349
18	16	A	Aberdeen	W	2-1	0-1	6	Johnston, Colquhoun	12,308
19	Jan 1	A	Hibernian	L	1-2	1-2	—	Pointon	14,872
20	6	A	Partick Th	W	1-0	0-0	6	McManus	4618
21	10	H	Motherwell	W	4-0	2-0	6	Fulton, Colquhoun, Johnston 2	9288
22	13	H	Falkirk	W	2-1	1-0	3	Robertson, Fulton	11,560
23	17	H	Celtic	L	1-2	1-0	—	Robertson	15,871
24	20	A	Rangers	W	3-0	1-0	3	Johnston 3	45,096
25	Feb 3	H	Raith R	W	2-0	1-0	3	Robertson, Locke	10,183
26	10	H	Aberdeen	L	1-3	1-2	4	Robertson	14,314
27	24	A	Kilmarnock	W	2-0	2-0	4	Colquhoun, Robertson	8022
28	Mar 2	A	Celtic	L	0-4	0-3	4		37,034
29	16	H	Hibernian	D	1-1	0-0	4	Mackay	14,923
30	23	H	Partick Th	L	2-5	1-2	4	Johnston, Eskilson	9610
31	30	A	Falkirk	W	2-0	1-0	4	Ritchie, Locke	5164
32	Apr 10	H	Rangers	W	2-0	1-0	—	Pointon, Johnston	15,350
33	13	A	Raith R	W	3-1	1-0	4	Cameron, Pointon, Mackay	4956
34	20	A	Aberdeen	D	1-1	0-0	4	Locke	11,303
35	27	H	Kilmarnock	W	1-0	1-0	3	McManus	11,329
36	May 4	A	Motherwell	D	1-1	1-0	4	Cameron	8301

Final League Position: 4

Honours
League Champions: Division I 1894-95, 1896-97, 1957-58, 1959-60. First Division 1979-80; *Runners-up:* Division I 1893-94, 1898-99, 1903-04, 1905-06, 1914-15, 1937-38, 1953-54, 1956-57, 1958-59, 1964-65. Premier Division 1985-86, 1987-88, 1991-92. First Division 1977-78, 1982-83.
Scottish Cup Winners: 1891, 1896, 1901, 1906, 1956; *Runners-up:* 1903, 1907, 1968, 1976, 1986, 1996.
League Cup Winners: 1954-55, 1958-59, 1959-60, 1962-63; *Runners-up:* 1961-62.

European: *European Cup* 4 matches (1958-59, 1960-61). *Cup Winners Cup:* 4 matches (1976-77). *UEFA Cup:* 34 matches (*Fairs Cup:* 1961-62, 1963-64, 1965-66. *UEFA Cup:* 1984-85, 1986-87, 1988-89, 1990-91, 1992-93, 1993-94).
Club colours: Shirt: Maroon. Shorts: White. Stockings: Maroon with white tops.

Goalscorers: *League (55):* Robertson 11 (1 pen), Johnston 9 (1 pen), Lawrence 5, Colquhoun 4, Locke 4, Millar J 4, Pointon 3, Cameron 2, Eskilsson 2, Fulton 2, Mackay 2, McManus 2, Bruno 1, Hagen 1, McPherson 1, Ritchie 1, own goal 1. *Scottish Cup (8):* Ritchie 2, Berry 1, Colquhoun 1, Johnston 1, Lawrence 1, McPherson 1, Robertson 1. *Coca-Cola Cup (9):* McPherson 3, Colquhoun 1, Hagen 1, Hamilton 1, Lawrence 1, Leitch 1, Robertson 1 (pen).

Smith H 3	Locke G 29	Wishart F 1	Levein C 1	McPherson D 22+4	Hamilton B 8+4	Colquhoun J 20+11	Mackay G 21+5	Hagen D 5+2	Johnston A 30+3	Lawrence A 17+9	Berry N 16+3	Leitch S 4+2	Winnie D 6	Robertson J 28+5	Jamieson W 2+3	Nelson C 4	Ritchie P 28	Miller C 2+1	Wright G 2	Millar J 16+4	O'Connor G 3	Pointon N 21+1	Fulton S 26	Roussel G 25	Smith P 4+5	Bruno P 22	Eskilson H 9+2	McManus A 16+1	Callaghan S —+1	Thomas K —+3	Cameron C 4	Hogarth M 1	Naysmith G —+1	Match No.
1	2	3[3]	4	5	6	7	8	9	10	11[2]	12	13																						1
1	2[2]			5	6	7			11[1]	10	8	4		12		3	9	13																2
1	2			5	6	7[1]	13	12	10	8	4			11[2]		3	9																	3
?				5	6[1]	7			11	10	12			8		4	9		1		3													4
	2[1]			5	6	13	7	11	8		12			9			3		1	4[2]	10													5
	2			5	6	12		11	8[1]		7			3			9		1	4	2	10												6
	2			5	12	7	4[1]	13	8		2	11[2]	6	9		3				10	1													7
	2			5	6	7[1]	12		8[2]	4				9		13	11	1		3	10													8
	2			5	6[1]	7			8	4				9	12		11	1		3	10													9
	2			5[1]		7	13		8	12			6	9	4		11			3[1]	10	1												10
	2				7	8[1]	5		9	13				3			11			10[2]	1	4	6	12										11
	2				7	5			9	3				11			10			1	4	6	8											12
	2				7	12	5		9[1]	3				11			10			1	4	6	8											13
				12	4	7			5	9[1]				3			11			10	1		6	8										14
	2			12	4[2]	7	9[1]	5						3			11			10	1	13	6	8										15
	2			13	12	4[1]	7	5		9				3			11			10[2]	1		6	8										16
	2			12[3]	14	4	7	5		9[2]				3			11			13	10[1]	1	6	8										17
				12	13	4	7		9					3			11			5	10[1]	1	6	8[2]	2									18
				13		4[1]	7	14	9					3			11			5[3]	10	1	12	6	8[2]	2								19
	2			9	4	7	8[1]	12						3			10			11	1		6	5										20
	2			12	8[3]	4[2]	7	14	9					3			11			10	1	13	6[1]	5										21
	2			13	8[1]	4	7	12	9					3			11[2]			10	1		6	5										22
	2			13	8	4	7	12	9[1]					3			11			10	1		6	5[2]										23
	2			4	8[2]	12	7	9	13					3			11			10	1		6[1]	5										24
	2			4	8	10	7	12	9[1]					3			11			1		13	6[2]	5										25
	2			4	8	10	7		9					3			12			11	1		6	5[1]										26
	2			4	7	6[2]	12	8[3]	9[1]					3			11			10	1	13	5	14										27
	2			4	9	6	7	8[2]	12		1			3			13			11	10		5[1]											28
	2			4	8	14	7	13	9					3			12			11[1]	10	1	6[3]	5[2]										29
				4	8	5	7	9[1]	13					3			11[2]			10	1	2[3]	6	12	14									30
	2			12	9[2]	8	7		4					3			11			10	1		6[1]	5	13									31
				5	14	4[1]	7	12	9[2]					3			11[3]			10	1		6	2	13	8								32
				5		4	7		9					3			11			10	1		6	2		8								33
	2			5	12	13	7		6					9			3[1]			11	10	1	4			8[2]								34
	2			5	8[3]	12	7[2]	14	6					9[1]			3			11	10	1	4			13								35
	2			5	14		7[1]	9[3]	6					12			3			11[2]	10		4			8	1	13						36

HIBERNIAN
Premier Division

Year Formed: 1875. *Ground & Address:* Easter Road Stadium, Albion Rd, Edinburgh EH7 5QG. *Telephone:* 0131 661 2159. *Fax:* 0131 659 6488.
Ground Capacity: total: 16,218. *Size of Pitch:* 112yd × 74yd.
Chairman: Douglas Cromb. *Secretary:* Cecil F. Graham, FIFA, MInst CM. *Commercial Manager:* Ian Erskine.
Manager: Alex Miller. *Assistant Manager and Coach:* John Scott.
Physio: Stewart Collie. *Coach Assistant:* Martin Ferguson.
Managers since 1975: Eddie Turnbull; Willie Ormond; Bertie Auld; Pat Stanton; John Blackley. *Club Nickname(s):*
Hibees. *Previous Grounds:* Meadows 1875-78, Powderhall 1878-79, Mayfield 1879-80, First Easter Road 1880-92, Second Easter Road 1892-.
Record Attendance: 65,860 v Hearts, Division I; 2 Jan, 1950.
Record Transfer Fee received: £1,000,000 for Andy Goram to Rangers (June 1991).
Record Transfer Fee paid: £420,000 for Keith Wright from Dundee.
Record Victory: 22-1 v 42nd Highlanders; 3 Sept, 1881.
Record Defeat: 0-10 v Rangers; 24 Dec, 1898.
Most Capped Player: Lawrie Reilly, 38, Scotland.
Most League Appearances: 446: Arthur Duncan.
Most League Goals in Season (Individual): 42: Joe Baker.
Most Goals Overall (Individual): 364: Gordon Smith.

HIBERNIAN 1995–96 LEAGUE RECORD

Match No.	Date	Venue	Opponents		Result	H/T Score	Lg. Pos.	Goalscorers	Atten- dance
1	Aug 26	A	Partick Th	D	1-1	0-0	—	O'Neill	5327
2	Sept 9	A	Kilmarnock	W	3-0	3-0	3	Wright 2, Evans	7014
3	16	H	Aberdeen	D	1-1	0-0	3	Jackson D	11,161
4	23	H	Rangers	W	1-0	0-0	3	Jackson D (pen)	44,221
5	Oct 1	H	Hearts	D	2-2	0-1	—	Donald, McGinlay	12,374
6	4	A	Raith R	L	0-3	0-1	—		6051
7	7	H	Falkirk	W	2-1	1-0	4	Jackson D, McAllister	8356
8	14	A	Celtic	D	2-2	1-1	4	Harper, Jackson D (pen)	31,738
9	21	H	Motherwell	W	4-2	3-0	4	Jackson D 2 (1 pen), Wright, O'Neill	9803
10	28	H	Kilmarnock	W	2-0	1-0	3	O'Neill, Wright	9888
11	Nov 4	A	Aberdeen	W	2-1	1-0	3	Wright, O'Neill	14,774
12	11	A	Falkirk	L	0-2	0-0	3		6046
13	19	A	Hearts	L	1-2	0-1	—	Jackson C	12,074
14	22	H	Partick Th	W	3-0	1-0	—	Jackson D, Weir, McAllister	6783
15	25	H	Rangers	L	1-4	1-2	3	Jackson C	13,558
16	Dec 2	A	Motherwell	W	2-0	0-0	3	Wright 2	5362
17	9	H	Celtic	L	0-4	0-2	3		13,626
18	16	H	Raith R	L	1-2	1-0	3	McGinlay	8507
19	30	A	Rangers	L	0-7	0-2	3		44,692
20	Jan 1	H	Hearts	W	2-1	2-1	—	O'Neill, Harper	14,872
21	8	H	Aberdeen	L	1-2	0-2	—	Harper	8191
22	13	A	Kilmarnock	L	2-3	2-0	4	O'Neill, Wright	6686
23	16	A	Partick Th	D	0-0	0-0	—		2811
24	20	H	Motherwell	D	0-0	0-0	8		7658
25	Feb 3	A	Celtic	L	1-2	1-0	5	Jackson D	36,976
26	10	A	Raith R	L	0-1	0-1	5		4832
27	24	H	Falkirk	W	2-1	0-0	5	Evans, Wright	7609
28	Mar 3	H	Rangers	L	0-2	0-1	—		11,923
29	16	A	Hearts	D	1-1	0-0	5	Dow	14,923
30	23	A	Aberdeen	L	1-2	1-0	5	McAllister	10,924
31	30	H	Kilmarnock	D	1-1	1-0	5	McAllister	8001
32	Apr 6	A	Motherwell	L	0-3	0-2	7		5964
33	14	H	Celtic	L	1-2	0-0	—	McGinlay	10,742
34	20	H	Raith R	D	1-1	0-0	7	McGinlay	7214
35	27	A	Falkirk	D	1-1	0-0	7	McGinlay	2813
36	May 4	H	Partick Th	W	1-0	0-0	5	Jackson D	6885

Final League Position: 5

Honours
League Champions: Division I 1902-03, 1947-48, 1950-51, 1951-52. First Division 1980-81. Division II 1893-94, 1894-95, 1932-33; *Runners-up:* Division I 1896-97, 1946-47, 1949-50, 1952-53, 1973-74, 1974-75.
Scottish Cup Winners: 1887, 1902; *Runners-up:* 1896, 1914, 1923, 1924, 1947, 1958, 1972, 1979.
League Cup Winners: 1972-73, 1991-92; *Runners-up:* 1950-51, 1968-69, 1974-75, 1993-94.

European: *European Cup:* 6 matches (1955-56 semi-finals). *Cup Winners Cup:* 6 matches (1972-73). *UEFA Cup:* 56 matches (*Fairs Cup:* 1960-61 semi-finals, 1961-62, 1962-63, 1965-66, 1967-68, 1968-69, 1970-71. *UEFA Cup:* 1973-74, 1974-75, 1975-76, 1976-77, 1978-79, 1992-93).
Club colours: Shirt: Green with white sleeves. Shorts: White. Stockings: Green with white trim.

Goalscorers: *League (43):* Jackson D 9 (3 pens), Wright 9, O'Neill 6, McGinlay 5, McAllister 4, Harper 3, Evans 2, Jackson C 2, Donald 1, Dow 1, Weir 1. *Scottish Cup (0) Coca-Cola Cup (3):* Jackson D 2 (1 pen), McGinlay 1.

Leighton J 36	Jackson C 19+4	Dods D 14+1	McGinlay P 30+1	Tweed S 31	Millen A 25	McAllister K 29+2	Donald G 2+11	Harper K 14+2	Jackson D 36	O'Neill M 26+2	Miller W 13	Hunter G 22	Evans G 12+11	Wright K 25+3	Weir M 5+4	Love G 10+4	Tortolano J 15+1	Miller G 1+3	Renwick M 1+1	Farrell D 7+1	McLaughlin J 9	Mitchell G 6	Dow A 8	Match No.
1	2	3	4	5	6	7	8	9	10	11														1
1	8	14	4	5	3	12			10²	11			2¹	6	7	9³	13							2
1	8		4	5	2			12	10	11			6	7¹	9	3								3
1	2		4	5	6	7		12	8¹	10	11				9	3								4
1	2		4	5			8¹	12	10	11			6	7	9	3								5
1	8		4	5		2¹	7		10	11			6	12	9	3								6
1	3	2	4	5		7¹	8		10	11			6		9	12								7
1	8²	2	4	5		7¹	14	9	10³	11			6	13	12	3								8
1	12	2	4	5²		7¹	13	8	10³	11			6	14	9	3								9
1		2	4	5		7	8		10	11			6		9	3								10
1	7	2	4	5		12		8¹	10	11			6		9	3								11
1	11²	2	4	5		7	13	8²	10				6	12	9¹	3	14							12
1	8		4	5	2	7			10¹	11			6	9	12	3								13
1	11	2	4³	5		8	7¹	13	10				6	12	9¹	3	14							14
1	8	2		5	4²	7	12		10¹	11			6	9³	13	3	14							15
1	3	2	4	5		8	7		10	11			6		9	3								16
1	3	2	4	5		8	7		10				6		9		11¹	12						17
1	8		4	5	2	7			10				6	12	9	13	3²	11¹						18
1	8		4	5	2	7	12		10				6	9	11¹	3								19
1			4	5	2	7		8¹	10	11			6	12	9	3								20
1			4	5	2	7		8	10	11			6	9		3								21
1	6		4	5	2	7		8¹	10	11				9		3		12						22
1	8		4	5¹	2	7			10	11				9	12	3	6							23
1	5		4		2	7		8	10	11				9	6	3								24
1	13		8			7			9¹	10	11	2		12						3	4	5	6²	25
1	12		8			7			10	11		2		9²	13					3	4	5	6¹	26
1			4		6	7¹			10	11		2	8²	9		12			13		5		3	27
1			4		6				10	11		2		12	9	7¹				8	5		3	28
1		6	4						10			2	12	7	9¹					8	5	3	11	29
1	12	6	4			7²			10	13		2¹		9						8	5	3	11	30
1			4					7	10	11		2	6	9						8	5	3		31
1	13		4	5		7			9¹	10	11	2		12		6				8			3²	32
1			4	5		8	7	13	10	11¹		2		9²		12	6						3	33
1	6¹		4	5		8	7	13	10	11²		2		12	9								3	34
1			4			8	7	12	10			7	6	11	9¹						5		3	35
1			4			8	7	13	10			2	6	12	9¹	11					5		3²	36

INVERNESS CALEDONIAN THISTLE
Third Division

Year Formed: 1994. *Ground & Address:* Telford Street Park, Inverness IV3 5LU. *Address for Correspondence:* 28 Greig St, Inverness IV3 5PX. *Telephone:* 01463 230274.
Ground Capacity: 5498, seated 498. *Size of Pitch:* 110 × 70yd.
President: Dugald McGilvray. *Hon. Life President:* John S.McDonald. *Secretary:* Jim Falconer. *Manager:* S.W.Paterson.
Assistant Manager: Alec Caldwell. *Physio:* Ian Manning. *Coach:* Alex Young.
Record Attendance: 4931, v Ross County, Third Division, 23 January 1996 [11,296, v Rangers, 9 March 1996; home tie at Tannadice Park, Dundee].
Record Victory: 6-1, v Albion Rovers, 21 October 1995.
Record Defeat: 0-4, v Queen's Park, Third Division, 20 August 1994 and v Montrose, Third Division, 14 February 1995.
Most League Appearances: 57, Michael Noble, 1994-96.
Most League Goals in Season: 23, Ian Stewart, 1995-96.
Club Colours: Shirts: Blue with white flashes; Shorts: White with blue flashes; Stockings: Blue.

INVERNESS CALEDONIAN THISTLE 1995–96 LEAGUE RECORD

Match No.	Date	Venue	Opponents	Result	H/T Score	Lg. Pos.	Goalscorers	Atten-dance
1	Aug 12	H	Livingston	L	0-3	0-2	—		1259
2	26	H	Brechin C	L	1-2	1-0	10	Stewart	1029
3	Sept 2	A	Albion R	D	2-2	2-1	9	Hercher 2	284
4	9	H	Queen's P	W	3-1	1-0	7	Stewart (pen), Green, Hercher	1141
5	16	A	Arbroath	L	1-2	0-1	8	Stewart	579
6	23	A	Alloa	W	5-0	2-0	6	Christie 3, Stewart 2	387
7	30	H	Ross Co	D	1-1	1-1	6	Hercher	3627
8	Oct 7	A	East Stirling	W	5-0	1-0	5	Brennan, Ross, Stewart 2, Mitchell	381
9	14	H	Cowdenbeath	W	3-2	2-1	4	Hercher, Hastings, Stewart	1378
10	21	H	Albion R	W	6-1	6-0	3	Stewart 3, Ross, Mitchell 2	1222
11	28	A	Brechin C	D	0-0	0-0	3		374
12	Nov 4	H	Arbroath	W	5-1	2-0	3	Hastings, Stewart 2, Christie 2	1525
13	11	A	Queen's P	W	3-0	2-0	2	Stewart 2, Hercher	597
14	18	A	Ross Co	L	0-2	0-1	3		4288
15	25	H	Alloa	D	1-1	0-0	4	Christie	1181
16	Dec 2	H	East Stirling	D	1-1	1-0	4	Ross	1142
17	16	A	Cowdenbeath	D	0-0	0-0	4		230
18	Jan 13	A	Alloa	W	2-0	1-0	5	Thomson, Christie	410
19	17	A	Livingston	W	2-0	0-0	—	Christie, Teasdale	2578
20	20	A	East Stirling	W	5-1	3-0	2	Scott, Stewart 3, Ross	353
21	23	H	Ross Co	D	1-1	1-0	—	Stewart	4931
22	Feb 3	A	Cowdenbeath	L	1-2	1-0	3	Christie	229
23	21	A	Arbroath	W	2-1	0-0		Stewart, Scott	703
24	24	H	Brechin C	L	0-1	0-1	5		2514
25	28	A	Albion R	W	2-0	1-0	—	Stewart (pen), Hercher	364
26	Mar 2	A	Livingston	D	2-2	0-1	3	Sinclair (og), Teasdale	2152
27	5	H	Queen's P	D	1-1	0-0	—	Hercher	1245
28	12	H	Alloa	D	0-0	0-0	—		1162
29	16	A	Ross Co	L	1-2	0-1	4	McAllister	3670
30	23	H	Arbroath	D	1-1	0-0	4	Hercher	1105
31	30	A	Queen's P	W	2-1	1-0	4	Stewart, Christie	526
32	Apr 6	H	East Stirling	L	0-3	0-3	4		1071
33	13	H	Cowdenbeath	W	2-0	1-0	3	Christie, Thomson	721
34	20	A	Albion R	D	1-1	1-1	3	Christie	769
35	27	A	Brechin C	W	1-0	1-0	3	Hercher	656
36	30	H	Livingston	L	1-2	0-1	3	Stewart	1403

Final League Position: 3

Honours
Scottish Cup: Quarter-finals 1996.

Goalscorers: *League (64):* Stewart 23 (2 pens), Christie 12, Hercher 10, Ross 4, Mitchell 3, Hastings 2, Scott 2, Teasdale 2, Thomson 2, Brennan 1, Green 1, McAllister 1, own goal 1. *Scottish Cup (6):* Hercher 2, Ross 1, Stewart 1, Teasdale 1, Thomson 1. *Coca-Cola Cup (1):* own goal 1. *League Challenge Cup (1):* MacMillan

McRitchie M 2	McGinlay D 9 + 13	McAllister M 15 + 5	Noble M 36	Benson R 3	Ross D 28 + 4	Mitchell C 12 + 9	Lisle M 7 + 5	Stewart I 33 + 3	Christie C 24 + 5	Green D 4 + 7	Bennett G 30 + 3	MacMillan N 3 + 5	Brennan D 11 + 3	Hastings R 28	Hercher A 30 + 4	Calder J 34	MacArthur I 24	Scott J 28 + 2	Teasdale M 19	Thomson B 16 + 4	McKenzie P — + 4	Match No.
1	2	3	4	5	6	7	8^1	9	10	11^2	12	13										1
1			4	5	6	12		9	10		8	7	2	3	11^1							2
			4	5	7	12		9^2	10	13	8	6^1	2	3	11	1						3
			5		7^1	12		9	10	6	4			3	11	1	2	8				4
			5		7			9	10	6	4			3	11	1	2	8				5
			5		7^3	14	13	9	10	6^1	4	12		3	11^2	1	2	8				6
	13		5		7		12	9^2	10		4	6^1		3	11	1	2	8				7
			5		6^1	10	7^2	9		12		13	2	3	11	1	4	8^2				8
	14		5		6	10^3	7^1	9		12	13		2	3	11	1	4	8^2				9
		6	5		7	10	14	9		12	4	13	2^3	3	11^2	1		8				10
	14	6^2	5		7	10^1		9	12	13	4		2	3	11^3	1		8				11
		6^1	5		7^3	10	13	9	12		4	14	2^2	3	11	1		8				12
	12	6^1	5		7^2	14		9	10	13	4		2	3^1	11			8				13
	12	6	5		7^1			9	10	13	4		2	3	11^2	1		8				14
	13	6^1	5		12		7	9	10		4		2	3	11^2	1		8				15
	11^2	6	5^1		7	12		9	10		4			3	13	1	2	8				16
	2		5		6			9	10		4			3	12	1		8	7	11^1		17
			5		6^1	12			10		4			3	11	1	2	8	7	9		18
			5		6^1	12			10		4			3	11	1	2	8	7	9		19
	2	14	5^3			12		9	10^1				13	3	11^2	1	4	8	7	6		20
			5		6^1			9	12		4			3	11	1	2	8	7	10		21
	6	12	5		11^1			9	10		4			3		1	2		7	8		22
			5		6			9			4			3	11	1	2	8	7	10		23
	12		5		6^1		13	9			4			3	11	1	2	8^2	7	10		24
	13	14	5		6^3	12		9			4			3	11	1	2	8	7^2	10^1		25
	14		5		6^1		13	9	12		4			3	11	1	2	8^2	7	10^3		26
	2		5^3			12	10^2	9			4		14	3	11	1		8^1	7	6	13	27
	12		5		10		13	9^2	14		4			3	11^3	1	2	8	7	6^1		28
	13	14	5		6^3			9^1	10		4			3	11	1	2	8	7^2	12		29
	11	3	5^1		6^2		7	9	10		4				12	1	2	13		8^3	14	30
	6	3	5		8			9	10		4		2^2		11	1			12	7^1	13	31
	6^1	3	5		13		8^2	9	10		4	14			11	1	2			7^3	12	32
		3	5		7			9^1	10						4	1	6	8	2	11	12	33
	14	3	5		7	8^1		9^2	10		12				4	1	6		2	11^3	13	34
	12	3	5^1		11		13		10		6				4	1	2	8	7	9^2		35
	14	3	5		11^3	8^1		9	10		4				12	1	2	6^2	7	13		36

KILMARNOCK
Premier Division

Year Formed: 1869. *Ground & Address:* Rugby Park, Kilmarnock KA1 2DP. *Telephone:* 01563 525184. *Fax:* 01563 522181.
Ground Capacity: total: 18,128 seated. *Size of Pitch:* 114yd × 72yd.
Chairman: James Moffat. *Secretary:* Kevin Collins. *Commercial Manager:* Denny Martin. *Stadium Manager:* G. Hollas.
Manager: Alex Totten. *Assistant Manager:* Kenny Thomson. *Physio:* Hugh Allan.
Managers since 1975: W. Fernie; D. Sneddon; J. Clunie; E. Morrison; J. Fleeting; T Burns. *Club Nickname(s):* Killie.
Previous Grounds: Rugby Park (Dundonald Road); The Grange; Holm Quarry; Present ground since 1899.
Record Attendance: 35,995 v Rangers, Scottish Cup; 10 March, 1962.
Record Transfer Fee received: £300,000 for Shaun McSkimming to Motherwell,1995.
Record Transfer Fee paid: £300,000 for Paul Wright from St Johnstone, 1995.
Record Victory: 11-1 v Paisley Academical, Scottish Cup; 18 Jan, 1930 (15-0 v Lanemark, Ayrshire Cup; 15 Nov, 1890).
Record Defeat: 1-9 v Celtic, Division I; 13 Aug, 1938.
Most Capped Player: Joe Nibloe, 11, Scotland.
Most League Appearances: 481: Alan Robertson, 1972-88.
Most League Goals in Season (Individual): 34: Harry 'Peerie' Cunningham 1927-28 and Andy Kerr 1960-61.
Most Goals Overall (Individual): 148: W. Culley; 1912-23.

KILMARNOCK 1995–96 LEAGUE RECORD

Match No.	Date		Venue	Opponents	Result		H/T Score	Lg. Pos.	Goalscorers	Attendance
1	Aug 26	A	Rangers	L	0-1	0-0	—		44,686
2	Sept 9	H	Hibernian	L	0-3	0-3	9		7014
3	16	A	Raith R	L	0-2	0-0	10		4441
4	23	H	Aberdeen	L	1-2	0-2	10	Brown	7198
5	30	A	Motherwell	L	0-3	0-1	10		6356
6	Oct 4	A	Partick Th	D	1-1	1-1	—	Watson (og)	3419
7	7	H	Hearts	W	3-1	2-1	9	Brown, McKee 2	6721
8	14	A	Falkirk	W	2-0	2-0	9	Mitchell, Wright	4878
9	21	H	Celtic	D	0-0	0-0	7		14,011
10	28	A	Hibernian	L	0-2	0-1	9		9888
11	Nov 4	H	Raith R	W	5-1	2-0	6	Henry 2, Wright 2, Brown	6440
12	8	H	Rangers	L	0-2	0-0	—		14,613
13	11	A	Hearts	L	1-2	0-0	8	McKee	10,442
14	18	H	Motherwell	D	1-1	1-1	9	Mitchell	6608
15	Dec 2	A	Celtic	L	2-4	2-2	10	Mitchell, Brown	33,660
16	9	H	Falkirk	W	4-0	2-0	8	Brown 2, Black, MacPherson	6017
17	13	A	Aberdeen	L	1-4	1-2	—	Wright	14,060
18	16	H	Partick Th	W	2-1	1-1	7	Wright 2	6581
19	26	A	Rangers	L	0-3	0-2	7		45,143
20	Jan 6	A	Raith R	D	1-1	0-1	7	Black	4781
21	13	H	Hibernian	W	3-2	0-2	7	Maskrey, Wright, Henry	6686
22	16	A	Motherwell	W	1-0	0-0	—	Wright	5781
23	20	H	Celtic	D	0-0	0-0	7		16,024
24	23	H	Aberdeen	D	1-1	0-1	—	Wright	6703
25	Feb 3	A	Falkirk	L	2-4	2-2	7	Wright 2	4143
26	10	A	Partick Th	W	1-0	1-0	7	Black	4857
27	24	H	Hearts	L	0-2	0-2	7		8022
28	Mar 2	A	Aberdeen	L	0-3	0-1	7		7177
29	16	H	Motherwell	L	0-1	0-1	8		7035
30	23	H	Raith R	W	2-0	0-0	7	McKee, Wright	6143
31	30	A	Hibernian	D	1-1	0-1	8	Wright	8001
32	Apr 10	A	Celtic	D	1-1	1-0	—	McIntyre	36,476
33	13	H	Falkirk	W	1-0	0-0	7	McIntyre	6505
34	20	H	Partick Th	W	2-1	0-0	5	Skilling, Black	7276
35	27	A	Hearts	L	0-1	0-0	6		11,329
36	May 4	H	Rangers	L	0-3	0-2	7		17,102

Final League Position: 7

Honours
League Champions: Division I 1964-65. Division II 1897-98, 1898-99; *Runners-up:* Division I 1959-60, 1960-61, 1962-63, 1963-64. First Division 1975-76, 1978-79, 1981-82, 1992-93. Division II 1953-54, 1973-74. Second Division 1989-90.
Scottish Cup Winners: 1920, 1929; *Runners-up:* 1898, 1932, 1938, 1957, 1960.
League Cup Runners-up: 1952-53, 1960-61, 1962-63.

European: *European Cup:* 1965-66. *UEFA Cup (Fairs):* 1964-65 (semi-finals), 1969-70, 1970-71.
Club colours: Shirt: Blue and white vertical stripes. Shorts: Blue. Stockings: Blue.

Goalscorers: *League (39):* Wright 13, Brown 6, Black 4, McKee 4, Henry 3, Mitchell 3, McIntyre 2, MacPherson 1, Maskrey 1, Skilling 1, own goal 1. *Scottish Cup (3):* Wright 2, Anderson 1. *Coca-Cola Cup (2):* Roberts 1, Wright 1.

Lekovic D 33	Skilling M 13+1	Black T 30	Montgomerie R 12+2	Whitworth N 28	Connor R 22+1	Mitchell A 29	Henry J 22+6	Wright P 35+1	Brown T 19+5	Reilly M 22+6	Roberts M 2+9	Geddes R 2	MacPherson A 35	McKee C 19+9	Findlay W 2+1	Anderson D 28	Maskrey S 14+8	Holt G 16+8	Meldrum C 1	Lauchlan J 5	McIntyre J 7	Match No.
1	2	3	4	5	6	7	8	9^1	10	11	12											1
	11	3	4	5	6^1	7	8	9^2	13	12	10		1	2								2
		8		4	5	6	7^2	10	13		3^1	9	1	2	11	12						3
1		8		5	4	7	12	10^1	11		3^1	13	2	9		6						4
1		8^2	3		5	4	7^1	10	11				2	9		6	12	13				5
1		4	3		5	8	7	9	10^1				2	11		6	12					6
1		4	3		5	8^1	7	9	10				2	11^2		6	13	12				7
1		4	3		5	8	7	9^1	10^2	13			2	11^3		6	14	12				8
1		4^3	3		5	8	13	9	10^2				2	11^1	7	6	14	12				9
1		3			5	8	10	13	9				2^2	11^1	7	6	12	4				10
1		3			5	8	7	4	9	10^2	13		2			6	11^1	12				11
1		3			5	8	7	4^2	9	10^1	13		2	11		6	12		1			12
1		3			5	8	7	4	9		12		2	11		6	10^1					13
1		3			5	8	7	4	9^1	10^1?			2^2	11		6	12	13				14
1		3			5	8^2	7	13	9^1	10	4		2	12		6	11					15
1		3			5	8^1	7	4	9^2	10	12		2			6	13	11				16
1					5	8	7	4	9	10	3		2			6		11				17
1					5	8	7	4	9	10	3		2			11		6				18
1					5	8	7	4	9	10	3		2			11		6				19
1		3			5	8^1	7	12	9		4	13	2			10^2	11	6				20
1		3^1			5		7	8	9		4		2	12		6	10	11				21
1		3	13		5		7	8	9^2		4		2	12		6	10^1	11				22
1		3			5		7	8	9		4		2	12		6	10^1	11				23
1		3			5		7	8	9	13	4		2	12		6	10^2	11^1				24
1		3			5		8	9	10^1	4	12		2	7		6		11				25
1		3	5				8	9	10	4			2	7		6		11				26
1		3^1	5				8	9	10	4	12		2	11		6						27
1		3	13	5	10	7	12	9^2	8^1	4			2	11		6						28
1	12	3^2	5			7	8	9	4^1	14			2	13		6	10^3	11				29
1	8		4	5^1			9	13	12		2		7			3	11^2	6			10	30
1		3	4				8	9	12	6			2	7		5	11^1				10	31
1		3	4				8	9		6			2	7		5	11				10	32
1		3	4				8	9		6			2	7		5	11				10	33
1	8	3	4			7		9^1	12	6			2	14		5	11^2	13			10^3	34
1	8	3	4		6	7^2		9		13			2	12			11^1			5	10	35
1	8^1	3	4		12	7		9		6	14		2	13			11^2			5	10^3	36

LIVINGSTON
Second Division

Year Formed: 1974. *Ground:* Almondvale Stadium, Almondvale Stadium Road, Livingston EH54 7DN. *Telephone:* 01506 417000. *Fax:* 01506 418888. Address for correspondence: Preston Farm, Preston Road, Prestonpans, EH32 9LB. *Fax:* 01875 811130.
Ground Capacity: total: 16,500. seated: 16,500. Main stand only used 7500. *Size of Pitch:* 105yd × 72yd.
Chairman: William P Hunter. *Secretary:* J.R.S.Renton. *Vice-chairman:* Hugh Cowan.
Manager: Jim Leishman. *Club Doctor:* Dr M. M. Morrison. *Physio:* Arthur Duncan. *Coach:* George McNeil.
Managers since 1975: John Bain; Alec Ness; Willie MacFarlane; Terry Christie; Michael Lawson. *Club Nickname(s):* Thistle; Wee Jags. *Previous Grounds:* None.
Record Attendance: 4000 v Albion Rovers, League Cup 1st rd; 9 Sept, 1974.
Record Transfer Fee received: £115,000 for John Inglis to St Johnstone (1990).
Record Transfer Fee paid: £28,000 for Victor Kasule from Albion Rovers (1987).
Record Victory: 6-0 v Raith R, Second Division; 9 Nov, 1985.
Record Defeat: 0-8 v Hamilton A. Division II; 14 Dec, 1974.
Most Capped Player (under 18): I. Little.
Most League Appearances: 446: Walter Boyd, 1979-89.
Most League Goals in Season (Individual): 21: John McGachie, 1986-87. *(Team):* 69; Second Division, 1986-87.
Most Goals Overall (Individual): 64: David Roseburgh, 1986-93.

LIVINGSTON 1995–96 LEAGUE RECORD

Match No.	Date	Venue	Opponents	Result		H/T Score	Lg. Pos.	Goalscorers	Attendance
1	Aug 12	A	Caledonian Th	W	3-0	2-0	—	Bailey 2, McLeod	1259
2	26	A	Arbroath	W	3-1	0-1	1	Young 2, Harvey	721
3	Sept 9	A	East Stirling	W	2-1	2-0	1	Young 2	409
4	16	H	Alloa	W	2-0	1-0	2	Williamson, Smart	249
5	20	H	Queen's P	W	2-0	0-0	—	McLeod, McMartin	223
6	23	H	Albion R	W	2-1	1-1	1	Williamson, McMartin	229
7	30	A	Cowdenbeath	W	1-0	1-0	1	Young	340
8	Oct 7	A	Ross Co	D	1-1	0-1	1	Young	2120
9	14	H	Brechin C	D	0-0	0-0	1		273
10	21	A	Queen's P	W	1-0	1-0	1	Young	540
11	28	H	Arbroath	L	0-1	0-0	1		236
12	Nov 4	A	Alloa	W	2-0	2-0	1	Duthie 2	548
13	11	H	East Stirling	D	1-1	0-0	1	Young	4000
14	18	H	Cowdenbeath	L	0-1	0-0	1		3880
15	25	A	Albion R	W	2-0	1-0	1	Young 2	433
16	Dec 2	H	Ross Co	D	0-0	0-0	1		3444
17	16	A	Brechin C	L	0-2	0-1	1		419
18	Jan 10	H	Queen's P	W	3-1	2-1	—	Harvey, Duthie, McLeod	1822
19	13	H	Albion R	L	0-1	0-0	1		2509
20	17	H	Caledonian Th	L	0-2	0-0	—		2578
21	Feb 3	H	Brechin C	L	0-1	0-0	5		2386
22	10	A	Alloa	W	1-0	1-0	2	Young	2066
23	13	A	Ross Co	D	2-2	1-2	—	Harvey, Young	2300
24	17	A	East Stirling	W	3-0	2-0	1	Young 2, Sinclair	472
25	24	A	Arbroath	W	2-1	1-0	1	McLeod, Alleyne	772
26	28	A	Cowdenbeath	W	3-0	1-0	—	Bailey, McMartin, Young	272
27	Mar 2	H	Caledonian Th	D	2-2	1-0	1	Young, Bailey	2152
28	9	A	Albion R	W	1-0	1-0	1	Alleyne	623
29	16	H	Cowdenbeath	W	2-1	0-0	1	Tierney, Sinclair	2147
30	23	A	Alloa	D	1-1	0-1	1	Bailey	541
31	30	H	East Stirling	D	1-1	0-0	2	Young	2084
32	Apr 6	H	Ross Co	W	2-1	1-1	1	Campbell, Sinclair	2333
33	13	A	Brechin C	W	1-0	0-0	1	Tierney	768
34	20	A	Queen's P	D	0-0	0-0	1		928
35	27	H	Arbroath	W	3-0	3-0	1	Young, Hislop, Campbell (pen)	2993
36	30	A	Caledonian Th	W	2-1	1-0	1	Laidlaw 2	1403

Final League Position: 1

Honours
League Champions: Second Division 1986-87. Third Division 1995-96; *Runners-up:* Second Division 1982-83. First Division 1987-88.
Scottish Cup: —. *League Cup:* Semi-finals 1984-85. *B&Q Cup:* Semi-finals 1992-93, 1993-94.
Club colours: Shirt: Amber with black trim. Shorts: Black. Stockings: Amber.

Goalscorers: *League (51):* Young 18, Bailey 5, McLeod 4, Duthie 3, Harvey 3, McMartin 3, Sinclair 3, Alleyne 2, Campbell 2 (1 pen), Laidlaw 2, Tierney 2, Williamson 2, Hislop 1, Smart 1. *Scottish Cup (5):* Harvey 3, Duthie 2. *Coca-Cola Cup (4):* Young 2, Bailey 1, McMartin 1. *League Challenge Cup (4):* Callaghan 1, McLeod 1, Sinclair 1, Young 1.

Stoute H 12	Smart C 31	McCartney C 4	Davidson G 32	Williamson S 23+3	Alleyne D 19+1	McMartin G 36	Bailey L 20+7	Young J 36	McLeod G 34	Duthie M 25+4	Harvey G 6+12	Sinclair C 17+4	Sorbie S 5+6	Martin C 1+1	Callaghan W 6+17	Graham T 15	Douglas R 24	Thorburn S 3+3	Campbell S 19	McBride J —+2	Coulston D —+1	Tierney G 16	Wright G 7+3	Hislop K 4	Laidlaw S 1	Match No.
1	2	3	4	5	6	7	8^1	9	10	11^2	12	13														1
1	2		4	5	10	7	8^2	9	6	3	13	11^1	12													2
1	2		4	5	10^2	7	8^1	9	6	11	12			13	3^3	14										3
1	10		4	2		7	8	9	6	3		11				5										4
1	10^2		4	2		7	8^1	9	6	3	12	11		13		5										5
1	10		4	2^1		7	8	9^2	6	3	12	11			13	5										6
1	2		4		6	7		8	10	3	12	11^1			9	5										7
1	6		4	2	8	7		9	10	3	12	11^1				5										8
1	8^3	11	4	2		7	10^2	9	6	3^1	12	13	14			5										9
1	8		4	2		7	11^1	9	6	3	12		10			5										10
	8		4	2	12	7	10	9^3	6	3	13	11^1	14		12	5^2	1									11
11			4	2	8	7	10	9	6	3						5	1									12
	6		4	5		7	11^2	9	10	3^1	13				8^3	14	1	2		12						13
	6		4	5		7	11^2	9	10	3^3	13				8^1	12	1	2		14						14
	8	3	4	2		7		9	6	11		10				5	1									15
	8^3		4	2	3	7	13	10^2	6	11	12			14	9^1	5	1									16
	2^1	4		3		7	13	9^2	6	11	10^3			14	8	5	1			12						17
			4	5	8	7		9	6	11	10^2				13		1	2	3^1	12						18
			4^2	5	8^3	7		9	6	11	10				13		1	2^1	3	14	12					19
1	8^1		4			7	12	9	6	10		11						2	3			5				20
1	6		4	2		7	12	8	10			11			9^1				3			5				21
	2		4		8	7		9	6	11^1	10				12		1		3			5				22
	2		4		8	7	13	9	6	11^1	10^2				12		1		3			5				23
	2		4^1	12	8	7	10^2	9	6			11			13		1		3			5				24
	2		4		8	7	10	9	6			11					1		3			5				25
	2		4		8	7	10	9^2	6			11			13		1		3			5	12			26
	2		4		8	7	10	9	6			11					1		3			5				27
	2		4		8^1	7	10	9^2	6			11			13		1		3			5	12			28
	2		4		8^1	7	10	9^2	6			11			13		1		3			5	12			29
	2		4	14		7	8^3	9^2	6	12		11^1			13		1		3			5	10			30
	2		4	12	10	7	8	9		13		11					1		3			5^1	6^2			31
	2			4		7^1		9^2	6		12	11			13		1		3			5	8	10		32
	2			4		7		9	6			11			12		1		3			5	8	10^1		33
	2			4		7		9	6	11^1					12		1		3			5	8	10		34
		6	4		7	14	9^2	10	12		11^1			13		1		3			5	2	8^2			35
			4		7	12	10		2		11			9^1		1	3				6			8		36

MONTROSE   Third Division

Year Formed: 1879. *Ground & Address:* Links Park, Wellington St, Montrose DD10 8QD. *Telephone:* 01674 673200.
Ground Capacity: total: 4338. seated: 1338. *Size of Pitch:* 113yd × 70yd.
Chairman: Michael Craig. *Secretary:* Malcolm J. Watters.
Manager: Dave Smith. *Physio:* Allan Borthwick.
Managers since 1975: A. Stuart; K. Cameron; R. Livingstone; S. Murray; D. D'Arcy; I. Stewart; C. McLelland; D. Rougvie; J. Leishman, J Holt, A. Dornan.
Club Nickname(s): The Gable Endies. *Previous Grounds:* None.
Record Attendance: 8983 v Dundee, Scottish Cup 3rd rd; 17 Mar, 1973.
Record Transfer Fee received: £50,000 for Gary Murray to Hibernian (Dec 1980).
Record Transfer Fee paid: £17,500 for Jim Smith from Airdrieonians (Feb 1992).
Record Victory: 12-0 v Vale of Leithen, Scottish Cup 2nd rd; 4 Jan, 1975.
Record Defeat: 0-13 v Aberdeen; 17 Mar, 1951.
Most Capped Player: Alexander Keillor, 2 (6), Scotland.
Most League Appearances: 343: Martin Allan, 1983-93.
Most League Goals in Season (Individual): 28: Brian Third, Division II; 1972-73.
Most Goals Overall (Individual): —.

MONTROSE 1995–96 LEAGUE RECORD

Match No.	Date	Venue	Opponents	Result		H/T Score	Lg. Pos.	Goalscorers	Atten- dance
1	Aug 12	A	Stirling A	L	0-3	0-1	—		752
2	26	H	Queen of the S	L	1-4	1-1	10	McGlashan	557
3	Sept 2	A	Stranraer	L	1-4	0-2	10	MacDonald	503
4	9	A	East Fife	L	0-3	0-2	10		702
5	16	H	Clyde	D	0-0	0-0	10		763
6	23	H	Ayr U	L	0-1	0-0	10		409
7	30	A	Forfar Ath	D	0-0	0-0	10		660
8	Oct 7	A	Stenhousemuir	L	1-3	0-3	10	Smith	521
9	14	H	Berwick R	L	1-3	1-1	10	McAvoy	503
10	21	H	Stirling A	D	2-2	0-2	10	McGlashan, Smith	629
11	28	A	Queen of the S	L	2-4	1-0	10	McGlashan 2	902
12	Nov 4	A	Clyde	L	0-3	0-0	10		849
13	11	H	East Fife	L	1-2	0-0	10	Masson P	802
14	18	H	Forfar Ath	W	1-0	0-0	10	Kennedy	730
15	25	A	Ayr U	L	0-2	0-2	10		1166
16	Dec 2	H	Stenhousemuir	L	1-4	0-3	10	McGlashan	504
17	16	A	Berwick R	D	2-2	1-1	10	Kennedy, Grant	314
18	23	A	Stirling A	L	0-2	0-0	10		1056
19	Jan 13	H	Ayr U	L	0-1	0-1	10		587
20	16	H	Stranraer	W	4-2	1-1	—	McGlashan 3, Taylor S	334
21	20	A	Stenhousemuir	L	1-3	1-2	10	McGlashan	378
22	23	A	Forfar Ath	L	1-2	0-1	—	McGlashan	589
23	Feb 3	H	Berwick R	L	1-2	0-0	10	McGlashan	520
24	21	A	East Fife	L	0-7	0-3	—		425
25	24	H	Queen of the S	L	0-6	0-1	10		545
26	Mar 2	A	Stranraer	W	2-1	1-1	10	Kennedy 2	436
27	9	A	Ayr U	L	0-2	0-0	10		1326
28	12	H	Clyde	L	2-3	0-3	—	MacDonald, McGlashan	226
29	16	H	Forfar Ath	W	3-1	2-0	10	McGlashan, Taylor S 2	585
30	23	A	Clyde	W	3-1	0-1	10	McGlashan, Taylor S 2	791
31	30	H	East Fife	L	0-1	0-1	10		696
32	Apr 6	H	Stenhousemuir	L	1-3	1-1	10	McGlashan	507
33	13	A	Berwick R	L	1-4	0-0	10	Mailer	367
34	20	H	Stirling A	L	0-3	0-0	10		824
35	27	A	Queen of the S	D	1-1	0-1	10	McGlashan	1227
36	May 4	H	Stranraer	L	0-1	0-1	10		347

Final League Position: 10

Rothmans Football Yearbook 1996–97   665

Honours
League Champions: Second Division 1984-85, *Runners-up:* 1990-91. Third Division, *Runners-up:* 1994-95.
Scottish Cup: Quarter-finals 1973, 1976.
League Cup: Semi-finals 1975-76.
B&Q Cup: Semi-finals 1992-93.
Club colours: Shirt: White, royal blue and yellow. Shorts: Royal blue. Stockings: White with royal blue and red tops.

Goalscorers: *League (33):* McGlashan 16, Taylor 5, Kennedy 4, MacDonald 2, Smith 2, Grant 1, McAvoy 1, Mailer 1, Masson P 1. *Scottish Cup (6):* McGlashan 3, Kennedy 2, Masson P 1. *Coca-Cola Cup (0) League Challenge Cup (3):* Grant 1, McGlashan 1, Masson P 1.

Larter D 33	Robertson I 11	Mailer C 32+1	Masson P 19+2	Grant D 24+1	Tosh J 18+1	Cooper C 19+3	MacDonald I 34	McGlashan C 33	Smith S 25+3	MacRonald C 3+1	Brown M —+1	Stephen L 22+3	Massie R 3	McAvoy N 12+1	Taylor S 11+16	Tindall K 17+3	Ferrie A 8+14	Garden M 1	Masson C 8+1	Craib M 26+1	Kennedy A 14+2	Kydd S 4+7	Haro M 19	Match No.
1	2	3	4	5	6	7	8	9	10[1]	11[2]	12	13												1
	2		4	5	6	7	8	9	10[2]	11[1]		3	1	12	13									2
	2		4	5	6	7	8		10[2]	13		3	1	11[1]	9[3]	12	14							3
1	2			5	6	7	4	9	10[2]	11[1]		3		8	13	12								4
1		6	4	5		7	10	9				3		11		2		8						5
1		4[2]	5	6		7[1]	8	9	10[3]			3		11	12	2	13	14						6
1	2	12		5	6[1]		8	9	10			4		11	7	3								7
1	2	12	14	5	6[1]		8	9	10			4[3]		11	7[2]	3				13				8
1	2	6	4	5		7[2]	8	9	10[1]			3		11	12	13								9
1	2	6	4	5	12	7[1]		9	10			3		11					8					10
1	2[2]	6	4	5	12	7[1]		9	10			3		11		13			8					11
1	2	6		5		7	8					3		11	9[1]	12			4		10			12
1	2	3	4		6	7				11[1]	13	12		5	8	10[2]	9							13
1	2	3	4		6	7	9			11				5	8	10[1]	12							14
1	2	3			6	7	9			4				11	5	8	10[1]	12[1]						15
1	2[1]	3	4		6	7	9			14		12	13	5	8	10[2]	11[1]							16
1		2	4	5	6	7	9	12				3	11	8	10[1]									17
1		2	4	5		7	9	13				12	3	11[1]	8	10[2]					6			18
1	8	4[2]	5	2		7	9	12				13	3	11	10[1]						6			19
1	8	4	5	2		7[2]	9[1]	10				13	12	3	11						6			20
1		5	4			7[3]	9	10[2]				11[1]	12	3	14	8	13				6			21
1	8	4[1]	5	2		7[2]	9					12	3	11	13	10					6			22
1	2		5		7[1]		9	10				4		11	3	12	8				6			23
		5	2		11		9	10[2]				4	1	12	3	8	7[1]	13			6			24
1	2	4	5				9	10				11[2]		12	3[1]	13	8	7			6			25
1	2					7	8	9	10			12		11		3	4	6[1]		5				26
1	2					7	8	9	10			11		5	3	4			6					27
1	2					7	8	9	10			12		11	5	3	6[1]		4					28
1	2		5			7	8	9	10			6		11	3				4					29
1	2		5			7[2]	8	9	10			12		6	11[1]	3	13		4					30
1	2		5			7	8	9	10			11[1]		6	12	3			4					31
1	2					7	8	9	10			11[1]		12	5	3	6		4					32
1	2	13	5[2]		7	8[1]	9	10	11			6[3]		3	12	14	4							33
1	2		7[2]		8	9	10	11[1]				6	3	12	5	13	4							34
1	2	6			7	8	9	10[2]	11[1]	13		3	12	5	4									35
1	2[1]	6		12	13	8	9	11				7	3	5	10[2]	4								36

MOTHERWELL   Premier Division

Year Formed: 1886. *Ground & Address:* Fir Park, Motherwell ML1 2QN. *Telephone:* 01698 333333. *Fax:* 01698 276333.
Ground Capacity: total: 13,742 all seated. *Size of Pitch:* 110yd × 75yd.
Chairman: John C. Chapman. *Secretary:* Alan C. Dick. *Commercial Manager:* John Swinburne.
Manager: Alex McLeish. *Assistant Manager:* Andy Watson. *Physio:* John Porteous. *Coach:* Jim Griffin.
Managers since 1975: Ian St. John; Willie McLean; Rodger Hynd; Ally MacLeod; David Hay; Jock Wallace; Bobby
Watson, Tommy McLean.
Club Nickname(s): The Well. *Previous Grounds:* Roman Road, Dalziel Park.
Record Attendance: 35,632 v Rangers, Scottish Cup 4th rd replay; 12 Mar, 1952.
Record Transfer Fee received: £1,750,000 for Phil O'Donnell to Celtic, September 1994.
Record Transfer Fee paid: £400,000 for Mitchell Van Der Gaag from PSV Eindhoven, March 1995.
Record Victory: 12-1 v Dundee U, Division II; 23 Jan, 1954.
Record Defeat: 0-8 v Aberdeen, Premier Division; 26 Mar, 1979.
Most Capped Player: George Stevenson, 12, Scotland; Tommy Coyne, 12, Republic of Ireland.
Most League Appearances: 626: Bobby Ferrier, 1918-37.
Most League Goals in Season (Individual): 52: Willie McFadyen, Division I; 1931-32.
Most Goals Overall (Individual): 283: Hugh Ferguson, 1916-25.

MOTHERWELL 1995–96 LEAGUE RECORD

Match No.	Date		Venue	Opponents		Result	H/T Score	Lg. Pos.	Goalscorers	Attendance
1	Aug 26		A	Hearts	D	1-1	0-0	—	Arnott	10,971
2	Sept	9	H	Partick Th	D	1-1	0-0	6	Walker (og)	6155
3		16	A	Celtic	D	1-1	0-1	7	Arnott	31,365
4		23	A	Falkirk	D	0-0	0-0	7		4246
5		30	H	Kilmarnock	W	3-0	1-0	5	Coyne 2 (1 pen), May	6356
6	Oct	3	A	Rangers	L	1-2	0-1	—	McSkimming	39,891
7		7	H	Raith R	L	0-2	0-1	6		5727
8		14	H	Aberdeen	W	2-1	1-1	6	Coyne, Lambert	6842
9		21	A	Hibernian	L	2-4	0-3	6	Hendry 2	9803
10		28	A	Partick Th	L	0-1	0-0	6		4029
11	Nov	4	A	Celtic	L	0-2	0-0	8		12,077
12		7	H	Hearts	D	0-0	0-0	—		5595
13		11	A	Raith R	D	0-0	0-0	7		4293
14		18	A	Kilmarnock	D	1-1	1-1	7	Burns	6608
15		25	H	Falkirk	D	1-1	0-1	7	Burns	5201
16	Dec	2	H	Hibernian	L	0-2	0-0	9		5362
17		9	A	Aberdeen	L	0-1	0-0	10		11,299
18		19	H	Rangers	D	0-0	0-0	—		10,197
19	Jan	6	A	Celtic	L	0-1	0-1	9		34,629
20		10	A	Hearts	L	0-4	0-2	—		9288
21		13	H	Partick Th	L	0-2	0-1	10		5226
22		16	H	Kilmarnock	L	0-1	0-0	—		5781
23		20	A	Hibernian	D	0-0	0-0	10		7658
24		23	A	Falkirk	W	1-0	1-0	—	McLaughlin (og)	3845
25	Feb 10		A	Rangers	L	2-3	0-1	10	Martin, Falconer	44,871
26		13	H	Aberdeen	W	1-0	0-0	—	Burns	5090
27		24	H	Raith R	W	1-0	0-0	8	Falconer	5569
28	Mar	2	A	Falkirk	W	1-0	1-0	8	Falconer	5037
29		16	A	Kilmarnock	W	1-0	1-0	7	Lambert (pen)	7035
30	Mar 23		H	Celtic	D	0-0	0-0	8		12,394
31		30	A	Partick Th	W	2-0	1-0	7	Davies, Van Der Gaag	4846
32	Apr	6	H	Hibernian	W	3-0	2-0	6	Falconer, Martin, Coyne	5964
33		13	A	Aberdeen	L	1-2	1-0	6	Falconer	8943
34		20	H	Rangers	L	1-3	0-2	8	Arnott	13,128
35		27	A	Raith R	L	0-2	0-1	8		3653
36	May	4	H	Hearts	D	1-1	0-1	8	Davies	8301

Final League Position: 8

Honours
League Champions: Division I 1931-32. First Division 1981-82, 1984-85. Division II 1953-54, 1968-69; *Runners-up:* Premier Division 1994-95. Division I 1926-27, 1929-30, 1932-33, 1933-34. Division II 1894-95, 1902-03. *Scottish Cup:* 1952, 1991; *Runners-up:* 1931, 1933, 1939, 1951.
League Cup: 1950-51. *Runners-up:* 1954-55 *Scottish Summer Cup:* 1944, 1965.
Club colours: Shirt: Amber with claret hoop and trimmings. Shorts: Claret. Stockings: Amber.

European: *UEFA Cup* 2 matches 1995-96

Goalscorers: *League (28):* Falconer 5, Coyne 4 (1 pen), Arnott 3, Burns 3, Davies 2, Hendry 2, Lambert 2 (1 pen), Martin 2, McSkimming 1, May 1, Van Der Gaag 1, own goals 2. *Scottish Cup (0) Coca-Cola Cup (4):* Arnott 3, Lambert 1.

Howie S 36	May E 28	McKinnon R 27	Roddie A 12 + 12	Martin B 33	McCart C 20	Lambert P 35	Dolan J 24 + 3	Burns A 14 + 14	Arnott D 23 + 4	Davies W 26 + 7	Philliben J 19 + 5	McSkimming S 13 + 2	Ritchie I 5 + 5	Coyne T 9 + 5	Krivokapic M 13	Denham G 11 + 2	Hendry J 8 + 8	McMillan S 10 + 2	Essandoh R — + 4	Ferguson P 1	McLeish A 1	Falconer W 15	Van Der Gaag M 12	Ross 1 1	McCulloch L — + 1	Match No.
1	2	3	4	5	6¹	7	8	9	10	11²	12	13														1
1	2		4	5		7	8	9	10	12	6	11	3¹													2
1	2	3	12	5	6	7	8		10		4	11¹		9												3
1	2		11	5	6	7	8¹		10	12	4	3		9												4
1	2	3²	13	5	6	7		12	10¹	8	4	11		9												5
1	2	3	13	5	6	7	8¹	14	10³	12	4	11⁷		9												6
1	2	3	11¹	5	6	7		12	10	8	4			9												7
1	2	3¹	12	5		7	8		10³	11²	4			9	6	13	14									8
1	2		3	5		7	8	12	10¹	11	6			9²	4		13									9
1			13	5	6	7	8	12		11⁷	2			9¹	4		10	3								10
1	2¹		13	5	6	7	8	14	10	11	4²		12				9³	3								11
1			10¹	5	6	7	8	9		11	2			4				3	12							12
1			10²	5	6	7	8	9	13	11	2¹			4	12		3									13
1		3	12	5		7		9³	10⁴	11¹			14			4	13	8		2	6					14
1		3	12	5		7	8¹	9	10¹	11⁷		2			4	6	13	14								15
1		3	11²			7	8¹	9	10	13		2	5		4	6	12									16
1	2	3	13	5		7	8²	9	10¹	11				4	6	12										17
1	2	3	10³	5¹		7	13	9		11²		8	12		4	6			14							18
1	2	3	12²	5		7	13	9	10	11		8¹			4	6										19
1	7	3	13	5²			8	9	10³	11¹		2			4	6		12	14							20
1	2	3	14			7³	8	10	9	13		5¹			4	6		11²	12							21
1	2²	3	11			7	8¹	12	9		5		13	4³	6	14			10							22
1	2	3		5		7		12	11	4				6	9¹	8			10							23
1	2	3		5		7		12	9	11	4			6		8			10							24
1	2	3		5	6	7	13		9¹			11			12	8²			10	4						25
1	2	3		5	6	7		13		14	12	11³			9²	8¹			10	4						26
1	2	3¹		5	6	7	8	13		12		11²		14	9³				10	4						27
1	2	3		5	6	7³	8	13		11				12	9¹				10	4						28
1	2	3		5	6	7	8	9¹		11				12					10	4						29
1	2	3		5		7	8	9²	13	11¹	6			12					10	4						30
1	2	3		5	6	7²		13	9	11¹	8			12					10	4						31
1	2	3²		5	6	7	8¹		13	11	12			9					10	4						32
1	2	3		5	6	7	8¹	13		9¹	11	12							10	4						33
1	2	3¹		5	6	7	8²	14	9³	11	13	12							10	4						34
1		8	5	8	7				11¹	2	3	12		9					10	4						35
1		2	5		7			11	6	3				9¹					10	4	8	12				36

PARTICK THISTLE   First Division

Year Formed: 1876. *Ground & Address:* Firhill Park, 80 Firhill Rd, Glasgow G20 7BA. *Telephone:* 0141 945 4811. *Fax:* 0141 945 1525
Ground Capacity: total: 21,776. seated: 9076. *Size of Pitch:* 110yd × 74yd.
Chairman: James Oliver. *Secretary:* Lorna Bryce. *Commercial Manager:* John Lawson.
Manager: Murdo MacLeod. *Assistant Manager:* Gordon Chisholm. *Physio:* Iain McFadyen.
Managers since 1975: R. Auld; P. Cormack; B. Rooney; R. Auld; D. Johnstone; W. Lamont; S. Clark; J. Lambie. *Club Nickname(s):* The Jags. *Previous Grounds:* Jordanvale Park; Muirpark; Inchview; Meadowside Park.
Record Attendance: 49,838 v Rangers, Division I; 18 Feb, 1922.
Record Transfer Fee received: £200,000 for Mo Johnston to Watford.
Record Transfer Fee paid: £85,000 for Andy Murdoch from Celtic (Feb 1991).
Record Victory: 16-0 v Royal Albert, Scottish Cup 1st rd; 17 Jan, 1931.
Record Defeat: 0-10 v Queen's Park, Scottish Cup; 3 Dec, 1881.
Most Capped Player: Alan Rough, 51 (53), Scotland.
Most League Appearances: 410: Alan Rough, 1969-82.
Most League Goals in Season (Individual): 41: Alec Hair, Division I; 1926-27.
Most Goals Overall (Individual): —.

PARTICK THISTLE 1995–96 LEAGUE RECORD

Match No.	Date	Venue	Opponents		Result	H/T Score	Lg. Pos.	Goalscorers	Attendance
1	Aug 26	H	Hibernian	D	1-1	0-0	—	Gibson	5327
2	Sept 9	A	Motherwell	D	1-1	0-0	7	McDonald	6155
3	16	H	Hearts	W	2-0	1-0	4	McWilliams, Docherty	5396
4	23	A	Raith R	L	1-3	0-2	6	McDonald	4342
5	30	H	Falkirk	D	1-1	0-0	6	Craig	4078
6	Oct 4	H	Kilmarnock	D	1-1	1-1	—	Craig	3419
7	7	A	Celtic	L	1-2	0-0	7	Smith	29,950
8	14	H	Rangers	L	0-4	0-2	8		16,066
9	21	A	Aberdeen	L	0-3	0-1	9		12,719
10	28	H	Motherwell	W	1-0	0-0	7	Docherty	4029
11	Nov 4	A	Hearts	L	0-3	0-1	9		10,094
12	11	H	Celtic	L	1-2	1-1	10	Docherty	12,223
13	18	A	Falkirk	W	1-0	0-0	8	Foster	4127
14	22	A	Hibernian	L	0-3	0-1	—		6783
15	25	H	Raith R	L	0-2	0-2	8		3503
16	Dec 2	H	Aberdeen	W	1-0	0-0	7	Smith	4286
17	9	A	Rangers	L	0-1	0-0	7		43,137
18	16	A	Kilmarnock	L	1-2	1-1	8	McWilliams	6581
19	Jan 6	H	Hearts	L	0-1	0-0	8		4618
20	9	H	Falkirk	L	0-3	0-2	—		2708
21	13	A	Motherwell	W	2-0	1-0	8	Turner, Watson	5226
22	16	H	Hibernian	D	0-0	0-0	—		2811
23	20	A	Aberdeen	L	0-1	0-0	8		9149
24	23	A	Raith R	W	2-0	0-0	—	McDonald R 2	3651
25	Feb 3	H	Rangers	L	1-2	1-2	8	McDonald R	16,488
26	10	H	Kilmarnock	L	0-1	0-1	9		4857
27	24	A	Celtic	L	0-4	0-2	10		36,421
28	Mar 2	H	Raith R	L	0-3	0-1	10		2336
29	16	A	Falkirk	W	2-1	1-0	9	Lyons 2	3711
30	23	A	Hearts	W	5-2	2-1	9	Lyons 2, Turner, Macdonald W, Cameron	9610
31	30	H	Motherwell	L	0-2	0-1	9		4846
32	Apr 13	A	Rangers	L	0-5	0-2	9		46,438
33	16	H	Aberdeen	D	1-1	1-1	—	McWilliams	4568
34	20	A	Kilmarnock	L	1-2	0-0	9	Turner	7276
35	27	H	Celtic	L	2-4	2-1	9	Henderson, Lyons	14,693
36	May 4	A	Hibernian	L	0-1	0-0	9		6885

Final League Position: 9

Honours
League Champions: First Division 1975-76. Division II 1896-97, 1899-1900, 1970-71; *Runners-up:* First Division 1991-92. Division II 1901-02.
Scottish Cup Winners: 1921; *Runners-up:* 1930.
League Cup Winners: 1971-72; *Runners-up:* 1953-54, 1956-57, 1958-59.

European: *UEFA Cup:* 10 matches (*Fairs Cup:* 1963-64. *UEFA Cup:* 1972-73, 1994-95).
Club colours: Shirt: Red and yellow broad vertical stripes. Shorts: Black. Stockings: Yellow with red turnover.

Goalscorers: *League (29):* Lyons 5, McDonald R 5, Docherty 3, McWilliams 3, Turner 3, Craig 2, Smith 2, Cameron 1, Foster 1, Gibson 1, Henderson 1, Macdonald W 1, Watson 1. *Scottish Cup (0) Coca-Cola Cup (10):* Craig 4, McWilliams 2, Curran 1, Foster 1, McDonald R 1, Pittman 1.

Walker N 33	Dinnie A 31	Pittman S 14	McWilliams D 25+2	Watson G 32	Welsh S 35	Gibson A 8+13	Craig A 9	Foster W 19	Curran H 3+4	Cameron J 32+3	McDonald R 12+4	Milne C 19+3	McKee K 10+1	Docherty S 19+5	Tierney G 1	Smith T 24+1	Shepherd A —+1	Turner T 20+2	Ayton S 1+4	MacLeod M 1	Macdonald W 11+6	Cairns M 3	Adams C 1+4	Henderson N 12+4	McMahon S —+1	Lyons A 9	McCue J 2+1	Slavin J 8	Stirling J 2	Match No.
1	2	3	4	5	6	7	8	9	10	11																				1
1	2	3	4[1]	6	5		8	9		11	7	10	12																	2
1	2	3	7	6	5		8	9[2]	12	11		10[1]	4	13																3
1	2		4		5	13		9[2]		11	7	3		10		6[1]	8	12												4
1	2			6	5	9[1]	8			12	7	3	4	11			10													5
1	7	11	6	5		9[1]	8[3]		14	13	7	3	4[2]	12			10													6
1	2		9	6	5		8			11	7[1]	3		12		4		10												7
1	2[2]		11	6	5	12	8			7[1]		3		9		4		10	13											8
1	2		13	6	5	12	8			14	7[1]	3	4[3]	9		11				10[2]										9
1	2	3	7	6	5	9				11				8		4		10[1]	12											10
1	2	3	7[1]	6	5	9	8	11		10				12		4														11
1	2	3	7[1]	6	5	13		9	12	10				11		4		8[2]												12
1	2	3	7	6	5	12		9[1]		10				11		4		8												13
1	2	3[1]	7	6	5	13		9[2]	14	10		12		11		4		8[3]												14
1	2	3	7[2]	6	5	13				10	9	4		11				8[1]				12								15
	2	3	7		5	9				10[3]		6		11		4		8			12	1								16
	2		7	6	5	12		9		10				3	11[1]	4		8					1							17
	2		7[3]	6	5	9				10				3[1]	11	4		8[2]	12		13	1	14							18
1	2		7[1]	6	5	13				10		3		11		4[2]		8			12									19
1	2			6	5	11[1]			7[2]	10	3					8					13		4	9	12					20
1	2			6	5					10	13	3		11		4		8[1]	12		7[3]		14	9[2]						21
1	2			6	5			8		10	12	3		11		4[1]					7			9						22
1	2			6	5			8		10	12	3		11[1]		4					7			9						23
1	2	4		6	5			8		10	11	3									7			9						24
1	2	11[1]		6	5			9		10	7			3	12	4					8									25
1	2	11[2]		6	5			9		10	7[1]	3			8	4		13						12						26
1	2	11[1]	12	6	5			9[2]		10	7			3	8	4								13						27
1	2	3		6	5			9		10	7[2]			8				12			4[1]			11	13					28
1	2	3		6				9[1]		10				4		8		7			12			11		5				29
1	2	9	3	6						10		12		4		8[1]		7						11		5				30
1	2	9	3[1]	6						10				4[1]		8		7			13	12		11		5				31
1		3	6	12						10			2	4		8[1]		7						9		11		5		32
1		4	3	6	12			8[1]		10		13	2[2]					7						9		11		5		33
1		4	3	6	12			8[1]		10		2		14		13		7[3]						9[2]		11		5		34
1		4		6	13					10			2					7			12			8[1]		11	9[2]	5	3	35
1		4	6							10	12	2				8								7[1]		11	9	5	3	36

QUEEN OF THE SOUTH   Second Division

Year Formed: 1919. *Ground & Address:* Palmerston Park, Dumfries DG2 9BA. *Telephone and Fax:* 01387 254853.
Ground Capacity: total: 8352. seated: 3549. *Size of Pitch:* 112yd × 73yd.
Chairman: Norman Blount. *Secretary:* Richard Shaw MBE. *Commercial Manager:* Robert McKinnel.
Co-managers: Rowan Alexander and Mark Shanks. *Coach:* Ian McChesney. *Physio:* Derek Kelly.
Managers since 1975: M. Jackson; G. Herd; A. Busby; R. Clark; M. Jackson; D. Wilson; W. McLaren; F. McGarvey; A.
MacLeod; W. McLaren. *Club Nickname(s):* The Doonhamers. *Previous Grounds:* None.
Record Attendance: 24,500 v Hearts, Scottish Cup 3rd rd; 23 Feb, 1952.
Record Transfer Fee received: £100,000 for K. McMinn to Rangers (1985).
Record Transfer Fee paid: —.
Record Victory: 11-1 v Stranraer, Scottish Cup 1st rd; 16 Jan, 1932.
Record Defeat: 2-10 v Dundee, Division I; 1 Dec, 1962.
Most Capped Player: Billy Houliston, 3, Scotland.
Most League Appearances: 619: Allan Ball; 1962-83.
Most League Goals in Season (Individual): 33: Jimmy Gray, Division II; 1927-28.
Most Goals Overall (Individual): 109, Andrew Thomson, 1989-94.

QUEEN OF THE SOUTH 1995–96 LEAGUE RECORD

Match No.	Date	Venue	Opponents	Result	H/T Score	Lg. Pos.	Goalscorers	Atten- dance
1	Aug 12	H	Stenhousemuir	D 2-2	1-1	—	Harris, Mallan	1300
2	26	A	Montrose	W 4-1	1-1	2	McLaren 2, Harris 2	557
3	Sept 2	H	Clyde	L 0-3	0-1	6		1897
4	9	H	Stranraer	L 0-3	0-2	8		1531
5	16	A	Forfar Ath	L 1-2	0-0	8	Cody	589
6	23	A	East Fife	L 1-2	1-0	8	Hope (og)	700
7	30	H	Berwick R	L 1-4	1-2	9	Harris	1056
8	Oct 7	H	Ayr U	D 0-0	0-0	9		1147
9	14	A	Stirling A	D 2-2	1-1	8	Campbell D, McLaren	748
10	21	A	Stenhousemuir	L 1-2	0-2	9	Bryce	509
11	28	H	Montrose	W 4-2	0-1	8	Bryce, Jackson, McLaren, Campbell D	902
12	Nov 4	H	Forfar Ath	D 1-1	0-0	8	Campbell D (pen)	1147
13	11	A	Stranraer	D 0-0	0-0	8		1006
14	21	A	Berwick R	D 0-0	0-0	—		324
15	25	H	East Fife	L 0-2	0-1	8		1081
16	Dec 2	A	Ayr U	L 0-2	0-1	9		1434
17	16	H	Stirling A	L 1-5	0-4	9	Mallan	1004
18	Jan 10	H	Stenhousemuir	D 3-3	1-2	—	Dobie, Mallan, Telfer	743
19	20	H	Ayr U	D 2-2	1-2	9	Mallan, Harris	1264
20	23	H	Berwick R	W 3-0	0-0	—	Mallan 2, Bryce	840
21	31	A	East Fife	W 2-1	1-1	—	Bryce, Mallan	732
22	Feb 3	A	Stirling A	L 1-4	0-1	9	Harris	1042
23	13	A	Forfar Ath	W 3-0	1-0	—	Mallan 2, Dobie	427
24	17	H	Stranraer	W 2-1	2-1	6	Duncan (og), McFarlane	1229
25	24	A	Montrose	W 6-0	1-0	7	Dobie 3, Mallan 2, McLaren	545
26	Mar 2	H	Clyde	W 2-1	1-1	6	Mallan, Wilson	877
27	5	A	Clyde	L 1-2	0-2	—	Bryce	776
28	9	H	East Fife	W 1-0	0-0	5	Harris	1476
29	16	A	Berwick R	L 1-4	0-3	7	Harris (pen)	363
30	23	H	Forfar Ath	W 4-1	1-0	5	Bryce 3, McLaren	1279
31	30	A	Stranraer	L 1-3	0-2	6	Harris	722
32	Apr 6	A	Ayr U	L 0-3	0-3	7		1764
33	13	A	Stirling A	L 0-7	0-4	8		1394
34	20	A	Stenhousemuir	W 3-1	0-0	7	Bryce 2, Wilson	471
35	27	H	Montrose	D 1-1	1-0	7	Dobie	1227
36	May 4	A	Clyde	D 0-0	0-0	7		1095

Final League Position: 7

Honours
League Champions: Division II 1950-51; *Runners-up:* Division II 1932-33, 1961-62, 1974-75. Second Division 1980-81, 1985-86.
Scottish Cup: —.
League Cup: —.
Club colours: Shirt: Royal blue. Shorts: White. Stockings: Royal blue with white tops.

Goalscorers: *League (54):* Mallan 12, Bryce 10, Harris 9 (1 pen), Dobie 6, McLaren 6, Campbell D 3 (1 pen), Wilson 2, Cody 1, Jackson 1, McFarlane 1, Telfer 1, own goals 2. *Scottish Cup (2):* Bryce 1 (pen), Mallan 1. *Coca-Cola Cup (3):* Campbell D 1, Harris 1, Mallan 1 (pen). *League Challenge Cup (0)*

Butter J 26	McKeown D 30 + 3	Brown J 9 + 6	McKeown B 30 + 1	Hetherington K 6	Ramsay S 16 + 10	Wilson S 19 + 5	Kennedy D 34 + 1	Campbell D 11 + 6	Harris C 25 + 8	Mallan S 27 + 5	Bryce T 35 + 1	Cody S 13 + 3	McFarlane A 23 + 2	McLaren J 10 + 13	Campbell C 15 + 1	McColm R 4	Jackson D 4 + 1	Lilley D 23	Telfer G — + 2	Millar J — + 1	Dobie M 17 + 1	Graham C — + 3	Leslie S 10 + 3	Burridge J 6	Allen C 1	McAllister J 2	Pettit S — + 1	Alexander R — + 1	Match No.
1	2¹	3	4³	5	6²	7	8	9	10	11	12	13	14																1
1	3	4	2	8¹	7	5	9		13	10	12	6²	11																2
1	3	4	2	11	7	5	14	9³	12		10¹	8	6			13													3
1	2²	3	4	14	7	5	9¹	12	11	10	8³	6				13													4
1	3		5	6	7	2	9		12	13	10	8	11²				4¹												5
12	3		2	5	6²	7	14	9³	10	11	8¹	13			4	1													6
1	13	3	5²	6¹	7	2	12	10	11	9	8						4												7
1	3²	13	6		2	7	9¹	10	11	8	5						4						12						8
1	3	13	6¹		2	7	9	10²	11	8	5			12			4												9
1	3	12	8	7	2	10¹	9²	6	11	5	13						4												10
1	3		2		7	8	9¹	12	10	6²	4				4		11	5	13										11
1	3		2		7¹	10	9	12	8	11	4	6	5					5											12
1	3	13	2		7¹	8	9	12	10	11	4	6²	5					5											13
1	3		2		7	8	9¹	12	6	10	11	4	5					5											14
1	3		2		7	8	9	12	13	6	14	10¹	4³	11²				5											15
1	3		2	6	12	7	11	10	8	9¹	4²							5	13										16
1	3		2	6²	13	10	12	7	11	9	8	4¹						5											17
1	3	4			7		9	11¹	6	8	2	5		12									10						18
1	3	6	2		7		9	10	4	11¹	5			8	12														19
1	3	13	6	12	2	7	9¹	10	4¹	11²	5			8	14														20
1	3	6	12		2	7	8	10	11	5	9			4¹															21
1	3	6	2		7	8	10	11	5	9¹	12	4																	22
1	3	6	4¹	12	2	7	10	8	11	13	5	9²																	23
1	3	6	4	2	7	10²	8¹	11	13	5	9	12																	24
1	3	6	4³	12	2	7	10²	8	11¹	13	5	9	14																25
1	3	6	4²	12	2	7¹	10	8	11	14	5	9³	13																26
1	3	6	12	7²	2	13	10	8	11	9	5	4¹																	27
	3	6	13	7²	2	5	10	8	11	9¹	12												4	1					28
	3	6			2	7	10	8	11		5							5			9		4	1					29
	3	6	14	13	2	7²	10¹	8	11	12	5							5			9		4³	1					30
	3	6	12		2	7	10	8	11²	13	5							5			9		4¹	1					31
	3	6	12	13	2	7	10²	8	11³	14	5			5¹							9		4	1					32
	3	11³	6	14	2	7	5	12	8	13	10¹				13						9²		4	1					33
	3	14	6	12	2	7	10³	8	11	13	5					1		5			9²		4¹						34
		13	6	12	7	4	10	8	11³	14	5					1		5			9²					2¹	3		35
	3	12	6	4	2	7	10³	8			5					1		5			9²		11¹		13	14			36

QUEEN'S PARK   Third Division

Year Formed: 1867. *Ground & Address:* Hampden Park, Mount Florida, Glasgow G42 9BA. *Telephone:* 0141 632 1275. *Fax:* 0141 636 1612.
Ground Capacity: total: 38,335 all seated. *Size of Pitch:* 115yd × 75yd.
President: H. Gordon Wilson. *Secretary:* Alistair Mackay. *Physio:* R.C.Findlay. *Coach:* Hugh McCann.
Coaches since 1975: D.McParland, J.Gilroy, E Hunter. *Club Nickname(s):* The Spiders. *Previous Grounds:* 1st Hampden (Recreation Ground); (Titwood Park was used as an interim measure between 1st & 2nd Hampdens); 2nd Hampden (Cathkin); 3rd Hampden.
Record Attendance: 95,772 v Rangers, Scottish Cup, 18 Jan, 1930.
Record for Ground: 149,547 Scotland v England, 1937.
Record Transfer Fee received: Not applicable due to amateur status.
Record Transfer Fee paid: Not applicable due to amateur status.
Record Victory: 16-0 v St. Peters, Scottish Cup 1st rd; 29 Aug, 1885.
Record Defeat: 0-9 v Motherwell, Division I; 26 Apr, 1930.
Most Capped Player: Walter Arnott, 14, Scotland.
Most League Appearances: 473: J. B. McAlpine.

QUEEN'S PARK 1995–96 LEAGUE RECORD

Match No.	Date		Venue	Opponents		Result	H/T Score	Lg. Pos.	Goalscorers	Atten- dance
1	Aug	12	A	Ross Co	L	0-2	0-0	—		1515
2		26	H	Cowdenbeath	W	3-1	2-0	6	McCusker 2, Edgar	444
3	Sept	9	A	Caledonian Th	L	1-3	0-1	8	Edgar	1141
4		16	H	East Stirling	W	1-0	0-0	6	Caven	627
5		20	A	Livingston	L	0-2	0-0	—		223
6		23	H	Brechin C	L	0-2	0-0	7		422
7		30	A	Albion R	L	1-3	1-3	8	McGoldrick	378
8	Oct	7	H	Alloa	D	0-0	0-0	9		483
9		17	A	Arbroath	D	1-1	0-1	—	Edgar	361
10		21	H	Livingston	L	0-1	0-1	8		540
11		28	A	Cowdenbeath	L	2-3	0-2	10	Edgar, Caven	222
12	Nov	4	A	East Stirling	W	2-1	1-0	8	Edgar, Caven	407
13		11	H	Caledonian Th	L	0-3	0-2	8		597
14		18	H	Albion R	W	4-1	2-0	8	Edgar, McGoldrick 2, Porter	467
15		25	A	Brechin C	L	0-1	0-0	8		306
16	Dec	2	A	Alloa	D	0-0	0-0	8		352
17		16	H	Arbroath	W	2-0	1-0	7	Callan, Ferry	464
18		30	H	Ross Co	D	1-1	0-1	7	Fraser	699
19	Jan	1	H	Albion R	W	5-1	2-0	—	Ferry 2, McGoldrick, Caven, Fraser	617
20		10	A	Livingston	L	1-3	1-2	—	Ferry	1822
21		13	H	Brechin C	D	0-0	0-0	7		505
22		20	H	Alloa	D	0-0	0-0	7		467
23	Feb	3	A	Arbroath	D	1-1	0-1	7	Orr	572
24		10	H	East Stirling	D	2-2	0-2	7+	Ferry, Orr	522
25		24	H	Cowdenbeath	W	2-1	0-0	7	McPhee, Graham	468
26	Mar	2	H	Ross Co	D	0-0	0-0	7		238
27		5	A	Caledonian Th	D	1-1	0-0	—	Graham	1245
28		9	A	Brechin C	L	0-4	0-1	7		363
29		16	A	Albion R	W	2-0	1-0	7	McGoldrick, Arbuckle	387
30		23	A	East Stirling	W	2-1	1-0	6	Maxwell 2	364
31		30	H	Caledonian Th	L	1-2	0-1	6	McPhee	526
32	Apr	6	A	Alloa	W	1-0	0-0	6	McGoldrick	403
33		13	H	Arbroath	D	0-0	0-0	6		401
34		20	H	Livingston	D	0-0	0-0	6		928
35		27	A	Cowdenbeath	W	3-2	2-0	6	McPhee 2, Meldrum (og)	231
36		30	A	Ross Co	W	1-0	1-0	6	McPhee	916

Final League Position: 6

Most League Goals in Season (Individual): 30: William Martin, Division I; 1937-38.
Most Goals Overall (Individual): 163: J. B. McAlpine.

Honours
League Champions: Division II 1922-23. B Division 1955-56. Second Division 1980-81.
Scottish Cup Winners: 1874, 1875, 1876, 1880, 1881, 1882, 1884, 1886, 1890, 1893; *Runners-up:* 1892, 1900.
League Cup: —.
FA Cup runners-up: 1884, 1885.
Club colours: Shirt: White and black hoops. Shorts: White. Stockings: White with black hoops.

Goalscorers: *League (40):* Edgar 6, McGoldrick 6, Ferry 5, McPhee 5, Caven 4, Fraser 2, Graham 2, McCusker 2, Maxwell 2, Orr 2, Arbuckle 1, Callan 1, Porter 1, own goal 1. *Scottish Cup (4):* Edgar 3, McGoldrick 1. *Coca-Cola Cup (1):* McPhee 1. *League Challenge Cup (0)*

Chalmers J 28	Graham D 32+1	McGoldrick K 36	McGrath D 5+1	Caven R 31	Maxwell I 29	McInally A 4+4	Arbuckle D 35	McCusker J 3+4	McPhee B 20+12	Matchett J 3+2	Kerr G 4+4	Brodie D 7+11	Porter C 6+10	Ferguson P 23	Elder G 26	Edgar S 28+5	Callan D 23+7	Wilson D 10+3	Smith M 1	Fraser R 13+3	Ferry D 9+8	McGinlay M —+1	Orr G 11+1	Kennedy K —+7	Bruce G 8	Ward J 1+1	Match No.
1	2	3	4	5	6	7¹	8		9¹	10²	11	12	13	14													1
1	2	11¹	4	8	6	12		9¹	14	13	7					3²	5	10									2
1	11	10	4	5	6		8		12					7¹		3	9	2									3
1	2	11		8	6	7²	4		9¹	12			14			3	5	10³	13								4
1	2	11	4		6	7³	8		13	10¹	12					3	5	9²	14								5
1	8	11¹		7	6	13	4		14	10³	12					3²	5	9	2								6
1	3	11	4¹	7	6		8		13	10²	12					5	9	14	2²								7
1	3	11		8	6		4		13		12		10²		5¹	9		2	7³	14							8
1	3	11			6		13	4		12		10¹	5		9	8	2		7²								9
1		11	5	6	14	4			12			13	10¹	3	9	8	2²		7¹								10
1	3		6	5	11²	4		13		12			8	9¹	10	7	2									11
1	3	11	5	6	4		10²		8		13			9	2	12	7¹									12
1	3³	11		8	6	4	10		12		13		5	9²	2		7¹	14								13
1	2	11	5	6		8	10		7²		14	3¹	4	9³	12	13										14
1	2¹	11	5	6		8	10					3⁴	4	9	12	7		13								15
1	3		5	6	11		10		9¹			4		2	8	12	7									16
1	14	11	5	6		3			12	10¹		4	9	2	8³	13	7²									17
1	6	11	5		3				7¹	12		4	9	2	8	10										18
1	6	11	14	5	3³				10	13		4	9²	2¹	8	7	12									19
1	6	11		5	3	12			7²			4	9	2	8	10¹	13									20
1	6	11		5	3	12			7	14		4	9³	2	8²	10	13									21
1	3	11	5		8	7³	14		13			6	4	9²	2¹	10	12									22
1	3	11	5		8	9¹			10²			6	4	12	2	13	7³	14								23
1	11	3	5		8¹	13			10²			6	4	9	2	12	7³	14								24
1	3	11²	5	4	8	12	13					6	9¹	2	10	7										25
1	8	11	5	4	3	10						6	9¹	2	12	7										26
1	3	11	5	4	8	10¹						6	9	2	12	7										27
1	3	11²	5	4	8	12	10²	13				6	9¹	2	14	7										28
	7	11	5	6	8	9						3	4	12	2	10¹							1				29
	7	11	5	6	8	9		13				3	4	12²	2	10¹							1				30
	8	11	5	6	7	9	14					3³	4	12	2²	13	10¹						1				31
	8	11³	5	6	7	9²		13				3	4	10¹	2	12							1	14			32
	8	3	5	6	7	9		12				4	10¹	13	2	11²	1										33
	8	11	5	7	9	12						6	4		2	13	10¹		1	3²							34
	11	3	5	7	9	6	4	12				2	8²	10¹	13		1										35
	11	3	5	7	9	6	4	10¹	13	2	8²		12	1													36

RAITH ROVERS Premier Division

Year Formed: 1883. *Ground & Address:* Stark's Park, Pratt St, Kirkcaldy KY1 1SA. *Telephone:* 01592 263514. *Fax:* 01592 642833.
Ground Capacity: total: 9300. seated: 3040. *Size of Pitch:* 113yd × 67yd.
Chairman: Alex Penman. *Company Secretary:* C.Cant. *General Manager:* W.McPhee.
Manager: Jimmy Thomson. *Assistant Manager:* Jim McInally. *Physio:* Gerry Docherty. *Coach:* Andy Harrow.
Managers since 1975: R. Paton; A. Matthew; W. McLean; G. Wallace; R. Wilson; F. Connor; J. Nicholl. *Club Nickname(s):* Rovers. *Previous Grounds:* Robbie's Park.
Record Attendance: 31,306 v Hearts, Scottish Cup 2nd rd; 7 Feb, 1953.
Record Transfer Fee received: £900,000 for S. McAnespie to Bolton Wanderers (Sept 1995).
Record Transfer Fee paid: £150,000 for J. McInally from Dundee United (July 1995).
Record Victory: 10-1 v Coldstream, Scottish Cup 2nd rd; 13 Feb, 1954.
Record Defeat: 2-11 v Morton, Division II; 18 Mar, 1936.
Most Capped Player: David Morris, 6, Scotland.
Most League Appearances: 430: Willie McNaught.
Most League Goals in Season (Individual): 38: Norman Haywood, Division II; 1937-38.
Most Goals Overall (Individual): 154: Gordon Dalziel (League), 1987-94.

RAITH ROVERS 1995–96 LEAGUE RECORD

Match No.	Date	Venue	Opponents	Result	H/T Score	Lg. Pos.	Goalscorers	Attendance
1	Aug 26	H	Celtic	L	0-1	0-0	—	9300
2	Sept 9	A	Rangers	L	0-4	0-3	10	43,284
3	16	H	Kilmarnock	W	2-0	0-0	8	Graham, Dair	4441
4	23	H	Partick Th	W	3-1	2-0	5	Cameron 2, Dair	4342
5	30	A	Aberdeen	L	0-3	0-2	7		13,983
6	Oct 4	H	Hibernian	W	3-0	1-0	—	Cameron 2, Sinclair	6051
7	7	A	Motherwell	W	2-0	1-0	5	Dair, Sinclair	5727
8	14	A	Hearts	L	2-4	0-2	5	Graham, Crawford	10,133
9	21	H	Falkirk	L	0-1	0-1	5		4715
10	28	H	Rangers	D	2-2	0-0	5	Lennon, Cameron	9300
11	Nov 4	A	Kilmarnock	L	1-5	0-2	5	Cameron	6440
12	8	A	Celtic	D	0-0	0-0	—		28,832
13	11	H	Motherwell	D	0-0	0-0	6		4293
14	18	H	Aberdeen	W	1-0	1-0	5	Lennon	5786
15	25	A	Partick Th	W	2-0	2-0	4	Graham, Crawford	3503
16	Dec 2	A	Falkirk	L	1-2	0-0	4	Graham	4442
17	9	H	Hearts	D	1-1	1-0	5	Lennon	6349
18	16	A	Hibernian	W	2-1	0-1	5	Crawford, Graham	8507
19	Jan 6	A	Kilmarnock	D	1-1	1-0	5	Lennon	4781
20	9	H	Celtic	L	1-3	0-2	—	Cameron	9300
21	13	A	Rangers	L	0-4	0-3	6		42,498
22	20	H	Falkirk	W	1-0	0-0	6	Sinclair	4123
23	23	H	Partick Th	L	0-2	0-0	—		3651
24	Feb 3	A	Hearts	L	0-2	0-1	6		10,183
25	7	A	Aberdeen	L	0-1	0-1	—		6628
26	10	H	Hibernian	W	1-0	1-0	6	Kirkwood	4832
27	24	A	Motherwell	L	0-1	0-0	6		5569
28	Mar 2	A	Partick Th	W	3-0	1-0	6	Cameron, Duffield, McCulloch (pen)	2336
29	16	A	Aberdeen	D	2-2	2-1	6	Kirk, Cameron	4932
30	23	A	Kilmarnock	L	0-2	0-0	6		6143
31	30	H	Rangers	L	2-4	1-1	6	Duffield, Kirkwood	9300
32	Apr 6	A	Falkirk	W	3-2	1-2	5	Rougier, Raeside, Duffield	3766
33	13	H	Hearts	L	1-3	0-1	5	Lennon	4956
34	20	A	Hibernian	D	1-1	0-0	6	Millar	7214
35	27	H	Motherwell	W	2-0	1-0	5	Duffield, Thomson SM	3653
36	May 4	A	Celtic	L	1-4	0-3	6	Duffield	37,318

Final League Position: 6

Honours
League Champions: First Division: 1992-93, 1994-95. Division II 1907-08, 1909-10 (shared), 1937-38, 1948-49; *Runners-up:* Division II 1908-09, 1926-27, 1966-67. Second Division 1975-76, 1977-78, 1986-87.
Scottish Cup Runners-up: 1913. *League Cup Winners: (Coca-Cola Cup):* 1994-95. *Runners-up:* 1948-49.
Club colours: Shirt: Navy blue, white trim. Shorts: White. Stockings: White.

European: *UEFA Cup* 6 matches 1995-96

Goalscorers: League (41): Cameron 9, Duffield 5, Graham 5, Lennon 5, Crawford 3, Dair 3, Sinclair 3, Kirkwood 2, Kirk 1, McCulloch 1 (pen), Millar 1, Raeside 1, Rougier 1, Thomson SM 1. *Scottish Cup (3):* Crawford 2, Lennon 1. *Coca-Cola Cup (3):* Kirkwood 2, Rougier 1.

Thomson S Y 26	Kirkwood D 25+3	Braddle J 23+4	McInally J 23+2	Dennis S 25	Sinclair D 31+1	Wilson B 8+5	Cameron C 30	Graham A 18+7	Crawford S 21+7	Rougier A 17+5	Lennon D 31+3	Raeside R 6+2	Coyle R 22+2	McAnespie S 2+1	Dair J 18+1	Nicholl J —+1	Taylor A 1+9	McMillan I 4+4	Buist M 2	Humphries M 9	McKilligan N 1+2	Forrest G —+1	Fridge L 1	Geddes R 9	McCulloch G 7	Thomson SM 9	Duffield P 9	Kirk S 6+1	Krivokapic M 5	Millar J 3	Bonar P 4+1	Landells G —+1	Dargo C —+1	Sellars N —+1	Match No.
1	2	3	4^2	5	6	7	8	9	10^1	11	12	13																							1
1	2	3	4^2	5	6	7^1	8^3	12	9	11	10				13	14																			2
1	6	3	13		5	7^1	8^3	9	14	12	10		4		7		11^2																		3
1	6^1	3	12		5	14	8	9^2	13	7^3	10		4		2		11																		4
1	2^3	3	4	5	6	7^1	8		9^2		10	13	12				11	14																	5
1	2	3	7	5	6		8	9			10		4		11																				6
1	2	3	7	5	6		8^1	9		12	10		4		11																				7
1	2	3	7^2	5	6		8^3	9		12	10		4		11			13	14																8
1	2^3	3	7^1	5	6		8	9		12	10	13	4		11																				9
1		3			6		8	12	9	11^1	10		4		7			13	5	2^2															10
1	2	3^1	7	5^2	6		8^3	9		12	10		4		11			14		13															11
1	2	3	7	5	6		8^1	9		12	10		4		11																				12
1	2	3	7	5	6		8	9		12	10^1		4		11^2			13																	13
1		3	2	5	6	12	8	9^1	7		10		4		11																				14
1	12	3	2	5	6		8	9	7		10^2		4		11^1																				15
1		3	2	5	6	11	8	9	7	12	10^2		4^1							13															16
1		3	2	5		11	8	9	7	12	10^1		4							6															17
1	12	3		5	13	14	8	9	7	11^3	10		4							6^2	2^1														18
1	11	3	2	5		12	8	9	7		10^1		4							6															19
1		3		5	6	7^2	8	9		11	10^2		4^1					13		2	12	14													20
1	12		2	5	6	7^2	8	9		11	10		4^1					13			3														21
1	12			5	6		8	9	7		10		4			11^1				2	3														22
1	12	13		5	6		8	9		11	10		4^1							7^2	2	3													23
	2	3^1		5	6		8	9^2	7	10	11		4					12		6	13		1												24
	2	13		5	6		8	12	9	11^1	10		4		7						3^2			1											25
	2	3		5	6		8	12	9^1	7	10		4		11									1											26
10	3^2	11^1			6		13	8			7		5	4		9	12							1	2										27
	3		4		6		8	9																1	2	7	10	11							28
	3		4		6		8	12	13	10^1			5											1	2	7	9^2	11							29
	3		4		6		8^1	12			10		5											1	2	7	9	11							30
	3		4						11^1	10			6					12		13				1	2	7	9	8^2	5						31
	3^1		4						11^1	10			6											1	2	7	9		5	8	12				32
									11^1	10								5^1	6					1	2	7	9	12	4	8	3				33
1	2			5	6				11^1	12														7	9	8^1	4	10	3						34
1	2		10^1	5	6				11^1	12														7	9	8	4		3						35
1	2		4	5	6				11^3	7				8^1											10	9					3^2	12	13	14	36

RANGERS
Premier Division

Year Formed: 1873. *Ground & Address:* Ibrox Stadium, Edminston Drive, Glasgow G51 2XD. *Telephone:* 0141 427 8500. *Fax:* 0141 427 2676.
Ground Capacity: total: 50,500. *Size of Pitch:* 115yd × 78yd.
Chairman: David Murray. *Secretary:* R. C. Ogilvie. *Commercial Manager:* Bob Reilly.
Manager: Walter Smith. *Assistant Manager:* Archie Knox. *Physio:* Grant Downie. *Coach:* David Dodds. *Reserve team coaches:* John McGregor, John Brown.
Managers since 1975: Jock Wallace; John Greig; Jock Wallace; Graeme Souness. *Club Nickname(s):* The Gers. *Previous Grounds:* Burnbank, Kinning Park.
Record Attendance: 118,567 v Celtic, Division I; 2 Jan, 1939.
Record Transfer Fee received: £5,580,000 for Trevor Steven to Marseille (Aug 1991).
Record Transfer Fee paid: £4.3 million for Paul Gascoigne from Lazio (July 1995).
Record Victory: 14-2 v Blairgowrie, Scottish Cup 1st rd; 20 Jan, 1934.
Record Defeat: 2-10 v Airdrieonians; 1886.
Most Capped Player: Alistair McCoist, 54, Scotland.
Most League Appearances: 496: John Greig, 1962-78.
Most League Goals in Season (Individual): 44: Sam English, Division I; 1931-32.
Most Goals Overall (Individual): 236: Bob McPhail; 1927-39.

RANGERS 1995–96 LEAGUE RECORD

Match No.	Date	Venue	Opponents	Result		H/T Score	Lg. Pos.	Goalscorers	Atten-dance
1	Aug 26	H	Kilmarnock	W	1-0	0-0	—	McCall	44,686
2	Sept 9	H	Raith R	W	4-0	3-0	1	McCoist 2, Miller, Robertson	43,284
3	16	A	Falkirk	W	2-0	1-0	1	Salenko, Robertson	11,480
4	23	H	Hibernian	L	0-1	0-0	2		44,221
5	30	A	Celtic	W	2-0	1-0	1	Cleland, Gascoigne	33,296
6	Oct 3	H	Motherwell	W	2-1	1-0	—	Gascoigne, McCoist	39,891
7	7	A	Aberdeen	W	1-0	0-0	1	Moore	20,351
8	14	A	Partick Th	W	4-0	2-0	1	Gough, Durie 3	16,066
9	21	H	Hearts	W	4-1	3-0	1	Gascoigne, Salenko 2, Durie	45,155
10	28	A	Raith R	D	2-2	0-0	1	Gough, Petric	9300
11	Nov 4	H	Falkirk	W	2-0	2-0	1	McCoist 2	42,059
12	8	A	Kilmarnock	W	2-0	0-0	—	McLaren, Salenko	14,613
13	11	H	Aberdeen	D	1-1	1-1	1	Salenko	45,427
14	19	H	Celtic	D	3-3	1-1	—	Laudrup, McCoist, McKinlay (og)	46,640
15	25	A	Hibernian	W	4-1	2-1	1	McCoist, Dods (og), Miller, Durie	13,558
16	Dec 2	H	Hearts	W	2-0	0-0	1	McCoist, Gascoigne	15,105
17	9	H	Partick Th	W	1-0	0-0	1	Durie	43,137
18	19	A	Motherwell	D	0-0	0-0	—		10,197
19	26	H	Kilmarnock	W	3-0	2-0	—	Salenko, Durie (pen), Gascoigne	45,143
20	30	H	Hibernian	W	7-0	2-0	1	Miller, Durie 4, Gascoigne, Salenko	44,692
21	Jan 3	A	Celtic	D	0-0	0-0	—		36,719
22	6	A	Falkirk	W	4-0	3-0	1	Durie, McCoist 2 (1 pen), Robertson	10,348
23	13	H	Raith R	W	4-0	3-0	1	McCoist, Durie 2, Ferguson	42,498
24	20	H	Hearts	L	0-3	0-1	1		45,096
25	Feb 3	A	Partick Th	W	2-1	2-1	1	Gascoigne 2	16,488
26	10	H	Motherwell	W	3-2	1-0	1	Ferguson, McLaren, McCoist (pen)	44,871
27	25	A	Aberdeen	W	1-0	1-0	—	Gascoigne (pen)	19,842
28	Mar 3	A	Hibernian	W	2-0	1-0	—	Mitchell (og), Laudrup (pen)	11,923
29	17	H	Celtic	D	1-1	1-0	—	McLaren	47,312
30	23	H	Falkirk	W	3-2	2-0	1	Gascoigne, Andersen 2	46,361
31	30	A	Raith R	W	4-2	1-1	1	McCoist 3 (1 pen), Durie (pen)	9300
32	Apr 10	A	Hearts	L	0-2	0-1	—		15,350
33	13	H	Partick Th	W	5-0	2-0	1	Andersen 3, McCall, Gough	46,438
34	20	A	Motherwell	W	3-1	2-0	1	McCall, Andersen, Gascoigne	13,128
35	28	H	Aberdeen	W	3-1	1-1	—	Gascoigne 3 (1 pen)	47,247
36	May 4	A	Kilmarnock	W	3-0	2-0	1	McCoist, Durie 2	17,102

Final League Position: 1

Honours
League Champions: (46 times) Division I 1890-91 (shared), 1898-99, 1899-1900, 1900-01, 1901-02, 1910-11, 1911-12, 1912-13, 1917-18, 1919-20, 1920-21, 1922-23, 1923-24, 1924-25, 1926-27, 1927-28, 1928-29, 1929-30, 1930-31, 1932-33, 1933-34, 1934-35, 1936-37, 1938-39, 1946-47, 1948-49, 1949-50, 1952-53, 1955-56, 1956-57, 1958-59, 1960-61, 1962-63, 1963-64, 1974-75. Premier Division: 1975-76, 1977-78, 1986-87, 1988-89, 1989-90, 1990-91, 1991-92, 1992-93, 1993-94, 1994-95, 1995-96; *Runners-up:* 23 times.
Scottish Cup Winners: (27 times) 1894, 1897, 1898, 1903, 1928, 1930, 1932, 1934, 1935, 1936, 1948, 1949, 1950, 1953, 1960, 1962, 1963, 1964, 1966, 1973, 1976, 1978, 1979, 1981, 1992, 1993, 1996; *Runners-up:* 16 times.
League Cup Winners: (19 times) 1946-47, 1948-49, 1960-61, 1961-62, 1963-64, 1964-65, 1970-71, 1975-76, 1977-78, 1978-79, 1981-82, 1983-84, 1984-85, 1986-87, 1987-88, 1988-89, 1990-91, 1992-93, 1993-94; *Runners-up:* 7 times.

European: *European Cup:* 81 matches (1956-57, 1957-58, 1959-60 semi-finals, 1961-62, 1963-64, 1964-65, 1975-76, 1976-77, 1978-79, 1987-88, 1989-90, 1990-91, 1991-92, 1992-93 final pool, 1993-94, 1994-95). Final pool 1995-96.
Cup Winners Cup Winners: 1971-72. 50 matches (1960-61 runners-up, 1962-63, 1966-67 runners-up, 1969-70, 1971-72 winners, 1973-74, 1977-78, 1979-80, 1981-82, 1983-84). *UEFA Cup:* 38 matches (*Fairs Cup:* 1967-68, 1968-69 semi-finals, 1970-71 *UEFA Cup;* 1982-83, 1984-85, 1985-86, 1986-87, 1988-89).
Club colours: Shirt: Royal blue with red and blue panels. Shorts: White with red and blue panels. Stockings: Red with black tops.

Goalscorers: *League (85):* Durie 17 (2 pens), McCoist 16 (3 pens), Gascoigne 14 (2 pens), Salenko 7, Andersen 6, Gough 3, McCall 3, McLaren 3, Miller 3, Robertson 3, Ferguson 2, Laudrup 2 (1 pen), Cleland 1, Moore 1, Petric 1, own goals 3. *Scottish Cup (24):* Durie 4 (1 pen), Cleland 3, Ferguson 3, Gascoigne 3, Laudrup 3, Miller 3, McCoist 1, Mikhailichenko 1, Robertson 1, Van Vossen 1, own goal 1. *Coca-Cola Cup (8):* McCoist 3, Hateley 2, Gascoigne 1, McCall 1, Salenko 1.

Goram A 30	Wright S 6	Robertson D 25	Gough R 29	McLaren A 36	Petric G 32+1	Steven T 5+1	Miller C 17+6	McCoist A 18+7	McCall S 19+2	Durie G 21+6	Currant I 6+9	Salenko O 14+2	Gascoigne P 27+1	Laudrup B 22	Moore C 9+2	Murray N 2+3	Mikhailichenko A 6+5	Cleland A 21+4	Ferguson I 16+2	Brown J 8+6	Scott C 3	Bollan G 4	Thomson W 1	McGinty B 2	McInnes D 5+1	Van Vossen P 3+4	Andersen E 6	Sneiders T 2	Shields G 1	Match No.
1	2	3	4	5	6	7¹	8²	9	10	11	12	13																		1
1	2	3	4	5	6	7	9					12	10	8	11¹															2
1		3	4	5	6	10³	14	8²		9	13	2¹	7	11	12															3
1	2		4²	5	6	7¹	9		13	10	8	11	12		3		11													4
1	2		4	5	6	12	9	7		10¹	8			3	11															5
1		4	5	6		9²	12	7	13		8¹	2	14	11¹²	3	10														6
1	2	3	4	5	6		10	11⁷	8¹	9¹		12	13	7																7
1	2	3	4¹	5	6		13	10	9²	8³		14	11	7	12															8
1	3¹	4²	5	6			10	13	9	8		2	11	7	12															9
1		4	5	6	12	9		11		10	8	2²	7	13	3¹															10
1		4	5	6	12	9	10	11	7			2	8¹			1	3													11
1		4	5	6		9²			7¹	10	8	13	2	11	12		1	3												12
1		4	5	6		13	10		12	9	8¹	11²	2	7	14	3³	1													13
1	3	4	5	6	13	12	10		9²	8		11	2	7¹																14
1		4	5	6	7¹	9		12	13	10	8	2			3	11²														15
1	3	4	5	6	10²	9	12	13		8	11	2			7¹															16
1	3	4	5	6	7	9		10	12		11	2¹			8															17
1	3	4	5	6	9		10			11			7	8	2															18
1	3	4	5	6	7	10²	13	9	8	11	2¹					12														19
1	3	4	5	6	7		10		9	8	11	2																		20
1	3	4	5	6	7		10		9¹	8	11	12	2																	21
1	3	4	5	6	9	10¹	12	8	7	2	11																			22
1	3	4	5	6	9	10	8¹	11	12	2	7																			23
1	3	4	5	6¹	7	10	9²	11	13	8	2	12																		24
1	3		5	6	9	10	8	11	12	2	4¹	7																		25
1	3		5	6	7	12	10	8	11	4	2	9¹																		26
1	3		5	4	7	10	8¹	11	2	13	9²	6	12																	27
1	3	4¹	5	6	13	14	10	8	11	2	12	7²	9³																	28
1		5	4	7	9	10	12	8	11	2¹	3	6																		29
	5	4	2¹	9²	10	13	8	11	12	3	6	1														7				30
	5	2	9	10	4	8	11	3²	12	6	13	7¹	1																	31
1	3	4	5	6²	7²	9	10	12	8	11	2¹	14	13																	32
1	3	4	5¹	12		10	7	8	11	2	6	9																		33
1	3	4	5	2		10	7	8	11	6	9																			34
1	3	4	5	13	2¹	12	10	7³	14	8	11	6	9¹																	35
	3	5	7¹	12	9	4	10	6	8	11¹²	13	1	2																	36

ROSS COUNTY   Third Division

Year Formed: 1929. *Ground & Address:* Victoria Park, Dingwall IV15 9QW. *Telephone:* 01349 862253. *Fax:* 01349 866277.
Ground Capacity: total 5400, seated 1520. *Size of Ground:* 110×75yd.
Secretary: Donald MacBean. *Office Secretary:* Mrs Cathie Caird. *Commercial Manager:* Brian Campbell.
Manager: Neale Cooper. *Assistant Manager:* Jim Kelly. *Physio:* Douglas Sim. *Record Attendance:* 8000, v Rangers, Scottish Cup, 28 February 1966.
Record Transfer Fee Received: £40,000 for Barry Wilson to Raith R, Sept.1994.
Record Transfer Fee Paid: £25,000 for Barry Wilson from Southampton, Oct.1992.
Record Victory: 11-0 v St Cuthbert Wanderers, Scottish Cup, Dec.1993.
Record Defeat: 1-10 v Inverness Thistle, Highland League.
Most League Appearances: 35, Robbie Williamson, 1994-95.
Most League Goals in Season: 12, Brian Grant, 1994-95.
Club Colours: Shirt: Dark Blue with White trim. Shorts: White. Stockings: Red.

ROSS COUNTY 1995–96 LEAGUE RECORD

Match No.	Date	Venue	Opponents	Result		H/T Score	Lg. Pos.	Goalscorers	Atten- dance
1	Aug 12	H	Queen's P	W	2-0	0-0	—	Milne, McPherson	1515
2	26	A	East Stirling	W	2-1	0-1	—	Bellshaw, McPherson	478
3	Sept 2	H	Arbroath	W	4-2	1-2	1	Bellshaw, Milne, McPherson, Connelly	1400
4	9	A	Brechin C	L	1-2	1-0	2	McPherson	479
5	16	H	Albion R	W	5-1	1-0	1	Milne 2, McPherson, Grant 2	1419
6	23	H	Cowdenbeath	D	2-2	1-0	3	Milne, McPherson	1571
7	30	A	Caledonian Th	D	1-1	1-1	3	McPherson	3627
8	Oct 7	H	Livingston	D	1-1	1-0	3	Milne	2120
9	14	A	Alloa	L	0-1	0-0	3		501
10	21	A	Arbroath	W	2-1	2-1	2	Connelly, Williamson	603
11	28	H	East Stirling	D	1-1	0-0	2	Furphy	1646
12	Nov 4	A	Albion R	W	4-3	2-1	2	Grant, Milne 2 (2 pens), Ferries	399
13	11	H	Brechin C	D	0-0	0-0	3		1653
14	18	H	Caledonian Th	W	2-0	1-0	2	McPherson 2	4288
15	25	A	Cowdenbeath	L	0-2	0-0	2		318
16	Dec 2	A	Livingston	D	0-0	0-0	2		3444
17	16	H	Alloa	D	2-2	1-0	3	Somerville, Golabek	1303
18	30	A	Queen's P	D	1-1	1-0	3	McPherson	699
19	Jan 10	H	Arbroath	D	0-0	0-0	—		944
20	13	H	Cowdenbeath	W	4-1	1-1	2	Milne, Grant 2, Connelly	1369
21	23	A	Caledonian Th	D	1-1	0-1	—	Milne	4931
22	Feb 3	A	Alloa	W	4-0	1-0	4	MacPherson, Milne 2, Williamson	373
23	13	H	Livingston	D	2-2	2-1	—	MacPherson, MacLeod	2300
24	17	A	Brechin C	D	0-0	0-0	4		506
25	24	A	East Stirling	W	4-2	1-0	3	Milne, Somerville, MacLeod, Ferries	353
26	Mar 2	A	Queen's P	D	0-0	0-0	4		238
27	6	H	Albion R	D	1-1	1-0	—	Milne	1031
28	9	A	Cowdenbeath	D	1-1	1-1	4	Golabek	290
29	16	H	Caledonian Th	W	2-1	1-0	3	MacLeod, Grant	3670
30	23	A	Albion R	W	3-0	2-0	3	Grant 3	364
31	30	H	Brechin C	L	1-2	0-1	3	Bradshaw	2362
32	Apr 6	A	Livingston	L	1-2	1-1	3	Milne (pen)	2333
33	13	H	Alloa	D	0-0	0-0	4		1068
34	20	A	Arbroath	D	1-1	0-1	4	Grant	439
35	27	H	East Stirling	L	1-3	0-2	3	Grant	914
36	30	H	Queen's P	L	0-1	0-1	4		916

Final League Position: 4

Goalscorers: *League (56).* Milne 15 (3 pens), MacPherson 12, Grant 11, Connelly 3, MacLeod 3, Bellshaw 2, Ferries 2, Golabek 2, Somerville 2, Williamson 2, Bradshaw 1, Furphy 1. *Scottish Cup (2):* Robertson 1, own goal 1. *Coca-Cola Cup (0) League Challenge Cup (2):* Connelly 1, Milne 1.

Hutchison S 32	Herd W 36	Mackay D 36	Williamson R 18 + 3	Bellshaw J 35	Furphy W 28 + 3	Ferries K 31 + 5	Grant B 16 + 18	Milne C 31 + 3	Connelly G 27 + 4	Crainie D 5	MacPherson J 19 + 5	McFee R — + 13	Somerville C 23 + 1	Watt V 2 + 3	MacLeod A 15 + 10	Robertson C 11 + 6	McMillan D 4	Golabek S 22	Ruickbie R 1 + 4	Bradshaw P 4 + 4	Stewart R — + 1	Match No.
1	2	3	4	5	6	7	8^1	9	10	11	12											1
1	2	3	4	5	6	7^2	12	9^1	10	11	8	13										2
1	2	3	4	5	6	7^3	13	9	10	11^1	8^2	12	14									3
1	2	3	4	5	6^1	7	14	9	10	11^2	8^3	13		12								4
1	2	3	4	5	6^1	7	13	9	10	11^3	8^2				12	14						5
1	2	3	4	5	6	7	12	9^1	10		8	13				11^2						6
1	2	3	4	5	6^2	7^1	12	9	10		8				13	11						7
1	2	3	4	5	6	7	8	9^2	10			13			12	11^1						8
1	2	3	4	5	6^1	7	13	9	10		8				12	11^2						9
1	2	3	4	5	6	7	12	9^1	10		8^2	13				11						10
	2	3	4	5	6	7	12	9	10		8^1	13				11^2	1					11
	2	3	4	5	6	7	8	9	10						12	11^3	1					12
1	4	3		5	6	7^2	8^1	9	10		13			2	12	11						13
	4	3		5	6	7	12	9^2	10		8^1			2	14	13	1	11^2				14
	4	3	13	5	6	7^2	12	9^1	10		8			2		14	1	11^3				15
1	7^1	3	4	5	6	14	8^2	13	10		9		7^3		12			11				16
1	4	3	13	5	6^2	7	14	9^1	10		8			2	12			11^1				17
1	4	3		5	6	7	12	9^1	10		8			2		13		11^2				18
1	2	3	14	5	6	7	8^2	12	10		9^1				13	4^3		11				19
1	4	3		5	6	12	8	9	13					2	10^2	7^1		11				20
1	4	3		5	6	12	8^1	9^2	10		13			2	7			11				21
1	7	3	4^1	5	6	12		9	10		8			2^2					11	13		22
1	4	3		5	6	12		9	10		8^1			2	7			11				23
1	4	3		5		7	12	9	10		8^1			2	6			11				24
1	4^3	3		5		7	12	9	10		8^1	13		2	14	6		11^2				25
1	4	3		5		7	8	9^1	10					2	6	13		11^2		12		26
1	4	3		5	12	7	8^1	9	10		13			2	6			11^2				27
1	4	3		5	6	7^2	12	9			13			2	8			11		10^1		28
1	4	3		5	6	7^2	12	9			13			2	8			11		10^1		29
1	4	3		5	6	7	8^2	9	12					2	10^1			11		13		30
1	4	3		5^2	6	7	8	9^1	13		14			2	10^2			11		12		31
1	4	3		5	6^1	7^3	8^2	9	12		14			2	10			11		13		32
1	8^3	3	4	5		7	13		10^2					2	6	12		11^1	14	9		33
1	10	3	4		12	7^3	8		14					2^1	6^2	9		11	5		13	34
1	6	3	4	5	12	7	8	13						2	10^1			11^2	14	9^3		35
1	6	3	4^3	5		7	8^2	9^1			13			2	12	10		11	14			36

ST JOHNSTONE
First Division

Year Formed: 1884. *Ground & Address:* McDiarmid Park, Crieff Road, Perth PH1 2SJ. *Telephone:* 01738 626961. *Fax:* 01738 625 771. *Clubcall:* 0898 121559.
Ground Capacity: total: 10,721. seated: 10,721. *Size of Pitch:* 115yd × 75yd.
Chairman: G.S.Brown. *Secretary and Managing Director:* Stewart Duff.
Manager: Paul Sturrock. *Sales Executive:* Helen Harcus. *Physio:* David Henderson. *Coach:* John Blackley. *Youth Development Coach:* Alistair Stevenson.
Managers since 1975: J. Stewart; J. Storrie; A. Stuart; A. Rennie; I. Gibson; A. Totten, J. McClelland. *Club Nickname(s):* Saints. *Previous Grounds:* Recreation Grounds, Muirton Park.
Record Attendance: (McDiarmid Park): 10,504 v Rangers, Premier Division; 20 Oct, 1990.
Record Transfer Fee received: £750,000 for Billy Dodds to Aberdeen, 1994.
Record Transfer Fee paid: £300,000 for Billy Dodds from Dundee, 1994.
Record Victory: 9-0 v Albion R, League Cup; 9 March, 1946.
Record Defeat: 1-10 v Third Lanark, Scottish Cup; 24 January, 1903.
Most Capped Player: Sandy McLaren, 5, Scotland.
Most League Appearances: 298: Drew Rutherford.
Most League Goals in Season (Individual): 36: Jimmy Benson, Division II; 1931-32.
Most Goals Overall (Individual): 114: John Brogan, 1977-83.

ST JOHNSTONE 1995–96 LEAGUE RECORD

Match No.	Date	Venue	Opponents	Result	H/T Score	Lg. Pos.	Goalscorers	Atten- dance
1	Aug 12	H	Dundee	L	0-2	0-1	—	5236
2	26	A	St Mirren	D	0-0	0-0	8	2430
3	Sept 2	H	Morton	L	0-2	0-1	9	3134
4	9	A	Hamilton A	W	3-0	2-0	9	O'Boyle, O'Neil 2	803
5	16	A	Dumbarton	W	4-1	2-0	4	O'Boyle, Twaddle, O'Neil, Farquhar	2273
6	23	H	Clydebank	D	2-2	0-0	6	Grant, O'Boyle	2482
7	30	A	Dunfermline Ath	L	1-2	1-0	7	O'Boyle	5737
8	Oct 7	H	Airdrieonians	W	1-0	1-0	6	Scott	2839
9	14	A	Dundee U	L	1-2	0-2	7	McQuillan	7572
10	21	A	Morton	L	0-4	0-2	7		3313
11	28	H	St Mirren	D	0-0	0-0	7		3028
12	Nov 4	A	Dumbarton	W	3-1	0-1	7	Twaddle 2, O'Boyle	1050
13	11	H	Hamilton A	W	2-0	1-0	5	O'Neil, Preston	2348
14	18	H	Dunfermline Ath	W	1-0	0-0	5	Twaddle	4559
15	25	A	Clydebank	L	0-2	0-2	7		923
16	Dec 2	A	Airdrieonians	D	1-1	0-0	7	Scott	1660
17	9	H	Dundee U	D	0-0	0-0	6		5966
18	16	A	Dundee	W	1-0	0-0	5	Scott	3034
19	Jan 6	H	Dumbarton	W	3-0	0-0	5	O'Boyle 2, Burns (og)	2448
20	9	H	Morton	W	6-1	3-0	—	O'Boyle 3, Scott, Sekerlioglu, Ferguson	3253
21	13	A	Hamilton A	L	1-2	0-1	5	Preston	1197
22	20	H	Airdrieonians	D	0-0	0-0	5		2761
23	23	H	Clydebank	W	3-1	1-1	—	Scott 2, O'Boyle	2167
24	Feb 3	A	Dundee U	W	3-1	2-0	5	O'Boyle 2, O'Neil	7478
25	13	H	Dundee	W	3-2	2-0	—	McGowne, Grant, O'Boyle	3960
26	24	A	St Mirren	W	3-1	1-1	4	Scott 2, O'Boyle	2568
27	28	A	Dunfermline Ath	L	2-3	2-1	—	Grant, O'Boyle	6348
28	Mar 2	A	Clydebank	W	2-1	2-0	3	Tosh, O'Neil	705
29	16	H	Dunfermline Ath	D	2-2	1-2	4	Griffin, Jenkinson	5239
30	23	A	Dumbarton	W	3-0	2-0	4	Jenkinson, O'Boyle, Grant	903
31	30	H	Hamilton A	W	4-1	1-0	4	McGowne, Sekerlioglu, Grant, O'Boyle	2614
32	Apr 6	A	Airdrieonians	W	3-1	1-1	3	McQuillan, O'Boyle 2	2018
33	13	H	Dundee U	W	1-0	1-0	3	Pressley (og)	9973
34	20	A	Morton	L	0-1	0-1	4		5808
35	27	H	St Mirren	W	1-0	1-0	4	O'Boyle	3687
36	May 4	A	Dundee	D	0-0	0-0	4		2710

Final League Position: 4

Honours
League Champions: First Division 1982-83, 1989-90. Division II 1923-24, 1959-60, 1962-63; *Runners-up:* Division II 1931-32. Second Division 1987-88.
Scottish Cup: Semi-finals 1934, 1968, 1989, 1991.
League Cup Runners-up: 1969.

European: *UEFA Cup:* 1971-72.
Club colours: Shirt: Royal blue with white trim. Shorts: White. Stockings: Royal blue, white trim.

Goalscorers: *League (60):* O'Boyle 21, Scott 8, O'Neil 6, Grant 5, Twaddle 4, Jenkinson 2, McGowne 2, McQuillan 2, Preston 2, Sekerlioglu 2, Farquhar 1, Ferguson 1, Griffin 1, Tosh 1, own goals 2. *Scottish Cup (5):* Scott 3, Grant 1, O'Boyle 1. *Coca-Cola Cup (1):* O'Boyle 1. *League Challenge Cup (2):* O'Neil 1, Scott 1.

Main A 34	McQuillan J 25	Donaldson E 15	Cherry P 13 + 2	Irons D 9 + 8	McGowne K 23	Scott P 28	Griffin D 22 + 9	Twaddle K 17 + 9	Grant R 19 + 8	Preston A 25 + 2	Ferguson 13 + 7	Farquhar G 10 + 5	Proctor M 2 + 4	McCluskey S 2	O'Neil J 34	O'Boyle G 35	Tosh S 8 + 1	McLean S 1 + 5	Weir J 29	English I — + 1	Whiteford A 3 + 1	Sekerlioglu A 17	Jenkinson L 18	Young S 1 + 3	Robertson S 2	Davidson C 1	Match No.
1	2	3	4	5	6	7^2	8^1	9	10	11	12	13															1
1	2		12			7^1	5	13	8^2	3		4	6		9	10	11										2
1	2		12	6		7	5	13	8^2	3	11	4^3			9^1	10	14										3
1	2			6	4	7	5^2	9^2	12	3	11	13			8	10^1		14									4
1	2				4	7	5^1	9^2	13	3	11	12			8	10^2		14	6								5
1	2	14			4	7^3	5	9	13	3	11^2				8^1	10		6	12								6
1	2		12		4^1	7	5	9^2		3	13	11			8	10		6									7
1	2	3		6	4	7	5^1	9^2	13		11	12			8	10											8
1	2			6	4		5	9	13	3	11^1	12^2			8	10		7									9
1	2		4	6^2		8	13	9	12	3	11				10		7^1		5								10
1	2	3	12		7	6	11	9^1	8	13					5	4	10^2										11
1	2^1	3		6	7	4	9		12		8				11	10			5								12
1		3		6	7	4	9^1	11							8	10			12	5	2						13
1		3		6	7	4	9^1	11							8	10			12	5	2						14
1		3	14	6	7	4	9^2	11	12						8^3	10			13	5	2^1						15
1		3	2	13	6	7	4	9	12	11^1					8^2	10			5								16
1		2		6	7		9		3						8	10			5			4	11				17
1		2		7	6	9			3	12					8	10^1			5			4	11				18
1		2	13	7^2	6		12	3	9^1						8	10			5			4^2	11	14			19
1		2		7^2	6		9^1	3	12						8	10			5			4	11	13			20
1		2	14		7	6^3		9^2	3	13	12				8^1	10			5			4	11				21
		2		4	7	6	11^1	13	3	9^2	12				8	10			5							1	22
1	2			6	7		13	9	3		12				8^1	10^2			5			4	11				23
1	2			6	7			9	3						8	10			5			4	11				24
1	2		4	6	7	12		9	3						8	10			5				11				25
1	2			6	7		12	9^1	3						8	10			5			4	11				26
1	2		12	6	7	14	13	9^2	3^3						8	10			5			4	11				27
1	2			6	12		9	3^1							8	10	7		5			4	11				28
1	2	3		6		5	12	9		7^1					8	10						4	11				29
1	2	3		6	14	12	9	13							8^3	10	7^1	5				4	11^2				30
1	2	3		6	13	12	9^1								8^3	10	7	5				4^2	11	14			31
1	2	3		6			9								8	10	7	5				4	11				32
1	2	3^1		6	7	12	9								8	10			5			4	11				33
1	2	3		6	7^3	13	12	9							8	10			5			4^2	11				34
1	2	3		6		12	9								8	10	7^1	5				4	11				35
		2		6	4							8			10	7	9^1	5	12				11	1	3		36

ST MIRREN   First Division

Year Formed: 1877. *Ground & Address:* St Mirren Park, Love St, Paisley PA3 2EJ. *Telephone:* 0141 889 2558/0141 840 1337. *Fax:* 0141 848 6444.
Ground Capacity: total: 15,410. seated 9395. *Size of Pitch:* 112yd × 73yd.
Chairman: Bob Earlie. *Secretary:* Jack Copland.
Manager: Jimmy Bone. *Physio:* Andrew Binning. *Coach:* Kenny McDowall.
Managers since 1975: Alex Ferguson; Jim Clunie; Rikki MacFarlane; Alex Miller; Alex Smith; Tony Fitzpatrick; David Hay. *Club Nickname(s):* The Buddies. *Previous Grounds:* Short Roods 1877-79, Thistle Park Greenhill 1879-83, Westmarch 1883-94.
Record Attendance: 47,438 v Celtic, League Cup, 20 Aug, 1949.
Record Transfer Fee received: £850,000 for Ian Ferguson to Rangers (1988).
Record Transfer Fee paid: £400,000 for Thomas Stickroth from Bayer Uerdingen (1990).
Record Victory: 15-0 v Glasgow University, Scottish Cup 1st rd; 30 Jan, 1960.
Record Defeat: 0-9 v Rangers, Division I; 4 Dec, 1897.
Most Capped Player: Godmundor Torfason, 29, Iceland.
Most League Appearances: 351: Tony Fitzpatrick, 1973-88.
Most League Goals in Season (Individual): 45: Dunky Walker, Division I; 1921-22.
Most Goals Overall (Individual): 221: David McCrae, 1923-24.

ST MIRREN 1995–96 LEAGUE RECORD

Match No.	Date	Venue	Opponents	Result	H/T Score	Lg. Pos.	Goalscorers	Atten- dance
1	Aug 12	A	Clydebank	D 1-1	1-0	—	Fullarton	1886
2	26	H	St Johnstone	D 0-0	0-0	4		2430
3	Sept 2	A	Airdrieonians	W 2-1	1-0	5	Bone, Lavety	2142
4	9	A	Dundee U	L 0-1	0-0	7		6159
5	16	H	Dunfermline Ath	L 0-2	0-1	9		3479
6	23	A	Hamilton A	D 2-2	2-2	8	Yardley, Boyd	1451
7	30	H	Morton	L 1-4	1-2	8	Boyd	5436
8	Oct 7	A	Dundee	L 1-3	0-1	9	Boyd	3555
9	14	H	Dumbarton	W 3-2	2-1	8	Dick, Archdeacon, Yardley	2377
10	21	H	Airdrieonians	L 1-2	1-1	8	Taylor	2459
11	28	A	St Johnstone	D 0-0	0-0	8		3028
12	Nov 4	A	Dunfermline Ath	D 1-1	1-0	8	McCathie (og)	4578
13	11	H	Dundee U	D 1-1	1-1	8	Gillies	3556
14	18	A	Morton	W 3-0	1-0	8	Yardley 2, Lavety	6217
15	25	H	Hamilton A	L 0-3	0-1	8		2546
16	Dec 2	H	Dundee	L 1-2	0-2	8	Lavety	2278
17	9	A	Dumbarton	D 0-0	0-0	8		1461
18	16	H	Clydebank	W 2-1	1-1	8	Yardley, Dick	1828
19	Jan 6	H	Dunfermline Ath	W 2-1	2-1	8	Hetherston, Gillies	3380
20	13	A	Dundee U	L 1-2	0-2	8	Lavety	6523
21	16	A	Airdrieonians	W 3-1	1-1	—	Hetherston, Yardley 2 (1 pen)	1554
22	20	A	Dundee	W 2-1	1-0	7	Fullarton, McMillan	2698
23	24	A	Hamilton A	L 0-3	0-1	—		1531
24	31	H	Morton	L 0-1	0-0	—		5312
25	Feb 3	H	Dumbarton	W 5-0	1-0	6	Lavety 2, Fenwick, Watson, Iwelumo	1838
26	10	A	Clydebank	W 2-1	1-0	6	Fenwick, Gillies	1515
27	24	H	St Johnstone	L 1-3	1-1	6	Yardley	2568
28	Mar 2	H	Hamilton A	L 0-1	0-1	6		1243
29	16	A	Morton	W 2-1	2-1	6	McLaughlin, Lavety	4204
30	23	A	Dunfermline Ath	D 2-2	0-2	6	Lavety 2	4936
31	30	H	Dundee U	L 1-3	0-3	6	McLaughlin	4347
32	Apr 6	H	Dundee	W 2-1	2-1	6	Fenwick, Taylor	2175
33	13	A	Dumbarton	W 1-0	1-0	6	Archdeacon	1139
34	20	H	Airdrieonians	W 2-1	2-1	6	Lavety, Taylor	2117
35	27	A	St Johnstone	L 0-1	0-1	6		3687
36	May 4	H	Clydebank	L 1-2	0-1	6	Lavety	1657

Final League Position: 6

Honours
League Champions: First Division 1976-77. Division II 1967-68; *Runners-up:* 1935-36.
Scottish Cup Winners: 1926, 1959, 1987. *Runners-up* 1908, 1934, 1962.
League Cup: Runners-up 1955-56.
B&Q Cup: Runners-up 1993-94 *Victory Cup:* 1919-20. *Summer Cup:* 1943-44. *Anglo-Scottish Cup:* 1979-80.

European: *Cup Winners Cup:* 1987-88. *UEFA Cup:* 1980-81, 1983-84, 1985-86.
Club colours: Shirt: Black and white vertical stripes. Shorts: Black. Stockings: Black with white trim. Change colours: Predominantly red.

Goalscorers: *League (46):* Lavety 11, Yardley 8 (1 pen), Boyd 3, Fenwick 3, Gillies 3, Taylor 3, Archdeacon 2, Dick 2, Fullarton 2, Hetherston 2, McLaughlin 2, Bone 1, Iwelumo 1, McMillan 1, Watson 1, own goal 1. *Scottish Cup (0) Coca-Cola Cup (1):* McLaughlin 1. *League Challenge Cup (3):* Lavety 2, Dawson 1 (pen).

Money C 13	Dawson R 8	Baker M 26	McWhirter N 17	Watson S 18+12	McLaughlin B 29+1	Law R 14+5	Fullarton J 19+3	Lavety R 27+2	Bone A 3+2	Boyd J 12+2	Gillies R 28+5	Taylor S 14+10	Combe A 20	McGrotty G 3+7	Dick J 24+2	Hetherston B 16+7	McIntyre P 20+6	Inglis G —+1	Archdeacon P 16+4	Smith B 6+6	Yardley M 29	Fenwick P 26	Makele J 1	Prentice A —+2	Scrimgour D 3	McMillan J —+8	Iwelumo C 2+3	Hringsson H —+1	Milne D 1+4	Galloway G 1	Love F —+1	Match No.
	2	3	4	5	6	7	8²	9¹	10	11	12	13																				1
	2	3	4	5	6	7³	8	9	10¹	11²	12	13	1		14																	2
	2	3	4²	5	6	7	8	9³	10¹	11	12	13	1		14																	3
	2	3	4	5¹	6	7³	8	9	10²	11	12	13	1		14																	4
	2	3	4	5	6	7	8	9	10¹	11²	12	13	1		14																	5
	2	3	4	5	6	7	8	9	10¹	11	12		1																			6
	2	3	4	5	6	7¹	8	9	10	11²	12	13	1																			7
	2	3¹	4	5	6	7	8	9	10	11	12		1																			8
		3		5	6	7²	8¹	10		11¹	12	13	1		2	14					9	4										9
		3		5	6	7²	8	10		11	12	13	1		2¹						9	4										10
		3²		5	6	7	8	10¹		11	12	13	1		2						9	4										11
		3²		5	6	7	8	10		11¹	12	13	1		2						9	4				14						12
		3		5¹	6	7	8	10²		11³	12	13	1		2						9	4				14						13
		3		5²	6	7	8³	10		11¹	12	13	1		2						9	4				14						14
		3		5¹	6	7	8	10		11²	12	13	1		2³						9	4				14						15
1		3		5¹	6	7²	8	10		11	12	13			2						9	4										16
1		3		5¹	6	7²	8	10		11²	12	13			2						9	4				14						17
1		3	4		6¹	7	8³	10		11	12	13			2						9²	5				14						18
1		3	4		6	7	8²	10		11¹	12	13			2						9	5										19
1		3	4	5¹	6	7	8²	10		11³	12	13			2			1			9					14						20
1		3	4		6¹	7	8³	10²		11	12	13			2						9	5				14						21
1		3	4		6	7	8	10²		11¹	12	13			2³						9	5				14						22
1		3	4		6¹	7²	8	10³		11	12	13			2						9	5				14						23
1		3	4		6²	7	8³	10		11¹	12	13			2						9	5				14						24
1		3	4²		6	7	8¹	10³		11	12	13			2						9	5				14						25
1		3	4		6¹	7	8	10²		11	12	13			2						9	5										26
1		3	4		6	7	8³	10		11²	12	13			2¹						9	5				14						27
1		3¹	4		6	7	8	10²		11	12	13			2						9	5										28
		3	4		6	7²	8	10		11¹	12	13	1		2						9	5										29
		3²	4		6	7	8	10		11¹	12	13	1		2						9	5										30
		3²	4		6¹	7	8	10		11²	12	13	1		2						9	5				14						31
		3	4		6	7	8²	10		11³	12	13	1		2						9¹	5				14						32
		3	4		6	7¹	8	10²		11³	12	13	1		2						9	5				14						33
		3	4²		6¹	7	8	10		11³	12	13	1		2						9	5				14						34
		3	4		6³	7²	8	10		11¹	12	13	1		2						9	5				14						35
		3	4³		6	7	8²	10		11¹	12	13	1		2						9	5				13	1		14			36

STENHOUSEMUIR Second Division

Year Formed: 1884. *Ground & Address:* Ochilview Park, Gladstone Rd, Stenhousemuir FK5 5QL. *Telephone:* 01324 562992.
Ground Capacity: total: 3520. seated: 310. *Size of Pitch:* 113yd × 74yd.
Chairman: A Terry Bulloch. *Secretary:* David O.Reid. *Commercial Manager:* John Sharp.
Manager: Terry Christie. *Assistant Manager:* Graeme Armstrong. *Physio:* Lee Campbell. *Coach:* Gordon Buchanan.
Managers since 1975: H. Glasgow; J. Black; A. Rose; W. Henderson; A. Rennie; J. Meakin; D. Lawson. *Club Nickname(s):* The Warriors. *Previous Grounds:* Tryst Ground 1884-86, Goschen Park 1886-90.
Record Attendance: 12,500 v East Fife, Scottish Cup 4th rd; 11 Mar, 1950.
Record Transfer Fee received: £30,000 for David Beaton to Falkirk (June 1989).
Record Transfer Fee paid: £7000 to Meadowbank T for Lee Bullen (Nov 1990).
Record Victory: 9-2 v Dundee U, Division II; 19 Apr, 1937.
Record Defeat: 2-11 v Dunfermline Ath. Division II; 27 Sept, 1930.
Most Capped Player: —.
Most League Appearances: 360: Archie Rose.
Most League Goals in Season (Individual): 32: Robert Taylor, Division II; 1925-26.
Most Goals Overall (Individual): —.

STENHOUSEMUIR 1995–96 LEAGUE RECORD

Match No.	Date	Venue	Opponents	Result		H/T Score	Lg. Pos.	Goalscorers	Attendance
1	Aug 12	A	Queen of the S	D	2-2	1-1	—	Little, Hutchison	1300
2	26	H	Stranraer	W	3-0	1-0	3	Little, Mathieson, Fisher	336
3	Sept 2	A	Forfar Ath	L	0-1	0-1	5		542
4	9	H	Stirling A	D	1-1	0-1	6	Little	674
5	16	A	Berwick R	L	1-3	0-1	7	Henderson	362
6	23	A	Clyde	W	1-0	0-0	6	Little	1088
7	30	H	East Fife	L	0-1	0-0	7		789
8	Oct 7	H	Montrose	W	3-1	3-0	6	Logan, Mathieson, Hutchison	521
9	14	A	Ayr U	W	2-1	0-1	4	Hutchison, Shepherd (og)	1106
10	21	H	Queen of the S	W	2-1	2-0	3	Hutchison, Little	509
11	28	A	Stranraer	L	1-2	0-1	5	Mathieson	566
12	31	H	Berwick R	W	4-1	3-0	—	Sprott 4	402
13	Nov 11	A	Stirling A	L	1-2	0-0	5	Sprott	903
14	18	A	East Fife	W	2-0	2-0	4	Little I, Mathieson	815
15	25	H	Clyde	L	0-1	0-1	4		714
16	Dec 2	A	Montrose	W	4-1	3-0	4	Little I, Mathieson 2, Hutchison	504
17	16	H	Ayr U	D	1-1	1-0	4	Mathieson	525
18	Jan 10	A	Queen of the S	D	3-3	2-1	—	Hutchison 2, Mathieson	743
19	13	A	Clyde	L	0-3	0-2	4		958
20	16	H	Forfar Ath	W	3-1	1-1	—	Bannon, Little I, Hunter	381
21	20	H	Montrose	W	3-1	2-1	3	Mathieson 2, Fisher	378
22	23	H	East Fife	D	2-2	1-1	—	Hunter, Hutchison	594
23	Feb 3	A	Ayr U	D	1-1	1-1	4	Hunter	1181
24	10	A	Berwick R	L	1-2	0-2	4	Sprott	333
25	24	H	Stranraer	W	2-0	0-0	4	Sprott, Aitken	406
26	27	H	Stirling A	L	0-1	0-0	—		864
27	Mar 2	A	Forfar Ath	L	1-3	0-2	4	Hutchison	371
28	9	H	Clyde	W	1-0	0-0	4	Sprott	674
29	16	H	East Fife	L	1-3	0-1	4	Hunter	621
30	23	H	Berwick R	L	0-3	0-2	4		419
31	30	A	Stirling A	W	1-0	0-0	4	Hunter	1132
32	Apr 6	A	Montrose	W	3-1	1-1	4	Hunter 2, Little I	507
33	13	A	Ayr U	L	0-1	0-1	4		559
34	20	H	Queen of the S	L	1-3	0-0	4	Hunter	471
35	27	A	Stranraer	D	0-0	0-0	4		503
36	May 4	H	Forfar Ath	L	0-2	0-0	4		431

Final League Position: 4

Honours

League Champions: —. *Scottish Cup:* Semi-finals 1902-03. Quarter-finals 1994-95 *League Cup:* Quarter-finals 1947-48, 1960-61, 1975-76. *League Challenge Cup:* Winners 1995-96.

Club colours: Shirt: Maroon with silver stripe. Shorts: White with maroon insert. Stockings: White.

Goalscorers: *League (51):* Mathieson 10, Hutchison 9, Little I 9, Hunter 8, Sprott 8, Fisher 2, Aitken 1, Bannon 1, Henderson 1, Logan 1, own goal 1. *Scottish Cup (6):* Little I 2, Hutchison 1, McGeachie 1, Mathieson 1, own goal 1. *Coca-Cola Cup (1):* Hutchison. *League Challenge Cup (8):* Hutchison 4, Little I 1, Logan 1, Mathieson 1, own goal 1.

McKenzie R 36	Bannon E 29	Haddow L 24+2	Armstrong G 34	McGeachie G 21+1	Christie M 18+1	Logan P 8+6	Fisher J 33	Mathieson M 30+1	Hutchison G 35+1	Little I 33	Clarke J —+1	Henderson J 6+5	Aitken N 7+14	Swanson D 1+3	Sprott A 30+1	Scott C 6+2	Hunter P 25+3	Brannigan K 11	Steel T 1+2	Roseburgh D 6+4	Little G 2+5	Match No.
1	2	3	4	5	6	7	8	9	10	11												1
1	2	3	4	5	6^2	7^1	8	9	10	11	12	13										2
1	2	3	4	5		7	8	9^2	10	11		13	6^1	12								3
1	2	3	4	5		7	8^1	9	10	11		6			12							4
1	2	3	4	5		7^1	8	9^2	10	11		13	12		6							5
1	2		4	5			8	9	10	11		12			6	3^1	7					6
1	2	3^1	4	5			8	9	10^2	11		13	12		6		7					7
1		3	4	5		6^2	8^1	9	10	11	12	13					7	2				8
1		3	4	5		6	8	9^2	10	11		12	13				7	2^1				9
1	2	3	4	5			8	9	10	11		12			6		7^1					10
1	2		4			13	8	9	10	11		12				3	7^2	5	6^1			11
1	2	3	4			13	8^1	9	10	11^2		5			6		7		12			12
1	2	3^2	4	5			8	9	10	11^1			14		6		7^2		13	12		13
1		3	4	5	6		8	9	10	11							7	2				14
1	7	3	4	5^2	6^1		8	9	10	11					2				13		12	15
1	7	3	4	5	6^1		8	9	10	11^2					2					13	12	16
1	7	3	4	5			8^1	9	10	11				12^2	2		6			13		17
1	7	3	4	5^1	6	12^2	8	9	10	11					2				13			18
1	7	3^1	4		6^3	14	8^2	9	10	11					2	13	12	5				19
1	3		4		6		8	9	10	11^1					2	12	7	5				20
1	7^1	3	4	12	6		8	9^2	10	11					2			5		13		21
1			4	6^2	12	8		10	11	7^1					2	5	9	3		13		22
1			4	5^1	6	8		10	11	12					2	9	3	7				23
1	3	12	4	6^2			10	11	13						2	8^3	9	5		7^1	14	24
1	3		4			8	9	10^1	11	12					2	7	5	6				25
1	3^1		4			8	9	10	11	6					2	7	5	12				26
1		3	4	5	6		8	13	12			7^1			2	11	9	10^2				27
1	3^1		4	5			8	10	11	12					2	7	9	6				28
1	13	3	4	5^2	6	8^1		9	10	11	12				2	7		3^1				29
1	5	8	4		6	12		9	10	11					2	7		3^1				30
1	5	3	4				8	9	10	11	6				2	7						31
1	5	3	4				8	9	10	11	6				2	7						32
1	5	3		12			8	9	10	11	6				2	4^1	7					33
1	5	3	4		6		8	9	10	11					2	7						34
1	3			5	6		8	9	10	11	4				2	7						35
1	3		4	5	6		8		10	11	9^1	12			2	7						36

STIRLING ALBION First Division

Year Formed: 1945. *Ground & Address:* Forthbank Stadium, Springkerse Industrial Estate, Stirling FK7 7UJ.
Telephone: 01786 450399. *Fax:* 01786 448592.
Ground Capacity: 3808. seated: 2508. *Size of Pitch:* 110yd × 74yd.
Chairman: Peter McKenzie. *Secretary:* Mrs Marlyn Hallam.
Manager: Kevin Drinkell. *Assistant Manager:* Ray Stewart. *Physio:* George Cameron.
Managers since 1975: A.Smith; G.Peebles; J.Fleeting, J.Brogan. *Club Nickname(s):* The Binos. *Previous Grounds:*
Annfield.
Record Attendance: 26,400 v Celtic, Scottish Cup 4th rd; 14 Mar, 1959.
Record Transfer Fee received: £70,000 for John Philliben to Doncaster R (Mar 1984).
Record Transfer Fee paid: £17,000 for Douglas Lawrie from Airdrieonians (Dec 1989).
Record Victory: 20-0 v Selkirk, Scottish Cup 1st rd; 8 Dec, 1984.
Record Defeat: 0-9 v Dundee U, Division I; 30 Dec, 1967.
Most Capped Player: —.
Most League Appearances: 504: Matt McPhee, 1967-81.

STIRLING ALBION 1995–96 LEAGUE RECORD

Match No.	Date	Venue	Opponents	Result	H/T Score	Lg. Pos.	Goalscorers	Atten- dance
1	Aug 12	H	Montrose	W 3-0	1-0	—	McCormick, Mitchell, Tait	752
2	26	A	Berwick R	L 0-3	0-2	5		434
3	Sept 2	H	East Fife	L 0-2	0-2	8		942
4	9	A	Stenhousemuir	D 1-1	1-0	7	Watson	674
5	16	H	Ayr U	W 2-0	0-0	6	Gibson, Taggart	760
6	23	A	Stranraer	D 0-0	0-0	7		658
7	30	H	Clyde	D 1-1	1-0	6	Taggart	1011
8	Oct 7	A	Forfar Ath	W 6-0	3-0	5	McCormick 3, McInnes 2, Taggart	624
9	14	H	Queen of the S	D 2-2	1-1	6	McLeod, Tait	748
10	21	A	Montrose	D 2-2	2-0	5	McQuilter, Bone	629
11	28	H	Berwick R	W 1-0	1-0	4	McCormick	811
12	Nov 4	A	Ayr U	W 2-1	1-1	3	Wood, Gibson	1233
13	11	A	Stenhousemuir	W 2-1	0-0	3	McInnes, Bone	903
14	18	A	Clyde	W 2-1	1-1	2	McCormick, Taggart	1200
15	25	H	Stranraer	D 1-1	0-0	3	Bone	811
16	Dec 2	H	Forfar Ath	W 4-1	2-0	2	McInnes, McCormick 2, McQuilter	734
17	16	A	Queen of the S	W 5-1	4-0	2	McCormick 3, Bone, Paterson G	1004
18	23	H	Montrose	W 2-0	0-0	2	McCormick 2	1056
19	Jan 13	A	Stranraer	D 2-2	1-1	2	Bone, Paterson G	587
20	17	A	East Fife	W 3-0	2-0	—	Taggart, Paterson G, Bone	1529
21	20	A	Forfar Ath	W 4-1	3-1	2	Taggart, Bone, McLeod, McCormick	611
22	24	H	Clyde	W 3-0	2-0	—	Bone 2, Tait	1068
23	Feb 3	H	Queen of the S	W 4-1	1-0	1	McCormick 3, Taggart	1042
24	14	H	Ayr U	W 2-0	2-0	—	McCormick, Bone	834
25	24	A	Berwick R	W 3-0	1-0	1	McCormick 2, Bone	483
26	27	A	Stenhousemuir	W 1-0	0-0	—	Gibson	864
27	Mar 2	H	East Fife	D 2-2	1-0	1	McQuilter, McCormick	1166
28	9	H	Stranraer	W 2-0	0-0	1	Tait, McCormick	1023
29	16	A	Clyde	W 3-1	2-1	1	Mitchell, Bone, McCormick	1183
30	23	A	Ayr U	D 2-2	0-1	1	McCormick, Tait	1732
31	30	H	Stenhousemuir	L 0-1	0-0	1		1132
32	Apr 6	H	Forfar Ath	W 1-0	0-0	1	Wood	788
33	13	A	Queen of the S	W 7-0	4-0	1	Bone 3, Gibson 2, Tait, Paterson G	1394
34	20	A	Montrose	W 3-0	1-0	1	Mailer (og), Taggart, Bone	824
35	27	H	Berwick R	W 4-3	2-2	1	Bone, Gibson, Tait, McCormick	1238
36	May 4	A	East Fife	W 1-0	0-0	1	Bone	1185

Final League Position: 1

Most League Goals in Season (Individual): 27: Joe Hughes, Division II; 1969-70.
Most Goals Overall (Individual): 129: Billy Steele, 1971-83.

Honours
League Champions: Division II 1952-53, 1957-58, 1960-61, 1964-65. Second Division 1976-77, 1990-91, 1995-96; *Runners-up:* Division II 1948-49, 1950-51.
Scottish Cup: —. *League Cup:* —.
Club colours: Shirt: Red with white sleeves. Shorts: White. Stockings: White.

Goalscorers: *League (83):* McCormick 25, Bone 18, Taggart 8, Tait 7, Gibson 6, McInnes 4, Paterson G 4, McQuilter 3, McLeod 2, Mitchell 2, Wood 2, Watson 1, own goal 1. *Scottish Cup (4):* McCormick 3, Mitchell 1. *Coca-Cola Cup (4):* McCormick 1, McLeod 1, Taggart 1, Tait 1. *League Challenge Cup (9):* McCormick 3, McLeod 2, Tait 2, Gibson 1, Taggart 1.

McGeown M 26	McKechnie M 3	Watson P 5 + 3	Mitchell C 32 + 4	McQuilter R 35	Tait T 28	McInnes I 15 + 1	Deas P 35	McCormick S 33	Taggart C 33 + 2	McLeod J 23 + 3	Farquhar A — + 3	Gibson J 18 + 11	Paterson A 33	Roberts P — + 3	Watters W — + 2	Monaghan M 10	Kirkham D — + 2	Bone A 27	Wood D 11 + 3	Paterson G 26	Bennett N 1 + 7	McGrotty G 2 + 4	Match No.
1	2	3	4	5	6	7	8	9¹	10	11	12												1
1	2	3	4	5	6	7	8¹	9	10	11	12												2
1	2¹	3²	4	5	6	7	8	9	10	11	13	12											3
1		3	4	5	6	7	8	9¹	10	11			2	12									4
1		3	4	5	6	7	8	9	10			11	2										5
1			4	5	6	7	8	9	10	11¹		3	2	12									6
			4	5	6	7	8	9	10	11¹		3	2		12	1							7
	13		4	5²	6¹	7	8	9	10	11		3	7³	14		1	17						8
	13		4	5	6	7	8	9¹	10	11²		3	2	12		1							9
	12		4	5	6¹			3	9	10		8	2			1		7	11				10
1			4	5				3	9	10		8	2			1	12	7	11¹	6			11
1			4	5		12		3	9	10		8	2			1		7	11¹	6			12
1			4	5		10		3	9			8	2			1		7	11	6			13
1			4	5		10		3	9	12		8	2			1		7	11¹	6			14
1			4	5		10		3	9	12		8	2			1		7	11¹	6			15
1		4²	5		8		3	9	10	12		13	2					7	11¹	6			16
1			4	5		8		3	9	10	12		2					7	11¹	6			17
1			4	5		8		3	9	10	12		2					7	11¹	6			18
1			4	5	8			3	9	10		11	2					7		6			19
1			4	5	8			3	9	10	11		2					7		6			20
1			4	5	8			3	9	10	11		2					7		6			21
1			4	5	8			3	9¹	10	11	12	2					7		6			22
1			4	5	8			3	9	10	11	12	2¹					7		6			23
1			4	5	8			3	9	10	11¹	12	2					7		6			24
1			4	5	8			3	9¹	10	11	12	2					7		6			25
1		4²	5	8			3	9	10			13	2					7	11¹	6	12		26
1		4¹	5	8			3	9	10	11²		12	2					7	13	6			27
1		4²	5	8			3	9	10¹	11		13	2					7		6	12		28
1			4	5	8			3	9¹	10	11	12	2					7		6			29
1			4	5	8			3	9	10¹	11	12	2					7		6			30
1			4²	5	8		3		10	11		9¹	2					7		6	13	12	31
1		12	5	8		3		10	11²			4	2¹					7	13	6	14	9³	32
1		13	5²	8		3¹		10	11			4	2					7³	14	6	12	9	33
1		13	5	8		3		9¹	10	11		4²	2					7		6	14	12	34
1		13	5	8		3		9	10	11¹		4	2²					7³		6	12	14	35
		5		8				9	10			4	2		1			7	11¹	6	3	12	36

STRANRAER   Second Division

Year Formed: 1870. *Ground & Address:* Stair Park, London Rd, Stranraer DG9 8BS. *Telephone:* 01776 703271.
Ground Capacity: total: 6100. seated: 1800. *Size of Pitch:* 110yd × 70yd.
Chairman/Secretary: Graham Rodgers. *Commercial Manager:* T. L. Sutherland.
Manager: Campbell Money. *Coach:* Jim Denny.
Managers since 1975: J. Hughes; N. Hood; G. Hamilton; D. Sneddon; J. Clark; R. Clark; A. McAnespie. *Club
Nickname(s):* The Blues. *Previous Grounds:* None.
Record Attendance: 6500 v Rangers, Scottish Cup 1st rd; 24 Jan, 1948.
Record Transfer Fee received: £30,000 for Duncan George to Ayr Utd.
Record Transfer Fee paid: £15,000 for Colin Harkness from Kilmarnock (Aug 1989).
Record Victory: 7-0 v Brechin C, Division II; 6 Feb, 1965.
Record Defeat: 1-11 v Queen of the South, Scottish Cup 1st rd; 16 Jan, 1932.
Most Capped Player: —.
Most League Appearances: 256: Danny McDonald.
Most League Goals in Season (Individual): 27: Derek Frye, Second Division; 1977-78.
Most Goals Overall (Individual): —.

STRANRAER 1995–96 LEAGUE RECORD

Match No.	Date	Venue	Opponents	Result		H/T Score	Lg. Pos.	Goalscorers	Attendance
1	Aug 12	H	Berwick R	D	0-0	0-0	—		507
2	26	A	Stenhousemuir	L	0-3	0-1	9		336
3	Sept 2	H	Montrose	W	4-1	2-0	7	Robertson, Grant 2, Walker	503
4	9	A	Queen of the S	W	3-0	2-0	5	Sloan, Henderson, Grant	1531
5	16	H	East Fife	W	2-0	0-0	4	Henderson, Ferguson	634
6	23	H	Stirling A	D	0-0	0-0	4		658
7	30	A	Ayr U	D	0-0	0-0	4		1455
8	Oct 7	A	Clyde	D	1-1	0-1	3	Henderson	1048
9	14	H	Forfar Ath	D	1-1	1-0	3	Grant	635
10	21	A	Berwick R	L	0-4	0-1	6		433
11	28	H	Stenhousemuir	W	2-1	1-0	6	Duncan, Reilly	566
12	Nov 4	A	East Fife	D	3-3	0-1	6	Kerrigan, Grant 2	850
13	11	H	Queen of the S	D	0-0	0-0	6		1006
14	18	H	Ayr U	W	2-0	1-0	5	Kerrigan, Duncan	891
15	25	A	Stirling A	D	1-1	0-0	5	Ferguson	811
16	Dec 2	H	Clyde	D	0-0	0-0	5		683
17	16	A	Forfar Ath	D	0-0	0-0	5		430
18	Jan 10	H	Berwick R	L	0-3	0-1	—		433
19	13	H	Stirling A	D	2-2	1-1	5	Sloan, Walker	587
20	16	A	Montrose	L	2-4	1-1	—	McAulay, McGuire	334
21	20	A	Clyde	D	2-2	2-1	5	Crawford, McConnell (og)	942
22	27	A	Ayr U	D	0-0	0-0	5		1919
23	Feb 3	H	Forfar Ath	W	1-0	0-0	5	Walker	476
24	10	H	East Fife	D	0-0	0-0	5		531
25	17	A	Queen of the S	L	1-2	1-2	5	Walker	1229
26	24	A	Stenhousemuir	L	0-2	0-0	5		406
27	Mar 2	H	Montrose	L	1-2	1-1	5	Kerrigan	436
28	9	A	Stirling A	L	0-2	0-0	8		1023
29	16	H	Ayr U	D	1-1	0-1	8	Hughes	806
30	23	A	East Fife	L	1-2	0-2	8	Duncan	738
31	30	H	Queen of the S	W	3-1	2-0	8	Kerrigan, McGuire, Bilsland	722
32	Apr 6	H	Clyde	D	2-2	0-0	8	Howard, Sloan	655
33	13	A	Forfar Ath	D	2-2	1-1	7	McMillan 2	388
34	20	A	Berwick R	L	0-1	0-0	8		373
35	27	H	Stenhousemuir	D	0-0	0-0	8		503
36	May 4	A	Montrose	W	1-0	1-0	8	Kerrigan	347

Final League Position: 8

Honours
League Champions: Second Division 1993-94.
Scottish Cup: —.
League Cup: —.
Qualifying Cup Winners: 1937.
Club colours: Shirt: Royal blue and red quarters. Shorts: White. Stockings: Royal blue.

Goalscorers: *League (38):* Grant 6, Kerrigan 5, Walker 4, Duncan 3, Henderson 3, Sloan 3, Ferguson 2, McGuire 2, McMillan 2, Bilsland 1, Crawford 1, Howard 1, Hughes 1, McAulay 1, Reilly 1, Robertson 1, own goal 1. *Scottish Cup (0) Coca-Cola Cup (0) League Challenge Cup (0)*

Ross G 27	Hughes J 32	McLean P 1+3	Robertson J 33+1	Howard N 28+2	Gallagher A 18+1	Sloan T 36	Walker T 29+3	Duncan G 29+4	McGuire D 5+10	Henderson D 20	Callaghan T 2+7	McCaffrey J 7	Grant A 18+4	McAulay I 23+2	Ferguson W 1+10	Millar G 19+2	McGowan N 1+3	Reilly R 14+9	Pickering M —+1	Kerrigan S 19+2	Skippen R —+1	Crawford D 12+2	Shepherd A 2	Bilsland B 4+6	Duffy B 9	McMillan J 4+2	Connelly D 3+2	Match No.
1	2	3	4	5	6	7	8	9	10¹	11	12																	1
1	2	14	4			7	9	3	12	11	6¹	5	8²	10³	13													2
1	2	12	4¹	5		7	9			11	13	6	8³	10²		3	14											3
1	3	14	2	5		7	9¹	12		11	13	6²	8³	10		4												4
1	3		2	5		7³	9	13		11		6	8¹	10²	12	4	14											5
1	3		2	5		7³	9	13		11		6	8¹	10²	14	4	12											6
1	3		2	5		7	9	12		11		6¹	8	10²		4	13											7
1	3		2	5		7	9¹	6		11	12		8³	10²	14	4	13											8
1	3	2²	5	4¹		7	9	6		11	13		8		12	10												9
1	3³	2¹	5			7	9	6		11	13		8		12	10²	14											10
1	3		5	4			9	6		11¹	2		8²	13	12	10												11
1	3	2³	5	4¹		7	10	6		11			8		13	12		9										12
1	3	2³	4			7	10			11	14	5²	8¹		12	6	13	9										13
1	3	2	4	5		7	8		10	11				13	12	6¹		9²										14
1	3	2³	4	5		7	9¹	10	14	11	13	6²			12			8										15
1		2	4	5		7²	8¹	6	13	11			12	3	9			10										16
1	3	2	4	5		7	8	6		11	12			10¹				9										17
1	3	2	4	5		7	8	6		11²	12			10¹			13	9										18
1	6	2	12	5		7	8	4		11								10		9¹		3						19
1	6	2		5		7	8	4		11¹	12						13	10		9²		3						20
1	6	2		5		7	8	4		11								10		9		3						21
1	6	2	4	5		7	8			11	12							10		9¹		3						22
1	6	2		5		7	10	4		11			8							9		3						23
1	6	2		5		7	10	4		11¹			8		12					9		3						24
1	6	2²	5¹			7	10	4		11			8		12		13			9		3						25
1	6	2				7	10	4		11		5		9¹	12							3		8				26
1	6	12	14	5³		7	10²	4		11	2						13			9		3¹		8				27
	3	2	5			7	14	4³		11	12	6²	8¹				13	10		9					1			28
	3	2¹	4	5	6	7	10	9		11			8				12								1			29
		2²		5	6	7	8	9		11				10¹	12	4	13					3			1			30
	3	2	5		6	7²	10	9		11			8¹				14					2³			1		13	31
	3	2	5		6	7²	8				12				12	4	14			9³					1	10¹	13	32
	3	2	5		6¹	7			13	11			14		12	4				9³					1	10	8²	33
		2	5		6³	7				11	12		14			4	13			9		3			1	10²	8¹	34
		2	5		6²	7			13	11			14	10¹		4				9		3³			1	12	8	35
		2	5		6	7			12	11						4	13			9		3¹			1	10²	8	36

SCOTTISH LEAGUE 1995–96

Premier Division

	P	W	D	L	F	A	W	D	L	F	A	Pt	GD
		Home			Goals		Away			Goals			
Rangers	36	13	3	2	47	16	14	3	1	38	9	87	+60
Celtic	36	12	5	1	40	12	12	6	0	34	13	83	+49
Aberdeen	36	11	1	6	31	17	5	6	7	21	28	55	+7
Hearts	36	10	2	6	33	26	6	5	7	22	27	55	+2
Hibernian	36	7	5	6	25	26	4	5	9	18	31	43	−14
Raith R	36	7	5	6	23	21	5	2	11	18	36	43	−16
Kilmarnock	36	8	4	6	25	21	3	4	11	14	33	41	−15
Motherwell	36	6	6	6	15	16	3	6	9	13	23	39	−11
Partick T	36	3	5	10	12	28	5	1	12	17	34	30	−33
Falkirk	36	4	4	10	17	26	2	2	14	14	34	24	−29

First Division

	P	W	D	L	F	A	W	D	L	F	A	Pt	GD
		Home			Goals		Away			Goals			
Dunfermline Ath	36	11	4	3	40	23	10	4	4	33	18	71	+32
Dundee U	36	11	3	4	47	18	8	7	3	26	19	67	+36
Greenock Morton	36	10	4	4	32	16	10	3	5	25	23	67	+18
St Johnstone	36	11	5	2	33	14	8	3	7	27	22	65	+24
Dundee	36	5	8	5	24	20	10	4	4	29	20	57	+13
St Mirren	36	6	2	10	23	30	7	6	5	23	21	47	−5
Clydebank	36	6	4	8	20	24	4	6	8	19	34	40	−19
Airdrieonians	36	4	7	7	24	25	5	4	9	19	29	38	−11
Hamilton A	36	5	3	10	22	26	5	3	10	18	31	36	−17
Dumbarton	36	2	1	15	10	36	1	1	16	13	58	11	−71

Second Division

	P	W	D	L	F	A	W	D	L	F	A	Pt	GD
		Home			Goals		Away			Goals			
Stirling Albion	36	12	4	2	36	15	12	5	1	47	15	81	+53
East Fife	36	8	6	4	27	17	11	4	3	23	12	67	+21
Berwick R	36	10	4	4	32	18	8	2	8	32	29	60	+17
Stenhousemuir	36	8	3	7	26	21	6	4	8	25	28	49	+2
Clyde	36	7	4	7	28	23	4	8	6	19	22	45	+2
Ayr U	36	7	6	5	26	18	4	6	8	14	22	45	0
Queen of the S	36	6	6	6	27	38	5	4	9	27	29	43	−13
Stranraer	36	6	10	2	21	14	2	8	8	17	29	42	−5
Forfar Ath	36	8	3	7	21	32	3	4	11	16	29	40	−24
Montrose	36	3	2	13	18	39	2	3	13	15	47	20	−53

Third Division

	P	W	D	L	F	A	W	D	L	F	A	Pt	GD
		Home			Goals		Away			Goals			
Livingston	36	8	5	5	21	14	13	4	1	30	10	72	+27
Brechin C	36	10	3	5	25	9	8	6	4	16	12	63	+20
Caledonian T	36	5	8	5	28	23	10	4	4	36	15	57	+26
Ross County	36	6	9	3	30	20	6	8	4	26	19	53	+17
Arbroath	36	6	7	5	22	21	7	6	5	19	20	52	0
Queen's Park	36	6	8	4	21	15	6	4	8	19	28	48	−3
East Stirling	36	6	3	9	26	32	5	8	5	32	30	44	−4
Cowdenbeath	36	7	5	6	26	23	3	3	12	19	36	38	−14
Alloa	36	5	3	10	18	37	1	8	9	8	21	29	−32
Albion R	36	5	4	9	20	28	2	4	12	17	46	29	−37

PLAY-OFF: Partick T (9th place, Premier Division) v Dundee U (runners-up, First Division)

12 MAY at Firhill
Partick T (1) 1 (*Lyons*)
Dundee U (0) 1 (*Dailly*)   10,414
Partick T: Walker; Milne, Watson, McWilliams (Smith), Slavin, Welsh, McDonald R, Macdonald W (Turner), McCue, Cameron, Lyons.
Dundee U: Maxwell; Dailly, Shannon, Pressley, Welsh, McKinnon (McSwegan), Winters, Bowman, McLaren (Coyle); Brewster, McQuilken.

16 MAY at Tannadice
Dundee U (0) 2 (*Welsh, Coyle*)
Partick T (0) 1 (*Cameron (pen)) aet*   12,120
Dundee U: Maxwell; Dailly, McQuilken, Pressley, Welsh, Dailly, Winters (Johnston), Bowman, McSwegan (Coyle); Brewster (McKinnon), McLaren.
Partick T: Walker; Milne, Watson, Smith, Slavin, Welsh, McDonald R, McWilliams (Dinnie), McCue (Henderson), Cameron, Lyons.

SCOTTISH LEAGUE 1890–91 to 1995–96

*On goal average/difference.   †Held jointly after indecisive play-off.   ‡Won on deciding match.
††Held jointly.   ¶Two points deducted for fielding ineligible player.
Competition suspended 1940–45 during war.   ‡‡Two points deducted for registration irregularities.

PREMIER DIVISION
Maximum points: 72

	First	Pts	Second	Pts	Third	Pts
1975–76	Rangers	54	Celtic	48	Hibernian	43
1976–77	Celtic	55	Rangers	46	Aberdeen	43
1977–78	Rangers	55	Aberdeen	53	Dundee U	40
1978–79	Celtic	48	Rangers	45	Dundee U	44
1979–80	Aberdeen	48	Celtic	47	St Mirren	42
1980–81	Celtic	56	Aberdeen	49	Rangers*	44
1981–82	Celtic	55	Aberdeen	53	Rangers	43
1982–83	Dundee U	56	Celtic*	55	Aberdeen	55
1983–84	Aberdeen	57	Celtic	50	Dundee U	47
1984–85	Aberdeen	59	Celtic	52	Dundee U	47
1985–86	Celtic*	50	Hearts	50	Dundee U	47

Maximum points: 88

	First	Pts	Second	Pts	Third	Pts
1986–87	Rangers	69	Celtic	63	Dundee U	60
1987–88	Celtic	72	Hearts	62	Rangers	60

Maximum points: 72

	First	Pts	Second	Pts	Third	Pts
1988–89	Rangers	56	Aberdeen	50	Celtic	46
1989–90	Rangers	51	Aberdeen*	44	Hearts	44
1990–91	Rangers	55	Aberdeen	53	Celtic*	41

Maximum points: 88

	First	Pts	Second	Pts	Third	Pts
1991–92	Rangers	72	Hearts	63	Celtic	62
1992–93	Rangers	73	Aberdeen	64	Celtic	60
1993–94	Rangers	58	Aberdeen	55	Motherwell	54

Maximum points: 108

	First	Pts	Second	Pts	Third	Pts
1994–95	Rangers	69	Motherwell	54	Hibernian	53
1995–96	Rangers	87	Celtic	83	Aberdeen*	55

FIRST DIVISION
Maximum points: 52

	First	Pts	Second	Pts	Third	Pts
1975–76	Partick T	41	Kilmarnock	35	Montrose	30

Maximum points: 78

	First	Pts	Second	Pts	Third	Pts
1976–77	St Mirren	62	Clydebank	58	Dundee	51
1977–78	Morton*	58	Hearts	58	Dundee	57
1978–79	Dundee	55	Kilmarnock*	54	Clydebank	54
1979–80	Hearts	53	Airdrieonians	51	Ayr U*	44
1980–81	Hibernian	57	Dundee	52	St Johnstone	51
1981–82	Motherwell	61	Kilmarnock	51	Hearts	50
1982–83	St Johnstone	55	Hearts	54	Clydebank	50
1983–84	Morton	54	Dumbarton	51	Partick T	46
1984–85	Motherwell	50	Clydebank	48	Falkirk	45
1985–86	Hamilton A	56	Falkirk	45	Kilmarnock	44

Maximum points: 88

	First	Pts	Second	Pts	Third	Pts
1986–87	Morton	57	Dunfermline Ath	56	Dumbarton	53
1987–88	Hamilton A	56	Meadowbank T	52	Clydebank	49

Maximum points: 78

	First	Pts	Second	Pts	Third	Pts
1988–89	Dunfermline Ath	54	Falkirk	52	Clydebank	48
1989–90	St Johnstone	58	Airdrieonians	54	Clydebank	44
1990–91	Falkirk	54	Airdrieonians	53	Dundee	52

Maximum points: 88

	First	Pts	Second	Pts	Third	Pts
1991–92	Dundee	58	Partick T*	57	Hamilton A	57
1992–93	Raith R	65	Kilmarnock	54	Dunfermline Ath	52
1993–94	Falkirk	66	Dunfermline Ath	65	Airdrieonians	54

Maximum points: 108

	First	Pts	Second	Pts	Third	Pts
1994–95	Raith R	69	Dunfermline Ath*	68	Dundee	68
1995–96	Dunfermline Ath	71	Dundee U*	67	Morton	67

SECOND DIVISION
Maximum points: 52

	First	Pts	Second	Pts	Third	Pts
1975–76	Clydebank*	40	Raith R	40	Alloa	35

Maximum points: 78

	First	Pts	Second	Pts	Third	Pts
1976–77	Stirling A	55	Alloa	51	Dunfermline Ath	50
1977–78	Clyde*	53	Raith R	53	Dunfermline Ath	48
1978–79	Berwick R	54	Dunfermline Ath	52	Falkirk	50
1979–80	Falkirk	50	East Stirling	49	Forfar Ath	46
1980–81	Queen's Park	50	Queen of the S	46	Cowdenbeath	45

1981–82	Clyde	59	Alloa*	50	Arbroath	50
1982–83	Brechin C	55	Meadowbank T	54	Arbroath	49
1983–84	Forfar Ath	63	East Fife	47	Berwick R	43
1984–85	Montrose	53	Alloa	50	Dunfermline Ath	49
1985–86	Dunfermline Ath	57	Queen of the S	55	Meadowbank T	49
1986–87	Meadowbank T	55	Raith R*	52	Stirling A*	52
1987–88	Ayr U	61	St Johnstone	59	Queen's Park	51
1988–89	Albion R	50	Alloa	45	Brechin C	43
1989–90	Brechin C	49	Kilmarnock	48	Stirling A	47
1990–91	Stirling A	54	Montrose	46	Cowdenbeath	45
1991–92	Dumbarton	52	Cowdenbeath	51	Alloa	50
1992–93	Clyde	54	Brechin C*	53	Stranraer	53
1993–94	Stranraer	56	Berwick R	48	Stenhousemuir*	47

Maximum points: 108

1994–95	Morton	64	Dumbarton	60	Stirling A	58
1995–96	Stirling A	81	East Fife	67	Berwick R	60

THIRD DIVISION

Maximum points: 108

1994–95	Forfar Ath	80	Montrose	67	Ross Co	60
1995–96	Livingston	72	Brechin C	63	Caledonian T	57

FIRST DIVISION to 1974–75

Maximum points: a 36; b 44; c 40; d 52; e 60; f 68; g 76; h 84.

	First	Pts	Second	Pts	Third	Pts
1890–91a	Dumbarton††	29	Rangers††	29	Celtic	21
1891–92b	Dumbarton	37	Celtic	35	Hearts	34
1892–93a	Celtic	29	Rangers	28	St Mirren	20
1893–94a	Celtic	29	Hearts	26	St Bernard's	23
1894–95a	Hearts	31	Celtic	26	Rangers	22
1895–96a	Celtic	30	Rangers	26	Hibernian	24
1896–97a	Hearts	28	Hibernian	26	Rangers	25
1897–98a	Celtic	33	Rangers	29	Hibernian	22
1898–99a	Rangers	36	Hearts	26	Celtic	24
1899–1900a	Rangers	32	Celtic	25	Hibernian	24
1900–01c	Rangers	35	Celtic	29	Hibernian	25
1901–02a	Rangers	28	Celtic	26	Hearts	22
1902–03b	Hibernian	37	Dundee	31	Rangers	29
1903–04d	Third Lanark	43	Hearts	39	Celtic*	38
1904–05d	Celtic‡	41	Rangers	41	Third Lanark	35
1905–06e	Celtic	49	Hearts	43	Airdrieonians	38
1906–07f	Celtic	55	Dundee	48	Rangers	45
1907–08f	Celtic	55	Falkirk	51	Rangers	50
1908–09f	Celtic	51	Dundee	50	Clyde	48
1909–10f	Celtic	54	Falkirk	52	Rangers	46
1910–11f	Rangers	52	Aberdeen	48	Falkirk	44
1911–12f	Rangers	51	Celtic	45	Clyde	42
1912–13f	Rangers	53	Celtic	49	Hearts*	41
1913–14g	Celtic	65	Rangers	59	Hearts*	54
1914–15g	Celtic	65	Hearts	61	Rangers	50
1915–16g	Celtic	67	Rangers	56	Morton	51
1916–17g	Celtic	64	Morton	54	Rangers	53
1917–18f	Rangers	56	Celtic	55	Kilmarnock*	43
1918–19f	Celtic	58	Rangers	57	Morton	47
1919–20h	Rangers	71	Celtic	68	Motherwell	57
1920–21h	Rangers	76	Celtic	66	Hearts	50
1921–22h	Celtic	67	Rangers	66	Raith R	51
1922–23g	Rangers	55	Airdrieonians	50	Celtic	46
1923–24g	Rangers	59	Airdrieonians	50	Celtic	46
1924–25g	Rangers	60	Airdrieonians	57	Hibernian	52
1925–26g	Celtic	58	Airdrieonians*	50	Hearts	50
1926–27g	Rangers	56	Motherwell	51	Celtic	49
1927–28g	Rangers	60	Celtic*	55	Motherwell	55
1928–29g	Rangers	67	Celtic	51	Motherwell	50
1929–30g	Rangers	60	Motherwell	55	Aberdeen	53
1930–31g	Rangers	60	Celtic	58	Motherwell	56
1931–32g	Motherwell	66	Rangers	61	Celtic	48
1932–33g	Rangers	62	Motherwell	59	Hearts	50
1933–34g	Rangers	66	Motherwell	62	Celtic	47
1934–35g	Rangers	55	Celtic	52	Hearts	50
1935–36g	Celtic	66	Rangers*	61	Aberdeen	61
1936–37g	Rangers	61	Aberdeen	54	Celtic	52
1937–38g	Celtic	61	Hearts	58	Rangers	49
1938–39g	Rangers	59	Celtic	48	Aberdeen	46

1946–47e	Rangers	46	Hibernian	44	Aberdeen	39
1947–48e	Hibernian	48	Rangers	46	Partick T	36
1948–49e	Rangers	46	Dundee	45	Hibernian	39
1949–50e	Rangers	50	Hibernian	49	Hearts	43
1950–51e	Hibernian	48	Rangers*	38	Dundee	38
1951–52e	Hibernian	45	Rangers	41	East Fife	37
1952–53e	Rangers*	43	Hibernian	43	East Fife	39
1953–54e	Celtic	43	Hearts	38	Partick T	35
1954–55e	Aberdeen	49	Celtic	46	Rangers	41
1955–56f	Rangers	52	Aberdeen	46	Hearts*	45
1956–57f	Rangers	55	Hearts	53	Kilmarnock	42
1957–58f	Hearts	62	Rangers	49	Celtic	46
1958–59f	Rangers	50	Hearts	48	Motherwell	44
1959–60f	Hearts	54	Kilmarnock	50	Rangers*	42
1960–61f	Rangers	51	Kilmarnock	50	Third Lanark	42
1961–62f	Dundee	54	Rangers	51	Celtic	46
1962–63f	Rangers	57	Kilmarnock	48	Partick T	46
1963–64f	Rangers	55	Kilmarnock	49	Celtic*	47
1964–65f	Kilmarnock*	50	Hearts	50	Dunfermline Ath	49
1965–66f	Celtic	57	Rangers	55	Kilmarnock	45
1966–67f	Celtic	58	Rangers	55	Clyde	46
1967–68f	Celtic	63	Rangers	61	Hibernian	45
1968–69f	Celtic	54	Rangers	49	Dunfermline Ath	45
1969–70f	Celtic	57	Rangers	45	Hibernian	44
1970–71f	Celtic	56	Aberdeen	54	St Johnstone	44
1971–72f	Celtic	60	Aberdeen	50	Rangers	44
1972–73f	Celtic	57	Rangers	56	Hibernian	45
1973–74f	Celtic	53	Hibernian	49	Rangers	48
1974–75f	Rangers	56	Hibernian	49	Celtic	45

SECOND DIVISION to 1974–75

Maximum points: a 76; b 72; c 68; d 52; e 60; f 36; g 44.

1893–94f	Hibernian	29	Cowlairs	27	Clyde	24
1894–95f	Hibernian	30	Motherwell	22	Port Glasgow	20
1895–96f	Abercorn	27	Leith Ath	23	Renton	21
1896–97f	Partick T	31	Leith Ath	27	Kilmarnock*	21
1897–98f	Kilmarnock	29	Port Glasgow	25	Morton	22
1898–99f	Kilmarnock	32	Leith Ath	27	Port Glasgow	25
1899–1900f	Partick T	29	Morton	28	Port Glasgow	20
1900–01f	St Bernard's	25	Airdrieonians	23	Abercorn	21
1901–02g	Port Glasgow	32	Partick T	31	Motherwell	26
1902–03g	Airdrieonians	35	Motherwell	28	Ayr U*	27
1903–04g	Hamilton A	37	Clyde	29	Ayr U	28
1904–05g	Clyde	32	Falkirk	28	Hamilton A	27
1905–06g	Leith Ath	34	Clyde	31	Albion R	27
1906–07g	St Bernard's	32	Vale of Leven*	27	Arthurlie	27
1907–08g	Raith R	30	Dumbarton*‡‡	27	Ayr U	27
1908–09g	Abercorn	31	Raith R*	28	Vale of Leven	28
1909–10g	Leith Ath‡	33	Raith R	33	St Bernard's	27
1910–11g	Dumbarton	31	Ayr U	27	Albion R	25
1911–12g	Ayr U	35	Abercorn	30	Dumbarton	27
1912–13d	Ayr U	34	Dunfermline Ath	33	East Stirling	32
1913–14d	Cowdenbeath	31	Albion R	27	Dunfermline Ath*	26
1914–15d	Cowdenbeath*	37	St Bernard's*	37	Leith Ath	37
1921–22a	Alloa	60	Cowdenbeath	47	Armadale	45
1922–23a	Queen's Park	57	Clydebank¶	50	St Johnstone¶	45
1923–24a	St Johnstone	56	Cowdenbeath	55	Bathgate	44
1924–25a	Dundee U	50	Clydebank	48	Clyde	47
1925–26a	Dunfermline Ath	59	Clyde	53	Ayr U	52
1926–27a	Bo'ness	56	Raith R	49	Clydebank	45
1927–28a	Ayr U	54	Third Lanark	45	King's Park	44
1928–29b	Dundee U	51	Morton	50	Arbroath	47
1929–30a	Leith Ath*	57	East Fife	57	Albion R	54
1930–31a	Third Lanark	61	Dundee U	50	Dunfermline Ath	47
1931–32a	East Stirling*	55	St Johnstone	55	Raith R*	46
1932–33c	Hibernian	54	Queen of the S	49	Dunfermline Ath	47
1933–34c	Albion R	45	Dunfermline Ath*	44	Arbroath	44
1934–35c	Third Lanark	52	Arbroath	50	St Bernard's	47
1935–36c	Falkirk	59	St Mirren	52	Morton	48
1936–37c	Ayr U	54	Morton	51	St Bernard's	48
1937–38c	Raith R	59	Albion R	48	Airdrieonians	47
1938–39c	Cowdenbeath	60	Alloa*	48	East Fife	48
1946–47d	Dundee	45	Airdrieonians	42	East Fife	31
1947–48e	East Fife	53	Albion R	42	Hamilton A	40

1948–49e	Raith R*	42	Stirling A	42	Airdrieonians*	41
1949–50e	Morton	47	Airdrieonians	44	Dunfermline Ath*	36
1950–51e	Queen of the S*	45	Stirling A	45	Ayr U*	36
1951–52e	Clyde	44	Falkirk	43	Ayr U	39
1952–53e	Stirling A	44	Hamilton A	43	Queen's Park	37
1953–54e	Motherwell	45	Kilmarnock	42	Third Lanark*	36
1954–55e	Airdrieonians	46	Dunfermline Ath	42	Hamilton A	39
1955–56b	Queen's Park	54	Ayr U	51	St Johnstone	49
1956–57b	Clyde	64	Third Lanark	51	Cowdenbeath	45
1957–58b	Stirling A	55	Dunfermline Ath	53	Arbroath	47
1958–59b	Ayr U	60	Arbroath	51	Stenhousemuir	46
1959–60b	St Johnstone	53	Dundee U	50	Queen of the S	49
1960–61b	Stirling A	55	Falkirk	54	Stenhousemuir	50
1961–62b	Clyde	54	Queen of the S	53	Morton	44
1962–63b	St Johnstone	55	East Stirling	49	Morton	48
1963–64b	Morton	67	Clyde	53	Arbroath	46
1964–65b	Stirling A	59	Hamilton A	50	Queen of the S	45
1965–66b	Ayr U	53	Airdrieonians	50	Queen of the S	47
1966–67a	Morton	69	Raith R	58	Arbroath	57
1967–68b	St Mirren	62	Arbroath	53	East Fife	49
1968–69b	Motherwell	64	Ayr U	53	East Fife*	48
1969–70b	Falkirk	56	Cowdenbeath	55	Queen of the S	50
1970–71b	Partick T	56	East Fife	51	Arbroath	46
1971–72b	Dumbarton*	52	Arbroath	52	Stirling A	50
1972–73b	Clyde	56	Dumfermline Ath	52	Raith R*	47
1973–74b	Airdrieonians	60	Kilmarnock	58	Hamilton A	55
1974–75a	Falkirk	54	Queen of the S*	53	Montrose	53

Elected to First Division: 1894 Clyde; 1895 Hibernian; 1896 Abercorn; 1897 Partick T; 1899 Kilmarnock; 1900 Morton and Partick T; 1902 Port Glasgow and Partick T; 1903 Airdrieonians and Motherwell; 1905 Falkirk and Aberdeen; 1906 Clyde and Hamilton A; 1910 Raith R; 1913 Ayr U and Dumbarton.

RELEGATED FROM PREMIER DIVISION

1974–75 No relegation due to league reorganization
1975–76 Dundee, St Johnstone
1976–77 Hearts, Kilmarnock
1977–78 Ayr U, Clydebank
1978–79 Hearts, Motherwell
1979–80 Dundee, Hibernian
1980–81 Kilmarnock, Hearts
1981–82 Partick T, Airdrieonians
1982–83 Morton, Kilmarnock
1983–84 St Johnstone, Motherwell
1984–85 Dumbarton, Morton
1985–86 *No relegation due to League reorganization*
1986–87 Clydebank, Hamilton A
1987–88 Falkirk, Dunfermline Ath, Morton
1988–89 Hamilton A
1989–90 Dundee
1990–91 None
1991–92 St Mirren, Dunfermline Ath
1992–93 Falkirk, Airdrieonians
1993–94 *See footnote*
1994–95 Dundee U
1995–96 Partick T, Falkirk

RELEGATED FROM DIVISION 1

1974–75 No relegation due to league reorganization
1975–76 Dunfermline Ath, Clyde
1976–77 Raith R, Falkirk
1977–78 Alloa Ath, East Fife
1978–79 Montrose, Queen of the S
1979–80 Arbroath, Clyde
1980–81 Stirling A, Berwick R
1981–82 East Stirling, Queen of the S
1982–83 Dunfermline Ath, Queen's Park
1983–84 Raith R, Alloa
1984–85 Meadowbank T, St Johnstone
1985–86 Ayr U, Alloa
1986–87 Brechin C, Montrose
1987–88 East Fife, Dumbarton
1988–89 Kilmarnock, Queen of the S
1989–90 Albion R, Alloa
1990–91 Clyde, Brechin C
1991–92 Montrose, Forfar Ath
1992–93 Meadowbank T, Cowdenbeath
1993–94 *See footnote*
1994–95 Ayr U, Stranraer
1995–96 Hamilton A, Dumbarton

RELEGATED FROM DIVISION 2

1994–95 Meadowbank T, Brechin C
1995–96 Forfar Ath, Montrose

RELEGATED FROM DIVISION 1 (TO 1973–74)

1921–22 *Queen's Park, Dumbarton, Clydebank
1922–23 Albion R, Alloa Ath
1923–24 Clyde, Clydebank
1924–25 Third Lanark, Ayr U
1925–26 Raith R, Clydebank
1926–27 Morton, Dundee U
1927–28 Dunfermline Ath, Bo'ness
1928–29 Third Lanark, Raith R
1929–30 St Johnstone, Dundee U
1930–31 Hibernian, East Fife
1931–32 Dundee U, Leith Ath
1932–33 Morton, East Stirling

1933–34 Third Lanark, Cowdenbeath
1934–35 St Mirren, Falkirk
1935–36 Airdrieonians, Ayr U
1936–37 Dunfermline Ath, Albion R
1937–38 Dundee, Morton
1938–39 Queen's Park, Raith R
1946–47 Kilmarnock, Hamilton A
1947–48 Airdrieonians, Queen's Park
1948–49 Morton, Albion R
1949–50 Queen of the S, Stirling A
1950–51 Clyde, Falkirk
1951–52 Morton, Stirling A

1952–53 Motherwell, Third Lanark	1963–64 Queen of the S, East Stirling
1953–54 Airdrieonians, Hamilton A	1964–65 Airdrieonians, Third Lanark
1954–55 No clubs relegated	1965–66 Morton, Hamilton A
1955–56 Stirling A, Clyde	1966–67 St Mirren, Ayr U
1956–57 Dunfermline Ath, Ayr U	1967–68 Motherwell, Stirling A
1957–58 East Fife, Queen's Park	1968–69 Falkirk, Arbroath
1958–59 Queen of the S, Falkirk	1969–70 Raith R, Partick T
1959–60 Arbroath, Stirling A	1970–71 St Mirren, Cowdenbeath
1960–61 Ayr U, Clyde	1971–72 Clyde, Dunfermline Ath
1961–62 St Johnstone, Stirling A	1972–73 Kilmarnock, Airdrieonians
1962–63 Clyde, Raith R	1973–74 East Fife, Falkirk

*Season 1921–22 – only 1 club promoted, 3 clubs relegated.

Scottish League championship wins: Rangers 45, Celtic 35, Aberdeen 4, Hearts 4, Hibernian 4, Dumbarton 2, Dundee 1, Dundee U 1, Kilmarnock 1, Motherwell 1, Third Lanark 1.

At the end of the 1993–94 season four divisions were created assisted by the admission of two new clubs Ross County and Caledonian Thistle. Only one club was promoted from Division 1 and Division 2. The three relegated from the Premier joined with teams finishing second to seventh in Division 1 to form the new Division 1. Five relegated from Division 1 combined with those who finished second to sixth to form a new Division 2 and the bottom eight in Division 2 linked with the two newcomers to form a new Division 3.

Ally McCoist of Rangers tests Swiss goalkeeper Marco Pascolo in the European Championship finals. (Colorsport).

SCOTTISH LEAGUE CUP FINALS 1946–96

Season	Winners	Runners-up	Score
1946–47	Rangers	Aberdeen	4-0
1947–48	East Fife	Falkirk	4-1 after 0-0 draw
1948–49	Rangers	Raith R	2-0
1949–50	East Fife	Dunfermline Ath	3-0
1950–51	Motherwell	Hibernian	3-0
1951–52	Dundee	Rangers	3-2
1952–53	Dundee	Kilmarnock	2-0
1953–54	East Fife	Partick T	3-2
1954–55	Hearts	Motherwell	4-2
1955–56	Aberdeen	St Mirren	2-1
1956–57	Celtic	Partick T	3-0 after 0-0 draw
1957–58	Celtic	Rangers	7-1
1958–59	Hearts	Partick T	5-1
1959–60	Hearts	Third Lanark	2-1
1960–61	Rangers	Kilmarnock	2-0
1961–62	Rangers	Hearts	3-1 after 1-1 draw
1962–63	Hearts	Kilmarnock	1-0
1963–64	Rangers	Morton	5-0
1964–65	Rangers	Celtic	2-1
1965–66	Celtic	Rangers	2-1
1966–67	Celtic	Rangers	1-0
1967–68	Celtic	Dundee	5-3
1968–69	Celtic	Hibernian	6-2
1969–70	Celtic	St Johnstone	1-0
1970–71	Rangers	Celtic	1-0
1971–72	Partick T	Celtic	4-1
1972–73	Hibernian	Celtic	2-1
1973–74	Dundee	Celtic	1-0
1974–75	Celtic	Hibernian	6-3
1975–76	Rangers	Celtic	1-0
1976–77	Aberdeen	Celtic	2-1
1977–78	Rangers	Celtic	2-1
1978–79	Rangers	Aberdeen	2-1
1979–80	Dundee U	Aberdeen	3-0 after 0-0 draw
1980–81	Dundee U	Dundee	3-0
1981–82	Rangers	Dundee U	2-1
1982–83	Celtic	Rangers	2-1
1983–84	Rangers	Celtic	3-2
1984–85	Rangers	Dundee U	1-0
1985–86	Aberdeen	Hibernian	3-0
1986–87	Rangers	Celtic	2-1
1987–88	Rangers	Aberdeen	3-3
		(Rangers won 5-3 on penalties)	
1988–89	Rangers	Aberdeen	3-2
1989–90	Aberdeen	Rangers	2-1
1990–91	Rangers	Celtic	2-1
1991–92	Hibernian	Dunfermline Ath	2-0
1992–93	Rangers	Aberdeen	2-1
1993–94	Rangers	Hibernian	2-1
1994–95	Raith R	Celtic	2-2
		(Raith R won 6-5 on penalties)	
1995–96	Aberdeen	Dundee	2-0

SCOTTISH LEAGUE CUP WINS

Rangers 19, Celtic 9, Hearts 4, Aberdeen 5, Dundee 3, East Fife 3, Dundee U 2, Hibernian 2, Motherwell 1, Partick T 1, Raith R 1.

APPEARANCES IN FINALS

Rangers 25, Celtic 21, Aberdeen 11, Hibernian 7, Dundee 6, Hearts 5, Dundee U 4, Partick T 4, East Fife 3, Kilmarnock 3, Dunfermline Ath 2, Motherwell 2, Raith R 2, Falkirk 1, Morton 1, St Johnstone 1, St Mirren 1, Third Lanark 1.

SCOTTISH COCA-COLA CUP 1995–96

FIRST ROUND

5 AUG

Albion R (0) 0
Cowdenbeath (1) 1 *(Scott)*   430
Albion R: Moonie; McDonald (Young), Gallagher, Strain, Ryan, Shanks, Duncan, Collins, Scott, Crawford, Seggie (McBride).
Cowdenbeath: Russell; Steven, Meldrum, Wood, Malloy, McMahon, Petrie, Bowmaker (Smith), Scott, Winter, De Melo (Wardell).

Alloa (1) 2 *(Moffat, Rixon)*
Forfar Ath (0) 1 *(Loney)*   512
Alloa: Graham; Newbigging, Bennett, McCormack, Lawrie, Kirkham, Cadden, Diver, Rixon, Moffat (Whyte), Morrison.
Forfar Ath: Arthur; Bowes, McPhee, Mann, McKillop, Craig, Morgan, McVicar, Ross (Loney), Hannigan (O'Neill), Bingham.

Berwick R (0) 1 *(Clegg)*
Caledonian T (0) 1 *(Valentine (og))* aet   482
Berwick R: Young; Valentine, Banks, Reid, Cowan, Fraser, Graham, Wilson, Forrester, Rutherford (Walton), Kane (Clegg).
Caledonian T: McRitchie; McGinlay, McAllister, Noble, Benson, Ross, Mitchell (Hastings), Lisle (Bennett), Stewart, Christie, Green.
(Berwick R won 5-3 on penalties)

Brechin C (1) 2 *(Brand 2)*
East Fife (1) 3 *(Scott 2, Hutcheon)* aet   476
Brechin C: Allan; Mitchell, Brown R, Cairney, Conway, Scott, McNeill (Vannett), Farnan, Price, Brand, Marr (Smith R).
East Fife: Robertson; McStay, Hamill, Cusick, Beaton, Sneddon (Allan), Hildersley, Balmain (Donaghy), Scott, Andrew (Hutcheon), Hope.

Clyde (1) 1 *(Annand)*
East Stirling (2) 2 *(Abercromby 2 (1 pen))*   834
Clyde: Hillcoat; Prunty (McConnell), Ferguson (Patterson), Watson, Knox, Brown, O'Neill, Nisbet, Annand, Harrison, Dickson.
East Stirling: McDougall; Orr, Neill, Stirling, Ross, Lee R, Millar, Hunter, Geraghty (McKenna), Abercromby (Scott), MacLean (Cuthbert).

Montrose (0) 0
Livingston (1) 2 *(Young, McMartin)*   636
Montrose: Larter; Robertson, Mailer, Tindal (Garden), Grant, Tosh, MacDonald, Stephen (Masson P), McGlashan, Taylor (Smith), MacRonald.
Livingston: Stoute; Smart, McCartney, Davidson, Williamson, Alleyne, McMartin, Bailey (Harvey), Young, McLeod, Duthie (Sinclair).

Queen of the S (2) 3 *(Campbell D, Harris, Mallan (pen))*
Queen's Park (0) 1 *(McPhee)*   1202
Queen of the S: Butter; McKeown D, Brown, McKeown B, Kennedy, Ramsay, Campbell D (McFarlane), Wilson, Harris, Bryce (Cody), Mallan.
Queen's Park: Bruce; Kerr, Graham, McGrath, Caven, Maxwell, Fraser, Arbuckle (Edgar), Brodie, McPhee, McInally (McGoldrick).

Ross Co (0) 0
Arbroath (0) 2 *(Lindsay, McCormick)*   1128
Ross Co: Hutchison; Somerville (Ferries), Campbell, Williamson, Bellshaw, Furphy, Mackay, MacPherson, Milne (Grant), Connelly, Herd.
Arbroath: Hinchcliffe; McMillan, Florence, Peters, Fowler, Clark, Lindsay, Porteous, McCormick, Kennedy (Pew), McAulay.

SECOND ROUND

19 AUG

Aberdeen (2) 3 *(Dodds, Booth 2)*
St Mirren (1) 1 *(McLaughlin)*   10,397
Aberdeen: Snelders; McKimmie, Ireland, McKinnon (Verveer), Inglis, Hetherston, Miller, Jess, Booth, Dodds, Glass.
St Mirren: Money; Dawson, Baker, Taylor, McLaughlin, Watson, Law, Fullarton, Gillies (Dick), Bone, Boyd (Lavety).

Ayr U (0) 0
Celtic (1) 3 *(Van Hooijdonk, Thom, Collins (pen))*   9128
Ayr U: Lamont; Tannock, Boyce, George (Wilson), Rolling, Sharples, Shepherd, McKilligan (MacFarlane), Bilsland, Stainrod, Moore.
Celtic: Marshall; Boyd, McKinlay, Vata, Hughes (Mackay), Grant, O'Donnell, Donnelly, van Hooijdonk, Thom (McLaughlin), Collins.

Berwick R (0) 0
Partick T (2) 7 *(Craig 2, McWilliams 2, McDonald R, Pittman, Curran)*   1120
Berwick R: Young; Valentine, Banks, Reid, Cowan, Fraser (Wilson), Forrester (Kane), Neil, Rutherford, Irvine, Graham (Walton).
Partick T: Walker; Dinnie, Pittman, McWilliams, Tierney, Welsh, McDonald R, Craig, Foster, Curran, Cameron.

Clydebank (1) 1 *(Robertson)*
Motherwell (0) 1 *(Arnott)* aet   2192
Clydebank: Matthews; Tomlinson, Sutherland (Crawford), Murdoch, Currie, Nicholls, Robertson, Connell, Eadie, Kerrigan (Teale), Bowman.
Motherwell: Howie; May (Philliben), McKinnon, Van Der Gaag (Woods), Martin, McSkimming, Lambert, Dolan (Roddie), Coyne, Arnott, Davies.
(Motherwell won 4-1 on penalties)

Cowdenbeath (0) 0
Dundee U (2) 4 *(McKinlay, Caldwell, Connolly 2)*   2077
Cowdenbeath: Russell; Maratea (Wardell), Meldrum, Wood, Malloy, McMahon, Steven, Winter, Scott (Buckley), Yardley, Smith (De Melo).
Dundee U: Maxwell; Perry, Shannon, Pressley, Welsh, Bowman, McLaren, McKinlay, Winters, Connolly, Caldwell.

Dunfermline Ath (2) 3 *(Moore, McCathie, Petrie)*
Stranraer (0) 0   3089
Dunfermline Ath: Van De Kamp; Den Bieman, Millar, McCathie, Tod, Smith, Moore, McNamara (McCulloch), Shaw, Petrie, Kinnaird (Fleming).
Stranraer: Ross; McLean, Hughes (McGowan), Robertson, Howard, McCaffrey, Sloan, Callaghan, Walker, Duncan (Grant), Henderson (McGuire).

East Fife (1) 2 *(Scott, Allan)*
Airdrieonians (0) 3 *(Boyle, Duffield, Cooper)*   1187
East Fife: Hamilton; McStay, Hamill, Cusick, Beaton, Donaghy, Balmain (Allan), Hildersley (Hutcheon), Scott (Archibald), Andrew, Hope.
Airdrieonians: Martin; Boyle, Jack, Sandison, McIntyre T (McIntyre J), Stewart, Davies, Harvey (Wilson), Cooper, Duffield, Smith.

East Stirling (0) 0
Dundee (3) 6 *(Wieghorst, Hamilton, McCann 4)*   1140
East Stirling: McDougall; Orr (McKenna), Lee R, Watt, Sneddon, Neill, Hunter (MacLean), Scott, Geraghty, Abercromby, Stirling (Dwyer).
Dundee: Pageaud; Bain (Anderson), Cargill, Manley, Wieghorst, Duffy C, Tosh, Vrto, Britton, Hamilton (Shaw), McCann.

Hearts (1) 3 *(Hamilton, McPherson, Leitch)*
Alloa (0) 0   7732
Hearts: Smith; Locke, Wishart, Levein, McPherson, Hamilton, Colquhoun, Mackay, Hagen, Johnston, Leitch (Callaghan).
Alloa: Graham; Newbigging, Bennett, McCormack, Lawrie, Little (McKenzie), Wylie (Cully), Diver, Moffat, Rixon (Whyte), Morrison.

Hibernian (1) 3 *(McGinlay, Jackson D 2 (1 pen))*
Stenhousemuir (0) 1 *(Hutchison)*   7053
Hibernian: Leighton; Donald, Mitchell, McGinlay, Tweed, Jackson C, Weir (McAllister), Millen, Harper (Miller), Jackson D, O'Neill.
Stenhousemuir: McKenzie; Bannon, Haddow, Armstrong, McGeachie, Christie (Swanson), Logan (Clarke), Fisher, Mathieson (Henderson), Hutchison, Little I.

Kilmarnock (0) 1 *(Roberts)*
Dumbarton (0) 0 *aet*   5011
Kilmarnock: Lekovic; MacPherson (Findlay), Black, Montgomerie, Whitworth, Skilling, Mitchell, Henry (Roberts), Wright, Connor, Brown (Reilly).
Dumbarton: MacFarlane; Burns, Fabiani, Marsland, Martin, King, Mooney, Meechan, McGivern (Gibson), McGarvey (Granger), Charnley.

Queen of the S (0) 0
Falkirk (1) 2 *(Johnston M, Henderson)*   2507
Queen of the S: Butter; Hetherington, Brown, McKeown B, Kennedy, Ramsay (Bryce), Wilson, Mallan, Harris (Friels), McFarlane, Campbell D (Cody).
Falkirk: Parks; Clark (Johnston F), Napier, Oliver, McLaughlin, Rice, McGowan, Kirk, McGraw (Henderson), Johnston M, Elliot.

Raith R (1) 2 *(Kirkwood 2)*
Arbroath (1) 1 *(McCormick)*   3012
Raith R: Thomson; Kirkwood, Broddle, McInally (Lennon), Dennis, Sinclair, Rougier, Cameron, Crawford, Taylor, Dair (Graham).
Arbroath: Hinchcliffe; McMillan, Crawford, Peters, Fowler, Clark, Pew (McAulay), Porteous, McCormick, Kennedy (McLean), Lindsay.

Rangers (2) 3 *(McCoist, Hateley, Gascoigne)*
Greenock Morton (0) 0   3396
Rangers: Goram; Wright (Cleland), Robertson, Gough, Moore, Ferguson, Miller (Durrant), Gascoigne, McCoist, Hateley, Mikhailichenko.
Greenock Morton: Wylie; Johnstone, Collins, Anderson, McCahill, Lindberg, Lilley, Mahood, Hawke (Laing), McInnes, Rajamaki (Blair).

St Johnstone (1) 1 *(O'Boyle)*
Livingston (1) 1 *(Bailey) aet*   2226
St Johnstone: Main; McQuillan, Preston, Griffin, Irons (Cherry), McGowne, Scott (O'Neil), Grant (McLean), Twaddle, O'Boyle, Farquhar.
Livingston: Stoute; Smart, McCartney (Sinclair), Davidson, Williamson, Alleyne, McMartin, Bailey (Harvey), Young, McLeod, Duthie.
(Livingston won 4-2 on penalties)

Stirling Albion (0) 2 *(Tait, McLeod)*
Hamilton A (0) 0   921
Stirling Albion: McGeown; McKechnie, Watson (Gibson), Mitchell, McQuilter, Tait, McInnes, Deas, McCormick (Farquhar), Taggart, McLeod.
Hamilton A: Cormack; Renicks, McInulty, Thomson, Paterson, McIntosh, Hartley, Clark (Baptie), McCormick (McCarrison), McQuade, Lorimer (McCulloch).

THIRD ROUND

29 AUG

Airdrieonians (2) 2 *(Tweed (og), Boyle)*
Hibernian (0) 0   3201
Airdrieonians: Martin; Boyle, McIntyre T, Sandison, Sweeney (Tait), Davies, Wilson, Harvey, McIntyre J (Cooper), Duffield, Smith.
(Hibernian): Leighton; Jackson C, Dods, McGinlay, Tweed, Hunter (Weir), McAllister (Donald), Millen, Harper, Jackson D, O'Neill.

Dundee U (1) 1 *(Winters)*
Motherwell (1) 2 *(Lambert, Arnott)*   6839
Dundee U: Maxwell; Perry, Shannon, Dailly, Pressley, Welsh, McLaren, McKinlay, Robertson (Connolly), Bett (Crabbe), Winters.
Motherwell: Howie; May, McKinnon, Roddie (Davies), Martin, Philliben, Lambert, Dolan, Burns, Arnott, McSkimming.

30 AUG

Dundee (0) 3 *(Shaw, Wieghorst, Hamilton)*
Kilmarnock (1) 1 *(Wright)*   3173
Dundee: Pageaud; Bain, Cargill (McQueen), Manley, Wieghorst, Duffy C, Shaw, Vrto (Anderson), Britton (Tosh), Hamilton, McCann.
Kilmarnock: Lekovic; Skilling, Black, Montgomerie, Whitworth, Connor, Mitchell, Henry (Holt), Wright, Brown, Reilly (Roberts).

Falkirk (1) 1 *(Johnston M)*
Aberdeen (2) 4 *(Booth, Clark (og), Woodthorpe, Miller)*   6387
Falkirk: Parks; Clark, Napier (Inglis), Oliver, McLaughlin, McKenzie (Rice), McGowan, Kirk, McDonald (Henderson), Johnston M, Elliot.
Aberdeen: Snelders; McKimmie, Woodthorpe, Hetherston (McKinnon), Inglis, Smith, Miller, Jess, Booth (Thomson), Dodds, Glass.

Hearts (1) 2 *(Hagen, McPherson)*
Dunfermline Ath (1) 1 *(Den Bieman)*   12,498
Hearts: Smith; Locke, Winnie, Levein (Berry), McPherson, Hamilton, Colquhoun (Lawrence), Mackay, Hagen, Johnston, Robertson.
Dunfermline Ath: Van De Kamp; Den Bieman, Millar, McCathie, Tod, Smith, Moore, McNamara, Shaw (Cooper), Petrie, McCulloch (Fleming).

Livingston (1) 1 *(Young)*
Partick T (0) 2 *(Craig 2)* 1280
Livingston: Stoute; Smart, Martin (Sinclair), Davidson, Williamson, Sorbie (Harvey), McMartin, Bailey (Callaghan), Young, Alleyne, Duthie.
Partick T: Walker; Dinnie, Pittman, McWilliams, Watson, Welsh, McDonald R, Craig, Foster, Turner, Cameron (Gibson).

Rangers (1) 3 *(Hateley, McCall, McCoist)*
Stirling Albion (0) 2 *(Taggart, McCormick)* 39,540
Rangers: Goram; Wright, Robertson, Gough, McLaren, Petric, McCall, Miller, McCoist, Hateley, Mikhailichenko.
Stirling Albion: McGeown; McKechnie (Armstrong), Watson, Mitchell, McQuilter, Tait, McInnes, Deas (Gibson), McCormick, Taggart, McLeod.

31 AUG

Celtic (0) 2 *(van Hooijdonk, Donnelly)*
Raith R (0) 1 *(Rougier) aet* 27,546
Celtic: Marshall; Boyd, McKinlay, Vata, Hughes, Grant, O'Donnell, McLaughlin (Donnelly), van Hooijdonk, Thom (Walker), Collins.
Raith R: Thomson; Kirkwood, Broddle, McInally (Graham), Dennis (Coyle), Sinclair, Rougier, Cameron, Crawford, Lennon, Dair (Wilson).

QUARTER-FINALS

19 SEPT

Celtic (0) 0
Rangers (0) 1 *(McCoist)* 32,803
Celtic: Marshall; Boyd, McKinlay, Vata, Hughes, Grant, Donnelly, McStay, Walker (van Hooijdonk), Thom (McLaughlin), Collins.
Rangers: Goram; Wright, Robertson (Cleland), Gough, McLaren, Petric, Miller, Gascoigne, McCoist, Salenko (Durie), Laudrup.

20 SEPT

Airdrieonians (1) 1 *(McIntyre J)*
Partick T (1) 1 *(Foster) aet* 4311
Airdrieonians: Martin; Stewart, Jack (Smith), Sandison, Sweeney, Black, Boyle, Davies, Cooper (Duffield), Harvey, McIntyre J.
Partick T: Walker; Dinnie, Pittman (Curran), McKee (McDonald R), Welsh, Watson, McWilliams, Craig, Foster, Milne, Cameron.
(Airdrieonians won 3-2 on penalties)

Dundee (2) 4 *(Shaw 2, Tosh, Wieghorst)*
Hearts (0) 4 *(McPherson, Colquhoun, Lawrence, Robertson (pen)) aet* 9528
Dundee: Pageaud; Farningham, McQueen, Cargill (Duffy J), Wieghorst, Duffy C, Shaw, Vrto (Bain), Tosh, Hamilton (Anderson), McCann.

Hearts: Smith; Locke, Winnie (Jamieson), Berry, McPherson, Hamilton, Colquhoun, Mackay (Leitch), Robertson, Hagen, Lawrence.
(Dundee won 5-4 on penalties)

Motherwell (1) 1 *(Arnott)*
Aberdeen (0) 2 *(Dodds, Inglis) aet* 9137
Motherwell: Howie; May, McKinnon (Davies), Philliben, Martin, McCart, Lambert (Roddie), Dolan, Coyne, Arnott (Burns), McSkimming.
Aberdeen: Watt; McKimmie, Woodthorpe, Hetherston (Christie), Inglis, Smith, Miller, Jess, Booth, Dodds, Glass (Shearer).

SEMI-FINALS

24 OCT at Hampden Park

Rangers (0) 1 *(Salenko)*
Aberdeen (0) 2 *(Dodds 2)* 26,131
Rangers: Goram; Wright, Brown, Moore (Durrant), McLaren, Petric, Cleland (Mikhailichenko), Gascoigne, McCoist, Salenko, Durie.
Aberdeen: Watt; McKimmie, Glass, Grant, Inglis, Smith, Miller (Hetherston), Bernard, Booth, Dodds, Jess.

25 OCT at McDiarmid Park

Dundee (1) 2 *(Tosh, McCann)*
Airdrieonians (0) 1 *(Duffield)* 8930
Dundee: Pageaud; Farningham, McQueen, Manley, Wieghorst, Duffy J, Shaw, Vrto, Tosh (Britton), Hamilton, McCann.
Airdrieonians: Martin; Stewart, Smith (Duffield), Sandison, Sweeney, Black, Boyle, Davies, Cooper, Harvey, McIntyre J.

FINAL

26 NOV at Hampden Park

Aberdeen (1) 2 *(Dodds, Shearer)*
Dundee (0) 0 33,096
Aberdeen: Watt; McKimmie, Glass, Grant, Inglis, Smith, Miller (Robertson), Shearer, Bernard, Dodds, Jess (Hetherston).
Dundee: Pageaud; Duffy J, McQueen, Manley, Wieghorst, Duffy C, Shaw, Vrto (Farningham), Tosh (Britton), Hamilton, McCann (Anderson).
Referee: L W Mottram (Forth)

SCOTTISH CUP FINALS 1874–1996

Year	Winners	Runners-up	Score
1874	Queen's Park	Clydesdale	2-0
1875	Queen's Park	Renton	3-0
1876	Queen's Park	Third Lanark	2-0 after 1-1 draw
1877	Vale of Leven	Rangers	3-2 after 0-0 and 1-1 draws
1878	Vale of Leven	Third Lanark	1-0
1879	Vale of Leven*	Rangers	
1880	Queen's Park	Thornlibank	3-0
1881	Queen's Park†	Dumbarton	3-1
1882	Queen's Park	Dumbarton	4-1 after 2-2 draw
1883	Dumbarton	Vale of Leven	2-1 after 2-2 draw
1884	Queen's Park‡	Vale of Leven	
1885	Renton	Vale of Leven	3-1 after 0-0 draw
1886	Queen's Park	Renton	3-1
1887	Hibernian	Dumbarton	2-1
1888	Renton	Cambuslang	6-1
1889	Third Lanark§	Celtic	2-1
1890	Queen's Park	Vale of Leven	2-1 after 1-1 draw
1891	Hearts	Dumbarton	1-0
1892	Celtic¶	Queen's Park	5-1
1893	Queen's Park	Celtic	2-1
1894	Rangers	Celtic	3-1
1895	St Bernard's	Renton	2-1
1896	Hearts	Hibernian	3-1
1897	Rangers	Dumbarton	5-1
1898	Rangers	Kilmarnock	2-0
1899	Celtic	Rangers	2-0
1900	Celtic	Queen's Park	4-3
1901	Hearts	Celtic	4-3
1902	Hibernian	Celtic	1-0
1903	Rangers	Hearts	2-0 after 1-1 and 0-0 draws
1904	Celtic	Rangers	3-2
1905	Third Lanark	Rangers	3-1 after 0-0 draw
1906	Hearts	Third Lanark	1-0
1907	Celtic	Hearts	3-0
1908	Celtic	St Mirren	5-1
1909	••		
1910	Dundee	Clyde	2-1 after 2-2 and 0-0 draws
1911	Celtic	Hamilton A	2-0 after 0-0 draw
1912	Celtic	Clyde	2-0
1913	Falkirk	Raith R	2-0
1914	Celtic	Hibernian	4-1 after 0-0 draw
1920	Kilmarnock	Albion R	3-2
1921	Partick T	Rangers	1-0
1922	Morton	Rangers	1-0
1923	Celtic	Hibernian	1-0
1924	Airdrieonians	Hibernian	2-0
1925	Celtic	Dundee	2-1
1926	St Mirren	Celtic	2-0
1927	Celtic	East Fife	3-1
1928	Rangers	Celtic	4-0
1929	Kilmarnock	Rangers	2-0
1930	Rangers	Partick T	2-1 after 0-0 draw
1931	Celtic	Motherwell	4-2 after 2-2 draw
1932	Rangers	Kilmarnock	3-0 after 1-1 draw
1933	Celtic	Motherwell	1-0
1934	Rangers	St Mirren	5-0
1935	Rangers	Hamilton A	2-1
1936	Rangers	Third Lanark	1-0
1937	Celtic	Aberdeen	2-1
1938	East Fife	Kilmarnock	4-2 after 1-1 draw
1939	Clyde	Motherwell	4-0
1947	Aberdeen	Hibernian	2-1
1948	Rangers	Morton	1-0 after 1-1 draw
1949	Rangers	Clyde	4-1
1950	Rangers	East Fife	3-0
1951	Celtic	Motherwell	1-0
1952	Motherwell	Dundee	4-0
1953	Rangers	Aberdeen	1-0 after 1-1 draw
1954	Celtic	Aberdeen	2-1
1955	Clyde	Celtic	1-0 after 1-1 draw
1956	Hearts	Celtic	3-1
1957	Falkirk	Kilmarnock	2-1 after 1-1 draw
1958	Clyde	Hibernian	1-0
1959	St Mirren	Aberdeen	3-1
1960	Rangers	Kilmarnock	2-0
1961	Dunfermline Ath	Celtic	2-0 after 0-0 draw
1962	Rangers	St Mirren	2-0
1963	Rangers	Celtic	3-0 after 1-1 draw
1964	Rangers	Dundee	3-1

Year	Winners	Runners-up	Score
1965	Celtic	Dunfermline Ath	3-2
1966	Rangers	Celtic	1-0 after 0-0 draw
1967	Celtic	Aberdeen	2-0
1968	Dunfermline Ath	Hearts	3-1
1969	Celtic	Rangers	4-0
1970	Aberdeen	Celtic	3-1
1971	Celtic	Rangers	2-1 after 1-1 draw
1972	Celtic	Hibernian	6-1
1973	Rangers	Celtic	3-2
1974	Celtic	Dundee U	3-0
1975	Celtic	Airdrieonians	3-1
1976	Rangers	Hearts	3-1
1977	Celtic	Rangers	1-0
1978	Rangers	Aberdeen	2-1
1979	Rangers	Hibernian	3-2 after 0-0 and 0-0 draws
1980	Celtic	Rangers	1-0
1981	Rangers	Dundee U	4-1 after 0-0 draw
1982	Aberdeen	Rangers	4-1 (aet)
1983	Aberdeen	Rangers	1-0 (aet)
1984	Aberdeen	Celtic	2-1 (aet)
1985	Celtic	Dundee U	2-1
1986	Aberdeen	Hearts	3-0
1987	St Mirren	Dundee U	1-0 (aet)
1988	Celtic	Dundee U	2-1
1989	Celtic	Rangers	1-0
1990	Aberdeen	Celtic	0-0 (aet)
		(Aberdeen won 9-8 on penalties)	
1991	Motherwell	Dundee U	4-3 (aet)
1992	Rangers	Airdrieonians	2-1
1993	Rangers	Aberdeen	2-1
1994	Dundee U	Rangers	1-0
1995	Celtic	Airdrieonians	1-0
1996	Rangers	Hearts	5-1

*Vale of Leven awarded cup, Rangers failing to appear for replay after 1-1 draw.
†After Dumbarton protested the first game, which Queen's Park won 2-1.
‡Queen's Park awarded cup, Vale of Leven failing to appear.
§Replay by order of Scottish FA because of playing conditions in first match, won 3-0 by Third Lanark.
¶After mutually protested game which Celtic won 1-0.
••Owing to riot, the cup was withheld after two drawn games – between Celtic and Rangers 2-2 and 1-1.

SCOTTISH CUP WINS

Celtic 30, Rangers 27, Queen's Park 10, Aberdeen 7, Hearts 5, Clyde 3, St Mirren 3, Vale of Leven 3, Dunfermline Ath 2, Falkirk 2, Hibernian 2, Kilmarnock 2, Motherwell 2, Renton 2, Third Lanark 2, Airdrieonians 1, Dumbarton 1, Dundee 1, Dundee U 1, East Fife 1, Morton 1, Partick T 1, St Bernard's 1.

APPEARANCES IN FINAL

Celtic 47, Rangers 43, Aberdeen 14, Queen's Park 12, Hearts 11, Hibernian 10, Kilmarnock 7, Vale of Leven 7, Clyde 6, Dumbarton 6, St Mirren 6, Third Lanark 6, Dundee U 7, Motherwell 6, Renton 5, Airdrieonians 4, Dundee 4, Dunfermline Ath 3, East Fife 3, Falkirk 2, Hamilton A 2, Morton 2, Partick T 2, Albion R 1, Cambuslang 1, Clydesdale 1, Raith R 1, St Bernard's 1, Thornlibank 1.

TENNENTS SCOTTISH CUP 1996

FIRST ROUND

9 DEC

Stranraer (0) 0
Livingston (2) 3 *(Harvey 2, Duthie)* 752
Stranraer: Ross; Robertson, Reilly (McGuire), Howard, Gallagher, Duncan, Sloan, Grant (Ferguson), Kerrigan, Walker (McAulay), Henderson.
Livingston: Douglas; Williamson, Alleyne, Davidson, Graham, McLeod, McMartin, Sorbie, Young, Harvey, Duthie (Thorburn).

12 DEC

Stenhousemuir (2) 2 *(McGeachie, Gardner (og))*
Arbroath (2) 2 *(McCormick, Pew)* 424
Stenhousemuir: McKenzie; Sprott, Haddow, Armstrong, McGeachie, Christie, Bannon, Fisher (Roseburgh), Mathieson, Hutchison, Little I.
Arbroath: Dunn; McAulay, Peters, Ward (McCabe), Florence, Crawford, Pew (Elliot), Elder, McCormick, Watters, Gardner.

16 DEC

Albion R (0) 0
Deveronvale (1) 2 *(Stewart, Heggie)* 484
Albion R: Moffat; McDonald, Gallacher, Deeley, Speirs, Shanks, Bell, Crawford (Ryan), Young, McBride (McEwan), Willock.
Deveronvale: Grant I; Humphries, Cameron, Rattray, Cormack (Ironside), Simmers, Bell (Wolecki), Grant A, Heggie, Stewart (Thornton), Dolan.

Glasgow U (0) 0
Spartans (1) 1 *(Burns)* 273
Glasgow U: Menzies; Mitchell (McLeod), Smith B, Welsh (Smith A), Duffy (McKinney), Gilchrist, Ventham, Guadagno, McIntosh, Sloan, Craig.
Spartans: Oliver; Burns, Ettles (Mitchell), Findlay, Thomson, McKeating, Nixon (Johnstone), Galbraith (MacKinnon), Govan, McGovern, Durkin.

FIRST ROUND REPLAY

18 DEC

Arbroath (0) 0
Stenhousemuir (0) 1 *(Mathieson)* 669
Arbroath: Hinchcliffe; Peters, Crawford, Middleton (Sexton), Ward, McAulay, Pew (Porteous), Elliot, McCormick, Watters, Gardner (McCabe).
Stenhousemuir: McKenzie; Sprott, Haddow, Armstrong, Bannon, Christie, Hunter (Aitken), Fisher, Mathieson, Hutchison, Little I.

SECOND ROUND

6 JAN

Ayr U (0) 0
Ross Co (0) 2 *(Robertson, Sharples (og))* 2053
Ayr U: Duncan; Clarke (Byrne), Traynor, George, Jamieson, Sharples, Smith, Steele, Dalziel, Balfour, Kinnaird (Wilson).
Ross Co: Hutchison; Herd, Mackay, Robertson, Bellshaw, Furphy (MacLeod), Ferries, Grant (Williamson), MacPherson (Milne), Connelly, Golabek.

Berwick R (2) 3 *(Reid, Fraser, Irvine)*
Annan Athletic (1) 3 *(Docherty 2, Muir)* 421
Berwick R: Young; Valentine, Banks, Reid, Cowan, Fraser, Wilson, Neil, Kane, Irvine, Graham,.
Annan Athletic: Burnett; Smith, Elliot, McGinlay, Hetherington, Sim, Patterson, Leslie, Docherty (Learmont), Adams, Muir.

Caledonian T (2) 3 *(Ross, Teasdale, Hercher)*
Livingston (0) 2 *(Duthie, Harvey)* 1923
Caledonian T: Calder; MacArthur, Hastings, Bennett, Noble, Ross, Teasdale, Scott, Thomson, Christie, Hercher.
Livingston: Douglas; Sorbie (Callaghan), Alleyne (Coulston), Davidson, Williamson, McLeod, McMartin, Bailey (Thorburn), Young, Harvey, Duthie.

Clyde (1) 2 *(Annand, Nicholas)*
Brechin C (2) 2 *(Mitchell, Cairney (pen))* 903
Clyde: Hillcoat; Knox, Angus, Harrison (McCarron), McConnell, McCheyne, Dickson (Falconer), Nicholas, Annand, Watson, Ferguson.
Brechin C: Allan; Mitchell, Brown, Cairney, Scott, Christie, McKellar, Farnan, Ross, Buick, McNeill (Smith).

Deveronvale (0) 0
Keith (0) 0 1333
Deveronvale: Grant I; Humphries, Cameron, Rattray, Cormack, Simmers, Bell (Schofield), Will, Heggie, Stewart (Morrison), Dolan.
Keith: Thain; Thow, Wilson, Watt, Woolley, Gibson, Thomson, Taylor S, Strachan (Cormie), Will (Nicol), Allan (Garden).

Forfar Ath (2) 3 *(Bowes, Inglis, Mann)*
Lossiemouth (0) 1 *(Clark)* 667
Forfar Ath: Arthur; Hamilton, Henderson (Heddle), Mann, Craig, McPhee, Morgan, Inglis, Higgins, Bowes, Irvine.
Lossiemouth: Pirie; Fiske, Cheyne, Masson, McKenzie, Gerrard (Kew), Still, Presslie (Shaw), Douglas (Kellas), Clark, Main.

Montrose (1) 2 *(Kennedy, Masson)*
Cowdenbeath (1) 1 *(Maratea)* 501
Montrose: Larter; Tosh, Tindal, Masson P, Grant, Haro, MacDonald, Mailer, McGlashan, Kennedy (Smith), Ferrie (Taylor).
Cowdenbeath: Russell; Maratea (Hamilton), Meldrum, Conn, Humphreys, Bowmaker, Steven, Millar (Brock), MacKenzie, Winter, Buckley (Soutar).

Queen of the S (2) 2 *(Mallan, Bryce (pen))*
Queen's Park (1) 4 *(Edgar 3, McGoldrick)* 1034
Queen of the S: Butter; McKeown B, Brown (Ramsay), Campbell C (Campbell D), McKeown D, Bryce, Wilson, Cody, Graham (Harris), Kennedy, Mallan.
Queen's Park: Chalmers; Callan, Arbuckle, Elder, Caven, Graham, Brodie (Orr), Fraser (Kennedy), Edgar, Ferry (McPhee), McGoldrick.

Spartans (0) 0
East Fife (0) 0 997
Spartans: Oliver; Burns, MacDonald, Findlay, Thomson, McKeating, Mitchell, Galbraith, Govan, McGovern (Nixon), Ettles (MacKinnon).
East Fife: Hamilton; McStay, Gibb, Dixon, Beaton, Donaghy, Hutcheon (Andrew), Archibald, Scott, Allan, Hamill.

Stirling Albion (0) 3 *(McCormick 2, Mitchell)*
Alloa (0) 1 *(Rixon)* 1256
Stirling Albion: McGeown; Paterson A, Deas, Mitchell, McQuilter, Paterson G, Bone, McInnes (Tait), McCormick, Taggart, McLeod.
Alloa: Balfour; McCormack, Bennett, Newbigging (Cully), McAneny, McAvoy, MacKay, Cadden (Whyte), Moffat, Gilmour (Hannah), Rixon.

Whitehill Welfare (1) 2 *(Gowrie (pen), Tulloch)*
Fraserburgh (1) 2 *(Killoh 2)* 932
Whitehill Welfare: Cantley; Purves, Gowrie, Bennett (McCulloch) (Cameron), Steel, Millar, Smith, Bird, Sneddon, Brown, Tulloch.
Fraserburgh: Gordon; Clark, Geddes, Young, Milne, Thomson, McCafferty (Norris), Killoh (McGruther), Keith, Hunter, Stephen.

7 JAN

East Stirling (0) 0
Stenhousemuir (1) 1 *(Little I)* 901
East Stirling: McDougall; Russell, Lee R, Watt (McBride), Sneddon (Stirling), Ross, Lee I, Hunter (MacLean), Dwyer, Lamont, Neill.
Stenhousemuir: McKenzie; Sprott, Haddow, Armstrong, McGeachie, Christie, Bannon, Fisher, Mathieson, Hutchison, Little I.

SECOND ROUND REPLAYS

13 JAN

Annan Athletic (0) 1 *(Sibbring)*
Berwick R (0) 2 *(Kane 2)* 1056
Annan Athletic: Burnett; Smith, Stanley Leslie, McGinlay, Hetherington, Sim (Middlemiss), Paterson (Sibbring), Darrell (Learmont), Docherty, Steven Leslie, Muir.
Berwick R: Young; Wilson, Valentine, Reid, Cowan, Fraser, Kane (Forrester), Neil, McGlynn, Irvine, Graham.

Fraserburgh (0) 1 *(Stephen)*
Whitehill Welfare (1) 2 *(Bird, Steel)* 2027
Fraserburgh: Gordon; Clark, Michie, Young, Milne, Thomson (McCafferty), Geddes, Killoh (Beaton), Keith, Hunter, Stephen.
Whitehill Welfare: Cantley; Purves, Gowrie, Bennett (Cameron), Steel, Millar, Middlemist (O'Rourke), Bird, Sneddon, Brown, Tulloch.

Keith (1) 2 *(Nicol, Maver)*
Deveronvale (0) 0 1899
Keith: Thain; Thow, Wilson, Watt, Woolley (Garden), Gibson, Thomson, Taylor S, Strachan (Maver), Nicol (McPherson), Allan.
Deveronvale: Grant I; Humphries, Cameron (Grant A), Rattray, Cormack, Simmers, Bell, Will (Morrison), Heggie, Stewart C (Stewart M), Dolan.

East Fife (0) 2 *(Gibb, Allan)*
Spartans (0) 1 *(Nixon)* 1135
East Fife: Hamilton; McStay, Gibb, Dixon, Beaton, Donaghy, Hamill, Hutcheon (Gartshore), Scott, Allan, Hope.
Spartans: Oliver; Burns, Ettles (Johnstone), Findlay, Thomson, McKeating, Mitchell (Harley), Galbraith, McGovern (Nixon), Govan, Durkin.

15 JAN

Brechin C (0) 1 *(Christie)*
Clyde (0) 3 *(McCheyne, McConnell, Annand)* aet 1033
Brechin C: Allan; Mitchell, Brown, Cairney, Christie, Ferguson, McKellar, Farnan, Ross (Smith), Scott, McNeill.
Clyde: Hillcoat; Knox, Angus, Thomson, McConnell, McCheyne, Prunty, Nicholas, Annand, Watson (Brownlie) (McCluskey), Ferguson (Harrison).

THIRD ROUND

27 JAN

Caledonian T (1) 1 *(Stewart)*
East Fife (0) 1 *(Dwarika)* 2320
Caledonian T: Calder; MacArthur, Hastings, Bennett, Noble, Thomson, Teasdale, Scott (Mitchell), Stewart, Christie, Hercher (McGinlay).
East Fife: Hamilton; McStay, Gibb, Dixon, Beaton, Donaghy, Cusick, Dwarika, Scott, Allan, Hamill.

Hibernian (0) 0
Kilmarnock (0) 2 *(Wright 2)* 8366
Hibernian: Leighton; Millen, Tortolano, Farrell, Love, Mitchell (Harper), McAllister (Weir), Jackson C, Wright, Jackson D, O'Neill.
Kilmarnock: Lekovic; MacPherson, Black (McKee), Reilly, Whitworth, Anderson, Mitchell, Henry, Wright (Montgomerie), Maskrey (Brown), Holt.

Keith (0) 1 *(Garden)* at Pittodrie Stadium
Rangers (6) 10 *(Ferguson 3, Cleland 3, Durie (pen), Robertson, Miller, Mikhailichenko)* 15,461
Keith: Thain; Thow, Wilson, Watt, Woolley, Gibson, Thomson, Taylor S, Strachan (Garden), Nicol (Taylor G), Allan (McPherson).
Rangers: Goram; Cleland (Durrant), Robertson, Gough (Brown), McLaren, Petric, Ferguson, McCall, Miller, Durie, Laudrup (Mikhailichenko).

Raith R (0) 3 *(Crawford 2, Lennon)*
Queen's Park (0) 0 2665
Raith R: Fridge; McMillan (McKilligan), Humphries, Kirkwood, Dennis, Sinclair (Coyle), Rougier, Cameron, Graham, Lennon, Crawford.
Queen's Park: Chalmers; Callan, Graham, Elder, Caven, Ferguson, Orr (Kennedy), Arbuckle, McPhee (Ferry), Brodie (Edgar), McGoldrick.

Ross Co (0) 0
Forfar Ath (1) 3 *(Bowes 2, Morgan)* 2283
Ross Co: Hutchison; Somerville (Williamson), Mackay, Herd, Bellshaw, Furphy, Ferries, MacLeod, Milne, Connelly, Golabek (Grant).
Forfar Ath: Arthur; Hamilton, McVicar, McPhee, Mann, Craig, Morgan, Allison (Glennie), Hannigan (Higgins), Bowes, Heddle.

28 JAN

Whitehill Welfare (0) 0 at Easter Road Stadium
Celtic (1) 3 *(Van Hooijdonk 2, Donnelly)* 13,313
Whitehill Welfare: Cantley; Purves, Gowne, Bennett, Steel, Millar, Middlemist (Smith), Bird (Cameron), Sneddon, Brown, Tulloch (O'Rourke).
Celtic: Marshall; McNamara, McKinlay, Boyd (O'Neil), Hughes, Grant, Wieghorst, McStay, Van Hooijdonk, Walker (Donnelly), Collins (McLaughlin).

30 JAN

Clydebank (0) 0
Stirling Albion (1) 1 *(McCormick)* 911
Clydebank: Matthews; Lovering, Sutherland, Murdoch, Currie, Nicholls, Robertson (Flannigan), Connell, Teale, Lansdowne (Melvin), Bowman.
Stirling Albion: McGeown; Paterson A (Gibson), Deas, Mitchell, McQuilter, Paterson G, Bone, Tait, McCormick, Taggart, McLeod.

Dumbarton (0) 1 *(Mooney)*
Airdrieonians (0) 3 *(Duffield 2, Smith)* 1076
Dumbarton: McFarlane; Burns, Fabiani (Granger), Melvin, Gow, Meechan, Mooney, McKinnon (McGarvey), Gibson, King, Ward (Dallas).
Airdrieonians: Rhodes; Boyle (Bonar), Stewart, Sandison, Sweeney, Black (McIntyre J), Davies, Wilson, Cooper, Duffield, Smith.

Falkirk (0) 0
Stenhousemuir (1) 2 *(Little I, Hutchison)* 3321
Falkirk: Parks; Weir, Munro (Kirk), Clark, James, Gray, McKenzie, Ferguson (Craig), Hagen, Johnston M, Elliot.
Stenhousemuir: McKenzie' Sprott, Scott (Roseburgh), Armstrong, Brannigan, Christie, Aitken, Fisher, Hunter, Hutchison, Little I.

Motherwell (0) 0
Aberdeen (1) 2 *(Windass, Shearer)* 6035
Motherwell: Howie; May, McKinnon, Philliben, Martin, Denham, Lambert, Dolan, Arnott, Burns, McSkimming (Hendry).
Aberdeen: Watt; McKimmie, Glass, Grant, Irvine, Smith, Miller, Shearer (Dodds), Bernard, Windass, Jess.

31 JAN

Clyde (2) 3 *(Nicholas, Harrison, Annand)*
Dundee (1) 1 *(Duffy C)* 2039
Clyde: Hillcoat; Knox, Angus (Nisbet), Gillies, Thomson, Prunty, O'Neill (McCluskey), Nicholas (Paterson), Annand, Harrison, Ferguson.
Dundee: Mathers; Smith, McQueen, Duffy C, Magee (Tosh), McKeown, Shaw, Vrto, Britton, Hamilton, Cargill (Tully).

Hamilton A (0) 0
St Johnstone (1) 1 *(Scott)* 1394
Hamilton A: Cormack; Hillcoat, Renicks, Thomson (Sherry), Baptie, Craig, Quitongo (McKenzie), McEntegart, Geraghty, Hartley, McInulty.
St Johnstone: Main; McQuillan, Preston, Sekerlioglu, Weir, McGowne, Scott, O'Neil, Grant, O'Boyle, Jenkinson.

Hearts (0) 1 *(Ritchie)*
Partick T (0) 0 13,770
Hearts: Rousset; Locke, Ritchie, McPherson, McManus, Bruno, Johnston, Colquhoun, Robertson, Mackay, Pointon.
Partick T: Walker; Dinnie, Milne, Pittman (McWilliams), Welsh, Watson, Macdonald W (Docherty), Foster, Henderson (Smith), Cameron, McDonald R.

12 FEB

Dunfermline Ath (1) 3 *(Bingham, Petrie, Smith A)*
St Mirren (0) 0 4899
Dunfermline Ath: Van De Kamp; Miller C, Fleming, Den Bieman, Tod, French, Moore, Robertson, Smith A (Shaw), Petrie, Bingham (Farrell).
St Mirren: Money; Smith, McIntyre, McWhirter, Fenwick, Archdeacon (Taylor) (McLaughlin), Law, Gillies, Yardley, Lavety, Watson (Iwelumo).

13 FEB

Greenock Morton (1) 1 *(Rajamaki)*
Montrose (0) 1 *(Kennedy)* 2707
Greenock Morton: Wylie; Collins, McArthur, Anderson, McCahill, Lindberg, Lilley, Mahood, Hawke, Cormack, Rajamaki.
Montrose: Larter; Tosh, Tindal, Stephen, Grant, Haro, Kennedy (Cooper), Craib, McGlashan, Smith, Taylor (Ferrie).

14 FEB

Berwick R (1) 1 *(Johnson (og))*
Dundee U (2) 2 *(Coyle 2)* 2077
Berwick R: McQueen; Valentine, Banks (Walton), Reid, Cowan, Fraser (Forrester), Wilson, Neil, Kane, Irvine, Graham.
Dundee U: Maxwell; Perry, Shannon, Pressley, Dailly, Johnson, Winters (McLaren), Robertson, McSwegan (Keith), Coyle, McQuilken.

THIRD ROUND REPLAYS

12 FEB

East Fife (0) 1 *(Scott)*
Caledonian T (0) 1 *(Hercher) aet* 1345
East Fife: Hamilton; McStay, Gibb (Gartshore), Dixon, Demmin (Hutcheon), Hope, Donaghy, Archibald (Andrew), Scott, Allan, Hamill.
Caledonian T: Calder; MacArthur, Hastings, Bennett, Noble, Thomson (Mitchell), Teasdale (Ross), Scott (McGinlay), Stewart, Christie, Hercher.
(Caledonian T won 3-1 on penalties)

14 FEB

Montrose (2) 3 *(McGlashan 3)*
Greenock Morton (2) 2 *(Cormack, Lilley)* 682
Montrose: Larter; Tosh, Tindal, Stephen, Grant, Haro, Kennedy (Ferrie), Craib, McGlashan, Smith, MacDonald.
Greenock Morton: Wylie; Collins, McArthur, Anderson, Johnstone, Lindberg, Lilley, Mahood (Blair), Hawke (Laing), Cormack, Rajamaki (McPherson).

FOURTH ROUND

15 FEB

Clyde (0) 1 *(Angus)*
Rangers (0) 4 *(Miller 2, Van Vossen, Gascoigne)* 5722
Clyde: Hillcoat; Knox, Angus, Gillies, Thomson, Harrison (Nisbet), O'Neil, Nicholas, Annand (Patterson), Watson, Ferguson (Prunty).
Rangers: Goram; Ferguson, Robertson, Moore, McLaren, Petric, Miller, Gascoigne, Van Vossen, McCall, Laudrup.

17 FEB

Airdrieonians (2) 2 *(Cooper, Duffield)*
Forfar Ath (1) 2 *(Inglis, Morgan)* 1410
Airdrieonians: Martin; Stewart, Smith, Sandison, Sweeney, Black, Boyle, Davies, Cooper, Harvey (Wilson), Duffield (McIntyre J).
Forfar Ath: Arthur (Donegan); Irvine (Heddle), McVicar, Hamilton, McKillop, Glennie, Morgan, Allison, Hannigan, Bowes, Inglis.

Celtic (2) 2 *(Thom, Donnelly)*
Raith R (0) 0 30,870
Celtic: Marshall; Boyd, McKinlay, McNamara, O'Neil, Grant, Donnelly (McLaughlin), McStay, Van Hooijdonk, Thom (Hay), Collins.
Raith R: Geddes; Kirkwood, Broddle, Coyle, Dennis, Sinclair, Rougier, Cameron, Crawford (Graham), Lennon (Dair), McInally.

Dundee U (0) 1 *(Brewster)*
Dunfermline Ath (0) 0 7342
Dundee U: Maxwell; Perry, Shannon, Pressley, Dailly, Malpas, Johnson, Robertson (McKinnon), McSwegan (Brewster), Coyle, Winters.
Dunfermline Ath: Van De Kamp; Miller C, Millar M, Den Bieman, Tod, French, Moore, Robertson, Smith, Petrie, Fleming (Shaw).

Kilmarnock (0) 1 *(Anderson)*
Hearts (0) 2 *(Ritchie, Berry)* 14,173
Kilmarnock: Lekovic; MacPherson, Black, Reilly, Montgomerie, Anderson, Mitchell, Henry, Wright, Brown, Holt (McKee).
Hearts: Rousset; Berry, Ritchie, McPherson, Mackay, Millar (McManus), Johnston (Robertson), Colquhoun, Lawrence, Fulton, Pointon.

St Johnstone (1) 3 *(Scott 2, Grant)*
Montrose (0) 0 3370
St Johnstone: Main; McQuillan, Preston, Sekerlioglu (Irons), Weir, McGowne, Scott, O'Neil (Farquhar), Grant (Twaddle), O'Boyle, Jenkinson.
Montrose: Larter; Tosh, Tindal, Stephen, Grant, Haro, Kennedy (Ferrie), Craib, McGlashan, Smith (Kydd), MacDonald (Taylor).

Stenhousemuir (0) 0
Caledonian T (0) 1 *(Thomson)* 1634
Stenhousemuir: McKenzie; Sprott, Bannon, Armstrong, Brannigan, Roseburgh (Hunter), Aitken, Fisher, Mathieson, Hutchison (Haddow), Little I.
Caledonian T: Calder; MacArthur, Hastings, Bennett, Noble, Thomson, Teasdale, Scott, Stewart, Christie, Hercher.

Stirling Albion (0) 0
Aberdeen (1) 2 *(Windass, Shearer)* 3808
Stirling Albion: McGeown; Paterson A, Deas, Mitchell, McQuilter, Paterson G, Bone, Tait (Wood), McCormick, Taggart, McLeod (Gibson).
Aberdeen: Watt; McKimmie, Glass, Grant, Irvine, Smith, Miller, Shearer, Windass, Dodds (Booth), Jess.

FOURTH ROUND REPLAY

27 FEB

Forfar Ath (0) 0
Airdrieonians (0) 0 *aet* 1632
Forfar Ath: Arthur; McKillop, McVicar, McPhee, Mann (Hamilton), Glennie, Morgan, Allison (Donegan), Hannigan, Bowes (Higgins), Inglis.
Airdrieonians: Martin; Stewart (Bonar), Smith, Sandison, Sweeney,
Davies, Boyle, Wilson, Cooper, Duffield, Harvey.
(Airdrieonians won 4-2 on penalties)

QUARTER-FINALS

7 MAR

St Johnstone (0) 1 *(O'Boyle)*
Hearts (1) 2 *(Lawrence, McPherson)* 9951
St Johnstone: Main; McQuillan, Preston, Sekerlioglu, Weir (Farquhar), McGowne, Griffin, O'Neil (Twaddle), Grant, O'Boyle, Jenkinson.
Hearts: Rousset; Locke, Ritchie, McPherson, Mackay (Johnston), Bruno, Lawrence, Colquhoun, Robertson (Millar), Fulton (McManus), Pointon.

9 MAR

Aberdeen (1) 2 *(Windass, Bernard)*
Airdrieonians (1) 1 *(Bonar)* 11,749
Aberdeen: Watt; Grant, Woodthorpe, Bernard, Irvine, Smith, Miller (Shearer), Windass, Booth, Dodds, Glass.
Airdrieonians: Martin; Stewart, Bonar, Sandison, Sweeney, Black (Wilson), Boyle, Davies, Cooper, Harvey, McIntyre J.

Caledonian T (0) 0 at Tannadice Park
Rangers (2) 3 *(Thomson (og), Gascoigne 2)* 11,296
Caledonian T: Calder; MacArthur, Hastings, Bennett (Mitchell), Noble, Thomson (Ross), Teasdale, Scott, Stewart, Christie, Hercher (McGinlay).
Rangers: Goram; Moore, Robertson, Petric (Cleland), McLaren, Brown, Van Vossen (Durrant), Gascoigne, McCoist, Miller, Laudrup.

10 MAR

Celtic (0) 2 *(Van Hooijdonk, McLaughlin)*
Dundee U (1) 1 *(Coyle)* 31,403
Celtic: Marshall; O'Neil (O'Donnell), McKinlay, McNamara, Hughes, Grant, Donnelly, McStay, Van Hooijdonk, Thom, McLaughlin.
Dundee U: Maxwell; Perry, Malpas, Pressley, Welsh, Johnson, Coyle, Bowman, McSwegan (McLaren), Brewster (McKinnon), Winters.

SEMI-FINALS

6 APR at Hampden Park

Aberdeen (0) 1 *(Shearer)*
Hearts (0) 2 *(Robertson, Johnston)* 27,785
Aberdeen: Watt; McKimmie, Woodthorpe, Glass, Inglis, Smith, Miller (Grant), Windass, Bernard, Dodds, Robertson (Shearer).
Hearts: Rousset; Locke, Ritchie, Mackay, McManus, Bruno, Johnston, Colquhoun, Lawrence (McPherson), Fulton (Robertson), Pointon.

7 APR at Hampden Park

Celtic (0) 1 *(Van Hooijdonk)*
Rangers (1) 2 *(McCoist, Laudrup)* 36,333
Celtic: Marshall; Boyd, McKinlay, McNamara, Hughes, Grant, Donnelly, McStay, Van Hooijdonk, Thom, McLaughlin (Wieghorst).
Rangers: Goram; Cleland, Robertson, Petric, McLaren, Brown, Durie (Steven), Gascoigne, McCoist, McCall, Laudrup.

FINAL at Hampden Park

18 MAY

Rangers (1) 5 *(Laudrup 2, Durie 3)*
Hearts (0) 1 *(Colquhoun)* 37,730
Rangers: Goram; Cleland, Robertson, Gough, McLaren, Brown, Durie, Gascoigne, Ferguson (Durrant), McCall, Laudrup.
Hearts: Rousset; Locke (Lawrence), Ritchie, McManus, McPherson, Bruno (Robertson), Johnston, Mackay, Colquhoun, Fulton, Pointon.
Referee: H Dallas (Motherwell).

SCOTTISH LEAGUE CHALLENGE CUP 1995–96

FIRST ROUND

19 AUG

Albion R (1) 2 *(McBride, Scott)*
Ross Co (0) 2 *(Milne, Connelly) aet*   315
Albion R: Moonie; Riley (McDonald), Gallagher, Shanks, Ryan, Strain, Deeley, Collins, Scott, McBride (Seggie), Young.
Ross Co: Hutchison; Somerville, Mackay, Williamson, Herd, Furphy (Campbell), Ferries (McPhee), Grant (MacPherson), Milne, Connelly, Crainie.
(Albion R won 3-2 on penalties)

22 AUG

Ayr U (1) 1 *(Bilsland)*
Dunfermline Ath (1) 2 *(McNamara, Millar) aet*   1209
Ayr U: Lamont; Tannock, Boyce, MacFarlane, Rolling, Sharples, Shepherd, Bilsland, Wilson, Stainrod (Connelly), Moore (Biggart).
Dunfermline Ath: Van De Kamp; Den Bieman, Millar, McCathie, Tod, Smith, Moore, McNamara (Cooper), Shaw (Fleming), Petrie, Kinnaird (McCulloch).

Caledonian T (1) 1 *(McMillan)*
Alloa (1) 2 *(Moffat, Diver)*   878
Caledonian T: McRitchie; Brennan, Hastings, Noble, Benson, MacMillan, Ross, Lisle (Bennett), Stewart, Christie, Green.
Alloa: Graham; Smith, Cully, McCormack, Lawrie, Bennett, Morrison (Wylie), Diver, Moffat, Rixon, McKenzie (Whyte).

Clyde (0) 0
St Johnstone (0) 2 *(Scott, O'Neil)*   1020
Clyde: Hillcoat; Watson, Angus (Ferguson), Gillies, Knox, Brown, O'Neill, Nicholas, Annand, Harrison, Parks (McConnell).
St Johnstone: Main; McQuillan, Preston, Proctor (Farquhar), Griffin, McGowne, Scott, Grant (Twaddle), O'Neil, O'Boyle, Tosh (Irons).

Clydebank (2) 2 *(Kerrigan 2)*
Arbroath (0) 0   345
Clydebank: Matthews; Tomlinson, Lovering, Murdoch, Currie, Nicholls, Kerrigan, Connell, Grady (Prior), Robertson (Teale), Bowman.
Arbroath: Dunn; McMillan, Florence, Clark, Fowler, Crawford, Pew, Porteous (McCormick), McLean, Kennedy, McAulay (Peters).

Dumbarton (0) 0
Brechin C (1) 1 *(Mearns)*   524
Dumbarton: MacFarlane; Burns, Fabiani, Gow (McKinnon), Martin, Marsland, Mooney, King, Gibson, Charnley (McGarvey), Granger (McGivern).
Brechin C: Allan; Mearns, Brown R, Cairney, Conway, Christie, Brand (Smith R), Farnan, Price, Scott, Ferguson.

East Fife (1) 2 *(Scott 2)*
Dundee (2) 4 *(Anderson, Hamilton 3)*   1157
East Fife: Hamilton; McStay, Hamill (Archibald), Cusick, Beaton, Donaghy, Hildersley, Allan, Scott, Andrew, Hope.
Dundee: Pageaud; Farningham, McQueen, Manley, Bain, Cargill, Anderson, Vrto (Wieghorst), Shaw, Hamilton (Britton), McCann (Tully).

East Stirling (0) 0
St Mirren (2) 3 *(Lavety 2, Dawson)*   648
East Stirling: McDougall; Cuthbert (Watt), Lee R, McBride, Sneddon, Neill, MacLean (Stirling), Scott, Geraghty, Abercromby, McKenna.
St Mirren: Combe; Dawson, Baker, Fullarton, Watson (Dick), Smith, Law, Hetherston, Lavety, Bone (McGrotty), Boyd (McMillan).

Hamilton A (0) 2 *(Clark 2)*
Airdrieonians (0) 2 *(Boyle, McIntyre J) aet*   883
Hamilton A: Cormack; McKenzie, McInulty, McEntegart, Paterson, McIntosh, Hartley (Baptie), Sherry, McCormick (McCarrison), McQuade, McCulloch (Clark).
Airdrieonians: Martin; Stewart, Jack (Boyle), Sandison, Sweeney, Black (Wilson), Connelly (McIntyre J), Davies, Cooper, Duffield, Smith.
(Hamilton A won 4-3 on penalties)

Montrose (0) 2 *(Grant, Masson P)*
Berwick R (1) 1 *(Cole)*   420
Montrose: Massie; Tindal, Stephen, Masson P, Grant, Tosh, MacDonald, McAvoy (Cooper), McGlashan, Smith, MacRonald.
Berwick R: Young; Valentine, Banks, Cole, Cowan, Fraser, Graham, Neil, Rutherford, Irvine, Walton (Forrester).

Queen of the S (0) 0
Forfar Ath (1) 1 *(Mann)*   1087
Queen of the S: Butter; Hetherington (Cody), Brown, McKeown B, Kennedy, Ramsay, Wilson, McFarlane, Harris (Jackson), Campbell D, Bryce (Mallan).
Forfar Ath: Arthur; Glennie, McVicar (O'Neill), Mann, McKillop, Craig, Morgan, Bowes, Hannigan, Bingham, Irvine (Paterson).

Stirling Albion (2) 3 *(Tait 2, McCormick)*
Queen's Park (0) 0   546
Stirling Albion: McGeown; McKechnie, Watson, Mitchell, McQuilter, Tait, McInnes, Deas, McCormick (Farquhar), Taggart, McLeod.
Queen's Park: Chalmers; Graham, McGoldrick, McGrath, Elder, Kennedy, Brodie (Porter), Caven, Edgar, McPhee (Ferguson), Matchett.

23 AUG

Livingston (1) 1 *(Callaghan)*
Greenock Morton (0) 0   303
Livingston: Stoute; Graham, Duthie, Davidson, Williamson, Smart, McMartin, Harvey, Callaghan, Alleyne, Sinclair (Sorbie).
Greenock Morton: Wylie; Johnstone (Blair), McArthur, Anderson, McCahill, Lindberg, Lilley (Hawke), Mahood, Laing, McInnes, Rajamaki.

Stranraer (0) 0
Dundee U (1) 2 *(Brewster, McKinlay)*   576
Stranraer: Ross; Hughes, Duncan, Robertson, McCaffrey, Callaghan (McGuire), Sloan, Ferguson (Grant), Walker, McAulay, Henderson.
Dundee U: Maxwell; Perry, Shannon, Pressley, Welsh, Bowman, McLaren, Robertson (McKinlay), Brewster, Crabbe (Connolly), Caldwell (Winters).

SECOND ROUND

11 SEPT

Dundee (2) 3 *(Cargill, Anderson, Shaw)*

Cowdenbeath (0) 0 1101

Dundee: Pageaud; Farningham, McQueen, Duffy C, Cargill, McBain (Teasdale), Shaw (O'Driscoll), Vrto, Tosh, Hamilton, Anderson (Bain).
Cowdenbeath: Russell; Winter (Petrie), Meldrum, Humphreys, McMahon (Smith), Malloy, Wood, Steven, Scott, Yardley, Buckley (Soutar).

12 SEPT

Albion R (1) 1 *(Crawford)*

Brechin C (2) 3 *(Brand 2, Brown R)* 214

Albion R: Osborne; McDonald, Gallagher, Strain, Ryan (Miller), Shanks, Collins (Seggie), Deeley, Crawford, McBride, Russell.
Brechin C: Allan; Mitchell, Brown R, Cairney, Conway, Christie, Smith R (Mearns), Farnan, Ross, Scott, Brand.

Alloa (1) 2 *(Moffat 2)*

Stirling Albion (1) 4 *(Gibson, Taggart, McLeod, McCormick)* 722

Alloa: Balfour; Hannah, Conway (Nelson), McCormack, Wylie, Gilmour, Kirkham, Diver, Moffat, Whyte, Cadden.
Stirling Albion: McGeown; Paterson A, Watson, Mitchell, McQuilter, Tait, Gibson (McKechnie), Deas, McCormick (Watters), Taggart, McLeod.

Clydebank (0) 3 *(Grady 2, Nicholls)*

St Johnstone (0) 0 560

Clydebank: Monaghan; Agnew (McLaughlin), Sutherland, Murdoch, Currie, Nicholls, Robertson, Connell, Flannigan (Teale), Grady, Bowman.
St Johnstone: Main; McQuillan, Preston, Proctor, Cherry, Irons, Scott (Grant), O'Neil, Twaddle (McLean), O'Boyle, Farquhar (Griffin).

Dundee U (1) 3 *(Connolly 2, Johnson)*

Hamilton A (0) 0 3512

Dundee U: O'Hanlon; Perry, Shannon, Pressley, Dailly, Malpas, Walker, McKinlay, Crabbe (Winters), Johnson, Connolly.
Hamilton A: Ferguson; Hillcoat, Renicks, McStay (Lorimer), Baptie, McIntosh, Clark, Sherry, McCarrison, McQuade (Hartley), McParland (McKenzie).

Dunfermline Ath (0) 2 *(Shaw, Tod)*

Forfar Ath (0) 1 *(Bingham)* 2083

Dunfermline Ath: Van De Kamp; Fenwick (Tod), Fleming (Kinnaird), McCathie, Robertson, Smith, Moore, McNamara, Shaw, Petrie, Millar (Den Bieman).
Forfar Ath: Arthur; O'Neill, McVicar, Mann, McKillop, Craig, Morgan, Bowes, Hannigan, Bingham, McPhee.

Stenhousemuir (2) 3 *(Hutchison 3)*

Montrose (0) 1 *(McGlashan)* 280

Stenhousemuir: McKenzie; Bannon, Haddow, Armstrong, McGeachie, Henderson (Sprott), Logan (Swanson), Aitken (Clarke), Mathieson, Hutchison, Little I.
Montrose: Larter; MacRonald (Cooper), Stephen, Smith, Grant, Tosh, MacDonald, McAvoy, McGlashan, Taylor, Ferrie.

13 SEPT

Livingston (0) 2 *(Young, Sinclair)*

St Mirren (0) 0 469

Livingston: Stoute; McCartney, Duthie, Davidson, Graham, McLeod, McMartin, Smart, Callaghan, Harvey (Young), Sinclair.
St Mirren: Combe; Dawson, Baker, Dick, Watson, McLaughlin, Law (Taylor), Fullarton, Gillies, Bone (Boyd), McGrotty (Hetherston).

QUARTER-FINALS

25 SEPT

Dundee (0) 1 *(Cargill)*

Stenhousemuir (1) 3 *(Bain (og), Little I, Mathieson)* 1128

Dundee: Mathers; Matheson, Hutchison (Shaw), Duffy J, Cargill, McBain, Anderson (Cadger), Bain, Dailly, Hamilton, McCann (Britton).
Stenhousemuir: McKenzie; Bannon, Haddow, Armstrong, McGeachie, Sprott, Hunter (Logan), Fisher, Mathieson, Hutchison, Little I (Henderson).

26 SEPT

Clydebank (0) 0

Dundee U (0) 1 *(Honeyman)* 835

Clydebank: Matthews; Tomlinson (Agnew), Sutherland, Lansdowne, Currie, Nicholls, Teale, Connell, Kerrigan (Flannigan), Grady, Bowman.
Dundee U: O'Hanlon; Perry, Shannon, Gray, Dailly, Malpas, Caldwell, Johnson, Walker, Honeyman, Gilmour.

Dunfermline Ath (1) 2 *(Shaw, Petrie)*

Brechin C (0) 0 2006

Dunfermline Ath: Van De Kamp; McNamara, Fleming, Fenwick, Tod, McCulloch (Den Bieman), Moore (Smith), Robertson, Shaw, Petrie, Kinnaird.
Brechin C: Allan; Mitchell, Brown R, Cairney, Conway, Christie, McKellar, Farnan, Ross, Mearns, Reid (McNeill).

28 SEPT

Livingston (0) 1 *(McLeod)*

Stirling Albion (0) 1 *(McLeod) aet* 283

Livingston: Stoute; Williamson, Duthie, Davidson, Graham, Smart, Alleyne (Sorbie), Harvey (Young), Callaghan (Bailey), McLeod, McMartin.
Stirling Albion: Monaghan; Paterson A, Gibson (Roberts), Mitchell, McQuilter, Tait, McInnes, Deas, McCormick (Watters), Taggart, McLeod.
(Stirling Albion won 4-2 on penalties)

SEMI-FINALS

4 OCT

Dunfermline Ath (0) 0

Dundee U (3) 4 *(Dailly, Winters 2, Johnson)* 4900

Dunfermline Ath: Van De Kamp; Den Bieman, Fleming, Tod, Fenwick (McCathie), Smith, McCulloch (Farrell), Robertson, Shaw, Petrie, Kinnaird.
Dundee U: O'Hanlon; Perry, Shannon, Gray, Dailly, Malpas, Winters, Robertson, Welsh, Johnson, McLaren (Walker).

Stirling Albion (0) 1 *(McCormick)*

Stenhousemuir (2) 2 *(Hutchison, Logan)* 1055

Stirling Albion: Monaghan; Paterson A, Gibson (Watters), Mitchell, McQuilter, Tait, McInnes (Roberts), Deas, McCormick, Taggart, McLeod.
Stenhousemuir: McKenzie; Bannon (Aitken), Sprott (Henderson), Armstrong, Brannigan, Logan (Swanson), Hunter, Fisher, Mathieson, Hutchison, Little I.

FINAL

5 NOV at McDiarmid Park

Stenhousemuir (0) 0

Dundee U (0) 0 7856

Stenhousemuir: McKenzie; Bannon, Haddow, Armstrong, McGeachie, Sprott, Hunter, Fisher (Steel), Mathieson, Hutchison, Little I.
Dundee U: Maxwell; Shannon, Malpas, Pressley, Dailly, McKinnon, McLaren (McQuilken), Johnson, McSwegan, Coyle (Brewster), Winters.
Referee: J Rowbotham (Kirkcaldy)
(Stenhousemuir won 5-4 on penalties)

WELSH FOOTBALL 1995–96

When Bobby Gould became the fourth Wales manager in eighteen months in August 1995, Welsh football heaved a huge sigh of relief. After the turmoil created by Terry Yorath's replacement by John Toshack, the man who won the FA Cup for Wimbledon in 1988 was given a two-year contract. A dispirited nation desperately needed a period of stability.

Failure to reach the 1994 World Cup Finals by the width of a crossbar had been exacerbated by Toshack's one-match reign and he was succeeded by the highly respected but ultimately unsuitable Mike Smith who was in charge for the second time. Dignified to the end, Smith was sacked after poor European Championship performances and replaced by the effervescent Gould. He took his adopted country to his heart and wore his Welshness on his sleeve.

Gould's enthusiasm for Welsh football cannot be faulted. He certainly talks a good game but a record of one win in five matches shows why the jury is still out on his achievements on the international stage. Wales beat Moldova (1-0) and lost to Germany (2-1) at home and drew in Albania (1-1) in the European Championship before going down in friendlies in Italy (3-0) and Switzerland (2-0).

Gould has shown a refreshing willingness to experiment—leaving out established players like Rush, Hughes and Southall for various reasons—and World Cup qualifying matches against San Marino, Holland, Turkey and Belgium, will provide a more realistic assessment of his progress in the coming season. He made an encouraging start with a 5-0 win over San Marino.

At one stage, it looked as if Barry Town would dominate Welsh domestic football. Having become the first League of Wales team to go full-time, they swept all before them with a 41-game unbeaten cup and league run first bringing them the championship title. Seventeen points behind came Newtown, who deservedly won a UEFA Cup spot, while third-placed Conwy United qualified for the much-maligned Intertoto Cup.

A mixture of experienced professionals and promising youngsters seemed likely to win Barry the treble but loss of form, coupled with the death in a road accident of 22-year-old midfielder Matthew Holtham, took their toll as the season drew to a close. Ebbw Vale knocked Barry out of the League Cup in the semi-finals and then little Llansantffraid beat them in a truly memorable Welsh Cup Final.

Llansantffraid's extraordinary success coincided with the three Welsh Endsleigh League clubs, Wrexham, Swansea and Cardiff, all being excluded from the Welsh Cup. As part of UEFA's campaign to make Welsh football more representative, only clubs playing in the Welsh pyramid could enter. Newport, Merthyr and Colwyn Bay, the three Welsh teams playing in England who UEFA say must return by 1997, all had mediocre league seasons but Colwyn Bay's FA Cup run took them to the second round before they lost to Blackpool.

In the Endsleigh League, Wrexham narrowly missed out on a Second Division promotion play-off place, Swansea were relegated to the Third where Cardiff had their worst-ever season.

With Barry already in the UEFA Cup as league champions, the small Mid Wales village team of Llansantffraid were assured a place in the European Cup Winners Cup—whatever the outcome of the Welsh Cup Final. Sheer determination to qualify as winners—in an all-round performance of no little skill—drove them on to a famous victory in an exciting penalty shoot-out. Three times they led in normal and extra-time, only to be pegged back by Barry.

They eventually triumphed 3-2 when keeper Andy Mulliner saved the last Barry penalty after an undistinguished display in the previous 120 minutes. Six years ago, Llansantffraid where an amateur village team but, under the guidance of manager Graham Breeze and his assistant, 38-year-old striker Tomi Morgan, the Saints will experience their fifteen minutes of fame in Europe this season.

Within three days of the final, Barry player-manager Paul Giles surprisingly resigned over a bonus dispute and along with brother David joined Ebbw Vale, Paul as assistant to John Lewis, the manager.

Spare a thought for Afan Lido, another small-time club who reached for the stars. Championship runners-up to Bangor City in 1994–95, they nearly became the first League of Wales side to reach the first round of any European competition but were narrowly beaten by RAF Yelgava from Latvia in the UEFA Cup. Last season, the bubble burst and they were relegated to the Office Visions Welsh League with Llanelli. All of Welsh football will be hoping the same fate does not befall Llansantffraid—population 954—after their European adventure.

GRAHAME LLOYD

LEAGUE OF WALES

	P	Home			Goals		Away			Goals			
		W	D	L	F	A	W	D	L	F	A	GD	Pts
Barry Town	40	17	2	1	50	10	13	5	2	42	13	+69	97
Newtown	40	12	5	3	32	7	11	6	3	37	18	+44	80
Conwy United	40	11	7	2	53	23	10	6	4	48	35	+43	76
Bangor City	40	12	5	3	40	27	9	1	10	32	38	+7	69
Flint Town United	40	9	6	5	35	28	10	3	7	41	29	+19	66
Caernarfon Town	40	9	7	4	38	23	7	6	7	39	36	+18	61
Cwmbran Town	40	8	6	6	30	24	6	9	5	28	25	+9	57
Inter Cardiff	40	11	6	3	41	27	3	6	11	21	35	0	54
Caersws	40	10	3	7	46	46	5	6	9	35	51	−16	54
Connah's Quay Nomads	40	9	6	5	46	32	4	8	8	22	31	+5	53
Ebbw Vale	40	7	5	8	35	28	7	6	7	24	28	+3	53
Llansantffraid	40	9	3	8	36	29	5	7	8	30	28	+9	52
Porthmadog	40	7	7	6	34	28	6	4	10	22	34	−6	50
Aberystwyth Town	40	7	7	6	32	30	6	2	12	28	38	−8	48
Cemaes Bay	40	11	5	4	45	28	2	2	16	18	52	−17	46
Holywell Town	40	8	3	9	32	34	4	4	12	21	40	−21	43
Briton Ferry Athletic	40	8	5	7	38	35	3	4	13	26	56	−27	42
Rhyl	40	6	5	9	23	31	5	4	11	24	52	−36	42
Ton Pentre	40	4	8	8	25	29	4	8	8	21	36	−19	40
Afan Lido	40	7	2	11	21	33	2	7	11	12	38	−38	36
Llanelli	40	5	5	10	31	38	3	4	13	19	50	−38	33

LEAGUE OF WALES

	Aberystwyth T	Afan Lido	Bangor City	Barry Town	Briton Ferry Ath	Caernarfon T	Caersws	Cemaes Bay	Connah's Quay	Conwy U	Cwmbran T	Ebbw Vale	Flint Town U	Holywell T	Inter Cardiff	Llanelli	Llansantffraid	Newtown	CPD Porthmadog	Rhyl	Ton Pentre
Aberystwyth T	—	1-1	2-1	0-1	3-1	3-3	1-1	1-3	1-0	2-0	1-1	1-1	2-4	1-2	1-0	2-2	2-2	1-4	4-1	1-2	2-0
Afan Lido	1-4	—	2-3	0-3	0-4	3-1	3-2	0-1	2-0	0-3	0-0	0-1	0-3	2-0	2-0	3-2	0-1	0-0	1-0	2-3	0-2
Bangor City	0-3	2-0	—	0-3	4-1	1-1	1-2	3-2	2-1	4-4	1-0	2-2	3-2	2-1	2-1	4-0	2-1	1-1	1-1	3-1	2-0
Barry Town	2-1	6-0	0-1	—	4-0	1-0	1-1	2-0	2-0	3-1	2-2	1-0	3-1	4-0	2-1	3-0	2-1	2-0	4-1	4-0	2-0
Briton Ferry Ath	3-1	1-1	4-1	1-6	—	3-1	2-3	1-1	1-1	2-5	0-5	3-1	0-2	2-0	1-1	5-0	2-1	0-1	5-1	1-1	1-2
Caernarfon T	2-1	1-0	1-2	0-2	1-1	—	2-0	1-0	1-4	2-2	3-1	0-0	1-1	1-1	3-1	4-0	3-3	0-1	2-2	8-1	2-0
Caersws	1-3	0-0	3-1	0-4	3-0	3-2	—	4-3	3-2	1-3	2-1	3-4	2-4	5-3	2-2	4-0	0-7	0-2	4-1	4-2	2-2
Cemaes Bay	2-2	2-2	3-2	2-1	5-1	0-4	2-2	—	7-1	0-2	1-1	2-1	3-0	4-1	1-2	2-0	0-0	2-4	2-1	2-1	3-0
Connah's Quay	1-0	4-0	1-2	0-0	8-3	4-1	6-3	3-3	—	2-4	5-1	1-1	0-3	1-4	3-1	3-1	0-0	0-2	1-1	2-1	1-1
Conwy U	5-2	5-0	4-0	0-2	1-1	1-1	7-3	3-0	2-2	—	2-3	4-0	2-1	1-1	1-0	2-0	2-2	1-1	1-0	7-2	2-2
Cwmbran T	1-0	0-0	0-0	0-0	2-1	1-2	2-1	3-1	1-1	2-2	—	1-3	4-2	1-0	3-0	2-3	3-1	1-2	0-1	1-2	2-2
Ebbw Vale	1-2	2-2	1-2	0-1	4-1	3-2	3-3	3-0	1-1	3-3	0-1	—	1-0	4-1	1-1	0-1	0-1	1-3	1-2	3-1	3-0
Flint Town U	4-0	0-3	3-2	5-1	4-0	3-2	1-1	2-1	0-0	2-2	1-3	1-1	—	1-2	1-1	2-1	0-5	2-1	2-0	0-1	1-1
Holywell T	2-1	2-0	0-1	0-2	2-2	1-2	3-4	2-1	1-3	1-1	2-0	3-1	3-5	—	2-3	4-2	2-1	0-3	1-0	0-1	1-1
Inter Cardiff	2-0	2-0	4-2	0-0	2-1	2-2	3-1	5-2	2-1	2-1	0-2	0-0	0-5	0-3	—	3-3	1-1	2-2	3-0	4-1	4-0
Llanelli	4-2	4-0	1-3	0-5	2-3	2-2	3-1	2-0	2-0	2-4	1-1	0-2	0-1	1-1	0-1	—	0-1	3-3	1-4	2-2	1-2
Llansantffraid	3-1	1-2	0-2	1-1	3-1	1-3	4-1	5-0	1-2	2-5	1-1	0-1	1-0	3-0	3-2	0-2	—	1-0	0-3	5-1	1-1
Newtown	1-1	1-0	2-1	0-0	3-0	0-0	4-0	3-0	0-0	3-0	0-0	1-2	0-2	2-0	2-0	2-0	3-0	—	0-1	2-0	3-0
CPD Porthmadog	1-0	3-1	4-1	2-3	1-2	1-2	1-1	4-0	1-1	1-2	0-2	3-1	1-1	2-0	1-1	4-1	1-1	0-5	—	0-0	3-3
Rhyl	1-2	1-0	0-3	1-5	2-1	1-5	1-2	3-0	1-1	0-1	2-2	1-0	1-1	1-1	3-2	1-1	3-0	0-1	0-1	—	0-2
Ton Pentre	1-2	0-0	3-2	1-2	2-2	2-3	1-3	2-0	0-1	1-3	1-1	1-2	2-3	2-0	1-1	0-0	2-1	1-1	1-1	1-1	—

OFFICE VISIONS WELSH LEAGUE

Division One

	P	W	D	L	F	A	Pts
Carmarthen Town	34	25	7	2	101	37	82
Haverfordwest	34	23	7	4	116	34	76
Maesteg Park	34	20	8	6	73	47	68
Cardiff Civil Service	34	19	6	9	82	47	63
Treowen	34	18	6	10	67	46	60
Llanwern	34	15	7	12	57	56	52
Penrhiwceiber	34	14	9	11	69	58	51
Taffs Well	34	14	9	11	66	63	51
Caldicot	34	14	4	16	60	68	46
AFC Porth	34	11	10	13	57	67	43
Pontypridd Town	34	12	7	15	58	73	43
Risca	34	12	6	16	50	67	42
Cardiff Corries	34	11	7	16	46	56	40
Aberaman	34	11	7	16	64	79	40
Abergavenny Thursdays	34	10	8	16	50	62	38
Brecon Corries	34	8	3	23	48	90	27
Ammanford	34	6	5	23	43	105	23
Caerleon	34	2	6	26	30	82	12

PA ROWLANDS CYMRU ALLIANCE

	P	W	D	L	F	A	Pts
Oswestry Town*	36	25	3	8	84	41	78
Welshpool	36	23	7	6	83	40	76
Brymbo	36	23	4	9	81	57	73
Llandudno	36	21	9	6	94	42	72
Rhydymwyn	36	21	8	7	73	40	71
Rhayader Town	36	20	5	11	66	44	65
Penrhyncoch†	35	18	10	7	74	45	64
Cefn Druids	36	19	4	13	82	57	61
Lex XI	36	18	4	14	67	49	58
Penycae	36	13	8	15	58	71	47
Llandrindod Wells	36	11	11	14	50	58	44
Mostyn	36	13	4	19	78	78	43
Rhos Aelwyd†	35	10	5	20	47	74	35
Knighton Town	36	11	2	23	52	83	35
Mold Alexandra**	36	10	6	20	61	90	33
Ruthin Town	36	9	6	21	42	71	33
Llanidloes Town	36	8	5	23	34	70	29
Buckley Town	36	7	6	23	38	107	27
Carno	36	6	3	27	42	89	21

* Oswestry Town will not be able to take up their place in the League of Wales because they are an English club. Welshpool will be promoted instead.
† The Penrhyncoch v Rhos Aelwyd game was not played on the last day of the season because of a transport breakdown incurred by Rhos Aelwyd en route.
** Three points deducted.

WELSH CUP 1995–96

Preliminary Round

Abercynon Athletic v Cambrian United	1-2
Bala Town v Penley	0-2
British Steel v Bryntirion Athletic	3-1
Grange Harlequins v Pontlottyn Blast Furnace	3-2
Panteg v Newport YMCA	0-2
Porthcawl Town v Llangeinor	2-2, 3-2
Porth Tywyn Suburbs v Pontyclun	6-0
Trelewis Welfare v Albion Rovers	0-5

First Round

Aberman Athletic v Risca United	3-1
Abergavenny Thursdays v Caerleon	1-0
Albion Rovers v Treowen Stars	0-2
Ammanford Town v Bridgend Town	2-0
Brecon Corinthians v Cardiff Corinthians	0-1
British Steel v BP Llandarcy	0-1
Buckley Town v New Brighton Villa	1-1, 3-0
Cambrian United v Newport YMCA	0-4
Carmarthen Town v Pontardawe Athletic	2-4
Carno v Rhayader Town	1-2
Cefn Druids v Oswestry Town	0-2
Ferndale Athletic v Taffs Well	1-12
Fields Park/Pontllanfraith v AFC Porth	2-2, 1-2
Goytre United v Haverfordwest	3-0
Grange Harlequins v Caldicot Town	5-1
Gresford Athletic v Chirk	1-2
Knighton Town v Llandrindod Wells	1-3
Llandudno v Llangefni Town	1-0
Llandyrnog United v Prestatyn Town	2-0
Llanrwst United v Rhyl Delta	3-2
Llanwern v Pontypridd	0-4
Maesteg Park v Caerau	2-1
Mostyn v Denbigh Town	3-2
Nantlle Vale v Nefyn Utd	2-1
New Broughton v Ruthin Town	1-3
Newcastle Emlyn v Morriston Town	1-5
Penley v Mold Alexandra	2-2, 2-5
Penparcau v Llanidloes	1-1, 3-2
Penrhiwceiber Rangers v Cardiff Civil Service	2-1
Penycae v Brymbo	1-6
Porthcawl Town v Porth Tywyn Suburbs	0-3
Port Talbot Athletic v Skewen	2-0
Rhos Aelwyd v Lex XI	0-2
Welshpool v Penrhyncoch	2-1

Second Round

Aberaman Athletic v Llandrindod Wells	1-1, 1-4
AFC Porth v Grange Harlequins	3-3, 2-3
Ammanford Town v Cardiff Corinthians	1-4
Briton Ferry Athletic v Pontardawe Athletic	3-0
Brymbo v Conwy United	1-3
Connah's Quay Nomads v Welshpool	5-1
Ebbw Vale v BP Llandarcy	3-1
Goytre United v Penrhiwceiber Rangers	4-2
Llandudno v Mostyn	3-2

Llandyrnog United v Buckley Town	2-1
Llanrwst United v Cemaes Bay	2-6
Maesteg Park Athletic v Morriston Town	2-1
Nantlle Vale v Caersws	1-3
Newport YMCA v Pontypridd Town	2-4
Oswestry Town v Chirk	1-0
Penparcau v Rhyl	0-2
Porthmadog v Mold Alexandra	2-1
Porth Tywyn Suburbs v Taffs Well	0-0, 0-1
Port Talbot Athletic v Aberystwyth Town	2-7
Rhayader Town v Abergavenny Thursdays	1-2
Ruthin Town v Lex XI	0-3
Treowen Stars v Llanelli	1-3

Third Round

Abergavenny Thursdays v Caersws	3-2
Aberystwyth Town v Newtown	1-1, 1-0
Bangor City v Cwmbran	2-3
Cemaes Bay v Maesteg Park Athletic	3-0
Connah's Quay Nomads v Llandudno	1-3
Conwy United v Barry Town	0-2
Ebbw Vale v Briton Ferry Athletic	1-0
Goytre United v Llanelli	8-2
Holywell Town v Grange Harlequins	0-2
Lex XI v Ton Pentre	0-0, 2-3
Llandrindod Wells v Afan Lido	1-0
Llansantffraid v Llandyrnog United	2-1
Oswestry Town v Flint Town United	2-1
Porthmadog v Cardiff Corinthians	1-0
Rhyl v Inter Cardiff	1-0
(Rhyl disqualified for fielding an ineligible player)	
Taffs Well v Pontypridd Town	0-1

Fourth Round

Aberystwyth Town v Oswestry Town	0-0, 2-3
Cwmbran Town v Gotyre United	3-0
Grange Harlequins v Ebbw Vale	1-2
Inter Cardiff v Llandudno	2-0
Llansantffraid v Abergavenny Thursdays	4-0
Pontypridd Town v Cemaes Bay	1-0
Porthmadog v Llandrindod Wells	2-1
Ton Pentre v Barry Town	0-1

Fifth Round

Cwmbran Town v Porthmadog	2-0
Ebbw Vale v Inter Cardiff	0-1
Oswestry Town v Barry Town	0-2
Pontypridd v Llansantffraid	1-2

Semi-finals (two legs)

Barry Town v Cwmbran Town	1-0
Cwmbran Town v Barry Town	3-2
(Barry won on away goals rule)	
Inter Cardiff v Llansantffraid	0-1
Llansantffraid v Inter Cardiff	3-1

Final: Llansantffraid 3, Barry Town 3
(aet; Llansantffraid won 3-2 on penalties)
(At National Stadium, Cardiff, 19 May 1996) Att: 2,666

Llansantffraid: Mulliner; Whelan J, Curtiss, Brown, Jones, O'Brien (Watt), Evans I (Nunnerly), Evans G, Morgan, Whelan C, Abercrombie.
Scorers: Morgan, Evans G, Whelan C.
Penalties: Whelan J, Morgan, Curtiss.
Barry Town: Ovendale; Evans, Lloyd, Mayer, Batchelor, Barnett (Griffith), Giles (Withers), Bird, Hunter (Pike), Jones, O'Gorman.
Scorers: Lloyd, Mulliner og, Bird.
Penalties: Lloyd, Ovendale.
Referee: R. Gifford (Llanbradach)

NORTHERN IRISH FOOTBALL 1995–96

Northern Ireland football experienced one of the most astonishing seasons since the establishment of the Irish FA. Promotion and relegation introduced in August proved a success yet it also created many problems.

First Division clubs found themselves in near bankruptcy with reduced attendances and no income from the traditional matches against crowd-pulling glamour teams. It was a hand-to-mouth existence with a few even on occasions opting not to publish a programme.

It was found that two divisions of eight did not really work. Clubs met each other too frequently, the air of anticipation vanished from derby games while style and tactics became so familiar that teams cancelled each other out.

Fortunately, this set-up is to be altered from season 1997–98 with the Premier Division increased to 10 teams and probably two junior sides introduced into the First Division. Already a few have expressed interest but they ponder on whether it is worth the additional expenditure – and risk.

Then there were the disputes between the clubs and the soccer authorities. Portadown became involved in a wrangle over a young player's registration while Glenavon found themselves forced to take legal action over using striker Marc Kenny while still serving a suspension imposed when with Bangor the previous season. "I hope this era is over and that in future any disagreements can be solved within football," said IFA president Jim Boyce.

Portadown proved to be the team of the year. They were the inaugural Premier Division champions. Ronnie McFall got the Manager of the Year Award, midfielder Peter Kennedy was named Player of the Year while striker Garry Haylock collected the leading scorer's Golden Boot with 41 goals.

Crusaders had to concede the title but finished second; Glentoran, under manager Tommy Cassidy, after a lean spell won the Bass Irish Cup and Cliftonville the Coca-Cola Floodlit Cup – their first trophy in 16 years.

For Linfield, whose supporters have been brought up on a diet of success for decades, it was a disastrous year with no success in any series. Manager Trevor Anderson put 10 on the transfer list, is now engaged on rebuilding his squad and realises there cannot be a repeat performance. Fans, who have revealed remarkable tolerance, simply will not accept such mediocrity.

Sponsorship has been maintained for all competitions apart from the Ulster Cup while negotiations are taking place for a new three-year deal, probably worth £300,000, for the televising of all Irish League tournaments.

Manager Bryan Hamilton expressed satisfaction with Northern Ireland's international performances. In fact, his squad narrowly missed qualifying for the European Championship finals after the away draw with Portugal, the 5-3 win over Austria, the Republic's surprise failures and, in retrospect, that 2-1 defeat by Latvia in May 1995 was the real knock-out blow.

Hamilton, however, is gradually moulding a promising side and, more important, there is an excellent flow of talent from the grass roots. "Our resources are limited but it is essential we utilise them to the best advantage," said Hamilton. "We are concentrating on development at all levels from mini-soccer to the senior squad. Things are now slotting into place but it is a process which must continue."

The Irish FA have appointed 16 development officers, and completed a £350,000 refurbishment and rebuilding programme at their Windsor Avenue, Belfast, headquarters, without resorting to capital investment. Now they have an ultra-modern administrative set-up comparable with any in Europe.

Northern Ireland next embarks on the World Cup campaign with matches in Group Nine against Ukraine, Armenia, Albania, Portugal and Germany and, with only one team qualifying it will be a formidable task to reach the France '98 finals. Who knows what will happen but the Irish FA at least have the satisfaction of collecting £1.5m from the televising of the series and, of course, a capacity attendance for the August 1997 World Cup tie with Germany which coincides with the opening of the multi-million pound stand at Windsor Park's Spion Kop.

MALCOLM BRODIE

WILKINSON SWORD LEAGUE CUP

Quarter-finals

Portadown v Linfield	0-0
(aet; Portadown won 5-4 on penalties)	
Carrick Rangers v Omagh Town	2-6
Cliftonville v Crusaders	0-0
(aet; Crusaders won 3-0 on penalties)	
Coleraine v Glenavon	0-3

Semi-finals

Crusaders v Omagh Town *(at The Oval)*	3-1
Portadown v Glenavon *(at Shamrock Park—venue selected by toss of coin)*	3-0

Final

Portadown 2 Crusaders 1 *(at Windsor Park)*
Portadown: Keenan; Fulton, Murray (Magee), Casey, Strain, Major, Boyle (Davidson), Russell, Haylock, Peebles, Kennedy.
Crusaders: McKeown; McMullan, McCartney, Dunlop, Callaghan, O'Brien (Hunter K), Murray, Dunne, Baxter, Hunter G, Burrows.
Scorers: Portadown—Haylock, Casey.
Crusaders—Burrows.
Referee: L. Irvine (Limavady).
Attendance: 2600.

SMIRNOFF IRISH LEAGUE

Premier Division

	P	W	D	L	F	A	Pts
Portadown	28	16	8	4	61	40	56
Crusaders	28	15	7	6	45	32	52
Glentoran	28	13	7	8	56	38	46
Glenavon	28	13	5	10	47	32	44
Linfield	28	11	8	9	34	35	41
Cliftonville	28	6	11	11	27	48	29
Ards	28	6	7	15	29	43	25
Bangor	28	3	5	20	23	54	14

First Division

	P	W	D	L	F	A	Pts
Coleraine	28	21	4	3	82	28	67
Ballymena United	28	13	10	5	38	25	49
Omagh Town	28	12	7	9	50	43	43
Distillery	28	10	7	11	35	34	37
Ballyclare Comrades	28	10	3	15	29	48	33
Carrick Rangers	28	9	3	16	32	56	30
Larne	28	7	7	14	31	36	28
Newry Town	28	7	5	16	31	58	26

IRISH LEAGUE CHAMPIONSHIP WINNERS

1891	Linfield	1910	Cliftonville	1934	Linfield	1961	Linfield	1981	Glentoran
1892	Linfield	1911	Linfield	1935	Linfield	1962	Linfield	1982	Linfield
1893	Linfield	1912	Glentoran	1936	Belfast Celtic	1963	Distillery	1983	Linfield
1894	Glentoran	1913	Glentoran	1937	Belfast Celtic	1964	Glentoran	1984	Linfield
1895	Linfield	1914	Linfield	1938	Belfast Celtic	1965	Derry City	1985	Linfield
1896	Distillery	1915	Belfast Celtic	1939	Belfast Celtic	1966	Linfield	1986	Linfield
1897	Glentoran	1920	Belfast Celtic	1940	Belfast Celtic	1967	Glentoran	1987	Linfield
1898	Linfield	1921	Glentoran	1948	Belfast Celtic	1968	Glentoran	1988	Glentoran
1899	Distillery	1922	Linfield	1949	Linfield	1969	Linfield	1989	Linfield
1900	Belfast Celtic	1923	Linfield	1950	Linfield	1970	Glentoran	1990	Portadown
1901	Distillery	1924	Queen's Island	1951	Glentoran	1971	Linfield	1991	Portadown
1902	Linfield	1925	Glentoran	1952	Glenavon	1972	Glentoran	1992	Glentoran
1903	Distillery	1926	Belfast Celtic	1953	Glentoran	1973	Crusaders	1993	Linfield
1904	Linfield	1927	Belfast Celtic	1954	Linfield	1974	Coleraine	1994	Linfield
1905	Glentoran	1928	Belfast Celtic	1955	Linfield	1975	Linfield	1995	Crusaders
1906	Cliftonville/	1929	Belfast Celtic	1956	Linfield	1976	Crusaders	1996	Portadown
	Distillery	1930	Linfield	1957	Glentoran	1977	Glentoran		
1907	Linfield	1931	Glentoran	1958	Ards	1978	Linfield		
1908	Linfield	1932	Linfield	1959	Linfield	1979	Linfield		
1909	Linfield	1933	Belfast Celtic	1960	Glenavon	1980	Linfield		

ULSTER CUP
SECTIONAL TABLES

Section A

	P	W	D	L	F	A	Pts
Crusaders	3	2	0	1	8	4	6
Glentoran	3	2	0	1	7	6	6
Carrick Rangers	3	1	1	1	6	6	4
Omagh Town	3	0	1	2	5	10	1

Section B

	P	W	D	L	F	A	Pts
Glenavon	3	3	0	0	9	0	9
Distillery	3	2	0	1	7	1	6
Cliftonville	3	1	0	2	7	4	3
Ballyclare Comrades	3	0	0	3	1	19	0

Section C

	P	W	D	L	F	A	Pts
Coleraine	3	2	1	0	5	1	7
Portadown	3	2	0	1	7	2	6
Bangor	3	1	1	1	3	6	4
Newry Town	3	0	0	3	1	7	0

Section D

	P	W	D	L	F	A	Pts
Ards	3	3	0	0	7	0	6
Linfield	3	2	0	1	5	2	6
Ballymena United	3	1	0	2	1	7	3
Larne	3	0	0	3	0	4	0

ULSTER CUP 1995–96

Quarter-finals

Crusaders v Distillery	1-1
(aet; Crusaders won 6-5 on penalties)	
Glenavon v Glentoran	2-0
Coleraine v Linfield	0-1
Ards v Portadown	1-2

Semi-finals

Linfield v Crusaders *(at The Oval)*	3-2
Portadown v Glenavon	3-2

Final

Linfield 2 Portadown 2 *(at Windsor Park, Belfast)*
(aet; 1-1 after 90 mins; Portadown won 5-3 on penalties)
Linfield: Crawford; Dornan, Crothers (Beatty), Ewing, Spiers, McCoosh, Campbell (Erskine), Gorman, Johnston, Knell (Fenlon) Bailie.
Portadown: Dalton; Fulton, Davidson, Casey, Byrne (Candlish), Stewart, Evans (Carlyle), Peebles, Haylock, Leitch, Kennedy.
Scorers: Portadown–Haylock, Peebles.
Linfield–McCoosh, Fenlon.
Referee: D. Magill (Belfast).
Attendance: 4061.

Winners

1949	Linfield	1959	Glenavon	1969	Coleraine	1979	"Linfield	1989	Glentoran
1950	Larne	1960	Linfield	1970	Linfield	1980	Ballymena U	1990	Portadown
1951	Glentoran	1961	Ballymena U	1971	Linfield	1981	Glentoran	1991	Bangor
1952		1962	Linfield	1972	Coleraine	1982	Glentoran	1992	Linfield
1953	Glentoran	1963	Crusaders	1973	Ards	1983	Glentoran	1993	Crusaders
1954	Crusaders	1964	Linfield	1974	Linfield	1984	Linfield	1994	Bangor
1955	Glenavon	1965	Coleraine	1975	Coleraine	1985	Coleraine	1995	Portadown
1956	Linfield	1966	Glentoran	1976	Glentoran	1986	Coleraine		
1957	Linfield	1967	Linfield	1977	Linfield	1987	Larne		
1958	Distillery	1968	Coleraine	1978	Linfield	1988	Glentoran		

CALOR COUNTY ANTRIM SHIELD

Semi-finals

Crusaders v Ballymena United *(at The Oval)*	2-0
Glenavon v Portadown *(at Shamrock Park, Portadown)*	
	4-1 *(aet)*

Final

Crusaders 0 Glenavon 3 *(at The Oval, Belfast)*
Crusaders: Wilson; McMullan (Livingstone), Carroll (McCartney), Dunlop, Lawlor R (Murray), Deecan, O'Brien, Dunne, Baxter, Hunter G, Callaghan.
Glenavon: O'Neill; Byrne, Glendinning, Murphy, Gauld, Smyth G, Johnstone, McCoy, Ferguson, McBride, Kenny (Collins).
Scorers: Glenavon–McBride 2, Kenny.
Referee: D. Magill (Belfast).
Attendance: 1700.

COCA-COLA IRISH LEAGUE FLOODLIT CUP

Semi-finals

Ards v Cliftonville *(at New Grosvenor Stadium)*	1-3
Portadown v Glenavon *(at Mourneview Park, Lurgan)*	
	2-1

Final

Cliftonville 3 Glentoran 1 *(at Windsor Park, Belfast)*
Cliftonville: Rice; Hill, Flynn, Tabb, Kerr, Heath, McCann, Sliney, Cross, Stokes, Donnelly (O'Neill).
Glentoran: Armstrong; Nixon, Smyth, Kennedy, Devine, Walker (Coyle), Quigley (Parker), Little, Cook, Batey, McBride.
Scorers: Cliftonville–McCann, Ross, Stokes.
Glentoran–Cook.
Referee: N. Cowie (Bangor).
Attendance: 1672.

BASS IRISH CUP 1995–96

Fifth Round (First Round Proper)
Chimney Corner v Ballymena United	0-1
Glentoran v Limavady United	4-1
Crusaders v Duneiven	4-0
Tobermore United v Ballyclare Comrades	2-3
Distillery v Larne Tech OB	4-2
Newry Town v Coleraine	2-1
Dungannon Swifts v Omagh Town	2-4
Crumlin United v Linfield	0-8
East Belfast v Malachians	4-1
Larne v Banbridge Town	3-0
Kilmore Rec v Cliftonville	0-3
RUC v Carrick Rangers	2-3
Ards v Cookstown United	10-0
Bangor v Portadown	0-4
Armagh City v Dundela	2-1
Glenavon v 1st Liverpool	12-1

Sixth Round
Linfield v East Belfast	1-0
Glenavon v Cliftonville	3-1
Ballyclare Comrades v Crusaders	0-1
Glentoran v Distillery	2-0
Portadown v Omagh Town	3-1

Ballymena United v Armagh City	4-0
Ards v Larne	1-0
Carrick Rangers v Newry Town	1-0

Quarter-finals
Crusaders v Linfield	2-0
Glentoran v Ballymena United	0-0, 4-2
Glenavon v Carrick Rangers	3-1
Portadown v Ards	2-1

Semi-finals
Crusaders v Glentoran *(at Windsor Park)*	2-2, 1-2
Glenavon v Portadown *(at The Oval, Belfast)*	1-1, 4-1

Final
Glentoran 1 Glenavon 0 *(at Windsor Park, Belfast)*
Glentoran: Devine D; Nixon, Finlay, Walker, Devine J, Parker, Smith T, Little, Coyle, Batey, McBride J.
Glenavon: Straney; Smyth J, Glendinning, Murphy, Gauld, Smyth G, Johnston, Shepherd, Ferguson, McBride (McCoy), Shipp.
Scorer: Glentoran–Little
Referee: A. Snoddy (Carryduff).
Attendance: 10,000.

IRISH CUP FINALS (from 1946–47)

1946–47	Belfast Celtic 1, Glentoran 0
1947–48	Linfield 3, Coleraine 0
1948–49	Derry City 3, Glentoran 1
1949–50	Linfield 2, Distillery 1
1950–51	Glentoran 3, Ballymena U 1
1951–52	Ards 1, Glentoran 0
1952–53	Linfield 5, Coleraine 0
1953–54	Derry City 1, Glentoran 0
1954–55	Dundela 3, Glenavon 0
1955–56	Distillery 1, Glentoran 0
1956–57	Glenavon 2, Derry City 0
1957–58	Ballymena U 2, Linfield 0
1958–59	Glenavon 2, Ballymena U 0
1959–60	Linfield 5, Ards 1
1960–61	Glenavon 5, Linfield 1
1961–62	Linfield 4, Portadown 0
1962–63	Linfield 2, Distillery 1
1963–64	Derry City 2, Glentoran 0
1964–65	Coleraine 2, Glenavon 1
1965–66	Glentoran 2, Linfield 0
1966–67	Crusaders 3, Glentoran 1
1967–68	Crusaders 2, Linfield 0
1968–69	Ards 4, Distillery 2
1969–70	Linfield 2, Ballymena U 1
1970–71	Distillery 3, Derry City 0

1971–72	Coleraine 2, Portadown 1
1972–73	Glentoran 3, Linfield 2
1973–74	Ards 2, Ballymena U 1
1974–75	Coleraine 1:0:1, Linfield 1:0:0
1975–76	Carrick Rangers 2, Linfield 1
1976–77	Coleraine 4, Linfield 1
1977–78	Linfield 3, Ballymena U 1
1978–79	Cliftonville 3, Portadown 2
1979–80	Linfield 2, Crusaders 0
1980–81	Ballymena U 1, Glenavon 0
1981–82	Linfield 2, Coleraine 1
1982–83	Glentoran 1:2, Linfield 1:1
1983–84	Ballymena U 4, Carrick Rangers 1
1984–85	Glentoran 1:1, Linfield 1:0
1985–86	Glentoran 2, Coleraine 1
1986–87	Glentoran 1, Larne 0
1987–88	Glentoran 1, Glenavon 0
1988–89	Ballymena U 1, Larne 0
1989–90	Glentoran 3, Portadown 0
1990–91	Portadown 2, Glenavon 1
1991–92	Glenavon 2, Linfield 1
1992–93	Bangor 1:1:1, Ards 1:1:0
1993–94	Linfield 2, Bangor 0
1994–95	Linfield 3, Carrick Rangers 1
1995–96	Glentoran 1, Glenavon 0

SUN-LIFE GOLD CUP
SECTIONAL TABLES

Section A	P	W	D	L	F	A	Pts
Crusaders	3	2	1	0	9	5	7
Linfield	3	1	2	0	5	3	5
Distillery	3	1	1	1	6	6	4
Newry Town	3	0	0	3	3	9	0

Section B	P	W	D	L	F	A	Pts
Glenavon	3	3	0	0	7	1	9
Bangor	3	2	0	1	4	2	6
Ballymena United	3	1	0	2	2	4	3
Coleraine	3	0	0	3	2	8	0

Section C	P	W	D	L	F	A	Pts
Portadown	3	2	1	0	9	4	7
Omagh Town	3	1	2	0	4	3	5
Ards	3	1	1	1	8	9	4
Ballyclare Comrades	3	0	0	3	0	5	0

Section D	P	W	D	L	F	A	Pts
Cliftonville	3	2	0	1	5	1	6
Glentoran	3	1	1	1	3	2	4
Carrick Rangers	3	1	1	1	3	5	4
Larne	3	1	0	2	1	4	3

SUN-LIFE GOLD CUP 1995–96

Quarter-finals

Linfield v Glentoran	2-2

(Linfield won 4-3 on penalties)

Crusaders v Bangor	2-1
Omagh Town v Portadown	4-2 *(aet)*
Cliftonville v Ballymena United	1-0

(Glenavon were eliminated from the competition for a registration offence)

Semi-finals

Crusaders v Omagh Town	1-0
Linfield v Cliftonville	2-1

Final

Crusaders 1 Linfield 0 *(at The Oval, Belfast, 13 February 1996)*
Crusaders: McKeown; McMullan, Lawlor M, Dunlop, Lawlor R, Murray, O'Brien, Dunne, Baxter, Carroll, Burrows.
Linfield: Lamont; Dornan, Easton, McCoosh (Ewing), Spiers, Knell (Rob Campbell), Ray Campbell, Johnston (Erskine), Millar, Fenlon, Bailie.
Scorer: Crusaders–O'Brien.
Referee: A. Snoddy (Carryduff).
Attendance: 3076.

WHERE THE TROPHIES WENT

	Winners	Runners-up
Smirnoff Irish League:		
Premier Division	Portadown	Crusaders
First Division	Coleraine	Ballymena United
Bass Irish Cup	Glentoran	Glenavon
Sun-Life Gold Cup	Crusaders	Linfield
Wilkinson Sword League Cup	Portadown	Crusaders
Ulster Cup	Portadown	Linfield
Calor County Antrim Shield	Glenavon	Crusaders
Coca-Cola Irish League Cup Final	Cliftonville	Glentoran
Calor Steel and Sons Cup Final	Ballymena United Res	Dromara Village
Wilkinson Sword B Division:		
Section 1	Loughgall	Dungannon Swifts
Section 2	Glentoran II	Bangor Res
Coca-Cola Irish Youth Cup	Kilmore Rec	Portadown Boys
Irish Intermediate Cup	Limavady United	H & W Welders
Wilkinson Sword (George Wilson Cup)	Coleraine Res	Bangor Res
McEwans Mid Ulster Cup	Bangor	Dungannon Swifts
Mid Ulster Shield	Newry Celtic	Gilford Crusaders
North West Senior Cup	Omagh Town	Coleraine
North West Junior Cup	Ballykelly United	Upperlands
North West Youth Cup	Oxford United	Institute
Bob Radcliffe Memorial Cup	Dungannon Swifts	Lurgan Celtic
Ormo Irish Junior Cup	Hill Street	Oxford United
Smirnoff Knock Out Cup	Limavady United	Banbridge Town
Irish Youth League Cup	Glentoran Colts	Linfield Rangers
Calor County Antrim Junior Shield	Grove United	Knockbreda Parish
Irish News Cup (inaugural year)	Coleraine	Omagh Town

Ulster Footballer of the Year—Castlereagh Glentoran Supporters Club—Peter Kennedy (Portadown).
NIFWA Player of the Year—Peter Kennedy (Portadown).
NIFWA Young Player of the Year—Glen Little (Glentoran).
Manager of the Year (Coaches Association)—Ronnie McFall (Portadown).
Jimmy Dubois Trophy—outstanding non-senior team—Oxford United Stars.
NIFWA Personality—Steve Lomas (Manchester City)
Sunday Life Goalscoring award—Smirnoff Irish League Premier Division—Garry Haylock (Portadown) 41.
First Division—Sammy Shiels (Coleraine) 27.

INTERNATIONAL DIRECTORY

The latest available information has been given regarding numbers of clubs and players registered with FIFA, the world governing body. Where known, official colours are listed. With European countries, League tables show a number of signs. * indicates relegated teams, + play-offs, *+ relegated after play-offs, ++ promoted.

When provisional members are added there will be 190 FIFA countries. The four home countries, England, Scotland, Northern Ireland and Wales, are dealt with elsewhere in the Yearbook; but basic details appear in this directory.

EUROPE

ALBANIA

Federation Albanaise De Football, Rruga Dervish Hima Nr. 31, Tirana.
Founded: 1930; *Number of Clubs:* 49; *Number of Players:* 5,192; *National Colours:* Red shirts, black shorts, red stockings.
Telephone: 00–355–42 27 877; *Cable:* ALBSPORT TIRANA; *Telex:* 2228 bfssh ab. *Fax:* 00 355–42 27 877.

International matches 1995
Moldova (h) 3-0, Georgia (a) 0-2, Moldova (a) 3-2, Bulgaria (h) 1-1, Bulgaria (1) 0-3, Wales (h) 1-1, Bosnia (h) 2-0.

League Championship wins (1945–96)
Dinamo Tirana 15; Partizani Tirana 15; 17 Nentori 8; Vllaznia 7; SK Tirana 2; Flamurtari 1; Labinoti 1; Teuta 1.

Cup wins (1948–96)
Partizani Tirana 13; Dinamo Tirana 12; 17 Nentori 6; Vllaznia 5; Flamurtari 2; SK Tirana 2; Labinoti 1; Elbasan 1; Teuta 1.

Final League Table 1995–96

	P	W	D	L	F	A	Pts
SK Tirana	34	19	10	5	52	22	55
Teuta	34	20	10	4	50	22	54
Partizani	34	16	9	9	43	24	46
Flamurtari	34	17	6	11	42	35	45
Olimpik	34	15	8	11	42	30	41
Apolonia	34	12	9	13	46	44	37
Besa	34	12	9	13	29	31	35
Sopoti	34	11	9	14	35	47	34
Shkumbini	34	12	9	13	43	40	33
Vllaznia	34	9	13	12	30	36	32
Albpetrol	34	12	7	15	30	48	32
Tomori	34	11	9	14	34	40	31
Laci	34	13	4	17	49	53	31
Elbasan	34	10	10	14	35	41	31
Skenderbeu	34	13	3	18	36	51	31
Shqiponia	34	11	6	17	36	42	31
Kastrioti	34	11	6	17	30	40	30
Beselidhja*	34	9	9	16	24	40	27

Three points for away win, two at home.
Top scorer: Čuko (Laci) 21.
Cup Final: SK Tirana 1, Flamurtari 1 aet.
SK Tirana won 4-3 on penalties.

ARMENIA

Football Federation of Armenia, 9, Abovian Str. 375001 Erevan, Armenia.
Number of Clubs: 956; *Number of Players:* 12,055.
Telephone: 00374 2/527014; *Telex:* 885–52 3376; *Fax:* 00374 2/151573.

International matches 1995
Spain (h) 0-2, Macedonia (h) 2-2, Spain (a) 0-1, Denmark (h) 0-2, Macedonia (a) 2-1, Belgium (h) 0-2, Denmark (a) 1-3.

League Championship wins 1992–94
Shirak Gyumri 2; Ararat Erevan 1.

Cup winners 1992–94
Ararat Erevan 2.

Final League Table 1994
Piunik Erevan 60; Shirak Gyumri 51; Erazank 44; Ararat 39; Tsement 39; Kotaik 36; Karabach 29; Van 24; Homenmen 21; Zankezour 17; Aragats* 15; Aznavour 2.
Cup Final: Pyunik 3, Kotaik 2.

AUSTRIA

Oesterreichischer Fussball-Bund, Wiener Stadion, Sektor A/F, Meierestrasse, A-1020 Wien.
Founded: 1904; *Number of Clubs:* 2,081; *Number of Players:* 253,576; *National Colours:* White shirts, black shorts, black stockings.
Telephone: 0043 1 727 18; *Cable:* FOOTBALL WIEN; *Telex:* 111919 oefb a; *Fax:* 0043 1 728 1632.

International matches 1995
Latvia(h) 5-0, Liechtenstein (h) 7-0, Eire (a) 3-1, Latvia (a) 2-3, Eire (h) 3-1, Portugal (h) 1-1, Northern Ireland (a) 3-5.

League Championship wins (1912–96)
Rapid Vienna 30; FK Austria 22; Admira-Energie-Wacker (prev. Sportklub Admira & Admira-Energie) 8; First Vienna 6; Tirol-Svarowski-Innsbruck (prev. Wacker Innsbruck) 7; Wiener Sportklub 3; Austria Salzburg 2; FAC 1; Hakoah 1; Linz ASK 1; Wacker Vienna 1; WAF 1; Voest Linz 1.

Cup wins (1919–96)
FK Austria 25; Rapid Vienna 14; TS Innsbruck (prev. Wacker Innsbruck) 7; Admira-Energie-Wacker (prev. Sportklub Admira & Admira-Energie) 5; First Vienna 3; Linz ASK 1; Wacker Vienna 1; WAF 1; Wiener Sportklub 1; Graz 1; Stockerau 1; Sturm Graz 1.

Final table 1995–96

	P	W	D	L	F	A	Pts
Rapid	36	22	7	7	68	38	73
Sturm Graz	36	20	7	9	61	35	67
Innsbruck	36	18	8	10	64	40	62
Graz	36	14	15	7	46	36	57
FK Austria	36	14	9	13	42	35	51
Linz ASK	36	13	9	14	36	35	48
Ried	36	11	14	11	47	53	47
Austria Salzburg	36	10	14	12	53	51	44
Admira Wacker+	36	7	13	16	35	61	34
Vorwaerts*	36	6	6	30	25	93	6

Top scorer: Vastic (Sturm Graz) 20.
Cup Final: Sturm Graz 3, Admira Wacker 1.

AZERBAIJAN

Association of Football Federations of Azerbaijan, Husu Haciyev kuc., 42, 37009 Baku, Azerbaijan.
Number of Clubs: 2,200. *Number of Players:* 131,000.
Telephone: 00994 12 94 49 16; *Fax:* 00994 12 98 93 93; *Telex:* 142349 affa su.

International matches 1995
Slovakia (a) 1-4, Romania (h) 1-4, Slovakia (h) 0-1, France (a) 0-10, Israel (a) 0-2, Poland (h) 0-0.

League Championship wins 1995
Kepez 1.

Cup wins 1995
Neftchi 1.

BELARUS

Belarus Football Association, 8–2 Kyrov Str. 220600 Minsk, Belarus.
Founded: 1992; *Number of Players:* 120,000.
Telephone: 007 0172 27 29 20; *Telex:*252175 athlet su; *Fax:* 007 0172 27 29 20.

International matches 1995
Czech Republic (a) 2-4, Malta (h) 1-1, Holland (h) 1-0, Lithuania (a) 1-1, Holland (a) 0-1, Czech Republic (h) 0-2, Luxembourg (a) 0-0, Malta (a) 2-0.

League Championship wins 1992–95
Dynamo Minsk 4.

Cup wins 1992–95
Dynamo Minsk 2; Neman 1; Dynamo 93 Minsk 1.
Cup Final: Dynamo Minsk 1, MPKC 4.

BELGIUM

Union Royale Belge Des Societes De Football; Eturl, Association, Rue De La Loi 43, Boite 1, B-1040 Bruxelles.
Founded: 1895; *Number of Clubs:* 2,120; *Number of Players:* 390,468; *National Colours:* Red shirts with tri-coloured trim, red shorts, red stockings with trim.
Telephone: 0032 2 477 12 11; *Cable:* UBSFA BRUX-ELLES; *Telex:* 23257 bvbfbf b; *Fax:* 0032 2 478 23 91.

International matches 1995
Spain (a) 1-1, USA (h) 1-0, Cyprus (h) 2-0, Macedonia (a) 5-0, Germany (h) 1-2, Denmark (h) 1-3, Armenia (a) 2-0, Cyprus (a) 1-1.

League Championship wins (1896–1996)
Anderlecht 24; Union St Gilloise 11; FC Brugge 10; Standard Liege 8; Beerschot 7; RC Brussels 6; FC Liege 5; Daring Brussels 5; Antwerp 4; Mechelen 4; Lierse SK 3; SV Brugge 3; Beveren 2; RWD Molenbeek 1.

Cup wins (1954–96)
Anderlecht 8; FC Brugge 7; Standard Liege 5; Beerschot 2; Waterschei 2; Beveren 2; Gent 2; Antwerp 2; Lierse SK 1; Racing Doornik 1; Waregem 1; SV Brugge 1; Mechelen 1; FC Liege 1.

Final League Table 1995–96

	P	W	D	L	F	A	Pts
FC Brugge	34	25	6	3	83	30	81
Anderlecht	34	22	5	7	83	37	71
Ekeren	34	15	8	11	53	37	53
RWD Molenbeek	34	13	14	7	39	29	53
Lierse	34	14	10	10	54	45	52
Standard Liege	34	13	12	9	51	46	51
Charleroi	34	13	11	10	59	53	50
CS Brugge	34	13	10	11	51	46	49
Lommel	34	14	6	14	40	45	48
Mechelen	34	12	8	14	40	46	44
Harelbeke	34	13	4	17	40	48	43
Aalst	34	12	10	12	55	50	42
Antwerp	34	11	9	14	38	46	42
Gent	34	10	11	13	38	49	41
St Truiden	34	11	7	16	42	60	40
Seraing	34	8	5	21	35	75	29
Beveren*	34	6	9	19	38	57	27
Waregem*	34	4	9	21	30	70	21

Aalst forfeited 4 points.
Top scorer: Stanic (FC Brugge) 20.
Cup Final: FC Brugge 2, CS Brugge 1.

BOSNIA HERZEGOVINA

Bosnia & Herzegovina Football Federation, D. Ozme 7/III, 71000 Sarajevo.
Telephone: 00387 71664836, 670345; *Satellite Telephone:* 0087 114/46271; *Fax:* 00387 71670738.

International matches 1995
Albania (a) 0-2.

BULGARIA

Bulgarian Football Union, Gotcho Gopin 19, 1000 Sofia.
Founded: 1923; *Number of Clubs:* 376; *Number of Players:* 48,240; *National Colours:* White shirts, green shorts, red stockings.
Telephone: 00359 2 87 74 90; *Cable:* BULFUTBOL; *Telex:* 23145 bfs bg; *Fax:* 00359 2 80 32 37.

International matches 1995
Argentina (a) 1-4, Wales (h) 3-1, Macedonia (a) 0-0, Moldova (a) 3-0, Germany (h) 3-2, Albania (a) 1-1, Albania (h) 3-0, Georgia (a) 1-2, Germany (a) 1-3.

League Championship wins (1925–96)
CSKA Sofia 27; Levski Sofia 19; Slavia Sofia 7; Vladislav Varna 3; Lokomotiv Sofia 3; Trakia Plovdiv 2; AS 23 Sofia 1; Botev Plovdiv 1; SC Sofia 1; Sokol Varna 1; Spartak Plovdiv 1; Tichka Varna 1; ZSZ Sofia 1; Beroe Stara Zagora 1; Etur 1.

Cup wins (1946–96)
Levski Sofia 18; CSKA Sofia 14; Slavia Sofia 7; Lokomotiv Sofia 4; Botev Plovdiv 1; Spartak Plovdiv 1; Spartak Sofia 1; Marek Stanke 1; Trakia Plovdiv 1; Spartak Varna 1; Sliven 1.

Final League Table 1995–96

	P	W	D	L	F	A	Pts
Slavia Sofia	30	20	7	3	51	14	67
Levski Sofia	30	19	5	6	49	22	62
Lokomotiv Sofia	30	17	7	6	55	24	58
Neftochimik	30	17	6	7	58	31	57
CSKA Sofia	30	16	8	6	50	26	56
Spartak Varna	30	13	2	15	47	52	41
Dobroudja	30	12	3	15	30	43	39
Levski Kustendil	30	10	7	13	27	37	37
Montana	30	9	9	12	33	35	36
Lokomotiv Plovdiv	30	10	5	15	25	50	35
Botev Plovdiv	30	9	6	15	30	38	33
Etur	30	9	6	15	21	37	33
Rakovski	30	9	5	16	33	41	32
Chumen*	30	9	5	16	28	45	32
Lovetch Lex*	30	7	9	14	29	40	30
Spartak Plovdiv*	30	7	4	19	24	55	25

Top scorer: Gueorguiev (Spartak Varna) 21.
Cup Final: Slavia Sofia 4, Levski Sofia 0.
Abandoned after 76 minutes.

CROATIA

Croatian Football Federation, Illica 21/11, CRO-41000 Zagreb, Croatia.
Telephone: 00385 1/4554100. *Fax:* 00385 41 42 46 39.

International matches 1995
Ukraine (h) 4-0, Lithuania (a) 0-0, Slovenia (h) 2-0, Ukraine (a) 0-1, Estonia (h) 7-1, Italy (h) 1-1, Slovenia (a) 2-1.

League Championship wins 1993–95
Hajduk Split 2; Croatia Zagreb 1.

Cup wins 1993–95
Hajduk Split 2, Croatia Zagreb 2.

Qualifying League Table 1995–96

	P	W	D	L	F	A	Pts
Croatia Zagreb	22	14	5	3	46	13	47
Osijek	22	13	4	5	40	17	43
Hajduk Split	22	11	6	5	39	21	39
Varteks	22	11	6	5	29	19	39
Zagreb	22	7	8	7	24	25	29
Segesta	22	8	4	10	32	35	28
Sibenik	22	7	6	9	25	28	27
Inker	22	7	6	9	28	38	27
Vinkovci	22	6	9	7	26	37	27
Marsonia	22	6	3	13	15	33	21
Rijeka	22	4	5	13	25	42	17
Istra Pola	22	3	8	11	16	37	17

Final League Table 1995–96

	P	W	D	L	F	A	Pts
Croatia Zagreb	10	7	0	3	28	14	26
Hajduk Split	10	7	1	2	25	14	26
Varteks	10	7	1	2	15	7	24
Osijek	10	4	0	6	13	13	15
Dragovoljac	10	1	3	6	8	23	7
Zagreb	10	1	1	8	7	25	5

Top scorer: Cvitanovic (Croatia Zagreb) 19.
Cup Final: Croatia Zagreb 2, 1, Varteks 0, 0.

CYPRUS

Cyprus Football Association, Stasinos Str. 1, Engomi 152, P.O. Box 5071, Nicosia.
Founded: 1934; *Number of Clubs:* 85; *Number of Players:* 6,000; *National Colours:* Sky blue shirts, white shorts, blue and white stockings.
Telephone: 00357 2 44 53 41; *Cable:* FOOTBALL NICOSIA; *Telex:* 3880 football cy; *Fax:* 00357 2 47 25 44.

International matches 1995
Greece (h) 2-3, Norway (h) 0-2, Estonia (h) 3-1, Sweden (h) 3-3, Denmark (h) 1-1, Belgium (a) 0-2, Denmark (a) 0-4, Spain (a) 0-6, Macedonia (h) 1-1, Belgium (h) 1-1.

League Championship wins (1935–96)
Omonia 17; Apoel 16; Anorthosis 7; AEL 5; EPA 3; Olympiakos 3; Apollon 2; Pezoporikos 2; Chetin Kayal 1; Trast 1.

Cup wins (1935–96)
Apoel 15; Omonia 10; AEL 6; EPA 5; Anorthosis 4; Apollon 4; Trast 3; Chetin Kayal 2; Olympiakos 1; Pezoporikos 1; Salamina 1.

Final League Table 1995–96

	P	W	D	L	F	A	Pts
Apoel	26	19	7	0	65	21	64
Omonia	26	16	5	5	66	29	53
Anorthosis	26	15	8	3	48	23	53
AEK	26	16	5	5	43	21	53
Apollon	26	10	10	6	42	29	40
Ethnikos	26	9	10	7	36	33	37
Paralimni	26	8	9	9	37	40	33
Salamina	26	10	3	13	37	48	33
Aris	26	7	10	9	34	36	31
Alki	26	8	7	11	42	46	31
Olympiakos	26	8	6	12	24	32	30
AEL*	26	6	6	14	37	29	24
Evagoras*	26	2	8	16	21	57	14
Aradippu*	26	0	2	24	18	86	2

Top scorer: Kiprich (Apoel) 25.
Cup Final: Apoel 2, AEK 0 aet.

CZECH REPUBLIC

Football Association of Czech Republic, Diskarska 100, 169 00 Prague 6, Czech Republic.
Number of Clubs: 3,562; *Number of Players:* 237,200; *National Colours:* Red shirts, white shorts, blue stockings.
Telephone: (General Secretary) 0042 2 20513575 (International and PR Dept) 0042 2 520156; *Fax:* 0042 2 35 27 84.

International matches 1995
Finland (h) 4-1, Belarus (h) 4-2, Holland (h) 3-1, Slovakia (a) 1-1, Luxembourg (a) 0-1, Norway (a) 1-1, Norway (h) 2-0, Belarus (a) 2-0, Luxembourg (h) 3-0.

League Championship wins (1926–93)
Sparta Prague 20; Slavia Prague 12; Dukla Prague (prev. UDA) 11; Slovan Bratislava 7; Spartak Trnava 5; Banik Ostrava 3; Inter-Bratislava 1; Spartak Hradec Kralove 1; Viktoria Zizkov 1; Zbrojovka Brno 1; Bohemians 1; Vitkovice 1.

Cup wins (1961–93)
Dukla Prague 8; Sparta Prague 8; Slovan Bratislava 5; Spartak Trnava 4; Banik Ostrava 3; Lokomotiv Kosice 3; TJ Gottwaldov 1; Dunajska Streda 1.
From 1993–94, there were two separate countries; the Czech Republic and Slovakia.

League Championship wins (1994–96)
Sparta Prague 3.

Cup wins (1994–96)
Viktoria Zizkov 1; Spartak Hradec Kralove 1; Sparta Prague 1.

Final League Table 1995–96

	P	W	D	L	F	A	Pts
Slavia Prague	30	23	1	6	68	28	70
Sigma Olomouc	30	19	4	7	54	33	61
Jablonek	30	16	5	9	45	26	53
Sparta Prague	30	14	7	9	56	35	49
Petra Drnovice	30	14	6	10	53	40	48
Kaucuk Opava	30	13	7	10	40	34	46
Slovan Liberec	30	12	8	10	34	30	44
Boby Brno	30	12	7	11	39	42	43
Viktoria Plzen	30	11	6	13	34	34	39
Viktoria Zizkov	30	9	10	11	38	43	37
Ceske Budejovice	30	10	7	13	35	47	37
Banik Ostrava	30	10	5	15	40	46	35
Union Cheb	30	8	9	13	35	47	33
Hradec Kralove	30	8	5	17	28	46	29
Svit Zlin*	30	6	9	15	17	38	27
Uherske Hradiste*	30	3	8	19	19	65	17

Top scorer: Drulak (Petra Drnovice) 12.
Cup Final: Sparta Prague 4, Petra Drnovice 0.

DENMARK

Dansk Boldspil Union, Ved Amagerbanen 15, DK-2300, Copenhagen S.

Founded: 1889; *Number of Clubs:* 1,555; *Number of Players:* 268,517; *National Colours:* Red shirts, white shorts, red stockings.
Telephone: 0045 31 95 05 11; *Cable:* DANSKBOLDSPIL COPENHAGEN; *Telex:* 15545 dbu dk; *Fax:* 0045 31 95 05 88.

International matches 1995
Saudi Arabia (a) 2-0, Mexico (h) 1-1, Argentina (h) 2-0, Canada (h) 1-0, Portugal (a) 0-1, Cyprus (a) 1-1, Macedonia (h) 1-0, Finland (a) 1-0, Cyprus (h) 4-0, Armenia (a) 2-0, Belgium (a) 3-1, Spain (h) 1-1, Armenia (h) 3-1.

League Championship wins (1913–96)
KB Copenhagen 15; B 93 Copenhagen 9; AB (Akademisk) 9; B 1903 Copenhagen 7; Frem 6; Esbjerg BK 5; Vejle BK 5; AGF Aarhus 5; Brondby 5; Hvidovre 3; Odense BK 3; B 1909 Odense 2; Koge BK 2; Lyngby 2; FC Copenhagen 1; Silkeborg 1, AaB Aalborg 1.

Cup wins (1955–96)
Aarhus GF 9; Vejle BK 6; Randers Freja 3; Lyngby 3; OB Odense 3; B1909 Odense 2; Aalborg BK 2; Esbjerg BK 2; Frem 2; B 1903 Copenhagen 2; Brondby 2; B 93 Copenhagen 1; KB Copenhagen 1; Vanlose 1; Hvidovre 1; B1913 Odense 1, FC Copenhagen 1.

Final League Table 1995–96

	P	W	D	L	F	A	Pts
Brondby	33	20	7	6	71	32	67
Aarhus	33	18	12	3	61	28	66
Odense	33	17	9	7	57	33	60
Lyngby	33	14	11	8	61	35	53
Aalborg	33	15	6	12	57	37	51
Silkeborg	33	14	7	12	44	42	49
FC Copenhagen	33	13	9	11	48	49	48
Viborg	33	9	11	13	47	67	38
Vejle	33	8	9	16	34	50	33
Herfolge	33	6	9	18	41	62	27
Ikast	33	5	10	18	28	63	25
Naestved	33	5	8	20	29	80	23

Top scorer: Thorninger (Aarhus) 20.
Cup Final: Aarhus 2, Brondby 0.

ENGLAND

The Football Association, 16 Lancaster Gate, London W2 3LW
Founded: 1863; *Number of Clubs:* 42,000; *Number of Players:* 2,250,000; *National Colours:* White shirts, navy blue shorts, white stockings.
Telephone: 0171 262 4542; *Cable:* FOOTBALL ASSOCI-ATION LONDON W2; *Telex:* 261110; *Fax:* 0171 402 0486.

ESTONIA

Estonian Football Association, Voidu 16, Tallinn EE 0012.
Number of Clubs: 40; *Number of Players:* 12,000.
Telephone: 00372 6/542715, 542716, 542717; *Telex:* 173236 sport su; *Fax:* 00372 6/542719.

International matches 1995
Vietnam (a) 0-1, Norway (a) 0-7, Cyprus (a) 1-3, Italy (a) 1-4, Slovenia (a) 0-3, Ukraine (h) 0-1, Latvia (a) 0-2, Lithuania (a) 0-7, Slovenia (h) 1-3, Lithuania (h) 0-1, Croatia (a) 1-7, Lithuania (a) 0-5.
League Championship wins (1992–95)
Norma Tallinn 2; Flora Tallinn 2; Lantana 1.

Cup wins (1992–95)
VMV Tallinn 1; Nikol Tallinn 1; Norma Tallinn 1, Lantana 1.

Final League Table 1995–96

	P	W	D	L	F	A	Pts
Lantana	10	6	2	2	21	7	37
Flora	10	6	2	2	14	3	31
Tevalte	10	6	0	4	13	13	28
Sadan	10	4	1	5	17	19	24
Trans	10	2	2	6	11	16	19
Tervis	10	2	1	7	10	28	16

Top scorer: Rajala (Flora) 16.

FAEROE ISLANDS

Fotboltssamband Foroya, The Faeroes' Football Assn., Gundalur, P.O. Box 1028, FR-110, Torshavn.

Founded: 1979; *Number of Clubs:* 16; *Number of Players:* 1,014.
Telephone: 00298 16 707; *Telex:* 81332 itrott FA; *Fax:* 00298 19 079.

International matches 1995
Finland (h) 0-4, Russia (a) 0-3, San Marino (h) 3-0, Scotland (h) 0-2, Russia (h) 2-5, San Marino (a) 3-1, Greece (a) 0-5.

League Championship wins (1942–95)
KI Klaksvik 15; HB Torshavn 14; TB Tvoroyri 7; GI Gotu 6; B36 Torshavn 5; B68 Toftir 3; SI Sorvag 1; IF Fuglafjordur 1; B71 Sandur 1.

Cup wins (1955–94)
HB Torshavn 23; TB Tvoroyri 5; KI Klaksvik 4; B36 Torshavn 2; GI Gotu 2; VB Vagur 1; NSI Runavik 1; B71 Sandur 1.

Final League Table 1995

	P	W	D	L	F	A	Pts
GI	18	13	2	3	41	16	41
HB	18	9	6	3	34	14	33
B68	18	9	3	6	43	21	30
B71	18	9	2	7	35	27	29
B36	18	8	2	8	23	35	26
FS	18	6	5	7	30	38	23
TB	18	6	4	8	23	29	22
KI	18	6	4	8	31	43	22
S/VB+	18	6	2	10	26	39	20
NSI*	18	2	2	14	13	37	8

Top scorer: Johannesen (B68) 24.

FINLAND

Suomen Palloliitto Finlands Bollfoerbund, Kuparitie 1, P.O. Box 29, SF-00441 Helsinki.
Founded: 1907; *Number of Clubs:* 1,135; *Number of Players:* 66,100; *National Colours:* White shirts, blue shorts, white stockings.
Telephone: 00358 0 701 01 01; *Cable:* SUOMIFOTBALL HELSINKI; *Telex:* 126033 spl sf; *Fax:* 00358 0 701 01 099.

International matches 1995
Trinidad & Tobago (a) 1-2, Trinidad & Tobago (a) 2-2, Czech Republic (a) 1-4, San Marino (a) 2-0, Faeroes (a) 4-0, Denmark (h) 0-1, Greece (h) 2-1, Russia (h) 0-6, Scotland (a) 0-1, Turkey (h) 0-0, Russia (a) 1-3.

League Championship wins (1949–95)
Helsinki JK 9; Turun Palloseura 5; Kuopion Palloseura 5; Valkeakosken Haka 5; Kuusysi 4; Lahden Reipas 3; IF Kamraterna 3; Ilves-Kissat 2; Kotkan TP 2; OPS Oulu 2; Torun Pyrkiva 1; IF Kronohagens 1; Helsinki PS 1; Kokkolan PV 1; Vasa 1; Jazz Pori 1; TPV Tampere 1.

Cup wins (1955–95)
Valkeakosken Haka 9; Lahden Reipas 7; Kotkan TP 4; Helsinki JK 4; Mikkeli 2; Kuusysi 2; Kuopion Palloseura 2; Ilves Tampere 2; TPS Turku 2; ; MyPa 2; IFK Abo 1; Drott 1; Helsinki PS 1; Pallo-Peikot 1; Rovaniemi PS 1.

Final League Table 1995

	P	W	D	L	F	A	Pts
Haka	26	18	5	3	56	17	59
MyPa	26	16	5	5	45	20	53
HJK Helsinki	26	14	10	2	44	18	52
Jazz Pori	26	12	6	8	43	29	42
Jaro	26	11	5	10	37	32	38
TPS Turku	26	10	6	10	33	32	36
Ilves	26	9	7	10	36	39	34
FinnPa	26	9	5	12	40	40	32
RoPS Rovaniemi	26	8	8	10	29	30	32
VPS	26	10	2	14	26	34	32
Mikkeli	26	7	7	12	23	35	28
TPV Tampere	26	6	6	14	33	48	24
Kuusysi	26	6	5	15	23	50	23
Ponnistus	26	6	3	17	19	63	21

Top scorer: Popovic (Haka) 21.
Cup Final: MyPa 1, Jazz Pori 0.

FRANCE

Federation Francaise De Football, 60 Bis A venue D'Iena, F-75783 Paris, Cedex 16.
Founded: 1919; *Number of Clubs:* 21,629; *Number of Players:* 1,692,205; *National Colours:* Blue shirts, white shorts, red stockings.
Telephone: 0033 1 44 31 73 00; *Cable:* CEFI PARIS 034; *Telex:* 640000 fedfoot f; *Fax:* 0033 1 47 20 82 96.

International matches 1995
Holland (a) 1-0, Israel (a) 0-0, Slovakia (h) 4-0, Norway (a) 0-0, Poland (h) 1-1, Azerbaijan (h) 10-0, Romania (a) 3-1, Israel (h) 2-0.

League Championship wins (1933–96)
Saint Etienne 10; Olympique Marseille 8; Nantes 7; Stade de Reims 6; AS Monaco 5; OGC Nice 4; Girondins Bordeaux 4; Lille OSC 3; Paris St Germain 2; FC Sete 2; Sochaux 2; Racing Club Paris 1; Roubaix-Tourcoing 1; Strasbourg 1; Auxerre 1.

Cup wins (1918–96)
Olympique Marseille 10; Saint Etienne 6; Lille OSC 5; Racing Club Paris 5; Red Star 5; AS Monaco 5; Olympique Lyon 4; Girondins Bordeaux 3; Paris St Germain 3; CA Genereaux 2; Nancy 2; OGC Nice 2; Racing Club Strasbourg 2; Sedan 2; FC Sete 2; Stade de Reims 2; SO Montpellier 2; Stade Rennes 2; Auxerre 2; AS Cannes 1; Club Français 1; Excelsior Roubaix 1; Le Havre 1; Olympique de Pantin 1; CA Paris 1; Sochaux 1; Toulouse 1; Bastia 1; Nantes 1; Metz 1.

Final League Table 1995–96

	P	W	D	L	F	A	Pts
Auxerre	38	22	6	10	56	30	72
Paris St Germain	38	19	11	8	65	36	68
Monaco	38	19	11	8	64	39	68
Metz	38	18	11	9	42	30	65
Lens	38	16	15	7	45	31	63
Montpellier	38	17	9	12	51	40	60
Nantes	38	14	13	11	44	42	55
Rennes	38	13	15	10	44	41	54
Strasbourg	38	14	12	12	46	44	54
Guingamp	38	13	14	11	34	33	53
Lyon	38	10	18	10	41	41	48
Nice	38	12	9	17	37	44	45
Le Havre	38	11	12	15	33	45	45
Cannes	38	12	8	18	45	51	44
Bastia	38	12	8	18	45	55	44
Bordeaux	38	11	9	18	44	52	42
Lille	38	9	12	17	27	50	39
Gueugnon*	38	8	14	16	27	46	38
St Etienne*	38	6	16	16	36	59	34
Martigues*	38	9	7	22	31	58	34

Top scorer: Anderson (Monaco) 21.
Cup Final: Auxerre 2, Nimes 1.

GEORGIA

Football Federation of Georgia, 5 Shota Iamanidze Str, Tbilisi 380012, Georgia.
Founded: 1992; *Number of Clubs:* 4050. *Number of Players:* 115,000.
Telephone: 007 8832 96 07 10; *Telex:* 340744. *Fax:* 00995 32/001128.

International matches 1995
Germany (h) 0-2, Albania (h) 2-0, Wales (a) 1-0, Germany (a) 1-4, Bulgaria (h) 2-1, Moldova (a) 2-3.

League Championship wins (1991–96)
Dynamo Tbilisi 6.

Cup wins (1993–1996)
Dynamo Tbilisi 6.

Final League Table 1995–96

	P	W	D	L	F	A	Pts
Dynamo Tbilisi	30	25	4	1	109	16	79
Samtredia	30	20	8	2	94	35	68
Margveti	30	22	2	6	85	36	68
Kolkheti	30	22	2	6	69	38	68
Metalurgi	30	22	0	8	70	36	66
Dynamo Batumi	30	16	6	8	68	28	54
Torpedo Kutaisi	30	15	7	8	70	49	52
Dila Gori	30	12	4	14	52	55	40
Iveria	30	9	4	17	31	57	33
Sioni	30	11	0	19	39	64	33
Dynamo Zugdidi	30	10	3	17	42	61	33
Shevardeni	30	9	3	18	40	61	30
Kakheti	30	8	3	19	29	68	27
Guria	30	8	0	22	30	73	24
Egrissi*	30	5	2	23	41	90	17
Duruji*	30	1	1	28	22	124	4

Cup Final: Dynamo Tbilisi 1, Batumi 0.

GERMANY

Deutsche Fussball-Bund, Otto-Fleck-Schneise 6, Postfach 710265, D-6000, Frankfurt (Main) 71.
Founded: 1900; *Number of Clubs:* 26,760; *Number of Players:* 5,260,320; *National Colours:* White shirts, black shorts, white stockings.
Telephone: 0049 69 678 80; *Cable:* FUSSBALL FRANKFURT; *Telex:* 416815 dfb d; *Fax:* 0049 69 678 82 66.

International matches 1995

Spain (a) 0-0, Georgia (a) 2-0, Wales (h) 1-1, Bulgaria (a) 2-3, Italy (h) 2-0, Switzerland (a) 2-1, Belgium (a) 2-1, Georgia (h) 4-1, Moldova (h) 6-1, Wales (a) 2-1, Bulgaria (h) 3-1, South Africa (a) 0-0.

League Championship wins (1903–96)

Bayern Munich 13; IFC Nuremberg 9; Schalke 04 7; SV Hamburg 6; Borussia Moenchengladbach 5; Borussia Dortmund 5; VfB Stuttgart 4; VfB Leipzig 3; Sp Vgg Furth 3; IFC Cologne 3; IFC Kaiserslautern 3; Werder Bremen 3; Viktoria Berlin 2; Hertha Berlin 2; Hanover 96 2; Dresden SC 2; Munich 1860 1; Union Berlin 1; FC Freiburg 1; Phoenix Karlsruhe 1; Karlsruher FV 1; Holsten Kiel 1; Fortuna Dusseldorf 1; Rapid Vienna 1; VfB Mannheim 1; Rot-Weiss Essen 1; Eintracht Frankfurt 1; Eintracht Brunswick 1.

Cup wins (1935–96)

Bayern Munich 8; IFC Cologne 4; Eintracht Frankfurt 4; IFC Nuremberg 3; SV Hamburg 3; Werder Bremen 3; Moenchengladbach 3; Dresden SC 2; Fortuna Dusseldorf 2; Karlsruhe SC 2; Munich 1860 2; Schalke 04 2; VfB Stuttgart 2; Borussia Dortmund 2; Kaiserslautern 2; First Vienna 1; VfB Leipzig 1; Kickers Offenbach 1; Rapid Vienna 1; Rot-Weiss Essen 1; SW Essen 1; Bayer Uerdingen 1; Hannover 96 1; Leverkusen 1.

Final League Table 1995–96

	P	W	D	L	F	A	Pts
Borussia Dortmund	34	19	11	4	76	38	68
Bayern Munich	34	19	5	10	66	46	62
Schalke	34	13	15	6	44	36	54
Moenchengladbach	34	15	8	11	52	51	53
Hamburg	34	12	14	8	52	47	50
Hansa Rostock	34	13	10	11	47	43	49
Karlsruhe	34	12	12	10	53	47	48
Munich 1860	34	11	12	11	52	46	45
Werder Bremen	34	10	15	9	39	41	45
Stuttgart	34	10	13	11	59	62	43
Freiburg	34	11	9	14	30	41	42
Cologne	34	9	13	12	33	35	40
Dusseldorf	34	8	16	10	40	47	40
Leverkusen	34	8	14	12	37	38	38
St Pauli	34	11	5	18	30	52	38
Kaiserslautern*	34	6	18	10	31	37	36
Eintracht Frankfurt*	34	7	11	16	43	68	32
Uerdingen*	34	5	11	18	33	56	26

Top scorer: Bobic (Stuttgart) 17.
Cup Final: Kaiserslautern 1, Karlsruhe 0.

GREECE

Federation Hellenique De Football, Singrou Avenue 137, Athens.
Founded: 1926; *Number of Clubs:* 4,050; *Number of Players:* 180,000; *National Colours:* White shirts, blue shorts, white stockings.
Telephone: 0030 1 933 88 50; *Cable:* FOOTBALL ATHENES; *Telex:* 215328 epo gr; *Fax:* 0030 1 935 96 66.

International matches 1995

Cyprus (a) 3-2, Romania (h) 1-0, Switzerland (h) 1-1, Russia (h) 0-3, Lithuania (a) 1-2, Finland (a) 1-2, Scotland (a) 0-1, San Marino (a) 4-0, Yugoslavia (h) 0-2, Russia (a) 1-2, Faeroes (h) 5-0.

League Championship wins (1928–96)

Olympiakos 25; Panathinaikos 18; AEK Athens 11; Aris Salonika 3; PAOK Salonika 2; Larissa 1.

Cup wins (1932–96)

Olympiakos 20; Panathinaikos 16; AEK Athens 10; PAOK Salonika 4; Aris Salonika 1; Ethnikos 1; Iraklis 1; Panionios 1; Kastoria 1; Larissa 1; Ofi Crete 1.

Final League Table 1995–96

	P	W	D	L	F	A	Pts
Panathinaikos	34	26	5	3	72	22	83
AEK Athens	34	25	6	3	87	22	81
Olympiakos	34	19	8	7	66	34	65
Iraklis	34	17	7	10	51	39	58
Ofi Crete	34	17	6	11	57	52	57
Xanthi	34	12	11	11	53	47	47
Aris Salonika	34	12	10	12	45	47	46
Ionikos	34	12	10	12	44	50	46
Edessiakos	34	12	8	14	50	59	44
Athinaikos	34	12	8	14	33	47	44
PAOK Salonika	34	10	11	13	42	46	41
Apollon	34	11	7	16	49	48	40
Paniliakos	34	10	10	14	46	51	40
Kalamata	34	9	12	13	41	46	39
Panachaiki	34	10	6	18	27	47	36
Larissa*	34	9	7	18	32	64	34
Panionios*	34	8	5	21	35	59	29
Ethnikos*	34	5	3	26	40	90	18

Top scorer: Tsartas(AEK Athens) 26.
Cup Final: AEK Athens 7, Apollon 1.

HOLLAND

Koninklijke Nederlandsche Voetbalbond, Woudenbergseweg 56, Postbus 515, NL-3700 AM, Zeist.
Founded: 1889; *Number of Clubs:* 3,097; *Number of Players:* 962,397; *National Colours:* Orange shirts, white shorts, orange stockings.
Telephone: 00343 499211; *Cable:* VOETBAL ZEIST; *Telex:* 40497 knvb nl; *Fax:* 00343 491487.

International matches 1995

France (h) 0-1, Portugal (h) 0-1, Malta (h) 4-0, Czech Republic (a) 1-3, Belarus (a) 0-1, Belarus (h) 1-0, Malta (a) 4-0, Norway (h) 3-0, Eire (h) 2-0.

League Championship wins (1898–96)

Ajax Amsterdam 26; Feyenoord 14; PSV Eindhoven 13; HVV The Hague 8; Sparta Rotterdam 6; Go Ahead Deventer 4; HBS The Hague 3; Willem II Tilburg 3; RCH Haarlem 2; RAP 2; Heracles 2; ADO The Hague 2; Quick The Hague 1; BVV Schiedam 1; NAC Breda 1; Eindhoven 1; Enschede 1; Volewijckers Amsterdam 1; Limburgia 1; Rapid JC Haarlem 1; DOS Utrecht 1; DWS Amsterdam 1; Haarlem 1; Be Quick Groningen 1; SVV Schiedam 1; AZ 67 Alkmaar 1.

Cup wins (1899–96)

Ajax Amsterdam 12; Feyenoord 10; PSV Eindhoven 8; Quick The Hague 4; AZ 67 Alkmaar 3; Rotterdam 3; DFC 2; Fortuna Geleen 2; Haarlem 2; HBS The Hague 2; RCH 2; VOC 2; Wageningen 2; Willem II Tilburg 2; FC Den Haag 2; Concordia Rotterdam 1; CVV 1; Eindhoven 1; HVV The Hague 1; Longa 1; Quick Nijmegen 1; RAP 1; Roermond 1; Schoten 1; Velocitas Breda 1; Velocitas Groningen 1; VSV 1; VUC 1; VVV Groningen 1; ZFC 1; NAC Breda 1; Twente Enschede 1; Utrecht 1.

Final League Table 1995–96

	P	W	D	L	F	A	Pts
Ajax	34	26	5	3	97	24	83
PSV Eindhoven	34	24	5	5	97	25	77
Feyenoord	34	18	9	7	66	36	63
Roda JC	34	15	12	7	51	35	57
Vitesse	34	15	8	11	48	44	53
Sparta	34	15	8	11	53	53	53
Heerenveen	34	14	11	9	66	68	53
NAC Breda	34	14	10	10	58	44	52
Groningen	34	12	13	9	48	43	49
Twente	34	14	6	14	46	55	48
RKC Waalwijk	34	11	11	12	44	44	44
Willem II	34	9	12	13	53	59	39
Fortuna Sittard	34	6	13	15	27	54	31
De Graafschap	34	6	11	17	37	66	29
Utrecht	34	6	10	18	27	59	28
Volendam+	34	6	9	19	29	65	27
NEC Nijmegen+	34	6	7	21	33	73	25
Go Ahead*	34	5	7	22	40	71	22

Top scorer: Nilis(PSV Eindhoven) 21.
Cup Final: PSV Eindhoven 5, Sparta 2.

HUNGARY

Magyar Labdarugo Szovetseg, Hungarian Football Federation, Nepkoztarsasag Utja 47, H-1061 Budapest VI.
Founded: 1901; *Number of Clubs:* 1944; *Number of Players* 95,986; *National Colours:* Red shirts, white

shorts, green stockings.
Telephone: 0036 1 252 92 96; *Cable:* MLSZ BUDAPEST; *Telex:* 225782 misz h; *Fax:* 0036 1 252 99 86.

International matches 1995
Latvia (h) 3-1, Switzerland (h) 2-2, Sweden (h) 1-0, Iceland (a) 1-2, Hungary (h) 0-2, Turkey (a) 0-2, Switzerland (a) 0-3, Iceland (h) 1-0.

League Championship wins (1901–96)
Ferencvaros (prev. FRC) 26; MTK-VM Budapest (prev. Hungaria, Bastay and Vörös Lobogo) 19; Ujpest Dozsa 19; Honved 13; Vasas Budapest 6; Csepel 3; Raba Gy{r}or (prev. Vasas Gy{r}or) 3; BTC 2; Nagyvarad 1; Vac 1.

Cup wins (1910–96)
Ferencvaros (prev. FRC) 17; MTK-VM Budapest (prev. Hungaria, Bastay and Vörös Lobogo) 9; Ujpest Dozsa 8; Raba Gy{r}or (prev. Vasas Györ) 4; Kispest Honved 4; Vasas Budapest 3; Diösgyör 2; Bocskai 1; III Ker 1; Kispesti AC 1; Soroksar 1; Szolnoki MAV 1; Siofok Banyasz 1; Bekescsaba 1; Pecs 1.
Cup not regularly held until 1964

Final League Table 1995–96

	P	W	D	L	F	A	Pts
Ferencvaros	30	21	3	6	56	25	66
BVSC	30	18	7	5	50	29	61
Ujpest	30	12	12	6	43	31	48
Debrecen	30	14	6	10	49	40	48
MTK	30	13	7	10	58	43	46
Kispest Honved	30	12	10	8	49	35	46
Vasas	30	12	10	8	44	40	46
Csepel	30	11	9	10	46	45	42
Stadler	30	8	12	10	35	41	36
Zalaegerszeg	30	8	10	12	42	48	34
Vac	30	7	12	11	39	46	33
Haladas	30	8	8	14	30	48	32
Fehervar 96	30	8	7	15	38	54	31
Bekescsaba	30	6	11	13	33	46	29
Gyori	30	6	9	15	34	54	27
Pecs	30	7	5	18	32	53	23

Pecs three points deducted.
Cup Final: BVSC 1, 0, Kispest Honved 0, 2.

ICELAND

Knattspyrnusamband Island, P.O. Box 8511, 128 Reykjavik.
Founded: 1929; *Number of Clubs:* 73; *Number of Players:* 23,673; *National Colours;* Blue shirts, white shorts, blue stockings.
Telephone: 00354 1 81 44 44; *Cable* KSI REYKJAVIK; *Telex:* 2314 isi is; *Fax:* 00354 1 68 97 93.

International matches 1995
Chile (a) 1-1, Sweden (a) 1-1, Hungary (h) 2-1, Switzerland (h) 0-2, Turkey (h) 0-0, Hungary (a) 0-1.

League Championship wins (1912–95)
KR 20; Valur 19; Fram 18; IA Akranes 16; Vikingur 5; IBK Keflavik 3; IBV Vestmann 2; KA Akureyri 1.

Cup wins (1960–95)
KR 9; Valur 8; Fram 7; IA Akranes 5; IBV Vestmann 3; IBA Akureyri 1; Vikingur 1; IBK Keflavik 1.

Final League Table 1995

	P	W	D	L	F	A	Pts
IA Akranes	18	16	1	1	50	15	49
KR	18	11	2	5	33	22	35
IBV	18	10	1	7	41	29	31
IBK	18	6	8	4	28	29	26
Leiftur	18	7	3	8	32	34	24
UBM	18	7	2	9	26	29	23
Valur	18	7	2	9	26	34	23
UBK	18	6	3	9	25	30	21
FH*	18	4	3	11	26	42	15
Fram*	18	2	3	13	17	40	9

Top scorer: Gunnlaugsson A (IA Akranes) 15.
Cup Final: KR Reykjavik 2, Fram 1.

REPUBLIC OF IRELAND

The Football Association of Ireland, (Cumann Peile Na H-Eireann), 80 Merrion Square, South Dublin 2.
Founded: 1921; *Number of Clubs:* 3,190; *Number of Players:* 124,615; *National Colours:* Green shirts, white shorts, green stockings.
Telephone: 00353 1 676 68 64; *Cable:* SOCCER DUBLIN; *Telex:* 91397 fai ei; *Fax:* 00353 1 661 09 31.

League Championship wins (1922–96)
Shamrock Rovers 15; Dundalk 9; Shelbourne 8; Bohemians 7; Waterford 6; Cork United 5; Drumcondra 5; St Patrick's Athletic 5; St James's Gate 2; Cork Athletic 2; Sligo Rovers 2; Limerick 2; Athlone Town 2; Dolphin 1; Cork Hibernians 1; Cork Celtic 1; Derry City 1, Cork City 1.

Cup wins (1922–96)
Shamrock Rovers 24; Dundalk 8; Drumcondra 5; Bohemians 5; Shelbourne 4; Cork Athletic 2; Cork United 2; St James's Gate 2; St Patrick's Athletic 2; Cork Hibernians 2; Limerick 2; Waterford 2; Derry City 2; Athlone Town 2; Sligo 2; Alton United 1; Cork 1; Fordsons 1; Transport 1; Finn Harps 1; Home Farm 1; UCD 1; Bray Wanderers 1; Galway United 1.

Final League Table 1995–96

	P	W	D	L	F	A	Pts
St Patrick's Ath	33	19	10	4	53	34	67
Bohemians	33	18	8	7	60	29	62
Sligo Rovers	33	16	7	10	45	38	55
Shelbourne	33	15	9	9	45	33	54
Shamrock Rovers	33	14	8	11	31	32	50
Derry City	33	11	13	9	50	38	46
Dundalk	33	11	9	13	38	39	42
UCD	33	12	6	15	38	39	42
Cork City	33	12	8	13	37	40	44
Athlone T*+	33	8	7	18	38	59	31
Drogheda U*	33	7	9	17	38	51	30
Galway U*	33	5	6	22	26	67	21

Cork City three points deducted.
Top scorer: Geoghegan (Shelbourne) 19.
Cup Final: Shelbourne 1, 2, St Patrick's 1, 1.

ISRAEL

Israel Football Association, 12 Carlibach Street, P.O. Box 20188, Tel Aviv 61201.
Founded: 1928; *Number of Clubs:* 544; *Number of Players:* 30,449; *National Colours:* White shirts, blue shorts, white stockings.
Telephone: 00972 3 570 59 99; *Cable:* CADUREGEL TEL AVIV; *Fax:* 00972 3 570 20 44.

International matches 1995
Luxembourg (h) 4-2, Turkey (a) 1-2, France (h) 0-0, Poland (a) 3-4, Brazil (h) 1-2, Romania (a) 1-2, Hungary (a) 2-0, Slovakia (a) 0-1, Uruguay (h) 3-1, Azerbaijan (h) 2-0, France (a) 0-2.

League Championship wins (1932–96)
Maccabi Tel Aviv 18; Hapoel Tel Aviv 12; Hapoel Petah Tikva 6; Maccabi Haifa 5; Maccabi Netanya 5; Beitar Jerusalem 2; Hakoah Ramat Gan 2; Hapoel Beersheba 2; Bnei Yehouda 1; British Police 1; Hapoel Kfar Sava 1; Hapoel Ramat Gan 1.

Cup wins (1928–96)
Maccabi Tel Aviv 19; Hapoel Tel Aviv 9; Beitar Jerusalem 5; Maccabi Haifa 4; Hapoel Haifa 3; Hapoel Kfar Sava 3; Beitar Tel Aviv 2; Bnei Yehouda 2; Hakoah Ramat Gan 2; Hapoel Petah Tikva 2; Maccabi Petah Tikva 2; British Police 1; Hapoel Jerusalem 1; Hapoel Lod 1; Maccabi Netanya 1.

Final League Table 1995–96

	P	W	D	L	F	A	Pts
Maccabi Tel Aviv	30	23	5	2	59	16	74
Maccabi Haifa	30	19	9	2	74	31	66
Beitar Jerusalem	30	19	7	4	65	31	64
Hapoel Haifa	30	19	7	4	66	33	64
Hapoel Tel Aviv	30	16	6	8	47	28	54
Maccabi Petah Tikva	30	13	10	7	43	37	49
Maccabi Herzliya	30	10	6	14	33	37	36
Hapoel Petah Tikva	30	7	15	8	31	40	36
Ironi Rishon	30	9	7	15	25	40	31
Hapoel Beersheba	30	6	11	13	32	36	29
Bnei Yehuda	30	7	7	16	46	65	28
Hapoel Kfar Sabah	30	8	4	18	29	53	28
Zafirim Holon	30	7	6	17	32	52	27
Hapoel Beit Shean	30	5	11	14	28	49	26
Beitar Tel Aviv*	30	6	6	18	30	63	24
Maccabi Jaffa*	30	6	5	19	24	53	23

Top scorer: Revivo (Maccabi Haifa) 26.
Cup Final: Maccabi Tel Aviv 4, Ironi Rishon 1.

ITALY

Federazione Italiana Giuoco Calcio, Via Gregorio Allegri 14, C.P. 2450, 1-00198, Roma.
Founded: 1898; *Number of Clubs:* 20,961; *Number of Players:* 1,420,160; *National Colours:* Blue shirts, white shorts, blue stockings, white trim.
Telephone: 0039 6 849 11 11; *Cable:* FEDERCALCIO ROMA; *Telex:* 611483 calcio i; *Fax:* 0039 6 849 12 526.

International matches 1995
Estonia (h) 4-1, Ukraine (a) 2-0, Lithuania (a) 1-0, Switzerland (h) 1-0, Germany (a) 0-2, Slovenia (h) 1-0, Croatia (a) 1-1, Ukraine (h) 3-1, Lithuania (h) 4-0.

League Championship wins (1898–1996)
Juventus 23; AC Milan 15; Inter-Milan 13; Genoa 9; Torino 8; Pro Vercelli 7; Bologna 7; Fiorentina 2; Napoli 2; AS Roma 2; Casale 1; Novese 1; Cagliari 1; Lazio 1; Verona 1; Sampdoria 1.

Cup wins (1922–96)
Juventus 9; AS Roma 8; Fiorentina 5; Torino 4; AC Milan 4; Sampdoria 4; Inter-Milan 3; Napoli 3; Bologna 2; Atalanta 1; Genoa 1; Lazio 1; Vado 1; Venezia 1; Parma 1.

Final League Table 1995–96

	P	W	D	L	F	A	Pts
AC Milan	34	21	10	3	60	24	73
Juventus	34	19	8	7	58	35	65
Lazio	34	17	8	9	66	38	59
Fiorentina	34	17	8	9	53	41	59
Parma	34	16	10	8	44	31	58
Roma	34	16	10	8	51	34	58
Internazionale	34	15	9	10	51	30	54
Sampdoria	34	14	10	10	59	47	52
Vicenza	34	13	10	11	36	37	49
Cagliari	34	11	8	15	34	47	41
Udinese	34	11	8	15	41	49	41
Napoli	34	10	11	13	28	41	41
Atalanta	34	11	6	17	38	50	39
Piacenza	34	9	10	15	31	48	37
Bari*	34	8	8	18	49	71	32
Torino*	34	6	11	17	28	46	29
Cremonese*	34	5	12	17	37	57	27
Padova*	34	7	3	24	41	79	24

Top scorers: Protti (Bari), Signori (Lazio) 24.
Cup Final: Fiorentina 1, 2, Atalanta 0, 0.

LATVIA

Latvian Football Federation, Augsiela, 1, LV-1009, Riga.
Founded: 1921; *Number of Clubs:* 50; *Number of Players:* 12,000.
National Colours: Carmine red shirts, white shorts, carmine red stockings.
Telephone: 00371 2 29 29 88; *Telex:* 161183 ritm su; *Fax:* 00371 8 82 83 31.
Cable: Augsiela 1, LV–1009, Riga.

International matches 1995
Hungary (a) 1-3, Austria (a) 0-5, Northern Ireland (h) 0-1, Estonia (h) 2-0, Lithuania (h) 2-0, Portugal (a) 2-3, Northern Ireland (a) 2-1, Austria (h) 3-2, Liechtenstein (h) 1-0, Eire (a) 1-2.

League Championship wins (1922–95)
ASK Riga 9; RFK Riga 8; Olympia Liepaya 7; Sarkanais Metalurgs Liepaya 7; VEF Riga 6; Skonto Riga 5; Energija Riga 4; Elektrons Riga 3; Torpedo Riga 3; Daugava Liepaya 2; ODO Riga 2; Khimikis Daugavpils 2; RAF Yelgava 2; Keisermezhs Riga 2; Dinamo Riga 1; Zhmilyeva Team 1; Darba Rezervi 1; REZ Riga 1; Start Brotseni 1; Venta Ventspils 1; Yurnieks Riga 1; Alfa Riga 1; Gauya Valmiera 1.

Cup wins (1937–95)
Elektrons Riga 7; Sarkanais Metalurgs Liepaya 5; ODO Riga 3; VEF Riga 3; ASK Riga 3; Tseltnieks Riga 3; RFK Riga 2; Daugava Liepaya 2; Start Brotseni 2; Selmash Liepaya 2; Yurnieks Riga 2; Khimikis Daugavpils 2; RAF Yelgava 2; Skonto Riga 2; Rigas Vilki 1; Dinamo Liepaya 1; Dinamo Riga 1; REZ Riga 1; Voulkan Kouldiga 1; Baltija Liepaya 1; Venta Ventspils 1; Pilot Riga 1; Lielupe Yurmala 1; Energija Riga 1; Torpedo Riga 1; Daugava SKIF Riga 1; Tseltnieks Daugavpils 1; Olympia Riga 1.

Final League Table 1995

Group A (for 1-6 places)						
	P	W	D	L	F	A	Pts
Skonto Riga	28	25	3	0	99	15	78
Vilan-D Daugavpils	28	16	3	9	45	30	51
RAF Yelgava	28	14	6	8	40	28	48
Starts Brotseni	28	11	5	12	31	43	38
Amstrig Riga	28	9	8	11	47	38	35
Vairogs Rezekne	28	7	7	14	35	52	28

Group B (for 7-10 places)						
	P	W	D	L	F	A	Pts
Skonto/Metals Riga	24	8	4	12	37	51	28
DAG-Liepaya	24	7	7	10	26	34	28
Olympia Riga	24	5	5	14	29	57	20
Kvadrats Riga	24	5	2	17	22	63	17

Top scorer; Astafyev (Skonto) 19.
Cup Final: Skonto Riga 3, DAG-Liepaya 0.

LIECHTENSTEIN

Liechtensteiner Fussball-Verband, Am schragen Weg 17, Postfach 165, 9490 Vaduz.
Founded: 1933; *Number of Clubs:* 7; *Number of Players:* 1,247; *National Colours:* Blue & red shirts, red shorts, blue stockings.
Telephone: 004175 233 24 28; *Cable:* FUSSBALLVER-BAND VADUZ; *Fax:* 004175 233 24 30.

International matches 1995
Austria (a) 0-7, Eire (h) 0-0, Portugal (h) 0-7, Latvia (a) 0-1, Northern Ireland (h) 0-4.
Liechtenstein has no national league. Teams compete in Swiss regional leagues.

Cup wins (1946–94)
Vaduz 25; Balzers 10; Triesen 8; Eschen/Mauren 4; Schaan 2.

LITHUANIA

Lithuanian Football Federation, Seimyniskiu str. 15, 2051 Vilnius. Championship of 14 teams.
Number of Clubs: 20; *Number of Players:* 16,600.
Telephone: 00370 2/723654/58; *Telex:* 0539-261518 lsr; *Fax:* 00370 2/723651.

International matches 1995
Poland (a) 1-4, Croatia (h) 0-0, Italy (h) 0-1, Greece (h) 2-1, Estonia (h) 7-0, Latvia (a) 0-2, Slovenia (h) 2-1, Belarus (h) 1-1, Estonia (a) 1-0, Ukraine (h) 1-3, Estonia (h) 5-0, Italy (a) 0-4.

League Championship wins (1922–96)
Kovas Kaunas 6; KSS Klaipeda 6; LFLS Kaunas 4; Zalgiris Vilnius 3; LGSF Kaunas 2; MSK Kaunas 1; Ekranas Panevezys 1; Romar Mazeikiai 1; Inkaras Grifas 1.

Cup wins (1992–96)
Zalgiris Vilnius 3; Inkaras 1; Kareda 1.

Final League Table 1995–96

	P	W	D	L	F	A	Pts
Inkaras	28	24	3	1	67	9	56
Kareda	28	22	2	4	67	17	52
Zalgiris	28	22	4	2	106	22	50
Kaunas	28	14	3	11	48	35	31
Panerys	28	13	2	13	40	47	29
Atlantas	28	12	4	12	42	34	25
Ekranas	28	7	8	13	39	46	19
Zalgiris 2	28	5	6	17	28	60	12

Top scorer: Jankauskas (Zalgiris) 25.
Cup Final: Kareda 2, Inkaras 1.

LUXEMBOURG

Federation Luxembourgeoise De Football, (F.L.F.), 50, Rue De Strasbourg, L-2560, Luxembourg.
Founded: 1908; *Number of Clubs:* 126; *Number of Players:* 21,684; *National Colours:* Red shirts, white shorts, blue stockings.
Telephone: 00352 48 86 65; *Cable:* FOOTBALL LUX-EMBOURG; *Telex:* 2426 flf lu; *Fax:* 00352 40 02 01.

International matches 1995
Israel (a) 2-4, Malta (a) 1-0, Norway (h) 0-2, Norway (a) 0-5, Czech Republic (h) 1-0, Malta (h) 1-0, Belarus (h) 0-0, Czech Republic (a) 0-3.

League Championship wins (1910–96)
Jeunesse Esch 23; Spora Luxembourg 11; Stade Dudelange 10; Avenir Beggen 7; Red Boys Differdange 6; US Hollerich-Bonnevoie 5; Fola Esch 5; US Luxembourg 5; Aris Bonnevoie 3; Progres Niedercorn 1.

Cup wins (1922–96)
Red Boys Differdange 16; US Luxembourg 10; Jeunesse Esch 9; Spora Luxembourg 8; Avenir Beggen 6; Stade Dudelange 4; Progres Niedercorn 4; Fola Esch 3; Alliance Dudelange 2; US Rumelange 2; Aris Bonnevoie 1; US Dudelange 1; Jeunesse Hautcharage 1; National Schiffige 1; Racing Luxembourg 1; SC Tetange 1; Hesperange 1, Grevenmacher 1.

Final Table 1995–96

	P	W	D	L	F	A	Pts
Jeunesse Esch	22	15	3	4	59	19	48
Grevenmacher	22	14	5	3	44	19	47
Union	22	12	6	4	43	18	42
F91 Dudelange	22	11	5	6	43	23	38
Sporting Mertzig	22	11	4	7	32	29	37
Avenir Beggen	22	9	4	9	38	33	31
Spora	22	7	6	9	35	34	27
Rodange	22	7	3	12	22	36	24
FC Wiltz 71	22	7	3	12	25	41	24
Aris	22	5	6	11	32	52	21
Petange	22	6	1	14	20	49	19
Red Boys	22	3	4	15	29	72	13

Top scorer: Zaritski (Avenir Beggen) 18.
Cup Final: Union 3, Jeunesse Esch 1.

MACEDONIA

Football Association of the Former Yugoslav Republic of Macedonia, VIII-ma Udarna Brigada 31A, MAC-91000Skopje.
Telephone: 00389 1 22 90 42; *Fax:* 00389 1 23 54 48.

International matches 1995
Bulgaria (h) 0-0, Denmark (a) 0-1, Armenia (a) 2-2, Belgium (h) 0-5, Armenia (h) 1-2, Cyprus (a) 1-1, Spain (a) 0-3.

League Championship wins (1994–95)
Vardar 2.

Cup wins (1995)
Sileks 1; Vardar 1.

Final League Table 1994–95
Sileks 70; Sloga 58; Vardar 57; Pelister 43; Pobeda 41; Makedonia 37; Sasa 37; Balkan 34; Belasica 33; Tikves 32; Cementarnica 32; Rudar 32; FK Ohrid* 31; Osogovo* 26; Ljuboten* 16.
Top scorer: Boskovski (Sileks) 24.

MALTA

Malta Football Association, 280 St. Paul Street, Valletta.

Founded: 1900; *Number of Clubs:* 252; *Number of Players:* 5,544; *National Colours:* Red shirts, white shorts, red stockings.
Telephone: 00356 22 26 97; *Cable:* FOOTBALL MALTA VALLETTA; *Telex:* 1752 malfa mw; *Fax:* 00356 24 51 36.

International matches 1995
Luxembourg (h) 0-1, Holland (a) 0-4, Belarus (a) 1-1, Norway (a) 0-2, Luxembourg (a) 0-1, Holland (h) 0-4, Belarus (h) 0-2.

League Championship wins (1910–96)
Floriana 25; Sliema Wanderers 23; Valletta 15; Hibernians 8; Hamrun Spartans 6; Rabat Ajax 2; St George's 1; KOMR 1.

Cup wins (1935–95)
Floriana 18; Sliema Wanderers 17; Valletta 7; Hamrun Spartans 6; Hibernians 5; Gzira United 1; Melita 1; Zurrieq 1; Rabat Ajax 1.

Final League Table 1995–96

	P	W	D	L	F	A	Pts
Sliema Wanderers	18	15	1	2	55	16	46
Valletta	18	13	3	2	49	11	42
Floriana	18	11	4	3	32	12	37
Hibernians	18	9	6	3	35	18	33
Hamrun Spartans	18	8	5	5	29	20	29
Birkirkara	18	6	3	9	23	26	21
Naxxar Lions	18	6	3	9	22	33	21
Rabat Ajax	18	4	2	12	27	50	14
St Patrick's*	18	3	0	15	15	52	9
Zurrieq*	18	1	1	16	12	62	4

Top scorer: Muscat (Sliema) 18.

MOLDOVA

Moldavian Football Federation, Bd Stefan cel Mare 73, 277001 Chisinau, Moldavia.
Number of Clubs: 143; *Number of Players:* 75,000.
Telephone: 00373 2 22 12 95. *Fax:* 00373 2 22 22 44. *Telex:* 64163218.

International matches 1995
Albania (a) 0-3, Bulgaria (h) 0-3, Albania (h) 2-3, Wales (a) 0-1, Germany (a) 1-6, Georgia (h) 3-2.
League champions 1993–94: Zimbru Chisinau.

Final League Table 1995–96
Zimbru Chisinau 81; Tiligul 74; Constructorul 74; Agro 63; Olimpia 63; Otaci 52; Spumante 47; MHM 93 45; Calarasi 38; CSS 34; Sperante 31; Bender 26; Torentul 20; Cioburciu 16; Briceni* 16; Bugeac* 1.
Cup Final: Constructorul 2, Tiligul 1.

NORTHERN IRELAND

Irish Football Association Ltd, 20 Windsor Avenue, Belfast BT9 6EG.
Founded: 1880; *Number of Clubs:* 1,555; *Number of Players:* 24,558; *National Colours:* Green shirts, white shorts, green stockings.
Telephone: 01232 66 94 58/59; *Cable:* FOOTBALL BELFAST; *Telex:* 747317 ifa ni g; *Fax:* 01232 66 76 20.

NORWAY

Norges Fotballforbund Ulleval Stadion, Postboks 3823, Ulleval Hageby, 0805 Oslo 8.
Founded: 1902; *Number of Clubs:* 1,810; *Number of Players:* 300,000; *National Colours:* Red shirts, white shorts, blue & white stockings.
Telephone: 0047 22 95 10 00; *Cable* FOTBALLFOR-BUND OSLO; *Telex:* 71722 nff n; *Fax:* 0047 22 95 10 10.

International matches 1995
Estonia (h) 7-0, Cyprus (a) 2-0, Luxembourg (a) 2-0, Luxembourg (h) 5-0, Ghana (h) 3-2, Malta (h) 2-0, France (h) 0-0, Czech Republic (h) 1-1, Czech Republic (a) 0-2, England (h) 0-0, Holland (a) 0-3, Jamaica (a) 1-1, Trinidad & Tobago (a) 2-3.

League Championship wins (1937–95)
Fredrikstad 9; Rosenborg Trondheim 9; Viking Stavanger 8; Lillestroem 6; Valerengen 4; Larvik Turn 3; Brann Bergen 2; Lyn Oslo 2; IK Start 2; Friedig 1; Fram 1; Skeid Oslo 1; Strömsgodset Drammen 1; Moss 1.

Cup wins (1902–95)
Odds Bk Skien 11; Fredrikstad 10; Lyn Oslo 8; Skeid Oslo 8; Sarpsborg FK 6; Rosenborg Trondheim 6; Brann Bergen 5; Orn F Horten 4; Lillestroem 4; Viking Stavanger 4; Strömsgodset Drammen 4; Frigg 3; Mjondalens F 3; Bodo Glimt 2; Mercantile 2; Grane Nordstrand 1; Kvik Halden 1; Sparta 1; Gjovik 1; Valerengen 1; Moss 1; Tromso 1; Byrne 1, Molde 1.
(Known as the Norwegian Championship for HM The King's Trophy).

Final League Table 1995

	P	W	D	L	F	A	Pts
Rosenborg	26	19	5	2	78	29	62
Molde	26	14	5	7	60	47	47
Bodo-Glimt	26	12	7	7	65	43	43
Lillestrom	26	11	8	7	50	36	41
Viking	26	12	4	10	55	42	40
Tromso	26	11	5	10	53	42	38
VIF Fotball	26	11	6	9	47	44	37
Start	26	11	1	14	51	52	34
Stabaek	26	9	6	11	36	40	33
Brann	26	9	5	12	40	50	32
Kongsvinger	26	7	8	11	37	54	29
Hodd*	26	8	4	14	38	57	28
Hamkam*	26	8	3	15	33	66	27
Strindheim*	26	4	5	17	36	77	17

VIF Fotball two points deducted.
Top scorer: Brattbakk (Rosenborg) 26.
Cup Final: Rosenborg 3, Brann 1.

POLAND

Federation Polonaise De Foot-Ball, Al. Ujazdowskie 22, 00-478 Warszawa.
Founded: 1923; *Number of Clubs:* 5,881; *Number of Players:* 317,442; *National Colours:* White shirts, red shorts, white & red stockings.
Telephone: 0048 22 6223398, 6211975; *Cable:* PEZETPEEN WARSZAWA; *Telex:* 815320 pzpn pl; *Fax:* 0048 22 629 24 89.

International matches 1995
Lithuania (h) 4-1, Romania (a) 1-2, Israel (h) 4-3, Slovakia (h) 5-0, Brazil (a) 1-2, France (a) 1-1, Romania (h) 0-0, Slovakia (a) 1-4, Azerbaijan (a) 0-0.

League Championship wins (1921–96)
Gornik Zabrze 14; Ruch Chorzow 13; Wisla Krakow 6; Legia Warsaw 6; Lech Poznan 5; Pogon Lwow 4; Cracovia 3; Widzew Lodz 3; Warta Poznan 2; Polonia Bytom 2; Stal Mielec 2; Garbarnia Krakow 1; Polonia Warsaw 1; LKS Lodz 1; Slask Wroclaw 1; Szombierki Bytom 1; Zaglebie Lubin 1.

Cup wins (1951–96)
Legia Warsaw 11; Gornik Zabrze 6; Zaglebie Sosnowiec 4; Lech Poznan 3; GKS Katowice 3; Ruch Chorzow 3; Slask Wroclaw 2; Gwardia Warsaw 1; LKS Lodz 1; Polonia Warsaw 1; Wisla Krakow 1; Stal Rzeszow 1; Arka Gdynia 1; Lechia Gdansk 1; Widzew Lodz 1; Miedz Legnica 1.

Final League Table 1995–96

	P	W	D	L	F	A	Pts
Widzew	34	27	7	0	84	22	88
Legia	34	27	4	3	92	21	85
Hutnik	34	15	7	12	48	43	52
LKS Lodz	34	13	10	11	44	38	49
Amica	34	13	9	12	35	37	48
Stomil	34	13	7	14	32	41	46
Lech	34	11	12	11	45	40	45
Zaglebie Lubin	34	11	11	12	34	35	44
Sokol	34	11	11	12	36	39	44
Rakow	34	12	8	14	33	36	44
Katowice	34	11	10	13	36	37	43
Gornik Zabrze	34	10	13	11	45	52	43
Slask	34	9	15	10	39	40	42
Pogon	34	11	9	14	33	41	42
GKS	34	12	6	16	40	54	42
Olimpia	34	11	7	16	39	59	40
Stal	34	8	4	22	31	65	28
Siarka	34	3	6	25	24	70	15

Top scorer: Koniarek (Widzew) 29.
Cup Final: Ruch 1, GKS 0.

PORTUGAL

Federacao Portuguesa De Futebol, Praca De Alegria N.25, Apartado 21.100, P-1128, Lisboa Codex.
Founded: 1914; *Number of Clubs:* 204; *Number of Players:* 79,235; *National Colours:* Red shirts, white shorts, red stockings.
Telephone: 00351 1 347 59 34; *Cable:* FUTEBOL LISBOA; *Telex:* 13489 fpf p; *Fax:* 00351 1 346 72 31.

International matches 1995
Canada (a) 1-1, Denmark (h) 1-0, Holland (a) 1-0, Eire (a) 0-1, Latvia (h) 3-2, Liechtenstein (a) 7-0, Northern Ireland (h) 1-1, Austria (a) 1-1, Eire (h) 3-0, England (a) 1-1.

League Championship wins (1935–96)
Benfica 30; Sporting Lisbon 16; FC Porto 15; Belenenses 1.

Cup wins (1939–96)
Benfica 23; Sporting Lisbon 12; FC Porto 8; Boavista 4; Belenenses 3; Vitoria Setubal 2; Academica Coimbra 1; Leixoes Porto 1; Sporting Braga 1; Amadora 1.

Final League Table 1995–96

	P	W	D	L	F	A	Pts
Porto	34	26	6	2	84	20	84
Benfica	34	22	7	5	57	27	73
Sporting Lisbon	34	19	10	5	70	27	67
Boavista	34	19	8	7	58	28	65
Guimaraes	34	19	5	10	55	39	62
Belenenses	34	14	9	11	53	33	51
Leiria	34	14	5	15	38	50	47
Braga	34	12	9	13	44	47	45
Maritimo	34	12	7	15	39	53	43
Farense	34	10	6	18	36	45	36
Salgueiros	34	7	15	12	39	49	36
Gil Vicente	34	9	9	16	31	49	36
Amadora	34	7	14	13	35	50	35
Chaves	34	9	7	18	38	56	34
Leca	34	9	7	18	29	54	34
Felgueiras	34	8	9	17	29	47	33
Campomairoense*	34	10	3	21	32	69	33
Tirsense*	34	7	10	17	30	54	31

Top scorer: Domingos(Porto) 25.
Cup Final: Benfica 3, Sporting Lisbon 1.

ROMANIA

Federatia Romana De Fotbal, Vasile Conta 16, Bucharest 70130.
Founded: 1908; *Number of Clubs:* 414; *Number of Players:* 22,920; *National Colours:* Yellow shirts, blue shorts, red stockings.
Telephone: 0040 1 617 33 43; *Cable:* SPORTROM BUCURESTI-FOTBAL; *Telex:* 10097 frf r; *Fax:* 0040 1 312 83 24

International matches 1995
Greece (a) 0-1, Turkey (a) 1-1, Poland (h) 2-1, Azerbaijan (a) 4-1, Israel (h) 2-1, Poland (a) 0-0, Brazil (a) 2-2, France (h) 1-3, Slovakia (a) 2-0.

League Championship wins (1910–96)
Steaua Bucharest (prev. CCA) 18; Dinamo Bucharest 14; Venus Bucharest 8; Chinezul Timisoara 6; UT Arad 6; Ripensia Temesvar 4; Uni Craiova 4; Petrolul Ploesti 3; Olimpia Bucharest 2; Colentina Bucharest 2; Arges Pitesti 2; ICO Oradea 2; Soc RA Bucharest 1; Prahova Ploesti 1; Coltea Brasov 1; Juventus Bucharest 1; Metalochimia Resita 1; Ploesti United 1; Unirea Tricolor 1; Rapid Bucharest 1.

Cup wins (1934–96)
Steaua Bucharest (prev. CCA) 18; Rapid Bucharest 9; Dinamo Bucharest 7; Uni Craiova 6; UT Arad 2; Ripensia Temesvar 2; Politehnica Timisoara 2; Petrolul Ploesti 2; Colentina 1; Metalochimia Resita 1; Stinta Cluj 1; CFR Turnu Severin 1; Chimia Ramnicu Vilcea 1; Jiul Petroseni 1; Progresul Bucharest 1; Progresul Oradea 1; Gloria Bistrita 1.

Final League Table 1995–96

	P	W	D	L	F	A	Pts
Steaua	34	21	8	5	79	30	71
National	34	18	6	10	60	44	60
Rapid Bucharest	34	18	5	11	59	33	59
Uni Craiova	34	17	6	11	45	30	57
Dinamo	34	15	7	12	40	37	52
Petrolul	34	16	3	15	44	38	51
Politehnica	34	14	7	13	58	47	49
Farul	34	15	4	15	56	49	49
Uni Cluj	34	14	6	14	41	40	48
Brasov	34	13	7	14	38	60	46
Gloria	34	14	3	17	41	38	45
Selena	34	15	0	19	40	58	45
Otelul	34	14	3	17	42	46	45
Sportul	34	12	7	15	33	35	43
Ceahlaul	34	13	4	17	34	46	43
Arges	34	12	6	16	39	52	42
Inter Sibiu*	34	10	7	17	29	48	37
Iasi*	34	9	3	22	27	74	30

Top scorer: Vladoiu (Steaua) 25.
Cup Final: Steaua 3, Gloria 1.

RUSSIA

Football Union of Russia; Luzhnetskaya Naberezyhnaja, 8. SU-119270 Moscow. *Telephone:* 0070 95 248 08 34; *Telex:* 411287 priz su; *Fax:* 0070 502 220 20 37; *Founded:* 1992; *Number of Clubs:* 43,700; *Number of Players:* 2,170,000.

International matches 1995
Slovakia (a) 1-2, Scotland (h) 0-0, Greece (a) 3-0, Faeroes (h) 3-0, Yugoslavia (a) 2-1, San Marino (a) 7-0, Finland (a) 6-0, Faeroes (a) 5-2, Greece (h) 2-1, Finland (h) 3-1.

League Championship wins (1945–95)
Spartak Moscow 14; Dynamo Kiev 13; Dynamo Moscow 11; CSKA Moscow 7; Torpedo Moscow 3; Dynamo Tbilisi 2; Dnepr Dnepropetrovsk 2; Saria Voroshilovgrad 1; Ararat Erevan 1; Dynamo Minsk 1; Zenit Leningrad 1; Spartak Vladikavkaz 1.

Cup wins (1936–96)
Spartak Moscow 11; Dynamo Kiev 10; Torpedo Moscow 7; Dynamo Moscow 7; CSKA Moscow 5; Donetsk Shaktyor 4; Lokomotiv Moscow 3; Dynamo Tbilisi 2; Ararat Erevan 2; Karpaty Lvov 1; SKA Rostov 1; Zenit Leningrad 1; Metallist Kharkov 1; Dnepr 1.

Final League Table 1995

	P	W	D	L	F	A	Pts
Vladikavkaz	30	22	5	3	64	21	71
Spartak Moscow	30	20	5	5	79	26	65
Lokomotiv Moscow	30	20	5	5	52	25	65
Dynamo Moscow	30	16	8	6	45	29	56
Torpedo Moscow	30	16	7	7	40	30	55
CSKA Moscow	30	16	5	9	56	36	53
Volgograd	30	11	6	13	62	52	39
Ekaterinbourg	30	12	3	15	43	47	39
Kamaz	30	9	8	13	33	32	35
Chernomorets	30	11	2	17	34	61	35
Tekstilchik Kamychin	30	9	7	14	37	41	34
Novgorod	30	6	11	13	28	42	29
Rostov	30	8	4	18	36	56	28
Sotchi	30	8	4	18	38	69	28
Krylia Sovekov	30	6	8	16	34	65	26
Gazovik	30	3	6	21	28	77	15

Top scorer: Veretennikov (Volgograd) 25.
Cup Final: Lokomotiv Moscow 3, Spartak Moscow 2.

SAN MARINO

Federazione Sammarinese Giuoco Calcio, Viale Campo dei Giudei, 14; 47031-Rep. San Marino.
Founded: 1931; *Number of Clubs:* 17; *Number of Players:* 1,033; *Colours:* Blue and white.
Telephone: 0039549 99 05 15; *Cable:* FEDERCALCIO SAN MARINO; *Telex:* 0505284 cogmar; *Fax:* 0039549 99 23 48.

International matches 1995
Finland (h) 0-2, Scotland (h) 0-2, Faeroes (a) 0-3, Russia (h) 0-7, Greece (h) 0-4, Faeroes (h) 1-3, Scotland (a) 0-5.

League Championship wins (1986–96)
Tre Fiori 4; Fiorita 2; Faetano 2; Domagnano 1; Montevito 1, Libertas 1.

Cup wins (1986–95)
Domagnano 3; Libertas 3; Faetano 1, Fiorita 1, Tre Fiori 1; Cosmos 1.

Final League Table 1995–96

	P	W	D	L	F	A	Pts
Cosmos	18	10	3	5	29	21	33
Murata	18	8	7	3	29	15	31
La Fiorita	18	8	5	5	24	17	29
San Giovanni	18	7	7	4	26	24	28
Folgore	18	7	6	5	22	18	27
Domagnano	18	7	5	6	22	16	26
Tre Fiori	18	8	2	8	23	25	26
Virtus	18	5	6	7	22	26	21
Cailungo	18	3	6	9	20	32	15
Faetano	18	3	1	14	16	39	10

Play-Offs
San Giovanni 0,Libertas 1; Murata 2, La Fiorita 4; Libertas 2, La Fiorita 2 (La Fiorita won 4-3 on penalties); San Giovanni 2, Murata 0.

Semi-finals
Cosmos 1, La Fiorita 0, Libertas 3, San Giovanni 0.

Final
Libertas 4, Cosmos 1.
Top scorer: Pancotti (San Giovanni) 11.

SCOTLAND

The Scottish Football Association Ltd, 6 Park Gardens, Glasgow G3 7YF.
Founded: 1873; *Number of Clubs:* 6,148; *Number of Players:* 135,474; *National Colours:* Dark blue shirts, white shorts, red stockings.
Telephone: 0141 332 6372; *Cable:* EXECUTIVE GLASGOW; *Telex:* 778904 sfa g; *Fax:* 0141 332 7559.

SLOVAKIA

Slovak Football Association, Junacka 6, 83280 Bratislava, Slovakia.
Number of Clubs: 2,140; *Number of Players:* 141,000.
Telephone: 0042 7 279 01 51; *Fax:* 0042 7 279 05 54.

International matches 1995
Brazil (a) 0-5, Russia (h) 2-1, Azerbaijan (h) 4-1, France (a) 0-4, Czech Republic (h) 1-1, Poland (a) 0-5, Argentina (a) 0-6, Peru (a) 0-1, Azerbaijan (a) 1-0, Israel (h) 1-0, Poland (h) 4-1, Romania (h) 0-2.

League Championship wins (1994–96)
Slovan Bratislava 3.

Cup wins (1994–96)
Tatran Presov 1; Inter 1; Humenne 1.

Final League Table 1995–96

	P	W	D	L	F	A	Pts
Slovan Bratislava	32	22	9	1	79	20	75
Kosice	32	21	2	9	62	33	65
Spartak Trnava	32	19	6	7	54	32	63
Dukla Bystrica	32	14	9	9	39	36	47
Tatran Presov	32	12	7	13	34	36	43
Bardejov	32	13	3	16	38	42	42

Promotion/Relegation Table 1995–96

	P	W	D	L	F	A	Pts
Humenne	32	13	5	14	50	44	44
Lokomotiv Kosice	32	13	2	17	37	49	41
Inter	32	11	7	14	42	45	40
Dunajska Streda	32	10	3	19	41	76	33
Nitra	32	10	3	19	41	76	33
Prievidza	32	7	4	21	31	65	25

Top scorer: Semenik (Kosice) 29.
Cup final: Humenne 2, Spartak Trnava 1.

SLOVENIA

Football Association of Slovenia, P.P. 3986, 1001 Ljubljana, Slovenia.
Founded: 1992; *Number of Clubs:* 232; *Number of Players:* 15,048.
Telephone: 00386 61 133 40 63; *Fax:* 00386 61 30 23 37.

International matches 1995
Estonia (h) 3-0, Croatia (a) 0-2, Lithuania (a) 1-2, Estonia (a) 3-1, Italy (a) 0-1, Ukraine (h) 3-2, Croatia (h) 1-2.

League Championship wins (1992–96)
SCT Olimpija 4; Gorica 1.

Cup wins (1992–96)
Branik Maribor 2; SCT Olimpija 2; Mura 1.

Final League Table 1995–96

	P	W	D	L	F	A	Pts
Gorica	36	18	13	5	49	22	67
Olimpija	36	19	7	10	79	39	64
Mura	36	15	13	8	43	29	58
Branik Maribor	36	14	11	11	47	32	53
Publikum	36	13	12	11	62	47	51
Beltinci	36	13	11	12	41	40	50
Rudar	36	13	10	13	46	37	49
Primorje	36	13	9	14	56	48	48
Korotan	36	11	9	16	44	46	42
Isola	36	1	5	30	13	140	8

Top scorer: Siljak (Olimpija) 28.
Cup Final: Olimpija 1, 1, Primorje 0, 1.

SPAIN

Real Federacion Espanola De Futbol, Calle Alberto Bosch 13, Apartado Postal 347, E-28014 Madrid.
Founded: 1913; *Number of Clubs:* 10,240; *Number of Players:* 408,135; *National Colours:* Red shirts, dark blue shorts, black stockings, yellow trim.
Telephone: 0034 1 420 13 62; *Cable:* FUTBOL MADRID; *Telex:* 42420 rfcf c; *Fax:* 0034 1 420 20 94.

International matches 1995
Uruguay (h) 2-2, Germany (h) 0-0, Belgium (h) 1-1, Armenia (a) 2-0, Armenia (h) 1-0, Cyprus (h) 6-0, Argentina (h) 2-1, Denmark (a) 1-1, Macedonia (h) 3-0.

League Championship wins (1945–96)
Real Madrid 26; Barcelona 14; Atletico Madrid 9; Athletic Bilbao 8; Valencia 4; Real Sociedad 2; Real Betis 1; Seville 1.

Cup wins (1902–96)
Athletic Bilbao 23; Barcelona 22; Real Madrid 17; Atletico Madrid 9; Valencia 5; Real Zaragoza 4; Real Union de Irun 3; Seville 3; Espanol 2; Arenas 1; Ciclista Sebastian 1; Racing de Irun 1; Vizcaya Bilbao 1; Real Betis 1; Real Sociedad 1, La Coruna 1.

Final League Table 1995–96

	P	W	D	L	F	A	Pts
Atletico Madrid	42	26	9	7	75	32	87
Valencia	42	26	5	11	77	51	83
Barcelona	42	22	14	6	72	39	80
Espanol	42	20	14	8	63	36	74
Tenerife	42	20	12	10	69	54	72
Real Madrid	42	20	10	12	75	51	70
Real Sociedad	42	17	12	13	62	53	63
Betis	42	16	14	12	61	54	62
La Coruna	42	16	13	13	63	44	61
Compostela	42	17	8	17	47	54	59
Celta	42	12	16	14	49	51	52
Zaragoza	42	11	15	16	51	59	48
Athletic Bilbao	42	11	15	16	44	55	48
Sevilla	42	11	15	16	42	54	48
Oviedo	42	12	12	18	48	67	48
Valladolid	42	11	14	17	57	62	47
Santander	42	11	14	17	47	69	47
Sporting Gijon	42	13	7	22	51	60	46
Rayo Vallecano+	42	12	8	22	47	75	44
Merida*	42	10	12	20	37	62	42
Albacete*+	42	10	12	20	55	81	42
Salamanca*	42	8	9	25	52	81	33

Top scorer: Pizzi (Tenerife) 31.
Cup Final: Atletico Madrid 1, Barcelona 0 aet.

SWEDEN

Svenska Fotbollfoerbundet, Box 1216, S-17123 Solna.
Founded: 1904; *Number of Clubs:* 3,250, *Number of Players:* 485,000; *National Colours:* Yellow shirts, blue shorts, yellow and blue stockings.
Telephone: 0046 8 735 09 00; *Cable:* FOOTBALL-S; *Telex:* 17711 fotboll s; *Fax:* 0046 8 27 51 47.

International matches 1995
Cyprus (a) 3-3, Turkey (a) 1-2, Hungary (a) 0-1, Iceland (h) 1-1, Brazil (a) 0-1, England (a) 3-3, Japan (n) 2-2, USA (h) 1-0, Switzerland (h) 0-0, Scotland (h) 2-0, Turkey (h) 2-2.

League Championship wins (1896–1995)
IFK Gothenburg 16; Oergryte IS Gothenburg 14; Malmo FF 14; IFK Norrköping 12; AIK Stockholm 9; Djurgaarden 8; GAIS Gothenburg 6; IF Helsingborg 5; Boras IF Elfsborg 4; Oster Vaxjo 4; Halmstad 2; Atvidaberg 2; IFK Ekilstune 1; IF Gavic Brynas 1; IF Gothenburg 1; Fassbergs 1; Norrköping IK Sleipner 1.

Cup wins (1941–95)
Malmo FF 13; IFK Norrköping 6; AIK Stockholm 5; IFK Gothenburg 4; Atvidaberg 2; Kalmar 2; GAIS Gothenburg 1; IF Helsingborg 1; Raa 1; Landskrona 1; Oster Vaxjo 1; Djurgaarden 1; Degerfors 1, Halmstad 1.

Final League Table 1995

	P	W	D	L	F	A	Pts
IFK Gothenburg	26	12	10	4	43	20	46
Helsingborg	26	12	6	8	42	46	42
Halmstad	26	11	8	7	40	32	41
Malmo	26	9	12	5	32	28	39
Orebro	26	10	8	8	35	29	38
Djurgaarden	26	10	8	8	33	33	38
Orgryte	26	9	8	9	22	26	35
AIK	26	7	11	8	34	31	32
Degerfors	26	7	11	8	32	45	32
Osters+	26	5	13	8	41	41	28
Norrköping+	26	7	7	12	28	44	28
Hammarby*	26	6	8	12	33	40	26
Frolunda*	26	5	10	11	35	45	25

Top scorer: Skoog (Frolunda) 17.
Cup Final: AIK 1, Malmo 0 aet.

SWITZERLAND

Schweizerisher Fussballverband. Haus des Schweizer Fussballs, Worbstrasse 48, 3074 Muri/BE. Mailing Address: PO Box 3000 Bern 15.
Founded: 1895; *Number of Clubs:* 1,473; *Number of Players:* 185,286; *National Colours:* Red shirts, white shorts, red stockings.
Telephone: 0041 31 950 81 11; *Cable:* SWISSFOOT BERNE; *Telex:* 912910 sfv ch; *Fax:* 0041 31 950 81 81.

International matches 1995
Greece (a) 1-1, Hungary (a) 2-2, Turkey (h) 1-2, Italy (h) 0-1, Germany (h) 1-2, Iceland (a) 2-0, Sweden (a) 0-0, Hungary (h) 3-0, England (a) 1-3.

League Championship wins (1898–1996)
Grasshoppers 24; Servette 16; Young Boys Berne 11; FC Zurich 9; FC Basle 6; Lausanne 7; La Chaux-de-Fonds 3; FC Lugano 3; Winterthur 3; FX Aarau 3; Neuchatel Xamax 2; FC Anglo-American 1; St Gallen 1; FC Brühl 1; Cantonal-Neuchatel 1; Biel 1; Bellinzona 1; FC Etoile Le Chaux-de-Fonds 1; Lucerne 1; Sion 1.

Cup wins (1926–96)
Grasshoppers 18; FC Sion 8; Lausanne 7; La Chaux-de-Fonds 6; Young Boys Berne 6; Servette 6; FC Basle 5; FC Zurich 5; Lucerne 2; FC Lugano 2; FC Granges 1; St Gallen 1; Urania Geneva 1; Young Fellows Zurich 1; Aarau 1.

Qualifying Table 1995–96

	P	W	D	L	F	A	Pts
Grasshoppers	22	13	4	5	38	22	43
Sion	22	13	3	6	37	28	42
Neuchatel Xamax	22	12	5	5	40	24	41
Lucerne	22	11	7	4	36	15	40
Basle	22	9	3	10	23	29	30
Servette	22	7	7	8	28	28	28
Aarau	22	7	6	9	36	27	27
St Gallen	22	6	9	7	26	24	27
Lausanne	22	6	9	7	25	25	27
Lugano	22	5	6	11	21	42	21
Zurich	22	4	6	12	17	32	18
Young Boys Berne	22	4	5	13	14	35	17

Top scorer: Moldovan (Neuchatel Xamax) 13.

Final Table 1996

	P	W	D	L	F	A	Pts
Grasshoppers	14	8	6	0	26	7	52
Sion	14	8	2	4	20	14	47
Neuchatel Xamax	14	5	7	2	21	16	43
Aarau	14	7	4	3	23	18	39
Lucerne	14	4	3	7	23	19	35
Basle	14	3	4	7	11	20	28
Servette	14	2	5	7	18	25	25
St Gallen	14	2	3	9	11	34	23

Promotion/Relegation 1996

	P	W	D	L	F	A	Pts
Young Boys Berne	14	10	3	1	28	13	33
Zurich	14	8	4	2	21	12	28
Lausanne	14	7	6	1	24	10	27
Lugano	14	4	5	5	13	17	17
Yverdon	14	3	4	7	16	22	13
Delemont	14	3	4	7	17	26	13
Kriens	14	2	5	7	14	22	11
Etoile Carouge	14	1	5	8	9	20	8

Top scorers: Aleksandrov (Lucerne), Moldovan (Neuchatel Xamax) 19.
Cup Final: Sion 3, Servette 2.

TURKEY

Federation Turque De Football, Konur Sokak No. 10, Ankara Kizilay.
Founded: 1923; *Number of Clubs:* 230; *Number of Players:* 64,521; *National Colours:* White shirts, white shorts, red and white stockings.
Telephone: 0090 212 282 70 10; *Cable:* FUTBOLSPOR ANKARA; *Fax:* 0090 212 282 70 15.

International matches 1995
Romania (h) 1-1, Israel (h) 2-1, Sweden (h) 2-1, Switzerland (a) 2-1, Canada (a) 3-1, Canada (a) 3-0, Honduras (h) 1-0, Paraguay (a) 0-0, New Zealand (h) 2-1, Chile (a) 0-0, Hungary (h) 2-0, Finland (a) 0-0, Iceland (a) 0-0, Sweden (a) 2-2.

League Championship wins (1960–96)
Fenerbahce 13; Galatasaray 10; Besiktas 10; Trabzonspor 6.

Cup wins (1963–96)
Galatasaray 11; Besiktas 5; Trabzonspor 5; Fenerbahce 4; Goztepe Izmir 2; Altay Izmir 2; Ankaragucu 2; Eskisehirspor 1; Bursapor 1; Genclerbirligi 1; Sakaryaspor 1.

Final League Table 1995–96

	P	W	D	L	F	A	Pts
Fenerbahce	34	26	6	2	68	19	84
Trabzonspor	34	26	4	4	78	24	82
Besiktas	34	22	3	9	74	46	69
Galatasaray	34	21	5	8	66	38	68
Kocaeli	34	16	11	7	61	43	59
Gaziantep	34	14	7	13	42	43	49
Antalya	34	13	6	15	45	55	45
Samsun	34	12	7	15	46	45	43
Bursa	34	10	11	13	50	48	41
Genclerbirligi	34	10	11	13	40	47	41
Ankaragucu	34	10	7	17	35	51	37
Altay	34	9	9	16	36	56	36
Istanbul	34	8	11	15	46	57	35
Van	34	8	11	15	32	50	35
Denizli	34	7	11	16	37	50	32
Kayseri*	34	7	11	16	41	60	32
Eskisehir*	34	10	2	22	39	68	32
Karsiyaka*	34	7	7	20	27	63	28

Top scorer: Arveladze (Trabzonspor) 25.
Cup Final: Galatasaray 1, 1, Fenerbahce 0, 1.

UKRAINE

Football Federation of Ukraine, Ulianovyh Street 1, P.O. Box 503, 252150 Kiev, Ukraine.
Founded: 1992; *Number of Teams:* 30,460; *Number of Players:* 757,758.
Telephone: 0070 44 264 72 98, 2691793; *Fax:* 0070 44 264 75 64, 269 25 50; *Telex:* 0680 631461 UFF+.

International matches 1995
Croatia (a) 0-4, Italy (h) 0-2, Estonia (a) 1-0, Croatia (h) 1-0, Lithuania (a) 3-1, Slovenia (a) 2-3, Italy (a) 1-3.

League Championship wins (1992–96)
Dynamo Kiev 4; Tavria Simferopol 1.

Cup wins (1992–96)
Chernomorets 2; Dynamo Kiev 2; Shakhtjor Donetsk 1.

Final League Table 1995–96

	P	W	D	L	F	A	Pts
Dynamo Kiev	34	24	7	3	65	17	79
Chernomorets	34	22	7	5	56	25	73
Dnepr	34	19	6	9	65	34	63
CSKA	34	15	11	8	47	27	56
Zirka	34	14	8	12	37	33	50
Metallurg	34	16	4	14	49	42	52
Torpedo	34	15	3	16	40	46	48
Karpaty	34	12	10	12	39	39	46
Kremen	34	14	4	16	46	56	46
Donetsk	34	13	6	15	44	43	45
Prekarpate	34	12	8	14	49	49	44
Tavria	34	12	8	14	46	46	44
Ternopol	34	13	3	18	37	42	42
Krivbass	34	11	9	14	43	52	42
Vinnitsa	34	11	7	16	28	36	40
Nikolaev	34	10	8	16	37	53	38
Volyn*	34	9	7	18	34	58	34
Zarja*	34	4	4	26	16	80	16

Top Scorer: Guseinov (Chernomorets) 20.
Cup Final: Dynamo Kiev 2, Vinnitsa 0.

WALES

The Football Association of Wales Limited, Plymouth Chambers, 3 Westgate Street, Cardiff.
Founded: 1876; *Number of Clubs:* 2,326; *Number of Players:* 53,926; *National Colours:* All red. *Telephone:* 01222 372325; *Telex:* 497 363 faw g; *Fax:* 01222 343961.

YUGOSLAVIA

Yugoslav Football Association, P.O. Box 263, Terazije 35, 11000 Beograd.
Founded: 1919; *Number of Clubs:* 6,532; *Number of Players:* 229,024; *National Colours:* Blue shirts, white shorts, red stockings.
Telephone: 00381 11 33 34 47; *Cable:* JUGOFUDBAL BEOGRAD; *Telex:* 11666 sfj yu; *Fax:* 00381 11 33 34 33.

International matches 1995
Hong Kong (h) 3-1, South Korea (h) 1-0, Uruguay (h) 1-0, Russia (h) 1-2, Greece (a) 2-0, El Salvador (a) 4-1, Mexico (a) 4-1.

League Championship wins (1923–96)
Red Star Belgrade 20; Partizan Belgrade 14; Hajduk Split 9; Gradjanski Zagreb 5; BSK Belgrade 5; Dynamo Zagreb 4; Jugoslavija Belgrade 2; Concordia Zagreb 2; FC Sarajevo 2; Vojvodina Novi Sad 2; HASK Zagreb 1; Zeljeznicar 1.

Cup wins (1947–96)
Red Star Belgrade 15; Hajduk Split 9; Dynamo Zagreb 8; Partizan Belgrade 7; BSK Belgrade 2; OFK Belgrade 2; Rijeka 2; Velez Mostar 2; Vardar Skopje 1; Borac Banjaluka 1.

Final League Table 1995–96
Group A

	P	W	D	L	F	A	Pts
Partizan Belgrade	18	13	3	2	51	17	60
Red Star Belgrade	18	9	5	4	27	16	48
Vojvodina	18	8	6	4	33	19	43
Becej	18	9	6	3	18	19	41
Mladost L	18	8	2	8	24	27	32
Cukariki	18	4	6	8	23	23	29
Rad	18	5	5	8	21	23	28
Proleter	18	6	3	9	24	28	27
Radnicki Nis*	18	4	5	9	19	37	26
Sloboda*	18	2	3	13	10	41	14

Group B

	P	W	D	L	F	A	Pts
Zemun	18	10	3	5	29	14	40
Borac	18	10	3	5	25	13	35
Hajduk Kula	18	8	4	6	20	20	34
Buducnost	18	8	5	5	15	14	32
Obilic	18	8	2	8	20	18	31
OFK Belgrade	18	7	4	7	23	23	29
Loznica	18	7	4	7	23	22	27
Mladost BJ	18	7	2	9	18	25	27
Napredak	18	5	9	9	22	27	24
Radnicki NB	18	2	4	12	13	32	17

Top scorer: Bidimirovic (Cukariki) 22.
Cup Final: Red Star Belgrade 3, 3, Partizan Belgrade 0, 1.

NEW PROVISIONAL MEMBER OF FIFA: PALESTINE.

SOUTH AMERICA

ARGENTINA
Asociacion Del Futbol Argentina, Viamonte 1366/76, 1053 Buenos Aires.
Founded: 1893; *Number of Clubs:* 3,035; *Number of Players:* 306,365; *National Colours:* Blue & white shirts, black shorts, white stockings.
Telephone: 00541 404 276; *Cable:* FUTBOL BUENOS AIRES; *Telex:* 17848 AFA AR; *Fax:* 54-1 3754410.

BOLIVIA
Edificio Federacion Boliviana De Futbol, Av. Libertador Bolivar No. 1148, Casilla de Correo 484, Cochabamba, Bolivia.
Founded: 1925; *Number of Clubs:* 305; *Number of Players:* 15,290; *National Colours:* Green shirts, white shorts, green stockings.
Telephone: 0059142 45889; *Cable:* FEDFUTBOL COCHABAMBA; *Telex:* 6239 FEDBOL; *Fax:* 0059142 82132.
League Champions 1995: San Jose.

BRAZIL
Confederacao Brasileira De Futebol, Rua Da Alfandega, 70, P.O. Box 1078, 20.070 Rio De Janeiro.
Founded: 1914; *Number of Clubs:* 12,987; *Number of Players:* 551,358; *National Colours:* Yellow shirts, blue shorts, white stockings, green trim.
Telephone: 005521 221 5937; *Cable:* DESPORTOS RIO DE JANEIRO; *Telex:* 2121509 CBDS BR; *Fax:* 005521 252 9294.
League Champions 1995: Botafogo.

CHILE
Federacion De Futbol De Chile, Avda. Quillin No. 5635, Casilla postal 3733, Correo Central, Santiago de Chile.
Founded: 1895; *Number of Clubs:* 4,598; *Number of Players:* 609,724; *National Colours:* Red shirts, blue shorts, white stockings.
Telephone: 00562 2849000; *Cable:* FEDFUTBOL SANTIAGO DE CHILE; *Telex:* 440474 FEBOL CZ; *Fax:* 00562 2843510.
League Champions 1995: Univ de Chile.

COLOMBIA
Federacion Colombiana De Futbol, Avenida 32, No. 16-22 piso 40. Apartado Aereo 17602, Santafe de Bogota.
Founded: 1925; *Number of Clubs:* 3,685; *Number of Players:* 188,050; *National Colours:* Red shirts, blue shorts, tricolour stockings.
Telephone: 00571 2853320, 2853145, 2855220; *Telex:* 45598 COLFU CO; *Fax:* 00571 2854340.
League Champions 1995: Junior.

ECUADOR
Federacion Ecuatoriana De Futbol, Calle Jose Mascote 1.103 (Piso 2), Luque, Casilla 7447, Guayaquil.
Founded: 1925; *Number of Clubs:* 170; *Number of Players:* 15,700; *National Colours:* Yellow shirts, blue shorts, red stockings.
Telephone: 005934 371674; *Cable:* ECUAFUTBOL GUAYAQUIL; *Telex:* 42970 FEECFU ED; *Fax:* 005934 373320.
League Champions 1995: Barcelona.

PARAGUAY
Liga Paraguaya De Futbol, Estadio De Sajonia, Calles Mayor Martinez Y Alejo Garcia, Asuncion.
Founded: 1906; *Number of Clubs:* 1,500; *Number of Players:* 140,000; *National Colours:* Red & white shirts, blue shorts, blue stockings.
Telephone: 0059521 81743; *Telex:* 627 PY FUTBOL; *Fax:* 0059521 81743.
League Champions 1995: Olimpia.

PERU
Federacion Peruana De Futbol, Estadio Nacional, Puerto No. 4, Calle Jose Diaz, Lima.
Founded: 1922; *Number of Clubs:* 10,000; *Number of Players:* 325,650; *National Colours:* White shirts, red trim, white shorts, white stockings.
Telephone: 005114 337070; *Cable* FEPEFUTBOL LIMA; *Fax:* 005114 335552; *Telex:* 20066 FEPEFUT PE.
League Champions 1995: Sporting Cristal.

URUGUAY
Asociacion Uruguaya De Futbol, Guayabo 1531, Montevideo.
Founded: 1900; *Number of Clubs:* 1,091; *Number of Players:* 134,310; *National Colours:* Light blue shirts, black shorts, black stockings.
Telephone: 00598442 407101; *Cable:* FUTBOL MONTE-VIDEO; *Fax:* 00598442 407873; *Telex:* AUF UY 22607.
League Champions 1995: Penarol.

VENEZUELA
Federacion Venezolana De Futbol, Avda Este Estadio Nacional, El Paraiso Apdo. Postal 14160, Candelaria, Caracas.
Founded: 1926; *Number of Clubs:* 1,753; *Number of Players:* 63,175; *National Colours:* Magenta shirts, white shorts, white stockings.
Telephone/Fax: 00582 4618010; *Cable:* FEVEFUTBOL CARACAS; *Telex:* 26140 FVFCS VC.
League Champions 1995: Caracas.

ASIA

AFGHANISTAN
The Football Federation of National Olympic Committee, Kabul.
Founded: 1922; *Number of Clubs:* 30; *Number of Players:* 3,300; *National Colours:* White shirts, white shorts, white stockings.
Telephone: 0093 20579; *Cable:* OLYMPIC KABUL.

BAHRAIN
Bahrain Football Association, P.O. Box 5464, Bahrain.
Founded: 1951; *Number of Clubs:* 25; *Number of Players:* 2,030; *National Colours:* White shirts, red shorts, white stockings.
Telephone: 00973 728218; *Cable:* BAHKORA BAHRAIN; *Telex:* 9040 FAB BN; *Fax:* 00973 729361.

BANGLADESH
Bangladesh Football Federation, Stadium, Dhaka 2.
Founded: 1972; *Number of Clubs:* 1,265; *Number of Players:* 30,385; *National Colours:* Orange shirts, white shorts, green stockings.
Telephone: 008802 236072; *Cable:* FOOTBALFED DHAKA; *Telex:* 642460 BHL BJ. *Fax:* 00880–2 863191.

BRUNEI
Brunei Amateur Football Association, P.O. Box 2010, Bandar Seri Begawan 1920, Brunei Darussalam.
Founded: 1959; *Number of Clubs:* 22; *Number of Players:* 830; *National Colours:* Gold shirts, black shorts, gold stockings.
Telephone: 006732 383883, 858585; *Cable:* BAFA BRUNEI; *Telex:* BU 2575 Attn: BAFA; *Fax:* 006732 382900.

BURMA (now Myanmar)
Myanmar Football Federation, Aung San Memorial Stadium, Kandawgalay Post Office, Yangon.
Founded: 1947; *Number of Clubs:* 600; *Number of Players:* 21,000; *National Colours:* Red shirts, white shorts, red stockings.

Telephone: 00951 75249; *Cable:* YANGON MYANMAR; *Telex:* 21218 BRCROS BRN.

CAMBODIA

Federation Khmere De Football Association, C.P. 101, Complex Sportif National, Phnom-Penh.
Founded: 1933; *Number of Clubs:* 30; *Number of Players:* 650; *National Colours:* Red shirts, white shorts, red stockings.
Telephone: 0085523 22469; *Cable:* FKFA PHNOM-PENH.

CHINA PR

Football Association of The People's Republic of China, 9 Tiyuguan Road, Beijing.
Founded: 1924; *Number of Clubs:* 1,045; *Number of Players:* 2,250,000; *National Colours:* Red shirts, white shorts, red stockings.
Telephone: 00861 07117018/9; *Cable:* SPORTSCHINE BEIJING; *Telex:* 22034 ACSF CN; *Fax:* 00861 07142533.

HONG KONG

The Hong Kong Football Association Ltd, 55 Fat Kwong Street, Homantin, Kowloon, Hong Kong.
Founded: 1914; *Number of Clubs:* 69; *Number of Players:* 3,274; *National Colours:* Red shirts, white shorts, red stockings.
Telephone: 00852 27129122; *Cable:* FOOTBALL HONG KONG; *Telex:* 40518 FAHKG HX; *Fax:* 00852 27604303.

INDIA

All India Football Federation Green Lawns, Talap, P.O. Box 429, Cannanore 670 002/ Kerala.
Founded: 1937; *Number of Clubs:* 2,000; *Number of Players:* 56,000; *National Colours:* Light blue shirts, white shorts, dark blue stockings.
Telephone: 0091497 500199; *Cable:* SOCCER CALCUTTA; *Telex:* 212216 MCPL IN; *Fax:* 0091 497500923.

INDONESIA

All Indonesia Football Federation, Main Stadium Senayan, Gate VII, P.O. Box 2305, Jakarta.
Founded: 1930; *Number of Clubs:* 2,880; *Number of Players:* 97,000; *National Colours:* Red shirts, white shorts, red stockings.
Telephone: 006221 581541; *Cable:* PSSI JAKARTA; *Telex:* 65739 as; *Fax:* 006221 584386.

IRAN

IR Iran Football Federation, Shahid Keshvari Sports Complex, Mirdamad Ave., Razan Jonoobi Str., Tehran 15875.
Founded: 1920; *Number of Clubs:* 6,326; *Number of Players:* 306,000; *National Colours:* Green shirts, white shorts, red stockings.
Telephone: 009821 2258151, 2258117, 2258118; *Cable:* FOOTBALL IRAN TEHRAN; *Fax:* 009821 2258123; *Telex:* 212691 nocir.

IRAQ

Iraqi Football Association, Olympic Committee Building, Palestine Street, Baghdad.
Founded: 1948; *Number of Clubs:* 155; *Number of Players:* 4,400; *National Colours:* White shirts, white shorts, white stockings.
Telephone: 009641 774 8261; *Cable:* BALL BAGHDAD; *Telex:* 214074 IRFA IK; *Fax:* 009641 7728424.

JAPAN

The Football Association of Japan, 2nd Floor, Gotoh Ikueikai Bldg, 1-10-7 Dogenzaka, Shibuya-Ku, Tokyo 150, Japan.
Founded: 1921; *Number of Clubs:* 13,047; *Number of Players:* 358,989; *National Colours:* Blue shirts, white shorts, blue stockings.
Telephone: 00813 3476211; *Cable:* SOCCERJAPAN TOKYO; *Telex:* 2422975 FOTJPN J; *Fax:* 00813 34762291.

JORDAN

Jordan Football Association, P.O. Box 1054, Amman.
Founded: 1949; *Number of Clubs:* 98; *Number of Players:* 4,305; *National Colours:* White shirts, white shorts, white stockings.
Telephone: 009626 624481; *Cable:* JORDAN FOOTBALL ASSOCIATION AM; *Telex:* 22415 FOBALL JO. *Fax:* 009626 624454.

KAZAKHSTAN

Football Association of the Republic of Kazakhstan, 44 Abai Street, 480072 Almaty, Kazakhstan.
Number of Clubs: 5,793; *Number of Players:* 260,000.
Telephone: 0073272 674492; *Fax:* 0073272 671885; *Telex:* 251347 TREK SU.

KOREA, NORTH

Football Association of The Democratic People's Rep. of Korea, Munsin-Dong 2, Dongdaewon Distr, Pyongyang.
Founded: 1928; *Number of Clubs:* 90; *Number of Players:* 3,420; *National Colours:* Red shirts, white shorts, red stockings.
Telephone: 008502 3998; *Cable:* DPR KOREA FOOTBALL PYONGYANG; *Telex:* 5472 KP; *Fax:* 008502 814403.

KOREA, SOUTH

Korea Football Association, 110-39, Kyeonji-Dong, Chongro-Ku, Seoul.
Founded: 1928; *Number of Clubs:* 476; *Number of Players:* 2,047; *National Colours:* Red shirts, red shorts, red stockings.
Telephone: 00822 7336764; *Cable:* FOOTBALLKOREA SEOUL; *Telex:* KFASEL K 25373; *Fax:* 00822 7352755.

KUWAIT

Kuwait Football Association, Udailiyya, BL. 4, Al-Ittihad St, P.O. Box 2029 (Safat), 13021 Safat.
Founded: 1952; *Number of Clubs:* 14 (senior); *Number of Players:* 1,526; *National Colours:* Blue shirts, white shorts, blue stockings.
Telephone: 00965 2555851 or 2555822; *Cable:* FOOTKUWAIT; *Telex:* FOOTKUW 22600 KT; *Fax:* 00965 2563737 or 2549955.

KYRGYZSTAN

Football Association of Kyrgyzstan, 17 Togolok Moldo Street, 720033 Bishkek, Kyrgyzstan.
Number of Players: 20,000.
Telephone: 00331 2/261752; *Fax:* 00331 2/227954; *Telex:* 251239 SALAM SU.

LAOS

Federation De Foot-Ball Lao, c/o Dir. Des Sports, Education, Physique Et Artistique, Vientiane.
Founded: 1951; *Number of Clubs:* 76; *Number of Players:* 2,060; *National Colours:* Red shirts, white shorts, blue stockings.
Telephone: 0085621 2741; *Cable:* FOOTBALL VIENTIANE.

LEBANON

Federation Libanaise De Football Association, P.O. Box 4732, Verdun Street, Bristol, Radwan Centre Building, Beirut.
Founded: 1933; *Number of Clubs:* 105; *Number of Players:* 8,125; *National Colours:* Red shirts, white shorts, red stockings.
Telephone: 009611 347157; *Cable:* FOOTBALL BEIRUT; *Telex:* 21404 LIBALL.

MACAO

Associacao De Futebol De Macau (AFM), P.O. Box 920, Macau.
Founded: 1939; *Number of Clubs:* 52; *Number of Players:* 800; *National Colours:* Green shirts, white shorts, green and white stockings.
Telephone: 00853 71996; *Fax:* 00853 260148; *Cable:* FOOTBALL MACAU.

MALDIVES REPUBLIC

Football Association of Maldives, Attn. Mr. Bandhu Ahamed Saleem, Sports Division, G. Banafsa Magu 20-04, Male.
Founded: 1986; *Number of Clubs: Number of Players:* *National Colours:* Green shirts, white shorts, green and white stockings.

Telephone: 0096032 5758; *Telex:* 77039 MINHOM MF; *Fax:* 0096032 4739.

MALAYSIA

Football Association of Malaysia, Wisma Fam, Tingkat 4, Jalan SS5A/9, Kelana Jaya, 47301 Petaling, Jaya Selangor.
Founded: 1933; *Number of Clubs:* 450; *Number of Players:* 11,250; *National Colours:* Black and gold shirts, white shorts, black and gold stockings.
Telephone: 00603 7763766; *Cable:* FOOTBALL PETALING JAYA SELANGO; *Telex:* FAM PJ MA 35701; *Fax:* 00603 7757984.

NEPAL

All-Nepal Football Association, Dasharath Rangashala, Tripureshwor, Kathmandu.
Founded: 1951; *Number of Clubs:* 85; *Number of Players:* 2,550; *National Colours:* Red shirts, blue shorts, blue and white stockings.
Telephone: 009771 15703; *Cable:* ANFA KATHMANDU; *Telex:* 2390 NSC NP.

OMAN

Oman Football Association, P.O. Box 6462, Ruwi-Muscat.
Founded: 1978; *Number of Clubs:* 47; *Number of Players:* 2,340; *National Colours:* White shirts, red shorts, white stockings.
Telephone: 00968 593840; *Cable:* FOOTBALL MUSCAT; *Telex:* 5320 FOOTBALL ON; *Fax:* 00968 593736.

PAKISTAN

Pakistan Football Federation, Mr. Hafiz Salman Butt, General Secretary, Punjab University Ground, Lahore 54000, Pakistan.
Founded: 1948; *Number of Clubs:* 882; *Number of Players:* 21,000; *National Colours:* Green shirts, white shorts, green stockings.
Telephone: 009242 5832786; *Cable:* FOOTBALL QUETTA; *Telex:* 47643 PFF PK; *Fax:* 009242 7281541.

PHILIPPINES

Philippine Football Federation, Room 207, Administration Building, Rizal Memorial Sports Complex, Vito Cruz, Metro Manila.
Founded: 1907; *Number of Clubs:* 650; *Number of Players:* 45,000; *National Colours:* Blue shirts, white shorts, blue stockings.
Telephone: 00632 594655; *Cable:* FOOTBALL MANILA; *Telex:* 65014 POC PACA PN; *Fax:* 00632 588317.

QATAR

Qatar Football Association, P.O. Box 5333, Doha.
Founded: 1960; *Number of Clubs:* 8 (senior); *Number of Players:* 1,380; *National Colours:* White shirts, maroon shorts, white stockings.
Telephone: 00974 351641, 454444; *Cable:* FOOTQATAR DOHA; *Telex:* 4749 QATFOT DH; *Fax:* 00974 411660.

SAUDI ARABIA

Saudi Arabian Football Federation, Al Mather Quarter (Olympic Complex), P.O. Box 5844, Riyadh 11432.
Founded: 1959; *Number of Clubs:* 120; *Number of Players:* 9,600; *National Colours:* White shirts, white shorts, white stockings.
Telephone: 009661 4022699; *Cable:* KORA RIYADH; *Telex:* 404300 SAFOTB SJ; *Fax:* 009661 4921276.

SINGAPORE

Football Association of Singapore, Jalan Besar Stadium, Tyrwhitt Road, Singapore 0820.
Founded: 1892; *Number of Clubs:* 250; *Number of Players:* 8,000; *National Colours:* Sky blue shirts, sky blue shorts, sky blue stockings.

Telephone: 0065 2931477; *Cable:* SOCCER SINGAPORE; *Fax:* 0065 2933728; *Telex:* SINFA RS 37683.

SRI LANKA

Football Federation of Sri Lanka, No. 2, Old Grand Stand, Race Course, Reid Avenue, Colombo 7.
Founded: 1939; *Number of Clubs:* 600; *Number of Players:* 18,825; *National Colours:* Maroon shirts, white shorts, white stockings.
Telephone: 00941 696179; *Cable:* SOCCER COLOMBO; *Telex:* 21537 METALIX CE; *Fax:* 00941 580721.

SYRIA

Association Arabe Syrienne De Football, General Sport Fed. Building, October Stadium, Damascus _ Baremke.
Founded: 1936; *Number of Clubs:* 102; *Number of Players:* 30,600; *National Colours:* White shirts, white shorts, white stockings.
Telephone: 0096311 3331511, 3335866, 3117423; *Cable:* FOOTBALL DAMASCUS; *Telex:* HOTECH 411935; *Fax:* 0096311 3331511, 2128526, 2123346.

TAJIKISTAN

Football Federation of Tajikistan, 44, Rudaki Ave., PB 26, 734012 Dushanbe, Tajikistan.
Number of Clubs: 1,804; *Number of Players:* 71,400.
Telephone: 0073772 223603; *Fax:* 0073772 230996; *Telex:* 116119 SAWDO SU.

THAILAND

The Football Association of Thailand, c/o National Stadium, Rama I Road, Bangkok.
Founded: 1916; *Number of Clubs:* 168; *Number of Players:* 15,000; *National Colours:* Crimson shirts, white shorts, crimson stockings.
Telephone: 00662 2141058; *Cable:* FOOTBALL BANGKOK; *Telex:* 20211 FAT TH; *Fax:* 00662 2154494.

TURKMENISTAN

Football Federation of Turkmenistan, 44 Engels Street, 744000 Ashkabad, Turkmenistan.
Number of Players: 75,000.
Telephone: 0073632 253844; *Fax:* 0073632 290646; *Telex:* 116175 TINTO SU.

UNITED ARAB EMIRATES

United Arab Emirates Football Association, P.O. Box 916, Abu Dhabi.
Founded: 1971; *Number of Clubs:* 23 (senior); *Number of Players:* 1,787; *National Colours:* White shirts, white shorts, white stockings.
Telephone: 00971 2/445600; *Cable:* FOOTBALL EMIRATES DUBAI; *Telex:* 22121 uefa em; *Cable:* FOOTBALL EMIRATES ABU DHABI; *Fax:* 00971 2/448558.

UZBEKISTAN

Football Federation of Uzbekistan, Karl Marx Street 32, 700047 Tashkent, Uzbekistan.
Number of Clubs: 15,000; *Number of Players:* 217,000.
Telephone: 0073712 322854; *Fax:* 0073712 443183; *Telex:* 116108 PTB SU.

VIETNAM

Association De Football De La Republique Du Viet-Nam, No. 36, Boulevard Tran-Phu, Hanoi. *Founded:* 1962; *Number of Clubs:* 55 (senior); *Number of Players:* 16,000; *National Colours:* Red shirts, white shorts, red stockings. *Telephone:* 00844 4867; *Cable:* AFBVN, 36, TRAN-PHU-HANOI.

YEMEN

Yemen Football Association, P.O. Box 908, Sana'a.
Founded: 1962; *Number of Clubs:* 26; *Number of Players:* 1750; *National Colours:* Green.
Telephone: 009672 215720. *Telex:* 2710 YOUTH YE

CONCACAF

ANTIGUA

The Antigua Football Association, P.O. Box 773, St. Johns.
Founded: 1928; *Number of Clubs:* 60; *Number of Players:* 1,008; *National Colours:* Gold shirts, black shorts, black stockings.
Telephone: 001809 4623945; *Cable:* AFA ANTIGUA; *Telex:* 2177 SIDAN AK; *Fax:* 001809 4622649.

ARUBA

Arubaanse Voetbal Bond, Schoenerstraat 2, PO Box 376, Oranjestad, Aruba.
Founded: 1932; *Number of Clubs:* 50; *Number of Players:* 1,000; *National Colours:* Yellow shirts, blue shorts, yellow stockings.
Telephone: 00297 828016; *Fax:* 00297 838438.

BAHAMAS

Bahamas Football Association, P.O. Box N 8434, Nassau, N.P.
Founded: 1967; *Number of Clubs:* 14; *Number of Players:* 700; *National Colours:* Yellow shirts, black shorts, yellow stockings.
Telephone: 001809 3233426; *Cable:* BAHSOCA NASSAU; *Fax:* 001809 3288006.

BARBADOS

Barbados Football Association, P.O. Box 833E, Bridgetown.
Founded: 1910; *Number of Clubs:* 92; *Number of Players:* 1,100; *National Colours:* Royal blue shirts, gold shorts, royal blue stockings.
Telphone: 001809 425 4667, 435 7909; *Cable:* FOOTBALL BRIDGETOWN; *Telex:* 2306 SHAMROCK WB; *Fax:* 001809 4292206.

BELIZE

Belize National Football Association, P.O. Box 1742, Belize City.
Founded: 1986; *National Colours:* Blue shirts, red & white trim, white shorts, blue stockings.
Telephone: 005012 30641 or 30642; *Telex:* 102 FOREIGN BZ.

BERMUDA

The Bermuda Football Association, P.O. Box HM 745, Hamilton 5 HM CX.
Founded: 1928; *Number of Clubs:* 30; *Number of Players:* 1,947; *National Colours:* Blue shirts, white shorts, white stockings.
Telephone: 001809 2952199; *Cable:* FOOTBALL BERMUDA; *Telex:* 3441 BFA BA; *Fax:* 001809 2959773.

CANADA

The Canadian Soccer Association, 1600 James Naismith Drive, Gloucester, Ont. K1B 5N4.
Founded: 1912; *Number of Clubs:* 1,600; *Number of Players:* 224,290; *National Colours:* Red shirts, red shorts, red stockings.
Telephone: 001613 7485667; *Cable:* SOCCANADA OTTAWA; *Telex:* 0533350; *Fax:* 001613 7451938.

CAYMAN ISLANDS

Cayman Islands Football Association, PO Box 178, Georgetown, Grand Cayman, Cayman Islands W1.
Number of Clubs: 25; *Number of Players:* 875.
Telephone: 001809 9497339. *Fax:* 001809 9492337.

COSTA RICA

Federacion Costarricense De Futbol, Apartado 670-1000, Calle 40, Avda CTL I, San Jose.
Founded: 1921; *Number of Clubs:* 431; *Number of Players:* 12,429; *National Colours:* Red shirts, blue shorts, white stockings.
Telephone: 00506 2221544; *Cable:* FEDEFUTBOL SAN JOSE; *Telex:* 3394 DIDER CR; *Fax:* 00506 2552674.

CUBA

Asociacion De Futbol De Cuba, c/o Comite Olimpico Cubano, Calle 13 No. 601, Esq. C. Vedado, La Habana, ZP4.
Founded: 1924; *Number of Clubs:* 70; *Number of Players:* 12,900; *National Colours:* White shirts, blue shorts, white stockings.
Telephone: 00537 403581; *Cable:* FOOTBALL HABANA; *Telex:* 511332 INDER CU.

DOMINICA

Dominica Football Association, P.O. Box 372, Roseau, Commonwealth of Dominica.
Number of Clubs: 30; *Number of Players:* 500.
Telephone: 00180944 87545; *Fax:* 00180944 81111.

DOMINICAN REPUBLIC

Federacion Dominicana de Futbol, Apartado De Correos No. 1953, Santo Domingo.
Founded: 1953; *Number of Clubs:* 128; *Number of Players:* 10,706; *National Colours:* Blue shirts, white shorts, red stockings.
Telephone: 001809542 6923. *Cable:* FEDOFUTBOL SANTO DOMINGO. *Fax:* 001809547 5363.

EL SALVADOR

Federacion Salvadorena De Futbol, Av. J.M. Delgado, Col. Escalon, Centro Espanol, Apartado 1029, San Salvador.
Founded: 1936; *Number of Clubs:* 944; *Number of Players:* 21,294; *National Colours:* Blue shirts, blue shorts, blue stockings.
Telephone: 00503 237362; *Cable:* FESFUT SAN SALVADOR; *Fax:* 00503 235893; *Telex:* 20484 FESFUT SAL.

GRENADA

Grenada Football Association, St. Juilles Street, P.O. Box 326, Grenada, West Indies.
Founded: 1924; *Number of Clubs:* 15; *Number of Players:* 200; *National Colours:* Green & yellow shirts, red shorts, green & yellow stockings.
Telephone: 001809 4401986; *Cable:* GRENBALL GRENADA; *Telex:* 3431 CW BUR; *Fax:* 001809 4401986.

GUATEMALA

Federacion Nacional De Futbol De Guatemala C.A., 12 Calle 4-09, Zona 9, Tercer Nivel, Ciudad de Guatemala.
Founded: 1933; *Number of Clubs:* 1,611; *Number of Players:* 43,516; *National Colours:* White/blue diagonal striped shirts, blue shorts, white stockings.
Telephone: 005022 600908, 600928, 600938; *Fax:* 005022 600918; *Cable:* FEDFUTBOL GUATEMALA.

GUYANA

Guyana Football Association, P.O. Box 10727 Georgetown.
Founded: 1902; *Number of Clubs:* 103; *Number of Players:* 1,665; *National Colours:* Green & yellow shirts, black shorts, white & green stockings.
Telephone: 005922 59458/9; *Cable:* FOOTBALL GUYANA; *Telex:* 2266 RICEBRD GY; *Fax:* 005922 52169.

HAITI

Federation Haitienne De Football, P.O. Box 2258, Port-Au-Prince.
Founded: 1904; *Number of Clubs:* 40; *Number of Players:* 4,000; *National Colours:* Red shirts, black shorts, red stockings.
Telephone: 00509 46450910; *Fax:* 00509 1573001; *Cable:* FEDHAFOOB PORT-AU-PRINCE.

HONDURAS

Federacion Nacional Autonoma De Futbol De Honduras, Apartado Postal 827, Costa Oeste Del Est. Nac, Tegucigalpa, De. C.
Founded: 1951; *Number of Clubs:* 1,050; *Number of Players:* 15,300; *National Colours:* Blue shirts, blue shorts, blue stockings.
Telephone: 00504 321897; *Cable* FENAFUTH TEGUCIGALPA; *Telex:* 1209 FENEFUTH; *Fax:* 00504 311428.

JAMAICA

Jamaica Football Federation, Attn. Anthony James, President, Room 8 INSPORTS, Independence Park, Kingston 6.
Founded: 1910; *Number of Clubs:* 266; *Number of Players:* 45,200; *National Colours:* Green shirts, black shorts, green & gold stockings.
Telephone: 001809 9290483; *Fax:* 001809 9622858; *Telex:* 2224 FEDLASCO JA; *Cable:* FOOTBALL JAMAICA KINGSTON.

MEXICO

Federacion Mexicana De Futbol Asociacion, A.C., Abraham Gonzales 74, C.P. 06600, Col. Juarez, Mexico 6, D.F.
Founded: 1927; *Number of Clubs:* 77 (senior); *Number of Players:* 1,402,270; *National Colours:* Green shirts, white shorts, green stockings.
Telephone: 00525 5662155; *Cable:* MEXFUTBOL MEXICO; *Telex:* 1771678 MSUTME; *Fax:* 00525 5667580.

NETHERLANDS ANTILLES

Nederlands Antiliaanse Voetbal Unie, P.O. Box 341, Curacao, N.A.
Founded: 1921; *Number of Clubs:* 85; *Number of Players:* 4,500; *National Colours:* white shirts, white shorts, red stockings.
Telephone:Cable: NAVU CURACAO; *Telex:* 1046 ENNIA NA; *Fax:* 005999 611173.

NICARAGUA

Federacion Nicaraguense De Futbol, Inst. Nicaraguense De Deportes, Apartado Postal 976 6 383, Managua.
Founded: 1968; *Number of Clubs:* 31; *Number of Players:* 160 (senior); *National Colours:* Blue shirts, blue shorts, blue stockings.
Telephone/Fax: 005052 664134; *Cable:* FEDEFOOT MANAGUA; *Telex:* 2156 IND NK.

PANAMA

Federacion Nacional De Futbol De Panama, Apartado Postal 8-391, Zona 8, Panama.
Founded: 1937; *Number of Clubs:* 65; *Number of Players:* 4,225; *National Colours:* Red & white shirts, blue shorts, red stockings.
Telephone: 00507 2130935; *Cable:* PANAOLIMPIC PANAMA; *Telex:* 2534 INDE PG; *Fax:* 00507 2130936.

PUERTO RICO

Federacion Puertorriquena De Futbol, Coliseo Roberto Clemente, P.O. Box 4355, Hato Rey, 00919-4355.
Founded: 1940; *Number of Clubs:* 175; *Number of Players:* 4,200; *National Colurs:* White & red shirts, blue shorts, white & blue stockings.
Telephone/Fax: 001809 7642025; *Cable:* BORIKENFPF; *Telex:* 3450296.

SAINT LUCIA

St Lucia National Football Union, PO Box 255, Castries, St Lucia.
Number of Clubs: 100; *Number of Players:* 4,000; *National Colours:* Blue and white striped shirts, black shorts, blue stockings.
Telephone: 001809 31519; *Fax:* 001809 4524127; *Telex:* 6394 FOR AFF LC.

SAINT KITTS AND NEVIS

St Kitts and Nevis Football Association, P.O. Box 465, Basseterre, St Kitts, West Indies.
Number of Clubs: 36; *Number of Players:* 600.
Telephone: 001809 4652521/ 4654086; *Fax:* 001809 4655501/ 4651042.

SAINT VINCENT & THE GRENADINES

St Vincent & The Grenadines Football Federation, PO Box 1278, Kingstown, St Vincent.
Number of Clubs: 500; *Number of Players:* 5,000.
Telephone: 001809 4561525; *Fax:* 001809 4571659, 4571381.

SURINAM

Surinaamse Voetbal Bond, Cultuuruinlaan 7, P.O. Box 1223, Paramaribo.
Founded: 1920; *Number of Clubs:* 168; *Number of Players:* 4,430; *National Colours:* Red shirts, white shorts, white stockings.
Telephone: 00597 473112; *Fax:* 00597 465832; *Cable:* SVB Paramaribo.

TRINIDAD AND TOBAGO

Trinidad & Tobago Football Association, Petrotrin Savannah Building 9, Queen's Park West, P.O. Box 400, Port of Spain.
Founded: 1906; *Number of Clubs:* 124; *Number of Players:* 5,050; *National Colours:* Red shirts, black shorts, red stockings.
Telephone: 001809 6271011/1013. *Cable:* TRAFA PORT OF SPAIN; *Telex:* 22652 TRAFA WG; *Fax:* 001809 6271007.

USA

United States Soccer Federation, U.S. Soccer House, 1801-1811 S. Prairie Avenue, Chicago, Illinois 60616.
Founded: 1913; *Number of Clubs:* 7,000; *Number of Players:* 1,411,500; *National Colours:* White shirts, blue shorts, red stockings.
Telephone: 001312 5784678; *Telex:* 450024 US SOCCER FED; *Fax:* 001312 5784636.

OCEANIA

AUSTRALIA

Soccer Australia, Sydney Football Stadium, Driver Avenue, P.O. Box 175, Paddington NSW 2021.
Founded: 1961; *Number of Clubs:* 6,816; *Number of Players:* 433,957; *National Colours:* Gold shirts, green shorts, white stockings.
Telephone: 0061 2/3806099; *Cable:* FOOTBALL SYDNEY; *Fax:* 0061 2/3806155.

COOK ISLANDS

Cook Islands Football Federation, PO Box 473, Rarotonga, Cook Islands.
Number of Clubs: 9; *Number of Players:* – .
Telephone: 00682 29410; *Fax:* 00682 29610.

FIJI

Fiji Football Association, Mr. J.D. Maharaj, Hon. Secretary, Government Bldgs, P.O.Box 2514, Suva.
Founded: 1946; *Number of Clubs:* 140: *Number of Players:* 21,300; *National Colours:* White shirts, black shorts, black stockings.

Telephone: 00679 300453; *Cable:* FOOTSOCCER SUVA; *Telex:* 2366 FJ; *Fax:* 00679 304642.

NEW ZEALAND

Soccer New Zealand, P.O. Box 11.357, Ellerslie, Auckland.
Founded: 1891; *Number of Clubs:* 312; *Number of Players:* 52,969; *National Colours:* White shirts, black shorts, white stockings.
Telephone: 00649 5256120; *Fax:* 00649 5256123; *Telex:* NZ 63007 NZFAOFC.

PAPUA NEW GUINEA

Papua New Guinea Football (Soccer) Association Inc., c/o National Sports Institute, P.O. Box 337, Goroka, EHP.
Founded: 1962; *Number of Clubs:* 350; *Number of Players:* 8,250; *National Colours:* Red shirts, black shorts, red stockings.
Telephone: 00675 722391; *Telex:* TOTOTRA NE 23436; *Fax:* 00675 721941.

SOLOMAN ISLANDS

Soloman Islands Football Federation, PO Box 532, Honiara, Soloman Islands.
Number of Players: 4,000; *National Colours:* Blue shirts, white shorts, white stockings.
Telephone: 00677 23553; *Fax:* 00677 20391; *Telex:* HQ 66349.

TAHITI

Federation Tahitienne de Football, Attn. Napoleon Spitz, B.P. 650, Papeete, Tahiti, French Polynesia.
Founded: 1938; *National Colours:* Red shirts, white shorts, white stockings.
Telephone: 00689 420410; *Fax:* 00689 421479; *Telex:* 454 FP.

TONGA

Tonga Football Association, C/O Tonga Amateur Sports Association, P.O. Box 1278, Nuku'alofa, Tonga.

Number of Clubs: 23; *Number of Players:* 350.
Telephone: 00676 21041, 24661; *Fax:* 00676 24127.

VANUATU

Vanuatu Football Federation, P.O. Box 226, Port Vila, Vanuatu.
Founded: 1934; *National Colours:* Gold shirts, black shorts, gold stockings.
Telephone: 00678 22009; *Fax:* 00678 23579.

WESTERN SAMOA

Western Samoa Football (Soccer) Association, Min. of Youth, Sports Culture, Private Bag, Apia.
Founded: 1986; *National Colours:* Blue shirts, white shorts, blue and white stockings.
Telephone: 00685 21420; *Fax:* 00685 24166; *Telex:* 230 SAMGAMES SX.

AFRICA

ALGERIA

Federation Algerienne De Futbol, Route Ahmed Ouaked, Boite Postale No. 39, Alger _ Dely Ibrahim.
Founded: 1962; *Number of Clubs:* 780; *Number of Players:* 58,567; *National Colours:* Green shirts, white shorts, red stockings.
Telephone: 00213 799943; *Cable:* FAFOOT ALGER; *Telex:* 61378. *Fax:* 00213 366181.

ANGOLA

Federation Angolaise De Football, B.P. 3449, Luanda.
Founded: 1977; *Number of Clubs:* 276; *Number of Players:* 4,269; *National Colours:* Red shirts, black shorts, red stockings.
Telephone: 002442 338635/338233; *Cable:* FUTANGO-LA; *Telex:* 4072 CIAM AN.

BENIN

Federation Beninoise De Football, B.P. 965, Cotonou.
Founded: 1968; *Number of Clubs:* 117; *Number of Players:* 6,700; *National Colours:* Green shirts, green shorts, green stockings.
Telephone: 00229 330537; *Cable:* FEBEFOOT COTO-NOU K; *Telex:* 5033 BIMEX COTONOU; *Fax:* 00229 312485.

BOTSWANA

Botswana Football Association, P.O. Box 1396, Gabarone.
Founded: 1976; *National Colours:* Sky blue shirts, white shorts, sky blue stockings.
Telephone: 00267 300279; *Cable:* BOTSBALL GABARONE; *Telex:* 2977 BD; *Fax:* 00267 372911.

BURKINA FASO

Federation Burkinabe De Foot-Ball, B.P. 57, Ouagadougou.
Founded: 1960; *Number of Clubs:* 57; *Number of Players:* 4,672; *National Colours:* Black shirts, white shorts, red stockings.
Telephone: 00226 302850; *Cable:* FEDEFOOT OUA-GADOUGOU.

BURUNDI

Federation De Football Du Burundi, B.P. 3426, Bujumbura.
Founded: 1948; *Number of Clubs:* 132; *Number of Players:* 3,930; *National Colours:* Red shirts, white shorts, green stockings.
Telephone: 00257 225160; *Fax:* 00257 212891 or 211431; *Cable:* FFB BUJA.

CAMEROON

Federation Camerounaise De Football, B.P. 1116, Yaounde.
Founded: 1960; *Number of Clubs:* 200; *Number of Players:* 9,328; *National Colours:* Green shirts, red shorts, yellow stockings.
Telephone: 00237 202538; *Cable:* FECAFOOT YAOUNDE; *Telex:* 8568 JEUNESPO KN.

CAPE VERDE ISLANDS

Federacao Cabo-Verdiana De Futebol, P.O. Box 234, Praia.
Founded: 1986; *National Colours:* Green shirts, green shorts, green stockings.
Telephone: 00238 611362; *Fax:* 00238 611362; *Cable:* FCF-CV; *Telex:* 6005 acs cv.

CENTRAL AFRICAN REPUBLIC

Federation Centrafricaine De Football, B.P. 344, Bangui.
Founded: 1937; *Number of Clubs:* 256; *Number of Players:* 7,200; *National Colours:* Grey & blue shirts, white shorts, red stockings.
Telephone: 00236 612433 or 611917; *Fax:* 00236 611637 or 610042; *Cable:* FOOTBANGUI BANGUI.

CONGO

Federation Congolaise De Football, B.P. 4041, Brazzaville.
Founded: 1962; *Number of Clubs:* 250; *Number of Players:* 5,940; *National Colours:* Red shirts, red shorts, white stockings.
Telephone: 00242 834885, 835306, 828736, 820582; *Cable:* FECOFOOT BRAZZAVILLE; *Telex:* 5210 KG; *Fax:* 00242 820582, 836464.

DJIBOUTI

Federation Djiboutienne de Football, B.P. 1916, Djibouti.
Number of Players: 2,000.
Fax: 00253 356830.

EGYPT

Egyptian Football Association, 5, Shareh Gabalaya, Guezira, Al Borg Post Office, Cairo.
Founded: 1921; *Number of Clubs:* 247; *Number of Players:* 19,735; *National Colours:* Red shirts, white shorts, black stockings.
Telephone: 00202 3401793; *Cable:* KORA CAIRO; *Fax:* 00202 3417817; *Telex:* 93504 kora un.

ETHIOPIA

Ethiopia Football Federation, Addis Ababa Stadium, P.O. Box 1080, Addis Ababa.
Founded: 1943; *Number of Clubs:* 767; *Number of Players:* 20,594; *National Colours:* Green shirts, yellow shorts, red stockings.
Telephone: 002511 514453/514321. *Cable:* FOOTBALL ADDIS ABABA; *Fax:* 002511 513345; *Telex:* 21377 NESCO ET.

GABON

Federation Gabonaise De Football, B.P. 181, Libreville.
Founded: 1962; *Number of Clubs:* 320; *Number of Players:* 10,000; *National Colours:* Blue shirts, white shorts, white stockings.
Telephone: 00241 744747; *Cable:* FEGAFOOT LIBRE-VILLE; *Telex:* 5642 GO.

GAMBIA

Gambia Football Association, Independence Stadium, Bakau, P.O. Box 523, Banjul.
Founded: 1952; *Number of Clubs:* 30; *Number of Players:* 860; *National Colours:* White & red shirts, white shorts, white stockings.
Telephone: 00220 95834; *Cable:* SPORTS GAMBIA BANJUL; *Fax:* 00220 29837; *Telex:* 2262 FISCO GV.

GHANA

Ghana Football Association, P.O. Box 1272, Accra.
Founded: 1957; *Number of Clubs:* 347; *Number of Players:* 11,275; *National Colours:* White shirts, white shorts, white stockings.
Telephone: 0023321 663924; *Cable:* GFA, ACCRA; *Fax:* 0023321 21662; *Telex:* 2519 SPORTS GH.

GUINEA

Federation Guineenne De Football, P.O. Box 3645, Conakry.
Founded: 1959; *Number of Clubs:* 351; *Number of Players:* 10,000; *National Colours:* Red shirts, yellow shorts, green stockings.
Telephone: 00224 445041; *Cable:* GUINEFOOT CONAKRY; *Telex:* 22302 MJ GE; Fax: 00224 442781.

GUINEA-BISSAU

Federacao De Football Da Guinea-Bissau, Rua4 No. 10-C, Apartado 375, 1035 Bissau Codex.
Founded: 1986; *National Colours:* Green shirts, green shorts, green stockings.
Telephone: 00245 201918; *Cable:* FUTEBOL BISSAU; *Telex:* 205 PUBLICO BI.

GUINEA, EQUATORIAL

Federacion Ecuatoguineana De Futbol, Malabo.
Founded: 1986; *National Colours:* All red.
Telephone: 00240 26523; *Telex:* 9991111 EG; *Cable:* FEGUIFUT/MALABO.

IVORY COAST

Federation Ivoirienne De Football, Stade Felix Houphouet Boigny, B.P. 1202, Abidjan.
Founded: 1960; *Number of Clubs:* 84 (senior); *Number of Players:* 3,655; *National Colours:* Orange shirts, white shorts, green stockings.
Telephone: 00225 242301; *Cable:* FIF ABIDJAN; *Telex:* 42344 FIF CI; *Fax:* 00225 244308.

KENYA

Kenya Football Federation, Nyayo National Stadium, P.O. Box 40234, Nairobi.
Founded: 1960; *Number of Clubs:* 351; *Number of Players:* 8,880; *National Colours:* Red shirts, red shorts, red stockings.
Telephone: 002542 501853; *Cable:* KEFF NAIROBI; *Fax:* 002542 501120; *Telex:* 25784 KFF.

LESOTHO

Lesotho Sports Council, P.O. Box 138, Maseru 100, Lesotho.
Founded: 1932; *Number of Clubs:* 88; *Number of Players:* 2,076; *National Colours:* Blue shirts, green shorts, white stockings.
Telephone: 00266 311291; *Cable:* LIPAPALI MASERU; *Fax:* 00266 310914; *Telex:* 4493.

LIBERIA

The Liberia Football Association, P.O. Box 1066, Monrovia 10.
Founded: 1962; *National Colours:* Blue & white shirts, white shorts, blue & white stockings.
Telephone: 00231 225947; *Cable:* LIBFOTASS MONROVIA; *Telex:* 44508 IFA LI. *Fax:* 00231 735003.

LIBYA

Libyan Arab Jamahiriya Football Federation, P.O. Box 5137, Tripoli.
Founded: 1963; *Number of Clubs:* 89; *Number of Players:* 2,941; *National Colours:* Green shirts, white shorts, green stockings.
Telephone: 0021821 46610; *Telex:* 20896 KURATP LY. *Fax:* 0021821 607016.

MADAGASCAR

Federation Malagasy De Football, c/o Comite Nat. De Coordination De Football, B.P. 4409, Antananarivo 101.
Founded: 1961; *Number of Clubs:* 775; *Number of Players:* 23,536; *National Colours:* Red shirts, white shorts, green stockings.
Telephone: 002612 28051; *Telex:* 22265 arosur mg; *Fax:* 00261 1/34464.

MALAWI

Football Association of Malawi, P.O. Box 865, Blantyre.
Founded: 1966; *Number of Clubs:* 465; *Number of Players:* 12,500; *National Colours:* Red shirts, red shorts, red stockings.
Telephone: 00265 636686; *Cable:* FOOTBALL BLANTYRE; *Telex:* 4526 SPORTS MI. *Fax:* 00265 636941.

MALI

Federation Malienne De Football, Stade Mamdou Konate, B.P. 1020, Bamako.
Founded: 1960; *Number of Clubs:* 128; *Number of Players:* 5,480; *National Colours:* Green shirts, yellow shorts, red stockings.
Telephone: 00223 224152; *Cable:* MALIFOOT BAMAKO; Telex: 1200/1202.

MAURITANIA

Federation De Foot-Ball De La Rep. Isl. De Mauritanie, B.P. 566, Nouakshott.
Founded: 1961; *Number of Clubs:* 59; *Number of Players:* 1,930; *National Colours:* Green and yellow shirts, blue shorts, green stockings.
Telephone/Fax: 00222 259057; *Telex:* 577 MTN NKTT RIM; *Cable:* FOOTRIM NOUAKSHOTT.

MAURITIUS

Mauritius Football Association, Chancery House, 14 Lislet Geoffroy Street, (2nd Floor, Nos. 303.305), Port Louis.
Founded: 1952; *Number of Clubs:* 397; *Number of Players:* 29,375; *National Colours:* Red shirts, white shorts, red stockings.
Telephone: 00230 2121418, 2125771; *Cable:* MFA PORT LOUIS; *Telex:* 4427 MSA IW; *Fax:* 00230 2084100.

MOROCCO

Federation Royale Marocaine De Football, Av. Ibn Sina, C.N.S. Bellevue, B.P. 51, Rabat.
Founded: 1955; *Number of Clubs:* 350; *Number of Players:* 19,768; *National Colours:* Red shirts, green shorts, red stockings.
Telephone: 002127 672706/08 or 67 26 07; *Cable:* FERMAFOOT RABAT; *Telex:* 32940 FERMFOOT M. *Fax:* 002127 671070

MOZAMBIQUE

Federacao Mocambicana De Futebol, Av. Samora Machel, 11-2, Caixa Postal 1467, Maputo.
Founded: 1978; *Number of Clubs:* 144; *National Colours:* Red shirts, red shorts, red stockings.
Telephone: 002581 26475; *Cable:* MOCAMBOLA MAPUTO; *Telex:* 6575 PERCO MO.

NAMIBIA

Namibia Football Federation, PO Box 1345, Independance Avenue, Juvenis Building – First Floor Windhoek, Namibia.
Number of Clubs: 244; *Number of Players:* 7320.
Telephone: 0026461 249441, 249442; *Fax:* 0026461 249442.

NIGER

Federation Nigerienne De Football, Stade du 29 Juillet, B.P. 10299, Niamey.
Founded: 1967; *Number of Clubs:* 64; *Number of Players:* 1,525; *National Colours:* Orange shirts, white shorts, green stockings.
Telephone: 00227 734705; *Fax:* 00227 735512; *Telex:* 5527 or 5349; *Cable:* FEDERFOOT NIGER NIAMEY.

NIGERIA

Nigeria Football Association National Sports Commission, National Stadium, P.O. Box 466, Lagos.

Founded: 1945; *Number of Clubs:* 326; *Number of Players:* 80,190; *National Colours:* Green shirts, white shorts, green stockings.
Telephone: 002341 5851970, 5851971, 5856268; *Cable:* FOOTBALL LAGOS; *Telex:* 26570 NFA NG; *Fax:* 002341 824912, 5451971, 263223, 2635847.

PALESTINE

Palestinian Football Federation, P.O. Box 98, Jerico.
Fax: 00972 2/922 304.

RWANDA

Federation Rwandaise De Foot-Ball Amateur, B.P. 2000, Kigali.
Founded: 1972; *Number of Clubs:* 167; *National Colours:* Red shirts, red shorts, red stockings.
Telephone: 00250 82605; *Cable:* MIJENCOOP KIGALI; *Telex:* 22504 PUBLIC RW; *Fax:* 00250 76574.

SENEGAL

Federation Senegalaise De Football, Stade De L'Amitie, Route De L'Aeroport De Yoff, B.P. 130 21, Dakar.
Founded: 1960; *Number of Clubs:* 75 (senior); *Number of Players:* 3,977; *National Colours:* Green shirts, yellow shorts, red stockings.
Telephone: 00221 243524; *Fax:* 00221 220241; *Telex:* 21741; *Cable:* SENEFOOT DAKAR.

SEYCHELLES

Seychelles Football Federation, P.O. Box 843, People's Stadium, Victoria-Mahe, Seychelles.
Founded: 1986; *National Colours:* Green shirts, yellow shorts, red stockings.
Telephone: 00248 323908; *Telex:* 2240 CULSPT SZ; *Fax:* 00248 323518.

ST. THOMAS AND PRINCIPE

Federation Santomense De Fut., P.O. Box 42, Sao Tome.
Founded: 1986; *National Colours:* Green shirts, green shorts, green stockings.
Telephone: 0023912 22311; *Telex:* 213 PUBLICO STP.

SIERRA LEONE

Sierra Leone Amateur Football Association, Siaka Stevens Stadium, Brookfields, P.O. Box 672, Freetown.
Founded: 1967; *Number of Clubs:* 104; *Number of Players:* 8,120; *National Colours:* Green shirts, white shorts, blue stockings.
Telephone: 0023222 41872; *Cable:* SLAFA FREETOWN; *Telex:* 3210 BOOTH SL. *Fax:* 0023222 224439.

SOMALIA

Somali Football Federation, C/O CAF, 5 Gabalaya Street, 11567, El Borg, Cairo, Egypt.
Founded: 1951; *Number of Clubs:* 46 (senior); *Number of Players:* 1,150; *National Colours:* Sky blue shirts, white shorts, white stockings.
Telephone: 0020 2/3412497; *Cable:* SOMALIA FOOTBALL CAIRO; *Telex:* 93162 caf un; *Fax:* 0020 2/3420114.

SOUTH AFRICA

South African Football Association, First National Bank Stadium, Nasrec; PO Box 910, Johannesburg 2000; South Africa.
Number of Teams: 51,944; *Number of Players:* 1,039,880.
Telephone: 002711 4943522; Fax: 002711 4943447.

SUDAN

Sudan Football Association, P.O. Box 437, Khartoum.
Founded: 1936; *Number of Clubs:* 750; *Number of Players:* 42,200; *National Colours:* White shirts, white shorts, white stockings.
Telephone: 0024911 776633 or 773786; *Cable:* ALKOURA,

KHARTOUM; *Fax:* 0024911 781160; *Telex:* 23007 KORA SD.

SWAZILAND

National Football Association of Swaziland, P.O. Box 641, Mbabane.
Founded: 1976; *Number of Clubs:* 136; *National Colours:* Blue and gold shirts, white shorts, blue and gold stockings.
Telephone: 00268 46852; *Telex:* 2245 EXP WD.

TANZANIA

Football Association of Tanzania, P.O. Box 1574, Dar Es Salaam.
Founded: 1930; *Number of Clubs:* 51; *National Colours:* Yellow shirts, yellow shorts, yellow stockings.
Telephone: 0025551 32334; *Telex:* 41873 TZ; *Cable:* FAT DAR ES SALAAM.

TOGO

Federation Togolaise De Football, C.P. 5, Lome.
Founded: 1960; *Number of Clubs:* 144; *Number of Players:* 4,346; *National Colours:* Red shirts, white shorts, red stockings.
Telephone: 00228 21412; *Cable:* TOGOFOOT LOME; *Telex:* 5015 CNOT TG. *Fax:* 00228 221413.

TUNISIA

Federation Tunisienne De Football, 2 rue Hamza Abderlmottaleb, El-Menzah VI, Tunis 1004.
Founded: 1957; *Number of Clubs:* 215; *Number of Players:* 18,300; *National Colours:* Red shirts, white shorts, red stockings.
Telephone: 002161 233303, 233544; *Cable:* FOOTBALL TUNIS; *Fax:* 002161 767929; *Telex:* 14783 FTFOOT TN.

UGANDA

Federation of Uganda Football Associations, P.O. Box 20077, Kampala, Uganda.
Founded: 1924; *Number of Clubs:* 400; *Number of Players:* 1,518; *National Colours:* Yellow shirts, black shorts, yellow stockings.
Telephone: 0025641 254477; *Cable:* FUFA KAMPALA; *Telex:* 61605; *Fax:* 0025641 258350; *Telegrams:* fufa lugogo stadium.

ZAIRE

Federation Zairoise De Football-Association, P.O. Box 1284, rue Dima No. 10, Kinshasa 1.
Founded: 1919; *Number of Clubs:* 3,800; *Number of Players:* 64,627; *National Colours:* Green shirts, yellow shorts, yellow stockings. *Cable:* FEZAFA KINSHASA; *Telex:* 63915. *Fax:* 0024312 506555.

ZAMBIA

Football Association of Zambia, P.O. Box 347 51, Lusaka.
Founded: 1929; *Number of Clubs:* 20 (senior); *Number of Players:* 4,100; *National Colours:* Green shirts, white shorts, black stockings.
Telephone: 002601 221145; *Cable:* FOOTBALL LUSAKA; *Telex:* 40204 FAZ ZA; *Fax:* 002601 225046.

ZIMBABWE

Zimbabwe Football Association, P.O. Box 8343, Causeway, Harare.
Founded: 1965; *National Colours:* White shirts, black shorts, black stockings.
Telephone: 002634 754933/6; *Cable:* SOCCER HARARE; *Telex:* 22299 SOCCER ZW; *Fax:* 00263 4/751470.

Other addition: CHAD (readmitted).

THE WORLD CUP 1930–94

Year	Winners		Runners-up		Venue	Attendance	Referee
1930	Uruguay	4	Argentina	2	Montevideo	90,000	Langenus (B)
1934	Italy	2	Czechoslovakia	1	Rome	50,000	Eklind (Se)
	(after extra time)						
1938	Italy	4	Hungary	2	Paris	45,000	Capdeville (F)
1950	Uruguay	2	Brazil	1	Rio de Janeiro	199,854	Reader (E)
1954	West Germany	3	Hungary	2	Berne	60,000	Ling (E)
1958	Brazil	5	Sweden	2	Stockholm	49,737	Guigue (F)
1962	Brazil	3	Czechoslovakia	1	Santiago	68,679	Latychev (USSR)
1966	England	4	West Germany	2	Wembley	93,802	Dienst (Sw)
	(after extra time)						
1970	Brazil	4	Italy	1	Mexico City	107,412	Glockner (EG)
1974	West Germany	2	Holland	1	Munich	77,833	Taylor (E)
1978	Argentina	3	Holland	1	Buenos Aires	77,000	Gonella (I)
	(after extra time)						
1982	Italy	3	West Germany	1	Madrid	90,080	Coelho (Br)
1986	Argentina	3	West Germany	2	Mexico City	114,580	Filho (Br)
1990	West Germany	1	Argentina	0	Rome	73,603	Codesal (Mex)
1994	Brazil	0	Italy	0	Los Angeles	94,194	Puhl (Hungary)

(Brazil won 3-2 on penalties aet)

GOALSCORING AND ATTENDANCES IN WORLD CUP FINAL ROUNDS

Venue	Matches	Goals (avge)	Attendance (avge)
1930, Uruguay	18	70 (3.9)	434,500 (24,138)
1934, Italy	17	70 (4.1)	395,000 (23,235)
1938, France	18	84 (4.6)	483,000 (26,833)
1950, Brazil	22	88 (4.0)	1,337,000 (60,772)
1954, Switzerland	26	140 (5.4)	943,000 (36,270)
1958, Sweden	35	126 (3.6)	868,000 (24,800)
1962, Chile	32	89 (2.8)	776,000 (24,250)
1966, England	32	89 (2.8)	1,614,677 (50,458)
1970, Mexico	32	95 (2.9)	1,673,975 (52,311)
1974, West Germany	38	97 (2.5)	1,774,022 (46,684)
1978, Argentina	38	102 (2.7)	1,610,215 (42,374)
1982, Spain	52	146 (2.8)	2,064,364 (38,816)
1986, Mexico	52	132 (2.5)	2,441,731 (46,956)
1990, Italy	52	115 (2.2)	2,515,168 (48,368)
1994, USA	52	141 (2.7)	3,567,415 (68,604)

LEADING GOALSCORERS

Year	Player	Goals
1930	Guillermo Stabile (Argentina)	8
1934	Angelo Schiavio (Italy)	
	Oldrich Nejedly (Czechoslovakia)	
	Edmund Conen (Germany)	4
1938	Leonidas da Silva (Brazil)	8
1950	Ademir (Brazil)	9
1954	Sandor Kocsis (Hungary)	11
1958	Just Fontaine (France)	13
1962	Drazen Jerkovic (Yugoslavia)	5
1966	Eusebio (Portugal)	9
1970	Gerd Muller (West Germany)	10
1974	Grzegorz Lato (Poland)	7
1978	Mario Kempes (Argentina)	6
1982	Paolo Rossi (Italy)	6
1986	Gary Lineker (England)	6
1990	Salvatore Schillaci (Italy)	6
1994	Oleg Salenko (Russia)	
	Hristo Stoichkov (Bulgaria)	6

1998 FIFA WORLD CUP

Qualifying draw for France 1998

OCEANIA (Members 10, Entries 10)
Either one or no team qualifies.

First Round (League System + 1 play-off match)
Melanesian Group: Papua New Guinea, Soloman Islands, Vanuatu;
Polynesian Group: Cook Islands, Tonga, Western Samoa.

Second Round (League System)
Group 1: Australia, Tahiti, winner of first Polynesian group and second in Melanesian group.
Group 2: New Zealand, Fiji, winner of the Melanesian group.

Third Round (Cup System)
Winner of group 1 v winner of group 2.
Third Round Winner plays team finishing fourth in Asia.

ASIA (Members 41 + 1, Entries 36)
Three or four teams qualify.

First Round (League System)
Group 1: Saudi Arabia, Malaysia, Bangladesh, Taiwan;
Group 2: Iran, Syria, Maldives, Kyrgyzstan;
Group 3: United Arab Emirates, Bahrain, Jordan;
Group 4: Japan, Oman, Nepal, Macao;
Group 5: Uzbekistan, Indonesia, Yemen, Cambodia;
Group 6: Korea Republic, Thailand, Hong Kong;
Group 7: Kuwait, Lebanon, Singapore;
Group 8: China, Turkmenistan, Vietnam, Tajikistan;
Group 9: Iraq, Kazakhstan, Pakistan;
Group 10: Qatar, India, Sri Lanka, Philippines.

Second Round (League System)
Two groups of five teams.

Third Round (Cup System)
Group winners and runners-up qualify for the semi-finals. The winners qualify for the finals, the losers compete in a play-off, the winner qualifying for the finals, the losing team meets the winners of the Oceania zone.

CONCACAF (Members 30, Entries 30, including 2 late entries Bermuda and Cuba)
Three teams qualify.

First Round (Cup System – Caribbean zone)
Dominican Republic 3, Aruba 2; Aruba 1, Dominican Republic 3; Bahamas withdrew v St Kitts & Nevis w.o.; Guyana 1, Grenada 2; Grenada 6, Guyana 0; Dominica 3, Antigua 3; Antigua 1, Dominica 3.

Second Round (Cup System – Caribbean zone)
Bermuda withdrew v Trinidad & Tobago w.o.; Puerto Rico 1, St Vincent & the Grenadines 2; St Vincent & the Grenadines 7, Puerto Rico 0; Cuba 1, Cayman Islands 0; Cayman Islands 0, Cuba 5; St Kitts & Nevis 5, St Lucia 1; St Lucia 0, St Kitts & Nevis 1; Haiti 6, Grenada 1; Grenada 0, Haiti 1; Surinam 0, Jamaica 1; Jamaica 1, Surinam 0; Dominica 0, Barbados1; Barbados 1, Dominica 0; Dominican Republic 2, Netherlands Antilles 1; Netherlands Antilles 0, Dominican Republic 0.

Third Round (Cup System – Caribbean zone)
Cuba 5, Haiti 1; Haiti 1, Cuba 1; Dominican Republic 1, Trinidad & Tobago 4; Jamaica 2, Jamaica 2, Barbados 0; St Kitts & Nevis 2, St Vincent 2; St Vincent 0, St Kitts & Nevis 0.

First Round (Cup System – Central American zone)
Nicaragua 0, Guatemala 1; Guatemala 2, Nicaragua 1; Belize 1, Panama 2; Panama 4, Belize 1.

Semi-final Round (League System)
Group 1: USA, Costa Rica, first Caribbean winner, winner of Nicaragua v Guatemala.
Group 2: Canada, El Salvador, winner of Belize v Panama, second Caribbean winner.
Group 3: Mexico, Honduras, winner of third Caribbean group, winner of fourth Caribbean group.

Final Round (League System)
The three winners and three runners-up form one group with the first three teams qualifying for the finals.

SOUTH AMERICA (Members 10, Entries 10)
Five teams qualify including Brazil as champions.
The nine competing teams play each other twice, the first four qualifying for the finals.

AFRICA (Members 51, Entries 38, Withdrawals 2)
Five teams qualify.

First Round (Cup System)
Sudan 2, Zambia 0; Namibia 2, Mozambique 0; Tanzania 0, Ghana 0; Swaziland 0, Gabon 1; Uganda 0, Angola 2; Mauritius 1, Zaire 5; Malawi 0, South Africa 1; Madagascar 1, Zimbabwe 2; Guinea-Bissau 3, Guinea 2; Rwanda 1, Tunisia 3; Congo 2, Ivory Coast 0; Kenya 3, Algeria 1; Burundi 1, Sierra Leone 0; Mauritania 0, Burkina Faso 0; Togo 2, Senegal 1; Gambia 2, Liberia 1.

Second Round (League System)
The sixteen winners plus Cameroon, Nigeria, Egypt and Morocco are divided into five groups of four teams. The group winners qualify for the finals.

EUROPE (Members 49 + 1, Entries 50)
Fifteen teams qualify including France as the host nation. The nine group winners and the best runner-up qualify. The eight other runners-up will be drawn in pairs, the four winners also qualifying for the final.

Group 1
Denmark, Greece, Croatia, Slovenia, Bosnia-Herzegovina.

24.04.96	Greece v Slovenia
01.09.96	Greece v Bosnia-Herzegovina
01.09.96	Slovenia v Denmark
09.10.96	Denmark v Greece
09.10.96	Bosnia-Herzegovina v Croatia
10.11.96	Croatia v Greece
29.03.97	Croatia v Denmark
02.04.97	Croatia v Slovenia
02.04.97	Bosnia-Herzegovina v Greece
30.04.97	Denmark v Slovenia
30.04.97	Greece v Croatia
08.06.97	Denmark v Bosnia-Herzegovina
20.08.97	Bosnia-Herzegovina v Denmark
06.09.97	Croatia v Bosnia-Herzegovina
10.09.97	Denmark v Croatia
10.09.97	Bosnia-Herzegovina v Slovenia
11.10.97	Greece v Denmark
11.10.97	Slovenia v Croatia

Group 2
Italy, England, Poland, Georgia, Moldova.

01.09.96	Moldova v England
05.10.96	Moldova v Italy
09.10.96	England v Poland
09.10.96	Italy v Georgia
09.11.96	Georgia v England
10.11.96	Poland v Moldova
12.02.97	England v Italy
29.03.97	Italy v Moldova
02.04.97	Poland v Italy
30.04.97	England v Georgia
30.04.97	Italy v Poland
07.06.97	Georgia v Moldova
14.06.97	Poland v Georgia
10.09.97	England v Moldova
10.09.97	Georgia v Italy
24.09.97	Moldova v Georgia
07.10.97	Moldova v Poland
11.10.97	Italy v England
11.10.97	Georgia v Poland

Group 3
Norway, Switzerland, Finland, Hungary, Azerbaijan

02.06.96	Norway v Azerbaijan
31.08.96	Azerbaijan v Switzerland
01.09.96	Hungary v Switzerland
06.10.96	Finland v Switzerland
09.10.96	Norway v Hungary
10.11.96	Switzerland v Norway
10.11.96	Azerbaijan v Hungary

02.04.97	Azerbaijan v Finland
30.04.97	Norway v Finland
30.04.97	Switzerland v Hungary
08.06.97	Finland v Azerbaijan
08.06.97	Hungary v Norway
20.08.97	Finland v Norway
20.08.97	Hungary v Switzerland
06.09.97	Switzerland v Finland
06.09.97	Azerbaijan v Norway
10.09.97	Hungary v Azerbaijan
10.09.97	Norway v Switzerland
11.10.97	Finland v Hungary
11.10.97	Switzerland v Azerbaijan

Group 4
Sweden, Scotland, Austria, Latvia, Belarus, Estonia

01.06.96	Sweden v Belarus
31.08.96	Austria v Scotland
31.08.96	Belarus v Estonia
01.09.96	Latvia v Sweden
05.10.96	Estonia v Belarus
05.10.96	Latvia v Scotland
09.10.96	Sweden v Austria
09.10.96	Estonia v Scotland
09.10.96	Belarus v Latvia
09.11.96	Austria v Latvia
10.11.96	Scotland v Sweden
29.03.97	Scotland v Estonia
02.04.97	Scotland v Austria
30.04.97	Austria v Estonia
30.04.97	Sweden v Scotland
30.04.97	Latvia v Belarus
18.05.97	Estonia v Latvia
08.06.97	Estonia v Sweden
08.06.97	Latvia v Austria
08.06.97	Belarus v Scotland
20.08.97	Estonia v Austria
20.08.97	Belarus v Sweden
06.09.97	Austria v Sweden
06.09.97	Scotland v Belarus
06.09.97	Latvia v Estonia
10.09.97	Sweden v Latvia
10.09.97	Belarus v Austria
11.10.97	Austria v Belarus
11.10.97	Scotland v Latvia
11.10.97	Sweden v Estonia

Group 5
Russia, Bulgaria, Israel, Cyprus, Luxembourg

01.09.96	Israel v Bulgaria
01.09.96	Russia v Cyprus
08.10.96	Luxembourg v Bulgaria
09.10.96	Israel v Russia
10.11.96	Cyprus v Israel
10.11.96	Luxembourg v Russia
14.12.96	Cyprus v Bulgaria
15.12.96	Israel v Luxembourg
29.03.97	Cyprus v Russia
30.03.97	Luxembourg v Israel
02.04.97	Bulgaria v Cyprus
03.04.97	Israel v Cyprus
30.04.97	Russia v Luxembourg
08.06.97	Bulgaria v Luxembourg
08.06.97	Russia v Israel
20.08.97	Bulgaria v Israel
07.09.97	Luxembourg v Cyprus
10.09.97	Bulgaria v Russia
11.10.97	Cyprus v Luxembourg
11.10.97	Russia v Bulgaria

Group 6
Spain, Czech Republic, Slovakia, Yugoslavia, Malta, Faeroe Islands

24.04.96	Yugoslavia v Faeroes
02.06.96	Yugoslavia v Malta
31.08.96	Faeroes v Slovakia
04.09.96	Faeroes v Spain
18.09.96	Czech Republic v Malta
22.09.96	Slovakia v Malta
06.10.96	Faeroes v Yugoslavia
09.10.96	Czech Republic v Spain
23.10.96	Slovakia v Faeroes
10.11.96	Yugoslavia v Czech Republic
13.11.96	Spain v Slovakia
14.12.96	Spain v Yugoslavia
18.12.96	Malta v Spain
12.02.97	Spain v Malta

31.03.97	Malta v Slovakia
02.04.97	Czech Republic v Yugoslavia
30.04.97	Yugoslavia v Spain
30.04.97	Malta v Faeroes
21.05.97	Slovakia v Czech Republic
08.06.97	Yugoslavia v Slovakia
08.06.97	Faeroes v Malta
08.06.97	Spain v Czech Republic
20.08.97	Czech Republic v Faeroes
06.09.97	Faeroes v Czech Republic
10.09.97	Slovakia v Yugoslavia
24.09.97	Malta v Czech Republic
24.09.97	Slovakia v Spain
11.10.97	Malta v Yugoslavia
11.10.97	Czech Republic v Slovakia
11.10.97	Spain v Faeroes

Group 7
Holland, Belgium, Turkey, Wales, San Marino

02.06.96	San Marino v Wales
31.08.96	Belgium v Turkey
31.08.96	Wales v San Marino
05.10.96	Wales v Netherlands
09.10.96	San Marino v Belgium
09.11.96	Netherlands v Wales
10.11.96	Turkey v San Marino
14.12.96	Belgium v Netherlands
20.03.97	Netherlands v San Marino
29.03.97	Wales v Belgium
02.04.97	Turkey v Netherlands
30.04.97	Turkey v Belgium
30.04.97	San Marino v Netherlands
07.06.97	Belgium v San Marino
20.08.97	Turkey v Wales
06.09.97	Netherlands v Belgium
10.09.97	San Marino v Turkey
11.10.97	Belgium v Wales
11.10.97	Netherlands v Turkey

Group 8
Romania, Republic of Ireland, Lithuania, Iceland, Macedonia, Liechtenstein

24.04.96	Macedonia v Lichtenstein
01.06.96	Iceland v Macedonia
31.08.96	Liechtenstein v Republic of Ireland
31.08.96	Romania v Lithuania
05.10.96	Lithuania v Iceland
09.10.96	Iceland v Romania
09.10.96	Republic of Ireland v Macedonia
09.10.96	Lithuania v Liechtenstein
09.11.96	Liechtenstein v Macedonia
10.11.96	Republic of Ireland v Iceland
14.12.96	Macedonia v Romania
29.03.97	Romania v Liechtenstein
02.04.97	Lithuania v Romania
02.04.97	Macedonia v Republic of Ireland
30.04.97	Liechtenstein v Lithuania
30.04.97	Romania v Republic of Ireland
07.06.97	Republic of Ireland v Liechtenstein
07.06.97	Macedonia v Iceland
11.06.97	Iceland v Lithuania
19.08.97	Liechtenstein v Iceland
20.08.97	Republic of Ireland v Lithuania
20.08.97	Romania v Macedonia
06.09.97	Iceland v Republic of Ireland
06.09.97	Liechtenstein v Romania
06.09.97	Lithuania v Macedonia
10.09.97	Romania v Iceland
10.09.97	Lithuania v Republic of Ireland
11.10.97	Iceland v Liechtenstein
11.10.97	Republic of Ireland v Romania
11.10.97	Macedonia v Lithuania

Group 9
Germany, Portugal, Northern Ireland, Ukraine, Albania, Armenia

31.08.96	Northern Ireland v Ukraine
31.08.96	Armenia v Portugal
05.10.96	Northern Ireland v Armenia
05.10.96	Ukraine v Portugal
09.10.96	Albania v Portugal
09.10.96	Armenia v Germany
09.11.96	Albania v Armenia
09.11.96	Germany v Northern Ireland
09.11.96	Portugal v Ukraine
14.12.96	Northern Ireland v Albania
14.12.96	Portugal v Germany

29.03.97	Albania v Ukraine
29.03.97	Northern Ireland v Portugal
02.04.97	Albania v Germany
02.04.97	Ukraine v Northern Ireland
30.04.97	Germany v Ukraine
30.04.97	Armenia v Northern Ireland
07.05.97	Ukraine v Armenia
07.06.97	Portugal v Albania
07.06.97	Ukraine v Germany
20.08.97	Northern Ireland v Germany
20.08.97	Portugal v Armenia
20.08.97	Ukraine v Albania
06.09.97	Germany v Portugal
06.09.97	Armenia v Albania
10.09.97	Albania v Northern Ireland
10.09.97	Germany v Armenia
11.10.97	Germany v Albania
11.10.97	Portugal v Northern Ireland
11.10.97	Armenia v Ukraine

SOUTH AMERICA

24.04.96	Argentina v Bolivia, Venezuela v Uruguay, Colombia v Paraguay, Ecuador v Peru.
02.06.96	Ecuador v Argentina, Uruguay v Paraguay, Venezuela v Chile, Peru v Colombia.
07.07.96	Peru v Argentina, Chile v Ecuador, Colombia v Uruguay, Bolivia v Venezuela.
01.09.96	Argentina v Paraguay, Colombia v Chile, Ecuador v Venezuela, Bolivia v Peru.

09.10.96	Venezuela v Argentina, Uruguay v Bolivia, Ecuador v Colombia, Paraguay v Chile.
10.11.96	Chile v Uruguay, Bolivia v Colombia, Paraguay v Ecuador, Peru v Venezuela.
15.12.96	Argentina v Chile, Uruguay v Peru, Venezuela v Colombia, Bolivia v Paraguay.
12.01.97	Uruguay v Argentina, Peru v Chile, Venezuela v Paraguay, Bolivia v Ecuador.
12.02.97	Colombia v Argentina, Ecuador v Uruguay, Paraguay v Peru, Bolivia v Chile.
02.04.97	Bolivia v Argentina, Uruguay v Venezuela, Paraguay v Colombia, Peru v Ecuador.
30.04.97	Argentina v Ecuador, Paraguay v Uruguay, Chile v Venezuela, Colombia v Peru.
08.06.97	Argentina v Peru, Ecuador v Chile, Uruguay v Colombia, Venezuela v Bolivia.
06.07.97	Paraguay v Argentina, Chile v Colombia, Peru v Bolivia, Venezuela v Ecuador.
20.07.97	Argentina v Venezuela, Bolivia v Uruguay, Colombia v Ecuador, Chile v Paraguay.
20.08.97	Uruguay v Chile, Colombia v Bolivia, Ecuador v Paraguay, Venezuela v Peru.
10.09.97	Chile v Argentina, Peru v Uruguay, Colombia v Venezuela, Paraguay v Bolivia.
12.10.97	Argentina v Uruguay, Chile v Peru, Paraguay v Venezuela, Ecuador v Bolivia.
16.11.97	Argentina v Colombia, Uruguay v Ecuador, Peru v Paraguay, Chile v Bolivia.

WORLD CUP – opening games

Athens, 24 April 1996, 9000
Greece (0) 2 *(Batista 56, Nikolaidis 66)*
Slovenia (0) 0

Greece: Atmatzidis; Apostolakis, Kassapis, Ouzounidis, Kalitzakis, Costantinidis (Alexandris 46), Zagorakis, Vrizas, Batista, Tsartas (Franzeskos 82), Donis (Nikolaidis 61).
Slovenia: Boskovic; Galic, Englaro, Milanic, Jermanis, Seh, Novak, Zidan (Gaiser 36), Udovic (Gliha 70), Gregor, Florjancic.
Referee: Pedersen (Denmark).

Skopje, 24 April 1996, 12,000
Macedonia (1) 3 *(Milosevski 5, Babunski 49 (pen), Zaharievski 80)*
Liechtenstein (0) 0

Macedonia: Celeski; Babunski, Markovski (Nikolovski 60), Jovanovski, Stojkovski, Milosevski, Milosavov, Gosev (Zaharievski 75), Ciric, Boskovski, Hristov (Naumovski 71).
Liechtenstein: Heeb; Hanselmann, Hasler, Stocker, Zech, Frick C, Frick D, Frick M, Hilti, Oehri, Telser (Sele 51).

Belgrade, 24 April 1996, 25,000
Yugoslavia (3) 3 *(Savicevic 3, 30, Milosevic 38)*
Faeroes (0) 1 *(Petersen 54)*

Yugoslavia: Kocic; Curcic (Mirkovic 75), Djorovic, Jokanovic, Brnovic, Mihajlovic (Pantic 40), Jugovic, Savicevic, Mijatovic, Stojkovic, Milosevic (Nadj 87).
Faeroes: Knudsen; Johannsen O, Hansen J, Hansen A, Johnsson J, Morkore A, Jarnskor H, Dam, Muller, Petersen, Rasmussen J E (Jarnskor M 75).
Referee: Bec (Liechtenstein).

Buenos Aires, 24 April 1996, 60,000
Argentina (2) 3 *(Ortega 8, 18, Batistuta 49)*
Bolivia (1) 1 *(Baldivieso 42)*

Argentina: Passet; Zanetti, Ayala, Sensini, Chamot, Simeone, Almeyda, Ortega, Morales, Caniggia (Balbo 72), Batistuta (Lopez C 87).
Bolivia: Barrero; Rimba, Pena, Paraba, Sanchez, Ramos (Castillo I 80), Coimbra (Paniagua 77), Tufino, Baldivieso, Etcheverry (Suarez 78), Castillo R.
Referee: Sanchez (Chile).

Barranquilla, 24 April 1996, 60,000
Colombia (0) 1 *(Asprilla 55)*
Paraguay (0) 0

Colombia: Mondragon; Perez (Estrada 69), Bermudez, Mendoza, Moreno, Alvarez, Serna, Valderrama, Rincon, Valenciano (Valencia 75), Asprilla.
Paraguay: Chilavert; Arce, Gamarra, Celso, Ayala, Rivarola, Jara (Sarabia 80), Acuna, Sotelo, Struway, Ferreira (Benitez 64), Campos (Rojas 69).
Referee: Castrilli (Argentina).

Guayaquil, 24 April 1996, 65,000
Ecuador (0) 4 *(Hurtado E 54, 90, Tenorio 65, Gavica 77)*
Peru (0) 1 *(Palacios 62)*

Ecuador: Morales; Rivera, Montano, Hurtado I (Obregon 84), Capurro, De Souza, Tenorio, Carabali W (Carabali H 46), Aguinaga, Fernandez (Gavica 76), Hurtado E.
Peru: Miranda; Solano, Reynoso, Marengo, Ferrari (Magallanes 67), Carranza, Jayo, Del Solar, Palacios, Maestri, Guadalupe (Ramirez 68).
Referee: Matto (Uruguay).

Caracas, 24 April 1996, 12,000
Venezuela (0) 0
Uruguay (0) 2 *(Otero 54, Poyet 71)*

Venezuela: Angelucci; Filosa, Gonzalez W, Tortolero, Gonzalez L, Vallenilla, Valiente (McIntosh 74), Hernandez, Castellin, Diaz (Rivas 55), Guerra.
Uruguay: Arbiza; Olivera, Herrera, Moas, Montero, Saralegui, Gutierrez, Bengoechea (Abeijon 90), Poyet, Otero (Cedres 87).
Referee: Tejada (Peru).

Stockholm, 1 June 1996, 30,014
Sweden (2) 5 *(Andersson K 20 (pen), 62, Dahlin 30, Andersson P 77, Larsson 88)*
Belarus (0) 1 *(Belkevich 75)*

Sweden: Andersson B; Nilsson R, Andersson P, Bjorklund, Sundgren, Ingesson (Mild 85), Thern, Zetterberg, Limpar, Dahlin (Larsson 77), Andersson K.
Belarus: Satsunkhevich; Gurenko, Khatskevich, Staniouk, Kachentsev (Koulty 63), Vergeichik, Belkevich, Maleiev, Romashchenko (Kachuro 57), Makovski, Baranov.
Referee: Harrel (France).

Reykjavik, 1 June 1996, 5000
Iceland (0) 1 *(Gudjohnsen A 63)*
Macedonia (0) 1 *(Memedi 62)*
Iceland: Kristinsson B; Sigurdsson, Gretarsson, Jonsson S, Adolfsson, Kristinsson R, Bergsson, Gudjohnsen A, Thordarsson (Stefansson 68), Gudjonsson T (Benediktsson 81), Gunnlaugsson B (Gylfason 29).
Macedonia: Celeski; Milosavov, Markovski, Nikolovski, Stojkovski, Sedloski, Memedi, Gosev, Kiric (Sakiri 36), Hristov (Borov 84), Milosevski.
Referee: Luinge (Holland).

Oslo, 2 June 1996, 14,012
Norway (2) 5 *(Solbakken 8, 46, Solskjaer 37, 90, Strandli 60)*
Azerbaijan (0) 0
Norway: Grodaas; Haaland, Berg, Johnsen, Bjornebye, Rudi, Solbakken (Larsen 79), Rekdal, Leonhardsen (Flo 46), Solskjaer, Strandli.
Azerbaijan: Jidkov; Gasimov, Getman, Ahmedov, Agayev (Nossenko 40), Idigov, Abusev (Asadov 79), Ryzalev (Kurbanov 46), Guseynov, Lichin, Suleimanov.\
Referee: Snoddy (Northern Ireland).

Belgrade, 2 June 1996, 20,000
Yugoslavia (3) 6 *(Milosevic 2, 68, Mijatovic 39, Stojkovic 45, Savicevic 71, 73)*
Malta (0) 0
Yugoslavia: Kocic; Mirkovic, Djorovic (Saveljic 85), Jokanovic, Djukic, Mihajlovic, Jugovic (Nadj 50), Savicevic, Mijatovic, Stojkovic, Milosevic (Kovacevic 79).
Malta: Cluett; Attard (Woods 46), Buhagiar, Vella, Debono, Zammit (Camilleri 75), Busuttil, Turner, Brincat, Cetcutti, Agius.
Referee: Albrecht (Germany).

Serravalle, 2 June 1996, 1613
San Marino (0) 0
Wales (3) 5 *(Melville 20, Hughes M 32, 43, Giggs 50, Pembridge 85)*
San Marino: Muccioli S; Gasperoni, Valentini M, Guerra, Gobbi, Manzaroli, Pasolini (Muccioli R 69), Mazza, Casadei (Peverani 74), Mularoni (Valentini V 46), Montagna.
Wales: Southall; Bowen, Melville, Coleman, Pembridge, Browning (Goss 74), Horne (Savage 81), Robinson (Legg 80), Hughes M, Saunders, Giggs.
Referee: Lubos (Slovakia).

Montevideo, 2 June 1996, 60,000
Uruguay (0) 0
Paraguay (1) 2 *(Arce 10, Rojas 89)*
Uruguay: Arbiza; Mendez, Herrera, Moas, Montero, Saralegui (Romero 46), Gutierrez (Dorta 69), Poyet, Bengoechea, Otero, Martinez (Cedres 60).
Paraguay: Chilavert; Arce, Rivarola, Ayala, Gamarra, Struway, Enciso, Bourdier, Acuna (Suarez 90), Baez E (Gonzalez 60), Baez R (Rojas 70).
*Referee:*Rezende (Brazil).

Quito, 2 June 1996, 55,000
Ecuador (0) 2 *(Montano 52, Hurtado E 89)*
Argentina (0) 0
Ecuador: Morales; Rivera, Hurtado I (Obregon 84), Tenorio, Capurro, Montano, Gavica (Fernandez 46), Aguinaga, Carabali, De Souza, Hurtado E.
Argentina: Bossio; Zanetti, Caceres, Sensini, Chamot, Almeyda, Simeone, Morales (Lopez 76), Ortega (Cardoso 71), Batistuta (Crespo 76), Caniggia.
Referee: Perez (Colombia).

Barinas, 2 June 1996, 9850
Venezuela (1) 1 *(Guerra 7)*
Chile (0) 1 *(Margas 90)*
Venezuela: Dudamel; McIntosh, Tortolero, Gonzalez L, Diaz (Hezzel 67) (Urdanetta 85), Hernandez S, Valiente, Hernandez F, Rivas, Guerra, Castellin (Savarese 67).
*Chile:*Tapia; Mendoza, Ramirez, Fuentes, Margas, Vilches (Nunez 73), Estay, Vega (Rozental 46), Valencia (Musrri 46), Zamorano, Salas.
Referee: Gonzales (Paraguay).

Lima, 2 June 1996, 45,000
Peru (0) 1 *(Reynoso 48)*
Colombia (0) 1 *(Aristizabal 60)*
Peru: Balerio; Marengo, Reynoso, Olivares, Legario, Carranza (Guadalupe 75), Solano, Del Solar, Maestri, Palacios, Zegarra (Aguinaga 79).
Colombia: Mondragon; Mendoza, Herrera, Bermudez, Valencia (Aristizabal 46), Estrada, Valderrama (Bolado 90), Asprilla, Rincon.
Referee: Rodas (Ecuador).

Santiago, 6 July 1996, 75,000
Chile (1) 4 *(Zamorano 21, 85, Salas 75, Estay 83)*
Ecuador (0) 1 *(Aguinaga 74)*
Chile: Tapia; Castaneda C, Gonzalez, Margas, Miranda, Musrri, Valencia (Estay 58), Vega (Sierra 76), Castaneda V (Mora 68), Salas, Zamorano.
Ecuador: Morales; Tenorio M (Gonzalez 78), Rivera, Montano (Tenorio B 46), Capurro, Hurtado I, Obregon (Fernandez 46), Carabali, Aguinaga, Gilson, Hurtado E.
Referee: Duran (Bolivia).

La Paz, 7 July 1996, 40,000
Bolivia (2) 6 *(Sandy 3, Etcheverry 27 (pen), Baldivieso 49, Coimbra 67, Suarez 77, Paniagua 80)*
Venezuela (0) 1 *(Tortolero 65 (pen))*
Bolivia: Trucco; Sanchez, Quinteros, Sandy, Rimba, Pena, Cristaldo, Castillo R (Suarez 75), Baldivieso, Etcheverry (Moreno 68), Coimbra (Paniagua 78).
Venezuela: Dudamel; Filosa, McIntosh, Tortolero, Hernandez S (Diaz 46), Vera, Gonzalez, Hernandez F, Rivas S (Urdaneta 46), Savarese (Miranda 46), Guerra.
Referee: Da Rosa (Uruguay).

Lima, 7 July 1996, 45,000
Peru (0) 0
Argentina (0) 0
Peru: Balerio; Solano, Reynoso, Soto, Olivares, Jayo, Zegarra (Magallanes 68), Carranza (Farfan 83), Palacios, Julinho, Maestri.
Argentina: Burgos; Zanetti, Ayala, Sensini, Chamot, Almeyda, Simeone, Morales (Bassedas 46), Ortega (Lopez 89), Caniggia (Paz 72).
Referee: Souza (Brazil).

Barranquilla, 7 July 1996, 40,000
Colombia (2) 3 *(Asprilla 10, Valderrama 22, De Avila 77)*
Uruguay (0) 1 *(Cedres 55)*
Colombia: Mondragon; Cabrera, Bermudez, Mendoza, Moreno, Alvarez, Serna, Rincon, Valderrama, Asprilla, Aristizabal (De Avila 64).
Uruguay: Arbiza; Oliveira (Bengoechea 36), Moas, Aguirregaray, Lima (Silva T 54), Pereyra, Dorta (Sosa H 71), Poyet, Saralegui, Cedres, Romero.
Referee: Ruscio (Argentina).

EUROPEAN FOOTBALL CHAMPIONSHIP
(formerly EUROPEAN NATIONS' CUP)

Year	Winners		Runners-up		Venue	Attendance
1960	USSR	2	Yugoslavia	1	Paris	17,966
1964	Spain	2	USSR	1	Madrid	120,000
1968	Italy	2	Yugoslavia	0	Rome	60,000
	After 1-1 draw					75,000
1972	West Germany	3	USSR	0	Brussels	43,437
1976	Czechoslovakia	2	West Germany	2	Belgrade	45,000
	(Czechoslovakia won on penalties)					
1980	West Germany	2	Belgium	1	Rome	47,864
1984	France	2	Spain	0	Paris	48,000
1988	Holland	2	USSR	0	Munich	72,308
1992	Denmark	2	Germany	0	Gothenburg	37,800

EUROPEAN CHAMPIONSHIP 1994–96
Qualifying Tournament

Group 1

Tel Aviv, 4 September 1994, 3500
Israel (1) 2 *(Harazi R 43, 58)*
Poland (0) 1 *(Kosecki 80)*
Israel: Ginzburg; Harazi A, Klinger, Balbul, Glam, Hazan, Berkovitch (Levi 86), Banin, Revivo, Rosenthal (Atar 89), Harazi R.
Poland: Wandzik; Bak, Szewczyk, Waldoch, Maciejewski, Lapinski, Jalocha (Czerwiec 46), Mielcarski (Gesior 58), Brzeczek, Kosecki, Kowalczyk.
Referee: Van den Wijngaert (Belgium).

Bratislava, 7 September 1994, 14,238
Slovakia (0) 0
France (0) 0
Slovakia: Molnar; Glonek, Stupala, Zeman, Tittel, Kinder, Tomaschek, Kristofik, Zvara (Penksa 63), Rusnak (Weiss 80), Moravcik.
France: Lama; Angloma, Blanc, Roche, Di Meco, Deschamps, Le Guen, Ginola, Djorkaeff (Lizarazu 82), Cantona, Pedros (Dugarry 63).
Referee: Mikkelsen (Denmark).

Bucharest, 7 September 1994, 10,000
Romania (1) 3 *(Belodedici 43, Petrescu 58, Raducioiu 88)*
Azerbaijan (0) 0
Romania: Stelea (Stingaciu 85); Petrescu, Prodan, Belodedici, Selymes (Carstea 82), Lupescu (Timofte D 75), Popescu, Munteanu, Lacatus, Raducioiu, Dumitrescu.
Azerbaijan: Jidkov; Allahverdiev, Asadov, Ahmedov T, Drozdov, Abusov, Diniyev, Huseynov Y (Agayev 80), Alekberov, Suleymanov (Rzayev 59), Kasumov.
Referee: Sedlacek (Austria).

St Etienne, 8 October 1994, 31,744
France (0) 0
Romania (0) 0
France: Lama; Blanc, Angloma, Roche, Lizarazu, Karembeu, Desailly, Loko (Dugarry 83), Pedros, Cantona, Ouedec (Zidane 71).
Romania: Stelea; Belodedici, Prodan, Petrescu, Lupescu, Timofte D (Lacatus 71), Popescu, Hagi, Selymes, Dumitrescu, Raducioiu (Panduru 80).
Referee: Sundell (Sweden).

Tel Aviv, 12 October 1994, 10,000
Israel (2) 2 *(Harazi R 23, Banin 32 (pen))*
Slovakia (2) 2 *(Rusnak 5, Moravcik 14)*
Israel: Ginzburg; Balbul, Glam, Klinger (Shelach 67), Harazi A, Hazan, Berkovitch, Banin (Nimni 60), Revivo, Harazi R, Rosenthal.

Slovakia: Molnar; Stupala, Tittel, Glonek, Kinder, Zeman, Kristofik, Dubovsky, Weiss (Kozak 75), Moravcik, Rusnak (Zvara 76).
Referee: Blankenstein (Holland).

Mielec, 12 October 1994, 10,000
Poland (1) 1 *(Juskowiak 44)*
Azerbaijan (0) 0
Poland: Wandzik; Waldoch, Jaskulski, Lapinski (Maciejewski 79), Kozminski (Fedoruk 70), Swierczewski P, Czereszewski, Brzeczek, Kosecki, Warzycha, Juskowiak.
Azerbaijan: Jidkov; Allahverdiev, Karimov, Ahmedov T, Asadov, Abusov (Gurbanov M 89), Huseynov Y, Diniyev, Mardanov, Kasumov, Alekberov.
Referee: Koho (Finland).

Bucharest, 12 November 1994, 15,000
Romania (1) 3 *(Popescu 7, Hagi 46, Prodan 80)*
Slovakia (0) 2 *(Dubovsky 56, Chvila 78)*
Romania: Stelea; Petrescu, Belodedici, Prodan, Munteanu, Lacatus (Timofte D 75), Popescu, Lupescu, Hagi, Raducioiu (Vladoiu 83), Dumitrescu.
Slovakia: Molnar; Stupala, Chvila, Tittel, Glonek, Kinder, Tomaschek, Kristofik, Moravcik, Penksa (Timko 46), Dubovsky.
Referee: Zhuk (Russia).

Zabrze, 16 November 1994, 20,000
Poland (0) 0
France (0) 0
Poland: Wandzik; Jaskulski, Czereszewski, Swierczewski M, Waldoch, Swierczewski P, Baluszynski (Gesior 80), Kozminski (Bak 28), Juskowiak, Kosecki, Warzycha.
France: Lama; Angloma, Blanc, Roche, Di Meco, Karembeu, Desailly, Le Guen, Ouedec (Dugarry 76), Cantona, Pedros (Djorkaeff 25).
Referee: Amendolia (Italy).

Trabzon, 16 November 1994, 3000
Azerbaijan (0) 0
Israel (1) 2 *(Harazi R 30, Rosenthal 51)*
Azerbaijan: Jidkov; Allahverdiev, Ahmedov T, Mayorov (Agayev 46), Cabarov, Asadov, Huseynov Y (Rzayev 77), Diniyev, Kasumov, Suleymanov, Alekberov.
Israel: Ginzburg; Balbul, Harazi A, Klinger, Glam, Hazan, Banin, Berkovitch (Nimni 66), Revivo, Harazi R (Shelah 83), Rosenthal.
Referee: Vagner (Hungary).

Tel Aviv, 14 December 1994, 40,000

Israel (0) 1 *(Rosenthal 84)*

Romania (0) 1 *(Lacatus 70)*

Israel: Ginzburg; Balbul, Klinger, Harazi A, Glam, Hazan, Berkovitch, Levi (Zohar 75), Revivo, Harazi R (Shelach 90), Rosenthal.

Romania: Stelea; Petrescu, Belodedici, Prodan, Selymes, Hagi, Popescu, Lupescu, Munteanu (Vladoiu 52), Lacatus, Dumitrescu (Galca 74).

Referee: Navarrete (Spain).

Trabzon, 14 December 1994, 4000

Azerbaijan (0) 0

France (1) 2 *(Papin 25, Loko 56)*

Azerbaijan: Jidkov (Hasanov 41); Allahverdiev, Vahabzadze, Abusov, Agayev, Cabarov, Asadov (Gadirov 78), Kasumov, Diniyev (Rzayev 78), Huseynov Y, Alekberov.

France: Lama; Angloma, Roche, Blanc, Di Meco, Desailly (Ferri 71), Le Guen, Cantona, Loko, Papin, Pedros (Martins 76).

Referee: Pedersen (Norway).

Bucharest, 29 March 1995, 22,000

Romania (1) 2 *(Raducioiu 45, Wandzik 55 (og))*

Poland (1) 1 *(Juskowiak 43 (pen))*

Romania: Stelea; Petrescu, Prodan, Belodedici, Selymes, Hagi (Vladoiu 88), Dumitrescu, Popescu, Munteanu, Lacatus (Lupu 46), Raducioiu.

Poland: Wandzik; Jaskulski, Swierczewski M, Waldoch, Swierczewski P, Nowak (Wieszczycki 58), Czereszewski (Sokolowski 73), Baluszynski, Warzycha, Juskowiak, Kosecki.

Referee: Rothlisberger (Switzerland).

Kosice, 29 March 1995, 12,400

Slovakia (3) 4 *(Tittel 35, Timko 40, 50, Dubovsky 45 (pen))*

Azerbaijan (0) 1 *(Suleymanov 80 (pen))*

Slovakia: Molnar; Stupala, Glonek, Zeman, Kinder, Kristofik, Tittel, Moravcik (Prazenica 73), Dubovsky, Timko, Penksa.

Azerbaijan: Hasanov; Aliyev (Gadirov 65), Vahabzadze, Abusov, Cabarov, Asadov, Huseynov Y, Agayev, Diniyev, Suleymanov, Kasumov (Alekberov 56).

Referee: Nikakis (Greece).

Tel Aviv, 29 March 1995, 45,000

Israel (0) 0

France (0) 0

Israel: Ginzburg; Halfon, Klinger, Harazi A, Glam, Hazan, Banin, Revivo, Berkovitch (Zohar 64), Rosenthal, Harazi R.

France: Lama; Angloma, Roche, Blanc, Di Meco, Desailly, Le Guen, Martins (Djorkaeff 78), Pedros, Loko, Ouedec (Ginola 66).

Referee: McCluskey (Scotland).

Zabrze, 25 April 1995, 5500

Poland (1) 4 *(Nowak 1, Juskowiak 50, Kowalczyk 55, Kosecki 62)*

Israel (2) 3 *(Rosenthal 37, Revivo 42, Zohar 77)*

Poland: Wandzik; Lapinski, Swierczewski M, Waldoch, Swierczewski P, Nowak (Bukalski 46), Kozminski, Baluszynski (Wieszczycki 46), Juskowiak, Kowalczyk, Kosecki.

Israel: Ginzburg; Halfon, Harazi A, Klinger, Glam, Hazan, Banin, Revivo, Berkovitch, Mizrahi (Zohar 73), Rosenthal.

Referee: Frisk (Sweden).

Trabzon, 26 April 1995, 500

Azerbaijan (1) 1 *(Suleymanov 4)*

Romania (2) 4 *(Raducioiu 1 (pen), 68, 76, Dumitrescu 38)*

Azerbaijan: Hasanov; Asadov, Getmam, Ahmedov T (Vahabzadze 21), Cabarov (Gadirov 75), Abusov, Huseynov Y, Diniyev, Lichkin, Suleymanov, Alekberov.

Romania: Stelea (Prunea 85); Petrescu, Prodan, Belodedici, Selymes, Popescu (Timofte D 81), Munteanu, Lupescu, Dumitrescu, Lacatus (Lupu 69), Raducioiu.

Referee: Momirov (Bulgaria).

Nantes, 26 April 1995, 26,000

France (2) 4 *(Kristofik 27 (og), Ginola 42, Blanc 57, Guerin 62)*

Slovakia (0) 0

France: Lama; Angloma, Blanc, Roche, Di Meco, Deschamps, Desailly, Guerin, Zidane (Djorkaeff 73), Loko, Ginola.

Slovakia: Molnar; Stupala, Zeman, Glonek, Kinder, Kristofik, Tittel, Tomaschek (Timko 46), Moravcik, Penksa (Maixner 73), Dubovsky.

Referee: Heynemann (Germany).

Zabrze, 7 June 1995, 20,000

Poland (1) 5 *(Juskowiak 10, 70, Wieszczycki 58, Kosecki 63, Nowak 70)*

Slovakia (0) 0

Poland: Szczesny; Jaskulski (Czereszewski 76), Zielinski, Bukalski, Waldoch, Kozminski, Swierczewski P, Nowak, Kosecki, Juskowiak, Kowalczyk, (Wieszczycki 46).

Slovakia: Vencel; Kozak (Penksa 60), Zeman, Glonek, Prazenica, Tomaschek, Solar, Kristofik (Weiss 71), Timko, Dubovsky, Moravcik.

Referee: Sedlacek (Austria).

Bucharest, 7 June 1995, 20,000

Romania (1) 2 *(Lacatus 16, Munteanu 65)*

Israel (0) 1 *(Berkovitch 50)*

Romania: Stelea; Petrescu, Prodan, Belodedici, Selymes, Munteanu, Lupescu, Lupu (Panduru 87), Dumitrescu (Vladoiu 63), Lacatus, Raducioiu.

Israel: Cohen; Halfon, Shelah (Balbul 65)(Zohar 74), Brumer, Amsalem, Hazan, Klinger, Mizrahi, Banin, Berkovitch, Driks.

Referee: Pedersen (Norway).

Trabzon, 16 August 1995, 50

Azerbaijan (0) 0

Slovakia (0) 1 *(Jancula 60)*

Azerbaijan: Sadygov; Getmam, Gadirov, Ahmedov T, Agayev (Asadov 71), Abusov, Huseynov Y, Diniyev (Mahmoud 46), Nosenko, Lichkin, Alekberov.

Slovakia: Molnar; Pecko, Tittel, Balis (Prazenica 89), Zeman, Kinder, Tomaschek, Simon, Moravcik (Faktor 75), Rusnak (Jancula 58), Dubovsky.

Referee: Hamer (Luxemburg).

Paris, 16 August 1995, 40,496

France (0) 1 *(Djorkaeff 85)*

Poland (1) 1 *(Juskowiak 35)*

France: Lama; Angloma (Karembeu 66), Thuram, Leboeuf (Djorkaeff 69), Lizarazu, Deschamps, Desailly, Guerin, Zidane, Dugarry, Ginola (Pedros 64).

Poland: Wozniak; Lapinski, Waldoch, Zielinski, Kozminski, Iwan, Swierczewski P, Nowak (Czerwiec 56), Kosecki (Wojtala 71), Juskowiak, Kowalczyk (Bukalski 60).

Referee: Diaz Vega (Spain).

Auxerre, 6 September 1995, 15,000

France (3) 10 *(Desailly 13, Djorkaeff 17, 78, Guerin 33, Pedros 49, Leboeuf 54, 74, Dugarry 65, Zidane 72, Cocard 90)*

Azerbaijan (0) 0

France: Lama; Angloma (Thuram 57), Desailly, Leboeuf, Lizarazu, Deschamps, Guerin, Djorkaeff, Zidane, Dugarry (Cocard 68), Pedros (Ginola 65).

Azerbaijan: Hasanov (Sadygov 38); Asadov, Getmam, Ahmedov T, Agayev, Abusov, Gadirov (Huseynov M 75), Diniyev, Gurbanov M (Alekberov 46), Huseynov Y, Lichkin.

Referee: Micallef (Malta).

Zabrze, 6 September 1995, 18,000

Poland (0) 0

Romania (0) 0

Poland: Wozniak; Jaskulski, Zielinski, Waldoch, Kozminski, Bednarz (Bukalski 62), Swierczewski P, Iwan (Czerwiec 76), Kosecki, Juskowiak, Wieszczicki (Podbrozny 67).

Romania: Stelea; Petrescu, Prodan, Popescu, Mihali, Selymes, Lupescu, Munteanu (Galca 76), Lacatus (Timofte I 85), Sabau, Vladoiu (Panduru 66).

Referee: Gallagher (England).

Kosice, 6 September 1995, 7810

Slovakia (0) 1 *(Jancula 54)*

Israel (0) 0

Slovakia: Molnar; Tittel, Pecko, Karhan, Kinder, Balis (Kostka 89), Simon (Faktor 82), Juriga, Moravcik, Jancula (Rusnak 66), Dubovsky.

Israel: Cohen; Brumer, Glam, Harazi A, Shelah, Hazan, Klinger (Rosenthal 46), Banin, Revivo, Mizrahi, Berkovitch (Driks 65).

Referee: Piraux (Belgium).

Bucharest, 11 October 1995, 25,000

Romania (0) 1 *(Lacatus 51)*

France (2) 3 *(Karembeu 29, Djorkaeff 41, Zidane 72)*

Romania: Stelea; Petrescu, Mihali (Lupu 46), Popescu, Prodan, Selymes, Lupescu, Hagi (Panduru 62), Munteanu, Lacatus, Dumitrescu (Vladoiu 46).

France: Barthez; Angloma, Leboeuf, Desailly, Di Meco, Karembeu, Deschamps, Guerin, Djorkaeff (Lizarazu 73), Dugarry (Madar 62), Zidane (Thuram 84).

Referee: Pairetto (Italy).

Bratislava, 11 October 1995, 12,000

Slovakia (1) 4 *(Dubovsky 31 (pen), Jancula 68, Ujlaky 78, Simon 83)*

Poland (1) 1 *(Juskowiak 19)*

Slovakia: Molnar; Karhan, Tittel, Zeman, Kinder, Balis, Juriga (Ujlaky 71), Simon, Moravcik, Jancula (Bochnovic 87), Dubovsky.

Poland: Wozniak; Lapinski, Zielinski, Waldoch, Kozminski (Bednarz 58), Iwan, Swierczewski P, Bukalski, Baluszynski (Czereszewski 79) Juskowiak, Kosecki.

Referee: Coroado (Portugal).

Tel Aviv, 11 October 1995, 8000

Israel (1) 2 *(Harazi R 31, 50)*

Azerbaijan (0) 0

Israel: Ginzburg; Halfon, Brumer, Shelah, Amsalem, Hazan, Banin, Berkovitch (Zohar 71), Revivo (Klinger 87), Harazi R (Atar 79), Rosenthal.

Azerbaijan: Jidkov; Asadov, Vahabzadze, Mayorov (Agayev 52), Ahmedov T, Abusov, Lichkin (Mamedov 70), Gadirov, Rzayev (Gurbanov M 70), Suleymanov, Kasumov.

Referee: Detruche (Switzerland).

Caen, 15 November 1995, 21,500

France (0) 2 *(Djorkaeff 69, Lizarazu 89)*

Israel (0) 0

France: Lama; Angloma, Desailly, Leboeuf, Di Meco (Lizarazu 63), Karembeu (Keller 90), Deschamps, Guerin, Zidane, Djorkaeff, Madar (Loko 63).

Israel: Cohen; Halfon, Brumer, Shelah, Glam (Zohar 79), Hazan, Klinger, Banin, Berkovitch (Atar 70), Rosenthal, Harazi R (Mizrahi 65).

Referee: Grabner (Austria).

Kosice, 15 November 1995, 8000

Slovakia (0) 0

Romania (0) 2 *(Hagi 68, Munteanu 82)*

Slovakia: Molnar; Pecko (Juriga 46), Tittel, Karhan, Kinder, Simon (Semenik 77), Balis, Tomaschek, Moravcik, Jancula (Ujlaky 69), Dubovsky.

Romania: Stelea; Petrescu, Prodan, Dobos, Selymes, Hagi (Panduru 85), Lupescu, Popescu, Munteanu, Lacatus (Dumitrescu 73), Moldovan (Timofte I 89).

Referee: Uilenberg (Holland).

Trabzon, 15 November 1995, 1000

Azerbaijan (0) 0

Poland (0) 0

Azerbaijan: Jidkov; Getman, Gaishumov, Ahmedov T, Vahabzadze, Abusov, Agayev, Rzayev (Gurbanov K 69), Nosenko (Gurbanov M 66), Suleymanov (Lichkin 86), Kasumov.

Poland: Wozniak; Jaskulski, Sokolowski, Bukalski (Lenart 71), Waldoch, Czereszewski, Wojtala, Swierczewski P, Baluszynski (Kuzba 64), Czerwiec, Majak (Siadaczka 46).

Referee: Mottram (Scotland).

	P	W	D	L	F	A	Pts
Romania	10	6	3	1	18	9	21
France	10	5	5	0	22	2	20
Slovakia	10	4	2	4	14	18	14
Poland	10	3	4	3	14	12	13
Israel	10	3	3	4	13	13	12
Azerbaijan	10	0	1	9	2	29	1

Group 2

Brussels, 7 September 1994, 11,000

Belgium (1) 2 *(Oliveira 3, Degryse 73)*

Armenia (0) 0

Belgium: Preud'homme; Genaux, De Wolf, Albert, Smidts, Staelens (Emmers 75), Van der Elst F, Van der Heyden (Boffin 67), Degryse, Oliveira, Weber.

Armenia: Arm. Petrossian; Art. Petrossian, Kerpasian, Tonoian, Hovsepian, Khachatrian V, Soukiassian, Oganesian, Shakhgeldian (Avetissian A 46), Grigorian, Mikhitarian.

Referee: Ferry (Northern Ireland).

Limassol, 7 September 1994, 12,000

Cyprus (1) 1 *(Sotiriou 35)*

Spain (2) 2 *(Higuera 18, 26)*

Cyprus: Panayiotou; Costa, Constandinou C, Christophi E, Charalambous M, Pittas, Ioannou D, Phasouliotis (Malekos 62), Savvides (Andreou 77), Gogic, Sotiriou.

Spain: Zubizarreta; Voro, Nadal, Camarasa, Sergi, Goicoechea, Hierro, Guerrero, Guardiola (Caminero 63), Higuera, Amavisca (Ciganda 78).

Referee: Batta (France).

Skopje, 7 September 1994, 22,000

Macedonia (1) 1 *(Stojkovski 4)*

Denmark (0) 1 *(Povlsen 87)*

Macedonia: Trajcev; Stanojkovic, Najdoski, Markovski, Jovanovski, Stojkovski, Boskovski (Serafimovski 82), Djurovski B, Babunski (Kanatlarovski 65), Pancev, Micevski.

Denmark: Schmeichel; Helveg, Rieper, Olsen, Friis-Hansen, Steen-Nielsen, Jensen J (Larsen 65), Vilfort (Povlsen 50), Christensen B, Laudrup M, Laudrup B.

Referee: Van der Ende (Holland).

Erevan, 8 October 1994, 6000

Armenia (0) 0

Cyprus (0) 0

Armenia: Abramian; Soukiassian, Khachatrian V (Kerpasian 46), Tonoian, Oganesian, Vardanian, Art. Petrossian, Grigorian, Adamian, Avetissian A, Mikhitarian (Avetissian Y 79).

Cyprus: Christophi M; Kalotheou, Pittas, Ioannou D, Stephani, Zembashis, Charalambous, Sotiriou, Gogic, Phasouliotis (Malekos 70), Savvides.

Referee: Bremisla (Poland).

Copenhagen, 12 October 1994, 40,000

Denmark (1) 3 *(Vilfort 35, Jensen J 72, Strudal 86)*

Belgium (1) 1 *(Degryse 31)*

Denmark: Schmeichel; Helveg, Olsen, Rieper, Friis-Hansen, Risager (Kjeldbjerg 78), Vilfort (Jensen J 72), Laudrup M, Steen-Nielsen, Laudrup B, Strudal.

Belgium: Bodart; Genaux, Van Meir, Albert, Smidts, Borkelmans (Oliveira 77), Verheyen, Van der Elst F, Staelens, Degryse, Weber.

Referee: Pairetto (Italy).

Skopje, 12 October 1994, 30,000

Macedonia (0) 0

Spain (2) 2 *(Julio Salinas 16, 25)*

Macedonia: Trajcev (Celeski 50); Stanojkovic, Stojkovski, Djurovski B, Najdoski, Jovanovski, Boskovski, Savevski, Babunski (Markovski 39), Djurovski M (Serafimovski 70), Micevski.
Spain: Zubizarreta; Ferrer, Abelardo, Alkorta, Caminero, Nadal, Hierro (Amavisca 76), Sergi, Luis Enrique, Higuera, Julio Salinas (Pier 65).
Referee: Grabner (Austria).

Brussels, 16 November 1994, 17,000

Belgium (1) 1 *(Verheyen 31)*

Macedonia (0) 1 *(Boskovski 54)*

Belgium: Preud'homme; Genaux, Crasson, Smidts, Boffin, Staelens, Van der Elst F, Walem (De Bilde 72), Verheyen, Degryse, Nilis.
Macedonia: Celeski; Stanojkovic, Djurovski B, Najdoski, Janevski, Jovanovski, Boskovski (Kanatlarovski 87), Markovski, Djurovski M (Serafimovski 80), Stojkovski, Micevski.
Referee: Kusainov (Russia).

Limassol, 16 November 1994, 8000

Cyprus (1) 2 *(Sotiriou 7, Phasouliotis 87)*

Armenia (0) 0

Cyprus: Christophi M; Andreou A, Ioannou D, Christophi E, Stephani, Zembashis (Elia 89), Malekos (Phasouliotis 68), Savvides, Pittas, Gogic, Sotiriou.
Armenia: Abramian; Tonoian, Oganesian, Vardanian, Kerpasian, Art. Petrossian, Grigorian, Mikhitarian (Avetissian V 85), Hovsepian, Soukiassian, Gsepian (Avetissian A 69).
Referee: Ashby (England).

Seville, 16 November 1994, 38,000

Spain (1) 3 *(Nadal 41, Donato 57, Luis Enrique 87)*

Denmark (0) 0

Spain: Zubizarreta; Ferrer, Belsue, Alkorta, Abelardo, Nadal, Luis Enrique, Caminero (Bakero 72), Sergi, Donato, Julio Salinas (Higuera 70).
Denmark: Schmeichel; Helveg, Rieper, Olsen, Risager, Friis Hansen (Christensen B 65), Steen-Nielsen (Jensen J 46), Vilfort, Strudal, Laudrup B, Laudrup M.
Referee: McCluskey (Scotland).

Skopje, 17 December 1994, 12,000

Macedonia (2) 3 *(Djurovski B 15, 36, 89)*

Cyprus (0) 0

Macedonia: Celeski; Stanojkovic, Janevski, Najdoski, Stojkovski, Markovski, Babunski (Jovanovski 72), Djurovski B, Boskovski (Serafimovski 86), Djurovski M, Micevski.
Cyprus: Christophi M; Kalotheou, Charalambous M, Ioannou D, Christophi E, Stephani, Charalambous C, Phasouliotis, Savvides (Malekos 67), Gogic, Sotiriou (Andreou 78).
Referee: Strampe (Germany).

Brussels, 17 December 1994, 25,000

Belgium (1) 1 *(Degryse 6)*

Spain (1) 4 *(Hierro 28, Donato 55 (pen), Julio Salinas 68, Luis Enrique 89)*

Belgium: Preud'homme; Genaux, Crasson, Albert, Smidts, Bettagno (Verheyen 46), Van der Elst F, Staelens, Boffin, Degryse, De Bilde.
Spain: Zubizaretta; Belsue, Abelardo, Nadal, Alkorta, Hierro, Sergi, Donato, Guerrero (Voro 57), Luis Enrique, Julio Salinas (Goicoechea 70).
Referee: Cakar (Turkey).

Seville, 29 March 1995, 27,000

Spain (1) 1 *(Guerrero 24)*

Belgium (1) 1 *(Degryse 25)*

Spain: Zubizaretta; Belsue, Abelardo, Nadal, Sergi, Hierro, Luis Enrique, Guerrero (Higuera 37), Donato, Julio Salinas (Pizzi 63), Amavisca.

Belgium: Bodart; Genaux, Medved, Renier, Smidts, Walem (Verheyen 68), Karagiannis (Crasson 83), Staelens, Degryse, De Bilde, Schepens.
Referee: Harrel (France).

Limassol, 29 March 1995, 15,000

Cyprus (1) 1 *(Agathocleous 45)*

Denmark (1) 1 *(Schjonberg 2)*

Cyprus: Panayiotou; Costa, Pittas, Ioannou D, Charalambous M, Christodolou G, Engomitis, Andreou A, Hadjilucas (Constandinou C 89), Gogic, Agathocleous.
Denmark: Schmeichel; Laursen, Rieper, Friis-Hansen (Helveg 46), Hogh, Schjonberg, Steen-Nielsen, Nielsen P, Laudrup M, Rasmussen, Laudrup B.
Referee: Shorte (Republic of Ireland).

Erevan, 26 April 1995, 40,000

Armenia (0) 0

Spain (0) 2 *(Amavisca 49, Goicoechea 63)*

Armenia: Abramian; Soukiassian, Hovsepian, Tonoian, Oganesian, Vardanian, Art. Petrossian, Grigorian (Takhmazian 65), Mikhitarian, Shakhgeldian, Adamian (Avetissian A 55).
Spain: Zubizarreta; Belsue, Alkorta, Karanka, Otero, Nadal, Donato (Camarasa 69), Luis Enrique, Goicoechea, Pizzi (Julio Salinas 58), Amavisca.
Referee: Porumboiu (Romania).

Copenhagen, 26 April 1995, 38,888

Denmark (0) 1 *(Nielsen P 70)*

Macedonia (0) 0

Denmark: Schmeichel; Laursen, Rieper, Hogh, Schjonberg, Thomsen, Steen-Nielsen, Rasmussen (Andersen 46), Laudrup M, Nielsen P (Helveg 78), Laudrup B.
Macedonia: Celeski; Stanojkovic, Stojkovski, Najdoski, Markovski (Memed 26), Jovanovski, Boskovski, Djurovski B, Micevski, Pancev, Serafimovski (Marjan Stojkovski 77).
Referee: Ihring (Slovakia).

Brussels, 26 April 1995, 13,000

Belgium (1) 2 *(Karagiannis 20, Schepens 47)*

Cyprus (0) 0

Belgium: Bodart; Renier, Medved, Grun, Smidts, Staelens, Karagiannis, Degryse, Schepens, Nilis, De Bilde (Goossens 81).
Cyprus: Panayiotou; Kalotheou, Charalambous M, Ioannou D, Pittas, Christodolou G, Gogic, Andreou A, Engomitis, Agathocleous (Larkou 62), Papavassiliou (Sotiriou 85).
Referee: Elleray (England).

Erevan, 10 May 1995, 12,500

Armenia (1) 2 *(Grigorian 21, 51)*

Macedonia (0) 2 *(Hristov 59, Markovski 70)*

Armenia: Abramian; Soukiassian, Hovsepian, Tonoian, Oganesian, Vardanian, Art. Petrossian, Grigorian, Mikhitarian (Gsepian 79), Shakhgeldian, Avetissian A (Tahmazian 69).
Macedonia: Celeski; Stanojkovic, Stojkovski, Najdoski, Markovski, Janevski (Kanatlarovski 69), Hristov, Babunski, Micevski (Memed 59), Pancev, Serafimovski.
Referee: Fajilstrom (Sweden).

Copenhagen, 7 June 1995, 40,199

Denmark (1) 4 *(Vilfort 45, 50, Laudrup B 58, Laudrup M 75)*

Cyprus (0) 0

Denmark: Schmeichel; Laursen, Rieper, Hogh, Schjonberg, Steen-Nielsen (Rasmussen 46), Jensen, Vilfort (Andersen 87), Beck, Laudrup M, Laudrup B.
Cyprus: Petrides; Costa, Pittas, Christodolou G, Charalambous M, Andreou A, Engomitis, Larkou, Hadjilucas (Phasouliotis 60), Gogic, Sotiriou (Andreou P 68).
Referee: Muller (Switzerland).

Seville, 7 June 1995, 20,000
Spain (0) 1 *(Hierro 64 (pen))*
Armenia (0) 0
Spain: Zubizarreta; Belsue, Aranzabal, Alkorta, Abelardo, Hierro, Goicoechea (Julio Salinas 46), Guerrero (Caminero 78), Nadal, Luis Enrique, Amavisca.
Armenia: Abramian; Soukiassian, Hovsepian, Tonoian, Nigoian (Ter-Petrossian 71), Vardanian, Art. Petrossian (Avetissian V 76), Tahmazian, Mikhitarian, Shakhgeldian, Avetissian A.
Referee: Philippi (Luxembourg).

Skopje, 7 June 1995, *
Macedonia (0) 0
Belgium (4) 5 *(Grun 15, Scifo 18, 60, Schepens 28, Versavel 43)*
Macedonia: Celeski; Stanojkovic, Najdovski, Stojkovski, Boskovski, Djurovski B (Hristov 61), Janevski, Babunski, Micevski, Pancev, Serafimovski (Memed 35).
Belgium: Bodart; Genaux, Renier, Grun, Smidts, Staelens, Karagiannis, Schepens (Leonard 83), Scifo, Versavel, De Bilde.
Referee: Wojciki (Poland).
*Match played behind closed doors as disciplinary punishment.

Erevan, 16 August 1995, 22,000
Armenia (0) 0
Denmark (1) 2 *(Laudrup M 34, Nielsen A 47)*
Armenia: Arm. Petrossian; Khachatrian V, Khachatrian A, Oganesian, Hovsepian, Tonoian, Art. Petrossian, Grigorian, Avetissian A (Avetissian V 80), Tahmazian (Ter-Petrossian 41), Shakhgeldian.
Denmark: Schmeichel; Laursen, Rieper, Hogh, Risager (Schjonberg 85), Thomsen, Jensen (Nielsen A 46), Steen-Nielsen, Beck, Laudrup M, Rasmussen.
Referee: Dardenne (Germany).

Brussels, 6 September 1995, 40,000
Belgium (1) 1 *(Grun 25)*
Denmark (2) 3 *(Laudrup M 19, Beck 21, Vilfort 70)*
Belgium: Bodart; Genaux, Medved, Grun, Smidts (Renier 76), Staelens (Nilis 12), Karagiannis, Scifo, Schepens (Foguenne 57), Degryse, De Bilde.
Denmark: Schmeichel; Risager, Rieper, Hogh, Laursen, Steen-Nielsen, Vilfort, Nielsen A, Laudrup M, Beck (Rasmussen 73), Laudrup B (Andersen 77).
Referee: Zhouk (Belarus).

Skopje, 6 September 1995 *
Macedonia (1) 1 *(Micevski 10)*
Armenia (0) 2 *(Grigorian 61, Shakhgeldian 78)*
Macedonia: Celeski; Nikolovski, Stojkovski, Jovanovski, Markovski, Babunski, Serafimovski, Memed, Savevski, Hristov, Micevski.
Armenia: Arm. Petrossian; Gsepian, Khachatrian V, Vardanian, Oganesian, Stepanian, Ter-Petrossian, Mikhitarian, Avetissian A, Grigorian, Shakhgeldian.
Referee: Pereira (Portugal).
*Match played behind closed doors as disciplinary punishment.

Grenada, 6 September 1995, 30,000
Spain (1) 6 *(Guerrero 45, Alfonso 51, Pizzi 74, 79, Hierro 78, Caminero 82)*
Cyprus (0) 0
Spain: Zubizarreta; Belsue, Aranzabal, Alkorta, Nadal, Hierro, Luis Enrique, Caminero (Manjarin 77), Caminero, Amavisca (Fran 54), Alfonso (Pizzi 61).
Cyprus: Panayiotou; Charalambous M, Panayi, Pittas, Christodolou G, Ashiotis, Andoniou (Kalotheou 79), Ioannou Y, Malekos (Sotiriou 57), Gogic, Hadjilukas (Ioannou D 75).
Referee: Jol (Holland).

Erevan, 7 October 1995, 5000
Armenia (0) 0
Belgium (2) 2 *(Nilis 28, 39)*
Armenia: Abramian; Gsepian, Khachatrian V, Khachatrian A, Soukiassian, Hovsepian, Grigorian (Avetissian V 46), Mikhitarian (Margarian 71), Art. Petrossian, Shakhgeldian, Avetissian A.
Belgium: De Wilde; Genaux, Crasson, De Boeck, Smidts, Staelens, Karagiannis (Vermant 80), Scifo, Schepens, De Bilde (Goossens 64), Nilis.
Referee: Mitrev (Bulgaria).

Copenhagen, 11 October 1995, 40,262
Denmark (0) 1 *(Vilfort 47)*
Spain (1) 1 *(Hierro 17 (pen))*
Denmark: Schmeichel; Laursen, Piechnik, Hogh, Rieper, Risager, Vilfort, Steen-Nielsen (Wieghorst 67), Laudrup M, Beck, Rasmussen.
Spain: Zubizarreta; Belsue, Abelardo, Alkorta, Nadal, Sergi, Luis Enrique, Hierro, Caminero (Francisco 30), Manjarin (Donato 62), Pizzi (Alfonso 46).
Referee: Krondl (Czech Republic).

Limassol, 11 October 1995, 15,000
Cyprus (0) 1 *(Agathocleous 90)*
Macedonia (1) 1 *(Jovanovski B 31)*
Cyprus: Petrides; Costa, Pittas, Christodolou G, Charalambous M, Kalotheou (Agathocleous 64), Engomitis (Papavassiliou 46), Sotiriou (Larkou 80), Gogic, Savvides, Malekos.
Macedonia: Celeski; Jovanovski B, Karadzov, Markovski, Nikolovski, Jovanovski Z, Veselinovski (Christov 84), Ciric, Serafimovski (Karanfilovski 77), Memed, Savevski.
Referee: Irvine (Republic of Ireland).

Elche, 15 November 1995, 34,000
Spain (1) 3 *(Kiko 8, Manjarin 72, Caminero 79)*
Macedonia (0) 0
Spain: Zubizarreta; Sergi, Nadal, Alkorta, Belsue, Amavisca (Ferrer 46), Caminero, Donato, Manjarin, Kiko (Goicoechea 75), Pizzi (Alfonso 46).
Macedonia: Celeski; Jovanovski B, Stojkovski, Serafimovski (Pecelinovski 52) (Hristov 78), Babunski, Jovanovski Z (Nikolovski 72), Karadzov, Memed, Boskovski, Ciric, Nikolovski.
Referee: Steinborn (Germany).

Copenhagen, 15 November 1995, 40,208
Denmark (2) 3 *(Schjonberg 19, Beck 35, Laudrup M 58)*
Armenia (0) 1 *(Art. Petrossian 47)*
Denmark: Schmeichel; Helveg, Rieper, Hogh, Risager, Schjonberg, Steen-Nielsen, Vilfort, Beck, Laudrup M, Rasmussen.
Armenia: Abramian; Artoian, Khachatrian V, Hovsepian, Vardanian, Gsepian (Kerpasian 80), Art. Petrossian, Avetissian V (Margarian 71), Mikhitarian, Nikolian, Avetissian A.
Referee: Veissiere (France).

Limassol, 15 November 1995, 10,000
Cyprus (1) 1 *(Agathocleous 18)*
Belgium (0) 1 *(De Bilde 66)*
Cyprus: Panayiotou; Costa, Pittas A, Christodolou G, Charalambous M, Engomitis, Gogic (Elia 86), Andreou A, Malekos (Larkou 49), Papavassiliou, Agathocleous (Zembashis 75).
Belgium: De Wilde; Genaux, Grun, De Boeck, Smidts (Schepens 77), Staelens, Karagiannis (Goossens 46), Boffin (Huysmans 58), Degryse, De Bilde, Nilis.
Referee: Cesari (Italy).

	P	W	D	L	F	A	Pts
Spain	10	8	2	0	25	4	26
Denmark	10	6	3	1	19	9	21
Belgium	10	4	3	3	17	13	15
Macedonia	10	1	4	5	9	18	7
Cyprus	10	1	4	5	6	20	7
Armenia	10	1	2	7	5	17	5

Group 3

Reykjavik, 7 September 1994, 15,000

Iceland (0) 0

Sweden (1) 1 *(Ingesson 37)*

Iceland: Kristinsson B; Kristinsson R, Jonsson K, Bergsson, Gislason, Gudjohnsen, Orlygsson (Gunnlaugsson B 60), Jonsson S, Stefansson, Gunnlaugsson A, Sverrisson.
Sweden: Ravelli; Nilsson R, Andersson P, Bjorklund, Ljung, Brolin, Mild, Schwarz, Ingesson, Dahlin (Larsson 67), Andersson K.
Referee: Mottram (Scotland).

Budapest, 7 September 1994, 10,000

Hungary (2) 2 *(Kiprich 4, Halmai 45)*

Turkey (0) 2 *(Hakan 66, Bulent K 70)*

Hungary: Petry; Telek, Meszoly, Lipcsei, Kozma, Halmai, Detari, Urban, Duro (Banfi 62), Kiprich (Wukovics 67), Kovacs K.
Turkey: Engin; Gokhan K (Arif 46), Recep, Bulent K, Ilker, Ogun, Oguz, Tugay, Orhan, Ertugrul (Abdullah 87), Hakan.
Referee: Pairetto (Italy).

Istanbul, 12 October 1994, 20,000

Turkey (3) 5 *(Saffet 11, 28, Hakan 30, 62, Sergen 65)*

Iceland (0) 0

Turkey: Engin (Rustu 87); Gokhan K, Recep, Bulent K, Orhan (Mutlu 3), Arif, Oguz, Ogun, Abdullah, Saffet, Hakan (Sergen 64).
Iceland: Kristinsson B (Finnbogason 5), Jonsson S, Kristinsson R, Bergsson, Gislason, Gudjohnsen, Orlygsson, Jonsson K, Stefansson (Gunnlaugsson B 85), Sverisson, Gunnlaugsson A (Gretarsson 72).
Referee: Levnikov (Russia).

Berne, 12 October 1994, 24,000

Switzerland (1) 4 *(Ohrel 36, Blomqvist 64 (og), Sforza 79, Turkyilmaz 81)*

Sweden (1) 2 *(Andersson K 6, Dahlin 61)*

Switzerland: Pascolo; Hottiger, Herr, Geiger, Thuler, Ohrel, Yakin (Henchoz 83), Sforza, Sutter A, Grassi (Turkyilmaz 69), Chapuisat.
Sweden: Ravelli; Nilsson R, Andersson P, Bjorklund, Kamark, Brolin, Thern (Mild 49), Schwarz, Blomqvist (Larsson 82), Dahlin, Andersson K.
Referee: Elleray (England).

Stockholm, 16 November 1994, 27,571

Sweden (1) 2 *(Brolin 44, Dahlin 70)*

Hungary (0) 0

Sweden: Ravelli; Nilsson R, Andersson P, Bjorklund, Kamark, Brolin (Rehn 70), Schwarz, Thern, Andersson K, Dahlin, Larsson.
Hungary: Petry; Banfi, Meszoly, Lorincz, Kozma, Lipcsei (Halmai 58), Urban, Detari, Duro (Kovacs K 75), Kiprich, Klausz.
Referee: Van der Ende (Holland).

Lausanne, 16 November 1994, 15,800

Switzerland (1) 1 *(Bickel 45)*

Iceland (0) 0

Switzerland: Pascolo; Hottiger, Henchoz, Geiger, Thuler, Ohrel, Sforza, Bickel, Sutter A, Grassi (Turkyilmaz 68), Chapuisat.
Iceland: Kristinsson B; Kristinsson R, Bergsson, Gislason (Ingolfsson 84), Jonsson K, Dervic, Gretarsson (Gunnlaugsson B 64), Orlygsson, Stefansson, Sverrisson, Gunnlaugsson A.
Referee: Kelly (Republic of Ireland).

Istanbul, 14 December 1994, 25,000

Turkey (1) 1 *(Recep 39)*

Switzerland (2) 2 *(Koller 7, Bickel 16)*

Turkey: Rustu; Recep, Bulent K, Gokhan K, Abdullah, Ogun, Oguz, Cengiz (Ilker 46), Arif (Sergen 75), Hakan, Saffet.

Switzerland: Pascolo; Hottiger, Herr, Geiger, Thuler, Ohrel, Sforza, Koller, Sutter A, Bickel (Bonvin 65), Subiat (Grassi 80).
Referee: Craciunescu (Romania).

Budapest, 29 March 1995, 13,000

Hungary (0) 2 *(Kiprich 50, Illes 72)*

Switzerland (0) 2 *(Subiat 73, 85)*

Hungary: Petry; Mracsko, Lorincz, Meszoly, Kovacs E, Kozma, Halmai, Salloi, Illes, Kiprich (Marton 69), Vincze (Klausz 82).
Switzerland: Pascolo; Hottiger, Herr, Geiger, Fernandez, Koller, Ohrel, Sforza, Bickel (Grassi 65), Sutter A, Subiat (Henchoz 89).
Referee: Wieser (Austria).

Istanbul, 29 March 1995, 20,000

Turkey (0) 2 *(Emre 64, Sergen 75)*

Sweden (1) 1 *(Andersson K 23 (pen))*

Turkey: Engin; Recep, Bulent K, Emre, Alpay, Abdullah, Metin, Tolunay, Sergen (Mutlu 77), Hakan, Ertugrul (Oguz 46).
Sweden: Ravelli; Nilsson R, Andersson P, Bjorklund, Ljung, Schwarz, Zetterberg (Rehn 81), Thern, Larsson (Blomqvist 75), Dahlin, Andersson K.
Referee: Trentalange (Italy).

Budapest, 26 April 1995, 10,000

Hungary (1) 1 *(Halmai 2)*

Sweden (0) 0

Hungary: Vegh; Csabi, Meszoly, Mracsko, Kozma, Halmai, Lipcsei, Illes, Salloi, Csertoi (Szlezak 86), Vincze (Urban 68).
Sweden: Ravelli; Nilsson R, Andersson P, Kamark, Ljung, Schwarz, Zetterberg, Mild (Andersson R 62), Ingesson, Alexandersson (Gudmundsson 82), Andersson K.
Referee: Lopez Nieto (Spain).

Berne, 26 April 1995, 24,000

Switzerland (1) 1 *(Hottiger 38)*

Turkey (1) 2 *(Hakan 17, Ogun 56)*

Switzerland: Pascolo; Hottiger, Herr, Geiger, Fernandez (Walker 75), Ohrel, Sforza, Bickel, Sutter A, Grassi, Bonvin (Zuffi 70).
Turkey: Engin; Emre, Bulent K, Alpay, Recep, Ogun, Oguz (Ertugrul 83), Tolunay, Sergen (Suat 79), Abdullah, Hakan.
Referee: Van den Wijngaert (Belgium).

Stockholm, 1 June 1995, 25,676

Sweden (1) 1 *(Brolin 16 (pen))*

Iceland (1) 1 *(Gunnlaugsson A 2)*

Sweden: Ravelli; Sundgren, Andersson P, Mattsson, Kamark, Brolin, Schwarz, Thern, Limpar (Larsson 51), Dahlin, Andersson K.
Iceland: Kristinsson B; Orlygsson, Bergsson, Adolfsson, Jonsson K, Gudjohnsen (Thordarson 90), Stefansson, Jonsson S, Kristinsson R, Sverrisson, Gunnlaugsson A (Gunnlaugsson B 78).
Referee: Ouzounov (Bulgaria).

Reykjavik, 11 June 1995, 4500

Iceland (0) 2 *(Bergsson 63, Jonsson S 69)*

Hungary (1) 1 *(Vincze 20)*

Iceland: Kristinsson B; Bergsson, Adolfsson, Jonsson K, Jonsson S, Kristinsson R, Gretarsson, Gunnlaugsson A, Thordarson (Gunnlaugsson B 68), Gudjohnsen, Sverrisson.
Hungary: Petry; Csabi, Meszoly, Lipcsei, Mracsko, Halmai, Illes (Marton 68), Salloi, Kozma, Csertoi, Vincze (Hamar 70).
Referee: Sars (France).

Reykjavik, 16 August 1995, 12,000

Iceland (0) 0

Switzerland (2) 2 *(Knup 4, Turkyilmaz 17)*

Iceland: Kristinsson B; Adolfsson, Jonsson K (Dervic 89), Jonsson S, Bergsson, Kristinsson R, Orlygsson, Thorvaldsson, Gunnlaugsson A, Sverrisson (Ingolfsson 67), Gunnlaugsson B.

Switzerland: Pascolo; Hottiger, Geiger, Henchoz, Quentin, Ohrel, Fournier, Sforza, Sutter A (Bickel 81), Knup, Turkyilmaz (Bonvin 84).
Referee: Wojcik (Poland).

Gothenburg, 6 September 1995, 40,505

Sweden (0) 0

Switzerland (0) 0

Sweden: Andersson B; Kamark, Andersson P, Bjorklund, Nilsson M, Alexandersson, Thern, Schwarz (Erlingmark 89), Brolin (Larsson 77), Andersson K, Dahlin.

Switzerland: Pascolo; Hottiger, Henchoz, Geiger, Quentin, Ohrel, Sforza, Fournier, Sutter A (Herr 46), Knup, Turkyilmaz (Grassi 90).
Referee: Ceccarini (Italy).

Istanbul, 6 September 1995, 35,000

Turkey (2) 2 *(Hakan 9, 32)*

Hungary (0) 0

Turkey: Rustu; Recep, Alpay, Ogun, Osman, Oguz, Tugay, Sergen (Tolunay 46), Abdullah, Hakan (Bulent K 88), Hami (Bulent U 85).

Hungary: Petry; Lipcsei, Telek, Meszoly, Kozma, Farkashazy, Arany, Illes (Klausz 46), Halmai, Nagy (Salloi 46), Kiprich.
Referee: Krondl (Czech Republic).

Zurich, 11 October 1995, 21,000

Switzerland (1) 3 *(Turkyilmaz 23, Sforza 56, Ohrel 89)*

Hungary (0) 0

Switzerland: Pascolo; Hottiger, Henchoz, Geiger, Quentin, Ohrel, Yakin, Sforza, Fournier (Bickel 81), Knup (Bonvin 90), Turkyilmaz (Sutter A 85).

Hungary: Hajdu; Halmai, Telek, Lipcsei, Urban, Mracsko, Simon (Jagodics 21), Nyilas (Monos 62), Illes (Arany 62), Jovan, Vincze.
Referee: Agius (Malta).

Reykjavik, 11 October 1995, 2308

Iceland (0) 0

Turkey (0) 0

Iceland: Kristinsson B; Bergsson, Gislason, Ingolfsson, Adolfsson, Jonsson S, Kristinsson R, Orlygsson, Gudjohnsen, Sverrisson (Gunnlaugsson B 80), Gunnlaugsson A.

Turkey: Rustu; Recep, Ogun, Osman, Tugay, Alpay, Oguz, Sergen (Tolunay 75), Abdullah, Ertugrul, Hami.
Referee: Strampe (Germany).

Budapest, 11 November 1995, 3000

Hungary (0) 1 *(Illes 55)*

Iceland (0) 0

Hungary: Hajdu; Monos, Banfi, Csabi, Szlezak, Nyilas, Illes (Zombori 89), Duro, Bukszegi, Orosz (Farkashazy 75), Vincze (Nagy 88).

Iceland: Kristinsson B; Jonsson K, Bergsson, Adolfsson, Gislason, Orlygsson, Gretarsson (Stefansson 81), Kristinsson R (Danielsson 84), Gunnlaugsson A, Sverrisson, Gudjohnsen.
Referee: Bikas (Greece).

Stockholm, 15 November 1995, 11,700

Sweden (1) 2 *(Alexandersson 24, Pettersson 63)*

Turkey (0) 2 *(Hakan 62, Andersson P 72 (og))*

Sweden: Ravelli; Lucic, Bjorklund, Andersson P, Alexandersson, Mild, Fursth, Pettersson (Sahlin 81), Schwarz, Dahlin, Brolin (Zetterberg 75).

Turkey: Rustu; Alpay, Ogun, Osman, Tayfur, Oguz (Ertugrul 68), Tolunay, Tugay, Ibrahim (Kemalettin 46), Hakan, Oktay (Arif 46).
Referee: Wojcik (Poland).

	P	W	D	L	F	A	Pts
Switzerland	8	5	2	1	15	7	17
Turkey	8	4	3	1	16	8	15
Sweden	8	2	3	3	9	10	9
Hungary	8	2	2	4	7	13	8
Iceland	8	1	2	5	3	12	5

Group 4

Tallinn, 4 September 1994, 1500

Estonia (0) 0

Croatia (1) 2 *(Suker 45, 72)*

Estonia: Poom; Lemsalu, Prins, Kaljend, Kallaste T, Alonen, Olumets (Reim 46), Klavan, Kristal, Kirs (Krom 75), Linnumae.

Croatia: Ladic; Turkovic, Bilic, Stimac, Jarni, Jerkan, Asanovic (Cvitanovic 90), Prosinecki, Boban, Suker, Boksic.
Referee: Krondl (Czech Republic).

Maribor, 7 September 1994, 18,000

Slovenia (1) 1 *(Udovic 13)*

Italy (1) 1 *(Costacurta 15)*

Slovenia: Simeunovic; Jermanis, Novak, Milanic, Galic, Englaro, Katanec (Binkovski 58), Zidan (Krizan 90), Ceh, Udovic, Gliha.

Italy: Pagliuca; Mussi, Baresi, Costacurta, Panucci, Donadoni, Dino Baggio (Evani 55), Albertini, Signori, Casiraghi, Zola (Berti 55).
Referee: Heynemann (Germany).

Kiev, 7 September 1994, 25,000

Ukraine (0) 0

Lithuania (0) 2 *(Ivanauskas 55, Skarbalius 61)*

Ukraine: Tiapushkin; Skrypnik, Sak (Kovalets 8), Yevtushok, Popov, Petrov I, Pokhlebayev (Nagornyak 59), Maksimov, Finkel, Protasov, Konovalov.

Lithuania: Stauce; Ziukas, Sukristovas, Tereskinas, Vainoras, Vaineikis (Stonkus 81), Gudaitis, Stumbrys, Suika (Zuta 54), Ivanauskas, Skarbalius.
Referee: Karlsson (Sweden).

Tallinn, 8 October 1994, 4000

Estonia (0) 0

Italy (1) 2 *(Panucci 19, Casiraghi 77)*

Estonia: Poom; Lemsalu, Kallaste T, Alonen, Klavan (Kallaste R 75), Kaljend, Kristal, Reim, Krom (Olumets 67), Linnumae, Kirs.

Italy: Pagliuca; Panucci, Favalli (Apolloni 87), Evani (Albertini 83), Costacurta, Maldini, Rambaudi, Dino Baggio, Casiraghi, Zola, Signori.
Referee: Muller (Switzerland).

Zagreb, 9 October 1994, 12,000

Croatia (0) 2 *(Jerkan 56, Kozniku 61)*

Lithuania (0) 0

Croatia: Ladic; Mladenovic, Jarni, Bilic, Jerkan, Stimac (Brajkovic 88), Jurcevic, Asanovic, Suker, Boban, Boksic (Kozniku 78).

Lithuania: Stauce; Ziukas, Mazeikis, Gudaitis, Tereskinas, Vainoras, Sukristovas, Stumbrys, Zuta (Poderis 76), Skarbalius, Vaineikis (Korsakovas 59).
Referee: Wieser (Austria).

Kiev, 12 October 1994, 12,000

Ukraine (0) 0

Slovenia (0) 0

Ukraine: Tiapushkin; Luzhnyi, Diryavka, Kuznetsov O, Shmatovalenko, Lezhentsev, Mikhailichenko (Petrov I 70), Mikhailenko, Konovalov (Guseynov 61), Kovalets, Leonenko.

Slovenia: Boskovic; Galic, Krizan, Milanic, Jermanis, Ceh, Novak (Kokol 75), Zidan, Benedejcic, Udovic (Gliha 65), Florjancic.
Referee: Oezenov (Bulgaria).

Kiev, 13 November 1994, 500

Ukraine (2) 3 *(Konovalov 31, Kirs 45 (og), Guseynov 76)*

Estonia (0) 0

Ukraine: Shovkovski (Suslov 83); Luzhnyi, Kuznetsov O, Lezhentsev, Popov, Bezhenar, Kovalets (Petrov I 75), Litovchenko, Orbu, Skachenko (Guseynov 46), Konovalov.
Estonia: Vessenberg; Lemsalu, Kirs, Linnumae, Kallaste R, Alonen, Olumets, Lindmaa, Pari, Kristal, Zelinski.
Referee: Schellings (Belgium).

Palermo, 16 November 1994, 33,570

Italy (0) 1 *(Dino Baggio 90)*

Croatia (1) 2 *(Suker 32, 60)*

Italy: Pagliuca; Negro, Costacurta, Maldini, Panucci, Lombardo, Albertini (Di Matteo 65), Dino Baggio, Rambaudi (Donadoni 46), Casiraghi, Roberto Baggio.
Croatia: Ladic; Brajkovic, Jarni, Bilic, Stimac, Asanovic, Jerkan, Prosinecki (Mladenovic 57), Boban, Suker, Jurcevic (Kozniku 90).
Referee: Quiniou (France).

Maribor, 16 November 1994, 2500

Slovenia (0) 1 *(Zahovic 90)*

Lithuania (0) 2 *(Sukristovas 64, Zuta 87)*

Slovenia: Boskovic; Galic, Krizan, Englaro (Polisak 46), Jermanis, Ceh, Zidan, Benedejcic (Binkovski 46), Zahovic, Florjancic, Gliha.
Lithuania: Stauce; Suika (Zuta 76), Sukristovas, Mazeikis, Tereskinas, Vainoras, Gudaitis, Stumbrys, Narbekovas, Ivanauskas, Apanavicius.
Referee: Ihring (Slovakia).

Zagreb, 25 March 1995, 30,000

Croatia (2) 4 *(Boban 13, Suker 21, 79, Prosinecki 71)*

Ukraine (0) 0

Croatia: Ladic; Jerkan, Bilic, Pavlicic, Jarni, Prosinecki, Boban, Asanovic, Jurcevic (Vlaovic 79), Boksic (Turkovic 75), Suker.
Ukraine: Tiapushkin; Luzhnyi, Shmatovalenko, Mizin, Telesnenko, Martynov (Orbu 46), Bukel, Kalitvintsev, Shevchenko, Leonenko, Konovalov.
Referee: Weber (Germany).

Salerno, 25 March 1995, 35,000

Italy (1) 4 *(Zola 45, 65, Albertini 58, Ravanelli 82)*

Estonia (0) 1 *(Reim 74)*

Italy: Peruzzi; Negro, Maldini, Minotti, Carboni, Albertini, Eranio (Lombardo 57), Dino Baggio, Del Piero (Berti 69), Zola, Ravanelli.
Estonia: Poom; Lemsalu, Kallaste T, Kirs, Kallaste R, Olumets, Lindmaa, Linnumae, Kristal, Lell (Pari 76), Krom (Reim 72).
Referee: Philippi (Luxembourg).

Vilnus, 29 March 1995, 9500

Lithuania (0) 0

Croatia (0) 0

Lithuania: Stauce; Ziukas, Sukristovas, Stonkus, Vainoras, Suika, Gudaitis, Zdancius (Zuta 70), Narbekovas (Pocius 69), Ivanauskas, Skarbalius.
Croatia: Ladic; Pavlicic (Mladenovic 46), Stimac, Bilic, Jarni, Soldo, Prosinecki, Brajkovic, Asanovic, Suker, Boksic.
Referee: Burge (Wales).

Kiev, 29 March 1995, 10,000

Ukraine (0) 0

Italy (2) 2 *(Lombardo 11, Zola 37)*

Ukraine: Tiapushkin; Luzhnyi (Bukel 60), Telesnenko, Khomin, Yevtushok, Orbu, Mizin, Kalitvintsev, Leonenko, Shevchenko, Konovalov (Pokhlebayev 76).
Italy: Peruzzi; Benarrivo, Apolloni, Minotti, Maldini, Albertini, Di Matteo, Zola, Berti, Lombardo (Conte 73), Casiraghi (Ravanelli 65).
Referee: Puhl (Hungary).

Maribor, 29 March 1995, 6000

Slovenia (1) 3 *(Zahovic 40, Gliha 53, Kokol 90)*

Estonia (0) 0

Slovenia: Boskovic; Galic, Milanic, Jermanis (Skaper 70), Englaro, Ceh, Novak, Zahovic (Kokol 68), Zidan, Florjancic, Gliha.
Estonia: Poom; Kallaste R, Kallaste T, Olesk, Arbeiter (Lell 77), Olumets, Linnumae, Lindmaa, Lepik, Reim, Kirs.
Referee: Mendes (Portugal).

Tallinn, 26 April 1995, 500

Estonia (0) 0

Ukraine (1) 1 *(Guseynov 17)*

Estonia: Poom; Lemsalu, Kirs, Kallaste T, Kallaste R, Alonen, Olumets, Reim (Pari 68), Krom (Lepa 46), Lell, Kristal.
Ukraine: Suslov; Luzhnyi, Shmatovalenko, Diryavka, Holovko, Orbu, Zhabchenko, Maksimov, Naduda (Yevtushok 85), Nagornyak (Konovalov 46), Guseynov.
Referee: Hollung (Norway).

Vilnius, 26 April 1995, 15,000

Lithuania (0) 0

Italy (1) 1 *(Zola 12)*

Lithuania: Stauce; Ziukas, Sukristovas, Vainoras, Tereskinas, Suika, Gudaitis (Poderis 70), Skarbalius, Apanavicius (Preiksaitis 46), Ivanauskas, Slekys.
Italy: Pagliuca; Benarrivo, Costacurta, Minotti, Maldini, Conte (Dino Baggio 24), Di Matteo, Crippa (Berti 85), Lombardo, Casiraghi, Zola.
Referee: McCluskey (Scotland).

Zagreb, 26 April 1995, 25,000

Croatia (1) 2 *(Prosinecki 17, Suker 90)*

Slovenia (0) 0

Croatia: Ladic; Jerkan, Bilic, Stimac, Jarni, Prosinecki, Boban, Asanovic, Jurcevic (Gabric 13), Suker (Pavlicic 90), Boksic.
Slovenia: Boskovic; Galic, Englaro, Milanic (Skaper 89), Binkovski, Jermanis, Novak, Zidan, Zahovic (Kokol 71), Florjancic, Gliha.
Referee: Saravan (Turkey).

Vilnius, 7 June 1995, 6000

Lithuania (0) 2 *(Stonkus 47, Suika 69)*

Slovenia (0) 1 *(Gliha 82)*

Lithuania: Stauce; Ziukas, Sukristovas, Tereskinas, Vainoras, Stonkus, Maciulevicius (Baltusnikas 75), Preiksaitis (Suika 68), Skarbalius, Slekys, Ivanauskas.
Slovenia: Boskovic; Galic (Krizan 78), Englaro, Milanic, Jermanis, Ceh, Novak (Skaper 58), Kokol, Zahovic, Florjancic, Gliha.
Referee: Vagner (Hungary).

Tallinn, 11 June 1995, 2000

Estonia (1) 1 *(Reim 27)*

Slovenia (1) 3 *(Novak 37, 68, Zahovic 78)*

Estonia: Poom; Lepa (Klavan 46), Kirs, Kallaste T, Olumets, Alonen, Pari, Linnumae, Kristal, Reim, Arbeiter (Rajala 59).
Slovenia: Boskovic; Galic, Englaro, Milanic, Novak, Jermanis (Cvikl 64), Kokol (Krizan 46), Ceh, Zahovic, Florjancic, Gliha.
Referee: Durkin (England).

Kiev, 11 June 1995, 8500

Ukraine (1) 1 *(Kalitvintsev 13)*

Croatia (0) 0

Ukraine: Suslov; Zhabchenko, Skripnik, Holovko, Maksimov, Orbu, Pokhlebayev, Kalitvintsev, Palyanitsa (Nagornyak 77), Horilyi, Guseynov (Shkapenko 46).
Croatia: Gabric; Pavlicic (Mrmic 28), Jarni, Soldo, Jerkan, Bilic, Asanovic (Pralija 48), Mladenovic, Suker, Boban (Butorovic 38), Boksic.
Referee: Rothlisberger (Switzerland).

Tallinn, 16 August 1995, 1500

Estonia (0) 0

Lithuania (0) 1 *(Maciulevicius 48)*

Estonia: Poom; Kallaste R, Lell, Kiisman (Krom 46), Lepa, Kirs, O'Konnel-Bronin (Olesk 73), Lemsalu, Reim, Lindmaa, Kristal.
Lithuania: Stauce; Ziukas, Sukristovas, Suika, Stonkus, Tereskinas, Vainoras, Maciulevicius, Ivanauskas, Skarbalius (Kanchelskis 77), Slekys (Zuta 67).
Referee: Nilsson (Sweden).

Zagreb, 3 September 1995, 25,000

Croatia (4) 7 *(Mladenovic 3, Suker 19 (pen), 58, 89, Boksic 29, Boban 42, Stimac 82)*

Estonia (1) 1 *(Reim 17)*

Croatia: Ladic (Mrmic 30); Mladenovic, Stimac (Turkovic 83), Jerkan, Bilic (Pralija 75), Jarni, Stanic, Boban, Prosinecki, Suker, Boksic.
Estonia: Poom; Kallaste R, Lemsalu, Kallaste T, Kirs, Kiisman (Lell 42), Lepa, Lindmaa, Rajala, Kristal, Reim.
Referee: Huzu (Romania).

Udine, 6 September 1995, 30,000

Italy (1) 1 *(Ravanelli 12)*

Slovenia (0) 0

Italy: Peruzzi; Ferrara, Costacurta, Tacchinardi, Carboni, Di Matteo, Albertini, Di Livio, Del Piero (Signori 46), Ravanelli (Dino Baggio 81), Zola (Roberto Baggio 61).
Slovenia: Zupan; Galic, Milanic, Polisak, Jermanis, Ceh, Kokol (Binkovski 46), Cvikl (Valentincic 77), Zahovic, Udovic, Gliha (Becaj 58).
Referee: Gadosi (Slovakia).

Vilnius, 6 September 1995, 6000

Lithuania (1) 1 *(Maciulevicius 16)*

Ukraine (0) 3 *(Guseynov 66, 71, Gussine 84)*

Lithuania: Stauce; Suika, Vainoras, Ziukas, Tereskinas (Preiksaitis 68), Stonkus, Sukristovas, Maciulevicius, Skarbalius (Zvingilas 77), Ivanauskas, Slekys.
Ukraine: Suslov; Luzhnyi, Holovko, Skripnik, Bezhenar, Zhabchenko (Pokhlebayev 66), Horilyi, Kalitvintsev, Orbu, Gussine, Guseynov (Yevtushok 87).
Referee: Shorte (Republic of Ireland).

Split, 8 October 1995, 40,000

Croatia (0) 1 *(Suker 48 (pen))*

Italy (1) 1 *(Albertini 29)*

Croatia: Ladic; Stimac, Jerkan, Pavlicic, Mladenovic, Boban, Asanovic, Stanic, Jurcevic (Kozniku 46), Boksic, Suker.
Italy: Bucci; Ferrara (Benarrivo 84), Apolloni, Costacurta, Maldini, Di Livio, Di Matteo, Albertini, Del Piero (Crippa 86), Zola (Toldo 9), Ravanelli.
Referee: Uilenberg (Holland).

Vilnius, 11 October 1995, 2000

Lithuania (4) 5 *(Maciulevicius 8, Suika 13, 19, Slekys 44, Ivanauskas 61)*

Estonia (0) 0

Lithuania: Stauce (Martinkenas 46); Suika (Zvingilas 74), Vainoras, Kanchelskis, Stonkus, Rimkus, Maciulevicius, Baltusnikas, Vencevicius, Slekys (Jankauskas 46), Ivanauskas.
Estonia: Poom; Lell (Reim 46) (Krom 80), Olesk, Kallaste T, Lindmaa, Zelinski, Lepa (Kristal 46), Kallaste R, Linnumae, Rajala, Oper.
Referee: Pauchard (France).

Ljubljana, 11 October 1995, 4000

Slovenia (0) 3 *(Udovic 50, 90, Zahovic 73)*

Ukraine (2) 2 *(Skripnik 23, Guseynov 45)*

Slovenia: Zupan; Galic, Englaro, Milanic, Rudonja, Ceh, Novak, Zahovic, Udovic, Florjancic (Cvikl 72), Gliha.
Ukraine: Suslov; Luzhnyi, Shmatovalenko (Polunin 88), Holovko, Zhabchenko, Skripnik, Orbu, Kalitvintsev, Bezhenar, Guseynov, Gussine (Nagornyak 51).
Referee: Coroado (Portugal).

Bari, 11 November 1995, 50,000

Italy (1) 3 *(Ravanelli 21, 48, Maldini 53)*

Ukraine (1) 1 *(Polunin 18)*

Italy: Peruzzi; Benarrivo, Costacurta, Ferrara, Maldini, Di Matteo, Albertini, Dino Baggio (Crippa 46), Del Piero (Carboni 87), Zola (Simone 65), Ravanelli.
Ukraine: Suslov; Luzhnyi, Skripnik, Bezhenar, Horilyi (Yevtushok 14), Polunin, Orbu, Kalitvintsev, Nagornyak (Pokhlebayev 71), Sharan (Popov 50), Guseynov.
Referee: Muhmenthaler (Switzerland).

Ljubljana, 15 November 1995, 15,000

Slovenia (1) 1 *(Gliha 36)*

Croatia (1) 2 *(Suker 40 (pen), Jurcevic 55)*

Slovenia: Zupan; Galic, Englaro, Krizan, Jermanis, Zulic (Cvikl 62), Novak, Udovic, Ceh, Florjancic (Rudonja 62), Gliha.
Croatia: Ladic; Jurcevic, Jarni, Soldo, Jerkan, Bilic, Pralija (Mladenovic 63), Prosinecki, Suker, Stanic, Mornar.
Referee: Goethals (Belgium).

Reggio-Emilia, 15 November 1995, 30,000

Italy (0) 4 *(Suika 52 (og), Zola 65, 81, Vainoras 82 (og))*

Lithuania (0) 0

Italy: Peruzzi; Mussi, Ferrara, Costacurta, Maldini (Carboni 72), Statuto (Zola 46), Albertini, Di Matteo, Del Piero, Casiraghi (Ravanelli 46), Simone.
Lithuania: Stauce; Stonkus, Rimkus, Vainoras, Ziukas, Tereskinas, Suika (Vencevicius 78), Preiksaitis, Skarbalius, Maciulevicius (Zvingilas 46), Ivanauskas (Zutautas 68).
Referee: Diaz Vega (Spain).

	P	W	D	L	F	A	Pts
Croatia	10	7	2	1	22	5	23
Italy	10	7	2	1	20	6	23
Lithuania	10	5	1	4	13	12	16
Ukraine	10	4	1	5	11	15	13
Slovenia	10	3	2	5	13	13	11
Estonia	10	0	0	10	3	31	0

Group 5

Prague, 6 September 1994, 10,226

Czech Republic (3) 6 *(Smejkal 6 (pen), Kubik 33, Siegl 35, 49, 81, Berger P 89)*

Malta (0) 1 *(Laferla 75)*

Czech Republic: Kouba; Suchoparek, Kubik, Novotny J, Latal (Vesely 87), Nemecek, Frydek (Berger P 83), Nemec, Smejkal, Kuka, Siegl.
Malta: Cluett; Vella S, Galea, Buttigieg, Buhagiar, Camilleri J, Gregory (Camilleri E 83), Brincat, Saliba, Laferla, Busuttil.
Referee: Loizou (Cyprus).

Luxembourg, 7 September 1994, 8200

Luxembourg (0) 0

Holland (1) 4 *(Roy 22, Ronald de Boer 62, 64, Jonk 90)*

Luxembourg: Koch; Ferron, Weis, Strasser, Birsens, Wolf, Holtz, Saibene, Groff, Cardoni (Morocutti 80), Langers (Theis 89).
Holland: De Goey; Valckx, Blind, Frank de Boer, Winter, Jonk, Rob Witschge, Overmars, Bosman, Ronald de Boer, Roy (Van Vossen 75).
Referee: Snoddy (Northern Ireland).

Oslo, 7 September 1994, 16,739

Norway (0) 1 *(Frigaard 88)*

Belarus (0) 0

Norway: Grodaas; Lydersen, Pedersen T, Berg H, Bjornebye, Flo (Frigaard 70), Mykland, Rekdal, Bohinen (Leonhardsen 46), Jakobsen, Fjortoft.
Belarus: Shantolosov; Gurenko, Sosnitski, Zygmantovich, Khatskevich, Yakhimovich, Gerasimets, Metlitsky, Kulanin (Kachuro 46), Antonovitch, Markhel.
Referee: Goethals (Belgium).

Valletta, 12 October 1994, 4000

Malta (0) 0

Czech Republic (0) 0

Malta: Cluett; Buttigieg, Galea, Vella S, Camilleri J, Saliba (Sant-Fournier 77), Brincat, Carabott (Camilleri E 90), Gregory, Busuttil, Laferla.
Czech Republic: Srnicek; Suchoparek, Kubik, Novotny J, Latal, Nemecek (Kadlec 44), Hasek, Nemec, Smejkal (Frydek 70), Skuhravy, Kuka.
Referee: Coroado (Portugal).

Oslo, 12 October 1994, 22,293

Norway (0) 1 *(Rekdal 52 (pen))*

Holland (1) 1 *(Roy 22)*

Norway: Thorstvedt; Lydersen, Berg, Pedersen, Bjornebye, Rushfeldt (Flo 63), Bohinen, Rekdal, Mykland, Leonhardsen, Fjortoft (Frigaard 77).
Holland: De Goey; Blind, Reiziger (Van Gobbel 77), Valckx, Frank de Boer, Winter, Jonk, Rob Witschge, Overmars, Bergkamp (Ronald de Boer 71), Roy.
Referee: McCluskey (Scotland).

Minsk, 12 October 1994, 5000

Belarus (0) 2 *(Romashchenko 67, Gerasimets 76)*

Luxembourg (0) 0

Belarus: Shantolosov; Gurenko, Rodnionok (Sosnitski 80), Yakhimovich, Zygmantovich, Gerasimets, Markhel (Antonovitch 65), Aleinikov, Romashchenko, Shukanov, Metlitsky.
Luxembourg: Koch; Ferron (Vanek 83), Strasser, Birsens, Wolf, Cardoni, Hellers, Weis, Holtz (Morocutti 58), Saibene, Fanelli.
Referee: O'Hanlon (Republic of Ireland).

Minsk, 16 November 1994, 8000

Belarus (0) 0

Norway (2) 4 *(Berg 34, Leonhardsen 39, Bohinen 52, Rekdal 83)*

Belarus: Shantolosov; Yaskovich, Zygmantovich, Rodnionok, Yakhimovich, Metlitsky, Markhel (Youssipets 82), Antonovitch, Romashchenko (Gurinovich 82), Gerasimets, Shukanov.
Norway: Grodaas; Halle, Berg, Johnsen R (Jakobsen 80), Bjornebye (Lydersen 42), Mykland, Leonhardsen, Bohinen, Rekdal, Rushfeldt, Fjortoft.
Referee: Spassov (Bulgaria).

Rotterdam, 16 November 1994, 40,000

Holland (0) 0

Czech Republic (0) 0

Holland: De Goey; Valckx, Blind, Frank de Boer, Rob Witschge (Numan 78), Winter, Roy, Jonk, Van Vossen, Mulder (Kluivert 70), Taument.
Czech Republic: Srnicek; Latal, Kadlec, Suchoparek, Hapal, Kubik, Nemec, Bilek, Kuka (Samec 90), Siegl, Poborsky (Berger 75).
Referee: Puhl (Hungary).

Rotterdam, 14 December 1994, 26,000

Holland (3) 5 *(Mulder 6, Roy 17, Jonk 40, Ronald de Boer 52, Seedorf 90)*

Luxembourg (0) 0

Holland: De Goey; Valckx, Blind, Frank de Boer, Winter (Van Hooydonk 75), Jonk, Numan, Overmars, Ronald de Boer, Mulder (Seedorf 46), Roy.
Luxembourg: Koch; Ferron, Weis, Wolf, Birsens, Strasser, Holtz, Hellers, Cardoni, Groff, Langers (Theis 61).
Referee: Roduit (Switzerland).

Ta Qali, 14 December 1994, 9000

Malta (0) 0

Norway (1) 1 *(Fjortoft 10)*

Malta: Cluett; Vella S, Woods, Buttigieg, Camilleri J, Brincat, Busuttil, Saliba (Scerri 82), Carabott (Buhagiar 60), Gregory, Laferla.
Norway: Grodaas; Halle, Berg, Johnsen R, Bjornebye, Mykland, Rekdal, Rushfeldt (Jakobsen 82), Flo, Bohinen (Solbakken 72), Fjortoft.
Referee: Beschin (Italy).

Valletta, 22 February 1995, 6000

Malta (0) 0

Luxembourg (0) 1 *(Cardoni 54)*

Malta: Cluett; Vella S, Brincat, Buttigieg, Buhagiar, Camilleri J, Busuttil, Suda (Sciberras 60), Carabott (Saliba 78), Gregory, Laferla.
Luxembourg: Koch; Vanek, Weis, Wolf, Deville, Saibene, Hellers, Birsens, Groff, Langers (Schneider 89), Cardoni (Holtz 87).
Referee: Berusan (Croatia).

Luxembourg, 29 March 1995, 3000

Luxembourg (0) 0

Norway (1) 2 *(Leonhardsen 35, Aase 80)*

Luxembourg: Rohmann; Ferron, Vanek, Birsens (Schneider 85), Strasser, Deville, Saibene (Feyder 78), Weis, Groff, Langers, Cardoni.
Norway: Thorstvedt; Haaland, Johnsen R, Berg, Bjornebye, Flo (Aase 46), Leonhardsen, Rekdal (Solbakken 84), Bohinen, Fjortoft, Jakobsen.
Referee: Levnikov (Russia).

Rotterdam, 29 March 1995, 34,000

Holland (1) 4 *(Seedorf 39, Bergkamp 77 (pen), Winter 80, Kluivert 85)*

Malta (0) 0

Holland: De Goey; Valckx, Blind, Frank de Boer, Jonk, Winter, Seedorf, Overmars, Ronald de Boer (Kluivert 76), Bergkamp, Roy (Van de Luer 58).
Malta: Cluett; Vella S (Gregory 90), Buhagiar, Galea, Woods, Camilleri J, Busuttil (Agius 88), Saliba, Sant-Fournier, Camilleri E, Laferla.
Referee: Orrason (Iceland).

Ostrava, 29 March 1995, 5549

Czech Republic (2) 4 *(Kadlec 5, Berger 18, 63, Kuka 69)*

Belarus (1) 2 *(Gerasimets 44 (pen), Gurinovich 88)*

Czech Republic: Srnicek; Repka, Kadlec, Latal, Frydek (Bilek 86), Nemecek, Berger, Hapal, Smejkal, Kuka, Siegl (Samec 89).
Belarus: Shantolosov; Yakhimovich (Rodnionok 77), Gurenko, Zygmantovich, Sosnitski, Juravel (Kachentsev 81), Taikov, Metlitsky, Youssipets, Gerasimets, Gurinovich.
Referee: Veissiere (France).

Minsk, 26 April 1995, 13,000

Belarus (0) 1 *(Taikov 53)*

Malta (0) 1 *(Carabott 72)*

Belarus: Marchoukel; Gurenko, Zygmantovich, Taikov, Juravel, Metlitsky (Rodnionok 70), Youssipets (Romashchenko 75), Shukanov, Gerasimets, Gurinovich, Antonovitch.
Malta: Cluett; Vella S, Buttigieg, Camilleri E, Woods, Saliba, Gregory (Agius 24), Laferla, Sant-Fournier, Carabott, Busuttil (Attard 88).
Referee: Gadosi (Slovakia).

Prague, 26 April 1995, 20,000

Czech Republic (0) 3 *(Skuhravy 49, Nemecek 57, Berger 62)*

Holland (1) 1 *(Jonk 7)*

Czech Republic: Kouba; Repka, Kadlec, Suchoparek, Berger, Hapal, Nemecek, Nemec, Frydek (Latal 46), Kuka (Siegl 89), Skuhravy.
Holland: De Goey; Valckx, Blind, Frank de Boer, Winter (Kluivert 65), Jonk, Seedorf, Numan, Overmars, Ronald de Boer, Van Vossen (Bosz 46).
Referee: Krug (Germany).

Oslo, 26 April 1995, 15,124

Norway (3) 5 *(Jakobsen 11, Fjortoft 12, Brattbakk 24, Berg 46, Rekdal 49)*

Luxembourg (0) 0

Norway: Grodaas; Berg (Haaland 76), Johnsen R, Nilsen, Halle, Bohinen (Solbakken 35), Rekdal, Leonhardsen, Jakobsen, Brattbakk, Fjortoft.

Luxembourg: Koch; Feyder, Vanek, Holtz (Theis 34), Strasser, Deville, Hellers, Saibene (Lamborelle 75), Langers, Cardoni, Groff.
Referee: Ferry (Northern Ireland).

Luxembourg, 7 June 1995, 1500
Luxembourg (0) 1 *(Hellers 90)*
Czech Republic (0) 0
Luxembourg: Koch; Vanek, Strasser, Weis, Birsens, Ganser (Cardoni 87), Hellers, Groff, Deville, Langers, Theis (Saibene 75).
Czech Republic: Kouba; Suchoparek, Repka (Frydek 69), Kadlec, Hapal, Latal, Nemec, Nemecek, Berger, Kuka, Skuhravy (Drulak 60).
Referee: Ashman (Wales).

Oslo, 7 June 1995, 15,000
Norway (1) 2 *(Fjortoft 43, Flo 88)*
Malta (0) 0
Norway: Thorstvedt; Haaland (Brattbakk 69), Johnsen R, Berg, Nilsen, Flo, Mykland, Solbakken, Rekdal (Ingebrigtsen 83), Fjortoft, Jakobsen.
Malta: Cluett; Vella S, Buhagiar (Saliba 76), Attard, Woods, Buttigieg (Camilleri E 28), Busuttil, Agius, Laferla, Sant-Fournier, Carabott.
Referee: Przesmycki (Poland).

Minsk, 7 June 1995, 12,000
Belarus (1) 1 *(Gerasimets 27)*
Holland (0) 0
Belarus: Shantolosov; Dovnar (Kachentsev 86), Taikov, Gurenko, Rodnionok, Zygmantovitch, Juravel, Youssipets, Romashchenko (Antonovitch 54), Kachuro, Gerasimets.
Holland: Van der Sar; De Kock, Blind (Winter 69), Valckx (Numan 64), Seedorf, Jonk, Van't Schip, Davids, Ronald de Boer, Kluivert, Overmars.
Referee: Porumboiu (Romania).

Oslo, 16 August 1995, 22,054
Norway (1) 1 *(Berg 27)*
Czech Republic (0) 1 *(Suchoparek 84)*
Norway: Thorstvedt; Haaland, Johnsen R, Berg, Loken, Flo, Bohinen, Leonhardsen, Fjortoft (Brattbakk 80), Solbakken, Jakobsen (Brandesather 69).
Czech Republic: Kouba; Latal (Poborsky 78), Kadlec, Suchoparek, Repka, Hapal, Nemec, Berger (Nedved 46), Frydek, Kuka, Drulak (Samec 78).
Referee: Koushainov (Russia).

Prague, 6 September 1995, 19,522
Czech Republic (1) 2 *(Skuhravy 6 (pen), Drulak 87)*
Norway (0) 0
Czech Republic: Kouba; Latal, Kadlec, Suchoparek, Repka, Nemecek, Frydek (Poborsky 71), Nemec, Nedved, Kuka (Drulak 19), Skuhravy (Lokvenc 81).
Norway: Thorstvedt; Loken, Johnsen R, Johnsen E, Berg, Flo, Bohinen (Rekdal 75), Solbakken, Leonhardsen, Jakobsen, Fjortoft (Brattbakk 70).
Referee: Rothlisberger (Switzerland).

Rotterdam, 6 September 1995, 22,000
Holland (0) 1 *(Mulder 83)*
Belarus (0) 0
Holland: Van der Sar; Reiziger, Blind, De Kock, Frank de Boer, Ronald de Boer, Winter, Richard Witschge (Numan 86), Eykelkamp (Mulder 64), Bergkamp, Overmars.
Belarus: Satsunkevich; Gurenko, Zygmantovitch, Dovnar, Rodnionok, Gerasimets, Taikov, Juravel (Vekhtev 89), Romashchenko (Vergeichik 85), Youssipets (Kachentsev 69), Kachuro.
Referee: Sedlacek (Austria).

Luxemburg, 6 September 1995, 4,700
Luxemburg (1) 1 *(Holtz 44)*
Malta (0) 0
Luxemburg: Koch; Vanek, Deville, Birsens, Strasser, Saibene, Hellers, Weis, Holtz (Cardoni 85), Langers, Groff (Theis 68).

Malta: Cluett; Delia (Agius 28) (Gregory 89), Buhagiar, Galea, Woods, Buttigieg, Busuttil, Saliba, Sant-Fournier, Laferla, Carabott.
Referee: Dubinskas (Lithuania).

Minsk, 7 October 1995, 9500
Belarus (0) 0
Czech Republic (1) 2 *(Frydek 25, Berger 84)*
Belarus: Shantolosov; Taikov, Gurenko, Dovnar, Rodnionok, Juravel, Gerasimets, Youssipets (Baranov 74), Belkevich, Kachuro, Kachentsev.
Czech Republic: Kouba; Kadlec, Repka, Nedved (Berger 73), Hapal, Latal, Nemecek (Hornak 15), Frydek (Poborsky 87), Nemec, Drulak, Kuka.
Referee: Frisk (Sweden).

Valletta, 11 October 1995, 8000
Malta (0) 0
Holland (0) 4 *(Overmars 52, 61, 65, Seedorf 80)*
Malta: Cluett; Attard (Galea 71), Buhagiar, Brincat, Woods, Zammit, Busuttil, Saliba, Laferla, Carabott, Agius (Sant Fournier 5).
Holland: Van der Sar; Reiziger, Blind (Trustfull 71), Frank de Boer, Ronald de Boer, Seedorf, Numan, Richard Witschge, Overmars, Kluivert, Mulder (Helder 64).
Referee: Nielsen (Denmark).

Luxemburg, 11 October 1995, 4500
Luxemburg (0) 0
Belarus (0) 0
Luxemburg: Koch; Vanek, Deville, Birsens, Strasser, Saibene, Hellers, Weis, Holtz (Lamborelle 90), Langers (Theis 81), Morocutti (Cardoni 72).
Belarus: Shantolosov; Gurenko, Dovnar, Rodnionok, Taikov, Youssipets, Juravel, Baranov, Belkevich, Kachentsev (Vergeichik 90), Kachuro.
Referee: Durkin (England).

Ta'Qali, 12 November 1995, 2500
Malta (0) 0
Belarus (0) 2 *(Gerasimets 79, 83)*
Malta: Cluett; Attard, Vella S, Woods, Saliba, Zammit, Busuttil, Buhagiar, Brincat (Sant-Fournier 48), Agius (Carabott 73), Laferla.
Belarus: Shantolosov; Gurenko, Zygmantovitch (Youssipets 51), Taikov, Dovnar, Khmelnitski (Belkevich 80), Baranov, Maleyev (Makovski 68), Melitski, Gerasimets, Kachuro.
Referee: Metin (Turkey).

Prague, 15 November 1995, 20,239
Czech Republic (1) 3 *(Drulak 37, 46, Berger 56)*
Luxemburg (0) 0
Czech Republic: Kouba; Hapal, Kadlec, Suchoparek, Latal, Nemecek (Poborsky 70), Frydek, Berger (Smicer 83), Nedved, Kuka (Lokvenc 86), Drulak.
Luxemburg: Koch; Ferron, Vanek, Weis, Strasser, Deville (Theis 58), Holtz (Ganser 75), Hellers, Saibene (Cardoni 89), Groff, Langers.
Referee: Vieser (Austria).

Rotterdam, 15 November 1995, 49,000
Holland (0) 3 *(Seedorf 48, Mulder 88, Overmars 89)*
Norway (0) 0
Holland: Van der Sar; Reiziger, Blind, Frank de Boer, Numan, Richard Witschge (Davids 56), Seedorf, Bergkamp (Mulder 78), Overmars, Ronald de Boer, Helder (De Kock 85).
Norway: Grodaas; Loken (Haaland 62), Johnsen E, Berg, Bjornebye, Flo, Mykland (Leonhardsen 58), Rekdal, Bohinen (Solbakken 82), Jakobsen, Fjortoft.
Referee: Gallagher (England).

	P	W	D	L	F	A	Pts
Czech Republic	10	6	3	1	21	6	21
Holland	10	6	2	2	23	5	20
Norway	10	6	2	2	17	7	20
Belarus	10	3	2	5	8	13	11
Luxembourg	10	3	1	6	3	21	10
Malta	10	0	2	8	2	22	2

Group 6

Windsor Park, 20 April 1994, 7000
Northern Ireland (3) 4 *(Quinn 5, 33, Lomas 25, Dowie 48)*
Liechtenstein (0) 1 *(Hasler 84)*
Northern Ireland: Wright; Fleming, Taggart, Donaghy, Worthington, Magilton (O'Neill 81), Wilson, Lomas, Hughes, Quinn, Dowie (Gray 78).
Liechtenstein: Oehry; Stocker, Frick C, Ospelt J, Moser, Quaderer, Ritter, Zech H, Telser, Matt (Hasler 70), Frick M.
Referee: Luinge (Holland).

Riga, 7 September 1994, 2200
Latvia (0) 0
Republic of Ireland (2) 3 *(Aldridge 16, 75 (pen), Sheridan 29)*
Latvia: Karavayev; Troicki, Sevliakovs, Lobanev, Zemlinsky, Astafyev, Mikutsky (Yeliseyev 62), Milevskis (Stepanov 46), Sharando, Bulders, Babichev.
Republic of Ireland: Kelly A; Kelly G, Babb, McGrath, Irwin, McAteer (McGoldrick 80), Sheridan, Townsend, Staunton, Aldridge, Quinn (Cascarino 70).
Referee: Frisk (Sweden).

Eschen, 7 September 1994, 5800
Liechtenstein (0) 0
Austria (3) 4 *(Polster 18, 45, 79, Aigner 22)*
Liechtenstein: Heeb; Moser, Hefti, Ospelt J, Quaderer, Telser, Zech H (Matt 68), Klaunzer, Ospelt W (Hanselmann 28), Frick M, Hasler.
Austria: Wohlfahrt; Schottel, Werner, Kogler J, Prosenik, Stoger, Pfeifenberger (Flogel 74), Feiersinger, Aigner, Ogris (Cerny 63), Polster.
Referee: Ziller (Germany).

Windsor Park, 7 September 1994, 6000
Northern Ireland (0) 1 *(Quinn 58 (pen))*
Portugal (1) 2 *(Rui Costa 8, Oliveira 81)*
Northern Ireland: Fettis; Fleming, Morrow (Taggart 81), McDonald, Worthington, Gillespie (O'Boyle 81), Magilton, Lomas, Hughes, Quinn, Gray.
Portugal: Vitor Baia; Joao Pinto I, Paulo Madeira, Paulinho Santos, Helder, Tavares, Paulo Sousa, Vitor Paneira (Folha 63), Figo, Rui Costa, Sa Pinto (Domingos 80).
Referee: Pedersen (Norway).

Riga, 9 October 1994, 2000
Latvia (0) 1 *(Monyak 88)*
Portugal (1) 3 *(Joao Pinto II 33, 72, Vigo 73)*
Latvia: Karavayev; Troicki, Astafyev, Zemlinsky, Sevliakovs, Sprogis (Monyak 69), Stepanov, Ivanov, Babichev, Glazov (Milevskis 46), Semenov.
Portugal: Vitor Baia; Joao Pinto I, Helder, Paulo Madeira, Nelo, Paulo Sousa, Vitor Paneira (Paulo Alves 60), Joao Pinto II, Figo (Tavares 81), Rui Costa, Domingos.
Referee: Blareau (Belgium).

Vienna, 12 October 1994, 20,000
Austria (1) 1 *(Polster 24 (pen))*
Northern Ireland (2) 2 *(Gillespie 3, Gray 36)*
Austria: Wohlfahrt; Kogler J, Schottel, Werner, Artner, Prosenik (Pfeifenberger 65), Stoger, Feiersinger, Hutter, Ogris (Hasenhuttl 45), Polster.
Northern Ireland: Kee; Fleming, Worthington, Taggart, McDonald, Lomas, Gillespie (O'Neill 66), Magilton, Dowie (Quinn 74), Gray, Hughes.
Referee: Lopez Nieto (Spain).

Dublin, 12 October 1994, 32,980
Republic of Ireland (3) 4 *(Coyne 2, 4, Quinn 30, 82)*
Liechtenstein (0) 0
Republic of Ireland: Bonner; Kelly G, Irwin (McLoughlin 46), McAteer, Kernaghan, Babb, McGoldrick, Coyne, Quinn, Sheridan, Staunton.

Liechtenstein: Heeb; Hefti, Telser, Ritter, Moser, Ospelt W, Hanselmann, Zech H, Haas (Klaunzer 77), Frick M, Heidegger (Matt 71).
Referee: Bergmann (Iceland).

Lisbon, 13 November 1994, 50,000
Portugal (1) 1 *(Figo 36)*
Austria (0) 0
Portugal: Vitor Baia; Joao Pinto I, Paulo Madeira, Helder, Paulinho Santos, Paulo Sousa, Figo, Oceano, Rui Costa (Domingos 84), Joao Pinto II, Sa Pinto (Vitor Paneira 70).
Austria: Konrad; Schottel, Furstaller, Kogler J, Feiersinger, Artner, Stoger, Winklhofer, Kuhbauer (Prosenik 46), Cerny (Hutter 70), Polster.
Referee: Mikkelsen (Denmark).

Eschen-Mauren, 15 November 1994, 1300
Liechtenstein (0) 0
Latvia (1) 1 *(Babichev 14)*
Liechtenstein: Heeb; Moser, Telser, Hefti, Ritter, Hilti, Zech H (Klaunzer 60), Ospelt W, Frick M, Heidegger (Oehri 59), Hasler.
Latvia: Karavayev; Troicki, Astafyev, Zemlinsky, Sevliakovs, Sprogis, Blagonadezhdin (Mikutsky 46), Ivanov, Semenov, Milevskis, Babichev (Sharando 71).
Referee: Werner (Poland).

Windsor Park, 16 November 1994, 10,336
Northern Ireland (0) 0
Republic of Ireland (3) 4 *(Aldridge 6, Keane 11, Sheridan 38, Townsend 54)*
Northern Ireland: Kee; Fleming, Worthington, Morrow, Taggart, O'Neill (Patterson 46), Gillespie (Wilson 62), Magilton, Dowie, Gray, Hughes.
Republic of Ireland: Kelly A; Kelly G, Irwin, Keane (McAteer 44), McGrath, Babb, Sheridan, Aldridge (Coyne 46), Quinn, Townsend, Staunton.
Referee: Muhmenthaler (Switzerland).

Lisbon, 18 December 1994, 30,000
Portugal (3) 8 *(Domingos 2, 11, Oceano 45, Joao Pinto II 56, Fernando Couto 72, Folha 74, Paulo Alves 75, 79)*
Liechtenstein (0) 0
Portugal: Vitor Baia; Joao Pinto I, Fernando Couto, Oceano, Paulinho Santos, Figo, Vitor Paneira (Paulo Alves 57), Rui Costa, Joao Pinto II (Secretario 70), Domingos, Folha.
Liechtenstein: Heeb; Telser, Hefti, Ospelt W (Oehri R 44), Moser, Hilti, Ritter, Zech H, Hasler (Matt 58), Frick M, Heidegger.
Referee: Pucek (Czech Republic).

Dublin, 29 March 1995, 32,200
Republic of Ireland (0) 1 *(Quinn 47)*
Northern Ireland (0) 1 *(Dowie 72)*
Republic of Ireland: Kelly A; Kelly G, Irwin, Keane, McGrath, Babb, Sheridan, Kelly D (McAteer 75), Quinn (Cascarino 82), Townsend, Staunton.
Northern Ireland: Fettis; Patterson, Worthington, Hill, Taggart, McDonald, Morrow, Magilton, Dowie, Hughes, Gillespie.
Referee: Van der Ende (Holland).

Salzburg, 29 March 1995, 5500
Austria (2) 5 *(Herzog 18, 58, Pfeifenberger 41, Polster 69 (pen), 90)*
Latvia (0) 0
Austria: Konrad; Furstaller, Kogler J, Feiersinger, Pfeifenberger, Marasek, Artner (Hutter 76), Kuhbauer, Herzog, Ogris (Ramusch 46), Polster.
Latvia: Laizan; Sevliakovs, Sprogis, Lobanev, Troicki, Astafyev, Zemlinsky (Mikutsky 66), Blagonadezhdin, Teplov, Monyak, Babichev (Shtolcers 74).
Referee: Agius (Malta).

Riga, 26 April 1995, 1560
Latvia (0) 0
Northern Ireland (0) 1 *(Dowie 69 (pen))*
Latvia: Laizan; Troicki, Astafyev, Zemlinsky, Sevliakovs, Sprogis, Stepanov, Blagonadezhdin (Butkus 30), Teplov, Babichev, Yeliseyev.
Northern Ireland: Fettis; Patterson, Worthington, Hunter, McDonald, Hill, Gillespie (O'Boyle 78), Wilson, Dowie (Quinn 80), Horlock, Hughes.
Referee: Lambek (Denmark).

Salzburg, 26 April 1995, 5700
Austria (3) 7 *(Kuhbauer 8, Polster 11, 53, Sabitzer 17, Purk 84, Hutter 87, 90)*
Liechtenstein (0) 0
Austria: Konrad; Feiersinger, Kogler J, Furstaller (Hutter A 71), Ramusch, Artner, Herzog, Kuhbauer, Marasek, Sabitzer (Purk 69), Polster.
Liechtenstein: Oehry; Moser, Stocker, Ospelt J, Ritter (Matt 66), Hilti, Telser, Zech H, Hasler, Oehri (Marxer 46), Burgmaier.
Referee: Melnitschuk (Ukraine).

Dublin, 26 April 1995, 33,000
Republic of Ireland (1) 1 *(Vitor Baia 45 (og))*
Portugal (0) 0
Republic of Ireland: Kelly A; Kelly G, Irwin, Townsend, McGrath, Babb, Sheridan, Houghton (Kenna 84), Aldridge (Cascarino 84), Quinn, Staunton.
Portugal: Vitor Baia; Joao Pinto I, Fernando Couto, Helder (Folha 64), Paulinho Santos, Jorge Costa, Paulo Sousa, Figo (Pedro Barbosa 76), Rui Costa, Joao Pinto II, Domingos.
Referee: Amendolia (Italy).

Porto, 3 June, 1995, 40,000
Portugal (3) 3 *(Figo 5, Secretario 19, Domingos 21)*
Latvia (0) 2 *(Rimkus 49, 83)*
Portugal: Vitor Baia; Nelson (Pedro Barbosa 79), Fernando Couto, Jorge Costa, Paulinho Santos, Figo, Secretario, Domingos, Folha, Paulo Sousa (Futre 46), Rui Costa.
Latvia: Laizan; Troicki, Sevliakovs, Teplov (Sprogis 59), Astafyev, Zemlinsky, Monyak, Valeriy, Zeiberlins, Rimkus, Bleidelis (Babichev 37).
Referee: Petrovic (Yugoslavia).

Eschen, 3 June 1995, 4500
Liechtenstein (0) 0
Republic of Ireland (0) 0
Liechtenstein: Heeb; Hasler, Hanselmann, Ospelt J (Zech J 32), Ritter, Zech H, Hilti, Telser, Ospelt W (Marxer 64), Burgmaier, Frick M.
Republic of Ireland: Kelly A; Kelly G, Irwin, McAteer (Kenna 73), McGrath, Babb, Sheridan, Aldridge, Quinn (Cascarino 60), Whelan, Staunton.
Referee: Agius (Malta).

Windsor Park, 7 June 1995, 6000
Northern Ireland (1) 1 *(Dowie 44)*
Latvia (0) 2 *(Zeiberlins 58, Astafyev 62)*
Northern Ireland: Fettis; McGibbon (Patterson 46), Worthington, Morrow, Taggart, McDonald, McMahon, Magilton, Dowie, Hughes, Rowland (Gillespie 64).
Latvia: Laizan; Monyak, Sprogis, Zakresevskis, Bleidelis, Troicki, Astafyev, Zeiberlins, Ivanov, Rimkus (Yeliseyev 69), Babichev (Teplov 82).
Referee: Roca (Spain).

Dublin, 11 June 1995, 33,000
Republic of Ireland (0) 1 *(Houghton 65)*
Austria (0) 3 *(Polster 69, 78, Ogris 72)*
Republic of Ireland: Kelly A; Kelly G, Irwin, Houghton, McGrath, Babb, Sheridan, Coyne, Quinn (Cascarino 57), Whelan, Staunton (Kenna 46).
Austria: Konsel; Pfeffer, Schottel, Furstaller, Kogler J, Prosenik, Kuhbauer, Pfeifenberger (Hutter 83), Masarek, Ramusch (Ogris 71), Polster.
Referee: Merk (Germany).

Eschen, 15 August 1995, 3500
Liechtenstein (0) 0
Portugal (3) 7 *(Domingos 25, Paulinho Santos 33, Rui Costa 41, 71 (pen), Paulo Alves 67, 73, 90)*
Liechtenstein: Heeb; Hasler, Hanselmann, Hilti, Zech J, Stocker (Frick C 46), Klaunzer (Marxer 46), Telser (Oehri 68), Moser, Zech H, Frick M.
Portugal: Alfredo (Rui Correa 82); Oceano (Sa Pinto 46), Fernando Couto, Jorge Costa, Dimas (Paulo Alves 55), Secretario, Paulinho Santos, Rui Costa, Rui Barros, Fohla, Domingos.
Referee: Poljak (Croatia).

Riga, 16 August 1995, 2600
Latvia (1) 3 *(Rimjus 11, 59, Zeiberlins 88)*
Austria (0) 2 *(Polster 68, Ramusch 78)*
Latvia: Laizan; Sevliakovs, Troicki, Zemlinsky, Zakresevskis (Monyak 82), Zeiberlins, Ivanov, Bleidelis, Babichev (Yeliseyev 75), Rimkus, Astafyev.
Austria: Konrad; Schottel, Kogler W, Pfeffer, Kogler J (Schopp 46), Prosenik (Stoger P 64), Feiersinger, Pfeifenberger, Marasek, Ogris (Ramusch 64), Polster.
Referee: Koho (Finland).

Oporto, 3 September 1995, 50,000
Portugal (0) 1 *(Domingos 47)*
Northern Ireland (0) 1 *(Hughes 66)*
Portugal: Vitor Baia; Secretario, Jorge Costa (Rui Barros 74), Fernando Couto, Paulinho Santos, Oceano, Paulo Sousa, Figo, Rui Costa (Paulo Alves 82), Domingos, Folha.
Northern Ireland: Fettis; Morrow, Worthington, Hunter, Hill, Lomas, Gillespie, Magilton (Rowland 79), Dowie (Gray 77), Lennon, Hughes.
Referee: Harrel (France).

Vienna, 6 September 1995, 24,000
Austria (1) 3 *(Stoger P 3, 64, 77)*
Republic of Ireland (0) 1 *(McGrath 74)*
Austria: Konsel; Furstaller, Schottel, Pfeffer, Schopp, Stoger P, Kuhbauer, Herzog, Marasek, Pfeifenberger, Polster (Cerny 78).
Republic of Ireland: Kelly A; Kelly G, Irwin, Keane, McGrath, Kernaghan, Houghton (Cascarino 67), Townsend, Quinn, Kennedy, Sheridan.
Referee: Cakar (Turkey).

Riga, 6 September 1995, 3800
Latvia (0) 1 *(Zeiberlins 83)*
Liechtenstein (0) 0
Latvia: Karavayev; Troicki, Zemlinsky, Sevliakovs, Astafyev, Bleidelis (Bulders 31), Ivanov, Zeiberlins, Babichev (Karachausks 74), Rimkus, Monyak.
Liechtenstein: Heeb; Frick C, Oehri R (Bicker 64), Hasler, Zech J, Telser, Stocker (Klaunzer 89), Hilti, Frick M, Schadler, Marxer (Frick D 74).
Referee: Henning (Norway).

Vienna, 11 October 1995, 44,000
Austria (1) 1 *(Stoger 21)*
Portugal (0) 1 *(Paulinho Santos 49)*
Austria: Konsel; Feiersinger, Schottel, Pfeffer, Schopp, Kuhbauer, Stoger, Herzog, Marasek, Pfeifenberger, Polster (Cerny 81).
Portugal: Vitor Baia; Nelson, Jorge Costa, Helder, Paulinho Santos, Secretario (Sa Pinto 59), Oceano, Paulo Sousa, Rui Costa, Joao Pinto II (Folha 46), Domingos (Jose Dominguez 72).
Referee: Levnikov (Russia).

Dublin, 11 October 1995, 33,000
Republic of Ireland (0) 2 *(Aldridge 61 (pen), 64)*
Latvia (0) 1 *(Rimkus 78)*
Republic of Ireland: Kelly A; Kelly G, Phelan, McAteer, McGrath, Babb, Staunton, Aldridge (Kelly D 79) (Kennedy 84), Quinn, Townsend, Kenna.

Latvia: Karavayev; Troicki, Astafyev, Sevliakovs, Stepanov, Zemlinsky, Babichev (Elisejev 75), Ivanov, Zakresevskis, Zieberlins, Rimkus.
Referee: Marin (Spain).

Eschen, 11 October 1995, 1100

Liechtenstein (0) 0

Northern Ireland (1) 4 *(O'Neill 36, McMahon 49, Quinn 55, Gray 72)*

Liechtenstein: Oehry; Telser, Hefti, Hasler, Frick C (Hanselmann 78), Hilti (Ospelt J 66), Klaunzer, Stocker (Sele 46), Zech H, Oehri, Schadler.
Northern Ireland: Fettis (Wood 75); Lomas, Worthington, McMahon (McGibbon 80), Hill, Hunter, O'Neill, Quinn, Gray, Lennon, Hughes (Rowland 89).
Referee: Lubos (Slovakia).

Lisbon, 15 November 1995, 80,000

Portugal (0) 3 *(Rui Costa 60, Helder 74, Cadete 89)*

Republic of Ireland (0) 0

Portugal: Vitor Baia (Neno 86); Secretario, Fernando Couto, Helder, Paulinho Santos, Oceano, Figo, Paulo Sousa, Rui Costa, Joao Pinto II (Folha 67), Domingos (Cadete 67).
Republic of Ireland: Kelly A; Kelly G, Irwin, McAteer, McGrath, Babb, Staunton (Kernaghan 78), Aldridge, Quinn, Kenna, Kennedy (Cascarino 75).
Referee: Ceccarini (Italy).

Belfast, 15 November 1995, 8400

Northern Ireland (2) 5 *(O'Neill 27, 78, Dowie 32 (pen), Hunter 53, Gray 64)*

Austria (0) 3 *(Schopp 56, Stumpf 70, Wetl 81)*

Northern Ireland: Fettis; Lomas, Worthington, Hunter, Hill, Gillespie, Hughes, Dowie (Quinn 81), Gray (McDonald 78), Lennon, O'Neill.
Austria: Konsel; Schopp, Kogler W, Feiersinger, Pfeiffer, Marasek, Pfeifenberger, Stoger, Kuhbauer (Stumpf 46), Herzog (Wetl 46), Polster.
Referee: Sundell (Sweden).

	P	W	D	L	F	A	Pts
Portugal	10	7	2	1	29	7	23
Republic of Ireland	10	5	2	3	17	11	17
Northern Ireland	10	5	2	3	20	15	17
Austria	10	5	1	4	29	14	16
Latvia	10	4	0	6	11	20	12
Liechtenstein	10	0	1	9	1	40	1

Group 7

Tbilisi, 7 September 1994, 40,000

Georgia (0) 0

Moldova (1) 1 *(Oprea 40)*

Georgia: Zoidze; Nemsadze, Tskhadadze, Shelia, Kavelashvili, Arveladze R (Revishvili 70), Arveladze A, Jamarauli, Arveladze S, Guruli (Inalishvili 46), Kinkladze.
Moldova: Coselev; Secu, Belous, Pogorelov, Stroenco A, Stroenco S (Rebeja 55), Curtianu, Nani, Clescenco, Oprea, Spiridon (Kosse 82).
Referee: Sakari (Turkey).

Cardiff Arms Park, 7 September 1994, 15,791

Wales (1) 2 *(Coleman 9, Giggs 67)*

Albania (0) 0

Wales: Southall; Williams, Melville, Coleman, Bodin, Goss (Pembridge 74), Phillips, Speed, Giggs, Rush, Blake (Roberts I 80).
Albania: Strakosha; Shulku, Xhumba, Vata, Kacaj, Kola A (Fortuzi 53), Bellai, Kola B, Demollari, Pano, Shehu (Dosti 81).
Referee: Beschin (Italy).

Kishinev, 12 October 1994, 12,000

Moldova (2) 3 *(Belous 9, Secu 29, Pogorelov 79)*

Wales (1) 2 *(Speed 6, Blake 70)*

Moldova: Coselev; Secu, Stroenco S, Nani, Pogorelov, Rebeja, Belous (Caras 86), Oprea, Curtianu, Spiridon, Miterev (Kosse 46).

Wales: Southall; Bowen M, Coleman, Symons, Williams, Horne, Phillips, Blake (Melville 87), Roberts, Pembridge, Speed.
Referee: Vad (Hungary).

Sofia, 12 October 1994, 45,000

Bulgaria (0) 2 *(Kostadinov 55, 62)*

Georgia (0) 0

Bulgaria: Popov; Kiriakov, Ivanov, Hubchev, Tsvetanov, Yankov, Borimirov (Kostadinov 55), Lechkov, Balakov, Sirakov (Penev 70), Stoichkov.
Georgia: Devadze; Revishvili, Tskhadadze, Shelia, Chikhradze, Kudinov, Nemsadze (Inalishvili 71), Gogichaishvili, Ketsbaia, Kinkladze, Arveladze S (Guruli 76).
Referee: Gadosi (Slovakia).

Tirana, 16 November 1994, 20,000

Albania (1) 1 *(Zmijani 32)*

Germany (1) 2 *(Klinsmann 18, Kirsten 46)*

Albania: Strakosha; Vata, Kacaj, Xhumba, Zmijani (Pano 65), Lekbello, Demollari (Kola B 55), Millo, Bellai, Kushta, Rraklli.
Germany: Kopke; Matthaus, Kohler, Berthold, Reuter, Eilts, Sammer (Strunz 46), Weber (Schuster 83), Moller, Kirsten, Klinsmann.
Referee: Melnitschuk (Ukraine).

Sofia, 16 November 1994, 50,000

Bulgaria (1) 4 *(Stoichkov 45, 85, Balakov 65, Kostadinov 88)*

Moldova (0) 1 *(Clescenco 60)*

Bulgaria: Mikhailov; Hubchev, Kiriakov, Ivanov, Tsvetanov, Penev (Sirakov 80), Yordanov, Lechkov (Stoilov 86), Balakov, Stoichkov, Kostadinov.
Moldova: Coselev; Stroenco S, Secu, Pogorelov, Nani, Rebeja, Belous, Curtianu (Kosse 86), Spiridon, Oprea, Clescenco.
Referee: McArdle (Republic of Ireland).

Tbilisi, 16 November 1994, 45,000

Georgia (2) 5 *(Ketsbaia 31, 49, Kinkladze 41, Gogrichiani 59, Arveladze S 67)*

Wales (0) 0

Georgia: Devadze; Gogichaishvili, Tskhadadze, Shelia, Chikhradze, Revishvili, Kinkladze, Nemsadze (Inalishvili 41), Ketsbaia (Kavelashvili 75), Gogrichiani, Arveladze S.
Wales: Southall; Neilson (Symons 46), Bowen M, Horne, Melville, Coleman, Phillips, Saunders, Rush, Hughes, Speed.
Referee: Sars (France).

Chisinau, 14 December 1994, 20,000

Moldova (0) 0

Germany (2) 3 *(Kirsten 7, Klinsmann 38, Matthaus 73)*

Moldova: Coselev; Secu, Stroenco S, Nani, Pogorelov, Rebeja (Testimitanu 81), Spiridon, Curtianu, Belous, Oprea (Gaidamasciuc 58), Clescenco.
Germany: Kopke; Berthold, Matthaus, Helmer, Reuter, Hassler, Sammer, Moller (Kuntz 79), Weber, Kirsten (Strunz 69), Klinsmann.
Referee: Van Vliet (Holland).

Cardiff, 14 December 1994, 20,000

Wales (0) 0

Bulgaria (2) 3 *(Ivanov 5, Kostadinov 15, Stoichkov 51)*

Wales: Southall; Phillips, Bowen M, Aizlewood, Coleman, Melville, Jones, Saunders, Rush, Hughes, Speed.
Bulgaria: Mikhailov; Kremenliev, Ivanov, Tsvetanov, Yankov, Yordanov, Lechkov, Balakov, Kostadinov (Sirakov 73), Penev (Kiriakov 73), Stoichkov.
Referee: Sundell (Sweden).

Tirana, 14 December 1994, 15,000

Albania (0) 0

Georgia (1) 1 *(Arveladze S 17)*

Albania: Strakosha; Dema, Vata (Shulku 30), Xhumba, Kacaj, Lekbello (Malko 46), Bellai, Rraklli, Demollari, Fortuzi, Kola B.

Georgia: Devadze; Revishvili, Shelia, Kudinov, Chikhradze, Gogichaishvili (Jishkariani 62), Inalishvili, Gogrichiani, Ketsbaia, Kinkladze, Arveladze S (Jamarauli 30).
Referee: Molnar (Hungary).

Kaiserslautern, 18 December 1994, 20,310

Germany (2) 2 _(Matthaus 8 (pen), Klinsmann 17)_

Albania (0) 1 _(Raklli 58)_

Germany: Kopke; Matthaus, Berthold, Helmer, Weber, Reuter, Sammer, Hassler (Strunz 77), Moller, Kirsten (Kuntz 59), Klinsmann.
Albania: Strakosha; Xhumba, Dema, Kajac, Shulku, Zmijani, Demollari, Malko, Bellai, Rraklli, Kola B (Zalla 62).
Referee: Christensen (Denmark).

Tbilisi, 29 March 1995, 75,000

Georgia (0) 0

Germany (2) 2 _(Klinsmann 24, 45)_

Georgia: Devadze; Revishvili, Tskhadadze, Shelia, Chikhradze, Gogichaishvili, Kudinov, Kinkladze, Jamarauli (Gogrichiani 70), Arveladze R (Kavelashvili 75), Arveladze S.
Germany: Kopke; Reuter, Kohler, Helmer, Babbel, Weber (Freund 46), Eilts, Basler, Moller, Klinsmann, Herrlich.
Referee: Bodenham (England).

Sofia, 29 March 1995, 60,000

Bulgaria (1) 3 _(Balakov 37, Penev 70, 82)_

Wales (0) 1 _(Saunders 83)_

Bulgaria: Mikhailov; Ivanov, Hubchev, Tsvetanov (Kiriakov 85), Balakov, Yankov, Kremenliev, Lechkov, Stoichkov, Penev, Kostadinov.
Wales: Southall; Phillips, Bowen M, Jones (Cornforth 78), Symons, Coleman, Speed, Horne, Saunders, Hartson, Giggs.
Referee: Piraux (Belgium).

Tirana, 29 March 1995, 20,000

Albania (2) 3 _(Kushta 32, 78, Kacaj 73)_

Moldova (0) 0

Albania: Strakosha (Nallbani 80); Malko, Xhumba (Fortuzi 66), Vata, Shulku, Kacaj, Bellai, Rraklli, Abazi, Kushta (Dalipi 88), Demollari.
Moldova: Coselev; Secu, Pogorelov, Belous, Gaidamasciuc (Stroenco A 66), Stroenco S, Oprea, Curtianu (Caras 72), Spiridon, Nani, Clescenco.
Referee: Meier (Switzerland).

Tbilisi, 26 April 1995, 20,000

Georgia (2) 2 _(Arveladze S 3, Ketsbaia 43)_

Albania (0) 0

Georgia: Devadze; Chikhradze, Gudushauri, Kudinov, Shelia (Lobjanidze 70), Ketsbaia, Gogichaishvili, Jamarauli, Kizilashvili (Arveladze A 59), Arveladze S, Inalishvili.
Albania: Strakosha; Mema, Vata, Xhumba, Kacaj, Fortuzi (Prenga 46), Malko, Dalipi, Demollari, Rraklli, Kushta (Dosti 87).
Referee: Luinge (Holland).

Chisinau, 26 April 1995, 17,000

Moldova (0) 0

Bulgaria (1) 3 _(Balakov 29, Stoichkov 54, 68)_

Moldova: Coselev; Secu, Fistican, Nani, Pogorelov, Caras (Gaidamasciuc 65), Rebeja, Oprea (Cibotaru 72), Belous, Curtianu, Clescenco.
Bulgaria: Mikhailov; Kremenliev (Kiriakov 82), Hubchev, Ivanov, Tsvetanov, Yankov, Lechkov, Balakov, Yordanov, Penev, Stoichkov (Mikhtarski 79).
Referee: Ulrich (Czech Republic).

Dusseldorf, 26 April 1995, 45,000

Germany (1) 1 _(Herrlich 42)_

Wales (1) 1 _(Saunders 7)_

Germany: Kopke; Reuter, Freund, Babbel, Eilts, Basler (Scholl 76), Hassler, Weber (Kuntz 86), Ziege, Herrlich, Klinsmann.

Wales: Southall; Phillips, Bowen M, Jones, Symons, Coleman (Williams 45), Horne, Hughes (Hartson 90), Rush, Saunders, Speed.
Referee: Encinar (Spain).

Sofia, 7 June 1995, 50,000

Bulgaria (1) 3 _(Stoichkov 45 (pen), 66 (pen), Kostadinov 69)_

Germany (2) 2 _(Klinsmann 18, Strunz 44)_

Bulgaria: Mikhailov; Hubchev, Ivanov, Tsvetanov, Yankov, Lechkov (Sirakov 80), Balakov, Yordanov (Kostadinov 65), Penev, Stoichkov.
Germany: Kopke; Helmer, Sammer, Babbel, Reuter, Eilts, Basler (Moller 80), Hassler, Strunz (Kirsten 89), Klinsmann, Herrlich.
Referee: Pairetto (Italy).

Cardiff, 7 June 1995, 6500

Wales (0) 0

Georgia (0) 1 _(Kinkladze 73)_

Wales: Southall; Phillips, Bowen M, Jones, Williams, Symons, Horne, Saunders (Pembridge 84), Rush, Cornforth, Hughes (Hartson 84).
Georgia: Devadze; Beradze, Tskhadadze, Shelia, Chikhradze, Inalishvili, Gogichashvili, Kinkladze, Ketsbaia, Kavelashvili (Tskitishvili 74), Arveladze S (Kilasonia 88).
Referee: Koho (Finland).

Chisinau, 7 June 1995, 7000

Moldova (2) 2 _(Curtianu 10, Clescenco 15)_

Albania (2) 3 _(Kushta 7, Bellai 25, Vata 71)_

Moldova: Ivanov; Secu, Fistican, Pogorelov, Rebeja (Kosse 74), Stroenko S, Stroenko A, Belous (Miterev 55), Nani, Curtianu, Clescenco.
Albania: Strakosha; Bano, Shulku, Malko, Vata, Kacaj, Kushta, Bellai, Kola B, Rraklli (Prenga 87), Demollari (Pano 79).
Referee: Schelings (Belgium).

Tirana, 6 September 1995, 10,000

Albania (1) 1 _(Rraklli 16)_

Bulgaria (1) 1 _(Stoichkov 8)_

Albania: Strakosha; Abazi, Vata, Xhumba, Shulku, Lekbello, Kushta, Bellai, Kola B (Shehu 65), Rraklli, Bozgo (Demollari 85).
Bulgaria: Mikhailov; Kremenliev, Ivanov, Hubchev, Tsvetanov, Lechkov (Chomakov 75), Balakov, Borimirov, Kostadinov, Penev (Sirakov 75), Stoichkov.
Referee: Agius (Malta).

Nuremburg, 6 September 1995, 40,000

Germany (1) 4 _(Moller 39, Ziege 57, Kirsten 62, Babbel 72)_

Georgia (1) 1 _(Ketsbaia 28)_

Germany: Kahn; Helmer, Kohler, Babbel, Freund, Hassler, Moller, Strunz, Ziege, Klinsmann, Kirsten.
Georgia: Devadze; Kudinov, Gujabidze, Shelia, Tskhadadze, Gogichaishvili (Arveladze A 67), Nemsadze, Kinkladze, Ketsbaia, Arveladze S, Kavelashvili (Kilasonia 46).
Referee: McCluskey (Scotland).

Cardiff, 6 September 1995, 5000

Wales (0) 1 _(Speed 55)_

Moldova (0) 0

Wales: Southall; Bowen M, Coleman, Williams, Symons, Pembridge, Horne, Speed, Nogan (Phillips 46), Rush (Hartson 69), Hughes.
Moldova: Ivanov; Fistican, Testimitanu, Culibaba, Rebeja, Stroenco S, Oprea, Belous, Nani (Soucharev 76), Cibotaru, Clescenco.
Referee: Orrason (Iceland).

Sofia, 7 October 1995, 25,000

Bulgaria (1) 3 _(Lechkov 14, Kostadinov 80, 82)_

Albania (0) 0

Bulgaria: Mikhailov; Kiriakov (Borimirov 87), Kremenliev, Ivanov, Tsvetanov, Lechkov, Yankov, Balakov, Kostadinov (Sirakov 86), Penev, Stoichkov.

Albania: Strakosha; Dema, Malko, Xhumba, Shulku, Zmijani, Bellai, Kola B, Abazi (Demollari 86), Kushta, Rraklli.
Referee: Hirvinemi (Finland).

Leverkusen, 8 October 1995, 18,300
Germany (3) 6 *(Stroenko S 16 (og), Helmer 18, Sammer 24, 71, Moller 47, 61)*
Moldova (0) 1 *(Rebeja 82)*
Germany: Kopke; Sammer (Worns 83), Babbel, Helmer, Eilts, Hassler, Freund, Moller (Scholl 78), Ziege, Klinsmann, Herrlich (Bobic 74).
Moldova: Ivanov; Culibaba, Seku, Stroenko S, Testimitanu, Rebeja, Belous, Nani (Chisinau 59) (Oprea 87), Curtianu, Gavriliuc, Clescenco.
Referee: Ziober (Poland).

Tbilisi, 11 October 1995, 45,000
Georgia (1) 2 *(Arveladze S 1, Kinkladze 46 (pen))*
Bulgaria (0) 1 *(Stoichkov 88)*
Georgia: Devadze; Kudinov, Shelia, Chikhradze, Nemsadze, Gudushauri (Beradze 46), Jamarauli, Kinkladze, Arveladze A (Kavelashvili 46), Arveladze S, Gogichaishvili.
Bulgaria: Mikhailov; Kiriakov, Ivanov, Tsvetanov, Balakov, Borimirov, Lechkov, Sirakov, Kostadinov, Penev, Stoichkov.
Referee: Meier (Switzerland).

Cardiff, 11 October 1995, 25,000
Wales (0) 1 *(Symons 78)*
Germany (0) 2 *(Kuntz 75, Klinsmann 80)*
Wales: Southall; Symons, Bowen M, Melville, Jenkins (Mardon 70), Blake (Williams G 82), Horne, Pembridge (Hodges 82), Saunders, Speed, Giggs.
Germany: Kopke; Babbel (Worns 46), Sammer, Helmer, Freund, Eilts, Moller, Ziege, Hassler, Klinsmann, Herrlich (Kuntz 73).
Referee: Craciunescu (Romania).

Berlin, 15 November 1995, 75,841
Germany (0) 3 *(Klinsmann 50, 76 (pen), Hassler 56)*
Bulgaria (0) 1 *(Stoichkov 47)*
Germany: Kopke; Babbel, Kohler (Strunz 46), Sammer, Freund, Helmer, Eilts, Basler, Hassler (Reuter 86), Klinsmann, Kuntz (Bobic 82).
Bulgaria: Popov; Kremenliev, Dartilov, Guentchev, Tsvetanov, Lechkov (Kiriakov 62), Yankov, Balakov (Borimirov 82), Kostadinov, Penev (Sirakov 79), Stoichkov.
Referee: Nikakis (Greece).

Tirana, 15 November 1995, 6000
Albania (1) 1 *(Kushta 4 (pen))*
Wales (1) 1 *(Pembridge 43)*
Albania: Strakosha; Zmijani, Shulku, Dema (Miloti 84), Vata, Lekbello, Kushta (Bushi 57), Malko, Bozgo (Zalla 80), Rraklli, Pano.
Wales: Southall; Young, Bowen M, Jenkins, Phillips, Melville, Taylor (Robinson 84), Pembridge, Saunders, Savage (Hughes C 63), Giggs.
Referee: Suheil (Israel).

Kichinev, 15 November 1995, 9000
Moldova (2) 3 *(Testimitanu 5, Miterev 17, 72)*
Georgia (0) 2 *(Dzhanashia 68, Culibaba 82 (og))*
Moldova: Coselev; Secu, Testimitanu, Culibaba, Nani, Oprea (Soukharev 54), Kirilov (Gavriliuc 80), Belous, Curtianu (Cibotaru 76), Clescenco, Miterev.
Georgia: Zoidze; Gudushauri (Dzhanashia 56), Kudinov, Beradze, Chikhradze, Gogichaishvili, Tsikarishvili, Jamarauli (Machavariani 62), Ketsbaia, Kinkladze, Arveladze S.
Referee: Van der Ende (Holland).

	P	W	D	L	F	A	Pts
Germany	10	8	1	1	27	10	25
Bulgaria	10	7	1	2	24	10	22
Georgia	10	5	0	5	14	13	15
Moldova	10	3	0	7	11	27	9
Wales	10	2	2	6	9	19	8
Albania	10	2	2	6	10	16	8

Group 8

Toftir, 7 September 1994, 2412
Faeroes (0) 1 *(Apostolakis (og) 89)*
Greece (2) 5 *(Saravakos 12, Tsalouhidis 18, 85, Alexandris 54, 60)*
Faeroes: Knudsen; Hansen T, Hansen A, Johannesen O, Jarnskor M, Hansen J, Morkore A (Rasmussen J E 85), Dam J, Muller, Jonsson, Hansen O (Jarnskor H 56).
Greece: Karkamanis; Apostolakis, Pavlopoulos, Kallitzakis, Karataidis, Hantzidis (Zagorakis 82), Tsalouhidis, Tsartas, Kostis (Markos 77), Alexandris, Saravakos.
Referee: Piraux (Belgium).

Helsinki, 7 September 1994, 12,845
Finland (0) 0
Scotland (1) 2 *(Shearer 29, Collins 66)*
Finland: Jakonen; Makela, Hyrylainen, Kanerva, Heinola (Holmgren 28), Suominen, Litmanen, Lindberg, Rantanen (Jarvinen 41), Paatelainen, Hjelm.
Scotland: Goram; McKimmie, Hendry, Levein (McCall 78), Boyd, McLaren, McStay, McAllister, Collins, Walker (Jess 65), Shearer.
Referee: Wocjik (Poland).

Hampden Park, 12 October 1994, 20,885
Scotland (3) 5 *(McGinlay 4, Booth 34, Collins 40, 72, McKinlay 61)*
Faeroes (0) 1 *(Muller 75)*
Scotland: Goram; McLaren, McKimmie, Levein, Hendry (McKinlay W 58), McStay, Boyd, Nevin, Booth (Walker 69), McGinlay, Collins.
Faeroes: Knudsen; Dam J (Joensen 53), Hansen T, Johannesen O, Hansen J, Hansen O (Rasmussen J 73), Jarnskor H, Morkore K, Jarnskor M, Muller, Jonsson.
Referee: Hauge (Norway).

Salonika, 12 October 1994, 30,000
Greece (1) 4 *(Markos 23, Batista 70, Mahlas 76, 90)*
Finland (0) 0
Greece: Atmatzidis; Apostolakis, Kassapis, Dabizas, Kallitzakis, Tsalouhidis, Zagorakis, Markos (Toursounidis 65), Mahlas, Tsartas, Vrizas (Batista 43).
Finland: Jakonen; Makela, Kanerva, Hyrylainen, Heinola (Holmgren 30), Suominen, Jarvinen (Sumiala 73), Lindberg, Hjelm, Litmanen, Paatelainen.
Referee: Leduc (France).

Moscow, 12 October 1994, 20,000
Russia (1) 4 *(Karpin 43, Kolyvanov 64, Nikiforov 65, Radchenko 67)*
San Marino (0) 0
Russia: Cherchesov; Kulkov (Tetradze 65), Nikiforov, Tsymbalar (Kolyvanov 55), Shalimov, Karpin, Onopko, Kanchelskis, Pyatnitski, Radchenko, Kiryakov.
San Marino: Benedettini; Gobbi, Gennari, Mazza M, Valentini M, Guerra (Della Valle 23), Manzaroli, Matteoni, Bacciocchi, Bonini, Francini (Canti 67).
Referee: Hamer (Luxembourg).

Helsinki, 16 November 1994, 2240
Finland (1) 5 *(Sumiala 37, Litmanen 51 (pen), 71, Paatelainen 75, 85)*
Faeroes (0) 0
Finland: Laukkanen; Makela, Kanerva, Eriksson, Helin, Litmanen, Ukkonen, Lindberg (Rajamaki 78), Sumiala (Ruhanen 90), Hjelm, Paatelainen.
Faeroes: Knudsen; Johannesen O, Rasmussen J, Hansen O (Rasmussen J E 80), Hansen T, Morkore K, Jarnskor M, Jarnskor H, Joensen D, Muller, Jonsson.
Referee: Orrason (Iceland).

Athens, 16 November 1994, 15,000
Greece (1) 2 *(Mahlas 21, Frantzeskos 84)*
San Marino (0) 0
Greece: Atmatzidis; Apostolakis, Dabizas, Kallitzakis, Kassapis, Maragos (Frantzeskos 46), Zagorakis, Toursounidis, Tsartas, Mahlas, Vrizas (Batista 70).

San Marino: Benedettini; Gobbi, Valentini M, Guerra, Gennari (Canti 46), Manzaroli, Della Valle (Gasperoni 75), Francini, Bonini, Bacciocchi, Gualtieri.
Referee: Lipkovitch (Israel).

Hampden Park, 16 November 1994, 31,254

Scotland (1) 1 *(Booth 19)*

Russia (1) 1 *(Radchenko 25)*

Scotland: Goram; McKimmie, Boyd, McCall, Levein, McLaren, McKinlay W (Nevin 83), McAllister, Booth, McGinlay (Spencer 63), Collins.
Russia: Cherchesov; Gorlukovich, Nikiforov, Kulkov, Shalimov, Kanchelskis, Karpin, Pyatniski (Tetradze 75), Onopko, Radimov, Radchenko.
Referee: Karlsson (Sweden).

Helsinki, 14 December 1994, 3140

Finland (2) 4 *(Paatelainen 24, 30, 85, 90)*

San Marino (1) 1 *(Della Valle 34)*

Finland: Laukkanen; Makela, Kanerva, Eriksson, Lindberg, Helin (Myyry 74), Ukkonen, Sumiala, Litmanen, Hjelm, Paatelainen.
San Marino: Benedettini; Canti, Gasperoni, Gobbi, Gennari, Bonini, Guerra, Manzaroli, Della Valle, Bacciocchi (Peverani 15), Mularoni (Gualtieri 60).
Referee: Albrecht (Germany).

Athens, 18 December 1994, 20,310

Greece (1) 1 *(Apostolakis 18 (pen))*

Scotland (0) 0

Greece: Atmatzidis; Apostolakis, Vlahos, Kallitzakis, Kassapis, Tsalouhidis, Zagorakis, Nioblias (Karassavidis 88), Toursounidis, Mahlas, Alexandris (Maragos 72).
Scotland: Goram (Leighton 78); McKimmie, Hendry, McLaren, Boyd, McCall, McAllister, Collins, McGinlay, McKinlay W (Spencer 46), Ferguson D.
Referee: Blankenstein (Holland).

Moscow, 29 March 1995, 25,000

Russia (0) 0

Scotland (0) 0

Russia: Kharine; Khlestov, Nikiforov, Kovtun, Karpin, Onopko, Dobrovolski, Shalimov (Radimov 69), Kanchelskis, Kiryakov, Radchenko (Pisarev 57).
Scotland: Leighton; McKimmie, Calderwood, Hendry, McLaren, McStay, Boyd, Collins, McAllister, McGinlay (McKinlay W 84), Jackson (Shearer 78).
Referee: Strampe (Germany).

San Marino, 29 March 1995, 1000

San Marino (0) 0

Finland (1) 2 *(Litmanen 45, Sumiala 65)*

San Marino: Benedettini; Gobbi, Valentini M, Guerra, Gennari, Mazza M (Matteoni 70), Manzaroli, Francini, Bonini, Montagna (Gualtieri 75), Mularoni.
Finland: Laukkanen; Makela (Hyypia 74), Ukkonen, Helin, Lindberg, Eriksson, Sumiala, Myyry, Litmanen, Hjelm, Jarvinen (Rajamaki 69).
Referee: Suheli (Israel).

Serravalle, 26 April 1995, 2738

San Marino (0) 0

Scotland (1) 2 *(Collins 19, Calderwood 85)*

San Marino: Benedettini; Manzaroli, Canti, Guerra, Gobbi, Gennari, Mazza M, Della Valle, Bonini (Matteoni 46), Mularoni (Gualtieri 72), Bacciocchi.
Scotland: Leighton; McLaren, Boyd, Calderwood, Hendry, Jackson, Collins, McGinlay, Shearer (Spencer 67), McAllister, Nevin (McKinlay W 78).
Referee: Loizou (Cyprus).

Salonika, 26 April 1995, 30,000

Greece (0) 0

Russia (1) 3 *(Nikiforov 36, Zagorakis 78 (og), Bestchastnikh 79)*

Greece: Atmatzidis; Apostolakis, Kallitzakis, Dabizas, Zagorakis, Tsalouhidis, Kassapis, Nioblias (Tsartas 46), Toursounidis, Mahlas (Nikolaidis 60), Donis.

Russia: Kharine; Kovtun, Nikiforov, Kulkov, Khlestov, Karpin, Onopko, Dobrovolski, Pyatnitski (Kiryakov 46), Radchenko (Mostovoi 77), Bestchastnikh.
Referee: Stafoggia (Italy).

Toftir, 26 April 1995, 1000

Faeroes (0) 0

Finland (0) 4 *(Hjelm 55, Paatelainen 75, Lindberg 78, Helin 83)*

Faeroes: Knudsen; Morkore A, Rasmussen J, Johannesen O, Hansen J, Hansen O, Johnsson, Morkore K, Joensen D, Jarnskor M (Jarnskor H 80), Jonsson.
Finland: Laukkanen; Makela, Ukkonen, Eriksson, Helin, Hyypia, Litmanen, Lindberg (Suominen 82), Sumiala (Kolkka 61), Hjelm, Paatelainen.
Referee: Howells (Wales).

Moscow, 6 May 1995, 9500

Russia (0) 3 *(Ketschinov 52, Pisarev 73, Moukhamadiev 80)*

Faeroes (0) 0

Russia: Cherchesov; Khlestov, Nikiforov, Kovtun, Tetradze, Kechinov, Onopko, Cheryshev, Pyatnitski (Lebed 22), Pisarev, Mukhamadiev.
Faeroes: Knudsen; Johannesen O, Hansen J, Rasmussen J, Morkore K, Joensen A, Jarnskor M, Hansen E, Jarnskor H (Joensen D 69), Jonsson, Rasmussen J E.
Referee: Kvartskelia (Georgia).

Toftir, 25 May 1995, 3452

Faeroes (2) 3 *(Hansen J 7, Rasmussen J E 9, Johnsson 62)*

San Marino (0) 0

Faeroes: Knudsen; Jarnskor H, Hansen J, Johannesen O, Rasmussen J, Hansen O, Johnsson, Morkore K, Jarnskor M, Jonsson, Rasmussen J E.
San Marino: Benedettini; Gasperoni, Gobbi, Valentini M, Gennari, Canti, Manzaroli, Bonini (Ugolini 72), Francini, Bacciocchi, Mularoni.
Referee: Shorte (Republic of Ireland).

Serravalle, 7 June 1995, 1400

San Marino (0) 0

Russia (2) 7 *(Dobrovolski 30 (pen), Gobbi 35 (og), Kiryakov 49, Shalimov 50, Bestchastnikh 59, Kolyvanov 65, Tcherychev 88)*

San Marino: Benedettini; Gobbi, Gennari, Mazza M, Valentini M, Guerra, Manzaroli, Della Valle (Canti 64), Francini, Montagna (Bonini 78), Bacciocchi.
Russia: Cherchesov; Kulkov, Tetradze, Kovtun, Karpin, Onopko, Shalimov, Dobrovolski (Radchenko 60), Kiryakov, Kolyvanov, Bestchastnikh (Cheryshev 84).
Referee: Bohunek (Czech Republic).

Toftir, 7 June 1995, 3881

Faeroes (0) 0

Scotland (2) 2 *(McKinlay W 25, McGinlay 29)*

Faeroes: Knudsen; Jarnskor H, Hansen T, Johannesen O, Rasmussen J, Hansen J, Johnsson, Jarnskor M (Joensen A 56), Hansen O, Rasmussen J E (Muller 75), Jonsson.
Scotland: Leighton; McKimmie, McLaren, Burley, Calderwood, McKinnon, McKinlay W, Jackson, Shearer (Robertson 86), McGinlay (Gemmill 75), Collins.
Referee: Hrinak (Slovakia).

Helsinki, 11 June 1995, 7000

Finland (1) 2 *(Litmanen 45 (pen), Hjelm 55)*

Greece (1) 1 *(Nikolaidis 6)*

Finland: Laukkanen; Makela, Tuomela, Holmgren, Helin, Lindberg, Sumiala (Jarvinen 63), Myyry, Hjelm, Litmanen, Paatelainen (Tiainen 85).
Greece: Michopoulos; Apostolakis, Kassapis, Dabizas, Alexiou, Tsalouhidis, Nikolaidis, Markos (Batista 57), Zagorakis, Tsartas (Mahlas 70), Donis.
Referee: Krug (Germany).

Helsinki, 16 August 1995, 14,200
Finland (0) 0
Russia (3) 6 *(Kulkov 32, 49, Karpin 40, Radchenko 43, Kolyvanov 67, 69)*
Finland: Laukkanen; Makela, Kanerva, Holmgren, Nieminen, Lindberg, Sumiala, Rantanen (Gronlund 65), Tiainen, Hjelm, Paatelainen.
Russia: Kharine (Cherchesov 74); Khlestov, Kovtun, Nikiforov, Tsymbalar, Karpin (Kanchelskis 54), Onopko, Kulkov, Mostovoi, Radchenko (Kiryakov 68), Kolyvanov.
Referee: Puhl (Hungary).

Hampden Park, 16 August 1995, 34,910
Scotland (0) 1 *(McCoist 72)*
Greece (0) 0
Scotland: Leighton; Burley, McKinlay W, Calderwood, McKimmie, Boyd, McCall, Jackson (Robertson), Shearer (McCoist 71), McAllister, Collins.
Greece: Atmatzidis; Kallitzakis, Karataidis, Dabizas, Zagorakis (Georgiadis G), Apostolakis, Tsalouhidis, Kassapis, Tsartas, Batista (Alexandris), Vrizas (Mahlas 30).
Referee: Mikkelsen (Denmark).

Hampden Park, 6 September 1995, 35,505
Scotland (1) 1 *(Booth 10)*
Finland (0) 0
Scotland: Leighton; McKimmie (McKinlay W 89), Boyd, McLaren, Calderwood, Hendry, McKinlay T, Collins, Booth (Jackson 80), McAllister, Spencer (McCoist 75).
Finland: Laukkanen; Rissanen, Kanerva, Holmgren, Suominen, Lindberg, Nieminen (Gronlund 63), Myyry, Litmanen, Hjelm, Jarvinen.
Referee: Melnichuk (Ukraine).

Toftir, 6 September 1995, 1792
Faeroes (1) 2 *(Jarnskor H 12, Jonsson T 55)*
Russia (1) 5 *(Mostovoi 10, Kiryakov 60, Kolyvanov 65, Tsymbalar 84, Shalimov 87)*
Faeroes: Knudsen; Johannesen O, Hansen T (Joensen A 81), Rasmussen J, Hansen J, Hansen O, Morkore K, Johnsson, Muller (Rasmussen J E 15), Jonsson, Jarnskor H.
Russia: Cherchesov; Kulkov (Mamedov 64), Kovtun, Nikiforov, Tsymbalar, Shalimov, Kanchelskis (Bestchastnikh 57), Onopko, Mostovoi, Radchenko (Kiryakov 46), Kolyvanov.
Referee: Snoddy (Northern Ireland).

Serrevalle, 6 September 1995, 1000
San Marino (0) 0
Greece (2) 4 *(Tsalouhidis 5, Georgiadis G H 31, Alexandris 61, Donis 81)*
San Marino: Muccioli; Gennari, Gobbi, Guerra, Mazza M, Matteoni, Manzaroli (Peverani 89), Della Valle, Francini (Canti 76), Bacciocchi, Mularoni (Montagna 79).
Greece: Atmatzidis; Apostolakis, Ouzounidis, Karataidis, Dabizas, Tsalouhidis, Zagorakis, Nikolaidis (Alexandris 46), Georgiadis G H (Georgatos 57), Mahlas (Batista 77), Donis.
Referee: Mitrovic (Slovenia).

Moscow, 11 October 1995, 40,000
Russia (1) 2 *(Ouzounidis 35 (og), Onopko 71)*
Greece (0) 1 *(Tsalouhidis 64)*
Russia: Kharine; Khlestov, Nikiforov, Kovtun, Karpin (Shalimov 76), Kulkov, Onopko, Mostovoi, Tsymbalar (Radchenko 69), Yuran (Kiryakov 46), Kolyvanov.
Greece: Mihopoulos; Apostolakis, Ouzounidis, Kallitzakis (Dabizas 46), Kassapis, Tsalouhidis, Tsartas (Georgatos 46), Zagorakis, Donis, Alexandris, Batista (Mahlas 71).
Referee: Graber (Austria).

San Marino, 11 October 1995, 1000
San Marino (0) 1 *(Valentini M 50)*
Faeroes (2) 3 *(Jonsson 40, 45, 62)*
San Marino: Muccioli; Valentini V, Gennari, Matteoni (Peverani 72), Valentini M, Guerra, Manzaroli, Mazza M (Mularoni 58), Bacciocchi, Francini, Montagna (Gasperoni 82).
Faeroes: Knudsen; Hansen A, Hansen J, Rasmussen J, Jarnskor H (Bertholdsen 89), Morkore A, Jarnskor M, Hansen O (Reynheim 82), Muller, Jonsson (Petersen 75), Dam J.
Referee: Beck (Liechtenstein).

Hampden Park, 15 November 1995, 30,306
Scotland (2) 5 *(Jess 30, Booth 45, McCoist 49, Nevin 71, Francini 90 (og))*
San Marino (0) 0
Scotland: Leighton; McLaren, Boyd, Calderwood, Hendry, Gemmill, Nevin, Jess, Booth (Jackson 66), McAllister (McCoist 48), Collins (McKinlay W 59).
San Marino: Muccioli; Manzaroli, Moroni, Guerra (Montagna 71), Valentini M, Gennari, Mazza M (Della Valle 82), Francini, Matteoni, Mularoni (Canti 52), Bacciocchi.
Referee: Bohunek (Czech Republic).

Moscow, 15 November 1995, 6000
Russia (1) 3 *(Radchenko 40, Kulkov 55, Kiryakov 70)*
Finland (1) 1 *(Suominen 45)*
Russia: Cherchesov; Khlestov, Nikiforov, Mamedov (Dobrovolski 46), Onopko, Tsymbalar, Kulkov, Karpin (Kanchelskis 75), Mostovoi, Yuran, Radchenko (Kiryakov 62).
Finland: Niemi; Rissanen, Nuorela, Hyrylainen, Nieminen, Lindberg, Sumiala (Kangaskorpi 76), Suominen (Yionen 88), Gronlund (Koskinen 70), Hjelm, Myyry.
Referee: Merk (Germany).

Iraklis, 15 November 1995, 12,000
Greece (0) 5 *(Alexandris 58, Nikolaidis 62, Mahlas 66, Donis 75, Tsartas 80)*
Faeroes (0) 0
Greece: Atmazidis; Apostolakis, Katzidis, Ouzounidis, Dabizas, Tsalouhidis (Nikolaidis 46), Zagorakis (Konstantinidis C 70), Alexandris (Georgatos 76), Mahlas, Tsartas, Donis.
Faeroes: Mikkelsen; Johannesen O, Hansen T, Hansen G, Hansen E (Bertoldsen 89), Morkore A, Jarnskor M, Jarnskor G, Muller (Petersen 84), Reynheim (Jonsson 55), Dam J.
Referee: Mitrev (Bulgaria).

	P	W	D	L	F	A	Pts
Russia	10	8	2	0	34	5	26
Scotland	10	7	2	1	19	3	23
Greece	10	6	0	4	23	9	18
Finland	10	5	0	5	18	18	15
Faeroes	10	2	0	8	10	35	6
San Marino	10	0	0	10	2	36	0

Play-off

Anfield, 13 December 1995, 40,000
Republic of Ireland (0) 0
Holland (1) 2 *(Kluivert 29, 89)*
Republic of Ireland: Kelly A; Kelly G, Irwin, Kenna, McGrath, Babb, Sheridan, Aldridge (Kernaghan 73), Cascarino, Townsend (McAteer 50), Phelan.
Holland: Van der Sar; Reiziger, Blind, Bogarde, Ronald de Boer, Seedorf, Bergkamp (De Kock 58), Davids, Overmars, Kluivert, Helder (Winter 79).
Referee: Zhuk (Belarus).

EUROPEAN CHAMPIONSHIP 1994–96
Finals

Hindsight – that happy condition of perfect vision – may well reflect on Euro 96 as being the 'nearly' competition. England nearly reached the final, the venues were almost full, there were few outbreaks of hooliganism and there was early – if unfulfilled – promise of some memorable performances.

England began unimpressively, drawing 1-1 with Switzerland, but on the second day, non-partizan observers might have been lulled into thinking that this was to be an outstanding tournament when Denmark, the holders, drew 1-1 with Portugal. Alas, neither team played as well as that in subsequent games and it was left to one or two of the unfancied contestants to cause a stir.

Notable among these were the Czech Republic, who were hard, determined and not a little skilful and Croatia, who were too laid back to really succeed, but had in Davor Suker an outstanding centre-forward. His audacious scoring attempt from the half-way line against Denmark was pure Pele at his best.

Among the huge disappointments were Holland and Italy. England may have trimmed down its Christmas tree, but Holland were suffering from Dutch Elm disease. Plagued with problems off the field, their display against England was a shambles and though England fully deserved their 4-1 win it perhaps presented an inflated opinion of Terry Venables' team. Italy really threw their chances away by resting some players against the Czechs and the French, who declined to enter the competition with Eric Cantona and David Ginola, gradually deteriorated.

After a quiet beginning, Spain gave England some uncomfortable moments before the inevitable penalty shoot-out ended their interest. The five England penalty kicks were as near perfect as could be expected and arguably bettered only by the five taken by Uruguay against Brazil in the 1995 Copa America final.

However, it was England's turn to lose on penalties against their eternal rivals Germany, Gareth Southgate being the unfortunate player to have his kick saved. Two of the quarter-finals and both semi-finals were decided by the farce of such penalties.

It was left to the disciplined Germans, of course, to reach the final, unfazed by either pre-match tabloid hostility or by conceding an early goal against England. They managed to avenge their defeat against Czechoslovakia in 1976, ironically then by penalty kicks. This time it was the only 'golden goal' of the tournament which separated the teams. There were claims that Oliver Bierhoff's winning effort was scored with another player standing offside, but the Czechs' penalty had been derived from an infringement outside the penalty box.

Afterwards, the Germans paid for an advertisement in *The Times* praising the treatment they had received in England. Perhaps we have many things to learn from them.

With goalscoring at a low ebb, it was defenders who took most of the honours. England won the Fair Play Award, the Dutch fans were proclaimed the most well-behaved, but the memory of the tournament as a quality event of outstanding football will quickly fade.

Alan Shearer finished as leading goalscorer in Euro 96 with five to his credit. Here he is congratulated with the first of these goals by Darren Anderton. (Colorsport)

Group A

Wembley, 8 June 1996, 76,567

England (1) 1 *(Shearer 23)*

Switzerland (0) 1 *(Turkyilmaz 83 (pen))*

England: Seaman; Neville G, Pearce, Ince, Southgate, Adams, Anderton, Gascoigne (Platt 74), Shearer, Sheringham (Barmby 67), McManaman (Stone 67).
Switzerland: Pascolo; Jeanneret, Vega, Henchoz, Quentin, Vogel, Geiger (Kollo 67), Sforza, Bonvin (Chapuisat 67), Grassi, Turkyilmaz.
Referee: Diaz Vega (Spain).

Villa Park, 10 June 1996, 34,363

Holland (0) 0

Scotland (0) 0

Holland: Van der Sar; Reiziger, De Kock, Bogarde, Davids, Ronald de Boer (Winter 68), Seedorf, Witschge (Cocu 76), Taument (Kluivert 61), Bergkamp, Jordi Cruyff.
Scotland: Goram; McKimmie (Burley 83), Boyd, McCall, Hendry, Calderwood, Durie, Gallagher (McKinlay W 55), Booth (Spencer 46), McAllister, Collins.
Referee: Sundell (Sweden).

Villa Park, 13 June 1996, 36,800

Switzerland (0) 0

Holland (0) 2 *(Jordi Cruyff 65, Bergkamp 78)*

Switzerland: Pascolo; Henchoz, Jeanneret, Vega, Hottiger (Comisctti 68), Sforza, Vogel, Quentin, Turkyilmaz, Grassi, Chapuisat.
Holland: Van der Sar; Reiziger, Blind, Seedorf (De Kock 25), Bogarde, Jordi Cruyff (Kluivert 82), Witschge, Winter, Ronald de Boer (Davids 80), Hoekstra, Bergkamp.
Referee: Ouzounov (Bulgaria).

Wembley, 15 June 1996, 76,864

Scotland (0) 0

England (0) 2 *(Shearer 53, Gascoigne 79)*

Scotland: Goram; McKimmie, Boyd, McCall, Hendry, Calderwood, Durie (Jess 85), McKinlay T (Burley 81), Spencer (McCoist 66), McAllister, Collins.
England: Seaman; Neville G, Pearce (Redknapp 46) (Campbell 84), Ince (Stone 79), Southgate, Adams, Anderton, Gascoigne, Shearer, Sheringham, McManaman.
Referee: Pairetto (Italy).

Wembley, 18 June 1996, 76,798

Holland (0) 1 *(Kluivert 77)*

England (1) 4 *(Shearer 23 (pen), 57, Sheringham 51, 62)*

Holland: Van der Sar; Reiziger, Bogarde, Seedorf, Blind, Ronald de Boer (Kluivert 72), Jordi Cruyff, Witschge (De Kock 46), Winter, Hoekstra (Cocu 72), Bergkamp.
England: Seaman; Neville G, Pearce, Ince (Platt 61), Southgate, Adams, Anderton, Gascoigne, Shearer (Fowler 76), Sheringham (Barmby 76), McManaman.
Referee: Grabher (Austria).

Villa Park, 18 June 1996, 34,926

Scotland (1) 1 *(McCoist 37)*

Switzerland (0) 0

Scotland: Goram; Burley, Boyd, McCall, Hendry, Calderwood, Durie, McKinlay T (Booth 60), McCoist (Spencer 83), McAllister, Collins.
Switzerland: Pascolo; Hottiger, Vega, Henchoz, Quentin (Comisetti 80), Vogel, Sforza, Koller (Fournier 46), Bonvin, Turkyilmaz, Chapuisat (Wicky 46).
Referee: Krondl (Czech Republic).

Group B

Elland Road, 9 June 1996, 26,006

Spain (0) 1 *(Munoz 73)*

Bulgaria (0) 1 *(Stoichkov 65 (pen))*

Spain: Zubizarreta; Belsue, Alkorta, Abelardo, Sergi, Caminero (Donato 82), Amor (Alfonso 72), Hierro, Luis Enrique, Guerrero (Amavisca 51), Pizzi.
Bulgaria: Mikhailov; Kischischev, Hubchev, Ivanov, Kiriakov (Tsvetanov 72), Lechkov, Iankov, Balakov, Kostadinov (Yordanov 72), Stoichkov, Penev (Borimirov 77).
Referee: Ceccarini (Italy).

St James' Park, 10 June 1996, 26,323

Romania (0) 0

France (1) 1 *(Dugarry 24)*

Romania: Stelea; Petrescu (Filipescu 77), Belodedici, Mihali, Selymes, Lupescu, Popescu, Munteanu, Lacatus (Ilie A 52), Raducioiu (Moldovan 46), Hagi.
France: Lama; Thuram, Blanc, Desailly, Di Meco (Lizarazu 68), Karembeu, Deschamps, Guerin, Zidane (Roche 79), Djorkaeff, Dugarry (Loko 68).
Referee: Krug (Germany).

St James' Park, 13 June 1996, 19,107

Bulgaria (1) 1 *(Stoichkov 3)*

Romania (0) 0

Bulgaria: Mikhailov; Kischischev, Iankov, Ivanov, Tsvetanov, Lechkov (Guentchev 89), Yordanov, Balakov, Kostadinov (Borimirov 31), Penev (Sirakov 71), Stoichkov.
Romania: Stelea; Petrescu, Belodedici, Prodan, Selymes, Lupescu (Galca 46), Popescu (Ilie A 76), Munteanu, Hagi, Lacatus (Moldovan 28), Raducioiu.
Referee: Mikkelsen (Denmark).

Elland Road, 15 June 1996, 35,626

France (0) 1 *(Djorkaeff 48)*

Spain (0) 1 *(Caminero 85)*

France: Lama; Angloma (Roche 65), Desailly, Blanc, Karembeu, Zidane, Deschamps, Guerin (Thuram 80), Lizarazu, Djorkaeff, Loko (Dugarry 73).
Spain: Zubizarreta; Otero (Kiko 58), Lopez, Abelardo, Sergi, Luis Enrique (Manjarin 55), Caminero, Hierro, Alkorta, Amavisca, Alfonso (Julio Salinas 82).
Referee: Zhuk (Belarus).

St James' Park, 18 June 1996, 26,976

France (1) 3 *(Blanc 20, Penev 63 (og), Loko 90)*

Bulgaria (0) 1 *(Stoichkov 69)*

France: Lama; Thuram, Blanc, Desailly, Lizarazu, Karembeu, Deschamps, Guerin, Zidane (Pedros 61), Djorkaeff, Dugarry (Loko 67).
Bulgaria: Mikhailov; Kremenliev, Ivanov, Hubchev, Tsvetanov, Lechkov, Yordanov, Iankov (Borimirov 77), Balakov (Donkov 77), Penev, Stoichkov.
Referee: Gallagher (England) Durkin (England 28).

Elland Road, 18 June 1996, 32,719

Romania (1) 1 *(Raducioiu 29)*

Spain (1) 2 *(Manjarin 11, Amor 85)*

Romania: Prunea; Dobos, Prodan (Lupescu 86), Galca, Petrescu, Stinga, Popescu, Hagi, Selymes, Raducioiu (Vladoiu 78), Ilie A (Munteanu 65).
Spain: Zubizarreta; Lopez, Alkorta, Abelardo (Amor 64), Sergi, Hierro, Nadal, Manjarin, Kiko, Amavisca (Guerrero 72), Pizzi (Alfonso 85).
Referee: Caker (Turkey).

Group A Final Table	P	W	D	L	F	A	Pts
England	3	2	1	0	7	2	7
Holland	3	1	1	1	3	4	4
Scotland	3	1	1	1	1	2	4
Switzerland	3	0	1	2	1	4	1

Group B Final Table	P	W	D	L	F	A	Pts
France	3	2	1	0	5	2	7
Spain	3	1	2	0	4	3	5
Bulgaria	3	1	1	1	3	4	4
Romania	3	0	0	3	1	4	0

Group C

Old Trafford, 9 June 1996, 37,300

Germany (2) 2 *(Ziege 25, Moller 31)*

Czech Republic (0) 0

Germany: Kopke; Reuter, Sammer, Kohler (Babbel 14), Helmer, Ziege, Hassler, Eilts, Moller, Bobic (Strunz 65), Kuntz (Bierhoff 82).
Czech Republic: Kouba; Kadlec, Hornak, Suchoparek, Latal, Frydek (Berger 46), Bejbl, Nemec, Nedved, Poborsky (Drulak 46), Kuka.
Referee: Elleray (England).

Anfield, 11 June 1996, 35,120

Italy (1) 2 *(Casiraghi 4, 52)*

Russia (1) 1 *(Tsymbalar 20)*

Italy: Peruzzi; Mussi, Costacurta, Apolloni, Maldini, Di Livio (Fuser 61), Albertini, Di Matteo, Del Piero (Donadoni 46), Casiraghi (Ravanelli 79), Zola.
Russia: Cherchesov; Tetradze, Bushmanov (Yanovski 46), Onopko, Kovtun, Mostovoi, Radimov, Karpin (Kiryakov 63), Tsymbalar (Dobrovolski 72), Kanchelskis, Kolyvanov.
Referee: Mottram (Scotland).

Anfield, 14 June 1996, 37,320

Czech Republic (2) 2 *(Nedved 4, Bejbl 35)*

Italy (1) 1 *(Chiesa 18)*

Czech Republic: Kouba; Hornak, Kadlec, Suchoparek, Latal (Nemecek 88), Nedved, Berger (Smicer 64), Bejbl, Nemec, Poborsky, Kuka.
Italy: Peruzzi; Mussi, Costacurta, Apolloni, Maldini, Fuser, Albertini, Dino Baggio (Carboni 38), Donadoni, Ravanelli (Casiraghi 58), Chiesa (Zola 78).
Referee: Lopez Nieto (Spain).

Old Trafford, 16 June 1996, 50,760

Russia (0) 0

Germany (0)3 *(Sammer 56, Klinsmann 77, 90)*

Russia: Kharine; Nikiforov, Kovtun, Onopko, Kanchelskis, Khokhlov (Simutenkov 66), Radimov (Karpin 46), Tetradze, Tsymbalar, Mostovoi, Kolyvanov.
Germany: Kopke; Helmer, Babbel, Sammer, Reuter, Hassler (Freund 66), Eilts, Moller (Strunz 87), Ziege, Bierhoff (Kuntz 84), Klinsmann.
Referee: Nielsen (Denmark).

Anfield, 19 June 1996, 21,128

Russia (0) 3 *(Mostovoi 49, Tetradze 54, Beschastnykh 85)*

Czech Republic (2) 3 *(Suchoparek 6, Kuka 19, Smicer 89)*

Russia: Cherchesov; Tetradze, Gorlukovich, Nikiforov, Yanovski, Karpin, Radimov, Khokhlov, Tsymbalar (Shalimov 67), Simutenkov (Mostovoi 46), Kolyvanov (Beschastnykh 46).
Czech Republic: Kouba; Kubik, Hornak, Suchoparek, Latal, Bejbl, Nedved, Berger (Nemecek 90), Nemec, Poborsky, Kuka (Smicer 68).
Referee: Frisk (Sweden).

Old Trafford, 19 June 1996, 53,740

Italy (0) 0

Germany (0) 0

Italy: Peruzzi; Mussi, Maldini, Carboni (Torricelli 77), Costacurta, Albertini, Fuser (Di Livio 80), Di Matteo (Chiesa 71), Casiraghi, Zola, Donadoni.
Germany: Kopke; Strunz, Sammer, Helmer, Freund, Ziege, Hassler, Eilts, Moller (Bode 88), Bobic, Klinsmann.
Referee: Goethals (Belgium).

Group C Final Table

	P	W	D	L	F	A	Pts
Germany	3	2	1	0	5	0	7
Czech Republic	3	1	1	1	5	6	4
Italy	3	1	1	1	3	3	4
Russia	3	0	1	2	4	8	1

Group D

Hillsborough, 9 June 1996, 34,993

Denmark (1) 1 *(Laudrup B 21)*

Portugal (0) 1 *(Sa Pinto 52)*

Denmark: Schmeichel; Helveg, Rieper, Hogh, Thomsen (Piechnik 83), Steen-Nielsen, Larsen (Vilfort 90), Risager, Laudrup B, Laudrup N, Beck.
Portugal: Vitor Baia; Paulinho Santos, Cristovao, Fernando Couto, Dimas, Oceano (Folha 37), Paulo Sousa (Tavares 77), Sa Pinto, Figo (Domingos 62), Rui Costa, Joao Pinto.
Referee: Van der Ende (Holland).

City Ground, 11 June 1996, 22,460

Turkey (0) 0

Croatia (0) 1 *(Vlaovic 86)*

Turkey: Rustu; Vedat, Rahim, Alpay, Ogun, Tolunay (Saffet 89), Abdullah, Tugay, Arif (Hami 82), Segen, Hakan.
Croatia: Ladic; Stimac, Jerkan, Bilic, Jarni, Asanovic, Boban (Soldo 57), Stanic, Prosinecki, Suker (Pavlicic 90), Boksic (Vlaovic 73).
Referee: Muhmenthaler (Switzerland).

City Ground, 14 June 1996, 22,670

Portugal (0) 1 *(Fernando Couto 66)*

Turkey (0) 0

Portugal: Vitor Baia; Paulinho Santos, Fernando Couto, Helder, Dimas, Sa Pinto (Cadete 65), Paulo Sousa, Figo, Rui Costa, Folha (Tavares 46), Joao Pinto (Porfirio 76).
Turkey: Rustu; Ogun (Rahim 46), Recep, Alpay, Vedat, Abdullah, Oguz (Arif 70), Tugay, Sergen, Hakan, Saffet (Tolunay 63).
Referee: Puhl (Hungary).

Hillsborough, 16 June 1996, 33,671

Croatia (0) 3 *(Suker 53 (pen), 90, Boban 81)*

Denmark (0) 0

Croatia: Ladic; Stanic, Asanovic, Bilic, Jerkan, Stimac, Prosinecki (Mladenovic 87), Boban (Soldo 83), Suker, Vlaovic (Jurcevic 82), Jarni.
Denmark: Schmeichel; Helveg (Laursen 46), Thomsen, Hogh, Rieper, Vilfort (Beck 58), Steen-Nielsen, Larsen (Tofting 68), Schjonberg, Laudrup B, Laudrup M.
Referee: Batta (France).

City Ground, 19 June 1996, 20,484

Croatia (0) 0

Portugal (2) 3 *(Vigo 4, Joao Pinto 33, Domingos 83)*

Croatia: Mrmic; Pavlicic, Bilic, Soldo, Jurcevic, Simic, Mladenovic (Asanovic 46), Pamic (Suker 46), Prosinecki (Boban 46), Vlaovic, Jarni.
Portugal: Vitor Baia; Secretario, Fernando Couto, Cristovao, Oceano, Rui Costa (Barbosa 61), Paulo Sousa (Tavares 70), Figo, Teixera, Joao Pinto, Sa Pinto (Domingos 46).
Referee: Heynemann (Germany).

Hillsborough, 19 June 1996, 28,951

Turkey (0) 0

Denmark (0) 3 *(Laudrup B 50, 84, Nielsen 70)*

Turkey: Rustu; Recep (Saffet 67), Alpay, Ogun, Vedat, Tayfun, Tugay, Abdullah, Orhan (Bulent 67), Hami, Hakan (Arif 46).
Denmark: Schmeichel; Helveg, Hogh, Thomsen, Rieper, Nielsen, Steen-Nielsen, Schjonberg (Larsen 46), Andersen E (Andersen S 88), Laudrup B, Laudrup M.
Referee: Levnikov (Russia).

Group D Final Table	P	W	D	L	F	A	Pts
Portugal	3	2	1	0	5	1	7
Croatia	3	2	0	1	4	3	6
Denmark	3	1	1	1	4	4	4
Turkey	3	0	0	3	0	5	0

QUARTER-FINALS

Wembley, 22 June 1996, 75,440

Spain (0) 0

England (0) 0

Spain: Zubizarreta; Belsue, Nadal, Alkorta (Lopez 73), Abelardo, Manjarin (Caminero 46), Hierro, Amor, Sergi, Kiko, Julio Salinas (Alfonso 46).
England: Seaman; Neville G, Pearce, Platt, Southgate, Adams, Anderton (Stone 109), Gascoigne, Shearer, Sheringham (Barmby 109), McManaman (Fowler 109).
aet; England 4-2 on penalties.
Referee: Batta (France).

Anfield, 22 June 1996, 37,465

France (0) 0

Holland (0) 0

France: Lama; Thuram, Blanc, Desailly, Lizarazu, Karembeu, Deschamps, Guerin, Zidane, Djorkaeff, Loko (Dugarry 61) (Pedros 80).
Holland: Van der Sar; Reiziger, Bogarde, Blind, De Kock, Ronald de Boer, Jordi Cruyff (Winter 68), Witschge (Mulder 80), Kluivert, Bergkamp (Seedorf 59), Cocu.
aet; France won 5-4 on penalties.
Referee: Nieto (Spain).

Old Trafford, 23 June 1996, 43,412

Germany (1) 2 *(Klinsmann 21 (pen), Sammer 58)*

Croatia (0) 1 *(Suker 51)*

Germany: Kopke; Reuter, Helmer, Sammer, Babbel, Moller, Scholl (Hassler 87), Eilts, Ziege, Bobic (Kuntz 46), Klinsmann (Freund 38).
Croatia: Ladic; Stanic, Bilic, Jerkan, Stimac, Jurcevic (Mladenovic 77), Asanovic, Boban, Suker, Vlaovic, Jarni.
Referee: Sundell (Sweden).

Villa Park, 23 June 1996, 26,832

Portugal (0) 0

Czech Republic (0) 1 *(Poborsky 53)*

Portugal: Vitor Baia; Secretario, Fernando Couto, Helder, Dimas, Oceano (Folha 65), Rui Costa, Paulo Sousa, Figo (Cadete 83), Joao Pinto, Sa Pinto (Domingos 46).
Czech Republic: Kouba; Kadlec, Hornak, Suchoparek, Latal, Bejbl, Nemecek (Berger 90), Nemec, Poborsky, Smicer (Kubik 85), Kuka.
Referee: Krug (Germany).

SEMI-FINALS

Wembley, 26 June 1996, 75,862

England (1) 1 *(Shearer 3)*

Germany (1) 1 *(Kuntz 16)*

England: Seaman; Southgate, Pearce, Platt, Ince, Adams, Anderton, Gascoigne, Shearer, Sheringham, McManaman.
Germany: Kopke; Babbel, Helmer (Bode 110), Sammer, Reuter, Freund (Strunz 119), Scholl (Hassler 76), Eilts, Ziege, Moller, Kuntz.
aet; Germany won 6-5 on penalties.
Referee: Puhl (Hungary).

Old Trafford, 26 June 1996, 43,877

France (0) 0

Czech Republic (0) 0

France: Lama; Thuram (Angloma 84), Blanc, Roche, Lizarazu, Lamouchi (Pedros 64), Desailly, Guerin, Zidane, Djorkaeff, Loko.
Czech Republic: Kouba; Kadlec, Hornak, Rada, Nedved, Nemecek, Nemec (Kubik 84), Novotny, Poborsky, Smicer (Berger 46), Drulak (Kotulek 70).
aet; Czech Republic won 6-5 on penalties.
Referee: Mottram (Scotland).

David Seaman's crucial fourth Spanish penalty save which ensured England a place in the European Championship semi-final. Nadal was the culprit. (Colorsport)

FINAL

WEMBLEY, 30 JUNE 1996, 73,611

Germany (0) 2 *(Bierhoff 73, 95)*

Czech Republic (0) 1 *(Berger 59 pen)*

Germany: Kopke; Helmer, Sammer, Scholl (Bierhoff 69), Hassler, Kuntz, Babbel, Ziege, Klinsmann, Strunz, Eilts (Bode 46).
Czech Republic: Kouba; Suchoparek, Nedved, Kadlec, Nemec, Poborsky (Smicer 88), Kuka, Bejbl, Berger, Hornak, Rada.
Score 1-1 after 90 minutes.
Germany won with first extra time (sudden death) goal.
Referee: Pairetto (Italy).

The German team celebrate after winning the European Championship final against the Czech Republic at Wembley. In doing so, they avenged a penalty shoot-out defeat against Czechoslovakia in the 1976 tournament. (Colorsport)

EURO 96 – the penalties

England v Spain
Shearer 1-0; Hierro hit bar 1-0; Platt 2-0; Amor 2-1; Pearce 3-1; Belsue 3-2; Gascoigne 4-2; Nadal saved 4–2

England v Germany
Shearer 1-0; Hassler 1-1; Platt 2-1; Strunz 2-2; Pearce 3-2; Reuter 3-3; Gascoigne 4-3; Ziege 4-4; Sheringham 5-4; Kuntz 5-5; Southgate saved 5-5; Moller 5-6

Holland v France
De Kock 1-0; Zidane 1-1; Ronald de Boer 2-1; Djorkaeff 2-2; Kluivert 3-2; Lizarazu 3-3; Seedorf saved 3-3; Guerin 3-4; Blind 4-4; Blanc 4-5

France v Czech Republic
Zidane 1-0; Kubik 1-1; Djorkaeff 2-1; Nedved 2-2; Lizarazu 3-2; Berger 3-3; Guerin 4-3; Poborsky 4-4; Blanc 5-4; Rada 5-5; Pedros saved; Kadlec 5-6

EURO 96 – the cards

Red
Bulgaria 1, Croatia 1, Czech Republic 1, Germany 1, Italy 1, Russia 1, Spain 1

Yellow
Czech Republic 18, Germany 16, Portugal 12, Spain 12, Switzerland 12, France 11, Croatia 10, England 9, Holland 9, Russia 9, Scotland 8, Turkey 8, Bulgaria 7, Romania 7, Italy 5, Denmark 4

EURO 96 – the top scorers

Shearer (England)	5
Stoichkov (Bulgaria)	3
Brian Laudrup (Denmark)	3

Klinsmann (Germany)	3
Suker (Croatia)	3

EURO 96 – the awards

Mastercard Man of the Match
Shearer, England v Switzerland
Stoichkov, Bulgaria v Spain
Sammer, Germany v Czech Republic
Schmeichel, Denmark v Portugal
McAllister, Scotland v Holland
Djorkaeff, France v Romania
Casiraghi, Italy v Russia
Prosinecki, Croatia v Turkey
Stoichkov, Bulgaria v Romania
Bergkamp, Holland v Switzerland
Couto, Portugal v Turkey
Bejbl, Czech Republic v Italy
Seaman, England v Scotland
Caminero, Spain v France
Klinsmann, Germany v Russia
Suker, Croatia v Denmark
Blanc, France v Bulgaria
Sergi, Romania v Spain

Sheringham, England v Holland
McCall, Scotland v Switzerland
Joao Pinto, Portugal v Croatia
Brian Laudrup, Denmark v Turkey
Kopke, Germany v Italy
Poborsky, Czech Republic v Russia
Seaman, England v Spain
Lama, France v Holland
Sammer, Germany v Croatia
Poborsky, Czech Republic v Portugal
Kadlec, Czech Republic v France
Eilts, Germany v England
Poborsky, Czech Republic v Germany

Fair Play Award
England

Crowd Assessment
Holland

EURO 96 – the crowds

1,268,201 for an average of 40,916

EURO 96 – in perspective

		Games	Crowds	Average	Goals
1960	France	4	78,958	19,739	17
1964	Spain	4	156,253	39,063	13
1968	Italy	5	260,936	52,187	7
1972	Belgium	4	107,326	26,831	10
1976	Yugoslavia	4	106,087	26,521	19
1980	Italy	14	350,655	25,046	27
1984	France	15	599,655	39,977	41
1988	Germany	15	809,844	53,989	34
1992	Sweden	15	906,946	37,789	32
1996	England	31	1,268,201	40,916	64

BRITISH AND IRISH INTERNATIONAL RESULTS 1872–1996

Note: In the results that follow, wc=World Cup, ec=European Championship, ui=Umbro International Trophy. For Ireland, read Northern Ireland from 1921.

ENGLAND v SCOTLAND

Played: 107; England won 43, Scotland won 40, Drawn 24. *Goals:* England 188, Scotland 168.

Year	Date	Venue	E	S	Year	Date	Venue	E	S
1872	30 Nov	Glasgow	0	0	1931	28 Mar	Glasgow	0	2
1873	8 Mar	Kennington Oval	4	2	1932	9 Apr	Wembley	3	0
1874	7 Mar	Glasgow	1	2	1933	1 Apr	Glasgow	1	2
1875	6 Mar	Kennington Oval	2	2	1934	14 Apr	Wembley	3	0
1876	4 Mar	Glasgow	0	3	1935	6 Apr	Glasgow	0	2
1877	3 Mar	Kennington Oval	1	3	1936	4 Apr	Wembley	1	1
1878	2 Mar	Glasgow	2	7	1937	17 Apr	Glasgow	1	3
1879	5 Apr	Kennington Oval	5	4	1938	9 Apr	Wembley	0	1
1880	13 Mar	Glasgow	4	5	1939	15 Apr	Glasgow	2	1
1881	12 Mar	Kennington Oval	1	6	1947	12 Apr	Wembley	1	1
1882	11 Mar	Glasgow	1	5	1948	10 Apr	Glasgow	2	0
1883	10 Mar	Sheffield	2	3	1949	9 Apr	Wembley	1	3
1884	15 Mar	Glasgow	0	1	wc1950	15 Apr	Glasgow	1	0
1885	21 Mar	Kennington Oval	1	1	1951	14 Apr	Wembley	2	3
1886	31 Mar	Glasgow	1	1	1952	5 Apr	Glasgow	2	1
1887	19 Mar	Blackburn	2	3	1953	18 Apr	Wembley	2	2
1888	17 Mar	Glasgow	5	0	wc1954	3 Apr	Glasgow	4	2
1889	13 Apr	Kennington Oval	2	3	1955	2 Apr	Wembley	7	2
1890	5 Apr	Glasgow	1	1	1956	14 Apr	Glasgow	1	1
1891	6 Apr	Blackburn	2	1	1957	6 Apr	Wembley	2	1
1892	2 Apr	Glasgow	4	1	1958	19 Apr	Glasgow	4	0
1893	1 Apr	Richmond	5	2	1959	11 Apr	Wembley	1	0
1894	7 Apr	Glasgow	2	2	1960	19 Apr	Glasgow	1	1
1895	6 Apr	Everton	3	0	1961	15 Apr	Wembley	9	3
1896	4 Apr	Glasgow	1	2	1962	14 Apr	Glasgow	0	2
1897	3 Apr	Crystal Palace	1	2	1963	6 Apr	Wembley	1	2
1898	2 Apr	Glasgow	3	1	1964	11 Apr	Glasgow	0	1
1899	8 Apr	Birmingham	2	1	1965	10 Apr	Wembley	2	2
1900	7 Apr	Glasgow	1	4	1966	2 Apr	Glasgow	4	3
1901	30 Mar	Crystal Palace	2	2	ec1967	15 Apr	Wembley	2	3
1902	3 Mar	Birmingham	2	2	ec1968	24 Jan	Glasgow	1	1
1903	4 Apr	Sheffield	1	2	1969	10 May	Wembley	4	1
1904	9 Apr	Glasgow	1	0	1970	25 Apr	Glasgow	0	0
1905	1 Apr	Crystal Palace	1	0	1971	22 May	Wembley	3	1
1906	7 Apr	Glasgow	1	2	1972	27 May	Glasgow	1	0
1907	6 Apr	Newcastle	1	1	1973	14 Feb	Glasgow	5	0
1908	4 Apr	Glasgow	1	1	1973	19 May	Wembley	1	0
1909	3 Apr	Crystal Palace	2	0	1974	18 May	Wembley	0	2
1910	2 Apr	Glasgow	0	2	1975	24 May	Wembley	5	1
1911	1 Apr	Everton	1	1	1976	15 May	Glasgow	1	2
1912	23 Mar	Glasgow	1	1	1977	4 June	Wembley	1	2
1913	5 Apr	Chelsea	1	0	1978	20 May	Glasgow	1	0
1914	14 Apr	Glasgow	1	3	1979	26 May	Wembley	3	1
1920	10 Apr	Sheffield	5	4	1980	24 May	Glasgow	2	0
1921	9 Apr	Glasgow	0	3	1981	23 May	Wembley	0	1
1922	8 Apr	Aston Villa	0	1	1982	29 May	Glasgow	1	0
1923	14 Apr	Glasgow	2	2	1983	1 June	Wembley	2	0
1924	12 Apr	Wembley	1	1	1984	26 May	Glasgow	1	1
1925	4 Apr	Glasgow	0	2	1985	25 May	Glasgow	0	1
1926	17 Apr	Manchester	0	1	1986	23 Apr	Wembley	2	1
1927	2 Apr	Glasgow	2	1	1987	23 May	Glasgow	0	0
1928	31 Mar	Wembley	1	5	1988	21 May	Wembley	1	0
1929	13 Apr	Glasgow	0	1	1989	27 May	Glasgow	2	0
1930	5 Apr	Wembley	5	2	ec1996	15 June	Wembley	2	0

ENGLAND v WALES

Played: 97; England won 62, Wales won 14, Drawn 21. *Goals:* England 239, Wales 90.

Year	Date	Venue	E	W	Year	Date	Venue	E	W
1879	18 Jan	Kennington Oval	2	1	1882	13 Mar	Wrexham	3	5
1880	15 Mar	Wrexham	3	2	1883	3 Feb	Kennington Oval	5	0
1881	26 Feb	Blackburn	0	1	1884	17 Mar	Wrexham	4	0

			E	W				E	W
1885	14 Mar	Blackburn	1	1	1934	29 Sept	Cardiff	4	0
1886	29 Mar	Wrexham	3	1	1936	5 Feb	Wolverhampton	1	2
1887	26 Feb	Kennington Oval	4	0	1936	17 Oct	Cardiff	1	2
1888	4 Feb	Crewe	5	1	1937	17 Nov	Middlesbrough	2	1
1889	23 Feb	Stoke	4	1	1938	22 Oct	Cardiff	2	4
1890	15 Mar	Wrexham	3	1	1946	13 Nov	Manchester	3	0
1891	7 May	Sunderland	4	1	1947	18 Oct	Cardiff	3	0
1892	5 Mar	Wrexham	2	0	1948	10 Nov	Aston Villa	1	0
1893	13 Mar	Stoke	6	0	wc1949	15 Oct	Cardiff	4	1
1894	12 Mar	Wrexham	5	1	1950	15 Nov	Sunderland	4	2
1895	18 Mar	Queen's Club,			1951	20 Oct	Cardiff	1	1
		Kensington	1	1	1952	12 Nov	Wembley	5	2
1896	16 Mar	Cardiff	9	1	wc1953	10 Oct	Cardiff	4	1
1897	29 Mar	Sheffield	4	0	1954	10 Nov	Wembley	3	2
1898	28 Mar	Wrexham	3	0	1955	27 Oct	Cardiff	1	2
1899	20 Mar	Bristol	4	0	1956	14 Nov	Wembley	3	1
1900	26 Mar	Cardiff	1	1	1957	19 Oct	Cardiff	4	0
1901	18 Mar	Newcastle	6	0	1958	26 Nov	Aston Villa	2	2
1902	3 Mar	Wrexham	0	0	1959	17 Oct	Cardiff	1	1
1903	2 Mar	Portsmouth	2	1	1960	23 Nov	Wembley	5	1
1904	29 Mar	Wrexham	2	2	1961	14 Oct	Cardiff	1	1
1905	27 Mar	Liverpool	3	1	1962	21 Oct	Wembley	4	0
1906	19 Mar	Cardiff	1	0	1963	12 Oct	Cardiff	4	0
1907	18 Mar	Fulham	1	1	1964	18 Nov	Wembley	2	1
1908	16 Mar	Wrexham	7	1	1965	2 Oct	Cardiff	0	0
1909	15 Mar	Nottingham	2	0	EC1966	16 Nov	Wembley	5	1
1910	14 Mar	Cardiff	1	0	EC1967	21 Oct	Cardiff	3	0
1911	13 Mar	Millwall	3	0	1969	7 May	Wembley	2	1
1912	11 Mar	Wrexham	2	0	1970	18 Apr	Cardiff	1	1
1913	17 Mar	Bristol	4	3	1971	19 May	Wembley	0	0
1914	16 Mar	Cardiff	2	0	1972	20 May	Cardiff	3	0
1920	15 Mar	Highbury	1	2	wc1972	15 Nov	Cardiff	1	0
1921	14 Mar	Cardiff	0	0	wc1973	24 Jan	Wembley	1	1
1922	13 Mar	Liverpool	1	0	1973	15 May	Wembley	3	0
1923	5 Mar	Cardiff	2	2	1974	11 May	Cardiff	2	0
1924	3 Mar	Blackburn	1	2	1975	21 May	Wembley	2	2
1925	28 Feb	Swansea	2	1	1976	24 Mar	Wrexham	2	1
1926	1 Mar	Crystal Palace	1	3	1976	8 May	Cardiff	1	0
1927	12 Feb	Wrexham	3	3	1977	31 May	Wembley	0	1
1927	28 Nov	Burnley	1	2	1978	3 May	Cardiff	3	1
1928	17 Nov	Swansea	3	2	1979	23 May	Wembley	0	0
1929	20 Nov	Chelsea	6	0	1980	17 May	Wrexham	1	4
1930	22 Nov	Wrexham	4	0	1981	20 May	Wembley	0	0
1931	18 Nov	Liverpool	3	1	1982	27 Apr	Cardiff	1	0
1932	16 Nov	Wrexham	0	0	1983	23 Feb	Wembley	2	1
1933	15 Nov	Newcastle	1	2	1984	2 May	Wrexham	0	1

ENGLAND v IRELAND

Played: 96; England won 74, Ireland won 6, Drawn 16. *Goals:* England 319, Ireland 80.

			E	I				E	I
1882	18 Feb	Belfast	13	0	1903	14 Feb	Wolverhampton	4	0
1883	24 Feb	Liverpool	7	0	1904	12 Mar	Belfast	3	1
1884	23 Feb	Belfast	8	1	1905	25 Feb	Middlesbrough	1	1
1885	28 Feb	Manchester	4	0	1906	17 Feb	Belfast	5	0
1886	13 Mar	Belfast	6	1	1907	16 Feb	Everton	1	0
1887	5 Feb	Sheffield	7	0	1908	15 Feb	Belfast	3	1
1888	31 Mar	Belfast	5	1	1909	13 Feb	Bradford	4	0
1889	2 Mar	Everton	6	1	1910	12 Feb	Belfast	1	1
1890	15 Mar	Belfast	9	1	1911	11 Feb	Derby	2	1
1891	7 Mar	Wolverhampton	6	1	1912	10 Feb	Dublin	6	1
1892	5 Mar	Belfast	2	0	1913	15 Feb	Belfast	1	2
1893	25 Feb	Birmingham	6	1	1914	14 Feb	Middlesbrough	0	3
1894	3 Mar	Belfast	2	2	1919	25 Oct	Belfast	1	1
1895	9 Mar	Derby	9	0	1920	23 Oct	Sunderland	2	0
1896	7 Mar	Belfast	2	0	1921	22 Oct	Belfast	1	1
1897	20 Feb	Nottingham	6	0	1922	21 Oct	West Bromwich	2	0
1898	5 Mar	Belfast	3	2	1923	20 Oct	Belfast	1	2
1899	18 Feb	Sunderland	13	2	1924	22 Oct	Everton	3	1
1900	17 Mar	Dublin	2	0	1925	24 Oct	Belfast	0	0
1901	9 Mar	Southampton	3	0	1926	20 Oct	Liverpool	3	3
1902	22 Mar	Belfast	1	0	1927	22 Oct	Belfast	0	2

Year	Date	Venue	E	I		Year	Date	Venue	E	I
1928	22 Oct	Everton	2	1		1962	20 Oct	Belfast	3	1
1929	19 Oct	Belfast	3	0		1963	20 Nov	Wembley	8	3
1930	20 Oct	Sheffield	5	1		1964	3 Oct	Belfast	4	3
1931	17 Oct	Belfast	6	2		1965	10 Nov	Wembley	2	1
1932	17 Oct	Blackpool	1	0		EC1966	20 Oct	Belfast	2	0
1933	14 Oct	Belfast	3	0		EC1967	22 Nov	Wembley	2	0
1935	6 Feb	Everton	2	1		1969	3 May	Belfast	3	1
1935	19 Oct	Belfast	3	1		1970	21 Apr	Wembley	3	1
1936	18 Nov	Stoke	3	1		1971	15 May	Belfast	1	0
1937	23 Oct	Belfast	5	1		1972	23 May	Wembley	0	1
1938	16 Nov	Manchester	7	0		1973	12 May	Everton	2	1
1946	28 Sept	Belfast	7	2		1974	15 May	Wembley	1	0
1947	5 Nov	Everton	2	2		1975	17 May	Belfast	0	0
1948	9 Oct	Belfast	6	2		1976	11 May	Wembley	4	0
wc1949	16 Nov	Manchester	9	2		1977	28 May	Belfast	2	1
1950	7 Oct	Belfast	4	1		1978	16 May	Wembley	1	0
1951	14 Nov	Aston Villa	2	0		EC1979	7 Feb	Wembley	4	0
1952	4 Oct	Belfast	2	2		1979	19 May	Belfast	2	0
wc1953	11 Nov	Everton	3	1		EC1979	17 Oct	Belfast	5	1
1954	2 Oct	Belfast	2	0		1980	20 May	Wembley	1	1
1955	2 Nov	Wembley	3	0		1982	23 Feb	Wembley	4	0
1956	10 Oct	Belfast	1	1		1983	28 May	Belfast	0	0
1957	6 Nov	Wembley	2	3		1984	24 Apr	Wembley	1	0
1958	4 Oct	Belfast	3	3		wc1985	27 Feb	Belfast	1	0
1959	18 Nov	Wembley	2	1		wc1985	13 Nov	Wembley	0	0
1960	8 Oct	Belfast	5	2		EC1986	15 Oct	Wembley	3	0
1961	22 Nov	Wembley	1	1		EC1987	1 Apr	Belfast	2	0

SCOTLAND v WALES

Played: 101; Scotland won 60, Wales won 18, Drawn 23. *Goals:* Scotland 238, Wales 111.

Year	Date	Venue	S	W		Year	Date	Venue	S	W
1876	25 Mar	Glasgow	4	0		1921	12 Feb	Aberdeen	2	1
1877	5 Mar	Wrexham	2	0		1922	4 Feb	Wrexham	1	2
1878	23 Mar	Glasgow	9	0		1923	17 Mar	Paisley	2	0
1879	7 Apr	Wrexham	3	0		1924	16 Feb	Cardiff	0	2
1880	3 Apr	Glasgow	5	1		1925	14 Feb	Tynecastle	3	1
1881	14 Mar	Wrexham	5	1		1925	31 Oct	Cardiff	3	0
1882	25 Mar	Glasgow	5	0		1926	30 Oct	Glasgow	3	0
1883	12 Mar	Wrexham	4	1		1927	29 Oct	Wrexham	2	2
1884	29 Mar	Glasgow	4	1		1928	27 Oct	Glasgow	4	2
1885	23 Mar	Wrexham	8	1		1929	26 Oct	Cardiff	4	2
1886	10 Apr	Glasgow	4	1		1930	25 Oct	Glasgow	1	1
1887	21 Mar	Wrexham	2	0		1931	31 Oct	Wrexham	3	2
1888	10 Mar	Edinburgh	5	1		1932	26 Oct	Edinburgh	2	5
1889	15 Apr	Wrexham	0	0		1933	4 Oct	Cardiff	2	3
1890	22 Mar	Paisley	5	0		1934	21 Nov	Aberdeen	3	2
1891	21 Mar	Wrexham	4	3		1935	5 Oct	Cardiff	1	1
1892	26 Mar	Edinburgh	6	1		1936	2 Dec	Dundee	1	2
1893	18 Mar	Wrexham	8	0		1937	30 Oct	Cardiff	1	2
1894	24 Mar	Kilmarnock	5	2		1938	9 Nov	Edinburgh	3	2
1895	23 Mar	Wrexham	2	2		1946	19 Oct	Wrexham	1	3
1896	21 Mar	Dundee	4	0		1947	12 Nov	Glasgow	1	2
1897	20 Mar	Wrexham	2	2		wc1948	23 Oct	Cardiff	3	1
1898	19 Mar	Motherwell	5	2		1949	9 Nov	Glasgow	2	0
1899	18 Mar	Wrexham	6	0		1950	21 Oct	Cardiff	3	1
1900	3 Feb	Aberdeen	5	2		1951	14 Nov	Glasgow	0	1
1901	2 Mar	Wrexham	1	1		wc1952	18 Oct	Cardiff	2	1
1902	15 Mar	Greenock	5	1		1953	4 Nov	Glasgow	3	3
1903	9 Mar	Cardiff	1	0		1954	16 Oct	Cardiff	1	0
1904	12 Mar	Dundee	1	1		1955	9 Nov	Glasgow	2	0
1905	6 Mar	Wrexham	1	3		1956	20 Oct	Cardiff	2	2
1906	3 Mar	Edinburgh	0	2		1957	13 Nov	Glasgow	1	1
1907	4 Mar	Wrexham	0	1		1958	18 Oct	Cardiff	3	0
1908	7 Mar	Dundee	2	1		1959	4 Nov	Glasgow	1	1
1909	1 Mar	Wrexham	2	3		1960	20 Oct	Cardiff	0	2
1910	5 Mar	Kilmarnock	1	0		1961	8 Nov	Glasgow	2	0
1911	6 Mar	Cardiff	2	2		1962	20 Oct	Cardiff	3	2
1912	2 Mar	Tynecastle	1	0		1963	20 Nov	Glasgow	2	1
1913	3 Mar	Wrexham	0	0		1964	3 Oct	Cardiff	2	3
1914	28 Feb	Glasgow	0	0		EC1965	24 Nov	Glasgow	4	1
1920	26 Feb	Cardiff	1	1		EC1966	22 Oct	Cardiff	1	1

1967	22 Nov	Glasgow	3	2	wc1977	12 Oct	Liverpool	2	0
1969	3 May	Wrexham	5	3	1978	17 May	Glasgow	1	1
1970	22 Apr	Glasgow	0	0	1979	19 May	Cardiff	0	3
1971	15 May	Cardiff	0	0	1980	21 May	Glasgow	1	0
1972	24 May	Glasgow	1	0	1981	16 May	Swansea	0	2
1973	12 May	Wrexham	2	0	1982	24 May	Glasgow	1	0
1974	14 May	Glasgow	2	0	1983	28 May	Cardiff	2	0
1975	17 May	Cardiff	2	2	1984	28 Feb	Glasgow	2	1
1976	6 May	Glasgow	3	1	wc1985	27 Mar	Glasgow	0	1
wc1976	17 Nov	Glasgow	1	0	wc1985	10 Sept	Cardiff	1	1
1977	28 May	Wrexham	0	0					

SCOTLAND v IRELAND

Played: 91; Scotland won 60, Ireland won 15, Drawn 16. *Goals:* Scotland 253, Ireland 81.

			S	I				S	I
1884	26 Jan	Belfast	5	0	1934	20 Oct	Belfast	1	2
1885	14 Mar	Glasgow	8	2	1935	13 Nov	Edinburgh	2	1
1886	20 Mar	Belfast	7	2	1936	31 Oct	Belfast	3	1
1887	19 Feb	Glasgow	4	1	1937	10 Nov	Aberdeen	1	1
1888	24 Mar	Belfast	10	2	1938	8 Oct	Belfast	2	0
1889	9 Mar	Glasgow	7	0	1946	27 Nov	Glasgow	0	0
1890	29 Mar	Belfast	4	1	1947	4 Oct	Belfast	0	2
1891	28 Mar	Glasgow	2	1	1948	17 Nov	Glasgow	3	2
1892	19 Mar	Belfast	3	2	1949	1 Oct	Belfast	8	2
1893	25 Mar	Glasgow	6	1	1950	1 Nov	Glasgow	6	1
1894	31 Mar	Belfast	2	1	1951	6 Oct	Belfast	3	0
1895	30 Mar	Glasgow	3	1	1952	5 Nov	Glasgow	1	1
1896	28 Mar	Belfast	3	3	1953	3 Oct	Belfast	3	1
1897	27 Mar	Glasgow	5	1	1954	3 Nov	Glasgow	2	2
1898	26 Mar	Belfast	3	0	1955	8 Oct	Belfast	1	2
1899	25 Mar	Glasgow	9	1	1956	7 Nov	Glasgow	1	0
1900	3 Mar	Belfast	3	0	1957	5 Oct	Belfast	1	1
1901	23 Feb	Glasgow	11	0	1958	5 Nov	Glasgow	2	2
1902	1 Mar	Belfast	5	1	1959	3 Oct	Belfast	4	0
1903	21 Mar	Glasgow	0	2	1960	9 Nov	Glasgow	5	2
1904	26 Mar	Dublin	1	1	1961	7 Oct	Belfast	6	1
1905	18 Mar	Glasgow	4	0	1962	7 Nov	Glasgow	5	1
1906	17 Mar	Dublin	1	0	1963	12 Oct	Belfast	1	2
1907	16 Mar	Glasgow	3	0	1964	25 Nov	Glasgow	3	2
1908	14 Mar	Dublin	5	0	1965	2 Oct	Belfast	2	3
1909	15 Mar	Glasgow	5	0	1966	16 Nov	Glasgow	2	1
1910	19 Mar	Belfast	0	1	1967	21 Oct	Belfast	0	1
1911	18 Mar	Glasgow	2	0	1969	6 May	Glasgow	1	1
1912	16 Mar	Belfast	4	1	1970	18 Apr	Belfast	1	0
1913	15 Mar	Dublin	2	1	1971	18 May	Glasgow	0	1
1914	14 Mar	Belfast	1	1	1972	20 May	Glasgow	2	0
1920	13 Mar	Glasgow	3	0	1973	16 May	Glasgow	1	2
1921	26 Feb	Belfast	2	0	1974	11 May	Glasgow	0	1
1922	4 Mar	Glasgow	2	1	1975	20 May	Glasgow	3	0
1923	3 Mar	Belfast	1	0	1976	8 May	Glasgow	3	0
1924	1 Mar	Glasgow	2	0	1977	1 June	Glasgow	3	0
1925	28 Feb	Belfast	3	0	1978	13 May	Glasgow	1	1
1926	27 Feb	Glasgow	4	0	1979	22 May	Glasgow	1	0
1927	26 Feb	Belfast	2	0	1980	17 May	Belfast	0	1
1928	25 Feb	Glasgow	0	1	wc1981	25 Mar	Glasgow	1	1
1929	23 Feb	Belfast	7	3	1981	19 May	Glasgow	2	0
1930	22 Feb	Glasgow	3	1	wc1981	14 Oct	Belfast	0	0
1931	21 Feb	Belfast	0	0	1982	28 Apr	Belfast	1	1
1931	19 Sept	Glasgow	3	1	1983	24 May	Glasgow	0	0
1932	12 Sept	Belfast	4	0	1983	13 Dec	Belfast	0	2
1933	16 Sept	Glasgow	1	2	1992	19 Feb	Glasgow	1	0

WALES v IRELAND

Played: 90; Wales won 42, Ireland won 27, Drawn 21. *Goals:* Wales 181, Ireland 126.

			W	I				W	I
1882	25 Feb	Wrexham	7	1	1886	27 Feb	Wrexham	5	0
1883	17 Mar	Belfast	1	1	1887	12 Mar	Belfast	1	4
1884	9 Feb	Wrexham	6	0	1888	3 Mar	Wrexham	11	0
1885	11 Apr	Belfast	8	2	1889	27 Apr	Belfast	3	1

			W	I
1890	8 Feb	Shrewsbury	5	2
1891	7 Feb	Belfast	2	7
1892	27 Feb	Bangor	1	1
1893	8 Apr	Belfast	3	4
1894	24 Feb	Swansea	4	1
1895	16 Mar	Belfast	2	2
1896	29 Feb	Wrexham	6	1
1897	6 Mar	Belfast	3	4
1898	19 Feb	Llandudno	0	1
1899	4 Mar	Belfast	0	1
1900	24 Feb	Llandudno	2	0
1901	23 Mar	Belfast	1	0
1902	22 Mar	Cardiff	0	3
1903	28 Mar	Belfast	0	2
1904	21 Mar	Bangor	0	1
1905	18 Apr	Belfast	2	2
1906	2 Apr	Wrexham	4	4
1907	23 Feb	Belfast	3	2
1908	11 Apr	Aberdare	0	1
1909	20 Mar	Belfast	3	2
1910	11 Apr	Wrexham	4	1
1911	28 Jan	Belfast	2	1
1912	13 Apr	Cardiff	2	3
1913	18 Jan	Belfast	1	0
1914	19 Jan	Wrexham	1	2
1920	14 Feb	Belfast	2	2
1921	9 Apr	Swansea	2	1
1922	4 Apr	Belfast	1	1
1923	14 Apr	Wrexham	0	3
1924	15 Mar	Belfast	1	0
1925	18 Apr	Wrexham	0	0
1926	13 Feb	Belfast	0	3
1927	9 Apr	Cardiff	2	2
1928	4 Feb	Belfast	2	1
1929	2 Feb	Wrexham	2	2
1930	1 Feb	Belfast	0	7
1931	22 Apr	Belfast	3	2
1931	5 Dec	Belfast	0	4
1932	7 Dec	Wrexham	4	1
1933	4 Nov	Belfast	1	1
1935	27 Mar	Wrexham	3	1

			W	I
1936	11 Mar	Belfast	2	3
1937	17 Mar	Wrexham	4	1
1938	16 Mar	Belfast	0	1
1939	15 Mar	Wrexham	3	1
1947	16 Apr	Belfast	1	2
1948	10 Mar	Wrexham	2	0
1949	9 Mar	Belfast	2	0
wc1950	8 Mar	Wrexham	0	0
1951	7 Mar	Belfast	2	1
1952	19 Mar	Swansea	3	0
1953	15 Apr	Belfast	3	2
wc1954	31 Mar	Wrexham	1	2
1955	20 Apr	Belfast	3	2
1956	11 Apr	Cardiff	1	1
1957	10 Apr	Belfast	0	0
1958	16 Apr	Cardiff	1	1
1959	22 Apr	Belfast	1	4
1960	6 Apr	Wrexham	3	2
1961	12 Apr	Belfast	5	1
1962	11 Apr	Cardiff	4	0
1963	3 Apr	Belfast	4	1
1964	15 Apr	Cardiff	2	3
1965	31 Mar	Belfast	5	0
1966	30 Mar	Cardiff	1	4
ec1967	12 Apr	Belfast	0	0
ec1968	28 Feb	Wrexham	2	0
1969	10 May	Belfast	0	0
1970	25 Apr	Swansea	1	0
1971	22 May	Belfast	0	1
1972	27 May	Wrexham	0	0
1973	19 May	Everton	0	1
1974	18 May	Wrexham	1	0
1975	23 May	Belfast	0	1
1976	14 May	Swansea	1	0
1977	3 June	Belfast	1	1
1978	19 May	Wrexham	1	0
1979	25 May	Belfast	1	1
1980	23 May	Cardiff	0	1
1982	27 May	Wrexham	3	0
1983	31 May	Belfast	1	0
1984	22 May	Swansea	1	1

OTHER BRITISH INTERNATIONAL RESULTS 1908–1996

ENGLAND

v ALBANIA

			E	A
wc1989	8 Mar	Tirana	2	0
wc1989	26 Apr	Wembley	5	0

v ARGENTINA

			E	A
1951	9 May	Wembley	2	1
1953	17 May	Buenos Aires	0	0
(abandoned after 21 mins)				
wc1962	2 June	Rancagua	3	1
1964	6 June	Rio de Janeiro	0	1
wc1966	23 July	Wembley	1	0
1974	22 May	Wembley	2	2
1977	12 June	Buenos Aires	1	1
1980	13 May	Wembley	3	1
wc1986	22 June	Mexico City	1	2
1991	25 May	Wembley	2	2

v AUSTRALIA

			E	A
1980	31 May	Sydney	2	1
1983	11 June	Sydney	0	0
1983	15 June	Brisbane	1	0
1983	18 June	Melbourne	1	1
1991	1 June	Sydney	1	0

v AUSTRIA

			E	A
1908	6 June	Vienna	6	1
1908	8 June	Vienna	11	1
1909	1 June	Vienna	8	1
1930	14 May	Vienna	0	0
1932	7 Dec	Chelsea	4	3
1936	6 May	Vienna	1	2
1951	28 Nov	Wembley	2	2
1952	25 May	Vienna	3	2
wc1958	15 June	Boras	2	2
1961	27 May	Vienna	1	3
1962	4 Apr	Wembley	3	1
1965	20 Oct	Wembley	2	3
1967	27 May	Vienna	1	0
1973	26 Sept	Wembley	7	0
1979	13 June	Vienna	3	4

v BELGIUM

			E	B
1921	21 May	Brussels	2	0
1923	19 Mar	Highbury	6	1
1923	1 Nov	Antwerp	2	2
1924	8 Dec	West Bromwich	4	0
1926	24 May	Antwerp	5	3
1927	11 May	Brussels	9	1
1928	19 May	Antwerp	3	1
1929	11 May	Brussels	5	1
1931	16 May	Brussels	4	1
1936	9 May	Brussels	2	3
1947	21 Sept	Brussels	5	2

			E	B
1950	18 May	Brussels	4	1
1952	26 Nov	Wembley	5	0
wc1954	17 June	Basle	4	4*
1964	21 Oct	Wembley	2	2
1970	25 Feb	Brussels	3	1
EC1980	12 June	Turin	1	1
wc1990	27 June	Bologna	1	0*

After extra time

v BOHEMIA			E	B
1908	13 June	Prague	4	0

v BRAZIL			E	B
1956	9 May	Wembley	4	2
wc1958	11 June	Gothenburg	0	0
1959	13 May	Rio de Janeiro	0	2
wc1962	10 June	Vina del Mar	1	3
1963	8 May	Wembley	1	1
1964	30 May	Rio de Janeiro	1	5
1969	12 June	Rio de Janeiro	1	2
wc1970	7 June	Guadalajara	0	1
1976	23 May	Los Angeles	0	1
1977	8 June	Rio de Janeiro	0	0
1978	19 Apr	Wembley	1	1
1981	12 May	Wembley	0	1
1984	10 June	Rio de Janeiro	2	0
1987	19 May	Wembley	1	1
1990	28 Mar	Wembley	1	0
1992	17 May	Wembley	1	1
1993	13 June	Washington	1	1
UI1995	11 June	Wembley	1	3

v BULGARIA			E	B
wc1962	7 June	Rancagua	0	0
1968	11 Dec	Wembley	1	1
1974	1 June	Sofia	1	0
EC1979	6 June	Sofia	3	0
EC1979	22 Nov	Wembley	2	0
1996	27 Mar	Wembley	1	0

v CAMEROON			E	C
wc1990	1 July	Naples	3	2*
1991	6 Feb	Wembley	2	0

v CANADA			E	C
1986	24 May	Burnaby	1	0

v CHILE			E	C
wc1950	25 June	Rio de Janeiro	2	0
1953	24 May	Santiago	2	1
1984	17 June	Santiago	0	0
1989	23 May	Wembley	0	0

v CHINA			E	C
1996	23 May	Beijing	3	0

v CIS			E	C
1992	29 Apr	Moscow	2	2

v COLOMBIA			E	C
1970	20 May	Bogota	4	0
1988	24 May	Wembley	1	1
1995	6 Sept	Wembley	0	0

v CROATIA			E	C
1996	24 Apr	Wembley	0	0

v CYPRUS			E	C
EC1975	16 Apr	Wembley	5	0
EC1975	11 May	Limassol	1	0

v CZECHOSLOVAKIA			E	C
1934	16 May	Prague	1	2
1937	1 Dec	Tottenham	5	4
1963	29 May	Bratislava	4	2
1966	2 Nov	Wembley	0	0
wc1970	11 June	Guadalajara	1	0
1973	27 May	Prague	1	1
EC1974	30 Oct	Wembley	3	0
EC1975	30 Oct	Bratislava	1	2
1978	29 Nov	Wembley	1	0
wc1982	20 June	Bilbao	2	0
1990	25 Apr	Wembley	4	2
1992	25 Mar	Prague	2	2

v DENMARK			E	D
1948	26 Sept	Copenhagen	0	0
1955	2 Oct	Copenhagen	5	1
wc1956	5 Dec	Wolverhampton	5	2
wc1957	15 May	Copenhagen	4	1
1966	3 July	Copenhagen	2	0
EC1978	20 Sept	Copenhagen	4	3
EC1979	12 Sept	Wembley	1	0
EC1982	22 Sept	Copenhagen	2	2
EC1983	21 Sept	Wembley	0	1
1988	14 Sept	Wembley	1	0
1989	7 June	Copenhagen	1	1
1990	15 May	Wembley	1	0
EC1992	11 June	Malmo	0	0
1994	9 Mar	Wembley	1	0

v ECUADOR			E	Ec
1970	24 May	Quito	2	0

v EGYPT			E	Eg
1986	29 Jan	Cairo	4	0
wc1990	21 June	Cagliari	1	0

v FIFA			E	FIFA
1938	26 Oct	Highbury	3	0
1953	21 Oct	Wembley	4	4
1963	23 Oct	Wembley	2	1

v FINLAND			E	F
1937	20 May	Helsinki	8	0
1956	20 May	Helsinki	5	1
1966	26 June	Helsinki	3	0
wc1976	13 June	Helsinki	4	1
wc1976	13 Oct	Wembley	2	1
1982	3 June	Helsinki	4	1
wc1984	17 Oct	Wembley	5	0
wc1985	22 May	Helsinki	1	1
1992	3 June	Helsinki	2	1

v FRANCE			E	F
1923	10 May	Paris	4	1
1924	17 May	Paris	3	1
1925	21 May	Paris	3	2
1927	26 May	Paris	6	0
1928	17 May	Paris	5	1
1929	9 May	Paris	4	1
1931	14 May	Paris	2	5
1933	6 Dec	Tottenham	4	1
1938	26 May	Paris	4	2
1947	3 May	Highbury	3	0
1949	22 May	Paris	3	1
1951	3 Oct	Highbury	2	2
1955	15 May	Paris	0	1
1957	27 Nov	Wembley	4	0
EC1962	3 Oct	Sheffield	1	1
EC1963	27 Feb	Paris	2	5
wc1966	20 July	Wembley	2	0
1969	12 Mar	Wembley	5	0
wc1982	16 June	Bilbao	3	1

			E	F
1984	29 Feb	Paris	0	2
1992	19 Feb	Wembley	2	0
EC1992	14 June	Malmo	0	0

v GERMANY

			E	G
1930	10 May	Berlin	3	3
1935	4 Dec	Tottenham	3	0
1938	14 May	Berlin	6	3
1991	11 Sept	Wembley	0	1
1993	19 June	Detroit	1	2
EC1996	26 June	Wembley	1	1

v EAST GERMANY

			E	EG
1963	2 June	Leipzig	2	1
1970	25 Nov	Wembley	3	1
1974	29 May	Leipzig	1	1
1984	12 Sept	Wembley	1	0

v WEST GERMANY

			E	WG
1954	1 Dec	Wembley	3	1
1956	26 May	Berlin	3	1
1965	12 May	Nuremberg	1	0
1966	23 Feb	Wembley	1	0
wc1966	30 July	Wembley	4	2*
1968	1 June	Hanover	0	1
wc1970	14 June	Leon	2	3*
EC1972	29 Apr	Wembley	1	3
EC1972	13 May	Berlin	0	0
1975	12 Mar	Wembley	2	0
1978	22 Feb	Munich	1	2
wc1982	29 June	Madrid	0	0
1982	13 Oct	Wembley	1	2
1985	12 June	Mexico City	3	0
1987	9 Sept	Dusseldorf	1	3
wc1990	4 July	Turin	1	1*

After extra time

v GREECE

			E	G
EC1971	21 Apr	Wembley	3	0
EC1971	1 Dec	Athens	2	0
EC1982	17 Nov	Athens	3	0
EC1983	30 Mar	Wembley	0	0
1989	8 Feb	Athens	2	1
1994	17 May	Wembley	5	0

v HOLLAND

			E	H
1935	18 May	Amsterdam	1	0
1946	27 Nov	Huddersfield	8	2
1964	9 Dec	Amsterdam	1	1
1969	5 Nov	Amsterdam	1	0
1970	14 Jun	Wembley	0	0
1977	9 Feb	Wembley	0	2
1982	25 May	Wembley	2	0
1988	23 Mar	Wembley	2	2
EC1988	15 June	Dusseldorf	1	3
wc1990	16 June	Cagliari	0	0
wc1993	28 Apr	Wembley	2	2
wc1993	13 Oct	Rotterdam	0	2
EC1996	18 June	Wembley	4	1

v HUNGARY

			E	H
1908	10 June	Budapest	7	0
1909	29 May	Budapest	4	2
1909	31 May	Budapest	8	2
1934	10 May	Budapest	1	2
1936	2 Dec	Highbury	6	2
1953	25 Nov	Wembley	3	6
1954	23 May	Budapest	1	7
1960	22 May	Budapest	0	2
wc1962	31 May	Rancagua	1	2
1965	5 May	Wembley	1	0
1978	24 May	Wembley	4	1

			E	H
wc1981	6 June	Budapest	3	1
wc1982	18 Nov	Wembley	1	0
EC1983	27 Apr	Wembley	2	0
EC1983	12 Oct	Budapest	3	0
1988	27 Apr	Budapest	0	0
1990	12 Sept	Wembley	1	0
1992	12 May	Budapest	1	0
1996	18 May	Wembley	3	0

v ICELAND

			E	I
1982	2 June	Reykjavik	1	1

v REPUBLIC OF IRELAND

			E	RI
1946	30 Sept	Dublin	1	0
1949	21 Sept	Everton	0	2
wc1957	8 May	Wembley	5	1
wc1957	19 May	Dublin	1	1
1964	24 May	Dublin	3	1
1976	8 Sept	Wembley	1	1
EC1978	25 Oct	Dublin	1	1
EC1980	6 Feb	Wembley	2	0
1985	26 Mar	Wembley	2	1
EC1988	12 June	Stuttgart	0	1
wc1990	11 June	Cagliari	1	1
EC1990	14 Nov	Dublin	1	1
EC1991	27 Mar	Wembley	1	1
1995	15 Feb	Dublin	0	1

(abandoned after 27 mins)

v ISRAEL

			E	I
1986	26 Feb	Ramat Gan	2	1
1988	17 Feb	Tel Aviv	0	0

v ITALY

			E	I
1933	13 May	Rome	1	1
1934	14 Nov	Highbury	3	2
1939	13 May	Milan	2	2
1948	16 May	Turin	4	0
1949	30 Nov	Tottenham	2	0
1952	18 May	Florence	1	1
1959	6 May	Wembley	2	2
1961	24 May	Rome	3	2
1973	14 June	Turin	0	2
1973	14 Nov	Wembley	0	1
1976	28 May	New York	3	2
wc1976	17 Nov	Rome	0	2
wc1977	16 Nov	Wembley	2	0
EC1980	15 June	Turin	0	1
1985	6 June	Mexico City	1	2
1989	15 Nov	Wembley	0	0
wc1990	7 July	Bari	1	2

v JAPAN

			E	J
UI1995	3 June	Wembley	2	1

v KUWAIT

			E	K
wc1982	25 June	Bilbao	1	0

v LUXEMBOURG

			E	L
1927	21 May	Luxembourg	5	2
wc1960	19 Oct	Luxembourg	9	0
wc1961	28 Sept	Highbury	4	1
wc1977	30 Mar	Wembley	5	0
wc1977	12 Oct	Luxembourg	2	0
EC1982	15 Dec	Wembley	9	0
EC1983	16 Nov	Luxembourg	4	0

v MALAYSIA

			E	M
1991	12 June	Kuala Lumpur	4	2

v MALTA

			E	M
EC1971	3 Feb	Valletta	1	0
EC1971	12 May	Wembley	5	0

		v MEXICO	E	M
1959	24 May	Mexico City	1	2
1961	10 May	Wembley	8	0
wc1966	16 July	Wembley	2	0
1969	1 June	Mexico City	0	0
1985	9 June	Mexico City	0	1
1986	17 May	Los Angeles	3	0

		v MOROCCO	E	M
wc1986	6 June	Monterrey	0	0

		v NEW ZEALAND	E	NZ
1991	3 June	Auckland	1	0
1991	8 June	Wellington	2	0

		v NIGERIA	E	N
1994	16 Nov	Wembley	1	0

		v NORWAY	E	N
1937	14 May	Oslo	6	0
1938	9 Nov	Newcastle	4	0
1949	18 May	Oslo	4	1
1966	29 June	Oslo	6	1
wc1980	10 Sept	Wembley	4	0
wc1981	9 Sept	Oslo	1	2
wc1992	14 Oct	Wembley	1	1
wc1993	2 June	Oslo	0	2
1994	22 May	Wembley	0	0
1995	11 Oct	Oslo	0	0

		v PARAGUAY	E	P
wc1986	18 June	Mexico City	3	0

		v PERU	E	P
1959	17 May	Lima	1	4
1962	20 May	Lima	4	0

		v POLAND	E	P
1966	5 Jan	Everton	1	1
1966	5 July	Chorzow	1	0
wc1973	6 June	Chorzow	0	2
wc1973	17 Oct	Wembley	1	1
wc1986	11 June	Monterrey	3	0
wc1989	3 June	Wembley	3	0
wc1989	11 Oct	Katowice	0	0
EC1990	17 Oct	Wembley	2	0
EC1991	13 Nov	Poznan	1	1
wc1993	29 May	Katowice	1	1
wc1993	8 Sept	Wembley	3	0

		v PORTUGAL	E	P
1947	25 May	Lisbon	10	0
1950	14 May	Lisbon	5	3
1951	19 May	Everton	5	2
1955	22 May	Oporto	1	3
1958	7 May	Wembley	2	1
wc1961	21 May	Lisbon	1	1
wc1961	25 Oct	Wembley	2	0
1964	17 May	Lisbon	4	3
1964	4 June	S~ao Paulo	1	1
wc1966	26 July	Wembley	2	1
1969	10 Dec	Wembley	1	0
1974	3 Apr	Lisbon	0	0
EC1974	20 Nov	Wembley	0	0
EC1975	19 Nov	Lisbon	1	1
wc1986	3 June	Monterrey	0	1
1995	12 Dec	Wembley	1	1

		v ROMANIA	E	R
1939	24 May	Bucharest	2	0
1968	6 Nov	Bucharest	0	0
1969	15 Jan	Wembley	1	1
wc1970	2 June	Guadalajara	1	0
wc1980	15 Oct	Bucharest	1	2
wc1981	29 April	Wembley	0	0
wc1985	1 May	Bucharest	0	0
wc1985	11 Sept	Wembley	1	1
1994	12 Oct	Wembley	1	1

		v SAN MARINO	E	SM
wc1992	17 Feb	Wembley	6	0
wc1993	17 Nov	Bologna	7	1

		v SAUDI ARABIA	E	SA
1988	16 Nov	Riyadh	1	1

		v SPAIN	E	S
1929	15 May	Madrid	3	4
1931	9 Dec	Highbury	7	1
wc1950	2 July	Rio de Janeiro	0	1
1955	18 May	Madrid	1	1
1955	30 Nov	Wembley	4	1
1960	15 May	Madrid	0	3
1960	26 Oct	Wembley	4	2
1965	8 Dec	Madrid	2	0
1967	24 May	Wembley	2	0
EC1968	3 Apr	Wembley	1	0
EC1968	8 May	Madrid	2	1
1980	26 Mar	Barcelona	2	0
EC1980	18 June	Naples	2	1
1981	25 Mar	Wembley	1	2
wc1982	5 July	Madrid	0	0
1987	18 Feb	Madrid	4	2
1992	9 Sept	Santander	0	1
EC 1996	22 June	Wembley	0	0

		v SWEDEN	E	S
1923	21 May	Stockholm	4	2
1923	24 May	Stockholm	3	1
1937	17 May	Stockholm	4	0
1947	19 Nov	Highbury	4	2
1949	13 May	Stockholm	1	3
1956	16 May	Stockholm	0	0
1959	28 Oct	Wembley	2	3
1965	16 May	Gothenburg	2	1
1968	22 May	Wembley	3	1
1979	10 June	Stockholm	0	0
1986	10 Sept	Stockholm	0	1
wc1988	19 Oct	Wembley	0	0
wc1989	6 Sept	Stockholm	0	0
EC1992	17 June	Stockholm	1	2
UI1995	8 June	Leeds	3	3

		v SWITZERLAND	E	S
1933	20 May	Berne	4	0
1938	21 May	Zurich	1	2
1947	18 May	Zurich	0	1
1948	2 Dec	Highbury	6	0
1952	28 May	Zurich	3	0
wc1954	20 June	Berne	2	0
1962	9 May	Wembley	3	1
1963	5 June	Basle	8	1
EC1971	13 Oct	Basle	3	2
EC1971	10 Nov	Wembley	1	1
1975	3 Sept	Basle	2	1
1977	7 Sept	Wembley	0	0
wc1980	19 Nov	Wembley	2	1
wc1981	30 May	Basle	1	2
1988	28 May	Lausanne	1	0
1995	15 Nov	Wembley	3	1
EC1996	8 June	Wembley	1	1

		v TUNISIA	E	T
1990	2 June	Tunis	1	1

v TURKEY		E	T
wc1984	14 Nov	Istanbul	8	0
wc1985	16 Oct	Wembley	5	0
EC1987	29 Apr	Izmir	0	0
EC1987	14 Oct	Wembley	8	0
EC1991	1 May	Izmir	1	0
EC1991	16 Oct	Wembley	1	0
wc1992	18 Nov	Wembley	4	0
wc1993	31 Mar	Izmir	2	0

v URUGUAY		E	U
1953	31 May	Montevideo	1	2
wc1954	26 June	Basle	2	4
1964	6 May	Wembley	2	1
wc1966	11 July	Wembley	0	0
1969	8 June	Montevideo	2	1
1977	15 June	Montevideo	0	0
1984	13 June	Montevideo	0	2
1990	22 May	Wembley	1	2
1995	29 Mar	Wembley	0	0

v USA		E	USA
wc1950	29 June	Belo Horizonte	0	1
1953	8 June	New York	6	3
1959	28 May	Los Angeles	8	1
1964	27 May	New York	10	0
1985	16 June	Los Angeles	5	0
1993	9 June	Foxboro	0	2
1994	7 Sept	Wembley	2	0

v USSR		E	USSR
1958	18 May	Moscow	1	1
wc1958	8 June	Gothenburg	2	2
wc1958	17 June	Gothenburg	0	1
1958	22 Oct	Wembley	5	0
1967	6 Dec	Wembley	2	2
EC1968	8 June	Rome	2	0
1973	10 June	Moscow	2	1
1984	2 June	Wembley	0	2
1986	26 Mar	Tbilisi	1	0
EC1988	18 June	Frankfurt	1	3
1991	21 May	Wembley	3	1

v YUGOSLAVIA		E	Y
1939	18 May	Belgrade	1	2
1950	22 Nov	Highbury	2	2
1954	16 May	Belgrade	0	1
1956	28 Nov	Wembley	3	0
1958	11 May	Belgrade	0	5
1960	11 May	Wembley	3	3
1965	9 May	Belgrade	1	1
1966	4 May	Wembley	2	0
EC1968	5 June	Florence	0	1
1972	11 Oct	Wembley	1	1
1974	5 June	Belgrade	2	2
EC1986	12 Nov	Wembley	2	0
EC1987	11 Nov	Belgrade	4	1
1989	13 Dec	Wembley	2	1

SCOTLAND

v ARGENTINA		S	A
1977	18 June	Buenos Aires	1	1
1979	2 June	Glasgow	1	3
1990	28 Mar	Glasgow	1	0

v AUSTRALIA		S	A
wc1985	20 Nov	Glasgow	2	0
wc1985	4 Dec	Melbourne	0	0
1996	27 Mar	Glasgow	1	0

v AUSTRIA		S	A
1931	16 May	Vienna	0	5
1933	29 Nov	Glasgow	2	2
1937	9 May	Vienna	1	1
1950	13 Dec	Glasgow	0	1
1951	27 May	Vienna	0	4
wc1954	16 June	Zurich	0	1
1955	19 May	Vienna	4	1
1956	2 May	Glasgow	1	1
1960	29 May	Vienna	1	4
1963	8 May	Glasgow	4	1
(abandoned after 79 mins)				
wc1968	6 Nov	Glasgow	2	1
wc1969	5 Nov	Vienna	0	2
EC1978	20 Sept	Vienna	2	3
EC1979	17 Oct	Glasgow	1	1
1994	20 Apr	Vienna	2	1

v BELGIUM		S	B
1947	18 May	Brussels	1	2
1948	28 Apr	Glasgow	2	0
1951	20 May	Brussels	5	0
EC1971	3 Feb	Liège	0	3
EC1971	10 Nov	Aberdeen	1	0
1974	2 June	Brussels	1	2
EC1979	21 Nov	Brussels	0	2
EC1979	19 Dec	Glasgow	1	3
EC1982	15 Dec	Brussels	2	3
EC1983	12 Oct	Glasgow	1	1
EC1987	1 Apr	Brussels	1	4
EC1987	14 Oct	Glasgow	2	0

v BRAZIL		S	B
1966	25 June	Glasgow	1	1
1972	5 July	Rio de Janeiro	0	1
1973	30 June	Glasgow	0	1
wc1974	18 June	Frankfurt	0	0
1977	23 June	Rio de Janeiro	0	2
wc1982	18 June	Seville	1	4
1987	26 May	Glasgow	0	2
wc1990	20 June	Turin	0	1

v BULGARIA		S	B
1978	22 Feb	Glasgow	2	1
EC1986	10 Sept	Glasgow	0	0
EC1987	11 Nov	Sofia	1	0
EC1990	14 Nov	Sofia	1	1
EC1991	27 Mar	Glasgow	1	1

v CANADA		S	C
1983	12 June	Vancouver	2	0
1983	16 June	Edmonton	3	0
1983	20 June	Toronto	2	0
1992	21 May	Toronto	3	1

v CHILE		S	C
1977	15 June	Santiago	4	2
1989	30 May	Glasgow	2	0

v CIS		S	C
EC1992	18 June	Norrkoping	3	0

v COLOMBIA		S	C
1988	17 May	Glasgow	0	0
1996	30 May	Miami	0	1

v COSTA RICA		S	CR
wc1990	11 June	Genoa	0	1

v CYPRUS		S	C
wc1968	17 Dec	Nicosia	5	0
wc1969	11 May	Glasgow	8	0
wc1989	8 Feb	Limassol	3	2
wc1989	26 Apr	Glasgow	2	1

v CZECHOSLOVAKIA			S	C
1937	22 May	Prague	3	1
1937	8 Dec	Glasgow	5	0
wc1961	14 May	Bratislava	0	4
wc1961	26 Sept	Glasgow	3	2
wc1961	29 Nov	Brussels	2	4*
1972	2 July	Porto Alegre	0	0
wc1973	26 Sept	Glasgow	2	1
wc1973	17 Oct	Prague	0	1
wc1976	13 Oct	Prague	0	2
wc1977	21 Sept	Glasgow	3	1

After extra time

v DENMARK			S	D
1951	12 May	Glasgow	3	1
1952	25 May	Copenhagen	2	1
1968	16 Oct	Copenhagen	1	0
EC1970	11 Nov	Glasgow	1	0
EC1971	9 June	Copenhagen	0	1
wc1972	18 Oct	Copenhagen	4	1
wc1972	15 Nov	Glasgow	2	0
EC1975	3 Sept	Copenhagen	1	0
EC1975	29 Oct	Glasgow	3	1
wc1986	4 June	Nezahualcayotl	0	1
1996	24 Apr	Copenhagen	0	2

v ECUADOR			S	E
1995	24 May	Toyama	2	1

v EGYPT			S	E
1990	16 May	Aberdeen	1	3

v ESTONIA			S	E
wc1993	19 May	Tallinn	3	0
wc1993	2 June	Aberdeen	3	1

v FAEROES			S	F
EC1994	12 Oct	Glasgow	5	1
EC1995	7 June	Toftir	2	0

v FINLAND			S	F
1954	25 May	Helsinki	2	1
wc1964	21 Oct	Glasgow	3	1
wc1965	27 May	Helsinki	2	1
1976	8 Sept	Glasgow	6	0
1992	25 Mar	Glasgow	1	1
EC1994	7 Sept	Helsinki	2	0
EC1995	6 Sept	Glasgow	1	0

v FRANCE			S	F
1930	18 May	Paris	2	0
1932	8 May	Paris	3	1
1948	23 May	Paris	0	3
1949	27 Apr	Glasgow	2	0
1950	27 May	Paris	1	0
1951	16 May	Glasgow	1	0
wc1958	15 June	Orebro	1	2
1984	1 June	Marseilles	0	2
wc1989	8 Mar	Glasgow	2	0
wc1989	11 Oct	Paris	0	3

v GERMANY			S	G
1929	1 June	Berlin	1	1
1936	14 Oct	Glasgow	2	0
EC1992	15 June	Norrkoping	0	2
1993	24 Mar	Glasgow	0	1

v EAST GERMANY			S	EG
1974	30 Oct	Glasgow	3	0
1977	7 Sept	East Berlin	0	1
EC1982	13 Oct	Glasgow	2	0
EC1983	16 Nov	Halle	1	2
1985	16 Oct	Glasgow	0	0
1990	25 Apr	Glasgow	0	1

v WEST GERMANY			S	WG
1957	22 May	Stuttgart	3	1
1959	6 May	Glasgow	3	2
1964	12 May	Hanover	2	2
wc1969	16 Apr	Glasgow	1	1
wc1969	22 Oct	Hamburg	2	3
1973	14 Nov	Glasgow	1	1
1974	27 Mar	Frankfurt	1	2
wc1986	8 June	Queretaro	1	2

v GREECE			S	G
EC1994	18 Dec	Athens	0	1
EC1995	16 Aug	Glasgow	1	0

v HOLLAND			S	H
1929	4 June	Amsterdam	2	0
1938	21 May	Amsterdam	3	1
1959	27 May	Amsterdam	2	1
1966	11 May	Glasgow	0	3
1968	30 May	Amsterdam	0	0
1971	1 Dec	Rotterdam	1	2
wc1978	11 June	Mendoza	3	2
1982	23 Mar	Glasgow	2	1
1986	29 Apr	Eindhoven	0	0
EC1992	12 June	Gothenburg	0	1
1994	23 Mar	Glasgow	0	1
1994	27 May	Utrecht	1	3
EC1996	10 June	Birmingham	0	0

v HUNGARY			S	H
1938	7 Dec	Glasgow	3	1
1954	8 Dec	Glasgow	2	4
1955	29 May	Budapest	1	3
1958	7 May	Glasgow	1	1
1960	5 June	Budapest	3	3
1980	31 May	Budapest	1	3
1987	9 Sept	Glasgow	2	0

v ICELAND			S	I
wc1984	17 Oct	Glasgow	3	0
wc1985	28 May	Reykjavik	1	0

v IRAN			S	I
wc1978	7 June	Cordoba	1	1

v REPUBLIC OF IRELAND			S	RI
wc1961	3 May	Glasgow	4	1
wc1961	7 May	Dublin	3	0
1963	9 June	Dublin	0	1
1969	21 Sept	Dublin	1	1
EC1986	15 Oct	Dublin	0	0
EC1987	18 Feb	Glasgow	0	1

v ISRAEL			S	I
wc1981	25 Feb	Tel Aviv	1	0
wc1981	28 Apr	Glasgow	3	1
1986	28 Jan	Tel Aviv	1	0

v ITALY			S	I
1931	20 May	Rome	0	3
wc1965	9 Nov	Glasgow	1	0
wc1965	7 Dec	Naples	0	3
1988	22 Dec	Perugia	0	2
wc1992	18 Nov	Glasgow	0	0
wc1993	13 Oct	Rome	1	3

v JAPAN			S	J
1995	21 May	Hiroshima	0	0

v LUXEMBOURG			S	L
1947	24 May	Luxembourg	6	0
EC1986	12 Nov	Glasgow	3	0
EC1987	2 Dec	Esch	0	0

		v MALTA	S	M
1988	22 Mar	Valletta	1	1
1990	28 May	Valletta	2	1
wc1993	17 Feb	Glasgow	3	0
wc1993	17 Nov	Valletta	2	0

		NEW ZEALAND	S	NZ
wc1982	15 June	Malaga	5	2

		v NORWAY	S	N
1929	28 May	Oslo	7	3
1954	5 May	Glasgow	1	0
1954	19 May	Oslo	1	1
1963	4 June	Bergen	3	4
1963	7 Nov	Glasgow	6	1
1974	6 June	Oslo	2	1
EC1978	25 Oct	Glasgow	3	2
EC1979	7 June	Oslo	4	0
wc1988	14 Sept	Oslo	2	1
wc1989	15 Nov	Glasgow	1	1
1992	3 June	Oslo	0	0

		v PARAGUAY	S	P
wc1958	11 June	Norrkoping	2	3

		v PERU	S	P
1972	26 Apr	Glasgow	2	0
wc1978	3 June	Cordoba	1	3
1979	12 Sept	Glasgow	1	1

		v POLAND	S	P
1958	1 June	Warsaw	2	1
1960	4 June	Glasgow	2	3
wc1965	23 May	Chorzow	1	1
wc1965	13 Oct	Glasgow	1	2
1980	28 May	Poznan	0	1
1990	19 May	Glasgow	1	1

		v PORTUGAL	S	P
1950	21 May	Lisbon	2	2
1955	4 May	Glasgow	3	0
1959	3 June	Lisbon	0	1
1966	18 June	Glasgow	0	1
EC1971	21 Apr	Lisbon	0	2
EC1971	13 Oct	Glasgow	2	1
1975	13 May	Glasgow	1	0
EC1978	29 Nov	Lisbon	0	1
EC1980	26 Mar	Glasgow	4	1
wc1980	15 Oct	Glasgow	0	0
wc1981	18 Nov	Lisbon	1	2
wc1992	14 Oct	Glasgow	0	0
wc1993	28 Apr	Lisbon	0	5

		v ROMANIA	S	R
EC1975	1 June	Bucharest	1	1
EC1975	17 Dec	Glasgow	1	1
1986	26 Mar	Glasgow	3	0
EC1990	12 Sept	Glasgow	2	1
EC1991	16 Oct	Bucharest	0	1

		v RUSSIA	S	R
EC1994	16 Nov	Glasgow	1	1
EC1995	29 Mar	Moscow	0	0

		v SAN MARINO	S	SM
EC1991	1 May	Serravalle	2	0
EC1991	13 Nov	Glasgow	4	0
EC1995	26 Apr	Serravalle	2	0
EC1995	15 Nov	Glasgow	5	0

		v SAUDI ARABIA	S	SA
1988	17 Feb	Riyadh	2	2

		v SPAIN	S	Sp
wc1957	8 May	Glasgow	4	2
wc1957	26 May	Madrid	1	4
1963	13 June	Madrid	6	2
1965	8 May	Glasgow	0	0
EC1974	20 Nov	Glasgow	1	2
EC1975	5 Feb	Valencia	1	1
1982	24 Feb	Valencia	0	3
wc1984	14 Nov	Glasgow	3	1
wc1985	27 Feb	Seville	0	1
1988	27 Apr	Madrid	0	0

		v SWEDEN	S	Sw
1952	30 May	Stockholm	1	3
1953	6 May	Glasgow	1	2
1975	16 Apr	Gothenburg	1	1
1977	27 Apr	Glasgow	3	1
wc1980	10 Sept	Stockholm	1	0
wc1981	9 Sept	Glasgow	2	0
wc1990	16 June	Genoa	2	1
1995	11 Oct	Stockholm	0	2

		v SWITZERLAND	S	Sw
1931	24 May	Geneva	3	2
1948	17 May	Berne	1	2
1950	26 Apr	Glasgow	3	1
wc1957	19 May	Basle	2	1
wc1957	6 Nov	Glasgow	3	2
1973	22 June	Berne	0	1
1976	7 Apr	Glasgow	1	0
EC1982	17 Nov	Berne	0	2
EC1983	30 May	Glasgow	2	2
EC1990	17 Oct	Glasgow	2	1
EC1991	11 Sept	Berne	2	2
wc1992	9 Sept	Berne	1	3
wc1993	8 Sept	Aberdeen	1	1
EC1996	18 June	Birmingham	1	0

		v TURKEY	S	T
1960	8 June	Ankara	2	4

		v URUGUAY	S	U
wc1954	19 June	Basle	0	7
1962	2 May	Glasgow	2	3
1983	21 Sept	Glasgow	2	0
wc1986	13 June	Nezahualcoyotl	0	0

		v USA	S	USA
1952	30 Apr	Glasgow	6	0
1992	17 May	Denver	1	0
1996	26 May	New Britain	1	2

		v USSR	S	USSR
1967	10 May	Glasgow	0	2
1971	14 June	Moscow	0	1
wc1982	22 June	Malaga	2	2
1991	6 Feb	Glasgow	0	1

		v YUGOSLAVIA	S	Y
1955	15 May	Belgrade	2	2
1956	21 Nov	Glasgow	2	0
wc1958	8 June	Vasteras	1	1
1972	29 June	Belo Horizonte	2	2
wc1974	22 June	Frankfurt	1	1
1984	12 Sept	Glasgow	6	1
wc1988	19 Oct	Glasgow	1	1
wc1989	6 Sept	Zagreb	1	3

		v ZAIRE	S	Z
wc1974	14 June	Dortmund	2	0

WALES

v ALBANIA		W	A
EC1994	7 Sept	Cardiff	2	0
EC1995	15 Nov	Tirana	1	1

v ARGENTINA		W	A
1992	3 June	Tokyo	0	1

v AUSTRIA		W	A
1954	9 May	Vienna	0	2
EC1955	23 Nov	Wrexham	1	2
EC1974	4 Sept	Vienna	1	2
1975	19 Nov	Wrexham	1	0
1992	29 Apr	Vienna	1	1

v BELGIUM		W	B
1949	22 May	Liège	1	3
1949	23 Nov	Cardiff	5	1
EC1990	17 Oct	Cardiff	3	1
EC1991	27 Mar	Brussels	1	1
wc1992	18 Nov	Brussels	0	2
wc1993	31 Mar	Cardiff	2	0

v BRAZIL		W	B
wc1958	19 June	Gothenburg	0	1
1962	12 May	Rio de Janeiro	1	3
1962	16 May	São Paulo	1	3
1966	14 May	Rio de Janeiro	1	3
1966	18 May	Belo Horizonte	0	1
1983	12 June	Cardiff	1	1
1991	11 Sept	Cardiff	1	0

v BULGARIA		W	B
EC1983	27 Apr	Wrexham	1	0
EC1983	16 Nov	Sofia	0	1
EC1994	14 Dec	Cardiff	0	3
EC1995	29 Mar	Sofia	1	3

v CANADA		W	C
1986	10 May	Toronto	0	2
1986	20 May	Vancouver	3	0

v CHILE		W	C
1966	22 May	Santiago	0	2

v COSTA RICA		W	CR
1990	20 May	Cardiff	1	0

v CYPRUS		W	C
wc1992	14 Oct	Limassol	1	0
wc1993	13 Oct	Cardiff	2	0

v CZECHOSLOVAKIA		W	C
wc1957	1 May	Cardiff	1	0
wc1957	26 May	Prague	0	2
EC1971	21 Apr	Swansea	1	3
EC1971	27 Oct	Prague	0	1
wc1977	30 Mar	Wrexham	3	0
wc1977	16 Nov	Prague	0	1
wc1980	19 Nov	Cardiff	1	0
wc1981	9 Sept	Prague	0	2
EC1987	29 Apr	Wrexham	1	1
EC1987	11 Nov	Prague	0	2
wc1993	28 Apr	Ostrava†	1	1
wc1993	8 Sept	Cardiff†	2	2

†Czechoslovakia played as RCS (Republic of Czechs and Slovaks).

v DENMARK		W	D
wc1964	21 Oct	Copenhagen	0	1
wc1965	1 Dec	Wrexham	4	2
EC1987	9 Sept	Cardiff	1	0
EC1987	14 Oct	Copenhagen	0	1
1990	11 Sept	Copenhagen	0	1

v ESTONIA		W	E
1994	23 May	Tallinn	2	1

v FINLAND		W	F
EC1971	26 May	Helsinki	1	0
EC1971	13 Oct	Swansea	3	0
EC1987	10 Sept	Helsinki	1	1
EC1987	1 Apr	Wrexham	4	0
wc1988	19 Oct	Swansea	2	2
wc1989	6 Sept	Helsinki	0	1

v FAEROES		W	F
wc1992	9 Sept	Cardiff	6	0
wc1993	6 June	Toftir	3	0

v FRANCE		W	F
1933	25 May	Paris	1	1
1939	20 May	Paris	1	2
1953	14 May	Paris	1	6
1982	2 June	Toulouse	1	0

v GEORGIA		W	G
EC1994	16 Nov	Tbilisi	0	5
EC1995	7 June	Cardiff	0	1

v GERMANY		W	G
EC1995	26 Apr	Dusseldorf	1	1
EC1995	11 Oct	Cardiff	1	2

v EAST GERMANY		W	EG
wc1957	19 May	Leipzig	1	2
wc1957	25 Sept	Cardiff	4	1
wc1969	16 Apr	Dresden	1	2
wc1969	22 Oct	Cardiff	1	3

v WEST GERMANY		W	WG
1968	8 May	Cardiff	1	1
1969	26 Mar	Frankfurt	1	1
1976	6 Oct	Cardiff	0	2
1977	14 Dec	Dortmund	1	1
EC1979	2 May	Wrexham	0	2
EC1979	17 Oct	Cologne	1	5
wc1989	31 May	Cardiff	0	0
wc1989	15 Nov	Cologne	1	2
EC1991	5 June	Cardiff	1	0
EC1991	16 Oct	Nuremberg	1	4

v GREECE		W	G
wc1964	9 Dec	Athens	0	2
wc1965	17 Mar	Cardiff	4	1

v HOLLAND		W	H
wc1988	14 Sept	Amsterdam	0	1
wc1989	11 Oct	Wrexham	1	2
1992	30 May	Utrecht	0	4

v HUNGARY		W	H
wc1958	8 June	Sanviken	1	1
wc1958	17 June	Stockholm	2	1
1961	28 May	Budapest	2	3
EC1962	7 Nov	Budapest	1	3
EC1963	20 Mar	Cardiff	1	1
EC1974	30 Oct	Cardiff	2	0
EC1975	16 Apr	Budapest	2	1
1985	16 Oct	Cardiff	0	3

v ICELAND		W	I
wc1980	2 June	Reykjavik	4	0
wc1981	14 Oct	Swansea	2	2
wc1984	12 Sept	Reykjavik	0	1
wc1984	14 Nov	Cardiff	2	1
1991	1 May	Cardiff	1	0

		v IRAN	W	I
1978	18 Apr	Teheran	1	0

		v REPUBLIC OF IRELAND	W	RI
1960	28 Sept	Dublin	3	2
1979	11 Sept	Swansea	2	1
1981	24 Feb	Dublin	3	1
1986	26 Mar	Dublin	1	0
1990	28 Mar	Dublin	0	1
1991	6 Feb	Wrexham	0	3
1992	19 Feb	Dublin	1	0
1993	17 Feb	Dublin	1	2

		v ISRAEL	W	I
wc1958	15 Jan	Tel Aviv	2	0
wc1958	5 Feb	Cardiff	2	0
1984	10 June	Tel Aviv	0	0
1989	8 Feb	Tel Aviv	3	3

		v ITALY	W	I
1965	1 May	Florence	1	4
wc1968	23 Oct	Cardiff	0	1
wc1969	4 Nov	Rome	1	4
1988	4 June	Brescia	1	0
1996	24 Jan	Terni	0	3

		v JAPAN	W	J
1992	7 June	Matsuyama	1	0

		v KUWAIT	W	K
1977	6 Sept	Wrexham	0	0
1977	20 Sept	Kuwait	0	0

		v LUXEMBOURG	W	L
EC1974	20 Nov	Swansea	5	0
EC1975	1 May	Luxembourg	3	1
EC1990	14 Nov	Luxembourg	1	0
EC1991	13 Nov	Cardiff	1	0

		v MALTA	W	M
EC1978	25 Oct	Wrexham	7	0
EC1979	2 June	Valletta	2	0
1988	1 June	Valletta	3	2

		v MEXICO	W	M
wc1958	11 June	Stockholm	1	1
1962	22 May	Mexico City	1	2

		v MOLDOVA	W	M
EC1994	12 Oct	Kishinev	2	3
EC1995	6 Sept	Cardiff	1	0

		v NORWAY	W	N
EC1982	22 Sept	Swansea	1	0
EC1983	21 Sept	Oslo	0	0
1984	6 June	Trondheim	0	1
1985	26 Feb	Wrexham	1	1
1985	5 June	Bergen	2	4
1994	9 Mar	Cardiff	1	3

		v POLAND	W	P
wc1973	28 Mar	Cardiff	2	0
wc1973	26 Sept	Katowice	0	3
1991	29 May	Radom	0	0

		v PORTUGAL	W	P
1949	15 May	Lisbon	2	3
1951	12 May	Cardiff	2	1

		v ROMANIA	W	R
EC1970	11 Nov	Cardiff	0	0
EC1971	24 Nov	Bucharest	0	2
1983	12 Oct	Wrexham	5	0
wc1992	20 May	Bucharest	1	5
wc1993	17 Nov	Cardiff	1	2

		v SAN MARINO	W	SM
wc1996	2 June	Serravalle	5	0

		v SAUDI ARABIA	W	SA
1986	25 Feb	Dahran	2	1

		v SPAIN	W	S
wc1961	19 Apr	Cardiff	1	2
wc1961	18 May	Madrid	1	1
1982	24 Mar	Valencia	1	1
wc1984	17 Oct	Seville	0	3
wc1985	30 Apr	Wrexham	3	0

		v SWEDEN	W	S
wc1958	15 June	Stockholm	0	0
1988	27 Apr	Stockholm	1	4
1989	26 Apr	Wrexham	0	2
1990	25 Apr	Stockholm	2	4
1994	20 Apr	Wrexham	0	2

		v SWITZERLAND	W	S
1949	26 May	Berne	0	4
1951	16 May	Wrexham	3	2
1996	24 Apr	Lugano	0	2

		v TURKEY	W	T
EC1978	29 Nov	Wrexham	1	0
EC1979	21 Nov	Izmir	0	1
wc1980	15 Oct	Cardiff	4	0
wc1981	25 Mar	Ankara	1	0

		v REST OF UNITED KINGDOM		
			W	UK
1951	5 Dec	Cardiff	3	2
1969	28 July	Cardiff	0	1

		v URUGUAY	W	U
1986	21 Apr	Wrexham	0	0

		v USSR	W	USSR
wc1965	30 May	Moscow	1	2
wc1965	27 Oct	Cardiff	2	1
wc1981	30 May	Wrexham	0	0
wc1981	18 Nov	Tbilisi	0	3
1987	18 Feb	Swansea	0	0

		v YUGOSLAVIA	W	Y
1953	21 May	Belgrade	2	5
1954	22 Nov	Cardiff	1	3
EC1976	24 Apr	Zagreb	0	2
EC1976	22 May	Cardiff	1	1
EC1982	15 Dec	Titograd	4	4
EC1983	14 Dec	Cardiff	1	1
1988	23 Mar	Swansea	1	2

NORTHERN IRELAND

v ALBANIA			NI	A
wc1965	7 May	Belfast	4	1
wc1965	24 Nov	Tirana	1	1
EC1982	15 Dec	Tirana	0	0
EC1983	27 Apr	Belfast	1	0
wc1992	9 Sept	Belfast	3	0
wc1993	17 Feb	Tirana	2	1

v ALGERIA			NI	A
wc1986	3 June	Guadalajara	1	1

v ARGENTINA			NI	A
wc1958	11 June	Halmstad	1	3

v AUSTRALIA			NI	A
1980	11 June	Sydney	2	1
1980	15 June	Melbourne	1	1
1980	18 June	Adelaide	2	1

v AUSTRIA			NI	A
wc1982	1 July	Madrid	2	2
EC1982	13 Oct	Vienna	0	2
EC1983	21 Sept	Belfast	3	1
EC1990	14 Nov	Vienna	0	0
EC1991	16 Oct	Belfast	2	1
EC1994	12 Oct	Vienna	2	1
EC1995	15 Nov	Belfast	5	3

v BELGIUM			NI	B
wc1976	10 Nov	Liège	0	2
wc1977	16 Nov	Belfast	3	0

v BRAZIL			NI	B
wc1986	12 June	Guadalajara	0	3

v BULGARIA			NI	B
wc1972	18 Oct	Sofia	0	3
wc1973	26 Sept	Sheffield	0	0
EC1978	29 Nov	Sofia	2	0
EC1979	2 May	Belfast	2	0

v CANADA			NI	C
1995	22 May	Edmonton	0	2

v CHILE			NI	C
1989	26 May	Belfast	0	1
1995	25 May	Edmonton	1	2

v COLOMBIA			NI	C
1994	4 June	Boston	0	2

v CYPRUS			NI	C
EC1971	3 Feb	Nicosia	3	0
EC1971	21 Apr	Belfast	5	0
wc1973	14 Feb	Nicosia	0	1
wc1973	8 May	London	3	0

v CZECHOSLOVAKIA			NI	C
wc1958	8 June	Halmstad	1	0
wc1958	17 June	Malmo	2	1*
*After extra time				

v DENMARK			NI	D
EC1978	25 Oct	Belfast	2	1
EC1979	6 June	Copenhagen	0	4
1986	26 Mar	Belfast	1	1
EC1990	17 Oct	Belfast	1	1
EC1991	13 Nov	Odense	1	2
wc1992	18 Nov	Belfast	0	1
wc1993	13 Oct	Copenhagen	0	1

v FAEROES			NI	F
EC1991	1 May	Belfast	1	1
EC1991	11 Sept	Landskrona	5	0

v FINLAND			NI	F
wc1984	27 May	Pori	0	1
wc1984	14 Nov	Belfast	2	1

v FRANCE			NI	F
1951	12 May	Belfast	2	2
1952	11 Nov	Paris	1	3
wc1958	19 June	Norrkoping	0	4
1982	24 Mar	Paris	0	4
wc1982	4 July	Madrid	1	4
1986	26 Feb	Paris	0	0
1988	27 Apr	Belfast	0	0

v GERMANY			NI	G
1992	2 June	Bremen	1	1
1996	29 May	Belfast	1	1

v WEST GERMANY			NI	WG
wc1958	15 June	Malmo	2	2
wc1960	26 Oct	Belfast	3	4
wc1961	10 May	Hamburg	1	2
1966	7 May	Belfast	0	2
1977	27 Apr	Cologne	0	5
EC1982	17 Nov	Belfast	1	0
EC1983	16 Nov	Hamburg	1	0

v GREECE			NI	G
wc1961	3 May	Athens	1	2
wc1961	17 Oct	Belfast	2	0
1988	17 Feb	Athens	2	3

v HOLLAND			NI	H
1962	9 May	Rotterdam	0	4
wc1965	17 Mar	Belfast	2	1
wc1965	7 Apr	Rotterdam	0	0
wc1976	13 Oct	Rotterdam	2	2
wc1977	12 Oct	Belfast	0	1

v HONDURAS			NI	H
wc1982	21 June	Zaragoza	1	1

v HUNGARY			NI	H
wc1988	19 Oct	Budapest	0	1
wc1989	6 Sept	Belfast	1	2

v ICELAND			NI	I
wc1977	11 June	Reykjavik	0	1
wc1977	21 Sept	Belfast	2	0

v REPUBLIC OF IRELAND			NI	RI
EC1978	20 Sept	Dublin	0	0
EC1979	21 Nov	Belfast	1	0
wc1988	14 Sept	Belfast	0	0
wc1989	11 Oct	Dublin	0	3
wc1993	31 Mar	Dublin	0	3
wc1993	17 Nov	Belfast	1	1
EC1994	16 Nov	Belfast	0	4
EC1995	29 Mar	Dublin	1	1

v ISRAEL			NI	I
1968	10 Sept	Jaffa	3	2
1976	3 Mar	Tel Aviv	1	1
wc1980	26 Mar	Tel Aviv	0	0
wc1981	18 Nov	Belfast	1	0
1984	16 Oct	Belfast	3	0
1987	18 Feb	Tel Aviv	1	1

v ITALY

			NI	I
wc1957	25 Apr	Rome	0	1
1957	4 Dec	Belfast	2	2
wc1958	15 Jan	Belfast	2	1
1961	25 Apr	Bologna	2	3

v LATVIA

			NI	L
wc1993	2 June	Riga	2	1
wc1993	8 Sept	Belfast	2	0
EC1995	26 Apr	Riga	1	0
EC1995	7 June	Belfast	1	2

v LIECHTENSTEIN

			NI	L
EC1994	20 Apr	Belfast	4	1
EC1995	11 Oct	Eschen	4	0

v LITHUANIA

			NI	L
wc1992	28 Apr	Belfast	2	2
wc1993	25 May	Vilnius	1	0

v MALTA

			NI	M
wc1988	21 May	Belfast	3	0
wc1989	26 Apr	Valletta	2	0

v MEXICO

			NI	M
1966	22 June	Belfast	4	1
1994	11 June	Miami	0	3

v MOROCCO

			NI	M
1986	23 Apr	Belfast	2	1

v NORWAY

			NI	N
EC1974	4 Sept	Oslo	1	2
EC1975	29 Oct	Belfast	3	0
1990	27 Mar	Belfast	2	3
1996	27 Mar	Belfast	0	2

v POLAND

			NI	P
EC1962	10 Oct	Katowice	2	0
EC1962	28 Nov	Belfast	2	0
1988	23 Mar	Belfast	1	1
1991	5 Feb	Belfast	3	1
EC1995	3 Sept	Lisbon	1	1

v PORTUGAL

			NI	P
wc1957	16 Jan	Lisbon	1	1
wc1957	1 May	Belfast	3	0
wc1973	28 Mar	Coventry	1	1
wc1973	14 Nov	Lisbon	1	1
wc1980	19 Nov	Lisbon	0	1
wc1981	29 Apr	Belfast	1	0
EC1994	7 Sept	Belfast	1	2
EC1995	3 Sept	Lisbon	1	1

v ROMANIA

			NI	R
wc1984	12 Sept	Belfast	3	2
wc1985	16 Oct	Bucharest	1	0
1994	23 Mar	Belfast	2	0

v SPAIN

			NI	S
1958	15 Oct	Madrid	2	6
1963	30 May	Bilbao	1	1
1963	30 Oct	Belfast	0	1
EC1970	11 Nov	Seville	0	3
EC1972	16 Feb	Hull	1	1
wc1982	25 June	Valencia	1	0
1985	27 Mar	Palma	0	0
wc1986	7 June	Guadalajara	1	2
wc1988	21 Dec	Seville	0	4
wc1989	8 Feb	Belfast	0	2
wc1992	14 Oct	Belfast	0	0
wc1993	28 Apr	Seville	1	3

v SWEDEN

			NI	S
EC1974	30 Oct	Solna	2	0
EC1975	3 Sept	Belfast	1	2
wc1980	15 Oct	Belfast	3	0
wc1981	3 June	Solna	0	1
1996	24 Apr	Belfast	1	2

v SWITZERLAND

			NI	S
wc1964	14 Oct	Belfast	1	0
wc1964	14 Nov	Lausanne	1	2

v TURKEY

			NI	T
wc1968	23 Oct	Belfast	4	1
wc1968	11 Dec	Istanbul	3	0
EC1983	30 Mar	Belfast	2	1
EC1983	12 Oct	Ankara	0	1
wc1985	1 May	Belfast	2	0
wc1985	11 Sept	Izmir	0	0
EC1986	12 Nov	Izmir	0	0
EC1987	11 Nov	Belfast	1	0

v URUGUAY

			NI	U
1964	29 Apr	Belfast	3	0
1990	18 May	Belfast	1	0

v USSR

			NI	USSR
wc1969	19 Sept	Belfast	0	0
wc1969	22 Oct	Moscow	0	2
EC1971	22 Sept	Moscow	0	1
EC1971	13 Oct	Belfast	1	1

v YUGOSLAVIA

			NI	Y
EC1975	16 Mar	Belfast	1	0
EC1975	19 Nov	Belgrade	0	1
wc1982	17 June	Zaragoza	0	0
EC1987	29 Apr	Belfast	1	2
EC1987	14 Oct	Sarajevo	0	3
EC1990	12 Sept	Belfast	0	2
EC1991	27 Mar	Belgrade	1	4

REPUBLIC OF IRELAND

v ALBANIA

			RI	A
wc1992	26 May	Dublin	2	0
wc1993	26 May	Tirana	2	1

v ALGERIA

			RI	A
1982	28 Apr	Algiers	0	2

v ARGENTINA

			RI	A
1951	13 May	Dublin	0	1
1979	29 May	Dublin	0	0*
1980	16 May	Dublin	0	1

* Not considered a full international

v AUSTRIA

			RI	A
1952	7 May	Vienna	0	6
1953	25 Mar	Dublin	4	0
1958	14 Mar	Vienna	1	3
1962	8 Apr	Dublin	2	3
EC1963	25 Sept	Vienna	0	0
EC1963	13 Oct	Dublin	3	2
1966	22 May	Vienna	0	1
1968	10 Nov	Dublin	2	2
EC1971	30 May	Dublin	1	4
EC1971	10 Oct	Linz	0	6
EC1995	11 June	Dublin	1	3
EC1995	6 Sept	Vienna	1	3

v BELGIUM			RI	B
1928	12 Feb	Liège	4	2
1929	30 Apr	Dublin	4	0
			RI	B
1930	11 May	Brussels	3	1
wc1934	25 Feb	Dublin	4	4
1949	24 Apr	Dublin	0	2
1950	10 May	Brussels	1	5
1965	24 Mar	Dublin	0	2
1966	25 May	Liège	3	2
wc1980	15 Oct	Dublin	1	1
wc1981	25 Mar	Brussels	0	1
EC1986	10 Sept	Brussels	2	2
EC1987	29 Apr	Dublin	0	0

v BOLIVIA			RI	B
1994	24 May	Dublin	1	0
1996	15 June	New Jersey	3	0

v BRAZIL			RI	B
1974	5 May	Rio de Janeiro	1	2
1982	27 May	Uberlandia	0	7
1987	23 May	Dublin	1	0

v BULGARIA			RI	B
wc1977	1 June	Sofia	1	2
wc1977	12 Oct	Dublin	0	0
EC1979	19 May	Sofia	0	1
EC1979	17 Oct	Dublin	3	0
wc1987	1 Apr	Sofia	1	2
wc1987	14 Oct	Dublin	2	0

v CHILE			RI	C
1960	30 Mar	Dublin	2	0
1972	21 June	Recife	1	2
1974	12 May	Santiago	2	1
1982	22 May	Santiago	0	1
1991	22 May	Dublin	1	1

v CHINA			RI	C
1984	3 June	Sapporo	1	0

v CROATIA			RI	C
1996	2 June	Dublin	2	2

v CYPRUS			RI	C
wc1980	26 Mar	Nicosia	3	2
wc1980	19 Nov	Dublin	6	0

v CZECHOSLOVAKIA			RI	C
1938	18 May	Prague	2	2
EC1959	5 Apr	Dublin	2	0
EC1959	10 May	Bratislava	0	4
wc1961	8 Oct	Dublin	1	3
wc1961	29 Oct	Prague	1	7
EC1967	21 May	Dublin	0	2
EC1967	22 Nov	Prague	2	1
wc1969	4 May	Dublin	1	2
wc1969	7 Oct	Prague	0	3
1979	26 Sept	Prague	1	4
1981	29 Apr	Dublin	3	1
1986	27 May	Reykjavik	1	0

v CZECH REPUBLIC			RI	C
1994	5 June	Dublin	1	3
1996	24 Apr	Prague	0	2

v DENMARK			RI	D
wc1956	3 Oct	Dublin	2	1
wc1957	2 Oct	Copenhagen	2	0
wc1968	4 Dec	Dublin	1	1
(abandoned after 51 mins)				
wc1969	27 May	Copenhagen	0	2

			RI	D
wc1969	15 Oct	Dublin	1	1
EC1978	24 May	Copenhagen	3	3
EC1979	2 May	Dublin	2	0
wc1984	14 Nov	Copenhagen	0	3
wc1985	13 Nov	Dublin	1	4
wc1992	14 Oct	Copenhagen	0	0
wc1993	28 Apr	Dublin	1	1

v ECUADOR			RI	E
1972	19 June	Natal	3	2

v EGYPT			RI	E
wc1990	17 June	Palermo	0	0

v ENGLAND			RI	E
1946	30 Sept	Dublin	0	1
1949	21 Sept	Everton	2	0
wc1957	8 May	Wembley	1	5
wc1957	19 May	Dublin	1	1
1964	24 May	Dublin	1	3
1976	8 Sept	Wembley	1	1
EC1978	25 Oct	Dublin	1	1
EC1980	6 Feb	Wembley	0	2
1985	26 Mar	Wembley	1	2
EC1988	12 June	Stuttgart	1	0
wc1990	11 June	Cagliari	1	1
EC1990	14 Nov	Dublin	1	1
EC1991	27 Mar	Wembley	1	1
1995	15 Feb	Dublin	1	0
(abandoned after 27 mins)				

v FINLAND			RI	F
wc1949	8 Sept	Dublin	3	0
wc1949	9 Oct	Helsinki	1	1
1990	16 May	Dublin	1	1

v FRANCE			RI	F
1937	23 May	Paris	2	0
1952	16 Nov	Dublin	1	1
wc1953	4 Oct	Dublin	3	5
wc1953	25 Nov	Paris	0	1
wc1972	15 Nov	Dublin	2	1
wc1973	19 May	Paris	1	1
wc1976	17 Nov	Paris	0	2
wc1977	30 Mar	Dublin	1	0
wc1980	28 Oct	Paris	0	2
wc1981	14 Oct	Dublin	3	2
1989	7 Feb	Dublin	0	0

v GERMANY			RI	G
1935	8 May	Dortmund	1	3
1936	17 Oct	Dublin	5	2
1939	23 May	Bremen	1	1
1994	29 May	Hanover	2	0

v WEST GERMANY			RI	WG
1951	17 Oct	Dublin	3	2
1952	4 May	Cologne	0	3
1955	28 May	Hamburg	1	2
1956	25 Nov	Dublin	3	0
1960	11 May	Dusseldorf	1	0
1966	4 May	Dublin	0	4
1970	9 May	Berlin	1	2
1975	1 Mar	Dublin	1	0†
1979	22 May	Dublin	1	3
1981	21 May	Bremen	0	3†
1989	6 Sept	Dublin	1	1
†v West Germany 'B'				

v HOLLAND			RI	N
1932	8 May	Amsterdam	2	0
1934	8 Apr	Amsterdam	2	5

			RI	H
1935	8 Dec	Dublin	3	5
1955	1 May	Dublin	1	0
1956	10 May	Rotterdam	4	1
wc1980	10 Sept	Dublin	2	1
wc1981	9 Sept	Rotterdam	2	2
EC1982	22 Sept	Rotterdam	1	2
EC1983	12 Oct	Dublin	2	3
EC1988	18 June	Gelsenkirchen	0	1
wc1990	21 June	Palermo	1	1
1994	20 Apr	Tilburg	1	0
wc1994	4 July	Orlando	0	2
EC1995	13 Dec	Liverpool	0	2
1996	4 June	Rotterdam	1	3

	v HUNGARY		RI	H
1934	15 Dec	Dublin	2	4
1936	3 May	Budapest	3	3
1936	6 Dec	Dublin	2	3
1939	19 Mar	Cork	2	2
1939	18 May	Budapest	2	2
wc1969	8 June	Dublin	1	2
wc1969	5 Nov	Budapest	0	4
wc1989	8 Mar	Budapest	0	2
wc1989	4 June	Dublin	2	0
1991	11 Sept	Gyor	2	1

	v ICELAND		RI	I
EC1962	12 Aug	Dublin	4	2
EC1962	2 Sept	Reykjavik	1	1
EC1982	13 Oct	Dublin	2	0
EC1983	21 Sept	Reykjavik	3	0
1986	25 May	Reykjavik	2	1

	v IRAN		RI	I
1972	18 June	Recife	2	1

	v N. IRELAND		RI	NI
EC1978	20 Sept	Dublin	0	0
EC1979	21 Nov	Belfast	0	1
wc1988	14 Sept	Belfast	0	0
wc1989	11 Oct	Dublin	3	0
wc1993	31 Mar	Dublin	3	0
wc1993	17 Nov	Belfast	1	1
EC1994	16 Nov	Belfast	4	0
EC1995	29 Mar	Dublin	1	1

	v ISRAEL		RI	I
1984	4 Apr	Tel Aviv	0	3
1985	27 May	Tel Aviv	0	0
1987	10 Nov	Dublin	5	0

	v ITALY		RI	I
1926	21 Mar	Turin	0	3
1927	23 Apr	Dublin	1	2
EC1970	8 Dec	Rome	0	3
EC1971	10 May	Dublin	1	2
1985	5 Feb	Dublin	1	2
wc1990	30 June	Rome	0	1
1992	4 June	Foxboro	0	2
wc1994	18 June	New York	1	0

	v LATVIA		RI	L
wc1992	9 Sept	Dublin	4	0
wc1993	2 June	Riga	2	1

	v LIECHTENSTEIN		RI	L
EC1994	12 Oct	Dublin	4	0
EC1995	3 June	Eschen	0	0

	v LITHUANIA		RI	L
wc1993	16 June	Vilnius	1	0
wc1993	8 Sept	Dublin	2	0

	v LUXEMBOURG		RI	I
1936	9 May	Luxembourg	5	1
wc1953	28 Oct	Dublin	4	0
wc1954	7 Mar	Luxembourg	1	0
EC1987	28 May	Luxembourg	2	0
EC1987	9 Sept	Dublin	2	1

	v MALTA		RI	M
EC1983	30 Mar	Valletta	1	0
EC1983	16 Nov	Dublin	8	0
wc1989	28 May	Dublin	2	0
wc1989	15 Nov	Valletta	2	0
1990	2 June	Valletta	3	0

	v MEXICO		RI	M
1984	8 Aug	Dublin	0	0
wc1994	24 June	Orlando	1	2
1996	13 June	New Jersey	2	2

	v MOROCCO		RI	M
1990	12 Sept	Dublin	1	0

	v NORWAY		RI	N
wc1937	10 Oct	Oslo	2	3
wc1937	7 Nov	Dublin	3	3
1950	26 Nov	Dublin	2	2
1951	30 May	Oslo	3	2
1954	8 Nov	Dublin	2	1
1955	25 May	Oslo	3	1
1960	6 Nov	Dublin	3	1
1964	13 May	Oslo	4	1
1973	6 June	Oslo	1	1
1976	24 Mar	Dublin	3	0
1978	21 May	Oslo	0	0
wc1984	17 Oct	Oslo	0	1
wc1985	1 May	Dublin	0	0
1988	1 June	Oslo	0	0
wc1994	28 June	New York	0	0

	v POLAND		RI	P
1938	22 May	Warsaw	0	6
1938	13 Nov	Dublin	3	2
1958	11 May	Katowice	2	2
1958	5 Oct	Dublin	2	2
1964	10 May	Kracow	1	3
1964	25 Oct	Dublin	3	2
1968	15 May	Dublin	2	2
1968	30 Oct	Katowice	0	1
1970	6 May	Dublin	1	2
1970	23 Sept	Dublin	0	2
1973	16 May	Wroclaw	0	2
1973	21 Oct	Dublin	1	0
1976	26 May	Poznan	2	0
1977	24 Apr	Dublin	0	0
1978	12 Apr	Lodz	0	3
1981	23 May	Bydgoszcz	0	3
1984	23 May	Dublin	0	0
1986	12 Nov	Warsaw	0	1
1988	22 May	Dublin	3	1
EC1991	1 May	Dublin	0	0
EC1991	16 Oct	Poznan	3	3

	v PORTUGAL		RI	P
1946	16 June	Lisbon	1	3
1947	4 May	Dublin	0	2
1948	23 May	Lisbon	0	2
1949	22 May	Dublin	1	0
1972	25 June	Recife	1	2
1992	7 June	Boston	2	0
EC1995	26 Apr	Dublin	1	0
EC1995	15 Nov	Lisbon	0	3
1996	29 May	Dublin	0	1

		v ROMANIA	RI	R
1988	23 Mar	Dublin	2	0
wc1990	25 June	Genoa	0	0*
After extra time				

		v RUSSIA	RI	R
1994	23 Mar	Dublin	0	0
1996	27 Mar	Dublin	0	2

		v SCOTLAND	RI	S
wc1961	3 May	Glasgow	1	4
wc1961	7 May	Dublin	0	3
1963	9 June	Dublin	1	0
1969	21 Sept	Dublin	1	1
ec1986	15 Oct	Dublin	0	0
ec1987	18 Feb	Glasgow	1	0

		v SPAIN	RI	S
1931	26 Apr	Barcelona	1	1
1931	13 Dec	Dublin	0	5
1946	23 June	Madrid	1	0
1947	2 Mar	Dublin	3	2
1948	30 May	Barcelona	1	2
1949	12 June	Dublin	1	4
1952	1 June	Madrid	0	6
1955	27 Nov	Dublin	2	2
ec1964	11 Mar	Seville	1	5
ec1964	8 Apr	Dublin	0	2
wc1965	5 May	Dublin	1	0
wc1965	27 Oct	Seville	1	4
wc1965	10 Nov	Paris	0	1
ec1966	23 Oct	Dublin	0	0
ec1966	7 Dec	Valencia	0	2
1977	9 Feb	Dublin	0	1
ec1982	17 Nov	Dublin	3	3
ec1983	27 Apr	Zaragoza	0	2
1985	26 May	Cork	0	0
wc1988	16 Nov	Seville	0	2
wc1989	26 Apr	Dublin	1	0
wc1992	18 Nov	Seville	0	0
wc1993	13 Oct	Dublin	1	3

		v SWEDEN	RI	S
wc1949	2 June	Stockholm	1	3
wc1949	13 Nov	Dublin	1	3
1959	1 Nov	Dublin	3	2
1960	18 May	Malmo	1	4
ec1970	14 Oct	Dublin	1	1
ec1970	28 Oct	Malmo	0	1

		v SWITZERLAND	RI	S
1935	5 May	Basle	0	1
1936	17 Mar	Dublin	1	0
1937	17 May	Berne	1	0
1938	18 Sept	Dublin	4	0
1948	5 Dec	Dublin	0	1
ec1975	11 May	Dublin	2	1

			RI	S
ec1975	21 May	Berne	0	1
1980	30 Apr	Dublin	2	0
wc1985	2 June	Dublin	3	0
wc1985	11 Sept	Berne	0	0
1992	25 Mar	Dublin	2	1

		v TRINIDAD & TOBAGO	RI	TT
1982	30 May	Port of Spain	1	2

		v TUNISIA	RI	T
1988	19 Oct	Dublin	4	0

		v TURKEY	RI	T
ec1966	16 Nov	Dublin	2	1
ec1967	22 Feb	Ankara	1	2
ec1974	20 Nov	Izmir	1	1
ec1975	29 Oct	Dublin	4	0
1976	13 Oct	Ankara	3	3
1978	5 Apr	Dublin	4	2
1990	26 May	Izmir	0	0
ec1990	17 Oct	Dublin	5	0
ec1991	13 Nov	Istanbul	3	1

		v URUGUAY	RI	U
1974	8 May	Montevideo	0	2
1986	23 Apr	Dublin	1	1

		v USA	RI	USA
1979	29 Oct	Dublin	3	2
1991	1 June	Boston	1	1
1992	29 Apr	Dublin	4	1
1992	30 May	Washington	1	3
1996	9 June	Boston	1	2

		v USSR	RI	USSR
wc1972	18 Oct	Dublin	1	2
wc1973	13 May	Moscow	0	1
ec1974	30 Oct	Dublin	3	0
ec1975	18 May	Kiev	1	2
wc1984	12 Sept	Dublin	1	0
wc1985	16 Oct	Moscow	0	2
ec1988	15 June	Hanover	1	1
1990	25 Apr	Dublin	1	0

		v WALES	RI	W
1960	28 Sept	Dublin	2	3
1979	11 Sept	Swansea	1	2
1981	24 Feb	Dublin	1	3
1986	26 Mar	Dublin	0	1
1990	28 Mar	Dublin	1	0
1991	6 Feb	Wrexham	3	0
1992	19 Feb	Dublin	0	1
1993	17 Feb	Dublin	2	1

		v YUGOSLAVIA	RI	Y
1955	19 Sept	Dublin	1	4
1988	27 Apr	Dublin	2	0

OTHER BRITISH AND IRISH INTERNATIONAL MATCHES 1995-96

Wembley, 6 September 1995, 20,038

England (0) 0

Colombia (0) 0

England: Seaman; Neville G, Le Saux, Redknapp (Barnes), Howey, Adams, Barmby, Gascoigne (Lee), Shearer (Sheringham), McManaman, Wise.
Colombia: Higuita; Santa, Bermudez, Mendoza, Perez, Lozano (Quinonez), Alvarez, Valderrama, Rincon, Asprilla, Valenciano.

Oslo, 11 October 1995, 21,006

Norway (0) 0

England (0) 0

Norway: Thorstvedt; Loken, Johnsen, Berg, Bjornebye, Bohinen, Leonhardsen (Solbakken), Rekdal, Jakobsen, Flo, Fjortoft (Brattbakk).
England: Seaman; Neville G, Pearce, Redknapp, Pallister, Adams, Lee, Barmby (Sheringham), Shearer, McManaman, Wise (Stone).

Stockholm, 11 October 1995, 19,121

Sweden (2) 2 *(Pettersson, Schwarz)*

Scotland (0) 0

Sweden: Andersson B; Lucic (Kamark), Andersson P, Bjorklund, Schwarz, Alexandersson, Brolin, Gudmundsson (Pringle), Nilsson, Andersson K (Erlingmark), Pettersson.
Scotland: Leighton (Goram); McKimmie, Burley (McKinlay W), McLaren, Hendry, Calderwood, Collins, Boyd, McGinlay (Jess), McAllister (Jackson), Robertson (Nevin).

Wembley, 15 November 1995, 29,874

England (1) 3 *(Quentin (og), Sheringham, Stone)*

Switzerland (1) 1 *(Knup)*

England: Seaman; Neville G, Pearce, Redknapp (Stone), Pallister, Adams, Lee, Gascoigne, Shearer, Sheringham, McManaman.
Switzerland: Pascolo; Hottiger, Geiger, Henchoz, Quentin (Vega), Ohrel, Sforza, Fournier (Wolf), Sutter A (Grassi), Knup, Turkyilmaz.

Wembley, 12 December 1995, 28,592

England (1) 1 *(Stone)*

Portugal (0) 1 *(Alves)*

England: Seaman; Neville G, Pearce (Le Saux), Stone, Howey, Adams, Barmby (McManaman), Gascoigne, Shearer, Ferdinand (Beardsley), Wise (Southgate).
Portugal: Neno; Secretario, Fernando Couto, Jorge Costa, Dimas, Paolo Sousa (Dominguez), Helder, Folha (Pedro), Figo (Alves), Joao Pinto (Dani), Sa Pinto.

Terni, 24 January 1996, 20,000

Italy (1) 3 *(Del Piero, Ravanelli, Casiraghi)*

Wales (0) 0

Italy: Peruzzi (Toldo); Ferrara (Torricelli), Apolloni, Costacurta, Carboni, Del Piero (Casiraghi), Albertini, Di Matteo (Conte), Di Livio (Crippa), Ravaneilli, Zola.
Wales: Southall; Phillips, Jenkins, Williams A, Symons, Coleman, Horne, Hodges (Browning), Rush (Taylor), Hughes M, Speed (Blake).

Wembley, 27 March 1996, 29,708

England (1) 1 *(Ferdinand)*

Bulgaria (0) 0

England: Seaman; Neville G, Pearce, Stone, Howey, Southgate, Ince, Gascoigne (Lee), Ferdinand (Platt), Sheringham (Fowler), McManaman.
Bulgaria: Mikhailov (Popov); Hubchev, Iankov, Ivanov, Kremenliev (Kishishev), Lechkov, Kiriakov, Guinchev (Guentchev), Yordanov (Borimirov), Penev (Sirakov), Kostadinov.

Belfast, 27 March 1996, 5343

Northern Ireland (0) 0

Norway (0) 2 *(Solskjaer, Ostenstad)*

Northern Ireland: Fettis; Lomas, Worthington (Rowland), Magilton (Patterson), Hill, McDonald, Gillespie, Lennon, Dowie, O'Neill (McMahon), Hughes.
Norway: Grodaas (Thorstvedt); Haaland, Johnsen, Berg, Bjornebye, Rudi, Rekdal, Solbakken (Lundekvam), Leonhardsen (Jakobsen), Fjortoft (Ostenstad), Solskjaer.

Dublin, 27 March 1996, 41,600

Republic of Ireland (0) 0

Russia (1) 2 *(Mostovoi, Kolyvanov)*

Republic of Ireland: Given; McAteer, Phelan, Kernaghan, McGrath, Staunton, Keane, Aldridge (Cascarino), Quinn (Coyne), Townsend (Kenna), Kennedy.
Russia: Cherchesov; Nikiforov, Onopko, Kovtun, Karpin, Kanchelskis, Mostovoi (Shalimov), Radimov (Radichenko), Tsymbalar (Tetradze), Kiryakov (Simutenkov), Kolyvanov.

Hampden Park, 27 March 1996, 20,608

Scotland (0) 1 *(McCoist)*

Australia (0) 0

Scotland: Leighton; Burley, Boyd, McStay (Gallacher), Hendry, O'Neil (Booth), Collins, McKinlay W (Jackson), McCoist (Nevin), McAllister, Spencer.
Australia: Bosnich; Tobin, Horvat, Popovic, Vidmar T, Slater, Vidmar A, Corica, Van Blerk, Arnold, Veart (Tiatto).

Wembley, 24 April 1996, 33,650

England (0) 0

Croatia (0) 0

England: Seaman; Neville G, Pearce, Stone, Wright, Ince, Platt, Gascoigne, Sheringham, Fowler, McManaman.
Croatia: Mrmic; Stimac (Soldo), Jerkan, Bilic, Pavlicic (Mladenovic), Asanovic, Boban (Stanic), Prosinecki, Jarni, Boksic (Panic), Suker.

Prague, 24 April 1996, 6118

Czech Republic (0) 2 *(Frydek, Kuka)*

Republic of Ireland (0) 0

Czech Republic: Kouba; Hornak (Rada), Kadlec (Kubik), Repka, Latal (Nedved), Frydek, Nemecek (Bejbl), Berger, Hapal, Drulak, Kuka (Kerbr).
Republic of Ireland: Given; Cunningham, Kenna, Babb (Daish), McGrath, Irwin (Fleming), Houghton, Townsend, Quinn, Kennedy, Moore.

Copenhagen, 24 April 1996, 23,031

Denmark (2) 2 *(Laudrup M, Laudrup B)*

Scotland (0) 0

Denmark: Schmeichel (Krogh); Helveg, Schjonberg, Rieper, Olsen, Risager, Thomsen, Laudrup M (Nielsen A), Steen-Nielsen, Laudrup B, Beck.
Scotland: Leighton (Goram); McKimmie, Boyd, Burley, Hendry (McKinlay W), McCall (Gemmill), Collins, McKinlay T, Spencer (McCoist), McAllister, Gallacher (Jackson).

Belfast, 24 April 1996, 5666

Northern Ireland (0) 1 *(McMahon)*

Sweden (1) 2 *(Dahlin, Ingesson)*

Northern Ireland: Davison; Patterson, Worthington (Quinn JS), Hill, Hunter, Morrow, McCarthy, Lomas, McMahon, O'Neill (O'Boyle), Rowland.
Sweden: Andersson B; Nilsson, Andersson P, Bjorklund, Sundgren, Schwarz, Wilbran (Zetterberg), Ingesson, Thern, Dahlin (Larsson), Andersson K (Pettersson).

Lugano, 24 April 1996, 8000

Switzerland (2) 2 *(Coleman (og), Turkyilmaz (pen))*

Wales (0) 0

Switzerland: Pascolo (Lehmann); Vogel (Hottiger), Vega, Henchoz, Quentin, Ohrel (Lombardo), Sforza, Wicky (Comisetti), Turkyilmaz (Koller), Grassi (Knup), Chapuisat (Sutter A).

Wales: Coyne (Marriott); Symons, Bowen, Coleman (Edwards), Robinson, Horne (Goss), Jones (Savage), Pembridge, Legg (Speed), Taylor (Davies), Hartson.

Wembley, 18 May 1996, 34,184

England (1) 3 *(Anderton 2, Platt)*

Hungary (0) 0

England: Seaman (Walker); Neville G, Pearce, Ince (Campbell), Wright (Southgate), Platt (Wise), Lee, Anderton, Ferdinand (Shearer), Sheringham, Wilcox.

Hungary: Petry; Hahn, Banfi, Plokai, Balog (Illes), Mracsko (Telek), Urban, Sebok, Nagy (Lisztes), Horvath (Aranyos), Vincze (Egressy).

Beijing, 23 May 1996, 65,000

China (0) 0

England (1) 3 *(Barmby 2, Gascoigne)*

China: Ou Quliang; Xu Hong, Wei Qun, Jiang Feng (Gao Zhangxun), Fan Ziyi, Xie Yuxing (Mi Ling), Li Bing (Peng Weiguo), Ma Mingyu, Li Hongjun, Gao Feng, Hao Haidong.

England: Flowers (Walker); Neville G, Neville P, Southgate, Adams (Ehiogu), Redknapp, Anderton, Gascoigne, Shearer (Fowler), Barmby (Beardsley), McManaman (Stone).

New Britain, 26 May 1996, 8526

USA (1) 2 *(Wynalda, Jones)*

Scotland (1) 1 *(Durie)*

USA: Sommer; Burns, Agoos, Lalas, Balboa, Jones, Harkes, Dooley (Kirovski), Reyna (McBride), Stewart, Wynalda.

Scotland: Leighton (Walker); Burley (McCall), Boyd, Calderwood, Hendry, Whyte, Jess, Gemmill (Collins), Durie (Spencer), Jackson (McAllister), Booth.

Hong Kong, 26 May 1996, 26,000

Hong Kong Golden Select (0) 0

England (1) 1 *(Ferdinand)*

Hong Kong Golden Select: Hesford; Grainger, Duxbury, Watson, Van der Sander (Leung Shing Kit), Lee Fook Wing, Bajkusa (Pang Kam Chuen), Grabo, Roberts, Fairweather, Bullen.

England: Seaman; Neville P, Pearce, Stone (Anderton), Howey (Campbell), Adams, Platt, Ince, Ferdinand (Shearer), Sheringham (Fowler), McManaman (Wilcox).

Belfast, 29 May 1996, 11,770

Northern Ireland (0) 1 *(O'Boyle)*

Germany (0) 1 *(Scholl)*

Northern Ireland: Fettis; Griffin, Worthington (Rowland), Magilton, Hunter, Hill, Gillespie (O'Boyle), Lomas, Dowie, McMahon, Hughes.

Germany: Kahn; Basler, Kohler, Helmer, Strunz, Eilts, Ziege (Bode), Scholl, Moller, Bierhoff (Bobic), Klinsmann (Kuntz).

Dublin, 29 May 1996, 26,576

Republic of Ireland (0) 0

Portugal (0) 1 *(Folha)*

Republic of Ireland: Given; Cunningham, Kenna, Kernaghan (Breen), Fleming, Phelan, McLoughlin, Farrelly (Savage), Cascarino (Quinn), Townsend, Connolly (O'Neill).

Portugal: Vitor Baia; Helder, Fernando Couto, Dimas, Paulinho Santos, Paneira (Sa Pinto), Oceano (Porfirio), Tavares, Cadete (Secretario), Joao Pinto, Folha.

Miami, 30 May 1996, 5000

Colombia (0) 1 *(Asprilla)*

Scotland (0) 0

Colombia: Mondragon; Ortiz (Herrera), Bermudez, Cassiani (Mendoza), Moreno, Mafla (Valderrama), Serna, Rincon, Estrada (Alvarez), Valenciano (Aristizabal), Valencia (Asprilla).

Scotland: Goram; Burley, Boyd, Calderwood, Hendry (McKimmie), McCall, Collins, McKinlay T, McCoist (Gallacher), McAllister, Spencer (Jess).

Dublin, 2 June 1996, 29,100

Republic of Ireland (1) 2 *(O'Neill, Quinn)*

Croatia (2) 2 *(Boban, Suker)*

Republic of Ireland: Given; Cunningham (Fleming), Phelan (Harte), Breen (Cascarino), Daish, Kenna (Kernaghan), McLoughlin (Savage), O'Neill (Moore), Quinn, Kennedy, O'Brien.

Croatia: Mrmic (Ladic); Stanic (Soldo), Bilic, Jerkan, Stimac, Asanovic, Vlaovic (Jurcevic), Suker, Boksic, Boban, Jarni.

Rotterdam, 4 June 1996, 15,002

Holland (1) 3 *(Bergkamp, Seedorf, Cocu)*

Republic of Ireland (1) 1 *(Breen)*

Holland: Van der Sar; Reiziger, Bogarde, Blind (De Kock), Ronald de Boer (Winter), Davids, Witschge, Jordi Cruyff (Cocu), Seedorf, Hoekstra (Taument), Bergkamp.

Republic of Ireland: Given; Kenna (Fleming), Phelan, Breen, Kernaghan, Harte, McLoughlin, O'Brien (Cunningham), Moore (Kennedy), Cascarino (O'Neill), Connolly (Quinn).

Boston, 9 June 1996, 25,332

USA (0) 2 *(Ramos, Rayna)*

Republic of Ireland (0) 1 *(Connolly)*

USA: Freidel; Burns, Dooley, Harkes, Ramos (Lassiter), Agoss, Jones, Balboa, Rayna (Kirovski), Lalas, Wynalda (Caligiuri).

Republic of Ireland: Given; Breen, Kernaghan, Cunningham, Kenna (Fleming), McLoughlin, O'Brien (Savage), Farrelly (Kennedy), Phelan, Quinn (O'Neill), Connolly.

New Jersey, 13 June 1996, 21,322

Mexico (1) 2 *(Garcia L 2 (1 pen))*

Republic of Ireland (1) 2 *(Connolly, Davino (og))*

Mexico: Sanchez; Suarez, Davino, De Olmo, Villa, Lara, Sol, Garcia R (Blanco), Alfaro, Garcia L, Palencia (Abundis).

Republic of Ireland: Bonner; Breen, Daish, Harte, Fleming, Savage, McLoughlin, Moore, Kennedy (Phelan), Connolly, O'Neill.

New Jersey, 15 June 1996, 14,624

Bolivia (0) 0

Republic of Ireland (3) 3 *(O'Neill 2, Harte)*

Bolivia: Sorio; Pena, Sanchez, Rimba, Castillo, Baldivieso, Etcheverry, Ramos (Cristalda), Cossio, Sandy, Moreno (Coimbra).

Republic of Ireland: Given (Bonner); Cunningham, Kernaghan (Breen), Harte, Fleming, Savage, O'Brien (McLoughlin), Phelan, Farrelly, O'Neill, Moore.

INTERNATIONAL APPEARANCES

This is a list of full international appearances by Englishmen, Irishmen, Scotsmen and Welshmen in matches against the Home Countries and against foreign nations. It does not include unofficial matches against Commonwealth and Empire countries. The year indicated refers to the season; ie 1994 is the 1993-94 season. Explanatory code for matches played by all five countries: A represents Austria; Alb, Albania; Alg, Algeria; An, Angola; Arg, Argentina; Aus, Australia; B, Bohemia; Bel, Belgium; Bol, Bolivia; Br, Brazil; Bul, Bulgaria; C,CIS; Ca, Canada; Cam, Cameroon; Ch, Chile; Chn, China; Co, Colombia; Cr, Costa Rica; Cro, Croatia; Cy, Cyprus; Cz, Czechoslovakia; CzR, Czech Republic; D, Denmark; E, England; Ec, Ecuador; Ei, Republic of Ireland; EG, East Germany; Eg, Egypt; Es, Estonia; F, France; Fa, Faeroes; Fi, Finland; G, Germany; Ge, Georgia; Gr, Greece; H, Hungary; Ho, Holland; Hon, Honduras; I, Italy; Ic, Iceland; Ir, Iran; Is, Israel; J,Japan; K, Kuwait; L, Luxembourg; La, Latvia; Li, Lithuania; Lie, Liechtenstein; M, Mexico; Ma, Malta; Mal, Malaysia; Mol, Moldova; Mor, Morocco; N, Norway; Ni, Ng, Nigeria; Northern Ireland; Nz, New Zealand; P, Portugal; Para, Paraguay; Pe, Peru; Pol, Poland; R, Romania; RCS, Republic of Czechs and Slovaks; R of E, Rest of Europe; R of UK, Rest of United Kingdom; R of W, Rest of World; Ru, Russia; S.Ar, Saudi Arabia; S, Scotland; Se, Sweden; Sm, San Marino; Sp, Spain; Sw, Switzerland; T, Turkey; Tr, Trinidad & Tobago; Tun, Tunisia; U, Uruguay; US, United States of America; USSR, Soviet Union; W, Wales; WG, West Germany; Y, Yugoslavia; Z, Zaire.
As at June 1995.

ENGLAND

Abbott, W. (Everton), 1902 v W (1)
A'Court, A. (Liverpool), 1958 v Ni, Br, A, USSR; 1959 v W (5)
Adams, T. A. (Arsenal), 1987 v Sp, T, Br; 1988 v WG, T, Y, Ho, H, S, Co, Sw, Ei, Ho, USSR; 1989 v D, Se, S.Ar.; 1991 v Ei (2); 1993 v N, T, Sm, T, Ho, Pol, N; 1994 v Pol, Ho, D, Gr, N; 1995 v US, R, Ei, U; 1996 v Co, N, Sw, P, Chn, Sw, S, Ho, Sp, G (45)
Adcock, H. (Leicester C), 1929 v F, Bel, Sp; 1930 v Ni, W (5)
Alcock, C. W. (Wanderers), 1875 v S (1)
Alderson, J. T. (C Palace), 1923 v F (1)
Aldridge, A. (WBA), 1888 v Ni; (with Walsall Town Swifts), 1889 v Ni (2)
Allen, A. (Stoke C) 1960 v Se, W, Ni (3)
Allen, A. (Aston Villa), 1888 v Ni (1)
Allen, C. (QPR), 1984 v Br (sub), U, Ch; (with Tottenham H), 1987 v T; 1988 v Is (5)
Allen, H. (Wolverhampton W), 1888 v S, W, Ni; 1889 v S; 1890 v S (5)
Allen, J. P. (Portsmouth), 1934 v Ni, W (2)
Allen, R. (WBA), 1952 v Sw; 1954 v Y, S; 1955 v WG, W (5)
Alsford, W. J. (Tottenham H), 1935 v S (1)
Amos, A. (Old Carthusians), 1885 v S; 1886 v W (2)
Anderson, R. D. (Old Etonians), 1879 v W (1)
Anderson, S. (Sunderland), 1962 v A, S (2)
Anderson, V. (Nottingham F), 1979 v Cz, Se; 1980 v Bul, Sp; 1981 v N, R, W, S; 1982 v Ni, Ic; 1984 v Ni; (with Arsenal), 1985 v T, Ni, Ei, R, Fi, S, M, US; 1986 v USSR, M; 1987 v Se, Ni (2), Y, Sp, T; (with Manchester U), 1988 v WG, H, Co (30)
Anderton, D. R. (Tottenham H), 1994 v D, Gr, N; 1995 v US, Ei, U, J, Se, Br; 1996 v H, Chn, Sw, S, Ho, Sp, G (16)
Angus, J. (Burnley), 1961 v A (1)
Armfield, J. C. (Blackpool), 1959 v Br, Pe, M, US; 1960 v Y, Sp, H, S; 1961 v L, P, Sp, M, I, A, W, Ni, S; 1962 v A, Sw, Pe, W, Ni, S, L, P, H, Arg, Bul, Br; 1963 v F (2), Br, EG, Sw, Ni, W, S; 1964 v R of W, W, Ni, S; 1966 v Y, Fi (43)
Armitage, G. H. (Charlton Ath), 1926 v Ni (1)
Armstrong, D. (Middlesbrough), 1980 v Aus; (with Southampton), 1983 v WG; 1984 v W (3)
Armstrong, K. (Chelsea), 1955 v S (1)
Arnold, J. (Fulham), 1933 v S (1)
Arthur, J. W. H. (Blackburn R), 1885 v S, W, Ni; 1886 v S, W; 1887 v W, Ni (7)
Ashcroft, J. (Woolwich Arsenal), 1906 v Ni, W, S (3)
Ashmore, G. S. (WBA), 1926 v Bel (1)
Ashton, C. T. (Corinthians), 1926 v Ni (1)
Ashurst, J. (Notts Co), 1923 v Se (2); 1925 v S, W, Bel (5)
Astall, G. (Birmingham C), 1956 v Fi, WG (2)
Astle, J. (WBA), 1969 v W; 1970 v S, P, Br (sub), Cz (5)
Aston, J. (Manchester U), 1949 v S, W, D, Sw, Se, N, F; 1950 v S, W, Ni, Ei, I, P, Bel, Ch, US; 1951 v Ni (17)
Athersmith, W. C. (Aston Villa), 1892 v Ni, 1897 v S, W, Ni; 1898 v S, W, Ni; 1899 v S, W, Ni; 1900 v S, W (12)
Atyeo, P. J. W. (Bristol C), 1956 v Br, Se, Sp; 1957 v D, Ei (2) (6)
Austin, S. W. (Manchester C), 1926 v Ni (1)

Bach, P. (Sunderland), 1899 v Ni (1)
Bache, J. W. (Aston Villa), 1903 v W; 1904 v W, Ni; 1905 v S; 1907 v Ni; 1910 v Ni; 1911 v S (7)
Baddeley, T. (Wolverhampton W), 1903 v S, Ni; 1904 v S, W, Ni (5)
Bagshaw, J. J. (Derby Co), 1920 v Ni (1)
Bailey, G. R. (Manchester U), 1985 v Ei, M (2)
Bailey, H. P. (Leicester Fosse), 1908 v W, A (2), H, B (5)
Bailey, M. A. (Charlton Ath), 1964 v US; 1965 v W (2)

Bailey, N. C. (Clapham Rovers), 1878 v S; 1879 v S, W; 1880 v S; 1881 v S; 1882 v S, W; 1883 v S, W; 1884 v S, W, Ni; 1885 v S, W, Ni; 1886 v S, W; 1887 v S, W (19)
Baily, E. F. (Tottenham H), 1950 v Sp; 1951 v Y, Ni, W; 1952 v A (2), Sw, W; 1953 v Ni (9)
Bain, J. (Oxford University), 1887 v S (1)
Baker, A. (Arsenal), 1928 v W (1)
Baker, B. H. (Everton), 1921 v Bel; (with Chelsea), 1926 v Ni (2)
Baker, J. H. (Hibernian), 1960 v Y, Sp, H, Ni, S; (with Arsenal) 1966 v Sp, Pol, N (8)
Ball, A. J. (Blackpool), 1965 v Y, WG, Se; 1966 v S, Sp, Fi, D, U, Arg, P, WG (2), Pol (2); (with Everton), 1967 v W, S, Ni, A, Cz, Sp; 1968 v W, S, USSR, Sp (2), Y, WG; 1969 v Ni, W, S, R (2), M, Br, U; 1970 v P, Co, Ec, R, Br, Cz (sub), WG, W, S, Bel; 1971 v Ma, EG, Gr, Ma (sub), Ni, S; 1972 v Sw, Gr; (with Arsenal) WG (2), S; 1973 v W (3), Y, S (2), Cz, Ni, Pol; 1974 v P (sub); 1975 v WG, Cy (2), Ni, W, S (72)
Ball, J. (Bury), 1928 v Ni (1)
Balmer, W. (Everton), 1905 v Ni (1)
Bamber, J. (Liverpool), 1921 v W (1)
Bambridge, A. L. (Swifts), 1881 v W; 1883 v W; 1884 v Ni (3)
Bambridge, E. C. (Swifts), 1879 v S; 1880 v S; 1881 v S; 1882 v S, W; 1883 v W; 1884 v S, W, Ni; 1885 v S, W, Ni; 1886 v S, W; 1887 v S, W (18)
Bambridge, E. H. (Swifts), 1876 v S (1)
Banks, G. (Leicester C), 1963 v S, Br, Cz, EG; 1964 v W, Ni, S, R of W, U, P (2), US, Arg; 1965 v Ni, S, H, Y, WG, Se; 1966 v Ni, S, Sp, Pol (2), WG (2), Y, Fi, U, M, F, Arg, P; 1967 v Ni, W, S, Cz; (with Stoke C), 1968 v W, Ni, S, USSR (2), Sp, WG, Y; 1969 v Ni, S, R (2), F, U, Br; 1970 v W, Ni, S, Ho, Bel, Co, Ec, R, Br, Cz; 1971 v Gr, Ma (2), Ni, S; 1972 v Sw, Gr, WG (2), W, S (73)
Banks, H. E. (Millwall), 1901 v Ni (1)
Banks, T. (Bolton W), 1958 v USSR (3), Br, A; 1959 v Ni (6)
Bannister, W. (Burnley), 1901 v W; (with Bolton W), 1902 v Ni (2)
Barclay, R. (Sheffield U), 1932 v S; 1933 v Ni; 1936 v S (3)
Bardsley, D. J. (QPR), 1993 v Sp (sub), Pol (2)
Barham, M. (Norwich C), 1983 v Aus (2) (2)
Barkas, S. (Manchester C), 1936 v Bel; 1937 v S; 1938 v W, Ni, Cz (5)
Barker, J. (Derby Co), 1935 v I, Ho, S, W, Ni; 1936 v G, A, S, W, Ni; 1937 v W (11)
Barker, R. (Herts Rangers), 1872 v S (1)
Barker, R. R. (Casuals), 1895 v W (1)
Barlow, R. J. (WBA), 1955 v Ni (1)
Barmby, N.J. (Tottenham H), 1995 v U (sub), Se (sub); (with Middlesbrough), 1996 v Co, N, P, Chn, Sw (sub), Ho (sub), Sp (sub) (9)
Barnes, J. (Watford), 1983 v Ni (sub), Aus (sub), Aus (2); 1984 v D, L (sub), F (sub), S, USSR, Br, U, Ch; 1985 v EG, Fi, T, Ni, R, Fi, S, I (sub), M, WG (sub), US (sub); 1986 v R (sub), Is (sub), M (sub), Ca (sub), Arg (sub); 1987 v Se, T (sub), Br; (with Liverpool), 1988 v WG, T, Y, Is, Ho, S, Co, Sw, Ei, Ho, USSR; 1989 v Se, Gr, Alb, Pol, D; 1990 v Se, I, Br, D, U, Tun, Ei, Ho, Eg, Bel, Cam; 1991 v H, Pol, Cam, Ei, T, USSR, Arg; 1992 v Cz, Fi; 1993 v Sm, T, Ho, Pol, US, G; 1995 v US, R, Ng, U, Se; 1996 v Co (sub) (79)
Barnes, P. S. (Manchester C), 1978 v I, WG, B1, W, S, II; 1979 v D, Ei, Cz, Ni (2), S, Bul, A; (with WBA), 1980 v D, W; 1981 v Sp (sub), Br, W, Sw (sub); (with Leeds U), 1982 v N (sub), Ho (sub) (22)
Barnet, H. H. (Royal Engineers), 1882 v Ni (1)
Barrass, M. W. (Bolton W), 1952 v W, Ni; 1953 v S (3)
Barrett, A. F. (Fulham), 1930 v Ni (1)
Barrett, E. D. (Oldham Ath), 1991 v Nz; 1993 v Br, G (3)

Barrett, J. W. (West Ham U), 1929 v Ni (1)

Barry, L. (Leicester C), 1928 v F, Bel; 1929 v F, Bel, Sp (5)

Barson, F. (Aston Villa), 1920 v W (1)

Barton, J. (Blackburn R), 1890 v Ni (1)

Barton, P. H. (Birmingham), 1921 v Bel; 1922 v Ni; 1923 v F; 1924 v Bel, S, W; 1925 v Ni (7)

Barton, W. D. (Wimbledon), 1995 v Ei; (with Newcastle U), Se, Br (sub) (3)

Bassett, W. I. (WBA), 1888 v Ni, 1889 v S, W; 1890 v S, W; 1891 v S, Ni; 1892 v S; 1893 v S, W; 1894 v S; 1895 v S, Ni; 1896 v S, W, Ni (16)

Bastard, S. R. (Upton Park), 1880 v S (1)

Bastin, C. S. (Arsenal), 1932 v W; 1933 v I, Sw; 1934 v S, Ni, W, H, Cz; 1935 v S, Ni, I; 1936 v S, W, G, A; 1937 v W, Ni; 1938 v S, G, Sw, F (21)

Batty, D. (Leeds U), 1991 v USSR (sub), Arg, Aus, Nz, Mal; 1992 v G, T, H (sub), F, Se; 1993 v Ni, S, Br; (with Blackburn R), 1994 v D (sub); 1995 v J, Br (17)

Baugh, R. (Stafford Road), 1886 v Ni; (with Wolverhampton W) 1890 v Ni (2)

Bayliss, A. E. J. M. (WBA), 1891 v Ni (1)

Baynham, R. L. (Luton T), 1956 v Ni, D, Sp (3)

Beardsley, P. A. (Newcastle U), 1986 v Eg (sub), Is, USSR, M, Ca (sub), P (sub), Pol, Para, Arg; 1987 v Ni (2), Y, Sp, Br, S; (with Liverpool), 1988 v WG, T, Y, Is, Ho, H, S, Co, Sw, Ei, Ho; 1989 v D, Se, S.Ar, Gr (sub), Alb (sub+1), Pol, D; 1990 v Se, Pol, I, Br, U (sub), Tun (sub), Ei, Eg (sub), Cam (sub), WG, I; 1991 v Pol (sub), Ei (2), USSR (sub); (with Newcastle U), 1994 v D, Gr, N; 1995 v Ng, Ei, U, J, Se; 1996 v P (sub), Chn (sub) (59)

Beasant, D. J. (Chelsea), 1990 v I (sub), Y (sub) (2)

Beasley, A. (Huddersfield T), 1939 v S (1)

Beats, W. E. (Wolverhampton W), 1901 v W; 1902 v S (2)

Beattie, T. K. (Ipswich T), 1975 v Cy (2), S; 1976 v Sw, P; 1977 v Fi, I (sub), Ho; 1978 v L (sub) (9)

Becton, F. (Preston NE), 1895 v Ni; (with Liverpool), 1897 v W (2)

Bedford, H. (Blackpool), 1923 v Se; 1925 v Ni (2)

Bell, C. (Manchester C), 1968 v Se, WG; 1969 v W, Bul, F, U, Br; 1970 v Ni (sub), Ho (2), P, Br (sub), Cz, WG (sub); 1972 v Gr, WG (2), W, Ni, S; 1973 v W (3), Y, S (2), Ni, Cz, Pol; 1974 v A, Pol, I, W, Ni, S, Arg, EG, Bul, Y; 1975 v Cz, P, WG, Cy (2), Ni, S; 1976 v Sw, Cy (48)

Bennett, M. (Sheffield U), 1901 v S, W (2)

Benson, R. W. (Sheffield U), 1913 v Ni (1)

Bentley, R. T. F. (Chelsea), 1949 v Se; 1950 v S, P, Bel, Ch, USA; 1953 v W, Bel; 1955 v W, WG, Sp, P (12)

Beresford, J. (Aston Villa), 1934 v Cz (1)

Berry, A. (Oxford University), 1909 v Ni (1)

Berry, J. J. (Manchester U), 1953 v Arg, Ch, U; 1956 v Se (4)

Bestall, J. G. (Grimsby T), 1935 v Ni (1)

Betmead, H. A. (Grimsby T), 1937 v Fi (1)

Betts, M. P. (Old Harrovians), 1877 v S (1)

Betts, W. (Sheffield W), 1889 v W (1)

Beverley, J. (Blackburn R), 1884 v S, W, Ni (3)

Birkett, R. H. (Clapham Rovers), 1879 v S (1)

Birkett, R. J. E. (Middlesbrough), 1936 v Ni (1)

Birley, F. H. (Oxford University), 1874 v S; (with Wanderers), 1875 v S (2)

Birtles, G. (Nottingham F), 1980 v Arg (sub), I; 1981 v R (3)

Bishop, S. M. (Leicester C), 1927 v S, Bel, L, F (4)

Blackburn, F. (Blackburn R), 1901 v S; 1902 v Ni; 1904 v S (3)

Blackburn, G. F. (Aston Villa), 1924 v F (1)

Blenkinsop, E. (Sheffield W), 1928 v F, Bel; 1929 v S, W, Ni, F, Bel, Sp; 1930 v S, W, Ni, G, A; 1931 v S, W, Ni, F, Bel; 1932 v S, W, Ni, Sp; 1933 v S, W, Ni, A (26)

Bliss, H. (Tottenham H), 1921 v S (1)

Blissett, L. (Watford), 1983 v WG (sub), L, W, Gr (sub), H, Ni, S (sub), Aus (1+1 sub); (with AC Milan), 1984 v D (sub), H, W (sub), S, USSR (14)

Blockley, J. P. (Arsenal), 1973 v Y (1)

Bloomer, S. (Derby Co), 1895 v S, Ni; 1896 v W, Ni; 1897 v S, W, Ni; 1898 v S; 1899 v S, W, Ni; 1900 v S; 1901 v S, W; 1902 v S, W, Ni; 1904 v S; 1905 v S, W, Ni; (with Middlesbrough), 1907 v S, W (23)

Blunstone, F. (Chelsea), 1955 v W, S, F, P; 1957 v Y (5)

Bond, R. (Preston NE), 1905 v Ni, W; 1906 v S, W, Ni; (with Bradford C), 1910 v S, W, Ni (8)

Bonetti, P. P. (Chelsea), 1966 v D; 1967 v Sp, A; 1968 v Sp; 1970 v Ho, P, WG (7)

Bonsor, A. G. (Wanderers), 1873 v S; 1875 v S (2)

Booth, F. (Manchester C), 1905 v Ni (1)

Booth, T. (Blackburn R), 1898 v W; (with Everton), 1903 v S (2)

Bould, S. A. (Arsenal), 1994 v Gr, N (2)

Bowden, E. R. (Arsenal), 1935 v W, I; 1936 v W, Ni, A; 1937 v H (6)

Bower, A. G. (Corinthians), 1924 v Ni, Bel; 1925 v W, Bel; 1927 v W (5)

Bowers, J. W. (Derby Co), 1934 v S, Ni, W (3)

Bowles, S. (QPR), 1974 v P, W, Ni; 1977 v I, Ho (5)

Bowser, S. (WBA), 1920 v Ni (1)

Boyer, P. J. (Norwich C), 1976 v W (1)

Boyes, W. (WBA), 1935 v Ho; (with Everton), 1939 v W, R of E (3)

Boyle, T. W. (Burnley), 1913 v Ni (1)

Brabrook, P. (Chelsea), 1958 v USSR; 1959 v Ni; 1960 v Sp (3)

Bracewell, P. W. (Everton), 1985 v WG (sub), US; 1986 v Ni (3)

Bradford, G. R. W. (Bristol R), 1956 v D (1)

Bradford, J. (Birmingham), 1924 v Ni; 1925 v Bel; 1928 v S; 1929 v Ni, W, F, Sp; 1930 v S, Ni, G, A; 1931 v W (12)

Bradley, W. (Manchester U), 1959 v I, US, M (sub) (3)

Bradshaw, F. (Sheffield W), 1908 v A (1)

Bradshaw, T. H. (Liverpool), 1897 v Ni (1)

Bradshaw, W. (Blackburn R), 1910 v W, Ni; 1912 v Ni; 1913 v W (4)

Brann, G. (Swifts), 1886 v S, W; 1891 v W (3)

Brawn, W. F. (Aston Villa), 1904 v W, Ni (2)

Bray, J. (Manchester C), 1935 v W; 1936 v S, W, Ni, G; 1937 v S (6)

Brayshaw, E. (Sheffield W), 1887 v Ni (1)

Bridges, B. J. (Chelsea), 1965 v S, H, Y; 1966 v A (4)

Bridgett, A. (Sunderland), 1905 v S; 1908 v S, A (2), H, B; 1909 v Ni, W, H (2), A (11)

Brindle, T. (Darwen), 1880 v S, W (2)

Brittleton, J. T. (Sheffield W), 1912 v S, W, Ni; 1913 v S; 1914 v W (5)

Britton, C. S. (Everton), 1935 v S, W, Ni, I; 1937 v S, Ni, H, N, Se (9)

Broadbent, P. F. (Wolverhampton W), 1958 v USSR; 1959 v S, W, Ni, I, Br; 1960 v S (7)

Broadis, I. A. (Manchester C), 1952 v S, A, I; 1953 v S, Arg, Ch, U, US; (with Newcastle U), 1954 v S, H, Y, Bel, Sw, U (14)

Brockbank, J. (Cambridge University), 1872 v S (1)

Brodie, J. B. (Wolverhampton W), 1889 v S, Ni; 1891 v Ni (3)

Bromilow, T. G. (Liverpool), 1921 v W; 1922 v S, W; 1923 v Bel; 1926 v Ni (5)

Bromley-Davenport, W. E. (Oxford University), 1884 v S, W (2)

Brook, E. F. (Manchester C), 1930 v Ni; 1933 v Sw; 1934 v S, W, Ni, F, H, Cz; 1935 v S, W, Ni, I; 1936 v S, W, Ni; 1937 v H; 1938 v W, Ni (18)

Brooking, T. D. (West Ham U), 1974 v P, Arg, EG, Bul, Y; 1975 v Cz (sub), P; 1976 v P, W, Br, I, Fi; 1977 v Ei, Fi, I, Ho, Ni, W; 1978 v I, WG (sub), H; 1979 v D, Ei, Ni, W (sub), S, Bul, Se (sub), A; 1980 v D, Ni, Arg (sub), W, Ni, S, Bel, Sp; 1981 v Sw, Sp, R, H; 1982 v H, S, Fi, Sp (sub) (47)

Brooks, J. (Tottenham H), 1957 v W, Y, D (3)

Broome, F. H. (Aston Villa), 1938 v G, Sw, F; 1939 v N, I, R, Y (7)

Brown, A. (Aston Villa), 1882 v S, W, Ni (3)

Brown, A. S. (Sheffield U), 1904 v W; 1906 v S (2)

Brown, A. (WBA), 1971 v W (1)

Brown, G. (Huddersfield T), 1927 v S, W, Ni, Bel, L, F; 1928 v W; 1929 v S; (with Aston Villa), 1933 v W (9)

Brown, J. (Blackburn R), 1881 v W; 1882 v Ni; 1885 v S, W, Ni (5)

Brown, J. H. (Sheffield W), 1927 v S, W, Bel, L, F; 1930 v Ni (6)

Brown, K. (West Ham U), 1960 v Ni (1)

Brown, W. (West Ham U), 1924 v Bel (1)

Bruton, J. (Burnley), 1928 v F, Bel; 1929 v S (3)

Bryant, W. I. (Clapton), 1925 v F (1)

Buchan, C. M. (Sunderland), 1913 v Ni; 1920 v W; 1921 v W, Bel; 1923 v F; 1924 v S (6)

Buchanan, W. S. (Clapham R), 1876 v S (1)

Buckley, F. C. (Derby Co), 1914 v Ni (1)

Bull, S. G. (Wolverhampton W), 1989 v S (sub), D (sub); 1990 v Y, Cz, D (sub), U (sub), Tun (sub), Ei (sub), Ho (sub), Eg, Bel (sub); 1991 v H, Pol (13)

Bullock, F. E. (Huddersfield T), 1921 v Ni (1)

Bullock, N. (Bury), 1923 v Bel; 1926 v W; 1927 v Ni (3)

Burgess, H. (Manchester C), 1904 v S, W, Ni; 1906 v S (4)

Burgess, H. (Sheffield W), 1931 v S, Ni, F, Bel (4)

Burnup, C. J. (Cambridge University), 1896 v S (1)

Burrows, H. (Sheffield W), 1934 v H, Cz; 1935 v Ho (3)

Burton, F. E. (Nottingham F), 1889 v Ni (1)

Bury, L. (Cambridge University), 1877 v S; (with Old Etonians), 1879 v W (2)

Butcher, T. (Ipswich T), 1980 v Aus; 1981 v Sp; 1982 v W, S, F, Cz, WG, Sp; 1983 v D, WG, L, W, Gr, H, Ni, S, Aus (3); 1984 v D, H, L, F, Ni; 1985 v EG, Fi, T, Ni, Ei, R, Fi, S, I, WG, US; 1986 v Is, USSR, S, M, Ca, P, Mor, Pol, Para, Arg; (with Rangers), 1987 v Se, Ni (2), Y, Sp, Br, S; 1988 v T, Y; 1989 v D, Se, Gr, Alb (2), Ch, S, Pol, D; 1990

v Se, Pol, I, Y, Br, Cz, D, U, Tun, Ei, Ho, Bel, Cam, WG (77)
Butler, J. D. (Arsenal), 1925 v Bel (1)
Butler, W. (Bolton W), 1924 v S (1)
Byrne, G. (Liverpool), 1963 v S; 1966 v N (2)
Byrne, J. J. (C Palace), 1962 v Ni; (with West Ham U), 1963 v Sw; 1964 v S, U, P (2), Ei, Br, Arg; 1965 v W, S (11)
Byrne, R. W. (Manchester U), 1954 v S, H, Y, Bel, Sw, U; 1955 v S, W, Ni, WG, F, Sp, P; 1956 v S, W, Ni, Br, Se, Fi, WG, D, Sp; 1957 v S, W, Ni, Y, D (2), Ei (2); 1958 v W, Ni, F (33)

Callaghan, I. R. (Liverpool), 1966 v Fi, F; 1978 v Sw, L (4)
Calvey, J. (Nottingham F), 1902 v Ni (1)
Campbell, A. F. (Blackburn R), 1929 v W, Ni; (with Huddersfield T), 1931 v W, S, Ni; 1932 v W, Ni, Sp (8)
Campbell, S. (Tottenham H), 1996 v H (sub), S (sub) (2)
Camsell, G. H. (Middlesbrough), 1929 v F, Bel; 1930 v Ni, W; 1934 v F; 1936 v S, G, A, Bel (9)
Capes, A. J. (Stoke C), 1903 v S (1)
Carr, J. (Middlesbrough), 1920 v Ni; 1923 v W (2)
Carr, J. (Newcastle U), 1905 v Ni; 1907 v Ni (2)
Carr, W. H. (Owlerton, Sheffield), 1875 v S (1)
Carter, H. S. (Sunderland), 1934 v S, H; 1936 v G; 1937 v S, Ni, H; (with Derby Co), 1947 v S, W, Ni, Ei, Ho, F, Sw (13)
Carter, J. H. (WBA), 1926 v Bel; 1929 v Bel, Sp (3)
Catlin, A. E. (Sheffield W), 1937 v W, Ni, H, N, Se (5)
Chadwick, A. (Southampton), 1900 v S, W (2)
Chadwick, E. (Everton), 1891 v S, W; 1892 v S; 1893 v S; 1894 v S; 1896 v Ni; 1897 v S (7)
Chamberlain, M (Stoke C), 1983 v L (sub); 1984 v D (sub), S, USSR, Br, U, Ch; 1985 v Fi (sub) (8)
Chambers, H. (Liverpool), 1921 v S, W, Bel; 1923 v S, W, Ni, Bel; 1924 v Ni (8)
Channon, M. R. (Southampton), 1973 v Y, S (2), Ni, W, Cz, USSR, I; 1974 v A, Pol, I, P, W, Ni, S, Arg, EG, Bul, Y; 1975 v Cz, P, WG, Cy (2), Ni (sub), W, S; 1976 v Sw, Cz, P, W, Ni, S, Br, I, Fi; 1977 v Fi, I, L, Ni, W, S, Br (sub), Arg, U; (with Manchester C), 1978 v Sw (46)
Charles, G. A. (Nottingham F), 1991 v Nz, Mal (2)
Charlton, J. (Leeds U), 1965 v S, H, Y, WG, Se; 1966 v W, Ni, S, A, Sp, Pol (2), WG (2), Y, Fi, D, U, M, F, Arg, P; 1967 v W, S, Ni, Cz; 1968 v W, Sp; 1969 v W, R, F; 1970 v Ho (2), P, Cz (35)
Charlton, R. (Manchester U), 1958 v S, P, Y; 1959 v S, W, Ni, USSR, I, Br, Pe, M, US; 1960 v W, S, Se, Y, Sp, H; 1961 v Ni, W, S, L, P, Sp, M, I, A; 1962 v W, Ni, S, A, Sw, Pe, L, P, H, Arg, Bul, Br; 1963 v S, F, Br, Cz, EG, Sw; 1964 v S, W, Ni, R of W, U, P, Ei, Br, Arg, US (sub); 1965 v Ni, S, Ho; 1966 v W, Ni, S, A, Sp, WG (2), Y, Fi, N, Pol, U, M, F, Arg, P; 1967 v Ni, W, S, Cz; 1968 v W, Ni, S, USSR (2), Sp (2), Se, Y; 1969 v S, W, Ni, R (2), Bul, M, Br; 1970 v W, Ni, Ho (2), P, Co, Ec, Cz, R, Br, WG (106)
Charnley, R. O. (Blackpool), 1963 v F (1)
Charsley, C. C. (Small Heath), 1893 v Ni (1)
Chedgzoy, S. (Everton), 1920 v W; 1921 v W, S, Ni; 1922 v Ni; 1923 v S; 1924 v W; 1925 v Ni (8)
Chenery, C. J. (C Palace), 1872 v S; 1873 v S; 1874 v S (3)
Cherry, T. J. (Leeds U), 1976 v W, S (sub), Br, Fi; 1977 v Ei, I, L, Ni, S (sub), Br, Arg, U; 1978 v Sw, L, I, Br, W; 1979 v Cz, W, Se; 1980 v Ei, Arg (sub), W, Ni, S, Aus, Sp (sub) (27)
Chilton, A. (Manchester U), 1951 v Ni; 1952 v F (2)
Chippendale, H. (Blackburn R), 1894 v Ni (1)
Chivers, M. (Tottenham H), 1971 v Ma (2), Gr, Ni, S; 1972 v Sw (1+1 sub), Gr, WG (2), Ni (sub), S; 1973 v W (3), S (2), Ni, Cz, Pol, USSR, I; 1974 v A, Pol (24)
Christian, E. (Old Etonians), 1879 v S (1)
Clamp, E. (Wolverhampton W), 1958 v USSR (2), Br, A (4)
Clapton, D. R. (Arsenal), 1959 v W (1)
Clare, T. (Stoke C), 1889 v Ni; 1892 v Ni; 1893 v W; 1894 v S (4)
Clarke, A. J. (Leeds U), 1970 v Cz; 1971 v EG, Ma, Ni, W (sub), S (sub); 1973 v S (2), W, Cz, Pol, USSR, I; 1974 v A, Pol, I; 1975 v P; 1976 v Cz, P (sub) (19)
Clarke, H. A. (Tottenham H), 1954 v S (1)
Clay, T. (Tottenham H), 1920 v W; 1922 v W, S, Ni (4)
Clayton, R. (Blackburn R), 1956 v Ni, Br, Se, Fi, WG, Sp; 1957 v W, Ni, Y, D (2), Ei (2); 1958 v S, W, Ni, F, P, Y, USSR; 1959 v S, W, Ni, USSR, I, Br, Pe, M, US; 1960 v W, Ni, S, Se, Y (35)
Clegg, J. C. (Sheffield W), 1872 v S (1)
Clegg, W. E. (Sheffield W), 1873 v S; (with Sheffield Albion), 1879 v W (2)
Clemence, R. N. (Liverpool), 1973 v W (2); 1974 v EG, Bul, Y; 1975 v Cz, P, WG, Cy, Ni, W, S; 1976 v Sw, Cz, P, W (2), Ni, S, Br, Fi; 1977 v Ei, Fi, I, Ho, L, S, Br, Arg, U; 1978 v Sw, L, I, WG, Ni, S; 1979 v D, Ei, Ni (2), S, Bul, A (sub); 1980 v D, Bul, Ei, Arg, W, S, Bel, Sp; 1981 v R, Sp,

Br, Sw, H; (with Tottenham H), 1982 v N, Ni, Fi; 1983 v L; 1984 v L (61)
Clement, D. T. (QPR), 1976 v W (sub+1), I; 1977 v I, Ho (5)
Clough, B. H. (Middlesbrough), 1960 v W, Se (2)
Clough, N. H. (Nottingham F), 1989 v Ch; 1991 v Arg (sub), Aus, Mal; 1992 v F, Cz, C; 1993 v Sp, T (sub), Pol (sub), N (sub), US, Br, G (14)
Coates, R. (Burnley), 1970 v Ni; 1971 v Gr (sub); (with Tottenham H), Ma, W (4)
Cobbold, W. N. (Cambridge University), 1883 v S, Ni; 1885 v S, Ni; 1886 v S, W; (with Old Carthusians), 1887 v S, W, Ni (9)
Cock, J. G. (Huddersfield T), 1920 v Ni; (with Chelsea), v S (2)
Cockburn, H. (Manchester U), 1947 v W, Ni, Ei; 1948 v S, I; 1949 v S, Ni, D, Sw, Se; 1951 v Arg, P; 1952 v F (13)
Cohen, G. R. (Fulham), 1964 v U, P, Ei, US, Br; 1965 v W, S, Ni, Bel, H, Ho, Y, WG, Se; 1966 v W, S, Ni, A, Sp, Pol (2), WG (2), N, D, U, M, F, Arg, P; 1967 v W, S, Ni, Cz, Sp; 1968 v W, Ni (37)
Cole, A. (Manchester U), 1995 v U (sub) (1)
Coleclough, H. (C Palace), 1914 v W (1)
Coleman, E. H. (Dulwich Hamlet), 1921 v W (1)
Coleman, J. (Woolwich Arsenal), 1907 v Ni (1)
Collymore, S. V. (Nottingham F), 1995 v J, Br (sub) (2)
Common, A. (Sheffield U), 1904 v W, Ni; (with Middlesbrough), 1906 v W (3)
Compton, L. H. (Arsenal), 1951 v W, Y (2)
Conlin, J. (Bradford C), 1906 v S (1)
Connelly, J. M. (Burnley), 1960 v W, N, S, Se; 1962 v W, A, Sw, P; 1963 v W, F; (with Manchester U), 1965 v H, Y, Se; 1966 v W, Ni, S, A, N, D, U (20)
Cook, T. E. R. (Brighton), 1925 v W (1)
Cooper, C. T. (Nottingham F), 1995 v Se, Br (2)
Cooper, N. C. (Cambridge University), 1893 v Ni (1)
Cooper, T. (Derby Co), 1928 v Ni; 1929 v W, Ni, S, F, Bel, Sp; 1931 v F; 1932 v W, Sp; 1933 v S; 1934 v S, H, Cz; 1935 v W (15)
Cooper, T. (Leeds U), 1969 v W, S, F, M; 1970 v Ho, Bel, Co, Ec, R, Cz, Br, WG; 1971 v EG, Ma, Ni, W, S; 1972 v Sw (2); 1975 v P (20)
Coppell, S. J. (Manchester U), 1978 v I, WG, Br, W, Ni, S, H; 1979 v D, Ei, Cz, Ni (2), W (sub), S, Bul, A; 1980 v D, Ni, Ei (sub), Sp, Arg, W, S, Bel, I; 1981 v R (sub), Sw, R, Br, W, S, Sw, H; 1982 v H, S, Fi, F, Cz, K, WG; 1983 v L, Gr (42)
Copping, W. (Leeds U), 1933 v I, Sw; 1934 v S, Ni, W, F; (with Arsenal), 1935 v Ni, I; 1936 v A, Bel; 1937 v N, Se, Fi; 1938 v S, W, Ni, Cz; 1939 v W, R of E; (with Leeds U), R (20)
Corbett, B. O. (Corinthians), 1901 v W (1)
Corbett, R. (Old Malvernians), 1903 v W (1)
Corbett, W. S. (Birmingham), 1908 v A, H, B (3)
Corrigan, J. T. (Manchester C), 1976 v I (sub), Br; 1979 v W; 1980 v Ni, Aus; 1981 v W, S; 1982 v W, Ic (9)
Cottee, A. R. (West Ham U), 1987 v Se (sub), Ni (sub); 1988 v H (sub); (with Everton) 1989 v D (sub), Se (sub), Ch (sub), S (7)
Cotterill, G. H. (Cambridge University), 1891 v Ni; (with Old Brightonians), 1892 v W; 1893 v S, Ni (4)
Cottle, J. R. (Bristol C), 1909 v Ni (1)
Cowan, S. (Manchester C), 1926 v Bel; 1930 v A; 1931 v Bel (3)
Cowans, G. (Aston Villa), 1983 v W, H, Ni, S, Aus (3); (with Bari), 1986 v Eg, USSR; (with Aston Villa), 1991 v Ei (10)
Cowell, A. (Blackburn R), 1910 v Ni (1)
Cox, J. (Liverpool), 1901 v Ni; 1902 v S; 1903 v S (3)
Cox, J. D. (Derby Co), 1892 v Ni (1)
Crabtree, J. W. (Burnley), 1894 v Ni; 1895 v Ni, S; (with Aston Villa), 1896 v W, S, Ni; 1899 v S, W, Ni; 1900 v S, W, Ni; 1901 v W; 1902 v W (14)
Crawford, J. F. (Chelsea), 1931 v S (1)
Crawford, R. (Ipswich T), 1962 v Ni, A (2)
Crawshaw, T. H. (Sheffield W), 1895 v Ni; 1896 v S, W, Ni; 1897 v S, W, Ni; 1901 v Ni; 1904 v W, Ni (10)
Crayston, W. J. (Arsenal), 1936 v S, W, G, A, Bel; 1938 v W, Ni, Cz (8)
Creek, F. N. S. (Corinthians), 1923 v F (1)
Cresswell, W. (South Shields), 1921 v W; (with Sunderland), 1923 v F; 1924 v Bel; 1925 v Ni; 1926 v W; 1927 v Ni; (with Everton), 1930 v Ni (7)
Crompton, R. (Blackburn R), 1902 v S, W, Ni; 1903 v S, W; 1904 v S, W, Ni; 1906 v S, W, Ni; 1907 v S, W, Ni; 1908 v S, W, Ni, A (2), H, B; 1909 v S, W, Ni H (2), A; 1910 v S, W; 1911 v S, W, Ni; 1912 v S, W, Ni; 1913 v S, W, Ni; 1914 v S, W, Ni (41)
Crooks, S. D. (Derby Co), 1930 v S, G, A; 1931 v S, W, Ni, F, Bel; 1932 v S, W, Ni, Sp; 1933 v Ni, W, A; 1934 v S, Ni, W, F, H, Cz; 1935 v Ni; 1936 v S, W; 1937 v W, H (26)
Crowe, C. (Wolverhampton W), 1963 v F (1)
Cuggy, F. (Sunderland), 1913 v Ni; 1914 v Ni (2)

Cullis, S. (Wolverhampton W), 1938 v S, W, Ni, F, Cz; 1939 v S, Ni, R of E, N, I, R, Y (12)
Cunliffe, A. (Blackburn R), 1933 v Ni, W (2)
Cunliffe, D. (Portsmouth), 1900 v Ni (1)
Cunliffe, J. N. (Everton), 1936 v Bel (1)
Cunningham, L. (WBA), 1979 v W, Se, A (sub); (with Real Madrid), 1980 v Ei, Sp (sub); 1981 v R (sub) (6)
Curle, K. (Manchester C), 1992 v C (sub), H, D (3)
Currey, E. S. (Oxford University), 1890 v S, W (2)
Currie, A. W. (Sheffield U), 1972 v Ni; 1973 v USSR, I; 1974 v A, Pol, I; 1976 v Sw; (with Leeds U), 1978 v Br, W (sub), Ni, S, H (sub); 1979 v Cz, Ni (2), W, Se (17)
Cursham, A. W. (Notts Co), 1876 v S; 1877 v S; 1878 v S; 1879 v W; 1883 v S, W (6)
Cursham, H. A. (Notts Co), 1880 v W; 1882 v S, W, Ni; 1883 v S, W, Ni; 1884 v W (8)

Daft, H. B. (Notts Co), 1889 v Ni; 1890 v S, W; 1891 v Ni; 1892 v Ni (5)
Daley, A. M. (Aston Villa), 1992 v Pol (sub), C, H, Br, Fi (sub), D (sub), Se (7)\ Danks, T. (Nottingham F), 1885 v S (1)
Davenport, P. (Nottingham F), 1985 v Ei (sub) (1)
Davenport, J. K. (Bolton W), 1885 v W; 1890 v Ni (2)
Davis, G. (Derby Co), 1904 v W, Ni (2)
Davis, H. (Sheffield W), 1903 v S, W, Ni (3)
Davison, J. E. (Sheffield W), 1922 v W (1)
Dawson, J. (Burnley), 1922 v S, Ni (2)
Day, S. H. (Old Malvernians), 1906 v Ni, W, S (3)
Dean, W. R. (Everton), 1927 v S, W, F, Bel, L; 1928 v S, W, Ni, F, Bel; 1929 v S, W, Ni; 1931 v S; 1932 v Sp; 1933 v Ni (16)
Deane, B. C. (Sheffield U), 1991 v Nz (sub + 1); 1993 v Sp (sub) (3)
Deeley, N. V. (Wolverhampton W), 1959 v Br, Pe (2)
Devey, J. H. G. (Aston Villa), 1892 v Ni; 1894 v Ni (2)
Devonshire, A. (West Ham U), 1980 v Aus (sub), Ni; 1982 v Ho, Ic; 1983 v WG, W, Gr; 1984 v L (8)
Dewhurst, F. (Preston NE), 1886 v W, Ni; 1887 v S, W, Ni; 1888 v S, W, Ni; 1889 v W (9)
Dewhurst, G. P. (Liverpool Ramblers), 1895 v W (1)
Dickinson, J. W. (Portsmouth), 1949 v N, F; 1950 v S, W, Ei, P, Bel, Ch, US, Sp; 1951 v Ni, W, Y; 1952 v W, Ni, S, A (2), I, Sw; 1953 v W, Ni, S, Bel, Arg, Ch, U, US; 1954 v W, Ni, S, R of E, H (2), Y, Bel, Sw, U; 1955 v Sp, P; 1956 v W, Ni, S, D, Sp; 1957 v W, Y, D (48)
Dimmock, J. H. (Tottenham H), 1921 v S; 1926 v W, Bel (3)
Ditchburn, E. G. (Tottenham H), 1949 v Sw, Se; 1953 v US; 1957 v W, Y, D (6)
Dix, R. W. (Derby Co), 1939 v N (1)
Dixon, J. A. (Notts Co), 1885 v W (1)
Dixon, K. M. (Chelsea), 1985 v M (sub), WG, US; 1986 v Ni, Is, M (sub), Pol (sub); 1987 v Se (8)
Dixon, L. M. (Arsenal), 1990 v Cz; 1991 v H, Pol, Ei (2), Cam, T, Arg; 1992 v G, T, Pol, Cz (sub); 1993 v Sp, N, T, Sm, T, Ho, US; 1994 v Sm (21)
Dobson, A. T. C. (Notts Co), 1882 v Ni; 1884 v S, W, Ni (4)
Dobson, C. F. (Notts Co), 1886 v Ni (1)
Dobson, J. M. (Burnley), 1974 v P, EG, Bul, Y; (with Everton), 1975 v Cz (5)
Doggart, A. G. (Corinthians), 1924 v Bel (1)
Dorigo, A. R. (Chelsea), 1990 v Y (sub), Cz (sub), D (sub), I; 1991 v H (sub), USSR; (with Leeds U), 1992 v G, Cz (sub), H, Br; 1993 v Sm, Pol, US, Br; 1994 v H (15)
Dorrell, A. R. (Aston Villa), 1925 v W, Bel, F; 1926 v Ni (4)
Douglas, B. (Blackburn R), 1958 v S, W, Ni, F, P, Y, USSR (2), Br, A; 1959 v S, USSR; 1960 v Y, H; 1961 v Ni, W, S, L, P, Sp, M, I, A; 1962 v W, Ni, S, Pe, L, P, H, Arg, Bul, Br; 1963 v S, Br, Sw (36)
Downs, R. W. (Everton), 1921 v Ni (1)
Doyle, M. (Manchester C), 1976 v W, S (sub), Br, I; 1977 v Ho (5)
Drake, E. J. (Arsenal), 1935 v Ni, I; 1936 v W; 1937 v H; 1938 v F (5)
Ducat, A. (Woolwich Arsenal), 1910 v S, W, Ni; (with Aston Villa), 1920 v S, W; 1921 v Ni (6)
Dunn, A. T. B. (Cambridge University), 1883 v Ni; 1884 v Ni; (with Old Etonians), 1892 v S, W (4)
Duxbury, M. (Manchester U), 1984 v L, F, W, S, USSR, Br, U, Ch; 1985 v EG, Fi (10)

Earle, S. G. J. (Clapton), 1924 v F; (with West Ham U), 1928 v Ni (2)
Eastham, G. (Arsenal), 1963 v Br, Cz, EG; 1964 v W, Ni, S, R of W, U, P, Ei, US, Br, Arg; 1965 v H, WG, Se; 1966 v Sp, Pol, D (19)
Eastham, G. R. (Bolton W), 1935 v Ho (1)
Eckersley, W. (Blackburn R), 1950 v Sp; 1951 v S, Y, Arg, P; 1952 v A (2), Sw; 1953 v Ni, Arg, Ch, U, US; 1954 v Ni, R of E, H (17)

Edwards, D. (Manchester U), 1955 v S, F, Sp, P; 1956 v S, Br, Se, Fi, WG; 1957 v S, Ni, Ei (2), D (2); 1958 v W, Ni, F (18)
Edwards, J. H. (Shropshire Wanderers), 1874 v S (1)
Edwards, W. (Leeds U), 1926 v S, W; 1927 v W, Ni, S, F, Bel, L; 1928 v S, F, Bel; 1929 v S, W, Ni; 1930 v W, Ni (16)
Ehiogu, U. (Aston Villa), 1996 v Chn (sub) (1)
Ellerington, W. (Southampton), 1949 v N, F (2)
Elliott, G. W. (Middlesbrough), 1913 v Ni; 1914 v Ni; 1920 v W (3)
Elliott, W. H. (Burnley), 1952 v I, A; 1953 v Ni, W, Bel (5)
Evans, R. E. (Sheffield U), 1911 v S, W, Ni; 1912 v W (4)
Ewer, F. H. (Casuals), 1924 v F; 1925 v Bel (2)

Fairclough, P. (Old Foresters), 1878 v S (1)
Fairhurst, D. (Newcastle U), 1934 v F (1)
Fantham, J. (Sheffield W), 1962 v L (1)
Fashanu, J. (Wimbledon), 1989 v Ch, S (2)
Felton, W. (Sheffield W), 1925 v F (1)
Fenton, M. (Middlesbrough), 1938 v S (1)
Fenwick, T. (QPR), 1984 v W (sub), S, USSR, Br, U, Ch; 1985 v Fi, S, M, US; 1986 v R, T, Ni, Eg, M, P, Mor, Pol, Arg; (with Tottenham H), 1988 v Is (sub) (20)
Ferdinand, L. (QPR), 1993 v Sm, Ho, N, US; 1994 v Pol, Sm; 1995 v US (sub); (with Newcastle U), 1996 v P, Bul, H (10)
Field, E. (Clapham Rovers), 1876 v S; 1881 v S (2)
Finney, T. (Preston NE), 1947 v W, Ni, Ei, Ho, F, P; 1948 v S, W, Ni, Bel, Se, I; 1949 v S, W, Ni, Se, N, F; 1950 v S, W, Ni, Ei, I, P, Bel, Ch, US, Sp; 1951 v W, S, Arg, P; 1952 v W, Ni, S, F, I, Sw, A; 1953 v W, Ni, S, Bel, Arg, Ch, U, US; 1954 v W, S, Bel, Sw, U, H, Y; 1955 v WG; 1956 v S, W, Ni, D, Sp; 1957 v S, W, Y, D (2), Ei (2); 1958 v W, S, F, P, Y, USSR (2); 1959 v Ni, USSR (76)
Fleming, H. J. (Swindon T), 1909 v S, H (2); 1910 v W, Ni; 1911 v W, Ni; 1912 v Ni; 1913 v S, W; 1914 v S (11)
Fletcher, A. (Wolverhampton W), 1889 v W; 1890 v W (2)
Flowers, R. (Wolverhampton W), 1955 v F; 1959 v S, W, I, Br, Pe, US, M (sub); 1960 v W, Ni, S, Se, Y, Sp, H; 1961 v Ni, W, S, L, P, Sp, M, I, A; 1962 v W, Ni, S, A, Sw, Pe, L, P, H, Arg, Bul, Br; 1963 v Ni, W, S, F (2), Sw; 1964 v Ei, US, P; 1965 v W, Ho, WG; 1966 v N (49)
Flowers, T. D. (Southampton), 1993 v Br; (with Blackburn R), 1994 v Gr; 1995 v Ng, U, J, Se, Br; 1996 v Chn (8)
Forman, Frank (Nottingham F), 1898 v S, Ni; 1899 v S, W, Ni; 1901 v S; 1902 v S, Ni; 1903 v W (9)
Forman, F. R. (Nottingham F), 1899 v S, W, Ni (3)
Forrest, J. H. (Blackburn R), 1884 v W; 1885 v S, W, Ni; 1886 v S, W; 1887 v S, W, Ni; 1889 v S; 1890 v Ni (11)
Fort, J. (Millwall), 1921 v Bel (1)
Foster, R. E. (Oxford University), 1900 v W; (with Corinthians), 1901 v W, Ni, S; 1902 v W (5)
Foster, S. (Brighton & HA), 1982 v Ni, Ho, K (3)
Foulke, W. J. (Sheffield U), 1897 v W (1)
Foulkes, W. A. (Manchester U), 1955 v Ni (1)
Fowler, R. B. (Liverpool), 1996 v Bul (sub), Cro, Chn (sub), Ho (sub), Sp (sub) (5)
Fox, F. S. (Millwall), 1925 v F (1)
Francis, G. C. J. (QPR), 1975 v Cz, P, W, S; 1976 v Sw, Cz, P, W, Ni, S, Br, Fi (12)
Francis, T. (Birmingham C), 1977 v Ho, L, S, Br; 1978 v Sw, L, I (sub), WG (sub), Br, W, S, H; (with Nottingham F), 1979 v Bul (sub), Se, A (sub); 1980 v Ni, Bul, Sp; 1981 v Sp, R, S (sub), Sw; (with Manchester C), 1982 v N, Ni, W, S (sub), Fi (sub), F, Cz, K, WG, Sp; (with Sampdoria), 1983 v D, Gr, H, Ni, S, Aus (3); 1984 v D, Ni, USSR; 1985 v EG, F (sub), Ni (sub), R, Fi, S, I, M; 1986 v S (52)
Franklin, C. F. (Stoke C), 1947 v S, W, Ni, Ei, Ho, F, Sw, P; 1948 v S, W, Ni, Bel, Se, I; 1949 v S, W, Ni, D, Sw, N, F, Se; 1950 v W, S, Ni, Ei, I (27)
Freeman, B. C. (Everton), 1909 v S, W; (with Burnley), 1912 v S, W, Ni (5)
Froggatt, J. (Portsmouth), 1950 v Ni, I; 1951 v S; 1952 v S, A (2), I, Sw; 1953 v Ni, W, S, Bel, US (13)
Froggatt, R. (Sheffield W), 1953 v W, S, Bel, US (4)
Fry, C. B. (Corinthians), 1901 v Ni (1)
Furness, W. I. (Leeds U), 1933 v I (1)

Galley, T. (Wolverhampton W), 1937 v N, Se (2)
Gardner, T. (Aston Villa), 1934 v Cz; 1935 v Ho (2)
Garfield, B. (WBA), 1898 v Ni (1)
Garratty, W. (Aston Villa), 1903 v W (1)
Garrett, T. (Blackpool), 1952 v S, I; 1954 v W (3)
Gascoigne, P. J. (Tottenham H), 1989 v D (sub), S.Ar (sub), Alb (sub), Ch, S (sub); 1990 v Se (sub), Br (sub), Cz, D, U, Tun, Ei, Ho, Eg, Bel, Cam, WG; 1991 v H, Pol, Cam; (with Lazio), 1993 v N, T, Sm, T, Ho, Pol, N; 1994 v Pol, D; 1995 v J (sub), Se (sub), Br (sub); (with Rangers), 1996 v Co, Sw, P, Bul, Cro, Chn, Sw, S, Ho, Sp, G (43)
Gates, E. (Ipswich T), 1981 v N, R (2)

Gay, L. H. (Cambridge University), 1893 v S; (with Old Brightonians), 1894 v S, W (3)
Geary, F. (Everton), 1890 v Ni; 1891 v S (2)
Geaves, R. L. (Clapham Rovers), 1875 v S (1)
Gee, C. W. (Everton), 1932 v W, Sp; 1937 v Ni (3)
Geldard, A. (Everton), 1933 v I, Sw; 1935 v S; 1938 v Ni (4)
George, C. (Derby Co), 1977 v Ei (1)
George, W. (Aston Villa), 1902 v S, W, Ni (3)
Gibbins, W. V. T. (Clapton), 1924 v F; 1925 v F (2)
Gidman, J. (Aston Villa), 1977 v L (1)
Gillard, I. T. (QPR), 1975 v WG, W; 1976 v Cz (3)
Gilliat, W. E. (Old Carthusians), 1893 v Ni (1)
Goddard, P. (West Ham U), 1982 v Ic (sub) (1)
Goodall, F. R. (Huddersfield T), 1926 v S; 1927 v S, F, Bel, L; 1928 v S, W, F, Bel; 1930 v S, G, A; 1931 v S, W, Ni, Bel; 1932 v Ni; 1933 v W, Ni, A, I, Sw; 1934 v W, Ni, F (25)
Goodall, J. (Preston NE), 1888 v S, W; 1889 v S, W; (with Derby Co), 1891 v S, W; 1892 v S; 1893 v W; 1894 v S; 1895 v S, Ni; 1896 v S, W; 1898 v W (14)
Goodhart, H. C. (Old Etonians), 1883 v S, W, Ni (3)
Goodwyn, A. G. (Royal Engineers), 1873 v S (1)
Goodyer, A. C. (Nottingham F), 1879 v S (1)
Gosling, R. C. (Old Etonians), 1892 v W; 1893 v S; 1894 v W; 1895 v W, S (5)
Gosnell, A. A. (Newcastle U), 1906 v Ni (1)
Gough, H. C. (Sheffield U), 1921 v S (1)
Goulden, L. A. (West Ham U), 1937 v Se, N; 1938 v W, Ni, Cz, G, Sw, F; 1939 v S, W, R of E, I, R, Y (14)
Graham, L. (Millwall), 1925 v S, W (2)
Graham, T. (Nottingham F), 1931 v F; 1932 v Ni (2)
Grainger, C. (Sheffield U), 1956 v Br, Se, Fi, WG; 1957 v W, Ni; (with Sunderland), 1957 v S (7)
Gray, A. A. (C Palace), 1992 v Pol (1)
Greaves, J. (Chelsea), 1959 v Pe, M, US; 1960 v W, Se, Y, Sp; 1961 v Ni, W, S, L, P, Sp, I, A; (with Tottenham H), 1962 v S, Sw, Pe, H, Arg, Bul, Br; 1963 v Ni, W, S, F (2), Br, Cz, Sw; 1964 v W, Ni, R of W, P (2), Ei, Br, U, Arg; 1965 v Ni, S, Bel, Ho, H, Y; 1966 v W, A, Y, N, D, Pol, U, M, F; 1967 v S, Sp, A (57)
Green, F. T. (Wanderers), 1876 v S (1)
Green, G. H. (Sheffield U), 1925 v F; 1926 v S, Bel, W; 1927 v W, Ni; 1928 v F, Bel (8)
Greenhalgh, E. H. (Notts Co), 1872 v S; 1873 v S (2)
Greenhoff, B. (Manchester U), 1976 v W, Ni; 1977 v Ei, Fi, I, Ho, Ni, W, S, Br, Arg, U; 1978 v Br, W, Ni, S (sub), H (sub); (with Leeds U), 1980 v Aus (sub) (18)
Greenwood, D. H. (Blackburn R), 1882 v S, Ni (2)
Gregory, J. (QPR), 1983 v Aus (3); 1984 v D, H, W (6)
Grimsdell, A. (Tottenham H), 1920 v S, W; 1921 v S, Ni; 1923 v W, Ni (6)
Grosvenor, A. T. (Birmingham), 1934 v Ni, W, F (3)
Gunn, W. (Notts Co), 1884 v S, W (2)
Gurney, R. (Sunderland), 1935 v S (1)

Hacking, J. (Oldham Ath), 1929 v S, W, Ni (3)
Hadley, N. (WBA), 1903 v Ni (1)
Hagan, J. (Sheffield U), 1949 v D (1)
Haines, J. T. W. (WBA), 1949 v Sw (1)
Hall, A. E. (Aston Villa), 1910 v Ni (1)
Hall, G. W. (Tottenham H), 1934 v F; 1938 v S, W, Ni, Cz; 1939 v S, Ni, R of E, I, Y (10)
Hall, J. (Birmingham C), 1956 v S, W, Ni, Br, Se, Fi, WG, D, Sp; 1957 v S, W, Ni, Y, D (2), Ei (2) (17)
Halse, H. J. (Manchester U), 1909 v A (1)
Hammond, H. E. D. (Oxford University), 1889 v S (1)
Hampson, J. (Blackpool), 1931 v Ni, W; 1933 v A (3)
Hampton, H. (Aston Villa), 1913 v S, W; 1914 v S, W (4)
Hancocks, J. (Wolverhampton W), 1949 v Sw; 1950 v W; 1951 v Y (3)
Hapgood, E. (Arsenal), 1933 v I, Sw; 1934 v S, Ni, W, H, Cz; 1935 v S, Ni, W, I, Ho; 1936 v S, Ni, W, G, A, Bel; 1937 v Fi; 1938 v S, G, Sw, F; 1939 v S, W, Ni, R of E, N, I, Y (30)
Hardinge, H. T. W. (Sheffield U), 1910 v S (1)
Hardman, H. P. (Everton), 1905 v W; 1907 v S, Ni; 1908 v W (4)
Hardwick, G. F. M. (Middlesbrough), 1947 v S, W, Ni, Ei, Ho, F, Sw, P; 1948 v S, W, Ni, Bel, Se (13)
Hardy, H. (Stockport Co), 1925 v Bel (1)
Hardy, S. (Liverpool), 1907 v S, W, Ni; 1908 v S; 1909 v S, W, Ni, H (2), A; 1910 v S, W, Ni; 1912 v Ni; (with Aston Villa), 1913 v S; 1914 v Ni, W, S; 1920 v S, W, Ni (21)
Harford, M. G. (Luton T), 1988 v Is (sub); 1989 v D (2)
Hargreaves, F. W. (Blackburn R), 1880 v W; 1881 v W; 1882 v Ni (3)
Hargreaves, J. (Blackburn R), 1881 v S, W (2)
Harper, E. C. (Blackburn R), 1926 v S (1)
Harris, G. (Burnley), 1966 v Pol (1)
Harris, P. P. (Portsmouth), 1950 v Ei; 1954 v H (2)
Harris, S. S. (Cambridge University), 1904 v S; (with Old Westminsters), 1905 v Ni, W; 1906 v S, W, Ni (6)

Harrison, A. H. (Old Westminsters), 1893 v S, Ni (2)
Harrison, G. (Everton), 1921 v Bel; 1922 v Ni (2)
Harrow, J. H. (Chelsea), 1923 v Ni, Se (2)
Hart, E. (Leeds U), 1929 v W; 1930 v W, Ni; 1933 v S, A; 1934 v S, H, Cz (8)
Hartley, F. (Oxford C), 1923 v F (1)
Harvey, A. (Wednesbury Strollers), 1881 v W (1)
Harvey, J. C. (Everton), 1971 v Ma (1)
Hassall, H. W. (Huddersfield T), 1951 v S, Arg, P; 1952 v F; (with Bolton W), 1954 v Ni (5)
Hateley, M. (Portsmouth), 1984 v USSR (sub), Br, U, Ch; (with AC Milan), 1985 v EG (sub), Fi, Ni, Ei, Fi, S, I, M; 1986 v R, T, Eg, S, M, Ca, P, Mor, Para (sub); 1987 v T (sub), Br (sub), S; (with Monaco), 1988 v WG (sub), Ho (sub), H (sub), Co (sub), Ei (sub), Ho (sub), USSR (sub); (with Rangers), 1992 v Cz (32)
Haworth, G. (Accrington), 1887 v Ni, W, S; 1888 v S; 1890 v S (5)
Hawtrey, J. P. (Old Etonians), 1881 v S, W (2)
Hawkes, R. M. (Luton T), 1907 v Ni; 1908 v A (2), H, B (5)
Haygarth, E. B. (Swifts), 1875 v S (1)
Haynes, J. N. (Fulham), 1955 v Ni; 1956 v S, Ni, Br, Se, Fi, WG, Sp; 1957 v W, Y, D, Ei (2); 1958 v W, Ni, S, F, P, Y, USSR (3), Br, A; 1959 v S, Ni, USSR, I, Br, Pe, M, US; 1960 v Ni, Y, Sp, H; 1961 v Ni, W, S, L, P, Sp, M, I, A; 1962 v W, Ni, S, A, Sw, Pe, P, H, Arg, Bul, Br (56)
Healless, H. (Blackburn R), 1925 v Ni; 1928 v S (2)
Hector, K. J. (Derby Co), 1974 v Pol (sub), I (sub) (2)
Hedley, G. A. (Sheffield U), 1901 v Ni (1)
Hegan, K. E. (Corinthians), 1923 v Bel, F; 1924 v Ni, Bel (4)
Hellawell, M. S. (Birmingham C), 1963 v Ni, F (2)
Henfrey, A. G. (Cambridge University), 1891 v Ni; (with Corinthians), 1892 v W; 1895 v W; 1896 v S, W (5)
Henry, R. P. (Tottenham H), 1963 v F (1)
Heron, F. (Wanderers), 1876 v S (1)
Heron, G. H. H. (Uxbridge), 1873 v S; 1874 v S; (with Wanderers), 1875 v S; 1876 v S; 1878 v S (5)
Hibbert, W. (Bury), 1910 v S (1)
Hibbs, H. E. (Birmingham), 1930 v S, W, A, G; 1931 v S, W, Ni; 1932 v W, Ni, Sp; 1933 v S, W, Ni, A, I, Sw; 1934 v Ni, W, F; 1935 v S, W, Ni, Ho; 1936 v G, W (25)
Hill, F. (Bolton W), 1963 v Ni, W (2)
Hill, G. A. (Manchester U), 1976 v I; 1977 v Ei (sub), Fi (sub), L; 1978 v Sw (sub), L (6)
Hill, J. H. (Burnley), 1925 v W; 1926 v S; 1927 v S, Ni, Bel, F; 1928 v Ni, W; (with Newcastle U), 1929 v F, Bel, Sp (11)
Hill, R. (Luton T), 1983 v D (sub), WG; 1986 v Eg (sub) (3)
Hill, R. H. (Millwall), 1926 v Bel (1)
Hillman, J. (Burnley), 1899 v Ni (1)
Hills, A. F. (Old Harrovians), 1879 v S (1)
Hilsdon, G. R. (Chelsea), 1907 v Ni; 1908 v S, W, Ni, A, H, B; 1909 v Ni (8)
Hine, E. W. (Leicester C), 1929 v W, Ni; 1930 v W, Ni; 1932 v W, Ni (6)
Hinton, A. T. (Wolverhampton W), 1963 v F; (with Nottingham F), 1965 v W, Bel (3)
Hirst, D. E. (Sheffield W), 1991 v Aus, Nz (sub); 1992 v F (3)
Hitchens, G. A. (Aston Villa), 1961 v M, I, A; (with Inter-Milan), 1962 v Sw, Pe, H, Br (7)
Hobbis, H. H. F. (Charlton Ath), 1936 v A, Bel (2)
Hoddle, G. (Tottenham H), 1980 v Bul, W, Aus, Sp; 1981 v Sp, W, S; 1982 v N, Ni, W, Ic, Cz (sub), K; 1983 v L (sub), Ni, S; 1984 v H, L, F; 1985 v Ei (sub), S, I (sub), M, WG, US; 1986 v R, T, Ni, Is, USSR, S, M, Ca, P, Mor, Pol, Para, Arg; 1987 v Se, Ni, Y, Sp, T, S; (with Monaco), 1988 v WG, T (sub), Y (sub), Ho (sub), H (sub), Co (sub), Ei (sub), Ho, USSR (53)
Hodge, S. B. (Aston Villa), 1986 v USSR (sub), S, Ca, P (sub), Mor (sub), Pol, Para, Arg; 1987 v Se, Ni, Y; (with Tottenham H), Sp, Ni, T, S; (with Nottingham F), 1989 v D; 1990 v I (sub), Y (sub), Cz, D, U, Tun; 1991 v Cam (sub), T (sub) (24)
Hodgetts, D. (Aston Villa), 1888 v S, W, Ni; 1892 v S, Ni; 1894 v Ni (6)
Hodgkinson, A. (Sheffield U), 1957 v S, Ei (2), D; 1961 v W (5)
Hodgson, G. (Liverpool), 1931 v S, Ni, W (3)
Hodkinson, J. (Blackburn R), 1913 v W, S; 1920 v Ni (3)
Hogg, W. (Sunderland), 1902 v S, W, Ni (3)
Holdcroft, G. H. (Preston NE), 1937 v W, Ni (2)
Holden, A. D. (Bolton W), 1959 v S, I, Br, Pe, M (5)
Holden, G. H. (Wednesbury OA), 1881 v S; 1884 v S, W, Ni (4)
Holden-White, C. (Corinthians), 1888 v W, S (2)
Holford, T. (Stoke), 1903 v Ni (1)
Holley, G. H. (Sunderland), 1909 v S, W, H (2), A; 1910 v W; 1912 v S, W, Ni; 1913 v S (10)
Holliday, E. (Middlesbrough), 1960 v W, Ni, Se (3)
Hollins, J. W. (Chelsea), 1967 v Sp (1)
Holmes, R. (Preston NE), 1888 v Ni; 1891 v S; 1892 v S; 1893 v S, W; 1894 v Ni; 1895 v Ni (7)

Lofthouse, J. M. (Blackburn R), 1885 v S, W, Ni; 1887 v S, W; (with Accrington), 1889 v Ni; (with Blackburn R), 1890 v Ni (7)
Lofthouse, N. (Bolton W), 1951 v Y; 1952 v W, Ni, S, A (2), I, Sw; 1953 v W, Ni, S, Bel, Arg, Ch, U, US; 1954 v W, Ni, R of E, Bel, U; 1955 v Ni, S, F, Sp, P; 1956 v W, S, Sp, D, Fi (sub); 1959 v W, USSR (33)
Longworth, E. (Liverpool), 1920 v S; 1921 v Bel; 1923 v S, W, Bel (5)
Lowder, A. (Wolverhampton W), 1889 v W (1)
Lowe, E. (Aston Villa), 1947 v F, Sw, P (3)
Lucas, T. (Liverpool), 1922 v Ni; 1924 v F; 1926 v Bel (3)
Luntley, E. (Nottingham F), 1880 v S, W (2)
Lyttelton, Hon. A. (Cambridge University), 1877 v S (1)
Lyttelton, Hon. E. (Cambridge University), 1878 v S (1)

McCall, J. (Preston NE), 1913 v S, W; 1914 v S; 1920 v S; 1921 v Ni (5)
McDermott, T. (Liverpool), 1978 v Sw, L; 1979 v Ni, W, Se; 1980 v D, Ni (sub), Ei, Ni, S, Bel (sub), Sp; 1981 v N, R, Sw, R (sub), Br, Sw (sub), H; 1982 v N, H, W (sub), Ho, S (sub), Ic (25)
McDonald, C. A. (Burnley), 1958 v USSR (3), Br, A; 1959 v W, Ni, USSR (8)
McFarland, R. L. (Derby Co), 1971 v Gr, Ma (2), Ni, S; 1972 v Sw, Gr, WG, W, S; 1973 v W (3), Ni, S, Cz, Pol, USSR, I; 1974 v A, Pol, I, W, Ni; 1976 v Cz, S; 1977 v Ei, I (28)
McGarry, W. H. (Huddersfield T), 1954 v Sw, U; 1956 v W, D (4)
McGuinness, W. (Manchester U), 1959 v Ni, M (2)
McInroy, A. (Sunderland), 1927 v Ni (1)
McMahon, S. (Liverpool), 1988 v Is, H, Co, USSR; 1989 v D (sub); 1990 v Se, Pol, I, Y (sub), Br, Cz (sub), D, Ei (sub), Eg, Bel, I; 1991 v Ei (17)
McManaman, S. (Liverpool), 1995 v Ng (sub), U (sub), J (sub); 1996 v Co, N, Sw, P (sub), Bul, Cro, Chn, Sw, S, Ho, Sp, G (15)
McNab, R. (Arsenal), 1969 v Ni, Bul, R (1+1 sub) (4)
McNeal, R. (WBA), 1914 v S, W (2)
McNeil, M. (Middlesbrough), 1961 v W, Ni, S, L, P, Sp, M, I; 1962 v L (9)
Mabbutt, G. (Tottenham H), 1983 v WG, Gr, L, W, Gr, H, Ni, S (sub); 1984 v H; 1987 v Y, Ni, T; 1988 v WG; 1992 v T, Pol, Cz (16)
Macaulay, R. H. (Cambridge University), 1881 v S (1)
Macdonald, M. (Newcastle U), 1972 v W, Ni, S (sub); 1973 v USSR (sub); 1974 v P, S (sub), W (sub); 1975 v WG, Cy (2), Ni; 1976 v Sw (sub), Cz, P (14)
Macrae, S. (Notts Co), 1883 v S, W, Ni; 1884 v S, W, Ni (6)
Maddison, F. B. (Oxford University), 1872 v S (1)
Madeley, P. E. (Leeds U), 1971 v Ni; 1972 v Sw (2), Gr, WG (2), W, S; 1973 v S, Cz, Pol, USSR, I; 1974 v A, Pol, I; 1975 v Cz, P, Cy; 1976 v Cz, P, Fi; 1977 v Ei, Ho (24)
Magee, T. P. (WBA), 1923 v W, Se; 1925 v S, Bel, F (5)
Makepeace, H. (Everton), 1906 v S; 1910 v S; 1912 v S, W (4)
Male, C. G. (Arsenal), 1935 v S, Ni, I, Ho; 1936 v S, W, Ni, G, A, Bel; 1937 v S, Ni, H, N, Se, Fi; 1939 v I, R, Y (19)
Mannion, W. J. (Middlesbrough), 1947 v S, W, Ni, Ei, Ho, F, Sw, P; 1948 v W, Ni, Bel, Se, I; 1949 v N, F; 1950 v S, Ei, P, Bel, Ch, US; 1951 v Ni, W, S, Y; 1952 v F (26)
Mariner, P. (Ipswich T), 1977 v L (sub), Ni; 1978 v L, W (sub), S; 1980 v W, Ni (sub), S, Aus, I (sub), Sp (sub); 1981 v N, Sw, Sp, Sw, H; 1982 v N, H, Ho, S, Fi, F, Cz, K, WG, Sp; 1983 v D, WG, Gr, W; 1984 v D, H, L; (with Arsenal), 1985 v EG, R (35)
Marsden, J. T. (Darwen), 1891 v Ni (1)
Marsden, W. (Sheffield W), 1930 v W, S, G (3)
Marsh, R. W. (QPR), 1972 v Sw (sub); (with Manchester C), WG (sub+1), W, Ni, S; 1973 v W (2), Y (9)
Marshall, T. (Darwen), 1880 v W; 1881 v W (2)
Martin, A. (West Ham U), 1981 v Br, S (sub); 1982 v H, Fi; 1983 v Gr, L, W, Gr, H; 1984 v H, L, W; 1985 v Ni; 1986 v Is, Ca, Para; 1987 v Se (17)
Martin, H. (Sunderland), 1914 v Ni (1)
Martyn, A. N. (C Palace), 1992 v C (sub), H; 1993 v G (3)
Marwood, B. (Arsenal), 1989 v S.Ar (sub) (1)
Maskrey, H. M. (Derby Co), 1908 v Ni (1)
Mason, C. (Wolverhampton W), 1887 v Ni; 1888 v W; 1890 v Ni (3)
Matthews, R. D. (Coventry C), 1956 v S, Br, Se, WG; 1957 v Ni (5)
Matthews, S. (Stoke C), 1935 v W, I; 1936 v G; 1937 v S; 1938 v S, W, Cz, G, Sw, F; 1939 v S, W, Ni, R of E, N, I, Y; 1947 v S; (with Blackpool), 1947 v Sw, P; 1948 v S, W, Ni, Bel, I; 1949 v S, W, Ni, D, Sw; 1950 v Sp; 1951 v Ni, S; 1954 v Ni, R of E, H, Bel, U; 1955 v Ni, W, S, F, WG, Sp, P; 1956 v W, Br; 1957 v S, W, Ni, Y, D (2), Ei (54)
Matthews, V. (Sheffield U), 1928 v F, Bel (2)
Maynard, W. J. (1st Surrey Rifles), 1872 v S; 1876 v S (2)
Meadows, J. (Manchester C), 1955 v S (1)

Medley, L. D. (Tottenham H), 1951 v Y, W; 1952 v F, A, W, Ni (6)
Meehan, T. (Chelsea), 1924 v Ni (1)
Melia, J. (Liverpool), 1963 v S, Sw (2)
Mercer, D. W. (Sheffield U), 1923 v Ni, Bel (2)
Mercer, J. (Everton), 1939 v S, Ni, I, R, Y (5)
Merrick, G. H. (Birmingham C), 1952 v Ni, S, A (2), I, Sw; 1953 v Ni, W, S, Bel, Arg, Ch, U; 1954 v W, Ni, S, R of E, H (2), Y, Bel, Sw, U (23)
Merson, P. C. (Arsenal), 1992 v G (sub), Cz, H, Br (sub), Fi (sub), D, Se (sub); 1993 v Sp (sub), N (sub), Ho (sub), Br (sub), G; 1994 v Ho, Gr (14)
Metcalfe, V. (Huddersfield T), 1951 v Arg, P (2)
Mew, J. W. (Manchester U), 1921 v Ni (1)
Middleditch, B. (Corinthians), 1897 v Ni (1)
Milburn, J. E. T. (Newcastle U), 1949 v S, W, Ni, Sw; 1950 v W, P, Bel, Sp; 1951 v W, Arg, P; 1952 v F; 1956 v D (13)
Miller, B. G. (Burnley), 1961 v A (1)
Miller, H. S. (Charlton Ath), 1923 v Se (1)
Mills, G. R. (Chelsea), 1938 v W, Ni, Cz (3)
Mills, M. D. (Ipswich T), 1973 v Y; 1976 v W (2), Ni, S, Br, I (sub), Fi; 1977 v Fi (sub), I, Ni, W, S; 1978 v WG, Br, W, Ni, S, H; 1979 v D, Ei, Ni (2), S, Bul, A; 1980 v D, Ni, Sp (2); 1981 v Sw (2), H; 1982 v N, H, S, Fi, F, Cz, K, WG, Sp (42)
Milne, G. (Liverpool), 1963 v Br, Cz, EG; 1964 v W, Ni, S, R of W, U, P, Ei, Br, Arg; 1965 v Ni, Bel (14)
Milton, C. A. (Arsenal), 1952 v A (1)
Milward, A. (Everton), 1891 v S, W; 1897 v S, W (4)
Mitchell, C. (Upton Park), 1880 v W; 1881 v S; 1883 v S, W; 1885 v W (5)
Mitchell, J. F. (Manchester C), 1925 v Ni (1)
Moffat, H. (Oldham Ath), 1913 v W (1)
Molyneux, G. (Southampton), 1902 v S; 1903 v S, W, Ni (4)
Moon, W. R. (Old Westminsters), 1888 v S, W; 1889 v S, W; 1890 v S, W; 1891 v S (7)
Moore, H. T. (Notts Co), 1883 v Ni; 1885 v W (2)
Moore, J. (Derby Co), 1923 v Se (1)
Moore, R. F. (West Ham U), 1962 v Pe, H, Arg, Bul, Br; 1963 v W, Ni, S, F (2), Br, Cz, EG, Sw; 1964 v W, Ni, S, R of W, U, P (2), Ei, Br, Arg; 1965 v Ni, S, Bel, H, Y, WG, Se; 1966 v W, Ni, S, A, Sp, Pol (2), WG (2), N, D, U, M, F, Arg, P; 1967 v W, Ni, S, Cz, Sp, A; 1968 v W, Ni, S, USSR (2), Sp (2), Se, Y, WG; 1969 v Ni, W, S, R, Bul, F, M, U, Br; 1970 v W, Ni, S, Ho, P, Bel, Co, Ec, R, Br, Cz, WG; 1971 v EG, Gr, Ma, Ni, S; 1972 v Sw (2), Gr, WG (2), W, S; 1973 v W (3), Y, S (2), Ni, Cz, Pol, USSR, I; 1974 v I (108)
Moore, W. G. B. (West Ham U), 1923 v Se (1)
Mordue, J. (Sunderland), 1912 v Ni; 1913 v Ni (2)
Morice, C. J. (Barnes), 1872 v S (1)
Morley, A. (Aston Villa), 1982 v H (sub), Ni, W, Ic; 1983 v D, Gr (6)
Morley, H. (Notts Co), 1910 v Ni (1)
Morren, T. (Sheffield U), 1898 v Ni (1)
Morris, F. (WBA), 1920 v S; 1921 v Ni (2)
Morris, J. (Derby Co), 1949 v N, F; 1950 v Ei (3)
Morris, W. W. (Wolverhampton W), 1939 v S, Ni, R (3)
Morse, H. (Notts Co), 1879 v S (1)
Mort, T. (Aston Villa), 1924 v W, F; 1926 v S (3)
Morten, A. (C Palace), 1873 v S (1)
Mortensen, S. H. (Blackpool), 1947 v P; 1948 v W, S, Ni, Bel, Se, I; 1949 v S, W, Ni, Se, N; 1950 v S, W, Ni, I, P, Bel, Ch, US, Sp; 1951 v S, Arg; 1954 v R of E, H (25)
Morton, J. R. (West Ham U), 1938 v Cz (1)
Mosforth, W. (Sheffield W), 1877 v S; (with Sheffield Albion), 1878 v S; 1879 v S, W; 1880 v S, W; (with Sheffield W), 1881 v W; 1882 v S, W (9)
Moss, F. (Arsenal), 1934 v S, H, Cz; 1935 v I (4)
Moss, F. (Aston Villa), 1922 v S, Ni; 1923 v Ni; 1924 v S, Bel (5)
Mosscrop, E. (Burnley), 1914 v S, W (2)
Mozley, B. (Derby Co), 1950 v W, Ni, Ei (3)
Mullen, J. (Wolverhampton W), 1947 v S; 1949 v N, F; 1950 v Bel (sub), Ch, US; 1954 v W, Ni, S, R of E, Y, Sw (12)
Mullery, A. P. (Tottenham H), 1965 v Ho; 1967 v Sp, A; 1968 v W, Ni, S, USSR, Sp (2), Se, Y; 1969 v Ni, S, R, Bul, F, M, U, Br; 1970 v W, Ni, S (sub), Ho (sub), Bel, P, Co, Ec, R, Cz, WG, Br; 1971 v Ma, EG, Gr; 1972 v Sw (35)

Neal, P. G. (Liverpool), 1976 v W, I; 1977 v W, S, Br, Arg, U; 1978 v Sw, I, WG, Ni, S, H; 1979 v D, Ei, Ni (2), S, Bul, A; 1980 v D, Ni, Sp, Arg, W, Bel, I; 1981 v R, Sw, Sp, Br, H; 1982 v N, H, W, Ho, Ic, F (sub), K; 1983 v D, Gr, L, W, Gr, H, Ni, S, Aus (2); 1984 v D (50)
Needham, E. (Sheffield U), 1894 v S; 1895 v S; 1897 v S, W, Ni; 1898 v S, W; 1899 v S, W, Ni; 1900 v S, Ni; 1901 v S, W, Ni; 1902 v W (16)
Neville, G. A. (Manchester U), 1995 v J, Br; 1996 v Co, N, Sw, P, Bul, Cro, H, Chn, Sw, S, Ho, Sp (14)
Neville, P. J. (Manchester U), 1996 v Chn (1)

Stephenson, C. (Huddersfield T), 1924 v W (1)
Stephenson, G. T. (Derby Co), 1928 v F, Bel; (with Sheffield W), 1931 v F (3)
Stephenson, J. E. (Leeds U), 1938 v S; 1939 v Ni (2)
Stepney, A. C. (Manchester U), 1968 v Se (1)
Sterland, M. (Sheffield W), 1989 v S.Ar (1)
Steven, T. M. (Everton), 1985 v Ni, Ei, R, Fi, I, US (sub); 1986 v T (sub), Eg, USSR (sub), M (sub), Pol, Para, Arg; 1987 v Se, Y (sub), Sp (sub); 1988 v T, Y, Ho, H, S, Sw, Ho, USSR; 1989 v S; (with Rangers), 1990 v Cz, Cam (sub), WG (sub), I; 1991 v Cam; (with Marseille), 1992 v G, C, Br, Fi, D, F (36)
Stevens, G. A. (Tottenham H), 1985 v Fi (sub), T (sub), Ni; 1986 v S (sub), M (sub), Mor (sub), Para (sub) (7)
Stevens, M. G. (Everton), 1985 v I, WG; 1986 v R, T, Ni, Eg, Is, S, Ca, P, Mor, Pol, Para, Arg; 1987 v Br, S; 1988 v T, Y, Is, Ho, H (sub), S, Sw, Ei, Ho, USSR; (with Rangers), 1989 v D, Se, Gr, Alb (2), S, Pol; 1990 v Se, Pol, I, Br, D, Tun, Ei, I; 1991 v USSR; 1992 v C, H, Br, Fi (46)
Stewart, J. (Sheffield W), 1907 v S, W; (with Newcastle U), 1911 v S (3)
Stewart, P. A. (Tottenham H), 1992 v G (sub), Cz (sub), C (sub) (3)
Stiles, N. P. (Manchester U), 1965 v S, H, Y, Se; 1966 v W, Ni, S, A, Sp, Pol (2), WG (2), N, D, U, M, F, Arg, P; 1967 v Ni, W, S, Cz; 1968 v USSR; 1969 v R; 1970 v Ni, S (28)
Stoker, J. (Birmingham), 1933 v W; 1934 v S, H (3)
Stone, S. B. (Nottingham F), 1996 v N (sub), Sw (sub), P, Bul, Cro, Chn (sub), Sw (sub), S (sub), Sp (sub) (9)
Storer, H. (Derby Co), 1924 v F; 1928 v Ni (2)
Storey, P. E. (Arsenal), 1971 v Gr, Ni, S; 1972 v Sw, WG, W, Ni, S; 1973 v W (3), Y, S (2), Ni, Cz, Pol, USSR, I (19)
Storey-Moore, I. (Nottingham F), 1970 v Ho (1)
Strange, A. H. (Sheffield W), 1930 v S, A, G; 1931 v S, W, Ni, F, Bel; 1932 v S, W, Ni, Sp; 1933 v S, Ni, A, I, Sw; 1934 v Ni, W, F (20)
Stratford, A. H. (Wanderers), 1874 v S (1)
Streten, B. (Luton T), 1950 v Ni (1)
Sturgess, A. (Sheffield U), 1911 v Ni; 1914 v S (2)
Summerbee, M. G. (Manchester C), 1968 v S, Sp, WG; 1972 v Sw, WG (sub), W, Ni; 1973 v USSR (sub) (8)
Sunderland, A. (Arsenal), 1980 v Aus (1)
Sutcliffe, J. W. (Bolton W), 1893 v W; 1895 v S, Ni; 1901 v S; (with Millwall), 1903 v W (5)
Swan, P. (Sheffield W), 1960 v Y, Sp, H; 1961 v Ni, W, S, L, P, Sp, M, I, A; 1962 v W, Ni, S, A, Sw, L, P (19)
Swepstone, H. A. (Pilgrims), 1880 v S; 1882 v S, W; 1883 v S, W, Ni (6)
Swift, F. V. (Manchester C), 1947 v S, W, Ni, Ei, Ho, F, Sw, P; 1948 v S, W, Ni, Bel, Se, I; 1949 v S, W, Ni, D, N (19)

Tait, G. (Birmingham Excelsior), 1881 v W (1)
Talbot, B. (Ipswich T), 1977 v Ni (sub), S, Br, Arg, U; (with Arsenal), 1980 v Aus (6)
Tambling, R. V. (Chelsea), 1963 v W, F; 1966 v Y (3)
Tate, J. T. (Aston Villa), 1931 v F, Bel; 1933 v W (3)
Taylor, E. (Blackpool), 1954 v H (1)
Taylor, E. H. (Huddersfield T), 1923 v S, W, Ni, Bel; 1924 v S, Ni, F; 1926 v S (8)
Taylor, J. G. (Fulham), 1951 v Arg, P (2)
Taylor, P. H. (Liverpool), 1948 v W, Ni, Se (3)
Taylor, P. J. (C Palace), 1976 v W (sub+1), Ni, S (4)
Taylor, T. (Manchester U), 1953 v Arg, Ch, U; 1954 v Bel, Sw; 1956 v S, Br, Se, Fi, WG; 1957 v Ni, Y (sub), D (2), Ei (2); 1958 v W, Ni, F (19)
Temple, D. W. (Everton), 1965 v WG (1)
Thickett, H. (Sheffield U), 1899 v S, W (2)
Thomas, D. (Coventry), 1983 v Aus (1+1 sub) (2)
Thomas, D. (QPR), 1975 v Cz (sub), P, Cy (sub+1), W, S (sub); 1976 v Cz (sub), P (sub) (8)
Thomas, G. R. (C Palace), 1991 v T, USSR, Arg, Aus, Nz (2), Mal; 1992 v Pol, F (9)
Thomas, M. L. (Arsenal), 1989 v S.Ar; 1990 v Y (2)
Thompson, P. (Liverpool), 1964 v P (2), Ei, US, Br, Arg; 1965 v Ni, W, S, Bel, Ho; 1966 v Ni; 1968 v Ni, WG; 1970 v S, Ho (sub) (16)
Thompson, P. B. (Liverpool), 1976 v W (2), Ni, S, Br, I, Fi; 1977 v Fi; 1979 v Ei (sub), Cz, Ni, S, Bul, Se (sub), A; 1980 v D, Ni, Bul, Ei, Sp (2), Arg, W, S, Bel, I; 1981 v N, R, H; 1982 v H, W, Ho, S, Fi, F, Cz, K, WG, Sp; 1983 v WG, Gr (42)
Thompson T. (Aston Villa), 1952 v W; (with Preston NE), 1957 v S (2)
Thomson, R. A. (Wolverhampton W), 1964 v Ni, US, P, Arg; 1965 v Bel, Ho, Ni, W (8)
Thornewell, G. (Derby Co), 1923 v Se (2); 1924 v F; 1925 v F (4)
Thornley, I. (Manchester C), 1907 v W (1)
Tilson, S. F. (Manchester C), 1934 v H, Cz; 1935 v W; 1936 v Ni (4)
Titmuss, F. (Southampton), 1922 v W; 1923 v W (2)

Todd, C. (Derby Co), 1972 v Ni; 1974 v P, W, Ni, S, Arg, EG, Bul, Y; 1975 v P (sub), WG, Cy (2), Ni, W, S; 1976 v Sw, Cz, P, Ni, S, Br, Fi; 1977 v Ei, Fi, Ho (sub), Ni (27)
Toone, G. (Notts Co), 1892 v S, W (2)
Topham, A. G. (Casuals), 1894 v W (1)
Topham, R. (Wolverhampton W), 1893 v Ni; (with Casuals) 1894 v W (2)
Towers, M. A. (Sunderland), 1976 v W, Ni (sub), I (3)
Townley, W. J. (Blackburn R), 1889 v W; 1890 v Ni (2)
Townrow, J. E. (Clapton Orient), 1925 v S; 1926 v W (2)
Tremelling, D. R. (Birmingham), 1928 v W (1)
Tresadern, J. (West Ham U), 1923 v S, Se (2)
Tueart, D. (Manchester C), 1975 v Cy (sub), Ni; 1977 v Fi, Ni, W (sub), S (sub) (6)
Tunstall, F. E. (Sheffield U), 1923 v S; 1924 v S, W, Ni, F; 1925 v Ni, S (7)
Turnbull, R. J. (Bradford), 1920 v Ni (1)
Turner, A. (Southampton), 1900 v Ni; 1901 v Ni (2)
Turner, H. (Huddersfield T), 1931 v F, Bel (2)
Turner, J. A. (Bolton W), 1893 v W; (with Stoke C) 1895 v Ni; (with Derby Co) 1898 v Ni (3)
Tweedy, G. J. (Grimsby T), 1937 v H (1)

Ufton, D. G. (Charlton Ath), 1954 v R of E (1)
Underwood A. (Stoke C), 1891 v Ni; 1892 v Ni (2)
Unsworth, D. G. (Everton), 1995 v J (1)
Urwin, T. (Middlesbrough), 1923 v Se (2); 1924 v Bel; (with Newcastle U), 1926 v W (4)
Utley, G. (Barnsley), 1913 v Ni (1)

Vaughton, O. H. (Aston Villa), 1882 v S, W, Ni; 1884 v S, W (5)
Veitch, C. C. M. (Newcastle U), 1906 v S, W, Ni; 1907 v S, W; 1909 v W (6)
Veitch, J. G. (Old Westminsters), 1894 v W (1)
Venables, T. F. (Chelsea), 1965 v Ho, Bel (2)
Venison, B. (Newcastle U), 1995 v US, U (2)
Vidal, R. W. S. (Oxford University), 1873 v S (1)
Viljoen, C. (Ipswich T), 1975 v Ni, W (2)
Viollet, D. S. (Manchester U), 1960 v H; 1962 v L (2)
Von Donop (Royal Engineers), 1873 v S; 1875 v S (2)

Wace, H. (Wanderers), 1878 v S; 1879 v W (3)
Waddle, C. R. (Newcastle U), 1985 v Ei, R (sub), Fi (sub), S (sub), I, M (sub), WG, US; (with Tottenham H), 1986 v R, T, Ni, Is, USSR, S, M, Ca, P, Mor, Pol (sub), Arg (sub); 1987 v Se (sub); Ni (2), Y, Sp, T, Br, S; 1988 v WG, Is, H, S (sub), Co, Sw (sub), Fi, Ho (sub); 1989 v Se, S.Ar, Alb (2), Ch, S, Pol, D (sub); (with Marseille), 1990 v Se, Pol, I, Y, Br, D, U, Tun, Ei, Ho, Eg, Bel, Cam, WG, I (sub); 1991 v H (sub), Pol (sub); 1992 v T (62)
Wadsworth, S. J. (Huddersfield T), 1922 v S; 1923 v S, Bel; 1924 v S, Ni; 1925 v S, Ni; 1926 v W; 1927 v Ni (9)
Wainscoat, W. R. (Leeds U), 1929 v S (1)
Waiters, A. K. (Blackpool), 1964 v Ei, Br; 1965 v W, Bel, Ho (5)
Walker, D. S. (Nottingham F), 1989 v D (sub), Se (sub), Gr, Alb (2), Ch, S, Pol, D; 1990 v Se, Pol, I, Y, Br, Cz, D, U, Tun, Ei, Ho, Eg, Bel, Cam, WG, I; 1991 v H, Pol, Ei (2), Cam, T, Arg, Aus, Nz (2), Mal; 1992 v T, Pol, F, Cz, C, H, Br, Fi, D, F, Se; (with Sampdoria), 1993 v Sp, N, T, Sm, T, Ho, Pol, N, US (sub), Br, G; (with Sheffield W), 1994 v Sm (59)
Walker, I. M. (Tottenham H), 1996 v H (sub), Chn (sub) (2)
Walden, F. I. (Tottenham H), 1914 v S; 1922 v W (2)
Walker, W. H. (Aston Villa), 1921 v Ni; 1922 v Ni, W, S; 1923 v Se (2); 1924 v S; 1925 v Ni, W, S, Bel, F; 1926 v Ni, W, S; 1927 v Ni, W; 1933 v A (18)
Wall, G. (Manchester U), 1907 v W; 1908 v Ni; 1909 v S; 1910 v S; 1912 v S; 1913 v Ni (7)
Wallace, C. W. (Aston Villa), 1913 v W; 1914 v Ni; 1920 v S (3)
Wallace, D. L. (Southampton), 1986 v Eg (1)
Walsh, P. (Luton T), 1983 v Aus (2 + 1 sub); 1984 v F, W (5)
Walters, A. M. (Cambridge University), 1885 v S, N; 1886 v S; 1887 v S, W; (with Old Carthusians), 1889 v S, W; 1890 v S, W (9)
Walters, K. M. (Rangers), 1991 v Nz (1)
Walters, P. M. (Oxford University), 1885 v S, Ni; (with Old Carthusians), 1886 v S, W, Ni; 1887 v S, W; 1888 v S, Ni; 1889 v S; 1890 v S, W (13)
Walton, N. (Blackburn R), 1890 v Ni (1)
Ward, J. T. (Blackburn Olympic), 1885 v W (1)
Ward, P. (Brighton & HA), 1980 v Aus (sub) (1)
Ward, T. V. (Derby Co), 1948 v Bel; 1949 v W (2)
Waring, T. (Aston Villa), 1931 v F, Bel; 1932 v S, W, Ni (5)
Warner, C. (Upton Park), 1878 v S (1)
Warren, B. (Derby Co), 1906 v S, W, Ni; 1907 v S, W, Ni; 1908 v S, W, Ni, A (2), H, B; (with Chelsea), 1909 v S, Ni, W, H (2), A; 1911 v S, Ni, W (22)
Waterfield, G. S. (Burnley), 1927 v W (1)

NORTHERN IRELAND

Aherne, T. (Belfast C), 1947 v E; 1948 v S; 1949 v W; (with Luton T), 1950 v W (4)
Alexander, A. (Cliftonville), 1895 v S (1)
Allen, C. A. (Cliftonville), 1936 v E (1)
Allen, J. (Limavady), 1887 v E (1)
Anderson, T. (Manchester U), 1973 v Cy, E, S, W; 1974 v Bul, P; (with Swindon T), 1975 v S (sub); 1976 v Is; 1977 v Ho, Bel, WG, E, S, W, Ic; 1978 v Ic, Ho, Bel; (with Peterborough U), S, E, W; 1979 v D (sub) (22)
Anderson, W. (Linfield), 1898 v W, E, S; 1899 v S (4)
Andrews, W. (Glentoran), 1908 v S; (with Grimsby T), 1913 v E, S (3)
Armstrong, G. (Tottenham H), 1977 v WG, E, W (sub), Ic (sub); 1978 v Bel, S, E, W; 1979 v Ei, D, Bul, E, Bul, E, S, W, D; 1980 v E, Ei, Is, S, E, W, Aus (3); 1981 v Se; (with Watford), P, S, P, S, Se; 1982 v S, Is, E, F, W, Y, Hon, Sp, A, F; 1983 v A, T, Alb, S, E, W; (with Real Mallorca), 1984 v A, WG, E, W, Fi; 1985 v R, Fi, E, Sp; (with WBA), 1986 v T, R (sub), E (sub), F (sub); (with Chesterfield), D (sub), Br (sub) (63)

Baird, G. (Distillery), 1896 v S, E, W (3)
Baird, H. (Huddersfield T), 1939 v E (1)
Balfe, J. (Shelbourne), 1909 v E; 1910 v W (2)
Bambrick, J. (Linfield), 1929 v W, S, E; 1930 v W, S, E; 1932 v W; (with Chelsea), 1935 v W; 1936 v E, S; 1938 v W (11)
Banks, S. J. (Cliftonville), 1937 v W (1)
Barr, H. H. (Linfield), 1962 v E; (with Coventry C), 1963 v E, Pol (3)
Barron, H. (Cliftonville), 1894 v E, W, S; 1895 v S; 1896 v S; 1897 v E, W (7)
Barry, H. (Bohemians), 1900 v S (1)
Baxter, R. A. (Cliftonville), 1887 v S, W (2)
Bennett, L. V. (Dublin University), 1889 v W (1)
Berry, J. (Cliftonville), 1888 v S, W; 1889 v E (3)
Best, G. (Manchester U), 1964 v W, U; 1965 v E, Ho (2), S, Sw (2), Alb; 1966 v S, E, Alb; 1967 v E; 1968 v S; 1969 v E, S, W, T; 1970 v S, E, W, USSR; 1971 v Cy (2), Sp, E, S, W; 1972 v USSR, Sp; 1973 v Bul; 1974 v P; (with Fulham), 1977 v Ho, Bel, WG; 1978 v Ic, Ho (37)
Bingham, W. L. (Sunderland), 1951 v F; 1952 v E, S, W; 1953 v E, S, F, W; 1954 v E, S, W; 1955 v E, S, W; 1956 v E, S, W; 1957 v E, S, W, P (2), I; 1958 v S, E, W, I (2), Arg, Cz (2), WG, F; (with Luton T), 1959 v E, S, W, Sp; 1960 v S, E, W; (with Everton), 1961 v E, S, W, WG (2), Gr, I; 1962 v E, Gr; 1963 v E, S, Pol (2), Sp; (with Port Vale), 1964 v S, E, Sp (56)
Black, J. (Glentoran), 1901 v E (1)
Black, K. (Luton T), 1988 v Fr (sub), Ma (sub); 1989 v Ei, H, Sp (2), Ch (sub); 1990 v H, N, U; 1991 v Y (2), D, A, Pol, Fa; (with Nottingham F), 1992 v Fa, A, D, S, Li, G; 1993 v Sp, D (sub), Alb, Ei (sub), Sp; 1994 v D (sub), Ei (sub), R (sub) (30)
Blair, H. (Portadown), 1931 v S; 1932 v S; (with Swansea), 1934 v S (3)
Blair, J. (Cliftonville), 1907 v W, E, S; 1908 v E, S (5)
Blair, R. V. (Oldham Ath), 1975 v Se (sub), S (sub), W; 1976 v Se, Is (5)
Blanchflower, R. D. (Barnsley), 1950 v S, W; 1951 v E, S; (with Aston Villa), F; 1952 v W; 1953 v E, S, W, F; 1954 v E, S, W; 1955 v E, S (with Tottenham H), W; 1956 v E, S, W; 1957 v E, S, W, I, P (2); 1958 v E, S, W, I (2), Cz (2), Arg, F, WG; 1959 v E, S, W, Sp; 1960 v E, S, W; 1961 v E, S, W, WG (2); 1962 v E, S, W, Gr, Ho; 1963 v E, S, Pol (2) (56)
Blanchflower, J. (Manchester U), 1954 v W; 1955 v E, S; 1956 v S, W; 1957 v S, E, P; 1958 v S, E, I (2) (12)
Bookman, L. O. (Bradford C), 1914 v W; (with Luton T), 1921 v S, W; 1922 v E (4)
Bothwell, A. W. (Ards), 1926 v S, E, W; 1927 v E, W (5)
Bowler, G. C. (Hull C), 1950 v E, S, W (3)
Boyle, P. (Sheffield U), 1901 v E; 1902 v E; 1903 v S, W; 1904 v E (5)
Braithwaite, R. S. (Linfield), 1962 v W; 1963 v P, Sp; (with Middlesbrough), 1964 v W, U; 1965 v E, S, Sw (2), Ho (10)
Breen, T. (Belfast C), 1935 v E, W; 1937 v E, W; (with Manchester U), 1937 v W; 1938 v E, S; 1939 v W, S (9)
Brennan, B. (Bohemians), 1912 v W (1)
Brennan, R. A. (Luton T), 1949 v W; (with Birmingham C), 1950 v E, S, W; (with Fulham), 1951 v E (5)
Briggs, W. R. (Manchester U), 1962 v W; (with Swansea T), 1965 v Ho (2)
Brisby, D. (Distillery), 1891 v S (1)
Brolly, T. (Millwall), 1937 v W; 1938 v W; 1939 v E, W (4)
Brookes, E. A. (Shelbourne), 1920 v S (1)
Brotherston, N. (Blackburn R), 1980 v S, E, W, Aus (3); 1981 v Se, P; 1982 v S, Is, E, F, S, W, Hon (sub), A (sub);

1983 v A (sub), WG, Alb, T, Alb, S (sub), E (sub), W; 1984 v T; 1985 v Is (sub), T (27)
Brown, J. (Glenavon), 1921 v W; (with Tranmere R), 1924 v E, W (3)
Brown, J. (Wolverhampton W), 1935 v E, W; 1936 v E; (with Coventry C), 1937 v E, W; 1938 v S, W; (with Birmingham C), 1939 v E, S, W (10)
Brown, W. G. (Glenavon), 1926 v W (1)
Brown, W. M. (Limavady), 1887 v E (1)
Browne, F. (Cliftonville), 1887 v E, S, W; 1888 v E, S (5)
Browne, R. J. (Leeds U), 1936 v E, W; 1938 v E, W; 1939 v E, S (6)
Bruce, W. (Glentoran), 1961 v S; 1967 v W (2)
Buckle, H. (Cliftonville), 1882 v E (1)
Buckle, H. R. (Sunderland), 1904 v E; (with Bristol R), 1908 v W (2)
Burnett, J. (Distillery), 1894 v E, W, S; (with Glentoran), 1895 v E, W (5)
Burnison, J. (Distillery), 1901 v E, W (2)
Burnison, S. (Distillery), 1908 v E; 1910 v E, S; (with Bradford), 1911 v E, S, W; (with Distillery), 1912 v E; 1913 v W (8)
Burns, J. (Glenavon), 1923 v E (1)
Butler, M. P. (Blackpool), 1939 v W (1)

Campbell, A. C. (Crusaders), 1963 v W; 1965 v Sw (2)
Campbell, D. A. (Nottingham F), 1986 v Mor (sub), Br; 1987 v E (2), T, Y; (with Charlton Ath), 1988 v Y, T (sub), Gr (sub), Pol (sub) (10)
Campbell, J. (Cliftonville), 1896 v W; 1897 v E, S, W; (with Distillery), 1898 v E, S, W; (with Cliftonville), 1899 v E; 1900 v E, S; 1901 v S, W; 1902 v S; 1903 v E; 1904 v S (15)
Campbell, J. P. (Fulham), 1951 v E, S (2)
Campbell, R. (Bradford C), 1982 v S, W (sub) (2)
Campbell, W. G. (Dundee), 1968 v S, E; 1969 v T; 1970 v S, W, USSR (6)
Carey, J. J. (Manchester U), 1947 v E, S, W; 1948 v E; 1949 v E, S, W (7)
Carroll, E. (Glenavon), 1925 v S (1)
Casey, T. (Newcastle U), 1955 v W; 1956 v W; 1957 v E, S, W, I, P (2); 1958 v WG, F; (with Portsmouth), 1959 v E, Sp (12)
Cashin, M. (Cliftonville), 1898 v S (1)
Caskey, W. (Derby Co), 1979 v Bul, E, Bul, E, D (sub); 1980 v E (sub); (with Tulsa R), 1982 v F (sub) (7)
Cassidy, T. (Newcastle U), 1971 v E (sub); 1972 v USSR (sub); 1974 v Bul (sub), S, E, W; 1975 v N; 1976 v S, E, W; 1977 v WG (sub); 1980 v E, Ei (sub), Is, S, E, W, Aus (3); (with Burnley), 1981 v Se, P; 1982 v Is, Sp (sub) (24)
Caughey, M. (Linfield), 1986 v F (sub), D (sub) (2)
Chambers, J. (Distillery), 1921 v W; (with Bury), 1928 v E, S, W; 1929 v E, S, W; 1930 v S, W; (with Nottingham F), 1932 v E, S, W (12)
Chatton, H. A. (Partick T), 1925 v E, S; 1926 v E (3)
Christian, J. (Linfield), 1889 v S (1)
Clarke, C. J. (Bournemouth), 1986 v F, D, Mor, Alg (sub), Sp, Br; (with Southampton), 1987 v E, T, Y; 1988 v Y, T, Gr, Pol, F, Ma; 1989 v Ei, H, Sp (1+1 sub); (with QPR), Ma, Ch; 1990 v H, Ei, N; (with Portsmouth), 1991 v Y (sub), D, A, Pol, Y (sub), Fa; 1992 v Fa, D, S, G; 1993 v Alb, Sp, D (38)
Clarke, R. (Belfast C), 1901 v E, S (2)
Cleary, J. (Glentoran), 1982 v S, W; 1983 v W (sub); 1984 v T (sub); 1985 v Is (5)
Clements, D. (Coventry C), 1965 v W, Ho; 1966 v M; 1967 v S, W; 1968 v S, E; 1969 v T (2), S, W; 1970 v S, E, W, USSR (2); 1971 v Sp, E, S, W, Cy; (with Sheffield W), 1972 v USSR (2), Sp, E, S, W; 1973 v Bul, Cy (2), P, E, S, W; (with Everton), 1974 v Bul, P, S, E, W; 1975 v N, Y, E, S, W; 1976 v Se, Y; (with New York Cosmos), W (48)
Clugston, J. (Cliftonville), 1888 v W; 1889 v W, S, E; 1890 v E, S; 1891 v W; 1892 v E, S, W; 1893 v E, S, W (14)
Cochrane, D. (Leeds U), 1939 v E, W; 1947 v E, S, W; 1948 v E, S, W; 1949 v S, W; 1950 v S, E (12)
Cochrane, M. (Distillery), 1898 v S, W, E; 1899 v E; 1900 v E, S, W; (with Leicester Fosse), 1901 v S (8)
Cochrane, T. (Coleraine), 1976 v N (sub); (with Burnley), 1978 v S (sub), E (sub), W (sub); 1979 v Ei (sub); (with Middlesbrough), D, Bul, E, Bul, E; 1980 v Is, E (sub), W (sub), Aus (1+2 sub); 1981 v Se (sub), P (sub), S, P, S, Se; 1982 v E (sub), F; (with Gillingham), 1984 v S, Fi (sub) (26)
Collins, F. (Celtic), 1922 v S (1)
Condy, J. (Distillery), 1887 v W; 1886 v E, S (3)
Connell, T. (Coleraine), 1978 v W (sub) (1)
Connor, J. (Glentoran), 1901 v S, E; (with Belfast C), 1905 v E, S, W; 1907 v E, S; 1908 v E, S; 1909 v W; 1911 v S, E, W (13)

Gara, A. (Preston NE), 1902 v E, S, W (3)
Gardiner, A. (Cliftonville), 1930 v S, W; 1931 v S; 1932 v E, S (5)
Garrett, J. (Distillery), 1925 v W (1)
Gaston, R. (Oxford U), 1969 v Is (sub) (1)
Gaukrodger, G. (Linfield), 1895 v W (1)
Gaussen, A. W. (Moyola Park), 1884 v E, S; 1888 v E, W; 1889 v E, W (6)
Geary, J. (Glentoran), 1931 v S; 1932 v S (2)
Gibb, J. T. (Wellington Park) 1884 v S, W; 1885 v S, E, W; 1886 v S; 1887 v S, E, W; 1889 v S (10)
Gibb, T. J. (Cliftonville), 1936 v W (1)
Gibson W. K. (Cliftonville), 1894 v S, W, E; 1895 v S; 1897 v W; 1898 v S, W, E; 1901 v S, W, E; 1902 v S, W (13)
Gillespie, K.R. (Manchester U), 1995 v P, A, Ei; (with Newcastle U) Ei, La, Ca, Ch (sub), La (sub); 1996 v P, A, N, G (12)
Gillespie, R. (Hertford), 1886 v E, S, W; 1887 v E, S, W (6)
Gillespie, W. (Sheffield U), 1913 v E, S; 1914 v E, W; 1920 v S, W; 1921 v E; 1922 v E, S, W; 1923 v E, S, W; 1924 v E, S, W; 1925 v E, S; 1926 v S, W; 1927 v E, W; 1928 v E; 1929 v E; 1931 v E (25)
Gillespie, W. (West Down), 1889 v W (1)
Goodall, A. L. (Derby Co), 1899 v S, W; 1900 v E, W; 1901 v E; 1902 v S; 1903 v E, W; (with Glossop), 1904 v E, W (10)
Goodbody, M. F. (Dublin University), 1889 v E; 1891 v W (2)
Gordon, H. (Linfield), 1891 v S; 1892 v E, S, W; 1893 v E, S, W; 1895 v E, W; 1896 v E, S (11)
Gordon, T. (Linfield), 1894 v W; 1895 v E (2)
Gorman, W. C. (Brentford), 1947 v E, S, W; 1948 v W (4)
Gowdy, J. (Glentoran), 1920 v E; (with Queen's Island), 1924 v W; (with Falkirk), 1926 v E, S; 1927 v E, S (6)
Gowdy, W. A. (Hull C), 1932 v S; (with Sheffield W), 1933 v S; (with Linfield), 1935 v E, S, W; (with Hibernian), 1936 v W (6)
Graham, W. G. L. (Doncaster R), 1951 v W, F; 1952 v E, S, W; 1953 v S, F; 1954 v E, W; 1955 v S, W; 1956 v E, S; 1959 v E (14)
Gray, P. (Luton T), 1993 v D (sub), Alb, Ei, Sp; (with Sunderland), 1994 v La, D, Ei, R, Lie (sub); 1995 v P, A, Ei, Ca, Ch (sub); 1996 v P (sub), Lie, A (17)
Greer, W. (QPR), 1909 v E, S, W (3)
Gregg, H. (Doncaster R), 1954 v W; 1957 v E, S, W, I, P (2); 1958 v E, I; (with Manchester U), 1958 v Cz, Arg, WG, F, W; 1959 v E, W; 1960 v S, E, W; 1961 v E, S; 1962 v S, Gr; 1964 v S, E (25)
Griffin, D. J. (St Johnstone), 1996 v G (1)

Hall, G. (Distillery), 1897 v E (1)
Halligan, W. (Derby Co), 1911 v W; (with Wolverhampton W), 1912 v E (2)
Hamill, M. (Manchester U), 1912 v E; 1914 v E, S; (with Belfast C), 1920 v E, S, W; (with Manchester C), 1921 v S (7)
Hamilton, B. (Linfield), 1969 v T; 1971 v Cy (2), E, S, W; (with Ipswich T), 1972 v USSR (1+1 sub), Sp; 1973 v Bul, Cy (2), P, E, S, W; 1974 v Bul, S, E, W; 1975 v N, Se, Y, E; 1976 v Se, N, Y; (with Everton), Is, S, E, W; 1977 v Ho, Bel, WG, E, S, W, Ic; (with Millwall), 1978 v S, E, W; 1979 v Ei (sub); (with Swindon T), Bul (2), E, S, W, D; 1980 v Aus (2 sub) (50)
Hamilton, J. (Knock), 1882 v E, W (2)
Hamilton, R. (Distillery), 1908 v W (1)
Hamilton, R. (Rangers), 1928 v S; 1929 v E; 1930 v S, E; 1932 v S (5)
Hamilton, W. (QPR), 1978 v S (sub); (with Burnley), 1980 v S, E, W, Aus (2); 1981 v Se, P, S, P, S, Se; 1982 v S, Is, E, W, Y, Hon, Sp, A, F; 1983 v A, WG, Alb (2), S, E, W; 1984 v A, T, WG, S, E, W, Fi; (with Oxford U), 1985 v R, Sp; 1986 v Mor (sub), Alg, Sp (sub), Br (sub) (41)
Hamilton, W. D. (Dublin Association), 1885 v W (1)
Hamilton, W. J. (Dublin Association), 1885 v W (1)
Hampton, H. (Bradford C), 1911 v E, S, W; 1912 v E, W; 1913 v E, S, W; 1914 v E (9)
Hanna, D. R. A. (Portsmouth), 1899 v W (1)
Hanna, J. (Nottingham F), 1912 v S, W (2)
Hannon, D. J. (Bohemians), 1908 v E, S; 1911 v E, S; 1912 v W; 1913 v E (6)
Harkin, J. T. (Southport), 1968 v W; 1969 v T; (with Shrewsbury T), W (sub); 1970 v USSR; 1971 v Sp (5)
Harland, A. I. (Linfield), 1923 v E (1)
Harris, J. (Cliftonville), 1921 v W (1)
Harris, V. (Shelbourne), 1906 v E; 1907 v E, W; 1908 v E, W, S; (with Everton), 1909 v E, W, S; 1910 v E, S, W; 1911 v E, S, W; 1912 v E; 1913 v E, S; 1914 v S, W (20)
Harvey, M. (Sunderland), 1961 v I; 1962 v Ho; 1963 v W, Sp; 1964 v S, E, W, U, Sp; 1965 v E, S, W, Sw (2), Ho (2), Alb; 1966 v S, E, W, M, Alb, WG; 1967 v E, S; 1968 v E, W; 1969 v Is, T (2), E; 1970 v USSR; 1971 v Cy, W (sub) (34)

Hastings, J. (Knock), 1882 v E, W; (with Ulster), 1883 v W; 1884 v E, S; 1886 v E, S (7)
Hatton, S. (Linfield), 1963 v S, Pol (2)
Hayes, W. E. (Huddersfield T), 1938 v E, S; 1939 v E, S (4)
Healy, F. (Coleraine), 1982 v S, W, Hon (sub); (with Glentoran), 1983 v A (sub) (4)
Hegan, D. (WBA), 1970 v USSR; (with Wolverhampton W), 1972 v USSR, E, S, W; 1973 v Bul, Cy (7)
Hehir, J. C. (Bohemians), 1910 v W (1)
Henderson, A. W. (Ulster), 1885 v E, S, W (3)
Hewison, G. (Moyola Park), 1885 v E, S (2)
Hill, C. F. (Sheffield U), 1990 v N, U; 1991 v Pol, Y; 1992 v A, D; (with Leicester C) 1995 v Ei, La; 1996 v P, Lie, A, N, Se, G (14)
Hill, M. J. (Norwich C), 1959 v W; 1960 v W; 1961 v WG; 1962 v S; (with Everton), 1964 v S, E, Sp (7)
Hinton, E. (Fulham), 1947 v S, W; 1948 v S, E, W; (with Millwall), 1951 v W, F (7)
Hopkins, J. (Brighton), 1926 v E (1)
Horlock, K. (Swindon T), 1995 v La, Ca (2)
Houston, J. (Linfield), 1912 v S, W; 1913 v W; (with Everton), 1913 v E, S; 1914 v S (6)
Houston, W. (Linfield), 1933 v W (1)
Houston, W. G. (Moyola Park), 1885 v E, S (2)
Hughes, M. E. (Manchester C), 1992 v D, S, Li, G; (with Strasbourg), 1993 v Alb, Sp, D, Ei, Sp, Li, La; 1994 v La, D, Ei, R, Lie, Co, M; 1995 v P, A, Ei (2) La, Ca, Ch, La; 1996 v P, Lie, A, N, G (31)
Hughes, P. (Bury), 1987 v E, T, Is (3)
Hughes, W. (Bolton W), 1951 v W (1)
Humphries, W. (Ards), 1962 v W; (with Coventry C), 1962 v Ho; 1963 v E, S, W, Pol, Sp; 1964 v S, E, Sp; 1965 v S; (with Swansea T), 1965 v W, Ho, Alb (14)
Hunter, A. (Distillery), 1905 v W; 1906 v W, E, S; (with Belfast C), 1908 v W; 1909 v W, E, S (8)
Hunter, A. (Blackburn R), 1970 v USSR; 1971 v Cy (2), E, S, W; (with Ipswich T), 1972 v USSR (2), Sp, E, S, W; 1973 v Bul, Cy (2), P, E, S, W; 1974 v Bul, S, E, W; 1975 v N, Se, Y, E, S, W; 1976 v Se, N, Y, Is, S, E, W; 1977 v Ho, Bel, WG, E, S, W, Ic; 1978 v Ic, Ho, Bel; 1979 v Ei, D, S, W, D; 1980 v Ei (53)
Hunter, B.V. (Wrexham), 1995 v La; 1996 v P, Lie, A, Se, G (6)
Hunter, R. J. (Cliftonville), 1884 v E, S, W (3)
Hunter, V. (Coleraine), 1962 v E; 1964 v Sp (2)

Irvine, R. J. (Linfield), 1962 v Ho; 1963 v E, S, W, Pol (2), Sp; (with Stoke C), 1965 v W (8)
Irvine, R. W. (Everton), 1922 v S; 1923 v E, W; 1924 v E, S; 1925 v E; 1926 v E; 1927 v E, W; 1928 v S; (with Portsmouth), 1929 v E; 1930 v S; (with Connah's Quay), 1931 v E; (with Derry C), 1932 v W (15)
Irvine, W. J. (Burnley), 1963 v W, Sp; 1965 v S, W, Sw, Ho (2), Alb; 1966 v S, E, W, M, Alb; 1967 v E, S; 1968 v E, W; (with Preston NE), 1969 v Is, T, E; (with Brighton), 1972 v E, S, W (23)
Irving, S. J. (Dundee), 1923 v S, W; 1924 v S, E, W; 1925 v S, E, W; 1926 v S, W; (with Cardiff C), 1927 v S, E, W; 1928 v S, E, W; (with Chelsea), 1929 v E; 1931 v W (18)

Jackson, T. (Everton), 1969 v Is, E, S, W; 1970 v USSR (1+1 sub); (with Nottingham F), 1971 v Sp; 1972 v E, S, W; 1973 v Cy, E, S, W; 1974 v Bul, P, S (sub), W (sub); 1975 v N (sub), Se, Y, E, S, W; (with Manchester U); 1976 v Se, N, Y; 1977 v Ho, Bel, WG, E, S, W, Ic (35)
Jamison, J. (Glentoran), 1976 v N (1)
Jennings, P. A. (Watford), 1964 v W, U; (with Tottenham H), 1965 v E, S, Sw (2), Ho, Alb; 1966 v S, E, W, Alb, WG; 1967 v S; 1968 v S, E, W; 1969 v Is, T (2), E, S, W; 1970 v S, E, USSR (2); 1971 v Cy (2), E, S, W; 1972 v USSR, Sp, S, E, W; 1973 v Bul, Cy, P, E, S, W; 1974 v P, S, E, W; 1975 v N, Se, Y, E, S, W; 1976 v N, Y, Is, S, E, W; 1977 v Ho, Bel, WG, E, S, W, Ic; (with Arsenal), 1978 v Ic, Ho, Bel; 1979 v Ei, D, Bul, E, Bul, E, S, W, D; 1980 v E, Ei, Is; 1981 v S, P, S, Se; 1982 v S, Is, E, W, Y, Hon, Sp, F; 1983 v Alb, S, E, W; 1984 v A, T, WG, S, W, Fi; 1985 v R, Fi, E, Sp, T; (with Tottenham H), 1986 v T, R, E, F, D, Mor, Alg, Sp, Br (119)
Johnston, H. (Portadown), 1927 v W (1)
Johnston, R. (Old Park), 1885 v S, W (2)
Johnston, S. (Distillery), 1882 v W; 1884 v E; 1886 v E, S (4)
Johnston, S. (Linfield), 1890 v W; 1893 v S, W; 1894 v E (4)
Johnston, S. (Distillery), 1905 v W (1)
Johnston, W. C. (Glenavon), 1962 v W; (with Oldham Ath), 1966 v M (sub) (2)
Jones, J. (Linfield), 1930 v S, W; 1931 v S, W, E; 1932 v S, E; 1933 v S, E, W; 1934 v S, E, W; 1935 v S, E, W; 1936 v E, S; (with Hibernian), 1936 v W; 1937 v E, W, S; (with Glenavon), 1938 v E (23)
Jones, J. (Glenavon), 1956 v W; 1957 v E, W, S (3)

Jones, S. (Distillery), 1934 v E; (with Blackpool), 1934 v W (2)
Jordan, T. (Linfield), 1895 v E, W (2)

Kavanagh, P. J. (Celtic), 1930 v E (1)
Keane, T. R. (Swansea T), 1949 v S (1)
Kearns, A. (Distillery), 1900 v E, S, W; 1902 v E, S, W (6)
Kee, P. V. (Oxford U), 1990 v N; 1991 v Y (2), D, A, Pol, Fa; (with Ards), 1995 v A, Ei (9)
Keith, R. M. (Newcastle U), 1958 v E, W, Cz (2), Arg, I, WG, F; 1959 v E, S, W, Sp; 1960 v S, E; 1961 v S, E, W, I, WG (2), Gr; 1962 v W, Ho (23)
Kelly, H. R. (Fulham), 1950 v E, W; (with Southampton), 1951 v E, S (4)
Kelly, J. (Glentoran), 1896 v E (1)
Kelly, J. (Derry C), 1932 v E, W; 1933 v E, W, S; 1934 v W; 1936 v E, S, W; 1937 v S, E (11)
Kelly, P. (Manchester C), 1921 v E (1)
Kelly, P. M. (Barnsley), 1950 v S (1)
Kennedy, A. L. (Arsenal), 1923 v W; 1925 v E (2)
Kernaghan, N. (Belfast C), 1936 v W; 1937 v S; 1938 v E (3)
Kirkwood, H. (Cliftonville), 1904 v W (1)
Kirwan, J. (Tottenham H), 1900 v W; 1902 v E, W; 1903 v E, S, W; 1904 v E, S, W; 1905 v E, S, W; (with Chelsea), 1906 v E, S, W; 1907 v W; (with Clyde), 1909 v S (17)

Lacey, W. (Everton), 1909 v E, S, W; 1910 v E, S, W; 1911 v E, S, W; 1912 v E; (with Liverpool), 1913 v W; 1914 v E, S, W; 1920 v E, S, W; 1921 v E, S, W; 1922 v E, S; (with New Brighton), 1925 v E (23)
Lawther, W. I. (Sunderland), 1960 v W; 1961 v I; (with Blackburn R), 1962 v S, Ho (4)
Leatham, J. (Belfast C), 1939 v W (1)
Ledwidge, J. J. (Shelbourne), 1906 v S, W (2)
Lemon, J. (Glentoran), 1886 v W; 1888 v S; (with Belfast YMCA), 1889 v W (3)
Lennon, N. F. (Crewe Alex), 1994 v M (sub); 1995 v Ch; 1996 v P, Lie, A; (with Leicester C), v N (6)
Leslie, W. (YMCA), 1887 v E (1)
Lewis, J. (Glentoran), 1899 v S, E, W; (with Distillery), 1900 v S (4)
Little, J. (Glentoran), 1898 v W (1)
Lockhart, H. (Rossall School), 1884 v W (1)
Lockhart, N. (Linfield), 1947 v E; (with Coventry C), 1950 v W; 1951 v W; 1952 v W; (with Aston Villa), 1954 v S, E; 1955 v W; 1956 v W (8)
Lomas, S. M. (Manchester C), 1994 v R, Lie, Co (sub), M (sub); 1995 v P, A; 1996 v P, Lie, A, N, Se, G (12)
Lowther, R. (Glentoran), 1888 v E, S (2)
Loyal, J. (Clarence), 1891 v S (1)
Lutton, R. J. (Wolverhampton W), 1970 v S, E; (with West Ham U), 1973 v Cy (sub), S (sub), W (sub); 1974 v P (6)
Lyner, D. (Glentoran), 1920 v E, W; 1922 v S, W; (with Manchester U), 1923 v E; (with Kilmarnock), 1923 v W (6)

McAdams, W. J. (Manchester C), 1954 v W; 1955 v S; 1957 v E; 1958 v S, I; (with Bolton W), 1961 v E, S, W, I, WG (2), Gr; 1962 v E, Gr; (with Leeds U), Ho (15)
McAlery, J. M. (Cliftonville), 1882 v E, W (2)
McAlinden, J. (Belfast C), 1938 v S; 1939 v S; (with Portsmouth), 1947 v E; (with Southend U), 1949 v E (4)
McAllen, J. (Linfield), 1898 v E; 1899 v E, S, W; 1900 v E, S, W; 1901 v W; 1902 v S (9)
McAlpine, W. J. (Cliftonville), 1901 v S (1)
McArthur, A. (Distillery), 1886 v W (1)
McAuley, J. L. (Huddersfield T), 1911 v E, W; 1912 v E, S; 1913 v E, S (6)
McAuley, P. (Belfast C), 1900 v S (1)
McBride, S. (Glenavon), 1991 v D (sub), Pol (sub); 1992 v Fa (sub), D (4)
McCabe, J. J. (Leeds U), 1949 v S, W; 1950 v E; 1951 v W; 1953 v W; 1954 v S (6)
McCabe, W. (Ulster), 1891 v E (1)
McCambridge, J. (Ballymena), 1930 v S, W; (with Cardiff C), 1931 v W; 1932 v E (4)
McCandless, J. (Bradford), 1912 v W; 1913 v W; 1920 v W, S; 1921 v E (5)
McCandless, W. (Linfield), 1920 v E, W; 1921 v E; (with Rangers), 1921 v W; 1922 v S; 1924 v W, S; 1925 v S; 1929 v W (9)
McCann, P. (Belfast C), 1910 v E, S, W; 1911 v E; (with Glentoran), 1911 v S; 1912 v E; 1913 v W (7)
McCarthy, J. D. (Port Vale), 1996 v Se (1)
McCashin, J. (Cliftonville), 1896 v W; 1898 v S, W; 1899 v S (4)
McCavana, W. T. (Coleraine), 1955 v S; 1956 v E, S (3)
McCaw, D. (Distillery), 1882 v E (1)
McCaw, J. H. (Linfield), 1927 v W; 1930 v S; 1931 v E, S, W (5)
McClatchey, J. (Distillery), 1886 v E, S, W (3)

McClatchey, R. (Distillery), 1895 v S (1)
McCleary, J. W. (Cliftonville), 1955 v W (1)
McCleery, W. (Linfield), 1930 v E, W; 1931 v E, S, W; 1932 v S, W; 1933 v E, W (9)
McClelland, J. (Arsenal), 1961 v W, I, WG (2), Gr; (with Fulham), 1966 v M (6)
McClelland, J. (Mansfield T), 1980 v S (sub), Aus (3); 1981 v Se, S; (with Rangers), S, Se (sub); 1982 v S, W, Y, Hon, Sp, A, F; 1983 v A, WG, Alb, T, Alb, S, E, W; 1984 v A, T, WG, S, E, W, Fi; 1985 v R, Is; (with Watford), Fi, E, Sp, T; 1986 v T, F (sub); 1987 v E (2), T, Is, Y; 1988 v T, Gr, F, Ma; 1989 v Ei, H, Sp (2), Ma; (with Leeds U), 1990 v N (53)
McCluggage, A. (Bradford), 1924 v E; (with Burnley), 1927 v S, W; 1928 v S, E, W; 1929 v S, E, W; 1930 v W; 1931 v E, W (12)
McClure, G. (Cliftonville), 1907 v S, W; 1908 v E; (with Distillery), 1909 v E (4)
McConnell, E. (Cliftonville), 1904 v S, W; (with Glentoran), 1905 v S; (with Sunderland), 1906 v E; 1907 v E; 1908 v S, W; (with Sheffield W), 1909 v S, W; 1910 v S, W, E (12)
McConnell, P. (Doncaster R), 1928 v W; (with Southport), 1932 v E (2)
McConnell, W. G. (Bohemians), 1912 v W; 1913 v E, S; 1914 v E, S, W (6)
McConnell, W. H. (Reading), 1925 v W; 1926 v E, W; 1927 v E, S, W; 1928 v E, W (8)
McCourt, F. J. (Manchester C), 1952 v E, W; 1953 v E, S, W, F (6)
McCoy, J. (Distillery), 1896 v W (1)
McCoy, R. (Coleraine), 1987 v Y (sub) (1)
McCracken, R. (C Palace), 1921 v E; 1922 v E, S, W (4)
McCracken, W. (Distillery), 1902 v E, W; 1903 v E; 1904 v E, S, W; (with Newcastle U), 1905 v E, S, W; 1907 v E; 1920 v E; 1922 v E, S, W; (with Hull C), 1923 v S (15)
McCreery, D. (Manchester U), 1976 v S (sub), E, W; 1977 v Ho, Bel, WG, E, S, W, Ic; 1978 v Ic, Ho, Bel, S, E, W; 1979 v Ei, D, Bul, E, Bul, W, D; (with QPR), 1980 v E, Ei, S (sub), E (sub), W (sub), Aus (1+1 sub); 1981 v Se (sub), P (sub); (with Tulsa R), S, P, Se; 1982 v S, Is, E (sub), F, Y, Hon, Sp, A, F; (with Newcastle U), 1983 v A; 1984 v T (sub); 1985 v R, Sp (sub); 1986 v T (sub), R, E, F, D, Alg, Sp, Br; 1987 v T, E, Y; 1988 v Y; 1989 v Sp, Ma, Ch; (with Hearts), 1990 v H, Ei, N, U (sub) (67)
McCrory, S. (Southend U), 1958 v E (1)
McCullough, K. (Belfast C), 1935 v W; 1936 v E; (with Manchester C), 1936 v S; 1937 v E, S (5)
McCullough, W. J. (Arsenal), 1961 v I; 1963 v Sp; 1964 v S, E, W, U, Sp; 1965 v E, Sw; (with Millwall), 1967 v E (10)
McCurdy, C. (Linfield), 1980 v Aus (sub) (1)
McDonald, A. (QPR), 1986 v R, E, F, D, Mor, Alg, Sp, Br; 1987 v E (2), T, Is, Y; 1988 v Y, T, Pol, F, Ma; 1989 v Ei, H, Sp, Ch; 1990 v H, Ei, U; 1991 v Y, D, A, Fa; 1992 v Fa, S, Li, G; 1993 v Alb, Sp, D, Alb, Ei, Sp, Li, La; 1994 v D, Ei; 1995 v P, A, Ei, La, Ca, Ch, La; 1996 v A (sub), N (52)
McDonald, R. (Rangers), 1930 v S; 1932 v E (2)
McDonnell, J. (Bohemians), 1911 v E, S; 1912 v W; 1913 v W (4)
McElhinney, G. (Bolton W), 1984 v WG, S, E, W, Fi; 1985 v R (6)
McFaul, W. S. (Linfield), 1967 v E (sub); (with Newcastle U), 1970 v W; 1971 v Sp; 1972 v USSR; 1973 v Cy; 1974 v Bul (6)
McGarry, J. K. (Cliftonville), 1951 v W, F, S (3)
McGaughey, M. (Linfield), 1985 v Is (sub) (1)
McGee, G. (Wellington Park), 1885 v E, S, W (3)
McGibbon, P. C. G. (Manchester U), 1995 v Ca (sub), Ch, La; 1996 v Lie (sub) (4)
McGrath, R. C. (Tottenham H), 1974 v S, E, W; 1975 v N; 1976 v Is (sub); 1977 v Ho; (with Manchester U), Bel, WG, E, S, W, Ic; 1978 v Ic, Ho, Bel, S, E, W; 1979 v Bul (sub), E (2 sub) (21)
McGregor, S. (Glentoran), 1921 v S (1)
McGrillen, J. (Clyde), 1924 v S; (with Belfast C), 1927 v S (2)
McGuire, E. (Distillery), 1907 v S (1)
McIlroy, H. (Cliftonville), 1906 v E (1)
McIlroy, J. (Burnley), 1952 v E, S, W; 1953 v E, S, W; 1954 v E, S, W; 1955 v E, S, W; 1956 v S, W; 1957 v E, S, W, I, P (2); 1958 v E, S, W, I (2), Cz (2), Arg, WG, F; 1959 v E, S, W, Sp; 1960 v E, S, W; 1961 v E, W, WG (2), Gr; 1962 v E, S, Gr, Ho; 1963 v E, S, Pol (2); (with Stoke C), 1963 v W; 1966 v S, E, Alb (55)
McIlroy, S. B. (Manchester U), 1972 v Sp, S (sub); 1974 v S, E, W; 1975 v N, Se, Y, E, S, W; 1976 v Se, N, Y, S, E, W; 1977 v Ho, Bel, WG, E, S, W, Ic; 1978 v Ic, Ho, Bel, S, E, W; 1979 v Ei, D, Bul, E, Bul, E, S, W, D; 1980 v E, Ei, Is, S, E, W; 1981 v Se, P, S, P, Se; 1982 v S, Is; (with Stoke C), E, F, S, W, Y, Hon, Sp, A, F; 1983 v A, WG, Alb, T, Alb, S, E, W; 1984 v A, T, S, E, W, Fi; 1985 v Fi, E, T; (with

Manchester C), 1986 v T, R, E, F, D, Mor, Alg, Sp, Br; 1987 v E (sub) (88)

McIlvenny, J. (Distillery), 1890 v E; 1891 v E (2)

McIlvenny, P. (Distillery), 1924 v W (1)

McKeag, W. (Glentoran), 1968 v S, W (2)

McKee, F. W. (Cliftonville), 1906 v S, W; (with Belfast C), 1914 v E, S, W (5)

McKelvie, H. (Glentoran), 1901 v W (1)

McKenna, J. (Huddersfield), 1950 v E, S, W; 1951 v E, S, F; 1952 v E (7)

McKenzie, H. (Distillery), 1923 v S (1)

McKenzie, R. (Airdrie), 1967 v W (1)

McKeown, H. (Linfield), 1892 v E, S, W; 1893 v S, W; 1894 v S, W (7)

McKie, H. (Cliftonville), 1895 v E, S, W (3)

McKinney, D. (Hull C), 1921 v S; (with Bradford C), 1924 v S (2)

McKinney, V. J. (Falkirk), 1966 v WG (1)

McKnight, A. (Celtic), 1988 v Y, T, Gr, Pol, F, Ma; (with West Ham U) 1989 v Ei, H, Sp (2) (10)

McKnight, J. (Preston NE), 1912 v S; (with Glentoran), 1913 v S (2)

McLaughlin, J. C. (Shrewsbury T), 1962 v E, S, W, Gr; 1963 v W; (with Swansea T), 1964 v W, U; 1965 v E, W, Sw (2); 1966 v W (12)

McLean, T. (Limavady), 1885 v S (1)

McMahon, G. J. (Tottenham H), 1995 v Ca (sub), Ch, La; 1996 v Lie, N (sub), Se, G (7)

McMahon, J. (Bohemians), 1934 v S (1)

McMaster, G. (Glentoran), 1897 v E, S, W (3)

McMichael, A. (Newcastle U), 1950 v E, S; 1951 v E, S, F; 1952 v E, S, W; 1953 v E, S, W, F; 1954 v E, S, W; 1955 v E, W; 1956 v W; 1957 v E, S, W, I, P (2); 1958 v E, S, W, I (2), Cz (2), Arg, WG, F; 1959 v S, W, Sp; 1960 v E, S, W (40)

McMillan, G. (Distillery), 1903 v E; 1905 v W (2)

McMillan, S. (Manchester U), 1963 v E, S (2)

McMillen, W. S. (Manchester U), 1934 v E; 1935 v S; 1937 v S; (with Chesterfield), 1938 v S, W; 1939 v E, S (7)

McMordie, A. S. (Middlesbrough), 1969 v Is, T (2), E, S, W; 1970 v E, S, W, USSR; 1971 v Cy (2), E, S, W; 1972 v USSR, Sp, E, S, W; 1973 v Bul (21)

McMorran, E. J. (Belfast C), 1947 v E; (with Barnsley), 1951 v E, S, W; 1952 v E, S, W; 1953 v E, S, F; (with Doncaster R), 1953 v W; 1954 v E; 1956 v W; 1957 v I, P (15)

McMullan, D. (Liverpool), 1926 v E, W; 1927 v S (3)

McNally, B. A. (Shrewsbury T), 1986 v Mor; 1987 v T (sub); 1988 v Y, Gr, Ma (sub) (5)

McNinch, J. (Ballymena), 1931 v S; 1932 v S, W (3)

McParland, P. J. (Aston Villa), 1954 v W; 1955 v E, S; 1956 v E, S; 1957 v E, S, W, P; 1958 v E, S, W, I (2), Cz (2), Arg, WG, F; 1959 v E, S, W, Sp; 1960 v E, S, W; 1961 v E, S, W, I, WG (2), Gr; (with Wolverhampton W), 1962 v Ho (34)

McShane, J. (Cliftonville), 1899 v S; 1900 v E, S, W (4)

McVickers, J. (Glentoran), 1888 v E; 1889 v S (2)

McWha, W. B. R. (Knock), 1882 v E, W; (with Cliftonville), 1883 v E, W; 1884 v E; 1885 v E, W (7)

Macartney, A. (Ulster), 1903 v S, W; (with Linfield), 1904 v S, W; (with Everton), 1905 v E, S; (with Belfast C), 1907 v E, S, W; 1908 v E, S, W; (with Glentoran), 1909 v E, S, W (15)

Mackie, J. (Arsenal), 1923 v W; (with Portsmouth), 1935 v S, W (3)

Madden, O. (Norwich C), 1938 v E (1)

Magill, E. J. (Arsenal), 1962 v E, S, Gr; 1963 v E, S, W, Pol (2), Sp; 1964 v E, S, W, U, Sp; 1965 v E, S, Sw (2), Ho, Alb; 1966 v S, (with Brighton), E, Alb, W, WG, M (26)

Magilton, J. (Oxford U), 1991 v Pol, Y, Fa; 1992 v Fa, A, D, S, Li, G; 1993 v Alb, D, Alb, Ei, Li, La; 1994 v La, D, Ei;(with Southampton), R, Lie, Co, M; 1995 v P, A, Ei (2), Ca, Ch, La; 1996 v P, N, G (32)

Maginnis, H. (Linfield), 1900 v E, S, W; 1903 v S, W; 1904 v E, S, W (8)

Maguire, E. (Distillery), 1907 v S (1)

Mahood, J. (Belfast C), 1926 v S; 1928 v E, S, W; 1929 v E, S, W; 1930 v W; (with Ballymena), 1934 v S (9)

Manderson, R. (Rangers), 1920 v W, S; 1925 v S, E; 1926 v S (5)

Mansfield, J. (Dublin Freebooters), 1901 v E (1)

Martin, C. J. (Glentoran), 1947 v S; (with Leeds U), 1948 v E, S, W; (with Aston Villa), 1949 v E; 1950 v W (6)

Martin, D. (Bo'ness), 1925 v S (1)

Martin, D. C. (Cliftonville), 1882 v E, W; 1883 v E (3)

Martin, D. K. (Belfast C), 1934 v E, S, W; 1935 v S; (with Wolverhampton W), 1935 v E; 1936 v W; (with Nottingham F), 1937 v S; 1938 v E, S; 1939 v S (10)

Mathieson, A. (Luton T), 1921 v W; 1922 v E (2)

Maxwell, J. (Linfield), 1902 v W; 1903 v W, E; (with Glentoran), 1905 v W, S; (with Belfast C), 1906 v W; 1907 v S (7)

Meek, H. L. (Glentoran), 1925 v W (1)

Mehaffy, J. A. C. (Queen's Island), 1922 v W (1)

Meldon, P. A. (Dublin Freebooters), 1899 v S, W (2)

Mercer, H. V. A. (Linfield), 1908 v E (1)

Mercer, J. T. (Distillery), 1898 v E, S, W; 1899 v E; (with Linfield), 1902 v E, W; (with Distillery), 1903 v S, W; (with Derby Co), 1904 v E, W; 1905 v S (11)

Millar, W. (Barrow), 1932 v W; 1933 v S (2)

Miller, J. (Middlesbrough), 1929 v W, S; 1930 v E (3)

Milligan, D. (Chesterfield), 1939 v W (1)

Milne, R. G. (Linfield), 1894 v E, S, W; 1895 v E, W; 1896 v E, S, W; 1897 v E, S; 1898 v E, S, W; 1899 v E, W; 1901 v W; 1902 v E, S, W; 1903 v E, S; 1904 v E, S, W; 1906 v E, S, W (27)

Mitchell, E. J. (Cliftonville), 1933 v S; (with Glentoran), 1934 v W (2)

Mitchell, W. (Distillery), 1932 v E, W; 1933 v E, W; (with Chelsea), 1934 v W, S; 1935 v S, E; 1936 v S, E; 1937 v E, S, W; 1938 v E, S (15)

Molyneux, T. B. (Ligoniel), 1883 v E, W; (with Cliftonville), 1884 v S, W; 1885 v E, W; 1886 v E, W, S; 1888 v S (11)

Montgomery, F. J. (Coleraine), 1955 v E (1)

Moore, C. (Glentoran), 1949 v W (1)

Moore, J. (Linfield Ath), 1891 v E, S, W (3)

Moore, P. (Aberdeen), 1933 v E (1)

Moore, T. (Ulster), 1887 v S, W (2)

Moore, W. (Falkirk), 1923 v S (1)

Moorhead, F. W. (Dublin University), 1885 v E (1)

Moorhead, G. (Linfield), 1923 v S; 1928 v S; 1929 v S (3)

Moran, J. (Leeds C), 1912 v S (1)

Moreland, V. (Derby Co), 1979 v Bul (2 sub), E, S; 1980 v E, Ei (6)

Morgan, F. G. (Linfield), 1923 v E; (with Nottingham F), 1924 v S; 1927 v E; 1928 v E, S, W; 1929 v E (7)

Morgan, S. (Port Vale), 1972 v Sp; 1973 v Bul (sub), P, Cy, E, S, W; (with Aston Villa), 1974 v Bul, P, S, E; 1975 v Se; 1976 v Se (sub), N, Y; (with Brighton & HA), S, W (sub); (with Sparta Rotterdam), 1979 v D (18)

Morrison, J. (Linfield Ath), 1891 v E, W (2)

Morrison, T. (Glentoran), 1895 v E, S, W; (with Burnley), 1899 v W; 1900 v W; 1902 v E, S (7)

Morrogh, E. (Bohemians), 1896 v S (1)

Morrow, S. J. (Arsenal), 1990 v U (sub); 1991 v A (sub), Pol, Y; 1992 v Fa, S (sub), G (sub); 1993 v Sp (sub), Alb, Ei; 1994 v R, Co, M (sub); 1995 v P, Ei (2), La; 1996 v P, Se (19)

Morrow, W. J. (Moyola Park), 1883 v E, W; 1884 v S (3)

Muir, R. (Oldpark), 1885 v S, W (2)

Mullan, G. (Glentoran), 1983 v S, E, W, Alb (sub) (4)

Mulholland, S. (Celtic), 1906 v S, E (2)

Mulligan, J. (Manchester C), 1921 v S (1)

Murphy, J. (Bradford C), 1910 v E, S, W (3)

Murphy, N. (QPR), 1905 v E, S, W (3)

Murray, J. M. (Motherwell), 1910 v E, S; (with Sheffield W), 1910 v W (3)

Napier, R. J. (Bolton W), 1966 v WG (1)

Neill, W. J. T. (Arsenal), 1961 v I, Gr, WG; 1962 v E, S, W, Gr; 1963 v E, W, Pol, Sp; 1964 v S, E, W, U, Sp; 1965 v E, S, W, Sw, Ho (2); Alb; 1966 v S, E, W, Alb, WG, M; 1967 v S, W; 1968 v S, E; 1969 v E, S, W, Is, T (2); 1970 v S, E, W, USSR (2); (with Hull C), 1971 v Cy, Sp; 1972 v USSR (2), Sp, S, E, W; 1973 v Bul, Cy (2), P, E, S, W (59)

Nelis, P. (Nottingham F), 1923 v E (1)

Nelson, S. (Arsenal), 1970 v W, E (sub); 1971 v Cy, Sp, E, S, W; 1972 v USSR (2), Sp, E, S, W; 1973 v Bul, Cy, P; 1974 v S, E; 1975 v Se, Y; 1976 v Se, N, Is, E; 1977 v Bel (sub), WG, W, Ic; 1978 v Ic, Ho, Bel; 1979 v Ei, D, Bul, E, Bul, E, S, W, D; 1980 v E, Ei, Is; 1981 v S, P, S, Se; (with Brighton & HA), 1982 v E, S, Sp (sub), A (51)

Nicholl, C. J. (Aston Villa), 1975 v Se, Y, E, S, W; 1976 v Se, N, Y, S, E, W; 1977 v W; (with Southampton), 1978 v Bel (sub), S, E, W; 1979 v Ei, Bul, E, Bul, E, W; 1980 v Ei, Is, S, E, W, Aus (3); 1981 v Se, P, S, P, S, Se; 1982 v S, Is, E, F, W, Y, Hon, Sp, A, F; 1983 v S (sub), E, W; (with Grimsby T), 1984 v A, T (51)

Nicholl, H. (Belfast C), 1902 v E, W; 1905 v E (3)

Nicholl, J. M. (Manchester U), 1976 v Is, W (sub); 1977 v Ho, Bel, E, S, W, Ic; 1978 v Ic, Ho, Bel, S, E, W; 1979 v Ei, D, Bul, E, Bul, E, S, W, D; 1980 v Ei, Is, S, E, W, Aus (3); 1981 v Se, P, S, P, S, Se; 1982 v S, Is, E; (with Toronto B), F, W, Y, Hon, Sp, A, F; (with Sunderland), 1983 v A, WG, Alb, T, Alb; (with Toronto B), S, E, W; 1984 v T; (with Rangers), WG, S, E; (with Toronto B), Fi; 1985 v R; (with WBA), Fi, E, Sp, T; 1986 v T, R, E, F, Alg, Sp, Br (73)

Nicholson, J. J. (Manchester U), 1961 v S, W; 1962 v E, W, Gr, Ho; 1963 v E, S, Pol (2); (with Huddersfield T), 1965 v W, Ho (2); Alb; 1966 v S, E, W, Alb, M; 1967 v S, W; 1968 v S, E, W; 1969 v S, E, W, T (2); 1970 v S, E, W, USSR (2); 1971 v Cy (2), E, S, W; 1972 v USSR (2) (41)

Nixon, R. (Linfield), 1914 v S (1)

Small, J. M. (Cliftonville), 1893 v E, S, W (3)
Smith, E. E. (Cardiff C), 1921 v S; 1923 v W, E; 1924 v E (4)
Smith, J. (Distillery), 1901 v S, W (2)
Smyth, R. H. (Dublin University), 1886 v W (1)
Smyth, S. (Wolverhampton W), 1948 v E, S, W; 1949 v S, W; 1950 v E, S, W; (with Stoke C), 1952 v E (9)
Smyth, W. (Distillery), 1949 v E, S; 1954 v S, E (4)
Snape, A. (Airdrie), 1920 v E (1)
Spence. D. W. (Bury), 1975 v Y, E, S, W; 1976 v Se, Is, E, W, S (sub); (with Blackpool), 1977 v Ho (sub), WG (sub), E (sub), S (sub), W (sub), Ic (sub); 1979 v Ei, D (sub), E (sub), Bul (sub), E (sub), S, W, D; 1980 v Ei; (with Southend U), Is (sub), Aus (sub); 1981 v S (sub), Se (sub); 1982 v F (sub) (29)
Spencer, S. (Distillery), 1890 v E, S; 1892 v E, S, W; 1893 v E (6)
Spiller, E. A. (Cliftonville), 1883 v E, W; 1884 v E, S, W (5)
Stanfield, O. M. (Distillery), 1887 v E, S, W; 1888 v E, S, W; 1889 v E, S, W; 1890 v E, S; 1891 v E, S, W; 1892 v E, S, W; 1893 v E, W; 1894 v E, S, W; 1895 v E, S; 1896 v E, S, W; 1897 v E, S, W (30)
Steele, A. (Charlton Ath), 1926 v W, S; (with Fulham), 1929 v W, S (4)
Stevenson, A. E. (Rangers), 1934 v E, S, W; (with Everton), 1935 v E, S; 1936 v S, W; 1937 v E, W; 1938 v E, W; 1939 v E, S, W; 1947 v S, W; 1948 v S (17)
Stewart, A. (Glentoran), 1967 v W; 1968 v S, E; (with Derby Co), 1968 v W; 1969 v Is, T (1+1 sub) (7)
Stewart, D. C. (Hull C), 1978 v Bel (1)
Stewart, I. (QPR), 1982 v F (sub); 1983 v A, WG, Alb, T, Alb, S, E, W; 1984 v A, T, WG, S, E, W, Fi; 1985 v R, Fi, Is, E, Sp, T; (with Newcastle U), 1986 v R, E, D, Mor, Alg (sub), Sp (sub), Br; 1987 v E, Is (sub) (31)
Stewart, R. H. (St Columb's Court), 1890 v E, S, W; (with Cliftonville), 1892 v E, S, W; 1893 v E, W; 1894 v E, S, W (11)
Stewart, T. C. (Linfield), 1961 v W (1)
Swan, S. (Linfield), 1899 v S (1)

Taggart, G. P. (Barnsley), 1990 v N, U; 1991 v Y, D, A, Pol, Fa; 1992 v Fa, A, D, S, Li, G; 1993 v Alb, Sp, D, Alb, Ei, Sp, Li, La; 1994 v La, D, Ei, R, Lie, Co, M; 1995 v P (sub), A, Ei (2), Ca, Ch, La (35)
Taggart, J. (Walsall), 1899 v W (1)
Thompson, F. W. (Cliftonville), 1910 v E, S, W; (with Bradford C), 1911 v E; (with Linfield), v W; 1912 v E, W; 1913 v E, S, W; (with Clyde), 1914 v E, S (12)
Thompson, J. (Belfast Ath), 1889 v S (1)
Thompson, J. (Distillery), 1897 v S (1)
Thunder, P. J. (Bohemians), 1911 v W (1)
Todd, S. J. (Burnley), 1966 v M (sub); 1967 v E; 1968 v W; 1969 v E, S, W; 1970 v S, USSR; (with Sheffield W), 1971 v Cy (2), Sp (sub) (11)
Toner, J. (Arsenal), 1922 v W; 1923 v W; 1924 v W, E; 1925 v E, S; (with St Johnstone), 1927 v E, S (8)
Torrans, R. (Linfield), 1893 v S (1)
Torrans, S. (Linfield), 1889 v S; 1890 v S, W; 1891 v S, W; 1892 v E, S, W; 1893 v E, S; 1894 v E, S, W; 1895 v E; 1896 v E, S, W; 1897 v E, S, W; 1898 v E, S; 1899 v E, W; 1901 v S, W (26)
Trainor, D. (Crusaders), 1967 v W (1)
Tully, C. P. (Celtic), 1949 v E; 1950 v E; 1952 v S; 1953 v E, S, W, F; 1954 v S; 1956 v E; 1959 v Sp (10)
Turner, E. (Cliftonville), 1896 v E, W (2)
Turner, W. (Cliftonville), 1886 v E; 1886 v S; 1888 v S (3)
Twoomey, J. F. (Leeds U), 1938 v W; 1939 v E (2)

Uprichard, W. N. M. C. (Swindon T), 1952 v E, S, W; 1953 v E, S; (with Portsmouth), 1953 v W, F; 1955 v E, S, W; 1956 v E, S, W, S, I, Cz; 1959 v S, Sp (18)

Vernon, J. (Belfast C), 1947 v E, S; (with WBA), 1947 v W; 1948 v E, S, W; 1949 v E, S, W; 1950 v E, S; 1951 v E, S, W, F; 1952 v S, E (17)

Waddell, T. M. R. (Cliftonville), 1906 v S (1)
Walker, J. (Doncaster R), 1955 v W (1)
Walker, T. (Bury), 1911 v S (1)
Walsh, D. J. (WBA), 1947 v S, W; 1948 v E, S, W; 1949 v E, S, W; 1950 v W (9)
Walsh, W. (Manchester C), 1948 v E, S, W; 1949 v E, S (5)
Waring, R. (Distillery), 1899 v E (1)
Warren, P. (Shelbourne), 1913 v E, S (2)
Watson, J. (Ulster), 1883 v E, W; 1886 v E, S, W; 1887 v S, W; 1889 v E, W (9)
Watson, P. (Distillery), 1971 v Cy (sub) (1)
Watson, T. (Cardiff C), 1926 v S (1)
Wattle, J. (Distillery), 1899 v E (1)
Webb, C. G. (Brighton), 1909 v S, W; 1911 v S (3)
Weir, E. (Clyde), 1939 v W (1)
Welsh, E. (Carlisle U), 1966 v W, WG, M; 1967 v W (4)
Whiteside, N. (Manchester U), 1982 v Y, Hon, Sp, A, F; 1983 v WG, Alb, T; 1984 v A, T, WG, S, E, W, Fi; 1985 v R, Fi, Is, E, Sp, T; 1986 v R, E, F, D, Mor, Alg, Sp, Br; 1987 v E (2), Is, Y; 1988 v T, Pol, F; (with Everton), 1990 v H, Ei (38)
Whiteside, T. (Distillery), 1891 v E (1)
Whitfield, E. R. (Dublin University), 1886 v W (1)
Williams, J. R. (Ulster), 1886 v E, S (2)
Williams, P. A. (WBA), 1991 v Fa (sub) (1)
Williamson, J. (Cliftonville), 1890 v E; 1892 v S; 1893 v S (3)
Willigham, T. (Burnley), 1933 v W; 1934 v S (2)
Willis, G. (Linfield), 1906 v S, W; 1907 v S; 1912 v S (4)
Wilson, D. J. (Brighton & HA), 1987 v T, Is, E (sub); (with Luton T), 1988 v Y, T, Gr, Pol, F, Ma; 1989 v Ei, H, Sp, Ma, Ch; 1990 v H, Ei, N, U; (with Sheffield W), 1991 v Y, D, A, Fa; 1992 v A (sub), S (24)
Wilson, H. (Linfield), 1925 v W (1)
Wilson, K. J. (Ipswich T), 1987 v Is, E, Y; (with Chelsea), 1988 v Y, T, Gr (sub), Pol (sub), F (sub); 1989 v H (sub), Sp (2), Ma, Ch; 1990 v Ei (sub), N, U; 1991 v Y (2), A, Pol, Fa; 1992 v Fa, A, D, S; (with Notts Co), Li, G; 1993 v Alb, Sp, D, Sp, Li, La; 1994 v La, D, Ei, R, Lie, Co, M; (with Walsall), 1995 v Ei (sub), La (42)
Wilson, M. (Distillery), 1884 v E, S, W (3)
Wilson, R. (Cliftonville), 1888 v S (1)
Wilson, S. J. (Glenavon), 1962 v S; 1964 v S; (with Falkirk), 1964 v E, W, U, Sp; 1965 v E, Sw; (with Dundee), 1966 v W, WG; 1967 v S; 1968 v E (12)
Wilton, J. M. (St Columb's Court), 1888 v E, W; 1889 v S, E; (with Cliftonville), 1890 v E; (with St Columb's Court), 1892 v W; 1893 v S (7)
Wood, T. J. (Walsall), 1996 v Lie (sub) (1)
Worthington, N. (Sheffield W), 1984 v W, Fi (sub); 1985 v Is, Sp (sub); 1986 v T, R (sub), E (sub), D, Alg, Sp; 1987 v E (2), T, Is, Y; 1988 v Y, T, Gr, Pol, F, Ma; 1989 v Ei, H, Sp, Ma; 1990 v H, Ei, U; 1991 v Y, D, A, Fa; 1992 v A, D, S, Li, G; 1993 v Alb, Sp, D, Ei, Sp, Li, La; 1994 v La, D, Ei, Lie, Co, M; (with Leeds U), 1995 v P, A, Ei (2), La, Ca (sub), Ch, La; 1996 v P, Lie, A, N, Se, G (64)
Wright, J. (Cliftonville), 1906 v E, S, W; 1907 v E, S, W (6)
Wright, T. J. (Newcastle U), 1989 v Ma, Ch; 1990 v H, U; 1992 v Fa, A, S, G; 1993 v Alb, Sp, Alb, Ei, Sp, Li, La; 1994 v La; (with Nottingham F), D, Ei, R, Lie, Co, M (sub) (22)
Young, S. (Linfield), 1907 v E, S; 1908 v E, S; (with Airdrie), 1909 v E; 1912 v S; (with Linfield), 1914 v E, S, W (9)

SCOTLAND

Adams, J. (Hearts), 1889 v Ni; 1892 v W; 1893 v Ni (3)
Agnew, W. B. (Kilmarnock), 1907 v Ni; 1908 v W, Ni (3)
Aird, J. (Burnley), 1954 v N (2), A, U (4)
Aitken, A. (Newcastle U), 1901 v E; 1902 v E; 1903 v E, W, 1904 v E; 1905 v E, W; 1906 v E; (with Middlesbrough), 1907 v E, W; 1908 v E; (with Leicester Fosse), 1910 v E; 1911 v E, Ni (14)
Aitken, G. G. (East Fife), 1949 v E, F; 1950 v W, Ni, Sw; (with Sunderland), 1953 v W, Ni; 1954 v E (8)
Aitken, R. (Dumbarton), 1886 v E; 1888 v Ni (2)
Aitken, R. (Celtic), 1980 v Pe (sub), Bel, W (sub), E, Pol; 1983 v Bel, Ca (1+1 sub); 1984 v Bel (sub), Ni, W (sub); 1985 v E, Ic; 1986 v W, EG, Aus (2), Is, R, E, D, WG, U; 1987 v Bul, Ei (2), L, Bel, E, Br; 1988 v H, Bel, Bul, L, S.Ar, Ma, Sp, Co, E; 1989 v N, Y, I, Cy, F, Cy, E, Ch; 1990 v Y, F, N; (with Newcastle U), Arg (sub), Pol, Ma, Cr, Se, Br; (with St Mirren), 1992 v R (sub) (57)
Aitkenhead, W. A. C. (Blackburn R), 1912 v Ni (1)

Albiston, A. (Manchester U), 1982 v Ni; 1984 v U, Bel, EG, W, E; 1985 v Y, Ic, Sp (2), W; 1986 v EG, Ho, U (14)
Alexander, D. (East Stirlingshire), 1894 v W, Ni (2)
Allan, D. S. (Queen's Park), 1885 v E, W; 1886 v W (3)
Allan, G. (Liverpool), 1897 v E (1)
Allan, H. (Hearts), 1902 v W (1)
Allan, J. (Queen's Park), 1887 v E, W (2)
Allan, T. (Dundee), 1974 v WG, N (2)
Ancell, R. F. D. (Newcastle U), 1937 v W, Ni (2)
Anderson, A. (Hearts), 1933 v E; 1934 v A, E, W, Ni; 1935 v E, W, Ni; 1936 v E, W, Ni; 1937 v G, E, W, Ni, A; 1938 v E, W, Ni, Cz, Ho; 1939 v W, H (23)
Anderson, F. (Clydesdale), 1874 v E (1)
Anderson, G. (Kilmarnock), 1901 v Ni (1)
Anderson, H. A. (Raith R), 1914 v W (1)
Anderson, J. (Leicester C), 1954 v Fi (1)
Anderson, K. (Queen's Park), 1896 v Ni; 1898 v E, Ni (3)

Cameron, J. (St Mirren), 1904 v Ni; (with Chelsea), 1909 v E (2)
Campbell, C. (Queen's Park), 1874 v E; 1876 v W; 1877 v E, W; 1878 v E; 1879 v E; 1880 v E; 1881 v E; 1882 v E, W; 1884 v E; 1885 v E; 1886 v E (13)
Campbell, H. (Renton), 1889 v W (1)
Campbell, Jas (Sheffield W), 1913 v W (1)
Campbell, J. (South Western), 1880 v W (1)
Campbell, J. (Kilmarnock), 1891 v Ni; 1892 v W (2)
Campbell, John (Celtic), 1893 v E, Ni; 1898 v E, Ni; 1900 v E, Ni; 1901 v E, W, Ni; 1902 v W, Ni; 1903 v W (12)
Campbell, John (Rangers), 1899 v E, W, Ni; 1901 v Ni (4)
Campbell, K. (Liverpool), 1920 v E, W, Ni; (with Partick T), 1921 v W, Ni; 1922 v W, Ni, E (8)
Campbell, P. (Rangers), 1878 v W; 1879 v W (2)
Campbell, P. (Morton), 1898 v W (1)
Campbell, R. (Falkirk), 1947 v Bel, L; (with Chelsea), 1950 v Sw, P, F (5)
Campbell, W. (Morton), 1947 v Ni; 1948 v E, Bel, Sw, F (5)
Carabine, J. (Third Lanark), 1938 v Ho; 1939 v E, Ni (3)
Carr, W. M. (Coventry C), 1970 v Ni, W, E; 1971 v D; 1972 v Pe; 1973 v D (sub) (6)
Cassidy, J. (Celtic), 1921 v W, Ni; 1923 v Ni; 1924 v W (4)
Chalmers, S. (Celtic), 1965 v W, Fi; 1966 v P (sub), Br; 1967 v Ni (5)
Chalmers, W. (Rangers), 1885 v Ni (1)
Chalmers, W. S. (Queen's Park), 1929 v Ni (1)
Chambers, T. (Hearts), 1894 v Ni (1)
Chaplin, G. D. (Dundee), 1908 v W (1)
Cheyne, A. G. (Aberdeen), 1929 v E, N, G, Ho; 1930 v F (5)
Christie, A. J. (Queen's Park), 1898 v W; 1899 v E, Ni (3)
Christie, R. M. (Queen's Park), 1884 v E (1)
Clark, J. (Celtic), 1966 v Br; 1967 v W, Ni, USSR (4)
Clark, R. B. (Aberdeen), 1968 v W, Ho; 1970 v Ni; 1971 v W, Ni, E, D, P, USSR; 1972 v Bel, Ni, W, E, Cz, Br; 1973 v D, E (17)
Clarke, S. (Chelsea), 1988 v H, Bel, Bul, S.Ar, Ma; 1994 v Ho (6)
Cleland, J. (Royal Albert), 1891 v Ni (1)
Clements, R. (Leith Ath), 1891 v Ni (1)
Clunas, W. L. (Sunderland), 1924 v E; 1926 v W (2)
Collier, W. (Raith R), 1922 v W (1)
Collins, J. (Hibernian), 1988 v S.Ar; 1990 v EG, Pol (sub), Ma (sub); (with Celtic), 1991 v Sw (sub), Bul (sub); 1992 v Ni (sub), Fi; 1993 v P, Ma, G, P, Es (2); 1994 v Sw, Ho (sub), A, Ho; 1995 v Fi, Fa, Ru, Gr, Ru, Sm, Fa; 1996 v Gr, Fi, Se, Sm, Aus, D, US (sub), Co, Ho, E, Sw (36)
Collins, R. Y. (Celtic), 1951 v W, Ni, A; 1955 v Y, A, H; 1956 v Ni, W; 1957 v E, W, Sp (2), Sw, WG; 1958 v Ni, W, Sw, H, Pol, Y, F, Par; (with Everton), 1959 v E, W, Ni, WG, Ho, P; (with Leeds U), 1965 v E, Pol, Sp (31)
Collins, T. (Hearts), 1909 v W (1)
Colman, D. (Aberdeen), 1911 v E, W, Ni; 1913 v Ni (4)
Colquhoun, E. P. (Sheffield U), 1972 v P, Ho, Pe, Y, Cz, Br; 1973 v D (2), E (9)
Colquhoun, J. (Hearts), 1988 v S.Ar (sub) (1)
Combe, J. R. (Hibernian), 1948 v E, Bel, Sw (3)
Conn, A. (Hearts), 1956 v A (1)
Conn, A. (Tottenham H), 1975 v Ni (sub), E (2)
Connachan, E. D. (Dunfermline Ath), 1962 v Cz, U (2)
Connelly, G. (Celtic), 1974 v Cz, WG (2)
Connolly, J. (Everton), 1973 v Sw (1)
Connor, J. (Airdrieonians), 1886 v Ni (1)
Connor, J. (Sunderland), 1930 v F; 1932 v Ni; 1934 v E; 1935 v Ni (4)
Connor, R. (Dundee), 1986 v Ho; (with Aberdeen), 1988 v S.Ar (sub); 1989 v E; 1991 v R (4)
Cook, W. L. (Bolton W), 1934 v E; 1935 v W, Ni (3)
Cooke, C. (Dundee), 1966 v W, I; (with Chelsea), P, Br; 1968 v E, Ho; 1969 v W, Ni, A, WG (sub), Cy (2); 1970 v A; 1971 v Bel; 1975 v Sp, P (16)
Cooper, D. (Rangers), 1980 v Pe, A (sub); 1984 v W, E; 1985 v Y, Ic, Sp (2), W; 1986 v W, EG, Aus (2), Ho, WG (sub), U (sub); 1987 v Bul, L, Ei, Br; (with Motherwell), 1990 v N, Eg (22)
Cormack, P. B. (Hibernian), 1966 v Br; 1969 v D (sub); 1970 v Ei, WG; (with Nottingham F), 1971 v D (sub), W, P, E; 1972 v Ho (sub) (9)
Cowan, J. (Aston Villa), 1896 v E; 1897 v E; 1898 v E (3)
Cowan, J. (Morton), 1948 v Bel, Sw; F; 1949 v E, W, F; 1950 v E, W, Ni, Sw, P, F; 1951 v E, W, Ni, A (2), D, F, Bel; 1952 v Ni, W, USA, D, Se (25)
Cowan, W. D. (Newcastle U), 1924 v E (1)
Cowie, D. (Dundee), 1953 v E, Se; 1954 v Ni, W, Fi, N, A, U; 1955 v W, Ni, A, H; 1956 v W, A; 1957 v Ni, W; 1958 v H, Pol, Y, Par (20)
Cox, C. J. (Hearts), 1948 v F (1)
Cox, S. (Rangers), 1949 v E, F; 1950 v E, F, W, Ni, Sw, P; 1951 v E, D, F, Bel, A; 1952 v Ni, USA, D, Se; 1953 v W, Ni, E; 1954 v W, Ni, E (24)
Craig, A. (Motherwell), 1929 v N, Ho; 1932 v E (3)

Craig, J. (Celtic), 1977 v Se (sub) (1)
Craig, J. P. (Celtic), 1968 v W (1)
Craig, T. (Rangers), 1927 v Ni; 1928 v Ni; 1929 v N, G, Ho; 1930 v Ni, E, W (8)
Craig, T. B. (Newcastle U), 1976 v Sw (1)
Crapnell, J. (Airdrieonians), 1929 v E, N, G; 1930 v F; 1931 v Ni, Sw; 1932 v E, F; 1933 v Ni (9)
Crawford, D. (St Mirren), 1894 v W, Ni; 1900 v W (3)
Crawford, J. (Queen's Park), 1932 v F, Ni; 1933 v E, W, Ni (5)
Crawford, S. (Raith R), 1995 v Ec (sub) (1)
Crerand, P. T. (Celtic), 1961 v Ei (2), Cz; 1962 v Ni, W, E, Cz (2), U; 1963 v W, Ni; (with Manchester U), 1964 v Ni; 1965 v E, Pol, Fi; 1966 v Pol (16)
Cringan, W. (Celtic), 1920 v W; 1922 v E, Ni; 1923 v W, E (5)
Crosbie, J. A. (Ayr U), 1920 v W; (with Birmingham), 1922 v E (2)
Croal, J. A. (Falkirk), 1913 v Ni; 1914 v E, W (3)
Cropley, A. J. (Hibernian), 1972 v P, Bel (2)
Cross, J. H. (Third Lanark), 1903 v Ni (1)
Cruickshank, J. (Hearts), 1964 v WG; 1970 v W, E; 1971 v D, Bel; 1976 v R (6)
Crum, J. (Celtic), 1936 v E; 1939 v Ni (2)
Cullen, M. J. (Luton T), 1956 v A (1)
Cumming, D. S. (Middlesbrough), 1938 v E (1)
Cumming, J. (Hearts), 1955 v E, H, P, Y; 1960 v E, Pol, A, H, T (9)
Cummings, G. (Partick T), 1935 v E; 1936 v W, Ni; (with Aston Villa), E; 1937 v G; 1938 v W, Ni, Cz; 1939 v E (9)
Cunningham, A. N. (Rangers), 1920 v Ni; 1921 v W, E; 1922 v Ni; 1923 v E, W; 1924 v E, Ni; 1926 v E, Ni; 1927 v E, W (12)
Cunningham, W. C. (Preston NE), 1954 v N (2), U, Fi, A; 1955 v W, E, H (8)
Curran, H. P. (Wolverhampton W), 1970 v A; 1971 v Ni, E, D, USSR (sub) (5)

Dalglish, K. (Celtic), 1972 v Bel (sub), Ho; 1973 v D (1+1 sub), E (2), W, Ni, Sw, Br; 1974 v Cz (2), WG (2), Ni, W, E, Bel, N (sub), Z, Br, Y; 1975 v EG, Sp (sub+1), Se, P, W, Ni, E, R; 1976 v D (2), R, Sw, Ni, E; 1977 v Fi, Cz, W (2), Se, Ni, E, Ch, Arg, Br; (with Liverpool), 1978 v EG, Cz, W, Bul, Ni (sub), W, E, Pe, Ir, Ho; 1979 v A, N, P, W, Ni, E, Arg, N; 1980 v Pe, A, Bel (2), P, Ni, W, E, Pol, H; 1981 v Se, P, Is; 1982 v Se, Ni, P (sub), Sp, Ho, Ni, W, E, Nz, Br (sub); 1983 v Bel, Sw; 1984 v U, Bel, EG; 1985 v Y, Ic, Sp, W; 1986 v EG, Aus, R; 1987 v Bul (sub), L (102)
Davidson, D. (Queen's Park), 1878 v W; 1879 v W; 1880 v W; 1881 v E, W (5)
Davidson, J. A. (Partick T), 1954 v N (2), A, U; 1955 v W, Ni, E, H (8)
Davidson, S. (Middlesbrough), 1921 v E (1)
Dawson, A. (Rangers), 1980 v Pol (sub), H; 1983 v Ni, Ca (2) (5)
Dawson, J. (Rangers), 1935 v Ni; 1936 v E; 1937 v G, E, W, Ni, A, Cz; 1938 v W, Ho, Ni; 1939 v E, Ni, H (14)
Deans, J. (Celtic), 1975 v EG, Sp (2)
Delaney, J. (Celtic), 1936 v W, Ni; 1937 v G, E, A, Cz; 1938 v Ni; 1939 v W, Ni; (with Manchester U), 1947 v E; 1948 v E, W, Ni (13)
Devine, A. (Falkirk), 1910 v W (1)
Dewar, G. (Dumbarton), 1888 v Ni; 1889 v E (2)
Dewar, N. (Third Lanark), 1932 v E, F; 1933 v W (3)
Dick, J. (West Ham U), 1959 v E (1)
Dickie, M. (Rangers), 1897 v Ni; 1899 v Ni; 1900 v W (3)
Dickson, W. (Dumbarton), 1888 v Ni (1)
Dickson, W. (Kilmarnock), 1970 v Ni, W, E; 1971 v D, USSR (5)
Divers, J. (Celtic), 1895 v W (1)
Divers, J. (Celtic), 1939 v Ni (1)
Docherty, T. H. (Preston NE), 1952 v W; 1953 v E, Se; 1954 v N (2), A, U; 1955 v W, E, H (2), A; 1957 v E, Y, Sp (2), Sw, WG; 1958 v Ni, W, E, Sw; (with Arsenal), 1959 v W, E, Ni (25)
Dodds, D. (Dundee U), 1984 v U (sub), Ni (2)
Dodds, J. (Celtic), 1914 v E, W, Ni (3)
Doig, J. E. (Arbroath), 1887 v Ni; 1889 v Ni; (with Sunderland), 1896 v E; 1899 v E; 1903 v E (5)
Donachie, W. (Manchester C), 1972 v Pe, Ni, E, Y, Cz, Br; 1973 v D, E, W, Ni; 1974 v Ni; 1976 v R, Ni, W, E; 1977 v Fi, Cz, W (2), Se, Ni, E, Ch, Arg, Br; 1978 v EG, W, Bul, W, E, Ir, Ho; 1979 v A, N, P (sub) (35)
Donaldson, A. (Bolton W), 1914 v E, Ni, W; 1920 v E, Ni; 1922 v Ni (6)
Donnachie, J. (Oldham Ath), 1913 v E; 1914 v E, Ni (3)
Dougall, C. (Birmingham), 1947 v W (1)
Dougall, J. (Preston NE), 1939 v E (1)
Dougan, R. (Hearts), 1950 v Sw (1)
Douglas, A. (Chelsea), 1911 v Ni (1)
Douglas, J. (Renfrew), 1880 v W (1)

Gray, D. (Rangers), 1929 v W, Ni, G, Ho; 1930 v W, E, Ni; 1931 v W; 1933 v W, Ni (10)

Gray, E. (Leeds U), 1969 v E, Cy; 1970 v WG, A; 1971 v W, Ni; 1972 v Bel, Ho; 1976 v W, E; 1977 v Fi, W (12)

Gray, F. T. (Leeds U), 1976 v Sw; 1979 v N, P, W, Ni, E, Arg (sub); (with Nottingham F), 1980 v Bel (sub); 1981 v Se, P, Is, Ni, Is, W; (with Leeds U), Ni, E; 1982 v Se, Ni, P, Sp, Ho, W, Nz, Br, USSR; 1983 v EG, Sw, Bel, Sw, W, E, Ca (32)

Gray, W. (Pollokshields Ath), 1886 v E (1)

Green, A. (Blackpool), 1971 v Bel (sub), P (sub), Ni, E; (with Newcastle U), 1972 v W, E (sub) (6)

Greig, J. (Rangers), 1964 v E, WG; 1965 v W, Ni, E, Fi (2), Sp, Pol; 1966 v Ni, W, E, Pol, I (2), P, Ho, Br; 1967 v W, Ni, E; 1968 v Ni, W, E, Ho; 1969 v W, Ni, E, D, A, WG, Cy (2); 1970 v W, E, Ei, WG, A; 1971 v D, Bel, W (sub), Ni, E; 1976 v D (44)

Groves, W. (Hibernian), 1888 v W; (with Celtic), 1889 v Ni; 1890 v E (3)

Guilliland, W. (Queen's Park), 1891 v W; 1892 v Ni; 1894 v E; 1895 v E (4)

Gunn, B. (Norwich C), 1990 v Eg; 1993 v Es (2); 1994 v Sw, I, Ho (sub) (6)

Haddock, H. (Clyde), 1955 v E, H (2), P, Y; 1958 v E (6)

Haddow, D. (Rangers), 1894 v E (1)

Haffey, F. (Celtic), 1960 v E; 1961 v E (2)

Hamilton, A. (Queen's Park), 1885 v E, W; 1886 v E; 1888 v E (4)

Hamilton, A. W. (Dundee), 1962 v Cz, U, W, E; 1963 v W, Ni, E, A, N, Ei; 1964 v Ni, W, E, N, WG; 1965 v Ni, W, E, Fi (2), Pol, Sp; 1966 v Pol, Ni (24)

Hamilton, G. (Aberdeen), 1947 v Ni; 1951 v Bel, A; 1954 v N (2) (5)

Hamilton, G. (Port Glasgow Ath), 1906 v Ni (1)

Hamilton, J. (Queen's Park), 1892 v W; 1893 v E, Ni (3)

Hamilton, J. (St Mirren), 1924 v Ni (1)

Hamilton, R. C. (Rangers), 1899 v E, W, Ni; 1900 v W; 1901 v E, Ni; 1902 v W, Ni; 1903 v E; 1904 v Ni; (with Dundee), 1911 v W (11)

Hamilton, T. (Hurlford), 1891 v Ni (1)

Hamilton, T. (Rangers), 1932 v E (1)

Hamilton, W. M. (Hibernian), 1965 v Fi (1)

Hannah, A. B. (Renton), 1888 v W (1)

Hannah, J. (Third Lanark), 1889 v W (1)

Hansen, A. D. (Liverpool), 1979 v W, Arg; 1980 v Bel, P; 1981 v Se, P, Is; 1982 v Se, Ni, P, Sp, Ni (sub), W, E, Nz, Br, USSR; 1983 v EG, Sw, Bel, Sw; 1985 v W (sub); 1986 v R (sub); 1987 v Ei (2), L (26)

Hansen, J. (Partick T), 1972 v Bel (sub), Y (sub) (2)

Harkness, J. D. (Queen's Park), 1927 v E, Ni; 1928 v E; (with Hearts), 1929 v W, E, Ni; 1930 v E, W; 1932 v W, F; 1934 v Ni, W (12)

Harper, J. M. (Aberdeen), 1973 v D (1+1 sub); (with Hibernian), 1976 v D; (with Aberdeen), 1978 v Ir (sub) (4)

Harper, W. (Hibernian), 1923 v E, Ni, W; 1924 v E, Ni, W; 1925 v E, Ni, W; (with Arsenal), 1926 v E, Ni (11)

Harris, J. (Partick T), 1921 v W, Ni (2)

Harris, N. (Newcastle U), 1924 v E (1)

Harrower, W. (Queen's Park), 1882 v E; 1884 v Ni; 1886 v W (3)

Hartford, R. A. (WBA), 1972 v Pe, W (sub), E, Y, Cz, Br; (with Manchester C), 1976 v D, R, Ni (sub); 1977 v Cz (sub), W (sub), Se, W, Ni, E, Ch, Arg, Br; 1978 v EG, Cz, W, Bul, W, E, Pe, Ir, Ho; 1979 v A, N, P, W, Ni, E, Arg, N; (with Everton), 1980 v Pe, Bel; 1981 v Ni (sub), Is, W, Ni, E; 1982 v Se; (with Manchester C), Ni, P, Sp, Ni, W, E, Br (50)

Harvey, D. (Leeds U), 1973 v D; 1974 v Cz, WG, Ni, W, E, Bel, Z, Br, Y; 1975 v EG, Sp (2); 1976 v D (2); 1977 v Fi (sub) (16)

Hastings, A. C. (Sunderland), 1936 v Ni; 1938 v Ni (2)

Haughney, M. (Celtic), 1954 v E (1)

Hay, D. (Celtic), 1970 v Ni, W, E; 1971 v D, Bel, W, P, Ni; 1972 v P, Bel, Ho; 1973 v W, Ni, E, Sw, Br; 1974 v Cz (2), WG, Ni, W, E, Bel, N, Z, Br, Y (27)

Hay, J. (Celtic), 1905 v Ni; 1909 v Ni; 1910 v W, Ni, E; 1911 v Ni, E; (with Newcastle U), 1912 v E, W; 1914 v E, Ni (11)

Hegarty, P. (Dundee U), 1979 v W, Ni, E, Arg, N (sub); 1980 v W, E; 1983 v Ni (8)

Heggie, C. (Rangers), 1886 v Ni (1)

Henderson, G. H. (Rangers), 1904 v Ni (1)

Henderson, J. G. (Portsmouth), 1953 v Se; 1954 v Ni, E, N; 1956 v W; (with Arsenal), 1959 v W, Ni (7)

Henderson, W. (Rangers), 1963 v W, Ni, E, A, N, Ei, Sp; 1964 v W, Ni, E, N, WG; 1965 v Fi, Pol, E, Sp; 1966 v Ni, W, Pol, I, Ho; 1967 v W, Ni; 1968 v Ho; 1969 v Ni, E, Cy; 1970 v Ei; 1971 v P (29)

Hendry, E. C. J. (Blackburn R), 1993 v Es (2); 1994 v Ma, Ho, A, Ho; 1995 v Fi, Fa, Gr, Ru, Sm; 1996 v Fi, Se, Sm, Aus, D, US, Co, Ho, E, Sw (21)

Hepburn, J. (Alloa Ath), 1891 v W (1)

Hepburn, R. (Ayr U), 1932 v Ni (1)

Herd, A. C. (Hearts), 1935 v Ni (1)

Herd, D. G. (Arsenal), 1959 v E, W, Ni; 1961 v E, Cz (5)

Herd, G. (Clyde), 1958 v E; 1960 v H, T; 1961 v W, Ni (5)

Herriot, J. (Birmingham C), 1969 v Ni, E, D, Cy (2), W (sub); 1970 v Ei (sub), WG (8)

Hewie, J. D. (Charlton Ath), 1956 v E, A; 1957 v E, Ni, W, Y, Sp (2), Sw, WG; 1958 v H, Pol, Y, F; 1959 v Ho, P; 1960 v Ni, W, Pol (19)

Higgins, A. (Kilmarnock), 1885 v Ni (1)

Higgins, A. (Newcastle U), 1910 v E, Ni; 1911 v E, Ni (4)

Highet, T. C. (Queen's Park), 1875 v E; 1876 v E, W; 1878 v E (4)

Hill, D. (Rangers), 1881 v E, W; 1882 v W (3)

Hill, D. A. (Third Lanark), 1906 v Ni (1)

Hill, F. R. (Aberdeen), 1930 v F; 1931 v W, Ni (3)

Hill, J. (Hearts), 1891 v E; 1892 v W (2)

Hogg, G (Hearts), 1896 v E, Ni (2)

Hogg, J. (Ayr U), 1922 v Ni (1)

Hogg, R. M. (Celtic), 1937 v Cz (1)

Holm, A. H. (Queen's Park), 1882 v W; 1883 v E, W (3)

Holt, D. D. (Hearts), 1963 v A, N, Ei, Sp; 1964 v WG (sub) (5)

Holton, J. A. (Manchester U), 1973 v W, Ni, E, Sw, Br; 1974 v Cz, WG, Ni, W, E, N, Z, Br, Y; 1975 v EG (15)

Hope, R. (WBA), 1968 v Ho; 1969 v D (2)

Houliston, W. (Queen of the South), 1949 v E, Ni, F (3)

Houston, S. M. (Manchester U), 1976 v D (1)

Howden, W. (Partick T), 1905 v Ni (1)

Howe, R. (Hamilton A), 1929 v N, Ho (2)

Howie, J. (Newcastle U), 1905 v E; 1906 v E; 1908 v E (3)

Howie, H. (Hibernian), 1949 v W (1)

Howieson, J. (St Mirren), 1927 v Ni (1)

Hughes, J. (Celtic), 1965 v Pol, Sp; 1966 v Ni, I (2); 1968 v E; 1969 v A; 1970 v Ei (8)

Hughes, W. (Sunderland), 1975 v Se (sub) (1)

Humphries, W. (Motherwell), 1952 v Se (1)

Hunter, A. (Kilmarnock), 1972 v Pe, Y; (with Celtic), 1973 v E; 1974 v Cz (4)

Hunter, J. (Dundee), 1909 v W (1)

Hunter, J. (Third Lanark), 1874 v E; (with Eastern), 1875 v E; (with Third Lanark), 1876 v E; 1877 v W (4)

Hunter, R. (St Mirren), 1890 v Ni (1)

Hunter, W. (Motherwell), 1960 v H, T; 1961 v W (3)

Husband, J. (Partick T), 1947 v W (1)

Hutchison, T. (Coventry C), 1974 v Cz (2), WG (2), Ni, W, Bel (sub), N, Z (sub), Y (sub); 1975 v EG, Sp (2), P, E (sub), R (sub); 1976 v D (17)

Hutton, J. (Aberdeen), 1923 v E, W, Ni; 1924 v Ni; 1926 v W, E, Ni; (with Blackburn R), 1927 v Ni; 1928 v W, Ni (10)

Hutton, J. (St Bernards), 1887 v Ni (1)

Hyslop, T. (Stoke C), 1896 v E; (with Rangers), 1897 v E (2)

Imlach, J. J. S. (Nottingham F), 1958 v H, Pol, Y, F (4)

Imrie, W. N. (St Johnstone), 1929 v N, G (2)

Inglis, J. (Kilmarnock Ath), 1884 v Ni (1)

Inglis, J. (Rangers), 1883 v E, W (2)

Irons, J. H. (Queen's Park), 1900 v W (1)

Irvine, B. (Aberdeen), 1991 v R; 1993 v G, Es (2); 1994 v Sw, I, Ma, A, Ho (9)

Jackson, A. (Cambuslang), 1886 v W; 1888 v Ni (2)

Jackson, A. (Aberdeen), 1925 v E, W, Ni; (with Huddersfield T), 1926 v E, W, Ni; 1927 v W, Ni; 1928 v E, W; 1929 v E, W, Ni; 1930 v E, W, Ni, F (17)

Jackson, C. (Rangers), 1975 v Se, P (sub), W; 1976 v D, R, Ni, W, E (8)

Jackson, D. (Hibernian), 1995 v Ru, Sm, J, Ec, Fa; 1996 v Gr, Fi (sub), Se (sub), Sm (sub), Aus (sub), D (sub), US (12)

Jackson, J. (Partick T), 1931 v A, I, Sw; 1933 v E; (with Chelsea), 1934 v E; 1935 v E; 1936 v W, Ni (8)

Jackson, T. A. (St Mirren), 1904 v W, E, Ni; 1905 v W; 1907 v W, Ni (6)

James, A. W. (Preston NE), 1926 v W; 1928 v E; 1929 v E, Ni; (with Arsenal), 1930 v E, W, Ni; 1933 v W (8)

Jardine, A. (Rangers), 1971 v D (sub); 1972 v P, Bel, Ho; 1973 v E, Sw, Br; 1974 v Cz (2), WG (2), Ni, W, E, Bel, N, Z, Br, Y; 1975 v EG, Sp (2), Se, P, W, Ni, E; 1977 v Se (sub), Ch (sub), Br (sub); 1978 v Cz, W, Ni, Ir; 1980 v Pe, A, Bel (2) (38)

Jarvie, A. (Airdrieonians), 1971 v P (sub), Ni (sub), E (sub) (3)

Jenkinson, T. (Hearts), 1887 v Ni (1)

Jess, E. (Aberdeen), 1993 v I (sub), Ma; 1994 v Sw (sub), I, Ho (sub), A, Ho (sub); 1995 v Fi (sub); 1996 v Se (sub), Sm, (with Coventry C) US, Co (sub), E (sub) (13)

Johnston, L. H. (Clyde), 1948 v Bel, Sw (2)

Johnston, M. (Watford), 1984 v W (sub), E (sub), F; 1985 v Y; (with Celtic), Ic, Sp (2), W; 1986 v EG; 1987 v Bul, Ei (2), L; (with Nantes), 1988 v H, Bel, L, S.Ar, Sp, Co, E; 1989 v N, Y, I, Cy, F, Cy, E, Ch (sub); (with Rangers), 1990 v F, N, EG, Pol, Ma, Cr, Se, Br; 1992 v Sw, Sm (sub) (38)

Johnston, R. (Sunderland), 1938 v Cz (1)

Johnston, W. (Rangers), 1966 v W, E, Pol, Ho; 1968 v W, E; 1969 v Ni (sub); 1970 v Ni; 1971 v D; (with WBA), 1977 v Se, W (sub), Ni, E, Ch, Arg, Br; 1978 v EG, Cz, W (2), E, Pe (22)

Johnstone, D. (Rangers), 1973 v W, Ni, E, Sw, Br; 1975 v EG (sub), Se (sub); 1976 v Sw, Ni (sub), E (sub); 1978 v Bul (sub), Ni, W; 1980 v Bel (14)

Johnstone, J. (Abercorn), 1888 v W (1)

Johnstone, J. (Celtic), 1965 v W, Fi; 1966 v E; 1967 v W, USSR; 1968 v W; 1969 v A, WG; 1970 v E, WG; 1971 v D, E; 1972 v P, Bel, Ho, Ni, E (sub); 1974 v W, E, Bel, N; 1975 v EG, Sp (23)

Johnstone, Jas (Kilmarnock), 1894 v W (1)

Johnstone, J. A. (Hearts), 1930 v W; 1933 v W, Ni (3)

Johnstone, R. (Hibernian), 1951 v E, D, F; 1952 v Ni, E; 1953 v E, Se; 1954 v W, E, N, Fi; 1955 v Ni, H; (with Manchester C), 1955 v E; 1956 v E, Ni, W (17)

Johnstone, W. (Third Lanark), 1887 v Ni; 1889 v W; 1890 v E (3)

Jordan, J. (Leeds U), 1973 v E (sub), Sw (sub), Br; 1974 v Cz (sub+1), WG (sub), Ni (sub), W, E, Bel, N, Z, Br, Y; 1975 v EG, Sp (2); 1976 v Ni, W, E; 1977 v Cz, W, Ni, E; 1978 v EG, Cz, W; (with Manchester U), Bul, Ni, E, Pe, Ir, Ho; 1979 v A, P, W (sub), Ni, E, N; 1980 v Bel, Ni (sub), W, E, Pol; 1981 v Is, W, E; (with AC Milan), 1982 v Se, Ho, W, E, USSR (52)

Kay, J. L. (Queen's Park), 1880 v E; 1882 v E, W; 1883 v E, W; 1884 v W (6)

Keillor, A. (Montrose), 1891 v W; 1892 v Ni; (with Dundee), 1894 v Ni; 1895 v W; 1896 v W; 1897 v W (6)

Keir, L. (Dumbarton), 1885 v W; 1886 v Ni; 1887 v E, W; 1888 v E (5)

Kelly, H. T. (Blackpool), 1952 v USA (1)

Kelly, J. (Renton), 1888 v E; (with Celtic), 1889 v E; 1890 v E; 1892 v E; 1893 v E, Ni; 1894 v W; 1896 v Ni (8)

Kelly, J. C. (Barnsley), 1949 v W, Ni (2)

Kelso, R. (Renton), 1885 v W, Ni; 1886 v W; 1887 v E, W; 1888 v E, Ni; (with Dundee), 1898 v Ni (9)

Kelso, T. (Dundee), 1914 v W (1)

Kennaway, J. (Celtic), 1934 v A (1)

Kennedy, A. (Eastern), 1875 v E; 1876 v E, W; (with Third Lanark), 1878 v E; 1882 v W; 1884 v W (6)

Kennedy, J. (Celtic), 1964 v W, E, WG; 1965 v W, Ni, Fi (6)

Kennedy, J. (Hibernian), 1897 v W (1)

Kennedy, S. (Aberdeen), 1978 v Bul, W, E, Pe, Ho; 1979 v A, P; 1982 v P (sub) (8)

Kennedy, S. (Partick T), 1905 v W (1)

Kennedy, S. (Rangers), 1975 v Se, P, W, Ni, E (5)

Ker, G. (Queen's Park), 1880 v E; 1881 v E, W; 1882 v W, E (5)

Ker, W. (Granville), 1872 v E; (with Queen's Park), 1873 v E (2)

Kerr, A. (Partick T), 1955 v A, H (2)

Kerr, P. (Hibernian), 1924 v Ni (1)

Key, G. (Hearts), 1902 v Ni (1)

Key, W. (Queen's Park), 1907 v Ni (1)

King, A. (Hearts), 1896 v E, W; (with Celtic), 1897 v Ni; 1898 v Ni; 1899 v Ni, W (6)

King, J. (Hamilton A), 1933 v Ni; 1934 v Ni (2)

King, W. S. (Queen's Park), 1929 v W (1)

Kinloch, J. D. (Partick T), 1922 v Ni (1)

Kinnaird, A. F. (Wanderers), 1873 v E (1)

Kinnear, D. (Rangers), 1938 v Cz (1)

Lambert, P. (Motherwell), 1995 v J, Ec (sub) (2)

Lambie, J. A. (Queen's Park), 1886 v Ni; 1887 v Ni; 1888 v E (3)

Lambie, W. A. (Queen's Park), 1892 v Ni; 1893 v W; 1894 v E; 1895 v E, Ni; 1896 v E, Ni; 1897 v E, Ni (9)

Lamont, D. (Pilgrims), 1885 v Ni (1)

Lang, A. (Dumbarton), 1880 v W (1)

Lang, J. J. (Clydesdale), 1876 v W; (with Third Lanark), 1878 v W (2)

Latta, A. (Dumbarton), 1888 v W; 1889 v E (2)

Law, D. (Huddersfield T), 1959 v W, Ni, Ho, P; 1960 v Ni, W; (with Manchester C), 1960 v E, Pol, A; 1961 v E, Ni; (with Torino), 1962 v Cz (2), E; (with Manchester U), 1963 v W, Ni, E, A, N, Ei, Sp; 1964 v W, E, N, WG; 1965 v W, Ni, E, Fi (2), Pol, Sp; 1966 v Ni, E, Pol; 1967 v W, E,

USSR; 1968 v Ni; 1969 v Ni, A, WG; 1972 v Pe, Ni, W, E, Y, Cz, Br; (with Manchester C), 1974 v Cz (2), WG (2), Ni, Z (55)

Law, G. (Rangers), 1910 v E, Ni, W (3)

Law, T. (Chelsea), 1928 v E; 1930 v E (2)

Lawrence, J. (Newcastle U), 1911 v E (1)

Lawrence, T. (Liverpool), 1963 v Ei; 1969 v W, WG (3)

Lawson, D. (St Mirren), 1923 v E (1)

Leckie, R. (Queen's Park), 1872 v E (1)

Leggat, G. (Aberdeen), 1956 v E; 1957 v W; 1958 v Ni, H, Pol, Y, Par; (with Fulham), 1959 v E, W, Ni, WG, Ho; 1960 v E, Ni, W, Pol, A, H (18)

Leighton, J. (Aberdeen), 1983 v EG, Sw, Bel, Sw, W, E, Ca (2); 1984 v U, Bel, Ni, W, E, F; 1985 v Y, Ic, Sp (2), W, E, Ic; 1986 v W, EG, Aus (2), Is, D, WG, U; 1987 v Bul, Ei (2), L, Bel, E; 1988 v H, Bel, Bul, L, S.Ar, Ma, Sp; (with Manchester U), 1989 v E; 1989 v N, Cy, F, Cy, E, Ch; 1990 v Y, F, N, Arg, Ma (sub, Cr, Se, Br; (with Hibernian), 1994 v Ma, A, Ho; 1995 v Gr (sub), Ru, Sm, J, Ec, Fa; 1996 v Gr, Fi, Se, Sm, Aus, D, US (74)

Lennie, W. (Aberdeen), 1908 v W, Ni (2)

Lennox, R. (Celtic), 1967 v Ni, E, USSR; 1968 v W, L; 1969 v D, A, WG, Cy (sub); 1970 v W (sub) (10)

Leslie, L. G. (Airdrieonians), 1961 v W, Ni, Ei (2), Cz (5)

Levein, C. (Hearts), 1990 v Arg, EG, Eg (sub), Pol, Ma (sub), Se; 1992 v R, Sm; 1993 v P, G, P; 1994 v Sw, Ho; 1995 v Fi, Fa, Ru (16)

Liddell, W. (Liverpool), 1947 v W, Ni; 1948 v E, W, Ni; 1950 v E, W, P, F; 1951 v W, Ni, E, A; 1952 v W, Ni, E, USA, D, Se; 1953 v W, Ni, E; 1954 v W; 1955 v P, Y, A, H; 1956 v Ni (28)

Liddle, D. (East Fife), 1931 v A, I, Sw (3)

Lindsay, D. (St Mirren), 1903 v Ni (1)

Lindsay, J. (Dumbarton), 1880 v W; 1881 v W, E; 1884 v W, E; 1885 v W, E; 1886 v E (8)

Lindsay, J. (Renton), 1888 v E; 1893 v E, Ni (3)

Linwood, A. B. (Clyde), 1950 v W (1)

Little, R. J. (Rangers), 1953 v Se (1)

Livingstone, G. T. (Manchester C), 1906 v E; (with Rangers), 1907 v W (2)

Lochhead, A. (Third Lanark), 1889 v W (1)

Logan, J. (Ayr U), 1891 v W (1)

Logan, T. (Falkirk), 1913 v Ni (1)

Logie, J. T. (Arsenal), 1953 v Ni (1)

Loney, W. (Celtic), 1910 v W, Ni (2)

Long, H. (Clyde), 1947 v Ni (1)

Longair, W. (Dundee), 1894 v Ni (1)

Lorimer, P. (Leeds U), 1970 v A (sub); 1971 v W, Ni; 1972 v Ni (sub), W, E; 1973 v D (2), E (2); 1974 v WG (sub), E, Bel, N, Z, Br, Y; 1975 v Sp (sub); 1976 v D (2), R (sub) (21)

Love, A. (Aberdeen), 1931 v A, I, Sw (3)

Low, A. (Falkirk), 1934 v Ni (1)

Low, T. P. (Rangers), 1897 v Ni (1)

Low, W. L. (Newcastle U), 1911 v E, W; 1912 v Ni; 1920 v E, Ni (5)

Lowe, J. (Cambuslang), 1891 v Ni (1)

Lowe, J. (St Bernards), 1887 v Ni (1)

Lundie, J. (Hibernian), 1886 v W (1)

Lyall, J. (Sheffield W), 1905 v E (1)

McAdam, J. (Third Lanark), 1880 v W (1)

McAllister, G. (Leicester C), 1990 v EG, Pol, Ma (sub); (with Leeds U), 1991 v R, Sw, Bul, USSR (sub), Sm; 1992 v Sw (sub), Sm, Ni, Fi (sub), US, Ca, N, Ho, G, C; 1993 v Sw, P, I, Ma; 1994 v Sw, I, Ma, Ho, A, Ho; 1995 v Fi, Ru, Gr, Ru, Sm; 1996 v Gr, Fi, Se, Sm, Aus, D, US (sub), Co, Ho, E, Sw (44)

McArthur, D. (Celtic), 1895 v E, Ni; 1899 v W (3)

McAtee, A. (Celtic), 1913 v W (1)

McAulay, J. (Dumbarton), 1882 v W; (with Arthurlie), 1884 v Ni (2)

McAulay, J. (Dumbarton), 1883 v E, W; 1884 v E; 1885 v W; 1886 v E; 1887 v E, W (8)

McAuley, R. (Rangers), 1932 v Ni, W (2)

McAvennie, F. (West Ham U), 1986 v Aus (2), D (sub), WG (sub); (with Celtic), 1988 v S.Ar (5)

McBain, E. (St Mirren), 1894 v W (1)

McBain, N. (Manchester U), 1922 v E; (with Everton), 1923 v Ni; 1924 v W (3)

McBride, J. (Celtic), 1967 v W, Ni (2)

McBride, P. (Preston NE), 1904 v E; 1906 v E; 1907 v E, W; 1908 v E; 1909 v W (6)

McCall, J. (Renton), 1886 v W; 1887 v E, W; 1888 v E; 1890 v E (5)

McCall, S. M. (Everton), 1990 v Arg, EG, Eg (sub), Pol, Ma, Cr, Se, Br; 1991 v Sw, USSR, Sm; (with Rangers), 1992 v Sw, R, Sm, US, Ca, N, Ho, G, C; 1993 v Sw, P (2); 1994 v I, Ho, A (sub), Ho; 1995 v Fi (sub), Ru, US, Gr, D, US (sub), Co, Ho, E, Sw (37)

McCalliog, J. (Sheffield W), 1967 v E, USSR; 1968 v Ni; 1969 v D; (with Wolverhampton W), 1971 v P (5)
McCallum, N. (Renton), 1888 v Ni (1)
McCann, R. J. (Motherwell), 1959 v WG; 1960 v E, Ni, W; 1961 v E (5)
McCartney, W. (Hibernian), 1902 v Ni (1)
McClair, B. (Celtic), 1987 v L, Ei, E, Br (sub); (with Manchester U), 1988 v Bul, Ma (sub), Sp (sub); 1989 v N, Y, I (sub), Cy, F (sub); 1990 v N (sub), Arg (sub); 1991 v Bul (2), Sm; 1992 v Sw (sub), R, Ni, US, Ca (sub), N, Ho, G, C; 1993 v Sw, P (sub), Es (2) (30)
McClory, A. (Motherwell), 1927 v W; 1928 v Ni; 1935 v W (3)
McCloy, P. (Ayr U), 1924 v E; 1925 v E (2)
McCloy, P. (Rangers), 1973 v W, Ni, Sw, Br (4)
McCoist, A. (Rangers), 1986 v Ho; 1987 v L (sub), Ei (sub), Bel, E, Br; 1988 v H, Bel, Ma, Sp, Co, E; 1989 v Y (sub), F, Cy, E; 1990 v Y, F, N, EG (sub), Eg, Pol, Ma (sub), Cr (sub), Se (sub), Br; 1991 v R, Sw, Bul (2), USSR; 1992 v Sw, Sm, Ni, Fi (sub), US, Ca, N, Ho, G, C; 1993 v Sw, P, I, Ma, P; 1996 v Gr (sub), Fi (sub), Sm (sub), Aus, D (sub), Co, E (sub), Sw (54)
McColl, A. (Renton), 1888 v Ni (1)
McColl, I. M. (Rangers), 1950 v E, F; 1951 v W, Ni, Bel; 1957 v E, Ni, W, Y, Sp, Sw, WG; 1958 v Ni, E (14)
McColl, R. S. (Queen's Park), 1896 v W, Ni; 1897 v Ni; 1898 v Ni; 1899 v Ni, E, W; 1900 v E, W; 1901 v E, W; (with Newcastle U), 1902 v E; (with Queen's Park), 1908 v Ni (13)
McColl, W. (Renton), 1895 v W (1)
McCombie, A. (Sunderland), 1903 v E, W; (with Newcastle U), 1905 v E, W (4)
McCorkindale, J. (Partick T), 1891 v W (1)
McCormick, R. (Abercorn), 1886 v W (1)
McCrae, D. (St Mirren), 1929 v N, G (2)
McCreadie, A. (Rangers), 1893 v W; 1894 v E (2)
McCreadie, E. G. (Chelsea), 1965 v E, Sp, Fi, Pol; 1966 v P, Ni, W, Pol, I; 1967 v E, USSR; 1968 v Ni, W, E, Ho; 1969 v W, Ni, E, D, A, WG, Cy (2) (23)
McCulloch, D. (Hearts), 1935 v W; (with Brentford), 1936 v E; 1937 v W, Ni; 1938 v Cz; (with Derby Co), 1939 v H, W (7)
MacDonald, A. (Rangers), 1976 v Sw (1)
McDonald, J. (Edinburgh University), 1886 v E (1)
McDonald, J. (Sunderland), 1956 v W, Ni (2)
MacDougall, E. J. (Norwich City) 1975 v Se, P, W, Ni, E; 1976 v D, R (sub) (7)
McDougall, J. (Liverpool), 1931 v I, A (2)
McDougall, J. (Airdrieonians), 1926 v Ni (1)
McDougall, J. (Vale of Leven), 1877 v E, W; 1878 v E; 1879 v E, W (5)
McFadyen, W. (Motherwell), 1934 v A, W (2)
Macfarlane, A. (Dundee), 1904 v W; 1906 v W; 1908 v W; 1909 v Ni; 1911 v W (5)
McFarlane, R. (Greenock Morton), 1896 v W (1)
Macfarlane, W. (Hearts), 1947 v L (1)
McGarr, E. (Aberdeen), 1970 v Ei, A (2)
McGarvey, F. P. (Liverpool), 1979 v Ni (sub), Arg; (with Celtic), 1984 v U, Bel (sub), EG (sub), Ni, W (7)
McGeoch, A. (Dumbreck), 1876 v E, W; 1877 v E, W (4)
McGhee, J. (Hibernian), 1886 v W (1)
McGhee, M. (Aberdeen), 1983 v Ca (1+1 sub); 1984 v Ni (sub), E (4)
McGinlay, J. (Bolton W), 1994 v A, Ho; 1995 v Fa, Ru, Gr, Ru, Sm, Fi; 1996 v Se (9)
McGonagle, W. (Celtic), 1933 v E; 1934 v A, E, Ni; 1935 v Ni, W (6)
McGrain, D. (Celtic), 1973 v W, Ni, E, Sw, Br; 1974 v Cz (2), WG, W (sub), E, Bel, N, Z, Br, Y; 1975 v Sp, Se, P, W, Ni, E, R; 1976 v D (2), Sw, Ni, W, E; 1977 v Fi, Cz, W (2), Se, Ni, E, Ch, Arg, Br; 1978 v EG, Cz; 1980 v Bel, P, Ni, W, E, Pol, H; 1981 v Se, P, Is, Ni, Is, W (sub), Ni, E; 1982 v Se, Sp, Ho, Ni, E, Nz, USSR (sub) (62)
McGregor, J. C. (Vale of Leven), 1877 v E, W; 1878 v E; 1880 v E (4)
McGrory, J. E. (Kilmarnock), 1965 v Ni, Fi; 1966 v P (3)
McGrory, J. (Celtic), 1928 v Ni; 1931 v E; 1932 v Ni, W, 1933 v E, Ni; 1934 v Ni (7)
McGuire, W. (Beith), 1881 v F, W (2)
McGurk, F. (Birmingham), 1934 v W (1)
McHardy, H. (Rangers), 1885 v Ni (1)
McInally, A. (Aston Villa), 1989 v Cy (sub), Ch; (with Bayern Munich), 1990 v Y (sub), F (sub), Arg, Pol (sub), Ma, Cr (8)
McInally, J. (Dundee U), 1987 v Bel, Br; 1988 v Ma (sub); 1991 v Bul (2); 1992 v US (sub), N (sub), C (sub); 1993 v G, P (10)
McInally, T. B. (Celtic), 1926 v Ni; 1927 v W (2)
McInnes, T. (Cowlairs), 1889 v Ni (1)
McIntosh, W. (Third Lanark), 1905 v Ni (1)
McIntyre, A. (Vale of Leven), 1878 v E; 1882 v E (2)

McIntyre, H. (Rangers), 1880 v W (1)
McIntyre, J. (Rangers), 1884 v W (1)
McKay, D. (Celtic), 1959 v E, WG, Ho, P; 1960 v E, Pol, A, H, T; 1961 v W, Ni; 1962 v Ni, Cz, U (sub) (14)
Mackay, D. C. (Hearts), 1957 v Sp; 1958 v F; 1959 v W, Ni; (with Tottenham H), 1959 v WG, E; 1960 v W, Ni, A, Pol, H, T; 1961 v W, Ni, E; 1963 v E, A, N; 1964 v Ni, W, N; 1966 v Ni (22)
Mackay, G. (Hearts), 1988 v Bul (sub), L (sub), S.Ar (sub), Ma (4)
McKay, J. (Blackburn R), 1924 v W (1)
McKay, R. (Newcastle U), 1928 v W (1)
McKean, R. (Rangers), 1976 v Sw (sub) (1)
McKenzie, D. (Brentford), 1938 v Ni (1)
Mackenzie, J. A. (Partick T), 1954 v W, E, N, Fi, A, U; 1955 v E, H; 1956 v A (9)
McKeown, M. (Celtic), 1889 v Ni; 1890 v E (2)
McKie, J. (East Stirling), 1898 v W (1)
McKillop, T. R. (Rangers), 1938 v Ho (1)
McKimmie, S. (Aberdeen), 1989 v E, Ch; 1990 v Arg, Eg, Cr (sub), Br; 1991 v R, Sw, Bul, Sm; 1992 v Sw, R, Ni, Fi, US, Ca (sub), N (sub), Ho, G, C; 1993 v P, Es (sub); 1994 v Sw, I, Ho, A, Ho; 1995 v Fi, Fa, Ru, Gr, Ru, Fa; 1996 v Gr, Fi, Se, D, Co (sub), Ho, E (40)
McKinlay, D. (Liverpool), 1922 v W, Ni (2)
McKinlay, T. (Celtic), 1996 v Gr, Fi, D, Co, E, Sw (6)
McKinlay, W. (Dundee U), 1994 v Ma, Ho (sub), A, Ho; 1995 v Fa (sub), Ru, Gr, Ru (sub), Sm (sub), J, Ec, Fa; 1996 v Fi (sub), Se (sub); (with Blackburn R), Sm (sub), Aus, D (sub), Ho (sub) (18)
McKinnon, A. (Queen's Park), 1874 v E (1)
McKinnon, R. (Rangers), 1966 v W, E, I (2), Ho, Br; 1967 v W, Ni, E; 1968 v Ni, W, E, Ho; 1969 v D, A, WG, Cy; 1970 v Ni, W, E, Ei, WG, A; 1971 v D, Bel, P, USSR, D (28)
McKinnon, R. (Motherwell), 1994 v Ma; 1995 v J, Fa (3)
MacKinnon, W. (Dumbarton), 1883 v E, W; 1884 v E, W (4)
McKinnon, W. W. (Queen's Park), 1872 v E; 1873 v E; 1874 v E; 1875 v E; 1876 v E, W; 1877 v E; 1878 v E; 1879 v E (9)
McLaren, A. (St Johnstone), 1929 v N, G, Ho; 1933 v W, Ni (5)
McLaren, A. (Preston NE), 1947 v E, Bel, L; 1948 v W (4)
McLaren, A. (Hearts), 1992 v US, Ca, N; 1993 v I, Ma, G, Es (sub + 1); 1994 v I, Ma, Ho, A; 1995 v Fi, Fa; (with Rangers), Ru, Gr, Ru, Sm, J, Ec, Fa; 1996 v Fi, Se, Sm (24)
McLaren, J. (Hibernian), 1888 v W; (with Celtic), 1889 v E; 1890 v E (3)
McLean, A. (Celtic), 1926 v W, Ni; 1927 v W, E (4)
McLean, D. (St Bernards), 1896 v W; 1897 v Ni (2)
McLean, D. (Sheffield W), 1912 v E (1)
McLean, G. (Dundee), 1968 v Ho (1)
McLean, T. (Kilmarnock), 1969 v D, Cy, W; 1970 v Ni, W; 1971 v D (6)
McLeish, A. (Aberdeen), 1980 v F, Ni, W, E, Pol, H; 1981 v Se, Is, Ni, Is, Ni, E; 1982 v Se, Sp, Ni, Br (sub); 1983 v Bel, Sw (sub), W, E, Ca (3); 1984 v U, Bel, EG, Ni, W, E, F; 1985 v Y, Ic, Sp (2), W, E, Ic; 1986 v W, EG, Aus (2), E, Ho, D; 1987 v Bel, E, Br; 1988 v Bel, Bul, L, S.Ar (sub), Ma, Sp, Co, E; 1989 v N, Y, I, Cy, F, Cy, E, Ch; 1990 v Y, F, N, Arg, EG, Eg, Cr, Se, Br; 1991 v R, Sw, USSR, Bul; 1993 v Ma (77)
McLeod, D. (Celtic), 1905 v Ni; 1906 v E, W, Ni (4)
McLeod, J. (Dumbarton), 1888 v Ni; 1889 v W; 1890 v Ni; 1892 v E; 1893 v W (5)
MacLeod, J. M. (Hibernian), 1961 v E, Ei (2), Cz (3)
MacLeod, M. (Celtic), 1985 v E (sub); 1987 v Ei, L, E, Br; (with Borussia Dortmund), 1988 v Co, E; 1989 v I, Ch; 1990 v Y, F, N (sub), Arg, EG, Pol, Se Br; (with Hibernian), 1991 v R, Sw, USSR (sub) (20)
McLeod, W. (Cowlairs), 1886 v Ni (1)
McLintock, A. (Vale of Leven), 1875 v E; 1876 v E; 1880 v E (3)
McLintock, F. (Leicester C), 1963 v N (sub), Ei, Sp; (with Arsenal), 1965 v Ni; 1967 v USSR; 1970 v Ni; 1971 v W, Ni, E (9)
McLuckie, J. S. (Manchester C), 1934 v W (1)
McMahon, A. (Celtic), 1892 v E; 1893 v E, Ni; 1894 v E; 1901 v W; 1902 v W (6)
McMenemy, J. (Celtic), 1905 v Ni; 1909 v Ni; 1910 v E, W; 1911 v Ni, W, E; 1914 v W, Ni, E; 1920 v Ni (12)
McMenemy, J. (Motherwell), 1934 v W (1)
McMillan, J. (St Bernards), 1897 v W (1)
McMillan, I. L. (Airdrieonians), 1952 v E, USA, D; 1955 v E; 1956 v E; (with Rangers), 1961 v Cz (6)
McMillan, T. (Dumbarton), 1887 v Ni (1)
McMullan, J. (Partick T), 1920 v W; 1921 v W, Ni, E; 1924 v E, Ni; 1925 v E; 1926 v W; (with Manchester C), 1926 v E; 1927 v E, W; 1928 v E, W; 1929 v W, E, Ni (16)
McNab, A. (Morton), 1921 v E, Ni (2)

McNab, A. (Sunderland), 1937 v A; (with WBA), 1939 v E (2)

McNab, C. D. (Dundee), 1931 v E, W, A, I, Sw; 1932 v E (6)

McNab, J. S. (Liverpool), 1923 v W (1)

McNair, A. (Celtic), 1906 v W; 1907 v Ni; 1908 v E, W; 1909 v E; 1910 v W; 1912 v E, W, Ni; 1913 v E; 1914 v E, Ni; 1920 v E, W, Ni (15)

McNaught, W. (Raith R), 1951 v A, W, Ni; 1952 v E; 1955 v Ni (5)

McNeil, H. (Queen's Park), 1874 v E; 1875 v E; 1876 v E, W; 1877 v W; 1878 v E; 1879 v E, W; 1881 v E, W (10)

McNeil, M. (Rangers), 1876 v W; 1880 v E (2)

McNeill, W. (Celtic), 1961 v E, Ei (2), Cz; 1962 v Ni, E, Cz, U; 1963 v Ei, Sp; 1964 v W, E, WG; 1965 v E, Fi, Pol, Sp; 1966 v Ni, Pol; 1967 v USSR; 1968 v E; 1969 v Cy, W, E, Cy (sub); 1970 v WG; 1972 v Ni, W, E (29)

McPhail, J. (Celtic), 1950 v W; 1951 v W, Ni, A; 1954 v Ni (5)

McPhail, R. (Airdrieonians), 1927 v E; (with Rangers), 1929 v W; 1931 v E, Ni; 1932 v W, Ni, F; 1933 v E, Ni; 1934 v A, Ni; 1935 v E; 1937 v G, E, Cz; 1938 v W, Ni (17)

McPherson, D. (Kilmarnock), 1892 v Ni (1)

McPherson, D. (Hearts), 1989 v Cy, E; 1990 v N, Ma, Cr, Se, Br; 1991 v Sw, Bul (2), USSR (sub), Sm; 1992 v Sw, R, Sm, Ni, Fi, US, Ca, N, Ho, G, C; (with Rangers), 1993 v Sw, I, Ma, P (27)

McPherson, J. (Clydesdale), 1875 v E (1)

McPherson, J. (Vale of Leven), 1879 v E, W; 1880 v E; 1881 v W; 1883 v E, W; 1884 v E; 1885 v Ni (8)

McPherson, J. (Kilmarnock), 1888 v W; (with Cowlairs), 1889 v E; 1890 v Ni, E; (with Rangers), 1892 v W; 1894 v E; 1895 v E, Ni; 1897 v Ni (9)

McPherson, J. (Hearts), 1891 v E (1)

McPherson, R. (Arthurlie), 1882 v E (1)

McQueen, G. (Leeds U), 1974 v Bel; 1975 v Sp (2), P, W, Ni, E, R; 1976 v D; 1977 v Cz, W (2), Ni, E; 1978 v EG, Cz, W; (with Manchester U), Bul, Ni, W; 1979 v A, N, P, Ni, E, N; 1980 v Pe, A, Bel; 1981 v W (30)

McQueen, M. (Leith Ath), 1890 v W; 1891 v W (2)

McRorie, D. M. (Morton), 1931 v W (1)

McSpadyen, A. (Partick T), 1939 v E, H (2)

McStay, P. (Celtic), 1984 v U, Bel, EG, Ni, W, E (sub); 1985 v I, Ic, Sp (2), W; 1986 v EG (sub), Aus, Is, U; 1987 v Bul, Ei (1+1 sub), L (sub), Bel, E, Br; 1988 v H, Bel, Bul, L, S.Ar, Sp, Co, E; 1989 v N, Y, I, Cy, F, Cy, E, Ch; 1990 v Y, F, N, Arg, EG (sub), Eg, Pol (sub), Ma, Cr, Se (sub), Br; 1991 v R, USSR, Bul; 1992 v Sm, Fi, US, Ca, N, Ho, G, C; 1993 v Sw, P, I, Ma, P, Es (2); 1994 v I (sub), Ho; 1995 v Fi, Fa, Ru; 1996 v Aus (73)

McStay, W. (Celtic), 1921 v W, Ni; 1925 v E, Ni, W; 1926 v E, Ni, W; 1927 v E, Ni, W; 1928 v W, Ni (13)

McTavish, J. (Falkirk), 1910 v Ni (1)

McWhattie, G. C. (Queen's Park), 1901 v W, Ni (2)

McWilliam, P. (Newcastle U), 1905 v E; 1906 v E; 1907 v E, W; 1909 v E, W; 1910 v E; 1911 v W (8)

Macari, L. (Celtic), 1972 v W (sub), E, Y, Cz, Br; 1973 v D; (with Manchester U), E (2), W (sub), Ni (sub); 1975 v Se, P (sub), W, E (sub), R; 1977 v Ni (sub), E (sub), Ch, Arg; 1978 v EG, Bul, Pe (sub), Ir (24)

Macauley, A. R. (Brentford), 1947 v E; (with Arsenal), 1948 v E, W, Ni, Bel, Sw, F (7)

Madden, J. (Celtic), 1893 v W; 1895 v W (2)

Main, F. R. (Rangers), 1938 v W (1)

Main, J. (Hibernian), 1909 v Ni (1)

Maley, W. (Celtic), 1893 v E, Ni (2)

Malpas, M. (Dundee U), 1984 v F; 1985 v E, Ic; 1986 v W, Aus (2), Is, R, E, Ho, D, WG; 1987 v Bul, Ei, Bel; 1988 v Bel, Bul, L, S.Ar, Ma; 1989 v N, Y, I, Cy, F, Cy, E, Ch; 1990 v Y, F, N, Eg, Pol, Ma, Cr, Se, Br; 1991 v R, Bul (2), USSR, Sm; 1992 v Sw, R, Sm, Ni, Fi, US, Ca (sub), N, Ho, G; 1993 v Sw, P, I (55)

Marshall, G. (Celtic), 1992 v US (1)

Marshall, H. (Celtic), 1899 v W; 1900 v Ni (2)

Marshall, J. (Middlesbrough), 1921 v E, W, Ni; 1922 v E, W, Ni; (with Llanelly), 1924 v W (7)

Marshall, J. (Third Lanark), 1885 v Ni; 1886 v W; 1887 v E, W (4)

Marshall, J. (Rangers), 1932 v E; 1933 v E; 1934 v E (3)

Marshall, R. W. (Rangers), 1892 v Ni; 1894 v Ni (2)

Martin, B. (Motherwell), 1995 v J, Ec (2)

Martin, F. (Aberdeen), 1954 v N (2), A, U; 1955 v E, H (6)

Martin, N. (Hibernian), 1965 v Fi, Pol; (with Sunderland), 1966 v I (3)

Martis, J. (Motherwell), 1961 v W (1)

Mason, J. (Third Lanark), 1949 v E, W, Ni; 1950 v Ni; 1951 v Ni, Bel, A (7)

Massie, A. (Hearts), 1932 v Ni, W, F; 1933 v Ni; 1934 v E, Ni; 1935 v E, Ni, W; 1936 v W, Ni; (with Aston Villa), 1936 v E; 1937 v G, E, W, Ni, A; 1938 v W (18)

Masson, D. S. (QPR), 1976 v Ni, W, E; 1977 v Fi, Cz, W, Ni, E, Ch, Arg, Br; 1978 v EG, Cz, W; (with Derby Co), Ni, E, Pe (17)

Mathers, D. (Partick T), 1954 v Fi (1)

Maxwell, W. S. (Stoke C), 1898 v E (1)

May, J. (Rangers), 1906 v W, Ni; 1908 v E, Ni; 1909 v W (5)

Meechan, P. (Celtic), 1896 v Ni (1)

Meiklejohn, D. D. (Rangers), 1922 v W; 1924 v W; 1925 v W, Ni, E; 1928 v W, Ni; 1929 v E, Ni; 1930 v E, Ni; 1931 v E; 1932 v W, Ni; 1934 v A (15)

Menzies, A. (Hearts), 1906 v E (1)

Mercer, R. (Hearts), 1912 v W; 1913 v Ni (2)

Middleton, R. (Cowdenbeath), 1930 v Ni (1)

Millar, A. (Hearts), 1939 v W (1)

Millar, J. (Rangers), 1897 v E; 1898 v E, W (3)

Millar, J. (Rangers), 1963 v A, Ei (2)

Miller, J. (St Mirren), 1931 v E, I, Sw; 1932 v F; 1934 v E (5)

Miller, P. (Dumbarton), 1882 v E; 1883 v E, W (3)

Miller, T. (Liverpool), 1920 v E; (with Manchester U), 1921 v E, Ni (3)

Miller, W. (Third Lanark), 1876 v E (1)

Miller, W. (Celtic), 1947 v E, W, Bel, L; 1948 v W, Ni (6)

Miller, W. (Aberdeen), 1975 v R; 1978 v Bul; 1980 v Bel, W, E, Pol, H; 1981 v Se, P, Is (sub), Ni, W, Ni, E; 1982 v Ni, P, Ho, Br, USSR; 1983 v EG, Sw (2), W, E, Ca (3); 1984 v U, Bel, EG, W, E, F; 1985 v Y, Ic, Sp (2), W, E, Ic; 1986 v W, EG, Aus (2), Is, R, E, Ho, D, WG, U; 1987 v Bul, E, Br; 1988 v H, L, S.Ar, Ma, Sp, Co, E; 1989 v N, Y; 1990 v Y, N (65)

Mills, W. (Aberdeen), 1936 v W, Ni; 1937 v W (3)

Milne, J. V. (Middlesbrough), 1938 v E; 1939 v E (2)

Mitchell, D. (Rangers), 1890 v Ni; 1892 v E; 1893 v E, Ni; 1894 v E (5)

Mitchell, J. (Kilmarnock), 1908 v Ni; 1910 v Ni, W (3)

Mitchell, R. C. (Newcastle U), 1951 v D, F (2)

Mochan, N. (Celtic), 1954 v N, A, U (3)

Moir, W. (Bolton W), 1950 v E (1)

Moncur, R. (Newcastle U), 1968 v Ho; 1970 v Ni, W, E, Ei; 1971 v D, Bel, W, P, Ni, E, D; 1972 v Pe, Ni, W, E (16)

Morgan, H. (St Mirren), 1898 v W; (with Liverpool), 1899 v E (2)

Morgan, W. (Burnley), 1968 v Ni; (with Manchester U), 1972 v Pe, Y, Cz, Br; 1973 v D (2), E (2), W, Ni, Sw, Br; 1974 v Cz (2), WG (2), Ni, Bel (sub), Br, Y (21)

Morris, D. (Raith R), 1923 v Ni; 1924 v E, Ni; 1925 v E, W, Ni (6)

Morris, H. (East Fife), 1950 v Ni (1)

Morrison, T. (St Mirren), 1927 v E (1)

Morton, A. L. (Queen's Park), 1920 v W, Ni; (with Rangers), 1921 v E; 1922 v E, W; 1923 v E, W, Ni; 1924 v E, W, Ni; 1925 v E, W, Ni; 1927 v E, Ni; 1928 v E, W, Ni; 1929 v E, W, Ni; 1930 v E, W, Ni; 1931 v E, W, Ni; 1932 v E, W, F (31)

Morton, H. A. (Kilmarnock), 1929 v G, Ho (2)

Mudie, J. K. (Blackpool), 1957 v W, Ni, E, Y, Sw, Sp (2), WG; 1958 v Ni, E, W, Sw, H, Pol, Y, Par, F (17)

Muir, W. (Dundee), 1907 v Ni (1)

Muirhead, T. A. (Rangers), 1922 v Ni; 1923 v E; 1924 v W; 1927 v Ni; 1928 v Ni; 1929 v W, Ni; 1930 v W (8)

Mulhall, G. (Aberdeen), 1960 v Ni; (with Sunderland), 1963 v Ni; 1964 v Ni (3)

Munro, A. D. (Hearts), 1937 v W, Ni; (with Blackpool), 1938 v Ho (3)

Munro, F. M. (Wolverhampton W), 1971 v Ni (sub), E (sub), D, USSR; 1975 v Se, W (sub), Ni, E, R (9)

Munro, I. (St Mirren), 1979 v Arg, N; 1980 v Pe, A, Bel, W, E (7)

Munro, N. (Abercorn), 1888 v W; 1889 v E (2)

Murdoch, J. (Motherwell), 1931 v Ni (1)

Murdoch, R. (Celtic), 1966 v W, E, I (2); 1967 v Ni; 1968 v Ni; 1969 v W, Ni, E, WG, Cy; 1970 v A (12)

Murphy, F. (Celtic), 1938 v Ho (1)

Murray, I. (Renton), 1895 v W (1)

Murray, J. (Hearts), 1958 v E, H, Pol, Y, F (5)

Murray, J. W. (Vale of Leven), 1890 v W (1)

Murray, P. (Hibernian), 1896 v Ni; 1897 v W (2)

Murray, S. (Aberdeen), 1972 v Bel (1)

Mutch, G. (Preston NE), 1938 v E (1)

Napier, C. E. (Celtic), 1932 v E; 1935 v E, W; (with Derby Co), 1937 v Ni, A (5)

Narey, D. (Dundee U), 1977 v Se (sub); 1979 v P, Ni (sub), Arg; 1980 v P, Ni, Pol, H; 1981 v W, E (sub); 1982 v Ho, W, E, Nz (sub), Br, USSR; 1983 v EG, Sw, Bel, Ni, W, E, Ca (3); 1986 v Is, R, Ho, WG, U; 1987 v Bul, E, Bel; 1989 v I, Cy (35)

Neil, R. G. (Hibernian), 1896 v W; (with Rangers), 1900 v W (2)

Neill, R. (Queen's Park), 1876 v W; 1877 v E, W; 1878 v W; 1880 v E (5)

Neilles, P. (Hearts), 1914 v W, Ni (2)

Shearer, R. (Rangers), 1961 v E, Ei (2), Cz (4)

Sillars, D. C. (Queen's Park), 1891 v Ni; 1892 v E; 1893 v W; 1894 v E; 1895 v W (5)

Simpson, J. (Third Lanark), 1895 v E, W, Ni (3)

Simpson, J. (Rangers), 1935 v E, W, Ni; 1936 v E, W, Ni; 1937 v G, E, W, Ni, A, Cz; 1938 v W, Ni (14)

Simpson, N. (Aberdeen), 1983 v Ni; 1984 v F (sub); 1987 v E; 1988 v E (4)

Simpson, R. C. (Celtic), 1967 v E, USSR; 1968 v Ni, E; 1969 v A (5)

Sinclair, G. L. (Hearts), 1910 v Ni; 1912 v W, Ni (3)

Sinclair, J. W. E. (Leicester C), 1966 v P (1)

Skene, L. H. (Queen's Park), 1904 v W (1)

Sloan, T. (Third Lanark), 1904 v W (1)

Smellie, R. (Queen's Park), 1887 v Ni; 1888 v W; 1889 v E; 1891 v E; 1893 v E, Ni (6)

Smith, A. (Rangers), 1898 v E; 1900 v E, Ni, W; 1901 v E, Ni, W; 1902 v E, Ni, W; 1903 v E, Ni, W; 1904 v Ni; 1905 v W; 1906 v E, Ni; 1907 v W; 1911 v E, Ni (20)

Smith, D. (Aberdeen), 1966 v Ho; (with Rangers), 1968 v Ho (2)

Smith, G. (Hibernian), 1947 v E, Ni; 1948 v W, Bel, Sw, F; 1952 v E, USA; 1955 v P, Y, A, H; 1956 v E, Ni, W; 1957 v Sp (2), Sw (18)

Smith, H. G. (Hearts), 1988 v S.Ar (sub); 1992 v Ni, Ca (3)

Smith, J. (Rangers), 1935 v Ni; 1938 v Ni (2)

Smith, J. (Ayr U), 1924 v E (1)

Smith, J. (Aberdeen), 1968 v Ho (sub); (with Newcastle U), 1974 v WG, Ni (sub), W (sub) (4)

Smith, J. E. (Celtic), 1959 v H, P (2)

Smith, Jas (Queen's Park), 1872 v E (1)

Smith, John (Mauchline), 1877 v E, W; 1879 v E, W; (with Edinburgh University), 1880 v E; (with Queen's Park), 1881 v W, E; 1883 v E, W; 1884 v E (10)

Smith, N. (Rangers), 1897 v E; 1898 v W; 1899 v E, W, Ni; 1900 v E, W, Ni; 1901 v Ni, W; 1902 v E, Ni (12)

Smith, R. (Queen's Park), 1872 v E; 1873 v E (2)

Smith, T. M. (Kilmarnock), 1934 v E; (with Preston NE), 1938 v E (2)

Somers, P. (Celtic), 1905 v E, Ni; 1907 v Ni; 1909 v W (4)

Somers, W. S. (Third Lanark), 1879 v E, W; (with Queen's Park), 1880 v W (3)

Somerville, G. (Queen's Park), 1886 v E (1)

Souness, G. J. (Middlesbrough), 1975 v EG, Sp, Se; (with Liverpool), 1978 v Bul, W, E (sub), Ho; 1979 v A, N, W, Ni, E; 1980 v Pe, A, Bel, P, Ni; 1981 v P, Is (2); 1982 v Ni, P, Sp, W, E, Nz, Br, USSR; 1983 v EG, Sw, Bel, Sw, W, E, Ca (2 + 1 sub); 1984 v U, Ni, W; (with Sampdoria), 1985 v Y, Ic, Sp (2), W, E, Ic; 1986 v EG, Aus (2), R, E, D, WG (54)

Speedie, D. R. (Chelsea), 1985 v E; 1986 v W, EG (sub), Aus, E; (with Coventry C), 1989 v Y (sub), I (sub), Cy (1+1 sub), Ch (10)

Speedie, F. (Rangers), 1903 v E, W, Ni (3)

Speirs, J. H. (Rangers), 1908 v W (1)

Spencer, J. (Chelsea), 1995 v Ru (sub), Gr (sub), Sm (sub), J; 1996 v Fi, Aus, D, US (sub), Co, Ho (sub), E, Sw (sub) (12)

Stanton, P. (Hibernian), 1966 v Ho; 1969 v Ni; 1970 v Ei, A; 1971 v D, Bel, P, USSR, D; 1972 v P, Bel, Ho, W; 1973 v W, Ni; 1974 v WG (16)

Stark, J. (Rangers), 1909 v E, Ni (2)

Steel, W. (Morton), 1947 v E, Bel, L; (with Derby Co), 1948 v F, E, W, Ni; 1949 v E, W, Ni, F; 1950 v E, W, Ni, Sw, P, F; (with Dundee), 1951 v W, Ni, E, A (2), D, F, Bel; 1952 v W; 1953 v W, E, Ni, Se (30)

Steele, D. M. (Huddersfield), 1923 v E, W, Ni (3)

Stein, C. (Rangers), 1969 v W, Ni, D, E, Cy (2); 1970 v A (sub), Ni (sub), W, E, Ei, WG; 1971 v D, USSR, Bel, D; 1972 v Cz (sub); (with Coventry C), 1973 v E (2 sub), W (sub), Ni (21)

Stephen, J. F. (Bradford), 1947 v W; 1948 v W (2)

Stevenson, G. (Motherwell), 1928 v W, Ni; 1930 v Ni, E, F; 1931 v E, W; 1932 v W, Ni; 1933 v Ni; 1934 v E; 1935 v Ni (12)

Stewart, A. (Queen's Park), 1888 v Ni; 1889 v W (2)

Stewart, A. (Third Lanark), 1894 v W (1)

Stewart, D. (Dumbarton), 1888 v Ni (1)

Stewart, D. (Queen's Park), 1893 v W; 1894 v Ni; 1897 v Ni (3)

Stewart, D. S. (Leeds U), 1978 v EG (1)

Stewart, G. (Hibernian), 1906 v W, E; (with Manchester C), 1907 v E, W (4)

Stewart, J. (Kilmarnock), 1977 v Ch (sub); (with Middlesbrough), 1979 v N (2)

Stewart, R. (West Ham U), 1981 v W, Ni, E; 1982 v Ni, P, W; 1984 v F; 1987 v Ei (2), L (10)

Stewart, W. E. (Queen's Park), 1898 v Ni; 1900 v Ni (2)

Storrier, D. (Celtic), 1899 v E, W, Ni (3)

Strachan, G. (Aberdeen), 1980 v Ni, W, E, Pol, H (sub); 1981 v Se, P; 1982 v Ni, P, Sp, Ho (sub), Nz, Br, USSR;

1983 v EG, Sw, Bel, Sw, Ni (sub), W, E, Ca (2 + 1 sub); 1984 v EG, Ni, E, F; (with Manchester U), 1985 v Sp (sub), E, Ic; 1986 v W, Aus, R, D, WG, U; 1987 v Bul, Ei (2); 1988 v H; 1989 v F (sub); (with Leeds U), 1990 v F; 1991 v USSR, Bul, Sm; 1992 v Sw, R, Ni, Fi (50)

Sturrock, P. (Dundee U), 1981 v W (sub), Ni, E (sub); 1982 v P, Ni (sub), W (sub), E (sub); 1983 v EG (sub), Sw, Bel (sub), Ca (3); 1984 v W; 1985 v Y (sub); 1986 v Is (sub), Ho, D, U; 1987 v Bel (20)

Summers, W. (St Mirren), 1926 v E (1)

Symon, J. S. (Rangers), 1939 v H (1)

Tait, T. S. (Sunderland), 1911 v W (1)

Taylor, J. (Queen's Park), 1872 v E; 1873 v E; 1874 v E; 1875 v E; 1876 v E, W (6)

Taylor, J. D. (Dumbarton), 1892 v W; 1893 v W; 1894 v Ni; (with St Mirren), 1895 v Ni (4)

Taylor, W. (Hearts), 1892 v E (1)

Telfer, W. (Motherwell), 1933 v Ni; 1934 v Ni (2)

Telfer, W. D. (St Mirren), 1954 v W (1)

Templeton, R. (Aston Villa), 1902 v E; (with Newcastle U), 1903 v W; 1904 v E; (with Woolwich Arsenal), 1905 v W; (with Kilmarnock), 1908 v Ni; 1910 v E, Ni; 1912 v E, Ni; 1913 v W (11)

Thomson, A. (Arthurlie), 1886 v Ni (1)

Thomson, A. (Third Lanark), 1889 v W (1)

Thomson, A. (Airdrieonians), 1909 v Ni (1)

Thomson, A. (Celtic), 1926 v E; 1932 v F; 1933 v W (3)

Thomson, C. (Hearts), 1904 v Ni; 1905 v E, Ni, W; 1906 v W, Ni; 1907 v E, W, Ni; 1908 v E, W, Ni; (with Sunderland), 1909 v W; 1910 v E; 1911 v Ni; 1912 v E, W; 1913 v E, W; 1914 v E, Ni (21)

Thomson, C. (Sunderland), 1937 v Cz (1)

Thomson, D. (Dundee), 1920 v W (1)

Thomson, J. (Celtic), 1930 v F; 1931 v E, W, Ni (4)

Thomson, J. J. (Queen's Park), 1872 v E; 1873 v E; 1874 v E (3)

Thomson, J. R. (Everton), 1933 v W (1)

Thomson, R. (Celtic), 1932 v W (1)

Thomson, R. W. (Falkirk), 1927 v E (1)

Thomson, S. (Rangers), 1884 v W, Ni (2)

Thomson, W. (Dumbarton), 1892 v W; 1893 v W; 1898 v Ni, W (4)

Thomson, W. (Dundee), 1896 v W (1)

Thornton, W. (Rangers), 1947 v W, Ni; 1948 v E, Ni; 1949 v F; 1952 v D, Se (7)

Thomson, W. (St Mirren), 1980 v Ni; 1981 v Ni (sub+1) 1982 v P; 1983 v Ni, Ca; 1984 v EG (7)

Toner, W. (Kilmarnock), 1959 v W, Ni (2)

Townsley, T. (Falkirk), 1926 v W (1)

Troup, A. (Dundee), 1920 v E; 1921 v W, Ni; 1922 v Ni; (with Everton), 1926 v E (5)

Turnbull, E. (Hibernian), 1948 v Bel, Sw; 1951 v A; 1958 v H, Pol, Y, Par, F (8)

Turner, T. (Arthurlie), 1884 v W (1)

Turner, W. (Pollokshields Ath), 1885 v Ni; 1886 v Ni (2)

Ure, J. F. (Dundee), 1962 v W, Cz; 1963 v W, Ni, E, A, N, Sp; (with Arsenal), 1964 v Ni, N; 1968 v Ni (11)

Urquhart, D. (Hibernian), 1934 v W (1)

Vallance, T. (Rangers), 1877 v E, W; 1878 v E; 1879 v E, W; 1881 v E, W (7)

Venters, A. (Cowdenbeath), 1934 v Ni; (with Rangers), 1936 v E; 1939 v E (3)

Waddell, S. S. (Queen's Park), 1891 v Ni; 1892 v E; 1893 v E, Ni; 1895 v E, Ni (6)

Waddell, W. (Rangers), 1947 v W; 1949 v E, W, Ni, F; 1950 v E, Ni; 1951 v E, D, F, Bel, A; 1952 v Ni, W; 1954 v Ni; 1955 v W, Ni (17)

Wales, H. M. (Motherwell), 1933 v W (1)

Walker, A. (Celtic), 1988 v Co (sub); 1995 v Fi, Fa (sub) (3)

Walker, F. (Third Lanark), 1922 v W (1)

Walker, G. (St Mirren), 1930 v F; 1931 v Ni, A, Sw (4)

Walker, J. (Hearts), 1895 v Ni; 1897 v W; 1898 v Ni; (with Rangers), 1904 v W, Ni (5)

Walker, J. (Swindon T), 1911 v E, W, Ni; 1912 v E, W, Ni; 1913 v E, W, Ni (9)

Walker, J. N. (Hearts), 1993 v G; (with Partick T), 1996 v US (sub) (2)

Walker, R. (Hearts), 1900 v E, Ni; 1901 v E, W; 1902 v E, W, Ni; 1903 v E, W, Ni; 1904 v E, W, Ni; 1905 v E, W, Ni; 1906 v Ni; 1907 v E, Ni; 1908 v E, W, Ni; 1909 v E, W; 1912 v E, W, Ni; 1913 v E, W (29)

Walker, T. (Hearts), 1935 v E, W; 1936 v E, W, Ni; 1937 v G, E, W, Ni, A, Cz; 1938 v E, W, Ni, Cz, Ho; 1939 v E, W, Ni, H (20)

Walker, W. (Clyde), 1909 v Ni; 1910 v Ni (2)

Wallace, I. A. (Coventry C), 1978 v Bul (sub); 1979 v P (sub), W (3)

Wallace, W. S. B. (Hearts), 1965 v Ni; 1966 v E, Ho; (with Celtic), 1967 v E, USSR (sub); 1968 v Ni; 1969 v E (sub) (7)

Wardhaugh, J. (Hearts), 1955 v H; 1957 v Ni (2)

Wark, J. (Ipswich T), 1979 v W, Ni, E, Arg, N (sub); 1980 v Pe, A, Bel (2); 1981 v Is, Ni; 1982 v Se, Sp, Ho, Ni, Nz, Br, USSR; 1983 v EG, Sw (2), Ni, E (sub); 1984 v U, Bel, EG; (with Liverpool), E, F; 1985 v Y (29)

Watson, A. (Queen's Park), 1881 v E, W; 1882 v E (3)

Watson, J. (Sunderland), 1903 v E, W; 1904 v E; 1905 v E; (with Middlesbrough), 1909 v E, Ni (6)

Watson, J. (Motherwell), 1948 v Ni; (with Huddersfield T), 1954 v Ni (2)

Watson, J. A. K. (Rangers), 1878 v W (1)

Watson, P. R. (Blackpool), 1934 v A (1)

Watson, R. (Motherwell), 1971 v USSR (1)

Watson, W. (Falkirk), 1898 v W (1)

Watt, F. (Kilbirnie), 1889 v W, Ni; 1890 v W; 1891 v E (4)

Watt, W. W. (Queen's Park), 1887 v Ni (1)

Waugh, W. (Hearts), 1938 v Cz (1)

Weir, A. (Motherwell), 1959 v WG; 1960 v E, P, A, H, T (6)

Weir, J. (Third Lanark), 1887 v Ni (1)

Weir, J. B. (Queen's Park), 1872 v E; 1874 v E; 1875 v E; 1878 v W (4)

Weir, P. (St Mirren), 1980 v Ni, W, Pol (sub), H; (with Aberdeen), 1983 v Sw; 1984 v Ni (6)

White, John (Albion R), 1922 v W; (with Hearts), 1923 v Ni (2)

White, J. A. (Falkirk), 1959 v WG, Ho, P; 1960 v Ni; (with Tottenham H), 1960 v W, Pol, A, T; 1961 v W; 1962 v Ni, W, E, Cz (2); 1963 v W, Ni, E; 1964 v Ni, W, E, N, WG (22)

White, W. (Bolton W), 1907 v E; 1908 v E (2)

Whitelaw, A. (Vale of Leven), 1887 v Ni; 1890 v W (2)

Whyte, D. (Celtic), 1988 v Bel (sub), L; 1989 v Ch (sub); 1992 v US (sub); (with Middlesbrough), 1993 v P, I; 1995 v J (sub), Ec; 1996 v US (9)

Wilson, A. (Sheffield W), 1907 v E; 1908 v E; 1912 v E; 1913 v E, W; 1914 v Ni (6)

Wilson, A. (Portsmouth), 1954 v Fi (1)

Wilson, A. N. (Dunfermline), 1920 v E, W, Ni; 1921 v E, W, Ni; (with Middlesbrough), 1922 v E, W, Ni; 1923 v E, W, Ni (12)

Wilson, D. (Queen's Park), 1900 v W (1)

Wilson, D. (Oldham Ath), 1913 v E (1)

Wilson, D. (Rangers), 1961 v E, W, Ni, Ei (2), Cz; 1962 v Ni, W, E, Cz, U; 1963 v W, E, A, N, Ei, Sp; 1964 v E, WG; 1965 v Ni, E, Fi (22)

Wilson, G. W. (Hearts), 1904 v W; 1905 v E, Ni; 1906 v W; (with Everton), 1907 v E; (with Newcastle U), 1909 v E (6)

Wilson, Hugh, (Newmilns), 1890 v W; (with Sunderland), 1897 v E; (with Third Lanark), 1902 v W; 1904 v Ni (4)

Wilson, I. A. (Leicester C), 1987 v E, Br; (with Everton), 1988 v Bel, Bul, L (5)

Wilson, J. (Vale of Leven), 1888 v W; 1889 v E; 1890 v E; 1891 v E (4)

Wilson, P. (Celtic), 1926 v Ni; 1930 v F; 1931 v Ni; 1933 v E (4)

Wilson, P. (Celtic), 1975 v Sp (sub) (1)

Wilson, R. P. (Arsenal), 1972 v P, Ho (2)

Wiseman, W. (Queen's Park), 1927 v W; 1930 v Ni (2)

Wood, G. (Everton), 1979 v Ni, E, Arg (sub); (with Arsenal), 1982 v Ni (4)

Woodburn, W. A. (Rangers), 1947 v E, Bel, L; 1948 v W, Ni; 1949 v E, F; 1950 v E, W, Ni, P, F; 1951 v E, W, Ni, A (2), D, F, Bel; 1952 v E, W, Ni, USA (24)

Wotherspoon, D. N. (Queen's Park), 1872 v E; 1873 v E (2)

Wright, K. (Hibernian), 1992 v Ni (1)

Wright, S. (Aberdeen), 1993 v G, Es (2)

Wright, T. (Sunderland), 1953 v W, Ni, E (3)

Wylie, T. G. (Rangers), 1890 v Ni (1)

Yeats, R. (Liverpool), 1965 v W; 1966 v I (2)

Yorston, B. C. (Aberdeen), 1931 v Ni (1)

Yorston, H. (Aberdeen), 1955 v W (1)

Young, A. (Hearts), 1960 v E, A (sub), H, T; 1961 v W, Ni; (with Everton), Ei; 1966 v P (8)

Young, A. (Everton), 1905 v E; 1907 v W (2)

Young, G. L. (Rangers), 1947 v E, Ni, Bel, L; 1948 v E, Ni, Bel, Sw, F; 1949 v E, W, Ni, F; 1950 v E, W, Ni, Sw, P, F; 1951 v E, W, Ni, A (2), D, F, Bel; 1952 v E, W, Ni, USA, D, Se; 1953 v W, E, Ni, Se; 1954 v W, Ni; 1955 v W, Ni, P, Y; 1956 v Ni, W, E, A; 1957 v E, Ni, W, Y, Sp, Sw (53)

Young, J. (Celtic), 1906 v Ni (1)

Younger, T. (Hibernian), 1955 v P, Y, A, H; 1956 v E, Ni, W, A; (with Liverpool), 1957 v E, Ni, W, Y, Sp (2), Sw, WG; 1958 v Ni, W, E, Sw, H, Pol, Y, Par (24)

WALES

Adams, H. (Berwyn R), 1882 v Ni, E; (with Druids), 1883 v Ni, E (4)

Aizlewood, M. (Charlton Ath), 1986 v S.Ar, Ca (2); 1987 v Fi; (with Leeds U), USSR, Fi (sub); 1988 v D (sub), Se, Ma, I; 1989 v Ho, Se (sub), WG; (with Bradford C), 1990 v Fi, WG, Ei, Cr; (with Bristol C), 1991 v D, Bel (2), L, Ei, Ic, Pol, WG; 1992 v Br, L, Ei, A, R, Ho, Arg, J; 1993 v Ei, Bel, Fa; 1994 v RCS, Cy; (with Cardiff C) 1995v Bul (39)

Allchurch, I. J. (Swansea T), 1951 v E, Ni, P, Sw; 1952 v E, S, Ni, R of UK; 1953 v S, E, Ni, F, Y; 1954 v S, E, Ni, A; 1955 v S, E, Ni, Y; 1956 v E, S, Ni, A; 1957 v E, S; 1958 v Ni, Is (2), H (2), M, Sw, Br; (with Newcastle U), 1959 v E, S, Ni; 1960 v S, E; 1961 v Ni, H, Sp (2); 1962 v E, S, Br (2), M; (with Cardiff C), 1963 v S, E, Ni, H (2); 1964 v E; 1965 v S, E, Ni, Gr, I, USSR; (with Swansea T), 1966 v USSR, E, S, D, Br (2), Ch (68)

Allchurch, L. (Swansea T), 1955 v Ni; 1956 v A; 1958 v S, Ni, EG, Is; 1959 v S; (with Sheffield U), 1962 v S, Ni, Br; 1964 v E (11)

Allen, B. W. (Coventry C), 1951 v S, E (2)

Allen, M. (Watford), 1986 v S.Ar (sub), Ca (1 + 1 sub); (with Norwich C), 1989 v Is (sub); 1990 v Ho, WG; (with Millwall), Ei, Se, Cr (sub); 1991 v L (sub), Ei (sub); 1992 v A; 1993 v Ei (sub); (with Newcastle U), 1994 v R (sub) (14)

Arridge, S. (Bootle), 1892 v S, Ni; (with Everton), 1894 v Ni; 1895 v Ni; 1896 v E; (with New Brighton Tower), 1898 v E, Ni; 1899 v E (8)

Astley, D. J. (Charlton Ath), 1931 v Ni; (with Aston Villa), 1932 v E; 1933 v E, S, Ni; 1934 v E, S; 1935 v S; 1936 v E, Ni; (with Derby Co), 1939 v E, S; (with Blackpool), F (13)

Atherton, R. W. (Hibernian), 1899 v E, S, Ni; 1903 v E, S, Ni; (with Middlesbrough), 1904 v E, S, Ni; 1905 v Ni (9)

Bailiff, W. E. (Llanelly), 1913 v E, S, Ni; 1920 v Ni (4)

Baker, C. W. (Cardiff C), 1958 v M; 1960 v S, Ni; 1961 v S, E, Ei; 1962 v S (7)

Baker, W. G. (Cardiff C), 1948 v Ni (1)

Bamford, T. (Wrexham), 1931 v E, S, Ni; 1932 v Ni; 1933 v F (5)

Barnes, W. (Arsenal), 1948 v E, S, Ni; 1949 v E, S, Ni; 1950 v E, S, Ni, Bel; 1951 v E, S, Ni, P; 1952 v E, S, Ni, R of UK; 1954 v E, S; 1955 v S, Y (22)

Bartley, T. (Glossop NE), 1898 v E (1)

Bastock, A. M. (Shrewsbury), 1892 v Ni (1)

Beadles, G. H. (Cardiff C), 1925 v E, S (2)

Bell, W. S. (Shrewsbury Engineers), 1881 v E, S; (with Crewe Alex), 1886 v E, S, Ni (5)

Bennion, S. R. (Manchester U), 1926 v S; 1927 v S; 1928 v S, E, Ni; 1929 v S, E, Ni; 1930 v S; 1932 v Ni (10)

Berry, G. F. (Wolverhampton W), 1979 v WG; 1980 v Ei, WG (sub), T; (with Stoke C), 1983 v E (sub) (5)

Blackmore, C. G. (Manchester U), 1985 v N (sub); 1986 v S (sub), H (sub), S.Ar, Ei, U; 1987 v Fi (2), USSR, Cz; 1988 v D (2), Cz, Y, Se, Ma, I; 1989 v Ho, Fi, Is, WG; 1990 v F, Ho, WG, Cr; 1991 v Bel, L; 1992 v Ei (sub), A, R (sub), Ho, Arg, J; 1993 v Fa, Cy, Bel, RCS; 1994 v Se (sub) (38)

Blake, N. A. (Sheffield U), 1994 v N, Se (sub); 1995 v Alb, Mol; 1996 v G (with Bolton W), I (sub) (6)

Blew, H. (Wrexham), 1899 v E, S, Ni; 1902 v S, Ni; 1903 v E, S; 1904 v E, S, Ni; 1905 v S, Ni; 1906 v E, S, Ni; 1907 v S; 1908 v E, S, Ni; 1909 v E, S; 1910 v E (22)

Boden, T. (Wrexham), 1880 v E (1)

Bodin, P. J. (Swindon T), 1990 v Cr; 1991 v D, Bel, L, Ei; (with C Palace), Bel, Ic, Pol, WG; 1992 v Br, G, L (sub); (with Swindon T), Ei (sub), Ho, Arg; 1993 v Ei, Bel, RCS, Fa; 1994 v R, Se, Es (sub); 1995 v Alb (23)

Boulter, L. M. (Brentford), 1939 v Ni (1)

Bowdler, H. E. (Shrewsbury), 1893 v S (1)

Bowdler, J. C. H. (Shrewsbury), 1890 v Ni; (with Wolverhampton), 1891 v S; 1892 v Ni; (with Shrewsbury), 1894 v E (4)

Bowen, D. L. (Arsenal), 1955 v S, Y; 1957 v Ni, Cz, EG; 1958 v E, S, Ni, EG, Is (2), H (2), M, Se, Br; 1959 v E, S, Ni (19)

Bowen, E. (Druids), 1880 v S; 1883 v S (2)

Bowen, J. P. (Swansea C), 1994 v Se (1)

Bowen, M. R. (Tottenham H), 1986 v Ca (2 sub); (with Norwich C), 1988 v Y (sub); 1989 v Ho (sub) Is, Se, WG (sub); 1990 v Fi (sub), Ho, WG, Se; 1992 v Br (sub), G, L, Ei, A, R, Ho (sub), J; 1993 v Fa, Cy, Bel (1 + sub), RCS

(sub); 1994 v RCS, Se; 1995 v Mol, Ge, Bul (2), G, Ge; 1996 v Mol, G, Alb, Sw, Sm (37)
Bowsher, S. J. (Burnley), 1929 v Ni (1)
Boyle, T. (C Palace), 1981 v Ei, S (sub) (2)
Britten, T. J. (Parkgrove), 1878 v S; (with Presteigne), 1880 v S (2)
Brookes, S. J. (Llandudno), 1900 v E, Ni (2)
Brown, A. I. (Aberdare Ath), 1926 v Ni (1)
Browning, M. T. (Bristol R), 1996 v I (sub), Sm (2)
Bryan, T. (Oswestry), 1886 v E, Ni (2)
Buckland, T. (Bangor), 1899 v E (1)
Burgess, W. A. R. (Tottenham H), 1947 v E, S, Ni; 1948 v E, S; 1949 v E, S, Ni, P, Bel, Sw; 1950 v E, S, Ni, Bel; 1951 v S, Ni, P, Sw; 1952 v E, S, Ni, R of UK; 1953 v S, E, Ni, F, Y; 1954 v S, E, Ni, A (32)
Burke, T. (Wrexham), 1883 v E; 1884 v S; 1885 v E, S, Ni; (with Newton Heath), 1887 v E, S; 1888 v S (8)
Burnett, T. B. (Ruabon), 1877 v S (1)
Burton, A. D. (Norwich C), 1963 v Ni, H; (with Newcastle U), 1964 v E; 1969 v S, E, Ni, I, EG; 1972 v Cz (9)
Butler, J. (Chirk), 1893 v E, S, Ni (3)
Butler, W. T. (Druids), 1900 v S, Ni (2)

Cartwright, L. (Coventry C), 1974 v E (sub), S, Ni; 1976 v S (sub); 1977 v WG (sub); (with Wrexham), 1978 v Ir (sub); 1979 v Ma (7)
Carty, T. – See McCarthy – (Wrexham).
Challen, J. B. (Corinthians), 1887 v E, S; 1888 v E; (with Wellingborough GS), 1890 v E (4)
Chapman, T. (Newtown), 1894 v E, S, Ni; 1895 v S, Ni; (with Manchester C), 1896 v E; 1897 v E (7)
Charles, J. M. (Swansea C), 1981 v Cz, T (sub), S (sub), USSR (sub); 1982 v Ic; 1983 v N (sub), Y (sub), Bul (sub), S, Ni, Br; 1984 v Bul (sub); (with QPR), Y (sub), S; (with Oxford U), 1985 v Ic (sub), Sp, Ic; 1986 v Ei; 1987 v Fi (19)
Charles, M. (Swansea T), 1955 v Ni; 1956 v E, S, A; 1957 v E, Ni, Cz (2), EG; 1958 v E, S, EG, Is (2), H (2), M, Se, Br; 1959 v E, S; (with Arsenal), 1961 v Ni, H, Sp (2); 1962 v E, S; (with Cardiff C), 1962 v Br, Ni; 1963 v S, H (31)
Charles, W. J. (Leeds U), 1950 v Ni; 1951 v Sw; 1953 v Ni, F, Y; 1954 v E, S, Ni, A; 1955 v E, Ni, Y; 1956 v E, S, A, Ni; 1957 v E, S, Ni, Cz (2), EG; (with Juventus), 1958 v Is (2), H (2) M, Se; 1960 v S; 1962 v E, Br (2), M; (with Leeds U), 1963 v S; (with Cardiff C), 1964 v S; 1965 v S, USSR (38)
Clarke, R. J. (Manchester C), 1949 v E; 1950 v S, Ni, Bel; 1951 v E, S, Ni, P, Sw; 1952 v S, E, Ni, R of UK; 1953 v S, E; 1954 v E, S, Ni; 1955 v Y, S, E; 1956 v Ni (22)
Coleman, C. (C Palace), 1992 v A (sub); 1993 v Ei (sub); 1994 v N, Es; 1995 v Alb, Mol, Ge, Bul (2), G; 1996 v Mol; (with Blackburn R), I, Sw, Sm (14)
Collier, D. J. (Grimsby T), 1921 v S (1)
Collins, W. S. (Llanelly), 1931 v S (1)
Conde, C. (Chirk), 1884 v E, S, Ni (3)
Cook, F. C. (Newport Co), 1925 v E, S; (with Portsmouth), 1928 v E, S; 1930 v E, S, Ni; 1932 v E (8)
Cornforth, J.M. (Swansea C), 1995 v Bul (sub), Ge (2)
Coyne, D. (Tranmere R), 1996 v Sw (1)
Crompton, W. (Wrexham), 1931 v E, S, Ni (3)
Cross, E. A. (Wrexham), 1876 v S; 1877 v S (2)
Cross, K. (Druids), 1879 v S; 1881 v E, S (3)
Crowe, V. H. (Aston Villa), 1959 v E, Ni; 1960 v E, Ni; 1961 v S, E, Ni, Ei, H, Sp (2); 1962 v E, S, Br, M; 1963 v H (16)
Cumner, R. H. (Arsenal), 1939 v S, Ni (3)
Curtis, A. (Swansea C), 1976 v E, Y (sub), S, Ni, Y (sub), E; 1977 v WG, S (sub), Ni (sub); 1978 v WG, E, S; 1979 v WG, S; (with Leeds U), Ni, Ma; 1980 v Ei, WG, T; (with Swansea C), 1982 v Cz, Ic, USSR, Sp, E, S, Ni; 1983 v N; 1984 v R (sub); (with Southampton), S; 1985 v Sp, Ni (1 + 1 sub); 1986 v H; (with Cardiff C), 1987 v USSR (35)
Curtis, E. R. (Cardiff C), 1928 v S; (with Birmingham), 1932 v S; 1934 v Ni (3)

Daniel, R. W. (Arsenal), 1951 v E, Ni, P; 1952 v E, S, Ni, R of UK; 1953 v S, E, Ni, F, Y; (with Sunderland), 1954 v E, S, Ni; 1955 v E, Ni; 1957 v S, E, Ni, Cz (21)
Darvell, S. (Oxford University), 1897 v S, Ni (2)
Davies, A. (Manchester U), 1983 v Ni, Br; 1984 v E, Ni; 1985 v Ic; (with Newcastle U), 1986 v H; (with Swansea C), 1988 v Ma, I; 1989 v Ho; (with Bradford C), 1990 v Fi, Ei (11)
Davies, A. (Wrexham), 1876 v S; 1877 v S (2)
Davies, A. (Druids), 1904 v S; (with Middlesbrough), 1905 v S (2)
Davies, A. O. (Barmouth), 1885 v Ni; 1886 v E, S; (with Swifts), 1887 v E, S; 1888 v E, Ni; (with Wrexham), 1889 v S; (with Crewe Alex), 1890 v E (9)
Davies, A. T. (Shrewsbury), 1891 v Ni (1)
Davies, C. (Brecon), 1899 v Ni; (with Hereford), 1900 v Ni (2)

Davies, C. (Charlton Ath), 1972 v R (sub) (1)
Davies, D. (Bolton W), 1904 v S, Ni; 1908 v E (sub) (3)
Davies, D. C. (Brecon), 1899 v Ni; (with Hereford); 1900 v Ni (2)
Davies, D. W. (Treharris), 1912 v Ni; (with Oldham Ath), 1913 v Ni (2)
Davies, E. Lloyd (Stoke C), 1904 v E; 1907 v E, S, Ni; (with Northampton T), 1908 v S; 1909 v Ni; 1910 v Ni; 1911 v E, S; 1912 v E, S; 1913 v E, S; 1914 v Ni, E, S (16)
Davies, E. R. (Newcastle U), 1953 v S, E; 1954 v E, S; 1958 v E, EG (6)
Davies, G. (Fulham), 1980 v T, Ic; 1982 v Sp (sub), F (sub); 1983 v E, Bul, S, Ni, Br; 1984 v R (sub), S (sub), E, Ni; 1985 v Ic; (with Manchester C), 1986 v S.Ar, Ei (16)
Davies, Rev. H. (Wrexham), 1928 v Ni (1)
Davies, Idwal (Liverpool Marine), 1923 v S (1)
Davies, J. E. (Oswestry), 1885 v E (1)
Davies, Jas (Wrexham), 1878 v S (1)
Davies, John (Wrexham), 1879 v S (1)
Davies, Jos (Newton Heath), 1888 v E, S, Ni; 1889 v S; 1890 v E; (with Wolverhampton W), 1892 v E; 1893 v E (7)
Davies, Jos (Everton), 1889 v S, Ni; (with Chirk), 1891 v Ni; (with Ardwick), v E, S; (with Sheffield U), 1895 v E, S, Ni; (with Manchester C), 1896 v E; (with Millwall), 1897 v E; (with Reading), 1900 v E (11)
Davies, J. P. (Druids), 1883 v E, Ni (2)
Davies, Ll. (Wrexham), 1907 v Ni; 1910 v Ni, S, E; (with Everton), 1911 v S, Ni; (with Wrexham), 1912 v Ni, S, E; 1913 v Ni, S, E; 1914 v Ni (13)
Davies, L. S. (Cardiff C), 1922 v E, S, Ni; 1923 v E, S, Ni; 1924 v E, S, Ni; 1925 v S, Ni; 1926 v E, Ni; 1927 v E, Ni; 1928 v S, Ni, E; 1929 v S, Ni, E; 1930 v E, S (23)
Davies, O. (Wrexham), 1890 v S (1)
Davies, R. (Wrexham), 1883 v Ni; 1884 v Ni; 1885 v Ni (3)
Davies, R. (Druids), 1885 v E (1)
Davies, R. O. (Wrexham), 1892 v Ni, E (2)
Davies, R. T. (Norwich C), 1964 v Ni; 1965 v E; 1966 v Br (2), Ch; (with Southampton), 1967 v S, E, Ni; 1968 v S, Ni, WG; 1969 v S, E, Ni, I, WG, R of UK; 1970 v S, Ni; 1971 v Cz, S, E, Ni; 1972 v R, E, S, N; (with Portsmouth), 1974 v E (29)
Davies, R. W. (Bolton W), 1964 v E; 1965 v E, S, Ni, D, Gr, USSR; 1966 v E, S, Ni, USSR, D, Br (2), Ch (sub); 1967 v S; (with Newcastle U), E; 1968 v S, Ni, WG; 1969 v S, E, Ni, I; 1970 v EG; 1971 v R, Cz; (with Manchester C), 1972 v E, S, Ni; (with Manchester U), 1973 v E, S (sub), Ni; (with Blackpool), 1974 v Pol (34)
Davies, S. I. (Manchester U), 1996 v Sw (sub) (1)
Davies, Stanley (Preston NE), 1920 v E, S, Ni; (with Everton), 1921 v E, S, Ni; (with WBA), 1922 v E, S, Ni; 1923 v S; 1925 v S, Ni; 1926 v S, E, Ni; 1927 v S; 1928 v S; (with Rotherham U), 1930 v Ni (18)
Davies, T. (Oswestry), 1886 v E (1)
Davies, T. (Druids), 1903 v E, Ni, S; 1904 v S (4)
Davies, W. (Wrexham), 1884 v Ni (1)
Davies, W. (Swansea T), 1924 v E, S, Ni; (with Cardiff C), 1925 v E, S, Ni; 1926 v E, S, Ni; 1927 v S; 1928 v Ni; (with Notts Co), 1929 v E, S, Ni; 1930 v E, S, Ni (17)
Davies, William (Wrexham), 1903 v Ni; 1905 v Ni; (with Blackburn R), 1908 v E, S; 1909 v E, S, Ni; 1911 v E, S, Ni; 1912 v Ni (11)
Davies, W. C. (C Palace), 1908 v S; (with WBA), 1909 v E; 1910 v S; (with C Palace), 1914 v E (4)
Davies, W. D. (Everton), 1975 v H, L, S, E, Ni; 1976 v Y (2), E, Ni; 1977 v WG, S (2), Cz, E, Ni; 1978 v K; (with Wrexham), S, Cz, WG, Ir, E, S, Ni; 1979 v Ma, T, WG, S, E, Ni, Ma; 1980 v Ei, WG, T, E, S, Ni, Ic; 1981 v T, Cz, Ei, T, S, E, USSR; (with Swansea C), 1982 v Cz, Ic, USSR, Sp, E, S, F; 1983 v Y (52)
Davies, W. H. (Oswestry), 1876 v S; 1877 v S; 1879 v E; 1880 v E (4)
Davies, W. O. (Millwall Ath), 1913 v E, S, Ni; 1914 v S, Ni (5)
Davis, G. (Wrexham), 1978 v Ir, E (sub), Ni (3)
Day, A. (Tottenham H), 1934 v Ni (1)
Deacy, N. (PSV Eindhoven), 1977 v Cz, S, E, Ni; 1978 v K (sub), S (sub), Cz (sub), WG, Ir, S (sub), Ni; (with Beringen), 1979 v T (12)
Dearson, D. J. (Birmingham), 1939 v S, Ni, F (3)
Derrett, S. C. (Cardiff C), 1969 v S, WG; 1970 v I; 1971 v Fi (4)
Dewey, F. T. (Cardiff Corinthians), 1931 v E, S (2)
Dibble, A. (Luton T), 1986 v Ca (1+1 sub); (with Manchester C), 1989 v Is (3)
Doughty, J. (Druids), 1886 v S; (with Newton Heath), 1887 v S, Ni; 1888 v E, S, Ni; 1889 v S; 1890 v E (8)
Doughty, R. (Newton Heath and Druids), 1888 v S, Ni (2)
Durban, A. (Derby Co), 1966 v Br (sub); 1967 v Ni; 1968 v E, S, Ni, WG; 1969 v EG, S, E, Ni, WG; 1970 v E, S, Ni, EG, I; 1971 v R, S, E, Ni, Cz, Fi; 1972 v Fi, Cz, E, S, Ni (27)

Dwyer, P. (Cardiff C), 1978 v Ir, E, S, Ni; 1979 v T, S, E, Ni, Ma (sub); 1980 v WG (10)

Edwards, C. (Wrexham), 1878 v S (1)
Edwards, C. N. H. (Swansea C), 1996 v Sw (sub) (1)
Edwards, G. (Birmingham C), 1947 v E, S, Ni; 1948 v E, S, Ni; (with Cardiff C), 1949 v Ni, P, Bel, Sw; 1950 v E, S (12)
Edwards, H. (Wrexham Civil Service), 1878 v S; 1880 v E; 1882 v E, S; 1883 v S; 1884 v Ni; 1887 v Ni (7)
Edwards, J. H. (Wanderers), 1876 v S (1)
Edwards, J. H. (Oswestry), 1895 v Ni; 1897 v E, Ni (3)
Edwards, J. H. (Aberystwyth), 1898 v Ni (1)
Edwards, L. T. (Charlton Ath), 1957 v Ni, EG (2)
Edwards, R. I. (Chester), 1978 v K (sub); 1979 v Ma, WG; (with Wrexham), 1980 v T (sub) (4)
Edwards, T. (Linfield), 1932 v S (1)
Egan, W. (Chirk), 1892 v S (1)
Ellis, B. (Motherwell), 1932 v E; 1933 v E, S; 1934 v S; 1936 v E; 1937 v S (6)
Ellis, E. (Nunhead), 1931 v S; (with Oswestry), E; 1932 v Ni (3)
Emanuel, W. J. (Bristol C), 1973 v E (sub), Ni (sub) (2)
England, H. M. (Blackburn R), 1962 v Ni, Br, M; 1963 v Ni, H; 1964 v E, S, Ni; 1965 v E, D, Gr (2), USSR, Ni, I; 1966 v E, S, Ni, USSR, D; (with Tottenham H), 1967 v S, E; 1968 v E, Ni, WG; 1969 v EG; 1970 v R of UK, EG, E, S, Ni, I; 1971 v R; 1972 v Fi, E, S, Ni; 1973 v E (3), S; 1974 v Pol; 1975 v H, L (44)
Evans, B. C. (Swansea C), 1972 v Fi, Cz; 1973 v E (2), Pol, S; (with Hereford U), 1974 v Pol (7)
Evans, D. G. (Reading), 1926 v Ni; 1927 v Ni, E; (with Huddersfield T), 1929 v S (4)
Evans, H. P. (Cardiff C), 1922 v E, S, Ni; 1924 v E, S, Ni (6)
Evans, I. (C Palace), 1976 v A, E, Y (2), E, Ni; 1977 v WG, S (2), Cz, E, Ni; 1978 v K (13)
Evans, J. (Oswestry), 1893 v Ni; 1894 v E, Ni (3)
Evans, J. (Cardiff C), 1912 v Ni; 1913 v Ni; 1914 v S; 1920 v S, Ni; 1922 v Ni; 1923 v E, Ni (8)
Evans, J. H. (Southend U), 1922 v E, S, Ni; 1923 v S (4)
Evans, Len (Aberdare Ath), 1927 v Ni; (with Cardiff C), 1931 v E, S; (with Birmingham), 1934 v Ni (4)
Evans, M. (Oswestry), 1884 v E (1)
Evans, R. (Clapton), 1902 v Ni (1)
Evans, R. E. (Wrexham), 1906 v E, S; (with Aston Villa), Ni; 1907 v E; 1908 v E, S; (with Sheffield U), 1909 v S; 1910 v E, S, Ni (10)
Evans, R. O. (Wrexham), 1902 v Ni; 1903 v E, S, Ni; (with Blackburn R), 1908 v Ni; (with Coventry C), 1911 v E, Ni; 1912 v E, S, Ni (10)
Evans, R. S. (Swansea T), 1964 v Ni (1)
Evans, T. J. (Clapton Orient), 1927 v S; 1928 v E, S; (with Newcastle U), Ni (4)
Evans, W. (Tottenham H), 1933 v Ni; 1934 v E, S; 1935 v E; 1936 v E, Ni (6)
Evans, W. A. W. (Oxford University), 1876 v S; 1877 v S (2)
Evans, W. G. (Bootle), 1890 v E; 1891 v E; (with Aston Villa), 1892 v E (3)
Evelyn, E. C. (Crusaders), 1887 v E (1)
Eyton-Jones, J. A. (Wrexham), 1883 v Ni; 1884 v Ni, E, S (4)

Farmer, G. (Oswestry), 1885 v E, S (2)
Felgate, D. (Lincoln C), 1984 v R (sub) (1)
Finnigan, R. J. (Wrexham), 1930 v Ni (1)
Flynn, B. (Burnley), 1975 v L (2 sub), H (sub), S, E, Ni; 1976 v A, E, Y (2), E, Ni; 1977 v WG (sub), S (2), Cz, E, Ni; 1978 v K (2), S; (with Leeds U), Cz, WG, Ir (sub), E, S, Ni; 1979 v Ma, T, S, E, Ni, Ma; 1980 v Ei, WG, E, S, Ni, Ic; 1981 v T, Cz, Ei, T, S, E, USSR; 1982 v Cz, S, E, Ni, F; 1983 v N; (with Burnley), Y, E, Bul, S, Ni, Br; 1984 v N, R, Bul, Y, S, N, Is (66)
Ford, T. (Swansea T), 1947 v S; (with Aston Villa), 1947 v Ni; 1948 v S, Ni; 1949 v E, S, Ni, P, Bel, Sw; 1950 v E, S, Ni, Bel; 1951 v S; (with Sunderland), 1951 v E, Ni, P, Sw; 1952 v E, S, Ni, R of UK; 1953 v S, E, Ni, F, Y; (with Cardiff C), 1954 v A; 1955 v S, E, Ni, Y; 1956 v S, Ni, E, A; 1957 v S (38)
Foulkes, H. E. (WBA), 1932 v Ni (1)
Foulkes, W. I. (Newcastle U), 1952 v E, S, Ni, R of UK; 1953 v E, S, F, Y; 1954 v E, S, Ni (11)
Foulkes, W. T. (Oswestry), 1884 v Ni; 1885 v S (2)
Fowler, J. (Swansea T), 1925 v E; 1926 v E, Ni; 1927 v S; 1928 v S; 1929 v E (6)

Garner, J. (Aberystwyth), 1896 v S (1)
Giggs, R. J. (Manchester U), 1992 v G (sub), I (sub), R (sub); 1993 v Fa (sub), Bel (sub + 1), RCS, Fa; 1994 v RCS, Cy, R; 1995 v Alb, Bul; 1996 v G, Alb, Sm (16)
Giles, D. (Swansea C), 1980 v E, S, Ni, Ic; 1981 v T, Cz, T (sub), E (sub), USSR (sub); (with C Palace), 1982 v Sp (sub); 1983 v Ni (sub), Br (12)

Gillam, S. G. (Wrexham), 1889 v S (sub), Ni; (with Shrewsbury), 1890 v E, Ni; (with Clapton), 1894 v S (5)
Glascodine, G. (Wrexham), 1879 v E (1)
Glover, E. M. (Grimsby T), 1932 v S; 1934 v Ni; 1936 v S; 1937 v E, S, Ni; 1939 v Ni (7)
Godding, G. (Wrexham), 1923 v S, Ni (2)
Godfrey, B. C. (Preston NE), 1964 v Ni; 1965 v D, I (3)
Goodwin, U. (Ruthin), 1881 v E (1)
Goss, J. (Norwich C), 1991 v Ic, Pol (sub); 1992 v A; 1994 v Cy (sub), R (sub), Se; 1995 v Alb; 1996 v Sw (sub), Sm (sub) (9)
Gough, R. T. (Oswestry White Star), 1883 v S (1)
Gray, A. (Oldham Ath), 1924 v E, S, Ni; 1925 v E, S, Ni; 1926 v E, S; 1927 v S; (with Manchester C), 1928 v E, S; 1929 v E, S, Ni; (with Manchester Central), 1930 v S; (with Tranmere R), 1932 v E, S, Ni; (with Chester), 1937 v E, S, Ni; 1938 v E, S, Ni (24)
Green, A. W. (Aston Villa), 1901 v Ni; (with Notts Co), 1903 v E; 1904 v S, Ni; 1906 v Ni, E; (with Nottingham F), 1907 v E; 1908 v S (8)
Green, C. R. (Birmingham C), 1965 v USSR, I; 1966 v E, S, USSR, Br (2); 1967 v E; 1968 v E, S, Ni, WG; 1969 v S, I, Ni (sub) (15)
Green, G. H. (Charlton Ath), 1938 v Ni; 1939 v E, Ni, F (4)
Grey, Dr W. (Druids), 1876 v S; 1878 v S (2)
Griffiths, A. T. (Wrexham), 1971 v Cz (sub); 1975 v A, H (2), L (2), E, Ni; 1976 v A, E, S, E (sub), Ni, Y (2); 1977 v WG, S (17)
Griffiths, F. J. (Blackpool), 1900 v E, S (2)
Griffiths, G. (Chirk), 1887 v Ni (1)
Griffiths, J. H. (Swansea T), 1953 v Ni (1)
Griffiths, L. (Wrexham), 1902 v S (1)
Griffiths, M. W. (Leicester C), 1947 v Ni; 1949 v P, Bel; 1950 v E, S, Bel; 1951 v E, Ni, P, Sw; 1954 v A (11)
Griffiths, P. (Chirk), 1884 v E, Ni; 1888 v E; 1890 v S, Ni; 1891 v Ni (6)
Griffiths, P. H. (Everton), 1932 v S (1)
Griffiths, S. (Wrexham), 1902 v S (1)
Griffiths, T. P. (Everton), 1927 v E, Ni; 1929 v E; 1930 v E; 1931 v Ni; 1932 v Ni, S, E; (with Bolton W), 1933 v E, S, Ni; (with Middlesbrough), F; 1934 v E, S; 1935 v E, Ni; 1936 v S; (with Aston Villa), Ni; 1937 v E, S, Ni (21)

Hall, G. D. (Chelsea), 1988 v Y (sub), Ma, I; 1989 v Ho, Fi, Is; 1990 v Ei; 1991 v Ei; 1992 v A (sub) (9)
Hallam, J. (Oswestry), 1889 v S (1)
Hanford, H. (Swansea T), 1934 v Ni; 1935 v S; 1936 v E; (with Sheffield W), 1936 v Ni; 1938 v E, S; 1939 v F (7)
Harrington, A. C. (Cardiff C), 1956 v Ni; 1957 v E, S; 1958 v S, Ni, Is (2); 1961 v S, E; 1962 v E, S (11)
Harris, C. S. (Leeds U), 1976 v E, S; 1978 v WG, Ir, E, S, Ni; 1979 v Ma, T, WG, E (sub), Ma; 1980 v Ni (sub), Ic (sub); 1981 v T, Cz (sub), Ei, T, S, E, USSR; 1982 v Cz, Ic, E (sub) (24)
Harris, W. C. (Middlesbrough), 1954 v A; 1957 v EG, Cz; 1958 v E, S, EG (6)
Harrison, W. C. (Wrexham), 1899 v E; 1900 v E, S, Ni; 1901 v Ni (5)
Hartson, J. (Arsenal), 1995 v Bul, G (sub), Ge (sub); 1996 v Mol (sub), Sw (5)
Hayes, A. (Wrexham), 1890 v Ni; 1894 v Ni (2)
Hennessey, W. T. (Birmingham C), 1962 v Ni, Br (2); 1963 v S, E, H (2); 1964 v E, S; 1965 v S, E, D, Gr, USSR; 1966 v E, USSR; (with Nottingham F), 1966 v S, Ni, D, Br (2), Ch; 1967 v S, E; 1968 v E, S, Ni; 1969 v WG, EG, R of UK; 1970 v EG; (with Derby Co), E, S, Ni; 1972 v Fi, Cz, E, S; 1973 v E (39)
Hersee, A. M. (Bangor), 1886 v S, Ni (2)
Hersee, R. (Llandudno), 1886 v Ni (1)
Hewitt, R. (Cardiff C), 1958 v Ni, Is, Se, H, Br (5)
Hewitt, T. J. (Wrexham), 1911 v E, S, Ni; (with Chelsea), 1913 v E, S, Ni; (with South Liverpool), 1914 v E, S (8)
Heywood, D. (Druids), 1879 v E (1)
Hibbott, H. (Newtown Excelsior), 1880 v E, S; (with Newtown), 1885 v S (3)
Higham, G. G. (Oswestry), 1878 v S; 1879 v E (2)
Hill, M. R. (Ipswich T), 1972 v Cz, R (2)
Hockey, T. (Sheffield U), 1972 v Fi, R; 1973 v E (2); (with Norwich C), Pol, S, E, Ni; (with Aston Villa), 1974 v Pol (9)
Hoddinott, T. F. (Watford), 1921 v E, S (2)
Hodges, G. (Wimbledon), 1984 v N (sub), Is (sub); 1987 v USSR, Fi, Cz; (with Newcastle U), 1988 v D; (with Watford), D (sub), Cz (sub), Se, Ma (sub), I (sub); 1990 v Se, Cr; (with Sheffield U), 1992 v Br (sub), Ei (sub), A; 1996 v G (sub), I (18)
Hodgkinson, A. V. (Southampton), 1908 v Ni (1)
Holden, A. (Chester C), 1984 v Is (sub) (1)
Hole, B. G. (Cardiff C), 1963 v Ni; 1964 v Ni; 1965 v S, E, Ni, D, Gr (2), USSR, I; 1966 v E, S, Ni, USSR, D, Br (2), Ch; (with Blackburn R), 1967 v S, E, Ni; 1968 v E, S, Ni, WG;

(with Aston Villa), 1969 v I, WG, EG; 1970 v I; (with Swansea C), 1971 v R (30)

Hole, W. J. (Swansea T), 1921 v Ni; 1922 v E; 1923 v E, Ni; 1928 v E, S, Ni; 1929 v E, S (9)

Hollins, D. M. (Newcastle U), 1962 v Br (sub), M; 1963 v Ni, H; 1964 v E; 1965 v Ni, Gr, I; 1966 v S, D, Br (11)

Hopkins, I. J. (Brentford), 1935 v S, Ni; 1936 v E, Ni; 1937 v E, S, Ni; 1938 v E, Ni; 1939 v E, S, Ni (12)

Hopkins, J. (Fulham), 1983 v Ni, Br; 1984 v N, R, Bul, Y, S, E, Ni, N, Is; 1985 v Ic (1 + 1 sub), N; (with C Palace), 1990 v Ho, Cr (16)

Hopkins, M. (Tottenham H), 1956 v Ni; 1957 v Ni, S, E, Cz (2), EG; 1958 v E, S, Ni, EG, Is (2), H (2), M, Se, Br; 1959 v E, S, Ni; 1960 v E, S; 1961 v Ni, H, Sp (2); 1962 v Ni, Br (2), M; 1963 v S, Ni, H (34)

Horne, B. (Portsmouth), 1988 v D (sub), Y, Se (sub), Ma, I; 1989 v Ho, Fi, Is; (with Southampton), Se, WG; 1990 v WG (sub), Ei, Se, Cr; 1991 v D, Bel (2), L, Ei, Ic, Pol, WG; 1992 v Br, G, L, Ei, A, R, Ho, Arg, J; (with Everton), 1993 v Fa, Cy, Bel, Ei, Bel, RCS, Fa; 1994 v RCS, Cy, R, N, Se, Es; 1995 v Mol, Ge, Bul, G, Ge; 1996 v Mol, G, I, Sw, Sm (54)

Howell, E. G. (Builth), 1888 v Ni; 1890 v E; 1891 v E (3)

Howells, R. G. (Cardiff C), 1954 v E, S (2)

Hugh, A. R. (Newport Co), 1930 v Ni (1)

Hughes, A. (Rhos), 1894 v E, S (2)

Hughes, A. (Chirk), 1907 v Ni (1)

Hughes, C. M. (Luton T), 1992 v Ho (sub); 1994 v N (sub), Se (sub), Es; 1996 v Alb (5)

Hughes, E. (Everton), 1899 v S, Ni; (with Tottenham H), 1901 v E, S; 1902 v Ni; 1904 v E, Ni, S; 1905 v E, Ni, S; 1906 v E, Ni; 1907 v E (14)

Hughes, E. (Wrexham), 1906 v S; (with Nottingham F), 1906 v Ni; 1908 v S, E; 1910 v Ni, E, S; 1911 v Ni, E, S; (with Wrexham), 1912 v Ni, E, S; (with Manchester C), 1913 v E, S; 1914 v N (16)

Hughes, F. W. (Northwich Victoria), 1882 v E, Ni; 1883 v E, Ni, S; 1884 v S (6)

Hughes, I. (Luton T), 1951 v E, Ni, P, Sw (4)

Hughes, J. (Cambridge University), 1877 v S; (with Aberystwyth), 1879 v S (2)

Hughes, J. (Liverpool), 1905 v E, S, Ni (3)

Hughes, J. I. (Blackburn R), 1935 v Ni (1)

Hughes, L. M. (Manchester U), 1984 v E, Ni; 1985 v Ic, Sp, Ic, N, S, Sp, N; 1986 v S, H, U; (with Barcelona), 1987 v USSR, Cz; 1988 v D (2), Cz, Se, Ma, I; (with Manchester U), 1989 v Ho, Fi, Is, Se, WG; 1990 v Fi, WG, Cr; 1991 v D, Bel (2), L, Ic, Pol, WG; 1992 v Br, G, L, Ei, R, Ho, Arg, J; 1993 v Fa, Cy, Bel, Ei, Bel, RCS, Fa; 1994 v RCS, Cy, N; 1995 v Ge, Bul, G, Ge; (with Chelsea), 1996 v Mol, I, Sm (60)

Hughes, P. W. (Bangor), 1887 v Ni; 1889 v Ni, E (3)

Hughes, W. (Bootle), 1891 v E; 1892 v S, Ni (3)

Hughes, W. A. (Blackburn R), 1949 v E, Ni, P, Bel, Sw (5)

Hughes, W. M. (Birmingham), 1938 v E, Ni, S; 1939 v E, Ni, S, F; 1947 v E, S, Ni (10)

Humphreys, J. V. (Everton), 1947 v Ni (1)

Humphreys, R. (Druids), 1888 v Ni (1)

Hunter, A. H. (FA of Wales Secretary), 1887 v Ni (1)

Jackett, K. (Watford), 1983 v N, Y, E, Bul, S; 1984 v N, R, Y, S, N, N, Is; 1985 v Ic, Sp, Ic, N, S, Sp, N; 1986 v S, H, S.Ar, Ei, Ca (2); 1987 v Fi (2); 1988 v D, Cz, Y, Se (31)

Jackson, W. (St Helens Rec), 1899 v Ni (1)

James, E. (Chirk), 1893 v E, Ni; 1894 v E, S, Ni; 1898 v S, E; 1899 v Ni (8)

James, E. G. (Blackpool), 1966 v Br (2), Ch; 1967 v Ni; 1968 v S; 1971 v Cz, S, E, Ni (9)

James, L. (Burnley), 1972 v Cz, R, S (sub); 1973 v E (3), Pol, S, Ni; 1974 v Pol, E, S, Ni; 1975 v A, H (2), L (2), S, E, Ni; 1976 v A; (with Derby Co), S, E, Y (2), Ni; 1977 v WG, S (2), Cz, E, Ni; 1978 v K (2); (with QPR), WG; (with Burnley), 1979 v T; (with Swansea C), 1980 v E, S, Ni, Ic; 1981 v T, Ei, T, S, E; 1982 v Cz, Ic, USSR, E (sub), S, Ni, F; (with Sunderland), 1983 v E (sub) (54)

James, R. M. (Swansea C), 1979 v Ma, WG (sub), S, E, Ni, Ma; 1980 v WG; 1982 v Cz (sub), Ic, Sp, E, S, Ni, F; 1983 v N, Y, E, Bul; (with Stoke C), 1984 v N, R, Bul, Y, S, E, Ni, N, Is; 1985 v Ic, Sp, Ic; (with QPR), N, S, Sp, N; 1986 v S, S.Ar, Ei, U, Ca (2); 1987 v Fi (2), USSR, Cz; (with Leicester C), 1988 v D (2); (with Swansea C), Y (47)

James, W. (West Ham U), 1931 v Ni; 1932 v Ni (2)

Jarrett, R. H. (Ruthin), 1889 v Ni; 1890 v S (2)

Jarvis, A. L. (Hull C), 1967 v S, E, Ni (3)

Jenkins, E. (Lovell's Ath), 1925 v E (1)

Jenkins, J. (Brighton), 1924 v Ni, E, S; 1925 v S, Ni; 1926 v E, S; 1927 v S (8)

Jenkins, R. W. (Rhyl), 1902 v Ni (1)

Jenkins, S. R. (Swansea C), 1996 v G; (with Huddersfield T), Alb, I (3)

Jenkyns, C. A. L. (Small Heath), 1892 v E, S, Ni; 1895 v E; (with Woolwich Arsenal), 1896 v S; (with Newton Heath), 1897 v Ni; (with Walsall), 1898 v S, E (8)

Jennings, W. (Bolton W), 1914 v E, S; 1920 v S; 1923 v Ni, E; 1924 v S, Ni; 1927 v S, Ni; 1929 v S (11)

John, R. F. (Arsenal), 1923 v S, Ni; 1925 v Ni; 1926 v E; 1927 v E; 1928 v E, Ni; 1930 v E, S; 1932 v E; 1933 v F, Ni; 1935 v Ni; 1936 v S; 1937 v E (15)

John, W. R. (Walsall), 1931 v Ni; (with Stoke C), 1933 v E, S, Ni, F; 1934 v E, S; (with Preston NE), 1935 v E, S; (with Sheffield U), 1936 v E, S, Ni; (with Swansea T), 1939 v E, S (14)

Johnson, M. G. (Swansea T), 1964 v Ni (1)

Jones, A. (Port Vale), 1987 v Fi, Cz (sub); 1988 v D, (with Charlton Ath), D (sub), Cz (sub); 1990 v Hol (sub) (6)

Jones, A. F. (Oxford University), 1877 v S (1)

Jones, A. T. (Nottingham F), 1905 v E; (with Notts Co), 1906 v E (2)

Jones, Bryn (Wolverhampton W), 1935 v Ni; 1936 v E, S, Ni; 1937 v S, Ni; 1938 v E, S, Ni; (with Arsenal), 1939 v E, S, Ni; 1947 v S, Ni; 1948 v E; 1949 v S (17)

Jones, B. S. (Swansea T), 1963 v S, E, Ni, H (2); 1964 v S, Ni; (with Plymouth Arg), 1965 v D; (with Cardiff C), 1969 v S, E, Ni, I (sub), WG, EG, R of UK (15)

Jones, Charlie (Nottingham F), 1926 v E; 1927 v S, Ni; 1928 v E; (with Arsenal), 1930 v E, S; 1932 v E; 1933 v F (8)

Jones, Cliff (Swansea C), 1954 v A; 1956 v E, Ni, S, A; 1957 v E, S, Ni, Cz (2), EG; 1958 v EG, E, S, Is (2); (with Tottenham H), 1958 v Ni, H (2), M, Se, Br; 1959 v Ni; 1960 v E, S, Ni; 1961 v S, E, Ni, Sp, H, Ei; 1962 v E, Ni, S, Br (2), M; 1963 v S, Ni, H; 1964 v E, S, Ni; 1965 v E, S, Ni, D, Gr (2), USSR, I; 1967 v S, E; 1968 v E, S, WG; (with Fulham), 1969 v I, R of UK (59)

Jones, C. W. (Birmingham), 1935 v Ni; 1939 v F (2)

Jones, D. (Chirk), 1888 v S, Ni; (with Bolton W), 1889 v E, S, Ni; 1890 v E; 1891 v S; 1892 v Ni; 1893 v E; 1894 v E; 1895 v E; 1898 v S; (with Manchester C), 1900 v E, Ni (14)

Jones, D. E. (Norwich C), 1976 v S, E (sub); 1978 v S, Cz, WG, Ir, E; 1980 v E (8)

Jones, D. O. (Leicester C), 1934 v E, Ni; 1935 v E, S; 1936 v E, Ni; 1937 v Ni (7)

Jones, Evan (Chelsea), 1910 v S, Ni; (with Oldham Ath), 1911 v E, S; 1912 v E, S; (with Bolton W), 1914 v Ni (7)

Jones, F. R. (Bangor), 1885 v E, Ni; 1886 v S (3)

Jones, F. W. (Small Heath), 1893 v S (1)

Jones, G. P. (Wrexham), 1907 v S, Ni (2)

Jones, H. (Aberaman), 1902 v Ni (1)

Jones, Humphrey (Bangor), 1885 v E, Ni, S; 1886 v E, Ni, S; (with Queen's Park), 1887 v E; (with East Stirlingshire), 1889 v E, Ni; 1890 v E, S, Ni; (with Queen's Park), 1891 v E, S (14)

Jones, Ivor (Swansea T), 1920 v S, Ni; 1921 v Ni, E; 1922 v S, Ni; (with WBA), 1923 v E, Ni; 1924 v S; 1926 v Ni (10)

Jones, Jeffrey (Llandrindod Wells), 1908 v Ni; 1909 v Ni; 1910 v S (3)

Jones, J. (Druids), 1876 v S (1)

Jones, J. (Berwyn Rangers), 1883 v S, Ni; 1884 v S (3)

Jones, J. (Wrexham), 1925 v Ni (1)

Jones, J. L. (Sheffield U), 1895 v E, S, Ni; 1896 v Ni, S, E; 1897 v Ni, S, E; (with Tottenham H), 1898 v Ni, E, S; 1899 v S, Ni; 1900 v S; 1902 v E, S, Ni; 1904 v E, S, Ni (21)

Jones, J. Love (Stoke C), 1906 v S; (with Middlesbrough), 1910 v Ni (2)

Jones, J. O. (Bangor), 1901 v S, Ni (2)

Jones, J. P. (Liverpool), 1976 v A, E, S; 1977 v WG, S (2), Cz, E, Ni; 1978 v K (2), S, Cz, WG, Ir, E, S, Ni; (with Wrexham), 1979 v Ma, T, WG, S, E, Ni, Ma; 1980 v Ei, WG, T, E, S, Ni, Ic; 1981 v T, Ei, T, S, E, USSR; 1982 v Cz, Ic, USSR, Sp, E, S, Ni, F; 1983 v N; (with Chelsea), Y, E, Bul, S, Ni, Br; 1984 v N, R, Bul, Y, S, E, Ni, N, Is; 1985 v Ic, N, S, N; (with Huddersfield T), 1986 v S, H, Ei, U, Ca (2) (72)

Jones, J. T. (Stoke C), 1912 v E, S, Ni; 1913 v E, Ni; 1914 v S, Ni; 1920 v E, S, Ni; (with C Palace), 1921 v E, S; 1922 v E, S, Ni (15)

Jones, K. (Aston Villa), 1950 v S (1)

Jones, Leslie J. (Cardiff C), 1933 v F; (with Coventry C), 1935 v Ni; 1936 v S; 1937 v E, S, Ni; (with Arsenal), 1938 v E, S, Ni; 1939 v E, S (11)

Jones, P. W. (Bristol R), 1971 v Fi (1)

Jones, R. (Bangor), 1887 v S; 1889 v E; (with Crewe Alex), 1890 v V (3)

Jones, R. (Leicester Fosse), 1898 v S (1)

Jones, R. (Druids), 1899 v S (1)

Jones, R. (Bangor), 1900 v S, Ni (2)

Jones, R. (Millwall), 1906 v S, Ni (2)

Jones, R. A. (Druids), 1884 v E, Ni, S; 1885 v S (4)

Jones, R. A. (Sheffield W), 1994 v Es (1)

Jones, R. S. (Everton), 1894 v Ni (1)

Jones, S. (Wrexham), 1887 v Ni; (with Chester), 1890 v S (2)

Jones, S. (Wrexham), 1893 v S, Ni; (with Burton Swifts), 1895 v S; 1896 v E, Ni; (with Druids), 1899 v E (6)
Jones, T. (Manchester U), 1926 v Ni; 1927 v E, Ni; 1930 v Ni (4)
Jones, T. D. (Aberdare), 1908 v Ni (1)
Jones, T. G. (Everton), 1938 v Ni; 1939 v E, S, Ni; 1947 v E, S; 1948 v E, S, Ni; 1949 v E, Ni, P, Bel, Sw; 1950 v E, S, Bel (17)
Jones, T. J. (Sheffield W), 1932 v Ni; 1933 v F (2)
Jones, V.P. (Wimbledon), 1995 v Bul (2), G, Ge; 1996 v Sw (5)
Jones, W. E. A. (Swansea T), 1947 v E, S; (with Tottenham H), 1949 v E, S (4)
Jones, W. J. (Aberdare), 1901 v E, S; (with West Ham U), 1902 v E, S (4)
Jones, W. Lot (Manchester C), 1905 v E, Ni; 1906 v E, S, Ni; 1907 v E, S, Ni; 1908 v S; 1909 v E, S, Ni; 1910 v E; 1911 v E; 1913 v E, S; 1914 v S, Ni; (with Southend U), 1920 v E, Ni (20)
Jones, W. P. (Druids), 1889 v E, Ni; (with Wynstay), 1890 v S, Ni (4)
Jones, W. R. (Aberystwyth), 1897 v S (1)

Keenor, F. C. (Cardiff C), 1920 v E, Ni; 1921 v E, Ni, S; 1922 v Ni; 1923 v E, Ni, S; 1924 v E, Ni, S; 1925 v E, Ni, S; 1926 v S; 1927 v E, Ni, S; 1928 v E, Ni, S; 1929 v E, Ni, S; 1930 v E, Ni, S; 1931 v E, Ni, S; (with Crewe Alex), 1933 v S (32)
Kelly, F. C. (Wrexham), 1899 v S, Ni; (with Druids), 1902 v Ni (3)
Kelsey, A. J. (Arsenal), 1954 v Ni, A; 1955 v S, Ni, Y; 1956 v E, Ni, S, A; 1957 v E, Ni, S, Cz (2), EG; 1958 v E, S, Ni, Is (2), H (2), M, Se, Br; 1959 v E, S; 1960 v E, Ni, S; 1961 v E, Ni, S, H, Sp (2); 1962 v E, S, Ni, Br (2) (41)
Kenrick, S. L. (Druids), 1876 v S; 1877 v S; (with Oswestry), 1879 v S; (with Shropshire Wanderers), 1881 v E (5)
Ketley, C. F. (Druids), 1882 v Ni (1)
King, J. (Swansea T), 1955 v E (1)
Kinsey, N. (Norwich C), 1951 v Ni, P, Sw; 1952 v E; (with Birmingham C), 1954 v Ni; 1956 v E, S (7)
Knill, A. R. (Swansea C), 1989 v Ho (1)
Krzywicki, R. L. (WBA), 1970 v EG, I; (with Huddersfield T), Ni, E, S; 1971 v R, Fi; 1972 v Cz (sub) (8)

Lambert, R. (Liverpool), 1947 v S; 1948 v E; 1949 v P, Bel, Sw (5)
Latham, G. (Liverpool), 1905 v E, S; 1906 v S; 1907 v E, S, Ni; 1908 v E; 1909 v Ni; (with Southport Central), 1910 v E; (with Cardiff C), 1913 v Ni (10)
Law, B. J. (QPR), 1990 v Se (1)
Lawrence, E. (Clapton Orient), 1930 v Ni; (with Notts Co), 1932 v S (2)
Lawrence, S. (Swansea T), 1932 v Ni; 1933 v F; 1934 v S, E, Ni; 1935 v E, S; 1936 v S (8)
Lea, A. (Wrexham), 1889 v S; 1891 v S, Ni; 1893 v Ni (4)
Lea, C. (Ipswich T), 1965 v Ni, I (2)
Leary, P. (Bangor), 1889 v Ni (1)
Leek, K. (Leicester C), 1961 v S, E, Ni, H, Sp (2); (with Newcastle U), 1962 v S; (with Birmingham C), v Br (sub), M; 1963 v E; 1965 v S, Gr; (with Northampton T), 1965 v Gr (13)
Legg, A. (Birmingham C), 1996 v Sw, Sm (sub) (2)
Lever, A. R. (Leicester C), 1953 v S (1)
Lewis, B. (Chester), 1891 v Ni; (with Wrexham), 1892 v S, E, Ni; (with Middlesbrough), 1893 v S, E; (with Wrexham), 1894 v S, E, Ni; 1895 v S (10)
Lewis, D. (Arsenal), 1927 v E; 1928 v Ni; 1930 v E (3)
Lewis, D. (Swansea C), 1983 v Br (sub) (1)
Lewis, D. J. (Swansea T), 1933 v E, S (2)
Lewis, D. M. (Bangor), 1890 v Ni, S (2)
Lewis, J. (Bristol R), 1906 v E (1)
Lewis, J. (Cardiff C), 1926 v S (1)
Lewis, T. (Wrexham), 1881 v E, S (2)
Lewis, W. (Bangor), 1885 v E; 1886 v E, S; 1887 v E, S; 1888 v E; 1889 v E, Ni, S; (with Crewe Alex), 1890 v E; 1891 v E, S; 1892 v E, S, Ni; 1894 v E, S, Ni; (with Chester), 1895 v S, Ni, E; 1896 v E, S, Ni; (with Manchester C), 1897 v E, S; (with Chester), 1898 v Ni (27)
Lewis, W. L. (Swansea T), 1927 v E, Ni; 1928 v E, Ni; 1929 v S; (with Huddersfield T), 1930 v E (6)
Lloyd, B. W. (Wrexham), 1976 v A, E, S (3)
Lloyd, J. W. (Wrexham), 1879 v S; (with Newtown), 1885 v S (2)
Lloyd, R. A. (Ruthin), 1891 v Ni; 1895 v S (2)
Lockley, A. (Chirk), 1898 v Ni (1)
Lovell, S. (C Palace), 1982 v USSR (sub); (with Millwall), 1985 v N; 1986 v S (sub), H (sub), Ca (1+1 sub) (6)
Lowrie, G. (Coventry C), 1948 v E, S, Ni; (with Newcastle U), 1949 v P (4)
Lowndes, S. (Newport Co), 1983 v S (sub), Br (sub); (with Millwall), 1985 v N (sub); 1986 v S.Ar (sub), Ei, U, Ca (2); (with Barnsley), 1987 v Fi (sub); 1988 v Se (sub) (10)

Lucas, P. M. (Leyton Orient), 1962 v Ni, M; 1963 v S, E (4)
Lucas, W. H. (Swansea T), 1949 v S, Ni, P, Bel, Sw; 1950 v E; 1951 v E (7)
Lumberg, A. (Wrexham), 1929 v Ni; 1930 v E, S; (with Wolverhampton W), 1932 v S (4)

McCarthy, T. P. (Wrexham), 1899 v Ni (1)
McMillan, R. (Shrewsbury Engineers), 1881 v E, S (2)
Maguire, G. T. (Portsmouth), 1990 v Fi (sub), Ho, WG, Ei, Se; 1992 v Br (sub), G (7)
Mahoney, J. F. (Stoke C), 1968 v E; 1969 v EG; 1971 v Cz; 1973 v E (3), Pol, S, Ni; 1974 v Pol, E, S, Ni; 1975 v A, H (2), L (2), S, E, Ni; 1976 v A, Y (2), E, Ni; 1977 v WG, Cz, S, E, Ni; (with Middlesbrough), 1978 v K (2), S, Cz, Ir, E (sub), S, Ni; 1979 v WG, S, E, Ni, Ma; (with Swansea C), 1980 v Ei, WG, T (sub); 1982 v Ic, USSR; 1983 v Y, E (51)
Mardon, P. J. (WBA), 1996 v G (sub) (1)
Marriott, A. (Wrexham), 1996 v Sw (sub) (1)
Martin, T. J. (Newport Co), 1930 v Ni (1)
Marustik, C. (Swansea C), 1982 v Sp, E, S, Ni, F; 1983 v N (6)
Mates, J. (Chirk), 1891 v Ni; 1897 v E, S (3)
Mathews, R. W. (Liverpool), 1921 v Ni; (with Bristol C), 1923 v E; (with Bradford), 1926 v Ni (3)
Matthews, W. (Chester), 1905 v Ni; 1908 v E (2)
Matthias, J. S. (Brymbo), 1896 v S, Ni; (with Shrewsbury), 1897 v E, S; (with Wolverhampton W), 1899 v S (5)
Matthias, T. J. (Wrexham), 1914 v S, E; 1920 v Ni, S, E; 1921 v S, E, Ni; 1922 v S, E, Ni; 1923 v S (12)
Mays, A. W. (Wrexham), 1929 v Ni (1)
Medwin, T. C. (Swansea T), 1953 v Ni, F, Y; (with Tottenham H), 1957 v E, S, Ni, Cz (2), EG; 1958 v E, S, Ni, Is (2), H (2), M, Br; 1959 v E, S, Ni; 1960 v E, S, Ni; 1961 v S, Ei, E, Sp; 1963 v E, H (30)
Melville, A. K. (Swansea C), 1990 v WG, Ei, Se, Cr (sub); (with Oxford U), 1991 v Ic, Pol, WG; 1992 v Br, G, L, R, Ho, J (sub); 1993 v RCS, Fa (sub); (with Sunderland), 1994 v RCS (sub), R, N, Se, Es; 1995 v Alb, Mol (sub), Ge, Bul; 1996 v G, Alb, Sm (27)
Meredith, S. (Chirk), 1900 v S; 1901 v S, E, Ni; (with Stoke C), 1902 v E; 1903 v Ni; 1904 v E; (with Leyton), 1907 v E (8)
Meredith, W. H. (Manchester C), 1895 v E, Ni; 1896 v E, Ni; 1897 v E, Ni, S; 1898 v E, Ni; 1899 v E; 1900 v E, Ni; 1901 v E, Ni; 1902 v E, S; 1903 v E, S, Ni; 1904 v E; 1905 v E, S; (with Manchester U), 1907 v E, S, Ni; 1908 v E, Ni; 1909 v E, S, Ni; 1910 v E, S, Ni; 1911 v E, S, Ni; 1912 v E, S, Ni; 1913 v E, S, Ni; 1914 v E, S, Ni; 1920 v E, S, Ni (48)
Mielczarek, R. (Rotherham U), 1971 v Fi (1)
Millership, H. (Rotherham Co), 1920 v E, S, Ni; 1921 v E, S, Ni (6)
Millington, A. H. (WBA), 1963 v S, E, H; (with C Palace), 1965 v E, USSR; (with Peterborough U), 1966 v Ch, Br; 1967 v E, Ni; 1968 v Ni, WG; 1969 v I, EG; (with Swansea T), 1970 v E, S, Ni; 1971 v Cz, Fi; 1972 v Fi (sub), Cz, R (21)
Mills, T. J. (Clapton Orient), 1934 v E, Ni; (with Leicester C), 1935 v E, S (4)
Mills-Roberts, R. H. (St Thomas' Hospital), 1885 v E, S, Ni; 1886 v E; 1887 v E; (with Preston NE), 1888 v E, Ni; (with Llanberis), 1892 v E (8)
Moore, G. (Cardiff C), 1960 v E, S, Ni; 1961 v Ei, Sp; (with Chelsea), 1962 v Br; 1963 v Ni, H; (with Manchester U), 1964 v S, Ni; (with Northampton T), 1966 v Ni, Ch; (with Charlton Ath), 1969 v S, E, Ni, R of UK; 1970 v E, S, Ni, I; 1971 v R (21)
Morgan, J. R. (Cambridge University), 1877 v S; (with Swansea T), 1879 v S; (with Derby School Staff), 1880 v E, S; 1881 v E, S; 1882 v E, S, Ni; (with Swansea T), 1883 v E (10)
Morgan, J. T. (Wrexham), 1905 v Ni (1)
Morgan-Owen, H. (Oxford University), 1901 v E; 1902 v S; 1906 v E, Ni; (with Welshpool), 1907 v S (5)
Morgan-Owen, M. M. (Oxford University), 1897 v S, Ni; 1898 v E; 1899 v S; 1900 v E, S; (with Corinthians), 1903 v S; 1906 v S, E, Ni; 1907 v E (12)
Morley, E. J. (Swansea T), 1925 v E; (with Clapton Orient), 1929 v E, S, Ni (4)
Morris, A. G. (Aberystwyth), 1896 v E, Ni, S; (with Swindon T), 1897 v E; 1898 v S; (with Nottingham F), 1899 v E, S; 1903 v E, S; 1905 v E, S; 1907 v E, S; 1908 v E; 1910 v E, S, Ni; 1911 v E, S, Ni; 1912 v E (21)
Morris, C. (Chirk), 1900 v E, S, Ni; (with Derby Co), 1901 v E, S, Ni; 1902 v E, S; 1903 v E, S, Ni; 1904 v Ni; 1905 v E, S, Ni; 1906 v S; 1907 v S; 1908 v E, S; 1909 v E, S, Ni; 1910 v E, S, Ni; (with Huddersfield T), 1911 v E, S, Ni (28)
Morris, E. (Chirk), 1893 v E, S, Ni (3)
Morris, H. (Sheffield U), 1894 v S; (with Manchester C), 1896 v E; (with Grimsby T), 1897 v E (3)
Morris, J. (Oswestry), 1887 v S (1)
Morris, J. (Chirk), 1898 v Ni (1)

Morris, R. (Chirk), 1900 v E, Ni; 1901 v Ni; 1902 v S; (with Shrewsbury T), 1903 v E, Ni (6)

Morris, R. (Druids), 1902 v E, S; (with Newtown), Ni; (with Liverpool), 1903 v S, Ni; 1904 v E, S, Ni; (with Leeds C), 1906 v S; (with Grimsby T), 1907 v Ni; (with Plymouth Arg), 1908 v Ni (11)

Morris, S. (Birmingham), 1937 v E, S; 1938 v E, S; 1939 v F (5)

Morris, W. (Burnley), 1947 v Ni; 1949 v E; 1952 v S, Ni, R of UK (5)

Moulsdale, J. R. B. (Corinthians), 1925 v Ni (1)

Murphy, J. P. (WBA), 1933 v F, E, Ni; 1934 v E, S; 1935 v E, S, Ni; 1936 v E, S, Ni; 1937 v S, Ni; 1938 v E, S (15)

Nardiello, D. (Coventry C), 1978 v Cz, WG (sub) (2)

Neal, J. E. (Colwyn Bay), 1931 v E, S (2)

Neilson, A. B. (Newcastle U), 1992 v Ei; 1994 v Se, Es; 1995 v Ge (4)

Newnes, J. (Nelson), 1926 v Ni (1)

Newton, L. F. (Cardiff Corinthians), 1912 v Ni (1)

Nicholas, D. S. (Stoke C), 1923 v S; (with Swansea T), 1927 v E, Ni (3)

Nicholas, P. (C Palace), 1979 v S (sub), Ni (sub), Ma; 1980 v Ei, WG, T, E, S, Ni, Ic; 1981 v T, Cz, E; (with Arsenal), T, S, E, USSR; 1982 v Cz, Ic, USSR, Sp, E, S, Ni, F; 1983 v Y, Bul, S, Ni; 1984 v N, Bul, N, Is; (with C Palace), 1985 v Sp; (with Luton T), N, S, Sp, N; 1986 v S, H, S.Ar, Ei, U, Ca (2); 1987 v Fi (2) USSR, Cz; (with Aberdeen), 1988 v D (2), Cz, Y, Se; (with Chelsea), 1989 v Ho, Fi, Is, Se, WG; 1990 v Fi, Ho, WG, Ei, Se, Cr; 1991 v D (sub), Bel, L, Ei; (with Watford), Bel, Pol, WG; 1992 v L (73)

Nicholls, J. (Newport Co), 1924 v E, Ni; (with Cardiff C), 1925 v E, S (4)

Niedzwiecki, E. A. (Chelsea), 1985 v N (sub); 1988 v D (2)

Nock, W. (Newtown), 1897 v Ni (1)

Nogan, L. M. (Watford), 1992 v A (sub); (with Reading), 1996 v Mol (2)

Norman, A. J. (Hull C), 1986 v Ei (sub), U, Ca; 1988 v Ma, I (5)

Nurse, M. T. G. (Swansea T), 1960 v E, Ni; 1961 v S, E, H, Ni, Ei, Sp (2); (with Middlesbrough), 1963 v E, H; 1964 v S (12)

O'Callaghan, E. (Tottenham H), 1929 v Ni; 1930 v S; 1932 v S, E; 1933 v Ni, S, E; 1934 v Ni, S, E; 1935 v E (11)

Oliver, A. (Blackburn R), 1905 v E; (with Bangor), S (2)

O'Sullivan, P. A. (Brighton), 1973 v S (sub); 1976 v S; 1979 v Ma (sub) (3)

Owen, D. (Oswestry), 1879 v E (1)

Owen, E. (Ruthin Grammar School), 1884 v E, Ni, S (3)

Owen, G. (Chirk), 1888 v S; (with Newton Heath), 1889 v S, Ni; 1893 v Ni (4)

Owen, J. (Newton Heath), 1892 v E (1)

Owen, Trevor (Crewe Alex), 1899 v E, S (2)

Owen, T. (Oswestry), 1879 v E (1)

Owen, W. (Chirk), 1884 v E; 1885 v Ni; 1887 v E; 1888 v E; 1889 v E, Ni, S; 1890 v S, Ni; 1891 v E, S, Ni; 1892 v E, S; 1893 v S, Ni (16)

Owen, W. P. (Ruthin), 1880 v E, S; 1881 v E, S; 1882 v E, S, Ni; 1883 v S; 1884 v E, S, Ni (12)

Owens, J. (Wrexham), 1902 v S (1)

Page, M. E. (Birmingham C), 1971 v Fi; 1972 v S, Ni; 1973 v E (1+1 sub), Ni; 1974 v S, Ni; 1975 v H, L, S, E, Ni; 1976 v E, Y (2), E, Ni; 1977 v WG, S; 1978 v K (sub+1), WG, Ir, E, S; 1979 v Ma, WG (28)

Palmer, D. (Swansea T), 1957 v Cz; 1958 v E, EG (3)

Parris, J. E. (Bradford), 1932 v Ni (1)

Parry, B. J. (Swansea T), 1951 v S (1)

Parry, C. (Everton), 1891 v S, Ni; 1893 v E; 1894 v E; 1895 v E, S; (with Newtown), 1896 v E, S, Ni; 1897 v Ni; 1898 v E, S, Ni (13)

Parry, E. (Liverpool), 1922 v S; 1923 v E, Ni; 1925 v Ni; 1926 v Ni (5)

Parry, M. (Liverpool), 1901 v E, S, Ni; 1902 v E, S, Ni; 1903 v E, S; 1904 v E, Ni; 1906 v E; 1908 v E, S, Ni; 1909 v E, S (16)

Parry, T. D. (Oswestry), 1900 v E, S, Ni; 1901 v E, S, Ni; 1902 v E (7)

Parry, W. (Newtown), 1895 v Ni (1)

Pascoe, C. (Swansea C), 1984 v N, Is; (with Sunderland), 1989 v Fi, Is, WG (sub); 1990 v Ho (sub), WG (sub); 1991 v Ei, Ic (sub); 1992 v Br (10)

Paul, R. (Swansea T), 1949 v E, S, Ni, P, Sw; 1950 v E, S, Ni, Bel; (with Manchester C), 1951 v E, S, E, Ni, P, Sw; 1952 v E, S, Ni, R of UK; 1953 v S, E, Ni, F, Y; 1954 v E, S, Ni; 1955 v S, E, Y; 1956 v E, Ni, S, A (33)

Peake, E. (Aberystwyth), 1908 v Ni; (with Liverpool), 1909 v Ni, S, E; 1910 v S, Ni; 1911 v Ni; 1912 v E; 1913 v E, Ni; 1914 v Ni (11)

Peers, E. J. (Wolverhampton W), 1914 v Ni, S, E; 1920 v E, S; 1921 v S, Ni, E; (with Port Vale), 1922 v E, S, Ni; 1923 v E (12)

Pembridge, M. A. (Luton T), 1992 v Br, Ei, R (with Derby Co), Ho, J (sub); 1993 v Bel (sub), Ei; 1994 v N (sub); 1995 v Alb (sub), Mol, Ge (sub); (with Sheffield W), 1996 v Mol, G, Alb, Sw, Sm (16)

Perry, E. (Doncaster R), 1938 v E, S, Ni (3)

Perry, J. (Cardiff C), 1994 v N (1)

Phennah, E. (Civil Service), 1878 v S (1)

Phillips, C. (Wolverhampton W), 1931 v Ni; 1932 v E; 1933 v S; 1934 v E, S, Ni; 1935 v E, S, Ni; 1936 v S; (with Aston Villa), 1936 v E, Ni; 1938 v S (13)

Phillips, D. (Plymouth Arg), 1984 v E, Ni, N; (with Manchester C), 1985 v Sp, Ic, S, Sp, N; 1986 v S, H, S.Ar, Ei, U; (with Coventry C), 1987 v Fi, Cz; 1988 v D (2), Cz, Y, Se; 1989 v Se, WG; (with Norwich C), 1990 v Fi, Ho, WG, Ei, Se; 1991 v D, Bel, Ic, Pol, WG; 1992 v L, Ei, A, R, Ho (sub), Arg, J; 1993 v Fa, Cy, Bel, Ei, Bel, RCS, Fa; (with Nottingham F), 1994 v RCS, Cy, R, N, Se, Es; 1995 v Alb, Mol, Ge, Bul (2), G, Ge; 1996 v Mol (sub), Alb, J (62)

Phillips, L. (Cardiff C), 1971 v Cz, S, E, Ni; 1972 v Cz, R, S, Ni; 1973 v E; 1974 v Pol (sub), Ni; 1975 v A; (with Aston Villa), H (2), L (2), S, E, Ni; 1976 v A, E, Y (2), E, Ni; 1977 v WG, S (2), Cz, E; 1978 v K (2), S, Cz, WG, E, S; 1979 v Ma; (with Swansea C), T, WG, S, E, Ni, Ma; 1980 v Ei, WG, T, S (sub), Ni, Ic; 1981 v T, Cz, T, S, E, USSR; (with Charlton Ath), 1982 v Cz, USSR (58)

Phillips, T. J. S. (Chelsea), 1973 v E; 1974 v E; 1975 v H (sub); 1978 v K (4)

Phoenix, H. (Wrexham), 1882 v S (1)

Poland, G. (Wrexham), 1939 v Ni, F (2)

Pontin, K. (Cardiff C), 1980 v E (sub), S (2)

Powell, A. (Leeds U), 1947 v E, S; 1948 v E, S, Ni; (with Everton), 1949 v E; 1950 v Bel; (with Birmingham C), 1951 v S (8)

Powell, D. (Wrexham), 1968 v WG; (with Sheffield U), 1969 v S, E, Ni, I, WG; 1970 v E, S, Ni, EG; 1971 v R (11)

Powell, I. V. (QPR), 1947 v E; 1948 v E, S, Ni; (with Aston Villa), 1949 v Bel; 1950 v S, Bel; 1951 v S (8)

Powell, J. (Druids), 1878 v S; 1880 v E, S; 1882 v E, S, Ni; 1883 v E, S, Ni; (with Bolton W), 1884 v E; (with Newton Heath), 1887 v E, S; 1888 v E, S, Ni (15)

Powell, Seth (WBA), 1885 v S; 1886 v E, Ni; 1891 v E, S; 1892 v E, S (7)

Price, H. (Aston Villa), 1907 v S; (with Burton U), 1908 v Ni; (with Wrexham), 1909 v S, E, Ni (5)

Price, J. (Wrexham), 1877 v S; 1878 v S; 1879 v E; 1880 v E, S; 1881 v E, S; (with Druids), 1882 v S, E, Ni; 1883 v S, Ni (12)

Price, P. (Luton T), 1980 v E, S, Ni, Ic; 1981 v T, Cz, Ei, T, S, E, USSR; (with Tottenham H), 1982 v USSR, Sp, F; 1983 v N, Y, E, Bul, S, Ni; 1984 v N, R, Bul, Y, S (sub) (25)

Pring, K. D. (Rotherham U), 1966 v Ch, D; 1967 v Ni (3)

Pritchard, H. K. (Bristol C), 1985 v N (sub) (1)

Pryce-Jones, A. W. (Newtown), 1895 v E (1)

Pryce-Jones, W. E. (Cambridge University), 1887 v S; 1888 v S, E, Ni; 1890 v Ni (5)

Pugh, A. (Rhostyllen), 1889 v S (1)

Pugh, D. H. (Wrexham), 1896 v S, Ni; 1897 v S, Ni; (with Lincoln C), 1900 v S; 1901 v S, E (7)

Pugsley, J. (Charlton Ath), 1930 v Ni (1)

Pullen, W. J. (Plymouth Arg), 1926 v E (1)

Rankmore, F. E. J. (Peterborough), 1966 v Ch (sub) (1)

Ratcliffe, K. (Everton), 1981 v Cz, Ei, T, S, E, USSR; 1982 v Cz, Ic, USSR, Sp, E; 1983 v Y, E, Bul, S, Ni, Br; 1984 v N, R, Bul, Y, S, E, Ni, N, Is; 1985 v Ic, Sp, Ic, N, S, Sp; 1986 v S, H, S.Ar, U; 1987 v Fi (2), USSR, Cz; 1988 v D (2), Cz; 1989 v Fi, Is, Se, WG; 1990 v Fi; 1991 v D, Bel (2), L, Ei, Ic, Pol, WG; 1992 v Br, G; (with Cardiff C), 1993 v Bel (59)

Rea, J. C. (Aberystwyth), 1894 v Ni, S, E; 1895 v S; 1896 v S, Ni; 1897 v S, Ni; 1898 v Ni (9)

Reece, G. I. (Sheffield U), 1966 v E, S, Ni, USSR; 1967 v S; 1969 v R of UK (sub); 1970 v I (sub); 1971 v S, E, Ni, Fi; 1972 v Fi, R, E (sub), S, Ni; (with Cardiff C), 1973 v E (sub), Ni; 1974 v Pol (sub), S, Ni; 1975 v A, H (2), L (2), S, Ni (29)

Reed, W. G. (Ipswich T), 1955 v S, Y (2)

Rees, A. (Birmingham C), 1984 v N (sub) (1)

Rees, J. M. (Luton T), 1992 v A (sub) (1)

Rees, R. R. (Coventry C), 1965 v S, E, Ni, D, Gr (2), I, R; 1966 v E, S, Ni, R, D, Br (2), Ch; 1967 v E, Ni; 1968 v E, S, Ni; (with WBA), WG; 1969 v I; (with Nottingham F), 1969 v WG, EG, S (sub), R of UK; 1970 v E, S, Ni, EG, I; 1971 v Cz, R, E (sub), Ni (sub), Fi; 1972 v Cz (sub), R (39)

Rees, W. (Cardiff C), 1949 v Ni, Bel, Sw; (with Tottenham H), 1950 v Ni (4)

Richards, A. (Barnsley), 1932 v S (1)

Richards, D. (Wolverhampton W), 1931 v Ni; 1933 v E, S, Ni; 1934 v E, S, Ni; 1935 v E, S, Ni; 1936 v S; (with Brentford), 1936 v E, Ni; 1937 v S, E; (with Birmingham), Ni; 1938 v E, S, Ni; 1939 v E, S (21)
Richards, G. (Druids), 1899 v E, S, Ni; (with Oswestry), 1903 v Ni; (with Shrewsbury), 1904 v S; 1905 v Ni (6)
Richards, R. W. (Wolverhampton W), 1920 v E, S; 1921 v Ni; 1922 v E, S; (with West Ham U), 1924 v E, S, Ni; (with Mold), 1926 v S (9)
Richards, S. V. (Cardiff C), 1947 v E (1)
Richards, W. E. (Fulham), 1933 v Ni (1)
Roach, J. (Oswestry), 1885 v Ni (1)
Robbins, W. W. (Cardiff C), 1931 v E, S; 1932 v Ni, E, S; (with WBA), 1933 v F, E, S, Ni; 1934 v S; 1936 v S (11)
Roberts, A. M. (QPR), 1993 v Ei (sub) (1)
Roberts, D. F. (Oxford U), 1973 v Pol, E (sub), Ni; 1974 v E, S; 1975 v A; (with Hull C), L, Ni; 1976 v S, Ni, Y; 1977 v E (sub), Ni; 1978 v K (1+1 sub), S, Ni (17)
Roberts, I. W. (Watford), 1990 v Ho; (with Huddersfield T), 1992 v A, Arg, J; (with Leicester C), 1994 v Se; 1995 v Alb (sub), Mol (7)
Roberts, Jas (Chirk), 1898 v S (1)
Roberts, Jas (Wrexham), 1913 v S, Ni (2)
Roberts, J. (Corwen), 1879 v S; 1880 v E, S; 1882 v E, S, Ni; (with Berwyn R), 1883 v E (7)
Roberts, J. (Ruthin), 1881 v S; 1882 v S (2)
Roberts, J. (Bradford C), 1906 v Ni; 1907 v Ni (2)
Roberts, J. G. (Arsenal), 1971 v S, E, Ni, Fi; 1972 v Fi, E, Ni; (with Birmingham C), 1973 v E (2), Pol, S, Ni; 1974 v Pol, E, S, Ni; 1975 v A, H, S, E; 1976 v E, S (22)
Roberts, J. H. (Bolton), 1949 v Bel (1)
Roberts, P. S. (Portsmouth), 1974 v E; 1975 v A, H, L (4)
Roberts, R. (Druids), 1884 v S; (with Bolton W), 1887 v S; 1888 v S, E; 1889 v S, E; 1890 v S; 1892 v Ni; (with Preston NE), S (9)
Roberts, R. (Wrexham), 1886 v Ni; 1887 v Ni (2)
Roberts, R. (Rhos), 1891 v Ni; (with Crewe Alex), 1893 v E (2)
Roberts, W. (Llangollen), 1879 v E, S; 1880 v E, S; (with Berwyn R), 1881 v S; 1883 v S (6)
Roberts, W. (Wrexham), 1886 v E, S, Ni; 1887 v Ni (4)
Roberts, W. H. (Ruthin), 1882 v E, S; 1883 v E, S, Ni; (with Rhyl), 1884 v S (6)
Robinson, J. R. C. (Charlton Ath), 1996 v Alb (sub), Sw, Sm (3)
Rodrigues, P. J. (Cardiff C), 1965 v Ni, Gr (2); 1966 v USSR, E, S, D; (with Leicester C), Ni, Br (2), Ch; 1967 v S; 1968 v E, S, Ni; 1969 v E, Ni, EG, R of UK; 1970 v E, S, Ni, EG; (with Sheffield W), 1971 v R, E, S, Cz, Ni; 1972 v Fi, Cz, R, E, Ni (sub); 1973 v E (3), Pol, S, Ni; 1974 v Pol (40)
Rogers, J. P. (Wrexham), 1896 v E, S, Ni (3)
Rogers, W. (Wrexham), 1931 v E, S (2)
Roose, L. R. (Aberystwyth), 1900 v Ni; (with London Welsh), 1901 v E, S, Ni; (with Stoke C), 1902 v E, S; 1904 v E; (with Everton), 1905 v S, E; (with Stoke C), 1906 v E, S, Ni; 1907 v E, S, Ni; (with Sunderland), 1908 v E, S; 1909 v E, S, Ni; 1910 v E, S, Ni; 1911 v S (24)
Rouse, R. V. (C Palace), 1959 v Ni (1)
Rowlands, A. C. (Tranmere R), 1914 v E (1)
Rowley, T. (Tranmere R), 1959 v Ni (1)
Rush, I. (Liverpool), 1980 v S (sub), Ni; 1981 v E (sub); 1982 v Ic (sub), USSR, E, S, Ni, F; 1983 v N, Y, E, Bul; 1984 v N, R, Bul, Y, S, E, Ni; 1985 v Ic, N, S, Sp; 1986 v S, S.Ar, Ei, U; 1987 v Fi (2), USSR, Cz; (with Juventus), 1988 v D, Cz, Y, Se, Ma, I; (with Liverpool), 1989 v Ho, Fi, Se, WG; 1990 v Fi, Ei; 1991 v D, Bel (2), L, Ei, Pol, WG; 1992 v G, L, R; 1993 v Fa, Cy, Bel (2), RCS, Fa; 1994 v RCS, Cy, R, N, Se, Es; 1995 v Alb, Ge, Bul, G, Ge; 1996 v Mol, I (73)
Russell, M. R. (Merthyr T), 1912 v S, Ni; 1914 v E; (with Plymouth Arg), 1920 v E, S, Ni; 1921 v E, S, Ni; 1922 v E, Ni; 1923 v E, S, Ni; 1924 v E, S, Ni; 1925 v E, S; 1926 v E, S; 1928 v S; 1929 v E (23)

Sabine, H. W. (Oswestry), 1887 v Ni (1)
Saunders, D. (Brighton & HA), 1986 v Ei (sub), Ca (2); 1987 v Fi, USSR (sub); (with Oxford U), 1988 v Y, Se, Ma, I (sub); 1989 v Ho (sub), Fi; (with Derby Co), S, Se, WG; 1990 v Fi, Ho, WG, Se, Cr; 1991 v D, Bel (2), L, Ei, Ic, Pol, WG; (with Liverpool), 1992 v Br, G, Ei, R, Ho, Arg, J; 1993 v Fa; (with Aston Villa), Cy, Bel (2), RCS, Fa; 1994 v RCS, Cy, R, N, Se; 1995 v Ge, Bul (2), G, Ge; (with Galatasaray), 1996 v G, Alb, Sm (52)
Savage, M. W. (Crewe Alex), 1996 v Alb (sub), Sw (sub), Sm (sub) (3)
Savin, G. (Oswestry), 1878 v S (1)
Sayer, P. (Cardiff C), 1977 v Cz, S, E, Ni; 1978 v K (2), S (7)
Scrine, F. H. (Swansea T), 1950 v E, Ni (2)
Sear, C. R. (Manchester C), 1963 v E (1)
Shaw, E. G. (Oswestry), 1882 v Ni; 1884 v S, Ni (3)
Sherwood, A. T. (Cardiff C), 1947 v E, Ni; 1948 v S, Ni; 1949 v E, S, Ni, P, Sw; 1950 v E, S, Ni, Bel; 1951 v E, S, Ni, P,

Sw; 1952 v E, S, Ni, R of UK; 1953 v S, E, Ni, F, Y; 1954 v E, S, Ni, A; 1955 v S, E, Y, Ni; 1956 v E, S, Ni, A; (with Newport Co), 1957 v E, S (41)
Shone, W. W. (Oswestry), 1879 v E (1)
Shortt, W. W. (Plymouth Arg), 1947 v Ni; 1950 v Ni, Bel; 1952 v E, S, Ni, R of UK; 1953 v S, E, Ni, F, Y (12)
Showers, D. (Cardiff C), 1975 v E (sub), Ni (2)
Sidlow, C. (Liverpool), 1947 v E, S; 1948 v E, S, Ni; 1949 v S; 1950 v E (7)
Sisson, H. (Wrexham Olympic), 1885 v Ni; 1886 v S, Ni (3)
Slatter, N. (Bristol R), 1983 v S; 1984 v N (sub), Is; 1985 v Ic, Sp, Ic, N, S, Sp, N; (with Oxford U), 1986 v H (sub), S.Ar, Ca (2); 1987 v Fi (sub), Cz; 1988 v D (2), Cz, Ma, I; 1989 v Is (sub) (22)
Smallman, D. P. (Wrexham), 1974 v E (sub), S (sub), Ni; (with Everton), 1975 v H (sub), E, Ni (sub); 1976 v A (7)
Southall, N. (Everton), 1982 v Ni; 1983 v N, E, Bul, S, Ni, Br; 1984 v N, R, Bul, Y, S, E, Ni, N, Is; 1985 v Ic, Sp, Ic, N, S, Sp, N; 1986 v S, H, S.Ar, Ei; 1987 v USSR, Fi, Cz; 1988 v D, Cz, Y, Se; 1989 v Ho, Fi, Se, WG; 1990 v Fi, Ho, WG, Ei, Se, Cr; 1991 v D, Bel (2), L, Ei, Ic, Pol, WG; 1992 v Br, G, L, Ei, A, R, Ho, Arg, J; 1993 v Fa, Cy, Bel, Ei, Bel, RCS, Fa; 1994 v RCS, Cy, R, N, Se, Es; 1995 v Alb, Mol, Ge, Bul (2), G, Ge; 1996 v Mol, G, Alb, I, Sm (86)
Speed, G. A. (Leeds U), 1990 v Cr (sub); 1991 v D, L (sub), Ei (sub), Ic, WG (sub); 1992 v Br, G (sub), L, Ei, R, Ho,Arg,J; 1993 v Fa, Cy, Bel, Ei, Bel, Fa (sub); 1994 v RCS (sub), Cy, R, N, Se; 1995 v Alb, Mol, Ge, Bul (2), G; 1996 v Mol, G, I, Sw (sub) (35)
Sprake, G. (Leeds U), 1964 v S, Ni; 1965 v S, D, Gr; 1966 v E, Ni, USSR; 1967 v S; 1968 v E, S; 1969 v S, E, Ni, WG, R of UK; 1970 v EG, I; 1971 v R, S, E, Ni; 1972 v Fi, E, S, Ni; 1973 v E (2), Pol, S, Ni; 1974 v Pol; (with Birmingham C), S, Ni; 1975 v A, H, L (37)
Stansfield, F. (Cardiff C), 1949 v S (1)
Stevenson, B. (Leeds U), 1978 v Ni; 1979 v Ma, T, S, E, Ni, Ma; 1980 v WG, T, Ic (sub); 1982 v Cz; (with Birmingham C), Sp, S, Ni, F (15)
Stevenson, N. (Swansea C), 1982 v E, S, Ni; 1983 v N (4)
Stitfall, R. F. (Cardiff C), 1953 v E; 1957 v Cz (2)
Sullivan, D. (Cardiff C), 1953 v Ni, F, Y; 1954 v Ni; 1955 v E, Ni; 1957 v E, S; 1958 v Ni, H (2), Se, Br; 1959 v S, Ni; 1960 v E, S (17)
Symons, C. J. (Portsmouth), 1992 v Ei, Ho, Arg, J; 1993 v Fa, Cy, Bel, Ei, RCS, Fa; 1994 v RCS, Cy, R; 1995 v Mol, Ge (sub), Bul, G, Ge; (with Manchester C), 1996 v Mol, G, I, Sw (22)

Tapscott, D. R. (Arsenal), 1954 v A; 1955 v S, E, Ni, Y; 1956 v E, Ni, S, A; 1957 v Ni, Cz, EG; (with Cardiff C), 1959 v E, Ni (14)
Taylor, G. K. (C Palace), 1996 v Alb, I (sub); (with Sheffield U), Sw (3)
Taylor, J. (Wrexham), 1898 v E (1)
Taylor, O. D. S. (Newtown), 1893 v S, Ni; 1894 v S, Ni (4)
Thomas, C. (Druids), 1899 v Ni; 1900 v S (2)
Thomas, D. A. (Swansea T), 1957 v Cz; 1958 v EG (2)
Thomas, D. S. (Fulham), 1948 v E, S, Ni; 1949 v S (4)
Thomas, E. (Cardiff Corinthians), 1925 v E (1)
Thomas, G. (Wrexham), 1885 v E, S (2)
Thomas, H. (Manchester U), 1927 v E (1)
Thomas, M. (Wrexham), 1977 v WG, S (1+1 sub), Ni (sub); 1978 v K (sub), S, Cz, Ir, E, Ni (sub); 1979 v Ma; (with Manchester U), T, WG, Ma (sub); 1980 v Ei, WG (sub), T, E, S, Ni; 1981 v Cz, S, E, USSR; (with Everton), 1982 v Cz; (with Brighton & HA), USSR (sub), Sp, E, S (sub), Ni (sub); 1983 (with Stoke C), v N, Y, E, Bul, S, Ni, Br; 1984 v R, Bul, Y; (with Chelsea), S, E; 1985 v Ic, Sp, Ic, S, Sp, N; 1986 v S; (with WBA), H, S.Ar (sub) (51)
Thomas, M. R. (Newcastle U), 1987 v Fi (1)
Thomas, R. J. (Swindon T), 1967 v Ni; 1968 v WG; 1969 v E, Ni, I, WG, R of UK; 1970 v E, S, Ni, EG, I; 1971 v S, E, Ni, R, Cz; 1972 v Fi, Cz, R, E, S, Ni; 1973 v E (3), Pol, S, Ni; 1974 v Pol; (with Derby Co), E, S, Ni; 1975 v H (2), L (2), S, E, Ni; 1976 v A, Y, E; 1977 v Cz, S, E, Ni; 1978 v K, S; (with Cardiff C), Cz (50)
Thomas, T. (Bangor), 1898 v S, Ni (2)
Thomas, W. R. (Newport Co), 1931 v E, S (2)
Thomson, D. (Druids), 1876 v S (1)
Thomson, G. F. (Druids), 1876 v S; 1877 v S (2)
Toshack, J. B. (Cardiff C), 1969 v S, E, Ni, WG, EG, R of UK; 1970 v EG, I; (with Liverpool), 1971 v S, E, Ni, Fi; 1972 v Fi, E; 1973 v E (3), Pol, S; 1975 v A, H (2), L (2), S, E; 1976 v Y (2), E; 1977 v S; 1978 v K (2), S, Cz; (with Swansea C), 1979 v WG (sub), S, E, Ni, Ma; 1980 v WG (40)
Townsend, W. (Newtown), 1887 v Ni; 1893 v Ni (2)
Trainer, H. (Wrexham), 1895 v E, S, Ni (3)
Trainer, J. (Bolton W), 1887 v S; (with Preston NE), 1888 v S; 1889 v E; 1890 v S; 1891 v S; 1892 v Ni, S; 1893 v E; 1894

v Ni, E; 1895 v Ni, E; 1896 v S; 1897 v Ni, S, E; 1898 v S, E; 1899 v Ni, S (20)
Turner, H. G. (Charlton Ath), 1937 v E, S, Ni; 1938 v E, S, Ni; 1939 v Ni, F (8)
Turner, J. (Wrexham), 1892 v E (1)
Turner, R. E. (Wrexham), 1891 v E, Ni (2)
Turner, W. H. (Wrexham), 1887 v E, Ni; 1890 v S; 1891 v E, S (5)

Van Den Hauwe, P. W. R. (Everton), 1985 v Sp; 1986 v S, H; 1987 v USSR, Fi, Cz; 1988 v D (2), Cz, Y, I; 1989 v Fi, Se (13)
Vaughan, Jas (Druids), 1893 v E, S, Ni; 1899 v E (4)
Vaughan, John (Oswestry), 1879 v S; 1880 v S; 1881 v E, S; 1882 v E, S, Ni; 1883 v E, S, Ni; (with Bolton W), 1884 v E (11)
Vaughan, J. O. (Rhyl), 1885 v Ni; 1886 v Ni, E, S (4)
Vaughan, N. (Newport Co), 1983 v Y (sub), Br; 1984 v N; (with Cardiff C), R, Bul, Y, Ni (sub), N, Is; 1985 v Sp (sub) (10)
Vaughan, T. (Rhyl), 1885 v E (1)
Vearncombe, G. (Cardiff C), 1958 v EG; 1961 v Ei (2)
Vernon, T. R. (Blackburn R), 1957 v Ni, Cz (2), EG; 1958 v E, S, EG, Se; 1959 v S; (with Everton), 1960 v Ni; 1961 v S, E, Ei; 1962 v Ni, Br (2), M; 1963 v S, E, H; 1964 v E, S; (with Stoke C), 1965 v Ni, Gr, I; 1966 v E, S, Ni, USSR, D; 1967 v Ni; 1968 v E (32)
Villars, A. K. (Cardiff C), 1974 v E, S, Ni (sub) (3)
Vizard, E. T. (Bolton W), 1911 v E, S, Ni; 1912 v E, S; 1913 v S; 1914 v E, Ni; 1920 v E; 1921 v E, S, Ni; 1922 v E, S; 1923 v E, Ni; 1924 v E, S, Ni; 1926 v E, S; 1927 v S (22)

Walley, J. T. (Watford), 1971 v Cz (1)
Walsh, I. (C Palace), 1980 v Ei, T, E, S, Ic; 1981 v T, Cz, Ei, T, S, E, USSR; 1982 v Cz (sub), Ic; (with Swansea C), Sp, S (sub), Ni (sub), F (18)
Ward, D. (Bristol R), 1959 v E; (with Cardiff C), 1962 v E (2)
Warner, J. (Swansea City), 1937 v E; (with Manchester U), 1939 v F (2)
Warren, F. W. (Cardiff C), 1929 v Ni; (with Middlesbrough), 1931 v Ni; 1933 v F, E; (with Hearts), 1937 v Ni; 1938 v Ni (6)
Watkins, A. E. (Leicester Fosse), 1898 v E, S; (with Aston Villa), 1900 v E, S; (with Millwall), 1904 v Ni (5)
Watkins, W. M. (Stoke C), 1902 v E; 1903 v E, S; (with Aston Villa); 1904 v E, S, Ni; (with Sunderland), 1905 v E, S, Ni; (with Stoke C), 1908 v Ni (10)
Webster, C (Manchester U), 1957 v Cz; 1958 v H, M, Br (4)
Whatley, W. J. (Tottenham H), 1939 v E, S (2)
White, P. F. (London Welsh), 1896 v Ni (1)
Wilcocks, A. R. (Oswestry), 1890 v Ni (1)
Wilding, J. (Wrexham Olympians), 1885 v E, S, Ni; 1886 v E, Ni; (with Bootle), 1887 v E; 1888 v S, Ni; (with Wrexham), 1892 v S (9)
Williams, A. (Reading), 1994 v Es; 1995 v Alb, Mol, G (sub), Ge; 1996 v Mol, I (7)
Williams, A. L. (Wrexham), 1931 v E (1)
Williams, B. (Bristol C), 1930 v Ni (1)
Williams, B. D. (Swansea T), 1928 v Ni, E; 1930 v E, S; (with Everton), 1931 v Ni; 1932 v E; 1933 v E, S, Ni; 1935 v Ni (10)

Williams, D. G. (Derby Co), 1988 v Cz, Y, Se, Ma, I; 1989 v Ho, Is, Se, WG; 1990 v Fi, Ho; (with Ipswich T), 1993 v Ei; 1996 v G (sub) (13)
Williams, D. M. (Norwich C), 1986 v S.Ar (sub), U, Ca (2); 1987 v Fi (5)
Williams, D. R. (Merthyr T), 1921 v E, S; (with Sheffield W), 1923 v S; 1926 v S; 1927 v E, Ni; (with Manchester U), 1929 v E, S (8)
Williams, E. (Crewe Alex), 1893 v E, S (2)
Williams, E. (Druids), 1901 v E, Ni, S; 1902 v E, Ni (5)
Williams, G. (Chirk), 1893 v S; 1894 v S; 1895 v E, S, Ni; 1898 v Ni (6)
Williams, G. E. (WBA), 1960 v Ni; 1961 v S, E, Ei; 1963 v Ni, H; 1964 v E, S, Ni; 1965 v S, E, Ni, D, Gr (2), USSR, I; 1966 v Ni, Br (2), Ch; 1967 v S, E, Ni; 1968 v Ni; 1969 v I (26)
Williams, G. G. (Swansea T), 1961 v Ni, H, Sp (2); 1962 v E (5)
Williams, G. J. J. (Cardiff C), 1951 v Sw (1)
Williams, G. O. (Wrexham), 1907 v Ni (1)
Williams, H. J. (Swansea), 1965 v Gr (2); 1972 v R (3)
Williams, H. T. (Newport Co), 1949 v Ni, Sw; (with Leeds U), 1950 v Ni; 1951 v S (4)
Williams, J. H. (Oswestry), 1884 v E (1)
Williams, J. J. (Wrexham), 1939 v F (1)
Williams, J. T. (Middlesbrough), 1925 v Ni (1)
Williams, J. W. (C Palace), 1912 v S, Ni (2)
Williams, R. (Newcastle U), 1935 v S, E (2)
Williams, R. P. (Caernarvon), 1886 v S (1)
Williams, S. G. (WBA), 1954 v A; 1955 v E, Ni; 1956 v E, S, A; 1958 v E, S, Ni, Is (2), H (2), M, Se, Br; 1959 v E, S, Ni; 1960 v E, S, Ni; 1961 v Ni, Ei, H, Sp (2); 1962 v E, S, Ni, Br (2), M; (with Southampton), 1963 v E, S, H (2); 1964 v E, S; 1965 v S, E, D; 1966 v D (43)
Williams, W. (Druids), 1876 v S; 1878 v S; (with Oswestry), 1879 v E, S; (with Druids), 1880 v E; 1881 v E, S; 1882 v E, S, Ni; 1883 v Ni (11)
Williams, W. (Northampton T), 1925 v S (1)
Witcomb, D. F. (WBA), 1947 v E, S; (with Sheffield W), 1947 v Ni (3)
Woosnam, A. P. (Leyton Orient), 1959 v S; (with West Ham U), E; 1960 v E, S, Ni; 1961 v S, E, Ni, Ei, Sp, H; 1962 v E, S, Ni, Br; (with Aston Villa), 1963 v Ni, H (17)
Woosnam, G. (Newton White Star), 1879 v S (1)
Worthington, T. (Newtown), 1894 v S (1)
Wynn, G. A. (Wrexham), 1909 v E, S, Ni; (with Manchester C), 1910 v E; 1911 v Ni; 1912 v E, S; 1913 v E, S; 1914 v E, S (11)
Wynn, W. (Chirk), 1903 v Ni (1)

Yorath, T. C. (Leeds U), 1970 v I; 1971 v S, E, Ni; 1972 v Cz, E, S, Ni; 1973 v E, Pol, S; 1974 v Pol, E, S, Ni; 1975 v A, H (2), L (2), S; 1976 v A, E, S, Y (2), E, Ni; (with Coventry C), 1977 v WG, S (2), Cz, E, Ni; 1978 v K (2), S, Cz, WG, Ir, E, S, Ni; 1979 v T, WG, S, E, Ni; (with Tottenham H), 1980 v Ei, T, E, S, Ni, Ic; 1981 v T, Cz; (with Vancouver W), Ei, T, USSR (59)
Young, E. (Wimbledon), 1990 v Cr; (with C Palace), 1991 v D, Bel (2), L, Ei; 1992 v G, L, Ei, A; 1993 v Fa, Cy, Bel, Ei, Bel, Fa; 1994 v RCS, Cy, R, N; (with Wolverhampton W) 1996 v Alb (21)

REPUBLIC OF IRELAND

Aherne, T. (Belfast C), 1946 v P, Sp; (with Luton T), 1950 v Fi, E, Fi, Se, Bel; 1951 v N, Arg, N; 1952 v WG (2), A, Sp; 1953 v F; 1954 v F (16)
Aldridge, J. W. (Oxford U), 1986 v W, U, Ic, Cz; 1987 v Bel, S, Pol; (with Liverpool), S, Bul, Bel, Br, L; 1988 v Bul, Pol, N, E, USSR, Ho; 1989 v Ni, Tun, Sp, F (sub), H, Ma (sub), H; 1990 v WG; (with Real Sociedad), Ni, Ma, Fi (sub), T, E, Eg, Ho, R, I; 1991 v T, E (2), Pol; (with Tranmere R), 1992 v H (sub), T, W (sub), Sw (sub), US (sub), Alb, I, P (sub); 1993 v La, D, Sp, D, Alb, La, Li; 1994 v Li, Ni, CzR, I (sub), M (sub), N; 1995 v La, Ni, P, Lie; 1996 v La, P, Ho, Ru (68)
Ambrose, P. (Shamrock R), 1955 v N, Ho; 1964 v Pol, N, E (5)
Anderson, J. (Preston NE), 1980 v Cz (sub), US (sub); 1982 v Ch, Br, Tr; (with Newcastle U), 1984 v Chn; 1986 v W, Ic, Cz; 1987 v Bul, Bel, Br, L; 1988 v R (sub), Y (sub); 1989 v Tun (16)
Andrews, P. (Bohemians), 1936 v Ho (1)
Arrigan, T. (Waterford), 1938 v N (1)

Babb, P. A. (Coventry C), 1994 v Ru, Ho, Bol, G, CzR (sub), I, M, N, Ho; (with Liverpool), 1995 v La, Lie, Ni (2), P, Lie, A; 1996 v La, P, Ho, CzR (20)
Bailham, E. (Shamrock R), 1964 v E (1)
Barber, E. (Shelbourne), 1966 v Sp; (with Birmingham C), 1966 v Bel (2)
Barry, P. (Fordsons), 1928 v Bel; 1929 v Bel (2)
Beglin, J. (Liverpool), 1984 v Chn; 1985 v M, D, I, Is, E, N, Sw; 1986 v Sw, USSR, D, W; 1987 v Bel (sub), S, Pol (15)
Bermingham, J. (Bohemians), 1929 v Bel (1)
Bermingham, P. (St James' Gate), 1935 v H (1)
Braddish, S. (Dundalk), 1978 v T (sub), Pol (2)
Bonner, P. (Celtic), 1981 v Pol; 1982 v Alg; 1984 v Ma, Is, Chn; 1985 v I, Is, E, N; 1986 v U, Ic; 1987 v Bel (2), S (2), Pol, Bul, Br, L; 1988 v Bul, R, Y, N, E, USSR, Ho; 1989 v Sp, F, H, Sp, Ma, H; 1990 v WG, Ni, Ma, W, Fi, T, E, Eg, Ho, R, I; 1991 v Mor, T, E (2), W, Pol, US; 1992 v H, Pol, T, W, Sw, Alb, I; 1993 v La, D, Sp, W, Ni, D, Alb, La, Li; 1994 v Li, Sp, Ni, Ru, Ho, Bol, CzR, I, M, N, Ho; 1995 v Lie; 1996 v M, Bol (sub) (80)

Bradshaw, P. (St James' Gate), 1939 v Sw, Pol, H (2), G (5)

Brady, F. (Fordsons), 1926 v I; 1927 v I (2)

Brady, T. R. (QPR), 1964 v A (2), Sp (2), Pol, N (6)

Brady, W. L. (Arsenal), 1975 v USSR, T, Sw, USSR, Sw, WG; 1976 v T, N, Pol; 1977 v E, T, F (2), Sp, Bul; 1978 v Bul, N; 1979 v Ni, E, D, Bul, WG; 1980 v W, Bul, E, Cy; (with Juventus), 1981 v Ho, Bel, F, Cy, Bel; 1982 v Ho, F, Ch, Br, Tr; (with Sampdoria), 1983 v Ho, Sp, Ic, Ma; 1984 v Ic, Ho, Ma, Pol, Is; (with Internazionale), 1985 v USSR, N, D, I, E, N, Sp, Sw; 1986 v Sw, USSR, D, W; (with Ascoli), 1987 v Bel, S (2), Pol; (with West Ham U), Bul, Bel, Br, L; 1988 v L, Bul; 1989 v F, H (sub), H (sub); 1990 v WG, Fi (72)

Breen, G. (Birmingham C), 1996 v P (sub), Cro, Ho, US, M, Bol (sub) (6)

Breen, T. (Manchester U), 1937 v Sw, F; (with Shamrock R), 1947 v E, Sp, P (5)

Brennan, F. (Drumcondra), 1965 v Bel (1)

Brennan, S. A. (Manchester U), 1965 v Sp; 1966 v Sp, A, Bel; 1967 v Sp, T, Sp; 1969 v Cz, D, H; 1970 v S, Cz, D, H, Pol (sub), WG; (with Waterford), 1971 v Pol, Se, I (19)

Brown, J. (Coventry C), 1937 v Sw, F (2)

Browne, W. (Bohemians), 1964 v A, Sp, E (3)

Buckley, L. (Shamrock R), 1984 v Pol (sub); (with Waregem), 1985 v M (2)

Burke, F. (Cork Ath), 1952 v WG (1)

Burke, J. (Cork), 1934 v Bel (1)

Burke, J. (Shamrock R), 1929 v Bel (1)

Byrne, A. B. (Southampton), 1970 v D, Pol, WG; 1971 v Pol, Se (2), I (2), A; 1973 v F, USSR (sub), F, N; 1974 v Pol (14)

Byrne, D. (Shelbourne), 1929 v Bel; (with Shamrock R), 1932 v Sp; (with Coleraine), 1934 v Bel (3)

Byrne, J. (Bray Unknowns), 1928 v Bel (1)

Byrne, J. (QPR), 1985 v I, Is (sub), E (sub), Sp (sub); 1987 v S (sub), Bel (sub), Br, L; 1988 v L, Bul (sub), Is, R, Y (sub), Pol (sub); (with Le Havre), 1990 v WG (sub), W, Fi, T (sub), Ma; (with Brighton & HA), 1991 v W; (with Sunderland), 1992 v T, W; (with Millwall), 1993 v W (23)

Byrne, P. (Shamrock R), 1984 v Pol, Chn; 1985 v M; 1986 v D (sub), W (sub), U (sub), Ic (sub), Cz (8)

Byrne, P. (Dolphin), 1931 v Sp; 1932 v Ho; (with Drumcondra), 1934 v Ho (3)

Byrne, S. (Bohemians), 1931 v Sp (1)

Campbell, A. (Santander), 1985 v I (sub), Is, Sp (3)

Campbell, N. (St Patrick's Ath), 1971 v A (sub); (with Fortuna, Cologne), 1972 v Ir, Ec, Ch, P; 1973 v USSR, F (sub); 1975 v WG; 1976 v N; 1977 v Sp, Bul (sub) (11)

Cannon, H. (Bohemians), 1926 v I; 1928 v Bel (2)

Cantwell, N. (West Ham U), 1954 v L; 1956 v Sp, Ho; 1957 v D, WG, E (2); 1958 v D, Pol, A; 1959 v Pol, Cz (2); 1960 v Se, Ch, Se; 1961 v N; (with Manchester U), S (2); 1962 v Cz (2), A; 1963 v Ic (2), S; 1964 v A, Sp, E; 1965 v Pol, Sp; 1966 v Sp (2), A, Bel; 1967 v Sp, T (36)

Carey, B. P. (Manchester U), 1992 v US (sub); 1993 v W; (with Leicester U), 1994 v Ru (3)

Carey, J. J. (Manchester U), 1938 v N, Cz, Pol; 1939 v Sw, Pol, H (2); 1946 v P, Sp; 1947 v E, Sp, P; 1948 v P, Sp; 1949 v Sw, Bel, P, Se, Sp; 1950 v Fi, E, Fi, Se; 1951 v N, Arg, N; 1953 v F, A (29)

Carolan, J. (Manchester U), 1960 v Se, Ch (2)

Carroll, B. (Shelbourne), 1949 v Bel; 1950 v Fi (2)

Carroll, T. R. (Ipswich T), 1968 v Pol; 1969 v Pol, A, D; 1970 v Cz, Pol, WG; 1971 v Se; (with Birmingham C), 1972 v Ir, Ec, Ch, P; 1973 v USSR (2), Pol, F, N (17)

Cascarino, A. G. (Gillingham), 1986 v Sw, USSR, D; (with Millwall), 1988 v Pol, N (sub), USSR (sub), Ho (sub); 1989 v Ni, Tun, Sp, F, H, Sp, Ma, H; 1990 v WG (sub), Ni, Ma; (with Aston Villa), W, Fi, T, E, Eg, Ho (sub), R (sub), I (sub); 1991 v Mor (sub),T(sub), E (2 sub), Pol (sub), Ch (sub), US; (with Celtic), 1992 v Pol, T; (with Chelsea), W, Sw, US (sub); 1993 v W, Ni (sub), D (sub), Alb (sub), La (sub); 1994 v Li (sub), Sp (sub), Ni (sub), Ru, Bol (sub), G, CzR, Ho (sub); (with Marseille), 1995 v La (sub), Ni (sub), P (sub), Lie (sub), A (sub); 1996 v A (sub), P (sub), Ho, Ru (sub), P, Cro (sub), Ho (63)

Chandler, J. (Leeds U), 1980 v Cz (sub), US (2)

Chatton, H. A. (Shelbourne), 1931 v Sp; (with Dumbarton), 1932 v Sp; (with Cork), 1934 v Ho (3)

Clarke, J. (Drogheda U), 1978 v Pol (sub) (1)

Clarke, K. (Drumcondra), 1948 v P, Sp (2)

Clarke, M. (Shamrock R), 1950 v Bel (1)

Clinton, T. J. (Everton), 1951 v N; 1954 v F, L (3)

Coad, P. (Shamrock R), 1947 v E, Sp, P; 1948 v P, Sp; 1949 v Sw, Bel, P, Se; 1951 v N (sub); 1952 v Sp (11)

Coffey, T. (Drumcondra), 1950 v Fi (1)

Colfer, M. D. (Shelbourne), 1950 v Bel; 1951 v N (2)

Collins, F. (Jacobs), 1927 v I (1)

Conmy, O. M. (Peterborough U), 1965 v Bel; 1967 v Cz; 1968 v Cz, Pol; 1970 v Cz (5)

Connolly, D. J. (Watford), 1996 v P, Ho, US, M (4)

Connolly, H. (Cork), 1937 v G (1)

Connolly, J. (Fordsons), 1926 v I (1)

Conroy, G. A. (Stoke C), 1970 v Cz, D, H, Pol, WG; 1971 v Pol, Se (2), I; 1973 v USSR, F, USSR, N; 1974 v Pol, Br, U, Ch; 1975 v T, Sw, USSR, Sw, WG (sub); 1976 v T (sub), Pol; 1977 v E, T, Pol (27)

Conway, J. P. (Fulham), 1967 v Sp, T, Sp; 1968 v Cz; 1969 v A (sub), H; 1970 v S, Cz, D, H, Pol, WG; 1971 v I, A; 1974 v U, Ch; 1975 v WG (sub); 1976 v N, Pol; (with Manchester C), 1977 v Pol (20)

Corr, P. J. (Everton), 1949 v P, Sp; 1950 v E, Se (4)

Courtney, E. (Cork U), 1946 v P (1)

Coyle, O. C. (Bolton W), 1994 v Ho (sub) (1)

Coyne, T. (Celtic), 1992 v Sw, US, Alb (sub), US (sub), I (sub), P (sub); 1993 v W (sub), La (sub); (with Tranmere R), Ni; (with Motherwell), 1994 v Ru (sub), Ho, Bol, G (sub), CzR (sub), I, M, Ho; 1995 v Lie, Ni (sub), A; 1996 v Ru (sub) (21)

Cummins, G. P. (Luton T), 1954 v L (2); 1955 v N (2), WG; 1956 v Y, Sp; 1958 v D, Pol, A; 1959 v Pol, Cz (2); 1960 v Se, Ch, WG, Se; 1961 v S (2) (19)

Cuneen, T. (Limerick), 1951 v N (1)

Cunningham, K. (Wimbledon), 1996 v CzR, P, Cro, Ho (sub), US, Bol (6)

Curtis, D. P. (Shelbourne), 1957 v D, WG; (with Bristol C), 1957 v E (2); 1958 v D, Pol, A; (with Ipswich T), 1959 v Pol; 1960 v Se, Ch, WG, Se; 1961 v N, S; 1962 v A; 1963 v Ic; (with Exeter C), 1964 v A (17)

Cusack, S. (Limerick), 1953 v F (1)

Daish, L. S. (Cambridge U), 1992 v W, Sw (sub); (with Coventry C), 1996 v CzR (sub), Cro, M (5)

Daly, G. A. (Manchester U), 1973 v Pol (sub), N; 1974 v Br (sub), U (sub); 1975 v Sw (sub), WG; 1977 v E, T, F; (with Derby Co), F, Bul; 1978 v Bul, T, D; 1979 v Ni, E, D, Bul; 1980 v Ni, E, Cy, Sw, Arg; (with Coventry C), 1981 v WG`B', Ho, Bel, Cy, W, Bel, Cz, Pol (sub); 1982 v Alg, Ch, Br, Tr; 1983 v Ho, Sp (sub); 1984 v Is (sub), Ma; (with Birmingham C), 1985 v M (sub), N, Sp, Sw; 1986 v Sw; (with Shrewsbury T), U, Ic (sub), Cz (sub); 1987 v S (sub) (48)

Daly, J. (Shamrock R), 1932 v Ho; 1935 v Sw (2)

Daly, M. (Wolverhampton W), 1978 v T, Pol (2)

Daly, P. (Shamrock R), 1950 v Fi (sub) (1)

Davis, T. L. (Oldham Ath), 1937 v G, H; (with Tranmere R), 1938 v Cz, Pol (4)

Deacy, E. (Aston Villa), 1982 v Alg (sub), Ch, Br, Tr (4)

De Mange, K. J. P. P. (Liverpool), 1987 v Br (sub); (with Hull C), 1989 v Tun (sub) (2)

Dempsey, J. T. (Fulham), 1967 v Sp, Cz; 1968 v Cz, Pol; 1969 v Pol, A, D; (with Chelsea), 1969 v Cz, D; 1970 v H, WG; 1971 v Pol, Se (2), I; 1972 v Ir, Ec, Ch, P (19)

Dennehy, J. (Cork Hibernians), 1972 v Ec (sub), Ch; (with Nottingham F), 1973 v USSR (sub), Pol, F, N; 1974 v Pol (sub); 1975 v T (sub), WG (sub); (with Walsall), 1976 v Pol (sub); 1977 v Pol (sub) (11)

Desmond, P. (Middlesbrough), 1950 v Fi, E, Fi, Se (4)

Devine, J. (Arsenal), 1980 v Cz, Ni; 1981 v WG`B', Cz; 1982 v Ho, Alg; 1983 v Sp, Ma; (with Norwich C), 1984 v Ic, Ho, Is; 1985 v USSR, N (13)

Donnelly, J. (Dundalk), 1935 v H, Sw, G; 1936 v Ho, Sw, H, L; 1937 v G, H; 1938 v N (10)

Donnelly, T. (Drumcondra), 1938 v N; (Shamrock R), 1939 v Sw (2)

Donovan, D. C. (Everton), 1955 v N, Ho, N, WG; 1957 v E (5)

Donovan, T. (Aston Villa), 1980 v Cz; 1981 v WG`B'(sub) (2)

Dowdall, C. (Fordsons), 1928 v Bel; (with Barnsley), 1929 v Bel; (with Cork), 1931 v Sp (3)

Doyle, C. (Shelbourne), 1959 v Cz (1)

Doyle, D. (Shamrock R), 1926 v I (1)

Doyle, L. (Dolphin), 1932 v Sp (1)

Duffy, B. (Shamrock R), 1950 v Bel (1)

Duggan, H. A. (Leeds U), 1927 v I; 1930 v Bel; 1936 v H, L; (with Newport Co), 1938 v N (5)

Dunne, A. P. (Manchester U), 1962 v A; 1963 v Ic, S; 1964 v A, Sp, Pol, N, E; 1965 v Pol, Sp; 1966 v Sp (2), A, Bel; 1967 v Sp, T, Sp; 1969 v Pol, D, H; 1970 v H; 1971 v Se, I,

A; (with Bolton W), 1974 v Br (sub), U, Ch; 1975 v T, Sw, USSR, Sw, WG; 1976 v T (33)
Dunne, J. (Sheffield U), 1930 v Bel; (with Arsenal), 1936 v Sw, H, L; (with Southampton), 1937 v Sw, F; (with Shamrock R), 1938 v N (2), Cz, Pol; 1939 v Sw, Pol, H (2), G (15)
Dunne, J. C. (Fulham), 1971 v A (1)
Dunne, L. (Manchester C), 1935 v Sw, G (2)
Dunne, P. A. J. (Manchester U), 1965 v Sp; 1966 v Sp (2), WG; 1967 v T (5)
Dunne, S. (Luton T), 1953 v F, A; 1954 v F, L; 1956 v Sp, Ho; 1957 v D, WG, E; 1958 v D, Pol, A; 1959 v Pol; 1960 v WG, Se (15)
Dunne, T. (St Patrick's Ath), 1956 v Ho; 1957 v D, WG (3)
Dunning, P. (Shelbourne), 1971 v Se, I (2)
Dunphy, E. M. (York C), 1966 v Sp; (with Millwall), 1966 v WG; 1967 v T, Sp, T, Cz; 1968 v Cz, Pol; 1969 v Pol, A, D (2), H; 1970 v D, H, Pol, WG (sub); 1971 v Pol, Se (2), I (2), A (23)
Dwyer, N. M. (West Ham U), 1960 v Se, Ch, WG, Se; (with Swansea T), 1961 v W, N, S (2); 1962 v Cz (2); 1964 v Pol (sub), N, E; 1965 v Pol (14)

Eccles, P. (Shamrock R), 1986 v U (sub) (1)
Egan, R. (Dundalk), 1929 v Bel (1)
Eglington, T. J. (Shamrock R), 1946 v P, Sp; (with Everton), 1947 v E, Sp, P; 1948 v P; 1949 v Sw, P, Se; 1951 v N, Arg; 1952 v WG (2), A, Sp; 1953 v F, A; 1954 v F, L, F; 1955 v N, Ho, WG; 1956 v Sp (24)
Ellis, P. (Bohemians), 1935 v Sw, G; 1936 v Ho, Sw, L; 1937 v G, H (7)

Fagan, E. (Shamrock R), 1973 v N (sub) (1)
Fagan, F. (Manchester C), 1955 v N; 1960 v Se; (with Derby Co), 1960 v Ch, WG, Se; 1961 v W, N, S (8)
Fagan, J. (Shamrock R), 1926 v I (1)
Fairclough, M. (Dundalk), 1982 v Ch (sub), Tr (sub) (2)
Fallon, S. (Celtic), 1951 v N; 1952 v WG (2), A, Sp; 1953 v F; 1955 v N, WG (5)
Fallon, W. J. (Notts Co), 1935 v H; 1936 v H; 1937 v H, Sw, F; 1939 v Sw, Pol; (with Sheffield W), 1939 v H, G (9)
Farquharson, T. G. (Cardiff C), 1929 v Bel; 1930 v Bel; 1931 v Sp; 1932 v Sp (4)
Farrell, P. (Hibernian), 1937 v Sw, F (2)
Farrell, P. D. (Shamrock R), 1946 v P, Sp; (with Everton), 1947 v Sp, P; 1948 v P, Sp; 1949 v Sw, P (sub), Sp; 1950 v E, Fi, Se; 1951 v Arg, N; 1952 v WG (2), A, Sp; 1953 v F, A; 1954 v F (2); 1955 v N, Ho, WG; 1956 v Y, Sp; 1957 v E (28)
Farrelly, G. (Aston Villa), 1996 v P, US, Bol (3)
Feenan, J. J. (Sunderland), 1937 v Sw, F (2)
Finucane, A. (Limerick), 1967 v T, Cz; 1969 v Cz, D, H; 1970 v S, Cz; 1971 v Se, I (1+1 sub); 1972 v A (11)
Fitzgerald, J. (Waterford), 1955 v Ho; 1956 v Ho (2)
Fitzgerald, P. J. (Leeds U), 1961 v W, N, S; (with Chester), 1962 v Cz (2) (5)
Fitzpatrick, K. (Limerick), 1970 v Cz (1)
Fitzsimons, A. G. (Middlesbrough), 1950 v Fi, Bel; 1952 v WG (2), A, Sp; 1953 v F, A; 1954 v F, L, F; 1955 v Ho, N, WG; 1956 v Y, Sp, Ho; 1957 v D, WG, E (2); 1958 v D, Pol, A; 1959 v Pol; (with Lincoln C), 1959 v Cz (26)
Fleming, C. (Middlesbrough), 1996 v CzR (sub), P, Cro (sub), Ho (sub), US (sub), M, Bol (7)
Flood, J. J. (Shamrock R), 1926 v I; 1929 v Bel; 1930 v Bel; 1931 v Sp; 1932 v Sp (5)
Fogarty, A. (Sunderland), 1960 v WG, Se; 1961 v S; 1962 v Cz (2); 1963 v Ic (2), S (sub); 1964 v A (2); (with Hartlepools U), Sp (11)
Foley, J. (Cork), 1934 v Bel, Ho; (with Celtic), 1935 v H, Sw, G; 1937 v G, H (7)
Foley, M. (Shelbourne), 1926 v I (1)
Foley, T. C. (Northampton T), 1964 v Sp, Pol, N; 1965 v Pol, Bel; 1966 v Sp (2), WG; 1967 v Cz (9)
Foy, T. (Shamrock R), 1938 v N; 1939 v H (2)
Fullam, J. (Preston NE), 1961 v N; (with Shamrock R), 1964 v Sp, Pol, N; 1966 v A, Bel; 1968 v Pol; 1969 v Pol, A, D; 1970 v Cz (sub) (11)
Fullam, R. (Shamrock R), 1926 v I; 1927 v I (2)

Gallagher, C. (Celtic), 1967 v T, Cz (2)
Gallagher, M. (Hibernian), 1954 v L (1)
Gallagher, P. (Falkirk), 1932 v Sp (1)
Galvin, A. (Tottenham H), 1983 v Ho, Ma; 1984 v Ho (sub), Is (sub); 1985 v M, USSR, N, D, I, N, Sp; 1986 v U, Ic, Cz; 1987 v Bel (2), S, Bul, L; (with Sheffield W), 1988 v L,

Bul, R, Pol, N, E, USSR, Ho; 1989 v Sp; (with Swindon T), 1990 v WG (29)
Gannon, E. (Notts Co), 1949 v Sw; (with Sheffield W), 1949 v Bel, P, Se, Sp; 1950 v Fi; 1951 v N; 1952 v WG, A; 1954 v L, F; 1955 v N; (with Shelbourne), 1955 v N, WG (14)
Gannon, M. (Shelbourne), 1972 v A (1)
Gaskins, P. (Shamrock R), 1934 v Bel, Ho; 1935 v H, Sw, G; (with St James' Gate), 1938 v Cz, Pol (7)
Gavin, J. T. (Norwich C), 1950 v Fi (2); 1953 v F; 1954 v L; (with Tottenham H), 1955 v Ho, WG; (with Norwich C), 1957 v D (7)
Geoghegan, M. (St James' Gate), 1937 v G; 1938 v N (2)
Gibbons, A. (St Patrick's Ath), 1952 v WG; 1954 v L; 1956 v Y, Sp (4)
Gilbert, R. (Shamrock R), 1966 v WG (1)
Giles, C. (Doncaster R), 1951 v N (1)
Giles, M. J. (Manchester U), 1960 v Se, Ch; 1961 v W, N, S (2); 1962 v Cz (2), A; 1963 v Ic, S; (with Leeds U), 1964 v A (2), Sp (2), Pol, N, E; 1965 v Sp; 1966 v Sp (2), A, Bel; 1967 v Sp, T (2); 1969 v A, D, Cz; 1970 v S, Pol, WG; 1971 v I; 1973 v F, USSR; 1974 v Br, U, Ch; 1975 v USSR, Sw, USSR, Sw; (with WBA), 1976 v T; 1977 v E, T, F (2), Pol, Bul; (with Shamrock R), 1978 v Bul, T, Pol, N, D; 1979 v Ni, D, Bul, WG (59)
Given, S. J. J. (Blackburn R), 1996 v Ru, CzR, P, Cro, Ho, US, Bol (7)
Givens, D. J. (Manchester U), 1969 v D, H; 1970 v S, Cz, D, H; (with Luton T), 1970 v WG; 1971 v Se, I (2), A; 1972 v Ir, Ec, P; (with QPR), 1973 v F, USSR, Pol, F, N; 1974 v Pol, Br, U, Ch; 1975 v USSR, T, Sw, USSR, Sw, WG; 1976 v T, N, Pol; 1977 v E, T, F (2), Sp, Bul; 1978 v Bul, N, D; (with Birmingham C), 1979 v Ni (sub), E, D, Bul, WG; 1980 v US (sub), Ni (sub), Sw, Arg; 1981 v Ho, Bel, Cy (sub), W; (with Neuchatel X), 1982 v F (sub) (56)
Glen, W. (Shamrock R), 1927 v I; 1929 v Bel; 1930 v Bel; 1932 v Sp; 1936 v Ho, Sw, H, L (8)
Glynn, D. (Drumcondra), 1952 v WG; 1955 v N (2)
Godwin, T. F. (Shamrock R), 1949 v P, Se, Sp; 1950 v Fi, E; (with Leicester C), 1950 v Fi, Se, Bel; 1951 v N; (with Bournemouth), 1956 v Ho; 1957 v E; 1958 v D, Pol (13)
Golding, J. (Shamrock R), 1928 v Bel; 1930 v Bel (2)
Gorman, W. C. (Bury), 1936 v Sw, H, L; 1937 v G, H; 1938 v N, Cz, Pol; 1939 v Sw, Pol (with Brentford) H; 1947 v E, P (13)
Grace, J. (Drumcondra), 1926 v I (1)
Grealish, A. (Orient), 1976 v N, Pol; 1978 v N, D; 1979 v Ni, E, WG; (with Luton T), 1980 v W, Cz, Bul, US, Ni, E, Cy, Sw, Arg; 1981 v WG'B', Ho, Bel, F, Cy, W, Bel, Pol; (with Brighton & HA), 1982 v Ho, Alg, Ch, Br, Tr; 1983 v Ho, Sp, Ic, Sp; 1984 v Ic, Ho; (with WBA), Pol, Chn; 1985 v M, USSR, N, D, Sp (sub), Sw; 1986 v USSR, D (45)
Gregg, E. (Bohemians), 1978 v Pol, D (sub); 1979 v E (sub), D, Bul, WG; 1980 v W, Cz (8)
Griffith, R. (Walsall), 1935 v H (1)
Grimes, A. A. (Manchester U), 1978 v T, Pol, N (sub); 1980 v Bul, US, Ni, E, Cy; 1981 v WG'B' (sub), Cz, Pol; 1982 v Alg; 1983 v Sp (2); (with Coventry C), 1984 v Pol, Is; (with Luton T), 1988 v L, R (18)

Hale, A. (Aston Villa), 1962 v A; (with Doncaster R), 1963 v Ic; 1964 v Sp (2); (with Waterford), 1967 v Sp; 1968 v Pol (sub); 1969 v Pol, A, D; 1970 v S, Cz; 1971 v Pol (sub); 1972 v A (sub) (13)
Hamilton, T. (Shamrock R), 1959 v Cz (2) (2)
Hand, E. K. (Portsmouth), 1969 v Cz (sub); 1970 v Pol, WG; 1971 v Pol, A; 1973 v USSR, F, USSR, Pol, F; 1974 v Pol, Br, U, Ch; 1975 v T, Sw, USSR, Sw, WG; 1976 v T (20)
Harrington, W. (Cork), 1936 v Ho, Sw, H, L; 1938 v Pol (sub) (5)
Harte, I. P. (Leeds U), 1996 v Cro (sub), Ho, M, Bol (4)
Hartnett, J. B. (Middlesbrough), 1949 v Sp; 1954 v L (2)
Haverty, J. (Arsenal), 1956 v Ho; 1957 v D, WG, E (2); 1958 v D, Pol, A; 1959 v Pol; 1960 v Se, Ch; 1961 v W, N, S (2); (with Blackburn R), 1962 v Cz (2); (with Millwall), 1963 v S; 1964 v A, Sp, Pol, N, E; (with Celtic), 1965 v Pol; (with Bristol R), 1965 v Sp; (with Shelbourne), 1966 v Sp (2), WG, A, Bel; 1967 v Sp, T, WG (32)
Hayes, A. W. P. (Southampton), 1979 v D (1)
Hayes, W. E. (Huddersfield T), 1947 v E, P (2)
Hayes, W. J. (Limerick), 1949 v Bel (1)
Healey, R. (Cardiff C), 1977 v Pol; 1980 v E (sub) (2)
Heighway, S. D. (Liverpool), 1971 v Pol, Se (2), I, A; 1973 v USSR; 1975 v USSR, T, USSR, WG; 1976 v T, N; 1977 v E, F (2), Sp, Bul; 1978 v Bul, N, D; 1979 v Ni, Bul; 1980 v Bul, US, Ni, E, Cy, Arg; 1981 v Bel, F, Cy, W, Bel; (with Minnesota K), 1982 v Ho (34)

Henderson, B. (Drumcondra), 1948 v P, Sp (2)
Hennessy, J. (Shelbourne), 1965 v Pol, Bel, Sp; 1966 v WG; (with St Patrick's Ath), 1969 v A (5)
Herrick, J. (Cork Hibernians), 1972 v A, Ch (sub); (with Shamrock R), 1973 v F (sub) (3)
Higgins, J. (Birmingham C), 1951 v Arg (1)
Holmes, J. (Coventry C), 1971 v A (sub); 1973 v F, USSR, Pol, F, N; 1974 v Pol, Br; 1975 v USSR, Sw; 1976 v T, N, Pol; 1977 v E, T, F, Sp; (with Tottenham H), F, Pol, Bul; 1978 v Bul, T, Pol, N, D; 1979 v Ni, E, D, Bul; (with Vancouver W), 1981 v W (30)
Horlacher, A. F. (Bohemians), 1930 v Bel; 1932 v Sp, Ho; 1934 v Ho (sub); 1935 v H;1936 v Ho, Sw (7)
Houghton, R. J. (Oxford U), 1986 v W, U, Ic, Cz; 1987 v Bel (2), S (2), Pol, L; 1988 v L, Bul; (with Liverpool), Is, Y, N, E, USSR, Ho; 1989 v Ni, Tun, Sp, F, H, Sp, Ma, H; 1990 v Ni, Ma, Fi, E, Eg, Ho, R, I; 1991 v Mor, T, E (2), Pol, Ch, US; 1992 v H, Alb, US, I, P; (with Aston Villa), 1993 v D, Sp, Ni, D, Alb, La, Li; 1994 v Li, Sp, Ni, Bol, G (sub), I, M, N, Ho; (with C Palace), 1995 v P, A; 1996 v A, CzR (66)
Howlett, G. (Brighton & HA), 1984 v Chn (sub) (1)
Hoy, M. (Dundalk), 1938 v N; 1939 v Sw, Pol, H (2), G (6)
Hughton, C. (Tottenham H), 1980 v US, E, Sw, Arg; 1981 v Ho, Bel, F, Cy, W, Bel, Pol; 1982 v F; 1983 v Ho, Sp, Ma, Sp; 1984 v Ic, Ho, Ma; 1985 v M (sub), USSR, N, I, Is, E, Sp; 1986 v Sw, USSR, U, Ic; 1987 v Bel, Bul; 1988 v Is, Y, Pol, N, E, USSR, Ho; 1989 v Ni, F, H, Sp, Ma, H; 1990 v W (sub), USSR (sub), Fi, T (sub), Ma; 1991 v T; (with West Ham U), Ch; 1992 v T (53)
Hurley, C. J. (Millwall), 1957 v E; (with Sunderland), 1958 v D, Pol, A; 1959 v Cz (2); 1960 v Se, Ch, WG, Se; 1961 v W, N, S (2); 1962 v Cz (2), A; 1963 v Ic (2), S; 1964 v A (2), Sp (2), Pol, N; 1965 v Sp; 1966 v WG, A, Bel; 1967 v T, Sp, T, Cz; 1968 v Cz, Pol; 1969 v Pol, D, Cz, (with Bolton W), H (40)
Hutchinson, F. (Drumcondra), 1935 v Sw, G (2)

Irwin, D. J. (Manchester U), 1991 v Mor, T, W, E, Pol, US; 1992 v H, Pol, W, US, Alb, US (sub), I; 1993 v La, D, Sp, Ni, D, Alb, La, Li; 1994 v Li, Sp, Ni, Bol, G, I, M; 1995 v La, Lie, Ni, E, Ni, P, Lie, A; 1996 v A, P, Ho, CzR (40)

Jordan, D. (Wolverhampton W), 1937 v Sw, F (2)
Jordan, W. (Bohemians), 1934 v Ho; 1938 v N (2)

Kavanagh, P. J. (Celtic), 1931 v Sp; 1932 v Sp (2)
Keane, R. M. (Nottingham F), 1991 v Ch; 1992 v H, Pol, W, Sw, Alb, US; 1993 v La, D, Sp, W, Ni, D, Alb, La, Li; (with Manchester U), 1994 v Li, Sp, Ni, Bol, G, CzR (sub), I, M, N, Ho; 1995 v Ni (2); 1996 v A, Ru (30)
Keane, T. R. (Swansea T), 1949 v Sw, P, Se, Sp (4)
Kearin, M. (Shamrock R), 1972 v A (1)
Kearns, F. T. (West Ham U), 1954 v L (1)
Kearns, M. (Oxford U), 1971 v Pol (sub); (with Walsall), 1974 v Pol (sub), U, Ch; 1976 v N, Pol; 1977 v E, T, F (2), Sp, Bul; 1978 v N, D; 1979 v Ni, E; (with Wolverhampton W), 1980 v US, Ni (18)
Kelly, A. T. (Sheffield U), 1993 v W (sub); 1994 v Ru (sub), G; 1995 v La, Ni, E, Ni, P, Lie, A; 1996 v A, La, P, Ho (14)
Kelly, D. T. (Walsall), 1988 v Is, R, Y; (with West Ham U), 1989 v Tun (sub); (with Leicester C), 1990 v USSR, Ma; 1991 v Mor, W (sub), Ch, US; 1992 v H; (with Newcastle U), I (sub), P; 1993 v Sp (sub), Ni; (with Wolverhampton W), 1994 v Ru, N (sub); 1995 v E, Ni; (with Sunderland), 1996 v La (sub) (20)
Kelly, G. (Leeds U), 1994 v Ru, Ho, Bol (sub), G (sub), CzR, N, Ho; 1995 v La, Lie, Ni (2), P, Lie, A; 1996 v A, La, P, Ho (18)
Kelly, J. (Derry C), 1932 v Ho; 1934 v Bel; 1936 v Sw, L (4)
Kelly, J. A. (Drumcondra), 1957 v WG, E; (with Preston NE), 1962 v A; 1963 v Ic (2), S; 1964 v A (2), Sp (2), Pol; 1965 v Bel; 1966 v A, Bel; 1967 v Sp (2), T, Cz; 1968 v Pol, Cz; 1969 v Pol, A, D, Cz, D, H; 1970 v S, D, H, Pol, WG; 1971 v Pol, Se (2), I (2), A; 1972 v Ir, Ec, Ch, P; 1973 v USSR, F, USSR, Pol, F, N (47)
Kelly, J. P. V. (Wolverhampton W), 1961 v W, N, S; 1962 v Cz (2) (5)
Kelly, M. J. (Portsmouth), 1988 v Y, Pol (sub); 1989 v Tun; 1991 v Mor (4)
Kelly, N. (Nottingham F), 1954 v L (1)
Kendrick, J. (Everton), 1927 v I; (with Dolphin) 1934 v Bel, Ho; 1936 v Ho (4)
Kenna, J. J. (Blackburn R), 1995 v P (sub), Lie (sub), A (sub); 1996 v La, P, Ho, Ru (sub), CzR, P, Cro, Ho, US (12)

Kennedy, M. (Liverpool), 1996 v A, La (sub), P, Ru, CzR, Cro, Ho (sub), US (sub), M, Bol (sub) (10)
Kennedy, M. F. (Portsmouth), 1986 v Ic, Cz (sub) (2)
Kennedy, W. (St James' Gate), 1932 v Ho; 1934 v Bel, Ho (3)
Keogh, J. (Shamrock R), 1966 v WG (sub) (1)
Keogh, S. (Shamrock R), 1959 v Pol (1)
Kernaghan, A. N. (Middlesbrough), 1993 v La, D (2), Alb, La, Li; 1994 v Li; (with Manchester C), Sp, Ni, Bol (sub), CzR; 1995 v Lie, E; 1996 v A, P (sub), Ho (sub), Ru, P, Cro (sub), Ho, US, Bol (22)
Kiernan, F. W. (Shamrock R), 1951 v Arg, N; (with Southampton), 1952 v WG (2), A (5)
Kinnear, J. P. (Tottenham H), 1967 v T; 1968 v Cz, Pol; 1969 v A; 1970 v Cz, D, H, Pol; 1971 v Se (sub), I; 1972 v Ir, Ec, Ch, P; 1973 v USSR, F; 1974 v Pol, Br, U, Ch; 1975 v USSR, T, Sw, USSR, WG; (with Brighton & HA), 1976 v T (sub) (26)
Kinsella, J. (Shelbourne), 1928 v Bel (1)
Kinsella, O. (Shamrock R), 1932 v Ho; 1938 v N (2)
Kirkland, A. (Shamrock R), 1927 v I (1)

Lacey, W. (Shelbourne), 1927 v I; 1928 v Bel; 1930 v Bel (3)
Langan, D. (Derby Co), 1978 v T, N; 1980 v Sw, Arg; (with Birmingham C), 1981 v WG`B', Ho, Bel, F, Cy, W, Bel, Cz, Pol; 1982 v Ho, F; (with Oxford U), 1985 v N, Sp, Sw; 1986 v W, U; 1987 v Bel, S, Pol, Br (sub), L (sub); 1988 v L (26)
Lawler, J. F. (Fulham), 1953 v A; 1954 v L, F; 1955 v N, H, N, WG; 1956 v Y (8)
Lawlor, J. C. (Drumcondra), 1949 v Bel; (with Doncaster R), 1951 v N, Arg (3)
Lawlor, M. (Shamrock R), 1971 v Pol, Se (2), I (sub); 1973 v Pol (5)
Lawrenson, M. (Preston NE), 1977 v Pol; (with Brighton), 1978 v Bul, Pol, N (sub); 1979 v Ni, E; 1980 v E, Cy, Sw; 1981 v Ho, Bel, F, Cy, Pol; (with Liverpool), 1982 v Ho, F; 1983 v Ho, Sp, Ic, Ma, Sp; 1984 v Ic, Ho, Ma, Is; 1985 v USSR, N, D, I, E, N; 1986 v Sw, USSR, D; 1987 v Bel, S; 1988 v Bul, Is (38)
Leech, M. (Shamrock R), 1969 v Cz, D, H; 1972 v A, Ir, Ec, P; 1973 v USSR (sub) (8)
Lennon, C. (St James' Gate), 1935 v H, Sw, G (3)
Lennox, G. (Dolphin), 1931 v Sp; 1932 v Sp (2)
Lowry, D. (St Patrick's Ath), 1962 v A (sub) (1)
Lunn, R. (Dundalk), 1939 v Sw, Pol (2)
Lynch, J. (Cork Bohemians), 1934 v Bel (1)

McAlinden, J. (Portsmouth), 1946 v P, Sp (2)
McAteer, J. W. (Bolton W), 1994 v Ru, Ho (sub), Bol (sub), G, CzR (sub), I (sub), M (sub), N, Ho (sub); 1995 v La, Lie, Ni (2 sub), Lie; (with Liverpool), 1996 v La, P, Ho (sub), Ru (18)
McCann, J. (Shamrock R), 1957 v WG (1)
McCarthy, J. (Bohemians), 1926 v I; 1928 v Bel; 1930 v Bel (3)
McCarthy, M. (Manchester C), 1984 v Pol, Chn; 1985 v M, D, I, Is, E, Sp, Sw; 1986 v Sw, USSR, W (sub), U, Ic, Cz; 1987 v S (2), Pol, Bul, Bel (with Celtic), Br, L; 1988 v Bul, Is, R, Y, N, E, USSR, Ho; 1989 v Ni, Tun, Sp, F, H, Sp; (with Lyon), 1990 v WG, Ni (with Millwall), W, USSR, Fi, T, E, Eg, Ho, R, I; 1991 v Mor, T, E, US; 1992 v H, T, Alb (sub), US, I, P (57)
McCarthy, M. (Shamrock R), 1932 v Ho (1)
McConville, T. (Dundalk), 1972 v A; (with Waterford), 1973 v USSR, F, USSR, Pol, F (6)
McDonagh, Joe (Shamrock R), 1984 v Pol (sub), Ma (sub); 1985 v M (sub) (3)
McDonagh, J. (Everton), 1981 v WG`B', W, Bel, Cz; (with Bolton W), 1982 v Ho, F, Ch, Br; 1983 v Ho, Sp, Ic, Ma, Sp; (with Notts Co), 1984 v Ic, Ho, Pol; 1985 v M, USSR, N, D, Sp, Sw; 1986 v Sw, USSR (with Wichita Wings) D (25)
McEvoy, M. A. (Blackburn R), 1961 v S (2); 1963 v S; 1964 v A, Sp (2), Pol, N, E; 1965 v Pol, Bel, Sp; 1966 v Sp (2); 1967 v Sp, T, Cz (17)
McGee, P. (QPR), 1978 v T, N (sub), D (sub); 1979 v Ni, E, D (sub), Bul (sub); 1980 v Cz, Bul; (with Preston NE), US, Ni, Cy, Sw, Arg; 1981 v Bel (sub) (15)
McGoldrick, E. J. (C Palace), 1992 v Sw, US, I, P (sub); 1993 v D, W, Ni (sub), D; (with Arsenal), 1994 v Ni, Ru, Ho, CzR; 1995 v La (sub), Lie, E (15)
McGowan, D. (West Ham U), 1949 v P, Se, Sp (3)
McGowan, J. (Cork U), 1947 v Sp (1)
McGrath, M. (Blackburn R), 1958 v A; 1959 v Pol, Cz (2); 1960 v Se, WG, Se; 1961 v W; 1962 v Cz (2); 1963 v S; 1964

v A (2), E; 1965 v Pol, Bel, Sp; 1966 v Sp; (with Bradford), 1966 v WG, A, Bel; 1967 v T (22)

McGrath, P. (Manchester U), 1985 v I (sub), Is, E, N (sub), Sw (sub); 1986 v Sw (sub), D, W, Ic, Cz; 1987 v Bel (2), S (2), Pol, Bul, Br, L; 1988 v L, Bul, Y, Pol, N, E, Ho; 1989 v Ni, F, H, Sp, Ma, H; (with Aston Villa), 1990 v WG, Ma, USSR, Fi, T, E, Eg, Ho, R, I; 1991 v E (2), W, Pol, Ch (sub), US; 1992 v Pol, T, Sw, US, Alb, US, I, P; 1993 v La, Sp, Ni, D, La, Li; 1994 v Sp, Ni, G, CzR, I, M, N, Ho; 1995 v La, Ni, E, Ni, P, Lie, A; 1996 v A, La, P, Ho, Ru, CzR (82)

McGuire, W. (Bohemians), 1936 v Ho (1)

McKenzie, G. (Southend U), 1938 v N (2), Cz, Pol; 1939 v Sw, Pol, H (2), G (9)

Mackey, G. (Shamrock R), 1957 v D, WG, E (3)

McLoughlin, A. F. (Swindon T), 1990 v Ma, E (sub), Eg (sub); 1991 v Mor (sub), E (sub); (with Southampton), W, Ch (sub); 1992 v H (sub), W (sub); (with Portsmouth), US, I (sub), P; 1993 v W; 1994 v Ni (sub), Ru, Ho (sub); 1995 v Lie (sub); 1996 v P, Cro, Ho, US, M, Bol (sub) (23)

McLoughlin, F. (Fordsons), 1930 v Bel; (with Cork), 1932 v Sp (2)

McMillan, W. (Belfast Celtic), 1946 v P, Sp (2)

McNally, J. B. (Luton T), 1959 v Cz; 1961 v S; 1963 v Ic (3)

Macken, A. (Derby Co), 1977 v Sp (1)

Madden, O. (Cork), 1936 v H (1)

Maguire, J. (Shamrock R), 1929 v Bel (1)

Malone, G. (Shelbourne), 1949 v Bel (1)

Mancini, T. J. (QPR), 1974 v Pol, Br, U, Ch; (with Arsenal), 1975 v USSR (5)

Martin, C. (Bo'ness), 1927 v I (1)

Martin, C. J. (Glentoran), 1946 v P (sub), Sp; 1947 v E; (with Leeds U), 1947 v Sp; 1948 v P, Sp; (with Aston Villa), 1949 v Sw, Bel, P, Se, Sp; 1950 v Fi, E, Fi, Se, Bel; 1951 v Arg; 1952 v WG, A, Sp; 1954 v F (2), L; 1955 v N, Ho, N, WG; 1956 v Y, Sp, Ho (30)

Martin, M. P. (Bohemians), 1972 v A, Ir, Ec, Ch, P; 1973 v USSR; (with Manchester U), 1973 v USSR, Pol, F, N; 1974 v Pol, Br, U, Ch; 1975 v USSR, T, Sw, USSR, Sw, WG; (with WBA), 1976 v T, N, Pol; 1977 v E, T, F (2), Sp, Pol, Bul; (with Newcastle U), 1979 v D, Bul, WG; 1980 v W, Cz, Bul, US, Ni; 1981 v WG`B', F, Bel, Cz; 1982 v Ho, F, Alg, Ch, Br, Tr; 1983 v Ho, Sp, Ma, Sp (52)

Meagan, M. K. (Everton), 1961 v S; 1962 v A; 1963 v Ic; 1964 v Sp; (with Huddersfield T), 1965 v Bel; 1966 v Sp (2), A, Bel; 1967 v Sp, T, Sp, T, Cz; 1968 v Cz, Pol; (with Drogheda), 1970 v S (17)

Meehan, P. (Drumcondra), 1934 v Ho (1)

Milligan, M. J. (Oldham Ath), 1992 v US (sub) (1)

Monahan, P. (Sligo R), 1935 v Sw, G (2)

Mooney, J. (Shamrock R), 1965 v Pol, Bel (2)

Moore, A. (Middlesbrough), 1996 v CzR, Cro (sub), Ho, M, Bol (5)

Moore, P. (Shamrock R), 1931 v Sp; 1932 v Ho; (with Aberdeen), 1934 v Bel, Ho; 1935 v H, G; (with Shamrock R), 1936 v Ho; 1937 v G, H (9)

Moran, K. (Manchester U), 1980 v Sw, Arg; 1981 v WG`B', Bel, F, Cy, W (sub), Bel, Cz, Pol; 1982 v F, Alg; 1983 v Ic; 1984 v Ic, Ho, Ma, Is; 1985 v M; 1986 v D, Ic, Cz; 1987 v Bel (2), S (2), Pol, Bul, Br, L; 1988 v L, Bul, Is, R, Y, Pol, N, E, USSR, Ho; (with Sporting Gijon), 1989 v Ni, Sp, H, Sp, Ma, H; 1990 v Ni, Ma; (with Blackburn R), W, USSR (sub), Ma, E, Eg, Ho, R, I; 1991 v T (sub), W, E, Pol, Ch, US; 1992 v Pol, US; 1993 v D, Sp, Ni, Alb; 1994 v La, Sp, Ho, Bol (71)

Moroney, T. (West Ham U), 1948 v Sp; 1949 v P, Se, Sp; 1950 v Fi, E, Fi, Bel; 1951 v N (2); 1952 v WG; (with Evergreen U), 1954 v F (12)

Morris, C. B. (Celtic), 1988 v Is, R, Y, Pol, N, E, USSR, Ho; 1989 v Ni, Tun, Sp, F, H (1+1 sub); 1990 v WG, Ni, Ma (sub), W, USSR, Fi (sub), T, E, Eg, Ho, R, I; 1991 v E; 1992 v H (sub) (sub), Pol, W, Sw, US (2), P; (with Middlesbrough), 1993 v W (35)

Moulson, C. (Lincoln C), 1936 v H, L; (with Notts Co), 1937 v H, Sw, F (5)

Moulson, G. B. (Lincoln C), 1948 v P, Sp; 1949 v Sw (3)

Mucklan, C. (Drogheda U), 1978 v Pol (1)

Muldoon, T. (Aston Villa), 1927 v I (1)

Mulligan, P. M. (Shamrock R), 1969 v Cz, D, H; 1970 v S, Cz, D; (with Chelsea), 1970 v H, Pol, WG; 1971 v Pol, Se, I; 1972 v A, Ir, Ec, Ch, P; (with C Palace), 1973 v F, USSR, Pol, F, N; 1974 v Pol, Br, U, Ch; 1975 v USSR, T, Sw, USSR, Sw; (with WBA), 1976 v T, Pol; 1977 v E, T, F (2), Pol, Bul; 1978 v Bul, N, D; 1979 v E, D, Bul (sub), WG; (with Shamrock R), 1980 v W, Cz, Bul, US (sub) (50)

Munroe, L. (Shamrock R), 1954 v L (1)

Murphy, A. (Clyde), 1956 v Y (1)

Murphy, B. (Bohemians), 1986 v U (1)

Murphy, J. (C Palace), 1980 v W, US, Cy (3)

Murray, T. (Dundalk), 1950 v Bel (1)

Newman, W. (Shelbourne), 1969 v D (1)

Nolan, R. (Shamrock R), 1957 v D, WG, E; 1958 v Pol; 1960 v Ch, WG, Se; 1962 v Cz (2); 1963 v Ic (10)

O'Brien, F. (Philadelphia F), 1980 v Cz, E, Cy (sub) (3)

O'Brien, L. (Shamrock R), 1986 v U; (with Manchester U), 1987 v Br; 1988 v Is (sub), R (sub), Y (sub), Pol (sub); 1989 v Tun; (with Newcastle U), 1992 v Sw (sub); 1993 v W; (with Tranmere R), 1994 v Ru; 1996 v Cro, Ho, US, Bol (15)

O'Brien, M. T. (Derby Co), 1927 v I; (with Walsall), 1929 v Bel; (with Norwich C), 1930 v Bel; (with Watford), 1932 v Ho (4)

O'Brien, R. (Notts Co), 1976 v N, Pol; 1977 v Sp, Pol; 1980 v Arg (sub) (5)

O'Byrne, L. B. (Shamrock R), 1949 v Bel (1)

O'Callaghan, B. R. (Stoke C), 1979 v WG (sub); 1980 v W, US; 1981 v W; 1982 v Br, Tr (6)

O'Callaghan, K. (Ipswich T), 1981 v WG`B', Cz, Pol; 1982 v Alg, Ch, Br, Tr (sub); 1983 v Sp, Ic (sub), Ma (sub), Sp (sub); 1984 v Ic, Ho, Ma; 1985 v M (sub), N (sub), D (sub), (with Portsmouth) E (sub); 1986 v Sw (sub), USSR (sub); 1987 v Br (21)

O'Connell, A. (Dundalk), 1967 v Sp; (with Bohemians), 1971 v Pol (sub) (2)

O'Connor, T. (Shamrock R), 1950 v Fi, E, Fi, Se (4)

O'Connor, T. (Fulham), 1968 v Cz; (with Dundalk), 1972 v A, Ir (sub), Ec (sub), Ch; (with Bohemians), 1973 v F (sub), Pol (sub) (7)

O'Driscoll, J. F. (Swansea T), 1949 v Sw, Bel, Se (3)

O'Driscoll, S. (Fulham), 1982 v Ch, Br, Tr (sub) (3)

O'Farrell, F. (West Ham U), 1952 v A; 1953 v A; 1954 v F; 1955 v Ho, N; 1956 v Y, Ho; (with Preston NE), 1958 v D; 1959 v Cz (9)

O'Flanagan, K. P. (Bohemians), 1938 v N, Cz, Pol; 1939 v Pol, H (2), G; (with Arsenal), 1947 v E, Sp, P (10)

O'Flanagan, M. (Bohemians), 1947 v E (1)

O'Hanlon, K. G. (Rotherham U), 1988 v Is (1)

O'Kane, P. (Bohemians), 1935 v H, Sw, G (3)

O'Keefe, E. (Everton), 1981 v W; (with Port Vale), 1984 v Chn; 1985 v M, USSR (sub), E (5)

O'Keefe, T. (Cork), 1934 v Bel; (with Waterford), 1938 v Cz, Pol (3)

O'Leary, D. (Arsenal), 1977 v E, F (2), Sp, Bul; 1978 v Bul, N, D; 1979 v E, Bul, WG; 1980 v W, Bul, N, Cy; 1981 v WG`B',Ho, Cz, Pol; 1982 v Ho, F; 1983 v Ho, Ic, Sp; 1984 v Pol, Is, Chn; 1985 v USSR, N, D, Is, E (sub), N, Sp, Sw; 1986 v Sw, USSR, D, W; 1989 v Sp, Ma, H; 1990 v WG, Ni (sub), Ma, W (sub), USSR, Fi, T, Ma, R (sub); 1991 v Mor, T, E (2), Pol, Ch; 1992 v H, Pol, T, W, Sw, US, Alb, I, P; 1993 v W (68)

O'Leary, P. (Shamrock R), 1980 v Bul, US, Ni, E (sub), Cz, Arg; 1981 v Ho (7)

O'Mahoney, M. T. (Bristol R), 1938 v Cz, Pol; 1939 v Sw, Pol, H, G (6)

O'Neill, F. S. (Shamrock R), 1962 v Cz (2); 1965 v Pol, Bel, Sp; 1966 v Sp (2), WG, A; 1967 v Sp, T, Sp; 1969 v Pol, A, D, Cz, D (sub), H (sub); 1972 v A (20)

O'Neill, J. (Everton), 1952 v Sp; 1953 v F, A; 1954 v F, L, F; 1955 v N, Ho, N, WG; 1956 v Y, Sp; 1957 v D; 1958 v A; 1959 v Pol, Cz (2) (17)

O'Neill, J. (Preston NE), 1961 v W (1)

O'Neill, K. P. (Norwich C), 1996 v P (sub), Cro, Ho (sub), US (sub), M, Bol (6)

O'Neill, W. (Dundalk), 1936 v Ho, Sw, H, L; 1937 v G, H, Sw, F; 1938 v N; 1939 v H, G (11)

O'Regan, K. (Brighton & HA), 1984 v Ma, Pol; 1985 v M, Sp (sub) (4)

O'Reilly, J. (Brideville), 1932 v Ho; (with Aberdeen), 1934 v Bel, Ho; (with Brideville), 1936 v Ho; Sw, H, L; (with St James' Gate), 1937 v G, H, Sw, F; 1938 v N (2), Cz, Pol; 1939 v Sw, Pol, H (2), G (20)

O'Reilly, J. (Cork U), 1946 v P, Sp (2)

Peyton, G. (Fulham), 1977 v Sp (sub); 1978 v Bul, T, Pol; 1979 v D, Bul, WG; 1980 v W, Cz, Bul, E, Cy, Sw, Arg; 1981 v Ho, Bel, F, Cy; 1982 v Tr; 1985 v M (sub); 1986 v W, Cz; (with Bournemouth), 1988 v L, Pol; 1989 v Ni, Tun; 1990 v USSR, Ma; 1991 v Ch; (with Everton) 1992 v US (2), I (sub), P (33)

Peyton, N. (Shamrock R), 1957 v WG; (with Leeds U), 1960 v WG, Se (sub); 1961 v W; 1963 v Ic, S (6)

Phelan, T. (Wimbledon), 1992 v H, Pol (sub), T, W, Sw, US, I (sub), P; (with Manchester C), 1993 v La (sub), D, Sp, Ni, Alb, La, Li; 1994 v Li, Sp, Ni, Ho, Bol, G, CzR, I, M, Ho; 1995 v E; 1996 v La; (with Chelsea), Ho, Ru, P, Cro, Ho, US, M (sub), Bol (35)

Quinn, N. J. (Arsenal), 1986 v Ic (sub), Cz; 1987 v Bul (sub), Br (sub); 1988 v L (sub), Bul (sub), Is, R (sub), Pol (sub), E (sub); 1989 v Tun (sub), Sp (sub), H (sub); (with Manchester C), 1990 v USSR, Ma, Eg (sub), Ho, R, I; 1991 v Mor, T, E(2) W, Pol; 1992 v H, W (sub), US, Alb, US, I (sub), P; 1993 v La, D, Sp, Ni, D, Alb, La, Li; 1994 v Li, Sp, Ni; 1995 v La, Lie, Ni, E, Ni, P, Lie, A; 1996 v A, La, P, Ru, CzR, P (sub), Cro, Ho (sub), US (60)

Reid, C. (Brideville), 1931 v Sp (1)
Richardson, D. J. (Shamrock R), 1972 v A (sub); (with Gillingham), 1973 v N (sub); 1980 v Cz (3)
Rigby, A. (St James' Gate), 1935 v H, Sw, G (3)
Ringstead, A. (Sheffield U), 1951 v Arg, N; 1952 v WG (2), A, Sp; 1953 v A; 1954 v F; 1955 v N; 1956 v Y, Sp, Ho; 1957 v E (2); 1958 v D, Pol, A; 1959 v Pol, Cz (2) (20)
Robinson, J. (Bohemians), 1928 v Bel; (with Dolphin), 1931 v Sp (2)
Robinson, M. (Brighton & HA), 1981 v WG`B', F, Cy, Bel, Pol; 1982 v Ho, F, Alg, Ch; 1983 v Ho, Sp, Ic, Ma; (with Liverpool), 1984 v Ic, Ho, Is; 1985 v USSR, N; (with QPR), N, Sp, Sw; 1986 v D (sub), W, Cz (24)
Roche, P. J. (Shelbourne), 1972 v A; (with Manchester U), 1975 v USSR, T, Sw, USSR, Sw, WG; 1976 v T (8)
Rogers, E. (Blackburn R), 1968 v Cz, Pol; 1969 v Pol, A, D, Cz, D, H; 1970 v S, D, H; 1971 v I (2), A; (with Charlton Ath), 1972 v Ir, Ec, Ch, P; 1973 v USSR (19)
Ryan, G. (Derby Co), 1978 v T; (with Brighton & HA), 1979 v E, WG; 1980 v W, Cy (sub), Sw, Arg (sub); 1981 v WG`B' (sub), F (sub), Pol (sub); 1982 v Br (sub), Ho (sub), Alg (sub), Ch (sub), Tr; 1984 v Pol, Chn; 1985 v M (18)
Ryan, R. A. (WBA), 1950 v Se, Bel; 1951 v N, Arg, N; 1952 v WG (2), A, Sp; 1953 v F, A; 1954 v F, L, F; 1955 v N; (with Derby Co), 1956 v Sp (16)

Savage, D. P. T. (Millwall), 1996 v P (sub), Cro (sub), US (sub), M, Bol (5)
Saward, P. (Millwall), 1954 v L; (with Aston Villa), 1957 v E (2); 1958 v D, Pol, A; 1959 v Pol, Cz; 1960 v Se, Ch, WG, Se; 1961 v W, N; (with Huddersfield T), 1961 v S; 1962 v A; 1963 v Ic (2) (18)
Scannell, T. (Southend U), 1954 v L (1)
Scully, P. J. (Arsenal), 1989 v Tun (sub) (1)
Sheedy, K. (Everton), 1984 v Ho (sub), Ma; 1985 v D, I, Is, Sw; 1986 v Sw, D; 1987 v S, Pol; 1988 v Is, R, Pol, E (sub), USSR; 1989 v Ni, Tun, H, Sp, Ma, H; 1990 v Ni, Ma, W (sub), USSR, Fi (sub), T, E, Eg, Ho, R, I; 1991 v W, E, Pol, Ch, US; 1992 v H, Pol, T, W; (with Newcastle U), Sw (sub), Alb; 1993 v La, W (sub) (45)
Sheridan, J. J. (Leeds U), 1988 v R, Y, Pol, N (sub); 1989 v Sp; (with Sheffield W), 1990 v W, T (sub), Ma, I (sub); 1991 v Mor (sub), T, Ch, US (sub); 1992 v H; 1993 v La; 1994 v Sp (sub), Ho, Bol, G, CzR, I, M, N, Ho; 1995 v La, Lie, Ni, E, Ni, P, Lie, A; 1996 v A, Ho (34)
Slaven, B. (Middlesbrough), 1990 v W, Fi, T (sub), Ma; 1991 v W, Pol (sub); 1993 v W (7)
Sloan, J. W. (Arsenal), 1946 v P, Sp (2)
Smyth, M. (Shamrock R), 1969 v Pol (sub) (1)
Squires, J. (Shelbourne), 1934 v Ho (1)
Stapleton, F. (Arsenal), 1977 v T, F, Sp, Bul; 1978 v Bul, N, D; 1979 v Ni, E (sub), D, WG; 1980 v W, Bul, Ni, E, Cy; 1981 v WG`B', Ho, Bel, F, Cy, Bel, Cz, Pol; (with Manchester U), 1982 v Ho, F, Alg; 1983 v Ho, Sp, Ic, Ma, Sp; 1984 v Ic, Ho, Ma, Pol, Is, Chn; 1985 v N, D, I, Is, E, N, Sw; 1986 v Sw, USSR, D, U, Ic, Cz (sub); 1987 v Bel (2), S (2), Pol, Bul, L; (with Ajax), 1988 v L, Bul; (with Derby Co), R, Y, N, E, USSR, Ho; (with Le Havre), 1989 v F, Sp, Ma; (with Blackburn R), 1990 v WG, Ma (sub) (71)

Staunton, S. (Liverpool), 1989 v Tun, Sp (2), Ma, H; 1990 v WG, Ni, Ma, W, USSR, Fi, T, Ma, E, Eg, Ho, R, I; 1991 v Mor, T, E (2), W, Pol, Ch, US; (with Aston Villa), 1992 v Pol, T, Sw, US, Alb, US, I, P; 1993 v La, Sp, Ni, D, Alb, La, Li; 1994 v Li, Sp, Ho, Bol, G, CzR, I, M, N, Ho; 1995 v La, Lie, Ni, E, Ni, P, Lie, A; 1996 v La, P, Ru (62)
Stevenson, A. E. (Dolphin), 1932 v Ho; (with Everton), 1947 v E, Sp, P; 1948 v P, Sp; 1949 v Sw (7)
Strahan, F. (Shelbourne), 1964 v Pol, N, E; 1965 v Pol; 1966 v WG (5)
Sullivan, J. (Fordsons), 1928 v Bel (1)
Swan, M. M. G. (Drumcondra), 1960 v Se (sub) (1)
Synnott, N. (Shamrock R), 1978 v T, Pol; 1979 v Ni (3)

Taylor, T. (Waterford), 1959 v Pol (sub) (1)
Thomas, P. (Waterford), 1974 v Pol, Br (2)
Townsend, A. D. (Norwich C), 1989 v F, Sp (sub), Ma (sub), H; 1990 v WG (sub), Ni, Ma, W, USSR, Fi (sub), T, Ma (sub), E, Eg, Ho, R, I; (with Chelsea), 1991 v Mor, T, E (2), W, Pol, Ch, US; 1992 v Pol, W, US, Alb, US, I; 1993 v La, D, Sp, Ni, D, Alb, La, Li; (with Aston Villa), 1994 v Li, Ni, Ho, Bol, G, CzR, I, M, N, Ho; 1995 v La, Ni, E, Ni, P; 1996 v A, La, Ho, Ru, CzR, P (60)
Traynor, T. J. (Southampton), 1954 v L; 1962 v A; 1963 v Ic (2), S; 1964 v A (2), Sp (8)
Treacy, R. C. P. (WBA), 1966 v WG; 1967 v Sp, Cz; 1968 v Cz; (with Charlton Ath), 1968 v Pol; 1969 v Pol, Cz, D; 1970 v S, D, H (sub), Pol (sub), WG (sub); 1971 v Pol, Se (sub+1), I, A; (with Swindon T), 1972 v Ir, Ec, Ch, P; 1973 v USSR, F, USSR, Pol, F, N; 1974 v Pol; (with Preston NE), Br; 1975 v USSR, Sw (2), WG; 1976 v T, N (sub), Pol (sub); (with WBA), 1977 v F, Pol; (with Shamrock R), 1978 v T, Pol; 1980 v Cz (sub) (42)
Tuohy, L. (Shamrock R), 1956 v Y; 1959 v Cz (2); (with Newcastle U), 1962 v A; 1963 v Ic (2); (with Shamrock R), 1964 v A; 1965 v Bel (8)
Turner, C. J. (Southend U), 1936 v Sw; 1937 v G, H, Sw, F; 1938 v N (2), (with West Ham U) Cz, Pol; 1939 v H (10)
Turner, P. (Celtic), 1963 v S; 1964 v Sp (2)

Vernon, J. (Belfast C), 1946 v P, Sp (2)

Waddock, G. (QPR), 1980 v Sw, Arg; 1981 v W, Pol (sub); 1982 v Alg; 1983 v Ic, Ma, Sp, Ho (sub); 1984 v Ma (sub), Ic, Ho, Is; 1985 v I, Is, E, N, Sp; 1986 v USSR; (with Millwall), 1990 v USSR, T (21)
Walsh, D. J. (Linfield), 1946 v P, Sp; (with WBA), 1947 v Sp, P; 1948 v P, Sp; 1949 v Sw, P, Se, Sp; 1950 v E, Fi, Se; 1951 v N; (with Aston Villa), Arg, N; 1952 v Sp; 1953 v A; 1954 v F (2) (20)
Walsh, J. (Limerick), 1982 v Tr (1)
Walsh, M. (Blackpool), 1976 v N, Pol; 1977 v F (sub), Pol; (with Everton), 1979 v Ni (sub); (with QPR), D (sub), Bul, WG (sub); (with Porto), 1981 v Bel (sub), Cz; 1982 v Alg (sub); 1983 v Sp, Ho (sub), Sp (sub); 1984 v Ic (sub), Ma, Pol, Chn; 1985 v USSR, N (sub), D (21)
Walsh, M. (Everton), 1982 v Ch, Br, Tr; 1983 v Ic (4)
Walsh, W. (Manchester C), 1947 v E, Sp, P; 1948 v P, Sp; 1949 v Bel; 1950 v E, Se, Bel (9)
Waters, J. (Grimsby T), 1977 v T; 1980 v Ni (sub) (2)
Watters, F. (Shelbourne), 1926 v I (1)
Weir, J. (Clyde), 1939 v H (2), G (3)
Whelan, R. (St Patrick's Ath), 1964 v A, E (sub) (2)
Whelan, R. (Liverpool), 1981 v Cz (sub); 1982 v Ho (sub), F; 1983 v Ic, Ma, Sp; 1984 v Is; 1985 v USSR, N, I (sub), Is, E, N (sub), Sw (sub); 1986 v USSR (sub), W; 1987 v Bel (sub), S, Bul, Bel, Br, L; 1988 v L, Bul, Pol, N, E, USSR, Ho; 1989 v Ni, F, H, Sp, Ma; 1990 v WG, Ni, Ma, W, Ho (sub); 1991 v Mor, E; 1992 v Sw; 1993 v La, W (sub), Li (sub); 1994 v Li (sub), Sp, Ru, Ho, G (sub), N (sub); (with Southend U), 1995 v Lie, A (53)
Whelan, W. (Manchester U), 1956 v Ho; 1957 v D, E (2) (4)
White, J. J. (Bohemians), 1928 v Bel (1)
Whittaker, R. (Chelsea), 1959 v Cz (1)
Williams, J. (Shamrock R), 1938 v N (1)

BRITISH AND IRISH INTERNATIONAL GOALSCORERS SINCE 1872

Where two players with the same surname and initials have appeared for the same country, and one or both have scored, they have been distinguished by reference to the club which appears *first* against their name in the international appearances section (pages 780–830). Unfortunately, four of the scorers in Scotland's 10-2 victory v Ireland in 1888 are unknown, as is the scorer of one of their nine goals v Wales in March 1878.

ENGLAND

Player	G	Player	G	Player	G	Player	G
A'Court, A.	1	Carter, H. S.	7	Grainger, C.	3	Hon. A. Lyttelton	1
Adams, T. A.	4	Carter, J. H.	4	Greaves, J.	44		
Adcock, H.	1	Chadwick, E.	3	Grovesnor, A. T.	2	Mabbutt, G.	1
Alcock, C. W.	1	Chamberlain, M.	1	Gunn, W.	1	Macdonald, M.	6
Allen, A.	3	Chambers, H.	5			Mannion, W. J.	11
Allen, R.	2	Channon, M. R.	21	Haines, J. T. W.	2	Mariner, P.	13
Anderson, V.	2	Charlton, J.	6	Hall, G. W.	9	Marsh, R. W.	1
Anderton, D. R.	5	Charlton, R.	49	Halse, H. J.	2	Matthews, S.	11
Astall, G.	1	Chenery, C. J.	1	Hampson, J.	5	Matthews, V.	1
Athersmith, W. C.	3	Chivers, M.	13	Hampton, H.	2	McCall, J.	1
Atyeo, P. J. W.	5	Clarke, A. J.	10	Hancocks, J.	2	McDermott, T.	3
		Cobbold, W. N.	7	Hardman, H. P.	1	Medley, L. D.	1
Bache, J. W.	4	Cock, J. G.	2	Harris, S. S.	2	Melia, J.	1
Bailey, N. C.	2	Common, A.	2	Hassall, H. W.	4	Mercer, D. W.	1
Baily, E. F.	5	Connelly, J. M.	7	Hateley, M.	9	Merson, P. C.	1
Baker, J. H.	3	Coppell, S. J.	7	Haynes, J. N.	18	Milburn, J. E. T.	10
Ball, A. J.	8	Cotterill, G. H.	2	Hegan, K. E.	4	Miller, H. S.	1
Bambridge, A. L.	1	Cowans, G.	2	Henfrey, A. G.	2	Mills, G. R.	3
Bambridge, E. C.	12	Crawford, R.	1	Hilsdon, G. R.	14	Milward, A.	3
Barclay, R.	2	Crawshaw, T. H.	1	Hine, E. W.	4	Mitchell, C.	5
Barmby, N. J.	2	Crayston, W. J.	1	Hirst, D. E.	1	Moore, J.	1
Barnes, J.	11	Creek, F. N. S.	1	Hitchens, G. A.	5	Moore, R. F.	2
Barnes, P. S.	4	Crooks, S. D.	7	Hobbis, H. H. F.	1	Moore, W. G. B.	2
Barton, J.	1	Currey, E. S.	2	Hoddle, G.	8	Morren, T.	1
Bassett, W. I.	7	Currie, A. W.	3	Hodgetts, D.	1	Morris, F.	1
Bastin, C. S.	12	Cursham, A. W.	2	Hodgson, G.	1	Morris, J.	3
Beardsley, P. A.	9	Cursham, H. A.	5	Holley, G. H.	8	Mortensen, S. H.	23
Beasley, A.	1			Houghton, W. E.	5	Morton, J. R.	1
Beattie, T. K.	1	Daft, H. B.	3	Howell, R.	1	Mosforth, W.	3
Becton, F.	2	Davenport, J. K.	2	Hughes, E. W.	1	Mullen, J.	6
Bedford, H.	1	Davis, G.	1	Hulme, J. H. A.	4	Mullery, A. P.	1
Bell, C.	9	Davis, H.	1	Hunt, G. S.	1		
Bentley, R. T. F.	9	Day, S. H.	2	Hunt, R.	18	Neal, P. G.	5
Bishop, S. M.	1	Dean, W. R.	18	Hunter, N.	2	Needham, E.	3
Blackburn, F.	1	Devey, J. H. G.	1	Hurst, G. C.	24	Nicholls, J.	1
Blissett, L.	3	Dewhurst, F.	11			Nicholson, W. E.	1
Bloomer, S.	28	Dix, W. R.	1	Ince, P. E. C.	2		
Bond, R.	2	Dixon, K. M.	4			O'Grady, M.	3
Bonsor, A. G.	1	Dixon, L. M.	1	Jack, D. N. B.	3	Osborne, F. R.	3
Bowden, E. R.	1	Douglas, B.	11	Johnson, D. E.	6	Own goals	23
Bowers, J. W.	2	Drake, E. J.	6	Johnson, E.	2		
Bowles, S.	1	Ducat, A.	1	Johnson, J. A.	2	Page, L. A.	1
Bradford, G. R. W.	1	Dunn, A. T. B.	2	Johnson, T. C. F.	5	Paine, T. L.	7
Bradford, J.	7			Johnson, W. H.	1	Palmer, C. L.	1
Bradley, W.	2	Eastham, G.	2			Parry, E. H.	1
Bradshaw, F.	3	Edwards, D.	5	Kail, E. I. L.	2	Parry, R. A.	1
Bridges, B. J.	1	Elliott, W. H.	3	Kay, A. H.	1	Pawson, F. W.	1
Bridgett, A.	3	Evans, R. E.	1	Keegan, J. K.	21	Payne, J.	2
Brindle, T.	1			Kelly, R.	8	Peacock, A.	3
Britton, C. S.	1	Ferdinand, L.	4	Kennedy, R.	3	Pearce, S.	4
Broadbent, P. F.	2	Finney, T.	30	Kenyon-Slaney, W. S.	2	Pearson, J. S.	5
Broadis, I. A.	8	Fleming, H. J.	9	Keown, M. R.	3	Pearson, S. C.	5
Brodie, J. B.	1	Flowers, R.	10	Kevan, D. T.	8	Perry, W.	2
Bromley-Davenport, W.	2	Forman, Frank	1	Kidd, B.	1	Peters, M.	20
Brook, E. F.	10	Forman, Fred	3	Kingsford, R. K.	1	Pickering, F.	5
Brooking, T. D.	5	Foster, R. E.	3	Kirchen, A. J.	2	Platt, D.	27
Brooks, J.	2	Francis, G. C. J.	3	Kirton, W. J.	1	Pointer, R.	2
Broome, F. H.	3	Francis, T.	12				
Brown, A.	4	Freeman, B. C.	3	Langton, R.	1	Quantrill, A.	1
Brown, A. S.	1	Froggatt, J.	2	Latchford, R. D.	5		
Brown, G.	5	Froggatt, R.	2	Latherton, E. G.	1	Ramsay, A. E.	3
Brown, J.	3			Lawler, C.	1	Revie, D. G.	4
Brown, W.	1	Galley, T.	1	Lawton, T.	22	Reynolds, J.	3
Buchan, C. M.	4	Gascoigne, P. J.	8	Lee, F.	10	Richardson, J. R.	2
Bull, S. G.	4	Geary, F.	3	Lee, J.	1	Rigby, A.	3
Bullock, N.	2	Gibbins, W. V. T.	3	Lee, R. M.	1	Rimmer, E. J.	2
Burgess, H.	4	Gilliatt, W. E.	3	Lee, S.	2	Roberts, H.	1
Butcher, T.	3	Goddard, P.	1	Le Saux, G. P.	1	Roberts, W. T.	4
Byrne, J. J.	8	Goodall, J.	12	Lindley, T.	15	Robinson, J.	3
		Goodyer, A. C.	1	Lineker, G.	48	Robson, B.	26
Camsell, G. H.	18	Gosling, R. C.	2	Lofthouse, J. M.	3	Robson, R.	4
		Goulden, L. A.	4	Lofthouse, N.	30	Rowley, J. F.	6

Royle, J.	2
Rutherford, J.	3
Sagar, C.	1
Sandilands, R. R.	2
Sansom, K.	1
Schofield, J.	1
Seed, J. M.	1
Settle, J.	6
Sewell, J.	3
Shackleton, L. F.	1
Sharp, J.	1
Shearer, A.	10
Shepherd, A.	2
Sheringham, E. P.	4
Simpson, J.	1
Smith, A. M.	2
Smith, G. O.	12
Smith, Joe	1
Smith, J. R.	2
Smith, J. W.	4
Smith, R.	13
Smith, S.	1
Sorby, T. H.	1
Southworth, J.	3
Sparks, F. J.	3
Spence, J. W.	1
Spiksley, F.	5
Spilsbury, B. W.	5
Steele, F. C.	1
Stephenson, G. T.	2
Steven, T. M.	4
Stewart, J.	1
Stiles, N. P.	1
Storer, H.	1
Stone, S. B.	2
Summerbee, M. G.	1
Tambling, R. V.	1
Taylor, P. J.	2
Taylor, T.	16
Thompson, P. B.	1
Thornewell, G.	1
Tilson, S. F.	6
Townley, W. J.	1
Tueart, D.	2
Vaughton, O. H.	6
Veitch, J. G.	3
Violett, D. S.	1
Waddle, C. R.	6
Walker, W. H.	9
Wall, G.	2
Wallace, D.	1
Walsh, P.	1
Waring, T.	4
Warren, B.	2
Watson, D. V.	4
Watson, V. M.	4
Webb, G. W.	1
Webb, N.	4
Wedlock, W. J.	2
Weir, D.	2
Weller, K.	1
Welsh, D.	1
Whateley, O.	2
Wheldon, G. F.	6
Whitfield, H.	1
Wignall, F.	2
Wilkes, A.	1
Wilkins, R. G.	3
Willingham, C. K.	1
Wilshaw, D. J.	10
Wilson, D.	1
Wilson, G. P.	1
Winckworth, W. N.	1
Windridge, J. E.	7
Wise, D. F.	1
Withe, P.	1
Wollaston, C. H. R.	1
Wood, H.	1
Woodcock, T.	16
Woodhall, G.	1
Woodward, V. J.	29
Worrall, F.	2
Worthington, F. S.	2
Wright, I. E.	5
Wright, M.	1
Wright, W. A.	3
Wylie, J. G.	1
Yates, J.	3

NORTHERN IRELAND

Anderson, T.	4
Armstrong, G.	12
Bambrick, J.	12
Barr, H. H.	1
Barron, H.	3
Best, G.	9
Bingham, W. L.	10
Black, K.	1
Blanchflower, D.	2
Blanchflower, J.	1
Brennan, B.	1
Brennan, R. A.	1
Brotherston, N.	3
Brown, J.	1
Browne, F.	2
Campbell, J.	1
Campbell, W. G.	1
Casey, T.	2
Caskey, W.	1
Cassidy, T.	1
Chambers, J.	3
Clarke, C. J.	13
Clements, D.	2
Cochrane, T.	1
Condy, J.	1
Connor, M. J.	1
Coulter, J.	1
Croft, T.	1
Crone, W.	1
Crossan, E.	1
Crossan, J. A.	10
Curran, S.	2
Cush, W. W.	5
Dalton, W.	6
D'Arcy, S. D.	1
Darling, J.	1
Davey, H. H.	1
Davis, T. L.	1
Dill, A. H.	1
Doherty, L.	1
Doherty, P. D.	3
Dougan, A. D.	8
Dowie, I.	8
Dunne, J.	4
Elder, A. R.	1
Emerson, W.	1
English, S.	1
Ferguson, W.	1
Ferris, J.	1
Ferris, R. O.	1
Finney, T.	2
Gaffkin, J.	5
Gara, A.	3
Gawkrodger, G.	1
Gibb, J. T.	2
Gibb, T. J.	1
Gibson, W. K.	1
Gillespie, K. R.	1
Gillespie, W.	12
Goodall, A. L.	2
Gray, P.	5
Halligan, W.	1
Hamill, M.	1
Hamilton, B.	4
Hamilton, W.	5
Hannon, D. J.	1
Harkin, J.	2
Harvey, M.	3
Hill, C. F.	1
Hughes, M.	2
Humphries, W.	1
Hunter, A. (*Distillery*)	1
Hunter, A. (*Blackburn R*)	1
Hunter, B. V.	1
Irvine, R. W.	3
Irvine, W. J.	8
Johnston, H.	2
Johnston, S.	2
Johnston, W. C.	1
Jones, S.	1
Jones, J.	1
Kelly, J.	4
Kernaghan, N.	2
Kirwan, J.	2
Lacey, W.	3
Lemon, J.	2
Lockhart, N.	3
Lomas, S. M.	1
Magilton, J.	4
Mahood, J.	2
Martin, D. K.	3
Maxwell, J.	7
McAdams, W. J.	7
McAllen, J.	1
McAuley, J. L.	1
McCandless, J.	3
McCaw, J. H.	1
McClelland, J.	1
McCluggage, A.	2
McCracken, W.	1
McCrory, S.	1
McCurdy, C.	1
McDonald, A.	3
McGarry, J. K.	1
McGrath, R. C.	4
McIlroy, J.	10
McIlroy, S. B.	5
McKnight, J.	2
McLaughlin, J. C.	6
McMahon, G. J.	2
McMordie, A. S.	3
McMorran, E. J.	4
McParland, P. J.	10
McWha, W. B. R.	1
Meldon, J.	1
Mercar, J.	1
Mercer, J. T.	1
Millar, W.	1
Milligan, D.	1
Milne, R. G.	2
Molyneux, T. B.	1
Moreland, V.	1
Morgan, S.	3
Morrow, S. J.	1
Morrow, W. J.	1
Murphy, N.	1
Neill, W. J. T.	2
Nelson, S.	1
Nicholl, C. J.	3
Nicholl, J. M.	2
Nicholson, J. J.	6
O'Boyle, G.	1
O'Hagan, C.	2
O'Kane, W. J.	1
O'Neill, J.	1
O'Neill, M. A.	4
O'Neill, M. H.	8
Own goals	5
Peacock, R.	2
Peden, J.	7
Penney, S.	2
Pyper, James	2
Pyper, John	1
Quinn, J. M.	12
Reynolds, J.	1
Rowley, R. W. M.	2
Sheridan, J.	2
Sherrard, J.	1
Simpson, W. J.	5
Sloan, H. A. de B.	4
Smyth, S.	5
Spence, D. W.	3
Stanfield, O. M.	9
Stevenson, A. E.	5
Stewart, I.	2
Taggart, G. P.	5
Thompson, F. W.	2
Tully, C. P.	3
Turner, E.	1
Walker, J.	1
Walsh, D. J.	5
Welsh, E.	1
Whiteside, N.	9
Whiteside, T.	1
Williams, J. R.	1
Williamson, J.	1
Wilson, D. J.	1
Wilson, K. J.	6
Wilson, S. J.	7
Wilton, J. M.	2
Young, S.	2

SCOTLAND

Aitken, R.	1
Aitkenhead, W. A. C.	2
Alexander, D.	1
Allan, D. S.	4
Allan, J.	2
Anderson, F.	1
Anderson, W.	4
Andrews, P.	1
Archibald, A.	1
Archibald, S.	4
Baird, D.	2
Baird, J. C.	2
Baird, S.	2
Bannon, E.	1
Barbour, A.	1
Barker, J. B.	4
Battles, B. Jr	1
Bauld, W.	2
Baxter, J. C.	3
Bell, J.	5
Bennett, A.	2
Berry, D.	1
Bett, J.	1
Beveridge, W. W.	1
Black, A.	3
Black, D.	1
Bone, J.	1
Booth, S.	5
Boyd, R.	2
Boyd, W. G.	1
Brackenridge, T.	1
Brand, R.	8
Brazil, A.	1
Bremner, W. J.	3
Brown, A. D.	6
Buchanan, P. S.	1
Buchanan, R.	1
Buckley, P.	1
Buick, A.	2
Burns, K.	1
Cairns, T.	1
Calderwood, C.	1
Calderwood, R.	2
Caldow, E.	4
Campbell, C.	1
Campbell, John (*Celtic*)	1
Campbell, John (*Rangers*)	4
Campbell, P.	2
Campbell, R.	1
Cassidy, J.	1

OTHER INTERNATIONAL RESULTS

SOUTH AMERICA

International matches 1995

Argentina
Japan (h) 5-1, Nigeria (h) 0-0, Denmark (h) 0-2, Bulgaria (h) 4-1, South Africa (a) 1-1, Peru (h) 1-0, Paraguay (h) 2-1, Slovakia (h) 6-0, Australia (h) 2-0, Bolivia (h) 2-1, Chile (n) 4-0, USA (n) 0-3, Brazil (n) 2-2, Spain (a) 1-2, Colombia (h) 0-0, Brazil (h) 0-1, Venezuela (h) 6-0.

Bolivia
Paraguay (h) 1-1, Paraguay (a) 0-0, Venezuela (a) 3-1, Peru (a) 4-1, Argentina (n) 1-2, USA (n) 1-0, Chile (n) 2-2, Uruguay (n) 1-2, Ecuador (h) 2-2.

Brazil
Slovakia (h) 5-0, Honduras (h) 1-1, Israel (a) 2-1, Sweden (h) 1-0, Japan (h) 3-0, England (a) 3-1, Poland (h) 2-1, Ecuador (n) 1-0, Peru (n) 2-0, Colombia (n) 3-0, Argentina (n) 2-2, USA (n) 1-0, Uruguay (n) 1-1, Japan (a) 5-1, South Korea (a) 1-0, Romania (h) 2-2, Uruguay (h) 2-0, Argentina (a) 1-0, Colombia (h) 3-1.

Colombia
South Korea (a) 0-1, Hong Kong (a) 3-1, Australia (a) 0-0, Australia (a) 1-0, Uruguay (h) 2-1, Nigeria (h) 1-0, Mexico (h) 0-0, USA (a) 0-0, Peru (n) 1-1, Ecuador (n) 1-0, Brazil (n) 0-3, Paraguay (n) 1-1, Uruguay (n) 0-2, USA (n) 4-1, England (a) 0-0, Argentina (a) 0-0, Mexico (h) 2-2, Brazil (a) 1-3.

Chile
Mexico (h) 2-1, Peru (a) 0-6, Iceland (h) 1-1, Northern

Ireland (h) 2-1, Canada (a) 2-1, New Zealand (h) 3-1, Paraguay (h) 0-1, Turkey (h) 0-0, USA (n) 1-2, Argentina (n) 0-4, Bolivia (n) 2-2, Canada (h) 2-0.

Ecuador
Scotland (h) 1-2, Japan (a) 0-3, Zambia (h) 4-1, Costa Rica (h) 2-1, Zambia (h) 1-0, Paraguay (a) 0-1, Brazil (n) 0-1, Colombia (n) 0-1, Peru (n) 2-1, Bolivia (a) 2-2.

Paraguay
Bolivia (a) 1-1, Bolivia (h) 0-0, Argentina (a) 1-2, Turkey (h) 0-0, Chile (a) 1-0, New Zealand (h) 3-2, Ecuador (h) 1-0, Mexico (n) 2-1, Uruguay (n) 0-1, Venezuela (n) 3-2, Colombia (n) 1-1, Japan (a) 3-1.

Peru
Uruguay (a) 0-1, Chile (h) 6-0, Argentina (a) 0-1, Slovakia (h) 1-0, Bolivia (h) 4-1, Colombia (n) 1-1, Brazil (n) 0-2, Ecuador (n) 1-2.

Uruguay
Spain (a) 2-2, Mexico (a) 0-1, Colombia (a) 1-2, USA (a) 2-2, England (a) 0-0, Yugoslavia (a) 0-1, Peru (h) 1-0, New Zealand (h) 7-0, New Zealand (h) 2-2, Venezuela (n) 4-1, Paraguay (n) 1-0, Mexico (n) 1-1, Boliv ia (n) 2-1, Columbia (n) 2-0, Brazil (n) 1-1, Israel (a) 1-3, Brazil (a) 0-2.

Venezuela
Bolivia (h) 1-3, Uruguay (n) 1-4, Mexico (n) 1-3, Paraguay (n) 2-3, Argentina (a) 0-6.

AFRICA

Algeria
Egypt (h) 1-0, Tanzania (a) 1-2, Ethiopia (h) 2-0, Sudan (a) 0-2, Sudan (h) 1-1, Egypt (a) 1-1, Tunisia (h) 2-1, Tanzania (h) 2-1, Mali (a) 2-0, Mauritania (h) 4-0, Tunisia (a) 0-2, Ivory Coast (h) 0-0, Cameroon (h) 4-0, Gabon (a) 1-2, Ivory Coast (a) 0-0.

Angola
Mozambique (h) 1-0, Botswana (a) 2-1, Namibia (a) 2-2, Guinea (h) 3-0, Mali (h) 1-0, Mozambique (a) 1-2, Botswana (h) 4-0.

Benin
Gabon (a) 0-7, Togo (a) 0-3.

Botswana
Mali (h) 1-3, Angola (h) 1-2, Guinea (a) 0-5, Mozambique (h) 0-3, Namibia (h) 1-1, Mali (a) 0-4, Angola (a) 0-4.

Burkina Faso
Ivory Coast (a) 2-2, Morocco (a) 0-0, Ivory Coast (h) 1-1, Tunisia (h) 2-2, Tunisia (a) 0-3, Gabon (h) 2-5.

Cameroon
Malawi (h) 0-0, Zimbabwe (a) 1-4, Zaire (a) 1-2, Lesotho (h) 4-1, Malwi (a) 3-1, Zimbabwe (h) 1-0, Gabon (a) 2-1, Algeria (a) 0-4, Ivory Coast (a) 1-2, Gabon (a) 0-0, Liberia (h) 1-0.

Cape Verde Islands
Mali (a) 1-0, Mauritania (a) 1-1, Gambia (a) 0-3, Sierra Leone (a) 0-2, Guinea-Bissau (h) 1-0.

Congo
Niger (h) 3-1, Ghana (a) 1-3, Gambia (a) 1-1, Sierra Leone (h) 0-2.

Egypt
Tunisia (a) 0-2, Algeria (a) 0-1, Uganda (a) 0-0, Sudan (h) 3-1, Tanzania (a) 2-1, Morocco (a) 0-0, Ethiopia (a) 2-0, Algeria (h) 1-1, Uganda (h) 6-0, Zimbabwe (a) 2-2, South Africa (a) 0-2, Zambia (a) 3-1.

Ethiopia
Tanzania (h) 1-0, Sudan (h) 2-0, Algeria (a) 0-2, Uganda (h) 0-0, Egypt (h) 0-2, Tanzania (a) 0-2, Sudan (a) 0-3, Tanzania (h) 2-2, Somalia (a) 5-0, Kenya (a) 1-2.

Gabon
Benin (h) 7-0, Zambia (a) 0-1, Togo (a) 0-1, Mauritius (a) 3-0, Sierra Leone (h) 1-0, Cameroon (h) 1-2, Ivory Coast (h) 0-2, Algeria (h) 2-1, Cameroon (h) 0-0, Burkina Faso (a) 5-2, Mali (a) 2-1.

Gambia
Sierra Leone (a) 0-2, Niger (a) 1-1, Congo (h) 1-1, Mauritania (a) 1-2, Mali (a) 0-1, Cape Verde Islands (h) 3-0.

Ghana
Congo (h) 3-1, Sierra Leone (a) 0-1, Niger (h) 1-0, Norway (a) 2-3, Australia (a) 1-2, Australia (a) 0-1, Australia (a) 1-0, Congo (a) 2-0, Sierra Leone (h) 2-0.

Guinea
Sierra Leone (h) 3-1, Namibia (h) 3-0, Botswana (h) 5-0, Angola (a) 0-1, Mozambique (a) 0-0, Namibia (a) 0-0, Mali (h) 4-1, Sierra Leone (a) 0-2, Senegal (a) 0-3, Guinea-Bissau (a) 1-2.

Guinea-Bissau
Senegal (a) 2-1, Sierra Leone (h) 0-2, Guinea (h) 2-1, Mauritania (a) 0-1, Cape Verde Islands (a) 0-1.

Ivory Coast
Togo (h) 0-0, Burkina Faso (h) 2-2, Mali (h) 0-1, Liberia (h) 1-1, Morocco (h) 2-0, Mali (a) 2-2, Burkina Faso (a) 1-1, Algeria (h) 0-0, Gabon (a) 2-0, Cameroon (h) 2-1, Algeria (h) 0-0, Mali (h) 2-1.

Kenya
Uganda (a) 0-0, Rwanda (a) 1-0, Ethiopia (h) 2-1.

Lesotho
Zaire (a) 0-3, Malawi (h) 0-2, Zimbabwe (h) 0-2, South Africa (h) 1-3, Cameroon (a) 1-4.

Liberia
Senegal (h) 1-1, Tunisia (a) 0-0, Togo (a) 0-0, Tunisia (h) 1-0, Ivory Cost (a) 1-1, Mauritania (h) 2-0, Senegal (a) 0-3, Sierra Leone (a) 0-1, Cameroon (a) 0-1.

Malawi
Cameroon (a) 0-0, Lesotho (a) 2-0, Zaire (h) 0-1, Zimbabwe (a) 1-1, Cameroon (h) 1-3.

Mali
Mauritania (h) 0-1, Botswana (a) 3-1, Mozambique (a) 0-1, Namibia (h) 2-0, Ivory Coast (a) 1-0, Angola (a) 0-1, Botswana (h) 4-0, Ivory Coast (h) 2-2, Guinea (a) 1-4, Algeria (h) 0-2, Morocco (a) 0-2, Cape Verde Islands (h) 0-1, Gambia (a) 1-0, Mauritania (a) 1-3, Ivory Coast (a) 1-2, Gabon (h) 1-2.

Morocco
Senegal (h) 2-0, Burkina Faso (h) 0-0, Egypt (h) 0-0, Ivory Coast (a) 0-2, Mali (h) 2-0.

Mauritania
Mali (a) 1-0, Togo (a) 0-0, Tunisia (a) 0-1, Senegal (h) 0-1, Liberia (a) 0-2, Togo (h) 2-1, Tunisia (h) 0-0, Algeria (a) 0-4, Tunisia (a) 1-2, Gambia (h) 2-1, Cape Verde Islands (h) 1-1, Mali (h) 3-1, Guinea-Bissau (h) 1-0, Sierra Leone (h) 0-0.

Mauritius
Zambia (h) 0-3, Gabon (h) 0-3, Zambia (a) 0-2.

Mozambique
Angola (a) 0-1, Namibia (h) 4-2, Mali (h) 1-0, Botswana (a) 3-0, Guinea (h) 0-0, Zimbabwe (h) 3-1, Angola (h) 2-1, Namibia (a) 0-0.

Namibia
Guinea (a) 0-3, Mozambique (a) 2-4, Angola (h) 2-2, Mali (a) 0-2, Botswana (a) 1-1, Guinea (h) 0-0, Mozambique (h) 0-0.

Niger
Congo (a) 1-3, Gambia (h) 1-1, Ghana (a) 0-1, Sierra Leone (a) 1-5.

Nigeria
Japan (h) 3-0, Argentina (a) 0-0, Mexico (h) 1-1, USA (a) 2-3, Colombia (a) 0-1, Mexico (a) 1-2, Uzbekistan (a) 3-2, Uzbekistan (h) 1-0.

Rwanda
Uganda (a) 0-0, Kenya (h) 0-1.

Senegal
Tunisia (h) 0-0, Liberia (a) 1-1, Mauritania (a) 1-0, Togo (h) 5-1, Tunisia (a) 0-4, Liberia (h) 3-0, Guinea-Bissau (h) 1-2, Guinea (a) 3-0, Sierra Leone (h) 1-1.

Sierra Leone
Guinea (a) 1-3, Ghana (h) 1-0, Congo (a) 2-0, Niger (h) 5-1, Gabon (a) 0-1, Ghana (a) 0-2, Guinea (h) 2-0, Guinea-Bissau (a) 2-0, Senegal (a) 1-1, Cape Verde Islands (h) 2-0, Mauritania (a) 0-0.

Somalia
Tanzania (a) 0-7, Ethiopia (h) 0-5.

South Africa
Lesotho (a) 3-1, Argentina (h) 1-1, Mozambique (h) 3-2, Zambia (h) 2-2, Egypt (h) 2-0, Zimbabwe (h) 2-0, Germany (h) 0-0.

Sudan
Uganda (h) 3-1, Ethiopia (a) 0-2, Egypt (a) 1-3, Tanzania (h) 2-1, Uganda (a) 0-2, Ethiopia (h) 3-0.

Tanzania
Ethiopia (a) 0-1, Algeria (h) 2-1, Uganda (a) 0-2, Egypt (h) 1-2, Sudan (a) 1-2, Ethiopia (h) 2-0, Algeria (a) 1-2, Ethiopia (a) 2-2, Somalia (h) 7-0.

Togo
Mauritania (h) 0-0, Ivory Coast (a) 0-0, Liberia (h) 0-0, Senegal (a) 1-5, Benin (h) 3-0, Gabon (h) 1-0, Tunisia (h) 0-1, Mauritania (a) 1-2.

Tunisia
Egypt (h) 2-0, Senegal (a) 0-0, Mauritania (h) 1-0, Liberia (h) 0-0, Liberia (a) 0-1, Togo (a) 1-0, Senegal (h) 4-0, Algeria (a) 1-2, Mauritania (a) 0-0, Burkina Faso (a) 2-2, Algeria (h) 2-0, Mauritania (h) 2-1, Burkina Faso (h) 3-0, Zambia (a) 0 2.

Uganda
Sudan (a) 1-3, Egypt (h) 0-0, Tanzania (h) 2-0, Ethiopia (a) 0-0, Algeria (a) 1-1, Sudan (h) 2-0, Egypt (a) 0-6, Rwanda (h) 0-0, Kenya (h) 0-0.

Zaire
Lesotho (h) 3-0, Malawi (a) 1-0, Cameroon (h) 2-1, Zimbabwe (h) 5-0.

Zambia
Mauritius (a) 3-0, Gabon (h) 1-0, Ecuador (a) 1-4, South Korea (a) 3-2, Ecuador (a) 0-1, Mauritius (h) 2-0, Jamaica (a) 1-3, Jamaica (a) 1-1, Jamaica (h) 1-0, Jamaica (h) 4-2, South Africa (a) 2-2, Zimbabwe (h) 1-1, Egypt (a) 1-3, Tunisia (h) 2-0.

Zimbabwe
Cameroon (h) 4-1, Lesotho (a) 2-0, Malawi (h) 1-1, Zaire (a) 0-5, Mozambique (a) 1-3, Cameroon (a) 0-1, Egypt (h) 2-2, Zambia (a) 1-1, South Africa (a) 0-2.

UEFA UNDER-21 CHAMPIONSHIP 1994–96

(Also used as qualification for Olympics)

Group 1
Israel 2, Poland 2
Romania 5, Azerbaijan 2
Slovakia 0, France 3
France 0, Romania 0
Israel 2, Slovakia 0
Poland 5, Azerbaijan 0
Romania 0, Slovakia 0
Poland 0, France 4
Azerbaijan 1, Israel 2
Israel 0, Romania 1
Azerbaijan 0, France 5
Israel 1, France 1
Romania 1, Poland 2
Slovakia 3, Azerbaijan 0
Poland 1, Israel 0
Azerbaijan 0, Romania 5
France 0, Slovakia 1
Poland 1, Slovakia 0
Romania 1, Israel 0
Azerbaijan 1, Slovakia 0
France 4, Poland 1
Slovakia 1, Israel 1
France 5, Azerbaijan 0
Poland 3, Romania 3
Israel 4, Azerbaijan 0
Romania 0, France 0
Slovakia 3, Poland 1
Slovakia 3, Romania 1
Azerbaijan 1, Poland 2
France 3, Israel 0

Group 2
Belgium 7, Armenia 0
Cyprus 0, Spain 6
Macedonia 5, Denmark 3
Armenia 1, Cyprus 2
Denmark 0, Belgium 1
Macedonia 0, Spain 1
Belgium 7, Macedonia 0
Spain 1, Denmark 0
Cyprus 2, Armenia 1
Belgium 3, Spain 3
Macedonia 1, Cyprus 0
Spain 1, Belgium 1
Cyprus 1, Denmark 5
Belgium 1, Cyprus 0
Denmark 5, Macedonia 2
Armenia 0, Spain 3
Armenia 2, Macedonia 0
Denmark 4, Cyprus 0
Spain 4, Armenia 0
Macedonia 3, Belgium 0
Armenia 2, Denmark 3
Belgium 2, Denmark 2
Spain 3, Cyprus 1
Macedonia 3, Armenia 2
Armenia 0, Belgium 3
Denmark 5, Spain 1
Cyprus 3, Macedonia 2
Denmark 4, Armenia 0
Spain 4, Macedonia 0
Cyprus 1, Belgium 1

Group 3
Hungary 2, Turkey 1
Iceland 0, Sweden 1
Switzerland 2, Sweden 5
Turkey 3, Iceland 0
Sweden 0, Hungary 1
Switzerland 2, Iceland 1
Turkey 1, Switzerland 1
Hungary 1, Switzerland 0
Turkey 0, Sweden 0
Hungary 2, Sweden 1
Switzerland 0, Turkey 2
Sweden 1, Iceland 0
Iceland 1, Hungary 1
Iceland 2, Switzerland 4
Sweden 1, Switzerland 0

Turkey 2, Hungary 1
Iceland 2, Turkey 3
Switzerland 2, Hungary 3
Hungary 3, Iceland 1
Sweden 6, Turkey 1

Group 4
Estonia 1, Croatia 2
Ukraine 3, Lithuania 2
Slovenia 1, Italy 1
Estonia 1, Italy 4
Croatia 2, Lithuania 0
Ukraine 1, Slovenia 0
Ukraine 3, Estonia 0
Slovenia 3, Lithuania 0
Italy 2, Croatia 1
Italy 7, Estonia 0
Croatia 1, Ukraine 0
Lithuania 0, Croatia 1
Slovenia 5, Estonia 0
Ukraine 2, Italy 1
Croatia 0, Slovenia 2
Estonia 2, Ukraine 5
Lithuania 0, Italy 2
Lithuania 1, Slovenia 2
Estonia 1, Slovenia 2
Ukraine 1, Croatia 1
Estonia 0, Lithuania 5
Croatia 1, Estonia 0
Lithuania 3, Ukraine 3
Italy 1, Slovenia 0
Croatia 2, Italy 2
Lithuania 3, Estonia 0
Slovenia 0, Ukraine 5
Italy 2, Ukraine 1
Slovenia 4, Croatia 2
Italy 0, Lithuania 0

Group 5
Czech Republic 1, Malta 0
Luxembourg 0, Holland 4
Norway 4, Belarus 0
Malta 0, Czech Republic 7
Norway 1, Holland 0
Belarus 3, Luxembourg 0
Holland 2, Czech Republic 2
Malta 2, Norway 3
Holland 3, Luxembourg 0
Malta 1, Luxembourg 0
Luxembourg 0, Norway 8
Holland 4, Malta 0
Czech Republic 2, Belarus 0
Norway 5, Luxembourg 0
Belarus 4, Malta 0
Czech Republic 2, Holland 2
Belarus 4, Norway 2
Luxembourg 0, Czech Republic 7
Norway 3, Malta 0
Belarus 3, Holland 1
Norway 3, Czech Republic 4
Luxembourg 0, Malta 0
Holland 3, Belarus 0
Czech Republic 1, Norway 2
Belarus 0, Czech Republic 3
Luxembourg 0, Belarus 5
Malta 0, Holland 2
Malta 1, Belarus 1
Holland 2, Norway 1
Czech Republic 4, Luxembourg 0

Group 6
England 0, Portugal 0
Latvia 1, Republic of Ireland 1
Latvia 0, Portugal 1
Austria 1, England 3
Portugal 2, Austria 0
England 1, Republic of Ireland 0
Republic of Ireland 0, England 2
Austria 0, Latvia 0
Republic of Ireland 1, Portugal 1
Latvia 0, England 1

Portugal 4, Latvia 0
Republic of Ireland 3, Austria 0
England 4, Latvia 0
Latvia 0, Austria 2
Portugal 2, England 0
Austria 1, Republic of Ireland 0
Austria 0, Portugal 1
Republic of Ireland 1, Latvia 0
England 2, Austria 1
Portugal 3, Republic of Ireland 1

Group 7
Georgia 3, Moldova 0
Bulgaria 1, Georgia 0
Moldova 1, Wales 0
Bulgaria 2, Moldova 0
Georgia 1, Wales 2
Wales 1, Bulgaria 1
Moldova 1, Germany 1
Bulgaria 3, Wales 1
Georgia 0, Germany 2
Germany 1, Wales 0
Moldova 0, Bulgaria 1
Bulgaria 2, Germany 0
Wales 5, Georgia 1
Germany 3, Georgia 0
Wales 1, Moldova 0
Germany 3, Moldova 1
Wales 1, Germany 5
Georgia 1, Bulgaria 2
Germany 7, Bulgaria 0
Moldova 2, Georgia 1

Group 8
Finland 1, Scotland 0
Greece 3, Finland 4
Russia 3, San Marino 0
Greece 4, San Marino 0
Scotland 2, Russia 1
Finland 4, San Marino 0
Greece 1, Scotland 2
San Marino 0, Finland 6
Russia 1, Scotland 2
Greece 0, Russia 1
San Marino 0, Scotland 1
San Marino 0, Russia 7
Finland 1, Greece 0
Finland 1, Russia 1
Scotland 3, Greece 0
San Marino 1, Greece 3
Scotland 5, Finland 0
Russia 0, Greece 1
Scotland 1, San Marino 0
Russia 3, Finland 0

Quarter-finals, First Leg
Hungary 2, Scotland 1
Germany 0, France 0
Spain 2, Czech Republic 1
Portugal 1, Italy 0

Quarter-finals, Second Leg
France 4, Germany 1
Scotland 3, Hungary 1
Czech Republic 1, Spain 2
Italy 2, Portugal 0

Semi-finals (in Spain)
Italy 1, France 0
Spain 2, Scotland 1

Third place
Scotland 0, France 1

Final
Spain 1, Italy 1 *aet*
(Spain won 4-2 on penalties)

OLYMPIC FOOTBALL

Previous medallists

Year	Venue		Year	Venue		Year	Venue	
1896	Athens*	1 Denmark	1932	Los Angeles		1968	Mexico City	1 Hungary
		2 Greece		no tournament				2 Bulgaria
1900	Paris*	1 Great Britain	1936	Berlin	1 Italy			3 Japan
		2 France			2 Austria	1972	Munich	1 Poland
1904	St Louis**	1 Canada			3 Norway			2 Hungary
		2 USA	1948	London	1 Sweden			3 E Germany/USSR
1908	London	1 Great Britain			2 Yugoslavia	1976	Montreal	1 East Germany
		2 Denmark			3 Denmark			2 Poland
		3 Holland	1952	Helsinki	1 Hungary			3 USSR
1912	Stockholm	1 England			2 Yugoslavia	1980	Moscow	1 Czechoslovakia
		2 Denmark			3 Sweden			2 East Germany
		3 Holland	1956	Melbourne	1 USSR			3 USSR
1920	Antwerp	1 Belgium			2 Yugoslavia	1984	Los Angeles	1 France
		2 Spain			3 Bulgaria			2 Brazil
		3 Holland	1960	Rome	1 Yugoslavia			3 Yugoslavia
1924	Paris	1 Uruguay			2 Denmark	1988	Seoul	1 USSR
		2 Switzerland			3 Hungary			2 Brazil
		3 Sweden	1964	Tokyo	1 Hungary			3 West Germany
1928	Amsterdam	1 Uruguay			2 Czechoslovakia	1992	Barcelona	1 Spain
		2 Argentina			3 East Germany			2 Poland
		3 Italy						3 Ghana

* No official tournament
** No official tournament but gold medal later awarded by IOC

OLYMPIC GAMES (ATLANTA 1996)

Qualifiers for the men's football.

Group A
USA, Argentina, Portugal, Tunisia

Group B
Spain, Saudi Arabia, France, Australia

Group C
Ghana, Korea Republic, Italy, Mexico

Group D
Brazil, Japan, Hungary, Nigeria

Qualifiers for the women's football.

Group E
USA, Denmark, Sweden, China

Group F
Norway, Brazil, Germany, Japan

(results in next year's edition)

12TH EUROPEAN UNDER-18 YOUTH CHAMPIONSHIP

Group 1
Austria 0, Yugoslavia 3
Georgia 1, Austria 3
Yugoslavia 3, Georgia 0

Group 2
Luxembourg 0, Switzerland 3
Switzerland 1, Greece 5
Luxembourg 0, Greece 2
Switzerland 1, Luxembourg 0
Greece 1, Switzerland 1
Greece 3, Luxembourg 0

Group 3
Italy 2, Bulgaria 0
Bulgaria 3, Malta 0
Italy 5, Malta 0
Bulgaria 0, Italy 1
Malta 0, Italy 1
Malta 0, Bulgaria 1

Group 4
Czech Republic 2, Russia 1
Russia 4, Czech Republic 1
Russia 1, Turkey 1
Turkey 0, Czech Republic 0
Czech Republic 0, Turkey 1
Turkey 2, Russia 3

Group 5
Israel 2, Azerbaijan 1
Azerbaijan 0, Hungary 3
Hungary 1, Israel 1

Group 6
Romania 0, Germany 1
Croatia 1, Romania 0
Germany 4, Croatia 2

Group 7
Belgium 3, Slovenia 1
Slovenia 2, Moldova 1
Moldova 2, Belgium 3

Group 8
Macedonia 0, Denmark 2
Portugal 3, Macedonia 0
Denmark 0, Portugal 1

Group 9
Cyprus 2, Holland 5
Armenia 0, Cyprus 1
Holland 9, Armenia 2

Group 10
Spain 2, Ukraine 1
Slovakia 1, Ukraine 4
Spain 0, Slovakia 0

Group 11
Faeroes 0, Poland 4
Norway 7, Faeroes 0
Poland 2, Norway 4

Group 12
Estonia 1, Lithuania 4
Scotland 4, Estonia 1
Lithuania 0, Scotland 1

Group 13
Sweden 3, Latvia 1
Latvia 0, England 2
England 6, Sweden 2

Group 14
Finland 2, Republic of Ireland 5
Wales 3, Finland 2
Republic of Ireland 0, Wales 0
Finland 0, Wales 2
Republic of Ireland 3, Finland 0
Wales 0, Republic of Ireland 3

Group 15
Northern Ireland 2, Belarus 0
Belarus 0, Iceland 0
Iceland 3, Northern Ireland 2

SECOND STAGE

Group 1
Italy 4, Greece 0
Greece 1, Italy 3
Greece 1, Austria 0
Italy 2, Austria 0
Austria 0, Greece 1
Austria 0, Italy 0

Group 2
Russia 2, Hungary 4
Hungary 1, Russia 0

Group 3
Germany 0, Belgium 0
Belgium 2, Germany 1

Group 4
Portugal 4, Holland 1
Holland 2, Portugal 0

Group 5
Spain 3, Norway 1
Norway 0, Spain 4

Group 6
Scotland 0, England 3
England 3, Scotland 0

Group 7
Republic of Ireland 2, Iceland 1
Iceland 1, Republic of Ireland 1

(in Ecuador, August 1995)

WORLD UNDER-17 CHAMPIONSHIP

Group A
Ecuador 2, USA 0
Ghana 1, Japan 0
Ecuador 1, Ghana 2
USA 1, Japan 2
Ecuador 0, Japan 0
USA 0, Ghana 2

Group B
Argentina 3, Portugal 0
Costa Rica 2, Guinea 0
Argentina 2, Costa Rica 0
Portugal 2, Guinea 3
Argentina 2, Guinea 0
Portugal 3, Costa Rica 0

Group C
Nigeria 1, Qatar 1
Australia 2, Spain 2
Nigeria 2, Australia 0
Qatar 0, Spain 1
Nigeria 2, Spain 1
Qatar 0, Australia 3

Group D
Brazil 3, Germany 0
Oman 2, Canada 1
Brazil 0, Oman 0
Germany 3, Canada 0
Brazil 2, Canada 0
Germany 0, Oman 3

Quarter-finals
Ghana 2, Portugal 0
Nigeria 1, Oman 2
Brazil 3, Australia 1
Argentina 3, Ecuador 1

Semi-finals
Ghana 3, Oman 1
Argentina 0, Brazil 3

Third place
Oman 0, Argentina 2

Final
Ghana 3, Brazil 2

(in Austria)

14th UEFA UNDER-16 CHAMPIONSHIP 1996

Group A
Eire 1, Austria 0
Portugal 3, Poland 0
Austria 0, Poland 0
Eire 0, Portugal 2
Austria 2, Portugal 2
Poland 0, Eire 1

Group B
Greece 2, Germany 1
Romania 0, Ukraine 1
Romania 0, Greece 1
Ukraine 1, Germany 6
Romania 1, Germany 4
Ukraine 1, Greece 1

Group C
France 2, Croatia 0
Spain 4, Switzerland 1
France 3, Spain 0
Croatia 2, Switzerland 1
Switzerland 0, France 1
Croatia 1, Spain 0

Group D
England 2, Slovakia 0
Turkey 3, Israel 0
England 2, Turkey 1
Slovakia 0, Israel 2
Israel 2, England 1
Slovakia 2, Turkey 1

Quarter-finals
Portugal 5, Croatia 1
France 0, Eire 0 *aet*
France won 5-4 on penalties
Greece 1, England 0
Israel 3, Germany 2 *aet*

Semi-finals
Portugal 3, Greece 0
France 1, Israel 0

Third Place
Israel 3, Greece 2

Final (in Vienna)
Portugal 1, France 0

ENGLAND UNDER-21 RESULTS 1976–96

EC UEFA Competition for Under-21 Teams

Year	Date		Venue	Eng	Opp
v ALBANIA				Eng	Alb
EC1989	Mar	7	Shkroda	2	1
EC1989	April	25	Ipswich	2	0
v ANGOLA				Eng	Ang
1995	June	10	Toulon	1	0
1996	May	28	Toulon	0	2
v AUSTRIA				Eng	Aus
1994	Oct	11	Kapfenberg	3	1
1995	Nov	14	Middlesbrough	2	1
v BELGIUM				Eng	Bel
1994	June	5	Marseille	2	1
1996	May	24	Toulon	1	0
v BRAZIL				Eng	B
1993	June	11	Toulon	0	0
1995	June	6	Toulon	0	2
1996	June	1	Toulon	1	2
v BULGARIA				Eng	Bul
EC1979	June	5	Pernik	3	1
EC1979	Nov	20	Leicester	5	0
1989	June	5	Toulon	2	3
v CROATIA				Eng	Cro
1996	Apr	23	Sunderland	0	1
v CZECHOSLOVAKIA				Eng	Cz
1990	May	28	Toulon	2	1
1992	May	26	Toulon	1	2
1993	June	9	Toulon	1	1
v DENMARK				Eng	Den
EC1978	Sept	19	Hvidovre	2	1
EC1979	Sept	11	Watford	1	0
EC1982	Sept	21	Hvidovre	4	1
EC1983	Sept	20	Norwich	4	1
EC1986	Mar	12	Copenhagen	1	0
EC1986	Mar	26	Manchester	1	1
1988	Sept	13	Watford	0	0
1994	Mar	8	Brentford	1	0
v EAST GERMANY				Eng	EG
EC1980	April	16	Sheffield	1	2
EC1980	April	23	Jena	0	1
v FINLAND				Eng	Fin
EC1977	May	26	Helsinki	1	0
EC1977	Oct	12	Hull	8	1
EC1984	Oct	16	Southampton	2	0
EC1985	May	21	Mikkeli	1	3
v FRANCE				Eng	Fra
EC1984	Feb	28	Sheffield	6	1
EC1984	Mar	28	Rouen	1	0
1987	June	11	Toulon	0	2
EC1988	April	13	Besancon	2	4
EC1988	April	27	Highbury	2	2
1988	June	12	Toulon	2	4
1990	May	23	Toulon	7	3
1991	June	3	Toulon	1	0
1992	May	28	Toulon	0	0
1993	June	15	Toulon	1	0
1994	May	31	Aubagne	0	3
1994	Sept	6	Leicester	0	0
1995	June	10	Toulon	0	2
v GERMANY				Eng	Ger
1991	Sept	10	Scunthorpe	2	1
v GREECE				Eng	Gre
EC1982	Nov	16	Piraeus	0	1
EC1983	Mar	29	Portsmouth	2	1
1989	Feb	7	Patras	0	1
v HOLLAND				Eng	H
EC1993	April	27	Portsmouth	3	0
EC1993	Oct	12	Utrecht	1	1
v HUNGARY				Eng	Hun
EC1981	June	5	Keszthely	2	1
EC1981	Nov	17	Nottingham	2	0
EC1983	April	26	Newcastle	1	0
EC1983	Oct	11	Nyiregyhaza	2	0
1990	Sept	11	Southampton	3	1
1992	May	12	Budapest	2	2
v ITALY				Eng	Italy
EC1978	Mar	8	Manchester	2	1
EC1978	April	5	Rome	0	0
EC1984	April	18	Manchester	3	1
EC1984	May	2	Florence	0	1
EC1986	April	9	Pisa	0	2
EC1986	April	23	Swindon	1	1
v ISRAEL				Eng	Isr
1985	Feb	27	Tel Aviv	2	1
v LATVIA				Eng	Lat
1995	April	25	Riga	1	0
1995	June	7	Burnley	4	0
v MALAYSIA				Eng	Mal
1995	June	8	Toulon	2	0
v MEXICO				Eng	Mex
1988	June	5	Toulon	2	1
1991	May	29	Toulon	6	0
1992	May	25	Toulon	1	1
v MOROCCO				Eng	Mor
1987	June	7	Toulon	2	0
1988	June	9	Toulon	1	0
v NORWAY				Eng	Nor
EC1977	June	1	Bergen	2	1
EC1977	Sept	6	Brighton	6	0
1980	Sept	9	Southampton	3	0
1981	Sept	8	Drammen	0	0
EC1992	Oct	13	Peterborough	0	2
EC1993	June	1	Stavanger	1	1
1995	Oct	10	Stavanger	2	2
v POLAND				Eng	Pol
EC1982	Mar	17	Warsaw	2	1
EC1982	April	7	West Ham	2	2
EC1989	June	2	Plymouth	2	1
EC1989	Oct	10	Jastrzebie	3	1
EC1990	Oct	16	Tottenham	0	1
EC1993	May	28	Zdroj	4	1
EC1993	Sept	7	Millwall	1	2
v PORTUGAL				Eng	Por
1987	June	13	Toulon	0	0
1990	May	21	Toulon	0	1
1993	June	7	Toulon	2	0
1994	June	7	Toulon	2	0
1995	Sept	2	Lisbon	0	2
1996	May	30	Toulon	1	3
v REPUBLIC OF IRELAND				Eng	RoI
1981	Feb	25	Liverpool	1	0
1985	Mar	25	Portsmouth	3	2
1989	June	9	Toulon	0	0
EC1990	Nov	13	Cork	3	0
EC1991	Mar	26	Brentford	3	0
1994	Nov	15	Newcastle	1	0
1995	Mar	27	Dublin	2	0
v ROMANIA				Eng	Rom
EC1980	Oct	14	Ploesti	0	4
EC1981	April	28	Swindon	3	0
EC1985	April	30	Brasov	0	0
EC1985	Sept	10	Ipswich	3	0
v RUSSIA				Eng	Rus
1994	May	30	Bandol	2	0
v SAN MARINO				Eng	SM
EC1993	Feb	16	Luton	6	0
EC1993	Nov	17	San Marino	4	0
v SENEGAL				Eng	Sen
1989	June	7	Toulon	6	1
1991	May	27	Toulon	2	1
v SCOTLAND				Eng	Sco
1977	April	27	Sheffield	1	0
EC1980	Feb	12	Coventry	2	1
EC1980	Mar	4	Aberdeen	0	0
EC1982	April	19	Glasgow	1	0
EC1982	April	28	Manchester	1	1

				Eng	Sco
EC1988	Feb	16	Aberdeen	1	0
EC1988	Mar	22	Nottingham	1	0
1993	June	13	Toulon	1	0
			v SPAIN	Eng	Spa
EC1984	May	17	Seville	1	0
EC1984	May	24	Sheffield	2	0
1987	Feb	18	Burgos	2	1
1992	Sept	8	Burgos	1	0
			v SWEDEN	Eng	Swe
1979	June	9	Vasteras	2	1
1986	Sept	9	Ostersund	1	1
EC1988	Oct	18	Coventry	1	1
EC1989	Sept	5	Uppsala	0	1
			v SWITZERLAND	Eng	Swit
EC1980	Nov	18	Ipswich	5	0
EC1981	May	31	Neuenburg	0	0
1988	May	28	Lausanne	1	1
			v USA	Eng	USA
1989	June	11	Toulon	0	2
1994	June	2	Toulon	3	0
			v TURKEY	Eng	Tur
EC1984	Nov	13	Bursa	0	0
EC1985	Oct	15	Bristol	3	0

				Eng	Tur
EC1987	April	28	Izmir	0	0
EC1987	Oct	13	Sheffield	1	1
EC1991	April	30	Izmir	2	2
1991	Oct	15	Reading	2	0
EC1992	Nov	17	Orient	0	1
EC1993	Mar	30	Izmir	0	0
			v USSR	Eng	USSR
1987	June	9	Toulon	0	0
1988	June	7	Toulon	1	0
1990	May	25	Toulon	2	1
1991	May	31	Toulon	2	1
			v WALES	Eng	Wales
1976	Dec	15	Wolverhampton	0	0
1979	Feb	6	Swansea	1	0
1990	Dec	5	Tranmere	0	0
			v WEST GERMANY	Eng	WG
EC1982	Sept	21	Sheffield	3	1
EC1982	Oct	12	Bremen	2	3
1987	Sept	8	Ludenscheid	0	2
			v YUGOSLAVIA	Eng	Yugo
EC1978	April	19	Novi Sad	1	2
EC1978	May	2	Manchester	1	1
EC1986	Nov	11	Peterborough	1	1
EC1987	Nov	10	Zemun	5	1

ENGLAND B RESULTS 1949–96

Year	Date		Venue		
			v ALGERIA	Eng	Alg
1990	Dec	11	Algiers	0	0
			v AUSTRALIA	Eng	Aust
1980	Nov	17	Birmingham	1	0
			v CIS	Eng	CIS
1992	April	28	Moscow	1	1
			v CZECHOSLOVAKIA	Eng	Cz
1978	Nov	28	Prague	1	0
1990	April	24	Sunderland	2	0
1992	Mar	24	Budejovice	1	0
			v FINLAND	Eng	Fin
1949	May	15	Helsinki	4	0
			v FRANCE	Eng	Fra
1952	May	22	Le Havre	1	7
1992	Feb	18	Loftus Road	3	0
			v WEST GERMANY	Eng	WG
1954	Mar	24	Gelsenkirchen	4	0
1955	Mar	23	Sheffield	1	1
1978	Feb	21	Augsburg	2	1
			v HOLLAND	Eng	Hol
1949	May	18	Amsterdam	4	0
1950	Feb	22	Newcastle	1	0
1952	Mar	26	Amsterdam	1	0
			v ICELAND	Eng	Ice
1989	May	19	Reykjavik	2	0
1991	April	27	Watford	1	0
			v ITALY	Eng	Italy
1950	May	11	Milan	0	5
1989	Nov	14	Brighton	1	1
			v LUXEMBOURG	Eng	Lux
1950	May	21	Luxembourg	2	1
			v MALAYSIA	Eng	Mal
1978	May	30	Kuala Lumpur	1	1
			v MALTA	Eng	Mal
1987	Oct	14	Ta'Qali	2	0

			v NEW ZEALAND	Eng	NZ
1978	June	7	Christchurch	4	0
1978	June	11	Wellington	3	1
1978	June	14	Auckland	4	0
1979	Oct	15	Leyton	4	1
1984	Nov	13	Nottingham	2	0
			v NORTHERN IRELAND	Eng	NI
1994	May	10	Sheffield	4	2
			v NORWAY	Eng	Nor
1989	May	22	Stavanger	1	0
			v REPUBLIC OF IRELAND	Eng	RoI
1990	Mar	27	Cork	1	4
1994	Dec	13	Liverpool	2	0
			v SCOTLAND	Eng	Sco
1953	Mar	11	Edinburgh	2	2
1954	Mar	3	Sunderland	1	1
1956	Feb	29	Dundee	2	2
1957	Feb	6	Birmingham	4	1
			v SINGAPORE	Eng	Sin
1978	June	18	Singapore	8	0
			v SPAIN	Eng	Sp
1980	Mar	26	Sunderland	1	0
1981	Mar	25	Granada	2	3
1991*	Dec	18	Castellon	1	0
			*Spanish Olympic XI		
			v SWITZERLAND	Eng	Swit
1950	Jan	18	Sheffield	5	0
1954	May	22	Basle	0	2
1956	Mar	21	Southampton	4	1
1989	May	16	Winterthur	2	0
1991	May	20	Walsall	2	1
			v USA	Eng	USA
1980	Oct	14	Manchester	1	0
			v WALES	Eng	Wales
1991	Feb	5	Swansea	1	0
			v YUGOSLAVIA	Eng	Yugo
1954	May	16	Ljubljana	1	2
1955	Oct	19	Manchester	5	1
1989	Dec	12	Millwall	2	1

BRITISH AND IRISH UNDER-21 TEAMS 1995–96

ENGLAND UNDER-21 INTERNATIONALS

2 Sept

Portugal (2) 2 *(Dani 2)*
England (0) 0   10,000
England: Gerrard; Neville P, Gordon, Beckham, Scimeca, Elliott, Butt (Bart-Williams), Thompson, Fowler, Shipperley, Sinclair.

10 Oct

Norway (1) 2 *(Solskjaer, Lund)*
England (0) 2 *(Campbell, Booth)*   2640
England: Watson D; Watson S (Neville P), Gordon, Pearce, Campbell (Bowyer), Unsworth, Roberts, Pollock (Holland), Shipperley, Booth (Dichio), Joachim.

14 Nov

England (2) 2 *(Fowler, Shipperley)*
Austria (1) 1 *(Cerny)*   13,496
England: Oakes; Watson S, Elliott, Campbell, Roberts, Unsworth, Butt, Pollock (Beckham), Shipperley, Bart-Williams (Holland), Fowler.

23 Apr

England (0) 0
Croatia (1) 1 *(Vucko)*   4376
England: Day (Davis); Brown, Briscoe, O'Connor (Plummer), Rufus, Thatcher (Carbon), Cooke, Ford (Hendrie), Gallen (Moore), Dyer, Holland.

24 May

England (1) 1 *(Slade)*
Belgium (0) 0   5000
England: Day; Plummer, Rufus, Stuart, Beckham, Holland, Brown, Bowyer, Cooke, Slade (Briscoe), Thornley (Moore).

28 May

England (0) 0
Angola (1) 2 *(Muhongo (pen), Costa)*   1600
England: Marshall; O'Connor (Holland), Challis, Plummer (Cooke), Rufus, Stuart, Beckham, Brown, Briscoe, Moore (Branch), Slade.

30 May

England (0) 1 *(Slade)*
Portugal (1) 3 *(Nuno, Beto (pen), Dani)*   2500
England: Davis; Brown, Challis (Plummer), Stuart, Rufus, Beckham, Bowyer, Cooke, Thornley, Slade, Moore.

1 June

England (0) 1 *(Moore)*
Brazil (0) 2 *(Alex, Abailcon)*   8000
England: Day; Rufus, Plummer, Stuart, O'Connor, Briscoe, Bowyer, Holland, Thornley, Slade, Moore.

SCOTLAND UNDER-21 INTERNATIONALS

15 Aug

Scotland (1) 3 *(McNamara, Liddell (pen), Donnelly)*
Greece (0) 0   2517
Scotland: Stillie; McNamara (McLoughlin), Gray, Fullarton (Murray), Pressley, Hannah, Miller, Glass, Crawford (Donnelly), Liddell, McCann.

6 Sept

Scotland (1) 5 *(Harper 3, Hamilton, Locke)*
Finland (0) 0   2571
Scotland: Stillie; Murray, Fullarton, Locke, Handyside, Dailly, McNamara, Glass, Liddell (Hamilton), Harper (Crawford), McCann.

14 Nov

Scotland (0) 1 *(Valentini (og))*
San Marino (0) 0   3000
Scotland: Stillie; McNamara (McNiven), Sheerin, Murray, Pressley, Handyside, Donnelly, Hamilton (Freedman), Liddell, Dailly, McCann (McLoughlin).

12 Mar

Hungary (1) 2 *(Szanyo (pen), Zavadszky)*
Scotland (1) 1 *(Glass)*   15,000
Scotland: Stillie; McNamara, Glass, Ritchie, Pressley, Dailly, Donnelly, Murray, Crawford (Fullarton), Liddell, Locke.

26 Mar

Scotland (1) 3 *(Dailly, Hamilton, Donnelly)*
Hungary (1) 1 *(Egressy)*   9173
Scotland: Stillie; McNamara (Hamilton), Gray, Marshall, Pressley, Dailly (Crawford), Donnelly, Murray (Baker), Liddell, Fullarton, McLoughlin.

28 May

Spain (2) 2 *(Oscar, De la Pena)*
Scotland (1) 1 *(Marshall)*   15,500
Scotland: Stillie; Dailly, Pressley, Marshall, McNamara, Miller, Gray (Fullarton), Glass, Donnelly, Jupp (Crawford), Johnston (Hamilton).

31 May

France (0) 1 *(Moreau)*
Scotland (0) 0   10,000
Scotland: Stillie (Meldrum); McNamara, Pressley, Marshall, Gray, Donnelly, Murray, Miller, Fullarton, Dailly (Crawford), Hamilton (Liddell).

**REPUBLIC OF IRELAND UNDER-21
INTERNATIONALS**

5 Sept

Austria (1) 1 *(Kauz)*
Republic of Ireland (0) 0   1500
Republic of Ireland: Given; Carr, Woods, Greene, Breen,
Boland, Kavanagh (Scully), Savage, Launders, Perkins,
Turner.

10 Oct

Republic of Ireland (1) 1 *(Moore)*
Latvia (0) 0   6000
Republic of Ireland: Colgan; Carr, Greene, Breen, Hardy,
Crawford (O'Halloran), Durkan, Savage, Launders,
Scully (O'Byrne), Moore (O'Sullivan).

14 Nov

Portugal (1) 3 *(Porfirio, Conceciao, Litos)*
Republic of Ireland (1) 1 *(Savage)*   10,000
Republic of Ireland: Given; Woods, Breen, Coll
(Greene), Hardy, Carsley, O'Sullivan, Savage
(Crawford), Farrelly, Scully, Launders (Turner).

26 Mar

Republic of Ireland (0) 0
Russia (1) 1 *(Semak)*   2500
Republic of Ireland: Murphy (Dempsey); Carr
(O'Byrne), Kilbane, Maher, Baker (Coll), Harte, Carey,
Turner (Scully), O'Neill, Launders (Foley), Farrelly.

30 May

Republic of Ireland (0) 1 *(Finnan)*
Norway (1) 1 *(Iversen)*   300
Republic of Ireland: Murphy; Carr, Kilbane, Worrell,
Coll, Harte, Finnan, Carey (Scully), Foley (Kelly), Delap,
Mahon.

B INTERNATIONALS

10 Oct

Sweden (0) 1 *(Andersson A)*
Scotland (1) 2 *(Shearer, Brown)*   1232
Scotland: Walker (Gunn); Martin, Whyte, Tweed,
McKinnon, Bernard, Rae, Gemmill, Telfer, Shearer
(Brown), Creaney (Harper).

23 Apr

Denmark (1) 3 *(Larsen 2, Andersen)*
Scotland (0) 0   3796
Scotland: Walker (Watt); McNamara, Whyte, Lambert,
Martin, O'Neil (Robertson), Nevin, Jess, McGinlay
(Booth), Durie (Shearer), Glass (Cameron).

MITRE UNDER-21 CHALLENGE

Huddersfield, 14 November 1995

Football League (1) 1 *(Moore)*
Italy Serie B (1) 1 *(Cammarata)*   8107
Football League: Watson; Makin (Smith J), Thatcher,
Makel, Rufus, Rowett, Smith M (Sturridge), Bullock
(Jones), Moore, Whalley, Gray (Lambert).
Italy Serie B: Brunner; Nicola, Colonnello, Ruliano,
Cardone, Cavallo, Tommasi, Torbidoni, Grabbi,
Tedesco, Cammarta.

INTERNATIONAL MANAGERS

England

Walter Winterbottom 1946–1962 (after period as coach);
Alf Ramsey 1963–1974; Joe Mercer (caretaker) 1974;
Don Revie 1974–1977; Ron Greenwood 1977–1982;
Bobby Robson 1982–1990; Graham Taylor 1990–1993;
Terry Venables (coach) 1994–1996; Glenn Hoddle from
May 1996.

Northern Ireland

Billy Bingham 1967–1971; Terry Neill 1971–1975; Dave
Clements (player-manager)1975–76; Danny Blanchflower
1976–1979; Billy Bingham 1980–1993; Bryan Hamilton
from February 1994.

Scotland

Bobby Brown 1967–1971; Tommy Docherty 1971–1972;
Willie Ormond 1973–1977; Ally MacLeod 1977–1978;

Jock Stein 1978–1985; Alex Ferguson (caretaker)
1985–1986; Andy Roxburgh (coach) 1986–1993; Craig
Brown from September 1993.

Wales

Mike Smith 1974–1979; Mike England 1980–1988; David
Williams (caretaker) 1988; Terry Yorath 1988–1993; John
Toshack 1994 for one match; Mike Smith 1994–1995;
Bobby Gould from August 1995.

Republic of Ireland

Liam Tuohy 1971–1972; Johnny Giles 1973–1980 (after
period as player-manager); Eoin Hand 1980–1985; Jack
Charlton 1986–1996; Mick McCarthy from February
1996.

UNDER-21 APPEARANCES 1976–1996

ENGLAND

Ablett, G. (Liverpool), 1988 v F (1)

Adams, A. (Arsenal). 1985 v Ei, Fi; 1986 v D; 1987 v Se, Y (5)

Adams, N. (Everton), 1987 v Se (1)

Allen, B. (QPR), 1992 v H, M, Cz, F; 1993 v N (sub), T, P, Cz (sub) (8)

Allen, C. A. (Oxford U), 1995 v Br (sub), F (sub) (2)

Allen, C. (QPR), 1980 v EG (sub); (with C Palace), 1981 v N, R (3)

Allen, M. (QPR), 1987 v Se (sub); 1988 v Y (sub) (2)

Allen, P. (West Ham U), 1985 v Ei, R; (with Tottenham H, 1986 v R (3)

Anderson, V. A. (Nottingham F), 1978 v I (1)

Anderton, D. R. (Tottenham H), 1993 v Sp, Sm, Ho, Pol, N, P, Cz, Br, S, F; 1994 v Pol, Sm (12)

Andrews, I. (Leicester C), 1987 v Se (1)

Ardley, N. C. (Wimbledon), 1993 v Pol, N, P, Cz, Br, S, F, 1994 v Pol (sub), Ho, Sm (10)

Ashcroft, L. (Preston NE), 1992 v H (sub) (1)

Atherton, P. (Coventry C), 1992 v T (1)

Atkinson, B. (Sunderland), 1991 v W (sub), Sen, M, USSR (sub), F; 1992 v Pol (sub) (6)

Awford, A. T. (Portsmouth), 1993 v Sp, N, T, P, Cz, Br, S, F; 1994 v Ho (9)

Bailey, G. R. (Manchester U), 1979 v W, Bul; 1980 v D, S (2), EG; 1982 v N; 1983 v D, Gr; 1984 v H, F (2), I, Sp (14)

Baker, G. E. (Southampton), 1981 v N, R (2)

Barker, S. (Blackburn R), 1985 v Is (sub), Ei, R; 1986 v I (4)

Barmby, N. J. (Tottenham H), 1994 v D; 1995 v P, A (sub) (3)

Bannister, G. (Sheffield W), 1982 v Pol (1)

Barnes, J. (Watford), 1983 v D, Gr (2)

Barnes, P. S. (Manchester C), 1977 v W (sub), S, Fi, N; 1978 v N, Fi, I (2), Y (9)

Barrett, E. D. (Oldham Ath), 1990 v P, F, USSR, Cz (4)

Bart-Williams, C. G. (Sheffield W), 1993 v Sp, N, T; 1994 v D, Ru, F, Bel, P; 1995 v P, A, Ei (2), La (2); (with Nottingham F) 1996 v P (sub), A (16)

Batty, D. (Leeds U), 1988 v Sw (sub); 1989 v Gr (sub), Bul, Sen, Ei, US; 1990 v Pol (7)

Bazeley, D. S. (Watford), 1992 v H (sub) (1)

Beagrie, P. (Sheffield U), 1988 v WG, T (2)

Beardsmore, R. (Manchester U), 1989 v Gr, Alb (sub), Pol, Bul, USA (5)

Beckham, D. R. J. (Manchester U), 1995 v Br, Mal, An, F; 1996 v P, A (sub), Bel, An, P (9)

Beeston, C (Stoke C), 1988 v USSR (1)

Bertschin, K. E. (Birmingham C), 1977 v S; 1978 v Y (2) (3)

Birtles, G. (Nottingham F), 1980 v Bul, EG (sub) (2)

Blackwell, D. R. (Wimbledon), 1991 v W, T, Sen (sub), M, USSR, F (6)

Blake, M. A. (Aston Villa), 1990 v F (sub), Cz (sub); 1991 v H, Pol, Ei (2), W; 1992 v Pol (8)

Blissett, L. L. (Watford), 1979 v W, Bul (sub), Se; 1980 v D (4)

Booth, A. D. (Huddersfield T), 1995 v La (2 subs); 1996 v N (3)

Bowyer, L. D. (Charlton Ath), 1996 v N (sub), Bel, P, Br (4)

Bracewell, P. (Stoke C), 1983 v D, Gr (1 + 1 sub), H; 1984 v D, H, F (2), I (2), Sp (2); 1985 v T (13)

Bradshaw, P. W. (Wolverhampton W), 1977 v W, S; 1978 v Fi, Y (4)

Breacker, T. (Luton T), 1986 v I (2) (2)

Brennan, M. (Ipswich T), 1987 v Y, Sp, T, Mor, F (5)

Brightwell, I. (Manchester C), 1989 v D, Alb; 1990 v Se (sub), Pol (4)

Briscoe, L. S. (Sheffield W), 1996 v Cro, Bel (sub), An, Br (4)

Brock, K. (Oxford U), 1984 v I, Sp (2); 1986 v I (4)

Brown, M. R. (Manchester C), 1996 v Cro, Bel, An, P (4)

Bull, S. G. (Wolverhampton W), 1989 v Alb (2) Pol; 1990 v Se, Pol (5)

Burrows, D. (WBA), 1989 v Se (sub); (with Liverpool), Gr, Alb (2), Pol; 1990 v Se, Pol (7)

Butcher, T. I. (Ipswich T), 1979 v Se; 1980 v D, Bul, S (2), EG (2) (7)

Butt, N. (Manchester U), 1995 v Ei (2), La; 1996 v P, A (5)

Butters, G. (Tottenham H), 1989 v Bul, Sen (sub), Ei (sub) (3)

Butterworth, I. (Coventry C), 1985 v T, R; (with Nottingham F), 1986 v R, T, D (2), I (2) (8)

Caesar, G. (Arsenal), 1987 v Mor, USSR (sub), F (3)

Callaghan, N. (Watford), 1983 v D, Gr (sub), H (sub); 1984 v D, H, F (2), I, Sp (9)

Campbell, K. J. (Arsenal), 1991 v H, T (sub); 1992 v G, T (4)

Campbell, S. (Tottenham), 1994 v D, Ru, F, US, Bel, P; 1995 v P, A, Ei; 1996 v N, A (11)

Carbon, M. P. (Derby Co), 1996 v Cro (sub) (1)

Carr, C. (Fulham), 1985 v Ei (sub) (1)

Carr, F. (Nottingham F), 1987 v Se, Y, Sp (sub), Mor, USSR; 1988 v WG (sub), T, Y, F (9)

Casper, C. M. (Manchester U), 1995 v Mal (1)

Caton, T. (Manchester C), 1982 v N, H (sub), Pol (2), S; 1983 v WG (2), Gr; 1984 v D, H, F (2), I (2) (14)

Challis, T. M. (QPR), 1996 v An, P (2)

Chamberlain, M. (Stoke C), 1983 v Gr; 1984 v F (sub), I, Sp (4)

Chapman, L. (Stoke C), 1981 v Ei (1)

Charles, G. A. (Nottingham F), 1991 v H, W (sub), Ei; 1992 v T (4)

Chettle, S. (Nottingham F), 1988 v M, USSR, Mor, F; 1989 v D, Se, Gr, Alb (2), Bul; 1990 v Se, Pol (12)

Clark, L. R. (Newcastle U), 1992 v Cz, F; 1993 v Sp, N, T, Ho (sub), Pol (sub), Cz, Br, S; 1994 v Ho (11)

Clough, N. (Nottingham F), 1986 v D (sub); 1987 v Se, Y, T, USSR, F (sub), P; 1988 v WG, T, Y, S (2), M, Mor, F (15)

Cole, A. A. (Arsenal), 1992 v H, Cz, F (sub); (with Bristol C), 1993 v Sm; (with Newcastle U), Pol, N; 1994 v Pol, Ho (8)

Coney, D. (Fulham), 1985 v T (sub); 1986 v R; 1988 v T, WG (4)

Connor, T. (Brighton & HA), 1987 v Y (1)

Cooke, R. (Tottenham H), 1986 v D (sub) (1)

Cooke, T. J. (Manchester U), 1996 v Cro, Bel, An (sub), P (4)

Cooper, C. (Middlesbrough), 1988 v F (2), M, USSR, Mor; 1989 v D, Se, Gr (8)

Corrigan, J. T. (Manchester C), 1978 v I (2), Y (3)

Cottee, A. (West Ham U), 1985 v Fi (sub), Is (sub), Ei, R, Fi; 1987 v Sp, P; 1988 v WG (8)

Couzens, A. J. (Leeds U), 1995 v Mal (sub), An, F (sub) (3)

Cowans, G. S. (Aston Villa), 1979 v W, Se; 1980 v Bul, EG; 1981 v R (5)

Cox, N. J. (Aston Villa), 1993 v T, Ho, Pol, N; 1994 v Pol, Sm (6)

Cranson, I. (Ipswich T), 1985 v Fi, Is, R; 1986 v R, I (5)

Croft, G. (Grimsby T), 1995 v Br, Mal, An, F (4)

Crooks, G. (Stoke C), 1980 v Bul, S (2), EG (sub) (4)

Crossley, M. G. (Nottingham F), 1990 v P, USSR, Cz (3)

Cundy, J. V. (Chelsea), 1991 v Ei (2); 1992 v Pol (3)

Cunningham, L. (WBA), 1977 v S, Fi, N (sub); 1978 v N, Fi, I (6)

Curbishley, L. C. (Birmingham C), 1981 v Sw (1)

Daniel, P. W. (Hull C), 1977 v S, Fi, N; 1978 v Fi, I, Y (2) (7)

Davis, K. G. (Luton T), 1995 v An; 1996 v Cro (sub), P (3)

Davis, P. (Arsenal), 1982 v Pol, S; 1983 v D, Gr (1 + 1 sub), H (sub); 1987 v T; 1988 v WG, T, Y, Fr (11)

Day, C. N. (Tottenham H), 1996 v Cro, Bel, Br (3)

D'Avray, M. (Ipswich T), 1984 v I, Sp (sub) (2)

Deehan, J. M. (Aston Villa), 1977 v N; 1978 v N, Fi, I; 1979 v Bul, Se (sub); 1980 v D (7)

Dennis, M. E. (Birmingham C), 1980 v Bul; 1981 v N, R (3)

Dichio, D. S. E. (QPR), 1996 v N (sub) (1)

Dickens, A. (West Ham U), 1985 v Fi (sub) (1)

Dicks, J. (West Ham U), 1988 v Sw (sub), M, Mor, F (4)

Digby, F. (Swindon T), 1987 v Sp (sub), USSR, P; 1988 v T; 1990 v Pol (5)

Dillon, K. P. (Birmingham C), 1981 v R (1)

Dixon, K. (Chelsea), 1985 v Fi (1)

Dobson, A. (Coventry C), 1989 v Bul, Sen, Ei, US (4)

Dodd, J. R. (Southampton), 1991 v Pol, Ei, T, Sen, M, F; 1992 v G, Pol (8)

Donowa, L. (Norwich C), 1985 v Is, R (sub), Fi (sub) (3)

Dorigo, A. (Aston Villa), 1987 v Se, Sp, T, Mor, USSR, F, P; 1988 v WG, Y, S (2) (11)

Dozzell, J. (Ipswich T), 1987 v Se, Y (sub), Sp, USSR, F, P; 1989 v Se, Gr (sub); 1990 v Se (sub) (9)

Draper, M. A. (Notts Co), 1991 v Ei (sub); 1992 v G, Pol (3)

Duxbury, M. (Manchester U), 1981 v Sw (sub), Ei (sub), R (sub), Sw; 1982 v N; 1983 v WG (2) (7)

Dyer, B. A. (Crystal Palace), 1994 v Ru, F, US, Bel, P; 1995 v P (sub); 1996 v Cro (7)

Dyson, P. I. (Coventry C), 1981 v N, R, Sw, Ei (4)

Eadie, D. M. (Norwich C), 1994 v F (sub), US (2)

Ebbrell, J. (Everton), 1989 v Sen, Ei, US (sub); 1990 v P, F, USSR, Cz; 1991 v H, Pol, Ei, W, T; 1992 v G, T (14)

Edghill, R. A. (Manchester C), 1994 v D, Ru; 1995 v A (3)

Ehiogu, U. (Aston Villa), 1992 v H, M, Cz, F; 1993 v Sp, N, T, Sm, T, Ho, Pol, N; 1994 v Pol, Ho, Sm (15)

Elliott, P. (Luton T), 1985 v Fi; 1986 v T, D (3)

Elliott, R. J. (Newcastle U), 1996 v P, A (2)

Fairclough, C. (Nottingham F), 1985 v T, Is, Ei; 1987 v Sp, T; (with Tottenham H), 1988 v Y, F (7)

Fairclough, D. (Liverpool), 1977 v W (1)

Fashanu, J. (Norwich C), 1980 v EG; 1981 v N (sub), R, Sw, Ei (sub), H; (with Nottingham F), 1982 v N, H, Pol, S; 1983 v WG (sub) (11)

Fear, P. (Wimbledon), 1994 v Ru, F, US (sub) (3)

Fenton, G. A. (Aston Villa), 1995 v Ei (1)

Fenwick, T. W. (C Palace), 1981 v N, R, Sw, Ei; (with QPR), R; 1982 v N, H, S (2); 1983 v WG (2) (11)

Fereday, W. (QPR), 1985 v T, Ei (sub). Fi; 1986 v T (sub), I (5)

Flitcroft, G. W. (Manchester C), 1993 v Sm, Hol, N, P, Cz, Br, S, F; 1994 v Pol, Ho (10)

Flowers, T. (Southampton), 1987 v Mor, F; 1988 v WG (sub) (3)

Ford, M. (Leeds U), 1996 v Cro (1)

Forster, N. M. (Brentford), 1995 v Br, Mal, An, F (4)

Forsyth, M. (Derby Co), 1988 v Sw (1)

Foster, S. (Brighton & HA), 1980 v EG (sub) (1)

Fowler, R. B. (Liverpool), 1994 v Sm, Ru (sub), F, US; 1995 v P, A; 1996 v P, A (8)

Froggatt, S. J. (Aston Villa), 1993 v Sp, Sm (sub) (2)

Futcher, P. (Luton T), 1977 v W, S, Fi, N; (with Manchester C), 1978 v N, Fi, I (2), Y (2); 1979 v D (11)

Gabbiadini, M. (Sunderland), 1989 v Bul, USA (2)

Gale, A. (Fulham), 1982 v Pol (1)

Gallen, K. A. (QPR), 1995 v Ei, La (2); 1996 v Cro (4)

Gascoigne, P. (Newcastle U), 1987 v Mo, USSR, P; 1988 v WG, Y, S (2), F (2), Sw, M, USSR (sub), Mor (13)

Gayle, H. (Birmingham C), 1984 v I, Sp (2) (3)

Gernon, T. (Ipswich T), 1983 v Gr (1)

Gerrard, P. W. (Oldham Ath), 1993 v T, Ho, Pol, N, P, Cz, Br, S, F; 1994 v D, Ru; 1995 v P, A, Ei (2), La (2); 1996 v P (18)

Gibbs, N. (Watford), 1987 v Mor, USSR, F, P; 1988 v T (5)

Gibson, C. (Aston Villa), 1982 v N (1)

Gilbert, W. A. (C Palace), 1979 v W, Bul; 1980 v Bul; 1981 v N, R, Sw, R, Sw, H; 1982 v N (sub), H (11)

Goddard, P. (West Ham U), 1981 v N, Sw, Ei (sub); 1982 v N (sub), Pol, S; 1983 v WG (2) (8)

Gordon, D. (Norwich C), 1987 v T (sub), Mor (sub), F, P (4)

Gordon, D. D. (Crystal Palace), 1994 v Ru, F, US, Bel, P; 1995 v P, A, Ei (2), La (2); 1996 v P, N (13)

Grant, A. J. (Everton), 1996 v An (sub) (1)

Gray, A. (Aston Villa), 1988 v S, F (2)

Haigh, P. (Hull C), 1977 v N (sub) (1)

Hall, R. A. (Southampton), 1992 v H (sub), F; 1993 v Sm, T, Ho, Pol, P, Cz, Br, S, F (11)

Hardyman, P. (Portsmouth), 1985 v Ei; 1986 v D (2)

Hateley, M. (Coventry C), 1982 v Pol, S; 1983 v Gr (2), H; (with Portsmouth), 1984 v F (2), I, Sp (2) (10)

Hayes, M. (Arsenal), 1987 v Sp, T; 1988 v F (sub) (3)

Hazell, R. J. (Wolverhampton W), 1979 v D (1)

Heaney, N. A. (Arsenal), 1992 v H, M, Cz, F; 1993 v N, T (6)

Heath, A. (Stoke C), 1981 v R, Sw, H; 1982 v N, H; (with Everton), Pol, S; 1983 v WG (8)

Hendon, I. M. (Tottenham H), 1992 v H, M, Cz, F; 1993 v Sp, N, T (7)

Hendrie, L. A. (Aston Villa), 1996 v Cro (sub) (1)

Hesford, I. (Blackpool), 1981 v Ei (sub), Pol (2), S (2); 1983 v WG (2) (6)

Hilaire, V. (C Palace), 1980 v Bul, S (1+1 sub), EG (2); 1981 v N, R, Sw (sub); 1982 v Pol (sub) (9)

Hill, D. R. L. (Tottenham H), 1995 v Br, Mal, An, F (4)

Hillier, D. (Arsenal), 1991 v T (1)

Hinchcliffe, A. (Manchester C), 1989 v D (1)

Hinshelwood, P. A. (C Palace), 1978 v N; 1980 v EG (2)

Hirst, D. (Sheffield W), 1988 v USSR, F; 1989 v D, Bul (sub), Sen, Ei, US (7)

Hoddle, G. (Tottenham H), 1977 v W (sub); 1978 v Fi (sub), I (2), Y; 1979 v D, W, Bul; 1980 v S (2), EG (2) (12)

Hodge, S. (Nottingham F), 1983 v Gr (sub); 1984 v D, F, I, Sp (2); (with Aston Villa), 1986 v R, T (8)

Hodgson, D. J. (Middlesbrough), 1981 v N, R (sub), Sw, Ei; 1982 v Pol; 1983 v WG (6)

Holdsworth, D. (Watford), 1989 v Gr (sub) (1)

Holland, C. J. (Newcastle U), 1995 v La; 1996 v N (sub), A (sub), Cro, Bel, An, Br (7)

Holland, P. (Mansfield T), 1995 v Br, Mal, An, F (4)

Horne, B. (Millwall), 1989 v Gr (sub), Pol, Bul, Ei, US (5)

Hucker, P. (QPR), 1984 v I, Sp (2)

Impey, A. R. (QPR), 1993 v T (1)

Ince, P. (West Ham U), 1989 v Alb; 1990 v Se (2)

Jackson, M. A. (Everton), 1992 v H, M, Cz, F; 1993 v Sm (sub), T, Ho, Pol, N; 1994 v Pol (10)

James, D. (Watford), 1991 v Ei (2), T, Sen, M, USSR, F; 1992 v G, T, Pol (10)

James, J. C. (Luton T), 1990 v F, USSR (2)

Jemson, N. B. (Nottingham F), 1991 v W (1)

Joachim, J. K. (Leicester C), 1994 v D (sub); 1995 v P, A, Ei, Br, Mal, An, F; 1996 v N (9)

Johnson, T. (Notts Co), 1991 v H (sub), Ei (sub); 1992 v G, T, Pol; (with Derby Co), M, Cz (sub) (7)

Johnston, C. P. (Middlesbrough), 1981 v N, Ei (2)

Jones, D. R. (Everton), 1977 v W (1)

Jones, C. H. (Tottenham H), 1978 v Y (sub) (1)

Jones, R. (Liverpool), 1993 v Sm, Ho (2)

Keegan, G. A. (Manchester C), 1977 v W (1)

Kenny, W. (Everton), 1993 v T (1)

Keown, M. (Aston Villa), 1987 v Sp, Mor, USSR, P; 1988 v T, S, F (2) (8)

Kerslake, D. (QPR), 1986 v T (1)

Kilcline, B. (Notts C), 1983 v D, Gr (2)

King, A. E. (Everton), 1977 v W; 1978 v Y (2)

Kitson, P. (Leicester C), 1991 v Sen (sub), M, F; 1992 v Pol; (with Derby Co), M, Cz, F (7)

Knight, A. (Portsmouth), 1983 v Gr, H (2)

Knight, I. (Sheffield W), 1987 v Se (sub), Y (2)

Lake, P. (Manchester C), 1989 v D, Alb (2), Pol; 1990 v Pol (5)

Langley, T. W. (Chelsea), 1978 v I (sub) (1)

Lee, D. J. (Chelsea), 1990 v F; 1991 v H, Pol, Ei (2), T, Sen, USSR, F; 1992 v Pol (10)

Lee, R. (Charlton Ath), 1986 v I (sub); 1987 v Se (sub) (2)

Lee, S. (Liverpool), 1981 v R, Sw, H; 1982 v S; 1983 v WG (2) (6)

Le Saux, G. (Chelsea), 1990 v P, F, USSR, Cz (4)

Lowe, D. (Ipswich T), 1988 v F, Sw (sub) (2)

Lukic, J. (Leeds U), 1981 v N, R, Ei, R, Sw, H; 1982 v H (7)

Lund, G. (Grimsby T), 1985 v T; 1986 v R, T (3)

McCall, S. H. (Ipswich T), 1981 v Sw, H; 1982 v H, S; 1983 v WG (2) (6)

McDonald, N. (Newcastle U), 1987 v Se (sub), Sp, T; 1988 v WG, Y (sub) (5)

McGrath, L. (Coventry C), 1986 v D (1)

MacKenzie, S. (WBA), 1982 v N, S (2) (3)

McLeary, A. (Millwall), 1988 v Sw (1)

McMahon, S. (Everton), 1981 v Ei; 1982 v Pol; 1983 v D, Gr (2); (with Aston Villa), 1984 v H (6)

McManaman, S. (Liverpool), 1991 v W, M (sub); 1993 v N, T, Sm, T; 1994 v Pol (7)

Mabbutt, G. (Bristol R), 1982 v Pol (2), S; (with Tottenham H), 1983 v D; 1984 v F; 1986 v D, I (7)

Makin, C. (Oldham Ath), 1994 v Ru (sub), F, US, Bel, P (5)

Marriott, A. (Nottingham F), 1992 v M (1)

Marshall, A. J. (Norwich C), 1995 v Mal, An (2)

Martin, L. (Manchester U), 1989 v Gr (sub), Alb (sub) (2)

Martyn, N. (Bristol R), 1988 v S (sub), M, USSR, Mor, F; 1989 v D, Se, Gr, Alb (2); 1990 v Se (11)

Matteo, D. (Liverpool), 1994 v F (sub), Bel, P (3)

Matthew, D. (Chelsea), 1990 v P, USSR (sub), Cz; 1991 v Ei, M, USSR, F; 1992 v G (sub), T (9)

May, A. (Manchester C), 1986 v I (sub) (1)

Merson, P. (Arsenal), 1989 v D, Gr, Pol (sub); 1990 v Pol (4)

Middleton, J. (Nottingham F), 1977 v Fi, N; (with Derby Co), 1978 v N (3)

Miller, A. (Arsenal), 1988 v Mor (sub); 1989 v Sen; 1991 v H, Pol (4)

Mills, G. R. (Nottingham F), 1981 v R; 1982 v N (2)

Mimms, R. (Rotherham U), 1985 v Is (sub), Ei (sub); (with Everton), 1986 v I (3)

Minto, S. C. (Charlton Ath), 1991 v W; 1992 v H, M, Cz; 1993 v T; 1994 v Ho (6)

Moore, I. (Tranmere R), 1996 v Cro (sub), Bel (sub), An, P, Br (5)

Moran, S. (Southampton), 1982 v N (sub); 1984 v F (2)

Morgan, S. (Leicester C), 1987 v Se, Y (2)

Mortimer, P. (Charlton Ath), 1989 v Sen, Ei (2)

Moses, R. M. (WBA), 1981 v N (sub), Sw, Ei, R, Sw, H; 1982 v N (sub); (with Manchester U), H (8)

Mountfield, D. (Everton), 1984 v Sp (1)

Muggleton, C. D. (Leicester C), 1990 v F (1)

Mutch, A. (Wolverhampton W), 1989 v Pol (1)

Myers, A. (Chelsea), 1995 v Br, Mal, An (sub), F (4)

Nethercott, S. (Tottenham), 1994 v D, Ru, F, US, Bel, P; 1995 v La (2) (8)

Neville, P. J. (Manchester U), 1995 v Br, Mal, An, F; 1996 v P, N (sub) (6)

Newell, M. (Luton T), 1986 v D (1 + 1 sub), I (1 + 1 sub) (4)

Newton, E. J. I. (Chelsea), 1993 v T (sub); 1994 v Sm (2)

Nicholls, A. (Plymouth Arg), 1994 v F (1)

Oakes, M. C. (Aston Villa), 1994 v D (sub), F (sub), US, Bel, P; 1996 v A (6)

Oakes, S. J. (Luton T), 1993 v Br (sub) (1)

O'Connor, J. (Everton), 1996 v Cro, An, Br (3)

Oldfield, D. (Luton T), 1989 v Se (1)

Olney, I. A. (Aston Villa), 1990 v P, F, USSR, Cz; 1991 v H, Pol, Ei (2), T; 1992 v Pol (sub) (10)

Ord, R. J. (Sunderland), 1991 v W, M, USSR (3)

Osman, R. C. (Ipswich T), 1979 v W (sub), Se; 1980 v D, S (2), EG (2) (7)

Owen, G. A. (Manchester C), 1977 v S, Fi, N; 1978 v N, Fi, I (2), Y; 1979 v D, W; (with WBA), Bul, Se (sub); 1980 v D, S (2), EG; 1981 v Sw, R; 1982 v N (sub), H; 1983 v WG (2) (22)

Painter, I. (Stoke C), 1986 v I (1)

Palmer, C. (Sheffield W), 1989 v Bul, Sen, Ei, US (4)

Parker, G. (Hull C), 1986 v I (2); (with Nottingham F), F; 1987 v Se, Y (sub), Sp (6)

Parker, P. (Fulham), 1985 v Fi, T, Is (sub), Ei, R, Fi; 1986 v T, D (8)

Parkes, P. B. F. (QPR), 1979 v D (1)

Parkin, S. (Stoke C), 1987 v Sp (sub); 1988 v WG (sub), T, S (sub), F (5)

Parlour, R. (Arsenal), 1992 v H, M, Cz, F; 1993 v Sp, N, T; 1994 v D, Ru, Bel, P; 1995 v A (12)

Peach, D. S. (Southampton), 1977 v S, Fi, N; 1978 v N, I (2) (6)

Peake, A. (Leicester C), 1982 v Pol (1)

Pearce, I. A. (Blackburn R), 1995 v Ei, La; 1996 v N (3)

Pearce, S. (Nottingham F), 1987 v Y (1)

Pickering N. (Sunderland), 1983 v D (sub), Gr, H; 1984 v F (sub + 1), I (2), Sp; 1985 v Is, R, Fi; 1986 v R, T; (with Coventry C), D, I (15)

Platt, D. (Aston Villa), 1988 v M, Mor, F (3)

Plummer, C. S. (QPR), 1996 v Cro (sub), Bel, An, P (sub), Br (5)

Pollock, J. (Middlesbrough), 1995 v Ei (sub); 1996 v N, A (3)

Porter, G. (Watford), 1987 v Sp (sub), T, Mor, USSR, F, P (sub); 1988 v T (sub), Y, S (2), F, Sw (12)

Pressman, K. (Sheffield W), 1989 v D (sub) (1)

Proctor, M. (Middlesbrough), 1981 v Ei (sub), Sw; (with Nottingham F) 1982 v N, Pol (4)

Ramage, C. D. (Derby Co), 1991 v Pol (sub), W; 1992 v Fr (sub) (3)

Ranson, R. (Manchester C), 1980 v Bul, EG; 1981 v R (sub), R, Sw (1 + 1 sub), H, Pol (2), S (10)

Redknapp, J. F. (Liverpool), 1993 v Sm, Pol, N, P, Cz, Br, S, F; 1994 v Pol, Ho (sub), D, Ru, F, US, Bel, P; 1995 v P, A (18)

Redmond, S. (Manchester C), 1988 v F (2), M, USSR, Mor, F; 1989 v D, Se, Gr, Alb (2), Pol; 1990 v Se, Pol (14)

Reeves, K. P. (Norwich C), 1978 v I, Y (2); 1979 v N, W, Bul, Sw; 1980 v D, S; (with Manchester C), EG (10)

Regis, C. (WBA), 1979 v D, Bul, Se; 1980 v S, EG; 1983 v D (6)

Reid, N. S. (Manchester C), 1981 v H (sub); 1982 v H, Pol (2), S (2) (6)

Reid, P. (Bolton W), 1977 v S, Fi, N; 1978 v Fi, I, Y (6)

Richards, D. I. (Wolverhampton W), 1995 v Br, Mal, An, F (4)

Richards, J. P. (Wolverhampton W), 1977 v Fi, N (2)

Rideout, P. (Aston Villa), 1985 v Fi, Is, Ei (sub), R; (with Bari), 1986 v D (5)

Ripley, S. (Middlesbrough), 1988 v USSR, F (sub); 1989 v D (sub), Se, Gr, Alb (2); 1990 v Se (8)

Ritchie, A. (Brighton & HA), 1982 v Pol (1)

Rix, G. (Arsenal), 1978 v Fi (sub), Y; 1979 v D, Se; 1980 v D (sub), Bul, S (7)

Roberts, A. J. (Millwall), 1995 v Ei, La (2); (with C Palace), 1996 v N, A (5)

Robins, M. G. (Manchester U), 1990 v P, F, USSR, Cz; 1991 v H (sub), Pol (6)

Robson, B. (WBA), 1979 v W, Bul (sub), Se; 1980 v D, Bul, S (2) (7)

Robson, S. (Arsenal), 1984 v I; 1985 v Fi, Is, Fi; 1986 v R, I (with West Ham U); 1988 v S, Sw (8)

Rocastle, D. (Arsenal), 1987 v Se, Y, Sp, T; 1988 v WG, T, Y, S (2), F (2 subs), M, USSR, Mor (14)

Rodger, G. (Coventry C), 1987 v USSR, F, P; 1988 v WG (4)

Rosario, R. (Norwich C), 1987 v T (sub), Mor, F, P (sub) (4)

Rowell, G. (Sunderland), 1977 v Fi (1)

Ruddock, N. (Southampton), 1989 v Bul (sub), Sen, Ei, US (4)

Rufus, R. R. (Charlton Ath), 1996 v Cro, Bel, An, P, Br (5)

Ryan, J. (Oldham Ath), 1983 v H (1)

Ryder, S.H. (Walsall), 1995 v Br, An, F (3)

Samways, V. (Tottenham H), 1988 v Sw (sub), USSR, F; 1989 v D, Se (5)

Sansom, K. G. (C Palace), 1979 v D, W, Bul, Se; 1980 v S (2), EG (2) (8)

Scimeca, R. (Aston Villa), 1996 v P (1)

Seaman, D. (Birmingham C), 1985 v Fi, T, Is, Ei, R, Fi; 1986 v R, F, D, I (10)

Sedgley, S. (Coventry C), 1987 v USSR, F (sub), P; 1988 v F; 1989 v D (sub), Se, Gr, Alb (2), Pol; (with Tottenham H), 1990 v Se (11)

Sellars, S. (Blackburn R), 1988 v S (sub), F, Sw (3)

Selley, I. (Arsenal), 1994 v Ru (sub), F (sub), US (3)

Sharpe, L. (Manchester U), 1989 v Gr; 1990 v P (sub), F, USSR, Cz; 1991 v H, Pol (sub), Ei (8)

Shaw, G. R. (Aston Villa), 1981 v Ei, Sw, H; 1982 v H, S; 1983 v WG (2) (7)

Shearer, A. (Southampton), 1991 v Ei (2), W, T, Sen, M, USSR, F; 1992 v G, T, Pol (11)

Shelton, G. (Sheffield W), 1985 v Fi (1)

Sheringham, T. (Millwall), 1988 v Sw (1)

Sheron, M. N. (Manchester C), 1992 v H, F; 1993 v N (sub), T (sub), Sm, Ho, Pol, N, P, Cz, Br, S, F; 1994 v Pol (sub), Ho, Sm (16)

Sherwood, T. A. (Norwich C), 1990 v P, F, USSR, Cz (4)

Shipperley, N. J. (Chelsea), 1994 v Sm (sub); (with Southampton) 1995 v Ei, La (2); 1996 v P, N, A (7)

Simpson, P. (Manchester C), 1986 v D (sub); 1987 v Y, Mor, F, P (5)

Sims, S. (Leicester C), 1977 v W, S, Fi, N; 1978 v N, Fi, I (2), Y (2) (10)

Sinclair, F. M. (Chelsea), 1994 v Ho, Sm, D, Ru, F, US, Bel, P (8)

Sinclair, T. (QPR), 1995 v P, Ei (2), La; 1996 v P (5)

Sinnott, L. (Watford), 1985 v Is (sub) (1)

Slade, S. A. (Tottenham H), 1996 v Bel, An, P, Br (4)

Slater, S. I. (West Ham U), 1990 v P, USSR (sub), Cz (sub) (3)

Small, B. (Aston Villa), 1993 v Sm, T, Ho, Pol, N, P, Cz, Br, S, F; 1994 v Pol, Sm (12)

Smith, D. (Coventry C), 1988 v M, USSR (sub), Mor; 1989 v D, Se, Alb (2), Pol; 1990 v Se, Pol (10)

Smith, M. (Sheffield W), 1981 v Ei, R, Sw, H; 1982 v Pol (sub) (5)

Smith, M. (Sunderland), 1995 v Ei (sub) (1)

Snodin, I. (Doncaster R), 1985 v T, Is, R, Fi (4)

Statham, B. (Tottenham H), 1988 v Sw; 1989 v D (sub), Se (3)

Statham, D. J. (WBA), 1978 v Fi, 1979 v W, Bul, Se; 1980 v D; 1983 v D (6)

Stein, B. (Luton T), 1984 v D, H, I (3)

Sterland, M. (Sheffield W), 1984 v D, H, F (2), I, Sp (2) (7)

Steven, T. (Everton), 1985 v Fi, T (2)

Stevens, G. (Brighton & HA), 1983 v H; (with Tottenham H), 1984 v H, F (1+1 sub), I (sub), Sp (1+1 sub); 1986 v I (8)

Stewart, P. (Manchester C), 1988 v F (1)

Stuart, G. C. (Chelsea), 1990 v P (sub), F, USSR, Cz; 1991 v T (sub) (5)
Stuart, J. C. (Charlton Ath), 1996 v Bel, An, P, Br (4)
Suckling, P. (Coventry C), 1986 v D; (with Manchester C), 1987 v Se (sub), Y, Sp, T; (with C Palace), 1988 v S (2), F (2), Sw (10)
Summerbee, N.J. (Swindon T), 1993 v P (sub), S (sub), F (3)
Sunderland, A. (Wolverhampton W), 1977 v W (1)
Sutton, C. R. (Norwich), 1993 v Sp (sub), T (sub + 1),Ho, P (sub), Cz, Br, S, F; 1994 v Pol, Ho, Sm, D (13)
Swindlehurst, D. (C Palace), 1977 v W (1)
Sutch, D. (Norwich C), 1992 v H, M, Cz; 1993 v T (4)

Talbot, B. (Ipswich T), 1977 v W (1)

Thatcher, B. D. (Millwall), 1996 v Cro (1)

Thomas, D. (Coventry C), 1981 v Ei; 1983 v WG (2), Gr, H; (with Tottenham H), I, Sp (7)
Thomas, M. (Luton T), 1986 v T, D, I (3)
Thomas, M. (Arsenal), 1988 v Y, S, F (2), M, USSR, Mor; 1989 v Gr, Alb (2), Pol; 1990 v Se (12)
Thomas, R. E. (Watford), 1990 v P (1)
Thompson, A. (Bolton W), 1995 v La; 1996 v P (2)
Thompson, G. L. (Coventry C), 1981 v R, Sw, H; 1982 v N, H, S (6)
Thorn, A. (Wimbledon), 1988 v WG (sub). Y, S, F, Sw (5)
Thornley, B. L. (Manchester U), 1996 v Bel, P, Br (3)
Tiler, C. (Barnsley), 1990 v P, USSR, Cz; 1991 v H, Pol, Ei (2), T, Sen, USSR, F; (with Nottingham F), 1992 v G, T (13)

Unsworth, D. G. (Everton), 1995 v A, Ei (2), La; 1996 v N, A (6)

Venison, B. (Sunderland), 1983 v D, Gr; 1985 v Fi, T, Is, Fi; 1986 v R, T, D (2) (10)
Vinnicombe, C. (Rangers), 1991 v H (sub), Pol, Ei (2), T, Sen, M, USSR (sub), F; 1992 v G, T, Pol (12)

Waddle, C. (Newcastle U), 1985 v Fi (1)
Wallace, D. (Southampton), 1983 v Gr, H; 1984 v D, H, F (2), I, Sp (sub); 1985 v Fi, T, Is; 1986 v R, D, I (14)
Wallace, Ray (Southampton), 1989 v Bul, Sen (sub), Ei; 1990 v Se (4)
Wallace, Rod (Southampton), 1989 v Bul, Ei (sub), US; 1991 v H, Pol, Ei, T, Sen, M, USSR, F (11)
Walker, D. (Nottingham F), 1985 v Fi; 1987 v Se, T; 1988 v WG, T, S (2) (7)
Walker, I. M. (Tottenham H), 1991 v W; 1992 v H, Cz, F; 1993 v Sp, N, T, Sm; 1994 v Pol (9)
Walsh, G. (Manchester U), 1988 v WG, Y (2)
Walsh, P. M. (Luton T), 1983 v D (sub), Gr (2), H (4)
Walters, K. (Aston Villa), 1984 v D (sub), H (sub); 1985 v Is, Ei, R; 1986 v R, T, D, I (sub) (9)
Ward, P. D. (Brighton & HA), 1978 v N; 1980 v EG (2)
Warhurst, P. (Oldham Ath), 1991 v H, Pol, W, Sen, M (sub), USSR, F (sub); (with Sheffield W), 1992 v G (8)
Watson, D. (Norwich C), 1984 v D, F (2), I (2), Sp (2) (7)
Watson, D. N. (Barnsley), 1994 v Ho, Sm; 1995 v Br, F; 1996 v N (5)
Watson, G. (Sheffield W), 1991 v Sen, USSR (2)
Watson, S. C. (Newcastle U), 1993 v Sp (sub), N; 1994 v Sm (sub), D; 1995 v P, A, Ei (2), La (2); 1996 v N, A (12)
Webb, N. (Portsmouth), 1985 v Ei; (with Nottingham F), 1986 v D (2) (3)
Whelan, P. J. (Ipswich T), 1993 v Sp, T (sub), P (3)
Whelan, N. (Leeds U), 1995 v A (sub), Ei (2)
White, D. (Manchester U), 1988 v S (2), F, USSR; 1989 v Se; 1990 v Pol (6)
Whyte, C. (Arsenal), 1982 v S (1+1 sub); 1983 v D, Gr (4)
Wicks, S. (QPR), 1982 v S (1)
Wilkins, R. C. (Chelsea), 1977 v W (1)
Wilkinson, P. (Grimsby T), 1985 v Ei, R (sub); (with Everton), 1986 v R (sub), I (4)
Williams, P. (Charlton Ath), 1989 v Bul, Sen, Ei, US (sub) (4)
Williams, P. D. (Derby Co), 1991 v Sen, M, USSR; 1992 v G, T, Pol (6)
Williams, S. C. (Southampton), 1977 v S, Fi, N; 1978 v N, I (1 + 1 sub), Y (2); 1979 v D, Bul, Se (sub); 1980 v D, EG (2) (14)
Winterburn, N. (Wimbledon), 1986 v I (1)
Wise, D. (Chelsea), 1991 v Sen, USSR (2)
Woodcook, A. S. (Nottingham F), 1978 v Fi, I (2)
Woods, C. C. E. (Nottingham F), 1979 v W (sub), Se; (with QPR), 1980 v Bul, EG; 1981 v Sw; (with Norwich C), 1984 v D (6)

Wright, A. G. (Blackburn), 1993 v Sp, N (2)
Wright, M. (Southampton), 1983 v Gr, H; 1984 v D, H (4)
Wright, W. (Everton), 1979 v D, W, Bul; 1980 v D, S (2) (6)

Yates, D. (Notts Co), 1989 v D (sub), Bul, Sen, Ei, US (5)

SCOTLAND

Aitken, R. (Celtic), 1977 v Cz, W, Sw; 1978 v Cz, W; 1979 v P, N (2); 1980 v Bel, E; 1984 v EG, Y (2); 1985 v WG, Ic, Sp (16)
Albiston, A. (Manchester U), 1977 v Cz, W, Sw; 1978 v Sw, Cz (5)
Archdeacon, O. (Celtic), 1987 v WG (sub) (1)
Archibald, S. (Aberdeen), 1980 v B, E (2), WG; (with Tottenham H), 1981 v D (5)

Bain, K. (Dundee), 1993 v P, I, Ma, P (4)
Baker, M. (St. Mirren), 1993 v F, M, E; 1994 v Ma, A; 1995 v Gr, M, F (sub), Sk (sub); 1996 v H (sub) (10)
Bannon, E. J. P. (Hearts), 1979 v US; (with Chelsea), P, N (2); (with Dundee U), 1980 v Bel, WG, E (7)
Beattie, J. (St Mirren), 1992 v D, US, P, Y (4)
Beaumont, D. (Dundee U), 1985 v Ic (1)
Bell, D. (Aberdeen), 1981 v D; 1984 v Y (2)
Bernard, P. R. J. (Oldham Ath), 1992 v R (sub), D, Se (sub), US; 1993 v Sw, P, I, Ma, P, F, Bul, M, E; 1994 v I, Ma (15)
Bett, J. (Rangers), 1981 v Se, D; 1982 v Se, D, I, E (2) (7)
Black, E. (Aberdeen), 1983 v EG, Sw (2), Bel; 1985 v Ic, Sp (2), Ic (8)
Blair, A. (Coventry C), 1980 v E; 1981 v Se; (with Aston Villa), 1982 v Se, D, I (5)
Bollan, G. (Dundee U), 1992 v D, G (sub), US, P, Y; 1993 v Sw, P, I, P, F, Bul, M, E; 1994 v Sw; 1995 v Cz; (with Rangers) v Ru, Sm (17)
Booth, S. (Aberdeen), 1991 v R (sub), Bul (sub + 1), Pol, F (sub); 1992 v Sw, R, D, Se, US, P, Y; 1993 v Ma, P (14)
Bowes, M. J. (Dunfermline Ath), 1992 v D (sub) (1)
Bowman, D. (Hearts), 1985 v WG (sub) (1)
Boyd, T. (Motherwell), 1987 v WG, Ei (2), Bel; 1988 v Bel (5)
Brazil, A. (Hibernian), 1978 v W (1)
Brazil, A. (Ipswich T), 1979 v N; 1980 v Bel (2), E (2), WG; 1981 v Se; 1982 v Se (8)
Brough, J. (Hearts), 1981 v D (1)
Burley, G. E. (Ipswich T), 1977 v Cz, W, Sw; 1978 v Sw, Cz (5)
Burley, C. (Chelsea), 1992 v D; 1993 v Sw, P, I, P; 1994 v Sw, I (sub) (7)
Burns, H. (Rangers), 1985 v Sp, Ic (sub) (2)
Burns, T. (Celtic), 1977 v Cz, W, E; 1978 v Sw; 1982 v E (5)

Campbell, S. (Dundee), 1989 v N (sub), Y, F (3)
Casey, J. (Celtic), 1978 v W (1)
Christie, M. (Dundee), 1992 v D, P (sub), Y (3)
Clark, R. (Aberdeen), 1977 v Cz, W, Sw (3)
Clarke, S. (St Mirren), 1984 v Bel, EG, Y; 1985 v WG, Ic, Sp (2), Ic (8)
Cleland, A. (Dundee U), 1990 v F, N (2); 1991 v R, Sw, Bul; 1992 v Sw, R, G, Se (2) (11)
Collins, J. (Hibernian), 1988 v Bel, E; 1989 v N, Y, F; 1990 v Y, F, N (8)
Connolly, P. (Dundee U), 1991 v R (sub), Sw, Bul (3)
Connor, R. (Ayr U), 1981 v Se; 1982 v Se (2)
Cooper, D. (Clydebank), 1977 v Cz, W, Sw, E; (with Rangers), 1978 v Sw, Cz (6)
Cooper, N. (Aberdeen), 1982 v D, E (2); 1983 v Bel, EG, Sw (2); 1984 v Bel, EG, Y; 1985 v Ic, Sp, Ic (13)
Crabbe, S. (Hearts), 1990 v Y (sub), F (2)
Craig, T. (Newcastle U), 1977 v E (1)
Crainie, D. (Celtic), 1983 v Sw (sub) (1)
Crawford, S. (Raith R), 1994 v A, Eg, P, Bel; 1995 v Fi, Ru,Gr, Ru, Sm, M, F (sub), Sk (sub), Br (sub); 1996 v Gr, Fi (sub), H (1 + sub), Sp (sub), F (sub) (19)
Creaney, G. (Celtic), 1991 v Sw, Bul (2), Pol, F; 1992 v Sw, R, G (2), Se (2) (11)

Dailly, C. (Dundee U), 1991 v R; 1992 v US, R; 1993 v Sw, P, I, Ic, P, F, Bul, M, E; 1994 v Sw, I, Ma, A, Eg, P, Bel; 1995 v Fi, Ru, Gr, Ru, Sm, M, F, Sk, Br; 1996 v Fi, Sm, H (2), Sp, F (34)
Dawson, A. (Rangers), 1979 v P, N (2); 1980 v B (2), E (2), WG (8)
Deas, P. A. (St Johnstone), 1992 v D (sub); 1993 v Ma (2)
Dennis, S. (Raith R), 1992 v Sw (1)
Dickov, P. (Arsenal), 1992 v Y; 1993 v F, M, E (4)

McNichol, J. (Brentford), 1979 v P, N (2); 1980 v Bel (2), WG, E (7)
McNiven, D. (Leeds U), 1977 v Cz, W (sub), Sw (sub) (3)
McNiven, S. A. (Oldham Ath), 1996 v Sm (sub) (1)
McPherson, D. (Rangers), 1984 v Bel; 1985 v Sp; (with Hearts), 1989 v N, Y (4)
McQuilken, J. (Celtic), 1993 v Bul, E (2)
McStay, P. (Celtic), 1983 v EG, Sw (2); 1984 v Y (2) (5)
McWhirter, N. (St Mirren), 1991 v Bul (sub) (1)
Main, A. (Dundee U), 1988 v E; 1989 v Y; 1990 v N (3)
Malpas, M. (Dundee U), 1983 v Bel, Sw (1+1 sub); 1984 v Bel, EG, Y (2); 1985 v Sp (8)
Marshall, S. R. (Arsenal), 1995 v Ru, Gr; 1996 v H, Sp, F (5)
May, E. (Hibernian), 1989 v Y (sub), F (2)
Meldrum, C. (Kilmarnock), 1996 v F (sub) (1)
Melrose, J. (Partick Th), 1977 v Sw; 1979 v US, P, N (2); 1980 v Bel (sub), WG, E (8)
Miller, C. (Rangers), 1995 v Gr, Ru; 1996 v Gr, Sp, F (5)
Miller, J. (Aberdeen), 1987 v Ei (sub); 1988 v Bel; (with Celtic), E; 1989 v N, Y; 1990 v F, N (7)
Miller, W. (Aberdeen), 1978 v Sw, Cz (2)
Miller, W. (Hibernian), 1991 v R, Sw, Bul, Pol, F; 1992 v R, G (sub) (7)
Milne, R. (Dundee U), 1982 v Se (sub); 1984 v Bel, EG (3)
Money, I. C. (St Mirren), 1987 v Ei; 1988 v Bel; 1989 v N (3)
Muir, L. (Hibernian), 1977 v Cz (sub) (1)
Murray, N. (Rangers), 1993 v P (sub), Ma, Ic, P; 1994 v Sw, I; 1995 v Fi, Ru, Gr, Sm; 1996 v Gr (sub), Fi, Sm, H (2), F (16)
Murray, R. (Bournemouth), 1993 v Ic (sub) (1)

Narey, D. (Dundee U), 1977 v Cz, Sw; 1978 v Sw, Cz (4)
Nevin, P. (Chelsea), 1985 v WG, Ic, Sp (2), Ic (5)
Nicholas, C. (Celtic), 1981 v Se; 1982 v Se; 1983 v EG, Sw, Bel; (with Arsenal), 1984 v Y (6)
Nicol, S. (Ayr U), 1984 v Se; 1982 v Se, D; (with Liverpool), I (2), E (2); 1983 v EG, Sw (2), Bel; 1984 v Bel, EG, Y (14)
Nisbet, S. (Rangers), 1989 v N, Y, F; 1990 v Y, F (5)

O'Donnell, P. (Motherwell), 1992 v Sw (sub), R, D, G (2), Se (1 + 1 sub); 1993 v P (8)
O'Neil, B. (Celtic), 1992 v D, G, Se (2); 1993 v Sw, P, I (7)
O'Neil, J. (Dundee U), 1991 v Bul (sub) (1)
O'Neill, M. (Clyde), 1995 v Ru (sub), F, Sk, Br (4)
Orr, N. (Morton), 1978 v W (sub); 1979 v US, P, N (2); 1980 v Bel, E (7)

Parlane, D. (Rangers), 1977 v W (1)
Paterson, C. (Hibernian), 1981 v Se; 1982 v I (2)
Payne, G. (Dundee U), 1978 v Sw, Cz, W (3)
Pressley, S. (Rangers), 1993 v Ic, F, Bul, M, E; 1994 v Sw, I, M, A, Eg, P, Bel; 1995 v Fi; (with Coventry C), Ru (2), Sm, M, F, Sk, Br; (with Dundee U), 1996 v Gr, Sm, H (2), Sp, F (26)
Provan, D. (Kilmarnock), 1977 v Cz (sub) (1)

Rae, A. (Millwall), 1991 v Bul (sub + 1), F (sub); 1992 v Sw, R, G (sub), Se (2) (8)
Redford, I. (Rangers), 1981 v Se (sub); 1982 v Se, D, I (2), E (6)
Reid, B. (Rangers), 1991 v F; 1992 v D, US, P (4)
Reid, C. (Hibernian), 1993 v Sw, P, I (3)
Reid, M. (Celtic), 1982 v E; 1984 v Y (2)
Reid, R. (St Mirren), 1977 v W, Sw, E (3)
Rice, B. (Hibernian), 1985 v WG (1)
Richardson, L. (St Mirren), 1980 v WG, E (sub) (2)
Ritchie, A. (Morton), 1980 v Bel (1)
Ritchie, P. R. (Hearts), 1996 v H (1)
Robertson, A. (Rangers) 1991 v F (1)
Robertson, C. (Rangers), 1977 v E (sub) (1)
Robertson, D. (Aberdeen), 1987 v Ei (sub); 1988 v E (2); 1989 v N, Y; 1990 v N, Y (7)
Robertson, H. (Aberdeen), 1994 v Eg; 1995 v Fi (2)
Robertson, J. (Hearts), 1985 v WG, Ic (sub) (2)
Robertson, L. (Rangers), 1993 v F, M (sub), E (sub) (3)
Roddie, A. (Aberdeen), 1992 v US, P; 1993 v Sw (sub), P, Ic (5)
Ross, T. W. (Arsenal), 1977 v W (1)
Russell, R. (Rangers), 1978 v W; 1980 v Bel; 1984 v Y (3)

Salton, D. B. (Luton T), 1992 v D, US, P, Y; 1993 v Sw, I (6)
Scott, P. (St Johnstone), 1994 v A (sub), Eg (sub), P, Bel (4)
Shannon, R. (Dundee), 1987 v WG, Ei (2), Bel; 1988 v Bel, E (2) (7)

Sharp, G. (Everton), 1982 v E (1)
Sharp, R. (Dunfermline Ath), 1990 v N (sub); 1991 v R, Sw, Bul (4)
Sheerin, P. (Southampton), 1996 v Sm (1)
Simpson, N. (Aberdeen), 1982 v I (2), E; 1983 v EG, Sw (2), Bel; 1984 v Bel, EG, Y; 1985 v Sp (11)
Sinclair, G. (Dumbarton), 1977 v E (1)
Skilling, M. (Kilmarnock), 1993 v Ic (sub); 1994 v I (2)
Smith, B. M. (Celtic), 1992 v G (2), US, P, Y (5)
Smith, G. (Rangers), 1978 v W (1)
Smith, H. G. (Hearts), 1987 v WG, Bel (2)
Sneddon, A. (Celtic), 1979 v US (1)
Speedie, D. (Chelsea), 1985 v Sp (1)
Spencer, J. (Rangers), 1991 v Sw (sub), F; 1992 v Sw (3)
Stanton, P. (Hibernian), 1977 v Cz (1)
Stark, W. (Aberdeen), 1985 v Ic (1)
Stephen, R. (Dundee), 1983 v Bel (sub) (1)
Stevens, G. (Motherwell), 1977 v E (1)
Stewart, J. (Kilmarnock), 1978 v Sw, Cz; (with Middlesbrough), 1979 v P (3)
Stewart, R. (Dundee U), 1979 v P, N (2); (with West Ham U), 1980 v Bel (2), E (2), WG; 1981 v D; 1982 v I (2), E (12)
Stille, D. (Aberdeen), 1995 v Ru (2), Sm, M, F, Sk, Br; 1996 v Gr, Fi, Sm, H (2), Sp, F (14)
Strachan, G. (Aberdeen), 1980 v Bel (1)
Sturrock, P. (Dundee U), 1977 v Cz, W, Sw, E; 1978 v Sw, Cz; 1982 v Se, I, E (9)
Sweeney, S. (Clydebank), 1991 v R, Sw (sub), Bul (2), Pol; 1992 v Sw, R (7)

Telfer, P. (Luton T), 1993 v Ma, P; 1994 v Sw (3)
Thomas, K. (Hearts), 1993 v F (sub), Bul, M, E; 1994 v Sw, Ma; 1995 v Gr (7)
Thomson, W. (Partick Th), 1977 v F (sub); 1978 v W; (with St Mirren), 1979 v US, N (2); 1980 v Bel (2), E (2), WG (10)
Tolmie, J. (Morton), 1980 v Bel (sub) (1)
Tortolano, J. (Hibernian), 1987 v WG, Ei (2)
Tweed, S. (Hibernian), 1993 v Ic; 1994 v Sw, I (3)

Walker, A. (Celtic), 1988 v Bel (1)
Wallace, I. (Coventry C), 1978 v Sw (1)
Walsh, C. (Nottingham F), 1984 v EG, Sw (2), Bel; 1984 v EG (5)
Wark, J. (Ipswich T), 1977 v Cz, W, Sw; 1978 v W; 1979 v P; 1980 v E (2), WG (8)
Watson, A. (Aberdeen), 1981 v Se, D; 1982 v D, I (sub) (4)
Watson, K. (Rangers), 1977 v E; 1978 v Sw (sub) (2)
Watt, M. (Aberdeen), 1991 v R, Sw, Bul (2), Pol, F; 1992 v Sw, R, G (2), Se (2) (12)
Whyte, D. (Celtic), 1987 v Ei (2), Bel; 1988 v E (2); 1989 v N, Y; 1990 v Y, N (9)
Will, J. A. (Arsenal), 1992 v D (sub), Y; 1993 v Ic (sub) (3)
Wilson, T. (St Mirren), 1983 v Sw (sub) (1)
Wilson, T. (Nottingham F), 1988 v E; 1989 v N, Y; 1990 v F (4)
Winnie, D. (St Mirren), 1988 v Bel (1)
Wright, P. (Aberdeen), 1989 v Y, F; (with QPR), 1990 v Y (sub) (3)
Wright, S. (Aberdeen), 1991 v Bul, Pol, F; 1992 v Sw, G (2), Se (2); 1993 v Sw, P, I, Ma; 1994 v I, Ma (14)
Wright, T. (Oldham Ath), 1987 v Bel (sub) (1)

WALES
Aizlewood, M. (Luton T), 1979 v E; 1981 v Ho (2)

Baddeley, L. M. (Cardiff C), 1996 v Mol (sub), G (sub) (2)
Balcombe, S. (Leeds U), 1982 v F (sub) (1)
Barnhouse, D. J. (Swansea), 1995 v Mol; 1996 v Mol, Sm (3)
Bater, P. T. (Bristol R), 1977 v E, S (2)
Bellamy, C. D. (Norwich C), 1996 v Sm (sub) (1)
Bird, A. (Cardiff C), 1993 v Cy (sub); 1994 v Cy (sub); 1995 v Mol, Ge (sub), Bul; 1996 v G (sub) (6)
Blackmore, C. (Manchester U), 1984 v N, Bul, Y (3)
Blake, N. (Cardiff C), 1991 v Pol (sub); 1993 v Cy, Bel, RCS; 1994 v RCS (5)
Bodin, P. (Cardiff C), 1983 v Y (1)
Bowen, J. P. (Swansea C), 1993 v Cy, Bel (2); 1994 v RCS, R (sub) (5)
Bowen, M. (Tottenham H), 1983 v N; 1984 v Bul, Y (3)
Boyle, T. (C Palace), 1982 v F (1)
Brace, D. P. (Wrexham), 1995 v Ge, Bul (2) (3)
Cegielski, W. (Wrexham), 1977 v E (sub), S (2)
Chapple, S. R. (Swansea C), 1992 v R; 1993 v Cy, Bel (2), RCS; 1994 v RCS; Bul (2) (8)

Charles, J. M. (Swansea C), 1979 v E; 1981 v Ho (2)
Clark, J. (Manchester U), 1978 v S; (with Derby Co), 1979 v E (2)
Coates, J. S. (Swansea C), 1996 v Mol, G (2)
Coleman, C. (Swansea C), 1990 v Pol; 1991 v E, Pol (3)
Coyne, D. (Tranmere R), 1992 v R; 1994 v Cy (sub), R; 1995 v Mol, Ge, Bul (2) (7)
Curtis, A. T. (Swansea C), 1977 v E (1)

Davies, A. (Manchester U), 1982 v F (2), Ho; 1983 v N, Y, Bul (6)
Davies, G. M. (Hereford U), 1993 v Bel, RCS; 1995 v Mol (sub), Ge, Bul (2); (with C Palace) 1996 v Mol (7)
Davies, I. C. (Norwich C), 1978 v S (sub) (1)
Deacy, N. (PSV Eindhoven), 1977 v S (1)
Dibble, A. (Cardiff C), 1983 v Bul; 1984 v N, Bul (3)
Doyle, S. C. (Preston NE), 1979 v E (sub); (with Huddersfield T), 1984 v N (2)
Dwyer, P. J. (Cardiff C), 1979 v E (1)

Ebdon, M. (Everton), 1990 v Pol; 1991 v E (2)
Edwards, C. N. H. (Swansea C), 1996 v G (1)
Edwards, R. I. (Chester), 1977 v S; 1978 v W (2)
Edwards, R. W. (Bristol C), 1991 v Pol; 1992 v R; 1993 v Cy, Bel (2), RCS; 1994 v RCS, Cy, R; 1995 v Ge, Bul; 1996 v Mol, G (13)
Evans, A. (Bristol R), 1977 v E (1)
Evans, P. S. (Shrewsbury T), 1996 v G (1)
Evans, T. (Cardiff C), 1995 v Bul (sub); 1996 v Mol, G (3)

Foster, M. G. (Tranmere R), 1993 v RCS (1)
Freestone, R. (Chelsea), 1990 v Pol (1)

Gale, D. (Swansea C), 1983 v Bul; 1984 v N (sub) (2)
Giggs, R. (Manchester U), 1991 v Pol (1)
Giles, D. C. (Cardiff C), 1977 v S; 1978 v S; (with Swansea C), 1981 v Ho; (with C Palace), 1983 v Y (4)
Giles, P. (Cardiff C), 1982 v F (2), Ho (3)
Graham, D. (Manchester U), 1991 v E (1)
Griffith, C. (Cardiff C), 1990 v Pol (1)
Griffiths, C. (Shrewsbury T), 1991 v Pol (sub) (1)

Hall, G. D. (Chelsea), 1990 v Pol (1)
Hartson, J. (Luton T), 1994 v Cy, R; 1995 v Mol, Ge, Bul; (with Arsenal), 1996 v G, Sm (7)
Hodges, G. (Wimbledon), 1983 v Y (sub), Bul (sub); 1984 v N, Bul, Y (5)
Holden, A. (Chester C), 1984 v Y (sub) (1)
Hopkins, J. (Fulham), 1982 v F (sub), Ho; 1983 v N, Y, Bul (5)
Huggins, D. S. (Bristol C), 1996 v Sm (1)
Hughes, D. R. (Southampton), 1994 v R (1)
Hughes, R. D. (Aston Villa), 1996 v Sm (1)
Hughes, I. (Bury), 1992 v R; 1993 v Cy, Bel (sub), RCS; 1994 v Cy, R; 1995 v Mol, Ge, Bul; 1996 v Mol (sub), G (11)
Hughes, L. M. (Manchester U), 1983 v N, Y; 1984 v N, Bul, Y (5)
Hughes, W. (WBA), 1977 v E, S; 1978 v S (3)

Jackett, K. (Watford), 1981 v Ho; 1982 v F (2)
James, R. M. (Swansea C), 1977 v E, S; 1978 v S (3)
Jarman, L. (Cardiff C), 1996 v Sm (1)
Jenkins, S. R. (Swansea C), 1993 v Cy (sub), Bel (2)
Jones, F. (Wrexham), 1981 v Ho (1)
Jones, L. (Cardiff C), 1982 v F (2), Ho (3)
Jones, P. L. (Liverpool), 1992 v R; 1993 v Cy, Bel (2), RCS; 1994 v RCS (sub), Cy, R; 1995 v Mol, Ge; 1996 v Mol, G (12)
Jones, R. (Sheffield W), 1994 v R; 1995 v Bul (2) (3)
Jones, V. (Bristol R), 1979 v E; 1981 v Ho (2)

Kendall, M. (Tottenham H), 1978 v S (1)
Kenworthy, J. R. (Tranmere R), 1994 v Cy; 1995 v Mol, Bul (3)
Knott, G. R. (Tottenham H), 1996 v Sm (1)

Law, B. J. (QPR), 1990 v Pol; 1991 v E (2)
Letheran, G. (Leeds U), 1977 v E, S (2)
Lewis, D. (Swansea C), 1982 v F (2), Ho; 1983 v N, Y, Bul; 1984 v N, Bul, Y (9)
Lewis, J. (Cardiff C), 1983 v N (1)
Loveridge, J. (Swansea C), 1982 v Ho; 1983 v N, Bul (3)
Lowndes, S. R. (Newport Co), 1979 v E; 1981 v Ho; (with Millwall), 1984 v Bul, Y (4)

McCarthy, A. J. (QPR), 1994 v RCS, Cy, R (3)
Maddy, P. (Cardiff C), 1982 v Ho; 1983 v N (sub) (2)

Margetson, M. W. (Manchester C), 1992 v R; 1993 v Cy, Bel (2), RCS; 1994 v RCS, Cy (7)
Marustik, C. (Swansea C), 1982 v F (2); 1983 v Y, Bul; 1984 v N, Bul, Y (7)
Meaker, M. J. (QPR), 1994 v RCS (sub), R (sub) (2)
Melville, A. K. (Swansea C), 1990 v Pol; (with Oxford U), 1991 v E (2)
Micallef, C. (Cardiff C), 1982 v F, Ho; 1983 v N (3)
Morgan, A. M. (Tranmere R), 1995 v Mol, Bul; 1996 v Mo

Nardiello, D. (Coventry C), 1978 v S (1)
Neilson, A. B. (Newcastle U), 1993 v Cy, Bel (2), RCS; 1994 v RCS, Cy, R (7)
Nicholas, P. (C Palace), 1978 v S; 1979 v E; (with Arsenal), 1982 v F (3)
Nogan, K. (Luton T), 1990 v Pol; 1991 v E (2)
Nogan, L. (Oxford U) 1991 v E (1)

Owen, G. (Wrexham), 1991 v E (sub), Pol; 1992 v R; 1993 v Cy, Bel (2); 1994 v Cy, R (8)

Page, R. J. (Watford), 1995 v Mol, Ge, Bul; 1996 v Mol (4)
Pascoe, C. (Swansea C), 1983 v Bul (sub); 1984 v N (sub), Bul, Y (4)
Pembridge, M. (Luton T), 1991 v Pol (1)
Perry, J. (Cardiff C), 1990 v Pol; 1991 v E, Pol (3)
Peters, M. (Manchester C), 1992 v R; (with Norwich C), 1993 v Cy, RCS (3)
Phillips, D. (Plymouth Arg), 1984 v N, Bul, Y (3)
Phillips, L. (Swansea C), 1979 v E; (with Charlton Ath), 1983 v N (2)
Pontin, K. (Cardiff C), 1978 v S (1)
Powell, L. (Southampton), 1991 v Pol (sub); 1992 v R (sub); 1993 v Bel (sub); 1994 v RCS (4)
Price, P. (Luton T), 1981 v Ho (1)
Pugh, D. (Doncaster R), 1982 v F (2) (2)
Pugh, S. (Wrexham), 1993 v Bel (2 subs) (2)

Ratcliffe, K. (Everton), 1981 v Ho; 1982 v F (2)
Ready, K. (QPR), 1992 v R; 1993 v Bel (2); 1994 v RCS, Cy (5)
Rees, A. (Birmingham C), 1984 v N (1)
Rees, J. (Luton T), 1990 v Pol; 1991 v E, Pol (3)
Roberts, A. (QPR), 1991 v E, Pol (2)
Roberts, D. (Hull C), 1983 v Bul (1)
Roberts, J. G. (Wrexham), 1977 v E (1)
Robinson, C. P. (Wolverhampton W), 1996 v Sm (1)
Robinson, J. (Brighton & HA), 1992 v R; (with Charlton Ath), 1993 v Bel; 1994 v RCS, Cy, R (5)

Rowlands, A. J. R. (Manchester C), 1996 v Sm (1)
Rush, I. (Liverpool), 1981 v Ho; 1982 v F (2)

Savage, R. W. (Crewe Alex), 1995 v Bul; 1996 v Mol, G (3)
Sayer, P. A. (Cardiff C), 1977 v E, S (2)
Searle, D. (Cardiff C), 1991 v Pol (sub); 1992 v R; 1993 v Cy, Bel (2), RCS; 1994 v RCS (6)
Slatter, N. (Bristol R), 1983 v N, Y, Bul; 1984 v N, Bul, Y (6)
Speed, G. A. (Leeds U), 1990 v Pol; 1991 v E, Pol (3)
Stevenson, N. (Swansea C), 1982 v F, Ho (2)
Stevenson, W. B. (Leeds U), 1977 v E, S; 1978 v S (3)
Symons, K. (Portsmouth), 1991 v E, Pol (2)

Taylor, G. K. (Bristol R), 1995 v Ge, Bul (2); 1996 v Mol (4)
Thomas, J. A. (Blackburn R), 1996 v Sm (1)
Thomas, Martin R. (Bristol R), 1979 v E; 1981 v Ho (2)
Thomas, Mickey R. (Wrexham), 1977 v E; 1978 v S (2)
Thomas, D. G. (Leeds U), 1977 v E; 1979 v E; 1984 v N (3)
Tibbott, L. (Ipswich T), 1977 v E, S (2)
Twiddy, C. (Plymouth Arg), 1995 v Mol, Ge; 1996 v G (sub) (3)

Vaughan, N. (Newport Co), 1982 v F, Ho (2)

Walsh, I. P. (C Palace), 1979 v E; (with Swansea C), 1983 v Bul (2)
Walton, M. (Norwich C.), 1991 v Pol (sub) (1)
Ward, D. (Notts Co), 1996 v Mol, G (2)
Williams, A. S. (Blackburn R), 1996 v Sm (1)
Williams, D. (Bristol R), 1983 v Y (1)
Williams, G. (Bristol R), 1983 v Y, Bul (2)
Williams, S. J. (Wrexham), 1995 v Mol, Ge, Bul (2) (4)
Wilmot, R. (Arsenal), 1982 v F (2), Ho; 1983 v N, Y; 1984 v Y (6)

Young, S. (Cardiff C), 1996 v Sm (1)

INTERNATIONAL RECORDS

MOST GOALS IN AN INTERNATIONAL

England	Malcolm Macdonald (Newcastle U) 5 goals v Cyprus, at Wembley	16.4.1975
	Willie Hall (Tottenham H) 5 goals v Ireland, at Old Trafford	16.11.1938
	G. O. Smith (Corinthians) 5 goals v Ireland, at Sunderland	18.2.1899
	Steve Bloomer (Derby Co) 5 goals* v Wales, at Cardiff	16.3.1896
	Oliver Vaughton (Aston Villa) 5 goals v Ireland, at Belfast	18.2.1882
Scotland	Charles Heggie (Rangers) 5 goals v Ireland, at Belfast	20.3.1886
Ireland	Joe Bambrick (Linfield) 6 goals v Wales, at Belfast	1.2.1930
Wales	James Price (Wrexham) 4 goals v Ireland, at Wrexham	25.2.1882
	Mel Charles (Cardiff C) 4 goals v Ireland, at Cardiff	11.4.1962
	Ian Edwards (Chester) 4 goals v Malta, at Wrexham	25.10.1978

* There are conflicting reports which make it uncertain whether Bloomer scored four or five goals in this game.

MOST GOALS IN AN INTERNATIONAL CAREER

		Goals	Games
England	Bobby Charlton (Manchester U)	49	106
Scotland	Denis Law (Huddersfield T, Manchester C, Torino, Manchester U)	30	55
	Kenny Dalglish (Celtic, Liverpool)	30	102
Ireland	Colin Clarke (Bournemouth, Southampton, QPR, Portsmouth)	13	38
Wales	Ian Rush (Liverpool, Juventus)	28	73
	Ivor Allchurch (Swansea T, Newcastle U, Cardiff C)	23	68
Republic of Ireland	Frank Stapleton (Arsenal, Manchester U, Ajax, Derby Co, Le Havre, Blackburn R)	20	70

HIGHEST SCORES

World Cup Match	New Zealand	13	Fiji	0	1981
European Championship	Spain	12	Malta	1	1983
Olympic Games	Denmark	17	France	1	1908
	Germany	16	USSR	0	1912
International Match	Germany	13	Finland	0	1940
	Spain	13	Bulgaria	0	1933
European Cup	Feyenoord	12	K R Reykjavik	2	1969
European Cup-Winners' Cup	Sporting Lisbon	16	Apoel Nicosia	1	1963
Fairs & UEFA Cups	Ajax	14	Red Boys	0	1984

GOALSCORING RECORDS

World Cup Final	Geoff Hurst (England) 3 goals v West Germany	1966
World Cup Final tournament	Just Fontaine (France) 13 goals	1958
Major European Cup game	Lothar Emmerich (Borussia Dortmund) v Floriana in Cup-Winners' Cup – 6 goals	1965
Career	Artur Friedenreich (Brazil) 1329 goals	1910–30
	Pelé (Brazil) 1281 goals	*1956–78
	Franz 'Bimbo' Binder (Austria, Germany) 1006 goals	1930–50

* *Pelé subsequently scored two goals in Testimonial matches making his total 1283.*

MOST CAPPED INTERNATIONALS IN BRITISH ISLES

England	Peter Shilton	125 appearances	1970–90
Northern Ireland	Pat Jennings	119 appearances	1964–86
Scotland	Kenny Dalglish	102 appearances	1971–86
Wales	Neville Southall	86 appearances	1982–96
Republic of Ireland	Paul McGrath	82 appearances	1984–96

TRANSFERS

Record British moves (UK only)

£8,500,000 Stan Collymore, Nottingham F to Liverpool, June 1995

£6,250,000 Andy Cole, Newcastle U to Manchester U, January 1995

£6,000,000 Les Ferdinand, QPR to Newcastle U, June 1995

£5,500,000 Andrei Kanchelskis, Manchester U to Everton, July 1995

£5,250,000 Nick Barmby, Tottenham H to Middlesbrough, August 1995

£5,000,000 Chris Sutton, Norwich to Blackburn R, July 1994

£4,500,000 Chris Armstrong, Crystal Palace to Tottenham H, June 1995

£4,500,000 Jason McAteer, Bolton W to Liverpool, September 1995

£4,200,000 Ruel Fox, Newcastle U to Tottenham H, October 1995

£4,000,000 Duncan Ferguson, Dundee U to Rangers, July 1993

£4,000,000 Duncan Ferguson, Rangers to Everton, December 1994

£4,000,000 Warren Barton, Wimbledon to Newcastle U, June 1995

Other British moves

£7,000,000 Paul Ince, Manchester U to Internazionale, June 1995

£6,500,000 David Platt, Bari to Juventus, May 1992

£5,500,000 David Platt, Aston Villa to Bari, July 1991

£5,500,000 Paul Gascoigne, Tottenham H to Lazio, May 1992

£5,200,000 David Platt, Juventus to Sampdoria, July 1993

£5,000,000 Trevor Steven, Rangers to Marseille, August 1991

£4,750,000 David Platt, Sampdoria to Arsenal, July 1995

£4,500,000 Chris Waddle, Tottenham H to Marseille, July 1989

£4,300,000 Paul Gascoigne, Lazio to Rangers, July 1995

£3,200,000 Ian Rush, Liverpool to Juventus, June 1987

£2,800,000 Ian Rush, Juventus to Liverpool, August 1988

£2,750,000 Gary Lineker, Everton to Barcelona, June 1986

World records

£13,000,000 Gianluigi Lentini, Torino to AC Milan, June 1992

£12,000,000 Gianluca Vialli, Sampdoria to Juventus, June 1992

£10,000,000 Jean-Pierre Papin, Marseille to AC Milan, June 1992

* *See also Stop Press*

FA SCHOOLS AND YOUTH GAMES 1995–96

ENGLAND UNDER-16

23 Oct

England 1 *(Owen (pen))*
Belgium 0
England: Stewart (Blackburn R); Cooper (Nottingham F), Ball (Everton), Haslam (Sheffield W), Brown (Manchester U), Day (Arsenal), Quinn (Sheffield W), Lunt (Crewe Alex), Jones (Aston Villa), Owen (Liverpool), Way (Norwich C) [Woodcock (Newcastle U)].

27 Oct

England 5 *(Owen 2, Brown, Jones, Quinn)*
Sweden 0
England: Stewart (Blackburn R); Cooper (Nottingham F), Ball (Everton), Haslam (Sheffield W), Brown (Manchester U), Day (Arsenal), Quinn (Sheffield W), [Stevenson (Notts Co)], Lunt (Crewe Alex), Jones (Aston Villa), Owen (Liverpool) [Hulbert (Everton)], Woodcock (Newcastle U) [Fenton (Manchester C)].

3 Feb

England 4 *(Owen 2, Ball, Quinn)*
Denmark 0
England: Stewart (Blackburn R); Cooper (Nottingham F), Ball (Everton), Haslam (Sheffield W), Owen K (QPR), Day (Arsenal), Quinn (Sheffield W), Woodcock (Newcastle U), Jones (Aston Villa), Owen (Liverpool), Way (Norwich C).
Subs all used: Lunt (Crewe Alex), Bray (Wolverhampton W), Gerrard (Liverpool), Brown (Manchester U).

20 Feb

England 2 *(Gerrard, Jevons)*
Republic of Ireland 1
England: Goodlad (Nottingham F); Haslam (Sheffield W), Fenton (Manchester C), Owen K (QPR), Fenton (Manchester C), Hulbert (Everton) [Day (Arsenal)], Purser (QPR) [Way (Norwich C)], Gerrard (Liverpool) [Harley (Chelsea)], Brown (Manchester U), Jevons (Everton), Ball (Everton).

9 Mar

Spain 2
England 0
England: Stewart (Blackburn R) [Bray (Wolverhampton W)]; Cooper (Nottingham F), Fenton (Manchester C) [Purser (QPR)], Haslam (Sheffield W) [Owen K (QPR)], Brown (Manchester U), Lunt (Crewe Alex), Quinn (Sheffield W) [Day (Arsenal)], Gerrard (Liverpool) [Marshall (Notts Co)], Jevons (Everton), Jones (Aston Villa), Ball (Everton).

29 Apr

England 2 *(Way, Owen)*
Slovakia 0
England: Stewart (Blackburn R); Cooper (Nottingham F), Ball (Everton), Haslam (Sheffield W), Brown (Manchester U), Day (Arsenal), Quinn (Sheffield W), Lunt (Crewe Alex), Jones (Aston Villa), Way (Norwich C), Owen (Liverpool).

1 May

England 2 *(Owen 2)*
Turkey 1
England: Stewart (Blackburn R); Cooper (Nottingham F) [Gerrard (Liverpool)], Ball (Everton), Haslam (Sheffield W), Brown (Manchester U), Day (Arsenal), Quinn (Sheffield W), Lunt (Crewe Alex), Jones (Aston Villa) [Jevons (Everton)], Owen (Liverpool), Way (Norwich C) [Marshall (Notts Co)].

3 May

England 1 *(Owen)*
Israel 2
England: Stewart (Blackburn R); Cooper (Nottingham F), Ball (Everton), Haslam (Sheffield W), Brown (Manchester U), Day (Arsenal), Quinn (Sheffield W), Lunt (Crewe Alex), Owen (Liverpool), Jevons (Everton), Fenton (Manchester C).

6 May

Greece 1
England 0
England: Stewart (Blackburn R); Cooper (Nottingham F), Ball (Everton), Haslam (Sheffield W), Brown (Manchester U), Day (Arsenal), [Marshall (Notts Co)], Quinn (Sheffield W) [Fenton (Manchester C)], Lunt (Crewe Alex), Jones (Aston Villa) Owen (Liverpool), Way (Norwich C).

ENGLAND UNDER-18

16 Nov

England 2 *(Heskey 2)*
Latvia 0
England: Lucas (Preston NE); Curtis (Manchester U), Crowe (Arsenal), Thompson (Liverpool) [Ducros (Coventry C)], Wallwork (Manchester U), Broomes (Blackburn R), Shepherd (Leeds U), Clemence (Tottenham H), Branch (Everton), Heskey (Leicester C), Quashie (QPR).
Subs also used: Piper (Wimbledon), Brayson (Newcastle U).

18 Nov

England 6 *(Piper 3, Wicks, Shepherd, 1 og)*
Sweden 2
England: Lucas (Preston NE); Curtis (Manchester U), Crowe (Arsenal), Thompson (Liverpool), Wallwork (Manchester U), Broomes (Blackburn R), Shepherd (Leeds U), Clemence (Tottenham H), Branch (Everton), Heskey (Leicester C), Piper (Wimbledon).
Sub used: Wicks (Manchester U).

28 Feb

France 1
England 1 *(Brayson)*
England: Dungey (Plymouth Arg); Curtis (Manchester U), Crowe (Arsenal), Blunt (Leeds U), Wallwork (Manchester U) [Ferdinand (West Ham U)], Jackson (Leeds U), Shepherd (Leeds U) [Cassidy (Liverpool)], Clemence (Tottenham H), Branch (Everton) [Brayson (Newcastle U)], Ducros (Coventry C), Piper (Wimbledon).

19 Mar

Scotland 0
England 3 *(Clemence, Ducros, 1 og)*
England: Lucas (Preston NE); Wallwork (Manchester U), Crowe (Arsenal), Shepherd (Leeds U), Curtis (Manchester U), Jackson (Leeds U) [Cassidy (Liverpool)], Barrett (Newcastle U), Clemence (Tottenham H), Branch (Everton) [Ducros (Coventry C)], Heskey (Leicester C), Piper (Wimbledon).

23 Apr

England 3 *(Clemence, Shepherd, Blunt)*
Scotland 0
England: Lucas (Preston NE); Wallwork (Manchester U), Crowe (Arsenal), Shepherd (Leeds U), Curtis (Manchester U), Jackson (Leeds U), Barrett (Newcastle U), Blunt (Leeds U), Branch (Everton), Heskey (Leicester C) [Ducros (Coventry C)], Clemence (Tottenham H) [Lampard (West Ham U)].

FROM THE CHAPLAIN

There were a couple of largely unheralded events during the last season that were particularly significant for those who feature on this page of the *Rothmans Yearbook*. Those who wholeheartedly embrace the cause of football chaplaincy, and indeed for those who still—somewhat surprisingly in the face of all its well publicised benefits—view the involvement of a chaplain at a football club with a measure of cynicism. Naturally enough the two events received little or no publicity, at the time or subsequently, but things to do with spiritual or pastoral issues seldom receive the attentions of the media and the football chaplains have never sought the glare of press or TV coverage although it is invariably laudatory when they are subjected to it.

Regular readers of *Rothmans* know that the football chaplains meet regularly. They hold a two-day national conference at least every other year though it is now becoming an annual event. The latest such took place last October—and it was held at Lilleshall and was sponsored in its entirety by the Premier League. This tacit endorsement by one of the sport's leading bodies was a tremendous encouragement to the chaplains themselves, whose dealings in the game are low-key by design and seldom extend beyond the contacts they have within their own clubs.

To know that their involvement in and contribution to the national sport is welcomed, appreciated and respected, certainly heartened the men concerned as well as sharpening their discussions together and stimulating their activities at their clubs. It was also greatly cheering to those who have long since advocated this form of Christian ministry within the Churches and the world of football. To have the concept of football chaplaincy endorsed and promoted in such a wholehearted manner was hugely encouraging to them, and the thanks of every Christian in football at any level today are due to the Premier League administration for their generous support.

The other event was somewhat more rarefied but provided further evidence of the significance and validity of football chaplaincy—this time within the Church. The Church has long been familiar with chaplains in education and the armed forces for example, but it has been rather guarded, in parts at least, in its acceptance of ministry within sport in general and football in particular.

However, one young theological student with a keen interest in our game was eager to explore the role of the chaplains at League clubs for part of a module in his training to do with non-parochial Christian work. Perhaps to the surprise of some, he was persistent enough to be allowed to seek the assistance in his project from the chaplain of a club near his theological college and the authorities were hugely impressed with the quality of the outcome which was the product of several lengthy discussions between the pair, as well as of meetings with and visits to other chaplains at a variety of different League outfits.

Not only has football taken public recognition of the chaplains that serve within its ranks, but even the Church has accepted and acknowledged that here is an authentic model of Christian service—and that certainly represents major progress!

THE REV

OFFICIAL CHAPLAINS TO FA PREMIERSHIP AND FOOTBALL LEAGUE CLUBS

Rev John Bingham—Chesterfield
Rev Richard Chewter—Exeter C
Rev Michael Lowe—AFC Bournemouth
Rev Andrew Taggart—Torquay U
Rev David Jeans—Sheffield W
Rev Nigel Sands—Crystal Palace
Rev Graham Spencer—Leicester C
Rev Phillip Miller—Ipswich T
Rev Allen Bagshawe—Hull C
Rev David Tully—Newcastle U
Rev Derek Cleave—Bristol C
Rev Brian Rice—Hartlepool U
Revs Andy Cowley and John Graham—Watford
Rev Michael Chantry—Oxford U
Rev Michael Futens—Derby C
Very Rev Brandon Jackson—Lincoln C
Rev Ken Hawkins—Birmingham C
Rev Simon Stevenette—Bristol R
Rev Michael Hunter—Grimsby T
Rev Dick Syms—York C
Rev Dennis Hall—Wigan Ath
Rev William Hall—Middlesbrough
Rev Canon John Hestor—Brighton & HA

Rev Mervyn Terrett—Luton T
Rev Jim Rushton—Carlisle U
Rev Robert de Berry—QPR
Rev Gary Piper—Fulham
Rev Peter Amos—Barnsley
Rev Barry Kirk—Reading
Rev Martin Short—Bradford C
Rev John Boyers—Manchester U
Rev Martin Butt—Walsall
Rev Steve Riley—Leeds U
Revs Alan Poulter and Gerald Courell—Tranmere R
Rev Mark Kichenside—Charlton Ath
Rev Owen Beament—Millwall
Rev Elwin Cockett—West Ham U
Rev Mick Woodhead—Sheffield U
Rev Alan Comfort—Leyton Orient
Rev John Hall-Matthews—Wolverhampton W
Rev Mark Cockayne—Doncaster R
Rev Peter Naylor—Northampton T
Rev John Knight—Barnet
Rev Richard Hayton—Gillingham
Rev Clive Andrews—Notts Co
Rev Chris Nelson—Preston North End
Rev Paul Brown—Wrexham

The chaplains hope that those who read this page will see the value and benefit of chaplaincy work in football and will take appropriate steps to spread the word where this is possible. They would also like to thank the editors of the Rothmans Yearbook *for their continued support for this specialist and growing area of work.*

The following addresses may be helpful; SCORE (Sports Chaplaincy Offering Resources and Encouragement), PO Box 123, Sale, Manchester M33 4ZA and Christians in Sport, PO Box 93, Oxford OX2 7YP.

FA WOMEN'S PREMIER LEAGUE 1995–96

National Division

	P	W	D	L	F	A	GD	Pts
Croydon	18	13	5	0	58	17	+41	44
Doncaster Belles	18	14	2	2	57	19	+38	44
Arsenal	18	11	4	3	54	12	+42	37
Everton	18	10	1	7	44	40	+4	31
Liverpool	18	9	2	7	36	27	+9	29
Wembley	18	7	5	6	43	21	+22	26
Millwall Lionesses	18	5	3	10	20	32	−12	18
Ilkeston Town	18	4	3	11	21	46	−25	15
Villa Aztecs	18	4	1	13	22	51	−29	13
Wolverhampton Wanderers	18	0	0	18	8	98	−90	0

Southern Division

	P	W	D	L	F	A	GD	Pts
Southampton Saints	18	13	2	3	52	21	+31	41
Berkhamsted Town	18	13	1	4	42	26	+16	40
Wimbledon	18	12	1	5	53	36	+17	37
Three Bridges	18	11	1	6	47	24	+23	34
Ipswich Town	18	8	1	9	36	35	+1	25
Brighton & Hove Albion	18	5	4	9	35	47	−12	19
Town & County	18	6	1	11	27	48	−21	19
Leyton Orient*	18	5	2	11	33	45	−12	16
Oxford United	18	4	4	10	24	46	−22	16
Brentford	18	3	3	12	29	50	−21	12

*Leyton Orient deducted 1 point for playing an ineligible player

Northern Division

	P	W	D	L	F	A	GD	Pts
Tranmere Rovers	16	14	2	0	73	11	+62	44
Huddersfield Town	16	12	3	1	60	23	+37	39
Garswood/St Helens	16	9	4	3	51	23	+28	31
Sheffield Wednesday	16	9	3	4	41	22	+19	30
Langford*	16	6	2	8	27	44	−17	17
RTM Newcastle Kestrels	16	3	4	9	21	43	−22	13
Notts County	16	4	1	11	18	43	−25	13
Kidderminster Harriers	16	4	1	11	27	53	−26	13
Bronte	16	0	2	14	11	67	−56	2

†Langford deducted 3 points

Play-offs – Southern Division
Semi-finals

Tottenham Hotspur (GL) v Swindon Town Spitfires (Sth)	8-0
Whitehawk (SE) v Canary Racers (E)	6-1

Final

Whitehawk v Tottenham Hotspur	6-0

Play-offs – Northern Division
Semi-finals

Bradford City (YH) v Manchester United (NW)	4-1
Calverton (EM) v Coventry City (WM)	2-1

Final

Calverton v Bradford City	1-2

Key: EM = East Midlands Regional, GL = Greater London Regional, WM = West Midlands Regional, Sth = Southern Region, YH = Yorkshire & Humberside, SE = South East Regional, NW = North West Regional, E = Eastern Region.

UK LIVING WOMEN'S FA CUP 1995–96

Preliminary Round

Hull City v Blackburn Rangers	4-2
Blackpool (Wren) Rovers v Scunthorpe Ironesses	0-4
Manchester Rangers withdrew v Winsford United w.o.	
Deans v Runcorn	0-4
Royal Strikers withdrew v Lowestoft Town w.o.	
West Ham v Great Wakering Rovers	5-0
Dulwich Hamlet v Hackney	8-1
Drayton Wanderers v Chelsea	0-4
Chesham United v Thames Valley	2-5
Sherborne v Tuffley Athletic	12-0
Hereford United v Cable-Tel (Newport)	1-5

First Round

Preston Rangers v Hull City	3-2
Able Town v Cleveland	7-0
Sheffield & Hallam v Haslingden	4-1
Sunderland v Leeds United	2-1
Darlington Spraire v Newcastle	3-13

Accrington Stanley v Doncaster Rovers	1-2
Brighouse v Wakefield	3-5
Kirklees v Barnsley	4-4, 0-1
Middlesbrough v South Shields	3-1
Lincoln United v Kilnhurst	0-4
Scunthorpe Ironesses v Bradford City	1-1, 1-5
Rochdale v Wigan	4-1
Manchester Belle Vue v Newsham PH	10-1
Radcliffe Borough v Chester City	12-0
Manchester United v Vernon-Carus	7-0
Leek Town v Bangor City	2-3
Blackburn Rovers v Derby County	4-2
Winsford United v Whalley Rangers	1-5
Highfield Rangers v Calverton MW	4-2
Nettleham v Wrexham	1-2
Warrington v Chesterfield	1-2
Manchester City v Oldham Athletic	0-1
Newcastle Town v Stockport County	4-5
Liverpool Feds v Rainworth MW	4-3

Stockport v Runcorn	10-1
Milton Keynes Athletic v Dunstable	1-1, 0-3
Rugby v Coventry City	0-12
Bedford Bells v Lowestoft Town	4-1
Cambridge City v Birmingham City	2-4
Rea Valley Rovers v Cambridge United	1-4
Tamworth v Leicester City	1-2
Leighton Linslade w.o.Atherstone failed to fulfil the tie	
Canary Racers v Pye	4-0
Chelsea v Hassocks	8-0
Watford v Fulham	1-4
Collier Row v Abbey Rangers	4-2
Tottenham Hotspur v Winchester & Ealing	9-0
Charlton v Whitehawk	2-5
Dulwich Hamlet v Surbiton Town	2-1
Colchester v Romford	3-2
Mill Hill United v Redbridge Wanderers	6-0
Crowborough Athletic v Barnet	2-3
Enfield v Sutton United	2-0
Palace Eagles v West Ham	1-0
Sittingbourne v Newham	0-7
(tie abandoned after 86 minutes game awarded to Newham)	
Edenbridge Town v Colchester Royals	3-4
Clacton w.o.Crystal Palace failed to fulfil the tie	
Gillingham v Harlow Town	3-7
St Georges v Teynham Gunners	5-0
Thames Valley w.o. Sturminster Newton withdrew	
Bournemouth v Bow Brickhill	3-0
Leatherhead v Aylesbury United	4-1
Gosport Borough v Thame United	2-5
Binfield v Portsmouth	3-0
Reading Royals v Farnborough Town	1-2
Bracknell Town v Slough Town	6-2
Winchester City v Camberley Town	0-9
Denham United v Newbury	3-1
Cable-Tel (Newport) v Plymouth Pilgrims	1-5
Elmore Eagles v Frome	0-7
Inter Cardiff v Clevedon	15-0
Newton Abbot v Barry	1-3
Swindon Town w.o. Cardiff Institute withdrew	
Clevedon United v Swindon Town Spitfires	0-6
Brislington v Sherborne	2-8
Truro City v Yate Town	1-0
Cheltenham YMCA v Freeway	12-1
Exeter Rangers v Worcester City	2-8

Second Round

Doncaster Rovers v Middlesbrough	0-3
Kilnhurst v Barnsley	5-1
RTM Newcastle Kestrels v Newcastle	0-1
Bronte v Preston Rangers	3-2
Amble Town v Huddersfield Town	1-5
Sheffield Wednesday v Sheffield Hallam United	6-0
Sunderland v Wakefield	0-2
Wrexham v Manchester United	1-3
Radcliffe Borough v Bangor City Girls	1-4
Leicester City v Oldham Athletic	1-5
Whalley Rangers v Highfield Rangers	0-4
Coventry City v Chesterfield	2-1
Garswood/St Helens v Bradford City	3-0
Liverpool Feds v Birmingham City	7-5
Dunstable v Blackburn Rovers	2-4
Stockport County v Stockport	2-1
Rochdale v Tranmere Rovers	0-9
Notts County v Manchester Belle Vue	1-3
Mill Hill United v Colchester Royals	4-2
Colchester v Langford	3-7
Camberley Town v Dulwich Hamlet	1-7
Denham United v Leighton Linslade	14-0
Barnet v St Georges	4-3
Brentford v Leyton Orient	2-3
Palace Eagles v Leatherhead	3-1
Cambridge United v Newham	0-1
Tottenham Hotspur v Enfield	5-4
Whitehawk v Wimbledon	1-0
Town & County v Chelsea	3-4
Bedford Bells v Collier Row	3-1
Clacton v Brighton & Hove Albion	1-5
Canary Racers v Harlow Town	6-0
Berkhamsted Town v Fulham	5-0
Ipswich Town v Three Bridges	3-1
Plymouth Pilgrims v Swindon Town	3-0
AFC Bournemouth v Thame United	0-2
Sherborne v Worcester City	18-0
Bracknell Town v Binfield	1-7

Swindon Town Spitfires v Farnborough Town	3-1
Bristol City v Southampton Saints	2-3
Truro City v Oxford United	0-1
Frome v Thames Valley	3-0
Cheltenham YMCA v Barry	2-2, 1-2
Inter Cardiff v Kidderminster Harriers	2-1

Third Round

Oldham Athletic v Liverpool Feds	1-0
Bangor City Girls v Huddersfield Town	1-6
Bronte v Stockport County	1-3
Blackburn Rovers v Manchester United	1-3
Middlesbrough v Manchester Belle Vue	2-1
Newcastle v Wakefield	2-1
Coventry City v Sheffield Wednesday	0-2
Kilnhurst v Highfield Rangers	2-4
Tranmere Rovers v Garswood/St Helens	2-3
Leyton Orient v Langford	2-3
Ipswich Town v Denham United	7-3
Canary Racers v Mill Hill United	2-1
Bedford Bells v Berkhamsted Town	0-6
Chelsea v Palace Eagles	3-1
Brighton & Hove Albion v Dulwich Hamlet	6-0
Barnet v Whitehawk	0-4
Newham v Tottenham Hotspur	0-6
Oxford United v Thame United	3-0
Swindon Town Spitfires v Southampton Saints	2-3
Plymouth Pilgrims v Barry	1-1, 3-4
Inter Cardiff v Sherborne	3-0
Frome v Binfield	1-4

Fourth Round

Oxford United v Everton	3-6
Millwall Lionesses v Langford	5-0
Arsenal v Manchester United	10-0
Binfield v Doncaster Belles	0-9
Chelsea v Newcastle	0-0, 0-3
Huddersfield Town v Berkhamsted Town	2-1
Liverpool v Garswood/St Helens	3-0
Oldham Athletic v Croydon	2-4
Ilkeston Town Rangers v Highfield Rangers	5-0
Southampton Saints v Whitehawk	1-2
Tottenham Hotspur v Villa Aztecs	3-4
Stockport County v Wembley	0-9
Sheffield Wednesday v Middlesbrough	2-3
Brighton & Hove Albion v Ipswich Town	0-1
Inter Cardiff v Wolverhampton Wanderers	1-2
Canary Racers v Barry	2-2, 4-1

Fifth Round

Liverpool v Middlesbrough	7-1
Croydon v Inter Cardiff	2-0
Canary Racers v Ipswich Town	1-3
Ilkeston Town v Millwall Lionesses	2-0
Arsenal v Wembley	2-1
Whitehawk v Newcastle	1-0
Huddersfield Town v Everton	5-5, 2-1
Villa Aztecs v Doncaster Belles	1-5

Sixth Round

Ilkeston Town v Arsenal	1-2
Huddersfield Town v Liverpool	0-9
Whitehawk v Ipswich Town	2-2, 1-2
Croydon v Doncaster Belles	1-0

Semi-finals

Liverpool v Arsenal	0-0
Liverpool won 5-4 on penalties	
Croydon v Ipswich Town	5-0

Final (at Millwall)

28 APR

Croydon (0) 1 *(Powell)*
Liverpool (1) 1 *(Burke)* 2500

Croydon: Cooper; Dines (Mulligan), Osborne (McGloin), Powell, Smith, Saunders, Mapes, Bampton (Cottier), Sempare, Davis, Proctor.
Liverpool: Brown; Taylor L, Griffiths (Formston), Taylor C, Thomas, Hayward, Burke, Easton (Duffy), Harper, Handley, McQuiggan (Holland).
Referee: S. Mathieson.

FA WOMEN'S LEAGUE CUP

First Round

Brentford v Tranmere Rovers	1-7
Ipswich Town v Berkhamsted Town	2-3
Kidderminster Harriers v Garswood/St Helens	0-5
Leyton Orient v Notts County	4-2
RTM Newcastle Kestrels v Langford	1-2
Southampton Saints v Sheffield Wednesday	3-1
Three Bridges v Oxford United	3-0
Town & County v Brighton & Hove Albion	1-0
Wimbledon v Huddersfield Town	3-2

bye: Bronte

Second Round

Garswood/St Helens v Southampton Saints	4-1
Bronte v Liverpool	0-13
Ilkeston Town Rangers v Croydon	1-2
Millwall Lionesses v Berkhamsted Town	2-1

byes: Arsenal, Doncaster Belles, Everton, Langford, Leyton Orient, Three Bridges, Town & County, Tranmere Rovers, Villa Aztecs, Wembley, Wimbledon and Wolverhampton Wanderers

Third Round

Leyton Orient v Town & County	5-2

Arsenal v Garswood/St Helens	5-0
Doncaster Belles v Langford	7-0
Three Bridges v Wimbledon	3-3
(Three Bridges won 5-3 on penalties)	
Wembley v Villa Aztecs	4-0
Tranmere Rovers v Wolverhampton Wanderers	5-1
Everton v Croydon	4-4
(Croydon won 7-6 on penalties)	
Millwall Lionesses v Liverpool	0-4

Fourth Round

Tranmere Rovers v Croydon	0-1
Leyton Orient v Doncaster Belles	0-10
Three Bridges v Arsenal	1-3
Liverpool v Wembley	1-3

Semi-finals

Arsenal v Wembley	1-4
Croydon v Doncaster Belles	1-3

Final (at Barnet)

Wembley v Doncaster Belles	2-2 aet
(Wembley won 5-3 on penalties)	

UEFA EUROPEAN CHAMPIONSHIP FOR WOMEN 1995–97

Group 3 (England results only)

England v Italy	1-1
England v Croatia	5-0
Portugal v England	0-5
Italy v England	2-1
Croatia v England	0-2
England v Portugal	3-0

EUROPEAN CUP

EUROPEAN CUP FINALS 1956–96

Year	Winners		Runners-up		Venue	Attendance	Referee
1956	Real Madrid	4	Reims	3	Paris	38,000	Ellis (E)
1957	Real Madrid	2	Fiorentina	0	Madrid	124,000	Horn (Ho)
1958	Real Madrid	3	AC Milan	2 *(aet)*	Brussels	67,000	Alsteen (Bel)
1959	Real Madrid	2	Reims	0	Stuttgart	80,000	Dutsch (WG)
1960	Real Madrid	7	Eintracht Frankfurt	3	Glasgow	135,000	Mowat (S)
1961	Benfica	3	Barcelona	2	Berne	28,000	Dienst (Sw)
1962	Benfica	5	Real Madrid	3	Amsterdam	65,000	Horn (Ho)
1963	AC Milan	2	Benfica	1	Wembley	45,000	Holland (E)
1964	Internazionale	3	Real Madrid	1	Vienna	74,000	Stoll (A)
1965	Internazionale	1	Benfica	0	Milan	80,000	Dienst (Sw)
1966	Real Madrid	2	Partizan Belgrade	1	Brussels	55,000	Kreitlein (WG)
1967	Celtic	2	Internazionale	1	Lisbon	56,000	Tschenscher (WG)
1968	Manchester U	4	Benfica	1 *(aet)*	Wembley	100,000	Lo Bello (I)
1969	AC Milan	4	Ajax	1	Madrid	50,000	Ortiz (Sp)
1970	Feyenoord	2	Celtic	1 *(aet)*	Milan	50,000	Lo Bello (I)
1971	Ajax	2	Panathinaikos	0	Wembley	90,000	Taylor (E)
1972	Ajax	2	Internazionale	0	Rotterdam	67,000	Helies (F)
1973	Ajax	1	Juventus	0	Belgrade	93,500	Guglovic (Y)
1974	Bayern Munich	1	Atletico Madrid	1	Brussels	65,000	Loraux (Bel)
Replay	Bayern Munich	4	Atletico Madrid	0	Brussels	65,000	Delcourt (Bel)
1975	Bayern Munich	2	Leeds U	0	Paris	50,000	Kitabdjian (F)
1976	Bayern Munich	1	St Etienne	0	Glasgow	54,864	Palotai (H)
1977	Liverpool	3	Moenchengladbach	1	Rome	57,000	Wurtz (F)
1978	Liverpool	1	FC Brugge	0	Wembley	92,000	Corver (Ho)
1979	Nottingham F	1	Malmo	0	Munich	57,500	Linemayr (A)
1980	Nottingham F	1	Hamburg	0	Madrid	50,000	Garrido (P)
1981	Liverpool	1	Real Madrid	0	Paris	48,360	Palotai (H)
1982	Aston Villa	1	Bayern Munich	0	Rotterdam	46,000	Konrath (F)
1983	Hamburg	1	Juventus	0	Athens	75,000	Rainea (R)
1984	Liverpool	1	Roma	1	Rome	69,693	Fredriksson (Se)
	(aet; Liverpool won 4–2 on penalties)						
1985	Juventus	1	Liverpool	0	Brussels	58,000	Daina (Sw)
1986	Steaua Bucharest	0	Barcelona	0	Seville	70,000	Vautrot (F)
	(aet; Steaua won 2–0 on penalties)						
1987	Porto	2	Bayern Munich	1	Vienna	59,000	Ponnet (Bel)
1988	PSV Eindhoven	0	Benfica	0	Stuttgart	70,000	Agnolin (I)
	(aet; PSV won 6–5 on penalties)						
1989	AC Milan	4	Steaua Bucharest	0	Barcelona	97,000	Tritschler (WG)
1990	AC Milan	1	Benfica	0	Vienna	57,500	Kohl (A)
1991	Red Star Belgrade	0	Marseille	0	Bari	56,000	Lanese (I)
	(aet; Red Star won 5–3 on penalties)						
1992	Barcelona	1	Sampdoria	0 *(aet)*	Wembley	70,827	Schmidhuber (G)
1993	Marseille*	1	AC Milan	0	Munich	64,400	Rothlisberger (Sw)
1994	AC Milan	4	Barcelona	0	Athens	70,000	Don (E)
1995	Ajax	1	AC Milan	0	Vienna	49,730	Craciunescu (Ro)
1996	Juventus	1	Ajax	1	Rome	67,000	Vega (Sp)
	(aet; Juventus won 4–2 on penalties)						

*Subsequently stripped of title.

EUROPEAN CUP 1995–96

Preliminary Round, First Leg
Anderlecht (0) 0, Ferencvaros (0) 1 *(Kuntics 58)* 20,000
Dynamo Kiev (0) 1 *(Pochlebajev 82)*, Aalborg (0) 0
61,000
Grasshoppers (0) 1 *(Ibrahim 50)*, Maccabi Tel Aviv (0) 1
(Kachentsev 55) 11,100
Legia Warsaw (0) 1 *(Podbrozny 49 (pen))*, IFK
Gothenburg (0) 0 15,000
Panathinaikos (0) 0, Hajduk Split (0) 0 45,000
Rangers (0) 1 *(Durie 68)*, Anorthosis (0) 0 43,519
Rosenborg (2) 3 *(Hoftun 22, Strand 27, Brattbakk 75)*
Besiktas (0) 0 14,352
Salzburg (0) 0, Steaua (0) 0 11,500

Preliminary Round, Second Leg
Aalborg (0) 1 *(Rasmussen 86)*, Dynamo Kiev (1) 3
(Kalitvintsev 36, Sjevtsjenko 49, 76) 10,100
Anorthosis (0) 0, Rangers (0) 0 9500
Besiktas (0) 3 *(Kuntz 8, 85 (pen), Mehmet 87)*,
Rosenborg (0) 1 *(Brattbakk 68)* 35,000
Ferencvaros (0) 1 *(Kopunovic 50)*, Anderlecht (0) 1
(De Bilde 65) 18,000
IFK Gothenburg (1) 1 *(Blomqvist 25)*, Legia Warsaw (0)
2 *(Pisz 73, Bednarz 90)* 11,017
Hajduk Split (1) 1, *(Stimac 4)*, Panathinaikos (0) 1
(Borelli 55) 11,000
Maccabi Tel Aviv (0) 0, Grasshoppers (1) 1
(Comisetti 4) 15,342
Steaua (1)1 *(Ilie 32)*, Salzburg (0) 0 22,000

CHAMPIONS LEAGUE

Group A
Dynamo Kiev (0) 1 *(Kossovski 61)*, Panathinaikos (0) 0
85,000
*(Dynamo Kiev banned from the competition for
alleged bribery of a match official. Replaced by
Aalborg)*
Nantes (0) 0, Porto (0) 0 25,000
Panathinaikos (2) 3 *(Georgiadis G H 17, Warzycha 30,
46)*, Nantes (0) 1 *(D'Doram 87)* 62,000
Porto (1) 2 *(Rui Barros 42, 63)*, Aalborg (0) 0 25,000
Porto (0) 0, Panathinaikos (1) 1 *(Markos 40)* 25,000
Nantes (1) 3 *(Ouedec 5, Pedros 56, Kosecki 75)*, Aalborg
(0) 1 *(Pedersen 46)* 30,000
Aalborg (1) 2 *(Andersen 7, Madsen 89)*, Panathinaikos
(1) 1 *(Warzycha 42)* 6100
Panathinaikos (0) 0, Porto (0) 0 62,000
Aalborg (0) 0, Nantes (1) 2 *(Guyot 10, Ouedec 69)*, 8000
Panathinaikos (2) 2 *(Alexoudis 1, Georgiadis G S 38)*,
Aalborg (0) 0 32,352
Porto (1) 2 *(Drulovic 11, Jose Carlos 56)*, Nantes (2) 2
(Pedros 3, 34) 25,000
Aalborg (1) 2 *(Andersen 10, Madsen 69)*, Porto (0) 2
(Emerson 62, 75) 3950
Nantes (0) 0, Panathinaikos (0) 0 30,000

Final table

	P	W	D	L	F	A	Pts
Panathinaikos	6	3	2	1	7	3	11
Nantes	6	2	3	1	8	6	9
Porto	6	1	4	1	6	5	7
Aalborg	6	1	1	4	5	12	4

Group B
Blackburn R (0) 0, Spartak Moscow (1) 1 *(Yuran 41)*
20,940
Legia Warsaw (0) 3 *(Pisz 64, 73, Staniek 69)*,
Rosenborg (0) 1 *(Jakobsen 63)* 10,000
Rosenborg (1) 2 *(Loken 29, Stensaas 86)*, Blackburn R
(0) 1 *(Newell 63)* 12,000
Spartak Moscow (1) 2 *(Nikiforov 14 (pen), Yuran 54)*,
Legia Warsaw (0) 1 *(Jozwiak 85)* 53,000
Legia Warsaw (1) 1 *(Podbrozny 25)*, Blackburn R (0) 0,
15,000

Rosenborg (2) 2 *(Loken 2, Brattbakk 45)*, Spartak
Moscow (0) 4 *(Alenitchev 59, Nikiforov 66, Kechinov
75, 82)* 12,000
Spartak Moscow (3) 4 *(Shmarov 1, Yuran 6, Tsymbalar
20, Tichonov 80)*, Rosenborg (0) 1 *(Loken 90)* 45,000
Blackburn R (0) 0, Legia Warsaw (0) 0 20,897
Spartak Moscow (1) 3 *(Alenichev 28, Nikiforov 47,
Mamedov 54)*, Blackburn R (0) 0 25,000
Rosenborg (2) 4 *(Strand 17, Brattbakk 45, Jakobsen 64,
Heggem 89)*, Legia Warsaw (0) 0 11,480
Blackburn R (4) 4 *(Shearer 16 (pen), Newell 31, 38, 40)*,
Rosenborg (1) 1 *(Iversen 30)* 20,677
Legia Warsaw (0) 0, Spartak Moscow (1) 1 *(Mamedov
40)* 15,000

Final table

	P	W	D	L	F	A	Pts
Spartak Moscow	6	6	0	0	15	4	18
Legia Warsaw	6	2	1	3	5	8	7
Rosenborg	6	2	0	4	11	16	6
Blackburn R	6	1	1	4	5	8	4

Group C
Steaua (0) 1 *(Prodan 84)*, Rangers (0) 0 26,000
Borussia Dortmund (1) 1 *(Moller 1)*, Juventus (2) 3
(Padovano 12, Del Piero 37, Conte 69) 35,800
Juventus (2) 3 *(Di Livio 35, Del Piero 39, Ravanelli 49)*,
Steaua (0) 0 35,000
Rangers (0) 2 *(Gough 62, Ferguson 72)* Borussia
Dortmund (1) 2 *(Herrlich 18, Kree 68)* 33,209
Juventus (3) 4 *(Ravanelli 14, 74, Conte 16, Del Piero 22)*,
Rangers (0) 1 *(Gough 77)* 50,000
Borussia Dortmund (0) 1 *(Ricken 58)*, Steaua (0) 0 35,000
Steaua (0) 0, Borussia Dortmund (0) 0 18,000
Rangers (0) 0, Juventus (1) 4 *(Del Piero 16, Torricelli 65,
Ravanelli 88, Marocchi 90)* 44,523
Rangers (1) 1 *(Gascoigne 32)*, Steaua (0) 1 *(Ilie 55)* 30,882
Juventus (0) 1 *(Del Piero 90)*, Borussia Dortmund (1) 2
(Zorc 30, Ricken 65) 40,000
Borussia Dortmund (1) 2 *(Moller 16, Riedle 48)*, Rangers
(1) 2 *(Laudrup 10, Durie 84)* 35,800
Steaua (0) 0, Juventus (0) 0 2500

Final table

	P	W	D	L	F	A	Pts
Juventus	6	4	1	1	15	4	13
Borussia Dortmund	6	2	3	1	8	8	9
Steaua	6	1	3	2	2	5	6
Rangers	6	0	3	3	6	14	3

Group D
Ajax (1) 1 *(Overmars 14)*, Real Madrid (0) 0 42,000
Grasshoppers (0) 0, Ferencvaros (0) 3 *(Lisztes 61, Vincze
78, 90)* 15,000
Ferencvaros (0) 1 *(Nyilas 59)*, Ajax (0) 5 *(Litmanen 57,
80 (pen), 88, Kluivert 67, Frank de Boer 84)* 18,000
Real Madrid (0) 2 *(Zamorano 68, 88)*, Grasshoppers (0) 0
62,000
Real Madrid (3) 6 *(Raul 23, 25, 84, Zamorano 34, 46,
Hierro 55)*, Ferencvaros (0) 1 *(Kopunovic 62)* 50,000
Ajax (1) 3 *(Kluivert 10, 68, George 87)*,
Grasshoppers (0) 0 42,000
Ferencvaros (1) 1 *(Albert 36)*, Real Madrid (0) 1
(Raul 74) 22,000
Grasshoppers (0) 0, Ajax (0) 0 20,000
Real Madrid (0) 0, Ajax (0) 2 *(Litmanen 63, Kluivert 75)*
85,000
Ferencvaros (2) 3 *(Albert 21, Lisztes 25, Nyilas 86 (pen))*,
Grasshoppers (1) 3 *(Subiat 22, Comisetti 48,
Ibrahim 64)* 18,000
Grasshoppers (0) 0, Real Madrid (0) 2 *(Raul 55,
Michel 67)* 20,100
Ajax (2) 4 *(Overmars 17, Ronald de Boer 21, Litmanen
61, 66)*, Ferencvaros (0) 0 45,000

Final table

	P	W	D	L	F	A	Pts
Ajax	6	5	1	0	15	1	16
Real Madrid	6	3	1	2	11	5	10
Ferencvaros	6	1	2	3	9	19	5
Grasshoppers	6	0	2	4	3	13	2

Quarter-finals, first leg

Borussia Dortmund (0) 0, Ajax (1) 2 *(Davids 8, Kluivert 83)*   35,800

Legia Warsaw (0) 0, Panathinaikos (0) 0   12,000

Nantes (1) 2 *(N'Doram 28, Ouedec 68)*, Spartak Moscow (0) 0   31,500

Real Madrid (1) 1 *(Raul 21)*, Juventus (0) 0   72,000

Quarter-finals, second leg

Ajax (0) 1 *(Musampa 74)*, Borussia Dortmund (0) 0   42,000

Juventus (1) 2 *(Del Piero 16, Padovano 55)*, Real Madrid (0) 0   70,000

Panathinaikos (1) 3 *(Warzycha 34, 58, Borrelli 72)*, Legia Warsaw (0) 0   75,000

Spartak Moscow (2) 2 *(Nikiforov 33,38)*, Nantes (0) 2 *(Ouedec 63, 85)*   30,000

Semi-finals, first leg

Ajax (0) 0, Panathinaikos (0) 1 *(Warzycha 87)*   42,000

Juventus (0) 2 *(Vialli 49, Jugovic 66)*, Nantes (0) 0   50,425

Semi-finals, second leg

Nantes (1) 3 *(Decroix 43, N'Doram 69, Renou 82)*, Juventus (1) 2 *(Vialli 17, Sousa 50)*   34,210

Panathinaikos (0) 0, Ajax (1) 3 *(Litmanen 4, 76, Wooter 86)*   77,433

Final

Ajax (1) 1, Juventus (1) 1

(in Rome, 22 May 1996, 67,000)

Ajax: Van der Sar; Silooy, Blind, Frank de Boer (Scholton 69), Bogarde, Ronald de Boer (Wooter 90), Litmanen, Davids, George, Kanu, Musampa (Kluivert 46).
Scorer: Litmanen 41.
Juventus: Peruzzi; Torricelli, Ferrara, Vierchowod, Pessotto, Conte (Jugovic 43), Sousa (Di Livio 58), Deschamps, Ravanelli (Padovano 77), Vialli, Del Piero.
Scorer: Ravanelli 13.
(aet; Juventus won 4-2 on penalties).
Referee: Vega (Spain).

Gianluca Vialli (Juventus) evades the despairing dive of Ajax goalkeeper Edwin Van der Sar, while defender Winston Bogarde watches proceedings in the European Cup Final. (Colorsport).

EUROPEAN CUP 1995–96 - BRITISH AND IRISH CLUBS

Preliminary Round, First Leg

9 AUG

Rangers (0) 1 *(Durie)*
Anorthosis (0) 0 43,519
Rangers: Goram; Wright, Robertson, Gough, McLaren, Reid (Durie), McCall, Gascoigne, Laudrup, Hateley, Ferguson (Miller).
Anorthosis: Panayiotou N; Stavrou, Panayi, Kastanis, Andreou, Panayiotou P (Melanarkitis), Assiotis, Kiriakov, Todorov, Ignatov (Chrisioforiou), Gogic.

Preliminary Round, Second Leg

23 AUG

Anorthosis (0) 0
Rangers (0) 0 9500
Anorthosis: Panayiotou N; Panayiotou A, Panayi, Kastanis, Assiotis (Pounas), Costas, Kiriakov, Todorov, Andreou, Ignatov (Thoma), Gogic.
Rangers: Goram; Wright, Robertson, Gough, McLaren, Petric, McCall, Gascoigne (Durrant), Durie (Murray), Hateley, Miller.

Group B

13 SEPT

Blackburn R (0) 0
Spartak Moscow (1) 1 *(Yuran)* 20,940
Blackburn R: Flowers; Berg, Le Saux, Batty, Hendry, Pearce, Ripley (Makel), Sherwood, Shearer, Newell, Atkins (Sutton).
Spartak Moscow: Cherchesov; Nikiforov, Mamedov, Onopko, Khlestov, Tikhonov, Kulkov, Piatnitsky, Tsymbalar, Shmarov (Kechinov), Yuran.

27 SEPT

Rosenborg (1) 2 *(Loken, Stensaas)*
Blackburn R (0) 1 *(Newell)* 12,000
Rosenborg: By Rise; Kvarme, Bragstad, Hoftun, Stensaas, Strand (Staurvik), Skammelsrud, Soltvedt, Loken (Iversen), Jakobsen, Brattbakk (Heggem).
Blackburn R: Flowers; Berg, Kenna, Batty, Hendry, Pearce, Newell, Sherwood (Warhurst), Shearer, Sutton, Makel (Ripley).

18 OCT

Legia Warsaw (1) 1 *(Podbrozny)*
Blackburn R (0) 0 15,000
Legia Warsaw: Szczesny; Jozwiak, Zielinski, Mandziejewicz, Lewandowski, Michalski, Pisz, Staniek, Bednarz, Podbrozny, Kucharski.
Blackburn R: Flowers; Berg, Kenna, Batty, Hendry, Pearce, Warhurst (Newell), Sherwood, Shearer, Sutton, Holmes.

1 NOV

Blackburn R (0) 0
Legia Warsaw (0) 0 20,897
Blackburn R: Flowers; Berg, Kenna, Batty, Hendry, Pearce, Ripley, Sherwood, Shearer, Newell (Sutton), Warhurst (Le Saux).
Legia Warsaw: Szczesny; Mandziejewicz, Jozwiak, Michalski, Lewandowski, Pisz, Jalocha, Wieszczycki, Bednarz, Podbrozny (Kucharski), Staniek.

22 NOV

Spartak Moscow (1) 3 *(Alenichev, Nikiforov, Mamedov)*
Blackburn R (0) 0 25,000
Spartak Moscow: Cherchesov; Mamedov, Onopko, Nikiforov, Khlestov, Alenichev, Kulkov, Tsymbalar (Piatnitsky), Tikhonov (Mukhamadiev), Shmarov, Yuran (Kechinov).
Blackburn R: Flowers; Kenna, Le Saux (Holmes), Batty, Hendry, Berg, Ripley (Sutton), Sherwood, Shearer, Newell, Warhurst.

6 DEC

Blackburn R (4) 4 *(Shearer (pen), Newell 3)*
Rosenborg (1) 1 *(Iversen)* 20,677
Blackburn R: Flowers; Berg, Kenna, Sherwood, Marker, Sutton, Ripley, Warhurst, Shearer, Newell, Holmes (Gallacher).
Rosenborg: By Rise; Kvarme, Bragstad (Staurvik), Hoftun, Stensaas, Iversen, Strand (Heggem), Skammelsrud, Soltvedt, Jakobsen, Brattbakk.

Group C

13 SEPT

Steaua (0) 1 *(Prodan)*
Rangers (0) 0 26,000
Steaua: Stelea; Csik, Dobos, Prodan, Pirvu, Militaru, Galca, Bucur (Filipescu), Raducan, Ilie A (Rosu), Vladoiu (Ilie S).
Rangers: Goram; Wright, Gough, McLaren, Cleland, Miller (Durie), Gascoigne, Petric, McCoist, Laudrup, Durrant (Murray).

27 SEPT

Rangers (0) 2 *(Gough, Ferguson)*
Borussia Dortmund (1) 2 *(Herrlich, Kree)* 33,209
Rangers: Goram; Wright, Petric, McCall, Gough, Cleland, Durie (Durrant), Gascoigne, McCoist, Laudrup (Ferguson), Miller.
Borussia Dortmund: Klos; Kohler, Sammer, Cesar (Schmidt), Reuter, Freund, Zorc, Kree, Herrlich, Moller (Tretschok), Ricken (Berger).

18 OCT

Juventus (3) 4 *(Ravanelli 2, Conte, Del Piero)*
Rangers (0) 1 *(Gough)* 50,000
Juventus: Peruzzi; Porrini (Carrera), Ferrara, Vierchowod, Torricelli, Conte (Tacchinardi), Sousa, Deschamps, Di Livio (Marocchi), Ravanelli, Del Piero.
Rangers: Goram; Wright (Brown), Robertson, McCall (Murray), Petric, Gough, Moore, Cleland, Durie, Salenko, McCoist.

1 NOV

Rangers (0) 0 42,523
Juventus (1) 4 *(Del Piero, Torricelli, Ravanelli, Marocchi)*
Rangers: Goram (Thomson); Wright (Durrant), Brown, Petric, Gough, McCall, Ferguson, Gascoigne, Miller (McCoist), Bollan, Salenko.
Juventus: Peruzzi; Torricelli, Carrera, Porrini (Ferrara), Pessotto, Di Livio, Conte, Sousa, Tacchinardi (Marocchi), Del Piero, Vialli (Ravanelli).

22 NOV

Rangers (1) 1 *(Gascoigne)*
Steaua (0) 1 *(Ilie A)* 30,882
Rangers: Goram; McLaren, Robertson, Brown (Bollan), Gough, Petric, McCall (Murray), Gascoigne, McCoist, Durrant (Miller), Laudrup.
Steaua: Stelea; Filipescu, Dobos, Prodan, Pirvu, Bucur, Lacatus (Raducan) Militaru (Rosu), Csik, Vladoiu, Ilie A (Nagy).

6 DEC

Borussia Dortmund (1) 2 *(Moller, Riedle)*
Rangers (1) 2 *(Laudrup, Durie)* 35,800
Borussia Dortmund: Klos; Reinhardt (Sosa), Kree, Freund, Franck, Gerger, Wolters, Zorc, Riedle (Kutowski), Moller, Herrlich.
Rangers: Goram; Cleland (Durrant), Robertson, Gough, McLaren, Bollan, Miller (McCoist) Gascoigne, Durie, McCall, Laudrup.

EUROPEAN CUP-WINNERS' CUP

EUROPEAN CUP-WINNERS' CUP FINALS 1961–96

Year	Winners		Runners-up		Venue	Attendance	Referee
1961	Fiorentina	2	Rangers	0 *(1st Leg)*	Glasgow	80,000	Steiner (A)
	Fiorentina	2	Rangers	1 *(2nd Leg)*	Florence	50,000	Hernadi (H)
1962	Atletico Madrid	1	Fiorentina	1	Glasgow	27,389	Wharton (S)
Replay	Atletico Madrid	3	Fiorentina	0	Stuttgart	45,000	Tschenscher (WG)
1963	Tottenham Hotspur	5	Atletico Madrid	1	Rotterdam	25,000	Van Leuwen (Ho)
1964	Sporting Lisbon	3	MTK Budapest	3 *(aet)*	Brussels	9000	Van Nuffel (Bel)
Replay	Sporting Lisbon	1	MTK Budapest	0	Antwerp	18,000	Versyp (Bel)
1965	West Ham U	2	Munich 1860	0	Wembley	100,000	Szolt (H)
1966	Borussia Dortmund	2	Liverpool	1 *(aet)*	Glasgow	41,657	Schwinte (F)
1967	Bayern Munich	1	Rangers	0 *(aet)*	Nuremberg	69,480	Lo Bello (I)
1968	AC Milan	2	Hamburg	0	Rotterdam	60,000	Ortiz (Sp)
1969	Slovan Bratislava	3	Barcelona	2	Basle	40,000	Van Ravens (Ho)
1970	Manchester C	2	Gornik Zabrze	1	Vienna	10,000	Schiller (A)
1971	Chelsea	1	Real Madrid	1 *(aet)*	Athens	42,000	Scheurer (Sw)
Replay	Chelsea	2	Real Madrid	1 *(aet)*	Athens	24,000	Bucheli (Sw)
1972	Rangers	3	Moscow Dynamo	2	Barcelona	35,000	Ortiz (Sp)
1973	AC Milan	1	Leeds U	0	Salonika	45,000	Mihas (Gr)
1974	Magdeburg	2	AC Milan	0	Rotterdam	5000	Van Gemert (Ho)
1975	Dynamo Kiev	3	Ferencvaros	0	Basle	13,000	Davidson (S)
1976	Anderlecht	4	West Ham U	2	Brussels	58,000	Wurtz (F)
1977	Hamburg	2	Anderlecht	0	Amsterdam	65,000	Partridge (E)
1978	Anderlecht	4	Austria/WAC	0	Paris	48,679	Adlinger (WG)
1979	Barcelona	4	Fortuna Dusseldorf	3 *(aet)*	Basle	58,000	Palotai (H)
1980	Valencia	0	Arsenal	0	Brussels	40,000	Christov (Cz)
	(aet; Valencia won 5-4 on penalties)						
1981	Dynamo Tbilisi	2	Carl Zeiss Jena	1	Dusseldorf	9000	Lattanzi (I)
1982	Barcelona	2	Standard Liege	1	Barcelona	100,000	Eschweiler (WG)
1983	Aberdeen	2	Real Madrid	1 *(aet)*	Gothenburg	17,804	Menegali (I)
1984	Juventus	2	Porto	1	Basle	60,000	Prokop (EG)
1985	Everton	3	Rapid Vienna	1	Rotterdam	30,000	Casarin (I)
1986	Dynamo Kiev	3	Atletico Madrid	0	Lyon	39,300	Wohrer (A)
1987	Ajax	1	Lokomotiv Leipzig	0	Athens	35,000	Agnolin (I)
1988	Mechelen	1	Ajax	0	Strasbourg	39,446	Pauly (WG)
1989	Barcelona	2	Sampdoria	0	Berne	45,000	Courtney (E)
1990	Sampdoria	2	Anderlecht	0	Gothenburg	20,103	Galler (Sw)
1991	Manchester U	2	Barcelona	1	Rotterdam	45,000	Karlsson (Se)
1992	Werder Bremen	2	Monaco	0	Lisbon	16,000	D'Elia (I)
1993	Parma	3	Antwerp	1	Wembley	37,393	Assenmacher (G)
1994	Arsenal	1	Parma	0	Copenhagen	33,765	Krondl (Czr)
1995	Zaragoza	2	Arsenal	1	Paris	42,424	Ceccarini (I)
1996	Paris St Germain	1	Rapid Vienna	0	Brussels	37,500	Pairetto (I)

EUROPEAN CUP-WINNERS' CUP 1995–96

Preliminary Round, First Leg
Apoel (2) 3 *(Andoniou 18, Ioannou 44, 66)*,
　Neftchi Baku (0) 0　14,000
DAG Liepaja (1) 1 *(Dobretsjev 6)*, Lantana Tallinn (1) 2
　*(Lapsa 18, Borisov 75) (match awarded 3-0 to DAG
　Liepaja as Lantana fielded an ineligible player)* 1500
Derry City (1) 1 *(McCourt 44)*, Lokomotiv Sofia (0) 0
　5500
Donetsk (3) 4 *(Ohtyurkin 10, Matvejev 20, Orbu 31, 90)*,
　Linfield (0) 1 *(Wing 48)*　30,000
Dynamo 93 Minsk (1) 1 *(Lobanov 37)*, Molde (0) 1
　(Sundgot 85)　10,000
Grevenmacher (1) 3 *(Jungbluth 8, 54, Andres Silva 58)*,
　KR Reykjavik (0) 2 *(Bibercic 52, Egilsson 84)* 1000
Katowice (2) 2 *(Bilski 26, Karwan 29)*,
　Ararat Erevan (0) 0　3000
Maccabi Haifa (2) 4 *(Mizrahi 8, 35, 82 (pen), Shitrit 56)*,
　KI Klakksvik (0) 0　8000
Obilic (0) 0, Dynamo Batumi (0) 1 *(Machutadze 71)* 1000
Tiligul (0) 0, Sion (0) 0　5000
TPS Turku (1) 1 *(Wallden 30)*, Teuta (0) 0　4200
Vac (0) 1 *(Romanek 90)*, Sileks (0) 1 *(Micevski 58)* 6000
Vaduz (0) 0, Hradec Kralove (3) 5 *(Cerny 15, Samec 30,
　49, 59, Ptacek 32)*　1300
Valletta (0) 0, Inter Bratislava (0) 0　2500
Wrexham (0) 0, Petrolul (0) 0　4308
Zalgiris (0) 2 *(Baltusnikas 53, Tereskinas 67)*, Mura
　Murska (0) 0　2000

Preliminary Round, Second Leg
Ararat Erevan (2) 2 *(Gspaian 23, Donoian 26)*, Katowice
　(0) 0 *Ararat won 5-4 on penalties*　10,000
Dynamo Batumi (0) 2 *(Machutadze 65, Mudzhiri 79)*,
　Obilic (2) 2 *(Tovic 8, Popovic 32)*　23,000
Hradec Kralove (5) 9 *(Samec 4, 9, 30, 53, Urban 15, 82
　(pen), Vrabel 37, 50 (pen), Smarda 64)*, Vaduz (1) 1
　(Ritter 27)　3558
Inter Bratislava (3) 5 *(Rupec 10, Tomko 15, 39, Saliba 79
　(og), Landerl 85)*, Valletta (0) 2 *(Doncic 61, Zarb 84)*
　2300
KI Klakksvik (0) 3 *(Danielsen 53, 63, 70)*, Maccabi Haifa
　(1) 2 *(Revivo 31, Shitrit 84)*　295
KR Reykjavik (1) 2 *(Biberic 45, Porca 62)*,
　Grevenmacher (0) 0　1600
Lantana (0) 0, DAG Liepaja (0) 0　700
Linfield (0) 0, Donetsk (0) 1 *(Voskoboynic 86)*　3000
Lokomotiv Sofia (2) 2 *(Slavchev 6, Hvoinev 29)*, Derry
　City (0) 0　3000
Molde (1) 2 *(Solskjaer 4, Stavsum 67)*, Dynamo 93 Minsk
　(1) 1 *(Skriptsjenko 19)*　2989
Mura Murska (0) 2 *(Kokol 11, Alihodzic 85)*, Zalgiris (0)
　1 *(Vencevicius 73)*　4500
Neftchi Baku (0) 0, Apoel (0) 0　5000
Petrolul (0) 1 *(Pirlog 59)*, Wrexham (0) 0　10,000
Sileks (2) 3 *(Memedi 15, 67, Borov 35)*, Vac (1) 1
　(Orguja 20)　12,000
Sion (3) 3 *(Moser 22, Herr 28, Bonvin 44)*, Tiligul (0) 2
　(Oprea 79, Popovitsj 90)　6500
Teuta (2) 3 *(Vila 8, Koca 19, Bushi 55)*, TPS Turku (0) 0
　5000

First Round, First Leg
AEK Athens (1) 2 *(Vlachos 45, Borbokis 70)*, Sion (0) 0
　25,000
Apoel (0) 0, La Coruna (0) 0　20,000
FC Brugge (0) 1 *(Spehar 87)*, Donetsk (0) 0　10,000
DAG Liepaja (0) 0, Feyenoord (1) 7 *(Larsson 2, Blinker
　47, 58, 62, Trustfull 61, Koeman 78, Obiku 88)* 3000
Dynamo Batumi (1) 2 *(Machutadze 9, Tugushi 66)*,
　Celtic (2) 3 *(Thom 21, 87, Donnelly 39)*　18,000
Dynamo Moscow (1) 3 *(Terjokin 45, 90, Stafronov 73)*,
　Ararat Erevan (0) 1 *(Stepanjan 71)*　7500
Hardec Cralove (2) 5 *(Samec 33, 76, Hinek 39, Cerny 52,
　Ptacek 90)*, FC Copenhagen (0) 0　4532
Inter Bratislava (0) 0, Zaragoza (1) 2 *(Morientes 43,
　Oscar 60)*　3000
KR Reykjavik (1) 2 *(Bibercic 36 (pen), 67 (pen))*,
　Everton (1) 3 *(Ebbrell 22, Unsworth 57 (pen),
　Amokachi 88)*　6000
Lokomotiv Sofia (2) 3 *(Marinov 40, Petkov 42 (pen),
　Donev 57)*, Halmstad (1) 1 *(Svensson 32)*　4000

Moenchengladbach (2) 3 *(Pflipsen 6, Effenberg 19,
　Klinkert 88)*, Sileks (0) 0　13,750
Molde (0) 2 *(Salkskjer 56, Stavrum 81)*, Paris St Germain
　(0) 3 *(Le Guen 76, Djorkaeff 78 (pen), Valdes 84)*
　3379
Rapid (1) 3 *(Barisic 45, 90, Ivanov 60)*, Petrolul (0) 1
　(Toader 65)　12,000
Sporting Lisbon (2) 4 *(Pedro Barbosa 7, 10, 50, Sa Pinto
　89)*, Maccabi Haifa (0) 0　35,000
Teuta (0) 0, Parma (0) 2 *(Zola 80, 85)*　15,000
Zalgiris (1) 2 *(Tereskinas 7, Mikoelenas 67)*, Trabzonspor
　(1) 2 *(Arveladze S 25, Abdullah 54*　3000

First Round, Second Leg
Ararat Erevan (0) 0, Dynamo Moscow (0) 1 *(Terekhin
　66)*　16,000
Celtic (2) 4 *(Thom 18, 20, Donnelly 46, Walker 90)*,
　Dynamo Batumi (0) 0　31,969
FC Copenhagen (1) 2 *(Tengstedt 28, Tur 72)*, Hradec
　Kralove (2) 2 *(Urbanek 8, Rehar 12)*　4432
Donetsk (0) 1 *(Voskoboynik 61)*, FC Brugge (0) 1
　(Stanic 60)　40,000
Everton (0) 3 *(Stuart 56, Grant 65, Rideout 87)*, KR
　Reykjavik (1) 1 *(Danielsson 20)*　18,422
Feyenoord (2) 6 *(Heus 37 (pen), Trustfull 43, Obiku 57,
　63, 65, Glaucio 61)*, DAG Liepaja (0) 0　13,000
Halmstad (1) 2 *(Andersson R 21, Andersson T 75)*,
　Lokomotiv Sofia (0) 0　3145
La Coruna (5) 8 *(Bebeto 16, 45, Radchenko 21, 28, 68,
　Beguiristain 43, Donato 60, Aldana 78)*, Apoel (0) 0
　21,000
Maccabi Haifa (0) 0, Sporting Lisbon (0) 0　7000
Paris St Germain (2) 3 *(Nouma 7, 13, Djorkaeff 77)*,
　Molde (0) 0　18,898
Parma (1) 2 *(Melli 8, Inzaghi 90)*, Teuta (0) 0　10,200
Petrolul (0) 0, Rapid (0) 0　12,000
Sileks (2) 3 *(Memedi 52, Boskovski 60)*,
　Moenchengladbach (1) 3 *(Effenberg 29, Dahlin 54,
　Nielsen 80)*　17,000
Sion (1) 2 *(Bonvin 20, Giallanza 85)*, AEK Athens (0) 2
　(Ketsbaja 84, Batista 87)　6900
Trabzonspor (0) 1 *(Hami 37)*, Zalgiris (0) 0　25,000
Zaragoza (1) 3 *(Poyet 11, Higuera 64, Dani 72)*, Inter
　Bratislava (1) 1 *(Obsitnik 77)*　14,000

Second Round, First Leg
Dynamo Moscow (0) 1 *(Kuzentsov 59)*, Hradec Kralove
　(0) 0　15,000
Everton (0) 0, Feyenoord (0) 0　27,526
Halmstad (2) 3 *(Gudmundsson 7, 31, Andersson R 36)*,
　Parma (0) 0　14,000
Moenchengladbach (0) 4 *(Dahlin 51, 92, Pflipsen 55,
　Wynhoff 67)*, AEK Athens (0) 1 *(Maladenis 79)*
　22,000
Paris St Germain (0) 1 *(Djorkaeff 76)*, Celtic (0) 0 30,010
Sporting Lisbon (2) 2 *(Pinto 14, Alvez 25)*,
　Rapid (0) 0　50,000
Trabzonspor (0) 0, La Coruna (0) 1 *(Donato 60)*　27,000
Zaragoza (2) 2 *(Aragon 28 (pen), Garcia 33)*, FC Brugge
　(0) 1 *(Staelens 73 (pen))*　26,000

Second Round, Second Leg
AEK Athens (0) 0, Moenchengladbach (0) 1 *(Effenberg
　71)*　23,000
FC Brugge (0) 0, Zaragoza (0) 1 *(Garcia 90)*　18,000
Celtic (0) 0, Paris St Germain (2) 3 *(Loko 36, 42,
　Nouma 68)*　34,822
Feyenoord (1) 1 *(Blinker 40)*, Everton (0) 0　40,000
Hradec Kralove (1) 1 *(Kaplan 14)*,
　Dynamo Moscow (0) 0　11,530
　(aet; Dynamo Moscow won 3-1 on penalties)
La Coruna (3) 3 *(Donato 21, Bebeto 38, 80)*, Trabzonspor
　(0) 0　28,000
Parma (2) 4 *(Inzaghi 1, Dino Baggio 38, Stoichkov 53,
　Andersson A 69 (og))*, Halmstad (0) 0　13,053
Rapid (1) 4 *(Kuhbauer 25, Stumpf 92, 104, Jancker 110)*,
　Sporting Lisbon (0) 0　25,000

Quarter-finals, First Leg
Dynamo Moscow (0) 0, Rapid (1) 1 *(Stumpf 34)*　7000
La Coruna (0) 1 *(Fernandez 69)*, Zaragoza (0) 0　15,000

Moenchengladbach (2) 2 *(Wynhoff 8, Kastenmaier 43*
  (pen)), Feyenoord (2) 2 *(Van Gastel 35,*
  Koeman 45 (pen))   51,000
Parma (0) 1 *(Stoichkov 59)*, Paris St Germain (0) 0 22,000

Quarter-finals, Second Leg
Feyenoord (0) 1 *(Trustfull 84)*, Moenchengladbach (0) 0
                                 22,000
Paris St Germain (2) 3 *(Rai 9 (pen), 69 (pen), Loko 38)*,
  Parma (1) 1 *(Melli 26)*   43,686
Rapid (0) 3 *(Jancker 48, 75, Stoeger 63)*, Dynamo
  Moscow (0) 0   44,000

Zaragoza (1) 1 *(Morientes 37)*, La Coruna (0) 1
                                32,000

Semi-finals, First Leg
Feyenoord (0) 1 *(Koeman 53 (pen))*, Rapid (0) 1
  (Jancker 67)   40,000
La Coruna (0) 0, Paris St Germain (0) 1 *(Djorkaeff 90)*
                                29,000

Semi-finals, Second Leg
Paris St Germain (0) 1 *(Loko 58)*, La Coruna (0) 0 43,965
Rapid (3) 3 *(Jancker 2, Stumpf 32, 34)*,
  Feyenoord (0) 0   49,000

Final: Paris St Germain (1) 1, Rapid (0) 0
(in Brussels, 8 May 1996, 37,500)

Paris St Germain: Lama; Roche, Le Guen, N'Gotty, Fournier (Llacer 77), Bravo, Guerin, Colleter, Loko, Rai (Dely Valdes 11), Djorkaeff.
Scorer: N'Gotty 29.
Rapid: Konsel; Schottel, Ivanov, Hatz, Heraf, Kuhbauer, Stoger, Guggi, Marasek, Stumpf (Barisic 46), Jancker.
Referee: Pairetto (Italy).

Youri Djorkaeff (Paris St Germain) and Peter Schottel (Rapid Vienna) about to demonstrate something akin to a military two-step during the Cup-Winners' Cup Final. (Colorsport).

EUROPEAN CUP-WINNERS' CUP 1995–96 – BRITISH AND IRISH CLUBS

Preliminary Round, First Leg

10 AUG

Derry City (1) 1 *(McCourt)*

Lokomotiv Sofia (0) 0   5500

Derry City: O'Dowd; Vaudequin, Curran, Gauld, McLoughlin, McCourt, Carlyle, Doolin, Mohan (Heaney), Fraser, Coyle.
Lokomotiv Sofia: Apostolev; Radivoevic, Velkov, Ofchev, Zafirov, Koelev, Marinov, Anguelov, Petkov, Hvoinev, Donnev.

Donetsk (3) 4 *(Atelkin, Matveev, Orbu 2)*

Linfield (0) 1 *(Ewing)*   20,000

Donetsk: Shutkov; Pyatenko, Koval, Chikhradze, Kochvar, Spivak, Orbu, Atelkin (Fedkov) (Voskoboynik), Petrov, Kriventzov, Matveev (Onopko).
Linfield: Lamont; Crothers, Easton, Ewing, McLean S, Beatty, Campbell, McGee, Erskine, Spiers, Bailie.

Wrexham (0) 0

Petrolul (0) 0   4308

Wrexham: Marriott; Brace, Hardy, Phillips, Hunter, Jones B, Futcher, Owen, Connolly, Watkin, Durkan.
Petrolul: Preda; Chirita, Leahu, Balaceanu, Grigore, Rachita, Pirlog (Bastina), Abaluta, Zafiris (Andreicut), Zmoleanu, Toader (Cadar).

Preliminary Round, Second Leg

24 AUG

Petrolul (0) 1 *(Pirlog)*

Wrexham (0) 0   10,000

Petrolul: Preda; Chirita, Leahu, Balaceanu, Grigore, Rachita, Pirlog, Abaluta, Zafiris (Toader), Zmoleanu (Bastina), Andreicut (Balasam).
Wrexham: Marriott; Thomas, Hardy, Phillips, Hunter, Jones B, Futcher (Barnes), Owen, Connolly, Watkin, Cross.

Linfield (0) 0

Donetsk (0) 1 *(Voskoboynic)*   3000

Linfield: Lamont; Dornan, Easton, Ewing (McCoosh), Spiers, Beatty (McLoughlin), Campbell, Gorman, Erskine, Fenlon, Bailie.
Donetsk: Nikitin; Pyatenko, Koval, Chikhradze, Popov, Kochvar, Orbu, Voskoboynik, Petrov (Shutkov), Kriventzov (Lenov), Matveev (Fedkov).

Lokomotiv Sofia (2) 2 *(Slavtchev, Hvoinev)*

Derry City (0) 0   4000

Lokomotiv Sofia: Apostolev; Radivoevic, Zafirov, Slavchev, Vokov, Anguelov, Petkov (Antonov), Koelev, Hvoinev, Donnev, Borisov (Marinov).
Derry City: O'Dowd; Vaudequin, Curran, Gauld, McLoughlin, McCourt (Tohill), Carlyle, Doolin, Hutton, Mohan, Coyle.

First Round, First Leg

14 SEPT

Dynamo Batumi (1) 2 *(Machutadze, Tugushi)*

Celtic (2) 3 *(Thom 2, Donnelly)*   18,000

Dynamo Batumi: Baladze; Malanya (Antidze), Shanidze, Mujiri, Shekiladze, Torgashvili, Makharadze, Machutadze, Tugushi (Glonti), Udjmaruridze (Marhazadze), Mindadze.
Celtic: Marshall; Boyd, McKinlay, Vata, Hughes, Grant, O'Donnell, Donnelly (Falconer), Walker (McLaughlin), Thom, Collins.

KR Reykjavik (1) 2 *(Bibercic 2 (2 pens))*

Everton (1) 3 *(Ebbrell, Unsworth (pen), Amokachi)* 6000

KR Reykjavik: Finnbogason; Jonsson S, Dervic, Adolfsson, Egilsson, Bjornsson, Porca, Gudjonsson, Danielsson, Bibercic, Benediktsson.
Everton: Southall; Jackson (Holmes), Ablett, Ebbrell, Watson, Unsworth, Limpar (Grant), Parkinson, Amokachi, Rideout, Hinchcliffe.

First Round, Second Leg

28 SEPT

Celtic (2) 4 *(Thom 2, Donnelly, Walker)*

Dynamo Batumi (0) 0   31,969

Celtic: Marshall; Vata, McKinlay, McStay, Boyd, Hughes, Donnelly (Hay), McLaughlin, Thom (Gray), Van Hooijdonk (Walker), Grant.
Dynamo Batumi: Tagonidze; Mindadze, Makharadze M, Shekiladze, Shanidze, Phutkaradze (Glonti), Torgashvili, Kantidze (Makharadze D), Mujiri, Tugushi, Udjmajuridze.

Everton (0) 3 *(Stuart, Grant, Rideout)*

KR Reykjavik (1) 1 *(Danielsson)*   18,422

Everton: Southall; Barrett, Hinchcliffe, Ebbrell, Short, Unsworth, Grant, Parkinson, Amokachi (Stuart), Rideout, Limpar.
KR Reykjavik: Finnbogason; Adolfsson, Jonsson S, Egilsson, Gunnarsson, Dervic, Bjornsson, Gudjonsson, Danielsson, Bibercic (Porca), Benediktsson (Haraldsson).

Second Round, First Leg

19 OCT

Everton (0) 0

Feyenoord (0) 0   27,526

Everton: Southall; Barrett, Unsworth, Jackson (Barlow), Short, Ablett, Samways, Horne, Stuart, Rideout, Limpar (Holmes).
Feyenoord: De Goey; Koeman, Zwijnenberg (Trustfull), Van Gobbel, Boateng, Van Bronchhorst, Larsson (Iwan), Maas, Witschge, Obiku, Blinka (Heus).

Paris St Germain (0) 1 *(Djorkaeff)*

Celtic (0) 0   30,010

Paris St Germain: Lama; Fournier (Llacer), Cobos, Le Guen, Colleter, Mahe, Rai (Nouma), Bravo, Guerin, Djorkaeff, Loko.
Celtic: Marshall; Vata, McKinlay, McStay, Boyd, Hughes, Grant, O'Donnell (Donnelly), Van Hooijdonk, Thom, Collins.

Second Round, Second Leg

2 NOV

Celtic (0) 0

Paris St Germain (2) 3 *(Loko 2, Nouma)*   34,822

Celtic: Marshall; Vata (Donnelly), McKinlay, Hughes, Boyd, McStay, Grant, Thom, Walker, Van Hooijdonk (McLoughlin), Collins.
Paris St Germain: Lama; Cobos, Le Guen, Mahe (Dieng), Colleter, Fournier (Llacer), Bravo, Guerin, Djorkaeff, Rai, Loko (Nouma).

Feyenoord (1) 1 *(Blinker)*

Everton (0) 0   40,000

Feyenoord: De Goey; Koeman, Boateng, Van Gobbel, Iwan, Bosz, Trustfull (Zwijnenberg), Heus, Blinker (Witschge), Larsson (Taument), Obiku.
Everton: Southall; Jackson, Hinchcliffe, Short, Watson, Ablett (Barlow), Stuart, Horne, Amokachi, Rideout, Ebbrell (Grant).

UEFA INTERTOTO CUP

Thirty-seven of UEFA's members were represented when the second Intertoto Cup began in June 1996; the notable absentees being English, Scottish and Portuguese clubs.
The eight places left vacant by these withdrawals were filled by additional teams from other countries, while Italy, Spain and Greece did not take up their entire allocation.
Three successful clubs gain access to the first round of the UEFA Cup.

Group 1
Aalborg 5, Hapoel Haifa 4
Cliftonville 0, Standard Liege 3
Hapoel Haifa 1, Cliftonville 1
Stuttgart 0, Aalborg 1
Cliftonville 1, Stuttgart 4
Standard Liege 2, Hapoel Haifa 2

Group 2
Apollon 0, Werder Bremen 2
Linz 2, Djurgaarden 0
Djurgaarden 8, Apollon 0
B68 0, Linz 4
Werder Bremen 3, Djurgaarden 2
Apollon 4, B68 1

Group 3
Maribor 3, FK Austria 0
Orebro 3, Keflavik 1
Keflavik 0, Maribor 0
FC Copenhagen 2, Orebro 2
Maribor 0, FC Copenhagen 1
FK Austria 6, Keflavik 0

Group 4
Charleroi 2, Silkeborg 4
Zaglebie Lubin 2, Ried 1
Conwy United 0, Charleroi 0
Silkeborg 0, Zaglebie Lubin 0
Zaglebie Lubin 3, Conwy United 0
Ried 0, Silkeborg 3

Group 5
Kaunas 1, Lillestrom 4
Sligo 0, Heerenveen 0
Lillestrom 4, Sligo 0
Nantes 3, Kaunas 1
Sligo 3, Nantes 3
Heerenveen 0, Lillestrom 1

Group 6
Hapoel Tel Aviv 0, Rennes 2
Orgryte 3, Lucerne 0
Lucerne 2, Hapoel Tel Aviv 0
Segesta 1, Orgryte 1
Rennes 1, Lucerne 2
Hapoel Tel Aviv 1, Segesta 3

Group 7
Ataka Aura 0, Volgograd 4
Basle 2, Donets 2
Antalya 2, Basle 5
Donets 1, Ataka Aura 2
Volgograd 4, Donets 1
Ataka Aura 0, Antalya 3

Group 8
Kamaz 3, LKS Lodz 0
Spartak Varna 2, 1860 Munich 1
Kaucuk 1, Kamaz 2
LKS Lodz 1, Spartak Varna 1
1860 Munich 5, LKS Lodz 0
Spartak Varna 0, Kaucuk 1

Group 9
Spartak Trnava 3, Cukarici 0
Uni Craiova 3, Daugava 0
Daugava 0, Spartak Trnava 6
Karlsruhe 1, Uni Craiova 0
Spartak Trnava 1, Karlsruhe 1
Cukarici 1, Daugava 3

Group 10
Groningen 1, Gaziantep 1
Vasas 2, Lierse 0
Trans Narva 1, Groningen 4
Gaziantep 3, Vasas 0
Lierse 1, Gaziantep 0
Vasas 4, Trans Narva 1

Group 11
Hibernians 2, Oralsmash 1
Kocaeli 1, CSKA Sofia 3
CSKA Sofia 4, Hibernians 1
Strasbourg 1, Kocaeli 1
Oralsmash 2, CSKA Sofia 1
Hibernians 0, Strasbourg 2

Group 12
Jaro 0, Guingamp 0
Zemun 2, Dinamo Bucharest 1
Dinamo Bucharest 0, Jaro 2
Kolcheti 2, Zemun 3
Guingamp 2, Dinamo Bucharest 1
Jaro 2, Kolcheti 0

(N.B. Competition still running)

EUROPEAN CUP-WINNERS' CUP 1994–95 – BRITISH AND IRISH CLUBS

Missing from last year's edition

Arsenal (1) 2 *(Wright (pen), Selley)*
Brondby (1) 2 *(Hansen, Eggen)* 32,290
Arsenal: Seaman; Dixon (Bould), Winterburn, Parlour, Keown, Adams, Jensen, Wright (Campbell), Smith, Mercer, Selley.
Brondby: Krogh; Hogh, Rieper, Eggen, Jensen (Colding), Bjur, Vilfort, Thogersen, Kristensen, Hansen, Strudal (Bagger).

FK Austria (0) 1 *(Narbekovas)*
Chelsea (1) 1 *(Spencer)* 25,000
FK Austria: Wohlfahrt; Zsak, Pfeffer, Kogler, Flogel, Zechner (Wagner), Prosenik, Belajic, Sekerlioglu, Narbekovas, Mjelde.
Chelsea: Kharine; Hall (Minto), Barness, Spackman, Johnsen, Myers, Rocastle (Hoddle), Spencer, Shipperley, Newton, Wise.

INTER-CITIES FAIRS & UEFA CUP

FAIRS CUP FINALS 1958–71
(Winners in italics)

Year	First Leg	Attendance	Second Leg	Attendance
1958	London 2 Barcelona 2	*45,466*	*Barcelona* 6 London 0	62,000
1960	Birmingham C 0 Barcelona 0	40,500	*Barcelona* 4 Birmingham C 1	70,000
1961	Birmingham C 2 Roma 2	21,005	*Roma* 2 Birmingham C 0	60,000
1962	Valencia 6 Barcelona 2	65,000	Barcelona 1 *Valencia* 1	60,000
1963	Dynamo Zagreb 1 Valencia 2	40,000	*Valencia* 2 Dynamo Zagreb 0	55,000
1964	*Zaragoza* 2 Valencia 1	50,000	(in Barcelona)	
1965	*Ferencvaros* 1 Juventus 0	25,000	(in Turin)	
1966	Barcelona 0 Zaragoza 1	70,000	Zaragoza 2 *Barcelona* 4	70,000
1967	Dynamo Zagreb 2 Leeds U 0	40,000	Leeds U 0 *Dynamo Zagreb* 0	35,604
1968	Leeds U 1 Ferencvaros 0	25,368	Ferencvaros 0 *Leeds U* 0	70,000
1969	Newcastle U 3 Ujpest Dozsa 0	60,000	Ujpest Dozsa 2 *Newcastle U* 3	37,000
1970	Anderlecht 3 Arsenal 1	37,000	*Arsenal* 3 Anderlecht 0	51,612
1971	Juventus 0 Leed U 0 *(abandoned 51 minutes)*	42,000		
	Juventus 2 Leeds U 2	*42,000*	*Leeds U* 1* Juventus 1	42,483

UEFA CUP FINALS 1972–96
(Winners in italics)

Year	First Leg	Attendance	Second Leg	Attendance
1972	Wolverhampton W 1 Tottenham H 2	45,000	*Tottenham H* 1 Wolverhampton W 1	48,000
1973	Liverpool 0 Moenchengladbach 0 *(abandoned 27 minutes)*	44,967		
	Liverpool 3 Moenchengladbach 0	41,169	Moenchengladbach 2 *Liverpool* 0	35,000
1974	Tottenham H 2 Feyenoord 2	46,281	*Feyenoord* 2 Tottenham H 0	68,000
1975	Moenchengladbach 0 Twente 0	45,000	Twente 1 *Moenchengladbach* 5	24,500
1976	Liverpool 3 FC Brugge 2	56,000	FC Brugge 1 *Liverpool* 1	32,000
1977	Juventus 1 Athletic Bilbao 0	75,000	Athletic Bilbao 2 *Juventus* 1*	43,000
1978	Bastia 0 PSV Eindhoven 0	15,000	*PSV Eindhoven* 3 Bastia 0	27,000
1979	Red Star Belgrade 1 Moenchengladbach 1	87,500	*Moenchengladbach* 1 Red Star Belgrade 0	45,000
1980	Moenchengladbach 3 Eintracht Frankfurt 2	25,000	*Eintracht Frankfurt* 1* Moenchengladbach 0	60,000
1981	Ipswich T 3 AZ 67 Alkmaar 0	27,532	AZ 67 Alkmaar 4 *Ipswich T* 2	28,500
1982	Gothenburg 1 Hamburg 0	42,548	Hamburg 0 *Gothenburg* 3	60,000
1983	Anderlecht 1 Benfica 0	45,000	Benfica 1 *Anderlecht* 1	80,000
1984	Anderlecht 1 Tottenham H 1	40,000	*Tottenham H* 1[1] Anderlecht 1	46,258
1985	Videoton 0 Real Madrid 3	30,000	*Real Madrid* 0 Videoton 1	98,300
1986	Real Madrid 5 Cologne 1	80,000	Cologne 2 *Real Madrid* 0	15,000
1987	Gothenburg 1 Dundee U 0	50,023	Dundee U 1 *Gothenburg* 1	20,911
1988	Espanol 3 Bayer Leverkusen 0	42,000	*Bayer Leverkusen* 3[2]Espanol 0	22,000
1989	Napoli 2 Stuttgart 1	83,000	Stuttgart 3 *Napoli* 3	67,000
1990	Juventus 3 Fiorentina 1	45,000	Fiorentina 0 *Juventus* 0	32,000
1991	Internazionale 2 Roma 0	68,887	Roma 1 *Internazionale* 0	70,901
1992	Torino 2 Ajax 2	65,377	*Ajax* 0* Torino 0	40,000
1993	Borussia Dortmund 1 Juventus 3	37,000	*Juventus* 3 Borussia Dortmund 0	62,781
1994	Salzburg 0 Internazionale 1	47,500	*Internazionale* 1 Salzburg 0	80,326
1995	Parma 1 Juventus 0	23,000	Juventus 1 *Parma* 1	80,750
1996	Bayern Munich 2 Bordeaux 0	62,000	Bordeaux 1 *Bayern Munich* 3	36,000

*won on away goals   [1]*Tottenham H won 4-3 on penalties aet*   [2]*Bayer Leverkusen won 3-2 on penalties aet*

UEFA CUP 1995–96

Preliminary Round, First Leg
Afan Lido (1) 1 *(Moore 30)*, RAF Yelgava (1) 2 *Karashauskas 21, Bogdan 58)* 2117
Apollon (1) 1 *(Blendar 41)*, Olimpija (0) 0 5000
Bangor City (0) 0, Widzew Lodz (2) 4 *(Czerwiec 25, 42, Koniarek 51, Koniarek 89)* 2600
Botev Plovdiv (1) 1 *(Guerov 45)*, Dynamo Tbilisi (0) 0 7000
Brondby (2) 3 *(Hansen 12, Bjur 44, Sand 81)*, Inkaras (0) 0 4000
Crusaders (0) 1 *(Hunter G 67)*, Silkeborg (1) 2 *(Fernandez 15, Larsen 46 (pen))* 1800
Dinamo Bucharest (0) 0, Levski (1) 1 *(Ivanov 29)* 6000
Dundalk (0) 0, Malmo (2) 2 *(Petterson 1, Andersson A 11)* 3400
Fenerbahce (0) 2 *(Bolic 71, Uygen 87)*, Partizani (0) 0 20,000
Glenavon (0) 0, Hafnarfjordur (0) 0 3500
Hibernians (1) 2 *(Lawrence 28, Sultana 87)*, Odessa (3) 5 *(Goeseinov 14, Asjkin 23, Darfenov 39, Koernijets 49, Motsjoelak 53)* 5000
Jeunesse Esch (0) 0, Lugano (0) 0 1700
Kapaz (0) 0, FK Austria (2) 4 *(Mjelde 30, Belajic 38, Flogel 49, Pacult 86)* 5000
Karlsruhe (0) 0, Bordeaux (1) 2 *(Dugarry 41, Dutuel 87)* 16,000
Kosice (0) 0, Ujpesti TE (1) 1 *(Tiefenbacher 41)* 6500
Lillestrom (1) 4 *(Ingelstad 44, Ingebrigtsen 61, Gulbrandsen 69, 88)*, Flora Tallinn (0) 0 7500
Motherwell (1) 1 *(McSkimming 9)*, MyPa (2) 3 *(Gronholm 13, Thiainen 31, Mahlia 55)* 8280
Omonia (1) 3 *(Stefan 40 (pen), Malekos 52, 75)*, Sliema Wanderers (0) 0 9000
Orebro (0) 0, Avenir Beggen (0) 0 5500
Raith Rovers (1) 4 *(Dair 40, Rougier 47, McAnespie 78, Cameron 80)*, GI Gotu (0) 0 5082
Red Star Belgrade (0) 0, Neuchatel Xamax (0) 1 *(Wittl 86)* 50,000
Shelbourne (0) 0, IA Akranes (1) 3 *(Gunnlaugsson A 22, 83, Reynisson 87)* 2500
Skonto Riga (1) 1 *(Babisjevs 12)*, Branik Maribor (0) 0 8000
Slavia Sofia (0) 0, Olympiakos (0) 2 *(Ivic 82, Juskowiak 90)* 4000
Slovan Bratislava (3) 4 *(Tittel 8, Rusnak 15, 41, Faktor 90)*, Osijek (0) 0 9000
Sparta Prague (2) 3 *(Nedved 18, 73, Lokvenc 23)*, Galatasaray(0) 1 *(Saunders 56)* 18,000
Sturm Graz (0) 0, Slavia Prague (0) 1 *(Beljbl 83 (pen)* 5000
Tampere (0) 0, Viking (0) 4 *(Gawara 47 (og), Ostenstad 57, Medalen 72, Serloth 86)* 2500
SK Tirana (0) 0, Hapoel Beer Sheva (1) 1 *(Zeiberlins 23)* 3000
Tirol (0) 1 *(Schiener 63)*, Strasbourg (1) 1 *(Sauzee 26)* 8300
Uni Craiova (0) 0, Dynamo Minsk (0) 0 20,000
Vardar Skopje (1) 1 *(Nikolovski 6)*, Samtredia (0) 0 12,750
Zaglebie Lubin (0) 0, Shirak Gumri (0) 0 6000
Zimbru Chisinau (1) 2 *(Gavrilioek 27, Rebeja 70)*, Hapoel Tel Aviv (0) 0 5000

Preliminary Round, Second Leg
IA Akranes (1) 3 *(Jonsson 45, Dunne 58 (og), Petursson 89)*, Shelbourne (0) 0 1500
Avenir Beggen (1) 1 *(Holtz 21)*, Orebro (0) 1 *(Birgirsson 88)* 1200
FK Austria (4) 5 *(Mjelde 10, 29, Ogris 18, 42, Glatzer 64)*, Kapaz (1) 1 *(Suleymanov 26)* 2000
Bordeaux (2) 2 *(Lizarazu 2 (pen), 10)*, Karlsruhe (1) 2 *(Fink 40, Schmitt 87)* 14,100
Branik Maribor (2) 2 *(Strebal 17, Fricelj 21)*, Skonto Riga (0) 0 1500
Dynamo Minsk (0) 0, Uni Craiova (0) 0 10,000
Dynamo Tbilisi (0) 0, Botev Plovdiv (1) 1 *(Vidulov 88)* 15,000
Flora Tallinn (0) 1 *(Korgalidze 52)*, Lillestrom (0) 0 1000
Galatasaray (1) 1 *(Saunders 4)*, Sparta Prague (1) 1 *(Nedved 23)* 28,000

GI Gotu (0) 2 *(Jarnskor H 65, Jarnskor M 87)*, Raith Rovers (1) 2 *(Lennon 30, Crawford 81)* 350
Hafnarfjordur (0) 0, Glenavon (0) 1 *(Johnston 67)* 500
Hapoel Beer Sheva (2) 2 *(Gusseijev 20, Avigdor 23)*, SK Tirana (0) 0 5000
Hapoel Tel Aviv (0) 0, Zimbru Chisinau (0) 0 3000
Inkaras (0) 0, Brondby (0) 3 *(Moller 52, 66, Risager 67)* 8000
Levski (0) 1 *(Vassilev 108)*, Dinamo Bucharest (0) 1 *(Lupu 70)* 18,000
Lugano (3) 4 *(Erceg 18, 45, 54, Espisito 34)*, Jeunesse Esch (0) 0 4800
Malmo (1) 2 *(Andersson 22, Fjellstrom 50)*, Dundalk (0) 0 4112
MyPa (0) 0, Motherwell (1) 2 *(Burns 28, Arnott 69)* 4200
Neuchatel Xamax (0) 0, Red Star Belgrade (0) 0 12,000
Odessa (1) 2 *(Kozakevitsj 34, Mussalitin 78)*, Hibernians (0) 0 4000
Olimpija (1) 3 *(Bozgo 11, 67, Zulic 81)*, Apollon (1) 1 *(Kola 2)* 2500
Olympiakos (1)1 *(Ivic 10)*, Slavia Sofia (0) 0 20,000
Osijek (0) 0, Slovan Bratislava (0) 2 *(Rusnak 54, Gomez 86) in Zagreb* 4000
Partizani (0) 0, Fenerbahce (2) 4 *(Yugen 16, Senturk 24, Bolic 59, Taskiran 88)* 8000
RAF Yelgava (0) 0, Afan Lido (0) 0 1100
Samtredia (0) 0, Vardar Skopje (2) 2 *(Serafimovsky 20, Petrovsky 39)* 26,000
Shirak Gumri (0) 0, Zaglebie Lubin (1) 1 *(Makhai 24)* 23,000
Silkeborg (1) 4 *(Larsen 10, Fernandez 55, Sommer 69, 75)*, Crusaders (0) 0 4339
Slavia Prague (1) 1 *(Hysky 45)*, Sturm Graz (0) 1 *(Haas 54)* 5430
Sliema Wanderers (1) 1 *(Suda 43)*, Omonia (0) 2 *(Valentin 70, Panayiotou 88)* 1500
Strasbourg (1) 6 *(Sauzee 16, 54, Mostovoj 65, Keller 67, 70, 90)*, Tirol (0) 1 *(Kirchler 51)* 22,000
Ujpest TE (0) 2 *(Berczy 55, Szanyo 81)*, Kosice (0) 1 *(Wiese 85)* 6000
Viking (2) 3 *(Bergersen 4, 41, Sorloth 63)*, Tampere (0) 1 *(Wiss 89 (pen)* 2354
Widzew Lodz (0) 1 *(Pikuta 84)*, Bangor City (0) 0 5300

First Round, First Leg
FK Austria (1) 1 *(Kogler 84)*, Dynamo Minsk (2) 2 *(Tsjoeravel 25, Tsjoekanov 41)* 4000
Bayern Munich (0) 0, Lokomotiv Moscow (0) 1 *(Tsjarlatsjev 71)* 16,000
Brondby (1) 3 *(Hansen 38, Eggen 57, Bjur 87 (pen))*, Lillestrom (0) 0 7686
Farense (0) 0, Lyon (1) 1 *(Giuly 6)* 10,000
Fenerbahce (0) 1 *(Aykut 74)*, Betis (1) 2 *(Cherubino 28, Sabas 79)* 15,000
Freiburg (0) 1 *(Todt 78)*, Slavia Prague (1) 2 *(Novotny 23, Penicka 75)* 18,000
Glenavon (0) 0, Werder Bremen (0) 2 *(Cardoso 60, Vier 88)* 4000
Guimaraes (1) 3 *(Gilmar 22, 88, Edinho 68)*, Standard Liege (1) 1 *(Schepens 32)* 5000
Hapoel Beer Sheva (0) 0, Barcelona (2) 7 *(De la Pena 4, Roger 45, 67, 78, Oscar 62, Figo 65, 81)* 15,000
Lazio (2) 5 *(Casiraghi 11, 16, 89, Rambaudi 53, Signori 55 (pen))*, Omonia (0) 0 20,000
Lens (2) 6 *(Camara 11, 49, Neyrieu 33, Tiehi 62, 74, Boli 70)*, Avenir Beggen (0) 0 13,437
Levski (0) 1 *(Vassilev 68)*, Aalst (0) 2 *(Markov 57 (og), Paas 77)* 20,000
Lierse (1) 1 *(Huysmans 39 (pen))*, Benfica (1) 3 *(Valdo 28 (pen), Marcelo 54, Bento 64)* 9300
Lugano (0) 1 *(Carrasco 67)*, Internazionale (1) 1 *(Roberto Carlos 12)* 13,000
Malmo (0) 2 *(Persson J 59, Andersson A 71)*, Nottingham F (1) 1 *(Woan 36)* 12,486
AC Milan (1) 4 *(Savicevic 19, Matchaj 46 (og), Weah 66, Boban 71)*, Zaglebie Lubin (0) 0 7629
Monaco (0) 0, Leeds U (1) 3 *(Yeboah 2, 65, 81)* 15,000
MyPa (1) 1 *(Mahlio 30)*, PSV Eindhoven (0) 1 *(Ronaldo 50)* 5000
Neuchatel Xamax (1) 1 *(Jenneret 13)*, Roma (1) 1 *(Moriero 19)* 13,500

Odessa (0) 1 *(Kazakevitsj 87)*, Widzew Lodz (0) 0 15,000
Olympiakos (0) 2 *(Juskowiak 51, Skartados 72 (pen))*,
  Branik Maribor (0) 0 25,000
Raith R (1) 3 *(Lennon 14, 66, Wilson 79)*, IA Akranes (1)
  1 *(Thordarson O 44)* 5284
Roda (4) 5 *(Van Galen 2, Roelofsen 23, Babanigida 34,
  Graef 44, De Kock 88 (pen))*, Olimpija (0) 0 10,500
Rota Volgograd (0) 0, Manchester U (0) 0 40,000
Sevilla (2) 2 *(Suker 30, 33)*, Botev Plovdiv (0) 0 35,000
Slovan Bratislava (1) 2 *(Tittel 28, Sobona 74)*,
  Kaiserslautern (0) 1 *(Hollerbach 64)* 20,000
Sparta Prague (0) 0, Silkeborg (1) 1 *(Fernandez 6)* 10,171
Spartak Vladikavkaz (1) 1 *(Kasimov 20)*, Liverpool (1) 2
  (McManaman 2, Redknapp 53) 43,000
Strasbourg (1) 3 *(Zitelli 7, Leboeuf 72 (pen), Baticle 74)*,
  Ujpest TE (0) 0 25,000
Vadar Skopje (0) 0, Bordeaux (1) 2 *(Bancarel 25, 75)*
  8000
Viking (0) 1 *(Ulfstein 55)*, Auxerre (1) 1 *(West 14)* 4097
Zimbru Chisinau (1) 1 *(Testimitanu 40)*, RAF Yelgava
  (0) 0 7000

First Round, Second Leg

Aalst (0) 1 *(Lamberg 59)*, Levski (0) 0 7500
IA Akranes (0) 1 *(Gunnlaugsson A 51)*, Raith R (0) 0
  2800
Auxerre (0) 1 *(Silvestre 47)*, Viking (0) 0 11,000
Avenir Beggen (0) 0, Lens (3) 7 *(Camara 20, Meyrieu 25,
  Boli 40, Delmotte 55, 73, Tiehi 57, 72)* 1200
Barcelona (2) 5 *(Guardiola 12, Hagi 27, Toni 51, Carreras
  62, Amor 65)*, Hapoel Beer Sheva (0) 0 18,000
Benfica (1) 2 *(Joao Pinto 24, Kenedy 60)*, Lierse (1) 1
  (Van Kerkhoven 33) 40,000
Betis (2) 2 *(Alexis 21, Canas 38)*, Fenerbahce (0) 0 25,000
Bordeaux (0) 1 *(Lizarazu 61 (pen))*, Vardar Skopje (0) 1
  (Serafimovski 38) 3000
Botev Plovdiv (0) 1 *(Ivanov 69)*, Sevilla (0) 1 *(Monchu
  57)* 10,000
Branik Maribor (0) 1 *(Karic (pen) 70)*, Olympiakos (1) 3
  (Ivic 38, Skartados 63 (pen), Hantzidis 83) 7500
Dynamo Minsk (0) 1 *(Belkevitch 90)*, FK Austria (0) 0
  12,000
Internazionale (0) 0, Lugano (0) 1 *(Carrasco 85)* 15,955
Kaiserslautern (2) 3 *(Wegmann 27, 56, Wollitz 38)*,
  Slovan Bratislava (0) 0 13,537
Leeds U (0) 0, Monaco (1) 1 *(Anderson 23)* 24,501
Lillestrom (0) 0, Brondby (0) 0 1090
Liverpool (0) 0, Spartak Vladikavkaz (0) 0 35,042
Lokomotiv Moscow (0) 0, Bayern Munich (4) 5
  (Klinsmann 26, 34, Herzog 38, Scholl 45, Strunz 78)
  20,000
Lyon (0) 1 *(Sassus 47)*, Farense (0) 0 8,000
Manchester U (0) 2 *(Scholes 59, Schmeichel 89)*, Rotor
  Volgograd (2) 2 *(Nidergaus 16, Veretennikov 24)*
  29,724
Nottingham F (0) 1 *(Roy 69)*, Malmo (0) 0 23,817
Olimpija (1) 2 *(Bozgo 37 (pen), Zulic 74 (pen)*, Roda (0)
  0 2500
Omonia (0) 1 *(Xiouroupos 68)*, Lazio (1) 2 *(Casiraghi 14,
  Di Vaio 75)* 5000
PSV Eindhoven (2) 7 *(Ronaldo 14, 45, 73, 83, Jonk 57, 71,
  Hoekstra 65)*, MyPa (1) 1 *(Keskitalo 16)* 10,800
RAF Yelgava (0) 1 *(Zuyev 76)*, Zimbru Chisinau (2) 2
  (Gavriloek 5, 25) 300
Roma (3) 4 *(Balbo 26, 35, Fonseca 32, Rueda 55 (og))*,
  Neuchatel Xamax (0) 0 18,953
Silkeborg (0) 1 *(Petersen 52)*, Sparta Prague (1) 2
  (Lokvinc 21, Nemec 51) 5200
Slavia Prague (0) 0, Freiburg (0) 0 9328
Standard Liege (0) 0, Guimaraes (0) 0 12,000
Ujpesti TE (0) 0, Strasbourg (1) 2 *(Mostovoi 9, Zitelli 77)*
  3000
Werder Bremen (4) 5 *(Hobsch 26, 35, 38, Basler 36 (pen),
  Borowka 67)*, Glenavon (0) 0 13,273
Widzew Lodz (0) 1 *(Michalczuk 80)*, Odessa (0) 0 *(aet;
  Odessa won 6-5 on penalties)* 13,000
Zaglebie Lubin (0) 1 *(Krzyzanowski 73)*, AC Milan (0) 4
  (Eranio 51, Simone 63, Boban 85, 90) 12,000

Second Round, First Leg

Auxerre (0) 0, Nottingham F (1) 1 *(Stone 23)* 20,000
Barcelona (1) 3 *(Kodro 44, 66, Celades 76)*, Guimaraes
  (0) 0 40,000
Benfica (0) 1 *(Panduro 78)*, Roda (0) 0 35,000

Bordeaux (0) 2 *(Histilloles 48, Witschge 90)*, Rotor
  Volgograd (1) 1 *(Huard 40 (og))* 10,000
Brondby (0) 0, Liverpool (0) 0 37,648
Kaiserslautern (0) 1 *(Koch 46)*, Betis (1) 3 *(Alfonso 45,
  73, Alexis 54)* 18,320
Leeds U (1) 3 *(Speed 6, Palmer 48, McAllister 72)*, PSV
  Eindhoven (3) 5 *(Eijkelkamp 11, Vink 35, Jonk 39,
  Nilis 83, 88)* 24,846
Lugano (0) 1 *(Shalimov 84)*, Slavia Prague (2) 2 *(Vagner
  20, Penicka 26)* 4000
Lyon (1) 2 *(Devaux 15, Deplace 66)*, Lazio (1) 1 *(Winter
  24)* 35,000
Odessa (0) 0, Lens (0) 0 10,000
Raith R (0) 0, Bayern Munich (1) 2 *(Klinsmann 6, 73)*
  12,818 *(at Hibernian)*
Roma (1) 4 *(Vandenhaege 6 (og), Van der Hoorn 51 (og),
  Balbo 69, Totti 77)*, Aalst (0) 0 20,000
Sevilla (0) 1 *(Juanito 90)*, Olympiakos (0) 0 30,000
Sparta Prague (2) 4 *(Frydek 19, Nedved 45 (pen), 57,
  Budka 58)*, Zimbru Chisinau (0) 3 *(Sucharev 56,
  Testimitsanu 62, 90 (pen))* 8147
Strasbourg (0) 0, AC Milan (0) 1 *(Simone 80)* 27,567
Werder Bremen (0) 5 *(Schtanjuk 53 (og), Basler 64, 83,
  Hobsch 72, Bode 88)*, Dynamo Minsk (0) 0 15,000

Second Round, Second Leg

Aalst (0) 0, Roma (0) 0 11,000
Bayern Munich (0) 2 *(Klinsmann 52, Babbel 64)*, Raith R
  (1) 1 *(Herzog 42 (og))* 27,000
Betis (0) 1 *(Jarni 55)*, Kaiserslautern (0) 0 40,000
Dynamo Minsk (0) 2 *(Hatskevich 76 (pen), Lukhvich 90)*,
  Werder Bremen (1) 1 *(Bode 25)* 8000
Guimaraes (0) 0, Barcelona (1) 4 *(Kodro 18, Oscar 61,
  Celades 66, Sergi 75)* 25,000
Lazio (0) 0, Lyon (1) 2 *(Maurice 22, Assadourian 59)*
  40,340
Lens (3) 4 *(Meyrieu 14, Vairelles 20, Dehu 26, Foe 77)*,
  Odessa (0) 0 31,000
Liverpool (0) 0, Brondby (0) 1 *(Eggen 78)* 35,878
AC Milan (2) 2 *(Roberto Baggio 28, 45 (pen))*,
  Strasbourg (0) 1 *(Sauzee 47)* 13,652
Nottingham F (0) 0, Auxerre (0) 0 28,064
Olympiakos (0) 2 *(Sabanis 72, Juskowiak 93)*, Sevilla (0)
  1 *(Suker 110)* 34,171
PSV Eindhoven (2) 3 *(Cocu 13, 74, Pemberton 43 (og))*,
  Leeds U (0) 0 25,750
Roda (0) 2 *(Hesp 60, Trost 72)*, Benfica (0) 2 *(Hassan 87,
  90)* 20,000
Rotor Volgograd (0) 0, Bordeaux (0) 1 *(Bancarel 83)*
  10,000
Slavia Prague (0) 1 *(Smicer 62)*, Lugano (0) 0 8800
Zimbru Chisinau (0) 0, Sparta Prague (1) 2 *(Koller 45,
  Vonasek 63)* 12,000

Third Round, First Leg

Bayern Munich (3) 4 *(Klinsmann 27, 32, 43, 46)*, Benfica
  (1) 1 *(Dimas 31)* 30,000
Bordeaux (1) 2 *(Dutuel 25, Croci 80)*, Betis (0) 0 18,000
Brondby (1) 2 *(Moller 45, Bjur 76)*, Roma (1) 1 *(Fonseca
  16)* 35,000
AC Milan (1) 2 *(Weah 33, 77)*, Sparta Prague (0) 0 12,758
Nottingham F (0) 1 *(McGregor 83)*, Lyon (0) 0 22,141
PSV Eindhoven (1) 2 *(Ronaldo 9 (pen), Nilis 84)*, Werder
  Bremen (0) 1 *(Bode 55)* 25,000
Sevilla (1) 1 *(Suker 45)*, Barcelona (0) 1 *(Hagi 69)* 45,000
Slavia Prague (0) 0, Lens (0) 0 8032

Third Round, Second Leg

Barcelona (0) 3 *(Bakero 61, Popescu 79, Roger 82)*,
  Sevilla (0) 1 *(Moya 80)* 80,000
Benfica (1) 1 *(Valdo 14)*, Bayern Munich (1) 3
  (Klinsmann 32, 67, Herzog 82) 20,000
Betis (2) 2 *(Alexis 30, Stosic 45)*, Bordeaux (1) 1 *(Zidane
  3)* 36,000
Lens (0) 0, Slavia Prague (0) 1 *(Poborsky 95)* 35,000
Lyon (0) 0, Nottingham F (0) 0 37,000
Roma (1) 3 *(Totti 23, Balbo 71, Carboni 89)*, Brondby (0)
  1 *(Moller 84)* 46,000
Sparta Prague (0) 0, AC Milan (0) 0 25,000
Werder Bremen (0) 0, PSV Eindhoven (0) 0 25,000

Quarter-finals, First Leg
Barcelona (1) 2 *(Bakero 21, Abelardo 70)*, PSV
   Eindhoven (1) 2 *(Nilis 4, 50)*   60,000
Bayern Munich (2) 2 *(Klinsmann 16, Scholl 45)*,
   Nottingham F (1) 1 *(Chettle 17)*   38,000
AC Milan (1) 2 *(Eranio 29, Roberto Baggio 75)*,
   Bordeaux (0) 0   25,670
Slavia Prague (1) 2 *(Poborsky 11, Vagner 51)*, Roma (0) 0
    14,377

Quarter-finals, Second Leg
Bordeaux (1) 3 *(Tholot 14, Dugarry 63, 69)*, AC Milan
   (0) 0   32,500
Nottingham F (0) 1 *(Stone 85)*, Bayern Munich (2) 5
   (Ziege 29, Strunz 43, Klinsmann 64, 79, Papin 72)
    28,844

PSV Eindhoven (1) 2 *(Zenden 43, Eykelkamp 65)*,
   Barcelona (2) 3 *(Bakero 3, Figo 22, Sergi 79)* 26,000
Roma (0) 3 *(Moriero 60, 99, Giannini 82)*, Slavia Prague
   (0) 1 *(Vavra 112)*   63,859

Semi-finals, First Leg
Bayern Munich (0) 2 *(Witeczek 52, Scholl 57)*, Barcelona
   (1) 2 *(Oscar 15, Hagi 77)*   63,000
Slavia Prague (0) 0, Bordeaux (1) 1 *(Dugarry 8)* 17,523

Semi-finals, Second Leg
Barcelona (0) 1 *(De la Pena 87)*, Bayern Munich (1) 2
   (Babbel 38, Witeczek 83)   100,000
Bordeaux (0) 1 *(Tholot 46)*, Slavia Prague (0) 0 31,500

Final First Leg

Bayern Munich (1) 2, Bordeaux (0) 0

(in Munich, 1 May 1996, 62,000)

Bayern Munich: Kahn; Kruezer, Matthaus (Frey 54), Helmer, Hamann, Sforza, Babbel, Scholl, Ziege, Papin (Witeczek
   68), Klinsmann.
Scorers: Helmer 35, Scholl 60.
Bordeaux: Huard; Grenet, Dogon, Friis-Hansen, Lizarazu, Bancarel, Croci, Dutuel, Lucas, Witschge, Tholot (Anselin
   89).
Referee: Muhmenthaler (Switzerland).

Final Second Leg

Bordeaux (0) 1, Bayern Munich (0) 3

(in Bordeaux, 15 May 1996, 36,000)

Bordeaux: Huard; Bancarel, Dogon, Friis-Hansen, Lizarazu (Anselin 31), Zidane, Croci (Dutuel 57), Lucas (Grenet
   80), Witschge, Tholot, Dugarry.
Scorer: Dutuel 76.
Bayern Munich: Kahn; Babbel, Matthaus, Helmer, Frey (Zickler 60), Strunz, Sforza, Ziege, Scholl, Kostadinov
   (Witeczek 75), Klinsmann.
Scorers: Scholl 53, Kostadinov 66, Klinsmann 78.
Referee: Zhuk (Belarus).

Bayern Munich players celebrate their UEFA Cup success against Bordeaux. They won this second leg game 3-1
for a 5-1 aggregate win. (Action Images).

UEFA CUP 1995–96 - BRITISH AND IRISH CLUBS

Preliminary Round, First Leg

8 AUG
Afan Lido (1) 1 *(Moore)*   2117
RAF Yelgava (1) 2 *(Karashauskas, Bogdan)*
Afan Lido: Thomas; Duggan (Jones D), Preece, Cook, Rickard, Glover, Moore, Evans, Radford, Bartley, Patton (Jones N).
RAF Yelgava: Oleinik; Ivanov, Erglis, Zakreshevsky, Dolgopolov, Gilis (Aizazars), Zuyev, Karashauskas, Sergeyev (Mikhalchouk), Savalnieks, Bogdan.

Bangor City (0) 0
Widzew Lodz (2) 4 *(Czerwiec 2, Koniarek 2)*   2600
Bangor City: Deegan; Jones K, Carberry (Jones A), Langley, Rutter, Humphreys (Parry D), Wiggins, Parry J (Barry), Mottram, Colville, Evans.
Widzew Lodz: Wozniak; Szymkowiak, Kapinski, Bogusz, Bajor (Bogus), Miaszkiewicz, Wyciszkiewicz (Podolski), Szarpak, Koniarek, Czerwiec (Michalczuk), Siadaczka.

Crusaders (0) 1 *(Hunter G)*
Silkeborg (1) 2 *(Fernandez, Larsen (pen))*   1800
Crusaders: McKeown; McMullan, McCartney, Dunlop, Callaghan, Hunter K (Morgan), Livingstone, Dunne, Baxter, Hunter G, Burrows.
Silkeborg: Kjaer; Petersen, Larsen, Laursen, Bruun, Katsbjerg, Bordinggaard, Sorensen, Reese, Thygesen (Knudsen), Fernandez (Hansen).

Glenavon (0) 0
Hafnarfjordur (0) 0   3500
Glenavon: O'Neill; Byrne, Glendinning, Doherty, Brown, Smyth G, McCoy, Johnston (Collins), Ferguson, McBride, Smyth J.
Hafnarfjordur: Arnarson A; Ragnarsson, Vijarrson, Sevensson, Marzek, Kristjansson H, Heljason, Toth (Erikkson), Magnusson, Arnarson H, Kristjansson O.

Motherwell (1) 1 *(McSkimming)*
MyPa (2) 3 *(Gronholm, Tiainen, Mahlio)*   8280
Motherwell: Woods; May, McKinnon, Van der Gaag, Martin, McCart, Lambert (Davies), Dolan, Coyne, Hendry (Essandoh), McSkimming.
MyPa: Jakonen; Huttunen, Viljanen, Hyypia, Jukka Koskinen, Mahlio, Gronholm (Keskitalo) (Hellsten), Kautonen, Tiainen, Kolkka, Pohja.

Raith R (1) 4 *(Dair, Rougier, McAnespie, Cameron)*
GI Gotu (0) 0   5082
Raith R: Thomson; McAnespie, Broddle, McInally, Dennis, Sinclair, Rougier (Graham), Cameron, Crawford (Lennon), Taylor, Dair.
GI Gotu: Knudsen; Justinussen A, Jarnskor H, Rasmussen, Enniggard (Hansen), Olsen, Jarnskor M (Tvorfoss), Jarnskor P, Justinussen S, Petersen J. Justinussen R.

Shelbourne (0) 0
IA Akranes (1) 3 *(Gunnlaugsson A 2, Reynisson)*   2500
Shelbourne: Gough; Flood, Duffy, Neville, Dunne, Byrne (Devereaux), Howlett, O'Rourke, Geoghegan D (Smith), Arkins, Geoghegan S.
IA Akranes: Thordarson T; Haraldsson, Adolfsson, Miljkovic, Gislason, Thordarson O (Petursson), Ingolfsson, Jonsson, Hognasson, Gunnlaugsson A, Gunnlaugsson B (Reynisson).

9 AUG
Dundalk (0) 0
Malmo (2) 2 *(Petterson, Anderson)*   3400
Dundalk: Van Boxtel; Futcher, Whelan, Doohan, Coady, Britton, McNulty, Kelly, Byrne, Withnell, Hanrahan.
Malmo: Fedel; Nylen, Ohlsson, Wirmola, Persson T, Persson J (Nilsson), Andersson D, Prytz, Fjellstrom, Andersson A, Pettersson J(Olsson).

Preliminary Round, Second Leg

22 AUG

GI Gotu (0) 2 *(Jarnskor H, Jarnskor M)*
Raith R (1) 2 *(Lennon, Crawford)*   350
GI Gotu: Knudsen; Justinussen A, Jarnskor H, Rasmussen, Tvorfoss, Olsen, Jarnskor M, Jarnskor P (Enniggard), Justinussen S, Petersen, Justinussen R.
Raith R: Thomson; Kirkwood, Broddle, Lennon, Dennis (Raeside), Sinclair, Rougier, Graham, Crawford, Taylor (Forrest), Cameron.

MyPa (0) 0
Motherwell (1) 2 *(Burns, Arnott)*   4200
MyPa: Jakonen; Huttunen, Viljanen, Hyypia, Jukka Koskinen, Mahlio, Gronholm, Kautonen, Tiainen, Kolkka, Keskitalo.
Motherwell: Howie; May, McKinnon, Roddie (McCulloch), Martin, McCart, Lambert, Dolan, Burns, Arnott, Davies.

RAF Yelgava (0) 0
Afan Lido (0) 0   1100
RAF Yelgava: Oleinik; Aizazars (Mikhalchouk), Erglis, Zakresevsky, Dolgopolov, Gilis, Zuyev, Karashauskas, Sergeyev (Shvans), Savalnieks, Bogdan.
Afan Lido: Thomas; Duggan, Evans D (Preece), Moore, Webber, Rickard, Patton, Glover, Bartley (Jones D), Radford, Jones N (Evans P).

Silkeborg (1) 4 *(Larsen, Fernandez, Sommer 2)*
Crusaders (0) 0   4339
Silkeborg: Kjaer; Knudsen, Larsen, Laursen, Bruun, Duus, Bordinggaard, Sorensen, Reese (Sommer), Thygesen, Fernandez.
Crusaders: McKeown; McMullan, McCartney, Dunlop, Callaghan, Hunter K (Dwyer), Livingstone, Dunne, Baxter (Morgan), Gardiner, Burrows.

Widzew Lodz (0) 1 *(Pikuta)*
Bangor City (0) 0   5300
Widzew Lodz: Muchinski; Szymkowiak, Kapinski (Bogus), Bogusz, Bagor, Miaszkiewicz, Wyciszkiewicz, Szarpak (Pikuta), Koniarek, Czerwiec (Michalczuk), Siadaczka.
Bangor City: Innes; Jones K, Parry D, Langley, Rutter, Jones A, Wiggins, Barnett, Mottram, Parry J (Evans), Noble.

23 AUG
IA Akranes (1) 3 *(Jonsson, Thordarson, Petursson)*
Shelbourne (0) 0   1500
IA Akranes: Thordarson T, Haraldsson, Adolfsson, Miljkovic, Gislason, Thordarson O (Petursson), Jonsson, Hognasson, Ingolfsson (Thordarson S), Gunnlaugsson A (Stojic), Gunnlaugsson B.
Shelbourne: Gough; Costello, Flood, Neville, Dunne, Devereaux, Howlett, Byrne, O'Rourke, Arkins, Geoghegan S.

Hafnarfjordur (0) 0
Glenavon (0) 1 *(Johnston)*   500
Hafnarfjordur: Arnarson A; Ragnarsson, Vijarrson, Sevensson, Marzek, Toth, Heljason, Kristjansson H, Magnusson, Arnarson H, Kristjansson O (Halldorsson).
Glenavon: O'Neill; Byrne, Glendinning, Doherty, Brown, Smyth G, McCoy, Johnston, Ferguson, McBride, Smyth J.

Malmo (1) 2 *(Andersson D, Fjellstrom)*
Dundalk (0) 0   4112
Malmo: Fedel; Ohisson, Persson T, Wirmola, Persson J,
Nylen, Andersson D, Thylander, Fjellstrom, Prytz,
Pettersson J.
Dundalk: Van Boxtel; Britton (Byrne M), Coady,
Doohan, Whelan, Futcher, Hanrahan (Long), McNulty,
Kelly, Byrne B, Withnell (Lopez).

First Round, First Leg

12 SEPT

Malmo (0) 2 *(Persson J, Andersson A)*
Nottingham Forest (1) 1 *(Woan)*   12,486
Malmo: Fedel; Nylen, Ohlsson, Wirmola, Persson T,
Persson J, Andersson D, Prytz, Fjellstrom (Thylander),
Pettersson J, Andersson A.
Nottingham Forest: Crossley; Lyttle, Pearce (Bart-
Williams), Cooper, Chettle, Stone, Phillips, Roy,
Campbell (Lee), Gemmill, Woan.

Monaco (0) 0
Leeds U (1) 3 *(Yeboah 3)*   15,000
Monaco: Piveteau (Delaroche) (Puel); Di Meco, Thuram,
Boli, Valery, Dumas, Dos Santos, Legwinski (Henry),
Scifo, Anderson, Wreh.
Leeds U: Lukic; Kelly, Dorigo (Beesley), Palmer,
Wetherall, Pemberton, Whelan, Yeboah, Deane,
McAllister, Speed.

Raith R (1) 3 *(Lennon 2, Wilson)*
IA Akranes (1) 1 *(Thordarson O)*   5284
Raith R: Thomson; McAnespie, Broddle, Kirkwood,
Dennis, Sinclair, Wilson (Coyle), Cameron, Crawford
(Graham), Lennon, Rougier (Dair).
IA Akranes: Thordarson T; Haraldsson, Hognasson,
Jonsson S, Adolfsson, Miljovic, Gunnlaugsson B,
Gislason, Gunnlaugsson A, Thordarson O, Ingolfsson
(Thordarson S).

Rotor Volgograd (0) 0
Manchester U (0) 0   40,000
Rotor Volgograd: Samorukov; Geraschenko, Junenko,
Shmarko, Estchenko, Esipov, Veretennikov,
Burlatchenko, Korniets, Nidergaus, Zernov (Krivov).
Manchester U: Schmeichel; Neville G, Irwin, Bruce,
Sharpe, Pallister, Butt, Keane (Davies), Scholes (Parker),
Beckham, Giggs.

Spartak Vladikavkaz (1) 1 *(Kasimov)*
Liverpool (1) 2 *(McManaman, Redknapp)*   43,000
Spartak Vladikavkaz: Khapov; Shelia, Tetradze,
Ianovski, Pageav (Timofeev), Djioev, Gorlukovich
(Komienko), Kasimov (Derkach), Tedeev, Kanichev,
Kavelashvili.
Liverpool: James; Jones, Harkness, Babb, Wright,
Ruddock, McManaman, Redknapp, Thomas, Barnes,
Collymore (Fowler).

13 SEPT

Glenavon (0) 0
Werder Bremen (0) 2 *(Cardoso, Vier)*   4000
Glenavon: O'Neill; Birney (Byrne), Murphy, Brown
(McCoy), Smyth G, Glendinning, Doherty, Johnston,
Smyth J (Collins), Ferguson, McBride.
Werder Bremen: Rost; Scholz, Baiano, Borowka, Bode,
Wiedener, Votava, Eilts, Cardoso (Schulz), Hobsch
(Neubarth), Bestchastnykh (Vier).

First Round, Second Leg

26 SEPT

IA Akranes (0) 1 *(Gunnlaugsson A)*
Raith R (0) 0   2800
IA Akranes: Thordarson T; Haraldsson, Hognasson,
Jonsson S, Adolfsson, Miljovic, Gunnlaugsson B,
Gislason, Gunnlaugsson A, Thordarson O, Ingolfsson
(Stojic).

Raith R: Thomson; McAnespie, Broddle, Coyle, Dennis,
Sinclair, Kirkwood, Cameron, Crawford (Wilson),
Lennon, Dair (McInally).

Leeds U (0) 0
Monaco (1) 1 *(Anderson)*   24,501
Leeds U: Lukic; Kelly, Beesley, Palmer, Wetherall,
Pemberton (Couzens), White (Tinkler), Yeboah, Deane,
McAllister, Speed.
Monaco: Barthez; Thuram, Boli, Dumas, Petit, Dos
Santos (Wreh), Puel, Viaud (Petersen), Scifo, Madar,
Anderson.

Liverpool (0) 0
Spartak Vladikavkaz (0) 0   35,042
Liverpool: James; Jones, Harkness, Babb, Wright,
Ruddock, McManaman, Redknapp, Thomas, Barnes,
Fowler (Rush).
Spartak Vladikavdaz: Khapov; Komienko (Timofeev),
Tetradze, Shelia, Pageav, Djioev, Kasimov, Ianovski,
Tedeev, Kanichev (Derkach), Suleimanov.

Manchester U (0) 2 *(Scholes, Schmeichel)*
Rotor Volgograd (2) 2 *(Nidergaus, Veretennikov)*   29,724
Manchester U: Schmeichel; Neville P, O'Kane (Scholes),
Bruce, Sharpe, Pallister, Butt, Keane, Cole, Beckham
(Cooke), Giggs.
Rotor Volgograd: Samorukov; Shmarko, Junenko,
Berketov, Estchenko (Tsarenko), Esipov, Veretennikov,
Burlatchenko, Korniets, Nidergaus (Krivov), Zernov
(Ilushin).

Nottingham F (0) 1 *(Roy)*
Malmo (0) 0   23,817
Nottingham F: Crossley; Lyttle, Pearce, Cooper, Chettle,
Stone, Bart-Williams, Roy (Silenzi), Bohinen (Gemmill),
Lee, Woan.
Malmo: Fedel; Nylen, Ohlsson, Wirmola, Persson T,
Andersson D (Dahistrom), Persson J, Prytz, Fjellstrom
(Olsson), Andersson A, Pettersson J.

27 SEPT

Werder Bremen (4) 5 *(Hobsch 3, Basler (pen), Borowka)*
Glenavon (0) 0   13,273
Werder Bremen: Reck; Scholz, Wolter, Borowka
(Beiersdorfer), Bode, Basler (Vier), Wiedener, Eilts,
Votava, Hobsch (Albayrak), Bestchastnykh.
Glenavon: O'Neill; Glendinning, Smyth G, Brown
(Murphy A), Byrne, McBride, Murphy D, Kenny
(McCoy), Johnston, Collins, Ferguson.

Second Round, First Leg

17 OCT

Auxerre (0) 0
Nottingham F (1) 1 *(Stone)*   20,000
Auxerre: Cool; Blanc (Rabarivony), Goma, Silvestre,
West, Saib, Lamouchi, Martins, Cocard, Laslandes
(Guivarch), Diomede (Tasfaout).
Nottingham F: Crossley; Lyttle, Pearce, Cooper, Chettle,
Stone, Bart-Williams, Gemmill, Haaland, Lee (Silenzi),
Woan.

Brondby (0) 0
Liverpool (0) 0   37,648
Brondby: Krogh; Colding, Eggen, Nielsen P, Risager,
Daugaard (Bagger), Ravn (Bjur), Vilfort, Nielsen A,
Sand, Moller (Thogersen).
Liverpool: James; Jones, Harkness, Scales, Wright, Babb,
McManaman, Redknapp, Rush, Barnes, Fowler
(Thomas).

Leeds U (1) 3 *(Speed, Palmer, McAllister)*
PSV Eindhoven (3) 5 *(Eijkelkamp, Vink, Jonk, Nilis 2)*   24,846
Leeds U: Lukic; Kelly, Dorigo (Beesley), Palmer,
Wetherall, Pemberton, Whelan (Wallace), Yeboah,
Deane, McAllister, Speed (Couzens).
PSV Eindhoven: Waterreus; Van der Weerden, Faber,
Valckx, Numan, Linskens, Vink (Pahlplatz), Jonk, Nilis,
Cocu, Eijkelkamp.

Raith R (0) 0 _(at Hibernian)_
Bayern Munich (1) 2 _(Klinsmann 2)_ 12,818
Raith R: Thomson; Coyle, Dennis, Sinclair, Kirkwood, Lennon, McInally (Rougier), Dair (Crawford), Broddle, Graham, Cameron.
Bayern Munich: Kahn; Kreuzer, Strunz, Helmer, Zickler, Hamann, Sforza, Herzog (Nerlinger), Ziege, Klinsmann, Scholl (Papin).

Second Round, Second Leg

31 OCT

Bayern Munich (0) 2 _(Klinsmann, Babbel)_
Raith R (1) 1 _(Herzog (og))_ 27,000
Bayern Munich: Kahn; Babbel, Hamann, Strunz, Helmer, Nerlinger, Zickler, Herzog (Witeczek), Papin, Sforza (Frey), Klinsmann.
Raith R: Thomson; Taylor (Kirkwood), Broddle, Coyle (McInally), Dennis, Sinclair, Rougier (Graham), Cameron, Crawford, Lennon, Dair.

Liverpool (0) 0
Brondby (0) 1 _(Eggen)_ 35,878
Liverpool: James; Jones (Collymore), Harkness (Kennedy), Scales, Wright, Babb, McManaman, Redknapp, Rush, Barnes, Fowler.
Brondby: Krogh; Colding, Eggen, Nielsen P, Risager, Bjur (Bagger), Vilfort, Ravn, Nielsen A, Thogersen (Daugaard), Sand (Moller).

Nottingham F (0) 0
Auxerre (0) 0 28,064
Nottingham F: Crossley; Lyttle, Pearce, Cooper, Chettle, Stone, Bart-Williams, Gemmill (Haaland), Roy (McGregor), Lee, Woan.
Auxerre: Cool; West, Silvestre, Goma, Rabarivony, Violeau, Saib, Lamouchi, Martins, Cocard (Tasfaout), Laslandes (Guivarch).

PSV Eindhoven (2) 3 _(Cocu 2, Pemberton (og))_
Leeds U (0) 0 25,750
PSV Eindhoven: Waterreus; Faber, Prommayon, Valckx, Numan, Vink (Pahlplatz), Linskens (Hoekstra), Jonk, Cocu, Nilis, Ronaldo.
Leeds U: Lukic; Kelly, Beesley (Ford), Palmer, Wetherall, Pemberton, Whelan (White), Bowman, Yeboah, McAllister, Speed (Sharp).

Third Round, First Leg

21 NOV

Nottingham F (0) 1 _(McGregor)_
Lyon (0) 0 22,141
Nottingham F: Crossley; Lyttle, Pearce, Cooper, Chettle, Stone, Bart-Williams, Gemmill, Silenzi (McGregor), Roy (Howe), Woan.
Lyon: Olmeta; Moulin, Sassus, Marcelo, Laville, Devaux, Deplace, Roy, Roche (Deguerville), Giuly, Maurice.

Third Round, Second Leg

5 DEC

Lyon (0) 0
Nottingham F (0) 0 37,000
Lyon: Olmeta; Sassus, Marcelo, Devaux, Rivenet (Assadourian), Deplace, Roy, Moulin, Giuly, Maurice, Bardon (Chavronder).
Nottingham F: Crossley; Lyttle, Pearce, Cooper, Chettle, Stone, Bart-Williams, Gemmill (Haaland), Howe, Lee (Silenzi), Woan.

Quarter-finals, First Leg

5 MAR

Bayern Munich (2) 2 _(Klinsmann, Scholl)_
Nottingham F (1) 1 _(Chettle)_ 38,000
Bayern Munich: Kahn; Strunz, Ziege, Kreuzer, Helmer, Nerlinger, Scholl, Sforza, Klinsmann, Matthaus, Zickler.
Nottingham F: Crossley; Phillips, Pearce, Haaland, Chettle, Stone, Bart-Williams, Gemmill, Campbell, Roy, Woan.

Quarter-finals, Second Leg

19 MAR

Nottingham F (0) 1 _(Stone)_ 28,844
Bayern Munich (2) 5 _(Ziege, Strunz, Klinsmann 2, Papin)_
Nottingham F: Crossley; Lyttle (Haaland), Pearce, Cooper, Chettle, Stone, Phillips, Roy, Campbell (Lee), Bart-Williams (McGregor), Woan.
Bayern Munich: Kahn; Babbel, Matthaus, Helmer, Strunz (Frey), Sforza (Nerlinger), Herzog, Scholl, Ziege (Kreuser), Papin, Klinsmann.

EUROPEAN CUP DRAWS 1996–97

EUROPEAN CUP
Qualifying Round
Maccabi Tel Aviv (Israel) v Fenerbahce (Turkey), Rangers v Vladikavkaz (Russia), Panathinaikos (Greece) v Rosenborg (Norway), Gothenburg (Sweden) v Ferencvaros (Hungary), Widzew Lodz (Poland) v Bronby (Denmark), Grasshoppers (Switzerland) v Slavia Prague (Czech Republic), FC Brugge (Belgium) v Steaua (Romania), Rapid Vienna (Austria) v Dynamo Kiev (Ukraine).

EUROPEAN CUP-WINNERS' CUP
Qualifying Round
Humenne (Slovakia) v Flamurtari (Albania), Sion (Switzerland) v Kareda (Lithuania), Olimpija (Slovenia) v Levski Sofia (Bulgaria), Red Star Belgrade (Yugoslavia) v Hearts, Karabakh (Azerbaijan) v MyPa (Finland), Kotaik (Armenia) v AEK (Cyprus), Constructorul (Moldova) v Hapoel Ironi Rishon (Israel), Valletta (Malta) v Gloria (Romania), MPCC (Belarus) v FC Reykjavik (Iceland), Brann (Norway) v Shelbourne, Llansantffraid v Ruch Chorzow (Poland), Kispest Honved (Hungary) v Sloga (Macedonia), Varteks (Croatia) v Union (Luxembourg), Universitate (Latvia) v Vaduz (Liechtenstein), Glentoran v Sparta Prague (Czech Republic), Dynamo Batumi (Georgia) v HB (Faeroes), Sadam (Estonia) v Vinnitsa (Ukraine).

UEFA Cup
Preliminary Round
Jeunesse Esch (Luxembourg) v Legia (Poland), Lantana (Estonia) v Vestmann (Iceland), Becej (Yugoslavia) v Mura (Slovenia), Zalgiris (Lithuania) v Crusaders, Newtown v Skonto Riga (Latvia), Tiligul (Moldova) v Dynamo 93 Minsk (Belarus), Khazri (Azerbaijan) v Hutnik (Poland), Portadown v Vojvodina (Yugoslavia), GI (Faeroes) v Jazz Pori (Finland), Akranes (Iceland) v Sileks (Macedonia), Bohemians v Dynamo Minsk (Belarus), Haka (Finland) v Flora (Estonia), Barry Town v Dinaburg (Latvia), Dynamo Tbilisi (Georgia) v Grevenmacher (Luxembourg), Maccabi Haifa (Israel) v Partizan Belgrade (Yugoslavia), Gorica (Slovenia) v Vardar (Macedonia), Croatia Zagreb (Croatia) v SK Tirana (Albania), Beitar Jerusalem (Israel) v Floriana (Malta), Pyunic (Armenia) v HJK Helsinki (Finland), Sandoyar (Faeroes) v Apoel (Cyprus), Lokomotiv Sofia (Bulgaria) v Neftchi Baku (Azerbaijan), Zimbru (Moldova) v Hajduk Split (Croatia), Slovan Bratislava (Slovakia) v St Patrick's Ath, Kosice (Slovakia) v Teuta (Albania), Anorthosis (Cyprus) v Shirak (Armenia), Margveti (Georgia) v Silema Wanderers (Malta), Slavia Sofia (Bulgaria) v Inkaras (Lithuania).

Summary of Appearances

EUROPEAN CUP (1955–96)

English clubs
12 Liverpool
7 Manchester U
3 Nottingham F, Leeds U
2 Derby Co, Wolverhampton W, Everton, Aston Villa, Arsenal
1 Burnley, Tottenham H, Ipswich T, Manchester C, Blackburn R

Scottish clubs
17 Rangers
15 Celtic
3 Aberdeen
2 Hearts
1 Dundee, Dundee U, Kilmarnock, Hibernian

Welsh clubs
1 Cwmbran

Northern Ireland clubs
18 Linfield
8 Glentoran
2 Crusaders, Portadown
1 Glenavon, Ards, Distillery, Derry C, Coleraine

Eire clubs
7 Shamrock R, Dundalk
6 Waterford
3 Drumcondra
2 Bohemians, Limerick, Athlone T, Shelbourne
1 Cork Hibs, Cork Celtic, Cork City, Derry C*, Sligo R, St Patrick's Ath

Winners: Celtic 1966–67; Manchester U 1967–68; Liverpool 1976–77, 1977–78, 1980–81, 1983–84; Nottingham F 1978–79, 1979–80; Aston Villa 1981–82

Finalists: Celtic 1969–70; Leeds U 1974–75; Liverpool 1984–85

EUROPEAN CUP-WINNERS' CUP (1960–96)

English clubs
6 Tottenham H
5 Manchester U
4 West Ham U, Liverpool
3 Arsenal, Chelsea, Everton
2 Manchester C
1 Wolverhampton W, Leicester C, WBA, Leeds U, Sunderland, Southampton, Ipswich T

Scottish clubs
10 Rangers
8 Aberdeen, Celtic
3 Dundee U
2 Dunfermline Ath
1 Dundee, Hibernian, Hearts, St Mirren, Motherwell, Airdrieonians

Welsh clubs
14 Cardiff C
8 Wrexham
7 Swansea C
2 Bangor C
1 Borough U, Newport Co, Merthyr Tydfil, Barry T

Northern Ireland clubs
7 Glentoran
4 Ballymena U, Coleraine, Glenavon
3 Crusaders, Linfield
2 Ards, Bangor
1 Derry C, Distillery, Portadown, Carrick Rangers, Cliftonville

Eire clubs
6 Shamrock R
3 Limerick, Waterford, Dundalk, Bohemians
2 Cork Hibs, Galway U, Shelbourne, Sligo R, Derry C*
1 Cork Celtic, St Patrick's Ath, Finn Harps, Home Farm, University College Dublin, Cork City, Bray W

Winners: Tottenham H 1962–63; West Ham U 1964–65; Manchester C 1969–70; Chelsea 1970–71; Rangers 1971–72; Aberdeen 1982–83; Everton 1984–85; Manchester U 1990-91; Arsenal 1993–94

Finalists: Rangers 1960–61, 1966–67; Liverpool 1965–66; Leeds U 1972–73; West Ham U 1975–76; Arsenal 1979–80, 1994–95

EUROPEAN FAIRS CUP & UEFA CUP (1955–96)

English clubs
9 Leeds U
8 Ipswich T, Liverpool
7 Manchester U
6 Everton, Arsenal, Aston Villa
5 Southampton, Tottenham H, Newcastle U, Nottingham F
4 Manchester C, Birmingham C, Wolverhampton W, WBA
3 Chelsea, Sheffield W
2 Stoke C, Derby Co, QPR
1 Burnley, Coventry C, Norwich C, London Rep XI, Watford, Blackburn R

Scottish clubs
17 Dundee U
14 Hibernian
11 Aberdeen
9 Celtic, Hearts
8 Rangers
5 Dunfermline Ath
4 Dundee
3 St Mirren, Kilmarnock
2 Partick T, Motherwell
1 Morton, St Johnstone, Raith R

Welsh Clubs
1 Inter Cardiff, Bangor C, Afan Lido

Northern Ireland clubs
11 Glentoran
6 Coleraine
5 Linfield
4 Glenavon
3 Portadown
2 Bangor, Crusaders
1 Ards, Ballymena U

Eire clubs
8 Bohemians
5 Dundalk
4 Shamrock R
3 Finn Harps, Shelbourne
2 Drumcondra, St Patrick's Ath, Derry C*, Cork City
1 Cork Hibs, Athlone T, Limerick, Drogheda U, Galway U

Winners: Leeds U 1967–68, 1970–71; Newcastle U 1968–69; Arsenal 1969–70; Tottenham H 1971–72, 1983–84; Liverpool 1972–73, 1975–76; Ipswich T 1980–81

Finalists: London 1955–58, Birmingham C 1958–60, 1960–61; Leeds U 1966–67; Wolverhampton W 1971–72; Tottenham H 1973–74; Dundee U 1986–87

* Now play in League of Ireland

FOOTBALL AND THE LAW

Nearly a decade ago, in 1988, on the eve of the first full-length Butterworth's 376 paged first edition of *Sport and the Law*, the late Ted Croker complained publicly that I had invented the subject with a *Sunday Telegraph* series in 1977, followed by a 76 paged 1978 booklet under the same title. He was concerned about police intervention on the playing fields, arguing that football should and could be left to look after its own affairs without legal intervention.

Last season proved how wrong he was. Duncan Ferguson was prosecuted to conviction and imprisonment for head-butting an opponent, John McStay, during a Scottish Premier League game for the same offence which was no less criminal than if it had occurred outside the ground. Off the field, Jean-Marc Bosman obtained a European Court of Justice judgement against the Belgian club Liege and UEFA, that the transfer system and UEFA's 3+2 rule were each in breach of the Treaty of Rome, and thereby as unlawful as Duncan Ferguson's breach of the criminal law.

Each offence could have been predicted from long-standing precedents. Criminal prosecutions for football violence have existed in the United Kingdom since as long as the two first ever prosecutions for football fatalities at the old Leicester Assizes, now the Leicester Crown Court, as *R-v-Bradshaw* in 1878 and *R-v-Moore* in 1898. In 1912 an Aston Villa professional player, Harry Kingaby, failed in a challenge to the Football League's retain and transfer system because his lawyers took the wrong legal route under common law case law.

In 1955, while publishing as *Corinthians and Cricketers*, to be re-issued later this year from Yore Publications, a schoolboy correspondence with England's centre-forward of Victorian England, G.O. Smith, raised the restraint of trade flag in Aldershot County Court for Ralph Banks who had played against Stanley Matthews in the 1953 Coronation Cup Final. The judge refused to tackle the claim in possession proceedings for Banks' Aldershot club house, but before an appeal could be launched, he gained the free transfer he had earlier been refused to Weymouth outside the Football League. Eight years later in 1963 it was George Eastham's blueprint for his London High Court ruling which outlawed the F.A. and Football League's retain and transfer system; and the Bosman judgement is a logical extension of it within the European Union.

Of equal significance within European Law has been the operation of yellow and red cards during the Euro '96 competition, graphically illuminated, appropriately in the *Sunday Telegraph* by Patrick Barclay, as I was reminded by Colin Malam, whose father's professional career as Albert Malam with the pre-war Huddersfield Town of Alf Young and Ken Willingham, was destroyed by a broken leg in a foul tackle. He wrote:

"No matter how many treats Euro '96 has in store, the Croatian substitute Goran Vlaovic's late winner against Turkey will go down among the goals of the tournament. It ought also to be hailed as a vindication of strict refereeing. The liberal use of yellow and red cards may be hurting, but this was a spectacular piece of evidence that it's working.

When Vlaovic burst over the halfway line, hurdling a rash challenge to earn a clear run at the Turkish goalkeeper, the only way he could have been stopped was for the pursuing Alpay Ozalan to stick out a leg, pull his shirt, or otherwise foul him. The thought must have crossed Alpay's mind like every other in a Nottingham stadium dominated by Turks. But the defender desisted, knowing he would be sure – not just likely – to incur dismissal and suspension from the next match.

Cynics argued afterwards that Alpay should have sacrificed himself nonetheless, that Turkey would probably have survived the consequent free-kick and cling on for a point with 10 men. How tiresome. How old-fashioned. The game's rulers should be congratulated on their campaign against such debilitating negativity, even if it seems to be taking an age for some observers to recognise the link between the hard line established in the 1994 World Cup and a perceptible tilting of the balance towards entertainment.

The complaining classes tend to forget how morally brutalised top-level football had become before FIFA, alarmed by the dull, fear-filled World Cup of 1990 and the distressing submission of a great player, Marco Van Basten, to the violent tackle from behind, at last resolved to act. So the odd case of excessively zealous refereeing is a price worth paying for what we have now. The tactical foul is almost an anachronism."

It wasn't when Pele was assaulted out of the 1966 World Cup in England by Bulgarian and Portuguese players without referee protection, all of whom he has named in *My Life and the Beautiful Game*. It is now, however, and those who trip over into deliberate and or reckless foul play during the coming season should realise what the late Ted Croker and Duncan Ferguson failed to understand. The law of the land does not stop at the touchline or the boardroom or other offences outside either of them. In 1996–97, sadly, will prove this with well publicised libel and criminal match fixing cases at least in the pipeline.

EDWARD GRAYSON
Founder President, British Association for Sport and the Law

WORLD CLUB CHAMPIONSHIP

Played annually up to 1974 and intermittently since then between the winners of the European Cup and the winners of the South American Champions Cup — known as the Copa Libertadores. In 1980 the winners were decided by one match arranged in Tokyo in February 1981 and the venue has been the same since. AC Milan replaced Marseille who had been stripped of their European Cup title in 1993.

1960	Real Madrid beat Penarol 0-0, 5-1
1961	Penarol beat Benfica 0-1, 5-0, 2-1
1962	Santos beat Benfica 3-2, 5-2
1963	Santos beat AC Milan 2-4, 4-2, 1-0
1964	Inter-Milan beat Independiente 0-1, 2-0, 1-0
1965	Inter-Milan beat Independiente 3-0, 0-0
1966	Penarol beat Real Madrid 2-0, 2-0
1967	Racing Club beat Celtic 0-1, 2-1, 1-0
1968	Estudiantes beat Manchester United 1-0, 1-1
1969	AC Milan beat Estudiantes 3-0, 1-2
1970	Feyenoord beat Estudiantes 2-2, 1-0
1971	Nacional beat Panathinaikos* 1-1, 2-1
1972	Ajax beat Independiente 1-1, 3-0
1973	Independiente beat Juventus* 1-0
1974	Atlético Madrid* beat Independiente 0-1, 2-0
1975	Independiente and Bayern Munich could not agree dates; no matches.
1976	Bayern Munich beat Cruzeiro 2-0, 0-0
1977	Boca Juniors beat Borussia Moenchengladbach* 2-2, 3-0
1978	Not contested

1995

1979	Olimpia beat Malmö* 1-0, 2-1
1980	Nacional beat Nottingham Forest 1-0
1981	Flamengo beat Liverpool 3-0
1982	Penarol beat Aston Villa 2-0
1983	Gremio Porto Alegre beat SV Hamburg 2-1
1984	Independiente beat Liverpool 1-0
1985	Juventus beat Argentinos Juniors 4-2 on penalties after a 2-2 draw
1986	River Plate beat Steaua Bucharest 1-0
1987	FC Porto beat Penarol 2-1 after extra time
1988	Nacional (Uru) beat PSV Eindhoven 7-6 on penalties after 1-1 draw
1989	AC Milan beat Atletico Nacional (Col) 1-0 after extra time
1990	AC Milan beat Olimpia 3-0
1991	Red Star Belgrade beat Colo Colo 3-0
1992	Sao Paulo beat Barcelona 2-1
1993	Sao Paulo beat AC Milan 3-2
1994	Velez Sarsfield beat AC Milan 2-0

*European Cup runners-up; winners declined to take part.

28 November in Tokyo

Ajax (0) 0
Gremio Porto Alegre (0) 0 60,000

Ajax: Van der Sar; Reiziger, Blind, Frank de Boer, George, Bogarde, Ronald de Boer, Davids, Litmanen (Reuser 95), Kluivert, Overmars (Kanu 69).
Gremio Porto Alegre: Danrlei; Francisco Arce, Rivarola, Adilson, Roger, Goiano, Dinho, Arilson (Luciano 62), Carlos Miguel (Gelson 97), Paulo Nunes, Jardel (Magno 79).
(aet; Ajax won 4-3 on penalties)
Referee: Elleray (England).

EUROPEAN SUPER CUP

Played annually between the winners of the European Champions' Cup and the European Cup-Winners' Cup. AC Milan replaced Marseille in 1993–94.

Previous Matches

1972	Ajax beat Rangers 3-1, 3-2
1973	Ajax beat AC Milan 0-1, 6-0
1974	Not contested
1975	Dynamo Kiev beat Bayern Munich 1-0, 2-0
1976	Anderlecht beat Bayern Munich 4-1, 1-2
1977	Liverpool beat Hamburg 1-1, 6-0
1978	Anderlecht beat Liverpool 3-1, 1-2
1979	Nottingham F beat Barcelona 1-0, 1-1
1980	Valencia beat Nottingham F 1-0, 1-2
1981	Not contested
1982	Aston Villa beat Barcelona 0-1, 3-0
1983	Aberdeen beat Hamburg 0-0, 2-0
1984	Juventus beat Liverpool 2-0
1985	Juventus v Everton not contested due to UEFA ban on English clubs
1986	Steaua Bucharest beat Dynamo Kiev 1-0
1987	FC Porto beat Ajax 1-0, 1-0
1988	KV Mechelen beat PSV Eindhoven 3-0, 0-1
1989	AC Milan beat Barcelona 1-1, 1-0
1990	AC Milan beat Sampdoria 1-1, 2-0
1991	Manchester U beat Red Star Belgrade 1-0
1992	Barcelona beat Werder Bremen 1-1, 2-1
1993	Parma beat AC Milan 0-1, 2-0
1994	AC Milan beat Arsenal 0-0, 2-0

1995–96

First Leg, 6 February 1996, Zaragoza
Zaragoza (1) 1 *(Aguado 29)*
Ajax (0) 1 *(Kluivert 71)* 23,000

Zaragoza: Juanmi Garcia; Belsue, Solana, Quartero, Aguado, Celada, Dani (Pardeza 76), Nayim, Fernando Morientes, Higuera, Gustavo Lopez (Berti 76).
Ajax: Van der Sar; Reiziger, Blind, Frank de Boer, Bogarde, Scholten, George, Ronald de Boer, Kluivert, Litmanen (Wooter 66), Musampa (Van den Berg 53).
Referee: Harrel (France).

Second Leg, 28 February 1996, Amsterdam
Ajax (1) 4 *(Bogarde 41, George 53, Blind 66 (pen), 69 (pen))*
Zaragoza (0) 0 22,000

Ajax: Van der Sar; Reiziger, Blind, Frank de Boer, Bogarde, Scholten (Van den Berg 79), George (Gehring 70), Davids, Kanu, Kluivert (Demtchenko 70), Silooy.
Zaragoza: Cedrun (Belman 64); Belsue, Sanjuan, Caceres, Oscar, Aguado, Gustavo Lopez, Aragon, Fernando Morientes (Quatero 81), Higuera, Dani.
Referee: Mottram (Scotland).

SOUTH AMERICA

COPA LIBERTADORES 1995
(Results continued from last edition)

Quarter-finals, First Leg
River Plate 1, Velez Sarsfield 1
At. Nacional 2, Millonarios 1
Emelec 3, Sporting Cristal 1
Gremio 5, Palmeiras 0

Quarter-finals, Second Leg
Velez Sarsfield 1, River Plate 1
(River Plate won 5-3 on penalties)
Millonairos 1, At. Nacional 1
Sporting Cristal 1, Emelec 1
Palmeiras 5, Gremio 1

Semi-finals, First Leg
At. Nacional 1, River Plate 0
Emelec 0, Gremio 0

Semi-finals, Second Leg
River Plate 1, At. Nacional 0
(At. Nacional won 8-7 on penalties)
Gremio 2, Emelec 0

Final First Leg
Gremio 3, Atletico Nacional 1

Final Second Leg
Atletico Nacional 1, Gremio 1

COPA LIBERTADORES 1996

Group 1

	P	W	D	L	F	A	Pts
Barcelona	6	4	1	1	11	8	13
Cerro Porteno	6	3	1	2	8	7	10
Espoli	6	2	0	4	7	10	6
Olimpia	6	1	2	3	4	5	5

Group 2

	P	W	D	L	F	A	Pts
Penarol	6	2	3	1	13	10	9
Defensor	6	1	4	1	6	6	7
Sporting Cristal	6	1	4	1	6	7	7
Universitario	6	2	1	3	7	9	7

Group 3

	P	W	D	L	F	A	Pts
America	6	4	0	2	11	2	12
Atletico Junior	6	3	1	2	8	6	10
San Jose	6	3	0	3	8	8	9
Guabira	6	1	1	4	7	16	4

Group 4

	P	W	D	L	F	A	Pts
Corinthians	6	4	1	1	13	6	13
Univ de Chile	6	4	1	1	9	5	13
Botafogo	6	1	1	4	8	12	4
Univ Catolica	6	1	1	4	6	13	4

Group 5

	P	W	D	L	F	A	Pts
River Plate	6	4	2	0	14	3	14
San Lorenzo	6	2	4	0	13	5	10
Minerven	6	1	2	3	8	16	5
Caracas	6	0	2	4	6	17	2

Second Round, First Leg
Espoli 1, Corinthians 3
Cerro Porteno 0, At. Junior 0
Univ de Chile 3, Defensor 2

Botafogo 1, Gremio 1
Minerven 1, America 1
San Lorenzo 3, Penarol 2
San Jose 1, Barcelona 0
Sporting Cristal 2, River Plate 1

Second Round, Second Leg
River Plate 5, Sporting Cristal 2
Barcelona 2, San Jose 1
(Barcelona won 4-2 on penalties)
Penarol 1, San Lorenzo 5
Corinthians 2, Espoli 0
Gremio 2, Botafogo 0
America 4, Minerven 1
At. Junior 1, Cerro Porteno 0
Defensor 2, Univ de Chile 1

Quarter-finals, First Leg
Corinthians 0, Gremio 3
San Lorenzo 1, River Plate 2
Univ de Chile 2, Barcelona 0
At. Junior 1, America 1

Quarter-finals, Second Leg
Barcelona 1, Univ de Chile 1
America 1, At. Junior 0
River Plate 1, San Lorenzo 1
Gremio 0, Corinthians 1

Semi-finals, First Leg
Gremio 1, America 0
Univ de Chile 2, River Plate 2

Semi-finals, Second Leg
America 3, Gremio 1
River Plate 1, Univ de Chile 0

Final, First Leg
America 1, River Plate 0

Final, Second Leg
River Plate 2, America 0

SOUTH AMERICAN SUPER CUP

First Round (league system)

Group A

	P	W	D	L	F	A	Pts
Sao Paulo	4	3	0	1	6	7	9
Olimpia	4	2	1	1	7	3	7
Boca Juniors	4	0	1	3	4	7	1

First Round, First Leg (Cup system)
Cruzeiro 1, Colo Colo 0
Nacional (Uru) 1, Estudiantes 0
Independiente 1, Santos 1
Velez Sarsfield 2, Flamengo 3

Penarol 2, River Plate 3
Argentinos Juniors 1, At. Nacional 3
Gremio 3, Racing 1

First Round, Second Leg
Estudiantes 2, Nacional (Uru) 2
Colo Colo 0, Cruzeiro 0
River Plate 2, Penarol 3
(River Plate won 7-6 on penalties)
Flamengo 3, Velez Sarsfield 0
Santos 2, Independiente 2
At. Nacional 2, Argentinos Juniors 0
Racing 3, Gremio 3

Quarter-finals, First Leg
Sao Paulo 0, Cruzeiro 1
Nacional (Uru) 0, Flamengo 1
At. Nacional 1, Independiente 0
Gremio 2, River Plate 1

Quarter-finals, Second Leg
Cruzeiro 1, Sao Paulo 0
(Cruzeiro won 4-1 on penalties)
Flamengo 1, Nacional (Uru) 0
Independiente 2, At. Nacional 1
River Plate 3, Gremio 2
(River Plate won 4-2 on penalties)

Semi-finals, First Leg
Cruzeiro 0, Flamengo 1
Independiente 2, River Plate 2

Semi-finals, Second Leg
Flamengo 3, Cruzeiro 1
River Plate 0, Independiente 0
(Independiente won 4-1 on penalties)

Final, First Leg
Independiente 2, Flamengo 0

Final, Second Leg
Flamengo 1, Independiente 0

CONMEBOL MASTERS CUP
Sao Paulo 7, Botafogo 3
Atletico Mineiro 0, Rosario Central 0
(Atletico Mineiro won 10-9 on penalties)

Final
Sao Paulo 3, Atletico Mineiro 0

CONMEBOL CUP

First Round, First Leg
America 3, Barcelona 1
Defensor 1, Rosario Central 3
Gimnasia 1, Sud America 0
Ciclista 4, Cobreloa 1
The Strongest 0, Colegiales 0
Ceara 1, Corinthians 0
Mineros 1, Independiente (Col) 0
Atletico Mineiro 1, Guarani 1

First Round, Second Leg
Guarani 0, Atletico Mineiro 1
Independiente (Col) 2, Mineros 1
(Mineros won 4-3 on penalties)
Colegiales 2, The Strongest 1
Barcelona 0, America 2
Cobreloa 7, Ciclista 2

Corinthians 2, Ceara 2
Sud America 4, Gimnasia 0
Rosario Central 2, Defensor 1

Quarter-finals, First Leg
Rosario Central 2, Cobreloa 0
Corinthians 2, America 1
Sud America 0, Colegiales 1
Atletico Mineiro 6, Mineros 0

Quarter-finals, Second Leg
Mineros 0, Atletico Mineiro 4
Colegiales 1, Sud America 2
(Colegiales won 4-3 on penalties)
America 3, Corinthians 1
Cobreloa 1, Rosario Central 3

Semi-finals, First Leg
Colegiales 0, Rosario Central 2
America 4, Atletico Mineiro 3

Semi-finals, Second Leg
Rosario Central 3, Colegiales 1
Atletico Mineiro 1, America 0
(Atletico Mineiro won 5-3 on penalties)

Final First Leg
Atletico Mineiro 4, Rosario Central 0

Final, Second Leg
Rosario Central 0, Atletico Mineiro 0

CONCACAF GOLD CUP
Group A
Mexico 5, St Vincent 0
Mexico 1, Guatemala 0
St Vincent 1, Guatemala 3

Group B
Canada 3, Honduras 1
Brazil 4, Canada 1
Brazil 5, Honduras 0

Group C
Trinidad 2, El Salvador 3
USA 3, Trinidad 2
USA 2, El Salvador 0

Semi-finals
Brazil 1, USA 0
Mexico 1, Guatemala 0

Third place
USA 3, Guatemala 0

Final
Brazil 0, Mexico 2

AFRICA

AFRICAN NATIONS CUP
(in South Africa, January 1996)

Group A
South Africa 3, Cameroon 0
Egypt 2, Angola 1
Cameroon 2, Egypt 1
Angola 0, South Africa 1
Angola 3, Cameroon 3
Egypt 1, South Africa 0

Group B
Zambia 0, Algeria 0
Sierra Leone 2, Burkina Faso 1
Algeria 2, Sierra Leone 0
Burkina Faso 1, Zambia 5
Sierra Leone 0, Zambia 4
Burkina Faso 1, Algeria 2

Group C
Gabon 1, Liberia 2
Zaire 0, Gabon 2
Liberia 0, Zaire 2
Nigeria withdrew

Group D
Ivory Coast 0, Ghana 2
Tunisia 1, Mozambique 1
Ghana 2, Tunisia 1
Mozambique 0, Ivory Coast 1
Mozambique 0, Ghana 2
Tunisia 3, Ivory Coast 1

Quarter-finals
South Africa 2, Algeria 1
Zambia 3, Egypt 1
Ghana 1, Zaire 0
Gabon 1, Tunisia 1

Semi-finals
South Africa 3, Ghana 0
Tunisia 4, Zambia 2

Third Place
Zambia 1, Ghana 0

Final
South Africa 2, Tunisia 0

VAUXHALL CONFERENCE 1995–96

VAUXHALL CONFERENCE TABLE 1995–96

		Home			Goals		Away			Goals		
	P	W	D	L	F	A	W	D	L	F	A	Pts
Stevenage Borough	42	13	6	2	51	20	14	4	3	50	24	91
Woking	42	16	5	0	47	13	9	3	9	36	41	83
Hednesford Town	42	13	3	5	38	21	10	4	7	33	25	76
Macclesfield Town	42	12	5	4	32	16	10	4	7	34	33	75
Gateshead	42	9	7	5	32	24	9	6	6	26	22	67
Southport	42	10	7	4	42	25	8	5	8	35	39	66
Kidderminster Harriers	42	13	4	4	49	26	5	6	10	29	40	64
Northwich Victoria	42	9	3	9	38	35	7	9	5	34	29	60
Morecambe	42	12	2	7	51	33	5	6	10	27	39	59
Farnborough Town	42	8	6	7	29	23	7	8	6	34	35	59
Bromsgrove Rovers	42	11	6	4	33	20	4	8	9	26	37	59
Altrincham	42	9	6	6	33	29	6	7	8	26	35	58
Telford United	42	8	7	6	27	23	7	3	11	24	33	55
Stalybridge Celtic	42	9	3	9	29	37	7	4	10	30	31	55
Halifax Town	42	8	7	6	30	25	5	6	10	19	38	52
Kettering Town	42	9	5	7	38	32	4	4	13	30	52	48
Slough Town	42	4	6	11	35	44	9	2	10	28	32	47
Bath City	42	9	4	8	29	31	4	3	14	16	35	46
Welling United	42	6	8	7	21	23	4	7	10	21	30	45
Dover Athletic	42	8	1	12	29	38	3	6	12	22	36	40
Runcorn	42	4	5	12	25	43	5	3	13	23	44	35
Dagenham & Redbridge	42	5	7	9	31	34	2	5	14	12	39	33

ATTENDANCES BY CLUB 1995–96

	Aggregate Attendance 1995–96	Average Attendance 1995–96	Average Attendance 1994–95	% Change
Altrincham	17,890	852	1,002	–15
Bath City	10,826	516	647	–20
Bromsgrove Rovers	22,499	1,071	1,130	–5
Dagenham & Redbridge	16,603	791	949	–17
Dover Athletic	21,042	1,002	1,101	–9
Farnborough Town	17,025	811	798	+2
Gateshead	13,083	623	693	–10
Halifax Town	17,600	838	974	–14
Hednesford Town	27,514	1,310	744	+76
Kettering Town	29,962	1,427	1,837	–22
Kidderminster Harriers	42,430	2,020	1,959	+3
Macclesfield Town	26,546	1,264	1,260	+1
Morecambe	23,727	1,130	746	+51
Northwich Victoria	17,103	814	944	–14
Runcorn	10,951	521	468	+11
Slough Town	19,379	923	825	+12
Southport	19,825	944	1,079	–13
Stalybridge Celtic	12,864	613	710	–14
Stevenage Borough	39,827	1,897	1,424	+33
Telford United	17,155	817	811	+1
Welling United	12,910	615	739	–17
Woking	50,056	2,384	1,815	+31

HIGHEST ATTENDANCES 1995–96

4583	Woking v Macclesfield Town	6.4.96		2874	Woking v Dagenham & Redbridge	26.12.95
4481	Kidderminster Harriers v Bromsgrove Rovers	1.1.96		2703	Kidderminster Harriers v Macclesfield Town	13.1.96
4398	Bromsgrove Rovers v Kidderminster Harriers	26.12.95		2679	Woking v Morecambe	4.11.95
				2637	Woking v Kettering Town	24.2.96
3976	Stevenage Borough v Woking	8.4.96		2556	Stevenage Borough v Morecambe	27.4.96
3194	Woking v Hednesford Town	30.3.96		2480	Hednesford Town v Telford United	11.9.95
3116	Woking v Farnborough Town	16.4.96				

VAUXHALL CONFERENCE LEADING GOALSCORERS 1995–96

Conf.			FAC	SCC	FAT
29	Barry Hayles *(Stevenage Borough)*	+	—	—	5
23	Joe O'Connor *(Hednesford Town)*	+	1	2	—
22	Carl Alford *(ex-Kettering Town)*	+	2	—	1
21	Mark West *(Slough Town)*	+	—	4	3
	Chris Boothe *(Farnborough Town)*	+	5	5	1
20	David Leworthy *(Dover Athletic)*	+	1	3	1
19	Steve Harkus *(Gateshead)*	+	—	1	—
18	Clive Walker *(Woking)*	+	1	—	—
17	Carwyn Williams *(Northwich Victoria)*	+	3	—	—
16	Andy Whittaker *(Southport)*	+	—	3	1
15	Corey Browne *(Stevenage Borough)*	+	1	—	—
14	Mike Bignall *(Runcorn)*	+	2	—	—
	Brian Butler *(Northwich Victoria)*	+	2	—	4
	Kim Casey *(Kidderminster Harriers)*	+	1	2	—
	Paul Davies *(Kidderminster Harriers)*	+	—	—	—
	Darran Hay *(Woking)*	+	4	—	—
	Junior Hunter *(Woking)*	+	—	—	—

FAC: FA Cup; SCC: Spalding Challenge Cup; FAT: FA Trophy.

CLUB REVIEW

	VC	FAT	SCC	FAC
Altrincham	12	2	2	1
1994-95	4	QF	QF	3
Bath City	18	QF	1	4q
	12	2	2	1
Bromsgrove Rovers	11	QF	W	1
	13	1	W	4q
Dagenham & Redbridge	22	1	1	3q
	15	1	SF	2q
Dover Athletic	20	2	QF	1q
	16	1	QF	4q
Farnborough Town	10	1	2	1
	14	2	2	4q
Gateshead	5	QF	QF	2q
	7	3	1	2q
Halifax Town	15	2	2	4q
	8	1	1	2
Hednesford Town	3	1	1	4q
Kettering Town	16	2	SF	4q
	6	2	F	1
Kidderminster Harriers	7	1	2	1
	11	F	2	1
Macclesfield Town	4	F	F	4q
	1	QF	SF	4q
Morecambe	9	1	QF	4q
Northwich Victoria	8	F	1	1
	10	1	2	1
Runcorn	21	1	2	1
	9	3	2	1
Slough Town	17	2	QF	1
Southport	6	1	SF	4q
	3	1	2	1
Stalybridge Celtic	14	1	1	4q
	18	1	QF	4q
Stevenage Borough	1	QF	2	1
	5	3	1	2q
Telford United	13	1	2	2
	19	2	1	4q
Welling United	19	2	1	2q
	17	2	1	2q
Woking	2	1	2	3
	2	F	QF	2

VC: Vauxhall Conference; FAT: FA Trophy; SCC: Spalding Challenge Cup; FAC: FA Cup.

HIGHEST AGGREGATE SCORES
Slough Town 5-4 Kidderminster Harriers 28.8.95
Morecambe 4-5 Woking 13.1.96

LARGEST HOME MARGINS
Macclesfield Town 7-0 Halifax Town 9.3.96
Morecambe 7-0 Altrincham 17.2.96
Southport 7-1 Farnborough Town 4.11.95
Farnborough Town 6-1 Macclesfield Town 30.9.95
Kidderminster Harriers 6-1 Halifax Town 18.3.96
Southport 6-1 Kettering Town 6.1.96

LARGEST AWAY MARGINS
Runcorn 0-8 Stevenage Borough 25.11.95
Kettering Town 1-6 Stalybridge Celtic 4.5.96
Slough Town 2-6 Stevenage Borough 12.3.96
Stalybridge Celtic 1-5 Northwich Victoria 25.4.96

MATCHES WITHOUT DEFEAT
17 Stevenage Borough
14 Woking
10 Macclesfield Town
 9 Farnborough Town, Kidderminster Harriers

MATCHES WITHOUT SUCCESS
10 Altrincham, Dover Athletic
 9 Dagenham & Redbridge, Runcorn
 8 Bath City, Dagenham & Redbridge, Kettering Town, Slough Town, Telford United, Welling United

CONSECUTIVE CONFERENCE VICTORIES
7 Woking
6 Macclesfield Town, Kidderminster Harriers, Woking
5 Altrincham, Hednesford Town, Stevenage Borough

CONSECUTIVE CONFERENCE DEFEATS
9 Dover Athletic
8 Kettering Town
7 Welling United
6 Bath City

VAUXHALL CONFERENCE 1995–96

APPEARANCES AND GOALSCORERS

Altrincham
Vauxhall Appearances: Allen, A. 3(5); Anderson, L. 7(2); Armstrong, D. 0(3); Bolland, P. 3(3); Butler, B. 31(2); Carmody, M. 27(2); Challender, G. 4(1); Clancy, M. 2; Cockram, D. 1(1); Collings, P. 25; Cross, S. 42; Daughtry, P. 2(1); Doherty, N. 15(1); France, P. 41(1); Green, A. 14(1); Hall, D. 3(1); Hardy, N. 26(7); Harris, R. 10(1); Heesom, D. 36(2); Horrigan, I. 2(2); Hughes, M. 6(4); John, J. 16(1); Jones, M. 1; Kelly, A. 9(1); Leitch, G. 1; Oliver, D. 10(5); O'Neill, S. 1(1); Pritchard, D. 10; Reid, A. 26; Royle, D. 4(11); Sharratt, C. 21; Terry, S. 40; Whalley, N. 20; Zumrutel, B. 3(1).
Goals (59): Allen 1, Bolland 1, Butler 2, Carmody 1, Doherty 5, France 4, Green 3, Hardy 10, Harris 2, Heesom 1, Kelly 1, Oliver 1, Pritchard 3, Royle 1, Sharratt 6, Terry 15, Whalley 1, og 1.

Bath City
Vauxhall Appearances: Adcock, P. 30; Birkby, D. 21; Brooks, N. 16; Challender, G. 6; Chenoweth, P. 11; Chiverton, E. 30; Cousins, R. 40; Croft, B. 1; Crowley, R. 10; Dicks, G. 42; Gill, J. 24; Graham, B. 6; Hedges, I. 31; Hervin, M. 3; James, S. 25; Lucas, J. 13; Micciche, M. 7; Mings, A. 28; Mogg, D. 42; Ricketts, A. 3; Saunders, N. 23; Scott, A. 10; Sherwood, J. 14; Smart, G. 38; Spencer, M. 12; Sugar, C. 16; Vernon, D. 22; Wigley, R. 4; Withey, G. 20; Walsh, A. 5.
Goals (45): Adcock 4, Birkby 3, Chiverton 4, Cousins 2, James 1, Mings 7, Scott 2, Smart 5, Spencer 1, Sugar 1, Vernon 4, Withey 10, og 1.

Bromsgrove Rovers
Vauxhall Appearances: Amos, N. 18(4); Brain, S. 3(8); Brighton, S. 18(3); Burgher, S. 5(1); Carter, R. 21(1); Clarke, N. 35(1); Crisp, M. 39; Dale, A. 20(14); Dowling, F. 2(24); Eades, G. 2; Gardner, R. 2(4); Gaunt, C. 33; Glasser, N. 4(10); Grocutt, D. 29(1); Humphrey, P. 3(3); Hunt, J. 24(2); Marlowe, A. 4(8); Olden, N. 2(1); Powell, R. 0(2); Radburn, C. 7(6); Randall, S. 18(2); Richardson, K. 36; Skelding, J. 37; Smith, A. 38; Taylor, C. 40; Trowman, W. 1(2); White, C. 2(1); Whitehead, S. 1(3); Whitehouse, A. 1; Young, L. 2(9).
Goals (59): Amos 3, Brighton 2, Carter 13, Clarke 1, Crisp 13, Dale 3, Gaunt 5, Grocutt 2, Hunt 5, Marlowe 1, Radburn 1, Skelding 5, Smith 4, og 1.

Dagenham & Redbridge
Vauxhall Appearances: Aldridge, M. 3; Alexander, T. 2(1); Bennett, G. 3(3); Bolder, B. 2; Jason, B. 28(2); Collins, D. 1(3); Creaser, G. 15; Cook, J. 3; Conner, S. 17(1); Crookes, D. 28; Culverhouse, D. 29; Davidson, J. 5(1); Derry, D. 11(3); Devereux, J. 1(2); Dyer, K. 11(8); Gammons, R. 6(3); Gothard, P. 18(3); Graham, D. 7; Greene, D. 8(2); Haag, K. 12; Healer, A. 0(2); Henry, L. 1; Hewes, N. 5(6); Hague, P. 7; Johnson, D. 0(1); Livett, S. 6(1); Matthews, N. 3; McDonough, R. 1(1); McParland, I. 1; Prindiville, S. 22; Reed, G. 15; Shipp, D. 7(1); Southon, J. 6; Stebbing, G. 31; Stringfellow, I. 20; Taylor, R. 32; Thompson, S. 13(1); Tripp, D. 5(1); Wallace, A. 1; Wells, M. 2; Williams, D. 22; Wilson, L. 32; Worthington, N. 20.
Goals (43): Aldridge 1, Bennett 2, Broom 1, Conner 1, Crookes 1, Derry 3, Dyer 1, Greene 1, Haag 3, Hewes 1, Matthews 2, Prindiville 4, Shipp 2, Stringfellow 7, Taylor 4, Wilson 1, Worthington 6, og 2.

Dover Athletic
Vauxhall Appearances: Bond, K. 1; Browne, C. 7; Budden, J. 37(1); Campbell, C. 26(3); Carruthers, M. 0(6); Chambers, P. 4(4); Dalli, J. 2; Daniels, S. 36; Darlington, J. 21(9); Donn, N. 19(14); Dixon, T. 0(1); Ebbli, E. 37(1); Ferney, M. 5(2); Foot, D. 10; Harris, J. 13(1); Hayes, M. 14(1); Jones, S. 0(11); Lawrence, S. 2(6); Lewis, J. 22(1); Leworthy, D. 30; Lindsey, S. 24(1); Milton, R. 26(4); Mitten, C. 5(4); Mosely, S. 8(2); O'Brien, P. 12(15); Pilkington, P. 22(6); Restarick, S. 13(5); Rogers, T. 18(3); Roget, L. 4; Southon, J. 0(2); Sowerby, C. 7(5); Strouts, J. 27(3); Taylor, P. 0(1); Theodosiou, A. 4(8); Walker, D. 8(1).
Goals (51): Carruthers 1, Chambers 1, Daniels 1, Darlington 2, Harris 5, Hayes 2, Lewis 2, Leworthy 20, Lindsey 1, Milton 3, Pilkington 2, Restarick 2, Sowerby 4, Strouts 2, Theodosiou 1, og 2.

Farnborough Town
Vauxhall Appearances: Baker, K. 24(2); Baker, S. 37; Boothe, C. 42; Coney, D. 12; Day, K. 34; Denny, R. 18(8); Gavin, P. 26; Harlow, D. 42; Hayward, D. 0(1); Horton, J. 9; Juryeff, I. 2(2); MacKenzie, S. 37; McAvoy, G. 20(3); Mintram, S. 3; Pratt, B. 2; Robson, D. 41; Rowe, A. 5(1); Senior, T. 13; Steadman, C. 0(2); Stemp, W. 39; Turkington, M. 0(1); Underwood, J. 18(1); Williams, R. 15(2); Wingfield, P. 23.
Goals (63): Baker 4, Boothe 21, Coney 1, Day 1, Denny 2, Gavin 9, Harlow 4, Horton 2, McAvoy 1, Robson 6, Senior 5, Underwood 2, Wingfield 5.

Gateshead
Vauxhall Appearances: Cramman, K. 31(1); Dobson, P. 3(9); Dowson, A. 11(7); Farrey, M. 10(9); Fell, G. 0(2); Harkus, S. 25(1); Hine, M. 32(7); Ketter, D. 2; Kitchen, S. 38(2); Lowe, K. 17(1); Marquis, P. 6; Musgrave, S. 12(1); Ord, D. 36(3); Parkinson, G. 1(2); Proudlock, P. 35(6); Robson, G. 9; Rowe, B. 40; Scaife, N. 2(1); Sherwood, S. 30; Thew, L. 3(7); Thompson, P. 20(20); Trott, D. 24(6); Watson, J. 34(3); Wrightson, J. 41.
Goals (58): Cramman 6, Dobson 1, Harkus 19, Hine 1, Lowe 1, Marquis 1, Ord 5, Proudlock 7, Thompson 8, Trott 8, Watson 1.

Halifax Town
Vauxhall Appearances: Annan, R. 20(3); Beddard, E. 8(14); Benn, W. 1; Brook, G. 11(5); Brown, J. 33(1); Buxton, N. 0(3); Cochrane, K. 16(8); Constable, S. 4(1); Daws, A. 5; Graham, D. 1; Griffiths, W. 0(4); Hart, I. 0(1); Hendrick, J. 25(4); Heyes, D. 17(12); Horner, N. 17(20); Johnson, S. 14(9); Lee, G. 4(3); Ludlow, L. 0(5); Megson, D. 0(2); Midwood, M. 36(5); Mudd, P. 6; Murray, N. 0(1); O'Regan, K. 40; Place, D. 0(1); Prindiville, S. 17(1); Sansam, C. 5(1); Scaife, N. 2; Smith, P. 27; Stoneman, P. 39; Thompson, S. 19(1); Thornber, S. 1; Timons, C. 14(1); Trotter, M. 36; Wilson, L. 2(3); Woods, A. 25(15); Worthington, G. 17(2).
Goals (49): Beddard 3, Brook 4, Brown 1, Cochrane 3, Daws 1, Hendrick 2, Horner 1, Johnson 6, Lee 1, Midwood 10, O'Regan 4, Sansam 1, Stoneman 3, Trotter 3, Worthington 5, og 1.

Hednesford Town
Vauxhall Appearances: Burr, S. 2(11); Carty, P. 25(5); Coates, D. 0(2); Collins, K. 37(2); Cooksey, S. 41; Devine, S. 37(3); Essex, S. 40; Fitzpatrick, G. 34(1); Freeman, M. 0(4); Foreman, D. 13(7); Hackett, B. 0(2); Hanson, D. 8; Harnett, D. 2(7); Jennings, G. 1(13); Lake, S. 5(15); Lambert, C. 27(2); McNally, B. 23; O'Connor, J. 40; Pierce, S. 1(4); Radburn, C. 0(1); Riddings, P. 4(2); Russell, K. 14; Simpson, W. 39; Street, T. 25(5); Titterton, D. 3(7); Williams, R. 1(2); Wright, H. 8(27); Yates, L. 32(4).
Goals (71): Burr 1, Carty 3, Collins 1, Devine 5, Essex 4, Fitzpatrick 2, Foreman 4, Hanson 3, Lake 4, Lambert 6, McNally 1, O'Connor 23, Riddings 2, Russell 4, Simpson 1, Street 3, Wright 1, Yates 2, og 1.

Kettering Town
Vauxhall Appearances: Alford, C. 32; Arnold, I. 4(4); Benjamin, I. 6(3); Birch, T. 0(1); Brown, R. 1; Brownrigg, A. 3; Cox, P. 7(1); Cullip, A. 3; Dowling, L. 1(5); Edwards, M. 2(1); Fowler, J. 16; Gynn, M. 13; Harmon, D. 23(5); Haworth, R. 8; Heffernan, L. 2; Holden, S. 21; Hunter, J. 15; Ibrahim, M. 8(5); Jones, D. 0(1); Judge, A. 34; King, E. 4(5); Kostka, M. 0(1); March, S. 38(15); McParland, I. 0(3); Miles, P. 0(10); Miller, C. 0(2); Mustafa, T. 31; Norman, C. 24(1); Nyamah, K. 34; Oxbrow, D. 22(2); Parsons, M. 2(6); Pope, N. 37; Rayment, P. 6(1); Rea, S. 4; Saddington, J. 1(5); Scott, I. 30(9); Shanahan, J. 1(1); Shoemake, K. 8(27); Stott, S. 18; Stringfellow, I. 16(7); Thomas, A. 6(2); Trigg, S. 1(2); Wilson, R. 0(1).
Goals (68): Alford 22, Benjamin 3, Dowling 2, Harmon 1, Haworth 2, Hunter 2, Mustafa 2, Norman 1, Nyamah 3, Oxbrow 5, Parsons 1, Pope 6, Scott 7, Stott 3, Stringfellow 6, Thomas 1, og 1.

Kidderminster Harriers

Vauxhall Appearances: Bancroft, P. 20(1); Brindley, C. 39; Cartwright, N. 22(3); Casey, K. 36(5); Davies, P. 38(1); Deakin, J. 25(2); Dearlove, M. 9(5); Eades, G. 1(5); Hodson, S. 40; Hughes, L. 32(3); May, L. 29(2); Purdie, J. 0(1); Robinson, S. 5; Rose, K. 4(1); Shepherd, M. 8(5); Steadman, D. 38; Webb, P. 33(2); Weir, M. 18(1); Willetts, K. 25(2); Yates, M. 40.
Goals (78): Brindley 2, Cartwright 2, Casey 14, Davies 14, Deakin 4, Dearlove 2, Hughes 12, May 13, Shepherd 4, Webb 1, Willetts 2, Yates 8.

Macclesfield Town

Vauxhall Appearances: Bradshaw, M. 30; Burr, S. 3(2); Cavell, P. 25(6); Clark, M. 3(5); Coates, M. 26(7); Edey, C. 20(4); Evans, G. 0(1); Gardiner, M. 20(2); German, D. 11; Hemmings, A. 26; Howarth, N. 38; Hulme, K. 16; Hutchinson, S. 4(7); Locke, S. 9(1); Lyons, D. 32(6); Marginson, K. 11(3); McDonald, M. 13; Middlemass, S. 2; Monk. I. 0(1); Morgan, P. 9; Payne, S. 38; Power, P. 21; Price, R. 22; Sorvel, N. 42; Tinson, D. 15; Tobin, S. 1(1); Williams, K. 11; Wood, S. 14(1).
Goals (66): Bradshaw 3, Cavell 9, Coates 11, Gardiner 1, Hemmings 4, Howarth 2, Hulme 4, Hutchinson 1, Lyons 9, Marginson 1, McDonald 1, Payne 1, Power 13, Tinson 1, Wood 3.

Morecambe

Vauxhall Appearances: Armstrong, R. 15; Banks, A. 8; Burns, P. 39; Cain, I. 30(4); Ceraolo, M. 14(15); Coleman, J. 27; Comstive, P. 23(4); Drummond, S. 1(1); Dullaghan, G. 5(6); Foley, S. 7; Grimshaw, A. 31(3); Harvey, J. 1(3); Hodgson, S. 0(1); Horrigan, I. 3(2); Hughes, A. 31; Jackson, J. 5(4); Johnstone, G. 19; Knowles, M. 28(7); Lavelle, B. 26; McCluskie, J. 25(11); McIlhargy, S. 15; Maddock, W. 10(2); Monk, I. 25(1); Norman, J. 14(9); Ruston, P. 25; Sang, N. 7(1); Stimpson, B. 2; Taylor, P. 0(2); Tomlinson, P. 25; West, P. 8; Withers, P. 2(4).
Goals (78): Armstrong 1, Burns 7, Cain 9, Ceraolo 11, Coleman 11, Comstive 1, Dullaghan 1, Grimshaw 3, Jackson 2, Knowles 2, McCluskie 11, Monk 9, Norman 8, Tomlinson 1, West 1.

Northwich Victoria

Vauxhall Appearances: Abel, G. 21(1); Ball, T. 5; Burgess, D. 36(3); Butler, B. 39(1); Clayton, P. 14(1); Cooke, I. 31(4); Cooper, L. 0(1); Cumiskey, P. 1; Duffy, C. 33(4); Edwards, M. 2; Greygoose, D. 35; Harwood, C. 0(1); Hilton, R. 7(1); Holden, S. 1; Hughes, G. 0(6); Humphreys, D. 12(3); Jones, M. 21(3); Logan, M. 0(1); MacAuley, H. 4(11); Newall, A. 2; Ogden, N. 2; Oghani, G. 2(21); Patterson, K. 0(1); Simpson, W. 23(5); Steele, L. 8(2); Sunderland, J. 3; Sweeney, R. 5(1); Tait, P. 8(1); Tinson, D. 24; Vicary, D. 37; Walters, S. 28; Ward, D. 27(1); Wilkinson, D. 0(1); Williams, D. 32(7).
Goals (72): Butler 15, Clayton 4, Cooke 6, Duffy 1, Humphreys 1, Jones 1, MacAuley 2, Oghani 1, Simpson 1, Steele 5, Tait 1, Vicary 9, Walters 6, Ward 2, Williams 17.

Runcorn

Vauxhall Appearances: Allen, G. 8; Anderson, G. 1(1); Bates, J. 31; Bignall, M. 33(3); Brady, I. 18(2); Byrne, P. 36; Carpenter, J. 11; Cartwright, M. 6; Clowes, L. 13(17); Daley, P. 2; Doherty, M. 24(3); Doherty, N. 21; Ellis, P. 34(1); Eyre, S. 19(1); Farrington, M. 5; Finley, A. 23; Furlong, C. 1(1); Hill, G. 0(1); Knapman, S. 0(3); Lee, A. 12; Livingstone, R. 1; McInerney, I. 16(5); Morris, M. 26; Okorie, K. 2(1); Robertson, P. 15; Ruffer, C. 30(8); Smith, M. 7(3); Stant, R. 2(1); Tait, P. 4; Taylor, C. 28(5); Thomas, K. 4(4); Thomson, A. 10; Warder, A. 17(1).
Goals (48): Allen 3, Bates 1, Bignall 15, Clowes 3, Doherty N. 4, Eyre 4, Farrington 3, Finley 1, Robertson 1, Ruffer 1, Smith 1, Taylor 9, Thomas 1, Warder 1

Slough Town

Vauxhall Appearances: Baron, T. 26; Bateman, S. 17(4); Blackman, G. 21(12); Blunden, M. 0(3); Bressington, G. 6; Bunting, T. 7; Bushay, A. 26(5); Catlin, K. 35(3); Clarke, D. 1; Clement, A. 27; Connor, B. 1(1); Fiore, M. 38(2); Gray, A. 5(3); Harvey, L. 28(3); Hercules, C. 16; Horner, C. 10(1); Horner, D. 0(1); Lay, D. 4(1); Lee, B. 31(5); Lomas, A. 1; McDermott, B. 2(4); McVie, G. 1; Miles, B. 15; Moussaddik, C. 3; Nolan, A. 4; Paris, A. 21; Pickett, R. 8(19); Preddie, D. 16; Pye, M. 21(1); Rake, B. 13(8); Saunders, M. 6; Smart, G. 8; Smith, R. 2(3); Stone, M. 1(1); West, M. 41.
Goals (63): Baron 4, Bateman 1, Blackman 6, Bushay 8, Catlin 5, Clement 2, Fiore 2, Harvey 1, Hercules 7, Lay 2, Pickett 2, Smart 1, West 21, og 1.

Southport

Vauxhall Appearances: Blackhurst, J. 3; Blackstone, I. 8(6); Blakeman, C. 1(1); Cavanagh, A. 1(9); Challender, G. 2(1); Clark, M. 29(1); Cochran, S. 16(2); Croasdale, P. 8; Cunningham, H. 9(2); Davenport, P. 34(5); Dove, L. 39; Farley, A. 26(1); Fuller, D. 25(3); Gamble, D. 31(6); Goulding, D. 40; Griffiths, B. 23(7); Haw, S. 19(10); Horner, P. 11; Howard, S. 1; Kelly, M. 1(1); Lodge, P. 36; McDonald, M. 19(2); McKenna, J. 33; Mitchell, N. 8; Thomas, G. 7(3); Ward, K. 3(2); Whittaker, A. 29(6).
Goals (77): Blackstone 3, Clark 2, Davenport 13, Dove 2, Farley 3, Fuller 2, Gamble 7, Goulding 1, Griffiths 6, Haw 9, Horner 1, Lodge 1, McDonald 4, Mitchell 4, Ward 1, Whittaker 16, og 2.

Stalybridge Celtic

Vauxhall Appearances: Arnold, I. 29; Bauress, G. 18(1); Booth, K. 1; Brown, R. 6; Burke, B. 42(1); Challender, G. 7(5); Coathup, I. 41(1); Dickson, K. 1; Edmonds, N. 13(12); Ellis, N. 14(10); Ellison, L. 3(2); Frain, D. 31(4); Goodacre, S. 21(13); Hall, D. 38(3); Higginbotham, P. 11(11); Holt, M. 0(1); Jones, A. 27; Jones, S. 29(3); Megson, K. 21(10); O'Shaughnessy, S. 29; Patterson, I. 2(6); Pearson, G. 3(5); Pearson, J. 4(1); Powell, C. 3(5); Quy, A. 4; Ryan, J. 27(4); Shaughnessy, S. 1(3); Shaw, N. 8(8); Sherwood, S. 10; Wheeler, P. 7(14); Willetts, H. 28; Wilson, P. 1(6).
Goals (59): Arnold 6, Burke 12, Coathup 2, Ellis 1, Ellison 1, Frain 2, Goodacre 12, Higginbotham 3, Jones A. 2, Jones S. 5, Megson 1, O'Shaughnessy 1, Powell 3, Ryan 3, Shaw 1, Wheeler 4.

Stevenage Borough

Vauxhall Appearances: Barrowcliff, P. 36(5); Bates, M. 0(7); Beeke, S. 1(7); Beevor, S. 14(14); Berry, S. 37; Browne, C. 31(2); Crawshaw, G. 12(7); Cretton, S. 6(13); Gallagher, D. 23(8); Grime, D. 0(1); Grime, N. 1(2); Haag, K. 0(1); Hayles, B. 38; Howell, D. 1(2); Lynch, A. 25(1); Marshall, S. 9(22); Mutchell, R. 35(1); Nugent, R. 10(2); Paris, A. 5(2); Phillips, M. 0(1); Simpson, P. 10(1); Sodje, E. 37(1); Smith, M. 39; Trebble, N. 6(2); Vier, M. 0(2); Venables, D. 29(5); Webster, K. 38; Wilmot, R. 19(17).
Goals (101): Barrowcliff 6, Beevor 2, Berry 2, Browne 15, Crawshaw 4, Hayles 29, Lynch 9, Marshall 4, Mutchell 1, Nugent 2, Smith 6, Sodje 4, Trebble 2, Venables 10, Webster 4, og 1.

Telford United

Vauxhall Appearances: Adams, C. 27; Bignot, M. 28(2); Clarke, W. 15(4); Crookes, D. 8(1); Davidson, J. 5(1); Dudley, D. J; Eccleston, S. 17(1); Ellitts, J. 6(6); Farrington, M. 2; Fereday, W. 5; Foster, S. 36(1); Fowler, L. 21(13); Gardiner, N. 4(4); Germaine, G. 10; Goodwin, N. 14(1); Gray, B. 41; Hughes, K. 15; Kearney, M. 29(2); Langford, T. 22(6); Moore, M. 0(2); Mutchell, R. 4; Myers, M. 33(2); Niblett, N. 24(1); Purdie, J. 5(4); Ramsey, P. 3; Robinson, L. 17(3); Simkin, D. 8; Straney, P. 2(1); Turner, M. 25; Warner, M. 10; Wassell, K. 1; Wilcox, R. 23(1).
Goals (51): Adams 4, Bignot 3, Clarke 5, Eccleston 1, Fereday 1, Gray 10, Langford 6, Myers 8, Niblett 3, Purdie 2, Robinson 1, Simkin 1, Turner 3, Wilcox 1, og 2.

Welling United

Vauxhall Appearances: Appiah, S. 3; Ash, J. 20(6); Barnes, S. 10; Berry, G. 41; Brown, D. 23(1); Brown, W. 19; Copley, P. 41; Dimmock, R. 3(3); Farley, J. 32(6); Gamble, B. 3; Gorman, P. 2(5); Gritt, S. 2; Hales, K. 1; Hanson, D. 12; Harris, A. 35; Henry, L. 14(2); Horton, D. 42; May, A. 1; Morah, O. 34; Rutherford, M. 35; Smith, D. 6(12); Sykes, P. 4(10); Tierling, L. 23; Wastell, J. 7(1); Watts, L. 27(4); Wordsworth, D. 22.
Goals (42): Barnes 3, Berry 1, Brown W. 2, Copley 2, Dimmock 1, Farley 3, Gamble 2, Gorman 1, Hanson 3, Henry 4, Morah 11, Rutherford 2, Wordsworth 4, og 4.

Woking

Vauxhall Appearances: Adams, D. 4(2); Alexander, T. 2(3); Baron, T. 7(2); Batty, L. 40; Brown, K. 41; Codner, R. 2(1); Crumplin, J. 36; Dowe, J. 1(2); Ellis, A. 42; Fielder, C. 42; Girdler, S. 3(8); Gordon, N. 1; Gregory, J. 2; Hay, D. 30(9); Henry, L. 2(1); Hoddle, C. 4; Hunter, J. 10(1); Kilner, A. 0(2); Omigie, J. 3(3); Peters, R. 1(4); Reid, N. 13(1); Steele, S. 36(1); Thompson, S. 24(2); Tierling, L. 3(3); Timothy, D. 13(6); Tucker, M. 33; Walker, C. 35(1); Wankes, P. 5; Wye, L. 27.
Goals (83): Adams 3, Baron 1, Brown 2, Crumplin 2, Ellis 7, Fielder 3, Girdler 1, Hay 14, Hunter 12, Peters 1, Reid 1, Steele 12, Thompson 1, Walker 18, Wanless 1, Wye 1, og 3.

VAUXHALL CONFERENCE: MEMBERS CLUBS SEASON 1996–97

Club: ALTRINCHAM
Colours: Red and white striped shirts, black
    shorts
Ground: Moss Lane, Altrincham, Cheshire
    WA15 8AP
Tel: 0161-928 1045
Year Formed: 1903
Record Gate: 10,275 (1925 v Sunderland Boys)
Nickname: The Robins
Manager: John King
Secretary: Graham Heathcote

Club: BATH CITY
Colours: Black and white striped shirts, white
    shorts
Ground: Twerton Park, Bath BA2 1DB
Tel: 01225 423087 and 313247
Year Formed: 1889
Record Gate: 18,020 (1960 v Brighton)
Nickname: City
Manager: Tony Ricketts
Secretary: Bob Twyford

Club: BROMSGROVE ROVERS
Colours: Green and white striped shirts, black
    shorts
Ground: Victoria Ground, Birmingham Road,
    Bromsgrove, Worcs. B61 0DR
Tel: 01527 876949
Year Formed: 1885
Record Gate: 7563 (1957–58 v Worcester City)
Nickname: Rovers
Manager: Brian Kenning
Secretary: Brian Hewings

Club: DOVER ATHLETIC
Colours: White shirts, black shorts
Ground: Crabble Athletic Ground, Lewisham
    Road, River, Dover, Kent CT17 0PB
Tel: 01304 822373
Year Formed: 1983
Record Gate: 4035 (1992 v Bromsgrove Rovers)
Nickname: The Lillywhites
Manager: Peter Taylor
Secretary: John Durrant

Club: FARNBOROUGH TOWN
Colours: Yellow and royal blue shirts, blue shorts
Ground: Cherrywood Road, Farnborough,
    Hampshire GU14 8UD
Tel: 01252 541469
Year Formed: 1967
Record Gate: 3069 (1991 v Colchester U)
Nickname: Boro
Manager: Alan Taylor
Secretary: Terry Parr

Club: GATESHEAD
Colours: Black and white halved shirts, black
    shorts
Ground: International Stadium, Neilson Road,
    Gateshead NE10 0EF
Tel: 0191-478 3883
Year Formed: 1977 (Reformed)
Record Gate: 20,752 (1937 v Lincoln C)
Nickname: Tynesiders
Manager: Colin Richardson
Secretary: Mark Donnelly

Club: HALIFAX TOWN
Colours: Blue and white shirts, white shorts
Ground: Shay Ground, Halifax HX1 2YS
Tel: 01422 345543 (330383 Match Days Only)
Year Formed: 1911
Record Gate: 36,885 (1953 v Tottenham
    Hotspur)
Nickname: The Shaymen
Manager: John Carroll
Secretary: Derek Newiss

Club: HAYES
Colours: Red and white shirts, black shorts
Ground: Townfield House, Church Road, Hayes,
    Middlesex UB3
Tel: 0181 573 2075
Year formed: 1909
Record Gate: 15,370 (1951 v Bromley)
Nickname: Missioners
Manager: Terry Brown
Secretary: John Price

Club: HEDNESFORD TOWN
Colours: White and black shirts with red trim,
    black shorts with red and white trim
Ground: Keys Park, Hill Street, Hednesford,
    Staffordshire
Tel: 01543 422870
Year Formed: 1880
Record Gate: 10,000 (1927 v Walsall)
Nickname: The Pitmen
Manager: John Baldwin
Secretary: Richard Murning

Club: KETTERING TOWN
Colours: Red shirts, red shorts
Ground: Rockingham Road, Kettering,
    Northants NN16 9AW
Tel: 01536 83028/410815
Year Formed: 1875
Record Gate: 11,536 (1947 v Peterborough)
Nickname: The Poppies
Manager: Gary Johnson
Secretary: Gerry Knowles

Club: KIDDERMINSTER HARRIERS
Colours: Red and white halved shirts, red shorts
Ground: Aggborough, Hoo Road, Kidderminster
    DY10 1NB
Tel: 01562 823931
Year Formed: 1886
Record Gate: 9155 (1948 v Hereford)
Nickname: The Harriers
Manager: Graham Allner
Secretary: Roger Barlow

Club: MACCLESFIELD TOWN
Colours: Royal blue shirts, white shorts
Ground: Moss Rose Ground, London Road,
    Macclesfield, Cheshire SK10 3JH
Tel: 01625 264686
Year Formed: 1875
Record Gate: 8900 (1968 v Stockport Co)
Nickname: The Silkmen
Manager: Sammy McIlroy
Secretary: Colin Garlick

Club: MORECAMBE
Colours: Red and white striped shirts, black
  shorts
Ground: Christie Park, Lancaster Road,
  Morecambe, Lancashire LA4 5TJ
Tel: 01524 411797
Year Formed: 1920
Record Gate: 9326 (1962 FA Cup Third Round
  Proper v Weymouth)
Nickname: The Shrimps
Manager: Jim Harvey
Secretary: Neil Marsdin

Club: NORTHWICH VICTORIA
Colours: Green and white shirts, white shorts
  with green trim
Ground: The Drill Field, Northwich, Cheshire
  CW9 5HN
Tel: 01606 41450
Year Formed: 1874
Record Gate: 11,290 (1949 v Witton A) 12,000
  (1977 v Watford FAC4)
Nickname: The Vics
Manager: Mark Hancock
Secretary: Derek Nuttall

Club: RUSHDEN & DIAMONDS
Colours: White shirts (red and blue trim), blue
  shorts
Ground: Nene Park, Station Road,
  Irthlingborough, Northants NN9 5QF
Tel: 01933 652000
Year Formed: 1992
Record Gate: 4664 (1996 v Merthyr Tydfil)
Nickname: Diamonds
Manager: Roger Ashby
Secretary: David Joyce

Club: SLOUGH TOWN
Colours: Amber shirts, navy blue shorts
Ground: Wexham Park Stadium, Wexham Road,
  Slough, Berkshire SL2 5QR
Tel: 01753 523358
Year Formed: 1980
Record Gate: 5000 (1982 v Millwall)
Nickname: The Rebels
Manager: Brian McDermott
Secretary: David Stanley

Club: SOUTHPORT
Colours: Old gold shirts, black shorts
Ground: Haig Avenue, Southport PR8 6JZ
Tel: 01704 533422
Year Formed: 1881
Record Gate: 20,010 (1932 v Newcastle United)
Nickname: The Sandgrounders
Manager: Steve Joel
Secretary: Roy Morris

Club: STALYBRIDGE CELTIC
Colours: Blue shirts, blue shorts
Ground: Bower Fold, Mottram Road,
  Stalybridge, Cheshire SK15 2RT
Tel: 0161-338 2828
Year Formed: 1911
Record Gate: 9753 (1922–23 v West Bromwich
  Albion)
Nickname: Celtic
Manager: Peter Wragg
Secretary: Martyn Torr

Club: STEVENAGE BOROUGH
Colours: White and red shirts, white with red
  trim shorts
Ground: Broadhall Way, Stevenage, Herts
  SG2 8RH
Tel: 01438 743322
Year Formed: 1976
Record Gate: 3976 (1996 v Woking)
Nickname: The Boro
Manager: Paul Fairclough
Secretary: Janice Hutchings

Club: TELFORD UNITED
Colours: White shirts, blue shorts
Ground: Bucks Head, Watling Street, Telford
  TF1 2NJ
Tel: 01952 223838
Year Formed: 1877
Record Gate: 13,000 (1935 v Shrewsbury)
Nickname: The Lillywhites
Manager: Wayne Clark
Secretary: Mike Ferriday

Club: WELLING UNITED
Colours: Red shirts, red shorts
Ground: Park View Road Ground, Welling, Kent
  DA16 1SY
Tel: 0181-301 1196
Year Formed: 1963
Record Gate: 4020 (1989 v Gillingham)
Nickname: The Wings
Manager: Kevin Hales
Secretary: Barrie Hobbins

Club: WOKING
Colours: Red and white halved shirts, black
  shorts
Ground: Kingfield Sports Ground, Kingfield,
  Woking, Surrey GU22 9AA
Tel: 01483 772470
Year Formed: 1889
Record Gate: 6000 (1978–79 v Swansea)
Nickname: The Cardinals
Manager: Geoff Chapple
Secretary: Phil Ledger, JP

VAUXHALL CONFERENCE RESULTS 1995–96

	Altrincham	Bath City	Bromsgrove Rovers	Dagenham & Redbridge	Dover Athletic	Farnborough Town	Gateshead	Halifax Town	Hednesford Town	Kettering Town	Kidderminster Harriers	Macclesfield Town	Morecambe	Northwich Victoria	Runcorn	Slough Town	Southport	Stalybridge Celtic	Stevenage Borough	Telford United	Welling United	Woking
Altrincham	—	1-2	3-0	3-1	2-2	2-2	1-1	3-2	2-1	1-3	1-1	0-4	3-0	3-4	2-2	0-1	1-0	1-0	0-2	1-0	1-0	2-0
Bath City	2-2	—	0-1	0-2	2-1	2-1	0-1	2-1	3-1	3-1	1-1	1-1	3-2	0-3	3-0	3-1	4-0	0-4	1-2	0-3	1-1	0-3
Bromsgrove Rovers	0-0	4-1	—	2-0	3-0	1-2	3-1	0-1	2-1	3-2	2-1	1-0	1-0	1-1	2-0	0-0	4-1	1-1	1-1	0-2	1-1	2-1
Dagenham & Redbridge	1-0	0-1	2-2	—	3-0	2-2	0-4	1-1	3-0	1-2	4-2	3-0	2-2	0-3	2-3	1-3	1-2	4-1	1-2	1-1	1-1	0-0
Dover Athletic	1-4	1-0	0-2	0-1	—	1-3	1-1	3-2	1-0	2-1	2-1	2-3	2-3	0-1	4-2	0-1	0-1	1-3	1-2	1-0	2-1	4-3
Farnborough Town	1-1	0-0	1-0	2-0	3-2	—	1-1	0-0	3-0	1-1	3-1	6-1	3-1	0-1	0-1	0-1	1-0	1-1	2-2	2-1	0-1	0-2
Gateshead	2-3	3-1	1-0	2-0	1-1	1-1	—	3-2	1-3	1-1	4-1	0-1	3-0	1-1	1-0	0-1	2-2	1-0	2-2	1-2	1-1	0-1
Halifax Town	1-1	3-1	1-1	3-0	1-0	0-0	2-0	—	0-3	2-0	0-2	1-0	3-0	2-0	1-0	2-1	2-2	2-3	2-2	0-0	2-1	2-2
Hednesford Town	2-1	2-1	4-2	0-0	2-2	4-1	0-1	3-0	—	1-0	1-3	0-1	1-1	2-1	1-3	1-2	2-1	0-1	2-1	4-0	1-1	2-1
Kettering Town	4-2	3-0	2-2	2-0	2-2	0-2	1-0	1-2	2-0	—	2-0	2-2	2-3	2-2	4-0	2-0	1-1	1-6	1-2	0-3	1-3	3-0
Kidderminster Harriers	1-1	1-2	1-0	5-1	1-1	3-3	1-1	6-1	3-1	1-0	—	0-4	4-2	2-1	4-1	4-3	2-3	3-0	0-1	2-0	3-0	2-0
Macclesfield Town	2-3	0-1	2-1	3-1	0-1	1-0	1-0	7-0	0-1	1-1	0-2	—	2-0	0-0	1-0	1-1	3-1	1-0	0-0	1-0	2-1	3-2
Morecambe	7-0	1-0	4-1	2-2	3-1	2-3	2-3	0-1	1-1	5-3	3-1	2-4	—	2-2	1-0	1-2	4-3	2-0	1-0	2-0	1-0	4-5
Northwich Victoria	2-1	2-2	2-2	1-0	1-2	2-3	2-3	1-1	0-2	6-2	5-2	1-2	2-1	—	4-3	0-3	1-2	1-0	1-3	2-0	1-2	3-0
Runcorn	0-1	1-0	0-0	2-0	1-0	3-0	1-1	0-1	2-2	4-2	0-1	0-0	1-3	3-4	—	4-3	1-1	0-1	0-8	2-3	1-3	2-3
Slough Town	1-2	1-1	2-3	5-0	3-2	1-1	1-2	2-3	0-2	1-2	5-4	2-2	1-1	1-1	0-1	—	1-1	2-1	2-6	1-2	0-0	2-3
Southport	1-2	2-1	1-2	2-1	0-0	7-1	1-0	0-0	2-2	6-1	0-2	1-1	1-1	2-2	1-1	2-0	—	5-3	0-1	3-2	2-0	2-2
Stalybridge Celtic	1-0	1-0	2-1	2-0	3-2	2-2	1-0	1-0	0-1	3-2	2-2	0-2	1-5	1-0	2-0	0-1	1-4	—	2-5	3-2	2-1	2-4
Stevenage Borough	1-1	2-0	3-3	1-0	3-2	0-0	1-1	2-0	1-0	5-1	4-1	4-0	1-1	5-1	4-1	3-1	1-3	2-2	—	0-1	4-1	4-0
Telford United	2-0	3-1	0-0	0-0	1-0	3-2	0-0	1-1	2-1	3-4	1-1	1-2	2-2	1-0	1-2	2-0	2-1	0-1	1-3	—	0-0	1-2
Welling United	1-1	2-1	5-2	0-0	1-0	0-1	1-2	0-0	0-3	1-0	0-0	1-0	1-0	1-1	1-1	0-3	0-1	1-1	0-3	3-1	—	3-2
Woking	2-0	2-0	1-1	2-2	1-0	2-0	2-0	2-0	1-1	3-0	0-0	3-0	3-0	0-0	2-1	3-0	4-0	2-1	4-1	5-1	3-2	—

SPALDING CHALLENGE CUP 1995–96

First Round *(two legs)*
Dagenham & Redbridge 0
Slough Town 3 *(Pickett, Bushay, Blackman)* 403

Slough Town 3 *(Bushay, West 2)*
Dagenham & Redbridge 0 456

Kidderminster Harriers 4 *(Brindley, Casey 2, May)*
Hednesford Town 1 *(Essex)* 1326

Hednesford Town 2 *(O'Connor 2)*
Kidderminster Harriers 0 1626

Bath City 0
Farnborough Town 3 *(Boothe 2, Day)* 257

Farnborough Town 3 *(Boothe 2, Denny)*
Bath City 2 *(Mings, Chiverton)* 385

Morecambe 4 *(Coleman, Ceraolo, Knowles, Norman)*
Stalybridge Celtic 1 *(Higginbotham)* 646

Stalybridge Celtic 5 *(Burke 2, Ryan 2, Goodacre)*
Morecambe 2 *(McCluskie, Ceraolo)* 454

Telford United 1 *(Wilcox)*
Northwich Victoria 2 *(Cooke, Walters)* 512

Northwich Victoria 0
Telford United 3 *(Clarke, Myers, Crooks)* 514

Welling United 1 *(O'Keefe)*
Dover Athletic 2 *(Leworthy 2)* 409

Dover Athletic 3 *(Restarick 2, Leworthy)*
Welling United 0 664

Byes to Second Round
Altrincham, Bromsgrove Rovers, Gateshead, Halifax Town, Kettering Town, Macclesfield Town, Runcorn, Southport, Stevenage Borough, Woking.

Second Round
Farnborough Town 1 *(Boothe)*
Dover Athletic 3 *(Restarick, Sowerby, Hayes)* 320

Kettering Town 2 *(Stringfellow, Harmon)*
Stevenage Borough 1 *(Bates)* 808

Macclesfield Town 4 *(Coates 2, Lyons, Cavell)*
Kidderminster Harriers 1 *(Hughes)* 566

Runcorn 1 *(Smith)*
Southport 5 *(Griffiths, Haw 2, Davenport 2)* 401

Bromsgrove Rovers 3 *(Amos, Grocutt, Crisp)*
Telford United 1 *(Clarke)* 548

Morecambe 6 *(Cain, McCluskie 3, Coleman, Knowles)*
Altrincham 4 *(Sharratt, Green, Hardy 2)* 546

Slough Town 3 *(West 2, Hercules)*
Woking 0 774

Gateshead 4 *(Wrightson, Proudlock, Harkus, Lowe)*
Halifax Town 0 229

Quarter-finals
Kettering Town 2 *(Pope, Harmon)*
Slough Town 0 646

Dover Athletic 0
Bromsgrove Rovers 1 *(Skelding)* 464

Morecambe 1 *(McCluskie)*
Macclesfield 4 *(Payne, Hulme 2, Hemmings)* 625

Southport 2 *(Haw, Whittaker)*
Gateshead 1 *(Thompson)* 315

Semi-finals *(two legs)*
Bromsgrove Rovers 2 *(Power, Dale)*
Kettering Town 0 650

Kettering Town 2 *(Gynn, Mustafa)*
Bromsgrove Rovers 1 *(Burgher)* 773

Southport 4 *(Davenport 2, Cunningham, Whittaker)*
Macclesfield Town 4 *(Sorvel, og, Hemmings, Power)* 561

Macclesfield Town 2 *(Coates, Power)*
Southport 1 *(Whittaker)* 510

Final *(two legs)*
Macclesfield Town 1 *(Coates)*
Bromsgrove Rovers 1 *(Howarth og)* 547

Bromsgrove Rovers 3 *(Grocutt, Hunt, Carter)*
Macclesfield Town 1 *(Sorvel)* 1341

UNIBOND LEAGUE

Premier Division

		Home					Away					Total	
	P	W	D	L	F	A	W	D	L	F	A		Pts
Bamber Bridge	42	9	8	4	43	26	11	8	2	38	23		76
Boston United	42	10	4	7	40	31	13	2	6	46	28		75
Hyde United	42	12	5	4	57	24	9	6	6	29	27		74
Barrow	42	10	7	4	36	20	10	6	5	33	22		73
Gainsborough Trinity	42	10	6	5	30	21	10	7	4	30	20		73
Blyth Spartans	42	11	8	2	46	24	6	5	10	29	37		64
Accrington Stanley	42	8	6	7	29	25	9	8	4	33	29		62
Emley	42	11	3	7	34	26	6	7	8	23	27		61
Spennymoor United	42	7	10	4	36	30	7	8	6	31	31		60
Guiseley	42	9	5	7	36	29	6	9	6	26	28		59
Bishop Auckland	42	7	7	7	31	28	9	4	8	29	27		59
Marine	42	10	6	5	34	22	5	8	8	25	32		59
Witton Albion	42	12	4	5	37	26	5	4	12	23	36		59
Chorley	42	9	7	5	31	27	5	2	14	36	47		51
Knowsley United	42	10	3	8	34	30	4	3	14	27	59		48
Winsford United	42	7	5	9	30	42	3	11	7	26	37		46
Leek Town	42	7	8	6	33	24	3	7	11	19	31		45
Colwyn Bay	42	2	13	6	18	24	6	8	7	25	33		45
Frickley Athletic	42	6	7	8	35	40	5	7	9	28	47		44
Buxton	42	5	3	13	22	36	4	8	9	21	36		38
Droylsden	42	6	4	11	31	43	4	4	13	27	57		38
Matlock Town	42	6	7	8	42	35	2	4	15	29	51		35

First Division

		Home					Away					Total	
	P	W	D	L	F	A	W	D	L	F	A		Pts
Lancaster City	40	15	3	2	44	19	9	8	3	35	19		83
Alfreton Town	40	14	2	4	47	28	9	7	4	32	19		78
Lincoln United	40	14	3	3	48	22	8	4	8	32	34		73
Curzon Ashton	40	9	4	7	31	25	11	3	6	42	28		67
Farsley Celtic	40	11	5	4	35	27	8	4	8	31	34		66
Radcliffe Borough	40	13	4	3	42	20	4	9	7	28	28		64
Eastwood Town	40	13	1	6	34	21	5	8	7	26	26		63
Whitley Bay	40	9	7	4	40	27	9	1	10	32	35		62
Ashton United	40	11	3	6	38	28	8	4	8	35	37		60
Atherton LR	40	9	7	4	31	24	6	5	9	29	37		57
Worksop Town	40	10	3	7	47	36	6	5	9	37	54		56
Gretna	40	8	5	7	43	31	5	8	7	32	34		52
Warrington Town	40	6	8	6	42	38	7	2	11	33	34		49
Leigh	40	9	6	5	28	23	5	1	14	25	36		49
Netherfield	40	4	8	8	23	32	9	2	9	41	41		49
Workington	40	8	6	6	30	23	3	6	11	20	39		45
Bradford PA	40	3	10	7	31	36	6	4	10	26	36		41
Congleton Town	40	6	6	8	19	24	5	5	10	17	35		41
Great Harwood Town	40	5	2	13	21	40	4	5	11	23	38		33
Fleetwood	40	4	5	11	20	35	3	5	12	21	46		31
Harrogate Town	40	3	4	13	31	61	4	6	10	23	35		31

Leading goalscorers

Premier Division

Lge	Cup	Tot	
23	9	32	Brian Ross (Chorley)
23	2	25	Nigel Evans (Droylsden)
21	14	35	Tony Carroll (Hyde United)
20	7	27	Jimmy Blackhurst (Marine)
19	3	22	Jock Russell (Winsford United)
17	6	23	Phil Brown (Boston United)
17	4	21	Mark Culley (Matlock Town)
17	3	20	Dave Leaver (Bamber Bridge)
16	15	31	Ged Kimmins (Hyde United)
16	11	27	Graham Roberts (Colwyn Bay)
16	4	20	Paddy Wilson (Knowsley United)
15	13	28	Liam Watson (Witton Albion)
15	6	21	Colin Little (Hyde United now Crewe Alex)
15	3	18	Chris Cook (Boston United)

First Division

Lge	Cup	Tot	
31	7	38	Billy O'Callaghan (Warrington Town)
26	6	32	Malcolm O'Connor (Curzon Ashton)
25	12	37	Kenny Clark (Worksop Town)
23	8	31	Tony Simmons (Lincoln United)
22	9	31	Phil Stafford (Alfreton Town)
21	8	29	Ian Lunt (Radcliffe Borough)
20	10	30	Mark Rookyard (Worksop T–7 + 6 for Lincoln)
20	7	27	Paul Heavey (Curzon A–6 + 2 for Warrington)
20	1	21	Andy Walker (Gretna)
19	10	29	Robbie Whellans (Farsley Celtic)
18	14	32	Stuart Diggle (Lancaster City)
16	6	22	Joey Dunn (Atherton LR)
16	4	20	Chris Shaw (Leigh)
16	2	18	Derek Townsley (Gretna)
16	-	16	Peter Borrowdale (Lancaster City)

UNIBOND LEAGUE—PREMIER DIVISION RESULTS 1995-96

	Accrington Stanley	Bamber Bridge	Barrow	Bishop Auckland	Blyth Spartans	Boston United	Buxton	Chorley	Colwyn Bay	Droylsden	Emley	Frickley Athletic	Gainsborough Trinity	Guiseley	Hyde United	Knowsley United	Leek Town	Marine	Matlock Town	Spennymoor United	Winsford United	Witton Albion
Accrington Stanley	—	1-2	1-1	2-1	1-2	0-2	1-0	7-3	3-1	0-2	0-0	2-1	2-1	0-1	1-1	4-2	0-0	0-0	2-1	0-0	1-2	1-2
Bamber Bridge	1-1	—	2-2	3-0	3-0	1-2	2-0	2-0	5-0	3-2	0-1	2-3	1-1	3-1	3-3	2-2	0-0	4-4	4-1	2-0	2-0	1-1
Barrow	0-3	2-2	—	0-0	2-1	2-0	1-0	6-2	1-1	3-3	0-0	1-1	0-1	0-2	2-1	7-0	1-0	2-0	3-1	1-1	1-1	3-0
Bishop Auckland	2-2	1-1	1-2	—	3-0	1-3	1-1	3-1	1-0	3-2	1-0	3-1	1-1	2-2	1-1	1-2	1-1	0-1	2-3	1-2	1-0	2-0
Blyth Spartans	2-2	1-1	1-2	3-0	—	0-3	1-1	3-2	2-0	2-1	0-0	1-1	0-0	3-3	5-1	4-1	2-1	2-2	3-0	3-1	3-2	2-0
Boston United	4-0	0-3	2-1	1-0	1-0	—	9-3	2-1	0-0	0-1	1-1	1-3	1-2	4-3	0-3	4-2	2-2	0-1	1-0	4-1	2-2	1-2
Buxton	0-1	1-2	0-0	1-2	2-1	0-3	—	5-2	0-1	6-0	1-2	1-0	1-2	0-0	0-1	3-2	1-2	1-3	3-1	1-1	1-3	0-4
Chorley	0-0	0-0	2-3	2-0	1-4	0-2	2-1	—	1-1	0-0	1-0	1-1	0-6	1-0	1-1	1-0	3-1	1-1	3-2	0-3	1-1	4-0
Colwyn Bay	1-2	1-1	0-1	1-3	0-0	3-1	1-1	1-1	—	1-1	1-0	1-3	0-0	1-2	1-3	0-0	0-0	0-0	3-3	2-3	1-1	1-1
Droylsden	1-2	1-2	0-4	1-4	2-2	2-5	1-3	0-6	1-1	—	3-0	2-2	1-2	1-2	0-2	5-1	0-0	2-0	3-0	1-1	1-1	2-1
Emley	1-3	1-1	1-2	1-1	1-3	2-0	2-1	0-3	4-1	4-0	—	5-2	1-0	1-0	1-0	1-3	0-1	1-1	3-2	0-2	1-0	1-0
Frickley Athletic	4-1	0-5	0-0	0-3	1-2	1-2	0-2	1-0	1-1	4-5	2-1	—	3-0	2-2	3-0	4-3	1-1	1-0	1-4	2-3	3-3	1-1
Gainsborough Trinity	1-1	2-1	2-0	1-0	4-0	2-1	1-0	1-0	2-2	7-1	0-3	0-2	—	0-2	1-1	2-1	1-0	2-4	2-2	0-1	0-0	1-0
Guiseley	1-3	4-0	1-3	2-0	1-1	4-2	0-3	0-3	1-0	3-0	7-2	3-0	1-3	—	0-2	1-1	3-1	4-0	4-2	2-2	1-1	0-1
Hyde United	0-0	2-3	1-3	3-1	4-1	2-4	3-1	3-1	0-3	1-1	1-3	4-1	1-2	1-1	—	5-0	3-2	2-1	1-1	3-2	0-1	1-0
Knowsley United	1-0	2-2	0-2	1-2	1-0	2-4	2-0	1-2	5-1	2-0	2-2	1-2	2-3	1-1	2-1	—	3-1	0-1	1-0	2-0	4-1	2-2
Leek Town	2-2	2-3	2-0	0-1	1-3	2-2	0-0	2-0	1-3	4-0	0-1	1-1	0-0	1-1	0-1	2-0	—	0-0	4-2	0-2	5-1	2-1
Marine	1-2	0-0	0-4	2-2	0-0	0-4	1-1	2-1	1-1	6-1	1-1	0-1	3-0	0-1	4-0	2-1	2-1	—	1-0	2-1	3-1	2-1
Matlock Town	2-0	0-1	1-1	1-0	3-3	0-2	0-1	3-2	1-4	2-2	2-0	6-0	0-2	3-0	1-3	8-0	1-0	3-3	—	1-1	1-1	5-2
Spennymoor United	3-4	4-2	1-1	1-1	2-1	2-3	0-0	2-2	0-0	2-0	0-4	2-2	1-1	0-0	0-1	1-4	4-2	2-2	1-1	—	3-3	3-1
Winsford United	2-2	1-4	4-3	0-4	2-4	1-0	1-1	0-2	1-3	3-2	0-4	4-1	1-1	1-2	1-4	0-1	0-0	1-0	3-1	2-2	—	2-1
Witton Albion	0-2	0-0	1-0	1-2	2-1	1-1	1-3	2-1	2-3	2-1	3-1	5-0	0-2	3-2	1-1	2-1	2-1	2-0	3-2	2-2	2-1	—

UNIBOND LEAGUE—FIRST DIVISION RESULTS 1995-96

	Alfreton Town	Ashton United	Atherton LR	Bradford Park Avenue	Congleton Town	Curzon Ashton	Eastwood Town	Farsley Celtic	Fleetwood	Great Harwood Town	Gretna	Harrogate Town	Lancaster City	Leigh	Lincoln United	Netherfield	Radcliffe Borough	Warrington Town	Whitley Bay	Workington	Worksop Town
Alfreton Town	—	3-0	1-2	3-2	2-1	3-2	2-2	2-3	1-0	4-1	4-0	2-0	1-6	1-0	2-1	4-1	1-0	5-1	2-3	2-1	2-2
Ashton United	2-1	—	2-1	0-1	2-0	1-4	2-1	2-1	3-0	1-2	1-1	1-4	1-1	3-2	1-1	5-0	1-1	3-1	2-3	3-1	1-2
Atherton LR	0-0	1-2	—	3-1	2-1	2-2	2-1	1-1	1-0	2-2	1-1	0-2	2-1	3-1	0-1	2-4	1-1	2-1	2-1	0-0	1-4
Bradford Park Avenue	1-1	0-1	2-2	—	0-0	2-3	2-2	1-1	2-2	1-3	2-2	1-1	0-3	1-0	2-3	0-2	2-2	1-0	2-3	3-0	4-4
Congleton Town	0-1	3-0	4-1	1-2	—	1-1	1-1	0-1	1-0	0-0	0-1	2-1	1-1	2-1	0-2	1-1	1-4	0-4	2-1	0-0	0-2
Curzon Ashton	0-1	4-2	2-3	0-1	0-0	—	0-0	1-0	1-1	4-1	2-2	2-1	0-3	1-0	1-2	2-1	1-2	2-1	1-3	3-0	3-0
Eastwood Town	2-0	2-1	1-0	0-1	3-0	2-3	—	1-2	3-0	1-0	3-1	1-1	1-2	2-1	4-2	1-0	2-1	2-1	0-2	2-1	2-3
Farsley Celtic	1-0	2-1	1-1	3-3	0-2	1-1	2-1	—	0-2	1-0	0-2	2-2	2-1	2-1	2-1	3-1	4-1	1-0	1-0	3-0	2-2
Fleetwood	0-2	3-0	1-0	3-2	0-2	0-1	1-0	1-3	—	1-2	2-1	1-2	2-1	0-4	1-1	1-2	1-0	0-1	0-0	1-1	1-4
Great Harwood Town	1-3	1-2	2-2	1-3	1-2	1-2	0-2	3-0	2-1	—	1-1	2-3	1-1	0-2	0-1	0-2	0-4	0-5	2-0	1-0	1-2
Gretna	0-0	1-1	1-1	1-1	2-1	3-4	1-3	7-1	7-1	0-2	—	4-1	2-3	3-1	3-3	1-4	1-0	1-3	1-3	1-1	6-0
Harrogate Town	0-3	1-4	0-2	1-2	1-1	0-2	2-2	1-6	2-2	3-2	0-5	—	2-2	1-2	2-5	4-6	2-2	1-3	2-3	0-3	3-2
Lancaster City	1-1	1-1	2-1	1-0	3-0	2-4	1-0	1-2	0-1	4-1	1-0	2-1	—	5-2	2-0	2-2	3-1	4-2	3-1	2-1	3-1
Leigh	1-1	3-2	3-1	3-0	1-1	2-1	2-0	0-0	2-0	3-1	1-3	2-0	0-1	—	2-0	1-4	1-1	2-2	0-1	4-2	1-1
Lincoln United	0-2	1-1	0-1	1-1	1-1	1-0	2-0	0-0	2-2	3-1	2-0	5-0	1-3	3-1	—	4-0	2-1	1-0	4-3	4-0	4-1
Netherfield	4-4	5-0	2-4	5-2	3-0	1-4	1-4	1-3	0-3	3-1	2-2	0-0	2-2	1-0	0-0	—	0-2	0-1	1-2	1-1	0-2
Radcliffe Borough	1-3	1-1	1-1	0-0	1-2	1-0	1-1	2-0	3-2	2-0	1-1	1-0	0-0	3-1	3-1	1-2	—	3-1	1-0	4-1	5-1
Warrington Town	2-2	3-1	2-1	3-0	4-1	2-1	2-0	5-1	3-3	1-1	3-4	2-2	1-1	0-1	4-2	3-6	1-1	—	2-1	2-3	3-2
Whitley Bay	0-5	2-3	2-1	1-1	1-2	0-2	2-1	5-2	6-0	0-0	1-1	1-1	0-1	3-1	2-0	2-1	1-1	3-1	—	1-2	3-3
Workington	1-2	3-1	0-0	3-2	2-0	0-1	1-2	2-1	3-0	0-2	2-2	2-0	0-2	0-3	1-2	1-0	1-1	2-1	1-0	—	6-2
Worksop Town	2-0	1-2	1-4	4-1	6-0	0-3	1-2	1-0	4-1	3-2	4-2	2-1	0-2	1-1	2-4	3-2	2-2	2-3	6-2	2-2	—

UNIBOND CHALLENGE CUP

First Round
Alfreton Town 4, Lincoln United 0
Blyth Spartans 2, Gretna 1
Bradford Park Avenue 2, Farsley Celtic 0
Congleton Town 1, Worksop Town 3
Curzon Ashton 1, Eastwood Town 2
Lancaster City 4, Fleetwood 2
Leigh 6, Great Harwood Town 4
Radcliffe Borough 0, Droylsden 3
Warrington Town 1, Ashton United 2
Whitley Bay 1, Harrogate Town 2
Workington 3, Netherfield 2

Second Round
Atherton LR 3, Winsford United 2
Barrow 3, Accrington Stanley 4
Colwyn Bay 3, Droylsden 1
Eastwood Town 3, Alfreton Town 2
Frickley Athletic 3, Bradford Park Avenue 1 (*after 1-1 draw*)
Guiseley 1, Blyth Spartans 0
Harrogate Town 0, Emley 2
Hyde United 4, Ashton United 1
Lancaster City 2, Knowsley United 0
Leek Town 1, Buxton 0
Leigh 0, Witton Albion 3 (*after 2-2 draw*)
Marine 4, Chorley 2 (*after 0-0 draw*)
Matlock Town 0, Gainsborough Trinity 1
Spennymoor United 3, Bishop Auckland 1 (*after 2-2 draw*)

Workington 0, Bamber Bridge 1
Worksop Town 0, Boston United 5

Third Round
Atherton LR 2, Witton Albion 5
Bamber Bridge 0, Lancaster City 1
Boston United 3, Guiseley 2
Colwyn Bay 2, Accrington Stanley 3
Gainsborough Trinity 4, Frickley Athletic 1
Hyde United 5, Marine 3
Leek Town 4, Eastwood Town 3
Spennymoor United 5, Emley 0

Fourth Round
Accrington Stanley 1, Leek Town 3 (*after 0-0 draw*)
Boston United 3, Spennymoor United 0
Gainsborough Trinity 3, Witton Albion 2
Hyde United 5, Lancaster City 1

Semi-finals (two legs)
Gainsborough Trinity 0, Hyde United 2
Hyde United 1, Gainsborough Trinity 0
(*Hyde United won 3-0 on aggregate*)
Boston United 1, Leek Town 2
Leek Town 2, Boston United 0
(*Leek Town won 4-1 on aggregate*)

Final
Hyde United 1, Leek Town 1 (*at Burnden Park*)
(*aet; Hyde United won 7-6 on penalties*)

UNIBOND LEAGUE PRESIDENT'S CUP

First Round
Ashton United 0, Buxton 1
Bamber Bridge 4, Warrington Town 1
Boston United 4, Alfreton Town 0 (*after 2-2 draw*)
Guiseley 4, Blyth Spartans 0
Hyde United 2, Leek Town 0 (*after 2-2 draw*)
Marine 2, Witton Albion 0
Radcliffe Borough 3, Spennymoor United 2
Worksop Town 3, Gainsborough Trinity 1

Second Round
Buxton 1, Guiseley 3 (*after 1-1 draw*)
Boston United 0, Worksop Town 2
Marine 0, Hyde United 3
Radcliffe Borough 1, Bamber Bridge 2 (*after 0-0 draw*)

Semi-finals (two legs)
Hyde United 0, Guiseley 2
Guiseley 1, Hyde United 1
(*Guiseley won 3-1 on aggregate*)
Worksop Town 1, Bamber Bridge 0
Bamber Bridge 2, Worksop Town 2
(*Worksop Town won 3-2 on aggregate*)

Final (two legs)
Guiseley 0, Worksop Town 1
Worksop Town 3, Guiseley 1
(*Worksop Town won 4-1 on aggregate*)

UNIFILLA FIRST DIVISION CUP

First Round
Atherton LR 3, Congleton Town 1
Farsley Celtic 2, Eastwood Town 1
Leigh 0, Curzon Ashton 1
Lincoln United 2, Bradford Park Avenue 0
Workington 3, Fleetwood 0 (*after 2-2 draw*)

Second Round
Curzon Ashton 0, Ashton United 2 (*after 1-1 draw*)
Farsley Celtic 1, Lancaster City 3 (*after 1-1 draw*)
Gretna 1, Whitley Bay 2
Lincoln United 1, Alfreton Town 4
Radcliffe Borough 0, Great Harwood Town 1
Warrington 0, Atherton LR 1
Workington 4, Netherfield 2
Worksop Town 5, Harrogate Town 1

Third Round
Alfreton Town 3, Ashton United 0
Great Harwood Town 2, Worksop Town 1 (*after 1-1 draw*)
Lancaster City 2, Whitley Bay 1
Workington 2, Atherton LR 3

Semi-finals (two legs)
Alfreton Town 0, Atherton LR 4
Atherton LR 1, Alfreton Town 2
(*Atherton LR won 5-2 on aggregate*)
Lancaster City 4, Great Harwood Town 1
Great Harwood Town 0, Lancaster City 2
(*Lancaster City won 6-1 on aggregate*)

Final
Atherton LR 0, Lancaster City 1
(*Played at Bamber Bridge FC*)

BEAZER HOMES LEAGUE 1995–96

Premier Division

	P	W	D	L	F	A	Pts
Rusden & Diamonds	42	29	7	6	99	41	94
Halesowen Town	42	27	11	4	70	36	92
Cheltenham Town	42	21	11	10	76	57	74
Gloucester City	42	21	8	13	65	47	71
Gresley Rovers	42	20	10	12	70	58	70
Worcester City	42	19	12	11	61	43	69
Merthyr Tydfil	42	19	6	17	67	59	63
Hastings Town	42	16	13	13	68	55	61
Crawley Town	42	15	13	14	57	56	58
Sudbury Town	42	15	10	17	69	71	55
Gravesend & Northfleet	42	15	10	17	60	62	55
Chelmsford City	42	13	16	13	46	53	55
Dorchester Town	42	15	8	19	62	57	53
Newport AFC	42	13	13	16	53	59	52
Salisbury City	42	14	10	18	57	69	52
Burton Albion	42	13	12	17	55	56	51
Atherstone United	42	12	12	18	57	75	48
Baldock Town	42	11	14	17	51	56	47
Cambridge City	42	12	10	20	56	68	46
Ilkeston Town	42	11	10	21	53	87	43
Stafford Rangers	42	11	4	27	58	90	37
VS Rugby	42	5	10	27	37	92	25

Midland Division

	P	W	D	L	F	A	Pts
Nuneaton Borough	42	30	5	7	82	35	95
King's Lynn*	42	27	5	10	85	43	84
Bedworth United*	42	24	10	8	76	42	81
Moor Green	42	22	8	12	81	47	74
Paget Rangers	42	21	9	12	70	45	72
Tamworth	42	22	3	17	97	64	69
Solihull Borough	42	19	9	14	77	64	66
Rothwell Town	42	17	14	11	79	62	65
Buckingham Town	42	18	9	15	74	62	63
Dudley Town	42	15	16	11	83	66	61
Stourbridge	42	17	8	17	60	63	59
Bilston Town	42	16	9	17	61	62	57
Sutton Coldfield	42	16	9	17	62	67	57
Grantham Town	42	17	5	20	71	83	56
Redditch United	42	14	11	17	57	77	53
Leicester United	42	13	13	16	58	72	52
Hinckley Town	42	14	7	21	62	83	49
Racing Club Warwick	42	10	13	19	67	90	43
Evesham United	42	11	6	25	59	94	39
Corby Town	42	9	7	26	52	95	34
Bury Town	42	8	8	26	57	95	32
Bridgnorth Town	42	7	6	29	53	112	27

Southern Division

	P	W	D	L	F	A	Pts
Sittingbourne	42	28	4	10	102	44	88
Ashford Town	42	25	9	8	75	44	84
Waterlooville	42	24	8	10	87	44	80
Havant Town*	42	23	11	8	73	42	80
Newport IOW	42	24	6	12	75	58	78
Weymouth	42	24	4	14	75	55	76
Forest Green Rovers	42	22	8	12	85	55	74
Braintree Town*	42	23	8	11	92	75	74
Trowbridge Town	42	18	8	16	86	51	62
Witney Town	42	17	11	14	65	53	62
Yate Town	42	17	8	17	85	71	59
Margate	42	18	5	19	68	62	59
Cinderford Town	42	17	8	17	76	77	59
Weston-super-Mare	42	16	9	17	78	68	57
Fisher	42	14	13	15	58	59	55
Bashley	42	14	11	17	63	61	53
Clevedon Town	42	15	6	21	70	80	51
Fleet Town	42	14	5	23	58	79	47
Tonbridge Angels	42	12	10	20	58	81	46
Fareham Town	42	12	5	25	71	97	41
Erith & Belvedere	42	4	4	34	38	111	16
Poole Town	42	0	1	41	17	188	1

* points deducted

LEADING GOALSCORERS
(League and Cup)

Premier Division

D. Collins (Rushden & Diamonds)	31
J. Smith (Cheltenham Town)	27
J. Eaton (Cheltenham Town)	24
I. Brown (Sudbury Town)	23
P. Evans (Merthyr Tydfil)	23
E. Wright (Halesowen Town)	23
S. Cuggy (Hastings Town)	21
M. Munday (Gravesend & Northfleet)	20
D. Taylor (Ilkeston Town)	18
D. Webley (Newport A.F.C.)	18
S. Norris (Worcester City)	17
O. Pickard (Dorchester Town)	17

Midland Division

R. Straw (Nuneaton Borough)	34
G. Piggott (Dudley Town)	33
I. Bennett (Tamworth)	31
I. Drewitt (Nuneaton Borough)	27
K. McGuire (Rothwell Town)	26
B. McNamara (King's Lynn)	25
P. Davies (Moor Green)	24
I. Perry (Bilston Town)	22
J. Symonds (Bedworth United)	21
J. Dowling (Solihull Borough)	19
J. Graham (Bedworth United)	19
M. Whitehouse (Tamworth)	19
M. Marshall (Buckingham Town)	18
S. Sinden (Hinckley Town)	18
A. Bullimore (Grantham Town)	17
P. McBean (Hinckley Town)	17
L. Palmer (Stourbridge)	17

Southern Division

M. Buglione (Margate)	34
P. Odey (Fareham Town)	33
D. Mitchell (Trowbridge Town)	31
D. Arter (Ashford Town)	27
W. Falana (Braintree Town)	27
S. Tate (Waterlooville)	25
C. Moore (Forest Green Rovers)	24
E. Fearon (Newport I.O.W.)	23
D. Powell (Weymouth)	22
T. Planck (Sittingbourne)	21
S. Lovell (Sittingbourne)	20
K. Bayliss (Forest Green Rovers)	19
D. Laws (Weymouth)	19
J. Smith (Fleet Town)	19
M. Frampton (Fleet Town)	18
G. Morgan (Clevedon Town)	17

DR MARTENS CUP

PRELIMINARY ROUND FIRST LEG
Cinderford Town 1, Merthyr Tydfil 4
Solihull Borough 2, Redditch United 4

PRELIMINARY ROUND SECOND LEG
Merthyr Tydfil 4, Cinderford Town 3
Redditch United 2, Solihull Borough 1

FIRST ROUND FIRST LEG
Bury Town 0, Baldock Town 2
Sittingbourne 1, Margate 3
Corby Town 2, Rothwell Town 2
Kings Lynn 0, Rushden & Diamonds 1
Gravesend & Northfleet 3, Chelmsford City 1
Crawley Town 1, Hastings Town 1
Tonbridge Angels 5, Ashford Town 3
Fisher 93 4, Erith & Belvedere 0
Forest Green Rovers 2, Clevedon Town 1
Newport AFC 2, Merthyr Tydfil 1
Waterlooville 1, Newport (IW) 1
Fareham Town 2, Fleet Town 2
Trowbridge Town 4, Yate Town 1
Bashley 3, Weymouth 0
Dorchester Town 1, Havant Town 0
Poole Town 0, Salisbury City 5
Nuneaton Borough 4, VS Rugby 2
Atherstone United 4, Tamworth 3
Buckingham Town 1, Braintree Town 0
Cambridge City 1, Sudbury Town 1
Weston Super Mare 1, Cheltenham Town 3
Witney Town 1, Gloucester City 0
Leicester United 0, Paget Rangers 3
Burton Albion 0, Gresley Rovers 2
Halesowen Town 0, Worcester City 2
Stourbridge 4, Dudley Town 2
Grantham Town 0, Ilkeston Town 3
Hinckley Town 1, Bedworth United 0
Redditch United 0, Evesham United 0
Bilston Town 3, Sutton Coldfield Town 0
Stafford Rangers 0, Bridgnorth Town 2
Racing Club Warwick 1, Moor Green 4

FIRST ROUND SECOND LEG
Baldock Town 1, Bury Town 1
Margate 1, Sittingbourne 0
Rothwell Town 1, Corby Town 0
Rushden & Diamonds 0, Kings Lynn 2
Chelmsford City 1, Gravesend & Northfleet 0
Hastings Town 1, Crawley Town 2
Ashford Town 1, Tonbridge Angels 1
Erith & Belvedere 0, Fisher 93 2
Clevedon Town 1, Forest Green Rovers 3
Merthyr Tydfil 1, Newport AFC 1
Newport (IW) 1, Waterlooville 3
Fleet Town 2, Fareham Town 0
Yate Town 2, Trowbridge Town 0
Weymouth 0, Bashley 0
Havant Town 0, Dorchester Town 1
Salisbury City 6, Poole Town 0
VS Rugby 1, Nuneaton Borough 2
Tamworth 2, Atherstone United 3
Braintree Town 0, Buckingham Town 0
Sudbury Town 1, Cambridge City 3
Cheltenham Town 4, Weston Super Mare 2
Gloucester City 3, Witney Town 0
Paget Rangers 5, Leicester United 3
Gresley Rovers 1, Burton Albion 2

Worcester City 4, Halesowen Town 1
Dudley Town 4, Stourbridge 4
Ilkeston Town 2, Grantham Town 2
Bedworth United 0, Hinckley Town 1
Evesham United 3, Redditch United 2
Sutton Coldfield Town 3, Bilston Town 3
Bridgnorth Town 3, Stafford Rangers 2
Moor Green 4, Racing Club Warwick 0

SECOND ROUND
Bashley 1, Trowbridge Town 1
replay: Trowbridge Town 2, Bashley 1
Bridgnorth Town 0, Moor Green 0
replay: Moor Green 2, Bridgnorth Town 1
Buckingham Town 1, Cambridge City 0
Cheltenham Town 4, Gloucester City 0
Evesham United 2, Bilston Town 2
replay: Bilston Town 5, Evesham United 2
Ilkeston Town 2, Hinckley Town 3
Waterlooville 4, Fleet Town 0
Baldock Town 1, Margate 0
Gravesend & Northfleet 1, Crawley Town 2
Tonbridge Angels 3, Fisher 93 0
Atherstone United 1, Nuneaton Borough 3
Rothwell Town 0, Kings Lynn 1
Paget Rangers 2, Gresley Rovers 3
Worcester City 3, Stourbridge 0
Forest Green Rovers 2, Newport AFC 4
Dorchester Town 1, Salisbury City 2

THIRD ROUND
Baldock Town 2, Kings Lynn 0
Crawley Town 3, Tonbridge Angels 0
Newport AFC 1, Waterlooville 0
Moor Green 3, Bilston Town 1
Trowbridge Town 1, Salisbury City 1
replay: Salisbury City 2, Trowbridge Town 1
Nuneaton Borough 3, Buckingham Town 1
Cheltenham Town 3, Gresley Rovers 3
replay: Gresley Rovers 2, Cheltenham Town 2
Worcester City 2, Hinckley Town 3

FOURTH ROUND
Baldock Town 1, Crawley Town 1
replay: Crawley Town 2, Baldock Town 2
Hinckley Town 0, Moor Green 4
Nuneaton Borough 4, Gresley Rovers 1
Salisbury City 2, Newport AFC 1

SEMI-FINAL FIRST LEG
Baldock Town 0, Salisbury City 0
Nuneaton Borough 2, Moor Green 0

SEMI-FINAL SECOND LEG
Salisbury City 1, Baldock Town 1
Moor Green 1, Nuneaton Borough 1

FINAL FIRST LEG
Nuneaton Borough 3, Baldock Town 1

FINAL SECOND LEG
Baldock Town 1, Nuneaton Borough 2

BEAZER HOMES LEAGUE—PREMIER DIVISION RESULTS 1995-96

Home \ Away	Worcester City	VS Rugby	Sudbury Town	Stafford Rangers	Salisbury City	Rushden & Diamonds	Newport AFC	Merthyr Tydfil	Ilkeston Town	Hastings Town	Halesowen Town	Gresley Rovers	Gravesend & Northfleet	Gloucester City	Dorchester Town	Crawley Town	Cheltenham Town	Chelmsford City	Cambridge City	Burton Albion	Baldock Town	Atherstone United
Atherstone United	1-1	4-1	0-0	2-2	3-1	1-3	0-0	0-2	3-3	1-0	0-1	1-2	2-0	2-1	3-4	2-1	1-2	1-2	2-2	0-3	2-2	—
Baldock Town	0-1	2-0	1-3	5-0	4-2	0-3	1-2	1-1	1-1	1-3	0-2	0-1	2-2	0-1	2-1	0-0	1-1	2-1	0-0	1-1	—	1-0
Burton Albion	2-0	0-0	2-3	5-1	0-1	4-2	0-1	1-3	1-2	1-1	0-1	1-1	1-2	1-0	1-0	2-1	3-2	1-1	0-0	—	2-1	3-2
Cambridge City	3-1	4-1	1-0	2-0	0-1	0-2	1-0	1-4	2-3	0-3	1-0	2-2	2-0	0-4	1-2	1-2	1-2	0-0	—	2-4	3-0	2-2
Chelmsford City	1-1	3-0	2-1	1-0	3-3	1-2	0-0	1-4	1-0	0-3	1-0	1-2	0-0	1-1	2-2	0-0	3-3	—	2-1	0-0	0-2	1-0
Cheltenham Town	1-1	4-0	1-1	4-0	3-3	0-2	2-0	1-0	4-0	1-2	2-2	1-1	0-0	0-0	1-1	1-1	—	4-1	2-1	1-1	3-1	1-1
Crawley Town	0-1	3-1	1-1	2-1	0-1	1-1	0-3	0-1	4-1	1-4	1-4	3-1	1-1	2-0	1-1	—	1-1	0-0	2-1	3-1	3-1	2-1
Dorchester Town	0-1	4-0	2-0	4-2	0-2	1-1	0-3	7-1	3-0	1-4	1-3	1-0	3-1	0-1	—	1-0	4-0	0-3	1-1	2-1	3-1	1-0
Gloucester City	0-2	3-1	1-0	3-2	2-0	2-2	0-3	7-1	3-1	0-2	0-2	5-0	3-1	—	1-0	1-1	4-0	0-3	3-1	2-0	3-1	0-2
Gravesend & Northfleet	2-1	1-1	3-3	0-3	1-1	1-3	4-0	1-0	3-1	4-0	0-1	1-1	—	0-0	1-0	3-1	1-0	1-0	2-0	1-2	1-1	2-1
Gresley Rovers	1-0	4-0	5-2	1-1	2-2	0-3	1-3	3-1	2-3	1-1	1-1	—	3-1	1-0	0-2	1-0	0-2	0-2	2-1	2-1	3-0	1-0
Halesowen Town	5-4	0-0	3-3	2-2	2-0	0-0	3-1	2-1	3-2	0-1	—	2-4	2-1	2-1	1-0	2-0	0-1	3-0	2-1	1-1	1-0	0-2
Hastings Town	5-0	2-2	2-1	0-2	6-2	0-1	1-1	2-1	—	1-0	0-2	1-1	1-3	2-0	1-1	2-0	4-1	2-3	3-1	0-3	5-0	2-1
Ilkeston Town	1-1	1-1	3-3	2-1	2-1	1-1	1-1	2-1	10-1	—	1-0	1-2	3-1	2-1	1-0	2-0	4-1	2-3	3-1	3-0	4-3	1-0
Merthyr Tydfil	4-0	1-1	1-2	3-1	1-0	0-1	0-1	—	2-1	0-1	1-1	2-1	3-1	1-0	7-1	1-0	4-0	0-3	1-2	1-3	1-1	0-2
Newport AFC	1-2	1-1	5-1	2-1	3-0	1-1	—	0-1	2-3	1-2	1-2	0-1	0-1	1-0	3-1	1-1	0-3	2-3	1-2	2-0	4-3	1-2
Rushden & Diamonds	7-3	6-1	3-0	2-1	3-0	—	3-0	3-2	3-0	3-4	2-3	1-4	0-0	3-2	0-1	3-1	4-1	2-1	1-0	2-1	5-1	2-0
Salisbury City	2-0	1-0	3-0	2-1	—	0-2	1-3	0-0	0-2	1-0	1-0	3-5	0-0	3-4	1-2	3-0	3-3	0-0	2-0	2-1	1-0	1-0
Stafford Rangers	1-4	2-1	0-1	—	2-1	0-4	6-1	1-2	0-2	1-1	1-0	3-1	1-0	3-4	0-3	3-0	0-3	3-0	2-4	2-3	2-1	2-0
Sudbury Town	0-1	3-2	—	3-1	3-3	4-1	3-1	1-2	1-0	1-1	1-2	5-3	5-3	0-2	0-0	1-2	3-4	2-0	1-1	3-0	1-2	4-0
VS Rugby	3-0	—	0-1	3-1	3-3	0-4	1-3	1-2	4-3	0-3	2-2	0-0	4-0	0-1	1-1	2-0	3-1	1-1	1-1	3-0	0-1	0-0
Worcester City	—	4-0	0-0	4-0	2-0	0-0	2-0	4-2	4-3	1-0	0-1	3-3	0-1	1-3	0-1	2-0	1-0	0-0	2-1	1-1	1-1	1-0

BEAZER HOMES LEAGUE—MIDLAND DIVISION RESULTS 1995-96

	Bedworth United	Bilston Town	Bridgnorth Town	Buckingham Town	Bury Town	Corby Town	Dudley Town	Evesham United	Grantham Town	Hinckley Town	King's Lynn	Leicester United	Moor Green	Nuneaton Borough	Paget Rangers	Racing Club Warwick	Redditch United	Rothwell Town	Solihull Borough	Stourbridge	Sutton Coldfield Town	Tamworth
Bedworth United		3-1	3-0	1-1	3-2	3-0	3-1	1-2	2-2	3-1	1-0	2-1	0-2	1-0	1-1	2-1	5-0	4-1	5-0	1-1	3-2	1-2
Bilston Town	0-1		1-0	0-0	2-1	1-0	0-3	3-1	3-4	4-3	2-0	3-0	0-4	0-2	0-2	1-1	2-2	3-0	2-1	3-0	0-1	0-3
Bridgnorth Town	0-5	1-0		0-3	2-1	3-3	1-2	3-1	4-1	2-5	2-3	3-3	2-3	1-0	0-2	2-4	1-4	1-3	1-4	2-4	1-2	1-4
Buckingham Town	0-2	0-2	3-0		2-2	5-0	0-2	3-1	1-0	1-2	0-4	3-3	2-0	2-3	2-4	2-2	0-0	1-1	3-1	0-2	3-0	2-1
Bury Town	0-1	0-1	5-1	2-1		1-2	1-3	2-2	2-4	1-3	1-5	0-1	0-1	1-3	1-2	2-5	2-0	1-4	2-0	1-0	1-5	1-1
Corby Town	2-3	3-1	0-0	2-3	1-2		6-1	0-1	2-4	1-1	1-1	0-1	0-2	1-3	1-2	4-0	1-2	0-2	2-1	1-5	2-2	1-0
Dudley Town	2-3	2-2	0-0	4-2	1-1	1-2		5-1	4-1	3-0	2-2	6-3	2-1	0-1	0-0	3-3	2-2	2-2	1-1	2-2	2-1	1-0
Evesham United	0-0	3-2	0-3	1-4	4-0	5-1	4-0		5-1	0-1	2-3	3-0	0-5	0-3	0-0	2-4	1-1	3-1	1-2	2-1	2-3	2-6
Grantham Town	1-1	1-1	4-1	1-0	2-0	1-1	3-0	4-0		5-1	2-3	0-3	2-1	0-3	0-0	1-1	5-3	0-6	3-4	1-3	1-0	3-1
Hinckley Town	0-0	2-4	4-0	0-4	3-2	1-3	0-1	0-1	0-1		4-3	1-0	4-3	0-3	2-0	1-1	3-4	0-6	2-3	2-1	2-1	3-2
King's Lynn	2-0	1-3	2-3	1-4	1-5	1-0	2-0	2-3	2-3	4-3		0-3	3-1	1-1	0-2	2-0	2-1	2-1	2-2	1-2	1-4	1-0
Leicester United	0-1	1-1	3-2	3-3	0-1	0-1	0-1	0-0	3-2	1-0	0-3		0-2	1-2	0-2	1-1	3-4	2-3	1-1	2-0	2-2	1-0
Moor Green	0-0	1-1	2-0	1-2	2-4	1-0	2-2	0-5	2-1	3-0	3-1	0-2		2-2	0-2	2-0	3-1	3-2	0-1	0-2	3-0	0-3
Nuneaton Borough	1-2	2-1	2-0	1-1	2-1	1-0	2-6	0-3	0-3	0-3	1-1	0-2	2-2		0-2	1-1	2-2	1-5	2-0	0-1	3-0	0-1
Paget Rangers	1-1	2-1	3-2	2-4	1-2	1-2	1-1	0-0	0-0	1-3	0-2	0-2	0-2	0-2		0-2	4-1	0-0	1-3	2-0	1-2	1-0
Racing Club Warwick	2-1	2-2	2-1	0-5	5-1	1-2	0-5	2-4	1-1	1-0	1-1	2-0	2-3	2-2	1-1		1-3	2-4	0-0	3-5	4-1	3-7
Redditch United	1-0	2-1	3-1	0-1	1-2	2-1	1-1	1-3	2-1	1-1	2-0	2-3	3-2	2-2	2-0	1-0		0-0	1-4	1-1	1-1	2-3
Rothwell Town	2-2	2-2	4-4	3-1	3-3	0-1	2-1	4-1	0-6	2-2	2-1	5-0	3-2	1-5	2-1	3-2	4-0		2-1	2-0	3-1	0-1
Solihull Borough	1-3	2-0	2-2	3-2	1-1	0-2	3-0	4-2	2-1	3-0	0-1	1-1	0-2	0-1	2-1	3-2	4-0	2-1		4-0	3-2	1-3
Stourbridge	3-0	1-0	3-0	2-0	1-0	1-0	1-1	3-0	1-5	1-1	1-2	0-5	0-2	0-1	3-2	0-0	1-0	2-0	4-0		0-1	3-2
Sutton Coldfield Town	2-0	1-0	3-0	0-2	3-2	2-0	1-0	3-0	1-0	1-1	1-2	2-2	0-5	0-3	0-1	0-0	1-0	2-0	2-2	3-2		2-0
Tamworth	1-2	3-5	4-0	6-0	3-0	7-0	3-2	7-2	3-1	3-2	1-0	2-4	1-5	0-3	3-1	2-0	2-3	2-2	1-3	1-2	3-0	

BEAZER HOMES LEAGUE—SOUTHERN DIVISION RESULTS 1995-96

	Ashford Town	Bashley	Braintree Town	Cinderford Town	Clevedon Town	Erith & Belvedere	Fareham Town	Fisher 93	Fleet Town	Forest Green Rovers	Havant Town	Margate	Newport I.O.W.	Poole Town	Sittingbourne	Tonbridge Angels	Trowbridge Town	Waterlooville	Weston-Super-Mare	Weymouth	Witney Town	Yate Town
Ashford Town	—	1-4	7-1	4-0	2-1	2-0	2-1	1-0	1-0	3-0	1-1	2-0	4-2	1-0	0-0	0-0	1-0	3-2	2-2	1-0	2-0	4-2
Bashley	2-0	—	3-4	3-0	1-2	2-1	3-0	2-0	2-1	1-2	2-3	3-0	0-1	2-0	0-1	0-2	1-1	2-2	1-2	2-3	0-1	1-2
Braintree Town	1-1	2-2	—	3-2	2-0	4-0	1-0	2-1	4-0	1-4	3-0	3-0	1-2	7-1	0-7	5-2	1-0	1-1	2-2	2-1	2-1	4-4
Cinderford Town	0-1	3-0	3-4	—	2-0	3-1	1-2	0-1	3-2	2-1	1-2	1-3	2-2	7-1	3-2	1-2	2-0	0-4	1-1	3-4	1-0	3-3
Clevedon Town	4-2	1-2	1-0	2-0	—	1-2	4-1	2-1	0-2	1-1	2-2	1-4	5-3	3-0	2-3	0-2	1-3	2-0	1-2	2-3	4-3	1-1
Erith & Belvedere	2-3	1-1	1-2	3-1	1-2	—	3-4	1-3	0-3	0-3	1-3	0-2	2-4	5-0	0-3	0-1	0-5	1-3	0-0	3-4	0-5	2-1
Fareham Town	0-3	1-2	2-2	2-1	3-0	5-1	—	0-2	0-3	2-2	1-3	0-2	2-7	5-0	0-2	3-3	0-5	0-3	0-3	1-1	3-3	2-1
Fisher 93	0-0	2-0	3-0	1-2	2-1	1-3	0-2	—	2-2	1-1	0-0	0-4	0-1	4-0	0-2	1-1	1-2	0-3	1-2	0-1	0-1	3-1
Fleet Town	3-2	2-2	2-1	3-2	0-2	3-0	0-3	1-3	—	1-1	2-0	2-0	3-1	2-1	0-5	1-0	1-0	1-0	2-0	3-2	1-0	1-4
Forest Green Rovers	2-3	2-1	1-0	2-1	1-1	0-3	2-2	1-1	1-1	—	1-1	2-0	0-5	6-0	2-2	3-0	2-0	4-2	3-3	2-0	5-1	1-0
Havant Town	2-1	1-2	3-1	1-2	2-2	1-3	1-3	0-0	2-0	1-1	—	2-0	0-5	7-1	2-2	4-1	1-0	0-1	1-0	2-1	1-1	2-1
Margate	0-1	2-1	3-0	1-3	1-4	0-2	0-2	0-4	2-0	2-0	2-0	—	2-2	6-0	1-2	2-2	1-3	2-1	0-3	2-1	1-1	2-1
Newport I.O.W.	2-1	1-1	1-3	2-2	5-3	2-4	2-7	0-1	1-1	5-2	0-5	2-2	—	1-0	3-1	2-0	1-3	2-1	0-3	2-0	0-0	2-1
Poole Town	0-4	1-1	4-0	7-1	3-0	5-0	5-0	4-0	2-1	6-0	7-1	6-0	1-0	—	0-5	8-1	0-8	8-1	7-0	6-0	2-0	8-0
Sittingbourne	4-0	0-0	1-0	0-3	2-3	1-0	3-0	2-3	3-1	3-1	0-5	3-1	0-5	8-1	—	3-1	0-8	0-2	0-2	0-3	0-5	2-2
Tonbridge Angels	2-1	2-3	1-0	1-2	1-1	1-1	1-8	1-1	1-2	2-3	1-1	3-1	1-2	8-1	1-4	—	3-1	2-2	3-2	0-1	0-1	3-4
Trowbridge Town	1-1	5-2	1-0	2-3	1-1	5-0	5-0	1-1	4-0	2-0	3-0	3-1	0-2	9-1	3-0	1-1	—	0-2	1-0	1-2	0-1	2-2
Waterlooville	1-1	2-0	3-0	3-0	2-1	6-0	1-0	0-1	6-0	1-2	3-0	0-4	8-1	8-1	1-0	4-1	1-2	—	3-1	1-0	3-2	1-1
Weston-super-Mare	1-1	2-0	2-3	3-2	2-0	1-6	2-1	0-1	1-6	0-3	0-0	4-3	5-0	7-0	1-2	2-0	1-5	0-3	—	1-1	2-2	6-1
Weymouth	0-2	2-0	5-1	2-0	2-4	2-1	2-1	2-0	2-0	1-2	1-2	2-0	6-0	6-0	0-3	2-1	0-1	2-1	2-2	—	1-0	1-0
Witney Town	1-2	2-1	2-3	4-1	2-1	0-1	5-1	1-0	1-1	1-0	0-0	3-2	2-0	2-0	0-2	1-1	2-1	0-1	0-1	1-1	—	2-0
Yate Town	0-1	0-3	1-1	4-1	1-4	1-4	2-0	1-2	3-1	2-0	2-1	3-2	3-0	8-0	2-2	4-0	2-1	1-3	2-1	1-5	3-0	—

ICIS FOOTBALL LEAGUE 1995–96

Premier Division

	P	W	D	L	F	A	W	D	L	F	A	Pts	GD
		Home			*Goals*		*Away*			*Goals*			
Hayes	42	12	7	2	41	16	12	7	2	35	16	86	44
Enfield	42	14	4	3	47	14	12	4	5	31	21	86	43
Boreham Wood	42	10	6	5	34	20	14	5	2	35	9	83	40
Yeovil Town	42	13	5	3	41	23	10	6	5	42	28	80	32
Dulwich Hamlet	42	11	7	3	42	27	12	4	5	43	32	80	26
Carshalton Athletic	42	10	7	4	38	22	12	1	8	30	27	74	19
St Albans City	42	13	4	4	43	16	7	8	6	27	25	72	29
Kingstonian	42	8	6	7	23	21	12	5	4	39	17	71	24
Harrow Borough	42	7	8	6	35	27	12	2	7	35	29	67	14
Sutton United	42	9	5	7	35	29	8	9	4	36	27	65	15
Aylesbury United	42	8	7	6	28	24	9	5	7	43	34	63	13
Bishop's Stortford	42	7	5	9	36	35	9	4	8	25	27	57	−1
Yeading	42	7	6	8	30	30	4	8	9	18	30	47	−12
Hendon	42	5	6	10	24	30	7	4	10	28	35	46	−13
Chertsey Town	42	8	2	11	26	37	5	4	12	19	34	45	−26
Purfleet	42	7	4	10	24	30	5	4	12	24	37	44	−19
Grays Athletic	42	8	4	9	25	29	3	7	11	18	34	44	−20
Hitchin Town	42	6	4	11	20	35	4	6	11	21	39	40	−33
Bromley	42	5	3	13	26	43	5	4	12	26	48	37	−39
Molesey	42	5	4	12	25	40	4	5	12	21	41	36	−35
Walton & Hersham	42	5	3	13	20	34	4	4	13	22	45	34	−37
Worthing	42	4	3	14	27	51	0	4	17	15	55	19	−64

Division One

	P	W	D	L	F	A	W	D	L	F	A	Pts	GD
		Home			*Goals*		*Away*			*Goals*			
Oxford City	42	14	5	2	48	27	14	2	5	50	33	91	38
Heybridge Swifts	42	17	3	1	62	15	10	4	7	35	28	88	54
Staines Town	42	12	7	2	50	31	11	4	6	32	28	80	23
Leyton Pennant	42	12	2	7	46	31	10	5	6	31	26	73	20
Aldershot Town	42	10	5	6	44	26	11	4	6	37	20	72	35
Billericay Town	42	10	5	6	31	24	9	4	8	27	34	66	0
Bognor Regis Town	42	10	7	4	37	20	8	4	9	34	33	65	18
Marlow	42	10	3	8	40	37	9	2	10	32	38	62	−3
Basingstoke Town	42	11	6	4	40	24	5	7	9	30	36	61	10
Uxbridge	42	7	9	5	22	21	9	3	9	24	28	60	−3
Wokingham Town	42	10	4	7	34	32	6	6	9	28	33	58	−3
Chesham United	42	9	6	6	29	17	6	6	9	22	27	57	7
Thame United	42	7	7	7	30	31	7	6	8	34	42	55	−9
Maidenhead United	42	8	4	9	27	31	4	10	7	23	32	50	−13
Whyteleafe	42	9	3	9	45	44	3	10	8	26	37	49	−10
Abingdon Town	42	8	4	9	36	33	5	5	11	27	47	48	−17
Barton Rovers	42	8	7	6	35	30	4	3	14	34	57	46	−18
Berkhamsted Town	42	5	6	10	25	30	6	5	10	27	38	44	−19
Tooting & Mitcham United	42	7	6	8	24	28	4	4	13	21	36	43	−19
Ruislip Manor	42	7	1	13	26	34	4	8	9	29	43	42	−22
Wembley	42	5	6	10	24	31	6	2	13	25	35	41	−17
Barking	42	2	5	14	21	45	2	7	12	14	45	24	−55

Division Two

	P	W	D	L	F	A	W	D	L	F	A	Pts	GD
		Home			*Goals*		*Away*			*Goals*			
Canvey Island	40	13	7	0	42	15	12	5	3	49	21	87	55
Croydon	40	15	1	4	41	18	10	5	5	37	24	81	36
Hampton	40	14	5	1	41	19	9	5	6	33	25	79	30
Banstead Athletic	40	11	7	2	41	18	10	4	6	31	18	74	36
Collier Row	40	9	5	6	40	29	12	6	2	33	12	74	32
Wivenhoe Town	40	13	3	4	53	25	8	5	7	29	32	71	25
Metropolitan Police	40	11	5	4	36	21	7	5	8	28	24	64	12
Bedford Town	40	11	5	4	40	28	7	5	8	27	31	64	8
Bracknell Town	40	12	2	6	42	25	6	6	8	27	25	62	19
Edgware Town	40	9	6	5	39	25	7	3	10	33	42	57	5
Tilbury	40	10	6	4	33	23	2	5	13	19	39	47	−10
Ware	40	8	5	7	33	34	5	3	12	22	46	47	−25
Chalfont St Peter	40	6	8	6	23	20	5	5	10	35	43	46	−5
Leatherhead	40	6	4	10	32	31	6	6	8	39	46	46	−6
Saffron Walden Town	40	5	6	9	33	35	6	6	8	23	23	45	−2
Cheshunt	40	5	5	10	21	41	5	7	8	35	49	42	−34
Hemel Hempstead	40	5	5	10	25	33	5	5	10	21	29	40	−16
Egham Town	40	7	1	12	20	37	5	2	13	22	37	39	−32
Witham Town	40	4	6	10	21	31	4	4	12	14	37	34	−33
Hungerford Town	40	4	5	11	22	36	5	2	13	22	43	34	−35
Dorking	40	5	1	14	24	48	3	4	13	20	56	29	−60

Division Three

	P	W	Home D	L	Goals F	A	W	Away D	L	Goals F	A	Pts	GD
Horsham	40	15	2	3	45	18	14	3	3	50	22	92	55
Leighton Town	40	16	1	3	60	18	12	4	4	35	16	89	61
Windsor & Eton	40	16	0	4	66	23	11	6	3	51	23	87	71
Wealdstone	40	11	4	5	51	24	12	4	4	53	15	77	65
Harlow Town	40	12	5	3	50	31	10	5	5	35	31	76	23
Northwood	40	11	6	3	49	27	9	3	8	27	29	69	20
Epsom & Ewell	40	10	6	4	59	25	8	8	4	36	32	68	38
Kingsbury Town	40	9	8	3	33	20	6	8	6	28	28	61	13
East Thurrock United	40	10	4	6	37	23	7	4	9	24	27	59	11
Aveley	40	8	7	5	26	20	8	3	9	36	33	58	9
Wingate & Finchley	40	9	4	7	41	27	7	3	10	33	43	55	4
Lewes	40	10	4	6	35	32	4	3	13	21	40	49	−16
Flackwell Heath	40	7	3	10	27	33	7	2	11	33	51	47	−24
Hornchurch	40	3	7	10	27	38	8	1	11	28	39	41	−22
Harefield United	40	6	3	11	22	39	5	4	11	27	50	40	−40
Tring Town	40	5	6	9	24	29	5	2	13	16	49	38	−38
Camberley Town	40	4	3	13	16	36	5	6	9	29	45	36	−36
Hertford Town	40	4	0	16	35	56	6	5	9	37	47	35	−31
Cove	40	6	6	8	19	35	2	4	14	18	54	34	−52
Clapton	40	7	2	11	31	44	2	4	14	17	45	33	−41
Southall	40	5	3	12	21	49	4	2	14	13	55	32	−70

LEADING GOALSCORERS

		Lge	GIC	CC/T
Premier Division				
29	Mark Xavier (Harrow Borough)	29		
26	Paul Whitmarsh (Dulwich Hamlet)	25	1	
25	Warren Patmore (Yeovil Town)	24		1
24	Andy Salako (Carshalton Athletic)	21	3	
	Dominic Feltham (Sutton United)	21		3
Division One				
33	Steve Darlington (Wokingham Town)	28	4	1
30	Paul Coombs (Basingstoke Town)	26	3	1
27	Mark Butler (Aldershot Town)	24	2	1
26	Matthew McDonnell (Marlow)	26		
Division Two				
28	Andy Jones (Canvey Island)	24	1	3
25	Simon Liddle (Banstead Athletic)	16	5	4
24	Jason Reed (Bedford Town)	23	1	
21	Alan Brett (Canvey Island)	16		5
Division Three				
36	Bradley Anderson (Leighton Town)	33	1	2
29	Stafford Browne (Lewes)	28		1
28	David Whitehead (Hertford Town)	28		
27	Andy Boxall (Epsom & Ewell)	27		

Lge: ICIS League; GIC: Guardian Insurance Cup; CC/T: Carlton Cup/Trophy

ATTENDANCES

Premier Divison
Aggregate: 222,603
Highest Individual average: Yeovil Town 2035

Division One
Aggregate: 126,211
Highest Individual average: Aldershot Town 1640

Division Two
Aggregate: 48,815
Highest Individual average: Bedford Town 390

Division One
Aggregate: 142,656
Highest Individual average: Wealdstone 295

PREVIOUS SEASONS

SEASON	CLUBS	GAMES	AGG	AVE
1988–1989	86	1764	323,197	183
1989–1990	87	1806	387,441	215
1990–1991	88	1848	404,703	219
1991–1992	86	1764	397,553	225
1992–1993	85	1724	430,518	247
1993–1994	87	1806	423,306	234
1994–1995	87	1806	433,703	240
1995–1996	86	1764	440,285	250

ICIS FOOTBALL LEAGUE PREMIER DIVISION 1995-96

	Aylesbury United	Bishop's Stortford	Boreham Wood	Bromley	Carshalton Athletic	Chertsey Town	Dulwich Hamlet	Enfield	Grays Athletic	Harrow Borough	Hayes	Hendon	Hitchin Town	Kingstonian	Molesey	Purfleet	St Albans City	Sutton United	Walton & Hersham	Worthing	Yeading	Yeovil Town
Aylesbury United	—	0-0	1-3	3-0	0-1	2-0	0-3	2-3	2-2	2-0	1-3	1-0	2-1	0-2	1-1	1-0	1-1	4-1	0-0	1-1	1-1	3-1
Bishop's Stortford	3-6	—	0-2	1-1	0-2	3-1	1-2	0-1	2-0	2-3	1-2	3-1	2-2	2-3	4-0	1-1	3-2	1-3	2-0	0-0	3-1	2-2
Boreham Wood	2-2	0-1	—	3-1	2-3	2-0	2-2	4-1	2-0	3-2	0-0	4-0	1-0	0-0	0-1	2-1	2-0	0-1	1-1	3-1	1-1	0-2
Bromley	0-3	0-2	3-1	—	1-2	3-3	0-2	0-1	2-2	5-1	0-1	2-5	0-2	1-1	1-3	0-2	1-0	2-3	3-2	3-2	1-0	1-5
Carshalton Athletic	3-1	2-0	0-0	1-2	—	3-1	2-2	1-1	3-1	0-1	0-3	1-1	1-1	0-3	4-0	3-1	1-1	1-2	5-2	4-0	2-0	2-1
Chertsey Town	0-3	3-0	0-3	0-2	0-1	—	0-1	0-3	2-0	1-6	1-3	3-1	2-1	2-1	3-0	2-1	1-2	1-1	1-3	2-1	1-1	1-3
Dulwich Hamlet	1-0	4-1	0-2	4-1	0-1	0-0	—	1-1	3-5	3-2	1-1	1-0	3-3	1-3	2-0	1-1	3-1	2-2	1-1	4-1	3-0	2-1
Enfield	3-3	0-1	4-1	5-0	2-1	0-0	1-0	—	3-0	3-0	1-1	2-0	3-0	2-1	2-0	3-0	2-2	0-2	4-0	5-1	2-0	2-1
Grays Athletic	2-2	2-0	2-0	2-2	3-1	2-0	3-5	3-0	—	3-0	5-1	0-0	1-0	1-0	1-0	1-0	1-1	0-0	1-4	1-1	0-1	1-0
Harrow Borough	2-0	2-3	3-2	5-1	0-1	1-6	3-2	3-0	0-2	—	2-1	0-2	1-5	0-1	0-1	0-2	4-0	2-2	1-2	1-2	1-2	0-0
Hayes	1-3	1-2	0-0	0-1	0-3	1-3	1-1	1-1	3-3	1-1	—	0-2	1-3	1-0	0-2	0-3	0-3	2-2	0-1	0-3	0-1	3-0
Hendon	4-2	3-1	4-0	2-0	1-1	3-1	1-2	2-0	0-0	2-2	3-1	—	1-2	0-1	1-2	2-3	3-1	2-3	1-0	0-5	0-0	4-1
Hitchin Town	0-3	1-1	1-0	0-2	2-5	2-1	3-3	3-0	1-2	1-2	1-1	1-2	—	0-1	2-1	1-1	5-1	4-0	4-1	2-0	2-0	1-1
Kingstonian	1-1	2-1	0-0	1-1	2-1	2-1	1-3	2-1	2-1	2-1	2-1	0-3	1-1	—	1-1	0-2	0-1	1-1	0-1	0-5	0-2	1-1
Molesey	1-4	4-0	0-1	1-3	4-0	3-0	2-0	2-0	3-1	2-0	2-0	2-0	0-1	1-1	—	0-2	1-0	2-0	3-3	4-4	2-2	3-2
Purfleet	1-2	1-1	2-1	0-2	3-1	2-1	1-1	3-0	2-0	2-2	2-4	2-0	1-1	2-3	0-2	—	3-0	1-0	1-2	1-2	3-1	2-1
St Albans City	2-0	3-0	2-0	1-0	1-1	1-2	3-1	2-2	0-3	0-0	1-2	0-0	4-1	1-1	0-1	0-1	—	2-2	0-1	1-2	2-1	1-1
Sutton United	2-3	2-1	0-1	2-3	1-2	1-1	2-2	0-2	1-2	0-0	0-4	1-0	2-2	0-5	2-1	2-2	2-2	—	1-1	5-2	2-2	0-0
Walton & Hersham	2-1	0-2	0-4	3-1	0-1	0-1	0-2	4-0	1-4	1-2	0-1	1-0	4-1	0-1	3-3	1-2	0-1	1-1	—	1-0	0-0	1-3
Worthing	1-3	0-1	0-2	2-2	2-3	1-2	1-3	5-1	1-1	1-2	0-3	0-5	2-0	0-5	4-4	1-2	1-5	5-2	1-0	—	2-1	3-2
Yeading	0-0	2-4	0-3	3-0	1-3	1-3	5-3	2-0	0-1	1-2	0-1	0-0	2-0	0-2	2-2	3-1	2-1	2-2	3-0	1-0	—	1-1
Yeovil Town	3-2	1-3	0-1	4-3	2-1	1-0	5-3	0-1	1-0	0-0	3-0	4-1	1-1	1-1	3-2	2-1	1-1	0-0	4-1	3-1	2-0	—

ICIS FOOTBALL LEAGUE DIVISION 1 1995-96

	Abingdon Town	Aldershot Town	Barking	Barton Rovers	Basingstoke Town	Berkhamsted Town	Billericay Town	Bognor Regis Town	Chesham United	Heybridge Swifts	Leyton Pennant	Maidenhead United	Marlow	Oxford City	Ruislip Manor	Staines Town	Thame United	Tooting & Mitcham United	Uxbridge	Wembley	Whyteleafe	Wokingham Town
Abingdon Town	—	1-2	4-0	4-2	1-0	2-0	1-2	1-2	0-0	3-1	2-2	1-1	3-4	4-2	2-2	0-2	1-2	2-1	0-2	0-2	1-3	3-1
Aldershot Town	5-1	—	5-1	6-2	1-1	2-1	0-1	1-1	1-0	1-1	4-1	0-1	2-3	0-2	0-1	3-3	1-0	3-1	4-0	0-3	3-0	2-2
Barking	1-5	0-4	—	1-4	2-2	1-2	0-1	1-1	0-2	1-2	1-2	1-1	2-0	2-3	1-2	1-2	1-4	1-1	0-2	1-0	2-2	1-3
Barton Rovers	0-1	0-3	0-0	—	1-2	5-2	1-1	0-5	0-0	1-4	2-2	4-0	2-1	1-0	1-0	0-2	3-3	2-0	1-1	5-1	4-0	2-2
Basingstoke Town	0-0	4-1	1-0	3-1	—	1-1	2-1	4-2	2-1	1-3	2-1	2-2	0-1	3-1	1-1	5-0	3-3	2-0	0-1	2-0	2-2	0-2
Berkhamsted Town	4-2	0-0	0-1	1-2	1-1	—	2-0	0-2	0-1	1-2	1-1	2-2	1-1	2-3	1-1	1-2	4-1	0-1	1-3	1-0	1-1	2-1
Billericay Town	1-3	1-2	3-0	1-6	2-2	2-0	—	3-1	2-0	2-0	0-3	1-1	2-0	1-0	4-1	2-1	1-2	1-0	0-0	0-1	1-1	0-0
Bognor Regis Town	2-0	1-0	1-1	3-0	4-1	3-0	4-0	—	3-0	1-3	3-2	0-0	0-1	3-1	1-1	3-1	0-1	3-2	0-2	1-1	2-2	2-0
Chesham United	4-0	1-0	1-1	4-0	2-2	1-1	0-1	3-0	—	1-1	0-1	1-0	1-1	0-2	3-2	2-0	0-0	1-0	1-0	3-0	2-2	2-0
Heybridge Swifts	3-0	2-0	7-0	3-1	3-1	0-1	3-2	0-1	1-1	—	0-0	1-1	3-1	2-4	3-0	3-0	5-1	4-1	4-0	4-1	2-0	2-0
Leyton Pennant	0-2	1-0	3-0	4-2	3-1	4-2	1-2	5-1	2-0	0-1	—	0-0	2-4	0-2	1-2	1-3	1-0	2-2	2-1	4-2	4-0	1-1
Maidenhead United	4-0	1-1	0-2	3-4	0-0	3-1	3-1	3-2	2-2	1-4	5-1	—	4-1	2-4	2-1	1-0	2-1	3-1	1-2	1-0	2-1	0-3
Marlow	2-1	0-3	2-0	2-0	3-3	1-1	1-4	0-1	0-1	1-0	4-1	5-1	—	1-3	3-2	2-3	4-6	3-1	2-3	0-2	2-0	1-1
Oxford City	3-3	1-3	1-0	3-0	3-2	1-0	4-1	3-0	1-0	4-3	2-2	3-0	2-4	—	2-4	2-3	5-0	2-1	0-1	5-1	2-0	2-0
Ruislip Manor	1-0	1-2	3-1	3-1	1-0	2-3	2-2	1-0	1-0	1-2	2-3	0-1	1-6	2-2	—	2-1	2-3	2-1	3-1	0-5	0-1	1-2
Staines Town	6-0	3-2	5-1	3-2	3-1	2-1	0-1	2-0	1-0	3-3	2-0	0-1	0-1	1-3	2-2	—	1-1	0-0	3-1	1-0	2-2	2-1
Thame United	1-1	2-2	1-0	3-1	1-0	2-2	0-1	2-3	3-3	1-0	2-3	2-5	3-1	4-6	2-3	1-1	—	1-1	1-0	1-1	1-1	4-3
Tooting & Mitcham United	1-0	0-2	5-1	0-0	1-3	2-0	2-2	1-0	1-2	1-1	2-0	1-1	0-3	3-1	3-3	1-1	1-0	—	1-0	0-4	0-5	1-2
Uxbridge	1-1	0-2	1-0	3-2	0-1	1-2	2-1	0-0	1-1	1-0	1-0	0-0	3-1	2-3	2-0	1-1	2-2	1-1	—	1-0	1-0	1-1
Wembley	1-1	1-2	2-2	3-0	0-2	2-2	3-0	2-1	0-0	0-3	0-1	0-1	1-2	4-2	1-1	1-1	2-2	1-0	1-0	—	2-2	3-1
Whyteleafe	4-2	0-6	2-0	3-3	2-0	1-1	2-1	2-4	0-2	4-1	1-3	2-1	3-1	2-0	2-1	0-1	1-2	0-2	0-2	0-4	—	1-2
Wokingham Town	3-4	1-0	1-1	1-1	3-3	1-2	3-0	0-5	0-3	1-0	0-1	2-1	2-0	2-0	2-2	0-3	2-0	2-1	3-1	2-0	1-1	—

ICIS FOOTBALL LEAGUE DIVISION 2 1995–96

	Banstead Athletic	Bedford Town	Bracknell Town	Canvey Island	Chalfont St Peter	Cheshunt	Collier Row	Croydon	Dorking	Edgware Town	Egham Town	Hampton	Hemel Hempstead	Hungerford Town	Leatherhead	Metropolitan Police	Saffron Walden	Tilbury	Ware	Witham Town	Wivenhoe Town
Banstead Athletic	—	2-0	1-1	0-3	6-1	0-0	2-4	1-0	2-2	2-2	3-1	1-1	2-1	6-0	2-1	0-0	2-0	1-1	3-0	3-0	2-0
Bedford Town	0-6	—	1-1	1-7	3-0	4-2	0-3	2-0	3-1	4-1	3-0	1-1	1-0	1-0	6-1	0-0	0-0	5-0	2-2	0-1	3-2
Bracknell Town	0-1	3-1	—	2-1	1-0	4-0	0-3	0-2	1-0	2-3	1-1	3-5	4-2	4-1	1-3	1-0	2-1	1-1	5-0	1-0	6-0
Canvey Island	1-0	2-2	2-1	—	2-0	1-1	2-1	0-0	4-0	2-0	5-1	3-3	1-0	3-0	1-1	2-0	1-0	3-2	4-1	2-0	3-3
Chalfont St Peter	1-1	1-0	0-0	2-0	—	4-1	1-1	0-1	2-2	2-0	1-1	2-0	0-1	3-0	2-2	1-2	1-3	1-0	0-0	0-0	0-3
Cheshunt	1-2	3-0	2-1	0-0	1-1	—	0-2	0-5	2-0	1-6	1-0	0-3	0-0	3-2	2-3	2-4	0-4	1-1	0-2	1-1	1-4
Collier Row	0-3	0-3	0-2	1-3	5-2	2-2	—	1-2	3-1	1-0	4-0	0-1	1-1	2-1	4-2	1-1	2-0	2-0	0-6	9-0	1-1
Croydon	0-0	4-1	2-1	0-2	4-0	3-2	1-2	—	2-1	0-1	1-0	1-0	2-0	3-0	2-1	4-1	2-0	2-1	5-2	2-0	1-2
Dorking	0-2	1-3	2-3	2-3	0-6	3-3	1-3	0-3	—	0-1	2-1	3-1	1-4	1-6	2-0	2-0	0-3	1-3	0-1	0-2	3-0
Edgware Town	1-2	3-1	3-1	1-1	2-1	0-3	1-3	1-4	7-0	—	0-2	4-2	0-0	2-2	2-3	2-0	1-1	0-0	5-0	1-0	3-1
Egham Town	1-0	0-2	0-4	0-4	3-1	2-4	1-1	2-3	1-0	3-2	—	0-2	2-2	0-1	1-4	0-2	1-0	2-1	0-2	2-1	0-1
Hampton	5-4	3-0	1-0	0-0	1-0	2-2	0-1	5-3	2-1	1-0	1-0	—	2-3	1-0	3-3	2-0	1-1	4-0	3-1	2-1	2-0
Hemel Hempstead	0-0	0-3	3-1	0-2	1-4	1-2	0-1	0-0	1-1	1-2	0-4	3-3	—	3-0	2-2	1-3	0-2	2-1	4-0	2-3	0-3
Hungerford Town	0-2	0-0	1-2	2-5	3-2	0-3	0-2	0-3	5-0	2-2	1-2	0-0	1-0	—	3-0	1-3	0-1	2-0	3-0	0-0	2-2
Leatherhead	0-2	1-1	1-3	2-4	2-2	2-2	0-1	2-2	2-3	7-1	2-0	1-1	4-0	2-1	—	0-2	1-1	4-2	3-1	1-0	0-1
Metropolitan Police	2-1	3-1	0-3	1-1	1-1	3-0	0-0	1-0	3-1	3-0	1-2	0-3	2-0	2-3	2-5	—	1-1	2-0	2-1	2-0	0-0
Saffron Walden	0-0	1-2	1-1	1-4	2-2	2-2	0-2	2-3	1-1	3-2	0-2	1-0	1-2	1-1	2-2	2-1	—	1-1	4-0	2-4	1-2
Tilbury	2-0	2-0	1-1	0-5	1-1	3-1	1-3	2-0	5-0	5-0	0-1	4-0	2-1	0-1	2-0	0-0	1-1	—	3-2	1-1	2-1
Ware	0-1	0-1	2-1	1-0	2-4	2-2	1-0	2-2	3-4	2-2	4-3	3-1	0-2	0-2	3-3	2-0	3-1	4-0	—	2-0	2-0
Witham Town	0-1	0-1	2-1	0-0	0-0	4-0	2-4	0-0	0-2	4-3	5-2	3-3	0-1	0-2	2-0	1-1	3-1	3-2	2-2	—	0-1
Wivenhoe Town	4-3	1-1	2-0	6-2	0-2	4-0	2-2	3-4	7-0	3-2	5-2	0-2	2-1	3-1	3-0	0-1	1-1	2-1	1-0	4-0	—

ICIS FOOTBALL LEAGUE DIVISION 3 1995–96

	Aveley	Camberley Town	Clapton	Cove	East Thurrock United	Epsom & Ewell	Flackwell Heath	Harefield United	Harlow Town	Hertford Town	Hornchurch	Horsham	Kingsbury Town	Leighton Town	Lewes	Northwood	Southall	Tring Town	Wealdstone	Windsor & Eton	Wingate & Finchley
Aveley	—	3-2	3-0	0-0	2-1	0-2	1-1	3-2	0-1	0-0	1-1	0-2	1-1	0-1	2-1	4-0	0-1	1-0	1-1	0-0	4-3
Camberley Town	1-2	—	1-0	0-1	0-4	0-2	1-4	1-2	1-3	4-3	0-1	0-2	1-1	1-5	2-1	0-1	0-0	0-3	1-2	1-1	0-2
Clapton	0-3	1-3	—	0-1	3-2	2-4	1-1	2-1	0-0	3-0	1-2	1-3	2-2	1-2	2-0	0-2	4-2	5-0	1-10	0-5	3-0
Cove	0-2	0-0	1-0	—	0-2	2-2	4-1	1-1	1-1	2-0	2-0	0-5	0-0	0-3	1-0	0-2	3-0	1-1	1-9	0-4	3-1
East Thurrock United	0-1	4-1	5-1	3-0	—	1-1	2-0	3-0	2-2	0-2	3-0	3-0	2-2	1-1	2-0	1-0	2-0	0-1	0-3	1-4	1-2
Epsom & Ewell	2-2	4-0	2-1	6-0	1-1	—	4-3	3-0	2-2	1-1	1-4	1-2	2-2	1-2	0-0	3-0	5-0	11-1	0-3	4-1	7-1
Flackwell Heath	1-0	1-4	1-1	3-2	1-1	1-2	—	3-0	0-1	2-3	1-3	2-1	1-2	1-0	2-4	1-2	4-2	1-0	0-0	0-3	1-2
Harefield United	1-3	2-1	1-0	2-1	2-0	1-2	3-0	—	1-3	1-3	1-0	0-6	0-1	1-4	0-1	2-2	0-0	0-2	1-2	0-3	4-3
Harlow Town	0-1	1-4	0-0	1-1	2-2	2-2	0-1	3-0	—	8-4	2-1	1-3	3-5	3-0	1-2	4-0	0-2	1-2	3-0	1-3	2-2
Hertford Town	0-0	4-3	3-0	2-0	0-2	0-2	2-3	1-3	1-3	—	2-1	2-3	3-2	3-0	4-3	1-1	5-0	3-0	3-3	1-4	1-7
Hornchurch	3-1	6-1	1-2	2-0	1-1	1-4	1-3	1-0	2-1	2-1	—	1-4	0-1	1-0	1-2	2-3	1-2	5-0	0-0	1-1	1-0
Horsham	0-2	2-2	1-0	1-0	2-3	1-2	3-4	0-1	1-3	2-6	2-1	—	0-4	1-4	2-1	2-2	3-1	5-0	1-2	1-4	4-0
Kingsbury Town	3-1	6-1	1-0	1-0	1-3	2-2	5-0	1-0	2-0	3-1	0-1	3-3	—	1-0	2-1	3-1	2-0	6-1	0-0	1-1	4-0
Leighton Town	3-2	6-0	3-0	3-0	2-3	1-2	3-1	3-0	2-0	3-0	1-0	3-3	2-0	—	1-1	5-0	5-0	2-0	0-2	4-3	0-1
Lewes	3-2	2-3	3-0	1-1	1-0	0-0	3-0	3-0	3-0	3-0	2-0	1-2	3-0	3-0	—	1-2	1-0	1-0	0-4	2-0	2-2
Northwood	3-1	2-2	2-1	3-2	3-0	3-0	2-1	2-2	0-2	1-1	3-1	2-2	3-1	5-0	1-2	—	2-1	2-1	0-5	1-1	2-2
Southall	2-1	2-1	4-0	2-1	0-1	5-0	2-1	0-1	2-1	5-0	2-0	3-1	2-0	5-0	1-0	2-1	—	0-1	9-0	6-1	3-0
Tring Town	0-0	0-0	2-1	1-1	2-0	1-3	4-0	0-2	1-0	3-0	0-1	0-1	1-3	1-1	5-1	0-2	0-1	—	1-0	0-3	3-1
Wealdstone	3-4	2-1	4-0	4-0	3-0	3-0	7-0	2-1	3-0	3-3	2-0	1-2	2-0	3-2	3-2	0-4	9-0	3-1	—	1-5	1-1
Windsor & Eton	2-1	3-0	0-1	5-3	2-0	4-1	2-1	0-3	1-3	1-4	1-1	1-4	1-1	4-3	2-0	1-1	0-3	0-3	1-5	—	3-1
Wingate & Finchley	1-3	1-0	7-0	8-1	0-2	3-0	3-2	4-3	2-2	1-7	1-0	4-0	4-0	0-1	2-3	2-0	3-0	2-3	2-0	1-2	—

GUARDIAN INSURANCE CUP 1995–96

Preliminary Round
Banstead Athletic 2, East Thurrock United 0
Bedford Town 2, Metropolitan Police 1
Bracknell Town 3, Cheshunt 1
Collier Row 0, Canvey Island 0 *aet*
  (at Canvey Island)
Croydon 4, Camberley Town 0
Dorking 3, Aveley 2
Edgware Town 2, Harlow Town 1
Egham Town 2, Hertford Town 0
Epsom & Ewell 2, Barton Rovers 3
Flackwell Heath 2, Wingate & Finchley 1
Hemel Hempstead 3, Tilbury 1 *aet*
Horsham 3, Oxford City 6
Hungerford Town W/O Newbury Town
  (Newbury Town suspended by Football Association)
Kingsbury Town 2, Cove 0
Leatherhead 3, Clapton 2 *aet*
Leighton Town 1, Hampton 2 *aet*
Lewes 1, Witham Town 2
Northwood 0, Harefield United 1
Saffron Walden Town 1, Hornchurch 2
Thame United 0, Chalfont St Peter 1
Ware 3, Tring Town 5
Windsor & Eton 2, Southall 1 *aet*
Wivenhoe Town 2, Wealdstone 5

Replay
Canvey Island 0, Collier Row 2
  (Collier Row removed from competition for playing an ineligible player.)

First Round
Aldershot Town 3, Chertsey Town 2
Aylesbury United 3, Maidenhead United 0
Banstead Athletic 6, Windsor & Eton 1
Berkhamsted Town 1, Kingsbury Town 2
Billericay Town 3, Hampton 1
Bracknell Town 3, Wokingham Town 5
Chesham United 4, Harrow Borough 1
Croydon 3, Witham Town 0
Dorking 1, Barton Rovers 5
Edgware Town 0, Bishop's Stortford 2
Egham Town 1, Ruislip Manor 1 *aet*
Enfield 4, Leyton Pennant 2
Flackwell Heath 1, Dulwich Hamlet 3 *aet*
Harefield United 0, Bromley 3
Hayes 0, Grays Athletic 1
Hitchin Town 4, Canvey Island 1
Hornchurch 1, Bedford Town 4
Kingstonian 2, Abingdon Town 1
Leatherhead 2, Hungerford Town 1
Marlow 2, Hemel Hempstead 1
Molesey 0, Basingstoke Town 1
Purfleet 0, Boreham Wood 1
St Albans City 2, Worthing 3
Staines Town 3, Oxford City 1 *aet*
Sutton United 2, Tring Town 0
Tooting & Mitcham United 4, Wealdstone 3
Uxbridge 0, Barking 1
Walton & Hersham 2, Chalfont St Peter 2 *aet*
Wembley 1, Carshalton Athletic 3
Whyteleafe 1, Heybridge Swifts 2
Yeading 0, Bognor Regis Town 3
Yeovil Town 1, Hendon 3

Replays
Chalfont St Peter 3, Walton & Hersham 5 *aet*
Ruislip Manor 2, Egham Town 0

Second Round
Aldershot Town 2, Grays Athletic 1
Barking 0, Kingstonian 6
Barton Rovers 0, Dulwich Hamlet 1
Basingstoke Town 2, Ruislip Manor 2 *aet*
Bedford Town 3, Tooting & Mitcham United 2
Bishop's Stortford 3, Staines Town 1
Bromley 3, Boreham Wood 3 *aet*
Carshalton Athletic 2, Bognor Regis Town 0
Chesham United 3, Aylesbury United 3 *aet*
Hendon 0, Croydon 1 *aet*
Heybridge Swifts 4, Billericay Town 3
Kingsbury Town 1, Walton & Hersham 1
  (Abandoned in extra time)
Leatherhead 0, Marlow 2
Sutton United 0, Hitchin Town 1
Wokingham Town 6, Banstead Athletic 3
  (Banstead Athletic removed from competition for playing an ineligible player.)
Worthing 1, Enfield 4

Replays
Boreham Wood 1, Bromley 0
Ruislip Manor 2, Basingstoke Town 3
Walton & Hersham 3, Kingsbury Town 1

Third Round
Aldershot Town 1, Boreham Wood 0
Aylesbury United 3, Carshalton Athletic 1
Basingstoke Town 6, Marlow 0
Bedford Town 1, Wokingham Town 2
Croydon 2, Walton & Hersham 1
Enfield 2, Kingstonian 2 *aet*
Heybridge Swifts 3, Dulwich Hamlet 2 *aet*
Hitchin Town 4, Bishop's Stortford 1 *aet*

Replay
Kingstonian 3, Enfield 0

Fourth Round
Aldershot Town 1, Basingstoke Town 0
Aylesbury United 2, Croydon 1 *aet*
Heybridge Swifts 2, Kingstonian 2 *aet*
Wokingham Town 2, Hitchin Town 3

Replay
Kingstonian 2, Heybridge Swifts 0

Semi-finals First Leg
Aylesbury United 1, Kingstonian 3
Hitchin Town 0, Aldershot Town 1

Semi-finals Second Leg
Aldershot Town 2, Hitchin Town 0
  (Aldershot Town won 3-0 on aggregate)
Kingstonian 2, Aylesbury United 1
  (Kingstonian won 5-2 on aggregate)

Final
Aldershot Town 1, Kingstonian 4
  (at Aldershot Town)

CARLTON CUP 1995–96

First Round
Aldershot Town 3, Bromley 0
Aylesbury United 3, Chesham United 1 *aet*
Barton Rovers 3, Heybridge Swifts 2 *(match void)*
Barton Rovers 0, Heybridge Swifts 1
Basingstoke Town 4, Whyteleafe 1
Berkhamsted Town 0, Yeading 3
Chertsey Town 0, Yeovil Town 2
Hendon 3, St Albans City 4
Molesey 0, Kingstonian 3
Purfleet 2, Hayes 0
Staines Town 0, Walton & Hersham 1
Thame United 4, Marlow 1
Uxbridge 1, Harrow Borough 0

Second Round
Aldershot Town 3, Maidenhead United 1
Aylesbury United 0, Purfleet 1
Bishop's Stortford 3, Hitchin Town 0
Bognor Regis Town 6, Worthing 0
Boreham Wood 3, Barking 1
Carshalton Athletic 2, Yeovil Town 1
Enfield 1, Yeading 2 *aet*
Grays Athletic 1, Billericay Town 2 *aet*
Heybridge Swifts 3, Uxbridge 1
Oxford City 1, Basingstoke Town 0
St Albans City 1, Ruislip Manor 2
Sutton United 3, Abingdon Town 0
Thame United 3, Dulwich Hamlet 0

Tooting & Mitcham United 4, Wokingham Town 3
Walton & Hersham 1, Kingstonian 3
Wembley 2, Leyton Pennant 3

Third Round
Aldershot Town 2, Bognor Regis Town 2 *aet*
  (Bognor Regis Town won 5-3 on penalties)
Carshalton Athletic 4, Thame United 0
Heybridge Swifts 0, Boreham Wood 2
Kingstonian 5, Oxford City 3
Leyton Pennant 5, Purfleet 1
Ruislip Manor 1, Billericay Town 4
Tooting & Mitcham United 1, Sutton United 3
Yeading 0, Bishop's Stortford 1

Fourth Round
Billericay Town 0, Bishop's Stortford 2
Bognor Regis Town 1, Sutton United 2 *aet*
Boreham Wood 5, Leyton Pennant 1
Kingstonian 2, Carshalton Athletic 3

Semi-finals
Boreham Wood 4, Bishop's Stortford 1
Sutton United 1, Carshalton Athletic 1 *aet*

Replay
Carshalton Athletic 1, Sutton United 4 *aet*

Final
Sutton United 2, Boreham Wood 2 *aet*
  (Sutton United won 4-3 on penalties)
  (at Purfleet)

CARLTON TROPHY 1995–96

First Round
Aveley 6, Harlow Town 2
Banstead Athletic 2, Windsor & Eton 0
Bracknell Town 1, Horsham 0
Chalfont St Peter 1, Croydon 0
Cove 2, Flackwell Heath 0
Hertford Town 0, East Thurrock United 2
Newbury Town v Metropolitan Police
  (Newbury Town removed from competition)
Southall 3, Saffron Walden Town 1
Wingate & Finchley 0, Harefield United 1
Witham Town 1, Clapton 4
Wivenhoe Town 5, Hornchurch 2

Second Round
Aveley 0, Ware 1
Banstead Athletic 6, Camberley Town 1
Bracknell Town 2, Harefield United 1 *aet*
Canvey Island 3, Collier Row 2
Cove 0, Hampton 4
Dorking 1, Hungerford Town 6
East Thurrock United 3, Cheshunt 2
Egham Town 1, Leatherhead 2
Epsom & Ewell 0, Lewes 1
Hemel Hempstead 3, Edgware Town 0
Kingsbury Town 2, Clapton 5
Metropolitan Police 2, Chalfont St Peter 6
Northwood 6, Southall 1
Tring Town 1, Tilbury 5
Wealdstone 1, Bedford Town 0
Wivenhoe Town 5, Leighton Town 3

Third Round
Banstead Athletic 2, Leatherhead 0
Bracknell Town 2, Lewes 0
Canvey Island 1, Clapton 0
East Thurrock United 2, Tilbury 2
  (Abandoned after 90 minutes due to weather condi-
  tions)
Hungerford Town 1, Hampton 0
Northwood 0, Wealdstone 2
Ware 3, Hemel Hempstead 1 *aet*
Wivenhoe Town 5, Chalfont St Peter 1

Replay
Tilbury 2, East Thurrock United 0

Fourth Round
Banstead Athletic 1, Bracknell Town 0
Tilbury 2, Ware 1
Wealdstone 1, Hungerford Town 2
Wivenhoe Town 1, Canvey Island 3

Semi-finals
Banstead Athletic 2, Tilbury 1 *aet*
Canvey Island 1, Hungerford Town 1 *aet*

Replay
Hungerford Town 1, Canvey Island 2

Final
Canvey Island 2, Banstead Athletic 1
  (at Aveley)

FA UMBRO TROPHY 1995–96

First Qualifying Round
Harrogate Town v Grantham Town	1-4
Farsley Celtic v Bedworth United	3-1
Droylsden v Matlock Town	0-3
Atherstone United v Lincoln United	2-1
Accrington Stanley v Bradford (Park Avenue)	2-2, 3-2
Atherton LR v Chorley	1-2
Sutton Coldfield Town v Bilston Town	1-1, 4-4, 1-2
Racing Club Warwick v Warrington Town	1-0
Bridgnorth Town v Leigh RMI	1-1, 0-7
Winsford United v Paget Rangers	1-1, 2-0
Curzon Ashton v Worksop Town	4-3
Knowlsley United v Moor Green	3-2
Alfreton Town v Congleton Town	5-0
Workington v Leicester United	1-1, 0-5
Barrow v Hinckley Town	3-0
Stourbridge v Frickley Athletic	1-2
Lancaster City v Solihull Borough	3-0
Fleetwood v Whitley Bay	2-1
Tamworth w.o. v Caernarfon Town withdrew	
Radcliffe Borough v Redditch United	3-1
Erith & Belvedere v Basingstoke Town	0-6
Leyton Pennant v Fleet Town	0-1
Hastings Town v Havant Town	2-2, 0-1
Chertsey Town v Poole Town	9-0
Bury Town v Trowbridge Town	1-2
Buckingham Town v Braintree Town	1-1, 0-1
Carshalton Athletic v Dulwich Hamlet	1-1, 1-1, 2-1
Ruislip Manor v Cinderford Town	3-1
Barton Rovers v Crawley Town	1-3
Salisbury City v Fisher	2-0
Weston-Super-Mare v Bognor Regis Town	2-6
Yate Town v Witney Town	3-2
Ashford Town v Sudbury Town	0-2
Billericay Town v Wembley	0-4
Fareham Town v Maidenhead United	2-4
Barking v Baldock Town	0-0, 2-3
Forest Green Rovers v Sittingbourne	1-2
Abingdon Town v Bishops Stortford	1-1, 1-5
Berkhamsted Town v Purfleet	1-2
Newport (IW) v Chesham United	1-3
Kings Lynn v Uxbridge	1-2
Staines Town v Wokingham Town	2-1
Weymouth v Tonbridge	4-0
Hendon v Waterlooville	2-2, 1-0
Whyteleafe v Tooting & Mitcham United	1-2
Harrow Borough v Marlow	1-1, 4-1
Worthing v Thame United	1-1, 0-2
Bashley v Margate	1-1, 2-1

Second Qualifying Round
Barrow v Winsford United	0-1
Tamworth v Netherfield	3-1
Bilston Town v Leicester United	5-2
Alfreton Town v Dudley Town	2-2, 0-2
Great Harwood Town v Frickley Athletic	3-2
Atherstone United v Accrington Stanley	1-3
Radcliffe Borough v Fleetwood	2-0
Eastwood Town v Chorley	0-1
Grantham Town v Farsley Celtic	1-3
Leigh RMI v Matlock Town	0-2
Emley v Racing Club Warwick	2-1
Curzon Ashton v Lancaster City	1-1, 0-3
Nuneaton Borough v Knowsley United	3-2
Carshalton Athletic v Weymouth	5-1
Braintree Town v Harrow Borough	4-0
Chertsey Town v Chesham United	2-2, 3-2
Staines Town v Havant Town	3-1
Walton & Hersham v Oxford City	0-0, 2-5
Trowbridge Town v Bishops Stortford	1-0
Clevedon Town v Worcester City	0-4
Crawley Town v Bashley	0-1
Evesham United v Aldershot Town	0-2
Newport AFC v Fleet Town	2-1
Tooting & Mitcham United v Baldock Town	2-1
Basingstoke Town v Uxbridge	0-2
Purfleet v Corby Town	6-1
Wembley v Ruislip Manor	1-1, 2-1
Bognor Regis Town v Sittingbourne	2-2, 2-1
Hendon v Gravesend & Northfleet	3-0
Salisbury City v Sudbury Town	2-2, 2-2, 2-3

Yate Town v Heybridge Swifts	1-2
Maidenhead United v Thame United	0-5

Third Qualifying Round
Spennymoor United v Nuneaton Borough	0-2
Halesowen Town v Bilston Town	0-0, 4-1
Burton Albion v Bamber Bridge	3-3, 3-2
Ashton United v Lancaster City	1-1, 2-0
Bishop Auckland v Witton Albion	0-0, 0-0, 3-1
Radcliffe Borough v Farsley Celtic	3-1
Emley v Great Harwood Town	3-1
Chorley v Winsford United	3-1
Stafford Rangers v Tamworth	1-1, 3-0
Matlock Town v Buxton	1-0
Blyth Spartans v Gretna	3-2
Dudley Town v VS Rugby	4-3
Accrington Stanley v Gresley Rovers	2-3
Leek Town v Boston United	0-0, 0-2
Ilkeston Town v Gainsborough Trinity	0-5
Chelmsford City v Yeading	2-1
Gloucester City v Aldershot Town	5-1
Boreham Wood v Heybridge Swifts	3-0
Bromley v Oxford City	1-1, 2-3
Worcester City v Aylesbury United	3-0
Chertsey Town v Purfleet	0-1
Molesey v Staines Town	2-2, 0-5
Carshalton Athletic v Braintree Town	1-1, 5-0
St Albans City v Thame United	4-2
Sutton United v Trowbridge Town	0-1
Wembley v Bashley	2-0
Rothwell Town v Uxbridge	3-2
Dorchester Town v Hayes	2-3
Hitchin Town v Bognor Regis Town	1-2
Newport AFC v Grays Athletic	1-0
Cambridge City v Hendon	2-0
Sudbury Town v Tooting & Mitcham United	2-0

First Round
Stalybridge Celtic v Gresley Rovers	1-1, 0-1
Stafford Rangers v Guiseley	1-1, 1-2
Colwyn Bay v Altrincham	3-3, 0-2
Halifax Town v Southport	2-1
Ashton United v Blyth Spartans	1-3
Dudley Town v Halesowen Town	4-2
Macclesfield Town v Runcorn	1-0
Burton Albion v Telford United	3-1
Gainsborough Trinity v Nuneaton Borough	4-1
Morecambe v Emley	2-2, 1-3
Hednesford Town v Northwich Victoria	1-1, 0-2
Kidderminster Harriers v Gateshead	0-0, 0-2
Marine v Hyde United	0-0, 0-0, 0-3
Boston United v Chorley	1-1, 1-2
Bromsgrove Rovers v Bishop Auckland	1-0
Radcliffe Borough v Matlock Town	3-2
Oxford City v Merthyr Tydfil	1-2
Rothwell Town v Welling United	2-2, 0-3
Bognor Regis Town v Worcester City	1-0
Dover Athletic v Cheltenham Town	2-2, 1-1, 1-0
Chelmsford City v Newport AFC	0-1
Bath City v Yeovil Town	1-1, 3-2
Gloucester City v Staines Town	5-0
Trowbridge Town v Sudbury Town	2-2, 1-1, 1-1, 3-4
Carshalton Athletic v Woking	3-1
Farnborough Town v Slough Town	1-1, 3-4
Rushden & Diamonds v Purfleet	0-1
Kettering Town v St Albans City	1-1, 3-2
Cambridge City v Boreham Wood	1-2
Hayes v Enfield	0-0, 2-2, 2-2, 2-0
Stevenage Borough v Dagenham & Redbridge	3-2
Wembley v Kingstonian	2-1

Second Round
Hyde United v Welling United	4-1
Sudbury Town v Gloucester City	3-1
Guiseley v Altrincham	4-0
Emley v Gateshead	1-2
Dudley Town v Merthyr Tydfil	1-2
Bognor Regis Town v Radcliffe Borough	1-3
Boreham Wood v Dover Athletic	2-1
Slough Town v Kettering Town	1-2
Chorley v Gainsborough Trinity	2-0

Bath City v Hayes	2-0
Macclesfield Town v Purfleet	2-1
Blyth Spartans v Gresley Rovers	1-2
Carshalton Athletic v Newport AFC	2-1
Stevenage Borough v Burton Albion	2-1
Wembley v Northwich Victoria	0-2
Halifax Town v Bromsgrove Rovers	0-1

Third Round

Guiseley v Gresley Rovers	1-2
Merthyr Tydfil v Northwich Victoria	1-1, 2-2, 0-3
Hyde United v Carshalton Athletic	3-2
Macclesfield Town v Sudbury Town	1-0
Boreham Wood v Chorley	1-1, 3-4
Radcliffe Borough v Gateshead	1-2
Stevenage Borough v Kettering Town	3-0
Bath City v Bromsgrove Rovers	1-1, 1-2

Fourth Round

Hyde United v Stevenage Borough	3-2
Gresley Rovers v Macclesfield Town	0-2
Bromsgrove Rovers v Northwich Victoria	0-1
Chorley v Gateshead	3-1

Semi-finals (two legs)

Hyde United v Northwich Victoria	1-2, 0-1
Macclesfield Town v Chorley	3-1, 1-1

FINAL (AT WEMBLEY)

19 MAY

Macclesfield Town (2) 3 *(Payne, Burgess (og), Hemmings)*

Northwich Victoria (0) 1 *(Williams)*　　8672

Macclesfield Town: Price; Edey, Howarth, Payne, Gardiner, Lyons, Sorvel, Wood (Hulme), Hemmings (Cavell), Coates, Power.
Northwich Victoria: Greygoose; Ward, Abel (Steele), Burgess (Simpson), Duffy, Williams, Butler, Walters, Vicary, Cooke, Humphreys.
Referee: M. Reed (Birmingham).

SEMI-PROFESSIONAL INTERNATIONALS

27 Feb

England 4 *(Alford, Hayles, Kimmins, 1 og)*
FAI National League 0　　1034

England: Ryan Price (Macclesfield Town); Paul Webb (Kidderminster Harriers), Nick Ashby (Rushden & Diamonds), Steve Stott (Rushden & Diamonds), Mark Smith (Stevenage Borough), Mark Tucker (Woking), David Venables (Stevenage Borough) [Colin Rose (Witton Albion)], Barry Hayles (Stevenage Borough) [Ged Kimmins (Hyde United)], Carl Alford (Kettering Town) [Phil Power (Macclesfield Town)], Ken Cramman (Gateshead), Lee Hughes (Kidderminster Harriers).

2 Apr

England 3 *(Stott, Alford, Hayles)*
The Netherlands 1　　1660

England: Ryan Price (Macclesfield Town); Paul Webb (Kidderminster Harriers), Nick Ashby (Rushden & Diamonds), Steve Stott (Rushden & Diamonds), Mark Smith (Stevenage Borough), Kevan Brown (Woking), Lee Endersby (Harrow Borough) [David Venables (Stevenage Borough)], Barry Hayles (Stevenage Borough), Carl Alford (Rushden & Diamonds) [Ged Kimmins (Hyde United)], Colin Rose (Witton Albion) [Phil Power (Macclesfield Town)], Lee Hughes (Kidderminster Harriers).

FA CARLSBERG VASE 1995–96

First Qualifying Round

Ponteland United v Billingham Town	4-3
Alnwick Town v Ryehope CA	1-1, 3-2
Eppleton CW v Seaton Delaval Amateurs	2-2, 2-2, 0-2
Jarrow Roofing Boldon CA v Evenwood Town	2-3
West Allotment Celtic v North Shields Athletic	1-0
Harrogate Railway v Shotton Comrades	0-0, 1-2
Shirebrook Town v Cheadle Town	1-3
Salford City v Sheffield	2-1
Castleton Gabriels v Wythenshawe Amateur	2-3
Garforth Town v Nuthall	1-1, 2-3
Maghull v Denaby United	2-3
Priory (Eastwood) withdrew v Harworth CI w.o.	
Grove United v Pontefract Collieries	3-3, 0-1
Heswall v Sandiacre Town	2-1
Tetley Walker v South Normanton Athletic	1-4
Rossington Main v Louth United	2-3
Maltby MW v Kimberley Town	4-2
Hallam v Selby Town	0-1
(at Selby Town)	
Kidsgrove Athletic v Formby	4-1
Hall Road Rangers v Nettleham	0-3
Glasshoughton Welfare v Atherton Collieries	0-0, 3-3, 0-2
Liversedge v Daisy Hill	3-0
Blackpool (Wren) Rovers v Newcastle Town	0-2
Eccleshill United v Worsbro Bridge MW	3-0
Long Eaton United v Merseyside Police	1-2
Tadcaster Albion v Ossett Town	1-2
Tividale v Stafford Town	0-3
Darlaston v Gedling Town	4-2, 3-2
(replay ordered: measurement of one of the goal posts was in breach of the Laws)	
Cradley Town v Holwell Sports	1-0
(at Holwell Sports)	
Boldmere St Michaels v Knypersley Victoria	6-0
Wellingborough Town v Pegasus Juniors	6-0
Rushall Olympic v Highgate United	3-1
Shifnal Town v Northfield Town	5-1
Stourport Swifts v Brierley Hill Town	4-0
Chasetown v Bloxwich Town	1-2
Rocester v Northampton Spencer	1-3
Tiptree United v Sawbridgeworth Town	2-3
Cornard United v Witham Town	1-4
Norwich United v Stamford	2-5
Fakenham Town v Sudbury Wanderers	2-0
(at Watton United)	
March Town United v Hullbridge Sports	4-0
Downham Town v Southend Manor	2-3
(at Southend Manor)	
Haverhill Rovers v Harwich & Parkeston	1-3
Brantham Athletic withdrew v Stowmarket Town w.o.	
Ford United v Tilbury	1-3
Kempston Rovers v Amersham Town	0-1
Milton Keynes v Edgware Town	1-2
Harlow Town v Beaconsfield Sycob	2-0
Hemel Hempstead v Stanstead	1-3
Wealdstone v East Ham United	10-0
Hanwell Town v Bedford Town	1-2
Harpenden Town v Ware	1-4
Totternhoe v Feltham	2-3
Romford v Tufnell Park	2-1
Kingsbury Town v Rayners Lane	2-1
Clapton v Leverstock Green	4-2
Bedfont v Ramsgate	2-3
Ashford Town (Middlesex) v Southwick	6-0
East Grinstead v Folkestone Invicta	1-4
Crowborough Athletic v Lancing	1-2
Bracknell Town v Redhill	2-0
Horsham YMCA v Epsom & Ewell	2-1
Merstham v Chichester City	1-4
Burgess Hill Town v Oakwood	3-0
Saltdean United v Sidley United	2-0
Chipstead v Beckenham Town	3-1
Dartford v Steyning Town	2-2, 4-0
(at Slade Green)	
Eastbourne Town v Littlehampton Town	0-1
(at Littlehampton Town)	
Portfield v Broadbridge Heath	2-0
Furness v Sheppey United	1-1, 3-0
Langney Sports v Mile Oak	3-2
Newhaven v Canterbury City	1-3
Swindon Supermarine v Downton	2-1
Abingdon United v BAT Sports	3-0
Carterton Town v Swanage Town & Herston	2-0

Bemerton Heath Harlequins v Kintbury Rangers	5-2
Didcot Town v Totton AFC	2-3
Sherborne Town v Portsmouth Royal Navy	5-3
Brockenhurst v Ryde	0-4
Cowes Sports v Gosport Borough	1-2
Odd Down v Hallen	1-0
Crediton United v Glastonbury	1-3
Chippenham Town v Clyst Rovers	2-0
St Blazey v DRG AFC	3-0
Shortwood United v Ilfracombe Town	4-0
Exmouth Town v Warminster Town	1-2
Fairford Town v Backwell United	2-3
Bridgwater Town v Larkhall Athletic	2-0

Second Qualifying Round

Easington Colliery v West Allotment Celtic	4-2
Alnwick Town v Esh Winning	1-2
Seaton Delaval Amateurs v Marske United	1-5
Pickering Town v Washington	3-4
Evenwood Town v Crook Town	1-3
Ashington v Darlington Cleveland Social	3-0
Penrith v Willington	0-1
Shotton Comrades v Morpeth Town	1-0
Anfield Plain v Norton & Stockton Ancients	2-1
Benfield Park v Whickham	2-3
Bedlington Terriers v Horden CW	5-1
Stockton v Ponteland United	0-1
Ferryhill Athletic v Yorkshire Amateur	0-1
Wythenshawe Amateur v Arnold Town	3-2
Oakham United v Blidworth MW	2-1
Flixton v Poulton Victoria	2-1
Darwen v Ossett Albion	0-3
Clitheroe v Immingham Town	4-0
Oldham Town v Prescot Cables	3-2
Liversedge v Newcastle Town	0-1
Denaby United v Ossett Town	0-1
Nettleham v Louth United	1-1, 1-0
Merseyside Police v North Ferriby United	2-3
Nantwich Town v Harworth CI	3-0
Selby Town v Armthorpe Welfare	2-0
Ashfield United v Heswall	5-1
Maltby MW v Nuthall	0-2
Salford City v Atherton Collieries	3-0
St Helens Town v Eccleshill United	4-0
Kidsgrove Athletic v Chadderton	3-0
Hatfield Main v Parkgate	7-1
Brigg Town v Rossendale United	9-0
Bootle v Grove United	2-1
Trafford v Staveley MW	4-2
Winterton Rangers v Rainworth MW	3-1
South Normanton Athletic v Hucknall Town	0-5
Heanor Town v Maine Road	2-2, 2-5
Borrowash Victoria v Cheadle Town	1-4
Stapenhill v West Midlands Police	1-2
Sandwell Borough v Lye Town	0-3
Long Buckby v Stourport Swifts	4-1
Shepshed Dynamo v Kings Heath	4-0
Darlaston v Northampton Spencer	4-1
Barwell v Stratford Town	1-0
Blakenall v Desborough Town	1-0
Rushall Olympic v Upton Town	3-1
Cradley Town v Halesowen Harriers	2-3
Shifnal Town v Bolehall Swifts	1-1, 3-1
Anstey Nomads v Radford	4-1
Westfields v Brackley Town	0-2
Knowle v Pershore Town	2-3
Meir KA v Walsall Wood	0-5
Friar Lane OB v Oldbury United	0-1
Stafford Town v Willenhall Town	2-4
(at Willenhall Town)	
Stewarts & Lloyds v Boldmere St Michaels	1-3
Banbury United v Burstall United	2-2, 3-1
Newport Pagnell Town v Wellingborough Town	3-3, 0-3
Bloxwich Town v Wednesfield	3-1
Coggenhoe United v Barrow Town	2-0
Lowestoft Town v Mildenhall Town	5-2
Wotton United v Stowmarket Town	0-1
Ipswich Wanderers v Gorleston	0-3
Warboys Town v March Town United	2-0
Long Sutton Athletic removed from competition v Brightlingsea United w.o.	
Felixstowe Port & Town v Harwich & Parkeston	1-2
Maldon Town v Burnham Ramblers	3-1
Saffron Walden Town v Swaffham Town	1-2

Histon v Fakenham Town	1-3
Woodbridge Town v Chatteris Town	5-0
Soham Town Rangers v Ely City	1-4
Bourne Town v Great Yarmouth Town	2-1
Holbeach United v Sawbridgeworth Town	1-4
Southend Manor v Newmarket Town	0-2
Stamford v St Neots Town	0-1
Great Wakering Rovers v Clacton Town	1-2
Wroxham v Somersham Town	7-3
Eynesbury Rovers v Mirrlees Blackstone	2-2, 1-2
Witham Town v Spalding United	1-1, 1-2
Hertford Town v Eton Manor	3-1
Kingsbury Town v Northwood	0-1
Wootton Blue Cross v Hillingdon Borough	4-3
Brentwood v Welwyn Garden City	1-1, 1-0
Harlow Town v East Thurrock United	5-4
Cockfosters v Edgware Town	1-2
Tilbury v Waltham Abbey	2-1
Hampton v Viking Town	3-0
Brimsdown Rovers v Romford	0-4
Langford v London Colney	3-2
Shillington v Clapton	2-4
Bedford Town v Brook House	1-0
Concord Rangers v Potters Bar Town	2-0
Potton United v Aveley	1-2
Greenwich Borough v Chalfont St Peter	0-1
Letchworth removed from the competition v Leighton Town w.o.	
Flackwell Heath v Hornchurch	1-0
Wealdstone v St Margaretsbury	1-1, 2-0
Cheshunt v Stanstead	1-0
Eton Wick v Stotfold	2-6
Feltham v Biggleswade Town	2-3
Ware v Bowers United	3-0
Southall v Royston Town	1-3
(at Royston Town)	
Amersham Town v Hoddesdon Town	0-0, 0-4
Tring Town v Wingate & Finchley	2-4
Barkingside v Harefield United	2-1
Horsham v Crockenhill	3-0
Dartford v Furness	1-3
Ash United v Shoreham	0-6
West Wickham v Eastbourne United	2-0
Lancing v Corinthian	2-3
Windsor & Eton v Folkestone Invicta	2-2, 5-4
Ramsgate v Hassocks	1-2
Pagham v Arundel	4-3
Thamesmead Town v Chipstead	1-0
Ringmer v Whitstable Town	2-3
Worthing United v Littlehampton Town	1-4
Chichester City v Canterbury City	1-0
Herne Bay v Cray Wanderers	1-0
Slade Green v Leatherhead	5-1
Cove v Wick	0-2
Chatham Town v Camberley Town	5-2
Godalming & Guildford v Three Bridges	1-0
Horsham YMCA v Faversham Town	0-0, 4-3
Croydon Athletic v Bracknell Town	0-0, 3-4
Hailsham Town v Portfield	4-0
Saltdean United v Corinthian-Casuals	3-2
Burgess Hill Town v Selsey	3-1
Cranleigh v Egham Town	3-1
Ashford Town (Middx) v Raynes Park Vale	2-1
Deal Town v Langney Sports	2-1
Netherne v Lewes	3-1
Bicester Town v Ryde	1-1, 1-3
Totton AFC v Milton United	2-1
Gosport Borough v Calne Town	3-1
Lymington AFC v Carterton Town	1-0
Hungerford Town v Wantage Town	3-1
Swindon Supermarine v Thatcham Town	2-1
First Tower United v Bournemouth	1-2
Sandhurst Town v Peppard	2-3
Andover v Abingdon United	3-1
Petersfield Town v North Leigh	0-1
Westbury United v Bemerton Heath Harlequins	0-1
Sherborne Town v Christchurch	3-1
St Blazey v Chippenham Town	0-3
Endsleigh v Bridgwater Town	0-1
Minehead v Warminster Town	0-1
Almondsbury Town v Devizes Town	1-2
Chard Town v Dawlish Town	2-0
Shortwood United v Tuffley Rovers	3-1
Cirencester Town v Old Georgians	1-5
Backwell United v Bristol Manor Farm	3-0
Frome Town v Torpoint Athletic	1-2
Porthleven v Keynsham Town	0-0, 2-4
Bishop Sutton v Welton Rovers	2-2, 1-0
Newquay v Bridport	0-3
Brislington v Torrington	0-2
Truro City v Cadbury Heath	6-2
Odd Down v Glastonbury	2-0
Wellington Town v Liskeard Athletic	2-4
Harrow Hill v Bideford	3-4
Melksham Town v Saltash United	0-1

First Round

Flixton v Glossop North End	3-0
Crook Town v Ashfield United	2-0
Oakham United v Washington	3-2
Eastwood Hanley v Shotton Comrades	2-0
Bedlington Terriers v Kidsgrove Athletic	4-0
Ponteland United v Thackley	2-5
Hatfield Main v Selby Town	0-2
Esh Winning v Winterton Rangers	2-5
Easington Colliery v Wythenshawe Amateur	2-1
Whickham v Marske United	3-2
Newcastle Town v Burscough	3-1
Ashington v North Ferriby United	0-3
Brigg Town v Stocksbridge Park Steels	2-1
Oldham Town v Anfield Plain	6-1
Ossett Town v Willington	7-3
Yorkshire Amateur v Cheadle Town	2-0
Trafford v St Helens Town	2-1
Brandon United v Ossett Albion	0-2
Salford City v Nuthall	0-1
Clitheroe v Bootle	5-1
Nettleham v Nantwich Town	2-0
South Shields v Maine Road	1-6
Hinckley Athletic v Wellingborough Town	3-2
Pelsall Villa v Halesowen Harriers	3-1
Anstey Nomads v Oldbury United	2-1
Oadby Town v Boldmere St Michaels	2-5
West Midlands Police v Pershore Town	3-4
Bloxwich Town v St Andrews	1-0
Rushall Olympic v Cogenhoe United	2-1
Boston Town v Shepshed Dynamo	2-6
Blakenall v Lye Town	1-4
Brackley Town v Banbury United	3-0
Barwell v Dunkirk	1-1, 2-1
Hucknall Town v Shifnall Town	2-1
Darlaston v Walsall Wood	1-1, 1-0
Willenhall Town v Long Buckby	1-0
Harlow Town v Barkingside	2-1
Wroxham v Lowestoft Town	2-0
Brightlingsea United v Newmarket Town	0-1
Clapton v Leighton Town	1-2
Edgware Town v Wingate & Finchley	4-1
Northwood v Stotfold	3-0
St Neots Town v Tilbury	1-4
Harwich & Parkeston v Warboys Town	2-0
Sawbridgeworth Town v Concord Rangers	1-0
Chalfont St Peter v Maldon Town	3-1
Royston Town v Cheshunt	1-2
Hadleigh United v Mirrlees Blackstone	4-2
Bourne Town v Bedford Town	0-1
Langford v Hoddesdon Town	3-1
Wealdstone v Hampton	0-3
Wootton Blue Cross v Flackwell Heath	2-2, 2-1
Romford v Fakenham Town	2-4
Halstead Town v Wisbech Town	1-2
Swaffham Town v Brentwood	2-3
Gorleston v Biggleswade Town	4-0
Collier Row v Clacton Town	8-1
Spalding United v Ely City	1-3
Ware v Basildon United	4-2
Stowmarket Town v Woodbridge Town	2-2, 1-2
Aveley v Hertford Town	2-1
Thamesmead Town v Ashford Town (Middx)	1-0
Slade Green v Saltdean United	5-1
Burgess Hill Town v Bournemouth	2-1
Shoreham v Gosport Borough	1-0
Lymington AFC v Croydon	3-0
Cranleigh v Peppard	3-2
Banstead Athletic v Chatham Town	1-0
Andover v Furness	1-4
Corinthian v Totton AFC	2-1
Whitehawk v Littlehampton Town	5-1
Whitstable Town v Ryde	4-0
Netherne v Bracknell Town	3-4
Stamco v Godalming & Guildford	1-2
Chichester City v Deal Town	2-0
Horsham YMCA v Wick	1-3
Pagham v Windsor & Eton	1-2
Horsham v Hassocks	6-3
West Whickham v Herne Bay	0-3

Tunbridge Wells v Hungerford Town	1-6
Eastleigh v Hailsham Town	2-1
Peacehaven & Telscombe v North Leigh	4-0
Falmouth Town v Liskeard Athletic	3-0
Poulton Rovers v Shortwood United	2-0
Backwell United v Bridport	1-2
Mangotsfield United v Truro City	3-0
Swindon Supermarine v Keynsham Town	1-2
Bideford v Tiverton Town	2-1
Chard Town v Saltash United	2-1
Elmore v Chippenham Town	1-4
Devizes Town v Bemerton Heath Harlequins	0-3
Torpoint Athletic v Odd Down	3-1
Warminster Town v Barnstable Town	3-2
Wimbourne Town v Old Georgians	2-1
Bridgwater Town v Bishop Sutton	1-2
Torrington v Sherbourne Town	3-0

Second Round

Guisborough Town v Crook Town	1-1, 2-1
Yorkshire Amateur v West Auckland Town	1-1, 1-2
Winterton Rangers v North Allerton 1994	1-0
Brigg Town v Tow Law Town	3-0
Selby Town v Billingham Synthonia	3-2
Shildon v Mossley	1-2
Hebburn v Ossett Albion	2-1
Chester Le Street Town v Whickham	5-1
North Ferriby United v Oldham Town	7-0
Durham City v Whitby Town	4-1
Clitheroe v RTM Newcastle	2-1
Seaham Red Star v Peterlee Newtown	2-1
Dunston FB v Cammell Laird	2-0
Prudhoe Town v Goole Town	2-0
Easington Colliery v Ossett Town	2-1
Murton v Consett	2-1
Thackley v Bedlington Terriers	0-1
Nettleham v Pershore Town	1-4
Anstey Nomads v Shepshed Dynamo	4-1
Armitage v Rushall Olympic	0-2
Nuthall v Boldmere St Michaels	1-3
Oakham United v Lye Town	1-4
Raunds Town v Hinckley Athletic	2-2, 3-0
Willenhall Town v Newcastle Town	3-1
Flixton v Hucknall Town	5-1
Belper Town v Bloxwich Town	3-1
Trafford v Darlaston	3-0
Maine Road v Eastwood Hanley	1-4
Pelsall Villa v Barwell	2-4
Northwood v Ely City	2-1
Hampton v Ware	5-2
Brackley Town v Aveley	2-3
Diss Town v Herne Bay	2-0
Burgess Hill Town v Wootton Blue Cross	3-2
Collier Row v Woodbridge Town	5-4
Cheshunt v Bedford Town	2-3
Wisbech Town v Wivenhoe Town	2-3
Slade Green v Newmarket Town	2-0
Arlesey Town v Thamesmead Town	1-2
Metropolitan Police v Canvey Island	1-3
Furness v Sawbridgeworth Town	0-0, 1-1, 2-1
Harwich & Parkeston v Tilbury	2-3
Langford v Whitstable Town	0-1
Wroxham v Brentwood	1-2
Whitehawk v Corinthian	3-1
Burnham v Windsor & Eton	0-4
Gorleston v Fakenham Town	3-2
Peacehaven & Telscombe v Harlow Town	2-0
Hadleigh United v Edgware Town	0-2
Leighton Town v Chalfont St Peter	1-1, 0-2
Keynsham Town v Chard Town	0-1
Lymington AFC v Warminster Town	2-0
Paulton Rovers v Bideford	2-0
Bridport v Bemerton Heath Harlequins	2-0
Horsham v Falmouth Town	0-2
Torpoint Athletic v Eastleigh	1-0
Shoreham v Chichester City	1-2
Dorking v Bishop Sutton	2-2, 0-2
Godalming & Guildford v Mangotsfield United	2-5
Wimborne Town v Torrington	1-2
Cranleigh v Banstead Athletic	0-2
Wick v Chippenham Town	0-1
Taunton Town v Bracknell Town	3-3, 2-1
bye Hungerford Town	

Third Round

Winterton Rangers v Flixton	0-4
Rushall Olympic v Bedlington Terriers	0-4
Brigg Town v Guisborough Town	2-0

Hebburn v Durham City	0-4
Seaham Red Star v Belper Town	1-2
Prudhoe Town v Dunston FB	1-2
North Ferriby United v Eastwood Hanley	4-2
Chester Le Street Town v Lye Town	1-3
Easington Colliery v Anstey Nomads	2-3
Boldmere St Michaels v Trafford	0-2
Barwell v Mossley	3-1
Merton v Selby Town	3-5
Clitheroe v West Auckland Town	6-0
Thamesmead Town v Brentwood	3-1
Willenhall Town v Chalfont St Peter	2-1
Whitstable Town v Peacehaven & Telscombe	0-1
Tilbury v Aveley	2-4
Slade Green v Diss Town	0-2
Northwood v Gorleston	0-1
Wivenhoe Town v Edgware Town	3-1
Raunds Town v Furness	1-1
(abandoned after 105 minutes; frozen pitch) 1-1, 5-2	
Canvey Island v Bedford Town	2-0
Hampton v Collier Row	0-1
Taunton Town v Chippenham Town	4-0
Bridport v Windsor & Eton	2-4
Lymington v Bishop Sutton	4-0
Whitehawk v Banstead Athletic	0-2
Burgess Hill Town v Pershore Town	2-1
Torpoint Athletic v Chard Town	4-2
Paulton Rovers v Falmouth Town	2-0
Torrington v Chichester City	1-2
Hungerford Town v Mangotsfield United	0-0, 1-5

Fourth Round

North Ferriby United v Anstey Nomads	2-3
Lye Town v Barwell	0-2
Clitheroe v Willenhall Town	3-0
Trafford v Selby Town	0-0, 1-1, 3-0
Flixton v Dunston FB	2-0
Durham City v Belper Town	2-3
Brigg Town v Bedlington Terriers	2-1
Burgess Hill Town v Collier Row	0-1
Windsor & Eton v Peacehaven & Telscombe	0-1
Diss Town v Banstead Athletic	1-2
Chichester City v Thamesmead Town	1-3
Wivenhoe Town v Aveley	4-0
Paulton Rovers v Mangotsfield United	0-3
Canvey Island v Gorleston	1-0
Raunds Town v Taunton Town	4-1
Lymington v Torpoint Athletic	1-3

Fifth Round

Raunds Town v Torpoint Athletic	2-0
Wivenhoe Town v Mangotsfield United	2-2, 0-3
Banstead Athletic v Peacehaven & Telscombe	2-3
Collier Row v Anstey Nomads	6-0
Brigg Town v Trafford	1-0
Flixton v Barwell	3-1
Thamesmead Town v Canvey Island	1-2
(at Slade Green)	
Belper Town v Clitheroe	0-3

Sixth Round

Brigg Town v Collier Row	2-0
Mangotsfield United v Raunds Town	2-2, 1-0
Clitheroe v Peacehaven & Telscombe	1-0
Flixton v Canvey Island	3-0

Semi-finals (two legs)

Brigg Town v Flixton	0-0, 1-0
Mangotsfield United v Clitheroe	1-0, 0-2

FINAL (AT WEMBLEY)

12 MAY

Brigg Town (1) 3 *(Stead C 2 (1 pen), Lampkin (og))*
Clitheroe (0) 0   7340

Brigg Town: Gawthorpe; Thompson, Buckley (Mail),
Greaves (Clay), Rogers, Elston, McLean, Stead C, Stead
N (McNally), Roach, Flounders.
Clitheroe: Nash; Rowbotham (Otley), Baron, Westwell,
Lampkin, Grimshaw, Butcher, Rouine, Hill (Dunn),
Darbyshire, Taylor (Smith).
Referee: S. Lodge (Sheffield & Hallam).

FA YOUTH CHALLENGE CUP 1995–96

Extra Preliminary Round
Guisborough Town v Hartlepool United	0-2
Shotton Comrades v Carlisle United	0-3
Marine v Rochdale	0-0, 1-0
Stalybridge Celtic v Southport	0-4
Leigh RMI v Huddersfield Town	0-9
Stockport County v Chorley	3-0
Hinckley Athletic v Chesterfield	2-1
Hinckley Town withdrew v Mansfield Town w.o.	
Bilston Town v Lye Town	1-1, 2-1
Brierley Hill Town v Pelsall Villa	4-1
Rushden & Diamonds v Raunds Town	1-1, 5-1
Saffron Walden Town withdrew v Bury Town w.o.	
Wivenhoe Town v March Town United	10-0
Potters Bar Town v Berkhamsted Town	2-1
St Albans City v Bedford Town	4-3
Southend Manor v Collier Row	1-1, 2-4
Brook House v Clapton	5-1
Hayes v Enfield	0-1
Staines Town v Newport Pagnell Town	4-1
Hillingdon Borough v Hampton	7-1
Tonbridge v Faversham Town	4-0
Ashford Town v Thamesmead Town	0-3
Tooting & Mitcham United v Stamco	3-1
Whitehawk v Bromley	1-2
Horsham YMCA v Crawley Town	1-2
Oakwood v Lewes	4-2
Wokingham Town v Woking	0-1
Walton & Hersham v Chipstead	6-1
Romsey Town v Camberley Town	3-2
(at Camberley Town)	
Havant Town v Bognor Regis Town	0-2
Abingdon Town v Aldershot Town	3-0
Maidenhead v Flackwell Heath	5-0
Mangotsfield United v Forest Green Rovers	2-4
Weston-Super-Mare v Cheltenham Town	2-0

Preliminary Round
Hartlepool United v Harrogate Town	8-0
Morecambe v Lancaster City	1-1, 0-3
Darlington v Scarborough	2-1
Darwen v Carlisle United	1-0
Marine v Bolton Wanderers	1-2
Chester City v Wigan Athletic	4-0
Chadderton v Warrington Town	1-1, 2-2
(aet; Chatterton won 5-3 on penalties)	
Trafford v Southport	0-1
Huddersfield Town v Bury	4-0
Immingham Town v Farsley Celtic	3-1
Port Vale v Northwich Victoria	6-1
Hall Road Rangers v Stockport County	2-2, 2-0
Hinckley Athletic v Lincoln City	1-1, 0-4
Bedworth United w.o. v Leicester United withdrew	
Worksop Town v Birstall United	2-3
Burton Albion v Mansfield Town	0-9
Bilston Town v Nuneaton Borough	1-4
Redditch United v Stourport Swifts	2-2, 1-0
Stratford Town v Chasetown	1-0
VS Rugby v Brierley Hill Town	3-2
Rushden & Diamonds v Corby Town	3-0
Bromsgrove Rovers v Banbury United	0-0, 0-3
Kidderminster Harriers v Kettering Town	1-3
Worcester City v Daventry Town	3-2
Bury Town v Wisbech Town	1-2
Hitchin Town v Royston Town	5-1
Braintree Town v Stevenage Borough	0-1
Bishop's Stortford v Wivenhoe Town	2-5
Potters Bar Town v Hemel Hempstead	5-1
Hornchurch v Cheshunt	2-0
Barnet v Wingate & Finchley	7-0
Hoddesdon Town v St Albans City	1-2
Collier Row v Basildon United	0-3
Concord Rangers withdrew v Waltham Abbey w.o.	
Billericay Town v Tilbury	0-1
Wembley v Canvey Island	3-0
Brook House v Harefield United	1-6
Northwood v Kingsbury Town	7-0
Eton Manor v Leyton Pennant	3-4
(at Barkingside)	
Viking Sports v Enfield	0-0, 0-9
Staines Town v Uxbridge	0-2

Bedfont v Beaconsfield Sycob	1-2
Ruislip Manor v Windsor & Eton	1-3
Bracknell Town v Hillingdon Borough	3-0
Tonbridge v Dover Athletic	3-1
Sittingbourne v Herne Bay	3-0
Hastings Town v Chatham Town	2-0
Gillingham v Thamesmead Town	9-1
Tooting & Mitcham United v Dartford	3-3, 2-1
Redhill v Whyteleafe	2-1
Three Bridges v Whitstable Town	0-3
Sutton United v Bromley	6-0
Crawley Town v Banstead Athletic	1-3
Shoreham v Ringmer	9-0
Carshalton Athletic v Peacehaven & Telscombe	4-0
Southwick v Oakwood	6-1
Woking v Raynes Park Vale	4-0
Croydon v Leatherhead	0-1
Kingstonian v Merstham	2-1
Corinthian-Casuals v Walton & Hersham	5-2
Romsey Town v Farnborough Town	1-4
(at Farnborough Town)	
Weymouth v Bashley	2-1
Waterlooville v Eastleigh	1-2
Bridport v Bognor Regis Town	0-2
Abingdon Town v Marlow	4-2
Thame United v Slough Town	1-6
Basingstoke Town w.o. v Newbury Town removed from competition	
Thatcham Town v Maidenhead United	0-3
Forest Green Rovers v Chippenham Town	3-0
Bristol Rovers v Oxford City	5-0
Gloucester City v Yate Town	6-1
Hereford United v Weston-Super-Mare	5-1

First Qualifying Round
Darwen v Darlington	3-3, 0-5
Lancaster City v Hartlepool United	0-6
Southport v Chadderton	3-0
Chester City v Bolton Wanderers	1-2
Hall Road Rangers v Port Vale	0-0, 1-2
Immingham Town v Huddersfield Town	1-9
(at Huddersfield Town)	
Mansfield Town v Birstall United	6-2
Bedworth United v Lincoln City	2-0
VS Rugby v Stratford Town	0-3
Redditch United v Nuneaton Borough	2-0
Worcester City v Kettering Town	1-5
Banbury United v Rushden & Diamonds	1-2
Wivenhoe Town v Stevenage Borough	2-0
Hitchin Town v Wisbech Town	7-1
St Albans City v Barnet	0-4
Hornchurch v Potters Bar Town	2-4
Wembley v Tilbury	4-3
Waltham Abbey v Basildon United	0-3
Enfield v Leyton Pennant	6-0
Northwood v Harefield United	1-9
Bracknell Town v Windsor & Eton	3-4
Beaconsfield Sycob v Uxbridge	2-5
Gillingham v Hastings Town	7-0
(at Hastings Town)	
Sittingbourne v Tonbridge	6-0
Sutton United v Whitstable Town	4-0
Redhill v Tooting & Mitcham United	0-4
Southwick v Carshalton Athletic	2-4
Shoreham v Banstead Athletic	2-4
Corinthian-Casuals v Kingstonian	2-2, 1-3
Leatherhead v Woking	1-2
Bognor Regis Town v Eastleigh	3-3, 0-1
Weymouth v Farnborough Town	1-6
Maidenhead United v Basingstoke Town	2-2, 2-1
Slough Town v Abingdon Town	5-1
Hereford United v Gloucester City	6-0
Bristol Rovers v Forest Green Rovers	1-2

Second Qualifying Round
Darlington v Hartlepool United	2-2, 1-1
(Hartlepool United won 3-1 on penalties)	
Southport v Bolton Wanderers	3-2
Port Vale v Huddersfield Town	1-1, 0-5
Mansfield Town v Bedworth United	2-1
Stratford Town v Nuneaton Borough	0-1

Kettering Town v Rushden & Diamonds	0-7
Wivenhoe Town v Hitchin Town	3-2
Barnet v Potters Bar Town	5-0
Wembley v Basildon United	1-2
Enfield v Harefield United	2-2, 3-1
Windsor & Eton v Uxbridge	2-4
Gillingham v Sittingbourne	2-1
Sutton United v Tooting & Mitcham United	4-1
Carshalton Athletic v Banstead Athletic	2-4
Kingstonian v Woking	0-5
Eastleigh v Farnborough Town	3-1
Maidenhead United v Slough Town	0-3
Hereford United v Forest Green Rovers	4-2

First Round

Rotherham United v Hartlepool United	1-0
Southport v Burnley	1-2
Tranmere Rovers v Wrexham	2-2, 3-1
Newcastle United v Blackpool	3-1
Grimsby Town v Oldham Athletic	3-4
Derby County v Scunthorpe United	3-1
Preston North End v Huddersfield Town	1-1, 1-2
Everton v Notts County	1-0
Blackburn Rovers v Sheffield Wednesday	2-0
Doncaster Rovers v Hull City	1-0
Leeds United v Barnsley	3-1
Basildon United v Chelsea	2-2, 1-0
Boreham Wood v Enfield	0-3
Wivenhoe Town v Northampton Town	0-1
Wycombe Wanderers v Watford	2-2, 1-3
Shrewsbury Town v Cambridge United	3-0
Wolverhampton Wanderers v Birmingham City	5-6
Leicester City v Nuneaton Borough	10-0
Walsall v Mansfield Town	1-1, 1-0
Barnet v Leighton Town	7-1
Boldmere St Michaels v Rushden & Diamonds	4-1
Cambridge v Luton Town	1-9
Colchester United v Peterborough United	2-4
AFC Bournemouth v Swansea City	1-2
Torquay United v Welling United	2-0
Southampton v Oxford United	1-1, 2-1
Woking v Croydon Athletic	5-1
Sutton United v Eastleigh	1-2
Reading v Cardiff City	0-2
Slough Town v Hereford United	2-4
Gillingham v Fulham	1-0
Dulwich Hamlet v Exeter City	0-0, 2-3
Uxbridge v Banstead Athletic	1-2
Plymouth Argyle v Charlton Athletic	1-4

(Charlton Athletic removed for fielding an ineligible player; Plymouth Argyle awarded the tie)

Second Round

Manchester City v Huddersfield Town	3-0
Leeds United v Middlesbrough	0-1
Everton v Tranmere Rovers	1-3
Oldham Athletic v York City	3-2
Sheffield United v Newcastle United	2-1
Sunderland v Crewe Alexandra	4-0
Manchester United v Rotherham United	3-1
Derby County v Doncaster Rovers	3-5
Burnley v Stoke City	1-0
Liverpool v Bradford City	4-2
Blackburn Rovers v Nottingham Forest	5-1
Ipswich Town v Walsall	0-0, 1-0
Peterborough United v Norwich City	1-1, 1-2
Barnet v Watford	0-4
Birmingham City v Basildon United	5-0
Tottenham Hotspur v Shrewsbury Town	4-1
West Ham United v Aston Villa	3-0
Leyton Orient v Enfield	0-2
Leicester City v Luton Town	1-2
Northampton Town v West Bromwich Albion	0-1
Coventry City v Arsenal	1-2
Boldmere St Michaels v Southend United	2-1
Wimbledon v Brighton & Hove Albion	1-0
Gillingham v Woking	1-3

Brentford v Exeter City	4-0
Swindon Town v Crystal Palace	0-2
Plymouth Argyle v Eastleigh	1-1, 3-1
Torquay United v Hereford United	0-1
Swansea City v Portsmouth	0-0, 1-3
Millwall v Southampton	3-2
Queens Park Rangers v Cardiff City	1-0
Bristol City v Banstead Athletic	2-1

Third Round

Norwich City v Burnley	2-1
Liverpool v Luton Town	5-0
Boldmere St Michaels v Manchester City	0-3
West Bromwich Albion v Sheffield United	1-2
Blackburn Rovers v Tranmere Rovers	0-2
Doncaster Rovers v Oldham Athletic	0-5
Sunderland v Manchester United	1-4
Ipswich Town v Middlesbrough	2-0
Queens Park Rangers v Brentford	2-0
Crystal Palace v Bristol City	7-0
Portsmouth v Watford	1-2
Hereford United v Enfield	1-1, 2-0
Plymouth Argyle v Tottenham Hotspur	2-1
Woking v West Ham United	0-3
Arsenal v Wimbledon	3-4
Millwall v Birmingham City	5-2

Fourth Round

Plymouth Argyle v Crystal Palace	0-2
Hereford United v Manchester City	1-2
Oldham Athletic v Millwall	2-0
Liverpool v Sheffield United	3-2
Manchester United v Norwich City	1-0
Queens Park Rangers v West Ham United	1-4
Wimbledon v Ipswich Town	2-2, 2-1
Tranmere Rovers v Watford	1-1, 1-4

Fifth Round

Liverpool v Manchester United	3-2
Oldham Athletic v West Ham United	1-2
Crystal Palace v Watford	2-0
Manchester City v Wimbledon	1-3

Semi-finals (two legs)

Liverpool v Crystal Palace	4-2, 3-3
West Ham United v Wimbledon	2-1, 3-2

FINAL FIRST LEG

30 APR

West Ham U (0) 0

Liverpool (1) 2 *(Newby, Larmour)*   15,386

West Ham U: Finn; Coyne, Ferdinand, Partridge, Moore, Omoyinmi, Lampard, McFarlane, Keith, Boylan, Hodges.
Liverpool: Naylor; Prior, Brazier, Carragher, Roberts, Quinn S, Thutson, Quinn M, Cassidy, Newby (Larmour), Parkinson.
Referee: M. Reilly (West Riding).

FINAL SECOND LEG

17 MAY

Liverpool (1) 2 *(Owen, Quinn S)*

West Ham U (1) 1 *(Lampard)*   20,600

Liverpool: Naylor; Prior, Brazier, Carragher, Roberts, Quinn S, Quinn M, Thompson, Cassidy (Turkington), Owen, Newby (Parkinson).
West Ham U: Finn; Moore, Coyne, McFarlane, Partridge (Bowen), Keith, Ferdinand, Lampard, Boylan (O'Reilly), Hodges, Omoyinmi.
Referee: M. Reilly (West Riding).

FA SUNDAY CUP 1995-96

First Round

Mitre withdrew v Stockton Roseworth Social w.o.	
A3 w.o. v Etnaward withdrew	
Albion Sports v Nenthead	3-0
Townley v Northwood	3-3, 2-4
Mode Force Boulevard v Boundary	3-2
Lobster v Eden Vale	0-4
Baildon Athletic v Seaton Sluice SC	2-5
Bolton Woods v Dock	1-1, 1-1
(Dock won 3-2 on penalties)	
Manfast v Sandon	0-1
Littlewoods Athletic v Clubmoor Nalgo	1-2
SDV v The Tiger	3-5
East Bowling Unity v Hartlepool Staincliffe Hotel	0-2
BRNESC v Nicosia	2-3
Dudley & Weetslade v Britannia	2-1
Croxteth & Gilmoss RBL v Fiddlers	4-1
Caldway v Almithak	3-2
Stanley Road v Walford Maritime	2-1
Salerno v Hartlepool Rovers	8-1
Waterloo Social Club Blyth withdrew v Queens Park AFC w.o.	
Grosvenor Park v Courage	1-1, 2-1
Leicester City Bus v Sawston Keys	1-4
Willen v BRSC Aiden	1-0
Erdington Cosmos Swan v Evesham WMC	8-1
Altone Steels v Marston Sports	1-6
Park Inn v Hemel Hempstead Social	5-0
Girton Eagles v Slade Celtic	0-2
Hanham Sunday v Celtic SC (Luton)	0-1
Hundred Acre w.o. v Sun Kislingbury withdrew	
Clifton Albion v Brookvale Athletic	1-1, 0-4
Birmingham Celtic v Ouzavich	1-2
St Clements Hospital v Watford Labour	2-1
Sandwell v Olympic Star	2-1
Dereham Hobbies v Roofwork	0-1
Poringland Wanderers v St Joseph's (South Oxhey)	2-1
Coach & Horses v Belstone	1-0
Melton Youth Old Boys v Heathfield	2-2, 0-2
Pitsea v Continental	3-1
Holderness United v Bedfont Sunday	1-0
Morden Nomads v St Joseph's (Bristol)	2-2, 0-0
(Morden Nomads won 4-3 on penalties)	
Reading Borough v Fryerns Community	0-4
Leavesden Sports & Social v Charlton Royal 89	6-1
Inter Royalle v Forest Athletic	1-2
Park Royals v Oakwood Sports	1-0
British Rail SA withdrew v Caversham Park w.o.	
Northfield Rangers v Cherry Tree (Warley)	0-3
Cavaliers v Hallen United	0-1
Ford Basildon v South Croydon	9-0
Merton Admiral withdrew v Oxford Road Social w.o.	
(byes: Berner United, Microgen Breakspear & Shankhouse United)	

Second Round

Park Inn v Hartlepool Lion Hotel	1-1, 1-2
Seaton Sluice SC v Caldway	5-1
Stanley Road v Newfield	5-1
Lodge Cottrell v Brook Vale Athletic	2-1
Dudley & Weetslade v Eden Vale	4-1
Sandon v Club Moor Nalgo	0-1
Croxteth & Gilmoss RBL v A3	3-0
Stockton Roseworth Social v Dock	4-0
Oakenshaw v Salerno	0-2

Allerton v Northwood	5-1
Hartlepool Staincliffe Hotel v Shankhouse United	0-2
Mode Force Boulevard v The Tiger	1-2
Humbledon Plains Farm v Nicosia	1-3
Seymour v Marston Sports	1-2
Lion Hotel v Queens Park AFC	0-0, 1-2
Albion Sports v Sandwell	4-2
Microgen Breakspear v Slade Celtic	0-3
Hundred Acre v Erdington Cosmos Swan	2-1
Berner United v Cherry Tree (Warley)	2-2, 2-1
Hammer v Roofwork	3-0
Heathfield v Coach & Horses	4-0
Pouringland Wanderers v Sawston Keys	1-3
Grosvenor Park v Fryerns Community	4-1
Caversham Park v Ouzavich	0-2
Park Royals v Oxford Road Social	2-1
Lebeq Tavern v Pitsea	3-1
Morden Nomads v St Clements Hospital	0-1
Hallen United v Capel Plough	0-2
Willen v Theale (Sunday)	3-2
Ford Basildon v Leavesden Sports & Social	6-2
Forrest Athletic v Holdeness United	3-0
Celtic SC (Luton) v St Josephs (Luton)	0-0, 2-6

Third Round

Queens Park AFC v Stanley Road	2-1
Nicosia v Lodge Cotterell	3-1
Marston Sports v Seaton Sluice SC	6-2
Shankhouse United v Dudley & Weetslade	0-7
Stockton Roseworth Social v Allerton	2-1
Croxteth & Gilmoss RBL v Albion Sports	5-1
The Tiger v Hartlepool Lyon Hotel	1-3
Salerno v Clubmoor Nalgo	1-0
Forest Athletic v Berner United	1-0
Willen v Hammer	2-0
Ford Basildon v Hundred Acre	2-1
St Clements Hospital v Heathfield	3-0
Ouzavich v Lebeq Tavern	2-2, 1-5
Grosvenor Park v St Josephs (Luton)	2-4
Capel Plough v Slade Celtic	4-1
Park Royals v Sawston Keys	4-1

Fourth Round

Croxteth & Gilmoss RBL v Stockton Roseworth Social	3-1
Nicosia v Marston Sports	1-0
Hartlepool Lion Hotel v Dudley & Weetslade	2-1
Salerno v Queens Park AFC	1-0
Lebeq Tavern v St Josephs (Luton)	1-2
Forest Athletic v Park Royals	1-6
Ford Basildon v Willen	0-3
St Clements Hospital v CapelPlough	1-0

Fifth Round

Hartlepool Lion Hotel v Croxteth & Gilmoss RBL	0-4
Salerno v Nicosia	1-0
Park Royals v St Josephs (Luton)	1-2
St Clements Hospital v Willen	1-2

Semi-finals

Croxteth & Gilmoss RBL v Salerno	4-3
St Josephs (Luton) v Willen	2-0

Final

St Josephs (Luton) v Croxteth & Gilmoss RBL	2-1

FA COUNTY YOUTH CHALLENGE CUP
1995–96

First Round

Cumberland v Lincolnshire	2-1
Nottingham v Lancashire	1-3
Westmorland v East Riding	2-4
Sheffield & Hallamshire v Birmingham	1-3
Cambridgeshire v Herefordshire	1-1, 2-3
Northamptonshire v Staffordshire	2-1
Berks & Bucks v London	2-0
Huntingdonshire v Oxfordshire	0-2
Sussex v Army	3-0
Kent v Bedfordshire	1-4
Gloucestershire v Dorset	1-0
Devon v Wiltshire	3-2

Second Round

Northumberland v West Riding	4-0
Liverpool v Manchester	6-0
Cumberland v Durham	0-4
Lancashire v Shropshire	4-1
East Riding v Cheshire	2-2, 0-1
Birmingham v North Riding	4-1
Herefordshire v Derbyshire	4-2
Northamptonshire v Worcestershire	1-1, 1-0
Berks & Bucks v Leicestershire & Rutland	5-0
Essex v Norfolk	6-2
Oxfordshire v Surrey	1-2
Sussex v Hertfordshire	3-3, 2-1
Bedfordshire v Suffolk	2-1

Gloucestershire v Middlesex	2-2
(abandoned in extra time), 4-0	
Devon v Hampshire	2-1
Cornwall v Somerset	1-2

Third Round

Durham v Herefordshire	3-1
Cheshire v Northumberland	3-3, 2-0
Liverpool v Lancashire	2-1
Birmingham v Northamptonshire	3-2
Surrey v Devon	2-1
Bedfordshire v Berks & Bucks	1-2
Essex v Sussex	5-1
Gloucestershire v Somerset	1-1, 4-1

Fourth Round

Durham v Berks & Bucks	3-0
Birmingham v Essex	4-3
Surrey v Liverpool	3-2
Gloucestershire v Cheshire	2-1

Semi-finals

Durham v Surrey	2-1
Gloucestershire v Birmingham	7-0

Final

Gloucestershire v Durham	0-1

FA XI REPRESENTATIVE MATCHES

14 Oct

FA XI 0

Northern Premier League 2   300

FA XI: Paul Collings (Altrincham) [Dean Greygoose]; Jamie Bates (Runcorn), Steve Prindiville (Halifax Town), Alex Jones (Stalybridge Celtic), Leroy Dove (Southport), Steve Haw (Southport) [David Gamble (Southport)], Stuart Terry (Altrincham), Martin McDonald (Macclesfield Town), Michael Midwood (Halifax Town) [Darren Lyons (Macclesfield Town)], Mick Carmody (Altrincham) [Brian Butler (Northwich Victoria)], Chris Sharratt (Altrincham).

9 Jan

FA XI 2 *(Carty, Street)*

British Students 0   301

FA XI: Darren Steadman (Kidderminster Harriers) [Nick Goodwin (Telford United)]; Marcus Bignot (Telford United) [Paul Carty (Hednesford Town)], Kevin Collins (Hednesford Town), John Deakin (Kidderminster Harriers), Wayne Simpson (Hednesford Town), Craig Gaunt (Bromsgrove Rovers), Adie Smith (Bromsgrove Rovers) [Martin Myers (Telford United)], Mark Yates (Kidderminster Harriers), John Hunt (Bromsgrove Rovers) [Paul Davies (Kidderminster Harriers)], Lee Hughes (Kidderminster Harriers) [Tyrone Street (Hednesford Town)], Joe O'Connor (Hednesford Town).

16 Jan

FA XI 1 *(Holmes)*

Combined Services 0   250

FA XI: Tony Pennock (Yeovil Town) [Russell Bowles (Cinderford Town)]; Jerry Gill (Bath City) [Lee Francis (Yeovil Town)], Micky Engwell (Yeovil Town), Chris Banks (Cheltenham Town) [Nick Dunphy (Cheltenham Town)], Mark Freeman (Gloucester City), Darren Wright (Cheltenham Town), Keith Knight (Gloucester City), Paul Chenoweth (Cheltenham Town), Jason Eaton (Cheltenham Town) [Lee Howell (Cheltenham Town)], Tommy Killick (Dorchester), David Holmes (Gloucester City).

UNIVERSITY FOOTBALL 1995–96

112th UNIVERSITY MATCH
(at Craven Cottage, Fulham, att 1260)
Oxford 2, Cambridge 1 (h-t 1-0)

Oxford: Novy; Parker, Buckley, Washington, Warman, Loosemore, Smith, Bissell, Hanssen J, Goff, Hanssen H. *Scorers:* Loosemore, Smith.
Cambridge: Park; Ball, Henderson, Budd, Thomson, White, Pett, Hayward, Evans, Miller, Morrow. *Scorer:* Miller *(pen).*
Cambridge have not won the fixture for eight years, but still lead Oxford by 45 wins to 42 with 25 drawn.

UNIVERSITY OF LONDON INTER-COLLEGIATE LEAGUE

Premier Division	P	W	D	L	F	A	Pts
Queen Mary Westfield College	14	11	1	2	47	18	34
Goldsmiths' College	14	10	3	1	39	7	33
London School of Economics	14	8	1	5	31	22	25
Royal Holloway College	14	6	2	6	31	19	20
King's College	14	5	1	8	21	36	16
Imperial College	14	4	3	7	27	37	15
University College	14	2	4	8	19	44	10
Ch. Cross & W'min. Hosp. Med. Sch.	14	2	1	11	13	45	7

Division One	P	W	D	L	F	A	Pts
Royal Holloway College Res.	18	15	0	3	53	18	45
Univ. Coll. & Middx. Hos. Med. Sch.	18	14	2	2	63	19	44
Queen Mary Westfield College Res.	18	13	2	3	54	17	41
Royal Holloway College 3rd	18	11	0	7	44	26	33
University College Res.	18	7	0	11	31	51	21
St George's Hospital Med. Sch.	18	4	6	8	25	41	18
London Sch. Economics Res.	18	5	1	12	39	68	16
R. Lon'n & St. Bart's Hos. M Colls.	18	4	3	11	29	43	15
Imperial College Res.	18	3	5	10	23	45	14
Royal Free Hosp. Sch. Med.	18	3	3	12	20	53	12

Division Two	P	W	D	L	F	A	Pts
King's College Hosp. Med. Sch.	18	14	1	3	65	19	43
U.M.D.S.	18	14	0	4	57	20	42
London Sch. Economics 3rd	18	11	0	7	45	33	33
Royal Veterinary College	18	11	0	7	41	37	33
St Mary's Hospital Med. Sch.	18	10	2	6	54	31	32
King's College Res.	18	10	1	7	38	42	31
Imperial College 3rd	18	5	2	11	27	44	17
Royal Holloway College 4th	18	5	1	12	30	47	16
Sch. Slavonic & E. Europ'n Studies	18	3	1	14	21	51	10
University College 3rd	18	2	2	14	21	75	8

Division Three–10 Teams–won by Goldsmiths' College Res.
Division Four–10 Teams–won by St George's Hospital MS Res.
Division Five–8 Teams–won by University College 6th
Division Six–9 Teams–won by Wye College, Kent

Challenge Cup–Goldsmiths' College 1*:5p, London School of Economics 1*:4p
Upper Reserves Cup–R. Holloway College 3rd 1*, Queen Mary Westfield College Res. 2*
Lower Reserves Cup–L.S.E. 5th 1, Royal Holloway College 5th 2
United Hospitals:
Senior Cup–St. Mary's Hospital Medical School 6, Charing Cross & Westminster Hospital Medical School 4

Junior Cup–Middlesex & University College Hospital Res. 6, U.M.D.S. 3rd 1

*(*after extra time)*

BRITISH UNIVERSITIES SPORTS ASSOCIATION CHAMPIONSHIP (Men)

Finals

First XI
Roehampton 2, Edinburgh 1 *aet*

Second XI
Crewe & Alsager 2, Luton 1

Third XI
Leeds 1, Staffordshire (Stoke) 0

Fourth XI
Chichester Inst 1, Loughborough 1
(Chichester Inst won 3-0 on penalties)

Home Nations Tournament
England 2, N Ireland 2

England 7, Scotland 1
England 2, Wales 1
N Ireland 1, Scotland 0
N Ireland 1, Wales 2
Scotland 0, Wales 3
Winners: England

BUSA Development Squad
(Reims, June 1996)
BUSA 0, German Universities 1
BUSA 3, Swiss Universities 1

Representative matches (Women)
England 1, Bradford City 4
Scotland 3, Wales 2
England 7, Scotland 1
England 7, Wales 1

SCHOOLS FOOTBALL 1995–96

ESFA FUJI FILM TROPHY

SEMI-FINALS:
Hackney & Tower Hamlets 1, Bury 2
Walsall 1, East Berkshire 0

FINAL: 1ST LEG
Bury 1, Walsall 0
Played at Bury FC 23 April

FINAL: 2ND LEG
Walsall 1, Bury 1
Played at Walsall FC 13 May

ESFA SNICKERS U.19 COMPETITION
(In association with Channel 4)

SEMI-FINALS:
Ridge Danyers College, Stockport 2, Franklin College, Grimsby 0
Palmers College, Grays 2, Fareham College 1

FINAL:
Ridge Danyers College, Stockport 2, Palmers College, Grays 3
Played at Stockport County FC on 16 April

ESFA GOODYEAR U.16 COMPETITION

SEMI-FINALS:
St Francis Xavier, Liverpool 3, George Stephenson, Newcastle 1
Larkmead School, Abingdon 1.3, Bungay High School 1.0

FINAL:
St Francis Xavier, Liverpool 0, Larkmead School, Abingdon 2
Played at Wolverhampton Wanderers FC on 28 April

ESFA PREMIER LEAGUE U.16 INTER COUNTY COMPETITION

SEMI-FINALS:
Hertfordshire 5, Devon 0
West Midlands 5, Humberside 3

FINAL:
Hertfordshire 2, West Midlands 0
Played at Sixfields Stadium, Northampton on 15 May

ESFA PREMIER LEAGUE U.19 INTER COUNTY COMPETITION

SEMI-FINALS:
Hampshire 2, Essex 3
Northumberland 5, Merseyside 0

FINAL:
Essex 1, Northumberland 1
Played at West Ham United FC on 23 April

ESFA VIMTO GIRLS U.16 COMPETITION

SEMI-FINALS:
West Bridgeford Comp 4, Archbishop Grimshaw 2
Sir John Bosco 1, Corfe Hills School 1
Sir John Bosco won on penalties

FINAL:
West Bridgeford Comp 3, Sir John Bosco 2
Played at Notts County FC on 1 May

ESFA WAGON WHEELS 5-A-SIDE COMPETITION

GIRLS FINAL:
Queens Park Community School, Brent 3, George Abbot School, Guildford 2

BOYS FINAL:
Bradon Forest School, Swindon 2, Woodside School, Newham 1
Staged at Aston Villa Sports Centre on 20 April

ESFA PREDATOR PREMIER 7-A-SIDE TROPHY

SEMI-FINALS:
Vale of White Horse 2, East Riding 0
Sutton 2, Wakefield 0

THIRD PLACE:
Wakefield 1, East Riding 0

FINAL:
Sutton 2, Vale of White Horse 0
Played at Wembley Stadium on 9 March

ESFA PREDATOR 6-A-SIDE TROPHY

SEMI-FINALS:
Kingmoor Junior School, Carlisle 1, Field End Junior School, Ruislip 1*
Grange Junior School, Swindon 0, Sneyd Green Primary, Stoke 2
* Won on corners gained

THIRD PLACE:
Kingmoor Junior School 3, Grange Junior School, Swindon 0

FINAL:
Sneyd Green Primary 3, Field End Junior School 0
Played at Old Trafford, Manchester on 4 May

BOODLE & DUNTHORNE INDEPENDENT SCHOOLS FA CUP 1995–96

FIRST ROUND:
Bye—Chigwell
Bye—Kimbolton
Repton 2 Winchester 2 *aet*
  (Winchester won 4-3 on penalties)
Charterhouse 0 Westminster 1
Bolton 3 Bradfield 0
Highgate 4 Hulme GS 5
QEGS, Blackburn 5 St Edmund's, Canterbury 0
Forest 6 Wellingborough 1
KES, Witley 0 Manchester GS 3

Shrewsbury 0 Brentwood 4
Bury GS 3 Batley GS 2 *aet*
Malvern 0 Ardingly 1
Latymer Upper 3 Oswestry 2
St Bede's 3 Aldenham 0
King's, Chester 0 Wolverhampton GS 1
Eton 0 Lancing 3

SECOND ROUND:
Bolton 1 Manchester GS 2 *aet*
QEGS, Blackburn 8 Winchester 2

Hulme GS 1 Wolverhampton GS 1 *aet*
(Hulme won 5-4 on penalties)
Latymer Upper 4 Kimbolton 0
Westminster 0 Brentwood 1
Bury GS 2 St Bede's 1
Ardingly 2 Forest 0
Lancing 4 Chigwell 1

THIRD ROUND:
Ardingly 0 Bury GS 1
Lancing 2 Latymer Upper 2 *aet*
(Latymer Upper won 4-3 on penalties)
Brentwood 2 Hulme GS 1
Manchester GS 1 QEGS, Blackburn 2

SEMI-FINALS:
QEGS, Blackburn 2 Latymer Upper 1 *aet*
Bury GS 1 Brentwood 1 *aet*
(Bury GS won 4-1 on penalties)

FINAL:
Bury GS (0) 0 *at Chester City FC*
QEGS, Blackburn (1) 1 *(McVerry)*
Bury GS: Willcock; Kirkby (Tomkinson), Cockcroft, Lawton, Grindod (Lingard), Watson (Jeffries), Mosawy, Smith, Tuke, Hyde, Rajasooriyar.
QEGS, Blackburn: Haworth; Connolly, Simpson, Gough, Hopkinson, Pimblett, Maclean (Collins), Peterson, McVerry, Fayomi, Penswick.
Referee: S. Lodge.

INTERNATIONAL PROGRAMME 1995–96

UNDER 15
England 2, Wales 1–Portsmouth, 2 February
England 0, N. Ireland 0–Middlesbrough, 23 February
England 2, Spain 3–Wembley 9 March
England 2, Hungary 3–Wolverhampton 15 March
England 1, Scotland 1–Kilmarnock, 28 March
England 1, Holland 0–Manchester, 4 May
England 0, Germany 3–Berlin, 7 May
England 1, France 2–Epernay, 29 May
Overall Record....Played 8, Won 2, Drew 2, Lost 4, Goals For 9, Goals Against 13
Goals: Wheatcroft (3), Parker (2), Taylor, Jeffers, Standing, Foster

UNDER 18
England 2, Belgium 2–Oostduinkerke, 21 February
England 3, Holland 3–Carlisle, 28 February
England 1, Switzerland 3–Gland, 26 March
England 4, Wales 0–Luton, 10 May
Overall Record....Played 4, Won 1, Drew 2, Lost 1, Goals For 10, Goals Against 8
Goals: Innes (3), Sutton (3), Fotiadis (2), Sadler, own goal

VICTORY SHIELD 1995–96

England 2, Wales 1–Portsmouth, 2 February
Wales 2, N. Ireland 1–Wrexham, 16 February
England 0, N. Ireland 0–Middlesbrough, 23 February
Wales 1, Scotland 4–Swansea, 8 March
N. Ireland 1, Scotland 0–Belfast, 22 March
Scotland 1, England 1–Kilmarnock, 28 March

	P	W	D	L	F	A	Pts
England	3	1	2	0	3	2	4
Scotland	3	1	1	1	5	3	3
N. Ireland	3	1	1	1	2	2	3
Wales	3	1	0	2	4	7	2

CENTENARY SHIELD 1995–96

Semi-finals
N. Ireland 2, Wales 1–Ballyclare, 15 March
Switzerland 3, England 1–Gland, 26 March

Play-off for 3rd place
England 4, Wales 0–Luton, 10 May

Final
N. Ireland 1, Switzerland 0–Belfast, 25 April

THE ENGLISH SCHOOLS' FA UNDER 18 INTERNATIONAL SQUAD 1995–96
Photographed during the final Coaching Weekend at Lilleshall National Sports Centre in February 1996
Back row: Craig Riley, Robert Walker, Mark Simpson, Jonathan Preston.
Middle row: Mr David Cook (Assistant Manager), Peter Sutton, David Sadler, Robert Clarke, Adam Clementson, Andrew Fotiadis, Mr Frank Melia (Physiotherapist), Mr Paul Brackwell (Team Manager).
Front row: Stuart Langrish, Russell Penn, Marc Burrow, Mr M.R. Duffield (ESFA Chairman), Mark Stevens, Andrew Potter, Steven Adams.

AVON INSURANCE COMBINATION

After the previous season's excitement when Tottenham Hotspur won the Avon Insurance Combination title by defeating Charlton Athletic in the very last match of the entire season, the 1995–96 Championship became a neck and neck struggle between Spurs, seeking to retain their title, and QPR who finally prevailed by a two point margin.

This was QPR's first Football Combination Championship since 1982–83 and was earned on the back of a run of 13 consecutive victories from January to April. Spurs put up a strong fight to win their fifth AIC title in the last decade and also put together a string of 11 wins in a row. However shock home defeats by Oxford United and Swindon Town put paid to their chances.

Arsenal and Wimbledon both had excellent seasons, finishing in third and fourth places respectively.

The main purpose of the Avon Insurance Combination is to provide a platform for the stars of the future and many players emerged who are likely to become household names.

Chris Plummer of QPR, Steve Slade of Spurs, Jason Euell of Wimbledon, Muzzie Izzet of Chelsea and David Connolly of Watford are just five of many who could be highlighted.

Established stars such as David Platt, Darren Anderton and Illie Dumitrescu also graced the Combination with their presence last season.

Norwich City won the Avon Insurance Enterprise award for the Family Night Football initiative, which saw an average crowd of over 2000 attracted to Carrow Road for AIC games, with two crowds in excess of 3000.

The 1996–97 season will see a restructuring of the Avon Insurance Combination, with Birmingham City, Plymouth Argyle and Torquay United and the three non-league teams, Bath City, Cheltenham Town and AFC Newport leaving the League and the three remaining AIC Division Two teams, Cardiff City, AFC Bournemouth and Swansea City joining a 23 team First Division. Teams will meet each other once. A Cup Competition will also be run and automatic promotion and relegation introduced, with the bottom seven teams being relegated to a newly reformed Division Two for the 1997–98 season along with other accepted high quality applicants.

Queens Park Rangers Avon Insurance Combination Champions

Appearances: Allen 7; Bardsley 3; Barker 2; Brazier 25+1; Brevett 5; Bruce 3+4; Challis 21+1; Charles 18+7; Conlon 1; Cross 16+3; Dichio 6; Dykstra 7; Gallen 8; Goodridge 25; Graham 28+5; Hateley 4; Hodge 12; Holloway 3; Hurst 8+1; Impey 3; Kingsmith 1+1; Langley +1; Lockwood 17+6; McDermott 34+4; McDonald 8; Maddix 5; Mahoney-Johnson 24+2; Murray F 2; Murray P 4+1; Nolan +1; Osborn 4; Parmenter 17+5; Penrice 6; Perry 2+1; Plummer 26; Power 18+1; Quashie 6+2; Ready 4; Roberts 23; Valk 1; Yates 9; Zelic 2.

Goals: Charles 11, Mahoney-Johnson 9, Parmenter 8, Gallen 6, Allen 5, Goodridge 5, Brazier 4, Plummer 4, Hateley 3, Penrice 3, Dichio 2, Graham 2, Hodge 2, Conlon 1, Lockwood 1, Murray P 1, Osborn 1, Perry 1, Quashie 1, Ready 1, Valk 1, Yates 1, own goals 4.

Division One

	P	W	D	L	F	A	Pts
Queens Park Rangers	38	27	3	8	77	43	84
Tottenham Hotspur	38	26	4	8	80	33	82
Arsenal	38	22	10	6	82	37	76
Wimbledon	38	21	5	12	82	57	68
Norwich City	38	20	7	11	72	48	67
Crystal Palace	38	16	12	10	50	41	60
Luton Town	38	17	7	14	56	48	58
West Ham United	38	15	9	14	60	63	54
Chelsea	38	14	11	13	50	47	53
Southampton	38	13	11	14	48	56	50
Charlton Athletic	38	14	8	16	52	65	50
Ipswich Town	38	13	10	15	62	62	49
Bristol City	38	13	8	17	41	52	47
Portsmouth	38	12	10	16	47	57	46
Millwall	38	11	10	17	53	68	43
Brighton & Hove Albion	38	10	8	20	48	76	38
Oxford United	38	8	12	18	50	86	36
Bristol Rovers	38	9	6	23	47	79	33
Swindon Town	38	6	13	19	35	66	31
Watford	38	8	6	24	46	74	30

Division Two

	P	W	D	L	F	A	Pts
AFC Bournemouth	16	10	3	3	36	17	33
Swansea City	16	9	4	3	32	21	31
Birmingham City	16	8	2	6	32	25	26
Plymouth Argyle	16	7	4	5	39	18	25
Cardiff City	16	5	8	3	24	22	23
Bath City	16	5	5	6	21	33	20
Torquay United	16	5	4	7	29	31	19
Newport County	16	4	4	8	16	33	16
Cheltenham Town	16	1	2	13	10	39	5

League Cup

Group A

	P	W	D	L	F	A	Pts
Plymouth Argyle	6	5	0	1	20	8	15
AFC Bournemouth	6	3	1	2	13	10	10
Torquay United	6	2	0	4	12	23	6
Bath City	6	1	1	4	9	13	4

Group B

	P	W	D	L	F	A	Pts
Birmingham City	8	5	1	2	21	8	16
Cheltenham Town	8	4	2	2	15	19	14
Newport County	8	3	1	4	12	16	10
Cardiff City	8	2	2	4	15	13	8
Swansea City	8	2	2	4	8	15	8

Cup Final

Plymouth Argyle 0, Birmingham City 1

PONTIN'S LEAGUE

Manchester United clinched the Pontin's League title, their second in three years on 24 April with a 2-0 win over Newcastle United. Jovan Kirovski and Desmond Baker were the goalscorers and although the team suffered a mini-crisis when only one point was taken from two games at the end of March, there was very little doubt that the Championship would go to Old Trafford.

Oddly enough on the same day, the A team had clinched the Lancashire League title by winning 6-1 at Bury. The Pontin's League side might have achieved their success earlier because on the previous Saturday, they had won 4-0 at Nottingham Forest, but on the Monday evening they were beaten 1-0 at Birmingham which kept the title on ice for two days.

United played a number of their reserve games at Bury's Gigg Lane and neighbours Manchester City used Witton Albion's facilities as did Oldham at Stalybridge, Wolverhampton at Telford and Aston Villa at Walsall.

For the 1996–97 season, the constitution of the Pontin's League will be changed, the competing teams split into four divisions as follows:

PONTIN'S LEAGUE CLUBS 1996/97 SEASON
Premier Division
Birmingham City
Bolton Wanderers
Derby County
Everton
Leeds United
Liverpool
Manchester United
Newcastle United
Nottingham Forest
Oldham Athletic
Sheffield Wednesday
Stoke City
Tranmere Rovers

Division 1
Aston Villa
Blackburn Rovers
Blackpool
Coventry City
Huddersfield Town
Middlesbrough
Notts County
Port Vale
Preston North End
Sheffield United
Sunderland
West Bromwich Albion
Wolverhampton Wanderers

Division 2
Barnsley
Bradford City
Burnley
Carlisle United
Grimsby Town
Hull City
Leicester City
Manchester City
Mansfield Town
Rotherham United
Stockport County
Wrexham
York City

Division 3
Bury
Chester City
Chesterfield
Darlington
Lincoln City
Rochdale
Scarborough
Scunthorpe United
Shrewsbury Town
Walsall
Wigan Athletic

Manchester United Pontin's League Appearances
Appearances: Appleton 20+8; Baker 8+5; Beckham 5+1; Butt 1; Byers +1; Cantona 1; Casper 24; Clegg 24+5; Cooke 28+1; Coton 8; Culkin 2; Curtis +1; Davies 26; Ford 1; Gibson 3; Giggs 2; Hall 4+3; Irwin 1; Keen 1; Kirovski 22; May 6; McClair 17; McGibbon 24; Mulryne 4+1; Murdock 7+4; Mustoe 12+7; Naylor 1; Neville G 1; Neville P 7+1; Notman 1; O'Kane 24; Parker 12; Pilkington 21; Prunier 1; Scholes 12; Sharpe 7; Smith +1; Thornley 8+1; Tomlinson 21+1; Twiss +1; Wallwork 4+2; Whittam 2; Wood 1+2.
Goals: Kirovski 20, Cooke 10, Tomlinson 8, Appleton 3, O'Kane 3, McGibbon 3, Scholes 3, Baker 2, Beckham 2, Casper 2, Davies 2, Giggs 2, Sharpe 2, Thornley 2, McClair 1, Mustoe 1, Neville G 1, Wallwork 1, Wood 1, own goals 2.

Division One

	P	W	D	L	F	A	Pts
Manchester United	34	22	5	7	71	35	71
Derby County	34	17	10	7	59	43	61
Stoke City	34	17	8	9	57	42	59
Leeds United	34	17	8	9	40	32	59
Liverpool	34	16	8	10	57	42	56
Tranmere Rovers	34	17	4	13	70	62	55
Everton	34	14	10	10	50	41	52
Oldham Athletic	34	12	11	11	55	54	47
Newcastle United	34	13	6	15	55	59	45
Bolton Wanderers	34	12	9	13	51	52	45
Birmingham City	34	13	5	16	57	64	44
Nottingham Forest	34	12	8	14	46	55	44
Sheffield Wednesday	34	11	8	15	66	63	41
Blackburn Rovers	34	9	13	12	48	44	40
Sheffield United	34	8	13	13	40	61	37
Wolverhampton Wanderers	34	10	5	19	42	48	35
Notts County	34	9	7	18	48	64	34
West Bromwich	34	5	6	23	33	84	21

Division Two

	P	W	D	L	F	A	Pts
Middlesbrough	34	23	5	6	80	31	74
Huddersfield Town	34	19	7	8	62	34	64
Sunderland	34	18	9	7	62	37	63
Preston North End	34	17	11	6	51	34	62
Coventry City	34	17	7	10	67	52	58
Blackpool	34	15	9	10	55	40	54
Port Vale	34	14	11	9	69	50	53
Aston Villa	34	14	11	9	62	46	53
Leicester City	34	13	13	8	64	42	52
Manchester City	34	13	11	10	40	39	50
Barnsley	34	14	6	14	61	59	48
Burnley	34	11	10	13	62	68	43
Grimsby Town	34	10	9	15	59	68	39
Rotherham United	34	9	7	18	35	57	34
Bradford City	34	10	3	21	47	75	33
York City	34	8	9	17	38	66	33
Hull City	34	5	4	25	19	68	19
Mansfield Town	34	2	6	26	35	102	12

Division Three

	P	W	D	L	F	A	Pts
Wrexham	28	20	2	6	74	36	62
Carlisle United	28	18	7	3	53	15	61
Stockport County	28	18	5	5	69	36	59
Shrewsbury Town	28	12	9	7	58	39	45
Bury	28	13	5	10	46	37	44
Wigan Athletic	28	12	7	9	59	43	43
Chesterfield	28	12	6	10	49	43	42
Walsall	28	12	5	11	40	39	41
Rochdale	28	9	8	11	64	70	35
Doncaster Rovers	28	10	4	14	42	49	34
Lincoln City	28	9	6	13	33	45	33
Scarborough	28	9	5	14	27	51	32
Chester City	28	6	7	15	39	54	25
Darlington	28	5	5	18	28	55	20
Scunthorpe United	28	4	1	23	34	103	13

NON-LEAGUE TABLES

MIDLAND FOOTBALL COMBINATION

Premier Division

	P	W	D	L	F	A	Pts
Bloxwich Town	38	31	4	3	122	45	97
Coventry Sphinx	38	25	5	8	87	43	80
Massey Ferguson	38	23	8	7	77	36	77
Knowle	38	21	10	7	87	49	73
Studley BKL	38	17	11	10	93	64	62
Kings Heath	38	18	6	14	63	65	60
Meir KA	38	15	10	13	77	72	55
Wellesbourne	38	15	10	13	55	60	55
Southam United	38	13	14	11	69	63	53
Coleshill Town	38	14	9	15	76	66	51
Chelmsley Town	38	14	8	16	65	62	50
Upton Town	38	14	6	18	68	72	48
Ansells	38	12	10	16	64	81	46
Olton Royale	38	12	8	18	56	71	44
West Midlands Fire Service	38	11	9	18	51	70	42
Alvechurch Villa	38	10	10	18	57	84	40
Highgate United	38	9	10	19	56	81	37
Handrahan Timbers	38	9	10	19	46	71	37
Shirley Town	38	8	8	22	51	74	32
Northfield Town	38	3	6	29	33	124	15

COMBINED COUNTIES

Premier Division

	P	W	D	L	F	A	Pts
Ashford Town	42	32	7	3	111	36	103
Chipstead	42	30	4	8	102	44	94
Peppard	42	23	8	11	86	58	77
Merstham	42	22	9	11	89	66	75
Farnham Town	42	20	12	10	71	52	72
Godalming/GFD	42	19	10	13	80	56	67
Reading Town	42	20	6	16	76	69	66
Feltham*	42	18	10	14	94	86	63
Bedfont**	42	18	6	18	67	64	63
Ash United	42	17	12	13	74	73	63
Westfield	42	17	11	14	69	67	62
Sandhurst Town	42	18	7	17	77	89	61
Netherne	42	16	12	14	78	64	60
DCA Basingstoke	42	15	6	21	56	73	51
Eton Wick	42	13	11	18	71	81	50
Hartley Wintney	42	13	6	23	47	88	45
Viking Sports**	42	11	9	22	58	85	43
Cranleigh	42	11	8	23	70	94	41
Cobham	42	12	4	26	59	84	40
Walton Casuals	42	10	8	24	46	67	38
Raynes Park Vale*	42	10	7	25	58	97	34
Horley Town	42	6	9	27	49	95	27

**Points awarded, games not played. *Points deducted, ineligible players

UNIJET SUSSEX COUNTY LEAGUE

Division One

	P	W	D	L	F	A	Pts
Peacehaven & Telscombe	38	32	5	1	133	23	101
Stamco	38	29	3	6	130	38	90
Shoreham	38	25	8	5	91	37	83
Wick	38	23	6	9	95	52	75
Hailsham Town	38	21	10	7	84	48	73
Pagham	38	20	3	15	59	59	63
Arundel	38	19	4	15	80	61	61
Hassocks	38	18	7	13	71	62	61
Langney Sports	38	17	9	12	70	52	60
Ringmer	38	16	6	16	70	59	54
Burgess Hill Town	38	14	10	14	66	66	52
Horsham YMCA	38	15	7	16	56	75	52
Portfield	38	15	5	18	65	81	50
Eastbourne Town	38	12	4	22	51	89	40
Southwick	38	10	9	19	38	75	39
Whitehawk	38	10	6	22	49	71	36
Mile Oak	38	9	6	23	48	93	33
Three Bridges	38	6	6	26	46	101	24
Oakwood	38	5	2	31	30	113	17
Crowborough Athletic	38	4	4	30	40	117	16

Division Two

	P	W	D	L	F	A	Pts
Saltdean United	34	25	6	3	87	40	81
Selsey	34	24	6	4	113	33	78
Chichester City	34	19	8	7	71	35	65
East Grinstead	34	19	8	7	76	53	65
Redhill	34	15	6	13	67	54	51
Newhaven	34	16	3	15	63	62	51
East Preston	34	13	10	11	63	55	49
Lancing	34	11	10	13	62	70	43
Worthing United	34	10	12	12	67	61	42
Steyning Town	34	11	9	14	61	76	42
Sidley United	34	10	10	14	45	56	40
Bexhill Town	34	11	6	17	65	59	39
Midhurst & Eastbourne	34	11	6	17	55	69	39
Withdean	34	11	6	17	57	81	39
Littlehampton Town	34	8	14	12	48	58	38
Broadbridge Heath	34	10	7	17	55	82	37
Bosham	34	10	4	20	65	103	34
Eastbourne United	34	3	7	24	33	106	16

HIGHLAND LEAGUE

	P	W	D	L	F	A	Pt	GD
Huntly	30	27	0	3	103	34	81	+69
Cove Rangers	30	20	5	5	74	35	65	+39
Lossiemouth	30	18	3	9	55	37	57	+18
Peterhead	30	16	7	7	74	51	55	+23
Fraserburgh	30	14	9	7	85	46	51	+39
Keith	30	14	6	10	59	40	48	+19
Elgin City	30	15	3	12	59	55	48	+4
Brora Rangers	30	12	5	13	40	50	41	−10
Wick Academy	30	12	4	14	43	63	40	−20
Deveronvale	30	12	3	15	47	53	39	−6
Clachnacuddin	30	9	7	14	45	51	34	−6
Buckie Thistle	30	8	8	14	45	61	32	−16
Forres Mechanics	30	6	8	16	38	51	26	−13
Fort William	30	8	2	20	27	72	26	−45
Rothes	30	4	7	19	39	75	19	−36
Nairn County	30	4	5	21	26	85	17	−59

LANCASHIRE FOOTBALL LEAGUE

Division One

	P	W	D	L	F	A	Pts
Manchester United A	30	21	3	6	70	22	66
Stoke City A	30	19	6	5	66	27	63
Crewe Alexandra Reserve	30	20	3	7	73	43	63
Everton A	30	16	6	8	70	51	54
Tranmere Rovers A	30	17	1	12	57	46	52
Blackburn Rovers A	30	14	7	9	57	40	49
Burnley A	30	14	6	10	48	38	48
Blackpool A	30	13	6	11	44	49	45
Preston North End A	30	11	8	11	45	48	41
Bury A	30	11	7	12	42	53	40
Wrexham A	30	11	6	13	68	60	39
Liverpool A	30	9	9	12	53	52	36
Oldham Athletic A	30	6	7	17	35	64	25
Manchester City A	30	5	6	19	30	58	21
Morecambe Reserves	30	5	5	20	39	82	20
Marine Reserve	30	4	2	24	20	84	14

Division Two

	P	W	D	L	F	A	Pts
Blackburn Rovers B	36	28	4	4	90	27	88
Manchester United B	36	25	6	5	104	39	81
Manchester City B	36	24	8	4	74	26	80
Liverpool B	36	23	2	11	93	43	71
Bolton Wanderers A	36	21	8	7	74	47	71
Crewe Alexandra A	36	20	4	12	82	57	64
Carlisle United A	36	18	9	9	74	46	63
Burnley B	36	15	5	16	61	66	50
Everton B	36	13	9	14	79	62	48
Tranmere Rovers B	36	14	5	17	48	60	47
Preston North End B	36	12	8	16	58	78	44
Chester City A	36	11	10	15	57	63	43
Blackpool B	36	11	8	17	48	72	41
Oldham Athletic B	36	9	11	16	44	62	38
Wigan Athletic A	36	9	9	18	56	71	36
Stockport County A	36	10	5	21	39	76	35
Marine Youth	36	5	6	25	23	102	21
Rochdale A	36	5	6	26	41	93	20
Bury B	36	4	8	24	33	88	20

NORTH WEST COUNTIES LEAGUE

Division One

	P	W	D	L	F	A	Pts
Flixton	42	28	8	6	85	30	92
Newcastle Town	42	26	7	9	88	42	85
Trafford	42	26	5	11	89	45	83
Mossley	42	24	8	10	87	59	80
Burscough	42	23	8	11	77	40	77
Bootle	42	23	5	14	74	55	74
Clitheroe	42	20	12	10	63	44	72
St Helens Town	42	19	13	10	71	53	70
Nantwich Town	42	20	7	15	64	59	67
Prescot Cables	42	17	11	14	70	66	62
Holker Old Boys	42	19	4	19	77	72	61
Glossop North End	42	15	15	12	55	48	60
Kidsgrove Athletic	42	15	9	18	61	64	54
Eastwood Hanley	42	12	15	15	60	57	51
Maine Road	42	12	14	16	60	71	50
Chadderton	42	14	8	20	52	69	50
Blackpool Rovers	42	11	9	22	49	74	42
Penrith	42	9	12	21	57	69	39
Darwen	42	9	10	23	57	77	37
Salford City	42	10	5	27	49	93	35
Rossendale United	42	6	10	26	32	114	28
Skelmersdale United	42	5	3	34	45	121	18

Division Two

	P	W	D	L	F	A	Pts
Vauxhall GM	34	28	4	2	112	25	88
Atherton Collieries	34	25	5	4	90	44	80
Tetley Walker	34	22	7	5	76	35	73
Castleton Gabriels	34	19	5	10	77	52	62
Nelson	34	17	9	8	78	55	60
Cheadle Town	34	17	5	12	67	49	56
Haslingden	34	15	9	10	69	45	54
Maghull	34	16	3	15	55	42	51
Oldham Town	34	14	8	12	75	74	50
Middlewich Athletic	34	12	7	15	45	74	43
Daisy Hill	34	12	4	18	46	66	40
Ramsbottom United	34	11	6	17	60	65	39
Formby	34	10	7	17	59	76	37
Stantondale	34	11	4	19	47	75	37
Blackpool Mechanics	34	8	8	18	56	74	32
Ashton Town	34	8	3	23	53	102	27
Squires Gate	34	5	7	22	37	82	22
Bacup Borough	34	4	3	27	35	102	15

VAUX WEARSIDE LEAGUE

Division One

	P	W	D	L	F	A	Pts
Marske United	30	22	3	5	97	29	69
Jarrow Roofing*	30	22	4	4	93	40	67
Sth Tyneside United	30	15	9	6	41	32	54
Birtley Town	30	15	6	9	60	49	51
Ryhope CW	30	14	8	8	53	31	50
Windscale	30	13	7	10	69	54	46
Boldon CA	30	12	6	12	59	50	42
Roker	30	12	5	13	56	55	41
Washington Nissan	30	11	7	12	44	40	40
Annfield Plain	30	12	4	14	50	47	40
Hartlepool BWOB	30	11	2	17	46	66	35
Wolviston	30	10	4	16	48	60	34
Cleadon SC	30	8	9	13	43	60	33
Jarrow	30	10	3	17	45	71	33
Nth Shields Athletic	30	7	5	18	34	74	26
SC Fulwell	30	5	0	25	36	116	15

*Points deducted

THE JEWSON SOUTH-WESTERN FOOTBALL LEAGUE

	P	W	D	L	F	A	Pts
Truro City	34	26	4	4	99	27	82
Torpoint Athletic	34	23	8	3	81	32	77
Falmouth Town	34	22	4	8	89	35	70
Launceston	34	20	9	5	95	29	69
Bodmin Town	34	18	10	6	91	36	64
Penzance	34	18	5	11	64	43	58
Newquay	34	18	4	12	73	54	58
Holsworthy	34	17	5	12	58	43	56
Wadebridge Town	34	16	5	13	65	55	53
Saltash United	34	14	8	12	66	67	50
Porthleven	34	13	5	16	62	66	44
St Austell	34	10	5	19	57	79	35
Millbrook	34	9	7	18	40	59	34
Liskeard Athletic	34	9	6	19	58	96	33
Appledore/BAAC	34	7	7	20	43	78	28
Tavistock	34	6	6	22	55	99	24
St Blazey	34	4	4	26	38	106	16
Okehampton Argyle	34	4	2	28	24	143	14

NORTHERN ALLIANCE LEAGUE

Premier Division

	P	W	D	L	F	A	Pts
Seaton Delaval	32	23	4	5	97	39	73
Carlisle City	32	19	10	3	85	23	67
Gillford Park	32	20	6	6	62	23	66
Benfield Park	32	21	3	8	73	41	66
Middlesbrough A	32	17	7	8	79	37	58
West Allotment Celtic	32	18	4	10	79	49	58
Ponteland United	32	15	7	10	73	39	52
Amble Town	32	15	6	11	81	58	51
Haltwhistle CP	32	14	5	13	52	58	47
Walker Central	32	13	5	14	59	62	44
St Columbas	32	12	7	13	56	55	43
Westerhope	32	13	4	15	58	68	43
Winlaton	32	9	9	14	59	56	36
Blyth Seahorse*	32	7	2	23	32	86	20
Spittal Rivers*	32	5	6	21	27	71	18
Longbenton	32	4	1	27	29	156	13
Heaton Stannington	32	3	2	27	34	114	11

*Points deducted

CARLSBERG WEST CHESHIRE

Division One

	P	W	D	L	F	A	Pts
Poulton Victoria	30	22	6	2	91	25	50
Heswall	30	17	10	3	77	38	44
Cammell Laird	30	17	9	4	82	37	43
Merseyside Police	30	14	9	7	61	42	37
Christleton	30	13	9	8	48	41	35
Mersey Royal	30	8	15	7	44	48	31
Vauxhall Motors	30	11	9	10	64	69	31
Capenhurst	30	8	14	8	52	50	30
Ashville	30	10	7	13	51	63	27
Bromborough Pool	30	9	6	15	36	44	24
Newton	30	8	8	14	52	71	24
General Chemicals	30	8	7	15	53	62	23
Moreton	30	8	7	15	47	61	23
Stork	30	8	5	17	44	71	21
Mond Rangers	30	7	7	16	39	68	21
Shell	30	5	6	19	41	92	16

BEEFEATER SHEFFIELD

Premier Division

	P	W	D	L	F	A	Pts
High Green Villa	26	21	3	2	74	20	66
Ash House Phoenix	26	17	4	5	63	21	55
Grimethorpe MW	26	15	4	7	54	36	49
A B M	26	14	5	7	57	45	47
Denaby & Cadeby	26	12	6	8	58	38	42
Frecheville CA	26	11	5	10	64	50	38
Parramore Sports	26	12	2	12	46	56	38
Worsbrough Bridge	26	9	8	9	43	40	35
Oughtibridge WM	26	9	7	10	38	41	34
Mexboro Main Street	26	7	9	10	46	46	30
Stocksbridge PS-6	26	8	5	13	44	46	23
Caribbean Sports	26	6	4	16	40	79	22
Penistone Church	26	6	1	19	37	62	19
Throstle Ridgeway	26	3	1	22	23	106	10

NOTTS FOOTBALL ALLIANCE

Senior Division

	P	W	D	L	F	A	Pts
Rainworth MW	30	19	8	3	83	40	65
Boots Athletic	30	20	4	6	75	41	64
Pelican	30	19	5	6	74	39	62
Hucknall R R	30	17	4	9	63	37	55
Greenwood Meadow	30	16	3	11	46	51	51
John Player	30	14	5	11	54	42	47
Notts Police	30	13	5	12	59	47	44
Keyworth United	30	11	10	9	46	46	43
Cotgrave CW	30	11	4	15	46	56	37
Ruddington United	30	10	5	15	59	79	35
Thoresby CW	30	9	7	14	39	46	34
Welbeck CW	30	10	3	17	42	58	33
Southwell City	30	10	3	17	39	58	33
Wollaton	30	8	6	16	40	65	30
Basford United	30	8	3	19	41	60	27
G P T FC	30	6	3	21	43	84	21

INTERLINK EXPRESS MIDLAND FOOTBALL ALLIANCE

	P	W	D	L	F	A	Pts
Shepshed Dynamo	36	22	10	4	90	37	76
Blakenall	36	19	11	6	60	36	68
Hinckley Athletic	36	21	4	11	78	54	67
Rocester	36	19	9	8	55	50	66
Knypersley Vics	36	18	8	10	73	43	62
Boldmere St Michaels	36	18	5	13	73	51	59
Sandwell Borough	36	17	5	14	56	50	56
Willenhall Town	36	16	7	13	52	62	55
Barwell	36	15	6	15	57	53	51
Oldbury United	36	14	8	14	49	41	50
Rushall Olympic*	36	15	5	16	57	65	47
Halesowen Harriers	36	13	7	16	54	62	46
Stratford Town	36	12	9	15	56	54	45
Pershore Town	36	12	9	15	58	73	45
West Midlands Police	36	11	11	14	49	55	44
Chasetown	36	10	10	16	44	52	40
Shifnal Town	36	8	9	19	38	60	33
Stapenhill	36	5	6	25	38	87	21
Bolehall Swifts	36	5	5	26	30	82	20

*Points deducted

MANCHESTER LEAGUE

Premier Division

	P	W	D	L	F	A	Pts
Little Hulton United	30	22	4	4	78	37	70
Springhead	30	18	7	5	61	36	61
Abbey Hey	30	19	3	8	62	38	60
Highfield United	30	17	5	8	59	39	56
BICC	30	14	10	6	60	43	52
Wythenshawe Town	30	16	4	10	50	33	52
Woodley Sports	30	12	8	10	49	41	44
Mitchell Shackleton	30	11	10	9	55	48	43
Wythenshawe Amateurs	30	12	7	11	50	44	43
East Manchester	30	10	12	8	54	51	42
Atherton Town	30	12	5	13	54	53	41
Dukinfield Town	30	9	6	15	39	58	33
Stockport Georgians	30	5	5	20	45	74	20
Monton Amateurs	30	5	5	20	37	73	20
Prestwich Heys	30	4	7	19	37	75	19
Sacred Heart	30	3	4	23	34	81	13

Division One

	P	W	D	L	F	A	Pts
Stand Athletic	26	18	5	3	83	25	59
Elton Fold	26	15	5	6	75	38	50
Manchester Royal	26	14	3	9	77	58	45
Breightmet United	26	12	9	5	59	42	45
Pennington	26	11	8	7	50	52	41
Whitworth Valley	26	11	7	8	68	66	40
Hollinwood	26	10	8	8	55	47	38
Old Altrincham's	26	9	7	10	52	46	34
Ashton Athletic	26	7	9	10	37	48	30
Whalley Range	26	8	5	13	58	83	29
Coldhurst United	26	7	6	13	53	79	27
Milton	26	6	7	13	51	66	25
New Mills	26	6	6	14	54	85	24
Gr Man Police	26	2	7	17	33	70	13

WINSTONLEAD KENT LEAGUE

Division One

	P	W	D	L	F	A	Pts
Furness	38	27	8	3	87	19	89
Dartford	38	26	11	1	71	21	89
Chatham Town	38	24	5	9	79	48	77
Herne Bay	38	18	10	10	74	44	64
Deal Town	38	17	13	8	72	52	64
Slade Green	38	17	12	9	66	46	63
Sheppey United	38	19	5	14	66	49	62
Whitstable Town	38	17	7	14	85	61	58
Thamesmead Town	38	17	7	14	59	51	58
Folkestone Invicta	38	15	11	12	82	56	56
Greenwich Borough	38	15	7	16	60	66	52
Cray Wanderers**	38	16	5	17	70	70	50
Canterbury City	38	14	6	18	48	59	48
Ramsgate	38	13	6	19	62	81	45
Tunbridge Wells	38	10	10	18	45	64	40
Beckenham Town	38	9	9	20	45	60	36
Corinthian	38	9	7	22	53	84	34
Crockenhill	38	8	8	22	51	92	32
Hythe United	38	8	6	24	58	101	30
Faversham Town	38	3	3	32	33	142	12

**Three points deducted

GREAT MILLS WESTERN LEAGUE

Premier Division

	P	W	D	L	F	A	Pts
Taunton Town	34	25	7	2	84	20	82
Tiverton Town	34	25	4	5	101	34	79
Mangotsfield United	34	22	7	5	88	23	73
Torrington	34	23	4	7	64	37	73
Brislington	34	17	4	13	60	41	55
Bideford	34	16	7	11	63	47	55
Backwell United	34	15	7	12	54	46	52
Paulton Rovers	34	14	10	10	59	53	52
Calne Town	34	14	9	11	41	40	51
Chippenham Town	34	11	12	11	53	41	45
Bridport	34	13	5	16	51	60	44
Bristol Manor Farm	34	11	6	17	55	69	39
Westbury United	34	9	9	16	39	53	36
Barnstaple Town	34	10	6	18	61	78	36
Odd Down Athletic	34	6	6	22	39	77	24
Elmore	34	6	6	22	30	91	24
Frome Town	34	5	7	22	30	84	22
Crediton United	34	3	6	25	18	96	15

Division One

	P	W	D	L	F	A	Pts
Bridgwater Town	36	29	3	4	93	29	90
Chard Town	36	28	6	2	65	17	90
Keynsham Town	36	22	7	7	69	35	73
Bishop Sutton	36	18	9	9	48	36	63
Clyst Rovers	36	18	7	11	74	52	61
Welton Rovers	36	15	11	10	52	43	56
Devizes Town	36	15	10	11	61	50	55
Dawlish Town	36	14	9	13	56	53	51
Melksham Town	36	13	11	12	59	54	50
Warminster Town	36	14	6	16	51	57	48
Glastonbury	36	12	10	14	45	54	46
Wellington	36	12	8	16	47	52	44
Pewsey Vale	36	10	6	20	34	71	36
Heavitree United	36	9	8	19	64	81	35
Larkhall Athletic	36	10	4	22	50	78	34
Amesbury Town	36	7	10	19	37	67	31
Minehead	36	8	7	21	41	73	31
Exmouth Town	36	9	3	24	44	67	30
Ilfracombe Town	36	6	11	19	43	64	29

JEWSON (EAST COUNTIES) LEAGUE

Premier Division

	P	W	D	L	F	A	Pts
Halstead Town	42	31	8	3	110	50	101
Diss Town	42	29	9	4	94	32	96
Wroxham	42	26	10	6	100	39	88
Stowmarket Town	41	23	7	11	67	44	76
Harwich & Parkeston*	39	21	9	9	87	51	53
Woodbridge Town	42	22	6	14	73	49	72
Newmarket Town	42	18	13	11	78	58	67
Felixstowe Town	42	16	11	15	60	57	59
Sudbury Wanderers	42	17	8	17	53	58	59
Tiptree United	42	17	8	17	56	67	59
Wisbech Town	42	16	9	17	76	67	57
Soham Town Rangers	42	16	9	17	76	78	57
Fakenham Town	42	17	5	20	67	67	56
Lowestoft Town	42	13	14	15	73	59	53
Clacton Town	42	14	10	18	72	84	52
Great Yarmouth Town	42	11	11	20	34	61	44
Hadleigh United	42	10	9	23	33	85	39
Sudbury Town Reserves	42	9	11	22	49	86	38
March Town United	42	10	7	25	39	67	37
Watton United	41	8	13	20	40	71	37
Haverhill Rovers	42	8	10	24	36	78	34
Cornard United	41	5	7	29	37	102	22

*19 points deducted

Division One

	P	W	D	L	F	A	Pts
Gorleston	32	26	4	2	100	30	82
Warboys Town	32	22	7	3	79	33	73
Ely City	32	19	6	7	82	40	63
Thetford Town	32	20	2	10	72	52	62
Ipswich Wanderers	32	17	8	7	87	41	59
Whitton United	32	15	10	7	67	43	55
Norwich United	32	14	7	11	58	46	49
Mildenhall Town	32	14	5	13	53	61	47
Swaffham Town	32	10	8	14	53	54	38
Brightlingsea United	32	8	11	13	44	61	35
Somersham Town	32	10	5	17	41	62	35
Downham Town	32	9	7	16	46	80	34
Histon	32	8	4	20	54	73	28
King's Lynn Reserves	32	8	4	20	46	91	28
Stanway Rovers	32	6	9	17	35	67	27
Chatteris Town	32	7	4	21	41	82	25
Bury Town Reserves	32	6	5	21	54	96	23

JOHN SMITH'S BITTER CENTRAL MIDLANDS LEAGUE

Supreme Division

	P	W	D	L	F	A	Pts
Oakham United	32	22	4	6	71	37	70
Glapwell	32	19	6	7	51	31	63
Heanor Town	32	19	5	8	70	41	62
Kimberley Town	32	17	6	9	70	56	57
Staveley Miners Welfare	32	16	8	8	52	43	56
Long Eaton United	32	16	4	12	69	52	52
South Normanton Athletic	32	14	7	11	47	40	49
Case Sports	32	14	7	11	52	51	49
Gedling Town	32	13	8	11	57	42	47
Sandiacre Town	32	11	7	14	52	58	40
Harworth Colliery Institute	32	12	3	17	55	76	39
Mickleover Sports	32	12	2	18	55	63	38
Rossington	32	10	7	15	49	59	37
Kiveton Park	32	9	5	18	40	61	32
Nettleham	32	5	13	14	34	55	28
Shirebrook Town	32	8	2	22	47	75	26
Thorne Colliery	32	6	4	22	26	57	22

Premier Division

	P	W	D	L	F	A	Pts
Killamarsh	34	26	3	5	111	46	81
Dunkirk	34	23	7	4	127	31	76
Graham Street Prims	34	20	7	7	67	36	67
Nuthall	34	18	12	4	74	36	66
Clipstone Welfare	34	18	4	12	83	51	58
Sneinton	34	18	4	12	87	62	58
Radford	34	16	8	10	66	48	56
Askern Welfare	34	17	4	13	77	65	55

	P	W	D	L	F	A	Pts
Shardlow St James	34	15	8	11	66	59	53
Hemsworth Town	34	15	5	14	63	58	50
Sheffield Hallam University	34	13	5	16	65	72	44
Mexborough Athletic (Oakhouse)	34	10	9	15	64	77	39
Derby Rolls Royce	34	11	5	18	62	78	38
Collingham	34	10	6	18	60	75	36
Stanton Ilkeston	34	10	5	19	54	79	35
Mickleover RBL	34	9	4	21	42	86	31
Blackwell Miners Welfare	34	2	8	24	44	125	14
Sheepbridge	34	2	2	30	34	162	8

LONDON SPARTAN FOOTBALL LEAGUE

Premier Division

	P	W	D	L	F	A	Pts
St Margaretsbury	30	18	7	5	51	29	61
Hillingdon Borough	30	17	8	5	55	28	59
Corinthian Casuals	30	15	6	9	49	30	51
Brimsdown Rovers	30	14	9	7	55	38	51
Cockfosters	30	14	7	9	61	43	49
Tottenham Omada	30	13	6	11	67	53	45
Croydon Athletic	30	13	6	11	50	51	45
Barkingside	30	11	6	13	48	46	39
Brook House	30	10	8	12	29	37	38
Tufnell Park	30	11	4	15	38	55	37
Hanwell Town	30	10	6	14	41	60	36
Woolwich Town	30	9	7	14	42	48	34
Waltham Abbey	30	8	10	12	27	45	34
Beaconsfield SYCOB	30	8	6	16	42	56	30
Willesden (Hawkeye)	30	7	7	16	37	44	28
Amersham Town	30	7	7	16	29	58	28

ESSEX SENIOR LEAGUE

Premier Division

	P	W	D	L	F	A	Pts
Romford	28	23	2	3	91	27	71
Great Wakering	28	20	4	4	67	28	64
Concord Rangers	28	20	3	5	67	31	63
Maldon Town	28	16	4	8	87	47	52
Ford United	28	14	6	8	59	53	48
Sawbridgeworth Town	28	13	5	10	59	43	44
Stansted	28	12	8	8	47	34	44
Southend Manor	28	12	7	9	50	49	43
Burnham Ramblers	28	13	3	12	63	48	42
Brentwood	28	13	2	13	56	53	41
Basildon United	28	5	8	15	31	52	23
Bowers United	28	5	6	17	28	57	21
Eton Manor	28	4	6	18	32	72	18
Hullbridge Sports	28	4	5	19	30	88	17
East Ham United	28	0	3	25	18	103	3

NORTHERN COUNTIES (EAST) LEAGUE

Premier Division

	P	W	D	L	F	A	Pts
Hatfield Main	38	22	9	7	77	45	75
Stocksbridge PS	38	21	10	7	59	36	73
North Ferriby United	38	21	9	8	78	33	72
Belper Town	38	20	10	8	66	39	70
Thackley	38	20	9	9	60	40	69
Denaby United	38	19	5	14	63	56	62
Brigg Town	38	17	8	13	65	50	59
Ashfield United	38	17	5	16	56	50	56
Liversedge	38	16	7	15	52	49	55
Ossett Albion	38	13	12	13	56	55	51
Armthorpe Welfare	38	13	11	14	53	47	50
Pickering Town	38	14	5	19	73	86	47
Goole Town	38	13	8	17	53	74	47
Arnold Town	38	13	7	18	51	57	46
Ossett Town	38	12	9	17	48	61	45
Hucknall Town	38	12	6	20	52	67	42
Hallam	38	11	7	20	41	68	40
Glasshoughton Welfare	38	10	9	19	45	62	39
Maltby MW	38	11	5	22	58	83	38
Sheffield	38	6	7	25	46	94	25

Division 1

	P	W	D	L	F	A	Pts
Selby Town	30	19	6	5	79	34	63
Pontefract Collieries	30	19	6	5	76	33	63
Garforth Town	30	18	7	5	63	27	61
Yorkshire Amateurs	30	18	6	6	51	30	60
Hall Road Rangers	30	17	5	8	65	34	56
Eccleshill United	30	18	1	11	74	53	55
Borrowash Victoria	30	13	5	12	59	46	44
Harrogate Railway	30	12	5	13	48	52	41
Winterton Rangers	30	11	6	13	44	51	39
Rossington Main	30	10	7	13	43	55	37
Worsbrough Bridge	30	9	5	16	48	60	32
Louth United	30	8	7	15	54	66	31
Blidworth Welfare	30	9	3	18	47	83	30
Tadcaster Albion	30	6	5	19	25	61	23
Parkgate	30	6	4	20	36	81	22
Brodsworth MW	30	2	12	16	23	69	18

BANKS'S BREWERY WEST MIDLANDS LEAGUE

Premier Division

	P	W	D	L	F	A	Pts
Wednesfield	36	28	6	2	95	30	90
Pelsall Villa	36	27	5	4	97	30	86
Lye Town	36	20	11	5	80	34	71
Stafford Town	36	19	10	7	79	35	67
Stourport Swifts	36	19	10	7	74	50	67
Bloxwich Strollers	36	17	9	10	67	50	60
Walsall Wood	36	16	8	12	61	42	56
Gornal Athletic	36	16	7	13	55	42	55
Westfields	36	16	6	14	86	73	54
Ludlow Town	36	14	9	13	68	71	51
Ettingshall HT	36	11	9	16	62	80	42
Tividale	36	10	9	17	65	80	39
Lichfield City	36	9	10	17	43	65	37
Malvern Town	36	9	9	18	34	67	36
Brierley Hill Town	36	10	4	22	49	73	34
Cradley Town	36	8	7	21	55	82	31
W'pton Casuals	36	9	4	23	53	108	31
Darlaston	36	5	11	20	40	86	26
Hill Top Rangers	36	4	6	26	34	99	18

SOUTH EAST COUNTIES LEAGUE

Division One

	P	W	D	L	F	A	Pts
West Ham United	30	22	4	4	79	37	48
Tottenham Hotspur	30	21	2	7	88	37	44
Watford	30	19	6	5	70	34	44
Arsenal	30	19	5	6	64	27	43
Norwich City	30	16	6	8	56	30	38
Millwall	30	14	3	13	44	46	31
Gillingham	30	10	9	11	49	59	29
Charlton Athletic	30	10	8	12	50	51	28
Leyton Orient	30	12	4	14	40	49	28
Chelsea	30	10	7	13	57	50	27
Ipswich Town	30	10	6	14	51	57	26
Queens Park Rangers	30	8	6	16	46	58	22
Southend United	30	6	9	15	36	60	21
Portsmouth	30	6	8	16	28	55	20
Cambridge United	30	5	6	19	42	96	16
Fulham	30	5	5	20	26	80	15

Division Two

	P	W	D	L	F	A	Pts
Crystal Palace	30	21	4	5	76	35	46
Luton Town	30	17	4	9	58	41	38
Wycombe Wanderers	30	17	4	9	54	39	38
Oxford United	30	17	3	10	64	38	37
Brighton & Hove Albion	30	14	5	11	40	37	33
Wimbledon	30	13	6	11	51	41	32
Southampton	30	13	5	12	51	28	31
Tottenham Hotspur	30	10	11	9	46	46	31
AFC Bournemouth	30	12	7	11	48	51	31
Barnet	30	9	9	12	38	41	27
Swindon Town	30	10	7	13	35	43	27

Brentford	30	10	7	13	37	51	27
Reading	30	8	7	15	33	69	23
Bristol City	30	7	8	15	39	50	22
Colchester United	30	6	8	16	37	67	20
Bristol Rovers	30	6	5	19	34	64	17

HELLENIC LEAGUE

Premier Division

	P	W	D	L	F	A	Pts
Cirencester Town	34	24	8	2	69	24	80
Brackley Town	34	19	12	3	60	32	69
Lambourn Sports	34	21	5	8	71	41	68
Tuffley Rovers	34	20	7	7	78	46	67
Burnham	34	20	4	10	66	37	64
Swindon Supermarine	34	20	3	11	82	33	63
Endsleigh	34	16	7	11	56	41	55
North Leigh	34	15	4	15	66	62	49
Carterton Town	34	13	9	12	57	59	48
Abingdon United	34	13	4	17	49	55	43
Fairford Town	34	10	10	14	49	52	40
Almondsbury Town	34	10	7	17	53	54	37
Shortwood United	34	10	5	19	53	82	35
Kintbury Rangers	34	8	9	17	45	74	33
Banbury United	34	8	6	20	40	66	30
Highworth Town	34	9	3	22	36	80	30
Didcot Town	34	7	7	20	39	88	28
Bicester Town	34	6	4	24	37	80	22

Division One

	P	W	D	L	F	A	Pts
Purton	34	22	6	6	79	40	72
Wantage Town	34	21	8	5	66	34	71
Milton United	34	18	8	8	102	63	62
Hallen	34	16	9	9	74	49	57
Harrow Hill	34	16	9	9	57	38	57
Pegasus Juniors	34	15	7	12	76	62	52
Kidlington	34	13	9	12	73	59	48
Cheltenham Saracens	34	14	6	14	71	71	48
Ardley United	34	13	6	15	47	60	45
Wootton Bassett	34	12	9	13	50	64	45
Clanfield	34	9	12	13	54	61	39
Bishops Cleeve	34	10	9	15	50	65	39
Rayners Lane	34	9	11	14	51	66	38
Easington Sports	34	9	10	15	45	64	37
Headington Amateurs	34	10	5	19	51	72	35
Letcombe	34	9	8	17	38	65	35
Yarnton	34	9	6	19	45	84	33
Cirencester United	34	8	8	18	53	66	32

MINERVA FOOTBALLS SOUTH MIDLANDS LEAGUE

Premier Division

	P	W	D	L	F	A	Pts
Arlesey Town	32	24	2	6	64	27	74
Hatfield Town	32	22	5	5	79	32	71
London Colney	32	21	5	6	88	34	68
Brache Sparta	32	20	8	4	56	24	68
Toddington Rovers	32	14	9	9	50	45	51
Royston Town*	32	13	11	8	48	36	47
Hoddesdon Town	32	12	8	12	49	44	44
Milton Keynes	32	13	4	15	55	70	43
Potters Bar Town	32	11	9	12	56	63	42
Biggleswade Town	32	12	5	15	51	50	41
Welwyn GC	32	11	7	14	53	62	40
Langford	32	10	8	14	30	48	38
Buckingham Athletic	32	9	6	17	43	63	33
Harpenden Town	32	8	8	16	42	56	32
Dunstable United	32	6	7	19	33	71	25
Shillington	32	5	9	18	43	60	24
Letchworth GC	32	1	9	22	33	88	12

*Three points deducted

Senior Division

	P	W	D	L	F	A	Pts
Holmer Green	26	19	5	2	71	31	62
Leverstock Green	26	17	6	3	63	26	57
Bedford United	26	16	3	7	57	32	51
New Bradwell SP	26	14	5	7	69	43	47
Totternhoe	26	13	6	7	52	44	45
Tring Athletic	26	13	4	9	66	37	43
Houghton Town	26	9	8	9	40	33	35
ACD	26	8	6	12	46	41	30
Winslow United	26	7	9	10	43	57	30
Risborough Rangers	26	7	7	12	35	56	28
Ampthill Town	26	7	6	13	39	62	27
Stony Stratford Town	26	6	5	15	39	66	23
The 61 FC Luton	26	5	4	17	28	71	19
Kent Athletic	26	3	5	18	31	78	14

EVERARDS BREWERY LEICESTERSHIRE SENIOR LEAGUE

Premier Division

	P	W	D	L	F	A	Pts
St Andrews	34	28	3	3	95	28	87
Oadby Town	34	27	2	5	122	40	83
Birstall United	34	21	7	6	60	37	70
Friar Lane OB	34	20	5	9	68	37	65
Kirby Muxloe	34	16	8	10	55	48	56
Ibstock Welfare	34	17	3	14	57	60	54
Burbage Old Boys	34	15	7	12	64	64	52
Barrow Town	34	15	6	13	80	76	51
Anstey Nomads	34	14	7	13	87	69	49
Holwell Sports	34	14	5	15	74	59	47
Cottesmore Amateurs	34	12	4	18	62	84	40
Asfordby Amateurs	34	11	6	17	44	61	39
Highfield Rangers	34	9	8	17	47	64	35
Downes Sports	34	10	4	20	54	79	34
Newfoundpool	34	9	5	20	45	76	32
Thringstone	34	8	7	19	40	69	31
Aylestone Park OB	34	8	6	20	48	76	30
North Kilworth	34	3	5	26	37	111	14

UNITED COUNTIES FOOTBALL LEAGUE

Premier Division

	P	W	D	L	F	A	Pts
Raunds Town	38	26	9	3	111	28	87
Stotfold	38	26	9	3	94	37	87
Desborough Town	38	25	4	9	104	56	79
Cogenhoe United	38	21	8	9	84	56	71
Eynesbury Rovers	38	19	9	10	64	39	66
Spalding United	38	19	8	11	62	51	65
Stamford	38	18	10	10	88	56	64
Long Buckby	38	17	10	11	80	63	61
Holbeach United	38	16	12	10	68	45	60
Boston Town	38	15	12	11	74	49	57
Mirrlees Blackstone	38	16	9	13	70	71	57
S & L Corby	38	15	8	15	90	77	53
Northampton Spencer	38	12	6	20	67	88	42
Wootton Blue Cross	38	11	9	18	54	78	42
St Neots Town	38	11	4	23	59	96	37
Potton United	38	9	9	20	46	76	36
Wellingborough Town	38	10	6	22	57	88	36
Bourne Town	38	8	9	21	49	103	33
Newport Pagnell Town	38	4	7	27	37	128	19
Kempston Rovers	38	1	4	33	32	105	7

Division One

	P	W	D	L	F	A	Pts
Ford Sports	36	27	5	4	105	42	86
Higham Town	36	27	4	5	94	33	85
Bugbrooke St M	36	25	6	5	91	31	81
Rothwell Cor	36	22	8	6	79	29	74
Olney Town	36	24	2	10	85	47	74
Northampton Vanaid	36	19	8	9	89	63	65
Whitworths	36	20	4	12	72	35	64
Ramsey Town	36	16	7	13	60	47	55
Burton Park Wanderers	36	13	8	15	50	46	47
Yaxley	36	10	12	14	51	67	42
Thrapston Venturers	36	12	5	19	64	70	41
Daventry Town	36	12	5	19	55	85	41
Cottingham	36	9	8	19	41	68	35

St Ives Town	36	7	12	17	50	62	33
Blisworth	36	8	8	20	59	103	32
Harrowby United	36	9	3	24	42	115	30
Sharnbrook	36	8	5	23	50	101	29
ON Chenecks	36	6	7	23	38	72	25
Irchester United	36	6	7	23	42	101	25

JEWSON WESSEX FOOTBALL LEAGUE

First Division

	P	W	D	L	F	A	Pts
Thatcham Town	40	28	8	4	73	27	92
Lymington AFC	40	28	7	5	100	31	91
Ryde	40	25	8	7	92	41	83
Eastleigh	40	21	13	6	83	50	76
Christchurch	40	21	8	11	66	49	71
Wimborne Town	40	20	6	14	85	61	66
Bournemouth	40	17	13	10	85	40	64
Bemerton HH	40	18	8	14	67	63	62
Andover	40	18	7	15	101	70	61
East Cowes Vics	40	17	8	15	60	60	59
Gosport Borough	40	16	9	15	59	58	57
Downton	40	16	6	18	65	73	54
Whitchurch United	40	12	13	15	66	76	49
Totton AFC	40	10	13	17	55	66	43
BAT	40	10	12	18	44	58	42
Cowes Sports	40	11	7	22	38	76	40
Portsmouth RN	40	10	8	22	52	84	38
Aerostructures	40	9	10	21	41	71	37
Brockenhurst	40	11	4	25	42	74	37
Petersfield Town	40	8	4	28	53	93	28
Swanage Tn & H	40	6	4	30	32	138	22

FEDERATION BREWERY NORTHERN LEAGUE

Division One

	P	W	D	L	F	A	Pts
Billingham Synthonia	38	24	8	6	78	34	80
Bedlington Terriers	38	22	12	4	90	37	78
Durham City	38	24	6	8	85	35	78
Tow Law Town	38	23	9	6	82	43	78
Whitby Town	38	21	8	9	100	58	71
Guisborough Town	38	20	8	10	80	54	68
Dunston Feds	38	20	8	10	75	52	68
West Auckland	38	19	5	14	66	57	62
Crook Town	38	17	9	12	59	41	60
Consett	38	17	7	14	76	64	58
Stockton	38	16	8	14	88	71	56
Shildon	38	16	3	19	74	75	51
Seaham Red Star	38	13	11	14	62	66	50
RTM Newcastle	38	13	7	18	69	58	46
Murton	38	11	12	15	56	53	45
Chester-le-Street	38	11	9	18	72	78	42
Whickham	38	11	8	19	43	77	41
Peterlee Newtown	38	5	4	29	40	96	19
Eppleton CW	38	2	3	33	26	153	9
Ferryhill Athletic	38	0	5	33	27	146	5

Division Two

	P	W	D	L	F	A	Pts
Morpeth Town	36	27	5	4	104	40	86
South Shields	36	25	4	7	89	34	79
Easington Colliery	36	23	7	6	86	40	76
Shotton Comrades	36	22	7	7	74	42	73
Northallerton	36	19	9	8	70	43	66
Ashington	36	18	9	9	66	48	63
Billingham Town	36	18	6	12	72	51	60
Evenwood Town	36	16	8	12	73	61	56
Prudhoe Town	36	17	4	15	75	69	55
Brandon United	36	16	6	14	59	55	54
Esh Winning	36	13	7	16	80	75	46
Hebburn	36	13	5	18	50	58	44
Willington	36	11	8	17	53	75	41
Washington*	36	14	4	18	71	74	40
Horden CW	36	12	3	21	65	75	39
Alnwick Town	36	10	6	20	47	65	36
Ryhope CA	36	6	5	25	40	83	23
Norton*	36	6	5	25	53	122	17
Darlington CS	36	0	4	32	34	152	4

*Points deducted

AMATEUR FOOTBALL ALLIANCE 1995–96

AFA SENIOR CUP

1st Round Proper
South Bank 1, Old Owens 0
Old Camdenians 1, Old Actonians Association 2
Ibis 0, Old Suttonians 4
Winchmore Hill 2, Old Salvatorians 1
Old Foresters 6*, Norsemen 4*
Old Vaughanians 1, Old Tiffinians 2
Old Wilsonians 1*, Carshalton 2*
Old Kingsburians 1*, Old Hamptonians 4*
Old Lyonian 6, Shene Old Grammarians 0
Enfield Old Grammarians 3, Crouch End Vampires 1
Mill Hill Village 1, Old Cholmeleians 3
Wake Green 5, Old Elizabethans 1
Hampstead Heathens 2, Witan 0
Old Meadonians 1, St Mary's College 2
Cardinal Manning Old Boys 4*, Hale End Athletic 5*
Old Tenisonians 3*:2, Old Westhamians 3*:1
Ulysses 1, London Airways 0
Corinthian-Casuals "A" 1, Wandsworth Borough 0
Old Manorians 2*, Broomfield 3*
Civil Service 2, Old Chigwellians 1
Lloyds Bank 3, Old Stationers 1
Pegasus Inner Temple 2, Nottsborough 5
Midland Bank 1, West Wickham 4
Southgate Olympic 1, Alleyn Old Boys 3
Old Isleworthians 2, Barclays Bank 4
Old Salesians 3, Old Tollingtonians 2
Parkfield 5*, Ealing Association 2*
Polytechnic 1, Glyn Old Boys 0
Old Parkonians 0:0, Bank of England 0:3
Cuaco 5, William Fitt 1
Old Ignatians 7, Old Alpertonians 0
Westerns 0, East Barnet Old Grammarians 2

2nd Round Proper
South Bank 2*, Old Actonians Association 3*
Old Suttonians 4, Winchmore Hill 1
Old Foresters 0, Old Tiffinians 4
Carshalton 2, Old Hamptonians 1
Old Lyonian 7, Enfield Old Grammarians 1
Old Cholmeleians 1, Wake Green 2
Hampstead Heathens 3, St Mary's College 2
Hale End Athletic 3, Old Tenisonians 6

Ulysses 3, Corinthian-Casuals "A" 1
Broomfield 1, Civil Service 3
Lloyds Bank 2, Nottsborough 1
West Wickham 3, Alleyn Old Boys 0
Barclays Bank 6, Old Salesians 2
Parkfield 2, Polytechnic 5
Bank of England 2*:1*, Cuaco 2*:0*
Old Ignatians 3, East Barnet Old Grammarians 2

3rd Round Proper
Old Actonians Association 2, Old Suttonians 0
Old Tiffinian 1, Carshalton 0
Old Lyonian 2*, Wake Green 3*
Hampstead Heathens 0, Old Tenisonians 4
Ulysses 2, Civil Service 3
Lloyds Bank 1, West Wickham 0
Barclays Bank 3, Polytechnic 0
Bank of England 0, Old Ignatians 2

4th Round Proper
Old Actonians Association 2, Old Tiffinian 0
Wake Green 1, Old Tenisonians 2
Civil Service 2, Lloyds Bank 0
Barclays Bank 1, Old Ignatians 3

Semi-finals
Old Actonians Association 1, Old Tenisonians 0
Civil Service 5, Old Ignatians 1

Final
Old Actonians Association 4, Civil Service 0

*(*after extra time)*

REPRESENTATIVE MATCHES

v Southern Olympian League	Lost	0-2
v Royal Marines	Won	5-2
v Southern Amateur League "B"	Won	2-1
v Old Boys' League	Lost	1-3
v Stock Exchange FA	Won	3-1
v Bristol Insurance Institute	Lost	0-3

AFA CUP RESULTS 1995-96

Senior
Old Actonians Association 4, Civil Service 0
Intermediate
Crouch End Vampires Res. 4, Old Actonians Assn Res. 2
Junior
Winchmore Hill 3rd 1, Old Actonians Assn 3rd 0
Minor
Polytechnic 4th 1, Old Meadonians 4th 0
Senior Novets
Civil Service 5th 0, Old Suttonians 5th 1
Intermediate Novets
Old Finchleians 6th 2, Old Tollingtonians 6th 3
Junior Novets
Norsemen 8th 0, Old Suttonians 7th 2
Veterans
City of London Veterans 2, Winchmore Hill Veterans 4
Open Veterans
Tate & Lyall Veterans 1, Port of London Authority
  Veterans 2

Essex Senior
Old Foresters 2, Old Chigwellians 1
Middlesex Senior
Crouch End Vampires 3, Old Ignatians 2
Surrey Senior
Carshalton 1, South Bank 2
Essex Intermediate
Old Chigwellians Res. 4, Old Parkonians Res. 0
Kent Intermediate
West Wickham Res. 1, Old Addeyans 1st 0
Middlesex Intermediate
Cardinal Manning O B Res. 2, Crouch End Vampires
  Res. 1
Surrey Intermediate
Old Dorkinians Res. 4, Kew Association Res. 2
W E Greenland Memorial
Old Chigwellians 2*, Witan 1*

*(*after extra time)*

LONDON OLD BOYS' CUPS

Senior
Phoenix Old Boys 3, Old Meadonians 1
Intermediate
Old Tenisonians 1, Cardinal Manning O B Res. 4
Junior
Old Tenisonians 3rd 2, Phoenix Old Boys 3rd 1
Minor
Old Actonians 4th 2, Albanian 4th 1
Novets
Old Suttonians 5th 4*:6*, Old Tollingtonians 5th 4*:3*

Drummond
Old Tollingtonians 6th 9, Old Suttonians 6th 1
Nemean
Old Addeyans 6th 2, Old Salvatorians 8th 1
Veterans'
Old Isleworthians Veterans. 2, Old Tenisonians
  Veterans. 1

*(*after extra time)*

OLD BOYS' INVITATION CUPS

Senior
Old Lyonians 2, Old Owens 0
Junior
Old Finchleians Res. 3*, E. Barnet O. Grammarians Res. 3*wp
Minor
Old Finchleians 3rd 1, Glyn Old Boys 3rd 3
4th XI
Old Stationers 4th 2*, Old Suttonians 4th 2*wp
5th XI
Old Finchleians 5th 2, Old Suttonians 5th 1
6th XI
Old Owens 6th 4, Old Finchleians 6th 1
7th XI
Old Latymerians 7th 3, Old Suttonians 7th 0
Veterans' XI
Old Tenisonians Veterans 3, Old Finchleians Veterans 0

*(*after extra time; wp – won on penalties)*

SOUTHERN OLYMPIAN LEAGUE

Senior Section

Division One	P	W	D	L	F	A	Pts
Old Owens	18	14	2	2	56	24	30
Southgate County	18	11	3	4	42	28	25
Hale End Athletic	18	11	3	4	48	39	25
Parkfield	18	8	3	7	40	33	19
Witan	18	6	6	6	43	32	18
Albanian	18	5	7	6	29	35	17
Nottsborough	18	5	4	9	33	35	14
Ulysses	18	5	2	11	36	38	12
St Mary's College	18	4	3	11	21	48	11
Old Grammarians	18	3	3	12	26	62	9

Division Two	P	W	D	L	F	A	Pts
Old Finchleians	20	16	3	1	87	31	35
Wandsworth Borough	20	11	4	5	62	39	26
City of London	20	11	2	7	46	37	24
Old Woodhouseians	20	11	2	7	50	43	24
Corinthian-Casuals "A"	20	9	4	7	39	36	22
Honourable Artillery Company	20	7	3	10	45	52	17
UCL Academicals	20	7	3	10	31	46	17
Hadley	20	7	3	10	30	51	17
Mill Hill Village	20	6	3	11	40	55	15
Ealing Association	20	5	3	12	36	49	13
Old Bealonians	20	5	0	15	38	65	10

Division Three	P	W	D	L	F	A	Pts
Old Simmarobians	20	15	3	2	70	18	33
Westerns	20	15	3	2	69	21	33
Fulham Compton Old Boys	20	14	3	3	74	19	31
Hampstead Heathens	20	15	1	4	64	18	31
BBC	20	12	0	8	52	47	24
Old Fairlopians	20	6	3	11	42	56	15
Duncombe Sports	20	5	4	11	33	38	14
London Welsh	20	5	3	12	42	71	13
Birkbeck College	20	4	4	12	37	69	12
Old Monovians	20	5	1	14	25	70	11
Pollygons	20	0	3	16	22	103	3

Division Four	P	W	D	L	F	A	Pts
Pegasus (Inner Temple)	18	14	0	4	50	23	28
Old Colfeians	18	13	0	5	40	21	26
Mayfield Athletic	18	10	3	5	45	37	23
Inland Revenue	18	9	4	5	40	34	22
London Airways	18	9	3	6	51	49	21
Brent	18	6	5	7	22	23	17
New Scotland Yard Comets	18	5	4	9	24	32	14
Centymca	18	4	3	11	26	37	11
Cardinal Pole Old Boys	18	3	3	12	28	39	9
Economicals	18	3	3	12	27	58	9

Intermediate Section:
Division One–10 Teams–won by Nottsborough Res.
Division Two–10 Teams–won by Southgate County Res.
Division Three–11 Teams–won by Honourable Artillery Company Res.
Division Four–9 Teams–won by Westerns Res.

Junior Section:
Division One–10 Teams–won by Old Finchleians 3rd
Division Two–10 Teams–won by Albanian 4th
Division Three–10 Teams–won by Old Woodhouseians 3rd
Division Four–10 Teams–won by Fulham Compton Old Boys 3rd

Minor Section:
Division "A"–10 Teams–won by BBC 4th
Division "B"–11 Teams–won by Ealing Association 5th
Division "C"–10 Teams–won by Old Owens 6th
Division "D"–9 Teams–won by Brent 4th
Division "E"–9 Teams–won by Old Fairlopians 3rd

Senior Challenge Bowl–won by Witan
Senior Challenge Shield–won by Ealing Association
Intermediate Challenge Cup–won by Nottsborough Res.
Intermediate Challenge Shield–won by Albanian Res.
Junior Challenge Cup–won by Old Finchleians 3rd
Junior Challenge Shield–won by Hampstead Heathens 3rd
Mander Cup–won by Albanian 4th
Mander Shield–won by Old Finchleians 4th
Burntwood Trophy–won by Parkfield 5th
Burntwood Shield–won by Albanian 5th
Thomas Parmiter Cup–won by Old Finchleians 6th
Thomas Parmiter Shield–won by Old Bealonians 7th
Veterans' Challenge Cup–won by City of London Veterans.
Veterans' Challenge Shield–won by Parkfield Veterans.

ARTHUR DUNN CUP

Old Brentwoods 1, Lancing Old Boys 4

ARTHURIAN LEAGUE

Premier Division	P	W	D	L	F	A	Pts
Old Foresters	16	14	0	2	67	26	25†
Old Chigwellians	16	11	3	2	39	23	25
Lancing Old Boys	16	10	3	3	54	25	23
Old Carthusians	16	8	2	6	41	30	18
Old Reptonians	16	7	1	8	33	35	15
Old Cholmeleians	16	6	1	9	45	43	13
Old Etonians	16	5	2	9	32	44	12
Old Malvernians	16	4	1	11	25	47	9
Old Aldenhamians	16	0	1	15	10	73	1

Division One	P	W	D	L	F	A	Pts
Old Brentwoods	16	14	1	1	63	18	29
Old Witleians	16	11	3	2	57	25	25
Old Salopians	16	10	3	3	44	24	23
Old Wellingburians	16	7	4	5	41	49	16†
Old Bradfieldians	16	6	3	7	33	37	15
Old Harrovians	16	5	2	9	30	43	12
Old Haileyburians	16	4	2	10	40	56	10
Old Haberdashers	16	2	3	11	22	51	7
Old Wykehamists	16	2	1	13	25	52	5

Division Two	P	W	D	L	F	A	Pts
Old Chigwellians Res.	16	13	1	2	74	22	27
Old Cholmeleians Res.	16	8	4	4	39	24	20
Old Etonians Res.	16	7	6	3	36	28	17
Old Carthusians Res.	16	7	3	6	31	32	17
Old Foresters Res.	16	9	0	7	32	38	15†
Old Cholmeleians 3rd	16	5	3	8	33	35	13
Lancing Old Boys Res.	16	6	3	7	36	44	13†
Old Chigwellians 3rd	16	4	4	8	18	36	12
Old Salopians Res.	16	2	1	13	25	65	3†

Division Three	P	W	D	L	F	A	Pts
Old Etonians 3rd	16	10	5	1	52	21	25
Old Harrovians Res.	16	9	3	4	41	27	21
Old Brentwoods Res.	16	8	4	4	37	29	20
Old Haberdashers Res.	16	7	2	7	30	45	16
Old Aldenhamians Res.	16	6	3	7	45	50	15
Old Westminsters	16	7	1	8	37	40	13†
Old Eastbournians	16	5	1	10	28	36	11
Old Malvernians Res.	16	3	5	8	26	40	11
Old Reptonians Res.	16	2	4	10	38	46	8†

(†Points deducted – breach of rule)

Division Four–won by Old Cholmeleians 4th
Division Five–won by Old Haileyburians Res.
Junior League Cup–Old Chigwellians Res. 3, Old Brentwoods Res. 0
Derrik Moore Veterans Cup–Old Cholmeleians Veterans 1*, Old Carthusians Veterans 0*
*(*after extra time)*

LONDON LEGAL LEAGUE

Division One	P	W	D	L	F	A	Pts
Grays Inn	18	17	0	1	73	13	34
Wilde Sapte	18	14	2	2	58	25	30
Pegasus (Inner Temple)	18	9	4	5	46	34	22
Linklaters & Paines	18	7	5	6	31	37	19
Gouldens	18	6	4	8	27	42	16
Nabarro Nathanson	18	4	7	7	37	44	15
Cameron Markby Hewitt	18	6	2	10	33	44	14
Clifford Chance	18	6	1	11	26	38	13
D.J. Freeman & Co	18	4	1	13	28	46	9
Slaughter & May	18	3	2	13	24	56	8

Division Two	P	W	D	L	F	A	Pts
Lovell White Durrant	18	15	3	0	74	20	33
Herbert Smith	18	9	5	4	45	26	23
Rosling King	18	9	3	6	63	35	21
S.J. Berwin	18	9	3	6	59	57	21
Macfarlanes	18	8	3	7	48	43	19
Norton Rose	18	8	3	7	40	42	19
Freshfields	18	8	2	8	48	38	18
Allen & Overy	18	4	3	11	30	78	11
Stephenson Harwood	18	5	0	13	38	54	10
Watson Farley & Williams	18	2	1	15	21	63	5

Division Three	P	W	D	L	F	A	Pts
Baker & McKenzie	14	13	1	0	67	16	27
Taylor Joynson Garrett	14	9	3	2	39	31	21
McKenna & Co	14	6	2	6	35	37	14
Simmons & Simmons	14	6	2	6	28	32	14
Titmuss Sainer	14	5	2	7	31	25	12
Denton Hall	14	4	4	6	25	36	12
Barlow Lyde & Gilbert	14	3	3	8	25	41	9
Richards Butler	14	0	3	11	16	48	3

League Challenge Cup–Gray's Inn 1, Stephenson Harwood 0
Weavers Arms Cup–Wilde Sapte 4*, Taylor Joynson Garrett 3*
Invitation Cup–Allen & Overy 2, Titmuss Sainer 1
Division 3 Cup–Barlow Lyde & Gilbert 3, Taylor Joynson Garrett 4

LONDON FINANCIAL FA

Senior Section

Division One	P	W	D	L	F	A	Pts
Sun Alliance	18	11	6	1	53	14	28
Royal Bank of Scotland	18	12	2	4	77	23	26
Morgan Stanley International	18	11	1	6	50	26	23
Bank America	18	9	5	4	38	24	23
Kleinwort Benson	18	8	5	5	49	26	21
Coutts	18	9	2	7	49	28	20
Chemical Bank	18	6	4	8	43	72	16
Citibank	18	4	2	12	29	64	10
Temple Bar	18	2	3	13	21	91	7
Liverpool Victoria	18	2	2	14	30	71	6

Division Two	P	W	D	L	F	A	Pts
Morgan Guaranty	14	12	2	0	54	13	26
Churchill Insurance	14	10	1	3	40	11	21
Allied Irish Bank	14	7	4	3	51	34	18
Granby	14	8	1	5	48	34	17
Eagle Star	14	5	2	7	30	33	12
Sedgwick	14	4	2	8	30	50	10
Salomon Brothers	14	2	1	11	20	67	5
Bardhill	14	0	3	11	14	45	3
Invesco				Withdrew after 11 matches			

Division Three	P	W	D	L	F	A	Pts
Bowring	16	14	1	1	62	25	29
Royal Bank of Scotland Res.	16	9	0	7	45	39	18
United Bank of Kuwait	16	8	1	7	52	45	17
Chase Manhattan Bank	16	5	5	6	49	46	15
Union Bank of Switzerland	16	8	2	6	37	31	14†
Sedgwick Noble Lowndes	16	6	1	9	39	40	13
Direct Line Insurance	16	5	3	8	41	54	13
ANZ Banking Group	16	5	2	9	24	43	12
Coutts Res.	16	3	3	10	31	57	9

Division Four	P	W	D	L	F	A	Pts
Vantage	18	14	2	2	75	23	30
Bankers Trust	18	13	3	2	56	26	29
Citibank Res.	18	7	8	3	28	15	22
Granby Res.	18	8	3	7	51	41	19
Bank America Res.	18	8	3	7	49	40	19
Lincoln National	18	7	4	7	39	45	18
Royal Bank of Scotland 3rd	18	7	2	9	37	41	16
Asphalia	18	5	3	10	30	47	13
U C B Home Loans	18	1	6	11	20	52	8
Temple Bar Res.	18	2	2	14	28	83	6

(†*Points deducted – breach of rule*)

Division Five–9 Teams–won by Credit Suisse Financial Products
Division Six–8 Teams–won by Bowring Res.
Challenge Cup–Lensbury 2, Barclays Bank 1
Senior Cup–Royal Bank of Scotland 6, Morgan Guaranty 1
Senior Plate–Chemical Bank 3*, Liverpool Victoria 1*
Junior Cup–United Bank of Kuwait 4, Royal Bank of Scotland 3rd 0
Junior Plate–Citibank Res. 2, Vantage 1
Minor Cup–Sun Alliance 3rd 5, St Paul International 2
Minor Plate–British Gas (Bromley) 7*, Standard Chartered Bank 5*
Veterans' Cup–Lensbury 4, Bank America 2
Veterans' Plate–Sedgwick 5, Coutts Bank 4
W A Jewell Memorial–Chemical Bank 5-a-Side
Saunders Shield–Morgan Guaranty 5-a-Side
Sportsmanship Shield–Kleinwort Benson

OLD BOYS' LEAGUE

Premier Division	P	W	D	L	F	A	Pts
Old Aloysians	20	15	1	4	56	16	31
Glyn Old Boys	20	11	5	4	42	23	27
Cardinal Manning Old Boys	20	11	5	4	44	29	27
Old Meadonians	20	12	2	6	41	20	26
Old Tenisonians	20	9	5	6	50	34	23
Old Hamptonians	20	9	2	9	43	27	20
Latymer Old Boys	20	7	6	7	42	38	20
Old Ignatians	20	6	6	8	41	31	18
Clapham Old Xaverians	20	6	3	11	28	42	15
Old Isleworthians	20	5	1	14	29	56	11
Old Danes	20	1	0	19	10	110	2

Senior Division One	P	W	D	L	F	A	Pts
Old Kingsburians	20	14	3	3	44	28	31
Old Vaughanians	20	12	6	2	44	23	30
Old Suttonians	20	11	4	5	39	28	26
Old Tiffinians	20	10	1	9	36	35	21
Old Wilsonians	20	9	2	9	34	40	20
Old Salvatorians	20	9	1	10	39	41	19
Old Manorians	20	6	5	9	41	47	17
Chertsey Old Salesians	20	7	2	11	39	48	16
Phoenix Old Boys	20	7	1	12	34	37	15
Old Tenisonians Res.	20	5	4	11	36	40	14
Shene Old Grammarians	20	5	1	14	37	56	11

Senior Division Two	P	W	D	L	F	A	Pts
Enfield Old Grammarians	20	14	1	5	60	29	29
Old Westhamians	20	12	2	6	46	26	26
Old Camdenians	20	10	6	4	43	28	26
Old Minchendenians	20	11	4	5	43	33	26
Old Tollingtonians	20	11	2	7	52	36	24
Latymer Old Boys Res.	20	8	5	7	33	31	21
Old Wokingians	20	7	6	7	41	44	20
Old Meadonians Res.	20	7	2	11	34	39	16
Mill Hill County Old Boys	20	4	5	11	28	49	13
Phoenix Old Boys Res.	20	5	1	14	27	61	11
Old Southallians	20	3	2	15	20	51	8

Senior Division Three	P	W	D	L	F	A	Pts
Old Buckwellians	20	13	3	4	64	29	29
Old Reigatians	20	12	5	3	47	23	29
Old Grocers	20	12	4	4	65	39	28
Old Dorkinians	20	10	4	6	62	30	24
Old Vaughanians Res.	20	8	5	7	41	41	21
Old Hamptonians Res.	20	8	3	9	42	45	19
Old Salvatorians Res.	20	6	6	8	32	45	18
Glyn Old Boys Res.	20	6	3	11	38	47	15
John Fisher Old Boys	20	5	5	10	28	46	15
Old Tollingtonians Res.	20	5	5	10	31	57	15
Old Ignatians Res.	20	2	3	15	22	70	7

Intermediate Division North–12 Teams–won by Wood Green Old Boys
Intermediate Division South–11 Teams–won by Old Addeyans
Division One North–10 Teams–won by Old Highburians
Division One South–12 Teams–won by Old Tenisonians 3rd
Division One West–11 Teams–won by Old Uffingtonians
Division Two North–11 Teams–won by Old Grocers Res.
Division Two South–11 Teams–won by Old Suttonians 3rd
Division Two West–9 Teams–won by Old Alpertonians Res.
Division Three North–10 Teams–won by Davenant Wanderers Old Boys
Division Three South–12 Teams–won by Old Suttonians 4th
Division Three West–11 Teams–won by Old Alpertonians 3rd
Division Four North–10 Teams–won by Leyton County Old Boys 4th
Division Four South–11 Teams–won by Old St Mary's Res.
Division Four West–10 Teams–won by Old Uffingtonians 3rd
Division Five North–11 Teams–won by Old Tollingtonians 6th
Division Five South–12 Teams–won by Old Tenisonians 5th
Division Five West–10 Teams–won by Old Manorians 5th
Division Six North–10 Teams–won by Wood Green Old Boys 5th
Division Six South–10 Teams–won by Old Suttonians 7th
Division Six West–8 Teams–won by Holland Park Old Boys Res.
Division Seven North–7 Teams–won by Old Egbertians 5th
Division Seven South–10 Teams–won by Old Meadonians 8th
Division Seven West–9 Teams–won by Old Magdalenians Res.
Division Eight South–9 Teams–won by Clapham O. Xaverians 6th
Division Eight West–9 Teams–won by Holland Park Old Boys 3rd
Division Nine South–10 Teams–won by Holland Park Old Boys 5th

SOUTHERN AMATEUR LEAGUE

Senior Section

First Division	P	W	D	L	F	A	Pts
Old Actonians Association	22	17	3	2	54	20	35†
Crouch End Vampires	22	12	6	4	46	30	30
South Bank Polytechnic	22	12	5	5	45	32	29
National Westminster Bank	22	11	6	5	42	31	28
Old Esthameians	22	9	7	6	38	29	25
Civil Service	22	9	4	9	47	42	22
West Wickham	22	7	6	9	37	39	20
Carshalton	22	6	8	8	29	37	20
East Barnet Old Grammarians	22	4	8	10	25	43	16
Norsemen	22	4	5	13	22	43	13
Kew Association	22	3	6	13	30	47	12
Winchmore Hill	22	4	4	14	24	46	12

Second Division	P	W	D	L	F	A	Pts
Old Parmiterians	22	15	5	2	52	31	35
Polytechnic	22	14	4	4	55	34	32
Barclays Bank	22	12	2	8	51	39	26
Lloyds Bank	22	10	5	7	35	28	25
Alexandra Park	22	10	3	9	42	39	23
Old Lyonians	22	11	1	10	43	41	23
Old Parkonians	22	8	5	9	26	25	21
Old Latymerians	22	7	6	9	42	40	20
Lensbury	22	8	4	10	40	43	20
Old Stationers	22	6	7	9	25	38	19
Midland Bank	22	8	1	13	36	47	17
Old Bromleians	22	1	1	20	23	65	3

Third Division	P	W	D	L	F	A	Pts
Old Salesians	20	15	3	2	64	20	33
Cuaco	20	12	6	2	43	19	30
Bank of England	20	12	2	6	56	28	26
Alleyn Old Boys	20	9	5	6	47	30	23
Brentham	20	9	3	8	45	46	21
Merton	20	8	4	8	46	49	20
Broomfield	20	7	5	8	43	44	19
Southgate Olympic	20	8	2	10	38	41	18
Ibis	20	4	4	12	29	55	12
Reigate Priory	20	4	3	13	19	53	11
Old Westminster Citizens	20	3	1	16	21	66	7

(†Points deducted – breach of rule)

MIDLAND AMATEUR ALLIANCE

Division One	P	W	D	L	F	A	Pts
Old Elizabethans	22	17	3	2	77	25	37
Lady Bay	22	16	4	2	77	30	36
Magdala Amateurs	22	15	3	4	85	36	33
Racing Toton	22	13	1	8	55	52	27
Bassingfield	22	11	2	9	65	52	24
Kirton B W	22	10	3	9	42	45	23
Beeston Town "A"	22	7	5	10	28	47	19
Derbyshire Amateurs	22	8	2	12	32	48	18
Old Bemrosians	22	5	5	12	38	51	15
County Nalgo	22	5	3	14	38	72	13
Arnold & Carlton College	22	4	2	16	33	55	10
Brunts Old Boys	22	4	1	17	28	85	9

Division Two	P	W	D	L	F	A	Pts
Old Elizabethans Res.	20	13	3	4	48	23	29
Magdala Amateurs Res.	20	12	4	4	50	25	28
Nottingham Univ. Postgraduates	20	11	4	5	63	36	26
Ilkeston Rangers	20	11	3	6	47	38	25
Tibshelf Old Boys	20	10	3	7	38	40	23
Chilwell	20	9	4	7	40	40	22
Nottinghamshire	20	6	6	8	44	41	18
Beeston Old Boys Assn.	20	8	2	10	32	40	18
Woodborough United	20	5	5	10	35	44	15
Keyworth AFC	20	2	4	14	29	48	8
Bassingfield Res.	20	2	4	14	26	77	8

Division Three	P	W	D	L	F	A	Pts
South Forest	18	12	5	1	61	18	29
Lady Bay Res.	18	13	2	3	62	22	28
Old Elizabethans 3rd	18	10	3	5	43	25	23
Brunts Old Boys Res.	18	8	4	6	43	37	20
Derbyshire Amateurs Res.	18	8	3	7	35	36	19
Old Bemrosians Res.	18	6	3	9	34	40	15
Arnold & Carlton College Res.	18	5	3	10	37	52	13
West-Clif	18	6	0	12	32	60	12
Nottinghamshire Res.	18	3	5	10	18	36	11
Tibshelf Old Boys Res.	18	5	0	13	27	66	10

Division Four	P	W	D	L	F	A	Pts
Magdala Amateurs 3rd	16	13	0	3	80	23	26
Beeston O B Assn.Res.	16	10	0	6	42	29	20
Derbyshire Amateurs 3rd	16	10	0	6	47	40	20
Ilkeston Rangers Res.	16	9	0	7	48	35	18
Old Elizabethans 4th	16	8	1	7	29	39	17
Racing Toton Res.	16	7	0	9	49	53	14
West-Clif Res.	16	5	1	10	35	51	11
Old Bemrosians 3rd	16	4	2	10	32	53	10
Nottinghamshire 3rd	16	3	2	11	29	68	8

League Cups:
Senior–Lady Bay 2*, Old Elizabethans 1*
Intermediate–Lady Bay Res. 1, Old Elizabethans Res. 0
Minor: Old Elizabethans 3rd 5, Nottinghamshire 3rd 3
Challenge Trophy–Lady Bay 1*:4p, Old Bemrosians 1*:2p
Division Two Challenge–Bassingfield Res. 1, Magdala Amateurs Res. 7
Division Three Challenge–West-Clif 3*, Old Elizabethans 3rd 2*
Division Four Challenge–Derbyshire Amateurs 3rd 1*:4p, Old Elizabethans 4th 1*:2p
Division Three Supplementary–Lady Bay Res. 2, South Forest 3
Division Four Supplementary–Beeston OBA Res. 2, Magdala Amateurs 3rd 1
H.B. Poole Trophy–Lady Bay 0, Magdala Amateurs 2

THE INTERNATIONAL FOOTBALL HALL OF FAME

Where Football Lives ...
Rugby Hall Of Fame, Pro-Football Hall Of Fame, Basketball Hall Of Fame, Ice-Hockey Hall Of Fame, Tennis Hall Of Fame ...
... as a football fan have you ever thought why so many major sports are represented by their own 'Hall Of Fame', except the world's favourite game?

Well relax, this travesty is about to be rectified. As befits the country that gave the world football, England will soon be the home to the one and only definitive 'International Football Hall Of Fame'. And for the supporter it won't be a dictatorial and arbitrary election process but one in which *you* play an integral part in how a player gets selected. Nor will it be biased towards any country or continent – as befits the global scope of 'the beautiful game' it is for the players and fans of every country.

First things first. For all you uninitiated out there asking just what is a 'Hall Of Fame' and why it's so important to our world game, we'll try and explain ...

The idea behind a 'Hall Of Fame' is to celebrate and commemorate the best sportsmen and women of a given sport. The first major one to establish itself was the Baseball Hall Of Fame which has been going since 1939 in Cooperstown, New York. Through an annual election process, retired players are selected by a group of established baseball journalists.

This is the principle by which most others have followed. But not football (or soccer depending on where you live). Sure there have been exhibitions and self-proclaimed 'museums' in which displays have been set up, yet nothing on a permanent basis that honours the very best players the game has produced. And what a choice there is.

The (unofficial) history of modern football spans well over a hundred years. In that time it has gone through many manifestations and changes in style (especially with the current economic upheaval that's taking place), but most importantly whatever team or country you support it's also produced some exhilarating moments and some magical players – and continues to foster exciting legends for the future.

That's why honouring our heroes in the 'International Football Hall Of Fame' is so necessary: an election process that includes football fans, ex-footballers and journalists from every playing country around the world; and a magnificent new building that will become a shrine for fans and an exciting new leisure complex in its own right.

Celebrating the spirit and enjoyment of the game itself, this will be a magnificent (or state-of-the-art building featuring a museum, film auditoriums, an interactive entertainment centre, a training area, a mini-stadium and, of course, at its heart the actual 'Hall Of Fame' itself – a showcase for the chosen few who can truly be called legends!

That's the 'International Football Hall Of Fame'. An inspirational new concept *and* leisure complex for the players and the fans.

It's been far too long in coming – but now it's become a reality!

The Voting System
The nomination and selection procedures to the **International Football Hall Of Fame** are designed to represent the views of the general public, the footballers, and the football journalists world-wide. The procedure will mean that it's not the decision of a small group of people – but that it is truly open to debate around the world. And becomes the definitive roll-of-honour for the greatest football players.

We feel that this provides the fairest and most democratic voting procedure.

Can anyone make a nomination?
Yes. Each year any person, anywhere in the world can make one nomination for a retired football player to the **International Football Hall Of Fame**.

Can any football player be nominated?
No, there are two criteria that have to be met.
(1) A player must have been retired from the professional game for three years from June 30th of the election year. In 1996, therefore, a player must have retired by June 30th 1993.
(2) A player must have played at full international level, gaining at least one cap for their country of origin.
Your nomination can include any player from throughout the history of the game and from any country, not just your own. But unless someone nominates a player they cannot be considered for the **International Football Hall Of Fame**.

How do you make a nomination?
Your nomination can be sent by post, by facsimile or by E-Mail, and must be made directly to the **International Football Hall Of Fame**. Only one nomination can be made each year. Your communication should include your name, address and country of residence. All nominations will be collated on a database from which a final list will be produced.

What happens to the list of nominations?
A Selection Committee comprised of an ex-player from each of the countries listed below and Chaired by a member of the Professional Footballers Association (PFA), who also has a vote, will select a shortlist of fifty candidates from the complete list of nominees.

England	Germany	France	Switzerland
Sweden	Italy	Spain	Mexico
Uruguay	Chile	Argentina	USA
Brazil	Japan	Morocco	Australia

The criteria for these participating countries is as follows: (1) those who have won or hosted the World Cup; (2) in addition, a representative nation from continents not represented through this will also be selected by the **International Football Hall Of Fame**.

This Selection Committee will be brought together during one weekend at the end of each year to produce the shortlist of fifty candidates.

How will a player be elected a 'Hall Of Fame'?
The shortlist of fifty nominees is sent to a selected sports journalist from every FIFA registered country. The journalists choose their top five players and send their selections back to the **International Football Hall Of Fame**. The five nominees who accumulate the most amount of journalists' votes are elected to the **International Football Hall Of Fame**. If, in any event, any players end up with the same amount of votes in that top five, then all those players will be elected.

To make your nomination write to:
The International Football Hall Of Fame
14a Eccleston Street, London SW1W 9LT
or E-Mail us at:
101531.323@compuserve.com
or visit us at:
http://www.int-foot-fame.com

RECORDS

Major British Records

HIGHEST WINS

First-Class Match		Arbroath *(Scottish Cup 1st Round)*	36	Bon Accord	0	12 Sept 1885
International Match		England	13	Ireland	0	18 Feb 1882
FA Cup		Preston NE *(1st Round)*	26	Hyde U	0	15 Oct 1887
League Cup		West Ham U *(2nd Round, 2nd Leg)*	10	Bury	0	25 Oct 1983
		Liverpool *(2nd Round, 1st Leg)*	10	Fulham	0	23 Sept 1986

FA PREMIER LEAGUE

	(Home)	Manchester U	9	Ipswich T	0	4 March 1995

FOOTBALL LEAGUE

Division 1	*(Home)*	WBA	12	Darwen	0	4 April 1892
		Nottingham F	12	Leicester Fosse	0	21 April 1909
	(Away)	Newcastle U	1	Sunderland	9	5 Dec 1908
		Cardiff C	1	Wolverhampton W	9	3 Sept 1955
Division 2	*(Home)*	Newcastle U	13	Newport Co	0	5 Oct 1946
	(Away)	Burslem PV	0	Sheffield U	10	10 Dec 1892
Division 3	*(Home)*	Gillingham	10	Chesterfield	0	5 Sept 1987
	(Away)	Halifax T	0	Fulham	8	16 Sept 1969
Division 3(S)	*(Home)*	Luton T	12	Bristol R	0	13 April 1936
	(Away)	Northampton T	0	Walsall	8	2 Feb 1947
Division 3(N)	*(Home)*	Stockport Co	13	Halifax T	0	6 Jan 1934
	(Away)	Accrington S	0	Barnsley	9	3 Feb 1934
Division 4	*(Home)*	Oldham Ath	11	Southport	0	26 Dec 1962
	(Away)	Crewe Alex	1	Rotherham U	8	8 Sept 1973
Aggregate Division 3(N)		Tranmere R	13	Oldham Ath	4	26 Dec 1935

SCOTTISH LEAGUE

Premier	*(Home)*	Aberdeen	8	Motherwell	0	26 March 1979
Division	*(Away)*	Hamilton A	0	Celtic	8	5 Nov 1988
Division 1	*(Home)*	Celtic	11	Dundee	0	26 Oct 1895
	(Away)	Airdrieonians	1	Hibernian	11	24 Oct 1950
Division 2	*(Home)*	Airdrieonians	15	Dundee Wanderers	1	1 Dec 1894
	(Away)	Alloa Ath	0	Dundee	10	8 March 1947

LEAGUE CHAMPIONSHIP HAT-TRICKS

Huddersfield T	1923–24 to 1925–26
Arsenal	1932–33 to 1934–35
Liverpool	1981–82 to 1983–84

MOST GOALS FOR IN A SEASON

		Goals	Games	Season
FA PREMIER LEAGUE				
	Newcastle U	82	42	1993–94
FOOTBALL LEAGUE				
Division 1	Aston V	128	42	1930–31
Division 2	Middlesbrough	122	42	1926–27
Division 3(S)	Millwall	127	42	1927–28
Division 3(N)	Bradford C	128	42	1928–29
Division 3	QPR	111	46	1961–62
Division 4	Peterborough U	134	46	1960–61
SCOTTISH LEAGUE				
Premier Division	Rangers	101	44	1991–92
	Dundee U	90	36	1982–83
	Celtic	90	36	1982–83
	Celtic	90	44	1986–87
Division 1	Hearts	132	34	1957–58
Division 2	Raith R	142	34	1937–38
New Division 1	Dunfermline Ath	93	44	1993–94
	Motherwell	92	39	1981–82
New Division 2	Ayr U	95	39	1987–88
New Division 3	Montrose	69	36	1994–95

FEWEST GOALS FOR IN A SEASON

FA PREMIER LEAGUE		Goals	Games	Season
	Manchester C	33	38	1995–96
	Crystal Palace	34	42	1994–95
FOOTBALL LEAGUE	(minimum 42 games)			
Division 1	Stoke C	24	42	1984–85
Division 2	Watford	24	42	1971–72
	Leyton Orient	30	46	1994–95
Division 3(S)	Crystal Palace	33	42	1950–51
Division 3(N)	Crewe Alex	32	42	1923–24
Division 3	Stockport Co	27	46	1969–70
Division 4	Crewe Alex	29	46	1981–82
SCOTTISH LEAGUE	(minimum 30 games)			
Premier Division	Hamilton A	19	36	1988–89
	Dunfermline Ath	22	44	1991–92
Division 1	Brechin C	30	44	1993–94
	Ayr U	20	34	1966–67
Division 2	Lochgelly U	20	38	1923–24
New Division 1	Stirling Alb	18	39	1980–81
	Dumbarton	23	36	1995–96
New Division 2	Berwick R	22	36	1994–95
New Division 3	Alloa	26	36	1995–96

MOST GOALS AGAINST IN A SEASON

FA PREMIER LEAGUE		Goals	Games	Season
	Swindon T	100	42	1993–94
FOOTBALL LEAGUE				
Division 1	Blackpool	125	42	1930–31
Division 2	Darwen	141	34	1898–99
Division 3(S)	Merthyr T	135	42	1929–30
Division 3(N)	Nelson	136	42	1927–28
Division 3	Accrington S	123	46	1959–60
Division 4	Hartlepools U	109	46	1959–60
SCOTTISH LEAGUE				
Premier Division	Morton	100	36	1984–85
	Morton	100	44	1987–88
Division 1	Leith Ath	137	38	1931–32
Division 2	Edinburgh C	146	38	1931–32
New Division 1	Queen of the S	99	39	1988–89
	Cowdenbeath	109	44	1992–93
New Division 2	Meadowbank T	89	39	1977–78
New Division 3	Albion R	82	36	1994–95

FEWEST GOALS AGAINST IN A SEASON

FA PREMIER LEAGUE		Goals	Games	Season
	Arsenal	28	42	1993–94
	Manchester U	28	42	1994–95
FOOTBALL LEAGUE	(minimum 42 games)			
Division 1	Liverpool	16	42	1978–79
Division 2	Manchester U	23	42	1924–25
	West Ham U	34	46	1990–91
Division 3(S)	Southampton	21	42	1921–22
Division 3(N)	Port Vale	21	46	1953–54
Division 3	Gillingham	20	46	1995–96
Division 4	Lincoln C	25	46	1980–81
SCOTTISH LEAGUE	(minimum 30 games)			
Premier Division	Rangers	19	36	1989–90
	Rangers	23	44	1986–87
	Celtic	23	44	1987–88
Division 1	Celtic	14	38	1913–14
Division 2	Morton	20	38	1966–67
New Division 1	Hibernian	24	39	1980–81
	Falkirk	32	44	1993–94
New Division 2	St Johnstone	24	39	1987–88
	Stirling Alb	24	39	1990–91
New Division 3	Brechin C	21	36	1995–96

MOST POINTS IN A SEASON

FOOTBALL LEAGUE	(under old system of two points for a win)	*Points*	*Games*	*Season*
Division 1	Liverpool	68	42	1978–79
Division 2	Tottenham H	70	42	1919–20
Division 3	Aston V	70	46	1971–72
Division 3(S)	Nottingham F	70	46	1950–51
	Bristol C	70	46	1954–55
Division 3(N)	Doncaster R	72	42	1946–47
Division 4	Lincoln C	74	46	1975–76
SCOTTISH LEAGUE				
Premier Division	Aberdeen	59	36	1984–85
	Rangers	73	44	1992–93
Division 1	Rangers	76	42	1920–21
Division 2	Morton	69	38	1966–67
New Division 1	St Mirren	62	39	1976–77
	Falkirk	66	44	1993–94
New Division 2	Forfar Ath	63	39	1983–84
FA PREMIER LEAGUE	(three points for a win)			
	Manchester U	92	42	1993–94
FOOTBALL LEAGUE				
Division 1	Everton	90	42	1984–85
	Liverpool	90	40	1987–88
Division 2	Chelsea	99	46	1988–89
Division 3	Bournemouth	97	46	1986–87
Division 4	Swindon T	102	46	1985–86
SCOTTISH LEAGUE				
Premier Division	Rangers	87	36	1995–96
New Division 1	Dunfermline Ath	71	36	1995–96
New Division 2	Stirling Alb	81	36	1995–96
New Division 3	Forfar Ath	80	36	1994–95

FEWEST POINTS IN A SEASON

FA PREMIER LEAGUE		*Points*	*Games*	*Season*
	Ipswich T	27	42	1994–95
FOOTBALL LEAGUE	(minimum 34 games)			
Division 1	Stoke C	17	42	1984–85
Division 2	Doncaster R	8	34	1904–05
	Loughborough T	8	34	1899–1900
	Walsall	31	46	1988–89
Division 3	Rochdale	21	46	1973–74
	Cambridge U	21	46	1984–85
Division 3(S)	Merthyr T	21	42	1924–25 & 1929–30
	QPR	21	42	1925–26
Division 3(N)	Rochdale	11	40	1931–32
Division 4	Workington	19	46	1976–77
SCOTTISH LEAGUE	(minimum 30 games)			
Premier Division	St Johnstone	11	36	1975–76
	Morton	16	44	1987–88
Division 1	Stirling Alb	6	30	1954–55
Division 2	Edinburgh C	7	34	1936–37
New Division 1	Queen of the S	10	39	1988–89
	Cowdenbeath	13	44	1992–93
New Division 2	Berwick R	16	39	1987–88
	Stranraer	16	39	1987–88

MOST WINS IN A SEASON

FA PREMIER LEAGUE		*Wins*	*Games*	*Season*
	Manchester U	27	42	1993–94
	Blackburn R	27	42	1994–95
FOOTBALL LEAGUE				
Division 1	Tottenham H	31	42	1960–61
Division 2	Tottenham H	32	42	1919–20
Division 3(S)	Millwall	30	42	1927–28
	Plymouth Arg	30	42	1929–30
	Cardiff C	30	42	1946–47
	Nottingham F	30	46	1950–51
	Bristol C	30	46	1954–55

Division 3(N)	Doncaster R	33	42	1946–47
Division 3	Aston V	32	46	1971–72
Division 4	Lincoln C	32	46	1975–76
	Swindon T	32	46	1985–86
SCOTTISH LEAGUE				
Premier Division	Rangers	27	36	1995–96
	Aberdeen	27	36	1984–85
	Rangers	33	44	1991–92
	Rangers	33	44	1992–93
Division 1	Rangers	35	42	1920–21
Division 2	Morton	33	38	1966–67
New Division 1	Motherwell	26	39	1981–82
New Division 2	Forfar Ath	27	39	1983–84
	Ayr U	27	39	1987–88
New Division 3	Forfar Ath	25	36	1994–95

RECORD HOME WINS IN A SEASON

Brentford won all 21 games
in Division 3(S), 1929–30

UNDEFEATED AT HOME

Liverpool 85 games (63
League, 9 League Cup, 7
European, 6 FA Cup), Jan
1978–Jan 1981

RECORD AWAY WINS IN A SEASON

Doncaster R won 18
of 21 games in Division 3(N),
1946–47

FEWEST WINS IN A SEASON

		Wins	Games	Season
FA PREMIER LEAGUE				
	Swindon T	5	42	1993–94
FOOTBALL LEAGUE				
Division 1	Stoke C	3	22	1889–90
	Woolwich Arsenal	3	38	1912–13
	Stoke C	3	42	1984–85
Division 2	Loughborough T	1	34	1899–1900
	Walsall	5	46	1988–89
Division 3(S)	Merthyr T	6	42	1929–30
	QPR	6	42	1925–26
Division 3(N)	Rochdale	4	40	1931–32
Division 3	Rochdale	2	46	1973–74
Division 4	Southport	3	46	1976–77
SCOTTISH LEAGUE				
Premier Division	St Johnstone	3	36	1975–76
	Kilmarnock	3	36	1982–83
	Morton	3	44	1987–88
Division 1	Vale of Leven	0	22	1891–92
Division 2	East Stirlingshire	1	22	1905–06
	Forfar Ath	1	38	1974–75
New Division 1	Queen of the S	2	39	1988–89
	Cowdenbeath	3	44	1992–93
New Division 2	Forfar Ath	4	26	1975–76
	Stranraer	4	39	1987–88
New Division 3	Albion R	5	36	1994–95

MOST DEFEATS IN A SEASON

		Defeats	Games	Season
FA PREMIER LEAGUE				
	Ipswich T	29	42	1994–95
FOOTBALL LEAGUE				
Division 1	Stoke C	31	42	1984–85
Division 2	Tranmere R	31	42	1938–39
	Chester C	33	46	1992–93
Division 3	Cambridge U	33	46	1984–85
Division 3(S)	Merthyr T	29	42	1924–25
	Walsall	29	46	1952–53
	Walsall	29	46	1953–54

Division 3(N)	Rochdale	33	40	1931–32
Division 4	Newport Co	33	46	1987–88

SCOTTISH LEAGUE

Premier Division	Morton	29	36	1984–85
Division 1	St Mirren	31	42	1920–21
Division 2	Brechin C	30	36	1962–63
	Lochgelly	30	38	1923–24
New Division 1	Queen of the S	29	39	1988–89
	Dumbarton	31	36	1995–96
	Cowdenbeath	34	44	1992–93
New Division 2	Berwick R	29	39	1987–88
New Division 3	Albion R	28	36	1994–95

HAT-TRICKS

Career   34 Dixie Dean (Tranmere R, Everton, Notts Co, England)
Division 1 (one season post-war)   6 Jimmy Greaves (Chelsea), 1960–61
Three for one team one match
West, Spouncer, Hooper, Nottingham F v Leicester Fosse, Division 1, 21 April 1909
Barnes, Ambler, Davies, Wrexham v Hartlepools U, Division 4, 3 March 1962
Adcock, Stewart, White, Manchester C v Huddersfield T, Division 2, 7 Nov 1987
Loasby, Smith, Wells, Northampton T v Walsall, Division 3S, 5 Nov 1927
Bowater, Hoyland, Readman, Mansfield T v Rotherham U, Division 3N, 27 Dec 1932

FEWEST DEFEATS IN A SEASON
(*Minimum 20 games*)

FA PREMIER LEAGUE		*Defeats*	*Games*	*Season*
	Manchester U	4	42	1993–94
FOOTBALL LEAGUE				
Division 1	Preston NE	0	22	1888–89
	Arsenal	1	38	1990–91
	Liverpool	2	40	1987–88
	Leeds U	2	42	1968–69
Division 2	Liverpool	0	28	1893–94
	Burnley	2	30	1897–98
	Bristol C	2	38	1905–06
	Leeds U	3	42	1963–64
	Chelsea	5	46	1988–89
Division 3	QPR	5	46	1966–67
	Bristol R	5	46	1989–90
Division 3(S)	Southampton	4	42	1921–22
	Plymouth Arg	4	42	1929–30
Division 3(N)	Port Vale	3	46	1953–54
	Doncaster R	3	42	1946–47
	Wolverhampton W	3	42	1923–24
Division 4	Lincoln C	4	46	1975–76
	Sheffield U	4	46	1981–82
	Bournemouth	4	46	1981–82
SCOTTISH LEAGUE				
Premier Division	Rangers	3	36	1995–96
	Celtic	3	44	1987–88
Division 1	Rangers	0	18	1898–99
	Rangers	1	42	1920–21
Division 2	Clyde	1	36	1956–57
	Morton	1	36	1962–63
	St Mirren	1	36	1967–68
New Division 1	Partick T	2	26	1975–76
	St Mirren	2	39	1976–77
	Raith R	4	44	1992–93
	Falkirk	4	44	1993–94
New Division 2	Raith R	1	26	1975–76
	Clydebank	3	26	1975–76
	Forfar Ath	3	39	1983–84
	Raith R	3	39	1986–87
	Livingston	6	36	1995–96
New Division 3	Forfar Ath	6	36	1994–95

MOST DRAWN GAMES IN A SEASON

FA PREMIER LEAGUE		*Draws*	*Games*	*Season*
	Manchester C	18	42	1993–94
	Sheffield U	18	42	1993–94
	Southampton	18	42	1994–95
FOOTBALL LEAGUE				
Division 1	Norwich C	23	42	1978–79
Division 4	Exeter C	23	46	1986–87
SCOTTISH LEAGUE				
Premier Division	Aberdeen	21	44	1993–94
New Division 1	East Fife	21	44	1986–87

MOST GOALS IN A GAME

FA PREMIER LEAGUE	Andy Cole (Manchester U) 5 goals v Ipswich T	4 Mar 1995
FOOTBALL LEAGUE		
Division 1	Ted Drake (Arsenal) 7 goals v Aston V	14 Dec 1935
	James Ross (Preston NE) 7 goals v Stoke	6 Oct 1888
Division 2	Tommy Briggs (Blackburn R) 7 goals v Bristol R	5 Feb 1955
	Neville Coleman (Stoke C) 7 goals v Lincoln C (away)	23 Feb 1957
Division 3(S)	Joe Payne (Luton T) 10 goals v Bristol R	13 April 1936
Division 3(N)	Bunny Bell (Tranmere R) 9 goals v Oldham Ath	26 Dec 1935
Division 3	Steve Earle (Fulham) 5 goals v Halifax T	16 Sept 1969
	Barrie Thomas (Scunthorpe U) 5 goals v Luton T	24 April 1965
	Keith East (Swindon T) 5 goals v Mansfield T	20 Nov 1965
	Alf Wood (Shrewsbury T) 5 goals v Blackburn R	2 Oct 1971
	Tony Caldwell (Bolton W) 5 goals v Walsall	10 Sept 1983
	Andy Jones (Port Vale) 5 goals v Newport Co	4 May 1987
	Steve Wilkinson (Mansfield T) 5 goals v Birmingham C	3 April 1990
Division 4	Bert Lister (Oldham Ath) 6 goals v Southport	26 Dec 1962
FA CUP	Ted MacDougall (Bournemouth) 9 goals v Margate (*1st Round*)	20 Nov 1971
LEAGUE CUP	Frankie Bunn (Oldham Ath) 6 goals v Scarborough	25 Oct 1989
SCOTTISH LEAGUE CUP	Jim Fraser (Ayr U) 5 goals v Dumbarton	13 Aug 1952
SCOTTISH LEAGUE		
Premier Division	Paul Sturrock (Dundee U) 5 goals v Morton	17 Nov 1984
Division 1	Jimmy McGrory (Celtic) 8 goals v Dunfermline Ath	14 Sept 1928
Division 2	Owen McNally (Arthurlie) 8 goals v Armadale	1 Oct 1927
	Jim Dyet (King's Park) 8 goals v Forfar Ath	2 Jan 1930
	John Calder (Morton) 8 goals v Raith R	18 April 1936
	Norman Hayward (Raith R) 8 goals v Brechin C	20 Aug 1937
SCOTTISH CUP	John Petrie (Arbroath) 13 goals v Bon Accord (*1st Round*)	12 Sept 1885

MOST LEAGUE GOALS IN A SEASON

		Goals	Games	Season
FA PREMIER LEAGUE	Andy Cole (Newcastle U)	34	40	1993–94
	Alan Shearer (Blackburn R)	34	42	1994–95
Division 1	Dixie Dean (Everton)	60	39	1927–28
Division 2	George Camsell (Middlesbrough)	59	37	1926–27
Division 3(S)	Joe Payne (Luton T)	55	39	1936–37
Division 3(N)	Ted Harston (Mansfield T)	55	41	1936–37
Division 3	Derek Reeves (Southampton)	39	46	1959–60
Division 4	Terry Bly (Peterborough U)	52	46	1960–61
FA CUP	Sandy Brown (Tottenham H)	15	8	1900–01
LEAGUE CUP	Clive Allen (Tottenham H)	12	9	1986–87
SCOTTISH LEAGUE				
Division 1	William McFadyen (Motherwell)	52	34	1931–32
Division 2	Jim Smith (Ayr U)	66	38	1927–28

MOST LEAGUE GOALS IN A CAREER

		Goals	Games	Season
FOOTBALL LEAGUE				
Arthur Rowley	WBA	4	24	1946–48
	Fulham	27	56	1948–50
	Leicester C	251	303	1950–58
	Shrewsbury T	152	236	1958–65
		434	619	
SCOTTISH LEAGUE				
Jimmy McGrory	Celtic	1	3	1922–23
	Clydebank	13	30	1923–24
	Celtic	396	375	1924–38
		410	408	

MOST CUP GOALS IN A CAREER

FA CUP (post-war)

Ian Rush 42 (Chester, Liverpool)
Pre-war: Henry Cursham 48 (Notts Co)

A CENTURY OF LEAGUE AND CUP GOALS IN CONSECUTIVE SEASONS

George Camsell	Middlesbrough	59 Lge	5 Cup	1926–27
(101 goals)		33	4	1927–28
Steve Bull	Wolverhampton W	34 Lge	18 Cup	1987–88
(102 goals)		37	13	1988–89

(Camsell's cup goals were all scored in the FA Cup; Bull had 12 in the Sherpa Van Trophy, 3 Littlewoods Cup, 3 FA Cup in 1987–88; 11 Sherpa Van Trophy, 2 Littlewoods Cup in 1988–89.)

LONGEST SEQUENCE OF CONSECUTIVE SCORING (Individual)

FA PREMIER LEAGUE
Mark Stein (Chelsea)   9 in 7 games   1993–94
FOOTBALL LEAGUE
RECORD
Dixie Dean (Everton)   23 in 12 games   1930–31

LONGEST WINNING SEQUENCE

FOOTBALL LEAGUE		*Games*	*Season*
Division 1	Tottenham H	13	1959–60 (2) and 1960–61 (11)
	Preston NE	13	1891–92
	Sunderland	13	1891–92
Division 2	Manchester U	14	1904–05
	Bristol C	14	1905–06
	Preston NE	14	1950–51
Division 3	Reading	13	1985–86
From Season's start			
Division 1	Tottenham H	11	1960–61
Division 3	Reading	13	1985–86

LONGEST WINNING SEQUENCE IN A SEASON

FOOTBALL LEAGUE		*Games*	*Season*
Division 1	Tottenham H	11	1960–61
Division 2	Manchester U	14	1904–05
Division 2	Bristol C	14	1905–06
Division 2	Preston NE	14	1950–51
SCOTTISH LEAGUE			
Division 2	Morton	23	1963–64

LONGEST UNBEATEN SEQUENCE

FOOTBALL LEAGUE		*Games*	*Seasons*
Division 1	Nottingham F	42	Nov 1977–Dec 1978

LONGEST UNBEATEN CUP SEQUENCE

Liverpool   25 rounds   League/Milk Cup   1980–84

LONGEST UNBEATEN SEQUENCE IN A SEASON

FOOTBALL LEAGUE		*Games*	*Season*
Division 1	Burnley	30	1920–21

LONGEST UNBEATEN START TO A SEASON

FOOTBALL LEAGUE		*Games*	*Season*
Division 1	Leeds U	29	1973–74
Division 1	Liverpool	29	1987–88

LONGEST SEQUENCE WITHOUT A WIN IN A SEASON

FOOTBALL LEAGUE		*Games*	*Season*
Division 2	Cambridge U	31	1983–84

LONGEST SEQUENCE WITHOUT A WIN FROM SEASON'S START

Division 1	Manchester U	12	1930–31

LONGEST SEQUENCE OF CONSECUTIVE DEFEATS

FOOTBALL LEAGUE		*Games*	*Season*
Division 2	Darwen	18	1898–99

GOALKEEPING RECORDS (WITHOUT CONCEDING A GOAL)

British record (all competitive games)
Chris Woods, Rangers, in 1196 minutes from 26 November 1986 to 31 January 1987.
Football League
Steve Death, Reading, 1103 minutes from 24 March to 18 August 1979.

PENALTIES

Most in a Season (individual)		*Goals*	*Season*
Division 1	Francis Lee (Manchester C)	13	1971–72
Most awarded in one game			
Five	Crystal Palace (4 – 1 scored, 3 missed) v Brighton & HA (1 scored), Div 2		1988–89
Most saved in a Season			
Division 1	Paul Cooper (Ipswich T)	8 (of 10)	1979–80

MOST LEAGUE APPEARANCES (750+ matches)

996 Peter Shilton (286 Leicester City, 110 Stoke City, 202 Nottingham Forest, 188 Southampton, 175 Derby County, 34
Plymouth Argyle, 1 Bolton Wanderers) 1966–95
824 Terry Paine (713 Southampton, 111 Hereford United) 1957–77
795 Tommy Hutchison (165 Blackpool, 314 Coventry City, 46 Manchester City, 92 Burnley 178 Swansea City, also 68
Alloa 1965–68) 1968–91
782 Robbie James (484 Swansea C, 48 Stoke C, 87 QPR, 23 Leicester C, 89 Bradford C, 51 Cardiff C)777 Alan Oakes
(565 Manchester City, 211 Chester City, 1 Port Vale) 1959–84
771 John Burridge (27 Workington, 134 Blackpool, 65 Aston Villa, 6 Southend U (loan), 88 Crystal Palace, 39 QPR, 74
Wolverhampton W, 6 Derby Co (loan), 109 Sheffield U, 62 Southampton, 67 Newcastle U, 65 Hibernian, 3
Scarborough, 4 Lincoln C, 3 Aberdeen, 3 Dumbarton, 3 Falkirk, 4 Manchester C, 3 Darlington, 6 Queen of the South)
1968–96
770 John Trollope (all for Swindon Town) 1960–80†
764 Jimmy Dickinson (all for Portsmouth) 1946–65
761 Roy Sproson (all for Port Vale) 1950–72
758 Ray Clemence (48 Scunthorpe United, 470 Liverpool, 240 Tottenham Hotspur) 1966–87
758 Billy Bonds (95 Charlton Ath, 663 West Ham U)
757 Pat Jennings (48 Watford, 472 Tottenham Hotspur, 237 Arsenal) 1963–86
757 Frank Worthington (171 Huddersfield T, 210 Leicester C, 84 Bolton W, 75 Birmingham C, 32 Leeds U, 195
Sunderland, 34 Southampton, 31 Brighton & HA, 59 Tranmere R, 23 Preston NE, 19 Stockport Co) 1966–88
† record for one club

Consecutive
401 Harold Bell (401 Tranmere R; 459 in all games) 1946–55

FA CUP
88 Ian Callaghan (79 Liverpool, 7 Swansea C, 2 Crewe Alex)

Most Senior Matches
1379 Peter Shilton (996 League, 86 FA Cup, 102 League Cup, 125 Internationals, 13 Under-23, 4 Football League XI, 53
others including European Cup, UEFA Cup, World Club Championship, various domestic cup competitions)

MOST FA CUP FINAL GOALS

Ian Rush (Liverpool) 5: 1986(2), 1989(2), 1992(1)

MOST LEAGUE MEDALS

Phil Neal (Liverpool) 8: 1976, 1977, 1979, 1980, 1982, 1983, 1984, 1986

OTHER RECORDS

YOUNGEST PLAYERS
FA Premier League   Neil Finn, 17 years 3 days, West Ham v Manchester C 1.1.96.
FA Premier League scorer   Andy Turner, 17 years 166 days, Tottenham H v Everton, 5.9.92.
Football League   Albert Geldard, 15 years 158 days, Bradford Park Avenue v Millwall, Division 2, 16.9.29; and Ken
Roberts, 15 years 158 days, Wrexham v Bradford Park Avenue, Division 3N, 1.9.51
Football League scorer
   Ronnie Dix, 15 years 180 days, Bristol Rovers v Norwich City, Division 3S, 3.3.28.
Division 1
   Derek Forster, 15 years 185 days, Sunderland v Leicester City, 22.8.84.
Division 1 scorer
   Jason Dozzell, 16 years 57 days as substitute Ipswich Town v Coventry City, 4.2.84
Division 1 hat-tricks
   Alan Shearer, 17 years 240 days, Southampton v Arsenal, 9.4.88.
   Jimmy Greaves, 17 years 10 months, Chelsea v Portsmouth, 25.12.57
FA Cup (any round)
   Andy Awford, 15 years 88 days as substitute Worcester City v Boreham Wood, 3rd Qual. rd, 10.10.87
FA Cup proper
   Scott Endersby, 15 years 288 days, Kettering v Tilbury, 1st rd, 26.11.77
FA Cup Final
   James Prinsep, 17 years 245 days, Clapham Rovers v Old Etonians, 1879
FA Cup Final scorer
   Norman Whiteside, 18 years 18 days, Manchester United v Brighton & Hove Albion, 1983

FA Cup Final captain
David Nish, 21 years 212 days, Leicester City v Manchester City, 1969
League Cup Final scorer
Norman Whiteside, 17 years 324 days, Manchester United v Liverpool, 1983
League Cup Final captain
Barry Venison, 20 years 7 months 8 days, Sunderland v Norwich City, 1985
OLDEST PLAYERS
Football League
Neil McBain, 52 years 4 months, New Brighton v Hartlepools United, Div 3N, 15.3.47 (McBain was New Brighton's manager and had to play in an emergency)
Division 1
Stanley Matthews, 50 years 5 days, Stoke City v Fulham, 6.2.65
FA Cup Final
Walter Hampson, 41 years 8 months, Newcastle United v Aston Villa, 1924
FA Cup
Billy Meredith, 49 years 8 months, Manchester City v Newcastle United, 29.3.24
International debutant
Leslie Compton, 38 years 2 months, England v Wales, 15.11.50
International
Billy Meredith, 45 years 229 days, Wales v England, 15.3 20

SENDINGS-OFF

Season	314 (League alone)	1994–95
Day	15 (3 League, 12 FA Cup*)	20 Nov 1982
	worst overall FA Cup total	
League	13	14 Dec 1985
Weekend	15	22/23 Dec 1990
FA Cup Final	Kevin Moran, Manchester U v Everton	1985
Wembley	Boris Stankovic, Yugoslavia v Sweden (Olympics)	1948
	Antonio Rattin, Argentina v England (World Cup)	1966
	Billy Bremner (Leeds U) and Kevin Keegan (Liverpool), Charity Shield	1974
	Gilbert Dresch, Luxembourg v England (World Cup)	1977
	Mike Henry, Sudbury T v Tamworth (FA Vase)	1989
	Lee Dixon, Arsenal v Tottenham H (FA Cup semi-final)	1993
	Peter Swan, Port Vale v WBA (play-offs)	1993
	Michael Wallace and Chris Beaumont (both Stockport Co) v Burnley (play-offs)	1994
Quickest	Mark Smith, Crewe Alex v Darlington (away) Div 3: 19 secs	12 March 1994
Division 1	Liam O'Brien, Manchester U v Southampton (away): 85 secs	3 Jan 1987
World Cup	Jose Batista, Uruguay v Scotland, Neza, Mexico (World Cup): 55 secs	13 June 1986
Most one game	Four: Northampton T (0) v Hereford U (4) Div 3	11 Nov 1992
	Four: Crewe Alex (2) v Bradford PA (2) Div 3N	8 Jan 1955
	Four: Sheffield U (1) v Portsmouth (3) Div 2	13 Dec 1986
	Four: Port Vale (2) v Northampton T (2) Littlewoods Cup	18 Aug 1987
	Four: Brentford (2) v Mansfield T (2) Div 3	12 Dec 1987

RECORD ATTENDANCES

FA Premier League	53,926	Manchester U v Nottingham F, Old Trafford	28.4.1996
Football League	83,260	Manchester U v Arsenal, Maine Road	17.1.1948
Scottish League	118,567	Rangers v Celtic, Ibrox Stadium	2.1.1939
FA Cup Final	126,047*	Bolton W v West Ham U, Wembley	28.4.1923
European Cup	135,826	Celtic v Leeds U, semi-final at Hampden Park	15.4.1970
Scottish Cup	146,433	Celtic v Aberdeen, Hampden Park	24.4.37
World Cup	199,854†	Brazil v Uruguay, Maracana, Rio	16.7.50

* It has been estimated that as many as 70,000 more broke in without paying.
† 173,830 paid.

ADDRESSES

The Football Association: R. H. G. Kelly, F.C.I.S., 16 Lancaster Gate, London W2 3LW

Scotland: J. Farry, 6 Park Gardens, Glasgow G3 7YE. *0141-332 6372*
Northern Ireland (Irish FA): D. I. Bowen, 20 Windsor Avenue, Belfast BT9 6EG. *01232 669458*
Wales: A. Evans, 3 Westgate Street, Cardiff, South Glamorgan CF1 1JF. *01222 372325*
Republic of Ireland (FA of Ireland): 80 Merrion Square South, Dublin 2. *003531 766864*

International Federation (FIFA): S. Blatter, FIFA House, Hitzigweg 11, CH-8032 Zurich, Switzerland. *00 411 384 9595. Fax: 00 411 384 9696*
Union of European Football Associations: G. Aigner, Chemin de la Redoute 54, Case Postale 303 CH-1260 Nyon, Switzerland. *01041 22 994 44 44. Fax: 0041 22 994 44 88*

THE LEAGUES

The Premier League: R. N. Parry, 16 Lancaster Gate, London W2 3LW. *0171-262 4542.*
The Football League: J. D. Dent, F.C.I.S., The Football League, Lytham St Annes, Lancs FY8 1JG. *01253-729421. Telex 67675*
The Scottish League: P. Donald, 188 West Regent Street, Glasgow G2 4RY. *0141-248 384415*
The Irish League: H. Wallace, 87 University Street, Belfast BT7 1HP. *01232 242888*
Football League of Ireland: E. Morris, 80 Merrion Square South, Dublin 2. *003531 765120*
Vauxhall Conference: J. A. Moules, Collingwood House, Schooner Court, Crossways, Dartford DA2 6QQ
Central League: A. Williamson, The Football League, Lytham St Annes, Lancs FY8 1JG. *01253 729421*
North West Counties League: M. Darby, 87 Hillary Road, Hyde, Cheshire SK14 4EB.
Eastern Counties League: C. Lamb, 26 Dunthorpe Road, Clacton, Essex CO12 8UJ. *01255 436398*
Football Combination: N. Chamberlain, 2 Vicarage Close, Old Costessey, Norwich NR8 5DL. *10603 743998*
Hellenic League: B. King, 83 Queens Road, Carterton, Oxon OX18 3YF. *01793 493502*
Kent League: R. Vinter, The Thatched Barn, Lower Hardres, Canterbury, Kent CT4 5PG
Lancashire Amateur League: R. G. Bowker, 13 Shores Green Drive, Wincham, Northwich, Cheshire CW9 6EE. *0161-480 7723*
Lancashire Football League: J. W. Howarth, 465 Whalley Road, Clapton-le-Moors, Accrington, Lancs BB5 5RP. *01254 398957*
Leicestershire Senior League: D. Jamieson, 48 King Georges Road, Loughborough, Leics LE11 2PA. *01509 263411*
London Spartan: D. Cordell, 24 Greenleas, Waltham Abbey, Essex EN9 1SZ. *01992 712428*
Manchester League: F. J. Fitzpatrick, 102 Victoria Road, Stretford, Manchester M32 0AD. *0161-865 2726*
Midland Combination: N. Harvey, 115 Millfield Road, Handsworth Wood, Birmingham B20 1ED.
Mid-Week Football League: N. A. S. Matthews, Cedar Court, Steeple Aston, Oxford. *01869 40347*

Northern Premier: R. D. Bayley, 22 Woburn Drive, Hale, Altrincham, Cheshire WA15 8LZ. *0161-980 7007*
Northern Intermediate League: G. Thompson, Clegg House, 253 Pitsmoor Road, Sheffield S3 9AQ. *01742 27817*
Northern League: J. H. McLackland, 92 Appletree Gardens, Walkerville NE6 4SX
North Midlands League: G. Thompson, 7 Wren Park Close, Ridgway, Sheffield.
Peterborough and District League: M. J. Croson, 44 Storrington Way, Werrington, Peterborough, Cambs PE4 6QP.
Isthmian League: N. Robinson, 226 Rye Lane, Peckham SE15 4NL. *0181-653 3903*
Southern Amateur League: S. J. Lucas, 23 Beaufort Close, North Weald Bassett, Epping, Essex CM16 6JZ. *0137882 3932*
South-East Counties League: A. Leather, 66 Green Acres, Chichester Road, Croydon, Surrey CR0 5UX. *0181-681 7100*
Southern League: D. J. Strudwick, 11 Welland Close, Durrington, Worthing, West Sussex BN13 3NR. *01903 267788*
South Midlands League: M. Mitchell, 26 Leighton Court, Dunstable, Beds LU6 1EW. *01582 667291*
South Western League: M. Goodenough, Rose Cottage, Horrelsford, Milton Damerel, Holsworthy, Devon EX22 7NJ. *01409 261402*
United Counties League: R. Gamble, 8 Bostock Avenue, Northampton. *01604 37766*
Wearside League: B. Robson, 12 Deneside, Howden-le-Wear, Crook, Co. Durham DL15 8JR. *01388 762034*
Western League: M. E. Washer, 16 Heathfield Road, Nailsea, Bristol BS19 1EB.
The Welsh League: K. J. Tucker, 16 The Parade, Merthyr Tydfil, Mid Glamorgan CF47 0ET. *01685 723884*
West Midlands Regional League: N. R. Juggins, 14 Badger Way, Blackwell, Bromsgrove, Worcs B60 1EX.
West Yorkshire League: W. Keyworth, 2 Hill Court Grove, Bramley, Yorks L13 2AP. *0113 74465*
Northern Counties (East): B. Wood, 6 Restmore Avenue, Guiseley, Nr Leeds LS20 9DG. *01943 874558*

COUNTY FOOTBALL ASSOCIATIONS

Bedfordshire: P. D. Brown, Century House, Skimpot Road, Dunstable, Beds LU5 4JU. *01582 565111*
Berks and Bucks: W. S. Gosling, 15a London Street, Faringdon, Oxon SN7 8AG. *01367 242099*
Birmingham County: M. Pennick, County FA Offices, Rayhall Lane, Great Barr, Birmingham B43 6JE. *0121-357 4278*
Cambridgeshire: A. K. Pawley, 3 Signet Court, Swanns Road, Cambridge CB5 8LA. *01223 576770*
Cheshire: A. Collins, The Cottage, Hartford Moss Rec Centre, Winnington, Northwich CW8 4BG.
Cornwall: Rev K. F. D. Trunks, 2 Knights Way, Mount Ambrose, Redruth, Cornwall TR15 1NL. *01209 215292*
Cumberland: R. Johnson, 98 Vulcans Lane, Workington, Cumbria CA14 2NX. *01900 872310*
Derbyshire: K. Compton, The Grandstand, Moorways Stadium, Moor Lane, Derby DE2 8FB. *01332 361422*
Devon County: C. Squirrel, County HQ, Coach Road, Newton Abbot, Devon TQ12 1EJ. *01626 332077*

Dorset County: P. Hough, County Ground, Blandford Close, Hamsworthy, Poole, Dorset BH15 4BF. *01202 682375*
Durham: J. R. Walsh, 'Codeslaw', Ferens Park, Durham DH1 1JZ. *0191 3848653*
East Riding County: D. R. Johnson, 52 Bethune Ave, Hull HU4 7EJ. *01482 647512*
Essex County: T. Alexander, 31 Mildmay Road, Chelmsford, Essex CM2 0DN. *01245 344430*
Gloucestershire: H. D. Boughton, Locquiers Farm, Mitcheldean, Glos GL17 0HQ. *01594 543186*
Guernsey: D. Dorey, Haut Regard, St. Clair Hill, St. Sampson's, Guernsey, GY2 4DT, CI. *01481 46231*
Hampshire: R. G. Barnes, 8 Ashwood Gardens, off Winchester Road, Southampton SO9 2UA. *01703 791110*
Herefordshire: F. R. Prescott, 7 Kirkland Close, Hampton Park, Hereford HR1 1XP. *01432 351134*

Hertfordshire: R. G. Kibble, 4 The Wayside, Leverstock-green, Hemel Hempstead, Herts HP3 8NR. *01707 256891*
Huntingdonshire: M. M. Armstrong, 1 Chapel End, Great Giddings, Huntingdon, Cambs PE17 5NP. *018323 293262*
Isle of Man: Mrs A. Garrett, P.O. Box 53, The Bowl, Douglas IOM IM99 1GY. *01624 615576*
Jersey: D. G. Speed, 93 Les Cinqchenes, Five Oaks, St. Saviour, Jersey JE2 7UE.
Kent County: K. T. Masters, 69 Maidstone Road, Chatham, Kent ME4 6DT. *01634 843824*
Lancashire: J. Kenyon, 31a Wellington St, St John's, Blackburn, Lancs BB1 8AU. *01254 264333*
Leicestershire and Rutland: R. E. Barston, Holmes Park, Dog and Gun Lane, Whetstone, Leicester LE8 3LJ. *01533 2867828*
Lincolnshire: F. S. Richardson, PO Box 26, 12 Dean Road, Lincoln LN2 4DP. *01522 524917*
Liverpool County: F. L. J. Hunter, 23 Greenfield Road, Old Swann, Liverpool L13 3EN. *0151-220 6089*
London: R. S. Ashford, Aldworth Grove, London SE13 6HY. *0181-690 9626*
Manchester County: F. Brocklehurst, Sports Complex, Brantingham Road, Chorlton, Manchester M21 1TG. *0161-881 0299*
Middlesex County: P. J. Clayton, 39 Roxborough Road, Harrow, Middx HA1 1NS. *0181-424 8524*
Norfolk County: R. J. Howlett, 153 Middleton Lane, Hellesdon, Norwich, Norfolk NR6 5SF. *01603 488222*
Northamptonshire: B. Walden, 2 Duncan Close, Red House Road, Moulton Park, Northampton NN3 1WL. *01604 670741*

North Riding County: P. Kirby, 284 Linthorpe Road, Middlesbrough TS4 2NN. *01642 224585*
Northumberland: R. E. Maughan, Seymour House, 10 Brenkley Way, Blezard Bus Park, Seaton Burn, Newcastle upon Tyne NE13 6DT. *0191 236 8020*
Nottinghamshire: W. T. Annable, 7 Clarendon Street, Nottingham NG1 5HS. *01602 9418954*
Oxfordshire: P. J. Ladbrook, 3 Wilkins Road, Cowley, Oxford OX4 2HY.
Sheffield and Hallamshire: G. Thompson, Clegg House, 5 Onslow Road, Sheffield S11 7AF. *01142 670068*
Shropshire: A. W. Brett, 5 Ebnal Road, Shrewsbury SY2 6PW. *01743 236145*
Somerset & Avon (South): Mrs H. Marchment, 30 North Road, Midsomer Norton, Bath BA3 2QQ. *01761 410280*
Staffordshire: B. J. Adshead, County Showground, Weston Road, Stafford ST18 0DB. *01785 256994*
Suffolk County: W. M. Steward, 2 Millfields, Haughley, Suffolk IP14 3PU. *01449 673481*
Surrey County: A. P. Adams, 321 Kingston Road, Leatherhead, Surrey KT22 7TU. *01372 373543*
Sussex County: D. M. Worsfold, County Office, Culver Road, Lancing, Sussex BN15 9AX. *01903 753547*
Westmorland: P. G. Ducksbury, 69 Hayclose Crescent, Kendal LA9 7NT. *01539 730946*
West Riding County: R. Carter, Fleet Lane, Woodlesford, Leeds LS26 8NX. *0113 2821222*
Wiltshire: E. M. Parry, 44 Kennet Avenue, Swindon SN2 3LG. *01793 529036*
Worcestershire: M. R. Leggett Fermain, 12 Worcester Road, Eyesham, Worcs WR11 4JV. *01905 612336*

OTHER USEFUL ADDRESSES

Amateur Football Alliance: W. P. Goss, 55 Islington Park Street, London N1 1QB. *0171-359 3493*
English Schools FA: M. R. Berry, 1/2 Eastgate Street, Stafford ST16 2NN. *01785 51142*
Oxford University: M. H. Matthews, University College, Oxford OX1 4BH.
Cambridge University: Dr A. J. Little, St Catherine's College, Cambridge CB2 1RL.
Army: Major T. C. Knight, Clayton Barracks, Aldershot, Hants GU11 2BG. *01252 348571/4*
Royal Air Force: Group Capt P. W. Hilton, 21 Overton Road, Cheltenham, Glos GL50 3BL. *01452 712612 Ext 5676*
Royal Navy: Lt-Cdr J. Danks, R.N. Sports Office, H.M.S. Temeraire, Portsmouth, Hants PO1 4QS. *01705 722671*
British Universities Sports Association: G. Gregory-Jones, Chief Executive: BUSA, 8 Union Street, London SE1 1SZ. *0171-357 8555*
Central Council of Physical Recreation: General Secretary, 70 Brompton Road, London SW3 1HE. *0171-584 6651*
British Olympic Association: 6 John Prince's Street, London W1M 0DH. *0171-408 2029*
National Federation of Football Supporters' Clubs: Chairman: Tony Kershaw, 87 Brookfield Avenue, Loughborough, Leicestershire LE11 3LN. *01509 267643 (and fax)*. National Secretary: Mark Agate, "The Stadium", 14 Coombe Close, Lordswood, Chatham, Kent ME5 8NU. *01634 863520 (and fax)*
National Playing Fields Association: Col R. Satterthwaite, O.B.E., 578b Catherine Place, London, SW1.
The Scottish Football Commercial Managers Association: J. E. Hillier (Chairman), c/o Keith FC Promotions Office, 60 Union Street, Keith, Banffshire, Scotland.
Professional Footballers' Association: G. Taylor, 2 Oxford Court, Bishopsgate, Off Lower Mosley Street, Manchester M2 3W2. *0161-236 0575*
Referees' Association: W. J. Taylor, Cross Offices, Summerhill, Kingswinford, West Midlands DY6 9JE. *01384 288386*

Women's Football Alliance: Miss H. Jeavons, 9 Wyllyotts Place, Potters Bar, Herts EN6 2JB. *01707 651840*
Commercial Managers Association: Olaf Dixon, 1ᴬ Chapel Court, Holly Walk, Leamington Spa, Warwickshire CV32 4YS. *01926 882313. Fax: 01926 886829*
Football Administrators Association: as above.
Institute of Football Management and Administration: as above.
Management Statts Association: as above.
League Managers Association: as above.
The Association of Football Statisticians: R. J. Spiller, 22 Bretons, Basildon, Essex SS15 5BY. *01268 416020*
The Football Programme Directory: David Stacey, 'The Beeches', 66 Southend Road, Wickford, Essex SS11 8EN.
England Football Supporters Association: Publicity Officer, David Stacey, 'The Beeches', 66 Southend Road, Wickford, Essex SS11 8EN. *01268 732041*
The Football League Executive Staffs Association: PO Box 52, Leamington Spa, Warwickshire.
The Ninety-Two Club: 104 Gilda Crescent, Whitchurch, Bristol BS14 9LD.
Scottish 38 Club: Mark Byatt, 6 Greenfields Close, Loughton, Essex IG10 3HG. *0181-508 6088*
The Football Trust: Second Floor, Walkden House, 10 Melton Street, London NW1 2EZ. *0171-388 4504*
The Football Supporters Association: PO Box 11, Liverpool L26 1XP. *0151-709 2594*
Association of Provincial Football Supporters' Clubs in London: Ian D. Todd, 8 Wyke Close, Isleworth, Middx TW7 5PE. *0181-847 2905 (and fax)*
World Association of Friends of English Football: PO Box 2221, D-30022 Hannover, Germany. *0049 511 885616*
Football Postcard Collectors Club: PRO: Bryan Horsnell, 275 Overdown Road, Tilehurst, Reading RG3 6NX. *01734 424448*

OTHER AWARDS 1995–96

FOOTBALLER OF THE YEAR

The Football Writers' Association Award for the Footballer of the Year went to Eric Cantona of Manchester United and France.

Past Winners

1947–48 Stanley Matthews (Blackpool), 1948–49 Johnny Carey (Manchester U), 1949–50 Joe Mercer (Arsenal), 1950–51 Harry Johnston (Blackpool), 1951–52 Billy Wright (Wolverhampton W), 1952–53 Nat Lofthouse (Bolton W), 1953–54 Tom Finney (Preston NE), 1954–55 Don Revie (Manchester C), 1955–56 Bert Trautmann (Manchester C), 1956–57 Tom Finney (Preston NE), 1957–58 Danny Blanchflower (Tottenham H), 1958–59 Syd Owen (Luton T), 1959–60 Bill Slater (Wolverhampton W), 1960–61 Danny Blanchflower (Tottenham H), 1961–62 Jimmy Adamson (Burnley), 1962–63 Stanley Matthews (Stoke C), 1963–64 Bobby Moore (West Ham U), 1964–65 Bobby Collins (Leeds U), 1965–66 Bobby Charlton (Manchester U), 1966–67 Jackie Charlton (Leeds U), 1967–68 George Best (Manchester U), 1968–69 Dave Mackay (Derby Co) shared with Tony Book (Manchester C), 1969–70 Billy Bremner (Leeds U), 1970–71 Frank McLintock (Arsenal), 1971–72 Gordon Banks (Stoke C), 1972–73 Pat Jennings (Tottenham H), 1973–74 Ian Callaghan (Liverpool), 1974–75 Alan Mullery (Fulham), 1975–76 Kevin Keegan (Liverpool), 1976–77 Emlyn Hughes (Liverpool), 1977–78 Kenny Burns (Nottingham F), 1978–79 Kenny Dalglish (Liverpool), 1979–80 Terry McDermott (Liverpool), 1980–81 Frans Thijssen (Ipswich T), 1981–82 Steve Perryman (Tottenham H), 1982–83 Kenny Dalglish (Liverpool), 1983–84 Ian Rush (Liverpool), 1984–85 Neville Southall (Everton), 1985–86 Gary Lineker (Everton), 1986–87 Clive Allen (Tottenham H), 1987–88 John Barnes (Liverpool), 1988–89 Steve Nicol (Liverpool), 1989–90 John Barnes (Liverpool), 1990–91 Gordon Strachan (Leeds U), 1991–92 Gary Lineker (Tottenham H), 1992–93 Chris Waddle (Sheffield W), 1993–94 Alan Shearer (Blackburn R), 1994–95 Jurgen Klinsmann (Tottenham H).

THE PFA AWARDS 1996

Player of the Year: Les Ferdinand (Newcastle U)
Previous Winners: 1974 Norman Hunter (Leeds U); 1975 Colin Todd (Derby Co); 1976 Pat Jennings (Tottenham H); 1977 Andy Gray (Aston Villa); 1978 Peter Shilton (Nottingham F); 1979 Liam Brady (Arsenal); 1980 Terry McDermott (Liverpool); 1981 John Wark (Ipswich T); 1982 Kevin Keegan (Southampton); 1983 Kenny Dalglish (Liverpool); 1984 Ian Rush (Liverpool); 1985 Peter Reid (Everton); 1986 Gary Lineker (Everton); 1987 Clive Allen (Tottenham H); 1988 John Barnes (Liverpool); 1989 Mark Hughes (Manchester U); 1990 David Platt (Aston Villa); 1991 Mark Hughes (Manchester U); 1992 Gary Pallister (Manchester U); 1993 Paul McGrath (Aston Villa); 1994 Eric Cantona (Manchester U); 1995 Alan Shearer (Blackburn R).

Young Player of the Year: Robbie Fowler (Liverpool).
Previous Winners: 1974 Kevin Beattie (Ipswich T); 1975 Mervyn Day (West Ham U); 1976 Peter Barnes (Manchester C); 1977 Andy Gray (Aston Villa); 1978 Tony Woodcock (Nottingham F); 1979 Cyrille Regis (WBA); 1980 Glenn Hoddle (Tottenham H); 1981 Gary Shaw (Aston Villa); 1982 Steve Moran (Southampton); 1983 Ian Rush (Liverpool); 1984 Paul Walsh (Luton T); 1985 Mark Hughes (Manchester U); 1986 Tony Cottee (West Ham U); 1987 Tony Adams (Arsenal); 1988 Paul Gascoigne (Tottenham H); 1989 Paul Merson (Arsenal); 1990 Matthew Le Tissier (Southampton); 1991 Lee Sharpe (Manchester U); 1992 Ryan Giggs (Manchester U); 1993 Ryan Giggs (Manchester U); 1994 Andy Cole (Newcastle U); 1995 Robbie Fowler (Liverpool).

Merit Award: Pele.
Previous Winners: 1974 Bobby Charlton CBE, Cliff Lloyd OBE; 1975 Denis Law; 1976 George Eastham OBE; 1977 Jack Taylor OBE; 1978 Bill Shankly OBE; 1979 Tom Finney OBE; 1980 Sir Matt Busby CBE; 1981 John Trollope MBE; 1982 Joe Mercer OBE; 1983 Bob Paisley OBE; 1984 Bill Nicholson; 1985 Ron Greenwood; 1986 The 1966 England World Cup team, Sir Alf Ramsey, Harold Shepherdson; 1987 Sir Stanley Matthews; 1988 Billy Bonds MBE; 1989 Nat Lofthouse; 1990 Peter Shilton; 1991 Tommy Hutchison; 1992 Brian Clough; 1993 the 1968 Manchester United team; 1994 Billy Bingham; 1995 Gordon Strachan.

THE SCOTTISH PFA AWARDS 1996

Player of the Year: Paul Gascoigne (Rangers).
Previous Winners: 1978 Derek Johnstone (Rangers); 1979 Paul Hegarty (Dundee U); 1980 Davie Provan (Celtic); 1981 Sandy Clark (Airdrieonians); 1982 Mark McGhee (Aberdeen); 1983 Charlie Nicholas (Celtic); 1984 Willie Miller (Aberdeen); 1985 Jim Duffy (Morton); 1986 Richard Gough (Dundee U); 1987 Brian McClair (Celtic); 1988 Paul McStay (Celtic); 1989 Theo Snelders (Aberdeen); 1990 Jim Bett (Aberdeen); 1991 Paul Elliott (Celtic); 1993 Ally McCoist (Rangers); 1993 Andy Goram (Rangers); 1994 Mark Hateley (Rangers); 1995 Brian Laudrup (Rangers).
Young Player of the Year: Jackie McNamara (Celtic).
Previous Winners: 1978 Graeme Payne (Dundee U); 1979 Graham Stewart (Dundee U); 1980 John MacDonald (Rangers); 1981 Francis McAvennie (St Mirren); 1982 Charlie Nicholas (Celtic); 1983 Pat Nevin (Clyde); 1984 John Robertson (Hearts); 1985 Craig Levein (Hearts); 1986 Craig Levein (Hearts); 1987 Robert Fleck (Rangers); 1988 John Collins (Hibernian); 1989 Bill McKinlay (Dundee U); 1990 Scott Crabbe (Hearts); 1991 Eoin Jess (Aberdeen); 1992 Phil O'Donnell (Motherwell); 1993 Eoin Jess (Aberdeen); 1994 Phil O'Donnell (Motherwell); 1995 Charlie Miller (Rangers).

SCOTTISH FOOTBALL WRITERS' ASSOCIATION

Player of the Year 1996 – Paul Gascoigne (Rangers)

1965 Billy McNeill (Celtic)	1981 Alan Rough (Partick Th)
1966 John Greig (Rangers)	1982 Paul Sturrock (Dundee U)
1967 Ronnie Simpson (Celtic)	1983 Charlie Nicholas (Celtic)
1968 Gordon Wallace (Raith R)	1984 Willie Miller (Aberdeen)
1969 Bobby Murdoch (Celtic)	1985 Hamish McAlpine (Dundee U)
1970 Pat Stanton (Hibernian)	1986 Sandy Jardine (Hearts)
1971 Martin Buchan (Aberdeen)	1987 Brian McClair (Celtic)
1972 Dave Smith (Rangers)	1988 Paul McStay (Celtic)
1973 George Connelly (Celtic)	1989 Richard Gough (Rangers)
1974 Scotland's World Cup Squad	1990 Alex McLeish (Aberdeen)
1975 Sandy Jardine (Rangers)	1991 Maurice Malpas (Dundee U)
1976 John Greig (Rangers)	1992 Ally McCoist (Rangers)
1977 Danny McGrain (Celtic)	1993 Andy Goram (Rangers)
1978 Derek Johnstone (Rangers)	1994 Mark Hateley (Rangers)
1979 Andy Ritchie (Morton)	1995 Brian Laudrup (Rangers)
1980 Gordon Strachan (Aberdeen)	

EUROPEAN FOOTBALLER OF THE YEAR 1995

George Weah (AC Milan) became the first non-European to win the award. Liberia born Weah was in his initial season with the Italian club and he was also voted FIFA's World Player of the Year.

Past winners

1956 **Stanley Matthews** (Blackpool)	1977 **Allan Simonsen** (Borussia Moenchengladbach)
1957 **Alfredo Di Stefano** (Real Madrid)	1978 **Kevin Keegan** (SV Hamburg)
1958 **Raymond Kopa** (Real Madrid)	1979 **Kevin Keegan** (SV Hamburg)
1959 **Alfredo Di Stefano** (Real Madrid)	1980 **Karl-Heinz Rummenigge** (Bayern Munich)
1960 **Luis Suarez** (Barcelona)	
1961 **Omar Sivori** (Juventus)	1981 **Karl-Heinz Rummenigge** (Bayern Munich)
1962 **Josef Masopust** (Dukla Prague)	
1963 **Lev Yashin** (Moscow Dynamo)	1982 **Paolo Rossi** (Juventus)
1964 **Denis Law** (Manchester United)	1983 **Michel Platini** (Juventus)
1965 **Eusebio** (Benfica)	1984 **Michel Platini** (Juventus)
1966 **Bobby Charlton** (Manchester United)	1985 **Michel Platini** (Juventus)
1967 **Florian Albert** (Ferencvaros)	1986 **Igor Belanov** (Dynamo Kiev)
1968 **George Best** (Manchester United)	1987 **Ruud Gullit** (AC Milan)
1969 **Gianni Rivera** (AC Milan)	1988 **Marco Van Basten** (AC Milan)
1970 **Gerd Muller** (Bayern Munich)	1989 **Marco Van Basten** (AC Milan)
1971 **Johan Cruyff** (Ajax)	1990 **Lothar Matthaus** (Inter-Milan)
1972 **Franz Beckenbauer** (Bayern Munich)	1991 **Jean-Pierre Papin** (Marseille)
1973 **Johan Cruyff** (Barcelona)	1992 **Marco Van Basten** (AC Milan)
1974 **Johan Cruyff** (Barcelona)	1993 **Roberto Baggio** (Juventus)
1975 **Oleg Blokhin** (Dynamo Kiev)	1994 **Hristo Stoichkov** (Barcelona)
1976 **Franz Beckenbauer** (Bayern Munich)	

THE CARLING AWARDS WINNERS 1995–96

The Carling No. 1 Awards panel

The panel that judges the Carling Manager of the Month, Carling Player of the Month and Carling No. 1 Awards represents all the game's key groups, including fans, making it the most representative judging panel ever assembled in football.

Terry Venables England coach; **Rick Parry** Chief Executive, FA Premier League; **Gordon Taylor** Chief Executive, Professional Footballers' Association; **Gordon Milne** Chief Executive, League Managers Association; **Bob Cass** Chairman, Football Writers' Association; **Brian Barwick** BBC – Editor Sportsnight; **Vic Wakeling** BSkyB – Head of Sport; **Trevor East** BSkyB – Executive Director of Sky Sports; **Alan Green** BBC Radio Sport; **Joe Melling** Football Writers' Association; **Alex Montgomery** Football Writers' Association; **Niall Sloane** Producer, Match of the Day; **Jonathan Pearce** Captial Radio; **Neil Midgley** President, Referees' Association; **Graham Kelly** Chief Executive, Football Association; **Tim Crabbe** Football Supporters' Association; **Tony Kershaw** The National Federation of Supporters' Clubs.

The Carling No. 1 Awards

The month-by-month guide to the Carling Premiership's top performing players and managers.

Carling Manager of the Month

August	Kevin Keegan	Newcastle United
September	Kevin Keegan	Newcastle United
October	Frank Clark	Nottingham Forest
November	Alan Ball	Manchester City
December	Roy Evans	Liverpool
January	Roy Evans	Liverpool
February	Alex Ferguson	Manchester United
March	Alex Ferguson	Manchester United
April	Dave Merrington	Southampton

Carling Manager of the Season Alex Ferguson   **Manchester United**

Carling Player of the Month

August	David Ginola	Newcastle United
September	Tony Yeboah	Leeds United
October	Trevor Sinclair	QPR
November	Robert Lee	Newcastle United
December	Robbie Fowler	Liverpool
January	Stan Collymore	Liverpool
	Robbie Fowler	Liverpool
February	Dwight Yorke	Aston Villa
March	Eric Cantona	Manchester United

Carling Player of the Season   Eric Cantona   **Manchester United**
(Carling sponsors of the Football Writers' Association)

Carling No. 1 Awards

Awarded for outstanding contributions to the national game.

September	**Eric Harrison**, Manchester United youth team coach – for his role in the club's incredibly successful youth policy.
January	**Alan Shearer**, Blackburn Rovers – for being the first player to score 100 goals in the Carling Premiership.
April	**Alan Shearer**, Blackburn Rovers – for scoring at least 30 Carling Premiership goals for the past three seasons – a feat not achieved since before the 2nd World War.

REFEREEING AND THE REFEREES

In a never ending quest for an improvement in fair play FIFA have again altered some of the Laws for the forthcoming season which took effect from the 1st July 1996. The most significant areas involve the 'advantage clause'; an increase in the number of substitutes who can be named and the re-titling of the word 'Linesman'. In addition there are some textual changes plus important instructions.

The most substantial of these changes is likely to occur under Law 5 relating to referees and their use of the 'advantage clause'. From now on a referee will have the rare discretion of applying the advantage but if such anticipated advantage does not materialise he/she can then penalise the original offence. The suggested time scale for credibility in making such a decision is 2/3 seconds. Should a second offence be committed by the offending team's player during the advantage period the referee must penalise the more serious offence.

In order more accurately to reflect the role of the linesman and to encourage more 'political correctness' the term 'Linesman' is replaced by the term 'Assistant Referee'. However this can only be applied to assistants who are qualified referees so unqualified club linesmen or those who are not neutral will remain linesmen as before. Of greater significance is the fact that for the first time the Linesman's/Assistant's duty is to indicate when an attacker is in an off-side position. Surprisingly for so long the previous text made no mention of such an important function.

Also created is a further enhancement of the role of the Fourth Official who will now submit misconduct reports if he sees any misconduct missed by the referee.

The current rule as to the number of substitutes who can be used is not changed, but now the choice can be made from seven who are named prior to the match rather than the previous five.

FIFA particularly remind referees to (a) strictly interpret the 4 step rule for goalkeepers (b) speed up restarts (c) ensure all stoppage time is added and (d) severely punish the unfair tackle from behind.

The National List of Referees appears below and David Allison remains the most senior official. There are ten new referees added to this List namely Messrs A Bates (last season's FA Cup Final Linesman); B Coddington; C T Finch; C J Foy; M R Halsey; T Jones; G Laws; D Pugh; J P Robinson; and R Styles. In addition Graham Barber and Mike Riley have been promoted to the List of Premier League Referees of whom there are nineteen.

KEN GOLDMAN

NATIONAL LIST OF REFEREES FOR SEASON 1996–97

* Alcock, P.E. (Redhill, Surrey)
  Allison, D.B. (Lancaster)
* Ashby, G.R. (Worcester)
  Bailey, M.C. (Impington, Cambridge)
  Baines, S.J. (Chesterfield)
* Barber, G.P. (Warwick)
  Barry, N.S. (Scunthorpe)
  Bates, A. (Stoke-on-Trent)
  Bennett, S.G. (Dartford)
* Bodenham, M.J. (East Looe, Cornwall)
  Brandwood, M.J. (Lichfield, Staffs)
* Burge, K.W. (Tonypandy)
  Burns W.C. (Scarborough)
  Butler, A.N. (Sutton-in-Ashfield)
  Cain, G. (Bootle)
  Coddington, B. (Sheffield)
  Cruikshanks, I.G. (Hartlepool)
* Danson, P.S. (Leicester)
* Dilkes, L.R. (Mossley, Lancs)
* Dunn, S.W. (Bristol)
* Durkin, P.A. (Portland, Dorset)
  D'Urso, A.P. (Billericay, Essex)
* Elleray, D.R. (Harrow-on-the-Hill)

Finch, C.T. (Bury St Edmunds)
Fletcher, M. (Warley, West Midlands)
Foy, C.J. (St Helens)
Frankland, G.B. (Middlesbrough)
Furnandiz, R.D. (Doncaster)
* Gallagher, D.J. (Banbury, Oxon)
  Halsay, M.R. (Welwyn Garden City, Herts)
  Harris, R.J. (Oxford)
  Heilbron, T. (Newton Aycliffe)
* Jones, P. (Loughborough)
  Jones, T. (Barrow-in-Furness)
  Kirkby, J.A. (Sheffield)
  Knight, B. (Orpington)
  Laws, D. (Whitley Bay)
  Laws, S. (Whitley Bay)
  Leach, K.A. (Wolverhampton)
  Leake, A.R. (Darwen, Lancashire)
* Lodge, S.J. (Barnsley)
  Lomas, E. (Manchester)
  Lunt, T. (Ashton-in-Makerfield, Lancs)
  Lynch, K.M. (Knaresborough)
  Mathieson, S.W. (Stockport)

Orr, D. (Iver, Bucks)
Pearson, R. (Peterlee, Durham)
Pierce, M.E. (Portsmouth)
* Poll, G. (Tring, Hertfordshire)
  Pooley, G.R. (Bishop's Stortford)
  Poulain, R. (Huddersfield)
  Pugh, D. (Wirral)
* Reed, M.D. (Birmingham)
  Rejer, P. (Tipton, West Midlands)
  Rennie, U.D. (Sheffield)
  Richards, P.R. (Preston)
* Riley, M.A. (Leeds)
  Robinson, J.P. (Hull)
  Singh, G. (Wolverhampton)
  Stretton, F.G. (Nottingham)
  Styles, R. (Waterlooville, Hants)
  Taylor, P. (Cheshunt, Hertfordshire)
  West, T.E. (Hull)
  Wiley, A.G. (Burntwood, Staffs)
  Wilkes, C.R. (Gloucester)
* Wilkie, A.B. (Chester-le-Street)
* Willard, G.S. (Worthing, W. Sussex)
* Winter, J.T. (Stockton-on-Tees)
  Wolstenholme, E.K. (Blackburn)
* Denotes Premier League Referee

ASSISTANT REFEREES

Adcock, D.J. (Long Eaton, Notts)
Armstrong, P. (Thatcham, Berks)
Ashman, J.J. (Swansea)
Atkins, G. (Bradford)
Babski, D.S. (Scunthorpe)
Baker, B.L. (Warminster, Wilts)
Baker, L. (Dulverton, Somerset)
Barnes, P.W. (Peterborough)
Bassindale, C. (Doncaster)
Beale, G.A. (Taunton)
Beeby, R.J. (Northampton)
Bello, B. (Manchester)
Binsley, D.E. (Sunderland)
Bishop, B.P. (Bath)
Blanchard, I. (Hull)
Bone, R. (Orpington, Kent)
Booth, D.A. (Barnsley)
Boulton, J.T. (Birmingham)

Boyeson, C. (Hull)
Brammer, D.S. (Weston-s-Mare)
Brand, S.R. (Wirral)
Breakspear, C.N. (Weybridge)
Breckell, A.S. (Accrington)
Brown, A.R. (Chorley)
Bryan, D.S. (Stamford)
Buller, K.R. (Bridgwater)
Burton, R. (Burton-upon-Trent)
Butler, A.N. (Wigan)
Cable, L.E. (Woking)
Cairns, M.J. (Burton-upon-Trent)
Canadine, P. (Rotherham)
Carrington, M. (Loughborough)
Castle, S. (Wolverhampton)
Charlton, D. (Huddersfield)
Clingo, S.G. (Wisbech, Cambs)
Clyde, A.L. (Doncaster)

Cockwill, N.R. (Barnstaple, N. Devon)
Cooper, M.A. (Walsall)
Cooper, R.J. (Tynemouth)
Copeland, J.F. (Wirral)
Cowburn, M.G. (Blackpool)
Coxhead, R. (Huntingdon, Cambs)
Crick, D.R. (Worcester Park, Surrey)
Cullen, P. (Dukinfield, Cheshire)
Curson, B. (Burbage, Leics)
Dean, M.L. (Wirral)
Dearing, M.D. (Northolt, Middlesex)
Devine, J.P. (Middlesbrough)
Dexter, M.C. (Thurmaston, Leics)
Douglas, M.J. (Blyth, Northumberland)
Dowd, P. (Stoke-on-Trent)
Downs, D.G. (Basingstoke)

Drysdale, D. (Waddington, Lincs)
Dyce, O. (Manchester)
Eastwood, P. (Manchester)
Edgeley, G. (Northwich)
Edwards, C.D. (Oldham)
Ellicott, B.P. (Redditch)
Elwick, P.A. (Boston)
Evans, E.M. (Manchester)
Evans, R.J. (Beckenham, Kent)
Francis, C.J. (Ely, Cambs)
Fraser, G.R. (Barrow-in-Furness)
French, S.J. (Wolverhampton)
Gagen, S.L. (New Malden, Surrey)
Gould, R. (Swadlincote, Derbyshire)
Gowers, W.G. (Shipston-on-Stour, Warks)
Green, A.J. (Hinckley, Leics)
Green, E.W. (Henley-on-Thames)
Green, N.E. (Stourport-on-Severn, Worcs)
Griffin, P.J. (Hornchurch, Essex)
Griffiths, J.H. (Chippenham)
Griffiths, S.J. (Macclesfield)
Griggs, P.J. (Dursley, Glos)
Habgood, S. (Swindon)
Hall, A.R. (Birmingham)
Hall, G.A. (Hixon, Nr Stafford)
Hall, M. (Whitley Bay)
Hancox, N. (Aldridge, W. Midlands)
Harding, P.D. (Crewe)
Harris, P.I. (Warrington)
Harteveld, A.C (York)
Harvey, A.C. (Croxley Green, Herts)
Hawkes, K.J. (Quedgeley, Glos)
Haxby, M.D. (New Brighton, Wirral)
Head, S. (Stokenchurch, Bucks)
Hegley, G.K. (Bishop's Stortford)
Hill, K.D. (Royston, Herts)
Hine, D.J. (Worcester)
Hogg, A.S. (Dronfield, Derbyshire)
Holbrook, J.H. (Telford)
Horlick, D.M. (Liverpool)
Horton, A.J. (Wolverhampton)
Howells, A.C. (Port Talbot)
Howes, T.P. (Norwich)
Hubbard, J.R. (Leicester)
Ingram, B. (Bath)
Ingram K.R. (Kingswinford)
Johnson, A.T. (Grantham)
Jones, C. (Pontypridd)
Jones, L.C. (Bournemouth)
Jones, M.J. (Chester)
Jordan, W.M. (Pinner, Middlesex)
Joslin, P.J. (Newark)
Joy, M.J. (Bristol)
Kaye, A. (Bradford)
Kellett, D.G. (Bradford)
Lee, G.M. (Corby, Northants)

Leech, J. (Wigan)
Legg, A.R. (East Grinstead, W. Sussex)
Lilley, S.J. (Bury St Edmunds)
Lockhart, R. (Newcastle-u-Tyne)
Lowe, B. (Doncaster)
McGee, A. (Liverpool)
McGregor, R.E. (Grimsby)
March, P. (Ramsgate)
Martin, A.J. (Stafford)
Martin, E.A.C. (Williton, Somerset)
Mellor, G.S. (Doncaster)
Messias, M.D. (York)
Millership, B.T. (Atherstone, Warks)
Mills, A.D. (Bristol)
Monk, J.C. (Grays, Essex)
Moore, J.F. (Norwich)
Morrall, D.A. (Sheffield)
Morrison, D.P. (Littleover, Derbys)
Mountain, M.J. (Mansfield)
Nind, K.J. (Bromsgrove)
Norbury, W.J. (Harlow)
Norman, P.V. (Bath)
North, M.J. (Wimborne)
Oldham, A.B. (Poulton-le-Fylde, Lancs)
Oliver, D.S. (Darlington)
Olivier, R.J. (Sutton Coldfield, W. Mids)
Oxley, P. (Rotherham)
Parish, G.B. (Harlow)
Parkes, T.A. (Birmingham)
Pashley, R.A. (Chesterfield)
Pawson, P.M. (Sheffield)
Payne, R.G. (Fitwick, Beds)
Peacock, D. (Redcar, Cleveland)
Pearce, J.E. (Dagenham)
Peeke, S. (Northfleet, Kent)
Penn, A.M. (Kinswinford)
Perkin, N.F. (Gravesend)
Perlejewski, A.J. (Yeovil)
Perry, M.J. (Wimborne, Dorset)
Pettitt, J.W. (Welling, Kent)
Phillips, D.C. (Bracknell, Berks)
Pike, K. (Gillingham, Dorset)
Pike, M.S. (Barrow-in-Furness)
Polkey, B.L. (Nottingham)
Pollard, T.J. (Bury St Edmunds)
Pollock, R.M. (Liverpool)
Postles, M.D. (Coneyhurst Common, W. Sussex)
Powell, K. (Hartlepool)
Priest, B.D. (Halesowen)
Prosser, P.J. (Albrighton, W. Mids)
Race, S. (Oldham)
Rawson, R.R. (Sheffield)
Reynolds, K.S. (East Barnet)
Rice, B.M. (Pershore, Worcs)

Richards, D.C. (Llanelli, Dyfed)
Roberts, P.A. (Belper)
Roberts, P.M. (Northampton)
Robinson, M.G. (Darlington)
Rogers, C.J. (Swindon)
Ross, J.J. (London)
Ryan, M. (Preston)
Saunders, R.L. (East Bergholt, Essex)
Sharp, P.R. (St Albans)
Shaw, G. (Oldham)
Shaw, I.D. (Crewe)
Sheffield, J.A. (Burntwood, Staffs)
Short, M.L. (Grantham, Lincs)
Sims, M.R. (Bristol)
Singh, M. (Coseley)
Smith, A.N. (Castleford, W. Yorks)
Smith, J.P. (Hyde, Cheshire)
Smith, R.A. (Loughborough)
Smith, S.J. (Ware, Herts)
Spicer, D.R. (Totten, Hampshire)
Spooner, G. (Sheffield)
Stobbart, M. (Guildford)
Stoddart, M.J. (Leeds)
Stones, G.A. (Swadlincote, Derbys)
Sutton, R. (Macclesfield)
Swift, M. (Sheffield)
Tarry, E.J. (Manchester)
Taylor, F. (Preston)
Thiarra, S.S. (Bedford)
Thornewill, C. (Chaddesden, Derby)
Thorpe, M. (Woodbridge, Suffolk)
Tiffin, R. (Houghton-le-Spring)
Tingey, M. (Lane End, Bucks)
Tomlin, S.G. (Lewes, E. Sussex)
Toms, W. [Mrs] (Poole)
Torrance, K.R. (Camberley, Surrey)
Unsworth, D. (Bolton)
Vosper, P.A. (London)
Walsh, E.J. (Rubery, Worcs)
Walton, P. (West Haddon, Northants)
Ward, J. (Ferryhill, Co Durham)
Ward, R.B. (Milton Keynes)
Wardle, K. (Houghton-le-Spring)
Warren, M.R. (Walsall)
Webb, A.J. (Winnersh, Berks)
Webb, H.M. (Rotherham)
Webster, C.H. (Chester-le-Street)
Wedgwood, S. (Burscough, Lancs)
Wesson, J.D. (Loughborough)
Whitehouse, I. (Calne, Wiltshire)
Williams, M.A. (Hereford)
Wing, P.B. (Peterborough)
Wood, A.R. (Birkenhead)
Wood, D. (Harrogate)
Wood, D.R. (Liverpool)
Woodhall, D.J. (Shipley)
Woolmer, K.A. (Kettering)
Zipfel, R.J. (Thetford, Norfolk)

OBITUARIES

Bert Adamson (b. Balbeggie 1913; d. 27.8.95). An inside-forward, Bert joined Hearts in 1931 and went on to play for Carlisle United, Wrexham, Dundee and East Fife.

Stan Aldous (b. Northfleet 10.2.23; d. 10.95). An excellent centre-half and captain of Leyton Orient, who made 302 League appearances for his one and only Football League club. Stan was 27 when he made his debut in 1950, having joined from Southern League Gravesend and Northfleet. He skippered 'the O's' to the Quarter-finals of the F.A. Cup as a Third Division (South) side in 1954 and to the Championship two years later.

Dennis Allen (b. Dagenham 2.3.39; d. 7.95). An inside forward who began at Charlton, for whom he signed in 1956. Dennis moved to Reading in June, 1961 and enjoyed nine years at Elm Park, making 335 League appearances and scoring 84 goals. In August, 1970 he joined Bournemouth, but injury curtailed his career after 17 League games and 3 goals. The brother of Les, the former Chelsea, Spurs and QPR star, and father of Pompey skipper, Martin. Nephews Bradley, Clive and Paul make up the other members of this famous football family.

Jimmy Allen (b. Poole 16.10.09; d. 2.95). A superb centre-half, signed by Portsmouth from Poole Town in 1930, he played for Pompey in the 1934 F.A. Cup final and represented England twice during the same season. In the summer of 1934, Jimmy joined Aston Villa for £10,775 - a record fee for a defender. Pompey used the transfer fee to build the North Stand at Fratton Park, which is still known as 'the Jimmy Allen' stand. At Villa, he skippered the side that won the Second Division Championship in 1938, but was missing from the team that lost to seven record-breaking Ted Drake goals in the defeat by Arsenal in December, 1935. After guesting for several clubs during the war, he retired in 1944.

Alec Ashworth (b. Southport 1.10.39; d. 6.95). Alec began at Everton in May, 1957 as an inside forward, where he scored 3 goals in 12 games before moving to Luton Town in 1960. At Kenilworth Road he teamed up with Gordon Turner and bagged 20 goals in 63 League games. Two years later he was snapped up by Northampton Town, where his 25 goals in 30 League games assured 'the Cobblers' of promotion from the Third Division. On the back of that strike rate, Preston North End signed him in 1963 and the following year he played in the F.A. Cup final against West Ham. An unfortunate injury six months later put him out of the game and he was forced to retire in 1966.

George Bargh (b. Bilsborrow 27.5.10; d. 13.9.95). A diminutive inside-forward who made his debut for Preston North End in 1928 and stayed until 1935, scoring 42 goals in 142 League games. He went on to play for Sheffield Wednesday, Bury and Chesterfield before the second world war intervened. After hostilities, he rejoined Bury, but managed only one League appearance before retiring. Between the mid-fifties and the early seventies he was a coach at Preston North End.

Dave Bowen (b. Maesteg 7.6.28; d. 25.9.95). Dave had two spells as a player with Northampton Town, sandwiched in between by 146 appearances as an oustanding defender with Arsenal. He won 19 caps for Wales and led his country to the quarter-finals of the 1958 World Cup, where he had the distinction of marking Pele. His playing career at the County Ground began in 1947 but, after three years and 12 appearances, he was signed by Arsenal. At Highbury he amassed 146 games in a nine year career before returning to Northampton for one season as a player. He then became the most successful manager in the club's history, guiding them from the Fourth to First Division between 1961 and 1965. In 1967, he was succeeded by Tony Marchi, but returned in 1969 and eventually became secretary and general manager, remaining until 1986. He also held a temporary post as manager of Wales.

Noel Brotherston (b. Belfast 18.11.56; d. 6.5.95). Noel signed for Spurs in 1974, but after only one League game he joined Blackburn Rovers three years later. With the Ewood Park club he made 317 League appearances and was leading goalscoring in his first season, which culminated in promotion to the Second Division. A tricky right-winger, Noel also won 27 caps for Northern Ireland. In the summer of 1987, he moved to Bury, then bowed out of League soccer in 1988-89 following a loan period at Scarborough.

Alan Brown (b. Corbridge 26.8.14; d. Biddecombe 9.3.96). Joined Huddersfield Town in 1933 and, like so many, saw his career interrupted by the war. After hostilities he signed for Burnley in February, 1946, became captain, and skippered 'the Clarets' to promotion from the Second Division. He also played in the 1947 F.A. Cup final, winning a runners-up medal following defeat by Charlton. In 1948 he signed for Notts County, but only made 13 League appearances. Alan turned to management by taking over the helm at Burnley in 1954. He stayed for three years before joining Sunderland. At Roker, he took the club to promotion in 1964. From Wearside he went to Sheffield Wednesday and was manager when 'the Owls' reached Wembley in 1966, losing 3-2 to Everton. He later managed Sunderland for a second time and also assisted Tony Waiters at Plymouth Argyle.

Vic Buckingham (b. Greenwich 23.10.15; d. 27.1.95). Vic signed for Spurs in 1935 and, although the war interrupted his career, he played 234 League games for his one and only League club. In June, 1951 he was appointed manager of Bradford Park Avenue, then two years later he went to West Bromwich Albion where he remained until 1959. A successful period with Ajax followed as the Dutch side won the League in 1960 and the Cup in 1961. At that time, Johan Cruyff was with the club's junior side and Vic helped to develop the youngster's early career. In May, 1961, he became boss at Sheffield Wednesday, but left three years later. In January, 1965 he took charge of Fulham, who were fighting for First Division survival, but left at the end of his three year contract a few months before the club were relegated. Vic went on to manage Ethnikos in Greece, became coach at Barcelona, where he led the club to victory in the 1971 Spanish Cup final, before finishing his managerial career with Seville in 1972.

Edward Calland (b. Lanchester 15.9.32; d. 25.5.95). The youngest of three brothers (Albert and Ralph) who all played for Torquay United. Ted joined Torquay from Fulham in 1952 and scored 22 times in 47 League games. After five years he was off to neighbours Exeter City where, as a bustling centre-forward he continued to be among the goals, scoring 49 in 106 League games. He completed his playing career in the early sixties with Port Vale and Lincoln City.

Johnny Carey (b. Dublin 23.1.19; d. 23.8.95). Known as 'Gentleman John', this supremely versatile player appeared in every position, but settled generally in a right-back role. He began his career in Ireland and was signed by Manchester United from St. James Gate as an inside forward. He went on to captain United's F.A. Cup winning side of 1948 and won a League Championship medal in 1952. In 1947 he captained The Rest of Europe against England and, in 1949, helped to inflict England's first home defeat by a non British country when Ireland won 2-0 at Goodison Park. That same year he was voted Footballer of the Year and won the Sportsman of the Year award in 1950. In all he won 29 caps for the Republic and 7 for Northern Ireland. In 1953, he was appointed manager of Blackburn Rovers, winning promotion to Division One in 1958. He then had a three year term at Everton before guiding Leyton Orient to promotion to the First Division in 1962. He then had a five year association with Nottingham Forest, briefly managed the Republic of Ireland team, before finishing his managerial career with Blackburn Rovers.

Eddie Clamp (b. Coalville 14.9.34; d. 11.95). A tough tackling half-back who made his name with the wonderful Wolves side who won back-to-back Championships in 1958 and 1959, plus the F.A. Cup in 1960. Eddie made 213 appearances for the club he served between 1952 and 1961, before moving on to Arsenal, Stoke City and Peterborough United, where he finished his playing career. He also made four England appearances.

John Cope (b. Ellesmere Port 1.8.08; d. 28.1.95). John was a half-back with Llanelly, Bury and Ipswich Town, for whom he played in 1938-39, Town's first season in the Football League.

George Cowell (b. Trimdon 5.12.22; d. 11.1.96). Bobby joined Newcastle United in 1943, but after making 289 appearances in the full-back position, he was forced to retire in 1956. In between he was a member of the 1948 Second Division promotion winning side and won three F.A. Cup winners' medals in 1951, 1952 and 1955.

Harry Cripps (b. East Dereham 29.4.41; d. 29.12.95). Will forever live in Millwall folklore. 'Arry Boy' as he was known at The Den began with West Ham in 1958, but moved to Millwall in 1961. He established himself in the left-back role and played a great part in Millwall's successive promotion winning campaigns which resulted in Second Division football. The air of expectation was evident whenever Harry received the ball on the left touchline as he began one of his famous overlapping runs. He always played with great enthusiasm and a determination that the Millwall faithful thrived on. He spent 14 seasons at the club and made 444 League and Cup appearances scoring 39 goals. He completed his playing career with neighbours Charlton, whom he joined in October, 1974, and went on to become assistant manager at the Valley.

Jimmy Davidson (b. Lanarkshire 8.11.25; d. 24.1.96). An accomplished centre-half who joined Partick Thistle in 1945 where he starred until 1960, playing in three League Cup finals (1954, 1957 and 1959). He also won nine caps for Scotland before departing to Inverness Caledonian in 1960.

Dirceu (b. Brazil 1952; d. 9.95). Superbly gifted midfielder who played in the 1974, 1978 and 1982 World Cup finals. Dirceu played for 14 clubs in a 21 year career, which spanned Ascoli, Como, Napoli, Verona and Atletico Madrid, plus America and Leon in Mexico and Brazil's Vasco da Gama.

Charlie Ferguson (b. Dunfermline 22.10.10; d. 16.4.95). Charlie played for Middlesbrough, Notts County and Aberdeen before the war and was the unfortunate manager of Gateshead when they went out of the League in 1960. He later went on to become a celebrated chief scout at Sunderland and was responsible for bringing no less than nine of the 1973 F.A. Cup winning side to Roker Park.

Lester Finch (b. Hadley 26.8.09; d. 20.11.95). A brilliant left-winger who won 16 English amateur caps between 1933 and 1939. He played for Great Britain at the 1936 Olympic Games and won an F.A. Amateur Cup winners' medal with Barnet in 1946, the club he served with great distinction for 20 years.

Dick Foss (b. Barking 28.11.12; d. 8.95). Played for Chelsea between 1937 and 1947 before becoming youth team coach at Stamford Bridge. He worked with youngsters Terry Venables, Barry Bridges, Peter Bonetti and Jimmy Greaves and guided the club to successive F.A. Youth Cup victories in 1960 and 1961.

Neil Franklin (born Stoke-on-Trent 24.1.22; d. 9.2.96). An outstanding centre-half who made his name with Stoke City immediately after the war and became a key figure with Billy Wright at the heart of the England defence. In 1950, he was expected to join England's preparations for the World Cup but he decided to join Sante Fe in Bogota, Colombia where, apparently, he was to receive 'ten times his English wages'. These days it is wholly acceptable for players to better their careers by playing abroad but Franklin was labelled 'greedy'for his decision to leave. Colombia were not FIFA registered in those days and when Neil returned to Britain disillusioned, two months later, he found himself banned until January, 1951. His career also took a downward turn - no First Division clubs were prepared to take him on and he signed for Second Division Hull City for a then massive £22,500. A crowd of 39,000 saw him make his debut, but he was sadly plagued by injuries and, after 95 League games, one of England's greatest ever talents departed for Crewe and then Stockport County. But Neil Franklin will be fondly remembered by all who saw him - a sublimely cultured defender who made 142 First Division appearances for Stoke - all too few in the top flight.

Willie Fraser (b. Australia 24.2.29; d. 7.3.96). A goalkeeper who early in his career played for Cowie F.C., Third Lanark and Airdrie. During his national service he played football the world over as skipper of the British Army team. In March, 1954 he joined Sunderland, for whom he made 128 League appearances, and during his time at Roker was capped twice by Scotland. He completed his playing career at Nottingham Forest.

Walter Galbraith (b. Glasgow 26.4.18; d. 11.95). A left back who played for Clyde immediately before and after the war and who also played for New Brighton between 1948 and 1951 making 109 League appearances. He spent two seasons with Grimsby (77 League games) before moving to Accrington Stanley as player-manager in 1953. Walter retired from playing a year later, but continued to manage Accrington until 1958. He then had managerial spells at Bradford, Tranmere, Hibernian, Bradford (as General Manager) and Stockport County.

Johnny Garvie (b. Bellshill 16.10.27; d. 3.1.96). A centre-forward who started out with Hibernian, then went to Preston in 1949. A year later he was transferred to Lincoln City and became an important member of the side that won the Division Three North in 1952. He hit 73 goals in 183 games for City before leaving for Carlisle United in 1956.

John 'Jack' Goodwin (b. Worcester 29.9.20; d. 6.5.95). Jackie was a right-winger who joined Birmingham City from Worcester City in May, 1946 for £1,000, a then record Southern League transfer fee. He played 32 League games and scored eight times for Birmingham before leaving for Brentford where he made 131 appearances and found the net on 23 occasions.

Alec Gordon (b. 1941; d. 2. 96). Alec began with Dundee United, had a spell with Bradford City, then returned to Scotland with St Johnstone. Able to play either in midfield or defence, he was an important member of the side and appeared in the 1969 League Cup final side that lost by a single goal to Celtic.

Don Green (b. Bramford 30.11.24; d. Ipswich, 5.96). Centre-half, he made 58 appearances for Ipswich from 1947 to 1952.

John Gregory (b. London 24.9.26; d. 10.10.95). Inside-forward who made 178 League appearances and scored 72 goals for West Ham, Scunthorpe and Aldershot. Began his career with Bromley.

Cliff Holton (Arsenal)

Neil Franklin (Stoke C)

William Harris (b. Dudley 1.12.18; d. 20.2.96). A goalkeeper who started with West Bromwich Albion before the war and joined Oldham immediately after hostilities. He made 32 appearances for 'the Latics' before signing for Accrington Stanley in 1947. He went on to make 99 appearances before joining Dudley Town in July, 1950 as player-coach.

Jack Hather (b. 1926; d. 1.1.96). A speedy left-winger who was an integral part of Aberdeen's Championship win of 1955, Jack also won three runners-up medals in Scottish Cup finals (1953, 1954 and 1959). He starred for the Dons between 1948 and 1960, playing 351 games and scoring 104 goals.

Cliff Holton (b. Oxford 29.4.29; d. 4.6.96). Joined Arsenal in November, 1947, initially as a full-back, but was converted to a centre-forward, and made his debut in 1950-51. Cliff played in the 1952 F.A. Cup final. In 198 League appearances for the Gunners, he amassed 82 goals, before moving to Watford. At Vicarage Road he broke the club's goalscoring record, hitting 42 goals in 45 appearances. His final tally was an incredible 84 strikes in 120 League games. In 1961, he signed for Northampton and broke their goalscoring record, too, hitting the net 36 times in 41 outings. A final total of 50 goals in 62 games for 'the Cobblers' persuaded Crystal Palace to sign him in December, 1962. A further 40 goals in 101 matches led him back to Watford (12 in 24 games), onto Charlton (7 in 18 games) and finally Orient (17 in 47 games).

Glyn Hughes (b. Llay 1932; d. 19.8.95). Glyn started out with Sheffield Wednesday in 1951, but didn't make a League appearance. In August, 1952, he signed for Wrexham where he had three productive seasons, playing 92 games and scoring 20 times in his centre-forward role. In July, 1955, he moved to Newport County, where he saw out his first class career.

Ernie Jackson (b. Sheffield 11.6.14; d. 2. 96). A talented half-back who made 229 League appearances for Sheffield United between 1933 and 1949. He played in the 1936 F.A. Cup final and was instrumental in the club's promotion to the First Division three years later. He subsequently became United's trainer but resigned from the post after giving 22 years unstinting service to the club.

Albert Johanneson (b. Johannesburg 13.3.40; d. 29.9.95). Arrived in England from Jo'burg's Germiston Callies in April, 1961 and made an immediate impression on his debut, making a goal for Jack Charlton. In the 1963-64 season, when Leeds won the Second Division title, he scored 13 times in 37 games, endearing himself to the Leeds faithful. The next season in the top flight, Albert enjoyed himself as United finished runners-up in the First Division and in the 1965 F.A. Cup final. In 1970, he left Elland Road after scoring 48 goals in 169 League games to join York City. There he played 26 times and hit three goals.

Cyril Jones (b. Ponciau 17.7.20; d. 21.11.95). A full-back who joined Wrexham before the second world war and whose career was ultimately disrupted by it. He made 166 wartime appearances and continued to play for Wrexham following hostilities, but he only had another 29 outings before his career was curtailed by injury.

George Jones (b. Sheffield 27.11.18; d. 10.3.95). A pacy winger who signed for his local club Sheffield United in 1936 and made 141 appearances, scoring 35 times before transferring to Barnsley in February, 1951. He made a further 23 appearances for 'the Tykes', scoring 6 goals.

William Jones (b. Liverpool 6.6.24; d. 4. 95). A forward, Bill began with Manchester City, for whom he made three appearances in the 1948-49 season. In June, 1951, he was transferred to Chester where he hit five goals in 30 League games before retiring from first class football.

Paul Jonquin (b. 1944; d. 29.8.95). Paul played 708 games for Airdrie, whom he served with great distinction between 1961 and 1979. During that period he had an amazing run of 196 consecutive appearances between April, 1967 and September, 1971. He won a Scottish Cup runners-up medal in 1975 and was Airdrie's longest serving player.

Bobby Keetch (b. Tottenham 25.10.41; d. 29.6.96). A centre-half, Bobby began at West Ham as an amateur before joining Fulham in April, 1959. At Craven Cottage he made 106 appearances, scoring twice. In November, 1966, he moved across London to Queens Park Rangers, where he had 51 outings.

William Keith (b. Stonehaven 1922; d. 1.96). Joined Clyde following the second world war and later played for Raith Rovers, Dunfermline Athletic, Stirling Albion and Cowdenbeath.

Jack Knight (b. Bolton 12.9.22; d. 28.1.96). Inside-forward who joined Burnley in 1938, moving to Preston ten years later in exchange for Andy McLaren. Was in Preston's championship winning team of 1951. Moved to Chesterfield, Exeter and Bath, working as a stonemason. 156 League appearances, 24 goals.

Bobby Langton (b. Burscough 8.9.18; d. 1.96). Bobby began at Blackburn, signing in September, 1938. A wonderful left-winger who possessed a blistering shot, he enjoyed a great debut season, scoring 14 goals in 34 matches, which culminated in Rovers winning the Second Division title. After the war he rejoined Blackburn and won the first of 11 England caps, scoring on his international debut in the 7-2 victory over Northern Ireland. In 1948, Preston snapped him up for £16,000. 55 appearances and 14 goals later he was off to Bolton, where he had 118 outings (16 goals) and played in the 1953 F.A. Cup final. He ended his first class playing career with Blackburn Rovers.

Captain Stanley Leonard O.B.E. (b. Hawarden 8.10.25; d. 1.8.95). Represented the navy at both soccer and rugby and made one League appearance for Chester in the 1946-47 season.

Denis Maffey (b. Sunderland 22.2.22; d. 8.95). A centre-forward who played for Ipswich Town in the 1947-48 season, making five appearances before joining then Southern League Colchester United.

John Marshall (b. 1979; d. Ormskirk 7.95). A graduate from the F.A. School of Excellence and an England Schoolboy international, John was about to sign for Everton when he tragically passed away.

Leslie Maskell (b. Cowes 30.11.18; d. 11.95). A goalscoring forward who signed for Norwich City in 1936 and hit a phenomenal 224 goals for the Canaries before and during the war. After hostilities he played in the Eastern Counties League for Lowestoft and Diss.

Len Martin (b. Queensland, Australia 1919; d. 21.8.95). The distinctive voice of BBC's Grandstand. Len was a integral part of Saturday tea-time for 37 years, reading the classified football results, after starting out on the Sportsview programme in October, 1958.

Bill Mason (b. London 31.10.08; d. 11.95). Bill played in goal for Fulham before the war, signing as an amateur in 1928, and going on to make 35 appearances before transferring to QPR in 1933. At Rangers he was a regular custodian making 154 League appearances.

Norman 'Norrie' McCathie (b. Edinburgh 23.3.61; d. 9.1.96). Norrie played more than 500 times for Dunfermline, whom he joined in 1981 from Cowdenbeath. He also skippered the club and won a Division Two Championship medal in 1986, plus a Scottish League Cup runners-up medal in 1992.

Ralph McDonald (b. 1933; d. 9.95). Father of Bobby McDonald (formerly of Aston Villa, Coventry, Manchester City and Oxford United), Ralph was himself a talented player, who represented Scotland Schoolboys in 1947 and was on the books of Aberdeen.

Dave McIntosh (b. Girvan 4.5.25; d. 7.95). Dave played 294 games in goal for Sheffield Wednesday between October, 1947 and January, 1958, before he moved on to Doncaster Rovers, for whom he made 15 League appearances.

Pat McKenna (b. Glasgow 25.4.20; d. 16.11.95). Joined Aberdeen in 1944 and played at left-back in the side that won the Scottish League Cup in 1946 and the Scottish Cup a year later. In August, 1952 he headed south west for Plymouth Argyle, but only made one League appearance before returning to Scotland to sign for Arbroath.

Michael Millett (b. Billinge 22.9.77; d. 22.9.95). With a wonderful career ahead of him Michael, a former England Schoolboy and Youth international, tragically died in a car crash on his 18th birthday. At the time he had already broken into the Wigan Athletic first team, having made his League debut at the tail end of the 1994-95 season.

Gilbert Mitton (b. Leyland 30.12.28; d. 1.5.95). Goalkeeper Gilbert began at Preston North End in 1950 but, after only two appearances in four years, he joined Carlisle United where he had 48 League outings.

Alex Muir (b. Inverkeithing 10.12.23; d. 4.9.95). Scottish winger who signed for Liverpool in July, 1947, but was only able to make four League appearances during 1947-48. Alex then went into non League football until he joined the Tranmere Rovers coaching staff in 1970 and spent the next 25 years at Prenton Park. He maintained an incredible level of fitness and when the Rovers reserves were a player short, 58 year-old Alex played the full 90 minutes!

Alan Nicholls (b. Birmingham 28.8.73; d. 26.11.95). Former England Under-21 goalkeeper who made 65 League appearances for Plymouth Argyle, before moving to Vauxhall Conference club, Stalybridge Celtic. Alan was tragically killed in a road accident.

Erik Nilsson (b. Sweden 1915; d. 9.95). Famous full-back who made 57 international appearances for Sweden and won a gold medal at the 1948 London Olympic Games.

Gunnar Nordahl (b. Sweden 1921; d. 1995). One of Sweden's greatest ever players and one of the top forwards in the world in his day, Gunnar starred for Norrkoping after the war and helped the club win four consecutive Swedish titles. He scored an incredible 93 goals in 92 matches which, not surprisingly, led to him being Norrkoping's top scorer every season and the League's leading marksman four times. In 33 internationals, he amassed 44 goals. In 1949, he signed for AC Milan and continued his wonderful strike rate, helping the club to two Championship wins in 1951 and 1955. The following year he moved on to Roma and eventually became trainer.

Sidney 'Skinner' Normanton (b. Barnsley 20.8.26; d. 24.4.95). A Barnsley boy through and through, Skinner was renowned as a tough tackling wing-half, who worked in the mines before being spotted in 1945 by Barnsley boss Angus

Seed. He went on to play 123 games for 'the Tykes', scoring twice. After nine years at Barnsley, he completed his playing career with Halifax Town, making 14 League appearances in the 1954-55 season.

J. Edgar Packard (b. Mansfield 7.3.19; d. 2.96). A solid centre-half, who signed for Sheffield Wednesday in 1936, but made his debut in 1946. He went on to make 124 appearances for 'the Owls', scoring once, before terminating his playing career with Halifax Town, whom he joined in 1952, and went on to have 85 outings.

Bob Paisley O.B.E. (b. Hetton 23.1.19; d. 14.2.96). After making 252 League appearances between 1946 and 1954 for Liverpool, his one and only club, Bob went on to become the most successful manager in British football. After his retirement from playing he became part of Liverpool's famous 'boot room', first as a physiotherapist, then a coach, before becoming assistant manager and, finally, manager - succeeding Bill Shankly in 1974. He won six League titles, three League Cups, three European Champions' Cups, one UEFA Cup, one European Super Cup and six F.A. Charity Shields, one of which was shared. He was awarded the O.B.E. in 1977.

Tommy Parker (b. Hartlepool, 13.2.24; d. Ipswich 18.3.96). An inside-forward or wing-half, he made 493 appearances and scored 100 goals for Ipswich and was Captain in seven seasons, 1945 to 1956.

Edward Parsons (b. Bristol 22.3.29; d. 1.96). A centre-forward, Ted had a tough time competing for the number nine shirt at Bristol Rovers with star man Geoff Bradford. Consequently, he only made five League appearances in the 1949-50 season, scoring twice, before moving to Barnstable Town.

Neil Paterson (b. 1916; d. 19.4.95). A Dundee United player before the second world war, Neil was the first amateur to skipper a professional club in Scotland. In the fifties he became a best selling author and film writer and won an Oscar for his screenplay of 'Room At The Top'.

James Pemberton (b. Wolverhampton 30.4.16; d. 2.96). A sturdy full-back who was an amateur with Birmingham City, then a professional with West Bromwich Albion in 1938. Jimmy made 162 League appearances for 'the Baggies' between 1946 and 1950 and was a member of the Albion side that won promotion from the Second Division in 1949. He suffered a serious injury at the outset of the 1950-51 season and was forced to retire from the game.

Cyril Poole (b. Mansfield 13.3.21; d. 11.2.96). When local lad Cyril made his debut against New Brighton on 27th February, 1937, he became the youngest ever, at 15 years and 351 days, to play for Mansfield Town. His next game, more than 12 years later, came during the 1950-51 season! In all, he made 16 appearances for 'the Stags', either in defence or up front, then soccer gave way to cricket. Cyril played 366 first class matches for Nottinghamshire County Cricket Club and on three occasions for England.

Harry Potts (b. Hetton-le-Hole 22.10.20; d. 16.1.96). An inside forward for Burnley between 1946 and 1950, for whom he made 165 appearances, Harry completed his playing career with Everton in the mid-fifties. In 1956 he accepted a post as coach at Wolves and a year later was in the hot seat at Shrewsbury. In 1958, he was back on his old stamping ground as manager of Burnley, where he enjoyed great success, blooding youngsters who were to become the club's mainstay. In 1960, Harry guided 'the Clarets' to the Championship and to a place in the F.A. Cup final two years later. In 1973, he became manager of Blackpool and, three years later, returned to Turf Moor as Chief Scout. In 1977, he took up his previous position as manager, staying until 1979.

George Poyser (b. Stanton Hill 6.2.10; d. 30.1.95). A full-back, George began with Wolves in 1928, then moved on to Stourbridge without having made a League appearance at Molineux. In 1930, he joined Mansfield but, before he could make his debut, left for Port Vale. After 73 games he was on the move again, this time to Brentford. He made his debut at the start of the 1934-35 season and had 150 League outings, plus another 201 during the second world war which included a 2-0 Wembley victory over Pompey in 1942. After hostilities, he signed for Plymouth Argyle, but only made three League appearances. Later in his career he managed Notts County and Manchester City.

John Price (b. Easington 25.10.43; d. 6.5.95). Short, stocky winger who joined Burnley from junior football in 1960. Transferred to Stockport in 1965 winning a Fourth Division medal two years later. To Blackburn in 1971 returning to Stockport in 1974. Died in tragic circumstances at 51. Over 350 League appearances.

Charles 'Jazz' Rattray (b. Fleetwood 10.5.11; d. 1.10.95). A tricky outside-right who played pre-war football for Blackpool, Watford, Mansfield, Port Vale and Accrington Stanley.

John Reid (b. Dunfermline 1930; d. 4.7.95). A right-winger with his local club, Dunfermline Athletic, and Queens Park, John was capped as an amateur by Scotland.

Stan Roberts (b. Wrexham 10.4.21; d. 3..4.95). Stan played for his local club, Wrexham, and made his debut on Chrismas Day, 1946. He bagged nine goals in 27 games before moving to New Brighton in July, 1948, where he had 105 outings and scored 25 goals.

William Ross (b. 1921; d. 14.11.95). Played 54 times for Queens Park between 1948 and 1955, before becoming club president and then treasurer, up until his death.

George Rumbold (b. Alton, Hampshire 10.7.11; d. Ipswich, 12.95). A full-back who played for Crystal Palace, Clapton Orient and Ipswich Town. He scored eight of nine penalty kicks for Ipswich from 1946 to 1950.

Edward Sandford (b. Birmingham 22.10.10; d. 14.5.95). Teddy won an F.A. Cup winners' medal with West Bromwich Albion in 1931 and went on to be capped by England. He won a runners-up medal in 1935 and towards the end of his playing career was converted from a forward to a defender. When he left the Albion in 1939, he had played 317 League games and hit 75 goals.

Helmut Schon (b. Dresden 15.12.16; d. Wiesbaden 22.2.96). West Germany coach between 1964 and 1978, he led them to victory in the 1974 World Cup finals, runners-up in 1966 and to third place in 1970. In the European Championship, he masterminded his country's victory in 1972 and saw his side narrowly beaten by Czechoslovakia on penalties four years later.

Frederick Scott (b. Fatfield 6.10.16; d. 9.95). Fred was a pacy outside right who made his debut for York City in the 1936-37 season. The war interrupted his career, but he resumed with 'the Minstermen' after hostilities. But after just two further appearances, York received a then record £4,500 from Nottingham Forest. The former England Schoolboy international went on to play 304 League games for Forest, scoring 39 times, and made his last appearance just 20 days short of his 40th birthday. Later in his career Fred scouted for Sunderland, Sheffield Wednesday, Southampton and Blackpool.

Alan Sealey (b. Canning Town 27.4.42; d. 2.96). Started out with Leyton Orient in 1959 and after just four League games and one goal he joined West Ham. Alan missed the 1964 F.A. Cup final victory over Preston, then a year later enjoyed the fame of scoring twice in the Cup-winners' Cup final win over TSV Munich. He left 'the Hammers' for Plymouth Argyle in 1967, but injury forced his premature retirement after only four League games. Latterly, he had returned to Upton Park to take up a scouting appointment.

Harold Shepherdson M.B.E. (b. Middlesbrough 28.10.18; d. 14.9.95). Harold signed for his local club, Middlesbrough, in 1934 and made his debut as a centre-half in 1937. War interrupted his career and he only made a further three appearances after hostilities. A transfer to Southend followed, but a knee injury terminated his playing career. Harold returned to Middlesbrough, where he became trainer and qualified as a coach. He was appointed by then England manager Walter Winterbottom as full-time trainer to the England team and continued in that role when Alf Ramsey took over the national team in 1963. The height of Harold's career came in 1966, of course, when he was trainer to the World Cup winning side. He received an M.B.E. in 1969.

Archie Smith (b. Larkhall 23.10.24; d. 5.95). A centre-forward with Exeter City, whom he joined in 1948, Archie hit 44 goals in 115 League games for 'the Grecians' before signing for Carlisle United in 1952. He saw out his first class career at Brunton Park, playing 31 League games and scoring on eight occasions.

Herbert Smith (b. Birmingham 17.12.22; d. 11.1.96). Herbert played 51 League games on the right wing for Aston Villa between 1949 and 1954, scoring eight times. In June, 1954, he moved to Southend United, where he had five League outings.

Leslie Smith (b. Ealing 13.3.18; d. Lichfield 20.5.95). A winger who signed professionally for Brentford in 1936 and made his debut for 'the Bees' at 18 and in May, 1939, replaced the injured Stanley Matthews for England against Romania. He played for Brentford during the war and scored both goals against Pompey in the London War Cup final at Wembley. In October, 1945, Leslie signed for Aston Villa and became a real favourite during his seven year stay, during which time he made 181 League appearances and scored 26 goals. He completed a wonderful playing career at Brentford, before retiring in 1953.

Sammy Stewart (b. 1920; d. 27.6.95). Sammy had a distinguished career as a left-back for East Fife between 1938 and 1959, setting up, at the time, a record of 521 appearances for the club. He also played in all three of the Fifers' League Cup successes in 1947-48, 1949-50 and 1953-54.

Reg Stockill (b. York 24.11.13; d. 12.95). Played in the inside-left position for his home town club, York City, in their first ever League match in August, 1929. It was a memorable debut - he scored 'the Minstermen's' first ever League goal - and at 15 years old to boot! Reg only played one more League match before leaving for Scarborough in 1931. Later that year he was snapped up by Arsenal, but only seven appearances resulted, in which he found the net on four occasions. The following year he was on his way to Derby County, where he enjoyed some superb times, including a hat-trick in the 9-3 demolition of West Brom. Then an unfortunate injury hindered his career and he was allowed to leave before the outbreak of war. During hostilities he saw out his playing career with Luton Town and York City.

Joseph Walter (b. Bristol 16.8.1895; d. 24.5.95). When Joe passed away only months before his 100th birthday, he was believed to have been the second oldest ex-professional footballer in England. He started out at Bristol Rovers, for whom he made 82 League appearances, scoring 12 goals, moved onto Herbert Chapman's Huddersfield Town, and won a Championship medal with the club during their first title success of 1924. In 1926, he was transferred to Blackburn, before returning to Bristol Rovers. He was a guest of honour at the opening match of Huddersfield's McAlpine Stadium in 1994.

Dai Ward (b. Barry 16.7.34; d. 1.96). A Welsh international who joined Bristol Rovers in November, 1954 and achieved a club record of scoring in eight consecutive matches. In 174 League games, he scored 90 goals which prompted a move to Cardiff City in 1961. His 17 goals in 31 League games during 1961-62 could not prevent Cardiff's relegation and he was surprisingly sold to Third Division Watford. At Vicarage Road he found the net 29 times during the following campaign, before Brentford bought him for £11,000 in October, 1963, and he played his part fully in their record League win to date, scoring twice in a 9-0 victory over Wrexham.

Billy Whare (b. Guernsey 14.5.24; d. 5.95). Billy was a one club man, making 300 League appearances for Nottingham Forest between his debut in 1949 and 1960. He won a Third Division South Championship medal in 1951, but the pinnacle of his career came in 1959, when he helped Forest beat Luton Town in the F.A. Cup final.

Kenneth Wilkins (b. Salford 24.10.28; d. 8.95). A forward, Ken had two spells with Southampton in the early fifties, sandwiched by a nine month stay at Exeter City. He completed his first class playing career with Fulham, without making any League appearances.

Dennis Woodhead (b. Sheffield 12.6.25; d. 26.7.95). A exciting left-winger, Dennis played 214 League games for Sheffield Wednesday, scoring 71 goals. In 1952, he was part of the side that won the Second Division Championship and was top scorer in 1953-54 with a total of 21 goals. In September, 1955, he moved to Chesterfield, scored 7 times in 15 outings, then left for Derby in January, 1956. A further 24 goals in 94 games followed from the touchline raider, but unfortunate injuries curtailed his career at his last League club, Southport, restricting him to just four appearances.

THE FA CARLING PREMIERSHIP
and NATIONWIDE FOOTBALL LEAGUE
FIXTURES 1996–97

Friday 16 August 1996
Nationwide Football League Division 1
Manchester C v Ipswich T (7:45)

Saturday 17 August 1996
FA Carling Premiership
Arsenal v West Ham U
Blackburn R v Tottenham H
Coventry C v Nottingham F
Derby Co v Leeds U
Everton v Newcastle U
Middlesbrough v Liverpool
Sheffield W v Aston Villa
Sunderland v Leicester C
Wimbledon v Manchester U

Nationwide Football League Division 1
Bradford C v Portsmouth
Grimsby T v Wolverhampton W
Huddersfield T v Charlton Ath
Norwich C v Swindon T
Oldham Ath v Stoke C
Port Vale v Bolton W
QPR v Oxford U
Reading v Sheffield U
Southend U v Tranmere R
WBA v Barnsley

Nationwide Football League Division 2
AFC Bournemouth v Watford
Blackpool v Chesterfield
Bristol R v Peterborough U
Bury v Brentford
Crewe Alex v Stockport Co
Gillingham v Bristol C
Luton T v Burnley
Millwall v Wrexham
Notts Co v Preston NE
Plymouth Arg v York C
Walsall v Rotherham U

Nationwide Football League Division 3
Brighton & HA v Chester C
Cambridge U v Barnet
Colchester U v Hartlepool U
Doncaster R v Carlisle U
Fulham v Hereford U
Hull C v Darlington
Leyton Orient v Scunthorpe U
Mansfield T v Exeter C
Scarborough v Cardiff C
Swansea C v Rochdale
Torquay U v Lincoln C
Wigan Ath v Northampton T

Sunday 18 August 1996
FA Carling Premiership
Southampton v Chelsea (4:00)

Nationwide Football League Division 1
Birmingham C v Crystal Palace (1:00)

Nationwide Football League Division 2
Shrewsbury T v Wycombe W (3:00)

Monday 19 August 1996
FA Carling Premiership
Liverpool v Arsenal (8:00)

Tuesday 20 August 1996
FA Carling Premiership
Leeds U v Sheffield W (7:45)

Nationwide Football League Division 1
Bolton W v Manchester C (7:45)

Wednesday 21 August 1996
FA Carling Premiership
Aston Villa v Blackburn R (7:45)
Chelsea v Middlesbrough (7:45)
Leicester C v Southampton (7:45)
Manchester U v Everton (8:00)
Newcastle U v Wimbledon (7:45)
Nottingham F v Sunderland (7:45)
Tottenham H v Derby Co (7:45)
West Ham U v Coventry C (7:45)

Friday 23 August 1996
Nationwide Football League Division 1
Portsmouth v QPR (7:45)
Tranmere R v Grimsby T (7:45)

Saturday 24 August 1996
FA Carling Premiership
Aston Villa v Derby Co
Chelsea v Coventry C
Leicester C v Arsenal
Liverpool v Sunderland
Newcastle U v Sheffield W
Nottingham F v Middlesbrough
Tottenham H v Everton
West Ham U v Southampton

Nationwide Football League Division 1
Bolton W v Norwich C
Charlton Ath v WBA
Crystal Palace v Oldham Ath
Ipswich T v Reading
Oxford U v Southend U
Sheffield U v Birmingham C
Stoke C v Manchester C
Swindon T v Port Vale
Wolverhampton W v Bradford C

Nationwide Football League Division 2
Brentford v Luton T
Bristol C v Blackpool
Burnley v Walsall
Chesterfield v Bury
Peterborough U v Crewe Alex
Preston NE v Bristol R
Rotherham U v Shrewsbury T
Stockport Co v Notts Co
Watford v Millwall
Wrexham v Plymouth Arg
Wycombe W v Gillingham
York C v AFC Bournemouth

Nationwide Football League Division 3
Barnet v Wigan Athletic
Cardiff C v Brighton & HA
Carlisle U v Hull C
Chester C v Cambridge U
Darlington v Swansea C
Exeter C v Scarborough
Hartlepool U v Fulham
Hereford U v Doncaster R
Lincoln C v Leyton Orient
Northampton T v Mansfield T

Rochdale v Colchester U
Scunthorpe U v Torquay U

Sunday 25 August 1996
FA Carling Premiership
Manchester U v Blackburn R (4:00)

Nationwide Football League Division 1
Barnsley v Huddersfield T (1:00)

Monday 26 August 1996
FA Carling Premiership
Leeds U v Wimbledon (8:00)

Tuesday 27 August 1996
Nationwide Football League Division 1
Charlton Ath v Birmingham C (7:45)
Crystal Palace v WBA (7:45)
Ipswich T v Grimsby T (7:45)
Oxford U v Norwich C (7:45)
Portsmouth v Southend U (7:45)
Sheffield U v Huddersfield T (7:45)
Tranmere R v Port Vale (7:45)

Nationwide Football League Division 2
Brentford v Gillingham (7:45)
Bristol C v Luton T (7:45)
Burnley v Shrewsbury T (7:45)
Chesterfield v Walsall (7:45)
Peterborough U v Notts Co
Preston NE v Crewe Alex (7:45)
Rotherham U v Blackpool (7:45)
Stockport Co v AFC Bournemouth
Watford v Plymouth Arg (7:45)
Wrexham v Bristol R
Wycombe W v Bury (7:45)
York C v Millwall

Nationwide Football League Division 3
Barnet v Brighton & HA (7:45)
Cardiff C v Wigan Ath
Carlisle U v Leyton Orient (7:45)
Chester C v Swansea C
Darlington v Colchester U
Exeter C v Doncaster R (7:45)
Hartlepool U v Mansfield T
Hereford U v Hull C
Lincoln C v Cambridge U
Northampton T v Torquay U (7:45)
Rochdale v Fulham
Scunthorpe U v Scarborough

Wednesday 28 August 1996
Nationwide Football League Division 1
Barnsley v Reading (7:45)
Stoke C v Bradford C (7:45)
Swindon T v Oldham Ath (7:45)
Wolverhampton W v QPR (7:45)

Friday 30 August 1996
Nationwide Football League Division 1
WBA v Sheffield U (7:45)

Nationwide Football League Division 3
Swansea C v Lincoln C

Saturday 31 August 1996
Nationwide Football League Division 1
Birmingham C v Barnsley
Bradford C v Tranmere R
Grimsby T v Portsmouth

Huddersfield T v Crystal Palace
Manchester C v Charlton Ath
Norwich C v Wolverhampton W
Oldham Ath v Ipswich T
Port Vale v Oxford U
Reading v Stoke C
Southend U v Swindon T

Nationwide Football League Division 2
AFC Bournemouth v Peterborough U
Blackpool v Wycombe W
Bristol R v Stockport Co
Bury v Bristol C
Crewe Alex v Watford
Gillingham v Chesterfield
Luton T v Rotherham U
Millwall v Burnley
Notts Co v York C
Plymouth Arg v Preston NE
Shrewsbury T v Brentford
Walsall v Wrexham

Nationwide Football League Division 3
Brighton & HA v Scunthorpe U
Cambridge U v Cardiff C
Colchester U v Hereford U
Doncaster R v Darlington
Fulham v Carlisle U
Hull C v Barnet
Leyton Orient v Hartlepool U
Mansfield T v Rochdale
Scarborough v Northampton T
Torquay U v Exeter C
Wigan Ath v Chester C

Sunday 1 September 1996
Nationwide Football League Division 1
QPR v Bolton W (1:00)

Monday 2 September 1996
FA Carling Premiership
Sheffield W v Leicester C (8:00)

Tuesday 3 September 1996
FA Carling Premiership
Wimbledon v Tottenham H (7:45)

Wednesday 4 September 1996
FA Carling Premiership
Arsenal v Chelsea (7:45)
Blackburn R v Leeds U (7:45)
Coventry C v Liverpool (7:45)
Derby Co v Manchester U (7:45)
Everton v Aston Villa (7:45)
Middlesbrough v West Ham U (7:45)
Southampton v Nottingham F (7:45)
Sunderland v Newcastle U (7:45)

Friday 6 September 1996
Nationwide Football League Division 1
Wolverhampton W v Charlton Ath
(7:45)

Saturday 7 September 1996
FA Carling Premiership
Aston Villa v Arsenal
Leeds U v Manchester U
Liverpool v Southampton
Middlesbrough v Coventry C
Nottingham F v Leicester C
Sheffield W v Chelsea
Tottenham H v Newcastle U
Wimbledon v Everton

Nationwide Football League Division 1
Bradford C v Norwich C
Grimsby T v Swindon T
Ipswich T v Huddersfield T
Manchester C v Barnsley
Oldham Ath v Sheffield U
Portsmouth v Port Vale
QPR v WBA
Southend U v Bolton W
Stoke C v Crystal Palace
Tranmere R v Birmingham C

Nationwide Football League Division 2
AFC Bournemouth v Crewe Alex
Blackpool v Walsall
Bristol C v Preston NE
Bury v Rotherham U
Chesterfield v Brentford
Gillingham v Burnley
Millwall v Bristol R
Plymouth Arg v Notts Co
Watford v Stockport Co
Wrexham v Peterborough U
Wycombe W v Luton T
York C v Shrewsbury T

Nationwide Football League Division 3
Barnet v Northampton T
Brighton & HA v Scarborough
Cambridge U v Torquay U
Cardiff C v Exeter C
Carlisle U v Swansea C
Chester C v Lincoln C
Doncaster R v Mansfield T
Fulham v Colchester U
Hereford U v Hartlepool U
Hull C v Rochdale
Leyton Orient v Darlington
Wigan Ath v Scunthorpe U

Sunday 8 September 1996
FA Carling Premiership
Sunderland v West Ham U (4:00)

Nationwide Football League Division 1
Reading v Oxford U (1:00)

Monday 9 September 1996
FA Carling Premiership
Blackburn R v Derby Co (8:00)

Tuesday 10 September 1996
Nationwide Football League Division 1
Barnsley v Stoke C (7:45)
Birmingham C v Oldham Ath (7:45)
Bolton W v Grimsby T (7:45)
Charlton Ath v Southend U (7:45)
Crystal Palace v Ipswich T (7:45)
Huddersfield T v Tranmere R (7:45)
Oxford U v Wolverhampton W (7:45)
Port Vale v Manchester C (7:45)
Sheffield U v Bradford C (7:45)
WBA v Reading (7:45)

Nationwide Football League Division 2
Brentford v Plymouth Arg (7:45)
Bristol R v AFC Bournemouth (7:45)
Burnley v Blackpool (7:45)
Crewe Alex v Bury (7:45)
Luton T v Gillingham (7:45)
Notts Co v Watford (7:45)
Peterborough U v Millwall (7:45)
Preston NE v York C (7:45)
Rotherham U v Chesterfield (7:45)
Shrewsbury T v Bristol C
Stockport Co v Wrexham
Walsall v Wycombe W (7:45)

Nationwide Football League Division 3
Colchester U v Brighton & HA (7:45)
Darlington v Wigan Ath
Exeter C v Fulham (7:45)
Hartlepool U v Carlisle U
Lincoln C v Hull C
Mansfield T v Barnet (7:45)
Northampton T v Leyton Orient
(7:45)
Rochdale v Chester C
Scarborough v Doncaster R
Scunthorpe U v Cambridge U
Swansea C v Hereford U
Torquay U v Cardiff C (7:45)

Wednesday 11 September 1996
Nationwide Football League Division 1
Norwich C v QPR (7:45)
Swindon T v Portsmouth (7:45)

Friday 13 September 1996
Nationwide Football League Division 1
Huddersfield T v Oldham Ath (7:45)

Saturday 14 September 1996
FA Carling Premiership
Coventry C v Leeds U
Derby Co v Sunderland
Everton v Middlesbrough
Manchester U v Nottingham F
Newcastle U v Blackburn R
Southampton v Tottenham H
West Ham U v Wimbledon

Nationwide Football League Division 1
Barnsley v QPR
Birmingham C v Stoke C
Bolton W v Portsmouth
Charlton Ath v Reading
Crystal Palace v Manchester C
Norwich C v Southend U
Oxford U v Bradford C
Port Vale v Grimsby T
Sheffield U v Ipswich T
Swindon T v Tranmere R

Nationwide Football League Division 2
Brentford v Blackpool
Bristol R v Watford
Burnley v Wycombe W
Crewe Alex v Wrexham
Luton T v Chesterfield
Notts Co v Millwall
Peterborough U v York C
Preston NE v AFC Bournemouth
Rotherham U v Bristol C
Shrewsbury T v Bury
Stockport Co v Plymouth Arg
Walsall v Gillingham

Nationwide Football League Division 3
Colchester U v Hull C
Darlington v Hereford U
Exeter C v Brighton & HA
Hartlepool U v Wigan Ath
Lincoln C v Barnet
Mansfield T v Leyton Orient
Northampton T v Cambridge U
Rochdale v Doncaster R
Scarborough v Carlisle U
Scunthorpe U v Cardiff C
Swansea C v Fulham
Torquay U v Chester C

Sunday 15 September 1996
FA Carling Premiership
Chelsea v Aston Villa (4:00)
Leicester C v Liverpool (3:00)

Nationwide Football League Division 1
WBA v Wolverhampton W (1:00)

Monday 16 September 1996
FA Carling Premiership
Arsenal v Sheffield W (8:00)

Friday 20 September 1996
Nationwide Football League Division 1
Ipswich T v Charlton Ath (7:45)

Saturday 21 September 1996
FA Carling Premiership
Aston Villa v Manchester U
Blackburn R v Everton
Leeds U v Newcastle U
Liverpool v Chelsea
Middlesbrough v Arsenal
Nottingham F v West Ham U
Sheffield W v Derby Co
Sunderland v Coventry C

Nationwide Football League Division 1
Bradford C v Bolton W
Grimsby T v Oxford U

Manchester C v Birmingham C
Oldham Ath v Barnsley
Portsmouth v Norwich C
QPR v Swindon T
Reading v Crystal Palace
Southend U v Port Vale
Tranmere R v WBA
Wolverhampton W v Sheffield U

Nationwide Football League Division 2
AFC Bournemouth v Notts Co
Blackpool v Shrewsbury T
Bristol C v Walsall
Bury v Luton T
Chesterfield v Burnley
Gillingham v Rotherham U
Millwall v Crewe Alex
Plymouth Arg v Bristol R
Watford v Peterborough U
Wrexham v Preston NE
Wycombe W v Brentford
York C v Stockport Co

Nationwide Football League Division 3
Barnet v Exeter C
Brighton & HA v Torquay U
Cambridge U v Scarborough
Cardiff C v Northampton T
Carlisle U v Darlington
Chester C v Scunthorpe U
Doncaster R v Swansea C
Fulham v Mansfield T
Hereford U v Rochdale
Hull C v Hartlepool U
Leyton Orient v Colchester U
Wigan Ath v Lincoln C

Sunday 22 September 1996
FA Carling Premiership
Tottenham H v Leicester C (4:00)

Nationwide Football League Division 1
Stoke C v Huddersfield T (1:00)

Monday 23 September 1996
FA Carling Premiership
Wimbledon v Southampton (8:00)

Friday 27 September 1996
Nationwide Football League Division 1
Swindon T v Wolverhampton W
  (7:45)

Saturday 28 September 1996
FA Carling Premiership
Arsenal v Sunderland
Chelsea v Nottingham F
Coventry C v Blackburn R
Derby Co v Wimbledon
Everton v Sheffield W
Leicester C v Leeds U
Southampton v Middlesbrough

Nationwide Football League Division 1
Barnsley v Grimsby T
Birmingham C v QPR
Bolton W v Stoke C
Charlton Ath v Oldham Ath
Crystal Palace v Southend U
Huddersfield T v Reading
Norwich C v Tranmere R
Oxford U v Portsmouth
Sheffield U v Manchester C
WBA v Ipswich T

Nationwide Football League Division 2
Brentford v York C
Bristol R v Chesterfield
Burnley v Bristol C
Crewe Alex v Plymouth Arg
Luton T v Blackpool
Notts Co v Wrexham
Peterborough U v Wycombe W
Preston NE v Millwall
Rotherham U v AFC Bournemouth

Shrewsbury T v Watford
Stockport Co v Gillingham
Walsall v Bury

Nationwide Football League Division 3
Colchester U v Doncaster R
Darlington v Fulham
Exeter C v Cambridge U
Hartlepool U v Chester C
Lincoln C v Cardiff C
Mansfield T v Hereford U
Northampton T v Brighton & HA
Rochdale v Leyton Orient
Scarborough v Wigan Ath
Scunthorpe U v Barnet
Swansea C v Hull C
Torquay U v Carlisle U

Sunday 29 September 1996
FA Carling Premiership
Manchester U v Tottenham H (4:00)
West Ham U v Liverpool (3:00)

Nationwide Football League Division 1
Port Vale v Bradford C (1:00)

Monday 30 September 1996
FA Carling Premiership
Newcastle U v Aston Villa (8:00)

Tuesday 1 October 1996
Nationwide Football League Division 1
Bradford C v Swindon T (7:45)
Grimsby T v Norwich C (7:45)
Ipswich T v Barnsley (7:45)
Oldham Ath v WBA (7:45)
Portsmouth v Crystal Palace (7:45)
Reading v Birmingham C (7:45)
Southend U v Sheffield U (7:45)
Stoke C v Charlton Ath (7:45)
Tranmere R v Oxford U (7:45)

Nationwide Football League Division 2
AFC Bournemouth v Walsall (7:45)
Blackpool v Crewe Alex –
  POSTPONED
Bristol C v Brentford (7:45)
Bury v Burnley (7:45)
Chesterfield v Shrewsbury T (7:45)
Crewe Alex v Blackpool
Gillingham v Notts Co (7:45)
Plymouth Arg v Peterborough U
  (7:45)
Watford v Preston NE (7:45)
Wrexham v Luton T
Wycombe W v Rotherham U (7:45)
York C v Bristol R

Nationwide Football League Division 3
Barnet v Scarborough (7:45)
Brighton & HA v Lincoln C (7:45)
Cambridge U v Darlington (7:45)
Cardiff C v Rochdale
Carlisle U v Colchester U (7:45)
Chester C v Northampton T
Doncaster R v Hartlepool U
Fulham v Torquay U (7:45)
Hereford U v Scunthorpe U
Hull C v Mansfield T (7:45)
Leyton Orient v Swansea C (7:45)
Wigan Ath v Exeter C (7:45)

Wednesday 2 October 1996
Nationwide Football League Division 1
QPR v Port Vale (7:45)
Wolverhampton W v Bolton W (7:45)

Nationwide Football League Division 2
Millwall v Stockport Co (7:45)

Friday 4 October 1996
Nationwide Football League Division 1
Stoke C v Norwich C (7:45)

Nationwide Football League Division 2
Wrexham v Shrewsbury T

Nationwide Football League Division 3
Swansea C v Colchester U

Saturday 5 October 1996
Nationwide Football League Division 1
Bradford C v Southend U
Charlton Ath v Barnsley
Grimsby T v QPR
Huddersfield T v Birmingham C
Ipswich T v Swindon T
Manchester C v WBA
Oldham Ath v Port Vale
Oxford U v Bolton W
Tranmere R v Portsmouth
Wolverhampton W v Reading

Nationwide Football League Division 2
Brentford v Rotherham U
Bristol R v Crewe Alex
Burnley v Stockport Co
Bury v Blackpool
Chesterfield v Bristol C
Gillingham v AFC Bournemouth
Luton T v Walsall
Plymouth Arg v Millwall
Preston NE v Peterborough U
Wycombe W v Notts Co
York C v Watford

Nationwide Football League Division 3
Barnet v Torquay U
Cambridge U v Hartlepool U
Carlisle U v Mansfield T
Chester C v Cardiff C
Darlington v Rochdale
Doncaster R v Leyton Orient
Hereford U v Scarborough
Hull C v Scunthorpe U
Lincoln C v Exeter C
Northampton T v Fulham
Wigan Ath v Brighton & HA

Sunday 6 October 1996
Nationwide Football League Division 1
Crystal Palace v Sheffield U (1:00)

Friday 11 October 1996
Nationwide Football League Division 1
Norwich C v Ipswich T (7:45)

Nationwide Football League Division 2
Bristol C v York C (7:45)

Saturday 12 October 1996
FA Carling Premiership
Blackburn R v Arsenal
Derby Co v Newcastle U
Everton v West Ham U
Leeds U v Nottingham F
Leicester C v Chelsea
Manchester U v Liverpool (11:15)
Tottenham H v Aston Villa
Wimbledon v Sheffield W

Nationwide Football League Division 1
Barnsley v Crystal Palace
Birmingham C v Bradford C
Bolton W v Oldham Ath
Port Vale v Stoke C
Portsmouth v Charlton Ath
QPR v Manchester C
Reading v Grimsby T
Sheffield U v Tranmere R
Swindon T v Oxford U
WBA v Huddersfield T

Nationwide Football League Division 2
AFC Bournemouth v Wycombe W
Blackpool v Gillingham
Crewe Alex v Brentford
Millwall v Chesterfield
Notts Co v Bristol R

Peterborough U v Bury
Rotherham U v Burnley
Shrewsbury T v Luton T
Stockport Co v Preston NE
Walsall v Plymouth Arg
Watford v Wrexham

Nationwide Football League Division 3
Brighton & HA v Cambridge U
Cardiff C v Barnet
Colchester U v Wigan Ath
Exeter C v Northampton T
Fulham v Doncaster R
Hartlepool U v Darlington
Leyton Orient v Hull C
Mansfield T v Swansea C
Rochdale v Carlisle U
Scarborough v Chester C
Scunthorpe U v Lincoln C
Torquay U v Hereford U

Sunday 13 October 1996
FA Carling Premiership
Coventry C v Southampton (4:00)

Nationwide Football League Division 1
Southend U v Wolverhampton W
(1:00)

Monday 14 October 1996
FA Carling Premiership
Sunderland v Middlesbrough (8:00)

Tuesday 15 October 1996
Nationwide Football League Division 1
Barnsley v Oxford U (7:45)
Birmingham C v Ipswich T (7:45)
Bolton W v Tranmere R (7:45)
Port Vale v Crystal Palace (7:45)
Portsmouth v Wolverhampton W
(7:45)
Reading v Manchester C (7:45)
Sheffield U v Charlton Ath (7:45)
Southend U v Grimsby T (7:45)

Nationwide Football League Division 2
AFC Bournemouth v Plymouth Arg
(7:45)
Blackpool v Wrexham
Bristol C v Wycombe W (7:45)
Crewe Alex v York C
Notts Co v Chesterfield (7:45)
Peterborough U v Brentford
Rotherham U v Bristol R (7:45)
Shrewsbury T v Gillingham
Stockport Co v Luton T
Walsall v Preston NE (7:45)
Watford v Burnley (7:45)

Nationwide Football League Division 3
Brighton & HA v Hereford U (7:45)
Cardiff C v Darlington
Colchester U v Barnet (7:45)
Exeter C v Carlisle U (7:45)
Fulham v Cambridge U (7:45)
Hartlepool U v Swansea C
Leyton Orient v Chester C (7:45)
Mansfield T v Wigan Ath (7:45)
Rochdale v Lincoln C
Scarborough v Hull C
Scunthorpe U v Northampton T
Torquay U v Doncaster R (7:45)

Wednesday 16 October 1996
Nationwide Football League Division 1
Norwich C v Oldham Ath (7:45)
QPR v Bradford C (7:45)
Swindon T v Huddersfield T (7:45)
WBA v Stoke C (7:45)

Nationwide Football League Division 2
Millwall v Bury (7:45)

Friday 18 October 1996
Nationwide Football League Division 1
Oxford U v Birmingham C (7:45)

Saturday 19 October 1996
FA Carling Premiership
Arsenal v Coventry C
Aston Villa v Leeds U
Chelsea v Wimbledon
Middlesbrough v Tottenham H
Nottingham F v Derby Co
Sheffield W v Blackburn R
Southampton v Sunderland
West Ham U v Leicester C

Nationwide Football League Division 1
Bradford C v Barnsley
Charlton Ath v Bolton W
Crystal Palace v Swindon T
Grimsby T v WBA
Huddersfield T v Southend U
Ipswich T v Portsmouth
Manchester C v Norwich C
Oldham Ath v Reading
Stoke C v Sheffield U
Wolverhampton W v Port Vale

Nationwide Football League Division 2
Brentford v Walsall
Bristol R v Blackpool
Burnley v Notts Co
Bury v Watford
Chesterfield v Crewe Alex
Gillingham v Millwall
Luton T v Peterborough U
Plymouth Arg v Bristol C
Preston NE v Shrewsbury T
Wrexham v AFC Bournemouth
Wycombe W v Stockport Co
York C v Rotherham U

Nationwide Football League Division 3
Barnet v Hartlepool U
Cambridge U v Rochdale
Carlisle U v Cardiff C
Chester C v Exeter C
Darlington v Mansfield T
Doncaster R v Brighton & HA
Hereford U v Leyton Orient
Hull C v Fulham
Lincoln C v Scarborough
Northampton T v Colchester U
Swansea C v Scunthorpe U
Wigan Ath v Torquay U

Sunday 20 October 1996
FA Carling Premiership
Liverpool v Everton (3:00)
Newcastle U v Manchester U (4:00)

Nationwide Football League Division 1
Tranmere R v QPR (1:00)

Friday 25 October 1996
Nationwide Football League Division 1
Barnsley v Bolton W (7:45)

Nationwide Football League Division 3
Cambridge U v Doncaster R (7:45)

Saturday 26 October 1996
FA Carling Premiership
Arsenal v Leeds U
Chelsea v Tottenham H
Coventry C v Sheffield W
Leicester C v Newcastle U
Middlesbrough v Wimbledon
Southampton v Manchester U
Sunderland v Aston Villa
West Ham U v Blackburn R

Nationwide Football League Division 1
Birmingham C v Norwich C
Charlton Ath v Oxford U
Crystal Palace v Grimsby T

Huddersfield T v Port Vale
Ipswich T v Tranmere R
Oldham Ath v Southend U
Reading v Swindon T
Sheffield U v QPR
Stoke C v Portsmouth
WBA v Bradford C

Nationwide Football League Division 2
Blackpool v Watford
Brentford v Millwall
Bristol C v Notts Co
Burnley v Plymouth Arg
Bury v Bristol R
Chesterfield v York C
Gillingham v Preston NE
Luton T v AFC Bournemouth
Rotherham U v Peterborough U
Shrewsbury T v Crewe Alex
Walsall v Stockport Co
Wycombe W v Wrexham

Nationwide Football League Division 3
Barnet v Carlisle U
Brighton & HA v Fulham
Cardiff C v Leyton Orient
Chester C v Hereford U
Exeter C v Hartlepool U
Lincoln C v Colchester U
Northampton T v Darlington
Scarborough v Mansfield T
Scunthorpe U v Rochdale
Torquay U v Swansea C
Wigan Ath v Hull C

Sunday 27 October 1996
FA Carling Premiership
Liverpool v Derby Co (4:00)

Nationwide Football League Division 1
Manchester C v Wolverhampton W
(1:00)

Monday 28 October 1996
FA Carling Premiership
Nottingham F v Everton (8:00)

Tuesday 29 October 1996
Nationwide Football League Division 1
Bolton W v Reading (7:45)
Bradford C v Crystal Palace (7:45)
Grimsby T v Oldham Ath (7:45)
Oxford U v Stoke C (7:45)
Port Vale v Barnsley (7:45)
Portsmouth v Birmingham C (7:45)
Southend U v Manchester C (7:45)
Tranmere R v Charlton Ath (7:45)

Nationwide Football League Division 2
AFC Bournemouth v Bristol C (7:45)
Bristol R v Brentford (7:45)
Crewe Alex v Rotherham U
Notts Co v Walsall (7:45)
Peterborough U v Shrewsbury T
Plymouth Arg v Gillingham (7:45)
Preston NE v Burnley (7:45)
Stockport Co v Chesterfield
Watford v Luton T (7:45)
Wrexham v Bury
York C v Wycombe W

Nationwide Football League Division 3
Carlisle U v Chester C (7:45)
Colchester U v Exeter C (7:45)
Darlington v Barnet
Doncaster R v Lincoln C
Fulham v Scunthorpe U (7:45)
Hartlepool U v Northampton T
Hereford U v Cambridge U
Hull C v Cardiff C (7:45)
Leyton Orient v Scarborough (7:45)
Mansfield T v Torquay U (7:45)
Rochdale v Brighton & HA
Swansea C v Wigan Ath

Wednesday 30 October 1996
Nationwide Football League Division 1
Norwich C v Sheffield U (7:45)
QPR v Ipswich T (7:45)
Swindon T v WBA (7:45)
Wolverhampton W v Huddersfield T
(7:45)

Nationwide Football League Division 2
Millwall v Blackpool (7:45)

Saturday 2 November 1996
FA Carling Premiership
Aston Villa v Nottingham F
Derby Co v Leicester C
Leeds U v Sunderland
Manchester U v Chelsea
Sheffield W v Southampton
Tottenham H v West Ham U
Wimbledon v Arsenal

Nationwide Football League Division 1
Bolton W v Huddersfield T
Bradford C v Oldham Ath
Norwich C v Charlton Ath
Oxford U v Ipswich T
Port Vale v Birmingham C
Portsmouth v WBA
QPR v Stoke C
Southend U v Reading
Swindon T v Manchester C
Tranmere R v Crystal Palace
Wolverhampton W v Barnsley

Nationwide Football League Division 2
AFC Bournemouth v Bury
Bristol R v Gillingham
Crewe Alex v Wycombe W
Millwall v Walsall
Notts Co v Shrewsbury T
Peterborough U v Blackpool
Plymouth Arg v Luton T
Preston NE v Rotherham U
Stockport Co v Bristol C
Watford v Brentford
Wrexham v Chesterfield
York C v Burnley

Nationwide Football League Division 3
Carlisle U v Wigan Ath
Colchester U v Cardiff C
Darlington v Scarborough
Doncaster R v Chester C
Fulham v Lincoln C
Hartlepool U v Brighton & HA
Hereford U v Barnet
Hull C v Cambridge U
Leyton Orient v Torquay U
Mansfield T v Scunthorpe U
Rochdale v Exeter C
Swansea C v Northampton T

Sunday 3 November 1996
FA Carling Premiership
Blackburn R v Liverpool (3:00)
Newcastle U v Middlesbrough (4:00)

Nationwide Football League Division 1
Grimsby T v Sheffield U (1:00)

Monday 4 November 1996
FA Carling Premiership
Everton v Coventry C (8:00)

Friday 8 November 1996
Nationwide Football League Division 1
Huddersfield T v Bradford C (7:45)

Saturday 9 November 1996
Nationwide Football League Division 1
Barnsley v Norwich C
Birmingham C v Bolton W
Charlton Ath v Grimsby T
Ipswich T v Southend U

Manchester C v Oxford U
Oldham Ath v Portsmouth
Reading v Tranmere R
Sheffield U v Swindon T
Stoke C v Wolverhampton W
WBA v Port Vale

Nationwide Football League Division 2
Blackpool v AFC Bournemouth
Brentford v Stockport Co
Bristol C v Millwall
Burnley v Crewe Alex
Bury v York C
Chesterfield v Preston North End
Gillingham v Wrexham
Luton T v Notts Co
Rotherham U v Watford
Shrewsbury T v Bristol R
Walsall v Peterborough U
Wycombe W v Plymouth Arg

Nationwide Football League Division 3
Barnet v Rochdale
Brighton & HA v Mansfield T
Cambridge U v Swansea C
Cardiff C v Fulham
Chester C v Hull C
Exeter C v Leyton Orient
Lincoln C v Darlington
Northampton T v Carlisle U
Scarborough v Hartlepool U
Scunthorpe U v Doncaster R
Torquay U v Colchester U
Wigan Ath v Hereford U

Sunday 10 November 1996
Nationwide Football League Division 1
Crystal Palace v QPR (1:00)

Friday 15 November 1996
Nationwide Football League Division 1
Tranmere R v Oldham Ath (7:45)

Saturday 16 November 1996
FA Carling Premiership
Aston Villa v Leicester C
Blackburn R v Chelsea
Everton v Southampton
Leeds U v Liverpool
Manchester U v Arsenal
Newcastle U v West Ham U
Tottenham H v Sunderland
Wimbledon v Coventry C

Nationwide Football League Division 1
Bolton W v Crystal Palace
Bradford C v Ipswich T
Grimsby T v Stoke C
Norwich C v Reading
Oxford U v Huddersfield T
Port Vale v Sheffield U
Portsmouth v Manchester C
QPR v Charlton Ath
Southend U v WBA
Swindon T v Barnsley
Wolverhampton W v Birmingham C

Sunday 17 November 1996
FA Carling Premiership
Derby Co v Middlesbrough (4:00)

Monday 18 November 1996
FA Carling Premiership
Sheffield W v Nottingham F (8:00)

Tuesday 19 November 1996
Nationwide Football League Division 2
AFC Bournemouth v Brentford (7:45)
Bristol R v Burnley (7:45)
Crewe Alex v Bristol C
Notts Co v Bury (7:45)
Peterborough U v Gillingham
Plymouth Arg v Chesterfield (7:45)
Preston NE v Luton T (7:45)
Stockport Co v Blackpool

Watford v Wycombe W (7:45)
Wrexham v Rotherham U
York C v Walsall

Nationwide Football League Division 3
Carlisle U v Cambridge U (7:45)
Colchester U v Scunthorpe U (7:45)
Darlington v Exeter C
Doncaster R v Northampton T
Fulham v Barnet (7:45)
Hartlepool U v Cardiff C
Hereford U v Lincoln C
Hull C v Torquay U (7:45)
Leyton Orient v Wigan Ath (7:45)
Mansfield T v Chester C (7:45)
Rochdale v Scarborough
Swansea C v Brighton & HA

Wednesday 20 November 1996
Nationwide Football League Division 1
Manchester C v Huddersfield T (7:45)

Nationwide Football League Division 2
Millwall v Shrewsbury T (7:45)

Friday 22 November 1996
Nationwide Football League Division 3
Chester C v Colchester U

Saturday 23 November 1996
FA Carling Premiership
Chelsea v Newcastle U
Coventry C v Aston Villa
Leicester C v Everton
Liverpool v Wimbledon
Middlesbrough v Manchester U
Nottingham F v Blackburn R
Southampton v Leeds U
Sunderland v Sheffield W
West Ham U v Derby Co

Nationwide Football League Division 1
Barnsley v Portsmouth
Birmingham C v Swindon T
Charlton Ath v Bradford C
Crystal Palace v Wolverhampton W
Huddersfield T v Grimsby T
Ipswich T v Port Vale
Manchester C v Tranmere R
Oldham Ath v Oxford U
Reading v QPR
Sheffield U v Bolton W
Stoke C v Southend U
WBA v Norwich C

Nationwide Football League Division 2
Blackpool v Notts Co
Brentford v Wrexham
Bristol C v Peterborough U
Burnley v AFC Bournemouth
Bury v Plymouth Arg
Chesterfield v Watford
Gillingham v York C
Luton T v Bristol R
Rotherham U v Millwall
Shrewsbury T v Stockport Co
Walsall v Crewe Alex
Wycombe W v Preston North End

Nationwide Football League Division 3
Barnet v Doncaster R
Brighton & HA v Carlisle U
Cambridge U v Leyton Orient
Cardiff C v Hereford U
Exeter C v Hull C
Lincoln C v Mansfield T
Northampton T v Rochdale
Scarborough v Swansea C
Scunthorpe U v Darlington
Torquay U v Hartlepool U
Wigan Ath v Fulham

Sunday 24 November 1996
FA Carling Premiership
Arsenal v Tottenham H (4:00)

Saturday 30 November 1996
FA Carling Premiership
Aston Villa v Middlesbrough
Blackburn R v Southampton
Derby Co v Coventry C
Everton v Sunderland
Manchester U v Leicester C
Newcastle U v Arsenal
Sheffield W v West Ham U
Wimbledon v Nottingham F

Nationwide Football League Division 1
Bolton W v Barnsley
Bradford C v WBA
Grimsby T v Crystal Palace
Norwich C v Birmingham C
Oxford U v Charlton Ath
Port Vale v Huddersfield T
Portsmouth v Stoke C
QPR v Sheffield U
Southend U v Oldham Ath
Swindon T v Reading
Tranmere R v Ipswich T
Wolverhampton W v Manchester C

Nationwide Football League Division 2
AFC Bournemouth v Luton T
Bristol R v Bury
Crewe Alex v Shrewsbury T
Millwall v Brentford
Notts Co v Bristol C
Peterborough U v Rotherham U
Plymouth Arg v Burnley
Preston NE v Gillingham
Stockport Co v Walsall
Watford v Blackpool
Wrexham v Wycombe W
York C v Chesterfield

Nationwide Football League Division 3
Carlisle U v Barnet
Colchester U v Lincoln C
Darlington v Northampton T
Doncaster R v Cambridge U
Fulham v Brighton & HA
Hartlepool U v Exeter C
Hereford U v Chester C
Hull C v Wigan Ath
Leyton Orient v Cardiff C
Mansfield T v Scarborough
Rochdale v Scunthorpe U
Swansea C v Torquay U

Sunday 1 December 1996
FA Carling Premiership
Leeds U v Chelsea (4:00)

Monday 2 December 1996
FA Carling Premiership
Tottenham H v Liverpool (8:00)

Tuesday 3 December 1996
Nationwide Football League Division 2
Blackpool v Plymouth Arg
Brentford v Notts Co (7:45)
Bristol C v Watford (7:45)
Burnley v Wrexham (7:45)
Bury v Preston NE (7:45)
Chesterfield v Peterborough U (7:45)
Gillingham v Crewe Alex (7:45)
Luton T v York C (7:45)
Rotherham U v Stockport Co (7:45)
Shrewsbury T v AFC Bournemouth
Walsall v Bristol R (7:45)
Wycombe W v Millwall (7:45)

Nationwide Football League Division 3
Barnet v Leyton Orient (7:45)
Brighton & HA v Darlington (7:45)
Cambridge U v Mansfield T (7:45)
Cardiff C v Swansea C
Chester C v Fulham
Exeter C v Hereford U (7:45)
Lincoln C v Carlisle U
Northampton T v Hull C (7:45)

Scarborough v Colchester U
Scunthorpe U v Hartlepool U
Torquay U v Rochdale (7:45)
Wigan Ath v Doncaster R (7:45)

Saturday 7 December 1996
FA Carling Premiership
Arsenal v Derby Co
Chelsea v Everton
Coventry C v Tottenham H
Leicester C v Blackburn R
Liverpool v Sheffield W
Middlesbrough v Leeds U
Southampton v Aston Villa
Sunderland v Wimbledon

Nationwide Football League Division 1
Barnsley v Southend U
Birmingham C v Grimsby T
Charlton Ath v Swindon T
Crystal Palace v Oxford U
Huddersfield T v Norwich C
Ipswich T v Wolverhampton W
Manchester C v Bradford C
Oldham Ath v QPR
Reading v Port Vale
Sheffield U v Portsmouth
Stoke C v Tranmere R
WBA v Bolton W

Sunday 8 December 1996
FA Carling Premiership
West Ham U v Manchester U (4:00)

Monday 9 December 1996
FA Carling Premiership
Nottingham F v Newcastle U (8:00)

Friday 13 December 1996
Nationwide Football League Division 2
Preston NE v Blackpool (7:45)

Nationwide Football League Division 3
Doncaster R v Cardiff C
Swansea C v Barnet

Saturday 14 December 1996
FA Carling Premiership
Arsenal v Southampton
Coventry C v Newcastle U
Derby Co v Everton
Leeds U v Tottenham H
Liverpool v Nottingham F
Middlesbrough v Leicester C
Sheffield W v Manchester U
West Ham U v Aston Villa
Wimbledon v Blackburn R

Nationwide Football League Division 1
Barnsley v Tranmere R
Birmingham C v WBA
Bolton W v Ipswich T
Bradford C v Reading
Charlton Ath v Port Vale
Manchester C v Grimsby T
Norwich C v Crystal Palace
Oxford U v Sheffield U
Portsmouth v Huddersfield T
QPR v Southend U
Stoke C v Swindon T
Wolverhampton W v Oldham Ath

Nationwide Football League Division 2
AFC Bournemouth v Millwall
Burnley v Brentford
Gillingham v Bury
Luton T v Crewe Alex
Notts Co v Rotherham U
Plymouth Arg v Shrewsbury T
Stockport Co v Peterborough U
Walsall v Watford
Wycombe W v Chesterfield
York C v Wrexham

Nationwide Football League Division 3
Brighton & HA v Hull C
Cambridge U v Wigan Ath
Chester C v Darlington
Fulham v Leyton Orient
Hereford U v Carlisle U
Lincoln C v Northampton T
Mansfield T v Colchester U
Rochdale v Hartlepool U
Scunthorpe U v Exeter C
Torquay U v Scarborough

Sunday 15 December 1996
FA Carling Premiership
Sunderland v Chelsea (4:00)

Nationwide Football League Division 2
Bristol C v Bristol R (1:00)

Wednesday 18 December 1996
Nationwide Football League Division 2
Millwall v Luton T (7:45)

Friday 20 December 1996
Nationwide Football League Division 2
Crewe Alex v Notts Co
Peterborough U v Burnley

Nationwide Football League Division 3
Colchester U v Cambridge U (7:45)
Northampton T v Hereford U (7:45)

Saturday 21 December 1996
FA Carling Premiership
Blackburn R v Middlesbrough
Chelsea v West Ham U
Everton v Leeds U
Leicester C v Coventry C
Manchester U v Sunderland
Nottingham F v Arsenal
Southampton v Derby Co
Tottenham H v Sheffield W

Nationwide Football League Division 1
Crystal Palace v Charlton Ath
Grimsby T v Bradford C
Huddersfield T v QPR
Ipswich T v Stoke C
Oldham Ath v Manchester C
Port Vale v Norwich C
Reading v Portsmouth
Sheffield U v Barnsley
Southend U v Birmingham C
Swindon T v Bolton W
Tranmere R v Wolverhampton W
WBA v Oxford U

Nationwide Football League Division 2
Blackpool v York C
Brentford v Preston NE
Bristol R v Wycombe W
Bury v Stockport Co
Chesterfield v AFC Bournemouth
Rotherham U v Plymouth Arg
Shrewsbury T v Walsall
Watford v Gillingham
Wrexham v Bristol C

Nationwide Football League Division 3
Barnet v Chester C
Cardiff C v Mansfield T
Carlisle U v Scunthorpe U
Darlington v Torquay U
Exeter C v Swansea C
Hartlepool U v Lincoln C
Hull C v Doncaster R
Scarborough v Fulham
Wigan Ath v Rochdale

Sunday 22 December 1996
FA Carling Premiership
Aston Villa v Wimbledon (4:00)

Nationwide Football League Division 3
Leyton Orient v Brighton & HA
(12:00)

Monday 23 December 1996
FA Carling Premiership
Newcastle U v Liverpool (8:00)

Thursday 26 December 1996
FA Carling Premiership
Aston Villa v Chelsea (3:00)
Blackburn R v Newcastle U (3:00)
Leeds U v Coventry C (3:00)
Liverpool v Leicester C (3:00)
Middlesbrough v Everton (3:00)
Nottingham F v Manchester U (3:00)
Sheffield W v Arsenal (5:45)
Sunderland v Derby Co (3:00)
Tottenham H v Southampton (12:00)
Wimbledon v West Ham U (12:00)

Nationwide Football League Division 1
Bradford C v Sheffield U (3:00)
Grimsby T v Bolton W (3:00)
Ipswich T v Crystal Palace (3:00)
Manchester C v Port Vale (3:00)
Oldham Ath v Birmingham C (1:00)
Portsmouth v Swindon T (3:00)
QPR v Norwich C (3:00)
Reading v WBA (3:00)
Southend U v Charlton Ath (3:00)
Stoke C v Barnsley (3:00)
Tranmere R v Huddersfield T (3:00)
Wolverhampton W v Oxford U (3:00)

Nationwide Football League Division 2
AFC Bournemouth v Bristol R (3:00)
Blackpool v Burnley (3:00)
Bristol C v Shrewsbury T (3:00)
Bury v Crewe Alex (3:00)
Chesterfield v Rotherham U (3:00)
Gillingham v Luton T (3:00)
Millwall v Peterborough U (3:00)
Plymouth Arg v Brentford (3:00)
Watford v Notts Co (12:00)
Wrexham v Stockport Co (3:00)
Wycombe W v Walsall (3:00)
York C v Preston NE (3:00)

Nationwide Football League Division 3
Barnet v Mansfield T (3:00)
Brighton & HA v Colchester U
(12:00)
Cambridge U v Scunthorpe U (3:00)
Cardiff C v Torquay U (3:00)
Carlisle U v Hartlepool U (3:00)
Chester C v Rochdale (3:00)
Doncaster R v Scarborough (3:00)
Fulham v Exeter C (12:00)
Hereford U v Swansea C (3:00)
Hull C v Lincoln C (3:00)
Leyton Orient v Northampton T
(3:00)
Wigan Ath v Darlington (3:00)

Saturday 28 December 1996
FA Carling Premiership
Arsenal v Aston Villa
Chelsea v Sheffield W
Coventry C v Middlesbrough
Derby Co v Blackburn R
Everton v Wimbledon
Leicester C v Nottingham F
Manchester U v Leeds U
Newcastle U v Tottenham H
Southampton v Liverpool
West Ham U v Sunderland

Nationwide Football League Division 1
Barnsley v Manchester C
Birmingham C v Tranmere R
Bolton W v Southend U
Charlton Ath v Wolverhampton W
Crystal Palace v Stoke C
Huddersfield T v Ipswich T

Norwich C v Bradford C
Oxford U v Reading
Port Vale v Portsmouth
Sheffield U v Oldham Ath
Swindon T v Grimsby T
WBA v QPR

Nationwide Football League Division 2
Brentford v Chesterfield
Bristol R v Millwall
Burnley v Gillingham
Crewe Alex v AFC Bournemouth
Luton T v Wycombe W
Notts Co v Plymouth Arg
Peterborough U v Wrexham
Preston NE v Bristol C
Rotherham U v Bury
Shrewsbury T v York C
Stockport Co v Watford
Walsall v Blackpool

Nationwide Football League Division 3
Colchester U v Fulham
Darlington v Leyton Orient
Exeter C v Cardiff C
Hartlepool U v Hereford U
Lincoln C v Chester C
Mansfield T v Doncaster R
Northampton T v Barnet
Rochdale v Hull C
Scarborough v Brighton & HA
Scunthorpe U v Wigan Ath
Swansea C v Carlisle U
Torquay U v Cambridge U

Wednesday 1 January 1997
FA Carling Premiership
Arsenal v Middlesbrough (3:00)
Chelsea v Liverpool (3:00)
Coventry C v Sunderland (3:00)
Derby Co v Sheffield W (3:00)
Everton v Blackburn R (5:45)
Leicester C v Tottenham H (3:00)
Manchester U v Aston Villa (8:00)
Newcastle U v Leeds U (3:00)
Southampton v Wimbledon (3:00)
West Ham U v Nottingham F (3:00)

Nationwide Football League Division 1
Barnsley v Oldham Ath (3:00)
Birmingham C v Manchester C (3:00)
Bolton W v Bradford C (3:00)
Charlton Ath v Ipswich T (3:00)
Crystal Palace v Reading (3:00)
Huddersfield T v Stoke C (3:00)
Norwich C v Portsmouth (3:00)
Oxford U v Grimsby T (3:00)
Port Vale v Southend U (3:00)
Sheffield U v Wolverhampton W
(3:00)
Swindon T v QPR (3:00)
WBA v Tranmere R (3:00)

Nationwide Football League Division 2
Brentford v Wycombe W (3:00)
Bristol R v Plymouth Arg (3:00)
Burnley v Chesterfield (3:00)
Crewe Alex v Millwall (3:00)
Luton T v Bury (3:00)
Notts Co v AFC Bournemouth (3:00)
Peterborough U v Watford (3:00)
Preston NE v Wrexham (3:00)
Rotherham U v Gillingham (3:00)
Shrewsbury T v Blackpool (3:00)
Stockport Co v York C (3:00)
Walsall v Bristol C (3:00)

Nationwide Football League Division 3
Colchester U v Leyton Orient (3:00)
Darlington v Carlisle U (3:00)
Exeter C v Barnet (3:00)
Hartlepool U v Hull C (3:00)
Lincoln C v Wigan Ath (3:00)
Mansfield T v Fulham (3:00)
Northampton T v Cardiff C (3:00)

Rochdale v Hereford U (3:00)
Scarborough v Cambridge U (3:00)
Scunthorpe U v Chester C (3:00)
Swansea C v Doncaster R (3:00)
Torquay U v Brighton & HA (3:00)

Saturday 4 January 1997
Nationwide Football League Division 2
AFC Bournemouth v Preston NE
Blackpool v Brentford
Bristol C v Rotherham U
Bury v Shrewsbury T
Chesterfield v Luton T
Gillingham v Walsall
Millwall v Notts Co
Plymouth Arg v Stockport Co
Watford v Bristol R
Wrexham v Crewe Alex
Wycombe W v Burnley
York C v Peterborough U

Nationwide Football League Division 3
Barnet v Lincoln C
Brighton & HA v Exeter C
Cambridge U v Northampton T
Cardiff C v Scunthorpe U
Carlisle U v Scarborough
Chester C v Torquay U
Doncaster R v Rochdale
Fulham v Swansea C
Hereford U v Darlington
Hull C v Colchester U
Leyton Orient v Mansfield T
Wigan Ath v Hartlepool U

Friday 10 January 1997
Nationwide Football League Division 1
Tranmere R v Swindon T (7:45)

Saturday 11 January 1997
FA Carling Premiership
Aston Villa v Newcastle U
Blackburn R v Coventry C
Leeds U v Leicester C
Liverpool v West Ham U
Middlesbrough v Southampton
Nottingham F v Chelsea
Sheffield W v Everton
Sunderland v Arsenal
Tottenham H v Manchester U
Wimbledon v Derby Co

Nationwide Football League Division 1
Bradford C v Oxford U
Grimsby T v Port Vale
Ipswich T v Sheffield U
Manchester C v Crystal Palace
Oldham Ath v Huddersfield T
Portsmouth v Bolton W
QPR v Barnsley
Reading v Charlton Ath
Southend U v Norwich C
Stoke C v Birmingham C
Wolverhampton W v WBA

Nationwide Football League Division 2
AFC Bournemouth v Rotherham U
Blackpool v Luton T
Bristol C v Burnley
Bury v Walsall
Chesterfield v Bristol R
Gillingham v Stockport Co
Millwall v Preston NE
Plymouth Arg v Crewe Alex
Watford v Shrewsbury T
Wrexham v Notts Co
Wycombe W v Peterborough U
York C v Brentford

Nationwide Football League Division 3
Barnet v Scunthorpe U
Brighton & HA v Northampton T
Cambridge U v Exeter C
Cardiff C v Lincoln C
Carlisle U v Torquay U

Chester C v Hartlepool U
Doncaster R v Colchester U
Fulham v Darlington
Hereford U v Mansfield T
Hull C v Swansea C
Leyton Orient v Rochdale
Wigan Ath v Scarborough

Saturday 18 January 1997
FA Carling Premiership
Arsenal v Everton
Chelsea v Derby Co
Coventry C v Manchester U
Leicester C v Wimbledon
Liverpool v Aston Villa
Middlesbrough v Sheffield W
Nottingham F v Tottenham H
Southampton v Newcastle U
Sunderland v Blackburn R
West Ham U v Leeds U

Nationwide Football League Division 1
Barnsley v Ipswich T
Birmingham C v Reading
Bolton W v Wolverhampton W
Charlton Ath v Stoke C
Crystal Palace v Portsmouth
Huddersfield T v Manchester C
Norwich C v Grimsby T
Oxford U v Tranmere R
Port Vale v QPR
Sheffield U v Southend U
Swindon T v Bradford C
WBA v Oldham Ath

Nationwide Football League Division 2
Blackpool v Crewe Alex
Brentford v Bristol C
Bristol R v York C
Burnley v Bury
Crewe Alex v Blackpool –
POSTPONED
Luton T v Wrexham
Notts Co v Gillingham
Peterborough U v Plymouth Arg
Preston NE v Watford
Rotherham U v Wycombe W
Shrewsbury T v Chesterfield
Stockport Co v Millwall
Walsall v AFC Bournemouth

Nationwide Football League Division 3
Colchester U v Carlisle U
Darlington v Cambridge U
Exeter C v Wigan Ath
Hartlepool U v Doncaster R
Lincoln C v Brighton & HA
Mansfield T v Hull C
Northampton T v Chester C
Rochdale v Cardiff C
Scarborough v Barnet
Scunthorpe U v Hereford U
Swansea C v Leyton Orient
Torquay U v Fulham

Saturday 25 January 1997
Nationwide Football League Division 2
Blackpool v Millwall
Brentford v Bristol R
Bristol C v AFC Bournemouth
Burnley v Preston NE
Bury v Wrexham
Chesterfield v Stockport Co
Gillingham v Plymouth Arg
Luton T v Watford
Rotherham U v Crewe Alex
Shrewsbury T v Peterborough U
Walsall v Notts Co
Wycombe W v York C

Nationwide Football League Division 3
Barnet v Darlington
Brighton & HA v Rochdale
Cambridge U v Hereford U
Cardiff C v Hull C

Chester C v Carlisle U
Exeter C v Colchester U
Lincoln C v Doncaster R
Northampton T v Hartlepool U
Scarborough v Leyton Orient
Scunthorpe U v Fulham
Torquay U v Mansfield T
Wigan Ath v Swansea C

Tuesday 28 January 1997
Nationwide Football League Division 1
Bradford C v Port Vale (7:45)
Grimsby T v Barnsley (7:45)
Ipswich T v WBA (7:45)
Oldham Ath v Charlton Ath (7:45)
Portsmouth v Oxford U (7:45)
Reading v Huddersfield T (7:45)
Southend U v Crystal Palace (7:45)
Tranmere R v Norwich C (7:45)

Wednesday 29 January 1997
Nationwide Football League Division 1
Manchester C v Sheffield U (7:45)
QPR v Birmingham C (7:45)
Stoke C v Bolton W (7:45)
Wolverhampton W v Swindon T
(7:45)

Friday 31 January 1997
Nationwide Football League Division 3
Colchester U v Torquay U (7:45)
Swansea C v Cambridge U

Saturday 1 February 1997
FA Carling Premiership
Aston Villa v Sunderland
Blackburn R v West Ham U
Derby Co v Liverpool
Everton v Nottingham F
Leeds U v Arsenal
Manchester U v Southampton
Newcastle U v Leicester C
Sheffield W v Coventry C
Tottenham H v Chelsea
Wimbledon v Middlesbrough

Nationwide Football League Division 1
Bolton W v Birmingham C
Bradford C v Huddersfield T
Grimsby T v Charlton Ath
Norwich C v Barnsley
Oxford U v Manchester C
Port Vale v WBA
Portsmouth v Oldham Ath
QPR v Crystal Palace
Southend U v Ipswich T
Swindon T v Sheffield U
Tranmere R v Reading
Wolverhampton W v Stoke C

Nationwide Football League Division 2
AFC Bournemouth v Blackpool
Bristol R v Shrewsbury T
Crewe Alex v Burnley
Millwall v Bristol C
Notts Co v Luton T
Peterborough U v Walsall
Plymouth Arg v Wycombe W
Preston NE v Chesterfield
Stockport Co v Brentford
Watford v Rotherham U
Wrexham v Gillingham
York C v Bury

Nationwide Football League Division 3
Carlisle U v Northampton T
Darlington v Lincoln C
Doncaster R v Scunthorpe U
Fulham v Cardiff C
Hartlepool U v Scarborough
Hereford U v Wigan Ath
Hull C v Chester C
Leyton Orient v Exeter C
Mansfield T v Brighton & HA
Rochdale v Barnet

Saturday 8 February 1997
Nationwide Football League Division 1
Barnsley v Port Vale
Birmingham C v Portsmouth
Charlton Ath v Tranmere R
Crystal Palace v Bradford C
Huddersfield T v Wolverhampton W
Ipswich T v QPR
Manchester C v Southend U
Oldham Ath v Grimsby T
Reading v Bolton W
Sheffield U v Norwich C
Stoke C v Oxford U
WBA v Swindon T

Nationwide Football League Division 2
Blackpool v Peterborough U
Brentford v Watford
Bristol C v Stockport Co
Burnley v York C
Bury v AFC Bournemouth
Chesterfield v Wrexham
Gillingham v Bristol R
Luton T v Plymouth Arg
Rotherham U v Preston NE
Shrewsbury T v Notts Co
Walsall v Millwall
Wycombe W v Crewe Alex

Nationwide Football League Division 3
Barnet v Hereford U
Brighton & HA v Hartlepool U
Cambridge U v Hull C
Cardiff C v Colchester U
Chester C v Doncaster R
Exeter C v Rochdale
Lincoln C v Fulham
Northampton T v Swansea C
Scarborough v Darlington
Scunthorpe U v Mansfield T
Torquay U v Leyton Orient
Wigan Ath v Carlisle U

Friday 14 February 1997
Nationwide Football League Division 3
Colchester U v Chester C (7:45)

Saturday 15 February 1997
FA Carling Premiership
Aston Villa v Coventry C
Blackburn R v Nottingham F
Derby Co v West Ham U
Everton v Leicester C
Leeds U v Southampton
Manchester U v Middlesbrough
Newcastle U v Chelsea
Sheffield W v Sunderland
Tottenham H v Arsenal
Wimbledon v Liverpool

Nationwide Football League Division 1
Bolton W v Sheffield U
Bradford C v Charlton Ath
Grimsby T v Huddersfield T
Norwich C v WBA
Oxford U v Oldham Ath
Port Vale v Ipswich T
Portsmouth v Barnsley
QPR v Reading
Southend U v Stoke C
Swindon T v Birmingham C
Tranmere R v Manchester C
Wolverhampton W v Crystal Palace

Nationwide Football League Division 2
AFC Bournemouth v Burnley
Bristol R v Luton T
Crewe Alex v Walsall
Millwall v Rotherham U
Notts Co v Blackpool
Peterborough U v Bristol C
Plymouth Arg v Bury
Preston NE v Wycombe W
Stockport Co v Shrewsbury T
Watford v Chesterfield

Wrexham v Brentford
York C v Gillingham

Nationwide Football League Division 3
Carlisle U v Brighton & HA
Darlington v Scunthorpe U
Doncaster R v Barnet
Fulham v Wigan Ath
Hartlepool U v Torquay U
Hereford U v Cardiff C
Hull C v Exeter C
Leyton Orient v Cambridge U
Mansfield T v Lincoln C
Rochdale v Northampton T
Swansea C v Scarborough

Saturday 22 February 1997
FA Carling Premiership
Arsenal v Wimbledon
Chelsea v Manchester U
Coventry C v Everton
Leicester C v Derby Co
Liverpool v Blackburn R
Middlesbrough v Newcastle U
Nottingham F v Aston Villa
Southampton v Sheffield W
Sunderland v Leeds U
West Ham U v Tottenham H

Nationwide Football League Division 1
Barnsley v Wolverhampton W
Birmingham C v Port Vale
Charlton Ath v Norwich C
Crystal Palace v Tranmere R
Huddersfield T v Bolton W
Ipswich T v Oxford U
Manchester C v Swindon T
Oldham Ath v Bradford C
Reading v Southend U
Sheffield U v Grimsby T
Stoke C v QPR
WBA v Portsmouth

Nationwide Football League Division 2
Blackpool v Stockport Co
Brentford v AFC Bournemouth
Bristol C v Crewe Alex
Burnley v Bristol R
Bury v Notts Co
Chesterfield v Plymouth Arg
Gillingham v Peterborough U
Luton T v Preston NE
Rotherham U v Wrexham
Shrewsbury T v Millwall
Walsall v York C
Wycombe W v Watford

Nationwide Football League Division 3
Barnet v Fulham
Brighton & HA v Swansea C
Cambridge U v Carlisle U
Cardiff C v Hartlepool U
Chester C v Mansfield T
Exeter C v Darlington
Lincoln C v Hereford U
Northampton T v Doncaster R
Scarborough v Rochdale
Scunthorpe U v Colchester U
Torquay U v Hull C
Wigan Ath v Leyton Orient

Friday 28 February 1997
Nationwide Football League Division 1
Tranmere R v Stoke C (7:45)

Nationwide Football League Division 3
Colchester U v Scarborough (7:45)
Doncaster R v Wigan Ath

Saturday 1 March 1997
FA Carling Premiership
Aston Villa v Liverpool
Blackburn R v Sunderland
Derby Co v Chelsea
Everton v Arsenal

Leeds U v West Ham U
Manchester U v Coventry C
Newcastle U v Southampton
Sheffield W v Middlesbrough
Tottenham H v Nottingham F
Wimbledon v Leicester C

Nationwide Football League Division 1
Bolton W v WBA
Bradford C v Manchester C
Grimsby T v Birmingham C
Norwich C v Huddersfield T
Oxford U v Crystal Palace
Port Vale v Reading
Portsmouth v Sheffield U
QPR v Oldham Ath
Southend U v Barnsley
Swindon T v Charlton Ath
Wolverhampton W v Ipswich T

Nationwide Football League Division 2
AFC Bournemouth v Shrewsbury T
Bristol R v Walsall
Crewe Alex v Gillingham
Millwall v Wycombe W
Notts Co v Brentford
Peterborough U v Chesterfield
Plymouth Arg v Blackpool
Preston NE v Bury
Stockport Co v Rotherham U
Watford v Bristol C
Wrexham v Burnley
York C v Luton T

Nationwide Football League Division 3
Carlisle U v Lincoln C
Darlington v Brighton & HA
Fulham v Chester C
Hartlepool U v Scunthorpe U
Hereford U v Exeter C
Hull C v Northampton T
Leyton Orient v Barnet
Mansfield T v Cambridge U
Rochdale v Torquay U
Swansea C v Cardiff C

Tuesday 4 March 1997
FA Carling Premiership
Arsenal v Manchester U (7:45)
Sunderland v Tottenham H (7:45)

Nationwide Football League Division 1
Barnsley v Swindon T (7:45)
Birmingham, C v Wolverhampton W (7:45)
Charlton Ath v QPR (7:45)
Crystal Palace v Bolton W (7:45)
Huddersfield T v Oxford U (7:45)
Ipswich T v Bradford C (7:45)
Oldham Ath v Tranmere R (7:45)
Reading v Norwich C (7:45)
Sheffield U v Port Vale (7:45)
WBA v Southend U (7:45)

Wednesday 5 March 1997
FA Carling Premiership
Chelsea v Blackburn R (7:45)
Coventry C v Wimbledon (7:45)
Leicester C v Aston Villa (7:45)
Liverpool v Leeds U (7:45)
Middlesbrough v Derby Co (7:45)
Nottingham F v Sheffield W (7:45)
Southampton v Everton
West Ham U v Newcastle U (7:45)

Nationwide Football League Division 1
Manchester C v Portsmouth (7:45)
Stoke C v Grimsby T (7:45)

Friday 7 March 1997
Nationwide Football League Division 3
Cambridge U v Colchester U (7:45)

Saturday 8 March 1997
FA Carling Premiership
Arsenal v Nottingham F
Coventry C v Leicester C
Derby Co v Southampton
Leeds U v Everton
Liverpool v Newcastle U
Middlesbrough v Blackburn R
Sheffield W v Tottenham H
Sunderland v Manchester U
West Ham U v Chelsea
Wimbledon v Aston Villa

Nationwide Football League Division 1
Barnsley v Sheffield U
Birmingham C v Southend U
Bolton W v Swindon T
Bradford C v Grimsby T
Charlton Ath v Crystal Palace
Manchester C v Oldham Ath
Norwich C v Port Vale
Oxford U v WBA
Portsmouth v Reading
QPR v Huddersfield T
Stoke C v Ipswich T
Wolverhampton W v Tranmere R

Nationwide Football League Division 2
AFC Bournemouth v Chesterfield
Bristol C v Wrexham
Burnley v Peterborough U
Gillingham v Watford
Luton T v Millwall
Notts Co v Crewe Alex
Plymouth Arg v Rotherham U
Preston NE v Brentford
Stockport Co v Bury
Walsall v Shrewsbury T
Wycombe W v Bristol R
York C v Blackpool

Nationwide Football Division 3
Brighton & HA v Leyton Orient
Chester C v Barnet
Doncaster R v Hull C
Fulham v Scarborough
Hereford U v Northampton T
Lincoln C v Hartlepool U
Mansfield T v Cardiff C
Rochdale v Wigan Ath
Scunthorpe U v Carlisle U
Swansea C v Exeter C
Torquay U v Darlington

Friday 14 March 1997
Nationwide Football League Division 3
Cardiff C v Doncaster R
Colchester U v Mansfield T (7:45)

Saturday 15 March 1997
FA Carling Premiership
Aston Villa v West Ham U
Blackburn R v Wimbledon
Chelsea v Sunderland
Everton v Derby Co
Leicester C v Middlesbrough
Manchester U v Sheffield W
Newcastle U v Coventry C
Nottingham F v Liverpool
Southampton v Arsenal
Tottenham H v Leeds U

Nationwide Football League Division 1
Crystal Palace v Norwich C
Grimsby T v Manchester C
Huddersfield T v Portsmouth
Ipswich T v Bolton W
Oldham Ath v Wolverhampton W
Port Vale v Charlton Ath
Reading v Bradford C
Sheffield U v Oxford U
Southend U v QPR
Swindon T v Stoke C
Tranmere R v Barnsley
WBA v Birmingham C

Nationwide Football League Division 2
Blackpool v Preston NE
Brentford v Burnley
Bristol R v Bristol C
Bury v Gillingham
Chesterfield v Wycombe W
Crewe Alex v Luton T
Millwall v AFC Bournemouth
Peterborough U v Stockport Co
Rotherham U v Notts Co
Shrewsbury T v Plymouth Arg
Watford v Walsall
Wrexham v York C

Nationwide Football League Division 3
Barnet v Swansea C
Carlisle U v Hereford U
Darlington v Chester C
Exeter C v Scunthorpe U
Hartlepool U v Rochdale
Hull C v Brighton & HA
Northampton T v Lincoln
Scarborough v Torquay U
Wigan Ath v Cambridge U

Sunday 16 March 1997
Nationwide Football League Division 3
Leyton Orient v Fulham (12:00)

Friday 21 March 1997
Nationwide Football League Division 3
Colchester U v Rochdale (7:45)
Doncaster R v Hereford U

Saturday 22 March 1997
FA Carling Premiership
Arsenal v Liverpool
Blackburn R v Aston Villa
Coventry C v West Ham U
Derby Co v Tottenham H
Everton v Manchester U
Middlesbrough v Chelsea
Sheffield W v Leeds U
Southampton v Leicester C
Sunderland v Nottingham F
Wimbledon v Newcastle U

Nationwide Football League Division 1
Birmingham C v Sheffield U
Bradford C v Wolverhampton W
Grimsby T v Tranmere R
Huddersfield T v Barnsley
Manchester C v Stoke C
Norwich C v Bolton W
Oldham Ath v Crystal Palace
Port Vale v Swindon T
QPR v Portsmouth
Reading v Ipswich T
Southend U v Oxford U
WBA v Charlton Ath

Nationwide Football League Division 2
AFC Bournemouth v York C
Blackpool v Bristol C
Bury v Chesterfield
Crewe Alex v Peterborough U
Gillingham v Wycombe W
Luton T v Brentford
Millwall v Watford
Notts Co v Stockport Co
Plymouth Arg v Wrexham
Shrewsbury T v Rotherham U
Walsall v Burnley

Nationwide Football League Division 3
Brighton & HA v Cardiff C
Cambridge U v Chester C
Fulham v Hartlepool U
Hull C v Carlisle U
Leyton Orient v Lincoln C
Mansfield T v Northampton T
Scarborough v Exeter C
Swansea C v Darlington
Torquay U v Scunthorpe U
Wigan Ath v Barnet

Sunday 23 March 1997
Nationwide Football League Division 2
Bristol R v Preston NE (3:00)

Friday 28 March 1997
Nationwide Football League Division 1
Ipswich T v Manchester C (7:45)

Nationwide Football League Division 2
Wrexham v Millwall (12:00)

Nationwide Football League Division 3
Cardiff C v Scarborough

Saturday 29 March 1997
FA Carling Premiership
Aston Villa v Sheffield W
Chelsea v Southampton
Leeds U v Derby Co
Leicester C v Sunderland
Liverpool v Middlesbrough
Manchester U v Wimbledon
Newcastle U v Everton
Nottingham F v Coventry C
Tottenham H v Blackburn R
West Ham U v Arsenal

Nationwide Football League Division 1
Barnsley v WBA
Bolton W v Port Vale
Charlton Ath v Huddersfield T
Crystal Palace v Birmingham C
Oxford U v QPR
Portsmouth v Bradford C
Sheffield U v Reading
Stoke C v Oldham Ath
Swindon T v Norwich C
Tranmere R v Southend U
Wolverhampton W v Grimsby T

Nationwide Football League Division 2
Brentford v Bury
Bristol C v Gillingham
Burnley v Luton T
Chesterfield v Blackpool
Peterborough U v Bristol R
Preston NE v Notts Co
Rotherham U v Walsall
Stockport Co v Crewe Alex
Watford v AFC Bournemouth
Wycombe W v Shrewsbury T
York C v Plymouth Arg

Nationwide Football League Division 3
Barnet v Cambridge U
Carlisle U v Doncaster R
Chester C v Brighton & HA
Darlington v Hull C
Exeter C v Mansfield T
Hartlepool U v Colchester U
Hereford U v Fulham
Lincoln C v Torquay U
Northampton T v Wigan Ath
Rochdale v Swansea C
Scunthorpe U v Leyton Orient

Monday 31 March 1997
Nationwide Football League Division 1
Birmingham C v Charlton Ath (3:00)
Bradford C v Stoke C (3:00)
Grimsby T v Ipswich (3:00)
Huddersfield T v Sheffield U (3:00)
Norwich C v Oxford U (3:00)
Oldham Ath v Swindon T (3:00)
Port Vale v Tranmere R (3:00)
QPR v Wolverhampton W (3:00)
Reading v Barnsley (3:00)
Southend U v Portsmouth (3:00)
WBA v Crystal Palace (3:00)

Nationwide Football League Division 2
Blackpool v Rotherham U (3:00)
Bristol R v Wrexham (3:00)
Bury v Wycombe W (3:00)
Crewe Alex v Preston NE (3:00)

Gillingham v Brentford (3:00)
Notts Co v Peterborough U (3:00)
Plymouth Arg v Watford (3:00)

Nationwide Football League Division 3
Brighton & HA v Barnet (3:00)
Cambridge U v Lincoln C (3:00)
Colchester U v Darlington (3:00)
Doncaster R v Exeter C (3:00)
Fulham v Rochdale (3:00)
Hull C v Hereford U (3:00)
Leyton Orient v Carlisle U (3:00)
Mansfield T v Hartlepool U (3:00)
Scarborough v Scunthorpe U (3:00)
Swansea C v Chester C (3:00)
Torquay U v Northampton T (3:00)
Wigan Ath v Cardiff C (3:00)

Tuesday 1 April 1997
Nationwide Football League Division 2
AFC Bournemouth v Stockport Co (7:45)
Luton T v Bristol C (7:45)
Shrewsbury T v Burnley
Walsall v Chesterfield (7:45)

Wednesday 2 April 1997
Nationwide Football League Division 2
Millwall v York C (7:45)

Friday 4 April 1997
Nationwide Football League Division 1
Tranmere R v Bradford C (7:45)

Saturday 5 April 1997
FA Carling Premiership
Aston Villa v Everton
Chelsea v Arsenal
Leeds U v Blackburn R
Leicester C v Sheffield W
Liverpool v Coventry C
Manchester U v Derby Co
Newcastle U v Sunderland
Nottingham F v Southampton
Tottenham H v Wimbledon
West Ham U v Middlesbrough

Nationwide Football League Division 1
Barnsley v Birmingham C
Bolton W v QPR
Charlton Ath v Manchester C
Crystal Palace v Huddersfield T
Ipswich T v Oldham Ath
Oxford U v Port Vale
Portsmouth v Grimsby T
Sheffield U v WBA
Stoke C v Reading
Swindon T v Southend U
Wolverhampton W v Norwich C

Nationwide Football League Division 2
Brentford v Shrewsbury T
Bristol C v Bury
Burnley v Millwall
Chesterfield v Gillingham
Peterborough U v AFC Bournemouth
Preston NE v Plymouth Arg
Rotherham U v Luton T
Stockport Co v Bristol R
Watford v Crewe Alex
Wrexham v Walsall
Wycombe W v Blackpool
York C v Notts Co

Nationwide Football League Division 3
Barnet v Hull C
Cardiff C v Cambridge U
Carlisle U v Fulham
Chester C v Wigan Ath
Darlington v Doncaster R
Exeter C v Torquay U
Hartlepool U v Leyton Orient
Hereford U v Colchester U
Lincoln C v Swansea C
Northampton T v Scarborough

Rochdale v Mansfield T
Scunthorpe U v Brighton & HA

Wednesday 9 April 1997
Nationwide Football League Division 1
Manchester C v Bolton W (7:45)

Friday 11 April 1997
Nationwide Football League Division 2
Rotherham U v Brentford (7:45)

Nationwide Football League Division 3
Colchester U v Swansea C (7:45)

Saturday 12 April 1997
FA Carling Premiership
Arsenal v Leicester C
Blackburn R v Manchester U
Coventry C v Chelsea
Derby Co v Aston Villa
Everton v Tottenham H
Middlesbrough v Nottingham F
Sheffield W v Newcastle U
Southampton v West Ham U
Sunderland v Liverpool
Wimbledon v Leeds U

Nationwide Football League Division 1
Barnsley v Charlton Ath
Birmingham v Huddersfield T
Bolton W v Oxford U
Norwich C v Stoke C
Port Vale v Oldham
Portsmouth v Tranmere R
QPR v Grimsby T
Reading v Wolverhampton W
Sheffield U v Crystal Palace
Southend U v Bradford C
Swindon T v Ipswich T
WBA v Manchester C

Nationwide Football League Division 2
AFC Bournemouth v Gillingham
Blackpool v Bury
Bristol C v Chesterfield
Crewe Alex v Bristol R
Millwall v Plymouth Arg
Notts Co v Wycombe W
Peterborough U v Preston NE
Shrewsbury T v Wrexham
Stockport Co v Burnley
Walsall v Luton T
Watford v York C

Nationwide Football League Division 3
Brighton & HA v Wigan Ath
Cardiff C v Chester C
Exeter C v Lincoln C
Fulham v Northampton T
Hartlepool U v Cambridge U
Leyton Orient v Doncaster R
Mansfield v Carlisle U
Rochdale v Darlington
Scarborough v Hereford U
Scunthorpe U v Hull C
Torquay U v Barnet

Saturday 19 April 1997
FA Carling Premiership
Arsenal v Blackburn R
Aston Villa v Tottenham H
Chelsea v Leicester C
Liverpool v Manchester U
Middlesbrough v Sunderland
Newcastle U v Derby Co
Nottingham F v Leeds U
Sheffield W v Wimbledon
Southampton v Coventry C
West Ham U v Everton

Nationwide Football League Division 1
Bradford C v Birmingham C
Charlton Ath v Portsmouth
Crystal Palace v Barnsley
Grimsby T v Reading

Huddersfield T v WBA
Ipswich T v Norwich C
Manchester C v QPR
Oldham Ath v Bolton W
Oxford U v Swindon T
Stoke C v Port Vale
Tranmere R v Sheffield U
Wolverhampton W v Southend U

Nationwide Football League Division 2
Brentford v Crewe Alex
Burnley v Rotherham U
Bury v Peterborough U
Chesterfield v Millwall
Gillingham v Blackpool
Luton T v Shrewsbury T
Plymouth Arg v Walsall
Preston NE v Stockport Co
Wrexham v Watford
Wycombe W v AFC Bournemouth
York C v Bristol C

Nationwide Football League Division 3
Barnet v Cardiff C
Cambridge U v Brighton & HA
Carlisle U v Rochdale
Chester C v Scarborough
Darlington v Hartlepool U
Doncaster R v Fulham
Hereford U v Torquay U
Hull C v Leyton Orient
Lincoln C v Scunthorpe U
Northampton T v Exeter C
Swansea C v Mansfield T
Wigan Ath v Colchester U

Sunday 20 April 1997
Nationwide Football League Division 2
Bristol R v Notts Co (3:00)

Tuesday 22 April 1997
FA Carling Premiership
Blackburn R v Sheffield W (7:45)
Leeds U v Aston Villa (7:45)
Sunderland v Southampton (7:45)
Wimbledon v Chelsea (7:45)

Wednesday 23 April 1997
FA Carling Premiership
Coventry C v Arsenal (7:45)
Derby Co v Nottingham F (7:45)
Everton v Liverpool (7:45)
Leicester v West Ham U (7:45)
Manchester U v Newcastle U (8:00)
Tottenham H v Middlesbrough (7:45)

Saturday 26 April 1997
Nationwide Football League Division 1
Barnsley v Bradford C
Birmingham v Oxford U
Bolton W v Charlton Ath
Norwich C v Manchester C
Port Vale v Wolverhampton W
Portsmouth v Ipswich T
QPR v Tranmere R
Reading v Oldham Ath
Sheffield U v Stoke C
Southend U v Huddersfield T
Swindon T v Crystal Palace
WBA v Grimsby T

Nationwide Football League Division 2
AFC Bournemouth v Wrexham
Blackpool v Bristol R
Bristol C v Plymouth Arg
Crewe Alex v Chesterfield
Millwall v Gillingham
Notts Co v Burnley
Peterborough U v Luton T
Rotherham U v York C
Shrewsbury T v Preston NE
Stockport Co v Wycombe W
Walsall v Brentford
Watford v Bury

Nationwide Football League Division 3
Brighton & HA v Doncaster R
Cardiff C v Carlisle U
Colchester U v Northampton T
Exeter C v Chester C
Fulham v Hull C
Hartlepool U v Barnet
Leyton Orient v Hereford U
Mansfield T v Darlington
Rochdale v Cambridge U
Scarborough v Lincoln C
Scunthorpe U v Swansea C
Torquay U v Wigan Ath

Saturday 3 May 1997
FA Carling Premiership
Arsenal v Newcastle U
Chelsea v Leeds U
Coventry C v Derby Co
Leicester C v Manchester U
Liverpool v Tottenham H
Middlesbrough v Aston Villa
Nottingham F v Wimbledon
Southampton v Blackburn R
Sunderland v Everton
West Ham U v Sheffield W

Nationwide Football League Division 2
Brentford v Peterborough U
Bristol R v Rotherham U
Burnley v Watford
Bury v Millwall
Chesterfield v Notts Co
Gillingham v Shrewsbury T
Luton T v Stockport Co
Plymouth Arg v AFC Bournemouth
Preston NE v Walsall
Wrexham v Blackpool
Wycombe W v Bristol C
York C v Crewe Alex

Nationwide Football League Division 3
Barnet v Colchester U
Cambridge U v Fulham
Carlisle U v Exeter C
Chester C v Leyton Orient
Darlington v Cardiff C
Doncaster R v Torquay U
Hereford U v Brighton & HA
Hull C v Scarborough
Lincoln C v Rochdale
Northampton T v Scunthorpe U
Swansea C v Hartlepool U
Wigan Ath v Mansfield T

Nationwide Football League Division 1
Bradford C v QPR (3:00)
Charlton Ath v Sheffield U (3:00)
Crystal Palace v Port Vale (3:00)
Grimsby T v Southend U (3:00)
Huddersfield T v Swindon T (3:00)
Ipswich T v Birmingham C (3:00)
Manchester C v Reading (3:00)
Oldham Ath v Norwich C (3:00)
Oxford U v Barnsley (3:00)
Stoke C v WBA (3:00)
Tranmere R v Bolton W (3:00)
Wolverhampton W v Portsmouth
  (3:00)

Sunday 11 May 1997
FA Carling Premiership
Aston Villa v Southampton (4:00)
Blackburn R v Leicester C (4:00)
Derby Co v Arsenal (4:00)
Everton v Chelsea (4:00)
Leeds U v Middlesbrough (4:00)
Manchester U v West Ham U (4:00)
Newcastle U v Nottingham F (4:00)
Sheffield W v Liverpool (4:00)
Tottenham H v Coventry C (4:00)
Wimbledon v Sunderland (4:00)

FA CARLING PREMIERSHIP FIXTURES 1996–97

	Arsenal	Aston Villa	Blackburn R	Chelsea	Coventry C	Derby Co	Everton	Leeds U	Leicester C	Liverpool	Manchester U	Middlesbrough	Newcastle U	Nottingham F	Sheffield W	Southampton	Sunderland	Tottenham H	West Ham U	Wimbledon
Arsenal	—	28.12	19.4	4.9	19.10	7.12	18.1	26.10	12.4	22.3	4.3	1.1	3.5	8.3	16.9	14.12	28.9	24.11	17.8	22.2
Aston Villa	7.9	—	21.8	26.12	15.2	24.8	5.4	19.10	16.11	1.3	21.9	30.11	11.1	2.11	29.3	11.5	1.2	19.4	15.3	22.12
Blackburn R	12.10	22.3	—	16.11	11.1	9.9	21.9	4.9	11.5	3.11	12.4	21.12	26.12	15.2	22.4	30.11	1.3	17.8	1.2	15.3
Chelsea	5.4	15.9	5.3	—	24.8	18.1	7.12	3.5	19.4	1.1	22.2	21.8	23.11	28.9	28.12	29.3	15.3	26.10	21.12	19.10
Coventry C	23.4	23.11	28.9	12.4	—	3.5	22.2	14.9	8.3	4.9	18.1	28.12	14.12	17.8	26.10	13.10	15.3	7.12	21.12	5.3
Derby Co	11.5	12.4	28.12	1.3	30.11	—	14.12	17.8	2.11	1.2	4.9	17.11	12.10	23.4	1.1	8.3	14.9	22.3	15.2	28.9
Everton	1.3	4.9	1.1	11.5	4.11	15.3	—	21.12	15.2	23.4	22.3	14.9	17.8	1.2	28.9	16.11	30.11	12.4	12.10	28.12
Leeds U	1.2	22.4	5.4	1.12	26.12	21.12	8.3	—	11.1	16.11	7.9	11.5	21.9	12.10	20.8	15.2	2.11	14.12	1.3	26.8
Leicester C	24.8	5.3	7.12	12.10	21.12	22.2	23.11	28.9	—	15.9	3.5	15.3	26.10	28.12	5.4	21.8	29.3	1.1	23.4	18.1
Liverpool	19.8	18.1	22.2	21.9	5.4	27.10	20.10	5.3	26.12	—	19.4	29.3	8.3	14.12	7.12	7.9	24.8	3.5	11.1	23.11
Manchester U	16.11	1.1	25.8	2.11	1.3	5.4	21.8	28.12	30.11	12.10	—	15.2	23.4	14.9	15.3	1.2	21.12	29.9	11.5	29.3
Middlesbrough	21.9	3.5	8.3	22.3	7.9	5.3	26.12	7.12	14.12	3.11	15.2	—	22.2	12.4	18.1	11.1	23.4	19.10	4.9	26.10
Newcastle U	30.11	30.9	14.9	23.11	15.3	19.4	29.3	1.1	26.10	8.3	23.4	22.2	—	11.5	21.9	26.10	21.12	19.10	16.11	21.8
Nottingham F	21.12	22.2	23.11	11.1	29.3	21.9	1.1	19.4	7.9	14.12	14.9	24.8	9.12	—	5.3	5.4	4.9	18.1	21.9	3.5
Sheffield W	26.12	17.8	19.10	28.12	26.10	1.1	28.9	22.3	5.4	7.12	15.3	18.1	21.9	5.3	—	22.2	23.11	8.3	30.11	12.10
Southampton	15.3	7.12	3.5	18.8	19.4	26.12	5.3	23.11	21.8	7.9	1.2	11.1	26.10	5.4	22.2	—	22.4	14.9	12.4	23.9
Sunderland	11.1	26.10	18.1	15.12	21.9	21.8	3.5	22.2	29.3	24.8	8.3	14.10	7.9	18.11	23.11	22.4	—	4.3	8.9	7.12
Tottenham H	15.2	12.10	29.3	1.2	11.5	22.3	12.4	15.3	1.1	3.5	29.9	19.10	19.4	18.1	8.3	22.4	4.3	—	2.11	3.9
West Ham U	29.3	14.12	26.10	8.3	21.8	23.11	19.4	18.1	23.4	11.1	11.5	4.9	16.11	21.9	30.11	12.4	8.9	2.11	—	14.9
Wimbledon	2.11	8.3	14.12	22.4	16.11	11.1	7.9	12.4	18.1	23.11	17.8	26.10	22.3	3.5	12.10	23.9	7.12	3.9	26.12	—

NATIONWIDE FOOTBALL LEAGUE FIXTURES 1996-97

Copyright © The Football League Ltd 1996. Copyright Licence No. NCH 10796. Compiled in association with SEMA Group.

DIVISION ONE

	Barnsley	Birmingham C	Bolton W	Bradford C	Charlton Ath	Crystal Palace	Grimsby T	Huddersfield T	Ipswich T	Manchester C	Norwich C	Oldham Ath	Oxford U	Port Vale	Portsmouth	QPR	Reading	Sheffield U	Southend U	Stoke C	Swindon T	Tranmere R	WBA	Wolverhampton W
Barnsley	—	5.4	25.10	26.4	12.4	12.10	28.9	25.8	18.1	28.12	9.11	1.1	15.10	8.2	23.11	14.9	28.8	8.3	7.12	10.9	4.3	14.12	29.3	22.2
Birmingham C	31.8	—	9.11	12.10	31.3	18.8	7.12	12.4	15.10	1.1	26.10	10.9	26.4	22.2	8.2	28.9	18.1	22.3	8.3	14.9	23.11	28.12	14.12	4.3
Bolton W	30.11	1.2	—	1.1	26.4	16.11	10.9	2.11	14.12	20.8	24.8	12.10	12.4	29.3	14.9	5.4	29.10	15.2	28.12	28.9	8.3	15.10	1.3	18.1
Bradford C	19.10	19.4	21.9	—	15.2	29.10	8.3	1.2	16.11	1.3	7.9	2.11	11.1	28.1	17.8	4.5	14.12	26.12	5.10	31.3	1.10	31.8	30.11	22.3
Charlton Ath	5.10	27.8	19.10	23.11	—	8.3	26.10	5.4	1.1	14.9	15.3	24.8	7.12	4.5	19.4	4.3	14.9	6.10	10.9	18.1	7.12	8.2	24.8	28.12
Crystal Palace	19.4	29.3	4.3	8.2	21.12	—	26.10	15.2	5.4	14.9	15.3	24.8	7.12	4.5	18.1	23.8	1.1	3.11	28.9	28.12	19.10	22.2	27.8	23.11
Grimsby T	28.1	1.3	10.9	8.3	26.10	26.10	—	15.2	30.11	12.10	4.5	29.10	21.9	11.1	19.10	12.4	19.4	31.3	4.5	16.11	7.9	22.3	19.10	7.12
Huddersfield T	22.3	5.10	2.11	1.2	29.3	5.4	15.2	—	28.12	16.10	7.12	13.9	21.9	11.1	31.8	5.10	28.9	11.1	19.10	1.1	4.5	10.9	19.10	17.8
Ipswich T	1.10	29.1	14.12	16.11	1.1	1.3	30.11	28.12	—	10.9	7.9	29.10	21.9	31.8	26.10	21.12	24.8	30.10	9.11	21.12	5.10	26.10	28.1	7.12
Manchester C	7.9	18.10	20.8	1.3	5.4	14.9	12.10	16.10	10.9	—	21.12	12.4	26.10	26.12	5.3	19.4	4.5	29.1	8.2	22.3	22.2	23.11	5.10	27.10
Norwich C	1.2	30.11	24.8	7.9	15.3	21.9	4.5	14.12	7.9	16.10	—	16.10	23.11	23.11	1.1	7.12	19.10	30.10	14.9	12.4	17.8	28.9	15.2	31.8
Oldham Ath	21.9	26.12	12.10	2.11	24.8	13.9	28.1	8.3	2.11	12.4	16.10	—	23.11	5.3	1.1	7.12	7.9	7.9	26.10	29.10	28.9	4.3	1.10	15.3
Oxford U	4.5	18.10	12.4	11.1	7.12	22.2	21.9	30.11	11.1	1.2	23.11	23.11	—	31.8	22.3	7.12	26.10	16.11	24.8	12.10	19.4	18.1	8.3	10.9
Port Vale	29.10	2.11	29.3	28.1	14.12	5.3	11.1	4.5	26.4	28.9	5.10	31.3	31.8	—	28.9	29.3	28.12	14.12	24.8	30.11	22.3	31.3	1.2	26.4
Portsmouth	15.2	29.10	14.9	17.8	19.4	18.1	28.12	16.11	30.10	26.12	21.9	1.1	22.3	28.9	—	28.12	1.3	1.3	1.1	2.11	26.12	12.4	2.11	15.10
QPR	11.1	29.1	1.9	16.10	16.11	23.8	21.12	8.3	26.12	15.10	7.12	7.9	18.1	23.8	22.3	—	15.2	30.11	27.8	31.8	21.9	26.4	7.9	31.3
Reading	31.3	1.10	8.2	15.3	1.10	1.1	22.3	28.1	22.3	15.10	26.10	7.12	21.12	7.12	22.2	23.11	—	17.8	22.2	31.8	26.10	9.11	26.12	12.4
Sheffield U	21.12	24.8	23.11	10.9	15.10	15.10	12.4	26.12	28.1	5.3	28.1	31.8	15.3	26.10	17.8	23.11	29.3	—	18.1	26.4	9.11	12.10	5.4	1.1
Southend U	1.3	21.12	7.9	26.4	26.4	26.4	28.1	16.10	12.12	30.11	11.1	26.4	2.11	21.9	31.3	31.3	2.11	1.10	—	15.2	31.8	17.8	16.11	13.10
Stoke C	26.12	11.1	28.8	1.10	7.9	7.9	5.3	22.9	8.3	19.4	4.10	9.3	8.2	19.4	26.10	22.2	5.4	19.10	23.11	—	14.12	31.3	30.10	9.11
Swindon T	16.11	15.2	18.1	2.11	28.12	2.11	26.10	16.10	30.11	24.8	2.11	15.11	12.10	9.11	11.9	20.10	30.11	1.2	5.4	15.3	—	14.9	30.10	27.9
Tranmere R	15.3	7.9	4.5	4.4	29.10	2.11	23.8	8.3	15.2	21.9	28.1	27.8	5.10	22.2	28.12	2.10	15.2	19.4	29.3	5.4	10.1	—	21.9	21.12
WBA	17.8	15.3	7.12	26.10	22.3	31.3	23.8	26.12	12.4	18.1	23.11	1.10	21.12	9.11	22.2	28.12	10.9	30.8	4.3	16.10	8.2	1.1	—	15.9
Wolverhampton W	2.11	16.11	2.10	24.8	6.9	15.2	29.3	12.10	1.3	14.12	5.4	18.1	26.12	19.10	4.5	28.8	5.10	21.9	19.4	1.2	29.1	8.3	11.1	—

NATIONWIDE FOOTBALL LEAGUE FIXTURES 1996–97

DIVISION TWO

	Blackpool	AFC Bournemouth	Brentford	Bristol C	Bristol R	Burnley	Bury	Chesterfield	Crewe Alex	Gillingham	Luton T	Millwall	Notts Co	Peterborough U	Plymouth Arg	Preston N E	Rotherham U	Shrewsbury T	Stockport Co	Walsall	Watford	Wrexham	Wycombe W	York C
Blackpool	—	9.11	4.1	22.3	26.4	26.12	12.4	17.8	18.1	12.10	11.1	25.1	23.11	8.2	3.12	15.3	31.3	21.9	22.2	7.9	26.10	15.10	31.8	21.12
AFC Bournemouth	1.2	—	19.11	29.10	26.12	15.2	2.11	8.3	7.9	21.12	30.11	14.12	21.9	31.8	15.10	4.1	11.1	1.3	1.4	1.10	17.8	26.4	12.10	22.3
Brentford	14.9	22.2	—	18.1	25.1	15.3	29.3	28.12	19.4	27.8	24.8	26.10	3.12	3.5	10.9	21.12	5.10	5.4	9.11	19.10	8.2	23.11	1.1	28.9
Bristol C	24.8	25.1	1.10	—	15.12	11.1	5.4	12.4	22.2	29.3	27.8	9.11	26.10	23.11	26.4	7.9	4.1	26.12	8.2	21.9	3.12	8.3	15.10	11.10
Bristol R	19.10	10.9	29.10	15.3	—	19.11	30.11	28.9	5.10	2.11	15.2	28.12	20.4	17.8	1.1	23.3	3.5	1.2	31.8	1.3	14.9	31.3	21.12	18.1
Burnley	10.9	23.11	14.12	28.9	19.11	—	18.1	1.1	9.11	28.12	15.2	5.4	19.10	8.3	26.10	25.1	19.4	27.8	5.10	24.8	3.5	3.12	14.9	8.2
Bury	5.10	8.2	17.8	26.10	9.11	18.1	—	22.3	19.10	5.4	29.3	3.5	22.2	19.4	23.11	3.12	7.9	4.1	21.12	11.1	19.10	25.1	31.3	9.11
Chesterfield	29.3	21.12	7.9	5.10	11.1	21.9	24.8	—	19.10	1.3	4.1	3.5	3.5	3.12	22.2	9.11	3.12	1.10	25.1	27.8	23.10	8.2	15.3	26.10
Crewe Alex	1.10	1.2	12.10	19.11	12.4	19.10	26.4	19.10	—	1.3	15.3	1.1	3.5	22.3	28.9	31.3	29.10	21.9	1.2	4.1	31.8	14.9	2.11	15.10
Gillingham	19.4	5.10	31.3	29.3	2.11	7.9	5.4	1.3	5.4	—	26.12	19.10	1.10	20.12	25.1	26.10	21.9	3.5	11.1	4.1	8.3	9.11	22.3	23.11
Luton T	28.9	30.11	24.8	27.8	15.2	11.1	29.3	4.1	15.3	26.12	—	18.12	26.12	18.1	5.4	19.11	12.10	24.8	15.10	1.10	25.1	18.1	28.12	3.12
Millwall	30.10	14.12	1.3	30.11	15.2	16.10	16.10	12.10	15.10	1.3	18.12	—	4.1	26.12	12.4	11.1	11.1	15.2	20.11	2.11	10.9	17.8	1.3	2.4
Notts Co	15.2	21.9	3.12	26.10	20.4	19.10	22.2	3.5	20.12	1.10	1.10	9.11	—	4.1	28.12	12.4	7.9	8.2	29.3	26.12	1.1	28.9	12.4	31.8
Peterborough U	2.11	3.5	8.3	23.11	17.8	8.3	11.1	23.11	18.1	20.12	18.1	12.4	11.1	—	18.1	1.10	26.10	22.3	25.1	9.11	31.3	28.12	28.9	14.9
Plymouth Arg	1.3	15.10	10.9	26.4	1.1	26.10	23.11	22.2	28.9	25.1	5.4	22.2	28.12	18.1	—	31.8	15.3	26.4	14.9	19.4	18.1	22.3	1.2	17.8
Preston N E	13.12	14.9	8.3	7.9	23.3	25.1	19.4	11.1	31.8	26.10	19.11	12.4	7.9	8.2	31.8	—	8.2	26.4	12.10	15.10	9.11	1.1	15.2	10.9
Rotherham U	27.8	28.9	11.4	14.9	5.10	19.4	7.9	26.4	12.10	15.10	15.10	11.2	26.10	25.1	26.10	8.2	—	22.3	1.3	8.2	17.8	22.2	18.1	26.4
Shrewsbury T	1.1	3.12	1.2	2.11	1.1	23.11	11.1	26.10	29.3	28.9	24.8	8.2	25.1	26.4	15.3	24.8	12.10	—	1.3	30.11	8.3	12.4	18.8	28.12
Stockport Co	19.11	27.8	1.2	2.11	19.11	26.10	15.10	18.1	14.9	12.10	12.10	18.1	24.8	14.12	14.9	15.10	15.10	1.3	—	30.11	28.12	10.9	26.4	1.1
Walsall	28.12	18.1	26.4	1.1	3.12	21.9	23.11	15.2	26.4	1.1	15.2	8.2	25.1	11.2	12.10	15.10	17.8	8.3	26.10	—	14.12	31.8	10.9	22.2
Watford	30.11	29.3	1.1	21.12	4.1	15.10	26.4	15.2	3.12	27.8	21.9	19.11	11.1	21.9	24.8	21.9	19.11	11.1	4.10	15.3	—	19.4	19.11	12.4
Wrexham	3.5	19.10	15.2	3.5	4.1	27.8	8.3	1.2	2.11	11.1	23.11	5.10	11.1	7.9	24.8	21.9	19.11	4.10	29.3	1.10	19.4	—	26.10	25.1
Wycombe W	5.4	19.4	21.9	3.5	8.3	22.2	26.12	5.4	8.2	22.3	26.12	26.12	19.10	22.2	1.2	29.3	22.2	30.11	19.10	5.4	19.4	26.10	—	29.10
York C	8.3	24.8	11.1	19.4	1.2	3.5	3.5	15.2	4.1	1.10	2.11	11.1	21.9	19.10	29.3	26.12	19.10	7.9	21.9	19.11	5.10	14.12	29.10	—

NATIONWIDE FOOTBALL LEAGUE FIXTURES 1996–97

Copyright © The Football League Ltd 1996. Copyright Licence No. NCH 10796. Compiled in association with SEMA Group.

DIVISION THREE

	Barnet	Brighton & H A	Cambridge U	Cardiff C	Carlisle U	Chester C	Colchester U	Darlington	Doncaster R	Exeter C	Fulham	Hartlepool U	Hereford U	Hull C	Leyton O	Lincoln C	Mansfield T	Northampton T	Rochdale	Scarborough	Scunthorpe U	Swansea C	Torquay U	Wigan Ath
Barnet	—	27.8	29.3	19.4	26.10	21.12	3.5	25.1	23.11	21.9	22.2	19.10	8.2	5.4	3.12	4.1	26.12	7.9	9.11	1.10	11.1	15.3	5.10	24.8
Brighton & H A	31.3	—	12.10	22.3	23.11	17.8	26.12	3.12	26.4	4.1	26.10	8.2	15.10	14.12	8.3	1.10	9.11	11.1	25.1	7.9	31.8	22.2	21.9	12.4
Cambridge U	17.8	19.4	—	31.8	22.2	22.3	7.3	1.10	25.10	11.1	3.5	5.10	25.1	8.2	23.11	31.3	3.12	4.1	19.10	21.9	26.12	9.11	7.9	14.12
Cardiff C	12.10	24.8	5.4	—	26.4	12.4	8.2	15.10	14.3	7.9	9.11	22.2	23.11	25.1	26.10	11.1	21.12	21.9	1.10	28.3	4.1	3.12	26.12	27.8
Carlisle U	30.11	15.2	19.11	19.10	—	29.10	20.12	18.1	29.3	3.5	29.10	15.2	29.10	2.11	15.2	27.8	1.3	28.9	26.4	28.12	5.4	19.11	1.1	5.10
Chester C	8.3	29.3	24.8	5.10	25.1	—	14.2	31.3	28.9	19.10	3.12	11.1	26.10	9.11	3.5	7.9	22.2	1.10	26.12	19.4	21.9	27.8	4.1	5.4
Colchester U	15.10	10.9	20.12	2.11	18.1	14.2	—	31.3	28.9	29.10	28.12	17.8	26.10	14.9	1.1	30.11	14.3	26.4	21.3	28.2	21.9	11.4	31.1	12.10
Darlington	29.10	1.3	18.1	3.5	1.1	15.3	31.3	—	5.4	19.11	28.9	17.8	31.8	29.3	1.1	1.2	19.10	30.11	5.10	28.2	15.2	24.8	21.12	10.9
Doncaster R	15.2	19.10	30.11	13.12	17.8	2.11	5.4	31.8	—	31.3	19.4	21.3	14.9	8.3	28.12	1.2	7.9	30.11	5.10	2.11	1.2	21.9	21.12	10.9
Exeter C	1.1	14.9	28.9	28.12	15.10	2.11	11.1	21.3	27.8	—	10.9	22.3	17.8	26.4	14.12	2.11	29.3	12.10	8.2	24.8	15.3	21.12	4.1	18.1
Fulham	19.11	30.11	15.10	1.2	19.11	2.11	10.9	5.4	27.8	10.9	—	22.3	24.8	29.3	12.4	29.10	7.9	8.3	4.1	26.12	1.2	21.9	1.10	15.2
Hartlepool U	26.4	2.11	12.4	19.11	3.5	28.9	22.3	17.8	18.1	22.3	2.11	—	28.12	1.1	14.12	2.11	27.8	29.10	15.3	1.2	22.3	15.10	15.2	14.9
Hereford U	2.11	3.5	29.10	15.2	14.12	30.11	11.1	31.8	7.9	1.3	27.8	7.9	—	27.8	19.10	19.11	11.1	8.3	21.9	5.10	1.10	26.12	19.4	1.2
Hull C	31.8	15.3	2.11	29.10	1.2	30.11	15.2	21.12	21.9	15.2	19.10	21.9	27.8	—	19.4	26.12	1.10	1.3	7.9	3.5	5.10	11.1	19.11	30.11
Leyton O	1.3	22.12	15.2	30.11	31.3	15.10	28.12	12.4	16.3	19.10	19.10	14.12	19.4	19.4	—	26.12	4.1	26.12	11.1	29.10	17.8	5.4	2.11	19.11
Lincoln C	14.9	18.1	27.8	3.12	31.3	28.12	28.12	2.11	31.8	5.10	19.10	5.4	28.12	12.10	24.8	—	23.11	14.12	3.5	19.10	19.4	5.4	29.3	1.1
Mansfield T	10.9	1.2	1.3	8.3	12.4	19.11	14.3	8.3	31.3	17.8	1.1	18.1	22.2	18.1	24.8	—	23.11	22.3	31.8	5.4	15.2	12.10	29.10	15.10
Northampton T	28.12	28.9	14.9	1.1	9.11	18.1	26.4	26.10	22.2	27.8	5.10	28.12	28.9	3.12	28.12	4.1	22.3	—	23.11	22.3	5.4	8.2	27.8	29.3
Rochdale	1.2	29.10	26.4	18.1	12.10	10.9	24.8	12.4	14.9	27.8	14.12	1.1	28.12	14.12	15.2	5.4	15.2	26.10	—	23.11	3.5	22.2	1.3	8.3
Scarborough	18.1	28.12	1.1	17.8	12.10	10.9	2.11	10.9	9.11	22.3	21.12	12.4	15.10	26.4	26.10	1.1	31.8	22.3	19.11	—	31.3	23.11	15.3	27.8
Scunthorpe U	28.9	5.4	31.1	1.3	28.12	1.1	10.9	19.4	1.1	15.10	26.10	8.2	30.8	19.4	2.11	26.4	8.2	15.10	26.10	31.3	—	26.4	24.8	28.12
Swansea C	13.12	19.11	31.1	1.3	28.12	31.3	1.1	28.12	8.2	1.1	30.8	19.4	10.9	28.9	18.1	2.11	31.3	15.2	17.8	25.1	19.4	—	30.11	29.10
Torquay U	12.4	1.1	31.1	10.9	14.9	8.3	22.3	21.12	30.8	8.2	8.2	22.2	17.8	25.1	30.8	17.8	25.1	19.4	17.8	15.2	22.3	26.10	—	26.4
Wigan Ath	22.3	5.10	15.3	31.3	8.2	31.8	19.4	1.1	28.12	4.1	9.11	26.10	22.2	21.9	19.4	3.5	17.8	31.3	21.12	11.1	7.9	25.1	19.10	—

OTHER FIXTURES – SEASON 1996–97

August
7 Wed   Euro Comps Prelim Rd (1)
10 Sat   Official Start of Season
11 Sun   Littlewoods FA Charity Shield
17 Sat   Commencement of FA Premier League and Football League
21 Wed   Euro Comps Prelim (2)
         FL Coca-Cola Cup 1st Rd (1)
26 Mon   Bank Holiday
28 Wed   FL Coca-Cola Cup 1st Rd (2)
31 Sat   FA Cup Sponsored by Littlewoods Prel Rd
         Austria v Scotland (WC)
         Wales v San Marino (WC)
         Liechtenstein v Republic of Ireland (WC)
         Northern Ireland v Ukraine (WC)

September
1 Sun   Moldova v England (WC)
4 Wed   International
7 Sat   FA Carlsberg Vase 1st Rd Qual
        FA Youth Cup Extra Prel Rd*
8 Sun   UK Living Women's FA Cup Preliminary Round
11 Wed   Euro Comps 1st Round (1)
14 Sat   FA Cup Sponsored by Littlewoods 1st Rd Qual
18 Wed   FA Coca-Cola Cup 2nd Rd (1)
21 Sat   FA Youth Cup Prel Rd*
25 Wed   Euro Comps 1st Round (2)
28 Sat   FA Cup Sponsored by Littlewoods 2nd Rd Qual
29 Sun   UK Living Women's FA Cup 1st Round

October
2 Wed   FL Coca-Cola Cup 2nd Rd (2)
5 Sat   FA Carlsberg Vase 2nd Rd Qual
       Latvia v Scotland (WC)
       Wales v Holland (WC)
       Northern Ireland v Armenia (WC)
9 Wed   England v Poland (WC)
       Estonia v Scotland (WC)
       Republic of Ireland v Macedonia (WC)
12 Sat   FA Cup Sponsored by Littlewoods 3rd Rd Qual
        FA Youth Cup 1st Rd Qual Rd*
        FA County Youth Cup 1st Rd*
16 Sat   Euro Comps 2nd Round (1)
19 Sat   FA Umbro Trophy 1st Rd Qual
23 Wed   FL Coca-Cola Cup 3rd Rd
26 Sat   FA Cup Sponsored by Littlewoods 4th Rd Qual
27 Sun   FA Sunday Cup 1st Round
30 Wed   Euro Comps 2nd Round (2)

November
2 Sat   FA Carlsberg Vase 1st Rd Proper
       FA Youth Cup 2nd Rd Qual*
3 Sun   UK Living Women's FA Cup 2nd Round
6 Wed   FL Coca-Cola Cup 3rd Rd replays
9 Sat   FA Umbro Trophy 2nd Rd Qual
       Georgia v England (WC)
       Holland v Wales (WC)
       Germany v Northern Ireland (WC)
10 Sun   Scotland v Sweden (WC)
       Republic of Ireland v Iceland (WC)
16 Sat   FA Cup Sponsored by Littlewoods 1st Rd Proper
20 Wed   Euro Comps 3rd Round (1)
23 Sat   FA Carlsberg Vase 2nd Rd Proper
       FA Youth Cup 1st Rd Proper*
       FA County Youth Cup 2nd Rd*
24 Sun   FA Sunday Cup 2nd Round
27 Wed   FA Cup Sponsored by Littlewoods 1st Proper Replays
       FL Coca-Cola Cup 4th Rd
30 Sat   FA Umbro Trophy 3rd Rd Qual

December
1 Sun   UK Living Women's FA Cup 3rd Round
4 Wed   Euro Comps 3rd Round (2)
7 Sat   FA Cup Sponsored by Littlewoods 2nd Rd Proper
14 Sat   FA Carlsberg Vase 3rd Rd Proper
       Wales v Turkey (WC) (prov)
       Northern Ireland v Albania (WC)
       FA Youth Cup 2nd Rd Proper*
15 Sun   FA Sunday Cup 3rd Round
       Wales v Turkey (WC) (prov)
18 Wed   FA Cup Sponsored by Littlewoods 2nd Rd Proper replays
       FL Coca-Cola Cup 4th Rd replays
21 Sat
26 Thu   Boxing Day
28 Sat

January 1997
1 Wed   New Years Day
4 Sat   FA Cup Sponsored by Littlewoods 3rd Rd Proper
5 Sun   UK Living Women's FA Cup 4th Round
8 Wed   FL Coca-Cola Cup 5th Rd
11 Sat   FA Carlsberg Vase 4th Rd Proper
       FA Youth Cup 3rd Rd Proper*
       FA County Youth Cup 3rd Rd*

12 Sun   FA Sunday Cup 4th Round
15 Wed   FA Cup Sponsored by Littlewoods 3rd Rd Proper replays
18 Sat   FA Umbro 1st Rd Proper
22 Wed   FL Coca-Cola Cup 5th Rd replays
25 Sat   FA Cup sponsored by Littlewoods 4th Rd Proper

February
1 Sat   FA Carlsberg Vase 5th Rd Proper
2 Sun   UK Living Women's FA Cup 5th Round
5 Wed   FA Cup Sponsored by Littlewoods 4th Rd Proper replays
8 Sat   FA Umbro Trophy 2nd Rd Proper
9 Sun   FA Sunday Cup 5th Round
12 Wed   England v Italy (WC)
15 Sat   FA Cup Sponsored by Littlewoods 5th Rd Proper
       FA Youth Cup 4th Rd Proper*
       FA County Youth Cup 4th Rd*
19 Wed   FL Coca-Cola Cup Semi-Finals (1)
22 Sat   FA Carlsberg Vase 6th Rd Proper
23 Sun   FL Coca-Cola Cup Semi-Finals (1)
26 Wed   FA Cup Sponsored by Littlewoods 5th Rd Proper replays

March
1 Sat   FA Umbro Trophy 3rd Rd Proper
2 Sun   UK Living Women's FA Cup 6th Round
5 Wed   Euro Comps QF (1)
8 Sat   FA Cup Sponsored by Littlewoods 6th Rd Proper
       FA Youth Cup 5th Rd Proper*
12 Wed   FL Coca-Cola Cup Semi-Finals (2)
15 Sat   FA Carlsberg Vase Semi-Final (1)
       FA County Youth Cup Semi-Finals*
16 Sun   FL Coca-Cola Cup Semi-Finals (2)
       FA Sunday Cup Semi-Final
19 Wed   Euro Comps QF (2)
       FA Cup Sponsored by Littlewoods 6th Rd Proper replays
22 Sat   FA Umbro Trophy 4th Rd Proper
       FA Carlsberg Vase Semi-Finals (2)
28 Fri   Good Friday
29 Sat   Scotland v Estonia (WC)
       Wales v Belgium (WC)
       Northern Ireland v Portugal (WC)
30 Sun   UK Living Women's FA Cup Semi-Finals
31 Mon   Easter Monday

April
2 Wed   Scotland v Austria (WC)
       Macedonia v Republic of Ireland (WC)
       Ukraine v Northern Ireland (WC)
5 Sat   FA Umbro Trophy Semi-Finals (1)
       FA Youth Cup Semi-Finals*
6 Sun   FL Coca-Cola Cup Final
9 Wed   Euro Comps SF (1)
12 Sat   FA Umbro Trophy Semi-Final (2)
13 Sun   FA Cup Sponsored by Littlewoods Semi-Finals
16 Wed   FA Cup Sponsored by Littlewoods Semi-Finals replays (prov)
19 Sat
23 Wed   Euro Comps SF (2)
       FA Cup Sponsored by Littlewoods Semi-Finals replays (prov)
26 Sat   FA County Youth Final (fixed date)
27 Sun   FA Sunday Cup Final
30 Wed   England v Georgia (WC)
       Sweden v Scotland (WC)
       Romania v Republic of Ireland (WC)
       Armenia v Northern Ireland (WC)

May
3 Sat   Final matches in Football League
4 Sun   UK Living Women's FA Cup Final
5 Mon   Bank Holiday
7 Wed   UEFA Cup Final 1st Leg
10 Sat   Final matches in FA Premier League
       FA Carlsberg Vase Final – Wembley Stadium
       FA Youth Cup Final*
11 Sun   FL Play off Semi-Finals (1)
14 Wed   European Cup Winners Cup Final
       FL Play off Semi-finals (2)
17 Sat   FA Cup Sponsored by Littlewoods Final – Wembley Stadium
18 Sun   FA Umbro Trophy Final – Wembley Stadium
21 Wed   UEFA Cup Final 2nd Leg
22 Thu   FA Cup Sponsored by Littlewoods Final replay – Wembley Stadium
24 Sat   FL Play off Final Division 3
25 Sun   FL Play off Final Division 2
26 Mon   FL Play off Final Division 1
       Bank Holiday
28 Wed   European Champions Cup Final
31 Sat   Poland v England (WC)

June
7 Sat   Republic of Ireland v Liechtenstein (WC)
8 Sun   Belarus v Scotland (WC)
16 Mon   Commencement of Close Season

* closing date of rounds

STOP PRESS

England bid for World Cup 2006 ... Keith Wiseman is new FA Chairman ... Middlesbrough pay £7m for Ravanelli ... Iron-age encampment at Orient's ground? ... Portsmouth want Venables as joint owner ... Graeme Souness becomes Southampton manager ... Threat of players strike over TV cash ... Newtown lose 4-1 to Skonto Riga in UEFA Cup ... Caspian Holdings seek Leeds takeover ... Newcastle's go-ahead for new ground ... and agree to pay world record fee of £15m to Blackburn for Alan Shearer.

Transfers:- Fabrizio Ravanelli, Juventus to Middlesbrough £7m; Roberto Di Matteo, Lazio to Chelsea £4.9m; Emerson, Porto to Middlesbrough £4m; Gary Speed, Leeds to Everton £3.5m; Alan Stubbs, Bolton to Celtic £3.5m; Karel Poborsky, Slavia Prague to Manchester U £3.5m; Andy Booth, Huddersfield T to Sheffield W £2.65m; Lee Bowyer, Charlton to Leeds £2.6m; Joachim Bjorklund, Vicenza to Rangers £2.6m; Darko Kovacevic, Sheffield W to Real Sociedad £2.5m; Frank Leboeuf, Strasbourg to Chelsea £2.5m; Michael Johansen, FC Copenhagen to Bolton W £2.5m; Florin Raducioiu, Espanol to West Ham U £2.4m; Ben Thatcher, Millwall to Wimbledon £1.9m; Marc Degryse, Sheffield W to PSV Eindhoven £1.8m; Ronnie Johnsen, Besiktas to Manchester U £1.5m; Ole Solskjar, Molde to Manchester U £1.5m; Fernando Nelson, Sporting Lisbon to Aston Villa £1.5m; Paul Furlong, Chelsea to Birmingham C £1.5m; Marcus Stewart, Bristol R to Huddersfield T £1.2m; Iwan Roberts, Leicester C to Wolverhampton W £1.1m; Dean Saunders, Galatasaray to Nottingham F £1m; Nikola Jerkan, Oviedo to Nottingham F £1m; Paolo Di Canio, AC Milan to Celtic £1m; Gianluca Vialli, Juventus to Chelsea Free; Paulo Futre, AC Milan to West Ham U Free.

Other Moves:- Derek Allan, Southampton to Brighton; Leo Cotterell, Ipswich to Bournemouth; David Greene, Luton T to Colchester U; Duncan Jupp, Fulham to Wimbledon; David Nurse, Manchester C to Millwall; Alex Rae, Millwall to Sunderland; Steve Bruce, Manchester U to Birmingham C; Jason Fowler, Bristol C to Cardiff C; Barry Horne, Everton to Birmingham C; George Donis, Panithaniakos to Blackburn R; Ian Rush, Liverpool to Leeds U; Les Sealey, West Ham U to Leyton Orient; Alvin Martin, West Ham U to Leyton Orient; John Collins, Celtic to Monaco; Joao Moreira, Benfica to Swansea C; Danny Sonner, Preussen Cologne to Ipswich T; Chris Tate, York C to Sunderland; Bobby Petta, Feyenoord to Ipswich T; Aljosa Asanovic, Hajduk Split to Derby Co; Jacob Laursen, Silkeborg to Derby Co; Mark Jones, Aston Villa to Wolverhampton W; Rudi Vata, Celtic to Marseilles; Kingsley Black, Nottingham F to Grimsby T; Johnny Vilstrup, Luton T to Aarhus; Gary Ablett, Everton to Birmingham C; Chris Allen, Oxford U to Nottingham F; Staale Solbakken, Lillestrom to Wolverhampton W; Dave Martin, Gillingham to Leyton Orient; Colin Scott, Rangers to Bradford C; Rhys Wilmot, Crystal Palace to Torquay U; Per Frandsen, FC Copenhagen to Bolton W; Ray Van der Gouw, Vitesse to Manchester U; Phil Masinga, Leeds U to St Gallen; Paul Hartley, Steve Crawford, Dave Sinclair and Jason Dair all Raith R to Millwall; Neil Thompson, Ipswich T to Barnsley; Andy Fensome, Preston NE to Rochdale; Glenn Cotterill, Leyton Orient to Fulham; Richard Hall, Southampton to West Ham U; Andy Payton, Barnsley to Huddersfield T; Andy Morrison, Blackpool to Huddersfield T; Mark Bowen, Norwich C to West Ham U; Danny Cullip, Oxford U to Fulham; Darren Freeman, Gillingham to Fulham; Paul McCarthy, Brighton to Wycombe W; Paul Bodin, Swindon T to Reading; Bobby Davison, Rotherham U to Halifax; Steve White, Hereford U to Cardiff C; Michael Hughes, Strasbourg to West Ham U; Justin Channing, Bristol R to Leyton Orient; Martin O'Connor, Walsall to Peterborough U; Scott Houghton, Wallsall to Peterborough U; Zeke Rowe, Chelsea to Peterborough U; Aidy Boothroyd, Mansfield T to Peterborough U; Steve Welsh, Partick T to Peterborough U; Tommy Widdrington, Southampton to Grimsby T; Matt Clarke, Rotherham U to Sheffield W; Muzzy Izzet, Chelsea to Leicester C; Alec Chamberlain, Sunderland to Watford; Steve Talboys, Wimbledon to Watford; Graeme Jones, Doncaster R to Wigan Ath; Malcolm McPherson, West Ham U to Brentford; Stuart Myall, Brighton to Brentford; Darren Purse, Leyton Orient to Oxford U; Nigel Spackman, Chelsea to Sheffield U; Steve Slade, Tottenham H to QPR; Paul Browne, Aston Villa to Raith R; Stuart Watkiss, Hereford U to Mansfield T; Chris Day, Tottenham H to Crystal Palace; Barry Hunter, Wrexham to Reading; Paul Conlon, Hartlepool U to Sunderland; Nigel Jemson, Notts Co to Oxford U; Charlie Bishop, Barnsley to Wigan Ath; Christian Dailly, Dundee U to Derby Co; Jeremy Goss, Norwich C to Charlton Ath; Nigel Worthington, Leeds U to Stoke C; Andy Hessenthaler, Watford to Gillingham; Gordon Cowans, Sheffield U to Bradford C; Paul Groves, Grimsby T to WBA; Ben Dixon, Lincoln C to Blackpool; Matty Appleby, Darlington to Barnsley; Shaun Goater, Rotherham U to Bristol C; Peter Kachuro, Dynamo Minsk to Sheffield U; Gary Monk, Torquay U to Southampton; Robert Ullathorne, Norwich C to Osasuna.

Administrative Moves:- Roger Brinsford replaces Ian Wilson as Bristol R secretary; John Howarth resigns as Blackburn R secretary; Mike Phelan Blackpool assistant manager; Phil Boersma Southampton assistant manager; coach Phil Holder leaves Reading; Gary Bennett is Scarborough player-coach.